BRITISH JEWRY
BOOK OF HONOUR

PART 1

LIEUT.-GEN. SIR JOHN MONASH, G.C.M.G., K.C.B.,
G.O.C. AUSTRALIAN CORPS.

[*Frontispiece*

British Jewry
Book of Honour

Edited by
REV. MICHAEL ADLER, D.S.O., S.C.F., B.A.

Organiser
MAX R. G. FREEMAN

Part One

The Naval & Military Press Ltd

Published by
The Naval & Military Press Ltd
Unit 10 Ridgewood Industrial Park,
Uckfield, East Sussex,
TN22 5QE England
Tel: +44 (0) 1825 749494
Fax: +44 (0) 1825 765701
www.naval-military-press.com

© The Naval & Military Press Ltd 2006

In reprinting in facsimile from the original, any imperfections are inevitably reproduced and the quality may fall short of modern type and cartographic standards.

Contents

	PAGE
LETTERS FROM DISTINGUISHED MEN	ix-xix
THE STORY OF BRITISH JEWRY IN THE WAR	1
RECORD OF LIEUT.-GENERAL SIR JOHN MONASH, G.C.M.G., K.C.B., V.D.	28
RECORDS OF THE SCHOOLS AND CLUBS	32
STORY OF THE EXPERIENCES OF A JEWISH CHAPLAIN ON THE WESTERN FRONT (WITH MAP)	33
THE JEWISH UNITS IN THE WAR, BY V. JABOTINSKY	59
THE PALESTINIAN BATTALION	66
ROLL OF HONOUR (*The Glorious Dead*)	68
OFFICIAL RECORDS OF GALLANT DEEDS (MILITARY CROSS AND DISTINGUISHED CONDUCT MEDAL)	127
RECORD OF HONOURS	157
ALPHABETICAL INDEX OF NOMINAL ROLLS	188
NOMINAL ROLL OF JEWS IN HIS MAJESTY'S FORCES	189
ROLL OF OFFICERS AND MEN TOO LATE FOR CLASSIFICATION	610
INDEX TO THE ILLUSTRATIONS	611

THE CHIEF RABBI THE VERY REV. DR. HERTZ.

THE CHIEF RABBI, THE VERY REV. DR. HERTZ.

OFFICE OF THE CHIEF RABBI.

" I earnestly hope that British Jewry's Book of Honour will find a place in every Jewish home throughout the Empire.

We owe it to the brave sons of Israel who so gladly gave their lives that Freedom and Righteousness prevail, to see to it that their names shall not be blotted out nor the memory of their heroic deeds forgotten.

This permanent written record of the part played by Anglo-Jewry in the Great War will help lovers of the Truth in their warfare against the malicious slander that the Jew shrinks from the sacrifices demanded of every loyal citizen in the hour of national danger.

The Jewish Community owes a deep debt of gratitude to the projectors and editors of this Book, as well as to its wise-hearted patrons—The Right Hon. the Earl of Reading, the Right Hon. Lord Rothschild, the Right Hon. Lord Bearsted, the Right Hon. Sir Alfred Mond, Bart., M.P., the Right Hon. Sir Herbert Samuel, Sir Edward Stern, Sir Adolph Tuck, Bart., Sir Robert Waley Cohen, Sir Stuart Samuel, Sir Samuel Instone, Major James de Rothschild, Colonel S. L. Mandelberg, J.P., and Messrs. Samuel Samuel, M.P., Raphael Abdella, Bernard Baron, Henry Van den Bergh, L. Levene-Davis, Sydney Frankenburg, Nathan Laski, J.P., A. M. Landauer, F. Millhoff, Harold Mosenthal, and S. Schneider & Sons, whose encouragement and munificence alone rendered its publication possible."

(Signed) J. H. HERTZ,
Chief Rabbi.

LIEUT.-GEN. SIR JOHN MONASH, G.C.M.G., K.C.B.,
G.O.C. AUSTRALIAN CORPS.

"To have been asked by the compilers of this Volume to write a few words by way of introduction to its pages is esteemed by me as a great privilege. In the stressful years through which the world has passed, and under the burdens which the leaders and the men of our Armies have had to bear, it needed strong impulses and great appeals to sustain the fortitude and endurance of us all. To me, when during the course of the War my responsibilities increased, one particular impetus became ever more paramount and dominating, and that was the recognition of the fact that a growing duty devolved upon me of helping my co-religionists to create and maintain the prestige, as worthy citizens, and as devoted soldiers, of the Jews of the Empire. The fortune of war, in my case a happy one, placed me in command of that splendid fighting instrument—the Australian Army Corps—and to the men of that Corps I owe all that has come to me. But not to them alone, for I owe much, also, to the many thousands of Jewish Soldiers, scattered throughout all His Majesty's Armies, who by their valour, their fortitude, and their devoted sacrifice have combined to achieve a story of Jewish service to our Country, which will still further enhance the prestige of every British Citizen of the Jewish faith, as second to no other in patriotism or in readiness and ability to bear his full share of all the burdens of the State. In gratitude for the services which have been rendered by them all, individually and collectively, by those who have succumbed, and by those who have survived—I commend to the public this Book of Honour, in the pages of which is enshrined the proud record of their performance."

(Signed) JOHN MONASH,
Lieut.-General.

EARL OF READING, G.C.B.

"It appears to me that your idea in compiling a British Jewry Book of Honour is excellent, and I was greatly interested in the copy of the work that you were recently good enough to show me.

I am sure that it will prove a valuable record of the services rendered to their country by the Jews of Great Britain. The list of achievements is a fine one, but the quality of it will cause no surprise when it is remembered how pre-eminent has been the example of this country in matters of civil and religious liberty, and how seriously the freedom of the world was threatened in the great war from which we have emerged victorious. Your book demonstrates to the full that British Jews were ready and eager to do battle for the preservation of that freedom and for the triumph of the country which has given to them such generous opportunity to share in its liberties.

I wish you all success in your undertaking."

(Signed) READING.

RT. HON. SIR ALFRED MOND, BART.

"I have been very interested to learn that you have succeeded in compiling so complete a record of the services in the Imperial Forces of members of the Jewish race. Though but a small community amidst the vast population of the British Empire, the record shows in proportion to their number that they gallantly responded to the call of the defence of an Empire whose generous and tolerant treatment has for generations made them feel an identity of devotion to its cause with all other citizens. This is a record of which we have a right to be proud as Jews and as citizens of the British Empire. I sincerely hope that the labour of love which you have devoted in compiling this work will have that great success which it deserves, and that the book will not only find a permanent place in all Jewish homes, but will find a wider distribution and become a testimony of the Jewish sacrifices and efforts on behalf of the British Empire in the world's greatest war."

(Signed)   ALFRED MOND.

SIR HERBERT SAMUEL, G.B.E.

"It is fitting that there should be published the war record of British Jews. A small community, they have taken their due share in the country's effort, and borne their full part in its sacrifice. One motive inspired them—their plain duty as citizens of the British Empire. One fact fortified them—the justice of the cause in which they were engaged. To those who employ aggressive force, force is the only possible reply. Peace-loving peoples found themselves obliged to engage in war for the sake of defending their future peace. Free peoples had to consent to the temporary surrender of much of their freedom in order to save their permanent liberties. Jews care for peace and for liberty as much as others; they are not less ready than others to fight, if need be, in their defence. This book furnishes the proof. It is a record, for ourselves and for our descendants, of those who fought and suffered, of those who won honourable distinctions by their service, and of those who, through their sacrifice of life itself, are the most honoured and distinguished of all."

(Signed)   HERBERT SAMUEL.

SIR ADOLPH TUCK, BART.

"The community no less than the country owes you a debt for the great work you have undertaken and have now happily completed.

The BRITISH JEWRY BOOK OF HONOUR with its proud record of devotion to duty, and of sacrifice on the part of the Jews of the British Empire, will ever stand out as an example to future generations and animate them to emulate that spirit of courage, loyalty and patriotism to which the pages of your volume give such eloquent testimony.

The great World War has indeed found England happy in all her sons, not the least among whom are those of Jewish blood who have responded to the call for the freedom of the world, as befits the ancient race from which they have sprung.

The sacrifices which they have made for civilisation and for freedom show that those who have been accorded equal liberties, irrespective of creed, have not been found wanting at a time when their country had most need of them."

(Signed)   ADOLPH TUCK.

HENRY VAN DEN BERGH, ESQ.

"I have perused with great interest the BRITISH JEWRY BOOK OF HONOUR of which you have sent me a copy, and I am glad to see that the valuable services rendered to the Empire by the Jewish Contingents of the British Forces have met with such commendation from their fellow-countrymen, and that the sacrifices they have made are to be so suitably placed on record.

Where all have done so admirably, it is a source of special pride that our Co-Religionists have played so worthy a part in the tremendous struggle for the supremacy of right over might.

I feel sure that every Jew would like to have a copy of the book, to be handed down to future generations as a record of the achievements of their brethren of what is, without doubt, one of the greatest events in the history of the world."

(Signed)   HENRY VAN DEN BERGH.

FIELD-MARSHAL EARL HAIG, K.T.

"The British Jewry Book of Honour is a striking testimony to a fact which every soldier will gladly recognise—namely, the loyalty with which British Jews of every class came forward to fight for the country of their adoption, and for the great human ideals which they shared with their Christian comrades in arms."

(Signed)   HAIG,
Field-Marshal.

MARQUIS OF CREWE, K.G.

"I am glad to know that the part taken by British Jews in the Great War is to be duly chronicled. Their services have been appreciated and recognised by their fellow-countrymen, and the value of such services rendered by the King's subjects all over the Empire has never admitted any thought of the race or origin of those who gave and risked their lives. But it is a natural and legitimate pride that inspires a special record such as this, and we may all be proud that the ancient traditions of Jewry have been revived all through the fight waged by the British Empire on behalf of liberty and justice."

(Signed) CREWE.

VISCOUNT NORTHCLIFFE

"Our British Jews have played a splendid part in the War. They have provided us with one of the finest Generals of all, Monash, the head of the Australian Army, and many other officers of distinction.

Although the Jewish population of the Empire is comparatively small, Jewry has to its credit 5 Victoria Crosses, 50 Distinguished Service Orders, 242 Military Crosses, 80 Distinguished Conduct Medals, 308 Military Medals, and 374 Mentioned in Dispatches.

Nearly 9,000 Jews in the British Army alone fell in Action or were wounded and missing, and missing, of course, means dead.

The Jews are a cautious people and not anxious to make war, but in this great conflict they waged it just as vigorously as they did in the wars of the Bible."

(Signed)   NORTHCLIFFE.

RIGHT HON. WINSTON CHURCHILL, M.P.

SECRETARY OF STATE FOR WAR.

WAR OFFICE,

WHITEHALL, S.W. 1,

6th March, 1920.

"It is with great pleasure that I accede to your request to contribute a message to the British Jewry Book of Honour. I feel, however, that any such message from me is unnecessary in view of the facts, which speak for themselves.

Although Jews form but a small proportion of the population of the British Empire, some 60,000 fought in the War in Europe, Africa and Asia. Of these, 2,324 gave their lives for the Cause and a further 6,350 became casualties. Five Jewish soldiers won the highest honour it is possible to obtain in our country, namely the Victoria Cross, while a further 1,533 obtained other honours.

I can truthfully say that this record is a great one, and British Jews can look back with pride on the honourable part they played in winning the Great War."

(Signed)   WINSTON S. CHURCHILL.

BRITISH JEWRY BOOK OF HONOUR

THE JEWS OF THE EMPIRE AND THE GREAT WAR.

"Their Name Liveth to all Generations."

IN those fatal and ever-memorable days of August, 1914, when the call came to the young men of the British Empire to give up all that they held most dear and go forth to fight in the battle for right against might, for justice against injustice, for freedom against tyranny, among the first who responded were men of the Jewish faith. In the mighty struggle which rent the world for nearly five long and weary years no fewer than fifty thousand Jews bore their part, and bore it nobly.

From all corners of the British Empire they came. From South Africa, from Canada, from Australia and New Zealand, they came in their thousands. Among them were men in every walk of life. They served in all the fields of the far-flung war, in all capacities, from that of the simple soldier or sailor to that of the commanding officer. Each made the supreme offering; his life, his wealth, his strength, his personal happiness were his response to the great call of duty. For themselves these men asked nothing. Obedience to duty, to the voice within speaking of righteousness, is the mark and sign of the children of Light. Never did the Sons of Israel prove more splendidly what is that righteousness which exalteth a nation than in those terrible five years.

British Jews have vindicated, once and for all time, their right to British citizenship. They have proved in an unmistakable manner that they are part and parcel of the Empire. Great Britain was the first country in the world completely to emancipate the Jews. This was in 1854. The opportunity to justify that emancipation did not come for sixty years, but when it did come—in August, 1914—the opportunity was seized with a spontaneity and enthusiasm that surprised even those who knew the loyalty of the British Jews.

WHAT IS THE BOOK OF HONOUR? The British Jewry Book of Honour has been planned as a permanent record of the services of all the fifty thousand Jews who, from all parts of the British Empire, served in the

Great War; so that, in days to come, all may have before them, in a permanent form, the remembrance of these men and know how to hold them in honour and lasting thankfulness. To do less, is to fail in duty to them.

More than this, it is to under-estimate a landmark in the history of the Jewish race. For nothing is more remarkable, in the whole course of their long history, than the way in which in the British Empire, wherever they were living, the sons of Israel came forward and bore their part, thinking only of the great cause at stake. In doing this they asserted before the eyes of all the world all that is great and permanent in the idea of nationality and showed, once more, that neither time, nor exile, nor oppression, can extinguish the sacred spark.

RECORDS. Every endeavour has been made to secure completeness in the records. As far as it has been possible no one has been forgotten. All the Chaplains and officiating clergymen working in different parts of the world have deposited their official records with the Editor, and all information sent to the Jewish Press has been carefully noted. The detailed lists which were prepared by the Jewish War Services Committee have been fully utilised, nominal rolls have been received from all the Dominions overseas, whilst information has poured into the editorial office from various sources, both public and private.

It has naturally hardly been possible to keep in touch with the frequent changes in rank of Officers, N.C.O.'s or men in a large number of instances, but whenever brought to the notice of the Editor these alterations in titles have been duly recorded.

It has been designed to place on permanent record details of the war services rendered by Jewish sailors and soldiers, who served in France, in Belgium, in Italy, in Mesopotamia, in Palestine, in North Russia, at the Dardanelles, in Salonica, in East and South Africa, and on the Seas. Of these over two thousand made the supreme sacrifice; thousands more have lost their health and strength which to many men mean as much as life itself; others, have been spared to return home and rejoice in the achievement common to them all.

JEWISH ENLISTMENTS. When war broke out the number of Jews attached to the Regular branches of His Majesty's Forces was comparatively small. There were about fifty in the Royal Navy; four hundred officers and men in the Army; and about six hundred in the Special Reserve and Territorial Forces. In response to the appeal for volunteers, Jews came from all classes and from all parts of the world to uphold England's cause. The number of Jews who were on active service before conscription came into force was about 10,000, of whom 1,140 were officers.

In the British Dominions, Canada, Australia, New Zealand, South Africa, in the British West Indies and other Colonies, the proportion of Jews who enlisted was very high. (For detailed lists see pages 549 to 596.) In Australia, for example, out of a total Jewish population of 17,000, there were 2,000 enlistments and 300 deaths in action. (See further, p. 21.)

Of the families of English birth, the proportion of voluntary enlistment was something approaching 90 per cent. of the available young men, whilst British-born sons of alien immigrants from countries like Russia and Poland contributed a large number to the ranks. Thus, from the well-known Jews' Free School in the East End of London about 1,200 old boys joined up, and the Jewish houses at the public schools of Clifton and Cheltenham can point to the proud record of practically every one of their present and past pupils of military age having taken a commission. It is further striking evidence of the enthusiasm of the English Jews in joining the forces at the outbreak of the War that the Jewish Lads' Brigade, which both in London and the provinces trained Jewish boys in military exercises without being regarded as a part of the Army, contributed 80 officers out of a total of 90 young men who were serving as officers of the Brigade at the time.

The complete record of the number of Jews who were on active service throughout the whole war will never be accurately known, owing to the difficulty of compiling the lists. The military authorities rendered from time to time, both abroad and in the United Kingdom, nominal rolls of Jews who were serving, and, in addition, the chaplains and officiating clergymen, in the course of their ministrations, discovered many other men, but the experience of all associated with the work showed that only two-thirds, if as large a proportion, of the actual number of men on service ever became known. All figures, therefore, relative to the number of men in the Army, number of casualties, number of honours and distinctions gained, must be qualified by this knowledge.

The total Jewish population of the United Kingdom is computed at 275,000. To these figures must be added the numbers in the Dominions from which men were recruited, a further 145,000, making in all a rough total of 420,000 for the British Empire, including women and children. Among the male population, a large proportion of Jews of alien birth were not available as soldiers, so that the exact total of acceptable men cannot be accurately ascertained. As far as existing records testify, some 50,000 Jews from the beginning to the end of the war were in some branch of His Majesty's Forces. The manner in which Jewish officers and men were distributed among the thousand and one units of the Forces renders the task of compiling exact records an unusually complicated one. The battalions and divisions recruited from the large centres of Jewish population in the United Kingdom, as London, Manchester, Liverpool, and Leeds, naturally contained the largest number of Jewish representatives, but they were also found scattered by ones and twos in every kind of formation.

CASUALTIES AND HONOURS. That men of the Jewish faith played their part in the great war nobly and well is proved by the number of casualties as well as by the many honours and distinctions gained.

The Casualties were as follows:—

Officers fallen in action or died on active service	334
Non-commissioned officers and men ditto	2,091
Wounded	6,500
Total	8,925

Detailed lists of the names of those who gave their lives in the great cause are set forth on pages 68 to 126. An examination of this

Roll of Honour to the undying memory of those who have fallen will reveal many interesting features. A glance at the record of dates will show that from the early days in 1914 until the hour of the Armistice in November, 1918, Jews were in the forefront of the fighting, and if the locations had been also indicated where these deaths took place, all of which are known, it would be found that in every area of the conflict, on the sea, on the land and in the air, Jewish men made the supreme sacrifice. It would, moreover, be noted that nearly every unit of H.M. Forces has contributed its quota of Jewish losses and that the men themselves came from all parts of the Empire, as well as from Egypt and Palestine.

The details given of the battalions, etc., to which the men belonged further demonstrate that the large majority of Jews on active service belonged to the fighting units and not to the administrative or departmental corps.

During the months of August, September and October, 1914, when the "Old Contemptibles" stemmed the onrush of the enemy, Jews in the Regular Army laid down their lives in the terrible struggles which first proved the superiority of the British soldier. On August 23rd and 24th, 1914, at the battle of Mons which began the war, Jews in the 4th Middlesex Regiment, the 1st Northumberland Fusiliers, 1st Norfolk Regiment, and 1st K.O.R. Lancaster Regiment, fell in action, and at the battles of the Marne in the month of September, Lieut. R. L. Q. Henriques was the first Jewish officer to fall, together with other Jewish soldiers. In the heroic fight of "L" Battery, R.H.A., on August 31st, at Néry,* where the one remaining gun fought against twelve German guns, a Jewish driver met his end, and similar lists could be compiled of the names of men who fell in the continuous fighting which would fully illustrate the statement that Jews took part in every phase of the War from the beginning to the end.

Our records reveal the fact that London families suffered heavy losses in the deaths of 186 officers and 1,046 N.C.O.'s and men, Manchester men who fell number 12 officers and 173 N.C.O.'s and

* See Lord E. Hamilton, "The First Seven Divisions," p. 84

DECORATIONS AND HONOURS

men, Liverpool contributed to the sad total 5 officers and 64 N.C.O.'s and men, Birmingham casualties are 9 officers and 37 N.C.O.'s and men, Glasgow mourns 3 officers and 44 N.C.O.'s and men, and Leeds lost 1 officer and 92 N.C.O.'s and men. From the great democracies of the Dominions, the Roll of Casualties is as follows:—Australia and New Zealand 27 officers and 229 N.C.O.'s and men; South Africa 4 officers and 57 N.C.O.'s and men; Canada 7 officers and 89 N.C.O.'s and men.

It is certain that the full roll of Jewish casualties in all parts of the world will never be known, though every effort has been made to ensure a complete record, each name having been officially confirmed. Jewish congregations throughout the Empire have been asked to supply their lists of casualties, schools, clubs and institutions have contributed their Rolls of Honour, mourning parents and relatives have sent full details concerning their lost children or kinsmen, whilst the military authorities have rendered every assistance in this important branch of the work. Photographs of a very large proportion of those whose names appear in our Roll of Honour will be found in the pages of this Book, thus ensuring a lasting record of Anglo-Jewry's young men who came not back from the field of battle. It is nevertheless certain that a small proportion of Jewish casualties is not here included—and it is estimated that at least a further 10 per cent. of names should be added to ensure a complete list. Photographs of War Memorials erected in various places will be found amongst the illustrations.

The decorations and honours awarded for services rendered were as follows:—

Victoria Cross	5
Order of St. Michael and St. George	15
Distinguished Service Order	49
Military Crosses	263
Distinguished Flying Cross	11
Order of the British Empire	144
Distinguished Conduct Medals	85
Military Medals	329

Meritorious Service Medals	66
Mentioned in Despatches	336
Foreign Honours	138
Mentioned in Home Despatches	155
Total	1,596

THE FIVE JEWISH V.C.'S. The official records of the exploits of the five V.C.'s are as follows. (For photographs see Plate I.)

Lieut. FRANK ALEXANDER DE PASS, late 34th Prince Albert Victor's Own Poona Horse.

"For conspicuous bravery near Festubert on November 24th, 1914. In entering a German sap and destroying a traverse in the face of the enemy's bombs and for subsequently rescuing, under heavy fire, a wounded man who was lying exposed in the open. Lieut. de Pass lost his life on this day in a second attempt to capture the aforesaid sap, which had been re-occupied by the enemy."

No. 168 Sgt. ISSY SMITH (SHMULOVITCH), 1st Battalion Manchester Regiment.

"For most conspicuous bravery on April 26th, 1915, near Ypres, when he left his company on his own initiative and went well forward towards the enemy's position to assist a severely wounded man whom he carried a distance of 250 yards into safety, whilst exposed the whole time to heavy machine-gun and rifle fire. Subsequently Sgt. Smith displayed great gallantry when casualties were very heavy in voluntarily assisting to bring in many more wounded men throughout the whole day, and attending them with the greatest devotion to duty regardless of personal risk."

No. 958 Pte. (later Lieut.) LEONARD KEYSOR, 1st Battalion Australian Imperial Force.

"For most conspicuous bravery and devotion to duty at Lone Point trenches in the Gallipoli Peninsula. On August 7th, 1915, he was in a trench which was being heavily bombed by the enemy. He picked up two live bombs and threw them back at the enemy at great risk to his own life, and continued throwing bombs, although himself wounded, thereby saving a portion of the trench which it was important to hold. On August 8th, at the same place, Pte. Keysor successfully bombed the enemy out of a position from which a temporary mastery over his own trench had been obtained, and was again wounded. Although marked for hospital he declined to leave, and volunteered to throw bombs for another company which had lost its bomb-throwers. He continued to bomb the enemy till the situation was relieved."

No. 18105 Pte. J. WHITE (WEISS), 6th King's Own Royal Lancs. Regiment.

"During an attempt to cross the river Diala (Mesopotamia) on March 7th, 1917, he saw the two pontoons ahead of him come under machine-gun fire, with disastrous results. When his own pontoon had reached mid-stream, with every man except himself either dead or wounded, finding that he was unable to control the pontoon, Pte. White promptly tied a telephone wire to the pontoon and towed it to the shore, thereby saving an officer's life and bringing to land the rifles and equipment of the other men in the boat, who were either dead or dying."

Captain ROBERT GEE, M.C., 2nd Royal Fusiliers.

"For most conspicuous bravery, initiative and determination when an attack by a strong enemy force pierced our line south-west of Cambrai on November 30th, 1917, and captured a brigade headquarters and ammunition dump. Captain Gee, finding himself a prisoner, killed one of the enemy with his spiked stick, and succeeded in escaping. He then organised a party of the Brigade Staff, with which he attacked the enemy fiercely, closely followed and supported by two companies of infantry. By his own personal bravery and prompt action he, aided by his orderlies, cleared the locality. Capt. Gee established a defensive flank on the outskirts of the village, then finding that an enemy machine gun was still in action, with a revolver in each hand, and followed by one man, he rushed and captured the gun, killing eight of the crew. At this time he was wounded, but refused to have the wound dressed until he was satisfied that the defence was organised."

As has been pointed out in dealing with the subject of Casualties, the full total of Honours and Distinctions gained cannot be ascertained with certainty, although every copy of the *London Gazette* with its record of awards published since the beginning of the War has been carefully scrutinised.

The number of five Jewish V.C.'s compares favourably with the total of 578 awarded among the six million men on active service. A large proportion of the D.S.O.'s, M.C.'s and M.M.'s were won by deeds of personal gallantry in the field, and Jews of all branches of the Forces are included in the lists. For detailed records of many of these deeds of heroism, see pp. 127 to 156.

JEWISH UNITS.* Early in October 1914, a movement was inaugurated in London to raise a battalion consisting entirely of Jews. The War Office approved of the idea and granted facilities for this proposal to be carried into effect. Public meetings were held, and recruiting was opened in the East End of London and other parts of the country on the lines of the " Pals " units, which had been so successful in some of the provincial cities. After a short time, however, the movement was abandoned owing to lack of support. Nothing further was heard of this proposal until the subject of the recruitment of Russian Jews was raised in 1917.

On the initiative of Mr. (later Lieut.) V. Jabotinsky, the War Office authorised the formation of a battalion in which Russian Jews could serve together, arrangements being made for Jewish observances to be maintained while the men were on service. A number of Jewish soldiers already serving were allowed to transfer to this battalion, which became the 38th Royal Fusiliers, under the command of Lieut.-Col. J. H. Patterson, D.S.O., of " Zion Mule Corps " fame (see below), and was officially gazetted as a unit of the British Army on August 24th, 1917.

* See Articles by V. Jabotinsky and H. Wolfensohn, pp. 59 to 67.

It was subsequently decided by the War Office to send these soldiers to help in the fighting in Palestine. This greatly stimulated recruiting, and the battalion was soon over strength, which led to the formation of the 39th battalion, under the command of Lieut.-Col. E. Margolin, D.S.O., who had previously served with the Australian forces. Under the presidency of the Rt. Hon. Lord Rothschild, a Regimental Care and Comforts' Fund was formed in London, with Mr. M. J. Landa as Hon. Sec., and various Committees administered the Fund in the interest of the Jewish soldiers.

Recruiting was also carried out in the United States for the Jewish battalions. About 2,000 men inspired by Zionist ideals came to England for this purpose, and they formed the greater part of the 40th battalion, which was organised early in 1918 under the command of Lieut.-Col. F. D. Samuel, D.S.O., recently transferred from the 3rd London Regiment, which had taken part in the battles on the Western front. In all, there were 6,500 men belonging to the three battalions of the Royal Fusiliers, and the 38th and 39th reached Palestine in time to take part in the final campaign of Field Marshal Viscount Allenby in September 1918. These battalions were placed on the right of the advance in the Jordan Valley, and were included in the praise awarded by the victorious Commander-in-Chief, in his dispatch upon the battle : " I would bring to notice the good fighting qualities shown by the newer units. These include . . . . . 38th and 39th (Jewish) Battalions of the Royal Fusiliers." Several officers obtained the M.C., a number of N.C.O.s and men received the Military Medal, and the battalions received many mentions in Despatches. A special cap badge in the form of a *Menorah* (The Temple Candelabra) with the Hebrew word *Kadima* (eastward) underneath was adopted by the War Office for these units, but, owing to the early cessation of hostilities, it was not distributed in time among the units then in Egypt and Palestine. (See Plate 102.)

At the time of the Armistice, there were some 2,000 men in England belonging to these battalions who were popularly known as the " Judeans." They were in training at the Depot at Saltash, Cornwall, under the command of Lieut.-Col. J. S. Miller, D.S.O., who had risen

JEWISH CHAPLAINS

from the ranks of the Guards to be a Staff Officer of an Irish Division, the second in command being Major W. Schonfield, T.D., 19th London Regiment. In Palestine itself, a battalion was raised from among the local Jewish inhabitants in which practically only Hebrew was spoken, and this unit of the Royal Fusiliers remained on duty after the war had concluded. (For nominal rolls of the "Judeans" see pp. 254 to 285; photographs will be found in different parts of the book. See Index.)

The only other specifically Jewish unit to be instituted took its rise in Egypt,* where some 700 men were recruited early in 1915 among Egyptian Jews and refugees from Palestine to serve as a unit of the Royal Army Service Corps. These men were known as the Zion Mule Corps and were commanded by Lieut.-Col. J. H. Patterson, D.S.O. They rendered valuable service in taking up supplies and ammunition to the forces engaged in the Dardanelles expedition, and wore on their caps the badge of the "Shield of David," the first unit in the British Army, apart from the Jewish Chaplains, to wear this emblem. Their history is recorded in detail in the book written by their Commanding Officer called "With the Zionists in Gallipoli." They lost several men in action, won a number of distinctions, and were highly commended for their services by Gen. Sir Ian Hamilton. At the close of the Dardanelles expedition early in 1916 the Corps was disbanded. (For nominal roll, see p. 512.)

JEWISH CHAPLAINS. As already mentioned, there were, prior to the outbreak of hostilities, about one thousand Jews in the Forces, and the Rev. Michael Adler, of the Central Synagogue, London, held a commission as Territorial Chaplain. From August, 1914, until January, 1915, Mr. Adler was in charge of religious work both in the United Kingdom and by correspondence with the men at the front. He organised the areas in the United Kingdom under the local Jewish Ministers, so that regular services could be held with Jewish soldiers under training. An abridged form of the Prayer Book was prepared and was accepted by the War Office. This book was later enlarged, under the editorship of the Chief Rabbi, and about 110,000 copies were printed and distributed. With the consent of the War Office, Mr.

* The unit owes its origin to the energy of the Chief Rabbi of Alexandria, Professor R. della Pergola, Dr. Lattis Bey, Messrs. E. Suares and J. de Picciotto Bey.

Adler paid a visit to the troops at the front in January, 1915, while the Rev. S. Lipson took charge of the work at home. He was thus the first Jewish Chaplain to be attached to a British Army on active service and discharged the duties of a Senior Chaplain on the Western Front until July, 1918.* As the area occupied by the British Army grew larger, the establishment of Jewish Chaplains abroad increased, until, during the last months of the war, there was a Chaplain for each of the five Army areas and three at the Bases—Boulogne, Etaples and Rouen—in addition to the Australian Chaplain who was attached to the Australian Corps.

The first Chaplain to follow Mr. Adler to France was the Rev. V. G. Simmons, and at brief intervals the work was continued in different parts of the front by the Revs. A. Barnett (later Senior Chaplain in succession to Mr. Adler), L. Morris, B. B. Lieberman, E. M. Levy, J. L. Geffen, D. Hirsch, I. Brodie, H. L. Price, N. Levine, and H. P. Silverman. Rev. D. I. Freedman, Minister of the Perth Congregation, Western Australia, served with the Army in Gallipoli and Egypt prior to coming to France in July, 1916. In 1918 he was succeeded by Rev. J. Danglow from St. Kilda, Victoria, who remained on duty with the Australians until the end of the war. In other parts of the war area the Rev. M. Gollop served in Salonica, and the Revs. L. Morris (transferred from France) and Walter Levin were with the troops in Italy. Mr. Levin afterwards proceeded to Egypt and Palestine, keeping in close touch with the Jewish units of the Royal Fusiliers in those countries. Attached to the Egyptian Expeditionary Force were the Revs. S. Grajewsky and I. Frankenthal, while the Rev. L. A. Falk, C.F., accompanied the 38th Battalion of the Royal Fusiliers to Palestine.

There were two Chaplains with the South African Jewish soldiers. In the fighting in German West Africa, the Rev. E. Lyons was attached to General Botha's troops and the Rev. I. Levinson served as Chaplain in the prolonged struggle against General Von Lettow-Vorbeck in East

* See story of Mr. Adler's "Experiences on the Western Front," with map, page 33.

Africa. Rabbi F. L. Cohen was the Senior Chaplain to the forces in the Australian Commonwealth, and Rabbi Dr. H. Abramowitz occupied the same position in Canada.

In England, the Rev. S. Lipson became Senior Chaplain, and the Rev. N. Goldston was appointed Chaplain to the troops in the Southern Command, whilst the Rev. V. G. Simmons, on returning from France, took charge of the Aldershot area. A number of officiating clergymen were appointed on the recommendation of the Jewish War Services Committee, and carried on their religious ministrations to the troops in the United Kingdom. The following gentlemen acted as Officiating Clergymen: Rev. Dr. J. Abelson, the late Rev. M. Abrahams, Rev. A. Cohen, Rev. B. I. Cohen, Rev. S. Frampton, Rev. L. Geffen, Rev. H. Goodman, Rev. A. A. Green, Rev. A. Gudansky, Rev. H. Jerevitch, Rev. W. Levin, Rev. E. M. Levy, Mr. D. L. Lipson, Rev. B. Paletz, Rev. E. P. Phillips, Rev. J. Phillips, Rev. H. Shandel, the late Rev. D. Wasserzug, and Rev. L. Wolfe. (See photograph of a number of Officiating Clergymen, Plate 201.)

In connexion with this work, mention should be made of the literature published under the editorship of the Chief Rabbi, which was freely distributed to the troops both at home and abroad. The following books were included in these publications, in addition to the Soldiers' Prayer Book :—

A Book of Jewish Thoughts, of which about 60,000 were distributed, including a special issue for the United States Jewish Welfare Board.

The Jewish Version of the Book of Psalms, from the American translation of the Bible.

A History of the Jews. By Paul Goodman.

Prayers for Trench and Base. By Captain B. L. Q. Henriques of the Tank Corps. In addition, the Rev. Prof. Dr. H. Gollancz circulated his version of *The Foundation of Religious Fear*, of which many thousands were issued.

The Rev. Michael Adler was awarded the D.S.O., and twice mentioned in Despatches, whilst the Revs. A. Barnett, M. Gollop and

S. Grajewsky were mentioned in Despatches, and the Rev. S. Lipson mentioned in Home Despatches:

HOSPITAL WORK. In addition to a large number of Jewish doctors and nurses serving with the Forces, special attention was devoted by Jews in this country to the establishment of Hospitals.

THE BEECH HOUSE MILITARY HOSPITAL. This was organised by the officers and members of the West Hampstead Division of the British Red Cross Society at The Avenue, Brondesbury, London, N.W., immediately after war was declared, and about 1,560 cases were treated until May, 1919, when the hospital was closed.

Beech House was mainly staffed by voluntary Jewish workers, who for two years conducted the work of the Hospital without the aid of any Government grant.

Dr. M. A. Dutch acted as Commandant, Mrs. Edith Marsden, R.R.C., was the matron, and the organisation and secretarial work were under the direction of Mrs. Elizabeth Davidson, M.B.E. The Matron, the sister-in-charge—Miss McDermott—and one V.A.D.—Mrs. Edith Abrahams—received the R.R.C., Mrs. Davidson was awarded the M.B.E., and seven members of the staff were "mentioned" for devotion to duty. Portraits of a number of the workers appear on Plate 68.

THE MOTE AUXILIARY MILITARY HOSPITAL, MAIDSTONE. This Hospital was presented to the War Office by Sir Marcus Samuel, Bart., and Lady Samuel acted as Commandant. It was opened in September 1914, and continued its activities till December 1918, during which period 445 seriously wounded non-commissioned officers were admitted. Sir Marcus and Lady Samuel bore the whole expense of maintenance and equipment, including an operating theatre, recreation room, motor ambulance, etc.,and received the cordial thanks of the War Office, Lady Samuel being mentioned in Home Despatches for her excellent work. A short time before the war, Sir Marcus presented an operating theatre and Röntgen Rays Installation to the West Kent General Hospital, Maidstone, where considerable numbers of wounded were tended.

In Lancashire, Mr. and Mrs. Walter Beer* established, at their own expense, the Bradstones Auxiliary Hospital at West Derby, over 600 patients passing through the institution, whilst Mr. John Howard presented for a similar purpose a Convalescent Home he had erected near Brighton. The " David L. Jacobs " Holiday Home at Broadstairs was also used as a Hospital throughout the whole period of the war.

TUDOR HOUSE MILITARY HOSPITAL. The only hospital which was intended exclusively for the use of Jewish soldiers was that established at Tudor House, Hampstead Heath, by Mrs. Bischoffsheim. It was opened in October, 1918, and received a large number of patients until the middle of 1919. Miss Janie Joseph, B.R.C.S., V.A.D,, London 76, was appointed Commandant and was decorated with the order of the M.B.E. in recognition of her valuable services. Dr. A. Gaster, M.D., and Dr. L. Lowenthal were the medical officers, and almost the whole of the nursing staff was constituted by Jewish ladies. The Hospital was visited by Her Majesty the Queen, who warmly commended the work carried on at the institution. (See illustrations, Plates 71 and 72.)

Large numbers of Jews were engaged in Red Cross work, and rose to prominent positions in this organisation. Major Arthur C. Abrahams, C.B.E., was an Administrator of the British Red Cross Society throughout the War at its Headquarters at Boulogne.

JEWISH WAR SERVICES COMMITTEE. During the first year of the war the administrative work in Great Britain on behalf of Jewish soldiers was carried on by the Chaplains and the Visitation Committee of the United Synagogue. But many questions having arisen concerning specifically Jewish needs a new Committee was formed at the end of 1915 at the request of the War Office. This was called the Central Jewish Recruiting Committee, and its headquarters were at the offices of Messrs. N. M. Rothschild & Sons, New Court, London.

The growth in the number of recruits and the general development

* Mrs. Beer was awarded the O.B.E. for her services.

of the work in connexion with the Jewish men in the Forces led to one representative Committee being established, in June 1916, under the name of the Jewish War Services Committee, which dealt with all matters of military interest to Jews, including the registration and enlistment of friendly aliens, and the nomination of Chaplains and officiating clergymen. It also kept records and supervised all religious ministrations to the troops both at home and abroad.

Mr. E. Sebag Montefiore, C.B.E., was the Chairman, Major Lionel de Rothschild, M.P., O.B.E., Vice-Chairman, and Mr. S. Stephany, Honorary Secretary. Major W. Schonfield, T.D., was appointed Officer-in-Charge of Administration, while the Chaplains' Department was in the hands of the Rev. S. Lipson, Senior Chaplain to the Forces. This Committee continued its useful labours until the end of 1919.

A branch of the Jewish War Services Committee was formed at Calcutta in order to supervise all matters concerning the welfare of Jewish soldiers in India and Burmah. The Rev. E. M. D. Cohen, of the "Magen David" Synagogue, acted as President, and Lieut. Herbert Loewe was the Supervising Officer. Every assistance was rendered by Army Headquarters to enable men to have leave for the Festivals and to receive the necessary religious ministrations, in spite of the wide area in which the troops were distributed.

Similar work was carried on by a Committee in Bombay; and other centres, where Jewish soldiers were permitted to assemble for Divine Service and the observance of their sacred days, were at Karachi, Bangalore, Cochin, Rangoon, Poona and Sialkot.

A small Jewish periodical called "Dabar B'Itto" ("A Word in Season") was published for the use of the troops, and also an English version of the Passover Evening Ritual, both of which emanated from the pen of Lieut. Loewe, and were circulated among the soldiers. It is calculated that there were about 350 Jews on active service in India belonging to all branches of the Forces, exclusive of the members of the native communities who held commissions or served in the ranks of the Indian Army. Among the latter was included a considerable number of the young men of the Bombay community, some of whom served in East Africa and Mesopotamia. A special unit of the St. John Ambulance Brigade was formed and received the name of No. 3 District Bombay Corps (Jewish Division). An almost complete list of the Bombay Jews who were on duty during the war is printed on page 595.

OTHER JEWISH AGENCIES. In the early days of the war it was realised that the needs of the Jewish soldier and his relatives with regard to questions of Allowances and Pensions would require special attention. Particularly was this so in cases where the English language was not thoroughly understood. Under the auspices of the United Synagogue, an office was opened in 1914 at the Jewish Institute, Mulberry Street, London, where the Revs. A. A. Green and B. N. Michelson were regularly in attendance to deal with applications from dependants. Many thousands of cases passed through their hands and they were enabled to afford valuable assistance to a very large number of soldiers and their relations. The official departments of the War Office dealing with claims, as well as the Regimental Paymasters, were in constant touch with this Committee in settlement of all financial matters that arose, and in addition, the Bureau conducted correspondence on behalf of relatives, with men serving in all parts of the world, traced missing soldiers, recovered effects, secured pensions, and looked after the welfare of widows and orphans. At the conclusion of the armistice claims for demobilisation and their presentation in proper form to the War Office also entailed a considerable amount of labour.

Similar work was carried on in other large cities—Liverpool, Manchester, Leeds and Glasgow—where the local Jewish Ministers, who were usually at the same time acting as Officiating Clergymen to the troops, attended to the needs of the Jewish men and their families. In Leeds, Mr. L. Rosenberg was very active both in recruiting and the care of soldiers and their dependants, and was the recipient of a personal presentation from about 500 Leeds Jewish soldiers in recognition of their appreciation of his labours. Through his efforts about 3,000 men were recruited in the Leeds area.

Early in 1916 there was formed the Jewish Naval and Military

Association with its premises at the West Central Men's Club, 113a, Tottenham Court Road, London, the most active members of which were Mrs. Brighten, Messrs. B. Mocatta, M. Harris, J. M. Ansell and H. Franks. The Association provided a number of beds and an excellent canteen, together with other conveniences of a temporary rest house. Thousands of soldiers of all denominations benefited by this most admirable work until May 1919. It was officially attached to the Y.M.C.A. as its Jewish Branch.

In the general work of the Y.M.C.A., both at home and abroad, English Jews took an active interest, considerable sums being raised both in Australia and the United Kingdom, and the cost of several Huts being contributed. The members of the Central Synagogue, London, subscribed for one Hut, and in recognition of the liberal spirit in which the Y.M.C.A. catered for the needs of the Jewish soldier, especially in allowing the regular use of their buildings for Jewish services, the Jews of the East End of London erected a Hut in the Mile End Road which proved very welcome to local soldiers.

In 1918 a Hut was opened in connexion with the Australian Branch of the Y.M.C.A. in the Strand, next to Australia House. The inauguration ceremony was performed by Lieut.-Gen. Sir John Monash, K.C.B., and the Hut served as a very useful centre for many months. A crowded Passover Evening Service was held in March 1919. The Hut was under the charge of Mr. L. P. Jacobs and Lieut. Harold Boas, the latter acting as the official representative of the Australian Y.M.C.A. in England and France. (See book, " With the Jewish Soldier of the Australian Imperial Force," by Lieut. Boas.)

When the war was drawing to a close, the desirability of co-ordinating the various agencies for the welfare of Jewish soldiers was recognised, and the Central Council for Jewish soldiers was opened at 167, Strand, London, W.C., under the chairmanship of Sir Robert Waley Cohen, K.B.E. This body proved very helpful, especially in assisting demobilised soldiers to return to work. It continued in active operation till September 1920.

SPECIAL CONSTABULARY. A considerable number of Jews ineligible for the Fighting Forces were enrolled in the Special Constabulary. In London, Mr. E. N. J. Jacobson was appointed to the Headquarter Staff and Chairman of the Discipline Board, being awarded the C.B.E. for his services.

THE JEW IN THE FIGHTING FORCES.

As already indicated, there was no section of the war area in which Jews were not found doing their duty.

ROYAL NAVY. On sea they took part in every action of importance and served in every kind of vessel afloat and under the sea. The nominal rolls on page 189 show that the number of Jews in the Royal Navy was comparatively small. This fact is easily explained. In the first place, the sea-port towns contained small Jewish congregations, and further there was a rule of the Admiralty that " persons born in His Majesty's Dominions of foreign parentage were ineligible for entry into the Naval Services, whether their parents were naturalised British subjects or not." This regulation excluded that class of Jewish recruit which poured by its thousands into all branches of the Army, and only a small number of men of foreign birth succeeded in eluding the official rule and performed valuable service with the senior branch of H.M. Forces.

In the famous naval operations for the blocking of Zeebrugge and Ostend, which took place in the Spring of 1918, several Jewish officers and men took part, and Lieut.-Commander R. Saunders was one of the seven officers who obtained the D.S.O. in recognition of gallantry on that occasion.

In the fighting around the British Isles, in the Heligoland Bight, the Battle of Jutland, where a Jewish Warrant Officer was yeoman of Signals on board the Admiral's Flagship, in the Battle of Coronel, the Battle of Falkland Islands, and in the Adriatic Sea, representatives of Jewry are known to have had a share. When H.M.S. " Highflyer " sank the raider " Kaiser Wilhelm der Grosse " off the coast of West Africa in August, 1914, a Jewish sailor was among the crew, whilst on board the cruiser H.M.S. " Glasgow," which alone escaped the disaster at Coronel, there was an old Stepney Jewish School lad who had been in the Navy prior to the war. One of the gunners of the "Saucy Arethusa" which led the way to victory in the Heligoland Bight on August 28th, 1914, was an ex-Jews' Orphan Asylum pupil, and a master gunner on H.M.S. "Lion" was transferred to the Royal Naval Division as Company-Sergeant Major, where he lost his life in the trenches in front of Havrincourt Wood (Bapaume sector). A Jewish Midshipman went down with H.M.S. "Monmouth" at Coronel, and in the attack on the town of Akaba, in the Red Sea, early in 1915, a Jewish warrant officer, of H.M.S. "Minerva," was in charge of one of the landing parties that took the town. In the landing at the Dardanelles, Admiral de Robeck, in the course of his despatch describing the stirring fight in Gallipoli on April 25th and 26th, 1915, recommended for gallant service in action a young sailor from the Jewish School in Stepney, London, E., by name Lewis Jacobs, belonging to H.M.S. "Lord Nelson." The Admiral reported that "Jacobs took his boat into 'V' Beach unaided, after all the remainder of the crew and the troops were killed or wounded. When last seen Jacobs was standing and endeavouring to pole the cutter to the shore. Whilst thus employed he was killed." On board the Australian cruiser H.M.S. "Sydney," when it destroyed the German raider, the "Emden," off the Cocos Islands in November, 1914, were two Jewish sailors; and in the Homeric struggle when the torpedo boat H.M.S. "Broke," together with the "Swift," defeated the enemy flotilla in the Downs in April, 1917, Jewish sailors were in action. A number of Jews served with the famous Dover patrol and with the Royal Marines at Antwerp and elsewhere, whilst the Royal Naval Volunteer Reserve and the Royal Naval Air Service included many representatives. Others were engaged in submarine work, mine-laying and mine-sweeping.

ON LAND. The operations on land likewise saw Jews in every part of the war area. When General Botha conquered German South-West Africa, in his army there was a considerable number of Jews from Cape Colony, Natal, Rhodesia and the Transvaal. A still larger force of Jews followed him to East Africa, whilst in the South African Brigade, which won such fame on the Western Front, many officers and men were included. In Cape Town, a unit was formed called the Cape Peninsular Garrison Regiment, which included sixty-eight Jewish members (see names in S. African lists marked C.P.G.R., pp. 568 to 579). Canadian Jews worthily played their part with the Canadian Expeditionary Forces, and Jews from New Zealand were at the capture of Samoa and in the Palestinian and French campaigns. The splendid record of the enlistment of Australian Jews, where, like in South Africa, compulsory service was never introduced, is already mentioned on page 3. In Egypt, Palestine, Gallipoli and France, Australian Jews won renown. The following statistics and record of achievements are taken from the book compiled by Lieut. Harold Boas (see p. 18), pages 50 and 51.

Comparative Statistics.

		Per cent.
Number of Jews in Australia	17,287	
Population of Australia	4,940,000	0.35
No. of Jews in A.I.F.	2,000	
No. of enlistments in A.I.F.	416,000	0.48
No. of Jews in Australia	17,287	
No. of Jews in A.I.F.	2,000	11.5
Population of Australia	4,940,000	
Enlistments in A.I.F.	416,000	9.2
No. of Jews in A.I.F.	2,000	
No. of Jews killed	300	15.0
No. of enlistments in A.I.F.	416,000	
No. of A.I.F. killed and missing	58,228	14.0

Officers.

The present records show that 192 commissioned ranks were held by Jews in the Australian Imperial Force, although this is likely to be increased considerably when verification is thoroughly completed. They rank as follows :—

Lieut.-General	1
Lieut.-Colonel	2
Major	24
Captain	50
Lieutenant	108
2nd Lieutenant	7

A large percentage of Jewish men also held non-commissioned rank in the Forces.

Honours.

So far as the Records show at this date, the proportion of honours gained by the Jewish personnel of the A.I.F. exemplifies in another way that their part was well played. Apart from the varied distinctions attained by Lieut.-General Sir John Monash, referred to in his biography, the following honours were gained :—

V.C. (Lieut. L. Keysor)	1
D.S.O.	4
Military O.B.E.	3
M.C.	15
M.C. and Bar	1
M.C. and two Bars	1
D.C.M.	5
M.M.	39
M.M. and Bar	1
M.S.M.	5

and, in addition, 20 officers and men were Mentioned in Despatches.

The highest position held by a Jewish officer throughout the war was occupied by an Australian, Lieut.-General Sir John Monash, G.C.M.G., K.C.B., whose career is set forth in detail on pages 28 to 31. The only other officer to reach the rank of General was Brigadier-Gen.

JEWISH HONOURS

H. J. Seligman, C.M.G., D.S.O., who was a regular officer attached to the Royal Artillery, and went through the war from beginning to end. Many other officers who served in the various campaigns deserve to be mentioned.

Lieut.-Col. E. H. L. Beddington, D.S.O., M.C., who first proceeded to France in August, 1914, as a captain in the 16th (The Queen's) Lancers, took part in all the early fighting and was afterwards appointed Staff Officer to the Fifth Army. Lieut.-Col. C. J. Elkan, D.S.O., of the Royal Irish Fusiliers, was also a regular officer who fought at Mons and later became a well-known Staff Officer, first at one of the bases and later at General Headquarters. Lieut.-Col. J. H. Levey, D.S.O., had originally been in the Regular Army as a private in the Scots Guards and had seen active service in South Africa. At the beginning of the war he was Sergeant-Major to the 3rd Scots Guards. He was given a commission in the Gordon Highlanders, but, before proceeding to his battalion, was appointed Chief Instructor to the Royal Naval Division, which saw active service in the Dardanelles, at Antwerp, and on the Western Front. Colonel Levey became a Commandant of a Corps School in France, was given command of a battalion, the 13th Royal Sussex Regiment, late in 1917, and won the D.S.O. in the battle for the Passchendaele Ridge.

Other officers of similar rank who gained distinction were: Lieut.-Col. H. E. Cohen, D.S.O., of the Australian Artillery; Lieut.-Col. Stanley G. Cohen, who led the 5th King's Liverpools into action; Lieut.-Col. H. J. Solomon, M.C., of the Royal Army Service Corps, who was in charge of the main Base Depot for the supply of the Army in the Field at Havre and later on at Salonica; Lieut.-Col. F. H. Kisch, D.S.O., and Lieut.-Col. R. H. Joseph, D.S.O., in the Royal Engineers; Lieut.-Col. H. Weisberg, D.S.O., of the City of London Yeomanry, who fought in Gallipoli and Palestine; Lieut.-Col. I. M. Heilbron, D.S.O., R.A.S.C., and his brother, Lieut.-Col. E. J. Heilbron, K.O.Y.L.I., attached to the West African Regiment; Lieut.-Col. W. H. Samuel, of the 11th Middlesex Regiment, and Lieut.-Col. C. Beddington, who was in command of the Divisional Mounted Troops of the 20th Division in France. Lieut.-Col. C. S. Myers, Royal Army Medical Corps, was one of the principal medical officers in France engaged on work in connection with nervous diseases and shell-shock, whilst Lieut.-Col. B. E. Myers was in charge of the New Zealand Hospitals in the United Kingdom. Lieut.-Col. R. Q. Henriques commanded the Engineers in the 60th London Division both in France and Palestine. Lieut.-Col. J. Waley Cohen, C.M.G., D.S.O., proceeded to the front with one of the first Territorial battalions to go to France, the 16th London Regiment (Queen's Westminster Rifles), and was later attached to Army Signals, in which service he held various commands, whilst his brother, Lieut.-Col. C. Waley Cohen, C.M.G., C.B.E., Royal Army Service Corps, held an important post in the Salonica Forces. Another example of an officer to rise from the ranks and become a Lieut.-Colonel of a battalion was J. S. Miller, D.S.O., who later was appointed in charge of the Depot of the Jewish Battalions in training in England.

Major Sir Philip Sassoon, Bart., M.P., C.M.G., of the Royal East Kent Yeomanry, proceeded to the Front as Private Military Secretary to the first Field-Marshal of the British Army in France, Lord French, and held the same important office throughout the whole war to Field-Marshal Sir Douglas Haig. Among the men to whom was due the invention of the Tank, which weapon played so important a part in bringing about a successful issue to the war, was Lieut.-Col. Sir Albert G. Stern, K.B.E., C.M.G., a member of the well-known banking firm of Stern Brothers, who has written a book upon the story of the Tank in the War. The first group of Tanks to be sent into action in September, 1916, was painted by the brush of Lieut.-Col. S. J. Solomon, the well-known artist of the Royal Academy. Lieut.-Col. Solomon was sent on a special mission to develop the art of camouflage at the Front, and he spent the whole of the period of the war in this work. He also established a school of instruction for this purpose in London, and published a work called "Strategic Camouflage." Another artist to proceed to France at the invitation of the War Office was Prof. W. Rothenstein, who was commissioned to paint pictures of the war area for the Government.

JEWISH HONOURS

Among the best-known families of Anglo-Jewry to send sons into the war were the Rothschilds, of whom all three sons of Mr. Leopold de Rothschild were on duty. Major Evelyn de Rothschild fell at the head of his men of the Royal Bucks Yeomanry in the campaign in Palestine, and Captain Anthony G. de Rothschild, of the same regiment, was wounded in action at Gallipoli. The Sassoon family contributed ten officers, of whom three won the M.C. The family of Sir Isidore Spielmann, C.M.G., and his relatives who were engaged in the war number forty-one, who were all commissioned officers, and of whom Captain H. L. I. Spielmann, of the Manchester Regiment, was killed in action at Gallipoli; two others fell in France and twelve were wounded. The Beddington family contributed thirty-seven members, and of the sons of Mrs. Arthur Sebag Montefiore all five held commissions. Captain Robert, the eldest, of the Royal East Kent Yeomanry, died of wounds received in action at Gallipoli, and Major Thomas, of the Royal Horse Artillery, won the D.S.O. and M.C. The second son of Sir Marcus Samuel, Bart., Lieut. Gerald Samuel, fell at the battle of Messines in June, 1917, and the elder son, Capt. Walter H. Samuel, gained the M.C. and served as a Staff Officer.

Jewish officers occupied important posts in the administration of the army both at home and abroad, serving as town majors, railway transport officers and interpreters, and were especially helpful in connection with Intelligence work. Officers and men alike won distinction by their gallant conduct in such hard-fought fields as the battles of Flanders and the Somme, in the Dardanelles and in Mesopotamia, and some were among the prisoners at the fall of Kut. Large numbers were met by the chaplains in the Expeditionary Forces in Italy and on the Salonica Front. Others were present at the capture of Baghdad, whilst in Palestine, in addition to the men in the Jewish Royal Fusilier units, there was a considerable body of Jewish soldiers in the 60th London Division who were at the taking of Jerusalem. A Jewish Palestinian, Captain A. Aaronson, won the D.S.O. for organising a spy system which proved of the utmost value to the British Intelligence Department in the campaign against the Turks. In the lesser operations of the British Army Jews were also to be found. As an illustration of this, one may mention the daring march of General Dunsterville's small force from Baghdad to Baku in 1917. This force held Baku for a short time, when it was almost overwhelmed by the enemy and obliged to evacuate the city. Among the survivors of this exploit were Jewish Sergeants in the Worcester and R. West Kent Regiments and two men of the Gloucester Regiment. Jewish regulars belonging to the South Wales Borderers co-operated with the Japanese Army at the taking of Tsing-tau, and in the Armoured Car Battery lent to the Emir Feisul in the Hedjaz, were two Jewish drivers who accompanied the Arab army in its northward advance to Palestine. A Jewish Sergeant was in charge of one of the Locker-Lampson armoured cars in their adventures in Russia and subsequently in Mesopotamia, and in the fighting against the Senoussi in Egypt South African Jews participated.

It is a striking fact, as already mentioned, that the large majority of Jews engaged on active service belonged to the fighting units of the Army, such as the Infantry, Artillery, Tanks, Machine Gun Units, and the special Brigades of the Royal Engineers who were in charge of the gas operations. In the Administrative Departments they appear to have been comparatively few in number. In the Royal Army Medical Corps there was a considerable number of Jewish doctors, several of whom were killed, and most of the rank and file are known to have acted as stretcher-bearers on the battlefields and performed extremely good work under the most dangerous conditions. Attached to the Medical Staff of the Second Army in France, and afterwards in Italy, was Major M. Coplans, D.S.O., Royal Army Medical Corps, whilst Lieut.-Col. H. Lightstone, D.S.O., Royal Army Medical Corps, was in charge of the important work of evacuating the wounded from the front areas during the whole Somme battles, July to October, 1916.

Aviation. The air fighting which led to the wonderful development of the Royal Flying Corps, afterwards called the Royal Air Force, attracted a large number of Jewish young men, many of whom gained distinction as aviators. In the first list published of the awards of the

Distinguished Flying Cross the names of Captain D. C. Bauer and Lieut. G. F. Hyams were included, and Major J. Kemper, M.B.E., who had risen from the ranks, was given charge of a large aircraft depot near one of the bases. Captain Desmond Tuck was attached to the French Flying Corps in the Salonica area, where he won the Croix de Guerre. In the first raid made upon a German aerodrome, Major R. L. Marix took part and won the D.S.O., and Captain J. I. Barnato flew one of the aeroplanes that dropped bombs on the city of Constantinople —feats which, in the early days of flying, created a great sensation. Among the rank and file was included a large number of Jewish tailors and other workmen who were engaged in preparing the different parts of the aeroplanes and in other departments of the R.A.F. (See also details of the awards of the D.F.C., p. 151.)

The extracts from the official documents and the lists of honours set forth in this book—no less than the sad Roll of the Glorious Dead—will fill out this brief story of the achievement of British Jewry in the Great War, constituting a record of which we have reason to be truly proud. By this record of patriotism and sacrifice, British Jewry will be judged in the years to come, and there need be no fear as to the verdict that will be pronounced. For the Jew of the British Empire has risen to the height of his opportunity during the greatest crisis in the history of England, and side by side with his compatriots of all other creeds and nationalities has materially contributed to the victory of the cause of the Allies.

Record of
Lieut.-Gen. Sir John Monash,
G.C.M.G., K.C.B., V.D.

THE story of General Monash's rapid rise to the highest commanding position in the Australian Forces will go down to posterity as one of the most remarkable developments of military genius. He is the first civilian soldier to have secured this coveted position. More than this, he is the first Jewish soldier to have risen to the rank of Lieut.-General.

This could never have been accomplished had it not been for his sound business and organising ability, supplemented by his military knowledge. His strength lay in these two attributes, and he leaves the army as one of its most successful and most popular officers.

Born in Melbourne on June 27th, 1865, of the family of an old Australian colonist, Sir John Monash was educated at Scotch College, Melbourne, of which he was Dux in the year 1881, also taking in the same year the Matriculation Exhibition in Mathematics, and first-class honours in Modern Languages.

In March 1882, entering the Melbourne University, he took the Arts Course and obtained his degree of B.A. Continuing, he took the engineering course, qualifying for the B.C.E. degree, and later secured his M.C.E. degree. In the final year of his study in engineering at the University, he secured the "Argus" Scholarship in Engineering with first-class honours.

For the time being this terminated his studies, and from 1885 until 1892 he practiced as a civil engineer. First of all he officiated as Assistant Engineer at the construction of the new Prince's Bridge, Melbourne, and was later employed in a similar capacity on the Falls Railway Bridge, and the Queen's Bridge, Melbourne. In 1887 he was appointed Engineer for the construction of the Outer Circle Railway, Melbourne, continuing as such until its completion in 1891. Following this, he acted in the capacity of Assistant Engineer to the Melbourne Harbour Trust. He continued to fulfil his duties in this connexion until 1893, when he commenced in private practice as a consulting engineer. During the last two years of his connexion with the Melbourne Harbour Trust, however, Sir John took the Law Course at the Melbourne University, obtaining the LL.B. degree.

He practiced as consulting Engineer in general railway, bridge and hydraulic engineering from 1893 until 1914, taking up in 1900 as a speciality, Reinforced Concrete Construction, which he introduced into the Southern Australian States, executing works for the Government and the municipalities to the value of over a million pounds sterling. During this period he was much in demand as an expert witness in litigation connected with drainage and water supply questions, also in actions for infringement of letters patent and in arbitration cases, frequently acting also as arbitrator.

He was admitted as Associate Member of the Institution of Civil Engineers, London, in 1895, and in 1902 was admitted to full membership of this institution.

He became a member of the Council of the Victorian Institute of Engineers in 1905 and officiated as President during 1911, 12 and 13.

Sir John Monash's business career accounts very largely for his success as a soldier. It is only possible to give a brief résumé of the many and varied positions which he has held.

In 1884, he entered the Victoria Militia, receiving a commission as Lieutenant in the Victorian Garrison Artillery in the year 1887, rising through all grades to the command of the North Melbourne Artillery in 1901.

In 1908 he was appointed to the Intelligence Corps as Lieut.-Colonel and promoted Colonel in command of 13th Infantry Brigade in 1913. In 1901 he won the first Gold Medal for military writings in the Commonwealth Journal.

At the outbreak of the European war, he was appointed Chief Censor for Australia, and was later appointed to command the Fourth Infantry Brigade of the A.I.F. He was in command of the second Australian convoy of 22 ships, landing in Egypt in January 1915. He commanded the Fourth

Brigade at the Landing at Gallipoli on April 25th, 1915, "Monash Valley" being named after him. He continued in command of the Fourth Brigade throughout the whole period of the occupation of Gallipoli, and was present at the evacuation. Subsequently he served with his Brigade in the Canal Zone, Egypt, until May 1916, and then took them to France.

In July 1916, being appointed to command the Third Australian Division, with the rank of Major-General, he proceeded to England, where he organised, equipped and trained this Division, taking them to France in November 1916, and he served there until the cessation of hostilities. He took part in the battle of Messines, June 1917, and the three phases of the third battle of Ypres, July to November 1917.

When in April 1918, General Sir William Birdwood was placed in charge of the Fifth Army, Sir John Monash was appointed to command the Australian Corps, with the rank of Lieut.-General. At this time, four of the Australian Divisions held the line near Villers-Bretonneux, blocking the way of the enemy to Amiens. In vain the enemy sought to break down the defence of the Australians, and in July the victory at Hamel was achieved which was the prelude to the great attack of August 8th. At Hamel, Sir John experimented with a series of new tactics in which Tanks were largely employed and achieved marked success.

When the great counter-attack of August 8th was commenced, Sir John was in charge of the Australian forces which broke through the German lines together with the British and Canadian Divisions on the Amiens front. His advance was wonderfully rapid. Péronne and Mont St. Quentin were taken by a brilliant charge of the Australian soldiers and for over 100 days the advance continued, Sir John leading his forces from victory to victory until the Armistice was declared. On his return to London, Sir John led the Australians through the streets of London and was everywhere acclaimed. He has written a graphic account of his battles in his book called "The Australian Victories in France in 1918." A famous critic wrote of this work, that, "it is a particularly shrewd and able book which will be read as eagerly for its real human interest as for its undoubted technical and historical value."

Lt.-Gen. Sir John Monash was created C.B. in September 1915, and

K.C.B. on January 1st, 1919, being seven times mentioned in despatches. He was created Grand Officer, Ordre de le Couronne (Belgium) on the 18th October, 1918. On November 18th, 1918, he was created Grand Officer, Legion d'Honneur, France. During November 1918 he was awarded the Belgian Croix de guerre, and also the French Croix de guerre avec Palme. In December 1918, he was appointed Director-General of Demobilisation and Repatriation, A.I.F., and took up his quarters in London. On 1st January, 1919, he was created G.C.M.G. In January 1919, the President of the United States of America conferred upon him the American Distinguished Service Medal. The London degree of D.C.L., Oxford and Cambridge were conferred on him in June and July 1919. On his return to Australia, he was received with every mark of honour and fêted as one of Australia's most distinguished soldiers.

RECORD OF WAR SERVICE OF SCHOOLS AND CLUBS

	ON ACTIVE SERVICE.		DIED.	
	Officers.	Men.	Officers.	Men.
Bayswater Jewish School, London, W.		141		9
Borough Jewish Schools, London, S.E.	3	160	No record kept.	
Grove House Club, Manchester		274		13
Hayes Industrial School for Boys	1	139	—	14
Hutchinson House Club, London, E.	19	328	2	18
Hebrew Schools, Liverpool	12	250	1	31
Hebrew Schools, Birmingham	6	258	1	23
Jewish House, Cheltenham	40	—	8	—
Jewish House, Clifton	132	6	24	—
Jewish Lads' Brigade	Cannot be ascertained		39	525
Jews' Hospital and Orphan Asylum, Norwood	4	135	1	14
Jewish Working Men's Club, Manchester	11	210	—	5
Jews' School, Manchester		464		21
Jewish Lads' Club, Notting Hill, London, W.	24	159	6	14
Jews' Free School, London, E.	19	1210	1	78
Stepney Jewish Lads' Club, London, E.	16	417	6	35
The Maccabeans	74	6	10	3
The Old Boys' Club, London, E.	10	115	11	
Victoria Working Boys' Club, London, E.		435	13	18
Westminster Jews' Free School, London, W.	7	290	16	

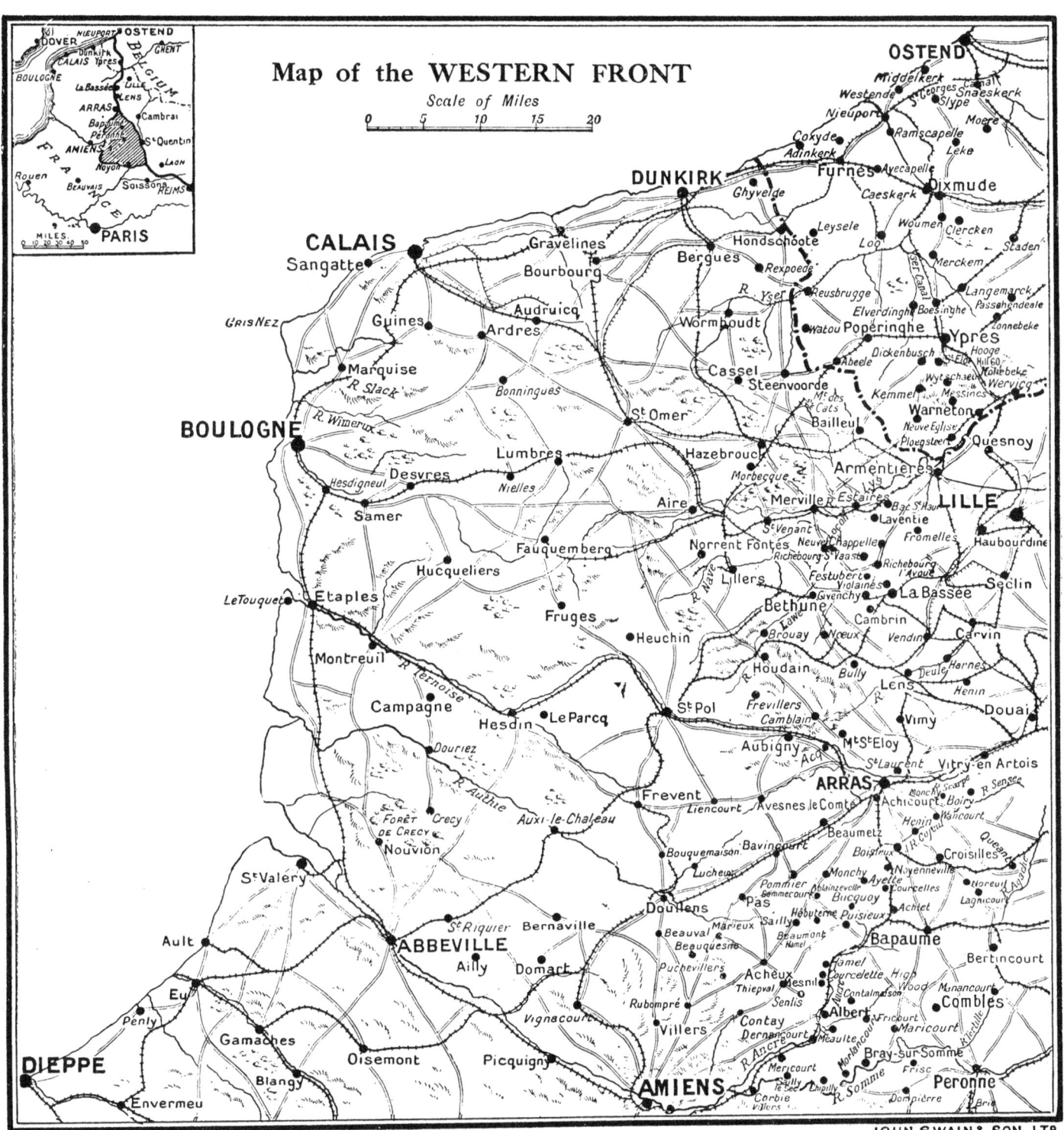

EXPERIENCES OF A JEWISH CHAPLAIN ON THE WESTERN FRONT (1915—1918).*

By Rev. MICHAEL ADLER, D.S.O.

DURING the recent Great War, for the first time in Anglo-Jewish history, Jewish Chaplains formed part of the British Army on active service. The demand for Jewish Chaplains to live at the front with their men became apparent in the early days of the War, in order to minister to "the large Jewish Community serving in the field," as Field-Marshal Lord French described them in one of his despatches. My work at home as a Territorial Chaplain soon proved to me that opportunities for valuable service in the war area would present themselves, if the necessary arrangements for proceeding abroad could be made. I therefore suggested that I should transfer my activities to France. This raised many difficulties, as the authorities at the War Office could find no precedent for a Jewish Chaplain being attached to an Army in the Field. Through the kind offices of the late Sir Charles Henry, Bart., M.P., however, it was decided that I should be allowed to pay a visit to the troops in order to ascertain whether there was any scope for religious work among the Jewish soldiers scattered in all parts of the front. The Chaplain-General, the Right Rev. Bishop Taylor-Smith, C.V.O., had previously shown his interest in my work by attending one of the Chanucah Military Services, and in many other ways, and now proved himself most helpful. When the question of my Chaplain's badge was considered, he readily approved of my proposal that the " Magen David " should be adopted in place of the customary Chaplains' badge.

Upon landing at Havre in January, 1915, the spirit of cordial helpfulness which marked our future relations throughout displayed itself immediately, when the Principal Chaplain of the British Expeditionary Force, the Rev. Dr. J. M. Simms, C.M.G., met me at the dock and accompanied me to report my arrival at Base Headquarters.

On board the ship I had met Lieut. Ernest Polack, who was thus the first Jewish officer on active service whom I encountered, and it was with great sorrow that in July, 1916, I learnt of his death in action.

* Reprinted from *The Jewish Guardian*.

On emerging from Base Headquarters, a soldier saluted me and asked if I was the Jewish Chaplain—as he had noticed the " Magen David " I was wearing. This badge, from the first hour of my landing, thus proved itself of the utmost value in drawing the attention of our men—and I later on had one fixed on the bonnet of my car.

A brief look round Havre with its hospitals, depots and camps scattered over a large area soon brought me face to face with what was going to prove a serious difficulty unless rapidly overcome. It was evident that the transport question had to be solved without delay, as I could not cover the ground by using the local trams or jumping on a motor lorry. With the Army authorities I could do nothing at this stage, but on the second day of my arrival, the friendly relations between the Y.M.C.A. and myself began, which continued both towards myself and all the other Chaplains during the whole period of the War. Mr. Pilkington, in charge of the office at Havre, lent me a small Ford car driven by a young curate, with whom I had many a pleasant conversation. The first service I held in France was in a Y.M.C.A. Hut at Harfleur Reinforcement Camp on Friday evening, January 29th, which date, I believe, also marks the opening of the first Y.M.C.A. hut in this great camp. Nominal rolls of Jews in the area had been obtained, notices were published in Base Orders, and invitations sent to all officers and men in Havre, with successful results.

My second service was held in the local Synagogue at Havre, the community taking considerable interest in this first gathering of Jewish soldiers. It was naturally part of my programme to get into close touch with the French Jews wherever possible, as I could not give personal attention to the Bases and the Front Areas single-handed. It was necessary to make arrangements with the local French communities to look after the religious interests of the Jewish soldiers in their areas and to arrange for burials, and this I proceeded to do in Havre, Rouen, Paris, Versailles and Boulogne. I must especially allude to the keen personal interest taken in the local British-Jewish soldiers by the authorities of the Rouen Congregation, headed by their President, M. Fernand Lang. Both to myself and to the other Chaplains stationed in Rouen they on all occasions extended the utmost kindness and helpful assistance. In Boulogne, the Rev. M. Weill, and in Havre, the venerable Rev. M. Cahen, proved themselves warm-hearted friends of the Jewish soldier.

On my first arrival at Rouen a surprise awaited me, as the Principal Chaplain showed me a letter from the Army Council in which it was laid down that I " was not to venture beyond the lines of communication on the chance of meeting with the adherents of my Faith." Dr. Simms at once expressed his agreement that this would limit my powers of usefulness to a considerable degree, and, through his kind intervention, I shortly afterwards received permission to visit G.H.Q., then at St. Omer, and made the acquaintance of the principal authorities there. The foundations of my future work were thus successfully laid.

During my first visit to the B.E.F. I went to Paris, where I came into close contact with the late Grand Rabbin M. Alfred Lévy, as I had a scheme to provide the Jewish soldiers in France with *Motzas* for the coming Passover. It was arranged that a local Jewish society should take the matter in hand as they were doing the same for the French Army. The expenses were raised in England, and I supplied a list of some 1,200 men to whom the food was to be forwarded. Unfortunately, the French Committee did not carry out my instructions, but sent the supplies to the main depot at Havre in a number of large crates. There they remained for a considerable time unopened, as I learnt to my annoyance later, when I received an official letter about three months after Passover, asking me what I wished to be done with the special food that was awaiting distribution ! No further attempt was made to supply *Motzas* to soldiers in the Field until after the Armistice, when the Chief Rabbi was able to forward large supplies to France.

On my return to London, I presented a report to the War Office, which resulted in my being informed that I could return to the Front for as long a period as necessary. I paid a second round of visits to nearly all the same areas, before taking up my residence in St. Omer, near G.H.Q., in a billet situated in a narrow street close to the Mairie, which was known as " Burlington Arcade " or the " Dardanelles." From here I organised a series of services along the whole front, which, in those days, extended from Ypres in in the north to Bethune in the south, and was occupied by the First and Second Armies, and also kept in touch with the widely-scattered camps and medical units of the forward districts.

With the help of Dr. Simms and G.H.Q., a motor car was placed at my disposal, which was certainly an exceptional privilege, but, naturally, was indispensable for my work over the huge area under my charge.

At the end of June, 1915, the Chief Rabbi paid a visit to France, when he had an interview with Sir John French, then in command of the Army, and dined at the house of Lieut.-General Sir Neville Macready, the Adjutant-General. From both of these distinguished soldiers, we heard words of commendation of the services rendered in the battle-field by men of the Jewish faith. After a service in the Soldiers' Club at St. Omer, I escorted Dr. Hertz to the Front areas where we visited Ypres a month after the great battle in which the enemy had first used gas in their attacks, and also to the stricken area south of Bethune, where we held a service in the square of Mazingarbe, well known to all soldiers who have been in the line in the Loos and Vermelles sectors. As the shells of the enemy were exploding quite near to us, I was very glad when the car took us safely out of this dangerous zone.

On our way to visit Ypres, we halted for lunch at a Casualty Clearing Station. This was situated in the famous Trappist Monastery of Mont-des-Cats, which stands at the top of a hill behind Bailleul, prominent for many miles round. From this building one could see clearly the ruins of Ypres and the whole line as far as Bethune. As we entered the gates and sent in our names through the sentry, we were met by Lieut.-Col. W. P. Peake, R.A.M.C., and the Chaplain, the Rev. Mr. Tate. We were received most hospitably, and the Chaplain, who had been trained in a Scottish school of theology, on learning that we were Jews, addressed us in Hebrew words of welcome. As I afterwards lived at this Monastery for some months, I learnt that Mr. Tate possessed a sound knowledge of the Hebrew language. I remember on the first visit that we examined the admission and discharge books of the C.C.S. to see if there were any Jewish patients there, and found a man by the name of Cohen entered as a member of the Church of England. We visited him and learnt that he was not a Jew, much to the surprise of Dr. Hertz. I had already come across several soldiers bearing the names of Cohen, Levy, Isaacs and Solomons who were Christians—a fact which put me on my guard against accepting any man as a Jew unless I was absolutely certain that he belonged to the Faith. A day's motor run from St. Omer took us to Rouen where the Chief Rabbi preached to a large congregation, after which we were entertained by the President, M. Lang. The visit closed with a service in Boulogne.

Arrangements were made in November, 1917, for the Chief Rabbi to pay a second visit to the Front; but, owing to unforeseen circumstances, this trip had to be abandoned at the last moment.

My work now developed by my deciding to leave G.H.Q. in order to live at the Mont-des-Cats Monastery—much nearer to the trenches. I wrote to Col. Peake asking him if he could find accommodation for me among his Mess, and he replied that "he would gladly do so if I would follow the doctrine of the Rechabites of the Bible." I replied that I was willing to do this as far as the custom of dwelling in a tent was concerned, but I could not bind myself to the other law of the Rechabites in regard to beverages. Until the Battle of Loos in September, I lived in a tent in the monks' garden, using as my office the bedroom of the Colonel—whose personal kindness to me, and to the Rev. V. G. Simmons, C.F., who succeeded me, will never be forgotten. My stay at this centre for many months was full of interest, for it was here that, at the invitation of the Colonel, I delivered two addresses to the officers and men of the unit at the Sunday afternoon services. I also held services here, in a room full of crucifixes, for the Jewish soldiers of Canadian and Imperial Divisions encamped round the hill.

A series of talks which I gave to the men of the C.C.S., dealing with the religion and history of the Jews, created considerable interest. I had already delivered similar addresses in Y.M.C.A. huts in Rouen, and later, when at Achiet-le-Grand, six lectures to crowded audiences were successfully given.

From Mont-des-Cats I was able to supervise the whole of the front line of the two Armies which were then in France, with occasional runs to the Bases when necessity arose. Shortly after I had taken up my residence in this forward area, I received a letter from a Chaplain, the Rev. Mr. Williams, sending me a nominal roll of Jews of the 17th Division to which he was attached. This act of courtesy led me to visit him in his billet at Reninghelst, near Poperinghe, where I lunched with a group of Chaplains of different denominations, and was asked to recite the Hebrew "Grace at Meals." Here I learnt that no objection would be taken at any Divisional Headquarters to my receiving these lists of Jews. These returns were therefore obtained two or three times a year, a privilege which was conceded to Jewish Chaplains alone, and of enormous help in the organisation of our work. Before a service could be conducted, arrangements were made through the Divisional Headquarters for the time and place, which would be any day of the week and any hour convenient for the men. Secret information was given concerning the location of troops and when they were not actually in the front line on duty. At G.H.Q. I was allowed to visit the O.B. (Order of

Battle) department and learn all necessary for my work. Staff officers were amused at seeing me write down the information about troops and movements in Hebrew, and the hope was expressed that no German understanding this language would capture my note-books. Orders were issued about the services in the Divisional Orders and a postcard was sent by me to every officer and man giving him details of the meetings, and these cards were distributed by the Divisional Headquarters. Notices of the services were placarded in Y.M.C.A. huts, and thus attracted the attention of stray soldiers. Their devotion to Judaism was exemplified by the eagerness of the men to attend these services under the most difficult conditions and frequently after long journeys, and the form of service I originated was based upon the Soldiers' Prayer Book, a work which was very greatly treasured by the men. Of this book, which I compiled in August, 1914, and the Chief Rabbi enlarged later, over 100,000 copies have been printed, and it has been used by the Army in all parts of the world. It has also served as a model for the American Military Prayer Book. A part of our service was in English, with familiar passages in Hebrew, as we desired to enlist the interest of those men who had no knowledge of the sacred tongue. Many a soldier whom I personally asked to come to the services informed me that he did not wish to attend, as he knew no Hebrew; but, upon my urging him not to absent himself, most of them presented themselves and never failed to come a second time. It was interesting to observe that the knowledge of Hebrew seemed better among soldiers from the large provincial cities than among London men—a difference which one could easily detect during the course of a service, and especially in the singing of hymns like *Adon Olam* and the *Yigdal*, which formed part of every ritual.

We held these services in all kinds of places—often in the open air and in Y.M.C.A. or Church Army huts; sometimes in barns or in ruined buildings destroyed by the enemy's shells, or in billets set apart for our convenience. On one occasion during the Somme battles of 1916, when visiting a R.A.F. balloon unit in Fricourt Wood, the C.O. ordered us to shelter in an old German dug-out as it was not safe where we were standing. In the village of Morlancourt, near Albert, an old disused church was utilised by me for a service; many a village town hall (or Mairie) witnessed a Jewish gathering for worship; on one occasion the 56th London Division Headquarters ordered a marquee to be specially erected for a service in the middle of a square of a destroyed village (Achicourt) near Arras. Many a time I would visit a group of men, however small, in some out-of-the-way place, much to their gratification, and a friendly chat and smoke always concluded with a brief religious service in which the men earnestly joined. Sometimes the orderly room would be clearly for my visit to the Jewish men of the unit, and, on one occasion, an adjutant who did not know what was happening walked suddenly into his orderly room to find, much to his astonishment, a Jewish Chaplain and twelve men engaged in prayer! I once met a party of fifty newly-arrived Jewish soldiers belonging to the 1/1st Bucks. Battalion—to which Lieut. D. Fallon, M.C., was attached—near a village called Bouzincourt, outside Albert. As the place was being bombarded, all troops were ordered into the open, and we found a vacant space in a cornfield where a square was formed and a brief service held. It was a very solemn occasion as it was the first time these men had seen and heard a shell explode, and they were due to begin their work in the trenches that same evening.

I well remember the surprise of the Mother Superior of the Hospice at Locre—famous for its battles in 1918 and for the grave of Major Willie Redmond being there—when I asked permission to use the central hall for a Jewish service after the Church of England and the Roman Catholics had already held meetings there, and we saw the nuns peeping at our gatherings as the Jewish boys lustily sang *Adon Olam* and the National Anthem.

Each soldier I met, whether singly or at a gathering, gave me his details and the address of his family, and a letter was written to his home, which led to a most interesting correspondence. My heavy post-bag at times was the standing joke of the local Army Post Office and of my Mess, and many hours were spent at the desk in keeping in touch by letter, both with the soldiers and their anxious relatives. The address, "Jewish Chaplain, France," was sufficient to find me, and one intelligent youth directed his letter to the "Commander-in-Chief of the Jewish Army in France!" I was also given the title of "O.C. Jews."

The Army authorities were of the utmost assistance in arranging our services, and from time to time I received letters from Christian Chaplains and from Officers Commanding Units in which Jewish soldiers were found asking me to arrange services for their men. I had often to travel long distances for these meetings, but all labour in connection with their organisation was more than amply repaid by the large number of men thus being enabled to meet other Jewish lads and to take part in some form of Jewish religious service under the peculiar conditions in which they lived.

It soon became evident that a second Chaplain was required, and it was with great pleasure that I learnt that, on the suggestion of the late Mr. Albert Jessel, K.C., the Rev. V. G. Simmons, of the West London Synagogue, had agreed to join me, and in August, 1915, he came to France and began his work in Boulogne. Later on, when I removed in April, 1916, to the Third Army, Mr. Simmons took my place at Mont-des-Cats, and his work at the Base was carried on by the third Chaplain, the Rev. Arthur Barnett, who ultimately in 1918 succeeded me as Senior Chaplain at the Front.

Everyone who has been on active service knows how precious the word " leave " was to the man longing to return home if only for a few days. This desire was emphasised on the part of the Jewish soldiers at the approach of the Sacred Festivals, and I therefore had an interview with the Assistant Adjutant General at G.H.Q. to consider if an order could be published to allow Jews to go home to observe at least the Day of Atonement. It soon became evident that there were insuperable obstacles in the way, but G.H.Q. issued a letter upon the subject to the B.E.F. in August, 1915, to the following effect: " The Jewish Chaplain has put forward a request that any Jewish soldier who in the ordinary course be granted leave of absence during the next two months may be permitted to select days including 17th and 18th September (the Jewish ' Day of Atonement '). I should be glad if you will give this matter such consideration as may be possible."

A similar letter was issued for Passover, 1916, but the results were far from satisfactory as there were so many difficulties in making suitable arrangements to set the Jewish soldiers free, and no further action was taken except to grant facilities to organise services in the field on all sacred days.

As I was alone in the Front areas during the New Year and Day of Atonement of 1915 and desired to arrange as many services as possible for the men in the lines, on the first day of the New Year I had a large gathering in a Soldiers' Club in St. Omer, and on the second day I met a crowd of Canadian soldiers and men from English divisions of the Second Army in a tent belonging to the 3rd Canadian Field Ambulance in "Aldershot" Camp close to Neuve Eglise, a short distance from " Plugstreet " Wood. The Padre of the unit made all preparations for our meeting, the officers' mess tent being cleared for the occasion. After the service, a Canadian staff-sergeant provided lunch for all the worshippers, many of whom had come from long distances. One man in the Belgian Armoured Cars had motored from Dunkirk, 40 miles away. I remember a Canadian soldier saying to me after the service how delighted he was to see a Jewish Chaplain so close to the line conducting religious services for the men, as he was under the impression that we lived at the Base, where alone Jewish soldiers received our ministrations. To these services I took a Scroll of the Law in a small box which served as an Ark, lent to me by my French friends from the Boulogne Synagogue. My orderly, Cpl. R. Friedlander, who was with me throughout the whole of my work and rendered invaluable service, made a white curtain for the Ark, with a Hebrew inscription upon it, and the ceremony of the Reading of the Law was made doubly impressive in the special circumstances in which the services were held.

Having thus allotted the days of the New Year to the areas of General Headquarters and the Second Army, I was anxious to meet the men of the First Army round Bethune for the Day of Atonement. I learnt that the 47th London Division, containing some 200 Jews, were in the line in this sector, and I was also aware that within a few days after the Day of Atonement (the 18th September) a great battle was to be fought. I therefore journeyed south to the Bethune area and decided to hold this service in the mining village of Nœux-les-Mines, which would enable all local troops in the front lines, some four miles away, to attend. This visit to Nœux-les-Mines to arrange the service with Divisional Headquarters will always be impressed upon my memory because it was on this occasion that I paid a visit with the Colonel of the 19th London Regiment to the front line trenches, opposite the Double Crassier of Loos, where the battle took place a week later. It was a very thrilling experience, especially to one who had not been through it before. The enemy's artillery was disagreeably active that night as we passed through the ruined village of Maroc and inspected the trenches of the London men, and I was greatly relieved when, at about two in the morning, I reached my billet in the forward village of Les Brebis and went to bed in a miner's cottage.

My first service on Yom Kippur in the Mairie of Nœux-les Mines was most inspiring. Men marched in fully-equipped straight from the lines, special orders having been issued to set them free, and we numbered about 200 congregants. Many of the officers and men who were present at this service, which lasted three hours, fell in action on the following Saturday when the Army " went over the top," and the knowledge that a fierce struggle was shortly about to take place seemed to add an air of solemnity to our prayers which no words of mine can adequately depict. The men of the 8th Division were too far away to join us on the Fast Day, and I therefore wired to the Divisional H.Q. that I would hold a service for these soldiers on Sunday, September 26th. To this, I received a reply as follows:—" Regret proposed service next Sunday impossible." It was the second day of the great battle of Loos.

In the Second Army area, near Poperinghe, Atonement Services were conducted by Staff Sergeant J. Canton-Cohen, R.A.M.C. (killed in action July, 1916), in a marquee lent by his O.C.

Whilst the battle of Loos was in progress I visited the Field Ambulances, Dressing Stations and the Casualty Clearing Stations in the area and saw for the first time the dreadful sight of thousands of wounded and dying men being brought in. In Bethune, I met Field-Marshal Viscount French on the third day of the battle, in a hospital, and also at my C.C.S. which he visited. I frequently acted as interpreter with German wounded, several of whom were Jews, and found many opportunities to be of help in the work of attending to the patients who poured into the three C.C.S.s at Lillers. I also called at every Battalion Headquarters to learn what casualties had occurred among our men, and met troops who had been relieved from the line to hear, at first hand, graphic descriptions of the fight.

In the orderly room of a Highland battalion the Sergeant-Major informed me that one of his Jewish men had been most helpful during the advance into the enemy trenches owing to his knowledge of German. I saw this soldier, who was a Russian, who had enlisted in Glasgow, and spoke very imperfect English. He narrated how his services were requisitioned by his friends to call into the German dug-outs to demand surrender, and his shout to the enemy was " Kim Arois " (Yiddish, " Come out")—and the Germans understood him!

During the week between Atonement Day and the battle, I decided to change my headquarters in the north and left Mont-des-Cats. I attached myself to No. 9 C.C.S. in Lillers in order to be near the area where active operations were in progress. I was still in sole charge of the whole Army front, having frequently to run up to the districts of Poperinghe and Bailleul, principally for funerals. Messages to officiate at funerals often led to long journeys being undertaken. Once, whilst living at Mont-des-Cats, I was called to attend a funeral of an Australian Medical Officer attached to a British regiment who had died of wounds in Abbeville, a distance of four hours of fast motoring each way. Again, shortly after the Third Army had taken over its new area in the Albert district, a Jewish officer was killed and I received a telegram calling for my services. I set out on the six hours' journey and unfortunately left my pass behind. In those days, in 1915, the Arras sector was occupied by the French Army, which thus lay between the First and Third British Armies, and I had considerable difficulty in passing the French sentries, being able to show only the official telegram as a reason of my journey. I ultimately reached the Field Ambulance in Millencourt where the body lay, and conducted one of the first Jewish funerals in the Somme district, which later grew so numerous owing to the severe fighting in this district.

It is interesting to note that the first funeral at which I officiated in France was in Rouen, where I buried a Jewish Zouave from Algiers—in the absence of the local French Rabbi on active service as a stretcher-bearer (Brancardier) and Chaplain near Verdun. The second funeral was that of a German prisoner, a young law student from Westphalia, who was buried at Le Treport. This was in May, 1915. I discovered in the same cemetery the grave of a Jewish soldier whom I had met at a service a month before in Havre. A cross had been erected over this grave, and upon my pointing this out to the Senior Medical Officer of the district, he gave permission, a very unusual proceeding, for the body to be disinterred in order that it should be placed in a row allotted to Jews. The London boy and the German soldier were thus laid next to each other. It had been my original intention to obtain the concession of a special plot or row of graves for Jews, and in some cemeteries, as at Rouen, Hazebrouck, Bailleul and Etaples, I was able to arrange this with the authorities. As a rule, however, we were obliged to bury our dead side by side with their comrades. The question of a suitable memorial at once arose, and at Le Treport a local Staff Sergeant of the Royal Engineers very kindly made a wooden " Magen David " to be placed over the British soldier's grave—which he declined to do for the German, agreeing only to set up a simple board with an inscription. At Rouen and Paris-Plage, my orderly had made memorials with the word " Shalom " inserted within the triangles, and erected them over graves we discovered there; but it soon became evident that this work would have to be carried out officially on a larger scale. When I first visited Lillers, I called at the Headquarters of the Graves Registration Commission, which then stationed in a chateau near the approach of the village. I saw Major, now Major-General, Sir Fabian Ware, and discussed with him the best form of Jewish memorial. At my suggestion he obtained the approval of the authorities for a standard " Magen David " to be erected over all Jewish graves, both English and German, and I had a branding-iron made in England with the word " Shalom " on it, which was used. Photographs of these memorials were readily given by the Graves Registration authorities to the next-of-kin of the fallen, especially of graves in cemeteries at some distance behind the line. In many cases, the units to which the deceased belonged made their own pattern of the "Shield of David" or erected a plain board, thus avoiding the design of the cross. This form of personal attention to their former comrades was but one piece of evidence as to the general regard and goodwill with which Jewish soldiers were treated by those side by side with whom they lived and fought and died.

I have frequently been asked whether there were any signs of anti-Semitism in the life of the great British Army, and I say without the slightest hesitation, that whatever indication of ill-feeling there was towards the Jew was so small as to be entirely negligible. The Christian soldier was warmly attached to his Jewish " pal," and the relations between the soldiers of all denominations were remarkably cordial. I received frequent letters from Christian soldiers telling me about their Jewish friends in most affectionate terms, and, almost without exception, Jewish men spoke very highly of their treatment by their brothers-in-arms. I can bring the same testimony with regard to the relations of the Jewish Chaplains to their colleagues of all other faiths. We received every possible form of assistance, and in response to requests frequently put forward, I had a short form of the Jewish burial service printed and widely distributed among the Christian Chaplains who, in cases of extreme urgency, buried Jewish soldiers and recited the Jewish Burial Service in English. Each case of this kind was reported at once to me, and many of the Chaplains themselves made the rough form of the " Shield of David " in order to mark a Jewish grave. The Jewish soldiers often reported to me acts of kindness performed towards them by Chaplains in battalions or hospitals, and no instance of attempted proselytising ever came to my notice. An officer once narrated to me how he lay seriously wounded in a C.C.S., and the Padre sought to comfort him by telling him, with the best intention in the world, that, if he died, the Jewish Service would be read over his body, if I was not within reach ! When the Chief Rabbi sent out his excellent books on Jewish literature, they were in great demand among the Christian Chaplains, to whom, as to other Christian officers, there is no doubt they came as a new revelation of Jewish ideals and Jewish teachings. Both at the bases and up the line, we were often invited to meetings of Chaplains and treated with every courtesy. The Revs. E. M. Levy and L. Geffen delivered addresses to their brother Chaplains on aspects of Jewish life. On one occasion, Major-General Mercer of the 3rd Canadian Division summoned a gathering of his Chaplains to discuss their respective duties. Though I was not officially attached to the Division, as I was working in the area, I received an invitation and spent a pleasant hour in the General's billet, where he presided over the meeting. General Mercer took the greatest interest in his Jewish Canadians, once stopping me in a village street to ask about our arrangements for certain services. It was with great regret that I heard of his death shortly afterwards in the Ypres salient.

The general conduct of the Jewish soldier won for him an excellent record throughout the Army, and tended in every way to reflect credit upon the Jewish name. The number of courts-martial which were brought to my notice throughout the war in which Jewish soldiers were involved was agreeably small. Upon four occasions, when men appealed to me for assistance, I engaged the services of Jewish officers in the respective areas who belonged to the legal profession, with satisfactory results. In one case, however, when a R.A.M.C. lad had been rude to his N.C.O. and disobeyed orders, there was no one in the district available, so that I had to act as " prisoner's friend " and did my best to defend him before the officers of the court-martial—I am sorry to say, without the success I had desired. I only heard of one case throughout the whole war of a Jewish soldier being shot for cowardice, and he was entered in his battalion as a member of the Church of England. All other offences with which Jews were charged belonged to the ordinary category of military misdemeanours.

In the early days of the war certain of our men attempted to conceal their identity by not reporting themselves as Jews. Some, whilst remaining Jews, changed their names, as in the classic example of Gunner Leib Kalmanovitch adopting the name of Louis Bonaparte, whilst the name of Smith became a favourite. I was once asked by a Colonel to discover if a certain soldier who had applied for Passover leave was a Jew, as his name was Private McKennell. The man seemed to know very little of Judaism, and I was rather puzzled at his ignorance, when I chanced to ask him where his father lived. "Oh," he replied, "my father, *Olov Ha-sholom* (Hebrew for *Peace be upon him*), is dead." This decided me. One day I met an Australian soldier with the un-Jewish name of McPaul. He was entered as a Jew, and I asked him if he was born in the faith. He was not, he stated, but as he was out of sympathy with Christianity, he had resolved not to attend religious worship. When attesting in Sydney, he had been asked, "What religion do you profess?" He answered, "What religions have you got?" and upon learning that Judaism was officially recognised, he answered, "Then put me down as a Jew!" At a certain service I held, the only man present who wore an "Arba Kanfoth" was entered as a Roman Catholic in his unit. On the whole, however, the number of Jewish soldiers who did not confess their faith publicly was small, so that our records are reliable as to the number of men on active service. The total for all the war areas, including the Labour Companies, is about 50,000.

A real "Chanucah Military Service" was held at Lillers in December, 1915, when we lit the festival candles in the local theatre with a congregation of about a hundred men. After the service we adjourned to a local *estaminet* where the arrangements had been made for a tea party by Regimental-Sergt.-Major R. Harris of the 4th London Regiment, which battalion always included a considerable group of East End boys. During the evening, a R.A.M.C. soldier suggested that a collection should be made on behalf of the distressed Jews in Poland, and the sum of £3 was sent to the Treasurer of the fund, Mr. Leopold de Rothschild.

In the spring of 1916 I came across a large number of Australian troops for the first time. They were drawn up awaiting inspection on their recent arrival from Gallipoli and Egypt, in a village behind Armentieres, where they afterwards took over the line. I was chatting with the two Chaplains of the brigade, when the Commander-in-Chief, Sir Douglas Haig, was seen approaching, attended by his Military Secretary, Sir Philip Sassoon. We three Chaplains stood at the end of the line, and Sir Douglas rode up to us and, shaking hands, asked which denominations we represented. " I am glad to see you working so well together," he said, " as you can help us greatly by teaching the men about the noble cause for which we are fighting."

To return to my wanderings—for I was known in France as the " Wandering Jew "*—I later removed to Beauval—a pretty village near Doullens, where my mess occupied rooms in a stately chateau—in order to be at hand during the coming Somme offensive—preparations for which I saw being made in all directions. Mr. Simmons took over my area in the north, and ministered to the Australian troops before the Rev. D. I. Freedman arrived from the East, where he had been on duty with the forces. I held services for every division which took part in the battle on July 1st, 1916, and the succeeding days, working the area of the Third Army from my centre at Beauval and taking each corps and divisional district in turn. The attack on the line from Foncquevillers to the north of Albert having failed, I left No. 4 C.C.S. as the inflow of wounded had ceased, and transferred my home to No. 21 C.C.S., which bore part of the burden of the heavy casualties of the continuous struggle round Albert. I found a lodging in a small cottage, which consisted of two rooms, in the village of Corbie, the centre of the C.C.S. and the camps of the Albert sector. This billet was a most uncomfortable one, as there was scarcely a whole pane of glass to the room in which I slept and did my work. Every division that marched down to take part in the Somme " push " passed my window day and night, the result being an atmosphere of dust and noise. As each division rested for a night or two on its way to take part in the great battle, in which all except two Divisions in France were engaged, I hastily organised meetings of our men, many of whom gave me messages for their kinsfolk to be sent home in the event of their not returning from the conflict. Here I came into contact for the first time with the South African soldiers who were attached to the 9th (Scottish) Division, and learnt of their wonderful doings in the battle of Delville Wood. I afterwards visited the scene of the fight, and was able to gather some idea of the terrible struggle that raged for months round this wood and the adjacent High Wood, in which large numbers of Jewish soldiers fell.

It was at High Wood that, in September, 1916, the tanks were first used, and I saw the first batch hidden in a wood near Acheux being prepared for the great experiment. I learnt later that the *camouflage* on the tanks had

* I find a note in my Diary recording that in August, 1916, I expended petrol for 1,670 miles.

been painted by Lieutenant-Colonel Solomon J. Solomon, R.A., whom I frequently met whilst he was engaged in his work at the front, utilising his artistic genius in aid of the great cause.

Shortly before the New Year Festival I ascertained that the 60th London Division had arrived in France, and taken over the line to the north of Arras. Each division had its lorries and other transport marked by some design in colour, all numbers being suppressed. Thus the First Division was indicated by the ace of hearts, the Twelfth by the ace of spades, the 56th (London) by an inverted sword, the 34th by a chess-board, the 37th by a golden horse-shoe, the 62nd (Yorkshire) by a pelican, and so on. When on my travels a new sign was observed, inquiries were at once set on foot. One day I saw a bee painted on a cart, and I was told that General Bulfin's 60th Division had arrived from England. I called for a nominal roll, as was customary as soon as a new division came out, and found that there were over 300 Jewish soldiers to be looked after. I therefore decided to remove from the Albert area for a short time, in order to get into close touch with these men and other troops in the district. On arriving at Aubigny, which was the railhead for Arras, the only billet the Town Major could find for me was in an undertaker's shop. After passing through rows of tombstones I reached my bedroom, on the walls of which hung a number of *immortelle* wreaths. " Monsieur will not mind these," explained my polite landlady, " as it is better to see them when one is alive than when dead ! "

I had very frequently to pass through Arras, which was daily under fire, the noble Cathedral and Hotel de Ville having already been laid in ruins. The most exciting visit I paid to this renowned city was in the month of May of that year, from Beauval, when the German line was less than a mile from the railway station. As I was accustomed to do, I had sent a message to the commanding officer of the battalion in which I knew a number of Jewish soldiers were included, asking if I could hold a service for the men. I received a reply that if I came to Arras on a certain morning I would be welcome. Definite instructions were given to me for the journey, as only one road was at all safe by which to enter the city by daylight, as it was under constant observation of the enemy's artillery and his snipers. The last two miles from Dainville to Arras were covered in record time by my driver, who realised the risk we were running. The service was held in a battered building used as a Soldiers' Club, near the ruined Cathedral in the heart of the city, amidst a constant din of guns, as many of our big guns were stationed in the city itself and the enemy replied vigorously. Anxious to see all I could on the occasion of my first visit, I walked to the railway station to find a high barricade of sandbags in front of it, and I was warned to leave as quickly as possible as many casualties had occurred near the station. I continued in touch with the Londoners of the 60th Division until they left in November for Salonica, where they distinguished themselves, both here and subsequently in Palestine.

The services of the New Year of 1916 were held on the First Day in the village of Acq, in the Arras sector, in a crowded cinema—to which places the soldiers gave the name of " Cinema-gogues." On the afternoon of the same day, I took my Ark and Sefer Torah into the car, and, after a two hours' run, met a large body of men belonging to the R.A.F. and local divisions in rest in the middle area near Doullens, where a hangar was lent to us, and a very impressive service was held. On the Second Day, an old barn called " The Empire Theatre," in Senlis, close to Albert, where the battle was still raging, was filled by a congregation drawn from men who had come direct from the trenches and who begged of me to come again on the Day of Atonement. I therefore arranged my first service on Kippur in Acq as on the New Year, and the second in the afternoon in Albert itself, some fifty miles distant. It was on this occasion when I was organising these services that Divisional Headquarters, through the D.A.A.G. of the 14th (Light) Division, suggested a plan which was afterwards carried out on every important holiday, of allotting a number of lorries to each unit, which met the men at a spot immediately behind the trenches and brought them to the services, and so saved them the fatigue of a long tramp. The institution of this scheme led to the numbers of men at our services being largely increased. The Day of Atonement was a busy day for me, for, after the service at Acq, where about 350 men attended in the morning, I made my way to Albert, thus holding the first Jewish service ever conducted within the walls of this city. We were over an hour late in arriving at Albert, as the car had to travel slowly owing to the roads being choked with marching troops and guns. The men, however, were patiently waiting in the cinema, although the city was being heavily shelled at the time. I learnt, to my regret, that the men of the 56th London Division, whom I had hoped would attend our gathering in large numbers, had gone "over the top" near High Wood that same morning; but we still had 300 men who attentively followed the service.

On the same day services were being held in other parts of the front area by my colleagues, the Rev. V. G. Simmons, the Rev. D. I. Freedman, of the Australian Forces, and the Rev. Arthur Barnett, whilst the Rev. L. Morris was active in Etaples and Boulogne. Unquestionably the most striking services which we held were in September and October of the following year, 1917, on the New Year and Day of Atonement, when attendances were remarkably large. Thus, in Poperinghe, near the great battle for the Passchendaele Ridge, the Y.M.C.A. hut in which Mr. Morris held his service was so crowded that many men could not obtain admission. By this time there was a Chaplain in each of the five Army areas and three at the bases.* Moreover, our organisation for getting into touch with the individual men in the scattered units and for obtaining lorries to bring them to the services had been perfected, with the result that at my services in Bapaume over 1,500 men gathered together. In this small town not a single habitable building had remained intact when the enemy evacuated the area in March, 1917. I had entered Bapaume for the first time with Lieut. E. X. Kapp, the cartoonist, four days after the enemy had retreated, after destroying the town. Many of the houses were still burning and we visited the Town Hall, of which two storys still remained standing. The following night this building was blown up by a delayed mine, and a number of people, including the two French Deputies of the town, were killed.

The winter of 1916 found me at Contay, near the Beaumont-Hamel fighting, where my billets in succession were a dark low-roofed apartment in an old farmhouse and the back-room of an *estaminet.* It was here that I was suspected by a zealous Scottish A.P.M. of being a spy, as he did not recognise my badge, and I escaped arrest through the intervention of the village Town Major.

The snow and subsequent thaw of this winter covered the roads and fields in which the camps and C.C.S. were pitched with a troublesome layer of thick mud, and many of the roads which before had been used chiefly for farmers' wagons broke up under the weight of the heavy army traffic. This greatly added to the difficulties of travelling. On one occasion, we left the main road

---

* The number of Chaplains on the Western Front was never adequate, the consequence being that each was allotted an area of far too wide an extent to be thoroughly worked by one Chaplain. In spite of numerous applications to the authorities none of my colleagues had a motor car allotted to him to enable him to journey as often as necessary through the length and breadth of his Army or Base. Some rode long distances on horseback or borrowed a motor ambulance or other conveyance to travel from place to place, whilst the R.A.F. units were especially helpful in lending a car whenever possible.

to make a détour across a narrow track and suddenly the car sank to its axles in a mass of mud, and had to be extricated by the horses of a ploughman near at hand. About January, 1917, the 62nd Division joined my Army and I found a considerable body of Leeds Jews in the ranks. These men took part in the rapid advance which followed upon the retreat of the enemy in March, 1917, and one Sunday during this month I proceeded to the village of Louvencourt to hold a service to find that the Division had suddenly moved off in pursuit. I followed the path of the advance through the ruins of Beaumont-Hamel eastward where the Canadian Railway troops were already laying down the lines in territory which a few days before was in hostile hands. I was able to assemble a number of men and take the service, but naturally the sudden change in the whole military situation disturbed my plans for some time. The arrival in February of the EHN (58th) London Division with its large contingent of Jewish soldiers added considerably to my work, especially as my car happened to break down, and over two weeks elapsed before a new one was supplied. In the meantime, Army H.Q., the R.A.F. and the D.M.S. (Director of Medical Service) lent me conveyances to travel long distances in the performance of my duties.

In the spring of 1917 I returned to the Arras sector in preparation for the battle of Vimy and the Arras struggle, which kept me very busily occupied. The Jewish casualties in this offensive were very severe, and in many a newly-opened cemetery I read the Burial Service over our brave lads who fell. From place to place I journeyed, as summoned by 'phone or wire, for example—upon the same day I officiated in the Arras cemetery, and in the afternoon some fifty miles away at La Chapellette, south of Peronne, which was then the extreme end of the British line. The Feast of Weeks (May 27th) was celebrated by two services, the first in the open field in the captured area at Mercatel on the Arras—Bapaume road, close to a line of old German trenches, the second in a marquee lent by the O.C. of No. 19 C.C.S. at Agnez-les-Duisans, west of Arras. My frequent visits to the areas devastated by the enemy in his retreat proved to me that my services were now needed in those districts east of the Arras-Peronne main road where all sign of human habitation had been destroyed—especially as the Third Army holding the line there included large numbers of our men in London and Leeds divisions and in battalions which contained most Jews like the Royal Fusiliers, Middlesex, Manchesters, Rifle Brigade and King's Royal Rifles. I therefore left my friends at No. 42 C.C.S. in the village of Aubigny where I had been most comfortable and took up my residence amid the tents of No. 49 C.C.S. in an Armstrong hut made of canvas stretched on wood. I remained there, throughout a severe winter, amid the ruins of Achiet-le-Grand, near Bapaume, until the great retreat of March, 1918. It was a new experience living away from any town or village in the open field, but the varied interest of my work made the life very absorbing, as it was continuously full of new developments. Moreover, I was especially fortunate in meeting in the mess of my C.C.S. a body of medical men who extended towards me the utmost cordiality and friendship. Their interest in Judaism and in Jewish history was very keen, and I delivered several lectures upon these subjects—both to officers, nurses and men. It is interesting to put to record that as a rule both my brother Chaplains and I found it most convenient for our work to be attached to medical units, both at the front and at the bases, and found many friends among the doctors and surgeons with whom we lived.

Bapaume was a very useful centre for the Third Army area, which extended from Arras to Peronne, about 50 miles, and the line ran about six miles in front, close to Bullecourt and Havrincourt Wood. Next to the ruined cathedral of Bapaume a building had been patched up to serve as a theatre, called by the Australians who had captured Bapaume, the " Fair Dinkum " Theatre, and I was very gratified on visiting the place to find that an Australian Sergeant was temporarily in charge who was a Jew. He was of the utmost assistance in making arrangements for the service. Special electric lights were fitted up for the Reading Desk, and everything passed off most satisfactorily. The vast congregations included, both on New Year and Atonement Day, a number of American Engineers who had recently been attached to the British Army, a party of Egyptian Jews with a Labour Company, and men from all parts of the Empire. The Shofar was blown by a soldier of the 4th London Regiment, who had been a bugler in the Jewish Lads' Brigade. Lieutenant-Colonel F. D. Samuel read part of the service on Kippur, and the local Town Major served out extra rations for a large number of men.

In the month following these impressive gatherings the whole front line was in action, when General Byng made his surprise attack upon the enemy near Cambrai, and again on November 30th, when we were obliged to surrender part of the captured ground, owing to a counter attack. On the day of the second Cambrai battle I had been called to bury two soldiers, one of whom was a German, in a cemetery at Ytres, near Havrincourt Wood. Large numbers of wounded men were pouring into the C.C.S., including a number of gunners, who reported that hand-to-hand fighting was taking place round the batteries. The noise of the bombardment was deafening, and arrangements were being made for evacuation of the field hospitals, as it was rumoured that the enemy was approaching. I had reached the village of Fins, which was near to the cemetery, when I learnt that the enemy were already on the outskirts of the village of Gouzeaucourt, about three miles away, and I saw the cavalry galloping up to drive back the advancing foe. It was therefore necessary to escape as quickly as possible, and my faithful chauffeur, Cpl. Macintosh, who was with me for three years, sent the car flying along the road home to Achiet-le-Grand. It was a very exciting time, and on reaching Bapaume, which was being heavily shelled, I learnt that a Jewish soldier had been killed the same day whilst standing at the railway station through which I had passed.

In making the arrangements for the services for the High Festivals at Bapaume, an incident occurred which is worth recording. A party of over 100 men from the 4th Infantry Labour Company, Middlesex Regiment, had been brought to the service from their camp a few miles away on the New Year Day, and they reported to me that they had been informed that no permission would be granted for them to attend on Yom Kippur. I accordingly visited their Commanding Officer a few days later and learnt that the report was true, and, in spite of my efforts to obtain leave for the men to attend the service the following week on the Fast Day, I was unsuccessful in moving the Colonel. I suggested that the men might be allowed to work for two Sundays if the Yom Kippur were given to them, and, whilst this offer was being considered, a Canadian Major walked into the hut, who, I was told, was in charge of the Jewish men of the Labour Unit. The decision was placed in his hands, and he informed me that his home was in Montreal. I thereupon asked him if he knew anything about the Jewish observances and the importance of the Fast Day. His reply was that he was a wholesale clothier at home, and that the majority of his workmen were Jews. He therefore strongly urged the Commanding Officer to give way, " else," he added, " he would never hear the end of the trouble."

A feature in the life at the front in which a considerable number of

Jewish soldiers were prominent is to be noted in the Divisional and Army concert parties which gave entertainments for the amusement of the men. The musical talent of the Jewish soldier was fully utilised, and I was present at many performances of very high merit, in which Jewish actors or singers or pianists received the hearty applause of crowded audiences. I also attended boxing competitions in which some of our men did extremely well, and won marked popularity by their fistic prowess.

From the month of December, 1917, to our retreat in March, 1918, the Bapaume sector, in which I lived, received the unwelcome attentions of the enemy airmen night after night, and it was not a pleasant experience to hear bombs exploding around one with no other protection than that afforded by a canvas or tin roof. One night, in my village of Achiet le-Grand, about 40 bombs were dropped, causing many casualties, among them a Jewish driver of the Army Service Corps, whom I had seen the evening before. At the beginning of the month of March an enemy offensive was expected. I held a number of services in the front area which were very well attended, one of them in a recreation shed in the village of Metz-en-Couture—which was in Havrincourt Wood, about 1,500 yards from the front line. It was an exceedingly noisy spot, as many of our " heavies " were hidden in the ruins of the village, and it was difficult to make one's voice heard amidst the continuous din. For Sunday, March 10th, I had arranged a service in Arras; but on the Saturday I received a message from Corps Headquarters to the effect that the service must be postponed. I learnt later that the men were " standing to," expecting the beginning of the offensive. As this did not happen, I was able to hold that service on the 17th March in Arras in the Y.M.C.A. hut, which had been erected on the ruins of the Hotel de Ville. Mr. E. W. Hornung, the novelist, was in charge of the hut, and was very interested in the arrangements I was making for the Passover meetings on March 28th, both here and in the Cinema at Bapaume.

Three days before the 21st, Professor W. Rothenstein, the famous artist, came to stay at my mess. He had previously lived at the C.C.S., where the Rev. H. L. Price resided in the 5th Army, and was engaged in painting scenes of the war area. As I had more than once in the course of my wanderings, especially when searching for graves, visited the old battle areas of the Somme and Ancre, I took the Professor round and pointed out the scenes of famous battles such as Thiepval, High Wood, Delville Wood, the

Butte de Warlencourt, etc., as suitable subjects for his brush. On the day before the great attack which led to our retreat, Professor Rothenstein, as though having some knowledge of what was about to happen, took his portfolio of paintings to G.H.Q. and so was not with us when the retreat began. The same night a piece of shrapnel penetrated the bed which he would have occupied, whilst another fragment pierced the wall of my hut. I was aroused about 5 o'clock in the morning of March 21st by a loud explosion close by. For weeks past the sky had been lit up every night by the flashes of the guns, and one never went to bed without hearing the noise of a bombardment to which one became accustomed. But this time the shells, coming from a few miles away, were exploding all round us, and some fell within the grounds of the two casualty clearing stations which stood close to the railway station at Achiet. No. 45 C.C.S., which was about 50 yards away, suffered 24 casualties in a few minutes, a shell striking a trench in which a large number of men had taken refuge. Fourteen native Indian labourers were killed on the road at the side of our camp. We were all ordered to resort to the dugout which had been constructed for the nurses, and it was one o'clock in the day before we could safely emerge, the shells coming over at regular intervals of about two minutes. We had then no knowledge that we were about to remove or that the enemy had been successful in his advance. On the afternoon of March 21st—so little did we suspect that we were about to be involved in a great retreat—that after tea the Colonel invited me to a game of chess, and we were about to begin when an orderly brought a message to the effect that the enemy had broken through and it was thought advisable to evacuate the C.C.S. at once. The sisters were sent away in lorries as soon as possible, and the wounded were packed off to the Base in a Red Cross train which was still running. The unit was ordered to move off early next morning and general activity prevailed.

The shelling began again in the evening and the enemy airmen hovered around us for many hours. That night we slept crowded together in the dugout. Two R.A.M.C. men were wounded by a bomb dropping in our C.C.S. area.—At this point I should like to give my testimony to the effect that, as a rule, German aviators did not attack British hospitals, but carefully avoided injuring them. One of the cases that came to my knowledge of a deliberate air raid on a hospital was in May, 1918, at the Canadian Hospital in Doullens, where terrible destruction was wrought. I had been summoned to bury a Jewish Sergeant of the U.S.A. infantry, who had died of wounds received during his first tour of instruction in the British trenches. I found the hospital in flames and Doullens being shelled. The cemetery was on the outskirts of the town, and we all wore our tin-hats during the ceremony at the graveside, as we were under continuous shell-fire. In most other cases where C.C.S.'s or hospitals were bombed, it was owing to the proximity of these places to railway lines or dumps or camps. Although the enemy, night after night for about three months, sought to destroy the railway line and the station at the important junction of Achiet, about 100 yards away from our C.C.S., it was extraordinary that, except on the night just mentioned, our C.C.S. was never touched by a bomb, although they fell round us, doing great damage to camps which were close by. Few other cases of wilful bombing of medical units came under my direct notice. I once visited the Rev. L. Morris—who had the Rev. D. Hirsch with him for the customary week's instruction as a new Chaplain—and saw the damage that had been done the night before when bombs had been dropped on their C.C.S. at Remy, outside Poperinghe—Mr. Morris's tent being perforated by pieces of shell. The Rev. E. M. Levy had been present when the hospitals at Etaples were both bombed and attacked by machine-gun fire, and next morning I passed that way and learned full details of this outrage.

About three in the morning of the 22nd of March we were roused and informed that we had to leave immediately, and then began our exodus amid a terrific bombardment, as the enemy was now pressing down the Cambrai-Bapaume road towards the latter town, which they captured two days later and thus prevented me from holding the Passover Service which had been arranged for March 28th. Our first halt was in a field next to Aveluy Wood, immediately outside Albert. We little thought that Albert itself would soon be captured, for the town had been partially rebuilt since the battles of the Autumn of 1916, and many shops were opened. That night I slept in a hut belonging to an Indian Labour Company, and next day was again on the move backwards together with our unit. Part of it marched and the rest travelled with what equipment we could rescue by the few lorries which were allotted to us. The enemy captured Achiet-le-Grand three days after we had left it. Passing through Doullens during the retreat, I saw the cars of Marshal Foch, Field-Marshal Sir Douglas Haig, Mr. Lloyd George and M. Clemenceau outside the Town Hall, when the famous decision was reached to appoint Marshal Foch as Generalissimo of the Allies.

EXPERIENCES OF A CHAPLAIN

The Seder evening found me in a wood near Auxi-le-Château, where I lived in a tent with a few members of the unit who had not become detached. During the meal, which consisted of bully and a few Motzas which I had managed to save from the loss of much of my property, I recited by the light of a candle the Seder Service from the Soldiers' Prayer Book, reading it aloud in English to my brother officers, who were deeply interested at the coincidence of our flight with that of the Exodus from Egypt. Meeting a Jewish soldier next day in Auxi, we observed the Second Night Seder together, with some fragments of Motza that were left, being allowed to stay in the Orderly Room of the unit to which the man belonged. The C.C.S. ultimately settled down in a field outside St. Riquier, near Abbeville, having moved 80 miles from our original home at Achiet nine days before. Our travels from place to place were full of interest and adventure. On the third day the men of the C.C.S. joined us and we were about to set up our camp near a village called Puchevillers, when there arrived some 1,700 wounded men hurriedly brought from the battlefield. It was midnight, and a long row of ambulances filled the sunken road which led to the field where we had halted. Nobody had retired to rest and a huge fire was kindled in order to prepare hot food for the wounded soldiers when a German aeroplane returning from a raid made straight for the flame and hurled five bombs, creating great havoc with one of the bombs which struck the line of ambulances within a few feet of the officers' lines, and near where my car was standing.

Whilst at St. Riquier, I held several services at Abbeville and the district, and I had frequently to journey to the front area where the battle was still swaying, in order to keep in touch with our soldiers whenever possible and to bury those of our men who had fallen. Abbeville itself was bombed again and again, and one Saturday night the Theatre on the Pont Neuf belonging to the Y.M.C.A., in which I held my services, was destroyed. Next morning another room in an adjoining building was made ready for me by the Y.M.C.A. authorities, who were unfailing in their courtesy and friendship.

The American troops were now pouring into the British camps. The 77th Division, consisting largely of Jewish soldiers from New York City, took up its abode in my immediate area for training purposes. The American staff readily accepted my proposal to act as Chaplain to these hundreds of American soldiers who had no Jewish Chaplain with them, and the men themselves welcomed me very warmly. It was a considerable time before any number of Jewish Chaplains from the United States came to France, and, in the meantime, my brother Chaplains and I did what we could to minister to the religious needs of our co-religionists from the States. The last important service I held before I fell ill was in a barn in the village of Pas, north-west of Arras, at which about 150 Americans and 150 British troops, including a group of tall New Zealanders, were assembled. The Americans assured me that the service appealed to them very strongly, and they were especially delighted to be associated with their English Jewish brethren. The relations that sprang up between English and American boys of the same Faith naturally became very cordial. In reply to my letters to the parents of the New York soldiers, I received the most grateful acknowledgments, and a short time afterwards a U.S.A. Chaplain, Rabbi D. Tannenbaum, visited me and began that work of co-operation which bound English and American Chaplains in a common bond of interest.

In the Australian hospital at Abbeville, I one day observed that one of the hut-lines was called Monash Avenue. This led to a friendship with the Colonel, who had once been the Senior Medical Officer of General Sir John Monash's Brigade in Gallipoli. Here I learned of the General's promotion to be G.O.C. Australian Corps, after Sir William Birdwood had been given charge of the Fifth Army, and accordingly visited Sir John in his Headquarters at Bertangles, near Amiens. I had previously made his acquaintance after the victory of the Third Australian Division at Messines in June, 1917, when I had tea with him in Bailleul, and he gave me a map illustrating the whole course of the successful battle. At Bertangles he showed me a copy of the Chief Rabbi's "Jewish Thoughts," where he had marked an extract from the History of Professor Graetz, who, he informed me, was a relative of his family.

It was with the deepest regret that I was obliged to leave France through a breakdown in health in July, 1918, immediately before the final counter-offensive of Marshal Foch which destroyed the power of the enemy. As one of my colleagues remarked, "After I left the Front, all went well!" I knew that in the capable hands of the Rev. A. Barnett, whom I had trained to be my successor, the work of ministering to the spiritual needs of our men would continue to flourish. My principal sources of satisfaction in looking back at my varied war experiences are afforded by two considerations, of which the first is that I found ample opportunities to perform useful work, and the second that the reputation of the Jewish soldier on the Western Front stood very high and reflected the fullest credit upon the good name of Anglo-Jewry.

The Jewish Units in the War.

By V. Jabotinsky.

(Hon. Lieut. in the " Judeans.")

THE Zion Mule Corps was formed in 1915, the 38th Royal Fusiliers (now the " 1st Judeans ") in 1917. The purpose of these attempts to create a nucleus of Jewish troops for service in Palestine was very simple. There was a group of Jewish nationalists who, from the beginning of the war, believed that it would inevitably result in the liberation of Palestine. At the same time, they felt assured that British public opinion would sympathise with the idea of a new Jewish Commonwealth in the Holy Land, and would realise the strategical and political value of Judea for the keepers of the Suez Canal. Discovering therefore a certain harmony of ideals and interests between Great Britain and scattered Israel, they strove to express it in the form of a Jewish Legion fighting, side by side with the British, for the redemption of Palestine. Since Palestine was destined to become again the national home of the Jewish people they wanted Jewish soldiers, officially recognised as such, to shed their blood on her soil for her freedom, and after the victory to assist the British in the defence of law and order within her boundaries.

Such was the aim of the initiators of the Jewish Legion movement; *mutatis mutandis*, such is still their aim in endeavouring to secure the existence of the " Judeans " as a permanent part of the British garrison in Palestine.

The outward history of the Jewish units in the Great War is told elsewhere in this book; I will only add a few features concerning their inner life. Of these features, the most striking was the rather uncommon spectacle of harmonious co-operation of Christians and Jews in a purely Jewish " show." At least a half of our officers (counting all the battalions) were Christians; so were, especially in the beginning, a great many of the N.C.O.'s. I should not like to betray emotion in writing for a publication of a purely military character; let me therefore describe my impression of what these

Christians did for the Jewish Legion by the term which is both the soberest and the highest word of praise: they "played the game," played it in a straight and whole-hearted way.

There was, however, at least one among them who did more than that: Lieutenant-Colonel J. H. Patterson, D.S.O., who commanded, and practically raised, both the Zion Mule Corps and the 38th Royal Fusiliers. With an extraordinary thoroughness of purpose he made our ideals his own; the harmony of British and Jewish war aims became an article of his creed; he kept watch over the Jewish honour, so deeply engaged in the success or failure of the unit, with a noble and keen jealousy of a brother, and he looked after his "boys" like a father. He studied their peculiar psychology, and found a way of treating them which went straight to their hearts. There was no trouble, no misunderstanding in the rank and file which a few simple, quiet words of the "Collonêll" could not settle. And he stood up for them, at the sacrifice of his own career. He fought every battle of his little troop—fought to get them Kosher food and Passover cakes, to secure the promised reward of a special Jewish name and badge, to overcome unfriendly attitudes in some high places, and above all, to make of his men real soldiers. The almost miraculous transformation of unwilling conscripts into cheerful and eager fighters was due, perhaps entirely, to his personal influence. Jewry seldom had such friends among our Christian neighbours; Colonel Patterson's name will be remembered and revered in Palestine for ever.

Another striking figure is Lieutenant-Colonel E. L. Margolin, D.S.O., the actual C.O. of the 1st Judeans in Palestine.* His career is remarkable and romantic. He is a Russian Jew by birth. As a boy he emigrated with his parents to Palestine. There, in the Jewish colony of Rehobot, near Jaffa, he became popular among Jews and Arabs alike as an untiring worker with the plough and a dare-devil on horseback. Legends about the prowess of "Hawâja Nazâr" (the Arab substitute for Eliezer) are still living among Fellaheen of that district, in spite of the fact that their hero left Palestine for Australia some twenty years since. In Australia he lived the life of a "bushman," changing places and professions, but always in the open air, always a hard toiler and a frank sportsman, liked and trusted by all. He joined the Australian militia, where, at the outbreak of the war, he held the rank of a Captain. He was among the first to volunteer for imperial service, and December

* After Colonel Patterson left Palestine, the 38th and 39th Battalions were amalgamated to form the 1st Judeans, with Colonel Margolin in charge.

THE JEWISH UNITS IN THE WAR

1914 found him already in Cairo with his battalion—the 16th Battalion of the A.I.F. He went through the Gallipoli campaign, where he saw the Zion Mule Corps men at work. As a Major, and second in command of the same battalion, he won his D.S.O. and his wound-stripe in France. It was in the autumn of 1917 in a London Military Hospital that he heard of the formation of Jewish infantry battalions and was offered the command of the 39th Royal Fusiliers. The Australian Army released him but reluctantly, and he still wears with pride the Rising Sun badge on his shoulder-straps. Palestinian Jewry received him and his battalion with a double enthusiasm: it was one of her own blood coming back to her forever. Colonel Margolin is a born soldier from tip to toe, both in appearance and mentality, a man of few words, a first-rate organiser.

It would be an unforgivable omission not to mention in this series of personal sketches one who lies buried in the hills of Galilee—Captain Joseph Trumpeldor. His life, if written, would read like a story of a mediæval knight-errant. He was born in the Caucasus, in 1880. He was a lawyer by education. When the Russo-Japanese war broke out in 1904, he was a private in the Russian Army, in the garrison of Port Arthur. There, during the famous siege, he lost his left arm in action; but, when released from hospital, he applied for permission to return to the firing line for fighting service. As he had already two St. George's crosses, permission was granted, and it was in the outer trenches that he, a cripple, won two more before the siege was over. He was the first and, at that time, only Jew granted the rank of officer in the Russian Army. But in 1912–1914 we find him in Palestine in the humble rôle of labourer in a co-operative agricultural colony. His exceptional physical strength, endurance, Spartan love of hardship, fanatical conscientiousness, made of him as good a farm-hand as a soldier. After Turkey's entry into the Great War he was expelled from Palestine to Egypt, and here, in Cairo, he assisted Colonel Patterson in forming the Zion Mule Corps. G.H.Q., in recognition of his military past, granted him, though an alien, an honorary captaincy. He went through the Gallipoli campaign as second in command, and for a time as O.C. of the Zion Mule Corps. He was wounded, but refused to be evacuated. Colonel Patterson and all who knew him bear witness to his cool and mocking fearlessness.

After various unsuccessful efforts to save the Corps from disbandment, or to form a new Jewish unit, Trumpeldor returned to Russia in 1917 and began negotiations with the Kerensky Government with the object of creating a large Jewish Army in free Russia. Assent was given in principle; the idea was of sending some 75,000 to 100,000 Jewish troops to the Caucasus front, to co-operate with the British forces in Palestine and Mesopotamia in crushing the Turk. The Bolshevik revolution destroyed this great scheme, with all the wonderful possibilities it implied.

The last act of Trumpeldor's life was his reappearance in Palestine, at the head of a small force of young Zionist workmen who, for over a month, defended the Jewish colonies of Upper Galilee against hordes of hostile Bedouins. There were neither British nor French troops in that zone—the result of some red-tape dissension on the question of Palestine's boundaries. Here, in a small Jewish hamlet called Tel-Hay—"the Hill of the Living"—Trumpeldor, with six of his friends, was killed in action in March 1920. A Hebrew song, composed shortly afterwards in the fortress-prison of Acre, says: "From Dan to Beersheba, from the Gilead to the Sea, there is no inch of our country but was redeemed by blood. With Jewish blood are sated hill and field and vale. But, from days of yore, never was there shed a purer blood than that of the ploughers of Tel-Hay. Between Ayèlet and Metulla, in a lonely grave, keeps guard on the frontiers of our country a one-armed hero—and ours, ours wilt thou yet be, O Crown of the Hermon."

Of our Anglo-Jewish officers I need not speak. They would not like me to praise them or their fine work in educating and leading their men, but this I may add, that any corps would be proud to possess such a body of officers.

The rank and file of the Judeans presented a real museum of Jewish ethnography. There were men from Russia, England, America, Palestine, Georgia, Bokhara, Argentine, and Morocco. Ninety-two Turkish Jews, prisoners of war in Egypt, were allowed to join. One thousand five hundred volunteers from Salonica applied to be enlisted, with the consent of the Hellenic authorities. The communities of Jewish hillmen from Daghestan (Caucasus) sent emissaries offering all their youth. Two thousand Transylvanian prisoners of war made the same application from Italy.

But the real backbone of the unit was made out of three elements: the "mule-drivers," the "Schneiders," and the Palestinians.

The history of the Zion Mule Corps is a remarkable record of Jewish tenacity and singleness of purpose. Immediately after Turkey's joining the war, the Ottoman authorities in Palestine began to "clear" the country of Zionists. Over 12,000 Jews were expelled and brought to Alexandria. The great majority were old people of the Halukka type—women and children—but there also was a number of able-bodied young men, mostly students and workmen. The refugees were camped in buildings provided by the British authorities. It was in one of these camps that the idea of a Jewish military unit was actually born, in a bare room lighted by a single candle and filled with an eager young crowd. They had listened to a gloomy report by a newly arrived exile: the Turks had closed the Jewish bank, Hebrew signboards had been prohibited, pogrom propaganda was going on freely among the rabble of Jaffa and Haifa. . . . To all this the healthy mind of Palestinian youth, with unerring instinct, found at once a reply—straight, simple, and effective: a Jewish Legion to fight for Palestine.

Then only the real trial began. The proposal was submitted to General Maxwell, G.O.C. Egypt at the time, but his answer was discouraging. Under the Army Act he could not enrol them as fighting troops, nor could he promise to take them to Palestine. But he could employ them as mule-drivers—in the Dardanelles. The disappointment was great. It is natural for civilians, who know nothing about warfare, to sneer at transport service as not sufficiently heroic. General Maxwell's proposal would have been rejected, but for the intervention of two soldiers: Lieutenant-Colonel Patterson, who just about that time had landed in Egypt, and Trumpeldor, who was himself among the exiles. They brought home to the men two essential military truths; first, that the soldier who carries ammunition to the trenches requires no less courage than the soldier who fires the rifle; second, that one can fight for Palestine in Gallipoli just as well as one can fight for England in Flanders. So the Zion Mule Corps was formed. Many Egyptian Jews joined it, but its core consisted of Palestinians. Its record will be found on another page.

Then came the evacuation of Gallipoli, and eventually the Corps was disbanded, in spite of numerous petitions to the contrary submitted by the men themselves. But there was among them a nucleus of die-hards who, though discharged, still clung to their initial purpose: a Jewish legion. Through innumerable vicissitudes and adventures (one was the torpedoing of their transport-ship off Crete) about 150 of them reached London in December 1915 as British soldiers enlisted in Egypt, and about half of them were posted to the 20th London Regiment. Here they found in Lieutenant-Colonel A. Pownall—now a member of the House of Commons—a patient and sympathetic C.O., to whom much of their further progress is due. They formed the " No. 16 Platoon "—a platoon in which ten languages were spoken, and probably the only platoon in the history of the British Army specially mentioned and discussed at a meeting of the Imperial War Cabinet. It was the meeting at which the decision was taken to form a Jewish regiment and to employ "No. 16 Platoon" as a nucleus of instructors for the new unit. The dream of the mule-drivers became a reality.

In the Jewish battalions, especially in the 38th Royal Fusiliers, commanded by their old C.O., Zion Mule Corps men were among the best instructors and section-leaders—and among the bravest too. "This is a ticklish job. I'll want a couple of Zion Mule Corps boys" was a phrase often used when men had to be found for a particularly unpleasant patrol or scout duty.

Socially, they belonged to the most different classes. Students (of the upper forms of the Jaffa College) and workmen have been mentioned before. Among the Egyptians, side by side with boys of good *bourgeois* families, there were quite a few representatives of the "navvy" type, practically unknown to Western Jewry—reckless, rough, troublesome, but splendid military material. The last three words can be applied to the great majority of the mule-drivers.

"Schneiders" (Yiddish for "tailors") was the nickname given to the East End recruits. In the beginning it was used disparagingly; but gradually we felt the sobriquet was losing its mocking sound, and by the time of the Jordan Valley offensive every officer pronounced it with respect. It is time that justice should be done to these men. There hardly ever was a more striking sequence of the renowned systems variously described as "muddling through," or "just missing," or "patchwork"—systems before which a humble foreign observer can only bow in respectful astonishment, but not, I fear, in admiration. At first, when alien Jews tried to enlist at the outbreak of the war, under the impression that the world was going to reform and even Russia was improving, they were rejected *qua* aliens. Later—just when Tzarist Russia had managed again to show its real face hideously tattooed with Jewish blood—the alien Jew in England was descried a shirker because he did not want to join. Proposals to raise a Jewish regiment had also been rejected —when the war was young and popular and enlistment voluntary; but when conscription was introduced, and enthusiasm, consequently, dismissed as bad form and as an encumbrance—then and then only was the Jewish regiment granted, obviously to share in the popularity of the compulsory system. In addition, its Jewish name and badge were withdrawn before it actually was formed, and what remained of it after this operation looked very much like a "segregation-battalion," for keeping bad sorts apart from good sorts.

When, in spite of all this, the young unit straightened out and, at last, sailed to Palestine, after a really enthusiastic march through Whitechapel—a stab in the back followed and reached it at Taranto, in the form of official news that no more "Russians" were to be enlisted in the Jewish Regiment. The confusion which followed was indescribable. Three-quarters of the contingent were "Russians." Those who were keen on the Regiment asked: "Is my brother worse than I am?" Those who were not protested: "If you don't want my brother, why do you keep me?"

It may all sound amusing and comical: it was not. The Jewish good name was at stake. A unit raised and trained under such influences was in danger of utter demoralisation. If, in spite of all, the "Schneiders" emerged out of this ordeal as they did—good average soldiers, second to none of the average—let it be said: there is still some mettle of manhood left in the slums of Israel.

Open-air life and military training brought this manhood to full expansion. They did not like the Army, never said they did; but they lived up to every duty given them, behaved splendidly under fire, and there was never among them any breach of military discipline. When demobilised, they dispersed to their countless little workshops, and speak with pride of their campaigning out in Palestine; and many of them will return to the ancient homeland as pioneers.

The Palestinians volunteered for enlistment immediately after the occupation of Jerusalem. They were Ottoman subjects, and, if captured by the Turks in their khaki uniforms, would have been hanged. Undeterred by this prospect, undismayed by official reluctance to accept their offer, they kept on sending applications and deputations until the Palestinian battalion was formed. In the Jaffa district, 10 per cent. of the Jewish population joined "the Legion": old women were seen crying if their sons were passed unfit. Now, after all other Jewish units have been demobilised, they remain as the real cadre of a future Jewish army in Palestine. Strictly speaking, their history is outside the province of this book; but the future historian of Jewish Palestine will reserve to them a page of honour.

The Palestinian Battalion.

By Lieutenant H. Wolfensohn.

Perhaps the most interesting of all the units of the British Army, from a Jewish point of view, was the Palestinian Battalion of the Jewish Regiment—the 40th (S) Palestinian Battalion Royal Fusiliers, which was raised in Palestine.

The Jews had learned by painful experience to detest the incompetent Turk. Their reception then of the delivering British Armies was all the more enthusiastic. They were not content with welcoming them, but they wished to join the Army to strike their blow for the freeing of their land.

This was not at first practicable, and so they had to be content with such useful work as serving on the Intelligence Staff, as in the case of the Aaronsohn and Schneerson families. With the arrival, however, of the 38th and 39th Battalions Royal Fusiliers great possibilities appeared. The desire to bind a Jewish Palestine with Britain was stronger than ever, and soon active recruiting was commenced by Major J. A. de Rothschild, D.C.M., and Captain Eric Waley, with Lieutenant S. M. Lipsey for Jerusalem district, and Lieutenant H. Wolfensohn for Jaffa and the colonies. The Recruiting H.Q. was at Tel Aviv.

The language spoken was Hebrew, and its use in the twentieth century for military commands was probably the first since the time of the Maccabees. Tremendous enthusiasm prevailed throughout the recruiting period. In Tel Aviv and the colonies some 200 women wished to be enrolled in auxiliary Jewish units, but it was found practicable to send only six as Red Magen David Nurses to a hospital at Gaza.

Recruiting began on June 10th, 1918, and queues awaited the recruiting officers daily. In Tel Aviv, N.C.O.'s classes were immediately commenced, and daily parades held for all recruits at the Beth Sephar Lebonoth, under the supervision and instruction of the recruiting staff. Elected representatives of the recruits greatly facilitated the work. In Jaffa, Messrs. Hos, Golomb, Smelansky,

THE PALESTINIAN BATTALION

Katznelson, and Kwashne were of the utmost use, and in Jerusalem Messrs. Spiegelman and Gutman.

The Jaffa area supplied 457 recruits, and Jerusalem 350. The enthusiasm was so great that a special medal was struck at the Bezalel School, and presented on July 3rd, 1918, to all the volunteers and the recruiting officers. Dr. Weizmann presented a flag,* and the Haham Bashi a Sephar Torah. On July 4th the recruits left Ludd for training in Egypt. Scenes of great enthusiasm on the part of the inhabitants were witnessed on the trains and at the stations en route.

After a week's segregation at Kantara, where training was continued, the recruits arrived at Helmieh (near Cairo), and joined Lieutenant-Colonel E. Margolin, D.S.O., and the 39th Royal Fusiliers, as the Palestinian Detachment, 39th Royal Fusiliers. Officers and N.C.O.'s were detached from the sister battalions for special duty with the detachment. On August 5th the first half of 39th Royal Fusiliers left for the line, and the Palestinians became more self-supporting. On August 11th Egyptian recruiting commenced at Cairo and Alexandria, and produced some 200 recruits. Meanwhile at a neighbouring Prisoners of War Camp (Heliopolis) there were some Turkish Jews, and on August 22nd ninety-two were attested as British soldiers by Major D. Hopkin, M.C., and Lieutenant H. Wolfensohn. On August 25th the remainder of the 39th Royal Fusiliers went up the line, and the Palestinian Detachment was left alone.

Lieutenant-Colonel F. D. Samuel arrived at Tel-el-Kebir on August 29th with the 40th Royal Fusiliers, most of whom consisted of Americans. The Palestinians moved to Tel-el-Kebir on September 19th, and eventually became, under Lieutenant-Colonel F. D. Samuel, D.S.O., the 40th (S) Palestinian Battalion Royal Fusiliers. Meanwhile the battalion was carrying on duties at the P.O.W. camps.

The 40th Royal Fusiliers still exists as the Judeans Regiment, and wears the Menorah, with the motto *Kadimah*, as its badge. Lieutenant-Colonel Margolin, D.S.O., is in command, and recruiting is open so that the battalion may continue to take its part in the garrisoning of the Holy Land.

* See photograph, Plate 97.

Roll of Honour.

"THE GLORIOUS DEAD."
"THEIR NAME LIVETH TO ALL GENERATIONS."

IN LOVING MEMORY OF THE SONS OF ISRAEL WHO HAVE FALLEN IN THE WAR.

Officers.

Name.	Regiment.	Date of Death.	Address.
2nd Lieut. ABECASIS, A. P.	6th Somerset L.I.	9/4/17	27, Kensington Court, London, W.
Sub.-Lieut. ABELSON, E. G.	R.M.L.I.	1/12/16	10, Kidderpore Gardens, London, N.W.
Lieut. ABENDANA, E. M.	Canadian Engineers	16/10/18	Port Antonio, Jamaica.
2nd Lieut. ABINGER, B. R. (M.C.)	2nd Royal Berks Regt.	25/9/15	London, W.
Lieut. ABRAHAMS, A. C. L.	3rd Coldstream Guards	13/4/18	18, Porchester Terrace, London, W.
Major ABRAHAMS, M. N.	16th Rifle Brigade	3/9/16	14, Avenue Road, London, N.W.
2nd Lieut. ABRAHAMS, R. B.	4th Yorks Regt.	15/9/16	"The Limes," Massie Road, London, N.
Lieut. ADES, S. A.	35th Australian Inf.	22/8/18	18, Lapwing Lane, West Didsbury, Manchester.
2nd Lieut. ALEXANDER, G. R.	14th R. Sussex Regt.	24/4/17	44, Earl's Court Square, London, S.W.
2nd Lieut. ALEXANDER, S. A.	4th Royal Welsh Fusiliers	2/11/18	7, Loudoun Road, London, N.W.
Lieut. ANSELL, A.	52nd Australian Inf.	23/10/16	C/o Commonwealth Bank of Australia, London, E.C.
Lieut. ARNHOLZ, R. H.	1st Herts Regt.	23/9/18	62, Fairhazel Gardens, London, N.W.6.
2nd Lieut. ARNOLD, A. L.	9th London Regt.	15/8/17	94, Dartmouth Road, London, N.W.2.
Sub.-Lieut. ARON, E. M.	R.N.V.R.	13/11/16	14, Frobisher Terrace, Falmouth.
Lieut. ARON, F. A.	2nd South Lancs. Regt.	24/8/18	South Villa, Victoria Park, Manchester.
Lieut. ASHER, J. H.	11th Australian Inf.	2/9/17	Mittagong, N.S.W.
Capt. BAMBERGER, C. D. W.	Royal Engineers	19/12/14	3, Lancaster Road, London, N.W.
2nd Lieut. BAMBERGER, W. E. W.	1/5th Gloucester Regt.	16/8/17	3, Lancaster Road, London, N.W.
Lieut. BARDER, S. G.	8th East Surrey Regt.	30/9/16	7, Garlinge Road, London, N.W.
Capt. BARNATO, J. I.	R.A.F.	26/10/18	10, Austin Friars, London, E.C.2.
2nd Lieut. BARNETT, G.	13th Royal Scots	3/11/15	62, Hamilton Terrace, London, N.W.
Capt. BARNETT, H. W.	13th London Regt.	9/5/15	62, Hamilton Terrace, London, N.W.
2nd Lieut. BARNETT, P.	4th Middlesex Regt.	2/7/16	"The Crown," College Street, Lambeth, London, S.E.
Lieut. BARNETT, V. B.	12th Northumberland Fus.	25/9/15	61, St. Gabriel's Road, Cricklewood, London, N.W.
Lieut. BARRON, L.	7th Border Regt.	19/7/16	24, Lower Camden Street, Dublin.

OFFICERS—Continued.

Name.	Regiment.	Date of Death.	Address.
Capt. BASWITZ, A. (M.C.)	1/22nd London Regt.	16/9/16	40, Tamworth Street, Fulham, London, W.
Capt. BAUER, D. C. (D.F.C.)	12th K.B. Coy., R.A.F.	3/11/18	Ruskin Manor, Denmark Hill, London, S.E.
Lieut. BEAVER, W. N.	60th Australian Regt.	26/9/17	48, Leinster Square, London, W.
Lieut. BEER, A. H. (M.C.)	275th Brigade R.F.A.	22/4/18	11, Livingston Drive, Liverpool.
Lieut. BEHRENS, R. P.	1st South Wales Borderers	26/4/15	Vron Yw, Denbigh.
2nd Lieut. BENCHER, G. A.	2/19th London Regt.	9/12/17	54, Dukes Avenue, Muswell Hill, London, N.
Capt. BENJAMIN, H. S.	1/8th Worcestershire Regt.	9/10/17	15, Pembridge Crescent, London, W.11.
Capt. BENJAMIN, J. A.	9th West Riding Regt.	2/7/16	81, Inverness Terrace, London, W.
Sub.-Lieut. BENJAMIN, N. H.	Drake Battalion R.N.D.	25/4/17	70, Cazenove Road, Stamford Hill, London, N.
Lieut. BENZECRY, S.	17th Royal Fusiliers	30/11/17	34, Inverness Terrace, London, W.
2nd Lieut. BERNSTEIN, M. L. (M.C.)	11th Lancashire Fusiliers	9/4/18	25, Albany Road, London, N.
Staff-Sister BERNSTEIN, DORAH	S. African M.S.	6/11/18	17, Caroline Street, Johannesburg, South Africa.
Lieut. BINGEN, C. A. M.	5th Royal Sussex Regt.	10/2/16	4, Kidderpore Gardens, London, N.W.
Capt. BLASHKI, R. H.	53rd Bgde. Australian Artil.	3/8/17	Equitable Buildings, Sydney, N.S.W.
2nd Lieut. BLOOM, B.	3rd King's Liverpool Regt.	30/6/18	Grenville Avenue, West Hartlepool.
Lieut. BLOOM, H.	12th Yorkshire Regt.	14/2/17	The Crescent, Linthorpe, Middlesbrough.
2nd Lieut. BOWMAN, C. H.	1/4th Oxford & Bucks. L.I.	16/8/17	36, Ashborne Avenue, Golders Green, London, N.W.
2nd Lieut. BRANDON, B. L.	7th Cheshire Regt.	5/9/18	Kingstown, Jamaica.
Capt. BRAUN, C. L.	Essex Regt.	19/8/18	Nasirabad, India.
Major BRODZIAK, C. E. M. (D.S.O.)	3rd Australian M.G. Bn.	31/8/18	9, Bridge Street, Sydney, Australia.
2nd Lieut. BROOKS, F. J.	4th South Staffs. Regt.	13/11/16	11, Alexandra Road, Edgbaston, Birmingham.
2nd Lieut. CANSINO, J. H.	22nd Manchester Regt.	2/6/16	64, Faulkner Street, Manchester.
Capt. CAPPER, E. C. (M.C.)	9th Essex Regt.	24/12/17	6, Cleve Road, London, N.W.
2nd Lieut. CARO, J. P.	2/17th London Regt.	2/5/18	21, Fairhazel Gardens, London, N.W.6.
2nd Lieut. CLEEF, H. V.	8th Queen's R.W. Surrey	6/12/17	63, Bethune Road, London, N.
2nd Lieut. COBURN, C.	18th K.R.R.C.	31/7/17	40, King's Gardens, London, N.W.
Lieut. COHEN, A. S.	R.A.M.C., attd. 8th Som.L.I.	25/9/15	94, Woodville Road, Cardiff.
Lieut. COHEN, B.	R.A.M.C.	3/7/17	5, Clynville Terrace, Capetown, S. Africa.
2nd Lieut. COHEN, B.	R.A.F.	20/5/18	Montreal.
Lieut. COHEN, C. H.	R.G.A.	18/11/18	Sydney, N.S.W.
2nd Lieut. COHEN, D. T.	7th Royal Sussex Regt.	20/11/17	Hatfield House, Great Titchfield Street, London, W.
2nd Lieut. COHEN, E. (M.C.)	12th Royal Fusiliers	1/8/17	65, St. Thomas's Road, London, N.E.
Lieut. COHEN, G. H.	5th King's Liverpool Regt.	16/5/15	The Priory, St. Michael's, Liverpool.
2nd Lieut. COHEN, H.	4th Royal Berks. Regt.	18/7/15	310, Oxford Street, Reading.
2nd Lieut. COHEN, M.	21st London Regt.	15/9/16	181, Portsdown Road, London.
Lieut. COHEN, M. (M.M.)	2nd Durham L.I.	24/9/18	32, Honeycroft Road, Clapham Park, London, S.W.
Lieut. COHEN, M. T. (M.C.)	42nd Canadian Inf.	3/11/17	588, Huron Street, Toronto.
2nd Lieut. COHEN, S. M.	1/12th London Regt.	9/9/16	18, St. Quintin's Avenue, N. Kensington, London.
2nd Lieut. COOK, N. G.	1/6th North Staffs. Regt.	29/6/17	Bailey's Hotel, Gloucester Road, London, S.W.
2nd Lieut. COOTE, P. E.	8th London Regt.	15/9/16	13, Alexandra Villas, Finsbury Park, London, N.
Lieut. CRICHTON, C. A.	3rd London Regt.	10/3/15	17, Portman Street, London, W.
2nd Lieut. CULLEN, R. N. (COHEN)	5th R. Irish Fusiliers	7/12/15	Keith House, Porchester Gate, London, W.
Lieut. CUMMINS, T. M.	2/3rd London Regt.	7/11/18	Johannesburg, S.A.

OFFICERS—Continued.

Name.	Regiment.	Date of Death.	Address.
2nd Lieut. DANZIGER, C. W. J.	21st Manchester Regt.	15/5/17	Edgcoombe, The Avenue, Kersal, Manchester.
2nd Lieut. DAVIES, H.	2nd Royal Berks. Regt.	10/4/16	86, Lordship Park, London, N.
2nd Lieut. DAVIS, B. C.	2/12th London Regt.	22/8/18	12, Upper Hamilton Terrace, London, N.W.
Lieut. DAVIS, B. R.	45th Squadron, R.A.F.	20/9/17	18, Wetherly Mansions, Earl's Court Sq., London, S.W.
Capt. DAVIS, C. J. B.	470th Field Coy. R.E.	29/9/17	Old Grove House, The Grove, Hampstead, London, N.W.
Lieut. DAVIS, H. N.	2nd London Field Coy. R.E.	22/2/15	Old Grove House, The Grove, Hampstead, London, N.W.
2nd Lieut. DAVIS, H. PINDER	12th Essex Regt.	29/7/16	7, Cavendish Road, Regent's Park, London, N.W.
2nd Lieut. DAVIS, L. E.	5th Manchester Regt.	6/8/15	36, Dale Street, Liverpool.
Capt. DAVIS, L. J.	1/19th London Regt.	15/9/16	11, Cleve Road, London, N.W.
Lieut. DIAMOND, J. (M.C.)	R.A.F.	8/10/17	43, Abbotsford Road, Glasgow.
2nd Lieut. DE GUNZBURG, Baron A. G.	Royal Horse Guards	6/11/14	199, Boulevard St. Germain, Paris.
2nd Lieut. DE PASS, C. A.	2nd Tank Corps	22/3/18	Cliffe House, Falmouth.
Lieut. DE PASS, F. A. (V.C.)	34th Poona Horse	26/11/14	23, Queen's Gate Terrace, London, S.W.
Lieut. DE PASS, W. H.	13th Middlesex Regt.	28/3/18	46, Queen's Gate, London, S.W.7.
Capt. DRESCHFIELD, H. T.	13th Manchester Regt.	19/2/16	4, Park Lane, Kersal, Manchester.
2nd Lieut. DUNDON, S. J.	13th King's Liverpool Rgt.	19/9/16	41, Victoria Street, Dublin.
Capt. DURLACHER, E. A. O. (M.C.)	5th Worcester Regt.	20/5/17	67, Parliament Hill Mansions, Highgate, London, N
Lieut. EMANUEL, O.	1st Wilts. Regt.	26/9/16	28, Belsize Park, London, N.W.
Capt. EZRA, D.	192nd Siege Battery, R.G.A.	6/8/18	Wood Lawn, Loose, Kent.
2nd Lieut. FINE, S.	15th Squadron, R.A.F.	18/5/18	28, Southchurch Road, Southend.
2nd Lieut. FINK, S. J.	2/5th South Lancs. Regt.	20/4/17	10, Duchess Road, Edgbaston, Birmingham.
Lieut. FINZI, E.	221 Squadron, R.A.F.	5/9/18	Eldon Street, London, E.
2nd Lieut. FLEET, L.	R.A.F.	27/10/17	14, Cawdor Road, Manchester.
2nd Lieut. FRANKAU, P. E.	20th Rifle Bde.	2/11/17	144, Mitcham Lane, London, S.W.16.
2nd Lieut. FRANKS, B. A.	8th W. Riding Rgt.	23/10/15	50, Russell Square, London, W.C.
2nd Lieut. FRANKS, L.	8th East Yorks. Regt.	5/5/17	18, Park Avenue, Hull.
2nd Lieut. FRANKENSTEIN, C. J.	13th Bn. Tank Corps	28/8/18	315, Great Clowes Street, Manchester.
2nd Lieut. FRANKENSTEIN, O. R.	5th Welsh Rgt.	26/3/17	25, Regent Court, London, N.W.
2nd Lieut. FREADMAN, Z. E.	Australian F.C.	9/9/17	13, Cromwell Road, Hawksburn, Victoria.
2nd Lieut. FRECE, C. R. de-	175th Brigade, R.F.A.	10/8/16	153, Abbey Road, London, N.W.
2nd Lieut. FREEMAN-COWEN, C.	1/9th Manchester Regt.	23/6/16	Chorley Wood Cottage, Chorley Wood.
2nd Lieut. FREEDMAN, B.	6th East Kent Regt.	3/7/17	Box 5842, Johannesburg, S. Africa.
2nd Lieut. FREEDMAN, P.	20th Northumberland Fus.	3/10/17	9, Anson Road, Cricklewood, London, N.W.
2nd Lieut. FRIEND, J.		9/9/17	4, West Garden Street, Glasgow.
Lieut. GLUCKMAN, P.	1/3rd London Regiment	8/10/16	P.O. Box 66, Vereeniging, South Africa.
Lieut. GOLDSELLER, L. D.	2/5th West Riding Regt.	15/4/17	28, Belfield Road, Didsbury, Manchester.
Capt. GOLLIN, E. B.	13th King's Liverpool Rgt.	14/5/17	Park Side, Livingstone Drive, Liverpool.
Lieut. GORFUNKLE, I.	1st Lancs. Fusiliers	13/8/18	96, Antrim Road, Belfast.
Lieut. GOSSCHALK, E. M.	2nd K.O.Y.L.I.	28/8/16	210, Anlaby Road, Hull.
Capt. GREEN, E. M.	14th Hampshire Regt.	3/9/16	26, Upper Hamilton Terrace, London, N.W.

OFFICERS—Continued.

Name.	Regiment.	Date of Death.	Address.
Lieut. GREENWOOD, I. H.	8th Middlesex Regt.	6/7/18	24, Palace Court, London, W.
2nd Lieut. GORODISSKY, A.	Zion Mule Corps.	11/9/15	Alexandria.
2nd Lieut. GROSSMAN, V. D.	24th Northumberland Fus.	16/9/16	53, Portland Court, London, W.
2nd Lieut. GUTMANN, W.	71st Brigade, R.F.A.	7/5/17	43, Carlton Hill, London, N.W.
Lieut. HAGGAR, E. N.	21st Australian Inf.	20/3/17	Sarsfield P.O., E. Gippsland, Victoria.
Capt. HAINS, C. C.	Aust. Army Med. Corps	14/4/19	"Llandillo," Patrick St. Hurstville, N.S.W.
2nd Lieut. HAINES, E. A.	9th East Surrey Regt.	3/9/16	55, Lansdowne Road, London, W.
Capt. HALDINSTEIN, F. W.	8th Div. Sig. Coy., R.E.	7/3/17	Thorpe Lodge, Norwich.
Lieut. HALLE, J.	13th Worcester. Regt.	26/7/16	2, Park Drive, Bradford.
Lieut. HALLENSTEIN, D. I.	12th Australian M.G.C.	2/9/18	Woosocket, Berkley Street, St. Kilda.
Lieut. HARRIS, A.	13th London Regt.	9/9/16	7, Hyde Park Mansions, London, W.
Lieut. HARRIS, C. M.	R.A.M.C. att. 7th R.Scots.F.	28/8/15	19, Edgware Road, Enmore, Sydney, N.S.W.
Lieut. HARRIS, H.	10th West Riding Regt.	5/10/16	56, Tavistock Square, London, W.C.
Capt. HARRIS, N. L., (M.C.)	9th R. Welsh Fusiliers	28/8/18	11, Field Road, Newport, Mon.
Capt. HART, A. C.	2nd Northumberland Fus.	8/5/15	34, Holland Park, London, W.
Lieut. HART, C.	2nd Bedford Regt.	23/10/18	10, Marlboro' Place, London, N.W.
Capt. HART, C. L.	2nd W. Riding Regt.	1/7/16	12, Alexandra Mansions, London, N.W.
Nurse HARTMAN, E.	V.A.D.	20/10/18	37, Botanical Road, Sheffield.
2nd Lieut. HENRIQUES, P. B.	8th K.R.R.C.	25/7/15	33, Grosvenor Place, London, S.W.
Lieut. HENRIQUES, R. L. Q.	2nd R. West Surrey Regt.	14/9/14	17, Sussex Square, London, W.
2nd Lieut. HENRY, A. R.	1st Middlesex Regt.	23/4/17	120, Portsdown Road, London, W.
Lieut. HENRY, C. C.	2nd Worcester Regt.	26/9/15	5, Carlton Gardens, London, S.W.
2nd Lieut. HERBERTSON, A. H.	7th K.R.R.C.	16/5/17	Conamure, Sandgate, Kent.
2nd Lieut. HERMAN, R. P.	1st Canterbury, N.Z., Rgt.	10/6/16	Remuera, Auckland, N.Z.
Capt. HEUMANN, R.	2nd London Regt.	10/7/16	22, Belsize Avenue, London, N.W.
Lieut. HITNER, V. J.	R.A.S.C.	20/7/18	40, Granville Road, Fallowfield, Manchester.
Capt. HOLT, L.	2/10th London Regt.	11/3/18	61, Portland Place, London, W.1.
2nd Lieut. HORWITZ, S. S.	1st Loyal North Lancs. Rgt.	21/10/16	14, Buccleugh Place, Edinburgh.
2nd Lt. HURSTBOURNE, W. (HIRSCHBEIN)	D/180 Brigade, R.F.A.	23/6/17	2, Inglewood Mansions, London, N.W.6.
Lieut. HYAMS, A. H.	6th (attd. 3rd) Royal Fus.	3/5/15	The Old House, Eastergate, Sussex.
Lieut. HYMAN, E. M.	Canadian Inf.	27/9/16	187, Charles Street, Belleville, Canada.
2nd Lieut. HYMAN, H. E.	11th South Lancashire Regt.	1/11/18	4, Clowes Street, Manchester.
2nd Lieut. HYMAN, R.	6th Duke of Cornwall's L.I.	22/8/17	35, Finchley Road, London, N.W.
Lieut. IMROTH, L.	11th Hampshire Regt.	20/11/18	Johannesburg, South Africa.
2nd Lieut. ISAACS, B. C.	89th Coy. M.G.C.	1/8/17	28, New Church Road, Hove, Sussex.
Lieut. ISAACS, F. H.	11th Royal Scots Fusiliers	30/9/18	44, King's Gardens, W. Hampstead, London, N.W.
2nd Lieut. JACOBS, D.	2/4th South Lancs. Regt.	10/4/17	60, Crediton Hill, London, N.W.
2nd Lieut. JACOBS, H.	1/8th K.O.R. Lancs. Regt.	6/7/18	13, Lansdowne Place, Hove.
2nd Lieut. JACOBS, J.	5th Yorkshire Regt.	20/7/16	Haringay, Walter Road, Swansea.
Sub. Lieut. JACOBS, T.	R.N.V.R.	4/2/17	32, Goldhurst Terrace, London, N.W.
Lieut. JACOB, V. V.	2nd Oxford & Bucks L.I.	26/9/15	3, Cleveland Square, London, W.
Capt. JAFFE, J.	R.A.M.C., att. 2/4 Som. L.I.	1/8/18	Addo Station, Uitenhage, C.P., South Africa.

71

OFFICERS—Continued.

Name.	Regiment.	Date of Death.	Address.
Captain JEFFREYS, A.	20th North. Fusiliers	7/11/16	56, Carlton Hill, London, N.W.
Lieut. JESSEL, V. A. Z.	15th D.L.I.	6/4/17	38, Banbury Road, Oxford.
2nd Lieut. JOSEPH, H.	8th Devon Regt.	20/7/17	91, Northgate, Regent's Park, London, N.
2nd Lieut. JOSEPH, W. F. G.	2nd R. Berks. Regt.	27/5/18	23, Clanricarde Gardens, London, W.2.
2nd Lieut. JOSEPH, W. G. A.	1/5th Norfolk Regt.	19/4/17	10, Frognal Lane, London, N.W.
2nd Lieut. JOSEPHS, J.	12th London Regt.	1/7/16	72, Highbury New Park, London, N.
2nd Lieut. JOYCE, P. S.	60th Squad. R.A.F.	6/3/17	1, Park Road, Moseley, Birmingham.
2nd Lieut. KAHN, E.	1st Leinster Regt.	4/5/15	53, Compayne Gardens, London, N.W.
Lieut. KATZ, S. G.	8th K.O.R. Lancs. Regt.	19/7/18	69, Greencroft Gardens, London, N.W.
2nd Lieut. KAUFFMAN, E.	A.S.C., M.T.	17/10/18	372, High Street, Stratford, London, E.
2nd Lieut. KEYZOR, H. L. A.	25th Royal Welsh Fus.	9/3/18	65, Lancaster Road, London, N.W.
2nd Lieut. KING, S.	23rd Northumberland Fus.	12/10/16	14, Kayes Road, London, N.W.
2nd Lieut. KLEAN, M. G.	16th Northumberland Fus.	1/7/16	26, Hatton Garden, London, E.C.
2nd Lieut. KLEIN, J.	9th Essex Regt.	14/10/18	39, Plympton Road, London, N.W.
2nd Lieut. KLEMANTASKI, L. A.	8th R. Berks. Regt.	28/5/16	2, Tanza Road, London, N.W.
2nd Lieut. KOHN, W. A.	11th East Lancashire Regt.	1/7/16	79, Queen's Gate, London, S.W.
2nd Lieut. KOHNSTAMM, J.	54th M.G.C.	29/6/16	41, Frognal, London, N.W.
Capt. KOHNSTAMM, N.	1/18th Manchester Regt.	23/3/18	41, Frognal, London, N.W.
2nd Lieut. KOSMINSKY, M. E.	7th Australian Inf.	19/8/16	St. Kilda, Melbourne, Australia.
2nd Lieut. KRAUSS, D. E.	1/5th North Staffs. Regt.	7/4/17	12, Marlboro Place, London, N.W.
Capt. KROLIK, E. (M.C.)	16th Rifle Brigade	23/10/17	72, Finchley Road, London, N.W.
Flight-Lieut. LAN-DAVIS, C. F.	R.N.A.S.	14/10/15	6, King's Bench Walk, London, E.C.
Capt. LANGDON, W. M.	10th Cheshire Regt.	24/4/16	Silverlands, Altrincham, Cheshire.
Capt. LAZARUS, C. H.	7th Leicester Regt.	27/5/18	Muizenberg, South Africa.
Lieut. LAZER, H. J.	33rd Australian Inf.	24/3/17	Lambeth Street, Glen Innes, N.S.W.
Lieut. LELAND, W. A.	1st R. Dublin Fusiliers	4/6/15	5, Kensington Court, London, W.
2nd Lieut. LEON, E. J.	8th London Regt.	7/10/16	4, Cleveland Gardens, London, W.
Capt. LEON, J. T.	R.A.M.C.	1916	London.
Lieut. LEVENE, N. N.	8th King's Liverpool Regt.	8/8/16	258, Hornby Road, Blackpool.
Lieut. LEVESON, R. M.	10th Durham L.I.	18/12/17	16, Lancaster Gate Terrace, London, W.
2nd Lieut. LEVI, F. J.	2/5th Lincoln Regt.	25/3/18	116, Pershore Road, Birmingham.
2nd Lieut. LEVI, H.	9th Royal Fusiliers	30/11/17	16, Scarisbrick New Road, Southport.
Capt. LEVI, K. M.	Australian Med. Corps	7/8/15	Liverpool Buildings, William Street, Melbourne.
2nd Lieut. LEVINE, M. G.	R.A.F.	8/5/18	3, Park Road, Cromer.
Lieut. LEVINSTEIN, G. E.	26th Manchester Regt.	12/10/16	12, Broomwater West, Teddington.
2nd Lieut. LEVY, A. G.	R.A.F.	25/4/18	1104, Kenmore Place, Brooklyn, New York.
2nd Lieut. LEVY, A. M.	4th Bedford Regt.	14/6/19	220, Clapham Road, London, S.E.
Lieut. LEVY, H. S.	35th Australian Inf.	12/10/17	38, Pitt Street, Sydney, N.S.W.
Capt. LEVY, M. B. (M.C.)	2nd Irish Guards	12/4/17	10, Porchester Terrace, London, W.
2nd Lieut. LEWINSTEIN, H.	1st Royal West Kent Regt.	22/7/16	22, Great Windmill Street, London, W.
2nd Lieut. LEWIS, H.	7th King's Liverpool Regt.	25/9/16	382, Edge Lane, Liverpool.
2nd Lieut. LEWIS, L. W.	165th M.G.C.	9/8/16	10, Porchester Terrace, London, W.

OFFICERS—Continued.

Name.	Regiment.	Date of Death.	Address.
Capt. LEZARD, A. G.	13th Rifle Brigade	31/1/16	1, Hyde Park Street, London, W.
Capt. LIEBSON, S. (M.C.)	S.A.M.C. attd. 4th Bn.	22/3/18	Waldeck's Plant, West Kimberley, South Africa.
2nd Lieut. LIFETREE, E. H.	16th Notts. and Derby Regt.	21/5/16	23, Crediton Hill, London, N.W.
Lieut. LION, N. I.	1st R.M.L.I.	28/4/17	126, Elgin Avenue, London, W.
Capt. LITTEN, R.	6th Royal Berks. Regt.	1/7/16	21, Pembridge Villa, London, W.
2nd Lieut. LOWENSTEIN, J. C.	R.A.F.	9/5/18	Vitspankraal, P.O., Heidelberg, Cape Province.
Capt. LOWY, W. A.	10th Hants Regt.	3/9/18	8, St. John's Wood Park, London, N.W.
2nd Lieut. LURY, G. H.	15th Auckland Bn. N.Z. In.	29/8/18	Auckland, N.Z.
Lieut. LUSCOMBE, E. L.	19th Australian Inf.	3/5/17	
Lieut. LYONE, A. M. (M.C.)	11th Northumberland Fus.	26/9/17	70, Matheson Avenue, Winnipeg, Canada.
2nd Lieut. LYONS, E. J.	1st E. Lancs. Regt.	5/10/17	68, Blenheim Gardens, London, N.W.
Lieut. MARKS, A. S.	9th Royal Sussex Regt.	25/10/18	33, Tisbury Road, Hove.
2nd Lieut. MARKS, C. B.	8th East Surrey Regt.	23/10/18	Heathfield, Cavendish Road, Sutton.
Capt. MARKS, C. H.	R.A.F.	25/10/15	5, Cavendish Square, London, W.
2nd Lieut. MARKS, I. D.	10th West Riding Regt.	20/7/16	8, Rotton Park Road, Birmingham.
Lieut. MARKS, J.	15th Durham L.I.	23/10/18	22, Queen's Road, Newcastle.
2nd Lieut. MARKS, J. A.	10th N. Staffs. Regt.	25/3/17	84, Fern Avenue, Jesmond, Newcastle-on-Tyne.
Lieut. MARKS, L. T.	R.A.F.	29/10/18	23, Dock Road, Cape Town.
2nd Lieut. MARKS, P. M.	4th Middlesex Regt.	29/9/15	Mount Coombe, Oakhill Grove, Surbiton.
Major MARKS, N.	1/23rd London Regt.	27/7/18	Beechcroft Mansions, Streatham, London, S.W.
2nd Lieut. MARTINSON, K. L.	R.F.A., attd. R.A.F.	1/6/17	8, Carlton Gardens, Herne Bay.
2nd Lieut. MELHADO O. S.	11th Yorks. Regt.	7/12/15	Kingston, Jamaica.
Lieut. MENDELSON, B. H.	55th Australian Inf.	20/7/16	6, Raglan Road, Mossman, N.S.W.
Lieut. MENDOZA, H. K.	52nd Australian Inf.	11/6/17	Fabershon, Witham Road, Hawkesbury, Victoria.
Capt. MEZA, J. DE (M.C.)	1/19th London Regt.	22/8/18	Rest Harrow, Palmeira Avenue, Hove.
Lieut. MERE, C. L.	6th King's O.R. Lancs.	10/8/15	Manchester.
Lieut. MICHAELIS, G. M.	East Anglian R.E.	23/9/15	Melbourne, Victoria.
Lieut. MONTAGU, R. H.	15th Hampshire Regt	20/9/17	34, Queen's Gardens, London, W.
Capt. MONTEFIORE, R.M. SEBAG.	R. East Kent Yeomanry	19/11/15	5, Balfour Place, London, W.
2nd Lieut. MORRIS, H. M.	15th Lancashire Fusiliers	16/8/18	2, Albany Road, Southport.
2nd Lieut. MOSES, F. S.	1/1st Welsh H.B., R.G.A.	31/8/18	29, St. George's Road, Kilburn, London, N.W.
2nd Lieut. MOSES, V. S.	Y. 11. M.T.M.B., R.F.A.	4/6/17	100, Greencroft Gardens, London, N.W.
Lieut. MOSS, H. A.	7th Middlesex Regt.	7/10/16	90, Priory Road, London, N.W.
Lieut. MOSS, A. H.	15th Australian Inf.	19/6/18	152, Wickenham Street, Valley, Brisbane.
Lieut. MOSS, J.	11th Australian Inf.	19/7/18	Heath Drive, Hampstead, London, N.W.
Nurse MUNRO, E. H.	V.A.D.	12/12/16	11, Russell Gardens, Hendon, London, N.W.
Major MYER, E. A.	6th London Regt.	4/4/15	30, Pembridge Gardens, London, W.
2nd Lieut. MYER, DENZIL G. A.	9th Wor. at.7th N.Staffs.R.	25/2/17	30, Pembridge Gardens, London, W.
Lieut. MYERS, A. F.	4th Hussars	3/3/18	3, St. Aubyn's Court, Hove.
Lieut. MYERS, F. M.	11 Suf. atd. 20th Sq. R.A.F.	14/2/17	P.O. Box 5834, Johannesburg, South Africa.
Lieut. NATHAN, D.	A/155 Bde. R.F.A.	2/8/17	87, Broadhurst Gardens, London, N.W.
2nd Lieut. NATHAN, L. C.	8th W. Riding Regt.	14/9/16	Oatefield, Bradford.

73

OFFICERS—Continued.

Name.	Regiment.	Date of Death.	Address.
Capt. NATHAN, R. P.	X. 36. T.M.B., R.F.A.	22/3/18	83, Greencroft Gardens, London, N.W.
2nd Lieut. NATHAN, W. S.	12th Royal Fusiliers	14/6/17	37, Cornwall Gardens, London, S.W.7.
2nd Lieut. NEWMAN, N.	10th H.L.I.	28/6/16	2, Birchington Road, London, N.W.
2nd Lieut. OHLMANN, G. A. L.	3rd Royal Fusiliers	29/9/15	55, Belsize Park, London, N.W.
2nd Lieut. OPET, T. H.	8th London Regt.	23/3/18	Withernsea, Yorks.
2nd Lieut. PAIBA, E. J. A.	2nd Royal Fusiliers	20/10/15	2, Inglewood Road, London, N.W.
Lieut. PHILLIPS, R. H.	15th R. Warwick Regt.	24/9/..	17, Lyttleton Road, Birmingham.
Capt. PIZA, D.	1st E. Yorks. Regt.	9/4/17	21, Fairhazel Gardens, London, N.W.6.
2nd Lieut. PLATNAUER, L. M.	16th W. Yorks. Regt.	3/5/17	P.O. Box 124, Capetown.
2nd Lieut. POLACK, B. J.	9th Worcester Regt.	9/4/16	1, Percival Road, Clifton.
Lieut. POLACK, E. E.	1/4th Gloucester Regt.	17/7/16	1, Percival Road, Clifton.
2nd Lieut. POSENER, P. J.	2nd Wilts. Regt.	9/7/16	3, Canfield House, London, N.W.
2nd Lieut. POSNER, P. E.	8th Lincoln Regt.	27/4/17	57, Durban Road, Watford.
2nd Lieut. RAPHAEL, H. G.	7th East Lancs Regt.	31/7/17	7, Belsize Park, London, N.W.
2nd Lieut. RAPHAEL, N. H.	2nd Royal Warwick Regt.	8/6/16	17, Stratton Street, London, W.
2nd Lieut. REESE, A. (M.C. and Bar)	2nd West Yorks. Regt.	1/8/17	17, Lordship Park, London, N.
Sub/Asst. Sgn. REUBEN, B.	Indian Med. Ser., Bombay	1916	Indian Medical Service, Bombay.
Lieut. RINTEL, H. L.	8th Australian Inf.	20/9/17	
Lieut. RODNEY, W. B.	11th R. West Kent Regt.	21/4/16	15, London Wall, London, E.C.
Lieut. ROSENBAUM, L. B.	1/2nd Monmouth Regt.	17/4/18	55, Church Street, Tredegar, Monmouthshire.
2nd Lieut. ROSENTHAL, A.	65th Squadron, R.A.F.	24/11/17	37, Beaufort Road, Edgbaston, Birmingham.
Lieut. ROSENTHAL, S.	58th Australian Inf.	27/9/17	Elizabeth Street, Melbourne.
Capt. ROTHBAND, J. E.	23rd Manchester Regt.	19/7/16	153, Cheetham Hill Road, Manchester.
Major ROTHSCHILD, E. A. DE	Bucks Yeomanry	17/11/17	New Court, St. Swithin's Lane, London, E.C.
Capt. ROZELAAR, S. L.	6th Royal Berks. Regt.	10/10/18	Synagogue Chambers, Bayswater, London, W.
Lieut. RUDELL, E. A.	16th Royal Warwick Regt.	27/9/18	20, York Road, Edgbaston, Birmingham.
Lieut. SALAMAN, E. A.	R.F.A.	18/12/16	6, Connaught Place, London, W.
Capt. SALOMONS, D. R. H. P.	R.E.	28/10/15	Broomhill, Tunbridge Wells.
2nd Lieut. SAMUEL, A. D.	R.A.S.C.	19/5/18	30, Abercorn Place, London, N.W.
2nd Lieut. SAMUEL, C. V.	8th R. Warwick Regt.	6/10/17	14, Neville Court, London, N.W.
2nd Lieut. SAMUEL, E. B.	16th Middlesex Regt	30/1/16	12, Palmeira Court, Hove, Sussex.
Lieut. SAMUEL, G. G.	10th R. W. Kent Regt.	7/6/17	The Mote, Maidstone.
2nd Lieut. SAMUEL, G. B.	D.L.I., attd. R.A.F.	1917	105, Brondesbury Road, London, N.W.
Major SAMUEL, L. J.	A/83rd Bde. R.F.A.	29/9/17	105, Brondesbury Road, London, N.W.
Capt. SAMUEL, W. G.	2nd Bedford Regt.	21/9/18	32, Sloane Gardens, London, S.W.1.
2nd Lieut. SASSOON, H.	R.E.	1/11/15	Hatfield, Kent.
Lieut. SCHAFFER, H.	7th Canadian Engineers	30/10/18	60 Chichele Road, London, N.W.2.
Capt. SCHIFF, M. E. H.	12th Suffolk Regt.	25/9/17	14, Hyde Park Square, London, W.
2nd Lieut. SCHLOSS, L. E.	44th M.G.C.	31/7/17	24, Seeley Road, Nottingham.
Capt. SCHONFIELD, E.	2/19th London Regt.	20/9/16	10, Royal Crescent, Glasgow.
Midn. SCHREIBER, V.G.S.	H.M.S. "Monmouth"	1/11/14	
Lieut. SCHUR, P.	9th Notts. & Derby Regt.	15/6/18	Bowerdorp, Namaqualand, South Africa.

OFFICERS—Continued.

Name.	Regiment.	Date of Death.	Address.
2nd Lieut. SCOTT-FORBES, J.	78th Siege By. R.G.A.	1/4/17	Mentone House, Hessle, E. Yorks.
2nd Lieut. SEGAL, M.	13th King's Liverpool	19/6/17	4, Mowbray Road, London, N.W.
2nd Lieut. SELBY, M. G.	Artists' Rifles & Essex R.	27/9/18	Royal Palace Hotel, London, W.
Lieut. SHALLBERY, J. R.	23rd Australian Inf.	7/8/15	8, Waterloo Street, Camberwell, Victoria.
Lieut. SHAPPERE, C. S.	3rd Australian Inf.	29/12/16	Blayney, N.S.W.
Lieut. SHAW, M.	26th Royal Fusiliers	15/9/16	74, Gresham House, London, E.C.
2nd Lieut. SHEKURY, C (M.C.)	2nd Bedford Regt.	16/4/18	Hong Kong.
Capt. SHEREK, P.	R.A.F.	1/10/18	17, Lisle Street, London, W.
Lieut. SILVERA, L. G.	British West Indian Regt.	1917	Kingstown, Jamaica.
Capt. SIMON, E. C.	2/5th Lancashire Fusiliers	17/8/15	Lythe Hall Farm, Hazlemere, Surrey.
Capt. SIMONS, L. (M.C.)	22nd Royal Fusiliers	17/2/17	29, Eastcombe Avenue, London, S.E.17.
2nd Lieut. SLOWE, A.	6th K.O.Y.L.I.	25/8/17	42, Brondesbury Park, London, N.W.
Lieut. SMITH, C. O.	36/33 Brigade, R.F.A.	20/8/17	98, Lyncroft Gardens, London, N.W.
Capt. SOLOMON, A. M.	87th Canadian Inf.	15/8/17	123, Holland Road, London, W.
Lieut. SOLOMON, B.	2/10th London Rgt, attd. 1/19th London Regt.	24/3/18	123, Holland Road, London, W.
2nd Lieut. SOLOMON, E. J.	R.A.F.	30/10/17	Johannesberg.
2nd Lieut. SOLOMON, L.	2nd South Lancs. Regt.	3/8/17	11, Pitt Street, Campden Hill, London, W.
Lieut. SOLOMONS, H. M.	1st K. O. S. Borderers	23/4/17	21, Hamilton Terrace, London, N.W.
Lieut. SOLOMONS, L. B.	Bedford Regt., attd. R.A.F.	5/12/18	Aldershot.
2nd Lieut. SONDHEIM, W.	2nd R. Fus., attd. R.A.F.	11/4/18	162, Upper New Walk, Leicester.
Lieut. SONNENBERG, M. C.	R.A.F.	4/3/18	P.O. Box 911, Johannesburg, S.A.
Capt. SPIELMANN, H. L. I.	35th Sq. R.A.F.	19/9/18	8, Lydford Street, London, N.W.
Lieut. SPIERS, A. L. C.	10th Manchester Regt.	13/8/15	56, Westbourne Terrace, London, W.
Lieut. STARFIELD, B.	7th King's Shropshire L. I.	26/9/17	13, Augustus Road, Edgbaston, Birmingham.
2nd Lieut. STERN, L. H.	20th Squadron, R.A.F.	19/1/18	Box 2065, Johannesberg, S. Africa.
Lieut. STERN, S.	1/13th London Regt.	9/5/15	Synagogue House, Rectory Square, London, E.
Lieut. STERN, S. L.	King's African Rifles	19/7/17	11, Hanover Terrace, London, N.W.
Lieut. STIEBEL, C.	R.A.F.	15/2/18	London.
Lieut. STROSS, D.	Indian Medical Service	2/2/17	Crosby Square, London, E.C.
Lieut. STRAUSS, V. A.	R.A.F.	12/3/17	53, Grange Avenue, Leeds.
Lieut. STUART-SMITH, P. J.	R.A.F.	12/3/17	1, Kensington Palace Gardens, London, W.
2nd Lieut. TANBURN, W. L.	74th Squadron, R.A.F.	8/5/18	23, Frognal, London, N.W.3.
2nd Lieut. TEBBITT, I. L.	Indian Army R. 2nd Gurkhas	13/4/17	11, Cornwall Terrace, Regent's Park, London, N.W.
Lieut. TELFER, C. W.	1/19th London Regt.	4/11/15	5, King's Gardens, London, N.W.
Lieut. TELFER, H. A.	1st K.O. Yorks. L.I.	8/11/18	16, Belsize Park, London, N.W.
Capt. TOBIAS, L. M.	9th King's Own Yorks. L.I., attd. 64th T.M.B.	2/7/16	16, Belsize Park, London, N.W.
2nd Lieut. ULLMAN, D. M.	25th Royal Welsh Fusiliers	25/2/19	72, Priory Road, London, N.W.25.
Lieut. VALENTINE, M.	24th Royal Fusiliers	23/4/17	87, Priory Road, London, N.W.
Lieut. VAN DEN BERGH, J. H.	2nd Q.R.W. Surrey Regt.	26/10/17	73, Moorgate Street, London, E.C.
Capt. VAN DEN BERGH, S. J. H.	6th London Brigade R.F.A.	21/5/16	8, Kensington Palace Gardens, London, W.
	1st County of London Yeo.	27/10/17	8, Kensington Palace Gardens, London, W.

75

OFFICERS—Continued.

No.	Rank.	Name.	Regiment.	Date of Death.	Address.
	2nd Lieut.	VAN DER LINDE, M. J. T.	9th London Regt.	30/8/18	16, Petherton Road, London, N.
	2nd Lieut.	VAN DER LINDE, S.	6th Bedford Regt.	18/10/17	16, Petherton Road, London, N.
	Lieut.	WALEY, A. J.	12th Royal Fusiliers	31/8/17	14, Seymour Street, London, W.
	2nd Lieut.	WALLACE, J.	1st Black Watch	9/5/15	Edinburgh.
	Sub-Lieut.	WEIL, L. B.	14th Wing, R.N.A.S.	8/4/17	3, Grosvenor Place, London, W.
	2nd Lieut.	WEILL, A.	1st Rifle Brigade.	8/8/16	9, Greville Road, London, N.W.
	Lieut.	WEISS, E. S.	13th Wing, R.A.F.	22/11/17	167 Willesden Lane, London, N.W.
	Lieut.	WERTHEIMER, A. T.	12th Australian Inf.	4/6/18	Bellerive, Tasmania.
	Lieut.	WOLFFE, B.	38th Royal Fusiliers	20/7/18	207, Elgin Avenue, London, N.W.
	Lieut.	WOOLF, W.	24th Welsh Regt.	21/9/18	Savoy Hotel, London, W.
	Lieut.	WOOLF, W. R. MORTIMER	2nd Border Regt.	26/9/15	Mayfield, Mortimer Crescent, London, N.W.
	Lieut.	WORKMAN, M. J.	75th Canadian Inf.	9/4/17	333, Kensington Avenue, Montreal.
	Lieut.	YOUKLES, I. B.	87th Canadian Infantry	15/8/17	1657, Mance Street, Montreal.

N.C.O.'s and Men.

No.	Rank.	Name.	Regiment.	Date of Death.	Address.
21877	Pte.	AARONS, E.	1st (Queen's) R. W. Surrey	12/12/16	3a, Brondesbury Road, London, N.W.
776	Tpr.	AARONS, H.	4th Australian L. Horse	6/8/15	59, Cowper Street, Footscray, Vic.
36067	Pte.	AARONS, H. D.	6th Yorks Regt.	10/10/17	30, Canonbury Park S, London, N.
233751	Pte.	AARONS, J.	2/2nd London Regt.	15/6/17	102, Ben Jonson Road, London, E.
2868	Pte.	AARONS, J. F.	16th Australian Inf.	11/7/17	6, King's Road, Subiaco, W. Australia.
2281	Pte.	AARONS, M. L.	16th Australian Inf.	8/8/15	357, Smith Street, Fitzroy, Vic.
514271	Pte.	AARONS, M. J.	1/14th London Regt.	23/8/18	20, Sutherland Road, Bow, London, E.
2026	Pte.	ABELSON, C.	40th Australian Inf.	31/1/17	9, Torrens Street, Adelaide.
5163	Pte.	ABELSON, J.	7th South African Inf.	14/7/17	62, Bell Street, Manchester.
12199	Pte.	ABRAHAMS, A.	2nd Northampton Regt.	7/7/16	339, Mare Street, London, N.E.
282873	Pte.	ABRAHAMS (DAVIES), B.			
27758	Rfm.	ABRAHAMS (SYMBERLIST), C.	1/4th London Regt.	4/11/18	36, Broad Street, London, W.
69352	Pte.	ABRAHAMS, D.	11th Rifle Brigade	17/2/17	29, New Road, London, E.
540236	Pte.	ABRAHAMS, E.	9th Royal Fusiliers	8/4/18	4, Oxford Street, Whitechapel, London, E.
6028	Pte.	ABRAHAMS, F. W.	6th London Regt.	26/2/19	65, Goldsmith Row, London, E.2.
12424	Pte.	ABRAHAMS, G.	17th Australian Inf.	31/8/18	Oxford Street, Burwood, N.S.W.
11900	Rfm.	ABRAHAMS, H.	9th Devonshire Regt.	25/9/15	15, Blackford Street, Birmingham.
2434	Pte.	ABRAHAMS, H.	1st K.R.R.C.	10/3/15	87, Ernest Street, London, E.
220451	Pte.	ABRAHAMS, H. A.	17th King's Liverpool Rgt.	12/10/16	26, Broom Lane, Broughton Park, Manchester.
3007	Pte.	ABRAHAMS, H. A.	2nd R. Berks. Regt.	14/10/18	41, Aston Street, London, E. 14.
423036	Pte.	ABRAHAMS, I.	13th London Regt.	9/5/15	53, Gloucester Gardens, London, W.
43250	Pte.	ABRAHAMS, I.	2/10th London Regt.	14/7/17	50, Nathaniel Buildings, London, E.1.
5560	Pte.	ABRAHAMS, J.	10th Northumberland Fus.	9/6/17	15, Wentworth Place, Newcastle.
	Pte.	ABRAHAMS, J. E.	2nd Leicester Regt.	15/5/15	8, Van Street, Leicester.

76

N.C.O.'S AND MEN—Continued.

No.	Rank.	Name.	Regiment.	Date of Death.	Address.
53664	Pte.	ABRAHAMS, L.	2nd Welsh Regt.	25/9/16	51, Birch Street, Manchester.
12953	L/Cpl.	ABRAHAMS, M.	13th King's Liverpool Rgt.	31/8/18	30, Elton Street, Manchester.
33385	Rfm.	ABRAHAMS, M.	18th K.R.R.C.	1/8/17	29, Cleve Buildings, Shoreditch, London, E.2.
122060	Pte.	ABRAHAMS, M.	R.A.M.C.	15/2/19	52, Montague Road, London, E.8.
3054	Tpr.	ABRAHAMS, M. G.	1st Life Guards	18/5/15	14, Duckett Road, Harringay, London, N.
7201	Pte.	ABRAHAMS, R.	1st South Wales Borderers	4/10/14	33, Queen's Terrace, Wigan.
2268	Rfm.	ABRAHAMS, S.	16th London Regt.	1/7/16	1, Riffell House, Riffell Road, London, N.W.
281753	Pte.	ABRAHAMS, S.	1/4th London Regt.	16/8/17	12, Exchange Buildings, London, E.
576157	Rfm.	ABRAHAMS, S.	1/17th London Regt.	29/11/17	51, Cambridge Road, London, E.1.
17388	Rfm.	ABRAHAMS, S.	12th Rifle Brigade	24/3/18	194, Euston Road, London, N.W.1.
296267	Pte.	ABRAHAMS, S.	12th Royal Scots Fus.	4/11/18	10, Fieldgate Street, London, E.
25351	Pte.	ABRAHAMS, S.	2nd W. Yorks. Regt.	27/5/18	14, Morien Street, Leeds.
242689	Pte.	ABRAHAMS, S.	1/6th W. Yorks. Regt.	9/10/17	278, Great Horner Street, Liverpool.
321546	Pnr.	ABRAHAMS (BROWN), S. C.	Sig. Depot, R.E.	27/5/18	214, Whitechapel Road, London, E.
S/17926	Rfm.	ABRAHAMS, W.	1st Rifle Brigade	21/10/18	8, Ruth Houses, Flower & Dean Street, London, E.
53549	Cpl.	ABRAMOVITCH, P. (M.M.)	2nd Aust. Div. Sig. Coy.	12/2/19	Brunswick, Vic.
445201	L/Cpl.	ABRAHAMSON, C. O.	54th Canadian Inf.	22/3/17	Rejelstoke, B.C., Canada.
J/548	Pte.	ABRAHAMSON, S.	38th Royal Fusiliers	14/8/18	93, West Parade, Spongate, Hull.
80076	Pte.	ACKSTONE, S.	10th Notts & Derby Regt.	23/4/17	21, Marlborough Road, Manchester.
41749	Pte.	ADDIS, I.	11th Lancashire Fusiliers	31/7/17	2, Melbourne Street, Manchester.
30894	Pte.	ADELSON, A.	2nd Devonshire Regt.	24/4/18	31, Ellingford Road, Hackney, London, E.
7201	Sergt.	ADLER, P. (M.M.)	11th Royal Fusiliers	17/2/17	38, Farleigh Road, London, N.
80334	Pte.	ADLER, W.	3rd Middlesex (Lab.) Regt.	25/5/17	50, Fordwych Road, London, N.W.
86	L/Cpl.	AHBUL, L. E. (M.M.)	41st Australian Inf.	11/12/16	316, Annandale Street, Annandale, Sydney, Australia.
1767	L/Cpl.	ALBERT, J.	2/10th London Regt.	14/6/17	22, Elder Street, Norton Folgate, London, E.
2196	Pte.	ALEXANDER, A.	36th Australian Inf.	6/5/18	P.O., Leyton, N.S.W.
61316	Pte.	ALEXANDER, A.	4th Middlesex Regt.	12/10/16	237, Brunswick Buildings, London, E.
18531	Pte.	ALEXANDER, D.	16th Middlesex Regt.	1/12/17	44, Brady Street Buildings, London, E.
11820	Pte.	ALEXANDER, H.	3rd East Surrey Regt.	1/10/18	145, Kensal Road, London, W.10.
J/3909	Pte.	ALEXANDER, M.	39th Royal Fusiliers	20/10/18	16, South Clerk Street, Edinburgh.
J/1110	Pte.	ALICK, N.	38th Royal Fusiliers	30/10/18	17a, Spelman Street, London, E.1.
401	Pte.	ALLEN, D. C.	58th Australian Inf.	20/8/16	58, Capel Street North, Melbourne.
	P.O.	ALLEN, E.	H.M.S. "Mignonette"	17/3/17	154, Chorley New Road, Horwich, Lancs.
115561	Gnr.	ALLEN, S.	R.G.A.	19/11/17	20, King Edward Road, London, E.9.
773	Pte.	ALLONOWITZ, L.	38th Royal Fusiliers	29/10/18	London.
3629	Pte.	ALTHUSEN, M.	1st K.O.R. Lancs. Regt.	1/7/16	28, Darnley Road, Hackney, London, N.E.
63656	Pte.	ALTMAN, H.	16th Lancashire Fusiliers	24/8/18	201, Thistle Street, Glasgow, S.S.
9756	Cpl.	ALTMAN, J.	1st Royal Irish Rifles	24/10/14	297, Argyle Street, Glasgow.
13375	Pte.	ALTMAN, L.	1st Bedford Regt.	29/6/17	63, Manor Road, Stoke Newington, London, N.
1134	Pte.	ALTMANN, C.	24th Australian Inf.	29/11/15	Mt, Duneed, Seelong.
1685	Pte.	ANDRADE, W. A.	4th London Regt.	15/3/15	45, Oban Street, Poplar, London, E.
12/14	Pte.	ANKER, A.	3rd Auckland Inf. N.Z.E.F.	9/6/15	310, High Street, Poplar, London, E.
6916	Pte.	ANNENBERG, A.	2nd Devonshire Regt.	8/11/16	287, Green Lanes, London, N.

77

N.C.O.'S AND MEN—Continued.

No.	Rank. Name.	Regiment.	Date of Death.	Address.
14751	Pte. ANNENBERG, H. B.	2nd Royal Sussex Regt.	27/9/16	8, Paddington Green, London, W.
4908	Pte. ANNENBERG (ASH-BERRY), B.	—	—	—
40407	Tpr. ANNENBERG (ASHBERRY), R.	13th London Regt.	9/4/17	26, Dean Road, Willesden Green, London, N.W.
41506	Pte. ANNENBERG, S.	1st City of London Yeo.	14/1/17	26, Dean Road, Willesden Green, London.
27687	L/Cpl. APTER, S.	17th West Yorks Regt.	17/4/17	23, Enfield Road, Roundhay Road, Leeds.
374231	Rfm. ARANOW, H.	8th Oxford & Bucks L.I.	22/10/17	27, Clevedon Road, Birmingham.
55309	Pte. ARONBERG, S.	8th London Regt.	7/6/17	87, Langdale Mansions, London, E.
4164	Rfm. ASSENHEIM, L.	12th Manchester Regt.	27/4/18	83, Great Ducie Street, Manchester.
676	Pte. ASHER, S.	17th K.R.R.C.	3/9/16	25, Harold Road, Upton Park, London, E.
2149	Pte. ASHER, 9.	9th York & Lancs. Regt.	3/10/16	8, Cuba Street, Sunderland.
476450	Sapper AVERBACK, J.	36th Australian Inf.	1917	67, Holt Street, Surrey Hills, N.S.W.
S/368410	Pte. AVNER, M.	461 W. Riding Fld.Co.R.E.	8/6/18	61, Concord Street, Leeds.
1145	Trooper AUERBACH, W. H.	R.A.S.C.	6/4/18	137, Elizabeth Street, Manchester.
J/2622	Pte. AZUZ, J.	1st K.E. Horse	23/5/15	7, Cheyne Road, Chelsea, London, S.W.
		39th Royal Fusiliers	4/7/18	Jerusalem.
40738	Pte. BAKER, D.	22nd Manchester Regt.	4/10/17	45, Bell Street, Manchester.
850609	Pte. BAKER, H. J.	20th Canadian Inf.	3/11/17	1211, Hazel Street, Pittsburg, U.S.A.
1146	Pte. BAKER, H. R.	1st South African Inf.	17/7/16	22, De Villiers Street, Cape Town.
267228	Pte. BAKER, N.	2/7th West Yorks. Regt.	4/9/17	19, Claremont Place, Claypit Lane, Leeds.
193802	Gnr. BALCHIN, W.	A/242 Brigade, R.F.A.	27/11/17	438, London Road, Westcliffe.
2403	Pte. BALON, I. E.	1/7th Manchester Regt.	29/5/15	15, Thorncliffe Grove, Manchester.
76378	Pte. BANDAS, A.	1st Northumberland Fus.	23/11/18	83, Ely Terrace, Hartford Street, London, E.
190856	Pte. BANKOFSKY, A.	258th Area Emp. Coy.	28/10/18	95, Stock Street, Cheetham, Manchester.
51694	Pte. BARBACK, M.	11th Royal Scots	19/8/18	282, High Street, Glasgow.
	Pte. BARDIN, D.	Zion Mule Corps	21/6/15	Alexandria.
11832	Pte. BARADOSKY, B.	8th East Yorks. Regt.	14/7/16	33, Adelaide Street, Hull.
60	Pte. BARGMEN, S.	Zion Mule Corps	7/6/15	Alexandria.
39575	Cpl. BARITZ, E.	2nd South Wales Borderers	27/4/17	8, Hodgson Street, Cheetham, Manchester.
678049	Rfm. BARKMAN, C.	21st London Regt.	15/6/18	394, Brixton Road, London, S.W.9.
1748	Gnr. BARMES, W.	11th Bgde. Australian Artil.	7/6/17	5, Algiers Road, Lewisham, London.
74576	L/Cpl. BARNARD, J. H.	7th Royal Fusiliers	4/4/18	"Corona," Victoria Road, London, N.
2045	Sergt. BARNARD, L.	5th King's Liverpool Regt.	8/8/16	2, Whitland Road, Fairfield, Liverpool.
1427	Pte. BARNARD, L.	8th Canadian Inf.	25/4/15	54, Fordwych Road, London, N.W.
9070	L/Cpl. BARNARD, S.	1st Royal Munster Fus.	21/11/17	95, Stoke Road, Gosport.
12843	Pte. BARNES, J.	3rd South African Inf.	20/9/17	20, Hatherley Street, Liverpool.
235277	Pte. BARNES, J.	15th R. Welsh Fus.	27/2/17	115, Bromsgrove Street, Birmingham.
9017	Pte. BARNET, G.	4th Royal Fusiliers	28/8/15	8, Blossom Street, Bishopsgate, London, E.C.
472596	Rfm. BARNETT, B.	12th London Regt.	5/5/17	29, Cleveley Road, Upper Clapton, London, E.5.
9170	Pte. BARNETT, C.	3rd Royal Fusiliers	3/5/15	20, Ralph Street, Borough, London, S.E.
J/2062	Pte. BARNETT, D.	39th Royal Fusiliers	1/11/18	15, Irwell Street, Strangeways, Manchester.
5411	Pte. BARNETT, E. B.	24th London Regt.	16/9/16	141, Graham Road, Dalston, London, N.E.

N.C.O.'S AND MEN—Continued.

No.	Rank.	Name.	Regiment.	Date of Death.	Address.
532898	Pte.	BARNETT, G.	15th London Regt.	7/6/17	19, Enfield Grove, Roundhay Road, Leeds.
5722	L/Cpl.	BARNETT, H.	2/4th London Regt.	16/6/17	35, Mildmay Park, London, N.
267006	Pte.	BARNETT, J.	2/1st Bucks. Regt.	22/8/17	21, Lower Chapman Street, London, E.
9186	Pte.	BARNETT, J.	2nd Scots Guards	26/10/14	16, Nelson Street, Dundee.
72910	1/A.M. Obsvr.	BARNETT, J.	Canadian R.A.F.	12/11/18	35, Malmesbury Road, London, E.3.
6236	Pte.	BARNETT, L.	4th Middlesex Regt.	12/7/15	14, Benson Buildings, Shoreditch, London, E.
7654	Rfm.	BARNETT, M.	12th London Regt.	10/5/17	21a, Chambord Street, Bethnal Green, London, E.
452180	Pte.	BARNETT, M.	2/11th London Regt.	22/5/17	28, St. Peter's Road, London, E.
66760	Pte.	BARNETT, M.	32nd Royal Fusiliers	5/12/17	11, Bengan Street, Liverpool.
5509	Rfm.	BARNETT, R.	1st Rifle Brigade	20/12/14	18, Church Street, Stoke Newington, London, N.
204305	Pte.	BARNETT, S.	2/1st London Regt.	21/3/18	9, Gordon Road, Stoke Newington, London, N.
S/7822	Cpl.	BARNETT, S.	1st Rifle Brigade	8/8/16	189, Hoe Street, Walthamstow, London, E.
14946	Pte.	BARNETT, W.	7th South Lancs. Regt.	20/7/16	53, New Bridge Street, Manchester.
7338	Pte.	BARNEY, J. G.	2nd H.A.C.	1/4/17	195, Kentish Town Road, London, N.W.
4554	Pte.	BARON, O.	24th Royal Fusiliers	31/7/16	19, Plymouth Grove, C.-on-M, Manchester.
14216	Pte.	BARONOWITCH, L.	1st Worcester Regt.	31/7/17	72, Barking Road, Canning Town, London, E.
611863	Pte.	BARZOLOI, L.	1/19th London Regt.	7/12/17	6, Butler Street, Spitalfields, London, E.
1602	Pte.	BASH, L.	10th Royal Fusiliers	10/4/17	32, Charles Street, Hatton Garden, London, E.C.
22701	L/Cpl.	BAUM, H.	1st Border Regt.	3/7/16	7, Dempsey Street, London, E.
32976	Pte.	BAUMGARD, S.	22nd Lancashire Fusiliers	15/9/16	27, Pimblett Street, Cheetham, Manchester.
8667	Rfm.	BAZINSKI, S.	1/21st London Regt.	26/8/17	22, Rothschild Buildings, London, E.1.
85174	Pte.	BEAR, C.	118th M.G.C.	25/9/17	68, Cadogan Terrace, Victoria Park, London.
6435	Pte.	BECKER, J.	2/5th Notts & Derby Regt.	4/5/17	17, Lamb Street, London, E.
32455	Pte.	BECKER, J.	1st East Surrey Regt.	8/5/17	17, Lamb Street, London, E.
62069	Pte.	BECKER, W.	9th Royal Fusiliers	3/5/17	17, Lamb Street, London, E.
13547	Cpl.	BECKERWICK, M.	4th Middlesex Regt.	15/10/14	Duck End, Ampthill, Beds.
15945	Pte.	BELCHER, C.	1st S. Battery R.G.A.	19/5/17	7, Varden Street, London, E.
322804	Rfm.	BELL, I.	6th London Regt.	24/11/17	5, Harold Road, Upton Park, London, E.
546	Pte.	BELMAN, A. M.	2/7th Lancashire Fusiliers	22/4/17	121, Lisvane Street, Cathays, Cardiff.
46109	Gnr.	BELMONT, D.	B/87th Brigade, R.F.A.	3/10/16	23, Sutton Street, London, E.
16316	L/Cpl.	BENDER, J.	8th Royal Fusiliers	20/7/15	241, Commercial Road, London, E.
27537	Pte.	BENJAMIN, A.	6th Northampton Regt.	10/8/17	38, Heber Road, London, N.W.
822	L/Cpl.	BENJAMIN, A. L.	24th Australian Inf.	29/7/16	Wangaratta Road, Richmond, Victoria, Australia.
9466	Rfm.	BENJAMIN, A.	1st Rifle Brigade	6/12/14	31, Ernest Street, London, E.
30903	Pte.	BENJAMIN, C.	2nd Devon Regt.	25/11/17	59, Irving Street, Birmingham.
12029	Pte.	BENJAMIN, H.	7th Norfolk Regt.	9/5/17	24, Grove Terrace, Leeds.
	Pte.	BENJAMIN, H.	R.A.S.C., M.T.	28/1/19	London.
3/22893	Pte.	BENJAMIN, H. B.	7th South Wales Borderers	18/9/18	19, St. Peter's Road, London, E.
111031	Pte.	BENJAMIN, H. E.	5th Canadian Mounted Rifles	3/6/16	Cumberland County, N.S., Canada.
32321	Pte.	BENJAMIN, K.	10th West Yorks. Regt.	23/4/17	11, Lovell Place, Leeds.
53793	Pte.	BENJAMIN, L.	23rd Cheshire Regt.	1/10/18	95, Halton Road, Islington, London.
4893	Rfm.	BENJAMIN, M.	1st K.R.R.C.	15/5/15	17, Dunbar Road, Forest Gate, London, E.
2002	Rfm.	BENJAMIN, P.	17th London Regt.	26/9/15	18, Chilton Street, London, E.

N.C.O.'S AND MEN—Continued.

No.	Rank.	Name.	Regiment.	Date of Death.	Address.
5177	Pte.	BENJAMIN, P. D.	3/5th Lancashire Fusiliers	17/3/17	48, Trafalgar Street, Manchester.
3959	Bdr.	BENJAMIN, S. O.	21st How. Bde. Austr. F.A.	23/11/16	10, Hereford Mansions, London, W.
7249	Pte.	BENSON, S.	11th Royal Fusiliers	26/9/16	241, Brunswick Buildings, London, E.
523486	Rfm.	BENTLEY, J. (M.M.)	6th London Regt.	10/3/19	148, Princes Road, London, S.E.
58359	Pte.	BENZIMRA, A. J.	3rd Hampshire Regt.	25/10/18	145, Beedell Avenue, Westcliff.
161851	Pnr.	BERGSON, M.	80th Sig. R.E.	22/10/17	101, Constable Street, Wellington, N.Z.
163534	Pte.	BERKOVITZ, I. M.	1st Canadian Inf.	9/7/16	89, Armstrong Avenue, Toronto, Canada.
1304	Sergt.	BERKSON, M.	1/4th Cheshire Regt.	21/8/15	233, Park Road, Tranmere, Cheshire.
88271	Pte.	BERLINER, H.	148th Labour Coy.	23/11/17	26, Hackney Road, London, N.E.
11802	Pte.	BERMAN, B. (SAVILLE, H.)			
J/1321	Pte.	BERMAN, J.	4th S. African Inf.	2/6/17	26, Downs Park Road, London, N.E.
4868	Pte.	BERMAN, L.	38th Royal Fusiliers	25/10/18	40, Cameron Place, Commercial Road, London, E.
699007	Pte.	BERMAN, P.	9th Royal Fusiliers	30/8/16	85, Paddington, Liverpool.
171	Gnr.	BERMAN, R.	1/22nd London Regt.	22/2/18	87, Curtain Road, London, E.C.
5835	Pte.	BERMAN, S. M.	S. African Heavy Artillery	3/4/17	Lester Road, Wynberg, South Africa.
200163	Rfm.	BERNARD, A.	9th Royal Scots	29/3/17	13, Drummond Street, Edinburgh.
1659A	Pte.	BERNARD, F. (F. H. LESNIE)	11th Rifle Brigade	22/6/17	4, Newman Street, London, E.
27043	S/Sgt.	BERNARD, L. (B. LEVY)	17th Australian Inf.	2/3/17	2, Little Titchfield Street, London, W.
908	Pte.	BERNAYS, R. M.	15th Canadian Inf.	9/10/16	65, Petherton Road, London, N.
L/12830	Pte.	BERNHARD, A.	3rd Australian Inf.	27/4/15	Parliament House, Brisbane.
307486	Pte.	BERNSTEIN, A.	9th Lancers	27/3/18	12, Withmill Road, Blackpool.
9660	Pte.	BERNSTEIN, C.	2/10th King's Liverpool Rg.	10/5/17	19, Clarence Street, Liverpool.
393106	Rfm.	BERNSTEIN, C. N.	1st Connaught Rangers	26/4/15	13, Keble Street, Liverpool.
35607	Pte.	BERNSTEIN, H.	9th London Regt.	14/4/17	26, Torbay Mansions, Willesden, London, N.W.
14073	Sergt.	BERNSTEIN, H.	15th Cheshire Regt.	12/8/18	18, East Street, Stockport.
	Pte.	BERNSTEIN, I.	7th K.O.R. Lancaster Regt.	31/7/16	4, St. John's Road, Higher Broughton, Manchester.
23334	Pte.	BERNSTEIN, J.	2nd Norfolk Regt.	20/11/16	London, E.
32334	Pte.	BERNSTEIN, L.	10th West Riding Regt.	7/6/17	24, Ashfield, Horton Road, Bradford.
59168	Pte.	BERNSTEIN, L.	7th East Surrey Regt.	20/11/17	12, Latimer Street, Stepney, London, E.
183044	Gnr.	BERNSTEIN, M.	22nd Field Amb. R.A.M.C.	4/3/17	12, Mowbray Road, Sunderland.
S/30729	Rfm.	BERNSTEIN, S.	C/52nd Brigade, R.F.A.	25/10/17	58, Wardour Street, London, W.
6983	Pte.	BERNSTEIN, S.	1st Rifle Brigade	12/10/17	30, Nottingham Place, London, E.
3088	Tpr.	BERNSTEIN, S. A.	39th Royal Fusiliers	24/10/18	3, Cowper Street, Leeds.
3425	L/Cpl.	BERSON, D.	Middlesex Imp. Yeomanry	8/9/15	Rose Cottage, Bow Road, London, E.
18156	Pte.	BERSON, W.	2/7th West Yorks. Regt.	4/7/17	10, Metz Place, Leeds.
56069	Gnr.	BERZANCE, L.	13th Essex Regt.	2/7/16	77, North Street, Leeds.
10584	Pte.	BEYFUS, C. S.	D/82nd Brigade, R.F.A.	6/11/17	595, Stretford Road, Manchester.
225	Rfm.	BEYFUS, H.	2nd H.A.C.	16/7/17	4, Park Place Villas, London, W.
	Pte.		1st L.R.B.	13/5/15	4, Park Place Villas, London, W.
J/1750	Pte.	BIENSTOCK, M.	38th Royal Fusiliers	31/10/18	243, Cable Street, London, E.
199045	Pte.	BIGOFSKI, E.	746 Area Employment Coy.	9/10/17	311, Hoe Street, Walthamstow, London, N.E.
6304	L/Sergt.	BINNES, J.	2/5th Royal Warwick. Rgt.	6/9/17	95, Bellott Street, Cheetham, Manchester.
6043	Rfm.	BIRNBAUM, M.	15th London Regt.	26/1/17	65, Alvington Crescent, Dalston, London, N.
243099	Pte.	BIRTLESTON, J.	1/5th K.O.R. Lancs. Regt.	30/11/17	34, Peter Street, Manchester.

N.C.O.'S AND MEN—Continued.

No.	Rank.	Name.	Regiment.	Date of Death.	Address.
1187	Pte.	BISHOP, S.	5th Australian Inf.	29/8/18	37, Percy Street, London, W.
8495	Sergt.	BLACK, D.	1st H.L.I.	19/12/14	24, Sauchiehall Street, Glasgow.
J/332	Pte.	BLACK, L.	38th Royal Fusiliers	17/10/18	58, Roseville Street, Leeds.
12992	Pte.	BLACK, M.	1st King's Liverpool Regt.	1/12/17	128, Broughton Lane, Manchester.
11/831	Pte.	BLACK, M.	11th East Yorks. Regt.	13/11/16	34, St. Luke's Street, Hull.
31090	Pte.	BLACKMAN, J.	56th M.G.C.	3/5/17	418, Commercial Road, London, E.
1751	Cpl.	BLACKMAN, M.	4th London Regt.	27/4/15	16, Cecil Street, London, E.
26008	Pte.	BLACKER, P.	2/6th Royal Sussex Regt.	12/7/18	38, Grafton Street, London, W.
10770	Pte.	BLACKSTONE, M.	7th Seaforth Highlanders	14/10/16	24, Briddon Street, Manchester.
2976	Rfm.	BLAIN, S. (M.M.)	1st K.R.R.C.	29/7/16	13, Petworth Street, Manchester.
139182	Pte.	BLASHKEY, A.	R.A.M.C.	16/3/18	60, Royal Terrace, Dunedin, N.Z.
8/3495	Pte.	BLAUBAUM, E.	New Zealand Inf.	3/6/16	26, Sedgwick Street, Bradford.
41923	Pte.	BLIEVERS, C.	10/11th H.L.I.	13/4/17	39a, South Portland Street, Glasgow.
32707	Pte.	BLINT, M.	13th Royal Scots	1/8/17	19, Queen Street, Melbourne.
34944	Gnr.	BLOCH, F. L.	6th Army Bde. Austr. F.A.	17/8/18	29, Webster Street, Ballarat, Victoria.
1574	Pte.	BLOCK, N. S.	14th Australian Inf.	8/6/15	1, Coburg Place, Cleveland Street, London, E.
301844	Stoker	BLOK, M.	H.M.S. "Lapwing"	21/12/16	8, Church Street, King's Lynn.
7182	L/Cpl.	BLOOM, H.	1st Norfolk Regt.	31/1/15	43, George Avenue, Leeds.
1440	Gnr.	BLOOM, H.	0/5th R.H. Artillery	2/6/18	15, Calthorpe Street, London, W.C.
1851	Rfm.	BLOOM, J.	4th Rifle Brigade	14/5/15	25, Gossitt Street, Bethnal Green, London, N.E.
4748	Pte.	BLOOM, J.	2/4th London Regt.	15/5/17	29, Church Street, Shoreditch, London, E.
34455	Cpl.	BLOOM, J.	2nd Essex Regt.	3/5/17	57, Dorothy Street, Liverpool.
18503	Gnr.	BLOOM, J. S.	264th Bde. R.F.A.	30/9/18	110, Bathurst Street, Sydney, N.S.W.
1817	Pte.	BLOOM, L. R.	2nd Australian Inf.	5/1/15	Hunter Street, Abbotsford, Melbourne, Vic.
201	Pte.	BLOOM, S.	16th Australian Inf.	27/4/15	74, Virginia Road, Shoreditch, London, E.
19870	Pte.	BLOOMENTHAL, M.	21st Middlesex Regt.	9/4/17	27, Brook Street, Manchester.
J/1055	L/Cpl.	BLOOMFIELD, E. (M.M.)	38th Royal Fusiliers	1/11/18	27, Apsley Place, Glasgow.
4422	Pte.	BLOSTIEN, P.	9th H.L.I.	27/5/17	5a, Ducal Street, Bethnal Green, London, E.
43172	Pte.	BLUESTEIN, J.	2nd Royal Dublin Fusiliers	5/8/17	47, Fieldgate Street, London, E.
6244	Pte.	BLUESTONE, M.	1/1st London Regt.	15/9/16	82, Nelson Street, Stepney, London, E.
60074	Rfm.	BLUMENTHAL, J.	101st Labour Coy.	16/5/18	27, Ellen Street, London, E.
17776	Pte.	BLUSTIN, J. A.	1st Rifle Brigade	4/5/17	2, Northampton Park, Canonbury, London, N.
4656	Pte.	BLUMENTHAL (KINGSLEY), A.	4th London Regt.	9/9/16	
8470					
32647	Pte.	BOAM, C.	1st Leicester Regiment	16/3/16	8, Baldwin Crescent, London, S.E.
G/75008	Pte.	BOBER, H.	8th York and Lancs. Regt.	25/5/17	11, Vandyke Street, Leeds.
26185	Rfm.	BOGARD, J.	11th Royal Fusiliers	2/4/18	No. 9 Flat, Slater Street Buildings, London, E.
63572	Pte.	BOGARD, M.	8th Rifle Brigade	4/4/18	47, Pereira Street, London, E.1.
17402	Pte.	BOLLER, J.	13th Royal Fusiliers	18/9/18	34, Somerford Street, Bethnal Green, London, E.
10460	Pte.	BOMBERG, I.	8th East Lancashire Regt.	29/6/16	57, Maylons Road, Lewisham, London.
1204	Pte.	BONNER, P. M.	2nd Yorks. Regt.	12/3/15	4, Lewins Buildings, Sidney Street, London, E.
3/2344	S/Sgt.-Maj.	BOOCK, B.	2nd H.A.C.	1/3/17	53, Belsize Avenue, London, N.W.
1345	Cpl.	BOODSON, L.	N.Z. Med. Corps	10/11/18	83, Aro Street, Wellington, N.Z.
			6th Manchester Regt.	24/6/15	14, Brunswick Street, Cheetham, Manchester.

N.C.O.'S AND MEN—Continued.

No.	Rank.	Name.	Regiment.	Date of Death.	Address.
7008	Rfm.	BOOKER, J.	1st Rifle Brigade	5/7/15	118, Blackwall Buildings, London, E.
27676	Pte.	BOOKSTEIN, J.	76th Labour Coy.	24/2/19	39, Langdale Street, London, E.
3925	Pte.	BOROWSKI, L. P.	48th Australian Inf.	28/3/18	
556827	Rfm.	BOSS, N.	1/16th London Regt.	30/11/17	26, Fitzroy Square, London, W.
8/3495	Pte.	BOWDEN, E.	2nd Otago Inf., N.Z.	3/7/16	60, Royal Terrace, Dunedin, N.Z.
13262	Pte.	BOWMAN, L. E.	4th Aus. Field Amb.	8/6/17	13, Somerset Street, N. Richmond, Victoria.
2926	Pte.	BRAHAM, C.	1/1st London Regt.	15/9/16	167, The Grove, Hammersmith, London, W.
21941	Pte.	BRAHAM, P.	20th King's Liverpool Rgt.	1/7/16	31, Madeleine Street, Liverpool.
565099	Rfm.	BRAVER, A.	1/16th London Regt.	14/8/17	92, Hogarth Houses, Christian Street, London, E.
201559	Pte.	BRAZIL, V.	1/4th K.O.R. Lancs. Regt.	31/7/17	104, Herbert Street, Manchester.
4965	Pte.	BRETMAN, J. G. (M.M.)	3rd Australian Inf.	19/4/19	78, Exmouth Street, London, E.
7243	Pte.	BREM, J.	13th Labour Coy.	19/6/17	6, Carlton Court, Glasgow.
J/2862	Pte.	BRESLAUER, J.	39th Royal Fusiliers	13/10/18	Tredegar Square, London, E.
1/1010	Pte.	BRICK, B.	38th Royal Fusiliers	14/10/18	119, Morgan Houses, Hessle Street, E.
M/336085	Cpl.	BRODIE, J.	R.A.S.C., M.T.	5/12/18	19, Vernon Street, Hightown, Manchester.
195728	Cpl.	BRODIE, M.	520th Labour Coy.	6/12/17	32, Elmwood Street, Leeds.
307067	Pte.	BROSGILL, W.	12th West Yorks. Regt.	7/6/17	62, Grafton Street, Leeds.
457100	Pte.	BROMET, M. J. H.	6oth Canadian Inf.	25/12/16	104, Gloucester Place, London, W.
12/1448	Pte.	BROWN, A.	8th East Yorks. Regt.	14/7/16	33, Adelaide Street, Hull.
472385	Rfm.	BROWN, H.	12th London Regt.	10/5/15	27, Hale Terrace, Tottenham, London, N.
10506	Pte.	BROWN, H.	2nd Royal Sussex Regt.	16/5/15	164, High Street, Tottenham, London, N.
8255	Pte.	BROWN, J.	1st Royal Fusiliers	14/8/16	1, Princes Square, London, E.
12033	Pte.	BROWN, M.	1st Coldstream Guards	30/9/15	9, Offley Road, Brixton, London.
534120	Pte.	BUCK, A. I.	1/12th London Regt.	6/9/17	46, Sothby Road, Highbury, London, N.
10593	Pte.	BURMAN, T. M.	2nd Northampton Regt.	14/3/15	344, Neepsend Lane, Sheffield.
46814	Pte.	BURNSTEIN, J.	13th Canadian Inf.	15/8/17	Glace Bay P.O.B. 795, Nova Scotia.
J/3856	Pte.	BURNS, M.	38th Royal Fusiliers	2/2/18	32, Prince of Wales Road, Swansea.
SS/4259	Pte.	BUSNACH, H.	R.A.S.C.	13/6/15	5, King's Block, Stoney Lane, London, E.
200663	Pte.	BUTLER, A.	7th Rifle Brigade	29/9/17	25, Saville Street, London, W.
6895	Pte.	BUTMAN, J.	1st Somerset L.I.	18/10/16	2, Buckle Street, London, E.
52865	Pte.	CADINSKY, H. B.	17th King's Liverpool Rgt.	24/4/17	28, Elm Street, Manchester.
25457	Pte.	CAIRNS, J.	18th Lancashire Fusiliers	30/7/16	15, Fleur de Lis Buildings, London, E.
24038	Pte.	CAMINER, A.	2nd Middlesex Regt.	2/11/17	34, Tillman Street, London, E.
18848	Dvr.	CAMP, H.	12th Bde. Australian Artil.	10/6/18	Miller Street N., Sydney, N.S.W.
2657	Pte.	CAMPBELL, C.	1/5th Royal Scots Regt.	27/9/15	5, Montgomery Place, Edinburgh.
532630	Pte.	CAMRASS, E.	15th London Regt.	8/12/17	30, High Street, Dublin.
	Pte.	CANARICK, C.	South African Inf.	19/7/17	289, Proes Street, Pretoria, S.A.
J/1119	Pte.	CANTER, H.	38th Royal Fusiliers	22/10/18	129, Teesdale Street, London, E.8.
35749	S/Sgt.	CANTON (COHEN), J.	142nd Field Amb. R.A.M.C.	14/7/16	40, Brunswick Street, Manchester.
993	Sgt.	CANTOR, B.	5th Australian Arty.	9/5/15	Peal Street, Collingwood, Vic.
S/34024	Rfm.	CAPLAN, F.	1st R.B, attd. 4th M.G.Bn.	16/4/18	75, Hanbury Street, London, E.
G/69807	Pte.	CAPLAN, J.	1st Royal Fusiliers	23/3/18	51, Stone Street, Newcastle-on-Tyne.
46612	Pte.	CARLIPH, S.	12th Manchester Regt.	23/3/18	375, Oxford Road, Manchester.

82

N.C.O.'S AND MEN—Continued.

No.	Rank.	Name.	Regiment.	Date of Death.	Address.
393300	Pte.	CARMEL, M.	302nd Labour Coy.	23/2/18	63, Cephas Street, London, E.
5662	Pte.	CARO, M. C.	2/13th London Regt.	2/8/16	Albert Street, Auckland, N.Z.
10303	Pte.	CAROLTEN, R.	2nd Yorks. Regt.	23/10/14	9, Tysoe Street, London, E.C.
33335	Pte.	CARP, L.	1/4th York & Lancs. Regt.	9/10/17	81, Wilkes Street, London, E.
19748	Pte.	CASSEL, E.	1st Royal Dublin Fus.	18/8/15	96, Falkner Street, Liverpool.
17547	Pte.	CASSELL, C. A.	2/1st Norfolk Yeomanry	20/5/18	154, Percy Road, Canning Town, London, E.
7023	Pte.	CASSONMAN, H.	1st Dorset Regt.	21/4/15	38, Winterton Street, London, E.
B/3305	Pte.	CASTLE, F.	26th Royal Fusiliers	7/10/16	23, Lansdowne Crescent, London, W.
09054	Sgt.	CASVENIR, R.	Egyptian Labour Corps	11/4/17	Alexandria.
472437	Rfm.	CATES, A.	1/12th London Regt.	27/11/17	24, Wiltshire Road, London, S.E.
322588	Pte.	CATS, L. V.	23rd London Regt.	26/5/18	Home Lodge, Lordship Park, London, N.
271022	Pte.	CAVE, E. M.	6th East Kent Regt.	29/9/18	55, Madrid Road, Barnes, London, S.W.
12081	Pte.	CHAIMOWITZ, M.	1st South African Inf.	21/9/17	2, Avenue, Springs, South Africa.
493113	Pte.	CHALFEN, J.	13th London Regt.	6/10/18	29, Brackley Road, Chiswick, London.
18697	Pte.	CHAPMAN, H.	15th Royal Scots	28/4/17	4, Parkhouse Lane, Glasgow.
1985	Pte.	CHART, B.	4th London Regt.	26/4/17	86, Erlanger Road, London, S.E.
13109	Pte.	CHESNEY, D.	1st Coldstream Guards	18/10/15	3, Tenter St. N., London, E.
221673	Dvr.	CHESSES, W.	31st Div. Signals, R.E.	30/10/18	58, Ashley Street, Birmingham.
45099	Rfm.	CHITRIN, H.	2nd K.R.R.C.	7/7/18	1, Sanders Street, Johannesburg.
42347	Pte.	CLAFF, R.	1st Somerset L.I.	14/6/18	45, Alexandra Road, Southport.
4775	Pte.	CLAPHAM, P.	4th Seaforth Highlanders	29/11/16	22, Darfield Street, Bradford.
710	Tpr.	CLARK, D.	1st Royal Dragoons	17/5/15	233, Cookson Street, Glasgow.
253709	Pte.	CLEVE, M.	3rd London Regt.	25/4/18	7, Kitchener Road, London, E.
878	Cpl.	CLINE, D.	4th South African Inf.	20/4/17	Twickenham Avenue, Johannesburg.
926	Pte.	CLINE, J.	4th South African Inf.	16/7/16	125, Sivewright Avenue, Doornfontein, S.A.
3837	Pte.	COHEN, A.	1st Queen's R.W. Surrey	29/9/15	85, Selkirk Road, London, S.W.
6728	Rfm.	COHEN, A.	17th London Regt.	26/12/17	107, Grove Street, London, E.
8369	Pte.	COHEN, A.	1st Northampton Regt.	20/11/14	35, Shepherdess Walk, London, E.C.
48599	Pte.	COHEN, A.	12th King's Liverpool Rgt	7/10/16	44, Carnarvon Street, Manchester.
7079	Pte.	COHEN, A.	2nd H.A.C.	11/10/16	2, Chichele Mansions, London, N.W.
6739	Pte.	COHEN, A.	16th Australian Inf.	26/9/17	Woodville Road N., Perth, Western Australia.
25070	Pte.	COHEN, A.	24/27 Northumberland Fus.	23/10/17	66, Byron Street, Leeds.
307060	Pte.	COHEN, A.	8th West Yorks. Regt.	26/3/18	57, St. Luke's Street, Leeds.
202702	L/Cpl.	COHEN, A.	2/4th Leicester Regt.	26/7/18	108, Netherwood Road, London, W.
4347	L/Cpl.	COHEN, A.	2nd Welsh Regt.	5/3/19	163, York Street, Leeds.
23891	Pte.	COHEN, A. E.	1st Lincoln Labour Coy.	3/1/19	39, Busfield Street, Leeds.
362	Pte.	COHEN, A. E.	2nd South African Inf.	19/7/16	Ott's Cluff, Natal.
2338	Sergt.	COHEN, A. G.	6th West Yorks. Regt.	19/12/15	11, Darley Street, Bradford.
A/200123	Rfm.	COHEN, A. J.	17th K.R.R.C.	21/10/16	6, Hawthorne Close, Sutton Garden Suburb, Surrey.
26196	Pte.	COHEN, B.	21st Manchester Regt.	1/7/16	146, Boughton Street, Manchester.
32978	Pte.	COHEN, B.	1st Bedford Regt.	28/6/17	10, Augustin Street, Northampton.
1712	Sergt.	COHEN, B.	5th King's Liverpool Regt.	20/9/17	6, Great Orford Street, Liverpool.

N.C.O.'S AND MEN—Continued.

No.	Rank.	Name.	Regiment.	Date of Death.	Address.
252426	Pte.	COHEN, B.	2/3rd London Regt.	26/10/17	72, Fernhead Road, London, W.
4024	Pte.	COHEN, D.	21st Manchester Regt.	14/7/16	39, Soho Street, Liverpool.
18296	Tpr.	COHEN, D.	4th Hussars	26/6/16	201, Melrose Avenue, London, N.W.
192	Pte.	COHEN, D.	22nd Royal Fusiliers	4/7/16	9, Cromwell Terrace, Hammersmith, London, W.
265897	Cpl.	COHEN, D. (M.M.)	6th Welsh Regt.	27/5/17	108, Gloucester Road, Newcastle.
203246	Cpl.	COHEN, D.	2nd London Regt.	27/8/18	139, Ernest Street, London, E.
8755	L/Cpl.	COHEN, E.	2nd Royal Welsh Fusiliers	22/8/16	15, Fleur de Lis Buildings, London, E.
5/221	Rfm.	COHEN, E.	1st Rifle Brigade	19/12/14	31, King David Lane, London, E.
460919	Pte.	COHEN, F.	12th Can. F. Amb. C.A.M.C.	4/9/18	341, Harold Avenue, Winnipeg.
269475	Pte.	COHEN, G.	2/7th King's Liverpool Rgt.	28/6/17	450, Great Cheetham Street, Manchester.
6300	Pte.	COHEN, G.	28th Australian Inf.	22/9/17	Gallipoli, Melbourne.
8252	Pte.	COHEN, H.	1st Royal Irish Rifles	5/1/15	155, Ernest Street, London, E.
998	Pte.	COHEN, H.	1st Cheshire Regt.	1/6/15	34, Bushfield Street, Leeds.
39576	Pte.	COHEN, H.	2nd South Wales Borderers	26/10/16	18, Clarence Street, Manchester.
915886	Gnr.	COHEN, H.	D/291 Brigade, R.F.A.	15/12/17	Askew House, Shepherd's Bush, London.
39564	Pte.	COHEN, H.	10th Lancashire Fusiliers	22/3/18	20, Howard Street, Manchester.
6540	Pte.	COHEN, H.	19th Australian Inf.	3/10/18	St. James' Square, Bristol.
18330	Pte.	COHEN (CLARK), H.	1st Canadian Infantry	24/4/15	Montreal.
58523	2/A.M.	COHEN, H. A.	R.A.F.	2/9/18	15, Alderney Road, London, E.
242414	Pte.	COHEN, I.	1st Middlesex Regt.	25/9/17	8, Shepherd's Bush Road, London, W.
77934	Pte.	COHEN, I.	24th Cheshire Regt.	11/11/18	31, Cruddock Street, Cardiff.
33237	L/Cpl.	COHEN, J. I.	2nd Wiltshire Regt.	31/7/17	105, Silver Street, London, E.
17176	Pte.	COHEN, J.	18th King's Liverpool Rgt.	1/7/16	109, Paddington, Liverpool.
5467	Rfm.	COHEN, J.	1st Rifle Brigade	1/7/16	86, Boundary Street, Shoreditch, London, E.
4091	Pte.	COHEN, J.	1/1st Bucks Regt.	15/8/16	10, Fremont Street, Hackney, London, N.E.
2142	L/Cpl.	COHEN, J.	17th London Regt.	30/10/16	6, Butler Street, London, E.
3500	Cpl.	COHEN, J.	24th Australian Inf.	4/3/17	110, Wilson Street N., Carlton, Victoria.
101789	Gnr.	COHEN, J.	185th Hy. Battery, R.G.A.	28/8/17	11, Victoria Road, Kilburn, London, N.W.
17909	Rfm.	COHEN, J.	1st Rifle Brigade	18/2/17	3, Southboro' Road, London, N.E.
1630	Pte.	COHEN, J.	59th Australian Inf.	26/9/17	93, Chapel Street, Balaclava, Victoria.
200942	Rfm.	COHEN, J.	13th Rifle Brigade	23/8/18	148, Stepney Green Buildings, London, E.
347688	Pte.	COHEN, J.	1st D.A.C. Canadian	18/8/18	152, Laval Avenue, Montreal.
24003	Pte.	COHEN, J.	2nd West Riding Regt.	29/8/18	8, Leopold's Road, Chapeltown, Leeds.
J/2626	Pte.	COHEN, J.	39th Royal Fusiliers	28/8/18	Alexandria.
233048	L/Cpl.	COHEN, J. (M.M.)	2/6th London Regt.	27/8/18	3, Morgan Terrace, Coborn Road, London, E.
252663	Pte.	COHEN, J.	2/6th Manchester Regt.	21/3/18	31, Exchange Street, Manchester.
54178	Sgt.	COHEN, L.	1st Royal Welsh Fusiliers	22/12/16	26, Croxteth Grove, Liverpool.
4120	Rfm.	COHEN, L.	2/9th London Regt.	1/3/17	171, Portsdown Road, London, W.
4100	Pte.	COHEN, L.	2/2nd London Regt.	15/6/17	6, Buckle Street Mansions, London, E.
901743	Dvr.	COHEN, L.	87th Brigade, R.F.A.	21/8/17	80, Penzance Street, Cheetham, Manchester.
64251	Pte.	COHEN, L. L.	2nd Welsh Regt.	24/10/18	17, Ullet Road, Liverpool.
201653	Pte.	COHEN, L. L.	2nd Suffolk Regt.	28/3/18	14, Grove Road, Brixton, London, S.W.9.
13469	Rfm.	COHEN, M.	19th K.R.R.C.	14/12/15	60, Samuel Street, Leeds.

N.C.O.'S AND MEN—Continued.

No.	Rank.	Name.	Regiment.	Date of Death.	Address.
615663	Pte.	COHEN, M.	1/19th London Regt.	14/12/17	5, Keats House, Lolesworth Street, London, E.
201649	Pte.	COHEN, M.	4/5th Black Watch	1/4/18	68, Hollingbury Road, Brighton.
J/5322	Pte.	COHEN, M.	40th Royal Fusiliers	22/1/19	London.
63170	Pte.	COHEN, M.	2nd Royal Welsh Fusiliers	27/5/17	20, Howard Street, Manchester.
28597	Pte.	COHEN, M.	Royal West Kent Regt.	15/11/18	96, Fordwych Road, London, N.W.
3546	Drummer	COHEN, M.	1/9th Lancashire Fusiliers	21/8/15	36, Great Cheetham Street, Manchester.
	S.S.M.	COHEN, M.	21st Australian Inf.	4/2/17	78, Nicholson Street, Fitzroy, Vic.
5691	Pte.	COHEN, M.	2/2nd London Regt.	16/6/17	81, Christian Street, London, E.
104509	Pte.	COHEN, M. H.	Devon Regt.	—	36, Riga Street, Portsmouth.
16138	Pte.	COHEN, N.	32nd Royal Fusiliers	22/10/18	26, Caroline Place, Stepney, London, E.
22470	Pte.	COHEN, O.	7th East Kent Regt.	20/12/16	47, West Green Road, London, N.15.
4332	Pte.	COHEN, P.	7th Royal Fusiliers	21/3/18	119, Grosvenor Road, Forest Gate, London, E.
6193	L/Cpl.	COHEN (KING, A.), P.	—	13/10/16	
52969	Pte.	COHEN, P.	1st Lincolnshire Regt.	1/11/14	106, Rutland Street, London, E.
019767	Pte.	COHEN, P. G.	13th Durham Light Inf.	13/5/17	6, Melville Place, Liverpool.
28253	Pte.	COHEN, R. J.	R.A.O.C.	14/1/18	10, Napier Street, Warrington.
37706	Pte.	COHEN (WISE), R.	7th Lancs. Fusiliers	29/10/18	651, Rochdale Road, Manchester.
201255	Rfm.	COHEN, S.	2nd Lancs. Fusiliers	23/10/16	6, Upper Camp Street, Manchester.
016316	Pte.	COHEN, S.	16th K.R.R.C.	13/4/18	68, Borough Road, London, S.E.
	Pte.	COHEN, S.	R.A.O.C.	24/2/19	Sherwin Street, Nottingham.
6310	Pte.	COHEN, S.	13th London Regt.	9/4/17	51, Chesnut Road, Tottenham, London, N.
42905	Pte.	COHEN, S.	2/5th Manchester Regt.	9/10/17	158, Sandringham Road, Dalston, London, N.E.
58007	Pte.	COHEN, S.	1/8th King's Liverpool	22/9/17	98, Bavington Road, Maida Hill, London, N.W.
3378	Pte.	COHEN, S.	55th Australian Inf.	1/9/18	37, Turner Street, Manchester.
42388	Rfm.	COHEN, S.	1st Royal Irish Rifles	16/1/18	11, Hutchison Avenue, London, E.1.
10983	Pte.	COHEN, S.	7th Seaforth Highlanders	12/10/16	139, Stock Street, Cheetham, Manchester.
6494	Pte.	COHEN, S.	16th Manchester Regt.	13/3/17	Ashlea, C.-on-M., Manchester.
6039	Pte.	COHEN, S. B.	2nd London Regt.	3/5/17	3, Morgan Terrace, Coborn Road, London, E.3.
5985	Pte.	COHEN, T.	2nd Australian Inf.	18/9/18	Stewart Town, N.S.W.
43	Pte.	COHEN, W.	14th Australian Inf.	30/4/15	93, Napier Street, Fitzroy, Vic.
6476	Pte.	COHN, C.	4th Australian Inf.	22/5/17	5, Northwood Street, London, N.
7746	Pte.	COHN, L.	5th Canadian Mntd. Rifles	2/2/16	50, Woodeycrest Avenue, Toronto.
8669	Cpl.	COLE, H.	1st South Wales Borderers	16/9/14	46, Edwards Road, London, E.
44849	2/A.M.	COLINSKY, J.	R.A.F.	23/5/18	5, Brady Buildings, Whitechapel, London, E.
17110	Pte.	COLLINS, B.	1st Grenadier Guards	19/10/17	42, Laleham Buildings, Shoreditch, London, E.2.
141385	Pte.	COLLINS, B.	51st M.G. Bn.	3/8/18	166, Elizabeth Street, Manchester.
31029	Pte.	COLLINS, D.	1st Grenadier Guards	11/10/18	7, Pagoda Avenue, Richmond, Surrey.
266145	Pte.	COLLINS, H.	2/7th West Yorks. Regt.	12/5/17	8, Busk Street, Leeds.
936	Pte.	COLLINS, L.	2nd Australian Inf.	29/3/15	Angledale, Bega, N.S.W.
48421	Pte.	COLLOCK, M.	19th King's Liverpool Rgt.	23/6/17	16, Clarence Street, Liverpool.
3174	Pte.	COLLY, H. D.	2nd South African Inf.	17/7/16	94, Tramway Street, Turffontein, Johannesburg.
482	Pte.	COLMANS, L.	23rd Middlesex Regt.	8/10/16	43, Milton Road, London, N.E.
A/288	Pte.	COMAROFF, H.	Brit. S. African Police	1915	Salisbury, South Africa.
725	L/Cpl.	COMOR, M.	Newfoundland Regt.	10/11/17	5, Brighton Parade, Blackpool.
285917	Pte.	CONN, J.	R.A.S.C., M.T., 706th Coy.	19/12/14	21, King Edward Lane, London, E.
32025	Sergt.	COOKE, C.	14th Northumberland Fus.	1/6/18	358, Strand, London, W.

85

N.C.O.'S AND MEN—Continued.

No.	Rank.	Name.	Regiment.	Date of Death.	Address.
16171	Pte.	COOPER, A.	6th Dorset Regt.	23/4/17	42, Penton Street, Pentonville, London, N.
1167	Pte.	COOPER, L.	1st South African Inf.	18/10/16	9, Warwick Street, Cape Town.
200041	Rfm.	COOPMAN, A.	17th K.R.R.C.	27/10/16	14, Riffel Road, London, N.W.
293199	Pte.	COOK, P.	3/10th Middlesex Regt.	9/10/17	19, Gore Road, Victoria Park, London, N.E.
2999	Pte.	CORNBLATT, S.	20th Royal Fusiliers	16/4/17	120, Back Church Lane, London, E.
21925	Gnr.	CORPER, W.	F. Battery, R.H.A.	11/9/18	84, Graham Road, London, N.E.
280729	Pte.	COSSACK, H.	2/7th Lancs. Fusiliers	9/10/17	9, Smedley Lane, Manchester.
12071	Pte.	COSSACK, M.	6th Loyal N. Lancs. Regt.	9/8/15	9, Smedley Lane, Manchester.
373987	Pte.	COSTA, H.	9th Inniskilling Fusiliers	12/5/17	26, South Block, Stepney Lane, London, E.1.
242688	Pte.	COSTA, J.	1st East Kent Regt.	16/10/17	81, Listria Road, London, N.
60109	Pte.	COSTER, H.	101st Labour Company	15/5/18	22, Eckstein Road, London, S.W.
38421	Pte.	COSTER, J.	2/8th Worcestershire Regt.	1/10/18	82, High Street, Kingsland, London, N.E.
467478	Spr.	COUPLAN, J.	461st Field Company, R.E.	12/3/18	24, Ramsden Terrace, Leeds.
10917	Sgt.	COUPLAN, M.	7th W. Riding Regiment	3/5/18	24, Ramsden Terrace, Leeds.
Z/L.4167	Petty-Officer	COWAN, A.	R.N.V.R. Anson Bn.	23/7/17	28, Carne Street, Pentee, South Wales.
3057	Rfm.	COWAN, L.	14th King's Liverpool Rgt.	27/3/16	35, Vine Street, Liverpool.
11780	Pte.	COWAN, A.	2nd Hampshire Regt.	13/8/15	53, Lanark Villas, Bayswater, London, W.
53879	Pte.	CRISTOLL, H. S.	11th R. Scots Fusiliers	22/7/18	7, Richmond Road, Bayswater, London, W.
4249	Rfm.	CROOK, A.	1/6th London Regiment	20/5/16	28, Cephas Street, Mile End, London, E.
6109	Cpl.	CROOK, M.	R.A.F.	5/2/19	13, Hedworth Terrace, Sunderland.
2635	Pte.	CROOK, S.	4th London Regt.	9/9/16	100, Acre Lane, London, S.W.
34134	Pte.	CROOP, M.	18th Manchester Regt.	30/7/17	73, Bignor Street, Hightown, Manchester.
4176	Pte.	CUCKLE, L.	4th Seaforth Highlanders	24/7/16	19, Great Lukes Street, Hull.
701703	Gnr.	CUSHELSON, J.	D/330 Brigade, R.F.A.	26/7/17	110, Stock Street, Manchester.
137541	Pte.	DA COSTA, J.	Royal Fusiliers	30/10/18	8, Chichester Houses, Great Eastern Street, London, E.C.
S/19776	Rfm.	DA COSTA, J.	2nd Rifle Brigade	1/8/17	15, Calverley Street, Stepney, London, E.
14851	Pte.	DA COSTA, L.	2nd Middlesex Rgt.	1/8/17	73, Walton Buildings, Shoreditch, London, E.
64877	Pte.	DAINOW, G.	2/4th London Regt.	26/10/17	16, Hutchinson Avenue, Aldgate, London, E.
49295	Pte.	DALINSKY, B.	1st Cheshire Regt.	10/3/18	16, Broughton Street, Cheetham, Manchester.
20944	Cpl.	DANCYGER, L.	7th K.O. Scottish Borderers	20/6/16	5, Kenealy Street, Camp Road, Leeds.
10737	Spr.	DANILER, H. J.	S. African Engineers	24/5/17	Ladysmith, S. Africa.
63262	Pte.	DASKEL, A.	3rd Canadian Inf.	15/8/17	795, St. Laurence Street, Montreal.
4180	Rfm.	DAVID, J.	1/16th London Regt.	1/7/16	123, Evering Road, London, N.
6486	Sgt.	DAVID, T. J.	15th Australian Inf.	11/4/17	Jubilee Street, Cooparoo, Brisbane, Australia.
760338	Pte.	DAVIDSON, E. H. L.	1/28th London Regt.	27/8/18	Borlases, Twyford, Berks.
20028	Pte.	DAVIDSON, H.	2nd R. Scots Fusiliers	22/3/18	219, Great Cheetham Street, Manchester.
23777	Pte.	DAVIDSON, H. M.	7th Oxford & Bucks L.I.	9/5/17	24, Cross Street, Oxford.
1747	Pte.	DAVIDSON, S.	1/7th Manchester Regt.	1/6/17	171, Elizabeth Street, Hightown, Manchester.
235221	Pte.	DAVIES, H.	19th King's Liverpool Rgt.	2/8/17	39, Birch Street, Hightown, Manchester.
4378	Pte.	DAVIES, H.	1/1st Bucks. Regt.	6/10/16	2, Eastman's Court, Wentworth Street, London, E.
27909	Pte.	DAVIES, J.	15th Royal Warwick. Regt.	15/4/18	176, Corporation Street, Birmingham.
1640	Pte.	DAVIES, S.	7th King's Liverpool Regt.	10/5/17	253, Hawthorn Road, Bootle, Lancs.
1480	Pte.	DAVIS, A.	22nd Australian Inf.	4/10/18	70, Westgarth Street, Northcote, Victoria.

N.C.O.'S AND MEN—Continued.

No.	Rank.	Name.	Regiment.	Date of Death.	Address.
10604	Pte.	DAVIS, A.	4th Middlesex Regt.	20/3/15	20, Trident Street, Rotherhithe, London, S.E.
2958	Dvr.	DAVIS, C.	141st Hy. Battery, R.G.A.	3/7/16	7, St. Dunstan's Road, Burdett Road, London, E.
S/17757	Rfm.	DAVIS, D.	11th Rifle Brigade	11/8/17	37, Robertson Road, London, E.
505090	Pte.	DAVIS, D. K.	13th London Regt.	6/5/17	1, Fane Street, West Kensington, London, W.
774	Pte.	DAVIS, E. P.	11th Australian Inf.	18/7/15	c/o Boan Bros., Perth, W.A.
	Pte.	DAVIS, G. L.	18th Royal Fusiliers	1916	1, Gresham Buildings, London, E.C.
9116	L/Cpl.	DAVIS, H.	2nd Royal Berks. Regt.	20/7/15	6, Aldeney Road, Bow, London, E.
5/434	Rfm.	DAVIS, H.	1st Rifle Brigade	26/4/15	24, Wellesby Street, Stepney, London, E.
4827	C.S.M.	DAVIS, H. S. (M.C.)	1st East Yorks. Regt.	1/7/16	6, St. Gabriel Road, London, N.W.
158939	Dvr.	DAVIS, I.	1/1 Leicester R.H.A.	30/1/18	15, Brunswick Terrace, Leeds.
58907	Pte.	DAVIS, I.	Royal Defence Corps	13/10/18	32, Harrington Square, London, N.W.
15167	Rfm.	DAVIS, J.	13th K.R.R.C.	10/7/16	42, Vallance Road, London, E.
575	Pte.	DAVIS, J.	R.M.L.I.	1915	London.
6003	Cpl.	DAVIS, J. I.	1st Border Regt.	6/6/15	9, Hornby Street, Manchester.
427099	Pte.	DAVIS, L.	28th Canadian Inf.	11/6/16	65, Ellen Street, London, E.
423062	Pte.	DAVIS, M.	2/10th London Regt.	31/8/18	54, Grove Dwellings, Adelina Grove, London, E.
68	Pte.	DAVIS, N.	10th Royal Fusiliers	25/5/16	101, Queen's Road, Richmond, Surrey.
442048	Pte.	DAVIS, R.	R.C.R.	12/1/16	Stellarton, Nova Scotia.
34891	Pte.	DAVISON, S.	1st Essex Regt.	8/10/18	27, Wellesley Street, London, E.
10138	Pte.	DAWSON, R. H.	2nd York & Lancs. Regt.	21/6/18	96, Fawcett Street, Sheffield.
1113	Pte.	DEAS, E. D.	54th Australian Inf.	15/5/17	60, Chin Chin Street, Islington, N.S.W.
29818	Pte.	DEHAAN, L.	9th Norfolk Regt.	28/4/17	62, Abington Buildings, Shoreditch, London, E.
J/1754	Pte.	DEITZ, M.	38th Royal Fusiliers	24/10/18	18, Josephine House, Thrawl Street, London, E.1.
T4/219570	Pte.	DELINSKY, I.	51st D.S.C., R.A.S.C.	29/1/18	169, Rothschild Buildings, London, E.
718573	Pte.	DETMOLD, A. H.	107th Canadian Pioneer Bn.	15/8/17	29, Alleyn Park, London, S.E.
5835	Pte.	DE YOUNG, L.	1st Somerset L.I.	19/12/14	27, Rampayne St., Vauxhall Bridge Rd., London, S.W.
R/31517	Rfm.	DIAMOND, A.	16th K.R.R.C.	2/12/17	Smith's Street, Stepney, London, E.
6572	Pte.	DIAMOND, J.	23rd Cheshire Regt.	1/10/18	34, Stanley Street, Cheetham, Manchester.
12683	Pte.	DIAMONDSTONE, J.	23rd Middlesex Regt.	8/7/18	6, Raven Row, London, E.
12341	Pte.	DION, J. (M.M.)	5th Northampton Regt.	27/3/18	7, Gray Street, London, E.1.
2909	Pte.	DION, J.	6th Royal Munster Fus.	15/8/15	4, Gray Street, London, E.1.
453048	Rfm.	DOBKIN, J.	2/11th London Regt.	23/9/17	1, Nathaniel Buildings, London, E.1.
35571	Pte.	DOBREE, A. R.	12th South Wales Borderers	21/4/17	2, Adeline Terrace, Mile End, London, E.1.
5025	Pte.	DOMBEY, W.	1/1st Bucks Battalion	23/8/16	4, College Grove, Mile End, London, E.
14228	Pte.	DORER, H.	20th Middlesex Regt.	3/1/17	48, Princes Square, Cable Street, London, E.
SR/7753	Sergt.	DOWNS, F.	8th Royal Fusiliers	27/8/16	4, Fenton's Road, Plaistow, London.
22915	L/Cpl.	DREEBIN, H.	1st K.O.S.B.	11/4/18	2, Sands Street S., Sunderland.
17848	Pte.	DREEZER, J.	1st Royal Dublin Fusiliers	30/6/15	68, Clifton Buildings, London, E.C.
32173	Rfm.	DUDINSKY, J.	2nd Rifle Brigade	2/12/17	29, Providence Street, London, E.
12925	Pte.	DUMAS, N.	1st South African Inf.	2/1/18	4, Boorhout Street, Troyeville, Johannesburg.
2363	Dvr.	DURLACHER, L.	4th Australian M.G. Bn.	16/2/19	10, Cambridge Gardens, Kilburn, London, N.W.
J/1648	C.S.M.	EAGLE, N.	39th Royal Fusiliers	18/11/18	108, Fieldgate Mansions, London, E.
Z/6943	Pte.	ECKSTEIN, D.	1st Devon Regt.	17/12/14	22, Collingwood Street, Bethnal Green, London, E.

87

N.C.O.'S AND MEN—Continued.

No.	Rank	Name	Regiment	Date of Death	Address
2062	Pte.	Edelsten, H. V.	37th Australian Inf.	8/6/17	Carapooee West, Victoiria.
31937	L/Cpl.	Edelston, S.	23rd Manchester Regt.	22/10/17	2, Thirlmere Street, Manchester.
T4/241166	Sergt.	Edwards, H.	R.A.S.C.	24/12/18	32, Park Street, Cheetham, Manchester.
58380	Pte.	Edwards, J.	11th King's Liverpool Rgt.	13/8/17	61, Berkeley Street, Strangeways, Manchester.
2150	Pte.	Edwards, R.	24th London Regt.	25/5/15	288, Earl's Court Road, London, W.
5203	Rfm.	Ehrenberg, J.	2/6th London Regt.	21/5/17	20, Alderney Road, London, E.
725	Sgt.	Ehrenberg, S. M.	5th Australian Inf.	25/4/15	8, Kerfew Place, Albert Park, N.S.W.
DM2/209276	Cpl.	Elias, B.	R.A.S.C., att. Tank Corps	14/12/17	4, South Mansions, Gondar Gardens, London, N.W.6.
5836	Pte.	Ellice, B. E.	11th Australian Inf.	27/9/17	Perth, W.A.
241939	Pte.	Ellis, N.	2/6th Notts & Derby Regt.	27/9/17	26, Portland Street, Hull.
36066	Pte.	Ellis, S.	2nd Yorks. Regt.	21/3/18	26, Portland Street, Hull.
1626	Pte.	Ellison, P. S.	3rd Royal Fusiliers	14/4/15	76, Plumbers' Row, London, E.
8234	Pte.	Ellison, S. J.	2nd Royal Irish Regt.	4/8/17	76, Plumbers' Row, London, E.
3455	Pte.	Elman, N.	4th South African Inf.	11/9/16	P.O. Box, 206, Benoni, Transvaal.
42609	Pte.	Emanuel, A.	1/5th W. Yorks. Regt.	30/9/18	313, Toller Lane, Heaton, Bradford.
69294	Pte.	Emanuel, J.	6th Royal W. Surrey Regt.	3/9/18	10, Russell Square, Brighton.
41460	L/Cpl.	Emanuel, M.	2nd R. Inniskilling Fusiliers	24/3/18	126, Maybury Road, Woking.
207815	Pte.	Emden, J.	16th Middlesex Regt.	1/12/17	60, Victoria Park Road, London, E.9.
23190	Cpl.	Erdman, H.	1st King's Liverpool Regt.	8/8/16	6, Bisley Street, Liverpool.
425584	Pte.	Erlick, L.	50th Canadian Inf.	1/5/17	Aberdeen, South Africa.
13185	Pte.	Esterman, A.	3rd South African Inf.	20/9/17	Ceres, Cape Province.
16822	Pte.	Ettinger (Edgar), B.	1st Hampshire Regt.	28/3/18	14, Soho Street, Islington, Liverpool.
13973	Pte.	Faber, J.	14th Hants. Regt.	3/9/17	10, Casson Street, London, E.
36527	Pte.	Fabian, A.	1st South Wales Borderers	25/9/16	13, Godfrey House, Thrawl Street, London, E.
12	Pte.	Faingott, A. W.	Zion Mule Corps	3/5/15	Alexandria.
33517	Pte.	Falk, A.	1st Australian Inf.	19/4/17	Sydney, N.S.W.
128680	Pte.	Falk, B.	8th Suffolk Regt.	18/2/17	12, Cephas Street, London, E.
17150	Pte.	Falk, L.	2/4th London Regt.	15/6/17	12, Cephas Street, London, E.
5002	Pte.	Falk, N.	1st R. Welsh Fusiliers	21/3/18	39, Soho Street, Liverpool.
82264	Pte.	Falk, H.	2/7 Middlesex, attd. L.R.B.	10/9/16	53, Elgin Avenue, London, W.
235867	Pte.	Farber, H. H.	20th Durham L.I.	14/9/18	66, Cheetham Hill Road, Manchester.
12297	Pte.	Farbstein, L.	2nd Lancashire Fusiliers	12/10/17	32, Rutland Street, London, E.
354910	Pte.	Fearn, B.	13th West Yorks. Regt.	19/7/16	44, Crawford Street, Leeds.
7502	Pte.	Feder, M.	7th London Regt.	1/9/18	15, Lorna Road, Brixton, London, S.W.
52385	Sig.	Feinberg, M.	2nd South African Inf.	12/10/16	14, Macdonald Street, Johannesburg.
157250	A/M.	Feldman, L.	A/92 Brigade, R.F.A.	7/12/18	14, Victoria Road, Ellscombe, Torquay.
38492	Pte.	Felperin, M.	R.A.F.	24/2/19	132, Chatsworth Road, Lower Clapton, London, N.E.
3722	Pte.	Fell, J.	1st Shropshire L.I.	11/8/18	17, Bright Street, Hull.
4789	Pte.	Fellerman, C.	2/2nd London Regt.	15/6/17	32, Patriot Street, Cambridge.
10278	Pte.	Fernandez, J. F.	45th Australian Inf.	13/10/17	67, Pittwater Road, Manly, Sydney.
S/35069	Cpl.	Ferner, A. (D.C.M.)	6th Yorks. Regt.	21/8/17	42, Heath Street, Stepney, London, E.
862334	Rfm.	Fidler, M.	16th Rifle Bde.	21/3/18	103, Slater Street, London, E.
	Pte.	Field, M.	4th Canadian Inf.	2/9/18	1633, Mance Street, Montreal.

N.C.O.'S AND MEN—Continued.

No.	Rank.	Name.	Regiment.	Date of Death.	Address.
27859	Pte.	FIFER, G.	6th Wiltshire Regt.	10/4/18	102, Charles Henry Street, Birmingham.
94370	Pte.	FIFER, D.	158th Coy. Labour	8/10/17	38, Blyth Road, Sheffield.
59057	Pte.	FIFER, R.	23rd Northumberland Fus.	17/10/17	Esperanza, Hampstead Garden Suburb, London.
2606	Rfm.	FIGGINS, J.	2nd Rifle Brigade	26/9/16	254, Kingsland Road, London, N.E.
202755	Pte.	FILAR, H.	10th Royal West Kent Rgt.	29/9/18	8, Challis Court, Cannon Street, London, E.
201829	Pte.	FINBERG, H.	4th East Lancashire Regt.	4/6/17	56, Montague Street, Blackburn.
5197	Pte.	FINEBERG, S.	1/7th Worcestershire Regt.	27/2/17	70, Umberstone Street, London, E.
674	Pte.	FINK, G.	16th Australian Inf.	2/5/15	352, Collin Street, Melbourne.
3200	Pte.	FINK, S.	12th Manchester Regt.	26/10/17	Northfield, Church Street, Manchester.
205015	Pte.	FINKELSTEIN, A.	3/4th R. West Surrey Regt.	4/10/18	63, Elizabeth Street, Cheetham, Manchester.
450	Pte.	FINKELSTEIN, H.	20th Australian Inf.	5/8/16	73, Teneriffe Street, Manchester.
66571	Pte.	FINSTEIN, S.	Worcestershire Regt.	30/10/18	15, Leeland Road S., Tottenham, London, N.
202842	Pte.	FIRSHT, J.	2/1st London Regt.	8/6/17	73, Cable Street, London, E.
260096	Sig.	FISHER, D.	2/1st Co. of London Yeo.	10/10/18	London.
266755	Pte.	FISHER, W.	1/1st Bucks. Battalion	25/8/16	64, Hanbury Street, London, E.
86614	Gnr.	FISHMAN, M.	A/64th Brigade, R.F.A.	5/10/18	1, St. Mark's Road, London, N.E.
27638	Pte.	FISHSTEIN, H.	13th Northumberland Fus.	16/6/17	192, Rothschild Buildings, London, E.2.
W.R.275675	Spr.	FITELSON, H.	2/78th Rly. Coy., R.E.	9/8/18	7, Upper Camp Street, Higher Broughton, Manchester.
R/23186	Rfm.	FLASHMAN, S.	9th K.R.R.C.	15/9/16	50, Pelham Street, London, E.
12535	Pte.	FLATON, S.	6th Bedfordshire Regt.	15/7/16	73, Somerford Street, London, N.E.
7568	Pte.	FOGELMAN, L.	4th London Regt.	26/1/17	17, Leyden Street, Spitalfields, London, E.
85138	Gnr.	FOOT, H.	A/84th Brigade, R.F.A.	20/10/18	46, Davis Mansions, London, E.
204325	Pte.	FOREMAN, M.	2/1st London Regt.	16/6/17	2, Colmar Street, Mile End, London, E.
57515	Pte.	FORDANSKI, C.	10th Worcester Regt.	24/5/18	88, Wrentham Street, Birmingham.
8712	Pte.	FORSTEIN (FOSTER), G.			
		J.			
4271	Rfm.	FOX, D.	1st Norfolk Regt.	24/8/14	69, Eric Street, Bow, London, E.
375	Rfm.	FOX, S.	1/15th London Regt.	21/5/16	234, Fieldgate Mansions, London, E.
288	Cpl.	FRANK, A.	2nd Rifle Brigade	14/3/15	8, Ely Place, Chicksand Street, London, E.
56504	2/A.M.	FRANK, F. A.	Zion Mule Corps	14/5/15	Jerusalem.
2027a	Cpl.	FRANKEL, S.	R.A.F.	30/12/17	43, Linthorpe Road, Stamford Hill, London, N.
B/377	Rfm.	FRANKLIN, F.	24th Australian Inf.	15/3/18	15, Richardson Street N., Carlton, Melbourne.
5973	Pte.	FRANKLIN, H.	11th Rifle Brigade	3/9/16	5, Dean Street, London, E.
X/172	Pte.	FRANKLIN, S.	4th London Regt.	7/10/16	465, Mile End Road, London, W.
203265	Pte.	FRANKLYN, H. O.	2nd South African Inf.	12/4/17	3, Randolph Road, London, W.
C/3249	Rfm.	FRANKS, A.	1st London Regt.	16/8/17	10, St. George's Road, London, N.W.
34136	Pte.	FRANKS, D.	17th K.R.R.C.	16/6/16	23, Bremen Street, London, N.E.
24280	Pte.	FRANKS, H.	6th West Riding Regt.	1/11/18	8, Warton Road, Stratford, London, E.
282370	Pte.	FRANKS, I.	15th Lancashire Fusiliers	1/6/18	253, Cheetham Hill Road, Manchester.
2150	Pte.	FRANKS, L. E.	2/4th London Regt.	4/6/17	29, Rothschild's Buildings, London, E.
2313	Pte.	FRANKS, R.	6th Northumberland Fus.	27/4/15	28, Bayley Street, Newcastle-on-Tyne.
2818	Rfm.	FRASER, A.	38th Australian Inf.	24/6/18	
202360	Sgt.	FRASER, H.	1st L.R.B.	9/1/16	96, Maida Vale, London, W.
30854	Pte.	FREEDMAN, A.	11th King's Liv'pool Regt.	21/3/18	17, Bannerman Street, Liverpool.
			10th Lancashire Fusiliers	12/5/17	25, Baker Street, London, E.

89

N.C.O.'S AND MEN—Continued.

No.	Rank.	Name.	Regiment.	Date of Death.	Address.
7244	Pte.	FREEDMAN, A.	13th Australian Inf.	11/6/18	Devilliers Street, Johannesburg, S. Africa.
12434	Pte.	FREEDMAN, B.	2nd S. African Inf.	8/12/17	Palace Hotel, Hartley, Rhodesia.
33872	Pte.	FREEDMAN, I.	5/6th Royal Scots	11/8/18	119e, Main Street, Gorbals, Glasgow.
58524	Pte.	FREEDMAN, J.	7th Rifle Bde.	23/7/15	5, Westgate Street, London, N.E.
235130	Pte.	FREEDMAN, J.	9th Yorks. L.I.	4/10/17	1, Victoria Street, Newark.
13105	Pte.	FREEDMAN, M. (M.M.)	10th West Riding Regt.	17/9/16	1, South Street, Huddersfield.
25410	Pte.	FREEDMAN, M.	7th East Yorks. Regt.	31/3/18	1, Victoria Street, Newark, Notts.
R/12202	Rfm.	FREEDMAN, M.	13th K.R.R.C.	16/4/18	34, Castletown Road, W.14.
203869	Pte.	FREEDMAN, D. M.	22nd Northumberland Fus.	21/3/18	40, Merchant Street, London, E.
19786	Pte.	FREEDMAN, R.	9th Essex Regt.	3/7/16	30, Buross Street, London, E.
55241	3/A.M.	FREEMAN, D.	R.A.F.	29/5/17	154, Nathaniel Buildings, London, E.1.
8402	Pte.	FREEMAN, I.	1st South African Inf.	16/9/16	Maitland, Cape Town.
15579	Pte.	FREEMAN, I. M.	17th H.L.I.	2/7/16	51, Aboca Street, Belfast.
J/1266	Pte.	FREEMAN, N.	38th Royal Fusiliers	27/10/18	14, Severn Street, Commercial Road, London, E.1.
J/1590	Pte.	FREINER, M.	38th Royal Fusiliers	5/11/18	122, Vallance Road, London, E.1.
474352	Rfm.	FRESCO, M.	12th London Regt.	9/4/17	19, Grey Eagle Street, London, E.
2896	Pte.	FREUDENBERG, B. C.	49th Australian Inf.	7/6/17	Bailey Street, West End, Brisbane.
	Pte.	FRIDJOHN, L.	South African M.C.	20/1/17	Port Elizabeth, South Africa.
124181	Pte.	FRIEDLANDER, D.	1/6th West Yorks. Regt.	11/10/18	19, New Inn Yard, Shoreditch, London, E.
40534	Rfm.	FRIEDMAN, H.	1/9th London Regt.	25/8/18	51, Brunswick Street, Manchester.
64149	Pte.	FRIEND, J.	15th Cheshire Regt.	14/10/18	68, Burlington Street, Manchester.
1504	Sgt.	FROMER, H.	24th Australian Inf.	1/9/18	177, Cripps Street, Abbotsford, Victoria.
M/317513	Pte.	FRY, A.	R.A.S.C.	20/10/18	3, Balstrode Road, Hounslow.
1450	Pte.	FUCHSBALG, M.	1st H.A.C.	10/6/15	21, Trinity Rise, Tulse Hill, London.
6868	Pte.	FURMAN, H.	4th East Yorks. Regt.	16/1/17	45, William Street, Hull.
5899	Rfm.	FURST, E.	1/9th London Regt.	16/9/16	31, St. Gonatts Road, Lewisham, London.
1155	Pte.	GABRIEL, H. M.	14th Royal Warwick. Regt.	30/7/16	126, Corporation Street, Birmingham.
396	Cpl.	GABRIELSON, M.	King Edward's Horse	10/12/18	3, Windermere Terrace, Liverpool.
31581	Pte.	GAFFIN, A	17th Lancashire Fusiliers	22/10/17	12, Elison Street, Manchester.
A/202488	Pte.	GALINSKY, A.	16th K.R.R.C.	12/4/18	21, Bancroft Road, London, E.
29459	Pte.	GALINSKY, H.	1st West Yorks. Regt.	12/10/16	6, Byron Street, Leeds.
635686	Pte.	GALINSKY, H.	2/20th London Regt.	19/2/18	21, Bancroft Road, London, E.1.
J/1186	Pte.	GALINSKY, M.	38th Royal Fusiliers	9/9/18	5, Pattison Street, London, E.
64548	L-Cpl.	GALLEWSKI, M.(M.M.)	100th Field Amb. R.A.M.C.	19/2/17	5, Bishopstown Street, Sunderland.
410102	Pte.	GALOVITCH, A.	38th Canadian Inf.	18/11/16	Russia.
203778	Pte.	GAMPLE, D.	2/7th West Yorks. Regt.	27/3/18	18, Coburg Street, Leeds.
14767	Pte.	GANS, J.	20th Middlesex Regt.	20/9/16	23, Smith Street, London, E.
1009050	Dvr.	GANTFORD, A.	6th Canadian Ry. Engrs.	17/11/18	Leeds.
T3/029421	Cpl.	GARBUTT, L.	199th Coy., R.A.S.C.	2/5/18	64, Yarm Lane, Stockton-on-Tees.
122577	Pte.	GARDNER, J.	8th M.G. Bn.	27/5/18	11, High Street, Shadwell, London, E.
136470	Pte.	GARFUNKEL, H.	42nd Canadian Inf.	22/6/16	12, Russell Street, Toronto, Canada.
15224	Pte.	GARRETT, G.	4th Royal Fusiliers	16/6/15	London.
5673	Pte.	GEFFEN, E.	2/13th London Regt.	8/12/17	2, Dawson Place, London, W.

N.C.O.'s AND MEN—Continued.

No.	Rank.	Name.	Regiment.	Date of Death.	Address.
4209	Cpl.	GELLER, H.	R.A.F.	5/11/18	96, Wandsworth Road, Fulham, London, S.W.
18620	L/Cpl.	GERBER, E.	16th Lancashire Fusiliers	1/7/16	16, Whitfield Street, Cheetham, Manchester.
3266	Pte.	GERBER, J. S.	8th Argyll & Suth. Hrs.	27/5/16	16, Whitfield Street, Cheetham, Manchester.
G/25435	Pte.	GERLISKY, L.	4th Royal Sussex Regt.	30/7/18	43, Wentworth Buildings, London, E.
27248	Pte.	GERSHMAN, R.	5th K.O.Y.L.I.	20/7/18	66, Fitzwilliam Street, Sheffield.
6890	Bdr.	GILBERT, H.	20/9th Brigade, R.F.A.	29/9/18	32, Upper Stanhope Street, Liverpool.
280268	Pte.	GILBERT, S.	1/4th London Regt.	28/5/18	18, Brady Street Buildings, London, E.
4421	L/Cpl.	GILBERT, S.	1/2nd London Regt.	1/7/16	21, Hawking Street, London, E.
200351	Cpl.	GILLIES, M.	5th Scottish Rifles	14/4/17	29, Hospital Street, Glasgow.
235140	Pte.	GILLIS, J.	4th Yorks. Regt.	28/4/17	7, Rectory Terrace, Sunderland.
70126	Pte.	GILLMAN, A.	16th Notts & Derby Regt.	9/10/16	1, Claremount Place, Leeds.
1540	Pte.	GINSBERG, D.	13th London Regt.	15/12/15	25, St. Ann's Road, London, W.
353746	Pte.	GINSBERG, J.	58th M.G. Bn.	17/4/18	216, Euston Road, London, N.W.1.
2102	Pte.	GINSBERG, S.	22nd Royal Fusiliers	1/8/16	47, Bexley Grove, Leeds.
353746	Pte.	GINSBURG, S.	2/7th London Regt.	17/4/18	67, Cambridge Road, London, E.1.
298021	Pte.	GINSBURG, B.	1/4th London Regt.	30/5/18	3, Convent Garden, Kensington Park Rd., London, W.
12536	Pte.	GLASBERG, A.	8th East Kent Regt.	10/12/16	70, Cheetham Hill Road, Manchester.
33950	Pte.	GLASBERG, J.	12th Manchester Regiment	2/3/17	11, Honey Street, Cheetham, Manchester.
29430	Pte.	GLASS, F.	2nd Manchester Regiment	14/4/17	1, Wickcliffe Street, St. George's Road, Bolton.
393347	L/Cpl.	GLASS, M.	R.A.M.C.	21/10/18	7, East Parade, Newcastle-on-Tyne.
22092	Cpl.	GLASSMAN, A.	13th King's Liverpool Regt.	27/10/18	62, Bamber Street, Liverpool.
5026	Pte.	GLASSMAN, D.	1st Duke of Cornwall's L.I.	15/6/15	46, Hood Street, Northampton.
19036	Cpl.	GLASSTONE, I.	1st Cheshire Regt.	11/8/16	2a, Dunluce Street, Walton, Liverpool.
40159	Pte.	GLATT, L.	2nd Loyal North Lancs. Rgt.	29/7/18	13, Marlboro Road, Manchester.
145686	Pte.	GLAZIER, A. M.	45th Canadian Inf.	3/9/18	903, Colonial Avenue, Montreal, Canada.
S/8078	Rfm.	GLUCK, A.	12th Rifle Brigade	25/9/15	53, Haberdasher Street, London, N.
J/125	Pte.	GLUCK, D.	38th Royal Fusiliers	17/11/18	14, Hillside Road, London, N.15.
42	Pte.	GLUCK, L. J.	11th Australian Inf.	2/5/15	Beaufort Street, Mt. Lawley, Perth, W.A.
6171	Pte.	GLUCKMAN, S.	3rd S. African Infantry	9/7/16	P.O. Box 66, Vereeniging, South Africa.
4380	Pte.	GLUCKSTEIN, C. S.	10th Middlesex Regiment	19/8/16	184, Westbourne Grove, London, W.
41542	Pte.	GLUCKSTEIN, C.S.(M.M.)	52nd Fld. Amb. R.A.M.C.	6/8/16	13, Leebank Road, Birmingham.
2057	Pte.	GOFBERRY, H. H.	20th Middlesex Regt.	1/8/16	3, Court, 11, House, Hurst Street, Birmingham.
	STEWARD	GOLD, D.	H.M.S. "Dido"	26/2/16	9, Philip Street, London, E.
11781	Pte.	GOLD, J.	1st King's Liverpool Regt.	28/8/16	64, Muirhead Street, Glasgow.
1149	Spr.	GOLDBAUM, B. H.	Kent Fortress Co. R.E.	28/10/15	26, Marvin Street, Poplar, London, E.
3499	Pte.	GOLDBAUM, P.	1/10th London Regiment	23/7/16	26, Marvin Street, Poplar, London, E.
472346	L/Cpl.	GOLDBERG, A.	12th London Regiment	26/4/18	82, Boundary Road, London, E.
9544	Pte.	GOLDBERG, A. J.	2nd S. W. Borderers	20/10/16	13, Crown Street, Port Talbot, S. Wales.
3867	Pte.	GOLDBERG, D. I.	8th Middlesex Regiment	11/9/18	69, Carysfoot Road, London, N.
85316	Pte.	GOLDBERG, E.	1st King's Liverpool Regt.	21/3/18	185, Brunswick Buildings, London, E.
41429	Pte.	GOLDBERG, E.	6th Yorkshire Regiment	29/9/18	30, Blandford Street, Newcastle-on-Tyne.
C/12695	L/Cpl.	GOLDBERG, H.	21st K.R.R.C.	11/6/16	69, Bayswater Place, Leeds.
25092	Dvr.	GOLDBERG, J.	128th Battery, R.F.A.	2/9/18	13, Caskett Street, London, E.
5429	Rfm.	GOLDBERG, L.	17th London Regiment	16/9/16	162, Hanley Avenue, London, N.

N.C.O.'s AND MEN—Continued.

No.	Rank.	Name.	Regiment.	Date of Death.	Address.
49757	Pte.	GOLDBERG, L.	1st Essex Regiment	4/11/18	73, Turner Street, London, E.
200168	Rfm.	GOLDBERG, M.	11th Rifle Brigade	4/4/17	37, Fulborne Street, London, E.
3230379	Pte.	GOLDBERG, L.	4th Canadian Inf.	30/8/18	3319, Dundas Street, Toronto, Canada.
S/40733I	Pte.	GOLDBERG, P.	R.A.S.C.	6/11/18	28, Dunk Street, London, E.1.
10269	Pte.	GOLDBERG, P.	4th Middlesex Regt.	23/8/14	26, Newcastle Street, London, E.
	Sergt.-Major	GOLDBERG, S.	South African S.C.	2/12/18	"Holmhurst," President Brand Street, Bloemfontein.
J/3726	Pte.	GOLDENBERG, J.	38th Royal Fusiliers	17/9/18	31, Greek Street, Liverpool.
25211	Pte.	GOLDFARB, C.	7th E. Kent Regiment	1/10/18	5, Staver Street, Canterbury.
3514	Pte.	GOLDIE, B.	1st R. Irish Fusiliers	22/10/16	24, Portland Place, Carlisle.
57252	L/Cpl.	GOLDING, J.	1/7th Manchester Regiment	5/4/18	19, Sycamore Street, Manchester.
10007	Pte.	GOLDING, S.	2nd West Riding Regt.	5/5/15	47, Roundhay Road, Leeds.
1211	Cpl.	GOLDMAN, A.	2nd Royal Warwick Regt.	25/9/15	253, Camden Street, Birmingham.
315819	Pte.	GOLDMAN, D.	15th Cheshire Regt.	29/9/18	28, Sherborne Street, Manchester.
10645	Pte.	GOLDMAN, H.	3rd King's Liverpool Regt.	13/12/16	3, Hobson Place, London, E.
14548	L/Cpl.	GOLDMAN, J.	17th Middlesex Regt.	13/11/16	56, Fuller Street, London, E.
52825	Pte.	GOLDMAN, L.S.	20th Royal Fusiliers	16/4/17	13, Yatford Street, London, E.
485	Rfm.	GOLDMAN, N.	21st Rifle Brigade	9/9/16	2, Parliament Terrace, Nottingham.
12899	Pte.	GOLDMAN, S.	1st Royal Inniskilling Fus.	27/1/17	10, Vallance Road, London, E.
22013	2A/M.	GOLDMAN, S.	R.A.F.	16/12/18	3, Elmwood Place, Leeds.
J/249	Pte.	GOLDRICH, J.	38th Royal Fusiliers	19/12/18	Liverpool.
8/578	Pte.	GOLDRING, G.	15th Australian Inf.	8/8/15	Union Bank Chambers, Pitt Street, Sydney, N.S.W.
59615	Pte.	GOLDSACK, A. A.	1st Otago N.Z. Regt.	26/1/16	19, London Road, Canterbury, Kent.
1995	Pte.	GOLDSCHMIDT, C.	9th Royal Fusiliers	30/11/17	Fern Bank, Didsbury, Manchester.
9668	Pte.	GOLDSMITH, B.	6th Canadian Field Amb.	16/5/18	48, Bury Old Road, Manchester.
422404	Cpl.	GOLDSMITH, G.	1st S. W. Borderers	7/10/14	18, Sedbright Gardens, London, N.E.
3106165	Pte.	GOLDSTEIN, A. (M.M.)	2/10th London Regt.	22/9/18	5, Great Alie Street, London, E.
48614	Spr.	GOLDSTEIN, A.	13th Canad. Ry. Engineers	7/6/18	62, Cable Street, London, E.
373528	Rfm.	GOLDSTEIN, B.	13th Rifle Brigade	6/9/18	62, Benthal Road, London, N.
S/24196	Pte.	GOLDSTEIN, B.	8th London Regt.	3/10/17	64, New Road, London, E.
48574	Rfm.	GOLDSTEIN, D.	1st Rifle Brigade	5/5/18	74, Well's Street, London, E.9.
58103	Gnr.	GOLDSTEIN, E.	73rd Battery R.F.A.	19/6/15	13, Hutchinson Avenue, London, E.C.
336901	Pte.	GOLDSTEIN, E.	1st Middlesex Regt.	25/9/18	62, Benthall Road, London, N.16.
281362	Gnr.	GOLDSTEIN, E. H.	3rd Bde. Canadian Fd. Artil.	15/8/17	555, Argyll Avenue, Montreal.
411	Pte.	GOLDSTEIN, F. A.	2/4th London Regt.	19/5/17	106, Lolesworth Buildings, London, E.1.
715842	A/B.	GOLDSTEIN, I.	H.M.S. "Defence"	4/7/16	43, Sheridan Street, London, E.
129784	Pte.	GOLDSTEIN, J.	25th Canadian Inf.	9/4/17	775, St. Lawrence B, Montreal.
5004	Pnr.	GOLDSTEIN, J.	No. 4 Coy. Spec. Bde. R.E.	11/5/17	88a, Nelson Street, London, E.
6974	Rfm.	GOLDSTEIN, J.	12th London Regt.	9/9/16	9, Solander Street, London, E.
17078	Pte.	GOLDSTEIN, M.	2nd Middlesex Regt.	12/3/17	144, Jubilee Street, London, E.
9043	L/Cpl.	GOLDSTEIN, P.	1st Royal Welsh Fusiliers	25/9/15	1a, Tenter Street, London, E.
252638	Rfm.	GOLDSTEIN, R.	9th K.R.R.C.	16/6/17	89, Mount Pleasant, Liverpool.
352433	Pte.	GOLDSTEIN, S.	1/3rd London Regt.	16/6/17	9, Solander Street, Shadwell, London, E.
	Pte.	GOLDSTEIN, S.	9th Royal Scots	9/4/17	29, Kingsburgh Road, Murrayfield, Midlothian.

N.C.O.'S AND MEN—Continued.

No.	Rank.	Name.	Regiment.	Date of Death.	Address.
2130	Rfm.	GOLDSTON, L. E.	21st London Regt.	30/5/15	2, Pepys Road, New Cross, London, S.E.
31116	Pte.	GOLDSTONE, M.	1st East Yorks. Regt.	9/4/17	362, Cleethorpe Road, Grimsby.
3556	Pte.	GOLDSTEIN, S. W.	1st H.A.C.	7/2/17	89, Finsbury Park Road, London, N.
887	Sergt.	GOLDSTONE, A.	37th Australian Inf.	9/6/17	45, Derby Street, Collingwood, Victoria.
333	Cpl.	GOLDWATER, N. I.	4th Australian Inf.	21/4/18	74, Leichardt Street, Waverley, N.S.W.
S/28001	Rfm.	GOLIZSKY, J.	10th Rifle Brigade	23/9/17	310, Brick Lane, London, E.
2819	Spr.	GOLLAND, A.	Royal Engineers	4/2/18	Bedford House, Ford Street, London, E.
573510	Rfm.	GOODFRIEND, H.	2/17th London Regt.	12/12/17	70, Settle Street, London, E.
6560	Pte.	GOODMAN, A.	1st Leicestershire Regt.	20/10/14	London.
25839	Pte.	GOODMAN, B.	14th Canadian Inf.	30/7/15	47, Church Street, Montreal.
148	Sgt.	GOODMAN, D. (D.C.M.)	111th Battery, R.F.A.	26/4/16	298, Belgrave Road, Birmingham.
87519	Pte.	GOODMAN, E.	62nd M.G. Bn.	17/10/18	86, Christian Street, London, E.
81981	Pte.	GOODMAN, J.	44th M.G.C.	24/3/17	70, Columbia Road, London, E.
82530	Gnr.	GOODMAN, J.	33rd Battery, R.F.A.	10/11/17	76, Dempsey Street, London, E.
19802	L/Cpl.	GOODMAN, L.	12th Rifle Brigade	22/8/17	73, Abingdon Buildings, London, E.
625006	Pte.	GOODMAN, M.	1/19th London Regt.	4/12/17	83 Greenfield Street, London, E.
9546	Pte.	GOODMAN, M.	1st West Yorks. Regt.	9/10/17	80, Byron Street, Leeds.
3408	Pte.	GOODMAN, R. G.	55th Australian Inf.	20/10/18	9, Cecilia Street, Subiaco, N.S.W.
23539	Pte.	GOODMAN, S.	2nd K.O.Y.L.I.	9/2/16	59, New Oxford Street, Stirchley, Birmingham.
267009	Pte.	GOODMAN, S.	1/1st Bucks. Bn.	16/8/17	11, Ramsden Terrace, Leeds.
406172	Pte.	GOODMAN, W.	25th K.R.R.C.	8/7/18	148, Irving Street, Birmingham.
192529	Pte.	GOODMAN, W.	24th Training Reserve	20/6/18	43, Maplin Street, London, E.
17797	Rfm.	GORDON, B. (WOOLF)	8th Rifle Brigade	3/10/16	26, Irene House, Flower & Dean Street, London, E
348943	Gnr.	GORDON, B.	2nd Bde. Canad. Fld. Art.	9/5/17	42, Osborne Road, Newcastle-on-Tyne.
1877	Cpl.	GORDON, C.	13th Rifle Brigade	19/5/16	46, Marylands Road, Paddington, London, W.
30093	Pte.	GORDON, D.	9th Loyal North Lancs. Rgt.	11/11/16	9, John Street, Blackburn.
6957	Pte.	GORDON, H. I.	2/4th London Regt.	18/5/17	14, Burdett Road, London, E.
49297	Pte.	GORDON, I.	1st Cheshire Regt.	20/11/16	151, Stock Street, Manchester.
1891	Sgt.	GORDON, M. M.	17th London Regt.	16/5/15	32, Jubilee Street, London, E.
2520	Rfm.	GORDON, M.	1/5th London Regt.	1/7/16	186, Dalston Lane, London, N.E.
37883	Pte.	GORDON, N.	2nd R. Berks Regt.	26/4/18	15, Station Street, Burton-on-Trent.
458020	Spr.	GORFUNKLE, H.	Northumberland R.E.	11/2/17	63, Chatham Street, Liverpool.
8891	Cpl.	GOSS, J.	2nd Somerset L.I.	17/8/18	31, Edward Street, Manchester.
302726	Rfm.	GOSSCHALK, L. B.	2/5th London Regt.	20/9/17	2, Heathfield Park, London, N.W.
47093	Rfm.	GOTLOP, E.	13th R. Irish Rifles	16/8/17	7, Kelfield Gardens, London, W.
622936	Pte.	GOULDING, B.	44th Canadian Inf.	25/10/16	Austin Street, Winnipeg, Man., Canada.
5022	Rfm.	GREEN, A.	6th London Regt.	15/9/16	92, Wilberforce Road, London, N.
89936	Pte.	GREEN, A.	25th M.G. Bn.	29/5/18	50, Merchant Street, London, E.
8718	Pte.	GREEN, A. B.	3rd S. African Infantry	19/10/16	P.O. Box, 1928, Johannesburg.
205	Pte.	GREEN, A. P.	14th R. Warwick Regt.	27/7/16	493, Coventry Road, Birmingham.
63636	Pte	GREEN, G.	4th Royal Fusiliers	18/9/18	36, Finch Street Buildings, London, E.
4038	Gnr.	GREEN, I.	A/121st R.F.A.	26/7/17	21, Victoria Street, Merthyr Tydvil, South Wales.
18661	L/Cpl.	GREEN, I.	20th Middlesex Regt.	22/8/16	50, Merchant Street, London, E.
178921	Pnr.	GREEN, L.	1st Bn. Special Bde. R.E.	24/8/16	53, Manor Road, London, N.

93

N.C.O.'S AND MEN—Continued.

No.	Rank.	Name.	Regiment.	Date of Death.	Address.
303855	Rfm.	GREEN, M. M.	1/5th London Regt.	16/8/17	174, Brunswick Buildings, London, E.
6006	Pte.	GREEN, T. R.	4th Australian Inf.	16/4/18	Inch Street, Lithgow, N.S.W.
374193	Rfm.	GREEN, W.	1/8th London Regt	16/8/16	73, Wentworth Street, London, E.
1111	Pte.	GREENBAUM, B.	2nd E. Kent Regt.	9/10/18	7, Princelet Street, London, E.
74404	Cpl.	GREENBERG, G.	6th (Lab.) Middlesex Regt.	18/12/18	80, Rectory Road, London, N.
242578	Pte.	GREENBERG, P.	1/6th W. Yorks Regt.	14/3/18	6a, Stamford Street, Leeds.
J/6427	Pte.	GREENBERG, P.	38th Royal Fusiliers	16/1/19	75, Walnut Street, Chelsea, Mass., U.S.A.
234169	Pte.	GREENBERG, R.	488th Labour Coy.	18/2/19	50, Walton Street, Manchester.
8716	Pte.	GREENBERG, S.	1st K.O.R. Lancs. Regt.	26/8/14	19, Edinboro' Road, Liverpool.
41569	Pte.	GREENBURY, W.	2nd Northants Regt.	15/10/18	56, Oxford Street, London, E.
7555	Pte.	GREENWALD, L.	22nd London Regt.	8/10/16	99, Roman Road, London, N.
J/901	Pte.	GREYMAN, S.	38th Royal Fusiliers	7/9/18	5, Amber Street, Leeds.
42543	Pte.	GRIECK, M.	2nd Worcester Regt.	2/11/16	50, Plumbers, London, E.
1398	Rfm.	GRIEW, B.	1/5th London Regt.	1/7/16	171, Amhurst Road, London, N.
1748	Cpl.	GRIMISH, A. B.	9th Australian Inf.	11/8/18	Cordelia Street S., Brisbane, Queensland.
8193	Pte.	GRODNER (LEWIS), C.	4th Royal Fusiliers	22/2/15	83, Ernest Street, London, E.
48924	Pte.	GRODZINSKY, H.	Royal Defence Corps	4/8/18	8, Yalford Street, London, E.
57831	Pte.	GROSSMAN, A.	20th Canadian Inf.	23/4/16	202, Mountain Street, Montreal.
204717	Pte.	GROUSE, A.	1st Lon. Rgt. att.167 T.M.B.	4/5/17	11, Oxford Gardens, London, W.
1827	Sgt.	GROUSE, R. C.	36th Australian Inf.	10/6/17	"Lyric," Euston Road, Hurlstone Park, N.S.W.
295215	Pte.	GROWER, A.	1/4th London Regt.	16/8/17	10, Nottingham Place, London, E.I.
10032	Pte.	GRUENBAUM, A.	2nd Royal Berks. Regt.	17/9/15	67, West Street, Leytonstone, London, N.E.
2308	Pte.	GUBBAY, J. M.	36th Australian Inf.	8/6/17	Turner Street, Hamilton, N.S.W.
2705	Gnr.	GURR, H.	13th Aust. Fld. Art. Bde.	22/8/17	Henley Beech Road, Torrensville, S. Australia.
9340	Pte.	GUTERMAN, A.	5th Durham L.I.	17/12/16	19, Gee Street, London, N.W.
160123	Pte.	HACKMAN, S.	4th Canadian Inf.	24/9/16	Rumsey, Alberta, Canada.
47879	Pte.	HAFT, I. G.	18th Manchester Regt.	23/4/17	29, Thirlmere Street, Manchester.
2922	Cpl.	HAFT, S.	17th H.L.I.	10/7/17	123, Heywood Street, Manchester.
531103	Rfm.	HAINES, L.	15th London Regt.	8/6/17	30, Laurel Gardens, Hanwell.
2150	Pte.	HAINS, M.	3rd Australian Inf.	7/8/15	83, East Terrace, Adelaide.
	Pte.	HALIMI, M.	Zion Mule Corps	9/6/15	Alexandria.
283366	Pte.	HAMBURG, N.	2/4th London Regt.	14/5/17	24, Spital Square, London, E.I.
6864	Pte.	HAMBURG, S.	1st Royal Scots Fusiliers	12/3/15	124, Stepney Green, London, E.
20630	L/Cpl.	HAMBURGER, J.	32nd Royal Fusiliers	7/10/16	43, Coram Street, London, W.C.
2604	Pte.	HAMMERSBERG, R. M.	14th Australian Inf.	11/4/17	Coleford, Glebe Road, Cheltenham, Victoria.
883	A/M	HANSMAN, E. E.	Aust. Flying Corps	28/12/17	Marion, St. Redfern, Sydney.
2578	Pte.	HANSMAN, H. J.	37th Australian Inf.	3/12/17	Marion Street, Redfern, Sydney.
9444	Pte.	HANSELL, A.	17th Manchester Regt.	1/7/16	27, Brunswick Street, Manchester.
2173	Pte.	HARBERT, G.	59th Australian Inf.	19/7/16	73, Sidney Street, London, E.
786	Pte.	HARBOUR, I.	22nd Royal Fusiliers	17/2/17	6, Kerbela Street, Bethnal Green, London, E.
48708	Pte.	HARRINGMAN, L.	8th Royal Fusiliers	1/7/17	37, Stayners Road, London, E.
9391	A/Cpl.	HARRIS, A.	1st Duke of Cornwall's L.I.	9/4/15	Castle Mount Square, Axminster.
55594	Gnr.	HARRIS, A.	21st Siege Battery, R.G.A.	17/11/15	5, Victoria Street, Craig-y-don, Llandudno.

N.C.O.'S AND MEN—Continued.

No.	Rank.	Name.	Regiment.	Date of Death.	Address.
67436	Pte.	HARRIS, A.	25th Field Amb. R.A.M.C.	6/5/18	44, Pleasant Street, Liverpool.
1799	Pte.	HARRIS, A. B.	11th Middlesex Regt.	20/5/16	46, Anthony Street, London, E.
31695	Pte.	HARRIS, G.	2nd H.L.I.	28/4/17	154, Oxford Street, Glasgow.
7442	A/Cpl.	HARRIS, H.	1st Duke of Cornwall's L.I.	27/11/14	33, Mazall Road, Herne Hill, London.
18268	Pte.	HARRIS, H.	2nd R. Irish Regt.	22/3/18	38, Wilkes Street, London, E.
40922	Pte.	HARRIS, J.	1/6th Gordon Highlanders	24/4/17	68, Wilberforce Road, London, N.
42551	Rfm.	HARRIS, J.	14th Royal Irish Rifles	16/8/17	379, Old Kent Road, London.
4908	Pte.	HARRIS, L.	1st Duke of Cornwall's L.I.	28/4/15	11, Havering Street, London, E.
43055	Pte.	HARRIS, M.	10th W. Yorks. Regt.	7/11/18	41, Cooper Street, Leeds.
24478	Pte.	HARRIS, M.	10th E. Kent Regt.	6/8/18	8, Grove Terrace, Leeds.
5396	Rfm.	HARRIS, M.	4th Rifle Brigade	25/5/15	9, Newling Street, London, E.
11927	Gnr.	HARRIS, M.	311th Bde. R.F.A.	20/4/18	4, Northfield Square, Leeds.
204434	Pte.	HARRIS, M.	2/1st London Regt.	16/6/17	31, Blakesley Street, London, E.
21268	Sgt.	HARRIS, M.	9th Essex Regt.	6/11/16	169, Highbury New Park, London, N.
263163	Pte.	HARRIS, M. M.	2nd R. Sussex Regt.	18/9/18	14, Gordon Mansions, London, W.C.
7411	Pte.	HARRIS, N.	1st Cameron Highlanders	11/11/14	11, Main Street, Glasgow.
S/16064	Rfm.	HARRIS, S.	1st Rifle Brigade	22/4/18	32, Sillwood Road, Brighton.
S/7885	Pte.	HARRIS, S. E.	11th Rifle Bde.	25/2/16	22, Shepherd Street, Buildings, London, E.
S/13699	Pte.	HARRIS, S. W.	8th S. Stafford Regt.	26/8/15	84, Glebe Street, Penarth, South Wales.
6444	Cpl.	HARRIS, W. D.	20th Australian Inf.	9/10/17	Glen Point, Sydney, Australia.
25636	Spr.	HARRIS, W. D. (HERSHON, I. J.)	1st Field Coy. R.E.	8/8/16	35, Minshull Street, Liverpool.
2135	Pte.	HARRISON, J.	12th Middlesex Regt.	11/3/16	28, Willesden Lane, London, N.W.
268013	Pte.	HARRISON, M.	1/17th W. Yorks.	17/10/17	28, Glover Street, Leeds.
1943	Sgt.	HART, C. A. H.	18th Australian Inf.	5/8/16	Lett Street, Lithgow, N.S.W.
R/21696	Rfm.	HART, D.	10th K.R.R.C.	15/9/16	32, Sonning Buildings, London, E.
109610	Bdr.	HART, E. A.	N. Riding, H.B., R.G.A.	17/9/18	9, Sheldon Road, London, N.W.
373346	Rfm.	HART, H.	1/8th LondonRegt.	11/8/18	3a, Hayfield Passage, London, E.
1354	L./Cpl.	HART, H. A.	7th Australian Inf.	8/5/15	105, Beavers Road, Northcote, Melbourne.
71	Cpl.	HART, H. E.	8th Australian Inf.	1915	Sydney, N.S.W.
33359	Cpl.	HART, H. E.	3 Wellington Rgt. N.Z. Inf.	14/6/17	110, Sutherland Avenue, London, W.
190	Pte.	HART, J.	30th Australian Inf.	19/7/16	61, Raglan Road, Mosman, N.S.W.
32265	Rfm.	HART, J.	8th K.R.R.C.	3/12/17	23, Queen's Block, London, E.
202780	L/Cpl.	HART, J.	1st London Regt.	8/8/18	7, Rosetta Court, London, E.
6465	Pte.	HART, J.	7th Australian Inf.	2/5/19	105, Beavers Road, Northcote, Melbourne.
267	Pte.	HART, L.	7th Australian Inf.	4/5/15	5, Union Street, Brunswick, N.S.W.
126978	Pte.	HART, M.	19th M.G.C.	28/3/18	1a, Vartry Road, London, N.5.
8719	L/Cpl.	HART, R.	9th K.O.R. Lancs. Regt.	6/1/17	1a, Vartry Road, London, N.
9521	Rfm.	HART, S.	1/5th London Regt.	1/7/16	19, Anson Road, London, N.W.
55385	Bdr.	HART, S.	A/102 Brigade, R.F.A.	1/2/17	4, Imperial Avenue, London, N.
J/977	Pte.	HART, S.	38th Royal Fusiliers	16/10/18	23, Harold Road, Upton Park, London, E.
573826	Pte.	HART, W.	1/17th London Regt.	7/6/17	4, Imperial Avenue, London, N.16.
45185	Pte.	HARTSTONE, M.	2nd South Wales Borderers	9/12/17	32, Woodhouse Street, Hull.

95

N.C.O.'S AND MEN—Continued.

No.	Rank.	Name.	Regiment.	Date of Death.	Address.
12/1047	Desp. Rider	HAYMAN, E. P.	Auckland, N.Z., Regt.	10/2/17	19, Pembridge Gardens, London, W.
209743	Gnr.	HAYMAN, H.	C/315th Bde. R.F.A.	30/8/18	14, Wolverton Gardens, London, W.
40095	Pte.	HECKER, J.	16th Middlesex Regt.	11/8/17	48, Tredegar Street, London, E.
78800	Bdr.	HEILBRON, V. (M.M.)	L/15th Brigade, R.H.A.	27/4/17	178, Sutherland Avenue, London, W.
41283	Pte.	HELLER, D.	1/28th London Regt.	3/9/18	144b, Union Street, London, S.E.
493751	Pte.	HENISON, M.	13th London Regt.	9/4/17	5, Newcastle Street, London, E.
11508	Pte.	HEPSTONE, J.	1st K.O. Royal Lancs. Rgt.	7/6/15	130, Waterloo Road, Manchester.
	Sgt.	HERBERTS, J.	M.G.C.	4/5/17	26, William Henry Street, Blackburn.
2910	Pte.	HERMAN, C. H.	58th Australian Inf.	23/10/17	305, Riley Street, Surrey Hills, N.S.W.
204260	Pte.	HERMAN, H.	1/5th West Yorks. Regt.	20/6/18	162, Jefferson Street, Newcastle.
1706	Pte.	HERMAN, H. E.	17th Australian Inf.	20/11/15	Waverley Crescent, Waverley, N.S.W.
6874	Rfm.	HERMAN, J.	9th London Regt.	25/9/16	105, Hope Street, Capetown.
12313	Pte.	HERMAN, J.	6th K.O.R. Lancs. Regt.	10/8/15	23, Exchange Street, Manchester.
4370	Pte.	HERMAN, M. P.	30th Australian Inf.	8/8/18	Victoria Street, Darlinghurst, N.S.W.
1054121	Pte.	HERMAN, S.	87th Canadian Inf.	5/9/18	240, McCord Street, Montreal.
1024	Cpl.	HERMAN, S.	10th Rifle Brigade	15/4/17	11, Southampton Street, London, W.
5602	Pte.	HERMAN, W. R.	26th Australian Inf.	25/5/18	Lawntown, Queensland.
1926	Rfm.	HERON, J.	21st London Regt.	25/5/15	304, Queen's Road, New Cross, London, S.E.
A/1498	Rfm.	HERTZBERG, N.	8th K.R.R.C.	20/5/17	72, Palace Road, Hackney, London, N.E.
531269	Sergt.	HERTZ, A.	1/15th London Regt.	3/9/17	40, Wenlake Buildings, Old Street, London, E.C.
202209	Pte.	HERZEL, M.	1/6th King's Liverpool Rgt.	20/9/17	50, Erskine Street, Liverpool.
22897	Pte.	HEWSON, J. R.	6th Border Regt.	30/9/16	7, Fleur-de-lis Buildings, London, E.
55807	2/A.M.	HEYMANN, B.	R.A.F.	31/8/18	20, Queen's Block, Houndsditch, London, E.
781350	Pte.	HILLIER, A.	26th Royal Fusiliers	21/10/18	10, New Street, Houndsditch, London, E.C.
75249	Dvr.	HILLIER, C. J.	2nd T.M.B., R.F.A.	12/4/18	15, Highbury New Park, London, N.5.
41635	Pte.	HILLMAN, L.	5/6th Royal Scots.	11/8/18	6, Commercial Road, London, E.1.
203842	Pte.	HIMMELSTEIN, H.	2/2nd London Regt.	21/3/18	94, Grove Street, Camberwell, London, S.E.
100390	Pte.	HINES, S. C.	66th Canadian Inf.	11/9/16	Grand Lake, Halifax, Canada.
16284	Rfm.	HIZER, L.	3rd Rifle Brigade	1/9/16	153, Grange Road, London, S.E.
39652	Pte.	HOCKIN, B.	1st East Lancs. Regt.	24/4/18	146, Waterloo Road, Cheetham, Manchester.
160123	Pte.	HOCKMAN, S.	4th Canadian Inf.	24/9/16	Rumsey, Alberta, Canada.
024080	Pte.	HOEPELMAN, H.	R.A.O.C.	4/3/17	76, Clissold Road, London, N.
242789	Pte.	HOFFMAN, E.	2nd West Riding Regt.	20/7/18	51, Courtney Street, Hull.
1421	Pte.	HOFFMAN, J.	3rd South African Inf.	9/4/17	Hibernia, N.S., U.S.A.
2/30116	Pte.	HOLBROOK, M.	1/6th London Regt.	25/4/18	London.
29461	Pte.	HOLLAND, L.	1st West Yorks. Regt.	30/5/17	17, Nile Street, Leeds.
602707	Pte.	HOLMAN, J.	34th Canadian Inf.	3/6/16	232, Clarence Street, London, Ontario, Canada
10632	Cpl.	HOLMES, J. G.	7th East Surrey Regt.	10/12/17	27, Myrtle Street, Leeds.
2063	Pte.	HOLTSBAUM, T. R.	33rd Australian Inf.	4/10/17	Kelly's Plain, Armidale, N.S.W.
J/2027	Pte.	HOPPEN, L.	39th Royal Fusiliers	23/10/18	7, Victoria Park Road, London, N.E.
2785	Pte.	HORNICK, M.	23rd Middlesex Regt.	15/9/16	71, New Town Road, Birmingham.
32289	Pte.	HORWICH, I.	1st Middlesex Regt.	29/9/18	17, Virginia Road, London, E.
2701	Gnr.	HOVSHA, H. R.	C/232 Brigade, R.F.A.	16/3/17	28, Prince George's Road, London, N.
12802	Cpl.	HULLES, M.	6th Bedford. Regt.	29/4/17	8, St. Saviour's Road, London, S.W.
109783	Pte.	HUNT, A.	11th Tank Corps	2/9/18	9, Cardigan Road, London, E.

N.C.O.'S AND MEN—Continued.

No.	Rank.	Name.	Regiment.	Date of Death.	Address.
3880	Rfm.	HUROVITCH, M.	2/7th West Yorks. Regt.	18/2/17	1, Tanfield Place, Leeds.
35077	Pte.	HURWITZ, L.	9th East Surrey Regt.	15/10/18	9, Rockley Road, London, W.14.
2999	Pte.	HURWITZ, M.	7th Notts & Derby Regt.	17/11/15	114, Arkwright Street, Nottingham.
3262	Pte.	HYAM, E.	4th East Yorks. Regt.	1918	Hull.
T/36657	Dvr.	HYAM, L. W.	R.A.S.C.	1918	London.
40411	Cpl.	HYAM, M.	230th P.O.W. Co. Lab. Co.	6/12/18	Marsham Court, Bournemouth.
S/2650	Rfm.	HYAMS, L.	13th Rifle Brigade	21/11/18	22, Mayland Street, London, E.
8011	Pte.	HYAMS, P.	2nd South African Inf.	24/9/17	29, Brand Road, Durban, South Africa.
2999	Pte.	HYAMS, W.	24th Australian Inf.	4/10/17	330, Canning Street N., Carlton, Australia.
5359	A.B.	HYMAN, A. L.	Nelson Battalion, R.N.D.	31/12/17	157, Runcorn Road, Balsall Heath, Birmingham.
R/1533	Pte.	HYMAN, B.	2nd Lincolnshire Regt.	19/4/17	12, Tavistock Place, Sunderland.
30723	Pte.	HYMAN, J.	9th West Yorks. Regt.	10/10/17	15, Wingham Terrace, Leeds.
37454	Pte.	HYMAN, J.	11th Scottish Rifles	8/5/17	400, Mile End Road, London, E.
30548	Pte.	HYMAN, R.	8th East Yorks. Regt.	30/3/17	12, Tavistock Place, Sunderland.
27229	Pte.	HYMAN, S.	9th E. Surrey Regt.	3/9/18	55, Hartley Street, Bethnal Green, London, E.
27262	Pte.	HYMANS, A.	23rd Field Amb., R.A.M.C.	6/10/17	147, Nevill Road, London, N.E.
90917	L/Cpl.	HYMANS, L. H.	2/6th London Regt.	21/9/17	147, Nevill Road, London, N.E.
493789	Pte.	IDSTEIN, V. F.	35th Australian Inf.	29/5/17	Adelaide Street, Murrurrundi, N.S.W.
2173	Pte.	ILLFIELD, I.	20th Autralian Inf.	2/3/17	253, High Street, West, Maitland, N.S.W.
5666	Pte.	INSTEIN, J.	6th East Kent Regt.	16/5/18	79, Cornwall Road, London, W.
26293	Stoker	P. O. ISAAC, H.	H.M.S. "Seagull"	30/9/18	185, Lymington Road, Upton, Torquay.
358211	Pte.	ISAAC, L.	34th Canadian Inf.	6/6/16	651, Rideau Street, Brandon, Man., Canada.
603191	Pte.	ISAACS, A.	1st Devon. Regt.	7/2/15	161, Cavendish Terrace, Torquay.
8698	Rfm.	ISAACS, A.	9th Rifle Brigade	6/1/16	1, Gloucester Court, London, E.
6044	Pte.	ISAACS, A. A.	2nd Middlesex Regt.	11/5/16	134, Lansdown Road, London, N.E.
8322	Pte.	ISAACS, A.	1/14th London Regt.	1/7/16	34, Tottenham Court Road, London, W.
5835	Pte.	ISAACS, A.	1st Worcester Regt.	18/10/18	22, Newton Road, South Tottenham.
14438	Rfm.	ISAACS, A.	15th Royal Irish Rifles	22/11/17	22, Tilley Street, London, E.
43213	Pte.	ISAACS, A. V.	12th London Regt.	15/2/15	113, Long Acre, London, W.
1716	Pte.	ISAACS, A.	5th Middlesex Regt.	6/9/17	London.
34007	Rfm.	ISAACS, B.	16th K.R.R.C.	24/9/18	75, Park Lane, Clissold Park, London, N.
655918	Rfm.	ISAACS, E.	23rd London Regt.	5/4/18	19, Birchington Road, London, N.W.
5143	Pte.	ISAACS, E. E.	2nd Worcester Regt.	15/4/18	New Falcon Hotel, Waltham Cross.
6966	Tpr.	ISAACS, E. J.	2nd Dragoon Guards	31/10/14	6a, Kingsgate Road, Kilburn, London, N.W.
6913	Pte.	ISAACS, H.	2nd Royal Sussex Regt.	10/9/14	13, Swindon Road, Horsham.
1893	Pte.	ISAACS, H.	10th Royal Fusiliers	16/7/16	Chiswell House, Finsbury Pavement, London, E.C.
R/19103	Rfm.	ISAACS, J.	21st K.R.R.C.	20/9/17	129, Petherton Road, London, N.E.
920075	Gnr.	ISAACS, J.	A/92nd Brigade, R.F.A.	7/12/18	1, Keyes Road, London, N.W.
M/302200	Pte.	ISAACS, J.	R.A.S.C.	22/2/19	24, Old Castle Street, London, E.
13309	Pte.	ISAACS, L.	48th M.G.C.	1916	59, Sixth Avenue, Manor Park, London, E.
28171	Pte.	ISAACS, L.	1st King's Liverpool Rgt.	25/7/15	13, New Bridge Street, Manchester.
35054	Pte.	ISAACS, M.	23rd Northumberland Fus.	8/4/17	115, Sudbourne Road, Brixton Hill, London.
31011	Pte.	ISAACS (JACKSON), C. M.	10th Aus. Field Art.	2/7/18	3, McAlpine Street Glasgow.

N.C.O.'S AND MEN—Continued.

No.	Rank. Name.	Regiment.	Date of Death.	Address.
862334	Pte. ISAACS, M. (FIELD)	4th Canadian Inf.	2/9/18	1633, Mance Street, Montreal, P.Q., Canada.
17144	Pte. ISAACS, N.	1st Essex Regt.	6/12/17	21, Calverley Street, London, E.
473221	Rfm. ISAACS, S.	1/12th London Regt.	26/9/17	18, Palmer Street, London, E.
14193	L/Cpl. ISAACS, S. M.	1st Gordon Highlanders	15/6/18	16, Cricketfield Road, London, E.5.
634466	Pte. ISAACS, S. E.	2/20th London Regt.	14/9/18	170, High Street, Slough, Bucks.
4138	Pte. ISAACS, W.	22nd Australian Inf.	20/8/16	35, Mary Street, St. Kilda, Victoria.
19161	Pte. ISAACSON, A.	9th Royal Sussex Regt.	13/9/18	12, Cornwall Buildings, Manchester.
G/53395	Pte. ISIDORE, D.	1st Middlesex Regt.	3/4/17	50, Fieldgate Street, London, E.
3076	Pte. ISRAEL, A.	33rd Australian Inf.	27/7/18	7, Henry Street, Leichardt, Sydney.
4999	L/Cpl. ISRAEL, G. R.	3rd South African Inf.	16/7/16	Miriamville, Francis Street, Bondi, Sydney, N.S.W.,
2704	L/Cpl. ISRAEL, L. C. M.	20th Australian Inf.	11/7/18	105, Glenmore Road, Paddington, N.S.W.
920076	Sig. ISSER, D.	307th Brigade, R.F.A.	2/11/18	13, Tyers Street, London, S.E.
38781	Sig. JACKOFF, M.	2nd Royal Scots	26/9/17	93, Cambridge Road, Glasgow.
3387	Pte. JACKS, A.	49th Australian Inf.	26/9/17	5, Moreton Avenue, Manchester.
10796	Pte. JACKSON, H.	2nd West Riding Regt.	17/10/17	21, Crimbles Street, Leeds.
2578	Pte. JACKSON, I.	7th Durham L.I.	15/5/15	1, Manor House Road, Jesmond, Sunderland.
3048	Pte. JACKSON, M.	6th Welsh Regt.	2/4/16	128, Kingsland Road, London, N.
8741	Pte. JACOBS, A.	4th Middlesex Regt.	29/9/15	161, Stepney Green Buildings, London, E.
2886	Pte. JACOBS, A.	7th London Regt.	20/10/15	3, Pellerin Road, Stoke Newington, London, N.
20103	Tpr. JACOBS, A. L.	1st R. West Kent Regt.	26/10/17	45, Northfield Road, London, N.16.
203447	Pte. JACOBS, A.	4th East Yorks. Regt.	19/7/17	8, Coberg Street, Leeds.
M2/269400	Pte. JACOBS, A. J.	R.A.S.C.	29/10/18	50, Linden Grove, London, S.E.
4453	Cpl. JACOBS, A. M.	27th Australian Inf.	2/3/17	73, Airlie Street, Adelaide.
2846	Pte. JACOBS, A. N.	2nd South African Inf.	17/7/16	Box 1113, Durban.
32617	Pte. JACOBS, B.	11th South Lancs. Regt.	24/3/18	18, Stoke Newington Common, London, N.
474177	Rfm. JACOBS, B.	12th London Regt.	9/4/17	33, Willows Street, London, E.
4762	Pte. JACOBS, C.	2nd Scots Guards	17/10/15	107, Orwell Road, Liverpool.
10283	Pte. JACOBS, D.	4th Middlesex Regt.	15/9/17	2a, Lombard Street, London, E.
19438	Rfm. JACOBS, D.	2nd K.R.R.C.	2/9/16	57, Brunswick Buildings, London, E.
3145	Bdr. JACOBS, F.	R.F.A.	19/9/14	Salisbury, Wilts.
67800	Spr. JACOBS, F. C.	154th Field Coy., R.E.	16/10/16	42, Listria Road, London, N.
39928	Sergt. JACOBS, G. (D.C.M.)	47th Field Amb., R.A.M.C.	10/10/16	9, The Elms, W. Sunderland.
19154	Rfm. JACOBS, H.	1st K.R.R.C.	5/9/18	8, Blanchard Street, London, N.E.
3462	L/Cpl. JACOBS, H. M.	3rd South African Inf.	21/9/17	2, The Terrace, Camden Square, London, N.W.
24472	L/Cpl. JACOBS, I.	12th Royal Scots	12/4/17	84, John Street, Glasgow.
1508	Pte. JACOBS, I. E.	15th Royal Warwick. Regt.	23/7/16	120, Sherlock Street, Birmingham.
10409	Pte. JACOBS, J.	2nd East Surrey Regt.	22/2/16	10, Burdett Road, London, E.
8445	Pte. JACOBS, J.	2/2nd London Regt.	23/3/17	14, Great Garden Street, London, E.
14688	Pte. JACOBS, J.	7th R. West Surrey Regt.	18/11/16	63, Gold Street, London, E.
B/200165	Rfm. JACOBS, J.	11th Rifle Brigade	11/6/18	37, Whitehorse Lane, London, E.
16711	Spr. JACOBS, J.	206th Field Coy., R.E.	3/12/18	12, Bacon Street, London, E.2.
1774	Pte. JACOBS, J.	2/4th Oxford & Bucks. L.I.	22/8/17	58, British Street, London, E.
114712	Pte. JACOBS, J.	R.A.M.C.	26/2/18	30, Berwick Street, London, W.

N.C.O.'S AND MEN—Continued.

No.	Rank.	Name.	Regiment.	Date of Death.	Address.
624995	Dvr.	JACOBS, J.	H.A.C. Amm. Col. R.F.A.	1/5/17	78, Eric Street, London, E.
1539	Tpr.	JACOBS (COLE), J.	2nd King Edward's Horse	15/11/16	29, Bickton Road, Canning Town, London, E.
J/4081	A/B.	JACOBS, L.	H.M.S. "Lord Nelson."	25/4/15	66c, Stepney Green Buildings, London, E.
492399	Rfm.	JACOBS, L.	2/13th London Regt.	6/11/17	56, Linthorpe Road, London, N.
2756	Pte.	JACOBS, L.	6th H.L.I.	11/9/15	4, Thistle Street, Glasgow.
8733	Rfm.	JACOBS, L.	5th K.R.R.C.	15/5/17	5, Essex Street, Hackney, London, N.E.
4950	Rfm.	JACOBS, L. E.	2/16th London Regt.	10/5/17	8, Castellain Road, London, W.
1772	Pte.	JACOBS, L. W.	7th Australian Inf.	3/10/15	49, Newcastle Street, Perth, W. Australia.
27643	Pte.	JACOBS, M.	1st Worcester Regt.	31/7/17	134, Varna Road, Edgbaston, Birmingham.
23260	Pte.	JACOBS, M.	7th West Kent Regt.	9/2/17	623, Rochdale Road, Manchester.
17494	Pte.	JACOBS, M.	1st Duke of Cornwall's L.I.	23/7/16	22, Heneage Street, London, E.
293024	Pte.	JACOBS, M.	2/7th North. Fusiliers	29/3/19	5, Court Street, London, E.
3060	Pte.	JACOBS (JAY), M.	17th K.R.R.C.	3/9/16	6, Crowstone Road, South Westcliffe.
40241	Pte.	JACOBS, N.	3rd Worcestershire Regt.	2/8/17	Belle Vue Road, Cinderford, Gloster.
675025	Pte.	JACOBS, P.	21st London Regt.	29/8/18	78, Eric Street, London, E.
325	Pte.	JACOBS, P. K.	43rd Australian Inf.	21/4/17	Blanche Street, Gawler, South Australia.
34481	Sergt.	JACOBS, R. B.	12th Manchester Regt.	16/9/17	269, Waterloo Road, Manchester.
2789	Rfm.	JACOBS, S.	18th London Regt.	5/10/15	119, Sunny Gardens, Hendon, London, N.W.
5146	Pte.	JACOBS, S.	2nd Middlesex Regt.	8/6/16	21, Victoria Road, Kilburn, London, N.W.
1459	Pte.	JACOBS, S. A.	1st Aus. Light Horse	1/6/16	
6046	Pte.	JACOBS, V. M.	16th Australian Inf.	11/4/17	168, Bank Street, Melbourne.
19935	Pte.	JACOBS, W. H.	10th Canadian Inf.	23/4/15	1st Underwood Block, W. Calgary, Canada.
31876	Pte.	JACOBSON, A.	1st West Yorks. Regt.	22/12/16	15, Sheepscar Place, Leeds.
52546	L/Cpl.	JACOBSON, H.	11th Middlesex Regt.	20/11/17	163, Faulkner Street, Liverpool.
19303	Gnr.	JACOBSON, R. E.	7th Australian Arty.	8/8/18	111, Darling Street, Balmain, N.S.W.
40838	Pte.	JAFFA, W.	2nd Suffolk Regt.	6/9/17	3, Northampton Street, London, E.
40596	Pte.	JAFFE, I.	9th K.O. Yorkshire L.I.	20/7/17	13, Glover Street, Camp Road, Leeds.
14667	Rfm.	JAFFE, J.	20th K.R.R.C.	20/8/16	19, Cloth Street, Leeds.
27858	Pte.	JESKI, R. L.	2nd Wilts Regt.	19/10/18	21, Bernard Street, Southampton.
317958	Pte.	JESSELL, H.	1/4th R. Berks. Regt.	16/8/17	518, Kingsland Road, London, E.
530535	Pte.	JOFFE, M.	1/15th London Regt.	7/6/17	69, De Beers Road, Kimberley, South Africa.
2278	Pte.	JONAS, A. R. B.	48th Australian Inf.	9/6/17	King Street, Alberton, S. Australia.
225	Sgt.	JONAS, B.	33rd Australian Inf.	11/5/19	82, Riley Street, Sydney, N.S.W.
2681	Pte.	JONAS, E.	1st Australian Pion.	6/10/17	Andrew Street, Northcote, Victoria.
B/191619	Pte	JONAS, F. J.	26th Royal Fusiliers	19/7/16	4, York Road, Edgbaston, Birmingham.
25709	Pte.	JONAS, J.	10th R. W. Surrey Regt.	5/9/18	39, Morrison Buildings, London, E.
R/38280	Rfm.	JONAS, S.	9th K.R.R.C.	31/3/18	17, Chatsworth Road, London, S.W.
336	Sgt.	JOSEPH, E.	14th R. Warwick Regt.	22/7/16	108, Cape Road, Port Elizabeth, South Africa.
4910	L/Cpl.	JOSEPH, J. O.	14th London Regiment	19/9/16	17, Chichele Road, London, N.W.
1055	Pte.	JOSEPH, J. P. D.	31st Australian Inf.	20/7/16	214, Cecil Street, South Melbourne, Victoria.
9965	Pte.	JOSEPH, M.	2nd H.A.C.	28/10/17	56, Portsdown Road, London, W.
2672235	Pte.	JOSEPH, M.	2/7th W. Yorks Regt.	20/4/18	67, Glover Street, Leeds.
4536	L/Cpl.	JOSEPH, M.	1st Yorks. and Lancs. Regt.	23/4/15	2, Casson Street, London, E.

99

N.C.O.'S AND MEN—Continued.

No.	Rank.	Name.	Regiment.	Date of Death.	Address.
6522	Sgt.	Josephs, S.	7th Australian Inf.	9/8/18	2, Hawksburn Avenue, Toorak, Victoria.
213	Q.M.S.	Judell, E. M.	9th Australian L. H.	9/8/15	Unley Park, Adelaide.
10497	Pte.	Julius, C.	13th R. Sussex Regt.	22/7/17	40, Cable Street, London, E.
J/8305	Pte.	Kadishewitz, I.	39th Royal Fusiliers	8/11/18	20, Second Avenue, New York.
204072	Pte.	Kaiser, S. L.	1/1st London Regt.	3/5/17	17, Redmans Road, London, E.
134	Pte.	Kafer, F.	53rd Australian Inf.	1/9/18	Carrington, N.S.W.
889	Pte.	Kalisker, A.	Egyptian Labour Corps	13/2/19	Alexandria.
J/9215	Pte.	Kallan, M.	39th Royal Fusiliers	8/5/19	London.
M/332189	Pte.	Kalminsky, J.	R.A.S.C.	27/10/18	13, Stutfield Street, London, E.
5951	Pte.	Kapelusnick, A. J.	3rd South African Inf.	21/9/17	Harrow Road, Yeovil, Johannesburg, S. Africa.
	Cadet	Kaplan, H. W.	Canadian R.A.F.	1917	Winnipeg.
8676	Pte.	Kaplan, V.	2nd S. African Inf.	22/3/18	39, St. Paul's Road, London, N.
44675	A/M.	Kaplansky, W. M.	R.A.F.	25/11/18	121, Queen Street, Sheffield.
S/15121	Rfm.	Karasek, H.	16th Rifle Bde.	16/10/16	26, Plumbers Row, London, E.1.
	Pte.	Karet, C.	South African A.S.C.	27/7/17	38, Bridge Street, Mile End, London, E.
10396	Cpl.	Karker, S.	1st S. Staffs. Regt.	14/7/16	16, Queen's Buildings, London, E.
R/2424	A/B.	Karlish, A.	63rd M.G. Bn. R.N.D.	10/10/18	85, Hanbury Street, London, E.
2456	Pte.	Katz, C.	4th London Regt.	9/9/16	58, Clifton Buildings, London, E.
9194	Pte.	Katzenstein, M.	2nd S. African Inf.	18/4/17	26, Kirkland Street, Newcastle, Natal.
625457	Pte.	Katzovitz, N.	20th London Regt.	2/3/18	11, Luntley Place, Chicksand Street, London, E.
157	Pte.	Katznelson, B.	Zion Mule Corps	30/5/15	Alexandria.
1329	L/Cpl.	Kaufman, C.	15th Australian Inf.	1/5/15	Queen Street, Melbourne.
51227	Pte.	Kaufman, E. (Elias)	Imp. Camel Corps	28/3/18	34, Fore Street, Edmonton, London, N.
6018	Pte.	Kaufman (Kaye), H.	10th King's Liv'pool Regt.	24/8/16	25, Norton Street, Liverpool.
2220	Pte.	Kaufman, K.	58th Australian Inf.	12/5/17	Little Collins Street, Melbourne.
12601	Rfm.	Kaufman, L.	7th K.R.R.C.	30/4/17	12, New Cleveland Street, Leeds.
37750	Pte.	Kavarsky, J.	1/5th K.O. Roy. Lanc. Rgt.	15/5/18	193, Bury New Road, Manchester.
300937	Pte.	Kay, I. M.	16th K.R.R.C.	16/4/18	34, Devonshire Street, London, W.C.
221120	Gnr.	Kaye, S. (M.M.)	B/24th Bde. R.F.A.	18/10/18	13, Adamson Road, London, N.W.3.
C/7146	Rfm.	Kemp, S.	18th K.R.R.C.	15/9/16	46, Heskey Street, London, N.E.
R/18620	Rfm.	Kingstone, J. W.	16th K.R.R.C.	27/9/17	32, Colling Place, London, N.
18568	Rfm.	Kirsch, H.	8th Rifle Brigade	21/9/16	44, Lambs Conduit Street, London, W.C.
159	Pte.	Kirzner, I.	Zion Mule Corps	11/6/15	Alexandria.
4943	Pte.	Kitofski, W.	2/7th Manchester Regt.	18/8/16	29, North Street, Manchester.
53826	Pte.	Klein, I.	171st M.G.C.	23/8/17	19, Chesterfield Road, London, E.
395147	Rfm.	Kleiner, D.	9th London Regt.	24/4/18	2, Broad Street, London, W.1.
2133	Sig.	Klein, J.	26th Australian Inf.	20/9/17	Leyton Green, Leyton, E.
28385	Rfm.	Kleps, L.	12th Rifle Brigade	17/11/17	17, Oley Place, London, E.1.
31593	Gnr.	Klingberg, H. T.	4th Australian Arty.	18/9/18	Quorn, S. Australia.
J/3243	L/Cpl.	Klugman, J.	39th Royal Fusiliers	7/10/18	East 100 Street, Cleveland, Ohio, U.S.A.
26101	Pte.	Knight, H.	8th Northumberland Fus.	10/10/18	1, Town Hall Buildings, Walthamstow, E.
2217	Pte.	Knopf, D.	4th S. African Inf.	27/5/16	Maine Street, Simons Town, South Africa.
66	Pte.	Kohn, S.	24th Australian Inf.	28/5/15	Merino, Victoria.

N.C.O.'S AND MEN—Continued.

No.	Rank.	Name.	Regiment.	Date of Death.	Address.
6827	Rfm.	KONYN, M.	2nd K.R.R.C.	3/11/14	7, Tenter Street, London, E.
25462	Pte.	KONINSKY (PHILLIPS), L.	10th Suffolk Regt.	30/7/16	8, Cambridge Road, London, E.
S/22343	Rfm.	KOPINSKY, J.	8th Rifle Brigade	27/12/16	125, Redmans Road, London, E.
M/274351	Pte.	KOSKI (CLAYTON), C.	R.A.S.C., M.T.	9/11/18	75, Grosvenor Road, London, N.5.
154122	Sig.	KOSKY, J.	B/59th Brigade, R.F.A.	9/4/17	72, Anthony Street, London, E.
5/5074	Rfm.	KOSKY, R.	2nd K.R.R.C.	25/9/15	2, Lydia Street, London, E.
1975	Pte.	KOSMAN, G. E.	2nd London Regt.	25/2/15	63, Dieppe Street, London, S.W.
Z/8316	A.B.	KOSSICK, L.	Hood Battn. R.N.V.R.	13/11/16	19, Ashfield Terrace, Newcastle.
36325	Pte.	KOSSICK, L.	26th Northumberland Fus.	5/6/17	30, Broughton Street, South Shields.
17782	Rfm.	KOSSICK, R.	13th K.R.R.C.	11/4/17	30, Broughton Street, South Shields.
1235	Pte.	KOTTON, M.	4th Australian Inf.	19/9/18	Chislett House, Chislett Road, London, N.W.
1336	Pte.	KRAILSHEIMER, J. S.	10th Royal Fusiliers	20/7/16	Montreal, Canada.
65103	Bdr.	KRAMER, F.	R.F.A.	15/12/14	88a, Nelson Street, London, E.1.
24021	Rfm.	KRATOSKY, D.	8th Rifle Brigade	8/12/17	Rotorua, N.Z.
50967	Dvr.	KRABIS, H.	Div. Train, A.S.C., N.Z.	22/10/18	11, St. James Mansions, London, N.W.
4161	Pte.	KREISMAN, J. H.	25th Australian Inf.	29/7/16	62, Johnson Street, Manchester.
2206	Pte.	KRELL, J.	1/7th Manchester Regt.	14/6/15	38, Greencroft Gardens, London, N.W.
62485	Pte.	KROHN, H.	10th Royal Fusiliers	23/4/17	160, Alexandra Road, London, N.W.
40462	Pte.	KROHN, S.	2nd Lincolnshire Regt.	19/4/17	99, Charles Street, Perth, W. Australia.
978	Pte.	KRUG, D.	44th Australian Inf.	23/8/18	226, Faraday Street, Carlton, Victoria.
5043	Pte.	KUNIN, J.	22nd Australian Inf.	18/9/17	43, Porters' Row, Edinburgh.
4753	Cpl.	KURTZMAN, H.	6th Northumberland Fus.	15/9/16	2, Adelphi Street, Glasgow.
9389	Sgt.	KURTZMAN (MACK), W.	2nd Seaforth Highlanders	30/5/17	48, Anthony Street, London, E.
32227	Pte.	KUTCHINSKY, A.	9th K.R.R.C.	21/3/18	163, Heywood Street, Cheetham, Manchester.
83103	Pte.	KYTE, A.	55th M.G.C.	3/5/17	
37569	Pte.	LABOR, S.	1st Cambridge Regt.	1/5/18	78, Queen's Place, Leeds.
18164	Pte.	LACK, L.	S.A.M.C.	15/1/19	22, Park Lane, Fordsburg, Transvaal.
282395	Pte.	LANCOME, C.	18th Lancashire Fusiliers	4/9/18	7, Fitzallum Embankment, Cardiff.
9897	Rfm.	LANDSBERG, G. G.	1st London Rifle Brigade	27/4/15	18, Randolph Crescent, London, W.
24674	Rfm.	LANDSBERG, N.	8th R.B.	2/5/17	288, Richmond Road, London, N.E.
3336	Pte.	LANDSLER, E.	53rd Australian Inf.	19/7/16	17, Belgrave Road, Essex, Ilford.
894	Pte.	LANDY, S. S.	R.N.D.	16/10/15	8, Brunswick Terrace, Leeds.
251374	Cpl.	LANE, S.	2/3rd London Regt.	16/5/17	4, Dudley Terrace, London, E.
B/1550	Cpl.	LANGER, S.	9th Rifle Brigade	30/7/15	22, Somerford House, Bethnal Green, London, E.
28072	Pte.	LAPIDUS, J.	1st Duke of Cornwall's L.I.	4/10/17	24, William Street, London, E.
16400	Pte.	LAPPIN, A.	7th R. W. Surrey Regt.	1/7/16	44, Colverstone Crescent, London, N.
2271	Rfm.	LAPPIN, J.	12th London Regt.	9/9/16	43, Hillside Road, London, N.
2107	Pte.	LAPPIN, M.	7th King's Liverpool Regt.	21/6/15	88, Smith Street, Liverpool.
125293	Pte.	LATTER, A.	25th M.G.C.	22/3/18	40, Daisy Street, Glasgow.
3314584	Pte.	LATTNER, D.	2nd Cent. Ont. Regt.	22/4/18	79, Wellington Street, Hamilton, Canada.
227107	Pte.	LATSKY, W. J.	M.T., R.A.S.C.	13/11/18	17, Princelet Street, London, E.1.
5102	Pte.	LAVENDER, A.	2/1st Oxford and B. L.I.	22/8/17	41, Grafton Street, London, E.

N.C.O.'S AND MEN—Continued.

No.	Rank. Name.	Regiment.	Date of Death.	Address.
5240	Pte. LAZARUS, A. C.	2nd H.A.C.	17/4/17	33, Belsize Park Gardens, London, N.W.
7207	Cpl. LAZARUS, A. E.	1st Royal Fusiliers	11/10/18	16, Grafton Street, London, E.
360136	Pte. LAZARUS, B.	10th K. Liverpool Regt.	7/8/18	8, Sigdon Road, London, N.E.
352526	L/Cpl. LAZARUS, H.	9th R. Scots Regt.	10/7/17	135, Mount Annan Drive, Glasgow.
378	Pte. LAZARUS, I.	7th Australian Inf.	8/5/15	202, Gertrude Street, Fitzroy, Vic.
205708	Pte. LAZARUS, J.	2nd London Regt.	27/8/18	24, Tulton Street, London, E.
3632	L/Cpl. LAZARUS, J. B.	2nd S. African Inf.	15/5/17	39, Esselwood Road, Durban, Natal.
311408	Spr. LAZARUS, J. S. (LAWRENCE), (M.M.)	R.E. atd. 103rd Bde. R.F.A.	15/6/18	32, Dawes Road, London, S.W.6.
102315	Gnr. LAZARUS, L.	R.G.A.	15/12/18	5, Wolverton Gardens, London, W.
355319	Pte. LAZARUS, M.	4th Middlesex Regt.	26/8/18	166, Stepney Green, London, E.
401344	Pte. LAZARUS, M.	38th Canadian Inf.	21/11/16	151, Langanchetier Street East, Montreal.
Z/36	Rfm. LAZARUS, R.	1st Rifle Brigade	12/3/15	73, Punderson Gardens, London, E.
7531	Pte. LAZER, L.	8th Australian Inf.	11/8/18	171, Lygon Street, St. Carlton, Vic.
9800	Pte. LAZOFF, S.	3rd Canadian Inf.	13/6/16	503, Asquith Street, Baltimore, Md. U.S.A.
7002	Pte. LEBOVITCH, M.	2nd Australian Inf.	6/5/18	177, King Street, Newtown, Australia.
1275	Pte. LEE, D.	14th Australian Inf.	27/4/15	Frimley Street, Mile End Road, London.
8696	Sgt. LEE, J.	2nd R. Berks Regt.	25/9/15	47, Camden Street, London, N.E.
2199	Pte. LEHMAN, A.	27th Australian Inf.	2/3/17	
15629	Rfm. LEHMANN, L. C.	2nd Rifle Brigade	18/8/16	14, Mill Lane, Cricklewood, London, N.W.
2137	Pte. LEHMANN, R. R.	1/6th Seaforth Highlanders	15/6/15	15, Exeter Mansions, London, N.W.
3106478	Pte. LEIBOVITCH, M.	50th Canadian Inf.	29/9/18	18, Eversley Street, Liverpool.
306862	Pte. LEIZERBRAM, P.	2/8th West Yorks. Regt.	28/8/18	44, Lincoln Street, Leeds.
7602	Pte. LEMCHEM, A.	3rd S. African Inf.	20/7/18	4, Woodville Gardens, London, W.
7264	Pte. LENNEBERG, F. B.	16th Australian Inf.	20/9/18	Edwin Street, Croydon, Sydney, N.S.W.
80689	Pte. LENSKY, N.	257th Labour Company	27/6/18	4, Grindlegate, Sheffield.
48399	Sergt. LENSKY, P.	214th M.G.C.	7/10/17	4, Grindlegate, Sheffield.
22383	Pte. LENSNOR, I.	6th Dorset Regt.	2/1/17	111, Davis Mansions, London, E.
235302	Pte. LERNER, D.	2nd S. Lancs. Regt.	22/3/18	74, Langdale Mansions, London, E.
235100	Pte. LESCHINSKY, M.	4th Northumberland Fus.	28/3/18	38, Parkfield Street, London, N.
8421	Pte. LETSKY, C.	2nd Durham L.I.	23/9/15	47, Villiers Street, Sunderland.
10589	Pte. LEVANTER, J.	2nd East Lancs. Regt.	14/3/15	111, Brady Street Buildings, London, E.
708	Pte. LEVENE (CONROY), D.	4th Australian Inf.	23/7/15	32, Uppington Terrace, Nottingham.
136744	Seaman LEVENE, M.	H.M.S. "Salta"	10/4/17	17, Havelock Road, Southampton.
470911	Spr. LEVENE, I.	210th Field Coy., R.E.	24/11/17	2, Poplar Crescent, Gateshead-on-Tyne.
130431	2/A.M. LEVENE, T.	R.A.F.	31/8/18	6, Leslie Road, Birmingham.
G/19213	Pte. LEVENE, M.	1/7th Middlesex Regt.	19/8/17	26, Burton Road, London, N.W.
Y/1163	Rfm. LEVENE, S.	8th K.R.R.C.	28/11/15	Paris Avenue, Booth Street, London, E. London.
S/11583	Rfm. LEVENSON, H.	1st K.R.R.C.	26/7/16	21, Brown's Square, Leeds.
1252	Pte. LEVENTHAL, L.	7th Rifle Brigade	15/9/16	62, Causewayside, Edinburgh.
1775	Pte. LEVEY, E. C.	2nd Seaforth Highlanders	6/5/15	15, Stanley Street, Waverley, N.S.W.
108477	Sergt. LEVEY, H.	25th King's Liverpool Rgt.	2/10/18	299, Bury New Road, Manchester.

102

N.C.O.'S AND MEN—Continued.

No.	Rank.	Name.	Regiment.	Date of Death.	Address.
242676	Pte.	LEVEY, I.	1/8th K.O. Royal Lancs.	22/8/18	24, Granton Street, Manchester.
63910	Pte.	LEVEY, J.	20th Royal Fusiliers	27/11/17	27, Scarborough Street, London, E.9.
308776	L/Cpl.	LEVEY, J.	1/6th King's Liverpool Rgt.	12/6/18	14, Saxony Road, Liverpool.
9541	Pte.	LEVI, A.	2nd Royal Fusiliers	4/7/16	8, Camphill Street, Hammersmith, London, W.
25660	Pte.	LEVI, B.	10th West Yorks. Regt.	30/10/16	13, St. Peter's Square, Leeds.
202279	Pte.	LEVI, E.	1/5th West Yorks. Regt.	9/10/17	13, St. Peter's Square, Leeds.
7960	L/Cpl.	LEVI, H.	2nd Lincoln Regt.	21/5/16	57, Tredegar Square, London, E.
202418	Pte.	LEVI, H.	2/8th Lancashire Fusiliers	28/3/18	6, Caroline Street, Manchester.
24065	Pte.	LEVI, L.	10th West Yorks. Regt.	3/7/16	9, St. Peter's Square, Leeds.
98373	Pte.	LEVI, S.	206th M.G.C.	26/10/17	132, Bridgegate, Glasgow.
53180	Pte.	LEVIN, A.	1st King's Liverpool Regt.	14/11/16	110, Bury New Road, Manchester.
7221	Pte.	LEVIN, M.	3rd South African Inf.	20/8/16	P.O. Box 49, Krugersdorp, South Africa.
10427	Pte.	LEVINE, B.	6th Duke of Cornwall's L.I.	16/9/16	31, Nile Street, Hoxton, London, N.
746	Pte.	LEVINE, B.	2nd R. Warwick Regt.	19/12/14	41, Bromsgrove Street, Birmingham.
60997	Pte.	LEVINE, C.	112th M.G.C.	27/5/17	3, Park Road, Cromer.
J/958	Sgt.	LEVINE, L.	39th Royal Fusiliers	28/3/19	12, Lewisham High Road, London, S.E.
6662	Pte.	LEVINE, M.	9th Black Watch	28/4/17	39, Birch Street, Manchester.
2293331	Pte.	LEVINSON, A.	Lord Strathcona Horse	10/11/18	137, Langside Street, Winnipeg, Canada.
39036	Pte.	LEVINSON, A.D.	2/8th Lancs. Fusiliers	9/10/17	18, Polwarth Gardens, Edinburgh.
2656	Pte.	LEVINSON, L.	2nd South African Inf.	12/4/17	3, Randolph Road, Maida Vale, London, W.
23351	Pte.	LEVISON, S.S.	8th Oxford and Bucks. L.I.	3/12/18	33, New Street, Houndsditch, London, E.
6550	Pte.	LEVY, A.	2nd Royal W. Surrey Rgt.	2/9/16	Tilford Road, Tilford, Surrey.
5198	Sgt.	LEVY, A.	21st Manchester Regt.	16/7/16	17, St. James' Place, Liverpool.
505	Sgt.	LEVY, A.	39th Australian Inf.	29/3/18	3, Park Street, St. Kilda, Victoria, N.S.W.
17441	Rfm.	LEVY, A.	7th Rifle Brigade	24/7/17	117, Bethnal Green Road, London, E.
98128	2/A.M.	LEVY, A.	R.A.F.	20/5/18	32, Apsley Place, Glasgow.
1218	Sgt.	LEVY, A.I.	2nd K.R.R.C.	23/7/16	123, Sutherland Avenue, London, W.
415512	L/Cpl.	LEVY, A.J.	60th Canadian Inf.	15/6/16	Digby Co., N.S., Canada.
26256	Pte.	LEVY, B.	7th King's Shropshire L.I.	26/9/17	7, Brunswick Street, Manchester.
348	Pte.	LEVY, B.	23rd Middlesex Regt.	1/1/18	32, Cookham Buildings, London, E.
615654	Pte.	LEVY, B.	1/19th London Regt.	1917	15, Hemming Street, London, E.
J/13	Sgt.	LEVY, B.M.	38th Royal Fusiliers	7/9/18	17, Gloucester Place, Brighton.
9793	Sergt.	LEVY, B.M.	3rd Connaught Rangers	23/9/16	7, Gratton Houses, Globe Road, London, E.
59009	Pte.	LEVY, C.	70th Field Amb., R.A.M.C.	31/12/15	123, Sutherland Avenue, London, W.
25562	Pte.	LEVY, C.	55th Australian Inf.	15/5/18	65, Cleveland Street, Redfern, Sydney.
16524	Rfm.	LEVY, C.	2nd Rifle Bde.	24/5/18	60, Blythe Street, London, E.
29938	Pte.	LEVY, D.	9th Norfolk Regt.	2/10/17	12, Green Dragon Yard, London, E.
4947	Rfm.	LEVY, D.	1/9th London Regt.	9/10/16	263, Caledonian Rd., London, N.
4812	Pte.	LEVY, E.M.	50th Australian Inf.	15/11/16	83, Halifax Street, Adelaide.
36749	C.S.M.	LEVY, E.	4/3rd N.Z. Rifle Brigade	12/10/17	Custom House Quay, Wellington, N.Z.
114	Cpl.	LEVY, E.H.	R.A.F.	13/2/19	98, Commercial Street, London, E.1.
7000	L/Cpl.	LEVY, F.S.	Impl. Camel Corps	19/4/17	26, Brownswood Park, London, N.4.
43382	Pte.	LEVY, G.	11th Australian Inf.	8/10/17	26, Brownswood Park, London, N.4.
	Pte.	LEVY, G.N.	15th Royal Scots	9/10/17	30, Lothian Street, Edinburgh.

N.C.O.'S AND MEN—Continued.

No.	Rank.	Name.	Regiment.	Date of Death.	Address.
415193	Rfm.	Levy, G.	1/9th London Regt.	22/12/17	23, Wellington Terrace, Falmouth.
153929	Pte.	Levy, G. S.	43rd Canadian Inf.	21/9/16	Boness Bridge, N.B.
34458	Rfm.	Levy, H.	6th London Regt.	28/12/17	53, Rutland Street, London, E.1.
10708	Pte.	Levy, H.	2nd H.A.C.	9/10/17	Home Farm, Hurst Green, Oxted.
10969	Pte.	Levy, H.	9th Royal Fusiliers	8/7/16	57, Tredegar Square, London, E.
19751	Pte.	Levy, H.	3rd Bucks. Regt.	14/11/16	95, Tarling Street, London, E.
12086	L/Cpl.	Levy, H.	9th Devon Regt.	1/7/16	1, Guy Cliff Cottage, Oakley Rd, Whetstone, Middlesex
39584	Pte.	Levy, H.	2nd South Wales Borderers	22/10/16	37, Thirlmere Street, Manchester.
10753	Pte.	Levy, H.	1st D.C.L.I.	24/4/18	3, Kay Street, London, E.
28395	Sergt.	Levy, H.	1st Royal Scots Fusiliers	28/3/18	32, Apsley Place, Glasgow.
7365	Pte.	Levy, H. A.	11th Australian Inf.	21/9/17	222, McDonald Street, Kalgoorlie, W.A.
3179	Pte.	Levy, H. M.	60th Australian Inf.		36, Clive Road, Auburn, Vic.
3531	Pte.	Levy, H. M.	8th Australian Inf.	19/7/16	17, Chitweny Street, North, Melbourne.
32022	Rfm.	Levy, I. (Lea)	11th Rifle Bde.	20/9/17	32, Charlotte Street, London, E.C.2.
37361	Pte.	Levy, J.	1/20th London Regt.	24/8/18	28, Parfett Road, London, E.
42353	Rfm.	Levy, J.	12th Royal Irish Rifles	31/10/18	14, Wellhouse Road, Barnoldswick, Yorks.
307909	Pte.	Levy, J.	16th Tank Corps	29/9/18	13, Scarboro Street, London, E.
1547	Pte.	Levy, J.	22nd Royal Fusiliers	17/7/16	15, Dunsmere Road, London, N.
10866	Pte.	Levy, J.	11th R. West Surrey Regt.	2/10/16	4, Gresham Road, Brixton, London, S.W.9.
29006	Pte.	Levy, J.	14th Highland L.I.	21/10/16	13, Francis Street, Reading.
6147	Pte.	Levy, J.	4th London Regt.	10/2/17	14, Campbell Road, London, E.
16496	Rfm.	Levy, J.	16th Rifle Brigade	25/6/17	60, Blythe Street, London, E.
169	L/Cpl.	Levy, J.	16th Northumberland Fus.	8/8/17	67, Frederick Street, South Shields.
J/1289	Pte.	Levy, J.	38th Royal Fusiliers	24/10/18	81, Ernest Street, Stepney, London, E.1.
18418	Pte.	Levy, L.	1st Hants. Regt.	1/7/16	132, Bridge Street, London, E.
36565	Pte.	Levy, L.	1st South Wales Borderers	6/5/18	193, St. Georges Street, London, E.
7701	Pte.	Levy, L.	51st Welsh Regt.	16/1/19	28, Thirlmere Street, Hightown, Manchester.
2209	Pte.	Levy, L.	56th Australian Inf.	29/9/18	"Avon," Dudley, Coogee, Sydney.
675	Pte.	Levy, L. L.	9th Scottish Rifles	16/8/16	46, Sardine Terrace, West Glasgow.
2870	Pte.	Levy, L. S.	53rd Australian Inf.	19/7/16	2, Elton Place, Redfern, Sydney.
4532	Pte.	Levy, M.	22nd London Regt.	22/6/17	193, St. Georges Street, London E.
22533	L/Cpl.	Levy, M.	23rd Manchester Regt.	19/7/16	36, Pemberton Street, Manchester.
147125	Pte.	Levy, M.	M.G.C.	24/11/18	106, Bridge Street, London, E.
R/595	A.B.	Levy, M. R.	Anson Battn., R.N.D.	30/12/17	26, Worcester Villas, Hove.
322327	Pte.	Levy, P.	2/6th London Regt.	15/6/17	263, Caledonian Road, London, N.
4962	Pte.	Levy, P. S.	2nd H.A.C.	6/12/16	16, Heber Road, London, N.W.
46560	L/Cpl.	Levy, P. M.	9th Yorks. Regt.	6/11/18	174, Linthorpe Road, Middlesboro.
61645	Pte.	Levy, R	6th R. West Surrey Regt.	20/4/18	32, Cookham Buildings, London, E.3.
15535	Pte.	Levy, R. L.	3rd Fld. Am. Austral. A.M.C.	8/3/18	54, Gurner Street, Paddington, Sydney.
2940	Pte.	Levy, R.	8th Argyll & Suther. Highrs.	19/12/16	186, Cheetham Hill Road, Manchester.
4635	L/Cpl.	Levy, R. A.	1st H.A.C.	22/4/17	94, Melrose Avenue, London, N.W.
S/750	Sergt.	Levy, S.	12th Rifle Brigade	7/6/16	7, Parkgate Avenue, Withington, Manchester.
236197	Pte.	Levy, S.	R.F.A.	14/8/18	48, York Buildings, Cheetham, Manchester.

N.C.O.'s AND MEN—Continued.

No.	Rank.	Name.	Regiment.	Date of Death.	Address.
57450	Pte.	LEVY, S.	2nd Middlesex Regt.	21/12/18	22, Ernest Street, London, E.
458	Pte.	LEVY, S. E. (MACK, W.)	10th Royal Fusiliers	21/2/16	14, Corsehill Street, Streatham, London, S.E.
3034718	Pte.	LEVY (LARVEY), S. L.	15th Canadian Inf.	13/10/18	51, Vine Street, Liverpool.
	Pte.	LEWIN, A.	1st Australian Inf.	23/7/15	Bradford.
10381	Pte.	LEWIS, A.	14th Northumberland Fus.	23/11/16	11, North View, Ashington, Northumberland.
29716	Rfm.	LEWIS, A.	11th Rifle Brigade	20/3/18	3, Watney Street, London, E.1.
53191	Cpl.	LEWIS, E. F.	15th Durham L.I.	9/4/17	39, Navarino Road, London, N.
7409	Pte.	LEWIS, H.	2nd South Staffs. Regt.	2/9/15	75, Smith Road, Erdington, Birmingham.
67908	Pte.	LEWIS, H.	51st M.G.C.	23/4/17	26, Hunton Street, London, E.1.
5137	Pte.	LEWIS, H.	10th Royal Fusiliers	18/11/16	26a, Carnarvon Street, Manchester.
127171	Gnr.	LEWIS, H.	A/177th Brigade, R.F.A.	1/8/17	11, Brunswick Terrace, Leeds.
45083	Rfm.	LEWIS, H.	10th Royal Irish Rifles	26/6/17	25, Graham Road, London, N.
1584	Rfm.	LEWIS, H. R.	12th London Regt.	17/2/15	74, Sutherland Avenue, London, W.
16801	Pte.	LEWIS, J.	8th Somerset L.I.	26/6/16	11, Sandfield Road, Aberavon, South Wales.
7163	Pte.	LEWIS, J.	2nd H.A.C.	13/1/17	16, Heathside, Finchley Road, London, N.W.
R/9463	Rfm.	LEWIS, J.	9th K.R.R.C.	28/5/16	Sandgate, Kent.
314	Pte.	LEWIS, L.	8th Australian Inf.	26/7/16	King Street, Cardiff.
9831	Pte.	LEWIS, M.	2nd Essex Regt.	6/8/15	London.
L/4929	A.B.	LEWIS, M. C.	H.M.S. "Bulwark."	26/11/14	52, High Street, Aldgate, London, E.
278729	Pte.	LEWIS, N.	7th Arg. and Suth. Hrs.	23/4/17	32, Darley Street, Leeds.
14268	Pte.	LEWIS, S.	9th Devon Regt.	30/9/15	25, Lucas Street, London, E.
4073	L/Cpl.	LEWIS, T.	23rd Royal Fusiliers	6/10/16	74, Sutherland Avenue, London, W.
A/410	Rfm.	LEWIS, W.	4th K.R.R.C.	8/5/15	2, St. Mark's Road, London, W.
623195	Pte.	LEXIER, M.	10th Canadian Inf.	23/4/17	192, Langside Street, Winnipeg.
7	Sgt.	LIGGI, R.	10th Aus. Light Horse	10/6/15	5, Falconer Street, Scarborough.
53675	Pte.	LIGHT, J.	90th Labour Corps	18/8/18	3, Exchange Street, Manchester.
81496	Pte.	LICHTENSTEIN, M.	46th M.G.C.	25/4/17	43, Osbaldstone Road, London, N.16.
20335	Pte.	LICHTENSTEIN, M. H.	2nd Lancashire Fusiliers	3/5/17	425, Cheetham Hill Road, Manchester.
48240	Rfm.	LIGHTSTONE, L.	2nd Rifle Brigade	27/4/18	24, Green Street, London, E.1.
S/15791	2/Act/Cpl.	LIGHTSTONE, S.	R.N.A.S.	20/7/17	31, Hanbury Street, London, E.1.
13578	Sgt.	LINDE, A.	8th Norfolk Regt.	19/7/16	16, Petherton Road, London, N.
7640	Rfm.	LION, A. J.	9th Rifle Brigade	22/6/15	100, Broadhurst Gardens, London, N.W.
39321	Pte.	LIPCHINSKY (LIPMAN), S. R.			
21617	L/Cpl.	LIPMAN, H.	7th West Yorks. Regt.	28/3/18	4, Crawford Street, Leeds.
5820	Pte.	LIPMAN, H.	23rd Middlesex Regt.	14/7/16	104, Old Montague Street, London, E.1.
S/22846	Rfm.	LIPMAN, H.	23rd London Regt.	19/7/16	2, Nottingham Place, London, E.1.
M/273185	Pte.	LIPMAN, I.	3rd Rifle Brigade	4/9/16	12, Cwn Donkin Terrace, Swansea.
461023	Pte.	LIPMAN, J.	25th S.B.A.C., R.A.S.C.	27/5/18	48, Eric Street, London, E.
1017C	Pte.	LIPMAN, M.	84th Labour Company	19/10/18	229, Long Lane, London, E.
29152	L/Cpl.	LIPMAN, S.	21st W. Yorks. Regt.	17/6/17	214, North Street, Leeds.
5978	Rfm.	LIPMAN, W. R.	1/4th L. N. Lancs. Regt.	8/5/18	31, Lime Street, Hightown, Manchester.
9321	Pte.	LIPPMAN, S.	17th London Regt.	8/11/16	63, Lolesworth Buildings, London, E.1.
			7th Border Regt.	23/4/17	11, Whitehouse Road, Sunderland.

N.C.O.'S AND MEN—Continued.

No.	Rank.	Name.	Regiment.	Date of Death.	Address.
16539	Pte.	LIPSON, S. W.	18th King's Liverpool Rgt.	1/11/16	148, Queen's Road, Liverpool.
351517	Pte.	LIPSHACK, M. W. (PHILLIPS, J.)	7th London Regt.	7/6/17	77, Cleveland Street, London, E.
17635	Pte.	LIPTON, S. H.	19th King's Liverpool Rgt.	30/6/16	52, Saxony Road, Liverpool.
5212	Pte.	LISBONA, N.	20th Royal Fusiliers	20/7/16	45, Lloyd Street, Manchester.
473006	Rfm.	LIST, H.	2/12th London Regt.	12/9/17	30, George Street, London, N.W.1.
J/3542	Pte.	LITHMAN, J.	40th Royal Fusiliers	8/1/19	69, Great Peter Street, London, S.W.
2944	L/Cpl.	LITTMAN, M.	1/11th London Regt.	21/4/17	108, Dalston Lane, London, N.
1647	Pte.	LITTMAN, S.	23rd Royal Fusiliers	27/7/16	64, Middlesex Street, London, E.1.
2403	Pte.	LITTMAN, S. (M.M.)	51st Australian Inf.	18/5/18	47, Highbury New Park, London, N.
77494	Pte.	LIVENSTEIN, A.	133rd Labour Corps	5/11/18	Bl. 6, Paris Avenue, Booth Street, London, E.
251486	Pte.	LIVINGSTONE, J.	1/6th Manchester Regt.	9/12/17	13, Saunders Street, Southport.
4837	Pte.	LOEWE, S.	15th Australian Inf.	9/7/18	56, Baptist Street, Redfern, N.S.W.
86007	Pte.	LOFTUS, A.	134th Fld. Amb., R.A.M.C.	1/11/17	59, Tredegar Square, London, E.
359227	Pnr.	LONGMAN, E.	No. 7 F. Raily. Coy., R.E.	21/10/18	18, Tisort Square, Graham Road, London, N.E.
	Cpl.	LORIE, S. W.	S. African A.S.C.	1916	Sandgate, Kent.
266998	L/Cpl.	LOTSKY, A.	2/1st Bucks. Battn.	22/8/17	34, Buross Street, London, E.1.
4824	Pte.	LOUIS (SAGAR), P.	2nd London Regt.	16/9/16	80, High Street, Stratford, London, E.15.
S/S/1568	L/Cpl.	LOVEGUARD, C.	R.A.S.C.	10/8/15	29, Brighton Road, Stoke Newington, London, N.E.
50895	Pte.	LUBEL, H.	8th North Staffs. Regt.	6/5/18	170, Clapham Road, London, S.W.9.
253570	Pte.	LUBERTZ, C.	2/3rd London Regt.	26/10/17	115, Brady Street Buildings, London, E.
200153	Rfm.	LUBINSKY, H.	11th Rifle Brigade	5/4/17	18, Laverdale Street, London, E.
33555	2nd A.M.	LUBINSKY, J.	No. 1 A.D., R.A.F.	8/2/19	47, Bancroft Road, London, E.
683036	Pte.	LUBINSKY, M. (LEVY).	2/22nd London Regt.	30/11/17	16, Louisa Gardens, London, E.
72465	Pte.	LUDSKI, E. B.	7th Res. London Regt.	31/10/18	79, Fordwych Road, London, N.W.
4572	Pte.	LUKIES, W.	1/1st Bucks. Battn.	23/7/16	Lower Road, Helston.
530998	Rfm.	LUMER, J.	2/15th London Regt.	20/2/18	56, Queen's Street, Ramsgate.
232394	Pte.	LUPINSKY, L.	2/2nd London Regt.	24/4/18	21, Rectory Square, London, E.
8687	Pte.	LURIE, C.	4th Middlesex Regt.	23/8/14	East End Dwellings, Columbia Road, London, E.
5067	Pte.	LURIE, I.	4th South African Inf.	5/6/16	59, Sherwell Street, Doomfontein, Johannesburg.
232394	Pte.	LUPINSKY, L.	1st Royal Scots Fusiliers	28/10/14	733, Gallowgate, Glasgow.
3975	L/Cpl.	LUSCOMBE, B. T.	4th Australian Inf.	18/4/17	Duntroas Street, Hurlston Park, N.S.W.
47083	Pte.	LUSTGARTEN, M.	16th Northumberland Fus.	5/12/17	292, Great Clowes Street, Manchester.
259	Pte.	LYNES, A.	18th Australian Inf.	30/8/15	283, Brixton Road, London, S.W.9.
37474	Pte.	LYONS, A. R.	Royal Fusiliers	1917	London.
282535	Pte.	LYONS, I.	1/4th London Regt.	28/3/18	1, Eaton Rise, Ealing, London, W.
124	Pte.	LYONS, S.	17th Australian Inf.	21/5/15	
11922	Rfm.	LYONS, S.	9th Rifle Brigade	13/7/15	19, Navarino Road, London, N.E.
P/10869	L/Cpl.	LYONS, S. J.	Military Foot Police	5/9/17	6, Portland Court, London, W.
106095	Cpl.	MACABORSKI, A.	186th Coy. Spec. Bde. R.E.	25/9/15	67, Stocks Street, Manchester.
201185	Rfm.	MAGINSKY, S.	2/5th King's Liverpool	9/5/17	6, Jermyn Street, Liverpool.
S/9979	Rfm.	MAGNUS, M.	7th Rifle Brigade	29/8/17	13, Guilford Road, London, E.14.

N.C.O.'S AND MEN—Continued.

No.	Rank.	Name.	Regiment.	Date of Death.	Address.
233638	Pte.	MALINSKY, S.	2/2nd London Regt.	16/6/17	18, Mocatta House, Brady Street, London, E.
J/401	Pte.	MALKIN, J.	38th Royal Fusiliers	19/10/18	6, Clarence Street, Liverpool.
10154	Pte.	MALNICK, G.	2nd E. Kent Regt.	16/5/15	2, High Street, Sittingbourne.
4653	Rfm.	MALNICK, J.	1/12th London Regt.	9/9/16	138, Jubilee Street, London, E.
658	Pte.	MANDELSON, H.	28th Australian Inf.	19/7/16	113, Renfrew Street, Glasgow.
305127	Pte.	MANHOFF, J.	2/10th London Regt.	9/8/18	32, Chatham Place, London, E.9.
10/2498	Sgt.	MANOY, R. L.	1st Wellington Bn. N.Z.	16/9/16	100, Albion Road, London, N.
232	L/Cpl.	MARCUS, D.	3rd Fld Amb., Can. A.M.C.	6/11/17	18, Broadway, Bromley, Kent.
2216	Rfm.	MARCUS, D. H.	1/12th London Regt.	1/7/16	76, Melrose Avenue, London, N.W.
S/25205	Pte.	MARCUS, H.	8th R. Innis. Fusiliers	5/8/17	29, Wellington Quay, Dublin.
1471	Gnr.	MARCUS, H.	132nd Hy. By. R.G.A.	15/8/16	100, Charles Street, London, E.
31286	Rfm.	MARCUS, I.	3rd Rifle Brigade	20/8/17	17, Beaumont Square, London, E.
1881	Pte.	MARCUS, M.	26th Royal Fusiliers	4/10/16	82, Victoria Road, London, N.W.
732	Pte.	MARCUS, R.	31st Australian Inf.	19/7/16	Queen Nithe, Seapoint, Cape Town.
88483	Pte.	MARGOLSKY, J.	148th Labour Corps.	30/9/17	5a, Hope Street, London, E.
87967	Pte.	MARIENBERG, A. G.	13th King's Liverpool Regt.	12/12/17	32, Crown Street, Port Talbot, South Wales.
3203	Pte.	MARK, W.	2/10th Middlesex Regt.	13/8/15	2, Winchester Street, London, E.
100170	L/Cpl.	MARKOVITCH, H.	13th Royal Fusiliers	8/10/18	26, Frostic Place, London, E.1.
17130	Pte.	MARKOVITZ, M.	10th Notts. and Derby Rgt.	12/11/15	High Street, Tideswell, Buxton.
8068	Pte.	MARKOWSKY, W.	2nd S. Staffs. Regt.	22/7/18	54, Malvern Road, London, E.16.
658	Sgt.	MARKS, A.	5th Australian Inf.	14/8/15	Beaconsfield Parade, St. Kilda, Victoria.
1077	Pte.	MARKS, A.	17th Middlesex Regt.	28/7/16	16, Chapel Street, Somers Town, London, E.
1568	Cpl.	MARKS, A. G.	1st Australian Inf.	19/5/15	Whitecliffe, N.S.W.
246	Pte.	MARKS, B. E.	10th Australian Inf.	28/4/15	North Terrace, Hackney, S. Australia.
669619	Pte.	MARKS, C. A.	3rd Canadian Inf.	30/8/18	132, High Street, Kingsland, London, N.E.
M2/042871	9 Pte.	MARKS, G. C.	R.A.S.C.	17/11/18	461, Bury New Road, Manchester.
3292	Pte.	MARKS, H.	6th London Regt.	9/2/16	26, Charing Cross Road, London, W.C.
11610	Pte.	MARKS, H.	1st Scots Guards	31/7/17	38, Laleham Buildings, London, E.
42302	Pte.	MARKS, H.	16th Manchester Regt.	27/4/18	12, Robin Hood Lane, London, E.
11208	Pte.	MARKS, H.	4th Middlesex Regt.	13/10/14	113, Carlisle Street, London, W.
2111	Pte.	MARKS, H. H. S.	41st Australian Inf.	1/9/18	Townville, Queensland.
3075	Sgt.	MARKS, H. W.	5th Aus. Pioneer Bn.	3/10/18	Wellington, N.S.W.
36780	Pte.	MARKS, J.	24th Northumberland Fus.	30/7/17	38, Powis Square, London, W.
48743	Pte.	MARKS, J.	13th King's Liverpool Rgt.	14/11/17	43, Bulver Road, Bradford.
13163	Rfm.	MARKS, J.	2nd K.R.R.C.	23/7/16	1, King's Road, London, E.
5290	Pte.	MARKS, J.	1st Devon Regt.	18/12/14	51, Highbury Street, Portsmouth.
4396	Pte.	MARKS, J.	4th London Regt.	16/4/17	62, Warwick Avenue, London, W.
20448	Pte.	MARKS, J. A.	22nd Royal Fusiliers	17/2/17	4, Pearcefold Street, London, N.W.
506693	Pte.	MARKS, L.	222 A.E. Coy. Labour Corps	5/12/18	35, British Street, London, E.
43714	Pte.	MARKS, L.	9th S. Lancs. Regt.	29/9/19	22, Vernon Street, Hightown, Manchester.
413	Sgt.	MARKS, L. D.	13th Australian Inf.	3/5/15	34, Milford Street, St. Kilda, Victoria.
GS/26028	L/Cpl.	MARKS, L. G.	17th Royal Sussex Regt.	11/10/18	Hazelhurst, Akenside Terrace, Newcastle.
23043	Pte.	MARKS, M.	2nd Royal Scots Fusiliers	30/7/16	32, Govan Street, Glasgow.
7099	Pte.	MARKS, M.	35th Australian Inf.	8/8/18	Thirroull, N.S.W.

107

N.C.O.'S AND MEN—Continued.

No.	Rank.	Name.	Regiment.	Date of Death.	Address.
7888	Pte.	MARKS, M. L.	1st Fld. Amb. Aus. A.M.C.	4/10/17	187, McKean Street, North Fitzroy, N.S.W.
J/2588	Pte.	MARKS, R.	38th Royal Fusiliers	28/8/18	57, Mildmay Park, London, N.
1429	Pte.	MARKS, S.	1st Manchester Regt.	26/4/15	22, Vernon Street, Manchester.
3790	Pte.	MARKS, S.	3rd London Regt.	16/5/17	4, Dudley Terrace, London, E.
31986	Pte.	MARKS, W.	2nd Manchester Regt.	5/4/17	125, Claremont Road, Manchester.
242775	Pte.	MARKS, W.	2/5th Yorks. & Lancs. Rgt.	3/5/17	28, Enneidale, Sunderland.
22878	Pte.	MARLINSKY, B.	15th Royal Welsh Fusiliers	10/7/16	36, Hazelwood Road, London, E.
180579	Pte.	MARSHOFSKY, A.	723rd Labour Company	5/11/18	19, Grimsby Street, London, E.
R/23364	Rfm.	MARMELSTEIN, S.	9th K.R.R.C.	15/12/17	26, Pelham Street, London, E.
454312	Pte.	MARKUS, H.	19th Canadian Inf.	16/4/16	1264, Bloor Street, Toronto.
1577	Pte.	MARQUIS, G.	13th Australian Inf.	17/8/15	1, Chestnut Street, Mt. Pleasant, Liverpool.
5169	Sergt.	MARTIN, A.	1st Royal Welsh Fusiliers	19/10/14	45, Tredegar Road, London, E.
	Dvr.	MARTIN, B.	L Battery, R.H.A.	1914	Stepney, London, E.
521	Pte.	MARTIN, M.	Canadian A.M.C.	12/4/17	1250, St. Lawrence Boulevard, Montreal.
2878	Pte.	MARZAN, W.	35th Australian Inf.	14/10/17	78, City Road, Sydney, N.S.W.
32122	Pte.	MASON, I.	14th Gloucester Regt.	22/10/17	46, Vernon Street, Manchester.
2873	Pte.	MAYER, H.	55th Australian Inf.	20/7/16	Mordale, N.S.W.
202041	Rfm.	MAZERKOFF, B.	5th King's Liverpool Regt.	31/7/18	22, Fortescue Street, Liverpool.
273165	Pte.	MAZERKOFF, M.	Canadian M.G.C.	29/12/18	Montreal.
204583	Pte.	MAZZIER, M.	1/2nd London Regt.	16/8/17	9, Weston Place, London, N.E.
203381	Pte.	MEISEL, H.	4th Northumberland Fus.	4/7/17	62, Ernest Street, London, E.
6765	Pte.	MELTZER, G.	7th London Regt.	12/1/17	59, Globe Road, London, E.
64462	Pte.	MELTZER, S.	108th Labour Coy.	22/3/18	15, Hewitt Street, Hightown, Manchester.
	Tpr.	MENDELSOHN, F.	S. African M. Transport	5/12/18	Cape Town, S. Africa.
172375	Sergt.	MENDELSOHN, H.	13th Canadian Artillery	1915	Montreal.
	Gnr.	MENDELSON, M.	1st Somerset Bty. R.H.A.	12/10/18	5, Causewayside, Edinburgh.
331159	Pte.	MENDELSSOHN, M.	9th H.L.I. attd. 100th M.G.C.	26/9/17	303, St. Vincent Steet, Glasgow.
3176	Tpr.	MENDES, H. J.	2nd Life Guards	14/1/16	350, Finchley Road, London, N.W.
43727	Pte.	MENDES DA COSTA, B.	1st Essex Regt.	5/4/18	56, Elizabeth Street, Manchester.
4673	Pte.	MENDOZA, V. M.	R.A.O.C.	11/12/17	181, Barry Road, Dulwich, London, S.E.
2525	Cpl.	MENSER, L. M.	55th Australian Inf.	10/4/17	58, Duxford Street, Paddington, N.S.W.
36830	Rfm.	MERBER, J.	2nd K.R.R.C.	10/7/17	21, Upper Orange Street, Cape Town.
1695	Pte.	MICHAEL, R. F.	18th Australian Inf.	3/5/17	Burranew Bay, N.S.W.
31586	Sgt.	MICHAELS, F. M.	Australian Field Artillery	14/5/17	Orwell, Robe Street, St. Kilda, Australia.
1323	Cpl.	MITCHELL, A. D.	1st Australian Inf.	5/5/15	"Leitelena," Farlight Street, Manly, Sydney.
6398	Pte.	MICHAELS, B.	4th London Regt.	13/5/17	2, Dunk Street, London, E.
77152	Dvr.	MICHAELS, D.	18th By. 3rd Bde. R.F.A.	27/4/15	48, Hogarth Houses, Batty Street, London, E.
152	Pte.	MICHAELS, H.	2nd South African Inf.	23/3/17	Brand Street, Kroonstad, O.F.S., South Africa.
99	Pte.	MICHAELS, L.	8th Royal Fusiliers	17/3/16	43, Sunbury Buildings, London, E.
22588	Pte.	MICHAELS, L.	9th Royal Fusiliers	30/11/17	25, Farleigh Road, London, N.E.
54958	Pte.	MICHAELS, M.	10th R. Welsh Fusiliers	3/1/17	9, Palmer Street, London, E.1.
67945	Pte.	MICHAELS, P.	25th Canadian Inf.	11/11/15	P.O. Box 144, Glace Bay, C.B, Canada.
30588	Pte.	MICHAELS, S.	1/5th L. N. Lancs. Regt.	17/10/18	36, Hogarth Houses, London, E.

N.C.O.'S AND MEN—Continued.

No.	Rank.	Name.	Regiment.	Date of Death.	Address.
47938	L/Cpl.	MICHAELSON, H.	22nd Manchester Regt.	4/10/17	7, Mount Pleasant, Bury New Road, Manchester.
J/1219	Pte.	MILDEMER, S.	38th Royal Fusiliers	22/9/18	94, Newark Street, London, E.
454573	Pte.	MILLAR, S.	21st Canadian Inf.	4/11/17	179, Heywood Street, Hightown, Manchester.
552609	Rfm.	MILLEM, H.	1/16th London Regt.	14/4/17	140, Melrose Avenue, London, N.W.
A/379	Rfm.	MILLER, E.	7th K.R.R.C.	5/7/15	60, Alexandra Road, Birmingham.
3984	Sgt.	MILLER, J. (D.C.M.)	21st Australian Inf.	26/8/16	Melrose Theatre Buildings, Perth, Australia.
26868	Pte.	MILLER, L.	7th Royal Fusiliers	29/4/17	684, Seven Sisters Road, London, N.
10957	Pte.	MILLER, M.	2nd R. Sussex Regt.	10/7/17	3, Moseley Buildings, London, E.1.
10368	Rfm.	MILLER, N.	7th Rifle Brigade	3/5/16	19, Clarence Street, Leicester.
276612	Pte.	MILLWARD, A.	1/7 Man. Rgt. att. 127 T.M.B.	18/4/18	19, Clarence Road, Withington, Manchester.
4135	Pte.	MINDEN, M.	11th Middlesex Regt.	12/4/17	50, British Street, London, E.
6051	Pte.	MINOR, D.	1st Australian Inf.	4/5/18	2809, 8th Avenue, New York City, U.S.A.
10114	Pte.	MINSK, H.	1st Connaught Rangers	23/11/14	9, Mocatta House, Brady Street, London, E.
2718	Pte.	MINSK, M.	17th London Regt.	26/10/15	9, Mocatta House, Brady Street, London, E.
B/200171	Rfm.	MOLDOFSKY, S.	11th Rifle Brigade	10/8/17	60, Davis Mansions, London, E.
64741	Pte.	MONTSOFF, H.	1/23rd London Regt.	13/8/18	7, Wilkes Street, London, E.1.
2083	Sgt.	MONTY, J.	2/10th London Regt.	1/6/17	19, Barrow's Buildings, London, E.1.
3181	Pte.	MOORE, J.	5th Aus. Pioneer Bn.	29/7/16	Carlsruhe Station, N.S.W.
181	Pte.	MOORE, M.	10th Royal Fusiliers	10/7/16	121, Walm Lane, London, N.W.
225	Pte.	MORACK, M.	10th East Yorks. Regt.	29/10/18	32, Pryne Street, Hull.
5960	Pte.	MORELL, I.	2/24th London Regt.	24/8/16	12, Gower Street, London, W.C.
51647	Pte.	MORRIS, A.	17th K. Liverpool Regt.	12/10/16	87, Bedford Street, South Liverpool.
202744	Pte.	MORRIS, B.	2/1st London Regt.	3/6/17	60, Richard Street, London, E.
53867	Cpl.	MORRIS, C.	63rd M.G., Bn. R.N.D.	30/9/18	447, Fulham Palace Road, London, S.W.
84819	Gnr.	MORRIS, D.	B/190 Brigade, R.F.A.	1917	570, High Road, Leytonstone, London, E. London.
4673	Rfm.	MORRIS, H.	2nd Rifle Brigade	14/5/15	20, Bellevue Street, Swansea.
35305	Pte.	MORRIS, J.	7th K.S.L.I.	28/3/18	53, Northfield Road, Stamford Hill, London, N.
50280	Pte.	MORRIS, J. W.	23rd Royal Fusiliers	29/4/17	33, Maple Street, Manchester.
34072	Pte.	MORRIS, N.	19th Manchester Regt.	18/8/16	12, Upper Dean Street, Birmingham.
11137	Sgt.	MORRIS, S.	2nd Ox. and Bucks. L.I.	30/7/16	391, Oxford Road, C.-on-M, Manchester.
48499	Gnr.	MORRIS, S.	351st S.B. R.G.A.	6/10/18	95, Mosley Street, Manchester.
202284	Pte.	MORYOSEPH, S.	2/5th Manchester Regt.	2/3/17	8, Spelman Street, London, E.1.
G/25408	Pte.	MOSCOVSKY, H.	1st E. Kent Regt.	4/8/18	68, Lincoln Street, London, E.3.
275217	Pte.	MOSELEY, A.	1/3rd London Regt.	21/3/18	Crosby Lodge, Crosby Road, Westcliffe.
27605	Pte.	MOSELY, M. S. C.	7th Border Regt.	23/4/17	12, Palmer Street, London, E.
87874	Pte.	MOSES, H.	147th Labour Company	21/4/18	C/o Commercial Bank, Melbourne.
497	L/Cpl.	MOSES, H. L.	44th Australian Inf.	1/8/17	67, Teesdale Street, London, N.E.
82659	Cpl.	MOSES, I.	257th Area Employ. Coy.	26/2/19	24, Prospect Terrace, London, E.
6965	Pte.	MOSES, J.	3rd London Regt.	9/4/17	59, Latimer Street, Birmingham.
140612	Gnr.	MOSES, L.	208th Siege Bty. R.G.A.	22/7/17	15, Code Street, London, E.
353020	Pte.	MOSES, N.	7th London Regt.	24/3/17	N. Melbourne, Victoria.
1612	Pte.	MOSS, A.	6th Australian Inf.	8/5/15	12, Dee Street, Hull.
61862	Spr.	MOSS, A. E.	82nd Fld. Coy. R.E.	26/8/15	
1585	Pte.	MOSS, E. C.	4th Australian Inf.	8/8/15	49, Cambridge Street, Stanmore, N.S.W.

N.C.O.'S AND MEN—Continued.

No.	Rank.	Name.	Regiment.	Date of Death.	Address.
56192	Pte.	Moss, L. H.	19th Canadian Inf.	15/9/16	28, Frognal, London, N.W.
762908	Rfm.	Moss, M. A.	1/28th London Regt.	30/10/17	116, Highlever Road, London, W.
8337	Pte.	Mossell, A.	1st Royal Fusiliers	19/4/16	8, Cleve Road, London, N.W.
198	Pte.	Muscovitz, D.	Zion Mule Corps	29/5/15	Cairo.
204441	Pte.	Myerovitz, R.	2/4th London Regt.	25/4/18	14, Wolsey Street, London, E.
13265	Pte.	Myers, A.	8th Army Cyclist Corps	2/6/17	21, Alfred Street, London, E.
15816	Rfm.	Myers, A.	1st Rifle Brigade	23/10/16	Weymouth Terrace, London, N.E.
41730	Rfm.	Myers, A.	16th K.R.R.C.	21/6/18	62, Middlesex Street, London, E.1.
145450	Pte.	Myers, B.	77th Canadian Inf.	18/11/16	Genl. Delivery, Parry Sound, Ontario.
1094	Pte.	Myers, E.	22nd Royal Fusiliers	21/10/16	52, Temple Road, Croydon.
52655	L/Cpl.	Myers, S.	32nd Royal Fusiliers	22/6/17	18, Russia Lane, London, N.E.
2250	Pte.	Myers, G.	7th London Regt.	16/9/15	16, Mowbray Road, London, N.W.
22637	Pte.	Myers, H.	9th Lancashire Fusiliers	17/6/17	24, Church Street, Wigan, Lancs.
16967	Pte.	Myers, H.	23rd Royal Fusiliers	20/7/17	14, Charlotte Place, Goodge Street, London, W.C.
42418	Pte.	Myers, H.	6th S. Wales Borderers	27/5/18	50, Lower Chapman Street, London, E.
403	Pte.	Myers, H. T.	1/5th R. Warwick Regt.	5/10/17	51, Approach Road, Margate.
652298	Sgt.	Myers, J.	1/21st London Regt.	2/9/18	75, Grosvenor Road, Forest Gate, London, E.
17981	Rfm.	Myers, J. (Mordecai)	8th Rifle Brigade	13/9/16	75, Grosvenor Road, Forest Gate, London, E.
11266	Rfm.	Myers, J.	1st K.R.R.C.	18/9/14	14, Kinoul Mansions, Rohill Road, London, N.E.
32917	Rfm.	Myers, J.	11th Rifle Brigade	20/11/17	31, Arbery Road, London, E.3.
4084	Pte.	Myers (Smith), L.	9th Royal Fusiliers	12/1/16	35, Bushberry Road, London, E.19.
572484	Rfm.	Myers, M. (M.M.)	1/17th London Regt.	3/12/17	44, British Street, London, E.
8189	Pte.	Myers, M.	1st East Surrey Regt.	6/11/14	24, Winthorp Street, London, E.1.
3848	A.B.	Myers, M.	4th Australian Inf.	20/10/16	16, Alexander Street, Paddington, Sydney.
2126	Pte.	Myers, M. H.	Royal Navy	1916	35, Bushberry Road, London, E.9.
2846	Pte.	Myers, P.	2nd S. African Inf.	17/7/16	120, Broadhurst Gardens, London, N.W.
628565	Pte.	Myers, P.	1st L. N. Lancs. Regt.	9/5/15	42, Nursery Street, Liverpool.
5900	Pte.	Myers, S.	16th Canadian Scottish	24/3/17	35, Bushberry Road, London, E.9.
35933	Pte.	Myers, S.	2nd London Regt.	2/10/16	5, Tudor Road, Upton Park, London, E.
146713	Pnr.	Myerson, N.	3rd Bn. Special Bd. R.E.	29/12/17	9, St. Nicholas Street, London, E.1.
15478	Pte.	Myron, M.	13th Argyll and Suth. Hrs.	23/7/17	2, Church Street, Middlesbrough.
				15/9/16	365, Sauchiehall Street, Glasgow.
37932	Pte.	Nacowitz, J.	1/4th R. Berks. Regt.	16/8/17	56, Quaker Street, London, E.
	Pte.	Nagavkar, R.	Bangalore Rifles	1916	Bombay.
491980	Pte.	Naphtali, H.	1/13th London Regt.	22/9/18	75, Earlham Grove, London, E.
7554	Pte.	Natali, H.	4th London Regt.	8/4/17	20, College Place, London, N.
16417	Pte.	Nathan, A.	8th Devonshire Regt.	26/10/17	16, Sunbury Buildings, London, E.
4909	Pte.	Nathan, A.	60th Australian Inf.	20/3/17	13, Ellison Street, London, E.
254176	Pte.	Nathan, C.	1/1st London Regt.	12/10/18	57, Jane Street, London, E.
60796	Pte.	Nathan, H.	19th Middlesex Regt.	30/9/18	29, St. Peter's Street, London, N.E.
267007	Pte.	Nathan, J.	2nd Oxford and Bucks. L.I.	10/10/18	57, Jane Street, London, E.
425697	Pte.	Negal, J.	Canadian Inf.	15/9/16	London.
51112	L/Cpl.	Neiberg, H.	1/8 King's Liverpool Regt.	20/11/17	13, Ellingfort Road, London, E.

N.C.O.'S AND MEN—Continued.

No.	Rank.	Name.	Regiment.	Date of Death.	Address.
5472	Cpl.	NEWMAN, C.	1st W. Yorks Regt.	24/7/17	38, Great Passage Street, Hull.
C/6683	Rfm.	NEWMAN, S.	17th K.R.R.C.	17/4/18	32, Prince of Wales Road, Swansea.
25548	Pte.	NEWMAN, S.	1st Scottish Rifles	20/7/16	20, Chapel Street, London, N.W.
1598	Pte.	NISSEN, I.	4th Royal Fusiliers	10/7/16	London.
18602	Pte.	NOCHAMOVITCH (TAYLOR), D.			
2191	Pte.	NORMAN, A. E.	12th Highland L.I.	26/9/15	188a, Main Street, S.S., Glasgow.
1303	Sgt.	NORMAN, A. S.	23rd London Regt	27/9/15	12, Woodberry Crescent, Muswell Hill, London, N.
25576	Pte.	NORMAN, C.	4th Australian Inf.	20/5/15	60, North End Road, London, W.
13052	Pte.	NORMAND, H.	1st Grenadier Guards	1/12/17	33, Camden Passage, Islington, London, N.
20670	Cpl.	NOSSEK (NORRIS), G.	4th Middlesex Regt.	14/10/14	Nankgyls, Nr. Newport, Monmouthshire.
29777	Pte.	NOVINSKI, I.	2nd Royal Scots	23/7/16	10, Fairclough Street, London, E.
422402	Pte.	NOVITZKY, H. M.	1/4th East Yorks. Regt.	27/5/18	4, Cambridge Terrace, Sunderland.
S/19086	Rfm.	NUNES VAZ, L.	2/10th London Regt.	8/8/18	21, Redcross Street, London, E.C.1.
7021	Pte.	NYMAN, A.	10th Rifle Brigade	26/11/17	15, Merchant Street, London, E.
3882	Pte.	NYMAN, C.	2nd Australian Inf.	12/9/18	114, Johnson Street, Collingwood, Victoria.
10975	Pte.	NYMAN, H.	8th Australian Inf.	18/8/16	Sydney, N.S.W.
			1st. W. Yorks. Regt.	15/1/17	12, Graythorne Terrace, Leeds.
S/26880	Rfm.	NYMAN, J.	2nd Rifle Brigade	21/4/17	782, Holloway Road, London, N.17.
67650	Pte.	O'GRADY, A.	3rd R. Welsh Fusiliers	13/2/18	14, Caldmore Road, Walsall.
51232	Pte.	OPPENHEIM, E.	19th Manchester Regt.	31/7/17	51, Wittingstall Street, London, S.W.
61383	Pte.	OPPENHEIMER, J. R.	1st Q. R. W. Surrey Regt.	13/5/18	70, Harley House, London, N.W.
9311	Sgt.	ORMAN, R.	1st S. W. Borderers	31/10/14	Crosskey, S. Wales.
3890	Pte.	ORMISTON, G. W.	6th Australian Inf.	5/6/18	Woy-Woy, N.S.W.
2372	Pte.	ORMISTON, J. H.	35th Australian Inf.	6/5/18	Woy-Woy, N.S.W.
200156	Rfm.	OSOSKI, N.	11th Rifle Brigade	4/4/17	45, Lincoln Street, London, E.
811844	A.B.	OSSEROFFSKI, L.	Royal Navy	1917	4, Chicksand Street, London, E.
21023	Pte.	PADLOFSKY, J.	9th K.R.R.C.	22/10/17	14, Great Pearl Street, London, E.
79685	Pte.	PADVA, S.	133rd Labour Coy.	9/9/17	19, Rue Vielle de Temple, Paris.
27277	Rfm.	PAMPEL, A.	11th K.R.R.C.	8/8/17	30, Gold Street, London, E.
13789	Rfm.	PARKER, S.	11th Rifle Brigade	3/9/16	10, Kyverdale Road, Stoke Newington, London, N.
4872	Pte.	PASVALSKY, L.	51st Australian Inf.	19/7/16	29, Lindsay Street, Perth, W. Australia.
40443	Cpl.	PATERSON, R. F.	8/10th Gordon Highlanders	10/4/17	9, Panmure Place, Edinburgh.
51313	Pte.	PATTIE, H.	16th Royal Scots	14/4/18	38, Criegie Street, Queen's Park, Glasgow.
S/8014	Pte.	PAYMAN, S.	1st Seaforth Highl.	5/11/17	94, Waterloo Road, Manchester.
423036	Pte.	PAYNE, A.	2/10th London Regt.	25/7/17	104, Cannon Street, London, E.
29876	Pte.	PEARLMAN, H.	7th E. Lancs. Regt.	14/6/17	39, Kinglake Street, Edgehill, Liverpool.
152371	Pte.	PEARLMAN, J.	R.E.	19/8/17	2, Salisbury Place, South Shields.
266747	Pte.	PEARLMAN, S.	1/1st Bucks. Bn.	24/4/18	148, Whitechapel Road, London, E.
614395	Pte.	PEARLSTEIN, L.	2/19th London Regt.	8/1/19	1, Norman Buildings, London, E.C.
47211	Pte.	PELLMAN, W.	22nd Northumberland Fus.	30/4/17	188, Addison Road, Blackburn.
203864	Pte.	PEPPER, M.	2/4th London Regt.	26/10/17	10, Alexander Buildings, London, E.

111

N.C.O.'S AND MEN—Continued.

No.	Rank.	Name.	Regiment.	Date of Death.	Address.
1799	Pte.	PEREIRA, E. M.	48th Australian Inf.	8/6/17	Bowden, S. Australia.
622794	Pte.	PERELES, N.	10th Canadian Inf.	17/8/18	405, Alexander Avenue, Winnipeg.
129660	Pte.	PERLBERG, M.	R.A.F.	7/1/19	216, High Street, Shadwell, London, E.
3592	L/Cpl.	PERLMAN, M.	3rd Northumberland Fus.	7/4/15	163, Stepney Green Buildings, London, E.
36288	L/Cpl.	PESTKA, L.	61st Labour Company	15/8/17	73, Crown Street, Liverpool.
193667	Pte.	PETERS, A.	376th Employment Coy.	1/9/18	22, Haworth Street, Manchester.
MT/131615	Pte.	PHILLIPS, A.	R.A.S.C. att. 99th Fd. Amb.	29/12/15	7, Soulden Road, Hammersmith, London, W.
245106	Pte.	PHILLIPS, A.	32nd Royal Fusiliers	5/8/17	262, Camden Road, London, N.W.1.
5885	Cpl.	PHILLIPS, A. J.	20th Australian Inf.	3/5/17	Surrey Hills, N.S.W.
5032	Pte.	PHILLIPS, B.	1/23rd London Regt.	16/9/16	2, Teesdale Street, London, E.
10234	Pte.	PHILLIPS, D.	2nd Border Regt.	22/10/14	14, Whitehorse Lane, London, E.
11161	Pte.	PHILLIPS, J.	8th W. Riding Regt.	18/6/17	6, Amber Street, Leeds.
15952	Pte.	PHILLIPS, J.	9th Black Watch	23/8/18	83, Marlborough Road, Manchester.
2422	Tpr.	PHILLIPS, M.	Household Bn.	12/10/17	8, Whitechapel Road, London, E.
29252	L/Cpl.	PHILLIPS, M.	1st East Lancs. Regt.	18/10/16	26, Polwarth Gardens, Edinburgh.
10315	Pte.	PHILLIPS, N. L.	6th Somerset L.I.	19/8/15	16, Branden Street, London, W.
197233	Sig.	PHILLIPS, P.	129th By. 42nd Bde. R.F.A.	28/3/18	7, Moseford Street, London, E.
201910	Pte.	PHILLIPS, S.	2/5th R. Warwick Regt.	19/11/7	397, Cheetham Hill Road, Manchester.
37685	Rfm.	PHILLIPS, S.	8th K.R.R.C.	8/12/17	34, Stayners Road, London, E.
7385	Pte.	PHILLIPS, S.	7th Royal Fusiliers	8/8/18	118, Bridge Street, London, E.3.
41641	Pte.	PINTO, H. E.	1st Cameron Highlanders	2/9/18	165, Sutherland Avenue, London, W.
22426	Pte.	PINTO, L.	15th H.L.I.	5/4/17	365, Bath Street, Glasgow.
10346	Sgt.	PISELEY, A. C.	1st E. Lancs. Regt.	1/7/16	1, Union Square, London, S.E.
1881	Pte.	PITT, H.	6th R. Warwick Regt.	1/7/16	Blucher Street, Birmingham.
1255	Pte.	PIVANSKI (HYMAN), I.	7th Manchester Regt.	18/8/17	8, Thirlmere Street, Manchester.
G/42968	Pte.	PIVANSKY, A.	2nd Middlesex Regt.	5/10/17	1, Thompson Street, Manchester.
5433	Pte.	PIZER, E.	14th Australian Inf.	26/9/17	27, Pakington Street, Geelong, Victoria.
51258	Trp.	PLATER, J.	10th Hussars atd. M.G. Sq.	11/4/17	82, Leeside Crescent, London, N.W.
5986	Pte.	POLACK, M.	4th London Regt.	18/4/17	67, Vallance Road, London, E.
6108	Gnr.	POLAK, G. E.	Australian Artillery	22/10/17	
15089	Rfm.	POLAKOFF, J.	2nd K.R.R.C.	1/7/16	41, Osbaldeston Road, London, N.
52456	Pte.	POLIKOFF, I.	1/5th W. Yorks. Regt.	18/4/18	233, Brunswick Buildings, London, E.
626151	Gnr.	POLLACK, D. S.	309th S.B., H.A.C.	26/3/18	48, West End Lane, London, N.W.
325988	Pte.	POLLACK, L.	9th D.L.I.	24/4/17	67, Avenue Road, London, N.15.
64658	Pte.	POLLOCK, A.	216th M.G.C.	18/11/17	97, Sea View Road, Sunderland.
492788	Pte.	POMERANCE, S.	1/13th London Regt.	17/4/17	51, Fieldgate Street, London, E.
225026	Pte.	POMERANTZ, I.	4th Special Company, R.E.	26/9/18	36, Brick Lane, London, E.
15007	Pte.	POMERANTZ, J.	2nd Leicester Regt.	25/9/15	45, Dyfalty Street, Swansea.
308479	Pte.	POSENOR, A.	11th Tank Corps	8/10/18	32, Clifton Buildings, London, E.1.
4650	Sgt.	PRAEGER, A.	9th Lancers	1/10/14	19, Thirlstone Street, Liverpool.
232850	Pte.	PRICE, B.	2/2nd London Regt.	26/9/17	99, Portobello Road, London, W.
306925	Rfm.	PRICE, L.	2/8th W. Yorks. Regt.	3/5/17	3a, Crimbles Place, Leeds.
279632	Pte.	PRIMACK, M.	49th Canadian Inf.	9/6/17	44, Blythe Street, London, E.
43905	Pte.	PRIMHAK, N.	1st Essex Regt.	26/8/18	4, Osbaldeston Road, London, N.
5801	Pte.	PRINS, A.	4th London Regt.	7/10/16	92, Newington Green Road, London, N.

N.C.O.'S AND MEN—Continued.

No.	Rank.	Name.	Regiment.	Date of Death.	Address.
63375	Pte.	PYKE, J. L.	13th Royal Fusiliers	5/4/18	3, Regency Square, Brighton.
R/29413	Pte.	RABINSON, B.	1st Rhodesian Regt.	7/2/15	Buluwayo, S. Africa.
50412	Rfm.	RABBINOWITZ, B.	8th K.R.R.C.	3/5/17	2, Holcroft Road, London, E.9.
1798	Pte.	RABBINOWITZ, I.	18th Training Reserve	1918	2, Holcroft Road, London, E.
17708	Pte.	RABINOVITCH, B.	59th Australian Inf.	19/7/16	45, Leslie Street, Balaclava, E. St. Kilda.
42375	Pte.	RABINOVITCH, E. H.	9th Fld. Amb. Aust. A.M.C.	31/8/18	Vincent Street, Adelaide.
18859	Pte.	RACIONZER, H. F.	27th Northumberland Fus.	3/5/17	66, Sinclair Drive, Glasgow.
32837	Pte.	RADOMAN, B.	1st Canadian Inf.	7/10/16	Montenegro.
1599	Cpl.	RAKUSEN, H.	1/6th West Yorks. Regt.	9/10/17	42, Glover Street, Leeds.
2401	Pte.	RAMUS, E. J.	9th London Regt.	1/7/16	23, Park Drive, Harrogate.
1890	Pte.	RAMUS, J.	8th London Regt.	25/5/15	62, Windsor Road, London, N.
1277	Pte.	RAPHAEL, F. J.	21st Australian Inf.	30/7/16	61, Blair Street, E. Brunswick, Melbourne.
1273	Sergt.	RAPHAEL, H. C.	1st South African Inf.	18/7/16	P.O. Box 1434, Cape Town.
69326	Pte.	RAPHAEL, S. F.	1st South African Inf.	19/7/16	P.O. Box 1434, Cape Town.
850736	Pte.	RAPOPORT, P.	12/13th Northd. Fusrs.	5/6/18	75, Rua 10 de Marco, Para, Brazil.
74241	Pte.	RAPORT, M. D.	43rd Canadian Inf.	8/8/18	34a, Bradshaw Street, Manchester.
2045	Pte.	RAPP, L.	30th Middlesex (Lab.) Regt.	27/3/19	30, Millar Crescent, Edinburgh.
163510	Pte.	RASKY, L. S.	2/5th Manchester Regt.	11/10/17	26, Nightingale Street, Manchester.
40524	Gnr.	RAYNER, B.	26th S.B., R.G.A.	6/10/18	12, North Place, Brighton.
J/496	Pte.	RECKLER, L.	6th Northampton Regt.	24/4/18	657, Rochdale Road, Manchester.
11839	Pte.	REDLIKH, G. G.	38th Royal Fusiliers	14/10/18	Alexandria, Egypt.
39512	Pte.	REINFLEISCH, A.	19th Middlesex Regt.	21/4/18	57, Brunswick Buildings, London, E.
33097	Pte.	REUBEN, E.	6th Man. Rgt. att. 11th L. Fu.	10/10/16	99, Great Ducie Street, Manchester.
40854	Pte.	REUBEN, M.	15th West Yorks. Regt.	3/5/17	29, Elmwood Street, Leeds.
470	Pte.	REVENSKY, H.	2nd Suffolk Regt.	14/6/17	14, Deal Street, London, E.
1617	L/Cpl.	RIBERO, I.	1/4th K.O.R. Lancs. Regt.	18/7/17	8, Wood Lane, London, S.W.6.
1963	Pte.	RICH, F. P.	4th Australian Inf.	16/4/18	15, The Grove, Hammersmith, London, W.
18530	Cpl.	RICHARDS, C. S.	38th Australian Inf.	28/5/17	Malvern, Victoria.
200956	Pte.	RICKAYZEN, H. S.	25th By. Australian F.A.	19/9/17	Normanville, Bondi Road, Sydney.
307056	Pte.	RIGGLE, P.	9th Durham L.I.	7/9/18	31, Morgan Street, London, E.
42377	Gnr.	RISSIDORE, F. D.	2/7th West Yorks. Regt.	27/5/18	44, Whirelock Street, Leeds.
53932	Gnr.	RISSIDORE, L. B.	3rd Bde. Canadian Artillery	15/6/16	Central Fire Hall, Hamilton, Ontario.
J/1078	Pte.	RITTENBAUM, F.	C/34 By. R.F.A.	26/7/17	21, Victoria Street, Merthyr Tydvil.
2002	Pte.	ROBIN, D. K.	38th Royal Fusiliers	19/12/18	26-30, Turk Street, Brick Lane, London, E.
5198	R.S.M.	ROBINSON, M.	18th Australian Inf.	16/4/16	88, Alice Street, Newtown, N.S.W.
G/21998	Pte.	ROBINSON-MOLIVER, S.	10th Lincoln Regt.	16/4/17	100, Granville Street, Grimsby.
9888	L/Cpl.	ROBSON (DAVIS), J.	2nd Royal Fusiliers	30/10/16	13, Beckton Road, Canning Town, London, E
147423	Pte.	RODIN, M.	2nd Yorks. & Lancs. Regt.	12/10/16	73, Woodbine Street, South Shields.
559017	Pte.	ROGALEK, M.	78th Canadian Inf.	29/10/16	390, Flora Avenue, Winnipeg.
2613	Pte.	ROLBIN, H.	100st Labour Coy.	9/11/18	91, Underwood Street, London, E.1.
322647	Rfm.	ROME, L.	3rd Australian Inf.	18/1/17	Bowles Farm, Middleton, Nr. Manchester.
9123	L/Cpl.	ROOD, M.	1/6th London Regt.	4/4/18	34, Greenwood Road, London, N.E.
			2nd Dorset Regt.	16/12/15	56, British Street, London, E.

N.C.O.'S AND MEN—Continued.

No.	Rank. Name.	Regiment.	Date of Death.	Address.
51881	Pte. ROOMS, M.	2nd Lincoln Regt.	10/9/18	54, Villers Terrace, Leeds.
27115	L/Cpl. ROSCOE, H.	8th Cheshire Regt.	5/4/16	13, Congress Street, Liverpool.
216	Pte. ROSE, A. S.	10th Royal Fusiliers	25/5/16	27, Glazbury Road, London, W.
203030	Pte. ROSE, S. L.	1/5th West Yorks. Regt.	8/4/18	37, Silver Street Head, Sheffield.
59173	Pte. ROSE, S.	1st Devon Regt.	15/4/17	81, Gough Road, Birmingham.
9269	Pte. ROSEMAN, M.	2nd West Yorks. Regt.	12/3/15	15, Lovell Street, Camp Road, Leeds.
226645	Pte. ROSEMER, S.	18th Canadian Inf.	12/4/17	13, Plateau Street, Montreal.
154720	L/Cpl. ROSEN, J.	Royal Engineers	25/11/18	45, Willow Street, London, E.
10304	Pte. ROSEN, M.	2nd Yorks. Regt.	2/11/14	7, Cameron Place, Nelson Street, London, E.
15258	Cpl. ROSEN, P.	19th Lancs. Fusiliers	14/10/17	32, Albert Road, Blackpool.
29528	Pte. ROSENBAUM, A.	1st West Yorks. Regt.	12/10/16	19, Alfred Place, Leeds.
38072	Pte. ROSENBAUM, A.	8th East Surrey Regt.	25/10/18	95, Coldharbour Lane, London, S.E.5.
63410	Gnr. ROSENBAUM, A.	R.G.A.	3/9/17	28, Rutland Street, London, E.
G/25788	Pte. ROSENBAUM (RUSSELL), A.	7th Royal Sussex Regt.	25/10/18	2, Maple Street, London, W.
6215	Rfm. ROSENBAUM (Rowson), D.	16th London Regt.	10/9/16	128, Elizabeth Street, Manchester.
203115	Pte. ROSENBAUM, S.	1st London Regt.	14/5/17	52, Dalston Lane, London, N.E.
444	Pte. ROSENBAUM, S.	16th Royal Warwick. Regt.	3/9/16	50, Belgrave Road, Birmingham.
266983	Pte. ROSENBAUM, S.	1/1st Bucks. Battn.	15/8/16	91, Church Street, London, E.
71449	Pte. ROSENBAUM (ROSE), W.	15th Notts. & Derby Regt.	19/8/17	5, Mount Pleasant, Nottingham.
A/205198	Rfm. ROSENBERG, A.	1st K.R.R.C.	1918	686, Romford Road, London, E.
S/28547	Rfm. ROSENBERG, B.	2nd Rifle Brigade	31/7/17	55, Umberston Street, London, E.1.
40025	Pte. ROSENBERG, B.	9th Irish Fusiliers	16/8/17	18, Preston Street, Roundhay Road, Leeds.
241630	Pte. ROSENBERG, B.	1/5th K.O. Royal Lancs.	2/8/17	Stead Road, Sheffield.
51060	L/Cpl. ROSENBERG, D.	17th Royal Fusiliers	30/4/17	21, Cumberland Street, Bristol.
J/2074	Pte. ROSENBERG, F.	39th Royal Fusiliers	22/10/18	7, St. George's Terrace, Leeds.
130243	Pte. ROSENBERG, F.	72nd Canadian Inf.	17/1/17	10, Melbourne Road, Brighton, England.
37761	Cpl. ROSENBERG, H.	10th K.O. Yorks. L.I.	4/10/17	277, Ecclesall Road, Sheffield.
34958	Pte. ROSENBERG, H.	51st M.G. Bn.	21/3/18	3, Stamford Street, Leeds.
10640	Pte. ROSENBERG (ROSS), H.	2nd West Riding Regt.	1/7/16	18, Preston Street, Roundhay, Leeds.
612000	Pte. ROSENBERG, I.	1/19th London Regt.	4/12/17	3, Little Alie Street, London, E.
22311	Pte. ROSENBERG, I.	1st K.O. Royal Lancs. Rgt.	1/4/18	87, Dempsey Street, London, E.1.
7292	Pte. ROSENBERG, J.	8th London Regt.	12/3/17	4, St. Thomas Road, London, N.E.
5200	Pte. ROSENBERG, L.	10th Royal Fusiliers	22/4/17	28, Park Street, Manchester.
18928	Pte. ROSENBERG, L.	3rd Worcestershire Regt.	9/12/15	94, Duke Street, Southport.
233855	L/Cpl. ROSENBERG, L.	2/2nd London Regt.	21/3/18	220, St. Georges Street, London, E.
3552	Pte. ROSENBERG (ROSEN), L.	6th Gloucester Regt.	22/8/16	24, Victoria Street, St. Paul's, Bristol.
1678	Pte. ROSENBERG, L. M.	7th Aust. Light Horse	5/8/16	Charles Street, Broken Hill, N.S.W.
88368	Pte. ROSENBERG, M.	1st London Regt.	4/9/18	10, Baker Street, London, E.
30191	Pte. ROSENBERG, S.	4/5th Loyal N. Lancs. Rgt.	26/10/17	104, Exmouth Street, London, E.1.
47156	Pte. ROSENBERG, S.	9th Royal Welsh Fusiliers	8/5/18	159, Irving Street, Birmingham.
J/303	Pte. ROSENBERG, S.	38th Royal Fusiliers	21/10/18	17, Carburton Street, London, W.

N.C.O.'s AND MEN—Continued.

No.	Rank.	Name.	Regiment.	Date of Death.	Address.
47203	Pte.	ROSENBLOOM, H.	12th Manchester Regt.	16/4/17	40, Mary Street, Manchester.
49052	Pte.	ROSENBLOOM, H.	11th Royal Scots	22/3/18	41, Willerfield Place, Edinburgh.
46994	Pte.	ROSENBLOOM, J. G.	17th Lancashire Fusiliers	17/8/17	34, Pembroke Crescent, Hove, Sussex.
23104	Pte.	ROSENBLOOM, M.	12th Royal Scots Fusiliers	20/9/18	49, Adelphi Street, Glasgow.
481219	Pte.	ROSENTHAL, A.	250 Div. Emp. Coy. Lab. Co.	10/11/18	12, Hungerford Street, London, E.
50	Tpr.	ROSENTHAL, A. K.	1st Aust. Light Horse	29/5/15	James Street, Manly, N.S.W.
2317	Pte.	ROSENTHAL, C.	4th London Regt.	10/5/15	80, Balls Pond Road, London, N.E.
53196	Pte.	ROSENTHAL, D.	41st M.G. Bn.	1/4/18	27, Waterloo Street, Manchester.
4062	Pte.	ROSENTHAL, G.	16th Northumberland Fus.	10/2/17	246, Westgate Road, Newcastle.
28/34	Pte.	ROSENTHAL, H.	16th Northumberland Fus.	22/7/16	42, Whitelock Street, Leeds.
628	L/Cpl.	ROSENTHAL, H.	2nd Manchester Regt	29/4/15	43, Rugby Road, Manchester.
219580	Pte.	ROSENTHAL, H. (M.M.)	Canadian Inf.	19/11/16	Bessarabia, Russia.
53905	Cpl.	ROSENTHAL (PAGE), J.	18th Canadian Inf.	10/4/16	89, Upton Lane, London, E.7.
484	Pte.	ROSENTHAL, L. M.	14th Royal Warwick. Regt.	23/7/16	37, Beaufort Road, Birmingham.
27547	Pte.	ROSENTHAL, M.	15th Lancashire Fusiliers	1/7/16	41, Exchange Street, Manchester.
343808	Dvr.	ROSENTHAL, M.	R.A.S.C.	15/7/18	254, Waterloo Road, Manchester.
	Cadet	ROSENTHAL, S.	R.A.F.	29/5/18	37, Mayor Street, Montreal.
244416	Gnr.	ROSENTHAL, T.	2/2nd Lancs. R.G.A.	29/11/18	198, Bury New Road, Manchester.
2236	Pte.	ROSENWAX, C. H.	19th Australian Inf.	3/5/17	331, Richardson Street, Melbourne, Victoria.
19066	Rfm.	ROSOFF, J.	3rd R.B.	31/7/17	London.
4998	Pte.	ROSS, J.	4th East Yorks. Regt.	15/9/16	146, Well Street, Hackney, London, N.E.
20210	Pte.	ROSSINSKY, S.	6th Royal Warwick. Regt.	4/2/17	22, Great Pearl Street, London, E.
1676	Pte.	ROSSOGSKY, I. P.	34th Australian Inf.	12/7/17	
235023	Pte.	ROTHBLATT, S.	2/5th Royal Warwick. Rgt.	3/12/17	35, Choir Street, Lr. Broughton, Manchester.
33238	L/Cpl.	ROTENBERG, B.	2nd Wilts Regt.	9/4/17	3, Kinnoull Mansions, Clapton, London, E.
6710	Pte.	ROTHFIELD, J.	10th Northumberland Fus.	14/10/17	1, Hedley Street, Gateshead-on-Tyne.
1107	Pte.	ROTHKUGEL, M.	1st South African Inf.	1915	Cape Town.
363	Pte.	ROTTMAN, J.	Zion Mule Corps	3/6/15	Cairo.
4583	Pte.	RUBIN, J.	1st South African Inf.	17/7/16	Cape Town, S.A.
41858	Rfm.	RUBENSTEIN, B.	12th K.R.R.C.	20/9/18	48, Gowers Walk, London, E.
235283	Pte.	RUBENSTEIN, H.	4th East Lancs. Regt.	21/3/18	153b, Kensington, Liverpool.
34041	Pte.	RUBENSTEIN, M.	19th Manchester Regt.	23/7/16	62, Heywood Street, Manchester.
22993	Pte.	RUBINSTEIN, P.	6/7th Royal Scots Fusiliers	9/4/17	13, Rutherglen Road, S.S. Glasgow.
47940	Pte.	RUDSTEIN, S.	18th West Yorks. Regt.	3/5/17	18, Back Benson Street, Leeds.
23804	L/Cpl.	RUFFELL, S.	1st Duke of Cornwall's L.I.	20/7/16	74, Sudbury Buildings, Mount Street, London, E.
350391	Pte.	RUSHMAN, J.	2/1 E.Lan.F.Am.R.A.M.C.	27/8/17	30, Clarence Street, Manchester.
4197	Bgr.	RUSSELL, H.	26th Australian Inf.	14/11/16	Goodna, Queensland.
57653	Pte.	RUTER, D.	13th Middlesex Regt.	9/10/18	314, Queen's Road, Upton Park, London, E.
4341	Spr.	SACKS, C.	13th Fld. Coy. Aus. Eng.	8/6/17	3, Green's Court, London, W.
24051	Rfm.	SACKSHIVER, J.	9th Rifle Brigade	26/3/17	34, Merchant Street, London, E.
28555	Pte.	SACOFSKY, M.	6th Leicester Regt.	15/11/17	22, Lovell Street, Leeds.
1180	A.B.	SALAMAN, L. H.	Hawke Batt. R.N.V.R.	18/6/15	4, Greenfield Terrace, Edgbaston, Birmingham.
36935	Pte.	SALTMAN, T.	6th Royal Berks. Regt.	4/8/17	100, Albert Street, Grimsby.

N.C.O.'S AND MEN—Continued.

No.	Rank.	Name.	Regiment.	Date of Death.	Address.
3749	Sgt.	SAMPSON, A. F.	4th B.W. Indies Regt.	5/2/17	1, Lissant Road, Kingstown, Jamaica.
96127	Pte.	SAMSON, E.	M.G. Sqn.	15/2/18	Lauriston Road, S. Hackney, London, N.E.
53894	Rfm.	SAMSON, I. S.	2nd K.R.R.C.	19/12/18	27, George Street, Baker Street, London, W.
3911	Pte.	SAMUEL, E.	59th Australian Inf.	19/7/16	113, Renfrew Street, Glasgow.
10314	Pte.	SAMUEL, F. J.	2nd H.A.C.	8/10/17	47, Goldhurst Terrace, London, N.W.
30871	Rfm.	SAMUEL, S.	3rd R.B.	3/9/17	138, Dalston Lane, London, E.8.
R/20985	Rfm.	SAMUELS, A.	7th K.R.R.C.	15/9/16	256, Burdett Road, London, E.
35566	Pte.	SAMUELS, A.	10th K.O. Yorkshire L.I.	24/10/17	33, Queen's Place, Leeds.
8748	Pte.	SAMUELS, A.	2nd Yorkshire Regt.	12/3/15	42, Aberdeen Road, London, N.
69609	Pte.	SAMUELS, B.	19th Northumberland Fus.	24/8/18	17, Pimlico Walk, London, S.W.
589	Pte.	SAMUELS, E.	39th Australian Inf.	28/1/17	C/o Thompson's Yard, Blackrod, Lancs.
5423	Cpl.	SAMUEL, G.	16th Australian Inf.	17/10/17	152, Newcastle Street, Perth, W. Australia.
40966	Pte.	SAMUELS, H.	1st S. Staffs. Regt.	26/10/17	105, Hanbury Street, London, E.
68477	Gnr.	SAMUELS, H.	151st Siege By. R.G.A.	26/4/17	64, Settles Street, London, E.
40483	Pte.	SAMUELS, J.	7th Bedford Regt.	3/4/18	67, Knight's Hill, London, S.
S/17768	Rfm.	SAMUELS, M. (M.M.)	1st Rifle Brigade	1/9/18	43, Turner Street, London, E.
26742	Pte.	SAMUELS, P.	7th Royal Fusiliers	13/10/16	7, Donaldson Road, London, N.W.
52957	Pte.	SANDALL, D.	13th D.L.I.	2/6/17	121, Lancaster Road, Preston.
2066	Sgt.	SANDERS, G. H.	9th Royal Fusiliers	16/7/16	61, Beresford Street, London, N.
SS/102037	Stoker	SANDERS, H.	H.M.S. "Dreadnought"	20/11/17	50, Richmond Road, Shepherd's Bush, London, W.
134976	Gnr.	SANDFORD, M. S.	335th Siege By. R.G.A.	27/7/17	43, South Moulton Street, London, W.
15603	Pte.	SANDYS, J.	3rd Cameron Highlanders	15/3/15	126, Romford Street, London, E.
202186	Pte.	SANOFSKI, J.	1/5th West Yorks. Regt.	24/4/18	20, Cooper Street. Leeds.
285047	Pte.	SANOFSKY, S.	9th Welsh Regt.	3/7/17	109, Prescot Street, Liverpool.
41458	Pte.	SAPERIA, L.	9th West Yorks. Regt.	26/1/18	10, Cloth Street, Regent Street, Leeds.
79609	Sgt.	SARFATY, J.	R.A.M.C.	12/3/17	5, Warwickshire Road, London, N.E.
5467	Pte.	SAUL, H. J.	9th Australian Inf.	15/4/17	Sandgate, Queensland.
16738	Cpl.	SAUNDERS, H.	Labour Corps	6/3/19	28, Great Garden Street, London, E.1.
9463	Pte.	SAUNDERS, J.	1st Northumberland Fus.	23/8/14	15, Portland Crescent, Leeds.
6831	Sergt.	SAUNDERS, S. A.	14th Australian M.G.C.	15/8/16	268, Ward Street, North Adelaide.
871298	Pte.	SAVILLE, E. J.	44th Canadian Inf.	2/6/17	156, Elgin Avenue, London, W.
12868I	Gnr.	SAVITZ, J.	232nd Siege By. R.G.A.	14/10/17	76, Vine Street, Liverpool.
J/8132	Pte.	SAVITZ, S.	38th Royal Fusiliers	19/1/19	
1852	Sergt.	SAXON, M.	12th H.L.I.	26/9/15	10, Great Portland Street, Glasgow.
27483	Pte.	SCHAFFER, F. G.	6th Somerset L.I.	22/8/17	25, Shiplake Buildings, London, E.
173	Pte.	SCHAEFER, T. J.	33rd Australian Inf.	7/6/17	Brodelay, N.S.W.
13851	Pte.	SCHEIN, J. (WARNER)	9th Worcester Regt.	28/2/17	124, Davis Mansions, London, E.
204187	Pte.	SCHIFF, B.	13th Royal Fusiliers	28/4/17	37, Pedley Street, London, E.
CH/15143	A/C.S.M.	SCHIFF, F. G.	1st R.M.L.I. R.N.D.	16/3/18	575, Green Lanes, Harringay, London, N.8.
2267	Pte.	SCHILLING, H.	7th London Regt.	24/5/16	16, Mount Street, London, E.2.
R/22227	Rfm.	SCHILLING, R.	8th K.R.R.C.	12/4/17	3, Ducal Street, Bethnal Green, London, E.
2764	Sgt.	SCHNEIDER (TAYLOR) D. J.	6th London Regt.	1/1/16	13, Montifiore House, Cannon Street, London, E.
22832	Pte.	SCHNEIDER, S.	5th Oxford & Bucks L.I.	28/8/16	7, St. Thomas Place, London, N.E.

N.C.O.'s AND MEN—Continued.

No.	Rank.	Name.	Regiment.	Date of Death.	Address.
R/37727	Rfm.	SCHNEIDERMAN, L.	11th K.R.R.C.	2/12/17	London, E.
29919	1st/A.M.	SCHNEIDERS, A. M.	16th Squadron, R.A.F.	26/3/18	69, Aberdare Gardens, London, N.W.
9261	Cpl.	SCHONBERG, B.	5th London Regt.	9/2/15	North Street, Rochford, Essex.
300003	C.Q.M.S.	SCHONEWALD, S.	2/5th London Regt.	20/9/17	60, Westbere Road, London, N.W.
31224	Pte.	SCHULEBERG, H.	1st Royal West Kent Regt.	2/9/18	28, Benfleet Street, London, E.
51285	Pte.	SCHWARTZ, B.	Imp. Camel Corps	4/10/18	289, Oxford Street, London, E.
7323	Pte.	SCHWARTZ, C. F.	23rd Australian Inf.	1/9/18	Smythesdale, Victoria.
13728	Pte.	SCHWARTZ, E.	6th Corps Cyclists	10/4/17	Russell Grange, Chingford Road, Chingford.
2384	Pte.	SCHWARTZ, I. (SOLOMONS)			
R/35577	Rfm.	SCHWARTZMAN, D.	4th Royal Fusiliers	5/6/15	35, Parliament Row, Hanley.
133159	Gnr.	SCHWEITZER, P.	17th K.R.R.C.	11/8/17	7, Ascot Street, Brick Lane, London, E.
491622	Pte.	SCOLNUCK, H.	R.G.A.	26/11/18	434, Abbeydale Road, Sheffield.
35358	Pte.	SEGAL, N.	24th Canadian Inf.	7/11/17	980, Cadieux Street, Montreal.
44518	Cpl.	SEGELMAN, P.	10th R. Welsh Fusiliers	16/8/16	4a, Newling Street, London, E.
56876	Pte.	SEIDEMAN, M.	16th Notts. & Derby Regt.	26/3/18	113, Victor Street, Grimsby.
8141	Cpl.	SEIGAR, P.	13th Welsh Regt.	9/2/17	210, Cheetham Hill Road, Manchester.
49003	Pte.	SELCOVITCH, H.	1st Dorset Regt.	3/3/15	London.
B/23001	Pte.	SELINE, J. J.	1st S. W. Borderers	15/9/18	39, Granton Street, Cheetham, Manchester.
63232	L/Cpl.	SELMAN, H. D.	26th Royal Fusiliers	7/10/16	Central Chambers, Fisher Street, Swansea,
J/322	Pte.	SERAMBER, C.	1/19th London Regt.	1/9/18	3, Crown's Hotel, Stoke Newington, London, N.
J/966	Pte.	SHAFT, J.	38th Royal Fusiliers	8/10/18	4, East Street, Stockpool.
34462	Pte.	SHALGOSKY, B.	38th Royal Fusiliers	1/3/18	95, Becker Street, Manchester.
14229	A/Sgt.	SHALL, I.	9th York and Lancs. Regt.	9/4/17	30, Nile Street, Hull.
2657	Pte.	SHAPERO, C.	1st S. African Inf.	22/3/18	18a, Lovers' Walk, Fordsburg, Johannesburg.
132092	Pte.	SHATGOFSKY, H.	5th Royal Scots	27/9/15	16, Viewfield Terrace, Dunfermline.
8118	Pte.	SHATZ, M.	8th M.G. Bn.	28/5/18	19, Booth Street, London, E.1.
33887	Rfm.	SHAW, J.	3rd S. African Inf.	23/1/18	4, Pretoria Buildings, Johannesburg.
162614	Gnr.	SHEARE, S.	17th K.R.R.C.	20/9/17	111, Cambridge Road, London, E.1.
17259	L/Cpl.	SHENOW, W.	1/1st Lowland H.B. R.G.A.	22/7/18	25, Campbell Street, Newcastle-on-Tyne.
206	Pte.	SHERMAN, G. J.	5th Royal Berks. Regt.	1/7/16	23, Freemont Street, London, N.E.
5108a	Pte.	SHERMAN, L.	9th Australian Inf.	25/4/15	The Wentworth, Bordi Broch, Syd., N.S.W.
5151	Rfm.	SHERMAN, S.	33rd Australian Inf.	2/10/17	Larissa, Nelson Street, Woollawra, Sydney.
15500	Cpl.	SHIBKO, I.	2/8th West Yorks. Regt.	31/1/17	10, Brunswick Terrace, Leeds.
204389	Pte.	SHILCO, E.	11th Welsh Regt.	18/9/18	231, Newport Road, Cardiff.
202619	Pte.	SHIMBERG, M.	7th Royal West Kent Regt.	8/11/18	24, Choir Street, Salford, Manchester.
12334	Pte.	SHOWMAN, S.	1/8th K.O.R. Lancs. Regt.	15/11/18	7, Exchange Street, Manchester.
31224	Pte.	SHULEBERG, S.	1st K.O.R. Lancs. Regt.	23/10/16	4, Broughton Street, Manchester.
27480	Pte.	SHULMAN, I.	1st Royal West Kent Regt.	2/9/18	8, Benfleet Place, London, N.
33292	Pte.	SHUSTER, D.	11th Essex Regt.	4/4/18	4/5, Josephine Houses, Thrawl Street, London, E.1.
33285	L/Cpl.	SHUSTER, M.	18th Lancashire Fusiliers	30/7/16	46, Weaver Street, London, E.C.
21348	Pte.	SHYMAN, W.	18th Lancashire Fusiliers	30/7/16	46, Weaver Street, London, E.C.
108294	Spr.	SIEGEL, H.	19th King's Liverpool Rgt.	24/4/18	9, Duchess Street, Manchester.
6365	Pte.	SILBERTHAU, R.	2nd Bn. Canad. Ry. Troops	8/11/17	Nevada Stock Farm, U.S.A.
6939	Pte.	SILDIN, D.	1st Australian Inf.	4/10/17	157, Enmoor Road, Newtown. N.S.W.
	Pte.		Royal Fusiliers	30/10/18	303, Newberry Avenue, Chicago, U.S.A.

117

N.C.O.'S AND MEN—Continued.

No.	Rank.	Name.	Regiment.	Date of Death.	Address.
10929	Pte.	SILLBERG, M.	9th West Riding Regt.	4/7/16	13, Elmwood Road, Leeds.
37400	L/Cpl.	SILVER, A.	2nd (Gar.) Bn. Bedford Rgt.	25/10/18	77, Augusta Road, Ramsgate.
7351	L/Cpl.	SILVER, B.	1st K.R.R.C.	27/7/16	17, Boulton Road, Southsea.
15524	Cpl.	SILVER, I.	8th Canadian Inf.	21/6/15	14, Pleasant Square, New Haven, U.S.A.
204380	Pte.	SILVER, J.	2/4th York & Lancs. Regt.	13/4/18	78, Manor Road, London, N.16.
21647	Cpl.	SILVER, R.	12th Middlesex Regt.	17/2/17	3, Guy Street, London, S.E.
2815	Pte.	SILVERMAN, A.	20th Australian Inf.	9/10/17	17, Thrush Road, Redeath by Sea, England.
652267	Rfm.	SILVERMAN, H.	1/21st London Regt.	4/11/17	48, Cephas Street London, E.
14994	Pte.	SILVERMAN, J.	14th Fld. Amb. Aus. A.M.C.	24/9/17	167, Newcastle Street, Perth, W.A.
R/25266	Rfm.	SILVERMAN, P.	18th K.R.R.C.	21/9/17	48, Cephas Street, London, E.
9662	Pte.	SILVERMAN, S.	1st Royal Berks. Regt.	17/2/15	12, Teesdale Street, London, E.
2176	Pte.	SILVERSTEIN, L. B.	23rd London Regt.	16/9/16	47c, Clifton Gardens, London, W.
186241	Cadet	SILVERSTEIN, H. M.	Canadian R.A.F.	10/2/18	32, Manor Road, Romford.
3/2743	Cpl.	SILVERSTONE, H.	9th Essex Regt.	3/7/16	465, High Road, Leyton, London.
R/22093	Rfm.	SILVERSTONE, L.	9th K.R.R.C.	27/5/17	79, Gold Street, London, E.
6508	Pte.	SILVERSTONE, M.	1st London Regt.	7/10/16	57, Imperial Avenue, London, N.
28489	Pte.	SILVERSTONE, M.	4th Bedford Regt.	19/7/18	56, Tudor Street, Hackney, London, N.E.
8342	Pte.	SILVERSTONE, S.	39th Royal Fusiliers	6/2/19	
J/35694	Pte.	SIMCOVITCH (WISE), M.	40th Royal Fusiliers	22/8/18	88, Waterloo Road, Manchester.
12990	Pte.	SIMLO, R.	11th King's Liv'pool Regt.	23/3/18	71, Heywood Street, Manchester.
3469	Pte.	SIMMONDS, D. J.	55th Australian Inf.	24/5/18	Yarra Street, Heidleberg, Vic.
2438	Pte.	SIMMONS, A. E.	50th Australian Inf.	25/4/18	White Park, Werrabarra, N.S.W.
77175	Pte.	SIMMONS, B. E.	16th Canadian Scottish Rgt.	8/8/18	136, Englefield Road, London, N.
5726	Pte.	SIMMONS, J.	23rd Royal Fusiliers	8/9/18	8, St. Thomas Road, Stepney, London, E.
6416	Pte.	SIMMONS, P.	20th Australian Inf.	21/5/18	4, Gotham Street, Glebe, Sydney.
572559	Rfm.	SIMMONS, S.	17th London Regt.	24/8/18	2, Argyle Road, London, E.
L/39250	Gnr.	SIMMONS, S.	B/77 Bde. R/F.A.	13/10/17	18, Duchess Street, London, E.
298299	Pte.	SIMON, B.	59th Aux.Pet.Co., R.A.S.C.	8/9/17	25, Conway Grove, Harehills, Leeds.
4809	Pte.	SIMONS, L. J.	18th Australian Inf.	29/9/17	54, Barden Street, Cook's River, N.S.W.
5913	Pte.	SIMON, M.	3rd South African Inf.	12/4/17	P.O. Denver, Johannesberg, S. Africa.
33653	Pte.	SIMON, M.	7th Loyal N. Lancs. Regt.	15/6/17	24, Devon Street, Liverpool.
105	Pte.	SIMON, O.	9th Australian Inf.	6/5/15	Scolta Place, Auckland, N.Z.
8456	Rfm.	SIMONS, A.	17th London Regt.	4/3/17	36, Varden Street, London, E.
24429	Flight-Sergt.	SIMONS, A. S.	44th Squadron, R.A.F.	9/11/18	73, Casland Road, S. Hackney, London, N.E.
1478	Pte.	SIMONS, L. J.	20th M.G. Bn.	10/1/17	London.
201704	Rfm.	SIMONS, P.	10th K.R.R.C.	20/9/17	London.
S/355	Rfm.	SINGER, E.	1st Rifle Brigade	7/11/14	11, Elm Flat, Windsor.
438	Rfm.	SINGER, P.	2nd Rifle Brigade	26/9/15	16, Wickes Street, London.
1621	Pte.	SINGER, S.	2nd Australian Inf.	24/7/16	167, Commonwealth Street, Surry Hills, Sydney.
21924	Cpl.	SIRWINSKY, J.	8th Canadian Inf.	20/5/15	Bialystok, Poland.
	Pte.	SISSENWAIN, L.	Canadian Inf.	1918	Toronto, Canada.
42874	Pte.	SLIFKIN, I.	17th King's Liverpool Rgt.	30/4/18	85, Prescott Street, Liverpool.
2265959	Spr.	SLONEMSKY, J.	Canadian Engineers	14/8/18	371, Freil Street, Ottawa, Ontario, Canada.
9433	Pte.	SMITH, H.	2nd South Staffs. Regt.	25/9/15	2, South Street, Cork.

N.C.O.'S AND MEN—Continued.

No.	Rank.	Name.	Regiment.	Date of Death.	Address.
47339	Pte.	SMITH, J. J.	22nd Northumberland Fus.	21/3/18	34, South Block, Houndsditch, London, E.C.
33412	Pte.	SMOLENSKI, C.	11th East Lancs. Regt.	5/9/18	23, Great Oxford Street, Liverpool.
33847	Pte.	SMULLEN, H.	16th Manchester Regt.	21/3/18	89, Stock Street, Manchester.
8643	Cpl.	SNIDER, J.	2nd Bedford Regt.	2/7/18	30, Belgrade Road, London, N.
284	Pte.	SNIDERS, S.	Royal Bucks. Hussars	21/3/15	Hope Villa, Wallace Road, London, N.
79638	Sgt.	SOBEL, M.	Lkr. Lampson's M.M.G.C.	10/3/18	30, Maple Street, London, W.
J/1095	Pte.	SOBORINSKY, P.	38th Royal Fusiliers	19/10/18	31, Heneage Street, London, E.1.
23/394	Pte.	SOLBERG, B.	10th Durham L.I.	23/8/17	7, Turley Street, Manchester.
26892	Cpl.	SOLKOW, A.	6th King's Shropshire L.I.	30/11/17	30, Edmund Street, Hanley.
1999	Pte.	SOLNICK, E.	22nd Australian Inf.	29/7/16	55, Nicholson Street, Carlton, Victoria.
251908	Pte.	SOLOMON, B.	1/6th Manchester Regt.	28/3/18	164, Conran Street, Manchester.
68993	Pte.	SOLOMON, F.	23rd Royal Fusiliers	1/10/18	52, Clarence Street, Gravesend, Kent.
9777	L/Cpl.	SOLOMON (SULLIVAN), H.	1st Border Regt.	11/6/15	25, Mossford Street, London, E.
47557	Pte.	SOLOMON, I.	26th Northumberland Fus.	24/4/17	24, Cephas Street, London, E.
6386	Cpl.	SOLOMON, J. (M.M.)	2nd Middlesex Regt.	31/10/16	7, Code Street, London, E.
267275	Sig.	SOLOMON, J.	1/4th Seaforth Highlanders	20/7/18	65, Ickburgh Road, London, N.E.
29058	Pte.	SOLOMON, J.	1/5th R. Warwick Regt.	10/8/17	39, Whitehorse Lane, London, E.
2418	Pte.	SOLOMON, L.	44th Australian Inf.	9/6/17	Jordancup, W. Australia.
15218	Pte.	SOLOMON, L. E.	13th Australian Arty.	16/10/17	Longford, Tasmania.
	W.O.	SOLOMON, M.	H.M.S. "Queen"	1916	
1367	Pte.	SOLOMON, M.	32nd Australian Inf.	18/8/16	47, Hay Street, Subiaco, N.S.W.
35042	Pte.	SOLOMON, M.	23rd Northumberland Fus.	9/4/17	9, Pannure Place, Edinburgh.
7449	Pte.	SOLOMON, M.	1st Scots Guards	17/9/14	19, Clive Terrace, Great Horton, Bradford.
34657	Pte.	SOLOMON, N. C.	15th R. W. Fusiliers	14/10/16	Jewish Cemetery, Plashet, London, E.
63810	A/C.Q.M.S.	SOLOMON, R.	Can. Inf. Brit. Col. Regt.	5/12/18	Vancouver.
2960	Sgt.	SOLOMONS, A.	12th Middlesex Regt.	26/9/16	6, Abersham Road, London N.
43440	Pte.	SOLOMONS, A.	10th Royal Dublin Fusiliers	28/4/17	1, Regal Place, London, E.
570657	L/Cpl.	SOLOMONS (SELMAN) B.			
40406	Pte.	SOLOMONS, C.	1/17th London Regt.	6/12/17	25, Sonning Buildings, London, E.
R/23189	L/Cpl.	SOLOMONS, F.	1/6th Seaforth Highlanders	25/10/18	8, Reade Avenue, Blackpool.
474071	Rfm.	SOLOMONS, H.	9th K.R.R.C.	21/3/18	12, Frostie Mansions, London, E.
5540	Rfm.	SOLOMONS, H.	1/12th London Regt.	2/12/17	34, Ivy Street, London, N.
324414	Rfm.	SOLOMONS, H.	6th London Regt.	21/2/17	15, Bancroft Road, London, E.
5/8830	Rfm.	SOLOMONS, I.	1/6th London Regt.	30/11/17	55, Wentworth Street Dwellings, London, E.
54863	2/A.M.	SOLOMONS, J.	1st Rifle Brigade	2/11/14	88d, Pelham Street, London, E.
8830	Rfm.	SOLOMONS (KNOWLES), J.	4th Sq. R.A.F.	6/1/18	3, Maidman Street, London, E.
J/3059	Sgt.	SOLOMONS, L.	1st Rifle Brigade	2/11/14	6, Thackeray Buildings, Russell Square, London, W.
R/9593	Rfm.	SOLOMONS, L.	40th Royal Fusiliers	21/8/18	45, High Street, Marylebone, London, W.
26368	Pte.	SOLOMONS, M.	1st K.R.R.C.	27/7/16	1, Buckle Street Buildings, London, E.
21318	L/Cpl.	SOLOMONS, M.	3rd Worcester Regt.	13/7/16	44, Rectory Square, London, E.
27226	Rfm.	SOLOMONS, M.	8th Middlesex Regt.	24/8/18	5, Cromer Street, London, W.C.
			2nd K.R.R.C.	31/3/18	276, Cambridge Road, London, N.E.

119

N.C.O.'S AND MEN—Continued.

No.	Rank. Name.	Regiment.	Date of Death.	Address.
5513	Pte. SOLOMONS, M.	13th London Regt.	16/7/16	16, Willow Buildings Road, London, N.
62478	Pte. SOLOMONS, S.	2nd Royal Fusiliers	20/10/18	39, Harman Street, London, N.
572664	Rfm. SOLOMONS, S.	17th London Regt.	6/2/18	4, Anglesea Street, London, E.
29116	Pte. SOLOMONS, T.	7th R. Dublin Fusiliers	8/6/17	18, Beach Street, Manchester.
	Steward SPANIER, M. H.	H.M.S. "Queen Mary"	1916	
194083	Gnr. SPEAKMASTER, E.	50th Bde. R.F.A.	2/10/18	110, Jamaica Street, London, E.1.
202776	Pte. SPEAR, M.	2/1st London Regt.	17/5/17	126, Wentworth Dwellings, London, E.
9437	Pte. SPERO, J.	1st Dorset Regt.	3/5/15	53, Artingworth Street, West Ham, London.
3141	Rfm. SPERO, M.	17th London Regt.	17/9/15	15, Cecil Street, London, E.
330253	Pte. SPILG, W.	9th Highland L.I.	28/5/17	64, Jamieson Street, Glasgow.
A/204188	Rfm. SPRINGER, M.	13th K.R.R.C.	4/11/18	35, Kyverdale Road, London, N.
302933	Rfm. SPURLING, M. W.	1/L.R.B.	15/8/17	67, Blenheim Gardens, London, N.W.2.
17809	Rfm. SPURLING, S.	1st Rifle Brigade	15/6/18	20c, Newcastle Place, London, E.1.
9731	Pte. STAAL, E.	2nd Royal Scots	26/11/14	5, Canrobert Street, London, E.
62526	2/A.M. STABINSKY, I.	R.A.F.	25/4/17	5, Tottenham Street, London, W.1.
2685	Rfm. STAHL, E. F.	21st London Regt.	25/5/15	118, Kennington Road, London, S.E.
36773	Sgt. STAHL, J.	7th E. Lancs. Regt.	23/9/17	1, Bellott Street, Manchester.
6427	Pte. STAMM, I. (WASHINGTON, C.)			
20831	Spr. STANDER, B.	1st King's Liv'pool Regt.	10/3/15	98, Wentworth Buildings, London, E.
491141	Pte. STAWGKRY, S. M.	23rd Fld. Coy. R.E.	9/5/15	16, Denmark Street, London, E.
84239	Gnr. STEIN, D.	42nd Canadian Inf.	9/4/17	Georgetown, Ontario, Canada.
24148	Pte. STEIN, L.	41st T.M.B., R.G.A.	18/5/18	64, Dixon Avenue, Glasgow.
2778	L/Cpt. STEIN, W.	20th Middlesex Regt.	23/11/17	16, Challis Court, London, E.
41604	Pte. STEINBERG, A.	58th Australian Inf.	12/5/17	102, Bull Street, Cook Hill, Newcastle, N.S.W.
2218a	Pte. STEINBERG, A. J.	17th W. Yorks. Regt.	31/8/17	17, Meanwood Street, Leeds.
23708	Pte. STEINBERG, E.	9th Australian Inf.	20/4/16	123, Queen Street, Brisbane, Queensland.
24046	Pte. STEINBERG, H.	15th D.L.I.	3/2/16	42, Donovan Road, Muswell Hill, London, N.
40287	Pte. STEINBERG, I.	2nd R. W. Surrey Regt.	11/12/16	4, Nile Street, Sunderland.
27348	A/Sgt. STEINBERG, J. I.	1st Cameron Highlanders	21/9/16	17, Meanwood Street, Leeds.
M/252777	Pte. STEINBERG, M. L.	R.A.F.	4/6/18	24, Leopold Terrace, Leeds.
20565	L/Cpl. STEINBERG, S. R.	1st Base D., M.T. R.A.S.C.	8/11/18	39, Trafalgar Street, Leeds.
41990	Pte. STEPHAM, S.	12th Middlesex Regt.	17/7/16	22, Brondesbury Park, London, N.W.
257	Pte. STERN, H.	2nd Bedford Regt.	1/7/18	10, Cavendish Place, Brighton.
	Stoker STERN, W.	Zion Mule Corps		Alexandria.
15720	Pte. STERN, M.	H.M.S. "Pathfinder"	5/9/14	Bell Lane, London, E.
319489	Pte. STERNHEIM, A. H.	8th S. L. I. attd. T.M.B.	19/8/17	100, Blenheim Street, Newcastle-on-Tyne.
39396	Pte. STIBBE, M.	R.A.S.C.	8/11/18	22, Gloucester Road, Newcastle-on-Tyne.
324	Pte. STIEBEL, L.	2nd Northumberland Fus.	12/10/18	5, Cleveland Gardens, London, E.
R/19682	L/Cpl. STODEL, I. A.	13th Australian Inf.	3/5/15	44, Garfield Street, Launceston, Tasmania.
10821	Pte. STODEL, J.	16th K.R.R.C.	25/9/17	95, High Street, Merton.
11479	Pte. STOMOFF, M.	8th West Riding Regt.	12/8/15	14, Whitelock Street, Leeds.
1060097	Pte. STONE, A.	23rd Middlesex Regt.	1/10/16	63, Bacon Street, London, E.
59875	Pte. STONE, H.	Royal Canadian Regt.	12/9/18	Yarmouth, S. Nova Scotia, Canada.
		1/6th Manchester Regt.	27/9/18	156, Dale Street, Liverpool.

N.C.O.'S AND MEN—Continued.

No.	Rank.	Name.	Regiment.	Date of Death.	Address.
33502	Pte.	STONE, R.	16th Manchester Regt.	23/4/17	11, Lancaster Buildings, Manchester.
204687	Pte.	STONE, W.	2/1st London Regt.	20/5/17	15, Woodland Terrace, Abercarn, Mon.
6550	Rfm.	STOTT, J.	1/8th London Regt.	7/10/16	22, Maple Street, London, W.
12721	Pte.	STRASSBERG, G. L.	1st K.O. Yorks. L.I.	23/7/15	105, Scotland Street, Sheffield.
2869	Rfm.	STRAUSS, A. L.	17th London Regt.	24/5/15	9a, Little Alie Street, London, E.
37746	Pte.	STRAUSS, I.	11th S. Wales Borderers	29/8/17	45, Heneage Street, London, E.
3325	Pte.	STRAUSS, R. A.	2nd London Regiment	13/11/15	2, Daleham Gardens, Hampstead, London, N.W.
S/17055	Rfm.	STRELITZ, L.	16th Rifle Brigade	16/10/16	331, Barking Road, London, E.
5980	Pte.	STRELLSOF, W.	4th London Regt.	9/9/16	2, Pacific Road, Canning Town.
J/915	L/Cpl.	STRONG, H.	38th Royal Fusiliers	2/11/18	243, Cornwall Road, Kensington, London, W.1.
3518	Cadet	STYER, W. B.	28th London Regt.	3/11/16	12, Wedderburn Road, London, N.W.
616149	Rfm.	SUCKLING, H.	1/19th London Regt.	1/9/18	95, Charles Street, London, E.
380311	Pte.	SUCKMAN, J.	13th King's Liverpool Rgt.	31/8/18	135, Redman's Road, London, E.
27829	L/Cpl.	SUGARMAN, M.	17th Manchester Regt.	30/7/16	142, Elizabeth Street, Salford.
4144	Pte.	SUGARMAN, M.	4th London Regt.	9/9/16	65, Newark Street, London, E.
10/1331	Pte.	SUGARMAN, S.	12th East Yorks. Regt.	15/8/16	Lake Hotel Buildings, Boksburg, Transvaal.
73302	Pte.	SULKIN, M.	184th M.G.C.	20/1/18	55, Teesdale Street, London, E.
30749	Gnr.	SULTAN, J.	90th M.G.C.	9/7/16	14, Great Passage Street, Hull.
276	Pte.	SUSMAN, J.	1/1st Bucks. Battn.	15/8/16	146, Brunswick Street, London, N.E.
80304	Pte.	SWANGER, C.	4th Middx. Inf. Lab. Coy.	28/11/18	30, Townley Street, Cheetham, Manchester.
5159	Pte.	SWEDLOFF, S.	1/7th London Regt.	24/2/17	109, Redman Road, London, E.
48423	Pte.	SWEDE, J. A. M.	14th Royal Warwick. Regt.	25/8/18	21, Albany Road, Liverpool.
612068	Pte.	SWERDLEN, H.	1/19th London Regt.	21/3/18	London.
2/6827	Pte.	SYKES, R.	2nd London Regt.	10/5/17	132, Amhurst Road, London, N.E.
41857	Pte.	SYMON, I. D.	1st K.O.S.B.	23/10/18	45, Great Patrick Square, Edinburgh.
2371	Pte.	SYMONS, E.	22nd Australian Inf.	4/10/17	3, Egal Street, Richmond, Victoria, Australia.
493415	Rfm.	TANNEN, P.	2/6th London Regt.	13/12/17	49, Sydney Road, Stoke Newington, London, N.E.
1898	Pte.	TARASOV, S.	34th Australian Inf.	8/5/18	3, Ellingham Road, Shepherd's Bush, London, W.
8347	L/Cpl.	TASCH, F. G.	1st Border Regt.	14/5/15	29, Crown Street, Glasgow.
41820	Pte.	TAYLOR, A.	2nd Royal Scots Fusiliers	30/9/18	21, Portland Road, Bradford.
1122	Cpl.	TAYLOR, J.	1st Lancashire Fusiliers	25/4/15	99, Brunswick Road, Birmingham.
5925	Pte.	TAYLOR, H.	25th Australian Inf.	6/10/17	45, Morning Lane, Hackney, London, N.E.
2552	Pte.	TETTELBAUM, A.	2/10th London Regt.	15/2/17	181, Vallance Road, London, E.
21/5008	Pte.	TENNENBAUM, J.	2nd London Regt.	8/9/16	1, Carlton Terrace, Swansea.
472499	Rfm.	TENNENS, J.	1/12th London Regt.	25/4/18	33, Turnham Green Terrace, London, N.
J/148	C.S.M.	TENNENS, P.	38th Royal Fusiliers	18/10/18	15, Winterton Street, London, E.
S/17779	Rfm.	THEOBALD, J.	1st Rifle Brigade	25/6/18	117, Bedford Street, London, E.
115200	Pte.	TOBIAS, J.	8th M.G. Bn.	25/3/18	6, Elsie House, Philip Street, London, E.
8/397	Rfm.	TOBIAS, J.	1st Rifle Brigade	1/7/16	29, St. Luke Street, North Street, Leeds.
267261	Pte.	TOMPOFSKI, M. (M.M.)	1/8th West Yorks. Regt.	28/9/18	29, Goulden Road, Withington, Manchester.
6968	Pte.	TORRES, S. D.	10th Royal Fusiliers	17/11/16	2, Somali Road, London, N.W.
J/2716	L/Cpl.	TRACHTENBERG, M. I.	39th Royal Fusiliers	12/10/18	

121

N.C.O.'S AND MEN—Continued.

No.	Rank. Name.	Regiment.	Date of Death.	Address.
146227	Cpl. TRAGHEIM, E.	4th Special Battn. R.E.	29/6/16	12, Battlefield Gardens, Langside, Glasgow.
775	Rfm. TRAGHEIM (TRAVERS), E.	8th Rifle Brigade	6/7/15	12, Battlefield Gardens, Langside, Glasgow.
66093	Pte. TRAPPLER, A. E.	10th Balloon Sect., R.A.F.	15/7/18	59, Lorna Road, Hove, Sussex.
72560	L/Cpl. TRESMAN, H. J.	2nd West Yorks. Regt.	26/5/18	171a, Mare Street, London, N.E.
1750	Pte. TRIGGER, S. W.	50th Australian Inf.	16/8/16	Hamilton, Victoria.
34327	Pte. TROTSKEY, S. R.	7th Fld. Amb. R.A.M.C.	14/6/17	105, Cambridge Road, London, E.
1246	Tpr. TRUEFITT, C. J.	Essex Yeomanry	14/5/15	32, Cranbourne Gardens, London, S.E.
J/647	Sergt. TRUEFITT, E. E.	39th Royal Fusiliers	29/8/18	9, Duke Street, London, W.1.
M/4068o	Pte. TUBB, J.	1144th Coy., R.A.S.C.	25/11/18	54, Barnsley Street, Bethnal Green, London, E.
16701	Pte. TYLER, A.	4th South African Inf.	1916	Park Hotel, Bethlehem, S. Africa.
17032	L/Cpl. TYMON, R.	1st Royal Welsh Fusiliers	21/5/18	128, West Leigh Lane, West Leigh, Lancs.
J/3904	Pte. UNAL, H.	38/40th Royal Fusiliers	22/3/19	18, Lord Street, Cheetham, Manchester.
204079	Pte. VALENCIA, H.	1/2nd London Regt.	16/8/17	40, South Grove, London, E
184984	Flight Cadet VALENTINE, J.	R.A.F.	18/8/18	Johannesburg, South Africa.
1030632	Pte. VALINS, S.	13th Canadian Inf.	8/8/18	28, Chaple Place, Liverpool.
2663	Pte. VALLANCE, D.	1st Black Watch	8/10/15	Fifeley Cabinet Works, Duntocher, Scotland.
43756	Pte. VANDERLIND, M. S.	R.A.M.C.	18/8/15	20, Northcote Road, Bournemouth.
14529	Pte. VAN ENGLE, S.	10th Essex Regt.	5/7/16	32, Eric Street, London, E.
139515	Bdr. VAN LEER, A.	D/331 Bde. R.F.A.	16/12/17	24, Bishop's Road, Cambridge Heath, London, N.E
5762	Pte. VAN LOCKEN, J. N.	2/1st London Regt.	14/5/17	123, Brunswick Buildings, Aldgate, London, E.
53146	Sgt. VAN PRAAG, B.	15th D.L.I.	4/10/17	101, Caledonian Road, London, N.1.
3448	Rfm. VAN RYN, D.	9th London Regt.	24/4/15	Willesden Cemetery, London, N.W.
2641	Rfm. VAN THAL, M. J.	2nd Rifle Brigade	9/5/15	91, Addison Gardens, London, W.
20110	Pte. VAN THAL, S.	24th Royal Fusiliers	26/4/17	100, Sutherland Avenue, London, W.
30783	Pte. VAN WHYE, S.	9th Lancashire Fusiliers	6/9/17	44, Yale Court, Honeybourne Road, London, N.W.
1730	Dvr. VERIEN, E.	6th D.A.C., R.F.A.	5/3/17	31, Tenter Street, London, E.
202834	Pte. VERBLOWSKY, H.	2/1st London Regt.	14/9/17	84, High Street, Whitechapel, London, E.
35722	Pte. VIGDOSKY, H.	11th S. W. Borderers	31/1/17	42, Jane Street, Commercial Road, London, E.1.
199890	L/Cpl. VINEFSKY, A.	70th Labour Company	13/4/18	36, Bedford Street, Commercial Road, London, E.
42509	Pte. VOGEL, E.	97th T.M.B.	9/7/17	106, Elizabeth Street, Cheetham, Manchester.
37561	Gnr. VORZANGER, B.	124th Hy. By. R.G.A.	15/7/16	144, Wellbourne Road, Tottenham, London, N.
4451	Cpl. WACHMAN, R.	48th Australian Inf.	11/4/17	179, Lake Street, Perth, W.A.
7800	Pte. WAGNER, H.	18th Army Cyclist Corps	21/10/17	80, Hedsor Buildings, London, E.2.
5421	Pte. WALLACK, M.	1/6th West Yorks. Regt.	11/10/18	5, Holme's Avenue, London, E.
557816	Pte. WANGER N.	102nd Labour Corps	15/9/18	67, Kingsland Road, London, E.
1783	Sgt. WARTMAN, A. E.	Canadian A.M.C.	16/10/16	Newburgh, Ontario, Canada.
461378	Pte. WASKEY, S.	44th Canadian Inf.	25/10/16	58, Powis Street, Woolwich, London, S.E.
3923	Pte. WATCHMAN, A. E.	50th Australian Inf.	16/8/16	Coromandel Valley, S. Australia.
1147	Sgt. WEIHS, L.	1st Royal Fusiliers	14/4/17	396, City Road, London, E.C.
6029	Rfm. WEIL, R. C.	9th London Regiment	24/9/16	102, Grosvenor Road, London, N.

N.C.O.'S AND MEN—Continued.

No.	Rank.	Name.	Regiment.	Date of Death.	Address.
30831	Pte.	WEIN, M.	1st R. W. Kent Regt.	27/9/18	8, Bruce Grove Road, Tottenham, London, N.
X/225	Pte.	WEINBERG, A.	S. African Medical Corps	17/10/18	Grand Hotel, Kimberley, S. Africa.
50008	Pte.	WEINBERG, H.	1st Garr. Bn. Bedford Rgt.	9/10/18	85, Bedford Street, London, E.
35757	Pte.	WEINBERG, H.	1st Manchester Regt.	9/1/17	79, Stocks Street, Manchester.
J/1042	Pte.	WEINBERG, W.	38th Royal Fusiliers	26/10/18	126, Vallance Road, London, E.1.
2538	Rfm.	WEINER, J. D.	1/5th London Regt.	1/7/16	25, Spital Square, London, E.
283399	Pte.	WEINER, P.	2/4th London Regt.	14/5/17	72, Nelson Street, London, E.
695	Pte.	WEINGOTT, A. A.	13th Australian Inf.	2/5/15	380, Annadale Street, Annadale, N.S.W.
127	Pte.	WEINGOTT, S.	1st Australian Inf.	5/6/15	380, Annadale Street, Annadale, N.S.W.
5748	Pte.	WEISBERG, J.	4th Middlesex Regt.	26/10/14	109, Albert Road, W. Kilburn, London, N.W.
260196	Pte.	WELT, H.	8th Worcester Regt.	27/8/17	12, Shepherd Street Buildings, London, E. Alexandria.
366	Pte.	WERTHEIMER, B.	Zion Mule Corps	10/8/15	South Port, Queensland.
1022	Pte.	WESTERBERG, E. A.	38th Australian Inf.	11/10/17	7, Adam Street, London, W.
252388	Cpl.	WHITE, G. B.	2/3rd London Regt.	15/5/17	59, Teneriffe Street, Manchester.
41866	Pte.	WHITE, J.	70th Labour Coy.	24/9/17	37, Elight Street, Vrededorp, S. Africa.
5469	Pte.	WHITE, J. R.	4th S. African Inf.	15/10/16	196, Royal Street, E. Perth, W.A.
545	Pte.	WHITE, M.	51st Australian Inf.	25/4/18	
1792	Sgt.	WHITEFIELD, C. S. (M.S.M.)	4th Australian Inf.	17/4/18	78, Voord Street, Johannesburg, S. Africa.
88839	Pte.	WHITEFIELD, L.	152nd M.G.C.	22/11/17	125, Hospital Street, Glasgow.
20655	Pte.	WHITESMAN, N.	10th R. Warwick Regt.	9/6/17	417, Mile End Road, London, E.
9526	Pte.	WILLIAMS, F.	2nd R. Irish Rifles	10/8/17	67, Tylacelyn Road, Penygraig, S. Wales.
442831	Pte	WILLIAMS, J.	2nd Canadian Inf.	3/9/16	65, 125th Street, New York, U.S.A.
141430	Pte.	WILLIAMS, N. A.	206th M.G.C.	21/3/18	172, Green Street, Bethnal Green, London, E.
2269	Pte.	WILSON, B. G.	57th Australian Inf.	5/3/18	Bennett Street, Long Gully, Bendigo, Victoria.
141927	Pte.	WINSTONE, J. (WAINSTAIN)	13th Brigade, R.F.A.	1916	62, Adelphi Street, Glasgow.
3963	Cpl.	WITTNER, H.	22nd Australian Inf.	21/2/17	Dalgety Street, St. Kilda, Victoria.
9118	Pte.	WOLF, H.	1st Royal Fusiliers	9/6/15	80, Canonbury Avenue, London, N.
21366	Pte.	WOLFE, S.	2nd Auckland I.B., N.Z.	1/9/18	36, Crown Street, Newcastle.
204304	Pte.	WOLFSBERGEN, H.	2/1st London Regt.	14/9/17	73, Stoke Newington Road, London, N.
115620	Pte.	WOLLMAN, M.	227th M.G.C.	25/11/17	30, Great Garden Street, London, E.
3619	Pte.	WOOD, B.	24th Royal Fusiliers	30/4/17	71, Tachbrook Street, London, S.W.
269457	Pte.	WOODMAN, M.	2/7th King's Liverpool Rgt.	26/6/17	216, Bury New Road, Manchester.
3230199	Pte.	WOODROW, A.	4th Canadian Inf.	31/8/18	695, Markham Street, Toronto.
2318	Pte.	WOODS, L.	3rd Australian Inf.	26/9/17	18, Dick Street, Chippendale, Sydney.
A/204003	Rfm.	WOOLF, B. J.	13th K.R.R.C.	23/8/18	2, Colberg Place, Stamford Hill, London, N.
332364	L/Cpl.	WOOLF, H.	9th King's Liverpool Regt.	28/8/18	35, Great Oxford Street, Liverpool.
G/68446	Pte.	WOOLF, H. B.	2/2nd London Regt.	26/10/17	128, Wheeler Street, Birmingham.
146370	Pnr.	WOOLF, H. L.	1st Bn. Special Bde., R.E.	1/7/16	22, Belsize Park Gardens, London, N.W.
43305	Rfm.	WOOLF, H.	15th Royal Irish Rifles	27/4/18	1, New Street, Upper Baker Street, London, N.W.
18845	Rfm.	WOOLF, J.	16th K.R.R.C.	12/8/16	130, Hogarth Houses, London, E.
43564	Pte.	WOOLF, J.	9th King's Own Yorks. L.I.	28/4/17	23, Brady Street Buildings, London, E.
43389	Pte.	WOOLF, J.	9th Royal Irish Rifles	21/8/17	19, Esmond Road, London, W.

123

N.C.O.'S AND MEN—Continued.

No.	Rank.	Name.	Regiment.	Date of Death.	Address.
1354	Pte.	WOOLF, J. L.	6th London Regt.	20/5/15	49, Mortimer Street, Kensal Rise, London, N.W.
52072	Pte.	WOOLF, L.	1st Cheshire Regt.	28/6/18	53, Rothschild Buildings, London, E.
42488	Pte.	WOOLF, M.	5th South Wales Borderers	7/6/18	24, Jaes Street, Covent Garden, London, W.
2520	Rfm.	WOOLF, N.	17th London Regt.	17/9/15	14, Lincoln Street London, E.
202430	Pte.	WOOLF, R.	3/5th Lancashire Fusiliers	10/10/17	37, Dow Street, Salford, Manchester.
C/3059	Sig.	WOOLF, S.	17th K.R.R.C.	20/9/17	68, Walsingham Road, Hove, Sussex.
30661	Pte.	WOOLFE, S.	13th Royal Scots Regt.	15/9/16	39, Apsley Place, Glasgow.
24700	Pte.	WOOLFSON, S.	1st Royal Warwick. Regt.	1/11/18	54, Leazes Park Road, Newcastle,
21290	Pte.	WOOLMAN, A.	15th Durham L.I.	16/9/16	14, Broomhall Street, Sheffield.
324771	Rfm.	WOLLMAN, E.	1/17th London Regt.	1/9/18	30, Great Garden Street, London, E.
4495	Pte.	WRIGHT, J.	1/1st Bucks, Battn.	8/9/16	66, Settles Street, London, E.
33602	Rfm.	WYLER, J. M.	1/15th London Regt.	23/3/18	6, Brandreth Road, Balham, London, S.W.
47208	Pte.	WYNE, J. B.	19th Manchester Regt.	2/8/17	37, Brompton Street, Manchester.
40310	Pte.	YAFFIN, J.	18th W. Yorks. Regt.	2/3/17	5, Russell Place, Woodhouse Lane, Leeds.
7028	Pte.	YUTKOVITCH, M.	1st London Regt.	7/4/17	18, Spital Street, London, E.
804	Pte.	ZANDER, C. O.	10th Australian Inf.	22/8/16	Alexandria.
29566	Pte.	ZAOUI, M.	Zion Mule Corps	17/5/15	66, Bridon Ferry Road, Neath, S. Wales.
270158	L/Cpl.	ZEILER, M.	1st R. Welsh Fusiliers	14/5/17	82, Grove Street, London, E.2.
7999	Pte.	ZELINSKY, A.	Canadian Inf.	14/10/18	21, Rodney Bridge, London, E.1.
423346	Pte.	ZEPPENFIELD, P.	2nd W. Riding Regt.	18/4/15	32, King Edward Street, London, N.E.
9881	Pte.	ZIEGELMAN, S.	2/10th London Regt.	4/8/17	60, Royal Arcade, Weston-Super-Mare.
C/6123	Pte.	ZIMMERMAN, H.	2nd Oxford and Bucks.L.I.	21/10/14	34, Kensington Gardens, Birmingham.
J/761	Rfm.	ZIMMERMAN, J.	16th K.R.R.C.	24/4/17	34, Kensington Gardens, Birmingham.
42533	Pte.	ZIMMERMAN, M.	39th Royal Fusiliers	8/10/18	34, Kensington Gardens, Birmingham.
267774	Pte.	ZIMMERMAN, N.	2nd Yorkshire Regt.	8/5/18	184, High Street, Shadwell, London, E.
14678	Pte.	ZIMMERMAN, S.	2/7th Notts. & Derby Regt.	21/3/18	34, Kensington Gardens, Birmingham.
584148	Pte.	ZISKIND, H.	5th Oxford and Bucks.L.I.	24/8/16	19, Belgravia Street, London, E.
11057	Pte.	ZODICKSON, H.	14th South Lancs. Regt.	4/11/18	11, Southampton Street, Fitzroy Square, London, W.
73055	L/Cpl.	ZOLOWSKI, E. (M.M.)	18th K. Liverpool Regt.	1/7/17	7a, King Edward Road, London, N.E.
204673	Pte.	ZOTNICK, M.	9th Notts. and Derby Regt.	4/11/18	80, Allen Street, Sheffield.
			2/5th Y. and Lanc. Regt.	11/4/18	

Roll of Honour.

Additional List.

Officers.

Name.	Regiment.	Date of Death.	Address.
Lieut. Feinhols, H.	Cape Corps	8/10/18	Kimberley, S. Africa.
Lieut. Joffe, W. (D.S.O.)	K.O.Y.L.I. attached R.A.F.	1/10/18	Kimberley, S. Africa.
Lieut. Josephi, E. H.	R.A.S.C.	23/1/17	North View, Granville Road, N. Finchley, N.
Cadet Levene-Davis, J. H.	Inns of Court O.T.C.	18/1/16	3, Cleve Road, London, N.W.
Lieut. Levy, J.	1/5th Norfolk Regt.	19/4/17	2, Thornfield Road, Linthorpe, Middlesbrough.
2nd-Lieut. Solomon, K. M. H.	11th Gloucestershire Regt.	18/9/15	c/o London Bank of Australia, 71, Old Broad Street, London, E.C.

N.C.O.'s and Men.

No.	Name.	Regiment.	Date of Death.	Address.
5227	Pte. Apple, A. N.	4th Cameron Hrs.	10/10/16	P.O. Box 75, Aluval North, Cape Province, S. Africa.
45217	Pte. Aronheim, S.	1st Essex Regt.	23/8/18	8, Newbold Street, E.1.
17446	Pte. Aronson, M.	9th Royal Fusiliers	30/11/17	90, White Horse Lane, Mile End, London, E.
1480	Sergt. Bamberg, M.	1st Northumberland Fus.	24/8/14	9, Queen's Block, Stoney Lane, London, E.
6738	Pte. Bennett, D.	R.A.M.C.	23/9/18	103, Foulden Road, London, N.16.
29303	Pte. Berman, S.	4th King's Liverpool Regt.	19/8/16	93, Linacre Road, Litherland, Liverpool.
	Pilot Best, D.	Mersey Pilot Service	29/12/18	70, Brunswick Road, Liverpool.
63121	Q.M.S. Conquy, J. S.	R.A.M.C.	27/12/18	50, Clifton Gardens, London, W.
27211	Pte. Copeland, P.	15th Hampshire Regt.	7/6/17	207, Waddell Street, Glasgow.

N.C.O.'S AND MEN—Continued.

No.	Name.	Regiment.	Date of Death.	Address.
J/58	Pte. Cregor, C.	38th Royal Fusiliers	3/6/19	56, Victoria Park Road, London, N.E.
282873	Pte. Davies, B.	1/4th London Regt	4/11/18	94, Fairholt Road, London, N.
13848	Pte. Davis, S.	Army Cyclist Corps	2/5/17	253, Hawthorne Road, Liverpool.
	S/Gnr. Emanuel (Kelly), J.	Royal Navy	6/1/19	4455, Dover Street, Chicago, U.S.A.
23802	Pte. Friedlander, H.	R.A.M.C.	14/7/16	86, Imperial Avenue, Stoke Newington, London, N.E.
451104	Pte. Furst (Hurst), H.	1/11th London Regt.	5/3/18	24, Burma Road, London, N.16.
901158	Gnr. Hart (Assenheim) P.	D/290 Bgde. R.F.A.	15/10/17	4, Russell Street, Brighton, Sussex.
491966	Pte. Isaacs, I. E.	2/13th London Regt.	25/5/17	39, Manor Road, London, N.16.
358589	Pte. Kafkevitch, E.	10th King's Liverpool Regt.	3/7/17	94, Stock Street, Cheetham, Manchester.
G/68140	Pte. Kitchenoff, W.	13th Royal Fusiliers	5/4/18	46c, Friar Stile Road, Richmond.
385113	Pte. Klein, M.	2/8th London Regt.	2/10/17	
	Pte. Kovanski, I. M.	2nd S. African Infy.	8/10/18	Kimberley, S. Africa.
11605	Pte. Leventhal, M.	1st Highland L. Infy.	19/12/14	62, Causewayside, Edinburgh.
46652	Pte. Levey, I.	16th Manchester Regt.	5/4/17	287, Bury New Road, Manchester.
1908	Cpl. Lipschitz, L.	S.A.M.C.	9/10/18	Kimberley, S. Africa.
9034	L/Cpl. Michaels, J.	2nd Somerset L. Infy.	20/6/19	42, Hogarth Houses, London, E.
42478	Pte. Miketansky, L.	11th Hampshire Regt.	17/5/18	10, Tottenham Street, London, W.C.
S/27256	Rfm. Nieman, E	16th Rifle Brigade	14/2/17	59, Shut Road, Fairfield, Liverpool.
39825	Pte. Newhouse, M.	14th Highland L. Infy.	24/11/17	119, Upper Adelaide Street, Blackpool.
23019	L/Cpl. Rose, H.	166th Coy. M.G.C.	30/11/17	24, Rosemount Avenue, Orangezicht, S. Africa.
11355	Pte. Slonimski, S.	8th C.M.R.	16/12/15	
27193	Pte. Smollen, D.	7th Training Res. Batt.	28/9/17	227, Newport Road, Middlesbrough
6184	Telegraphist Solomon, M.	R.N.V.R.	4/10/18	4, Colberg Place, Stamford Hill, London, N.16.
24001	Cpl. Steinberg, E.	2nd R.W. Surrey Regt.	27/10/18	4, Donovan Road, Muswell Hill, London, N.
6817	L/Cpl. Stern, P. (M.M.)	10th Northumberland Fus.	29/10/18	100, Blenheim Street, Newcastle-on-Tyne.
42618	Pte. Vander Molen, S.	1/8th Royal Scots	2/1/19	56, Cressy Houses, Stepney, London, E.
126694	Gnr. Wolfe, S.	165 A.A. Batty. R.G.A.	18/12/18	15, Cobb Street, Boston, Mass, U.S.A.
17470	Pte. Worman, A. A.	7th East Kent Regt.	4/8/18	5, Doveton Street, London, E.1.

OFFICIAL RECORDS OF GALLANT DEEDS

From the "London Gazette."

MILITARY CROSS.

Capt. Daniel S. Aarons, Australian Infantry.
"For conspicuous gallantry and devotion to duty. He took command of his company and led his men forward with great gallantry. Later, he went back under the most intense fire to report the situation." †

Capt. Everard Cecil Abraham, M.B., Royal Army Medical Corps.
"For conspicuous gallantry and devotion to duty when in charge of a bearer division during seven days' operations. The rapid and efficient clearing of wounded from the field was largely due to his efforts. During a heavy gas shell bombardment he led his bearers through the barrage to rescue men affected by the gas."

Sec.-Lieut. Leslie Abraham, Yeomanry.
"For conspicuous gallantry and devotion to duty. When the enemy attacked his position, by his skilful leadership he beat off three separate attacks inflicting heavy casualties on the enemy, and maintained his position intact."

Lieut. Frank Abrahams, Royal Field Artillery.
"For conspicuous gallantry and devotion to duty. As battery signalling officer, regardless of personal safety, he superintended the mending of wires under heavy shell fire, encouraging the signallers and men of the battery in their task by his example of energy and devotion to duty."

Lieut. Ernest Ansell, 1st Bn. Canadian Infantry.
"During the operations near Upton Wood on 30th August, 1918, he led his platoon with great skill and gallantry in face of heavy fire and captured two machine guns, with 15 prisoners, and killed many others. When his company commander became a casualty he took command, and beat off a determined counter-attack. His courage and leadership throughout the operation inspired his men with the greatest confidence."

† Also awarded bar to M.C.

Sec.-Lieut. Sampson Adler, 10th Bn. Cheshire Regiment, attd. 9th Bn.

"For conspicuous gallantry and good leadership during operations near Jenlain on the 3rd November, 1918, on the occasion of an enemy withdrawal. After his company commander and the other officers had become casualties, he reorganised the company and pushed forward under intense shell fire though out of touch on both flanks, making ground and capturing prisoners. He remained in command of his company for a considerable time after being wounded."

Sec.-Lieut. Cecil Aserman, Royal Garrison Artillery (Anti-Aircraft).

"For conspicuous gallantry and devotion to duty. When his gun came under heavy fire he called for volunteers, and removed it. Thirty seconds later a shell pitched on the spot where the gun had been standing, and eight more within five yards. By his coolness and prompt action the gun and lorry escaped untouched. His quick decision and cool bearing have been noteworthy at all times."

Major Ernest Y. Benjamin, Canadian Infantry.

"For conspicuous gallantry and devotion to duty. He was detailed to establish visual communication. He displayed great courage and determination and succeeded in establishing his post in close proximity and maintaining visual communication under most trying circumstances."

Sec.-Lieut. Felix Joseph Benzimra, Machine Gun Corps.

"For conspicuous gallantry and devotion to duty when commanding his section of guns in a forward position. He maintained his ground in spite of intense enemy fire and hostile counter attacks, by his timely aid greatly assisting to defeat the latter. Although twice buried and gassed, he refused to leave his post, and only reported sick on his return to camp on the following day."

Sec.-Lieut. Maurice Leon Bernstein,* 11th Lancashire Fusiliers.

"For conspicuous gallantry and devotion to duty. He led his platoon with great skill and dash to the attack and capture of an enemy position. Although wounded before the final assault, he led his men and captured thirty prisoners, afterwards helping to reorganise, until sent to the Dressing Station."

Lieut. Arthur Henry Beer,* Royal Field Artillery.

"For conspicuous gallantry and devotion to duty. When all communications were cut and runners could not get through to the batteries this officer volunteered to go forward, and at great personal risk went round all the batteries, collecting information and arranging for reinforcements. Later, while reconnoitering new positions he was severely wounded."

Note.—An asterisk after name denotes killed in action.

MILITARY CROSS

Capt. Roy Neville Benjamin, 12th Bn., attd. 10th Bn. Royal Fusiliers.

"For conspicuous gallantry and devotion to duty. When the enemy counter-attacked and almost surrounded his company, he formed a defensive flank and drove the enemy back. For 48 hours he was continuously attacked, and four times he launched counter-attacks, depriving the enemy of any ground he had gained. Though he and his men were exhausted they held on and consolidated the position, chiefly thanks to his indomitable spirit of endurance."

Capt. Philip Barnett Berliner, 2/7th London Regiment.

"For conspicuous gallantry in action. He was leading his company with great determination through the enemy's front lines when he was severely wounded in the leg, but he struggled on for a thousand yards with the help of his runner, encouraging and directing the men. All the other officers had become casualties, and his courage and endurance were of particular value to the success to the attack."

Capt. Abraham Benzecry, Machine Gun Corps.

"On September 19th, 1918, at El Tireh (Palestine), Lieut. Benzecry brought his section into action in the open, under heavy fire, to cover the advance of the infantry. The effective fire which he brought to bear on the enemy's posiions greatly contributed to the success of the attack. Throughout the day he showed the greatest gallantry and initiative in pushing his guns forward at once under heavy fire to support the infantry's advance."

Capt. Eric Philip Blashki, M.B., Royal Army Medical Corps.

"For conspicuous gallantry and devotion to duty. He went forward during an engagement and established a dressing station in an advance position. He remained at his post under heavy shelling and collected the wounded from an area swept by machine gun fire. He showed the greatest courage and resource."

Sec.-Lieut. Edward Beddington Behrens, Royal Field Artillery.

"For conspicuous gallantry and devotion to duty. During the very heavy bombardment of his battery he showed the greatest courage and promptitude in extinguishing fires amongst camouflage and ammunition. He also brought under cover a sergeant who was badly wounded. His energy prevented the destruction of much ammunition and material."

BAR TO M.C.

"For conspicuous gallantry and devotion to duty. Whilst acting as forward observation officer he maintained his communications for four hours under a heavy barrage, and sent back much useful information. On the infantry being forced to withdraw, he manned a trench with his observation post party, in addition to which he maintained communication with his battery, which was thus able to do great execution in the enemy ranks. On the following day, although all communication was cut, he succeeded in keeping the line in working order for a period of ten hours, thus enabling artillery fire to be brought to bear on hostile attacks. His fearlessness and determination were magnificent and his energy unremitting."

MILITARY CROSS

Lieut. Glynn Henry Reginald Barton, 15th Bn. Tank Corps.
"Having reached his objective with his Tank, he noticed the infantry were running short of ammunition. He got out of his Tank and distributed some 3,000 rounds of his own ammunition among them, moving about under very heavy fire from the enemy's machine-guns. When his Tank was disabled by a direct hit, he got out his Hotchkiss gun and ammunition, and with his crew joined the infantry and advanced with them. Throughout the day he set a fine example of gallantry, and his leadership and ability greatly contributed to the success of the operations."

Lieut. B. Lewis Barnett, Royal Engineers.
"For conspicuous gallantry and devotion to duty. During seven days' hard fighting this officer, who was signalling officer to the brigade, was continually out under heavy fire, superintending the laying and repairing of lines, and on one occasion, when the battalions were in front of the front line, it was owing to his devotion to duty that the brigade seldom lost communication with them. The buried cable was cut by shell fire, and he at once went out and repaired several breaks, which he located in an area exposed to the very heaviest fire and to reach which he had to traverse a barrage of intense description. His gallantry and disregard of danger were conspicuous."

Capt. W. B. L. Bonn, Welch Guards.
"For conspicuous gallantry and devotion to duty. He had his company headquarters completely destroyed by a shell at the commencement of a very heavy bombardment, he himself being buried and wounded in the arm. Nevertheless he remained at duty throughout the action and set a splendid example of grit and coolness to all ranks."

Sec.-Lieut. C. E. Barnett, 1/15th Bn. London Regt.
"For conspicuous gallantry and devotion to duty. During a critical time he collected a party of stragglers from other units and led them out under heavy machine gun and shell fire, and for seven hours held the line at a point where a break had threatened until the position was firmly established. He has previously shown great courage and resource in time of stress."

Sec.-Lieut. Edward Cohen,* 12th Royal Fusiliers.
"For conspicuous gallantry and devotion to duty. He led his platoon with great determination and skill, under heavy machine gun fire, against enemy dugouts, which he successfully bombed, taking prisoners and capturing the machine gun. He has previously done very fine work."

Lieut. Ellis James Castello, Royal Field Artillery.
"For conspicuous gallantry and devotion to duty. With the enemy at close quarters on his flank and in rear, he worked all day in the open on communications under constant machine gun and rifle fire. He restored and maintained communications that were frequently broken, and when the enemy was around the battery positions his energy and fearlessness inspired all ranks."

MILITARY CROSS

Capt. Ernest Raphael Capper,* 9th Essex Regiment.

"For conspicuous gallantry and devotion to duty. After the enemy had secured a footing in a portion of our trench he organized a bombing attack with his platoon and cleared them out, and when his original bombers had sustained causalties and were too tired to throw bombs accurately, he collected a fresh squad of men from another unit and attacked again. His excellent leading, clear orders, and great coolness under fire, very largely contributed to the success of the attack."

Sec.-Lieut. Manfred Cohen, Royal Engineers.

"For conspicuous gallantry and devotion to duty. He was in charge of a party carrying signal stores forward. His party came under very heavy fire, but he rallied his men and got the stores to their destination, making two journeys through an enemy barrage. He then established and maintained communications with very few men, working with untiring energy under heavy fire. During the withdrawal which followed he rallied parties of men, and helped to organise the new line. He showed great determination and contempt of danger, which were an example to all ranks."

Lieut. Myer Tutzer Cohen,* 42nd Canadian Infantry.

"For conspicuous gallantry and devotion to duty. While out with a patrol close to the enemy's lines he attacked a party of the enemy, killing three of them and capturing three prisoners. He remained out in No Man's Land with his men, and about two hours later he observed another party of the enemy. He again attacked and captured three more prisoners, and brought the whole of his patrol in without a casualty. He showed magnificent leadership and resource."

Lieut. W. Joseph Cowen, Canadian Cavalry.

"For conspicuous gallantry and devotion to duty as second in command of his squadron which charged an enemy battery two miles in the rear of their lines. Though badly wounded he led his men on and brought back six prisoners."

Lieut. Gerald Louis Davidson, Dorset Regiment.

"For conspicuous gallantry in attack. He led an attack across the open in daylight to take a strongly fortified 'stop.' His attack was successful and enabled the whole trench to be seized and consolidated. He was twice wounded."

C.S.-Maj. Harry Davis* (4827), 1st Bn. East Yorkshire Regiment.

"For conspicuous gallantry and devotion to duty during a violent enemy bombardment and raid. At great personal risk he carried out his duties, giving great assistance to his company commander, and by his coolness and vigilance set an excellent example to all."

Lieut. Julius Diamond,* K.O. Scottish Borderers, and Royal Flying Corps.

"For conspicuous gallantry and devotion to duty in co-operating with our artillery often under most adverse conditions. On two occasions he ranged our siege batteries on hostile battery positions causing numerous fires and explosions."

Capt. S. Davis, 4th London Regiment.

"For conspicuous gallantry and devotion to duty when in command of his company when in an attack. He was quick to grasp situations as they arose, and always kept his commanding officer fully informed of all that happened on his front. Though severely wounded during an enemy counter-attack he remained in command of his company, and it was largely owing to his courage and fine example that the position was held and consolidated."

Capt. Eric Alexander Ogilvie Durlacher,* 5th Worcester Regiment.

"For conspicuous gallantry and devotion to duty during a raid on the enemy's trenches. He carried out the task allotted to him with conspicuous success, displaying great courage and initiative throughout the raid."

Sec.-Lieut. H. William Durlacher, London Regiment.

"For conspicuous gallantry and devotion to duty in leading his platoon forward to reinforce the attacking troops who had suffered heavily and been driven back. He was constantly immersed in mud and water, and it was only by his grit and determination that a serious situation was overcome."

Capt. R. Graham Davis, Middlesex Regt. and Tank Corps.

"For conspicuous gallantry and devotion to duty. When his Tank broke down it was surrounded by the enemy and three of the gunners were wounded. When the enemy had been driven off, he went on foot and brought two gunners from another Tank to replace the casualties. He also went on foot to the assistance of another Tank which had broken down. He set a splendid example of courage and contempt of danger."

Lieut. G. H. Frederick Engel, Australian Engineers.

"For conspicuous gallantry and devotion to duty. Whilst laying a guiding tape forward he discovered a strong enemy patrol and indicated it to the garrison of the line, who counter-attacked it successfully. While marking out a communication trench to the captured position he and another officer located an enemy machine-gun post, and with a small party rushed it, capturing the garrison and two machine-guns. He rendered very valuable service."

Capt. W. H. Enoch, Oxford & Bucks. Light Infantry.

"For conspicuous gallantry and devotion to duty in a raid. As adjutant he worked out every detail with great thoroughness, and was of great assistance to companies while forming up. During the raid he advanced with battalion headquarters into the enemy front line, and by his coolness inspired all ranks with confidence."

MILITARY CROSS

Lieut. David Fallon, 1/1st Oxford and Bucks Light Infantry.
"For conspicuous gallantry in action. Although wounded, he carried out a daring reconnaissance, and obtained most valuable information. He set a splendid example throughout."

Sec.-Lieut. Donald Henry D. Freeman, Royal Field Artillery.
"For conspicuous gallantry and devotion to duty. When acting as F.O.O. he was wounded early in the day. He continued to perform his duties, and it was entirely owing to his information that the enemy counter-attacks were completely broken up."

Sec.-Lieut. Lionel Alfred Furst, Labour Corps.
"For conspicuous gallanry and devotion to duty. He marched his working party in heavy shell fire to their work, which was successfully carried out under shell, rifle and machine-gun fire, and getting them back again with but one casualty. Many of his party had never been under shell fire before. His control of inexperienced men under such condtiions was quite exceptional, and his display of coolness and courage undoubtedly caused the success of the task and the very low casualties sustained."

Capt. Charles Friend, 5th Bn. West Yorks. Regt., attd. H.Q. 185th Infantry Brigade.
"As Brigade Intelligence officer he went forward to tape out an assembly and position in advance of a line. This was done under heavy and continuous machine-gun and shell fire, and it was largely due to his courage and zeal that the troops were lined up in time for attack. During a later attack he went forward under heavy fire and established an observaion post, from which his clear and concise reports were most valuable."

Lieut. George Moss Montefuri Finsberg, 3rd (Light) Bn. Tank Corps.
"For conspicuous gallantry and devotion to duty near Estrees on the 3rd October, 1918. When the infantry were held up by two hostile strong points, although wounded in five places, he continued to drive his whippet tank in the face of the attack on this strong point. After enemy machine-gun fire had been brought to bear on him at 50 yards range, his car became ditched, and he was taken prisoner. Later he escaped and got back, although wounded in 17 places. It was largely due to his total disregard of personal safety that the enemy were forced to evacuate the strong points."

Lieut. Theodore Henri Fligelstone, 38th Bn. Royal Fusiliers.
"For conspicuous gallantry and ability. At Umm Esh Shert (Palestine), on the 22nd September, 1918, he worked his machine gun very successfully, and drove the enemy from off two miles of our front. He rendered very valuable service."

Lieut. Norman Franks, Canadian Infantry.
"For conspicuous gallantry and devotion to duty. He assembled his company for the attack in a difficult position with great skill, and showed great courage and resource in leading them to the objective, in spite of strong opposition and heavy fire. He set a splendid example throughout."

MILITARY CROSS

Lieut. C. Joseph Falk, Wiltshire Regiment.

"For conspicuous gallantry and initiative during an attack east of Noyelles on 4th November, 1918. The officers commanding the two leading companies early became casualties, and the companies became somewhat disorganised. He immediately moved forward his support company, reorganised the line and reached and consolidated the final objective, commanding all three companies until relieved by the arrival of the C.O. He has done consistent good work."

Lieut. Wilfred Maurice Guttmann, Middlesex Regiment.

"For conspicuous gallantry and devotion to duty. During a critical stage he organised a company, disposed them for defence, and by his coolness and courage kept them well under control. This timely action saved the situation, not only on his own front, but also on his left flank. Throughout the 10 days' operations he showed untiring energy and was a fine example to all ranks."

Lieut. Samuel Montague Gluckstein, Royal Field Artillery.

"For conspicuous gallantry and devotion to duty during a severe air raid in Dunkirk, when three fires were caused on the docks by the explosion of bombs. He was in a dugout, but at once proceeded with another officer while bombs were falling to extinguish the fires."

Capt. Herbert Myer Goldstein, New Zealand Medical Corps.

"For conspicuous gallantry and devotion to duty in establishing a forward aid post in our advanced lines over a mile in front of his regimental aid post. By his courageous decision to remain there in spite of heavy shelling, and his great gallantry and devotion in attending to the wounded, all the casualties were evacuated before the battalion was relieved."

Capt. Leslie Haden Guest, Royal Army Medical Corps.

"For conspicuous gallantry and devotion to duty. On the night of an attack he gallantly led his stretcher squads under heavy shell fire and collected who were lying out on newly-captured grounds. By his courageous example and disregard of danger he was the means of saving many wounded men."

Capt. R. Goldberg, Machine Gun Corps (Motor).

"For conspicuous gallantry and devotion to duty. Owing to his skill and ingenuity a howitzer was brought from a distance of twenty-four miles into action against the enemy. On another occasion he carried out a reconnaissance over difficult country under fire, and brought back valuable information."

Sec.-Lieut. L. Isaac Goldman, Royal Engineers.

"For conspicuous gallantry and devotion to duty in the Mormal Forest on 4th and 5th November, 1918. He was in command of a Tank, laying telephone lines. Two pairs of cables were carried forward through the enemy barrage and into Mormal Forest, and were maintained throughout the first night. Next morning the lines were extended to within 800 yards of Hatchette Farm, where the Tank became ditched. He immediately completed the lines to Hatchette Farm by hand and opened up an advanced signal office."

Capt. Robert Gee, V.C., Royal Fusiliers (see also page 8).
" For conspicuous gallantry in action. He encouraged his men during the attack by fearlessly exposing himself and cheering them on. When wounded he refused to retire, and urged his men on till, after being blown into the air by a shell, he was carried in half unconscious."

Capt. Nathan Leonard Harris,* 9th Royal Welsh Fusiliers.
" For conspicuous gallantry and devotion to duty as acting adjutant in an attack. When the enemy forced the front line back from some high ground he went forward and led his men in the face of the enemy's fire and recaptured the position. It was greatly due to his gallant conduct in moving along the line to reorganise regardless of the enemy's fire that the battalion was ready to meet an attack which was delivered shortly afterwards."

Lieut. M. M. Hirschfield, R.N.D., R.N.V.R.
" For conspicuous gallantry and devotion to duty. When all communications had broken down he organised a series of patrols and messengers, by means of which touch was regained with the units of the brigade at a very critical time. In addition to making excellent arrangements, he showed the greatest skill and courage in leading one of these patrols through heavy shell fire to the unit it was most necessary to warn."

Lieut. P. Henry Hart, Yorkshire Regiment.
" He led his two Stokes' guns in the attack on Neuvilly village on the night of October 10th—11th, 1918, with great gallantry and determination. When all the officers had become casualties he took over command of the company and displayed sound judgment, and after commanding for two days brought the company out, bringing also his two Stokes' guns. He showed fine leadership, and his services were invaluable to his company."

Capt. D. W. Isaacs, 4th Bn. Australian Infantry.
" For conspicuous gallantry and confident leadership near Chuignes on 23rd August, 1918. He handled his platoon successfully in the attack, and by his grasp of the situation was able to give useful assistance to the battalion on his left. His courage and resource were reflected in the work of his men."

Sec.-Lieut. Alan Edward A. Jacobs, 8th Bn. East Surrey Regiment.
" For conspicuous gallantry on several occasions, notably when, after having been for the moment forced back by a very superior number of the enemy, he rallied his platoon, and led them in a counter-attack, by which the enemy were driven back again."

Capt. Cyril Jacobs, M.B., Royal Army Medical Corps.

BAR TO M.C.

"For conspicuous gallantry and devotion to duty in forming his dressing station under heavy fire. It was once blown in on top of him and five casualties occurred, but he remained at his post and managed to evacuate all wounded. On the following day he cleared the battlefield in spite of heavy fire, and brought back twenty wounded cases."

Lieut. Ivan Albert Jacobs, East Kent Regiment.

"For conspicuous gallantry and devotion to duty as acting brigade transport officer in charge of a mule convoy carrying rations for four battalions. Guides could not be provided, the ground was quite unknown to him, the roads forward were very bad, and the night was pitch dark. In spite of heavy shelling he brought the convoy successfully to the rendezvous, after a journey lasting six hours."

Capt. Ben Jacobs, 2/5th Bn. Royal Lancaster Regiment.

"For conspcuous gallantry and good leadership. He led his company in an attack, capturing a village and repulsed several counter-attacks. Though twice wounded he remained with his men, showing utter contempt of danger. Later, he took command of another company which lost all its officers, and commanded both companies with great skill until relieved."

Capt. Henry Michael Joseph, M.B., Royal Army Medical Corps, attd. 9th Bn. Essex Regiment.

"During operations 8th—10th August, 1918, near Morlancourt, this medical officer displayed great courage and energy in dealing with the wounded. On 10th August, he moved forward immediately behind the fighting troops and saved many lives by timely action. When the objectives were gained, and battle patrols went out, the enemy's machine-gun fire was especially heavy; he nevertheless went forward and dealt with cases, carrying one badly-wounded man to a place of safety on his back under heavy fire."

Lieut. Harold Leslie Jacobs, 11th Brigade, Australian Field Artillery.

"For conspicuous gallantry and devotion to duty during the action near Montbrehain on the 5th October 1918. Two guns were knocked out by heavy enemy fire, the other section commander killed, and several casualties on detachments inflicted. Throughout this most trying period he continued to control the service of his guns and maintain the barrage fire so urgently necessary to the attacking infantry."

Major Sydney Jennings, Canadian Labour Battalion.

"For conspicuous gallantry and devotion to duty. When sections of the light railway in charge of his battalion were heavily shelled and broken in a number of places, he went the whole length of the line gathering up repairing parties from various dugouts in which they had taken shelter and effected all repairs, so enabling the traffic to proceed."

MILITARY CROSS

Lieut. Edwin George Joseph, Royal Berkshire Regiment.
"For conspicuous gallantry and devotion to duty during a night raid, when, although severely wounded while leaving the trenches he refused to go back, but remained with his platoon until they had reached their final objectives. It was mainly due to his courage and successful leadership that the operation was successful and a machine gun and several prisoners captured."

Sec.-Lieut. Lionel Jellinek, Royal Field Artillery.
"For conspicuous gallantry and devotion to duty. He cleared a refilling point under heavy shell fire and got his wagons away with very few casualties. Though the advancing enemy were close, he got the ammunition away successfully and so ensured a more sufficient supply for all guns in action during the retirement. Throughout the operations he showed increasing devotion to duty and rendered excellent service."

Lieut. David Albert Jacobs, Royal Berkshire Regiment.
"For conspicuous gallantry and devotion to duty. During an advance a good many of his men lost touch owing to the mist, but he collected as many as possible and, entirely on his own, pushed forward and took the objective, capturing and killing many of the enemy. Throughout the operations his courageous and steady leadership contributed largely to the success achieved."

C.S.M. Ernest Jacobs (7755), K.O. Yorks. L.I.
"For conspicuous gallantry in action. He assumed command and led two companies with great courage and initiative, capturing two lines of trenches and many prisoners. He remained in command for thirty-six hours, and set a splendid example to his men."

Sec.-Lieut. J. H. Jacobs, Royal Fusiliers.
"For conspicuous bravery and ability in attack. He was the only officer not wounded, but, with wonderful energy, he maintained control of his company. His splendid example inspired his men."

Lieut. L. H. Jacobson, Royal Field Artillery.
"For conspicuous gallantry in action. He established and maintained lamp signalling under heavy fire. Later, he returned to Battalion Headquarters and reported the situation. He has previously done fine work. He was wounded."

Lieut. George Jessel, East Kent Regiment.
"For distinguished service in the field in Mesopotamia."

Lieut. Morris Jacob (M.M.), 15th Bty. 6th Bde. Canadian Field Artillery.
"For conspicuous gallantry and initiative during the operations of Aug. 26th, at Monchy. He worked far ahead of the battery and kept touch at all times with the advancing infantry, and under heavy fire continued to send back most important information by wire until his wire was cut to pieces.

He then got hold of a lamp and continued to send until it was smashed, when he continued to get information back by orderlies. Later, in front of Cherisy, he again got back information which allowed the artillery to alter the protective barrage to conform with the retirement of our infantry."

Bar to M.C.

".For marked gallantry and devotion to duty on the morning of 27th September, 1918. When the battery was in action between Buissy and Inchy-en-Artois, firing the final barrage, it came under severe counter battery fire for several hours, causing many casualties. Although wounded he remained at the guns, encouraging and assisting the gunners to keep the guns in action. Throughout the whole day his conduct assisted materially in keeping all the guns of the battery in action."

Capt. Ernest Royalton Kisch, 13th London Regiment.

" For conspicuous gallantry and devotion to duty. For six nights prior to the advance he reconnoitred the road to be followed by the brigade, and it was due to his efforts that the brigade reached the position of deployment in schedule time. He then led his company to the assault with marked ability and courage in the face of heavy fire, and having gained his objective drove off three hostile counter-attacks with complete success."

Capt. Elliot Krolik,* 16th Rifle Brigade.

" For conspicuous gallantry and devotion to duty. He showed splendid leadership and skill in leading his company in an attack. When the advance was in danger of being held up by unexpected resistance from an enemy strong point, with great courage and determination he captured it and led his company forward to their objective."

Sec.-Lieut. J. Kohn, Australian Infantry.

" For conspicuous gallantry and devotion to duty in rushing a hostile machine-gun and putting it out of action. He then rallied his men again, leading them to their final objective. The success of the operation was largely due to his excellent leadership."

Capt. Stephen Liebson,* South African Medical Corps.

" For conspicuous gallantry and devotion to duty when attending the wounded during operations. Though himself wounded and with nothing but a small trench to work in, he carried on during several days under heavy shell and sniping fire with the greatest courage."

Lieut. De Symons Lewis-Barned, 1st Royal West Kent Regiment.

" For conspicuous gallantry and devotion to duty. When all company officers, save one, had become casualties, he was sent forward to report on the situation. The information which he obtained was of the greatest value, and he was again sent forward to collect stragglers and secure the right flank of the battalion, which he did most successfully. He also repaired and made available for action three Lewis guns which had been rendered useless."

MILITARY CROSS

Sec.-Lieut. Lionel Cyril Leapman, London Regiment.
"In spite of considerable opposition from machine-gun fire, he covered the flank of the division with his platoon, capturing 150 prisoners and several machine-guns, and then took command of the line of skirmishers, and led them forward to their objectives, where he consolidated. The next day, when the advance was held up, he took charge of the flank and led a considerable force of our own and Allied troops forward to their objective. He set a very fine example of determination and gallant leadership and great endurance during the two days' operations."

Sec.-Lieut. Sigmund Lotheim, 7th Royal Sussex Regiment.
"For conspicuous gallantry and devotion to duty. He showed great courage in reorganizing his company, which was heavily shelled when moving up the line, and after his three senior officers were casualties, he collected and brought on the company in a very short time without delaying the battalion. Later, though severely wounded, he stayed with his company until they had been collected and sent off to their new position, and personally reported that they had passed through and were all accounted for."

Capt. Morris Lewis, Australian Infantry.
"For conspicuous gallantry and devotion to duty when the enemy delivered a counter-attack and penetrated part of the line. This officer led a party and drove them out, inflicting severe casualties. He set an excellent example to his men."

Lieut. Maitland Ben Levy,* 1st Welch Guards.
"For conspicuous gallantry and devotion to duty. It was mainly due to his splendid powers as a leader that the attack was so successful. He formed and held a strong point under heavy artillery fire.

Sec.-Lieut. Alex Martin Lyone,* 11th Northumberland Fusiliers.
"For conspicuous gallantry and devotion to duty. In charge of a patrol he reconnoitred the country over four hundred yards in front of the Brigade sector, and bombed dug-outs, killing several of the enemy, and brought back a prisoner and most valuable information."

Sec.-Lieut. Harold B. L. Levy, London Regiment.
"For conspicuous gallantry and determination during an attack. Throughout he was foremost in the fighting, leading his men with great dash and skill. When the final objective was reached he was the only officer left in the battalion. His courage, personal example, and leadership were admirable."

Lieut. W. Wolf Lubelski, 37th Bn., Machine Gun Corps.
"For marked ability and able handling of his section and fighting limbers on the morning of October 6th, 1918, in the attack on Briseux Wood. The instant that the Masnieres-Beaurevoir line was taken, he rushed his section and limbers up in front of the advancing infantry, got his guns into action

under heavy machine-gun fire, and directing his fire on the enemy in the vicinity of Hurtebrise Farm East, caused heavy casualties. Later a hostile artillery limber was seen retiring towards Hurtebrise Farm. He engaged it at once, and after the advance the limber was found abandoned, and the horses with it dead."

Lieut. Arthur Louis Levy, Canadian Infantry.

"For conspicuous gallantry in action. He carried out a valuable reconnaissance under heavy fire. Later, he guided the attacking company with great skill and continued with the company until the objective had been gained."

Capt. Albert Percy Myers, 1st King's Own Royal Lancs. Regiment.

"For conspicuous gallantry in action. He led his section forward with great dash, and, when they had all become casualties, he went back and collected stragglers and led them on to the attack. Though wounded early in the day, he refused to leave his battalion, and set a fine example throughout."

Lieut. Francis Michael Myers,* Suffolk Regiment and R.A.F.

"For conspicuous gallantry in action. He carried out a daring raid with great courage and skill. Previously he did some valuable patrol work."

Major L. C. Mandleberg, 14th Lancashire Fusiliers.

"During a raid, despite the failure to explode two Bangalore torpedoes, he personally directed the laying of a third torpedo under heavy machine-gun fire. When the party laying this became casualties he at once reconnoitred for another means of entry through the hostile wire. Before returning to our lines, he carried back the body of one of the men killed, in the face of heavy machine-gun fire at close range. He displayed the highest courage and powers of leadership."

BAR TO M.C.

"For conspicuous gallantry and devotion to duty during an attack. He led his company with great dash to the most forward line reached, collecting stragglers on the way. Later, he assumed the duties of second in command, and organised parties to carry forward rations and ammunition. His utter disregard of danger had a marked effect on the spirits of the men."

Sec.-Lieut. Harold Victor Marks, 1st Northumberland Fusiliers.

"For conspicuous gallantry and devotion to duty. This officer's platoon, holding two advanced posts in trenches running towards the enemy's line, was heavily attacked at both blocks, and threatened from the rear also. In this critical situation he, although wounded, set such a fine fighting example to his men that the enemy was completely repulsed wih heavy loss."

Lieut. David Assur Henry Moses, Royal Army Medical Corps.

"For conspicuous gallantry and devotion to duty in working continuously at his aid post during three days' operations under heavy shelling. Frequently shells dropped close up killing and wounding several men, but he remained at work and showed the utmost indifference to danger."

Lieut. Charles Bernard Marks, 8th East Surrey Regt.

"For conspicuous gallantry and devotion to duty in action at Albert on 22nd August, 1918. His platoon was responsible for mopping up a large area of the town, and at one point came across vigorous opposition. He organised an immediate attack, capturing the post with 50 prisoners, and clearing his area within the scheduled time."

Capt. John Davis Marks, New Zealand Medical Corps.

"For conspicuous gallantry during operations near Ruyaulcourt on the 4/5th September. While his R.A.P. was twice shelled and several casualties occurred he continued at duty, binding men up and shifting them to shelter in spite of the heavy bombardment. Again on the 7th September, when the R.A.P. had been established on the edge of Havrincourt Wood, near Quotient Avenue, the enemy bombarded the place heavily. Under this fire, which had inflicted a number of casualties, he continued with his work. On both occasions his devotion to duty was admirable."

Lieut. J. Mayer, 2nd Bty. New Zealand Field Artillery.

"For conspicuous gallantry and devotion to duty on the 6th September, 1918, near Neuville, in command of a forward section of guns. He got them close up to the infantry in face of intense machine-gun fire, and kept them in action all day in close co-operation with the infantry, dealing with field guns and machine guns near Havrincourt Wood. One of his guns was put out of action, and he had heavy casualties to men and horses. This is not the first time he has distinguished himself."

Lieut. Ernest W. Michelson, Special List.

"For distinguished service in connection with Military Operations in North Russia."

Lieut. Ernest H. Meyers, Australian Infantry.

"For conspicuous gallantry and devotion to duty. He led his platoon in the attack with great dash and initiative, showing his qualities of leadership. When the final objective was captured he carried out reconnaissances in front of the position, and worked untiringly to secure the position against counter-attacks. When all the other officers had become casualties he took command of his company and held on under severe fire until relieved."

BAR TO M.C.

"Near Lihons on August 10th, 1918, he organised sections of various companies with marked ability, thus saving many casualties. He and another officer went forward and located a strong point which was holding up the advance, and which was at once dealt with. Next day he filled up a gap in the line, having to pass through Auger Wood, which had not been mopped up. He showed conspicuous gallantry and leadership." †

† Also awarded second bar to M.C.

Capt. Oscar Sydney Marks, 2/22nd Bn. London Regiment.

"For conspicuous gallantry and devotion to duty when in command of his company. He showed great initiative in handling his company and set a splendid example of courage which materially assisted in the success of the operations."

Bar to M.C.

"During the operations near Werbicq on October 14th, 1918, he led his company with great skill and dash to its final objective. During the advance his men became scattered owing to the smoke and mist, and were temporarily held up by machine-gun fire. He personally collected his men and led a rush of some machine-gun positions. Owing to his dash and initiative he captured many prisoners and machine guns, and reached his final objective. His fine courage and leadership contributed largely to the success of the attack."

Capt. H. C. Moses, Canadian Army Medical Corps, att. No. 5 Field Amb.

"For conspicuous gallantry and devotion to duty in charge of the advanced post of the right section during operations round Neuville, Vitasse, Wancourt, and Cherisy, August 26th—27th, 1918. He was exposed to frequent enemy shelling, bombing and machine gun fire from aeroplanes, and when a shell exploded among a number of wounded awaiting evacuation he directed the adjustment of the masks on the wounded and succeeded in protecting them from all effects of the gas."

Bar to M.C.

"During the operations north of Cambrai, 9th October, 1918, he was in charge of the stretcher-bearers evacuating the wounded of an attacking infantry Brigade. He personally led his parties close behind the advancing infantry under severe shell and machine-gun fire. Owing to his fine example of cool courage and energy the evacuation of wounded from difficult and dangerous positions was rapidly accomplished."

Capt. Harris Mendelsohn, 6th Field Ambulance, Australian A.M.C.

"During operations in the vicinity of Montbrehain, on the 5th October, 1918, soon after the attack had been launched, he pushed his aid-post forward under heavy shell fire, and established it at a most advanced position. Throughout the day he worked unceasingly, showing fearless devotion to duty, and was the means of saving many lives."

Sec.-Lieut. Cecil F. Nathan, Royal Air Force.

"For conspicuous gallantry and devotion to duty as observer. When information was urgently required during an attack, and several attempts to obtain it had been unsuccessful, owing to exceptionally bad weather conditions, he went out with his pilot and succeeded in gaining the necessary information, flying at a height of about 50 feet under heavy rifle and machine-gun fire. He had already made a flight under similar conditions on the same day. He showed great courage and determination."

MILITARY CROSS

Sec.-Lieut. Frank H. Nathan, 11th Bn. Manchester Regiment.

"For marked gallantry and good work during the operations north-west of Cambrai between the 27th September and 3rd October, 1918. When the advance was checked by machine-gun nests he took his platoon to a flank and bombed a nest of machine guns which had been holding up the flank, thus enabling the advance to continue. He and his platoon took three machine guns and many prisoners."

Sec.-Lieut. Lawrence G. Nathan, 49th Bn. Machine Gun Corps.

"On 1st November, 1918, near Aulney, he showed great courage and leadership—the advance of infantry was held up by machine-gun fire. He took his section forward on the left flank where there was a gap and succeeded in capturing two heavy machine guns and their crews. He penetrated the village and captured a further thirty prisoners. The capture of these heavy enemy machine guns materially assisted the advance of the infantry."

Sec.-Lieut. William Price, 2nd Royal Inniskilling Fusiliers.

"For conspicuous gallantry and devotion to duty. Whilst in charge of a special patrol, with great dash and gallantry he mopped up a trench and drove the enemy before him into a lock. He then took up a position commanding the lock and prevented the enemy from bringing their machine-guns into action, during which period he and his patrol were uder continual machine-gun fire from the village."

Capt. Richard James Pinto, Coldstream Guards, att. T.M. Battery.

"For conspicuous gallantry and devotion to duty when in command of three trench mortar batteries of the division firing a barrage. With great skill and resource he got his guns and ammunition into position the previous night, in spite of a sea of mud and enemy shelling. His barrage completely demoralised the enemy."

Major E. R. H. Pollak, R.F.A. and R.A.F.

"For conspicuous gallantry and devotion to duty. Whilst observing a shoot on a hostile battery, he was attacked by two enemy tri-planes, one of which he engaged and succeeded in driving off. On the second machine attacking him, his observer being wounded and his forward machine gun being out of action, he put his machine into a spin down to within 500 feet of the ground, during which time flames began to come out of the engine. These ceased, however, when his machine was once again on a level keel, and on their breaking out again he landed his machine, and was partially successful in extinguishing them. He has always shown great coolness and determination under the most trying circumstances."

Bar to M.C.

"For conspicuous gallantry and devotion to duty in reconnaissance work during a fight lasting three and a half hours. Throughout he scarcely flew at a height greater than 200 feet; he attacked enemy infantry and dropped messages on our batteries which enabled them to shoot with good effect on the enemy as they advanced; he also shot down one machine out of control. On returning to the aerodrome it was found that his own machine was riddled with bullets."

Major L. A. Pollak, London Regt., att. Machine Gun Corps.

BAR TO M.C.

"For conspicuous gallantry and devotion to duty. He commanded a company with great success during severe fighting lasting ten days. He never failed to respond cheerfully to any calls made upon him, inspiring his men, who were at times shaken and weary, with his own energy and determination. His personal reconnaissances and quick appreciation of a situation enabled him to render valuable services. He set a splendid example."

Lieut. Joseph B. Platnauer, Royal Engineers.

"For conspicuous gallantry and devotion to duty. During an important gas operation this officer displayed great energy and initiative in a sudden emergency. Owing to railway difficulties the plan of attack had to be changed, and, by prompt action on his part, an apparent failure was turned into a success. He has a fine record with his company, and his duties, though often difficult and dangerous, are always performed with zeal and energy."

Sec.-Lieut. Maurice A. Pyke, Royal Field Artillery.

"For conspicuous gallantry and devotion to duty while in charge of a forward section. Under heavy shell and machine-gun fire he fought his guns for hours, till the enemy was within 250 yards. He behaved splendidly."

Lieut. Abraham Rothfield, 14th Durham Light Infantry.

"For conspicuous gallantry and devotion to duty. Although exhausted by illness he successfully led a daylight raid into the enemy trenches, inspiring everyone by his unexpected presence, and taking all his objectives with the greatest skill and gallantry. He has previously done very fine work of the same description."

BAR TO M.C.

"For conspicuous gallantry and devotion to duty when in command of a company which was heavily attacked three times. During the bombardment he walked along the top of the trench to reorganise the men. He was badly wounded, but continued to direct operations until unable to do so through loss of blood."

Lieut. Isaac Rothfield, 10th Bn. Liverpool Regt., att. 4th Bn.

"During the period October 10th—12th, 1918, he displayed conspicuous gallantry and skill in leadership. In particular, on the night of the 11th instant, he took a patrol to reconnoitre ground on the south-west outskirts of Neuvilly. The patrol was repeatedly under heavy machine-gun fire, but he persisted and successfully brought back information as to the enemy positions, which was of great value and enabled suitable dispositions to be made."

MILITARY CROSS

Sec.-Lieut. Arnold Reese,* 2nd West Yorkshire Regiment.

" For conspicuous gallantry and devotion to duty. On perceiving an enemy machine gun about to go into action he opened such fire with his own section as prevented the enemy from mounting their gun. He finally collected a small party and rushing forward captured the hostile gun and one prisoner."

Bar to M.C.

" For conspicuous gallantry and devotion to duty when in charge of a successful raid. After all arrangements had been completed, he was compelled to alter them at a moment's notice, owing to his line of advance being bombed by the enemy, whereupon he moved round and gained the enemy's position from the rear, afterwards withdrawing his party safely to our own lines with only two slight casualties, in spite of a heavy bombardment and rifle fire."

Lieut. Albert Abram Robinson, King's Liverpool Regiment and R.A.F.

" For conspicuous gallantry and devotion to duty. During the attack on the enemy's position he took command of his company when his three senior officers had become casualties, and gained his objective under very adverse conditions, displaying the greatest gallantry and energy throughout the operation." †

† Also awarded bar to M.C.

Sec.-Lieut. Wilfred Rosen, London Regiment.

" For conspicuous gallantry and devotion to duty during an attack on a village. He was the first to enter the village, leading the firing line of his company with dash and vigour. Later, under heavy machine-gun fire, he pulled the line together, charged forward, and captured eighteen prisoners."

Capt. George Henry L. Samuel, Royal Field Artillery.

" For conspicuous gallantry and devotion to duty. When acting as F.O.O. during the attack he sent in much valuable and accurate information. He approached within one hundred yards of the enemy trench, and from this dangerous position gained much important information."

Capt. Siegfried Lorraine Sassoon, 3rd (att. 1st) Bn. Royal Welch Fusiliers.

" For conspicuous gallantry during a raid on the enemy trenches. He remained for one and a half hours under rifle and bomb fire collecting and bringing in our wounded. Owing to his courage and determination all the killed and wounded were brought in."

Sec.-Lieut. Cecil Shekury,* 2nd Bedford Regiment.

" For conspicuous gallantry and devotion to duty. He carried out a difficult reconnaissance under very heavy fire and brought back most valuable information. He set a fine example of courage and determination."

Capt. Kenneth Lionel Spiers, Worcestershire Regiment.

"For conspicuous gallantry in action. On three separate occasions he led his company forward with great dash under heavy fire. He also showed great skill and energy in occupying a position in the enemy's trench and organising the defence."

Capt. Mark Summerfield, 9th King's Royal Rifle Corps.

"For conspicuous gallantry in action. He led his men most gallantly in the attack. He was largely responsible for driving off an enemy counter attack. He set a fine example."

Capt. J. B. Solomon, Oxford and Bucks. L.I. and Royal Flying Corps.

"He carried out a patrol lasting nearly three hours in a very high wind and low clouds, flying at an average height of 500 feet, and brought back a valuable report. During this flight he attacked and drove down an enemy 'two-seater machine under heavy rifle and machine-gun fire from the ground. He also made a valuable reconnaissance in very bad weather, flying at an average height of 100 feet, under fire from a hostile battery, with his machine gun. He set a splendid example of courage and determination."

Capt. Leon Simons,* 22nd Royal Fusiliers.

"For conspicuous gallantry in action. He organized and pushed forward his strong points with great courage and skill under very heavy fire. He set a splendid example throughout."

Sec.-Lieut. Leopold Benjamin Seligmann, 18th Manchester Regiment.

"For conspicuous gallantry and devotion to duty. When the enemy were turning the left flank of the battalion, he collected a small party of men and led them, and actually entered the enemy's trench, one of his N.C.O.'s capturing two machine guns. By his example and daring he saved what might have been a critical situation. He continued to inflict casualties on the enemy until he fell wounded."

Sec.-Lieut. Heinrich Leon Seligsohn, London Regiment.

"For conspicuous gallantry and devotion to duty. Having brought up a party of men from the transport lines, he took up a line in front of a village, where he was attacked in great force. He held out for many hours, but was finally driven back. He rallied his men on the other side of the village, and with the greatest dash and determination led a charge through the village and captured the line, thereby undoubtedly saving a very serious situation."

Bar to M.C.

"For conspicuous gallantry in action. With a small party of Headquarter details he attacked the enemy in the wood, killing and making prisoners of several, and capturing many machine guns. His splendid example, until he was seriously wounded and unable to carry on, had a most inspiring effect on all ranks."

MILITARY CROSS

Lieut. Reginald Ellice Sassoon, Irish Guards.
"For conspicuous gallantry and devotion to duty. During an attack, when his company was held up by hostile machine-gun fire, he organised and led a party to the capture of a concrete strong point and of a machine-gun and trench mortar. He was then subjected to machine-gun fire from another strong point, which he promptly and successfully attacked from the flank, capturing another machine-gun and killing and capturing several of the enemy. His dash and initiative at a critical moment were worthy of the highest praise."

Lieut. A. C. Solomon, South African Artillery.
"For conspicuous gallantry and devotion to duty. When an ammunition dump and a truck full of ammunition were set on fire by enemy shells, with a small party he went to the spot and extinguished the fire, in spite of several explosions, after 15 minutes work, thereby saving many lives and a large quantity of ammunition."

Capt. E. D. Samuel, Middlesex Regiment.
"For conspicuous gallantry and devotion to duty. He led his company in an attack, and although they suffered heavy casualties and were held up by machine-gun fire he endeavoured to continue the advance with the survivors. He entered a village with two N.C.O.'s, himself killing four of the enemy and taking two prisoners. In the reorganisation of his line he worked untiringly under heavy fire."

Sec.-Lieut. T. A. S. Samuel, London Regiment.
"For conspicuous gallantry and devotion to duty in action, when he greatly assisted in maintaining the line intact under very heavy shell fire, although the flank was turned. Later he displayed great courage and devotion to duty in directing operations against enemy battalions at night under circumstances of considerable difficulty."

Lieut. Sidney Slavitz, Gloucestershire Regiment.
"For conspicuous gallantry and devotion to duty. When ordered to retire this officer collected his platoon and sent it away under an N.C.O., while he remained behind under intense machine-gun fire to cover the withdrawal. Before leaving he killed four of the enemy with his revolver. He did fine service."

Capt. Charles A. Stiebel, Lancashire Fusiliers.
"For conspicuous gallantry and devotion to duty. In a skilful reconnaissance he discovered an enemy shelter about 700 yards in front of the line. He returned and organised a raid party, and dividing them into three sections attacked the shelter, taking two prisoners and killing six of the enemy. He then successfully brought back his party and the two prisoners. He did fine work."

Lieut. Sydney Morris Samuel, 26th Bn. Royal Fusiliers.

"During the advance of September 26th, 29th and 30th, 1918, on Comines, he carried out his duties as battalion intelligence officer untiringly, and with utter disregard of personal danger. On several occasions he carried out a reconnaissance of the forward posts and of the position of units on the flank, though continually exposed to snipers and machine-gun fire. The information he sent back was accurate and contributed to the success of the advance."

BAR TO M.C.

"For conspicuous gallantry and devotion to duty on the night of 13th—14th October, 1918. Near Gheluwe he taped out the forming-up positions for units of the brigade preparatory to the attack on the morning of the 14th October. It was largely due to the success of his efforts under heavy fire that the attack was so successful. Later, he carried out a daring reconnaissance of our own front line and enemy positions on the banks of the River Lys near Menin and brought back valuable information."

Lieut. Louis Samuels, 1st Bde. Australian Field Artillery.

"For gallantry and devotion to duty at Jeancourt on 1st September, 1918. He was in charge of the F.O.O. party, and throughout the whole advance maintained communications with Group Headquarters; his lines were often the only ones available for both artillery and infantry use. Advancing with the company commanders, he sent valuable information as to progress made and location of enemy artillery and infantry."

Capt. Edwin Henry Shrager, 23rd Bn. Middlesex Regiment.

"At Houthem on September 29th, 1918, he was in command of a company when the battalion was heavily counter-attacked, he put up a great defence, and inflicted heavy casualties on the enemy. Subsequently he successfully brought his company to a fresh position in perfect order. He set a fine example of courage and devotion to duty. Two days afterwards he again led his company in the attack with the greatest gallantry."

Sec.-Lieut. Montague Levy Tebbitt, Royal Field Artillery.

"For conspicuous gallantry and devotion to duty. With another officer he acted as advance intelligence officer for the brigade. He established communications and was successful in keeping in touch with the batteries during the operations. He also sent back valuable information. Through his gallantry and determination under heavy shell fire and very trying conditions communications were kept up."

Lieut. V. R. Ullman, 21st Bn. Canadian Infantry.

"Though badly wounded early in the attack he continued to lead his company forward in face of heavy fire to the objective, which he captured after a severe struggle, in which he accounted for several o fthe enemy with his revolver. His conspicuous gallantry and skill and endurance carried his men forward with splendid dash."

MILITARY CROSS

Major Henry Barnard van Praagh, R.M.L.I.
" For conspicuous gallantry and devotion to duty. During an enemy counter attack he led forward a small party through an intense barrage to garrison a position under fire from snipers. He also carried out a reconnaissance under fire."

Sec. Lieut. E. M. Wolf, Royal Irish Regt., att. Tank Corps.
" He commanded his Tank with the greatest skill and gallantry in very difficult ground, and although it became 'bellied' early in the day, held on to his position in front of the infantry and kept the enemy fire down with his Lewis guns. Although 26 hours in action and very exhausted, he and his crew completely broke up a hostile counter-attack, and saved a critical situation. He displayed throughout the day a magnificent example of courage and endurance."

Lieut. Sigismund David Waley, 22nd London Regiment.
" For conspicuous gallantry and devotion to duty. He took out a small daylight patrol and brought back valuable information about the condition of the enemy trenches and positions of his posts and machine-guns. Later, he reconnoitred some bridges and brought in most valuable information, enabling a post to be established on the only bridge which infantry could cross. He did very fine work."

Capt. Bernard Montague Woolf, 9th Batt. Tank Corps.
" During the action near Mormal Forest, on 4th November, 1918, he showed great skill and judgment in reconnoitering a difficult approach march. Under a very heavy enemy barrage he led the tanks of his company forward on foot. He then followed up the tanks in action, collecting and sending back most valuable information. He set a splendid example throughout of fearless devotion to duty."

Sec. Lieut. Harry Wisnekowitz, Royal Air Force.
" For conspicuous gallantry and devotion to duty. On one occasion, during a very thick mist, he and his pilot, by flying very low, despite very heavy machine gun fire, succeeded in locating the enemy's position. Though his machine was hit in all the vital parts, it was flown back to the aerodrome in safety. On a later occasion, when on contact patrol, during failing light, they succeeding in locating accurately the position of the enemy. They have shown the utmost gallantry and skill during recent operations, and have carried out their duties with the greatest courage and determination."

Major Richard J. Weil, Royal Field Artillery.
" For conspicuous gallantry and devotion to duty. His battery was heavily shelled throughout the day while in action, and heavy casualties were caused. He nevertheless kept up the prescribed rates of fire throughout the day, although finally there were only one officer and several men working the guns. The success of the battery was entirely due to his influence and example under heavy fire."

Major Julien Weinberg, K.O.R. Lancs. Regt.
" For distinguished service in the field in Mesopotamia."

DISTINGUISHED FLYING CROSS.

Lieut. Victor Dreschfield, Royal Air Force.

"This officer invariably shows the greatest gallantry and devotion to duty. During recent operations he has frequently engaged troops and transport, causing heavy casualties. On one occasion, at an altitude of 700 feet, two enemy aeroplanes were set alight by tracer ammunition fired from his Lewis gun. He has taken part in many successful bombing raids and long distance reconnaisances."

Capt. Roy Manzer, Royal Air Force.

"While carrying out a solitary patrol he observed a two-seater below him; diving on it he opened fire, and following it down to 1,000 feet, caused it to land outside the aerodrome. During his return to our lines he saw a hostile kite balloon; attacking it as it was being hauled down he closed to point blank range at 300 feet altitude; on reaching the ground the balloon burst into flames. In addition to the above, this officer has accounted for seven enemy machines, four of which were destroyed and three driven out of control."

Capt. Carl Frederick Falkenberg, Quebec Regiment.

"A bold and skilful airman, he has destroyed four enemy machines and driven down four out of control. In addition, he has performed many gallant deeds in attacking troops, transport, etc., on the ground."

Bar to D.F.C.

"A gallant and skilful fighter he, since he was awarded the Distinguished Flying Cross, has destroyed four enemy machines and one balloon, and has also driven down two more machines out of control, making in all 14 enemy aircraft and one balloon to his credit. He has further rendered gallant service in attacking ground targets and reconnoitering lines."

Capt. Solomon Clifford Joseph, Sea Patrol.

"A gallant pilot he has accounted for eight enemy aircraft within the past four months. On many occasions the enemy were numerically superior to Lieutenant Joseph's patrol, but this did not prevent his attaining success."

Bar to D.F.C.

"A very gallant and skilful officer. He led his formation under a very large force of enemy aircraft with a view to inducing them to descend to attack him. In this *ruse de guerre* he was successful, and, in accordance with arrangements previously made, another formation of our machines then appeared on the scene, and a combined attack was made on the enemy, resulting in the destruction of four aeroplanes and three more being brought down completely out of control. Since the award of the Distinguished Flying Cross was conferred on this officer less than two months ago he has personally

DISTINGUISHED FLYING CROSS

destroyed one enemy machine, brought down another out of control and has helped to destroy a third. Captain Joseph was wounded on the occasion of the combined attack."

Lieut. Albert Abram Robinson, Liverpool Regiment (France).
" On 6th September this officer's balloon was attacked by enemy aircraft and riddled with bullets, and he was compelled to make a parachute descent. On landing he at once obtained permission to reascend in another balloon and carry on his observation, displaying marked determination and devotion to duty. During the last month 2nd Lieut. Robinson has been forced to parachute three times."

Capt. Duncan Ross Solomon, Royal Field Artillery (France).
" During the operations between the 21st, August and 1st October this officer has spent over 70 hours in the air in all weathers, and has afforded valuable assistance to our artillery. His gallantry, initiative, and skill in handling his balloon has been most noteworthy."

DISTINGUISHED CONDUCT MEDAL.

Sgt.-Major F. Ableson (24086), 13th Canadian Infantry.
" For conspicuous gallantry. His company held the extreme left of the British line, and when the enemy broke through the line held by the troops on our immediate left, he rendered invaluable service to his Company Commander by rallying some native troops and getting them back to their trenches. He also directed their fire, as well as that of his own men. He showed the greatest bravery and coolness in the performance of his duties under very heavy fire, and in trying conditions, and ultimately was wounded."

Cpl. I. E. Balaban (106100), 187th Company, Royal Engineers.
" For conspicuous gallantry. During an attack, when his partner was incapacitated and the parapet had been blown in, he stuck to his position, although fully exposed, and conducted himself in a very gallant manner."

B./Sgt./Major M. Beards (87102), Canadian Artillery.
" For conspicuous gallantry and devotion to duty. He has at all times displayed untiring perseverance and initiative, setting a fine example to the men in his battery."

Sgt. M. Baker, M.M. (95318), 152nd Field Company, Royal Engineers.
" During the period 25th February to 16th September, 1918, he has done most excellent work under trying conditions. He has throughout shown great coolness and indifference to danger, and the good work done by his section on several occasions has been largely due to his courage and excellent example."

Sgt. H. Caminer (19113), Canadian Infantry.

"For conspicuous gallantry and devotion to duty. He took command of his own platoon and collected the men of another who were without leaders. He led these men and captured and consolidated his position. He showed the utmost courage and ability throughout."

Sgt. A. Cohen (18/16709), 18th Liverpool Regiment.

"For conspicuous gallantry. When an enemy bomb fell in the trench he rushed forward and detonated the fuse with his feet, thus stopping the explosion of the bomb and saving several casualties."

Sgt. P. M. Coriat (96143), Machine Gun Corps.

"For conspicuous gallantry and devotion to duty. He galloped his sub-section forward under fire, on his own initiative, to assist in an advance, and got his machine-guns into action with excellent effect. He showed splendid initiative and skill."

Sapper A. L. Caselberg (4/363), Signal Troop, New Zealand Mounted Rifle Brigade.

"For conspicuous gallantry on the night of 22nd August, 1915, at Kaiajik Aghala (Hill 60, Dardanelles). At the close of the day a number of detached parties were scattered in advance of the fire trenches. The firing was very heavy, and in the darkness these parties did not know how to get back. Sapper Caselberg, on his own initiative, went out several times, searching for them, and guided them back on each occasion. His total disregard of personal danger and devotion to duty were most marked."

L/Cpl. H. O. Cohn (11820), 1st King's Royal Rifle Corps.

"For conspicuous gallantry near Cambrai on the night of the 24th November, 1915. When the Germans had exploded a mine, killing or wounding most of the garrison of a crater, Lance-Corporal Cohn volunteered to lead forward a fresh party of bombers to meet the enemy's attack. He occupied the crater, repulsed the enemy's bomb attack, and by his coolness and fine example kept his men together and held on till daybreak, when all was quiet."

Pte. J. Cowan (5060), 2nd Border Regiment.

"For conspicuous gallantry during a heavy bombardment. He dug out two comrades, who had been buried, regardless of personal risk, and later carried several messages under heavy fire."

Pte. S. Diamond (926), 6th Australian Imperial Force.

"For conspicuous gallantry and ability on the 25th and 26th April, 1915, near Gabe Tepe (Dardanelles). When, on one occasion during the operations, most of the officers having been killed or wounded, and part of the line commenced to retire, Private Diamond showed the greatest courage and decision of character in assisting to stop the retirement and in leading the men forward again under heavy fire. He also frequently carried messages over open ground swept by a heavy fire, and exhibited a splendid example of devotion to duty."

Sapper H. Epstein (19673), 59th Field Coy., Royal Engineers.
"For conspicuous gallantry on the 8th May, 1915, at Ypres, when he assisted an officer to lay a charge against a German barricade. This barricade was loopholed, and they were actually between our own and the German barricade when ours was blown up as a signal for the assaulting party."

Pte. S. Flansberg (477307), R. Canadian Regt. (att. 4th Bn. C.M.R.).
"For consistent good work in face of the enemy. He is always the first volunteer for dangerous duties, and his gallant example inspires confidence among the men."

Cpl. A. Ferner* (10278), 6th York Regiment.
"For conspicuous gallantry and devotion to duty. During the advance, he moved the line in the open under machine-gun fire, directing and encouraging his platoon, and later when ordered with his machine gun section to outflank a strong point, he moved up his gun, and though all his men were disabled, and he himself was wounded, continued to fire it until it was put out of action. His pluck and coolness were deserving of the highest praise."

Pte. N. Freshwater (14865), Royal Army Medical Corps.
"For gallantry, on 22nd October, 1914, in leading a party of stretcher-bearers in daylight, under heavy rifle fire over a quarter of a mile, to bring back a wounded sergeant."

C.S.M. J. Gilbert (26619), 16th Bn. Manchester Regiment.
"For conspicuous gallantry and devotion to duty. When all the machine and Lewis gunners became casualties, he mounted a Lewis gun under a hail of rifle and machine-gun fire, and effectually held up the enemy's enveloping attack on the flank. His coolness greatly encouraged the men, who put up a splendid fight until reinforcements arrived and the crisis was passed."

Sgt. A. Gold (320966), (M.M.), 6th London Regt.
"For conspicuous gallantry and devotion to duty. He showed great daring and skill in penetrating through five belts of the enemy's wire while on patrol. He located the position of a hostile dug-out and returned with valuable information. On the following night he went out with three others and attacked the dug-out. The party killed or wounded six of the enemy and returned without a casualty. He set a splendid example of courage and initiative."

Cpl. J. J. Goodman (10657), 2nd Bn. King's Royal Rifle Corps.
"For gallant work in the trenches, and for constantly carrying messages under fire."

Cpl. M. Grouchkowsky, Zion Mule Corps.
"On 5th May during operations near Krithia, for gallantry in delivering ammunition and food to the trenches. His mules stampeded under heavy fire, but although wounded in both arms by shrapnel bullets, Private Grouchkowsky kept hold of the animals and delivered the ammunition."

C.Q.M.S, I. Jacks (2/7676), 2nd R. Munster Fusiliers.
"For conspicuous gallantry and devotion to duty throughout the whole campaign. In every action he has displayed great courage and resource, and his fine example has inspired all ranks."

Sgt, G. Jacobs* (39928), Royal Army Medical Corps.
"For conspicuous gallantry during operations. When his stretcher-bearers were dazed by the intense shell fire he jumped on the parapet, and with the assistance of an orderly carried the first case through the barrage. The other bearers at once followed his lead."

Cpl. H, Jacobs (1346), 10th London Regiment.
"For conspicuous gallantry. When left out at night in an enemy observation post, with one man, he defended the post when the enemy came to occupy it, and finally, in a very gallant manner, brought in his companion who had been wounded."

Sgt. W. C. Jacobs (15/976), Royal Warwickshire Regiment.
"For conspicuous gallantry and devotion to duty as a linesman. He continually went out and repaired broken lines under very intense artillery fire. It was greatly owing to his splendid work that communication was maintained at critical moments."

Sgt. E. Joseph (9189), Worcester Regiment.
"As signalling sergeant to the battalion, he has carried out his duties with conspicuous gallantry and devotion to duty. During the retirement from the Somme in March and April, 1918, it was entirely due to his untiring efforts that forward communications were maintained. At Rosieres, on 27th March, he on numerous occasions, under heavy shell and machine-gun fire, went out along the lines and repaired breakages and maintained communications."

Cpl. H. F. Kettle (10420), K.O. Shropshire Light Infantry.
"For conspicuous gallantry and devotion to duty. He has displayed great courage and determination in patrol work. On one occasion he led a patrol along the enemy wire to search for a missing officer, under very heavy fire."

Sgt. J. Lacy (809), 2/3rd London Field Company, Royal Engineers.
"For consistent good work at all times. He has shown coolness and courage in the management of working parties."

Cpl. H. Lewis (553679), 1/16th London Regiment.
"For conspicuous gallantry and devotion to duty during an enemy attack. He fired his Lewis gun at the advancing enemy from an exposed position, and inflicted very heavy casualties. When his gun was destroyed and his team put out of action, he went back to the trench, found another gun

whose team had all become casualties, returned to his forward position, and continued to fire with great effect. He showed splendid initiative and determination."

Pte. D. Lazarus, M.M. (418), 2nd Bn. Australian Machine Gun Corps.
" For fine courage during the operations at Montbrehain on 6th October 1918, he captured an enemy machine gun single-handed. The crew of eight enemy fired on him with machine gun and rifle while he crossed 40 yards of open ground. He shot two of the crew with his revolver and compelled the remaining six to surrender."

Pte. I. Levy (F/172), Middlesex Regiment.
" For conspicuous gallantry in action. He took a machine-gun forward under intense fire. Later, although himself wounded in five places, he rescued and carried in many wounded men."

Rfm. (later Sec.-Lt.) E. Michael (2186), 17th London Regiment.
" For conspicuous gallantry; he displayed great skill in the maintenance of the communications, and on several occasions carried messages to detached companies under heavy fire."

C.S.M. J. Prooth (G/11160), 13th Royal Fusiliers.
" For conspicuous gallantry during a successful raid on the enemy trenches. Later he assisted the medical officer to carry in a wounded man. He has frequently done fine work."

Pte. A. E. Samuels (72474), Machine Gun Corps.
" For conspicuous gallantry and devotion to duty. When in charge of two Lewis guns he and three other men showed the greatest fearlessness in pushing forward to within a short distance of enemy machine-gun positions, in order to frustrate any hostile attempt to enfilade an infantry advance which was in progress. These men were able to gain their objective owing to the daring reconnaisances which they had previously carried out on three nights in succession. Pte. Samuels afterwards took his guns into action, crossing a heavy hostile barrage at a critical moment to replace teams that had become casualties. He and his men showed the most splendid example of soldierly qualities and devotion to duty."

Staff-Sgt. G. Simons (31150), Royal Army Medical Corps.
" For conspicuous and continuous gallantry with a bearer party. On one occasion he was struck on the face by shrapnel and twice was buried by shells, but he persisted in carrying on his work, frequently under very heavy fire, regardless of all personal danger."

Pte. S. Salberg (51885), 1st/9th Bn. Royal Scots.
"During the attack on Vendin le Viele on 12th October 1918, his platoon commander became a casualty. He then took command of a number of men in the vicinity who were held up in marshy ground, and reorganized them and led an attack on an enemy machine gun, personally killing the leader of the crew, and by great dash and gallantry carried the attack forward and captured the position."

Cpl. S. Schultz (19637), 10th Canadian Battalion.
"For conspicuous gallantry and devotion while acting as medical orderly on the night of 24th—25th April, 1915, when he remained at the dressing station after it had been practically blown to pieces, and took charge until every wounded man had been removed, displaying great courage throughout."

Cpl. G. G. Zissman (435039), 2/1st (S. Mid.) Field Ambulance, R.A.M.C.
"For conspicuous gallantry and devotion to duty. On 26th October, 1918, in the attack on the river at St. Martin Bridge, during the temporary absence of their medical officer, he dressed many men, moved them to a place of safety, and subsequently got them away without further injury. On the same day, near La Folie Farm, on the Bermerain-Ruesnes road, he took charge of all the wounded, dressing them, and subsequently clearing them to the car post under heavy fire. Throughout these operations his behaviour was admirable."

O.B.E. AWARDED FOR GALLANTRY

Lieut. Liova Shneerson, Resident of Palestine.
Whilst in the employ of the Intelligence Department of the Egyptian Expeditionary Force, he displayed marked courage and ability in the performance of his duties, which included two trips in disguise across the enemy lines. He undertook voluntarily to secure information by this means, and on both occasions undoubtedly carried his life in his hands. His services were of the greatest use to Intelligence at all times, and in various ways he exhibited conspicuous patriotism and devotion to the cause which he had at heart.

Lieut. Jussef Davidesco, Resident of Palestine.
He exhibited marked courage and ability whilst in the employ of Intelligence E.E.F. He volunteered to cross the Turkish lines with a view of carrying out important secret service work. He succeeded in passing through the lines and remained in the enemy's country several days in disguise. On his return, he volunteered to go a second time, but narrowly escaped capture by the Turks in the neighbourhood of Jiljuliah, and had to return. On both occasions he carried his life in his hands. His services were of the greatest use to Intelligence, and at all times and in various ways he exhibited conspicuous patriotism and devotion to the cause which he had at heart.

Record of Honours.

G.C.M.G.

Rank.	Name.	Regiment.
Lieut.-Gen.	MONASH, Sir JOHN, K.C.B.	G.O.C. Australian Corps.

K.C.M.G.

Col. HARRIS, Sir D., V.D.		South African Defence Force.
OPPENHEIMER, Sir F.		

C.M.G.

Lieut.-Col. BEDDINGTON, E. H. L. (D.S.O., M.C.)	General Staff.
Col. CARLEBACH, P.	London Regiment.
Lieut.-Col. COHEN, H. E. (D.S.O.)	Australian Artillery.
Lieut.-Col. COHEN, C. WALEY-	Royal Army Service Corps.
Lieut.-Col. COHEN, J. WALEY, (D.S.O.)	16th Queen's Westminster R. & Staff.
Col. JESSELL, Sir H. M., Bart. (C.B.)	Special List.
Lieut.-Col. MYERS, B. E.	New Zealand Medical Corps.
Col. NATHAN, W. S.	Royal Engineers.
Maj. SASSOON, Sir P. A. G. D., Bart., M.P.	Royal East Kent Yeomanry.
Brig.-Gen. SELIGMAN, H. S. (D.S.O.)	Royal Artillery.
Lieut.-Col. STERN, Sir A. G. (K.B.E.)	Special List.
Lieut.-Col. WALL, G.	Australian Imperial Forces.

Victoria Cross (See p. 7).

Lieut. DE-PASS, F. A.*	34th Poona Horse, Indian Cavalry.
Capt. GEE, R. (M.C.)	2nd Royal Fusiliers.
Pte. (later Lieut.) KEYSOR, L.	1st Australian Infantry.
Sgt. SMITH, I.	1st Manchester Regiment.
Pte. WHITE, J.	6th King's Own Royal Lancaster Regt

RECORD OF HONOURS.

D.S.O.

Rank. Name.	Regiment.
Capt. AARONSOHN, A.	Egyptian Force.
Major ABRAHAMS, J. J.	Royal Army Medical Corps.
The Rev. ADLER, MICHAEL	Senior Chaplain.
Major BAMBERGER, A. P. W.	Army Service Corps.
Capt. BARNETT, W. H. L.	Bedford Regiment.
Lieut.-Col. BEDDINGTON, E. H. L. (M.C.)	Lancers and General Staff.
Capt. BONN, W. B. L.	Welsh Guards.
Major BRODZIAK, C. E. M.*	Australian Imperial Force.
Lieut.-Col. COHEN, H. E.	Australian Artillery.
Lieut.-Col. COHEN, J. WALEY (C.M.G.)	London Regiment and Staff.
Major COHEN, L. (M.C.)	South African Horse.
Major COPLANS, M. (O.B.E.)	Royal Army Medical Corps.
Capt. DAVIS, A. H.	Royal Army Service Corps.
2nd Lieut. DE PASS, G. E.	Dragoon Guards.
Lieut.-Col. ELKAN, C. J. (O.B.E.)	Royal Irish Fusiliers.
Capt. GOLDBERG, R.	Machine Gun Corps.
Major HARRIS, E. M.	Canadian Army Service Corps.
Lieut.-Col. HARRIS, O. M.	Royal Field Artillery.
Lieut.-Col. HEILBRON, I. M.	Royal Army Service Corps.
Major HIRSCH, H. A.	South African Permanent Force.
Major HYMAN, E. M. (M.C.)	Australian Imperial Force.
Capt. JACOBS, L. M.	South African Infantry.
Lieut.-Col. JOSEPH, R. H.	Royal Engineers.
Capt. KINO, A. R.	East Yorkshire Regiment.
Lieut.-Col. KISCH, F. H.	Royal Engineers.
Major LANDSBERG, H. J.	Royal Field Artillery.
Lieut.-Col. LEVEY, J. H. (O.B.E.)	Gordon Highlanders.
Major LEVY, W. H.	Royal Army Service Corps.
Lieut.-Col. LIGHTSTONE, H. H. (M.C.)	Royal Army Medical Corps.
Major LOWE, S. J.	Royal Fusiliers.
Major MANDLEBERG, L. C. (M.C.)	Lancashire Fusiliers.
Lieut.-Col. MARGOLIN, E. A.	Australian Imp. Force & Royal Fus.
Flight-Commander MARIX, R. L.	Royal Flying Corps.
Colonel MARKS, D. G. (M.C.)	Australian Imperial Force.
Lieut.-Col. MILLER, J. S.	Scots Guards and Royal Fusiliers.
Commander MOCATTA, J. E. A.	Royal Navy.
Capt. MONTAGU, The Hon. L. S.	R.M.L.I., R.N.D.
Major MONTEFIORE, T. H. SEBAG (M.C.)	Royal Horse Artillery.
Lieut.-Col. OPPENHEIM, J.	King's Royal Rifles.
Capt. PARKER, G. A. (M.C.)	Northampton Regt. & Royal Air Force.
Major RICHARDSON, A. N. (M.C.)	Machine Gun Corps.
Major ROTHSCHILD, G. F. (M.C.)	Royal Sussex Regiment.
Capt. SAGAR, A. L.	East Lancashire Regiment.
Lieut.-Col. SAMUEL, F. D. (Bar)	London Regiment and Royal Fusiliers.
Lieut.-Commander SAUNDERS, R.	Royal Naval Volunteer Reserve.
Brig.-General SELIGMAN, H. S. (C.M.G.)	Royal Field Artillery.
Capt. SPEYER, A. W.	General Staff.
Lieut.-Col. WEISBERG, H.	County of London Yeomanry.
Major WOLFF, A. J.	Royal Engineers.

RECORD OF HONOURS.

Distinguished Flying Cross.

Rank.	Name.	Regiment.
Capt.	BAUER, D. C.*	Royal Air Force.
Capt.	DRESCHFELD, V.	Royal Air Force.
Capt.	FALKENBERG, F. C. (Bar)	Royal Air Force.
Lieut.	HYAMS, G. F.	Royal Air Force.
Capt.	JOSEPH, S. C. (Bar)	Royal Air Force.
Capt.	MANZER, R.	Royal Air Force.
Lieut.	ROBINSON, A. A. (M.C. and Bar)	Royal Air Force.
Capt.	SOLOMON, D. R.	Royal Air Force.
Lieut.	VINEBERG, H. A.	Royal Air Force.

Military Cross.

Capt. AARONS, D. S. (Bar)		Australian Infantry.
Lieut. ABINGER, B. R.*		Royal Berkshire Regiment.
Capt. ABRAHAM, C.		Indian Army.
Capt. ABRAHAM, E. C.		Royal Army Medical Corps.
Lieut. ABRAHAMS, F.		Royal Field Artillery.
2nd Lieut. ABRAHAM, L.		Yeomanry.
2nd Lieut. ADLER, S.		Cheshire Regiment.
Lieut. ANSELL, E.		Canadian Infantry.
Lieut. ANSLEY, S. S.		Royal Horse Artillery.
2nd Lieut. ASERMAN, C.		Royal Garrison Artillery.
Capt. BAMBERGER, H. T.		Middlesex Regiment.
Lieut. BARNETT, B. L.		Royal Engineers.
2nd Lieut. BARNETT, C. E.		London Regiment.
Capt. BARNETT, G.		Royal Army Service Corps.
Lieut. BARTON, G. H. R.		Tank Corps.
Capt. BASWITZ, A.*		London Regiment.
Lieut.-Col. BEDDINGTON, E. H. L. (D.S.O.)		Lancers and General Staff.
Major BEECHMAN, F. J.		M.G.C.
Capt. BEECHMAN, N. A.		East Surrey Regiment.
Lieut. BEER, A. H.*		Royal Field Artillery.
2nd Lieut BEHRENS, E. B. (Bar)		Royal Field Artillery.
Major BENJAMIN, E. V.		Canadian Army.
Capt. BENJAMIN, M. A.		Royal Flying Corps.
Capt. BENJAMIN, R. N.		Royal Fusiliers.
Capt. BENTWICH, N. de M.		Imperial Camel Corps.
Capt. BENZECRY, A.		Machine Gun Corps.
2nd Lieut. BENZIMRA, F. J.		Machine Gun Corps.
Capt. BERGER, S. J. D.		Notts and Derby Regiment.
Major BERLANDINA, H. H.		Royal Engineers.
Capt. BERLINER, A.		Royal Garrison Artillery.
Capt. BERLINER, P. B.		London Regiment.
2nd Lieut. BERNSTEIN, M. L.*		Lancashire Fusiliers.
Capt. BLASHKI, E. P.		Royal Army Medical Corps.
Lieut. BLOCH, L.		Intelligence Corps.
Capt. BONN, W. B. L.		Welsh Guards.
Capt. CAPPER, E. R.*		Essex Regiment.
Lieut. CASTELLO, E. J.		Royal Field Artillery.
Capt. CASTELLO, S. M.		Intelligence Corps.
Lieut. CAZES, P. J.		King's African Rifles.
Lieut. CHAPMAN, E. J. C.		Royal Army Service Corps.
Capt. COHEN, A. F.		Australian Engineers.
2nd Lieut. COHEN, E.*		Royal Fusiliers.

RECORD OF HONOURS. M.C. (continued).

Rank. Name. Regiment.

Rank	Name	Regiment
Major	COHEN, L. (D.S.O.)	South African Horse.
2nd Lieut.	COHEN, M.	Royal Engineers.
Lieut.	COHEN, M. T..*	Canadian Infantry.
Major	CORDOVA, V. L., DE	King's Own Royal Lancaster Regt.
Lieut.	COWEN, W. J.	Canadian Cavalry.
Lieut.	DAVIDSON, G. L.	Dorset Regiment.
Capt.	DAVIDSON, N. L.	Northumberland Fusiliers.
Coy.-Sgt.-Major	DAVIS, H.*	East Yorkshire Regiment.
Capt.	DAVIS, R. G.	Tank Corps.
Capt.	DAVIS, S.	London Regiment.
Lieut.	DIAMOND, J.*	K.O.S.B. and R.A.F.
Capt.	DURLACHER, E. A. O.*	Border Regiment.
Lieut.	DURLACHER, B. R.	Worcestershire Regiment.
2nd Lieut.	DURLACHER, H. W.	London Regiment.
2nd Lieut.	DURLACHER, P. A.	Machine Gun Corps.
2nd Lieut.	EDELSTON, J.	Royal Garrison Artillery.
Lieut.	ENGEL, G. H. F.	Australian Engineers.
Capt.	ENOCH, A. J.	Tank Corps.
Capt.	ENOCH, W. H.	Oxford and Bucks. Light Infantry.
2nd Lieut.	FALK, C. J.	Wiltshire Regiment.
Lieut.	FALLON, D.	Oxford and Bucks Light Infantry.
Lieut.	FINSBERG, G. M.	Tank Corps.
Lieut.	FLIGELSTONE, T. H.	Royal Fusiliers.
2nd Lieut.	FRANK, E.	Royal Field Artillery.
Lieut.	FRANKS, N.	Canadian Infantry.
2nd Lieut.	FREEMAN, H. A.	Royal Welsh Fusiliers.
2nd Lieut.	FREEMAN, D. H. D.	Royal Field Artillery.
Capt.	FRIEND, C.	West Yorkshire Regiment.
2nd Lieut.	FURST, L. A.	King's Own Scottish Borderers.
Capt.	GEE, R. (V.C.)	Royal Fusiliers.
Lieut.	GLUCKSTEIN, S. M.	Royal Field Artillery.
Capt.	GOLDBERG, R.	Machine Gun Corps.
2nd Lieut.	GOLDMAN, L.	Royal Engineers.
Capt.	GOLDSTEIN, H. M.	New Zealand Medical Corps.
Capt.	GUEST, L. H.	Royal Army Medical Corps.
Capt.	GUTTMAN, W.	Royal Berkshire Regiment.
Lieut.	GUTTMANN, W. M.	Middlesex Regiment.
Lieut.	HADIDA, P.	Gloucester Regiment.
Lieut.-Col.	HALFORD, M. W.	Gloucester Regiment.
Lieut.	HARRIS, B.	South Lancashire Regiment.
Capt.	HARRIS, L. G. R.	West Riding Regiment.
Lieut.	HARRIS, M.	Middlesex Regiment.
Capt.	HARRIS, N. L.*	Royal Welsh Fusiliers.
Capt.	HART, A. R.	King's Own Royal Lancaster Regt.
Lieut.	HART, B.	Australian Infantry.
2nd Lieut.	HART, J. A.	East Surrey Regiment.
Lieut.	HART, P. H.	Yorkshire Regiment
Lieut.	HARTOG, D. H.	Gloucester Regiment.
Lieut.	HIRSCHFIELD, M. M.	Royal Naval Volunteer Reserve.
2nd Lieut.	HYAMS, H. D.	London Regiment.
Capt.	HYMAN, E. M. (D.S.O.)	Australian Infantry.
Major	INFELD, H.	London Regiment & Royal Engineers.
Capt.	ISAACS, D. W.	Australian Imperial Force.
Capt.	ISAACS, M.	R.N.D.
Lieut.	ISAACS, R. M.	Australian Engineers.

RECORD OF HONOURS. M.C. (continued).

Rank. Name. Regiment.

Lieut. JACOB. M. (M.M.) (Bar) - Canadian Field Artillery.
2nd Lieut. JACOBS, A. E. - East Surrey Regiment.
Capt. JACOBS, B. - King's Own Royal Lancs. Regiment.
Lieut. JACOBS, B. - East Surrey Regiment.
Capt. JACOBS, C. (Bar) - Royal Army Medical Corps.
Lieut. JACOBS, D. A. - Royal Berkshire Regt.
Coy.-Sgt.-Major JACOBS, E. - King's Own Yorkshire Light Infantry.
2nd Lieut. JACOBS, H. - Royal Fusiliers.
Lieut. JACOBS, H. L. - Australian Field Artillery.
Lieut. JACOBS, I. A. - East Kent Regiment.
Lieut. JACOBS, S. - Queen's Royal West Surrey Regt.
Lieut. JACOBS, S. R. - King's Own Royal Lancs Regiment.
Lieut JACOBSON, L. H. - Royal Field Artillery.
2nd Lieut. JELLINEK, L. - Royal Field Artilery.
Major JENNINGS, S. - Canadian Infantry.
Lieut. JESSEL, G. - East Kent. Regiment.
Lieut. JOEL, G. J. - Royal West Kent Regiment.
Capt. JOSEPH, C. H. - Australian Infantry.
2nd Lieut. JOSEPH, E. - Gloucestershire Regiment.
Lieut. JOSEPH, E. G. - Royal Berkshire Regiment.
Capt. JOSEPH, H. M. - R.A.M.C. attd. Essex Regiment.
Capt. JOSEPH, R. L. - Royal Berkshire Regiment.

Sgt.-Major KAUFMAN, A. - Royal Army Medical Corps.
Major KENNARD, G. C. - Royal Engineers.
Capt. KEESING, H. M. - New Zealand Rifle Brigade.
Capt. KINO, A. J. - Royal Field Artillery.
Capt. KISCH, E. R. - London Regiment.
2nd Lieut. KOHN, J. - Australian Infantry.
Major KROHN, V. R. - Royal Field Artillery.
Capt. KROLIK, E.* - Rifle Brigade.

Lieut. LEAPMAN, L. C. - London Regiment.
Capt. LEEDMAN, C. H. - Australian Army Medical Corps.
Lieut. LEVIEN, E. - New Zealand Mounted Rifles.
Lieut. LEVINSON, L. F. - Dragoon Guards.
Lieut. LEVY, A. L. - Canadian Infantry.
2nd Lieut. LEVY, E. V. - Royal Fusiliers.
2nd Lieut. LEVY, H. B. L. - London Regiment.
2nd Lieut. LEVY, J. - Royal Fusiliers.
Capt. LEVY, M. B.* - Welch Guards.
Capt. LEVY, R. P. - Middlesex Regiment.
Capt. LEWIS, M. R. - Australian Infantry.
Capt. LEWIS, W. - London Regiment.
Lieut. LEWIS-BARNED, DE S. H. - Royal West Kent Regt.
Capt. LIEBSON, S.* - South African Medical Corps.
Lieut.-Col. LIGHTSTONE, H. H. (D.S.O.) - Royal Army Medical Corps.
2nd Lieut. LOTHEIM, S. - Royal Sussex Regiment.
Lieut. LUBELSKI, W. W. - Machine Gun Corps.
2nd Lieut. LYONE, A.M.* - Northumberland Fusiliers.

Capt. MANDLEBERG, J. H. - South Lancashire Regiment.
Capt. MANDLEBERG, L. C. (Bar) - Lancashire Fusiliers.
Lieut. MARKS, C. B. - East Surrey Regiment.
Major MARKS, D. G. (D.S.O.) - Australian Infantry.
Lieut. MARKS, H. H. - Durham Light Infantry.
2nd Lieut. MARKS, H. V. - Northumberland Fusiliers.
Capt. MARKS, J. D. - New Zealand Medical Corps.
Lieut. MARKS, L. D. - Royal Field Artillery.
Capt. MARKS, O. S. (Bar) - London Regiment.

RECORD OF HONOURS. M.C. (continued).

Rank. Name.	Regiment.
Lieut. MAYER, J.	New Zealand Field Artillery.
Capt. MENDELSOHN, H.	Australian Medical Corps.
Lieut. MEYERS, E. H. W. (2 Bars)	Australian Infantry.
Capt. MEZA, J. DE*	London Regiment.
Lieut. MICHELSON, E. W.	General List.
Major MONTEFIORE, T. H. SEBAG (D.S.O.)	Royal Field Artillery.
Capt. MONTEFIORE, W. SEBAG	Lancers.
Capt. MORRIS, F.	Army Ordnance Corps.
Lieut. MOSES, D. A. H.	Royal Army Medical Corps.
Capt. MOSES, H. C. (Bar)	Canadian Army Medical Corps.
Capt. MOSS-VERNON, S. R.	London Regiment.
Capt. MYERS, A. P.	King's Own Royal Lancaster Regt.
Lieut. MYERS, F. M.*	Suffolk Regt. and Royal Flying Corps.
2nd Lieut. NATHAN, C. F.	Royal Air Force.
2nd Lieut. NATHAN, E. G. P.	Royal Field Artillery.
2nd Lieut. NATHAN, F. H.	Manchester Regiment.
2nd Lieut. NATHAN, L. G.	Machine Gun Corps.
Lieut. NATHAN, R. P.*	Royal Field Artillery.
Capt. NATHAN, L.	Canadian Infantry.
Capt. PARKER, G. A. (D.S.O.)	Northampton Regt. & Royal Air Force.
Capt. PHILLIPS, F. R.	Surrey Yeomanry.
Capt. PHILLIPS, J. S.	South Staffordshire Regiment.
Lieut. PHILLIPS, L. H.	Royal Field Artillery.
Capt. PINTO, R. J.	Coldstream Guards.
Lieut. PLATNAUER, J. B.	Royal Engineers.
Major POLLAK, E. R. H. (Bar)	Royal Field Artillery and R.A.F.
Major POLLAK, L. A. (Bar)	Machine Gun Corps.
2nd Lieut. PRICE, W.	Royal Inniskilling Fusiliers.
Capt. PYKE, C. A.	Australian Army Service Corps.
2nd Lieut. PYKE, M. A.	Royal Field Artillery.
Major RAPHAEL, R. A.	Royal Warwickshire Regiment.
Lieut. RATHBONE, V.	King Edward's Horse.
2nd Lieut. REESE, A. (Bar)*	West Yorkshire Regiment.
Major RICHARDSON, A. N. (D.S.O.)	Machine Gun Corps.
Lieut. ROBINSON, A. A. (Bar)	King's Liverpool and Royal Air Force.
Lieut. ROLO, C.	Zion Mule Corps.
Lieut. ROSEN, L. W.	Australian Infantry.
2nd Lieut. ROSEN, W.	London Regiment.
Lieut. ROTHFIELD, A. (Bar)	Durham Light Infantry.
Lieut. ROTHFIELD, I.	King's Liverpool Regiment.
Major ROTHSCHILD, G. F. (D.S.O.)	Royal Sussex Regiment.
2nd Lieut. SALMON, S. A.	Royal Field Artillery.
Capt. SAMUEL, E. D.	Middlesex Regiment.
Lieut. SAMUEL, E. L.	Honorable Artillery Company.
Lieut. SAMUEL, S. M. (Bar)	Royal Fusiliers.
2nd Lieut. SAMUEL, T. A. S.	London Regiment.
Capt. SAMUEL, W.	West Kent Yoemanry.
Lieut. SAMUEL, G. H. L. M.	Royal Field Artillery.
2nd Lieut SAMUELS, F. A.	East Surrey Regiment.
Lieut. SAMUELS, L.	Australian Imperial Force.
Capt. SASSOON, A. M.	Hussars.
Lieut. SASSOON, R. E.	Irish Guards.
Capt. SASSOON, S. L.	Royal Welsh Fusiliers.
2nd Lieut. SELIGMANN, L. B.	Manchester Regiment.
2nd Lieut. SELIGSOHN, H. L. (Bar)	London Regiment.
2nd Lieut. SHEKURY, C.*	Bedford Regiment.
2nd Lieut. SHERMAN, E. H.	Essex Regiment.

RECORD OF HONOURS. M.C. (*continued*).

Rank.   Name.   Regiment.

Capt. SHRAGER, E.	Middlesex Regiment.
Capt. SIMONS, E. (Bar)	South Wales Borderers.
Capt. SIMONS, L.*	Royal Fusiliers.
Major SINAUER, E. M.	Royal Engineers.
Lieut. SLAVITZ, S.	Gloucestershire Regt.
Lieut. SOLOMON, A. C.	South African Infantry.
Lieut.-Col. SOLOMON, H. J.	Royal Army Service Corps.
Capt. SOLOMON, J. B.	Oxford and Bucks. L. I. and R.A.F.
Major SOLOMON, P. H.	Royal Air Force.
Capt. SOLOMON, R. B.	Royal Field Artillery.
Major SPIELMAN, C. M.	Royal Engineers.
Capt. SPIERS, K. L.	Worcester Regiment.
Capt. STAHL, A.	Royal Field Artillery.
Lieut. STEIN, I. R.	King Edward's Horse.
Major STERN, F. C. (O.B.E.)	County of London Yeomanry.
Capt. STERN, T. H.	Royal Engineers.
Capt. STIEBEL, C. A.	Lancashire Fusiliers.
Capt. STRAUSS, B. L.	East Kent Regiment.
Capt. SUMMERFIELD, M.	King's Royal Rifle Corps.
Capt. and Adj. SUTTON, D.	London Regiment.
2nd Lieut. TALLERMAN, K. H.	Royal Field Artillery.
2nd Lieut. TEBBITT, M. L.	Royal Field Artillery.
Capt. TRIEFUS, P.	Royal Field Artillery.
Capt. ULLMAN, R. B.	Royal Field Artillery.
Lieut. ULLMAN, V. R.	Canadian Infantry.
Major VAN PRAAGH, H. B.	Royal Marine Light Infantry.
Major WALEY, A. S.	Royal Engineers.
Capt. WALEY, F. R.	South Lancashire Regiment.
Lieut. WALEY, S. D.	London Regiment.
Major WEIL, R. J.	Royal Field Artillery.
Major WEINBERG, J.	King's Own Royal Lancaster Regt.
2nd Lieut. WISNEKOWITZ, H.	Royal Air Force.
Capt. WOLF, E. M.	Tank Corps.
Capt. WOOLF, B. M.	Tank Corps.
Lieut. WYLER, E. J.	Royal Army Medical Corps.

Order of the British Empire.

G.B.E.

READING, ALICE EDITH, Countess of

D.B.E.

Mrs. SAMUEL, L. V. — War Refugees Committee.

K.B.E.

Sir ROBERT WALEY COHEN
Sir P. G. HENRIQUES
Sir S. F. MENDL
Lieut.-Col. Sir F. L. NATHAN
Lieut.-Col. Sir A. G. STERN, C.M.G. — Special List.

C.B.E.

Major ABRAHAMS, A. C.	Red Cross Society.
ᵐLieut.-Col. COHEN C. WALEY.	Army Service Corps.
Dr. EICHHOLZ, A. (H.M.I.)	
JACOBSON, E. N. J.	Special Constabulary.
LEBUS, H. A. H.	
ᵐCol. MARKS, A. H. (D.S.O.)	Australian Imperial Force.
MARKS, G.	Army and Navy Canteen Board.

ᵐ Military Division.

RECORD OF HONOURS. **C.B.E.** (*continued*).

Rank. Name.	Regiment.
Montefiore, Sebag, E.	Home Office.
mLieut.-Col. Myers, C. S.	R.A.M.C.
Richardson, L.	South Africa.
mLieut.-Col. Rose, E. A.	Royal Army Service Corps.
Mrs. Rothschild, Leopold, de	Red Cross Society.
Major Salmon, I.	War Pensions Committee.
Mrs. Sassoon, Arthur	Officers' Families Association.

O.B.E.

Rank. Name.	Regiment.
mCapt. Abramson, A.	Special List.
mMajor Abrahams, A.	Royal Army Medical Corps.
Beddington, R.	Metropolitan Special Constabulary.
Mrs. Beer, Walter	Founder and Commandant, Bradstones Auxiliary Hospital.
mMajor Berlandina, H. H. (M.C.)	Royal Engineers.
Major Sir Cohen, H. B., Bart.	Royal West Kent Regiment.
Miss Cohen, H. F.	West Kent Women's War Agricultural Committee.
Cohen, P.	Red Cross Society.
mMajor Coplans, M. (D.S.O.)	Royal Army Medical Corps.
mLieut. Davidesco, J.	Intelligence Corps, Egypt.
mMajor Ehrmann, A.	Royal Army Medical Corps.
mLieut.-Col. Elkan, C. J. (D.S.O.)	Royal Irish Fusiliers.
mCapt. Ezra, E.	Indian Army.
Foa, F. E.	Foreign Office.
Franklin, L. B., J.P.	
mMajor Gluckstein, M.	Royal Engineers.
Gluckstein, J.	War Refugees Work.
Goldsmid, F. L.	
*Major Goldsmith, F.	Suffolk Yeomanry.
Gollin, Alfred	
*Goodman, C.	Victory Loan Campaign.
Major Halford, E. S.	Royal Air Force.
Hart, P. T.	Ministry of National Service.
mCapt. Harris, L. J.	Royal Engineers.
mCapt. Hoffnung-Goldsmid, C. J.	Lancers.
Hollander, L.	South Africa.
mMajor Hyman, A. E. W.	Australian Imperial Force.
Infield, L.	
Isaacs, H. M.	Ministry of Food.
mMajor Isaacs, I. B.	Royal Army Service Corps.
Mrs. Isaacs, M.	
mMajor Jacobs, J.	Royal Field Artillery.
Jacobs, J., J.P.	Ex Soldiers' Employment work.
mMajor Joel, H. C.	Royal Army Ordnance Corps.
Major Joseph, E. M.	Army Canteen Department.
Kalker, E.	War Refugees Work.
Kaufman, L.	Victory Loan Campaign.
Keyser, M. M.	Ministry of Munitions.
Landau, H.	War Refugees Work.
mCapt. Landau, H.	Special List.
Lazarus, S. L.	Australian Patriotic Society.
mMajor Leon, J.	Royal Army Service Corps.
mLieut.-Col. Levey, J. H. (D.S.O.)	Gordon Highlanders.
mMajor Lowe, S. J. (D.S.O.)	Royal Fusiliers.
mMajor Marks, E. S.	General List.
Marks, G.	
mCapt. and Brevet Major Mocatta, V. E.	Hussars.
mCapt. Montagu, V. C.	Honorable Artillery Company.
Capt. Montefiore, C. E.	Indian Army.

RECORD OF HONOURS. O.B.E. (continued).

Rank. Name. Regiment.

*m*Capt. MONTEFIORE, L. N.	Hampshire Regiment.
MYERS, L.	
Capt. NATHAN, E. J.	Special List.
Mrs. NATHAN, S.	New Zealand.
Lieut.-Commr. NATHAN, G. E.	Royal Naval Volunteer Reserve.
PHILLIPS, F. S.	
QUASS, P.	Ministry of Food.
ROSE, F.	
*m*Major ROTH, A. A.	Army Ordnance Corps.
Major ROTHSCHILD, L. N. De. M.P.,	Buckinghamshire Yeomanry.
Mrs. SAMUEL, GILBERT.	
*m*Capt. SASSOON, A. M. (M.C.)	Hussars.
SCHIFF, E. H.	War Refugees Work.
*m*Surg.-Lieut. SCHLESINGER, E. G.	Royal Navy.
m Lieut. SHNEERSON, L.	Intelligence Corps, Egypt.
*m*Capt. SIMONSON, P. W.	Australian Imperial Forces.
*m*Lieut.-Col. SOLOMON, H. J. (M.C.)	Royal Army Service Corps.
SPIERS, F. S.	
*m*Major STERN, F. C. (M.C.)	County of London Yeomanry.
SUTRO, A.	
*m*Major VAN DEN BERGH, H. E.	Army Canteen Department.
m Major WALEY, E. G. S.	16th London Regiment.
*m*Capt. WARBURG, O. E.	Royal Garrison Artillery.
*m*Lieut.-Col. WOLFF, H. P.	Labour Corps.
WOOLF, ALBERT M.	War Refugees Work.
WOOLF, MORTIMER	War Refugees Work.
*m*Major WOOLF, E. S.	Royal Army Service Corps.
*m*Lieut.-Col. WOLFF, M. A.	Canadian Infantry.
Paymr. Lieut. Commander WOOLF, T. A.	Royal Navy.

M.B.E.

ABRAHAMS, J. E.	War Refugee Work.
*m*Capt. ADLER, H. M.	R.A.S.C.
Mrs. BASCH, B.	
Mrs. BENJAMIN, F. S.	
*m*Lieut. CARO, P.	Australian Engineers.
DA COSTA, A., J.P.	West Indies.
Mrs. DAVIDSON, E.	V.A.D.
Mrs. DE CORDOVA, M.	West Indies.
FOX, J. J.	
Mrs. EDWARDS, R. G.	Commandant V.A.D.
GOLANCE, E. M.	War Trade Department.
*m*2nd Lieut. GOLDMAN, J. I.	Royal Army Service Corps.
GOLLIN, W. J.	Metropolitan Special Constabulary.
Mrs. HENOCHSBERG, E. M.	Nairobi Medical Service.
ISAACS, ELLIS	Glasgow Military Tribunal.
*m*Capt. ISAACS, D. N.	New Zealand Medical Corps.
*m*Lieut. JABOTINSKY, V.	38th Royal Fusiliers.
Miss JACOBS, D. I.	Foreign Office.
JACOBS, L.	Public Trustee Office.
Miss JOSEPH, J.	Commandant, Tudor House M. Hosp.
JOSEPH, D.	
*m*Major KEMPER, J.	Royal Air Force.
*m*Lieut. KLEIN, A. B. L.	Norfolk Regiment.
2nd Lieut. LEVEY, B. A.	R.A.F.
LEVI, L.	
*m*Sergt.-Major LEVY, J.	Royal Army Medical Corps.
Miss LEVY, J. A.	Women's League.

m Military Division.

RECORD OF HONOURS. M.B.E. (continued).

Rank. Name.	Regiment.
Cpl. LEVY, T.	Australian Mounted Police.
ᵐLieut. LEVY, T. H.	New Zealand Force.
LIPMAN, S. N.	
ᵐStaff-Sergt. LONDON, E.	Expeditionary Force Canteens.
LYONS, H.	War Work, Nottingham.
MAINZ, E.	War Refugees' Work.
Capt. MONTEFIORE, SEBAG, G. E.	Lancers.
Capt. MYERS, N. C.	I.A.R.O.
Lieut. MYERS, H. C.	Board of Trade.
MYERS, Hon. H. V.	Jamaica Legislative Council.
Miss NATHAN, S. C.	New Zealand Red Cross Society.
ᵐLieut. NATHAN, S. J.	Royal Engineers.
Mrs. RUBENSTEIN, V.	Women's Royal Naval Service.
ᵐCapt. SANDELSON, D. I.	Army Pay Department.
SCHIFF, O.	War Refugees Work.
SCHLESINGER, R. A.	War Refugees Work.
Mrs. STRAUS, B.	War Hospital Supply Depot.
TURK, E.	War Refugees Work.
WOLFFE, E. M.	London Ambulance Column.
YELLIN, D.	Palestine.

D.C.M.

Rank. Name.	Regiment.
Sgt.-Major ABLESON, F.	Canadian Infantry.
Pte. ABRAHAMS, H. W.	South African Infantry.
Cpl. ABRAHAMS, L. O.	Durham Light Infantry.
Pte. ADLER, D.	London Regiment.
Sgt.-Major BROOKS, H. (M.S.M.)	5th Manchester Regiment.
Sgt. BAKER M. (M.M.)	Royal Engineers.
Cpl. BALABAN, I. E.	Royal Engineers.
Pte. BARNETT, G.	Royal Army Medical Corps.
L/Cpl. BASS, E.	King's Royal Rifle Corps.
B/Sgt.-Major BEARDS, M.	Canadian Field Artillery.
S/Sgt. BERG, L. A. (M.M.)	New Zealand Infantry.
Sgt. BLACK, D.	Durham Light Infantry.
Sgt. CAMINER, H.	Canadian Infantry.
Sapper CASTELBERG, A. L.	New Zealand Rifle Brigade.
Sgt. COHEN, A.	Liverpool (and Welsh) Regiment.
L/Cpl. COHEN, H. O.	King's Royal Rifle Corps.
Sgt. CORIAT, P. M.	Machine Gun Corps.
Pte. COWEN, J.	Border Regiment.
Pte. (later Lieut.) DIAMOND, S.	Australian Infantry.
Sapper EPSTEIN, H.	Royal Engineers.
Sgt. ERSCHOVITZ, C.	Zion Mule Corps.
Cpl. FERNER, A.*	Yorkshire Regiment.
Pte. FISHMAN, W.	Northampton Regiment.
Sgt. FLANSBERG, S.	Canadian Infantry.
Pte. FRESHWATER, N.	Royal Army Medical Corps.
C.S.M. GILBERT, J.	Manchester Regiment.
Pte. GLUCKSTEIN, R.	Royal Marines.
Sgt. GOLD, A. (M.M.)	London Regiment.
Sgt. GOLDSTEIN, J. (Bar)	South Wales Borderers.
Sgt. GOODMAN, D.*	Royal Field Artillery.

RECORD OF HONOURS. D.C.M. (continued).

Rank. Name. — Regiment.

Cpl. Goodman, J. — King's Royal Rifle Corps.
Pte. Gottlieb, H. A. (M.M.) — Australian Infantry.
Cpl. Grouchkowsky, M. — Zion Mule Corps.

Pte. (later Lieut.) Hirschfeld, F. (M.M.) — Worcester Regiment.

Pte. (later Lieut.) Israel, N. — Australian Imperial Force.

C.Q.M.S. Jacks, I. — Royal Munster Fusiliers.
Sgt. Jacobs, G.* — Royal Army Medical Corps.
Cpl. Jacobs, H. — London Regiment.
Pte. Jacobs, M. J. (M.M.) — Royal Army Medical Corps.
Sgt. Jacobs, W. C. — Royal Warwickshire Regiment.
Sgt. Joseph, E. — Worcester Regiment.
Sgt. Keswell, I. — Australian Imperial Force.
Cpl. Kettle, H. — King's Shropshire Light Infantry.
Sgt. Kohn, H. D. — King's Royal Rifles.

Sgt. Lacy, J. — Royal Engineers.
Pte. Lazarus, D. (M.M.) — Australian Machine Gun Corps.
Pte. Lazarus, H. (M.M.) — Leicester Regiment.
Sgt. Levy, B. — London Regt.
Cpl. Levy, I. — Middlesex Regiment.
Cpl. Lewis, H. L. — Queen's Westminster Rifles.

Lieut. Marks, E. — New Zealand Infantry.
Sgt. Marks, M. J. — Coldstream Guards.
Cpl. Marks, R. — Australian Machine Gun Corps.
S/Sgt. Menkin, H. — Royal Field Artillery.
Sgt. Meyerstein, W. C. — Canadian Infantry.
Rfm. (later 2nd Lieut.) Michaels, E. — County of London Regiment.
Pte. Miller, D. (M.M.) — Manchester Regiment.
Cpl. Moses, C. — Royal Garrison Artillery.
Sgt. Moses, C. H. — Royal Engineers.
Pte. Myers, P. — London Regiment.

L/Sgt. Nathan, P. S. — Middlesex Regiment.

Sgt. Olsen, C. (Bar) (M.M.) — Lancashire Fusiliers.
Cpl. Ovitch, M. — Northumberland Fusiliers.

Sgt. Persoff, S. — Royal Berkshire Regiment.
Coy.-Sgt.-Major Prooth, J. — Royal Fusiliers.

Sgt. Reinovitch, M. — Australian Infantry.
Cpl. Rosen, H. (M.M.) — Royal Engineers.
Cpl. Rosenthal, I. — Royal Field Artillery.
Major Rothschild, J. de — R. Canadian Dragoons and R. Fusiliers.

Cpl. Sadaski S. — Canadian Infantry.
Pte. Salberg, S. A. — Royal Scots.
Pte. Samuel, H. (M.M.) — Machine Gun Corps.
Pte. Samuels, A. — Machine Gun Corps.
Gnr. Sapier, D. — Royal Field Artillery.
Sgt. Schultz, S. — Canadian Army Medical Corps.
L/Cpl. Sillender, I. — Cheshire Regiment.
S/Sgt. Simons, G. — Royal Army Medical Corps.
Pte. Simons, S. (M.M.) — Essex Regiment.
Pte. Stankiewitz, S. — Canadian Infantry.

Pte. Van Cleef, A. — London Scottish.

RECORD OF HONOURS. **D.C.M.** (*continued*).

Rank. Name. Regiment.

Sgt. WARTMAN, E.* - - - - - Canadian Medical Service.
Pte. WELLENSKY, B. - - - - - South African Infantry.

Cpl. ZISSMAN, G. G. - - - - - Royal Army Medical Corps.

Meritorious Service Medal

Sgt. ABRAHAMS, J. J. - - - - - Australian Infantry.
C.Q.M.S. ALEXANDER, H. T. - - - Royal Engineers, West Riding.
Regt.-Sgt.-Major ASHER, C. (M.M.) - - New Zealand Field Artillery.

Pte. BACHRACH, S. E. - - - - Royal Army Medical Corps.
Sgt. BAMBERGER, A. E. - - - - Labour Corps.
L/Cpl. BARNETT, R. C. S. - - - - Royal Army Service Corps.
C.Q.M.S BLOUSTEIN, H. M. - - - Australian Imperial Force.
Sgt.-Major BROOKS, H. (D.C.M.) - - - Manchester Regiment.

Sgt. DAVIS, D. T. - - - - - Royal Air Force.

Yeoman of Signals EMANUEL, A. - - - Royal Navy.
S/Sgt. EMANUEL, E. - - - - - Royal Army Service Corps.
Sgt. ENOCH, E. A. - - - - - Machine Gun Corps.

Sgt. FINEBERG, A. - - - - - South African Service Corps.
Sgt.-Maj. FRANKFORD, E. - - - - Australian Infantry.
Sgt. FRANKS, S. - - - - - - Bedford Regiment.

Sapper GOODMAN, E. - - - - - Royal Engineers.

C.S.M. HARRIS, G. S. - - - - - Labour Corps.
Spr.-Clerk. HART, S. A. - - - - - Royal Engineers.

Sgt. ISAACS, C. - - - - - - Royal Army Service Corps.
C.Q.M.S. ISAACS, D. J. - - - - Australian Machine Gun Corps.
A/S.M. ISAACS, G. - - - - - Royal Army Service Corps.

Sgt. JACOBS, C. V. R. - - - - - Royal Engineers.
Sgt. JACOBS, D. A. - - - - - Royal Engineers.
S/Sgt.-Major JACOBS, H. W. - - - Army Pay Corps.
R.S.M. JACOBS, S. - - - - - Royal Army Medical Corps.
R.Q.M.S. JACOBS, S. J. - - - - Canadian Infantry.
Dvr. JACOBS, S. M. - - - - - Royal Field Artillery.
Sgt. JACOBS, W. T. G. - - - - - Labour Corps.
S/Sgt.-Major JELLEN, J. - - - - Royal Army Service Corps.
Chief Clerk JOSEPH, A. - - - - - Labour Corps.

S/Sgt.-Major LAVENTHAL, S. - - - Indian Army.
C.S.M. LEVEY, O. S. H. - - - - London Regiment.
Flight-Sgt. LEVY, E. - - - - - Royal Air Force.
Sgt. LIEBERMAN, R. - - - - - Labour Corps.
C.Q.M.S. LIEBERMANN, W. J. - - - Oxford and Bucks Light Infantry.

Warrant-Officer LIPMAN, L. B. - - - Australian Imperial Force.
Sgt. MARKS, G. - - - - - - Royal Garrison Artillery.
Sgt. MENDEL, F. W. - - - - - London Regiment.
Coy.-Sgt.-Major MINTZ, J. D. - - - Labour Corps.
Sgt. MORDECAI, M. J. - - - - - Royal Army Medical Corps.
Pte. MOSES, H. D. - - - - - Royal Army Medical Corps.
S/Sgt. MOSS, H. L. - - - - - Royal Army Medical Corps.
Sgt. MOSS, J. E. - - - - - - Royal Garrison Artillery.

RECORD OF HONOURS. M.S.M. (continued).

Rank.	Name.	Regiment.
S/Sgt. Major	Moss, W. F.	Royal Army Medical Corps.
Gnr.	Myers, J.	Royal Garrison Artillery.
S/Sgt.-Major	Myers, O. B.	Royal Army Medical Corps.
Mech.-S/Sgt.	Myers, S. W.	Royal Army Service Corps.
Sgt.-Major	Pyser, R.	Royal Engineers.
S/Sgt.	Reuben, D. B.	Royal Fusiliers.
Pte.	Roberts, H. I.	Royal Fusiliers.
Sgt.	Rosenbaum, M.	Canadian Engineers.
Sgt.-Major	Rosenberg, W. F. H.	London Regiment.
Batty.-Sgt.-Major	Sagar, J. E.	Royal Garrison Artillery.
Sgt.	Samuels, M.	London Regiment.
L/Cpl.	Schulmovitch, S.	Labour Corps.
Sgt.	Schwartz, S.	Prisoner of War Section.
S/Sgt.	Silverberg, E. A.	Royal Army Ordnance Corps.
2nd Cpl.	Simons, G. E.	Royal Engineers.
Sgt.	Solomon, A. F.	Royal Fusiliers.
Pte.	Solomon, W. J. C.	Royal Warwickshire Regiment.
C.Q.M.S.	Somper, J.	Royal Army Service Corps.
Pte.	Somper, H.	
L/Cpl.	Spiers, F.	Australian Army Service Corps.
S/Sgt.	Ungar, Isidore, I.	Royal Army Medical Corps.
Sgt.	Whitefield, C. S.*	Australian Infantry.
Sgt.	Woodburn, L. (twice)	Worcester Regiment.
Sgt.	Woolf, E.	Middlesex Regiment.
S/Sgt.	Woolf, I.	Royal Army Medical Corps.

Military Medal

Rank.	Name.	Regiment.
L/Cpl.	Aaron, H.	Royal Warwickshire Regiment.
Sgt.	Aarons, J.	East Yorkshire Regiment.
Sgt.	Abrahams, D.	Rifle Brigade.
Sgt.	Abrahams, G.	Australian Infantry.
Sgt.	Abrahams, K. D.	Royal Field Artillery.
L/Cpl.	Abrahams, J.	Royal Army Medical Corps.
Pte.	Abrahams, J. H.	Oxford and Bucks. Light Infantry.
Pte.	Abrahams, J.	Gloucester Regiment.
Sgt.	Adler, P.*	Royal Fusiliers.
Pte.	Adolphus, B.	London Regiment.
L/Cpl.	Ahbul, L. E.*	Australian Infantry.
Cpl.	Abramovitch, P.	Australian Engineers.
Pte.	Angel, J.	Royal Fusiliers.
Pte.	Ansell, C. H.	Royal Field Artillery.
Pte.	Aron, C. J. (Bar)	Royal Fusiliers.
Cpl.	Arbeid, A.	Rifle Brigade.
Regt.-Sgt.-Major	Asher, C. (M.S.M.)	New Zealand Field Artillery.
L/Cpl.	Babitzky, H.	Rifle Brigade.
Pte.	Baker, H.	Scottish Rifles.
Sgt.	Baker, M. (D.C.M.)	Royal Engineers.
Sgt.	Bamberger, E. L.	Royal Engineers.
Sgt.	Barkman, G.	King's Liverpool Regiment.
Pte.	Barnes, I.	Gordon Highlanders.
Pte.	Barnett, J.	Canadian Infantry.
Sgt.	Barnett, L. F.	Machine Gun Corps.
Pte.	Baron, J. B.	Machine Gun Corps.

RECORD OF HONOURS. M.M. (continued).

Rank.	Name.	Regiment.
Pte.	Barrow, A.	Royal Army Service Corps.
Sgt.	Baum, B.	Essex Regiment.
Cpl.	Baum, R. W. (Bar)	Canadian Infantry.
Rfm.	Belkin, B.	King's Royal Rifle Corps.
Bombr.	Benjamin, B.	Royal Field Artillery.
L/Sgt.	Benjamin, E.	Australian Infantry.
Bombr.	Benjamin, F.	Royal Horse Artillery.
Pte.	Benjamin, H.	Welsh Regiment.
Pte.	Benjamin, H.	Gloucester Regiment.
Rfm.	Bentley, J.*	London Regiment.
Cpl.	Berg, L. A.	New Zealand Infantry.
Cpl.	Bernstein, A.	Royal Berkshire Regiment.
Coy.-Sgt.-Major	Bitton, B.	London Regiment.
Sgt.	Black, M.	Royal Fusiliers.
Rfm.	Blain, S.*	King's Royal Rifle Corps.
Pte.	Block, I.	Border Regiment.
Pte.	Bloom, H.	Rifle Brigade.
Sgt.	Bloom, I.	Royal Army Medical Corps.
Cpl.	Bloom, M.	38th Royal Fusiliers.
L/Cpl.	Bloomberg, G.	York and Lancaster Regiment.
Pte.	Blostein, P.*	Royal Dublin Fusiliers.
Pte.	Bogard, P.	South Wales Borderers.
Sgt.	Bonas, C. W. (Bar)	East Yorkshire Regiment.
Pte.	Bond, J.	Canadian Infantry.
Bombr.	Brandon, M.	Royal Garrison Artillery.
Pte.	Breitman, J. G.*	Australian Infantry.
Sgt.	Burke, S.	Royal Army Medical Corps.
Pte.	Caminer, H. (D.C.M.)	Canadian Infantry.
Sgt.	Camm, H.	R.A.S.C.
Pte.	Cantor, W.	New Zealand Medical Corps.
Cpl.	Casbourne, G.	Essex Regiment.
Pte.	Casher, B.	Worcestershire Regiment.
Dvr.	Cashman, G. A.	Royal Field Artillery.
Pte.	Chetminski, H.	Royal Fusiliers.
Sig.	Child, W.	Machine Gun Corps.
Pte.	Cohen, A.	Royal Fusiliers.
Pte.	Cohen, A.	Middlesex Regiment.
Pte.	Cohen, A.	Canadian Infantry.
Pte.	Cohen, A. H.	Canadian Infantry.
2nd A/M.	Cohen, D.	Royal Air Force.
Cpl.	Cohen, D.*	Welsh Regiment.
Rfm.	Cohen, E.	London Regiment.
S/Major	Cohen, H.	Labour Corps.
Pte.	Cohen, H.	Canadian Highlanders.
L/Cpl.	Cohen, J.*	London Regiment.
Pte.	Cohen, M.	Oxford and Bucks Light Infantry.
Sgt.	Cohen, M.	Middlesex Regiment.
Sgt. (later 2nd Lieut.)	Cohen, M.*	Durham Light Infantry.
Gnr.	Cohen, P.	Royal Garrison Artillery.
Pte.	Cohen, P. S.	Australian Infantry.
L/Cpl.	Cohen, R.	King's Royal Rifle Corps.
Pte.	Conbisley, A.	Canadian Infantry.
Gnr.	Coss, B.	Royal Field Artillery.
Sgt.	Davis, I.	R.A.S.C.
Cpl.	Davis, P.	Machine Gun Corps.
Pte.	Davis, R.	Royal Fusiliers.

RECORD OF HONOURS. M.M. (continued).

Rank. Name. Regiment.

Rank & Name	Regiment
Dvr. Diamond, A. S.	Honourable Artillery Company.
Pte. Dion, J.*	Northampton Regiment.
Cpl. Drapkin, I. A.	Royal Fusiliers.
L/Cpl. Elfman, M.	38th Royal Fusiliers.
Pte. Elias, H.	Royal Scots.
L/Cpl. Elias, J.	Royal Welsh Fusiliers.
Sgt. Emanuel, J.	Australian Infantry.
B/Cpl. Emanuel, J.	Welsh Guards.
Bdr. Falk, W.	Royal Field Artillery.
Act.-L/Cpl. Feldman, J.	Canadian Infantry.
Cpl. Field, R.	Rifle Brigade.
Sgt. Flatow, J. W.	East Yorkshire Regiment.
Cpl.-Sig. Fleisig, M. (Bar)	Canadian Infantry.
Sgt. Frankenberg, G.	Royal Engineers.
Pte. Franks, A. J.	East Kent Regiment.
Gnr. Franks, F.	Canadian Infantry.
Spr. Fraser, R. E.	Royal Engineers.
Cpl. Freedman, H.	Royal Field Artillery.
Pte. Freedman, M.*	West Riding Regiment.
Pte. Friedman, I.	Notts and Derby Regiment.
Cpl. Frieze,, M.	Canadian Field Artillery.
Sgt. Furst, R. M.	Royal Scots Fusiliers.
Sgt. Fyman, A	Northumberland Fusiliers.
L/Cpl. Gallewski, M.*	Royal Army Medical Corps.
Sgt. Glazier, L.	Canadian Infantry.
Pte. Gluckstein, C. S.*	Royal Army Medical Corps.
Pte. Godfrey, E. S.	London Yeomanry.
L/Cpl. Glynn, S.	Manchester Regiment.
Sgt. Gold, A. (D.C.M.)	London Regiment.
Pte. Goldberg, S.	Royal West Kent Regiment.
Pte. Goldstein, A.	London Regiment.
Pte. Goldstone, L.	Royal Fusiliers.
Pte. Goldstone, L.	Royal Irish Rifles.
Pte. Gollop, A.	Duke of Cornwall's Light Infantry.
Pte. Gordon, A.	Canadian Infantry.
Pte. Gordon, C.	Royal Fusiliers.
Pte. Gottlieb, H. A. (D.C.M.)	Australian Infantry.
Pte. Gourevitch, R.	Canadian Infantry.
Gnr. Green, I.	Royal Field Artillery.
Bombr. Green, M.	Royal Field Artillery.
Sgt. Greenburg, J.	Notts and Derby Regiment.
L/Cpl. Grodner, A.	Duke of Cornwall's Light Infantry.
Rfm. Haagman, E.	London Regiment.
Pte. Harris, D.	London Regiment.
Pte. Harris, L.	Rifle Brigade.
L/Cpl. Harris, M.	Royal Army Medical Corps.
Cpl. Harris, M. J. H.	Canadian Infantry.
Cpl. Hart, E. A.	Royal Fusiliers.
A.B. Hart, H.	R.N.D.
L/Cpl. Hart, W. H.	London Regiment.
Gnr. Hartsilver, C. D.	Royal Field Artillery.
Cpl. Hassan, V.	London Regiment.
Cpl. Hayes, M.	Gloucester Regiment.
Gnr. Heilbron, V. H.*	Royal Horse Artillery.
Rfm. Hernberg, D.	London Regiment.
Sgt. Himmell, H.	Northumberland Fusiliers.

RECORD OF HONOURS. M.M. (*continued*).

Rank. Name. Regiment.

Rank & Name	Regiment
Pte. (later Lieut.) HIRSCHFELD, F. (D.C.M.)	Worcestershire Regiment.
Spr. HIRSCHKOP, C.	Royal Engineers.
Pte. HOFFMAN, S.	Royal Irish Rifles.
Pte. HYAMS, F.	West Yorkshire Regiment.
Pte. HYAMS, H. C.	Royal Fusiliers.
Bombr. HYAMSON, J.	Royal Field Artillery.
Pte. HYMAN, A.	Leicester Regiment.
Pte. ISAACS, P. J.	Canadian Infantry.
Cpl. JACKSON, A.	Royal Army Service Corps.
Sgt. JACKSON, B.	Northumberland Fusiliers.
Pte. JACOBS, A. A.	London Regiment.
Pte. JACOBS, A. N.	Australian Army Medical Corps.
Gnr. JACOBS, B.	Royal Field Artillery.
Pte. JACOBS, C.	Machine Gun Corps.
Pte. JACOBS, C. I.	South African Medical Corps.
L/Cpl. JACOBS, C. J.	Australian Infantry.
Pte. JACOBS, C. R.	Lincolnshire Regiment.
Sgt. JACOBS, G.	Royal Engineers.
Pte. JACOBS, G. H.	Durham Light Infantry.
Flight-Sgt. JACOBS, J.	Royal Air Force.
Spr. JACOBS, S.	Canadian Engineers.
Cpl. JACOBS, S. F.	Machine Gun Corps.
Cpl. JACOBSON, A.	Australian Infantry.
Spr. JACOBSON, O.	Canadian Engineers.
Cpl. JONAS, L. M.	Canadian Infantry.
Pte. (later Lieut.) JONES, M.	Australian Infantry.
L/Cpl. JOSHUA, W.	Welsh Regiment.
Sgt. KAUFMAN, H.	Manchester Regiment.
Gnr. KAYE, S.	Royal Field Artillery.
Sgt. KEMPLER, H. W.	Middlesex Regiment.
Pte. KLEIN, F. W.	Australian Infantry.
Cpl. KLEIN, W. T.	Royal Warwickshire Regiment.
Cpl. KRAFT, J. H.	Royal Field Artillery.
Pte. KRAMER, M.	London Regiment.
Pte. KREMER, I.	Leicestershire Regiment.
Pte. KRONENBURG, N.	Welsh Regiment.
Pte. KUSHNER, L.	Canadian Infantry.
Pte. LAWRENCE, H.	Middlesex Regiment.
Spr. LAWRENCE, S. J.*	Royal Engineers.
Pte. LAZARUS, C. M.	South African Infantry.
Pte. LAZARUS, D. (D.C.M.)	Australian Machine Gun Corps.
Pte. LAZARUS, H. (D.C.M.)	Leicestershire Regiment.
Pte. LAZARUS, P.	London Regiment.
C.-S.-M. LEBELSKI, I.	Manchester Regiment.
Sgt. LEVEY, R.	Canadian Infantry.
C.-S.-M. LEVEY, S. M.	London Regiment.
Sgt. LEVI, A.	Royal Inniskilling Fusiliers.
Pte. LEVIE, A.	Middlesex Regiment.
Sgt. LEVIN, F.	Royal Fusiliers.
Cpl. LEVIN, W.	Machine Gun Corps.
Pte. LEVINSON, L.*	South African Infantry.
Pte. LEVITT, A. E.	Royal Fusiliers.
Cpl. LEVY, A.	Royal Army Medical Corps.
Sgt. LEVY, A.*	Australian Infantry.
Pte. LEVY, B. R. (Bar)	Canadian Infantry.
Rfm. LEVY, E.	London Regiment.
Pte. LEVY, E. F.	Hampshire Regiment.

RECORD OF HONOURS. M.M. (continued).

Rank.	Name.	Regiment.
Pte.	LEVY, H. S.	Australian Army Medical Corps.
Sgt.	LEVY, I. (Bar)	Duke of Wellington's Regiment.
Pte.	LEVY, L.	Manchester Regiment.
Pte.	LEVY, S.	King's Liverpool Regiment.
Cpl.	LEWIN, W.	Machine Gun Corps.
L/Cpl.	LEWIS, M.	Australian Infantry.
Sgt.	LEWIS, M.	Royal Fusiliers.
Pte.	LIPMAN, A.	London Regiment.
A.B.	LIPMAN, H.	R.N.D.
Pte.	LITTMAN, S.*	Australian Infantry.
L/Cpl.	LOBEL, F.	Middlesex Regiment.
L/Cpl.	LYONS, A.	Canadian Infantry.
Cpl.	LYONS, H. J.	London Regiment.
Pte.	LYONS, J. M.	Notts. and Derby Regiment.
Pte.	MALATSKI, M.	Duke of Wellington's Regiment.
Dvr.	MARKS, A.	Canadian Field Artillery.
Pte.	MARKS, C. H.	Australian Infantry Force.
Pte.	MARKS, H. E.	Australian Infantry.
Pte.	MARKS, J.	Canadian Infantry.
Pte.	MARKS, L. Y.	Royal Warwickshire Regiment.
Sgt.	MARKS, M. H.	Royal Field Artillery.
L/Cpl.	MARTIN, B.	Royal Fusiliers.
Cpl.	MAYER, G.	Rifle Brigade.
Cpl.	MENDOZA, R.	Royal Engineers.
Pte.	MEYER, P.	Canadian Infantry.
Sgt.	MICHAELS, S.	Canadian Infantry.
Sgt.	MILCOVITCH, M.	London Regiment.
Pte.	MILLER, D. (D.C.M.)	Manchester Regiment.
L/Cpl.	MIRON, G.	King's Royal Rifle Corps.
Pte.	MITCHELL, P.	Middlesex Regiment.
Sgt.	MORRIS, J. L.	2nd Canadian M.G.C.
Miss	MOSELEY, R. G.	F.A.N.Y.
L/Cpl.	MOSES, D.	Durham Light Infantry.
Cpl.	MOSES, G.	Royal Field Artillery.
Sgt.	MOSS, A.	Duke of Cornwall's Light Infantry.
Pte.	MYERS, C.	Canadian Infantry.
Pte.	MYERS, C.	Royal Irish Fusiliers.
L/Cpl.	MYERS, J. J.	Royal Engineers.
Pte.	MYERS, J. M.	London Regiment.
Cpl.	MYERS, P.	London Regiment.
Cpl.	MYERS, S.	Hampshire Regiment.
Pte.	MYERS, S.	Canadian Infantry.
Pte.	MYERS, T.	King's Royal Rifle Corps.
Sgt.	NATHAN, L.	London Regt.
Pte.	NORMAN, M.	Labour Corps.
L/Cpl.	OBERMAN, P.	Royal Fusiliers.
Sgt.	OLSEN, C. (D.C.M.)	Lancashire Fusiliers.
Sgt.	OPPENHEIM, R.	Royal Engineers.
Cpl.	PHILLIPS, H. G.	Middlesex Regiment.
Bdr.	PHILLIPS, B.	Canadian Artillery.
Sgt.	PHILLIPS, J.	Gloucester Regiment.
Cpl.	PHILLIPSON, L. G.	Machine Gun Corps.
Gnr.	POLAK, G. E.*	Australian Field Artillery.
Pte.	PYZER, W. (Bar)	Lincoln Regiment.

RECORD OF HONOURS. M.M. (continued).

Rank.	Name.	Regiment.
Gnr.	RAISMAN, M.	Royal Garrison Artillery.
Pte.	RAPHAEL, H.	Essex Regiment.
1st Class A.M.	RAPHAEL, H. S.	Australian Imperial Force.
L/Cpl.	REECE, W.	London Regiment.
L/Cpl.	ROBINSON, A. J.	38th Royal Fusiliers.
Sgt.	ROSEN, H. (D.C.M.)	Royal Engineers.
Pte.	ROSENBERG, J. M.	Australian Infantry.
Pte.	ROSENTHAL, H.*	Canadian Infantry.
Pte.	RUBENS, L.	Liverpool Regiment.
Sgt.	RUDA, M.	Royal Fusiliers.
Cpl.	SAGAR, H.	Machine Gun Corps.
Pte.	SAMUEL, A. (D.C.M.)	Machine Gun Corps.
Sgt.	SAMUEL, J. H. (Bar)	Royal Field Artillery.
Cpl.	SAMUEL, J. M.	Royal Field Artillery.
Pte.	SAMUEL, S.	East Lancashire Regiment.
Pte.	SAMUELS, H. (D.C.M.)	Machine Gun Corps.
Gnr.	SAMUELS, M.	Royal Garrison Artillery.
Pte.	SAMUELS, M.*	Rifle Brigade.
L/Cpl.	SANKEWITZ, P.	London Regiment.
Cpl.	SCHIMKOVITZ, E.	Australian Infantry.
C.S.M.	SCHOTTLANDER, S.	East Yorkshire Regiment.
Pte.	SCHRAM S.	Canadian Infantry.
L/Cpl.	SCHUMANN, J. D.	Australian Infantry.
Cpl.	SEFTON, L.	York and Lancaster Regt.
Pte.	SELIG, O. M.	Australian Infantry.
Pte.	SEPIACHVILE, R.	38th Royal Fusiliers.
Pte.	SHAPERO, L.	East Yorkshire Regiment.
Pte.	SHERMAN, H.	South African Infantry.
L/Cpl.	SHERWIN, M.	Rifle Brigade.
Sgt.	SHINE, N.	Northampton Regiment.
Sgt.	SHOCK, C. H.	Royal Army Service Corps.
Pte.	SHULMAN, S.	Royal Fusiliers.
Pte.	SIDERMAN, W. W.	Royal Army Service Corps.
Rfm.	SILVER, L.	Rifle Brigade.
S/Sgt.	SILVERSTONE, D.	Royal Army Service Corps.
Pte.	SIMMONS, J. R.*	Australian Infantry.
Sgt.	SIMONS, P.	London Regiment.
Pte.	SIMONS, S. (D.C.M.)	Essex Regiment.
Sgt.	SOLLY, I.	Middlesex Regiment.
Sgt.	SOLOMON, B.	Royal Scots.
Pte.	SOLOMON, M.	York and Lancaster Regiment.
L/Cpl.	SOLOMONS, G. (Bar)	London Regiment.
Cpl.	SOLOMONS, J.*	Middlesex Regiment.
L/Cpl.	SOLOMONS, M.	Machine Gun Corps.
Pte.	SOLWAY, I.	Royal Welsh Fusiliers.
Sgt.	SPILG, G. (Bar)	Glasgow Highlanders.
L/Cpl.	STANLEY H.	Highland Light Infantry.
Pte.	STEINBERG, V. N.	King's Own Yorkshire Light Infantry.
Sgt.	STEINGOLD, N.	Royal Field Artillery.
L/Cpl	STERN, P.	Northumberland Fusiliers.
Pte.	SWERSKI, A.	Durham Light Infantry.
Sgt.	SYMMONS, L. F. A.	Royal Army Medical Corps.
Pte.	SYMONDS, M. H. V.	Royal Marine Light Infantry.
L/Cpl.	SYMONS, H.	Royal Army Medical Corps.
L/Cpl.	TOBIAS, R. R.	Canadian Infantry.
Pte.	TOBIAS, W.	Leicester Regiment.

RECORD OF HONOURS. M.M. (continued).

Rank. Name. Regiment.

Cpl. Toff, J.		Middlesex Regiment.
Rfm. Tompofsky, M.*		West Yorkshire Regiment.
L/Cpl. Ullman, G. D.		Canadian Corps.
Pte. Valentine, S.		West Yorkshire Regiment.
Sgt. Vickers, G.		Royal Engineers.
Pte. Weisberg, T. (Bar)		London Regiment.
Cpl. White, L. W.		Manchester Regiment.
Sgt. Winter, M.		London Regiment.
Pte. Woolf, D.		London Regiment.
Rfm. Zimmerman, L.		Rifle Brigade.
Pte. Zuidema, L.		Canadian Infantry.
L/Cpl. Zolowski, E.*		Notts. and Derby Regiment.

Mentioned in Despatches

Lieut. Aaronsohn, A.	Intelligence Corps, Egypt.
Major Abrahams, A. C.	British Red Cross.
Capt. Abrahams, R.	Cheshire Regiment.
2nd Lieut. Abrahams, S.	38th Royal Fusiliers.
Capt. Abrahamson, A.	Intelligence Corps.
Rev. Adler, Michael, D.S.O. (twice)	Senior Chaplain, France.
2nd Lieut. Alexander, G. R.*	Royal Sussex Regiment.
Lieut. Alexander, S. A.*	Royal Welsh Fusiliers.
Capt. Andrade, E. N. da C.	Royal Garrison Artillery.
Capt. Balcon, P. C.	Royal Engineers.
Rev. Barnett, A.	Senior Chaplain, France.
Lieut.-Col. Beddington, C.	Westmoreland and Cumberland Yeo.
Lieut.-Col. Beddington, E. H. L. (6 times)	Lancers and General Staff.
Lieut. Beer, A. H.*	West Lancs. Royal Field Artillery.
Lieut. Beer, A. I.	London Regiment.
2nd Lieut. Behrend, A. F.	East Lancashire Regiment.
Lieut. Behrens, W.	Royal Field Artillery.
Capt. Benjamin, A.	Royal Army Medical Corps.
Lieut. Benzecry, S.*	Royal Fusiliers.
Capt. Bergman, R. H.	Royal Army Service Corps.
Major Berlandina, H. H. (M.C.)	Royal Engineers.
Capt. Beyfus, G. H.	West Riding Regiment.
Lieut. Birnstingl, H. J.	Royal Engineers.
Capt. Blashki, R. H.*	Australian Field Artillery.
Capt. Blond, N. L. (twice)	General List.
Capt. and Adjt. Brilliant, L.	Indian Army.
Capt. Caro, P.	Australian Engineers.
2nd Lieut. Castello, S. M.	Intelligence Corps.
Lieut. Chapman, E. J. C. (M.C.)	Royal Army Service Corps.
Capt. Cohen, A. F.	Australian Engineers.
Surg.-Lieut. Cohen, B.	R.N.V.R.
Lieut. Cohen, C. D.	West Yorkshire Regiment.
Capt. Cohen, D. D. M.	Royal Field Artillery.
Capt. Cohen, E. G.	Royal Engineers.
Capt. Cohen, E. V.	Royal Army Service Corps.
Major Cohen, J. B. B.	King's Liverpool Regiment.
Lieut.-Col. Cohen, C. Waley (twice)	Royal Army Service Corps.
Capt. Cohen, J. M.	South African S.C.
Lieut.-Col. Cohen, H. E. (D.S.O.)	Australian Field Artillery.
Lt.-Col. Cohen, J. Waley (D.S.O.) (6 times)	London Regiment.
Major Cohen, L. (D.S.O., M.C.)	South African Defence Corps.

RECORD OF HONOURS. Mentioned (continued).

Rank.	Name.	Regiment.
Lieut.	COHEN, M. (M.C.)	Royal Engineers.
Lt./Qmr.	COHEN, M.	Royal Army Medical Corps.
Lieut.	COHEN, M.	Royal Army Medical Corps.
Sgt. (later Lieut.)	COHEN, M.*	Durham Light Infantry.
Capt.	COHEN, W. S.	Hertfordshire Yeomanry.
Capt.	COHN, J. D.	British Red Cross Society.
Lieut.	COPLANS, J.	Royal Army Medical Corps.
Major	COPLANS, M. (D.S.O.) (4 times)	Royal Army Medical Corps.
2nd Lieut.	DACOSTA, R.	Duke of Wellington's Regiment.
Lieut	DAVIES, A. A.	South African Infantry.
Lt.-Col.	D'AVIGDOR-GOLDSMID, O. E. (twice)	Royal Army Service Corps.
Lieut.	DEFRIES, F.	Middlesex Regiment.
Capt.	DELGADO, A. E.	Royal Army Medical Corps.
Lieut.	DE PASS, F. A. (V.C.)*	34th Poona Horse.
Lieut.	DE PASS, R. D.	Royal Air Force.
Lieut.	DIAMOND, J. (M.C.)	Royal Air Force.
Lieut.	DURLACHER, B. R.	Border Regiment.
Lieut.-Col.	ELKAN, C. J. (D.S.O.) (5 times)	Royal Irish Fusiliers.
Lieut.	ESPIR, I. J.	R.A.S.C.
Lieut.	EZRA, E.	I.A.R.O.
Capt.	FELDMAN, I.	Royal Army Medical Corps.
Capt.	FINZI, N. S.	Royal Army Medical Corps.
Cpl.	FLATOW, F. W.	East Yorkshire Regiment.
Capt.	FRANKLIN, E. A.	King's Own Yorkshire Light Infantry.
Asst.-Paymaster	FRANKLIN, J. E.	Royal Naval Reserve.
Rev.	FREEDMAN, D. I.	Chaplain, Australian Forces.
Capt.	GEE, R. (V.C., M.C.)	Royal Fusiliers.
Lieut.	GENESE, J. D.	Royal Army Medical Corps.
Lieut.	GINGOLD, F. M.	Army Pay Corps.
Major	GLASS, J. N.	Royal Army Veterinary Corps.
Capt.	GLUCKSTEIN, I. M.	London Regiment.
Lieut.	GLUCKSTEIN, L. H.	Suffolk Regiment.
Lieut.	GOLDBERG, G. H. A.	Indian Army.
Capt.	GOLBIE, J. M.	Welsh Regiment.
Capt.	GOLDBERG, R. (M.C.)	Machine Gun Corps.
Rev.	GOLLOP, M.	Chaplain, Salonica.
Rev.	GRAJEWSKY, S.	Chaplain, Egypt.
Capt.	GREEN, S. M.	London Regiment.
Lieut.	HADIDA, P.	Gloucestershire Regiment.
Major	HALFORD, E. S.	Royal Flying Corps.
Major	HARRIS, A. I.	Royal Army Service Corps.
Capt.	HARRIS, L. G. R. (M.C.)	West Riding Regiment.
Lieut.	HARRIS, L. J.	Royal Engineers.
Lieut.-Col.	HARRIS, O. M. (D.S.O.)	Royal Horse Artillery.
Capt.	HART, A. C.*	Northampton Regiment.
Capt.	HART, C. L.*	West Riding Regiment.
Lieut.	HART, H. R.	King's Own Royal Lancaster Regt.
2nd Lieut.	HART, L. V.	Royal Engineers.
Lieut.	HARTOG, D. H. (M.C.)	Gloucestershire Regiment.
Lieut.	HARVEY-SAMUEL, G. D.	Middlesex Regiment.
Lieut.-Col.	HEILBRON, I. M. (3 times)	Royal Army Service Corps.
Capt.	HENRIQUES, B. L. Q. (twice)	Tank Corps.
Capt.	HENRIQUES, P. Q.	Royal Engineers.
Lieut.-Col.	HENRIQUES, R. Q. (twice)	Royal Engineers.
Major	HENRIQUES, W. Q. (3 times)	Machine Gun Corps.
Capt.	HOFFNUNG-GOLDSMID, C. J.	Lancers.

RECORD OF HONOURS. Mentioned (continued).

Rank. Name.	Regiment.
Major HORE-BELISHA, I. L.	Army Service Corps.
Lieut. HYAMS, G. S.	King's Own Royal Lancaster Regt.
Major HYMAN, E. M. (D.S.O.) (twice)	Australian Imperial Force.
Major ISAACS, I. B.	Royal Army Service Corps.
Capt. ISAACS, M. (M.C.)	Royal Naval Division.
Lieut. ISAACS, W. D.	Australian Infantry.
Lieut. JACOBI, M. R.	Canadian Infantry.
Capt. JACOBS, C. (M.C., Bar) (twice)	Royal Army Medical Corps.
Capt. JACOBS, H.	Australian Infantry.
Capt. JACOBS, H. W.	Tank Corps.
2nd Lieut. JACOBS, D.*	South Lancashire Regiment.
Capt. JACOBS, R.	Royal Army Medical Corps.
Lieut. JACOB, V. V.*	Oxford and Bucks. Light Infantry.
Lieut. JACOBSON, A. R.	New Zealand Force.
Major JONAS, H. D.	Special List.
Lieut.-Col. JOSEPH, R. H. (D.S.O.)	Royal Engineers.
Lieut. JOSEPHS, S. H.	Royal Engineers.
Lieut. JUDAH, D. A.	Indian Army.
Lieut. KAYE, M. M.	Royal Air Force.
Major KENNARD, G. C. (M.C.) (twice)	Royal Engineers.
Lieut.-Col. KISCH, F. H. (D.S.O.) (twice)	Royal Engineers. Indian Army.
Capt. KROLIK, E. (M.C.)*	Rifle Brigade.
Lieut. LADENBURY, A.	Intelligence Corps.
Capt. LANDSBERG, H. V.	Yeomanry.
Major LAZARUS, K. M.	Worcester Regiment.
Major LEON, J.	Royal Army Service Corps.
Capt. LEVENSON, G. R. F.	Royal Inniskilling Fusiliers.
Lieut.-Col. LEVEY, J. H. D.S.O. (3 times)	Gordon Highlanders.
Lieut. LEVY, J. M. D'A.	Royal Air Force.
Capt. LEVI, K. M.*	Australian Army Medical Corps.
2nd Lieut. LEVY, J. (M.C.)	Royal Fusiliers.
Lieut. LEVY, L. A.	Special List.
Lieut. LEVY, P. P.	Intelligence Corps.
Capt. LEVY, T. H.	Australian Provost Corps.
Major LEVY, W. H. (D.S.O.)	Royal Army Service Corps.
Lieut.-Col. LIGHTSTONE, H. H.	R.A.M.C.
Lieut. LION, B. S.	Royal Engineers.
Lieut. LIPSEY, S. M.	London Regt. and Royal Fusiliers.
Lieut. LOTINGA, A. G.	Northumberland Field Coy., R.E.
Intell. Agent LOWENBERG, F. R.	South African Intelligence Department.
Major MARKS, D. G. (M.C.)	Australian Infantry.
Lieut. MARKS, J. S.	Royal Engineers.
Lieut. MARKS, P.	R.A.S.C.
Lieut. MARSH, L.	Canadian Infantry.
Qrmr. and Hon. Capt. MARKS, R.	Australian Infantry.
Lieut. MARKS, R. M	Indian Army
Lieut. MARSDEN, E.	Rifle Brigade.
Capt. MEZA, J. de (M.C.)*	London Regiment.
2nd Lieut. MELHADO, O. S.*	King's Own Yorkshire Light Infantry.
Lieut.-Col. MICHOLLS, W. H.	Hussars.
Capt. and Bt. Major MOCATTA, V. E.	Hussars.
Lt.-Gen. MONASH, Sir J., G.C.M.G. (6 times)	Australian Corps.
Capt. MONTAGU, The Hon. L. S. (D.S.O.)	Royal Naval Division.
Major MONTEFIORE, T. H. SEBAG (D.S.O., M.C.)	Royal Horse Artillery.
Major MONTEFIORE, C. E. SEBAG (M.B.E.)	Lancers.

RECORD OF HONOURS. Mentioned (continued).

Rank. Name.	Regiment.
Capt. MONTEFIORE, L. N. (O.B.E.)	Hampshire Regiment.
Capt. MONTEFIORE, W. SEBAG (M.C.)	Lancers.
Capt. MORDECAI, L. R.	Lancashire Fusiliers.
2nd Lieut. MORRIS, H.	38th Royal Fusiliers.
Lieut. MOSES, D. A. H. (M.C.)	Royal Army Medical Corps.
Lieut. MOSES, W. J.	Royal Field Artillery.
Capt. MOSS, L.	Royal Army Service Corps.
Lieut. MYERS, N. C.	Royal Engineers.
Lieut.-Col. MYERS, C. S. (C.B.E.)	Royal Army Medical Corps.
Qmr. and Capt. NATHAN, A.	Royal Army Service Corps.
Capt. NATHAN, A. A.	Herts. Yeomanry and R.A.F.
Capt. NATHAN, A. F.	General List.
Capt. NATHAN, E. G.	General List.
2nd Lieut. NATHAN, R. P.	Royal Field Artillery.
Capt. PHILLIPS, J. S.	South Staffordshire Regiment.
Capt. PIZA, D.*	East Yorkshire Regiment.
2nd Lieut. POLACK, B. J.*	Worcestershire Regiment.
Lieut. POLLAK, L.	London Regiment.
2nd Lieut. Price, W.	Royal Inniskilling Fusiliers
Capt. PYKE, W. T.	Hampshire Regiment.
Capt. RACIONZER, J. L.	39th Royal Fusiliers.
Major RAPHAEL, R. A. (M.C.)	Royal Warwickshire Regiment.
Lieut. RAPPOPORT, F. G.	Indian Army.
Major RICHARDSON, A. N. (D.S.O., M.C.) (twice)	King's Own Yorkshire Light Infantry.
Lieut. ROLO, C.	Zion Mule Corps.
Capt. ROSEBERY, S. S.	Royal Army Medical Corps.
Lieut. ROTHSCHILD, A. G. DE	Bucks. Yeomanry.
Major ROTHSCHILD, E. A. DE* (4 times)	Bucks. Yeomanry.
Major ROTHSCHILD, F.	Royal Sussex Regiment.
Capt. ROTHSCHILD, G.	Royal Army Service Corps.
Capt. SALAMAN, R. N.	Royal Army Medical Corps.
2nd Lieut. SAMUEL, E. B.*	Middlesex Regiment.
Lieut.-Col. SAMUEL, F. D. (D.S.O.) (three times).	London Regiment.
Capt. SAMUEL, L.	Royal Field Artillery.
Capt. SAMUEL, S. G.	Australian Infantry.
Lieut.-Col. SAMUEL, W. H.	Middlesex Regiment.
Lieut. SASSOON, A. M.	Hussars.
Capt. SASSOON, Sir P. Bart., M.P., (four times).	Yeomanry.
2nd Lieut. SCHAVERIN, S.	Yorks and Lancaster Regiment.
Brig.-Gen. SELIGMAN, H. S. (D.S.O.) (four times).	Royal Field Artillery.
Lieut. SIMONS, H. B.	Indian Army.
Major SISMAN, L.	Royal Army Service Corps.
Capt. SOLOMON, D. C.	Middlesex Regiment.
Lieut.-Col. SOLOMON, H. J. (M.C.) (four times).	Royal Army Service Corps.
Qmr. and Hon. Lieut. SOLOMON, J.	Royal Sussex Regiment.
Major SOLOMON, J. B. (M.C.)	Oxford & Bucks. L.I. and R.A.F.
Capt. SOLOMON, J. C.	London Regiment.
Capt. SOLOMON, P. H.	Royal Field Artillery.
Capt. SOLOMON, R. B. (M.C.) (twice)	Royal Field Artillery.
2nd Lieut. SPANIER, E. J.	Honorable Artillery Company.
Lieut.-Col. STERN, A. G. (C.M.G.)	Special List.

RECORD OF HONOURS. Mentioned (continued).

Rank. Name.	Regiment.
Capt. STERN, B.	K. Liverpool Regt. and Div. Staff.
Major STERN, F. C., (O.B.E.) (M.C.)	County of London Yeomanry.
Capt. SUMMERFIELD, M.	King's Royal Rifle Corps.
Lieut. TRIEFUS, A.	R.H.A. and Intelligence Corps.
Lieut. VAN DEN BERGH, J. S.	R.A.S.C.
Major WALEY, E. G. S.	London Regiment.
Major WALEY, A. (M.C.	Royal Engineers.
Capt. WALTERS, A. B.	London Regiment.
Lieut.-Col. WEISBERG, H. (D.S.O.)	City of London Yeomanry.
Lieut. WOOLF, A. S.	Army Cyclist Corps.
Capt. WOOLF, E. S.	Royal Army Service Corps.
Lieut. WOLFFE, B.*	38th Royal Fusiliers.
Clerk ABRAHAM, J.	Indian Veterinary Corps.
Sgt. ABRAHAMS, H. E.	Royal Engineers.
Pte. ABRAHAMS, J.	Yeomanry.
Rfm. ABRAHAMS, S.*	Queen's Westminster Rifles.
Sgt. ADLER, P. (M.M.)*	Royal Fusiliers.
Pte. ANGEL, J.	39th Royal Fusiliers.
S.S.M. BARNETT, J.	R.A.S.C.
L/Cpl. BENJAMIN, C. A.	Canadian Infantry.
Sgt. BENJAMIN, J.	Australian Army Service Corps.
L/Cpl. BENPORATH, F. .H	Australian Infantry.
Cpl. BENJAMIN, W.	Royal Fusiliers.
Pte. BANET, L.	South Rhodesian Vol.
Sgt. BERGER, C. H.	Uganda Medical Service.
Rfm. BROD, H.	Rifle Brigade.
Coy.-Sgt.-Maj. BLACK, C.	Royal Fusiliers.
Pte. BLATTNER, C.	Royal Scots Fusiliers.
Sgt. BLOOMFIELD, F.	Norfolk Regiment.
Pte. BLUMENTHAL, J.	38th Royal Fusiliers.
Sgt. BOODSON, D.	Manchester Regiment.
C.S.M. BOONER, J. T.	39th Royal Fusiliers.
Rfm. BROD, H.	Royal Irish Rifles.
Cpl. CLEEF, I. V.	Labour Corps.
Sgt. COHEN, A. (D.C.M.)	Welsh Regiment.
Sgt. COHEN, A.	Royal Army Service Corps.
Sgt. COHEN, F. G.	Royal Warwickshire Regiment.
Pte. COHEN, H.	39th Royal Fusiliers.
Pte. COHEN, M.	Bucks. Regiment.
Sgt. COHEN, P.	Royal Engineers (Nyasaland).
Pte DAVIES, J.	Royal Sussex Regiment.
Miss DAVIS, J.	V.A.D.
Pte. EDELSTEIN, H.	Australian Infantry.
S/Sgt. EMMANUEL, E.	Royal Army Service Corps.
Pte. ERSHCOVITZ, M.	Zion Mule Corps.
S/Sgt.-Major FEIGENBAUM, S. S.	Labour Company.
C.Q.M.S. FINERMAN, H.	R.A.S.C.
Sgt. FRANKEL, F. D.	H.Q. Australian Forces.
Sgt. GENESE, J.	Royal Field Artillery.
Pte. GLASER, P. W.	Middlesex Labour Company.
Pte. GOLDBERG, M.	Royal Army Service Corps.

RECORD OF HONOURS. Mentioned (continued).

Rank. Name.	Regiment.
Pte. GOLDWATER, S. A.	London Regiment.
Flight-Sgt. GOODMAN, E.	Royal Air Force.
Staff-Sgt. GOODMAN, R.	R.A.S.C.
Cadet GOODMAN, S. F.	R.A.M.C.
Cpl. Clerk GOLDSTON, S. J.	Royal Air Force.
Pte. GREENBAUM, A.	Labour Corps.
Sgt. GREENBAUM, E. V.	39th Royal Fusiliers.
Sgt.-Major HARRIS, M.	London Regiment.
Cpl. HARRIS, M. J. H. (M.M.)	Canadian Infantry.
Sgt. HIRSCHFELD, F.	Worcestershire Regiment.
Sgt. ISAACS, A.	Royal Welsh Fusiliers.
Sub. Comdr. ISAACS, G.	Army Ordnance Corps.
Sgt. ISAACS, S.	Mounted Police.
Pte. ISAACS, S. J.	Royal Army Service Corps.
Sgt. ISRAEL, M. S.	Royal Engineers.
C.Q.M.S. JACKS, I.	Royal Munster Fusiliers.
L/Cpl. JACOBS, A.	Military Foot Police.
Cpl. JACOBS, H.	London Regiment.
Cpl. JACOBS, H.	Labour Corps.
Sgt. JACOBS, H. H.	Royal Flying Corps.
A.B. JACOBS, L.*	H.M.S. "Lord Nelson."
Sgt.-Maj. JACOBS, M.	Canadian Artillery.
L/Cpl. JACOBSON, F.	King's Own Scottish Borderers.
Staff Sgt.-Maj. JELLEN, J. (twice)	Royal Army Service Corps.
R.S.M. JENKINS, M.	Royal Field Artillery.
Cpl. JOSEPH, J. W.	Royal Engineers.
Sgt. JOSEPH, R.	Royal Garrison Artillrey.
Pte. KARSTADT, W.	38th Royal Fusiliers.
Sgt. KAUFMAN, H.	Lancashire Fusiliers.
Pte. LANDAU, R. C.	East African Force.
Cpl. LEVEY, G. T.	Royal West Kent Regiment.
Sister LEVEY, M. V., Miss	A.R.R.C.
Rgt.-Qmr.-Sgt. LEVY, E.	Royal Berkshire Regiment.
C.S.M. LEVY, S.	Labour Corps.
Sgt. LIEBERMAN, C. E.	Oxford & Bucks Light Infantry.
S/Sgt. LION, H. M.	Royal Army Medical Corps.
Sgt. LYON, C. C.	London R.E.
Pte. MARKS, H. A.	Australian Army Medical Corps.
L/Cpl. MICHAEL, J.	Highland Light Infantry.
Sgt. MORDECAI, M. J.	Royal Army Medical Corps.
MOSELEY, Miss R. G.	F.A.N.Y.
Cpl. MOSES, G.	Yeomanry.
Sgt. MYERS, A.	Royal Engineers.
R.Q.M.S. MYERS, G.	Rifle Brigade.
Pte. NEWMAN, S.	King's Liverpool Regiment.
Sgt. NOSCOVITCH, S.	Machine Gun Corps.
Staff Nurse OPPENHEIMER, Miss E.	Queen Alexandra's Imp. Nursing Serv.
Sgt. OVITCH, J.	Northumberland Fusiliers.
Bombr. PHILLIPS, B.C.	Canadian Artillery.
Cpl. PLATER, J.	R.A.S.C.
Sgt. PYZER, R.	Royal Engineers.
Pte. RAPHAEL, H. L.	City of London Yeomanry.

RECORD OF HONOURS. Mentioned (continued).

Rank. Name.	Regiment.
Pte. REGARDIE, B.	R.A.S.C.
Sgt. ROMAIN, H. E.	Royal Army Medical Corps.
Pte. ROSEMAN, M.	Durham Light Infantry.
Pte. ROSEN, L.	Royal Army Medical Corps.
Bombr. ROSENBERG, H. A.	Royal Field Artillery.
Sgt. ROSENBAUM, M. (M.S.M.)	Canadian Infantry.
Pte. ROSENBERG, N.	Zion Mule Corps.
Sgt. ROSENBERG, S.	London Regiment.
S/Major ROSENBERG, W. H.	London Regiment.
Sgt. ROSENBLOOM, F. S.	Egyptian Labour Corps.
Sister ROSENTHAL, L. (R.R.C.)	Australian Nursing Service.
Sgt. ROUSSIN, I.	38th Royal Fusiliers.
Pte. SAMSON, KHAN SAHEB. R.	Head Clerk, Kukee Arsenal, India.
Pte. SAMUEL, E.*	Australian Infantry.
Sgt. SAMUEL, R. B.	Middlesex Regiment.
Pte. SAPERIA, M.	Labour Corps.
Sgt. SCHIFF, A.	Border Regiment.
L/Cpl. SILVERA, L. L.	British West Indian Regiment.
L/Cpl. SILVERBERG, E. A.	Royal Army Ordnance Corps.
Flight-Sgt. SIMONS, A. S.	Royal Air Force.
Pte. SIMONS, A. C.	Royal Army Medical Corps.
Cpl. SIMONS, A. G.	Royal Engineers.
Sgt. SIMONS, G. E.	R.A.S.C.
Gnr. SIMONS, R.	Royal Field Artillery.
Sgt. STROUD, E. F.	Middlesex Labour Company
Sgt. SYMONS, C. L.	Yeomanry.
L/Cpl. TOBIAS, J.	R.A.S.C.
S.M. WASS, M.	Royal Army Medical Corps.
Pte. WHITE, J. (V.C.)	King's Own Royal Lancaster Regt.
Sgt. WOOLFSTEIN, P.	Northumberland Fusiliers.
Sgt. ZAKTRAGER, M.	Royal Engineers.

Foreign Honours.

LEGION D'HONNEUR (FRENCH).

Lieut.-Col. BEDDINGTON, E. H. L. (D.S.O., M.C.)	Lancers.
Lieut.-Col. COHEN, C. WALEY,	Royal Army Service Corps.
Lieut.-Col. ELKAN, C. J. (D.S.O.)	General Staff.
Major ENOCH, C. D., T.D.	London Regiment.
Major GOLDSMITH, F. (O.B.E.)	Suffolk Yeomanry.
Lieut.-Col. LIGHTSTONE, H. (D.S.O., M.C.)	Canadian A.M.C.
Capt. LUMLEY, C. H.	South Lancashire Regiment.
Lieut.-Gen. MONASH, Sir J. (K.C.B.)	G.O.C. Australian Corps.
Major SASSOON, Sir P. A. G. D., Bart.	
Bdr.-Gen. SELIGMAN, H. S. (D.S.O.)	Royal Artillery.
Lieut.-Col. STERN, A. G., K.B.E., C.M.G.	Special List.

RECORD OF HONOURS.

FRENCH CROIX DE GUERRE AND PALME.

Rank.   Name.   Regiment.

Lieut. ABRAHAMS, H. - - - - Royal Army Medical Corps.
Lieut.-Col. MICHOLLS, W. H. M. - - Hussars.
Lieut.-General MONASH, Sir J. - - - G.O.C. Australian Corps.
Major SOLOMON, J. B. (M.C.) - - - Royal Air Force.
Capt. SPERO, S. - - - - - - Royal Engineers.

FRENCH CROIX DE GUERRE.

2nd Lieut. ABRAHAMS, F. - - - - Royal Air Force.
Capt. ALBU, W. G. - - - - - Royal Air Force.
Lieut. BENNETT, I. D. - - - - Royal Air Force.
Bomb. CASSIMER, W. - - - - - Royal Field Artillery.
Capt. CASTELLO, L. B. - - - - Norfolk Regiment.
Lieut.-Col. COHEN, J. WALEY, (D.S.O.) - London Regiment.
Major CORDOVA, V. L. de (M.C.) - - King's O. Royal Lancaster Regiment.
Sgt. CORIAT, P. M. (D.C.M.) - - - Machine Gun Corps.
Lieut. DIAMOND, S. (D.C.M.) - - - Australian Infantry.
Pte. ELIAS, H. - - - - - - Royal Scots.
Capt. FALCKE, J. - - - - - Norfolk Regiment.
Sgt. FISHER, W. - - - - - Middlesex Regiment.
Sgt. FRANKEL, G. - - - - - Royal Army Medical Corps.
Lieut. FRIEND, C. (M.C.) - - - - West Yorkshire Regiment.
Lieut. FURST, L. A. (M.C.) - - - King's Own Scottish Borderers.
Cadet GOODMAN, S. F. - - - - R.A.M.C.
Pte. HARRIS, J. - - - - - - Royal Garrison Artillery
Lieut.-Col. HARRIS, O. M. (D.S.O.) - - Royal Field Artillery.
Sgt. HOROWITZ, S. - - - - - Middlesex Regiment.
Sgt. JACOBS, D. A. - - - - - Royal Engineers.
Lieut. JACOBS, J. H. - - - - - South African Defence Corps.
Lieut.-Col. KISCH, F. H. (D.S.O.) - - Royal Engineers.
Major LOWE, S. J. (D.S.O.) - - - Royal Engineers.
Lieut. LANDAU, R. C. - - - - South African Forces.
Despatch Rider MARKS, B. - - - - Royal Army Service Corps.
Lieut. MARKS, P. - - - - - R.A.S.C.
Lieut.-Gen. MONASH, Sir J. - - -
Cpl. MYERS, S. M. - - - - - Royal Field Artillery.
Major POLLAK, E. R. H. (M.C.) - - - Royal Air Force.
Major POLLAK, L. A. (M.C.) - - - Machine Gun Corps.
Sgt. RAPHAEL, W. - - - - - Gordon Highlanders.
Pte. ROSEN, M. - - - - - - Rifle Brigade.
Major SASSOON, Sir P. A. G. D., Bart. -
Sgt. SCHUMANN, H. B. - - - - H.A.C. attd. Intelligence Corps.
L/Cpl. SCHWABACHER, L. M. - - - R.F. attd. Intelligence Corps.
Capt. SOLOMON, R.B. (M.C.) (Gold Star) - Royal Field Artillery.
Capt. TUCK, D. A. - - - - - Royal Air Force.
Capt. VOS, P. - - - - - - Norfolk Regiment.

MEDAILLE MILITAIRE D'HONNEUR (FRENCH).

S.Q.M.S. ASHER, A. - - - - - Royal Army Service Corps.
Sgt.-Major BAMBERGER, L. (M.M.) - - Royal Engineers.
Sgt. CAMINER, H. (D.C.M., M.M.) - - Canadian Infantry.
Pte. HART, L. L. - - - - - Intelligence Corps.
Sgt. HARTSILVER, C. (M.M.) - - - Royal Field Artillery.
Tpr. JACOBS, D. - - - - - - South African Horse.
Bdr. JACOBS, G. L. - - - - - Royal Field Artillery.
S.Q.M.S. JELLEN, J. - - - - - Royal Army Service Corps.
Major KEMPER, J. - - - - - Royal Air Force.
1st/A.M. SALTZBERG, J. - - - - Royal Air Force.
Pte. SAMUEL, G. A. - - - - - Honorable Artillery Company.

RECORD OF HONOURS.

CHEVALIER ORDER DU MERITE AGRICOLE (FRENCH).

Rank.	Name.	Regiment.
Capt.	ISAACS, M.	Royal Naval Division.

ORDER OF THE BLACK STAR (FRENCH).

Major. SASSOON, Sir P. A. G. D., Bart. (C.M.G.)

AMERICAN DISTINGUISHED SERVICE MEDAL.

Lieut.-Gen. MONASH, Sir J. (K.C.B.)

ORDER OF THE REDEEMER (GREEK).

Capt. COHEN, W. S. - Herts. Yeomanry.
Lieut.-Col. HEILBRON, I. M. (D.S.O.) - Royal Army Service Corps.

ORDER OF THE NILE (EGYPTIAN)

Major WALEY, E. G. S. (O.B.E.) - 16th London Regiment.

MEDAL FOR MILITARY MERIT (GREEK).

Capt. COHEN, W. S. - Herts. Yeomanry.
Pte. SAMUELS, S. - King's Own Royal Lancaster Regt.

ORDER OF THE SACRED TREASURE (JAPANESE).

Lieut.-Col. KISCH, F. H. (D.S.O.) - Royal Engineers.

COMMANDER OF THE ORDER OF AVIS (PORTUGUESE).

Lieut.-Col. BEDDINGTON, E. H. L. (C.M.G., D.S.O., M.C.) - General Staff.

RED CROSS MEDAL (PORTUGUESE).

Major ABRAHAMS, A. C. (O.B.E.) - British Red Cross.

ORDER OF ST. SAVA (SERBIA).

SWAYTHLING, Rt. Hon. Lord
GINGOLD, Mrs. H.

ORDER OF ST. STANISLAUS (RUSSIAN).

Lieut.-Col. SOLOMON, S. J. - Royal Engineers.

ORDER OF ST. GEORGE (RUSSIAN).

Petty-Officer HYAMS, I. - Royal Naval Air Service.
Sgt. SMITH, I. (V.C.) - Manchester Regiment.
Pte. WOOLFE, D - Royal Army Medical Corps.

ORDER OF LEOPOLD (BELGIAN)

Col. JESSEL, Sir H. M. (C.M.G.) - Special List.
Lieut.-Col. NATHAN, Sir F. L. (K.B.E.) - Royal Engineers.
Major SASSOON, Sir P. A. G. D. (C.M.G.) - Yeomanry.
Rt. Hon. SAMUEL, H. L. - (Grand Cross.)

ORDER OF THE CROWN OF BELGIUM.

Lieut.-Gen. MONASH, Sir J. (K.C.B.)
DELARA, I.
FRANKLIN, L. B. (O.B.E.)
SWAYTHLING, Rt. Hon. Lord
BROWN, LEWIS

RECORD OF HONOURS.

BELGIAN CROIX DE GUERRE.

Rank. Name. Regiment.

Pte. BARROW, A.	Royal Army Service Corps.
Sgt. CARPELL, R.	New Zealand Infantry.
Major COPLANS, M. (D.S.O.)	Royal Army Medical Corps.
Capt. DE PASS, F. C.	Royal Army Service Corps.
Sgt. FURST, R. M. (M.M.)	Royal Scots Fusiliers.
Sgt. LEVY, A. J.	Royal Marine Artillery.
Lieut. LEVY, P. P.	Oxford and Bucks Light Infantry.
Lieut.-Gen. MONASH, Sir J. (K.C.B.)	
Lieut. OPPENHEIM, H.	Royal Field Artillery
Major SASSOON, Sir P. A.	
Major SOLOMON, J. B. (M.C.)	Royal Air Force.
Cpl. SUNDERLAND, A.	Royal Fusiliers.

COMMANDER OF THE ORDER OF LEOPOLD II.

The Very Rev. HERTZ, J. H. (Ph.D.)	Chief Rabbi

CHEVALIERS OF ORDER OF LEOPOLD.

HAYMAN, H. L.	Consulate Service.
MYERS, A.	Consulate Service.
WOOLF, A. M.	Vice-Chairman, Jewish War Refugees' Committee.
WOOLF, M.	War Refugees' Committee.

MEDAILLE DE LA REINE ELISABETH (BELGIAN).

Mrs. HILDA BARNETT.
Miss FREDA COHEN.
Miss LILY ESSINGER.
Mrs. FRANCESCA GLUCKSTEIN.
Mrs. HENRIETTA IRWELL.
Mrs. MARIE JOLOWICZ.
Mrs. ETTA LEFFMAN.
Miss KITTY PERRY.
Mrs. ROWENA ROZELAAR.
Mrs. S. ERNEST SAMUELS.
Miss MARIE STRIDE.
Miss SYBIL TUCK.
Mrs. GERTRUDE WOOD.
Mrs. PERCY WORMS.

BELGIAN MILITARY CROSS (2ND CLASS).

Cpl. JOSEPH, C. J.	South African Medical Corps.
Sergt.-Major LENENBERG, S.	South African Motor Dispatch Rider.

ORDER OF ST. MAURICE AND ST. LAZARUS (ITALIAN)

Col. NATHAN, W. S. (C.M.G.)	Royal Engineers.
Capt. ADES, S.	Royal Field Artillery.
Lieut. NATHAN, C.	Wiltshire Regiment.

ITALIAN CROCE DI GUERRA.

Major COPLANS, M. (D.S.O., O.B.E.)	Royal Army Medical Corps.
Capt. HOFFNUNG-GOLDSMID, C. J. (O.B.E.)	Lancers.
Major LOWE, S. J. (D.S.O., O.B.E.)	Royal Fusiliers

ITALIAN BRONZE AND SILVER MEDAL.

Capt. HOFFNUNG-GOLDSMID, C. J.	Lancers.
Capt. HENRIQUES, B. L. Q.	Tank Corps.
Cpl. LEVY, I. (D.C.M.)	Middlesex Regt.
Dis. Rider MARKS, B.	British Red Cross Society.
War Correspondent. PRICE, J. M.	
Seaman PULVERNESS, A.	Royal Navy.
Pte. SOLOMONS, J.	British Red Cross Society.
Pte. TAYLOR, H. R.	British Red Cross Society.
Pte. WHITE, J. (V.C.)	King's Own R. Lancs. Regt.

RECORD OF HONOURS.
Commended for Home War Service.

Rank. Name.	Regiment.
Mrs. AARONS, R.	
Mrs. ABRAHAMS, E. (R.R.C.) (twice)	V.A.D.
ABRAHAMS, J. W.	
2nd Lieut. ABRAHAMS, L. A.	Royal Fusiliers.
By.Q.M.S. ABRAHAMS, S.	Royal Garrison Artillery.
Mrs. ABRAHAMS	V.A.D.
Sgt. ABRAHAMS, T. W.	London Regiment.
Capt. ADLER, H. M.	Royal Army Service Corps.
Capt. ADLER, S. M.	Royal Fusiliers, att. O. Cadet Batt.
Sister BAKER, Bessie	V.A.D.
Lieut. BARNETT, J. H. N.	General List.
BARON, B.	
Lieut. BARUCH, H.	Northumberland Fusiliers.
Capt. BEDDINGTON, J. L.	War Office.
Mrs. BEER, W.	Bradstones Aux. Hosp., Lancs.
Lieut.-Col. BEHREND, F. D.	Border Regiment.
Major BEHRENS, C.	North Riding Volunteer Regt.
The Hon. Mrs. BEHRENS, E.	Nursing Service.
Capt. BEHRENS, E. C. (twice)	Royal Army Service Corps.
A/C.S.M. Instructor BERG, L. W.	Army Gymnastic Staff.
Capt. BESSO, R. A.	Yeomanry.
S.M. BIRLEY, O.	R.A.F.
2nd Lieut. BOAS, H.	Royal West Surrey Regt.
Lieut. BOAS, H. A.	Australian Y.M.C.A.
Col. CARLEBACH, P.	London Regiment.
Cpl. CARLEBACH, R.	Middlesex Labour Coy.
Staff Sgt. COHEN, B.	Royal Army Ord. Corps (War Office).
Capt. COHEN, B. S.	Royal Air Force.
Lieut.-Col. COHEN, D. de LARA,	London Regiment.
Pte. COHEN, E.	Royal Army Service Corps.
Major COHEN, Sir H. B. (Bart.)	Royal West Kent Regiment.
Miss COHEN, IRENE (A.R.R.C.)	Commandant, V.A.D.
COHEN, L.	War Office.
COHEN, P. B.	Red Cross Society.
COHEN, R.	Special Constabulary.
Mrs. DAVIDSON, E. (M.B.E.)	V.A.D.
D'AVIGDOR, D. C. A.	War Office.
DAVIS, G.	Special Constabulary.
Major DEFRIES, C.	Royal Flying Corps.
Miss DE LAREDO, S.	War Office.
DESART, ELLEN, Countess of	
DONNERSTEIN, L.	Special Constabulary.
Major DRUCQUER, M. N.	War Office.
Dr. DUTCH, M. A.	Medical Services.
Lieut. DUNKELS, E.	Royal Army Service Corps.
Lieut. ELIAS, F.	Suffolk Regiment.
The Hon. Mrs. ELIOT-YORKE,	
ELKIN, J. J.	Army Ordnance Department.
Cpl. FALK, H.	Middlesex Labour Regiment.
Major FAUDEL-PHILLIPS, H.	Lancers.
Sgt. FREEDMAN, S.	Special Constabulary.

RECORD OF HONOURS. Home Mentions (continued).

Rank. Name.	Regiment.
Mrs. Gabriel, A. C.	War Office.
Capt. Ginsbery, J. W.	London Regiment.
Capt. Goldman, A. C.	Royal Fusiliers.
Sgt. Goldman, I.	Royal Fusiliers.
Sgt. Goldman, P.	Royal Army Service Corps.
Sgt. Goldstein, A.	Special Constabulary.
Lieut. Gosschalk, F.	Yorkshire Regiment.
Capt. Green, F. M.	Royal Air Force.
Sergt.-Maj. Grossman, J.	Royal Army Medical Corps.
C.Q.M.S. Grossman, M.	Royal Fusiliers.
Cadet Col. Halstead, E. M.	Jewish Lads' Brigade.
Flight Sgt. Hamburger, F.	Royal Air Force.
L/Cpl. Harris, J.	Royal Fusiliers.
Capt. Hayman, L. F.	Royal Army Medical Corps.
Mrs. Henochsburg, E. M.	Nairobi Medical Service.
L/Cpl. Isaacs, B. A.	Royal Army Ordnance Corps.
Capt. Isaacs, D. N. (M.B.E.)	New Zealand Medical Corps.
S.M. Isaacs, F. J.	Royal Air Force.
Cpl. Isaacs, H.	Rifle Brigade.
Sgt. Isaacs, H. H.	Special Constabulary.
Mrs. Isaacs, M.	V.A.D.
Miss Isaacs	V.A.D.
Capt. Jacob, E. F.	Hampshire Regiment.
A/Sgt. Jacob, R. V.	Essex Regiment.
Miss Jacobs, D. B.	
Jacobs, E.	Medical Services.
Cpl. Jacobs, W.	Royal Fusiliers.
Hon. Col. Sir Jessel, H. M.	London Regiment.
Miss Jessell, N.	Q.A.M.H.
Major Joel, H. C. (twice) (O.B.E.)	Army Ordnance Department.
Capt. Joseph, C. H.	Australian Imperial Force.
Cadet Lt.-Col. Joseph, E. M. (O.B.E.)	Jewish Lads' Brigade.
Lieut.-Col. Joseph, R. H. (D.S.O.)	Royal Engineers.
Miss Joseph, J. (M.B.E.)	V.A.D.
A/Sgt. Joseph, W. G.	Labour Corps.
Capt. Keesing, H. M. (M.C.)	New Zealand Infantry.
Lieut.-Col. Kisch, F. H. (D.S.O.)	Royal Engineers.
Major Langdon, G. H.	Royal Army Service Corps.
Miss Lazarus, L.	V.A.D.
Miss Levy, D. E.	V.A.D.
Levy, F. L.	Labour Corps. Record Office.
Levy, H. S.	War Office.
Miss Levy, J. A.	Women's Legion.
Major Levy, L.	Royal Engineers.
Sister Levy, M. V.	Q.A.I., M.N.S.R.
Miss Levy, S.	War Office.
Levy, W. W.	
Mrs. Lewis, A.	
Lieut. Linden, P. L.	Royal Army Service Corps.
Lieut. Lipman, A. A.	Australian Imperial Force.
Rev. Lipson, S.	Senior Chaplain.
Sgt. Luper, M.	Royal Fusiliers.
Major Magnus, L.	Royal Defence Corps.
Cpl. Maier, J. D.	Middlesex Labour Regiment.
Lieut.-Col. Mandelberg, S. L.	Territorial Force, Reserve.
Engr. Marks, F. E.	British Red Cross Society.

RECORD OF HONOURS. Home Mentions (continued).

Rank Name.	Regiment.
Mrs. Marsden, E. (R.R.C.)	V.A.D.
Capt. Maurice, F. J.	Essex Regt.
Miss Meller, A.	Q.A.M.H.
Mendl, M. H.	War Office.
Capt. and Adj. Meredith, H. A.	Royal Defence Corps.
Capt. Michelson, A.	Special List.
Lieut. Mocatta, O. E.	R.A.S.C.
Miss Moses, J.	War Office.
Lieut. Moss, A. E.	Royal Fusiliers.
Lieut. Moss, V. A.	Royal Army Service Corps.
Capt. Myer, S.	Royal Army Service Corps.
Myers, B.	Medical Services.
Lieut.-Col. Myers, B. E. (M.D.)	New Zealand Medical Corps.
Capt. Myers, D. F.	New Zealand Medical Corps.
Bt. Col. Sir Nathan, F. L. (K.B.E.)	Reserve of Officers.
Sgt. Niman, H.	Royal Army Medical Corps.
Phillips, B. M.	Special Constabulary.
Raphael, R. R.	Royal Army Clothing Department.
C.S.M. Rosenthal, D.	Labour Corps.
Inspector Rothschild, A.	Special Constabulary.
Major Rothschild, L. de, M.P. (O.B.E.)	Territorial Force Res. Bucks. Yeo.
Mrs. Rothschild, Leopold de	Red Cross.
Instructor Rubens, A.	Rifle Brigade attached A.G.S.
Capt. Samuel, B. B.	R.A.M.C.
Mrs. Samuel, D.	War Office.
Lady Samuel, F. E.	The Mote Private Hospital (see p. 14).
C.S.M. Instructor Samuel, J. M.	Corps of Musketry.
Mrs. Samuels, D.	Reg. Assistant, London Regiment.
Miss Sandberg, J.	Queen Mary's Army Auxiliary Corps.
Miss Schiff, M.	V.A.D.
Mrs. Singer, I.	V.A.D.
Capt. Sington, G. H. A.	Royal Engineers.
A/Mech./S/Sgt. Solomon, H. T.	Royal Army Service Corps.
Spurling, S. J.	War Office.
Capt. Steinberg, H. E.	Royal Air Force.
S/Sgt. Stephany, M.	Royal Army Service Corps.
Sgt. Steinweis, J.	South African Mounted Rifles.
Cpl. Strauss, J.	Middlesex Labour Regiment.
Cpl. Strauss, O.	Middlesex Labour Regiment.
C.S.M. Instructor Symons, G.	Royal Fusiliers attd. A.G.S.
Van Thal, M.	War Office.
A/Capt. Wacholder, A. (twice)	Royal Fusiliers.
Capt. Walters, A. B.	Royal Air Force.
Capt. Weil, B.	Royal Air Force.
Sgt.-Maj. Wigoder, L.	Officers' Training Corps.
Wolfsberger, M.	War Office.
Miss Woolf, A. G. (Royal Red Cross)	V.A.D.
Lieut. Woolf, E. S.	Bedford Yeomanry.

Note.—An asterisk against a name denotes Killed in Action or Died on Active Service.

Alphabetical Index of Nominal Rolls

Regiment/Corps	PAGE
Air Force, Royal	535
Argyll and Sutherland Highlanders	379
Army Medical Corps, Royal	516
Army Ordnance Corps, Royal	529
Army Pay Corps, Royal	533
Army Service Corps, Royal	492
Army Veterinary Corps, Royal	532
Artillery, Royal	199
Australian Corps	549
Bedfordshire Regiment	303
Berkshire Regiment, Royal	343
Black Watch (Royal Highlanders)	334
Border Regiment	325
British West India Regiment	594
Cambridgeshire Regiment	458
Cameron Highlanders	377
Canadian Corps	579
Cavalry	193
Cheshire Regiment	310
Connaught Rangers	379
Cornwall's Light Infantry, Duke of	323
Cyclists' Battalions	387
Defence Corps, Royal	491
Devonshire Regiment	294
Dorsetshire Regiment	330
Dublin Fusiliers, Royal	380
Durham Light Infantry	371
Engineers, Royal	223
Essex Regiment	337
Gloucestershire Regiment	318
Gordon Highlanders	376
Guards (Grenadier, Coldstream, Scots, Irish, Welch)	233
Hampshire Regiment	328
Herefordshire Regiment	490
Hertfordshire Regiment	490
Honourable Artillery Company	221
Highland Light Infantry	374
Indian Army	595
Inniskilling Fusiliers, Royal	317
Irish Regiment, Royal	305
Irish Fusiliers, Royal	379
Irish Rifles, Royal	377
"Judeans" (38th, 39th, 40th Royal Fusiliers)	254
Kent Regiment, East (Buffs)	238
Kent Regiment, Royal West	344
King's Royal Rifle Corps	356
Labour Corps	414
Lancashire Fusiliers	307
Lancashire Regiment, East	320
Lancashire Regiment, Loyal North	341
Lancashire Regiment, South	331
Lancaster Regiment, King's Own Royal	239
Leicestershire Regiment	305
Leinster Regiment	380
Lincolnshire Regiment	293
Liverpool Regiment, King's	286
London Regiment	459
Machine Gun Corps	389
Manchester Regiment	363
Middlesex Regiment	348
Monmouthshire Regiment	458
Munster Fusiliers, Royal	380
Naval Division, Royal	192
Navy, Royal	189
New Zealand Forces	566
Norfolk Regiment	292
Northamptonshire Regiment	342
Northumberland Fusiliers	241
Nottingham and Derbyshire Regiment	340
Oxfordshire and Buckinghamshire Light Infantry	334
Rifle Brigade	381
Royal Fusiliers	246
Royal Fusiliers (Judeans)	254
Royal Fusiliers (Palestinians)	603
Royal Scots	234
Scots Fusiliers, Royal	310
Scottish Borderers, King's Own	316
Scottish Rifles	316
Seaforth Highlanders	376
Shropshire Light Infantry, King's Own	347
Somerset Light Infantry	296
South African Forces	568
Staffordshire Regiment, North	369
Staffordshire Regiment, South	329
Suffolk Regiment	295
Surrey Regiment, East	321
Surrey Regiment, Royal West (The Queen's)	236
Sussex Regiment, Royal	326
Tank Corps	396
Training Reserve Battalions	397
Various Units	597
Wales Borderers, South	314
Warwickshire Regiment, Royal	244
Welch Regiment	332
Welch Fusiliers, Royal	312
West Kent Regiment, Royal	344
West Riding Regiment	324
Wiltshire Regiment	363
Worcestershire Regiment	319
York and Lancaster Regiment	369
Yorkshire Light Infantry, King's Own	345
Yorkshire Regiment	306
Yorkshire Regiment, East	302
Yorkshire Regiment, West	297
Zion Mule Corps	512

OFFICERS, N.C.O.'s AND MEN TOO LATE FOR CLASSIFICATION - 610

Nominal Rolls

OF

Officers, N.C.O'S, and Men in H.M. Forces.

(Arranged according to the Navy, Army and Air Lists.)

ROYAL NAVY.

OFFICERS.

Capt. ABRAHAMS, G. H. F., H.M.S. "Calypso."
Lieut. ABRAHAMS, A. N., R.N.V.R.
Comr. BRANDON, G., H.M.S. "Queen."
Comr. BRANDON, V. R., H.M.S. "Cornwall."
Lieut. BONN, M., R.N.V.R.
Sub. Lieut. COHEN, L. R., R.N.V.R.
Sub.-Lieut. COHEN, R. W., R.N.V.R.
Surgeon COWEN, H., R.N.V.R.
Sub. Lieut. DUVEEN, G., R.N.V.R.
Sub. Lieut. DUVEEN, H. D., R.N.V.R.
Lieut. DE PASS, H., H.M.S. "Indomitable."
Sub. Lt. DAVIDSON, J. L., H.M.S. "Agamemnon."
Lt. Paym. FRANKLIN, J. A., H.M.S. "Defence."
Asst. Paym. FRANKLIN, S. E., R.N.R.
Lieut. FILEMAN, F. E., H.M.S. "Valiant."
Mid. GOLDREICH, R., H.M.S. "Thunderer."
Lieut. JACOB, E. E., R.N.V.R.
Sub. Lieut. KAMINSKA, C., H.M.S. "Himalaya."
Asst. Paym. LANG, A., H.M.S. "Columbelle."
Lieut. MAKOWER, W., R.N.V.R.
Sub. Lieut. MOSES, G. S., R.N.V.R.
Flt. Surg. MANDEL, L., H.M.S. "Donegal.'
Sub-Lieut. MELHADO, A.
Lieut. PYKE, L., R.N.V.R.
Surg.-Lieut. SCHLESINGER, E. G. (O.B.E.).
Lieut. SALMON, H., R.N.V.R.
Surgeon SINGTON, H., R.N.V.R.
Mid. SCHREIBER,* V. G. S., H.M.S. "Monmouth."
Surg. Lieut. SPERO, G. E., H.M.S. "Manners."
Mid. SPERO, L. P., H.M.S. "Prince."
Lieut. SUSMAN, A. S., H.M.S. "Powerful."
Sub. Lieut. SAMUEL, B., R.N.R.
Lieut. SASSOON, E. V., R.N.V.R.
Sub. Lieut. SYDNEY, C. A., R.N.V.R.
Sub. Lieut. SYDNEY, J. R., R.N.V.R.
Lieut. WARBURG, H. D., H.M.S. "Research."
Asst. Paym. WOLF, G. E.
Sub. Lieut. WOLFF, J., H.M.S. "Puepehu."
Sub. Lieut. WILKES, G., R.N.V.R.
Sub. Lieut. WEIL, L. B., R.N.V.R.
Paymr. Lt. Commander WOOLF, T. A. (O.B.E.).

OTHER RATINGS.

A.B. ABRAHAMS, A., 12th Bn. R.M. Bde.
Seaman ABRAHAMS, H., H.M.S. "Vincent."
1st Cl. Mech. ABRAHAMS, B., R.N.A.S.
P.O. ALLEN,* E., H.M.S. "Mignonette."
O.S. ANCHELL, H., H.M.S. "Antrim."
Sig. AITKEN, L., H.M.S. "Duke of Cornwall."
O.S. ANGEL, A., H.M.S. "Ganges II."
P.T.I. ABRAHAMS, L., R.N.A.S.
A.B. BAMBERG, J., S.B.S., H.M.S. "Dalhousie."
Pte. BANDALL, W., H.M.S. "Princess Royal."
Pte. BARGAD, J., H.M.S. "Yarmouth."
Seaman BENHAM, A., H.M.S. "Dido."
A.B. BENJAMIN, E., H.M.S. "Benbow."
Seaman BERNSTEIN, I., H.M.S. "Albemarle."
Stoker BLOK,* I. M., H.M.S. "Lapwing."
Seaman BLOOM, M., H.M.S. "Pembroke."
Stoker BRAHAM, S., H M.S. "Ambrose."
1st Cl. Stoker BRIGHT, C., H.M.S. "Acteon."
W.O. BRIGHT, M. M., H.M.S. "Minerva."
Stoker BROOK, J., H.M.S. "Sealark."
218394 C.P.O. BROCK, M. J. E., H.M.S. "Eaglet."
Seaman BLOOM, H., H.M.S. "Beaver."
Stoker BLOCK, M. N., H.M.S. "Contest."
Stoker BRIGHT,—, H.M.S. "Bacclante."
S/Steward BARNETT, W., Torpedo Boat 19.
A.B. BLITZ, W., H.M.S. "Agamemnon."
Seaman BEYFUS, H. M., H.M.S. "St. George."
S/Seaman BLOOM, M., H.M.S. "Dido."
Seaman BLACKMAN, N., H.M.S. "Orian."
Seaman BARNETT. A., R.N.V.R.
A.B. CASH, H., R.M.L.I.
P.O. COEVORDEN, M., H.M.S. "Ophir."
Telegraphist COHEN, E., H.M.S. "Centaur."
Stoker COHEN, H., H.M.S. "Victory."
P.O. Stoker COHEN, H., H.M.S. "Achilles."
A.B. COHEN, I., H.M.S. "St. Vincent."
Stoker, COHEN, J., H.M.S. "Sparrowhawk."
A.B. COHEN, J., H.M.S. "Cressy."
A.B. COHEN, J., H.M.S. "Zealandia."
Seaman COHEN, M., H.M.S. "Ruthenia."
A.B. COHEN, M. A., H.M.S. "Antrim."
A.B. COHEN, S., H.M.S. "Birmingham."

* Killed in Action or died on Active Service.

Royal Navy.—*Continued.*

A.B. COHEN, W., H.M.S. "Achilles."
Stoker COLLINS, J., H.M.S. "Indomitable."
Ldg. Stoker COOPER, C. F., H.M.S. "Titania."
A.B. CORNBLATT, S., H.M.S. "Colossus."
A.B. COSTA, R., H.M.S. "Lord Nelson."
Chief Writer COEVORDEN, M., H.M.S. "Ophir."
A.B. COOPER, C., H.M.S. "Inconstant."
A.B. DA COSTA, S., H.M.S. "Vernon."
Stoker DANIELS, I., H.M.S. "Bedford."
1st Cl. Stoker DAVIS, G., H.M.S. "Indomitable."
A.B. DAVIS, H., H.M.S. "Irresistible."
Stoker DAY, G. (WEIL), H.M.S. "Imelda."
Stoker DECKER, A. F., H.M.S. "Bustard."
Stoker DE FRIEND, H. I., H.M.S. "Curacoa".
A.B. DEITZ, H., R.M.L.I., H.M.S. "Albion."
A.B. DE MEZA, E., Naval Service Corps.
A.B. DE MEZA, J., Naval Service Corps.
Stoker DANIEL, E., H.M.S. "Apollo."
O.S. DAVIS, M., H.M.S. "Prince Rupert."
Seaman DAVIS, S., H.M.S. "Pembroke."
Stoker DECKER, A., H.M.S. "Bustard."
Chief Gunner DURRANT, A., H.M.S. "Nelson."
Pte. DEWILD, M., R.M.L.I.
Pte. DAVIS, S., R.M.L.I.
A.B. ENGLAND, B. M., H.M.S. "Spartiate."
Yeoman of Signals EMANUEL, A. (M.S.M.).
Pte. ERIERA, A., Royal Marines.
Stoker FORSTEIN, H., H.M.S. "Devonshire."
1st Stoker FORD, M., H.M.S. "Arethusa."
1st Stoker FOSTER, H., H.M.S. "Marlborough."
Chief P.O. FRANKS, L., H.M.S. "Vanguard."
P.O. FREEDMAN, S., R.N. Air Service.
A.B. FELDMAN, J., H.M.S. "Ismailia."
Act. Ldg. Seaman FRIEND, L.
A.B. GARRATT, A., H.M.S. "Dominion."
Stoker GLOHOFF, A., H.M.S. "Duncan."
A.B. GLUCKSTEIN, L., R.M. Brigade.
A.B. GOLDBERG, A., H.M.S. "Hecla."
Stoker GOLDBERG, B., H.M.S. "Inflexible."
3rd Writer GOLDBERG, J. J., H.M.S. "Antrim."
A.B. GOODMAN, A., R.N.D. Wireless Tel.
Steward GOLD,* D., H.M.S. "Dido."
A.B. GOLDSTEIN,* I., H.M.S. "Defence."
Signalman GOLDSTEIN, S. M., Dover Patrol.
1st Cl. Sto. GOLDSTEIN, P., H.M.S. "Inflexible."
A.B. GOLDSTONE, A., H.M.S. "Leviathan."
A.B. GOMPERTZ, A., H.M.S. "Southwark."
1st Cl. Stoker GOULD, S., H.M.S. "Monarch."
A.B. GREEN, B., H.M.S. "Intrepid."
A.B. GREEN, S., R.M.L.I.
A.B. GREENFIELD, H.M.S. "Leviathan."
Sig. GILBERT, I., H.M.S. "Emprise."
R/3395 A.B. GLAN, W., R.N.V.R.
Sig. GOTTSCHALK, A. G., H.M.S. "Formidable."
S.B.S. GROSSMAN, A., S.S. "Thermoschles."
Seaman GORDON, H., H.M.S. "Carnation."

A. B. HARBOUR, S., H.M.S. "Drake."
Seaman HAMMEL, W., H.M.S. "Parramatta."
A.B. HARRIS, G. A., H.M.S. "Victory."
Stoker HOLLANDER, L., H.M.S. "Vernon."
P.O. HYAMS, I., R.N.A.S.
1st Cl. Stoker HYAM, J., H.M.S. "Foxhound."
Stoker HYAMS, P., H.M.S. "Rhododendron."
Stoker HARRIS, J., H.M.S. "Gloucester Castle."
Stoker HYAMS, J., H.M.S. Submarine A15.
O.S. LZ/4891 HYAMS, H., R.N.
A.B. HARRIS, D. M., H.M.S. "Floande."
P.O. HANDLER, S., H.M.S. "Minesweeper."
Seaman HARRIS, S. C., R.N.
P.O. HOUGH, —, H.M.S. "Australia."
Stoker HURSTFIELD, H. T., Torpedo Boat No. 2.
A.B. ISAACS, A., H.M.S. "Mars."
Stoker ISAACS, A. L., H.M.S. "Erne."
A.B. ISAAC, W., R.M.L.I.
S.B.A. ISAACS, N.
Steward ISAACS, —, Mess 222, R.N.
A.B.S. ISAACS, B., H.M.S. "China."
358211 Sto. P.O. ISAAC, H.,* H.M.S. "Seagull."
Ldg. Stoker JACOBS, B., H.M.S. "Lord Nelson."
O.S. JACOBS, H., H.M.S. "Vernon."
A.B. JACOBS, H., H.M.S. "Donegal."
A.B. JACOBS, J. H., R.N.V.R.
A.B. JACOBS,* L., H.M.S. "Lord Nelson."
J/408 A.B. JACOBS, L., H.M.S. "Jupiter."
Seaman JACOBS, M., H.M.S. "Dunluce Castle."
A.B. JACOBSON, L., R.N. Air Station, Dundee.
A.B. JONAS, A., H.M.S. "Diligence."
1st Cl. Shipwright JONES, F., H.M.S. "Mars."
A.B. JOSEPH, A., H.M.S. "Kenilworth Castle."
A.B. JOSEPH, M., R.N.V.R.
A.B. JOSEPHS, H.M.S. "Africa."
A.S. JONES, A. J., 3rd Res. Batt. R.N.V.R.
Seaman JACOBS, —, H.M.S. "Ganges."
Stoker JONAS, H., H.M.T.B. "35."
1st Cl. P.O. JONES, F., H.M.S. "Russell."
A.B. JACOBS, J. A., R.N.V.R.
Seaman KAMINSKA, C., H.M.S. "Himalaya."
1st Cl. Stoker KEESING, J., H.M.S. "Illustrious."
Sea. Gnr. KELLY,* J. (JACOBS), H.M.S. "Lion."
W.O. KING, B., R.M.L.I.
Sto. KING, S. (KOSKI).
A.B. KLEIN, A. A., R.N.V.R.
1st Cl. P.O. KOSKI, S., H.M.S. "Talisman."
A.B. KURTZMAN, A., H.M.S. "Duncan."
2nd A.M. KARLITZ, L., R.N.A.S.
Seaman KAPLAN, J., H.M.T. "Franklin."
2nd Cl. P.O. KRAMINSKI, H.M.S. "Coast Guard."
Wire. O. LACKMAKER, S., H.M.S. "Irresistible."
Ldg. S. LATHWELL, A., H.M.S. "Birmingham."
Stoker LACK, S., H.M.S. "Athenic."
1st Cl. Stoker LAZARUS, S., H.M.S. "Laverock."
Seaman LENDER, A., H.M.S. "Vivid."
Ldg. Stoker LEVEY, N., H.M.S. "Broke."

Royal Navy.—*Continued.*

A.B. LEVY, B., H.M.S. "Cæsar."
3rd Writer LEVY, M. (M. 27128).
A.B. LEVY, S., H.M.S. "Sir John Moore."
A.B. LEWIS,* M. C., H.M.S. "Bulwark."
Gnr. LEWIS, S., Royal Marine Artillery.
A.B. LIMBURG, A., H.M.S. "Pekin."
A.B. LOWY, F. L., R.N.V.R.
2nd A/Cpl. LIGHTSTONE, S.,* R.N.A.S.
S.S.A. LAZARUS, M., "H.M.S. "Actaeon."
5936 A.B. LEVY, S. R., H.M.S. "Victorious."
Seaman LEVY, H., H.M.S. "Centaur."
Seaman LEVINE, D., H.M.S. "Victoria."
Stoker LEVEY, M., H.M.S. "Quidre."
T2/9859 O.S. LEVI, A., R.N.
52737 Pte. LEWIS, G., H.M.S. "Takada."
Seaman LINDSAY, L., H.M.S. "Impregnable."
Seaman LEVESON, A., H.M.S. "President."
Stoker LANARD, J., H.M.S. "Drake."
Stoker LAZARUS, —, H.M.S. "Goliath'"
Seaman LEVENE, M.,* H.M.S. "Salta."
A.B. MAGNUS, S., H.M.S. "Princess Royal."
1st Stoker MARCUS, S. L., H.M.S. "Cornwall."
2nd Boy MARKS, C. J., H.M.S. "Powerful."
Stoker MARKS, J., H.M.S. "Vindictive."
A.B. MARKS, J. J., H.M.S. "Canterbury."
1st Stoker MARKS, J., H.M.S. "Cornflower."
Stoker MARKS, L. J., H.M.S. "Wildfire."
A.B. MARKS, C., H.M.S. "Niobe."
A.B. MARSHALL, R. M. A., H.M.S. "Illustrious."
Stoker MARTIN, H.M.S. "Grafton."
Sig. MELINSKA, A., H.M.S. "Alcantara."
1st Stoker MICHAELS, M., H.M.S. "Essex."
Wireless Tel. MICKLER, L., H.M.S. "Europe."
Seaman MILLER, E., H.M.S. "New Zealand."
A.B. MIRANDA, I., R.N.V.R.
W.O. MISTOFSKY, J., H.M.S. "Gascony."
A.B. MISTOFSKY, M., H.M.S. "Sealda."
A.B. MORGENSTERN, A., H.M.S. "Shannon."
A.B. MORRIS, B., R.M.L.I.
A.B. MORRISON, A. A., R.M.L.I.
A.B. MORSE, P., R.M.L.I.
A.B. MYER, S., S.S. "Ballarat."
A.B. MYERS, M., T.B.D.
1st Stoker MYERS, F., Submarine E.7.
Ch. S. Cook MYERS, J., H.M.S. "K. George II."
A.B. MYERS, S., H.M.S. "Dominion."
A./Stoker P.O. MYERS, W., H.M.S. "Ivy."
A.B. MYERS, M. F., H.M.S. "Iphigenia."
O.S. MANDELSOHN, H. A., H.M.S. "Victory."
Stoker MYERS, I., H.M.S. "Sappho."
Stoker MYERS, J., H.M.S. "Handy."
Stoker MYERS, W., H.M.S. "Sparrowhawk."
C.P.O. MYERS, J. J., H.M.S. "Hyacinth."
Stoker MULLEN, S., H.M.S. "Superb."
S.M. MOSES, L., R.N.
C.P.O. MOSS, A., R.N.V.R.
A.B. NATHAN, A., H.M.S. "Birmingham."
A.B. NELSON, S., H.M.S. "Lancaster."
A.B. NIGHTINGALE, J., H.M.S. "Cæsar."
Pte. NIGHTINGALE, S., H.M.S. "Tiger."
Stoker NEWMARK, P. E., H.M.S. "Cyclops."
Stoker OSSER, N., H.M.S. "Vanguard."
Ldg. Stoker OSSER, L., H.M.S. "Inflexible."
811844 A.B. OSSEROFFSKI,* L., H.M.S. "Queen Mary."
W.O. PASCH, A. H., H.M.S. "Benbow."
A.B. PEREZ, A., H.M.S. "Marlborough."
A.B. PHILLIPS, A., R.N.V.R.
229683 1st Clerk PORTER, E., R.N.A.S.
A.B. PHILIPP, J., S.B.A.
A.B. PHILIP, J., R.M.L.I.
1st Cl. Sto. PHILLIPS, M., H.M.S. "Cornwallis."
A.B. POLLAND, A. R., H.M.S. "Hindustan."
1st Cl. Sto. PRESSMAN, J., H.M.S. "Majestic."
A.B. RABINOVITZ, S., H.M.S. "Triumph."
Pte. ROBINSON, H.M.S. "Terror."
Ldg./Stoker ROSE, J. M., H.M.S. "Kent."
Stoker ROCKMAN, M., H.M.S. "Broke."
A.B. RODIN, E., H.M.S. "Hind."
1st Cl. Stoker ROMAN, S., H.M. T.B. No. 25.
P.O. ROSE, J., H.M.S. "King Edward VII."
A.B. ROSE, J., R.N.S. "Asturias."
Sig. ROSE, J., R.N.V.R.
A.B. ROSENBERG, S., H.M.S. "Sydney."
2nd Cl. Boy ROSENTHAL, L. M., H.M.S. "Impregnable."
A.B. SAMPSON, L., R.M.A.
1st Cl. Stoker SANDERS, A., H.M.S. "Lucia."
Seaman SAUNDERS, E., H.M. T.B. 9.
102037 1st Cl. Stoker SANDERS, H.,* H.M.S. "Dreadnought."
A.B. SAUNDERS, H., H.M.S. "Virtue."
1st Cl. Stoker SAUNDERS, J., H.M.S. "Actaeon."
Stoker P.O. SAMUEL, M., H.M.S. "Bristol."
A.B. SCHNEIDERMAN, M., H.M.S. "St. Vincent."
Stoker SCHWARTZ, H. W., H.M.S. "Lowestoft."
A.B. SEAWOOD, A., H.M.S. "Vernon."
A.B. SHABERMAN, S., H.M.S. "Monarch."
Asst. Vict. SHINEGOLD, H., H.M.S. "Glory."
Stoker SILVER,* S., H.M.S. "Inflexible."
1st Cl. Sto. SILVERSTONE, A., H.M.S. "Queen.."
A.B. SILVERSTON, H., H.M.S. "Protector."
1st Cl. Sto. SILVERSTONE, H., H.M.S. "Implacable."
Stoker SILVERSTONE, J., H.M.S. "Impregnable."
A.B. SIMMONDS, J., H.M.S. "Princess Royal."
A.B. SIMONDS, C., H.M.S. "Liverpool."
A.B. SIMONS, D., H.M.S. "Ganges."
1st Cl. Stoker SOLOMONS, M., H.M.S. "King George V."
W.O. SOLOMON,* M., H.M.S. "Queen."
Steward SPANIER,* M. H., H.M.S. "Queen Mary."
Stoker STANFORD, H., H.M.S. "Carmania."
A.B. STEINGOLD, F., R.M.L.I.

Royal Navy.—Continued.

Probationer STERNE, W., P.S.B.A.
A.B. STERN, W.,* H.M.S. "Pathfinder."
A.B. STEVENSON, B., H.M.S. "Sir John Moore."
A.B. STOKES, J., H.M.S. "Leander."
Sig. SUGARMAN, H. E., H.M.S. "Dolphin."
1st Cl. Stoker SWART, A., H.M.S. "Cressy."
1st Cl. Stoker SWART, L., H.M.S. "Antrim."
Sig. SUMMERFIELD, G., H.M.S. "Goodward."
222 SIMONS, M., R.N.R.
Stoker STEIN, M., H.M.S. "Blanche."
1/W.O. SOLOMON, D., H.M.S. "Takada."
P.O. SAMUEL, M., H.M.S. "Bristol."
P.O. SAMUELS, A., H.M.S. "Vincent."
A.B. SUMMERFIELD, I., R.N.V.R.
1st Cl. Stoker TAVELL, S., H.M.S. "Sable."
Chief P.O. TAYLOR, C., H.M.S. "Inflexible."
Mechanic TERRY, P., H.M.S. "Riviera."
Stoker P.O. WALLER, A. E., H.M.S. "Birmingham."
2nd Cl. Sto. WALTERS, L., H.M.S. "Dominion."
Ch. Sto. WEINBERG, L., H.M.S. "Patrol."
1st Cl. Sto. WENSTONE, A., H.M.S. "Glasgow."
Seaman WOODS, J., H.M.S. "Highflyer."
A.B. WOOLF, D., R.M.L.I.
Schoolmaster WOOLMAN, W., R. Naval Barracks,
Sig. WALTERS, H., H.M.S. "Ringdove."
A.B. WEILL, M., H.M.S. "Imelda."
Seaman WALMAN, J., H.M.S. "Reliable."
G/S. WOLFE, B., H.M.S. "Acteon."
Gnr. YULES, R. L., R.M.A.
A.B. ZAUSMER, H., H.M.S. "Gorgon."
C.P.O. ZUCKER, S. E., H.M.S. "Naivana."

* Killed in Action or died on Active Service.

ROYAL NAVAL DIVISION.

OFFICERS.

Sub. Lieut. ARON, E. M.,* R.N.V.R.
Sub. Lieut. ABELSON, E. G.,* R.M.L.I., att. 190th M.G.C.
Sub. Lieut. BENJAMIN, N. H.,* Drake Bn.
Sub-Lieut. BARNEY, S. D., R.N.D.
Lieut. FURTADO, A. G. M., R.M.L.I.
Capt. ISAACS, M., (M.C.), H.Q.
Sub. Lieut. JACOBS, T.,* R.N.V.R.
Lieut. LION, N. I.,* 1st R.M.L.I.
Capt. Hon. MONTAGU, L. (M.C.), 2nd Hood Bn.
Lieut.-Col. ORD, G. P., R.M.L.I.
Major OPPENHEIM, G. O., R.M.L.I.
Sub. Lieut. POLITZER, E., Hawke Bn.
T./Sub.-Lieut. RAPHAEL, A. A., Hood Bn.
Major VAN PRAAGH, H. B. (M.C.).

OTHER RATINGS.

Pte. A. S. ABRAHAMS, L., R.M.L.I.
1057 Pte. ABRAHAMS, L.
24410 P.O. ALION, D.
Pte. ABEE, W., R.M.L.I.
Pte. ABRAHAMS, A., R.M.L.I.
Pte. ABRAHAMS, B., R.M.S.M.
Pte. ABRAHAMS, J. A., Drake Bn.
MZ/874 A.B. ASHLEY, S., att. 63rd M.G.C.
S/4050 Pte. ALEXANDER, I., R.N.D.
R/253 A.B. ASHLEY, N. J., 63rd R.N.D.
C/27590 A.B. AITKIN, L., R.N.D.
O/695 Pte. BARGER, J.
Pte. BOCHBINDER, H., R.N.A.S.
Ldg. Seaman BAKESEF, E., R.N.D.
1765 A.C. BAKESEF, J.
18779 Pte. BURLEY, M., R.M.L.I.
Pte. BAKESEF, N., R.N.D.
ZM/695 A.B. BLOOM, L., 2nd Hood Bn.
L/Z/5143 A.B. BARZOLAI, J., Hood Bn.
R/3881 A.B. BIRNSTEIN, W.
A.B. BLOOMFIELD, N., R.N.D.
Z/L/4167 P.O. COWAN, A.,* Anson Bn.
L2/1823 A.B. COHEN, J. W., 63rd M.G.C.
A.B. COHEN, F., R.N.V.R.
R/4051 A.B. CISSOFSKI, H., Hood Bn.
A.B. CASTLE, H. M., R.N.V.R.
R/250 A.B. COHEN, P., R.N.V.R
222276 2/A.M. CAPLAN, M., R.N.D.
2888 P.O. COOK, S., R.N.D.
S/5575 Sap. COHEN, M., R.N.D.
255821/A.M. COTT, C.
16022 2/A.M. CLAYTON, S.
15844 A.C.T. CRAIG, A.
99 Instr. COHEN, M.
Seaman COZENBRIGHT, B., Naval Res.
125194 Pte. DAVIDSON, S., 63rd M.G.C.
575 Pte. DAVIS, J.,* R.M.L.I.
R/2411 A.B. DAVIS, D., 2nd Res. Bn.
R/185 O.S. DEMANT, I., 3rd Res. Bn.
Pte. DEITZ, H., R.M.L.I.
28760 O.S. FRANKLIN, S.
8205 Pte. FESS, H., 2nd R.M.L.I.
18125 A.B. FROOMBERG, B., R.N.A.S.
2/A.M. FRASER, J., R.N.A.S.
10630 1/A.M. GOLD, M.
11262 A.M. GOLDHILL, C.
Ch215/5 Pte. GOLDMAN, S., R.M.L.R.
13254 Pte. GREENBLATT, A., R.M.L.I.
O.S. GALLEWSKI, S., R.M.S.M.
T2/9030 A.B. GOLDBERG, H., 2nd Hood Bn.
PO/17516 Pte. GLUCKSTEIN, R., (D.C.M.), 1st R.M. Bn.
R/3398 A.B. GLASS, W., Hawke Bn.
S/3994 A.B. GREEN, B., 1st F. Amb. R.N.D.
R/2846 A.B. GOWEN, F. J., Anson Bn.
A.B. GEARS, R.N.D.

Royal Naval Division.—*Continued.*

R/1533 A.B. HYMAN, A. L.,* Nelson Bn.
M2/695 A.B. HOOD, L., Hood Bn.
A.B. HART, H. (M.M.), R.N.D.
A.B. HYAM, H., R.N.V.R.
R/4739 A.B. ISRAEL, N., R.N.D.
L/Cpl. JACKSON, S., R.M.L.I.
Z/8316 A.B. KOSSICK, L.,* 2nd Hood Bn.
R/2424 A.B. KARLISH, A.,* 63rd M.G. Bn.
2420 A.B. KING, P., Drake Bn.
Z.C/3319 L.S.M. KENT, J., Hawke Bn.
S/3992 A.B. LEVY, M., 1st F. Amb. R.N.D.
R/3400 A.B. LESSER, A.
R/2293 A.B. LIPMAN, H. (M.M.), Hawke Bn.
894 A.B. LANDY, S. S.,* Ports. Bn.
2800 A.B. LE VOI, D., Benbow Bn.
R/595 A.B. LEVY, M. R.,* Anson Bn.
CH/482 Pte. LEWIS, J., R.M.L.I.
994 L/G. LAMBERT, H., R.N.D.
2623 O.S. LEENARD, J., R.N.D.
Gnr. LEWIS, S., R.M.A.
ZL./2230 A.B. MUSAPHIA, J., 2nd Hood Bn.
R/2436 A.B. MALIN, N., Drake Bn.
R/3319 A.B. MOSKOWITZ, H., Nelson Bn.
53867 Cpl. MORRIS, C.,* 63rd M.G. Bn.
Gnr. MARSHAL, R.M.A.
A.B. MICHAELS, S., R.M.I.
1912 Pte. MYERS, I., R.M.A.
6/22206 A.M. 2 NYKERK, N.
A.B. NATHAN, W., R.N.
99 Pte. OWEN, M., 1st R.M. Bn.
3315 A.B. ODERBERG, M., Nelson Bn.
1st W.O. PERLOW. A.
P/25635 A.M.1 PRICE, H. J.
L.Z./2011 A.B. PARSLOE, E., Nelson Bn.
170 A.B. PHILLIPS, J.
R/3397 A.B. RADIN, O., Hawke Bn.
PO/8207 Pte. SEFF, H., 1st R.M. Bn.
1180 A.B. SALAMAN, L. H.,* Hawke Bn.
CH/15143 A/C.S.M. SCHIFF, F. G.,* 1st R.M. Bn
R/3400 A.B. SISSER, A., Hawke Bn.
R/5772 A.B. STARSMORE, W., Hood Bn.
131 A.B. SEYMOUR, F., R.M.L.I.
Spr. SOLOMON, T. H., Div. Engineers.
A/18797 Pte. SILVER, L., R.N.D.
S/4345 Pte. SACK, S., R.N.D.
Pte. SYMONDS, M. H. V. (M.M.), R.M.L.I
38486 A.C.2 SPIERS, L.
3655 P.O. SMITH, M.
131680 Gnr. SINGER.
1816 O.S. STONE, J., R.N.D.
A.B. SILVER, J., Anson Bn.
Pte. SINDERS, P., R.M.L.I.
Pte. SPIERS, H., R.M.L.I.
Pte. SILVER, L., R.M.L.I.
Pte. STEINGOLD, L., R.M.L.I.
Pte. SEELIG, J., R.N.D.
Pte. SUTRO, C., R.N.D.

8426 Ldg. Seaman TURNBULL, S. H.
A.B. VOS, M. J., R.N.D.
R/3884 A.B. VAUGHAN, A.
Seaman WILKS, G., R.N.V.R.
B/Z/667 A.B. WILLIAMS, I., Hood Bn.
R/2313 A.B. WISEMAN, H., Drake Bn.
PO/17392 L/Cpl. WALTERS, A., 3rd R.M. Bn.
Ch/21054 Pte. WAY, A., R.M.L.I.
1005 Pte. ZEN, J. C.

* Killed in Action or died on Active Service.

CAVALRY.

OFFICERS.

2nd Lieut. ABRAHAMS, L., King Edward's Horse. (M.C.).
Lieut.-Col. BEDDINGTON, C., H.Q., 20th D.M.T.
Lieut. BEDDINGTON, W. R., 2nd Dragoon Guards.
Lieut.-Col. BEDDINGTON, E. H. L. (D.S.O., M.C.), 16th Lancers.
2nd Lieut. BENJAMIN, A. L., 21st Lancers.
Capt. BESSO, R. A., Lincoln Yeomanry.
Capt. COHEN, W. S., Hertfordshire Yeomanry.
Lieut. COHEN, M. D., 1st Dragoon Guards.
Lieut. DEFRIES, A. G., 8th Cav. Indian Army.
2nd Lieut. DE GUNZBURG,* Baron, A. G., Royal Horse Guards.
Capt. DE PASS, E. A., 3rd Co. London Yeo.
Lieut. DE PASS, G. E., (D.S.O.), 4th Dragoon Guards.
Lieut. DE PASS, H., 6th Dragoons.
Capt. DE ROTHSCHILD, A. G., Bucks. Yeo.
Major DE ROTHSCHILD, E. A. DE,* Bucks Yeo.
Major DE ROTHSCHILD, L. (O.B.E.), Bucks. Yeo.
Lieut. ELKAN, A. J. C., 13th Hussars.
Lieut. FRIEND, M., Yeomanry.
Major GOLDSMITH, F. (O.B.E.), Suffolk Yeo.
2nd Lieut. HART, R. H., Kent Yeomanry.
Capt. HENRY, C. J., Leicester Yeomanry.
Lieut. HYAMS, R. S., 4th Res. Regt. M.G.C.
Capt. HOFFNUNG-GOLDSMID, C. J. (O.B.E.), 9th Lancers.
Lieut. HOFFNUNG-GOLDSMID, R. G., 12th Lancers.
Lieut. JACOBS, A., 17th Lancers.
Lieut. JOEL, H. J., 15th Hussars.
Capt. LEVINSON, L. F. (M.C.), Dragoon Guards.
Lieut. LAZARUS, 21st Lancers.
Capt. MICHOLLS, M. G., 17th Lancers.
Major MICHOLLS, W. H. M., 20th Hussars.
Capt. MONTEFIORE, G. E. SEBAG (M.B.E.), 21st Lancers.
Capt. MONTEFIORE, R. M. SEBAG,* R. East Kent Yeomanry.
Lieut. MONTEFIORE, W. SEBAG (M.C.), 5th Irish Lancers.

Cavalry.—Continued.

Lieut. MYERS, A. F.,* 4th Hussars.
Major MOCATTA, V. E. (O.B.E.), 14th Hussars.
Capt. PHILLIPS, F. R. (M.C.), Surrey Yeomanry.
Major PHILLIPS, H., Yorks. Yeomanry.
Lieut. RATHBONE, V. (M.C.), 1st K. E. Horse.
Major SALAMAN, M. H., R. Devons. Hussars.
St. Capt. SAMUEL, W. H. (M.C.), West Kent Yeo.
Capt. SASSOON, A. M. (O.B.E., M.C.), 13th Hussars.
Lieut. SASSOON, E., 5th Dragoon Guards.
Lieut. SASSOON, Sir P. A. G. D., Bt., C.M.G., R. East Kent Yeo.
Capt. SASSOON, S. J., 6th Dragoon Guards.
2nd Lieut. SHERWINTER, S., 1/3rd Scottish Hrse.
Major STERN, F. C. (O.B.E., M.C.), 2nd Co. of London Yeo.
Major STERN, H. J., S. Irish Horse.
2nd Lieut. STRUMP, R., 4th Hussars.
Capt. TAMWORTH, L., Montgomery Yeomanry.
Capt. TUCK, D. A., 3rd Co. of London Yeo.
Major TUCK, W. R., 3rd Co. of London Yeo.
Capt. VAN DEN BERGH, S. J.,* Co. of Lond. Yeo.
Capt. WALFORD, W., 2nd C. of Lond. Yeo.
Lieut. WEISS, H. E., 3rd City of Lond. Yeo.
2nd Lieut. WEINGOTT, F. F., Middlesex Yeo.
Lieut.-Col. WEISBERG, H. (D.S.O.), Lond. Yeo.
Lieut. WOOLF, J., City of London Yeo.

N.C.O.'s AND MEN.

39877 Pte. ABRAHAMS, A., M.G.C. Cav.
Tpr. ABRAHAMS, M. L., K. E. H.
3054 Tpr. ABRAHAMS, M. G.,* 1st Life Gds.
231005 Pte. ABRAMS, J., Dorset Yeom.
D/23554 Pte. ALBERT, M., Norfolk Yeom.
236291 L/Cpl. ALBERGE, C. H., 2nd R. Glouc. H.
2272 Pte. ALEXANDER, A., Hants Yeo.
53755 Dvr. ASHER, D., R.H.A.
37161 Pte. APPLEBAUM, J., 3rd C. of Lon. Yeo.
H/38140 Pte. ANSCHEL, J., R. Wilts. Yeo.
50530 Pte. ARNOLD, E., 250th N. Irish Horse.
40407 Trp. ASHBERRY, R.,* 1st C. of L. Yeom.
1145 Tpr. AUERBACH, W. H.,* 1st K. E. H.
31231 Pte. BAKER, 5th Res. Cav.
33535 Pte. BANIN, 1st Res. Cav. 3rd Hussars.
22693 Pte. BARNETT, B., 6th Res. Regt.
76374 Pte. BARNETT, G., 2/1st Derby Yeom.
41047 Tpr. BARNETT, H., 2/1st London, Yeom.
76374 Tpr. BARNETT, I., 2/1st Derby. Yeom.
1918 Tpr. BARNETT, K. E. H.
1918 Tpr. BARNETT, Res. Sqdn. K. E. H.
3971 Pte. BARNETT, L., Staffs. Yeom.
36814 Pte. BARNETT, S., 20th Worc. Hussars.
42592 L/Cpl. BASSELL, H., Northumb. Hussars.
51620 Pte. BALON, J., 4th Hussars.
18891 Pte. BALSON, J. J., 1st C. of London Yeo.
76216 Tpr. BAYNARD, M., 2/1st Derby. Yeom.
720 Tpr. BARNARD, L., Royal Horse Guards.
H/38110 Pte. BARCHIN, I., R. Wilts. Yeo.
Tpr. BEDDILL, Pembroke Yeomanry.
1104 Tpr. BERCOVITZ, S., 1st K. E. Horse.
1050 Pte. BERWITZ, M., N. Irish H.
31161 Pte. BERG, B., 20th Hussars.
L/12830 Pte. BERNHARD, A.,* 9th Lancers.
27931 Pte. BERNHARD, V., C. of L. Yeom.
31159 Tpr. BERNSTEIN, M., 20th Hussars.
3088 Tpr. BERNSTEIN, S. A.,* Middl. Imp. Y.
996 Tpr. BECKMAN, G., K. E. H.
37073 Pte. BERLOFSKY, J., 3rd Co. of Lon. Yeo.
101147 Pte. BESTOW, Hampshire Yeo.
3513 Pte. BERMAN, A., Rough Riders.
266260 Pte. BERMAN, N., C. of L. Yeom.
75101 Tpr. BENJAMIN, B., 2/1st Glam. Yeo.
40727 Pte. BENJAMIN, H., C. of L. Yeom.
Tpr. BENJAMIN, L. A., King Edward's H.
6943 Pte. BENSON, A., 9th Lancers.
Pte. BENSON, J., 16th Lancers.
1758 Pte. BENHALM, 1st K E. Horse.
23409 Tpr. BECKER, W., 17th Lancers.
Tpr. BERMAN, R., Lanc. Yeo.
43182 Pte. BIERMAN, 2/1st West Som. Yeo.
Tpr. BLACKMAN, H., 18th Hussars.
Pte. BLANKSEE, S. L., 1st C. of Lond. Yeo.
35725 Tpr. BLACK, A., 2/1st Lanark. Yeom.
Pte. BLACKMAN, S., 18th Hussars.
27275 Pte. BLOOM, M., 19th Hussars.
27477 Pte. BLOOM, H., 19th Hussars.
Pte. BLOOM, I., 18th Hussars.
Pte. BLOOM, I., 4th Dragoon Guards.
41007 Pte. BLOOM, S., C. of L. Yeom.
Pte. BLOND, N. L., D. of L. Own Yeom.
Pte. BLOCK, A., 7th Hussars.
15507 S/Sgt. BLOCK, S. S., 14th Res. Cav.
120629 L/Cpl. BARNETT, I., 2/2nd Lovatt Scouts.
Pte. BARNETT, S. C., 2/2nd Scott. Horse.
305526 Pte. BLOCH, E., 2/1st Suffolk Yeom.
24748 Tpr. BLOCH, 10th Res. Cav. Regt.
2129 Cpl. BLOND, N., R.H. Guards.
5333 Pte. BLUESTONE, J., Pembroke Yeom.
1951 Pte. BENNETT, I., 3rd Co. of Lond. Yeo.
52146 Pte. BERG, 4th Hussars.
80349 L/Cpl. BRAHAM, H., 2/1st West Lond. Y.
295661 L/Cpl. BROWN, B., 2/1st West Som. Y.
5177 Pte. BROWN, K., 3/1st Pembroke Yeom.
2038 Pte. BROWN, M., 1st K.E.H.
3968 Pte. BROOKSTEIN, G., Staffs. Yeom.
Tpr. BURAS, C. of London Yeo.
34707 Pte. BRICK, R., 5th Res. Regt.
Tpr. BRILLIANT, H., Middlesex Yeo.
Tpr. BOWMAN, M. L., Royal Bucks. Hus.
100834 Pte. BOWMAN, M. L., 2nd M. G. Sqdn.
Tpr. BRILLIANT, L., 1st C. of Lond. Yeo.
37118 Pte. BUSKIN, H., C. of L. Yeom.

Cavalry.—*Continued.*

- Tpr. BUNTMAN, B., Imp. Light Horse.
- Tpr. BULLER, A., 5th Dragoon Guards.
- 33251 Pte. CARLSON, F., 4th Hussars.
- 265263 Pte. CANTOR, M., Co. of London Yeo.
- 121394 Pte. CAISOR, V. G., Dragoon Guards.
- 35502 Pte. CAPLAN, J., Reserve Cavalry.
- 21746 Pte. CAPLAN, M., 4th Dragoon Guards.
- 433 Tpr. CAPPER, A. J., 2nd K. E. H.
- H/285293 Pte. CLAYTON, L., Oxford Hussars.
- 17547 Pte. CASSELL, C. A.,* 2/1st Norfolk Yeo.
- H/42592 Pte. CASSELL, H., 1/1st North. H.
- 12545 Tpr. COHEN, A., Royal Horse Guards.
- 6009 Cpl. CARR, S. J., 7th Hussars.
- 18296 Tpr. COHEN, D.,* 4th Hussars.
- 7413 Pte. CARDIGAN, B., 3rd Hussars.
- 710 Tpr. CLARK, D.,* 1st Royal Dragoons.
- 2864 Tpr. CLAYTON, 3/1st Oxford Yeomanry.
- 29506 Pte. COUZINS, 14th Res. Cav. Regt.
- 125496 Tpr. COHEN, A., 2/1st Lovat Scouts.
- 24054 Tpr. CEDERBAUM, 8th Res. Cav. Regt.
- 331448 Pte. CLAYMAN, M., 2/1st Hussars.
- 2831 Pte. COLMAN, I., 10th Hussars.
- 170636 Pte. COTT, N., 2/1st Sussex Yeomanry.
- 76347 Pte. CUTNER, H., 2/1st Yeomanry.
- 2307 L/Cpl. GOFFMAN, B., 1st R. Berks. Yeo.
- 40955 Pte. CHECKTER, J., 2/1st Yeomanry.
- 24749 Tpr. COWEN, 10th Res. Cav. Regt.
- Pte. CROOK, J., Yeomanry.
- 5303 Tpr. COHEN, H. E., 3/1st Pembroke Y
- 1772 Tpr. COHEN, J., 2nd K. E. H.
- 265931 Pte. COHEN, M., 5th Res. Cavalry.
- Pte. COHEN, V., 4th R. Irish Dragoons.
- 240402 Pte. COHEN, J., 2/1st R.E.K. Mtd. Rifles.
- 46239 Pte. COHEN, S., 2/1st Surrey Yeomanry.
- 3086 Pte. COHEN, R., Sussex Yeomanry.
- 1983 Pte. COHEN, L., 3rd Yeomanry.
- 3126 Pte. COHEN, M., 1st Life Guards.
- 43203 Pte. CLAFF, 2/1st West Somerset Yeo.
- H/38961 Pte. COHEN, H., R. Wilts. Yeo.
- H/38787 Pte. COHEN, M., R. Wilts. Yeo.
- 38227 Pte. COHEN, S., 2/1st Denbigh Yeo.
- 2397 Pte. COHEN, R., Berks. Yeo.
- 48179 Pte. DAVIES, 5th Reserve Cavalry.
- Pte. DAVIES, O., Royal Sussex Yeo.
- 5221 Pte. DAVIS, A., Pembroke Yeomanry.
- Pte. DAVIS, E., Imp. Light Horse.
- Pte. DAVIS, M., 4th Hussars.
- 2325 Pte. DAVIS, M., 2nd King Ed.'s Horse.
- Pte. DAVIS, M., 19th Hussars.
- 37119 Pte. DAVIS, L. M., 3rd Co. of Lon. Yeo.
- Pte. DAVIS, L., Royal Bucks. Yeo.
- Pte. DAVIS, H., 8th Royal Lancers.
- 24684 Pte. DAVIS, J. W., 13th Hussars.
- Pte. DAVIS, P., Royal Sussex Yeo.
- Pte. DALE, H., 11th Hussars.
- 1888 Pte. DAVIDS, B., West Kent Yeomanry.
- 236398 Pte. DYSCH, H., 1st R. Gloucester Hrs.
- 46223 Pte. DICKS, L., 2/1st Surrey Yeomanry.
- 27788 Pte. DUSBOWIN, P., 10th Hussars.
- Pte. DE FRIES, A. G., Co. of Lond. Yeo.
- Pte. DIAMOND, A., 19th Hussars.
- Pte. DOMBEY, F., 2nd Co. of Lond. Yeo.
- Pte. DOVE, M., 20th Hussars.
- Pte. DRESMAN, 1st Co. of Lond. Yeo.
- Tpr. DRESSER, L., 21st Lancers.
- 34241 Pte. DA COSTA, J., 5th Res. Regt.
- 29085 Pte. DONSKIE, I., 2/1st Glamorgan Yeo.
- 266060 Pte. DIAMOND, L., 3rd Co. of Lon. Yeo.
- 37178 Pte. DA COSTA, A., 3rd Co. of Lon. Yeo.
- 37179 Pte. DEFRIES, I., 3rd Co. of Lond. Yeo.
- 7768 Tpr. EMANUEL, 21st Lancers.
- Tpr. EFFERMAN, E., 21st Lancers.
- 1903 Tpr. EDWARDS, 2nd K. E. H.
- Tpr. ELIAS, A., 3rd C. of Lond. Yeo.
- Pte. EATON, A., King Edward's Horse.
- Pte. EPSTEIN, P., 5th Dragoon Guards.
- 265948 Pte. EISON, D., 3rd Co. of Lon. Yeo.
- 153159 Pte. EPULE, J., 2/2nd Scottish Horse.
- 245618 Pte. EDLEMAN, R. I., 2/1st W. K. Yeo.
- 2071 Pte. ELIAS, A., Co. of London Yeo.
- 1492 Pte. EPSTEIN, M., Sussex Yeomanry.
- 290180 Pte. ESTREY, M., Pembroke Yeomanry.
- 6857 Pte. EPRILE, J., Scottish Horse.
- Cpl. EMANUEL, H., Warwick Yeomanry.
- Pte. ELLISON, 4th Hussars.
- Tpr. ELKAN, J. C., Middlesex Yeomanry.
- Tpr. ESSENBERG, J., 20th Hussars.
- 2659 Tpr. FABER, J., R. H. Guards.
- Tpr. FAGEW, I., Pembroke Yeo.
- Tpr. FAIGENBAUM, J., 11th Hussars.
- 71184 Pte. FREEDMAN, S., 2/1st Berks. Yeo.
- 7165 Pte. FREEDMAN, J., S. Notts Hussars.
- 331008 Pte. FREEDMAN, N., Yorks. Hussars.
- 18294 Pte. FREEDMAN, P., 2/1st Berks. Yeo.
- 17989 Pte. FREIDMAN, 4th Dragoon Guards.
- 11097 Pte. FISH, 8th Res. Regt.
- 16010 Pte. FREEMAN, 1st Dragoon Guards.
- 27497 Pte. FOOTING, 14th Res. Cav.
- Pte. FRANKEL, W., 3rd Dragoon Guards.
- H/38115 Pte. FOLUS, B., R. Wilts. Yeo.
- 260996 Sig. FISHER, D.,* 2/1st Co. of Lon. Yeo.
- Pte. FRANKS, H., 1st Royal Dragoons.
- 135698 Pte. FRANKS, J., 2/1st Montgomery Yeo.
- 30033 Pte. FRANKLIN, S., Dragoon Guards.
- 41192 Pte. FRANKEL, J., C. of L. Yeo.
- 29173 Pte. FELDMAN, J., Yeomanry.
- 5281 Pte. FINESTONE, J., 3/1st Pembroke Yeo.
- 2632 Pte. FEINSTEIN, M., 10th Yeomanry.
- 61260 Pte. FINKLESTEIN, M., 2/1st Dorset Yeo.
- 18682 Pte. FREED, M., 1st Reserve Cavalry.
- 5223 Pte. FREISLER, J., Pembroke Yeo.
- 76244 Pte. FINEMAN, S., 2/1st Derby Yeo.
- Pte. FINK, S., D. of Lanc. Own Yeo.
- Pte. FIREMAN, J., 9th Lancers.
- Tpr. FOX, P. J., 4th Hussars.

Cavalry.—*Continued.*

	Tpr. FONSECA, S., 1st Co. of London Yeo.
	Tpr. FRESSNER, I., Pembroke Yeo.
	Tpr. FREEMAN, A., Ayreshire Yeo.
396	Pte. GABRIELSON, M.,* 1st K. E. H.
1313	Pte. GARDINER, E., 2nd K. E. H.
506714	Pte. GABLOSKY, 3rd Res. Cavalry.
261155	Pte. GAFFINOVITCH, J., 2/10th M. H.
265281	Tpr. GARTMAN, T., 1/3rd Co. of Lon. Y.
	Pte. GARCIA, J. R., 5th Lancers.
215628	Pte. GLASS, P., 2/1st W. Kent Yeo.
	Pte. GODFREY, E. S. (M.M.), London Yeo.
290159	Pte. GLASS, W., 2/1st Pembroke Yeo.
61257	Pte. GLASS, H., 2/1st Dorset Yeo.
100963	Pte. GELLER, Hampshire Yeo.
8739	Tpr. GILBERT, H., 5th Dragoon Guards.
251023	Pte. GINSBERG, J., Lancs. Hussars.
1547	Pte. GLICKMAN, A., West Kent Yeo.
	Tpr. GLICK. R., Queen's O. O. H.
29724	Pte. GLUCK, J., 19th Hussars.
71150	Pte. GOLDSTEIN, L., 2/1st Berks. Yeo.
3602	Pte. GOLDSTEIN, L., 11th Yeo.
2312	Pte. GOLDSTEIN, N., 3rd Yeomanry.
65721	Pte. GOLDSTEIN, L., N. Irish Horse.
36987	Pte. GOLDSTEIN, J., R. Glouc. Hussars
100930	Tpr. GOLDBERG, J., 1/3rd Co. of Lon. Y
H/38978	Pte. GOLDBERG, S., R. Wilts. Yeo.
295659	Pte. GOLDSTEIN, S., 2/1 W. Somerset Y.
241481	Pte. GOLDBERG, N., 2/1st Q.O. Ox. Hrs.
29179	Pte. GOLDBERG, A., 8th Res. Cavalry.
25221	Pte. GOLDBERG, L., Yeomanry.
146225	Pte. GOLDBERG, I., 4th Dragoon Guards.
51349	Pte. GOLDBERG, S., 2/1st Yorks. Hussars.
215268	Pte. GOLDMAN, I., Denbigh Yeo.
742	Pte. GOLD, I., Yeomanry.
37188	Pte. GOLD, S., 3rd Co. of Lon. Yeo.
58905	L/Cpl. GOLDMAN, H., 25th N. Irish Horse
	Tpr. GOLD, H., 14th Hussars.
1068	Tpr. GOODMAN, 12th Lancers.
965	Tpr. GOODMAN, S., Household Bn.
43145	Pte. GOWLER, 2/1st West Somerset Yeo.
201648	Pte. GOODFIELD, S., 2/1st Pembroke Y.
59804	Pte. GORDON, J., 2/1st Pembroke Yeo.
1941	Tpr. GREEN, M., 2nd K. E. H.
3967	Pte. GREEN, B., 3/1st Staffs. Yeo.
24004	Tpr. GRESNER, 8th Res. Cav. Regt.
38684	Pte. GREENBAUM, L., 2/1st West K. Yeo
39206	Sig. GROSSMAN, H., 1st K. E. H.
24056	Pte. GROBAZTEIN, J., 16th Lancers.
24685	Tpr. GREENBAUM, 10th Res. Cav. Regt.
31683	Pte. GRODENTZ, M., 20th Hussars.
	Sgt. HADIDA, A. H., 5th D. Guards.
27762	Pte. HANELLA, 14th Res. Cav.
14869	Pte. HARRIS, S. H. R., 19th Hussars.
	Pte. HARRIS, A., 5th Dragoon Guards.
	Sgt. HARRIS, E., 2nd Co. of Lond. Yeo.
	Pte. HARRIS, G., 1st Co. of Lond. Yeo.
	Tpr. HARRIS, J., 5th Dragoon Guards.
170643	Pte. HARRIS, S., 2/1st Sussex Yeomanry.
	Pte. HARRIS, G., 7th Hussars.
14869	Pte. HARRIS, S., 19th Hussars.
240896	Pte. HARRIS, M., N. Somerset Yeo.
	Pte. HARRISON, A., Norfolk Yeomanry.
3649	Tpr HARDY, A., 3/1st Yorks. D.
	Cpl. HARDY, D., 2nd Dragoon Guards.
	Pte. HART, A., 3rd Co. of London Yeo.
23217	L/Cpl. HART, W., 21st Lanark Yeo.
	Tpr. HESS, H., Middlesex Hussars.
	Tpr. HART, H. R., Royal East Kent. Y.
2270	Tpr. HART, L., 13th Hussars.
	Pte. HART, A., 11th Hussars.
29394	Pte. HART, B., Dragoon Guards.
28353	Pte. HERZFIELD, S., 2/1st Q.O. Oxf. Hus.
48822	Pte. HERMAN, C., 3rd Reserve Cavalry.
23003	Tpr. HEILBRON, L., 21st Lancers.
	Tpr. HEITNER, A., 5th Dragoon Guards.
221030	Tpr. HEILBUTH, C., 5th Hussars.
76181	Pte. HECKER, J., 2/1st Glamorgan Yeo.
63221	Pte. HECKER, 3rd Hussars.
3290	Pte. HERSON, J., 2/1st Fife Forfar Yeo.
	Pte. HILL, H., 11th Hussars.
4606	Tpr. HOLLANDER, H., Queen's Bays.
15344	Pte. HUNT, W., 5th Lancers.
28280	Pte. HYMAN, 11th Reserve Cavalry.
37393	Pte. HYMAN, R., 9th Lancers.
27569	Pte. HYAM, S., 1st Reserve Cavalry Regt.
3055	Pte. HYAMS, A., Bucks. Hussars.
	Pte. ISRAEL, P., 11th Hussars.
2127	Pte. ISRAEL, D., 1/1st R. Wilts. Yeo.
	Pte. ISAACS, A., 21st Lancers.
	Pte. ISAACS, A., Welsh Horse.
6966	Tpr. ISAACS, E. J.,* 2nd Dragoon Guards.
	Pte. ISAACS, R., 21st Cavalry.
	Pte. ISAACS, S., 16th Lancers.
	Pte. ISAACS, S., Hertford Yeomanry.
	Pte. ISAACS, J., 7th Hussars.
58438	Pte. ISAACS, M., 2/1st W. Kent. Yeo.
2093	Pte. ISRAEL, L. L., 3/3rd Co. of Lon. Yeo.
115581	Tpr. ISAAC, E., 1/2nd Co. of Lon. Yeo.
15719	Pte. IZENSTEIN, Hampshire Yeomanry.
15406	Pte. JACOBS, J., 5th Reserve Cavalry.
245631	Pte. JACOBS, M., 2/1st W. Kent. Yeo.
46380	Pte. JACOBS, G. F., 2/1st Surrey Yeo.
30	Sgt. JACOBS, H. D., 1st K. E. H.
	Tpr. JACOBS, H., 10th Hussars.
	Tpr. JACOBS, J., 14th Hussars.
290165	Sgt. JACOBS, S., 2/1st Pembroke Yeo.
1539	Tpr. JACOBS (COLE), J.,* 2nd K. E. H.
205769	Pte. JACOBS, A., Bucks. Hussars.
33785	Pte. JACOBS, H. L., 3rd Hussars.
	L/Cpl. JACOBS, F. C., 5th Royal Irish Ls.
15896	Pte. JACOBS, J., Dragoon Guards.
1675	Pte. JACKSON, S., Bucks. Hussars.
	L/Cpl. JACOBS, J. A., 16th Co. of Lond.

Cavalry.—*Continued.*

15628	Pte. Jacobs, 14th Res. Cav.		
T/406482	Pte. Jacobson, G., 1st Cav. Res.		
	Pte. Jackson, J., 18th Hussars.		
4766	Tpr. Jaffe, I., Yeomanry.		
	Pte. Jewell, E. M., 12th Lancers.		
2071	Tpr. Joel, 2nd King Edward's Horse.		
23472	Tpr. Joel, T., 19th Hussars.		
240722	Pte. Joseph, W., N. Somerset Yeo.		
260603	Pte. Joseph, M., Co. of Lon. Yeo.		
31298	Pte. Jacob, A., 20th Hussars.		
2430	Pte. Joseph, A., 3/1st Glamorgan Yeo.		
	Tpr. Joseph, P., Imperial Yeomanry.		
296208	Pte. Joseph, A., Lanark. Yeomanry.		
48996	Pte. Josephs, M., 3rd Hussars.		
251028	Pte. Jacobson, M., Lancs. Hussars.		
37124	Pte. Joseph, T. M., Co. of London Yeo.		
1305	Tpr. Judah, R. J., 2nd K. E. H.		
474297	Pte. Judeson, H., Yeomanry.		
L/19576	Pte. Katz, 17th Lancers.		
37055	Pte. Kambish, P., 2/1st London Yeo.		
57915	Pte. Kaufman, L., Norfolk Yeomanry.		
261290	Pte. Kempner, A. A., Yeomanry.		
2609	Pte. Keiz, J., Royal Irish Horse.		
110822	Pte. Kershaw, R., 1/1st London Yeo.		
20334	L/Cpl. King, W., Dragoon Guards.		
20803	Pte. Kosky, O., 4th Dragoon Guards.		
21710	Pte. Koch, P., 3rd Dragoon Guards.		
2564	Pte. Krotoski, C., 3/1st E. Riding Yeo.		
	Sgt. Kurman, L., 2nd Dragoon Guards.		
34226	Pte. Kenrick, S., 5th Res. Cav.		
4526	Sgt. Kershaw, D. of Lancs. O. Y.		
1316	Tpr. Krohn, D. of Lancs. O. Y.		
38253	Pte. Kohler, L., 2/1st Denbigh Yeo.		
16400	Pte. Lappin, A., 3rd Hussars.		
5323	Pte. Lazarus, M., Pembroke Yeo.		
5275	Pte. Lazarus, P., Pembroke Yeo.		
203567	Pte. Lawrence, A., Pembroke Yeo.		
100837	Cpl. Langer, Hampshire Yeomanry.		
	Pte. Lazarus, A., 2nd Dragoon Guards.		
39583	Tpr. Lazarus, B., 3/1st Pembroke Yeo.		
1975	Pte. Lebovitch, W., King Edward's H.		
2252	Tpr. Lee, H., Scots Greys.		
2252	Pte. Lee, H., 2nd Dragoon Guards.		
2241	Tpr. Leopold, A., North Irish Horse.		
106368	Pte. Lerner, B., 2/1st Herts Yeomanry.		
5322	Pte. Lesser, A., Pembroke Yeo.		
46347	Pte. Lesser, R. W., 2/1st Surrey Yeo.		
32645	Pte. Levene, I., Worcester Yeo.		
241366	Pte. Levene, P., 2/1st Q.O. Oxford Hus.		
D/3424	Pte. Levine, J., 1st Royal Dragoons.		
326241	Pte. Levine, L., 2/1st Q.O. Leic. Hus.		
4165	Tpr. Levine, L., 12th Yeomanry.		
	Pte. Levi, H., 2nd Dragoon Guards.		
	Pte. Levi, A. E., 4th Dragoon Guards.		
460809	Pte. Levy, 5th Cav. Res.		
76807	Pte. Levy, A., Surrey Yeo.		
	Pte. Levy, A., Dragoon Guards.		
295695	Cpl. Levy, J. T., 2/1st W. Somerset Yeo.		
170645	Pte. Levy, B., 2/1st Sussex Yeomanry.		
2045	Pte. Levy, 2/2nd Co. of Lon. Yeo.		
21517	Pte. Levy, J., 6th **Dragoons.**		
17929	Pte. Levy, M., 2/1st Essex Yeomanry.		
16598	Pte. Levy, S., 1st Cavalry Regt.		
16767	Pte. Levy, J., Dragoon Guards.		
9093	Pte. Levy, A., 6th Dragoons.		
19751	Tpr. Levy, H.,* Bucks. Hussars.		
40123	Tpr. Levy, M., M.G. Squadron.		
21528	Tpr. Levy, V. L., 13th Hussars.		
7105	Tpr. Levy, 6th Res. Regt.		
31772	Tpr. Levy, 10th Res. Regt.		
2379	Sgt. Levy, M., 6th Light Horse.		
90083	Pte. Levy, T. A., 6th Dragoons.		
295695	L/Cpl. Levy, 2/1st West Somerset Yeo.		
356903	Pte. Levy, C., 15th Hussars.		
1940	Tpr. Levey, South Irish Horse.		
	Tpr. Leviseur, E. A., K. E. H.		
266117	Sgt. Lewis, W. M., 3rd Co. of Lon. Y.		
4235	Sgt. Lewis, D. of Lancs. Own Yeo.		
2102	Pte. Lewis, H., K.E.H.		
2050	Tpr. Lewinstein, 3/3rd Co. of Lon. Y.		
266106	L/Cpl. Lewin, F. M., 3rd C. of Lon. Y.		
43214	L/Cpl Lichstein, 2/1st West S. Yeo.		
2391	Pte. Lilliman, S., 5th Lancers.		
24044	Pte. Limburg, B., Derbyshire Yeo.		
2228	Pte. Linder, M., 2/1st Hussars.		
37855	Pte. Lion, P. R., 3rd Res. Hussars.		
51534	Pte. Lipman, I., 3rd Cavalry Depot.		
4388	Pte. Lipman, L., O.O. Yorks. D. Guards.		
101091	Tpr. Lipetz, A., 2/1st L. & B. Hussars.		
2421	Tpr. Lisman, South Irish Horse.		
205768	Pte. Litroen, E. N., 3rd Hussars.		
	Tpr. Littman, H., 7th Dragoon Guards.		
2156	Pte. Litrim, E. M., 2/1st Hussars.		
23443	Pte. Longman, S., Lancers.		
11156	Pte. Longman S., 16th Lancers.		
5535	Tpr. Lottries, A., 10th Hussars.		
166368	Pte. Lumar, B., 2/1st Herts. Yeo.		
1815	Tpr. Lupinsky, W., Royal H. Guards.		
22387	Pte. Lubinsky, D., 1st Dragoons.		
2108	L/Cpl. Lubelski,, W., 2/1st Sussex Y.		
33478	Pte. Lyons, H., 3rd Hussars.		
51151	Pte. Lyons, S., City of London Yeo.		
11418	Tpr. Mark, L., 4th Hussars.		
5245	Tpr. Marks, L., 3/1stPembroke Yeo.		
3328	Cpl. Marks, J., 12th Lancers.		
6154	Pte. Marks, R., 1st Dragoon Guards.		
2211	Pte. Marks, S., 2/1st Berks. Yeo.		
2941	Pte. Marks, A., 3/1st Shropshire Yeo.		
2986	Pte. Mason, I., 3/1st Shropshire Yeo.		
5276	Pte. Mason, P., Pembroke Yeomanry.		
	Sdlr. Cpl. Martin, D., 18th Hussars.		
	Tpr. McIntyre, 2nd K. E. H.		
5127	Pte. Mednick, Co. of London Yeo.		
286224	L/Cpl. Mendoza, M., 2/1 Q.O. Oxf. H.		
295978	Pte. Mendelson, A., Surrey Yeomanry.		

Cavalry.—*Continued.*

34227	Pte. MEARS, A., 5th Res. Cav.
100068	Pte. MELLER, A., 9th Cav. Bde.
1341	Pte. MERKIN, R., 1st K. E. H.
3176	Tpr. MENDES, H. J.,* 2nd Life Guards.
836	Tpr. MILLER, M., 2nd K. E. H.
2038	Tpr. MITCHELL, 2nd K. E. H.
11412	Tpr. MORRIS, J., 4th Hussars.
2031	Tpr. MORRIS, 2nd K. E. H.
2185	Pte. MORRIS, M., Northants. Yeomanry.
	Tpr. MORDECAI, A., Essex Yeom.
	Tpr. MYERS, A. A., 3/2nd C. of Lon. Yeo.
	Pte. MALINSKY, 4th Hussars.
	Tpr. MORRIS, H. I.
D/10913	Pte. MORACK, J., 2nd Drag. Guards.
47456	Pte. MORTON, H., M.G.C. Cavalry.
27645	Pte. MOSS, H., Gloucester Yeo.
1919	Pte. MUSCOVITCH, M., 2/1st Dorset Yeo.
2505	Pte. MUSCOVITCH, A., 2/1st Dorset Yeo.
56541	Pte. MUSAPHIA, H., 21st Norfolk Yeo.
4061	Tpr. MYERS, A., 1st Middlesex Yeo.
302	Tpr. MYERS, C. D., Gloucester Yeo.
95445	Pte. MYRON, H., 2/1st Q.O.R.G. Yeo.
27267	Pte. MYERS, R. M., 3rd Hussars.
12997	Pte. NEWMAN, S., Yeomanry.
6939	Tpr. NEWMAN, 21st Lancers.
985	Pte. NORTON, H., 15th Hussars.
51191	Pte. NOVINSKY, I., 2/1st E. Riding Yeo.
76093	Pte. NIGHTINGALE, L., Derby Yeo.
5314	Pte. OPPER, H., Pembroke Yeomanry.
331221	Pte. ORNARDLE, C., Yorks. Hussars.
	Pte. OZAREOFF, A., Dragoon Guards.
	Tpr. PARKER, S., 20th Lancers.
29141	Pte. PERETZKER, A., 2/1st Essex Yeo.
5647	Pte. PELLER, G., 2/1st Pembroke Yeo.
14257	Tpr. PEZARO, B., 8th Hussars.
27594	Pte. PETERS, P., Co. of Lon. Yeo.
266238	Pte. PHILLIPS, H., 3rd Co. of Lon. Yeo.
42151	Tpr. PHILLIPS, J., 1/1st Yorks. Hussars.
2082	Tpr. PHILLIPS, Buckinghamshire Yeo.
224	Tpr. PHILLIP, H., 12th Lancers.
1170	Tpr. PIZER, E. J., 1st K. E. H.
	Sgt. PUINE, M., Middlesex Yeom.
51258	Tpr. PLATER, J.,* 10th Hussars.
20806	Pte. POLLARD, A., 4th Dragoons.
7678	Pte. POLLACK, A. E., 6th Dragoons.
1301	L/Cpl. POLLACK, L., 2/1st W. Kent Yeo.
34205	Pte. POLIKOFF, T. J., 5th Lancers.
	Pte. POSNER, 14th Hussars.
4650	Sgt. PRAEGER, A.,* 9th Lancers.
2958	Pte. PRESS, S., 3/1st Shropshire Yeo.
48857	Pte. PRESS, P., 3rd Res. Hussars.
43741	Pte. PRESS, H., 15th Hussars.
5219	Tpr. PRESS, A., 20th Hussars.
1458	Tpr. RABIN, 1st K. E. H.
293187	Pte. RADIN, D., Pembroke Yeo.
2662	Pte. RAPHAEL, A., 2/1st Hussars.
265963	Pte. REIS, V. C., 3rd Co. of Lon. Yeo.
5274	Tpr. RESNICK, S., Pembroke Yeomanry.
38243	Pte. REUBEN, S., 2/1st Denbigh Yeo.
2963	Pte. RICH, P., 3/1st Shropshire Yeo.
60871	Tpr. ROSENBERG, C., 2/1st Y. Hussars.
2933	Pte. ROSENBERG, M., 6th Res. Cav. Regt.
83214	Pte. ROSENBEERG, S., 4th Hussars.
	Tpr. RAPP, L., 1st I. L. Horse.
208800	Pte. ROSENBURG, J., 3rd Hussars.
11341	Pte. ROSENBLOOM, 21st Lancers.
56401	Pte. RUBENSTEIN, J., 2/1st Norfolk Yeo.
51128	Pte. ROSENSTON, A., Yeomanry.
	Pte. ROSENCROWN, L. N., Hussars.
43162	Pte. ROSENTHAL, 2/1st W Som. Yeo.
1513	Pte. ROSEN, M., Yeomanry.
2003	Tpr. ROOMS, South Irish Horse.
22080	Tpr. ROSS, M., 5th Dragoon Guards.
34732	Pte. RUDA, 5th Res. Cav. Regt.
1196	Pte. RUECROFT, J. W., K. E. H.
206114	Pte. RUBINS, H., 13th Hussars.
5184	Pte. SAGAR, H., 18th Hussars.
206633	Pte. SALMAN, R. H., Bucks. Hussars.
42595	Tpr. SAMUELS, A. L., Warwick. Yeo.
5680	Cpl. SAMUELS, A., 20th Hussars.
311294	Pte. SAMUELS, 5th Reserve Cavalry.
24055	Pte. SANINA, A., 16th Lancers.
56839	Tpr. SAPHER, M., 2/1st Hussars.
281721	Pte. SAVILLE, W., 2/1st Hussars.
1901	Tpr. SCLARE, 2nd King's Edward Horse.
	Tpr. SCHOENFIELD, G., Q.O. Glasg. Yeo.
14283	Tpr. SCHNEIDER, E., 20th Hussars.
37150	Pte. SCHNEIDER, I., 3rd Co. of Lon. Yeo.
	Tpr. SCOTT, A., 19th Lancers.
326700	Pte. SEAGER, W., 2/1 Q.O. Worc. Hrs.
46235	Pte. SEIGENBERG, E., 2/1st Surr. Yeo.
5212	Tpr. SELIGSON, W., Pembroke Yeo.
	Tpr. SELINE, N. J., 7th Dragoon Guards.
	Tpr. SEFTON, L., 19th Hussars.
	Tpr. SEIDLITZ, S., R. Bucks Hussars.
15211	Pte. SHADOSKI, B., 3rd Dragoon Guards.
27297	Tpr. SHAETZEN, 9th Res. Regt.
235714	Tpr. SHANE, M., Gloucester Yeo.
1350	Pte. SHANE, N. M., R.G.H. Yeo.
6261	Pte. SHAPIRO, J., 3/2nd Scottish Horse.
51416	Pte. SHARE, R., 2/1st E.R. Yeo.
	Tpr. SHAFFER, H., D. of Lancs. Own Yeo.
170794	Pte. SHINEMAN, L. J., 2/1st Sussex Yeo.
190218	Pte. SHERMAN, J., Glamorgan Yeo.
2819	Pte. SHERMAN, I., 2/1st Glamorgan Yeo.
1073	Pte. SHIERS, A., Chesters. Imp. Yeo.
	Tpr. SHEREK, P., 2nd C. of Lond. Yeo.
	Tpr. SHRIFREEN, L., R. Bucks. Hussars.
3801	Pte. SILVERMAN, P., 4th Dragoon Guards.
27345	Tpr. SILVERSTEIN, M., 3rd Scottish Horse.
35044	Tpr. SILVERSTONE, J., 7th Queen's Husrs.
40113	L/Cpl. SIMMONS, J., Yeomanry.
18485	Sig. SIMPSON, A. E., 17th Lancers.
3619	Tpr. SIMPSON, 3/1st City of Lon. Yeo.
29698	Pte. SINGER, J., 19th Hussars.

Cavalry.—Continued.

153429 Pte. SINTLER, N., 1st K.E.H.
Pte. SILVER, D., 3rd Reserve Cavalry.
2236 Pte. SISS, A., 1st Dragoon Guards.
Tpr. SKIBB, A. J., Dragoons.
243 Tpr. SLOMAN, B., 2nd K. E. H.
Tpr. SMITH, A., 20th Hussars.
5007 Tpr. SMITH, C., 15th Hussars.
5063 Tpr. SNIPPER, A., Pembroke Yeo.
284 Pte. SNIDERS, S.,* R. B. Hussars.
23995 Tpr. SONNENFIELD, 8th Res. Cav. Regt.
2438 Tpr. SOLOMON, 3/3rd Co. of Lon. Yeo.
Tpr. SOLOMON, W., 2nd King Edw. H.
3429 Pte. SOLKOW, A. P., Mont Yeom.
461071 Pte. SPRING, 5th Reserve Cavalry.
2708 Pte. SPRINGER, P., 2/1st Hussars.
290630 Pte. SPIEGELMAN, 2/1st W. Somerset Yeo.
24057 Pte. STENCEL, C. N., 16th Lancers.
206379 L/Cpl. STERNHEIM, 5th Cavalry Res.
Pte. STERNHEIM, S., R. Bucks Hussars.
44820 Pte. STEPHENSON, 5th Reserve Cavalry.
Tpr. STERN, S. L., Lanarkshire Yeo.
5952 Tpr. SEGAR, M., 2/2nd Lovat Scouts.
Pte. STONE, D., Yorks. Hussars.
Tpr. STRUBLER, L., 4th Hussars.
Sgt. STRAUSSLER, H., C. of London Yeo.
Tpr. STRAUSLER, B., C. of London Yeo.
Tpr. SUPPER, H., Royal Bucks Hussars.
266059 Pte. SUGARMAN, I., 3rd Co. of Lon. Yeo.
286225 L/Cpl. SYMONS, J., 2/1 Q.O. Oxford Hrs.
1544 L/Sgt. SZAPIRA, S., Lincs. Yeo.
Pte. SOLOMONS, A., 1st Life Guards.
2933 Pte. TAYLOR, G., Herts. Yeo.
90529 Pte. TANCHAN, P., 2/1st Glam. Yeo.
326576 Pte. TEOFIL, R., 2/1 Q.O. Worcs. Hrs.
1246 Tpr. TRUEFITT, C. J.,* Essex Yeo.
1454 Sig. TOBIAS, N., King Edward's Horse.
3383 Tpr. TOOMIN, M., 3/1st City of Lon. Yeo.
46247 Pte. TOWER, A., 2/1st Surr. Yeo.
1098 Pte. VALLENTINE, P., 1st K. E. H.
2940 Pte. VAN PRAAGH, H., Royal H. G.
175951 Pte. VINEFSKY, H., 2/1st Yeomanry.
27422 Pte. VINCENT, S., 2/1st Yeomanry.
1183 Tpr. WHITE, E. V., 2nd K. E. H.
D/16145 Pte. WINTER, J., 2nd Dragoon G.
255549 L/Cpl. WACKS, P., Leicester Yeo.
15548 Pte. WALTERS, H., 16th Lancers.
1148 Tpr. WHITE, S., 13th Hussars.
27788 Tpr. WEISBOOM, P., 19th Hussars.
40628 Pte. WINDER, J., Yeomanry.
260395 Pte. WEINGOTT, A., Middlesex Yeo.
24781 Tpr. WEINTAUB, 10th Res. Cav. Regt.
5102 Pte. WOOD, S., Royal Horse Guards.
5100 Tpr. WOOD, H., Royal Horse Guards.
5101 Tpr. WOOD, I., Royal Horse Guards.
3039 Tpr. WOOD, M., Royal Horse Guards.
2928 Tpr. WOOD, H., R. Horse Guards.
46179 Tpr. WOOLF, B., R. Horse Guards.
Pte. WOOLF, J., 7th Hussars.
48805 Pte. WOOLFE, S., 3rd Res. Hussars.
298186 Pte. WINNE, S., 2/1st Pembroke Yeo.
3031013 Pte. WOLFSON, L., 2nd C. of L. Yeo.
38678 Pte. WEINTROP, S., 2/1st Norfolk Yeo.
90224 L/Cpl. WEISBOND, L., 2/1st Glam. Yeo.
6398 Tpr. WOBER, M., 2/2nd Scots Hussars.
328992 Pte. YELOWITZ, S., Wilts Yeomanry.
2162 Pte. ZELIGMAN, A., 2/1st Hussars.
Pte. ZARADI, J., 1st K. D. Guards.
L/Cpl. ZIMMERMAN, P., Scott. Horse.

* Killed in Action or died on Active Service.

ROYAL REGIMENT OF ARTILLERY.

OFFICERS.

Lieut. ABRAHAMS, F. (M.C.), R.F.A.
Lieut. ALBU, V. S., 26th Bde. Amn. Col. R.F.A.
Capt. ASH, A. S., D/86th Bde., R.F.A.
Lieut. ASERMAN, C. (M.C.), R.G.A.
Lieut. ALEXANDER, S., 46th D.A.C.
Capt. ANSLEY, S. S. (M.C.), R.H.A., 1/1st Berks.
Lieut. ABRAMS, L. M., R.H. and R.F.A.
Capt. ABRAHAM, J., R.H. and R.F.A.
2nd Lieut. BURMAN, J., R.G.A., 188th S. Batt.
Lieut. BEDDINGTON, H. L. V., R.F.A., B/229th B.
Lieut. BARNS, H. C., R.G.A.
Capt. BARNATO, W. J., 80th Bde., R.F.A.
Lieut. BEER, A. H.* (M.C.), 1st W. Lancs. F.A.
Lieut. BERNSTEIN, M. H., 38th Div. Amn. Col.
Capt. BENJAMIN, L. A., 239th Sge. Bty. R.G.A.
Lieut. BARRON, H. C., 23rd How. Bty.
2nd Lieut. BOODSON, H., R.F.A.
2nd Lieut. BEILES, H. L., R.G.A.
Capt. BERLINER, A. (M.C.), R.G.A.
2nd Lieut. BENEDICTUS, J. H., R.F.A.
2nd Lieut. BEHRENS, E. B. (M.C. and Bar), R.F.A.
Lieut. BENVENISTI, J. L., R.G.A.
Major BLUMENTHAL, A. Z., R.H. and R.F.A.
2nd Lieut. BROMET, W. G. H., R.F.A.
Lt.-Col. BEHREND, H. D., R.G.A.
Capt. and Adjt. BEHREND, A. F., R.G.A.
Capt. COHEN, D. D. M., 113th Bty. R.F.A.
Lieut. CHATHAM, H. A., R.G.A., "G" A.A. Bty.
Lieut. CONWAY, F. J., R.F.A.
Lieut. CASTELLO, E. J. (M.C.), R.F.A.
Lieut. COHEN, C. H.,* R.G.A.
2nd Lieut. CAPPER, S. M., R.G.A.
2nd Lieut. CHRISTIAN, E.
Capt. COHEN, G. E., R.F.A.
2nd Lieut. CIVVEN, F.
Lieut. DREYFUS, T. H., 49th T.M. Bty. R.F.A.

Royal Regiment of Artillery.—*Continued.*

Lieut. DAVIS, L. S., 24th D.A.C.
Lieut. DAVIS, S. F., R.F.A.
Lieut. DREYFUS, E., R.F.A.
2nd Lieut. DAVIES, S., R.G.A.
2nd Lieut. DREYFUS, L., R.G.A.
2nd Lieut. DAVIS, L., R.F.A.
2nd Lieut. DAVIS, R. G.
2nd Lieut. DUNKLEY, H. A., R.H. and R.F.A.
Lieut. EPPENHEIM, H. N., D/91st Bde. R.F.A.
2nd Lieut. ELLOWITZ, J., 236th Bde. R.F.A.
Capt. EZRA, D.,* 192nd Siege Bty.
Lieut. EHRMANN, J. P., R.G.A.
Lieut. ESPIR, L., R.F.A.
Lieut. EDELSTON, J. (M.C.), R.G.A.
Lieut. FREEMAN, D. H. D. (M.C.), R.F.A.
Lieut. FRANKLIN, A. P., R.H. and R.F.A.
2nd Lt. FREEMAN-COWEN, C.,* 175th Bde. R.F.A.
2nd Lieut. FRANKS, E. (M.C.).
Capt. FRISCHER, L., R.F.A.
Major FALCKE, J., R.H. and R.F.A.
2nd Lieut. FRIEDMAN, J. J.
2nd Lieut. FRIEDLANDER, W., R.G.A.
2nd Lieut. GOLDWATER, H. G., 256th Siege Bty.
Lt. GREENFIELD, E. R., 242nd Army Bde. R.F.A.
2nd Lieut. GOODSON, H., B/148th Bde.
2nd Lt. GORDON, A., No. 3 Sect. D.A.C., R.G.A.
Capt. GOLDSTEIN, B. A., 154th Sge. Bty. R.G.A.
Capt. GREENBERG, G. R., R.G.A.
2nd Lieut. GUTMANN, W.,* 71st Bde. R.F.A.
Lt. GOLDMAN, S. R., 58th D.A.C., R.H. & R.F.A.
Lt. GOLDSTEIN, L., 2/12 T.M.B., R.H. and R.F.A.
Lieut. GOLDMAN, A. H., 3rd D.A.C., R.F.A.
Lieut. GOODMAN, J. H., R.F.A.
Capt. GUNDLE, A. M., 123rd Bde. R.H. and R.F.A.
Lieut. GLUCKSTEIN, S. (M.C.), 40th D.A.C.
Capt. GOLDSTEIN, A., R.F.A.
Lieut. GOLDBERG, N. P., R.G.A.
Capt. HONOUR, W., R.H. and R.F.A.
2nd Lieut. HERSCH, L. H. J., R.F.A.
Lieut. HERNE, D. J., R.G.A.
Lieut. HART, W. L. D'ARCY, 26th Bty. R.F.A.
2nd Lt. HURSTBOURNE, W. H.,* 180th Bde. R.F.A.
Lieut. HEREFORD, S. B., 156th Sge. Bty. R.G.A.
Capt. HIME, P. J., A/56th Bde. R.F.A.
2nd Lieut. HENRIQUES, E. F. Q., R.F.A.
Capt. HALFORD, E. S., R.G.A.
2nd Lieut. HOCKMAN, J. S., R.G.A.
Lieut.-Col. HARRIS, O. M. (D.S.O.), R.H.A.
Lieut. HART, I. B., R.G.A.
2nd Lieut. ISAACS, J., 125th H.B., R.G.A.
Lieut. ISAAC, A. A., R.F.A.
Lieut. JACOBS, C. J., 130/30th Bde. R.F.A.
2nd Lieut. JACOBS, S., 288th Siege Bty. R.G.A.
2nd Lieut. JOEL, W., R.G.A.
Lieut. JELLINEK, L. (M.C.), R.F.A.
Lieut. JACKSON, E. J., R.F.A.
Lieut. JACKSON, L. H. (M.C.), R.F.A.
Lieut. JACOBS, F., R.F.A.
Major JACOBS, J. (O.B.E.). R.F.A.
Lieut. JACOBS, M., R.F.A.
Capt. KINO, A. J. (M.C.), R.F.A.
Major KAYE, G. S., R.F.A.
2nd Lieut. KAMM, G. E., R.F.A.
Major KROHN, V. R., (M.C.), R.F.A.
Major LEWIS-BARNED, H. B., R.G.A.
Lieut. LAZARUS, J., 70th Bde. R.F.A.
Lieut. LEVY, K. A., 285th Bde. R.F.A.
Capt. LIPSCHITZ, J., D/108th Bde. R.F.A.
Lieut. LIPSCHITZ, J. M., R.F.A.
Lieut. LANDSBERG, J., R.G.A.
Lieut. LINDO, G. M., 5th London F.A. Bde.
Lieut. LAZARUS, G. M., 307th Bty. R.G.A.
Lieut. LEWIS, M. S., 10th Bde. R.G.A.
2nd Lieut. LIBSTEIN, H. S., 178th T.M.B.
2nd Lieut. LEVY, H., R.G.A.
Capt. LUBBOCK, I., R.G.A.
2nd Lieut. LUCAS, R. H., R.F.A.
2nd Lieut. LEVINSON, B. A., R.G.A.
2nd Lt. MICHAELIS, R. L., 282nd Sge. Bty. R.G.A.
Major MAAS, N. N., 40th Bde. R.G.A.
2nd Lieut. MONTEFIORE, C. E. M. SEBAG, 106th Bty. R.G.A.
2nd Lieut. MOSS, W. J., A/179th Bde. R.F.A.
Capt. MOCATTA, F. E., 17th Bde. R.F.A.
Lieut. MARKS, H., D/47th Bde. R.F.A.
Lieut. MOSS, W. J., R.F.A.
Lieut. MILLER, C. A. M., R.H.A.
Lieut. MORLAND, S., D/190th Bde. R.F.A.
2nd Lt. MOSES, F. S.,* 22nd Heavy Bty. R.G.A.
Major MONTEFIORE, T. H. SEBAG (D.S.O., M.C.), R.F.A.
Major MONTAGUE, J. E. F., R.F.A.
2nd Lieut. MELHADO, D. I., R.F.A.
Lieut. MARCUS, E. V. H., 290th Bde. R.F.A.
2nd Lieut. MOSES, V. S.,* 11th M.T.M.B.
2nd Lt. MONTEFIORE, J SEBAG, 49th Bde. R.F.A.
Lieut. MICHAELIS, A. L., R.F.A.
Lieut. MARKS, L., R.F.A.
2nd Lieut. MARTINSON, K. L.,* R.F.A.
Lieut. MARSDEN, D. H., R.F.A.
2nd Lieut. MOSES, R. S., R.G.A.
Lieut. MARKS, L. D. (M.C.), R.F.A.
Lieut. MARIANS, R. M., R.F.A.
2nd Lieut. MENDES, H. J. C., R.G.A.
Lieut. NATHAN, C. J., A/162nd Bde. R.F.A.
Lieut. NATHAN, D.,* A/155th Bde. R.F.A.
Capt. NATHAN, R. P.* (M.C.), X/36th T.M.B., R.F.A.
Capt. NATHAN, E. G. P., (M.C.), R.F.A.
Lieut. PAGET, A. L., 528th Sge. Bty. R.G.A.
2nd Lieut. PYKE, E. J., 2nd Bde., R.F.A.
Lieut. PYKE, M. A. (M.C.). R.F.A.
Lieut. PHILLIPS, L. H. (M.C.), 190th Bde. R.F.A.

Royal Regiment of Artillery.—*Continued.*

2nd Lieut. PHILLIPS, J. P., R.F.A.
Major POLLAK, E. R. H. (M.C. and Bar), R.F.A.
Capt. PLATNAUER, M., R.G.A. and Staff.
2nd Lieut. ROTHSCHILD, L. J., 22nd Bty. R.G.A.
2nd Lieut. ROSSDALE, S. J., R.F.A.
2nd Lieut. ROBINSTEIN, M., R.F.A.
2nd Lieut. ROSE, T. E. D., R.F.A.
Capt. REITLINGER, H. S., R.F.A.
2nd Lieut. SPERO, A., 328th Sge. Bty. R.G.A.
Major SAMUEL, L. J.,* A/83rd Bde. R.F.A.
Capt. and Adjt. SANDEMAN, G., B/90th Bde. R.F.A.
Lieut. SAMUEL, G. H. L. M. (M.C.), A/158th Bde. R.F.A. and Staff.
Lieut. SAMUEL, C. M., 49th Bde. R.F.A.
Brig.-General SELIGMAN, H. S. (C.M.G., D.S.O.), R.F.A.
2nd Lieut. SAMUEL, S. A., 63rd Bde. R.F.A.
Capt. SOLOMON, R. B. (M.C.), A/153rd Bde. R.F.A. and Staff.
Lieut. SINGTON, A. J., R.F.A.
Lieut. SOMAN, S. G., 241st Bde. R.F.A.
2nd Lieut. SCHWERSEE, S. G., 1/48th D.A.C.
Lieut. SYDNEY, A. L., H.Q. 94th Bde. R.G.A.
Major SASSOON, F., 13/25th Bde. R.F.A.
2nd Lieut. SCOTT-FORBES, J.,* 78th Siege Bty., R.G.A.
2nd Lieut. SMITH, C. O.,* 361/33rd Bde., R.F.A.
Lieut. SAMUEL-YATES, J., R.G.A.
Lieut. SAALFELD, A. E., R.G.A.
Lieut. SALAMAN, E.,* R.F.A.
Lieut. SALMON, S. A. (M.C.), R.F.A.
Lieut. SAMUEL, E. L., R.F.A.
Major SAMUELS, G. E., R.F.A.
Lieut. SIMON, H., R.F.A.
Major SIMON, P. B., R.F.A.
2nd Lieut. SALAMAN, A. E., R.F.A.
Lieut. STRAUS, R.F.A.
Capt. STAHL, A. (M.C.), R.F.A.
2nd Lieut. STROSS, D., R.F.A.
Lieut. SELIGMAN, E. W., R.F.A.
2nd Lieut. SAMUEL, N. S., R.G.A.
Lieut. STEINFIELD, E. L., R.F.A.
2nd Lieut. SHERWOOD, H., R.G.A.
Capt. and Adjt. TUTEUR, M. P., R.F.A.
Capt. TRIEFUS, P. (M.C.), R.F.A.
Lieut. TEBBITT, M. L. (M.C.), B/77th A.F.A.B.
Lieut. TALLERMAN, K. H. (M.C.), R.F.A.
Capt. ULLMAN, R. B. (M.C.).
Lt. VAN DEN BERGH, J. H.,* 6th Lon. Bde. R.F.A.
2nd Lieut. VYNER, F., R.F.A.
2nd Lieut. VAN-GEUNS, J. L., R.G.A.
Lieut. WISE, L., C/113th Bde. R.F.A.
2nd Lt. WARBURG, F. J., 186th Sge. Bty. R.G.A.
Capt. WARBURG, O. E. (O.B.E.), R.G.A. and Staff.
2nd Lieut. WOOLF, E., 256th Sge. Bty.
2nd Lieut. WHITE, R. ,L., 74th L.T.M.B. R.G.A.
2nd Lieut. WEIL. R. G. (M.C.), R.G.A.
2nd Lieut. WERTHEIMER, F., R.F.A.
Capt. and Adj. WOLFF, J. D., R.G.A.

N.C.O.'s AND MEN.

67469 Gnr. ALBERT, G., 9th Battery.
387 Dvr. ABRAHAMS, A., 3nd Battery.
41789 Gnr. ASHWORTH, 87th Bde. Amn. Col.
048053 Bdr. ABRAM, B.
60237 Dvr. ALEXANDER, R., Div. Amn. Col.
44844 Dvr. ABRAHAMS, J., 189th Bde.
Sgt. ABRAHAMS, K. O. (M.M.), R.F.A.
45193 Bdr. ABELSON, B., 190th Bde.
1312 Pte. ABRAHAMS, A., 60th Div. T.M.
1676 Dvr. ABRAHAMS, A., 70th Bde.
36967 Bdr. ABRAHAMS, L., A/Bde.
720008 Gnr. ALEXANDER, V., 66th D.A.C.
210421 Dvr. ABRAHAMS, M., B/93 A.F.A.
53735 Dvr. ASHER, D., "K" Bt. R.H.A.
64754 Gnr. ABRAHAMS, A., 128th Sge. Bty.
841183 Gnr. ABRAHAMS, A., 49/40th Bde.
128065 Gnr. ALVEREZ, H., 159th H. Bty.
112110 Gnr. ASHTON, N., 31st D.A.C.
239172 Gnr. AARON, J., 156th Bde.
236403 Gnr. APPLEBAUM, H. L., C/171st Bde.
187016 Gnr. ASH, V., C/119th Army F.A.
43139 Gnr. ALLEN, G.,
195737 Gnr. ALTER, H., R.F.A.
386 Dvr. ABRAHAMS, M., 32nd R.F.A.
Dvr. ALLEN, N. A., 18th R.F.A.
253974 Sig. ALVAREZ, J., Sig. Train. Centre.
197969 Dvr. ANDORSKY, H., 7th D.A.C.
3869 Gnr. ABRAHAMS, R.H.A.
226408 Pte. APPLEBAUM, R.F.A.
236403 Pte. APPLEBAUM, H. L., R.F.A.
210527 Dvr. AARON, S.,
120289 Dvr. ALLPORT, I., R.H.A.
36967 Cpl. ABRAHAMS, R.F.A.
5001 Pte. ALBERT, C., 72nd Bty. R.F.A.
Pte. ABRAHAMS, 68th Bty. R.F.A.
140345 Gnr. ANGEL, L., R.G.A.
115561 Gnr. ALLEN, S.,* R.G.A.
153869 Gnr. ABRAHAMS, R.H.A.
208985 Gnr. ABRAHAMS, D. R., R.G.A.
212195 Gnr. ANDERSON, A., R.F.A.
199758 Dvr. ABRAHAMS, V., R.F.A.
393291 Dvr. ABRAHAMS, R., 41st R.F.A.
181149 Dvr. ABRAHAMS, A.
160436 Gnr. ASKINS, L., R.F.A.
195274 Gnr. ARROW, J.
195696 Gnr. ALEXANDER, H. J., R.F.A.
195274 Pte. ARROWN, J., R.F.A.
21042 Dvr. ABRAHAMS, E.
130357 C.Q.M.S. ABRAHAMS, S., R.F.A.
881554 Pte. ABRAHAMS, P., R.F.A.
134599 Cpl. ADLER, I., R.G.A.
60401 Gnr. ADDLESTONE, S., R.G.A.
123329 Dvr. ASTBURY, R.

Royal Regiment of Artillery.—*Continued.*

36506	Dvr. ACKERMAN, L.	
144355	Gnr. AMMATT, J. G.	
181164	Dvr. ABRAHAMOVITCH, A.	
153252	Gnr. ANNIS, M.	
261410	Pte. AHAIS, J., R.F.A.	
194510	Gnr. ABRAHAMS, S., R.G.A.	
	Pte. ANSELL, C. H. (M.M.), R.F.A.	
181938	Gnr. ABRAHAMS, L., R.F.A.	
115300	Pte. ABRAHAMS, M., R.G.A.	
257785	Pte. ABRAHAMS, J., R.H.A.	
26140	Pte. ATTIS, J.	
222260	Dvr. BARNETT, B., R.F.A.	
111849	Gnr. BERTRAM, I., R.F.A.	
56069	Gnr. BERZANCE, L.,* 82nd Bde. R.F.A.	
	Pte. BARRETT, J., 33rd R.F.A.	
	Pte. BENSON, H., 119th R.F.A.	
	Gnr. BLANCKENSEE, C., 24th By. R.F.A.	
125143	Dvr. BLOOM, J.,	
39689	Gnr. BURMAN, N., 241st Bde. R.F.A.	
308467	Gnr. BARNETT, H., 229th Bty. R.G.A.	
296161	Dvr. BLOOM, A., 90th H. Bty.	
497	Dvr. BREWER, A., 58th D.A.C.	
79830	Gnr. BERLYN, J., 199th Heavy Battery.	
111213	Dvr. BARNETT, H., 177th Heavy Battery.	
110832	Gnr. BENDETH, R.G.A.	
78757	Gnr. BENJAMIN, M., 159th Siege Battery.	
88385	Cpl. BEWLEY, J., R.G.A.	
745698	Pte. BERKHAM, M., R.F.A.	
631973	Gnr. BONN, D., R.F.A.	
198657	Dvr. BRODIE, M., R.F.A.	
202950	Sig. BAKER, N. L., R.F.A.	
214681	Gnr. BLOOMBERG, S., R.H.A.	
	Gnr. BARNARD, H. B., R.G.A.	
112020	Bdr. BROSGARTH, N., A/26th Bde.	
157071	Gnr. BLOOMBERG, M., 132nd H. Bty.	
161135	Gnr. BARLOW, 5th Bty. R.F.A.	
140109	Sig. BLOOMBERG, J. H., R.G.A.	
11708	Bdr. BENJAMIN, M., R.F.A.	
3034	Gnr. BROWN, L., 104th How. Bty.	
47121	Cpl. BERG, S., 41st Div. D.A.C.	
153317	Bdr. BROWN, I., 234th Bde.	
156282	Dvr. BLASKEY, S., 50/34th Bde.	
1562	Dvr. BENJAMIN, P., 64th Bde.	
3587	Dvr. BENJAMIN, B., D/306th Bde.	
211273	Dvr. BUCKNER, J., C/307th Bde.	
127254	Dvr. BLOOMBERG, S., 11th D.A.C.	
10747	Dvr. BERLINSKY, S., 9th D.A.C.	
116196	Dvr. BLOOM, M., 156th Bde.	
123583	Gnr. BISHOP, M., B/104th Bde.	
67404	Gnr. BLACKMAN, J., 42nd H.A. Group.	
60575	Gnr. BAKER, M., 1st H.A. Group, R.G.A.	
439	Bdr. BEDELSTEIN, A., 43rd H.A. Group, R.G.A.	
6959	Gnr. BLOOM, P. R., 90th How. Bty.	
606315	Gnr. BARNETT, S., 293rd Bde.	
1544	Gnr. BENNETT, D., 251st Bde.	
841033	R.Q.M.S. BOODSON, H., H.Q. Div. Art.	
79032	Gnr. BARNARD, P. L., 12th Amn. Sub. Pk. R.G.A.	
30774	Pte. BARNETT, B., 2nd T.M.B.	
	Pte. BLOCH, M., 120th T.M.B.	
686514	Cpl. BOGGINS, M. E., 92nd Bde.	
77425	Gnr. BERNSTONE, A. E., 135th Sge. Bty.	
686360	Dvr. BLOOMBERG, P., 466/65 A.F.A. Bde.	
128648	Bdr. BEAVER, P., 232nd Sge. By. R.G.A.	
338287	Gnr. BENTON, W., 157th Sge. By. R.G.A.	
115231	Gnr. BERNSTEIN, S., 194th Siege Bty.	
79830	Gnr. BERLYNE, J., 2nd Siege Bty.	
182511	Dvr. BISS, J., 33/55th Bde.	
1440	Bdr. BLOOM, H.,* 14th Bde. R.H.A.	
30551	Dvr. BARRETT, S., 45th Bde.	
89808	Dvr. BERSTEIN, P., 52nd Bde.	
46190	Gnr. BELMONT, D.,* D/87th Bde.	
50733	Gnr. BLACKMAN, T., 100th Bde.	
17055	Dvr. BRACKMAN, J., 22nd Div. Amn. Col.	
52662	Dvr. BEARMAN, N., D. Bty. 107th Bde.	
5845	Dvr. BROOKSTEIN, F., 24th Div. Amn. Cl.	
92060	Gnr. BROWNLOW, B/89th Bty.	
	Dvr. BUTT, A., 125th Bty.	
47313	Dvr. BERMAN, J., 21st Div. Amn. Col.	
35264	Dvr. BEBBER, L., 21st Div. Amn. Col.	
43832	Bdr. BASKIN, J., 5th Bde. 64th Bty.	
16811	Gnr. BARNETT, A., B/109th Bde.	
12149	Pte. BLOOMER, S., 146th T.M.B.	
92140	Dvr. BERNSTEIN, A., Guards Div.	
11708	Gnr. BENJAMIN, M. J., 156th Bde.	
22771	Gnr. BENDER, J., 35th Div. Amn. Col.	
187056	Gnr. BENNETT, J., C/157th Bde.	
35361	Gnr. BAKER, C., 154th Bde.	
2603	Gnr. BROWN, J., 1/3rd London.	
24956	Dvr. BURMAN, L., A/46th Bde. Amn. Col.	
L/43010	Dvr. BENSON, J., 180th Bde.	
	Bombr. BRANDON, M. (M.M.), R.G.A.	
L/36214	Dvr. BENDER, F., C/180th Bde.	
L/37691	Dvr. BERLINSON, L., 180th Bde.	
38883	Dvr. BERGER, A. A., D/182nd Bde.	
46420	Gnr. BRANDON, S., 56th Sge. Bty. R.G.A.	
27291	Cpl. BIERMAN, A., 1/L T.M.B.	
149688	Gnr. BROADY, L., 112th H.B., R.G.A.	
169443	Gnr. BERLINER, F., 139th Sub. Sect.	
337379	Gnr. BERG, H., 146th H. Bty. R.G.A.	
311432	Gnr. BROWN, H., 110th H. Bty. R.G.A.	
197885	Gnr. BUIKANT, J., 1st D.A.C.	
755205	Gnr. BENNETT, L., 50th Div. Amn. Col.	
195893	Dvr. BURSTOFF, J., A/106th Bde.	
192844	Gnr. BROWN, V. H., A/88th F.A. Bde.	
110957	Pte. BLOOM, J., No. 10 A.A. Coy.	
1770190	Dvr. BERG, S., R.H.A. "Z" Bty.	
1093	Bdr. BROWN, R., 72nd Siege Bty.	
193482	Gnr. BENJAMIN, J., 135th Siege Bty.	
81109	Gnr. BERNFIELD, J., 84th Bde.	
30009	Dvr. BEANSOCK, B., 34th Bde. R.F.A.	
111829	Gnr. BLACK, L., 72nd A.F.A.	
203070	Gnr. BROWN, O., D/83rd Bde.	
111849	Gnr. BERMAN, F., 54/39th Bde.

Royal Regiment of Artillery.—*Continued.*

103505 Gnr. BLACK, J., 118th Siege Bty.
149210 Gnr. BLIEVERS, B/58th Siege Bty.
70417 Sgt. BROWN, M., 169th Siege Bty.
119832 Gnr. BENDETH, B., 333rd Siege Bty.
140195 Gnr. BAKER, H., 19th A.A. Bty.
2830 Dvr. BARRETT, W., 18th Div. Amn. Col.
6955 Gnr. BALL, J., 37th How. Bty.
193802 Gnr. BALCHIN, D. W.,* R.F.A.
18503 Gnr. BLOOM, J.,* 264th Bde. R.F.A.
945571 Gnr. BERNSTEIN, C.,
97247 Gnr. BARNETT, N. M., R.G.A.
214681 Gnr. BLOOMBERG, R.H.A.
164720 Gnr. BITTON, N., R.G.A.
114181 Gnr. BERNHARDT, R.G.A.
328171 Gnr. BECK, L. H., Siege Park.
396346 Gnr. BLACK, S., R.G.A.
945463 Gnr. BREWER, A.
111849 Gnr. BURMAN, I.,
966660 Dvr. BESSER, L., 387th Bde. R.F.A.
68205 Dvr. BROMBERG, A., 123rd Bde.
181773 Gnr. BARDOLFSKY, A., R.F.A.
70417 Cpl. BROOM, M., 12th R.F.A.
73162 Dvr. BYATT, W. A., R.H.A.
208573 Gnr. BARBANEL, D., D/246th Bde.
236849 Gnr. BLONSTEN, "B" Bty. 320th Bde.
15945 Pte. BELCHER, C.,* 1st Bty. R.G.A.
183044 Gnr. BERNSTEIN, M.,* C/52nd Bde.
2558 Dvr. BLOOMBERG, 3/3rd W. Lancs. Bde.
223862 Dvr. BERG, B., R.H.A.
223852 Gnr. BERG, J., R.H.A.
122240 Dvr. BOTIBOL, J.
5490 Dvr. BLOOM, E. H.
147229 Dvr. BERGMAN, M.
166265 Pte. BANIN, R., R.F.A.
108332 Dvr. BEBERVITCH, J., R.H.A.
Pte. BENSON, B., 82nd Bde. R.F.A.
16664 Gnr. BERNSTEIN, J., 169th Bde.
148306 Gnr. BARUCH, P., R.F.A.
127252 Dvr. BERKOVITCH, L., R.F.A.
81419 Dvr. BERGER, H., R.F.A.
198045 Dvr. BARNETT, M., R.F.A.
130128 Gnr. BEAR, S.
211741 Gnr. BENJAMIN, I., 53rd Bty
221847 Gnr. BAROVITCH, S., R.F.A., 6th Res. Bde.
Cadet BENEDICTUS, B., R.F.A.
22924 Gnr. BARNETT, S. L.
935778 Pte. BROWN, J., R.F.A.
124174 Bdr. BUDNER, S., 342nd Sge. By. R.G.A.
208718 Gnr. BOSTON, H., R.G.A.
167267 Gnr. BERNEY, M.
175976 Gnr. BLACK, P.
180046 Dvr. BERNSTEIN, J.
175978 Dvr. BERMAN, R., R.F.A.
631973 Dvr. BROWN, D., R.F.A.
165226 Dvr. BRILL, M., R.F.A.
197734 A/Bdr. BLACKSTONE, E., R.F.A.

199873 Dvr. BAARS, H.
76793 Pte. BERKOVITCH,
311432 Gnr. BROWN, H.
27346 Pte. BOELAND, L., 303rd Bty.
22771 Gnr. BENDER, J., R.F.A.
43309 Gnr. BECKMANN, M.
14236 Dvr. BERGMAN, S.
181823 Dvr. BROOKS, J.
50553 Pte. BERNSTEIN, L.
20295 Pte. BOOKER, M. L., R.F.A.
127252 Pte. BERKOVITCH, L., R.F.A.
234954 Pte. BARNETT, J., R.F.A.
8608 Cpl. BETHOLD, L., R.G.A.
15328 Dvr. BENJAMIN, S., 21st Bty.
191885 Gnr. BEHRMAN, G.
Dvr. BLACKERM, P., 252nd Bty.
111922 S/Major BERNARD, B.
209041 Gnr. BOADENSKY, S., R.G.A.
801073 Gnr. BLOOM, H.
Gnr. BOORMAN, P., R.G.A.
365896 Gnr. BERLINSKY, J.
200118 Gnr. BENJAMIN, H.
125124 Gnr. BETHM, B.
229085 Dvr. BLOOM, S., R.G.A.
164036 Gnr. BARKMAN, H., R.G.A.
221231 Gnr. BERNSTEIN, S.
182357 Gnr. BLOOM, P.
Bombr. BENJAMIN, F. (M.M.) R.H.A.
Gnr. BUTLER, P., R.F.A.
Gnr. BERNSTOCK, M., R.F.A.
Gnr. BARRON, B., R.F.A.
Gnr. BIRK, H., R.F.A.
36106 Dvr. COHEN, H., 34th Bde. Amn. Col.
3250 Gnr. COHEN, A., 109th Bty.
96423 Dvr. COHEN, A., 109th Bty.
26848 Gnr. COHEN, P., 14th Bde. R.H.A.
82150 Cpl. COLLINSON, D., 70th Bde.
80750 Dvr. COOPER, D. H., 79th Bde.
2106 Gnr. CAMPBELL, H., 1/3rd W.R. Bde.
60064 Dvr. COHEN, M., 116th Bde.
2125 Spr. COOTE, J. H., 18th Lond. Bty. 7 Bde.
Staff-Sgt. COHEN, M., 88th Bty.
L37716 Gnr. COHEN, D., 180th Bde.
L36051 Gnr. COOPER, A., 180th Bde.
L37722 Dvr. COHEN, S., D/180th Bde.
33036 Dvr. COHEN, H., 170th Bde.
32285 Sgt. COHEN, J., 176th Bde. Amn. Col.
21401 Gnr. CASHER, C., 172nd Bde.
4993 Dvr. COHEN, J., 189th Bde.
3480 Gnr. COHEN, A. E., A/302nd Bde.
3481 Dvr. CLAYMAN, H. A., A/302nd Bde.
856 Dvr. COHEN, A., D/302nd Bde.
1932 Dvr. CLEIN, B., D/303rd Bde.
859 Dvr. CAPLIN, J., 60th D.A.C.
82803 Dvr. COHEN, W., C/84th Bde.
706255 Gnr. COWAN, S., 33rd D.A.C.
18323 Dvr. COHEN, S., 30th D.A.C.

Royal Regiment of Artillery.—*Continued.*

901743 Dvr. COHEN, L.,* 87th Bde.
514 Gnr. COHEN, P. (M.M.), 121st Sge. Bty.
30180 Gnr. COHEN, S., 185th Siege Bty.
2044 Gnr. COHEN, S., 161st Sge. Bty. R.G.A.
109053 Gnr. COHEN, A., 4th H.A. Group R.G.A.
931 Gnr. COHEN, N., 1/1st Essex Bty. R.G.A.
1477 Gnr. COHEN, F.M., 1/1 Essex By. R.G.A.
915886 Gnr. COHEN, H.,* 291st Bde.
116678 Gnr. COHEN, J., 383/179 Bde.
701703 Gnr. CUSHELSON, J.,* 330th Bde.
945319 Dvr. CASSELL, M., 58th D.A.C.
36248 Gnr. CONN, W., 180th D.A.C.
11809 Gnr. COHEN, H., 7th D.A.C.
208022 Dvr. COSTAR, S., 32nd D.A.C.
283082 Pte. COHEN, A., 168th T.M.B.
3250 Gnr. COHEN, A., 281st Bde.
82971 Gnr. CALISHER, W., 19th S.B. R.G.A.
131338 Sgt. COHEN, L., 4th Sge. Amn. Col.
7420 Dvr. COHEN, N., 153rd H.B. R.G.A.
101789 Gnr. COHEN, J.,* 38th Hvy. Bty. R.G.A.
109750 Gnr. COOPER, B., 38th Heavy Bty.
23937 Gnr. COUPLAND, P., M/87th A.A. Sect.
58679 Bdr. COHEN, J., 117th Siege Bty.
105310 Gnr. COHEN, S., 141st H.B.
120188 Gnr. CALMANSON, J., 175th Siege Bty.
76810 Gnr. CLEEBAUER, L., 4th Siege Bty.
  Bdr. CHEVITT, B/155th Bde.
117669 Dvr. COHEN, D., 14th D.A.C.
626114 Gnr. CHARATAN, B,. 309th Siege Bty.
166336 Gnr. COHEN, S., 57th Siege Bty.
104991 Gnr. CROSS, J., 152nd Siege Bty. R.G.A.
77365 Sgt. COWAN, C., 139th Sub. Sect.
775272 Dvr. COHEN, J. B., 245th (W.R.) Bde.
185520 Dvr. COHEN, N., 50th Div. Amn. Col.
236806 Gnr. COSTA, A., 2nd Bde.
111145 Dvr. COSS, A., C/160th Bde.
26848 Gnr. COHEN, E., Y/24th T.M.B.
157643 Gnr. COHEN, R., D/306 Bde.
22654 Gnr. COHEN, D., C/52 Army Bde.
327003 Fitter COHEN J., 46th Siege Bty.
1101 Gnr. CLAIN, H., 74th Siege Bty.
1151 Bdr. CANARD, H., 74th Siege Bty.
348234 Gnr. COHEN, P., 12th Bde. R.G.A.
344241 Gnr. CROSS, H. M., 359th Siege Bty.
37706 Dvr. CLASS, S., B.A.C.
146901 Dvr. COHEN, H. J.
85903 Gnr. COHEN, J., R.G.A.
139949 Dvr. COWAN, F., R.H.A.
110109 Dvr. CHESTER, M., R.F.A.
182403 Dvr. COHEN, J., 36th Bty.
233586 Gnr. COHEN, J., R.F.A.
44467 Dvr. COHEN, H., 177th Bn.
167145 Gnr. CAPLAN, D.,
64737 Pte. COHEN, P., 131st Bn. R.F.A.
  Gnr. COLE, J., 140th Bn. R.F.A.
21925 Gnr. CORPER, W. H.,* R.H.A.
175531 Dvr. COLEMAN, E., 13th Res. Bn.

111869 Gnr. COHEN, J., 7th D.A.C.
1435 Gnr. COHEN, B., 291st Bde.
346 Dvr. CASSELL, M., 58th D.A.C.
211079 Gnr. COHEN, H., R.G.A.
194043 Gnr. COPELAND, J. H., R.H.A.
196424 Gnr. CLASS, R., R.F.A.
214994 Dvr. COHEN, R.F.A.
11769 Dvr. COHEN, D., R.F.A.
961087 Gnr. CLAYMAN, H. A., R.F.A.
33006 Pte. CONN, H., R.F.A. C/75.
318778 Pte. COHEN, M.
268969 Gnr. COOK, L. C., R.G.A.
197810 Gnr. CRONENBERG, S.,
173907 Gnr. CLEINER, 29th Bty. R.F.A.
114726 Dvr. COHEN, 29th Bty. R.F.A.
146901 Gnr. COHEN, 30th Bty. R.F.A.
  Pte. COHEN, M., 135th Bty. R.F.A.
1285 Pte. COBDEN, J., R.F.A.
64737 Dvr. COHEN, C., R.F.A., 101st Bty.
80750 Gnr. COOPER, W., R.F.A.
195834 Pte. CRISS, J.,
61088 Pte. COHEN, A. S., R.G.A.
51818 Pte. COHEN, J., R.G.A.
76810 Gnr. CLEEBAUM, L., R.G.A.
189623 Dvr. COHEN, A., R.F.A.
198579 Dvr. CARO, M., 65th Army Bde.
109054 Dvr. COHEN, A., R.F.A.
177332 Gnr. CROOK, F., R.F.A.
199870 Gnr. CAPLAN, H., R.G.A.
116328 Dvr. COHEN, J.,
196182 Gnr. COHEN, S.,
907612 Dvr. CAPLIN, J., R.F.A.
219970 Pte. COHEN, J., R.G.A.
115304 Gnr. COVERMAN, P., R.G.A.
289943 Gnr. COHEN, H., 343rd Bde.
208117 Gnr. COHEN, L., 343rd Bde.
167038 Sgn. COHEN, C., 250th Bde.
284789 Pte. COHEN, H., 169th R.F.A.
197122 Pte. COHEN, J., 46th Sge. Bty. R.G.A.
4451 Pte. COHEN, J., 57th T.M.Bty.
198075 Pte. COHEN, H.
110102 Pte. COSGROVE, D.
41507 Dvr. COLLINSON, C.
2006 Dvr. COHEN, I.
86873 Gnr. COHEN, L., R.G.A.
167810 Dvr. CRAMMER, I., R.F.A.
41040 Dvr. CLARE, S., R.F.A.
36445 Dvr. CLACK, A., R.F.A.
30882 Gnr. CLARK, J., R.F.A.
40925 Dvr. COHEN, C., R.F.A.
631944 Dvr. COHEN, H., R.F.A.
198579 Dvr. CONN, M., R.F.A.
3218 Gnr. CAVE, J.
199889 Gnr. COHEN, H.
220975 Gnr. COHEN, S.
220943 Dvr. COHEN, H.
91837 Dvr. COWELL, J., R.H.A.
3459 Artr. COHEN, J., R.G.A.

Royal Regiment of Artillery.—*Continued.*

Gnr. Coss, B. (M.M.), R.F.A.
233297 Gnr. Caplin, H., R.F.A.
40725 Dvr. Cohen, S., R.F.A.
3042 Gnr. Cornofsky, L., R.F.A.
111205 Dvr. Cowen, P., R.F.A.
142715 Gnr. Crammer, Art. Training School.
17781 Gnr. Cohen, B.
170653 Gnr. Canter, A., R.G.A.
142175 Gnr. Crammer, R.F.A.
153419 Gnr. Cohl, H. A., R.G.A.
62563 Pte. Caron, M., R.F.A.
25168 Pte. Capper, I., R.F.A.
1510 Gnr. Cohen, L., R.F.A.
231776 Gnr. Cohen, W., R.F.A.
115558 Gnr. Caplin, A., R.G.A.
134949 Gnr. Cohen, M., R.G.A.
198142 Pte. Cohen, J., R.F.A.
199800 Pte. Cohen, I., R.F.A.
20137 Gnr. Cobb, E., 4th Sge. Bde. R.G.A.
109925 Gnr. Cohen, S., 53rd Bty.
235205 Sig. Cooper, H. N., 54th Bde.
191115 Bdr. Caplan, S., R.G.A.
66257 Pte. Cohen, A., R.F.A.
19155 Pte. Cohen, M., R.F.A.
9059 Pte. Cohen, S., R.G.A.
Cadet Chetham, R.H.A.
20920 Gnr. Cohen, D., 9th Bty.
69420 Sadler Sgt. Currey, G., 4th R.F.A.
165218 Gnr. Combles, E., 4th R.F.A.
233663 Pte. Conise, M., R.F.A.
253580 Gnr. Cohen, P., R.F.A.
196182 Gnr. Cohen, S., R.G.A.
890909 Gnr. Capaloff, B., R.F.A.
82971 Gnr. Calischer, B.
237055 Dvr. Carpel, L.
Dvr. Cashman, G. A. (M.M.), R.F.A.
125483 Gnr. Cohen, D.
787707 Pte. Continho, I., R.G.A.
131538 Gnr. Covely, J., R.G.A.
194842 Dvr. Canter, R.F.A.
117871 Bdr. Charles, A.
179950 Dvr. Colquhon, F.
214995 Gnr. Carson, S., R.G.A.
195978 Gnr. Canter, S., R.F.A.
249924 Gnr. Cliffe, K., R.F.A.
101301 Gnr. Conn, D., R.G.A.
125199 Gnr. Cohen, J.
90278 Dvr. Collins, H., R.H.A.
17781 Gnr. Cohen, B.
211641 Pte. Cohen, A.
115607 Gnr. Corbett, H. E., R.G.A.
358520 Gnr. Cohen, J., R.G.A.
127962 Gnr. Carton, H., R.G.A.
176938 Gnr. Claff, L., R.H.A.
75282 Cpl. de Wilde, G., 43rd Bde. Amn. Col.
87225 Gnr. Driver, J., 129th Bty.
40912 Bdr. Davis, J., C/125th Bty.

1845 Dvr. Da Costa, B., 6th London, B.A.C.
94049 Gnr. De Bock, H., 73rd Bty. 5th Bde.
44823 Gnr. Daniels, D., C/75th Bde.
L/40079 Dvr. Da Costa, H., C/180th Bde.
42362 Bdr. Davis, L., 371st Battery.
117408 Dvr. Davies, S. H, 124th Bty. 28th Bde. R.F.A.
L/1513 Gnr. Druker, A., 113th Bty. 1st Div.
861 Gnr. Daniels, S., Z/60th H.T.M.B.
927 Gnr. Diamond, L., 60th D.A.C.
128491 Gnr. Davis, J. M., D/95th Bde.
124556 Dvr. Davis, A., A/149th Bde.
931119 Dvr. Davis, F., 291st Bde.
64361 Cpl. Diamond, L., 88th Bde.
935922 Gnr. Driver, B., 280th Bde.
308717 Gnr. Dunn, S., 1/1st Welsh H.B.
171704 Pte. De Kromme, J. J., B/AA Bty.
148636 Gnr. Diamondstein, H., 36th Sge. Bty.
319062 Gnr. Drapkin, W., 219th R.G.A.
367927 Gnr. De Hass, F., 176th R.G.A.
128656 Gnr. Davidson, A., 162nd Siege Bty.
158274 Gnr. Davidson, R., 162nd Siege Bty.
198160 Gnr. De Haan, N., B/276th Bde.
30474 Gnr. Dagul, G., 42nd Bde.
97036 Bdr. Dunitz, L., 245th " S " Bty. R.G.A.
573924 Gnr. Dembinski, 140th Bde.
940959 Gnr. Da Costa, A., 24th B.A.C., R.F.A.
145477 Gnr. Da Costa, W., 307th Bde. R.F.A.
1430 Gnr. Davis, C., 125th Siege Bty.
625862 Dvr. Diamond, A. S., 120th Army Bde.
945571 Gnr. Drewstein, C/119th Bde.
46148 Gnr. Davis, N., 61st Bty.
88345 Gnr. Dehaan, L., R.G.A.
199891 Pte. Decker, L., R.F.A.
182598 Gnr. De Metz, H., R.F.A.
Gnr. Davies, H., 87th Coy.
Gnr. Davis, C. T., R.F.A.
Pte. Davis, C. J., 143rd Bty. R.F.A.
237326 Gnr. David, J. H., No. 8 Res. Bde.
1777 Pte. Devine, G., 106th Provisional Bty.
36112 Dvr. Davis, A., 180th Bde. R.F.A.
116312 Gnr. Davies, R., 105/22nd Bde.
2375 Dvr. Davis, P., 291st Bde.
204030 Gnr. Davis, A., R.F.A.
117408 Dvr. Davis, S. H., R.F.A.
43010 Gnr. Denson, J., D Bty.
182598 Gnr. De Merz, H.
168372 Gnr. Driver, M., A/174th Bde.
Pte. De Meza, C., R.A.
113560 Gnr. Dabreem, J., R.G.A.
970614 Gnr. Daniels, S., R.F.A.
40148 Gnr. Davis, J., R.G.A.
15923 Gnr. Dumosel, D. C., 10th R.G.A.
661375 A/Bdr. Donn, L., R.F.A.
2958 Dvr. Davis, C.,* 141st Hy. Bty., R.G.A.
158939 Dvr. Davis, I.,* 1/1st Leicester R.H.A.
27491 Gnr. Dansky, S.
159635 Dvr. Davies, P.

Royal Regiment of Artillery.—*Continued.*

183148 Gnr. DEFFENT, J.
321428 Bdr. DANIEL, T. L.
  2144 Pte. DE GRASSE, H.
  2353 Gnr. DAVIDSON, R.G.A.
181162 Gnr. DAVAROFF, I.
156266 Cpl. DONNE, C.
337063 Gnr. DRUCKER, R.F.A.
195076 Sgt. DAVIES, T., R.G.A.
       Pte. DEFRIES, A., R.G.A.
       Pte. DE YOUNG, M. J., R.F.A.
       Pte. DORIN, S., R.G.A.
130945 Gnr. DA COSTA, 331st Sge. Bty. R.G.A.
179233 Gnr. DUNITZ, W., R.G.A.
640959 Gnr. DA COSTA,
221025 Gnr. DRUMLITZ, H.
273464 Dvr. DAVIES, J.
173659 Cadet DANIELS, M., R.G.A.
197970 Gnr. DOWSETT, G.
199842 Gnr. DAVIES, J.
195689 Gnr. DAVIS, M.
1976172 Gnr. DICK, M.
103050 Dvr. DREW, B. C., R.F.A.
199893 Dvr. DUINKER, C.
131385 Gnr. DAGUTSKI, A., R.G.A.
139215 Gnr. DAVIS, S.
 61416 Gnr. DE LAREDO, M. A., R.H.A.
  1874 Gnr. DAVIS, J., R.F.A.
  1396 Gnr. DAVIS, J., R.F.A.
124891 Gnr. DE FRIES, D., R.F.A.
 78206 Gnr. DIGHT, H., R.G.A.
345302 Dvr. DIDIASHIVILLE, M., R.F.A.
 19846 Pte. DEANSFERTIE, J., R.F.A
111922 Gnr. DENNIS, B., R.F.A.
150203 Gnr. DAVIS, J., R.G.A.
 86058 Dvr. ERIERA, M., 63rd Bde.
  1412 Bdr. EMANUEL, M., 6th London F.A.B.
 97932 Dvr. ELKIN, J. H., 48th Bde.
 59893 Gnr. ENGLEMAN, M., 15th Bde.
  1555 Dvr. ELLIS, A., 60th D.A.C.
182974 Bdr. EMANUEL, L., R.F.A.
 87007 Dvr. EFFERSON, E., 18th D.A.C.
 76926 Gnr. ENFIELD, F., 40th Bty.
 84945 Gnr. ELSTEIN, M., 193rd Siege Bty.
232725 Gnr. EPSTEIN, L., A/147th Bde.
253579 Gnr. EVANS, J., 246th (W.R.) Bde.
233287 Dvr. ELLISON, J. S., "B" Bty. R.H.A.
176955 Gnr. EAGLE, H., R.H.A.
159685 Gnr. EPSTEIN, N., R.F.A.
158105 Gnr. ELEMAN, P. W., 39th D.A.C.
 80046 Pte. ELLIS, F., R.F.A.
       Gnr. ENGOLD, 1 Depot, R.F.A.
 30605 Cpl. ESTERSON, B. R., 63rd Bty. R.F.A.
117814 Dvr. EINSTEIN, N., R.F.A.
223849 Sgt. EPSTANE, L., R.H.A., "W" Bty.
229810 Dvr. ELLISON, L., A/307th Bde. R.F.A.
 76585 Pte. EMDEN, P., 119th Bty. R.G.A.
268349 Gnr. EPSTEIN, G., 11th By. R.G.A.
228940 Fitter EDELMAN, E. H., 76th Bde. A. Col.
131594 Gnr. ENDLEMAN, M., R.G.A.
 72225 Bdr. ELKIN, C.
224357 Gnr. EDWARDS, E., 53rd Bty. R.F.A.
       Gnr. ELSTEIN, M.
       Cadet ELMAN, B. J.
197703 Gnr. EPSTEIN, J., R.F.A.
197695 Gnr. EPSTEIN, D., R.F.A.
136518 Gnr. EVANTHAL, H., R.F.A.
165613 Gnr. EKER, A., R.G.A.
253359 Gnr. EISENBLATT, J., R.F.A.
640961 Gnr. EPSTEIN, I., R.F.A.
188244 Gnr. ERSLERE, H., R.G.A.
146427 Pte. ENGLISH, L.
181323 Dvr. EDELMAN, R., R.F.A.
       Gnr. EPRILE, R.F.A.
       A/Sgt. EDELSBERG, E., R.F.A.
371209 Gnr. EVANS, E., R.G.A.
 56523 Cpl. FREEDMAN, H. (M.M.), 9th Bty.
 86614 Gnr. FISHMAN, M.,* 64th Bde.
 80137 Dvr. FLYNN, M., 70th Bde.
 50210 A/Bdr. FRY, H., 86th Bde.
 52385 Sig. FELDMAN, L. F.,* D/92nd Bde.
 55141 Gnr. FORD, A., 104th Bde.
 17646 Dvr. FREEMAN, L., 110th Bde. Amn. Col.
 66743 Dvr. FRASER, A., 25th Div. Amn. Col.
 13323 Dvr. FREEDMAN, J., 35th Div. Amn. Col.
  1997 Gnr. FREEDMAN, H., B/282nd Bde.
 71210 Gnr. FREEDMAN, J., 41st Bde.
  1118 Dvr. FRIEDSON, M., 40th D.A.C.
112825 Gnr. FINE, G., 51st Bty.
 85138 Dvr. FOOT, H.,* C/84th Bde.
 50208 Dvr. FREEMAN, S., A/110th Bde.
125041 Gnr. FOOT, A., A/48th Bde.
 13559 Dvr. FROME, L., 31st D.A.C.
189884 Gnr. FRIEND, M., 251st Bde.
111818 Dvr. FLOWERS, H., 71st Bde.
930888 Gnr. FREEDMAN, H., 281st Bde.
 60236 Bdr. FREEDMAN, V., B/A.A. Bty.
334660 Gnr. FINKELSTEIN, M., 358th Siege Bty.
 77459 Gnr. FALK, A. G., 135th Siege Bty.
106026 Bdr. FLEMHOOD, L., 219th Siege Bty.
  1274 Gnr. FINKLESTONE, 1/1 Lond. H. Bty.
169735 Gnr. FOX, C., 13th Siege Bty.
125225 Gnr. FISHSTEIN, D., D/58th Bde.
151000 Gnr. FAIRLIE, C., 144th Heavy Bty.
626418 Gnr. FRANK, H. A., 309th Siege Bty.
183268 Gnr. FREEDMAN, A., 154th S. By. R.G.A.
 11803 Pte. FRANKS, A. B., 11th T.M.B.
144140 Dvr. FINK, L., A/88th F.A. Bde.
194118 Gnr. FINK, M., 15th D.A.C.
 54313 Bdr. FISH, 63rd Bde.
 88355 Gnr. FREEDMAN, H., 1/1st Lowland H.B.
  1084 Dvr. FEDER, D., 34th Bde. R.F.A.
 81318 Cpl. FOX, J., 138th Hy. Bty. R.G.A.
 65533 Pte. FREEMAN, M., 2nd Cav. D.A.C.
143098 Dvr. FREEMAN, G., R.F.A.
 14508 Gnr. FINE, J., 53/2 T.M.B.

Royal Regiment of Artillery.—*Continued.*

116175	Gnr. FOUNTAIN, G., 28th Siege Bty.
127945	Gnr. FEATHER, S., R.G.A.
	Gnr. FRITSH, L., No. 1 Depot.
	Gnr. FAULKNER, J., 17th Coy.
	Bdr. FOGELMAN, 79th Bty. R.F.A.
2281	Pte. FLACH, I. W., 106th Provisional By.
1662	Gnr. FREEDMAN, M., R.F.A.
149361	Gnr. FREEDMAN, H., 176th Bty. R.G.A.
42286	Pte. FREEDMAN, C., 4th R.G.A.
645	Dvr. FRIEDESON, 58th D.A.C.
2L/279	Gnr. FRANCIS, E., R.G.A.
183268	Gnr. FREEDMAN, A., R.G.A. 153rd S. By.
730702	Dvr. FEINBERG, "X" Bty. R.H.A.
62087	Gnr. FREEDMAN, D., 216 S.
631857	Dvr. FELDMAN, J.
961090	Dvr. FREEDMAN, D., R.F.A.
89092	Gnr. FRIEZE, N., R.G.A. 61st Coy.
182590	Gnr. FONSECA, A.
292997	Pte. FISH, A., R.G.A. 51st Hy.
	Bdr. FROST, H., R.F.A.
22964	Bdr. FISHER, N. C., R.G.A.
	Pte. FREEMAN, I., 97th Bty. R.F.A.
640910	Gnr. FOREMAN, H., 108th Bty.
235971	Pte. FIELDMAN, M., R.F.A.
46040	Sdr. FRIEDLAND, H., R.F.A.
191283	Gnr. FREEDMAN, J., C/342nd Bde. R.F.A
165220	Gnr. FREIZE, L., 354th Bde. R.F.A.
122200	Gnr. FISHER, S., 250th Bde.
194084	Dvr. FILZ, A., R.F.A.
43756	Sig. FIDLER, J. S., R.F.A.
13896	Dvr. FREDMAN, C.
175442	Gnr. FLETCHER, H., 99th Bde. R.F.A.
199849	Dvr. FINEGOLD, M., R.F.A.
163315	Dvr. FLETCHER, A. G., 106th Sge. Bty.
94940	Dvr. FRANCIS, L., 54th Bty. R.F.A.
110057	Gnr. FREEDMAN, J.
	Cadet FRIEDLANDER, W., R.G.A.
20109	Dvr. FIRSTAT, A., 8th Bde.
123544	Gnr. FELTZ, M., 4th R.F.A.
71815	Gnr. FRANK, N., 169th Hy. Bty. R.G.A.
198012	Gnr. FREDMAN, S.
3485	Dvr. FREEDMAN, L.
6049	Pte. FALK, M.
1615	Pte. FRANKS, R., R.F.A.
165267	Dvr. FREEDMAN, A., R.F.A.
195699	Gnr. FRAM, R., R.F.A.
646336	C.Q.M.S. FRIEND, S., 64th D.A.C.
83664	Bdr. FINE, M., R.G.A.
129990	Gnr. FROMBERG, A., R.G.A.
36043	Bdr. FINESEN, C., R.F.A.
117810	Pte. FITLEMAN, P., R.F.A.
138202	Dvr. FLOWERS, S., R.F.A.
40990	Dvr. FRANKS, J., R.F.A.
40275	A/Cpl. FRANKS, P., R.F.A.
2220	Dvr. FRIEDER, R.F.A.
198760	Gnr. FERGUSSON, S., R.F.A.
241538	Gnr. FINESTEIN, S., R.F.A.
125200	A/Bdr. FARR, W.
640986	Gnr. FRIAM, R., R.F.A.
337278	Gnr. FRANKS, W., R.F.A.
68743	Bdr. FROOMBERG, J.
197938	Dvr. FREEDMAN, S., R.F.A.
300894	Pte. FELDMAN, S., R.G.A.
111172	Gnr. FREEDMAN, M.
92705	Gnr. FIENSTEIN, M.
235417	Pte. FRANKS, H.
147265	Gnr. FLIGG, D., R.F.A.
180210	Gnr. FINE, I., R.G.A.
	Gnr. FIFER, J., R.F.A.
	Gnr. FRANKS, S., R.G.A.
	Bdr. FALK, W. (M.M.), R.F.A.
108757	Gnr. GOLDMAN, J., 143rd Siege Bty.
	Dvr. GLUCKSTEIN, 23rd Sge. Bty. R.G.A.
132286	Gnr. GREENSWEIG, P., 217th Siege Bty.
84751	Gnr. GOLDBERG, L., 231st Siege Bty.
170369	Gnr. GOLDBERG, H., 236th Siege Bty.
101349	Gnr. GLASSER, M., 126th B.A.C., A.F.A.
176939	Dvr. GOLDSTEIN, W., "O" Bty., R.H.A.
186319	Gnr. GREEN, B., 290th Sge. Bty. R.G.A.
258076	Gnr. GREENBERG, J., 118th S. By., R.G.A.
115323	Gnr. GOSHKORVZ, M., 111th Siege Bty.
194907	Gnr. GOLDSTEIN, N., 87th Sub. Sect.
182693	Dvr. GREEN, J., 40th Bty.
25092	Gnr. GOLDBERG, J.,* 4th D.A.C.
24773	Gnr. GINSBURG, S., D/124th Bde.
195912	Dvr. GOLDSTEIN, L., A/87th F.A. Bde.
154191	Gnr. GOLDBLATT, M., D/92nd Bde.
701391	Gnr. GOLD, S. G., 50th Bde.
228917	Gnr. GRANECK, J., 38th D.A.C.
11959	Dvr. GREENBERG, H., 25th D.A.C.
961091	Dvr. GREEN, G., 161st Bde.
143804	Gnr. GOODMAN, G., 12th Bde.
169525	Gnr. GLEED, W., 18th D.A.C.
68690	Gnr. GILBERT, H.,* 20/9th Bde.
168460	Gnr. GOLDBERG, S., 142nd Bty. R.G.A.
89392	Gnr. GOODMAN, B., C/256th Bde.
863	Gnr. GOLDBERG, A., W/60/Hy. T.M.B.
890	Dvr. GOLDBERG, C., 60th D.A.C.
864	Dvr. GOLDBERG, S., 60th D.A.C.
866	Dvr. GOLDSTEIN, D., 60th D.A.C.
865	Dvr. GOLDSTEIN, M., 60th D.A.C.
862	Dvr. GANTZ, J., 60th D.A.C.
96345	Bdr. GODDARD, S., 94th Bde.
121566	Bdr. GOODMAN, L. L., 11th D.A.C.
4298	Dvr. GREEN, M., D/310th Bde.
137803	Gnr. GREENFIELD, A., 23rd D.A.C.
16303	Gnr. GOLDMAN, M., 24th T.M.B.
76009	Gnr. GREENBERG, H., 66th Siege Battery.
44822	Gnr. GOLD, L., D/48th Bde.
1995	Gnr. GOLD, G. J., 93/280th Bde.
25092	Dvr. GOLDBERG, J.,* att. No. 7 G.H.Q. Ammunition Park R.F.A.
111926	Gnr. GOLDSTEIN, H., att. No. 8 G.H.Q. Ammunition Park.
925492	Gnr. GREENBERG, I., 290th Bde. R.F.A.

Royal Regiment of Artillery.—*Continued.*

901161 Gnr. GARCIA, S., 293rd Bde.
696417 Gnr. GOLDBERG, W., 57th D.A.C.
696116 Gnr. GOLDBERG, M., 57th D.A.C.
178327 Dvr. GOODMAN, J., 66th D.A.C.
155877 Gnr. GOODWIN, P., 66th D.A.C.
925851 Gnr. GOLD, J., 50th D.A.C.
208683 Dvr. GOLDSTEIN, M., 48th D.A.C.
188563 Gnr. GREEN, A., 33rd D.A.C.
1109 Gnr. GOSSCHALK, M., 125th Siege Bty.
    Gnr. GOODMAN, J., 86th Bty.
166489 Gnr. GALLEWSKI, J., 46th D.A.C.
    Pte. GROSS, H., 45th Coy.
    Gnr. GREEN, I. (M.M.), R.F.A.
    Tpr. GLAZEBROOK, A. W. E., 117th Bty.
50533 Pte. GOLDMAN, J., 22nd Bty. R.F.A.
181868 Gnr. GOLDSMAN, A. D., No. 8 Res. Bde.
36219 Gnr. GREENHALG, J., 180th Bde. R.F.A.
36333 Dvr. GORDON, A., 180th Bde. R.F.A.
    Dvr. GREEN, R., 85th Bde. R.F.A.
36036 Pte. GOLDBERG, H., P.B. Bty.
60962 Gnr. GARLICK, I., R.G.A.
22414 Gnr. GREENBERG, R.H.A.
207666 Gnr. GOLDBERG, A., R.G.A.
970616 Dvr. GOLDBERG, A., R.F.A.
951410 Gnr. GOLDSTEIN, D., R.F.A.
42431 Dvr. GARDIE, L., R.F.A.
147160 Gnr. GOLDSTEIN, B., R.F.A.
318474 Dvr. GEVER, G., R.F.A.
235690 L/Bdr. GARSTIN, I., R.F.A.
129991 Gnr. GONSKY, L.
177563 Dvr. GELARDE, J., 5th Bty. R.F.A.
227910 Gnr. GREENBERG, H., R.G.A.
65921 Dvr. GREEN, G. A., 14th Bde. R.F.A.
54501 Sgt. GREENBERG, D., 93rd Bty. R.F.A.
45318 Dvr. GILLETT, M., 5th Bty. R.F.A.
    Dvr. GOODMAN, A., 62nd Bde. R.F.A.
2806 Dvr. GARRETT, D., 50th By. E. Sub. Sect.
69521 A/Bdr. GREEN, J., 2nd Bde.
148 Sgt. GOODMAN, D.,* (D.C.M.), 111th Bty.
82530 Gnr. GOODMAN, J.,* 33rd Bty.
88853 Dvr. GOODMAN, A., 62nd Bde.
60332 Dvr. GOLDMAN, R., R.F.A.
68260 Dvr. GLASS, J., 17th Div. Amn. Col.
    Sgt. GOLDSTEIN, A/Bty. 83rd Bde.
17277 Sgt. GARCIA, J., 58/1 T.M. By. 58th Bde.
82118 Bdr. GLICKMAN, S., "C" Bty. 129th Bde.
5 Bdr. GOLDBERG, R., 49th Div. Amn. Col.
52848 Dvr. GRAD, J., H.Q. 106th Bde.
31426 Dvr. GOLDBERG, J., 177th Bde. Amn. Col.
L/36082 Gnr. GORON, L., B/180th Bde.
82179 Dvr. GOULD, H., 37th D.A.C.
4038 Gnr. GREEN, I.,* D/120th Bde.
    Dvr. GOODMAN, I., C/256th Bde.
71777 Gnr. GOODMAN, B., 47th Bde.
60232 Dvr. GOLDING, R., 48th Bde.
30606 Gnr. GREEN, C., 36th Div. Amn. Col.
35492 Dvr. GINSBERG, 36th Div. Amn. Col.

44750 Dvr. GOLDACRE, 189th Bde.
86250 Dvr. GARRETT, D., 34th Bde.
111810 Gnr. GOLDMAN, M., 29th Bde.
44289 Dvr. GREENSTEIN, G., 40th D.A.C.
863 Gnr. GOLDBERG, A., W/60th H.T.M.B.
222841 Dvr. GAROFF, L., R.F.A.
60703 Bdr. GLICKMAN, J. S., R.F.A.
242469 Gnr. GORDON, P. S., R.F.A.
776962 Bdr. GREEN, M. (M.M.), R.F.A.
115322 Gnr. GORDON, P., B/84th Bde.
83179 Dvr. GOULD, H.
135670 Gnr. GREEN, I., R.G.A.
111146 Dvr. GOODMAN, M., 547th How. Bty.
140729 Gnr. GOLD, J., No. 2 Sect. Welsh R.G.A.
741574 Dvr. GOLDBLATT, L., "B" By. 342nd Bde.
745731 Gnr. GRINSBERG, S., 343rd Bde. R.F.A.
48574 Gnr. GOLDSTEIN, E.,* 73rd Bty., R.F.A.
701397 Dvr. GOLD, A. L., R.F.A.
262547 Gnr. GREENBURGH, H., R.F.A.
164434 Gnr. GOLDSTONE, J., R.G.A.
920218 Gnr. GALVIDENSKY, J., 53rd Bty. R.F.A.
29934 Dvr. GARDNER, J., 440th Bty. R.F.A.
249231 Gnr. GOODMAN, G., R.F.A.
273578 Dvr. GRANT,
3487 Gnr. GREEN, G.
195547 Gnr. GOLDBERG, M.
199830 Gnr. GROSSMAN, L.
269090 Gnr. GRANAR, L.
199851 Gnr. GISH, A.
174918 Gnr. GOLDSTEIN, A., R.F.A.
189652 Gnr. GOODMAN, G., R.F.A.
234550 Gnr. GOLDSTEIN, B., R.F.A.
656956 Cpl. GODWIN, W. D., R.F.A.
224515 Gnr. GOTTLIB, M., R.F.A.
194720 Dvr. GOLDMAN, S. O.
110973 Gnr. GILLISPIE, J., A.A.R.H.A.
163831 Gnr. GERSHON, J., R.F.A.
32543 Dvr. GORDON, C., R.F.A.
1667 Gnr. GILBERT, M., R.G.A.
860096 Dvr. GOLDFAR, C., R.F.A.
195857 Dvr. GOLDSTEIN, D.
44803 Dvr. GILBERT,
651782 Dvr. GOLDBERG, J.
207200 Dvr. GANTEN, J., R.F.A.
174669 Bdr. GOULD, J., R.F.A.
127680 Pte. GOLDMAN, M., R.G.A.
174669 Pte. GOULD, J., R.G.A.
243665 Pte. GREENSTONE, M. J., R.F.A.
25373 Gnr. GOLDRICH, L., R.G.A.
168709 Gnr. GREEN, J. F., R.F.A.
152120 Gnr. GOLDMAN, M., R.G.A.
1328 Bdr. GOLINSKY, B., 39th Bde.
199215 Dvr. HARRIS, A., 4th D.A.C.
111820 Dvr. HARRIS, J., No. 2 Sect. 34th D.A.C.
23443 Dvr. HAMBURGER, M., B. 149th Bde.
751 Dvr. HENOCHSBERG, D., 73rd Sge. Bty.
127 Gnr. HILL, S., 72nd Siege Bty.

Royal Regiment of Artillery.—*Continued.*

158295 Dvr. HART, M., 66th D.A.C.
45286 Gnr. HOLMAN, W., 124th Hy. Bty.
109610 A/Bdr. HART, E. A., 144th Hy. Bty., R.G.A.
338580 Cpl. HYAMS, D., 286th Siege Bty.
       Gnr. HENSHER, W., R.F.A.
7281 Bdr. HARRIS, H., 69th Bty., R.F.A.
78800 Gnr. HEILBRON, V.* (M.M.), R.H.A.
47890 Gnr. HERMAN, G. J.
208735 Dvr. HARRISON, A., 63rd Res. Bty.
38574 Dvr. HART, N., 83rd Res. Bty.
172364 Gnr. HYAMS, S., 8th Res. Bde.
209550 Pte. HERMAN, D.,
12556 Gnr. HOFFMAN, J., 241st Bde. R.F.A.
53479 Gnr. HARTSTEIN, R.F.A.
53036 Gnr. HEILBRON, H., R.G.A.
25301 Gnr. HARRING, M., R.F.A.
2716 Gnr. HART, P., 293rd Bde.
2261 Dvr. HART, J., 58th D.A.C.
116057 Gnr. HATTER, D., R.G.A., 47th Coy.
177607 Dvr. HELLER, G., R.F.A.
67178 Gnr. HUST, R.G.A., 49th Coy.
961107 Gnr. HERMAN, H., R.F.A.
211642 Dvr. HYMANS, R.F.A.
90415 Bdr. HARRIS, L., 51st Bde.
98879 Dvr. HERDMAN, J., 70th Bde.
35284 Gnr. HARRIS, J., 148th Bty. 20th Bde.
81273 Dvr. HARRIS, I., B/124th Bde.
1337 Dvr. HARRIS, J. W., 2nd Non. Bde.
30848 Dvr. HART, J., D/75 Bde.
64575 Dvr. HARRIS, J., 111th Bde.
52782 Dvr. HOSMER, A., B.A.C. 107th Sde.
53479 Gnr. HARTSILVER, C. D. (M.M.), 5th Bde. 81st Bty.
40501 Bdr. HARTOG, J., 177th Bde.
       Gnr. HELMAN, A., 1st Welch Bde.
2262 Gnr. HARRIS, M., 2nd Welch Bde.
111819 Bdr. HARRIS, G., 168th Bde. Anm. Col.
954 Dvr. HAAGMAN, A., C/280th Bde.
40532 Dvr. HOGANI, A. M., C/183rd Bde.
40815 Dvr. HART, N., 189th Bde.
111812 Gnr. HYMAN, A., 29th Bde.
L/29850 Dvr. HAAGMAN, L., 178th Bde.
42379 Bdr. HARRIS, J., A/188th Bde.
4832 Bdr. HAMP, F. V., A/188th Bde.
966117 Sgt. HYAMS, B., Hdq. 303rd Bde. R.F.A.
901 Dvr. HARRIS, L. B., 60th D.A.C.
10536 Dvr. HART, A., 6/40th Bde.
22300 Dvr. HART, G., How. Bde.
       Dvr. HARRIS, D., 62nd D.A.C.
48282 Dvr. HELLIER, J., H.Q. 85th Bde.
64577 Dvr. HARRIS, H., 12th D.A.C.
55385 Bdr. HART, S.,* A/102nd Bde.
43752 Dvr. HARRIS, J., A/110th Bde.
2023 Gnr. HARRIS, E., 161st Sge. Bty. R.G.A.
95383 Dvr. HYAMSON, T., Lahore D.A.C.
1071 Dvr. HART, J., C/282nd Bde.

901158 Gnr. HART, P., 290th Bde. R.F.A.
209743 Gnr. HAYMAN, H.,* 38th D.A.C.
2701 Gnr. HOVSHA, H. R.,* C/232nd Bde.
944630 Dvr. HARRIS, H., D/210th Bde.
4750 Gnr. HENDRY, B., L/54th T.M.B.
925364 Dvr. HAAGMAN, A. E., 280th Bde.
945894 Gnr. HART, S., B/51st Bde.
13171 Gnr. HARRIS, H., 99th Siege Bty.
153466 Bdr. HARRIS, G., 413rd Sge. Bty. R.G.A.
176201 Gnr. HORWITZ, M. J., 276th Siege Bty.
168362 Gnr. HART, D., 6th Bty., R.F.A.
190146 Gnr. HARRIS, E., A/330th Bde.
625942 Gnr. HARRIS, H. M., 309th Sge. Bty.
157157 Gnr. HEISER, J., 259th Siege Bty.
796855 Dvr. HANIS, B., 311th Bde.
24227 Gnr. HAYMAN, D., B.A.C.
169914 Gnr. HARRIS, H., 236th S.B. R.G.A.
470642 Gnr. HARRIS, L. A., R.G.A.
220146 Sig. HARRIS, J. L., R.G.A. 523rd Sge. By.
210460 Gnr. HUNT, I. A., R.F.A.
228298 Dvr. HARRIS, A. A., R.F.A.
145776 Gnr. HORWITZ, M., R.F.A., 96th Bde.
12284 Gnr. HUNDLER, H., 2nd D.A.C.
156411 Gnr. HERMANN, H. B., R.G.A.
23336 Gnr. HYAMS, P.
42379 Cpl. HARRIS, I., R.H.A.
200248 Gnr. HARRISON, N.
240700 Gnr. HYMES, J., R.F.A.
35248 Gnr. HARRIS, J., 148th Bty. R.F.A.
252255 Gnr. HARRIS, A., 22nd Bty. R.F.A.
12282 Gnr. HANDBEAR, H.
       Dvr. HERTZBERG, M., R.F.A.
2261 Dvr. HART, S., 58th Bde.
55594 Gnr. HARRIS, A.,* 21st Biege By. R.G.A.
11927 Gnr. HARRIS, M.,* 311th Bde., R.F.A.
75249 Gnr. HILLIER, C. J.,* 2nd T.M.B.
194122 Gnr. HOBDAY, A., R.F.A.
22300 Gnr. HART, R., 67th Bty. R.F.A.
59142 Dvr. HYAM, T., R.F.A.
       Gnr. HUNTLEY, M. S., R.F.A.
198047 Dvr. HYMAN, R.F.A.
184233 Gnr. HARRIS, L., R.F.A.
9765 Sgt. HYAMS, H., 4th Sge. Bde. R.G.A.
525660 Gnr. HARRIS, E. J.
920342 L/Bdr. HARRIS, E. E., 53rd Bty. R.F.A.
159659 Dvr. HARRIS, E., R.F.A.
132817 Gnr. HARRIS, E., R.G.A.
3299 Gnr. HARRIS, J.
93288 Gnr. HARBURY, F.
960962 Gnr. HARRIS, J.
153981 Dvr. HARRIS, H. B., R.F.A.
11929 Gnr. HARRIS, M.,* R.F.A.
124420 Gnr. HARRIS, H., R.F.A.
235016 Dvr. HAUTMAN, E., R.F.A.
178498 Gnr. HYMAN, L., R.G.A.
83543 Gnr. HARCOURT, P. B., R.G.A.
1887 Dvr. HORROWITZ, A., 2/1st Bty.
651439 Bdr. HUTLEY, M., R.F.A.

Royal Regiment of Artillery.—*Continued.*

217601 Gnr. HALPERN, J. N., R.F.A.
   882 Gnr. HANDELAAR, H., R.F.A.
181402 Dvr. HARRIS, L., R.G.A.
881893 Gnr. HARRIS, H., R.F.A.
166820 Gnr. HERRING, G., R.F.A.
144714 Gnr. HYAMS, J.
134664 Gnr. HERTZOG, L.
273279 Gnr. HAUFMAN, M., R.F.A.
236839 Gnr. HERZKOVITZ, R.F.A.
131180 Bdr. HYDE, J., R.G.A.
 51930 Gnr. HALL, A. I., R.G.A.
154108 Gnr. HEGDES, B.
 37791 Gnr. HYMAN, J., 5th Bty.
143811 Gnr. HART, J.
      Bombr. HYAMSON, J. (M.M.), R.F.A.
 88534 Gnr. HITMAN, H.
 40569 Dvr. HERMAN, J., R.F.A.
 40609 Dvr. HERMAN, P., R.F.A.
123543 Dvr. HORWICH, J., R.F.A.
 99576 Gnr. HARRIS, J., R.F.A.
 99954 Gnr. HARRIS, A., R.G.A.
147007 Gnr. HYAMS, D.
225149 Gnr. HURST, B. L.
147778 Gnr. HARTZ, W.
182256 Gnr. HYAMS, D. W., R.F.A.
160901 Bdr. HERBERT, S., R.F.A.
202491 Bdr. HERMAN, G., R.F.A.
182177 Dvr. HERMAN, A., R.F.A.
159554 Dvr. HARRIS, W., R.G.A.
234084 Dvr. HARRIS, A., R.F.A.
  2261 Dvr. HART, S.
232785 Dvr. HOFMAN, L., 45th Bty.
  1399 Gnr. HARRIS, R.
 35172 Gnr. IZEN, A., 1/4th N.M. Bde.
   867 Gnr. ISRAEL, G., 54th Siege Bty.
353857 Dvr. ISAACS, D., 154th H.B.
169619 Gnr. ISAACS, J., 526th Sge. Bty. R.G.A.
210293 Dvr. ISAACS, N., D/84th Bty.
252985 Dvr. ISRAEL, B., S.A.A. 14th D.A.C.
920076 Gnr. ISSER, D.,* 307th Bde.
 19161 Gnr. ISAACSON, A., 73rd L.T.M.B.
189399 Gnr. ISSAMAN, W., B/88th Bde. F.A.
920075 Sig. ISAACS, J.,* A/92nd Bde.
199233 Gnr. INSTALL, W.
  2915 Gnr. ISENBERG, S., R.G.A.
  3584 Gnr. ISAACS, S., 106th Prov. Bn.
 85511 Dvr. ISAACS, J., D.A.C.
136962 Dvr. ISAACS, R.F.A., 102nd Bty.
182677 Gnr. ISAACS, C., R.F.A.
206991 Gnr. ISAACS, M., R.F.A.
156183 Dvr. ISAACS, 29th Bty. R.F.A.
148026 Dvr. ISRAEL, J.
218167 Gnr. ISAACS, C.
 76093 Gnr. ISAACS, M., R.G.A.
 43085 Gnr. ISAACS, H., R.F.A.
188574 Gnr. INGER, W., R.F.A.
155117 Gnr. ISAACS, I., R.F.A.

253563 Gnr. ISAACS, A.
236839 Gnr. ITZCOVITZ, S., R.F.A.
192524 Dvr. ISAACS, L. L., R.F.A.
297988 Gnr. ISAACS, E., R.F.A.
168469 Gnr. ISAACS, A. H., R.F.A.
253259 Gnr. ISENBLITT, J., R.F.A.
 49725 Dvr. JONES, B., "A" Bty. R.H.A.
 86887 Dvr. JOSEPH, J., 63rd Bde.
 38686 Bdr. JOSEPH, J., C/85th Bde.
 50961 Gnr. JOSEPH, A., 99th Bde.
   430 Gnr. JACOBS, L. G., 5th London F.A.B.
 39537 Dvr. JOSEPH, A., D/110th Bde.
 49153 Sig. JACOBS, D., D/79th Bde.
      Cpl. JACOBS, H. H., 4th Welsh Bde.
 11689 Dvr. JOEL, A., 156th Bde.
 25034 Dvr. JACOBS, H., 172nd Bde.
  1392 Bdr. JACOB, L., C/282nd Bde.
  2169 Gnr. JACOBS, A., 29th Div. Amn. Col.
  1874 Dvr. JACOBS, S., A/46th Bde.
 52820 Gnr. JACOB, H. V., 15th Bde. R.H.A.
 40580 Gnr. JACOBS, L. C., 187th Bde.
 94340 Dvr. JACOBS, S., 5th D.A.C.
 81508 Dvr. JACOBS, N., 4th D.A.C.
  2792 Gnr. JOSEPH, H. D., W/60th H.T.M.B.
   868 Dvr. JEFFREYS, H., 60th D.A.C.
132467 Gnr. JACOBSEN, W., A/103rd Bde.
 51925 Dvr. JOSEPHS, A., A/110th Bde.
 87890 Dvr. JASPER, H., Lahore D.A.C.
950364 Gnr. JACOBS, O. G., 235th Bde.
696871 Gnr. JACOBS, H., 62nd D.A.C.
113537 A/C.S.M. JACOBS, H. W., L. Siege Pk.
 91904 Gnr. JACOB, H., C/190th Bde.
187301 Gnr JACOBS, H., A/178th Bde. R.F.A.
119118 Gnr. JACOBS, H., 38th Hy. Bty.
 46956 Gnr. JACOBS, A., 388th Sge. Bty. R.G.A.
 71622 Gnr. JACOBS, C., 150th H.B. R.G.A.
143107 Gnr. JACOBSON, H., 194th S. B.
172095 Gnr. JANNER, B., 355th S. B.
136732 Dvr. JACOBS, M., 139th Hy. Bty.
156396 Gnr. JOSEPH, D., 111th Siege Bty.
 86370 Gnr. JOSEPH, J., 139th Sub. Sect.
211875 Gnr. JACOBS, H., V/XII T.M.B.
730900 Dvr. JULIUS, D., 32nd Bde. R.F.A.
138324 Gnr. JACOBWITZ, L., 6th D.A.C.
796871 Gnr. JACOBS, H., R.G.A.
139341 A/Sgt. JOSEPHS, J. R., 64th H.A. Group.
  1510 Dvr. JACOBS, I., 25th D.A.C.
 75223 Gnr. JACOBS, S., 69th Sge. Bty. R.G.A.
 77677 Gnr. JACOBS, D., 160th Sge. Bty. R.G.A.
 83150 Dvr JACOBS, W. C., 1/2nd Lancs. H. By.
 26879 Gnr. JACKSON, B., 32nd Siege Bty.
191981 Gnr. JACOBS, M., R.G.A.
624995 Dvr. JACOBS, J.,* R.F.A.
776703 Gnr. JEDELMAN, B.,
 77854 Gnr. JACOB, K., R.G.A.
235796 Gnr. JACOBS, D., "A" Bty. R.H.A.
      Gnr. JOHNSTON, R., R.G.A.
      Gnr. JOSEPH, S., R.G.A.

Royal Regiment of Artillery.—*Continued.*

196801	A/Bde.	JACKSON, M., 346th Bde. R.F.A.
39218	Gnr.	JACKSON, L., 180th Bde. R.F.A.
161082	Dvr.	JACOBSON, S., 7th D.A.C.
225051	Gnr.	JACOBOWITZ, A. E., 103rd Bde.
79829	Gnr.	JACOBSON, A., 199th Hy. Bty.
127964	Gnr.	JACOBS, E., R.G.A.
22465	Gnr.	JACOBS, H., R.F.A.
91904	Gnr.	JACOB, A., R.F.A.
134753	Bdr.	JOEL, W., 355th Bty. R.F.A.
143107	Gnr.	JACOBSON, H., 194th R.G.A.
9965	Dvr.	JOSEPH, P., R.H.A.
8595	Gnr.	JACOBS, S., R.F.A.
740532	Gnr.	JACOBS, H., R.F.A.
956333	Gnr.	JOSEPH, H. D., R.F.A.
	Gnr.	JACOBS, L., R.F.A.
	Gnr.	JOSEPH, L., 63rd Bde. R.F.A.
236362	Gnr.	JAFFA, S., 4th Depot R.F.A.
256723	Dvr.	JACOBS, B., 4th Res. Bde. R.F.A.
172196	Gnr.	JACOBS, M., 2/1st Highland, R.G.A.
881498	Gnr.	JACOBS, R., 354th Bde. R.F.A.
730990	Dvr.	JULIUS, D., 355th Bde. R.F.A.
3145	Bdr.	JACOBS, F.,* R.F.A.
111825	Gnr.	JACOBS, D., 4th Div. Amm. Col.
45907	Gnr.	JACOBS, M. S.
65738	Gnr.	JACOBS, S., R.F.A.
203955	Gnr.	JAMES, B., R.G.A.
	Gnr.	JACOBS, B. (M.M.), R.F.A.
189384	Gnr.	JACOBS, M., 54th Bty. R.F.A.
8881	Bdr.	JACQUES, H.
26760	Gnr.	JACOBS, G. N., 9th Bde.
125067	Gnr.	JUDELSON, T., 4th R.F.A.
179579	Dvr.	JOSEPH, E., 169th D.A.C.
133016	Gnr.	JOSEPH, I.
16215	Gnr.	JACOBS, L., R.F.A.
108501	Gnr.	JACOBS, H., R.G.A.
52677	R.S.M.	JENKINS, M., 13th Bty. R.F.A.
77854	Gnr.	JACOBS, K., R.G.A.
159841	Gnr.	JACKSON, C. F., R.G.A.
207683	Gnr.	JACOBS, H., R.G.A.
115322	Gnr.	JORDON, P.
63385	Gnr.	JACKS, C., R.G.A.
67293	Gnr.	JACOBS, E. L., R.G.A.
83150	Dvr.	JACOBS, W. C., R.G.A.
253723	Dvr.	JACOBS, B., R.F.A.
220986	Dvr.	JOSEPH, S., R.F.A.
98579	Gnr.	JOSEPH, J. J.
247272	Gnr.	JACOB, A., R.F.A.
119118	Gnr.	JACOBS, R.G.A.
235131	Gnr.	JACOBS, S., R.F.A.
235395	Bdr.	JAFFE, L., R.F.A.
203955	Bdr.	JAMES, B., R.G.A.
	Dvr.	JACOBS, S. M. (M.S.M.), R.F.A.
32706	Dvr.	KING, H., 134th Bty.
74916	Dvr.	KEPPELL, G., R.G.A.
39612	Gnr.	KEMPNER, D., A/106th Bde.
86250	Bdr.	KARET, J., 50th Bty.
39758	Gnr.	KAYS, J., D/182nd D.A.C.
167145	Gnr.	KAPLAN, D., D/182nd D.A.C.
21293	Gnr.	KOSKY, J., 172nd Bde.
1281	Dvr.	KEESING, H., 41st D.A.C.
146	Gnr.	KENERICK, A., B/301st Bde.
	Dvr.	KRAMER, L. E., H.Q. 112th Bde.
450823	Rfm.	KRENGEL, Light T.M.B.
87511	Dvr.	KITCHENOFF, P., 21st Bde.
901313	Dvr.	KAPINSKY, A., 33rd D.A.C.
114524	Gnr.	KEYS, J., 180th Siege Bty.
71548	Gnr.	KAUFMAN, H., 35th Hy. Bty.
211564	Dvr.	KEMLETT, M., B/58th Bde.
85034	Cpl.	KAUFMAN, L., 111th Siege Bty.
177902	Gnr.	KAHN, L., 87th Sub. Sect.
134859	Gnr.	KOSKY, B., 279th Ciege By. R.G.A.
208734	Gnr.	KAUFMAN, A., 311th Bde.
12407	Dvr.	KLEINBURG, S., C/56th Bde.
212115	Dvr.	KOKIA, E., Bde. Amn. Col., R.F.A.
221120	Gnr.	KAYE, S.,* (M.M.), 24th Bde.
41337	Gnr.	KAUFMAN, A., 184th Siege Bty.
696	Gnr.	KINGHAM, W., 174th Siege Bty.
40928	Dvr.	KENDRICK, J., R.H.A.
233877	Dvr.	KROHN, P., R.G.A.
3492	Gnr.	KLOEGMAN, J., A/252 Bde.
29669	Gnr.	KONCOPSKI, L., R.F.A.
200124	Gnr.	KING, M., R.F.A.
575225	Dvr.	KARS, J., R.H.A.
197650	Dvr.	KING, M., R.H.A.
26736	Dvr.	KASS, J.,
146880	Gnr.	KING, J.J., R.F.A.
731558	Gnr.	KERSH, J., 73rd D.A.C.
154122	Sig.	KOSKY, J.,* B/59th Bde., R.F.A.
65103	Bdr.	KRAMER, F.,* R.F.A.
213377	Bdr.	KENDRICK, R., R.F.A.
300920	Gnr.	KRAKANER, H., R.G.A.
178532	Dvr.	KEMPNER, H., 17th D.A.C.
83623	Gnr.	KLINEBERG, H., R.G.A.
293303	Sgt.	KLEMENTASKI, B. L., 185th Hw. By.
970624	Dvr.	KERSTEIN, M., 12th R.F.A.
24926	Dvr.	KALINSKY, A., 8th Bde.
	Cpl.	KRAFT, J. H. (M.M.), R.F.A.
252203	Gnr.	KREVER, M.
171021	Dvr.	KRAMER, H., R.F.A.
198130	Gnr.	KOLOSKY, H., 71st D.A.C.
211467	Dvr.	KORBINSKY, S., R.F.A.
139018	Gnr.	KAUFMAN, M. C.
30951	Dvr.	KAUFMAN, R., 36th Bde.
308893	Cpl.	KELLER, H., R.G.A.
100046	Gnr.	KING, C., R.F.A.
202041	Gnr.	KAISERMAN, J., R.G.A.
395410	Dvr.	KARASERK, W., 4th R.G.A.
37020	Dvr.	KING, J., R.F.A.
181156	Dvr.	KISNER, S., R.F.A.
182756	Bdr.	KATZ, J., R.F.A.
211929	Gnr.	KEMPNER, R.F.A.
216894	Gnr.	KLOOT, A.
970620	Dvr.	KLANE, J., R.F.A.
63499	Dvr.	LEVY, W., 30th D.A.C.
2473	Gnr.	LITTMAN, G., A/142/1 L.T.M.B.

Royal Regiment of Artillery.—*Continued.*

2118 Dvr. LEVY, H. A., 7th London Bde.
2368 Gnr. LEWIS, S. C., 1/3rd London R.F.A.
59614 Gnr. LEAKE, D., 22nd Bde.
44987 Gnr. LEFTWICH, H., 31st Bty.
460595 Gnr. LEVY, J., 31st Bty.
36502 Dvr. LEWIS, B., A/183rd Bde.
30221 Dvr. LEVENSTEIN, 189th Bde.
297 Gnr. LEVENE, R., 75th Siege Bty.
790 Gnr. LORRIMER, J. F. S., 75th Sge. Bty.
50940 Gnr. LYONS, G., 36th Bde.
13503 Dvr. LYONS, J., 36th Bde.
L/30061 Dvr. LYONS, S., 178th Bde.
35777 Dvr. LEVY, S., C/188th Bde.
111932 Gnr. LEVINE, S., 113th Bty. 39th Bde.
877 Dvr. LEFTWICH, A., C/301st Bde.
2769 Gnr. LEE, J., A/302nd Bde.
2863 Gnr. LAVENDER, L. L., B/302nd Bde.
2318 Sdr. LEVI, J., B/305th Bde.
145976 Bdr. LAZARUS, E., 94th Bde.
39803 Dvr. LAIKER, J., C/53rd Bde.
89050 Dvr. LEVY, N., B/84th Bde.
40282 Gnr. LEWIS, F., B/85th Bde.
93213 Dvr. LIEBERMAN, E., 84th D.A.C.
5535 Bdr. LEVITT, C., 155th Bde.
43753 Dvr. LEWIS, J., 25th D.A.C.
60671 Gnr. LEE, S., 66th Sge. Bty.
1052 Gnr. LEVY, D., 163rd Sge. Bty. R.G.A.
78784 Gnr. LONDON, L., 158th Sge. Bty.
151 Gnr. LAVENSKY, S. N., R.G.A.
120178 Gnr. LAURENCE, B. W., Siege Park.
201914 Dvr. LEVISON, R.
Dvr. LEVITT, J., R.G.A.
Gnr. LEWIS, C., R.G.A.
Dvr. LIPMAN, W., 17th Bde. R.F.A.
881682 Dvr. LEVENSTEIN, D., 346th Bde. R.F.A.
217737 Bdr. LEVINE, C., Sig. Training Centre.
125074 Sig. LASSMAN, A., Sig. Training Centre.
206961 Dvr. LEVY, G. G.
36565 Gnr. LEVY, L., P.B. Battery.
3144 Gnr. LIPNOFSKY, 72nd Div. Artillery.
2847 Gnr. LEAPMAN, A. C., 291st Bde.
111070 Gnr. LIEGLER, A., 180th Heavy Bty.
89915 Gnr. LEVY, M., R.G.A. "A" Company.
12541 A/Sgt. LESLIE, R., R.G.A., 43rd Coy.
265522 Gnr. LEVENE, R.F.A.
178251 Gnr. LIFTSHITZ, L., R.F.A.
95603 Gnr. LEVY, C., R.F.A.
139953 Sig. LAZARICK, R.H.A.
268971 Gnr. LASKI, N., R.G.A.
706673 Dvr. LEE, W., 148th Bde. R.F.A.
86600 Sgt. LEVIN, B., R.G.A.
109528 Gnr. LEIMER, N., R.G.A.
143777 Gnr. LYONS, B., R.G.A.
31245 Gnr. LEFCOVITCH, H., R.F.A.
136704 Gnr. LANDA, A., R.G.A.
209106 Dvr. LEVI, J., R.G.A.
134071 Dvr. LEVI, S., R.G.A.
140187 Gnr. LEVY, S., R.G.A.
178236 Dvr. LEVY, S., 17th D.A.C.
124910 Dvr. LEWIS, N., 78th Bde.
172839 Gnr. LESTER, S., 164th Siege Bty.
631245 Dvr. LEFCOVITCH, 242nd Army Bde.
111959 Gnr. LIEBMAN, J., 213th Siege Bty.
146627 Dvr. LEVY, C., 47th D.A.C.
383834 Dvr. LEVINE, E., No. 6 A.A. Coy.
146627 Dvr. LEVY, C., 236th Bde.
140616 Dvr. LEVY, N., 27th Bde.
154081 Dvr. LEVIN, A., D.A.C.
931483 Gnr. LEAPMAN, A., C/170th Bde.
177772 Gnr. LEVENE, A., C/170th Bde.
911515 Dvr. LEWINSTEIN, J., A/38 B.A.C., R.F.A.
153051 L/Bdr. LEVY, J., 9th D.A.C.
624572 Dvr. LEVY, J., 120th Army Bde.
313387 Gnr. LEAVY, H., 1/1st Highland Hy. By.
134974 Gnr. LEVENE, S., H.T.M.B.
189627 Dvr. LUBRICK, H., 9th Div. A.C.
93537 Dvr. LAZARUS, J., 13th Bde., R.G.A.
651961 Dvr. LIPTON, N., 169th A.F.A.
102279 Gnr. LEVY, A. N., R.G.A.
79799 Gnr. LEVY, H., 142nd Bty. R.G.A.
52593 Gnr. LYONS, J., 69th Bty.
31217 Gnr. LENNARD, H., C/117th Bde.
Gnr. LEVISON, A., R.H.A.
196197 Gnr. LEVISON, A. J.
21682 Gnr. LINKE, M., B/251st.
24348 Gnr. LEAVY, M. L., 114th T.M.B.
116678 Gnr. LESKS, A., 174th Bde.
706828 Dvr. LEVY, J., 330th Bde.
720359 Gnr. LEFKOWITCH, A., 66th D.A.C.
720378 Gnr. LYONS, J., 66th D.A.C.
78712 Gnr. LINK, J.
173472 Dvr. LEVY, J. F. S., 12th D.A.C.
L/14645 Dvr. LISSNER, J., 40th D.A.C.
41982 Gnr. LEVINE, S., 163rd Bty.
162804 Gnr. LEVINE, H., V/20th T.M.B.
307541 Gnr. LEWIS, J., 126th Hy. Bty.
143294 Gnr. LAZARUS, I., 19th S.B., R.G.A.
179467 Gnr. LEWIS, A., L. Siege Pk.
51375 Gnr. LEVINE, M., A/AA Bty.
61230 Dvr. LEWIS, H., 38th Hy. Bty.
135069 Gnr. LEVY, G. M., 23rd Siege By. R.G.A.
337310 Bdr. LINSKILL, C., 1/1st Wessex Bty., R.G.A.
129704 Gnr. LYONS, S., 101st Siege Bty.
191661 Gnr. LETOVITCH, P., 23rd Bde.
707383 Dvr. LEE, L., 37th D.A.C.
17825 Gnr. LEEF, L. J., 177th Siege Bty.
172118 Gnr. LEVINE, S., 33rd Siege Bty.
178691 Gnr. LEVEY, L., 126th Siege Bty.
144521 L/Bdr. LEWIS, H., 3rd Siege Bty.
34087 Bdr. LUPER, J., 108th Bty.
14573 Bdr. LUPER, M., 50th Bde.
28027 Dvr. LEVER, A., 50th Bde.
95161 Dvr. LUCAS, N., 52nd Bde.

Royal Regiment of Artillery.—*Continued.*

77125 Dvr. LEVER, L., A/91st Bde.
39142 Dvr. LYONS, J., 101st Bde.
48447 Gnr. LEE, H., 2/23rd T.M.B.
84913 Dvr. LAUDER, J. H., Amn. Col.
34466 Dvr. LALINSKY, E., Amn. Col.
219970 Dvr. LEWIS, A., 48th Div. Amn. Col.
35032 Dvr. LEWIS, W., A/96th Bde.
7144 A/Bdr. LEVY, B., D/96th Bde.
28720 Dvr. LEVY, N., C/96th Bde.
61116 Dvr. LEWIS, D., 26th Div. Amn. Col.
122 Dvr. LEVY, H., 47th Lond. Div. Amn. Cl.
60628 Dvr. LEWIS, J., D/110th Bde.
60870 Gnr. LYONS, P. I., 112th Bde.
46198 Bdr. LIPTON, I., 18th Bde. 59th Bty.
127171 Gnr. LEWIS, H.,* A/177th Bde.
L/40077 Gnr. LEWIS, J., C/180th Bde.
40673 Dvr. LEVY, S., D/180th Bde.
242054 Gnr. LEVEY, W., 2nd Bty. R.F.A.
651691 Gnr. LUPTON, M., R.F.A.
179001 Gnr LYONS, M., R.F.A.
267759 L/Bdr. LEVEY, R. B., R.F.A.
135069 Gnr. LEVY, M., R.G.A.
139632 Cpl. LISSACK, M., R.G.A.
89050 Dvr. LEVY, H., B/84th.
39162 Gnr. LANG, H., R.F.A.
337310 Gnr. LINSKILL, W., 199th. Bde.
89915 Gnr. LEVY, M.,
173472 Dvr. LEVY, J. F. S., R.F.A.
211188 Pnr. LIGHTMAN, A., R.G.A.
126119 Gnr. LEWIS, M., 10th Bde.
537019 Pte. LANGIN, M., 10th Bde.
84418 Dvr. LELYVELD, J., R.G.A.
960729 Bdr. LEE, J., R.F.A.
241077 Gnr. LANGER, P., 20th Bde.
236535 Gnr. LEVY, M., 250th Bde.
832112 Sdlr. LEVI, J., 306th Bde.
102315 Gnr. LAZARUS, L.,* R.G.A.
236197 Gnr. LEVY, S.,* R.F.A.
3316 Dvr. LEVENE, J., 3/1st.
142166 Gnr. LEVENTHAL, R.F.A.
731105 Gnr. LEVI, R.F.A.
T1/3079 Dvr. LEVER, C., 31st D.A.C.
67972 Gnr. LEBERMAN, A., 85th Sge. Bty.
881681 Dvr. LEVY, 89th Bde. R.F.A.
59862 Gnr. LAMB, C. H., H.Q., R.A.
16682 Gnr. LEVY, D., R.F.A.
184785 Dvr. LEVY, C., R.G.A.
15972 Dvr. LAZOURSA, D., R.F.A.
296452 Bdr. LESSER, J., R.G.A.
180808 Gnr. LEWIS, S., R.F.A.
254515 Gnr. LEE, E., R.F.A.
109551 Gnr. LOUIS, C., R.F.A.
211283 Gnr. LANDESMAN, H., 24th Sge. Bty.
112574 Gnr. LEVISON, J., R.F.A.
236888 Gnr. LEWIS, J., 9th D.A.C.
198135 Dvr. LEVY, H., R.F.A.
211389 Dvr. LAX, S., R.F.A.

225760 Gnr. LAUDEMAN, H., 4th Sge. By. R.G.A.
248070 Gnr. LEVIN, J.
218996 Gnr. LEVY, L., 53rd Bty. R.F.A.
40409 Cadet LESTWICK, R.
332112 Sdlr. LEVY, J., R.F.A.
194581 Gnr. LEVY, J., S.B.A.C.
706828 Dvr. LEVY, J., R.F.A.
28720 Dvr. LEVY, N., R.F.A.
57255 Dvr. LEVY, A., 57th L.T.M.B.
203082 Dvr. LEVINE, W., 126th L.T.M.B.
47696 Gnr. LEVEY, A., 217th Bde. H.Q.
253387 Dvr. LEVENE, B. P., 210th Bde. R.F.A.
804 Dvr. LEVY, R.H.A.
131540 Bomb. LANDES, H., R.G.A.
199888 Dvr. LYONS, L.
127776 Dvr. LINSKILL, I.
20446 B.S.M. LEAVEY, G. R., R.F.A.
36941 Gnr. LEE, S., R.F.A.
191074 A/Bdr. LIBERSON, S., R.F.A.
2706 Gnr. LEVAN, H., R.G.A.
83156 Gnr. LEVENE, L., R.G.A.
114393 Dvr. LEVENSTON, M., R.F.A.
58681 Gnr. LEVISON, R., R.G.A.
6922 Gnr. LEVY, A., R.F.A.
37779 Bdr. LEVY, H., R.F.A.
13146 Gnr. LEVY, J., R.F.A.
89915 Gnr. LEVY, M., R.G.A.
83297 Gnr. LEVY, P., R.G.A.
44669 Dvr. LEWIS, L., R.F.A.
956419 Dvr. LEFTURCH, A., R.F.A.
233677 Dvr. LASSMAN, R., R.F.A.
61584 Dvr. LAZARNICK, J., R.H.A.
77676 Bdr. LEWIS, H. B.
102279 Gnr. LEVY, A. M., R.G.A.
61116 Dvr. LEWIS, D., R.F.A.
44967 Gnr. LISSUCK, A., R.F.A.
146642 Gnr. LARNA, M.
197881 Gnr. LATOFSKY, H., R.F.A.
111959 Gnr. LIEBMAN, J., R.G.A.
46059 Gnr. LEVY, I., R.F.A.
876 Dvr. LIEBERMAN, E., 3/2nd D.A.C.
106311 Gnr. LEMAN, N., R.F.A.
216943 Gnr. LOVEGUARD, A. J., R.F.A.
144059 Dvr. LIPETZ, S.
181876 Gnr. LANGBEBEN, R.
181175 Dvr. LAVASCHILLI, J.
37108 Dvr. LOWER, J., R.F.A.
198136 Dvr. LEVENE, S.
5915 Dvr. LEVY, A., R.F.A.
7994 Gnr. LEVI, S., R.F.A.
115972 Dvr. LANZOUSSE, D., R.F.A.
317737 Gnr. LEVINE, C., R.F.A.
95161 Dvr. LUCAS, M., R.F.A.
195686 Gnr. LECHEM, E., R.F.A.
127171 Gnr. LEWIS, H., R.F.A.
155437 Gnr. LEWIS, A., R.F.A.
241883 Gnr. LINES, L., R.F.A.
211523 Gnr. LEWIS, E., R.F.A.

Royal Regiment of Artillery.—*Continued.*

661300 Gnr. LIPNOFSKY, S., R.F.A.
125043 Gnr. LEOPOLD, R.F.A.
211524 Dvr. LEVEY, B., R.G.A.
263535 Gnr. LEVY, M., R.F.A.
970085 Gnr. LEVY, H., R.F.A.
168294 Gnr. LEVINE, M., R.F.A.
198136 Gnr. LEVENE, S.
272787 Gnr. LAZARUS, T., R.F.A.
60671 Gnr. LEE, S., R.G.A.
81167 Sig. LAMB, A., R.G.A.
21186 Gnr. LANDERMAN, H., R.G.A.
162160 Gnr. LEVY, J., R.F.A.
50946 Dvr. LUGATER, M., R.F.A.
146641 Dvr. LEVENE, B.
80057 Gnr. MYEROWITZ, L., 141st Siege Bty.
142647 Gnr. MORRIS, R., 290th Bde.
405405 Gnr. MOMSHER, 178th T.M.B.
210730 Dvr. MUSTIN, A., A/173 Bde.
203750 Rfm. MARKSON, B., 17th L.T.M.B.
211930 Dvr. MORITZ, L., C571st Bde.
236779 Gnr. MILLER, D., 51st Bde.
189 Gnr. MOSS, J., 125th Siege Bty.
47682 Gnr. MATTHEWS, J., 170th Bde.
59858 Dvr. MALEM, L., 23rd D.A.C.
78260 Gnr. MANOF, I., No. 5 G.H.Q. Amn Pk.
41725 Dvr. MORRIS, L., 109th Heavy Bty.
139943 Gnr. MAIN, A., R.H.A.
75746 Gnr. MORLEY, J. E., D/119th.
S/Sgt. MENKIN, H. (D.C.M.), R.F.A.
38529 Gnr. MARKS, H., "T" Bty. R.H.A.
94098 Gnr. MORRIS, A., R.H.A.
54759 Dvr. MICHAEL, 18th Div. Amn. Col.
890915 Gnr. MENDELOWITCH, J. C., 230th Bde.
1471 Gnr. MARCUS, H.,* R.G.A., 132nd Bty.
81158 Gnr. MARKS, D., R.G.A.
Sig. MARCUSON, H.
211654 Dvr. MARK, K. M., R.F.A.
168565 Gnr. MARKOFSKY, D., R.F.A.
Pte. MEYERS, J., R.G.A.
77152 Dvr. MICHAELS, D.,* 18th Bty. R.F.A.
810105 Bdr. MILLER, M., Sig. Training Centre.
200126 Dvr. MYERS, P., 31/35th Bde.
156217 Gnr. MYERS, S., H.Q. R.G.A.
158019 Gnr. MORRIS, W., 317th Bty. R.G.A.
125619 Gnr. MILLINGS, M., 19th H. By. R.G.A.
83036 Gnr. MITCHELL, M., 2nd Bde.
51745 Bdr. MOSELEY, S., 24th Bde.
89817 Dvr. MYERSON, H., 52nd Bde.
98889 Dvr. MAXFIELD, A., 9th Div. Amn. Col.
57853 Dvr. MALLIN, L., 102nd Bde.
89554 Gnr. MINTZ, H., C/102nd Bde.
55253 Dvr. MINTZ, J., 23rd Div. Amn. Col.
67992 Dvr. MARKS, J., 19th D.A.C.
1666 Dvr. MARKS, S., 1st W.R. Bde.
17899 Dvr. MARCUS, D., 110th Bde. Amn. Col.
39541 Dvr. MILLER, J., 159th Bde.
Dvr. MARTISENSKIE, N., D/159th Bde.

L/21352 Sgt. MARKS, M. H. (M.M.), D/172nd Bde.
L/30404 Dvr. MORRIS, H., 173rd Bde.
41513 Dvr. MESSIAS, B/186th Bde.
83036 Gnr. MICHAEL, M., 2nd Bde.
30688 Gnr. MUSCOVITCH, J., 36th Div. Am. Col.
22366 Gnr. MORRIS, S., 56th Sge. Bty. R.G.A.
45890 Dvr. MYERS, A., 189th Bde.
651914 Dvr. MINSKY, J., 41st D.A.C.
84819 Gnr. MORRIS, D.,* B/190th Bde.
T/1/4764 Gnr. MORRIS, A., B/65th Bde.
2896 Gnr. MOSS, 12th D.A.C.
3495 Gnr. MARCUS, A., B/302nd Bde.
3496 Dvr. MARCUS, A., B/302nd Bde.
2662 Dvr. MOSS, J., B/302nd Bde.
177560 Gnr. MENDELEFSKY, A., C/310th Bde.
17890 Dvr. MARCUS, L., 166th Bde.
L/9835 Dvr. MILLER, R., 30th D.A.C.
217465 Gnr. MARKSON, L., V/24th T.M.B.
60436 Gnr. MARKS, M., 121st Siege Bty.
73671 Gnr. MARKS, B., H.Q., 24th H.A. Group.
125040 Gnr. MYERS, A., B/152nd Bde.
9237 Gnr. MOSES, J., 160th Bde.
Cpl. MOSES, G. (M.M.), R.F.A.
940585 Gnr. MYERS, S., 293rd Bde.
173523 Spr. MILLER, E., 330th Bde.
720409 Gnr. MITCHELL, M., 66th D.A.C.
720403 Gnr. MILLER, P., 66th D.A.C.
5251 Dvr. MORRIS, E., 36th D.A.C.
386051 Gnr. MOSS, J., 62nd Bde.
2264 Gnr. MYERS, 2nd T.M.B.
147043 Gnr. MIDOVITCH, P., V/1 T.M.B.
134291 Gnr. MORRIS, H., 335th Siege Bty.
284134 Gnr. MYERS, J., B/AA Bty.
139551 Cpl. MYERS, L., N. Amn. Pk.
180045 Sig. MISHON, H., C/174th R.F.A.
140692 Bdr. MOSCOVITCH, E., 101st Siege. Bty.
153244 Gnr. MICHAELS, 283rd Sge. Bty. R.G.A.
62812 Gnr. MORRIS, A., 12th A.S.P.
172176 Gnr. MOOCHNICK, L., 48th Siege Bty.
179920 Dvr. MOLEN, A., 169th A.F.A.
781828 Dvr. MARKS, 49th D.A.C.
210973 Gnr. MORRIS, L., 109th Hy. Bty.
134473 Gnr. MICOSKI, J., 131st Hy. Bty.
77854 Gnr. McKENNELL, J., 208th Bty., R.G.A.
133090 Gnr. MEYER, E., R.G.A. "G" A.A. By.
84865 Gnr. MOSS, J., 199th Hy. Bty.
96214 Gnr. MILLER, R.G.A.
6644 Gnr. MANNASSAH, F., R.F.A.
104039 Gnr. MORRIS, J.,
156064 Gnr. MORRIS, R., R.F.A.
961077 Gnr. MARCUS, C., R.F.A.
961098 Dvr. MARCUS, A., R.F.A.
180251 Dvr. MILKOVITCH, J., R.F.A.
197731 Dvr. MARTIN, P., R.F.A.
173130 Sgt. MOSS, M. R., 86th Sge. Bty. R.G.A.
236835 Gnr. MARRICK, S., R.F.A.
288661 Gnr. MACNICK, D., R.H.A.
81158 Gnr. MARKS, D., R.G.A.

Royal Regiment of Artillery.—*Continued.*

130950 Gnr. MEBER, 2/1st Hy. Bty. R.F.A.
246844 Gnr. MAGNUS, B.,
165906 Gnr. MORAN, 5th Bty. R.F.A.
731115 Dvr. MOSLEN, G., R.A.A.
139551 Cpl. MILES, R.F.A.
227727 Gnr. MEST, A., R.F.A.
182215 Gnr. MENDOZA, M., 5th T.M.B.
249100 Dvr. MORRIS, J. A.,
2407 Gnr. MELNICK, A., R.F.A.
64536 Gnr. MENDOZA, S., R.G.A.
19643 Gnr. MORRIS, H., 10th R.G.A.
Cpl. MEAKIN, 146th Bde. R.F.A.
1251 Dvr. MARTIN, S., R.F.A.
147839 Gnr. MORRIS, G., R.F.A.
232811 Gnr. MACNIFKA, J., R.F.A.
21889 Dvr. MARKS, H., R.F.A.
178490 Gnr. MARCHINSKY, I., 2nd Welsh R.G.A.
Dvr. MARTIN, B.,* L. Bty., R.H.A.
48499 Gnr. MORRIS, S.,* 351st Sge. By. R.G.A.
3031 Gnr. MARSHACK, R.F.A.
221859 Gnr. MILLER, A., R.F.A.
178958 Gnr. MORTON, T. N.
178998 Dvr. MILLER, M., 42nd Bty. R.F.A.
14843 Bdr. MENKIN, H., R.F.A.
Gnr. MYERS, J. (M.S.M.), R.G.A.
122458 Dvr. MYERS, A., R.F.A.
21889 Dvr. MARKS, H., R.F.A.
154492 Gnr. MUSKATT, L., 19th Bty. R.F.A.
251601 Spr. MALAMED, W., 69th Bde. H.Q.
69753 Gnr. MOSES, A., 71st Hy. Bty.
44242 Gnr. MICHAELS, J., R.F.A.
745755 Bdr. MINEVSKY, G., R.F.A.
200013 Gnr. MENDELSON, M.
152436 Sig. MILLER, B., 52nd Bty. R.F.A.
170678 Dvr. MOSS, B., 4th R.F.A.
174534 Gnr. MENCOFSKY, H., 211th Bde.
85768 Gnr. MOSES, M., 163rd Sge. Bty. R.G.A.
195688 Gnr. MARKS, S.
6252 Dvr. MARKS, S. F., R.H.A.
147043 Gnr. MEDOVITCH, P. B., T.M.B., R.F.A.
178249 Gnr. MEROPOLSKY, H., R.G.A.
207338 Gnr. MASCAVITZ, G.
45610 Gnr. MENDELSOHN, H.
207338 Dvr. MOSCOVITZ, G.
87391 Dvr. NEWMAN, S., 64th Bde.
189641 Dvr. MALDOFSKY, R.F.A.
Sgt. MARKS, G. (M.S.M.), R.G.A.
190045 Dvr. MISDON, H. T., R.F.A.
144048 Gnr. MEYER, R., R.G.A.
177096 Gnr. MENDOZA, M. G., R.G.A.
173522 Gnr. MILLER, E., R.F.A.
45890 Gnr. MYERS, A., R.F.A.
91803 Dvr. MUMMATT, M., R.F.A.
172375 Gnr. MENDELSSOHN, M.,* R.H.A.
41513 Dvr. MESSIAS, R., R.F.A.
84819 Gnr. MORRIS, D., R.F.A.
210730 Dvr. MUSLIN, H., R.F.A.

178911 Gnr. MORDEN, S., R.G.A.
149943 Dvr. MAYREM, A., R.H.A.
122524 Dvr. MARCHANT, J., R.F.A.
107543 Gnr. MARCUSON, P., R.G.A.
245039 Dvr. MILLER, M., R.F.A.
236635 Bdr. MARRICK, S., R.F.A.
81158 Gnr. MARKS, D., 20th R.G.A.
32366 Bdr. MORRIS, S., R.G.A.
180376 Dvr. MEIDER, G., R.F.A.
125091 Gnr. MYERS, A. S., R.F.A.
Cpl. MOSES, C. (D.C.M.).
313624 Gnr. MICHAELOVSKY, F., R.G.A.
400258 Dvr. MARKS, J., L.T.M.B.
259350 Gnr. MENDELSOHN, A., R.F.A.
245111 Gnr. MICHINSKY, I., R.F.A.
235470 Gnr. MOSS, H., R.F.A.
299601 Gnr. MARKS, H., R.F.A.
Gnr. MALHOLLAND, A., R.F.A.
Sgt. MOSS, J. E. (M.S.M.), R.G.A.
Gnr. MASTERS, H., R.F.A.
258993 Gnr. MARDER, S.
88711 Gnr. MARTIN, M., R.F.A.
122524 Dvr. MARCHANT, J., R.F.A.
140612 Gnr. MOSES, L.,* R.G.A.
6178 Dvr. NATHAN, A., B/156th Bde.
302543 Rfm. NORMAN, G. F. N., 169th Bde.
79138 Gnr. NATHAN, M., 135th Sge. Bty. R.G.A.
307023 Gnr. NATHAN, N. S., 111st Sge. By. R.G.A.
41978 Gnr. NEIMAN, G., 251st Sge. Bty.
624113 Dvr. NATHAN, G., 120th Army Bde.
72076 Gnr. NORDWIND, 169th Bty. R.G.A.
68417 Gnr. NATHAN, B., 157th Sge. Bty. R.G.A.
230 Gnr. NATHAN, N., R.G.A.
B/95161 Dvr. NATHAN, L., 50th Bty.
15825 Gnr. NATHAN, A.
85183 Dvr. NELSON, R.H.A.
125125 Gnr. NATHAN, M., 3rd "C" R. Bde.
52635 Dvr. NATHAN, J., R.G.A., 29th Bde.
43711 Dvr. NATHAN, H., R.F.A.
178958 Dvr. NEDELMAN, J. M., R.G.A.
164910 Gnr. NEWMAN, M.
180445 Dvr. NEWMAN, A., C/321st Bde. R.F.A.
194056 Gnr. NORVICK, R., R.F.A.
86886 Gnr. NATHAN, R., R.G.A.
204079 Gnr. NATHAN, A.
Gnr. NATHAN, R. E., 32nd Coy. R.G.A.
197966 Gnr. NATHAN, I.
222 Bdr. NATHAN, V. J., R.H.A.
200403 Dvr. NILLES, P., 66th D.A.C.
301861 Gnr. NIMAN, M., R.G.A.
186462 Dvr. NEWMAN, L., R.F.A.
181161 Dvr. NAZAROFF, E., R.F.A.
45909 Dvr. NATHAN, L., R.F.A.
197812 Gnr. NELSON,
22827 Gnr. NEWMAN, J. H., R.F.A.
876739 Dvr. NEWMAN, J., R.F.A.
102376 Dvr. NEIDER, J., R.F.A.
272760 Gnr. NEWMAN, I.

Royal Regiment of Artillery.—*Continued.*

71815 Gnr. NATHAN, F., R.G.A.
48208 Cpl. OLIVE, N., 103rd Bde.
146 Gnr. OSCAR, J., 54th Bty.
45495 Gnr. OWEN, S., 40th Div. Amn. Col.
154030 Gnr. OXENBURGH, M., 276th Bde.
494 Gnr. OPPENHEIM, H. C., 43rd H.A.G. R.G.A.
200018 Gnr. O'KERR, S., 51st Bde. R.F.A.
11881 Gnr. OPITZ, H., 105th Howit. Bty.
32713 Gnr. OSTROFF, I., R.G.A.
119950 Dvr. O'ROURKE, J.
810004 Gnr. OSTERMAN, L., R.F.A.
127983 Gnr. ORENSTEIN, J., R.F.A.
191837 Gnr. OSTERMAN, H., R.G.A.
68261 Dvr. PRICE, L., 17th Div. Amn. Col.
47068 Bdr. PHILLIPS, H., 18th Bde. 59th Bty.
1063 Sgt. PEARCE, M., 5th London F.A.B.
972 Gnr. PEARLMAN, J., 12th Motor M.G. By
27017 Dvr. PELIKANSKE, N., A/159th Bde.
107400 Dvr. POLLACK, M., A/179th Bde.
158152 Dvr. PHILLIPS, H., 311th Bde.
71208 Gnr. PARKS, S., 116th Sge. Bty. R.G.A.
926034 Staff-Sgt. PHILLIPS, J., 290th Bde.
821306 Gnr. PEARL, L., 59th D.A.C.
947731 Gnr. PHILLIPS, J., 40th Amn. Sub. Pk.
236508 Gnr. PEREZ, M. R., B/186th Bde. R.F.A.
2210172 Dvr. PARK, J., B/295th Bde.
39891 Gnr. POSNER, N., 94th Siege Bty.
197233 Sig. PHILLIPS, P.,* 42nd Bde.
156824 Gnr PAPIER, A., 147th Sge Bty. R.G.A.
76658 Cpl. PHILLIPS, 23rd Bde. R.G.A.
10336 Bdr. POPKINS, D/69th Bde.
239950 Gnr. PICKERCHICK, J. E., 26th By. R.F.A.
103803 Gnr. PEARLMAN, L., 21st Heavy Bty.
159669 Gnr. PAYMAN, S., 177th Bde.
70503 Gnr. PHILLIPS, M., 14th Heavy Bty.
61225 Dvr. PHILLIPS, S.
183245 Gnr. PRINS, A., R.F.A.
Gnr. PHILLIPS, B.
646693 Gnr. PLIENER, T., No. 8 R. Bde. R.H.A.
253380 Sig. PERETZ, J., Sig. Training Centre.
172906 Sig. PLIENER, J., Sig. Training Centre.
181322 Dvr. POLLONSKY, J., 22nd Res. Bty.
181165 Dvr. PIVKO, I.
225054 Gnr. PHILLIPS, H., "D" Bty 102nd Bde.
125200 A/Bdr. PARR, F. C., 3rd "C" R. Bde.
58844 Dvr. PASKIN, R.F.A. 296th Bde.
88427 Dvr. PRAR, R.F.A. 1094th Bty.
195536 Dvr. PASS, G., R.F.A.
169211 Gnr. PRESSMAN, W., 23rd R.F.A.
104419 Gnr. PURTON, D., R.F.A.
881898 Gnr. POLLOCK, M., R.F.A.
208635 Dvr. PARK, J., A/291 Bde.
236508 Gnr. PERCY, M. R.
211848 Gnr. PHILLIPS, R., R.G.A.
542197 Dvr. POSNER, J., R.F.A.
3213 Dvr. PHILLIPS, A. E., 3/3rd W. Lancs. Bde. R.F.A.

802615 Dvr. PARKIN, H., R.F.A.
58615 Dvr. PARISH, P., R.F.A.
144726 Gnr. PHILLIPS, R., R.F.A.
86616 Dvr. PLOTZE, H., R.F.A.
165497 Gnr. PHILLIPS, D., R.G.A.
22561 Gnr. PHILLIPS, P. D., 23rd R.F.A.
197808 Gnr. PRONT, S.
198044 Gnr. POSTER, H.
2961 B.S.M. POWELL, B.
173490 Dvr. PHILLIPS, W.
195687 Gnr. PHILLIPS, R., R.F.A.
197882 Gnr. PALASTINE, I., R.F.A.
195856 Dvr. POLACK, L., D.A.C.
225024 Gnr. PHILLIPS, H.
84851 Gnr. PETERS, L., 79th Bty. R.G.A.
2/925 Bdr. POOL, M. P., R.F.A.
197944 Dvr. PHILLIPS, M., R.H.A.
1955 Dvr. PHILLIPS, J. E., R.F.A.
234972 Gnr. PENN, J., 38th Bde. R.F.A.
165271 Dvr. PLIENER, J., R.F.A.
741580 Dvr. PLOTTEL, J., R.F.A.
53932 Gnr. PESIDORE, P., R.F.A.
237069 Dvr. PERLSTONE, J., R.F.A.
133145 Gnr. PRINS, A., R.F.A.
178338 Gnr. PHILLIPS, S., R.F.A.
235625 Dvr. POWER, J., R.F.A.
144370 Gnr. PHILLIPS, A. M., R.G.A.
209061 Gnr. PHILLIPS, A. P., R.G.A.
234008 Dvr. PICKLE, R.F.A.
169173 Gnr. PLASKOFSKY, A., R.F.A.
198927 Gnr. POLLICOFF, J., R.F.A.
199695 Gnr. PROVOST, J., R.F.A.
154921 Gnr. PHILLIPS, P., R.G.A.
200001 Dvr. PEREZE, M., R.F.A.
39653 Gnr. ROSE, J., 45th Sge. Bty. R.G.A.
L/6171 Gnr. ROSENBERG, L., D/250th Bde.
139008 Cpl. RAISMAN, M. (M.M.), 285th Sge. Bty. R.G.A.
19390 Dvr. RAPHAEL, S., 187th Bde.
Gnr. ROBINSON, F., 1/1st Low. R.G.A.
L/39396 Bdr. ROSENBERG, H. A., R.F.A.
139942 Gnr. ROSE, P., R.H.A.
36106 Dvr. REISS, I., R.F.A.
163510 Gnr. RAYNER, B.,* R.G.A.
215502 Dvr. ROSENBERG, S., 44th Bde.
83207 Gnr. ROSE, M.,
57854 Gnr. REDWOOD, M., 41st Bty. R.F.A.
Dvr. ROSE, H., R.F.A.
3842 Dvr. RUBINSTEIN, B., 106th Prov. Bty.
136204 Sig. ROSENBURG, Y., Sig. Train. Centre.
36107 Gnr. ROSENGARD, M., 180th Bde. R.F.A.
209382 Dvr. RUBIN, J., 24th Bty.
201128 Gnr. ROSEN, D., R.G.A.
D/205603 Gnr. RUBIN, L., "V" Bty. R.G.A.
142768 A/Bdr. RADJES, B. G., 72nd Div. Artilly.
2974 Gnr. ROSS, G., 291st Bde.
208834 Dvr. RENOVITCH, R., R.F.A.

Royal Regiment of Artillery.—*Continued.*

127447 Gnr. ROSENBERG, R., R.F.A.
120403 Gnr. ROSENTHAL, R.G.A.
211947 Dvr. RAINS, J., R.F.A.
30156 Gnr. RUSSELL, J., R.F.A.
690213 Bdr. RICHMOND, A., R.F.A.
156284 Dvr. ROSENBLUM, M., 29th Bty. R.F.A.
186799 Sgt. RICHMAN, A., R.F.A.
81288 Cpl. RABINOVITCH, J. E., 9th Div. R.F.A.
83489 Gnr. ROSENTHAL, S., 20th Div. Amn. Cl.
53932 Gnr. RISIDORE, L. B.,* 98th Bde.
55136 Gnr. RUBEN, A., 105th Bde.
66099 Dvr. ROSEN, A., A/108th Bde.
62811 Dvr. REES, A., 18th Bde. 59th Bty.
L/9760 Dvr. RALPH, H., B/169th Bde.
17890 Dvr. RAPHAEL, S., 171st Bde.
44796 Bdr. ROSEN, B., 189th Bde.
46348 Dvr. RUBINSTEIN, M., 40th Div. Amn. Cl.
660 Gnr. REUBENS, L., N. Riding Hy. Bty.
  Dvr. ROSE, A., D/95th Bde.
161795 Gnr. RADNONSKI, S., A/51st Bde.
208834 Dvr. RENOVITCH, D., 18th D.A.C.
178994 Dvr. REEMER, M., 87th Bde.
7725 Bdr. ROZELAR, J., 4th H.A. Group, R.G.A.
127415 Dvr. ROSENHEA, S., D.A.C.
931608 Gnr. ROSS, G., 291st Bde.
147009 Gnr. ROSENTHAL, H., H.Q. Div. Art.
137531 Gnr. ROSENBERG, G., 80th Bty.
27317 Gnr. ROSS, J., 121st T.M.B.
195621 Gnr. ROSENBERG, D., 2nd D.A.C.
H/2/138763 Gnr. ROSENTHAL, A., 28th S.B.A. Cl.
143480 Bdr. ROSENBERG, A., 6th Siege. Bty. R.G.A.
49031 Gnr. ROSEN, L., "O." A.A. Bty. 107th S.
143454 Gnr. ROBINSON, M., 47th Bde. R.F.A
72595 Gnr RIFKIN, B., 129th Siege Bty.
750189 Cpl. ROSENTHAL, J., 504th Bty.
145597 Gnr. ROSTOWSKI, 17th Hy. Bty. R.G.A.
147643 Gnr. REICHMAN, B., 158th Siege Bty.
248299 Sig. REFSON, R., R.F.A.
273569 Dvr. REEVES, J., R.F.A.
960104 Dvr. RICHLANDS, S., R.F.A.
SR/346 Gnr. ROSE, W., R.G.A.
236848 Gnr. ROSENBERG, 320th Bde. R.F.A.
189707 Gnr. ROSENBERG, R.F.A.
244416 Gnr. ROSENTHAL, T.,* R.G.A.
183145 Gnr. RINS, A., R.F.A.
111814 Gnr. ROSENBERG, H., R.F.A.
136557 Bdr. RUBINSTEIN, S., R.F.A.
879 Gnr. RITTER, A., R.F.A.
2519 Gnr. REUBEN, M., R.F.A.
111827 Dvr. RIDLEY, R.F.A.
148135 Fitter ROSENFELD, L., R.F.A.
2038 Dvr. RUDSTON, A., R.F.A.
78774 Gnr. RICHLAND, M., R.G.A.
137415 Dvr. ROSENHEAD, S.
77133 Gnr. ROSE E., R.G.A.
319061 Gnr. RUSSELL, F. G., R.G.A.
193370 Gnr. ROSENZWEIG, J.
127337 Gnr. ROSENHEAD, L.
152006 A/Bdr. ROUTLEDGE, G. E., R.F.A.
228537 Dvr. RUDELL, P. S., R.F.A.
104833 Gnr. RAYMON, R.G.A.
461423 Dvr. ROTHENBERG, H., R.F.A.
78719 Gnr. RAPAPORT, B., R.G.A.
133182 Gnr. RICHMOND, L., R.G.A.
86096 Gnr. ROSE, J., R.G.A.
63997 Gnr. REVEL, W., R.G.A.
  Gnr. RUNCIMAN, W. M., R.F.A.
311312 Gnr. RUBINS, L., R.G.A.
  Bdr. ROSENBLOOM, S., R.F.A.
44798 Bdr. ROSEN, R.F.A.
18359 Dvr. RONOFF, C., R.F.A.
031999 Gnr. ROSENTHAL, N., R.F.A.
291842 Dvr. REUBEN, S., R.H.A.
194110 Gnr. ROSSEN, H., R.F.A.
136087 Gnr. ROSENBAND, I., R.F.A.
178551 Dvr. RITCHES, R.F.A.
  Bdr. RIFFKIN, A., R.G.A.
881633 Dvr. REUBENS, A.
12737 Dvr. ROSENBERG, L.
45777 Gnr. REEVES, C.
176063 Gnr. ROSENBERG, I.
170372 Dvr. REUBEN, G.
20746 Bdr. RICHE, J., R.F.A.
242932 Gnr. ROSENBERG, A.
91974 Gnr. ROSENBERG, D.
91544 Gnr. ROSE, L.
91341 Gnr. ROTHBERG, A.
307031 Cpl. ROBINSON, F.
192117 Dvr. ROSE, A.
  Cpl. ROSENTHAL, I. (D.C.M.), R.F.A.
91954 Gnr. RICHES, M.
193048 Dvr. ROSE, G.
20104 Gnr. ROSEN, M. L., R.F.A.
170604 Dvr. ROTH, M., R.F.A.
177984 Dvr. REES, H.
166860 Gnr. ROMAIN, A.
1324 Gnr. RICKLER, M.
636729 Dvr. ROGAT, J. A., R.F.A.
189707 Dvr. ROSERBURG, R.F.A.
181913 Dvr. RUDDLINDER, A., R.F.A.
83159 Dvr. ROSINOW, C., R.F.A.
173212 Gnr. ROSENBERG, M.
139542 Gnr. RONALD, J.
139008 Bdr. RUSMAN, M.
104998 Gnr. ROSENSTEIN, M.
63410 Gnr. ROSENBAUM, A.,* R.G.A.
31183 Dvr. SOLOMON, M., 3rd D.A.C.
5542 Dvr. SOLOMONS, J., 173rd T.M.B.
140696 Gnr. SYMON, A., 62nd Bde.
194716 Gnr. SIMMONDS, S., 12th D.A.C.
130850 Dvr. SIMMONDS, R., 16th D.A.C.
221089 Gnr. SOLOMON, L., 168th Bde.
311626 Gnr. SAFFER, J., 9th H.B., R.G.A.

Royal Regiment of Artillery.—*Continued.*

138892 Dvr. SEIGLEMEN, J., B/AA Bty.
71948 Dvr. SUSWIN, J., 25th Heavy Bty.
135071 Gnr. SHUMAN, A., 23rd Siege Bty.
128681 Gnr. SAVITZ, J.,* 232nd Sge. Bty. R.G.A.
146642 Gnr. SARNA, M., 2/1st N. Midland H. By.
112040 Gnr. SCHNEIDER, R., 240th Sge. Bty.
167715 Gnr. SHALGOSKY, I., 244th Sge. Bty.
128134 Gnr. SILVER, D., 25th Siege Bty.
154215 Gnr. SAKOSHANSKY, J., 219th Sge. Bty.
Dvr. SILVERSTONE, P., D/293rd A.F.A.
182350 Bdr. STONE, H., A/307th R.F.A.
Batty.-Sgt.-Major SAGAR, J. E. (M.S.M.), R.G.A.
69898 Gnr. STEIN, L., H.Q. A.A. 3rd Army.
54974 Gnr. STEPINSKY, B., 76th T.M.B.
127295 Gnr. SHERIDAN, E. 11th D.A.C.
153701 Gnr. STAAL, S., 7th Sge. Bty. R.G.A.
169550 Gnr. SESENWINE, W., 32nd Siege Bty.
330068 Bdf. STONE, J., "Q" A.A.Bty.
944038 Gnr. SINGER, M., D/147th Bdr.
53451 Gnr. SAMUELS, M. (M.M.), 28th Bde. R.G.A.
223566 Gnr. SINGER, L., R.F.A.
141828 Gnr. SOLOMON, J., D/11 Bty. R.F.A.
235857 Gnr. SHIELS, H., 96th Bde. R.F.A.
237149 Dvr. SCHWARTZ, M., B/153 Bde. R.F.A.
68181 Gnr. SUMMERFIELD, J., 107th Bty.
14286 Dvr. STONE, S., 7th Div. Amn. Col.
86088 Dvr. SILVER, R., 63rd Bde.
83939 Dvr. SOLOMON, A., 3rd Sec. Div. Am. C.
37801 Dvr. SHANK, J., 84th Bde.
14532 Dvr. SPILLMAN, L., 101st Bde.
44509 Gnr. SYMONS, A., 20th Hy. By. R.G.A.
Dvr. SUGAR, H., 23rd Div. Amn. Col.
49686 Bdr. SEGER, A., "A" Bty. 107th Bde.
90603 Dvr. SIMMONS, M., 148th Bty.
42005 Dvr. SOLOMON, A. M., 25th Div. Am. C.
L/43011 Dvr. SIMMONS, N., B/180th Bde.
L/39250 Gnr. SIMMONS, S.,* C/180th Bde.
10676 Dvr. SINGER, D., 30th D.A.C.
L/43713 Bdr. SOLOMONS, A. E., B/161st Bde.
13256 Dvr. SPIERS, C., B/162nd Bde.
19314 Dvr. SAMPSON, H., C/163rd Bde.
1875 Cpl. SHAPIRO, H. R., 119th Bde. Am. C.
42 Dvr. SHENKEN, I., D/256th Bde.
1212 Dvr. SIPPETT, S., C/281st Bde.
210349 Gnr. SPARK, S., 29th Bde. R.F.A.
248568 Gnr. SELBY, M. H., 19th H.T.M.
180055 Dvr. SANGER, B., 84th Army Bde.
1743 Gnr. SACKE, J., 74th Siege Bty.
200960 Gnr. SNYDER, M., 275th Siege Bty.
79587 Gnr. SAMUELS, S., 239th Siege Bty.
159503 Gnr. SIMSOHN, H., 72nd Bde. R.G.A.
68477 Gnr. SAMUELS, H.,* 151st S. By. R.G.A.
60453 Gnr. SLESINGER, F., 20th Div. Amn. Pk.
83933 Dvr. SOLOMON, A., 18th Div. Amn. Pk.
11628 Gnr. SALTER, J., 24th Bty.

Gnr. SAMUELS, I., 171st Light T.M.B.
84239 Gnr. STEIN, D.,* 158th Bty.
169226 Dvr. SHENKINS, L., 11th D.A.C.
Gnr. STONE, D., R.G.A.
207200 Dvr. SANTEN, J.
83200 Gnr. SAMUELS, J., R.G.A.
Gnr. SEEGAR, W., R.G.A.
Gnr. SHINOWSKY, R.G.A.
Dvr. STIRLING, G., R.F.A.
Dvr. SAUNDERS, G., 33rd Bty. R.F.A.
Dvr. SAMUEL, M., 114th Bty. R.F.A.
S/Maj. SAPERE, M., R.H.A.
Pte. SUGARMAN, R., R.H.A.
165510 Dvr. SILBERG, A., 346th Bde. R.F.A.
18510 Dvr. SULLIVAN, L., No. 17 Res. Bty.
83042 Gnr. STIRLING, H., D.A.C.
36444 Dvr. SIMMONS, H., C/183rd Bde.
44866 Dvr. STONE, A., 189th Bde.
30545 Dvr. SCHNEIDER, A., 190th Bde.
178529 Bdr. SCHIFF, O., 2nd D.A.C.
L/29969 Dvr. SHAER, S. J. R., 178th Bde.
3507 Gnr. SHERMAN, N., C/302nd Bde.
3505 Gnr. SNELVA, M., C/302nd Bde.
3058 Gnr. SILVERMAN, J., C/302nd Bde.
1722 Gnr. SHERMAN, L., 60th T.M.B.
822 Gnr. SOLOMONS, S., 60th D.A.C.
88305 Gnr. SPALTER, J., "O" Bty. R.H.A.
118479 Dvr. STILLMAN, A., 11th D.A.S.P.
26799 Dvr. SLOWAY, B., 18th D.A.C.
111865 Gnr. SAPIER, D., 104th Bde.
155800 Gnr. SCHLAGER, M., 104th Bde.
28874 Gnr. SNIDERMAN, J., 30th T.M.B.
2172 Dvr. SHAER, M., 32nd T.M.B.
43713 Bdr. SOLOMONS, H. S., 161st Bde.
189902 Gnr. SAPIRO, M., A/112th Bde.
514 Gnr. SHRADER, H. L., 43rd H.A. G. R.G.A.
6621 Dvr. SHEPPHERD, W., 30th A.S.P.
111972 Dvr. SAPERIA, H., 500th How. Bty.
L/9239 Gnr. SANDERSON, T., 169th Bde.
Cpl. SAMUEL, J. M. (M.M.), R.F.A.
925703 Gnr. SLUIS, J., 290th Bde.
931483 Gnr. SEAPMAN, A., 291st Bde.
940364 Dvr. SILVERSTONE, R., 293rd Bde.
875 Cpl. SHIPRO, H., A/122nd Bde.
94403 Gnr. SINGER, M., 332nd Bde.
156642 Dvr. SMORODINSKY, R., 66th D.A.C.
181320 Dvr. SPECKTOR, M., 24th Res. Bty.
181321 Dvr. SPECKTOR, C. A., 24th Res. Bty.
173382 Gnr. SANTZ, H., 13th Res. Bty.
210064 Dvr. SHELTER, H., A/103rd Bde.
203913 Gnr. STONE, L., T/48 T.M. Bty.
101338 Gnr. SAMUELS, S., 197th S Bty. R.G.A.
168091 Gnr. SOLLER, B., 3rd "C" Bde.
156843 Dvr. SPEAGAL, E., 3rd "C" Bde.
399 Dvr. SEGAL, N., 58th D.A.C.
42263 Dvr. SOLOMONS, 199th Heavy Bty.
210562 Dvr. SADOVITCH, R.F.A., 1094th Bty.

Royal Regiment of Artillery.—*Continued.*

111822 Dvr. STAMBOIS, R.F.A. "A" 16th Bde.
92389 Sgt. SOLOMON, R.G.A. 9th Bde.
173826 Dvr. SKIBBEN, L., R.G.A.
111333 Gnr. SAUNDERS, R.G.A., 9th Bde.
88669 Dvr. SMITH, H., R.F.A.
160909 Dvr. SYMONS, L., R.F.A.
29705 Gnr. SAUNDERS, J., R.G.A. 11th Coy.
72806 Gnr. SHARR, I., R.G.A.
210527 Dvr. SAUNDERS, R., R.F.A.
173382 Gnr. SANTY, H., R.F.A.
63648 Gnr. STEIN, J., 96th A.C.
292098 Gnr. SAMUELS, M., R.G.A.
    Gnr. SOLOMON, H., R.G.A.
107390 Dvr. STONE, J., R.F.A.
98582 Gnr. SHIMPOT, I., R.G.A., 43rd Sge. Bty.
1428 Gnr. SMITH, W. C., L.T.M.B.
19713 Dvr. SMITH, G. W., R.F.A.
17044 Gnr. SILVERMAN, S., 64th T.M.B.
83042 Dvr. STIRLING, H., D/83 R.F.A.
    Gnr. SINGER, S. B., 93rd Bde. R.F.A.
232386 Gnr. SOLOMON, M., R.G.A.
156237 Dvr. SILVER, 29th Bty. R.F.A.
162614 Gnr. SHEARE, S.,* R.G.A.
17486 Gnr. SYMONDS, L.T.M.B.
241357 Dvr. STERN, R.F.A.
200014 Sig. SIMONS, D., R.F.A.
19837 Dvr. SAMUEL, R.F.A.
896171 Gnr. SILBERG, A., H.T.M.
130850 Sig. SIMMONDS, R.
881565 Gnr. SHAFRAN, A., R.G.A.
    Gnr. SAMUEL, M., 114th Bty. R.F.A.
966659 Dvr. SIMLER, T., R.F.A. 336th Bde.
133159 Gnr. SCHWEITZER, P.,* R.G.A.
17922 Dvr. SAPIER, S., R.F.A.
201089 Gnr. SEIGELMAN, J., R.F.A.
7220 Sgt. STONEFIELD, G., 88th Squad. R.G.A.
252524 Cpl. SOLOMONS, J., 173rd L.T.M.B.
134976 Gnr. SANDFORD, M. S.,* 335th Siege Bty.
194083 Gnr. SPEAKMASTER, E.,* 50th Bde.
194085 Dvr. SILVER, C., R.F.A.
87598 Bdr. SMITH, H. G., 41st Bde. R.F.A.
961106 Dvr. SNELL, M., R.F.A.
166450 Gnr. STEINBERG, M., R.F.A.
2619 Dvr. STERNHEIM, A., R.F.A.
109152 Gnr. STERN, A. M., 153rd Hr. By. R.G.A.
6473 B.Q.M.S. SHERWOOD, J., 153rd Hr. Bty.
675867 Gnr. STILLER, M., 3/1st West Lancs. R.F.A.
161601 Gnr. SAMUEL, H. A., 331st S. Bty.
180055 Dvr. SOUBER, B., A/84th Army Bde.
156027 Gnr. SAFINSKI, J., 145th Hr. Bty.
116579 Dvr. SIMMONS, B., R.F.A.
43011 Dvr. SIMMONS, N., R.F.A.
89764 Gnr. SULLY, G., R.F.A.
2799 Gnr. SOLOSKY, J., 7th Res. Bde. R.F.A.
198266 Gnr. SCHINEBERG, 4th Siege Art.

752118 Gnr. SHINEBAERG, L., 54th Bty. R.F.A.
197600 Cadet SAMUEL, E. H., R.F.A.
237716 Gnr. SHIMMEN, S., 8th T.M.B.
205202 Gnr. SEEMAN, H., 285th Bde. R.F.A.
198015 Gnr. SCHNERKIN, A.
199798 Gnr. SILVERSTEIN, I.
198131 Gnr. SOLOMONS, C.
197715 Gnr. SOLOMONS, J.
173125 Gnr. SAENS,
200020 Gnr. SPIRO, H.
200033 Gnr. SCHLASNEY, H.
1427 Gnr. SIMMONS,
139426 Dvr. SPRINGER, R.H.A.
29544 Gnr. SALAMAN, A.
4649 Gnr. SEIGAR, H.
387 L/Cpl. SAADJOFFE, A.
216925 Gnr. SILVERMAN, H.
88448 Gnr. SCHOLKE, E., R.G.A.
636737 Dvr. SOLOMONS, N., R.F.A.
631250 Bdr. SPINK, D., R.F.A.
31615 Cpl. SNIPP, H., R.F.A.
178534 Dvr. STEPHANY, R.F.A.
221089 Gnr. SOLOMON, L., R.F.A.
149129 Gnr. SMOLLEN, H., R.F.A.
169227 Gnr. SHANKER, J.
111843 Dvr. STONEFIELD, L., 11th D.A.C.
234204 Dvr. SKYLINSKY, S., R.F.A.
115980 Dvr. STONE, B.
779103 Dvr. SELDIS, J.
195904 Dvr. STABINSKY, C.
    Sgt. SAMUEL, J. H. (M.M. and Bar), R.F.A.
179854 Gnr. SEMAINE, W.
961106 Dvr. SNEL, M.
199853 Dvr. SANDGROUND, L., R.F.A.
2758 Dvr. SHENKIN, A., R.F.A.
2227 Gnr. SMITH, P., R.F.A.
34466 Dvr. SALINSKY, E., R.F.A.
134926 Gnr. SPIRO, A., R.G.A.
181158 Gnr. SIMENTO, A., R.F.A.
    Gnr. SHERWOOD, H., 2/3rd Essex R.G.A.
247476 Gnr. SINGER, A., R.F.A.
935071 Gnr. SHUMAN, A., R.G.A.
36980 Gnr. STONE, H., R.F.A.
159681 Gnr. SOLOMON, L., R.G.A.
187924 Bdr. SYKES, B., R.G.A.
214491 Gnr. SOLOMONS, J., R.F.A.
237415 Gnr. SKITTEN, M., R.F.A.
135104 Gnr. SIMMON S, M., R.G.A.
593 Gnr. SIMONS, M.
144850 Dvr. SMITH, J., R.F.A.
181170 Dvr. SCHETER, D.
236839 Gnr. STYCOVITZ, S., R.F.A.
362689 Gnr. SHEFFMAN, S., R.G.A.
    Gnr. SAPIER, D. (D.C.M.), R.F.A.
238513 Gnr. SACOFF, M., R.F.A.
237069 Dvr. SILBERG, A., R.F.A.
101245 Gnr. SILVERTON, B., R.G.A.

Royal Regiment of Artillery.—*Continued.*

179162 Gnr. SOLOMONS, G., R.G.A.
236718 Gnr. SCHANIN, W., R.F.A.
241561 Dvr. STRASKING, I., R.G.A.
166575 Gnr. SOLOMONS, J., R.G.A.
L/29969 Gnr. SHAW, S. J., R.F.A.
       Dvr. SPRINGER, J., R.H.A.
119143 Gnr. SOLOMONS, G., R.G.A.
214589 Gnr. SMOLLON, M., R.G.A.
197965 Dvr. SLOTHENSKY, M., R.G.A.
155115 Gnr. STOLLOFF, R.F.A.
115980 Dvr. STONE, B., R.F.A.
190857 Dvr. SUMMERS, R.F.A.
353819 Gnr. STERNHEIM, H., R.G.A.
169396 Gnr. SALBSTEIN, H., R.G.A.
525157 Gnr. SCHOLTZ, W., R.F.A.
172834 Gnr. SIMON, S., R.G.A.
291477 Gnr SCHNEIDER, H., R.F.A.
144850 Dvr. SMITH, A. J., R.F.A.
663220 Dvr. SIMONS, M.
139336 Gnr. STONE, D., R.G.A.
  9227 Dvr. SHENKIN, I., R.F.A.
       Sgt. STEINGOLD, N. (M.M.), R.F.A.
269137 Rfm. SANKEWITZ, A.
233431 Dvr. SOMERFIELD, A.
225270 Gnr. SYMONS, L.
135785 Gnr. SAMUELS, N., R.F.A.
   557 Gnr. SEDER, H., R.G.A.
88659 Cpl. SAUNDERS, J., R.G.A.
135769 Gnr. SILVERBLATT, M., R.F.A.
197965 Gnr. SHOTLINSKY, D., R.F.A.
187344 Dvr. SENKER, W., R.G.A.
       Gnr. SAMOVITCH, W.
       Gnr. SWYER, M., R.F.A.
       Gnr. SWERLING, S., R.F.A.
       Gnr. STEINGOLD, M. L., R.F.A.
127587 Dvr. SINGER, D., 147th H.B.
22950 Dvr. TURNER, J., 162nd Bde.
44931 Dvr. TRAVERS, H., C/183rd Bde.
144851 Gnr. TEEMAN, M., C/86th Bde.
95794 Bdr. THORNYCROFT, T., 54th A.A. Bty.
135039 Gnr. TROTSKY, L., 261st Siege Bty.
205202 Bdr. TEEMAN, H., C/285th R.F.A.
104837 Gnr. TAVROGIS, A., 227th Siege Bty.
54118 Gnr. TEBBITT, A., 364th Bty.
31506 Gnr. TULLMAN, A., 125th Bty.
159709 Gnr. THANESON, A., 3rd "C" R. Bde.
146000 Dvr. TAYLOR, R., 3rd "C" R. Bde.
162607 Gnr. TAYLOR, S., R.F.A.
295129 Sig. TAYLOR, J., 127th T.M.B.
53660 Gnr. TOBIAS, A., 3rd T.M.B.
       Gnr. TELBUTH, M., Amn. Pk.
205202 Bdr. TIEMAN, H., 285th Bde.
50333 Gnr. TEACHER, S., 10th R.G.A.
194077 Gnr. TAYLOR, P., R.F.A.
124820 Gnr. TOWER, L., R.G.A.
182390 Dvr. TENENBAUM, S., R.F.A.
234160 Gnr. TUCHMAN, J., R.F.A.

340378 Gnr. TANCHAN, J.
225822 Gnr. TAYLOR, B., R.F.A.
  1628 Dvr. TISH, A., R.G.A.
78999 Gnr. TOSHINSKY, L., R.G.A.
906690 Gnr. TALBOT, H. H., R.G.A.
23016 Gnr. TAYLOR, F., R.G.A.
181057 Gnr. TREIP, J., R.F.A.
111593 Gnr. ULLMAN, J., 301st Siege Bty.
130850 Gnr. UNIA, V., 25th Hy. Bty.
168959 Gnr. URSERMAN, J., R.G.A., 64th Coy.
135097 Gnr. UTKES, S.
39240 Dvr. VIDOFSKY, L., 49th D.A.C.
286029 L/Bdr. VANDYK, L., 146th Siege Bty.
139207 Dvr. VAY, H. N., B/71st Bde.
187016 Gnr. VICTOR, A. L., R.F.A.
24216 Gnr. VYNER, G., 28th R.G.A.
37561 Gnr. VORZANGER, B.,* R.G.A.
154552 Gnr. VELINSKI, R.G.A., 337th S. Bty.
308893 Cpl. VELLER, H., R.G.A.
44333 Gnr. VYE, S., P/251st.
255706 Gnr. VANGELDER, S., R.F.A.
890930 Gnr. VALENTINE, M. S., 73rd D.A.C.
139515 Bdr. VAN LEER, A.,* D/331st Bde.
  1730 Dvr. VERIEN, E.,* 60th D.A.C., R.F.A.
42509 Gnr. VOGEL, E.,* 97th T.M.B.
179920 Dvr. VANDERMOLEN, A.
177017 Gnr. VEDENBOHN, J., R.G.A.
139505 Bdr. VANHIER, A., R.F.A.
198044 Dvr. VOSTER, H.
246776 Gnr. VIDOVSKY, S., R.F.A.
181163 Gnr. VISINI, S., R.F.A.
  5298 B./Q.M./Sgt. WOOLLEY, F. J., 14th Bde., R.H.A.
98825 Gnr. WILKS, J., 37th Bde.
80200 Dvr. WOLFSON, J., 46th Bde.
114135 Dvr. WERNICK, L., A/108th Bde.
76224 Gnr. WEINBERG, D., 85th Bty.
L/37797 Bdr. WILSON, J., B/180th Bde.
13253 Bdr. WOOLF, E., 162nd Bde.
15081 Dvr. WAVROUSCH, W., 162nd Bde. A.C.
  1472 Dvr. WATERS, M., 24th Bde.
30742 Dvr. WALLIS, A., 36th Div. Amn. Col.
41926 Dvr. WILLOUGHBY, F., 33rd Bde.
123083 Gnr. WOOLF, H., 47th Bty., 41st Bde.
   885 Dvr. WERNICK, S., 60th Div. Amn. Col.
   888 Dvr. WOOLF, M., 60th Div. Amn. Col.
 1071 Dvr. WARSHAWSKY, M., 60th D.A.C.
 1126 Dvr. WEINTROB, R., 61st D.A.C.
45936 Gnr. WERNER, M. A., 33rd D.A.C.
25201 Gnr. WALLERS, A., 59th T.M.B.
940584 Gnr. WOLFSON, S., 293rd Bde.
 3181 Gnr. WEIDER, J., 167th T.M.B.
111881 Dvr. WEINER, B., 133rd Bde. Army F.A.
238957 Gnr. WINTER, S., 41st D.A.C.
 8494 Bdr. WOOLF, J., 77th Sge. Bty., R.G.A.
 1634 Gnr. WOLFSON, M., 4th R.M.A.
134729 Gnr. WOLFSBERGEN, D., 276th Sge. Bty.
526901 Gnr. WHITTIER, M., 1st Can. Heavy.

Royal Regiment of Artillery.—*Continued.*

195327	Gnr. WIESBERG, K., 194th Siege Bty.
28064	Dvr. WOLF, S., 26th Bde. Amn. Col.
283494	Cpl. WOOLFE, J., 528th Siege Bty.
172663	Gnr. WORMAN, H., 301st Siege Bty.
182316	Gnr. WILKS, N., 256th Bde.
237280	Gnr. WEINER, M., B/70th Bde.
159723	Gnr. WEINSTEIN, H., 109th Hy. Bty., R.G.A.
37779	Gnr. WILSON, J., B/180th Bde.
123083	Gnr. WOOLF, H., 23rd D.A.C.
1551186	Gnr. WINSTONE, D., 353rd S. Bty., R.G.A.
661229	Gnr. WOLFSON, H., 169th Bde.
220885	Dvr. WEINER, J. P., R.F.A.
193070	Gnr. WOOLF, H., 156th Hy. R.G.A.
1144	Gnr. WOOLF, J., R.G.A., B.D.
86718	Bdr. WORMS, J., R.F.A.
59713	Gnr. WILLIAMSON, A., 5th D.A.C.
173529	Sig. WEISBERG, A., Sig. Train. Centre.
36108	Dvr. WEBB, C., 180th Bde. R.F.A.
970629	Gnr. WOOLF, A. I., 13th Res. Bty.
175910	Gnr. WINSTONE, H., 316th S. By. R.G.A.
156981	Gnr. WALTERFREDA, A., 3rd "C" R. Bde.
36606	Dvr. WARSHOWER, M., 3rd "C" R. Bde.
1519	Gnr. WOLFSON, P., 293rd Bde.
80521	Gnr. WEIWOW, B., R.G.A. 47th Coy.
89093	Gnr. WHITE, S. H., R.G.A.
	Gnr. WELF, W., R.H.A.
845852	Dvr. WEINTROP, 24th D.A.C.
195327	Gnr. WISEBERG, H., 194th S. By. R.G.A.
200374	Dvr. WOLFE, S., "A" Bty.
146409	A/Cpl. WOLFF, 5th Bty. R.F.A.
234662	Gnr. WOOLF, H. B., R.F.A.
845261	Gnr. WILLIAMS, E. E., R.F.A.
970630	Dvr. WOOLFE, M. R., R.F.A.
141937	Gnr. WINSTONE, J.,* 13th Bde. R.F.A.
197188	Gnr. WOLDMAN, M. M., R.G.A.
77968	Dvr. WOLFE, R., 9th Bde. R.F.A.
132176	Dvr. WATSON, H., R.F.A.
36108	Dvr. WEFF, C., 68th Bde. R.F.A.
190729	Sgt. WERNSTEIN, D., R.G.A.
166296	Gnr. WOLLRANCH, J., R.G.A.
40148	Gnr. WEILL, H.
166817	Dvr. WOOLF, J., 53rd Bty. R.F.A.
178913	Gnr. WRIGHT, T. F., R.F.A.
197712	Gnr. WELLER, J.
19731	Dvr. WOODNICK, B., R.F.A.
76225	Dvr. WISBERG, D., R.F.A.
29632	Dvr. WOOLF, J.
30780	Gnr. WEINSTEIN, L., R.F.A.
24517	Dvr. WITTY, N., R.F.A.
209106	Gnr. WOOLF, T., R.F.A.
39352	Gnr. WAXMAN, H., R.G.A.
28064	Dvr. WOLFE, S., R.F.A.
30742	Bdr. WALLACE, A., 36th D.A.C.
129776	Gnr. WYNNE, J., R.F.A.
	Gnr. WALTERS, A., R.F.A.
69508	Gnr. WAGERSTEIN, S., R.F.A.
128065	Gnr. WAREY, H., R.F.A.
313684	Gnr. WILLIAMS, J., R.G.A.
45936	Gnr. WERNER, M., R.F.A.
T/1589	S/Sgt. WOOD, P., R.G.A.
156239	Gnr. WARNER, R.G.A.
166699	Gnr. WHITEHOUSE, H., R.G.A.
173346	Gnr. WOOLF, H., R.F.A.
195209	Gnr. WILLING, J., R.F.A.
166266	Gnr. WARRAUCH, J., R.G.A.
209253	Gnr. WERSCHKER, F., R.G.A.
49540	Gnr. WEITZENSANG, N., R.G.A.
776703	Dvr. YOUDLEMAN, B., 313th Bde.
176903	Gnr. YAFFE, M., R.G.A.
1149	Dvr. ZAUSMAN, G., 1/1st Lond. R.F.A.
111070	Gnr. ZEIGLER, A., 191st Siege Bty.
314049	Cpl. ZOLTY, B., 1/1st War Hy. Bty.
76110	Gnr. ZIMMERMAN, B., 117th Siege Bty.
40957	Gnr. ZUCKER, A., 63rd Coy. R.G.A.
28668	Gnr. ZEIZERAN, D., 13th Bty. R.G.A.
671812	Gnr. ZELKOVITCH, J., R.F.A.
208312	Gnr. ZALMANOVITCH, J., 4th Depot R.F.A.
	Bdr. ZIMBLER, J., R.F.A.
135051	Gnr ZONENACHWITCH, A., R.G.A.
246645	Dvr. ZLOTNICK, 7th Res. Art.
132497	Gnr. ZLOTNICK, S.
385839	Dvr. ZILTMAN, S., R.F.A.
147133	Gnr. ZAVASKI, L.
192461	Gnr. ZIVE, L.
236689	Gnr. ZENFTMAN, S.
52109	Gnr. ZISMAN, M., R.G.A.
85031	Gnr. ZOINS, D., R.G.A.
165226	Dvr. ZIVIL, N., R.F.A.
137646	Gnr. ZARENSKY, W., R.F.A.

* Killed in Action or died on Active Service.

HONOURABLE ARTILLERY COMPANY.
OFFICERS.

2nd Lieut. ALBERTS, J. S.
2nd Lieut. BARNEY, L. V.
2nd Lieut. HART, J. N., 1/1st Bn.
Capt. MONTAGU, V. (O.B.E.), 2nd Bn.
Capt. SAMUEL, E. L. (M.C.), 1st Bn.
2nd Lieut. SPANIER, E. J.
2nd Lieut. SCHIFF, M. N.

N.C.O.'s AND MEN.

10731	Pte. ADES, E. D., 2nd Bn.
4364	Pte. ALBERGE, E. J., 1st Bn.
1051	Dvr. ALEXANDER, H.
2975	Pte. ARON, C. J., 1st Bn.
	Pte. ARBIB, N. D.
	Pte. BARTON, G.
9408	Pte. BARNETT, A.
3719	Pte. BARNEY, L., 1st Bn.
625139	Pte. BARNETT, S.,
7338	Pte. BARNEY, J. G.,* 2nd Bn.
	Pte. BERLINER, A.

Honourable Artillery Company.—*Continued.*

	Pte. Belasco, E.
10584	Pte. Beyfus, C.,* 2nd Bn.
10174	Pte. Blankensee, A. J., 2nd Bn.
9222	Pte. Boss, P.
1204	Pte. Bonner, P. M.,* 2nd Bn.
5174	Pte. Bonner, W. G., 1st Bn.
624165	Gnr. Braham, G. M.
2441	Pte. Castello, S. M.
626114	Pte. Charatan, D.
3597	Pte. Clozenberg, G. R.
7079	Pte. Cohen, A.,* 2nd Bn.
11511	Pte. Cross, P., 1st Bn.
	Dvr. Davis, H. S.
	Dvr. Davis, M.
	Dvr. Davis, S.
5402	Dvr. Davis, P. C.
	Dvr. Davies, H.
	Dvr. Davidson, H. L.
	Dvr. Davidson, N.
2/B/625862	Dvr. Diamond, A. S. (M.M.).
624147	Staff Sgt. Dutch, S. L.
11405	Pte. Emanuel, L., 1st Bn.
	Pte. Ettlinger, A. F.
11220	Pte. Feldman, H. M., 1st Bn.
6823	Pte. Finsberg, M., 2nd Bn.
3041	Pte. Flatau, E. S., 1st Bn.
	Pte. Fox, A.
	Pte. Freeman, D. H.
626674	Gnr. Franklin, C. M. E.
1450	Pte. Fuchsbalg, M.,* 1st Bn.
3797	Pte. Green, H., 1/9th Bn.
7552	Pte. Goodman, M.
3556	Pte. Goldstein, S. W.,* 1st Bn.
1563	Pte. Hart, J. A., 1st Bn.
625942	Sig. Harris, H. M.
9423	Pte. Hemmings, H. W., 2nd Bn.
	Pte. Henriques, H. C.
	Pte. Herbert, A. E.
	Pte. Hirschland, H. E.
	Pte. Hess, I. F.
2283	Pte. Heyman, J. H.
1902	Pte. Hopkins, A., 1st Bn.
	Pte. Hyams, P. J.
4099	Pte. Hyams, L., 1st Bn.
3407	Pte. Isaacs, C., 1st Bn.
11594	Pte. Isaacs, E. M., 1st Bn.
	Pte. Isaacs, G.
9563	Pte. Isaacs, J.
4527	Gnr. Israel, A.
1053	Pte. Jacobs, A. C.
4755	Pte. Jacobs, E. L., 1st Bn.
624995	Pte. Jacobs, J.,* Artillery.
626240	Pte. Joel, B. B.
7469	Pte. Joel, L.
	Pte. Jolowitz, P.
10455	Pte. Josephs, S., 2nd Bn.
9965	Pte. Joseph, M.,* 2nd Bn.
6965	Pte. Kaufman, B. S.,
1753	Sgt. Krauss, N. D., 1st Bn.
5240	Pte. Lazarus, A. C.,* 2nd Bn.
7695	Pte. Levi, E.
37734	Pte. Levi, I.
4962	Pte. Levy, P. S.,* 2nd Bn.
10708	Pte. Levy, H.,* 2nd Bn.
624572	Dvr. Levy, J., Artillery.
4635	Pte. Levy, R. A.,* 1st Bn.
7163	Pte. Lewis, J.,* 2nd Bn.
5419	Gnr. Leapman, H., 2nd Bn.
	Pte. Lemkin, W., 2nd Bn.
	Pte. Lumley, A.
9998	Pte. Marks, L., 1st Bn.
11610	Dvr. Marks, D.
2848	L/Cpl. Mattana, J., 2nd Bn.
	Pte. Marcus, A. E.
	Dvr. Melbourne, H.
7561	Pte. Moss, J. L., 1st Bn.
375	Cpl. Moss, V.
7086	Pte. Mosely, M. P. H., 2nd Bn.
3480	Pte. Myer, K., 2nd Bn.
5153	Pte. Myers, M., 1st Bn.
3688	Pte. Myers, L., 1st Bn.
	Pte. Myers, H.
289	Sgt.-Maj. Nathan, A. J.
705	Sgt. Nathan, G., 1st Bn.
624113	Dvr. Nathan, G., Artillery.
5675	Sgt. Nathan, I.
	Bomb. Nathan, V. J., Artillery.
3428	Pte. Pinto, R., 1st Bn.
626151	Gnr. Pollack, D. S.,* 309th Sge. Bty.
3629	Pte. Rodney, G. W., 2nd Bn.
	Pte. Rosselli, H.
	Pte. Rosenwald, C.
2748	Pte. Samuel, G. H., 1st Bn.
10314	Pte. Samuel, F. J.,* 2nd Bn.
624996	Gnr. Sandford, M.
	Pte. Schaw, F.
	Pte. Schlesinger, A. L.
	Sgt. Schuman, H. B.
6812	Pte. Shaffer, B. L., 2nd Bn.
	Pte. Sherwood, J.
	Pte. Sinclair, H.
3480	Pte. Simmons, M.
	Pte. Simmons, K. J.
7121	Pte. Slowe, A., 21st Bn.
	Pte. Speyer, C. A.
9151	Pte. Solzbury, A.
	Pte. Solomon, R. B.
	Pte. Sonnenthal, E. F.
	Pte. Sutton, D.
6829	Pte. Tom, L., 2nd Bn.
7264	Pte. Tobias, W., 2nd Bn.
7354	Pte. Ullman, A. M.
7068	Pte. Woolf, D. L., 2nd Bn.
4313	Pte. Woolf, J. H., 2nd Bn.

* Killed in Action or died on Active Service.

ROYAL ENGINEERS.

OFFICERS.

2nd Lieut. ALBU, C., 255th Tunnelling Coy.
2nd Lieut. ABRAHAMS, L.
2nd Lieut. ASH, H. S.
2nd Lieut. ADLER, H.
Lieut. BARNETT, B. L., (M.C.), 59th Div. Sig. Coy.
Capt. BAMBERGER, C. D. W.*
2nd Lieut. BERNSTINGL, C. A.
Major BEHRENS, T. T.
Major BERLANDINA, H. (O.B.E., M.C.).
Capt. BRANDON, O. G.
2nd Lieut. COHEN, M. (M.C.), 8th Div. Sig. Coy.
2nd Lieut. COHEN, I. J., 11th Area Sig. Det.
Capt. COLLINGS, C. J., I.W.T.
Lieut. DE CASSERES, A.
Lieut. COHEN, S. S.
Capt. DAVIS, C. J.,* 470th Fld. Coy.
Lieut. DAVIS, H. N.,* 2nd London Fld. Coy.
Capt. DAVIS, P. W., 234th Fld. Coy.
2nd Lieut. ELLIS, N., Sig. School.
Capt. FRIEND, C., Signal Coy.
Major GLUCKSTEIN, M. (O.B.E.).
2nd Lieut. GOLDMAN, L. (M.C.).
Lieut. HART, H. M.
Lieut. HART, L., 69th Fld. Coy.
Capt. HARRIS, L. (O.B.E.), 5th Army.
Capt. HALDINSTEIN, F. W.* 8th Div. Sig.
Lieut.-Col. HENRIQUES, R.Q., 60th Div.
2nd Lieut. HAYMAN, H. L.
Capt. HENRIQUES, P. Q.
Lieut. HART, V.
Lieut. HUMPHREYS, J., Inland Water Transport.
Capt. INFELD, H., 4th Spec. Bn.
Lieut. Col. JOSEPH, R. H. (D.S.O.), 1st Lond. Fld. Coy.
Lieut. JACOBS, B. A.
Maj. KENNARD, G. (M.C.), O.C. 56th Div. Sig. Co.
2nd Lieut. KOPE, G. S., 257th Tunnelling Coy.
2nd Lieut. KRUGER, E. N.
2nd Lieut. KALKER, L. E.
Lieut. LION, B.S., H.Q. 93rd Bde.
2nd Lieut. LEINKIND, D. H., 86th Fld. Coy.
Capt. LUCK.
Lieut. MORRIS, A. E., 182nd Tun. Coy.
2nd Lieut. MORRIS, S., 3rd Res. Bn.
2nd Lieut. MEYER, J. V.
Lieut. MICHAELIS, G. M.,* East Anglian.
Lieut. NEWHOUSE, F., 15th Fld. Coy.
Lieut. NATHAN, R. F.
Lieut. NATHAN, S. J. (M.B.E.).
Lieut. PHILLIPS, J. E.
Lieut. POLACK. A. I.
Lieut. PLATNAUER, J. B. (M.C.).
2nd Lieut. PRAAG, I. C.
2nd Lieut. PYSER, M. E., I.W.T.

Lieut. RATHBONE.
Capt. REIS, P. H.
Major SPIELMAN. C. M. (M.C.), 100th Fld. Coy.
2nd Lieut. STEIN, H. K., 4th Ar. Sig. Sch.
Capt. STERN, T. H. (M.C.).
Capt. SCHWAB, M. H.
Major SEBAG MONTEFIORE, C., O.C. 459th F. Co.
Capt. SINAUER, E. M. (M.C)
Lieut SINGTON, G. H. A.
Capt. SPERO, S.
Hon. Col. SALOMONS, Sir D., Sub. Mining.
2nd Lieut. SASSOON, H.*
Lieut. SCHWARZ, W. H., 1st London.
Capt. SIMON, V. H.
2nd Lieut. SOLOMON, L.
Major SINGTON, J.
Lieut. Col. SOLOMON, S. J.
Capt. SALOMONS, D. R. H. P.*
Capt. WOLFF,
Major WALEY, A. S. (M.C.).
2nd Lieut. WILLIAMS, A.

N.C.O.'s AND MEN.

191627 Cpl. ABRAHAMS, M., Sig. Coy. Guards D.
161667 Dvr. ARKUSZ, J., 32nd Div. Sig. Hdqs.
170802 Pnr. ABBOT, H. M., 4th Spec. Bn.
482181 C.Q.M.S. ALEXANDER, H. T. (M.S.M.), 62nd Div. Sig. Coy.
3289 Spr. AVERBACK, I.,* 461st West Riding Fld. Coy.
1091 Dvr. ABRAHAMS, J. A., 2/1st Lond. F. Co.
476339 Dvr. ALEXANDER, B., 455th Fld. Coy.
306845 Pte. ARK, M., 460th Fld. Coy.
546211 Dvr. ABRAHAMS, J., 512nd Fld. Coy.
248565 Pnr. ABELSON, B., R.E. Sigs., att. 65th B.
477763 Pnr. ASHBERG, A., 4th Fld. Surrey Bn.
236902 Spr. ALEXANDER, A., R. Corps Sig. Coy.
2§10556 Spr. AGSTOL, R., 11th L.R.O.S.
27711 Spr. ANNOSKI, J., 432nd Fld. Coy.
21500 Spr. ANNENBERG, J., R.E. 3rd Field Trp.
L/Cpl. ALLENSTEIN, J., c/o C.R.E.
WR/291738 Spr. APHA, S., R.O.D.
WR/600261 Spr. AMSTELL, S., 1st I.W.T.
2274 Cpl. AARONS, L.
335279 Pnr. ASCHER, J.
286692 Spr. ABRAHAMS, G.
466096 2/Cpl. ALBERT, A.,
299460 Spr. APTER, D.
299460 Pte. AEIDER, A.
548092 Spr. ALBERT, I., 642nd Fld. Coy.
430728 Pte. ALEXANDER, L.
341877 Pnr. ALEXANDER, N.
300220 Spr. ARONSOUN, S.
2017 Spr. ARTHUR, J.
180963 Pte. ABRAHAMS, A.
95318 Sgt. BAKER, M. (M.M., D.C.M.). 152nd Fld. Coy.

Royal Engineers.—*Continued.*

1112	Spr. BLOCK, M., Div. Sig. Coy.
1203	Cpl. BENJAMIN, S., 2/1st Lond. Fld. Coy.
179359	Pnr. BLACKMAN, P., 4th Special Bn.
187251	Pnr. BLITZEN, I., 2nd Special Bn.
106100	Cpl. BALABAN, I. E. (D.C.M.), 2nd Spec. Bde.
195989	Pnr. BERNSTEIN, W., 1st Spec. Bde.
209515	Pnr. BLOOM, F. H., 5th Spec. Bde.
44435	Spr. BLOOMFIELD, E. R., 78th Fld. Coy.
558051	Spr. BLOCK, M., 57th Div. Sig. Coy.
251350	Spr. BRIDGER, H., 34th L.R.O.C.
241267	Pte. BERNSTEIN, H., 8th Army Tram. Co.
358670	Pte. BERNSTEIN, H., H.Q. "C" Sector Forways Def. Line.
224974	Pnr. BERNER, M. M., "M" Spec. Coy.
166081	Spr. BARNETT, S., 4th Sig. Con. Coy.
268201	Spr. BENJAMIN, B., Wireless Observ. Gp.
518268	Spr. BLITZ, E., 560th Coy. A.T.
518299	Spr. BLITZ, W., 560th A.T. Coy.
194847	Spr. BLOOM, E., 1st Army Sig. Coy.
362706	Spr. BENSON, J., att. 45th Bde. H.Q.
361917	Spr. BLUM, L., 15th Corps Signals.
204840	Spr. BEAUMONT, C. S., H.Q. Sig. Sect.
182316	Pnr. BAGEL, L., Sig. Coy.
276349	Pnr. BENSUSAN, D., 26th Lt. Ry. Coy.
321546	Pnr. BROWN, S. G.,* 4th Special Bde.
7214	Spr. BERGER, J., 6th Field Coy.
161851	Pnr. BERGSON, M.,* 80th Sig. Depot.
113942	Pnr. BEAGLE, M., 32nd Inf. Bde. H.Q.
	Pte. BLOM, R.
207129	Spr. BROWN, H., 26th Fld. Sig. Coy.
145495	Spr. BLINT, J.,
25261	Spr. BAKER, I., Base Depot.
42446	Pte. BEAGLE, J., 343rd R.C.C.
1280	L/Cpl. BARNETT, J.
820	Sgt. BACHRACK, 5th Coy.
238093	Spr. BERLYNE, M.
184249	Spr. BUSCOVITCH, L.
154676	Spr. BORSTEIN, A.
553087	Pnr. BLONDIN, H.
275014	Pnr. BUFFMAN, S.
457650	L/Cpl. BARNETT, J.
287650	Spr. BENDA, H. M.
264148	Spr. BARNETT, N.
244981	Spr. BRAUDE, J. N.
289031	Pnr. BLOOM, I.
106245	Pte. BARSTEIN, A.
519710	Pte. BERMAY, D., 79th Fld. Coy.
215842	Spr. BERG, S.
6053	Pte. BLUESTEIN, A.
14985	Pte. BELKIN, 9th Fld. Coy.
237512	Spr. BRANSHUNG, B., Signal Coy.
	Cpl. BLITZ, A.
341865	Spr. BOLTON, T.
290146	Spr. BENJAMIN, S., R.O.D.
537	Int. BACAHA, D.
564078	Spr. BENJAMIN, A.
	Pnr. BARMAN, H. J.
38	Spr. BLOOM, C.
281377	Spr. BELL, J.
18447	Spr. BERNSTONE, M.
264148	Spr. BARNETT, W.
359266	Pnr. BERWALD, J.
209327	Dvr. BARNETT, S.
232230	Spr. BLASHKY, S.
560690	Pnr. BLOOM, J.
290145	Spr. BENJAMIN, S.
422424	Pnr. BERNSTEIN, I.
277381	Spr. BOVINSKY, H.
285107	Spr. BORSTEIN, M.
301170	Spr. BERMAN, J.
3362	Spr. BARNETT, N.
237608	Pnr. BLOCK, J.
279399	Pte. BURNS, A., Signal Co.
9941	Dvr. BLUMENTHAL, A.
204789	Spr. BAKER, A.
25343	Dvr. BLACKMAN, H.
54624	Cpl. BENJAMIN,
560689	Pnr. BLANDIS, S.
163761	Pnr. BOSS, E.
348358	Pnr. BERNSTEIN, N.
312176	Spr. BERNARD, B.
344692	Pte. BERNSHEIM, H.
330720	Spr. BROWN, H.
344245	Spr. BRAVA, B.
334243	Spr. BETH, J.
329494	Spr. BARNETT, H.
238943	Spr. BERGER, I.
351913	Pnr. BARNARD, H. J.
329629	Spr. BLOOM, J.
322424	Pnr. BERSNTEIN, I.
22269	Spr. BROOKS, R.
410989	Spr. BLUESTEIN, G.
192291	Spr. BAKER, I.
214432	Pnr. BASCOVITCH, B.
332493	Spr. BERMAN, L.
357652	Pte. BLOOM, M.
320153	Spr. BARRON, S.
343358	Pte. BERNSTEIN, K.
2863	Pte. BRAVERMAN, M.
3112	Pte. BLIKE.
	Pte. BADER, H.
40495	Pte. BLACK, S.
366187	Pte. BOWMAN, S.
329564	Spr. BACKMINDER, S.
	Sgt. BAMBERGER. E. L. (M.M.).
	Pte. BENJAMIN, H.
	Pte. BENJAMIN, J.
	Pte. BLITZ, M.
	Pte. BLASTON, S.
	Pte. BLACK, R.
83840	Pte. COSS, H., 210th Fld. Coy.
335285	Pnr. COHEN, S., 206th Fld. Coy.
106130	Cpl. COHEN, E., 4th Spec. Bn.
120669	Cpl. COHEN, P., 4th Spec. Bn.

Royal Engineers.—*Continued.*

178920	Pnr. COHEN, E., 4th Spec. Bn.
85922	Sgt. COSTA, R., 212th Fld. Coy.
193023	Pnr. COPPLEMAN, J., 1st Spec. Coy.
467478	Spr. COUPLAN, J.,* 461st W. Riding F. C.
	Dvr. COHEN, J., 457th W. Riding F. Coy.
160576	Spr. COHEN, J., 68th Fld. Coy.
113567	Spr. COHEN, L., 3rd Spec. Bde.
113147	Sgt. CHAYTOW, J., Met. Sec. 4th Army.
206654	Pnr. COHEN, J., 2nd Spec. Bde.
3540	Spr. CALLEW, F., 2/2nd (Non.) Fld. Coy.
5446690	Spr. COHEN, M., 509th Lond. Fld. Coy.
32025	Pte. COHEN, M., 460th Fld. Coy.
546326	Spr. CAPLAN, N., 350th E. & M. Coy.
	Sgt. COWAN, Inf. Bde.
459681	Spr CALLEN, F., 446th Fld. Coy.
256266	Pnr. COHEN, J., R.O.D.
268348	Pnr. COHEN, I., 17th Div. Sig. Coy.
W2/278417	Pnr. COHEN, A., 340th R.C.C.
WR/42824	Pnr. CHYTOVITCH, J., 304th R.C.C.
254357	Spr. COHEN, M., Sig. Sub. Sect.
652077	Spr. COHEN, S., R.C.C.
277217	Spr. CLEMENTS, M., 26th Fld. Coy.
518457	Spr. COHEN, B., 520th Fld. Coy.
478568	Spr. COHEN, A., 511th Fld. Coy.
221673	Dvr. CHESSES, W.,* 31st Div. Sig. Coy.
259728	Pnr. COHEN, H., 34th Div. Sig. Coy.
168913	Spr. COHEN, J., R.O.D.
209875	Spr. CHALK, M., 1st L. Ry. Coy.
3412	Spr. COHEN, M., 3/1st.
37484	Sig. COHEN, J., att. 157th Bde.
198165	Sgt. COHEN, O. H.
202208	Pte. CIRELSTAIN, D. A.
120308	Pnr. COHEN, S., 1st Bn.
168913	Spr. COWAN, J., R.O.D. Loco. Dept.
277380	Spr. COWAN, P.
4809	Pte. COHEN, N., 22nd.
152778	Spr. COHEN, B., 239th Coy.
161658	Pnr. COHEN, M.
67316	Pte. CLENE, P.
307699	Spr. COHEN, S.
221710	Dvr. COHEN, W., Signal Co.
WR/291737	Spr. CITRIN, R.O.D.
254357	Spr. COHEN, A.
321524	Pte. COHEN, H., 46th Div. Sigs.
480266	Dvr. COHEN.
127824	Spr. COLEMAN, S., 15th Div. Sig. Corps.
81221	Spr. COHEN, S., R.E. Training Centre.
177129	Spr. CURLENDER, M. E.
301082	Spr. CLANOWITCH, L.
167141	Pte. CALLER, N., 2nd Res. Bn.
	Cpl. COHEN, C., 186th Coy.
	Cpl. COHEN, L., 186th Coy.
	Sig. COPELAND, P., 24th Fortress Coy.
	Cpl. CHADWICK, Wireless.
246698	Sap. COHEN, J. L.
512662	Pte. COHEN, L., 791st Coy.
282003	Spr. COHEN, G., 3rd Sig. Coy.
361586	Spr. CLAFF, L.
221719	Spr. COHEN.
328093	Pte. CAPLAN, H.
198165	Sgt. COHEN, H., Sig. Coy.
244188	Spr. COHEN, M., Sig. Coy.
300265	Spr. COLTINSKIE, T.
DM2/112634	Pte. CHARICK, E.
255780	Pnr. CRONS, D.
WR/330272	Spr. COHEN, A. V.
WR/26193	Spr. CRYSTOL, R.
167511	Pte. CLENETS, N.
200737	Pte. COHEN, B.
178920	Pte. COHEN, C.
106358	Cpl. COHEN, J.
168913	Spr. COHEN, J.
447207	Pnr. COHEN, I.
324314	Pnr. COHEN, A.
286224	Spr. COHEN, M.
152280	Spr. CRAIG, D.
278279	Pte. COHEN, J.
507563	Spr. COHEN, S.
73040	Cpl. CUTWELL, F.
276688	Spr. CORPER, M.
291208	Spr. CAMPBELL, I.
198574	Pnr. COHEN, S.
39442	Motor Cyc. CASSELL, C.
268091	Pnr. CITRIN, I.
264300	Spr. COHEN, H.
225090	Pnr. COHEN, D.
346482	Spr. CHARLES, R.
340296	Spr. CAMBERG, N.
277380	Spr. COHEN, P.
273569	Spr. COOPER, J.
202208	Spr. CIRELSTEIN, D. A.
301288	Spr. CHURNER, G.
73937	Cpl. COHEN, H.
595993	Spr. CAMBERG, W.
447205	Pnr. CAHN, S.
227498	Pte. CROSS, J.
369459	Spr. COHEN, M., R.E.P.S.
66	Spr. DURION, A. J.
69581	Spr. DAVIS, D., Det. 141st A.T. Coy.
46516	Dvr. DOUGLAS, J., 11th Div. Sig. Coy.
78128	Spr. DIAMOND, M., 6th Corps Sigs.
148320	Cpl. DIAMOND, J., 39th Div. Sig. Coy.
C/1890	Pte. DA COSTA, E., "K" Coy.
167399	Pnr. DEFRIES, S., 3rd Special Bde.
17299	Pnr. DAVIES, H., 29th Light Ry. Coy.
34532	L/Cpl. DRUCE, L., 4th G.B.D.
70715	Spr. DE KEYSER, J., "L" Sigs. Bn.
20028	Spr. DAVIES, A., 177th Tunnelling Coy.
1658	Spr. DAVIES, H., 1st Sect., 251st Coy.
7673	L/Cpl. DAVIES, E., 1st Sect., 251st Coy.
20886	Pte. DORAN, D.
12398	Spr. DANCYGER, B.
371468	Pte. DAVIS, B., 9th Corps.
335221	Pnr. DEFRIES, R.
262730	Pte. DAVIS, T., 578th Sussex Works Cy.

Royal Engineers.—*Continued.*

252858	Linesman	DAVIS, J.
272724	Spr.	DIAMOND, J., Sig. Section.
236901	Spr.	DE SWARTE, A., Sig. Coy.
935	Spr.	DAVIES, F., 12th Fld. Coy.
303996	Spr.	DOBBE, A., 224th Fld. Coy.
167217	Spr.	DOLIVASKY, M.
341585	Pnr.	DAVIDSON, A. L.
264321	Spr.	DREEZER, J.
457	Spr.	DAMEL, F.
246606	Pnr.	DA COSTA, R.
346472	Spr.	DONIGER, J.
396288	Pnr.	DAVIS, P.
176563	Pnr.	DALFIELD, W.
303302	Spr.	DAVIES, P.
309	Pte.	DAVIS, F.
	Spr.	DE FRIES, J.
2098	Pte.	DACIS, M.
4439	Pte.	DEENE, E.
4705	Pte.	DA COSTA, J.
338739	Pte.	DAVIS, M.
	Pte.	DAVEY, W. C.
	Pte.	DAVIS, N.
	Pte.	DE WILDE, G.
19637	L-Cpl.	EPSTEIN, H. (D.C.M.), 59th Fld. Co
106060	Cpl.	ELLOWITZ, J., 4th Spec. Bn.
560564	Spr.	ECKER, S., 3rd Army Sig. Coy.
188670	Pnr.	EDELBERG, E., 3rd Special Bde.
28833	Spr.	EMDEN, E., 207th Fld. Coy.
268349	Pnr.	EPSTEIN, C., Sig. Sub. Sect.
WR/278846	Spr.	EMANUEL, D., 35th L.R.O. Cy.
549810	Spr.	EPRILE, C. J., 1st Fld. Survey Coy.
176009	Spr.	ELLIS, J., 4th G.B.D.
556392	Spr.	ELIAS, M.
34958	Pte.	ERENBERG, S.
324392	Pte.	ELFORD, A.
231178	Pte.	EPSTEIN, J.
4584	Sig.	EMANUEL, H.
360269	Spr.	EPPSON, L.
1102	Spr.	FREEDMAN, J., 1st Durham Coy.
42435	Spr.	FOWLER, G., 18th Div. Signal Coy.
46390	Spr.	FREEDMAN, A., 154th Fld. Coy.
733	Spr.	FOX, M., 1/2nd Lond. Fld. Coy.
191804	Pnr.	FREEMAN, G., H.Q.Sig.
176566	Spr.	FREEDMAN, H., 1st Special Bde.
49005	Sgt.	FINK, A., 467th N. Midland Fld. Cy.
438659	Cpl.	FREEDMAN, A., 66th Div.
WR/275675	Spr.	FITELSON, H.,* 278th Ry. Coy
244943	Spr.	FISHEL, P., "V" Corps Signals.
258813	Spr.	FRIEND, L., I.W.T.
548052	Spr.	FOX, M., 510th Fld. Coy.
192018	Spr.	FREEMAN, C., 3rd Special Bde.
	Pnr.	FRENCHMAN, J., 4th G.B.D.
303299	Pte.	FALKSON, 3rd Foreways Coy.
28789	Cpl.	FIELD, H., 3rd Sig. Coy.
277517	Pnr.	FINKLESTEIN, L.
277378	Spr.	FILCHER, S.
	Spr.	FRANK, S.
311751	Spr.	FORWAINE, I.
46522	Pte.	FINEBERG, L.
160113	Spr.	FREEMAN, E.
278296	Spr.	FINKLESTEIN, D.
222259	Pte.	FISHMAN, C. S., Wireless Section.
55595	Pte.	FREEDMAN, H.
18	L/Cpl.	FERRIS, Signal Troop.
356414	Pte.	FINN, Signal Section.
466877	Spr.	FLEISIG, C.
470596	Spr.	FREEDMAN, J.
285527	Spr.	FRANKS, I., Essex (F) Coy.
189144	Spr.	FINSTONE, G.
600456	Spr.	FINKELSTEIN, H.
353789	Spr.	FINKELSTONE, J., Sig. Coy.
448413	Spr.	FRANKLIN, E.
182236	Cpl.	FRIEND, C., Sig. Coy.
	Dvr.	FERNBACK,
279359	Pnr.	FREEMAN, B. J.
324354	Pnr.	FREEMAN, L.
324356	Pnr.	FAGILE, D.
166750	Pnr.	FOREMAN, G.
450504	Spr.	FREEMAN, H.
	Sgt.	FRANKENBERG, G. (M.M.).
553901	Spr.	FERMO, R., Corps Sig.
503424	Spr.	FRITZ, A.
382	Sig.	FRANKEL, A. P., H.Q. Sig. Sect.
547909	Spr.	FISHER, J., 113th Coy.
303946	Pnr.	FRANKENBERG, W. E.
472331	Pnr.	FELDMAN, M.
285144	Spr.	FREIDER, J.
388288	Spr.	FISHER, J.
324390	Pnr.	FRIEZE, I.
488413	Spr.	FRANKLYN, E.
3355	Spr.	FREEDMAN, A.
560	Spr.	FREEDMAN, H.
169885	Spr.	FREEDMAN, R.
208707	L/Cpl.	FERNBERG, L. B.
264314	Spr.	FREEDLAND, H.
478684	Spr.	FREEDMAN.
287228	Spr.	FREEDER, J.
335901	Spr.	FERMO, R.
904407	Spr.	FREIDMAN,
353335	Pnr.	FELDMAN, J.
341110	Spr.	FLORENCE, A.
191636	Spr.	FIELDMAN, A.
258813	Spr.	FRIEND, R.
	Spr.	FRASER, R. E. (M.M.).
47211	Spr.	FELDMAN, M.
443999	Spr.	FIMEBERG, L.
764324	Spr.	FERMIS.
334921	Spr.	FRANKLIN, J.
281686	Spr.	FLETCHER, W. E.
329561	Spr.	FREEDMAN, E.
	Spr.	FRAENKEL, L.
61729	Pnr.	GOLD, A., 77th Fld. Coy.
40742	Spr.	GALLEWSKI, M., 61st Fld. Coy.
9760	Pnr.	GORDON, H., 31st Div. Sig. Coy.
113138	Sgt.	GOLDSTEIN, A. A., 4th Spec. Bn.

Royal Engineers.—*Continued.*

145936 Spr. GOODMAN, E. (M.S.M.), 84th Fld. Co.
480170 Spr. GRAYMAN, P., 457th Fld. Coy.
161659 Spr. GALLON, I.
178921 Pnr. GREEN, L.,* 1st Special Bde.
179455 L/Cpl. GREEN, H., 3rd Special Bde.
129784 Pnr. GOLDSTEIN, J.,* 5th Special Bde.
192525 Pnr. GOLDMAN, J., 3rd Special Bde.
129064 Pnr. GORDON, J., 4th Special Bde.
438001 C.Q.M.S. GILT, H., 427th Fld. Coy.
95 Spr. GOLLANCE, R. S., 354th Elec. & Mec. Coy.
31342 Pnr. GOLDMAN, J., R.E. Sig., att. H.Q. 1st Brigade.
26416 Spr. GLASSER, B., 438th Fld. Coy.
152760 Spr. GOLDSTEIN, M., 3rd R.E. Wkshps.
244938 Spr. GRUBSTEIN, J., 8th Corps Sig. Coy.
471902 Spr. GREENBAUM, J., "L" Corps Sig. Cy.
153856 Spr. GOLDSTEIN, S., 84th Fld. Coy.
176095 Pnr. GALLANT, J., 4th G.B.D.
170011 Spr. GOLDSTONE, A., 2nd Prov. Coy.
3115 Dvr. GUTTENBERG, L., 3/1st Lond. Div. Sig. Coy.
28150 Sgt. GOODMAN, F., "L" Signal Coy.
113136 Cpl. GESTETNER, S., 188th Coy. Special B.
29056 Cpl. GOODMAN, O., 4th Signal Troop.
174303 Dvr. GINSBERG, L.
277379 Spr. GOODMAN, J.
Spr. GILCHRIST, c/o C.R.E.
507054 Spr. GOLDSTEIN, L.
5344 Pte. GOLDZWEIG, L., Signal Coy.
70226 Pte. GOTTLIEB, B.
285193 Pte. GARSON, S.
358230 Spr. GOLDBERG, S., 4th Fld. Survey Bde
303925 Spr. GOLDBERG, S. N.
459680 Spr. GOLDSTEIN, C., 41st Coy. N.
90233 Dvr. GORE, M.
188503 Spr. GORDON, B.
217638 Spr. GOLDMAN, C.
223614 Pte. GOLDBERG, J.
295772 Pte. GREENBERG, R., 58th Field Coy.
262910 Spr. GOLDSTEIN, J., 547th Fld Coy.
458020 Spr. GORFUNKLE, H.*
2819 Spr. GOLLAND, A.*
HR/205483 Pte. GOLDSTEIN, U.
530 Cpl. GREENBERG, H, 2nd Sig. Troop.
85151 Pte. GOLDSTONE, P.
277560 Pnr. GREEN, A.
255742 Spr. GILBERT, H. G.
355328 Pnr. GREENBAUM, H.
348587 Pnr. GOLDSTEIN, W.
324349 Pnr. GREENBAUM, S.
217638 Spr. GOLDMAN, S.
276245 Spr. GATES, J.
324318 Pnr. GOLDBERG, I.
348598 Pnr. GOLDSTEIN, H.
205483 Pnr. GOLDSTEIN, N.
210218 Pnr. GOLDBERG, H.

38684 Pte. GOLDBERG, S.
278420 Pte. GOLDBERG, I.
273858 Pte. GOLDBERG, H., 254th E. & M. Coy.
217103 Pte. GOODMAN, H.
232279 Spr. GOLDSTONE, J.
201809 Spr. GOULDSTON.
425 Spr. GREEN, E.
125103 Spr. GREENBERG, B.
128204 Pnr. GISH, A.
178921 Spr. GREEN, C.
264147 Spr. GOLDSTONE, J.
546953 Sgt. GOLDNER, C.
190608 Dvr. GLASS, A.
262910 Spr. GOLDSTEIN, I.
194023 Spr. GOLDSTONE, R.
246903 Spr. GITTLESON, A.
224532 Spr. GLASSMAN, M.
222261 Pnr. GLADSTONE, B.
553084 Spr. GOLDENBERG, M.
341100 Spr. GELLERSTEIN, R.
344600 Spr. GROSE, A.
349731 Spr. GREEN, H. L.
270854 Spr. GINSBERG, D. M.
344267 Spr. GRELEB, M.
210331 Pte. GALES, H.
208713 Pte. GOLDBERG, I.
280957 Spr. GORFUNKLE, J.
279379 Spr. GOODFIELD, J.
295772 Spr. GOLDSTEIN, L.
703634 Spr. GILDFORD, D.
242748 Spr. GETZIG, R.
244912 Spr. GLASS, J.
Pnr. GOLDSTEIN, A.
Spr. GLOSSER, B.
276245 Spr. GATES, J.
205483 Spr. GOLDSTEIN, N.
223828 Spr. GOLDBERG, R.
545600 Spr. GOLDBERG, M.
236830 Spr. GREEN, M.
16320 Spr. GUSOFSKY, P.
367861 Spr. GIBSON, H.
288876 Spr. GINOFSKY, J.
134997 Spr. GOLDMAN, S.
1149 Spr. GOLDBAUM, B. H.,* Kent Fortess C.
56492 Cpl. HOBSBAUM, H., 23rd G.H.Q.
107982 Spr. HARRIS, S., 284th A.T. Coy.
159859 Spr. HEISER, A., H.Q. Sig.
169503 Pnr. HADIDA, J., 4th Spec. Bn.
146475 Pnr. HOPPENSTADT, M., 4th Spec. Bn.
154672 Spr. HUDALY, L., 98th Fld. Coy.
102434 Spr. HALEY, J., 179th Coy.
129165 Pnr. HARBOUR, B., 2nd Special Bde.
2/11406 Pte. HESSEY, F. N., 12th Pontoon Pk.
165410 Spr. HOLTZ, M.
2254125 Spr. HESS, A. J., Wireless Sec. Sig. Cy.
7820 Spr. HARRIS, E., No. Ry. Tel. Coy.
277462 Pte. HERTZOG, H., 9th Army Tram. Coy.
151303 L/Cpl. HORNE, A., 253rd Tunnelling Cy.
332489 Spr. HYAMS, D.

Royal Engineers.—*Continued.*

103922 Spr. Harris, L., "C" Corps Sig. Coy.
558654 Cpl. Harrison, P., "A" Corps Sig. Coy.
WR/264194 Spr. Hartstone, A., 20th Light Ry. Sig. Coy.
172352 Spr. Harris, D., Sig. Depot.
178233 Spr. Harris, J., P. No. 2 Coy.
64816 Spr. Harris, W., Signal Depot.
25636 Spr. Harris, W. D.,* 1st Fld Coy.
152797 Spr. Hoffman, D., 239th Army Tps. Cy.
Spr. Hirschkop, C. (M.M.), Signals.
WR/552020 Cpl. Harris, J., 1st W.T.
300339 L/Cpl. Holtz, L. A., 56th Div. Sig. Cy.
186277 Dvr. Halpern, A., Sig. Sect.
550237 Sgt. Harris, W. R., 83rd Bde.
Spr. Hershon,
552337 Dvr. Howard, J.
359035 L/Cpl. Hertzog.
329587 Spr. Hymanson, S.
154671 L/Cpl. Hyman, H.
105949 Cpl. Harris, J.
6810 Pte. Hart, L.
286400 Spr. Hadlereich, J.
1722787 Pte. Hepner, J.
300793 Spr. Harris, C.
552339 Dvr. Howard, J.
305222 Pte. Himmelfarb, J.
343405 Spr. Harris, D.
103922 Spr. Harris, R.
Spr.-Clerk Hart, S. A. (M.S.M.).
345138 Pte. Hashman, H. H.
298403 Pte. Harris, B.
Pte. Harris, G.
Pte. Hyams, B.
804321 Dvr. Isaacs, H., 32nd Div. Army Trps.
176563 Pnr. Infeld, W., 4th Spec. Bn.
282 Dvr. Isaacs, H., A.T. Coy.
278082 Pte. Isaacs, B., 9th Tramway Coy.
302135 Pnr. Isaacs, I., Sig.
359596 Spr. Isaacs, S., 2nd Field Survey Bn.
WR/319924 Spr. Isaacs, S., 221st Trans. Coy.
80432 Dvr. Isaacs, H., 63rd Fld. Coy.
4/24507 Pte. Isaacs, A., 303rd R.C.C.
415019 Pte. Isbit, A., 258th Coy.
32330 Pte Isaacs, S., att. 222nd A.T. Coy.
220251 Pnr. Isaacs, J. H.
549705 Pte. Isaacs.
364413 Pte. Israelovitch, W.
291706 Pte. Isaacs, J.
345140 Spr. Isaacs, S.
Spr. Israels, G.
27202 Sgt. Jacobs, A., L. Signal Coy.
161660 Dvr. Josephs, J., 32nd Div. Sigs. H.Q.
192606 Pnr. Jasper, H., 4th Spec. Bn.
105067 Spr. Jacobs, J., 230th A.T. Coy.
259198 Pte. Joel, L. I.
547905 Spr. Juweiler, A., "C" Corps Sig. Coy.
033879 Pte. Jacobowiez, N., Wireless T. Corps.

250844 Pnr. Jackson, B.
232310 Spr. Jacobs, J., 17th Div. Sig. Coy.
WR/43202 Pnr. Jackson, D., 340th R.C.C.
397690 Sgt. Jacobs, D. A. (M.S.M.), 1st Sge. Coy.
551976 Spr. Jacobs, L. G., 47th Div. Sig. Coy.
161341 Pnr. Jopper, S., 40th Div. Sig. Coy.
360336 Spr. Jacobs, J. Z., 497th Fld. Coy.
16711 Spr. Jacobs, J.,* 206th Fld. Coy.
67800 Spr. Jacobs, F. C.,* 154th Fld. Coy.
128477 Pnr. Jenkins, H., 3rd Special Bde.
167897 Sgt. Jacobs, A. I., 174th Tunn. Coy.
164041 Pte. Jacobs, R. C., 8th Pontoon Park.
167439 Pnr. Chem. Jacobs, J. M.
WR/279286 Pte. Jacobs, B.
263185 Spr. Joseph, D., 7th Fld. Coy.
259288 Pnr. Jones, A. P.
33183 Cpl. Jacobs, J.
Sgt. Jacobs, M. C., Signal Bn.
347991 Pnr. Jacobs, B.
324664 Spr. Jacobson, J.
161660 Spr. Joseph, S.
297043 Pte. Jacobson, J.
480400 Spr. Jacobs, Army Sigs.
232288 Pte. Jagger, B.
205076 Pte. Jockelson, S.
391833 Pte. Jacobs, B.
357671 Pte. Jaffe, S.
330131 Pnr. Joseph, J.
31816 L/Cpl. Jacobs, W. A.
302166 Pnr. Jay, G. E.
289780 Spr. Jacobs, M.
325708 Pnr. Jacobs, G.
3591 Spr. Jacobs, M.
Sgt. Jacobs, C. V. R. (M.S.M.).
167644 Spr. Jacobs, A.
263851 Dvr. Jacobs, S. A.
W2/509971 Pnr. Jacobs, C. H.
167887 Spr. Jacobs, E.
33542 Spr. Jacobs, G.
Sgt. Jacobs, G. (M.M.).
342602 Spr. Josephs, J.
69617 L/Cpl. Jacobs, J.
Spr. Joseph, F.
1269 Spr. Kossick, D., 2nd Non. Fld. Coy.
Sgt. Kitching, M., 92nd Inf. Bde. H.Q.
70657 Spr. Kelly, T. H., 3rd Army Sig. Coy.
471662 Spr. Kaufman, D., Sig. Coy. H.Q.
165283 Pnr. Koffer, L., 1st Sig. Coy.
171199 Spr. Klem, D., 1st Army R.E. Wkshp.
6783 Pte. Kasanoski, W., 511th Fld. Coy.
171568 Spr. Klebensky, J., 261st R.C.C.
9690 Dvr. Kaplan, L., "P" Corps. Sigs.
198220 Spr. Kuchner, A., Wireless Section.
Pte. Korzilski, L., 8th Army Tram. Co.
28211 Cpl. Krauss, D. E., "L" Signal Coy.
358686 Spr. Karnofsky, L., 8th Fld. Corps.
301452 Pte. Kutchinsky, A.
335384 Pte. Kates, H.

Royal Engineers.—Continued.

203682 Spr. KAPLAN, H.
201196 Spr. KARMINSKY, J.
Cpl. KLOOT, H. E.
264317 Spr. KEMP, I.
WR/43111 Pnr. KINSLER, S., 312th R.C.C.
348481 Pnr. KRUSLER, S.
347463 Pnr. KRAMER, N.
163791 Spr. KEIBSMAN, B. J.
425 Dvr. KROTSKY, P.
98738 Dvr. KAUFMAN, E.
4807 Cpl. KENYON, A. J.
210296 Pte. KENNAR, S.
114102 Spr. KOSKY, C.
344808 Pnr. KELLETT, G.
9608 Spr. KEPHAN, W.
40330 Spr. KAYOPKIS, S.
733843 Spr. KARAGANSKY, B.
3125557 Spr. KAMENSKY, S.
908 Sgt. LACY, J., (D.C.M.) 2/3rd London.
63966 Spr. LANGDON, A., 103rd Fld. Coy.
Spr. LYONS, D., 4th Lond. Fld. Coy.
2329 Spr. LYON, H. M., 1/2nd Lond. Fld. Coy.
141737 Dvr. LEVANE, R., 32nd Div. Army Trps.
106079 Cpl. LOB, R., 1st Spec. Bn.
154823 Pnr. LEVY, P., 4th Spec. Bn.
74360 Spr. LIVINGSTONE, H. N., 35th Airline S.
220295 Spr. LEVY, V., 1st Special Bde.
186355 Pnr. LEVINE, B., 1st Special Bde.
195942 Pnr. LEVINE, A. E., 3rd Special Bde.
1976467 Pnr. LEWIS, A., 3rd Special Bde.
214747 Pnr. LEVY, S., 5th Special Bde.
554014 Sgt. LYON, C. C., 511th Fld. Coy.
191819 Spr. LEVY, C. A., 42nd Div. Sig. Coy.
552484 Dvr. LYONS, C. J., 518th Fld. Coy.
560358 L/Cpl. LEE, A. A., 47th Div. Sig. Coy.
249953 Spr. LEVY, B., Sig. Coy.
470911 Spr. LEVENE, I.,* 210th Fld. Coy.
126698 Spr. LEWIS, N., Sp. Wireless, 1st Army.
Spr. LAZARUS, S., R.E.D. Troops.
257087 Spr. LICHSTEIN, M., R.O.D.
37569 Pte. LOBER, S., 8th Army Tramway Coy.
211188 Pnr. LIGHTMAN, A., Signal Sub. Sect.
67129 Spr. LAVENE, S., 458th Fld. Coy.
WR/24760 Pnr. LYONS, J., 334th R.C.C.
WR/277457 L/Cpl. LAWRENCE, H. L., 29th L.R. Operating Coy.
WR/278380 Pnr. LIEBGLICK, A., 29th L.R. Operating Coy.
157990 Spr. LAURENCE, M., 121st Fld. Coy.
T/330204 Dvr. LEVENE, H., 346th R.C.C.
3634 Spr. LAURENCE, B. H., Northd. Fld. Coy.
106131 Cpl. LEVER, D., 186th Coy.
Sgt. LINDE, H., 79th Fld. Coy.
31036 Spr. LEVY, H., 2nd Ind. Field Squad.
23679 Spr. LEVY, L.
220295 Pnr. LEVY, V. W.
381765 Pte. LEVINSON, H., 2nd Corps Camouflege Park.
141737 Spr. LEVENE, R.
480198 Spr. LAPPING, D., 457th Fld. Coy.
155545 Pnr. LIPITZ, H.
L/Cpl. LOUIS, J.
206948 Spr. LEDERER, R.
259395 Pnr. LEON M., 29th Div.
259737 Pnr. LEVERTON, S. C., Wireless Sect.
46979 Spr. LEE, M. J.
Pnr. LAWRENCE, F., Sig. Coy.
WR/20516 Spr. LESCHINSKY, R.O.D.
353094 Spr. LEVY, M., R.O.D.
552484 Dvr. LYONS, C. S., 548th Fld. Coy.
359227 Pnr. LONGMAN, E.,* 7th F. R. Coy.
522650 Spr. LEDERMAN, J.
342268 Spr. LEVY, E.
152745 Spr. LEVY.
145860 Spr. LEVENE, M
209106 Spr. LEVY, T.
243901 Spr. LARAINE, I.
WR/288860 Spr. LEVY, M., 1st Field Squad.
266339 Spr. LIVINGSTONE, I. G.
564127 Spr. LANDSTONE, J. E.
311408 Spr. LAZARUS (LAWRENCE), J. S.* (M.M.).
Pte. LANDSTONE, A.
281627 Spr. LEVY, J.
546160 L/Cpl. LEVY, D.
WR/260853 L/Cpl. LEVY, S., Signal Coy.
Cpl. LEAVY, W., 20th Motor Cyclist Coy.
546049 Spr. LAWTON, A. E., 642nd Fld. Coy.
289286 Spr. LEVY, J.
HR/205483 Dvr. LAZARUS, J. L.
356283 Pte. LEVI, I.
594600 Pte. LEIBSHUTZ, I.
208117 Pnr. LEECH, W.
279290 Pnr. LUBOVSKY, J.
251290 Spr. LATHAM, R. J.
106052 Sgt. LAKTRAGER, M.
355334 Pnr. LEVENE, J.
356283 Spr. LEVI, A. E.
138087 L/Cpl. LAZARUS, L.
324237 Pnr. LEIBOVITCH, B.
29936 Rfm. LUMBERMAN, H.
151527 Spr. LAZARUS, H. A.
322383 Pte. LEWRY, H.
527977 Pnr. LAZARUS, C., 8th Foreway Coy.
430 Pnr. LEVENE, J., R.C. Coy.
209156 Dvr. LEVI, J.
328015 Pte. LUKOVSKY, J.
312013 Spr. LESTER, A.
250704 Spr. LEVY, I.
706828 Pnr. LEVY, S.
61940 Spr. LATHAN, R. J.
23679 Pte. LEVY, L.
567557 Spr. LEVINSON, B.
238000 Pnr. LEWIS, H. P.
106131 Cpl. LEVER, D.

Royal Engineers.—*Continued.*

960 L/Cpl. LEVY, D.
169525 L/Cpl. LYNES, C. J.
2372 Dvr. LYONS, C. S.
316918 Spr. LAZARUS, B.
341200 Spr. LEVINE, J.
430728 Pnr. LIPMAN, A.
281939 Pte. LUPOVITCH, W., Wireless.
226981 Pte. LYONS, J.
322383 Pnr. LEVY, H.
241333 Spr. LOGITCH, H.
67129 Spr. LEVINE, G.
553015 Spr. LIPSCHITZ, S.
145860 Spr. LEVINE, H. M.
HR/151527 Spr. LAZARUS, H. A.
343867 Spr. LEVIN, N.
342268 Spr. LEVEY, L.
101085 Spr. LEACHINSKY, J.
595992 Cpl. LAWRENCE, J.
53009 Dvr. MEADER, P., 18th Div. Sig. Coy.
80058 Dvr. MARKS, J., 94th Fld. Coy.
480287 Dvr. MOSS, D., 457th Fld. Coy.
129821 Spr. MILLER, D., 1st Special Bde.
179588 Spr. MOSES, E., 1st Special Bde.
146713 Pnr. MYERSON, N.,* 3rd Special Bde.
476 Cpl. MORRIS, H., "Y" Corps Sig. Coy.
554187 Spr. MORRIS, A., 511th Fld. Coy.
215323 Spr. MARGRETT, A., R.E.D. Troops.
236907 Spr. MAZZIER, I., Q. Sec. Wireless, 15th Corps.
434417 Spr. MENKIN, C. S., 88th Motor Air. Sec.
M2/048719 Pte. MARKS, G., 1st Army Sig. Coy.
310557 Spr. MARKS, S., Sig.
43859 Spr. MORRIS, H. F., 458th Fld. Coy.
324248 Pnr. MILLER, S., R.O.D.
42423 Pnr. MAGNUS, J. W., 337th R.C.C.
210722 Pnr. MICHAELS, L., 3rd Corps H.A. Sig.
WR/42392 Pnr. MILNER, J., 334th R.C.C.
312036 Spr. MOSS, S., 289th Army Troops Coy.
267648 L/Cpl. MEISNER, E., 14th Signal Coy.
78738 Spr. MARSHALL, J. J., T.T. Cable Sect.
377616 Pte. MARKS, H., att. R.E. Sigs. 198th Inf.
224920 Pnr. MYERSON, J., 3rd Special Bde.
249102 Cpl. MENDOZA, R. (M.M), 18th Sig. Coy.
176055 Spr. MITCHELL, J., 4th G.B.D.
28151 Sgt. MYERS, R., "L" Signal Coy.
106095 Cpl. MACABORSKI, A. H.,* 186th Coy. Special Bde.
58484 Pte. MARKS, M., 43rd Coy.
Pte. MOSES, W.
187964 Spr. MOSCOW, J.
300711 Spr. MILLER, J., 487th Fld. Coy.
223668 Spr. MOSES, M., 487th Fld. Coy.
61862 Spr. MOSS, A. E.,* 82nd Fld. Coy.
16029 Pte. MENDOZA.
51816 Pte. MARKSON, B.
WR/291010 Spr. MORRIS, G., R.O.D.
299300 Pte. MARKS, E.
132713 Spr. MARCHANT, J. A.
152710 Spr. MARCHANT, S.
284732 Spr. MYERS, C.
L/Cpl. MYERS, J. J. (M.M.).
236798 Spr. MILLER, A.
27824 Spr. MOSCOVITCH, M.
218077 Spr. MILLER, F.
12333 Pte. MANN, A.
196005 Pnr. MOREYNO, S.
2655 Pte. MORRIS, S.
161189 L/Cpl. MICHAEL, G. C.
548963 Pnr. MYERS, J.
Sgt. MOSES, C. H. (D.C.M.).
343101 Spr. MARKS, E.
519703 Spr. MORRIS, S.
301390 Pnr. MORRIS, J.
298375 Spr. MILSTONE, P.
184249 Spr. MUSCOVITCH, L.
400238 Spr. MARKS, I.
341076 Pnr. MARCHIN, G. A.
312763 Spr. MANLICH, J.
458305 Pnr. MARCUS, H.
117650 C.S.M. MARTIN, C.
184616 Pnr. Chemist MEERSON, R.
33239 Spr. MORRISON, A.
277060 Spr. MEERSKIN, H.
79683 Sgt. MALAROF, M.
347432 Pte. MAY, H.
343498 Pnr. MILLER, I.
L/Cpl. MOSS, H.
Dvr. MANDELSTAN, J.
34020 Pte. MANCOF, M.
30253 Cpl. NORDWALD, L., "L" Signal Coy.
161354 Pnr. NATHAN, A.
87005 Spr. NATHAN, H. E., 73rd Fld. Coy.
23532 Spr. NORMAN, D., 29th L.R. Oper. Coy.
277254 Spr. NEWMAN, P.
214238 L/Cpl. NIEBERG, A.
285888 Spr. NEWRICK, D.
286400 Spr. NADLEREICH, J.
T4/232806 Dvr. NATANIELOV, N.
570130 Spr. NATHAN, A. I., Postal Service.
296918 Spr. NATHAN, N., 94th Bde. Hrs.
43952 Pnr. NEASY, T.
338794 Spr. NEWMARK, E. L.
324249 Spr. NEDDLEMAN, D.
324294 Pnr. NEEDLEMAN, D.
128210 Pte. NEWMAN, M.
300790 Pte. NERVA, M.
151947 Spr. OESTERMAN, H., 5th Army Sig. Coy.
149175 Cpl. OLSWANG, M., 4th Army Tps. S. Co.
Sgt. OPPENHEIM, R. (M.M.).
327679 Spr. OYZER, P.
1706 Dvr. PHILLIPS, H., 3rd Lond.
81908 Spr. PLATT, D., 200th Fld. Coy.
66780 Spr. PHILLIPS, S., 90th Fld. Coy.
129481 Pnr. PRESS, I. J., 2nd Special Bde.
197233 Spr. PHILLIPS, P., Div. Sig. Coy.

Royal Engineers.—*Continued.*

225026	Pnr. POMERANTZ, I.,* 4th Spec. Coy.
152720	2/Cpl. POU, P., 239th A.T. Coy.
M/296625	Pte. PHILLIPS, H., 1st Sig. Const. Co.
107496	C.S.M. PYSER, R. (M.S.M.), Met. Sect.
342331	Pnr. POSNER, S., 256th Tunnelling Coy.
560697	Pnr. POLLEN, H., 3rd Special Bde.
550085	Spr. PEARSE, J., 203rd Coy.
76658	Cpl. PHILLIPS, C., "C" A. Cp. Sigs.
	Spr. PARK, A., R.E. Wireless Cav. Corps Signals.
167277	Spr. POLVANSKY, M. H.
104790	Spr. PYSER, M., I.W.T.
58631	Spr. PELLMAN, W.
163146	Dvr. PASS, G.
	Pnr. PRICE, P.
152371	Pte. PEARLMAN, J.*
157845	Pnr. PLATKIN, G.
200167	Pnr. PETERS, A.
205723	Spr. PHILLIPS,
WR/291086	Spr. PARK, J., R.O.D.
160539	Spr. PINTO, J.
475984	Pte. PORTH, U., R.O.D.
77658	Cpl. PHILLIPS, P.
	Pte. PLOTSKY, S.
	Cpl. PLOTSKY, J.
62259	C.Q.M.S. PERKS, S. C.
51271	Spr. PAYMAN, S.
244943	Spr. PAUL, F., 2nd Sect. Wireless.
192220	Pte. PRUSKY, M.
138297	Spr. PRICE, M.
316392	Pnr. PIECHNER, S.
223793	Spr. PHILLIPS, N.
317371	Pte. PHILLIPS, B.
326562	Pte. POLTINS, J.
28912	Spr. RICKARDS, F., 9th Fld. Coy.
50582	Dvr. ROGERS, H., 21st Div. Sig. Coy.
70244	Spr. ROTHMAN, W., 3rd Army Sig. Coy.
154720	Pnr. ROSEN, J.,* 4th Spec. Bn.
154678	Spr. ROSE, J., 128th Fld. Coy.
480424	Dvr. REISS, B., 2/3rd W. Riding F. Coy.
184618	Pnr. RINDER, L., 1st Special Bde.
120637	Cpl. RUDOLF, M. E. S., 2nd Special Bde.
246053	Spr. ROSENBERG, M., "C" Corps Sig. Cy.
166187	Spr. ROSENBERG, J., 34th Div. Sig. Coy.
251763	Spr. ROUSSAK, J., Sig. Coy.
161343	Pnr. REBUCK, P., 17th Div. Sig. Coy.
224976	Spr. ROSENTHAL, M., "E" Special Coy.
360069	Spr. ROUTLEDGE, G. E.
94422	Sgt. ROBINSON, E. H.
34850	Spr. ROSENTHAL, J., 51st Div. Sig. Coy.
312017	Spr. RUSSELL, L., 4th Fld. Surrey Bn.
164201	Spr. ROSENTHAL, J. S., 15th Sig. Coy.
341654	Spr. ROSANSKY, A. J., 15th Sig. Coy.
206747	Pnr. ROSEN, P., 4th Special Bde.
172071	Cpl. ROSEN, D., 2nd Sig. Squad.
173212	Pte. ROSENBERG, M.
1458	Pte. ROBBIN, B.
289987	Pnr. RUFFMAN, S., 1st L.O.R. Corps.
54830	Spr. ROSENTHAL, J., Signal Coy.
186765	Gnr. ROSENWEIN, W., "C" Special Coy.
364712	L/Cpl. RIFKIN, I.
42473	Pte. ROGINSKY, A.
WR/553298	Spr. ROSS, O., 1st W.T.
265237	Spr. ROMAIN, M. A., 17th Div. Signals.
145394	Spr. ROSENBERG, I.
450433	Pnr. RUBENSTEIN, E.
172071	Cpl. ROSEN, D.
166752	Spr. ROSENBERG, H., "A" Coy.
53353	Pte. REUBEN, E. T.
312190	Spr. ROBERTS, S.
324315	Spr. ROSENBERG, W.
324391	Pnr. ROSEGARD, J. M.
562266	L/Cpl. ROGOFF, J.
57407	Pte. ROSENBLOOM, H., G.R. Coy.
222682	Cpl. ROSEN, H.
208334	Spr. ROSS, A.
276220	Spr. RICHMAN, J.
264301	Spr. ROSENTHALL, V.
161747	Spr. ROSENFELDT, M.
192220	Pnr. RUSKY, M.
525241	Pte. ROTHBAND, D., 362nd Coy.
278292	Pnr. ROSEN, I.
341654	Spr. ROSE, M. J.
166752	Spr. ROSENBERG, A.
184989	Spr. ROSENTHAL, S.
434485	Pte. ROSENBERG, W.
25231	L/Cpl. RECTOR, M.
300958	Spr. ROSEN, H. B.
1585	Spr. ROSENBERG, W.
404626	Spr. REDMAN, M.
552996	Spr. ROLANDS, E. A.
342520	Pnr. REDWOOD, I.
	Sgt. ROSEN, H. (D.C.M., M.M.).
345322	Spr. ROSENTHAL, H.
346054	Spr. ROBERTS, S.
91904	Pte. RICHER.
2354	Pte. ROSENWICK, J.
210793	Spr. RACKIND, S.
321604	Spr. RAYLER, J.
348057	Spr. RUH, L.
347404	Spr. ROSENTHAL, P.
58356	Spr. SHALGOSKY, M., 20th Sig. Coy.
1586	Spr. SILVERMAN, A., 4th London.
1586	Spr. SILVERMAN, A., 4th Lond. Fld. Coy.
966	Spr. SOLOMON, G., 1/2nd Lond. Fld. Cy.
1415	Cpl. SAMSON, V.A., 47th Div. Sig. Coy.
76699	Pnr. SHULMAN, S., 16th Sig. Coy.
154721	Pnr. SILVERSTON, C. J., 4th Spec. Bn.
131769	Pnr. SMOLLEN, B., 236th A.T. Coy.
1256	L/Cpl. SALOMAN, A. J.
742	Spr. STONE, S., 2nd Glam. A.T. Coy.
3377	Spr. SOLOMAN, A., 461st W. Riding F. C.
120576	Cpl. SAPPER, M., 1st Special Bde.
192826	Pnr. SOLOMON, A., 1st Special Bde.
94455	Spr. SPRINGER, M., 2nd Sig. Coy.

Royal Engineers.—*Continued.*

- 83841 Spr. SUMRIE, C., 210th Fld. Coy.
- 476555 Spr. SOLOMON, A., 458th W.R. Fld. Coy.
- 444100 Dvr. SALOMON, E., 42nd Div. Sig. Coy.
- 203239 Rfm. SILVERSTONE, A., 154th Fld. Coy.
- 221984 Pnr. STONE, M., Sig. Coy.
- 267508 Pnr. SIMMONS, M., R.O.D.
- 267507 Pnr. SIMMONS, S., R.O.D.
- 26809 Spr. SALTER, H.
- 9314 Spr. SABER, F., 15th Corps Signals.
- WR/42475 Pte. SILVERMAN, S., 331st R.C.C.
- WR/42927 Pte. SIMONOVITCH, M., 331st R.C.C.
- 549753 Pnr. SLUIS, J., 58th Div. Sig. Coy.
- 244655 A/L/Cpl. SHAFFIR, B. L., 4th Fld. Survey
- 170017 A/Cpl. SOLOMON, J., 9th Pontoon Park.
- 199557 Dvr. SILVERBERG, M., 209th Fld. Coy.
- 2730 L/Cpl. SOLOMON, J., 60th Inf. Bde. H.Q.
- 358105 Spr. SLANWEIT, M. M., "A" Corps Sig.
- 129774 Pnr. SPENCER, H., 4th Spec. Coy.
- 24493 Spr. SANIMA, E., Wireless Sect.
- 246021 Spr. SYTERCEL, C. M., Wirelss Section.
- 424320 Pnr. SUGARMAN, I., 3rd Special Bde.
- 78399 Spr. SIMMONS, H., "C" A. Corps Sigs.
- 222877 Spr. STAAL, L., I.W.T.
- 176053 Spr. STANTON, J., G.B.D. 8th Coy.
- 148948 Spr. SABEL, C.
- 20831 Spr. STANDER, B.,* 23rd Fld. Coy.
- 172235 Pnr. SEGENFIELD, I., Signal Depot.
- 203338 Spr. SEIGENBERG, E.
- 125510 Spr. SIMONS, W., L.B.
- Pte. SILVER, P.
- 192818 Pnr. SHANK, J., Spec. Bde.
- 244950 Spr. SIPPERT, S., 3rd Corps Sig.
- 458021 Spr. SUSS, H. M., 124th Fld. Coy.
- 509951 Pnr. SALMON, M. J.
- 337 Pte. SCHWARTZGLASS, S.
- 213259 Spr. SALOMON, M.
- 187781 Spr. SAWYER, J.
- 59951 Spr. SALMON, N.
- 457957 Spr. SHLESINGER, S.
- 96016 Spr. SEGAL, H.
- 213295 Spr. SOLOMON, W., 459th Fld. Coy.
- 548091 Spr. SPIELSINGER, J., 642nd Fld. Coy.
- 558503 Spr. SIMMONS, A., 642nd Fld. Coy.
- 169422 Spr. SUSS, M.
- 221771 Pnr. STEINLOFT, J.
- 199876 Spr. SOLOMON, T.
- 161333 Pnr. SHORE, H. A'.
- 216216 Sig. SCHEWATSCHUK, S. E.
- 190271 Spr. SALVEST, M.
- 825193 Spr. SARSON, S.
- 79686 Pnr. SEGALL, G.
- 208242 Spr. SMITH, L.
- 357135 Spr. STERN, B.
- 562418 Cpl. SCHAMASCH, M. C.
- 15765 Dvr. SOLOMON, V.
- 254515 Spr. SPIALTER, S., Wireless.
- 537888 Spr. SALAMON,
- 324350 Pnr. SUGAR, J.
- 324304 Pte. SHUTER, A.
- 357003 Dvr. SPIELSINGER, J.
- 301395 Spr. SHAPIRO, I.
- 342079 Spr. STERN, N.
- 329595 Spr. STONE,
- 276555 Spr. SOLOMON, A.
- 552303 Spr. SILVERMAN, A.
- 216566 Spr. SKOTNICKI, J.
- 300921 Spr. SUNSHINE.
- 961107 Spr. SHERMAN, N.
- 148949 L/Cpl. SABEL, J.
- 326612 Spr. SCHWARTZ, S.
- 350780 Pnr. SAUL, M.
- HR/205244 Spr. SEGAR, H.
- 347937 Pte. SIMON, M.
- 151069 Pte. SAMUELS.
- 354036 Spr. STEPHENSON, F., R.O.D.
- 515276 Spr. STAROSELSKI, Sig. Coy.
- 537808 Spr. SALOMON.
- 167513 Spr. SOLOWAY, A. A.
- 218125 Spr. SHOOLMAN, I.
- 339816 Spr. SASNER, C.
- 339816 Spr. SASUER, C.
- 348005 Pte. SUGARMAN, D.
- V/392 Spr. SELYER, N.
- 2nd Cpl. SIMONS, G. E. (M.S.M.).
- 257053 Spr. SOMOLOVITCH, S.
- 242455 Spr. SOLOMON, R. E.
- 347936 Pnr. SCHOLEPSKY, S.
- 324304 Spr. SHECHTER, A.
- 611970 Pte. SHIERS, L., 218th Coy.
- 334932 Pte. SAMUEL, D. L., H. Spec. Coy.
- 32187 L/Cpl. SPIRO, L. L.
- 87189 Dvr. SAMPSON, R.
- 546240 Cpl. SAMUEL, B.
- 548094 Spr. SOLOMON, J. G.
- 4864 Sgt. SAMPSON, A., Tel. Sect.
- 2587 Pnr. SIMMONS,
- 166914 Spr. SIMONS, N.
- 2336 Spr. SOLOMONS, S.
- 242455 Spr. SOLOMON, R.
- 330659 Spr. SHAPNISTSKY, R.
- 330115 Spr. SLABOTKIE, H.
- 871189 Dvr. SAMPSON, R.
- 216566 Spr. SCOTT, J.
- 9320103 Spr. SHULMAN.
- 315263 Spr. STEIN, H.
- Spr. SAMPSON, R.
- 347402 Spr. SOLOMONS, I.
- 358105 Spr. STANDISH, M.
- 348937 Pnr. SIMON, M.
- 108815 Pte. SAMUELS, L.
- Sig. SAVILLE, A.
- 476568 Spr. TOMPOFSKY, D., 461st W.R. F. Coy.
- 146227 Cpl. TRAGHEIM,* E., 4th Special Bde.
- 225060 Pnr. TAYLOR, M., Met. Sect.
- 361712 Pnr. TCHOUDNOWSKY, S., Met. Sect.

Royal Engineers.—*Continued.*

341155	Pnr.	TANCHON, 31st Div. Sig. Coy.
161341	Pnr.	TOPPER, S., Sig. Depot. Adv. Base.
	Sig.	TAYLOR, J.
78852	Spr.	TOBIAS, J.
324151	Pnr.	TERREBAUM, S. S.
553901	Spr.	TERUS, R.
222420	Spr.	TOCHINSKY, H.
224982	Spr.	TRESMAN, J. J.
351818	Pnr.	TOBE, M.
129129	Sgt.	VICKERS, G. (M.M.), 4th Spec. Bn.
106550	Cpl.	VAN JEUNS, J. L., 2nd Spec. Bn.
3505	Spr.	VANBROKE, J., 2/1st Lond. Fld. Coy.
161661	Pnr.	VELLIMAN, J. J., Signal Coy.
31055	Cpl.	VANE, M.
304795	Pte.	VINEBERG, H.
340827	Pnr.	VAN STRAATEN, E.
330036	Spr.	VINER, L.
413475	Pnr.	VAN BULLEN.
449	L/Cpl.	WOOLFE, E., 1st Lond. Fld. Coy.
154678	Dvr.	WRIGHTMAN, N., 106th Fld. Coy.
125510	Spr.	WOOLF, S., 3rd Lab. Bn.
146370	Pnr.	WOOLF,* H. L., 1st Special Bde.
176564	Pnr.	WELDMAN, J., 4th Special Bde.
438619	Spr.	WINEBERG, J., 66th Div.
	Spr.	WEISWALL, S., R.O.D.
165437	Spr.	WOOLMAN, J., 13th Corps H.A. Sig. Section.
89098	L/Cpl.	WISE, R., 7th Army Tram. Coy.
54631	Dvr.	WOLFE, E., 509th Fld. Coy.
516	Spr.	WALNITZ, 1/1st E. Riding Fld. Coy.
18794	Spr.	WOOLMAN, H.
411729	Pte.	WYSER, A.
544847	Pte.	WOOD, H., 248th.
WR/288651	Spr.	WISEMAN, I.
166745	Spr.	WOOLF, J., 2nd R.B.
170787	L/Cpl.	WEISBLOOM, P. D.
350026	Pnr.	WEBER, H.
249076	Pte.	WACKER, S.
G/506730	Pte.	WORTMAN, A. H.
3033872	Pte.	WIZOKSKY.
341834	Spr.	WOLFE, C. D.
D.M.2/221372	Pnr.	WOLFSON, S.
322555	Spr.	WOOLFE, M.
355744	Spr.	WOLFSON, H. A.
289014	Pnr.	WELLS, J., L. Spec. Coy.
490182	Dvr.	WILLIAMS, J.
142996	Spr.	WALDMAN, L.
161552	Pnr.	WALROCK, C.
3218	L/Cpl.	WEINBERG, J.
169416	Spr.	WOLFSBERGEN, B.
142996	Spr.	WEILDMAN' J.
344335	Spr.	WARKAWSKY, I.
208974	Pte.	WINTER, S.
438169	Spr.	WOOLF, H.
246670	Pte.	WOLFSBERGER, I.
548964	Pte.	WOLFE, J.
424170	Spr.	WHITEFIELD, S.
349751	Pnr.	WINSTON, L.
3218	Pnr.	WIMBERG, J.
259584	Pnr.	YUDKEVITCH, R., 11th Div.
255427	Spr.	ZAND, M., 20th Sig. Coy.
106052	Sgt.	ZAKTRAGER, M., 1st Spec. Bde.
324617	Spr.	ZASS, H., 245th (Guernsey) A.T. Cy.
42533	Pte.	ZIMMIRMAN, V., 2nd.
72227	A/Cpl.	ZIELINSKY, J.
327209	Spr.	ZAITAN, A.
213629	Spr.	ZARTMAN, C.
301066	Spr.	ZELLER, A.

* Killed in Action or died on Active Service.

FOOT GUARDS.

OFFICERS.

Lieut. ABRAHAMS, A. C. L.,,* 3rd Coldstream Gds.
Capt. BONN. W. A. L. (M.C.), Welch Guards.
Lieut. JACOBS, J. H.
Capt. LEVY, M.,* 2nd Irish Guards.
2nd Lieut. LEVY, P. R., Irish Guards.
2nd Lieut. MONTAGU, The Hon. S. A. S., 2nd Grenadier Guards.
Lieut. PINTO, R. J. (M.C.), 3rd Coldstream Gds.
Lieut. RAPHAEL, C. E., 3rd Coldstream Guards.
Capt. SEELEY, M. G., Coldstream Guards.
Capt. SASSOON, R. E. (M.C.), Coldstream Guards.

N.C.O.'s AND MEN.

20990	Dmr.	ALEXANDER, L., 1st Gren. Gds.
12033	Pte.	BROWN, M.,* 1st Coldstreams Gds.
720	Tpr.	BARNARD, L., R. Horse Guards.
	Pte.	BAKER, J. I., 2nd Grenadier Guards.
15834	Pte	BAKER, D., 3rd Grenadier Gds.
9186	Pte.	BARNETT, J.,* 2nd Scots Guards.
25432	Pte.	CASTLE, R., 5th Grenadier Gds.
29406	Pte.	CHALCROFT, H., 1st Grenadier Gds.
3848	Dmr.	CHYTE, Household Bn.
	Pte.	CHARIG, A., 2nd Grenadier Gds.
13109	Pte.	CHESNEY, D.,* 1st Coldstream Gds.
3126	Pte.	COHEN, M., Machine Gun Gds.
2968	Pte.	COHEN, J., Welch Guards.
15048	Pte.	COBDEN, L., Scots Guards.
23202	Pte.	COLLINS, J., 4th Grenadier Gds.
31029	Pte.	COLLINS, D.,* 1st Grenadier Gds.
17110	L/Cpl.	COLLINS, B.,* 1st Gren. Gds.
12320	Pte.	CRASTEN, D., Irish Guards.
8292	Pte.	CURTIS, R. J., 2nd Scots Guards.
15286	Cpl.	DANCYGER, B., 1st Coldstream Gds.
27407	Pte.	DE COSTA, M., 1st Grenadier Gds.
	Pte.	DOCKA, Gren. Gds.
	B/Cpl.	EMANUEL, J. (M.M.), Welch Gds.
170	Sgt.	EPSTEIN, J., 1st Welch Guards.
20424	Pte.	FERNANDEZ, B., Grenadier Gds.
18589	Pte.	FIELD, H., 5th Coldstream Gds.

Foot Guards.—Continued.

18587 Pte. FIELD, J. S., 1st Coldstream Gds.
8571 Pte. FILES, J., 2nd Scots Gds.
15771 Pte. FISHEL, P., 3rd Scots Gds.
11054 Pte. GAFFIN, T., Irish Gds. attd. 1st Guards Bde. M.G.C.
19260 Pte. GOTTCLIFFE, H., 2nd Cold. Gds.
1068 Tpr. GOODMAN, S. 1st Life Gds.
27593 Pte. GOLDBERG, L., Grenadier Gds.
24755 Pte. GOLDINSKY, Grenadier Gds.
22466 Pte. GLAZER, W., Coldstream Guards.
10889 Pte. HARRIS, J., 1st Coldstream Gds.
8701 Pte. HART, I., Scots Guards.
21084 Pte. HERMAN, S., 4th Grenadier Gds.
9813 L/Cpl. HYMAN, J., 1st Bn.
Pte. HYAMS, S. A., Grenadier Gds.
4762 Pte. JACOBS, C.,* 2nd Scots Gds.
25157 Pte. JENNENS, W., 5th Grenadier Gds.
Pte. JOSEPH, D., 3rd Scots Guards.
20083 Pte. JOSEPH, C. S., 3rd Gren. Gds.
12326 Pte. KRASTNER, D., 3rd Bn.
15225 Pte. LAZARUS, J., 2nd Scots Gds.
2344 Pte. LEWIS, L., 1st Welch Gds.
28561 L/Cpl. LEVYVELD, J., Coldstream Gds.
32408 Pte. LYONS, L.
29540 Pte. LYONSON, L., 3rd Grenadier Gds.
11610 Pte. MARKS, H.,* 1st Scots Gds.
5705 Sgt. MARKS, M. J., (D.C.M.), 3rd Coldstream Guards.
2263 Gdsm. MARKS, B., 4th Bn.
27760 Gdsm. MAZARKOFF, A., 5th Gren. Gds.
26479 Cpl. MARTIN, J., Grenadier Gds.
7901 Pte. MENDELSSOHN, J., 3rd Gren. Gds.
19093 Cpl. MENDOZA, E., 2nd Gren. Gds.
13154 Pte. MICKLER, Irish Guards.
Pte. MALLIS, J., Coldstream Guards.
Pte. MORRISON, A., 5th Grenadier Gds.
14456 Pte. MOSS, R., 1st Grenadier Gds.
Pte. MYERS, B., 5th Grenadier Gds.
7301 Pte. MYERS, L., 5th Grenadier Gds.
5598 Pte. NALTOSCHAY, M., 1st Bn. Scots Gds
Pte. NATHAN, J. S., Coldstream Gds.
24320 Pte. NASH, H., 5th Grenadier Gds.
Pte. NEWMAN, I., Scots Guards.
11610 Pte. NEEDLE, M., 1st Scots Gds.
25576 Pte. NORMAN, C.,* 1st Grenadier Gds.
5906 Gdsm. PARKS, A., Welch Guards.
25281 Pte. PARKER, I., Grenadier Gds.
2422 Tpr. PHILLIPS, M.,* Household Bn.
15658 Pte. ROSENBLOOM, 1st Scots Gds.
7880 L/Cpl. ROSENTHAL, C., 1st Scots G.
Sgt. ROSENBERG, 2nd Scots Gds.
4888 Pte. ROSEN, M., 1st Irish Gds.
Pte. SACKS, M., Scots Guards.
25027 Pte. SCHWARTZ, L., Grenadier Gds.
28132 Pte. SHERMAN, L., Grenadier Gds.
17901 Pte. SINGER, 4th Grenadier Gds.
Pte. SIMMONS, P., 3rd Scots Guards.

16148 Pte. SILVERSTONE, A., 2nd Gren. Gds.
19605 Pte. SIDENSTAT, M., 3rd Cold. Gds.
17584 Pte. SMOLLEN, B., 1st Gren. Guards.
Pte. SOLOMONS, I., 1st Scots Guards.
7449 Pte. SOLOMON, M.,* 1st Scots Gds.
18364 Pte. SPIEGAL, S., Coldstream Guards.
7666 Pte. SULLIVAN, M., 2nd Scots Gds.
25157 Pte. TENNENS, N., 4th Gren. Gds.
2940 Pte. VAN PRAAGH, H.
6604 Pte. WALTERS, B., Irish Gds.
17392 Pte. WEBB, H., 1st Grenadier Gds.
25562 Pte. WILSON, S., 5th Grenadier Gds.
17074 Tpr. WILSON, J., Grenadier Gds.
16145 Pte. WINTER, J., 2nd Gren. Gds.
5120 Pte. WOOD, S., Machine Gun Gds.
1603 Pte. ZAUSMER, S., Welch Guards.

* Killed in Action or died on Active Service.

THE ROYAL SCOTS (LOTHIAN REGIMENT).

OFFICERS.

Lieut. ANCILL, G. C.
2nd Lieut. BARNETT, G.,* 13th Bn.

N.C.O.'s AND MEN.

47766 Pte. ALTMAN, D., 13th Bn.
44381 Pte. ABRAHAM, S., 1/9th Bn.
2517 Pte. AITKEN, A., 2nd Bn.
36063 L/Cpl. ABRAHAMS, J., 2nd Bn.
5117 Pte. ADELMAN, A., 2/7th Bn.
3723 Pte. ASHER, H., 2/7th Bn.
49819 Pte. ALLEN, S., 2/9th Bn.
2603 Pte. BIALECK, S., 1/5th Bn.
5835 Pte. BERMAN, S.,* 9th Bn.
30551 Pte. BENJAMIN, A., 16th Bn.
32707 Pte. BLINT, M.,* 13th Bn.
30551 Pte. BENJAMIN, A., 12th Bn.
250637 Pte. BRAJECK, S., 5/6th Bn.
51694 Pte. BARBACK, M.,* 11th Bn.
80553 Pte. BROWN, G., 2nd Bn.
5897 Pte. BERMAN, R., 8th Bn.
31185 L/Cpl. BAKER, W., 2nd Bn.
34565 Pte. BLOCK, L., 11th Bn.
2636 Pte. BAKER, A., 9th Bn.
31301 Pte. BERNSTEIN, J., 1st Bn.
37477 Pte. BROMBERG, R. & A., 2nd Bn.
2/21911 Pte. BROOMBERG, A., 18th Bn.
2798 Pte. BLUMENTHAL, S., 2/8th Bn.
4946 Pte. BAKER, B., 2/8th Bn.
47492 Pte. BRODIE, A., 1st Bn.
Pte. BERNSTEIN, M., 9th Bn.
Pte. BLACK, H., 5th Bn.
53111 Pte. BARONWITZ, A., 1/9th Bn.
18697 Pte. CHAPMAN, H.,* 15th Bn.

Royal Scots.—*Continued.*

2657	Pte. CAMPBELL, C.,*	1/5th Bn.
276135	Cpl. CLINE, M.,	2nd Bn.
51144	Pte. CARTOON, R.,	17th Bn.
41714	Pte. COHEN, P.,	8th Bn.
44399	Pte. COHEN, J.,	9th Bn.
376832	L/Cpl. CRAMER, A.,	2/10th Bn.
2616	Pte. CALLINSKY, I.,	2/8th Bn.
330174	Pte. COHEN, H.,	9th Bn.
30687	Pte. COHEN, M.,	16th Bn.
	Pte. CARSON, V. G.,	2nd Bn.
	Pte. DIAMOND, J.,	1st Bn.
40069	Pte. DA COSTA, H.,	16th Bn.
5235	Pte. DOBRIN, D.,	2/7th Bn.
	Pte. DAVIDSON, I.	
2684	Pte. EPPEL, B.,	1/5th Bn.
34686	Pte. EPPEL, D.,	2nd Bn.
51524	Pte. EDELMAN, M.,	12th Bn.
350760	Pte. EPRILE, H.,	9th Bn.
202901	Pte. ELIAS, H. (M.M.),	2/5th Bn.
42924	Pte. EPSTEIN, H.	
7373	Pte. FRANKS, A.,	15th Bn.
33872	Pte. FREEDMAN, I.,*	5/6th Bn.
250164	Pte. FACTOR, A.,	5/6th Bn.
202149	Pte. FEDDY, F.,	1st Bn.
182480	Pte. FRANKS, B.	
9806	Pte. FISHMAN, N.,	4th Bn.
5955	Pte. FRIESMAN, H.,	2/8th Bn.
5248	Pte. FINBERG, M.,	2/4th Bn.
48923	Pte. FRANKS, M.	
	Pte. FINN, H.,	2/9th Bn.
3725	Pte. GOODSTONE, B.,	2/8th Bn.
330715	Cpl. GOLDSTEIN, A.,	9th Bn.
26148	Pte. GALBES, J.,	13th Bn.
352433	Pte. GOLDSTEIN, S.,*	9th Bn.
43013	GERBER, A.,	11th Bn.
41267	Pte. GROSSMAN, C.,	13th Bn.
270323	Pte. GROWS, H.,	11th Bn.
335466	Pte. GOLDSTEIN, H.,	1/9th Bn.
42635	Pte. GOODMAN, W.,	1/8th Bn.
41734	Pte. GREEN, F.,	1st Bn.
	Pte. GOLD, J.,	3rd Bn.
65433	Pte. GOLDFINE, J.,	3rd Bn.
48249	Pte. HARRIS, A.,	11th Bn.
41635	Pte. HILLMAN, L.,*	5/6th Bn.
42583	Pte. HUSSIES, L.,	12th Bn.
43583	Pte. HARRIS, B.,	1/8th Bn.
49808	Pte. HARTZ, W.,	2/7th Bn.
9102	Pte. HYMAN, S.,	2/8th Bn.
5833	Pte. ISAACS, J.,	1st Bn.
352632	Pte. ISAACS, B.,	2/9th Bn.
46984	Pte. JACOBS, A.,	2nd Bn.
31187	Pte. JACOBS, S.,	13th Bn.
38781	Pte. JACKOFF, M.,*	2nd Bn.
24472	L/Cpl. JACOBS, I.,*	12th Bn.
31097	Pte. JACOBS, H.,	1st Bn.
42587	Pte. KREITZMAN, H.,	1/8th Bn.
286201	Pte. KOMINSKY, I.,	2nd Bn.
31122	Pte. KINALATZ, H.,	1st Bn.
43382	Pte. LEVY, E.,*	15th Bn.
352526	L/Cpl. LAZARUS, H.,*	9th Bn.
47887	Pte. LURIE, J.,	11th Bn.
43382	Pte. LEVY, G.,*	15th Bn.
23154	L/Cpl. LIPMAN, S.,	2nd Bn.
675	Pte. LEVY, L. F.,	5th Bn.
351742	Pte. LAPIDUS, L.,	2/9th Bn.
47887	Pte. LEWIS, J.	
43382	Pte. LEVY, J.,	15th Bn.
	Pte. LEWIN, I.,	6th Bn.
	Pte. LIPETZ, S.	
18520	Pte. MACKIE, O.,	2nd Bn.
270112	Pte. MARKS, A.,	8th Bn.
31386	Pte. MARKS, H.,	12th Bn.
20670	Cpl. NORRIS, G.,*	2nd Bn.
	Pte. OLIVER, A.,	2nd Bn.
350774	Pte. POLUVANSKY, M.,	9th Bn.
330713	Sig. PRICE, L.,	11th Bn.
47581	Pte. PORTUGAL, W.,	16th Bn.
38340	Pte. POLLACK, M.,	13th Bn.
51313	Pte. PATTIE, H.,*	16th Bn.
3724	Pte. PRICE, E. M.,	2/7th Bn.
H/0976	Pte. PETERKOVSKY, R.,	17th Bn.
38716	Pte. REUBEN, J.,	15th Bn.
49052	Pte. ROSENBLOOM, H.,*	11th Bn.
23859	Pte. ROSENFIELD, H.,	13th Bn.
16381	Sgt. SOLOMON, B. (M.M.),	13th Bn.
38943	Pte. SAYERS, A.,	12th Bn.
4619	Pte. SOLOMON, M.,	13th Bn.
9731	Pte. STAAL, E.,*	2nd Bn.
350774	Pte. SOLIWANSKY, M.,	1/9th Bn.
57885	Pte. SALBERG, S. (D.C.M.),	1/9th Bn.
302660	Pte. SMITH, S.,	1/8th Bn.
42602	Pte. SCHAAPWELL, J.,	2nd Bn.
59709	Pte. SCHWARZMAN, J.,	2nd Bn.
28466	Cpl. STANLEY, H.,	1/7th Bn.
30597	Pte. SAMUELS, A.,	2nd Bn.
16381	Pte. SOLOMON, D.,	13th Bn.
201238	Cpl. SAMUELS, I. I.,	2/5th Bn.
13965	Pte. SPERO, P.,	2nd Bn.
51186	Pte. STOTT, E. M.,	1st Bn.
3705	Pte. SAFFER, J.,	2/7th Bn.
315014	Pte. SALMON, J.,	15th Bn.
6077	Pte. SILVERMAN, J.,	2/8th Bn.
301146	Pte. SIGAR, M.,	9th Bn.
48176	Pte. SHAKOWSKY, V.,	17th Bn.
31362	Pte. SIMON,	11th Bn.
2657	Pte. SHAPERO, C.,*	5th Bn.
3905	Pte. TAYLOR, L.,	2/4th Bn.
8097	Pte. TAGGER, J.,	2/8th Bn.
251275	Pte. TOBIAS, D.,	2/4th Bn.
201420	Pte. TOCHER, A.,	16th Bn.
42618	Ptt. VANDEMOLEN, S.,*	1/8th Bn.
4265	Cpl. VINESTOCK, J.,	5/6th Bn.
330793	Pte. WITTENBERG, J.,	9th Bn.
33192	Pte. WOLFSON, B.,	11th Bn.
30661	Pte. WOOLFE, S.,*	13th Bn.

Royal Scots.—Continued.

8218 Pte. WOLFSON, W., 8th Bn.
34408 Pte. WOLFSON, S. W., 16th Bn.
5889/8 Pte. WITTENBERG, H., 9th Bn.
5890/8 Pte. WITTENBERG, B., 9th Bn.
53926 Pte. WEINBAUM, J., 11th Bn.
39917 Pte. ZANCOFF, R. J., 19th Bn.

* Killed in Action or died on Active Service.

THE QUEEN'S (ROYAL WEST SURREY REGIMENT).

OFFICERS.

2nd Lieut. CLEEF, H. V.,* 8th Bn.
2nd Lieut. DAVIS, N. V., 6th Bn.
2nd Lieut. HENRIQUES, R. L. Q.,* 2nd Bn.
Lieut. HIGHAM, F. D.
2nd Lieut. JONAS, L. N., 8th Bn.
Lieut. JACOBS, S. (M.C.).
2nd Lieut. JOLOWICZ, P.
2nd Lieut. LYONS, S. E., 10th Bn.
Lieut. LEWIS, H., 2nd Bn.
Lieut. MICHOLLS, R. M. B.
Capt. SOLOMON, B.
2nd Lieut. VALENTINE, M.,* 2nd Bn.
2nd Lieut. WILKS, C.
Lieut. WAGNER, R. H., 22nd Bn.

N.C.O.'s AND MEN.

30534 Pte. ABRAHAMS, M., 19th Bn.
85015 Pte. ASHER, M., 2/4th Bn.
35236 Pte. AARONS, J.
20280 Pte. ABRAHAMS, H., 14th Bn.
21877 Pte. AARONS, E.,* 1st Bn.
3886 Pte. ABRAHAMS, S., 22nd Bn.
5864 Pte. ASH, A., 22nd Bn.
Pte. ABRAHAMS, A. B., 2/5th Bn.
141933 Pte. ALEXANDER, A., 10th Bn.
30409 Pte. ABRAHAMS, P., 6th Bn.
3/22 Pte. ATKINS, L., 3/22nd Bn.
14236 Pte. BERGMAN, S., 12th Bn.
42622 Pte. BERNSTEIN, M., 10th Bn.
36664 Pte. BARNETT, M.
5484 Pte. BYWATER, J. C.
69541 Pte. BERNOFSKY, J., 6th Bn.
24206 Pte. BURNS, L., 8th Bn.
26952 Pte. BEROLOVITCH, L.
4515 Pte. BRYER, M., 22nd Bn.
5844 Pte. BAKER, L. S., 2/5th Bn.
9774 Sgt. BRAINE, H., 3rd Bn.
266062 Pte. BARNARD, D. H., 19th Bn.
19994 Cpl. BARNETT, J., 2nd Bn.
152766 Pte. BLOODSTEIN,
Pte. BECKMEN, M., 8th Bn.

11730 Pte. COHEN, B., 11th Bn.
203328 Pte. COHEN, M. E., 10th Bn.
202361 Pte. COHEN, L., 11th Bn.
14218 Pte. CHAPLIN, W., 12th Bn.
14686 Pte. COHEN, A.
17111 Pte. COHEN, S.
82456 Sgt. CRECHTON, 10th Bn.
3837 Pte. COHEN, A.,* 1st Bn.
14307 Pte. COHEN, E., 12th Bn.
20715 Pte. COHEN, A., 14th Bn.
6750 Pte. CYMBALEST, M., 22nd Bn.
3741 Pte. COHEN, L., 22nd Bn.
22/5939 Pte. COHEN, H., 22nd Bn.
5828 Cpl. CROWN, H., 2/4th Bn.
5859 Pte. CLERNOFSKY, S., 2/5th Bn.
4956 Pte. COHEN, L., 2/4th Bn.
36193 Pte. CLEVE, P.
37726 Pte. COLLINS, L. C., 7th Bn.
19116 Pte. COSTER, H.
202705 Pte. DAVIS, J., 3/4th Bn.
G/60918 Pte. DRAPKIN, A. A., 2/4th Bn.
203639 Pte. DICKS, L., 6th Bn.
68095 Pte. DAVIDSON, S., 11th Bn.
21466 Pte. DAVIS, H., 11th Bn.
42121 Pte. DIAMONDSTEIN, B., 8th Bn.
65549 Pte. DAVIS, M., 26th Bn.
242480 Pte. DELMONT, S., 7th Bn.
84011 Pte. DAVIS, S.
Pte. DE HANN, M. G., 3rd Bn.
Pte. DORBINSKY, M.
22787 Pte. ESTERMAN, J., 6th Bn.
69294 Pte. EMANUEL, J., 6th Bn.
16636 Pte. ESSENBERG, J. W., 7th Bn.
6966 Pte. ENGLEMAN, J.
Pte. ELLIS, M. G., 2nd Bn.
Pte. EPSTEIN, M., 2nd Bn.
G/1209 Pte. FREEMAN, D., 7th Bn.
14687 Pte. FREEDBERG, R., 7th Bn.
205015 Pte. FINKLESTEIN, A.,* 3/4th Bn.
68418 Pte. FRANKS, M., 10th Bn.
44185 Sgt. FREEMAN, M., 16th Bn.
51431 Pte. FRANKLIN, G., 29th Bn.
85445 Pte. FRANKEL, B. L., 2/4th Bn.
54358 Pte. FOREMAN, S.
204989 Pte. FINCBERG, S., 3/4th Bn.
8147 Pte. FREEDMAN, M.
Pte. FORREST, W., 9th Bn.
7370 Pte. GARCIA, M., 7th Bn.
48013 Pte. GISH, A., 17th Bn.
42138 Pte. GILBERT, H., 11th Bn.
78776 Pte. GOLDSTEIN, M. A., 24th Bn.
8714 Pte. GREEN, M., 2nd Bn.
38871 Pte. GRENWALD, R., 16th Bn.
68100 Pte. GOROWITZ, S., 1st Bn.
258218 Pte. GERSHONT, S.
41623 Pte. GOLDSTEIN, J. D.
267199 Pte. GREMOVITCH, A., 4th Bn.
48059 Pte. GOLDSMITH, D., 2nd Bn.

Royal West Surrey Regiment.—*Continued.*

17576 Pte. GOLDNER, S., 13th Bn.
43969 Pte. GOLDSTEIN, M.
8595 Pte. GOLDMAN, A., 25th Bn.
25578 Pte. GERBER, J., 1st Bn.
24/6360 Pte. GREENBAUM, H., 22nd Bn.
4512 Pte. GOODMAN, H., 22nd Bn.
8225 Pte. HYAMS, J., 6th Bn.
24211 Pte. HUNT, M., 8th Bn.
61477 Pte. HARRIS, J., 6th Bn.
28218 Pte. HARRIS, J., 11th Bn.
207553 Pte. HYAMS, J., 10th Bn.
47247 Pte. HELNICK, I., 25th Bn.
61477 Pte. HARRIS, J., 6th Bn.
83072 Cpl. HARRIS, 10th Bn.
6698 Pte. HARTOG, J., 22nd Bn.
4896 Pte. HERMAN, D., 8th Bn.
17826 Pte. HYMAN, M.
5665 Pte. HERMAN, J., 3/4th Bn.
26700 Pte. HARRIS, H.
42535 Pte. HERSKOVITCH, J., 9th Bn.
32121 Pte. ISAACS, E., 2nd Bn.
16712 Cpl. ISRAEL, I.
78409 Pte. ISRAEL, R., 3rd Bn.
38681 Pte. ISAAC, C., 16th Bn.
14695 Pte. ISAACS, H., 1st Bn.
35497 Pte. ISAACSON, C., 16th Bn.
5480 Pte. ISAACS, M., 2/5th Bn.
27653 Pte. ISAACSON, M., 15th Bn.
84124 Pte. ISAACS, M. J.
14688 Pte. JACOBS, J.,* 7th Bn.
40199 Cpl. JACOBS, P., 7th Bn.
202788 Pte. JOSEPH, M., 3/4th Bn.
G/60711 Pte. JOEL, I., 2/4th Bn.
17455 Pte. JACOBS, G., 13th Bn.
14540 Pte. JACOBSON, H., 1st Bn.
52090 Pte. JACOBS, H.
85472 Pte. JACOBS, V. D., 2/4th Bn.
25578 Pte. JERBER, J., 1st Bn.
2978 Pte. JACOBS, M., 2/7th Bn.
81853 Pte. JACOBSON, L.
35274 Pte. JAFFA, S.
49081 Pte. JOEL, B.
27367 Pte. JACOBS, A.
25709 Pte. JONAS, J.,* 10th Bn.
21959 Pte. KITCHENOFF, M., 8th Bn.
17680 Pte. KLINE, A., 3/4th Bn.
212163 Pte. KIFTON, J., 1st Bn.
800600 Pte. KRIEGSBURG, J., 11th Bn.
241639 Pte. KASSIMER.
39048 Pte KELLMAN, 16th Coy
4530 Pte. KARTUM, 22nd Bn.
4581 Pte. KAPLAN, 22nd Bn.
22/4540 Pte. KIRSTEIN, L., 4th Bn.
22170 Pte. KLEIN, E., 3/4th Bn.
24838 Pte. LAZARUS, L., 2nd Bn.
10866 Pte. LEVY, J.,* 11th Bn.
9421 Pte. LEVY, E. G., 11th Bn.
61645 Pte. LEVY, R.,* 6th Bn.
69072 Pte. LEVEY, H., 1st Bn.
66655 Pte. LEAVER, J., 1st Bn.
 Cpl. LAZARUS, R., 2nd Bn.
23052 Pte. LIVINGSTONE, H., 10th Bn.
 L/Cpl. LAZARUS, J., 21st Bn.
4591 Pte. LAPIDOTH, S., 10th Bn.
7500 Pte. LEVY, S., 10th Bn.
14689 Pte. LEVY, E., 1st Bn.
42137 Pte. LAZARUS, M., 8th Bn.
25586 Pte. LEVENE, M., 1st Bn.
51869 Pte. LEVY, S.
16400 Pte. LAPPIN, A.,* 7th Bn.
6371 Pte. LEVY, L., 22nd Bn.
4552 Pte. LEVY, M., 22nd Bn.
4494 Pte. LEVEY, S., 22nd Bn.
6054 Pte. LUBINSKY, M., 22nd Bn.
43375 Pte. LEVY, A.
36277 Pte. LANCASTER, M.
16247 Pte. LEVY, P.
39040 Pte. LUBINSKY, L., 16th Bn.
49535 Pte. LEVY, J.
86779 Pte. LUKEMAN, P., 2/4th Bn.
10498 Pte. LESTWICK, J.
43058 Pte. LEVY, A.
54447 Pte. LEWIS, C., 4th Bn.
29147 Pte. LEVY, A., 14th Bn.
42120 Pte. LIGHTSTONE, J.
42472 Pte. LEVY, 2nd Bn.
207089 Pte. LEVENE, R., 2nd Bn.
79476 Pte. LEVY, A.
4967 Pte. LISS, H., 7th Bn.
6550 Pte. LEVY, A.,* 2nd Bn.
202375 Pte. MOOS, C. A. G., 3/4th Bn.
23681 Pte. MYERS, L., 3/4th Bn.
4671 Pte. MIRCHER, N., 20th Bn.
24 L/Cpl. MARTIN, A., 7th Bn.
24004 Pte. MOSES, A., 1st Bn.
 Pte. MILLEM, M., 16th Bn.
65109 Pte. MARKS, A.
32395 Pte. MARORITY, L., 1st Bn.
70373 Pte. MINSKI, W., 1st Bn.
20630 Pte. MOSES, J., 14th Bn.
4511 Pte. MORRIS, 22nd Bn.
4526 Pte. MAGNUM, A., 22nd Bn.
4504 Pte. MILLER, 22nd Bn.
5566 Pte. MARCHINSKI, G., 2/5th Bn.
79485 Pte. MORRIS, M., 25th Bn.
6147 Pte. MORRIS, H., 3/4th Bn.
25003 Pte. MICHAELS, D. M.
26115 Pte. MARCOVITCH, L., 14th Bn.
10748 Pte. MICHAELS, B.
35965 Pte. NEWMAN, L., 5th Bn.
G/28212 Pte. NATHAN, L., 4th Bn.
47247 A/C OPPENHEIMER, G. S., 16th Bn.
61383 Pte. OPPENHEIMER, J. R.,* 1st Bn.

Royal West Surrey Regiment.—*Continued.*

- 4539 Pte. OTTOR, 22nd Bn.
- 5940 Pte. OLOFSKY, M.D., 22nd Bn.
- 7315 Pte. PRINCE, W., 10th Bn.
- 36970 Cpl. PHILLIPS, G.
- 45150 Pte. PEZARO, A., 11th Bn.
- 5494 Pte. PHILLIPS, C., 2/5th Bn.
- 45365 Cpl. PICHARCHICK, E.
- 6069 Pte. ROSENTHAL, S., 7th Bn.
- 202418 Pte. ROSENBAUM, J., 3/4th Bn.
- 242668 Pte. RETINSKY, A., 10th Bn.
- G/49864 Pte. ROSENTHAL, H., 10th Bn.
- 17759 Pte. RUBENSTEIN, I., 13th Bn.
- 59621 Cpl. RUBENSTEIN.
- 85673 Pte. RICARDO, M., 2/4th Bn.
- 3842 Pte. RUBENSTEIN, B., 22nd Bn.
- 27214 Pte. ROOD, N.
- 52952 Pte. ROSANSKY, S.
- 43338 Pte. RUSSELL, G.
- 243151 Pte. ROGENSTEIN, S., 2/5th Bn.
- 51560 Pte. ROGERS, S.
- 6791 Pte. ROWSGA, H., 22nd Bn.
- 4526 Pte. RAVENSKY, 22nd Bn.
- 64564 Pte. ROTHSTEIN, S., 13th Bn.
- 7001 Pte. ROSENTHAL, E., 1st Bn.
- 24001 Pte. STEINBERG, C., 2nd Bn.
- 21991 Pte. SUMMERS, F., 6th Bn.
- 67782 Pte. SHOCKETT, J., 11th Bn.
- 19427 Pte. SHROOT, M., 13th Bn.
- 46196 Pte. SIMONS, D. A., 11th Bn.
- 38561 Pte. SOLOMONS, M. M., 2nd Bn.
- 67781 Pte. SUGARMAN, L., 2nd Bn.
- 32624 Cpl. SACHS, S.
- Pte. STEIN, B.
- 159533 Pte. SCHOLTE, S.
- 159894 Pte. SOLOMON, H.
- 60723 Pte. SOLOMONS, S.
- 68136 Pte. SHIEL, J., 3rd Bn.
- 84916 Pte. STERN, F., 2/4th Bn.
- 54280 Pte. SALISBURY, H. B.
- 34965 Pte. SAMUELS, W. S.
- 70400 Pte. SILVERMAN, J.
- 20099 Pte. SACKS, 14th Bn.
- 22046 Pte. STEINBERG, H.,* 2nd Bn.
- 14693 Pte. SHOMINSKY, W.
- 45139 Pte. SHARPES, H., 22nd Bn.
- 14597 Sgt. SHAPIRA, B., 1st Bn.
- 6621 Pte. SHEPHERD, W., 9th Bn.
- 26613 Pte. SOLOSKY, I., 14th Bn.
- 2430 Pte. STERN, L., 2/5th Bn.
- 681586 Pte. SMITH, J., 22nd Bn.
- 22797 Pte. SKURMICK, S.
- 65803 Pte. SLIFKIN, S.
- 69219 Pte. SMITH, M., 6th Bn.
- 20338 Pte. SEIGENBERG, E., 7th Bn.
- 156186 Pte. SILVER, S., 53rd Bn.
- 51208 Pte. SMOYAS, J., 28th Bn.
- 65257 Pte. STRELITZ, J.
- 8783 Pte. SCHNEIDER, A., 1st Bn.
- 78626 Cpl. TAYLOR, M. L., 24th Bn.
- 2526 Rfm. TUCKER, C.
- 85801 Pte. TISINBOM, J., 2/4th Bn.
- 54332 Pte. TERRY, M.
- 22/4493 Pte. TAFFA, M., 22nd Bn.
- 55943 Pte. TISCHLER, A., 25th Bn.
- 205731 Pte. VAN PRAAGH, S. J., 3/4th Bn.
- 24409 Pte. WOOLFE, H., 2nd Bn.
- 230614 Pte. WILKINS, J., 10th Bn.
- Pte. WOOLF, C. D., 9th Bn.
- 17599 Pte. WEYBERG, D., 13th Bn.
- 59862 L/Cpl. WINSTON, 13th Bn.
- 156241 Pte. WITTY, N.
- 55952 Pte. WATSON, F.
- 39232 Pte. WEISBERG, P.
- 14694 Pte. WYNSCHANK, B., 1st Bn.
- 426653 Pte. WORMS, H., 1st Bn.
- 4967 Pte. ZISS, H., 8th Bn.

* Killed in Action or died on Active Service.

THE BUFFS (EAST KENT REGIMENT).

OFFICERS.

- 2nd Lieut. BOAS, H., 8th Bn.
- Capt. FINE, H., 7th Bn.
- 2nd Lieut. FREEDMAN, P.,* 6th Bn.
- 2nd Lieut. FREEDMAN, S., 8th Bn.
- Lieut. ISAACS, H. B., 2nd Bn.
- Lieut. JESSELL, G. (M.C.).
- 2nd Lieut. JACOBS, I. A. (M.C.), 7th Bn.
- 2nd Lieut. PEARCE, H., 3rd Bn.
- 2nd Lieut. PHILLIPS, R. E., 17th Bn.
- Capt. STEINMAN, B. P., 5th Bn.
- Capt. STRAUSS, B. L. (M.C.).

N.C.O.'s AND MEN.

- 5185 Pte. ABRAHAMS, D., 2/4th Bn.
- Pte. ABRAHAMS, J., 2nd Bn.
- 265017 Pte. ALEX, A., 10th Bn.
- 20435 Pte. ALEX, A., 10th Bn.
- 8149 Pte. BROWN, J., 6th Bn.
- 5497 Pte. BARRS, S., 8th Bn.
- 12523 Pte. BERMAN, G. E., 8th Bn.
- 12672 Cpl. BRIGHTMAN, H. G., 1st Bn.
- 19483 Pte. BASS, E. A., 7th Bn.
- Pte. BRESH, W., 8th Bn.
- Pte. BERG, J., 8th Bn.
- 12531 Pte. COHEN, B., 8th Bn.
- 22470 Pte. COHEN, O.,* 7th Bn.
- 242688 Pte. COSTA, J.,* 1st Bn.
- 242406 Pte. COHEN, A. S., 1st Bn.
- 6992 Pte. COHEN, A., 10th Bn.
- 25317 Pte. COHEN, M., 1st Bn.

Royal West Surrey Regiment.—*Continued.*

- 242456 Pte. COHEN, A., 1st Bn.
- 20272 Pte. COHEN, 1/5th, 1st Res. Bn.
- 271022 Pte. CAVE, E. M.,* 6th Bn.
- 26290 Pte. COHEN, L. N.
- 25038 Pte. COHEN, H., 3rd Bn.
- 5359 Pte. DE GROOT, 2/4th Bn.
- 241749 Pte. DAVIES, H., 2/5th Bn.
- 3/38926 Pte. DELACOVITCH, M., 3rd Bn.
- 27414 Pte. ECKET, E., 3rd Bn.
- 25333 Pte. ELLIS, L., 1st Bn.
- Pte. FERBER, M., 1/5th Bn.
- 29727 Pte. FRANKS, H., 2nd Bn.
- Pte. FRANKLIN, I., 2/5th Bn.
- Pte. FRANKS, A. J. (M.M.).
- 202356 Pte. FING, M., 2/4th Bn.
- 1111 Pte. GREENBAUM, B.,* 2nd Bn.
- 12536 Pte. GLASBERG, A.,* 8th Bn.
- 25058 Pte. GOLD, J., 1st Bn.
- 4149 Pte. GOULD, M., 2/1st Bn.
- 5487 Pte. GLASIN, L.
- 25211 Pte. GOLDFARB, C.,* 7th Bn.
- Pte. GOLDSTEIN, S., 3rd Bn.
- G/3449 Pte. HYMAN, W., 7th Bn.
- 2444 Pte. HYAMS, B., 8th Bn.
- 24478 Pte. HARRIS, M.,* 10th Bn.
- 2448 Pte. HYMAN, 7th Bn.
- 242689 Pte. HYAMS, 2/5th Bn.
- 2568 Pte. HARRIS, H., 13th Bn.
- 26293 Pte. INSTEIN, J.,* 6th Bn.
- G/1677 Pte. JAYE, J. E., 7th Bn.
- G/3640 Pte. JONES, L., 7th Bn.
- 3646 Pte. JONES, N., 7th Bn.
- 8734 Pte. JACOBS, M., 8th Bn.
- 242691 Pte. JACOBS, L. B., 2/5th Bn.
- 23047 Pte. JOSEPH, H.
- 25384 Pte. KASHENBAUM, L., 7th Bn.
- 25069 Pte. KIRSHBAUM, J.
- 241714 Pte. LAYTON, J., 2/5th Bn.
- 25333 Pte. LAWRENCE, E., 1st Bn.
- G/25408 Pte. MOSCOVSKY, H.,* 1st Bn.
- 12551 Pte. MELROSE, I., 8th Bn.
- 2770 Pte. MAYHEW, W., 7th Bn.
- 10154 Pte. MALNICK, G.,* 2nd Bn.
- 24772 Cpl. MILWALL, S. L., 2/5th Bn.
- Pte. MARTIN, D. A., 2/5th Bn.
- 3426 Pte. NATHAN, S., 8th Bn.
- 3904 Pte. NIMNI, J.
- 22798 Pte. NETTLER, M.
- 7149 Pte. OLEESKY, M., 7th Bn.
- 5319 Pte. PRICE, W., 6th Bn.
- Pte. PINKUS, J., 8th Bn.
- 19950 Pte. PERRY, 1st Bn.
- 266118 Pte. POPPLESDORFF, J., 1st Bn.
- 2222 Pte. REUBINS, H., 8th Bn.
- 23874 Pte. RIDZ, A. S., 7th Bn.
- 5267 Pte. ROTAPPLE, J., 1/5th Bn.
- 242668 Pte. ROTHKINSKY, A., 19th Bn.
- 13704 Pte. REMOVITCH, 6th Bn.
- Pte. ROSENBERG, L., 8th Bn.
- Pte. ROSENBERG, S., 3rd Bn.
- 18307 Pte. SOMERS, H., 2nd Bn.
- 25825 Pte. SHONE, H.
- 12348 Pte. SCHOOLBERG, H.
- 242521 Pte. SILVERMAN, B., 2/5th Bn.
- 12568 Pte. VALESKY, M., 8th Bn.
- 242251 Pte. VEIN, P., 4th Bn.
- 17470 Pte. WORMAN, A., 7th Bn.
- 379058 Pte. WOLFE, M.
- 14050 Pte. WOLFSON, M., 6th Bn.
- 9/23882 Pte. WERSCHKER, A.

* Killed in Action or died on Active Service.

THE KING'S OWN (ROYAL LANCASTER REGIMENT).

OFFICERS.

- Lieut. AARONSON, A., 2nd Bn.
- 2nd Lieut. ABRAHAMS, 4th Bn.
- Major CORDOVA, V. L. I. E. (M.C.).
- Capt. HART, H. R., 1/4th Bn.
- 2nd Lieut. HYAMS, G. S., 8th Bn.
- Capt. JACOBS, B. (M.C.), 2/5th Bn.
- 2nd Lieut. JACOBS, H.,* 1/8th Bn.
- Lieut. JACOBS, S. R. (M.C.).
- Lieut. KATZ, S. G.,* 8th Bn.
- Lieut. KINGSLEY, H. H.
- Lieut. LEVI, U., 6th Bn.
- Lieut. MERE, C. L.,* 6th Bn.
- Capt. MYERS, A. P. (M.C.), 1st Bn.
- Capt. SPIRA, S., 9th Bn.
- 2nd Lieut. SCIAMA, A., 1st Bn.
- 2nd Lieut STERNBERG, E. A.
- Capt. WALEY, F. R., 11th Bn.
- Capt. WEINBERG, J., 6th Bn.

N.C.O.'s AND MEN.

- 3629 Pte. ALTHUSEN, M.,* 1st Bn.
- 24730 Pte. AUERBACH, W., 1/5th Bn.
- 2844 Pte. ANSELL, D., 8th Bn.
- 36855 Pte. ABIL, J., 3rd Bn.
- 49044 Pte. ALEXANDRA, J., 3rd Bn.
- Pte. BARNETT, J.
- 17588 Pte. BARNETT, H., 2nd Bn.
- 36858 Pte. BARAKONSKY, A., 3rd Bn.
- Pte. BERNSTEIN, A.
- 14073 Sgt. BERNSTEIN, H.,* 7th Bn.
- 29019 Pte. BENNER, M., 8th Bn.
- 28498 Pte. BECKER, S., 11th Bn.
- 26313 Pte. BENJAMIN, J., 9th Bn.
- 3465 L/Cpl. BENOFF, H., 2nd Bn.
- 243099 Pte. BIRTLESTEIN, J.,* 1/5th Bn.
- Pte. BLUNN.

Royal Lancaster Regiment.—*Continued.*

	Pte. BLOOM, B., 7th Bn.
235055	Pte. BLACK, R. J., 7th Bn.
235158	Pte. BOAM, M., 8th Bn.
27665	Pte. BROWN, J. J., 1st Bn.
244505	L/Cpl. BRAHAM, A., 1/4th Bn.
43516	Rfm. BRADLAW, L., 9th Bn.
	Pte. BURSK, S., 2/4th Bn.
279283	Pte. BUKSON, J., 3rd Bn.
35841	Pte. BURMAN, N., 4th Bn.
37016	Pte. BURMAN, M., 2/5th Bn.
201559	Pte. BRAZIL, V.,* 1/4th Bn.
5553	Pte. CARTER, H., 12th Bn.
39208	Pte. COVEL, J., 7th Bn.
62007	Pte. COOKLIN, S., 4th Bn.
37799	L/Cpl. COLLACK, H., 2/5th Bn.
30609	Pte. COHEN, L., 8th Bn.
3914	Pte. COHEN, S., 8th Bn.
26868	Pte. COHEN, H.
38591	Pte. COHEN, C., 4th Bn.
38910	Pte. COUSINS, T., 8th Bn.
14767	Pte. CROSSLEY, 3rd Bn.
2973	Pte. DA COSTA, E., 3rd Bn.
34320	Pte. DAVIES, 6th Bn.
202601	Pte. DAMBOVSKY, M., 4th Bn.
	Pte. DEANE, A.
3639	Pte. DELEW, M., 2nd Bn.
35442	Pte. DE HAAS, S.
4557	Pte. ELBOZ, R., 1/4th Bn.
202601	Pte. EMBOVSKY, M. D., 1/4th Bn.
2668	Pte. EPSTEIN, H., 2nd Bn.
10749	Pte. FEATHERS, A., 2nd Bn.
477307	Sgt. FLANSBERG, S.
202606	Pte. FOX, W., 4th Bn.
12312	Pte. FRANKS, H.
18286	L/Cpl. GELMAN, A., 1st Bn.
242334	Pte. GLASKIE, E., 1/5th Bn.
91473	Pte. GLASSER, B., 25th Bn.
24245	Pte. GLICK, J., 2nd Bn.
51150	Pte. GOLDSTONE, J.
12335	Pte. GOLDSTONE, S.
437285	Pte. GOLDWASSER, A.
30561	Pte. GOLDSTEIN, A., 8th Bn.
12338	Pte. GOLDBERG, A., 4th Bn.
380213	Cpl. GOLDMAN, S., 25th Bn.
30615	Pte. GORDIE, E., 1/4th Bn.
380098	Cpl. GOULD, M., 25th Bn.
8716	Pte. GREENBERG, S.,* 1st Bn.
202655	Pte. HARRIS, H., 6th Bn.
3371	Pte. HARRIS, J., 1st Bn.
8719	L/Cpl. HART, R.,* 9th Bn.
18015	Pte. HERMAN, L., 1st Bn.
30581	Pte. HEINBERG, D., 8th Bn.
5198	Pte. HERMAN, B., 5th Bn.
11508	Pte. HEPSTONE, J.,* 1st Bn.
12313	Pte. HERMAN, J.,* 6th Bn.
26344	Pte. HARRIS, S., 9th Bn.
202698	Pte. ISAACS, M., 7th Bn.
12275	Pte. ISRAEL, J.
19573	Sgt. JACOBS, C., 1st Bn.
19893	Pte. JAFFE, M., 6th Bn.
12274	Pte. JOSEPH, B.
36322	L/Cpl. JACOBSON, H., 11th Bn.
17814	L/Cpl. KAUFMAN, E., 1st Bn.
40848	Pte. KARSTADT, 17th Bn.
37750	Pte. KAVARSKY, J.,* 1/5th Bn.
3/7957	Pte. LAZARUS, H., 6th Bn.
3324	L/Cpl. LAWRENCE, A., 1/4th Bn.
22491	Pte. LERG, M., 1st Bn.
17742	Pte. LEICESTER, E.
37502	Pte. LEFCOVITCH, A.
242676	Pte. LEVEY, I.,* 1/8th Bn.
5411	Pte. LEVY, J., 1st Bn.
242478	Pte. LEVY, I., 8th Bn.
22649	Pte. LEVEY, M., 11th Bn.
28498	Pte. LEVENSON, B., 11th Bn.
61504	Pte. LEVENE, J., 1/4th Bn.
38696	Pte. LEVEN, H., 3rd Bn.
235160	Pte. LEMBERG, D., 8th Bn.
37350	Pte. LIND, S., 4th Bn.
201459	Pte. LIPSKIE, A., 1/4th Bn.
16092	Pte. LEWIS, J.
	Pte. LEVY, M., 15th Bn.
	L/Cpl. MARKS, J., 12th Bn.
25509	Pte. MARKS, J., 1st Bn.
B/10162	Sgt. MICHAELS, H., 8th Bn.
5194	Pte. MOSS, D., 5th Bn.
27645	Pte. MOSES, D., 1st Bn.
16092	L/Cpl. MENDOZA, A., 6th Bn.
5/5289	Pte. MIDDLEMAN, I., 4th Bn.
202265	Pte. MICHAELSON, S., 4th Bn.
242691	Pte. NEVITSKIE, I.
6939	Pte. NEWMAN, A.
24243	Pte. NEVITSKIE, S., 3rd Bn.
230582	Pte. NIMAN, 6th Bn.
202185	Pte. NAGELKOP, L.
202509	Pte. OLENSKY, M., 4th Bn.
5823	Pte. PHILLIPS, D., 6th Bn.
22311	Pte. ROSENBERG, I.,* 1st Bn.
241630	Pte. ROSENBERG, B.,* 1/5th Bn.
24459	Pte. ROSENBERG, M., 7th Bn.
470	Pte. RIBERO, I.,* 1/4th Bn.
D/23153	Pte. ROBINSON, H., 8th Bn.
10009	Pte. ROSEN, E., 13th Bn.
	Pte. REECE, S.
242341	Pte. ROSENFELD, J., 2/5th Bn.
22021	Pte. RHEINHIMER, A. F., 8th Bn.
1531	Pte. ROSENFELD, J., A. Coy.
30304	Pte. RUBENSTEIN, C., 3rd Bn.
26162	Pte. REUBEN, C., 9th Bn.
26486	Pte. SAMUELS, S., 9th Bn.
38017	Pte. SALKOWER, 1st Bn.
202160	Sgt. SEGAR F., 1/4th Bn.
21348	Pte. SHYMAN, W., 13th Bn.
12334	Pte. SHOWMAN, S.,* 1st Bn.
202619	Pte. SHIMBERG, M.,* 1/8th Bn.

Royal Lancaster Regiment.—*Continued.*

36666 Pte. SHOWMAN, M., 3rd Bn.
202038 Pte. SHUMBERG, M. S., 4tth Bn.
37719 Pte. SHAPIRO, L., 4th Bn.
3931 Pte. SHERMANSKI, J., 2/4th Bn.
11484 Pte. SILVERMAN, I., 1st Bn.
37348 Pte. SIMCOVITCH, M.
17873 Pte. SILVERT, 1st Bn.
17868 Sgt. SILVERSTONE, H., 2nd Bn.
242375 Pte. SILVERBURG, 5th Bn.
36803 Pte. SIMON, D., 9th Bn.
 Pte. SINGER, M., 3rd Bn.
9705 L/Cpl. SOLOMON, S., 2nd Bn.
12250 Pte. STARR, L.
38303 Pte. TAYLOR, M., 1/4th Bn.
43684 Pte. TYNAS, H., 2/4th Bn.
17867 Pte. UNGER, B., 1st Bn.
26097 Pte. VASS, A., 1/4th Bn.
26935 Pte. VANDERBERG, A., 1st Bn.
28129 Pte. WEINBERG, L., 7th Bn.
18105 Pte. WHITE, J., (V.C.) 6th Bn.
34236 Pte. WOLFF, 6th Bn.
12235 Pte. WISE, E.
37965 Pte. YOUNGERMAN, S., 4th Bn.
202038 Pte. ZACKS, C. L., 4th Bn.

* Killed in Action or died on Active Service.

THE NORTHUMBERLAND FUSILIERS.
OFFICERS.

Lieut. BARNETT, V. B.,* 12th Bn.
Capt. DAVIDSON, N. L. (M.C.), 14th Bn.
Capt. DAVIS, A. M., 30th Bn.
2nd Lieut. FRIEND, J.,* 20th Bn.
2nd Lieut. GROSSMAN, V. D.,* 24th Bn.
Capt. HART, A. C.,* 2nd Bn.
Capt. JEFFREYS, A. H.,* 20th Bn.
2nd Lieut. KLEAN, M. G.,* 16th Bn.
2nd Lieut. KING, S.,* 23rd Bn.
Lieut. LYONE, A. M. (M.C.),* 11th Bn.
Lieut. MARKS, C. V. 5th Bn.
Lieut. MARKS, H. V. (M.C.).
2nd Lieut. WOOLF, A. S., 3rd Bn.

N.C.O.'s AND MEN.

1066 Pte. ABRAHAMS, M., 19th Bn.
43250 Pte. ABRAHAMS, I.,* 10th Bn.
235552 Pte. ABRAHAM, J., 9th Bn.
7593 Pte. AARONS, H., 2/5th Bn.
7176 Pte. AARONS, M., 2/6th Bn.
5/9824 Pte. APPLEBAUM, A., 52nd Bn.
 Pte. ALLAR, S., 2nd Bn.
18771 Pte. ASH, R.
5408 Pte. ABRAHAMS, S.
6570 Pte. ALEXANDER, 2/7th Bn.
6695 Pte. ANGEL, R., 2/7th Bn.
291607 Pte. APPLEBY, L., 2/7th Bn.

67813 Pte. ANTINE, M., 13th Bn.
45700 Pte. ASHMAN, M., 15th Bn.
59027 Pte. AARONS, H., 23rd Bn.
53060 Pte. ALLEN, J., 3rd Bn.
96900 Pte. ALLIN, B., 52nd Bn.
201299 Pte. ANNIS, A., 18th Bn.
11/7452 Cpl. BERNSTEIN, F., 10th Bn.
34329 Pte. BERG, B., 16th Bn.
235330 Pte. BAKER, L., 16th Bn.
366019 Pte. BERNSTONE, J., 16th Bn.
29779 Pte. BERGSON, A., 23rd Bn.
61300 Pte. BERNSTEIN, S., 85th Bn.
45111 Pte. BARNETT, S. M., 18th Bn.
 L/Cpl. BARNETT, L., 1st Bn.
1480 Sgt. BAMBERG, M.,* 1st Bn.
 Pte. BARNETT, D., 2nd Bn.
6771 Pte. BERMAN, B., 1/7th Bn.
32783 Pte. BERNSTONE, D., 18th Bn.
8848 Pte. BOAS, D., 2/4th Bn.
8882 Pte. BEER, M., 2/4th Bn.
6120 Pte. BARNETT, M., 2/3th Bn.
6042 Pte. BENJAMIN, P., 2/5th Bn.
7449 Pte. BLOOMBERG, I., 2/6th Bn.
7499 Pte. BOSSICK, S., 2/6th Bn.
60730 Cpl. BENJAMIN, B., 12/13th Bn.
292436 Pte. BALCON, M., 2/7th Bn.
292004 Pte. BLOOMBERG, M., 2/7th Bn.
 Pte. BISHOP, L., 1st Bn.
 Pte. BERNSTEIN, A.
76378 Pte. BANDAS, A.,* 1st Bn.
316545 Pte. BLACK, M.
266961 Pte. BLOOMBERG, D.
158595 Pte. BLOOM, P.
7791 Pte. BERLIND, B., 4th Bn.
7452 Cpl. BERNSTEIN, M., 11th Bn.
11214 Pte. COHEN, V., 13th Bn.
3041 Pte. CHADWICK, A. C., 13th Bn.
204492 Pte. COLSTER, L., 4th Bn.
32666 Pte. COWAN, A., 9th Bn.
47742 Pte. COHEN, I., 26th Bn.
261307 Pte. COHEN, D., 19th Bn.
25070 Pte. COHEN, A.,* 24/27th Bn.
29314 Pte. COHEN, C., 15th Bn.
61530 Pte. COHEN, A., 36th G. Bn.
5418 Pte. COHN, J., 2/6th Bn.
34232 Pte. COWAN, D., 27th Bn.
46403 Pte. COHEN, S., 9th Bn.
203716 Pte. CONDOR, H., 2/4th Bn.
4918 Pte. COHEN, L., 2/4th Bn.
32025 Sgt. COOKE, C.,* 14th Bn
6285 Pte. COHEN, N., 2/5th Bn.
6063 Pte. COHEN, H., 2/5th Bn.
7184 Pte. COHEN, M., 2/6th Bn.
5430 Pte. COHEN, J., 2/7th Bn.
6013 L/Cpl. COHEN, L., 4th Bn.
29314 Pte. COHEN, C., 15th Bn.
32462 Pte. CRAFCHENSKI, M., 30th Bn.
41368 Pte. CRESWELL, T., 16th Bn.

Northumberland Fusiliers.—*Continued.*

6619 Pte. COHEN, A., 2/7th Bn.
5108 Pte. COHEN, A.
266747 Pte. COHEN, M., 10th Bn.
5412 Pte. COHEN, P., 2/7th Bn.
5/161006 Pte. COHEN, J., 53rd Bn.
39026 Pte. DAVIDSON, S., 21st Bn.
301845 Pte. DAVIS, M., 5th Bn.
Rfm. DAVIES, J., 14th Bn.
55507 Rfm. DONIGER, I., 11th Bn.
4919 Pte. DAVIS, M., 2/4th Bn.
6265 Pte. DAVIS, 2/6th Bn.
46309 Pte. DEEKER, 2nd Bn.
7723 Pte. DOBLER, M.
292496 Pte. ELLIS, J., 2/7th Bn.
6708 Pte. ESTERMAN, J., 2/7th Bn.
316012 Pte. EREIRA, D., 35th Bn.
203661 Pte. ENGLEMAN, B., 1/4th Bn.
1977 Pte. FRANKS, M., 6th Bn.
24881 Sgt. FYMAN, A. (M.M.), 24th Bn.
241609 Pte. FLAXMAN, C., 14th Bn.
27638 Pte. FISHSTEIN, H.,* 13th Bn.
44493 Pte. FREEDMAN, S., 25th Bn.
203505 Pte. FREEDMAN, H., 27th Bn.
203869 Pte. FREEDMAN, W.,* 22nd Bn.
59057 Pte. FIFER, R.,* 23rd Bn.
64307 L/Cpl. FINSTEIN, S., 1st Bn.
5965 Pte. FISHKIN, F., 6th Bn.
44464 Pte. FLAXMAN, J., 25th Bn.
267784 Pte. FREEDMAN, C., 11th Bn.
8852 Pte. FREEDMAN, M., 2/4th Bn.
4744 Pte. FINGERMAN, P., 2/4th Bn.
8705 Pte. FREEDMAN, C., 2/6th Bn.
26355 Cpl. FISHER, 2nd Bn.
2150 Pte. FRANKS, L. E.,* 6th Bn.
69275 Pte. FREEDMAN. B.
292821 Pte. FINEGARD, J., 2/7th Bn.
28774 Pte. FRENDENBERG, D., 3rd Bn.
28783 Pte. FRENDENBERG, L., 3rd Bn.
45027 L/Cpl. GOLDBERG, J., 14th (Pioneers).
61437 Pte. GLASS, A., 36th G. Bn.
49942 Pte. GOLLARD, 1st Bn.
285024 Pte. GOTTLIEB, E., 6th Bn.
4850 Pte. GLICK, V., 2/4th Bn.
8849 Pte. GORDON, L., 2/4th Bn.
8846 Pte. GILBERT, D., 2/4th Bn.
4790 Pte. GROSSMAN, H., 2/4th Bn.
7792 Pte. GOLDMAN, B., 2/5th Bn.
6222 Pte. GOLDSMID, M., 2/5th Bn.
7235 Pte. GOLDBERG, N., 2/6th Bn.
77234 Pte. GLOBE, B.,
33954 L/Cpl. GEORGE, L., 3rd Bn.
88154 Pte. GOLDBERG, H., 37th Bn.
19011 Pte. GOLDSTEIN, M., 2/7th Bn.
5058 Pte. GOLDSTEIN, A.
50990 Pte. GOPLD, J.
Pte. GOLDBERG, A., 25th Bn.
Cpl. GILLIS, L., 3rd Bn.

32462 Pte. GRAFINSKY, N.
23232 Pte. GREEN, H.
32407 Pte. GREEN, J.
32407 Pte. GROUT, G. E.
30724 Pte. GILLIES, L.
341197 Pte. GALANSKY, H.
56212 Pte. GOLDRING, H., 2/1st Bn.
316548 Pte. GRABINE, B., 12th Bn.
Pte. GILLESPIE, H., 1st Bn.
121 Pte. HYAMS, J., 16th Bn.
122 Pte. HARRIS, L., 16th Bn.
41973 Pte. HARRIS, H., 10th Bn.
40316 Pte. HAYMAN, J., 3rd Bn.
8846 Pte. HART, S., 2/4th Bn.
7506 Pte. HERMANN, J., 2/5th Bn.
28162 Pte. HERMAN, H., 3rd Bn.
56169 Sgt. HIMMEL, H. (M.M.), 22nd Bn.
26645 Pte. HALPERN, B.
292922 Pte. HEISER, D.
121 Pte. HYMES, I. I.
16630 Pte. HARRIS, J., 2nd Bn.
Pte. HARRIS, D., 2nd Bn.
14/28 Pte. HARRIS, S., 4th Bn.
35054 Pte. ISAACS, M.,* 23rd Bn.
56120 Pte. ISAACS, J., 21st Bn.
34391 Pte. IMBER, A., 26th Bn.
Pte. ISAACS, W., 2nd Bn.
8610 Pte. INGELLMAN, B., 2/4th Bn.
73233 Pte. ISAACS, D., 37th Bn.
2512 Pte. ISAACS, D.
28007 Pte. ISAACS, J., 4th Bn.
53355 Pte. ISAACS, J. H., 2nd Bn.
82122 Pte. ISAACS, M.
35271 Pte. JAFFE, S., 12th Bn.
3600 Pte. JOSEPH, J., 16th Bn.
266771 Pte. JACOBOVITCH, H., 10th Bn.
35058 Pte. JOSEPHSON, J., 23rd Bn.
59074 Pte. JACOBS, 23rd Bn.
69664 Pte. JACOBSON, J., 19th Bn.
46539 Sgt. JACKSON, B. (M.M.), 10th Bn.
6496 Pte. JEMENEFSKY, S. B., 2/5th Bn.
6499 Pte. JEMENEFSKY, A. B., 2/5th Bn.
7133 Pte. JACOBOVITCH, H., 2/6th Bn.
298027 Pte. JACOBS, B.,* 2/7th Bn.
294232 Pte. JOSEPHS, A., 2/7th Bn.
62589 Pte. JACOBS, M., 3rd Bn.
Pte. JACOBY, E., 27th Bn.
235371 Pte. KAUFMAN, P. K., 16th Bn.
203320 Pte. KLEVANSKI, J., 4th Bn.
55541 Pte. KLEIN, J., 11th Bn.
35438 Pte. KINEBERG, J., 12th Bn.
4753 Cpl. KURTZMAN, H.,* 6th Bn.
8670 Pte. KERSH, M., 2/4th Bn.
26731 Pte. KONYN, 2nd Bn.
63915 Pte. KRASNEY, A., 36th Bn.
26101 Pte. KNIGHT, H.,* 8th Bn.
36325 Pte. KOSSICK, L.,* 26th Bn.
6827 Pte. LOWENBERG, B., 6th Bn.

Northumberland Fusiliers.—*Continued.*

169 L/Cpl. LEVY, J.,* 16th Bn.
427 Sgt. LEVINE, L., 16th Bn.
34562 Pte. LEVY, L., 1st Bn.
34517 Pte. LAGATER, L., 1st Bn.
580 L/Cpl. LYONS, I., 16th Bn.
47083 Pte. LUSTGARTEN, M.,* 16th Bn.
6826 Drm. LEVEY, E., 6th Bn.
202633 Pte. LASSMAN, J., 6th Bn.
235100 Pte. LESCHINSKY, M.,* 4th Bn.
235093 Pte. LEIBERT, B., 4th Bn.
37888 Pte. LIPMANOVITCH, S., 21st Bn.
13578 Sgt. LINDE, A.,* 8th Bn.
38052 Pte. LIVINGSTONE, A., 23rd Bn.
41000 Pte. LEWIS, J., 27th Bn.
35832 Pte. LIPSEDGE, 26th Bn.
31521 Pte. LUBELSKI, I., 3rd Bn.
34893 Pte. LIPSIDE, P., 26th Bn.
10381 Pte. LEWIS, A.,* 14th Bn.
3634 Pte. LAWRENCE, M.
34395 Pte. LASSMAN, P., 11th Bn.
4920 Pte. LYSCHINSKY, H., 2/4th Bn.
8851 Pte. LEVY, D., 2/4th Bn.
90925 Pte. LEVENE, L., 35th Bn.
26732 Pte. LOWE, 2nd Bn.
51501 Pte. LEVI, P., 2nd Bn.
73683 Pte. LATNER, L., 1st Bn.
58233 Pte. LEVI, J., 3rd Bn.
7547 Pte. LANDSMAN, H., 2/5th Bn.
50712 Pte. LEVY, J., 2nd Bn.
6890 Pte. LEFCOVITCH, 6th Bn.
20816 Pte. LESSER, I., 15th Bn.
43209 Pte. LEAKE, C., 1st Bn.
7067 Pte. LANDMAN, J., 2/5th Bn.
4516 Pte. LEVY, P., 2nd Bn.
Pte. LEVY, S., 2/5th Bn.
10/19465 Pte. MARKS, H., 10th Bn.
34470 Pte. MAY, H., 1st Bn.
34321 Pte. MASCOTH, I., 12th Bn.
203381 Pte. MEISEL, H.,* 4th Bn.
204628 Pte. MUSCOVITCH, S., 4th Bn.
33941 Pte. MALLINSON, F. G., 20th Bn.
36780 Pte. MARKS, J.,* 24th Bn.
32468 Pte. MARKOVITCH, L., 30th Bn.
1666 Pte. MARKS, H. V., 6th Bn.
285039 Pte. MORRIS, N., 16th Bn.
8830 Pte. MERKOVITCH, H., 2/4th Bn.
7827 Pte. MYERSON, S., 2/5th Bn.
7566 Pte. MARKOVITCH, J., 2/5th Bn.
7179 Pte. MAGNUS, 2/6th Bn.
43585 L/Cpl. MARKS, A., 3rd Bn.
7078 Pte. MOSES, W.,* 2nd Bn.
79603 Pte. MORRIS, S., 1st Bn.
76381 Pte. MORORITZ, H., 1st Bn.
4943 Pte. MORRIS, I., 2/7th Bn.
8097 Pte. MORRIS, L.
417613 Pte. MERSKEY, A., 4th Bn.
285039 Pte. MORRIS, L., 23rd Bn.

203382 Pte. MIDDLEBURGH, B.
19465 Pte. MARKS, M., 12th Bn.
204629 Pte. NOSCOVITCH, S., 4th Bn.
60096 Pte. NYAM, J., 7th Bn.
6914 Pte. NATHAN, N., 2/7th Bn.
59244 Pte. NUNAR, A., 53rd Bn.
7853 Pte. NEISEL, H., 4th Bn.
32380 Pte. OVENDEN, E. T.
Cpl. OVITCH, M. (D.C.M.).
6825 Pte. PHILLIPS, 5th Bn.
47211 Pte. PELLMAN, W.,* 22nd Bn.
242058 Pte. PHILLIPS, J., 7th Bn.
61785 Pte. PATRICK, A., 36th G. Bn.
Pte. PHILLIPS, H., 4th Bn.
3592 L/Cpl. PEALMAN, M.,* 3rd Bn.
285047 Pte. POSNESKY, A., 6th Bn.
27119 Pte. PEARLMAN, 2nd Bn.
50520 Pte. PELTER, H., 36th Bn.
5136 Pte. PICK, M., 2/7th Bn.
6710 Pte. ROTHFIELD, J.,* 10th Bn.
Pte. RICHMAN, M., 16th Bn.
42375 Pte. RACIONZER, H.,* 27th Bn.
19432 Pte. REUBEN, S., 19th Bn.
4062 Pte. ROSENTHAL, G.,* 16th Bn.
44485 Cpl. RUDSTEIN, M., 16th Bn.
52835 Pte. ROSENBERG, D., 6th Bn.
2834 Pte. ROSENTHAL, H.,* 16th Bn.
69326 Pte. RAPOPORT, P.,* 12/13th Bn.
292657 Pte. ROCKLIN, M., 7th Bn.
28836 Pte. RUBENSTEIN, C., 25th Bn.
32745 Pte. ROSENBERG, A., 25th Bn.
36401 Pte. ROSENBLUM, A., 8th Bn.
25321 L/Cpl. RECTOR, M., 1st Gar. Bn.
27967 Pte. RICHMOND, J., 25th Bn.
4411 Pte. RUBINSTEIN, H., 4th Bn.
5463 Pte. ROSENSTEIN, I.
5463 Pte. ROSEN, J.
203714 Pte. REASH, M.
158253 Pte. ROSENBERG, M.
48681 Pte. RICARDO, H.
48663 Pte. ROSEN, M.
Pte. ROSENTHAL, D. E., 2nd Bn.
3138 Pte. ROSENTHAL, J., 2nd Bn.
271307 Pte. ROBERTS, 2/7th Bn.
52670 Pte. ROTAPPLE, F., Gar. Bn.
39424 Pte. RUBINSTEIN, L., 3rd Bn.
291382 Pte. SOLSTEIN, A., 2/7th Bn.
293004 Pte. SERLIN, J., 2/7th Bn.
292904 Pte. SCHWACHMAN, A., 2/7th Bn.
38976 Pte. STONEFIELD, S., 3rd Bn.
39396 Pte. STIBBE, M.,* 2nd Bn.
10/6817 L/Cpl. STERN, P. (M.M.), 10th Bn.
6860 Pte. SILLANDER, I., 12th Bn.
7369 Pte. STRELITZER, W. H., 4th Bn.
34471 Pte. SAMPSON, R., 1st Bn.
34472 Pte. SAMPSON, R., 1st Bn.
46145 Pte. STEIN, M., 12th Bn.
267102 Pte. SEGAL, W., 6th Bn.

Northumberland Fusiliers.—Continued.

- 47338 Pte. SILVERMAN, S., 20th Bn.
- 39471 Pte. SELINSKY, J., 20th Bn.
- 37960 Pte. SCHULTZ, H., 23rd Bn.
- 35042 Pte. SOLOMON, M.,* 23rd Bn.
- 41630 Pte. SAFFER, A., 24th Bn.
- 47557 Pte. SOLOMON, I.,* 26th Bn.
- 57690 Pte. SOLOMON, J., 18th Bn.
- 266447 L/Cpl. SELTZER, L., 1st Bn.
- 32471 Pte. STAAL, M., 3rd Bn.
- 204837 Pte. SCHWATHING, F., 1st Bn.
- 40837 Pte. SOLOMONS, B., 1st Bn.
- 47339 Pte. SMITH, J. J.,* 22nd Bn.
- 9463 Pte. SAUNDERS, J.,* 1st Bn.
- 69609 Pte. SAMUELS, B.,* 19th Bn.
- 63915 Pte. STRESNEY, A., 36th Gar. Bn.
- 85064 Pte. SILVERSTONE, A., 36th Gar. Bn.
- Pte. SOLOMONS, I., 2nd Bn.
- 47747 L/Cpl. SALZEDO, I. L., 23rd Bn.
- 17505 Pte. STONE, J., 27th Bn.
- 51279 Pte. SCHUMACHER, D., 25th Bn.
- 8847 Pte. STERN, M., 2/4th Bn.
- 7803 Pte. SOLOVITCH, A., 2/5th Bn.
- 6309 Pte. SELTZER, L., 2/6th Bn.
- 8887 Pte. SAPERIA, M., 2/4th Bn.
- 6865 Pte. SCHWARTZ, 2/7th Bn.
- 18994 Pte. SEILIN, 2/7th Bn.
- 4744 Pte. SINGERMAN, P., 2/4th Bn.
- 32470 Pte. SCHUNSTER, A. A., 20th Bn.
- 4218 Pte. SENIOR, S., 2/5th Bn.
- 32381 Pte. SHIEL, W., 21st Bn.
- 17505 Pte. STONE, J., 30th Bn.
- 315745 Pte. STEINBERG, M., 35th Bn.
- 41923 Pte. SANGOR, S., 4th Bn.
- 8889 Pte. TURITZ, J., 2/4th Bn.
- Pte. TAYLOR, S., 1st Bn.
- 8770 Pte. TANGAR, N., 2/4th Bn.
- 57141 Pte. TRAGER, J., 2nd Bn.
- 29234 Pte. TEMPLE, S., 2/7th Bn.
- 34423 Pte. WOOLFSTEIN, P., 8th Bn.
- 46179 L/Cpl. WOOLF, B., 8th Bn.
- 9551 Pte. WHITE, M., 1st Bn.
- 32473 Pte. WEXLER, C.
- Pte. WEINER, S.
- 51488 Pte. WHITFIELD, I., 19th Bn.
- 35438 Pte. WEINBERG, J. W., 19th Bn.
- 204349 Pte. WILKES, G., 10th Bn.
- 8928 Pte. WOOLF, G., 2/4th Bn.
- 4792 Pte. WINTER, L., 2/4th Bn.
- 392322 Pte. WINANSKE, A., 2/7th Bn.
- 292881 Pte. WEINBERG, J., 2/7th Bn.
- 9941 Pte. WILKES, J.
- 7906 Pte. WEINSTEIN, E., 4th Bn.
- 242864 Pte. WYERSON, S.
- 35271 Pte. YAFFE, S., 12/13th Bn.
- 340460 Pte. YALES, H., 36th Bn.
- 291412 Pte. ZIFF, J., 2/7th Bn.

* Killed in Action or died on Active Service.

THE ROYAL WARWICKSHIRE REGIMENT.

OFFICERS.

- 2nd Lieut. ABRAHAMS, D. S., 3rd Bn.
- Lieut. BARRON, L., 2/6th Bn.
- 2nd Lieut. BENOLIEL, S. H., 10th Bn.
- Lieut. BLOCK, R. A., 8th Bn.
- 2nd Lieut. BLAIBERG, H. E., 16th Bn.
- 2nd Lieut. NATHAN, G.
- Lieut. PHILLIPS, R. H.,* 15th Bn.
- 2nd Lieut. RAPHAEL, N. H.,* 2nd Bn.
- 2nd Lieut. RUDELL, E. A.,* 16th Bn.
- Major RAPHAEL, R. A. (M.C.), 4th Bn.
- 2nd Lieut. STUART, D., 16th Bn.
- Lieut. SAMUEL, P. C., 11th Bn.
- 2nd Lieut. SAMUEL, C. V.,* 8th Bn.
- 2nd Lieut. SAMUEL, R. C., 12th Bn.
- 2nd Lieut. WALEY, G. F., 11th Bn.

N.C.O.'s AND MEN.

- 633 Pte. ARNOLD, L., 15th Bn.
- L/Cpl. AARON, H. (M.M.).
- 30024 Pte. AARONS, J., 2nd Bn.
- 28994 Pte. AROTSKY, V., 1/5th Bn.
- 260078 Pte. APPLEBAUM, H., 1/6th Bn.
- 201768 Pte. ABRAMS, H. J., 1/6th Bn.
- 260276 Pte. ABRAHAMS, H. G., 1/6th Bn.
- 330594 Pte. ABRAHAMS, D., 18th Bn.
- Pte. BLACK, B., 2nd Bn.
- 6304 L/Sgt. BINNES, J.,* 2/5th Bn.
- 1216 Pte. BLUMENTHAL, E., 2/5th Bn.
- 28243 Cpl. BERG, A., 1st Bn.
- 260084 Pte. BENJAMIN, J., 1/6th Bn.
- 569921 Pte. BERG, J., 1/7th Bn.
- 30001 Pte. BLANK, J., 2nd Bn.
- 6457 Pte. BOLDBERG, L., 5th Bn.
- 26424 Pte. BROWN, M., 1st Bn.
- Pte. BENJAMIN, N.
- 153 Pte. COHEN, A., 14th Bn.
- 901 Pte. COLEMAN, L., 15th Bn.
- 16/297 Pte. COHEN, H., 16th Bn.
- 5493 Pte. COPLER, A. E., 2/5th Bn.
- 2708 Pte. COHEN, H., 6th Bn.
- 5109 Pte. COTTON, M., 6th Bn.
- 35067 Pte. COHEN, W., 2/7th Bn.
- 240605 L/Cpl. COHEN, H., 1/6th Bn.
- 260290 Pte. COHEN, A., 1/6th Bn.
- 786 Pte. DAVIS, S., 15th Bn.
- 27909 Pte. DAVIES, J., 15th Bn.
- 28254 Pte. DAVIS, H., 1st Bn.
- 27370 Pte. DAVIS, H., 10th Bn.
- 6229 Pte. DAVIES, J., 2/9th Bn.
- 1768 Pte. EPHRON, L., 15th Bn.
- 34300 Pte. FITZPATRICK, M., 15th Bn.
- 43228 Pte. FISHER, B., 2/7th Bn.
- 230259 Pte. FOGLE, A., 2/6th Bn.
- 202212 Pte. FLANCEBAUM, H., 2/6th Bn.
- 330487 Pte. FROCKMAN, B., 18th Bn.

Royal Warwickshire Regt.—*Continued.*

	Pte. FISHER, M.
3516	Pte. GARNER, H., 6th Bn.
2320	L/Cpl. GOODMAN, G., 6th Bn.
4710	Pte. GEBER, M., 5th Bn.
206	Pte. GREENBERG, M. S., 14th Bn.
205	Pte. GREEN, A. P.,* 14th Bn.
1155	Pte. GABRIEL, H. M.,* 14th Bn.
517	Pte. GOLDSTEIN, J., 15th Bn.
9267	Sgt. GOLDMAN, H., 1st Bn.
1211	Cpl. GOLDMAN, A.,* 2nd Bn.
	Pte. GOLD, 4th Bn..
202013	Pte. GOLDBERG, L., 16th Bn.
72908	Pte. GOLDSTEIN, 9th Bn.
22910	Pte. GRANT, A. D., 9th Bn.
406172	Pte. GOODMAN, W.,* 14th Bn.
4710	Pte. GEBER, M., 5th Bn.
22908	Pte. GOLDSTONE, J.
35553	Pte. GYINSKY, J., 3rd Bn.
7	L/Cpl. HERMON, D., 15th Bn.
2901	C/Sgt.-Maj. HYMAN, C., 2/5th Bn.
201651	Pte. HYAM, J., 1/6th Bn.
201743	Pte. HASSELL, J., 2/5th Bn.
4926	L/Sgt. HOFF, H., 5th Bn.
7524	Pte. HARRIS, H., 5th Bn.
39601	Pte. HARRIS, J., 1st Bn.
38376	Pte. HARRIS, H., 15th Bn.
24507	Pte. ISAACS, A., 1st Bn.
1705	L/Cpl. ISAACS, S. G., 11th Bn.
2706	L/Cpl. ISAACS, F., 6th Bn.
42242	Pte. ISAACS, H. L., 5th Bn.
13680	Pte. ISAACS, J., 1st Bn.
41745	Pte. IZON, J., 14th Bn.
336	Sgt. JOSEPH, E.,* 14th Bn.
1508	Pte. JACOBS, I. E.,* 15th Bn.
841	Pte. JOSEPHS, H., 16th Bn.
11457	Pte. JACOBS, D., 2nd Bn.
21327	Pte. JACOBS, P.
	Sgt. JACOBS, W. C. (D.C.M.).
976	Pte. JACOBS, C.
25452	Pte. JACOBS, S., 1st Bn.
	Pte. JACOBS, E. S.
	Pte. JACOBSON, I. E.
28626	Pte. KAYE, H., 53rd Bn.
	Cpl. KLEIN, W. T. (M.M.).
45762	Pte. KAMINSKI, H., 3rd Bn.
20460	Pte. LEWIS, B. L., 7th Bn.
2579	Pte. LEVY, A., 2/5th Bn.
746	Pte. LEVINE, B.,* 2nd Bn.
22005	Pte. LEVINE, J., 10th Bn.
268203	Pte. LEWIS, B. L., 1/7th Bn.
34995	Pte. LEVY, H. G., 1/6th Bn.
5229	Pte. LAZARUS, P., 7th Bn.
6247	Pte. LANDY, H. W.
23585	Pte. LOYNES, M., 3rd Bn.
29727	Pte. LEDERMAN, 2/8th Bn.
17757	Pte. LEVI, B., 13th Bn.
403	Pte. MYERS, H. T.,* 1/5th Bn.
18308	Pet. MILLER, C., 14th Bn.
5609	Pte. MARKS, S., 2/5th Bn.
260076	Pte. MILLER, S., 2/6th Bn.
28363	Pte. MALINSKY, L., 10th Bn.
29267	Pte. MAHONEY, C., 1/6th Bn.
34141	Pte. MARKS, L. Y. (M.M.), 15th Bn.
44116	Pte. MARKOSKI, E., 1/7th Bn.
15698	Cpl. MORRIS, M., 11th Bn.
331110	Pte. MARKS, M., 18th Bn.
17354	L/Cpl. MOSES, M., 1st Bn.
28280	Pte. ORLESS, H., 1st Bn.
1881	Pte. PITT, H.,* 6th Bn.
15/780	Sig. PHILLIPS, E., 15th Bn.
6276	Pte. PHILLIPS, G., 2/5th Bn.
4537	Pte. PRESS, H., 10th Bn.
5229	Pte. PHILLIP, L., 7th Bn.
60684	Pte. PERITLY, L., 15th Bn.
201910	Pte. PHILLIPS, S.,* 2/5th Bn.
20210	Pte. ROSINSKY, S.,* 6th Bn.
235023	Pte. ROTHBLATT, S.,* 2/5th Bn.
484	Pte. ROSENTHAL, L. M.,* 14th Bn.
1611	Pte. ROSENTHAL, A., 14th Bn.
444	Pte. ROSENBAUM, S.,* 16th Bn.
687	Pte. ROSENTHAL, C. H., 16th Bn.
29966	Pte. ROSINSKY, H. S., 2nd Bn.
	Pte. ROSE, S., 10th Bn.
50541	Pte. RABINOWITZ, E., 10th Bn.
22004	Pte. ROSENBAUM, A., 15th Bn.
20804	L/Cpl. RENOVITCH, H., 11th Bn.
	Pte. ROBERTS, J., 2nd Bn.
	Pte. RACKMULLIS, L.
20788	L/Cpl. ROSENBLATT, W., 3rd Bn.
89	Pte. SCHLESSER, H., 16th Bn.
48423	Pte. SWEDE, J. A. M.,* 14th Bn.
5414	Pte. SALAMAN, E., 2/8th Bn.
5426	Pte. SHARP, J. M., 2/8th Bn.
23584	Pte. SIMONS, J., 1/5th Bn.
	Pte. SOLOMON, W. J. C. (M.S.M.).
29053	Pte. SHOMACK, J., 1/5th Bn.
16/1341	Pte. SOLOMON, L., 16th Bn.
19200	Pte. STEBAMAN, A., 11th Bn.
29058	Pte. SOLOMON, J.,* 1/5th Bn.
20214	Pte. SOLOMON, H., 1/6th Bn.
23498	Pte. SOLOMONS, A., 1/6th Bn.
43214	Cpl. SYMONS, J., 3rd Bn.
330533	Dvr. SCHNEIDER, H., 18th Bn.
523200	Pte. STONE, J., 3rd Bn.
3003	L/Cpl. SINGER, L., 1st Bn.
40509	Pte. SIMON, H., 5th Bn.
	Pte. SANDERS, H., 20th Bn.
	Pte. SPIERS, K. L.
	Pte. SPIEGELMAN, I.
39515	Pte. WOOLF, 15th Bn.
20655	Pte. WHITESMAN, N.,* 10th Bn.
24700	Pte. WOOLFSON, S.,* 1st Bn.
18029	Pte. WOLFSON, H., 3rd Bn.
29945	Pte. ZAUSMER, M., 2nd Bn.

* Killed in Action or died on Active Service.

THE ROYAL FUSILIERS (CITY OF LONDON REGIMENT).

For 38th, 39th, 40th Royal Fusiliers (Jewish) see pp. 254 to 285.

OFFICERS.

Capt. ADLER, S. M., 13th Bn.
Capt. BENJAMIN, A. L., 32nd Bn.
Capt. BENJAMIN, R. N. (M.C.), 12th Bn.
Lieut. BENZECRY, S.,* 17th Bn.
2nd Lieut. BENJAMIN, C., 1st Bn.
Lieut. BARNETT, A. H.
Lieut. COWAN, A. R.
2nd Lieut. COHEN, E.* (M.C.), 12th Bn.
Capt. CRONBACK, R. C. L.
2nd Lieut. DAVIS, D. L., 2nd Bn.
Capt. GEE, R. (V.C., M.C.), 2nd Bn.
2nd Lieut. GOLDSMITH, D.
Lieut. HYAMS, A. H.,* 4th Bn.
2nd Lieut. HYMAN, G.
2nd Lieut. ISRAEL, D. D. G., 26th Bn.
2nd Lieut. JACOBS, H. (M.C.), 6th Bn.
2nd Lieut. KLEAN, R. M. A., 4th Bn.
2nd Lieut. KENNER, F., 32nd Bn.
2nd Lieut. LEVY, J. (M.C.), 13th Bn.
2nd Lieut. LEVY, E. V. (M.C.).
2nd Lieut. LAWRENCE, H. B., 22nd Bn.
2nd Lieut. LEVI, H.,* 9th Bn.
2nd Lieut. LIGHT, B., 2nd Bn.
2nd Lieut. LEVY, F., 26th Bn.
2nd Lieut. MILTCH, L. S.
2nd Lieut. MYERS, J. W., 3rd Bn.
2nd Lieut. MOSES, B.
2nd Lieut. MENDES, E. G., 42nd Bn.
2nd Lieut. MARKS, E., att. 111th T.R.B.
2nd Lieut. NATHAN, W. S.,* 12th Bn.
2nd Lieut. OHLMANN, G. A. L.,* 3rd Bn.
2nd Lieut. PHILLIPS, C., 26th Bn.
2nd Lieut. PHILLIPS, H. F.
2nd Lieut. PAIBA, E. J.,* 2nd Bn.
2nd Lieut. PEZARO, B.
Lieut. SOLOMON, L. B.,* 2nd Bn.
Lieut. SAMUELS, S. M. (M.C. and Bar), 26th Bn.
Lieut. SHAW, M.,* 26th Bn.
Lieut. STEINMANN, B. B., 6th Bn.
Capt. SIMONS, L.* (M.C.), 22nd Bn.
2nd Lieut. ULLMANN, D. M.,* 24th Bn.
2nd Lieut. VANDYK, A., 12th Bn.
Lieut. WALEY, A. J.,* 12th Bn.
Capt. WALEY, J. D.
Lieut. WEIL, F. B.

N.C.O.'s AND MEN.

7201 L/Sgt. ADLER, P.* (M.M.), 11th Bn.
3213 Pte. AHRONSBERG, S., 23rd Bn.
4419 L/Cpl. ARNOLD, S., 23rd Bn.
1773 Pte. ALLEN, L., 10th Bn.
44454 Pte. ABRAHAMS, A., 10th Bn.
480167 Pte. ALLUM, J. W., 43rd Bn.
8858 Pte. ABRAHAMS, M., 4th Bn.
7230 Pte. ADLER, W., 11th Bn.
22964 Pte. ALLMAN, D., 7th Bn.
69916 Pte. AARONS, J., 1st Bn.
69352 Pte. ABRAHAMS, D.,* 9th Bn.
17446 Pte. ARONSON, M.,* 9th Bn.
49339 Pte. ARON, C. (M.M. and Bar), 17th Bn.
G.182 Pte. AVERBACH.
114775 L/Cpl. ABRAHAMS, A., 23rd Bn.
253987 Pte. ALLEN, M., 3rd Bn.
1455 Pte. ALLEN, S., 10th Bn.
228799 Pte. ABRAHAMS, H., 4th Bn.
8661 L/Cpl. AXELBRAD, A., 3rd Bn.
2508 Pte. ABRAHAMS, J., 6th Bn.
2414 Pte. ALBERGA, E., 31st Bn.
855 Pte. ANGEL.
8255 Pte. BROWN, J.,* 1st Bn.
1572 Pte. BRODER, P. A., 10th Bn.
626 Pte. BURMAN, A. J., 10th Bn.
5962 Pte. BOWMAN, M., 13th Bn.
2400 Pte. BASS, A., 4th Bn.
Pte. BARTLETT, S., 4th Bn.
7249 Pte. BENSON, S.,* 11th Bn.
59 Pte. BERGL, B., 17th Bn.
1233 Pte. BEMBERGER, W., 18th Bn.
4466 Sgt. BERNSTEIN, J., 20th Bn.
711 Pte. BENAZON, J., 22nd Bn.
2639 Pte. BENJAMIN, C., 24th Bn.
3817 Pte. BECK, S., 23rd Bn.
1805 Pte. BLENDIS, S., 26th Bn.
G/47492 Pte. BRODIE, A., 26th Bn.
4511 Pte. BEARMAN, J. H., 32nd Bn.
G/51360 Pte. BAKESEF, I., 17th Bn.
Q.M.S. BRAHAM, A., 2nd Bn.
4808 Pte. BROWN, H., 9th Bn.
B/62069 Pte. BECKER, W.,* 9th Bn.
55165 Pte. BARNETT, S., 7th Bn.
1602 Pte. BASH, L.,* 10th Bn.
63572 Pte. BOGARD, M.,* 13th Bn.
4606 Pte. BLOOMBAUM, A., 7th Bn.
55263 Pte. BLUESTONE, H., 7th Bn.
13972 Pte. BATES, H., 22nd Bn.
67833 Pte. BERNSTEIN, J., 32nd Bn.
37241 L/Cpl. BENJAMIN, 37th Bn.
Sgt. BLACK, M. (M.M.).
31223 Pte. BARNETT, L., 34th Bn.
9017 Pte. BARNETT, G.,* 4th Bn.
Pte. BERGMAN, M., 11th Bn.
Pte. BROWN, S., 11th Bn.
1959 Pte. BRIGGS, H. A., 23rd Bn.
21612 Pte. BRANDRINK, T. P., 8th Bn.
42793 Cpl. BENNETT, S., 36th Bn.
6053 Pte. BLUESTEIN, A., 2nd Bn.
109252 Pte. BYCOFSKY, H., 43rd Bn.
515764 Pte. BAER, S.
G/25376 Pte. BRAUDMAN, M., 16th Bn.

Royal Fusiliers.—*Continued.*

78535 Pte. BANNGART, M., 5th Bn.
73443 Pte. BEARMAN, F., 23rd Bn.
75498 Pte. BATEMAN, A., 4th Bn.
3687 Pte. BAROFKA, N., 47th Bn.
110957 Pte. BLOOM, J., 44th Bn.
18683 Pte. BECKER, S., 3rd Bn.
Pte. BENJAMIN, M., 11th Bn.
4719 Pte. BLACKMAN, J., 30th Bn.
25006 L/Cpl. BENJAMIN, H., 3rd Bn.
9170 Pte. BARNETT, C.,* 3rd Bn.
66760 Pte. BARNETT, M.,* 32nd Bn.
4554 Pte. BARON, O.,* 24th Bn.
16316 L/Cpl. BENDER, J.,* 8th Bn.
4868 Pte. BERMAN, L.,* 9th Bn.
G/75008 Pte. BOBER, H.,* 11th Bn.
G/95488 Pte. BLOMMEKOPER, A., 10th Bn.
1608 Cpl. BRADBERRY, T. R., 23rd Bn.
1799 C.S.M. BLANKFIELD, H., Army Gym. S.
10149 Pte. BERLINSKI, A., 43rd G.B.
8026 Pte. BREWER, H., 2nd Bn.
5636 Pte. BROWN, A., 4/3rd Bn.
107975 Pte. BERGSON, J., 43rd Bn.
87475 Pte. BUCK, 6th Bn.
63767 Pte. BLANKSTONE, S.
66760 Pte. BARNETT, M.
10698 Pte. BENJAMIN, S., 6th Bn.
79651 Pte. BRATT, H.
14667 Pte. BARON, M., 4th Bn.
1779 Pte. BLOOM, L., 4/4th Bn.
8329 Sgt. BLUMBERG, M., 29th Bn.
4656 Pte. BLUSTIN, I. A., 4/4th Bn.
2928 Pte. BOGARD, T.
19022 Pte. BONN, D., 6th Bn.
6382 Pte. BONSTRAFF, S., 4/4th Bn.
50759 Pte. BARNETT, 42nd Bn.
1060 L/Cpl. BERLINER, M., 42nd Bn.
1654 Pte. BRAVERMAN, M., 42nd Bn.
265304 Sgt. BEARMAN, H., 42nd Bn.
19159 Pte. BLUMENSON, C., 42nd Bn.
1357 Pte. BUDOCK, M., 42nd Bn.
3114 Pte. BRILL, J., 42nd Bn.
62113 Pte. BRODSKY, S., 42nd Bn.
3484 Pte. BIRENTAAN, M., 42nd Bn.
29300 Pte. BERRYBISKI, F., 42nd Bn.
49716 Pte. BANCROFT, H., 2nd Bn.
6111 Pte. BERNSTEIN, M.
Pte. BERNSTEIN, L.
1752 Sig. BLACK, R., 2nd Bn.
50137 Pte. BILLING, D., 1st Bn.
Pte. BARON, H., 30th Bn.
Pte. BALLSON, D., 4th Bn.
L/Cpl. BARNETT, B.
Pte. BOHAR, G., 4th Bn.
Pte. BONMASH, J., 6th Bn.
Pte. BOAS, C. P.
Pte. BAILEY, C., 4th Bn.
Pte. BUTCHER, W., 4th Bn.
Pte. BUCKLEY, 24th Bn.
Pte. BENTICK, E., 4th Bn.
2816 Pte. BENJAMIN, J., 26th Bn.
2784 Pte. BARBITSKY, L., 26th Bn.
3260 Pte. BLUMENKRANTZ, S., 26th Bn.
3747 Pte. BREDSKI, P., 26th Bn.
5677 Pte. BEDISH, W., 26th Bn.
3005 Pte. BENE, N., 26th Bn.
74576 L/Cpl. BARNARD, J. H.,* 7th Bn.
195989 Pte. BERNSTEIN, W.
B/3305 Pte. CASTLE, F. S.,* 26th Bn.
1839 Pte. COHEN, I., 4th Bn.
1985 Pte. CHART, B., 4th Bn.
9223 Pte. COHEN, R.,* 8th Bn.
7269 Pte. CAPLAN, B., 18th Bn.
1366 Pte. COHEN, A. J., 18th Bn.
4667 Sgt. COHEN, M., 20th Bn.
192 Pte. COHEN, D.,* 22nd Bn.
3521 Pte. CITROEN, C. T., 24th Bn.
131217 Pte. COHEN, J., 2nd Bn.
22119 Pte. COHEN, A., 32nd Bn.
3737 Pte. CHETMINSKI, H. (M.M.), 23rd Bn.
2999 Pte. CORBLATT, S.,* 20th Bn.
10974 Pte. COHEN, C. M., 1st Bn.
9647 Pte. COHEN, A., 1st Bn.
66984 Pte. CHAPLIN, W., 9th Bn.
G/68695 Pte. COHEN, A., 24th Bn.
68337 Pte. COHEN, R., 13th Bn.
229725 Pte. COHEN, R. J., 13th Bn.
69369 Pte. COHEN, S., 9th Bn.
78689 Pte. COHEN, S., 2nd Bn.
64191 Pte. CROSKY, N., 26th Bn.
60109 L/Cpl. COSTER, H., 34th Bn.
39511 Pte. CAPLIN, D. H., 35th Bn.
26944 Pte. COHEN, A., 7th Bn.
16138 Pte. COHEN, N.,* 32nd Bn.
51730 Pte. CORPER, A., 2nd Bn.
4809 Pte. COHEN, M., 22nd Bn.
3097 Pte. CAMINSKY, J., 3rd Bn.
P.S/9952 Pte. CAPLAN, P. I.
71213 Pte. CAPLAN, J.
24161 Pte. CLEMENTS, M., 14th Bn.
206221 Cpl. COHEN, G., 42nd Bn.
G/69807 Pte. CAPLAN, J.,* 1st Bn.
4332 Pte. COHEN, P.,* 7th Bn.
73037 Pte. COWAN, J., 5th Bn.
226151 Pte. CAMPLIN, 5th Bn.
Pte. COHEN, A. (M.M.).
2473 Pte. CLOFFEM, I., 42nd Bn.
1405 Pte. COHEN, A., 42nd Bn.
1305 Pte. COHEN, S., 42nd Bn.
1896 L/Cpl. COHEN, A., 42nd Bn.
2877 Pte. COHEN, H., 42nd Bn.
Pte. COHEN, I., 42nd Bn.
Pte. COPPLE,
281979 Pte. COHEN, D., 1/4th Bn.
22938 Pte. CHAPMAN, H., 2nd Bn.
2431 Pte. CAPLAN, P., 26th Bn.

Royal Fusiliers.—*Continued.*

- 2450 Pte. COHEN, M. H., 26th Bn.
- 2815 Pte. CHUDNOSKY, C., 26th Bn.
- 3010 Pte. COON, A.
- 150527 Pte. COHEN, P., 5th Bn.
- 102132 Pte. CORNBLATT, G., 26th Bn.
- 123098 Pte. CARNEL, C., 47th Bn.
- 3890 Pte. CHART, L., 6th Bn.
- 2040 Pte. COHEN, D., 2/7th Bn.
- 5913 Pte. COHEN, H., 4/1st Bn.
- 6179 Pte. COHEN, J., 4/7th Bn.
- 16086 Pte. COHEN, J., 33rd Bn.
- 43974 Pte. CAKLAN, H. A.
- 8162 Pte. COPELAND, M., 22nd Bn.
- 32781 Pte. COHEN, A.
- 12756 Pte. COTTON, J.
- 8971 Pte. COPELAND, L., 28th Bn.
- 19022 Pte. CONN, D., 6th Bn.
- 1408 Sgt. COHEN, M., 4th Bn.
- 30582 Pte. COHEN, B., 6th Bn.
- 8755 L/Cpl. COHEN, L., 2nd Bn.
- G/70121 Pte. CLAPPAM, M.
- G/426 Pte. COHEN, N.
- 43202 Pte. COHEN, S.
- 201649 Pte. COHEN, M., 4/5th Bn.
- 292742 Pte. COHEN, J., 1/7th Bn.
- 58186 Pte. COHEN, B.
- 58483 Pte. CHAPMAN, L.
- 225012 Pte. COHEN, M. G.
- 64163 Pte. COHEN, L.
- 137541 Pte. DA COSTA, J.*
- 68 Pte. DAVIS, N.,* 10th Bn.
- 1905 Pte. DAVIS, C., 4th Bn.
- 1419 Pte. de BEER, A., 18th Bn.
- 2034 Cpl. DAVIS, L. H. B., 24th Bn.
- 482 Pte. DEFRIES, H. G., 23rd Bn.
- 49739 Cpl. DRAPKIN, I. A. (M.M.), 32nd Bn.
- 82042 L/Cpl. DAVIS, J., 26th Bn.
- 55903 Pte. DONIGER, I., 37th Bn.
- 49224 Pte. DUFRESNOY, A., 37th Bn.
- 35518 Pte. DIAMOND, M., 35th Bn.
- 38483 Pte. DECKER, S., 37th Bn.
- Pte. DE LEWE, J., 4th Bn.
- 228166 Cpl. DAVIES, P. A., 26th Bn
- 77563 Pte. DAVIES, J. H., 23rd Bn.
- G.S/478 Pte. DEVRIES, A., 9th Bn.
- Pte. DAVIES, R., 25th Bn.
- 24529 Pte. DESON, E.
- 44540 Pte. DICKERMAN, H., 4th Bn.
- Pte. DAVIS, G. L.,* 18th Bn.
- SR/7753 Sgt. DOWNS, F.,* 8th Bn.
- Pte. DA COSTA, M., 11th Bn.
- 32797 Pte. DAILES, B., 3rd Bn.
- 43756 Pte. DAVIDSON, I.
- 44485 Pte. DE SMITH, J.
- 3248 Pte. DAVIS, D. P., 4/2nd Bn.
- 8223 Pte. DILLER, 1st Bn.
- 18701 Pte. DAVIS, D., 2nd Bn.
- 15725 Pte. DENNEY, S. J., 4th Bn.
- 210470 Rfm. DAVIS, M., 25th Bn.
- 2295 Pte. DELETSKY, R., 42nd Bn.
- 2043 Pte. DOMBY, G., 11th Bn.
- 3127 Pte. DENNIS, L., 42nd Bn.
- 19126 Pte. DAVIS, A.
- 3418 Pte. DAGMAN, J., 42nd Bn.
- Pte. DENTSCH, R.
- Pte. DA COSTA, B., 3rd Bn.
- Pte. DAVIS, S., 13th Bn.
- Pte. DE FRIES, J., 8th Bn.
- Pte. DAVIS, H., 13th Bn.
- Pte. DAVIS, R. (M.M.).
- Pte. DE SOLLA, A., 3rd Bn.
- Pte. DE SOLLA, G., 3rd Bn.
- Pte. DE YOUNG.
- L/Cpl. DIAMOND, J., 5th Bn.
- Pte. DUDLEY, J., 10th Bn.
- 65549 Pte. DAVIES, M.
- 16636 Pte. ESSENBERG, J., 8th Bn.
- 4792 Pte. EPSTEIN, B., 20th Bn.
- 5120 Pte. EPSTEIN, D., 10th Bn.
- 4891 Pte. ENNESS, H. W., 13th Bn.
- 77910 Pte. ELLIS, S., 10th Bn.
- 1626 Pte. ELLISON, P. S.,* 3rd Bn.
- 202362 Sgt. EMDEN, J., 1st Bn.
- 4178 Pte. EMDEN, H., 3rd Bn.
- 53165 Pte. ELMAN, D., 10th Bn.
- 3223 Pte. EPSTEIN, M., 42nd Bn.
- 3167 Pte. ERIDEN, A., 42nd Bn.
- 381 Pte. EPSTEIN, J., 42nd Bn.
- 57623 Pte. ELLISON, W., 25th Bn.
- Pte. ELMAN, D., 21st Bn.
- Pte. EDELSTEIN, J., 2/4th Bn.
- Pte. EAGLE, H.
- 15722 Pte. FINEBERG, H., 4th Bn.
- 1096 Pte. FRIEND, L. M., 22nd Bn.
- 10919 Pte. FISHER, L. G., 23rd Bn.
- 57224 Pte. FREITAG, W., 12th Bn.
- 66160 Pte. FREEDMAN, C., 10th Bn.
- 54591 Pte. FRANKS, J., 34th Bn.
- 593818 Pte. FRASER, E. M.
- 6624 Pte. FINE, H., 8th Bn.
- 54204 Pte. FOREST, W., 34th Bn.
- Pte. FREEDMAN, 3rd Bn.
- Pte. FELDMAN, L., 11th Bn.
- 55807 Pte. FOBB, L., 12th Bn.
- 6249 Pte. FISHMAN, J., 1st Bn.
- 12188 Pte. FOLEDER, J., 12th Bn.
- 4594 Pte. FISHER, M., 10th Bn.
- 18129 Pte. FORESTER, S., 5th Bn.
- 781880 Pte. FORSTEIN, J., 11th Bn.
- 151519 Pte. FRIEDLANDER, A., 26th Bn.
- 55481 Pte. FOREST, P.
- Pte. FOSTER, G. J., 1st Bn.
- Pte. FIFER, A.
- G/95638 Pte. FRIEDSON, N., 10th Bn.
- G/93901 Pte. FELDMAN, S.

Royal Fusiliers.—*Continued.*

6780 Pte. Felix, A.
47500 Pte. Freeman, E., 6th Bn.
Cadet Frankel, R.
6397 Pte. Fellor, 1/4th Bn.
1278 Pte. From, H.
75638 Pte. Feldman, T.
1114 Pte. Frusht, I., 42nd Bn.
91202 Pte. Framberg, 42nd Bn.
3654 Pte. Finklestein, J., 26th Bn.
3391 Pte. Flowers, D., 26th Bn.
3364 Pte. Foot, J., 26th Bn.
3653 Pte. Foreman, M., 26th Bn.
16360 Pte. Glick, I. J., 4th Bn.
9665 Pte. Goodyear, A., 8th Bn.
Pte. Gordon, C. (M.M.).
Pte. Greenfield, E., 10th Bn.
4481 Pte. Goldman, B., 4th Bn.
14212 Pte. Garfinkel, E., 12th Bn.
2780 Pte. Goldman, H., 8th Bn.
7193 Pte. Goodman, M., 21st Bn.
2102 Pte. Ginsberg, S.,* 22nd Bn.
242558 Pte. Goldstein, H., 22nd Bn.
4804 Pte. Guterman, J., 9th Bn.
28652 Pte. Groffman, A., 7th Bn.
1986 Pte. Goldstein, G., 10th Bn.
6046 Pte. Green, G., 20th Bn.
10025 Pte. Goldstone, C., 20th Bn.
52825 Pte. Goldman, L. S.,* 20th Bn.
59615 Pte. Goldshmidt, C.,* 9th Bn.
65629 Pte. Goldstein, E., 10th Bn.
67828 Pte. Gradish, E., 32nd Bn.
39338 Pte. Goldberg, E., 35th Bn.
27322 Pte. Ginsberg, F., 35th Bn.
8007 Sgt. Green, H., 11th Bn.
2260 Pte. Gold, P., 4th Bn.
62502 Pte. Goldstein, L., 36th Bn.
32548 Pte. Grayrirski, J., 36th Bn.
Pte. Garnett, G., 1st Bn.
16111 Pte. Goldberg, A., 1st Bn.
1986 Pte. Goldstein, M., 10th Bn.
Pte. Goldmein, H., 8th Bn.
69387 Pte. Goldstone, L. (M.M.), 9th Bn.
614700 Sgt. Golding, J., 28th Bn.
95753 Pte. Goldberg, A., 10th Bn.
1195 Rct. Glucksman, A.
137177 Pte. Goldhill, B.
72237 Pte. Goldring, H., 31st Bn.
3824 Pte. Gushinoff, L., 42nd Bn.
G/95691 L/Cpl. Gosinney, M., 10th Bn.
151938 Pte. Gold, M., 26th Bn.
233933 Pte. Gordon, J.,
15224 Pte. Garrett, G.,* 4th Bn.
59615 Pte. Goldschmidt, C.,* 9th Bn.
63636 Pte. Green, G.,* 4th Bn.
100587 Cpl. Goldsmid, J., 2nd Bn.
203215 L/Cpl. Grose, H., 1st Bn.
64191 Drum. Grisky, 26th Bn.

23633 Pte. Goldstein, 2/2nd Bn.
28697 Pte. Goldstein, H., 7th Bn.
4573 Pte. Goldstein, I., 4th Bn.
6383 Pte. Goldstein, H., 4th Bn.
4702 Pte. Goldman, M., 4/3rd Bn.
4823 Pte. Galizer, H., 4/3rd Bn.
2174 Pte. Gonshaw, M.
3517 Pte. Goldie, B., 1st Bn.
64326 Pte. Goldberg, I., 32nd Bn.
66105 Pte. Gladstone, J.
G/560 Pte. Garfinkle, A.
2764 Pte. Goldberg, P., 5th Bn.
71217 Pte. Goddard, H. C., 5th Bn.
3438 Pte. Greenberg, J., 26th Bn.
2455 Pte. Glenternick, R., 26th Bn.
3468 Pte. Goldston, D., 26th Bn.
3346 Pte. Galbier, B., 26th Bn.
3897 Pte. Goldstein, S., 26th Bn.
3957 Pte. Goldberg, H., 26th Bn.
1335 Pte. Harburg, S., 10th Bn.
1195 Pte. Haber, A. V., 10th Bn.
712 Pte. Hoffman, M., 10th Bn.
4798 R.S.M. Harris, R., 4th Bn.
786 Pte. Harbour, I.,* 22nd Bn.
4170 Pte. Hecker, S., 24th Bn.
B/20365 Pte. Harris, S., 26th Bn.
20630 L/Cpl. Hamburger, J.,* 32nd Bn.
H/52508 Pte. Hassan, F. J., 4th Bn.
22481 Pte. Hillman, S., 32nd Bn.
G/4122 Pte. Heiser, A., 13th Bn.
49554 Pte. Hart, P. D., 13th Bn.
48708 Pte. Harringman, L.,* 8th Bn.
39376 Pte. Hassnovitch, J. J., 35th Bn.
8098 Pte. Harris, S., 7th Bn.
Pte. Hyams, H. C. (M.M.).
54350 Pte. Hyman, I., 34th Bn.
22481 Pte. Hillman, S., 32nd Bn.
57944 Pte. Hemp, G. W.
225688 Pte. Harris, J., 3rd Bn.
103264 Pte. Hafiel, L., 5th Bn.
25750 Pte. Hart, H., 16th Bn.
228789 Pte. Harris, V.
3013 Pte. Harris, A., 26th Bn.
781350 Pte. Hillier, A.,* 26th Bn.
3891 Cpl. Hendel, M.
6031 Pte. Hankin, H. J., 2nd Bn.
953 L/Cpl. Herbert, J., 17th Bn.
57159 Pte. Hoffman, C., 5th Bn.
6417 Pte. Hymans, L. H., 4/1st Bn.
136481 Pte. Harrison, M.
4072 Pte. Hamlyn, J., 2/2nd Bn.
2438 Sgt. Harris, D., 4/4th Bn.
18682 Pte. Haring, J.
Cpl. Hart, E. A. (M.M.).
3224 Pte. Haimovitch, S.
3758 Pte. Hyams, L., 42nd Bn.
Pte. Hargreaves, H. J., 18th Bn.
Pte. Haldinski, F., 2nd Bn.

Royal Fusiliers.—*Continued.*

3431 Pte. Harris, M., 26th Bn.
Pte. Isaacs, S., 10th Bn.
Pte. Isaacs, E.
7270 Pte. Isaac, B. C., 18th Bn.
897 Pte. Isaacs, H., 22nd Bn.
781865 Pte. Isaacs, A., 26th Bn.
22117 Pte. Israel, G., 32nd Bn.
G/47480 Pte. Isaacs, H., 24th Bn.
62481 Pte. Israel, L., 20th Bn.
1893 Pte. Isaacs, H.,* 10th Bn.
202131 Pte. Isaacs, H., 4th Bn.
47489 Pte. Isaacs, W.
32362 L/Cpl. Isaacs, M., 5th Bn.
10665 Pte. Isaacs, J., 4th Bn.
657 Pte. Joseph, M,. 17th Bn.
6480 Pte. Jacobs, J., 20th Bn.
2190 Cpl. Joseph, I., 24th Bn.
B/191619 Pte. Jonas, F. J.,* 26th Bn.
B/20109 Pte. Josephs, H., 26th Bn.
8290 Pte. Joseph, L., 9th Bn.
62413 Pte. Josephs, R., 9th Bn.
96147 Pte. James, B., 5th Bn.
62226 Pte. Jameson, P., 4th Bn.
57900 Pte. Jacobs, H., 17th Bn.
49765 Pte. Junnix, J., 3rd Bn.
93139 Pte. Joseph, G., 24th Bn.
95490 Sgt. Jacobs, F. R., 10th Bn.
58271 Pte. Jacobs, J.
35794 Pte. Jacobs, M.
54223 Pte. Jacobs, A. H.
82215 Sgt. Jacobs, 23rd Bn.
Pte. Jacobs, S., 13th Bn.
Pte. Jaffe, I.
Pte. Jacobs, K. E., 3rd Bn.
2478 Pte. Josephs, H., 26th Bn.
L/Cpl. Jacobs, G. J., 3rd Bn.
1336 Pte. Krailsheimer, J.,* 10th Bn.
Pte. Keen, M., 20th Bn.
4125 Pte. Kay, W., 21st Bn.
62485 Pte. Krohn, H.,* 10th Bn.
69181 Pte. Kusherman, E., 2nd Bn.
47138 Pte. Krupp, H., 26th Bn.
L/15999 Pte. Kriger, G., 7th Bn.
L/Cpl. Kay, L. H., 42nd Bn.
126407 Pte. Kruger, J., 5th Bn.
107329 Pte. Kavonic, I., 43rd Bn.
325644 Rfm. Kleinberg, H., 23rd Bn.
3602 Pte. Kroskafsky,
93908 Pte. Kneesburg, L., 5th Bn.
443344 L/Cpl. Keppner, L.
4753 Pte. Krans, A., 6th Bn.
3932 Pte. Krotoski, S., 6th Bn.
73009 Pte. Kerr, M., 31st Bn.
12803 Pte. Kosky, E.
68806 Pte. Kosky, C., 24th Bn.
204905 Pte. Kadish, M., 1stBn.
228102 Pte. Klein, G., 26th Bn.

1374 Pte. Kaplan, I., 42nd Bn.
2372 Pte. Kupferblatt, W., 26th Bn.
3329 Pte. Kelkovitz, H., 26th Bn.
8019 Pte. Lewis, H., 4th Bn.
149 Pte. Lansberg, N., 10th Bn.
1064 Sgt. Lion, F. J., 10th Bn.
1047 Pte. Lotheim, S., 10th Bn.
7207 Cpl. Lazarus, A. E.,* 1st Bn.
7538 Pte. Levinger, P., 11th Bn.
10969 Pte. Levy, H.,* 9th Bn.
7173 Pte. Leitz, H., 18th Bn.
612 Pte. Lindo, H. F., 19th Bn.
5125 Pte. Lichtenstein, M., 20th Bn.
9541 Pte. Levi, A.,* 2nd Bn.
6922 Pte. Levy, A., 21st Bn.
1547 Pte. Levy, J.,* 22nd Bn.
2015 Pte. Levy, P., 24th Bn.
1647 Pte. Littman, S.,* 23rd Bn.
523 Sgt. Lewis, M. (M.M.), 23rd Bn.
4073 L/Cpl. Lewis, T.,* 23rd Bn.
226 Pte. Lipman, J., 2nd Bn.
14567 L/Cpl. Lever, J., 2nd Bn.
9334 Pte. Langston, W., 7th Bn.
5137 Pte. Lewis, H.,* 10th Bn.
48757 Cpl. Levine, S., 20th Bn.
65488 Pte. Levy, J., 26th Bn.
49423 Pte. Levie, F., 32nd Bn.
271714 Sig. Leyton, J., 22nd Bn.
266453 Pte. Levy, B., 13th Bn.
70724 Pte. Lyons, M. L., 2nd Bn.
480165 Pte. Levene, H., 43rd Bn.
29439 Pte. Levy, A. L., 35th Bn.
43887 Pte. Leberman, G., 35th Bn.
32000 L/Cpl. Lonsdale, J., 34th Bn.
2065 Pte. Lewis, J. H., 8th Bn.
63193 Pte. Lazarus, J., 36th Bn.
8167 Pte. Levy, S., 4th Bn.
31223 Pte. Lazarus, B., 34th Bn.
13752 Pte. Levenston, H., 1st Bn.
Pte. Lewis, D., 1st Bn.
Pte. Levitt, A. E. (M.M.).
51053 Pte. Latman, P., 17th Bn.
76934 Pte. Levy, E., 9th Bn.
25754 Pte. Levy, J., 16th Bn.
Sig. Levy, B., 13th Bn.
Pte. Lissack, C., 4th Bn.
205806 Pte. Lewis, J.
69038 Pte. Layton, J., 23rd Bn.
63190 Pte. Levey, J.,* 20th Bn.
9541 Pte. Levi, A.,* 2nd Bn.
5212 Pte. Lisbona, N.,* 20th Bn.
100044 Pte. Lipschitz, M., 4th Bn.
232394 Pte. Lubinsky, G. L.
102975 Pte. Levy, J.
3299 Pte. Lazarus, H.
3025 Pte. Lefcovitch, I., 17th Bn.
93001 Pte. Lukes, L., 43rd Bn.
Sgt. Levin, F. (M.M.).

Royal Fusiliers.—*Continued.*

275294 Pte. LEVITT, M., 22nd Bn.
4221 Cpl. LEAPMAN, B., 4/1st Bn.
22005 Pte. LEVINE, J., 10th Bn.
53114 Pte. LEHMANN, L. 20th Bn.
J/69227 Pte. LEVITT, H., 22nd Bn.
63910 Pte. LEVY, J., 20th Bn.
58202 Pte. LANDY, B.
202146 Pte. LUBELSKI, M., 20th Bn.
17603 C.Q.M.S. LEGATT, C., 26th Bn.
6041 L/Cpl. LEVY, H.
26943 Pte. LEVY, J., 5th Bn.
2587 Pte. LEVY, L., 4th Bn.
27086 Pte. LYONS, L., 6th Bn.
Pte. LIBBERKLANG, M.
2429 Pte. LEWIN, G. M., 31st Bn.
4132 Pte. LEWIN, H., 29th Bn.
5231 Pte. LIGHT, B., 30th Bn.
5594 Pte. LUNZER, R., 2/3rd Bn.
62323 Pte. LAZARUS, 9th Bn.
3744 Pte. LEWIS, N., 42nd Bn.
50031 Pte. LANDSBERG, M., 11th Bn.
4238 Pte. LEVENSKY, H.
6358 Pte. LUTON, A., 42nd Bn.
Pte. LUMLEY, A. E., 10th Bn.
2740 Pte. LECANSKI, L., 26th Bn.
3562 Pte. LAKOFSKY, S., 26th Bn.
2422 Pte. LIPMAN, K., 26th Bn.
8193 Pte. LEWIS, C.* (GRODNER), 4th Bn.
37474 Pte. LYONS, A. R.*
14667 L/Cpl. MARTIN, B. (M.M.), 4th Bn.
8337 Pte. MOSSEL, A.,* 1st Bn.
181 Pte. MOORE, M.,* 10th Bn.
1805 Dvr. MARKS, 4th Bn.
99 Pte. MICHAELS, L.,* 8th Bn.
193 Pte. MISCH, C., 17th Bn.
677 Pte. MARKS, J., 17th Bn.
6346 Pte. MARKS, E., 19th Bn.
5343 Pte. MORRIS, M. H., 20th Bn.
1418 Pte. MORRIS, D., 22nd Bn.
21998 Pte. MOLIVER, S. R.,* 2nd Bn.
Pte. MORRIS, A., 5th Bn.
1881 Pte. MARCUS, M.,* 26th Bn.
16967 Pte. MYERS, H., 23rd Bn.
4084 Pte. MYERS, L.* (SMITH), 9th Bn.
22068 Pte. MEIDER, H., 32nd Bn.
22408 Pte. MYERS, L., 32nd Bn.
20480 Pte. MORRIS, J., 32nd Bn.
50280 Pte. MORRIS, J. W.,* 23rd Bn.
2367 Pte. MILLER, A., 17th Bn.
22588 Pte. MICHAELS, L.,* 9th Bn.
60178 Pte. MARCOVITCH, L., 34th Bn.
87 Pte. MICHAELS, A., 8th Bn.
64176 L/Cpl. MOSELEY, M. E., 26th Bn.
G/96374 Pte. MORTON, G., 44th Bn.
16899 Pte. MINDEN, J., 33rd Bn.
Pte. MARTIN, E. N., 4th Bn
Pte. MOSS, G. W.
109246 Pte. MYERS, G. H., 43rd Bn.
88673 Sgt. MOSCOW, E., 4th Bn.
79389 Pte. MOSS, J., 9th Bn.
16967 Pte. MYERS, H.,* 23rd Bn.
26868 Pte. MILLER, L.,* 7th Bn.
1094 Pte. MYERS, E.,* 22nd Bn.
52655 L/Cpl. MYERS, S.,* 32nd Bn.
56359 Pte. MOSES, L.
5071 Pte. MILLER, H., 3rd Bn.
458 Pte. MACK, W. (S. E. LEVI),* 10th Bn.
100170 L/Cpl. MARKOVITCH, H.,* 13th Bn.
20448 Pte. MARKS, J. A.,* 22nd Bn.
87720 Pte. MILLER, L., 24th Bn.
2584 Pte. MYERS, M., 3rd Bn.
49062 Pte. MALNICK, J., 6th Bn.
54830 Pte. MAXWELL, G., 4th Bn.
49124 Pte. MOSES, M. 10th Bn.
75194 Pte. MELAMER, I., 24th Bn.
52655 L/Cpl. MYERS, G., 32nd Bn.
50279 Pte. MORRIS, A., 2nd Bn.
2328 Pte. MILLER, F., 31st Bn.
5982 Pte. MODLIN, S., 4/4th Bn.
16967 Pte. MYERS, H.
3528 Pte. MYERS, L., 32nd Bn.
233337 Cpl. MYERS P.
5940 Pte. MANTSBAUM, J., 3rd Bn.
2402 Pte. MORRIS, J., 31st Bn.
2429 Pte. MARCUS, M., 31st Bn.
2486 Pte. MULAFSKY, I.
2957 Pte. MATUSOFF, 42nd Bn.
91113 Pte. MILLER, 42nd Bn.
2102 Pte. MENINSKY, B., 42nd Bn.
3283 Pte. MISENBERG, M., 42nd Bn.
68841 Pte. MORRIS, A., 42nd Bn.
1678 Pte. MALINSKY, J., 42nd Bn.
3317 Pte. MEYER, J., 42nd Bn.
3881 Pte. MILLER, M., 42nd Bn.
3416 Pte. MUSLIN, H., 42nd Bn.
3194 Pte. MOSKOWITZ, H., 42nd Bn.
Pte. MARKS, L., 42nd Bn.
4311 Pte. MESSON, 42nd Bn.
6760 Pte. MUSCOVITCH, G., 26th Bn.
3008 Pte. MOLDAJSKI, A., 26th Bn.
8168 Pte. NYMAN, J., 4th Bn.
1598 Pte. NISSEN, I.,* 4th Bn.
G/61613 Pte. NATHAN, S., 24th Bn.
4394 Pte. NELSON, R., 8th Bn.
62892 Pte. NORCEROVITCH, J., 13th Bn.
6240 Pte. NICKELSKY, H., 20th Bn.
6232 Pte. NEEDLESTICHER, 20th Bn.
38859 Pte. NELSON, A., 5th Bn.
21929 Pte. NATHAN, M.
3317 L/Cpl. OBERMAN, P. (M.M.), 12th Bn.
7149 Pte. OLEESKY, M., 18th Bn.
26878 Pte. OSOSKI, L., 2nd Bn.
87202 Pte. OLCHEST, G., 5th Bn.
2710 Pte. ORLANS, A., 42nd Bn.

Royal Fusiliers.—*Continued.*

Pte. ORENSTEIN, S.
11160 C.S.M. PROOTH, J. (D.C.M.), 13th Bn.
7385 Pte. PHILLIPS, S.,* 9th Bn.
245106 Pte. PHILLIPS, A.,* 32nd Bn.
2089 Pte. PRAAGH, A. VAN, 32nd Bn.
4240 Pte. PINKUS, M., 23rd Bn.
26771 Pte. PASS, G. J., 7th Bn.
63375 Pte. PYKE, J. L.,* 13th Bn.
4666 Pte. PUBECK, H. R., 20th Bn.
5117 Pte. PRESSMAN, H., 7th Bn.
45117 Pte. PRESSMAN, A., 8th Bn.
96070 Pte. PENDRY, J., 7th Bn.
Pte. PHILLIPS, T., 17th Bn.
9675 Pte. PETERS, G., 3rd Bn.
54402 Pte. PODORANSKY, 37th Bn.
232831 Pte. PARK, L., 11th Bn.
245106 Pte. PHILLIPS, A.,* 32nd Bn.
1032 L/Cpl. PESTON, S., 42nd Bn.
205870 L/Cpl. PHILLIPS, 42nd Bn.
6208 Pte. PEARSON, M., 3rd Bn.
67882 Pte. PHILLIPS, O.
4352 Pte. PHILLIPS, J.
5801 Pte. PRINS, A., 4th Bn.
65039 Pte. PERILLY, M.
801300 Pte. POSENER, H.
6117 Pte. PRICE, B., 20th Bn.
5949 Pte. PINKUS, A., 4th Bn.
6115 Pte. PEARLSTONE, A., 4th Bn.
557 Pte. PRISNALL, W. J., 42nd Bn.
J/415 L/Cpl. PHILLIPS, M., 42nd Bn.
J/3463 Pte. PARKUS, A., 42nd Bn.
67882 Pte. PHILLIPS, C., 7th Bn.
Pte. PILAR, 42nd Bn.
7148 Pte. PRINS, B., 1st Bn.
69420 Pte. PRINCE, T., 9th Bn.
67021 Pte. PHILLIPS, H., 23rd Bn.
5001 Pte. PALMER, H., 42nd Bn.
Pte. PALLEY, S.
218 Sgt. ROTHSCHILD, G. F., 10th Bn.
60 Pte. ROSE, S., 9th Bn.
7205 Sgt. ROSENBERG, J., 11th Bn.
4457 Pte. ROSENBLOOM, M., 13th Bn.
7834 Pte. ROSENTHAL, M. H., 21st Bn.
5196 Pte. RASHMAN, G., 26th Bn.
51060 L/Cpl. ROSENBERG, D.,* 17th Bn.
5125 Pte. ROSENBERG, H., 8th Bn.
216 Pte. ROSE, A. S.,* 10th Bn.
5200 Pte. ROSENBERG, L.,* 10th Bn.
5201 Pte. ROSENBLOOM, L., 10th Bn.
34510 Pte. RAPHAEL, S., 2nd Bn.
S/Sgt. REUBEN, O. B. (M.S.M.)
39659 Pte. ROUNDSTEIN, H., 35th Bn.
4666 Pte. RUBECK, H., 20th Bn.
4478 A/Sgt. ROSENTHAL, D., 11th Bn.
2703 Cpl. RUBNER, C., 4th Bn.
231981 Pte. ROSS, E., 2nd Bn.
267075 Pte. RIDZ, J., 2nd Bn.

G.S/2064 Pte. ROSE, T., 9th Bn.
5251 Pte. RAISMAN, M., 30th Bn.
112427 Pte. ROSENBLOOM, B., 5th Bn.
52835 Pte. ROSENBERG, D., 2nd Bn.
320889 Rfm. ROSENBERG, J.
G/21998 Pte. ROBINSON-MOLIVER S.,* 2nd Bn.
G/96123 Pte. ROSENBERG, M., 10th Bn.
69181 Pte. RUSHMAN, E., 2nd Bn.
21557 Pte. ROBERTS, G. J. S.
Sgt. RUDA, M. (M.M.)
57051 Pte. ROBBINS, W. A.
56108 Pte. ROSENBERG, I., 42nd Bn.
1900 Pte. RICHENBERG, L., 42nd Bn.
239 Pte. ROLBIN, N., 42nd Bn.
539 Pte. RACKMAN, A., 42nd Bn.
Pte. REBUCK, I., 42nd Bn.
3382 Pte. REZNICK, Z., 42nd Bn.
Pte. ROSENBERG, S.
Pte. ROSENTHAL, A.
Pte. ROMAIN, D. A.
Pte. ROBERTS, H. I. (M.S.M.)
Pte. REUBENS, A., 10th Bn.
62824 Pte. SOLOMONS, E., 20th Bn.
6477 Pte. SOLOMON, S., 20th Bn.
65580 Pte. SILVERMAN, W., 2nd Bn.
(65512 Pte. SCHWARTZMAN, M., 2nd Bn.
8152 Pte. SAUNDERS, H., 2nd Bn.
5207 Pte. STEINLOFT, 26th Bn.
5208 Cpl. SUNDERLAND, A., 26th Bn.
228354 Pte. SILVERMAN, S., 26th Bn.
52685 Pte. SOMAN, B., 32nd Bn.
241786 Pte. SUGARMAN, J., 32nd Bn.
77023 Pte. SHULMAN, S. (M.M.), 24th Bn.
62478 Pte. SOLOMONS, S.,* 2nd Bn.
5608 Pte. SELIGMAN, H. J., 20th Bn.
387142 Pte. SOLOMONS, N., 43rd Bn.
54243 Pte. SIMONS, W., 37th Bn.
39036 Pte. STEWART, H., 35th Bn.
29770 Pte. SELIG, M., 37th Lab. Bn.
74665 Pte. SAMUELS, E., 7th Bn.
10039 Pte. SYMONS, J., 4th Bn.
15774 Pte. STENOFF, C., 1st Bn.
16381 Sgt. SOLOMONS, F., 8th Bn.
68993 Pte. SOLOMONS, F.,* 23rd Bn.
L/Cpl. SIGMUND, L., 10th Bn.
4783 Pte. SCHIFERN, G., 20th Bn.
64327 Pte. SUGARMAN, J., 7th Bn.
Pte. SILVERBLATT, J., 8th Bn.
Pte. SOLOMON, J., 8th Bn.
Pte. SOLOMON, H., 8th Bn.
Pte. SYMONS, A., 8th Bn.
136 Pte. SMITH, H., 9th Bn.
8538 Pte. SIMMONDS, W., 4th Bn.
3110 Pte. SILVERBLATT, R., 4th Bn.
5726 Pte. SIMMONS, J.,* 23rd Bn.
240 Pte. SOLOMON, S., 10th Bn.
524 Pte. SCHARP, E. C., 10th Bn.
4122 Pte. SUGARMAN, M., 4th Bn.

Royal Fusiliers.—*Continued.*

3257 Pte. SELIGMAN, W. L., 21st Bn.
953 L/Cpl. STRAUS, J., 17th Bn.
2039 Pte. SHUR, P., 18th Bn.
2027 Pte. SAMUEL, C.V., 18th Bn.
2028 Pte. SAMUEL, R. J., 18th Bn.
4326 Pte. SHEKURY, C., 19th Bn.
5637 L/Cpl. SILVERSTONE, A. A., 20th Bn.
5608 Pte. SELIGMAN, H. J., 20th Bn.
4783 Pte. SHIFFREN, E.,* 20th Bn.
9114 Pte. SOLOMON, E. J., 21st Bn.
2018 Pte. SLOMAN, D., 24th Bn.
3447 Pte. SMITH, D. A., 24th Bn.
3864 Pte. SOLOMON, L., 24th Bn.
4042 Pte. SNIDERS, A., 23rd Bn.
B/23001 Pte. SELINE, J. J.,* 26th Bn.
18397 Cpl. SHARP, H., 32nd Bn.
G/52091 Cpl. SILVER, S., 24th Bn.
2924 Pte. SHEFFRIN, B., 23rd Bn.
2066 Sgt. SANDERS, G. J.,* 9th Bn.
26742 Pte. SAMUELS, P.,* 7th Bn.
25815 Pte. SCHNEIDER, C., 7th Bn.
8538 Pte. SIMMONDS, W., 4th Bn.
C/97706 Pte. SOLOMON, A. F., 5th Bn.
304 Pte. SCHNITZER, J., 16th Bn.
17995 Pte. SOLOMONS, A., 5th Bn.
52685 Pte. SIMON, B., 13th Bn.
102076 Pte. SEGAL, G., 43rd Bn.
8012 Pte. SIMONS, J.
8459 Pte. STAFFKEY, J.
54854 L/Cpl. SLOMAN, D., 23rd Bn.
G/107072 Pte. SOLOMON, M., 15th Bn.
42837 Pte. SONFIELD, S. H.
55501 Pte. STARR, J.
283753 Pte. SCHATT, H.
204187 Pte. SCHIFF, B.,* 13th Bn.
2384 Pte. SCHWARTZ, I.,* 4th Bn.
26742 Pte. SAMUELS, P.,* 7th Bn.
6939 Pte. SILDIN, P.*
J.3059 L/Cpl. SOLOMONS, L., 42nd Bn.
72505 C.S.M. SANSON, A., 2nd Bn.
100552 Pte. SHMERLSON, M., 2nd Bn.
Pte. SCHWARTZ, J. K.
P045 Pte. SOLOMONS, W., 3rd Bn.
4785 Pte. SINER, N., 3rd Bn.
61616 Pte. SHEPHERD, J., 3/5th Bn.
5935 Pte. SALKIND, R., 1/3rd Bn.
59567 Pte. SIMONS, N., 5th Bn.
58309 Pte. SANDOVITCH, I.
4848 Pte. SAMUELS, H., 4/4th Bn.
5974 Pte. SOLOMONS, J., 4/4th Bn.
10039 Pte. SYMONS, D., 6th Bn.
16381 Pte. SOLOMON, B., 13th Bn.
56841 Pte. SPRAGE, M.
7584 Pte. SOLOMONS. M., 4th Bn.
255154 Pte. SUGAR, M.
16619 Pte. SPIERS, A.
405155 Pte. STEINE, L.

225374 Pte. SYMONS, A., 11th Bn.
286 Sgt. SHAMROCK, P., 42nd Bn.
3232 Pte. SEGAL, D., 42nd Bn.
Sgt. SOLOMON, A. F. (M.S.M.).
1896 Pte. SCHWARTZ, V., 42nd Bn.
295585 Pte. SIMMONS, A., 1/4th Bn.
558753 Pte. SIDLER, E.
282858 Pte. SHERKISKY, D., 1/4th Bn.
3813 Pte. SELINSKY, S., 42nd Bn.
215 Cpl. STEINBERG, J., 42nd Bn.
19448 L/Cpl. SHULMAN, 26th Bn.
1640 Pte. SOLOMONS, J., 42nd Bn.
3607 Pte. SEGASKY, S., 42nd Bn.
852 Pte. STEIN, S., 42nd Bn.
3169 Pte. SMILES, S., 42nd Bn.
Pte. STUDENT, A., 42nd Bn.
6486 Pte. SHAPERO, M., 8th Bn.
Pte. SPIVAK, C., 6th Bn.
Pte. SCHIFREEN, R., 30th Bn.
6968 Pte. TORRES, S. D.,* 10th Bn.
G/20110 Pte. THAL, V., 24th Bn.
35973 Pte. TANNENBAUM, I., 37th Bn.
49809 Pte. TURNER, J., 9th Bn.
56282 Pte. TOBIAS, V.
62563 Pte. TOOMIN, M.
234154 Pte. TROBE, J.
12188 Pte. TOLEDOR, J., 6th Bn.
910 Pte. TARNOLPOSKY, A., 42nd Bn.
2418 Pte. TOBIN, M., 2/4th Bn.
91202 Pte. TRAMBURG, 42nd Bn.
Pte. TALKOVITCH, S., 42nd Bn.
46646 Pte. TAYLOR, J., 42nd Bn.
587 Pte. TIMANOFF, M., 42nd Bn.
2944 Pte. TEPR, L., 42nd Bn.
5928 Pte. VALENTINE, M., 13th Bn.
50319 Pte. VALENTINE, I., 2nd Bn.
39353 Pte. VAN GELDER, M., 35th Bn.
4785 L/Cpl. VINER, H., 3rd Bn.
20110 Pte. VAN THALL, M. J.,* 24th Bn.
282682 Pte. VANGROVE, S.
3882 Pte. VICE, T. G., 26th Bn.
61181 Pte. VOGEL, M., 19th Bn.
471 Pte. VAISOFCHICK, J., 42nd Bn.
Pte. VOLUMBERG, J., 42nd Bn.
3533 Pte. VAN RAALTE, E., 42nd Bn.
3420 Pte. VOLCH, H., 42nd Bn.
Pte. WEISBERG, J., 10th Bn.
3784 Pte. WARENBERG, J., 24th Bn.
3619 Pte. WOOD, B.,* 24th Bn.
85 Pte. WILSON, J., 22nd Bn.
65296 Pte. WOOLF, F., 4th Bn.
6246 Pte. WEITZMAN, W., 20th Bn.
1147 Sgt. WEIHS, L.,* 1st Bn.
66451 Pte. WENZEREL, M., 37th Bn.
54327 Pte. WOOLF, F. J., 37th Bn.
39062 Pte. WEITZMAN, S., 35th Bn.
28789 Pte. WANDERLOVITCH, B., 37th Bn.
54432 Pte. WHACKER, S., 35th Bn.

Royal Fusiliers.—*Continued.*

68822 Pte. WOLFE, F., 23rd Bn.
14251 Pte. WOOD, H.
   Pte. WILSON, J., 8th Bn.
   Pte. WOOLF, R., 42nd Bn.
9118 Pte. WOOLF, H.,* 1st Bn.
100540 Pte. WILKS, A., 2nd Bn.
5113 Pte. WOOLFSON, N., 3rd Bn.
54776 Pte. WINSBERG, J., 36th Bn.
65296 Pte. WOOLF, B., 4th Bn.
43389 Pte. WOOLF, I.
70057 Pte. WESENSKY, M.

225727 Pte. WILLIAM, M.
56965 Pte. WARSHAWSKY, M.
35294 Pte. WOOLF, N., 18th Bn.
377435 Pte. WEISS, H. T., 13th Bn.
33674 Pte. WINETROBE, L., 10th Bn.
198 Pte. WAINWRIGHT, S., 42nd Bn.
   Pte. YERNAN, 22nd Bn.
51053 Pte. ZATMAN, P., 17th Bn.
G/95670 Pte. ZEEHANDELAAR, W., 10th Bn.
17175 Pte. ZAIDNER, M.

* Killed in Action or died on Active Service.

JEWISH UNITS.
(See p. 9).

38th BATTALION ROYAL FUSILIERS ("JUDEANS")

Officers.

Lt.-Col. PATTERSON, J. H. (D.S.O.).
2nd Lieut. ABRAHAMS, S.
Lieut. CROSS, H. B.
2nd Lieut. DALTROFF, E. M.
2nd Lieut. FLIGELSTONE, T. H. (M.C.).
Lieut. GROSS, L. A.
2nd Lieut. HARRIS, E.
Capt. HARRIS, H. H.

Capt. HYAMS, G. S.
Hon. Lieut. JABOTINSKY, V.
Lt. JAFFE, I. (Lewis Gun Officer).
Lieut. LIPSEY, S. M.
2nd Lieut. MENDES, M.
2nd Lieut. MORRIS, H.
Lieut. NEVILLE, J. H.
Lieut. PHILLIPS, I. G. E.
Lieut. SAMUEL, H. B.

2nd Lieut. SIMMONS, H.
Capt. VANDYK, E.
2nd Lieut. WOLFENSOHN, H.
Lieut. WOLFFE, B.*
2nd Lieut. WOLFFE, L. D.
2nd Lieut. FREEMAN, H.
2nd Lieut. HARRIS, H.
2nd Lieut. COUSSIN, T.

N.C.O's and Men.

No.	Rank.	Name.	No.	Rank.	Name.	No.	Rank.	Name.
J 1351	Pte.	ANSLEVITCH, M.	J 258	Pte.	ABRAHAMS, S.	J 1043	Pte.	BLUMENTHAL, A.
J 1372	Pte.	ASHER, C.	J 773	Pte.	ALLONOWITZ, L.*	J 1295	Pte.	BEER, M.
J 1758	Pte.	ABBOTT, C. L.	J 1110	Pte.	ALICK, N.*	J 1321	Pte.	BERMAN, J.*
J 396	Pte.	ARONOFF, S.	J 1129	Pte.	ADELMAN, M.	J 1692	Pte.	BENJAMIN, D.
J 421	Pte.	ANDREWS, H.	19360	Pte.	ANGEL, J.	J 266	Pte.	BITOFSKY, B.
J 707	Pte.	ABRAHAMS, M.	J 83	L/Cpl.	ABRAHAMS, I.	J 1430	Pte.	BROOKS, S.
J 1039	Pte.	ALVAREZ, A.	J 255	Pte.	ADELMAN, P.	J 1456	Pte.	BARON, B.
J 630	Pte.	ABLESON, W.	J 48	Pte.	APTER, J.	J 1492	Pte.	BENJAMIN, A.
J 1038	Pte.	ABRAHAMS, S. M.	201812	Pte.	ALTON, GEORGE E.	J 1556	Pte.	BLASHKI, B.
J 548	Pte.	ABRAHAMSON, S.*		Pte.	ARONORSKY, ISRAEL.	J 1559	Pte.	BARR, S.
J 831	Pte.	ADLER, A.		Pte.	ADELMAN, ALFRED.	200291	Pte.	BLOCK, R.
J 855	Pte.	ANGEL, D.		Pte.	ALTMAN, PHILIP.	J 152	A/Cpl.	BLASENSTEIN, C.
J 888	Pte.	ANTIN, P.		Pte.	ABILL, BARNETT.	201485	Pte.	BROWN, J. H.
201687	Pte.	ASPDEN, P.	J 265	Pte.	BALOTIN, S.	J 176	Pte.	BALARSKY, J.
J 876	Pte.	AUSTIN, R. M.	J 332	Pte.	BLACK, L.*	J 367	Pte.	BERMAN, H.
J 316	Pte.	ABRAHAMS, D.	J 1010	Pte.	BRICK, B.*	J 375	Pte.	BERKOVITCH, J.

"Judeans." N.C.O.'s AND MEN—Continued.

J 427	Pte. Borstein, W.	J 1054	Pte. Bernstein, S.	J 36	Pte. Cooper, A.
290040	Pte. Blackburn, S.	J 1070	Pte. Bearman, S.	J 939	Pte. Cohen, P.
J 43	Pte. Boudic, A.	J 1108	Pte. Brackman, S.	J 58	A/Sgt. Cregor, C.*
J 149	Pte. Barbuk, M.	J 1161	Pte. Bransky, A.	J 800	Pte. Comras, H.
J 436	Pte. Bloomberg, I. R.	J 1176	Pte. Byginsky, L.	J 1037	Pte. Carlson, C.
J 445	Pte. Berson, M.	J 1198	Pte. Bromberg, M.	J 160	Pte. Cohen, H.
J 554	Pte. Beil, J.	J 1232	Pte. Baker, H.	J 435	Pte. Cooperberg, A.
J 632	Pte. Bloom, R.	J 1443	Pte. Brook, B.	J 426	Pte. Cohen, N.
J 1036	Pte. Blumberg, J. J.	J 1595	Pte. Belskie, M.	J 431	Pte. Cohen, I.
J 1338	Pte. Baum, J.	J 1750	Pte. Bienstock, M.*	J 498	Pte. Canter, W.
J 1468	Pte. Bootnitsky, B.	J 1107	Pte. Bernstein, L.	J 557	Pte. Cohen, J.
J 715	Pte. Barasauckas, S.	J 1109	Pte. Beinstein, I.	J 704	Pte. Cohen, J.
J 864	Pte. Bakesef, I.	J 1127	Pte. Braverman, M.	J 811	Pte. Cohen, S.
J 1225	Pte. Berton, H.	J 1149	Pte. Bratt, P.	J 1017	Pte. Cohen, H.
J 1606	Pte. Block, A.	J 1202	Pte. Brodie, S.	J 1050	Pte. Cohen, H.
J 1689	Pte. Bernstein, D.	203867	Pte. Borthwick, J. R.	J 1443	Pte. Cohen, I.
J 31	A/Sgt. Bondar, A.		Pte. Block, H.	J 1685	Pte. Chalfren, B.
J 841	Pte. Barnett, V.	205195	A/C.S.M. Black, C.	J 491	Pte. Cohen, P.
J 1021	Pte. Benjamin, W.	J 70	Pte. Berliner, A.	J 706	Pte. Cohen, J.
J 660	Pte. Berner, M.	J 150	Pte. Buznik, M.	J 1051	Pte. Cohen, J.
J 797	Pte. Barnett, H. D.	J 185	Pte. Bardfield, M.	J 1122	Pte. Cohen, H.
J 840	Pte. Bronstein, W.	J 245	Pte. Brown, G.	J 1304	Pte. Cohen, M.
J 899	Pte. Barrett, M.	J 18	L/Cpl. Beer, M. H.	J 1313	Pte. Cohen, J.
J 908	Pte. Black, S.	J 44	Pte. Bougnic, W.	32497	Pte. Cohen, H.
J 920	Pte. Black, D.	J 74	Pte. Blatt, J.	J 609	Pte. Cohen, P.
J 936	Pte. Bernstein, J.	J 180	Pte. Balen, J.	J 751	Pte. Cohen, A.
J 1069	Pte. Benjamin, L.	J 186	Pte. Berkman, M.	J 783	Pte. Cottler, H.
J 1260	Pte. Berezorsky, J.	J 243	Pte. Billyack, A.	201858	Pte. Chadwick, F.
J 1324	Pte. Beck, D.		Pte. Bartenbat, R.	J 645	L/Cpl. Caplen, M.
J 1378	Pte. Bresloff, L.		Pte. Brochodski, C.	J 685	Pte. Cohen, M.
J 926	Pte. Benjamin, L.		Pte. Bloom, Chain.	J 792	Pte. Coram, A.
J 947	Pte. Belinsky, A.		Pte. Berkman, Joseph.	J 1028	Pte. Cainer, G.
J 1022	Pte. Benstein, M.	J 43	Pte. Boudnik, Baron.	J 824	Pte. Chiren, D.
J 1056	Pte. Banylas, F.		Pte. Blass, Louis.	J 838	Pte. Cohen, S.
J 1197	Pte. Brooksban, M.		Pte. Blandestein, M.	J 903	Pte. Cohen, J.
J 1447	Pte. Bogoslovsky, B.	J 1043	Pte. Blumenthal, J.	J 1264	Pte. Creager, I.
J 1759	Pte. Bernstein, H.		Pte. Barnes, Joseph.	J 1323	Pte. Canter, J.
J 1763	Pte. Blond, H. L.	J 1457	Pte. Black, Barnett.	J 1483	Pte. Caplan, J.
J 1764	Pte. Belonkronitsky, M.	J 936	Pte. Bernstien, J.	J 528	Pte. Cohen, J. J.
203887	Pte. Brown, J.	J 675	Pte. Best, David.	J 573	Pte. Cohen, H.
202746	Pte. Bittiner, J.		Pte. Beaber, Israel.	J 681	Pte. Cohen, J.
J 4	A/Cpl. Berman, Y.	J 1161	Pte. Barodonsky, A.	J 1767	Pte. Cohen, S.
J 66	L/Cpl. Birland, I.		Pte. Berinzweig, I.	J 752	Pte. Cohen, S.
J 214	Pte. Black, J.		Sgt. Bobeoff, Henoke.	J 1007	Pte. Canter, N.
J 772	Pte. Bondoniski, H.		Pte. Berber, Alex.	J 1178	Pte. Cohen, M.
J 788	Pte. Bergbaum, H.	J 683	Pte. Bischoff, A.	J 1607	Pte. Cohen, L.
J 943	Pte. Bernzwig, J.	J 937	Pte. Boot, Isaac.	J 1711	Pte. Cohen, N.
J 1004	Pte. Brier, J.		Pte. Blanes, Armand.	Recruit	Chesler, M.
J 1011	Pte. Bland, J. I.		Pte. Bicklem, Jack.	Recruit	Clapper, B.
J 1055	Pte. Bloomenthall, M.*		Pte. Benderik.	J 1119	Pte. Canter, H.*
J 1975	Pte. Bass, M.		Pte. Benjamin, E.	J 1141	Pte. Casselheim, R.
72402	Pte. Bernstein, J.	J 345	Pte. Coleman, E.	J 1193	Pte. Cohen, W.
J 1457	L/Cpl. Black, C.	J 608	Pte. Cohen, M.	J 1646	Pte. Cobrin, W.
J 353	Pte. Bloom, B.	J 928	Pte. Cresswell, J. J.		Pte. Chilovitch, L.
J 541	Pte. Burenstein, I.	J 1271	Pte. Chaplitsky, I.	205124	A/R.S.M. Carmell, J.
J 576	Pte. Bodenitz, N.	J 1485	Pte. Cliff, A.	J 136	A/Cpl. Cohen, J.
J 900	Pte. Berlinsky, A.	J 274	Pte. Craskin, M.	J 873	A/Cpl. Cripps, H.

"Judeans." N.C.O.'s AND MEN—Continued.

J	312	L/Cpl. COHEN, H.	J	898	Pte. FREEDMAN, S.	J	229	Pte. FINKELSTEIN, G.
J	56	A/R.Q.M.S. CALLEN, J.	J	1490	Pte. FINKELSTONE, M.			Pte. FINKELSTEIN, M.
J	120	A/Cpl. COHEN, J.	J	1497	Pte. FELDMAN, S.			Pte. FRIEND, LOUIS.
J	913	L/Cpl. CALMUS, I.	J	1555	Pte. FINKELSTEIN, A.			Pte. FELDMAN, HYMAN.
J	143	Pte. CHELMINSKI, M. A.	J	1619	Pte. FLEXER, L.			Pte. FRANKEL, DAN.
		Pte. CHARVONIA, ISRAEL.	J	361	Pte. FELDSTEIN, B.			Pte. FRANK, JACOB.
		Pte. CHAYTON, ISRAEL.	J	969	Pte. FALK, M.			Pte. FRIEDMAN, B.
		Pte. CHARING, HARRY.	J	1489	Pte. FRESCO, D.			Pte. FIRKLE, SAM.
		Pte. CHASKELOW, MAX.	J	1491	Pte. FOGEL, I.			Pte. FIELD, JACK.
		Pte. CLEMENTS, MORRIS.	J	1801	Pte. FIFER, C.			Pte. FELDMAN, NATHAN.
		Pte. CHESTER, MORRIS.		201649	Pte. FULLER, R.			Pte. FINEMAN, N. E.
J	740	Pte. COHEN, DAVID.	J	386	Pte. FERNANDEZ, B.			Pte. FAUST, JOSEPH.
		Pte. CHASHKES, ELIC.		75807	Pte. FISHER, J.			Pte. FISHEL, HARRY.
J	277	Pte. DORFMAN, J.	J	416	Pte. FIELDMAN, S.	J	323	Pte. GORDON, A. I.
J	281	Pte. DANSKY, N.	J	433	Pte. FEDDY, S.	J	970	Pte. GOLD, S.
J	288	Pte. DANIEL, L.	J	472	Pte. FISHMAN, J.	J	1191	Pte. GOTZ, C.
J	1431	Pte. DAVIS, H.	J	515	Pte. FORD, L.	J	1267	Pte. GELPSMAN, J.
J	1618	Pte. DAVIS, H.	J	1600	Pte. FRAUM, J.	J	1422	Pte. GOULDBAUM, H.
J	896	Pte. DENNIS, M. J.	J	1622	Pte. FINKELSTEIN, I.	J	380	Pte. GOLDBERG, H.
J	1212	Pte. DANIEL, W.	J	547	Pte. FLASHER, M,	J	487	Pte. GOLDBERG, G.
J	687	Pte. DELMONTE, L.	J	712	Pte. FISHER, L.	J	1222	Pte. GOLDBERG, A.
		Pte. DEGWEDRON, A.	J	724	Pte. FINE, H.	J	1269	Pte. GOLDMAN, H.
J	902	Pte. DRUYAN, I.	J	62	A/Sgt. FREEMAN, H.	J	1420	Pte. GNESSON, M.
J	1288	Pte. DOBROZYSKI, I.	J	807	A/Sgt. FIRKSKER, A.	J	1462	Pte. GOLDBERG, S.
J	1293	Pte. DEITCH, S.	J	812	A/Cpl. FRIEDEL, L.	J	1697	Pte. GREENBAUM, J.
J	1211	Pte. DUDAKOFF, R.	J	849	A/Cpl. FLAXMAN, H.	J	124	L/Sgt. GOLDBERG, H.
J	1242	Sgt. DOE, S. W.		205314	A/Cpl. FREEMAN, S. M.	J	655	Pte. GLASIN, L.
J	24	A/Cpl. DEITZ, M.	J	694	Pte. FERRER, S.	J	391	Pte. GOOBLER, M.
J	718	L/Sgt. DAVIS, J.	J	406	Pte. FREEMAN, J.	J	118	L/Sgt. GREENBERG, S.
J	1159	Pte. DOBRIN, D.	J	1266	Pte. FREEMAN, N.*	J	313	Pte. GOODMAN, D.
J	650	Pte. DOSAVITCH, J.	J	1319	Pte. FRIEND, H.	J	365	Pte. GILLIES, I.
J	1123	Pte. DON, S.	J	967	Pte. FOX, R.	J	368	Pte. GLADSTONE, D.
J	1256	Pte. DREHER, I.	J	1298	Pte. FRANKLIN, L. D.	J	865	Pte. GLICK, J. I.
J	1754	DEITZ, M.*	J	1312	Pte. FIDLER, M.	J	1282	Pte. GREEN, A.
J	1586	Pte. DAVIS, L.	J	154	L/Sgt. FOX, L. H.	J	1658	Pte. GOLDBERG, S.
		Pte. DEANSFERTIG, C.	J	189	Pte FREEDMAN, S.	J	1703	Pte. GREENBERG, S.
J	36	A/Cpl. DAVIS, J.	J	392	Pte. FISHER,, B.	J	1713	Pte. GOLDMAN, I.
J	52	Pte. DAVARASHVILI, J. S.	J	409	Pte. FLACKS, I.	J	1723	Pte. GLUCKSTEIN, M.
J	236	Pte. DIESLER, H.	J	159	Sgt. FREEDMAN, C.	J	482	Pte. GILDE, G.
J	27	Pte. DICHTAIR, J.	J	290	Pte. FAITELBERG, R.	J	560	Pte. GARFINKLE, A.
J	55	Pte. DAPISEMODASHVILI, M.	J	725	Pte. FELDMAN, D.	J	1706	Pte. GOODMAN, D.
			J	1128	Pte. FREDZON, M.	J	9716	Pte. GOLDMAN, A.
J	1449	Pte. ELFMAN, M.	J	1246	Pte. FRANKLIN, S.	J	249	Pte. GOLDRICH, J.*
	202639	Pte. EDWARDS, D. J.	J	1284	Pte. FISHBERG, S.	J	963	Pte. GROUNDLER, M.
J	641	Pte. ELSBURY, H. I.	J	1415	Pte. FISHMAN, S.	J	659	Pte. GOLDMAN, I.
J	626	Pte. ECKMAN, J.	J	1580	Pte. FREED, J.	J	790	L/Cpl. GILLIS, L.
	883	A/C.Q.M.S. EDWARDS, C.	J	1590	Pte. FREINER, M.*	J	611	Pte. GILBERT, J.
	202402	Pte. EDWARDS, A. V.	Recruit		FELICIENT, H.	J	691	Pte. GRIZIBOWSKI, D.
Recruit		EPSTEIN, P.	J	1185	Pte. FRANKEL, I.	J	771	Pte. GOLDRICH, S.
J	45	Pte. EPREMASHVILI, J. L.	J	1205	Pte. FRANK, M.	J	780	Pte. GOLDBERG, S.
J	103	Pte. ERPERT, S.	J	1344	Pte. FISHER, S.	J	819	Pte. GOLDEN, C.
J	867	A/Cpl. ELLIS, A.	J	1568	Pte. FREEMAN, S.	J	846	Pte. GREENBERG, A.
J	107	L/Cpl. EDGAR, L.	J	121	A/Sgt. FINEMAN, M.	J	1019	Pte. GARDNER, M.
		Pte. EHRENGOTT, HARRY.	J	128	Pte. FRIEDMAN, H.	J	1335	Pte. GLASER, N.
J	289	Pte. ENTIN, ISRAEL.	J	874	A/Sgt. FILLINGHAM, J.	J	1474	Pte. GILDENHARSH, D.
		Pte. EPSTEIN, LIPMAN.	J	19	A/Cpl. FROUG, E.	J	901	Pte. GREYMAN, S.*
J	845	Pte. FINEMAN, S.	J	37	Pte. FREEDMAN, J.	J	931	Pte. GOLD, A.

"Judeans." N.C.O.'s AND MEN—Continued.

J 1086	Pte. GOLDMAN, M.		Pte. GOULD, HYMAN.	J 470	Pte. JOSEPH, C.
J 1257	Pte. GILLMAN, B.		Pte. GOLDSTEIN, ABE.	822	Pte. JACOBSON, A.
J 1277	Pte. GALINSKY, R.		Pte. GOLDSTEIN, ISAAC.	J 988	Pte. JANETSKY, S.
J 1286	Pte. GOLDMAN, M.		Pte. GREENBERG, ISAAC.	48831	Pte. JACOBS, J. D.
J 1334	Pte. GNESSON, B.		Pte. GILBERT, WOOLF.	777	Pte. JACOBS, F.
J 1563	Pte. GOODMAN, T.		Pte. GOLDING, HARRY.	700	Pte. JARASHEFSKY, J.
J 1693	Pte. GLASS, J.		Pte. GALINSKY, ISSY.	J 1332	Pte. JOSEPHS, A.
J 1714	Pte. GOLLOM, N.		Pte. GILBERT, SOLOMON.	962	Pte. JACOBS, A.
J 1839	Pte. GOLDSTEIN, M.		Pte. GOUCHER, SAMUEL.	J 1294	Pte. JACOBOWITZ, M.
47866	Pte. GLINTERNICK, S.	J 313	Pte. GOODMAN, DAVID.	201548	Pte. JOHN, H. O.
J 39	Pte. GERSON, B.	J 1703	Pte. GREENBERG, SAM.	524	Pte. JACKSON, B.
J 477	Pte. GREENBLATT, I.		Pte. GOLDUPPER, A.	J 781	Pte. JACOBS, P.
201525	Pte. GIMBERT, R. W.	J 1450	Pte. HYMAN, R.	461625	Pte. JACOBS, R. P.
201718	Pte. GAWTHROP, J.	J 1255	Pte. HARRIS, S.	J 697	Pte. JACOBS, L.
	Pte. GASAWSKY, I.	J 633	Pte. HYMAN, D.	205313	Pte. JONES, H. E.
J 125	Pte. GLUCK, D.*	J 564	A/Sgt. HYMAN, S.	267814	Pte. JONES, E.
J 348	Pte. GOLDSTEIN, B.	J 475	Pte. HARRIS, S.	J 100	A/Sgt. JABLONSKY, A.
J 951	Pte. GORDON, S.	J 977	Pte. HART, S.*	J 122	A/Sgt. JACOBSON, M.
J 1105	Pte. GELMOFSKY, R.	1280	Pte. HOCKRAD, A.		Pte. JACOBOVITCH, S.
J 1115	Pte. GARCOVITCH, S.	1477	Pte. HASFIELD, M.		Pte JUDELOVITCH, ISAAC.
J 1113	Pte. GUTMACHER, H.	513	Pte. HENKIN, G.	202655	(Trans.) Pte. JONES, G.
J 1138	Pte. GREEN, L.	673	Pte. HART, H. L.		Pte. JABLONSKY, MAX.
J 1186	Pte. GALINSKY, M.*	1633	Pte. HARRIS, N.		Pte. JENKINS, ADOLPH.
J 1203	Pte. GLOGOWSKI, S.	314	Pte. HAZEL, G.	J 371	Pte. KERSHENBLAT, S.
J 1487	Pte. GREENBERG, M.	500	Pte. HARING, M.	1424	Pte. KADISH, S.
J 1636	Pte. GRUMKIN, I.	J 1247	A/C.Q.M.S. HATTON, F. R.	1458	Pte. KERBOR, H.
	Pte. GOLD, A.			1558	Pte. KRASNANSKY, D.
	Pte. GUBBERMAN, I.	J 1700	Pte. HYAMS, S.	298	Pte. KAIRIS, A.
J 1116	Pte. GOLDSHAFT, J.	J 1762	Pte. HEPPNER, L.	1435	Pte. KOMINSKY, A.
J 1177	Pte. GANCHEROWSKI, N.	J 1493	Pte. HARRIS, V. L.	J 192	C.S.M. KARO, M.
J 1195	Pte. GLICKMAN, I.	1254	Pte. HARTZ, W.	201476	Pte. KENYON, M.
J 1234	Pte. GREENFIELD, W.	1076	Pte. HORNSTEIN, D.	924	Pte KAUFFMAN, M.
J 1251	Pte. GARLEK, D.	J 1067	Pte. HIRSHBEIN, H.	359	Pte. KRASNOFSKY, D.
J 1469	Pte. GREENSPAN, M.	204250	Pte. HAYDOCK, H.	481	Pte. KONTROVITZ, S.
	Pte. GLASSOW, S.	J 206	Pte. HORWITCH, C.	629	Pte. KOSKEY, J.
J 6427	Pte. GREENBAUM, P.*	J 1066	Pte. HERSHBERG, N.	1571	Pte. KUTCHINSKY, A.
J 29	Pte. GORODENTCHIK, Z.	1156	Pte. HERTZBERG, P.	628	Pte. KORPER, A.
J 81	Pte. GERGEL, I.	J 1149	Pte. HAILPERIN, A.	1532	Pte. KLIEMAN, H.
J 204	Pte. GOLDEN, M.	201823	Pte. HAWORTH, T.	1593	Pte. KALISH, B.
J 212	Pte. GOLD, M.	J 1594	Pte. HOFFMAN, S.	656	Pte. KURTZMAN, B.
J 226	Pte. GOLDBERG, E.	J 877	A/Sgt. HARRIS, E.	794	Pte. KOSOFSKY, H.
J 642	A/Sgt. GILBERT, M.	J 140	L/Sgt. HARRIS, J.	20	L/Sgt. KRETCHMER, S.
J 33	L/Sgt. GLASSMAN, C.	J 57	L/Cpl. HUTCHINSON, W.	643	L/Cpl. KROTTOSKY, M.
J 927	A/Cpl. GILLINSON, S.	J 15	L/Cpl. HANNAUX, H.	658	Pte. KERSH, W.
J 22	L/Cpl. GORNSTEIN, W.	J 157	A/Sgt. HARRIS, S.	802	Pte. KOENIGSBERG, A.
J 60	L/Cpl. GARFINKLE, J.		Pet. HERTZ, JULIUS.	836	Pte. KLEINBERG, A.
J 111	Pte. GELLER, A.		Pte. HERMAN, JACK.	930	Pte. KATZ, M.
	Pte. GINSBERG, HARRY.		Pte. HILLMAN, ISAAC.	1363	Pte. KIRSTEIN, J.
J 1234	Pte. GREENFIELD, W.	TR4/36304	Pte. HARRIS, SAMUEL.	1403	Pte. KRISTER, C.
	Pte. GRAZOFSKY, M.	380281	Pte. HARRIS, SAMUEL B.	1326	Pte. KAPELNICOFF, L.
	Pte. GRIFFITHS, DAVIS.	25	L/Sgt. ISRAEL, A.	1342	Pte. KOOR, H.
	Pte. GOODSTONE, H.	J 863	A/Cpl. ISAACS, L.	1353	Pte. KOOR, S.
	Pte. GINSBERG, ARCHIE.	117	Pte. ISENSTEIN, A.	1434	Pte. KRAKOWIAK, S.
	Pte. GROSSMITH, D.	J 1509	Pte. ISAACS, S.	123	Pte. KONETZKI, L.
	Pte. GOLDFORT, M.	J 1620	Pte. JACKSON, A	341	Pte. KUNES, B.
	Pte. GLENOVITCH, LAZ.	J 417	Pte. JACKSON, P.	612	Pte. KRIEDZER, S.
	Pte. GOLDBAND, SALMON.	J 466	Pte. JAFFE, A.	J 10	A/Sgt. KOFFMANN, L.

"Judeans." N.C.O.'s AND MEN—Continued.

J 49	A/Cpl. KOFFMAN, H.	
J 1147	Pte. KALINSKY, P.	
J 1182	Pte. KOPELMAN, S.	
J 1259	Pte. KURLANDER, H.	
J 1576	Pte. KAPUSHINSKY, I.	
J 1647	Pte. KELMAN, I.	
J 1189	Pte. KATZ, D.	
J 1257	Pte. KERSCHENBAUM, I.	
J 1613	Pte. KAUFFMAN, W.	
	Pte. KHESSIN, C.	
J 79	Pte. KAPLAN, L.	
J 217	Pte. KOENZATKY, M.	
J 104	L/Cpl. KIRSH, K. C.	
J 46	Pte. KRASNIANSKY, M.	
J 53	Pte. KRIVISHERFF, N.	
J 216	Pte. KLEINER, M.	
J 246	Pte. KISSMAN, I.	
	Pte. KRAPSCHINSKI, L.	
	Pte. KOSKY, CHARLES.	
	Pte. KRISCH, HENRY.	
	Pte. KOSKY, NATHAN.	
	Pte. KRETCHMAS, LEIB.	
	Pte. KLEINGLASS, J. A.	
	Pte. KABINSKI, AARON.	
	Pte. KOSNER, MORRIS.	
	Pte. KIRSCHENBAUM, H.	
	Pte. KROCHMALIEK, B.	
	Pte. KAUFMAN, SAMUEL.	
	Pte. KOBLINSKY, JACOB.	
	Pte. KIRSH, KAUFMAN.	
	Pte. KROSNISKY, R.	
J 325	Pte. LEWIS, E.	
J 356	Pte. LEWIS, H.	
J 1314	Pte. LANDAU, H.	
J 1399	Pte. LANDSMAN, H.	
J 1454	Pte. LEE, A.	
J 1645	Pte. LEVINE, J.	
J 282	Pte. LEIB, E.	
J 480	Pte. LEWIS, A.	
J 531	Pte. LATTER, A.	
J 826	Pte. LIPMAN, J. H.	
J 1207	Pte. LANDAU, M.	
J 1397	Pte. LITTMAN, M.	
J 1423	Pte. LEADERMAN, A.	
J 1644	Pte. LEFCOVITCH, P.	
J 1690	Pte. LEVY, J. L.	
J 638	A/Cpl. LEVY, S.	
J 959	A/Cpl. LEVY, L.	
J 364	Pte. LANDMAN, L.	
J 1809	Pte. LESSAR, S.	
202620	Pte. LETHBRIDGE, C. H.	
J 429	L/Cpl. LEVY, N.	
J 419	Pte. LEBUS, H.	
J 519	Pte. LEVENSON, S.	
J 566	Pte. LEVY, S.	
J 674	Pte. LAZARUS, R. D.	
J 501	Pte. LANDMAN, S.	
J 973	Pte. LABOFSKY, A.	
J 1570	Pte. LEVINE, L.	
J 795	A/Cpl. LEVY, D.	
J 699	Pte. LEE, I.	
J 719	Pte. LEVY, A. M.	
J 769	Pte. LEVI, T. H.	
49709	Pte. LUDZKER, B.	
J 184	Pte. LEVIN, L.	
570	Pte. LURIE, A.	
J 754	Pte. LYONS, N.	
J 961	Pte. LEVINE, D.	
1001	Pte. LEVENE, P.	
1023	Pte. LEVENTHAL, E.	
1048	Pte. LEVENE, L.	
1074	Pte. LITVINE, M.	
1414	Pte. LEMBERG, M.	
1498	Pte. LEVY, L.	
1056	Pte. LEVY, S.	
1072	Pte. LEWIS, J.	
1289	Pte. LEVY, I.	
1375	Pte. LEWIS, S.	
1396	Pte. LEVY, L.	
1412	Pte. LEVENE, I.	
1534	Pte. LUX, N.	
J 1664	Pte. LICHTENSTEIN, B.	
201823	Pte. LLOYD, A.	
J 13	Sgt. LEVY, B.	
J 884	L/Cpl. LAZARUS, M. D.	
74313	Pte. LEVY, C.	
J 352	Pte. LEE, H.	
J 622	Pte. LIEBERMAN, L.	
J 731	Pte. LEVINE, M.	
J 234	Pte. LEVINE, S.	
J 478	Pte. LEVINSKY, I.	
J 839	Pte. LANDSMAN, D.	
J 921	Pte. LEWIS, A.	
J 1130	Pte. LEFKAWITCH, J.	
J 1135	Pte. LEVENE, J.	
J 1170	Pte. LINDEN, S.	
S19775	Pte. LEVEY, C.	
	Pte. LOOCHIN, M.	
J 1113	Pte. LECKSTEIN, S.	
J 1132	Pte. LEWIS, S.	
J 1157	Pte. LEVIN, N. S.	
J 1164	Pte. LEVI, N.	
205198	A/Sgt. LEVINSON, B. H.	
J 144	Pte. LINSKILL, J.	
J 879	A/Sgt. LINFORD, J. C.	
	Pte. LEVI, MAURICE.	
	Pte. LIPSHITZ, A.	
J 973	Pte. LUBINSKY, ALEC.	
	Pte. LIPMAN, BARNETT.	
	Pte. LEVY, MORTIMER.	
	Pte. LEVY, JOSEPH.	
	Pte. LESSEL, MARKS.	
J 310	Pte. LEDERMAN, LOUIS.	
	Pte. LISOZORSKY, I.	
	Pte. LEEMAN, R.	
	Pte. LAZARUS, R.	
	Pte. LEVINE, AARON.	
J 1289	Pte. LEVY, JACK.*	
	Pte. LEVITT, JACK.	
	Pte. LEVISON, J.	
	Pte. LABUSCHINSKY, J.	
	Pte. LETMAN, WOOLFE.	
	Pte. LEHRMAN, NATHAN.	
J 273	Pte. MATTENBERG, N.	
J 1219	Pte. MILDERNER, S.	
J 1476	Pte. MARKS, H.	
J 1698	Pte. MARKS, J.	
J 350	Pte. MUSSMAN, S.	
J 621	Pte. MALNICK, M.	
J 559	Pte. MICHAELS, A.	
J 349	Pte. MARCHOFSKY, M.	
J 457	Pte. MESSENGER, L.	
J 895	A/Cpl. MYERS, B.	
J 358	Pte. MORRIS, G.	
J 395	Pte. MATZN, N.	
J 401	Pte. MALKIN, J.*	
J 506	Pte. MILLER, J.	
J 1536	Pte. MORRIS, C.	
J 703	Pte. MALINSKY, H.	
J 942	Pte. MILLER, M.	
J 1268	Pte. MANSELL, S.	
J 1537	Pte. MILLER, L.	
201517	Pte. MORGAN, D.	
J 414	Pte. MEIZENBERG, M.	
J 692	Pte. MILMAN, S.	
J 737	Pte. MICHAELS, J.	
J 620	Pte. MASSER, L.	
J 917	Pte. MICHAELS, H.	
J 947	Pte. MITTENBERG, W.	
J 1115	Pte. METCHICK, J.	
J 1535	Pte. MALMAN, B.	
J 1665	Pte. MOSES, A.	
J 47	Pte. MAKHNIOWKER, W.	
J 75	Pte. MULOVITCH, M.	
J 135	A/C.Q.M.S. MARKS, J.	
J 16	A/Cp. MORDECOVITCH, L.	
J 63	A/Cpl. MOSCOW, P.	
J 14	L/Cpl. MOCHOCHVILE, L. P.	
J 80	Pte. MOST, I.	
J 198	Pte. MILLER, M.	
J 205	Pte. MARDER, H.	
J 833	Pte. MARDER, B.	
J 907	Pte. MACROVITCH, N.	
J 1029	Pte. MENDOZA, J.	
J 1226	Pte. MARGOTT, B.	
	Pte. MINTZ, P.	
J 869	Sgt. MOORE, W. B.	
J 796	L/Cpl. MILLER, E.	
J 227	L/Cpl. MORRIS, C.	
J 1089	Pte. MAERTHALL, P. R.	

"Judeans."

N.C.O.'s AND MEN—Continued.

J	1272	Pte. MATTERMAN, P.	J	1661	Pte. PERLSTONE, S.	J	1560	Pte. REUBEN, I.
J	1540	Pte. MALCUS, B.	J	1728	Pte. POPLOVITCH, A.	J	859	Pte. ROWMAN, P.
J	1270	Pte. MILLER, A.	J	535	L/Cpl. PHILLIPS, J.	J	1002	Pte. ROSE, A.
J	1356	Pte. MYERS, B.	J	952	Pte. PELTZ, M.	J	1473	Pte. ROMANER, N.
J	1628	Pte. MENDLOVITCH, M.	J	1080	Pte. POBEREFSKY, B.	205191	A/Cpl. ROGOFF, A.
J	1659	Pte. MISEL, I.	J	1153	Pte. POLSKY, W.	J	1078	Pte. RITTENBAUM, F.*
		Pte. MOSS, A.			Pte. PENN, J.	J	1048	Pte. REUBEN, M.
J	50	Pte. MATFOIOFF, A.	J	1171	Pte. POMERANTZ, S.	J	1440	Pte. RUDETSKY, A.
		Pte. MARSHALL, S.	J	1187	Pte. POSNER, H.	J	1519	Pte. ROGANSKY, L.
		Pte. MAGALOFSKY, I.	J	1283	Pte. PERKOFF, W.			Pte. RABBINOVITZ, H.
		Pte. MEERKIN, MAX.			Pte. PLOTKIN, A. B.			Pte. ROSENBERG, M.
		Pte. MACHINSKY, M.			Pte. PRESS, RUEBEN.			Pte. RUBINOVITCH, P.
	11083	Pte. MARKOVITCH, D.			Pte. PEREL, J.			Pte. RUBENSTEIN, R.
		Pte. MILLMAN, ELLIS.			Pte. PLATT, Ch. D.			Pte. ROSENBLOOM, N.
		Pte. MOCHUMOVITZ, N.			Pte. PORTNER, JOE M.			Pte. ROGERNISKY, M.
		Pte. MUSWENSKI, M.			Pte. PALTNOI, SOLOMON.			Pte. ROMAIN, LEWIS.
		Pte. MILLER, A. SAM.			Pte. PHILLIPS, A.			Pte. ROSENFELDT, V.
		Pte. MARBLACKNICK, A.			Pte. PAPISIMEDIAS, I. M.			Pte. RABINOVITCH, M.
		Pte. MAEROVITCH, N.			Pte. PIEMASH, H.			Pte. RUBENSTEIN, H.
	293	Pte. NEWMAN, M.			Pte. QUINT, LAZARUS.			Pte. ROSENBERG, LOUIS.
	402	Pte. NOCHUMORVITZ, N.	J	12	L/Sgt. RICH, W.			Pte. ROSEN, M.
	413	Pte. NATHAN, B.	J	17	A/Cpl. RABON, V. G.			Pte. RABIN, BAMKLI, G.
J	532	A/Sgt. NEDVITCH, S.	J	230	Pte. REODNER, G. L.	J	191	A/Sgt. SHANOCK, L.
J	529	Pte. NOCKAMOVITCH, M.	J	11	A/R.Q.M.S. ROUSSIN, I.	J	7	A/Cpl. STOUKALIN, D.
J	747	A/Cpl. NORMAN, A.	J	387	L/Sg. ROSENBLATT, A. D.	J	88	A/Cpl. SEGAL, A.
J	666	Pte. NADELL, H.	J	138	A/Cpl. ROTH, D.	J	5	L/Cpl. SCHIFF S.
J	709	Pte. NISHMAN, I.	J	496	Pte. REDLIKH, G.*	205196	L/Cpl. SOLOMONS, O.
J	749	L/Cpl. NOVOSELSKY, M.	J	324	Pte. ROSE, L.	J	347	L/Cpl. SOLOMON, N.
J	723	Pte. NELSON, B.	J	1224	Pte. RABBINOVITCH, S.	J	54	Pte. SEPIACHVILE, R.
J	430	Pte. NISKY, G.	J	1310	Pte. REDHOUSE, B.			(M.M.)
J	1384	Pte. NYGAE, B.	H	1765	Pte. ROSE, M.	J	68	Pte. SHIOVITZ, P.
		Pte. NEDVITCH, DAVID.	J	162	L/Cpl. ROBINSON, A. J.	J	242	Pte. SIDLIN, A.
		Pte. NEEDLEMAN, M.			(M.M.)	J	263	Pte. SHAPIRO, S.
		Pte. NATHAN, ALICK.	J	487	L/Cpl. RUBENS, H.	J	9	Pte. SHOKHET, B.
J	1190	Pte. OSOVITCH, N.	J	21	L/Cpl. RIBKISS, S.	J	145	Pte. SAMUELS, W.
J	1341	Pte. ORLOFF, H.	J	974	L/Cpl. ROSENBERG, A. J.	J	235	Pte. STOLBERG, G.
J	1573	Pte. OXENHORNE, N.	J	87	Pte. RITCHIE, H. Z.	J	240	Pte. SMITH, J.
J	890	Pte. OLINSKI, J.	J	303	Pte. ROSENBERG, S.*	J	297	Pte. SELIG, D.
J	1531	Pte. OKMAN, M.	J	370	Pte. ROSENZWEEG, D.	J	946	Pte. STORCH, S. L.
J	118	A/Sgt. PHILLIPS, S.	J	220	A/Sgt. RASKY, D.		1124	Pte. SCHNEIDERSON, J.
J	264	Pte. PLATT, S.	J	886	A/Sgt. RICE, A.		1208	Pte. SOLOMONS, I.
J	928	Pte. PASS, H.	J	126	A/Cpl. ROSENBERG, J.		1237	Pte. STROPOTOFF, A.
J	1354	Pte. PEARLOFF, J.	J	213	Pte. RUDZMASKAS, J.		1488	Pte. SHINE, W.
J	1480	Pte. PELENOFSKY, J.	J	464	Pte. ROSENBERG, N.		1561	Pte. SCHULTZ, S.
J	1800	Pte. PODOLSKY, S.	J	485	Pte. ROSENBAUM, J.		296	Pte. SELIG, J.
J	880	A/Sgt. PORTER, E. A.	J	627	Pte. RAYMOND, J.		331	Pte. STRATTON, J.
	203169	Pte. PRITCHARD, W.	J	1494	Pte. RUBNER, M.		975	Pte. SWERNER, H.
J	469	Pte. PECHANSKY, L.	J	476	Pte. RUME, H.		1014	Pte. SHOWMAN, M.
J	503	Pte. POSVETNANSKY, L. F.	J	530	Pte. ROSENBAUM, S.		1210	Pte. SUDIC, M.
J	971	Pte. PRAGUE, I.	J	590	Pte. RAPHAEL, S.		1292	Pte. SUSSMAN, J.
J	1217	Pte. PELHAM, M.	J	1445	Pte. RACHLIS, G.	J	1451	Pte. SOLOWITZ, B.
J	1709	Pte. PAWLAHEZ, J.		202769	Pte. ROBERTS, F. G.		267671	Pte. SHUTT, J.
J	1472	Pte. PHILLIPS, H.	J	821	A/Cpl. ROSENBERG, J.	J	153	A/St. SCHLAFFERMAN, A.
J	1241	A/C.S.M. PLANT, G.	J	793	L/Cpl. ROBINSON, J.	J	922	A/Sgt. SCHIFREEN, R.
J	814	L/Cpl. PRINCE, W.		200279	Pte. ROBERTS, D. T.	J	196	Pte. SMITITSKY, R.
J	905	Pte. PERES, J.	J	1218	Pte. REUBIN, J.	J	866	A/C.Q.M.S. SIMONS, N.
J	1031	Pte. PHILLIPS, J.	J	1296	Pte. RUBIN, L.	J	631	L/Cpl. SAMSON, P.

"Judeans." N.C.O.'s AND MEN—Continued.

J 166 Pte. Solomons, J.	J 858 Pte. Smith, F.	J 870 C.S.M. Turner, C. R.
J 193 Pte. Schwartz, B.	J 915 Pte. Strong, H.*	J 372 Pte. Taylor, H.
J 461 Pte. Segal, M.	J 1053 Pte. Shnyder, J.	J 615 Pte. Taylor, D.
J 509 Pte. Sherman, S.	J 1065 Pte. Steiner, S.	202824 Pte. Thomas, A.
J 538 Pte. Simons, S.	203883 Pte. Sawyer, A.	J 1088 Pte. Trashansky, G.
J 654 Pte. Siger, M.	J 26 L/Cpl. Silberstein, P.	J 1152 Pte. Toffel, I.
J 716 Pte. Stark, M.	J 748 L/Cpl. Solomons, L.	66590 Pte. Thornber, J. B.
J 744 Pte. Saltman, M.	J 1184 L/Cpl. Schloss, N.	Pte. Trashensky, S.
J 759 Pte. Schneider, B.	J 187 Pte. Schneider, S.	Pte. Tolchinsky, S.
J 1062 Pte. Spiezyk, J.	J 525 Pte. Soble, W.	Pte. Teitelbaum, Isaac.
J 1036 Pte. Stanuilis, J.	J 782 Pte. Similovitch, H.	Pte. Tomkins, Jacob.
J 1315 Pte. Sabel S.	J 1003 Pte. Sherman, M.	Pte. Taylor, Barnet.
J 1370 Pte. Spielman, P.	J 1058 Pte. Sporn, I.	37996 Sgt. (O.R.S.) Viveash, L. H.
J 1452 Pte. Schnack, M.	J 1077 Pte. Schaffer, L.	
J 1560 Pte. Schultz, D.	J 1087 Pte. Shyowitz, J.	J 147 A/Cpl. Vallance, L.
J 1574 Pte. Schkrob, H.	J 1118 Pte. Shuter, S.	J 51 Pte. Velder, S.
J 505 Pte. Shawn, W.	J 1151 Pte. Shuter, M.	J 1799 Pte. Valinsky, L.
J 518 Pte. Stillman, T.	J 1188 Pte. Schneiderman, M.	J 432 Pte. Vigdor, B.
J 616 Pte. Shufleder, B.	J 1192 Pte. Sanderwitch, M.	J 447 Pte. Veltman, M.
J 743 Pte. Silverstein, H.	J 1320 Pte. Stern, M.	J 637 Pte. Vedenbohm, S.
J 746 Pte. Steinberg, H. S.	J 1095 Pte. Soborinsky, P.*	J 499 A/Cpl. Vilgerslosky, J. D.
J 798 Pte. Starolitis, A.	J 1137 Pte. Stalovilsky, I.	
J 1035 Pte. Seligman, C.	J 1145 Pte. Smoliransky, J.	J 406 Pte. Valensky, A.
J 1068 Pte. Segal, J.	J 1154 Pte. Sanderwick, I.	Pte. Vimbour, Hyman.
J 1214 Pte. Spindler, L.	J 1173 Pte. Swenetsky, S.	Pte. Vichnick, Joseph.
J 1281 Pte. Sherman, D.	Pte. Shulman, Hyman.	Pte. Varsofehick, J.
J 1358 Pte. Sugarman, E.	Pte. Steen, Julius.	J 317 A/Sgt. Wolfson, S. W.
J 1387 Pte. Spiegelman, I.	Pte. Simon, Joseph.	200589 Sgt. Williams, J. W.
J 59 A/Sgt. Steinberg, M.	Pte. Shamfram, Ab.	J 69 Pte. Wilfin, J.
J 567 A/Cpl. Shanker, S.	Pte. Sharpstone, H.	J 1215 Pte. Weiner, S.
J 817 L/Cpl. Shodoski, P.	Pte. Stein, Barnett.	J 1411 Pte. Wittle, S.
J 1027 L/Cpl. Sherman, J.	Pte. Saporynitk, Isaac.	J 1642 Pte. Wiseman, L.
J 203 Pte. Schervinsky, A.	Pte. Stein, Abram.	75801 Pte. Wilkins, H. J.
J 571 Pte. Saroginsky, R.	Pte. Sevelovitch, P.	J 437 Pte. Wineberg, H.
J 614 Pte. Selminsky, M.	Pte. Seager, William.	J 463 Pte. Winer, J.
J 701 Pte. Straskin, I.	Pte. Sevelovitch, P.	J 985 Pte. Wise, M.
J 646 A/Sgt. Spero, M.	Pte. Shutt, Israel.	J 374 Pte. Waterman, N.
J 322 Pte. Seramber, C.*	Pte. Sumner, Myer.	J 376 Pte. Winer, M.
J 522 Pte. Shapiro, M.	Pte. Symonds, Abram.	J 527 Pte. Weiner, N.
J 574 Pte. Silverman, S.	Pte. Spilman, Pincus.	J 556 Pte. Walters, B.
J 582 Pte. Symonds, K.	J 827 A/Sgt. Tschaikov, A.	J 1466 Pte. Weiner, S.
J 680 Pte. Stone, J.	J 95 L/Cpl. Tistchenko, W.	J 1660 Pte. Walport, N.
J 728 Pte. Sherman, A.	J 23 Pte. Tzvernnashvile, J.	J 1455 Pte. Ward, A. D.
J 739 Pte. Sacrovitch, A.	J 188 Pte. Tregunsky, L.	J 789 Pte. Wineberg, J.
J 891 Pte. Saperia, H.	J 77 Pte. Taretzky, S.	203180 Pte. Williams, J. O.
J 966 Pte. Shaft, J.*	J 260 Pte. Teeman, I.	J 727 Pte. Winestein, D.
J 1309 Pte. Silverstein, H.	J 383 Pte. Trager, C.	J 785 Pte. Weltman, W.
J 1348 Pte. Scher, J.	J 1216 Pte. Tinn, I.	J 1209 Pte. Weisblatt, J.
J 1437 Pte. Solomons, J.	J 148 A/Sgt. Tennens, P.*	J 1238 Pte. Weiner, S.
J 1467 Pte. Schneider, J.	J 389 Pte. Turek, A.	J 1538 Pte. Wolcovitch, S.
J 805 Pte. Shuster, M.	J 412 Pte. Tray, C.	J 1042 Pte. Weinberg, W.*
J 843 Pte. Sandler, I.	J 455 Pte. Thickmatch, H.	J 1546 Pte. Wicherofsky, R.
J 851 Pte. Speyer, J.	J 1307 Pte. Turnofsky, M.	J 1649 Pte. Woolf, M. ?
J 894 Pte. Share, R.	J 1046 Pte. Taylor, J.	Pte. Weitzman, H.
J 911 Pte. Sapirstein, N.	202663 Pte. Thompson, J. G.	J 133 Pte. White, S.
J 919 Pte. Solomons, S.	J 1059 Pte. Tynas, I.	J 354 Pte. Weinstein, A.
J 1653 Pte. Shantell, L.	J 810 Pte. Teofil, R.	J 1146 Pte. Wasserman, A. K.

"Judeans."

N.C.O.'s AND MEN—Continued.

J 1361	Pte. WARENBERG, A.	J 1416	Pte. YAFFA, M.	J 580	Pte. ZIFF, S.		
201783	Pte. WHITNEY, C.	J 158	L/Cpl. YAFFIE, S.	J 1279	Pte. ZUMANOVITZ, I.		
Recruit.	WILLINSKY, J.	J 1520	Pte. YASNICK, S.	J 1492	Pte. ZIMMERMAN, E.		
J 1134	Pte. WEINBERG, M.	J 1329	Pte. YARBLACKNICK, H.	J 1024	Pte. ZEMMELL, H.		
J 1148	Pte. WELTMAN, B.	J 670	L/Cpl. YOUNGMAN, P.	J 1073	Pte. ZWRE, M.		
J 1181	Pte. WELLER, H.		Pte. YUDCOVSKY, M.	J 1172	Pte. ZIMMERMAN, A.		
J 1300	Pte. WALKIN, L.	J 97	Pte. YAVOULOUNSVITCH, A.	J 1626	Pte. ZEFF.		
	Pte. WALCOTT, C.				Pte. ZILBERSTEIN, P.		
	Pte. WEISS, M.	J 730	Pte. ZEIGMAN, H.		Pte. ZERMAN, J.		
	Pte. WINCESTEIN, .	J 1223	Pte. ZEIDERMAN, H.		Pte. ZARILSKI, M.		
	Pte. WINCESTEIN, L.	J 1459	Pte. ZAIDNER, M.		Pte. ZUPRANSKY, H.		
	Pte. WEINER, JOE.	J 507	Pte. ZEIDMAN, J.		Pte. ZIOLNICK, JOSEPH.		
	Pte. WALCOVITCH, D.	J 1482	Pte. ZALKIN, I.		Pte. ZIEDMAN, H.		
	Pte. WASSERMAN, SAM.	J 659	Pte. ZEMMILL, L.				

39th BATTALION ROYAL FUSILIERS ("JUDEANS")

Officers.

Lt.-Col. MARGOLIN, E. L. (D.S.O.)
Major ROTHSCHILD, J. A. E. DE (D.C.M.), (Capt. R. Canadian Dragoons).
Capt. & Adjt. RACIONZER, J. L.
Capt. SAMUELSON, B. G.
Capt. REED, A. W. J.
Capt. BARNETT, A. E.

Lieut. SOMAN, H. D.
Lieut. RUBIN, H. DE V.
Lieut. LEVY, M.
Lieut. HARRIS, B. B.
2nd Lieut. GREEN, H.
2nd Lieut. FRANKS, A.
2nd Lieut. SAMUEL, E. H.
2nd Lieut. BROWN, H.

2nd Lieut. STONE, L.
2nd Lieut. ARNOLD, M. P.
2nd Lieut. PHILLIPS, H.
2nd Lieut. SALMON, H. W.
2nd Lieut. SPURLING, S. S.
2nd Lieut. COWEN, A.
2nd Lieut. HAGUE, H.
2nd Lieut. JACOBS, J.

N.C.O.'s and Men.

J 1550	Pte. AGRAS, J.	J 2882	Pte. ABRAHAM, L. P.	J 2187	Pte. BRENNER, V.
J 1419	Pte. ABRAHAMS, L.	J 483	Pte. AARONVITCH, J.	J 2208	Pte. BARNOVITCH, H.
J 1806	Pte. ASSINOFSKY, M.	J 1276	Pte. ALSCHWANG, L.	J 2210	Pte. BESS, S.
J 2075	Pte. AZERMAN, E. M.	J 1788	Pte. ANSHELVITZ, S.	J 2218	Pte. BRASLAVSKY, H.
J 2149	Pte. ADOLPH, L.	J 2149	Pte. ADOLPH, L.	J 2277	Pte. BOXER, M.
J 2712	Pte. ASHER, T.	J 71	Pte. ADELMAN, B.	J 2336	Pte. BLOOMBERG, M.
J 2199	Pte. ABRAHAMS, M.	J 1167	Pte. ABRAHAMS, H.	J 2399	Pte. BRILL, W.
J 2206	Pte. AGIN, J.	J 1262	Pte. ALEMBRICK, M.	J 2413	A/Sgt. BLOOMBAUM, M.
J 2254	Pte. ABRAHAMSON, S.	J 2011	Pte. APPLEBAUM, H.	J 2416	Pte. BIERMAN, A.
J 2262	Pte. ABRAHAMS, I.	J 1976	Pte. APPLESON, A.	J 2417	Pte. BERNSTEIN, L. E.
J 2276	Pte. ANDERSON, B.	J 2	A/Sgt. BLITSTEIN, F.	J 2442	Pte. BORITZKY, L.
J 2325	Pte. ABRAHAMS, D.	J 8	Cpl. BAK, S.	J 2470	Pte. BRADFIELD, R.
J 2341	L/Cpl. ANCILL, R.	J 91	Cpl. BRAND, S.	J 2724	L/Cpl. BERNSTEIN, A.
J 2356	Pte. ALBERT, M.	J 422	L/Cpl. BERNSTEIN, S.	J 292	Pte. BOEDLSKI, H.
J 2376	Pte. ARCHAVSKY, I.	J 6983	Pte. BERNSTEIN, S.*	J 1815	Pte. BERSON, J.
J 1523	Pte. APPLEMAN, L.	J 1111	Pte. BESAK, L.	J 1826	Pte. BENDER, D.
J 2490	Pte. APPLEBOOM, C.	J 1285	Pte. BERMAN, N.	J 1896	Pte. BERGER, H.
J 2742	A/L/Cpl. APPLEBAUM, J.	J 1587	Pte. BLOOM, J.	J 2275	Pte. BLOOMBERG, S.
J 1734	Pte. ASSINOFSKY, H.	J 1873	Pte. BEER, M.	J 2304	Pte. BAILIN, M.
J 1831	Pte. ABRAMS, S.	J 2022	Pte. BLACK, H.	J 2313	Sgt. BROWN, J.
J 1940	Pte. ADLER, L.	J 2062	Pte. BARNETT, D.*	J 872	Pte. BOTTING, H. T.
J 1830	Pte. ARON, B.	J 2148	Pte. BAUM, I.	J 1308	Pte. BARTENBLAT, R.
205307	L/Sgt. APPLETON, W.	J 2155	Pte. BARABAS, M.	J 1840	Pte. BERSON, B.

"Judeans." N.C.O.'s AND MEN—Continued.

J 1897 Pte. BERNHARDT, H.	J 2350 Pte. COHEN, W.	205862 A/L/Cpl. DAVIS, B.
205190 Pte. BOORER, J. T.	J 2378 Pte. COHEN, H.	J 1163 Pte. DELOW, L.
J 1327 Pte. BIDDOCK, M.	J 2396 A/Cpl. COLLINS, L. C.	J 2843 Pte. DAVIES, D.
J 2793 Pte. BLACK, M.	J 2357 Pte. COHEN, M.	J 1810 Pte. DAVYATSKI, S.
J 441 Pte. BERNSTEIN, J.	J 2439 Pte. COTLER, J.	J 1359 L/Cpl. DEITCHMAN, J.
J 458 Pte. BARON, N.	J 2459 L/Sgt. CHARNEY, B.	J 1807 Pte. DANIELS, H.
J 1112 Pte. BAROFSKY, W.	J 2489 A/Cpl. COHEN, S.	J 1407 Pte. DOPOLSKY, I.
J 1438 Pte. BRACKMAN, P.	J 2735 Pte. CHIMANOVITCH, L.	J 934 L/Cpl. EPSTEIN, L.
J 1460 Pte. BACKER, H. L.	J 2749 Pte. COOKLIN, S.	J 1331 Pte. EREICH, D.
J 2059 Pte. BERKAN, M.	733 Pte. CRYSTAL, A. D.	1648 A/C.S.M. EAGLE, N.*
J 2300 Pte. BENKOFSKI, M.	875 A/Sgt. CARTER, J.	J 2224 Pte. ERLICHMAN, M.
J 2353 Pte. BLOCK, A.	1866 Pte. CUCKILL, H.	J 2243 Pte. EILGOT, R.
610 Pte. BERCOVITCH, M.	J 2273 Pte. COHEN, A.	J 2736 Pte. ELGASHAVITCH, L.
644 Pte. BALOFSKY, B.	1865 Pte. COHEN, B.	J 103 Pte. ERPERT, S.
778 Cpl. BERNSTEIN, S.	J 1811 Pte. COHEN, C.	619 A/Cpl. ERNSTEIN, A.
1461 Pte. BORADOCK, I.	205199 A/Sgt. COHEN, M.	1792 Pte. ESTRIN, M.
1484 Pte. BERNSTEIN, B.	205655 Pte. CRUGMAN, S.	1852 Pte. EPSTEIN, L.
1527 Pte. BASS, N.	205827 L/Sgt. COLLINS, M.	2203 Pte. ENGLISHMAN, H.
1857 Pte. BERMAN, P.	J 741 Pte. COHEN, L.	J 38 Pte. EPSTEIN, J.
1987 Pte. BENKOVITCH, W. L.	1745 Pte. COHEN, W.	2185 Pte. ESNER, I.
2267 Pte. BROWN, I.	2819 Sgt. CLEMPERT, J.	708 Pte. FARBEY, N.
2268 Pte. BYDER, N.	2826 Pte. COHEN, H.	756 A/L/Cpl. FELDMAN, I.
70 Pte. BERLINER, A.	2844 Pte. GROSSMAN, A.	889 Sgt. FOX, J.
1783 Pte. BYER, A.	914 Pte. COHEN, M.	893 Pte. FOX, J.
1864 Pte. BECHMAN, W.	1303 Pte. CALIPH, M.	1085 Pte. FRAZENSKY, H.
2274 Pte. BLATT, J.	1405 Pte. COHEN, L.	2023 Pte. FREEDMAN, E.
1836 Pte. BENNETT, I.	1464 Pte. CUPPITMAN, I.	2058 Pte. FLETCHER, I. J.
2842 Pte. BLOOM, E.	2424 Pte. COHEN, L.	2104 Pte. FLORENCE, I.
2247 Pte. BROWN, A.	1782 Pte. CLOUD, M.	2140 Pte. FINEGOLD, S.
495 A/L/Cpl. CASSOFSKY, L.	93 Pte. COPPEL, M.	2194 Pte. FINEBERG, I.
521 A/L/Cpl. CAPLAN, P.	1583 Pte. CABAZALVITCH, S.	2198 Pte. FLITMAN, S.
580 Pte. COHEN, J.	1119 Pte. CANTER, J.	2222 Pte. FYNE, M.
736 Pte. CONNICK, D.	1845 Pte. COHEN, M.	2311 Pte. FIFER, E.
837 Pte. COWAN, A.	2077 Pte. CAPLAN, M.	2348 Pte. FREEDMAN, I.
1051 Pte. COHEN, J.	1861 Pte. CLYNE, J.	2428 Pte. FRIEDLANDER, I.
1143 Pte. COHEN, I.	181 Pte. COOPER, B.	2432 Pte. FAGNE, H.
1612 Pte. CHESNICK, M.	339 Pte. CORRICK, L.	2469 Pte. FREEDMAN, S.
1740 Pte. COHEN, I.	1408 Pte. COOK, M.	2474 A/Sgt. FREEDMAN, B.
1755 A/L/Cpl. COHEN, S.	2143 Pte. COHEN, S.	2744 Pte. FILBURY, M.
1984 Pte. CROMWELL, M.	2166 Pte. CAZIN, M.	453 Pte. FINE, M.
2016 Pte. COHEN, S.	2285 Pte. CHINSKY, N.	1568 Pte. FREEMAN, S.
2043 Pte. COWAN, M. J.	275 Pte. CARUSO, R.	1666 Pte. FINKLESTEIN, J.
2044 L/Cpl. CORB, I.	1122 Pte. COHEN, H.	1817 Pte. FRANKS, A.
2052 A/Cpl. COWEN, E.	2176 Pte. COHEN, J.	1981 Pte. FRANK, CHARLES.
2152 Pte. COHEN, S.	1417 Pte. CHAYTON, I.	1991 Pte. FIRST, S. Y.
2161 Pte. CASSOFSKI, S.	671 Pte. DAVIS, A.	1344 Pte. FISHER, L.
2177 A/L/Sgt. COHEN, J.	1316 Pte. DANIELS, J.	1250 Pte. FELDMAN, H.
2193 Pte. CAPLAN, A.	1989 Pte. DINKIN, R.	2823 Cpl. FOX, J.
2213 Pte. COHEN, J.	2189 Pte. DUBIN, I.	625 Pte. FIELD, J.
2220 Pte. COHEN, I.	2327 Pte. DRAYER, J.	1106 Pte. FORMAN, H.
2221 Pte. COHEN, S.	2397 Sgt. DICK, R.	1278 Pte. FRUM, H.
2269 Pte. CANTER, S.	2144 Pte. DEGRASSE, H.	1591 Pte. FERRER, D.
2289 Pte. COHEN, H.	2440 Pte. DUZELMAN, C.	1580 Pte. FREED, J.
2291 Pte. COHEN, M.	2457 Sgt. DENNETT, A.	2060 Pte. FREEDMAN, H.
2292 Pte. COHEN, J.	2747 Pte. DAVIS, M.	2266 Pte. FINEBERG, H.
2322 Pte. COHEN, H.	676 A/Sgt. DEUTCH, B.	J 1243 A/Sgt. FRIES, F.
J 2335 A/Cpl. CONDOR, H.	J 1860 Pte. DAVIES, M.	37829 Pte. FOX, H.

"Judeans." N.C.O.'s AND MEN—Continued.

J 35 Sgt. GREENBERG, M.	J 1611 Pte. GLUCKSTEIN, H.	J 1311 Pte. JACKNOVITCH, I.
319 A/L/Sgt. GREENBAUM, E.	J 1627 Pte. GROSSMOUNT, I.	J 1624 Pte. JACOBCHICK, W.
393 Pte. GOLDMAN, I.	J 1979 Pte. GREENSTEIN, A.	J 2358 Pte. JACOBS, H.
669 A/Cpl. GOLDMAN, H. L.	J 2061 Pte. GONCHER, S.	J 2379 Pte. JACOBI, H.
916 A/L/Sgt. GOLDBERG, H.	J 2223 Pte. GOODMAN, S.	J 2475 Cpl. JACOBS, L. L.
986 Pte. GOLDSTEIN, R.	J 1970 Pte. GLOBUSS, S.	J 2718 Pte. JULIAS, R.
1325 A/L/Sgt. GRALNICK, S.	202799 Pte. GLASS, A.	J 1013 L/Cpl. JACOBS, A.
1726 A/N.Q.M.S. GROSE, A.	J 1442 Pte. GREENBRG, L.	J 1844 Pte. JACOBOVITCH, H.
1349 Pte. GOLD, M.	J 2241 Pte. GOSCOVITCH, B.	J 1849 Pte. JOSEPH, J.
2018 Pte. GOODMAN, A.	J 2719 Pte. GREEN, M.	J 2821 Pte. JACKSON, B.
2026 Pte. GARSTEN, L.	J 1990 Pte. GRUNDLAND, S. J.	205860 Pte. JACKSON, I. L.
2038 Pte. GOLDSTEIN, J.	J 2056 Pte. GOODMAN, M.	J 112 Pte. JOSEFOVITCH, A.
2066 Pte. GOLDWATER, I.	J 2057 Pte. GILBERT, L.	J 1044 Pte. JACOBINSKY, P.
2089 Pte. GINSBERG, L.	J 2083 Pte. GOTHALPH, J.	J 2098 Pte. JACOBS, L.
2105 Pte. GRANT, K.	J 1794 Pte. GASTWICH, D.	J 2153 Pte. JACOBIN, S.
2229 Pte. GOTTLIEB, N.	J 1797 Pte. GASTWICH, B.	J 2107 Pte. JOHNSON, J.
2230 Pte. GOODMAN, P.	J 1346 Pte. GOLD, S.	J 90 Cpl. KAPLAN, S.
2246 Pte. GOLDING, H.	J 1581 Pte. GOLD, L.	J 689 Pte. KRAVITZ, A.
2255 Pte. GREENBLATT, B.	J 2844 Pte. GROSSMAN, A.	J 1084 Pte. KARENBERG, M.
2302 Pte. GOODHEART, B.	J 151 A/Sgt. HARRIS, S.	J 1273 Pte. KATANKA, H.
2365 Pte. GORDON, H.	J 575 Pte. HYRAT, I.	J 1287 A/Cpl. KIZER, H. W.
2409 L/Cpl. GOLDSTEIN, L.	J 828 L/Cpl. HARRISON, J. V.	J 1330 Pte. KATZ, H.
2427 Pte. GOLDING, M.	J 1398 Pte. HOFMAN, B.	J 1524 Pte. KADZ, A.
2448 Pte. GOLDMAN, A.	J 1982 Pte. HEMMERFIELD, B.	J 1553 Pte. KULMAN, I.
2493 Pte. GERSHON, I.	J 2027 Pte. HOPPEN, L.*	J 1610 Pte. KAPOTA, H.
34 A/Sgt. GERSBERG, A.	J 2253 Pte. HYMAN, B.	J 1699 Pte. KARCHINSKIE, J.
291 Pte. GLICK, R.	J 2464 Pte. HARRINGHAM, D.	J 1708 Pte. KOBELSKY, M.
467 Pte. GREENBERG, M.	J 2496 Pte. HANNICK, M.	J 1816 Pte. KNOBEL, H.
779 Pte. GLENOVITCH, L.	J 2750 A/Sgt. HARRIS, H.	J 2032 Pte. KAUFMAN, D.
1777 Pte. GREENBERG, G.	J 1743 Pte. HARTZBERG, L.	J 2037 Pte. KATZ, H.
1783 Pte. GROSS, M.	J 1785 Pte. HARRIS, S.	J 2180 Pte. KATZ, H.
1813 Pte. GETZ, S.	J 1786 A/L/Cp. HAMBORGER, H.	J 2200 Pte. KOPKIN, J.
1833 A/L/Cpl. GINSBERG, H.	J 1809 A/L/Cpl. HART, S.	J 2231 Pte. KRAWITZ, A.
1841 A/L/Cpl. GARBER, H.	J 639 Pte. HARRIS, S.	J 2257 Pte. KROMINSKY, A.
1847 Pte. GEDALOVITCH, B.	J 1843 Pte. HEPSTEIN, I.	J 2280 Pte. KAIZER, L. M.
1935 Pte. GELLMAN, I.	J 2272 Pte. HAROVITCH, M.	J 2393 Pte. KOFFMAN, L.
1971 Pte. GREENSPAN, L.	205267 A/Sgt. HARRIS, A. H.	J 225 Pte. KRETCHMER, L.
1426 Pte. GOLDSTEIN, S.	J 2814 Pte. HARRIS, W.	J 262 Pte. KOTLER, A.
1469 Pte. GREENSPAN, H.	953 Pte. HYMAN, D.	J 1823 Pte. KOSKY, C.
1855 Pte. GORDON, R.	J 1390 Pte. HAMBURGER, J.	J 1825 Pte. KRAMEN, H.
1306 Pte. GRODZINSKY, J.	J 2072 Pte. HYMANSON, H.	J 1915 Pte. KRIGER, M.
2820 Pte. GOLDSTEIN, M.	J 2337 L/Cpl. HARRIS, J.	J 1932 Pte. KADACHWITZ, H.
205864 A/Sgt. GRATTON, S. H.	J 2441 A/C.S.M. HELLINGS, S.	J 2315 Pte. KOSKIE, D.
2824 A/Cpl. GOLDBERG, M.	205645 Pte. HARRIS, B.	J 820 L/Sgt. KAY, L. H.
2828 Pte. GODLOVE, M.	J 2449 Pte. HARRIS, M. S.	J 1861 Pte. KLINE, J.
108 A/Sgt. GOLDSTEIN, A.	J 2711 Pte. HARRIS, E.	205863 A/L/Sgt. KIRK, H. R.
231 Pte. GORDON, A.	J 2712 Pte. HALPERN, L.	J 1543 Pte. KAUFFMAN, S.
252 Pte. GREENBERG, S.	J 1064 Pte. HESKOVITCH, M.	J 2008 Pte. KALESNIKOV, M.
305 L/Cpl. GOLDING, A.	J 2236 Pte. HUBERMAN, P.	J 2301 Pte. KOMINSKY, M.
328 Pte. GRAPMAN, M.	J 398 Pte. ISAAC, N.	J 1821 Pte. KLAPFISH, A.
511 Pte. GORDON, J.	J 2201 Pte. ISAACS, B.	J 1861 Pte. KLINE, J.
1015 Pte. GILBERT, S.	J 2339 Cpl. ISAACS, J.	J 61 Pte. KOZMINSKY, M.
1239 Pte. GELNER, B.	J 2344 Pte. ISAACS, I.	J 1479 Pte. KRAM, A.
1322 Pte. GOLDSTEIN, J.	J 1999 Cpl. IZON, R.	J 2028 Pte. KREEJER, A.
1328 Pte. GOLINSKY, B.	J 164 Pte. ISAACS, A.	J 2264 Pte. KLINE, J.
1402 Pte. GEDALOVITCH, A.	J 1819 Pte. ISAACS, I.	J 2298 Pte. KOPKIN, A.
1528 Pte. GREENSTEIN, S.	J 271 A/C.S.M. JACOBSON, M.	J 1382 Pte. KRITENBERG, J.

"Judeans." N.C.O.'s AND MEN—Continued.

J 1317	Pte. Krafchinsky, S.	J 2006	Pte. Medalger, J.	2150	Pte. Ornadel, W.
J 1435	Pte. Kaminsky, A.	J 2045	Cpl. Michaelson, S.	J 1190	Pte. Osavitch, H.
J 2088	Pte. Kessler, M.	J 2073	Pte. Myerthal, S.	J 2748	Pte. Overs, S.
J 228	Pte. Levine, J.	J 2147	Pte. Merotchnik, M.	J 423	Pte. Price, N.
J 248	Pte. Lawrence, A.	J 2164	Pte. Margolis, S.	829	Pte. Polinski, I.
J 321	Pte. Lipshitz, M.	1283	Pte. Meda, S.	1049	Pte. Powser, J.
J 826	Pte. Lipman, J. H.	2191	Pte. Muscovitch, W.	1481	Pte. Prager, J.
J 983	L/Cpl. Lazarus, J.	2214	Pte. Marks, I.	1729	Pte. Pock, M.
J 1206	Pte. Lesnie, J. H.	2303	Pte. Mallinger, D.	1803	A/C.Q.M.S. Platt, C.
1516	Pte. Levy, I.	2349	Pte. Montanjees, M.	2137	Pte. Paskovitch, H.
1869	Pte. Lipshitz, S.	2488	Pte. Michaelson, H.	2239	Pte. Pogrand, I.
2069	Pte. Levine, A.	J 1617	A/L/Sgt. Marks, H.	2244	Pte. Pick, B.
2169	Pte. Levine, N.	1798	Pte. Mundlack, M.	2324	Pte. Price, E.
2225	Pte. Levinson, M.	1822	Pte. Miller, M.	J 2400	Pte. Perlstone, J.
2234	Pte. Levy, M.	1829	Pte. Mintz, N.	2481	Pte. Perner, A.
2320	Pte. Linz, A.	1853	Pte. Molotick, J.	1848	Pte. Piltz, H.
2326	Pte. Levitt, L.	1928	Pte. Moscovitch, A.	2031	Pte. Predisky, L.
2411	Pte. Landy, H. W.	2394	Pte. Morgan, D.	678	L/Cpl. Pressman, I.
2414	AL/Cpl. Lebovitch, W.	2370	Sgt. Mullens, C. A.	1766	A/L/Sgt. Primack, H.
2734	Pte. Lerner, S. F.	1340	Pte. Miller, M.	1091	Pte. Popko, J.
958	A/Cpl. Levene, L.*	J 1884	Pte Miller, M.	280615	Cpl. Price, S. W.
1804	C.Q.M.S. Lamond, H. D.	205304	A/L/Cpl. Marcus, J.	2799	Sgt. Pryce, F.
1820	Pte. Ludensky, H.	205838	Pte. Marcus, B.	2796	Pte. Phillips, A.
1828	Pte. Levien, B. M.	J 2792	Pte. Meltzer, H. N.	494	Pte. Pshirovski, M.
1930	Pte. Lubman, M.	823	A/Sgt. Myers, J. W.	1302	Pte. Pickle, M.
760	Pte. Lipman, B.	956	L/Cpl. Minkovitch, E.	1725	Pte. Pavin, B.
520	Pte. Levy, M.	1983	Pte. Moskinsky, A.	1121	Pte. Plotka, I.
161	Pte. Lubinsky, A.	1270	Pte. Miller, J.	1263	Pte. Phillips, M.
2818	A/Sgt. Ludzker, A.	2102	Pte. Meninsky, B.	2731	Pte. Park, J.
2829	Pte. Langleben, N.	2430	Pte. Marcus, J.	1832	Pte. Press, J.
306	Pte. Levene, L.	2713	Cpl. Myers, P.	1942	Pte. Quinter, M.
378	Pte. Levine, J.	311	L/Cpl. Menzeretsky, J.	190	Pte. Rapstone H.
604	Pte. Labushinsky, J.	1261	Pte. Mallach, H.	394	Pte. Rosenblatt, J.
1236	Pte. Lupping, L.	1401	Pte. Magaziner, B.	502	Pte. Rhudstein, J.
1623	Pte. Luchinsky, J.	1522	Pte. Mashenberg, P.	J 599	A/Sgt. Reuben, D. B. (M.S.M.)
2211	Pte. Lebrach, J.	1579	Pte. Maron, A.		
237	Pte. Lipman, S.	2002	Pte. Malinofsky, S.	J 871	A/C.S.M. Robertson, C.
1432	Pte. Lisogorsky, I.	2101	Pte. Muscovitch, S.	1463	Pte. Reiner, H.
1955	Pte. Loufer, S.	2146	Pte. Mendleovitz, H.	1465	Pte. Richter, M. M.
2015	Pte. Levine, A.	2237	Pte. Myers, H.	1616	Pte. Rosenbrg, J.
203	Pte. Levine, I.	1721	Pte. Nathan, H.	1814	Pte. Rapstone, L.
2242	Pte. Lempert, E.	2029	Pte. Naftel, I.	2033	Pte. Rais, S.
2355	L/Cpl. Levin, L. G.	2067	Pte. Newman, J.	2154	Pte. Radin, I.
1784	Pte. Lungel, A.	2136	Pte. Nessell, E.	2157	Pte. Rosenbloom, A.
2012	Pte. Levine, M.	2165	Pte. Newman, J.	2170	Pte. Rosenberg, L.
86	Pte. Millings, J.	2174	Pte. Nelson, A.	2182	Pte. Rich, J.
98	Pte. Mordockovitch, B. Z.	2196	Pte. Newman, H.	2186	Pte. Rosen, S.
		2245	Pte. Newdall, A.	2249	Pte. Reeves, S.
146	A/Sgt. Mercer, M.	2270	Pte. Nearkin, M.	2252	Pte. Rose, S.
603	A/L/Cpl. Mendoza, J.	32	A/L/S. Noichovitch, J.	2260	Pte. Rabinovitch, S.
705	Pte. Myers, P.	1099	Pte. Nelson, B.	2369	Pte. Rabbinovitch, J.
1071	Pte. Mancha, H.	2141	Pte. Nathan, J.	2381	Pte. Rosenbloom, H.
1347	Pte. Millman, B.	2319	A/C.S.M. Nelson, W.	2408	Pte. Rontal, B. A.
1569	Pte. Marks, L.	2367	Pte. Nagelkop, L.	2426	Pte. Rosenthall, I.
1669	Pte. Merkin, R.	1274	Pte. Nadel, A.	2467	Pte. Rayner, H.
1702	Pte. Markovitch, S.	2263	Pte. Oppel, S.	2483	Sgt. Ryan, M. W.
1870	Pte. Moses, M.	102	Pte. Orenstein, S.	J 2732	A/L/C. Rosenberg, M.
				J 377	Pte. Ross, D.

"Judeans." — N.C.O.'s AND MEN—Continued.

No.	Rank & Name
J 1470	Pte. RUKOVITZER, N.
J 1808	Pte. ROCK, S.
J 1851	Pte. ROSENFELD, J.
J 1881	Pte. ROCK, N.
J 2017	Pte. ROSENBLOOM, M.
J 2074	Pte. ROSENBERG, F.
J 1850	Pte. KADNANSKY, A.
205192	A/C.S.M. ROME, S.
231982	L/Cpl. ROSS, E.
J 2825	Pte. ROSENBAUM, A.
J 239	Pte. ROLBIN, N.
J 618	Pte. RIFKIN, W.
J 2017	Pte. ROSENBLOOM, M.
J 2410	Pte. ROSENFELD, J.
J 1796	Pte. ROSEN, J.
J 1850	Pte. RADNANSKY, A.
J 342	Pte. RUBINOVITCH, P.
J 1120	Pte. RUBIN, M.
J 1179	Pte. RUBENSTEIN, H.
J 1371	Pte. RABBINOVITCH, G. V.
J 1668	Pte. ROSENBERG, S.
J 2055	Pte. ROGINSKY, M.
J 2240	Pte. ROSEN, M.
J 2329	Pte. ROSEN, I.
J 1548	Pte. ROTHBERG, J.
J 1081	Pte. ROSE, B.
28	L/Cpl. STEPHANSKY, R.
139	A/Sgt. SELLER, N.
309	A/Cpl. STRUMP, N.
317	A/Sgt. SAMUELS, A.
327	Pte. STAVERTSKY, S.
588	Pte. SEABERG, H.
J 735	Pte. STONE, R.
881	Sgt. SEAR, J. E.
965	L/Cpl. SERREE, N.
J 1510	Pte. SONTAG, H.
J 1588	Pte. SARNA, L.
J 1614	Pte. SINGER, I.
J 1630	Pte. SCOP, M.
J 1747	L/Cpl. SILVERSTONE, M.
J 1761	Pte. SHONE, H.
J 2020	Pte. SHNECK, A.
J 2021	Pte. SOLOVISCHICK, J.
J 2024	Pte. SVELMAN, D.
J 2035	Pte. SMITH, J.
J 2036	Pte. SHEAR, J.
J 2039	Pte. SNELWAR, M.
J 2063	Pte. SHALCOFSKY, B.
J 2071	Pte. SILVER, A.
J 2090	Pte. SHERR, M.
J 2091	Pte. STERN, H.
J 2113	Pte. SIMON, L.
J 2159	Pte. SHATZ, L.
J 2171	Pte. SILVERSTONE, H.
J 2217	Pte. SHECTOR, B.
J 2256	Pte. STONE, W.
J 2265	Pte. SUMNER, M.
J 2271	Pte. SIMMONS, L.
J 2287	Pte. SHMERLING, H.
J 2288	Sgt. SALZEDO, S.
J 2293	Pte. SHEINKER, C.
J 2306	Pte. SHEINKER, P.
J 2310	Pte SPIERS, I.
J 2330	Pte. SAPPERSTONE, S.
J 2352	Pte. SIFF, I.
J 2363	Pte. SCHULMAN, P. S.
J 2384	Pte. SIMMONS, H.
J 2404	Pte. SHELDM, J.
J 2415	Pte. SATTIN, L.
J 2425	Pte. SHAPIRA, M.
J 407	Pte. SOLOMON, I.
J 2447	Pte. SILVERGLEIT, H.
J 2468	Pte. SCHAPIRO, W.
J 2715	Pte. STONE, S.
J 2745	Pte. SILVERMAN, V.
J 2752	Sgt. SHIPMAN, J.
562	L/Cpl. SALANT, I.
J 1393	Pte. SHULTZ, M.
J 1781	Pte. SHAPSON, D.
J 1789	A/L/Cpl. SELNER, L.
J 1827	Pte. STRANSMAN, L.
J 1834	A/L/Cpl. SEGAL, I.
J 1923	Pte. STEINBERG, A.
J 1941	Pte. SUMMERS, S.
J 2310	Pte. SPIERS, I.
J 1093	Pte. SOLOMON, C.
J 1227	Pte. SAPOSHNIK, V.
J 1760	Pte. SCHNEIDER, H.
J 702	Pte. SALLIT, J.
J 2070	Pte. SAWODNICK, A.
205308	L/Cpl. SCHNEIDER, J.
J 301	Pte. SCHNITZER, J.
J 2798	A/L/Cpl. SUMROY, B.
J 2827	A/L/Cpl. SHAPIRO, B.
J 2830	Pte. SHULMAN, S.
J 2831	L/Sgt. SPYER, S. M.
J 218	Pte. STARCOVITSKY, W.
J 1377	Pte. SANGER, I.
J 1717	Pte. SPELKI, B.
J 1722	Pte. SHAPIRO, N.
J 1948	Pte. SANK, B.
J 2007	Pte. SINGER, L.
J 2092	Pte. SHRATER, L.
J 2212	Pte. STEIN, J. H.
J 2228	Pte. SIDDLER, E.
J 2278	Pte. SACKS, M.
J 2286	Pte. SHEAD, A.
J 2297	Pte. SACKS, A.
J 2375	Pte. SOLOMONS, H.
J 2472	A/L/Sgt. SIMPSON, R.
J 945	Pte. SEAGER, B.
J 1787	Pte. SILVERSTEIN, L.
J 1790	Pte. SILVERSTEIN, B.
J 1818	Pte. SHERBERKOFF, A.
J 2438	Pte. STARADOVSKY, I.
J 1584	Pte. SHAMPAN, A.
J 2042	Pte. STONE, B.
J 2334	Pte. SILVERMAN, L.
J 168	Pte. SIMKIN, A.
J 172	Pte. STEIN, A.
J 809	Pte. SEAGER, W.
J 1052	Pte. SLIVKIN, H.
J 1144	Pte. SILBERSTEIN, A.
J 1150	Pte. SHARE, S.
J 1592	Pte. SHERMAN, S.
J 1637	Pte. STUDENT, A.
J 1670	Pte. STEINMAN, S.
J 1871	Pte. SENTNER, I.
J 2076	Pte. SAMUELS, R.
J 2100	Pte. SILVERSTEIN, D.
J 2106	Pte. SHEIN, H.
J 2138	Pte. SILVER, J.
J 2216	Pte. SHUR, H.
J 2235	Pte. SCHNEIDER, W.
J 2238	Pte. SILVER, S.
J 2248	Pte. SUMROY, N.
J 1006	Pte. SAPORNIKOFF, F.
J 1980	Pte. SHATZ, H.
J 1228	Pte. SCHNEIDERMAN, L.
J 1365	Pte SAPIRO, S.
667	Pte. SLESS, R.
668	Pte. SLESS, A.
J 1768	Pte. SCHMELZINGER, S.
J 2383	Pte. SARNER, W.
647	A/Sgt. TRUEFITT, E.*
J 1174	Pte. TONDOSKY, M.
J 1778	Pte. TURNER, R.
J 1838	Cpl. TETTENBAUM, A.
J 2068	Pte. TENEBAUM, L.
J 2156	Pte. TABATSKY, S.
J 2173	Pte. TAYLOR, J.
J 2190	Pte. TAYLOR, P.
J 2192	Pte. TINGER, L.
J 2197	Pte. TAYLOR, I.
J 2202	Cpl. TISCOESKY, A.
J 2209	Pte. TATTENBAUM, J.
J 2446	L/Cpl. TANCHAM, J. P.
J 2716	Pte. TRACHTENBERG, M.I.*
J 2790	Pte. TOBIAS, D.
J 1846	Pte. TEPPER, H.
J 2034	Pte. TURSHIN, J.
J 2054	Pte. TEITLEBAUM, I.
J 2412	Pt.e TOMPOWSKI, E.
J 720	Pte. TAYLOR, I.
J 1719	Pte. TORSH, A.
J 2195	Pte. TAYLOR, A.
J 2233	Pte. TENENBAUM, L.
J 1920	Pte. URSHINABSKI, H.
J 2158	Pte. VELINSKY, M.
J 2175	Pte. VILENSKY, J.
J 2250	Pte. VICTOR, S.

"Judeans." N.C.O.'s AND MEN—Continued.

J 2259	Pte. VILOFSKY, B.	J 1741	Pte. WISE, H.	J 2160	Pte. YAFFA, J.
J 1575	Pte. VERBOSKY, S.	J 1805	C.Q.M.S. WELLS, A. R.	J 1824	Pte. YOSKOVITCH, J.
J 2840	Pte. VIRBICKAS, Y.	J 609	Pte. WYSE, I.	J 844	A/Sgt. ZEIFF, C.
J 468	Pte. WEINSTEIN, L.	J 1909	Pte. WINTINSKY, L.	J 2443	Pte. ZURBLISS, A.
J 1265	A/Cpl. WOOLF, H.	J 1920	Pte. WISNNEWSKY, H.	J 2454	Pte. ZIGGLES, M.
J 1343	Pte. WEINSTOCK, L.	J 2800	Sgt. WHITE, J.	J 761	Pte. ZIMMERMAN, M.
J 1565	Pte. WARTSKI, J.	J 617	Pte. WEINSTEIN, B.	205826	Pte. ZEALANDER, N.
J 1993	Pte. WEINER, H.	J 1352	Pte. WEISENBERG, N.	J 508	Pte. ZAGUE, S.
J 2135	L/Cpl. WINTER, R. Z.	J 652	L/Cpl. WEISBROD, A.	J 2065	Pte. ZAMOVSKY, N.
J 2139	Pte. WEITZANSANG, C.	J 1148	Pte. WELTMAN, B.	J 2382	Pte. ZALHASKV, A.
J 2258	Pte. WOOLFSON, L.	J 1718	Pte. WEISBLATT, H.	J 1100	Pte. ZEIDMAN, I.
J 2429	A/L/S. WOOLFSON, J.	J 565	Pte. WOLFSOHN, N.	J 405	Pte. ZEMMEL, J.
J 2486	Pte. WEINTRAUB, M.	J 1877	Pte. WAXMAN, P.	J 2791	Pte. ZELLMAN, I.
J 2714	Pte. WINE, I.	J 2215	Pte. WEINSTEIN, L.		
J 384	Pte. WEINBAUM, M.	J 390	Pte. YUDCOVSKY, M.		

Embarkation Roll.

40th (S) BATTALION ROYAL FUSILIERS ("JUDEANS")

Officers.

Lt.-Col. SAMUEL, F. D. (D.S.O.).	2nd Lieut. ROTH, L.	2nd Lieut. EINSTEIN, M.
Major MYER, H. D.	2nd Lieut. COHEN, J. D.	2nd Lieut. SINCLAIR, A. D.
Capt. LION, F. J.	2nd Lieut. ROE, B. V.	2nd Lieut. KROHN, A. J.
Capt. REISS, J. M.	2nd Lieut. GLUCKMANN, B.	2nd Lieut. BERNSTEIN, A.
Lieut. MELHADO, C. S. H.	2nd Lieut. LAZARUS, M.	2nd Lieut. GOODMAN, D.
Lieut. JACOB, P.	2nd Lieut. LAZARUS, L. H.	2nd Lieut. KISCH, A. M.
2nd Lieut. ROSKIN, N.	2nd Lieut. BLITZ, J.	2nd Lieut. WOLFSON, J.
2nd Lieut. HANBURY, A.	2nd Lieut. LEVINSON, S.	2nd Lieut. ARTARAS, H.
2nd Lieut. FIRTH, M.	2nd Lieut. RATHBONE, M.	
2nd Lieut. ALEXANDER, G. G.	2nd Lieut. TAYLOR, G.	

N.C.O.'s and Men.

4001	Pte. ACKERMAN, J.	3909	Pte. ALEXANDER, M.*	1551	Pte. ARINSKY, B.
4002	Pte. ADER, P.	2852	Pte. ADLERSTEIN, W.	3074	Pte. ABRAHAMS, J.
4006	Pte. ALPHER, D.	4005	Pte. ALKOVE, H.	3447	Pte. ABRAHAMSON, W. M.
4011	Pte. ARUMS, I.	4008	Pte. ALPERSON, H.	428	Pte. ALLEN, S.
5750	Pte. ABRAHAMS, W.	4010	Pte. APHER, S.	2041	Pte. ANDORSKY, J.
5752	Pte. ADDIS, S.	4004	Pte. AGRONSKY, G.	4000	Pte. ABERMAN, P.
5753	Pte. AISEN, S.	5542	Pte. AARONS, J.	4003	Pte. ADLER, A.
5754	Pte. ALIEFSKY, L.	5552	Pte. AXELROD, R.	247	Pte. ANNENBERG, M.
5755	Pte. ALPHER, D.	5572	Pte. AARONSON, P.	2219	Cpl. BOGGIN, A. M.
5758	Pte. ARONOV, S.	5571	Pte. AZIKOFF, S.	4012	Pte. BAKER, J.
5759	Pte. ARONOVITZ, L.	5756	Pte. ALPER, L.	4013	Pte. BARTON, J.
5760	Pte. ARONOW, A.	5587	Pte. AARON, S.	4014	Pte. BASHKOW, A. J.
5761	Pet. AXELROD, E.	5589	Pte. ALMAN, E.	4015	Pte. BASHKOW, M.
5762	Pte. AXELROD, I.	2057	Pte. ABIS, J.	4017	Pte. BAUMGARTEN, H.
5588	Pte. ABRAMS, A.	3397	Pte. ADELMAN, J.	4018	Pte. BEEBER, M.
5757	Pte. ALTSHEULAR, N.	3656	Pte. ALTMAN, A.	4020	Pte. BENDICK, S.

"Judeans." N.C.O.'s AND MEN—Continued.

4024	Pte. BERGER, V.	4032	Pte. BISHKOVE, H.	4030	Pte. BERNSTEIN, P.
4025	Pte. BERGER, W.	4034	Pte. BLIEFIELD, B.	4038	Pte. BLUMENGARTEN, J.
4026	Pte. BERKOWITZ, A.	4037	Pte. BLUM, M.	4040	Pte. BOGIN, N.
4027	Pte. BEROLSKY, H.	4041	Pte. BRAININ, J.	4043	Pte. BRAND, H. G.
4029	Pte. BERNSTEIN, J.	4042	Pte. BRAININ, J.	4044	Pte. BRAND, H.
4038	Pte. BLICK, D.	4051	Pte. BRODSKY, Y.	4047	Pte. BRENNER, N.
4035	Pte. BLOOM, W.	5553	Pte. BOUDAREWSKY, I.	4052	Pte. BRONSTEIN, B.
4036	Pte. BLOOMBERG, S. J.	5554	Pte. BEN-COHEN, A.	4053	Pte. BROWN, J.
4039	Pte. BOGARD, B.	5555	Pte. BEN ZEVIE, I.	4057	Pte. BURAK, J.
4045	Pte. BRAUNSTEIN, A.	5556	Pte. BERKOWITZ, N.	5663	Pte. BOGASKI, H.
4046	Pte. BREGMAN, J.	5557	Pte. BERNBAUM, J. H.	5677	Pte. BEDISH, W.
4050	Pte. BRODSKY, I.	5558	Pte. BARNETT, F.	733	Pte. CRYSTAL, A.
4054	Pte. BRYKMAN, J.	5559	Pte. BROCKSTEIN, A.	2465	L/Cpl. COHEN, A. H.
4056	Pte. BURACK, A.	5562	Pte. BOGDANOFF, L.	2489	Sgt. COHEN, S.
4058	Pte. BURLACK, J.	3102	Pte. BLER, A.	4063	Pte. CHAZANOVITZ, H.
4049	Pte. BRINKER, S.	3981	Sgt. BLOOMFIELD, T. J.	4064	Pte. CHEMEROW, H.
2487	Sgt. BROOKS, H.	4484	Pte. BACHOFSKY, R.	4065	Pte. CHESEN, H.
2708	Cpl. BAUM, J.	5591	Pte. BARKIN, H.	4066	Pte. CHUM, P.
5764	Pte. BAER, S.	5593	Pte. BAYEFSKY, S.	4070	Pte. COHEN, D.
5765	Pte. BALBER, J. A.	649	Cpl. BUTLER, J.	4072	Pte. COHEN, M.
5766	Pte. BARR, A.	2064	Pte. BLACK, S.	4074	Pte. COLODNY, D. C.
5767	Pte. BASEL, M.	2780	Pte. BERKMAN, L.	4075	Pte. COOPER, R.
5768	Pte. BASS, G.	3350	Pte. BELFER, M.	4077	Pte. COTTLER, N.
5769	Pte. BENBOW, M.	3393	Pte. BURSTOFF, H.	6112	C.Q.M.S. CORAM, H. W.
5770	Pte. BEN-GURION, D.	3472	Pte. BRODSKY, S.	155	C.S.M. COPELAND, M.
5771	Pte. BERESKIN, M.	3516	Pte. BESSER, H.	5788	Pte. CAHAN, I.
5772	Pte. BERMAN, B.	3603	Pte. BERGER, J.	5789	CAISERMAN, M.
5773	Pte. BERSCHAD, M.	3483	Pte. BULL, B.	5794	Pte. COHEN, H.
5774	Pte. BLASKI, J.	3690	Pte. BERLINSKY, A. L.	5795	Pte. COHEN, H.
5775	Pte. BLOOM, J. J.	3697	Cpl. BREWER, H.	5796	Pte. COHEN, I.
5776	Pte. BLUESTONE, L.	3735	Pte. BENDERSKY, A.	5797	Pte. COHEN, J.
5777	Pte. BLUM, H.	3747	Pte. BREDSKIE, P.	5799	Pte. COHEN, N.
5778	Pte. BODFSKY, S.	3777	C.S.M. BITTON, B.	5800	Pte. COHEN, V. H.
5779	Pte. BOGEN, A.	346	Cpl. BLASKY, S.	5801	Pte. COHOS, A.
5780	Pte. BOUGARD, H.	403	Pte. BLANKSTEIN, M.	3591	Pte. COHEN, F. H.
5781	Pte. BOOKMAN, H.	879	Pte. BERLINSKI, J.	5875	Pte. CADESKY, W.
5782	Pte. BOYARS, G.	1566	Pte. BLOCH, C.	3772	Pte. COHEN, G.
5783	Pte. BREGMAN, L.	1671	Pte. BUCKSTEIN, D.	5598	Pte. COHEN, H.
5784	Pte. BRISKER, S.	2353	Pte. BLOCK, A.	5596	Pte. CHAITMAN, B.
5786	Pte. BUDER, J.	2351	Pte. BRANDT, S.	5599	Pte. COHN, B.
5787	Pte. BULLUSKY, S.	2452	Cpl. BLUMENTHAL, J.	5597	Pte. CIGLEN, P.
1652	L/Sgt. BLACK, R.	2499	Pte. BESSER, S.	5802	Pte. CRETZ, C.
3005	Pte. BENE, N.	2784	Pte. BARBITSKY, L.	5595	Pte. CAPLAN, S.
3947	Pte. BERMAN, H.	2816	Pte. BENJAMIN, J.	3805	Pte. COHEN, J.
3327	Pte. BERG, E.	2835	Pte. BERNSTEIN, H.	3852	Pte. COHEN, D.
5592	L/Cp. BARLIPAN, J. B. D.	3114	Pte. BRILL, L. J.	3921	Pte. COHEN, C.
5590	Pte. BALANSKY, M.	3356	Pte. BROOKES, W.	3937	Pte. COHEN, E.
5594	Pte. BERNSTEIN, M.	3360	Pte. BLUMENKRANTZ, S.	2877	Pte. COHEN, H.
3867	Pte. BRAILOVSKY, A.	3797	Sgt. BARNETT, S.	3386	L/Sgt. COWEN, J.
4019	Pte. BELKIN, S.	2366	Pte. BIALICK, D.	3738	Pte. COMERVITCH, J.
4055	Pte. BUDIN, L.	T/364627	Dvr. BROWN, F.	3836	Pte. CHTWA, J.
1631	Cpl. BERNSTEIN, I.	3102	Pte. BLEI, A.	4060	Pte. CAHAN, L.
3106	Pte. BERKOWITZ, D.	3981	Sgt. BLOOMFIELD, T. J.	4073	Pte. COHEN, W.
3441	Sgt. BURNETT, L.	3984	Pte. BLACK, W.	4076	Pte. COOPER, R.
4021	Pte. BENDOW, I.	4016	Pte. BASS, S.	4078	Pte. CRADE, W.
4023	Pte. BERG, L	4022	Pte. BERASS, W.	5512	Pte. COPLAN, B.
4031	Pte. BIBERMAN, M.	4028	Pte. BERNSTEIN, H.	5549	Pte. CHIRNIS, I. L.

"Judeans."

N.C.O.'s AND MEN—Continued.

5550	Pte. COHEN, J.	4083	Pte. DIAMOND, P.	3501	Sgt. EBBLEWHITE, J. W.
5551	Pte. CARMEL, L. J.	4084	Pte. DIRECTOR, B.	4093	Pte. EDELSON, L.
5560	Pte. COSSEY, M. G.	4088	Pte. DUBINSKY, M.	4099	Pte. EINSIEDLER, S.
5561	Pte. COHN, M.	2460	Cpl. DAVIS, J.	4101	Pte. ELKUSHY, N.
5564	Pte. CITRON, C.	5804	Pte. DISCOUNT, D.	3448	Pte. ENTSMAN, M.
5570	Pte. CRUSHE, I.	5805	Pte. DORFINAN, A.	2492	L/Cpl. FRANKS, J.
5793	Pte. COHEN, A.	5679	L/Cpl. DUNN, M.	4106	Pte. FEDERBUSH, I.
5798	Pte. COHEN, J.	4089	Pte. DUNN, J. A.	4108	Pte. FEINBERG.
5545	Pte. COHEN, J.	5784	Pte. DRESSLER, J.	4109	Pte. FEINMAN, L.
5600	Pte. COOPER, M.	3835	Pte. DIAMOND, C.	4110	Pte. FIELDSTONE, P.
5601	Pte. COOPERSMITH, A.	3839	Pte. DAVIS, H.	4113	Pte. FINEGOLD, J.
5602	Pte. CUTLER, R. E.	3884	Pte. DREEBIN, M.	4114	Pte. FINK, S.
1252	Pte. COHEN, J.	4080	Pte. DAVIDSON, A.	4115	Pte. FINKELSTEIN, N.
1782	Pte. CLOUD, M.	4081	Pte. DENCHEUSKY, S.	4118	Pte. FISH, D.
1945	Pte. COHEN, A.	4082	Pte. DERZAWITZ, Z.	4120	Pte. FOREMAN, I.
3006	Pte. COHEN, S.	4087	Pte. DRIEG, S.	4122	Pte. FRANKELL, H. W.
3010	Pte. COON, A.	5565	Pte. DUBOFF, H.	4124	Pte. FREEMAN, P.
3351	Pte. COHEN, A.	5803	Pte. DALINSKY, N.	4128	Pte. FRIEDMAN, M.
3559	Pte. COHEN, D.	2723	C.Q.M.S. DAVEY, W. T.	4129	Pte. FRIED, S. D.
3599	Pte. COHEN, M.	3500	Pte. DAVIS, F.	3821	Pte. FREEMAN, H.
3704	Pte. COHEN, L.	1952	Sgt. DAVIDSON, A.	1243	Sgt. FRIES, F.
3718	Pte. COHEN, S.	2795	Pte. DARER, D.	5812	Pte. FEDER, D.
3727	Pte. COLEMAN, A.	3127	Pte. DENNIS, L.	5814	Pte. FEINBERG, M.
3734	Pte. CLIFF, M.	3485	Pte. DAVIS, H.	5815	Pte. FELMAN, S.
3736	Pte. COHEN, R. R.	3996	Pte. DRYER, W.	5817	Pte. FIGOWITZ, J.
3759	Pte. COMN, A.	3004	Pte. DEMBINSKY, S. T.	5818	Pte. FINE, M.
2760	Pte. COHEN, S.	2846	Cpl. DOLMAN, J.	5820	Pte. FINEGOLD, F.
1405	Pte. COHEN, A.	4085	Pte. DOLEN, H.	5822	Pte. FRANK, F.
1773	Pte. COHEN, S.	4086	Pte. DOREGOY, D.	5823	Pte. FRANKEL, A.
1863	Pte. COHEN, P.	4091	Pte. EDELMAN, G.	5824	Pte. FRIEDMAN, S.
2390	Pte. COHEN, J.	4092	Pte. EDELMAN, S.	5825	Pte. FREEHOREN, J.
2401	Pte. COHEN, H.	4095	Pte. EDRICH, E. E.	5826	Pte. FREDLAND, D.
2431	Pte. CAPLAN, P.	4097	Pte. EINHORN, A.	5827	Pte. FURMAN, M.
2437	Pte. CASH, H.	4098	Pte. EISENMAN, A.	3969	Pte. FRANKLIN, B.
2450	Pte. COHEN, H.	4100	Pte. EISENSTAT, H.	2739	Pte. FALK, J.
2726	Pte. COHEN, H.	4102	Pte. ELLENHORN, S.	2741	Pte. FALK, S.
2729	Pte. CITRON, J.	4104	Pte. ESTRIN, P.	3435	A/C.Q.M.S. FAGLEMAN, B.
2783	Pte. COOPER, H.	5806	Pte. EISENBERG, W.		
2815	Pte. CHUDNOSKY, C.	5807	Pte. ELLIS, D.	5606	Pte. FREEDER, H.
3308	Pte. CRINSKY, H.	5808	Pte. EPSTEIN, C.	4105	Pte. FALK, E. M.
3321	Pte. COHEN, B.	5810	Pte. EPSTEIN, M.	4107	Pte. FEIGENBAUM, H.
3385	Pte. COHEN, A.	5811	Pte. EPSTEIN, S.	4117	Pte. FISCHER, L.
3586	Pte. CLAPISH, M.	5604	Pte. ELSON, B.	4123	Pte. FRANKEL, M.
3592	Pte. COHEN, H.	4096	Pte. EDRICH, I.	4127	Pte. FRIEDMAN, J.
3597	Pte. CRASTER, C.	4499	Pte. ENGLEMAN, A.	4488	Pte. FISHER, M.
3698	Cpl. COHEN, M. G.	5809	Pte. EPSTEIN, L.	5537	Pte. FELDMAN, A.
3926	Pte. COHEN, D. W.	5603	Pte. EIZENBERG, S.	5548	Pte. FREEDMAN, J.
2495	Pte. COHEN, M.	3458	Pte. EPSTEIN, M.	5716	Sgt. FERRABY, H.
4059	Pte. COGOW, J.	3504	Sgt. EVANS, A.	5816	Pte. FENKELL, C.
4061	Pte. CANTOR, A.	3558	Pte. ESTERSON, E.	5819	Pte. FINEBERG, L.
4067	Pte. CLAYTON, R.	3609	Pte. ELLEN, B.	5821	Pte. FLAXMAN, P.
4070	Pte. COHEN, D.	2433	Pte. ERLICKMAN, S.	5605	Pte. FINKLESTEIN, F.
4071	Pte. COHEN, H.	2480	Pte. ELITZSKY, J.	5607	Pte. FREEMAN, H.
5583	Pte. COHEN, H. M.	3512	Pte. EPSTEIN, S.	1369	Pte. FRIEDMAN, K. I.
5709	Pte. CRASHINSKY, H.	4090	Pte. ECHTEL, J.	2797	Pte. FREEMAN, S.
1318	Pte. COHEN, M.	4103	Pte. EPSTEIN, B.	3041	Pte. FOX, L.
4079	Pte. DAVIDOWITZ, I.	6113	C.S.M. ELKIN, B.	3559	Pte. FLETCHER, D.

"Judeans."

3422	Sgt.	FIELD, W. C.
3380	Pte.	FIDLER, S.
3496	Pte.	FREEDMAN, S.
3653	Pte.	FOREMAN, M.
3654	Pte.	FINKLESTEIN, I.
3668	Pte.	FARRANT, F.
1985	Pte.	FREEDMAN, H.
2388	Pte.	FELDMAN, M.
2759	Pte.	FINKLESTEIN, S.
3091	Pte.	FREEDMAN, J.
3364	Pte.	FOOT, I.
3391	Pte.	FLOWERS, D.
4112	Pte.	FILGER, L.
4111	Pte.	FINSTONE, H.
4116	Pte.	FINMAN, I.
4119	Pte.	FLINTMAN, M.
4121	Pte.	FRANKEL, A.
4130	Pte.	FURDANS, M.
5646	L/Cpl.	FRANKS, M.
5725	Pte.	FASHT, J.
211	Pte.	FREEDMAN, S.
976	Cpl.	GREENWOOD, I.
4131	Pte.	GACH, S.
4132	Pte.	GAININ, B.
4135	Pte.	GARB, M.
4138	Pte.	GILMAN, A.
4142	Pte.	GISHES, J. S.
4145	Pte.	GLAZER, B.
4146	Pte.	GLAZER, L.
4147	Pte.	GLOSSER, S.
4149	Pte.	GOLD, L.
4150	Pte.	GOLD, M.
4151	Pte.	GOLDBERG, A.
4152	Pte.	GOLDBERG, L.
4153	Pte.	GOLDBERG, M.
4155	Pte.	GOLDEN, N.
4158	Pte.	GOLDMAN, Z.
4159	Pte.	GOLDSTEIN, D.
4160	Pte.	GOLDSTEIN, M.
4165	Pte.	GURLAND, A.
4166	Pte.	GUTBETER, M. Y.
2484	Cpl.	GLASS, W.
3788	Sgt.	GODBEE, A. W.
5828	Pte.	GALLER, S.
5829	Pte.	GELLEN, I.
5830	Pte.	GERESHAUSON, J.
5831	Pte.	GERWYTZ, M.
5832	Pte.	GINN, E.
5833	Pte.	GINSBERG, E.
5836	Pte.	GOLD, A.
5837	Pte.	GOLD, A.
5838	Pte.	GOLD, S.
5839	Pte.	GOLDBERG, B.
5840	Pte.	GOLDENHAR, S.
5841	Pte.	GOLDENHORN, S.
5852	Pte.	GOLDFARB, A.
8376	Pte.	SPIZER, S.

N.C.O.'s AND MEN—Continued.

5844	Pte.	GOLDZWEIG, L.
5845	Pte.	GOODE, J.
5846	Pte.	GOODMAN, J.
5847	Pte.	GOOTMAN, M.
5848	Pte.	GORCHOU, H.
5849	Pte.	GORDON, J.
5850	Pte.	GORFINKEL, S.
5851	Pte.	GORKIN, H.
5853	Pte.	GREENBERG, N.
5854	Pte.	GREENGRASS, M. H.
5857	Pte.	GROBER, V.
5858	Pte.	GROSS, B.
5859	Pte.	GRUENENKLEE, J.
6015	Pte.	GLASS, A.
6027	Pte.	GOLDEN, H.
5835	Pte.	GOFFINAN, J.
3723	Pte.	GOLDMAN, S.
1950	L/Cpl.	GOLD, J.
5612	Pte.	GORDON, L.
5614	Pte.	GREENBERG, B.
5608	Pte.	GELFAND, B.
5610	Pte.	GOLDBAUM, M.
5543	Pte.	GOOREVITCH, C. L.
3837	Pte.	GOLDMAN, I.
5852	Pte.	GREBERG, N.
3789	Sgt.	GOODMAN, J.
3831	Pte.	GOLDBERG, D.
3846	Pte.	GOLDSTEIN, L.
3897	Pte.	GOLDSTEIN, S.
3962	Pte.	GOULD, H.
3973	Pte.	GREEN, A.
3997	Pte.	GERSHMAN, A.
3871	Pte.	GOLDBERG, J.
4134	Pte.	GARB, G.
4136	Pte.	GELLOR, H.
4139	Pte.	GIMBLE, M.
4141	Pte.	GINSBERG, J.
4144	Pte.	GLAUBMAN, M.
4157	Pte.	GOLDMAN, S.
4161	Pte.	GOODMAN, B.
4164	Pte.	GRIFFIN, A.
4487	Pte.	GOGAL, D.
5513	Pte.	GOLDMAN, L.
5514	Pte.	GOLDSCHILD, D.
5530	Pte.	GOLDBERG, H. C.
5532	Pte.	GLASSER, S.
5534	Pte.	GREENBERG, M.
5535	Pte.	GOORVITCH, J.
5536	Pte.	GORSKY, H.
5539	Pte.	GOTBETTER, B.
5609	Pte.	GOLD, D.
5611	Pte.	GOLDSTEIN, I.
5615	Pte.	GRINSPAN, S.
5613	Pte.	GORDON, M.
5855	Pte.	GREENGARD, J.
5860	Pte.	GRUNES, S.
6045	Pte.	GORELICK, E.

6114	Sgt.	GATES, S.
1770	Pte.	GOLDBERG, S. S.
2498	Pte.	GREEN, H.
3084	Pte.	GORBULEFSKY, D.
3346	Pte.	GALBRER, L.
3551	Pte.	GRITZ, S.
3612	Pte.	GROSS, A.
3615	Pte.	GOLDBERG, D.
3633	Pte.	GOLDSTONE, I.
3639	Pte.	GLASS, S.
3655	Pte.	GLUCKSTEIN, I.
3660	Pte.	GOODSTONE, H.
3720	Pte.	GOODSON, J.
3721	Pte.	GOULD, H.
3726	Pte.	GOLDENBERG, J.*
3746	Pte.	GOLDSTONE, E.
200	Pte.	GARFINKLE, H.
1165	Cpl.	GELLMAN, I.
1233	Pte.	GOLDMAN, A.
1367	Pte.	GINSBERG, A.
2151	Pte.	GLEEK, E.
2299	Pte.	GREENBERG, J.
2455	Pte.	GLINTERNICK, I.
3367	Pte.	GOLDSTEIN, M.
3427	Pte.	GREENBERG, S.
3438	Pte.	GREENBERG, J.
3468	Pte.	GOLDSTON, D.
3494	Pte.	GREITSMAN, R. H.
3957	Pte.	GOLDBERG, H.
4493	Pte.	GROSS, S. A.
4140	Pte.	GINSBERG, I.
4154	Pte.	GOLDBERG, R.
5850	Pte.	GORFINKLE, S.
2730	Pte.	GROOPMAN, S.
177	Cpl.	GOODMAN, H.
4133	Pte.	GALPERN, C.
4148	Pte.	GOFF, W. S.
4156	Pte.	GOLDMAN, L. I.
4162	Pte.	GRABSTEIN, I.
4163	Pte.	GREENSTEIN, H.
4165	Pte.	GURLAND, A.
244	Pte.	GOLDSTEIN, E.
1835	Cpl.	HYMAN, A. S.
4167	Pte.	HALBRECHT, C.
4168	Pte.	HALIGMAN, M.
4169	Pte.	HALIGMAN, S.
4170	Pte.	HALPERIN, J.
4171	Pte.	HARRIS, S. D.
4174	Pte.	HELBRANT, M.
4177	Pte.	HOLDSBERG, H.
4181	Pte.	HURWITZ, I.
4182	Pte.	HURWITZ, M.
4183	Pte.	HURWITZ, P.
4184	Pte.	HURWITZ, S.
5616	Pte.	HARRIS, R. N.
3832	Cpl.	HART, J.
5861	Pte.	HABER, H.

"Judeans."

N.C.O.'s AND MEN—Continued.

5863	Pte. Haze, H.		992	Cpl. Isaacs, S. D.		5540	Pte. Krikow, S.
5864	Pte. Hill, M.		4186	Pte. Ikin, M.		5541	Pte. Kaplan, M.
5865	Pte. Hirshenson, R.		5654	Pte. Israel, H.		5544	Pte. Kurland, B.
5866	Pte. Holzinan, P.		4194	Pte. Julien, S.		5546	Pte. Kovish, J.
5867	Pte. Hurwitz, M.		3339	Pte. Jenkins, S.		5547	Pte. Kuvant, P.
5868	Pte. Hurwitz, N.		5872	Pte. Jacobson, M.		5621	Pte. Katz, A.
5869	Pte. Hyman, A.		2751	Pte. Jacobs, H.		5622	Pte. Keldofsky, L.
5870	Pte. Hyman, B.		7162	Sgt. James.		5623	Pte. Kramer, I.
5618	Pte. Hoffman, G.		5873	Pte. Jaffe, H.		5624	Pte. Kramer, M.
3928	Pte. Hill, N.		2476	Cpl. Jacobs, M. J.		5878	Pte. Kapultkin, M.
3960	Pte. Himmelfelb, B.		4190	Pte. Jaffe, J.		6013	Pte. Kemp, M.
4495	Sgt. Harris, D.		2478	Pte. Joseph, H.		4197	Pte. Kaminkowitz, L.
3130	Pte. Heirwitz, J.		3612	Pte. Jellan, B.		4198	Pte. Kaminsky, J.
4173	Pte. Heim, M.		3083	Pte. Joseph, L.		4200	Pte. Kaplan, J.
4175	Pte. Heller, B.		411	Pte. Jackson, S.		4201	Pte. Kaplan, L.
4178	Pte. Horwitz.		4191	Pte. Jaffe, S.		4203	Pte. Kash, M.
4185	Pte. Hymowitz, S.		4129	Pte. Janewitz, S.		4206	Pte. Katz, A. J.
4179	Pte. Hurvitz, J.		4195	Pte. Kaitz, D.		4210	Pte. Kaufman, L.
5617	Pte. Hendin, B.		4196	Pte. Kahanovsky, J.		4214	Pte. Ketcher, H.
5862	Pte. Hannock, M.		4202	Pte. Karp, J.		4223	Pte. Kowarsky, H.
696	Pte. Harris, M.		4205	Pte. Katkovsky, A.		4227	Pte. Kroopnick, I.
2371	Sgt. Hinchcliffe, G. H.		4207	Pte. Katz, J.		5515	Pte. Kaplan, N.
3307	Pte. Hyman, M.		4208	Pte. Katz, S.		991	Pte. Kosner, M.
3329	Pte. Hilkowitz, H.		4209	Pte. Kaufman, M.		1557	Pte. Krotoski, R.
3430	Pte. Harris, M.		4211	Pte. Kay, H.		1889	Pte. Kitchenoff, H.
3489	Pte. Hilkowitz, H.		4215	Pte. Kirshner, M.		2707	Pte. Krietzman, M.
3430	Pte. Harris, M.		4216	Pte. Klaiman, I.		1962	Pte. Kloss, S.
3489	Pte. Harries, S.		4218	Pte. Kolke, D.		3372	Pte. Kupferblatt, W. D.
3571	Pte. Hines, S.		4226	Pte. Kron, S.		3315	Pte. Karabalnick, I.
3751	Pte. Howrovitz, H.		5744	C.S.M. Knight, T. L.		3507	Pte. Kaufman, S.
994	Pte. Hantman, J.		5876	Pte. Kadish, J. L.		3650	Pte. Koninsky, W.
1868	Pte. Herman, J.		5879	Pte. Katz, I. M.		3708	Pte. Kassovitch, W.
2755	Pte. Hyman, P.		5880	Pte. Katz, N.		3732	Pte. Korn, M.
2838	Pte. Hess, P.		5883	Pte. Kerman, J. J.		3053	Pte. Kaufman, M.
3009	Pte. Harris, I.		5884	Pte. Kernerman, S. C.		3796	Pte. Kavaritch, A. L.
3035	Pte. Harris, N.		5885	Pte. Kirson, V.		4228	Pte. Kushin, W.
3431	Pte. Harris, M.		5886	Pte. Klapkin, M.		5719	Pte. Klyne, J.
3471	Pte. Hyman, S.		5887	Pte. Kotler, L.		A2424	A/Sgt. Kilby, T. V.
742	Sgt. Harris, A.		5888	Pte. Kovinsky, S.		2933	Pte. Karnofsky, C.
1769	Cpl. Hoffman, A.		5889	Pte. Kramer, M.		5577	Pte. Kersch, M.
982	Cpl. Hyams, S.		5891	Pte. Kuperman, A.		5719	Pte. Klien, J.
4172	Pte. Hartenstein, A.		5892	Pte. Kuskin, N.		1701	Sgt. Levine, P.
4176	Pte. Himnelforb, J.		3495	Pte. Kreger, J.		3768	Sgt. Levy, J.
4180	Pte. Hurvitz, J.		5620	Pte. Kapshut, C.		4230	Pte. Leavitt, R.
5582	L/Cpl. Hansell, M.		5890	Pte. Krinsky, A.		4232	Pte. Lefkowitz, S.
3791	Sgt. Holdgate, L.		5881	Pte. Kazennik, M.		4234	Pte. Levinbuck, M.
2441	R.S.M. Hellings, F.		3865	Pte. Kosminsky, S.		4244	Pte. Lilienthal, A.
577	Cpl. Hoffman, A.		3983	Pte. Kramaranka, B.		4251	Pte. Livingstone, A.
4187	Pte. Itkin, P.		3936	Pte. Kwartz, H.		4252	Pte. Lubin, L.
4188	Pte. Israely, D.		2930	Pte. Kellman, S.		6014	Pte. Lane, J.
5871	Pte. Israel, H.		3502	Sgt. Keeton, E.		6026	Pte. Levine, L.
3376	Pte. Isaacs, E.		4199	Pte. Kanet, S.		5893	Pte. Lackman, S.
3477	Pte. Isaacs, M.		4204	Pte. Kaspy, M.		5894	Pte. Latner, J.
3917	Pte. Israel, M.		4212	Pte. Kenschofski, A.		5895	Pte. Lerman, J.
5529	Pte. Isaacs, B.		4213	Pte. Kerrick, T.		5896	Pte. Leveton, B.
5619	Pte. Isenberg, L.		4220	Pte. Koran, A.		5897	Pte. Levine, H.
3068	Pte. Isaacs, A.		4222	Pte. Kouches, I.		5898	Pte. Levine, S.

"Judeans."

N.C.O.'s AND MEN—Continued.

5899 Pte. Lewis, I.	2794 Pte. Levy, A.	6018 Pte. Moerschen, A. J.
5800 Pte. Lieberman, M.	3078 Pte. Lazarus, M.	5908 Pte. Mandelbaum, C.
5901 Pte. Lifshitz, A.	3410 Pte. Lazarus, S.	5909 Pte. Marcus, H.
5902 Pte. Lindenbum, N.	3562 Pte. Lakofski, H.	5910 Pte. Markowitz, J.
5903 Pte. Lipner, J.	3659 Pte. Lesser, L.	5911 Pte. Mayer, S.
5904 Pte. Lipshitz, H.	3728 Pte. Landa, H.	5912 Pte. Miller, I.
5905 Pte. Livshitz, L.	3731 Pte. Levy, C.	5913 Pte. Milstein, P.
5906 Pte. Lotinsky, J.	536 Pte. Lebbish, H.	5914 Pte. Mirvis, W.
5907 Pte. Lubetsky, R.	679 L/Sgt. Levy, W.	5915 Pte. Mortkowitz, B.
2740 Pte. Lecansky, L.	906 Pte. Lippa, A.	5917 Pte. Murchin, L.
3303 Pte. Levy, I.	1696 Pte. Levy, B.	5918 Pte. Murman, I.
3636 Pte. Lipman, M.	2010 Pte. Levine, L.	6031 Pte. Mintz, H.
3725 Pte. Lustgarten, S.	2360 Pte. Levy, W. J.	4257 Sgt. Manoff, Z.
3338 Sgt. Lewis, S.	2461 Pte. Lourence, M.	4262 Pte. Mar-Heim, E.
989 Cpl. Lubofsky, A.	2770 Pte. Lee, M.	5628 Pte. Mendels, A.
5626 Pte. Levy, S.	3023 Pte. Lefcovitch, J.	4268 Pte. Mendelsohn, D.
4248 Pte. Lipshitz, H.	3082 Pte. Levi, M.	4287 Pte. Moznain, J.
6024 Pte. Levin, E.	3098 Pte. Lubin, P.	4281 Pte. Mirel, S.
4240 Pte. Levitzky, H.	3311 Pte. Levy, A.	6030 Pte. Miller, F.
3816 Pte. Lewin, L.	3316 Pte. Lipschitz, S.	3790 Pte. Marks, H.
3855 Pte. Levey, J.	3400 Pte. Levinsky, S.	3860 Pte. Michaels, S.
3870 Pte. Lazarus, M.	3576 Pte. Levy, L.	3911 Pte. Michaels, H.
3887 Pte. Lewis, J.	3638 Pte. Libgott, L.	3993 Pte. Mauzig, M.
3934 Pte. Luberoff, S. W.	3666 Pte. Levy, H.	3408 C.S.M. McEvoy, J.
3952 Pte. Levy, B.	3863 Pte. Levin, J.	4255 Pte. Maisel, N.
3963 Pte. Lazarus, L.	5672 Pte. Libbert, M. H.	4258 Pte. Marche, S.
3994 Pte. Lazarus, L.	5673 Pte. Landamski, M.	4271 Pte. Meyers, M.
1888 Sgt. Landau, S.	4247 Pte. Lipman, L.	4272 Pte. Meyer, S.
3778 Cpl. Linder, M.	67 Pte. Levy, J.	4276 Pte. Miller, H.
3816 Pte. Levine, L.	2145 Pte. Lieberman, J.	4284 Pte. Mosgin, I.
3995 Pte. Libman, A.	2422 Pte. Lipman, K.	4286 Pte. Mostofsky, H.
4231 Pte. Lebovitz, H.	1931 Pte. Levy, M.	5502 Pte. Miransky, D.
4236 Pte. Levine, H.	5495 Pte. Lizar, J.	5504 Pte. Miritsky, H.
4239 Pte. Levinson, L. H.	5710 Pte. Lelzman, Z.	5518 Pte. Mintz, L.
4249 Pte. Liss, J.	5717 Pte. Levine, H.	5526 Pte. Masolsky, Z.
5525 Pte. Levin, W.	5720 Pte. Levine, M.	5573 Pte. Meckler, B.
5531 Pte. Leibson, N.	6052 Pte. Levine, H.	5575 Pte. Maritzer, H.
5567 Pte. Lebovitch, J.	1996 Pte. Levitsky, M.	5629 Pte. Mintz, L.
5625 Pte. Layewsky, J.	4253 Pte. Magalois, M.	5630 Pte. Mirsky, E.
5627 Pte. Lubliner, S.	4254 Pte. Magdoff, B.	4278 Pte. Miller, S.
6044 Pte. Levin, A.	4256 Pte. Malawsky, M.	5503 Pte. Manchester, H.
6097 Pte. Levin, B. D.	4259 Pte. Marcus, J.	594 Pte. Maurice, L.
4229 Pte. Lachanis, D.	4261 Pte. Marcusin, J. H.	705 Pte. Myers, P.
4233 Pte. Leidecker, C.	4263 Pte. Markowitz, A.	1441 Pte. Melnekoff, R.
4235 Pte. Levine, A.	4264 Pte. Matusenko, S.	2418 Pte. Marks, J.
4237 Pte. Levine, S.	4266 Pte. Melukoff, A.	3008 Pte. Moldofsky, A.
4238 Pte. Levinsky, H.	4267 Pte. Melofsky, H.	3424 Sgt. Mendoza, D.
4241 Pte. Levy, L.	4269 Pte. Mendlewitz, G.	3616 Pte. Moses, M.
4242 Pte. Levy, M.	4270 Pte. Meshel, S.	241 Pte. Mackay, A.
4243 Pte. Liberty, D.	4274 Pte. Midner, L.	1018 Pte. Markovitch, S.
4245 Pte. Linkoff, J.	4275 Pte. Miller, D.	1682 Pte. Marcassin, W.
4246 Pte. Lipkofsky, ?.	4279 Pte. Milson, J. H.	1756 Pte. Messias, B.
4250 Pte. Lissitza, J.	4282 Pte. Mizel, J.	2430 Pte. Marcus, J.
65 Pte. Levison, I.	4283 Pte. Mizrochi, B.	2434 Pte. Morgan, M.
167 Pte. Levy, M.	4285 Pte. Moshel, P.	2435 Pte. Markson, D.
378 Pte. Levine, J.	4290 Pte. Meishtat, A.	2494 Pte. Mendelsohn, J.
978 L/Cpl. Leafschutz, I.	3087 Sgt. Morris, J.	3079 Pte. Myers, P.

"Judeans."

N.C.O.'s AND MEN—Continued.

3451	Pte. Morris, H.		4314	Pte. Piser, S. M.		5681	Pte. Pokenjohn, M.
3476	Pte. Miller, M.		4321	Pte. Polinsky, S.		1158	Sgt. Rosenbloom, E.
3798	Pte. Morris, J.		4322	Pte. Pollock, M.		4331	Pte. Rabinovitz, N.
4278	Pte. Miller, S.		4323	Pte. Portugal, R.		4332	Pte. Rabinovitz, S.
5707	Pte. Moreberg, A.		4325	Pte. Powell, A.		4334	Pte. Radom, I. A.
T/364514	Dvr. Millward, J.		4326	Pte. Pregosin, A.		4338	Pte. Rechtman, J.
T/365191	Dvr. Matley, J.		4327	Pte. Pressman, S.		4339	Pte. Reiser, M.
4288	Pte. Murray, E.		4330	Pte. Putterman, J.		4340	Pte. Reisfeld, A.
5524	Pte. Markel, H.		6001	Pte. Pitts, L.		4343	Pte. Resenick, H.
955	Pte. Matthews, S.		6022	Pte. Poriels, M.		4344	Pte. Resnick, S.
2436	Pte. Musaphia, J.		6023	Pte. Paticoff, H.		4352	Pte. Rosen, R. S.
2497	Pte. Messias, A. A.		6025	Pte. Pensky, F.		4353	Pte. Rosen, Z.
3857	Cpl. Marks, H.		5919	Pte. Parker, C.		4356	Pte. Rosenblum, S.
5645	Pte. Manus, H.		5920	Pte. Paszermy, M.		4357	Pte. Rosengarten, M.
6068	Pte. Myers, A.		5921	Pte. Parsowith, S.		4359	Pte. Ross, C.
4290	Pte. Neistat, A.		5922	Pte. Paul, H.		3341	Cpl. Rogoff, P.
4292	Pte. Newman, E. J.		5924	Pte. Pearlstein, J.		3719	Cpl. Rainsburg, S.
4299	Pte. Nutkis, D.		5925	Pte. Petrofsky, P.		6017	Pte. Rodoff, M.
6000	Pte. Nessenbaum, M.		5926	Pte. Pollack, H.		6019	Pte. Rosinsky, F.
6009	Pte. Niditch, S.		5927	Pte. Posner, S.		5929	Pte. Rafael, L.
6010	Pte. Nagdman, J.		2839	Pte. Prager, S.		5931	Pte. Rice, H.
6012	Pte. Natanson, C.		3893	Pte. Pearson, N.		5932	Pte. Richman, M. B.
6032	Pte. Naff, S.		3940	Pte. Pearce, E.		5933	Pte. Rickles, A.
6033	Pte. Newstone, S.		4303	Pte. Palbaum, W.		5934	Pte. Rifkin, A.
4297	Pte. Nidorf, L.		4304	Pte. Paigman, S.		5935	Pte. Rogers, H.
4289	Pte. Naiberg, I.		4305	Pte. Pearson, M.		5936	Pte. Rogg, H.
4291	Pte. Nelson, I.		4306	Pte. Peisner, S.		5937	Pte. Rosenbaum, N.
4293	Pte. Newman, M.		4308	Pte. Perlman, S.		5939	Pte. Rosenweig, W.
4294	Pte. Newman, N.		4316	Pte. Pleet, W.		5940	Pte. Rosov, S.
4296	Pte. Newton, S.		4317	Pte. Plotsky, W.		5941	Pte. Rothberg S.
4295	Pte. Newman, W. I.		4318	Pte. Rogoler, H.		5942	Pte. Rotburd, J.
2317	Pte. Nurishken, N.		4324	Pte. Posner, H.		5943	Pte. Rudnitsky, B.
2367	Pte. Nazelkop, L.		4329	Pte. Price, L.		6037	Pte. Raices, B.
2850	Pte. Noar, M.		5517	Pte. Pascal, A. D.		6039	Pte. Richter, Z. H.
3657	Pte. Newfield, H.		5574	Pte. Platter, H.		3032	Sgt. Rosenthal, S. L.
3283	Pte. Nirenberg, M.		5923	Pte. Pate, D.		3076	Pte. Rosenthal, J.
3511	Pte. Nasson, L.		4302	Pte. Pedowitz, E.		3384	Pte. Robinson, A.
T/406115	Dvr. Newbold, E.		4309	Pte. Perlin, B.		3445	Pte. Ritblat, J. R.
5676	Pte. Nimni, J.		4319	Pte. Polack, B.		2817	Pte. Rosenthal, H.
3474	Sgt. Owen, A.		4320	Pte. Polakoff, L.		5634	Pte. Rosen, M.
4301	Pte. Ornshkes, H.		4328	Pte. Price, J.		4439	Pte. Roch, I.
6034	Pte. Olin, J.		5528	Pte. Pontonwitz, C.		5930	Pte. Ravetz, H.
6035	Pte. Osofsky, S.		494	Pte. Pshirovski, M.		6040	Pte. Ross, H.
6036	Pte. Ouzil, N.		3205	Pte. Posner, H.		3803	Pte. Rosen, S.
3953	Pte. Oelbaum, C.		4303	Pte. Portner, H.		3905	Pte. Rosenberg, J.
5527	Pte. Ohlbaum, R.		3437	Pte. Phillips, L.		3933	Pte. Rogofski, J.
4300	Pte. Orkin, W.		3463	Pte. Parkus, A.		3099	Pte. Rubenstein, M.
1882	Pte. Obermeister, B.		3497	Pte. Phillips, I.		3950	Pte. Rubenstein, M.
2748	Pte. Overs, S.		3604	Pte. Platkin, H. S.		3966	Pte. Rifkin, S.
3764	Pte. Oesterman, H.		3673	Sgt. Pearse, W. S.		3979	Pte. Rosenson, I.
1927	Pte. Orlinsky, H.		1032	Cpl. Peston, S.		3851	Pte. Rosenbloom, J. N.
3308	Pte. Orinsky, H.		2466	Pte. Prager, B.		3710	Sgt. Roberts, W.
770	Cpl. Plisky, S.		3022	Pte. Phillips, J. R.		4333	Pte. Rachel, S.
4307	Pte. Penziner, L.		4312	Pte. Pine, H.		4336	Pte. Raskin, N.
4310	Pte. Perrybisky, F.		4315	Pte. Pizer, I.		4342	Pte. Reisma,n H.
4311	Pte. Pilzer, M.		2097	Pte. Pentlevitch, I.		4345	Pte. Richenstein, J.
4313	Pte. Pines, J.		2373	Pte. Polonsky, H.		4346	Pte. Richmond, D.

"Judeans." N.C.O.'s AND MEN—Continued.

4347 Pte. ROBINOVITZ, S.	4395 Pte. SHEITELMAN, S.	5637 Pte. SENKOLAW, B.
4358 Pte. ROSENTHAL, R. H.	4397 Pte. SHERRY, H.	5636 Pte. STEIN, S.
4362 Pte. RUBIN, L.	4401 Pte. SHULKIN, H.	4399 Pte. SHEIMAN, M.
4486 Pte. ROOSE, S.	4406 Pte. SIEGEL, M.	4384 Pte. SEGALL, J.
5523 Pte. RAVITZ, S.	4408 Pte. SILVER, H.	4417 Pte. SKUY, E.
5631 Pte. RACHWALSKY, J.	4412 Pte. SIMON, H.	4424 Pte. SOLIG, H.
5633 Pte. REISLER, H.	4413 Pte. SINGER, A.	5945 Pte. SALKOFF, B.
5638 Pte. ROSENFELD, D.	4414 Pte. SINGER, A.	6007 Pte. SILVERSTEIN, P.
6038 Pte. REISS, S.	4415 Pte. SINGER, I.	4410 Pte. SIMKIN, H.
6098 Pte. ROSENBUCK, D. W.	4416 Pte. SINGER, J.	4411 Pte. SIMKIN, J. I.
3282 Pte. RESNICK, Z.	4418 Pte. SLOANE, S.	3879 Cpl. SHOUFIELD, L.
5632 Pte. RACHWALSKY, J.	4419 Pte. SLOMOVITCH, S.	3920 Pte. SEGAL, J.
4335 Pte. RAPPERPORT, M.	4423 Pte. SOIBEL, S.	3974 Pte. SYMONS, A.
4337 Pte. RATMAN, H.	4425 Pte. SPERLING, E.	4494 Pte. SUTHERLAND, H.
4348 Pte. ROBBIN, J.	4426 Pte. SPERLING, M.	4496 Pte. SCHLOTT, H.
4350 Pte. RODNER, J.	4427 Pte. SPIEGAL, A.	4497 Pte. SHOOLMAN, C.
4355 Pte. ROSENBERG, I.	4430 Pte. STEIN, E.	4498 Pte. SILVERSTONE, M.
4360 Pte. ROTBERG, C.	4435 Pte. STRUSNSKY, I.	1552 Cpl. SUGARMAN, S.
4361 Pte. RUBIN, H. S.	4439 Pte. SUSSMAN, J. M.	3048 Sgt. STEINGOLD, B. L.
5516 Pte. ROSEN, R.	4440 Pte. SWARTZ, P.	3503 Sgt. STOLOFF, A. J.
3017 Pte. ROSENTHAL, J.	4441 Pte. SWILLING, M.	3730 L/Sgt. SILVER, M. A.
3080 Pte. ROSEN, D.	5635 Pte. SANTMAN, H. E.	4371 Pte. SARMDERS, H.
3632 Pte. ROSENBLOOM, B.	3930 Cpl. SCORA, S.	4373 Pte. SAZEWITZ, H.
3640 Pte. RICH, D.	5951 Pte. SCHNEIDER, H.	4374 Pte. SCHAPIRA, I.
3643 Pte. RUBENSTEIN, L.	5953 Pte. SCHREIBER, W. M.	4385 Pte. SEGEL, B.
868 Sgt. RANCE, R. S. T.	5954 Pte. SCHMIDT, M.	4386 Pte. SELIGSOHN, M. B.
1301 Pte. ROZENBARN, L.	5955 Pte. SHAPIRO, M.	4394 Pte. SHAPIRO, S.
1986 Pte. RHUDSTEIN, H.	5956 Pte. SHARPSTEIN, B.	4398 Pte. SHESHEN, K.
2389 Pte. ROSENBERG, J.	5957 Pte. SHEINBERG, R. L.	4400 Pte. SHGREEN, B.
2463 Pte. ROSEN, L.	5958 Pte. SHIFRIS, M.	4404 Pte. SHWRIFF, P.
2760 Pte. ROTH, I.	5959 Pte. SHULIM, D.	4405 Pte. SIEGEL, B.
2764 Pte. ROSENHEAD, L.	5960 Pte. SHUMSKY, M.	4429 Pte. STAYMAN, M.
2774 Pte. REUBEN, B.	5961 Pte. SIEGEL, A.	4431 Pte. STEINBERG, B.
2429 Sgt. ROSENBERG, A.	5962 Pte. SIEGEL, H.	4433 Pte. STRASBERG, J.
3854 Pte. REISERMAN, I.	5966 Pte. SISLER, M.	4434 Pte. STRAUSS, H.
3880 Pte. ROLAND, S.	5967 Pte. SLAVIN, I.	4436 Pte. SUSHANSKY, S.
4364 Pte. SACKS, M.	5969 Pte. SMITH, N.	4437 Pte. SUSSMAN, J.
4365 Pte. SACKS, R.	5971 Pte. SPIGEL, S.	4438 Pte. SUSSMAN, J.
816 Cpl. SOLOMONS, C.	5972 Pte. STRAUSMAN, H.	5505 Pte. SCHWARTZBAUM, I.
972 Cpl. SAFFER, E.	5973 Pte. STERNBERG, R.	5506 Pte. SCHRESHEFSKY, N. D.
3707 Cpl. SOLOMONS, M.	5974 Pte. STEINBERG, S.	5519 Pte. SEGAL, M.
4364 Pte. SACKS, M.	5975 Pte. SUGURMAN, H.	5520 Pte. STULBERG, S.
4365 Pte. SACKS, R.	5976 Pte. SUGENTMAN, I.	5521 Pte. SOLOF, A. L.
4366 Pte. SANDERS, M.	5977 Pte. SWARTZ, M.	5566 Pte. SAUNDERS, A.
4367 Pte. SAPERIA, S.	6002 Pte. SETORSKY, L.	5568 Pte. SOKOLZSKY, H.
4372 Pte. SAK, I.	6003 Pte. SCHWARTZ, B.	5569 Pte. SOLOMON, A.
4376 Pte. SCHNEIDERMAN, H.	6004 Pte. STARK, L.	5638 Pte. SILVER, S.
4377 Pte. SCHNITZER, I.	6005 Pte. STARWIN, B.	5639 Pte. STERIN, S.
4379 Pte. SCHUCKMAN, S.	5944 Pte. SAGAUMSKY, S.	5641 Pte. STRELZIN, M.
4380 Pte. SCHWARTZ, A.	5946 Pte. SAUL, J.	5680 Pte. SHAPIRO, M.
4382 Pte. SCHWARTZ, W. S.	5947 Pte. SCHARNKIN, S.	5968 Pte. SMITH, C.
4387 Pte. SELIGSON, S.	5948 Pte. SCHATZ, A. D.	6042 Pte. STALLAND, A.
4389 Pte. SENOR, M.	5949 Pte. SCHEINHOLZ, J.	4368 Pte. SAR, J.
4390 Pte. SHACK, M.	5950 Pte. SCHERER, H.	4369 Pte. SARE, L. H.
4391 Pte. SHAPIRO, A.	6041 Pte. SNYDER, H.	4375 Pte. SCHEIN, Z. L.
4392 Pte. SHAPIRO, I.	3002 Pte. SANKERIVITZ, I.	4378 Pte. SCHORR, H.
4393 Pte. SHAPIRO, J.	6043 Pte. STAWISKY, M.	4383 Pte. SCHWETZKY, P.

18

"Judeans."

N.C.O.'s AND MEN—Continued.

No.	Rank & Name
4388	Pte. SCLINKOFF, S.
4402	Pte. SHULMAN, N.
4407	Pte. SIEGAL, W.
4409	Pte. SILVERMAN, E.
4420	Pte. SIMLER, S.
4422	Pte. SOFIAN, I.
4428	Pte. SHRANK, H.
357	Pte. SEGAL, H.
998	Pte. SILVERSTONE, M.
1694	Pte. SACKS, I.
1919	Pte. SCHERBERKOFF, A.
2204	Cpl. SPEYER, J.
2452	Pte. SILVESTONE, J.
3015	Pte. SCHEFFER, N.
3059	Sgt. SOLOMON, L.*
3085	Pte. SKARLOFF, L.
3363	L/Sgt. SHAFRANSKY, T.
3454	Pte. SILVER, L.
3613	Pte. SILVERSTONE, A.
3627	Pte. SMITH, M.
3647	Pte. SMITH, S.
3683	Pte. SHERATSKY, M.
3733	Cpl. SILVER, M.
3765	Pte. SHAPIRO, I.
304	Pte. SCHNEIDER, C.
1751	Pte. SINKOVITCH, M.
2003	Pte. SCOLNICK, J.
2009	Pte. SOLOMONS, L.
2168	Pte. SINGER, J.
2251	Pte. SCHAFFER, L.
2343	Pte. SCHLOSKI, S. A.
2398	Pte. STALL, L.
2705	Pte. SCHIOVITZ, I.
2701	Pte. SALTER, J.
2737	Pte. STRACHAN, D.
3052	Pte. SCHLOM, B.
3488	Sgt. SILKOVITCH, L.
3980	Pte. STONEMAN, A. W.
T4/198194	Dvr. SELF, A. W.
T/394460	Dvr. SAKER, J.
950	Pte. STEEN, J.
980	Pte. SCHMERKIN, H.
2721	R.Q.M.S. SMITHSON, G.
3684	L/Cpl. SCHAFRAN, M. E.
3793	Sgt. SIMON, A.
3907	L/Sgt. SMITH, J.
5674	Pte. SAMNEL, S.
6096	Pte. SILVERSTEIN, S.
1643	Pte. SOLOMON, J.
4442	Pte. TALKOWSKY, J.
4444	Pte. TARSHISH, I.
4446	Pte. TEPLITZKY, I.
4447	Pte. TOHILL, H.
5745	Sgt. TAYLOR, L.
5652	Pte. THOMPSON, L. B.
4453	Pte. TRUSKER, L.
4448	Pte. TOPOL, N.
4449	Pte. TRACHTENBERG, S.
4450	Pte. TUCKER, J.
4451	Pte. TUCKER, L.
5501	Pte. TROPP, M.
6006	Pte. TUSCHNEIDER, M.
4452	Pte. TUROVITZ, A.
738	Pte. TERNOFSKY, M.
3439	Pte. TYTZ, D.
3762	Pte. TEPER, H.
1679	Pte. TROTSKY, A.
2733	Pte. TAYLOR, H.
4443	Pte. TANKUNOFF, J.
T/329442	Dvr. TREVASSO, S. C.
3027	Sgt. TRIGGER, J.
5576	Pte. TAYLOR, M.
5980	Pte. UTCH, M.
4695	Pte. USHEVITZ, M.
3381	Cpl. USDEN, M.
4455	Pte. VINER, H.
4456	Pte. VOLOD, S.
5981	Pte. VILDAVSKY, S.
3853	Cpl. VALENTINE, R.
3882	Pte. VICE, T. G.
4454	Pte. VAYDA, S.
5982	Pte. VILOFSKY, V.
3398	Pte. VALENSKY, P.
3669	Pte. VOLUMBERG, J.
5678	Pte. VILLENSKY, D. B.
4457	Pte. WALD, J.
4465	Pte. WEISSMAN, M.
4468	Pte. WENTRUB, W.
4469	Pte. WERTH, P.
4470	Pte. WOLF, A.
3086	Sgt. WOOLF, N.
5983	Pte. WAINGOLD, J.
5984	Pte. WASMAN, L.
5985	Pte. WATMAN, J.
5986	Pte. WEINBERG, D.
5989	Pte. WEISS, H.
5990	Pte. WEISSBERG, P.
5991	Pte. WINKLER, B.
5993	Pte. WISHNEFF, L.
5994	Pte. WITT, B.
5995	Pte. WOLF, H.
5996	Pte. WOLFSON, I.
5997	Pte. WEWFERRON, M.
6008	Pte. WALDSTEIN, S.
2746	Sgt. WILLIAMS, J. I.
3029	Cpl. WANSKER, H.
4458	Pte. WALDMAN, I.
3804	Pte. WEISBAUM, I.
3849	Pte. WOOLF, D.
3885	Pte. WISEMAN, H.
3968	Pte. WILLIAMS, P.
3986	Pte. WISEMAN, D.
4459	Pte. WARBERG, M.
4460	Pte. WEBBER, M.
4462	Pte. WEINSTEIN, F.
4464	Pte. WEISSAMN, M.
4465	Pte. WEISMAN, M.
4471	Pte. WRUBEL, J.
5500	Pte. WEIGENSBERG, I.
5507	Pte. WOEKELMAN, H.
5508	Pte. WAGNER, K.
5509	Pte. WEINSTOCK, H.
5510	Pte. WERGENSBERG, A.
5511	Pte. WEINGARDEN, A.
6099	Pte. WEINBERG, S.
4461	Pte. WEINER, A.
4467	Pte. WEKSTER, J.
2030	Pte. WACHMAN, B.
2340	Pte. WALDENBERG, S.
3490	Pte. WIENER, L.
2283	Pte. WINCHINSKY, R.
3066	Pte. WALTERS, H.
3480	Pte. WOOLF, H.
4466	Pte. WITZMAN, W.
5694	Pte. WISE, H.
T/325854	Drv. WHITEHEAD, A.
4354	Pte. WARD, A. R.
1621	Pte. WEINGROVE, A.
2706	Cpl. WALTERS, L.
6057	Pte. WILKS, M.
4472	Pte. YACHNITZ, H.
6011	Pte. YUSAN, L.
5998	Pte. YOCHELSON, C.
3967	Pte. YUDELMANN, C.
4193	Pte. YANKNER, M.
6028	Pte. YOZEVOVITCH, M.
3464	Pte. YAFFEE, G.
1654	Pte. YAROVITCH, H.
3415	Pte. YANOVITCH, S.
4473	Pte. ZALIS, M.
4474	Pte. ZAROWSKY, N.
4475	Pte. ZETLAN, A.
4476	Pte. ZETLAND, M.
4477	Pte. ZETLAND, R.
3028	Cpl. ZEFF, W. W.
5999	Pte. ZUCKERMAN, D.
6016	Pte. ZUBOW, A.
6029	Pte. ZWICK, H. R.
5020	Pte. ZICHLINSKY, S. A.
3510	Pte. ZIMMERMAN, I.
3674	Pte. ZERETSKY, B.
4483	Pte. ZWEIG, M.
4478	Pte. ZIMMERMAN, H.
4479	Pte. ZITMAN, M.
4481	Pte. ZOUNSKY, M.
4482	Pte. ZUKES, M.
4480	Pte. ZITOMUSKY, J.
2321	Pte. ZELIGHSON, I.

ROLL OF MEN AT THE DEPOT

38th—40th BATTALIONS ROYAL FUSILIERS ("JUDEANS") FEBRUARY, 1919.

3555	Pte. AMSTER, SAMUEL.	3687	Pte. BAROFKA, NATHAN.	5735	Pte. BLAND, S.
3763	Pte. ASH, ELI.	3739	Pte. BROOKSTONE, E.	2230	Pte. BRESKY, J. J.
3868	Pte. ABRAHAMS, C.	3748	Pte. BROSKY, DAVID.	993	A/Cpl. BOORMAN, D.
3890	Pte. ARSON, GERALD....	3862	Pte. BRITZ, MORRIS.	3355	Pte. BASS, HARRY.
4491	L/Cpl. ABRAHAMS, C. V.	3874	Pte. BIERMAN, ABEL.	3869	Pte. BRESH, ABRAHAM, J.
3491	A/Cpl. ABRAHAMOVIE, H.	3938	Pte. BROWN, REUBEN.	5563	Pte. BARANISKY, H.
3493	A/Cpl. APPLEBAUM, B.	3942	Pte. BERNSTEIN, A.	5659	Pte. BENSTEIN, H.
3802	Pte. ABRAHAMS, LOUIS.	3989	Pte. BURBEY, ISRAEL L.	2458	Pte. BROWN, I.
3794	Pte. ABEL, JACOB.	5578	Pte. BROWN, MYER.	3067	Pte. BECKNOFSKY, S.
5586	Pte. ARGUSH, S.	3450	Pte. BELGINSKY, C.	688	Pte. BOXMAN, H.
101	Pte. AUSTRYAK, S.	3635	Pte. BLANCK, A.	1460	Pte. BACKER, H. L.
6049	Pte. ABRAHAMS, A. L.	6953	Pte. BERG, CHAS. NOAH.	3840	Pte. BLACK, I.
3715	Pte ABRAHAMS, S.	6070	Pte. BROWN, H.	1639	Pte. BLACKSTEIN, A.
1506	Pte. AITMAN, A.	5563	Pte. BARANISKY, M.	3344	Pte. BUTKOWSKY, K.
3382	Pte. AROSKIN, P.	3487	Pte. BLAZZIS, J.	6046	Pte. BRAHAM, B.
543	A/Cpl. ABBEY, M.	3377	Pte. BOWER, A.	6058	Pte. BLOOMFIELD, L.
3478	Pte. AISENSTARK, A.	3945	Pte. BEGON, A.	6476	Pte. BUCHWARTZ, S.
343	Pte. ABRAHAMS, I.	3554	Pte. BILLIS, H.	6518	Pte. BLOOM, SOLOMON.
5651	Pte. ABRAHAMS, S.	2284	A/L/Sgt. BLACK, M.	6519	Pte. BARNETT, HARRY.
3818	Pte. ABRAHAMS, A.	2323	Pte. BERNARD, J.	6530	Pte. BURMAN, GEORGE.
3423	Pte. ARRUAS, F.	3807	Pte. BENZIMRA, G. H.	6537	Pte. BLOOMENFIELD, W.
182	Sgt. AVERBACH, M.	3484	Pte. BERENBAUM, M.	6751	Pte. BURSTEIN, SCHAJA.
6108	Pte. APATOFF, N.	381	L/C. BEO, C. L. D.	6550	Pte. BIERMAN, HYAM.
6107	Pte. AMSTELL, H.	6081	Pte. BROOKES, LESLIE.	6761	Pte. BRAVERMAN, ISRAEL.
6158	Pte. ABRAHAMS, HARRIS.	6087	Pte. BROWN, HARRY.	2485	Pte. BERENBAUM, D.
6274	Pte. AARONS, M.	6082	Pte. BLOOM, DAVID.	6804	Pte. BERCOVITZ, JACOB.
99	Pte. ANGEL, M.	999	Pte. BATTALION, S.	6827	Pte. BERMAN, SAMUEL.
6357	Pte. ALEXANDER, H.	3925	Pte. BARRON, A.	6821	Pte. BERNSTEIN, B.
5657	Pte. AARONS, A.	3689	Pte. BENCOVITCH, S.	6875	A/Cpl. BLOOM, H.
6484	Pte. ABRAHAMS, J.	3034	Pte. BARUCH, A.	6856	Pte. BURNS, MICHAEL.
6529	Pte. ALLEN, HARRY.	1201	A/Cpl. BESTOW, S.	6851	Pte. BRESLOFF, DAVID.
3353	A/L/Cpl. ALVAREZ, B.	3826	Sgt. BENNETT, H. A.	6874	Pte. BLASKEY, D.
6092	Pte. ABRAHAMS, A.	6169	Pte. BARLOW, GEO.	6891	Pte. BROWN, WOOLF.
6091	Pte. AARONS, L.	6165	Pte. BRAVERMAN, H.	6890	Pte. BRENNER, M. F.
6755	Pte ACKERMAN, SIMON.	6298	Pte. BASS, A.	8174	Pte. BERNARD, ABRAHAM.
6786	Pte. ALLMAN, S.	6288	Pte. BENJAMIN, SAM.	1327	Pte. BIDOK, M.
6824	Pte. AARONS, REUBEN.	6359	Pte. BRIGHT, DANIEL.	8228	Pte. BOTVINICK, I.
6861	Pte. APPEL, MAX.	6187	Pte. BLAZ, B.		Pte. BLOOM, S. H.
6879	Pte. ABRAHAMS, S.	6192	Pte. BRADY, L.	8251	Pte. BASS, ISIDORE.
3715	A/Cpl. ABRAHAMS, S.	6156	Pte. BAYLEY, J.	8253	Pte. BLUME, S. S.
8171	Pte. ALTERMAN, MAX.	6335	Pte. BERMAN, MARK.	8274	Pte. BECKER, J. J.
8233	Pte. AARONS, LEO.	6377	Pte. BLASKEY, BENJ.	8279	Pte. BERENSON, LEON.
8241	Pte. ALLEN, SOLOMON.	6366	Pte. BROWN, LOUIS.	8281	Pte. BINGER, LOUIS.
8250	Pte. AARONS, GERALD.	6367	Pte. BLACK, ABY.	8284	Pte. BENTMAN, PETER.
6939	Sgt. ALGER, W. G.	6372	Pte. BASS, ISRAEL.	8285	Pte. BERGMAN, IRWIN.
2011	Pte. APPLEBAUM, H.	6374	Pte. BURNS, SYDNEY.	8288	Pte. BOB, ISAAC.
8970	A/Cpl. AMMER, W.	3565	Pte. BARR, A.	8292	Pte. BENOVITZ, SIMON.
8589	Pte. ABRAHAMS, JACOB.	3526	Pte. BERMAN, J.	8299	Pte. BRICKMAN, HARRY.
8757	Pte. ALPERN, RALPH.	3534	Pte. BERNSTEIN, H.	6903	Pte. BLOOM, DAVID.
9003	Pte. ARNOLD, SIDNEY.	6391	Pte. BENDOFF, ISAAC.	6902	Pte. BROMBERG, MICH.
9344	Pte. ALTMAN, ISRAEL.	6111	Pte. BERNSTEIN, M.	6899	Pte. BURMAN, ELI.
9362	Pte. ASH, S. D.	6407	Pte. BLEICHMAN, S.	6907	Pte. BERNSTEIN, MORRIS.
6164	Pte. ANGEL, HYMAN.	3706	Cpl. BROWN, F.	6906	Pte. BLUMENSTEIN, M.

"Judeans." N.C.O.'s AND MEN—Continued.

72	Pte. BERKMAN, JOSEPH.	3578	Pte. COHEN, PHIL.	3539	Pte. COHEN, D.
1527	Pte. BASS, N.	3572	Pte. COHEN, SAMUEL.	6171	Pte. COPELOVITCH, I.
576	Pte. BODENITZ, N.	3605	Pte. COHEN, LEWIS.	6313	Pte. COHEN, BARNET.
2523	Pte. BRASS, D.	3637	Pte. CLAF, JOSHUA.	6194	Pte. COHEN, BEN.
6926	Pte. BUNGE, IRVING W.	3976	Pte. CARRIER, MARCUS.	6196	Pte. COHEN, ISAAC.
6916	Pte. BERMAN, MORRIS.	3977	A/Cpl. COHEN, NATHAN.	6356	Pte. COHEN, HYMAN.
6964	Pte. BLOOM, M.	2332	Pte. CANIN, H.	6347	Pte. COHEN, SAMUEL.
6948	Pte. BERISOFSKY, MYER.	3319	L/Cpl. COHEN, J. B.	6350	Pte. CAPATOFSKY, A.
6957	Pte. BLOCK, HYMAN J.	3466	Pte. COHEN, J. B.	3465	Pte. COHEN, H.
3331	Pte. BILKUS, S.	3466	Pte. COHEN, H.	6491	Pte. COHEN, HARRY.
6973	Pte. BURNAM, HARRY.	3467	Pte. COFFER, J.	6488	Pte. COHEN, PHILLIP.
7000	Pte. BARKIN, VIVIAN.	3375	Pte. COHEN, ISRAEL.	6490	Pte. CALLON, ROBERT.
8390	Pte. BENJAMIN, JOSEPH.	3556	Pte. CAPLAN, HYMAN.	5790	Pte. CARLTON, H.
8392	Pte. BROWNSTEIN, B.	3744	Pte. CAPLAN, SOLOMON.	6507	Pte. COLLINS, HARRY.
8385	Pte. BRANSKY, A.	3742	Pte. CROOK, SIDNEY, S.	6506	Pte. COLLINS, JOSEPH.
18	L/Cpl. BEER, M.	3745	Pte. COHEN, AUBREY.	6526	Pte. CLEAR, EDWARD.
8405	Pte. BOSMAN, LOUIS.	3455	Pte. COHEN, ISAAC.	6502	Pte. COHEN, WOOLFE.
8518	Pte. BUNYAN, JACOB.	270	A/Sgt. COHEN, C.	6763	Pte. COHEN, CHARLES.
8448	Pte. BRENNER, JACOB.	3049	Pte. CHATOW, M.	6767	Pte. COHEN, HARRY.
8475	Pte. BERMAN, JOSEPH.	2473	Pte. CLIFF, I.	6807	L/Cpl. CAPLIN, P.
8483	Pte. BOWMAN, JOHN.	5729	Pte. COLLINS, J.	6795	Pte. COHEN, JOSEPH.
8471	Pte. BLOOMBERG, LOUIS.	6064	Pte. COUSEN, I.	6801	Pte. COHEN, MYER.
8468	Pte. BOZINSKY, REUBEN.	6053	A/Cpl. COHEN, M.	6839	Pte. CRAMMER, MARK.
8517	Pte. BLUMENTHAL, JACK.	5715	Pte. COWAN, N. F.	6818	Pte. CHODICK, MORRIS.
	Pte. BARUSKIN, WILLIAM.	3626	Pte. CLEMENTS, N.	6854	Pte. COHEN, ISAAC.
	Pte. BLOCK, HY. ISAAC.	3539	Pte. COHEN, D.	2762	Pte. COHEN, A.
8747	Pte. BIRENBON, PHILIP.	3406	Pte. COPELAND, J.	6876	Pte. COHEN, ABRAHAM.
	Pte. BENJAMIN, SAMUEL.	3830	Pte. COOK, L.	6911	Pte. CRYSTAL, ASHER.
8739	Pte. BORDEN, JACOB.	3825	Pte. CRUGMAN. B.	8197	Pte. COHEN, ABRAHAM.
8790	Pte. BLOOM, CARL.	3987	Pte. COMINSKY, H.	8220	Pte. COHEN, SAM.
8862	Pte. BERNSTEIN, A.	996	Pte. COHEN, M.	8291	Pte. COHEN, GEORGE.
8841	Pte. BRONSTEIN, W.	3436	Pte. COHEN, B.	6896	Pte. COHEN, DAVID.
8902	Pte. BRESSLOFF, MYER.	3374	A/Cpl. CAPLAN, W.	6897	Pte. COHEN, HARRY.
8920	Pte. BRUNSTEIN, HIRSCH.	584	Pte. COHEN, I.	6894	Pte. CLEPS, ISRAEL.
9075	Pte. BERGINSKY, JOSHUA.	1583	Pte. CABAZALVITCH, S.	8369	Pte. CAPLAN, LEO.
9060	Pte. BENJAMIN, M.	2810	Pte. COLEMAN, S.	6912	Pte. CLEMENTS, JACK.
9139	Pte. BELSKY, SOLOMON.	2078	Pte. CHARING, H.	6965	A/Cpl. CORFMAN, D
9141	Pte. BERNSTEIN, LOUIS.	914	L/Cpl. COHEN, M.	1695	Pte. COHEN, M.
9136	Pte. BENNETT, H. C.	335	Pte. CAPLAN, S.	6967	Sgt. COE, T.
9138	Pte. BRAHINSKY, ALEX.	6090	Pte. CRAMMER, NATHAN.	5793	Pte. COHEN, ABRAHAM.
8520	Pet. BERNSTEIN, W.	3556	Pte. CAPLAN, H.	8377	Pte. CHIPKIN, DAVID.
8941	Pte. BLACK, JOSEPH.	3646	Pte. CAPLAN, W.	8408	Pte. CIPIN, ABEY.
9332	Pte. BROKIES, JACOB.	2768	Pte. CAPLAN, H.	8400	L/Cpl. COHEN, LEWIS.
8596	Pte. BLOCK, H. S.	3585	Pte. COHEN, R.	8449	Pte. COHEN, REUBEN.
8987	Pte. BEABROOK, ISAAC.	2377	L/Cpl. COHEN, J.	5647	Pte. COHEN, PERCY.
6132	Pte. BROMBERG, WOOLF.	3479	Sgt. COHEN, F.	8469	Pte. COHEN, MORRIS.
9349	Pte. BLACK, M.	5791	Pte. CASSEL, M.	8501	Pte. COWAN, JAMES.
9345	Pte. BLOCK, ISAAC.		Pte. COHEN, B.	6997	Pte. CHADWICK, W.
	Pte. BERNSTEIN, A.	4068	Pte. COHEN, A.	8535	Pte. CHOWCHETT, B.
2208	Pte. BARNOVITCH, H.	6110	Pte. COHEN, M.	8528	Pte. CHAPMAN, JACOB.
8945	Pte. BERNSTEIN, M.	2871	Pte. COHEN, J. L.	8815	Pte. COHEN, DAVID.
9365	Pte. BARONQUE, D. E.	2377	Pte. COHEN, J.	8835	Pte. CORMAN, CHAIN.
6874	Pte. BLASKEY, D. B.	6176	Pte. CASTLE, A.	8921	Pte. COHEN, DAVID.
9364	Pte. BERNSTEIN, M.	6123	L/Cpl. COHEN, M.	9005	Pte. CANIN, MONROE.
153	Pte. BLAZENSTEIN, C.	6162	Pte. COHEN, ABRAHAM.	9145	Pte. COHEN, SIMON.
3265	Pte. BERGER, M. A.	6148	Pte. COLLINS, W.	9147	Pte. CARP, JACOB.
3560	Pte. COHEN, DAVID M.	6279	Pte. COHEN, DAVID.	9149	Pte. CLEIN, ABE.

"Judeans."   N.C.O.'s AND MEN—Continued.

No.	Rank & Name
9157	Pte. CLUMPUS, MORRIS.
9330	Pte. CHAPNITSKY, H.
9325	Pte. COHEN, MORRIS.
8961	Pte. COHEN, MAURICE.
8961	Pte. COHEN, JACK.
8964	Pte. CARASOV, SAMUEL.
8989	Pte. CARPIN, NATHAN.
8993	Pte. CLAFF, ALEC.
8994	Pte. COHEN, JACOB.
93	Pte. COPPEL, M.
9340	Pte. COHEN, NATHAN.
9348	Pte. CRAVITZ, C. I.
849	Pte. CURASH, J.
5703	Pte. COHEN, H.
8949	Pte. COHEN, I.
5695	Pte. COHEN, M.
9134	Pte. CHEPLOVE, A. P.
3809	L/Cpl. CADEROFSKY, S.
8394	Pte. CANTER, ALEX.
9051	Pte. CANTER, SAMUEL.
8485	L/Cpl. CAPLAN, MYER.
6549	Pte. COHEN, ALEC.
6816	Pte. COHEN, N.
6341	Pte. COPELAND, JACK.
6318	Pte. CAPLIN, BENJAMIN.
3894	Pte. DIAMOND, JOSEPH.
3330	Pte. DRAGOVITCH, I.
385	Pte. DOVODOSKY, H.
3782	Pte. DAVIS, A.
6047	Pte. DAVIS, S.
5747	Pte. DAVIS, I. M.
6073	Pte. DORSET, S.
5731	Pte. DACOSTA, G.
5704	Pte. DOBBIN, J.
6084	L/Cpl. DAGUL, PHILLIP.
671	L/Cpl. DAVIS, A.
6147	Pte. DAVIES, WILLIAM.
1359	Pte. DEITCHMAN, J.
6155	Pte DESMOND, M.
6152	A/L/Cpl. DAVIS, G. A.
3449	Pte. DAVIS, E.
6315	Pte. DIAMOND, JOSEPH.
6349	A/Cpl. DROBINER, A.
6198	Pte. DANISHEFSKY, B.
6345	Pte. DOOKER, SAMUEL.
6364	Pte. DAVIS, JOE.
6368	Pte. DORMAN, JACK.
3024	Pte. DRAPKIN, I.
6757	Pte. DAVIS, HYMAN.
6777	Pte. DIMDONE, H.
6776	Pte. DAVIS, J.
6835	Pte. DAVIS, JOSEPH.
6870	Pte. DEGROOT, ISAAC.
8172	Pte. DIAMOND, ALFRED.
8224	Pte. DALE, N.
6941	Pte. DANZIGER, JACK.
1211	Pte. DUDAKOFF, R.
6975	Pte. DENTACH, RUEBEN.
6993	Pte. DANSICK, ISAAC.
8441	Pte. DAVIS, NORMAN.
8444	Pte. DARKE, JOSEPH.
8462	Pte. DROBCHINSKY, P.
8450	Pte. DAVIS, MYER.
8512	Pte. DA COSTA, ASHER.
8500	Pte. DAVIS, JACK.
8518	Pte. DAVIS, JACOB.
8546	Pte. DAIAN, DAVID.
8885	Pte. DUBOVIS, MEYER.
9023	Pte. DUBINSKY, LOUIS.
9063	Pte. DUNCAN, JNO.
9073	Pte. DUBOSKY, ARTHUR.
8990	Pte. DEMSKY, HYMAN.
8991	Pte. DONITZ, JOE.
1379	Pte. DAVIS, J. J.
6198	Pte. DANISHEFSKY, B.
8943	Pte. DAVIDSON, J. T.
	Dvr. DANZIG, L.
953	Pte. DAVIS, N.
2354	Pte. DAVIS, H. L.
4492	Pte. ERENBERG, ISAAC.
3413	Pte. EPSTEIN, W.
5660	Pte. ELFSKY, J.
3043	Pte. ELLIS, W. H.
535	Pte. EMMETT, G.
2887	Pte. ELIASOV, M.
3167	Pte. EVIDEN, A.
1994	Pte. ETROFF, S.
2773	Pte. ELLIS, M.
4094	Pte. EDLIN, H.
6417	Pte. EPSTEIN, M.
6871	Pte. EASENER, M.
8170	Pte. EDELMAN, PHILIP.
6769	Pte. ELLENBOGEN, S.
6980	Pte. EITMAN, JOS. SAM.
8389	Pte. ELSTER, MORRIS.
8415	Pte. EAUELINSKY, JOS.
8481	L/Cpl. EPRILE, REUBEN.
8900	Pte. ENGEL, SAMUEL.
9216	Pte. ELLISON, ISIDORE H.
8940	Pte. ELLIS, W.
9366	Pte. EDELMAN, J.
3581	Pte. FRESHFIELD, W. D.
3872	Pte. FRANKEL, LOUIS.
3915	Pte. FOX, ASHER.
2890	Pte. FRASIER, J.
5580	Pte. FIELDSTEIN, ROBT.
2757	Pte. FOGLEMAN, R.
3569	Pte. FREED, MARK.
3975	Pte. FREEDMAN, MYER.
3749	Pte. FLASHER, GEORGE.
5713	Pte. FARBY, S.
3771	A/Sgt. FOX, C. A.
1580	Pte. FREED, J.
1380	Pte. FLACKS, G.
653	A/L/Cpl. FELDMAN, N.
3033	Pte. FISHENBAUM, M.
3811	Pte. FIFER, G. H.
3444	Pte. FRIEDMAN, M.
6077	Pte. FREEDMAN, M.
6079	Pte. FINKLESTEIN, A.
5726	Pte. FREEDMAN, B.
5727	Pte. FROMSVITCH, A.
5737	Pte. FLINSKY, J.
6094	Pte. FISHER, H.
6095	Pte. FOX, S.
898	Pte. FREEDMAN, S.
1567	Pte. FISHER, M.
592	Sgt. FRIEDMAN, B.
1278	Pte. FRUM, H.
1106	Pte. FOREMAN, H.
2348	Pte. FREEDMAN, I.
5721	A/Cpl. FISHER, M.
496	Pte. FRIEND, L.
6059	Pte. FALK, N.
6116	Pte. FIVAS, H.
6177	Pte. FARBER, M.
6168	Pte. FREEDMAN, NATHAN.
3577	Sgt. FYMAN, A.
6292	Pte. FINEBERG, HARRIS.
6295	Pte. FINEBERG, ISAAC.
6319	Pte. FRIEND, ALFRED.
6202	Pte. FINEBERG, M. J.
6160	Pte. FRANKENSTEIN, I. I.
3691	Pte. FIELDCOVITCH, H.
6514	Pte. FRIEZE, HYMAN.
6515	Pte. FRIEDLANDER, M.
6528	Pte. FRIEDMAN, M.
6544	Pte. FREEMAN, LEON.
6524	Pte. FINKLESTEIN, M.
6780	Pte. FELIX, A.
4125	Pte. FREEDMAN, M.
6805	Pte. FELDMAN, SAMUEL.
6789	Pte. FRIEDMAN, SIDNEY.
6877	Pte. FINEGOLD, HARRY.
8057	Pte. FINKEL, JACOB.
8249	Pte. FEINSTEIN, JACK.
6918	Pte. FOONK, ABRAHAM.
6917	Pte. FINKLESTONE, I.
6919	Pte. FISHER, SOLOMON.
6986	Pte. FREEDMAN, PHILIP.
1936	Pte. FINEBERG, H.
8373	Pte. FOGLEMAN, B. R.
6996	Pte. FEINSON, ISRAEL.
6998	Pte. FEFFERBERG, ISRAEL.
5705	Pte. FIFER, A.
8404	Pte. FORMINSKY, I.
8416	Pte. FINEBERG, MAURICE.
8420	Pte. FOX, SOLOMON.
8419	Pte. FREEMAN, I. L.
8414	Pte. FULLHAM, JAMES.
8402	L/Cpl. FOX, N.

"Judeans." N.C.O.'s AND MEN—Continued.

5696	Pte. Frankel, S.	6074	Pte. Graham, A.	6781	Pte. Goldstein, Jacob.
8445	Pte. Freedman, Walter.	3877	Pte. Goldberg, S. L.	6521	Pte. Gingold, W.
8474	Pte. Finklestein, Jos.	3595	A/Cpl. Goldwater, H.	5837	Pte. Gold, A.
8489	Pte. Fivas, Alexander.	511	Pte. Gordon, J.	6784	Pte Goldstein, Judah.
8597	Pte. Fredman, J. B	3328	Pte. Goldberg, A. I.	2776	Pte. Greenberg, Julius.
8538	Pte. Fogal, Israel.	2103	Pte. Gausten, S.	6329	Pte. Gruberman, A.
8768	Pte. Falkovitz, Bennie.	3629	Pte. Gibkansky M.	3670	Pte. Green, J.
8831	Pte. Fifer, H.	5668	Pte. Gershon, S.	5829	Pte. Gellen, I.
8854	Pte. Figelman, Herman.	2479	Pte. Goldman, J.	1406	Pte. Goldstein, S.
9090	Pte. Finklestein, A.	3678	Pte. Goldman, M.	6806	Pte. Gordon, Abraham.
9042	Pte. Feldman, Julius.	462	Pte. Goodstone, N.	6814	Pte. Goldberg, Barney.
9160	Pte. Fisher, Abraham.	3020	Pte. Greenberg, H.	6836	Pte. Gordon, Harry.
8600	Pte. Freemin, Maurice.	3064	Pte. Godfrey, I.	6833	Pte. Glassman, Max.
8976	Pte. Freedman, S.	2188	Pte. Greengrass, H.	6830	Pte. Goldberg, Jacob.
9861	Pte. Faigin, I.	3761	Pte. Glantz, S.	6826	Pte. Goodman, Louis.
9338	Pte. Freedman, E.	6083	Pte. Greer, William.	6822	Pte. Green, Joe.
	Pte. Falkowitz, N.	201	Pte. Gabrielow, S.	6838	Pte. Goldstone, Frank.
	Pte. Flazman, P.	1911	L/Cpl. Goldberg, M.	8056	Pte. Gerson, Abraham.
547	Pte. Flasher, A.	5856	Pte. Greenspan, A.	8201	Pte. Glisk, Morris.
1128	Pte. Fredson, M.	3546	Pte. Goldblatt, H.	8202	Pte. Gochman, Benj.
1625	Pte. Friede, T.	1944	Pte. Goodman, J.	8205	Pte. Greenberg, H.
3641	Pte. Ginsberg, Reuben.	6120	Pte. Groginsky, G. H.	8217	Pte. Gordon, Julius.
3642	Pte. Goldman, H.	2462	Pte. Greenberg, I.	8219	Pte. Gollop, Michael.
3766	Pte. Goldberg, Mark.	5834	Pte. Glassman, A.	8225	Pte. Gold, Harry.
3815	Pte. Goodman, Israel.	2479	Pte. Goldman, J.	8227	Pte. Goldstein, Sam.
3822	Pte. Goldstein, A.	6174	Pte. Grabarsky, A.	8262	Pte. Ginsberg, Jacob.
3824	Pte. Goldberg, David.	6140	Pte. Goldstein, Louis.	8269	Pte. Grossman, Benj.
3829	Pte. Goldstone, Mark.	6137	Pte. Goldberg, Lewis.	8296	Pte. Goulin, Harry.
3956	Pte. Goodman, Isaac.	6282	Pte. Goller, J. S.	6900	Pte. Garber, Barnett.
3970	Pte. Goldman, Eli.	1891	Pte. Gerstein, B.	6898	Pte. Gibson, Len.
3820	Pte. Goldman, I.	6497	Cpl. Gold, H.	6910	Pte. Goldstein, Myer.
3486	Pte Glass, A.	3864	Pte. Gustinsky, S.	6934	Pte. Gottlier, David.
3814	Pte. Goldenberg, R.	6178	Pte. Gould, A. E.	6949	Pte. Green, Gustave.
3834	Pte. Gushinoff, Louis.	6283	Pte. Glassman, M.	6956	Pte. Goldstone, A.
3630	Pte. Gilbert, Nathan.	6323	Pte. Goldberg, Henry.	3189	Pte. Goldberg, I.
3700	Pte. Goldapple, L.	6321	Pte. Goldberg, Jacob.	6988	Pte. Greenbaum, Isaac.
3895	Pte. Gilbert, Jacob.	6322	Pte. Gillman, S. H.	2809	Pte. Goodman, H.
3916	Pte. Gould, Abraham.	6314	Pte. Goldberg, Mich.	6991	Pte. Goldstein, S.
5689	Pte. Greeph, M.	6317	Pte. Grossman, B.	8379	Pte. Ginsberg, Isaac.
5666	Pte. Grundland, W. S.	6331	Pte. Goldstein, Harry.	8407	Pte. Goodman, M.
5667	Pte. Goldberg, E.	6330	Pte. Goldstein, Chas.	8413	Pte. Gilbert, Sidney.
3099	A/C.Q.M.S. Grossmark, M.	6346	Pte. Gordon, Barnett.	1362	Pte. Goldapper, A.
		6342	Pte. Greenfield, M.	8454	Pte. Goldsmith, S.
834	A/Sgt. Greenfield, H.	6365	Pte. Guberman, Joseph.	8482	Pte. Goldberg, John.
1957	A/O.R.S. Goldman, I.	6375	L/Cpl. Glassen, M.	8492	Pte. Goodman, M.
2241	A.L/Cp. Gorovitch, B.	6373	Pte. Goldring, Sydney.	8516	Pte. Gevell, Max.
669	A/Cpl. Goldman, H. L.	3470	Cpl. Graves, M.	8499	Pte. Greenbaum, Jack.
1402	Pte. Gedslovitch, A.	3998	Pte. Goldstein, M.	8531	Pte. Greenberg, H.
3999	Pte. Gonsky, I.	3367	Pte. Goldstein, M.	8975	A/Cpl. Green, W.
2096	A/L/Cpl. Goldetneck, H. I.	1328	Pte. Golinsky, S.	8953	Pte. Greenstone, H.
		6430	Pte. Gluckman, N.	8590	Pte. Green, Dick.
5682	Pte. Golding, I.	6510	Pte. Gould, Matthew.	8729	Pte. Goldstein, M.
1030	Cpl. Goldstein, M.	6501	Pte. Gordon, M.	8774	Pte. Glodberg, Myer.
6051	A/L/Cpl. Green, H.	6516	Pte. Golding, J.	8731	Pte. Goldberg, Harry.
5736	Pte. Green, J.	6504	Pte. Glimbotski, H.	8786	Pte. Goodman, Irving.
6055	A/Cpl. Goldston, A. B.	6536	Pte. Goldberg, Peter.	8848	Pte. Goldshine, Harry
6089	Pte. Goobler, A.	6535	Pte. Gold, Sidney.	9029	Pte. Gordon, Harry.

"Judeans." N.C.O.'s AND MEN—Continued.

No.	Rank	Name
9041	Pte.	GRETZ, NATHAN.
9045	Pte.	GRUND, PHILIP.
9040	Pte.	GOLDBERG, JOSEPH.
9046	Pte.	GINGOLD, PHILIP.
9163	Pte.	GORDON, JACK.
9084	Pte.	GRESSEL, ARTHUR.
9331	Pte.	GOLDBERG, M.
9326	Pte.	GEEN, JOSEPH.
8960	Pte	GOLD, BARNETT.
8981	Pte.	GREENBERG, M.
2702	Pte.	GREENBERG, J.
1839	Pte.	GOLDSTEIN, M.
8978	Pte.	GORDON, A.
6539	Pte.	GOLDENBERG, R.
	Pte.	GINSBERG, M.
9360	Pte.	GREENBERG D.
	Pte.	GOLDSTEIN, ELIAS.
9352	Pte.	GILDSTEIN, S.
8947	Pte.	GORNSTEIN, S.
	Pte.	GEEN, L.
1322	Pte.	GOLDSTEIN, J.
	Pte.	GROSOFSKY, B.
3702	Pte.	HARRIS, SYDNEY.
3891	A/Cpl.	HANDEL, M.
3903	Pte.	HYMOVITCH, P.
3958	Pte.	HART, JOHN, J.
3892	Pte.	HAROWITZ, S. L.
3255	Pte.	HOLLICK, J.
2362	Pte.	HART, J.
3481	Pte.	HERTZ, HARRY.
3676	Pte.	HUDDLESTON, M.
156	A/Sgt.	HERMAN, J.
5698	Pte.	HARRIS, S.
1390	Pte.	HAMBURGER, J.
2711	AA/L/Cpl.	HARRIS, E.
285	Pte.	HARRIS, M.
2337	L/Cpl.	HARRIS, J.
5685	Pte.	HELLER, A.
2763	Pte.	HARRIS, H.
3844	Pte.	HYMAN, S.
3094	Pte.	HAMAIN, E. T.
1204	Sgt.	HOROWITZ, S.
3543	Pte.	HERBERT L,
3781	Sgt.	HALLAM, H.
2336	Pte.	HUBERMAN, P.
3758	Pte.	HYMAN, L.
1712	Pte.	HUBBERSGILT, O.
2712	Pte.	HALPERIN, L.
714	Pte.	HIRSHMAN, H.
3453	Pte.	HOROWITZ, N.
6103	Pte.	HICKS, J.
76	Pte.	HAMMER, B.
6173	Pte.	HYMAN, HARRY.
6170	Pte.	HARRIS, J. C.
2449	A/Cpl.	HARRIS, M. S.
6281	A/L/Cpl.	HARRIS, D.
6280	Pte.	HARRIS, I.
6210	Pte.	HARRIS, H.
3401	Cpl.	HATTON, J.
1651	Pte.	HOFFMANN, A.
6384	Pte.	HARDY, ISODORE.
6520	Pte.	HARRIS, ALBERT.
6779	Pte.	HERSCOVITCH, J.
6829	Pte.	HART, JACK.
6846	Pte.	HIRSCHSOHN, H.
8058	Pte.	HAFT, JACOB.
8180	Pte.	HANIGMAN, M.
8186	Pte.	HAIMOWITZ, JOE.
6908	Pte.	HARSHFIELD, S.
6922	Pte.	HAFT, SOLOMON.
6952	Pte.	HYAMS, GEORGE.
6985	Pte.	HEMMERDINGER, B. M.
6994	Pte.	HARRIS, MARK.
8378	Pte.	HAMAIN, VICTOR.
8393	Pte.	HART, JUDAH.
8383	Pte.	HART, MEYER.
8406	Pte.	HERMAN, ALEX.
8412	Pte.	HURWITZ, ISAAC.
8425	Pte.	HIZER, ALFRED.
8443	Pte.	HEXT, HYMAN.
8480	Pte.	HENRY, B.
9026	Pte.	HARRIS, ALFRED.
9044	Pte.	HARRIS, JOSEPH.
9078	Pte.	HOFFMAN, JACK.
9233	Pte.	HURVITZ, HARRY.
8988	Pte.	HART, HYMAN.
8946	Pte.	HARRIS, C.
9367	Pte.	HADDAD, A.
500	Pte.	HARRING, M.
3959	Pte.	INKER, HARRY.
5706	Pte.	ISAACS, J.
3808	Pte.	ISAACSON, B. A.
3057	Pte.	ISAACS, I.
117	Pte.	ISENSTEIN, I.
6327	Pte.	ISON, J.
6383	Pte.	ISAACS, MAX.
6522	Pte.	ISRAEL, ISRAEL.
6774	Pte.	ISRAELI, I. R.
6775	Pte.	ISENBERG, MORRIS.
6872	Pte.	ISAACS, J.
8182	Pte.	ITALIAN, ISAAC.
8461	Pte.	ISAACS, EMANUEL.
8456	Pte.	ISRAEL, SAMUEL.
8593	Pte.	ISAACS, HYMAN, M.
8781	Pte.	ISAACS, MEYER.
9166	Pte.	ISAACS, REGINALD.
3574	Pte.	JACOBS, RAPHAEL.
3900	L/Cpl.	JACOBS, M.
3910	Pte.	JACOBS, SOLOMON.
3941	Pte.	JACOBOVITCH, S.
3060	Pte.	JACOBOVITCH, M.
3314	Pte.	JOLKA, S.
2476	A/L/Cpl.	JACOBS, M.
4189	Pte.	JACOBS, A.
6078	Pte.	JACOBS, L.
5671	Pte.	JACOBS, A.
5690	Pte.	JOSEPH, P.
784	Pte.	JACKSON, L.
112	Pte.	JOSEPOVITCH, A.
3069	Cpl.	JACOBS, W.
6119	Pte.	JACKSON, JOE.
6143	Pte.	JACKSON, HARRY.
6179	L/Cpl.	JACOBS I,.
6306	Pte.	JONES, ARTHUR.
4166	Sgt.	JAY, P. P.
6339	A/Cpl.	JOSEPHS, A.
5874	Pte.	JOSEPHS, M.
3014	Pte.	JACOBS, J.
6532	Pte.	JACKSON, HARRY.
6538	Pte.	JACKSON, PERCY.
9350	A/Sgt.	JOEL, S.
6889	Pte.	JACOBS, C. S.
6927	Pte.	JACOBS, ALFRED.
6931	Pte.	JACOBS, M.
6950	Pte.	JACOBS, S.
6961	Pte.	JACOBS, H.
6977	Pte.	JACOBS, J.
3856	Pte.	JONES, B. R.
8439	Pte.	JOSEPH, JACK.
8452	Pte.	JACOBS, I.
8968	A/Cpl.	JONES, W.
3693	A/Sgt.	JONES, R. E.
9083	Pte.	JACOBSON, I.
9082	Pte.	JABINSKY, S.
9088	Pte.	JACOBSON, R.
9015	Pte.	JOSEPH, MAX.
9328	Pte.	JACOBS, HARRY.
8998	Pte.	JABLONSKY, P.
8977	Pte.	JACOBS, HARRIS.
8155	Pte.	JOSEPHOVITCH, S.
3083	Pte.	JOSEPH, L.
2592	Pte.	JACKSON, J.
3651	Pte.	KESSIN, C.
3705	A/Cpl.	KIRSCH, HYMAN.
3709	Pte.	KOCH, ALLEN.
3623	A/Cpl.	KUSHMAN, M.
3914	Pte.	KAMINSKY, HARRY.
2932	Pte.	KAPLAN, A.
3248	Pte.	KANE, FRED.
3935	Pte.	KOSAFSKI, L.
2923	Pte.	KITCHENER, H.
3051	Pte.	KELSON, S.
3409	A/Cpl.	KLEINBERG, S.
3460	Pte.	KORBINSKY, M.
3825	Pte.	KATERINSKY, S.
1499	Pte.	KURLANDER, I.
3519	Pte.	KAUFMAN, MYER.
5579	Pte.	KLEINMAN, JULIUS
3313	A/Cpl.	KEMPNER, S.
3411	Pte.	KLEMBOARD, W.

"Judeans."   N.C.O.'s AND MEN—Continued.

3568	Pte. Krupp, Reuben.	8135	Pte. Katz, Max.	1716	Pte Luboshitz, R.
3865	Pte. Kosminsky, S.	8307	Pte. Kalmanovitz, Sol.	2211	Pte. Lebrach, Jacob.
3011	Pte. Kayles, A.	8308	Pte. Kahn, Samuel.	5644	Pte. Levy, S.
3842	Pte. Kleinberg, J.	8322	Pte. Koplan, Max.	1541	Pte. Lazarus, I.
4224	Pte. Krantzman, H.	6901	Pte. Krupp, Morris.	1236	Pte. Lapping, L.
3779	Sgt. Klein, J.	8353	Pte Kozak, J.	2093	Pte. Levine, I.
5714	L/Cpl. Klein, A. J.	1435	Pte. Koninsky, A.	1663	Pte. Lassman, S.
5711	Pte. Kaminkavitch, G.	6923	Pte. Kudlatz, S.	3363	Pte. Lipkin, B.
1025	Pte. Kreike, S.	6944	Pte. Kleinberg, B.	5644	Pte. Levy, S.
1602	Pte. Kereisberg, C.	6958	Pte. Kurtz, L.	5734	Pte. Lowe, J.
4490	Pte. Kinsler, S.	6979	Pte. Kalinsky, M.	5732	Pte. Lowe, S.
4217	Pte. Klaver, L.	6978	Pte. Kosner, L.	6067	Pte. Levy, M.
5723	Pte. Kram, J.	8395	Pte. Kronenberg, A.	3741	Pte. Levine, E.
6072	Pte. Kingsley, S.	8396	Pte. Kronenberg, J.	3949	Pte. Levy, K.
3352	Pte. Kahn, D.	8423	Pte. Koppenhagen, H.	2338	Pte. Lazarus, A.
3518	Pte. Kosky, F.	6392	Pte. Kohen, Simon.	163	L/Cpl. Levy, H.
3679	Pte. Kaufman, J.	4224	Pte. Krantman, H.	3740	Pte. Lewis, H.
3602	Pte. Kroshofsky, S.	8511	Pte. Kafton, Hyman.	2771	Pte. Lee, S.
1543	Pte. Kaufman, S.	8505	Pte. Koenick, Harris.	3047	Cpl. Levy, S.
1382	Pte. Kritenberg, I.	8522	Pte. Kosky, Harry.	860	Pte. Lyons, M.
1317	Pte Krafchinsky, S.	8713	Pte. Klonsky, S.	3901	Pte. Lorensky, J.
2028	Pte. Kreiger, A.	9184	Pte. Kelsky, S.	2788	Pte. Lippitch, A.
3090	Pte. Krafshak, H.	9231	Pte. Katz, Isadore.	5650	Pte. Lempke, M.
113	Pte. Kossler, I.	9234	Pte. Krieger, Woolf.	5649	Pte. Lazarus, A.
6141	Pte. Kaplin, S.	9238	Pte. Kosky, Bert.	1901	Pte. Lappertin, L.
6125	Pte. Kohn, B.	9270	Pte. Koch, Jacob.	1396	Pte. Levy, L.
2932	Pte. Kaplin, S.	8955	Pte. Krayterkraft, H.	237	Pte. Lipman, S.
1374	Pte. Kaplan, I.	8992	Pte. Kanarick, S.	306	Pte. Levine, S.
1547	Pte. Koblinsky, J.	1673	Pet. Krimkoff, J.	5675	Pte. Levy, F.
6159	Pte. Kempner, G.		Pte. Katz, Ben.	3943	Pte. Levy, L.
2374	L/Cpl. Kolinsky, M.	9363	Pte. Kletofsky, A.	3523	Pte. Levy, J.
61	Cpl. Kosminsky.	3563	Pte. Levy, A.	3544	Pte. Lissack, A.
6316	Pte. Klein, Abraham.	3589	Pte. Levy, S.	5584	Pte. Levy, J.
6312	Pte. Katz, Siegfried.	3686	Pte. Lincovitch, I.	6056	Pte. Lewis, Joseph.
6221	Pte. Kapshut, H.	3753	Pte. Lifsbitz, Jacob.	5581	Pte. Lewis, J.
6334	Pte. Kurland, Max.	3806	Pte. Levy, S.	269	Sgt. Lewis, S.
5683	Pte. Kerstein, M.	3886	L/Sgt. Lebrovitch, S.		Pte. Levitsky, M.
6378	Pte. Knight, L.	3929	Pte. Levene, Nathan.		Pte. Lyons, J. J.
6379	Pte. Kline, H.	3964	Pte. Levine, J.	1683	Pte. Leiter, S.
6485	Pte. Kopple, Samuel.	3954	Pte. Levitt, M.	6109	Pte. Levy, Z.
6508	Pte. Kramer, Joseph.	2717	Pte. Lewis, H.	6127	Pte. Levy, A.
6549	Pte. Kelmanofsky, S.	3394	Pte. Lewis, P.	6128	A/Sgt. Luber, M.
6753	Pte. Kirschenbaum, A. M.	3542	Pte. Lithman, J.*	2491	L/Cpl. Lubel, J.
5877	Pte. Kanbrowitz, S.	3664	Pte. Longman, S. H.	3750	Pte. Latner, A.
6753	Pte. Karminsky, A.	3990	Pte. Levison, Woolf.	6278	Pte Lebanofsky, H.
6785	Pte. Kellen, Joseph.	1033	Cpl. Levy, B.	3299	Pte. Lazarus, H. R.
6812	Pte. Kaufman, Reuben.	3301	Pte. Lutsky, E.	6146	Pte. Lewis, Isaac.
6823	Pte. Kales, Samuel.	3528	Pte. Latinsky, E.	6157	Pte. Lambert, C. H.
6843	Pte. Katz, Benjamin.	3508	Pte. Liansky, M.	6483	Pte. Levinson, S.
6858	Pte. Koningberg, N.	3459	Pte. Levy, I.	3309	L/Cpl. Lishak, A.
1647	Pte. Kalman, I.	3499	Pte. Lazarus, L.	6184	Pte. Lipshitz, M.
6141	Pte. Kaplin, S.	3887	A/Cpl. Lewis, Jack.	6285	Pte. Laber, S.
4221	Pte. Koblowitz, N.	3713	Cpl. Lyons, I.	6179	Pte. Laskie, William.
6882	Pte. Kleinhorn, Max.	2944	Pte. Lindenauer, Max.	3652	Pte. Levy, H.
6936	Pte. Kirsch, Abraham.	3680	Pte. Lazarus, M.	6284	Pte. Lass, A.
8088	Pte. Kassel, Abraham.	283	A/Cpl. Levy, M.	6293	Pte. Lichter, Charles.

"Judeans."   **N.C.O.'s AND MEN**—Continued.

6309	Pte. LEWIS, ISAAC.	6955	Pte. LOVE, MAURICE.	635	Pte. MARKS, M.
6310	Pte. LESSMAN, JOSEPH.	3873	Pte. LIPNER, ISAAC.	3557	Pte. MYLOSKI, L.
6303	Pte. LEVY, A.	6984	Pte. LEWIS, SAM.	6063	Pte. MALINA, S.
1886	Pte. LEVENE, S.	6982	Pte. LEVY, LIONEL.	5741	Pte. MUNCHICK, S. A.
6229	Pte. LIPSHITZ, A.	8411	Pte. LECASKY, LEWIS.	5735	Pte. MORRIS, S.
6230	Pte. LEDERMAN, N.	8403	L/Cpl. LIBGATE, H.	5748	Pte. MASSING, M.
6150	Pte. LYONS, ISAAC.		Pte. LAZARUS, L.	6068	Pte. MYERS, A.
6333	Pte. LEVY, MORRIS.	8440	Pte. LISABRAM, BEN.	3361	C.S.M. MORRIS, B.
6340	Pte. LACEY, JACK.	8435	Pte. LEVINE, B.	3581	L/Cpl. MOSES, J.
6363	Pte. LEWIS, HARRY.	8437	Pte. LEFCOVITCH, M.	3694	Pte. MARKOVITCH, J.
6376	Pte. LYONS, ARNOLD.	2012	Pte. LEVINE, MAX.	3540	Pte. MICHAELS, H.
6354	Pte. LANG, ROBERT.	8473	Pte. LEVY, ISAAC.	3881	Pte. MILLER, M.
815	Sgt. LAZARUS, R.	3995	Pte. LIBMAN, A.	3046	A/Sgt. MARCUS, S.
6389	Pte. LEBOR, BARNEY.	2445	Pte. LIEBISKI, L.	3801	Pte. MORRIS, N.
3617	Pte. LEVY, J.	8466	L/Cpl. LEVINSKY, ALEC.	2453	A/Sgt. MORRIS, G. H.
6388	Pte. LASKY, I.	8524	Pte. LUBELSKY, WOOLF.	5708	Pte. MOSBAUM, A.
6393	Pte. LERNER, S.	8503	Pte. LEVY, CHARLES.	956	L/Cpl. MINCOVITCH, B.
6496	Cpl. LEWIS, E.	8490	Pte. LICKERMAN, P.	355	Pte. MATUSIAK, H.
6487	Pte. LUSTIG, A. J.	8536	Pte. LOCKSPEISER, J.	2775	Pte. MARCUS, H.
6489	Pte. LEVY, PHILIP.	8534	Pte. LEWIS, MYER.	1884	Pte. MILLER, M.
1623	Pte. LUTCHINSKY, J.	8530	Pte. LIPSCHITZ, MORRIS.	1261	Pte. MALLACH, H.
3919	Pte. LEVY, I.	8870	Pte. LERNER, SAMUEL.	2792	L/Cpl. MELTZER, M.
6505	Pte. LEVINS, ABE.	8871	Pte. LEVIN, SAM.	2811	Pte. MELNICK, D.
6545	Pte. LERNER, HARRY.	8928	Pte. LIBIEN, MORTIMER.	5724	Pte. MASS, W.
6541	Pte. LEON, ALBERT.	8874	Pte. LEVI, SOLOMON.	6118	Pte. MICHAELSON, H.
5538	Pte. LICHENSTEIN, M.	9295	Pte. LISMAN, MAX.	1678	Pte. MELNICK, J.
	Pte. LEVY, MORRIS.	9301	Pte. LEWIS, IRVING.	4260	Pte. MARCUS, N.
6796	Pte. LYONS, GILBERT.	9256	Pte. LANDSMAN, JOSEPH.	1746	A/Cpl. MONOSSOHN, S.
1117	Pte. LESSEL, M.	9310	Pte. LEVY, JNO.	3895	Pte. MICHAELIS, L.
6828	Pte. LEVY, ABRAHAM.	9324	Pte. LEVY, NATHAN.	6172	Pte. MENDELSOHN, M.
6841	Pte. LEVY, SAMUEL.	9323	Pte. LAVAN, MAX.	6142	Pte. MILLER, JOSEPH.
1867	Pte. LEVY, J.	8962	Pte. LIBERMAN, ASHER.	6135	Pte. MOSES, HARRY.
6857	Pte. LEVY, JULIUS.	9346	Pte. LEWIS, HARRY.	3786	A/Cpl. MOSS, J.
6869	L/Cpl. LEVY, NORMAN.	9359	Pte. LITMAN, I.	6167	Pte. MARCUS, HARRY.
2015	Pte. LEVENE, AARON.	3606	Pte. LEVEY, E.		Pte. MUSLIN, H.
5743	Pte. LOGITCH, HYMAN.	9369	Pte. LESTER, J.	6287	Pte. MORRIS, L.
3754	Pte. LEFCOVITCH, H.		Pte. LADERMAN, D.	6311	Pte. MARTIN, BERNARD.
1090	Pte. LIPSHITZ, A.	570	Pte. LURIE, A.	3432	Pte. MYEROVITCH, R.
2767	Pte. LEVINE, S.	3587	Pte. MANN, HARRY.	6234	Pte. MISKIN, S.
6864	Pte. LEVY, B.	3648	Pte. MICKLEVITCH, M.	6370	Pte. MOSS, HARRY.
6887	Pte. LEVY, SAMUEL.	3672	Pte. MOSES, ABRAHAM.	6371	Pte. McIVER, SAM.
6886	Pte. LEVINE, MAX.	3757	Pte. MYERS, J.	2385	Sgt. MELLOR, R.
6892	Pte. LEVY, ISAAC.	3861	Pte. MENDELSON, A.	6380	Pte. MINX, N.
8041	Pte. LEBMAN, MORRIS.	3896	Pte. MORRIS, DAVID.	6394	Pte. MILOFSKY, HARRY.
8043	Pte. LEVINE, SAMUEL.	3142	Pte. MENKES, J.	6398	Pte. MARTINOFF, J.
8050	Pte. LIPSKI, ABE.	3541	Pte. MASSER, B.	6361	Pte. MORRIS, ALFRED.
8066	Pte. LEWIS, NATHAN.	3332	Pte. MARKS, S.	6500	Pte. MELNIKOFF, D.
8069	Pte. LUBERT, LOUIS.	3520	Pte. MARCOVITCH, B.	6531	Pte. MOSCOVITCH, B.
8310	Pte. LANGNER, EDWARD.	3795	Pte. MICHAELS, ISAAC.	1579	Pte. MARON, A.
8311	Pte. LEON, HARRY.	2951	Pte. MATUSOFF, S.	6765	Pte. MORRIS, EMANUEL.
6992	Pte. LESSER, DAVIES.	5643	Pte. MENDICK, E.	6832	Pte. MARKS, JOSEPH.
3658	Pte. LEWIS, G.	2471	Pte. MASHLACK, A.	6820	Pte. MOSS, J. S.
352	Pte. LEE, H.	3575	Pte. MEYERS, A.	6844	Pte. MORRIS, MAURICE.
6913	Pte. LEWIS, REUBEN.	3021	Pte. MANTZ, B.	2781	Pte. MITNO, M.
1943	Pte. LIPSKY, LOUIS.	2713	Sgt. MYERS, P.		L/Cpl. MITCHELL, W.
6951	Pte. LEADER, HARRY.	1537	Pte. MILLER, M.	2394	Pte. MORGAN, D.
6954	Pte. LUKOFSKY, S.	2102	Pte. MENVINSKY, B.	6881	Pte. MARSH, SOLLY.

"Judeans." N.C.O.'s AND MEN—Continued.

6893	Pte. Moses, Max.	3692	A/L/Sgt. Nickeas, J. T.	6382	Pte. Price, Israel.
8124	Pte. Magid, Solomon.	6117	Pte. Nagus, S.	6451	Pte. Parenson, N.
8345	Pte. Magonet, Louis.	923	Pte. Newman, S.	6453	Pte. Panzick, H.
8346	Pte. Militzky, Victor.	2753	Pte. Newman, J.	6509	Pte. Pliskin, Simon.
8082	Pte. Michilowitz, C.	3838	Pte. Ninom, M.	6756	Pte. Palchitsky, Isaac.
8370	Pte. Miller, Samuel.	5585	Pte. Nunes-Vaz, M.	1249	Pte. Palache, A.
6928	Pte. Margolsky, M.	299	Pte. Nordwin, E.	6848	Pte. Plotzker, Jacob.
6921	Pte. Mendoza, Elias.	6304	Pte. Newman, J.	9354	Cpl. Panter, W.
6933	Pte. Mechanik, A.	6239	Pte. Nosbrack, S.	8029	Pte. Paine, Joseph.
941	Pte. Mittenberg, W.	6338	Pte. Nathan, Henry.	8335	Pte. Piper, Jacob.
6962	Pte. Michaels, Henry.	4295	Pte. Newman, W. J.	8366	Pte. Pessah, Elie.
6963	Pte. Myers, Bernard.	6482	C.Q.M.S. Notari, W.	6942	Pte. Price, Abraham.
6960	Pte. Michaels, Harry.	5691	Pte. Newblatt, C.	8372	A/Sgt. Passmore.
3511	Pte. Masson, L.	6508	Pte. Novidovsky, I.	6929	Pte. Press, Jack.
3432	Pte. Myerovitch, L.	3620	Pte. Nedovitch, N.	8388	Pte. Polak, A. L.
3317	Pte. Meyer, G.	8093	Pte. Naftalin, E. M.	8502	Pte. Pressman, Hyman.
6966	Sgt. McIvor, N.	8397	Pte. Nadoff, Mark.	8497	Pte. Park, Henry.
6987	Pte. Morris, Solomon.	8470	Pte. Newman, A.	8537	Pte. Phillips, Sidney.
6983	Pte. Marcovitch, S.	8646	Pte. Nathanson, N.		Pte. Povidler, B.
8374	A/Cpl. Matz, A.	8882	Pte. Nyman, Joseph.	8588	Pte. Podgourski, N.
8391	Pte, Moses, G. W.	9236	Pte. Nowick, Morris.	8691	Pte. Polick, Sam.
8384	Pte. Marcofsky, Jacob.	1969	Pte. Nedvitch,	8711	Pte. Pody, Ralph.
8401	Pte. Marks, Julius.	2710	Pte. Orlans, A.	9287	Pte. Porton, Joseph.
8380	Pte. Marcus, C.	5652	Pte. Oxenberg.	9283	Pte. Podrushnick, J.
8381	Pte. Monasirsky, J. S.	6770	Pte. Oleesky, M.	9291	Pte. Pivarotsky, I.
8427	Pte. Morris, Nathan.	2703	Pte. Osterman, J.	9299	Pte. Pecksr, Irving.
8429	L/Cpl. Main, A.	8409	Pte. Ourash, Jacob.	9294	Pte. Paskin, Phillip.
8436	Pte. Morris, A. R.	8523	Pte. Oldman, Israel.	9302	Pte. Pavlow, Ernest.
3583	Pte. Miller, D.	8695	Pte. Ostanoff, Samuel.	8952	Pte. Pearlman, R.
4280	Pte. Minsky, L.	8696	Pte. Oliff, Julius.	8996	Pte. Perkoff, Joseph.
8484	Pte. Marks, M.	9241	Pte. Ostrer, Morris.	8365	Pte. Perzwick, A.
8493	Pte. Michaelson, M.	9240	Pte. Oleesky, B.	9351	Pte. Pilkin, Morris.
8509	Pte. Marks, Harold.	9365	Pte. Olswang, Lewis.	8399	Pte. Pariser, S.
8515	Pte. Minsky, Charles.	9307	Pte. Orinsky, Isaac.	1368	Pte. Quint, L.
8504	Pte. Mapper, Jack.	9368	Pte. Okin, L.	3628	Pte. Rubenstein, N.
8519	Pte. Marks, M. L.		Pte. Oldman, S.	3582	Pte. Rosenblit, Mark.
2237	Pte. Myers, H.	3567	Pte. Prager, S.	3685	Pte. Rosenthal, T.
	Pte. Myers, G.	3675	Pte. Providler, David.	3800	Pte. Rosenberg, S.
	Pte. Miller, F. M.	3820	Pte. Fanasiewich, K.	3923	Pte. Rosenberg, A.
8633	Pte. Mendelssohn, D.	3843	Pte. Pyzer, Herbert.	3969	Pte. Robotkin, David.
8653	Pte. Minnaker, Irving.	3946	Pte. Phillips, Isadore.	3988	Pte. Rosenbloom, I.
8706	Pte. Morrison, C.	3446	A/Sgt. Pickles, H.	3671	Pte. Rosenthal, I.
8823	Pte. Malmuth, Eddie.	1302	Pte. Pickle, M.	3498	Pte. Ritz, Hyman.
9245	Pte. Mills, Emanuel.	2423	Pte. Pyser, Mark.	3521	Pte. Rothman, A.
9248	Pte. Morris, Bernard.	2309	Pte. Penn, Joseph.	3624	Pte. Roundstein, J.
	Pte. Meahouse, M. M.	1707	Pte. Pagel, R.	3452	A/Sgt. Rubenstein, C. E.
9336	Pte. Margolis, S.	5722	L/Sgt. Phillips, A.		
1522	Pte. Mashenberg, P.	6065	Pte. Pickle, V.	5669	Pte. Rosenberg, D.
9342	Pte. May, J.	6066	Pte. Pickle, J. S.	239	Pte. Rolbin, Nathan.
	Pte. Masson, L.	3982	Pte. Pam, Jacob.	197	Pte. Rosen, Jack.
5575	Pte. Maritzer, B.	1554	Pte. Pelerovitch, B.	2722	Pte. Ross, F. W.
2500	Pte. Moses, E. H.	320	Pte. Padolsky, A.	3985	A/Cpl. Richardson, T.
3461	Pte. Newbury, S.	6246	Pte. Pensky, L.	3302	Pte. Rosenbaum, I.
5699	Pte. Negan, J.	3699	Pte. Paradise, B.	539	Pte. Rockman, A.
885	Pte. Neve, N. W.	6050	Pte. Perrysoff, M.	3335	Pte. Richman, S.
2753	Pte. Newman, J.	3304	Pte. Press, M.	6048	A/L/Cpl. Rubens, C.
4298	Pte. Nozyk, J.	6021	Pte. Primach, J.	6062	Pte. Richman, A.

"Judeans."

N.C.O.'s AND MEN—Continued.

5742	Pte. Rose, Morris.	8433	L/Cpl. Rose, B.	286	A/Sgt. Shannock, P.
5522	Pte. Rosenberg, W.	8428	Pte. Ravinsky, A.	1502	Pte. Stillerman, H.
1961	Pte. Rosenfield, M.	8442	Pte. Rich, Albert, A.	2375	Pte. Solomons, H.
142	Pte. Rosen, N.	8434	Pte. Rabin, Simon.	2217	Pte. Shecter, B.
2789	Pte. Rothfarb, M.	8460	Pte. Rosenswike, A.	41	A/L/Cpl. Schlugleit, H.
3368	Pte. Rappaport, E.	8453	Pte. Rosenswig, S.	1092	Pte. Semansky, B.
1428	Pte. Rock, M.	8478	Pte. Rosenberg, S.	1722	Pte. Shapiro, N.
6085	Pte. Rogers, Sydney.	8507	Pte. Ritterband, L.	4403	Pte. Sliner, S.
1736	Pte. Rosenberg, G.	8506	Pte Rosenberg, Isaac.	3833	Pte. Solomons, David.
561	Sgt. Reese, J.	8527	Pte. Ruckovitch, I.	3847	Pte. Sarewski, S.
6105	Pte. Rosenberg, P.	8525	Pte. Rubinski, S.	2738	A/Sgt. Sefton, L.
3927	Pte. Raver, D.	8525	Pte. Rayner, Lewis.	3827	Sgt. Smith, J. S.
5684	Pte. Rebuck, P.	8599	Pte. Richland, A.	3475	Pte. Stockton, J.
6115	Pte. Rosenfield, L.	342	Pte. Rabinovitch, P.	6050	Pte. Samuels, M.
6808	Pte. Rose, D.	8954	Pte. Regnik, Isaac.	6080	Pte. Shaer, A.
6130	Pte. Rosenberg, M.	8598	Cpl. Raitz, Henry.	5738	Pte. Sterne, N.
6136	Pte. Roder, Isaac.	8682	Pte. Resnick, Louis.	5740	Pte. Sietta, S. A.
6134	Pte. Rosenthal, A.	8703	Pte. Raymond, John.	5739	Pte. Shoebinski, W.
6076	Pte. Rose, M.	9198	Pte. Rudnick, Charles.	6093	Pte. Stifman, L.
1275	Pte. Rosen, M.	9271	Pte. Rapporport, J.	4370	Pte. Satilowsky, N.
6286	Pte. Raven, Maurice.	9278	Pte. Resnick, Dave.	2986	Pte. Secher, J.
5712	Pte. Rhine, L.	8939	Pte. Rankchstas, C.	3407	Pte. Solomons, H.
3845	L/Cpl. Rosenhead, L.	8973	A/Cpl. Reeley, G.	2212	Pte. Stein, J. H.
3888	Pte. Reitzman, A.	8986	Pte. Rontal, Mark.	1956	Pte. Starkman, C.
6301	Pte. Rosenbaum, S.	8985	Pte. Ritterband, S.	3026	Pte. Siroke, H.
6337	Pte. Rosenberg, M.	9343	Pte. Rosenberg, B.	3737	L/Cpl. Simmons, H.
6324	L/Cpl. Rosenberg, H.		Pte. Rose, Alex.	2092	Pte. Shrater, L.
4363	Pte. Rushkish, H.	9358	Pte. Rushblack, A.	753	Pte. Simmons, C.
6390	Pte. Rubin, Louis.	9341	Pte. Rick, H.	1879	Pte. Singler, B.
6523	A/Cpl. Rothman, S.	1900	Pte. Richenberg, L.	3600	Pte. Silverman, M.
6534	Pte. Reid, Alfred.		Pte. Rosenthal, H.	5694	Pte. Silverman, S.
6752	Pte. Rudofsky, B.		Pte. Rosenthal.	317	Sgt. Samuels, A.
1668	Pte. Rosenberg, S.	3553	Pte. Solomons, S.	2701	Pte. Sassoon, A.
6302	Pte. Rdyer, N.	3564	Pte. Shatz, Harry.		Pte. Schwartz, I.
6793	Pte. Reuben, Henry.	3588	Pte. Shock, S. M.		Pte. Student, A.
6798	Pte. Rosen, Abraham.	3618	L/Cpl. Solomons, H.		Pte. Stein, H.
6865	Pte. Rose, Louis.	3817	Pte. Schneider, A.		Pte. Sandverg, C.
6847	Pte. Rockfeller, N.	3878	Pte. Simons, David.		Pte. Shear, H.
6800	Pte. Rosenberg, J.	3889	Pte. Schliffowitz, R.		Pte. Shapiro, S.
6860	Pte. Rashner, Gerald.	3908	Pte. Sigarman, Jacob.	721	Pte. Scolnick, B.
6878	Pte. Raisman, Jacob.	3951	L/Cpl. Saxton, Lionel.	3812	Pte. Schlean, J.
2765	Pte. Reuben, Israel.	3971	Pte. Segal, David.	6101	Pte. Sussman, P.
8005	Pte. Rubin, Gustave.	3598	Pte. Samuels, M.	6102	L/Cpl. Simmons, R.
8007	Pte. Rosenzweig, I.	3770	A/Sgt. Sterling, L.	5965	Pte. Silverstein, I.
8017	Pte. Rudenko. Abe.	3524	Pte. Sckolsky, H.	6088	Pte. Smith, Edward.
8018	Pte. Rosen, Harry.	3347	Pte. Shutsky, Louis, J.	6086	Pte. Sullivan, John.
8106	Pte. Rothschild, I.	3799	Pte. Simmons, A.	5749	Pte. Shapiro, A.
8114	Pte. Rosenberg, M.	3944	Pte. Soube,r Gershon.	1605	Pte. Schenawsky, M.
8138	Pte. Rolinsky, Harry.	3992	Pte. Stanley, A. M.	3016	Pte. Seiner, F.
6909	Pte. Rentovitch, I.	3418	Pte. Sagman, J.	2720	L/Cpl. Schloss, L.
6905	Pte. Rosenberg, Jack.	3509	Pte. Semp, I.	2349	A/Cpl. Samuels, S.
6932	Pte. Rabbinovitz, M.	3622	Pte. Segal, Nathan.	215	Cpl. Steinberg, J.
6914	Pte. Rabinovitz, S.	3823	Pte. Schwartz, B.	6104	Pte. Simmons, L.
	Pte. Rabin, Simon.	3948	Pte. Stein, Hyman.	5670	Pte. Schmerowitz, J.
6974	Pte. Rosenberg, M.	2472	A/Sgt. Simpson, R.	5718	L/Cpl. Sunlight, A.
8836	Pte. Reuben, J.	3931	Pte. Sherwin, A. V.	3221	Pte. Shor, L.
8410	Pte. Rubenstein M.	569	Pte. Sewelson, S.		

"Judeans." N.C.O.'s AND MEN—Continued.

1675	Pte. SHEFFRIN, D.	6543	Pte. SEDRUCK, LOUIS.	5978	Pte. SZOTEN, CHACKEL.
2094	L/Cpl. SCHFREEN, H.	6788	Pte. SIMBLIST, M.	8438	Pte. STONE, HARRY.
2281	A.Cpl. STEINSCHNEIDER, M.	6787	Pte. SPENOVEITCH, A.	8446	L/Cpl. STERNE, R.
537	L/Cpl. SCHWARTZGLASS, S.	5520	Pte. STUHLBERG, S.	1601	Pte. SILVER, P.
		1604	Pte. STEIN, B.	8455	Pte. STARAGOFSKY, A.
5648	Pte. SMITH, RAPHAEL.	6773	Pte. SOCOLE, JULIUS.	8459	Pte. STOFSKY, J.
4420	Pte. SMILER, D.	6791	Pte. SADICK, L.	8457	Pte. SATTEN, BARNETT.
5700	L/Cpl. SALMON, L.	6792	Pte. SEDLOFSKY, A. G.	8451	Pte. SONNENTAG, JOHN.
6126	A/Sgt. SEAGER, M.	6799	Pte. SWEETMAN, CHAS.	8486	Pte. SHAPIRO, LAZARUS.
6131	Pte. SYMONS, ALFRED.	6811	Pte. STOPNOTSKY, L.	8472	Pte. SIMPSON, GEORGE.
6149	Pte. STANTON, SAMUELS.	6813	Pte. SMOLASK, S.	8463	Pte. SAUNDERS, A.
6133	Pte. SCHMEROWITZ, M.	6809	Pte. SCHNEIDERMAN, S.	8513	Pte. SPERO, E.
6166	Pte. SCHWARTZ, MOSSY.	6837	Pte. SHERMAN, HYMAN.	8491	Pte. SAMUELS, J.
6163	Pte. SULKOYITCH, H.	6805	Pte. SCHNEIDERMAN, L.	8494	Pte. SONDAK, A.
6153	A/L/Cpl. SINCLAIR, J.	6840	Pte. STARR, MORRIS.	8508	Pte. SINGER, B.
3991	Pte. SHARKEY, B.	6842	Pte. SILVERMAN, SOLLY.	8505	Pte. SOLDEN, S.
3662	Pte. SALTMAIN, J.	6817	Pte. SEFF, J.	8521	Pte. SMITH, J.
3902	Pte. SYMONS, S.	6862	Pte. SARNER, NATHAN.	8496	Pte. SILDEN, D.
3412	Pte. SIMMONS, S.	6863	Pte. STATMAN, JOE.	8587	Pte. STEINGOLD, A.
6129	Pte. SIMON, ELI. G.	6880	Pte. SELTZER, MARK.	8625	Pte. SOKOLOFF, H.
6181	Pte. SOLOMONS, J.	3517	Pte. SKLAIR, HENRY.	8686	Pte. SCHIFF, SIDNEY.
6182	Pte. SUSMAN, MORRIS.	5963	Pte. SILVER, B.	8687	Pte. SCHWARZ, M.
6180	Pte. SHOWMAN, HARRY.	6888	Pte. SKIBA, A. G.	8644	Pte. SENDROWSKY, S.
3378	Pte. STEVELMAN, J.	2100	Pte. SILVERSTEIN, D.	8772	Pte. SHER, ABRAHAM.
2405	Pte. SILVERMAN, S.	8097	Pte. SCHUMUCKLERMAN,	9095	Pte. SOCKALL, LOUIS.
6290	Pte. SAMBURG, W.	8102	Pte. STEIN, HARRY.	9097	Pte. SEIGEL, CHARLES.
6297	Pte. SHERMAN, L.	8113	Pte. SCHLACK, JACOB.	9099	Pte. SILVER, A.
2076	Pte. SAMUELS, R.	8116	Pte. SMITH, MYER.	9103	Pte. SOURASKY, H.
6289	Pte. STURE, HYMAN.	8123	Pte. SIGNER, MORRIS.	9178	Pte. SAMUELS, J.
6308	Pte. SABINSKY, JACOB.	8127	Pte. SOKOL, HARRY.	9100	Pte. SARNER, H.
6307	Pte. SCHUMAN, W.	8140	Pte. SHER, MARTIN.	9108	Pte. SOCOLOFF, L.
6276	Pte. SMOLLAN, N.	8143	Pte. STEEN, JACOB.	9112	Pte. SHULMAN, I.
6254	Pte. STEIN, L.	8164	Pte. SILBERMAN, JACOB.	9114	Pte. STERN, S.
6256	Pte. SNERSON, H.	8212	Pte. SUSKIN, JOSEPH.	9116	Pte. SHORE, M. A.
6261	Pte. SILVER, G.	8317	Pte. SPARKS, THOMAS.	9120	Pte. SAMUELS, L.
6265	Pte. SILVER, A.	8332	Pte. SOLOMON, VICTOR.	9174	Pte. SIMBAL, MAX.
6243	Pte. SUCHOSTAWES, M.	1923	Pte. STEINBERG, A.	8958	Pte. SHAER, S.
775	Cpl. SMITH, C.	6904	Pte. SZLUMPER, S.	8983	Pte. SILVERMAN, J.
6381	Pte. STONE, L.	2979	Pte. SEIB, I.	9000	Pte. SHOWMAN, S.
6385	Pte. SCHNEIDER, D.	6924	Pte. SHECKTMAN, MARK.	8963	Pte. SHINBERG, E.
6387	Pte. SPERO, LEWIS.	6925	Pte. SPECTOR, PHILIP.	8995	Pte. SOLOMON, LOUIS.
6400	Pte. STEVENS, JACK.	6930	Pte. SILVERMAN, M.	9335	Pte. SHAPIRO, M.
6364	Pte. SCHAAPOOL, G.	6946	Pte. SHEIN NATHAN.	8944	Pte. SIRATA, A.
6360	Pte. STONE, ALFRED.	4368	Pte. SAR, J.		Pte. SIRMAN, H.
6486	Pte. SHAPIRO, MORRIS.	3607	Pte. SEGASKY, S.	4407	Pte. SIEGAL, W.
6463	Pte. SEIGEL, M.	6959	Pte. STADALINK, JOSEPH.	4405	Pte. SCHUSTER, M.
6464	Pte. SOLOMON, S.	6972	Pte. SOLOMONS, H.	1228	Pte. SCHNEIDERMAN, L.
6512	Pte. SELIGSON, DAVID.	6981	Pte. SASSIENI, NATHAN.	3222	Pte. SIMON, H.
6527	Pte. SMITH, BERT.	6976	Pte. SARULNICK, A.	3663	L/Cpl. TARSHISH, N. M.
6513	Pte. SINGER, ELLIS.	6971	Pte. SOLOMONS, I.	3348	Pte. TAYLOR, A.
6546	Pte. SINKOWITCH, H.	6990	Pte. SPECTOROVSKI, L.	3492	Pte. TOMIN, A.
6540	Pte. SHONN, MAURICE.	8375	Pte. STANGER, ISAAC.	3841	Pte. TUCKER, SIMON.
3813	Pte. SELINSKY, S.	6797	Pte. SILVERSTONE, J.	3561	Pte. TIMPOFSKY, D.
6762	Pte. SILVER, A.	8376	Pte. SPIZER, S.	720	Pte. TAYLOR, I.
6759	Pte. SABIAN, AARON.	1790	Pte. SILVERSTEIN, B.	6075	Pte. TAYLOR, E.
3552	Pte. SOLOMON, H.	8421	Pte. SMITH, MAURICE.	2999	Pte. TSINOWAY, L.
		8417	Pte. SHUBERT, ISAAC.	4445	Pte. TEPER, L.

"Judeans." N.C.O.'s AND MEN—Continued.

1795	Pte. TELCOVITCH, S.	6970	Pte. VECHT, M. M.	8465	Pte. WHITE, HARRY.
3366	Pte. TAYLOR, J.	8423	Pte. VANCLIFFE, J.	8477	Pte. WHITE, BENJAMIN.
440	Pte. TATE, I.	8498	Pte. VRONOFSKY, J.	8479	Pte. WOLFISH, MARKS.
6138	Pte. TARRAGIS, M.	9176	Pte. VACLENITZKI, ABE.	8467	Pte. WHITE, HARRY.
3965	Pte. TRAMBERG, H.	3866	Pte. WOOLF, JUDAH.	8594	Pte. WINEBERG, B.
6291	Pte. TRUMAN, M.	5658	L/Cpl. WIENER, F.	8526	Pte. WILLIAMS, JACK
6006	Pte. TUCKSCHNEIDER, M.	3543	Pte. WALTERS, I.	8532	Pte. WARSHAWSKI, S.D.
338	Pte. TROPPER, M.	3354	Pte. WOOLFSTEIN, S.	8965	A/L/Sgt. WATSON, J.
6764	Pte. TANTZER, CHARLES.	3462	Pte. WIGGINS, P.		A/L/Cpl. WEINBERG, J.
6778	Pte. TOBIN, J.	3667	Pte. WEINBERG, R.	8655	Pte. WEINSTEIN, GEO.
6873	Pte. TUROVSKY, S. S.	3608	Pte. WOOD, SOLLY.	8723	Pte. WATERMAN, IZZY.
2054	Pte. TEITLEBAUM, I.	3714	Cpl. WOLLAM, E.	8880	Pte. WEISMAN, GEO.
8160	Pte. TROGASH, LOUIS.	1352	Pte. WEISENBERG, M.	9201	Pte. WEINER, ALEX.
8162	Pte TESHKOFSKY, A.	6060	Pte. WILLIAMS, J.	9188	Pte. WEINER, BENJ.
6945	Pte. TAYLOR, MAX.	6061	Pte. WARSHAWSKY, M.	9202	Pte. WATCHMAN, MYER.
6943	Pte. TUGENBERG, JACK.	6071	Pte. WOLFSON, H.	9329	Pte. WEITZENFELD, M.
6947	Pte. TOUCHKNSKY, MAX.	565	Pte. WOOLFSON, N.	8972	A/Cpl. WEIR, D.
8398	Pte. TAVRAGIS, ISRAEL.	5702	Pte. WAGNER, D.	9333	Pte. WEINER, B.
8464	Pte. TARTARSKY, LEWIS.	2727	Pte. WEINSTEIN, A.	9337	Pte. WERNICK, E.
8458	Pte. TOITZ, HARRY.	1720	Pte. WESTOFF, N.		Pte. WEINBURG, B.
8487	Pte. TITTON, JULIUS.	6144	Pte. WATSON, FRANK.	2992	Pte. WALK, M.
9033	Pte. TOPOLSKY, MM.	6145	Pte. WHITE, JACK.	9347	Pte. WHITE, MICHAEL.
9096	Pte. TAUB, ALBERT.	3961	Pte. WISEPART, A.	968	A.Sgt YOUNGERMAN, H.
9186	Pte. TRAEHTENBERG, J.	2706	Sgt. WALTERS, A.L.	1824	Pte. YOSKEVITCH, J.
9204	Pte. TINKOFF, LOUIS.	617	Pte. WEINSTEIN, B.	6539	Pte. YELLICKINS, M.
9327	Pte. THOMAS, SOLOMON.	6294	Pte. WEXSLER, G.	3913	Pte. YARETSKY, LOUIS.
8982	Pte. TEITLEBAUM, M.	6395	Pte. WEINER, ISAAC.	3042	Pte. YASNEY, H.
8096	Pte. TRACHTMAN, C.	5992	Pte. WISE, A.	6999	Pte. YOUNG, MORRIS.
	Pte. TANNER, A. J.	6399	Pte. WILSON, JOSHUA.	8382	Pte. YAFFA, A.
3904	Pte. UNAL, HARRY.*	3876	Pte. WOOLFSON, S.	8476	Pte. YAFFE, S. DAVID.
452	Pte. UDOLOVITCH, I.	3434	Pte WEINER, L.	3955	Pte. ZEFFMAN, AARON.
8997	Pte. UDIN, ALEC.	6499	L/Cpl. WISESERG, A.	5661	Pte. ZEFF, M.
3333	Pte. VINETSK, A.	6533	Pte. WHITE, P.	508	Pte. ZAGUE, S.
585	A/Cpl. VOSK, I.	6542	Pte. WOOLF, L.	2382	Cpl. ZALHASKE, A.
3336	Pte. VITKINSKY, D.	6754	Pte. WATKIN, J.	3972	A/L/Cpl. ZELLERT, A.
471	Pte. VARSOFCHICK, J.	6768	Pte. WOOLF, R.	6272	Pte. ZIMMERMAN, P.
373	Pte. VINBAUM, H.	6790	Pte. WALDMAN, M.	6273	Pte. ZAREINSKY, D.
3533	Pte. VAN RAALTE, E.	6819	Pte. WEINER, HYMAN.	2998	Pte. ZALSFASS, T.
2766	Pte. VENITSKY, H.	6850	Pte. WEBBES, ISAAC.	6386	Pte. ZARNISH, MORRIS.
3420	Pte. VOLSK, H.	6883	Pte. WOOLOFYANOFSKY, H.	1404	Pte. ZUKER, H.
6185	Pte. VINETROUBE, M. J.			3724	Pte. ZELKOWITZ, D.
2364	Pte. VARTELSKY, G.	3918	Pte. WHITE, J.	8154	Pte. ZIDMAN, FRANK.
6275	Pte. VANGELDEN, G.	8084	Pte. WEISS, HARRY.	8349	Pte. ZUCKER, HYMAN.
6320	Pte. VALLEN, ALFRED.	8151	Pte. WEIN, IRVING.	8360	Pte. ZELIKOVITCH, E.
6332	Pte. VIDLER, HARRY.	8158	Pte. WALL, ISIDORE.	8362	Pte. ZADOLL, BENJAMIN.
6772	Pte. VOSK, B.	8347	Pte. WEINER, JM.	1100	Pte. ZEIDMAN, ISAAC.
6494	Pte. VALENTINE, J. E.	8357	Pte. WEINER, LOUIS.	2095	Pte. ZIMBACH, ISAAC.
6492	Pte. VINGRAD, CASSEL.	1922	L/Cpl. WOLFISH, H.	8426	Pte. ZULTAG, PHILIP.
6783	Pte. VAGEL, PHILIP.	6332	Pte. WIGLER, AARON.	8533	Pte. ZOUMERFELD, B.
6782	Pte. VERATSKY, W.	1131	Pte. WEISS, J.	9311	Pte. ZELDIN, MORRIS.
6834	Pte. VIDOFSKY, DAVID.		Pte WEINSTONE, B.	8956	Pte. ZEFFERT, SOLOMON.

* Killed in Action or died on Active Service.

THE KING'S (LIVERPOOL) REGIMENT.

OFFICERS.

2nd Lieut. AMSCHEWITZ, J., 7th Bn.
Capt. ANDRADE, F. J., 1st Bn.
2nd Lieut. BALABAN, I. E., 1st Bn.
2nd Lieut. BERWITZ, C., 19th Bn.
2nd Lieut. BLOOM, B.,* 3rd Bn.
Lieut.-Col. COHEN, S. S. G., 2/5th Bn.
Lieut. COHEN, G. H.,* 5th Bn.
Major COHEN, J. B. BRUNEL, 5th Bn.
2nd Lieut. DUNDON,* J., 13th Bn.
Lieut. FLIGELSTONE, B. I.
2nd Lieut. FRAMPTON, G. M., 5th Bn.
Capt. GOLLIN,* E. B., 13th Bn.
2nd Lieut. HYAM, H. (M.M.), 5th Bn.
Lieut. LEVENE,* N. N., 8th Bn.
Capt. LEVY, W. L., 5th Bn.
2nd Lieut. LEVY, H. W., 1/5th Bn.
2nd Lieut. LEWIS,* H., 7th Bn.
Lieut. LEBELL, F. B., 4th Bn.
2nd Lieut. MICHAELIS, R., 17th Bn.
2nd Lieut. MORRIS, F., 1/9th Bn.
Lieut. ROTHFIELD, I. (M.C.)., 4th Bn.
Capt. ROSE, P., 7th Bn.
Lieut. ROBINSON, A. A. (D.F.C., M.C. & Bar).
Capt. STERN, B., 17th Bn.
2nd Lieut. STERN, J., 1/7th Bn.
2nd Lieut. SEGAL,* M., 13th Bn.
Lieut. SAMUEL, W.
Capt. SAMUEL, F. G., 9th Bn.
2nd Lieut. ZERADI, D., 1st Bn.

N.C.O.'s AND MEN.

Pte. ASH, M.
12953 L/Cpl. ABRAHAMS, M.,* 13th Bn.
21438 Pte. ABRAHAMS, S., 19th Bn.
24595 Pte. ABRAHAMS, M., 1/7th Bn.
7/2434 Pte. ABRAHAMS,* H., 17th Bn.
801410 Pte. ABRAHAMS, E. C., 25th Bn.
86187 Pte. ABRAHAMS, 1/7th Bn.
 Sgt. ABRAHAMS, C. F., 11th Bn.
801299 Pte. ABRAHAMS, H., 25th Bn.
106832 Pte. ABRAM, T. H., 53rd Bn.
3087 Rfm. ARBIS, A., 5th Bn.
65789 Pte. ABSE, R., 4th Bn.
11044 Cpl. ALEXANDER,, A., 1st Bn.
1195 Pte. ARBITER, L., 1st Bn.
 Pte. ASKERWITCH, J., 7th Bn.
380269 Pte. AGULSKY, P., 25th Bn.
203554 Rfm. ALEXANDER, L., 5th Bn.
 Sgt. BARKMAN, G. (M.M.).
1344 Sig. BARNARD, A., 5th Bn.
2099 Pte. BARNARD, C. J., 5th Bn.
2045 Sgt. BARNARD,* L., 5th Bn.
2247 Pte. BARNARD, V., 8th Bn.
267781 Pte. BARNETT, A., 7th Bn.
296443 Pte. BARNETT, A., 7th Bn.
202356 Pte. BARRETT, A., 13th Bn.
68589 Pte. BARNETT, B.,
5288 Pte. BARNETT, H., 2/5th Bn.
65665 Pte. BARRETT, J., 9th Bn.
3685 Rfm. BANDELL, H., 2/6th Bn.
8/7299 Pte. BARRON, J., 7th Bn.
15738 Pte. BARISH, J., 17th Bn.
59803 Pte. BARGER, S., 53rd Bn.
405774 Pte. BARTELSTEIN, S., 2/8th Bn.
380713 Pte. BERNARD, A., 25th Bn.
90496 Pte. BERNARD, L.
27327 Pte. BENNETT, J.
227599 Pte. BENNETT, G., 18th Bn.
 Pte. BENJAMIN, J., 1/7th Bn.
241355 Pte. BENJAMIN, D., 7th Bn.
48517 Cpl. BENJAMIN, J., 4th Bn.
41160 L/Cpl. BERNSTEIN, D., 3rd Bn.
16507 Pte. BERNSTEIN, R., 2/5th Bn.
21835 Pte. BERNSTEIN, M., 3rd Bn.
307486 Pte. BERNSTEIN,* A., 2/10th Bn.
51679 Pte. BERNSTEIN, J., 19th Bn.
86952 Pte. BERNSTEIN, H., 3rd Bn.
5/5634 Pte. BERNSTEIN, S., 5th Bn.
86686 Pte. BERENBAUM, D., 5th Bn.
269443 Pte. BERENBAUM, J.
 Pte. BENSON, R., 14th Bn.
 Pte. BENSON, H.
1466 Pte. BENSON, J., 9th Bn.
359516 Pte. BENVER, 10th Bn.
 Pte. BEESLEY, J. P.
50573 Pte. BERLIN, J., 4th Bn.
29303 Pte. BERMAN, S., 4th Bn.
6997 Pte. BEAVER, P., 2/8th Bn.
8176 Pte. BEROFSKI, M., 2/7th Bn.
12992 Pte. BLACK,* M., 1st Bn.
48522 L/Cpl. BLACK, S., 52nd Bn.
91609 Pte. BLACK, N., 11th Bn.
5111 Pte. BLACK, B., 2/5th Bn.
2727 Pte. BLANKSTONE, M., 9th Bn.
5/5512 Pte. BLACKSTONE, J., 5th Bn.
8311 Pte. BLANK, H., 2/7th Bn.
359516 Pte. BLINDER, M.
4333 Pte. BLOOM, A., 2/9th Bn.
2925 Sgt. BLOOM, B., 2/7th Bn.
267867 Pte. BORITZKY, L., 19th Bn.
11250 Pte. BORKIN, J., 1/5th Bn.
380754 Pte. BORKIN, S., 25th Bn.
62608 Pte. BOWMAN, H.,
11237 Pte. BOANER, J., 2nd Bn.
128976 Pte. BOGARD, I., 23rd Bn.
15706 Pte. BRAHAM, H., 17th Bn.
21941 Pte. BRAHAM,* P., 20th Bn.
48635 Pte. BREMBAUM, S., 20th Bn.
6/1220 Rfm. BRESLAU, H., 6th Bn.

King's (Liverpool) Regt.—*Continued.*

68052 Pte. BROODY, J., 3rd Bn.
380635 Pte. BROWN, A., 25th Bn.
7/7927 Pte. BRODMAN, H., 7th Bn.
269256 Pte. BRODMAN, Z., 7th Bn.
57522 Pte. BUTCHARD, W., 1st Bn.
6202 Pte. BURNELL, A., 9th Bn.
37016 Pte. BURMAN, M., 4th Bn.
38541 Pte. BURMAN, N., 4th Bn.
52904 Pte. BYE, A., 19th Bn.
Pte. BROWN, A.
C.Q.M.S. COHEN, J., 16th Bn.
Pte. CHRISTIE, M., 11th Bn.
365074 Pte. CAPITEL, B., 5th Bn.
58539 Pte. CAPLAN, J., 2nd Bn.
203268 Rfm. CASSOFSKI, J., 2/5th Bn.
52865 Pte. CADINSKY,* H. B., 17th Bn.
80437 Pte. CHERNICK, J.
4001 Pte. CHRISTY, J., 1/8th Bn.
66136 Pte. CLEMENTS, I.
74044 Pte. CLICK, A., 18th Bn.
57708 Pte. CLICK, J., 18th Bn.
28029 Pte. COHEN, P., 1st Bn.
1712 Sgt. COHEN,* B., 5th Bn.
16709 Sgt. COHEN, A. (D.C.M.), 18th Bn.
17176 Pte. COHEN,* J., 18th Bn.
58007 Pte. COHEN,* S., 1/8th Bn.
58006 Pte. COHEN, M., 17th Bn.
37303 L/Cpl. COHEN, S., 1/9th Bn.
91883 Pte. COHEN, S., 11th Bn.
2569 L/Cpl. COHEN, J., 2/6th Bn.
269475 Pte. COHEN,* G., 2/7th Bn.
355023 Pte. COHEN, A., 10th Bn.
37691 Pte. COHEN, H., 4th Bn.
37605 Pte. COHEN, S., 4th Bn.
240790 Rfm. COHEN, J., 2/6th Bn.
108243 Pte. COHEN, H., 25th Bn.
71056 Pte. COHEN, I.,
90627 Pte. COHEN, J.
48599 Pte. COHEN,* A., 12th Bn.
Cpl. COHEN, L., 1st Bn.
5/5568 Pte. COHEN, M., 5th Bn.
8968 Pte. COHEN, H., 10th Bn.
292019 Pte. COHEN, P., 25th Bn.
200228 Pte. COHEN, B., 1/4th Bn.
38970 Pte. COHEN, J., 23rd Bn.
46796 Cpl. COHEN, S. S., 23rd Bn.
18596 Pte. COHEN, C., 4th Bn.
380300 Pte. COHN, R., 25th Bn.
Pte. COWAN, S., 4th Bn.
3057 Pte. COWAN,* L., 14th Bn.
2872 Pte. COLLINS, M., 5th Bn.
48421 Pte. COLLOCK,* M., 19th Bn.
35940 Pte. COPPELOV, A., 1/10th Bn.
4897 Pte. CRUGMAN, S., 2/6th Bn.
Pte. COPNER, A., 8th Bn.
37799 Pte. COLLOCK, H., 4th Bn.

97273 Pte. COLEMAN, A., 5th Bn.
129032 Pte. COPELAND, B.
25376 Rfm. COLLHO, S., 10th Bn.
53047 Pte. COVEL, H., 1st Bn.
1658 Pte. DAVIS, H., 7th Bn.
31156 Pte. DAVIS, M., 17th Bn.
5128 Pte. DAVIS, P., 17th Bn.
1449 Rfm. DAVIS, M., 2/10th Bn.
2806 Pte. DAVIS, A., 8th Bn.
Pte. DAVIS, J., 3rd Bn.
115215 Pte. DAVIS, J., 5th Bn.
5435 Rfm. DAVIES, S.
S/426 Rfm. DAVIES, B., 2/6th Bn.
1640 Pte. DAVIES,* S., 7th Bn.
235221 Pte. DAVIES,* H., 19th Bn.
5554 Pte. DAVIES, P., 9th Bn.
242715 Pte. DAVIES, C. S., 7th Bn.
241355 Pte. DAVIES, B., 7th Bn.
305817 Pte. DAVIES, A., 7th Bn.
82976 Pte. DAVIDSON, G.
331864 Pte. DANIELS, G., 7th Bn.
Pte. DANIELS, 9th Bn.
16524 Pte. DE HAAS, R., 18th Bn.
16525 Pte. DE HAAS, S., 18th Bn.
48251 Rfm. DEMBOSKI, A., 13th Bn.
202601 Pte. DEMBOSKY, J., 4th Bn.
86751 Rfm. DEAMOUR, J., 5th Bn.
75958 Pte. DEMBOVITCH, M. H.
6798 Pte. DEUTCH, S., 25th Bn.
86751 Pte. DIAMOND, G., 5th Bn.
Pte. DIMON, I., 14th Bn.
5128 Pte. DOV, P., 8th Bn.
5536 Pte. DOWN, 9th Bn.
6193 Pte. DONN, V., 1/9th Bn.
70300 Pte. DOBINSKY, S.,
11901 Cpl. DOWNES, G. H. W., 1/6th Bn.
87069 Rfm. DOVOVSKY, L., 5th Bn.
269723 Pte. DOBKIN, M., 7th Bn.
73273 Pte. DORDOWSKY, H., 23rd Bn.
58380 Pte. EDWARDS,* J., 11th Bn.
2231 Rfm. EPSTEIN, J. A., 6th Bn.
23190 Cpl. ERDMAN,* H., 1st Bn.
269467 Pte. EPRILE, L., 18th Bn.
5716 Pte. ELSHER, M., 2/9th Bn.
5705 Pte. ELLIS, B., 2/9th Bn.
67918 Pte. ELLIS, I., 10th Bn.
95362 Rfm. EMANUEL, H., 1/5th Bn.
Pte. ENTBINDER, 8th Bn.
307739 Pte. EICKE, J. W., 7th Bn.
269593 Pte. EPRILE, R., 7th Bn.
452444 Pte. FASS, H., 22nd Bn.
82288 Pte. FALK, S., 53rd Bn.
82289 Pte. FALK, J., 53rd Bn.
65829 Pte. FAUST, H.,
8/5098 Pte. FABIAN, J., 7th Bn.
82431 Pte. FAGIM, H.
380604 Pte. FEIGENBAUM, H., 25th Bn.

King's (Liverpool) Regt.—*Continued.*

6040	Pte. FISHER, W., 1/8th Bn.
3340	Pte. FINEBERG, M., 2/6th Bn.
94609	Pte. FIVENSTEIN, R., 4th Bn.
5299	Rfm. FINESTONE, H., 2/5th Bn.
202365	Pte. FINESTONE, W., 7th Bn.
111566	Pte. FINKLESTEIN, M., 7th Bn.
43815	Pte. FISHER, J. L., 24th Bn.
73273	Pte. FORDONSKI, H.
87267	Pte. FOX, S., 1/10th Bn.
356967	Pte. FOX, L., 2/10th Bn.
202606	Pte. FOX, W., 4th Bn.
13630	Pte. FRIEDEL, L., 11th Bn.
202360	Sgt. FRASER,* H., 11th Bn.
4853	Pte. FRIEDMAN, J., 2/6th Bn.
6/4848	Pte. FREEDMAN, J., 5th Bn.
	Pte. FRANK, J., 3rd Bn.
20/29289	Pte. FRANKS, S. M., 22nd Bn.
69652	Pte. FRANKS, B., 23rd Bn.
201956	Pte. FREEMAN, S., 1/5th Bn.
95356	Pte. FREEMAN, W., 1/5th Bn.
94615	Pte. FREEMAN, J., 1/6th Bn.
40768	Pte. FREEMAN, N., 23rd Bn.
15226	Cpl. FREEMAN, H. B., 13th Bn.
203246	Pte. FREEMAN, S., 2/5th Bn.
	Pte. FREEMAN, H., 1st Bn.
5/4179	Pte. FREEMAN, L. F., 5th Bn.
381555	Pte. FREEMAN, J., 7th Bn.
242280	Rfm. FREEMAN, J., 5th Bn.
108448	Pte. FRIEDSON, M., 25th Bn.
	Pte. FRIEDLANDER, C., 11th Bn.
70053	Pte. FRASER, I., 23rd Bn.
94615	Pte. FRUMIN, I., 5th Bn.
332504	Pte. FRYMAN, H., 7th Bn.
13018	Pte. FYNBERGE, H., 11th Bn.
22690	Pte. FYNE, S., 20th Bn.
	Pte. FYNE, I., 4th Bn.
	Cpl. GERSON, V., 7th Bn.
112726	Pte. GEUSE, H., 7th Bn.
858	Pte. GILL, R., 4th Bn.
204357	Pte. GILBERT, H., 7th Bn.
	Pte. GILLMAN, A., 3rd Bn.
10566	Pte. GILLETT, A., 1st Bn.
57708	Pte. GLICK, J., 18th Bn.
8213	Pte. GLICKMAN, D., 2/7th Bn.
5120	Pte. GLASKIE, E., 5th Bn.
269497	Pte. GLUCKMAN, D., 2/6th Bn.
4275	Pte. GLASS, J., 4th Bn.
23326	Pte. GLASS, P., 5th Bn.
90253	Pte. GLASS, W., 5th Bn.
32061	Pte. GLASS, G., 1st Bn.
91473	Pte. GLASSER, B., 25th Bn.
41679	Pte. GLASSMAN, D., 21st Bn.
22092	Cpl. GLASSMAN,* A., 13th Bn.
91523	Pte. GLASSBERG, E.
80261	Pte. GLACK, S., 29th Bn.
1781	Pte. GOLD,* J., 1st Bn.
22542	Pte. GOLDBERG, I.
58399	Pte. GOLDBERG, P., 13th Bn.
113189	Pte. GOLDBERG, J., 7th Bn.
85316	Pte. GOLDBERG,* E., 1st Bn.
64923	Pte. GOLDMAN, A., 1/8th Bn.
10645	Pte. GOLDMAN,* H., 3rd Bn.
380213	Pte. GOLDMAN, S., 25th Bn.
87057	Rfm. GOLDMAN, B., 5th Bn.
44268	Pte. GOLDSTONE, M. H., 2/10th Bn.
4788	Rfm. GOLDSTONE, P.,
242176	Pte. GOLDSTONE, L., 2/6th Bn.
380399	Pte. GOLDSTONE, J., 25th Bn.
37150	Pte. GOLDSTONE, J., 4th Bn.
51561	Pte. GOLDSTONE, A., 17th Bn.
240091	Pte. GOULDSTONE, L., 5th Bn.
94417	Pte. GOLDSTEIN, B., 13th Bn.
94417	Pte. GOLDSTEIN,
3/42599	Rfm. GOLDWATER, S. H., 18th Bn.
37283	Pte. GOLDWASSER, 4th Bn.
359272	Pte. GOODMAN, H., 2/10th Bn.
45191	Pte. GOODMAN, H., 23rd Bn.
37518	Pte. GOODMAN, E., 4th Bn.
	Sgt. GOODMAN, J.,
202589	Pte. GOODBREAD, G., 7th Bn.
62324	Pte. GOULD, H.
51679	L/Cpl. GORDON, T., 2/6th Bn.
380098	Cpl. GOULD, M., 25th Bn.
37613	Pte. GORDON, H., 4th Bn.
81744	Pte. GRED, N.
358577	Pte. GREENBAUM, S., 1/10th Bn.
202417	Pte. GREENBERG, R., 2/5th Bn.
49352	Rfm. GUNDER, M., 4th Bn.
	Pte. GREENBAUM, A., 2nd Bn.
	Pte. GRABOIS, L., 9th Bn.
359741	Pte. GROSSMAN, 10th Bn.
381076	Pte. GRUGMAN, D., 25th Bn.
68841	Pte. GREENBERG, J., 23rd Bn.
68501	Pte. GREENBERG, H., 23rd Bn.
267783	Pte. GREEN, S., 7th Bn.
112342	Pte. GREENBERG, P., 5th Bn.
13002	Pte. HARRIS, L., 11th Bn.
51678	Pte. HARRIS, J. H., 19th Bn.
357619	Pte. HARRIS, H. A., 2/10th Bn.
2447	Pte. HARRIS, J., 8th Bn.
381787	Pte. HARRIS, A., 25th Bn.
3467	Cpl. HARRIS, I.,
55306	Pte. HARRIS, R., 25th Bn.
380201	Pte. HARRIS, S., 25th Bn.
3044	Pte. HARRIS, J., 6th Bn.
8932	Pte. HARRIS, T., 10th Bn.
5/2110	Rfm. HARRIS, L., 5th Bn.
202387	Pte. HARRISON, S.
37701	Pte. HALPIN, J., 4th Bn.
	Cpl. HAMPTON, J., 2nd Bn.
68697	Cpl. HERWALD, R.
8984	Pte. HEWITSON, J., 1st Bn.
31156	Pte. HERMAN, L., 17th Bn.

King's (Liverpool) Regt.—*Continued.*

52943	Rfm. HERMAN, L. D., 2/7th Bn.
202209	Pte. HERZEL,* M., 1/6th Bn.
	Pte. HELLER, J., 2nd Bn.
2755	Pte. HEILBRON, G., 6th Bn.
91967	Pte. HILLMAN, L., 5th Bn.
5601	Pte. HORNBY, G. C., 1/7th Bn.
87357	Pte. HUFF, A., 13th Bn.
42173	Pte. HYAM, S.
1096	Sgt. HYAM, H., 6th Bn.
380651	Pte. HYAMS, H., 25th Bn.
4572	Rfm. HYMAN, H., 6th Bn.
107777	Pte. HYMAN, 5th Bn.
45004	Pte. ISAACSON, 23rd Bn.
28171	Pte. ISAACS,* L., 1st Bn.
29832	Pte. ISAACS, E., 12th Bn.
96412	L/Cpl. ISAACS, F. J., 1/5th Bn.
235588	Rfm. ISAACS, J., 1/5th Bn.
202608	Pte. ISAACS, 4th Bn.
15544	Pte. ISAACS, F. H., 18th Bn.
82139	Pte. INGRAM, W., 7th Bn.
8412	Pte. ISRAEL, C., 2/7th Bn.
331702	Pte. JACOBS, M., 1/9th Bn.
106829	Pte. JACOBS, E., 5th Bn.
	Pte. JACOBS, E. P., 2nd Bn.
2738	Pte. JACOBS, A., 6th Bn.
7/8064	Pte. JACOBS, M., 7th Bn.
405990	Pte. JACOBS, 26th Bn.
	Pte. JACOBS, I., 3rd Bn.
358922	Pte. JACOBSON, M., 2/10th Bn.
64444	Pte. JACOBSON, B., 22nd Bn.
	Pte. JACOBSON, A. D.
51675	Pte. JACOBSON, S., 19th Bn.
357296	Pte. JACOBSON, J. M., 2/10th Bn.
11790	Cpl. JALOFSKY, H.
	Pte. JACKSON, A., 5th Bn.
204838	Pte. JAY, P. S., 5th Bn.
2282	Pte. JOSEPH, I., 5th Bn.
74556	Pte. JOSEPHS, J., 23rd Bn.
269687	Pte. KAZER, I., 2/7th Bn.
8315	Pte. KAVONIC, I., 2/7th Bn.
68469	Pte. KARAVITCH, J., 3rd Bn.
37750	Pte. KAVEASKY, J., 4th Bn.
6018	Pte. KAYE,* H., 10th Bn.
380273	Pte. KERSHNER, S., 25th Bn.
77591	Pte. KELLETT, G., 23rd Bn.
8170	Pte. KITOFSKI, S., 2/7th Bn.
40183	Pte. KIMERLANSKI, H., 3rd Bn.
380592	Pte. KLEIN, J., 25th Bn.
67164	Pte. KNIT, E.,
34674	Pte. KRELL, S., 3rd Bn.
380279	Pte. KROLL, M., 25th Bn.
6204	Pte. KUDANSKI, H., 17th Bn.
2107	Pte. LAPPIN,* M., 7th Bn.
359297	Pte. LAPPIN, B., 1/10th Bn.
332697	Pte. LAZARUS, A., 1/6th Bn.
360136	Pte. LAZARUS,* B., 1/10th Bn.
	Pte. LAZARUS, A., 2nd Bn.
65296	Pte. LAZARUS, H.
2727	Pte. LAZARUS, J., 6th Bn.
35454	Pte. LANSKIN, J., 23rd Bn.
44307	Pte. LAGINSKY, S., 24th Bn.
332697	Rfm. LAZAROVITCH, L., 1/6th Bn.
11790	Pte. LABOFSKY, H., 1st Bn.
38298	Pte. LEVI, H.,
68205	Pte. LEVY, H., 23rd Bn.
4755	Pte. LEVY, L., 9th Bn.
68309	Pte. LEVY, J., 3rd Bn.
108477	Sgt. LEVY, H., 25th Bn.
82758	Pte. LEVY, D., 25th Bn.
201466	Q.M.S. LEVY, A.
5198	Pte. LEVY, A., 3/5th Bn.
66051	Pte. LEVY, H., 7th Bn.
358452	Pte. LEVY, S. (M.M.), 1/10th Bn.
202790	Sgt. LEVEY, L., 1/5th Bn.
35963	Pte. LEVEY, A., 1/10th Bn.
108477	Sgt. LEVEY,* H., 25th Bn.
308776	L/Cpl. LEVEY,* J., 1/6th Bn.
8152	Pte. LIVINGSTONE, N.
56859	Pte. LEVINE, A., 3rd Bn.
68206	Pte. LEVINE, S., 23rd Bn.
23333	L/Cpl. LEVINE, A., 4th Bn.
5/5558	Rfm. LEVINE, D., 5th Bn.
53180	Pte. LEVIN,* A., 1st Bn.
37502	Pte. LEVCOVITCH, A., 4th Bn.
42964	Pte. LEVINSKY, S., 3rd Bn.
44307	Pte. LEGINSKY, S., 23rd Bn.
18972	Pte. LEBA, H.
	Pte. LEDERMAN, D., 1st Bn.
	L/Cpl. LEWIS, H., 6th Bn.
87283	Rfm. LECOUSKY, 5th Bn.
8479	Rfm. LEES, R., 5th Bn.
36681	Pte. LERN, F., 23rd Bn.
73370	Pte. LEAKE, A. C.
2544	Pte. LEWIS, A., 1/9th Bn.
35824	Pte. LEFT, D., 18th Bn.
59090	L/Cpl. LIZA, M., 14th Bn.
16539	Pte. LIPSON,* S., 18th Bn.
17635	Pte. LIPTON,* S. H., 19th Bn.
4087	Pte. LINDER, P., 19th Bn.
51713	Pte. LIPSON, H., 20th Bn.
358933	Pte. LIBERMAN, M., 1/10th Bn.
5384	Pte. LIZARS, H., 4th Bn.
94609	Pte. LIVINGSTONE, H., 4th Bn.
68444	Pte. LIPSHAW, C., 3rd Bn.
34616	Pte. LIEBESCHITZ, R., 21st Bn.
37350	Pte. LIND, S., 4th Bn.
405828	Pte. LOMONOSOFF, I., 23rd Bn.
57213	Pte. LUSTGARTEN, S., 3rd Bn.
22763	Pte. LONDON, M., 20th Bn.
5057	Cpl. LOVESTONE, H., 2/10th Bn.
	Pte. LYONS, B., 1st Bn.
70404	Pte. LYONS, S., 23rd Bn.
307103	Pte. MARKS, H., 7th Bn.
48743	Pte. MARKS,* J., 13th Bn.
4766	Pte. MARKS, H., 1/8th Bn.

King's (Liverpool) Regt.—*Continued.*

11249	L./Cpl. MAYBLOOM, S., 1st Bn.
201185	Rfm. MAGINSKY,* S., 2/5th Bn.
204358	Rfm. MATHESON, H., 1/5th Bn.
2647	Pte. MAURICE, L., 9th Bn.
51529	Pte. MARCUS, B., 4th Bn.
5560	Pte. MAGGID, A., 9th Bn.
87967	Pte. MARIENBERG,* A. G., 13th Bn.
202041	Rfm. MAZAKOFF,* B., 5th Bn.
112822	Pte. McKENNA, K.
243872	Rfm. MESLOFF, S., 7th Bn.
5717	Rfm. MEROVITCH, M., 2/9th Bn.
86052	Pte. MENDEL, S.
90658	Pte. MENDELSON, H., 7th Bn.
380626	Pte. MENTEL, M., 12th Bn.
86278	Pte. MESSIAS, J., 18th Bn.
90208	Pte. MILLER, N., 5th Bn.
84916	Rfm. MICHAELS, M., 3rd Bn.
22773	Pte. MICHAEL, D.
46224	Pte. MIHALLOVITCH, D.
5525	Rfm. MISTOPSKI, L., 2/9th Bn.
332503	L/Cpl. MICKALOFSKY, H., 1st Bn.
29198	Pte. MORRIS, G., 17th Bn.
4132	Rfm. MORRIS, M., 1/6th Bn.
51647	Pte. MORRIS,* A., 17th Bn.
53038	Pte. MORRIS, L., 17th Bn.
	Pte. MORRIS, I., 9th Bn.
20253	Pte. MORRIS, W., 5th Bn.
69429	Pte. MOSES, D., 23rd Bn.
82880	Pte. MOSES, L., 25th Bn.
60410	Pte. MORED, D.,
90208	Pte. MULLEIN, 5th Bn.
47264	Rfm. MUSCOVITCH, A., 2/6th Bn.
9064	Pte. MYERS, J., 9th Bn.
	Cpl. MYERS, M., 1st Bn.
49339	Pte. MYERS, A., 4th Bn.
202381	Pte. MYERS, H., 1st Bn.
29288	Pte. MYERS, B., 22nd Bn.
5316	Rfm. MYERS, H., 2/5th Bn.
78365	Pte. MYERSON, H.
204355	Rfm. NATHANSON, H., 5th Bn.
202188	Rfm. NAGELKOP, 4th Bn.
12997	Rfm. NEWMAN, S., 11th Bn.
11250	Rfm. NEWMAN, S., 11th Bn.
6683	Rfm. NEY, S. R. C., 2/10th Bn.
51112	L/Cpl. NEIBERG,* H., 1/8th Bn.
105505	Pte. NELSON, R., 1/7th Bn.
4691	Rfm. NEURICK, I., 5th Bn.
4204	Rfm. NIEMEER, R., 1/6th Bn.
97383	Pte. NIMAN, I., 25th Bn.
	Pte. NICHOLSON, M., 10th Bn.
242508	Rfm. NIEMAN, R., 5th Bn.
51343	Rfm. NOSSEL, H., 1/7th Bn.
58039	Pte. NOORDON, E., 17th Bn.
	Pte. OWENS, J., 2nd Bn.
5538	Pte. ORMIANA, D., 8th Bn.
	Pte. PALMER, J., 2nd Bn.
45065	L/Cpl. PASERSKY, A., 23rd Bn.
61785	Pte. PATNICK, A., 25th Bn.
46612	Pte. PEARL, I., 1st Bn.
5293	Rfm. PETER, H., 2/5th Bn.
380859	Pte. PETER, P., 25th Bn.
4876	Rfm. PEARSON, W., 2/6th Bn.
106782	Pte. PILNICK, H., 53rd Bn.
87285	Rfm. PICKLE, M., 5th Bn.
45066	Pte. PHILLIPS, J., 23rd Bn.
11351	Pte. PHILLIPS, H., 1st Bn.
10489	Pte. PHILLIPS, C., 3rd Bn.
37158	Pte. PHILLIPS, D., 4th Bn
108215	Pte. POSNER, M., 13th Bn.
	Pte. POSNER, B., 5th Bn.
55084	Pte. POLLICK, J., 23rd Bn.
44336	Pte. POSKIN, H., 24th Bn.
38261	Pte. RAMM, I., 14th Bn.
21348	Pte. RABBINOVITCH, A.
204723	Pte. RAPPAPORT, A.
30265	Pte. RABINOWITZ, J., 19th Bn.
5078	Pte. RAISMAN, L., 2/6th Bn.
77292	Pte. RASHMAN, H.
8315	Pte. RAVONICK, I., 2/7th Bn.
360244	Pte. RAPHAEL, B., 10th Bn.
81387	Pte. REECE, R., 23rd Bn.
4878	Pte. RESNIK, J., 2/6th Bn.
45951	L/Cpl. REUBEN, M.
61907	Pte. RHINE, L.
52311	L/Cpl. RIFKIN, I., 1st Bn.
92097	Pte. RICH, S., 5th Bn.
	Pte. ROSEN, E., 13th Bn.
78334	Pte. ROSEBAND, J.
57996	Pte. RUBENS, L. (M.M.), 1/6th Bn.
405489	Pte. ROSETE, W., 4th Bn.
269604	Pte. ROSETE, R., 4th Bn.
	Pte. ROSENBLOOM, I.
8222	Pte. ROSENBERG, J., 2/7th Bn.
6496	Pte. ROSENBERG, M., 2/10th Bn.
5492	Pte. ROSENTHAL, C., 9th Bn.
86860	Pte. ROSENTHAL, M., 8th Bn.
380611	Pte. ROSENTHAL, P., 25th Bn.
65319	Pte. ROSENFELD, A., 3rd Bn.
7/6357	Pte. ROSENBLOOM, A., 7th Bn.
5543	Pte. ROSENBLOOM, H., 9th Bn.
5/5131	Pte. ROSENFIELD, J., 4th Bn.
	Pte. ROBINSON, B.
87434	Pte. ROBINSON, J., 5th Bn.
44116	Pte. ROTTERMAN, J., 24th Bn.
203384	Pte. RUBINSTEIN, H., 1/7th Bn.
357599	Pte. RUBENS, E., 2/10th Bn.
204360	Pte. SAVITZ, S., 7th Bn.
201238	Rfm. SAMUELS, I., 2/5th Bn.
	L/Cpl. SAMUELS, S., 12th Bn.
2824	L/Cpl. SAMUELS, W., 5th Bn.
65674	Pte. SAMUEL, H. E.,
3/46574	Pte. SALOMAN, E., 25th Bn.
113213	Pte. SAFFER, G., 27th Bn.
55488	Pte. SAVITZ, L., 23rd Bn.
36854	Pte. SANKEY, J., 8th Bn.

King's (Liverpool) Regt.—*Continued.*

22522 Pte. SCHILLER, J., 13th Bn.
58045 Rfm. SCON, B., 18th Bn.
359442 Cpl. SCHLESS, A., 1/10th Bn.
        Pte. SCHWARTZ, D., 1st Bn.
47265 Pte. SCHWABE, S.
115352 Pte. SEIGLE, I., 5th Bn.
14/18972 Pte. SEBA, H. A., 14th Bn.
47252 Pte. SHEAR, 2nd Bn.
381301 Pte. SHAPIRO, I., 25th Bn.
380287 Pte. SHAPIRO, S. M., 25th Bn.
49340 Rfm. SHEAR, A., 1/6th Bn.
130777 Pte. SHIFTER, S.
359449 Pte. SHEPPARD, B., 1/10th Bn.
21348 Pte. SHYMAN,* W., 19th Bn.
37719 Pte. SHAPIRA, L., 4th Bn.
58044 Pte. SHAVINSKY, S., 19th Bn.
70254 Pte. SHILCO, A.
67693 L/Cpl. SORSKY, D., 2nd G.B.
90633 Pte. SUGARWHITE, 2nd G.B.
49352 Pte. SUNDER, M., 2rd Bn.
380311 Pte. SUCKMAN, J.,* 13th Bn.
38017 Pte. SOLKOWEN, 4th Bn.
37348 Pte. SIMCOVITCH, 4th Bn.
38297 Pte. STONE, J., 4th Bn.
202254 Rfm. SOLOMON, 5th Bn.
11228 Pte. SMOLANSKI, P., 1st Bn.
2313 Pte. SILVERBERG, S., 5th Bn.
80043 Pte. SIMBORSKY, I.
242376 Pte. SILVERBERG, T.
84984 Pte. STEINBERG, S., 3rd Bn.
        Sgt. STERN, J., 6th Bn.   Pte. SIMS, R.
        Pte. SIMON, I., 14th Bn.
6427 Pte. STAMM, I.* (WASHINGTON, C.), 1st Bn.
12963 Pte. SILVERMAN, I., 11th Bn.
12990 Pte. SIMLO,* R., 11th Bn.
9039 Pte. SOLDEN, S., 11th Bn.
14/19289 Pte. SIMONS, J., 14th Bn.
5007 Pte. SYMONS, A., 1/8th Bn.
58519 Pte. STAHL, F., 1st Bn.
42874 Pte. SLIFKIN,* I., 17th Bn.
22264 Pte. STILLMAN, J., 20th Bn.
204143 Rfm. SIMON, N., 1/5th Bn.
2273 Cpl. SIMON, A., 2/5th Bn.
3147 Rfm. SIMON, D., 2/5th Bn.
5282 Rfm. SWEDE, H., 2/6th Bn.
6100 Rfm. SIMMONS, J., 2/10th Bn.
27006 Sgt. SOLK, S., 1st Bn.
105501 Rfm. SPRINGER, L., 1/6th Bn.
28977 Pte. SWITZER, F., 4th Bn.
53231 Pte. SIMONOVITCH, M., 4th Bn.
59970 Pte. SILVESTEIN, A.
65967 Pte. SILVERSTONE, A., 3rd Bn.
381994 Pte. SOLOMONS, H. M., 25th Bn.
380311 Pte. SUCKMAN,* J., 13th Bn.
71074 Pte. SKEIN, S.

50190 L/Cpl. SILVER, J., 2nd Bn.
65821 Pte. SIDEBOTTOM, B.
63969 Pte. SAVITCH, H.
61067 Sgt. SMOLLAN, P.
        Pte. SAMUELS, P., 5th Bn.
        Pte. SIMMONS, A. B., 5th Bn.
2829 Pte. SHANNOCK, B. L., 6th Bn.
4269 L/Cpl. SVARSKY, S., 3/5th Bn.
        Pte. SAQUI, A. J.
200820 Cpl. SAMUELS, 5th Bn.
6/4850 Rfm. SANTER, N., 5th Bn.
5/5161 Rfm. SOLOMON, J., 5th Bn.
5/5028 Rfm. SANOFSKY, S., 5th Bn.
332504 Pte. SILVERMAN, S., 7th Bn.
360296 Pte. SLOMAN, W., 10th Bn.
74373 Pte. SHIVAN, S., 23rd Bn.
8932 Pte. TABOLISKI, H., 10th Bn.
        Pte. TAYLOR, M., 4th Bn.
        Pte. TAYLOR, H.,
115341 Pte. TEIGER, W., 5th Bn.
79343 Pte. TIKLIN, M.
24389 Pte. TIPPER, M., 19th Bn.
1962 Rfm. TOBIAS, S., 6th Bn.
250374 L/Cpl. TORRES, 5th Bn.
11864 Pte. TROPP, P., 4th Bn.
        Pte. TREAGER, J., 4th Bn.
        Pte. TREAGER, E., 5th Bn.
10035 Pte. TUDOR, 2nd Bn.
50401 Pte. UNAL, W., 4th Bn.
92913 Pte. VINGAN, M.
71356 Pte. VALENSKY, S.
359419 Pte. VYNER, G., 1/10th Bn.
202963 Pte. WAINSHANKIN, K.
8367 Rfm. WASSESSON, W. B., 2/7th Bn.
71032 Rfm. WARM, J., 48472 Pte. WHITE, E.
17521 C.S.M. WILKINSON, R., 19th Bn.
5834 Rfm. WEINSHANKER, G., 1/5th Bn.
5441 L/Cpl. WOLFE, H., 2/9th Bn.
4757 Rfm. WOLFSON, J., 2/6th Bn.
269457 Pte. WOODMAN,* M., 2/7th Bn.
        Pte. WOOLF, J.
        Rfm. WEINBERG, 3rd Bn.
        Rfm. WALLACE, D., 3rd Bn.
4299 Rfm. WILSON, H. (GOLDBERG), 8th Bn.
5/4939 Rfm. WOLFSON, F., 5th Bn.
242209 L/Cpl. WOLFSON, J., 5th Bn.
332364 L/Cpl. WOOLF,* H., 9th Bn.
359942 Pte. WHITTIER, J., 10th Bn.
94626 Pte. WEISS, L., 5th Bn.
90617 Pte. WOODMAN, A., 5th Bn.
5472 Pte. YABLONSKI, M., 2/9th Bn.
        Pte. YELSKI, 22nd Bn.
37965 Pte. YOUNGERMAN, 4th Bn.
11057 Pte. ZODICKSON,* H., 18th Bn.
4844 Pte. ZODICKSON, M., 17th Bn.
782286 Pte. ZEFFERT, W. 82420 Pte. ZACKS, C.
59809 Pte. ZALHASKO, A., 53rd Bn.

THE NORFOLK REGIMENT.

OFFICERS.

Lieut. DAVIS, E. P., 8th Bn.
2nd Lieut. JOSEPH, W. G. A.,* 1/5th Bn.
Lieut. KLEIN, A. B. L. (M.B.E.).
2nd Lieut. KONTILI, H.
2nd Lieut. VOS, B., 8th Bn.

N.C.O.'s AND MEN.

203952 Pte. ABRAHAMS, L., 2/4th Bn.
72676 Pte. ANSLOW, J., 1st Bn.
12199 Pte. ABRAHAMS, R.,* 2nd Bn.
12029 Pte. BENJAMIN, H.,* 7th Bn.
26183 Pte. BACKHOUSE, J. D., 9th Bn.
30795 Pte. BARRETT, B., 2/5th Bn.
7182 L/Cpl. BLOOM, H.,* 1st Bn.
47004 L/Cpl. BRISCOE, M., 1/4th Bn.
14457 Pte. BLOCK, A., 1/4th Bn.
21528 Pte BROOKS, P., 1st Gar. Bn.
Pte. BERNSTEIN, I.,* 2nd Bn.
9153 Pte. BRILL, A., 7th Bn.
Pte. BLOOM, L.
37195 Pte. COHEN, J., 9th Bn.
15117 Pte. CARNES, K. Y. M., 9th Bn.
6343 Pte. COHEN, C., 2/4th Bn.
6361 Pte. COHEN, A., 2/5th Bn.
21442 Pte. COPPLEMAN, I., 2/5th Bn.
204072 Pte. CHESTER, E., 2/4th Bn.
330071 Pte. COLEMAN, J., 1/4th Bn.
230535 Pte. CRYSTAL, J., 1/4th Bn.
30932 Pte. COHEN, E., 1/4th Bn.
35835 Pte. CROOK, J. J., 3rd Bn.
32156 Pte. COPPLEMAN, A., 3rd Bn.
28117 Pte. CARNESKY, M., 3rd Bn.
6029 Pte. DAVIS, S., 2/5th Bn.
29818 Pte. DEHAAN, L.,* 9th Bn.
328992 Pte. DAVIS, I., 1/4th Bn.
328504 Pte. DE FRIEND, L., 1/4th Bn.
6348 Pte. DA COSTA, B., 2/4th Bn.
35874 Pte. DONNE, W., 4th Bn.
73900 L/Cpl. DEFFRIES, E., 13th Bn.
34418 Pte. FELDMAN, I., 1/6th Bn.
32143 Pte. FRESHMAN, I., 3rd Bn.
8712 Pte. FOSTER, G. J.,* 1st Bn.
7784 Pte. FINKLE, S., 2/5th Bn.
14061 Pte. GOLDBERG, H., 88th Bn.
Pte. GREENBERG, S., 2nd Bn.
242575 Pte. GOLDSTEIN, S., 2/5th Bn.
330405 Pte. GREEN, H. D., 1/4th Bn.
10716 Pte. GREMBLATT, A., 1/1st Bn.
34443 Pte. GORDON, E., 1/6th Bn.
7872 Pte. GARDNER, M., 2/4th Bn.
7728 Pte. GLASS, A.
12261 Pte. HARRIS, J., 1st Bn.
34639 Pte. HOFFBERG, L., 1/4th Bn.
35808 Pte. HARRIS, H., 3rd Bn.
2003 Pte. HARRISON, A. M., 6th Bn.
6076 Pte. HYAMS, A. L., 2/5th Bn.
30941 Pte. HYMAN, M., 1/4th Bn.
L/Cpl. HAMBERG, S.
13680 Pte. ISAACS, J., 1/5th Bn.
13455 L/Cpl. JACOBS, M., 1/4th Bn.
42276 Pte. JACOBY, D., 1st Bn.
21152 Pte. JACOBS, S., 1st Gar. Bn.
32744 Pte. JACOBS, H. L., 3rd Bn.
Pte. JONES, H. L., 5th Bn.
201922 Pte. KOSHEROFF, I., 2/4th Bn.
243091 Pte. KERSTEIN, I., 2/5th Bn.
302517 Pte. KAPLAN, S., 1/4th Bn.
28124 Pte. KIDDELL, F. C., 3rd Bn.
39585 Pte. KLETOPSKY, W., 3rd Bn.
13578 Cpl. LINDE, A.,* 8th Bn.
29938 Pte. LEVY, D.,* 9th Bn.
Pte. LEE, J., 2/5th Bn.
21652 Sgt. LAZARUS, A., 1st Bn.
32347 Pte. LANCHINSKY, S., 3rd Bn.
34192 Pte. LEE, A., 1/6th Bn.
39640 Pte. LEVY, B. E., 3rd Bn.
34189 Pte. LAZARUS, S., 1/6th Bn.
204308 Pte. LEVENE, L.
35917 L/Cpl. LEOPOLD, G., 9th Bn.
14030 Pte. MORRIS, M., 1/4th Bn.
30954 Pte. MARKS, M., 1/4th Bn.
7323 Pte. LANDO, B., 2/5th Bn.
6438 Pte. MENDELSON, B., 2/5th Bn.
6830 Pte. MATZ, H. N., 3rd Bn.
6289 Pte. MILLWARD, S. L., 2/4th Bn.
34440 Pte. NATHAN, G., 1/6th Bn.
21662 L/Cpl. POSENER, H., 1st Gar. Bn.
41223 L/Cpl. PHILLIPS, D., 1st Bn.
34445 Pte. PRESS, L., 1/6th Bn.
41712 Pte. PELLER, G., 12th Bn.
41718 Pte. PELLOW, S., 12th Bn.
Pte. POOLE, W. J., 4th Bn.
34870 Cpl. RENOVITCH, H., 2/6th Bn.
242186 Pte. ROSENBERG, M., 2/5th Bn.
13761 Pte. RABINOVITCH, K., 1/4th Bn.
252082 Pte. RAFPORT, J., 1/4th Bn.
37242 Pte. ROSE, W. J., 3rd Bn.
76594 Pte. RUBENSTEIN, M., 3rd Bn.
Pte. ROSENBERG, L., 7th Bn.
8/30908 Sgt. RICHENBERG, H.
27249 Pte. SMAJE, H., 7th Bn.
42254 Pte. SHINEMAN, L. J., 7th Bn.
328478 Pte. STEIN, M., 1/4th Bn.
5644 Pte. SHEFFRIN, J., 1/4th Bn.
25457 Pte. SILVER, H., 3rd Bn.
6492 Pte. SUGARMAN, H. W., 2/5th Bn.
28539 Pte. SOLOMON, S., 2/4th Bn.
41269 Pte. SCOTT, D., 9th Bn.
23869 Pte. SCHWATLING, J., 2/5th Bn.
6449 Pte. SOLOMON, O., 2/5th Bn.

The Norfolk Regt.—*Continued.*

5610 Pte. SANDEY, M., 2/5th Bn.
47259 Pte. SCHNEIDER, H., 2nd Bn.
34205 Pte. SIMONS, J., 1/5th Bn.
263837 Pte. SABELINSKY, L.
12120 Pte. TAYLOR, L., 7th Bn.
6734 Pte. TICHNER, D., 2/4th Bn.
34454 Ptt. VENITSKY, N., 1/6th Bn.
9153 Pte. WORMS, M., 7th Bn.
202415 Pte. WOOLF, H., 2/4th Bn.
201868 Pte. WILKINS, V. H., 2/4th Bn.
241365 L/Cpl. WERNER, J., 2/4th Bn.

* Killed in Action or died on Active Service.

THE LINCOLNSHIRE REGIMENT.

OFFICERS.

2nd Lieut. COLLINS, J. 2nd Bn.
2nd Lieut. GIDEON, T. R., 1st Bn.
Lieut. LOEWE, H. M. J., 1st Bn.
2nd Lieut. LEVI, F. J.,* 2/5th Bn.
2nd Lieut. MENDAL, B. F., 2/4th Bn.
2nd Lieut. MYERS, J. C.
2nd Lieut. POSNER, P. E.,* 8th Bn.
2nd Lieut. PHILLIPS, S., 7th Bn.

N.C.O.'s AND MEN.

26971 Pte. ALTMAN, P., 6th Bn.
49550 Pte. ACKMAN, B., 3rd Bn.
42509 Pte. BARNARD, D., 10th Bn.
43024 Pte. BURMAN, J., 3rd Bn.
82903 Pte. BRESLAW, H., 10th Bn.
30384 Pte. BENDELL, E.
Pte. BLUMB, J., 3rd Bn.
8075 Pte. COHEN, S., 1st Bn.
6689 Pte. CRASHINSKY, B., 2/4th Bn.
36838 Pte. CLINE, H., 13th Bn.
6193 L/Cpl. COHEN, P.* (KING), 1st Bn.
Pte. CASNER, H., 2nd Bn.
R3/30940 Pte. CHILD, W., 3rd Bn.
71037 Pte. COHEN, G., 7th Bn.
71056 Pte. COHEN, I.
265048 L/Cpl. CANIN, S., 6th Bn.
202658 Pte. CRASHINSKY, P., 1st Bn.
5954 Pte. COHERNEY, J. T., 4th Bn.
62603 Pte. COHEN, L.
20702 Pte. COHEN, A., 2/4th Bn.
26482 Pte. DAVIES, W.
8073 Pte. DELEW, M., 12th Bn.
202662 Pte. DONSKIE, J., 8th Bn.
26482 Sgt. DAVIES, J., 2nd Gar. Bn.
2351 Pte. DALEFUENTA, L., 8th Bn.
6346 Pte. DONNER, A., 4th Bn.
44275 Pte. DONBOSKY, M.
52116 Pte. ESHWIGE,

29804 Pte. FREEDMAN, C., 14th Bn.
47027 Cpl. FLATTON, 7th Bn.
7986 Pte. FRANKLIN, J., 1st Bn.
41942 Pte. FREEDMAN, B., 6th Bn.
39804 Pte. FIELDMAN, C., 14th Bn.
44717 Pte. FRASER, A.
41245 Pte. GOLDNER, A., 10th Bn.
6869 Pte. GLANTS, M., 2/4th Bn.
235288 Pte. GOODMAN, H., 2/4th Bn.
202666 Pte. GOODMAN, A., 2/4th Bn.
202822 Pte. GOLDBERG, J., 4th Bn.
30723 Pte. HYMAN, B.,* 2nd Bn.
235190 Pte. HERMAN, S., 8th Bn.
39943 Pte. HENRY, N., 15th Bn.
241355 Pte. ISSITT, G., 8th Bn.
7146 Cpl. HARDING, A., 1st Bn.
5996 Pte. HOFFMAN, H., 4th Bn.
19611 Pte. ISAACS, A., 1st Gar. Bn.
266530 Pte. JACKSON, G., 13th Bn.
Pte. JACOBS, C. R. (M.M.).
38388 Pte. JONES, H., 3rd Bn.
Pte. JACOBS, M., 9th Bn.
8069 Pte. JOSEPH, G., 3rd Bn.
40462 Pte. KROHN, S.,* 2nd Bn.
43696 Pte. KAUFMAN, 10th Bn.
29527 L/Cpl. KWARTZ, J., 12th Bn.
Pte. KELMAN, C., 1st Bn.
57544 Cpl. KAUFMAN, E., 1st Bn.
8206 Pte. LEVINSON, J., 2nd Bn.
5851 L/Cpl. LAZARUS, R., 2nd Bn.
7960 L/Cpl. LEVI, H.,* 2nd Bn.
8026 Pte. LEVISON, R., 2nd Bn.
3/7957 Pte. LAZARUS, H., 6th Bn.
44157 Pte. LEVY, N., 8th Bn.
39797 Pte. LUBESK, I., 14th Bn.
42102 Pte. LEES, W., 7th Bn.
50057 Pte. LEVINE, B.
265184 Pte. LOUIS, L., 15th Bn.
42084 Pte. LIBERMAN, W.
235627 Pte. MOSCOW, A., 10th Bn.
5743 Pte. MASSON, B., 2/4th Bn.
241977 Pte. MICHAELS, S., 2/5th Bn.
43110 Pte. MORRIS, P., 7th Bn.
203684 Pte. MORRIS, J., 4th Bn.
42162 Pte. NATHAN, 10th Bn.
6720 Pte. NEWFIELD, S., 2/4th Bn.
280133 L/Cpl. NIMAN, D., 2nd Gar. Gn.
8050 Pte. POLLOCK, S., 6th Bn.
9484 Pte. PYZER, J., 1st Bn.
39525 Pte. PHILLIPS, L.
Pte. PYZER, W. (M.M. and Bar).
5198 R.S.M. ROBINSON, M.,* 10th Bn.
5188 Pte. ROOMS, M.,* 2nd Bn.
508 Sgt. ROSENBERG, I., 10th Bn.
266499 Pte. ROSENBERG, A., 13th Bn.
42026 Pte. ROSENFIELD, H., 1st Bn.
44485 Pte. RUDSTEIN, M., 1/15th Bn.
42317 Pte. STONE, M., 10th Bn.

The Lincolnshire Regt.—Continued.

31629 Pte. SILVERMAN, M., 3rd Bn.
11/19017 Pte. SALTMAN, I., 11th Bn.
28691 Pte. SAMUELS, W., 3rd Bn.
24742 Pte. SAMUEL, H., 1/5th Bn.
6742 Pte. SOLOMONS, S., 1st Bn.
36832 Pte. SOLOMONS, M., 13th Bn.
35133 Pte. SLIPKIN, J., 8th Bn.
Pte. SCHNEIDER, J., 2nd Bn.
202706 Cpl. SOLOMON, H. E., 8th Bn.
41822 Pte. SACKSHIVER, A., 2/4th Bn.
92763 Pte. SOLOMONS, J., 3rd Bn.
28028 Pte. SUGARMAN, J., 2nd Gar. Bn.
32902 Pte. SOLOMAN, A., 2nd Bn.
11/1883 Pte. WOOD, I., 11th Bn.
11/1884 Pte. WOOD, M., 11th Bn.
9235 Pte. ZEREFSKY, H., 12th Bn.

* Killed in Action or died on Active Service.

THE DEVONSHIRE REGIMENT.

OFFICERS.

2nd Lieut. JOSEPH, H.,* 8th Bn.
Lieut. MOSES, 6th Bn.
Lieut. RICHARDSON, F. S., 16th Bn.
Lieut.-Col. SAMUEL, W. H., 52nd Bn.
Lieut. VOS, A., 2/6th Bn.

N.C.O.'s AND MEN.

12424 Pte. ABRAHAMS, G.,* 9th Bn.
6916 Pte. ANNENBERG, A.,* 2nd Bn.
30894 Pte. ADELSON, A.,* 2nd Bn.
460726 Pte. ABRAHAMS, B.
28998 Pte. ABRAHAMS, A., 13th Bn.
42312 Pte. ANDERS, A., 13th Bn.
39583 Pte. BRUIKS, L.
30903 Pte. BENJAMIN, C.,* 2nd Bn.
67438 Pte. BASS, 2/6th Bn.
Pte. BLANCKENSEE, L. R.
500942 Pte. BERSTEIN, H.
33773 Pte. BLOOM, J., 1st Bn.
52977 Pte. BRODIE, L. J., 13th Bn.
58240 Pte. BENJAMIN, A., 13th Bn.
31626 Pte. BAUM, H., 15th Bn.
63537 Pte. BRAND, C.
91857 Pte. BLOOM, J.
19785 Cpl. BERMAN, 1st Bn.
0994 Pte. BENSON, J. W.
Pte. BENJAMIN, I.
52425 Pte. CRASHINSKY, A.

60700 Pte. COHEN, A.
47326 Pte. COHEN, S.
104509 Pte. COHEN, M. H.,* 21st Bn.
67001 Sgt. COHEN, F., 2/7th Bn.
30010 Pte. COHEN, L.
460734 Pte. COHEN, H.
43141 Pte. COHEN, A., 13th Bn.
40931 Pte. COHEN, J., 14th Bn.
19371 Pte. COHEN, M.
292149 Pte. CASIMER, C., 1/4th Bn.
8160 Pte. DAVIS, T., 2nd Bn.
69162 Pte. DE FRIEND, H., 2nd Bn.
66550 Pte. DONNE, I., 1/7th Bn.
46058 L/Cpl. DELKANHO, E., 13th Bn.
6943 Pte. ECKSTEIN, D.,* 1st Bn.
298597 Pte. EPSTEIN, S., 1st Bn.
18428 Pte. FISHER, H. C.
39304 Pte. FRANKEL, H.
36743 Pte. FLEIGLEMAN, B., 13th Bn.
52810 Pte. FILER, J., 13th Bn.
36313 Pte. FISHER, E.
62160 Pte. FRIEDMAN, S., 15th Bn.
80769 Pte. FOX, S., 3rd Bn.
47897 Pte. GRODINSKY, M.
12372 Pte. GEPSTEIN, S., 9th Bn.
128336 Pte. GARODENTCHICK, A.
12463 Pte. HARRIS, D., 9th Bn.
16334 Pte. HARRIS, J., 1st Bn.
65124 Pte. HERSHAFT, W. M., 2/7th Bn.
32064 Pte. HENRY, N., 2nd Bn.
8698 Pte. ISAACS, A.,* 1st Bn.
9844 Pte. ISAACS, G., 1st Bn.
31390 Pte. JACOBSON, G., 8th Bn.
33364 L/Cpl. JACOBS, L., 3rd Bn.
440871 Pte. JACOBS, M.
267333 Pte. JORDAN, P., 1/6th Bn.
13799 Pte. KROTSKY, A., 3rd Bn.
46175 Pte. KYZER, J. R., 13th Bn.
28956 Pte. KANTOROVITCH, J.
52433 Pte. KURASH, J., 13th Bn.
466760 Pte. KAMINSKY, I., 1st Bn.
14268 Pte. LEWIS, S.,* 9th Bn.
43237 Pte. LEVY, V. E., 9th Bn.
58326 Pte. LEVIACHVILI, H., 8th Bn.
19541 Sgt. LAZARUS, J.
65125 Pte. LEVY, A., 2/7th Bn.
12086 L/Cpl. LEVY, H.,* 9th Bn.
80504 Pte. LERKOFF, M.
28301 Pte. LAMBERT, D., 2nd Bn.
43268 Pte. LIPMAN, H., 2nd Bn.
46152 Pte. LYONS, N., 13th Bn.
43567 Pte. LESSER, P., 13th Bn.
92880 Pte. LESSER, N., 14th Bn.
62447 Pte. LIPMAN, R., 2nd Bn.
41481 Pte. LUMBERG, A. J., 13th Bn.
17698 Pte. LENSHAW, H., 3rd Bn.
30854 Pte. LINGER, S., 2nd Bn.

The Devonshire Regt.—Continued.

- 30101 L/Cpl. MILLER, D., 9th Bn.
- 5290 Pte. MARKS, J.,* 1st Bn.
- 6956 Pte. MYERS, J., 1st Bn.
- 58332 Pte. MAISELS, N., 8th Bn.
- 465098 L/Cpl. MARKS, L. A.
- 61835 Pte. MILNER, J.
- 46632 Pte. MARGOLINS, S., 13th Bn.
- 143394 Pte. MORRIS, A., 2nd Bn.
- 461107 Pte. MINOFF, A., 16th Bn.
- 30101 L/Cpl. MILLER, H., 9th Bn.
- Pte. MICHAELS, D., 9th Bn.
- 16317 Pte. NATHAN, A.,* 8th Bn.
- 69301 Pte. NOBLE, S., 2/7th Bn.
- 8063 Pte. OSOSKI, L., 15th Bn.
- 465100 Pte. OPPENHEIM, H.
- 292142 Pte. PHILLIPS, B., 1/7th Bn.
- 172784 Pte. PULVERMACKER, P., 20th Bn.
- 292175 Pte. POGOLOVITCH, B., 1/7th Bn.
- 41301 Pte. ROSENBLATT, H., 8th Bn.
- 8/1688 Pte. ROSANSKY, M. T.
- 80431 Pte. ROSENBERG, N.
- 36801 Pte. ROOD, S., 13th Bn.
- 42952 Pte. RAGOFF, W., 13th Bn.
- 59173 Pte. ROSE, S.,* 1st Bn.
- 1858 Pte. SILVERSTON, J., 9th Bn.
- 30854 Pte. SINGER, L., 2nd Bn.
- 28759 Pte. SOLOMONS, S., 16th Bn.
- 50527 Pte. SHOCK, C.
- 39453 Pte. STONE, H.
- 67437 Pte. STEINBERG, 2/6th Bn.
- 292057 Pte. SCHOENTHAL, H., 1/7th Bn.
- 19242 Pte. SILK, B., 2nd Bn.
- 23812 Pte. STEINBERG, H., 13th Bn.
- 46147 Pte. SIMONS, I., 13th Bn.
- 22978 Pte. SPERBER, M., 13th Bn.
- 69164 Pte. SOLOMONS, J., 13th Bn.
- 60713 Pte. SILVERMAN, H., 13th Bn.
- 49198 Pte. SWATCENBERG, D. C., 13th Bn.
- 63433 Pte. SOLOMONS, K., 13th Bn.
- 29543 Pte. SPECTERMAN, A., 1/7th Bn.
- 291157 Pte. SPECTERMAN, M., 1/7th Bn.
- 43268 Pte. STEINBERG, H., 2nd Bn.
- 292179 Pte. SAVINSON, J. D., 1/17th Bn.
- 69241 Pte. SCHNEIDERMAN, B., 3rd Bn.
- 71758 Pte. SEGAL, J., 3rd Bn.
- 01710 Pte. SCHARNICK, S. W., 1st Bn.
- Pte. SILVERSTEIN, A.
- Pte. SWATSKI, L., 13th Bn.
- 291137 Pte. TROYNA, M., 9th Bn.
- 46660 Pte. TENTSHER, J., 13th Bn.
- 1520 Pte. VICTOR, M., 9th Bn.
- Pte. WHITE, J., 8th Bn.
- 29632 Pte. WOLFE, J., 13th Bn.

* Killed in Action or died on Active Service.

THE SUFFOLK REGIMENT.

OFFICERS.

- 2nd Lieut. BARNETT, G. B., 11th Bn.
- 2nd Lieut. COHEN, J.
- Lieut. GLUCKSTEIN, L. H., 2/5th Bn.
- Lieut. MYERS, F. M.,* (M.C.), 11th Bn.
- Lieut. SIMMONS, J., 7th Bn.
- Capt. SCHIFF, M. E. H.,* 12th Bn.
- Lieut. TRAVERS, H., 7th Bn.

N.C.O.'s AND MEN.

- 24595 Pte. ABRAHAMS, S., 2nd Bn.
- 65408 Pte. ABRAHAMS, B., 3rd Bn.
- 51239 Pte. ANSELL, I., Res. Bn.
- 66651 Pte. ABRAHAMS, M.
- 22225 Pte. BLOOMBERG, S. I., 12th Bn.
- 22173 Pte. BOVET, M., 12th Bn.
- 41649 Pte. BEN ELISHA, S., 12th Bn.
- 4820 Pte. BARNETT, J., 2/5th Bn.
- 242799 Pte. BURMAN, J., 2nd Bn.
- Pte. BERLINER, H., 1st Gar Bn.
- 51302 Pte. BERMAN, J., 3rd Bn.
- 66670 Pte. BLOOM, S., 3rd Bn.
- 14761 Pte. BIERMAN, G., 14th Bn.
- 51330 Pte. BLOOMBERG, S., Res Bn.
- 290843 Pte. BAKER, L., 14th Bn.
- 49210 Pte. BIERMAN, A., 1/6th Bn.
- 49209 Pte. BERG, M., 1/6th Bn.
- 47004 L/Cpl. BRISCOE, M.
- 66670 Pte. BLOOM, T.
- 49548 Pte. BARTLETT, S., 4th Bn.
- 39046 Pte. BARNETT, A., 18th Bn.
- 39464 Pte. BRILLESLYPER, J., 1st. Bn.
- 39310 Pte. BLANK, L., 1st Bn.
- 35140 Sgt. BOSS, J., 1st Bn.
- 39469 Pte. BOHN, B., 1st Bn.
- 201653 Pte. COHEN, L. L.,* 2nd Bn.
- 57392 Pte. COHEN, I., 12th Bn.
- 241614 Pte. COHEN, D., 2/5th Bn.
- 242800 Pte. CARTZ, L., 2/5th Bn.
- 64486 Pte. COHEN, P., 3rd Bn.
- 61644 Pte. COHEN, N., 14th Bn.
- 45509 Pte. CAIDEN, H. A.
- 21781 Pte. COHEN, H.
- 204072 Pte. CHESTER, E.
- 52110 Pte. CHRANOY, S.
- 47447 Pte. COHEN, M., 1/5th Bn.
- 41188 Pte. DAVID, I., 11th Bn.
- 31467 L/Cpl. DANSER, H., 11th Bn.
- 5368 Pte. DELAFUENTE, L., 4th Bn.
- 65135 Pte. DOLMAN, J.
- 65327 Pte. DONN, Y.
- 62055 Pte. EMANUEL, M., 1st Bn.
- 242009 Pte. EDGAR, L., 2/5th Bn.
- 49227 Pte. EMDLEMAN, D., 1/6th Bn.
- 57578 Pte. FREEDSON, M., 12th Bn.

The Suffolk Regt.—Continued.

265704 Pte. FEINSTEIN, A., 1/6th Bn.
33517 Pte. FALK, B.,* 8th Bn.
39434 Pte. FREEDMAN, A.
24355 Pte. FINKEL, S., 10th Bn.
1956 Pte. FRIEDMAN, 7th Bn.
5059 C.Q.M.S. FRIEND, D., 10th Bn.
21667 Pte. GREENBURG, W. 12th Bn.
50625 Pte. GOSCINNY, M., 2nd Bn.
41643 Pte. GILBERG, S., 12th Bn.
50253 Pte. GOLDSTEIN, H., 2nd Bn.
63135 Pte. GREEN, D., 12th Bn.
51815 Pte. GOLDSTEIN, S., 2nd Bn.
28729 Pte. GOLDSTEIN, H., 10th Bn.
45488 Pte. GOLDMAN, J.
52113 Pte. GOURVISH, A.
51859 Pte. GOLDING, H.
29164 L/Cpl. GREENSTONE, E.
46043 Pte. GOLLOP, E., 1st Bn.
19294 Pte. GILLS, J. J., 2nd Bn.
39229 Pte. GLUCKSTEIN, J., 1st Bn.
39435 Pte. GROSSE, J.
51759 Pte. GOBELL, G.
230611 Sgt. GARCIA, L., 14th Bn.
5268 Pte. HERMAN, S., 4th Bn.
39029 Pte. HENISON, I., 1st Gar. Bn.
320635 Pte. HARRISON, A., 15th Bn.
51322 Pte. HARRIS, D. G., 3rd Bn.
45945 Pte. HARRISON, M.
39480 Pte. HELPER, A.
41188 Pte. ISAACS, D., 11th Bn.
242010 Pte. ISAACS, J., 2/5th Bn.
57471 Pte. JEFFENER, 14th Bn.
40838 Pte. JAFFA, W.,* 2nd Bn.
52219 Pte. JACOBS, H., 1st Bn.
33044 L/Cpl. KOSSLOFF, B., 1st Bn.
52180 Pte. KASSEL, L., 12th Bn.
39486 Pte. KRASNY, C., 1st Bn.
45863 Pte. KIBEL, M., Res. Bn.
290801 Pte. KAUFMAN, P., 14th Bn.
41641 Pte. LEVY, C., 12th Bn.
28999 Pte. LAZARUS, J., 4th Bn.
241636 L/Cpl. LUBEL, J. L., 2/5th Bn.
242338 Pte. LUSTY, N., 2/5th Bn.
683657 Pte. LEBROVITCH, N., 2/5th Bn.
49266 Pte. LUSCOFSKY, J., Res. Bn.
37802 Pte. LILMAN, B., 14th Bn.
57542 Pte. MOSES, L., 12th Bn.
63237 Pte. MATLIN, J., 12th Bn.
24342 Pte. MAYERS, S., 10th Bn.
29613 Pte. METZER, S., 2nd Bn.
4823 Pte. MORRIS, C. L., 2/5th Bn.
65636 Pte. NAPPER, E.
42660 Pte. NIMMO, W., 11th Bn.
49921 Pte. NEGUS, D., 11th Bn.
345042 Pte. OTTOLANGUI, D.
62082 Pte. PRINCE, E., 3rd Bn.
25462 Pte. PHILLIPS, L.,* 10th Bn.

57357 Pte. PERILLY, M., 12th Bn.
243015 Pte. POSNER, B., 2/5th Bn.
27317 Pte. ROSS, J., 12th Bn.
44123 Pte. ROSENBLATT, T., 4th Bn.
21530 Pte. ROSS, L., 12th Bn.
52251 Pte. ROCKFALLER, N.
63437 Pte. ROSENBAUM, J., 12th Bn.
40854 Pte. REVENSKY, H.,* 2nd Bn.
242772 Cpl. ROSENFELT, H., 2/5th Bn.
39054 Pte. ROSEN, B.
51464 L/Cpl. RICHMAN, J., 3rd Bn.
290651 Pte. ROTH, D., 14th Bn.
22118 L/Cpl. SELMAN, H., 12th Bn.
63338 Pte. SILVER, H., 12th Bn.
242796 Pte. SAUNDERS, M., 2/5th Bn.
46163 Pte. SHOOP, M., 1st Bn.
51559 Pte. SOBEL, J., 2nd Bn.
51309 Pte. SIMMONS, L. A., Res. Bn.
47259 Pte. SCHNEIDER, H.
42666 L/Cpl. SIMONS, J.
39430 Pte. SILVERSTEIN, H., 1st Bn.
39770 Pte. SHERMAN, H.
34471 Pte. SAMPSON, R.
22118 L/Cpl. SELMAN, H. D., 12th Bn.
47747 L/Cpl. SOLJEDO, S.
2669 Pte. SEGALOFF, M., 1st Bn.
52027 L/Cpl. SHINDLER, P.
29027 Pte. TOBIAS, M., 10th Bn.
5007 Pte. WINEBERG, J. M., 2/5th Bn.
39052 Pte. WAXMAN, H., 1st Bn.
6260 Pte. WOOLF, A., 2/5th Bn.
29262 Pte. WOODRICH, J., 1/6th Bn.
52109 Pte. ZISMAN, M., 1st Bn.
52117 Pte. ZELKOWITZ, D., 1st Bn.
57575 Pte. WILLIAMS, H., 12th Bn.
39326 L/Cpl. WELLING, J., 12th Bn.
9892 Pte. WURMS, S., 3rd Bn.
49265 Pte. WEINSHINK, C., Res. Bn.

* Killed in Action or died on Active Service.

PRINCE ALBERT'S (SOMERSET LIGHT INFANTRY).

OFFICERS.

2nd Lieut. ABECASIS, A. P.,* 6th Bn.
2nd Lieut. HARBURG, J. H., 7th Bn.
Capt. SCHLESINGER, G. L., 8th Bn.

N.C.O.'s AND MEN.

265497 Pte. ALEXANDRA, B., 11th Bn.
Pte. ABRAHAMS, B.
6895 Pte. BUTMAN, J.,* 1st Bn.
265212 Pte. BROCKMAN, N., 11th Bn.
39159 Pte. BROZOL, J., 12th Bn.
39278 Pte. BELASCO, B., 12th Bn.
18058 Pte. BRENNER, J., 11th Bn.
40695 Pte. BERNS, F., 4th Bn.
33771 Pte. BERNSTOCK, P., 2/4th Bn.
41293 Pte. BAUM, S.

Somerset Light Infantry.—Continued.

6906 Pte. COHEN, S., 1st Bn.
16593 Pte. COHEN, H., 8th Bn.
32610 L/Sgt. COHEN, F., 10th Bn.
42347 Pte. CLAFF, R.,* 1st Bn.
39214 Pte. CASH, P., 12th Bn.
6820 Pte. COLE, H., 1st Bn.
5835 Pte. DE YOUNG, L.,* 1st Bn.
204109 Pte. FRANKS, J., 8th Bn.
3883 Pte. FIFER, D., 10th Bn.
8891 Cpl. GOSS, J.,* 2nd Bn.
Pte. GOLDFISH, M., 2nd Bn.
37657 Pte. GREEN, J., 215th Bn.
Pte. GOLDSTEIN, S.
465462 Pte. GOLDBERG, B.
204112 Pte. HORNE, M., 8th Bn.
209569 L/Cpl. HERNBERG, D., 6th Bn.
28754 Pte. HARRIS, H., 18th Bn.
39593 Pte. JOSEPH, L., 11th Bn.
38892 Pte. JACOBS, S., 3rd Bn.
15173 L/Sgt. ISAACS, A., 8th Bn.
265599 Pte. ISAACS, P., 11th Bn.
27588 Pte. KRISLOVSKY, A., 1st Bn.
62783 Pte. KREISBERG, J., 3rd Bn.
16801 Pte. LEWIS, J.,* 8th Bn.
52433 Cpl. LEVY, 6th Bn.
53866 Pte. LEVY, 6th Bn.
39259 Pte. LEVY, J., 12th Bn.
8443 L/Cpl. LIPWICK, H., 2nd Bn.
54641 Pte. LEVY, J., 4th Bn.
20419 L/Cpl. LAZARUS, J., 8th Bn.
43214 Pte. LICHSTEIN, N.
9034 L/Cpl. MICHAELS, J., 2nd Bn.
32417 Pte. MARKS, L., 3rd Bn.
0152 Pte. MARGOLIS, L., 1st Bn.
19098 Pte. MAYSEY, A. J.
?19099 Pe. NEDVITCH, S., 3rd Bn.
27471 Pte. POSTER, L., 6th Bn.
10315 Pte. PHILLIPS, N. L.,* 6th Bn.
8465 L/Cpl. POSNER, G., 2nd Bn.
41188 Pte. ROTH, C., 11th Bn.
41392 Pte. ROSENBERG, M., 4th Bn.
265038 Pte. RAASH, J., 13th Bn.
15720 Pte. STERN, M.,* 8th Bn.
27483 Pte. SCHAFFER, E.,* 6th Bn.
52469 Pte. SPIEGLEMAN, 6th Bn.
52488 Pte. SILVERSTON, 6th Bn.
39168 Pte. SIMMONS, H., 12th Bn.
290091 Pte. SHAPIRO, M., 12th Bn.
32398 Pte. SHAPIRO, N., 3rd Bn.
Sgt. SIMMONS, 1st Gar. Bn.
32256 Pte. SOLOMONS, J., 3rd Bn.
9468 Pte. TRAPLER, D., 1st Bn.
33815 L/Cpl. WOOLF, J., 8th Bn.
17904 Pte. WAGENHEIM, J., 11th Bn.
36198 Pte. WITOUSKI, A., 2nd Bn.
32729 Pte. YESKI, A., 11th Bn.

* Killed in Action or died on Active Service.

THE PRINCE OF WALES'S OWN (WEST YORKSHIRE REGIMENT).

OFFICERS.

2nd Lieut. BENJAMIN, R., 5th Bn.
Lieut. COHEN, C. D.
2nd Lieut. CROSS, H. B., 2/5th Bn.
Capt. FRIEND, C. (M.C.), 2/5th Bn.
2nd Lieut. FRANKLIN, 5th Bn.
2nd Lieut. GREEN, G., 2/5th Bn.
Lieut. LOTINGA, C. G., 12th Bn.
2nd Lieut. LOWY. F. L., 11th Bn.
Lieut. LEVY, S. A. J.,
2nd Lieut. MENDES, M., 15th Bn.
2nd Lieut. PLATNAUER, L. M.,* 16th Bn.
2nd Lieut. REESE, A.,* (M.C. and Bar), 2nd Bn.
2nd Lieut. ROBINSON, H. W., 6th Bn.
2nd Lieut. SAMUEL, H. B., 2/5th Bn.

N.C.O.'s AND MEN.

28812 Pte. ABRAHAMS, H., 2nd Bn.
25351 Pte. ABRAHAMS, S.,* 2nd Bn.
40163 Pte. ARLUCK, L., 12th Bn.
4874 Pte. ARK, M., 2/8th Bn.
235431 Pte. ANCILL, R., 2/5th Bn.
34815 L/Cpl. ABRAHAMS, M., 15th Bn.
32317 Pte. ABER, H., 16th Bn.
242689 Pte. ABRAHAMS, S.,* 1/6th Bn.
48885 Pte. APPLESON, L., 2/6th Bn.
202826 Pte. ASHBERG, A., 1/5th Bn.
28000 Pte. ADDLESTONE, B., 14th Bn.
20/277 Pte. ABRAHAMS, L., 20th Bn.
35091 Pte. ABRAHAMS, A., 1st Bn.
5895 Pte. ADLEMAN, S., 1/7th Bn.
41506 Pte. ANNENBERG, S.,* 17th Bn.
42017 L/Cpl. ANCILL, R., 2/8th Bn.
10382 Pte. ABRAHAMS, 1st Bn.
39887 Pte. ADELMAN, M., 3rd Bn.
94851 Pte. ABRAHAMS, L.
6719 Pte. ABRAHAMS, M., 1/6th Bn.
14/28069 Pte. ALBERTS, L.
4747 Pte. ANNENBERG, I., 5th Bn.
5719 Pte. ABRAHAMSON, S., 5th Bn.
53529 Pte. AIEKIN, L., 21st Bn.
Pte. BAKER, A., 1/7th Bn.
17122 Cpl. BROSGILL, D., 17th Bn.
27785 Pte. BENJAMIN, B., 17th Bn.
307067 Pte. BROSGILL, W.,* 12th Bn.
32315 Pte. BLUMBERG, M., 12th Bn.
3425 L/Cpl. BERSON, D.,* 2/7th Bn.
267228 Rfm. BAKER, N.,* 2/7th Bn.
5083 Rfm. BENJAMIN, A., 2/7th Bn.
5121 Rfm. BENJAMIN, H., 2/7th Bn.
5067 Rfm. BLAND, H., 2/7th Bn.
267497 Sig. BAKER, B., 2/8th Bn.
4856 Rfm. BERNSTEIN, M., 2/8th Bn.
4694 Rfm. BAKER, D., 2/8th Bn
5148 L/Cpl. BENJAMIN, I., 2/8th Bn.

West Yorkshire Regt.—*Continued.*

- 37172 Pte. BENJAMIN, S., 16th Bn.
- 242587 Pte. BROWN, M., 18th Bn.
- 267921 Pte. BLUMENTHAL, N., 1/7th Bn.
- 48813 Pte. BROSGILL, P., 1/7th Bn.
- 32321 Pte. BENJAMIN, K.,* 10th Bn.
- 52025 Pte. BOSSICK, J., 2/5th Bn.
- 29444 Pte. BERNSTEIN, 10th Bn.
- 33715 Pte. BERNSTEIN, H., 9th Bn.
- 242683 Pte. BENDELSKI, H., 1/6th Bn.
- L/Cpl. BLACK, B., 1st Bn.
- 28896 Pte. BLAKEY, W.
- 9170 Sgt. BARNETT, P., 2nd Bn.
- Pte. BENJAMIN, L.
- 200156 Pte. BROOKS, J. H., 51st Bn.
- 205298 Pte. BLASKEY, S. M., 5th Bn.
- 267308 Rfm. BICKLER, E., 2/7th Bn.
- 5592 Pte. BOCHELL, N., 12th Bn.
- 5360 Pte BEAVEY, 8th Bn.
- 3186 Pte. BROMBERG, E., 13th Bn.
- 48407 Pte. BERNSTEIN, 1/5th Bn.
- 48401 Pte. BETH, 1/5th Bn.
- 62578 Pte. BENKOVITCH, I., 1/5th Bn.
- 39319 L/Cpl. BAKER, I., 3rd Bn.
- 30300 Pte. BRONKS, J., 22nd Bn.
- 4736 Pte. BLUMENTHAL, W., 5th Bn.
- 268045 Pte. BLOOMER, S., 1/7th Bn.
- 6716 Pte. BAKER, 1/7th Bn.
- 306831 Rfm. BERNSTEIN, A., 2/8th Bn.
- 55160 Rfm. BLOCK, J., 7th Bn.
- 31456 Pte. BACOVITCH, S., 4th Bn.
- 5481 Pte. BAKER, B., 7th Bn.
- 4753 Pte. BAKER, C., 5th Bn.
- 4672 Pte. BAKER, I., 5th Bn.
- 5910 Rfm. BAKER, I., 7th Bn.
- 5085 Rfm. BAKER, N., 2/7th Bn.
- 5341 Rfm. BARKER, H., 7th Bn.
- 28961 Pte. BELINSKY, B., 13th Bn.
- 33286 Pte. BELOVITCH, A., 13th Bn.
- 34880 Pte. BOAM, C., 13th Bn.
- 5247 Pte. BROWN, M., 3/8th Bn.
- 28906 Pte. BROWN, A., 13th Bn.
- 89727 Rfm. BELFER, J., 53rd Bn.
- Rfm. BAILEY, J.
- Rfm. BROWNE, A.
- Rfm. BLOOMER, S., 7th Bn.
- 204122 Rfm. BLOUNT, A., 1/6th Bn.
- 60861 Pte. CRANARDLE, C., 15th Bn.
- 9343 Pte. CAPLAN, I., 2nd Bn.
- 6510 Rfm. COPE, D., 1/7th Bn.
- 31866 Pte. COHEN, A., 1st Bn.
- 31878 Pte. COHEN, B., 1st Bn.
- 259 Pte. COLLINS, J., 21st Bn.
- 28569 Pte. COHEN, S., 12th Bn.
- 5097 Rfm. Christie, W., 2/7th Bn.
- 5162 Rfm. COHEN, A.,* 2/7th Bn.
- 266145 Rfm. COLLINS, H.,* 2/7th Bn.
- 5063 Rfm. COHEN, D., 2/7th Bn.
- 307060 Rfm. COHEN, A.,* 8th Bn.
- 5156 Rfm. CLUBMAN P., 2/8th Bn.
- 300069 Pte. CHAIN, H., 18th Bn.
- 38023 L/Cpl. COCHIN, M., 18th Bn.
- A/204946 Pte. COHEN, L., 10th Bn.
- 267680 Pte. COPLAN, L., 1/6th Bn.
- 41148 Pte. COHEN, S., 11th Bn.
- 268001 Pte. COHEN, H., 1/7th Bn.
- 35262 Pte. CANTOR, J.
- 32729 Pte. COHEN, H., 13th Bn.
- 42100 Rfm. COHEN, M., 22nd Bn.
- 2338 Sgt. COHEN, A. G.,* 1/6th Bn.
- 30367 Pte. COHEN, A., 22nd Bn.
- 202393 Pte. COHEN, A., 5th Bn.
- 267287 Rfm. COPLIN, M. C., 2/7th Bn.
- 42380 Rfm. COHEN, V., 2/8th Bn.
- 46447 Pte. COHEN, H., 22nd Bn.
- 267663 Pte. COHEN, A., 8th Bn.
- 5186 Pte. COHEN.
- 26415 Pte. COHEN, N., 4th Bn.
- 26214 Pte. CANTER, I. L., 13th Bn.
- 14/32428 Pte. CAPLIN, 14th Bn.
- 8441 Pte. CHURNIN, M., 4th Bn.
- 32470 Pte. COHEN, H.
- 5321 Pte. COHEN, I., 7th Bn.
- 5216 Rfm. COHEN, S., 2/8th Bn.
- 122322 Rfm. CRENSTEIN, J., 53rd Bn.
- 251949 Pte. COHEN, A., 5th Bn.
- 5875 Pte. COHEN, A., 1st Bn.
- 270890 Pte. COHEN, D.
- 46447 Pte. COHEN, H.
- 48468 Pte. COLLINS, L., 3rd Bn
- 2813 Rfm. DRESSLER, J., 1/7th Bn.
- 8330 L/Cpl. DAVIS, B., 9th Bn.
- L/Cpl. DANIELS, J., 21st Bn.
- 26150 Pte. de MEZA, A., 12th Bn.
- 9268 Pte. DAVIS, M., 2nd Bn.
- Pte. DEFRIES, 2nd Bn.
- 307034 Pte. DAVIES, I., 11th Bn.
- 58719 Rfm. DUNN, S.
- 25809 Pte. DONIGEN, S., 9th Bn.
- 28960 Pte. DIAMOND, I., 13th Bn.
- 53269 Pte. DONNE, T., 21st Bn.
- 5154 Rfm. ELLINGER, M., 2/8th Bn.
- 42609 Pte. EMANUEL, A.,* 1/5th Bn.
- 52877 Pte. EREIRA, I., 1st Bn.
- 12297 Pte. FEARN, B.,* 13th Bn.
- 2230 Rfm. FREEMAN, J., 1/7th Bn.
- 353 L/Cpl. FRIEDER, S., 15th Bn.
- 1940 Pte. FRIEDER, P., 15th Bn.
- 9144 Pte. FLEXER, L., 1st Bn.
- 265427 Pte. FREEMAN, J., 2nd Bn.
- 306837 Pte. FREEMAN, S., 2nd Bn.
- 424 Pte. FREEDMAN, L., 21st Bn.
- 5089 Rfm. FELDMAN, D., 2/7th Bn.
- 5095 Rfm. FRANKS, E., 2/7th Bn.
- 5155 Rfm. FREEDMAN, A., 2/8th Bn.
- 4842 Rfm. FEARN, J., 2/8th Bn.

West Yorkshire Regt.—*Continued.*

	Rfm. FRAIS, 2/8th Bn.
4863	Rfm.. FREEDMAN S., 2/8th Bn.
41513	Pte. FRANKS, D., 16th Bn.
35132	Pte. FREEZE, M., 20th Bn.
60511	Rfm. FRANKS, G., 2/7h Bn.
41241	Rfm. FARBER, N., 11th Bn.
29542	Pte. FISHER, D.
33928	Pte. FREEDMAN, E., 14th Bn.
49397	L/Cpl. FISHER, I., 15th Bn.
41120	Rfm FRIEZE, 11th Bn.
9192	Pte. FINESTEIN, B., 2nd Bn.
203076	Pte. FRIEZE, J., 5th Bn.
124181	Pte. FRIEDLANDER, D.,* 1/6th Bn.
5837	Pte. FREEDMAN, H., 5th Bn.
5080	Rfm. FALK, H., 2/7th Bn.
27110	Pte. FROMANCHICK.
	Pte. FOX, P., 5th Bn.
6598	Pte. GREENBERG, D., 1/6th Bn.
267201	Pte. GARDNER, M., 2nd Bn.
27765	Pte. GOLDSTEIN, A., 2nd Bn.
306823	Pte. GOODSTONE, D., 2nd Bn.
242578	Pte. GREENBERG, P.,* 1/6th Bn.
36810	Pte. GOLDMAN, I., 9th Bn.
5153	Rfm. GOLDBERG, J., 2/8th Bn.
267223	L/Cpl. GOLDSTEIN, M., 2/7th Bn.
5127	Rfm. GOLDSBERG, S., 2/7th Bn
5094	Rfm. GOLDBERG, D., 2/7th Bn.
5156	Rfm. GOLDBERG, B., 2/7th Bn.
37614	Sig. GLASS, G., 2/5th Bn.
7848	Rfm. GOLDBERG, E., 2/5th Bn.
6052	Rfm. GOLDSTONE, B., 2/6th Bn.
66707	Pte. GLUCK, J., 15th Bn.
205045	Pte. GOODMAN, H., 1/8th Bn.
42447	Rfm. GOLDWATER, H., 2/7th Bn.
212435	Rfm. GIBBERTSON, J., 2/8th Bn.
41486	Pte. GOLDBERG, A., 17th Bn.
202222	Pte. GINSBERG, A., 1/5th Bn.
202164	Pte. GOLDSTONE, I., 1/5th Bn.
32328	Pte. GOLDMAN, C., 9th Bn.
4896	Pte. GOLDBERG, H., 5th Bn.
35023	Pte. GABER, L., 20th Bn.
11637	Rfm. GOLDMAN, J., 2nd Bn.
27778	Pte. GOLDMAN, M., 2nd Bn.
38179	Pte. GOULD, J., 17th Bn.
9546	Pte. GOODMAN, M.,* 1st Bn.
9473	Pte. GOLDBERG, I., 1st Bn.
5761	Pte. GRIFFINS, H., 5th Bn.
203778	Pte. GAMPLE, D.,* 2/7th Bn.
107836	L/Cpl. GOLDBERG, A., 51st Bn.
21592	Pte. GOODSTONE, N., 1/7th Bn.
41510	Pte. GRIFFINS, H., 17th Bn.
203150	Cpl. GOODMAN, M., 1/5th Bn.
53462	Pte. GOLDBERG, R. B., 10th Bn.
4676	Pte. GAFFIN, J., 1/6th Bn.
4680	Pte. GINSBURG, D., 5th Bn.
5689	Pte. GOLDBERG, A., 5th Bn.
28139	Pte. GOLDMAN, I., 13th Bn.
30899	Pte. GOLDMAN, J., 2nd Bn.
4682	Rfm. GOLDMAN, S., 3/5th Bn.
4675	Pte. GOLDSTEIN, S., 5th Bn.
28032	Rfm. GOODMAN, M., 13th Bn.
267268	Rfm. GOLDBERG, S., 1/5th Bn.
6117	L/Cpl. GLASSMAN, M., 4th Bn.
49900	Rfm. GOLDSTONE, P., 7th Bn.
48883	Pte. GOLDBERG, J., 3rd Bn.
60404	Pte. GOMBERG, L., 7th Bn.
29459	Pte. GALINSKY, H.,* 1st Bn.
	Cpl. GOLDBERG, M., 12th Bn.
62106	Cpl. GOLDBERG, R.
268013	Rfm. HARRISON, M.,* 1/17th Bn.
41512	Pte. HARRIS, B., 17th Bn.
25295	Pte. HARRIS, S., 1st Bn.
3880	Rfm. HUROMITCH, M.,* 2/7th Bn.
5091	Rfm. HARRIS, H., 2/7th Bn.
235384	Rfm. HYAMS, F., 2/6th Bn.
4870	Rfm. HARRIS, S., 2/8th Bn.
37454	Rfm. HYMAN, J.,* 9th Bn.
40155	Pte. HARRIS, H., 15th Bn.
7304	Pte. HOFFMAN, C., 1/8th Bn.
43055	Pte. HARRIS, L.,* 10th Bn.
42350	Pte. HYMAN, L., 2/5th Bn.
306848	Pte. HARRIS, S., 1/5th Bn.
45909	Pte. HYMAN, R., 2nd Bn.
204260	Pte. HERMAN, H.,* 1/5th Bn.
2230	Rfm. HERMAN, J., 1/7th Bn.
32321	Pte. HEBER, B., 14th Bn.
	Pte. HYAMS, F. (M.M.).
2542	L/Cpl. HONC, L., 3rd Bn.
29461	Pte. HOLLAND, L.,* 1st Bn.
8303	Pte. HUNTER, A., 1st Bn.
108295	Pte. HYMAN, H., 51st Bn.
267890	Rfm. HARRIS, M., 5th Bn.
5709	Pte. HARRIS, H.
60515	Pte. HERSHMAN, J. P., 9th Bn.
39297	Pte. HALL, J. W. R., 2/7th Bn.
4678	Pte. HARRIS, H., 5th Bn.
5772	Pte. HARRIS, I., 3/6th Bn.
14/28079	Pte. HELLER, S., 14th Bn.
38080	Pte. HARRIS, M. A., 16th Bn.
39277	Rfm. HALL, T. R. D., 2/7th Bn.
54423	Pte. ISRAEL, A.
	L/Cpl. ISAACS, H.
4676	Pte. JAFFIN, J., 1/5th Bn.
31876	Pte. JACOBSON, A.,* 1st Bn.
41646	Pte. JACKSON, L., 17th Bn.
34283	Rfm. JACKLIN, B., 9th Bn.
267235	Pte. JOSEPH, M.,* 2/7th Bn.
29512	Pte. JACKSON, A., 1st Bn.
235559	Dvr. JEMENFSKY, S. B., 11th Bn.
235560	Dvr. JEMENFSKY, V. B., 11th Bn.
331421	Rfm. JACOBS, A. S.
267249	Pte. KAMENKA, M., 11th Bn.
5107	Rfm. KAMINSKI, H., 2/7th Bn.
51612	Rfm. KASHDAM, D., 11th Bn.
29638	Pte. KLINE, A., 13th Bn.

West Yorkshire Regt.—*Continued.*

28938 Pte. KLINE, D., 19th Bn.
26933 Pte. KLINEBERG, S.
      Pte. KOPLEMAN, N., 8th Bn.
6579 Pte. LUDSKI, N., 1/6th Bn.
8532 Cpl. LYONS, B., 1st Bn.
8327 Pte. LEWIS, J., 1st Bn.
34856 Pte. LEWDALL, P., 1st Bn.
29513 Pte. LEVY, L., 1st Bn.
28930 Pte. LUDSKI, H., 2nd Bn.
10170 Pte. LIPMAN, M.,* 21st Bn.
37621 L/Cpl. LEVY, H., 9th Bn.
37312 Rfm. LAZARUS, A. N., 11th Bn.
5074 Rfm. LEVINSON, H., 2/7th Bn.
627297 Rfm. LEE, R., 2/7th Bn.
      Rfm. LEWIS, B., 2/7th Bn.
50571 Rfm. LEADER, 2/7th Bn.
43058 Rfm. LEVY, A., 2/6th Bn.
306862 Pte. LEIZERBRAM, P.,* 2/8th Bn.
3692 Rfm. LIDSKY, S., 2/8th Bn.
1994 Pte. LEVI, S., 1st Bn.
29527 Pte. LEVI, H., 15th Bn.
38576 Pte. LEVEY, L., 15th Bn.
8558 Pte. LAZARUS, L., 16th Bn.
202279 Pte. LEVI, E.,* 1/5th Bn.
39321 Pte. LIPMAN, S.,* 7th Bn.
267659 Rfm. LEVY, G., 2/8th Bn.
77775 Rfm. LEVY, S., 2/8th Bn.
242685 Pte. LEVI, D., 1/6th Bn.
39321 Rfm. LIPCHINSKY, S.,* 1/7th Bn.
39246 Rfm. LEVY, P., 1/7th Bn.
41119 Pte. LEVY, B., 11th Bn.
263038 Pte. LEWIS, J., 1/6th Bn.
34773 Pte. LIPMAN, W., 14th Bn.
27139 Pte. LESTCHICK, J., 22nd Bn.
31445 Pte. LEVI, J., 22nd Bn.
9898 Pte. LACHOWITCH, E., 2nd Bn.
5914 Pte. LIPMAN, B., 7th Bn.
107235 Pte. LEVINE, S., 51st Bn.
4899 Pte. LEVI, F., 1/5th Bn.
268819 Pte. LEVY, H., 1/7th Bn.
41945 Pte. LEVY, L. C., 2/6th Bn.
24065 Pte. LEVI, L.,* 10th Bn.
5683 Pte. LEVI, D., 5th Bn
38832 Pte. LIPSIDGE, P., 4th Bn.
58567 Rfm. LURVE, A., 7th Bn.
267219 Pte. LEVINSON, 1/5th Bn.
204174 Pte. LEBOFSKY, A., 2/8th Bn.
208265 Pte. LEVINSON, M.
5360 Rfm. LEAVEY, 8th Bn.
51911 Rfm. LEVI, S.
235389 Pte. LEVY, L.
30913 Pte. LIPSON, H., 2nd Bn.
5896 Rfm. LUBMAN, D., 7th Bn.
29526 Pte. LEWIS, S.
4681 Pte. LEVY, A., 5th Bn.
5235 Rfm. LEWIS, I., 7th Bn.
31789 Pte. LIEBERMAN, R., 4th Bn.

6113 Pte. LEWIS, J., 15th Bn.
25660 Pte. LEVI, B.,* 10th Bn.
18555 Pte. MASSEY, M., 10th Bn.
8332 Pte. MORRIS, T., 11th Bn.
3796 Rfm. MELTZ, N., 1/7th Bn.
31877 Pte. MENDLESON, M., 1st Bn.
306826 Cpl. MOSES, H., 2nd Bn.
34021 Rfm. MENCROFT, M., 9th Bn.
34020 Rfm. MENSCOFSKI, M., 6th Bn.
267 Rfm. MICHAELOFSKI, E., 2/th Bn.
5090 Rfm. MARKS, H., 2/7th Bn.
5168 Rfm. MARKS, L., 2/7th Bn.
39035 Rfm. MAZEIKO, J., 2/5th Bn.
4998 Rfm. MYERSON, M., 2/8th Bn.
8825 Sgt. MARKS, D., 1st Bn.
307510 Sig. MODOULAY, L., 1/8th Bn.
42055 Pte. MARKS, A., 2/5th Bn.
242535 Pte. MINKIN, B., 1/6th Bn.
27737 Pte. MORRIS, J., 22nd Bn.
27736 Pte. MORRIS, L., 22nd Bn.
8659 Cpl. MASSON, G., 2nd Bn.
      Sgt. MOSS, 1st Bn.
23532 Pte. MORMAN, D., 17th Bn.
10031 Pte. MORRIS, H., 1st Bn.
5701 Pte. MOSES, B., 5th Bn.
107382 Pte. MUNROE, W., 7th Bn.
268021 Rfm. MINSK, J., 1/7th Bn.
267408 Pte. MORRIS, B., 1/7th Bn.
203577 Pte. MARKS, E.
28937 L/Cpl. MARKS, J., 19th Bn.
267233 Pte. MARKS, H., 5th Bn.
38090 Pte. MARKS, H., 17th Bn.
14/28044 L/Cpl. McKENNELL, M., 14th Bn.
3567 Pte. MOSCOVITCH, 19th Bn.
5472 Pte. MYERS, E., 7th Bn.
34855 Pte. MYER, R.
4874 Pte. MYER, A., 2/8th Bn.
14/12540 Cpl. MARKS, C., 14th Bn.
10975 Pte. NYMAN, H.,* 1st Bn.
4955 Rfm. NEWMAN, M., 2/8th Bn.
41146 Pte. NATHAN, S., 11thBn.
35011 Pe. NATHAN, M., 20th Bn.
5472 Cpl. NEWMAN, C.,* 1st Bn.
7851 Pte. NIMAN, W., 3/5th Bn.
203576 Pte. NIMAN, P., 3/5th Bn.
39034 Rfm. OGONE, P., 2/5th Bn.
60861 Pte. ORANARDLE, C., 15th Bn.
122322 Pte. ORENSTEIN, L.
15586 Sgt. PEARCE, H., 1st Bn.
5222 Pte. PURVIN, R. M., 1/7th Bn.
43115 Rfm. PHILLIPS, A., 6th Bn.
      Rfm. PEEL, H., 2/7th Bn.
306925 Rfm. PRICE, L.,* 2/8th Bn.
324205 Pte. PIMS, B. L., 18th Bn.
10199 Sgt. PILE.
52456 Pte. POLIKOFF, I.,* 1/5th Bn.
202200 Pte. PURVIN, S., 1/5th Bn.
34924 Pte. PLETZ, L., 13th Bn.

West Yorkshire Regt.—*Continued.*

27096 Pte. PHILLIPS, H., 22nd Bn.
27095 Pte. PHILLIPS, J., 22nd Bn.
10075 Pte. POSNER, S., 1st Bn.
5768 Pte. PASACOVITCH, H., 5th Bn.
21689 L/Cpl. PUSEY, A. A., 9th Bn.
32441 Pte. PRICEMAN, H.
5657 Pte. PERELSTEIN, J., 7th Bn.
203030 Pte. ROSE, S. L.,* 1/5th Bn.
7390 Rfm. ROSENBLOOM, L., 1/7th Bn.
4832 Pte. ROSENTHAL, S., 1/6th Bn.
34855 Pte. REUBEN, M., 1st Bn.
286 L/Cpl. RICHE, S., 18th Bn.
27999 Pte. ROSENBERG, J., 9th Bn.
5136 Rfm. ROSENBLUM, S., 2/7th Bn.
267284 Rfm. RUBENSTEIN, M., 2/7th Bn.
5005 Rfm. RIGGLE, S., 2/7th Bn.
33097 Pte. REUBEN, M.,* 15th Bn.
47940 Pte. RUDSTEIN, S.,* 18th Bn.
32837 Sig. RAKUSEN, H.,* 1/6th Bn.
5348 Pte. ROSE, M., 1/8th Bn.
28871 Pte. ROSENBERG, R., 10th Bn.
268406 Rfm. ROSENBLOOM, C., 1/7th Bn.
62578 Pte. RENKOVITCH, I., 1/5th Bn.
268066 Rfm. REISS, M., 1/7th Bn.
34322 Pte. ROSENBERG, B., 4th Bn.
5121 Pte. ROCKMAN, W., 2/5th Bn.
32832 Pte. RAPPAPORT, M., 14th Bn.
5712 Rfm. ROSENBERG, H., 5th Bn.
5772 Rfm. ROSENSTEIN, B., 5th Bn.
200160 Pte. ROSE, J. E., 5th Bn.
5236 Pte. ROFOFSKI, D., 1/5th Bn.
307056 Pte. RIGGLE, P.,* 2/7th Bn.
1415 Sgt. RAMUS, A. J., 5th Bn.
267308 Pte. RICKLER, E., 2/7th Bn.
9269 Pte. ROSEMAN, M.,* 2nd Bn.
29528 Pte. ROSENBAUM, A.,* 1st Bn.
77884 Pte. ROSENSTONE, W., 2nd Bn.
3768 Pte. ROSENSTEIN, D., 17th Bn.
26304 Cpl. RUDSTEIN, M., 13th Bn.
28029 Pte. RUBENSTEIN, P., 2nd Bn.
14/33949 Pte. REEZIN, 14th Bn.
2815 Pte. RICHMOND, R., 7th Bn.
2213 L/Cpl. ROTENBERG, B.
20210 Pte. ROSSINSKY, S.,* 6th Bn.
3026 Pte. SHEDLOW, H., 1/7th Bn.
25734 Pte. SUDASKY, M., 17th Bn.
41604 Pte. STEINBERG, A.,* 17th Bn.
32316 Pte. SHOOLER, A., 16th Bn.
16177 Pte. SAPERIA, M., 12th Bn.
40156 Rfm. SACKS, S., 9th Bn.
41458 Rfm. SAPERIA, L.,* 9th Bn.
267221 Rfm. SHERENSKI, E., 2/7th Bn.
617216 Rfm. SHATTNER, C., 2/7th Bn.
5080 L/Cpl. SOLK, H., 2/7th Bn.
7849 Rfm. SHERMAN, I., 2/5th Bn.
306580 Rfm. STONE, B., 2/8th Bn.
5076 Rfm. SOLOMAN, M., 2/8th Bn.
39032 Rfm. SALAKAS, 2/5th Bn.
5151 Rfm. SHERMAN, S.,* 2/8th Bn.
4868 Rfm. SLESS, M., 2/8th Bn.
Rfm. SILVER, 2/8th Bn.
20262 Pte. SEGALMAN, W., 12th Bn.
268811 Rfm. SHAFFNER, M., 2/7th Bn.
202186 Pte. SANOFSKI, J.,* 1/5th Bn.
203580 Pte. SHARMAN, I., 1/5th Bn.
5312 Pte. SOLOMON, S., 1/7th Bn.
325084 Pte. SHULTZ, A., 1/8th Bn.
43063 L/Cpl. STONE, L., 10th Bn.
54271 L/Cpl. SAUNDERS, B., 1/6th Bn.
267344 Rfm. STONE, J., 1/7th Bn.
36616 Pte. SLOMAN, W., 11th Bn
42772 Pte. SAMUEL, P., 11th Bn.
5088 Pte. SABIN, B., 3/5th Bn.
33869 Pte. SONENBERG, W., 15th Bn.
41630 Pte. SAFFER, B., 3rd Bn.
5592 Pte. SOCHALL, D., 1/5th Bn.
Pte. SHEPIRO, S.
4699 Pte. SCHULTZ, M., 5th Bn.
271421 Pte. SILVERMAN, M., 51st Bn.
242590 Pte. SILVERMAN, S., 5th Bn.
4876 Pte. SOLOMONS, S., 6th Bn.
29555 Pte. SHEDLOW, M.,, 3rd Bn.
5648 Pte. SEGELMAN, W., 5th Bn.
267409 Rfm. SOLOMON, S., 1/7th Bn.
48980 Pte. SILVERSTONE, M., 2/8th Bn.
6331 Rfm. SWITZ, L., 15th Bn.
29617 Pte. SEIGLEMAN, D. L., 13th Bn.
4071 Pte. SIMCOVITCH, M.
4667 Pte. STONE, D., 5th Bn.
4677 Pte. SOCHALL, A., 5th Bn.
28360 Pte. SMOLLEN, P.
55228 Pte. SHIRE, B., 7th Bn.
47294 Pte. SIMON, T. ,18th Bn.
54734 Pte. STONE, H., 7th Bn.
49983 Pte. SPIWACH, W., 7th Bn.
30684 Pte. SPERO, M., 5th Bn.
Pte. SANDERS, H., 1st Bn.
51914 Pte. SOLOMON, L., 2/8th Bn.
Pte. SHINDLER, W. D., 6th Bn.
Pte. SIMON, D., 3rd Bn.
6618 L/Cpl. TAYLOR, A., 1/6th Bn.
267261 Pte. TOMPOFSKI, M.* (M.M.), 1/8th Bn.
41914 Pte. TERRACE, H., 1/7th Bn.
72560 L/Cpl. TRESMAN, H. J.,* 2nd Bn.
29144 Pte. TENNYSON, J., 13th Bn.
29629 Pte. TAYLOR, C., 13th Bn.
24436 Pte. TAYLOR, W., 11th Bn.
Rfm. VATES, I., 2/7th Bn.
31824 Pte. VEDENBOHN, I.
Pte. VALENTINE, S. (M.M.).
27063 Pte. VITKUNSKI, M.
32406 Pte. VINER, L., 14th Bn.
Pte. VYNER, S., 7th Bn.
4961 Rfm. WOLFE, H., 2/8th Bn.
5421 Pte. WALLACK, M.,* 1/6th Bn.

West Yorkshire Regt.—*Continued.*

5694 Pte. WINSTON, 6th Bn.
94717 Pte. WOLFSON, M.
210103 Pte. WINESTOCK, C.
5084 Pte. WOLFSON, H., 5th Bn.
266781 Pte. WELTZ, A.
54777 Rfm. WILKS, M., 7th Bn.
31758 Pte. WHITE, J., 13th Bn.
4892 Pte. WOLFF, H., 5th Bn.
14/35283 Pte. WYORSKY, S. D., 14th Bn.
242729 Sgt. WAXMAN, B., 6th Bn.
31879 Pte. YARMOSKY, J., 1st Bn.
184 Pte. YAFFE, B., 17th Bn.
40310 Pte. YAFFIN, J.,* 18th Bn.
25392 Pte. YARMOFSKY, J.
34856 Pte. YEWDALL, P., 1st Bn.
21889 Pte. ZISSMAN, S. S., 5th Bn.
267224 L/Cpl. ZALK, H., 15th Bn.
31014 Pte. ZABITT, A., 2nd Bn.

* Killed in Action or died on Active Service.

THE EAST YORKSHIRE REGIMENT.

OFFICERS.

2nd Lieut. FRANKS,* L., 8th Bn.
Major GOSSCHALK, H. J., 4th Bn.
2nd Lieut. GREEN, G.
Capt. GOSSCHALK, F., 4th Bn.
2nd Lieut. HARRIS, A., 11th Bn.
2nd Lieut. HARRIS, C. E., 13th Bn.
Lieut. MARGOLIES, I., 13th Bn.
Capt. PIZA, D.,* 1st Bn.
Capt. SCHOTTLANDER, A., 5th Bn.

N.C.O.'s AND MEN.

832 Sgt. AARONS, J. (M.M.), 11th Bn.
25645 Pte. ALLEN, D., 8th Bn.
175941 Pte. ALLEN, J., 8th Bn.
28847 Pte. ADLER, D.
241990 Pte. ANDERSON, C.
12662 Pte. BLASHKER, L., 7th Bn.
11/831 Pte. BLACK, M.,* 11th Bn.
25645 Pte. BENNETT, S., 8th Bn.
11832 Pte. BARADOSKY, B.,* 8th Bn.
12/1448 Pte. BROWN, A.,* 8th Bn.
28972 Pte. BERNSTINE, S., 1st Bn.
12/910 Pte. BROWN, H., 12th Bn.
23694 Pte. BASS, A., 15th Bn.
25071 Pte. BARRETT, H., 1st Bn.
35955 Pte. BODESKY, 1st Bn.
23666 Pte. BENNETT, H., 2nd Bn.
33494 Pte. BLOOM, P.
Pte. BARNETT, H., 15th Bn.
Pte. BAUM, S., 2nd Bn.
159 Pte. CASSON, D., 11th Bn.
14/24 Pte. CUTNER, M., 12th Bn.
24487 Pte. COHEN, J., 4th Bn.
23937 Pte. COUPLAND, P., 13th Bn.
225981 Pte. CARRIER, I., 1/4th Bn.
Pte. CRAMMER, E.
36848 Pte. COWEN, E., 3rd Bn.
50912 Pte. COHEN, H., 11th Bn.
33790 Pte. COHEN, A.
29494 Pte. CROSBY, M.
59918 Pte. COHEN, 1st Bn.
4827 C.S.M. DAVIS H. S.,* (M.C.), 1st Bn.
39704 Pte. DIAMOND, J., 3rd Bn.
Pte. DAVIS, E.
Pte. DAVIES, J., 2nd Bn.
Pte. DAVIS, M., 2nd Bn.
9304 Sgt. FREEMAN, A., 8th Bn.
25410 Pte. FREEDMAN, M.,* 7th Bn.
25489 Pte. FISHER, W., 10th Bn.
6868 Pte. FURMAN, H.,* 4th Bn.
41725 Sgt. FLATTOW, J. W. (M.M.), 11th Bn.
41413 Cpl. FREEDMAN, E., 6th Bn.
28302 Pte. FOX, C., 7th Bn.
22008 Pte. FINKLESTONE, H., 1st Bn.
9703 Pte. FREEMAN, B., 2nd Bn.
446 Pte. FELDMAN, J., 10th Bn.
9/26102 Pte. FLAXMAN, J., 9th Bn.
205346 Pte. FIELDMAN, S., 4th Bn.
7692 Sgt. GOODMAN, J., 7th Bn.
9988 Sgt. GOLDSTEIN, A., 2nd Bn.
517 Pte. GRABINE, S., 12th Bn.
31116 Pte. GOLDSTONE, M.,* 1st Bn.
220040 Pte. GRABINE, W., 4th Bn.
8835 Sgt. GOBES, A., 7th Bn.
49648 Pte. GORDON, M., 3rd Bn.
Pte. GOLDSTEIN, A., 1st Bn.
34456 Pte. GREEN, L., 11th Bn.
5398 Pte. GOLDSTEIN, D., 4th Bn.
38240 Pte. GRABINE, H., 3rd Bn.
205530 Pte. GROSSER, C., 4th Bn.
26162 Pte. GRAHAM, J.
7692 Sgt. GOODMAN, H., 7th Bn.
14/235 Pte. HARRIS, 12th Bn.
710 Pte. HARRIS, A. C., 10th Bn.
27229 Pte. HYMAN, R.,* 8th Bn.
14128 Pte. HARRIS, S., 4th Bn.
3262 Pte. HYAM, E.,* 4th Bn.
44277 Pte. HART, J., 11th Bn.
Pte. HARRIS, A., 5th Bn.
27071 Pte. HARRIS, M., 2nd Bn.
Pte. HARRIS, H., 3rd Bn.
42598 Pte. HERSHWITZ, E., 1st Bn.
226081 Pte. HARRIS, R., 5th Bn.
10/1404 Pte. HARKSTONE, M., 10th Bn.
175639 Pte. HARDY, A., 4th Bn.
15535 Pte. ISAACS, S., 7th Bn.
12662 Pte. ISAACS, L., 7th Bn.
8123 Sgt. JACKSON, E., 8th Bn.

East Yorkshire Regt.—Continued.

36773	Sgt. JACKSON, S., 7th Bn.
203447	Pte. JACOBS, A.,* 4th Bn.
52721	Pte. JACOBS, W., 1st Bn.
35754	Pte. JACKSON, 1st G.B.
876	Pte. KERSH, A., 10th Bn.
33434	Pte. KAUFFMAN, I., 13th Bn.
	Pte. KRAMMER, E., 3rd Bn.
35319	Pte. KNOWLES, H.
S4/145979	Sgt. KITCHING, M.
563	Pte. LANCH, J., 12th Bn.
5288	Pte. LEVINE, S., 4th Bn.
23934	Pte. LIPMANOVITCH, J., 7th Bn.
	Pte. LESSER, 1st Bn.
42598	Sig. LEWIS, E., 8th Bn.
20589	Pte. LEVY, 1st Bn.
	Sgt. LEWIS, S. J.
12802	Pte. LUKES, L., 4th Bn.
23645	Pte. LESHSKY, T. A., 14th Bn.
225	Pte. MOROCK, M.,* 10th Bn.
929	Pte. MOSS, B. B., 10th Bn.
940	Pte. MAGNER, E., 11th Bn.
29803	Pte. MOSSESSON, E., 6th Bn.
41692	Pte. MOSS, H.,
29777	Pte. NOVINSKI, I.,* 4th Bn.
22401	Pte. NEEDLER, M., 14th Bn.
1374	Pte. QUESKY, N. J., 10th Bn.
3/23948	Pte. QUESKEY, H., 10th Bn.
1045	Pte. REUBEN, J., 10th Bn.
317	Pte. RAPSTONE, M., 11th Bn.
4998	Pte. ROSS, J.,* 4th Bn.
	Pte. ROSE, P., 3rd Bn.
3579	Pte. ROSENBERG, S., 4th Bn.
25498	Pte. ROFOFSKIE, H., 3rd Bn.
28914	Pte. RAPPAPORT, J., 8th Bn.
26695	Pte. ROSEN, H., 15th Bn.
588	Pte. SHAPERO, L. (M.M.), 10th Bn.
664	C.S.M. SCHOTTLANDER, S. (M.M.), 10th B.
14/221	Pte. SEGAL, S., 12th Bn.
10/1331	Pte. SUGARMAN, S.,* 12th Bn.
10/371	Pte. SHEPHERD, L., 12th Bn.
4206	Pte. SMITH, G., 4th Bn.
23367	Pte. SLIMMER, L., 7th Bn.
33407	Pte. SUGAR, A., 7th Bn.
27881	Pte. SHALGOSKY, W., 13th Bn.
220132	Pte. SMITH, G., 12th Bn.
29208	Pte. STANLEY, M., 7th Bn.
1371	Pte. SHAPERO, S., 10th Bn.
25064	Pte. SELTZER, P., 14th Bn.
22387	Pte. SULTAN, J., 14th Bn.
9751	Pte. SLIMMER, H., 2nd Bn.
26127	Pte. SUMROY, B., 3rd Bn.
225408	Pte. SOLK, E., 5th Bn.
27013	L/Cpl. SELTZER, A., 3rd Bn.
50700	Cpl. SILVERMAN, S., 1st Bn.
22400	Pte. SHALGOSKY, B., 14th Bn.
234577	Pte. TOBIAS, M., 3rd Bn.
38	Pte. WACHOLDER, H. M., 10th Bn.
739	Pte. WOLFE, S. M., 11th Bn.
28901	Pte. WOLFSON, I., 8th Bn.
28847	Pte. WOODHEAD, W., 8th Bn.
143250	Pte. WEINOW, B., 14th Bn.
6254	Pte. WILSON, G., 3rd Bn.
57708	Pte. WHITE, B.
38010	Pte. WILLIAMSON, H., 2nd Bn.
205881	Pte. VIGODSKY, L., 10th Bn.
6429	Pte. WINETRAUBE, L. R., 3rd Bn.
21575	Pte. WOLFF, J., 9th Bn.
22694	Pte. WOOD. L., 12th Bn.

* Killed in Action or died on Active Service.

THE BEDFORDSHIRE REGIMENT.

OFFICERS.

Capt. HART, S. L., 6th Bn.
Capt. HART, C. H.,* 2nd Bn.
Lieut. HARBURG, S. H., 52nd Bn.
Lieut. JOLOWICZ, H. F.
2nd Lieut. LEVY, A. M.,* 4th Bn.
Lieut. MICHAELS, 2nd Bn.
Lieut. NATHAN.
2nd Lieut. ROMAIN, J. A., 4th Bn.
2nd Lieut. SCHLESINGER, F. D., 9th Bn.
Lieut. SOLOMON, H. M.,* 6th Bn.
2nd Lieut. SHEKURY, C.* (M.C.), 2nd Bn.
Lieut. SAMUEL,, W. G.,* 2nd Bn.
2nd Lieut. VAN DER LINDE, S.,* 6th Bn.
Major WOLFF, C. H., 1st Bn.

N.C.O.'s AND MEN.

378	L/Cpl. ABRAHAMS.
67447	Pte. ABRAHAMS, M.
13375	Pte. ALTMAN, L.,* 1st Bn.
7177	Pte. ALTMAN, P., 2/5th Bn.
35068	Pte. BARRS, 3rd Bn.
8203	Pte. BEAR, G., 1st Bn.
14643	Pte. BEAR, J., 1st Bn.
35634	Sgt. BENZIMRA, H. V., 3rd Bn.
29133	Pte. BROTSKY, E., 3rd Bn.
7186	Pte. BREWER, H., 2/5th Bn.
204374	Pte. BURNS, P., 2/5th Bn.
35743	Pte. BOSS, R. G., 3rd Bn.
	Sgt. BENJAMIN, 3rd Bn.
	Pte. BRAHAM, S.
23389	Pte. BLOWFIELD, J., 2nd Bn.
2503	Pte. BUIRSKI, S., 3rd Bn.
36732	Pte. CANTOR, J., 13th Bn.
13476	Pte. CARNANA, T., 6th Bn.
39424	Pte. CHEEK, E., 3rd Bn.

The Bedfordshire Regt.—*Continued.*

6758 Pte. COHEN, J., 2/5th Bn.
66897 L/Cpl. COHEN, S.
21568 Pte. COHEN, L. G., 3rd Bn.
28305 Pte. COHEN, S., 3rd Bn.
45941 Pte. COHEN, A. L., 51st Bn.
32978 Pte. COHEN, B.,* 1st Bn.
50765 Pte. COHEN, V., 1st Bn.
64287 Sgt. COHEN, H., 1st Bn.
27278 Pte. COHEN, D., 9th Bn.
5328 Pte. COSTA, M., 52nd Bn.
203402 Pte. CRAVITZ, M., 2/5th Bn.
Pte. DAVIES, P., 1st Bn.
201655 Pte. EPSTEIN, M., 2/5th Bn.
240835 Pte. EPHRAIM, H., 11th Bn.
49963 Pte. ELLIS, W., 1st Bn.
Sgt. FRANKS, S. (M.S.M.).
12535 Pte. FLATON, S.,* 6th Bn.
494610 Pte. FARBSTEIN, I.
203015 Pte. FINEBRG, H., 2/5th Bn.
201654 Pte. FINEMAN, N. E., 2/5th Bn.
201690 Pte. FORREST, C., 2/5th Bn.
Pte. FLAGON, S.
50275 Pte. FRASER, M., 3rd Bn.
201759 Pte. FREEDMAN, S., 2/5th Bn.
292032 Pte. FREEMAN, 3rd Bn.
26473 Pte. GARFINCLE, S., 4th Bn.
208953 Pte. GODINSKI, J., 13th Bn.
48715 Pte. GOODMAN, M., 3rd Bn.
12736 L/Cpl. GROSSMAN, E., 6th Bn.
49968 Pte. HARRIS, P., 1st Bn.
38769 Pte. HART, M.
33024 Pte. HENDLICK, J., 2nd Bn.
35744 Pte. HERMAN, B., 2nd Bn.
36872 Cpl. HERSHMAN, P., 13th Bn.
36831 Sgt. HEATHER, J., 12th T.E.
27159 Pte. HORWICH, H., 3rd Bn.
12802 Cpl. HULLES, M.,* 6th Bn.
Pte. HYAMS, W.
6853 Pte. JACOBS, A., 2/5th Bn.
12507 Pte. JACOBS, S., 6th Bn.
35662 L/Cpl. JONES, F., 2nd Bn.
Pte. JOSEPH, M., 2nd Bn.
201711 Pte. JOSEPH, R., 2/5th Bn.
19759 Pte. KAMOVITZ, J., 6th Bn.
39017 Pte. KINSLER, S., 13th Bn.
Pte. KOHN, P., 3rd Bn.
32075 Pte. LANCER, H., 4th Bn.
37917 Pte. LAWLER, 3rd Bn.
45509 Pte. LANDSTER, A. S., 3rd Bn.
5157 Pte. LEVY, B., 2/1st Bn.
8629 Pte. LEVY, J., 2nd Bn.
Pte. LEE, S., 2nd Bn.
24587 Pte. LOWE, J., 1st Bn.
7391 Pte. LYONS, H., 1st Bn.
34566 Pte. LINKE, H., 12th Bn.
24329 Pte. LEVENS, H., 1st Bn.
33054 Pte. MAYERS, J., 6th Bn.

65565 Cpl. MEADOWS, C.
268282 L/Cpl. MORRIS, D., 1st Bn.
6960 Pte. MORRIS, I., 2/5th Bn.
6962 Pte. MYERS, J., 2/5th Bn.
35757 Pte. MYERS, 2nd Bn.
38931 Pte. MOSS, F., 3rd Bn.
340660 Pte. MOSCOVITCH, J., 12th Bn.
45852 Pte. NEEDLEMAN, D.
41201 Pte. NEWMAN, H., 3rd Bn.
4391 Pte. NOBLE, S.
67512 Pte. OTOLANGUI, W. J.
Pte. PARKER, A., 7th Bn.
240955 Pte. PELLER, G., 11th Bn.
21878 Pte. PHILLIPS, D., 3rd Bn.
425861 Pte. PHILLIPS, W., 7th Bn.
28300 Pte. PRIMHACK, N., 3rd Bn.
48760 Pte. REITIS, J., 3rd Bn.
1834432 Pte. ROOD, N., 13th Bn.
201656 Dmr. ROSENBERG, H., 2/5th Bn.
32072 Pte. ROSENBERG, S., 3rd Bn.
67206 Pte. ROSENTHAL, A.
40483 Pte. SAMUELS, J.,* 7th Bn.
6320 Pte. SHINE, A., 2nd Bn.
37400 L/Cpl. SILVER, A.,* 2nd Bn.
27405 Pte. SILVER, 2nd Bn.
28489 Pte. SILVERSTONE, M.,* 4th Bn.
203400 Pte. SILVERSTONE, P., 2/5th Bn.
Pte. SIMONS, S., 2nd Bn.
32074 Pte. SHWECKLER, A., 3rd Bn.
3369 Pte. SMOLENSKY, A., 3rd Bn.
Pte. SNIDERS, S., 2nd Bn.
41990 Pte. STEPHEN, S., 2nd Bn.
35127 L/Cpl. STATMAN, 3rd Bn.
60957 Pte. SCHWAREMBERG, J., 3rd Bn.
46887 Pte. SCHRIERS, S.
Pte. SOLOMON, 1st Bn.
8693 Cpl. SNIDER, J.,* 2nd Bn.
48686 Pte. SILVERMAN, S., 3rd Bn
41990 Pte. STEPHAM, S.,* 2nd Bn.
36520 Sgt. STEINBERG, J., 12th Bn.
21883 Pte. STICKLER, K., 1/5th Bn.
50033 Pte. SQUISKY, 1st Bn.
Pte. SURDEN, J., 1st Bn.
13471 Pte. WOOLF, B., 1st Bn.
6905 Pte. WOOLF, F. J., 2/5th Bn.
Pte. WINEBERG, J. M., 9th Bn.
67694 Pte. WEINER, L.
36395 Pte. WOLSTENCROFT, A., 2rd Bn.
50008 Pte. WEINBERG, H.,* 1st Bn.
30008 Pte. WEINBERG, T., 1st Bn.
65003 Pte. ZEEGAN, L.

* Killed in Action or died on Active Service.

THE LEICESTERSHIRE REGIMENT.

OFFICERS.

2nd Lieut. COLEMAN, L. G., 7th Bn.
Lieut. DOVE, M., 8th Bn.
2nd Lieut. FISHER, L. H., 7th Bn.
Capt. LAZARUS, C. H.,* 7th Bn.
2nd Lieut. RUBINSTEIN, J. E., 6th Bn.

N.C.O.'s AND MEN.

5560 Pte. ABRAHAM, J. E.,* 2nd Bn.
526063 Pte. ABRAHAMSON, S., 51st Bn.
39062 Pte. ALENALASHVILI, B., 3rd Bn.
202239 Pte. ALEXANDER, H., 4th Bn.
25413 Pte. BROWN, H., 7th Bn.
25481 Pte. BROWN, Z. C., 7th Bn.
7147 Pte. BECK, A., 2/4th Bn.
242216 Pte. BARNARD, D., 2/5th Bn.
43164 Pte. BALKIN, W., 1s Bn.
42973 L/Cpl. BARNETT, B., 7th Bn.
5347 Pte. BUCKLER, F.
7197 Pte. COHEN, A., 2/4th Bn.
202702 L/Cpl. COHEN, A.,* 2/4th Bn.
529997 Pte. COHEN, S. S., 52nd Bn.
62493 Pte. COHEN, D., 53rd Bn.
526682 Pte. CLEVEN, J., 51st Bn.
6219 Pte. COTSON, J., 2/4th Bn.
37818 Pte. DANIEL, F., 6th Bn.
18091 Pte. ELLIOT, J., 9th Bn.
37281 Pte. FREEDMAN, B., 3rd Bn.
Pte. FRANKLIN, E., 4th Bn.
6560 Pte. GOODMAN, A.,* 1st Bn.
40341 Pte. GOLDMAN, M., 6th Bn.
46467 Pte. GREY, E., 11th Bn.
326490 Pte. GRAJEWSKY, B., 5th Bn.
34003 Pte. HOFBRAND, P., 52nd Bn.
Pte. HYMAN, A. (M.M.).
35110 Pte. HARRIS, M.
8444 Pte. JACOBS, A., 1st Bn.
24224 Pte. JOSEPH, M., 52nd Bn.
39388 Pte. JONES, H., 7th Bn.
43179 Pte. KREMER, I. (M.M.), 1st Bn.
8470 Cpl. KINGSLEY, A.,* 1st Bn.
36091 L/Cpl. LANDANSKI, B., 7th Bn.
41756 Pte. LAZARUS, H. (M.M., D.C.M.), 8th Bn.
418838 Pte. LESSER, R., 7th Bn.
8891 Pte. MILLER, H., 1st Bn.
203188 Pte. MEYERS, G., 4th Bn.
5619 Pte. MILLER, F., 6th Bn.
23675 Cpl. MARTIN, L., 10th Bn.
43281 Pte. OKEN, 11th Bn.
15007 Pte. POMERANTZ, J.,* 2nd Bn.
45717 Pte. PALLEY, B.
37871 Pte. SOLWAY, J., 1st Bn.
24364 Cpl. SAPPERSTONE, H.
327300 Pte. SYKES, W., 5th Bn.
110766 L/Cpl. SORKIN, A., 5th Bn.

024801 Cpl. SONFIELD, C.
031502 L/Cpl. SMITH, L. J.
367245 Pte. SMALLEN, M., 51st Bn.
40893 Pte. SHERWINTER, L., 51st Bn.
35692 Pte. SCHIBLER, H., 13th Bn.
39062 Pte. SCHAVILLE, B. A., 3rd Bn.
44407 Pte. SIMMONS, M., 1st Bn.
28555 Pte. SACOFSKY, M.,* 6th Bn.
28557 Pte. TAYLOR, L., 7th Bn.
41583 Pte. TOBIAS, W. (M.M.), 7th Bn.
10946 Pte. WACKS, J., 6th Bn.
10950 Pte. WOODWARD, E. W., 6th Bn.
226670 Pte. WOLFBERGEN, I., 6th Bn.
39241 Pte. WHITE, B.
50826 Pte. WOOLF, H., 4th Bn.
235263 Pte. ZISSMAN, M., 2/4th Bn.
309351 Pte. ZARBECK, S., 51st Bn.

* Killed in Action or died on Active Service.

THE ROYAL IRISH REGIMENT.

OFFICERS.

Capt. BLANCKENSEE, G., 1st Bn.
2nd Lieut. SAMUELS, A. P. I., 18th Bn.
Lieut. JOSEPH, S., 5th Bn.
Capt. WOLF, G., 4th Bn.
2nd Lieut. WOLF, C.
2nd Lieut. WOLF, E. M.,

N.C.O.'s AND MEN.

41807 Pte. AZEN, J., 7th Bn.
43525 Pte. ANSELL, S., 9th Bn.
20194 Pte BENJAMIN, M.
42202 Pte. BENJAMIN, B., 12th Bn.
7476 Pte. BELMON, A., 3rd Bn.
42388 Pte. COHEN, S., 1st Bn.
C.Q.M.S. COHEN, H., 11th Bn.
Pte. DAVIS, J., 2nd Bn.
Pte. DAVIS, P., 8th Bn.
8234 Pte. ELLISON, S. J.,* 2nd Bn.
Pte. EFFERMANN, J., 8th Bn.
3978 Pte. FREEDMAN, H., 2nd Bn.
44195 Pte. GREEN, A., 8th Bn.
18268 Pte. HARRIS, H.,* 2nd Bn.
18910 Pte. HART, M., 2nd Bn.
5317 Pte. HYMAN, H., 2nd Bn.
4003 Pte. JACOBS, J., 2nd Bn.
3985 Pte. KALMAN, H., 2nd Bn.
3884 Pte. LAPSEIN, J. H., 2nd Bn.
11640 Pte. LEVINSTONE, A.
5504 Pte. LEVY, J., 5th Pion. Bn.
8456 Pte. LUBINSKY, M., 2nd Bn.
3882 Pte. MARKS, D., 2nd Bn.
30995 Pte. MARCUS, V., 7th Bn.

Royal Irish Regt.—Continued.

44661 Pte. MEDNIKOFF, M., 16th Bn.
5228 Pte. MILSTONE, H., 5th Bn.
41692 Pte. MOSS, H.
8248 L/Cpl. ROBERTS, J., 18th Bn.
5325 Pte. SEBA, W., 8th Bn.
5236 Pte. SHAPERA, J., 5th (Pion.) Bn.
4001 Pte. SILVER, L.
Pte. SOLOMON, J., 2nd Bn.
72182 Pte. TEIMAN, J., 1/2nd Bn.
5236 L/Cpl. ZAPIRA, L., 5th Bn.

* Killed in Action or died on Active Service.

ALEXANDRA, PRINCESS OF WALES'S OWN (YORKSHIRE REGIMENT).

OFFICERS.

2nd Lieut. ABRAHAMS, R. B.,* 4th Bn.
Lieut. BLOOM, H.,* 12th Bn.
Lieut. HART, P. H. (M.C.).
2nd Lieut. JACOBS, J.,* 5th Bn.
2nd Lieut. MELHADO, O. S.,* 11th Bn.
Capt. ROSKIN, H., 1st Gar. Bn.
2nd Lieut. SAMUEL, P. C., 8th Bn.
Lieut. WACHOLDER, A., 2nd Bn.

N.C.O.'s AND MEN.

Pte. ASH, B., 4th Bn.
36067 Ptt. AARONS, H. D.,* 6th Bn.
48885 Pte. APPLESON, L.
63257 Pte. ADDLESTONE, D.
10424 Pte. BRIGGS, J., 2nd Bn.
31477 L/Cpl. BERSON, M.
10460 Pte. BOMBERG, J.,* 2nd Bn.
34381 Pte. BENOLIEL, M., 9th Bn.
25859 Pte. COSSICK, J., 8th Bn.
43007 Pte. COHEN, L., 4th Bn.
27036 Pte. COHEN, H., 8th Bn.
Sgt. COHEN, G., 2nd Bn.
10303 Pte. CAROLTEN, R.,* 2nd Bn.
201909 Pte. COHEN, J., 4th Bn.
5077 Pte. CROSS, H. B., 5th Bn.
242560 Pte. COHEN, J.
203400 Pte. COLMER, C., 4th Bn.
61362 Pte. DRAMOND, M., 9th Bn.
25509 Pte. DAVIS, J., 8th Bn.
35756 L/Cpl. DYSCH, H.
202154 Pte. DAVIES, H., 2/4th Bn.
36066 Pte. ELLIS, S.,* 2nd Bn.
235352 Pte. ENGLEMAN, B., 9th Bn.
10278 Cpl. FERNER, A.* (D.C.M.), 6th Bn.
241691 Pte. FINBERG, H., 5th Bn.
243798 Pte. FREEDMAN, 2/5th Bn.

10489 L/Cpl. GILDER, B., 2nd Bn.
43034 Pte. GILLER, W., 4th Bn.
235140 Pte. GILLIS, J., 4th Bn.
6117 Pte. GLASSMAN, M., 4th Bn.
34080 Pte. GOLDSTEIN, H., 7th Bn.
41429 Pte. GOLDBERG, E.,* 6th Bn.
Pte. GOLDSTEIN, S., 3rd Bn.
Bdsm. GARCIA, H., 1st Bn.
21864 Sgt. GOLDBERG, 1st Gar. Bn.
25954 Pte. GIRN, H., 7th Bn.
41597 Pte. HILL, H., 9th Bn.
235586 Pte. HARDY, A., 13th Bn.
62899 Pte. HARRIS, L., 3rd Bn.
26554 Ptt. HUSH, E., 3rd Bn.
61234 Pte. HARRIS, S., 18th Bn.
Pte. ISAACS, S.
29583 Pte. KOSSICK, J., 8th Bn.
243205 Pte. KERSH, 2/5th Bn.
24342 L/Cpl. KAY, J. J., 18th Bn.
9553 Pte. KANBROOCH, S., 2/4th Bn.
8532 Pte. LESKIE, H., 1/5th Bn.
33168 Pte. LEVY, S., 10th Bn.
235427 Pte. LYSCHINSKA, H., 8th Bn.
2435 Pte. LEVY, I., 4th Bn.
13464 Pte. LEVINSON, T., 16th Bn.
46560 L/Cpl. LEVY, P. M.,* 9th Bn.
2479 Pte. LAZARUS, H., 1/4th Bn.
40587 Pte. LEVY, M., 17th Bn.
32167 Pte. LEVY, L., 10th Bn.
29868 Sgt. MARGOLIES, I., 13th Bn.
23498 Pte. MORRIS, J., 8th Bn.
49437 Pte. MUSLIN, S., 9th Bn.
31799 Pte. MARKS. D. H.
43250 Pte. MILLER, M., 17th Bn.
42745 Pte. MENDOZA, J., 2nd Bn.
202619 Pte. MOSSESOM, E., 2/4th Bn.
43115 Pte. PHILLIPS, A., 9th Bn.
42424 Pte. PEARLMAN, M., 2nd Bn.
30731 Pte. PLOTTEL, F., 6th Bn.
204648 Pte. PESCHANSKY, M., 4th Bn.
260009 Pte. PERLMAN, J., 6th Bn.
62277 Pte. PLOTZSKY, G., 9th Bn.
10304 Pte. ROSEN, M.,* 2nd Bn.
28914 Pte. RAPPAPORT, J., 8th Bn.
61586 Pte. ROUNDSKIN, J., 9th Bn.
37283 Pte. ROSENTHAL, A., 15th Bn.
34277 Pte. REECE, J., 9th Bn.
5284 Pte. ROSSENBLEIM, L., 10th Bn.
8434 L/Cpl. SIMONS, J., 9th Bn.
42459 Pte. STONE, H., 9th Bn.
5524 Pte. SMALLEN, J., 4th Bn.
34947 Pte. SOLOMONS, S., 8th Bn.
42930 Pte. SAMUELS, N., 16th Bn.
8748 Pte. SAMUELS, A.,* 2nd Bn.
8540 Pte. STAMBER, D., 4th Bn.
11878 Pte. SHAW, L., 7th Bn.
44314 Pte. SALIT, 2/5th Bn.
243171 Pte. SELWYN, 2/5th Bn.

Yorkshire Regt.—*Continued*.

6170 Pte. SUGARMAN.
61364 Pte. SAVILLE, R., 48th Bn.
41168 Cpl. SUPPERSTONE, H., 17th Bn.
30301 Pte. SAPERIA, A., 2nd Bn.
63716 Pte. SAGLOWATCH, A., 18th Bn.
65889 Pte. SHALGOSKY, A., 18th Bn.
     Pte. SHLESSER, C.
24436 Pte. TAYLOR, N., 10th Bn.
43049 Pte. TAYLOR, O., 12th Bn.
43173 Pte. TUKEMAN, S., 17th Bn.
21533 Sgt. VANDERVELDE, 1st Gar. Bn.
62139 Pte. VYMAN, D,. 18th Bn.
23667 Pte. WHITEMAN, A. A., 13th Bn.
22694 Pte. WOOD, L., 12th Bn.
34336 Pte. WANDERLOVITCH, J., 8th Bn.
3561 Pte. WEBB, C., 5th Bn.
266766 Pte. WALDMAN, A., 18th Bn.
42574 Pte. WILLIAMS, T., 9th Bn.
204140 Pte. WILKS, E., 4th Bn.
42533 Pte. ZIMMERMAN, N.,* 2nd Bn.

* Killed in Action or died on Active Service.

THE LANCASHIRE FUSILIERS.

OFFICERS.

2nd Lieut. ANCILL, G. C., 2/6th Bn.
2nd Lieut. BERNSTEIN, M. L.* (M. C.), 11th Bn.
2nd Lieut. BIRNSTINGL, H., 17th Bn.
2nd Lieut. GORFUNKLE, I.,* 1st Bn.
2nd Lieut. GOLDSMITH, 2/6th Bn.
2nd Lieut. JOSEPH, K. M., 16th Bn.
Capt. LASKI, N. J., 1/6th Bn.
Capt. LEVI, V. N., 1/6th Bn.
Capt. MANDLEBERG, L. C. (M.C. & Bar), 15th Bn.
Col. MANDLEBERG, S. L., 2/8th Bn.
2nd Lieut. MORITZ, A., 9th Bn.
2nd Lieut. MORDECAI, L. R., 2/5th Bn.
Lieut. MORLAND, H. M., 9th Bn.
2nd Lieut. MORRIS, H. M.,* 15th Bn.
2nd Lieut. NATHAN, J. A., 11th Bn.
2nd Lieut. REISS, P. Q.
Capt. ROTHBAND, B. H., 2/5th Bn.
Capt. ROTHBAND, P. L., 4th Bn.
Capt. SAMUEL, C., 12th Bn.
2nd Lieut. SCHAFFER, H., 16th Bn.
2nd Lieut. SAGER, N., 1st Bn. attd 86th T.M.B
Capt. SIMON, E. C.,* 2/5th Bn.
2nd Lieut. SIMON, R., 6th Bn.
2nd Lieut. SINGTON, E. E., 7th Bn.
Capt. STIEBEL, C. O. (M.C.).

N.C.O.'s AND MEN.

20272 Pte. ABRAMS, M., 9th Bn.
5459 Pte. ADDIS, H., 3/5th Bn.
41749 Pte. ADDIS, I.,* 1 1st Bn.
5460 Pte. ADDIS, S., 3/5th Bn.
24779 Cpl. APPLEBOOM, C., 10th Bn.
1395 Pte. AARONS, B., 2nd Bn.
8850 Sgt. ASKINS, M., 2nd Bn.
63656 Pte. ALTMAN, H.,* 16th Bn.
15/5241 Pte. ANDREWS, I.
22678 Pte. ALEXANDER, H.
22/32950 Pte. ALEXANDER, J., 12th Bn.
252968 Pte. ALEXANDER, S., 2/5th Bn.
53858 Pte. AROZKIN, P., 4th Bn.
4/4077 Pte. ASH, M.
204895 Pte. AGULSKY, D., 5th Bn.
     Pte. ABRAHAMS, F. I., 8th Bn.
     Pte. ALPERN, A., 2/8th Bn.
29272 Pte. ABRAHAMS, M., 9th Bn.
     L/Cpl. BEAVER, J., 15th Bn.
1202x Pte. BLACKSTONE, M., 15th Bn.
4320 Pte. BLOOM, H., 2/5th Bn.
5177 Pte. BENJAMIN, P. D.,* 3/5th Bn.
32976 Pte. BAUMGARD, S.,* 22nd Bn.
3257 Sgt. BOWMAN, L., 2/7th Bn.
4597 Pte. BOWMAN, P., 2/7th Bn.
281904 Pte. BURMAN, S., 2/7th Bn.
546 Pte. BELMAN, A.,* 2/7th Bn.
202216 Pte. BLOOM, H., 1st Bn.
62680 Pte. BLACK, N., 19th Bn.
45758 L/Cpl. BERNBAUM, M., 1st Bn.
253569 Pte. BERNSTEIN, L., 2/3rd Bn.
63052 Pte. BLACK, 16th Bn.
6/13127 Pte. BARUCH, J., 6th Bn.
281832 Cpl. BONAM, P., 2/7th Bn.
2080 Pte. BERG, E., 6th Bn.
J/6 Sgt. BOBROFF, H., 6th Bn.
51250 Pte. BLOCK, P., 4th Bn.
3750 Pte. BLACK, H., 3rd Bn.
204807 Pte. BERMAN, I., 5th Bn.
     Pte. BINES, J., 8th Bn.
38103 Sgt. COSSACK, S., 20th Bn.
25457 Pte. CAIRNS, J.,* 18th Bn.
39564 Pte. COHEN, H.,* 10th Bn.
40358 Pte. CHECK, E., 1/5th Bn.
4624 Pte. COHEN, B., 1/7th Bn.
4465 Pte. COHEN, M., 1/8th Bn.
280729 Pte. COSSACK, H.,* 2/7th Bn.
37882 Pte. CHAPMAN, A., 2nd Bn.
32841 Pte. CARDSON, 17th Bn.
     Pte. COHEN, P., 2nd Bn.
3914 Pte. COHEN, S., 8th Bn.
306717 Pte. COHEN, M., 1/8th Bn.
66788 L/Cpl. COHEN, G., 15th Bn.
3593 Pte. CYPRUS, W., 3/8th Bn.
290065 Pte. COHEN, H., 2nd Bn.
22/3542 Pte. COHEN, B., 12th Bn.
22/32948 Pte. CREMERS, S., 4th Bn.
22/33871 Pte. COHEN, J., 12th Bn.
3526 Pte. CHAPMAN, J., 3/8th Bn.
62551 Pte. COHEN, M., 1/7th Bn.
3546 Drm. COHEN, M. M.,* 9th Bn.
251310 Pte. COHEN, H., 2/1st Bn.

The Lancashire Fusiliers.—*Continued.*

4/31954 Pte. COHEN, I., 4th Bn.
31936 Pte. COHEN, G., 4th Bn.
53532 Pte. COHEN, B., 4th Bn.
281839 Pte. COHEN, B., 7th Bn.
343511 Pte. COHEN, H., 6th Bn.
38103 Pte. COSSACK, S., 12th Bn.
28253 Pte. COHEN, R. J.,* 7th Bn.
40425 Pte. DON, G., 1/5th Bn.
5135 Pte. DAVIES, A. J., 2/8th Bn.
32910 Pte. DUBNER, J.
25798 Pte. DENNES, M., 10th Bn.
681214 Pte. DUDLEY, F. D., 2/8th Bn.
307274 Pte. DAVIES, J., 2/8th Bn.
48114 L/Cpl. DE HAAS, S. J., 19th Bn.
1861 Pte. DAVIS, 8th Bn.
435584 Pte. EHRLICK, L., 50th Bn.
17326 Pte. FERBER, H., 19th Bn.
4039 Pte. FRANKS, A., 15th Bn.
30854 Pte. FREEDMAN, A.,* 10th Bn.
12129 Pte. FINE, W., 1/6th Bn.
38112 Pte. FOX, F., 17th Bn.
20805 Pte. FILEMAN, H., 1st Bn.
745374 Pte. FREIT, H., 2nd Bn.
235867 Pte. FARBSTEIN, L.,* 2nd Bn.
Pte. FRIEDLANDER, J., 4th Bn.
26050 Pte. FRANKS, L.
3/24280 Pte. FRANKS, H.,* 15th Bn.
47743 Pte. FRYMAN, H. 2/5th Bn.
4581 Pte. FITELSON, A., 3/7th Bn.
5188 Pte. FRIEND, D., 4th Bn.
4/53865 Pte. FIDLER, S., 4th Bn.
18465 Pte. FREEMAN, J., 7/7th Bn.
Pte. FABER, M., 7th Bn.
Pte. FELDMAN, I., 19th Bn.
22273 Pte. GUINESS, S., 18th Bn.
31581 Pte. GAFFIN, A.,* 17th Bn.
18620 L/Cpl. GERBER, E.,* 16th Bn.
243276 Pte. GOLDSTONE, I.. 1/8th Bn.
12297 Pte. GOLDBERG, L., 2/6th Bn.
38446 Pte. GREENFIELD, L., 1st Bn.
3454 Pte. GLASS, S. G., 2nd Bn.
811579 Pte. GALETZ, L., 49th Bn.
2273 Pte. GOLDSTEIN, B., 2nd Bn.
63537 Pte. GOLDSTONE, J., 16th Bn.
45678 Pte. GERSCHOR, I., 4th Bn.
18286 L/Cpl. GELLMAN, A., 1st Bn.
204987 Pte. GOLDENBERG, T., 5th Bn.
53852 Pte. GOULD, J., 4th Bn.
6336 Pte. GOLDING, J., 2/5th Bn.
53874 Pte. GOLDENFIELD, M., 4th Bn.
54223 Pte. GOLDENBERG, J., 4th Bn.
53866 Pte. GOLDSTONE, M., 4th Bn.
29539 Pte. HANSELL, W., 15th Bn.
12389 L/Cpl. HYMAN, M., 2/6th Bn.
38801 Pte. HALFORD, H., 2/7th Bn.
348102 Pte. HELLER, S.
458574 Pte. HEISY, M., 60th Bn.

1600 Pte. HARRIS, D., 2nd Bn.
2626 Pte. HURDEN, M., 2nd Bn.
235861 Pte. HASSBERG, A.
57569 Pte. HYMAN, D., 16th Bn.
12140 Sgt. HORSFIELD, E., 16th Bn.
13/28772 Pte. HYMAN, R., 13th Bn.
30964 Pte. HAYES, M., 3rd Bn.
Pte. HELSTEIN, M.
3165 Pte. HOLMES, A., 2/8th Bn.
17614 Sgt. ISAACS, L., 19th Bn.
4089 Pte. ISAACS, A., 6th Bn.
37753 Pte. ISAACS, S., 3rd Bn.
39375 L/Cpl. JACOBS, M., 16th Bn.
300036 Pte. JACOBS, M., 1/7th Bn.
47003 Pte. JOSEPHS, H., 17th Bn.
42275 Pte. JOSEPHSON, M., 2/5th Bn.
60995 Pte. JACOBS, S., 23rd G. Bn.
1843 Pte. JACKSON, H., 2nd Bn.
33023 Pte. JACOBS, M., 9th Bn.
204996 Pte. JACOBS, L,. 15th Bn.
41181 Pte. JACOBS, H.
1043 Pte. JACOBS, H., 3rd Bn.
19963 Cpl. KAUFMAN, H., 20th Bn.
30818 Pte. KLEIN, L., 9th Bn.
306759 Pte. KINNERLASKI, H., 1/8th Bn.
40848 Pte. KARSTADT, D., 17th Bn.
47746 Pte. KROWL, M., 11th Bn.
34689 Pte. KING, H. M., 13th Bn.
33038 Pte. KERSCH, H., 3/5th Bn.
53853 Pte. KOZLOSS, L., 1st Bn.
242259 L/Cpl. KYMON, M., 2/6th Bn.
35181 Pte. KUNER, I.
53853 Pte. KOSLUFF, G., 4th Bn.
32304 Pte. LAZERSON, M., 20th Bn.
6937 Pte. LEON, I., 2/5th Bn.
12547 Pte. LEVY, M., 19th Bn.
36858 Pte. LEVINSON, H., 19th Bn.
3443 Pte. LEWIS, W., 9th Bn.
5803 Pte. LEVY, H., 1/5th Bn.
40372 Pte. LANDSLER, A. S., 1/5th Bn.
49076 Pte. LIPSHAW, B., 1/7th Bn.
Pte. LENG, S., 2/7th Bn.
281764 Pte. LABOVITZ, M., 1/7th Bn.
5150 Pte. LEVI, H. A., 3/5th Bn.
202418 Pte. LEVI, H.,* 2/8th Bn.
5333 Pte. LACOME, S., 2/7th Bn.
4444 Pte. LEVY, A. J., 2/8th Bn.
20335 Pte. LICHTENSTEIN, M. H.,* 2nd Bn.
38538 Pte. LEVY, H., 1st Bn.
282395 Pte. LANCOME, C.,* 18th Bn.
39036 Pte. LEVINSON, A. D.,* 2/8th Bn.
34668 Pte. LEVINE, L., 13th Bn.
28736 Pte. LUSTGARTEN, M., 13th Bn.
Sgt. LOVERMAN, D.
34761 Pte. LANDANSKI, B., 13th Bn.
4848 Pte. LERMAN, H., 8th Bn.
623195 Pte. LEXIER, M., 10th Bn.
27669 Pte. LIPSKIE, L., 1st Bn.

The Lancashire Fusiliers.—Continued.

31376 Pte. LEFCOVTCH, A., 16th Bn.
300153 Pte. LEVITZ, J., 1/7th Bn.
306710 Pte. LEVY, S. J., 8th Bn.
61353 Pte. LAZARUS, S., 1st Bn.
38335 Pte. LEVY, A.
282013 Pte. LERMAN, A., 1/7th Bn.
33157 Pte. LEVY, A., 12th Bn.
4/31486 Pte. LEVY, M.
53000 Pte. LEVINE, J., 11th Bn.
5725 Pte. LIPSCHAW, D., 3/9th Bn.
22637 Pte. MYERS, H.,* 9th Bn.
233635 Pte. MALINSKY, S.,* 2nd Bn.
33516 Pte. MARLOW, B., 20th Bn.
235647 Cpl. MOSCOW, A., 10th Bn.
4410 Pte. MIDDLEMAN, L., 1/8th Bn.
2367 Pte. MILLER, L., 17th Bn.
3/41446 Pte. MYERS, B., 3rd Bn.
32793 Pte. MILES, I.
23/49729 Pte. MOSES, L., 3rd Bn.
235422 Pte. MICHAELSON, S., 19th Bn.
33666 Pte. MALAMED, W., 21st Bn.
30436 Pte. MARKS, M., 4th Bn.
33671 Pte. MOSS, H., 21st Bn.
22/34422 Pte. MICHAELOVITCH, D., 4th Bn.
53863 Pte. MIZERITSKY, B., 4th Bn.
32978 Pte. MYERS, L., 13th Bn.
202346 Pte. NATHAN, M., 2/7th Bn.
6939 Pte. NEWMAN, A., 9th Bn.
205013 Pte. NIEMAN, H., 9th Bn.
Pte. NATHAN, H., 15th Bn.
239167 Pte. OCKRENT, L., 2/7th Bn.
40867 Pte. OTTOLANGUI, E., 20th Bn.
235571 Sgt. OLSEN, C. (D.C.M., M.M.), 1/5th Bn.
30765 A/Sgt. POSNANSKY, A., 2/5th Bn.
242091 Pte. PHILLIPS, W., 1/6th Bn.
57816 Sgt. POPPLESDORFF, J., 15th Bn.
28934 Cpl. PEARLSTONE, I., 18th Bn.
140900 Sig. PLOTTEL, P.
25462 Pte. PHILLIPS, L., 18th Bn.
15258 Pte. ROSEN, P.,* 19th Bn.
3672 Pte. ROSS, L., 2/8th Bn.
46994 Pte. ROSENBLOOM, J. G.,* 17th Bn.
57867 Pte. ROSENBAUM, D., 2/5th Bn.
19431 Pte. ROSENTHAL, A., 9th Bn.
27547 Pte. ROSENTHAL, M.,* 15th Bn.
52606 Pte. RUBENSTEIN, J., 1st Bn.
19432 Pte. REUBEN, S., 19th Bn.
4538 Pte. ROSEWAY, W., 8th Bn.
28722 Pte. REUBEN, H., 13th Bn.
105918 Pte. ROSS, S., 5th Bn.
42375 Pte. RISIDORE, W. W., 11th Bn.
S/443320 Pte. ROBINOVITCH, A., 2nd Bn.
25657 Pte. ROSENBAUM, J., 3rd Bn.
4538 Pte. ROSENWEIN, W., 8th Bn.
343250 Pte. ROSENFELDT, L.
42511 Pte. ROBINSON, A., 4th Bn.
36404 Pte. ROSENBERG, A.

48696 Pte. RATHENBERG, S., 4th Bn.
54149 Pte. ROTTSMAN, J.
205219 Pte. ROSENSON, J., 5th Bn.
204930 Pte. ROSENTHALL, P., 8th Bn.
Pte. ROSENTHAL, S., 21st Bn.
Pte. ROBIN, A., 2nd Bn.
33292 Pte. SHUSTER, D.,* 18th Bn.
33285 L/Cpl. SHUSTER, M.,* 18th Bn.
21392 Pte. SAMPSON, A., 9th Bn.
235752 Pte. SINGER, H., 10th Bn.
15638 Pte. STOBOFF, I., 10th Bn.
40405 Pte. SMOLANSKI, F., 1/5th Bn.
42289 Pte. SHONICK, H., 1/5th Bn.
4083 Pte. SILVERT, H., 1/8th Bn.
204718 Cpl. SAMUELS, D., 17th Bn.
60979 Pte. SAPIERA, M., 23rd G. Bn.
305644 Pte. SLATER, H., 2/8th Bn.
48072 Pte. SILVERMAN, A., 2nd Bn.
Pte. SCHWABE, M., 2nd Bn.
30551 Pte. SWEDE, I. A., 2/5th Bn.
21342 Pte. SIMPSON, R., 9th Bn.
37753 Pte. SAMUEL, J., 10th Bn.
3/18636 Pte. STOBOFF, J., 3rd Bn.
40405 Pte. SMOLENSKY, A., 1/5th Bn.
32969 Pte. SHIMBERG, S., 3rd Bn.
3770 Pte. SAMUELS, S., 12th Bn.
64607 Pte. SUSMAN, M., 1st Bn.
45676 Pte. SCHAFT, J., 4th Bn.
51019 Pte. SINGER, M.
58045 Pte. SION, B.
30551 Pte. SOOCH, A. P.
53474 Pte. SHEDNETSKY, I., 4th Bn.
67796 Pte. SHAPERO, M., 4th Bn.
300153 Pte. TURITZ, J., 1/7th Bn.
3/41486 Pte. TISCOFRY, A., 3rd Bn.
1848 Pte. TRAYER, H., 8th Bn.
1122 Cpl. TAYLOR, J., 1st Bn.
53864 Pte. USDEN, M., 4th Bn.
30783 Pte. VAN WHYE, S.,* 9th Bn.
26097 Pte. VELLINSKY, S., 15th Bn.
3435 Pte. WISE, J., 9th Bn.
202430 Pte. WOOLF, R.,* 3/5th Bn.
27210 Pte. WAGNER, R., 28th Bn.
410666 Pte. WISEBERG, M., 38th Bn.
898484 Pte. WALKOFF, A., 10th Bn.
37706 Pte. WISE, R.,* 2nd Bn.
204372 Pte. WISE, 2/8th Bn.
41444 Pte. WEINBERG, S., 3rd Bn.
42276 Pte. WEINBERG, L., 4th Bn.
53597 Pte. WEISBERG, N., 4th Bn.
28129 Cpl. WEINBERG, L., 7th Bn.
3/41445 Pte. YELLIN, S., 3rd Bn.
29259 Pte. YESNER, I., 4th Bn.
3863 Pte. ZAIDE, J.
36333 Pte. ZERMANSKY, M., 21st Bn.
82948 Pte. ZENTNER, P., 44th Bn.
34417 Pte. ZANG, 4th Bn.

* Killed in Action or died on Active Service.

THE ROYAL SCOTS FUSILIERS.

OFFICERS.

Capt. COHEN, D. H., 10th Bn.
2nd Lieut. GERSTENBERG, R. A., 1st Bn.
Lieut. ISAACS, F. H.,* 11th Bn.
2nd Lieut. KEYSER, M., 1st Bn.

N.C.O.'s AND MEN.

296267 Pte. ABRAHAMS, S.,* 12th Bn.
       Pte. ALTMAN, D., 13th Bn.
50667 Pte. ALLSEBURSANG, J.
50936 Pte. ACKERMAN, T., 11th Bn.
535593 Pte. BLATTNER, C., 1st Bn.
48267 Pte. BARNES, B., 11th Bn.
52549 Pte. BANCROFT, J.
119233 Pte. BRADBROOK, J., 6th Bn.
       Pte. BARNETT, M., 2nd Bn.
       Pte. BROWNE, H., 3rd Bn.
202483 Pte. CLAFF, H., 1st Bn.
33181 Pte. COHEN, J., 1st Bn.
41714 Pte. COHEN, M., 1st Bn.
59216 Pte. COHEN, H., 11th Gar. Bn.
       Pte. COWAN, S., 2nd Bn.
50909 Pte. CHALK, C.
53879 Pte. CRISTOL, H. S.,* 11th Bn.
266202 Pte. COHEN, A., 11th Bn.
47009 Pte. COMRAS, H., 3rd Bn.
20028 Pte. DAVIS, H., 2nd Bn.
20028 Pte. DAVIDSON, H.,* 2nd Bn.
20230 Pte. EGGINGTON, E., 12th Bn.
202149 Pte. FEDDY, F. M., 1st Bn.
265481 L/Cpl. FREEDMAN, 9th Bn.
9806 Pte. FISHMAN, M.
295398 Pte FREEMAN, A., 12th Bn.
202047 Pte. FREEDMAN, J., 2nd Bn.
61658 Pte. FELDMAN, J.
       Sgt. FURST, R. M. (M.M.).
59764 Pte. FRIESNER, M.
13914 L/Cpl. GLASKIE, H., 8th Bn.
16111 Pte. GOLDBERG, A., 1st Bn.
41734 Pte. GREEN, F., 1st Bn.
296234 Pte. GOLDSTEIN, M., 12th Bn.
28978 Pte. GROSSMAN, C., 3rd Gar. Bn.
51787 L/Cpl. GLASS, 1st Gar. Bn.
206824 Pte. GISH, A., 2/4th Bn.
28863 Cpl. GOLDBERG, M., 3rd Bn.
49122 Pte. GREENBAUM, J.
292609 Pte. HITZEL, B., 12th Bn.
6864 Pte. HAMBURG, S.,* 1st Bn.
266260 Pte. HEIMAN, T., 11th Bn.
50968 Pte. INKEMAN, S., 13th Bn.
266232 Pte. ISAACS, M., 11th Bn.
20407 Pte. JOSEPHALL, B., 2nd Bn.
31097 Pte. JACOBS, H., 3rd Bn.
24472 Cpl. JACOBS, I., 3rd Bn.
296201 Pte. KOMINSKI, I., 12th Bn.
40139 Pte. LEVI, A., 6/7th Bn.
28395 Sgt. LEVY, H.,* 1st Bn.
201557 Pte. LEVERSON, D., 1st Bn.
59235 Pte. LEVENSON, M., 11th Gar. Bn.
5504 Pte. LEVY, N., 5th Bn.
5645 Pte. LURINSKY, L.,* 1st Bn.
30071 Pte. LEVINE, I., 3rd Bn.
24154 L/Cpl. LIPMAN, I., 2nd Bn.
50058 Pte. LEHMAN, N.
       Pte. LIVINGSTONE, B.
23043 Pte. MARKS, M.,* 2nd Bn.
201566 Pte. MASSER, M., 2nd Bn.
50081 Pte. MISELL, D.
50102 Pte. MARKS, J.
50081 Pte. MISCH, D., 3rd Bn.
       Pte. MYERS, J. H.
296218 Pte. NATHAN, N., 12th Bn.
296256 Pte. PICK, M., 12th Bn.
59310 Pte. PAYNE, H., 11th Gar. Bn.
13230 Pte. PELIKANSKY, J.
23104 Pte. ROSNBLOOM, M.,* 12th Bn.
22993 Pte. RUBINSTEIN, P.,* 6/7th Bn.
48064 Pte. RYCHMAN, I.
24536 Pte. RAPP, L., 3rd Bn.
23859 Pte. ROSENFELD, H. P., 3rd Bn.
54468 Pte. RIFFKIN, J.
38716 Pte. REUBEN, J.
9667 Cpl. SHINEWELL, D., 1st Bn.
5236 Pte. SCHAPIRA, S., 5th Bn.
46510 Pte. SPERO, F., 3rd Bn.
23154 L/Cpl. SHIPMAN, L., 3rd Bn.
30099 Pte. SIMON, I., 3rd Bn.
37425 Pte. SLAGER, J., 10th Bn.
240200 Pte. SCHNIEDERMAN, I., 15th Bn.
50929 Pte. TAYLOR, I., 1st Bn.
1284 Pte. TERRY, M., 2/4th Bn.
41820 Pte. TAYLOR, A.,* 2nd Bn.
22994 Pte. WOLFSON, P., 1st Bn.
53926 Pte. WEINBAUM, J., 11th Bn.
43963 Pte. WHITE, M., 1st Bn.
50435 Pte. ZACK, S., 11th Gar. Bn.

* Killed in Action or died on Active Service.

THE CHESHIRE REGIMENT.

OFFICERS.

2nd Lieut. ABRAHAMS, M. L., 16th Bn.
2nd Lieut. ADLER, S. (M.C.), 9th Bn.
2nd Lieut. BRANDON, B. L.,* 7th Bn.
Capt. COHEN, M., 13th Bn.
Capt. LANGDON, W. M.,* 10th Bn.
Lieut. MOSES, E., 12th Bn.
Capt. YOUNG, A. H. E.

The Cheshire Regt.—Continued.

N.C.O.'s AND MEN.

- 10368 Pte. ABRAHAMS, C., 11th Bn.
- 292323 Pte. ASH, I., 4th Bn.
- 22001 Pte. BARNETT, A. L., 17th Bn.
- 67972 Pte. BARDOSKY, H., 23rd Bn.
- T2/016526 Pte. BERLIN, J., 17th Bn.
- 53793 Pte. BENJAMIN, L.,* 23rd Bn.
- 70013 Pte. BERMAN, S., 1st Bn.
- 267720 Pte. BEIL, J., 2/6th Bn.
- 315664 Pte. BENZIMRA, J., 23rd Bn.
- 1304 Sgt. BERKSON, M.,* 1/4th Bn.
- 3/35607 Pte. BERNSTEIN, H.,* 15th Bn.
- 2144 Pte. BERNSTEIN, G., 4th Bn.
- 292918 Pte. BLACKSTONE, J., 2/7th Bn.
- 39153 Pte. BLOOM, S., 19th Bn.
- 46692 Pte. BLACKSTONE, H., 17th Bn.
- 315381 Pte. BLOOM, G. E., 23rd Bn.
- 55286 Pte. BRONKHURST, 53rd Bn.
- 315796 Pte. BYE, E., 23rd Bn.
- 38868 Pte. COHEN, S., 19th Bn.
- 998 Pte. COHEN, H.,* 1st Bn.
- 315385 Pte. COHEN, I., 2/3rd Bn.
- 37134 Pte. COHEN, A., 18th Bn.
- 61242 Pte. COHEN, M., 19th Bn.
- 216765 Pte. COHEN, J.
- 77934 Pte. COHEN, I.,* 24th Bn.
- 24272 L/Cpl. CRAMER, A., 2/5th Bn.
- 55542 Pte. CLYNES, L., 22nd Bn.
- 49295 Pte. DALINSKY, B.,* 1st Bn.
- 83993 Sgt. DEMPSKY, E.
- 6572 Pte. DIAMOND, J.,* 23rd Bn.
- 1877 Pte. DIAMOND, G., 17th Bn.
- 12084 Pte. DRIVER, M., 1/17th Bn
- 38840 L/Cpl. EFFENBAUM, H., 19th Bn.
- 38704 Pte. ERENBERG, S., 19th Bn.
- 267648 Pte. ESTERSON, E., 2/6th Bn.
- 4719 Pte. FRANKLIN, S., 17th Bn.
- 4758 Pte. FINE, W., 2/7th Bn.
- 15012 Pte. FLAX, M., 6th Bn.
- 292386 Pte. FRIEZE, H., 2/7th Bn.
- 53842 Pte. FROBE, J., 23rd Bn.
- 64149 Pte. FRIEND, J., 15th Bn.
- 15012 Pte. FLOX, M., 6th Bn.
- 6715 Pte. FRIEDE, L.
- 504443 Pte. GLASS, J., 4th Bn.
- 19036 Cpl. GLASSTONE, I.,* 1st Bn.
- 39167 L/Cpl. GLASSMAN, M., 19th Bn.
- 45762 Pte. GLOBE, B., 23rd Bn.
- Pte. GOLDMAN, J., 1st Bn.
- 315819 Pte. GOLDMAN, D.,* 15th Bn.
- 47667 Pte. GOLDMAN, E., 21st Bn.
- 4746 Pte. GORDON, E., 2/7th Bn.
- 49297 Pte. GORDON, I.,* 1st Bn.
- 315817 Pte. GORDAN, A., 23rd Bn.
- 46648 Pte. GREENBURG, S., 17th Bn.
- 4847 Pte. HARRIS, E., 1/5th Bn.
- 50409 Pte. HARRIS, G., 16th Bn.
- 40892 Pte. HEILBREN, L., 1/4th Bn.
- 316306 Pte. HERZFIELD, S., 3rd Bn.
- 1288 Pte. HIBBERT, F., 6th Bn.
- 23421 Pte. HILLISON, E., 17th Bn.
- 9553 L/Cpl. HYMAN, A., 2nd Bn.
- 4488 Pte. HYMAN, R., 3/5th Bn.
- 34182 Pte. JACOBS, L., 3rd Bn.
- Pte. JACOBS, M., 15th Bn.
- 36370 L/Cpl. JACOBS, H., 12th Bn.
- 241700 Pte. JOSEPH, S., 5th Bn.
- 84866 Pte. KARP, S., 9th Bn.
- 50680 Pte. KARBARON, H.,
- 29086 Pte. KERSTEIN, L.
- 6162 Pte. KETOFSKY, I., 5th Bn.
- 315668 Pte. KELSEY, E., 3rd Bn.
- 42486 Pte. KERDANSKI, J., 18th Bn.
- 12287 Cpl. KNOWELS, A., 1st Bn.
- 60495 Pte. KONIGSBERG. G., 9th Bn.
- 29478 Pte. KRACKER, E.
- 3884 Pte. LAPSEIN, J., 23rd Bn.
- 9210 Sgt. LEVENSTON, H., 2nd Bn.
- 8055 Pte. LEVY, M., 17th Bn.
- 80770 Pte. LEVY, H., 3rd Bn.
- 315842 Pte. LEVY, P., 23rd Bn.
- 69003 Pte. LEVY, H., 52nd Bn.
- 267204 Pte. LEACH, W., 23rd Bn.
- 315842 Pte. LEVY, N.
- 315265 Pte. LEVY, S., 23rd Bn.
- 58497 Pte. LEVY, I. J., 12th Bn.
- 50920 Pte. LEWIS, I. M.
- 206951 Pte. LEWIS, N., 4th Bn.
- 4933 Pte. LEVISON, M., 2/4th Bn.
- 267625 Pte. LEARNER, D., 2/6th Bn.
- 4791 Pte. LITTLEBAUM, M., 23rd Bn.
- 49224 Pte. MARKS, A., 13th Bn.
- 6119 Pte. MAGNUS, E. D., 2/6th Bn.
- 67920 Pte. MATZ, H. P., 5th Bn.
- 4702 Pte. MITCHELL, H., 2/6th Bn.
- 315868 Pte. MOSEVITCH, I., 23rd Bn.
- 38843 C.Q.M.S. MOSCOW, H., 19th Bn.
- Pte. MILLER, S., 1st Bn.
- Pte. MORRIS, J., 3rd Bn.
- 34820 Pte. MOSS, R., 1st Bn.
- 9127 Pte. MORRIS, L., 8th Bn.
- 4987 Pte. MYERS, J. H., 3rd Bn.
- 7625 A/Sgt. NATHAN, R., 17th Bn.
- 268361 Pte. NIMAN, A., 3rd Bn.
- 41670 Pte. OLINSKY, A., 20th Bn.
- 4673 Pte. PAUL, M.
- 4748 Pte. PAYMAN, L.
- 14/35911 Pte. PETERS, E.
- 23452 Pte. POLICOVSKY, B., 53rd Bn.
- 49217 Pte. PRESS, S., 13th Bn.
- 41912 Pte. PHILLIPS, S., 9th Bn.
- 78967 Pte. PRICE, S.

The Cheshire Regt.—Continued.

- 39131 L/Cpl. ROSENBAUM, E., 19th Bn.
- 27115 L/Cpl. ROSCOE, H.,* 8th Bn.
- 10160 Pte. ROSE, C., 3rd Bn.
- 6151 Pte. RUSHNICK, 2/5th Bn.
- Pte. SAKS, S., 4th Bn.
- 267167 Pte. SANDLER, J., 23rd Bn.
- Pte. SAMUELS, H. E.
- 57779 Pte. SEMP, S., 20th Bn.
- 25905 Pte. SEIGAL, J., 9th Bn.
- 243490 Pte. SHENKER, S.
- 45382 Pte. SILVERSTONE, S., 23rd Bn.
- 41008 Pte. SILVERMAN, I., 17th Bn.
- 51880 Pte. SIMONS, M.
- 316172 Sgt. SIMON, J., 23rd Bn.
- 60338 Pte. SIMLO, 8th Bn.
- 9/6860 L/Cpl. SILLENDER, I. (D.C.M.), 9th Bn.
- 41114 L/Cpl. SMOLENSKI, M., 17th Bn.
- 49295 Sgt. SPIRO, A., 16th Bn.
- 193879 Pte. SOLOMON, M.
- 61014 Pte. STONE, L., 23rd Bn.
- 30485 Pte. SYMONS, H., 16th Bn.
- 38384 Pte. TAYLOR, H., 19th Bn.
- 53842 Pte. TROBE, J., 23rd Bn.
- 51269 Pte. TRAVERS, J., 1st Bn.
- 46117 Pte. WARSHAWSKI, H., 17th Bn.
- 53329 Pte. WANFORD, A. M., 5th Bn.
- 293398 Pte. WEINGLASS, I., 2/7th Bn.
- 9553 Pte. WOOD, J., 9th Bn.
- 52072 Pte. WOOLF, L.,* 1st Bn.
- 201701 Pte. WINEBERG, H., 1/4th Bn.
- 193713 Pte. WOLFSON, N.
- 77820 Cpl. WATTS, H.
- 20133 Pte. YAFFA, A., 1/7th Bn.

* Killed in Action or died on Active Service.

THE ROYAL WELCH FUSILIERS.

OFFICERS.

- Lieut. ALEXANDER, S. A.,* 1/4th Bn.
- 2nd Lieut. BUCKLAND, T., 7th Bn.
- 2nd Lieut. BLAIBERG.
- Capt. EIDINOW, W., 1st Bn.
- 2nd Lieut. FREEMAN, H. A. (M.C.).
- 2nd Lieut. FIRTH, M., 3rd Bn.
- Capt. HARRIS, N. L.,* (M.C.) 9th Bn.
- 2nd Lieut. HIGHAM, R. H.
- 2nd Lieut. KEYZOR, H. L. A.,* 25th Bn.
- Capt. KING, J.
- Capt. LEWIS, S.
- Lt.-Col. MARKS. C. J. S., 19th Bn.
- Lieut. MORRIS, F. A., 17th Bn.
- Lieut. PRICE, L. L., 1st Bn.
- 2nd Lieut. PHILLIPS, L. B.
- 2nd Lieut. PINTO, V. de S.
- 2nd Lieut. ROSS, R., 13th Bn.
- 2nd Lieut. SASSOON, S. L. (M.C.), 3rd Bn.
- Capt. TOBIAS, L. M.,* 25th Bn.

N.C.O.'s AND MEN.

- Pte. ABRAHAMS, H., 2nd Bn.
- 204264 Pte. ASHLEY, D., 2/4th Bn.
- 61897 L/Cpl. ABRAHAMS, S., 6th Bn.
- 63057 Pte. ALEXANDER, N., 3rd Bn.
- 3917 Pte. AARONOVITCH, A., 2/5th Bn.
- 38805 Pte. ABRAMS, H., 2nd Bn.
- 38804 Pte. ABRAMS, A., 2nd Bn.
- 67560 Cpl. ALEXANDER, S. J., 3rd Bn.
- 51186 Pte. ANCHELL, J., 14th Bn.
- 21753 Cpl. BLACK, L., 17th Bn.
- 55968 Pte. BABINSKY, R. B., 15th Bn.
- 59703 L/Cpl. BEERMAN, J., 7th Bn.
- 266744 Pte. BURGESS, A., 24th Bn.
- 269461 Pte. BEROFSKI, M., 4th Bn.
- 291744 Pte. BARRITZ, J., 15th Bn.
- 54549 Pte. BLUESTONE, J. H., 10th Bn.
- 56900 Pte. BROWN, K.
- 54169 Pte. BYR, J., 1st Bn.
- 68803 Pte. BRODIE, S., 2/4th Bn.
- 39446 Pte. BLACK, H., 20th Bn.
- 63212 Pte. BERNARD, M., 3rd Bn.
- 66623 Pte. BEBERASKERLI, E., 3rd Bn.
- 66722 Pte BRANSON, J. J., 3rd Bn.
- 67020 Pte. BERNSTEIN, H., 3rd Bn.
- 4673 Pte. BLARBERG, I., 2/6th Bn.
- 4335 Pte. BERGER, S., 2/6th Bn.
- 4815 Pte. BARRITZ, E., 2/7th Bn.
- 71913 Pte. BARNETT, N., 3rd Bn.
- 72705 Pte. BROCKMAN, J., 3rd Bn.
- 42153 Pte. BICOFF, J., 3rd Bn.
- 243200 Pte. BLOOM, M., 6th Bn.
- 34417 Pte. BINDER, S., 3rd Bn.
- Pte. BEAUMONT, S., 15th Bn.
- Pte. BROOKE, H., 18th Bn.
- Pte. BRUNSWICK, G., 1st Bn.
- Pte. BALKIN, E., 14th Bn.
- 235277 Pte. BARNES, J.,* 15th Bn.
- 10151 Pte. CHARNEY, B., 2nd Bn.
- 8755 L/Cpl. COHEN, E.,* 2nd Bn.
- 54718 Pte. COHEN, L.,* 1st Bn.
- 242636 Pte. COHEN, B., 24th Bn.
- 63545 Pte. COHEN, A., 4th Bn.
- 976321 Pte. COHEN, D., 2nd Bn.
- 456312 Pte. COHEN, H., 2nd Bn.
- 63170 Pte. COHEN, M.,* 2nd Bn.
- 235520 Pte. COHEN, L., 1st Bn
- Pte. COHEN, S., 11th Bn.
- 63377 Pte. COHEN, S. S., 3rd Bn.
- 62690 Pte. COHEN, S., 3rd Bn.
- 66527 Pte. COHEN, J., 3rd Bn.
- 66542 Pte. COMELANSKY, S., 3rd Bn.
- 66885 Pte. CHIVALL, W. S., 3rd Bn.

Royal Welch Fusiliers.—Continued.

66854	Pte. COHEN, B., 3rd Bn.
71073	L/Cpl. COHEN, H., 3rd Bn.
27160	Pte. COHEN, A., 3rd Bn.
315669	Pte. COBB, 2nd Bn.
2212	Pte. DURLACHER, L., 15th Bn.
22477	Pte. DAVIES, H., 14th Bn.
22092	L/Cpl. DAVIS, J., 17th Bn.
18649	Pte. DAVID, H., 13th Bn.
34593	Pte. DAVIS, N., 9th Bn.
267898	Pte. DAVIS, H., 4th Bn.
267058	Pe. DAVIDSON, A. L., 4th Bn.
66300	Pte. DIAMOND, W., 3rd Bn.
243554	Pte. DAVIS, W. M., 6th Bn.
67652	Pte. DAVIES, M., 3rd Bn.
	L/Cpl. ELIAS, J. (M.M.).
67050	Pte. EPSTEIN, E. M., 3rd Bn.
4825	Pte. EPHRAIM, E., 2/7th Bn.
	Pte. ELLIS, J., 15th Bn.
42286	Pte. FREEDMAN, C., 4th Bn.
62499	Pte. FRASER, R., 6th Bn.
52657	Pte. FIRSKER, A., 3rd Bn.
66897	Pte. FENSTONE, J., 3rd Bn.
17150	Pte. FALK, N.,* 1st Bn.
66770	Pte. FURZ, M., 3rd Bn.
71192	Pte. FRIEND, J., 3rd Bn.
55789	Cpl. FEIGENBAUM, A., 16th Bn.
43314	Cpl. FURFANSOFSKY, M., 9th Bn.
7772	Pte. FRANKS, J., 1/4th Bn.
16663	Pte. FRASER, I., 2/4th Bn.
28322	Pte. FINKLESTEIN, H., 4th Bn.
3964	Pte. FREEDMAN, M.
71854	Pte. FREEDMAN, A.
60496	Pte. FRANKS, J., 10th Bn.
5638	Pte. FREEDMAN, H., 2/7th Bn.
782227	Pte. FREEMAN, H., 4th Res. Bn.
71820	Pte. FINE, J., 3rd Bn.
35717	L/Cpl. FOX, P., 2nd Bn.
	Pte. FOX, N., 15th Bn.
17078	L/Cpl. GOLDSTEIN, P.,* 1st Bn.
25867	Cpl. GOODMAN, P., 17th Bn.
27777	Pte. GARFIELD, D., 16th Bn.
55047	Pte. GRUPMAN, G. M., 10th Bn.
45793	Pte. GOLDSTEIN, G. E., 19th Bn.
17277	Pte. GAROLD, J., 9th Bn.
46417	Pte. GOLDSTONE, R., 16th Bn.
10498	Pte. GOODFIELD, A., 4th Bn.
267134	Pte. GOLDSTONE, S., 4th Bn
316912	Pte GOLDBERG, F., 1/4th Bn.
3967	Pte. GOODMAN, L., 2/5th Bn.
4930	Pte. GERLINSYK, A.
345694	Pte. GENATTA, A., 24th Bn.
4911	Pte. GOLDSTONE, S., 4th Bn.
62808	Pte. GROFFENBERG, M.
54449	Pte. GOLDSTONE, B., 2nd Bn.
4926	Pte. GINSBERG, R., 2/6th Bn.
266973	Pte. GOLDMAN, M., 4th Bn.
267191	Pte. GRENOVITCH, A., 4th Bn.
59913	Pte. GREENFIELD, H., 1/7th Bn.
62523	Pte. GARBUTT, J., 6th Bn.
42291	L/Cpl. GORODKIN, H., 2nd Bn.
316914	Pte. GOLDBERG, I., 4th Bn.
63924	Pte. GENOFSKY, J., 3rd Bn.
63374	Pte. GINSBERG, S., 3rd Bn.
708118	Pte. GAFFIN, J., 3rd Bn.
17277	Sgt. GARCIA.
70821	Sgt. GREENBERG, S., 3rd Bn.
315328	Pte. GENOPSKI, H., 23rd Bn.
43317	Pte. GREENBAUM, H.
4236	Pte. GREENBERG, S., 2/3rd Bn.
20497	Pte. GILBERT, H., 3rd Bn.
54778	L/Cpl. GINSBERG, W., 17th Bn.
61683	Pte. GLATT, L., 6th Bn.
34081	Pte. GREENBERG, A.
22503	Pte. HART, J., 15th Bn.
53626	Pte. HYMAN, H., 1st Bn.
266935	Pte. HERTZBERG, J., 1/4th Bn.
34907	Pte. HARRIS, R., 4th Bn.
60540	Pte. HELLER, J., 17th Bn.
53036	Pte. HEILBRON, G., 4th Bn.
62808	Pte. HOFFENBERG, N., 3rd Bn.
4646	Rfm. HANSELL, J.
838080	Pte. HARRIS, M., 16th Bn.
355687	L/Sgt. ISAACS, A., 25th Bn.
4/10535	Pte. ISAACS, H., 4th Bn.
9873	Pte. INGHAM, F., 2/4th Bn.
315264	Pte. ISAACS, A., 23rd Bn.
29437	Pte. JACKSON, C., 4th Bn.
62674	Pte. JOSEPH, S., 3rd Bn.
77518	Pte. JACOBS, E., 14th Bn.
	Pte. JACOBY, J., 18th Bn.
38299	Pte. KERSH, H., 1st Bn.
235482	Pte. KERBLE, S., 17th Bn.
204721	Pte. KLAPISH, S., 4th Bn.
67803	Pte. KERDANSKI, D. O., 3rd Bn.
67164	Pte. KNIT, E., 3rd Bn.
27076	L/Cpl. KLINE, P., 13th Bn.
45577	Pte. LYONS, A., 19th Bn.
28182	Pte. LEVY, S., 15th Bn.
59127	Pte. LEVY, S., 13th Bn.
10552	Pte. LABELSKY, M., 4th Bn.
60495	Pte. LYONS, J., 10th Bn.
345560	L/Cpl. LAZARUS, W., 24th Bn.
54111	Pte. LUPPER, I. B., 2nd Bn.
61577	Pte. LEVY, I., 8th Bn.
204347	Pte. LERMON, R., 2/4th Bn.
75293	Pte. LEVY, L., 2/4th Bn.
68779	Pte. LUKEWARM, P., 2/4th Bn.
62644	Pte. LEVY, L., 3rd Bn.
63868	Pte. LEWIS, A., 3rd Bn.
66122	Pte. LEVY, B., 3rd Bn.
63869	Pte. LEVY, H., 3rd Bn.
71828	Pte. LAGERMAN, C., 3rd Bn.
76973	Pte. LEVINE, N., 3rd Bn.
71905	Pte. LEVY, L., 3rd Bn.

Royal Welch Fusiliers.—*Continued.*

4546	Pte. Lasof, S.	
67693	Pte. Lorsky, D., 3rd Bn.	
268122	Pte. Librock, D.	
52158	Pte. Lewis, S., 9th Bn.	
22878	Pte. Marlinsky, B.,* 15th Bn.	
26521	Pte. Morris, J., 16th Bn.	
235505	Pte. Maxwell, B., 1st Bn.	
66123	Pte. Morris, J. J., 9th Bn.	
57483	Pte. Mendoza, J., 4th Bn.	
95430	Pte. Maber, I., 23rd Bn.	
204687	Pte. Michaelovitch, 8th Bn.	
52410	Pte. Myers, R., 3rd Bn.	
66757	L/Cpl. Meller, R., 3rd Bn.	
34349	Pte. Mandel, J., 3rd Bn.	
54958	Pte. Michaels, M.,* 10th Bn.	
5169	Sgt. Martin, A.,* 1st Bn.	
63020	Cpl. Moses, H., 3rd Bn.	
87668	Pte. Marks, L., 3rd Bn.	
4017	Pte. Marks, N., 2/5th Bn.	
23205	Pte. Marcovitch, L., 16th Bn.	
241571	Pte. Myers, J., 1/5th Bn.	
4983	Pte. Morris, S., 2/6th Bn.	
4393	Pte. Maisner, S., 3/6th Bn.	
26790	Cpl. Moyulas, H., 19th Bn.	
5789	Pte. Mendoza, G., 26th Bn.	
235528	Pte. Nathan, B., 1st Bn.	
91631	Pte. Nash, I. B., 23rd Bn.	
21719	Pte. Owen, 15th Bn.	
67650	Pte. O'Grady, A.,* 3rd Bn.	
2.3992	Pte. Olsberg, W., 17th Bn.	
72190	Pte. Olanitskie, I., 3rd Bn.	
241653	Pte. Olinsky, J., 2/5th Bn.	
73622	Pte. Phillips, E., 9th Bn.	
52923	L/Sgt. Phillips, S., 3rd Bn.	
64089	Pte. Prager, 3rd Bn.	
291744	Pte. Paritz, J., 4th Bn.	
47156	Pte. Rosenberg, S.,* 9th Bn.	
14232	Pte. Ringelheim, S., 11th Bn.	
63897	Pte. Rose, B., 9th Bn.	
	Drm. Rosenberg, E., 26th Bn.	
267075	Pte. Ridy, G., 4th Bn.	
42346	Pte. Rosenberg, L., 4th Bn.	
267149	Pte. Rosenberg, S., 1/4th Bn.	
4061	Pte. Rubenstein, A., 2/5th Bn.	
64564	Pte. Rothstein, S., 13th Bn.	
96868	Pte. Radam, H., 2nd Bn.	
4/12685	Cpl. Rose, P., 4th Bn.	
75729	Pte. Richman, T., 13th Bn.	
5235	Pte. Rhines, H., 2/7th Bn.	
37491	Pte. Rose, R., 3/6th Bn.	
22004	Pte. Rosenbaum, A., 3rd Bn.	
4963	Pte. Rymer, J., 2/5th Bn.	
44422	Pte. Robins, N., 11th Bn.	
34657	Pte. Solomons, N. C.,* 15th Bn.	
45582	Pte. Saunders, L., 19th Bn.	
9592	Pte. Snipper, I. B., 1/4th Bn.	
35213	Pte. Shechter, M. H., 1/4th Bn.	
35358	Pte. Segal, N.,* 10th Bn.	
267076	Pte. Shirlog, R., 1st Bn.	
57353	Cpl. Saiet, A., 4th Bn.	
45582	Pte. Saunders, L., 19th Bn.	
45013	Pte. Smutonsky, M., 15th Bn.	
22831	Pte. Solk, M., 15th Bn.	
	Pte. Solway, I. (M.M.), 14th Bn.	
58139	Pte. Standard, D., 13th Bn.	
80186	Pte. Solomons, Z., 134th Bn.	
242670	Pte. Seigal, J., 1/7th Bn.	
243336	Pte. Shattenstein, W., 2nd Bn.	
267188	Pte. Sydney, B., 4th Bn.	
26741	Sgt. Stone, A., 3rd Bn.	
52651	Pte. Smolensky, M., 3rd Bn.	
67689	Pte. Schinker, R., 3rd Bn.	
63969	Pte. Sievitch, H., 3rd Bn.	
63517	Pte. Sugarwhite, B., 3rd Bn.	
66146	Pte. Sternberg, J., 3rd Bn.	
241658	Pte. Selkovitch, W., 2nd Bn.	
24472	Pte. Shapiro, A., 3rd Bn.	
4068	Pte. Skenker, J.	
66885	Pte. Samuel, W. S.	
	Pte. Spanjor, S., 18th Bn.	
63347	Pte. Tropp, W. W., 3rd Bn.	
17032	L/Cpl. Tymon, R.,* 1st Bn.	
66770	Pte. Tury, M.	
4826	Pte. Tennenbaum, S.	
52066	Pte. Verbloski, H., 1st Bn.	
67564	Pte. Venolopsky, N.	
44725	Pte. Valensky, P., 23rd Bn.	
66499	C.S.M. Wilkinson, R., 3rd Bn.	
63371	Pte. Woodman, A., 3rd Bn.	
95396	Pte. Wolfyansky, H.	
5041	Pte. Wander, G., 2/6th Bn.	
885	Pte. Wernick, S., 19th Bn.	
29566	L/Cpl. Zeiler, M.,* 1st Bn.	

* Killed in Action or died on Active Service.

THE SOUTH WALES BORDERERS.

OFFICERS.

Lieut. Behrens, R. P.,* 1st Bn.
Capt. Simons, E. (M.C. and Bar).

N.C.O.'s AND MEN.

7201	Pte. Abrahams, R.,* 1st Bn.	
9675	Pte. Adelberg, C., 1st Bn.	
46304	Pte. Andrews, A., 3rd Bn.	
31980	Pte. Arnovitch, B., 10th Bn.	
45034	Pte. Alexander, A., 7th Bn.	
28382	Pte. Aronovitch, A. M., 4th Bn.	
36095	Pte. Ansell, R.	
39575	Cpl. Baritz, E.,* 2nd Bn.	
35573	Pte. Barnett, M., 12th Bn.	
22897	Pte. Braham, M., 1st Bn.	

South Wales Borderers.—*Continued.*

Pte. BOGARD, P. (M.M.).
36243 Pte. BERLINER, I., 1st Bn.
Sgt. BALLINS, F., 1st Bn.
3/22893 Pte. BENJAMIN, H. B.,* 7th Bn.
326526 Pte. BUSNACK, L., 8th Bn.
40816 Pte. BARNETT, P., 53rd Bn.
202948 Pte. BROOKSTEIN, T., 1/5th Bn.
174088 Pte. BRAHAM, J.
36100 Pte. COHEN, C., 1st Bn.
8669 Pte. COLE, H.,* 1st Bn.
30576 Pte. COHEN, H.,* 2nd Bn.
44659 Pte. COHEN, A., 2nd Bn.
36344 Pte. COHEN, H., 12th Bn.
36185 Pte. CROWN, J., 3rd Bn.
44310 Cpl. CURLENDER, M. E., 1st Bn.
36035 Pte. COHEN, S., 8th Bn.
110468 Pte. CAPLIN, S.
268301 Pte. COHEN, H., 10th Bn.
30286 Pte. COHEN, S., 3rd Bn.
35571 Pte. DOBREE, A. R.,* 12th Bn.
24408 Pte. DAVIS, L., 2nd Bn.
265238 Pte. DAVIS, A. A., 5th Bn.
260218 Pte. DAVIS, A., 5th Bn.
62853 Pte. DORRIS, J., 3rd Bn.
49549 Pte. DAVIES, W., 5th Bn.
TR4/6276 Pte. DAVIES, D., 51st Bn.
TR4/40060 Pte. DRIBBON, E., 51st Bn.
TR4/7041 Pte. DAVIEZ, H., 51st Bn.
36239 Pte. DAVIS, B., 7th Bn.
41244 Pte. DAVIES, B. S.
37747 Pte. DOLNIC, 8th Bn.
36395 Pte. EVALANKA, J., 1st Bn.
86735 Pte. EVANS, D.
36527 Pte. FABIAN, A.,* 1st Bn.
44742 Pte. FRENCH, A. S., 1st Bn.
44742 Pte. FRANK, A., 1st Bn.
45531 Pte. FRIEZE, 1st Bn.
66829 Pte. FREEDENTHAL, H.
22901 Pte. FISTAL, B., 7th Bn.
9544 Pte. GOLDBERG, A. J.,* 2nd Bn.
36036 Pte. GOLDBERG, H., 1st Bn.
22632 Pte. GOLDBERG, F., 1st Bn.
8937 Pte. GREENBERG, J., 1st Bn.
9668 Cpl. GOLDSMITH, G.,* 1st Bn.
45552 Pte. GINSBERG, 1st Bn.
Pte. GEMBITSKI, I.
202232 Pte. GROSSMAN, J., 51st Bn.
14136 Pte. GOLDSTEIN, P., 8th Bn.
14/36006 Pte. GOLDSTEIN, H., 17th Bn.
Pte. GOULSTON, H., 2nd Bn.
Sgt. GOLDSTEIN, J. (D.C.M. and Bar).
Pte. GOLDSTON, A., 1st Bn.
260058 Pte. HOFFMAN, M., 1st Bn.
45185 Pte. HARTSTONE, M.,* 2nd Bn.
13084 Cpl HUNT, W.
14/35814 Pte. HAILPRY, H. G., 8th Bn.

3/36017 Pte. HIMMELFALT, S., 7th Bn.
26903 Pte. HARRIS, M., 11th Bn.
M2/060354 Pte. HUMPHREYS, A. B., 5th Bn.
146264 Pte. HARRIS, J., 8th Bn.
36005 Pte. ISAACS, S., 1st Bn.
39774 Pte. ISAAC, J., 2nd Bn.
36099 Pte. JACOBS, H., 11th Bn.
34081 Pte. JACOBS, B. A., 7th Bn.
30285 Pte. JOSEPH, L., 3rd Bn.
3043 Pte. KRONENBERG, E., 5th Bn.
40330 Pte. KAYOFSKY, S., 10th Bn.
Pte. KONYON, 1st Bn.
5025 Pte. KAMINKAVITCH, I., 3rd Bn.
35594 Pte. LUBINSKY, H., 1st Bn.
28695 Pte. LEVINE, M., 7th Bn.
39584 Pte. LEVY, H.,* 2nd Bn.
36565 Pte. LEVY, L.,* 1st Bn.
39655 Pte. LESSER, S., 2nd Bn.
31712 Pte. LAURENCE, E., 3rd Bn.
31687 Pte. LATNER, S., 3rd Bn.
30477 Pte. LITTLESTONE, J., 3rd Bn.
34732 Pte. LESCHINSKY, T. J., 3rd Bn.
66722 L/Cpl. LIVINGSTONE.
36008 L/Cpl. LEVY, E., 10th Bn.
3/44170 Pte. LEWIS, S., 8th Bn.
14/23277 Pte. LEVEY, B., 7th Bn.
42453 Pte. LEVENE, L., 5th Bn.
36096 Pte. LEVY, W., 2nd Bn.
31838 Pte. LASSMAN, M., 8th Bn.
36578 Pte. LEVY, J.
Pte. LEVY, A. H.
18314 Pte. MICHAEL, M., 5th Bn.
3548 Pte. MORRIS, M., 12th Bn.
4149 Pte. MOSESON, M., 6th Bn.
42418 Pte. MYERS, H.,* 6th Bn.
266365 Pte. MORRIS, W., 3/4th Bn.
46112 Pte. MOSS, C., 1st Bn.
36021 Pte. MILLER, M., 8th Bn.
34355 Pte. MUSCOVITCH, B., 3rd Bn.
34726 Pte. MARKS, D., 3rd Bn.
41064 Pte. MIDDLEMAN, J. M., 18th Bn.
67818 Pte. MENDLESOHN, J., 52nd Bn.
58448 Pte. MICHAELSON, 3rd Bn.
48263 Pte. MARKS, H. J., 8th Bn.
36463 Pte. NYKIRK, J.
27528 Pte. NATHAN, L., 8th Bn.
14/36015 Pte. NATHAN, H., 8th Bn.
32092 Pte. NAGUS, S.
36479 Pte. NATHAN, 14th Bn.
36009 Pte. NATHAN, A., 3rd Bn.
9311 Sgt. ORMAN, R.,* 1st Bn.
Pte. POSNER, J., 12th Bn.
36038 Pte. POSENEX, J., 1s Bn.
36007 Pte. PYZER, H., 1st Bn.
22839 Pte. PYE, D., 11th Bn.
3459 Pte. PHILLIPS, S., 52nd Bn.
35576 Sgt. PLATT, H., 8th Bn.

South Wales Borderers.—*Continued.*

36564 Pte. Pyzer, J., 3rd Bn.
67196 Pte. Price, J.
45860 Pte. Reubens, H., 4th Bn.
30236 Pte. Robins, H.
41688 Pte. Rudofski, G., 5th Bn.
67401 Sgt. Roseolsky, S., 53rd Bn.
39586 Cpl. Rosenbloom, L., 2nd Bn.
25577 Pte. Roundstein, R., 2nd Bn.
64053 Pte. Rose, S. W., 8th Bn.
36098 Pte. Rosenfield, I., 8th Bn.
36011 Pte. Sanshiver, A., 2nd Bn.
33093 Pte. Stern, J., 10th Bn.
39299 Pte. Simpson, H., 5th Bn.
37746 Pte. Strauss, I.,* 11th Bn.
36041 Pte. Silverstein, L., 1st Bn.
49003 Pte. Selkovitch, H.,* 1st Bn.
9088 L/Cpl. Saunders, J., 1st Bn.
45793 Pte. Sinclair, M., 1st Bn.
35876 Pte. Swatts, F. J., 2nd Bn.
260196 Pte. Safinovitch, M., 5th Bn.
29878 Pte. Shepherd, S., 6th Bn.
75013 Pte. Stone, A., 3rd Bn.
8238 Pte. Scareff, M. V., 1st Bn.
41921 Pte. Standard, D., 5/3rd Bn.
35642 Pte. Sampson, A., 12th Bn.
TR4/3210 Pte. Selcovitch, N., 51st Bn.
66912 Pte. Seigelman, H.
3/36014 Pte. Shonnick, D., 8th Bn.
3/37747 Pte. Solnick, V., 8th Bn.
35722 Pte. Vigdosky, H.,* 11th Bn.
35815 Pte. White, M., 1st Bn.
24159 Sgt. Wilde, E., 6th Bn.
42488 Pte. Woolfe, M.,* 5th Bn.

* Killed in Action or died on Active Service.

28846 Pte. Cowan, B., 6th Bn.
20944 Cpl. Dancyger, L.,* 7th Bn.
28901 Pte. Darters, S., 16th Bn.
242259 Pte. Daitsh, B., 2/5th Bn.
22915 L/Cpl. Dreebin, H.,* 1st Bn.
25567 Pte. Fierstein, J., 6th Bn.
 L/Cpl. Fetel, A.
202613 Pte. Freeman, J., 1st Bn.
25853 Pte. Freedman, A. B., 3rd Bn.
32298 Pte. Goldberg S., 6th Bn.
20480 Pte. Harrison, J., 6th Bn.
358922 Pte. Jacobson, M. J., 10th Bn.
202857 Pte. Latter, A.
44829 Pte. Lewis, L., 10th Bn.
13/51604 Pte. Michaels, L., 2/5th Bn.
S/13883 Pte. Ockrent, H., 3rd Bn.
 Cyc. Phillips, J.
12347 Pte Quinn, J., 6th Bn.
 Pte. Rosenheim, J., 4th Bn.
16981 L/Cpl. Rosenston, E., 8th Bn.
32694 Pte. Rosenbaum, B., 2nd Bn.
 Pte. Ross, B., 2nd Bn.
40698 Pte. Samuels, L., 10th Bn.
202810 Pte. Salberg, A. H.
200033 Pte. Schlosberg, H., 95th Bn.
 Pte. Shields, J., 3rd Bn.
 Pte. Shinley, H.
12726 Pte. Silver, S., 6th Bn.
 Pte. Simon, E.
38763 Cpl. Smith, E., 10th G. B.
26904 Pte. Stone, A., 11th Bn.
32732 Pte. Sunderland, P., 3rd Bn.
41857 Pte. Symon, I. D.,* 1st Bn.
34696 Pte. Taylor, M., 3rd Bn.
23706 Pte. Tait, L., 9th Bn.
33192 Pte. Wolfson, B., 2nd Bn.
22969 Pte. Wolbrom, G., 6th Bn.

* Killed in Action or died on Active Service.

THE KING'S OWN SCOTTISH BORDERERS.

OFFICERS.

Lieut. Diamond, J.* (M.C.).
2nd Lieut. Furst, L. A. (M.C.).
2nd Lieut. Solomon, L.,* 1st Bn.

N.C.O.'s AND MEN.

19058 Pte. Barr, S., 1st Bn.
41560 Pte. Baron, H., 1st Bn.
32560 Pte. Barnett, 7/8th Bn.
242662 Pte. Barnett, N., 1/5th Bn.
12641 Pte. Best, D., 2/5th Bn.
16912 Pte. Benson, D., 8th Bn.
407726 Pte. Butler, J.
18930 Pte. Caplan, H., 1st Bn.
28075 Pte. Cohen, S., 2nd Bn.

THE CAMERONIANS (SCOTTISH RIFLES).

N.C.O.'s AND MEN.

40335 Pte. Baker, A., 1st Bn.
9911 Pte. Bloom, L., 9th Bn.
33686 Pte. Baker, H. (M.M.), 5/6th Bn.
43304 Pte. Bloom, S., 18th Bn.
9844 Pte. Baker, J., 2nd Bn.
 Pte. Bennett, F. G., 2nd Bn.
 Pte. Besser, A., 2nd Bn.
42975 Pte. Black, A., 1/8th Bn.
9857 Bdr. Bearman, H.
 Pte. Boyd, J., 4th Bn.
203803 Pte. Cohen, E., 5/6th Bn.
201727 Pte. Conley, L., 5th Bn.

Scottish Rifles.—Continued.

34524	Pte. CARLTON, A., 5/6th Bn.
560	Rfm. CONEKY, 10th Bn.
30689	Pte. COHEN, M., 16th Bn.
26994	Pte. DAVIS, C., 14th Bn.
49121	Pte. DIAMOND, H., 4th Bn.
36366	Pte. DAVIS, M., 3rd Bn.
109173	Pte. DA COSTA, E.
	Pte. DIAMOND, J., 3rd Bn.
26473	Pte. ESTERSON, P., 9th Bn.
33560	Pte. ELIAS, D., 7th Bn.
36117	Pte. ESTERMAN, H., 4th Bn.
265481	L/Cpl. FREEDMAN, W., 2nd Bn.
316005	Pte. FREEDMAN, S., 15th Bn.
204313	Pte. FOX, I., 2/5th Bn.
4842	Rfm. FERN, J.
200351	Cpl. GILLIES, M.,* 5th Bn.
16484	Pte. GOLDBERG, M., 9th Bn.
26433	Pte. GLICKMAN, M. G., 1st Bn.
37728	Pte. GORDON, H., 10th Bn.
41987	Pte. GOLDSTONE, C., 2nd Bn.
8461	Pte. GOULSTON, M.
33627	Pte. GOODSON, B., 1/8th Bn.
45846	Pte. GOLDSTEIN, J., 18th Bn.
25043	Pte. HYMAN, D., 1st Bn.
292025	Pte. HOLLAND, J., 1/8th Bn.
27041	Pte. HARRIS, M., 14th Bn.
30548	Pte. HYMAN, J.,* 11th Bn.
10044	Pte. HYAMS, J. C., 2nd Bn.
22011	Pte. HERMER, I., 4th Bn
	Pte. HANLEY, H., 2nd Bn.
	Pte. JOSEPH, I., 1st Bn.
11548	Pte. JACOBOVITCH, H., 10th Bn.
10099	Pte. KLEIN, B., 1st Bn.
36203	Pte. KESNICK, B., 4th Bn.
675	Pte. LEVY, L. E.,* 9th Bn.
200526	Rfm. LEVY, N., 9th Bn.
34455	Pte. LEVI, E., 4th Bn.
63630	Rfm. LEVI, J., 1st Bn.
202686	Pte. MARCUSAN, C., 5/6th Bn.
41752	Pte. MANN, C., 2nd Bn.
5329	Pte. MORGAN, M., 1st Bn.
9366	Pte. MORGAN, J.
127355	Pte. MONITZ, S. L., 4th Bn.
316021	Pte. MARKS, M., 15th Bn.
41166	L/Cpl. NORMAN, J. H., 9th Bn.
25548	Pte. NEWMAN, S.,* 1st Bn.
26982	Pte. OCKRINT, H., 14th Bn.
18945	Pte. PRIMACK, H., 9th Bn.
	Pte. RUBENSTEIN, J.
1480	Rfm. SEROCHENSKY, D., 5th Bn.
41798	Pte. SAMUEL, A., 2nd Bn.
291684	Rfm. SYMON, J., 1/8th Bn.
41910	Pte. SELBERG, A., 1st Bn.
24821	Pte. SARDASKY, I., 2nd Bn.
10205	Cpl. STANLEY, H. (M.M.), 2nd Bn.
315014	Cpl. SALMON, J., 15th Bn.
36545	Pte. SCHNEIDER, H., 2/5th Bn.
9715	Pte. SAYERS, J., 2/5th Bn.
22594	Pte. STRASCHAN, A.
1595	Pte. SELLARS, H., 7th Bn.
33437	Pte. SIGAR, A., 3rd Bn.
19895	Pte. SIMON, I., 4th Bn.
	Pte. STEIN, D., 8th Bn.
316132	Pte. SHUGAR, M., 15th Bn.
36638	Pte. SHERMAN, J., 4th Bn.
29276	Pte. VERBLOVE, C., 4th Bn.
44982	Pte. WOLFF, S., 12th Bn.
31593	Pte. WEINBAUM, J., 15th Bn.
15022	Sgt. WEBBER, M., 11th Bn.
26984	Pte. WOOLFSON, H., 14th Bn.
9374	Pte. WOOLF, H., 2nd Bn.
32911	Pte. ZARAKSAS, F., 2nd Bn.

* Killed in Action or died on Active Service.

THE ROYAL INNISKILLING FUSILIERS.

OFFICERS.

2nd Lieut. PRICE, W. (M.C.).

N.C.O.'s AND MEN.

49484	Pte. AARON, M., 1st Bn.
4279	Pte. APPLE, M., 1st Bn.
373987	Pte. COSTA, H.,* 9th Bn.
51954	Pte. COHEN, I.
30582	Pte. COHEN, B., 6th Bn.
8408	Pte. ERLINSKY, M., 11th Bn.
41460	L/Cpl. EMANUEL, M.,* 2nd Bn.
	Pte. FINEBERG, S., 6th Bn.
32232	Pte. FISHMAN, H., 2nd Bn.
	Pte. FINKLE, M., 6th Bn.
	Pte. GLOVER, M.
12899	Pte. GOLDMAN, S.,* 1st Bn.
29573	Pte. GOLDSTEIN, 4th Bn.
114155	Pte. GOLDBLUM, H. G., 13th Bn.
28672	Sig. GOODMAN, H. N., 7th Bn.
29573	Pte. GOEVIE, D., 14th Bn.
	Pte. HIGHLAND, W., 2nd Bn.
43852	Pte. ISAAC, M.
43564	Pte JACOBS, J., 10th Bn.
42141	Pte. JOSEPHS, W., 9th Bn.
49803	Pte. LEVY, 13th Bn.
54616	Sgt. LEVI, A. (M.M.), 13th Bn.
S/25205	Pte. MARCUS, H.,* 8th Bn.
8275	Pte. MERCADO, B., 9th Bn.
13477	Pte. MOSS, H., 6th Bn.
34870	Pte. OPPENHEIM, H., 8th Bn.
40525	Pte. ROSENBERG, B., 13th Bn.
376569	Pte. ROSENBLOOM, M., 13th Bn.
59541	L/Cpl. ROTENBERG, G., 11th Bn.
32180	Pte. ROCKFELLER, H.
49772	Pte. SHULMAN, J., 13th Bn.

Royal Inniskilling Fusiliers.—*Continued.*

12726 Pte. SILVER, S., 1st Bn.
449917 Pte. SOLOMONS, A., 11th Bn.
30535 Pte. SILVERMAN, S., 5th Bn.
18449 Pte. SONEMBURG, W., 13th Bn.
5/30546 Pte. SIMONS, J., 5th Bn.
43314 Pte. TYANOFSKY, M., 9th Bn.
40628 L/Cpl. WINDER, J., 2nd Bn.
422102 Pte. WOLFSON, W., 13th Bn.
47887 Pte. WOLFSON, I., 7/8th Bn.
32189 L/Cpl. WOLFERS, P., 2nd Bn.
30643 Pte. ZETTER, I., 6th Bn.

* Killed in Action or died on Active Service.

THE GLOUCESTERSHIRE REGIMENT.

OFFICERS.

2nd Lieut. BAMBERGER W. E. W.,* 1/5th Bn.
Capt. DAVIES, J. F., 13th Bn.
Capt. ENRIQUEZ, H. S., 10th Bn.
2nd Lieut. GALLICK, N. D.
Lieut. HADIDA, P. (M.C.).
Capt. HARTOG, D. H. (M.C.), 6th Bn.
Lieut.-Col. HALFORD, M. W., 1st Bn.
2nd Lieut. LEVY, H. V., 8th Bn.
2nd Lieut. LEVY, L. A., 1/6th Bn.
2nd Lieut. MYERS, W.
2nd Lieut. MOSS, W. C., 13th Bn.
Lieut. POLACK, E. E.,* 1/4th Bn.
Capt. RUBINSTEIN, R. F., 1/5th Bn.
Lieut. SLAVITZ, S. (M.C.).
Lieut. SOLOMON, K. M., 11th Bn.

N.C.O.'s AND MEN.

S/Sgt. ABRAHAMS, B. S.
4195 Pte. ABRAMS, S., 6th Bn.
Pte. ABRAHAMS, J. (M.M.).
4039 Pte. ALBERT, H., 6th Bn.
266805 Pte. ANFLICK, H., 13th Bn.
203523 Pte. BALL, C., 2/6th Bn.
44678 Pte. BARENTY, J. L., 8th Bn.
32199 Pte. BENJAMIN, H. (M.M.), 1st Bn.
6210 Pte. BLACK, W. H., 4th Bn.
31942 Pte. BLACK, H., 9th Bn.
204194 Pte. CAMPBELL, H., 4th Bn.
202628 Pte. CANDY, A. G., 2/4th Bn.
27935 Pte. CASTELLO, G., 4th Bn.
202837 Pte. CANTER, J., 4th Bn.
6216 Pte. CIRELSTAIN, D. R., 4th Bn.
21630 Pte. COHEN, L., 14th Bn.
14480 Pte. COHEN, D., 12th Bn.
Pte. COHEN, J., 8th Bn.
3566 Pte. COHEN, B., 1/6th Bn.
206807 Pte. COBURG, H., 2/6th Bn.
54035 Pte. CROWN, J., 17th Bn.
27935 Pte. CUTNA, H., 4th Bn.
35076 Pte. EPSTEIN, J., 12th Bn.
202841 Pte. FELL, J., 4th Bn.
10461 Pte. FERGUSON, M., 1st Bn.
24571 Pte. FINE, J., 1/4th Bn.
34699 Pte. FRIEDLANDER, I.
25859 Pte. GODDARD, R., 8th Bn.
Pte. GOODMAN, H., 2nd Bn.
291144 Pte. GOLDBERGH, B. H., 17th Bn.
33835 Pte. GOLDSMID, 7th Bn.
35203 Pte. GLASSMAN, 12th Bn.
204172 Pte. GREENBAUM, S., 1/6th Bn.
23369 Pte. GLUCK, R., 1/4th Bn.
285057 Pte. HARRINGMAN, S., 1/6th Bn.
20537 Cpl. HAYES, M. (M.M.), 12th Bn.
291141 Pte. HARRIS, A., 17th Bn.
5470 Pte. HOFFMAN, H., 6th Bn.
291178 Pte. ISAACS, J., 17th Bn.
4082 Pte. JACOBS, H., 93rd Bn.
20277 Pte. KAHN, P. R., 12th Bn.
14097 Sgt. LEVY, L., 12th Bn.
14098 Pte. LEVY, S., 12th Bn.
Pte. LEVY, H., 8th Bn.
36650 Pte. LEIKIN, B., 1st Bn.
L/Cpl. LEWBITZ, A., 2nd Bn.
11807 L/Cpl. MORRIS, S., 2nd Bn.
32122 Pte. MASON, I.,* 14th Bn.
22911 Pte. MUSAPHIA, G., 3rd Bn.
293920 Pte. MUSLIN, L., 1/4th Bn.
5215 Pte. NEWMAN, A., 4th Bn.
43271 Pte. OHEN, L., 11th Bn.
Sgt. PHILLIPS, J. (M.M.).
42246 Pte. PEARLMAN, C., 3rd Bn.
27352 Pte. PEARSON, S., 9th Bn.
33580 Pte. PEREZ, E., 1/4th Bn.
290783 Pte. ROSE, J., 17th Bn.
3552 Pte. ROSEN, L.,* 6th Bn.
26817 Pte. ROSENBERG, S., 3rd Bn.
291145 Pte. ROSENBERG, M., 17th Bn.
55224 Pte. ROSENBURG, A., 3rd Bn.
237005 Pte. ROSENTHAL, M., 1/5th Bn.
Pte. SAUNDERS, H., 11th Bn.
32771 Pte. SCHAVINSKY, A.
32772 Pte. SCHNEIDER, A.
37566 Pte. SHONWICK, W., 14th Bn.
27565 Pte. SIMONS, M., 14th Bn.
36942 Pte. SILKOVITCH, B. H., 10th Bn.
29280 Pte. SPERLING, M., 3rd Bn.
5468 Pte. SPIEGEL, C., 6th Bn.
25914 Cpl. TAYLOR, F., 4th Bn.
32718 Pte. VIGNESKIE, N., 7th Bn.
11601 L/Cpl. WALTERS, S., 1st Bn.

* Killed in Action or died on Active Service.

THE WORCESTERSHIRE REGIMENT.

OFFICERS.

Capt. BENJAMIN, H. S.,* 1/8th Bn.
2nd Lieut. COLEMAN, P. N., 1/8th Bn.
2nd Lieut. DAVIS, E. L., 12th Bn.
Capt. DURLACHER, E.,* 15th Bn.
Lieut. DURLACHER, B. R. (M.C.).
Lieut. GODFREY, J. H. L., 14th Bn.
Lieut. HENRY, C. C.,* 2nd Bn.
Lieut. HIRSCHFELD, F. (D.C.M., M.M.).
Lieut. HALLE, J.,* 13th Bn.
Lieut. LAZARUS, C. L., 3rd Bn.
Lieut. LAZARUS, E. L., 6th Bn.
Lieut. MYER, D. G. A.,* 9th Bn.
2nd Lieut. POLACK, B. J.,* 9th Bn.
Capt. SPIERS, K. L. (M.C.), 6th Bn.
Lieut. SAMUEL, J. H., 10th Bn.
2nd Lieut. SOLOMON, G. D., 8th Bn.
Lieut. WINTER, H. G., 8th Bn.

N.C.O.'s AND MEN.

18707 Pte. ABRAHAMS, R. A., 10th Bn.
26316 Pte. ABRAHAMS, B., 1st Bn.
43375 L/Cpl. ACKERMAN, M., 3rd Bn.
5/9093 Pte. ASTLEY, H., 6th Bn.
62988 Pte. ABRAHAM, J., 15th Bn.
62102 Pte. ARCHER, J., 15th Bn.
51027 Pte. AARONS, A., 3rd Bn.
       L/Cpl. ALDERWICK, 10th Bn.
24680 Pte. BETTS, S., 4th Bn.
14216 Pte. BARONOVITCH, L.,* 1st Bn.
40118 Pte. BURGESS, D., 10th H.Q.
26843 Pte. BRADFIELD, R. E., 10th H.Q.
576121 L/Cpl. BAKER, J., 17th G Bn.
42840 Pte BARRATT, J.
4953 L/Cpl. BRAND, S., 7th Res. Bn.
39487 Pte. BERMEL, D., 15th Bn.
29771 Pte. BARNETT, B., 6th Bn.
66399 Pte. BLOOMFIELD, C.
       Pte. COHEN, W., 3rd Bn.
13287 Pte. CRASH, M., 3rd Bn.
576148 Pte. COHEN, H., 17th Gar. Bn.
23268 Pte. COHEN, L., 3rd Bn.
242317 Pte. COHEN, P., 1/8th Bn.
38421 Pte. COSTER, J.,* 2/8th Bn.
37062 Pte. COHEN, J., 9th Bn.
       Pte. CASHER, B. (M.M.).
42472 Pte. CHESSES, N., 5th Bn.
26886 Pte. CAMERON, D., 6th Bn.
62489 Pte. COHEN, M., 16th Bn.
59184 Pte. CORFAN, L., 5th Bn.
12166 L/Cpl. COFEMAN, J., 10th Bn.
62168 Pte. DAVIS, M., 16th Bn.
50539 Pte. DAVIS, H. M., 1st Bn.
57515 Pte. FORDANSKI, C.,* 10th Bn.
26309 Pte. FLETCHER, D. L., 13th Bn.

       Pte. FORDANSKI, J., 2nd Bn.
22669 L/Cpl. FRENCHMAN, E., 1st Bn.
66571 Pte. FINSTEIN, S.*
5197 Pte. FINEBERG, S.,* 7th Bn.
61367 Pte. FREEDMAN, S., 13th Bn.
42651 Cpl. FREEDMAN, E., 5th Bn.
41314 Pte. FRESHMAN, I., 1/7th Bn.
29647 L/Cpl. FREEMAN, M. J., 6th Bn.
50327 Pte. FINKLESTEIN, A.
       Pte. GOLDMAN, R., 6th Bn.
27634 Pte. GOLDMAN, N., 2nd Bn.
42543 Pte. GRIECK, M.,* 2nd Bn.
203591 Pte. GOODFRIEND, T., 1/7th Bn.
26982 Pte. GOODMAN, S., 13th Bn.
64948 Pte. GERILLY, I., 14th Gar. Bn.
33444 Pte. GOODFRIEND, I., 2nd Bn.
45344 Pte. GREEN, H., 5th Bn.
61758 Pte. GOLDBERG, M., 5th Bn.
62378 Pte. GOLDBERG, J., 16th Bn.
       Pte. GODFREY, G. H., 7th Bn.
50332 Pte. GOLDSTON, L., 1st Bn.
51100 Pte. HYMAN, D., 4th Bn.
26839 Pte. HAMBURGER, B., 6th Bn.
45411 Pte. HARONS, C.
62480 Pte. HARRIS, M., 16th Bn.
14438 Pte. ISAACS, A.,* 1st Bn.
30198 Pte. ISAACS, H., 6th Bn.
5143 Pte. ISAACS, E. E.,* 2nd Bn.
40241 Pte. JACOBS, N.,* 3rd Bn.
14438 Pte. JACOBOWITZ, E., 1st Bn.
69948 Pte. JOSEPH, J., 3rd Bn.
27643 Pte. JACOBS, M.,* 1st Bn.
58040 Pte. JACOBOVITZ, H.
       Sgt. JOSEPH, E. (D.C.M.), 2nd Bn.
38629 Pte. JOSEPH, W., 3rd Bn.
       Pte. JOSEPH, S., 5th Bn.
42538 L/Cpl. KAPPEL, J., 2nd Bn.
51057 Cpl. KENT, C. G., 1/8th Bn.
51064 Pte. KREPS, P. S., 1/8th Bn.
59346 Pte. KAPLAN, T., 1/8th Bn.
62475 Pte. KASSALITIS, G., 16th Bn.
45375 L/Cpl. KERMON, M., 5th Bn.
57255 Pte. LEVY, A., 3rd Bn.
57419 Pte. LEVNIE, A., 3rd Bn.
50946 Pte. LEARER, S., 2/th Bn.
51059 Pte. LEVY, M., 1/8th Bn.
51063 Pte. LIST, S., 1/8th Bn.
4721 Pte. LYONS, M. A., 16th Bn.
       Pte. LEVINE, L., 2nd Bn.
576226 Pte. MUSGRAVE, F., 17th Gar. Bn.
46025 Pte. MERCER, J., 4th Bn.
29581 Cpl. MINSKY, I. C., 9th Bn.
50166 Pte. MILLER, A., 16th Bn.
8599 Pte. NASH, W., 5th Bn.
42472 Pte. NEWMAN, C., 14th Bn.
45520 Pte. OSSENSTEIN, H., 8th Bn.
576404 Pte. PERILLY, T., 17th Gar. Bn.
       Pte. PERSOFF, C.

Worcestershire Regt.—*Continued.*

18928	Pte. ROSENBERG, L.,*	3rd Bn.
41728	Pte. REICHENBERG, D.,	14th Bn.
26046	Pte. RHODES, M.,	13th Bn.
26983	Pte. ROSENBERG, M.,	13th Bn.
31057	Pte. RICH,	9th Bn.
	Cpl. RUDELSTEIN, A.	
29938	Pte. RENOVITCH, P.,	11th Bn.
36851	Pte. ROSE, S.,	1st Bn.
3003	L/Cpl. SINGER, L.,	3rd Bn.
26368	Pte. SOLOMON, M.,*	3rd Bn.
24344	Pte. SNIDAL, F.,	4th Bn.
41776	Pte. STODEL, E.,	14th Bn.
51002	Pte. SIMONS, A.,	14th Bn.
51572	Pte. SOLOMONS, M.,	6th Bn.
296295	Pte. SHAFFREEN, L.,	1/1st Bn.
13851	Pte. SCHEIN, J.,*	9th Bn.
50305	Pte. SMITH, I.,	5th Bn.
31762	Pte. SIMMONS, L.,	1st Bn.
61101	L/Cpl. SINGER, J.,	2/8th Bn.
50536	Pte. STONSFIELD, J.,	1st Bn.
52137	Pte. SEFF, J.,	5th Bn.
	Pte. SILVER,	13th Bn.
	Pte. SHAW, J. (SHILKOFF),	3/7th Bn.
	Pte. SHOTLAND, M.	
	Pte. SILVERMAN, E.,	3rd Bn.
	A/Cpl. TURNER, G.,	4th Bn.
87801	Pte. THEOBALD,	2nd Bn.
68329	Pte. VAN KEMP,	1st Bn.
18484	Sgt. WOODBURN, L.,	10th Bn.
33858	L/Cpl. WEINBERG, A.,	1st Bn.
260196	Pte. WELT, H.,*	8th Bn.

* Killed in Action or died on Active Service.

THE EAST LANCASHIRE REGIMENT.

OFFICERS.

Capt. BEHREND, A., 4th Bn.
2nd Lieut. FORMAN, M., 3rd Bn.
2nd Lieut. KOHN, W. A.,* 11th Bn.
2nd Lieut. LOB, H., 8th Bn.
2nd Lieut. LYONS, E. J.,* 1st Bn.
2nd Lieut. RAPHAEL,* H. G., 7th Bn.
Lieut. SOULAL, J., 1st Bn.
2nd Lieut. WALLERSTEIN, L. D. J., 1st Bn.

N.C.O.'s AND MEN.

442143	Pte. ALEXANDER, B.	
21799	Pte. ABRAMS, J. B.,	1st Bn.
19483	Pte. BASS, E.,	2nd Bn.
124464	Pte. BARNETT, L.,	13th Bn.
17402	Pte. BOLLER, J.,*	8th Bn.
235690	Pte. BELL, D.,	2nd Bn.
	Pte. BARADSKY, B.,	2nd Bn.
	Pte. BESSO, E. M.,	7th Bn.
	Pte. BESSO, A.,	7th Bn.
29788	Pte. COHEN, D.,	7th Bn.
706255	Pte. COWAN, S.,	3/2nd Bn.
15306	Pte. CUNLIFFE, F.,	11th Bn.
12/24943	Pte. COBB, L.,	9th Bn.
54037	Pte. CORNFIELD, M.	
201831	Pte. DAVIES, H.,	1/2nd Bn.
30735	Pte. DELMONTE, J.,	2/4th Bn.
3/38926	Pte. DELACOVITCH, M.,	3rd Bn.
	Pte. FELDMAN, L.,	7th Bn.
2032	Pte. FRESCO, J.,	1st Bn.
79676	Pte. FIELDMAN, J.,	12th Bn.
201829	Pte. FINBERG, H.,*	4th Bn.
79367	Pte. FAW, J.,	12th Bn.
	Pte. FREEMAN, M.,	1st Bn.
29727	Pte. FRANKS, H.,	2nd Bn.
12307	Pte. GORDON, D.,	7th Bn.
29516	Pte. GOLDSTONE, A.,	8th Bn.
27163	Pte. GORDON, B.,	11th Bn.
29316	Pte. GOLDSTEIN,	8th Bn.
79678	Pte. GHENKIN, S.,	12th Bn.
21109	Pte. GOODMAN, P.,	1st Bn.
30832	Pte. GOLDSTEIN, I.,	1st Bn.
3/23494	Pte. GOLDSTEIN, L.,	9th Bn.
203335	Pte. GOLDSTONE, M.,	13th Bn.
10/23841	Pte. GOLDBERG, N. D.,	10th Bn.
38207	Pte. GIEL, N.	
	Pte. GOLDMAN, H.,	3rd Bn.
29518	Pte. HYMAN,	8th Bn.
5277	Pte. HARRISON, S.,	4th Bn.
39652	Pte. HOCKIN, B.,*	1st Bn.
158295	Pte. HART, M.,	6/6th Bn.
	Pte. HERBERTS, J.,	4th Bn.
	Pte. HARRIS, H.	
36322	Pte. JACOBSON, H.,	11th Bn.
2073	Pte. JACKSON,	2nd Bn.
39703	Pte. JACOBS, J.,	2nd Bn.
3/35307	Pte. JACOBSON, M.,	3rd Bn.
9/13302	Sgt. JACKSON, H.,	9th Bn.
764	Pte. JACOBS, H.,	2/2nd Bn.
	Pte. JOEL, C.,	1st Bn.
31400	Pte. KNIT, M.,	11th Bn.
13645	Pte. KELMAN, L.,	7th Bn.
6/14820	Pte. KOTCHER, S.,	9th Bn.
203655	Pte. LEWIS, H.,	2/4th Bn.
235421	Pte. LOFFMAN, A.,	1st Bn.
422002	Pte. LEVINSTEIN, S.,	13th Bn.
21273	Pte. LEVEY, H.,	13th Bn.
39518	Pte. LESSER, I.,	1st Bn.
51869	Pte. LEVY, S.,	12th Bn.
10589	Pte. LEVANTER, J.,*	2nd Bn.
29535	Pte. LANDSMAN, R. W.,	8th Bn
39022	Pte. LINSKIE,	6th Bn.
32147	Pte. LEVY, E.,	11th Bn.
4218	Pte. LEON, I.,	3/8th Bn.
33023	Pte. LEVY, S.,	13th Bn.
145752	Pte. LYONS, E.,	1st Bn.

East Lancashire Regt.—Continued.

- 29766 Pte. MUSCOVITCH, L., 11th Bn.
- 3/27500 Pte. MARGOLINS, S., 3rd Bn.
- C.Q.M.S. MARKS, R.
- 22658 Pte. MARKSON, H., 10th Bn.
- 801341 L/Cpl. MONTAGUE, M.
- 4683 Pte. NEWMAN, J., 1st Bn.
- 57538 Pte. NYBURG, J., 1st Bn.
- 10092 L/Cpl. ORMAN, J., 1st Bn.
- 62855 Pte. ORIENSTEIN, J., 12th Bn.
- 29876 Pte. PEARLMAN, H., 7th Bn.
- 10346 Sgt. PISELEY, A. C.,* 1st Bn.
- 29252 L/Cpl. PHILLIPS, M.,* 1st Bn.
- 10446 Pte. PEARLMAN, M.,* 8th Bn.
- 51833 Pte. POMERANTZ, A., 3rd Bn.
- 235283 Pte. RUBENSTEIN, H.,* 4th Bn.
- 38275 Pte. RAPPAPORT, B., 1/4th Bn.
- 30750 Pte. ROSENBERG, H., 2nd Bn.
- 22491 L/Cpl. RILEY, 6th Bn.
- 32052 Pte. RUBINSKY, M., 1/5th Bn.
- 350391 Pte. RUSHMAN, J.
- 18530 Pte. SHIERS, A., 2nd Bn.
- 16529 Pte. SHIERS, E., 2nd Bn.
- 36773 Sgt. STAHL, J.,* 7th Bn.
- 5684 Sgt. STOKER, I., 2/5th Bn.
- 47264 Pte. SOLOMON, M., 1st Bn.
- 33412 Pte. SMOLENSKI, C.,* 11th Bn.
- 87998 Pte. SYMON, R., 12th Bn.
- 260006 Cpl. SUMMERS, E., 1/4th Bn.
- 2588 Pte. STERN, H. S., 7th Bn.
- Pte. SAMUEL, S. (M.M.).
- 205377 Pte. SMITH, H.
- Pte. STERNSHIRE, J.
- 87978 Pte. SEMOUR, R., 8th Bn.
- 202767 Pte. TEGLISS, M., 4th Bn.
- 3/39471 Pte. WYNER, M., 1st Bn.
- 57326 Pte. WEAVER, R.
- Pte. WOOLF, E., 1st Bn.
- 3/22030 Pte. WILLESTONE, H., 9th Bn.
- 202717 Pte. YEGLISS, H., 2/4th Bn.
- 49337 Pte. ZELKIN, H., 2nd Bn.
- 34386 Pte. ZIGMOND, A.

* Killed in Action or died on Active Service.

THE EAST SURREY REGIMENT.

OFFICERS.

- 2nd Lieut. ABRAHAM, R. C., 10th Bn.
- 2nd Lieut. BARDER, D. M., 7th Bn.
- 2nd Lieut. BARDER, S. G.,* 8th Bn.
- 2nd Lieut. ELKIN, R. S., 5th Bn.
- 2nd Lieut. HAINES, E. A.,* 9th Bn.
- 2nd Lieut. HART, J. A. (M.C.).
- 2nd Lieut. JACOBS, A. E. (M.C.).
- 2nd Lieut. LYONS, C. W. F., 8th Bn.
- 2nd Lieut. MARKS, C. B.,* (M.C.), 8th Bn.
- 2nd Lieut. SAMUELS, F. A. (M.C.).

N.C.O.'s AND MEN.

- 13053 Pte. ABRAHAMS, L. G., 13th Bn.
- 20679 Pte. ABRAHAMSON, V., 8th Bn.
- 35173 Pte. AILION, B., 9th Bn.
- 11820 Pte. ALEXANDER, H.,* 3rd Bn.
- 9654 Pte. ANDERSON, A., 2nd Bn.
- 29269 Pte. ABRAHAMS, M., 8th Bn.
- 4928 Pte. AARONVITCH, J., 2/6th Bn.
- 33927 Pte. ABRAHAMS, D.
- Pte. ASSENDRIVER, E.
- G/5374 Pte. BERWALD, B., 8th Bn.
- 32455 Pte. BECKER, J.,* 1st Bn.
- 32334 Pte. BERNSTEIN, L.,* 7th Bn.
- 34038 Pte. BENJAMIN, N., 1st Bn.
- 12492 Pte. BUTLER, E., 13th Bn.
- 23292 Pte. BURNS, A., 4th Bn.
- 20473 Pte. BARNARD, H. J., 3rd Bn.
- 5099 Pte. BURR, M., 2/5th Bn.
- 4418 Pte. BERNBAUM, E., 2/5th Bn.
- Pte. BURRILL, P., 8th Bn.
- Pte. BURMAN, J.
- 5374 Pte. BERMAN, B.
- 25645 Pte. BENNETT, S., 13th Bn.
- 10767 Pte. COHEN, E., 1st Bn.
- Pte. COOPER, H., 1st Bn.
- 23940 Pte. COHEN, J., 3rd Bn.
- Pte. CUTNER, A., 2/6th Bn.
- 12140 Pte. COHEN, S., 3rd Bn.
- 26382 Pte. COHEN, J., 3rd Bn.
- 36435 Pte. COHEN, J., 4th Bn.
- 36445 Pte. COCHINSKI, A., 4th Bn.
- 49101 Pte. COWAN, A., 3rd Bat..
- 202064 Pte. CROSKEY, N., 2/5th Bn.
- 19389 Pte. COHEN, J., 11th Bn.
- 5058 Pte. COHEN, L., 2/5th Bn.
- 24205 Pte. COHEN, O.
- 1006 Cpl. COLLINS, D.
- 5142 Pte. CORAN, A., 2/6th Bn.
- 269 Pte. CREAMER, J. A., 3rd Bn.
- 32593 Pte. COHEN, D., 4th Bn.
- 20218 Pte. DOLIMAN, J., 5th Bn.
- 9681 Pte. DAVIDSON, W. L., 11th Bn.
- 4956 Pte. DORMAN, J., 2/5th Bn.
- 202077 Pte. DOBKIN, H., 2/5th Bn.
- Pte. DRIVER, C., 1st Bn.
- 23952 Pte. ELGART, D., 3rd Bn.
- 31532 Pte. FELDBERG, A., 7th Bn.
- 26157 Pte. FELDERMAN, T., 1st Bn.
- 28146 Pte. FEVERMAN, J., 3rd Bn.
- 27231 Pte. FINKLE, J., 9th Bn.
- 4976 Pte. FREEDMAN, M., 2/5th Bn.

East Surrey Regt.—*Continued.*

29175	Pte. FELDMAN, M., 2/5th Bn.
26612	Pte. FRANKS, A., 4th Bn.
	Pte. FARBKEL, J.
4231	Pte. GOLDSTEIN, H., 2nd Bn.
11194	Pte. GOULD, H., 8th Bn.
	Pte. GIVANT, R., 1st Bn.
26811	Pte. GLUCK, 13th Bn.
10787	Pte. GREENSTOCK, H.,* 1st Bn.
5145	Pte. GLASS, P., 2/6th Bn.
5302	Pte. GOLDCROWN, J., 2/6th Bn.
4300	Pte. GOLDBERG, I., 2/6th Bn.
4965	Pte. GOODMAN, W., 2/6th Bn.
4357	Pte. GLASIN, S., 2/5th Bn.
789	Pte. GOLDBERG, B., 5th Bn.
37764	Pte. GREITZER, H., 3rd Bn.
49102	Pte. GREEN, B., 3rd Bn.
	Pte. GAYTON, A., 2/5th Bn.
10632	Cpl. HOLMES, J. G.,* 7th Bn.
27262	Pte. HYMAN, S.,* 9th Bn.
35077	Pte. HURWITZ, L.,* 9th Bn.
	Pte. HYAMS, M., 1st Bn.
14447	Pte. HAZEL, G., 4th Bn.
20058	L/Cpl. HEILBUTH, L. P., 11th Bn.
5152	Pte. HARRISON, I. A., 2/8th Bn.
4971	Pte. HARRIS, B., 2/5th Bn.
11958	Pte. HART, H. L.
19189	Pte. HERSHAM, P., 3rd Bn.
9743	Pte. HEWSON, J.
30302	Pte. IDE, A., 4th Bn.
49093	Pte. ISRAEL, A., 3rd Bn.
49393	Pte. IYYARD, W., 3rd Bn.
20955	Pte. ISAACS, S., 7th Bn.
19832	Pte. ISAACS, G.
21645	L/Cpl. JOSEPH, A., 12th Bn.
26160	Pte. JACOBSON, M., 1st Bn.
10409	Pte. JACOBS, J.,* 2nd Bn.
24199	Pte. JACOBS, D., 4th Bn.
4299	Pte. JACOBS, S., 2/6th Bn.
202377	Pte. JACOBS, H.
4555	Pte. JACOBS, N., 2/6th Bn.
4927	Pte. JACOBS, A.
	Pte. JEWELL, H. A. M., 6th Bn.
	Pte. JOSEPHS, J., 1st Bn.
18237	Pte. KANTRAWITZ, J., 13th Bn.
26062	Pte. KNOLL, D., 1st Bn.
36885	Pte. KOGKINSKY, A., 4th Bn.
	Pte. KELLY, J., 8th Bn.
4927	Pte. KAPLOBELAH, W., 2/6th Bn.
5040	Pte. KROSLINSKY, S., 2/5th Bn.
G/39439	Pte. KINSKY, T.
34566	Sgt. KELLER, J.
48883	Pte. KOBRINSKY, T.
933	Pte. LEVY, N., 7th Bn.
12941	Pte. LAZARUS, 12th Bn.
34816	Pte. LEWIS, H., 8th Bn.
8378	Pte. LAURENCE, V., 1st Bn.
36603	Pte. LEVY, B., 4th Bn.
5331	Pte. LYONS, S.
31624	Pte. LEVISON, J., 4th Bn.
	Pte. LEWIS, A., 8th Bn.
	Pte. LEWIS, S., 2/6th Bn.
9309	Pte. MOSS, A., 9th Bn.
32288	Pte. MARKS, S., 9th Bn.
8189	Pte. MYERS, M.,* 1st Bn.
25104	Pte. MIRANDA, D., 1st Bn.
701718	L/Cpl. MATHIAN, J., 3rd Bn.
39470	Pte. MARKS, J., 3rd Bn.
5159	Pte. MARGRETT, M., 2/6th Bn.
5127	Pte. MELNICK, M., 2/5th Bn.
35880	Pte. MARKS, B.
	Pte. MARKS, A., 2/5th Bn.
	Pte. NATHAN, L., 1st Bn.
B/7030	Pte. NATHAN, J., 3rd Bn.
53939	Pte. OLIVER, R., 3rd Bn.
254670	Pte. OSOVITCH, H., 1st Bn.
7983	Pte. PARCEZAR, A., 2/5th Bn.
31378	Pte. PERILLY, S., 10th Bn.
22587	Pte. PYZER, B.
	Pte. PLOTKIN, J., 4th Bn.
	Pte. PHILLIPS, J., 2/5th Bn.
	Pte. PHILLIPS, M., 2/5th Bn.
23409	Pte. PIZER, M., 4th Bn.
204006	Pte. PAIN, J., 5th Bn.
55680	Pte. PUE, F., 3rd Bn.
22119	Pte. REYNOLDS, T. J. N., 8th Bn.
39210	Pte. ROSENBURG, R., 9th Bn.
956	Pte. REYNOLDS, F., 1st Bn.
201786	Pte. ROSENBAUM, S., 2/5th Bn.
38072	Pte. ROSENBAUM, A.,* 8th Bn.
19941	Pte. RABBINOBITZ, 11th Bn.
4939	Pte. ROSENBERG, S., 2/6th Bn.
38034	Pte. REUBEN, S., 3rd Bn.
49284	Pte. ROSENBERG, L.
	Pte. ROAT, R., 4th Bn.
	Pte. RANDALL, H., 2/6th Bn.
12603	Cpl. SHIELMAN, A., 12th Bn.
25382	Pte. SOMERS, M., 12th Bn.
203061	Pte. SCHAETZEN, L., 1st Bn.
19917	Pte. SOLOMONS, J.
204733	Pte. SEGIL, J., 1st Bn.
32378	Pte. SHEELLER, M., 4th Bn.
19355	Pte. SAMUELS, A., 4th Bn.
38435	Pte. SUSSMAN, P., 3rd Bn.
13604	Pte. SILVER, L., 3rd Bn.
36615	Pte. SONBERG, H., 4th Bn.
GG/38976	Pte. STONE, J., 3rd Bn.
35056	Pte. SCHARTZ, D., 2nd Bn.
5127	Pte. SCHAAPWOL, J.
3172	Pte. SPIEZEL, J., 2/6th Bn.
5300	Pte. SECUNDA, M.
5436	Pte. STOLERWITZSKY, I.
202018	Pte. SOLOMON, J., 2/5th Bn.

East Surrey Regt.—Continued.

4919 Pte. SUGARMAN, J.
240813 Pte. SPIRO, J., 2/6th Bn.
35636 Pte. SILVERMAN, V., 9th Bn.
Pte. SMITH, H., 1st Bn.
Pte. SCOTT, J.
14903 L/Sgt. TENNENS, P., 4th Bn.
49051 Pte. UNGER, H., 3rd Bn.
2049 Pte. VAN PRAAGH, B., 10th Bn.
26153 Pte. VINSLOVSKI, H., 1st Bn.
8118 Sgt. WILLIAMS, J., 7th Bn.
36563 Sgt. WILKS, S., 1st Bn.
26164 Pte. WARMBARDT, R., 1st Bn.
Pte. WOOLF, R., 1st Bn.
8437 Sgt. WOOLF, M., 1st Bn.
32658 L/Cpl. YOUNG, A., 13th Bn.
21182 Pte. YAROSHEFSKY, I.
5206 Pte. ZACK, S., 2/6th Bn.

* Killed in Action or died on Active Service.

THE DUKE OF CORNWALL'S LIGHT INFANTRY.

OFFICERS.

2nd Lieut. HYMAN,* R. L., 6th Bn.
Lieut. SCALLARD, F., 6th Bn.
2nd Lieut. TOMLINSON, S., 7th Bn.
10641 L/Cpl. ARCHER, M., 3rd Bn.
27426 Pte. ADELMAN, A., 3rd Bn.
Pte. AXELBAND, M.
Pte. ARTHUR, M., 6th Bn.
Pte. BERLIS, J., 2nd Bn.
Cpl. BROOKS, D., 1st Bn.
Pte. BENOLIEL, J.
17648 Pte. COHEN, D., 7th Bn.
Pte. COHEN, L., 2nd Bn
38601 Pte. COMERVITCH, J., 3rd Bn.
38467 Pte. COMBERG.
01463 Pte. CREGOR, A., 1st Bn.
01436 Pte. CAME, A. I., 1st Bn.
28013 Pte. DOBIN, D., 3rd Bn.
Pte. DANCYGER, H.
18078 Pte. ENGLEMAN, L., 8th Bn.
12244 Pte. FOX, H., 7th Bn.
B/23782 Pte. FELLS, I., 10th Bn.
19323 Pte. FREEDMAN, J., 3rd Bn.
Pte. FRANKS, B.
Pte. FLAMBERG, L., 3rd Bn.
18193 Pte. GOLDSTEIN, J., 8th Bn.
17489 L/Cpl. GRODNER, A. (M.M.), 10th Bn.
5026 Pte. GLASSMAN, D.,* 1st Bn.

23240 Pte. GRATZ, A., 7th Bn.
9803 Pte. GOODGLASS, P., 1st Bn.
Pte. GOLLOP, A. (M.M.).
5347 Pte. GREEN, A.
5710 Pte. GORDON, E.
Pte. GOODMAN, H., 3rd Bn.
10424 Pte. HOW, M., 6th Bn.
15973 Pte. HORNE, H., 8th Bn.
9391 A/Cpl. HARRIS A.,* 1st Bn.
7442 A/Cpl. HARRIS, H.,* 1st Bn.
4908 Pte. HARRIS, J.,* 1st Bn.
461089 Pte. HIRSCH, L.
436796 Pte. HONIGMAN, S.
Pte. HARRIS, D.
17494 Pte. JACOBS, M.,* 1st Bn.
19616 Pte. JACOBS, A., 1st Bn.
22566 Pte. JACOBS, J., 7th Bn.
Pte. JACOBS, L. L., 2nd Bn.
29853 Pte. KOSSICK, J., 1/5th Bn.
10427 Pte. LEVINE, B.,* 6th Bn.
18680 Pte. LEVY, C., 2nd Bn.
14628 Pte. LEVINE, H., 7th Bn.
28072 Pte. LAPIDUS, J.,* 1st Bn.
29221 Pte. LEWIS, H., 1st Bn.
17150 Pte. LEVY, S., 6th Bn.
L/Cpl. LEVENE, A.
10753 Pte. LEVY, H.,* 1st Bn.
37127 Pte. LASKER, L., 1/4th Bn.
20467 Pte. LAWRENCE, J.
L/Cpl. LAZARUS, J.
40946 Pte. LEVY, J., 7th Bn.
21519 Pte. LEVINSON, M., 8th Bn.
147434 Pte. LEE, R., 8th Bn.
10969 Sgt. MOSS, A. (M.M.), 7th Bn.
Pte. MARTIN, D.
Pte. MORRIS, M., 2nd Bn.
4987 Pte. MYERS, J. H., 3rd Bn.
28203 Pte. MEARS, M., 6th Bn.
Pte. NATHAN, J., 6th Bn.
18576 Pte. OLNEY, D., 1st Bn.
18575 Pte. PLOTTS, A., 1st Bn.
53517 Pte. PENER, N., 7th Bn.
24741 Pte. PHILLIPS, H., 8th Bn.
41006 Pte. ROSE, A., 1/5th Bn.
23804 L/Cpl. RUFFELL, S.,* 1st Bn.
4580 Pte. ROSE, J., 1st Bn.
53197 Pte. RABINOMBY, A., 15th Bn.
12070 Pte. ROSENBERG, 6th Bn.
36604 Pte. SIMANTON, A., 1/5th Bn.
35878 Pte. SIMONS, S.
19304 Pte. SIMMONS, H., 2nd Bn.
46091 Pte. SIROTA, A., 3rd Bn.
512457 Pte. ULPH, C., 3rd Bn.
37954 Pte. VINCENT, C.
27425 Pte. WILLIAMS, A., 1st Bn.
46094 Pte. WOLKOVITCH, A., 3rd Bn.

* Killed in Action or died on Active Service.

THE DUKE OF WELLINGTON'S (WEST RIDING REGIMENT).

OFFICERS.

Capt. BENJAMIN, J. A.,* 9th Bn.
2nd Lieut. DA COSTA, M. R., 1/5th Bn.
2nd Lieut. FOSTER, H., 10th Bn.
Lieut. FLATOW, E. W., 1/4th Bn.
2nd Lieut. FRANKS, B. A.,* 8th Bn.
Lieut. GOLDSELLER, L. D.,* 2/5th Bn.
Capt. HART, C. L.,* 2nd Bn.
Lieut. HARRIS, H.,* 10th Bn.
Capt. HARRIS, L. G. M. (M.C.), 1/7th Bn.
2nd Lieut. LISMAN, W.
2nd Lieut. MARKS, I. D.,* 10th Bn.
2nd Lieut. MENDES, M., 15th Bn.
2nd Lieut. NATHAN, L. C.,* 8th Bn.

N.C.O.'s AND MEN.

242281 Pte. ALTMAN, A., 1/5th Bn.
426506 Pte. ABRAHAMS, H., 13th Bn.
597801 Sgt. ABRAHAMS, T., 2nd Bn.
11036 Pte. ABELMAN, A., 3rd Bn.
41786 Pte. ABRAHAMS, H., 3rd Bn.
305760 Pte. AINLEY, B., 1/7th Bn.
10877 L/Cpl. ALATSKI, N. A.
23334 Pte. BERNSTEIN, J.,* 10th Bn.
5671 Pte. BLASHKY, I.
471179 Pte. BARNETT, M., 13th Bn.
10252 Pte. BACOVITCH, L., 2nd Bn.
7516 Pte. BAKER, J., 2nd Bn.
9951 Pte. BURMAN, J., 2nd Bn.
235367 Pte. BOAS, D., 10th Bn.
6611 Pte. BROWN, M., 6th Bn.
265212 Pte. BROCKMAN, W., 13th Bn.
33063 Pte. BENJAMIN, J.
12231 Pte. BERGMAN, S., 7th Bn.
56131 Pte. BLACK, D.
10917 Cpl. COUPLAN, M.,* 8th Bn.
24003 Pte. COHEN, J.,* 2nd Bn.
268011 Pte. COHEN, M., 1/6th Bn.
33677 Pte. COHEN, H., 1/6th Bn.
13864 Pte. COLLINS, J., 2nd Bn.
20040 Pte. COHEN, 1st Bn.
53327 Pte. COPPLE, L., 4th Bn.
39140 Pte. COHEN, H.
       Cpl. COUPLAN, A.
4797 Pte. COHEN, J., 3/7th Bn.
39038 Pte. CHAPMAN, C., 4th Bn.
401204 Pte. CIPKIN, M., 1st Bn.
17290 Pte. DAVIS, H., 9th Bn.
15300 Pte. DAVIS, J., 8th Bn.
204393 Pte. DEVOLOVITCH, H., 8th Bn.
26136 Pte. DIAMOND, M., 1/6th Bn.
       Pte. DAVIS, M., 7th Bn.
56113 Pte. ELLIS, A., 2nd Bn.
13105 Pte. FREEDMAN, M.* (M.M.), 10th Bn.
347344 Pte. FERBER, C., 1/4th Bn.
34136 Pte. FRANKS, D.,* 1/6th Bn.
       Pte. FINEBERG, J., 10th Bn.
205228 Pte. FINBURGH, H., 4th Bn.
34140 Pte. FELD, M., 1/6th Bn.
25690 Pte. FELDHEIN, M., 9th Bn.
405 Pte. FREEMAN, I., 1/1st Bn.
32571 Pte. FRANKS, J., 4th Bn.
26464 Pte. FURLEY, P., 2/5th Bn.
       Pte. FLAXMAN, H.
       Pte. FORDHAM, S.
       Pte. FINEBERG, S.
       Pte. FRIEZE, I.
11009 Pte. GOLDMAN, A., 2nd Bn.
6143 Pte. GROSSMAN, S., 1/5th Bn.
10919 Pte. GOODMAN, M., 9th Bn.
235384 Pte. GILBERT, D., 10th Bn.
4769 Pte. GOLDBERG, S., 1/7th Bn.
203277 Pte. GOODMAN, M., 1/4th Bn.
426498 Pte. GREEN, M., 13th Garr. Bn.
10007 Pte. GOLDING, S.,* 2nd Bn.
6661 Pte. GOLDBERG, E., 4th Bn.
33748 Pte. GAUSTENFAST, M., 1/7th Bn.
77705 Pte. GOLDMAN, 2/3rd Bn.
242789 Pte. HOFFMAN, E.,* 2nd Bn.
16780 Pte. HERMAN, J., 2nd Bn.
43292 Cpl. HYAMS, J. A., 13th Bn.
       Pte. HARRIS, L., 9th Bn.
23174 Pte. HART, E., 4th Bn.
204401 Pte. HART, E.
10796 Pte. JACKSON, H.,* 2nd Bn.
480400 Spr. JACOBS.
31038 Pte. JACKSON, 1st Bn.
8194 Pte. JOFFE, J.
10936 Pte. JACOBSON, S., 2nd Bn.
4766 Pte. JAFFE, I., 3/7th Bn.
       Pte. JACOBS, H.
10936 Pte. JACOBSON, W., 3rd Bn.
203286 Pte. KLYNE, J. A., 1/4th Bn.
       Pte. KAUFFMAN, E., 3rd Bn.
26902 Cpl. KLEIN, E.
12961 Pte. KOHLER, W., 8th Bn.
10639 Pte. LEVI, A., 2nd Bn.
11766 Pte. LEVINE, H., 10th Bn.
11760 Pte. LIPMAN, A., 10th Bn.
17726 Pte. LESSER, J., 2nd Bn.
5453 Pte. LAPP, S., 2/5th Bn.
16694 Pte. LONDSLER, J., 8th Bn.
10151 Pte. LEE, M., 8th Bn.
268243 Pte. LEVIN, L. D., 1/6th Bn.
26691 Pte. LIZERBRAM, R., 1/5th Bn.
       Pte. LEVER, L., 3rd Bn.
8247 Pte. LEVY, H., 6th Bn.
235400 Pte. LEVY, D., 10th Bn.
53383 Pte. LEVY, L.
235629 Sgt. LEVY, I. (M. M. and Bar), 5th Bn.
42021 Pte. LANDA, S., 53rd Bn.

West Riding Regt.—Continued.

6435	Rfm. LIPSEY, S. M., 2nd Bn.	
32636	Pte. LEWIS, H., 4th Bn.	
10877	Pte. MALTASKI, M. (M.M.), 8th Bn.	
412083	Pte. MOSES, S., 13th Bn.	
432360	L/Cpl. MILLER, H., 13th Bn.	
58584	Pte. MORRIS, M. I.	
49308	Pte. MARKS, M., 13th Bn.	
11761	Pte. NAGLEY, J. B., 10th Bn.	
16441	Pte. NEWMAN, A., 10th Bn.	
33906	Pte. NISINBAUM, H., 1/7th Bn.	
11161	Pte. PHILLIPS, J.,* 8th Bn.	
39585	Pte. PRESSMAN, D., 4th Bn.	
	Pte. PILVERBERG, M., 4th Bn.	
49374	Pte. PADWORTH, G., 13th Bn.	
	Pte. PEYNT, J.	
29594	Pte. PEARLMAN, A., 3rd Bn.	
	L/Cpl. RAE, J., 9th Bn.	
13118	Pte. RAISMAN, J., 10th Bn.	
10640	Pte. ROSS, H.* (ROSENBERG), 2nd Bn.	
26146	Pte. ROUNDSTEIN, R., 1/6th Bn.	
480424	Pte. REISS, 3rd Bn.	
53862	Pte. ROSE, A., 2nd Bn.	
11764	Pte. SWERSKI, A., 10th Bn.	
10929	Pte. SILLBERG, M.,* 9th Bn.	
10821	Pte. STODEL, J.,* 8th Bn.	
204702	Pte. SAMUEL, L., 8th Bn.	
42772	Pte. SAMUEL, P., 10th Bn.	
268012	Pte. SEARLMAN, J. B., 1/6th Bn.	
40509	Pte. SIMON, K., 5th Bn.	
5453	Pte. SAPP, S., 2/5th Bn.	
42060	Pte. SPILLMAN, S., 13th Bn.	
33143	Pte. STONE, G., 4th Bn.	
10638	Pte. SHILANSKY, B., 2nd Bn.	
205010	Pte. SINOVITCH, I., 4th Bn.	
4917	Pte. SCHOLES, A., 2/5th Bn.	
16880	L/Cpl. SUGARMAN, S.	
17505	Pte. STONE, J., 3rd Bn.	
32635	Pte. SOLOMONS, M., 4th Bn.	
405405	Pte. SHERR, M., 13th Bn.	
11534	Pte. TAYLOR, M., 10th Bn.	
307084	Pte. TAYLOR, B., 1/7th Bn.	
506728	Pte. TRAGER, H. E., 13th Bn.	
241603	L/Cpl. TAYLOR, J., 2/5th Bn.	
10656	Pte. WINEBERG, G., 2nd Bn.	
235441	Cpl. WEISBERG, P., 8th Bn.	
10395	Pte. WOLFE, M., 2nd Bn.	
267079	Pte. WALLS, B., 2/6th Bn.	
31034	Pte. WRIGHT, 1st Bn.	
25460	Pte. WEINSTEIN, L., 1/7th Bn.	
35025	Pte. WOLFSON, M., 4th Bn.	
26464	Pte. YUREY, P., 2/4th Bn.	
10916	Pte. ZABIT, A., 2nd Bn.	
7999	Pte. ZEPPENFIELD, P.,* 2nd Bn.	

* Killed in Action or died on Active Service.

THE BORDER REGIMENT.
OFFICERS.

Lieut. BARRON, L.,* 7th Bn.
Capt. DURLACHER, E. A. O.* (M.C.).
2nd Lieut. DREACHFELD, W. G.
2nd Lieut. ROBINSON, C. F., 5th Bn.
Lieut. WOOLF, W. R. M.,* 2nd Bn.
Capt. WOOLF, H. M.

N.C.O.'s AND MEN.

	Pte. ANNENBERG, M., 2nd Bn.	
32335	Pte. APPELBAUM, L., 6th Bn.	
27146	Pte. ARLEZARK, 2nd Bn.	
10254	Pte. ALLAN, M., 2nd Bn.	
34136	Pte. AARONSON, A., 3rd Bn.	
36405	Pte. BARNETT, B.	
22909	Pte. BLOCK, I. (M.M.), 1st Bn.	
22701	L/Cpl. BAUM, H.,* 1st Bn.	
26517	Pte. BRODIE, S., 1st Bn.	
13092	Sgt. BERRY, M., 7th Bn.	
35694	Pte. BRAHAM, 1/4th Bn.	
30500	Pte. BLUMBERG, M., 7th Bn.	
26518	Pte. CASSEL, E., 3rd Bn.	
5060	Pte. COWAN, J., (D.C.M.) 2nd Bn.	
22749	L/Cpl. COLLINS, B., 1st Bn.	
202113	Pte. CRAMMER, 2/4th Bn.	
32072	Pte. DAVIS, J., 8th Bn.	
6003	Cpl. DAVIS, J. I.,* 1st Bn.	
33621	Pte. DAVIS, M., 1st Bn.	
	Pte. DAVIES, S., 3rd Bn.	
10724	Pte. DIAMOND, M., 2nd Bn.	
13964	Pte. EGLASH, A.	
26407	Pte. FIRESTONE, J., 3rd Bn.	
26986	Pte. FINKELSTEIN, M., 8th Bn.	
203139	L/Cpl. FRANKS, A., 2nd Bn.	
11207	Pte. FRANKS, H., 6th Bn.	
24091	Pte. FREEMAN, M., 12th Bn.	
38930	Pte. GERSCHON, S., 3rd Bn.	
8337	Pte. GOLDBERG, I., 2nd Bn.	
28756	Pte. GINSBERG, G., 1st Bn.	
203340	Pte. GOLDSTONE, C., 1st Bn.	
29827	Pte. GOODSON, J., 1st Bn.	
34468	Pte. GOLDSTONE, G., 8th Bn.	
203350	Pte. GOLDSTEIN, C., 4th Bn.	
4335	Pte. HARRIS, E., 5th Bn.	
7351	Pte. HARRIS, G., 2nd Bn.	
26903	Pte. HARRIS, M., 11th Bn.	
241882	Pte. HARRIS, S., 2nd Bn.	
4043	Pte. HERMAN, A., 5th Bn.	
	Pte. HENSON, R.	
22897	Pte. HEWSON, R.,* 6th Bn.	
	Pte. HYMAN, T., 1st Bn.	
	Pte. HYMAN, H. M., 1st Bn.	
29870	L/Cpl. JACOBS, F. N., 1st Bn.	
5004	Pte. KERSHAW, M., 1st Pn.	
26708	Pte. KOBEROFSKY, 1st Bn.	
	Pte. KING, A., 1st Bn.	
27098	Pte. LEON, I., 2nd Bn.	

The Border Regt.—Continued.

- 7828 L/Cpl. LEVY, J., 1st Bn.
- 9321 Pte. LIPPMAN, S.,* 7th Bn.
- 9259 Pte. LIPMAN, A., 1st Bn.
- 34646 Pte. LIVINGSTONE, H., 3rd Bn.
- 36703 Pte. LEVY, A., 4th Bn.
- 10297 Pte. LEVENE, L., 2nd Bn.
- 7391 Pte. LYONS, H., 1st Bn.
- 26408 Pte. LERMAN, S., 3rd Bn.
- 202147 L/Cpl. LEVENTHAL, 2/4th Bn.
- 22894 Pte. MARKS, C., 1st Bn.
- 27605 Pte. MATTHEWS, M. N., 1st Bn.
- 9776 Pte. MARKS, H., 2nd Bn.
- 51578 Pte. MELANDOVITCH, M.
- 200013 Pte. MENDESON, M., 35th Bn.
- 29233 Pte. MARKINSON, N., 2nd Bn.
- S/38913 Pte. MANACKERMAN, M., 2nd Bn.
- 202059 Pte. MARSHUCK, 2/4th Bn.
- 1025 Pte. MORRICE, A.
- 41495 Pte. MOSESON, M., 16th Bn.
- 27605 Pte. MOSELY, C.,* 7th Bn.
- 30431 L/Cpl. MOSCOVITCH, M., 2nd Bn.
- 34355 Pte. MUSCOVITCH, 2/4th Bn.
- 114598 Pte. NEWMAN, A., 1st Bn.
- 203147 Pte. PASERSKY, H., 4th Bn.
- 33462 Cpl. PACY, J., 8th Bn.
- 10234 Pte. PHILLIPS, D.,* 2nd Bn.
- 27210 Pte. ROSE, M., 2nd Bn.
- 241854 Pte. ROSENSTON, M., 1/5th Bn.
- Pte. ROSENBERG, M., 1st Bn.
- 25106 Pte. REPULKIS, P., 11th Bn.
- 34169 Pte. SAMSON, P., 3rd Bn.
- 26408 Pte. SERMAN, S., 2nd Bn.
- 241856 Pte. SEGAL, B., 5th Bn.
- 26527 Pte. SHAPIRO, M., 3rd Bn.
- 34187 Pte. SHAPIRO, J., 3rd Bn.
- 11291 Cpl. SILVER, A., 2nd Bn.
- Pte. SMITH, S., 1st Bn.
- Pte. SMITH, D., 3rd Bn.
- 8330 Pte. SMITH, I., 1st Bn.
- 241882 Pte. SOLOMON, H., 2nd Bn.
- 33539 Pte. SOLOMONS, E., 11th Bn.
- Pte. SOLOMONS, H., 1st Bn.
- 4418 L/Cpl. SOLLY, G., 2nd Bn.
- Pte. SOLLY, F., 3rd Bn.
- 30033 Pte. SCHLOSBERG, H., 35th Bn.
- 33666 Pte. SPLUNT, S., 7th Bn.
- 33790 Pte. SPYER, S., 1st Bn.
- 38978 Pte. STONEFIELD, S., 3rd Bn.
- 26904 Pte. STONE, M., 2nd Bn.
- 9777 L/Cpl. SULLIVAN, H.,* 1st Bn.
- 7115 Sgt. TAYLOR, J., 2nd Bn.
- 8347 L/Cpl. TASCH, G.,* 1st Bn.
- 5313 Pte. TRAY, M., 4th Bn.
- 29558 Pte. WEIFELD, A.
- 37824 Pte. WEINBERG, D., 1st Bn.
- 241943 Pte. WILLIAMS, L., 1/5th Bn.

* Killed in Action or died on Active Service.

THE ROYAL SUSSEX REGIMENT.

OFFICERS.

- 2nd Lieut. ALEXANDER, G. R.,* 14th Bn.
- Capt. BARNETT, R. L.
- Lieut. BINGEN, C. A. M.,* 5th Bn.
- 2nd Lieut COHEN, D. T.,* 7th Bn.
- 2nd Lieut. DAVIES, P. A., 4th Bn.
- 2nd Lieut. FRASER, H. J., 3rd Bn.
- 2nd Lieut. CARLISH, E., 1/5th Bn.
- 2nd Lieut. HARRIS, A. V., 9th Bn.
- 2nd Lieut. KAPP, E., 11th Bn.
- 2nd Lieut. LOTHEIM, S. (M.C.), 7th Bn.
- Lieut. LOEWE, L. L., 6th Bn.
- Lieut. MARKS, A. S.,* 9th Bn.
- Lieut. MARKS, L., 4th Bn.
- Major ROTHSCHILD, F. G. (D.S.O., M.C.), 12th Bn.
- Lieut. SAXTON, G.

N.C.O.'s AND MEN.

- 19402 Pte. ATLEN, L., 7th Bn.
- 108470 Pte. ABRAHAMS, M., 53rd Bn.
- 14751 Pte. ANNENBERG, H. B.,* 2nd Bn.
- 42644 Pte. ALLEN, L., 51st Bn.
- 1982 Pte. ABRAHAMSON, L., 3/6th Bn.
- 5100 Pte. ABRAHAMOVITCH, I., 3rd Bn.
- 265759 Pte. BARNETT, 2/6th Bn.
- 10506 Pte. BROWN, H.,* 2nd Bn.
- 42729 Pte. BRESTON, D., 51st Bn.
- 10487 Pte. BURTON, C., 10th Bn.
- 18551 Pte. BERNSTEIN, M., 3r Bn.
- 28458 Pte. BERMEL, H. 52nd Bn.
- 42654 Pte. BOBSI, H.
- 2554 Pte. BROCKMAN, S.
- 12622 Pte. BENSUSAN, D.
- 24709 Pte. BENKOVITCH, I., 3rd Bn.
- 22523 L/Cpl. BLOOMBERG, S., 1/6th Bn.
- 28784 Pte. BRESLAW, D., 1st Bn.
- 18564 Pte. BARON, H., 2nd Bn.
- 23758 Pte. BEARMAN, J., 17th Bn.
- 19170 Pte. BERENTHALL, M., 9th Bn.
- 26008 Pte. BLACKER, P., 2/6th Bn.
- 20053 Pte. COPELAND, N., 7th Bn.
- 18578 Pte. COHEN, S., 2nd Bn.
- 47454 Pte. COHEN, R., 1/5th Bn.
- 28779 Pte. CANE, A. G., 8th Bn.
- 265813 Pte. COHEN, A., 2/6th Bn.
- 29210 Pte. COHEN, A., 10th Bn.
- 109204 Pte. COLLINS, W., 53rd Bn.
- 108901 Pte. COOPER, L., E. Coy.
- 1433 Pte. COHEN, I.
- 46154 Pte. COHEN, H., 52nd Bn.
- 24830 Pte. CHERNOWITZ, I., 3rd Bn.
- 24716 Pte. CLARKE, L., 3rd Bn.
- 45656 Pte. COHEN, J., 3rd Bn.
- 25702 Pte. COHEN, S., 3rd Bn.
- 23553 Pte. CAPLIN, J., 15th Bn.

Royal Sussex Regt.—*Continued.*

- 2347 Pte. COHEN, N., 1/2nd Bn.
- 2759 Pte. DIAMOND, V. S., 5th Bn.
- 2792 Pte. DAVIES, 9th Bn.
- 20320 Pte. DAVIDSON, L. N., 7th Bn.
- 25227 Pte. DAVIES, S., 3rd Bn.
- 109173 Pte. DA COSTA, E., C. Co.
- 20686 Pte. DA COSTA, M., 3rd Bn.
- 16579 Pte. DE POVER, 9th Bn.
- G/16908 Pte. EMANUEL, J., 11th Bn.
- 260013 Pte. EASTERMAN, S., 5th Bn.
- 9906 Pte. EPSTEIN, G.
- 2684 Pte. EPPEL, J., 5th Bn.
- 2407 Pte. FILEMAN, J., 12th Bn.
- 22529 Pte. FLACK, I., 2/6th Bn.
- 266031 Pte. FERNBACK, L., 2/6th Bn.
- 266104 Pte. FERNBACK, H., 2/6th Bn.
- 24542 Pte. FOGEL, S., 3rd Bn.
- 25911 Pte. FARBEY, N., 1/6th Bn.
- 41864 Pte. FREEDMAN, B., 51st Bn.
- 47119 Pte. FINEGOLA, A., 52nd Bn.
- 1070 Pte. FRANKS, J.
- 29105 Pte. FREEDMAN, P.
- 34465 Pte. FINEGOLD, A., 3rd Bn.
- G/10336 L/Cpl. GONSKY, A., 4th Bn.
- G/22175 Pte. GASTER, A. E., 4th Bn.
- G/25435 Pte. GERLISKY, L.,* 4th Bn.
- Pte. GOLD, J., 3/6th Bn.
- 20562 Pte. GOODMAN, M., 7th Bn.
- 22093 Pte. GOLDBERG, R., 2/6th Bn.
- 24205 Pte. GILBERT, S., 3rd Bn.
- 201427 Pte. GOLDSTEIN, M., 3rd Bn.
- 42590 Pte. GARFINCLE, K., 53rd Bn.
- 109485 Pte. GREENGRASS, I.
- 24721 Pte. GREENBAUM, L., 3rd Bn.
- 21143 Pte. GOLDSTEIN, J.
- 24757 Pte. GOLD, A., 3rd Bn.
- 24766 Pte. GOLDSTEIN, T., 3rd Bn.
- 109499 Pte. GONSHAW, J., 5/2nd Bn.
- 56481 Pte. GOLDBERG, A., 1/8th Bn.
- Sgt. HARMER, 9th Bn.
- 355765 Pte. HARRIS, F., 17th Bn.
- Pte. HERMAN, H.
- 4/34757 Pte. HARRIS, S. J., 5th Bn.
- 263163 Pte. HARRIS, M. M.,* 2nd Bn.
- 263163 Pte. HARRIS, M. F.,* 2nd Bn.
- 108445 Pte. HYAMS, M., 53rd Bn.
- 9791 Pte. HART, S. L.
- 6913 Pte. ISAACS, H.,* 2nd Bn.
- 19161 Pte. ISAACSON, A.,* 9th Bn.
- 11548 Pte JACOBITZ, H., 11th Bn.
- 7396 Pte. JOSEPH, B., 7th Bn.
- 265238 L/Cpl. JACOBS, M., 2/6th Bn.
- 266323 Pte. JACOBSON, C., 2/6th Bn.
- 182167 Pte. JACOBSON, M.
- 10497 Pte. JULIUS, C.,* 13th Bn.
- 9859 Pte. JACOB, P., 10th Bn.
- 27840 Pte. JESSEL, N.
- 57471 Pte. JESSENS, A., 14th Bn.
- 9742 Pte. JONES, A. P.
- Pte. KOLINSKY, L.
- 108796 L/Cpl. KADISHEWITZ, R., 53rd Bn.
- L/Cpl. KORSDORLD, S.
- 24681 Pte. KREEGER, J., 3rd Bn.
- 42781 Pte. KIRSHBOAM, I., 3rd Bn.
- 25766 Pte. KIRSH, A., 3rd Bn.
- 9798 Pte. KUTNER, N.
- 9904 Pte. KRASTER, A.
- 25702 Pte. KRIESKY, S., 3rd Bn.
- 34878 Pte. KERSH, J.
- 19170 Pte. LOWENTHAL, M., 9th Bn.
- 19590 L/Cpl. LAWRENCE, H. L., 8th Bn.
- 1116 Pte. LYONS, F., 10th Bn.
- 29133 Pte. LEVY, J., 10th Bn.
- 27868 Pte. LEVY, N., 52nd Bn.
- 28154 Pte. LEVY, M., 52nd Bn.
- 13725 Pte. LEVY, I., 1st Bn.
- 183945 Pte. LAPSHI, W., 53rd Bn.
- 109735 Pte. LAZARUS, L., 53rd Bn.
- 17046 Pte. LEVI, J., 12th Bn.
- 108051 Pte. LEAR, H.
- 7429 Pte. LEWIS, H., 3rd B.n
- 11116 Pte. LYONS, H., 10th Bn.
- 24762 Pte. LYONS, N., 3rd Bn.
- 10398 Cpl. LEVINE, L.
- 9792 Sgt. LEVY, A.
- 24762 Pte. LAZARUS, A., 3rd Bn.
- 4794 Pte. MENDOZA, J., 2nd Bn.
- G/2035 Pte. MENDOZA, R., 8th Bn.
- 10957 Pte. MILLER, M.,* 2nd Bn.
- GS/26028 Pte. MARKS, L. G.,* 17th Bn.
- 577926 Pte. MICHAELOVITCH, M., 17th Bn.
- 7490 Pte. MYERS, G., 17th Bn.
- 2035 Cpl. MENDOZA, 8th Bn.
- 202843 Pte. MARKS, 2/6th Bn.
- 24438 Pte. MALNICK, C., 3rd Bn.
- 108851 Pte. MECCABERG, H., 53rd Bn.
- 2484 Pte. MOSKOVITZ, H., 1/6th Bn.
- 108851 Pte. MARENBERG, H.
- 4194 Pte. MADOUYA, J.
- 266340 Pte. MORRELL, A.
- 18298 Pte. NIOSE, J., 53rd Bn.
- 9910 Pte. NORDA, L.
- 2232 Pte. NOVELL, A., 1/6th Bn.
- 2485 Pte. ODERBERG, M., 1/6th Bn.
- 17610 Pte. POPPLESDORF, 9th Bn.
- G/16579 Pte. POWER, J., 9th Bn.
- 182808 Pte. PRESTON, R., 16th Bn.
- 20848 Cpl. PHILLIPS, S., 1st Bn.
- 42851 Pte. PLATMAN, P., 51st Bn.
- 8359 Pte. ROSE, W., 7th Bn.
- Pte. RICH, B., 7th Bn.
- 20557 Pte. ROCKITTER, S., 11th Bn. ...
- 577948 Pte. ROSENBERGER, W., 17th Bn.
- 181015 Pte. ROBMAN, J., 3rd Bn.
- 18649 Pte. ROSELAAR, A., 9th Bn.

Royal Sussex Regt.—*Continued.*

20857 Pte. ROCKMAN, 1st Bn.
G/25788 Pte. RUSSELL, A.,* 7th Bn.
108553 Pte. ROSENBERG, I.
41911 Pte. ROSENBLOOM, H., 51st Bn.
10245 Pte. RADSTONE, S. H.
21519 Pte. REICHENBERG, D., 15th Bn.
13414 Pte. SCHWARTZBERG, D., 12th Bn.
240901 Pte. SALAMAN, V., 5th Bn.
G/22246 Pte. SHINEROCK, H., 3rd Bn.
577971 Pte. SARNA, J., 17th Bn.
8908 Pte. SCHULEBERG, H., 3rd Bn.
24736 Pte. SAUNDERS, B., 3rd Bn.
320403 Pte. SYMONS, E.
184025 Pte. SOLOMONS E., 53rd Bn.
46410 Pte. SHIFFERBLATT, B., 51st Bn.
42725 Pte. SUMMERFIELD, N.
37753 Pte. SAMUELS, A., 5th Bn.
9534 Pte. SACKS, S.
9915 Pte. SHOBEN, D. L.
9718 Pte. SILK, L.
Pte. SAMUEL, L. M.
326305 Pte. SALANT, S.
3936 Pte. STEPHENS, S., 11th Bn.
25807 Pte. SPRICE, J., 3rd Bn.
Pte. SILVERMAN, L., 6th Bn.
19045 Pte. TABRISKY, D., 9th Bn.
108464 Pte. USHERVITCH, J., 53rd Bn.
19221 Pte. VICTOR, M., 9th Bn.
29172 Pte. VANCLIFFE, B.
21509 Pte. VOGEL, L., 3rd Bn.
99913 Pte. VINIFSKY, A.
A/26491 Pte. WOLFE, 12th Bn.
19045 Pte. WABRISKY, O., 9th Bn.
22959 Pte. WALDEN, W., 7th Bn.
265729 R.S.M. WOOLLEY, R. C., 2/6th Bn.
Pte. WEINER, J.
132862 Pte. WEINRICH, E., 53rd Bn.
109605 Pte. WEINBERG, E., 53rd Bn.
Pte. WARSHAVSKI, A., 53rd Bn.
9899 Pte. WOOLF, H.
10037 Pte. WEBBER, S.
10245 Pte. WOLOSKY, D. L.
70978 Pte. ZIPPMAN, H., 2/11th Bn.
23539 Pte. ZEIDERMAN, M., 15th Bn.

* Killed in Action or died on Active Service.

THE HAMPSHIRE REGIMENT.

OFFICERS.

2nd Lieut. AFRIAT, A. M., 15th Bn.
2nd Lieut. CRAWCOUR, J.
Capt. GREEN, E. M.,* 14th Bn.
2nd Lieut. HART, J., 2/4th Bn.
Lieut. IMROTH, L.,* 11th Bn.
2nd Lieut. ISAACS, C. S., 3rd Bn.
2nd Lieut. ISAACS, G., 3rd Bn.
Capt. LOWY, W. A.,* 10th Bn.
Capt. MONTAGU, R. H.,* 15th Bn.
Capt. MONTEFIORE, N. N. (O.B.E.).
2nd Lieut. ROSENBERG, B., 1st Bn.
2nd Lieut. SHEARN, E., 1st Bn.
Lieut. SPERO, C., 15th Bn.

N.C.O.'s AND MEN.

33191 Pte. ALEXANDER, B., 14th Bn.
444668 Pte. ARAAS, I., 3rd Bn.
Pte. ASHER, J., 6th Bn.
45159 Pte. BACHARACH, J., 3rd Bn.
203942 Pte. BARNETT, J., 1/5th Bn.
22335 Pte. BERNSTEIN, I., 15th Bn.
31673 Pte. BERNSTEIN, N.
52402 Pte. BENAZERAF, M., 3rd Bn.
58359 Pte. BENZIMRA, A. J.,* 3rd Bn.
381066 Bdsm. BLAN, N., 2/1st Bn.
53418 Pte. BLOOMER, 3rd Bn.
Pte. BOGNOR, J.
L/Cpl. BENTATA, A. L., 3rd Bn.
22335 Pte. BUNSTEAD, L., 2nd Bn.
355148 L/Cpl. BURNS, J.
46723 Pte. CAPLIN, H., 1st Bn.
290794 Pte. CAPES, L. J., 2/1st Bn.
24113 Pte. COHEN, S.
10433 Pte. COHEN, M. L., 2/5th Bn.
29054 Pte. COHEN, L., 2nd Bn.
54522 Pte. CONN, D., 2nd Bn
27211 Pte. COPRIAND, P., 16th Bn.
11780 Pte. COWAN, A.,* 2nd Bn.
38771 Pte. DAVIS, A., 1/4th Bn.
16822 Pte. EDGAR, B.,* 1st Bn.
56591 Pte. ELIZANSTAN, E.
13973 Pte. FABER, J.,* 14th Bn.
356414 Pte. FIRM, H., 1/9th Bn.
43448 Pte. FINEBERG, R., 3rd Bn.
07820 Pte. FISHER, E., 11th Bn.
25942 Pte. FILER, J., 3rd Bn.
290540 Pte. FREEMAN, P., 2/1st Bn.
11803 Pnr. FRANKS, B., 11th Bn.
42634 Pte. FORDANSKY, B., 4th Bn.
54850 Pte. GINSBERG, H., 3rd Bn.
15860 Pte. GOLDSTEIN, M., 1st Bn.
31687 Pte. GREINS, S. J., 2nd Bn.
15605 Pte. GROSKY, A., 2nd Bn.
Pte. HARRIS, B., 10th Bn.
18267 Pte. HARRIS, R., 2nd Bn.
281622 Pte. HAMER, M., 6th Bn.
58292 Pte. HASSELL, D., 3rd Bn.
39349 Pte. HYMAN, H., 3rd Bn.
22708 Pte. HYMAN, S., 14th Bn.
50309 Pte. HYMAN, D., 9th Bn.
0616 Pte HYAMS, C., 3rd Bn.
29878 Pte. JACOBS, L., 15th Bn.
290929 Pte. JOSEPHS, W., 2/1st Bn.

The Hampshire Regt.—Continued.

- 27211 Pte. KLEIN, M., 15th Bn.
- 45020 Pte. KOHEN, S., 3rd Bn.
- 44892 Pte. KOHEN, H., 3rd Bn.
- 2003 Pte. LANDY, J., 5th Bn.
- Cpl. LEVY, E. F. (M.M.).
- 100837 Pte. LANGER, B. L., 2/1st Bn.
- 24579 Pte. LEVY, C., 1st Bn.
- 18418 Pte. LEVY, L.,* 1st Bn.
- 44842 Pte. LEIBOVITCH, H., 3rd Bn.
- 27949 Pte. LEWIS, J., 2nd Bn.
- Pte. LEWIS, L., 1st Bn.
- 31986 Pte. LIMM, C., 12th Bn.
- 2246 Pte. MARKS, S., 5th Bn.
- 23747 Pte. MARKSON, P., 17th Bn.
- Pte. MOSS, L., 17th Bn.
- 23262 Pte. MYERS, J., 1st Bn.
- Cpl. MYERS, S. (M.M.).
- 32857 Pte. MYERS, E., 18th Bn.
- 28119 Pte. NATHAN, H., 11th Bn.
- 255743 Pte. PALLY, S., 1/6th Bn.
- 37869 Pte. PERCY, E., 18th Bn.
- 291002 Pte. PIMS, B. L., 2/1st Bn.
- 4239 Pte. REUBENS, A., 2nd Bn.
- 32973 Pte. ROTH, L., 1st Bn.
- 11438 Cpl. ROBINSON, E. B., 14th Bn.
- 29911 Pte. ROOD, S., 11th Bn.
- 5796 Pte. ROSENBERG, J. W., 3rd Bn.
- Pte. ROFF, S., 12th Bn.
- TR8/30679 Pte. ROSE, 3rd Bn.
- Pte. SAUNDERS, Y., 2nd Bn.
- Pte. SHULMAN, R. J.
- Pte. SHASFRON, H., 18th Bn.
- 27867 Pte. SHOCK, C., 2nd Bn.
- 26536 Pte. SIMMONDS, L., 1st Bn.
- 356445 Pte. SPRING, 1/9th Bn.
- 1251 Pte. STAAL, L., 1/6th Bn.
- 23294 Pte. STANLEY, J. H., 1st Bn.
- Sgt. TUKER, 1/9th Bn.
- 45021 Pte. VENTURA, A., 3rd Bn.
- 32746 Pte. WARMAN, H., 1st Bn.
- 33435 Pte. WITMOND, C., 11th Bn.
- 26491 Pte. WOLFF, L., 14th Bn.
- 381266 Pte. WOLLRAND, G.
- 141053 Pte. WYNCHANKS, 1/9th Bn.
- 16154 Pte. WINGER, M., 10th Bn.
- 241582 Pte. YESKIE, 2/5th Bn.

* Killed in Action or died on Active Service.

THE SOUTH STAFFORDSHIRE REGIMENT.

OFFICERS.

- 2nd Lieut. BROOKS, F. J.,* 4th Bn.
- Lieut. BAUMAN, A.
- 2nd Lieut. DAVIS, A. D. S., 7th Bn.
- Lieut. GORDON, C. J.
- 2nd Lieut. DREYFUS, M., 5th Bn.
- Capt. PHILLIPS, J. S. (M.C.), 9th Bn.
- 2nd Lieut. ROSENBERG, C. M., 9th Bn.
- 2nd Lieut. SEEGER, L. E., 2nd Bn.

N.C.O.'s AND MEN.

- 240546 Cpl. ASTELL, F., 6th Bn.
- Pte. ABRAHAMS, B.
- 38961 Pte. ARTHUR, L., 3rd Bn.
- 3259 Pte. BROOKSTEIN, T., 5th Bn.
- 28955 Pte. BECKWITH, H.
- 27114 Pte. BROWN, H., 12th Bn.
- 202946 Pte. BROOKSTEIN, J.
- 14091 L/Cpl. COHEN, A., 9th Bn.
- 41886 Pte. CLAYMAN, M., 1st Bn.
- 43506 Pte. CAPLAN, A., 2nd Bn.
- 10536 Cpl. CALMAN, J., 7th Bn.
- 41514 Pte. CASTLE, G., 8th Bn.
- 17911 Pte. DAVIS, A., 7th Bn.
- 34443 Pte. DOBBER, 1st Bn.
- Pte. DAVIS, J.
- Pte. EVANS, J. S.
- 14899 Pte. FRIEDLANDER, B., 9th Bn.
- 302017 Sgt. FRIEND, L., 8th Bn.
- 3342 Pte. GREEN, B., 5th Bn.
- 32116 Pte. GOODMAN, L., 1st Bn.
- 39296 Pte. GOLDSTEIN, I., 3rd Bn.
- 48438 Pte. GOLDWATER, L., 1st Bn.
- 46603 Pte. HUMPHREY, 4th Bn.
- S/13699 Pte. HARRIS, S. E.,* 8th Bn.
- 19448 L/Cpl. HANNAFORD, R., 3rd Bn.
- 40943 L/Cpl. ISAACS, W., 1st Bn.
- 8/41564 Pte. JOSEPHSON, H., 8th Bn.
- 35096 Pte. JACOB, 1st Bn.
- 34655 Pte. KROLL, 1st Bn.
- 10396 Cpl. KARKER, S.,* 1st Bn.
- Pte. KOUN, L., 3rd Bn.
- 32999 Pte. LASSMAN, A., 5th Bn.
- 31838 Pte. LASSMAN, M., 8th Bn.
- 7409 Pte. LEWIS, H.,* 2nd Bn.
- 34456 Pte. LIPSON, 1st Bn.
- 9783 Pte. LIPMAN, H.
- Pte. LUTZES, A., 7th Bn.
- 3273 Pte. MICHAELOFSKI, L., 5th Bn.
- 40831 Pte. MILLER, A., 1st Bn.
- 19581 Sgt. MINSKY, 1st Bn.
- 321960 Pte. MON, W., 5th Bn.
- 8068 Pte. MARKOWSKY, W.,* 2nd Bn.
- 9848 Pte. NATHAN, J., 5th Bn.
- 563 Pte. PILNICK, W., 5th Bn.
- 11236 Pte. PAREEZER, S., 1st Bn.
- 18132 Pte. ROSEN, J., 1st Bn.
- 9341 Pte. SILVERMAN, H., 5th Bn.
- 2930 Pte. SCHLANOFFSKY, J., 2/5th Bn.
- 9433 Pte. SMITH, H.,* 2nd Bn.
- 3280 Pte. STEBAURMAN, L., 1/5th Bn.
- 40966 Pte. SAMUELS, H.,* 1st Bn.

South Staffordshire Regt.—*Continued.*

	Pte. SOCOL, J., 1st Bn.
304333	Cpl. SHAER, 1st Bn.
32258	Pte. SILVERSTONE, H., 3rd Bn.
43408	Pte. SEGAL, W., 2nd Bn.
10458	Pte. SMITH, L.
59916	Pte. STEIN, W., 3rd Bn.
45382	Pte. STERNE, K., 4th Bn.
	Pte. SOLOMON, S.
39136	Pte. TAYLOR, H.
519	S./Instr. TURGILL, J., 9th Bn.
46636	Pte. TAYLOR, J., 3rd Bn.
202974	Pte. WITTENBERG, I., 5th Bn.
34313	Pte. WOLFSON, 1st Bn.
203541	Pte. ZUSSMAN, M., 5th Bn.

* Killed in Action or died on Active Service.

THE DORSETSHIRE REGIMENT.

OFFICERS.

Lieut. DAVIDSON, G. L. (M.C.).
2nd Lieut. HYAM, C. E., 2nd Bn.
Lieut. POOL, M. L., 4th Bn.

N.C.O.'s AND MEN.

	Pte. ASHLEY, H.
	Pte. BROWN, A., 1st Bn.
26029	Pte. BERWELD, W., 2nd Bn.
41082	Pte. BOGATCH, H. L., 8th Bn.
16171	Pte. COOPER, A.,* 6th Bn.
7007	L/Cpl. CLEMENTS, J. P., 1st Bn.
28744	Pte. COHEN, N., 4th Bn.
7023	Pte. CASSONMAN, H.,* 1st Bn.
13244	Pte. CALINSKY, C., 3rd Bn.
15479	L/Cpl. COHEN, H., 7th Bn.
	Pte. CONLAN, H., 1st Bn.
25648	Pte. CONN, P., 3rd Bn.
6783	Pte. DAVIES, A., 1st Bn.
26027	Pte. DONSKIE, R., 1st Bn.
291597	Pte. EPSTEIN, S. S., 1/7th Bn.
203510	Pte. FREEDMAN, M., 1st Bn.
29147	Gnr. FIELDMAN, S.
41081	Pte. FINKLESTEIN, H., 3rd Bn.
26566	Pte. FRAZER, H., 2nd Bn.
19748	Pte. GRODINSKY, M., 6th Bn.
44255	Pte. GOLDGEWICHT, P., 3rd Bn.
13003	Pte. GEFFERT, J., 6th Bn.
10965	Pte. HAMBLING, S., 1st Bn.
13088	Pte. HARRIS, J., 6th Bn.
14700	Pte. HAMBLING, H., 1st Bn.
22708	Pte. HYAMS, S., 1st Bn.
27977	Pte. HIRSCHMAN, S.
15159	Pte. HART, J., 3rd Bn.
26459	Pte. HYMES, J., 1st Bn.
4967	Pte. ISAACS, P., 4th Bn.
	Pte. JOHNSON, S.
30751	Pte. JESKI, R., 3rd Bn.
	Pte. JACOBS, D.
	Pte. JACOBS, A., 3rd Bn.
14005	Pte. KAY, A., 5th Bn.
31280	Pte. KONIGSBERG, B., 3rd Bn.
38162	Pte. KUPFERBLATT, W., 3rd Bn.
534983	Pte. KIMMELBLATT, K., 3rd Bn.
22383	Pte. LENSNOR, I.,* 6th Bn.
14915	Pte. LEWIS, J., 5th Bn.
203266	Pte. LAZARUS, P., 2nd Bn.
18985	Pte. LEWIS, J., 7th Bn.
13122	Pte. LEWIS, S., 5th Bn.
15914	L/Cpl. LAZARUS, F., 3rd Bn.
	Pte. MORRIS, A.
9660	Pte. MARKHAM, J., 5th Bn.
13460	L/Sgt. MARKS, H., 3rd Bn.
14341	L/Cpl. MORRIS, J., 3rd Bn.
5017	Pte. MENDELSOHN, E., 4th Bn.
	Pte. MARKS, J., 10th Bn.
5829	Pte. NATHAN, J., 3rd Bn.
9015	Pte. OSBORNE, J., 1st Bn.
7861	Cpl. PHILLIPS, E., 1st Bn.
43020	Pte. PEARLMUTTER, H., 3rd Bn.
7313	Pte. RILEY, F., 1st Bn.
9123	L/Cpl. ROOD, M.,* 2nd Bn.
27159	Pte. RADSTONE, 1/11th Bn.
204161	Pte. ROSE, 2nd Bn.
4508	Pte. ROSENTHAL, E., 4th Bn.
25405	Pte. SHANACK, H., 6th Bn.
24364	Pte. SIPPERT, S., 3rd Bn.
9814	Cpl. SAUNDERS, H., 1st Bn.
9395	Pte. STONE, P., 1st Bn.
6878	Pte. SCOTT, H., 1st Bn.
9437	Pte. SPERO, J.,* 1st Bn.
8141	Cpl. SEIGER, P.,* 1st Bn.
20445	Pte. SHIFFERBLATT, B., 1st Bn.
22313	Cpl. SAUNDERS, M.
6976	L/Cpl. SOLLY, E.
17486	Pte. SIMONS, J., 3rd Bn.
16082	Pte. SYMON S, B., 1st Bn.
17486	Pte. SIMONS, J., 3rd Bn.
31274	Pte. SADICK, L., 3rd Bn.
	Pte. SOLOMON, P.
5914	Pte. WASS, B.
5857	Pte. WISE, C., 1st Bn.
13244	Pte. VALINSKY, I., 3rd Bn.
31257	Pte. WALKER, J., 1st Bn.
16343	Pte. WEINER, L. L., 7th Bn.

* Killed in Action or died on Active Service.

THE PRINCE OF WALES'S VOLUNTEERS (SOUTH LANCASHIRE REGIMENT).

OFFICERS.

Capt. and Adj. ABRAHAMS, D. C., 4th Bn.
Lieut. ARON, F. A.,* 2nd Bn.
2nd Lieut. FINK, S. J.,* 2/5th Bn.
Lieut. GREEN, B. M., 8th Bn.
Lieut. HARRIS, B. (M.C.).
2nd Lieut. HYMAN, H. E.,* 11th Bn.
Lieut. HURWITZ, W., 9th Bn.
2nd Lieut. JACOBS, D.,* 2/4th Bn.
Lieut. LUMLEY, C. H., 7th Bn.
Capt. MANDLEBERG, J. H. (M.C.), 4th Bn.
Lieut. NOVE, S., 1/4th Bn.
2nd Lieut. PHILLIPS, M. G., 9th Bn.
Capt. ROTHBAND, P. L., 4th Bn.
2nd Lieut. SOLOMON, E. J.,* 2nd Bn.
2nd Lieut. SAVILLE, S.
2nd Lieut. SPIEGAL, S. L., 9th Bn.
2nd Lieut. SEMKIN, W., 7th Bn.
Capt. WALEY, F. R. (M.C.), 8th Bn.

N.C.O.'s AND MEN.

50027 Pte. ADDLESTONE, B., 6th Bn.
49259 Pte. AHRENFIELD, L., 11th Bn.
44242 Pte. ASH, S., 4th Bn.
266575 Pte. ABRAHAMS, D.
60017 Pte. ABRAHAMS, M.
265854 Pte. ALEXANDER, A., 14th Bn.
64486 Pte. ABRAMOVITCH, H., 16th Bn.
3506 Rfm. BRADY, J., 5th Bn.
14946 Pte. BARNETT, W.,* 7th Bn.
202386 L/Cpl. BURMAN, W., 1/4th Bn.
36480 Pte. BLACKSTONE, W,. 2nd Bn.
49222 Pte. BLOOM, J., 11th Bn.
44873 Pte. BARNETT, L., 4th Bn.
44254 Pte. BAKER, M., 4th Bn.
17823 Pte. BAUM, S., 7th Bn.
36683 Pte. BYE, A., 3rd Bn.
60090 Cpl. BARNETT, M., 15th Bn.
Pte. BARASMIAN, A.
30730 Pte. BLUMENOW, H.
38602 Pte. BERNSTEIN, M., 1st Bn.
39076 Pte. COHEN, Z. J., 1/5th Bn.
39075 Pte. COHEN, J., 1/5th Bn.
242796 Pte. COTTON, J., 2/5th Bn.
36704 Pte. COHEN, S., 6th Bn.
203086 L/Cpl. CANTOR, A., 3/4th Bn.
64769 Pte. COVEL, J., 16th Bn.
204161 Pte. CLUMPUS, R., 4th Bn.
204073 Pte. CREME, M., 4th Bn.
44704 Pte. COCKLIN, S., 4th Bn.
44035 Pte. COHEN, L., 2nd Bn.
15071 Pte. CASSENBAUM, A., 1st Bn.
17947 Pte. CANTOR, J., 10th Bn.
63324 Pte. COHEN, A., 15th Bn.
14621 Pte. DAMESICK, J., 8th Bn.
203691 Pte. DEAL, A., 4th Bn.
Pte. EISENBARG, N.
40724 Rfm. FRANKFORT, P., 1/4th Bn.
266340 Pte. FREEDMAN, M., 2nd Bn.
265998 Pte. FINK, 6th Bn.
265299 Pte. FINCHERY, 6th Bn.
44807 Pte. FRUMIN, S., 4th Bn.
44273 Pte. FROINBERG, S., 4th Bn.
265294 Pte. FINEBERG, D., 14th Bn.
1683 L/Cpl. GERRAGHTY, W,. 5th Bn.
4726 Rfm. GOLDSMITH, H., 1/5th Bn.
32668 Pte. GILBERT, J., 11th Bn.
31194 Pte. GERMAN, M. A., 2/4th Bn.
44723 Pte. GOLDSTONE, I., 4th Bn.
45364 Pte. GOODALL, H., 4th Bn.
63461 Pte. GOLDBERG, L., 15th Bn.
13923 Pte. HARRIS, J., 9th Bn.
Pte. HURWITZ, W., 9th Bn.
49116 L/Cpl. HYAMS, J., 11th Bn.
20449 Pte. HAMISHVILLE, J., 4th Bn.
45104 Pte. HALPERN, S.
265860 Pte. ISAACS, B., 14th Bn.
203764 Pte. JACOBS, S., 2/4th Bn.
32617 Pte. JACOBS, B.,* 11th Bn.
24706 Pte. JACOBS, F., 12th Bn.
Sgt. JACKSON, 8th Bn.
44566 L/Cpl. JAY, P., 4th Bn.
9109 Pte. KRASEY, C., 2nd Bn.
8885 Pte. KUTNER, 1st Bn.
204420 Pte. KLEMENTASKI, L. P.; 4th Bn.
70003 L/Cpl. KERSH, J., 2nd Bn.
10152 Pte. LANDOW, J., 2nd Bn.
13923 Pte. LEWIS, J. W., 9th Bn.
61504 Rfm. LEVINE, J., 1/4th Bn.
31894 Pte. LASSMAN, J., 2nd Bn.
31992 Pte. LERMAN, M., 8th Bn.
203941 Pte. LEWIS, J., 4th nn.
43385 Pte. LYONS, L., 11th Bn.
10152 Sgt. LEVENE, H., 2nd Bn.
C.Q.M. Sgt. LIPSON, H. S.
46660 Pte. LEVINE, H., 4th Bn.
60771 Pte. LASOF, M., 15th Bn.
235302 Pte. LERNER, D.,* 2nd Bn.
242771 Rfm. MARKS, M., 1/5th Bn.
19335 Pte. MIDDLEMAN, M.
L/Cpl. MASON, S., 4th Bn.
50202 Sgt. MIDDLEBROOK, S. B., 6th Bn.
203875 Pte. MILLER, G., 4th Bn.
63670 Pte. MYERS, J., 3rd Bn.
63654 Pte. MOSS, B., 15th Bn.
43714 Pte. MARKS, L.,* 9th Bn.
18148 L/Cpl. NEWMAN, 2nd Bn.
7203 Pte. OWENS, J., 1st Bn.
36443 Rfm. OSTERMAN, R. H., 7th Bn.
8642 Pte. POLSON, J., 1st Bn.
24395 L/Cpl. PRAX, J., 12th Bn.
43854 Pte. PHILLIPS, M., 2nd Bn.
65233 Pte. ROBINSON, B. L., 2/4th Bn.

South Lancashire Regt.—Continued.

202963	Pte. ROBINSON, L.,	2/5th Bn.
37871	Pte. ROSENBERG, M.,	1st Bn.
36729	Pte. RUBEN, A.,	6th Bn.
44370	Pte. ROSENBLOOM, N.,	4th Bn.
44355	Pte. ROSENBLOOM, S.,	4th Bn.
44353	Pte. ROBINSON, H.,	4th Bn.
37753	Pte. SAMUEL, A.,	7th Bn.
10272	Pte. SMITH, H.,	2nd Bn.
10011	Pte. SHINE, J.,	2nd Bn.
9171	L/Sgt. SOLOMON, M.,	2nd Bn.
	Pte. SHOTLAND, V.,	2nd Bn.
32276	Pte. SLOTMAN,	6th Bn.
66231	Pte. STEAD W.,	16th Bn.
28708	Pte. SHAPIRO, A.,	6th Bn.
50446	Pte. SEWELSON, B.,	7th Bn.
	Pte. SHUMSKER, D.	
	Pte. SINGER, M.	
17909	Pte. TREY, M.,	7th Bn.
43684	Pte. TYNAS, H.,	2/4th Bn.
44396	Pte. TOBE, M.,	4th Bn.
17472	Pte. WHITE, J.,	9th Bn.
	Pte. WOLFE, W.,	1st Bn.
242109	Pte. WEINBERG, J.,	4th Bn.
203735	Pte. WERNER, E.,	4th Bn.
44978	Pte. WEISS, L.,	4th Bn.
584148	Pte. ZISKIND, H.,*	14th Bn.

* Killed in Action or died on Active Service.

THE WELCH REGIMENT.

OFFICERS.

2nd Lieut. FRANKENSTEIN, O. R.,* 5th Bn.
Capt. GOLDBERG, J. M., 6th Bn.
Lieut. GREEN, C. D.
Lieut. HART, M. A.
2nd Lieut. SOLOMON, W. E. G., 12th Bn.
Lieut. WOOLF, W.,* 24th Bn.

N.C.O.'s AND MEN.

51186	Pte. ANCHELL, J.,	14th Bn.
10815	Sgt. ABRAHAMS, T.,	2nd Bn.
	Pte. ABRAHAMS, S.	
53664	Pte. ABRAHAMS, L.,*	2nd Bn.
3085	Sgt. AARON, C.,	2/7th Bn.
64015	Pte. ABRAHAMS, H.,	11th Bn.
40217	Pte. ASH, M.,	21st Bn.
62449	Pte. ABREMOVITCH, H.,	4th Bn.
5177	Pte. BROWN, H.,	13th Bn.
31034	Pte. BELL, J.,	19th Bn.
31347	Pte. BENTKEN, W.,	19th Bn.
53666	Pte. BADDIEL, H.,	2nd Bn.
	Pte. BENJAMIN, H. (M.M.).	
48920	Pte. BARNETT, H. J.,	19th Bn.
46249	Pte. BERNSTEIN, L.,	24th Bn.
220492	Pte. BLACK, J.,	24th Bn.
54549	Pte. BLUESTONE, J.,	10th Bn.
	Pte. BROCKMAN, S.	
54326	Pte. BROWN, G.,	3rd Bn.
267805	Pte. BAKER, I.,	5th Bn.
285616	Pte. BETSON, T.,	6th Bn.
	Pte. BLOMBERG, W.,	6th Bn.
	Pte. BLACK, L.	
2906	Pte. COHEN, L.,	6th Bn.
30288	Pte. COHEN, S.,	19th Bn.
57400	Pte. COHEN, H.,	1/6th Bn.
5109	Pte. COTTON, M.,	1/6th Bn.
5905	Pte. COHEN, M.,	1/6th Bn.
58671	Pte. COHEN, B.,	2nd Bn.
53670	Pte. COHEN, E.,	2nd Bn.
53669	Pte. COHEN, H. E.,	2nd Bn.
4347	L/Cpl. COHEN, A.,*	2nd Bn.
56857	Pte. COHEN, M.,	13th Bn.
54319	Pte. COHEN, M. E.,	16th Bn.
30288	Pte. COHEN, L.,	19th Bn.
78286	Sgt. COHEN, A. (D.C.M.),	18th Bn.
64251	Pte. COHEN, L.,*	2nd Bn.
29332	Pte. CRABB, J. E.,	14th Bn.
98285	Pte. COHEN, L. S.	
53671	Pte. COWEN, B.,	2nd Bn.
265897	L/Cpl. COHEN, D.* (M.M.),	6th Bn.
63276	Pte. CASIMER, D.,	2nd Bn.
63545	Pte. COHEN, A.,	4th Bn.
TR4/21143	Pte. CLYNES, L.,	51st Bn.
237556	Pte. COHEN, H.,	52nd Bn.
34541	Cpl. CHARNEY, B.,	52nd Bn.
86307	Sgt. COHEN, M.,	51st Bn.
55430	Pte. COHEN, H.,	13th Bn.
204077	Pte. COHEN, L.,	16th Bn.
63276	Pte. CASINTH, L.,	2/7th Bn.
73015	Pte. COHEN, E.,	15th Bn.
48389	Pte. COLLINS, H.,	3rd Bn.
76392	Pte. CAPLAN, M.,	9th Bn.
63251	Pte. COHL, L.	
52221	Pte. DAVIS, A.,	13th Bn.
56861	Pte. DAVIS, S.,	13th Bn.
56899	Pte. DAVIES, W.,	13th Bn.
79088	Pte. DONSKIE, A.,	18th Bn.
	Pte. DAVIS, M.,	1st Bn.
34636	Pte. DORSHT, M.,	52nd Bn.
60927	Pte. DA COSTA, M.,	9th Bn.
54711	Pte. DAVIS, N.,	10th Bn.
202286	Pte. ENSTEIN, M.,	6th Bn.
17194	Pte. FRANKS, J.,	14th Bn.
15236	Pte. FLIGELSTONE, T. H.,	11th Bn.
56898	Pte. FRAZEN, I.,	13th Bn.
290298	Sgt. FIKLEBLECH, S.,	52nd Bn.
2992	Pte. FRIEDMAN,	6th Bn.
266186	Pte. FREEDMAN, P.,	11th Bn.
267232	Pte. FELDMAN, D.,	5th Bn.
	Pte. FISHER, P.	
15256	L/Cpl. GREEN, G.,	11th Bn.

The Welch Regt.—*Continued.*

56863 Pte. GLICK, W., 13th Bn.
L/Cpl. GOROVITCH, S.
Pte. GREEN, M., 1st Bn.
20213 Pte. GOLDBERG, L., 2/6th Bn.
79185 Pte. GOLDBERG, L., 18th Bn.
31042 Pte. GLAZIER, D., 51st Bn.
267212 Pte. GLASSIN, D., 52nd Bn.
63291 Pte. GOODMAN, S., 2/7th Bn.
63295 Pte. GORDON, S., 2/7th Bn.
86332 Pte. GLASS, B., 51st Bn.
59804 Pte. GORDON, J., 15th Bn.
59831 Pte. GOODFIELD, S., 15th Bn.
235384 Pte. GILBER, D., 1/16th Bn.
202187 Pte. GINSBERG, P., 5th Bn.
241631 Pte. GOODMAN, L.
55057 Pte. GEUPMAN, A.
50940 Pte. HUTTEL, W., 2nd Bn.
53686 Pte. HARRIS, D., 2nd Bn.
53687 Pte. HARRIS, I., 2nd Bn.
6304 Sgt. HYAMS, M., 1st Bn.
47626 Pte. HARRIS, A., 15th Bn.
61198 Pte. HOLTER, S., 18th Bn.
51753 Pte. HERMAN, 8th Bn.
45104 Pte. HOLPERN, S. D., 3rd Bn.
9551 Pte. HARRIS, B., 52nd Bn.
106119 Pte. HYMAN, J. H., 53rd Bn.
76772 Pte. HAIMAN, V., 53rd Bn.
Pte. HARRIS, J., 1st Bn.
3048 Pte. JACKSON, M.,* 6th Bn.
14747 Pte. JACOBS, A. V., 11th Bn.
59227 L/Cpl. JAFFA, L., 10th Bn.
L/Cpl. JACOBS, J., 7th Bn.
290489 Pte. JOY, P.
L/Cpl. JOSHUA, W. (M.M.).
58490 Pte. JOSEPH, 15th Bn.
Sig. JOSEPH, W.
42215 Pte. JACOBS, M., 23rd Bn.
27858 Pte. JESKE, R., 9th Bn.
39516 Pte. JACOBS, H., 21st Bn.
Pte. JONES, H., 2nd Bn.
Pte. JACOBS, I., 2nd Bn.
Pte. JACOBS, B., 7th Bn.
1920 Pte. KRONENBERG, N. (M.M.), 6th Bn.
2666 Pte. KRONENBERG, A., 6th Bn.
290292 Pte. KROTOSKY, P. R., 15th Bn.
3227 Pte. KRONENBERG, I., 3/6th Bn.
60632 Pte. KRENER, I., 10th Bn.
45789 Pte. KROTOSKY, M., 15th Bn.
5233 Pte. LEVINSON, D., 13th Bn.
24348 Pte. LEAVY, M., 14th Bn.
53643 Pte. LAGERMAN, C., 2nd Bn.
7701 Pte. LEVY, L.,* 51st Bn.
52521 Pte. LEVY, J., 15th Bn.
285463 Pte. LEVY, S., 15th Bn.
55673 Pte. LANCHINSKI, S., 6th Bn.
320484 Pte. LAZARUS, M., 24th Bn.
936 L/Cpl. LYONS, P., 7th Bn.

320486 Pte. LEWIS, P., 7th Bn.
5250 Cpl. LYONS, C. L., 4th Bn.
42200 Pte. LEWIS, N. W., 23rd Bn.
79489 Pte. LYONS, J., 19th Bn.
507910 Pte. LANDSMAN, W.
203567 Pte. LAURENCE, A.
2174 Pte. MORRIS, M., 6th Bn.
5276 Pte. MASON, S., 13th Bn.
33205 Pte. MARCOVITCH, L., 16th Bn.
6639 L/Cpl. MANCHESTER, I., 1/6th Bn.
53648 Pte. MARKS, L., 2nd Bn.
53649 Pte. MILLER, I., 2nd Bn.
56901 Pte. MASON, P., 13th Bn.
285579 Pte. MARKS, I., 13th Bn.
57463 Pte. MARKS, M., 19th Bn.
Pte. MELNICK, A.
897 Pte. MAXWELL, B., 2/7th Bn.
242149 Pte. MARSHALL, H., 4th Bn.
22591 Pte. MARGOLISS, H., 2/1st Bn.
52764 Pte. MICHAELSON, S.
37391 Pte. NIELDS, M., 11th Bn.
53671 Pte. OWAN, B. O.
14320 Pte. PHILLIPS, H., 6th Bn.
L/Cpl. PHILLIPS, H.
130561 Pte. PHILLIPS, M., 11th Bn.
Pte. PHILLIPS, I.
Pte. PEARSON, J., 11th Bn.
L/Cpl. PETERS, L., 9th Bn.
14711 Pte. REDHOUSE, J., 11th Bn.
28210 Pte. ROSSINSKY, H. S., 1/6th Bn.
Pte. ROTHSTEIN, J., 18th Bn.
77070 Pte. RAPHAEL, 18th Bn.
57426 Pte. ROSENBAUM, H., 6th Bn.
65248 Pte. RUBENSTEIN, A., 9th Bn.
Pte. RICHMOND, J., 1st Bn.
62304 Pte. ROSENBERG, 8th Bn.
Pte. RUBENSTEIN, N., 2nd Bn.
80332 Pte. ROSENWEY, M., 52nd Bn.
Pte. ROSENBERG, L.
320493 Pte. RESNICK, S., 24th Bn.
320491 Pte. ROSENBURG, C., 24th Bn.
Pte. REED, R.
290956 Pte. RATHSTEIN, 18th Bn.
44422 Pte. ROBINS, N., 11th Bn.
Pte. ROSKIN, N., 1st Bn.
26878 Pte. ROSE, J., 7th Bn.
2323 L/Cpl. SAMUELS, D., 6th Bn.
Pte. SAMUELS, J.
15500 Cpl. SHIBKO, I.,* 11th Bn.
5222 L/Cpl. SELIGSON, W., 13th Bn.
23250 Pte. SPIRO, H. L., 16th Bn.
20214 Pte. SOLOMON, H., 1/6th Bn.
53658 Pte. SNIPPER, A., 2nd Bn.
36041 Pte. SILVERSTEIN, I., 2nd Bn.
47879 Pte. SCHNEIDER, I., 10th Bn.
56876 Pte. SEIDEMAN, M.,* 13th Bn.
85471 Pte. SHULASKY, J., 15th Bn.
84795 Pte. SOLOMON, D. M., 52nd Bn.

The Welch Regt.—Continued.

- 84796 Pte. SIMONS, S., 52nd Bn.
- 44642 Pte. SNIPPER, B. I., 12th Bn.
- 57426 Pte. SHARP, L., 2nd Bn.
- 60630 Pte. SHENKER, K., 10th Bn.
- 285047 Pte. SANOFSKY, S.,* 9th Bn.
- 57353 L/Cpl. SAUL, A., 4th Bn.
- 85957 Pte. SIMMONS, J., 51st Bn.
- 62661 Pte. SHAPIRO, M., 13th Bn.
- 58872 Pte. SHVALBA, M., 11th Bn.
- 5178 Pte. TRAGER, I., 13th Bn.
- 53660 Pte. TOBIAS, A., 2nd Bn.
- 242166 Pte. TENNYSON, F. R., 1st Bn.
- 20016 Pte. TYNAS, H.
- 320454 Pte. VOLUSKY, G., 24th Bn.
- 27371 Pte. WOOLF, J., 19th Bn.
- 47631 Pte. WHIPMAN, J., 18th Bn.
- 34401 Pte. WEINSTEIN, B., 52nd Bn.
- 61290 Pte. WOOLFSON, S., 18th Bn.
- 63837 Pte. WANDER, M., 1st Bn.
- 14900 L/Cpl. ZEITLIN, J., 11th Bn.

* Killed in Action or died on Active Service.

THE BLACK WATCH (ROYAL HIGHLANDERS).

OFFICERS.

2nd Lieut. WALLACE, J.,* 1st Bn.

N.C.O.'s AND MEN.

- 292726 Pte. ANCILL, N., 1/7th Bn.
- 3804 Pte. BROWN, H., 3/6th Bn.
- Pte. BROWN, B., 1st Bn.
- 91857 Pte. BLOOM, J.
- 13904 Pte. BREM, P., 3rd Bn.
- 292242 Pte. COHEN, J., 1/7th Bn.
- Pte. CALLER, P., 9th Bn.
- 201649 Pte. COHEN, M.,* 4/5th Bn.
- 9270 Pte. COUSIN, B., 2/4th Bn.
- 7300 Pte. CLAYMAN, E., 4/5th Bn.
- Pte. DAVIS, V., 2nd Bn.
- 13323 Pte. DAVIS, J., 3rd Bn.
- 11246 Pte. DAVIES, J.
- 17585 Pte. FREEMAN, B., 1/7th Bn.
- 203367 Pte. FREEDMAN, 14th Bn.
- 12030 Pte. GLICK, M., 8th Bn.
- 5251 Pte. GOLDSTEIN, A., 2/4th Bn.
- 201542 Pte. GOLDSTEIN, B., 9th Bn.
- 7363 Pte. GOLDSMITH, D., 4/5th Bn.
- L./Cpl. HARRIS, T. H.
- 1249 Pte. LAPMAN, A., 2/4th Bn.
- 31750 Pte. LABOFSKY, B., 2nd Bn.
- 6662 Pte. LEVINE, M.,* 9th Bn.
- 12031 Pte. MITCHELL, P., 8th Bn.
- 266692 Pte. McGREGOR, C., 1/6th Bn.
- 18194 Pte. NATHAN, J., 1st Bn.
- 201706 Sgt. ORNSTEIN, A., 4/5th Bn.
- 15952 Pte. PHILLIPS, J.,* 9th Bn.
- Pte. ROSENBERG, G.
- Pte. ROSENBURG, M.
- 43196 Pte. RUTENBERG, T., 8th Bn.
- 2240 Pte. ROMAVITZ, N., 2/7th Bn.
- 203188 Pte. ROBERTSON, D. A., 4/5th Bn.
- 3805 Pte. SOLOMON, J., 1/6th Bn.
- 14973 Pte. SILVERMAN, G.
- 2663 Pte. VALLANCE, D.,* 1st Bn.
- 12035 Pte. WRIGHT, H., 8th Bn.

* Killed in Action or died on Active Service.

THE OXFORDSHIRE AND BUCKINGHAMSHIRE LIGHT INFANTRY.

OFFICERS.

- 2nd Lieut. BOWMAN, C. H.,* 1/4th Bn.
- 2nd Lieut. FALLON, D. (M.C.), 1/1st Bucks. Bn.
- Lieut. JACOB, V. V.,* 2nd Bn.
- Lieut. JOSEPHS, 8th Bn.
- Lieut. LOEWE, L., 2/4th Bn.
- Lieut. LEVY, P. P.
- Capt. MERTON, J., 1st Bn. G.B.
- 2nd Lieut. PIPERNO, J. H., 1/1st Bn.
- Capt. SOLOMON, J. B. (M.C.).
- Capt. SIMPSON, B. L., 7th Bn.
- 2nd Lieut. STERN, H., 2/1st Bn.
- 2nd Lieut. SIMMONS, E. E.

N.C.O.'s AND MEN.

- 266996 Pte. ARLICK, R., 4th Bn.
- 4468 Cpl. ABRAHAMS, L., 2/1st Bn.
- 22228 Pte. AARONS, J.
- Pte. ABRAHAMS, J. H. (M.M.).
- 25471 Pte. ABRAHAMS, I., 2nd Gar. Bn.
- 27687 L/Cpl. APTER, S.,* 8th Bn.
- 5051 Pte. ARLICK, H.
- 5023 Pte. ABRAHAMS, H., 1/1st Bn.
- L/Cpl. ABRAHAMS, F. C., 2nd Bn.
- 22314 Pte. ADLEMAN, 1st Bn.
- 266979 Pte. ABRAHAMS, H., 2/4th Bn.
- 5024 Pte. BENSUSAN, B., 1/1st Bn.
- 5009 Pte. BERG, I., 1st Bn.
- 5034 Pte. BLOOMSTEIN, M., 1st Bn.
- 4488 Pte. BERNSTEIN, M., 1st Bn.
- 203032 Pte. BERNBAUM, L., 2nd Bn.
- 267006 Pte. BARNETT, J.,* 2/1st Bn.
- 5020 Pte. BLOCH, C., 1/1st Bn.
- 266997 Pte. BERGER, J., 4th Bn.
- 36493 L/Cpl. BENJAMIN, L., 3rd Bn.

Oxford and Bucks. L.I.—*Continued.*

24316	Pte.	BROOKSTEIN, F.
23071	Pte.	BENJAMIN, N., 1st Bn.
5045	Pte.	BERGER, J., 2/1st Bn.
22313	Bglr.	BARNETT, J., 2nd Bn.
22546	Cpl.	BERNSTEIN, P., 3rd Bn.
4509	Pte.	BENJAMIN, W., 3rd Bn.
27694	Pte.	BLOOM, H.
22859	Pte.	BLANK, J.
241267	Pte.	BERNSTEIN, H., 10th Bn.
3733	Cpl.	BEARMAN, J., 2/1st Bn.
4470	Pte.	BERWALD, S.
30001	Pte.	BLACK, I., 9th Bn.
4091	Pte.	COHEN, J.,* 1/1st Bn.
267670	Pte.	COHEN, M. (M.M.), 2nd Bn.
5005	Pte.	COHEN, B., 1/1st Bn.
5002	Pte.	COHEN, M., 1/1st Bn.
4511	Pte.	COHEN, G., 1/1st Bn.
5071	L/Cpl.	CASSEBAUM, A., 1/1st Bn.
4512	Pte.	CREGO, M., 1/1st Bn.
3868	Pte.	COHEN, S., 1/1st Bn.
267456	Pte.	CLARFELT, S., 1/1st Bn.
5173	Pte.	COHEN, I.
21873	Pte.	COHEN, 1st Bn.
267008	Pte.	CASSENBAUM, J., 1st Bn.
7046	Pte.	COHEN, H., 4th Bn.
5027	Pte.	CRAMER, J.,
22547	L/Cpl.	COHEN, A., 3rd Bn.
4079	L/Cpl.	CLAYTON, L. V., 2/4th Bn.
20577	Pte.	CARIERSTRAUSS, L.
3817	Pte.	COHEN, N.
33895	Pte.	COHEN, J., 2nd Bn.
6518	Pte.	COHEN, M.
22787	Pte.	COHEN, N., 3rd Bn.
23481	Pte.	COHEN, D., 1st Bn.
25166	Sgt.	COHEN, J., 2nd Bn.
5000	Pte.	DENNENBERG, P., 1/1st Bn.
5025	Pte.	DOMBEY, W.,* 1/1st Bn.
202990	L/Cpl.	DIDSBURY, A., 4th Bn.
267037	Pte.	DAVIS, H., 2/4th Bn.
23777	Pte.	DAVIDSON, H. M.,* 3rd Bn.
33456	Pte.	DA COSTA, D. 6th Bn.
29638	Pte.	DAINOW, 1st Bn.
46481	Pte.	DONSKIE, I., 3rd Bn.
5041	Pte.	DAGGERS, R.
22812	Pte.	DAVIDSON, M.
5787	Pte.	DAVIS, S.
4378	Pte.	DAVIES, H.,* 1/1st Bn.
22508	Pte.	EZELNICK, S., 3rd Bn.
285221	Pte.	ENES, C. M., 2/1st Bn.
6518	Pte.	EBIN, I., 4th Bn.
4518	Pte.	FISHER, W., 1/1st Bn.
5049	Pte.	FINEBERG, H., 1/1st Bn.
5394	Pte.	FORDANSKY, J., 1/1st Bn
4491	L/Cpl	FRANKLIN, P., 1/1st Bn.
24571	Pte.	FINE, J., 4th Bn.
37988	Pte.	FRANKS, 1st Bn. G.B.
21116	Pte.	FIELD, J., 1st Bn.
4990	Pte.	FLEVANT.
240969	Sig.	FISHMAN, 2nd Bn.
5162	Pte.	FILNER, H.
4476	Pte.	FISHER, A.
	Pte.	FAFFLER, A.
	Pte.	FELD, R., 7th Bn.
266755	Pte.	FISHER, W.,* 1/1st Bn.
7620	Pte.	GLUCK, R., 4th Bn.
267009	Pte.	GOODMAN, S.,* 1/1st Bn.
4350	Pte.	GELDER, J., 1/1st Bn.
5004	Pte.	GRIVER, M., 1/1st Bn.
5014	Pte.	GLASSMAN, M., 1/1st Bn.
4993	Pte.	GREEN, A., 1/1st Bn.
5038	Pte.	GOLDBERG, A. 1/1st Bn.
	Pte.	GOLDSTEIN, L., 1/1st Bn.
4086	Pte.	GOODMAN, L., 1/1st Bn.
4149	Cpl.	GOULD, M., 2/1st Bn.
20414	Pte.	GROSS, L., 2/1st Bn.
5031	Pte.	GATES, M., 1/1st Bn.
4516	Pte.	GALINSKY, A., 2/1st Bn.
24315	Pte.	GORISH, A., 2nd Bn.
6967	Cpl.	GERSHON, S. S., 4th Bn.
22312	Pte.	GOLD, J., 3rd Bn.
203629	Pte.	GOLDWATER, P., 3/4th Bn.
22845	Pte.	GOTTLIEB, M., 3rd Bn.
30039	Pte.	GLICK, H.
22851	Pte.	GREEK, M.
197996	Pte.	GOLDSTEIN, H., 9th Bn.
4471	Pte.	GELMAN, S.
204570	Pte.	GOULD, L., 4th Bn.
266988	Pte.	GOLDSTEIN, I.
44932	Pte.	GOLDBERG, J., 2nd Bn.
197996	Pte.	GOLDSTEIN, H., 7th Bn.
5065	Pte.	HARRIS, A., 1/1st Bn.
12516	Pte.	HASSELL, S., 5th Bn.
13641	Pte.	HALL, J., 6th Bn.
7091	Cpl.	HARRIS, M., 4th Bn.
22227	Pte.	HARBOUR, S.
22083	Pte.	HART, J., 3rd Bn.
28353	Pte.	HERTZFELD, S., 3rd Bn.
4510	Pte.	HOOKEY, M.
11138	Pte.	IZON, M., 2nd Bn.
4481	Pte.	ISRAEL, L., 1/1st Bn.
202209	Pte.	JAFFE, L., 1/4th Bn.
266491	Sgt.	JACOBS, H.
4461	Pte.	JACOBS, P., 4th Bn.
4517	Pte.	JACOBS, J.
3966	Cpl.	JACOBS, A., 1/1st Bn.
4460	Pte.	JACOBS, M. V., 1/1st Bn.
1774	Pte.	JACOBS, J.,* 2/4th Bn.
6825	Pte.	JACOBS, A., 2/4th Bn.
266741	Pte.	KURTZ, M., 2/1st Bn.
5027	Pte.	KRAMER, I., 1/1st Bn.
4910	Pte.	KROLL, E., 1/1st Bn.
5169	Pte.	KARMECK, A., 1/1st Bn.
5170	Pte.	KOLSKY, J., 1st Bn.
20494	Pte.	KING, D., 2/1st Bn.
	Pte.	KADESH, M.

Oxford and Bucks. L.I.—Continued.

- 26316 Pte. KAPLINSKY, L., 1st Bn.
- 4480 Pte. KLEINBERG, S., 2/1st Bn
- 22846 L/Cpl. KAPPEL, J.
- 4911 Pte. LEVY, I., 1/1st Bn.
- 203022 Pte. LYMAN, J., 2/4th Bn.
- 5048 L/Cpl. LEWIS, S., 1/1st Bn.
- 5102 Pte. LAVENDER, A.,* 2/1st Bn.
- 203083 Pte. LYNN, G., 2/1st Bn.
- 4504 Pte. LIPMAN, I., 1/1st Bn.
- 4141 Pte. LENARTE, A., 1/1st Bn.
- 266998 L/Cpl. LOTSKY, A.,* 2/1st Bn.
- 23847 Cpl. LEVY, L., 5th Bn.
- 203032 Pte. LYNN, J., 5th Bn.
- 29460 Pte. LEWIS, J., 2nd Bn.
- 253038 Pte. LAUTENBERG, M., 2nd Bn.
- 4515 Pte. LEVENE, A.
- 4056 Pte. LAZARUS, J., 2/1st Bn.
- 29644 Pte. LEFCOVITCH, 1st Bn.
- 20015 Spr. LEIHMAN, C. E., 1/4th Bn.
- 241015 Pte. LEVY, J., 1st Bn.
- 4990 Pte. LEVART, F.
- Sgt. LEE, J., 3rd Bn.
- 4572 Pte. LUKIES, W.,* 1/1st Bn.
- 16836 Pte. LEVINSON, S., 8th Bn.
- 266932 Pte. LEWIS, C., 1st Bn.
- 49948 Pte. LEVY, M.
- C.Q.M.S. LIEBERMANN, W. J. (M.S.M.).
- 46671 Pte. LIGHT, J.
- 26532 Pte. LEVY, S., 7th Bn.
- 240883 Pte. LEVY, D., 3rd Bn.
- 111932 Pte. LEVENE, S.
- 22847 Pte. LEWIS, R.
- 23351 Pte. LEVISON, S. S.,* 8th Bn.
- 19751 Pte. LEVY, H.,* 3rd Bn.
- 20466 Pte. MUSLIN, L., 4th Bn.
- 5046 Pte. MUSCOVITCH, L., 1/1st Bn.
- 5008 Pte. MARKOSKI, E., 1/1st Bn.
- 11137 Sgt. MORRIS, S.,* 2nd Bn.
- 5061 Pte. MILLER, J., 2/1st Bn.
- 238044 Pte. MARGUERITE, W., 2nd Bn.
- L/Cpl. MORRIS, J., 5th Bn.
- 203845 Pte. MORDEN, M., 2/4th Bn.
- 7126 Pte. MUSCOVITCH, J., 2/4th Bn.
- 20577 Pte. MARIENSTRAUS, 1st Bn. G.B.
- 7035 Pte. MARGOLINSKY, H., 4th Bt.
- 34153 Pte. MUSCOVITCH, A., 2/4th Bn.
- 266991 Pte. MUSCOVITCH, H.
- 65/363 Pte. MILLER, F., 3rd Bn.
- 22229 Pte. MUSCOVITCH, S., 3rd Bn.
- 5011 L/Cpl. NEPORENT, M., 1/1st Bn.
- 5016 Pte. NATHAN, H. J., 1/1st Bn.
- 266743 Pte. NAVENSKY, 1/1st Bn.
- 4478 Pte. NAVENSKY, J., 2/1st Bn.
- 267007 Pte. NATHAN, J.,* 2nd Bn.
- 5070 Pte. NATHAN, J., 2/1st Bn.
- 203545 Pte. NANBOOLEN, R., 2/4th Bn.
- 4487 Pte. NARMSKY, J., 1st Bn.
- 34862 Pte. PHILLIPS, L., 2nd Bn.
- 5161 Pte. PLESKIN, L., 1st Bn.
- 4567 Pte. PELHAM, J., 1/1st Bn.
- 5633 Pte. POLIER, E., 1/1st Bn.
- 5003 Pte. PRICE, B., 1/1st Bn.
- 266747 Pte. PEARLMAN, S.,* 1/1st Bn.
- 20419 Pte. POSNER, M., 1/1st Bn.
- 266744 Pte. PADOLSKY, H., 2/1st Bn.
- 35580 Pte. PEREZ, E., 1/1st Bn.
- 253038 Pte. POLLOCK, L., 2/1st Bn.
- 5171 Pte. PHILLIPS, H., 3/1st Bn.
- 5163 Pte. POSNER, S., 3/1st Bn.
- 23483 Pte. PRICE, C. S., 1st Bn.
- 267397 Pte. POSNER, I. M., 2/1st Bn.
- 5015 Cpl. RAPHAEL, J., 1/1st Bn.
- 266983 Pte. ROSENBAUM, S.,* 1/1st Bn.
- 5066 Pte. ROSEN, J., 1/1st Bn.
- 5026 Pte. ROSEWOOD, A., 1/1st Bn.
- 4989 L/Cpl. ROSEN, P., 1/1st Bn.
- 5183 Pte. RODSTONE, V. J., 1/1st Bn.
- 240613 Pte. RUBINOVITCH, 1st Bn.
- 34178 Pte. ROSE, E., 2/4th Bn.
- 26316 Pte. RAPLINSKY, L., 1st Bn.
- 5234 Pte. RABINOWITZ, S., 4th Bn.
- 7212 Pte. RADSTONE, V. J., 4th Bn.
- 233510 Pte. ROSENBLUM, 8th Bn.
- 22702 Pte. ROSENSKY, S.
- 5164 Pte. RUBINSTEIN, M., 1st Bn.
- 22847 Pte. RABNER, L.
- 2923 Pte. ROSENBLOOM, H. C.
- 31651 Pte. STALL, J., 1/1st Bn.
- 276 Pte. SUSMAN, J.,* 1/1st Bn.
- 5073 L/Cpl. SMITH, J., 1/1st Bn.
- 5056 L/Cpl. SHAER, I., 1/1st Bn.
- 5057 L/Cpl. SHULMAN, B., 1/1st Bn.
- 203010 L/Cpl. SCHOOLING, A., 1/1st Bn.
- 22832 Pte. SCHNEIDER, S.,* 5th Bn.
- 203526 Pte. SOLOMONS, A., 2/4th Bn.
- 4480 L/Cpl. STEINBERG, S., 2/1st Bn.
- 267472 Pte. SHING, D., 2/1st Bn.
- 4477 Pte. SALTMAN, M., 1/1st Bn.
- 4519 Pte. SULKIN, M., 1/1st Bn.
- 5036 Pte. SCHOTT, D., 1/1st Bn.
- 280459 Pte. SIMONSON, J., 1/1st Bn.
- 5120 Pte. SULKIN, I., 3/1st Bn.
- 4514 Pte. STEINBERG, D.
- 3342 Pte. SILVERSTEIN, M., 6th Bn.
- 285509 Pte. SIMONS, J., 1/1st Bn.
- 266754 Pte. SHINEBOAM, A., 2/1st Bn.
- 6109 Sgt. SPYER, S. M., 3/4th Bn.
- 203141 Pte. SOLOMON, H., 1st Bn.
- 5119 Pte. SILVERMAN, M. S.
- 22230 Pte. SIMMONS, L., 3rd Bn.
- 22280 Pte. SIMONS, E., 3rd Bn.
- 4513 Pte. SIMONS, I., 3/1st Bn.
- 21809 Pte. STONIES, M.
- 286225 L/Cpl. SYMONS, J.
- 266998 L/Cpl. SOTSKY, A., 1/1st Bn.

Oxford and Bucks. L.I.—*Continued.*

49937 Pte. SILVERMAN, A. A.
77625 Pte. SILVERMAN, P., 8th Bn.
27345 Pte. SILVERSTEIN, M., 6th Bn.
266999 Pte. SHALO, I., 1/1st Bn.
4608 Pte. TAFFLER, A., 1/1st Bn.
4909 Pte. TAVROGES, M. L., 1st Bn.
4906 Pte. TEGLIN, M., 2/1st Bn.
19436 Pte. VINCENT, S., 3rd Bn.
13552 C.S.M. VANDERHOOK, S. S., 8th Bn.
7796 Pte. VANBOOLEN, R., 2/4th Bn.
4495 Pte. WRIGHT, J.,* 1/1st Bn.
5045 Pte. WEINBAUM, H., 1/1st Bn.
5067 L/Cpl. WEINER, L., 1/1st Bn.
12946 Pte. WINEBERG, J., 11/1st Bn.
5047 Pte. WARREN, S., 2/1st Bn.
266992 L/Cpl. WARREN, S., 2/1st Bn.
11949 Pte. WEISENBERG, S., 6th Bn.
4096 Pte. WEGLIN, M., 1/1st Bn.
14678 Pte. ZIMMERMAN, S.,* 5th Bn.
25196 Pte. ZASS, S., 2nd Garr. Bn.
22306 Cpl. ZAND, J., 5th Bn.
9881 Pte. ZIMMERMAN, H.,* 2nd Bn.
71809 Pte. ZAUSMER, M.

* Killed in Action or died on Active Service.

THE ESSEX REGIMENT.

OFFICERS.

Lieut. ARNHOLZ, R. H. P., 2/6th Bn.
Capt. BRAUN, C.,* 2nd L. ...
2nd Lieut. BALCON, S.
Capt. CAPPER, E. R.* (M.C.), 9th Bn.
Lieut. DAVIS, E. P., 10th Bn.
Lieut. DAVIS, H. P.,* 12th Bn.
2nd Lieut FREEDMAN, G., 1/4th Bn.
2nd Lieut. KLEIN, J.,* 9th Bn.
Lieut. LITTMAN, H., 2nd Bn.
2nd Lieut. LEVY, M. A., 12th Bn.
2nd Lieut. MYERS, H. C., 5th Bn.
2nd Lieut. SPERO, S.
2nd Lieut. SONNENTHAL.
2nd Lieut. SHERMAN, E. H. (M.C.), 13th Bn.
Lieut. TELFER, R. L., 1st Bn.

N.C.O.'s AND MEN.

L/Cpl. ABRAHAMS, C.
60118 Pte. ARTHUR, J., 4th Bn.
4706 Pte. ANNENBERG, H. B., 2/7th Bn.
16016 Pte. ABRAHAMS, R., Mil. Rys.
Pte. ABRAHAMS, C.
48846 Pte. ABRAHAMS, A.
34845 Pte. ABRAHAMS, J., 1st Bn.
45217 Pte. ARONHEIM, S., 1st Bn.
267495 Pte. ANSELL, I., 2/5th Bn.
302492 Pte. ABRAHAMS, G., 2/7th Bn.
31028 Pte. ABRAHAMS, S., 2nd Bn.
50287 Pte. ABRAHAMS, S. M., 237th Bn.
253040 Pte. ANSCHELL, T., 1/7th Bn.
400648 Pte. APPLEBAUM, J., 17th Bn.
43019 Pte. ARGEBAND, M., 3rd Bn.
3212 Sgt. BENJAMIN, J., 13th Bn.
18156 Pte. BERSON, W.,* 13th Bn.
34455 Cpl. BLOOM, J.,* 2nd Bn.
6622 Pte. BRUSKE, L., 2/6th Bn.
5399 Pte. BERNSTEIN, L.,
4945 Pte. BLOOMBERG, A., 2/5th Bn.
Sgt. BAUM, B. (M.M.).
55718 Pte. BARNETT, A., 15th Bn.
9856 Pte. BRANDT, L., 2nd Bn.
360200 Pte. BARBECK, L., 15th Bn.
252560 Pte. BRODER, I., 2/5th Bn.
252929 Pte. BARDOFSKY, R., 2/5th Bn.
302264 L/Cpl. BOGDIN, E., 2/7th Bn.
39139 Pte. BERGE, G., 2/6th Bn.
267845 Pte. BERWALD, J. K., 2/5th Bn.
301617 Pte. BROWN, H., 2/7th Bn.
40758 Cpl. BRAMS, C., 9th Bn.
44118 Pte. BAKER, M., 10th Bn.
471179 Pte. BARNETT, M., 15th Bn.
400324 Pte. BENJAMIN, S., 17th Bn.
45148 Pte. BENJAMIN, L., 17th Bn.
45151 Pte. BENJAMIN, J., 17th Bn.
7642 Pte. BARCUM, L., 16th Bn.
351040 Pte. BERL, L., 15th Bn.
2369 Pte. BENJAMIN, C., 24th Bn.
375959 Pte. BEVERLEY, L. G.
5394 Pte. BLOOM, J., 2/7th Bn.
28525 Pte. BAKER, J., 3rd Bn.
60640 Pte. BAMBERG, G. L., 3rd Bn.
10183 Pte. BOWDEN, W., 2nd Bn.
Pte. BLATTMAN, C.
16782 Pte. COHEN, M., 1st Bn.
316032 Pte. COHEN, M., 1st Bn.
316506 Pte. COHEN, F. M., 1st Bn.
5316 Pte. COHEN, L., 2/7th Bn.
55994 Pte. COSTA, M., 15th Bn.
10294 Pte. COHEN, S., 2nd Bn.
252964 Pte. CARCOSKI, S., 2/5th Bn.
36877 Pte. COHEN, L., 2/6th Bn.
302562 Pte. COHEN, E., 2/7th Bn.
262500 Pte. COHEN, J., 2/5th Bn.
Pte. COHEN, N.
301579 Pte. COHEN, L., 2/7th Bn.
302501 Pte. COGGIN, P., 2/7th Bn.
38690 Pte. COLLINS, A. J., 3rd Bn.
8904 L/Cpl. COHEN, S., 3rd Bn.

The Essex Regt.—*Continued.*

46447	Pte. COOPER, H., 4th Bn.
26443	Pte. CROWN, L., 4th Bn.
49109	Cpl. CASBOURNE, G. (M.M.), 1st Bn.
24023	Pte. DA COSTA, M., 2nd Bn.
18735	Pte. DA COSTA, J., 13th Bn.
34891	Pte. DAVISON, S.,* 1st Bn.
34820	Pte. DE HAAN, R., 9th Bn.
21745	Pte. DAVIES, J., 9th Bn.
302423	Pte. DAVIS, J., 2/7th Bn.
400929	Pte. DAVIS, M., 17th Bn.
	Pte. DION, H., 11th Bn.
	Pte. DRIVEE, M., 12th Bn.
5269	Pte. EDGAR, E. S., 2/7th Bn.
4869	Pte. ELWIN, R., 2/5th Bn.
55731	Pte. EPHRAIM, H., 15th Bn.
14795	Pte. EMANUEL, J., 11th Bn.
252928	Pte. ESNER, J., 2/5th Bn.
19786	Pte. FREEDMAN, R.,* 9th Bn.
14508	Pte. FINE, J., 10th Bn.
16987	Pte. FRANKS, S., 1st Bn.
55660	Pte. FRIEDLANDER, R., 15th Bn.
252394	Pte. FRANKENSTEIN, W., 2/5th Bn.
252858	Pte. FIDER, S. F., 2/5th Bn.
252932	Pte. FINKEL, A., 2/5th Bn.
252921	Pte. FRANKEL, I., 2/5th Bn.
267712	Pte. FALKSON, J., 2/6th Bn.
277713	Pte. FALKSON, S., 2/7th Bn.
302510	Pte. FINKLESTEIN, D., 2/7th Bn.
400619	Pte. FINKLESTEIN, E., 17th Bn.
36619	Pte. FRANKS, M., 1/7th Bn.
16188	Pte. FRANKS, F., 3rd Bn.
37539	Pte. FELINSON, I., 2/6th Bn.
3407	Pte. FILEMAN, J., 12th Bn.
45775	Pte. FREEDMAN, A., 1/7th Bn.
1704	Pte. GOLDBERG, A., 10th Bn.
23697	Pte. GOLD, J., 10th Bn.
49757	Pte. GOLDBERG, L.,* 1st Bn.
41171	L/Cpl. GREY, W. J., 10th Bn.
34907	Pte. GALLER, H., 11th Bn.
11366	Pte. GOLD, C., 10th Bn.
1675	Cpl. GOLDSTEIN, L., 3rd Bn.
303067	Pte. GREENBERG, S., 2/7th Bn.
302512	Pte. GORDON, J., 2/7th Bn.
56047	Pte. GRIZZARG, S., 1/8th Bn.
204066	Pte. GANKER, A., 2nd G.B.
400618	Pte GNESSEN, M., 17th Bn.
28040	Pte. GOLDSTONE, H., 13th Bn.
4481	Pte. GOLDMAN, B., 16th Bn.
20517	Pte. GOLDSMITH, H. D., 3rd Bn.
1457	Pte. GOLDSTEIN, M., 2/8th Bn.
45077	Pte. GATES, B.
376059	Pte. GARCIA, L., 16th Bn.
11426	Pte. GOODMAN, R. G., 1st Bn.
40483	Pte. GOLDBLUTT, D., 9th Bn.
44277	Pte. HART, J., 11th Bn.
277462	Pte. HERTZOG, H., 2/6th Bn.
55306	Pte. HARRIS, D., 15th Bn.
303061	Pte. HARRIS, L., 2/7th Bn.
301580	Pte. HART, A., 2/7th Bn.
21268	Sgt. HARRIS, M.,* 9th Bn.
301575	Pte. HARRIS, S., 2/7th Bn.
27454	Pte. HARRIS, A., 3rd Bn.
45050	Pte. HARRIS, W. D., 17th Bn.
3/2867	Sgt. HARRIS, T., 3rd Bn.
17144	Pte. ISAACS, N.,* 1st Bn.
42034	Pte. ISAAC, S., 11th Bn.
278082	Cpl. ISAAC, B., 2/6th Bn.
278057	Pte. ISAACS, D., 2/6th Bn.
22086	L/Cpl. ISAACS, I., 2nd Bn.
25693	L/Cpl. ISAACS, J. R., 2nd Bn.
45129	Pte. ISAACS, J. R., 17th Bn.
18326	Pte. JOSEPH, A., 13th Bn.
26600	Pte. JACOBSON, I., 2nd Bn.
267514	L/Cpl. JACOBS, P., 2/7th Bn.
303320	L/Cpl. JACOBS, H., 2/7th Bn.
267513	L/Cpl. JOEL, S. L., 2/6th Bn.
252902	Pte. KAUFFMAN, I., 2/5th Bn.
50374	Pte. KIRVITZ, V., 237th Inf. Bn.
13775	Pte. LEVY, J., 10th Bn.
302445	Pte. LATEN, S., 9th Bn.
33906	Pte. LEE, A., 11th Bn.
55644	Pte. LEMMETT, H., 15th Bn.
	Pte. LITTMAN, S., 3rd Bn.
45769	Pte. LEWIS, H., 3rd Bn.
9831	Pte. LEWIS, M.,* 2nd Bn.
252679	Pte. LAYMAN, L., 2/5th Bn.
252639	Pte. LONGMAN, E., 2/5th Bn.
303055	Pte. LUBITZ, J., 2/7th Bn.
301646	Pte. LANDAU, R. S., 2/7th Bn.
45124	Pte. LEVENBERG, J., 9th Bn.
50381	Pte. LEVY, A., 237th Inf. Bn.
50402	Pte. LEVINE, M., 237th Inf. Bn.
44854	Pte. LISCUSKY, J., 3rd Bn.
	Pte. LEE, J., 6th Bn.
37012	Pte. LECHAM, L., 1/4th Bn.
321657	L/Cpl. LAWSON, P. L., 17th Bn.
5525	Pte. LESTER, W., 16th Bn.
5253	Pte. LEARER, J., 16th Bn.
39377	L/Cpl. LEVY, L., 15th Bn.
5813	Pte. LEVY, T.
46500	Pte. LAZARUS, R., 4th Bn.
	Pte. LIPMAN, D., 14th Bn.
	Pte. LEVY, S., 2/5th Bn.
14795	Cpl. MILLER, E., 11th Bn.
29444	Pte. MAZIN, I., 1st Bn.
39355	L/Cpl. MARKS, J., 15th Bn.
43727	Pte. MENDES DA COSTAS, B.,* 1st Bn.
8559	Pte. MILLER, S.,
252926	Pte. MOSCOW, A., 2/5th Bn.
276351	Pte. MOSES, H., 2/6th Bn.
277489	Pte. MORRIS, B., 2/6th Bn.
	Pte. MILLER, B.
301253	Pte. MYERS, S., 2/7th Bn.
301878	Pte. MARKSON, B., 2/6th Bn.
14738	Pte. MIDDLEMAN, H., 237th Inf. Bn.

The Essex Regt.—*Continued.*

23516 Pte. MULLEN, S., 3rd Bn.
34306 Pte. MEADOWS, E., 3rd Bn.
87 Pte. MICHAELS, A. S., 2/5th Bn.
2767 Pte. MARKS, L. A. H., 1st Bn.
24065 Pte. MILLER, L., 3rd Bn.
23263 Pte. MORDECAI, L., 3rd Bn.
26553 Pte. MARKS, J., 14th Bn.
Pte. MENDELSOHN, I.
Pte. NYMAN, D., 10th Bn.
35156 Pte. NEIMAN, M., 10th Bn.
6/6801 Pte. NARCOVITCH, I., 4th Bn.
82145 Pte. NELSON, A., 10th Bn.
5241 Pte. OPPENHEIMER, R. J., 16th Bn.
3317 Pte. OBERMAN, P., 12th Bn.
71249 Pte. OLERSKY, M., 18th Bn.
15807 Pte. OPPENHEIM, D., 1/6th Bn.
6790 Pte. PARKS, H., 2/6th Bn.
6040 Pte. PORTRAITE, S., 16th Bn.
375517 Pte. PHILLIPS, A. B., 16th Bn.
46829 Pte. PRICE, J., 2nd Bn.
43905 Pte. PRIMHAK, N.,* 1st Bn.
50520 Pte. PELTER, H., 15th Bn.
252937 Pte. PAM, S., 2/5th Bn.
37715 Pte. PRESSMAN, I., 2/6th Bn.
303168 Pte. PECKAR, E., 2/7th Bn.
17934 Pte. RATHBONE, S., 13th Bn.
21304 Pte. ROSENTHAL, S., 13th Bn.
35513 Pte. RABINOVITZ, A., 10th Bn.
34968 Pte. ROSE, H., 11th Bn.
252640 Pte. RUBENSTEIN, L., 2/5th Bn.
252930 Pte. RUBENSTEIN, I., 2/5th Bn.
252934 Pte. ROSOFF, S., 2/5th Bn.
252931 Pte. RUBINOWITZ, H., 2/5th Bn.
277316 Pte. ROSENKRANTZ, L., 2/6th Bn.
276381 Pte. RUBENSTEIN, I., 2/6th Bn.
267823 Pte. RICHES, H., 2/7th Bn.
Pte. ROSENSTEIN, M., 1/8th Bn.
267741 Pte. RYNER, M., 2/7th Bn.
35876 L/Cpl. ROSENBERG, H., 3rd Bn.
45123 Pte. RAPHAEL, H. (M.M.), 17th Bn.
54800 Pte. REEVE, F., 3rd Bn.
55973 Pte. RYNER, M., 3rd Bn.
5471 Cpl. ROSEN, H.
7042 Pte. ROGENSTEIN, S., 2/7th Bn.
13033 Cpl. SHERMAN, E., 2nd Bn.
13144 Pte. SILVERMAN, H., 2nd Bn.
12334 Pte. SHOWMAN, S., 2nd Bn.
3/2743 Cpl. SILVERSTONE, H.,* 9th Bn.
13509 L/Cpl. SIMONS, S. (D.C.M., M.M.), 9th Bn.
H/5815 Pte. SMITH, H., 35th Bn.
27480 Pte. SHENNAN, J., 11th Bn.
46102 Pte. SHEINBAUM, J., 1st Bn.
55272 Pte. SONBERG, H., 15th Bn.
29486 Pte. SULLIVAN, M., 1st Bn.
Cpl. SHONTHAL, H., 1st Bn.
8226 Pte. SNIDER, E., 2/5th Bn.
36419 Pte. SCOTT, D. S., 2/6th Bn.

276993 Sig. SALTIEL, J. F., 2/6th Bn.
302338 Pte. SAMUELS, H., 2/7th Bn.
267836 Cpl. SHALSON, R. A., 2/7th Bn.
271444 Pte. SYMON, A., 2/7th Bn.
42019 Pte. SCHWEITZER, J. H., 9th Bn.
50419 Pte. SPURANCE, A.
45127 Pte. SIELES, L., 17th Bn.
46887 Pte. SCHRIER, I., 11th Bn.
15129 Pte. SPRINGER, M., 2/7th Bn.
9751 Pte. SLIMER, H., 3rd Bn.
4926 Pte. SUGARMAN, T., 2/5th Bn.
5273 Pte. SIMONS, W., 2/7th Bn.
46506 Pte. SLASBURG, M., 4th Bn.
45815 Pte. SMITH, A., 2nd Bn.
3879 Pte. SCHAVER, L., 3/4th Bn.
7664 Pte. SOLOMONS, A.
11306 Pte. SAMUEL, A., 1st Bn.
Pte. SAMUEL, J., 3rd Bn.
Pte. SOLOMON, S., 10th Bn.
27480 Pte. SHULMAN, I.,* 11th Bn.
252815 Pte. TOBIAS, W., 2/5th Bn.
36450 Pte. TOBIAS, R., 2/6th Bn.
15138 Pte. TEILEBAUM, S., 237th Inf. Bn.
38420 Pte. TRESCO, D., 3rd Bn.
5057 Pte. TROMER, A., 2/5th Bn.
23594 Pte. TULL, A., 4th Bn.
20057 Pte. TOMLINSON, H., 1/4th Bn.
252904 Pte. VECHT, M. M., 2/5th Bn.
252933 Pte. VALENSKY, P., 2/5th Bn.
37685 Pte. VELENSKY, H., 3rd Bn.
15827 Pte. WAIS, R., 2nd Bn.
13007 L/Cpl. WORMS, H., 1st Bn.
26399 Pte. WOLFF, L., 3rd Bn.
252516 Pte. WELT, H., 2/5th Bn.
302360 Pte. WOOLF, J., 2/7th Bn.
34369 L/Cpl. WOOLFE, M., 1st Bn.
35396 Pte. WOOLF, M., 3rd Bn.
14529 Pte. VAN ENGEL, S.,* 10th Bn.
Pte. WOLFERS, S., 3rd Bn.
5315 Pte. WARREN, H., 2/7th Bn.
1324 Pte. WILKINS, J., 16th Bn.
7667 Pte. WILKINSON, W., 16th Bn.
5535 Pte. YAELSHON, B., 16th Bn.
45774 Pte. YANTIEN, M., 10th Bn.
375675 Pte. YEOLSON, D., 16th Bn.
5509 Pte. YABLOWSKY, C., 4th Bn.
55644 Pte. ZIMMEL, H., 15th Bn.
7639 Pte. ZISSMAN, L., 16th Bn.
19823 Pte. ZILTER, T. W.
46532 Pte. ZELKIN, H., 4th Bn.
40122 Pte. ZOLOWSKI, A., 2nd Bn.
350882 Pte. ZIMMERMAN, J., 15th Bn.

* Killed in Action or died on Active Service.

THE SHERWOOD FORESTERS (NOTTINGHAM AND DERBYSHIRE REGIMENT).

OFFICERS.

Capt. Berger, F. J. D. (M.C.).
Capt. Cohen, D. H., 16th Bn.
Lieut. Eichholz, R. N., 13th Bn.
Lieut. Groner, R. E., 2nd Bn.
2nd Lieut. Lifetree, E. H.,* 16th Bn.
2nd Lieut. Posener, W., 13th Bn.
2nd Lieut. Schlesinger, A. L., 5th Bn.
2nd Lieut. Saunders, J. A., 14th Bn.
Capt. Simon, H., 7th Bn.
Lieut. Schur, P.,* 9th Bn.

N.C.O.'s AND MEN.

80076 Pte. Ackstone, S.,* 10th Bn.
6434 Pte. Abrahams, B., 2/5th Bn.
5353 Pte. Alexander, L., 8th Bn.
Pte. Appleton, A., 1/8th Bn.
306596 Pte. Alexander, A. E.
28006 Pte. Brill, A., 17th Bn.
6435 Pte. Becker, J.,* 2/5th Bn.
6432 Pte. Bensusan, M., 2/5th Bn.
80399 Pte. Brill, S., 2nd Bn.
83088 Pte. Bull, S., 2nd Bn.
75072 Pte. Baynard, M., 1st Bn.
73484 Pte. Block, A., 15th Bn.
49664 Pte. Blashkey, P., B. Coy.
47005 Pte. Bloom, J., 20th Bn.
96011 Pte. Barnard, M., 10th Bn.
54795 Pte. Baker, M., 10th Bn.
104353 Pte. Black, D., 3rd Bn.
55856 Pte. Brooker, S., 4th Bn.
3252 Pte. Bowman, M., 2/1st Bn.
38303 Pte. Cohen, J., 2nd Bn.
202808 Pte. Cohen, A., 9th Bn.
Pte. Caskey, P. B., 16th Bn.
Pte. Cohen, J., 16th Bn.
6/52157 Pte. Cohen, N., 52nd Bn.
75032 Pte. Cohen, D., 16th Bn.
73754 Pte. Cohen, P., 12th Bn.
200197 L/Cpl. Cohen, J., 10th Bn.
14/39315 Cpl. Copeland, M., 4th Bn.
72996 Pte. Donne, D. S., 15th Bn.
19429 Pte. Deitch, D., 52nd Bn.
72999 Pte. Davis, L., 15th Bn.
241939 Pte. Ellis, N.,* 2/6th Bn.
71854 Pte. Friedman, I. (M.M.), 11th Bn.
6191 L/Cpl. Fisher, D., 1s Bn.
25119 Pte. Friedman, A., 51st Bn.
6/50355 Pte. Frieze, S., 52nd Bn.
70126 Pte. Gillman, A.,* 16th Bn.
Sgt. Greenburg, J. (M.M.).
42160 Pte. Glassman, S., 1st Bn.
Pte. Greenberg, S., 2nd Bn.
72237 Pte. Golding, S. R., 10th Bn.

38304 Sgt. Galansky, I., 15th Bn.
39641 Pte. Goldman, A., 3rd Bn.
2182 Arm/S/Sgt. Harris, J., 2/5th Bn.
895 Pte. Harris, W., 2nd Bn.
117105 Pte. Herman, M., 8th Bn.
2999 Pte. Hurwitz, M.,* 7th Bn.
48024 Pte. Hoberts, S., 20th Bn.
96325 Pte. Harris, S.
44976 Ptet. Isaacs, C. B., 10th Bn.
93670 Pte. Jacobs, E. J., 12th Bn.
103324 Pte. Kohn, E., 16th Bn.
6363 Pte. Krost, I., 2/5th Bn.
102168 Pte. Kimberlaski, H., 2nd Bn.
202817 Pte. Krost, I., 2/5th Bn.
72685 Pte. King, S., 2nd Bn.
41165 Pte. Kemp, J.
11890 L/Cpl. Levy, W., 2nd Bn.
55741 Pte. Levy, J., 10th Bn.
6433 Pte. Lazarus, F., 2/5hth Bn.
24776 Pte. Lolowski, E., 11th Bn.
73872 Pte. Lando, B., 8th Bn.
72594 Pte. Levy, H., 15th Bn.
6/25392 Sgt. Lesser, M. S., 51st Bn.
Pte. Lyons, J. M. (M.M.).
103272 Pte. Lingmond, A., 15th Bn.
3518 Cpl. Livingstone, J., 3rd Bn.
74120 Pte Lubelski, M., 10th Bn.
123985 Pte. Lux, S., 53rd Bn.
117432 Pte. Lubing, H.
17890 Sgt. Levy, H., 2nd Bn.
70185 Sgt. Marks, C., 11th Bn.
6392 Pte. Marks, A. H., 2/5th Bn.
70186 Cpl. McKennel, 11th Bn.
49702 Pte. Marks, J.
14572 Dmr. Morris, H., 10th Bn.
12594 Pte. Morris, D., 11th Bn.
76483 Pte. Milberg, J., 17th Bn.
17130 Pte. Markovitz, M.,* 16th Bn.
7615 Pte. Mendelson, S., 51st Bn.
5872 Pte. Nesserbaum, I., 2/6th Bn.
72520 Pte Oppenheim, J., 16th Bn.
39316 Pte. Peterkovsky, D., 2nd Bn.
14730 Pte. Peres, H., 51st Bn.
306987 Pte. Pam, G., 2/7th Bn.
331636 Pte. Pearlman, A., 3rd Bn.
26225 Pte. Rosenberg, H., 17th Bn.
71449 Pte. Rose, W.,* 15th Bn.
281471 Pte. Renovitch, D., 10th Bn.
72549 L/Cpl. Rainsburg, S., 17th Bn.
48137 Pte. Ruthstein, 20th Bn.
6/15651 Pte. Reeves, J.
203115 Pte. Simberg, E., 5th Bn.
17833 Pte. Schaverien, J., 2/5th Bn.
75072 Pte. Solomon, C., 1st Bn.
67131 Pte. Samuels, H., 1st Bn.
15350 Pte. Shibko, M., 51st Bn.
6/15248 Pte. Solk, S. S., 52nd Bn.
44518 Cpl. Segelman, P.,* 16th Bn.

Sherwood Foresters.—*Continued.*

72997 Pte. SAUNDERS, M.
73800 Pte. SHAPIRO, I., 12th Bn.
60076 Pte. SOLOMON, H., 3rd Bn.
108352 Pte. SILVERMAN, R., 2nd Bn.
121832 Pte. SPARK, A., 53rd Bn.
123986 Pte. SIMONS, A., 53rd Bn.
7340 Pte. SARNO, A. J., 21st Bn.
3248 Pte. SHIFREEN, L., 2/1st Bn.
69601 Pte. SAMUELS, B. J., 19th Bn.
92369 Dvr. SILVERSTONE, J., 2/5th Bn.
42060 Dvr. SPELLMAN, S., 51st Bn.
102335 Pte. WEINSHANKER, G., 1st Bn.
6687 Pte. WOOLF, J., 5th Bn.
Pte. WILSON, R., 1st Bn.
205405 Pte. WALLMAN, A., 1st Bn.
266809 Pte. WARRENER, A., 1st Bn.
203092 Pte. WOOLF, I., 7th Bn.
73055 L/Cpl. ZOLOWSKI, E.,* (M.M.), 9th Bn.
267774 Pte. ZIMMERMAN, N.,* 2/7th Bn.
103272 Pte. ZIGMOND, A., 15th Bn.

* Killed in Action or died on Active Service.

THE LOYAL NORTH LANCASHIRE REGIMENT.

OFFICERS.

2nd Lieut. HENRIQUES, L. Q., 4th Bn.
2nd Lieut. HORWITZ, S. S.,* 1st Bn.
Capt. LEVERSON, B. A. D., 7th Bn.
Lieut. LUMLEY, C. H., 7th Bn.
2nd Lieut. MORRIS, H. M., 11th Bn.
Capt. PHILLIPS, B. J., 1/5th Bn.
2nd Lieut. SONNENTHAL, E. F.
2nd Lieut. ZEITLIN, F. I., 11th Bn.

N.C.O.'s AND MEN.

42578 Pte. AARON, L.
36561 Pte. ALLEN, A. L., 13th Bn.
33639 Pte. ALTMAN, A., 7th Bn.
40556 Pte. ANCIKAITES, F., 1/5th Bn.
266542 Pte. BALABAN, H., 2nd Bn.
35580 Pte. BENJAMIN, J., 9th Bn.
9836 L/Cpl. BERGER, M., 2/5th Bn.
40033 Pte. BIANCS, I., 2/4th Bn.
30718 Pte. BLACK, L., 2/5th Bn.
30300 Pte. BROOKS, J., 22nd Bn.
10207 Pte. BROSKY, B., 2/5th Bn.
55214 Pte. BYE, A., 15th Bn.
39927 Pte. COBRIN, W., 3rd Bn.
29766 Pte. COHEN, S., 9th Bn.
235124 Pte. COHEN, M., 4/5th Bn.
241869 Pte. COHEN, N., 4/5th Bn.
36067 Pte. COHEN, J., 1st Bn.
18030 Pte. COHEN, A., 1/1st Bn.
4715 Pte. COHEN, S.
40106 Pte. COHEN, S. W., 6th Bn.
36681 Pte. COHEN, L., 13th Bn.
36503 Pte. COHEN, W., 13th Bn.
12071 Pte. COSSACK, M.,* 6th Bn.
242796 Pte. COTTON, J., 7th Bn.
34342 Pte. CRANGLE, S., 2nd Bn.
36501 Pte. CROSS, J., 13th Bn.
39206 Pte. CROSSMAN, H., 1st Bn.
35616 Pte. DON, G., 13th Bn.
36693 Pte. ECKMAN, J., 13th Bn.
23313 Pte. ELLIS, I. H., 3rd Bn.
28380 Pte. ESTREY, M., 8th Bn.
Pte. FEINBERG, 2nd Bn.
30615 Pte. GARDIE, R., 1/4th Bn.
36591 Pte. GERSHON, A., 13th Bn.
38124 Pte. GILBERT, S., 3rd Bn.
40159 Pte. GLATT, L.,* 2nd Bn.
55547 Pte. GOODMAN, S., 15th Bn.
40440 Pte. GOODMAN, J., 3rd Bn.
30093 Pte. GORDON, D.,* 9th Bn.
34342 Pte. GRANGLE, S., 2nd Bn.
36501 Pte. GROSS, J., 13th Bn.
39206 Pte. GROSSMAN, H., 1st Bn.
39206 Pte. GROSMAN, H., 1st Bn.
30313 Pte. HARRIS, C., 3rd Bn.
Pte. HESSE, E. W.
34530 Pte. HORNOFSKY, L. L., 8th Bn.
27150 Pte. HORWICK, H., 8th Bn.
33270 Pte. HORWITCH, J., 7th Bn.
28904 Pte. HYAM, S., 2/5th Bn.
27157 Pte. HYMAN, H., 13th Bn.
10257 Pte. JACOBS, M., 2/5th Bn.
254144 Pte. JACOBS, J., 1/4th Bn.
50225 Pte. JOEL, J., 6th Bn.
35580 Pte. JOSEPH, B., 9th Bn.
23314 Pte. KAUFMAN, D., 3rd Bn.
22889 Pte. KAUFFMAN, L., 6th Bn.
25786 Pte. KOFFMAN, J., 13th Bn.
38516 Pte. KORPER, A., 13th Bn.
34133 Pte. LACK, S., 8th Bn.
34361 Pte. LAZAROVITCH, P., 2nd Bn.
38524 Pte. LAZARUS, P., 13th Bn.
205161 Ptt. LESSER, I., 15th Bn.
40544 Pte. LEVY, M.
2811 Cpl. LEWIS, I., 15th Bn.
29152 L/Cpl. LIPMAN, S.,* 14th Bn.
3/46238 Pte. LIPSHITZ, H., 4th Bn.
34122 Pte. MALAMED, W., 8th Bn.
1928 Pte. MARKS, M.
Pte. MARKS, H. L., 3rd Bn.
38900 Pte. MELROSE, 9th Bn.
38382 Pte. MENDEL, S., 8th Bn.
33516 Pte. MARLOW, B., 9th Bn.
30588 Pte. MICHAELS, S.,* 1/5th Bn.
4728 Pte. MILLER, J., 1st Bn.
11484 Pte. MILTZER, S., 1st Bn.

Loyal North Lancs. Regt.—*Continued.*

2846 Pte. MYERS, P.,* 1st Bn.
43728 Pte. OLIN, H., 1st Bn.
203642 Pte. OWEN, J., 10th Bn.
1869 Pte. PHILLIPS, M., 1st Bn.
39905 Pte. POWSER, J., 3rd Bn.
36377 Pte. RAYMOND, J., 13th Bn.
      Pte. RAPPAPORT, J., 2/4th Bn.
45083 Pte. REUBEN, S., 15th Bn.
27175 Pte. ROSENBURG, S., 8th Bn.
30191 Pte. ROSENBERG, S.,* 4/5th Bn.
20450 Pte. ROSENBERG, F., 2nd Bn.
244947 Pte. ROSENBERG, J., 2/5th Bn.
33634 Pte. ROSENBERG, J., 3rd Bn.
1925 Pte. ROSENTHAL, H., 4th Bn.
40443 Pte. ROTHSTEIN, T., 3rd Bn.
35786 Pte. ROSSMAN, J., 13th Bn.
34133 Pte. SACKS, S., 3rd Bn.
35579 Pte. SCHLENSKY, J., 3rd Bn.
33646 Pte. SEGELMAN, M., 7th Bn.
39870 Pte. SHERLOG, J., 4th Bn.
33653 Pte. SIMON, M.,* 7th Bn.
32276 Pte. SLOTMAN, A., 6th Bn.
38124 Pte. SOLOMON, S., 3rd Bn.
41237 Pte. STOUR, M., 1st Bn.
260006 A/Cpl. SUMMERS, E., 1/4th Bn.
40863 Pte. TOMPOSKI, A., 1st Bn.
38569 Pte. WHITE, H.
235723 Pte. WILKINS, V., 12th Bn.
26956 Pte. YELSKI, A., 1st Bn.

* Killed in Action or died on Active Service.

THE NORTHAMPTONSHIRE REGIMENT.

OFFICERS.

Capt. PARKER, G. A. (D.S.O., M.C.).
2nd Lieut. PHILLIPS, P. G., 9th Bn.
Lieut. PHILLIPS, P. F., 3rd Bn.
Lieut. TUCKEY, A. W., 1st Bn.

N.C.O.'s AND MEN.

13484 Pte. ASHER, J., 6th Bn.
30804 Pte. ABRAHAMS, I., 1st Bn.
38200 Pte. ALEXANDER, S.
19000 Pte. ABRAHAMS, J., 3rd Bn.
204813 Pte. BENNETT, H. S., 1st Bn.
2735 Pte. BERNBAUM, B., 2nd Bn.
27537 Pte. BENJAMIN, A.,* 6th Bn.
48579 Pte. BURMAN, J., 9th Bn.
10593 Pte. BURMAN, T. M.,* 2nd Bn.
59924 Pte. BROOKS, H., 3rd Bn.
241267 Pte. BERNSTEIN, H., 2/4th Bn.
31616 Pte. BLASKY, M., 2nd Bn.
49664 Pte. BLACK, R., 3rd Bn.
23922 Pte. BOSWELL, M., 1st Bn.
204818 Pte. COHEN, E. L., 1st Bn.
6063 Pte. CASSELL, R., 2/4th Bn.
33874 Pte. COHEN, S., 6th Bn.
60352 Pte. COHEN, A., 3rd Bn.
202796 Pte. COHEN, W., 2/4th Bn.
27955 Pte. COPPERMAN, B., 3rd Bn.
36911 Pte. COHEN, M.
      Pte. CAREY, J., 2nd Bn.
49273 Pte. COHEN, B., 4th Bn.
29397 Pte. COSSICK, S., 2nd Bn.
8369 Pte. COHEN, A.,* 1st Bn.
      Pte. DYAN, P., 5th Bn.
12341 Pte. DION, J.,* (M.M.), 5th Bn.
12231 Sgt. DAVIS, 5th Bn.
47464 Pte. DAVIDS, C., 7th Bn.
3500 Pte. DOBKIN, R., 2/4th Bn.
20081 Pte. EDELSTEIN, D., 2nd Bn.
48600 Pte. FINKLESTEIN, L., 3rd Bn.
25942 Pte. FILER, J., 3rd Bn.
51603 Pte. FORDER, A., 29th Bn.
      Pte. FREEMAN, E.
      Pte. FIELDMAN, P., 2nd Bn.
27958 Pte. FREEDMAN, J., 3rd Bn.
      Pte. FISHMAN, W. (D.C.M.), 1st Bn.
5557 Pte. FREEDMAN, D., 2/4th Bn.
27638 Pte. FISHSTEIN, N., 13th Bn.
12239 Pte. GOODMAN, P., 5th Bn.
12286 Pte. GOLDMAN, H., 5th Bn.
41569 Pte. GREENBURY, W.,* 2nd Bn.
201608 Pte. GOLDSTEIN, I., 2/4th Bn.
202676 Pte. GOODMAN, V., 2/4th Bn.
20291 Pte. GOMPERTZ, A., 2nd Bn.
40893 Pte. GOLDSTEIN, S., 6th Bn.
30964 Pte. GLASSMAN, H.
49284 Pte. GOLD, A., 4th Bs.
48449 Pte. GOLDSTEIN, L. H., 6th Bn.
5521 Pte. GUTERMAN, A., 2/4th Bn.
12291 Pte. HARRIS, J., 1st Bn.
201777 L/Cpl. HARRIS, A., 2/4th Bn.
29861 Pte. HILLIER, S., 2nd Bn.
89786 Pte. HART, J., 9th Bn.
90020 Pte. HYMAN, D., 9th Bn.
30564 Pte. HARRIS, L., 2nd Bn.
36498 Pte. HYAMS, A., 9th Bn.
25948 Pte. JOSEPH, W., 2nd Bn.
8876 Pte. JOSEPHS, S., 9th Bn.
89873 Pte. JOEL, J., 9th Bn.
5616 Pte. JACOBS, D., 2/4th Bn.
6504 Pte. JACOBS, E.
1482 S/M. JACKSON.
47336 Pte. KUPFERROTH, J., 5th Bn.
29609 Pte. KRONITZKY, M., 2nd Bn.
26036 Pte. KARNOVSKY, L. S., 2/4th Bn.
48852 Pte. KREGER, M., 4th Bn.
204098 Pte. KOVNOFF, C., 4th Bn.
59980 Pte. KURASCH, E.

Northamptonshire Regt.—Continued.

- 49542 Pte. LESSER, A., 3rd Bn.
- 17553 Pte. LAMBERT, B., 2nd Bn.
- 16400 Pte. LEVINE, L., 5th Bn.
- 2668 Pte. LEVINE, S., 3/8th Bn.
- 18045 Pte. LIPMAN, M., 2nd Bn.
- 51620 Pte. LEVY, G., 29th Bn.
- 201640 Pte. LAZARUS, C., 2/4th Bn.
- 26932 Pte. LEWIS, J., 7th Bn.
- 20505 Pte. LAZARUS, M., 2nd Bn.
- 20083 Pte. LASKEY, W. H., 2nd Bn.
- 59066 Pte. LEVENE, M., 1/4th Bn.
- 89686 Pte. LEVY, H. E., 9th Bn.
- 5638 Pte. LINKE, H., 2/4th Bs.
- 38871 Pte. LEFF, H., 1/4th Bn.
- 25778 Pte. LEWIS, M. P.
- 50595 Pte. LINDER, L., 3rd Bn.
- 205008 Pte. MARKS, L., 2nd Bn.
- 52189 Pte. MILLER, N., 6th Bn.
- 201657 Pte. MORRIS, J., 2/4th Bn.
- 201654 Pte. MARKS, M., 2/4th Bn.
- 28164 Pte. MORRIS, M., 1st Bn.
- 5843 Pte. MYERS, I., 2/3rd Bn.
- 88064 Pte. NATHAN, I.
- 225738 Pte. NEWMAN, H., 9th Bn.
- 38373 Pte. OESTERMAN, L.
- 60507 Pte. PARITSKY, A., 3rd Bn.
- 201859 Pte. PHILLIPS, L., 2/4th Bn.
- 48575 Pte. PIZER, J., 9th Bn.
- 205335 Pte. PHILLIPS, R., 1/4th Bn.
- 23483 Pte. PRICE, C. S., 1/4th Bn.
- 31471 Pte. PRICE.
- 41759 Pte. ROSS, J., 2nd Bn.
- 205014 Pte. ROSENSTEIN, W., 2nd Bn.
- 40524 Pte. RECKLER, L.,* 6th Bn.
- 48681 Pte. RICKARDO, H., 6th Bn.
- 5226 Pte. REECE, H. J., 2nd Bn.
- 201691 Pte. ROSE, J. E., 2/4th Bn.
- 35240 Pte. ROSENBERG, F., 5th Bn.
- 48663 Pte. ROSEN, M., 6th Bn.
- 29653 Pte. ROSNER, D., 2nd Bn.
- 29669 Pte. ROTHCHILD, H., 2nd Bn.
- 32731 Pte. ROSENTHAL, S.
- 30070 Pte. RITTERLAND, J., 2nd Bn.
- 36101 Pte. RUBENS, H.
- 12292 Pte. SYMONS, J., 5th Bn.
- 12180 Sgt. SHINE, N. (M.M.), 5th Bn.
- 204337 Pte. SOLOMON, B., 1st Bn.
- 201693 Pte. SARNA, J., 2nd Bn.
- 48604 Pte. STRENFIELD, M., 9th Bn.
- 60183 Pte. SOLOMON, H., 3rd Bn.
- 49834 Pte. SEIGLEMAN, B., 3rd Bn.
- 201710 Pte. SIMMONS, A. J., 2/4th Bn.
- 158021 Spr. SUSS, H. M., 54th Bn.
- 38730 Pte. STURGE, M., 5th Bn.
- 26568 Pte. SOLOMONS, B., 2nd Bn.
- 29865 L/Cpl. SIMS, N., 2nd Bn.
- 29680 Pte. SCHNEIDER, J., 2nd Bn.
- 5771 Pte. SHAW, J., 2/4th Bn.
- 29395 Pte. SEGALOVITCH, A., 2nd Bn.
- 5767 Pte. SAMUELS, R.
- 50292 Pte. SACHS, B., 4th Bs.
- 204079 Pte. SILVERMAN, P., 11th Bn.
- Pte. SHELLER, M., 3rd Bn.
- 50291 Pte. TROSKINSKY, L., 4th Bn.
- 22261 Pte. TVERGO, S.
- 203453 L/Cpl. WEST, L., 1/4th Bn.
- 204873 Pte. WEINER, S., 1st Bn.
- 201745 Pte. WOOLFE, C. D., 2/4th Bn.
- 89849 Pte. WENSERAL, H., 9th Bn.
- 49271 Pte. ZIGGLES, H., 3rd Bn.

* Killed in Action or died on Active Service.

PRINCESS CHARLOTTE OF WALES'S (ROYAL BERKSHIRE REGIMENT).

OFFICERS.

- 2nd Lieut. ABINGER, B. R.* (M.C.), 2nd Bn.
- 2nd Lieut. COHEN, H.,* 4th Bn.
- 2nd Lieut. DAVIES, H.,* 2nd Bn.
- Capt. GUTTMAN, W. M. (M.C.), 2nd Bn.
- Lieut. JACOBS, D. A. (M.C.).
- Lieut. JOSEPH, E. G., 5th Bn.
- 2nd Lieut. JOSEPH, W. F. G.,* 2nd Bn.
- Capt. JOSEPH, R. L. (M.C.).
- 2nd Lieut. KLEMANTASKI, L. A.,* 8th Bn.
- Capt. LITTEN, R.,* 6th Bn.
- Capt. ROZELAAR, S. L.,* 6th Bn.

N.C.O.'s AND MEN.

- 32317 Pte. ABRAHAMS, H., 1st Bn.
- 220451 Pte. ABRAHAMS, H.,* 2nd Bn.
- 12063 Pte. BERNSTEIN, H., 6th Bn.
- 73433 Pte. BEARMAN, G., 1st Bn.
- L/Cpl. BEAVER, H.
- 18954 Pte. BLACKMAN.
- Pte. BOLLE, A.
- Cpl. BERNSTEIN, A. (M.M.).
- 10944 Pte. BROWN, J., 5th Bn.
- 7291 Pte. BRIGHTMAN, H., 1st Bn.
- 38432 Pte. BROOKS, J. R., 1st Bn.
- 43683 Pte. BUTLER, A., 8th Bn.
- 38693 Pte. BROMBERG A.
- 24113 Pte. COHEN, S.
- 33083 L/Cpl. COHEN, L., 1st Bn.
- 33572 Pte. COHEN, S., 1st Bn.
- 24008 Pte. COHEN, S., 3rd Bn.
- 2920 Pte. COHEN, A. L., 4th Bn.
- 2922 Pte. COHEN, G., 4th Bn.
- 38230 Pte. CONSHAW, L.
- 41649 Pte. DAVATASHVILLE, J.
- 44392 Pte. DANIELS, T. H., 2/4th Bn.
- 9116 L/Cpl. DAVIS, H.,* 2nd Bn.

Royal Berkshire Regt.—*Continued.*

	Pte. EDELSTEIN, H., 8th Bn.
266994	Pte. FINEBERG, H., 1st Bn.
34281	Pte. FIFER, D.
28321	Pte. GILLINSON, S., 3rd Bn.
38230	Pte. GONSHAW, L., 8th Bn.
43779	Pte. GREENBAUM, J., 5th Bn.
41239	Pte. GOLDMAN, 10th Bn.
12979	L/Cpl. GOLDMAN, A., 6th Bn.
36036	Pte. GOLDBERG, H., 10th Bn.
45171	Cpl. GOLDBERG, A., 2nd Bn.
37883	Pte. GORDON, N.,* 2nd Bn.
21907	Pte. GREEN, S., 1st Bn.
31429	Pte. GRODSINSKY, H., 1st Bn.
10032	Pte. GRUENBAUM, A.,* 2nd Bn.
5210874	Pte. HARING, B., 20th Bn.
15356	Pte. HARRIS, B., 6th Bn.
	Cpl. HARRIS, R.
	Pte. HARRIS, J., 17th Bn.
	Pte. HARRIS, I., 1st Bn.
41381	Pte. JANOFF, 5th Bn.
12051	Pte. JACOBS, M., 6th Bn.
12737	Pte. JACOBS, J., 6th Bn.
	Pte. JACOBS, S.
317958	Pte. JESSEL, H.,* 1/4th Bn.
9981	Pte. JOEL, A., 1st Bn.
41234	Pte. KORMAN, I. C., 5th Bn.
11420	Pte. LAMBERT, A., 2nd Bn.
14284	Pte. LANGDON, A. N., 2nd Bn.
8696	Sgt. LEE, J.,* 2nd Bn.
5853	Pte. LESSER, I., 1st Bn.
	Cpl. LEVY, H. T., 6th Bn.
9154	Pte. LEVY, S., 2nd Bn.
36565	Pte. LEVY, L.
13420	Pte. LUBICK, S., 7th Bn.
9638	Pte. LUSTIG, M., 5th Bn.
220712	Pte. LUMER, B., 1st Bn.
17667	Rfm. MICHAELS, S., 16th Bn.
	Pte. MORRIS, W., 6th Bn.
29631	Pte. MUSCOVITCH, S., 1st Bn.
9538	Pte. MYERS, J., 3rd Bn.
37932	Pte. NACOWITZ, J.,* 1/4th Bn.
13446	Cpl. PALMER, S., 7th Bn.
	Sgt. PERSOFF, S. (D.C.M.).
	Pte. PRESTON, A., 2nd Bn.
5411	Pte. PULRERMACHER, P., 4th Res. Bn.
38880	Pte. ROSENBLOOM, R., 2/4th Bn.
12082	Pte. ROSS, A., 6th Bn.
6372	Pte. ROSEBAUM, H., 2nd Bn.
1907	Pte. SALTMAN, J., 6th Bn.
36935	Pte. SALTMAN, T.,* 6th Bn.
37954	Pte. SCHAVERIEN, C., 1/4th Bn.
202855	Pte. SHINEBOAM, 5th Bn.
7221	Pte. SHINEBAUM, H., 4th Res. Bn.
41234	Pte. SHEX, I., 2nd Bn.
98782	Pte. SHORE, H.
17259	L/Cpl. SHENOW, W.,* 5th Bn.
9662	Pte. SILVERMAN, S.,* 1st Bn.
13454	Pte. SOLOMON, H. M., 8th Bn.
15223	Pte. STRAWBAUM, L., 5th Bn.
25268	Pte. TAYLOR, M., 6th Bn.
41381	Pte. TAUFFS, J., 5th Bn.
46117	L/Cpl. WARSHAWSKY, 13th Bn.
39032	Pte. WERNICK, H., 5th Bn.
44155	Pte. WILDES, H., 2/4th Bn.
1884	Pte. WOOD, M., 6th Bn.
1883	Pte. WOOD, J., 6th Bn.

* Killed in Action or died on Active Service.

THE QUEEN'S OWN (ROYAL WEST KENT REGIMENT).

OFFICERS.

Major COHEN, A. M., 1/4th Bn.
Major COHEN, SIR H. B. (O.B.E.), 1/4th Bn.
2nd Lieut. HARRIS, B. B., 4th Bn.
2nd Lieut. ISAACS, H. B., 3rd Bn.
2nd Lieut. LEWINSTEIN, H.,* 1st Bn.
Lieut. LEWIS-BARNED, DE S. H. (M.C.), 1st Bn.
2nd Lieut. RODNEY, W. B.,* 11th Bn.
Lieut. SAMUEL, G. G.,* 10th Bn.
Lieut. STIEBEL, A., 6th Bn.
Lieut. STERN, D. C., 5th Bn.
2nd Lieut. SOLOMONS, L. P., 4th Bn.
2nd Lieut. WALEY, R. P. S.

N.C.O.'s AND MEN.

20201	Pte. AARONS, M., 1st Bn.
G/26851	Sgt. ABRAHAMS, J., 15th Bn.
20053	Pte. BLACKSTON, H., 7th Bn.
G/30532	Pte. BARNETT, S., 7th Bn.
G/6832	Pte. BENSON, H., 3rd Bn.
18960	Pte. BERNARD, G. H., 10th Bn.
267128	Pte. BERNSTEIN, C., 2/1st Bn.
203455	Pte. BARNETT, E., 2/4th Bn.
	Pte. BROWN, H. C., 8th Bn.
	Pte. BUCKWELL, P., 8th Bn.
	Pte. BUCKWELL, J., 8th Bn.
G/6992	Pte. COHEN, A., 10th Bn.
G/9280	Ptt. COHEN, H., 10th Bn.
203993	Pte. CHARIG, H. M., 3/4th Bn.
G/18784	Pte. COHEN, A., 11th Bn.
13407	Pte. CLARKE, C., 6th Bn.
267289	Pte. COLEMAN, A. M.
684531	Pte. COHEN, M., 8th Bn.
24939	Pte. CAPLAN, W., 2nd Bn.
10010	Pte. COHEN, D., 9th Bn.
24945	Pte. COHEN, R.
26773	Pte. CONRADE, E. L., 1st Bn.
28597	Pte. COHEN, M.,* 2nd Bn.
7669	Pte. DAVIDS, B., 1st Bn.
102319	Pte. DURAM, 1/4th Bn.
7453	Pte. DANN, R., 8th Bn.

Royal West Kent Regt.—*Continued.*

203432 Pte. Davis, G., 2/4th Bn.
26706 Pte. Defries, A.
      Pte. Ditkofsky.
24962 Pte. Emanuel, 2nd Bn.
9950 Pte. Ellis, A. R.
6047 Pte. Fenburn, A., 8th Bn.
9120 Pte. Feldham, H., 3rd Bn.
202755 Pte. Filar, H.,* 10th Bn.
G/13667 Pte. Frankel, J., 1st Bn.
203211 Pte. Friedenberg, H., 6th Bn.
202356 Pte. Fine, A., 2/4th Bn.
12798 Pte. Frankel, I.
16303 Pte. Goldman, M., 8th Bn.
266326 Pte. Goldstein, M., 1st Bn.
9200 Pte. Green, J., 3rd Bn.
25111 Pte. Goldberg, S. (M.M.), 7th Bn.
44641 Pte. Goldstone, H., 16th Bn.
G/6801 Pte. Hart, H. L., 10th Bn.
27375 Pte. Hyams, J., 3/4th Bn.
25783 Pte. Hyams, 2nd Bn.
40155 Pte. Harris, H., 15th Bn.
G/12943 Pte. Harris, J., 1st Bn.
G/13805 Pte. Hayes, M., 1st Bn.
G/30089 Pte. Hyams, H., 3rd Bn.
3557 Pte. Halle, L., 3/5th Bn.
204707 Pte. Hyman, J., 3/4th Bn.
24995 Pte. Isaacs, A.
      Pte. Isaacs, J., 2/5th Bn.
242192 Pte. Jacobs, D., 10th Bn.
6270 Pte. Jacobs, A.
23260 Pte. Jacobs, M.,* 7th Bn.
20103 Pte. Jacobs, A. L.,* 1st Bn.
24623 Pte. Joseph, R., 4th Bn.
G/14221 Pte. Josephs, H., 1st Bn.
G/11184 Pte. Jones, M., 1st Bn.
4910 Pte. Jacob, B., 3/4th Bn.
      Pte. Krersy, J., 2/5th Bn.
7200 Pte. King, F.
      Pte. Kusby, A., 8th Bn.
11536 Pte. Levy, M. H., 8th Bn.
20524 Pte. Lawton, H., 6th Bn.
203032 Pte. Littlestone, B., 3/4th Bn.
203031 Pte. Littlestone, S., 3/4th Bn.
21163 Pte. Lederbaum, J., 11th Bn.
20312 Pte. Loskey, M., 10th Bn.
54231 Pte. Lazarus, B., 8th Bn.
G/10492 Pte. Lyons, J., 3rd Bn.
25803 Pte. Lederman, 2nd Bn.
26976 Pte. Levy, S.
15269 Pte. Lyons, M., 3rd Bn.
2505 Pte. Lehmann, H.
9303 Pte. Lee, H. V., 2nd Bn.
30071 Pte. Levy, J., 6th Bn.
18210 Pte. Marks, A., 7th Bn.
9063 Cpl. Morris, S., 3rd Bn.
10495 Pte. Marks, A., 3rd Bn.
25029 Pte. Mordecai, B., 2nd Bn.

G/13687 L/Cpl. Mendoza, E., 1st Bn.
242046 Pte. Moodnick, B., 7th Bn.
70373 Pte. Minski, H., 1st Bn.
558 Pte. Marks, M., 3/4th Bn.
31357 Pte. Natelski, A., 1st Bn.
28212 L/Cpl. Orlofsky, 2nd Bn.
7935 Pte. Ottalangui, 1/4th Bn.
17658 Pte. Pints, 1/4th Bn.
16776 Pte. Podcarney, W., 3rd Bn.
204464 L/Cpl. Rosenberg, J., 3/4th Bn.
G/19758 Pte. Rosenfelt, A., 10th Bn.
11484 Pte. Rosenberg, S., 3rd Bn.
      Pte. Rose, H., 5th Bn.
11444 Pte. Rednick, 2/4th Bn.
203138 Pte. Sandler, H., 7th Bn.
13364 Pte. Somers, B., 6th Bn.
204389 Pte. Shilco, E.,* 7th Bn.
202279 Pte. Stern, B., 3/4th Bn.
G/6821 L/Cpl. Scharff, V., 3rd Bn.
25808 L/Cpl. Stecklyn, 2nd Bn.
27133 L/Cpl. Sklanowitz, 1/5th Bn.
241072 Pte. Scoble, H., 1/5th Bn.
G/13707 Pte. Solomons, M., 1st Bn.
31224 Pte. Schuleberg, H.,* 1st Bn.
3760 Pte. Smith, S., 3/5th Bn.
3791 Pte. Smith, W.
4403 Pte. Seninsky, J., 5th Bn.
      L/Cpl. Shonick, W., 7th Bn.
6047 Pte. Tenbourne, A., 8th Bn.
20164 A/Sgt. Valentine, P., 1st Bn.
3068 Pte. Wolfers, J., 8th Bn.
17445 Pte. Williams, H., 1st Bn.
202377 Pte. Weiner, L., 6th Bn.
30559 Pte. Weintrop, S., 8th Bn.
17996 Pte. Wagner, 1/4th Bn.
G/31068 Pte. Woolfe, H., 3rd Bn.
30831 Pte. Wein, M.,* 1st Bn.
240927 Cpl. Wolfe, H., 4th Res. Bn.
4993 Pte. Weinbaum, J., 2/5th Bn.
4432 Pte. Winestone, E., 2/5th Bn.

* Killed in Action or died on Active Service.

THE KING'S OWN (YORKSHIRE LIGHT INFANTRY).

OFFICERS.

Capt. and Adj. Beddington, J., 7th Bn.
Capt. Franklin, E. A., 10th Bn.
Capt. Goldman, S., Hqrs. 70th Bde.
2nd Lieut. Goldman, A. C., 3rd Bn.
Lieut. Gosschalk, E. M.,* 2nd Bn.
2nd Lieut. Gaster, V., 2nd Bn.
Lieut. Goldblatt, 38th Bde.
2nd Lieut. Holford, R. F. 9th Bn.
2nd Lieut. Lobel, F., 12th Bn.

Yorkshire Light Infantry.—*Continued.*
Major MICHOLLS, W. M., 6th Bn.
2nd Lieut. PHILLIPS, J. P., 2/4th Bn.
Major RICHARDSON, A. N., 9th Bn.
2nd Lieut. SLOWE, A.,* 6th Bn.
Lieut. TELFER, H. A.,* 9th Bn.
Lieut. TELFER, C. W.,* 1st Bn.
2nd Lieut. WOLFF, M. A.

N.C.O.'s AND MEN.

28787 Pte. ARONWITCH, S., 2nd Bn.
204477 Pte. ABRAHAMS, M., 12th Bn.
39816 Pte. ALEXANDER, B., 12th Bn.
234449 Pte. ABRAHAMS, A. R., 2/4th Bn.
36817 Pte. ASH, S. D., 1/5th Bn.
63733 Pte. ABRAMS, H., 9th Bn.
99515 Pte. BENSON, J.
22946 Pte. BLACKSTONE, M., 2nd Bn.
6507 Pte. BLASHKEY, A., 1/4th Bn.
32783 Pte. BERNSTONE, D., 2nd Gar. Bn.
93235 Pte. BERGSON, I., 52nd Bn.
24812 Pte. BLASKY, 1st Bn.
42925 L/Cpl. BRILLIANT, H., 1st Bn.
2027 Sgt. COYNE, S., 9th Bn.
36640 Pte. CRAMMER, S., 9th Bn.
27036 Pte. COHEN, H., 8th Bn.
235330 Pte. COHEN, J., 1/4th Bn.,
86996 Cpl. COUPLAN, A.
34349 Pte. COHEN, L., 8th Bn.
235456 Pte. COHEN, L.
64955 Pte. COHEN, M., 9th Bn.
25509 Pte. DAVIS, J., 8th Bn.
93125 Pte. DAVIS, I., 52nd Bn.
240774 Pte. DAVIES, A.
46464 Pte. DAVISON, L. H.
64430 L/Cpl. ESTERMAN, 15th Bn.
235130 Pte. FREEDMAN, J., 9th Bn.
28845 L/Cpl. FISHER, J., 2nd Bn.
235130 Pte. FREEDMAN, J.,* 9th Bn.
235282 Pte. FINKLESTEIN, E., 2nd Bn.
Pte. FREEMAN, A.
69505 Pte. GARBER, H.
32422 Pte. GALINSKY, Z., 16th Bn.
241339 Pte. GRAHAM, B., 14th Bn.
26421 Pte. GOLDMAN, D., 1st Bn.
Pte. GOLDSTEIN, S.
23539 Pte. GOODMAN, S.,* 2nd Bn.
33465 Pte. GORDON, A., 2/4th Bn.
34104 Pte. GOLDSTEIN, A., 7th Bn.
27248 Pte. GERSHMAN, R.,* 5th Bn.
2116 Cpl. HOFFMAN, H., 6th Bn.
28611 Pte. HARRISON, H., 2nd Gar. Bn.
396352 Pte. HIRSCOVITZ, 15th Bn.
Pte. HOFFMAN, M., 3rd Bn.
240560 Pte. HARRIS, A., 6th Bn.
24544 Pte. HARRIS, D., 3rd Bn.
L/Cpl. HIRSCH, A., 5th Bn.
58308 Pte. HOFFMAN, A., 15th Bn.

44963 Pte. IROPSKY, M., 16th Bn.
39082 Pte. JACOBS, H. C.
C.S.M. JACOBS, E. (M.C.).
86963 Pte. JACOBS, W., 52nd Bn.
40596 Pte. JAFFE, I.,* 9th Bn.
62314 Pte. JALOSKY, S., 2nd Bn.
49804 Pte. KATZ, I.
235310 Pte. KARNOVITZ, J., 52nd Bn.
204429 Pte. KRAMER, J., 9th Bn.
83320 Pte. KIRSCHNER, S., 51st Bn.
9324 L/Cpl. LENSKY, T., 1st Bn.
32405 C.Q.M.S. LEWIS, S., 2nd Bn.
36667 Pte. LIGHTSTONE, L., 10th Bn.
7583 Pte. LAZARUS, J., 1/4th Bn.
38717 Pte. LABOFSKY, 9th Bn.
9324 Pte. LASKY, P., 1st Bn.
48863 Pte. LEVY, J., 2nd Bn.
64011 Pte. LEWIS, M.
263184 Pte. LURIE, A.
5619 L/Cpl. MYERSON, D. S., 4th Bn.
42069 Pte. MALL, J., 10th Bn.
58347 Pte. MALLACH, M., 16th Bn.
24735 Pte. MARKS, H., 3rd Bn.
34987 Pte. MYERS, J., 2/4th Bn.
45305 Pte. NARITSKY, M., 14th Bn.
35848 Pte. NEEDLER, M., 8th Bn.
93604 Pte. NISENBAUM, H.
43512 Pte. NIMAN, A., 9th Bn.
34178 Pte. OSOSKI, H., 8th Bn.
260009 Pte. PEARLMAN, J. B., 5th Bn.
44976 Pte. PHILLIPS, A., 14th Bn.
203932 Pte. PELTENSON, J.
11064 Pte. POGRUND, S., 2nd Bn.
35612 Pte. PLOTTEL, F., 10th Bn.
Pte. ROSENBERG, S., 1st Bn.
6204 Pte. RABINOVITCH, M., 1/4th Bn.
29652 Pte. ROSE, N., 11th Bn.
1626 Pte. ROSEN, G., 12th Bn.
44941 Pte. ROSENBERG, L., 14th Bn.
45073 Pte. ROSENBERG, W., 14th Bn.
12194 L/Cpl. ROSENBERG, A., 15th Bn.
220135 Pte. ROSENBERG, B., 51st Bn.
37761 Cpl. ROSENBERG, H.,* 10th Bn.
58338 Pte. ROSENTHAL, E., 15th Bn.
11878 Pte. SHAW, L., 7th Bn.
36639 Pte. SILVERMAN, S., 9th Bn.
45411 Pte. SILVERMAN, T., 9th Bn.
43052 Pte. SAGER, J., 10th Bn.
35666 Pte. SAMUEL, A.,* 10th Bn.
403817 Pte. SHATZ, H., 2/4th Bn.
34947 Pte. SOLOMONS, L., 8th Bn.
12721 Pte. STRASSBERG, G. L.,* 1st Bn.
41427 Pte. SINGER, L., 6th Bn.
28862 Pte. SILVER, J., 2nd Bn.
205448 Sig. STRASSBERG, H., 2nd Bn.
24709 Pte. STEINBERG, N. (M.M.), 2/4th Bn.
40370 Pte. SOLOMON, S., 7th Bn.
62437 Pte. SAUNDERS, P., 1/4th Bn.

Yorkshire Light Infantry.—Continued.

64430 Pte. STANGER, J., 15th Bn.
74759 Pte. STIBBS, J., 15th Bn.
30602 Pte. SUMMERS, J., 2nd Bn.
       Pte. SOMMERPLAAG, M., 2nd Bn.
5967 Pte. SCHWEITZER, A. S., 4th Bn.
80470 Pte. SELTZER, P., 51st Bn.
85958 Pte. SORKIN, J., 52nd Bn.
205276 Pte. SHOVSKI, P., 4th Bn.
38602 Pte. SUMMERS, J., 2nd Bn.
40387 Pte. SCHABY, H., 3rd Bn.
51856 Pte. STONE, A., 2/4th Bn.
25893 Pte. SERELLA, J., 9th Bn.
83017 Pte. SILVER, P.
92058 Pte. SULTAN, A.
92234 Pte. STONE, A.
65028 Pte. SPURLING, 2/4th Bn.
9795 Pte. TAYLOR, J., 1st Bn.
202989 Pte. TAYLOR, G., 2/5th Bn.
36683 Pte. TREISMAN, C. H. J., 10th Bn.
20358 Pte. TAVROGIS, I., 51st Bn.
6542 Pte. TAYLOR, J., 4th Bn.
28814 L/Cpl. VERTES, I., 2nd Bn.
42509 Pte. VOGEL, E.,* 2nd Bn.
41015 Pte. WAGGONHEIM, J., 14th Bn.
40108 Pte. VENDENBANN, S., 14th Bn.
12014 Cpl. WATSSMAN, A., 7th Bn.
47607 Pte. WEISBERG, F. A., 2/4th Bn.
40369 Pte. WEINBERG, S.
       Pte. WILLIAMS, J., 2nd Bn.
43564 Pte. WOOLF, J.,* 9th Bn.
45305 Pte. ZARIBSKY, M., 14th Bn.

* Killed in Action or died on Active Service.

THE KING'S (SHROPSHIRE LIGHT INFANTRY).

OFFICERS.

2nd Lieut. DAVIS, W. L., 3rd Bn.
Lieut. SPIERS, A. L. C.,* 7th Bn.

N.C.O.'s AND MEN.

237873 Pte. ARBIS, 4th Bn.
275084 Pte. ABRAHAMS, L., 1st Bn.
4963 Pte. BERNSTEIN, A., 1/4th Bn.
       Pte. BEITCH,
2963 Pte. BIRCH, P., 4th Bn.
45377 Pte. BROWN, F., 4th Bn.
5014 Pte. CAMBERG, L., 2/4th Bn.
4835 Pte. COTTON, I., 2/4th Bn.
202344 Pte. CLAFF, R., 2/4th Bn.
6906 Pte. COHEN, S., 7th Bn.
4831 Pte. COPELAND, C.
45376 Pte. CROSS, J., 4th Bn.
24408 Pte. DAVIS, L., 7th Bn.

143765 Pte. DE HAAS, H., 4th Bn.
237975 Pte. ERFERMAN, E., 1st Bn.
40011 Pte. FREEDMAN, E., 9th Bn.
43314 L/Cpl. FURFANSAFSKY, M. T., 9th Bn.
38492 Pte. FELL, J.,* 1st Bn.
201952 Pte. FRIEZE, S., 5th Bn.
238194 Pte. FRIEDEL, L., 5th Bn.
5288 Pte. FINN, H., 1/5th Bn.
23095 Pte. FINEBERG, I., 9th Bn.
5040 Pte. FINKLESTEIN, A.
4728 Pte. FRIEND, J., 2/4th Bn.
22518 Pte. GARBUTT, J., 9th Bn.
202301 Pte. GOLDBERG, G., 2/4th Bn.
201662 Pte. GROSSMAN, J., 2/4th Bn.
201486 Pte. GOODFIELD, S., 2/4th Bn.
5046 Pte. GLASBURG, R., 2/4th Bn.
33997 Pte. GITTLESOHN, A.
49278 Pte. GOLDSTEON, M., 2/4th Bn.
38449 Pte. HARRIS, J., 1st Bn.
       Pte. HARRISON.
45506 Pte. HYMAN, M., 4th Bn.
28413 Pte. ISAAC, 7th Bn.
24439 Pte. ISAACS, J., 2nd Bn.
225387 L/Cpl. JACOBS, 1st Bn.
1353 Pte. JACOBS, C., 3rd Bn.
25383 Pte. KAYOFSKI, S.
10420 Cpl. KETTLE, H. (D.C.M.), 7th Bn.
23563 Pte. KIMM, J., 7th Bn.
5077 Pte. KAY, H., 2/4th Bn.
4744 Pte. KERBELL, S., 2/4th Bn.
237994 Pte. KING, H., 3rd Bn.
34532 Pte. KEMP, L., 3rd Bn.
27211 Pte. LITTLESTONE, J., 4th Bn.
26256 Pte. LEVY, B.,* 7th Bn.
22550 Pte. LEVI, J.
5081 Pte. LEVY, B., 2/4th Bn.
       Pte. LEVI, J., 9th Bn.
43578 Pte. LEVY, H., 7th Bn.
201662 Pte. LICHSTEIN, N., 2/4th Bn.
25815 Pte. LINDO, R., 2nd Bn.
204435 Pte. LEVENE, H., 4th Bn.
45509 Pte. LEVY, A., 4th Bn.
       Pte. MENDLESON, 4th Bn.
4914 Pte. MARCS, M., 2/4th Bn.
62232 Pte. MUSCOHITZ, S., 3rd Bn.
45429 Pte. MORRIS, J., 4th Bn.
46059 Pte. MARKS, E., 2nd Bn.
45873 Pte. MALINA, J.
35305 Pte. MORRIS, J.,* 7th Bn.
201669 Pte. NATHAN, L., 2/4th Bn.
       Pte. NOBLE, H.
2433 Pte. PRAG, A. J., 4th Bn.
22553 Pte. PAYMAN, L.
22918 Pte. POLAK, P., 6th Bn.
202633 Pte. POLIKOFF, 2/4th Bn.
33371 Pte. PODGUR, H., 3rd Bn.
6137 Pte. PEARLMAN, H. E., 2/4th Bn.
45375 Pte. PEARL, M., 4th Bn.

Shropshire Light Infantry.—*Continued.*

32926	Pte. ROBINSON, J., 4th Bn.
5114	Pte. RUSHNOCK, M.
200781	Pte. RAG, A.
26892	Cpl. SOLKOW, A. P.,* 6th Bn.
230573	Pte. SPIERS, A., 10th Bn.
275084	Pte. SHIENBERG, 1st Bn.
34932	Pte. SIPPERT, M., 3rd Bn.
45508	Pte. SAUNDERS, A., 4th Bn.
4963	Pte. SILCOVITCH, B. H., 2/4th Bn.
5123	Pte. SKEIN, I., 2/4th Bn.
	Pte. STARGETT, M., 2nd Bn.
22577	Pte. TEITLEBAUM, M.
201698	Pte. WILKS, B., 7th Bn.
4982	Pte. WINEBERG, H.
22516	Pte. YOUNGERMAN, H., 9th Bn.

* Killed in Action or died on Active Service.

THE DUKE OF CAMBRIDGE'S OWN (MIDDLESEX REGIMENT).

OFFICERS.

Lieut. BAER, A. M., 18th Bn.
2nd Lieut. BAMBERGER, H. T. (M.C.), 5th Bn.
2nd Lieut. BARNETT, A. E., 14th Bn.
2nd Lieut. BARNETT, P.,* 4th Bn.
2nd Lieut. DAVIS S., 1/8th Bn.
Lieut. DE PASS, W. H.,* 13th Bn.
Lieut. DAVIS, E. M., 2nd Bn.
Capt. DAVIDSON, I.
Lieut. DE PASS, D. R., 2/10th Bn.
2nd Lieut. GOLDBERG, P., 21st Bn.
Capt. GREENWOOD, H. I., 8th Bn.
Capt. GUTTMAN, W. M. (M.C.), 10th Bn.
2nd Lieut. GASTER, P. A., 2nd Bn.
Lieut. GROSS, L., 15th Bn.
2nd Lieut. GOLDBERG, P. G., 9th Bn.
Lieut. GAFFMAN, W., 4/10th Bn. attd 2nd R. B.
Lieut. GREENWOOD, I. H.,* 8th Bn.
Major HARRIS, H. J., 26th Bn.
Lieut. HARRIS, M. (M.C.).
Lieut. HARVEY-SAMUEL, G., 3/10th Bn.
2nd Lieut. HENRY, A. R.,* 1st Bn.
2nd Lieut. HENRY, J. L.,
Lieut. ISAACS, A.,
2nd Lieut. KLEAN, R. M. A.
Lieut. KEYSER, H. A.
Capt. and Adjt. LEVY, R. P. (M.C.), 1/8th Bn.
Lieut. MOSS, H. A.,* 7th Bn.
2nd Lieut. MARCUS, D. S.
Lieut. MARKS, P. M.,* 4th Bn.
2nd Lieut. MORYJOSEPH, E. C., 4th Bn.
2nd Lieut. PAIBA, R. I., 15th Bn.
Lieut. ROSENTHAL, J., 18th Bn.
2nd Lieut. ROSENFIELD, E., 19th Bn.
Lieut.-Col. SAMUEL, W. H., 11th Bn.
2nd Lieut. SAMUEL, E. B.,* 16th Bn.
Capt. SHRAGER, E. (M.C.), 2nd Bn.
Capt. SOLOMON, D. C., 19th Bn.
2nd Lieut. SOLOMONS, H., 16th Bn.
Capt. SAMUEL, E. D. (M.C.).
2nd Lieut. SINCLAIR, R. G., 15th Bn.
2nd Lieut. STONE, L., 6th Bn.
Lieut. TABBUSH, C. W., 21st Bn.
Lieut. WALEY, A. J., 12th Bn.
Lieut. WOLFFE, J., 18th Bn.
2nd Lieut. WOLFFE, B., 14th Bn.

N.C.O.'s AND MEN.

18531	Pte. ALEXANDER, D.,* 16th Bn.
52681	Pte. ARNOLD, E., 18th Bn.
315997	Pte. ASHER, A., 16th Bn.
62071	Pte. ADLEMAN, M., 20th Bn.
62058	Pte. APPLEBOAM, S., 20th Bn.
80356	Pte. AUERBACH, M., 11th Bn.
84186	Pte. ABRAHAMS, H.
266322	Pte. ABRAHAMS, 9th Bn.
84108	L/Cpl. ANSELL, P.
169631	L/Cpl. ALMBAUM, S., 2nd Bn.
25541	Pte. ANSELL, I., 15th Bn.
35496	Pte. ANTIVE, M.
G/33463	Pte. ALBERGE, J., 5th Bn.
17388	Rfm. ABRAHAMS, S., 15th Bn.
26851	Pte. ALLEN, J., 15th Bn.
G/32692	Pte. ALSCHWANG, L., 6th Bn.
G/32649	Pte. ASCHENFARB, M., 6th Bn.
80266	Pte. ADLER, D., 6th Bn.
175088	Pte. ALLEN, D., 2/10th Bn.
61316	Pte. ALEXANDER, A.,* 4th Bn.
103937	Pte. ABRAHAMS, S. B., 52nd Bn.
168234	Pte. ABRAHAMS, D., 53rd Bn.
128763	Pte. ABRAHAMS, B., 53rd Bn.
7236	Pte. AARONS, J., 3/8th Bn.
6904	Pte. ACKER, M., 3/10th Bn.
5348	Pte. AARONSON, M., 2/9th Bn.
7682	Pte. ANDERSON, C., 3/8th Bn.
288271	Pte. AUTINE, M., 22nd Bn.
168234	Pte. ABRAHAMSON, D.
11703	Pte. ABRAHAMS, I., 6th Bn.
30978	Pte. ACHERET, A. J.
24587	Pte. ADLER, M. H.
4952	Pte. ARNOLD, B., 2/7th Bn.
393358	Pte. ALTERMAN, J.
	Pte. ANDERSON, C., 3/8th Bn.
2458	Pte. ADLER, M. A., 7th Bn.
	Pte. ANGEL, E., 10th Bn.
89014	Pte. APPLEBAUM, J., 5th Bn.
4712	Pte. BLITZ, P., 13th Bn.
14270	Pte. BRIDGER, H., 20th Bn.
18718	Pte. BROWN, A., 20th Bn.

Middlesex Regt.—*Continued.*

14957	Pte. BARRS, W., 20th Bn.	
19870	Pte. BLOOM, S.,* 21st Bn.	
15645	L/Cpl. BIRD, J. M., 21st Bn.	
3077	Pte. BENNY, H. B., 1/7th Bn.	
F/2324	Pte. BLACK, W., 23rd Bn.	
20736	Pte. BENJAMIN, H., 13th Bn.	
11310	Pte. BLOOM, H., 13th Bn.	
6762	Pte. BASH, A., 8th Bn.	
G/52703	Pte. BUITEKANT, M., 3/10th Bn.	
62129	Pte. BURMAN, G., 20th Bn.	
6236	Pte. BARNETT, L.,* 4th Bn.	
36826	Pte. BARON, J., 16th Bn.	
	Pte. BENSON, C., 1st Bn.	
G/17597	Pte. BENJAMIN, A., 6th Bn.	
241886	L/Cpl. BASH, A., 4th Bn.	
28854	Pte. BLOOMFIELD, H. N., 13th Bn.	
31189	Pte. BARD, L., 2nd Bn.	
60005	Pte. BROWN, 9th Bn.	
7008	Pte. BARNETT, M., 1st Bn.	
38231	Pte. BARNETT, A., 1st Bn.	
70057	Pte. BARNETT, S., 1st Bn.	
38994	Pte. BARNETT, N., 1st Bn.	
G/51771	Pte. BLOOMSTEIN, 1/9th Bn.	
35044	Pte. BENSUSAN, D.	
G/36826	Pte. BARON, J., 5th Bn.	
80429	Pte. BROWN, H., 6th Bn.	
74376	Pte. BERNSTEIN, J., 4th Bn.	
266968	Pte. BARNETT, W., 1/9th Bn.	
90837	Pte. BRATT, H., 29th Bn.	
	Pte. BECKER, N.	
	Pte. BROTMAN, H.	
13547	Cpl. BECKERWICK, M.,* 4th Bn.	
2428	Cpl. BEARMAN, C., 16th Bn.	
30920	Pte. BASS, J., 29th Bn.	
48829	Pte. BENJAMIN, J., 3rd Bn.	
50379	Pte. BESSER, B. M., 3rd Bn.	
316009	Pte. BRICKMAN, I., 32nd Bn.	
80062	Pte. BRICKLES, L., 4th Bn.	
242545	Pte. BOAM, M., 2/8th Bn.	
20799	Pte. BROOD, N., 29th Bn.	
80163	Pte. BERLIN, J., 4th Bn.	
84076	Pte. BILFORD, S., 4th Bn.	
74442	Pte. BOXER, B., 4th Bn.	
128606	Pte. BROWN, F., 53rd Bn.	
129055	Pte. BELSON, D., 20th Bn.	
80262	Pte. BRANDSTATER, 4th Bn.	
80188	Pte. BLAUSTEIN, A., 4th Bn.	
83003	Pte. BIRNBAUM, N., 4th Bn.	
11310	Pte. BLOOM, H., 12th Bn.	
74351	Pte. BERGMAN, P., 2/6th Bn.	
74678	Pte. BILANTZ, D., 4th Bn.	
35481	Pte. BENNS, A., 1st Bn.	
4957	Pte. BARR, W., 20th Bn.	
24090	Pte. BERGMAN, H., 28th Bn.	
2800	L/Cpl. BENZIMRA, H. V., 9th Bn.	
1673	Pte. BERNSTEIN, L., 23rd Bn.	
37730	Pte. BETH, J., 29th Bn.	
54459	Pte. BAUMGART, M., 53rd Bn.	
129055	Pte. BELSON, D., 53rd Bn.	
74261	Pte. BUCKLER, 20th Bn.	
24358	Pte. BOSTOCK, A., 20th Bn.	
27194	Pte. BUTLER, E., 28th Bn.	
93782	Pte. BROWN, J. M.	
	Pte. BENJAMIN, B., 13th Bn.	
	Pte. BUSH, W., 17th Bn.	
	Pte. BRILL, H., 11th Bn.	
	Pte. BLOOMBERG, H.	
	Pte. BARNETT, B. N., 4/8th Bn.	
	Pte. BOWMAN, H.	
	Pte. BOWMAN, S., 11th Bn.	
	L/Cpl. BEARMAN, C.	
482	Pte. COLMANS, L.,* 23rd Bn.	
9183	Pte. CONRADI, E., 13th Bn.	
G/11811	Pte. COHEN, W. G., 19th Bn.	
14654	Cpl. CRUSKALL, H., 20th Bn.	
24317	Pte. COHEN, S., 20th Bn.	
24351	Pte. COHEN, G., 20th Bn.	
24038	Pte. CAMINER, A.,* 2nd Bn.	
242414	Pte. COHEN, I.,* 1st Bn.	
293199	Pte. COOR, P.,* 3/10 Bn.	
12306	Pte. COHEN, J., 17th Bn.	
14208	Pte. CLARKE, H. V., 20th Bn.	
33459	Pte. COCLAN, J., 4th Bn.	
19908	Pte. COOPER, D., 21st Bn.	
57395	Pte. COHEN, W., 2nd Bn.	
54327	Pte CHINKIN, S., 2nd Bn.	
118494	L/Cpl. COHEN, E., 4th Bn.	
884	Pte. COHEN, I., 11th Bn.	
14870	L/Cpl. COHEN, G., 6th Bn.	
32598	Pte. CANTOR, H., 16th Bn.	
57395	Pte. COHEN, M., 2nd Bn.	
35495	Pte. COHEN, S., 1st Bn.	
26840	Pte. COHEN, J., 15th Bn.	
12215	Pte. CLARKE, T., 1st Bn.	
12225	Pte. COWAN, S., 1st Bn.	
	Pte. CORINALDI, L. O.	
171790	Pte. COHEN, S.	
316278	Pte. COHEN, W.,* 20th Bn.	
14851	Pte. DA COSTA, L.,* 2nd Bn.	
16787	Pte. CAIRNS, J., 22nd Bn.	
24232	Pte. CASSOFF, L., 28th Bn.	
2934	Pte. CHISSICK, L. D., 2nd Bn.	
	Sgt. COHEN, M. (M.M.)	
80191	Pte. COHEN, J. L.	
45514	Pte. CLAYTON, L., 29th Bn.	
181014	Pte. COHEN, A. (M.M.), 29th Bn.	
50683	Pte. COHEN, J., 52nd Bn.	
16390	Sig. COBELSKY, 10th Bn.	
50813	Pte. COHEN, M., 52nd Bn.	
80038	Pte. COMOR, W.	

Middlesex Regt.—*Continued.*

37341	Pte. Corby, D., 1st Bn.
87097	Pte. Cohen, J. A., 5th Bn.
1151	Pte. Cohen, H., 19th Bn.
11806	Pte. Coleman, R.
2428	Pte. Cook, A., 23rd Bn.
93196	Pte. Cohn, H., 5th Bn.
14208	Sgt. Clarke, H. V., 20th Bn.
83439	Pte. Callam, J., 4th Bn.
G/14228	Pte. Dorer, H.,* 20th Bn.
18701	Pte. Davis, D., 20th Bn.
15198	L/Sgt. Daniels, J., 21st Bn.
15446	L/Cpl. Davis, J. J., 21st Bn.
G/24571	Pte. Davis, H., 13th Bn.
51056	Pte. Drapkin, C., 16th Bn.
31061	Pte. De Haan, E., 11th Bn.
12683	Pte. Diamondstone, J.,* 23rd Bn.
60953	Pte. Drielson, V., 19th Bn.
201831	Pte. Davies. M. D., 1/8th Bn.
18516	Pte. Deutch, B., 20th Bn.
	Pte. Drapkin, H., 2nd Bn.
11324	Pte Davis. S., 1st Bn.
265778	Sgt. Dainow, M., 1/9th Bn.
22080	Pte. Diamondstein, H., 14th Bn.
G/25398	Cpl. Davis, J., 5th Bn.
G/331404	Pte. Duynkerk, S., 6th Bn.
59444	Pte. Dailes, B., 5th Bn.
14208	Pte. Davies, J., 5th Bn.
94335	Pte. Dresner, M.
2081	Pte. Davis, H., 9th Bn.
G/104416	L/Cpl. Defries, J., 19th Bn.
91008	Pte. Davies, J., 29th Bn.
52238	Pte. Davies, J., 53rd Bn.
171258	Pte. Donn, L., 53rd Bn.
	Sgt. Dubeno, V.
	Pte. Dyson, J., 2nd Bn.
	Pte. Drapin, A., 2nd Bn.
72049	Pte. Diamondstone, A., 3/10th Bn.
235226	Pte. Davies, P.
24318	Pte. Daniels, A., 28th Bn.
21947	Pte. Davies, P., 14th Bn.
2711	Pte. Davis, J., 23rd Bn.
1932	Pte. Denry, A., 27th Bn.
11325	Pte. Diamond, S., 6th Bn.
24108	Pte. Dixon, G., 28th Bn.
17665	Pte. Driver, D., 15th Bn.
15466	Cpl. Davis, J., 21st Bn.
301722	Pte. Dew, C., 27th Bn.
	L/Cpl. Drukker, H. S., 7th Bn.
	Pte. Demetz, S.
	Pte. Delafunte, J., 11th Bn.
	Sgt. Duke, W., 4th Bn.
10604	Pte. Davis, A.,* 4th Bn.
258	Pte. Ereira, G., 1st Bn.
3877	Pte. Emden, J., 1/8th Bn.
7646	Sgt. Evans, C., 3rd Bn.
204109	Pte. Emanuel, E. M., 16th Bn.
23698	Pte. Esterman, J., 14th Bn.
34829	Pte. Elboz, R., 14th Bn.
207815	Pte. Emden, J.,* 16th Bn.
5035	Pte. Emanuel, E. M., 3/9th Bn.
73281	Pte. Edelstein, D., 29th Bn.
15453	Pte. Ert, J., 21st Bn.
80314	Pte. Emanuel, V., 4th Bn.
	Pte. Elliston, A., 4th Bn.
	Pte. Eckstein,
89038	Pte. Evans, A., 8th Bn.
7957	Sgt. Fisher, W., 1st Bn.
6173	L/Cpl. Freshwater, F., 3rd Bn.
T/17044	Sgt. Fox, M., 23rd Bn.
C/2511	Pte. Fifer, S., 23rd Bn.
34651	Pte. Finstein, S., 11th Bn.
293208	Pte. Fingleson, H., 3/10th Bn.
242870	Pte. Fior, L., 23rd Bn.
50474	Pte. Feldman, J., 20th Bn.
74215	Pte. Fleisig, N.
266972	Pte. Fishbim, 9th Bn.
86007	Pte. Fishenbaum, 1/10th Bn.
92804	Pte. Finberg, S., 1/10th Bn.
24045	Pte. Freelander, A., 6th Bn.
58099	Pte. Freshwater, 8th Bn.
74303	Pte. Fifer, R., 1st Bn.
	Pte. Freedman, W., 1/9th Bn.
30357	L/Cpl. Finer, S., 29th Bn.
83862	Pte. Franklin, J., 29th Bn.
35541	Pte. Franks, D., 51st Bn.
5002	Pte. Falk, H.,* 2/7th Bn.
G/91050	Pte. Fynburgh, H., 29th Bn.
54358	Pte. Foreman, S., 29th Bn.
315547	Pte. Freeman, S. M., 32nd Bn.
80053	Pte. Flower, S., 3rd Bn.
	Pte. Fry, E., 4th Bn.
	Pte. Farbstein, L., 2/8th Bn.
680066	Pte. Frankel, J.
80262	Pte. Fribich, H., 4th Bn.
80449	Pte. Freudenberg, I., 3rd Bn.
51516	Pte. Freshwater, L.
80464	Pte. Freeman, A.
260996	Pte. Fisher, V.
36743	Pte. Flugleman, C., 10th Bn.
74034	Pte. Finegold, N., 3rd Bn.
71248	Pte. Fordansky, A., 5th Bn.
24332	Pte. Fishelbon, L., 28th Bn.
16082	Pte. Frankenstein, 22nd Bn.
24348	Pte. Freeman, H., 28th Bn.
243226	Pte. Freeman, S., 28th Bn.
26651	Pte. Fasieux, H., 5th Bn.
4712	Pte. Flatter, J., 1/10th Bn.
	Pte. Friedenberg, E. M., 9th Bn.
	Pte. Friedeberg, H. J., 9th Bn.
	Pte. Franks, M., 22nd Bn.
	Pte. Feuerman, S., 14th Bn.
	Pte. Flatter, I., 14th Bn.
6974	Pte. Goldstein, M.,* 2nd Bn.

Middlesex Regt.—*Continued.*

1789	Pte. GOLDSTEIN, H., 2nd Bn.
18661	L/Cpl. GREEN, I.,* 20th Bn.
14100	Pte. GOLDSMITH, D. A., 20th Bn.
13286	Pte. GRAHAM, H., 20th Bn.
14767	Pte. GANS, J.,* 20th Bn.
1970	Pte. GONSHAW, G., 16th Bn.
3867	Pte. GOLDBERG, D.,* 1/8th Bn.
21567	Sgt. GOODMAN, J. W. R., 23rd Bn.
1715	Pte. GLASS, J., 12th Bn.
G/60117	Pte. GOLDSTEIN, J., 18th Bn.
9634	Pte. GOLDBERG, H., 8th Bn.
14547	Pte. GRANDIS, W., 23rd Bn.
26299	Pte. GOLDBERG, D. M., 8th Bn.
62035	Pte. GLECK, J., 20th Bn.
27726	L/Cpl. GOLDMAN, H., 13th Bn.
C/54507	Pte. GOULD, J., 19th Bn.
5323	Cpl. GOLDSTEIN, I., 6th Bn.
3262	Pte. GOLDSTONE, J., 12th Bn.
84334	Pte. GERBER C.
G/5783	Pte. GOLDBERG, R., 1/9th Bn.
G/51669	Pte. GREENBERG, M., 1/9th Bn.
32741	Pte. GOODMAN, A., 1st Bn.
252858	Pte. GOLDMAN, L., 5th Bn.
38098	Pte. GARCIA, P., 20th Bn.
79952	Pte. GOLDSTEIN, J., 29th Bn.
92099	Pte. GELLMAN, A., 6th Bn.
74492	Pte. GOOTLIEB, M., 6th Bn.
84323	Pte. GOLDBURG, S., 6th Bn.
14548	L/Cpl. GOLDMAN, J.,* 17th Bn.
4380	Pte. GLUCKSTEIN, C. S.,* 10th Bn.
10269	Pte. GOLDBERG, P.,* 4th Bn.
58103	Pte. GOLDSTEIN, E.,* 1st Bn.
93797	Pte. GILBERT, B., 5th Bn.
27786	Pte. GIDALOVITCH, 3rd Bn.
129362	Pte. GAUSENFAST, M. S., 53rd Bn.
168017	Pte. GORDON, A., 53rd Bn.
30976	Pte. GELLMAN, G., 20th Bn.
	Pte. GOLDSMID, L., 1st Bn.
233933	Pte. GORDON, J., 29th Bn.
75257	Pte. GOLDMAN, A., 29th Bn.
75240	Pte. GORDON, J., 29th Bn.
58097	Pte. GOLDERSTEIN, H., 20th Bn.
355291	Pte. GROSMITH, D., 3/10th Bn.
80637	Pte. GOLDING, H., 29th Bn.
26269	Pte. GOLDSTEIN, A., 2/7th Bn.
80197	Pte. GREENWOOD, J. M., 4th Bn.
128415	Pte. GLUCK, H., 53rd Bn.
292064	Pte. GOLDSTEIN, H., 2/10th Bn.
128265	Pte. GOLDSTEIN, E.
92035	Pte. GOULD, T., 51st Bn.
245380	Pte. GILLINAY, H., 1/7th Bn.
84260	Pte. GOTTLIEB, S.
3181	Pte. GOLDENBERG, M.
7079	Pte. GOLDSTEIN, A., 2/7th Bn.
24400	Pte. GOLDMAN, I., 28th Bn.
129362	Pte. GANSENPART, M.
15960	Pte. GOLD, J., 14th Bn.
24327	Pte. GOLDBERG, R., 28th Bn.
27575	Pte. GOLDMAN, A., 15th Bn.
24297	Pte. GOLDSTEIN, J., 28th Bn.
5656	Pte. GOULD, M., 17th Bn.
24294	Pte. GOODMAN, H., 28th Bn.
24717	Pte. GORDON, J., 15th Bn.
24352	Pte. GORDON, J., 28th Bn.
24312	Pte. GRADIST, J., 28th Bn.
3288	Pte. GREENHOLTZ, J., 27th Bn.
27786	Pte. GROTALOVITCH, A., 3rd Bn.
353663	Pte. GOLDSECKER, L., 1/8th Bn.
58152	Cpl. GOLDFIELD, G., 6th Bn.
2057	Pte. GOFBERRY, H. H.,* 20th Bn.
208035	Pte. HEINAN, H. P., 6th Bn.
74028	Pte. HIRSCH, M., 5th Bn.
90839	Pte. HALL, C., 29th Bn.
88231	Pte. HARRIS, W., 29th Bn.
76580	Pte. HYMAN, M., 29th Bn.
10649	L/Cpl. HOROWITZ, S., 1st Bn.
1450	L/Cpl. HARRIS, J., 1st Bn.
1799	Pte. HARRIS, A. B.,* 11th Bn.
14620	Cpl. HEALEY, L., 20th Bn.
14590	Cpl. HILL, C., 20th Bn.
18634	Pte. HARRIS, A., 20th Bn.
18555	Pte. HYMAN, H., 20th Bn.
18708	Pte. HYMANS, D., 20th Bn.
24379	Pte. HARRIS, H., 20th Bn.
14628	Pte. HARRIS, J., 20th Bn.
14840	Pte. HARRIS, B., 20th Bn.
2785	Pte. HORNICK, M.,* 23rd Bn.
32289	Pte. HORWICH, I.,* 1st Bn.
40086	Pte. HECKER, H., 16th Bn.
42657	Pte. HONIGBAUM, L., 17th Bn.
242924	Pte. HARRISON, A., 8th Bn.
21691	Pte. HARTOG, H., 14th Bn.
9487	Pte. HAKWARD, E., 1st Bn.
10785	Pte. HILSUM, 5th Bn.
8768	Pte. HYMAN, 5th Bn.
21832	Pte. HAYES, M. M., 14th Bn.
35526	Pte. HARRIS, E., 14th Bn.
35499	Pte. HAUPT, A., 14th Bn.
35439	Pte. HUIS, J., 14th Bn.
12770	Pte. HARRIS, M., 6th Bn.
	Pte. HAYMAN, E., 1st Bn.
23794	Cpl. HALLETT, A. E., 51st Bn.
2135	Pte. HARRISON, J.,* 12th Bn.
40095	Pte. HECKER, J.,* 16th Bn.
12306	Pte. HARRIS, J., 53rd Bn.
90839	Pte. HALL, C., 29th Bn.
31799	Pte. HOFFBERG, J., 29th Bn.
	Pte. HARVEY, H., 3/10th Bn.
	Pte. HOLT, D.
	Pte. HERBOR, A., 7th Bn.
293167	Pte. HARVEY, H., 7th Bn.
40024	Pte. HARRIS, G.
71397	Pte. HERRMAN, L., 4th Bn.
80416	Pte. HOLT, N., 4th Bn.
262553	Pte. HEINBERG, D., 2/8th Bn.

Middlesex Regt.—*Continued.*

31158	Pte. HART, H.
15784	Pte. HILDERBRAND, J. C., 29th Bn.
177996	Pte. HARRIS, P. C.
77056	Pte. HYMAN, J., 29th Bn.
31779	Pte. HOFFBERG, J., 29th Bn.
4712	Pte. HATTER, J., 1/10th Bn.
28829	Pte. HARRIS, P., 5th Bn.
2472	Pte. HASSAN, I., 27th Bn.
84360	Pte. HARRIS, S., 6th Bn.
804177	Cpl. HART, L.
8322	Pte. ISAACS, A. A.,* 2nd Bn.
952	L/Cpl. ISAACS, H., 11th Bn.
4660	Pte. ISAACS, J., 13th Bn.
5876	Pte. ISAACS, L., 13th Bn.
952	Sig. ISAACS, D. S., 11th Bn.
4662	Pte. ISAACS, J., 13th Bn.
293263	Pte. ISAACS, A., 3/10th Bn.
24120	Pte. IRVING, H., 28th Bn.
19823	Pte. ISAACS, G., 14th Bn.
7100	Pte. ISAACS, A., 4th Bn.
17933	Pte. ISAACS, 9th Bn.
71497	Pte. INESTEIN, J.
35401	Pte. ISADORE, D., 51st Bn.
	Pte. ISAACS, A.,* 5th Bn.
7354	Pte. ISAACS, A.
292900	Pte. ISAACS, J., 7th Bn.
8741	Pte. JACOBS, A.,* 4th Bn.
10283	Pte. JACOBS, D.,* 4th Bn.
10283	Pte. JACOBS, O., 3rd Bn.
F/2319	Pte. JACOBS, L., 23rd Bn.
5146	Pte. JACOBS, S.,* 2nd Bn.
243103	Pte. JACOBS, R., 16th Bn.
52546	L/Cpl. JACOBSON, H.,* 11th Bn.
292907	Pte. JONES, E., 3/10th Bn.
5316	Cpl. JACOBS, G., 2nd Bn.
G/17433	Pte. JOSEPH, H., 6th Bn.
G/17688	Pte. JOEL, G., 6th Bn.
26865	Pte. JOEL, L. S., 15th Bn.
26864	Pte. JACOBS, P., 15th Bn.
	Pte. JONES S., 14th Bn.
G/28692	Pte. JACOBS, C., 6th Bn.
354707	Pte. JAY, H., 5th Bn.
G/104461	Pte. JONAS, S., 19th Bn.
31798	Sgt. JOEL, S., 29th Bn.
169414	Pte. JACOBS, A., 51st Bn.
104462	Pte. JACOBS, S., 52nd Bn.
128532	Pte. JACOBS, I., 53rd Bn.
168529	Pte. JACOBS, S., 53rd Bn.
52807	Pte. JACOBS, D., 53rd Bn.
9429	Pte. JACOBS, 4th Bn.
1590	Pte. JACOBS, J. W., 1st Bn.
7237	Pte. JACOBS, M.
36229	Pte. JERICHOWER, S. S.
19349	Pte. JACOBS, F. L., 6th Bn.
4220	Sgt. JACOBS, E. E., 3/9th Bn.
6296	Pte. KING, M., 2nd Bn.
21775	Pte. KAMOVITCH, I., 20th Bn.
16390	Sig. KOVALESKY, J., 20th Bn.
292292	Pte. KLEIN, B., 3/10th Bn.
G/13964	Pte. KASSIMER, J., 6th Bn.
17749	Pte. KONYN, 5th Bn.
24388	Pte. KEMPTON, G., 20th Bn.
35523	Pte. KROGEMAN, S., 14th Bn.
715064	Pte. KANE, H., 6th Bn.
73470	Pte. KENERICK, S. J., 1st Bn.
170592	Pte. KAUFMAN, C., 53rd Bn.
31628	Pte. KING, A. A., 32nd Bn.
	Sgt. KEMPLER, H. W. (M.M.).
46891	Pte. KOLINSKY, L., 29th Bn.
58182	Pte. KEMPNER, A., 18th Bn.
	Pte. KREMNER, S.
	Pte. KLETSAL, A.
80390	Sig. KRAM, E.
80147	Pte. KLEIN, A., 4th Bn.
80252	Pte. KAUFMAN, S., 4th Bn.
104671	Pte. KAUFFMAN, G., 52nd Bn.
2434	Pte. KAY, J. J., 28th Bn.
33482	Pte. KAUTZ, J.
352687	Pte. KOSMINSKY, M., 1/8th Bn.
24038	Pte. KAMINER, A., 20th Bn.
7266	Pte. KOLINSKY, H., 3/10th Bn.
72615	Pte. KRAKAUER, J.
877	Pte. LEVY, W. T., 4th Bn.
7568	L/Cpl. LOBEL, F. (M.M.), 2nd Bn.
3883	Pte. LAZARUS, H., 1/8th Bn.
2088	Pte. LASSMAN, N., 11th Bn.
12727	Pte. LEVY, P., 3rd Bn.
8660	Pte. LEVINE, L., 3rd Bn.
1418	Pte. LAZARUS, J., 7th Bn.
G/21617	L/Cpl. LIPMAN, H.,* 23rd Bn.
F/348	Pte. LEVY, B.,* 23rd Bn.
F/172	Pte. LEVI, J., 23rd Bn.
A/6926	Cpl. LYONS, L., 23rd Bn.
35904	Pte. LEVY, B., 23rd Bn.
20027	Pte. LEVY, H., 21st Bn.
14044	Pte. LEFTOVITCH, J., 20th Bn.
18620	Pte. LEVENE, H., 20th Bn.
24389	Pte. LEVY, P., 20th Bn.
202678	Pte. LEWIS, H., 4th Bn.
40681	Pte. LEVY, H. M., 12th Bn.
3584	Pte. LYONS, S., 1st Bn.
34884	Pte. LEAPMAN, H., 1st Bn.
	Pte. LAURENCE, H. (M.M.).
34890	Pte. LAZARUS, M., 1st Bn.
19213	Pte. LEVENE, M.,* 7th Bn.
14440	Pte. LEVIE, 20th Bn.
60382	Pte. LEVY, W., 18th Bn.
354071	L/Cpl. LEVYVELD, B., 4th Bn.
54563	Pte. LEE, N., 23rd Bn.
12081	Pte. LYFORD, C., 23rd Bn.
1845	Pte. LEVY, G. D., 16th Bn.
	Pte. LAURIE, C., 4th Bn.
9343	Pte. LEWIS, C., 4th Bn.
	Pte. LEVY, I., 4th Bn.

Middlesex Regt.—*Continued.*

G/17746	Pte. Levene, H., 6th Bn.
240941	L/Cpl. Lazarus, H. A., 8th Bn.
28928	Pte. Levinson, I., 12th Bn.
31590	Pte. Levy, J.
89216	Pte. Lassinsky, L., 5th Bn.
35643	Pte. Lipman, B., 1st Bn.
267512	Pte. Lewis, H., 1/9th Bn. D.
84499	Pte. Levy, A., 6th Bn.
25052	Pte. Lafinsky, H., 14th Bn.
G/33450	Pte. Lewis, E., 6th Bn.
105964	Pte. Layrus, M., 5th Bn.
57450	Pte. Levy, S.,* 2nd Bn.
355319	Pte. Lazarus, M.,* 4th Bn.
	Pte. Levy, I., 17th Bn.
P S/1845	Pte. Levy, G., 16th Bn.
81683	Pte. Lazarus, A., 29th Bn.
47558	Pte. Levy, B., 29th Bn.
35528	Pte. Lipman, D., 29th Bn.
34375	Pte. Lawton, H., 51st Bn.
8687	Pte. Lurie, C.,* 4th Bn.
35214	Pte. Lewis, M., 12th Bn.
60833	Pte. Landa, H., 6th Bn.
157330	Pte. Lipert, A. I., 29th Bn.
37559	Pte. Lassman, J., 6th Bn.
18620	Pte. Levene, H., 5th Bn.
7972	Pte. Locker, J., 5th Bn.
80442	Pte. Lewin, R. E., 3rd Bn.
80450	Pte. Labinsky, W., 3rd Bn.
80268	Pte. Landsman, B., 4th Bn.
72138	Pte. Levy, M., 1st Bn.
86852	Pte. Levy, A.
51122	Pte. Lower, S., 52nd Bn.
G/19213	Pte. Levene, M.
	Pte. Levie, A. (M.M.).
4467	L/Cpl. Lewis, A.
80499	Pte. Lang, A., 4th Bn.
25754	Pte. Levy, J.
266342	Pte. Levy, J., 2/9th Bn.
266453	Pte. Levy, B., 2/9th Bn.
412727	Pte. Levy, P., 3rd Bn.
16205	Pte. Lehvin, M., 22nd Bn.
38104	Pte. Levene, S., 29th Bn.
11608	Pte. Levy, S., 6th Bn.
18455	Pte. Lewis, H., 20th Bn.
11324	Pte. Lewis, L., 6th Bn.
11666	Pte. Lyons, H., 5th Bn.
47558	Pte. Levy, P., 29th Bn.
	Pte. Loveguard, N.
	Cpl. Levy, I. (D.C.M.).
242637	Pte. Levy, D., 29th Bn.
1845	Pte. Levy, C., 10th Bn.
34890	Pte. Lazarus, M., 6th Bn.
40681	Pte. Levy, H. M., 12th Bn.
18426	Pte. Levison, S., 20th Bn.
G/90992	Pte. Lipert, S., 29th Bn.
39377	L/Cpl. Levey, E., 16th Bn.
169108	Pte. Lazarus, M., 51st Bn.
43746	Pte. Lyons, S., 1st Bn.
52561	Pte. Lewis, N., 53rd Bn.
88196	Pte. Lewis, D., 29th Bn.
46134	Pte. Lancer, H., 29th Bn.
26886	Pte. Levene, B., 29th Bn.
266313	Pte. Loffman, A., 2/7th Bn.
4640	Pte. Levy, B., 2/9th Bn.
14749	Pte. Levy, J., 20th Bn.
14612	Pte. Levy, L., 20th Bn.
14968	Pte. Lyons, B., 28th Bn.
14767	Pte. Lans, I., 20th Bn.
31590	Pte. Levey, J.
35729	Pte. Levy, A. A., 25th Bn.
8217	Pte. Lazarus, J., 3rd Bn.
4135	Pte. Minden, M.,* 11th Bn.
8186	Pte. Myers, J., 2nd Bn.
231	Pte. Mercado, J., 11th Bn.
9045	Pte. Moses, S., 11th Bn.
2598	Pte. Mathews, E., 16th Bn.
1077	Pte. Marks, A.,* 17th Bn.
F/2237	Pte. Minsky, H., 23rd Bn.
12720	L/Cpl. Michaels, I., 2nd Bn.
42824	Pte. Mardell, E., 4th Bn.
21886	Pte. Millman, N., 1st Bn.
33369	Pte. Main, A., 1st Bn.
33760	Pte. Martin, A., 13th Bn.
205300	Pte. Myers, M., 13th Bn.
89056	Pte. Moss, M., 13th Bn.
8168	Cpl. Myers, J., 17th Bn.
24283	Pte. Martin, D., 28th Bn.
6836	Pte. Marks, L., 3rd Bn.
87332	Cpl. Margand, P. M., 23rd Bn.
G/33204	Pte. Mansell, A., 5th Bn.
89678	Pte. Morris, N., 23rd Bn.
18941	Pte. Magnus, J. W., 29th Bn.
88089	Pte. Michaels, A., 29th Bn.
51552	Pte. Moses, B. P., 2/10th Bn.
	Pte. Mitchell, P. (M.M.).
35416	Pte. Miller, M., 51st Bn.
35859	Pte. Margollis, M., 51st Bn.
3203	Pte. Mark, W.,* 2/10th Bn.
39355	Pte. Marks, J., 16th Bn.
35594	Pte. Muller, C., 52nd Bn.
169612	Pte. Masaphia, C., 52nd Bn.
168185	Pte. Moses, B., 53rd Bn.
44328	Pte. Moses, J., 29th Bn.
56359	Pte. Moses, L., 29th Bn.
11208	Pte. Marks, H.,* 4th Bn.
1939	Cpl. MacOwens, 19th Bn.
80113	Pte. Morris, I., 31st Bn.
291656	Pte. Marks, B. J., 1/9th Bn.
241977	Pte. Margollis, S., 1/8th Bn.
42824	Pte. Margell, E., 4th Bn.
27301	Pte. Mendlesohn, 5th Bn.
	Pte. Menter, E., 6th Bn.
6676	Pte. Myers, M., 7th Bn.
128606	Pte. Masters, A. A.

Middlesex Regt.—*Continued.*

24338	Pte. MILLER, M., 28th Bn.
174296	Pte. MARKS, M. F., 1st Bn.
27736	Pte. MORRIS, L., 4th Bn.
35206	Pte. MARKS, A., 29th Bn.
12728	Pte. MICHAELS, D., 14th Bn.
1652	Pte. MILLER, D., 23rd Bn.
25007	Cpl. MUSCOVITCH, L., 5th Bn.
225	Pte. MUSGRAVE, F., 22nd Bn.
85950	Pte. MERKER, M., 29th Bn.
12594	Pte. MORRIS, D., 20th Bn.
21864	Pte. MARCUS, B., 14th Bn.
4529	Pte. MARKS, B., 3/10th Bn.
4528	Pte. MARKS, I., 4/10th Bn.
7103	Pte. MARCHOFSKY, 7th Bn.
51860	Pte. MOSCOW, A., 32nd Bn.
86049	Pte. MICHAELSON, J.
	Pte. NEWBLATT, S., 1/8th Bn.
4582	Pte. NOLET, H., 2nd Bn.
G/60796	Pte. NATHAN, H.,* 19th Bn.
1328	Pte. NEWMAN, W., 12th Bn.
393265	Pte. NEWSTONE, D., 52nd Bn.
	L/Sgt. NATHAN, P. S. (D.C.M.).
70955	Pte. NAPHALI, G., 28th Bn.
84176	Pte. NEWMAN, N., 6th Bn.
13052	Pte. NORMAND, H.,* 4th Bn.
24243	Pte. NOSSEL, H., 28th Bn.
1800	L/Cpl. NEST, J., 14th Bn.
81245	Pte. NELSON, A., 29th Bn.
2329	Pte. NIECOP, T.
218886	Pte. NILMAN, M., 4th Bn.
F/1939	L/Sgt. OWENS, M., 23rd Bn.
74147	Pte. OPPER, H., 4th Bn.
45876	Pte. ORGEL, S., 3rd Bn.
G/1348	Pte. OPPENHEIM, E., 15th Bn.
24240	Pte. ORLITSKY, M., 28th Bn.
24241	Pte. OSCAR, H., 28th Bn.
24383	Pte. OBTO, H., 28th Bn.
24301	Pte. OWEN, H., 20th Bn.
7935	Pte. OTTOLANGER, M.
76475	Pte. OTTOLANGER, A., 29th Bn.
	Pte. OLSWANG, H., 9th Bn.
	Pte. OSWICK, H., 2/8th Bn.
1415	Cpl. PEZARO, J., 11th Bn.
G/42968	Pte. PIVANSKI, A.,* 2nd Bn.
	Sgt. POSNER, J., 26th Bn.
292933	Pte. PESKOFF, L., 3/10th Bn.
292850	Pte. PARK, L., 3/10th Bn.
13309	Pte. PURKISS, E., 8th Bn.
95112	Pte. PARKER, G. W., 20th Bn.
615617	Pte. PHILLIPS, W., 4th Bn.
95448	Pte. PORT, F., 2nd Bn.
162791	Pte. PRECHNER, S., 29th Bn.
	Pte. PREGARO, J., 15th Bn.
G/76430	Pte. PERILLY, S., 29th Bn.
	Cpl. PHILLIPS, H. G. (M.M.).
169400	Pte. POLLOCK, J. I., 51st Bn.
39459	Pte. POLINSKY, H., 29th Bn.
6754	Pte. PARK, S., 3/10th Bn.
4163	Pte. PRYOR, W. H., 2/10th Bn.
18807	Pte. PHILLIPS, R.
71689	L/Cpl. PECK, J.
4998	L/Cpl. PASS, C. S., 7th Bn.
70556	Pte. QUANTEL, H., 4th Bn.
G/11839	Pte. REINFLEISCH, A.,* 19th Bn.
24293	Pte. ROSINSKY, S., 20th Bn.
24705	Pte. RUBENSTEIN, J., 18th Bn.
231095	Pte. RASCH, J., 20th Bn.
96589	Pte. ROSENBERG, S., 13th Bn.
2377	Pte. ROSENBERG, J., 23rd Bn.
71552	Pte. REMSTEN, M., 4th Bn.
G/28180	Pte. ROSALKIE., J., 6th Bn.
616778	Pte. RAPHAEL, L., 5th Bn.
28207	Pte. ROSENBLOOM, S., 5th Bn.
841791	Pte. RAPPAPORT.
71723	Pte. ROSENTHAL, D., 29th Bn.
85210	Pte. RANDALL, H., 29th Bn.
G/91060	Pte. ROSENBERG, R., 29th Bn.
	Drm. ROGER, G.
	Pte. ROSENTHAL, I.
168649	Pte. RUDA, 53rd Bn.
171573	Pte. RUBENSTEIN, M., 53rd Bn.
57653	Pte. RUTER, D.,* 13th Bn.
29669	Pte. ROTHSCHILD, H., 29th Bn.
80424	Pte. RAPP, J.
70556	Pte. RUERSHOL, A., 4th Bn.
953	Pte. ROGERS, A., 23rd Bn.
92003	Pte. REICH,
16120	Pte. ROSEN, B., 22nd Bn.
25545	Pte. ROSE, E., 15th Bn.
93199	Pte. ROSE, J.
16794	Cpl. ROSS, J., 22nd Bn.
2202	Pte. ROTHENBERG, R., 29th Bn.
38596	Pte. RADVANT, P., 29th Bn.
	Pte. RADZWILLER, I. G., 20th Bn.
58101	Pte. ROSENBERG, G., 20th Bn.
G/74388	Pte. ROSE, P., 3rd Bn.
80185	Pte. RAMULT, H., 3rd Bn.
6386	Cpl. SOLOMON, J.* (M.M.), 2nd Bn.
1614	Pte. SILVER, N., 11th Bn.
2960	Sgt. SOLOMONS, A.,* 12th Bn.
1355	C.Q.M.S. SAFFERTY, A., 13th Bn.
4559	Pte. SOLOMONS, J., 16th Bn.
12201	Sgt. SUGARMAN, C., 13th Bn.
7972	Pte. SOCKER, J., 13th Bn.
24148	Pte. STEIN, L.,* 20th Bn.
24197	Pte. STRYPEK, H., 20th Bn.
24153	Pte. SOLOMONS, D., 20th Bn.
24398	Pte. SYMONS, M., 20th Bn.
18585	Pte. STONE, J., 20th Bn.
14939	Pte. STONE, H., 20th Bn.
18610	Pte. SMITH, H., 20th Bn.
18718	Pte. SANDERS, H., 20th Bn.
	Sgt. SOLLY, I. (M.M.).
21318	L/Cpl. SOLOMONS, M.,* 21st Bn.
11479	Pte. STOMOFF, M.,* 23rd Bn.

Middlesex Regt.—*Continued.*

2902	Pte. SOMERS, M., 23rd Bn.
21647	Cpl. SILVER, R.,* 12th Bn.
8980	Pte. SOLOMON, L., 17th Bn.
G/26651	L/Cpl. SASIENI, J. H., 17th Bn.
261102	Pte. STEPHENSON, I., 20th Bn.
G/54460	Pte. SOLOMON, J., 19th Bn.
G/54473	Pte. SHOLMAN, M., 19th Bn.
2876	Pte. SOLOMON, W., 12th Bn.
	Pte. SIMMONS, G., 3rd Bn.
17851	Pte. STONE, A., 5th Bn.
L/10957	Pte. SCHOFIELD, 6th Bn.
G/8980	Pte. SOLOMON, G., 6th Bn.
G/13900	Pte. SHEIN, R., 6th Bn.
2536	Pte. SOLOMONS, J., 2nd Bn.
38704	Pte. SCHALHY, J.
11734	Pte. SERENO, M., 4th Bn.
92126	Pte. SANTER, J., 6th Bn.
51859	Pte. SMITH, H., 32nd Bn.
148948	Pte. SUTTELL, C., 3rd Bn.
	Pte. SILVERSTONE, H. S., 15th Bn.
G/28192	Pte. SLOWE, M., 6th Bn.
84280	Pte. SCHNEIDERMAN, H., 6th Bn.
92126	Pte. SANTER, J., 6th Bn.
93560	Pte. SONNENFIELD, H., 5th Bn.
30978	Pte. SHEREX, A. J.
93141	Pte. SEFTON, I.
	Pte. SHULKIND, M. J.
2876	Pte. SOLOMONS, W., 12th Bn.
2960	Cpl. SOLOMONS, 12th Bn.
G/103287	Pte. SANDERS, A. F., 7th Bn.
48319	L/Cpl. SHITH, S., 29th Bn.
35453	Pte. SOCKER, H., 51st Bn.
35914	Pte. SHULMAN, S., 51st Bn.
20565	L/Cpl. STEINBERG, S. R.,* 12th Bn.
88411	Pte. SOLOMON, N., 29th Bn.
54280	Pte. SALISBURY, H. B., 29th Bn.
34956	Pte. SAMUEL, W., 29th Bn.
42827	Pte. SONFIELD, S. H., 29th Bn.
55501	Pte. STARR, J., 29th Bn.
88198	Pte. SOLOMON, A., 29th Bn.
54460	Sig. SOLOMON, S., 19th Bn.
204725	Pte. SINGER, H., 2/7th Bn.
30133	Pte. SCHNEIDER, H., 29th Bn.
70020	Pte. SCHWARTZ, J., 3rd Bn.
74317	Pte. SILVERMAN, L., 4th Bn.
80173	Pte. STEIN, S., 4th Bn.
74389	Pte. SEIR, J. B., 4th Bn.
128910	Pte. SOLOMON, C.
129257	Pte. SHMELSINGER, S.
5043	Sgt. SCHASTZEN, J., 25th Bn.
35453	Pte. SOCKER, H., 51st Bn.
84162	Pte. SCHNEIDER, J.
68218	Sgt. SEGAL, S.
67812	Pte. SHONE, S., 29th Bn.
30904	Pte. SCHRIER, A.
128801	Pte. SMIDLOFF, H.
38451	Pte. SARDE, J., 29th Bn.
169420	Pte. SANDERS, A. W., 51st Bn.
	L/Cpl. SCHEIN, A.
	Pte. SANDERS, J.
170944	Pte. SAFARTY, J., 52nd Bn.
105514	Pte. SIEGLE, H., 52nd Bn.
104766	Pte. SIMONS, M., 52nd Bn.
168218	Pte. SEGAL, S., 53rd Bn.
92023	Pte. SHONMAN, C. L.
205731	Pte. SCHNEIDER, J., 7th Bn.
24353	Pte. SILVERSTEIN, S., 28th Bn.
24336	Pte. SMOLY, N., 28th Bn.
14642	Pte. SOLOMONS, N., 20th Bn.
36299	Pte. SOLOMONS, I., 27th Bn.
24384	Pte. SAMUEL, I., 28th Bn.
18718	Pte. SANDERS, H., 20th Bn.
24339	Pte. SCHAFFER, J., 28th Bn.
29777	Pte. SCHARER, A. J., 29th Bn.
4267	Pte. SCHNEIDER, J., 3/10th Bn.
14975	Pte. SCHARE, H., 20th Bn.
45819	Pte. STERN, M., 29th Bn.
30924	Pte. SMITH, M.
9/7368	L/Cpl. SOBEL, F., 5th Bn.
2398	Pte. STERN, H., 6th Bn.
77279	Pte. SILVERSTONE, S., 29th Bn.
80364	Pte. SHAPIRO, P., 4th Bn.
74303	Pte. SEGAL, J., 1st Bn.
G/51467	Pte. SURIMAMER, L., 26th Bn.
291968	Pte. SOLOMONS, L., 2/10th Bn.
9623	Pte. SPRINGHALL, J., 13th Bn.
35873	Pte. STOVIC, J., 29th Bn.
G/28778	Pte. STRAUSS, H., 2nd Bn.
70660	Pte. SERENS, M., 4th Bn.
153627	Pte. SCHNEIDER, 15th Bn.
	Pte. SELLER, J., 9th Bn.
	Pte. SIMON, H. D.
	Pte. SOMAN, D., 9th Bn.
	Pte. STATMAN, R. 22nd Bn.
	Pte. SHEARWOOD, W., 8th Bn.
6844	Cpl. TOFF, J. (M.M.), 2nd Bn.
2920	Pte. TASCH, M. A., 7th Bn.
	Pte. TOUMS, J., 4th Bn.
G/103356	Drm. TEACHER, A., 7th Bn.
90761	Pte. TYNAS, H., 29th Bn.
63149	Pte. TOMLINSON, J., 51st Bn.
G.28193	Pte. TOURNOFF, L., 3rd Bn.
72186	Pte. TITLEBOAM, S., 29th Bn.
56282	Pte. TOBIAS, V., 29th Bn.
17494	Pte. TOPALIAN, H. D., 29th Bn.
98238	Pte. TUCHVERDERBER, J., 29th Bn.
93685	Pte. TAFFEL, A., 2/9th Bn.
24337	Pte. VOGELSOHN, A., 16th Bn.
25709	L/Cpl. VANDERSLUIS, S., 16th Bn.
15091	Pte. VALENTINE, E., 13th Bn.
89282	Pte. VAN-DAM, 2nd Bn.
12817	Pte. VAN RAALTE, A., 1st Bn.
48393	Pte. VOSS, A., 4th Bn.
557442	Sgt. VAN DULERNS.
G/25709	Pte. VANDERSTEIN, S. B., 15th Bn.

Middlesex Regt.—Continued.

80138	L/Cpl. VINE, J.,	4th Bn.
5904	Pte. WALMAN, S.,	13th Bn.
1653	L/Sgt. WESTON, H.,	19th Bn.
28461	Pte. WEST, D.,	19th Bn.
40036	Pte. WOOLF, A.,	12th Bn.
293121	Pte. WARSHAWSKY, N.,	3/10th Bn.
5843	Pte. WILLIAMS, F.,	12th Bn.
	Pte. WHITE, M.	
80024	Pte. WHITESON, J. H.,	21st Bn.
11839	Pte. WOOD, G.,	28th Bn.
80452	Pte. WEBBER, J. M.,	1st Bn.
93037	Pte. WASSERMAN, T.	
84255	Pte. WETZLAR, M. M.	
G/25581	Cpl. WOLFE, C.,	5th Bn.
291850	Pte. WISEMAN, I.,	10th Bn.
31589	Pte. WEINER, J.,	4th Bn.
7446	Pte. WEINER, I.,	4th Bn.
169406	Pte. WOLF, J.,	52nd Bn.
169214	Pte. WOLF, J. B.,	52nd Bn.
21077	Pte. WHITE, J.	
5953	Pte. WEDELL, F.,	3/10th Bn.
25582	Pte. WILLIAMS, H.,	1st Bn.
45514	Pte. WOOF, S.,	29th Bn.
80382	Pte. WASSERBERG, D.,	3rd Bn.
80395	Pte. WINKLER, J.,	3rd Bn.
28771	Pte. WEINBERG, J.	
60382	Pte. WOOLF, L.,	6th Bn.
G/38985	Pte. WEINER, L.,	29th Bn.
24319	Pte. WOOD, J.,	28th Bn.
24088	Pte. WOOLF, L.,	28th Bn.
48355	Pte. WISEBERG, L.	
75298	Pte. WALKENBERG, L.	
61782	Pte. WHITE, J.,	6th Bn.
5748	Pte. WEISBERG, J.,*	4th Bn.
17876	Pte. YEGLISS, N.,	5th Bn.
G/91137	Pte. YOUNGERMAN, H.,	29th Bn.
2474	L/Cpl. ZEILER, B.,	16th Bn.
58196	Pte. ZEALANDER, H.,	18th Bn.
74407	Pte. ZEMBA, A.	
70081	Pte. ZIMMER, D.,	3rd Bn.
95038	Pte. ZAKTRAGER, J.	
38451	Pte. ZAIDE, J.,	29th Bn.
31918	Pte. ZAMARIN,	29th Bn.
30366	Pte. ZUCKER, A.,	4th Bn.

* Killed in Action or died on Active Service.

THE KING'S ROYAL RIFLE CORPS.

OFFICERS.

Lieut. BASS, E. (D.C.M.), 2nd Bn.
2nd Lieut. BEDDINGTON, F., 13th Bn.
Lieut. BOAS, 52nd Bn.
2nd Lieut. COBURN, C.,* 18th Bn.
2nd Lieut. DRAPKIN, I. A., (M.M.) 2nd Bn.
2nd Lieut. FREEDMAN, B.
2nd Lieut. HARRIS, I. M., 1st Bn.
2nd Lieut. HERBERTSON, A. H.,* 7th Bn.
2nd Lieut. HENRIQUES, P. B.,* 8th Bn.
2nd Lieut. JACOBS, P., 13th Bn.
2nd Lieut. LEVY, H. G., 21st Bn.
2nd Lieut. MARKS, L., 9th Bn.
2nd Lieut. MAUDERN, A., 67th Bn.
Capt. MYERS, L. M., 18th Bn.
2nd Lieut. MOSS H. M.
Lieut. MANNERS, J. E., 1st Bn.
2nd Lieut. PEZARO, L.
2nd Lieut. PRAAGH, R. B.
2nd Lieut. PRICE, J. S., 9th Bn.
2nd Lieut. RAPHAEL, Sir H. H.
2nd Lieut. SASSOON, R. E., 18th Bn.
Capt. SPERO, C. N., 6th Bn.
Capt. SPERO, L., 16th Bn.
Capt. SUMMERFIELD, M. (M.C.), 9th Bn.
Lieut. TENENBAUM, L., 13th Bn.
2nd Lieut. WALEY, F. R., 6th Bn.

N.C.O.'s AND MEN.

7533	Rfm. ABRAHAMS, A. M.,	23rd Bn.
28774	Rfm. ABRAHAMS, D.	
11886	Cpl. ABRAHAM, N.,	2nd Bn.
Y/1498	Rfm. ABRAHAMS, B.,	7th Bn.
11900	Rfm. ABRAHAMS, H.,*	1st Bn.
33385	Rfm. ABRAHAMS, M.,*	18th Bn.
A/201694	Rfm. ABRAHAMS, S.,	10th Bn.
38624	Rfm. ABRAHAMS, J.,	21st Bn.
R/36263	Rfm. ABRAHAMS, M.,	9th Bn.
R/12617	Rfm. ABRAHAMS, L.,	6th Bn.
R/38734	Rfm. ABRAHAMS, D.,	17th Bn.
15164	Rfm. ABRAHAMS, S.	
A/198	Rfm. ADDIS, M.,	8th Bn.
28092	Rfm. ALEXANDER, M.,	7th Bn.
21747	Rfm. ALEXANDER, M.,	3rd Bn.
32415	Rfm. ANNUS, J.,	11th Bn.
28751	Rfm. APPELBAUM, C.	
22775	Rfm. ASHER, A.,	14th Bn.
534269	Rfm. AGUS, G. H.	
32456	Rfm. ANGEL, H.,	5th Bn.
204361	Rfm. ADLER, W.	
393319	Rfm. ALBERT, H.,	
32456	Rfm. ANGEL, H.,	1st Bn.
34293	Rfm. ANNIS, J.,	11th Bn.
4164	Rfm. ASSENHEIM, L.,*	17th Bn.
63146	Rfm. BARRETT, H.,	52nd Bn.
55718	Rfm. BARNETT, A.,	25th Bn.
68444	Rfm. BARNETT,	52nd Bn.
C/6331	Sgt. BARNES, H.,	18th Bn.
426157	Rfm. BAVITZ, B.,	25th Bn.
397702	Rfm. BAROFSKI, M.,	25th Bn.
4823	Rfm. BARNETT, H.,	2nd Bn.
12547	Rfm. BALL, G.,	5th Bn.

King's Royal Rifle Corps.—*Continued.*

29305	Cpl. BASSBOGEN, S., 20th Bn.
R/36493	L/Cpl. BENJAMIN, L., 3rd Bn.
4892	Rfm. BENJAMIN, J., 1st Bn.
2830	Rfm. BENJAMIN, L., 10th Bn.
4893	Rfm. BENJAMIN, M.,* 1st Bn.
38717	Pte. BENJAMIN, B., 10th Bn.
R/32242	Rfm. BENJAMIN, A., 5th Bn.
51963	Rfm. BENJAMIN, E., 2nd Bn.
27248	Rfm. BENJAMIN, B., 23rd Bn.
39338	Rfm. BENJAMIN, T., 13th Bn.
22364	Rfm. BERNSTEIN, L.
15966	Rfm. BERNSTEIN, A., 2nd Bn.
4843	Rfm. BERNSTEIN, L., 2nd Bn.
C/4553	Rfm. BERNSTEIN, M., 16th Bn.
R/21459	Sgt. BERG, J., 51st Bn.
TRL/3/54950	Rfm. BURKE, L., 51st Bn.
201453	Rfm. BROOKS, D., 9th Bn.
33664	Rfm. BLAU, M., 1st Bn.
27172	Rfm. BETTS, J., Res Bn.
35451	Rfm. BLUMENTHAL, I., 17th Bn.
38362	Rfm. BLUMENTHAL, M., Res. Bn.
31189	Rfm. BLOOMBERG, D., 6th Bn.
15768	Rfm. BARRISH, J.
21860	Rfm. BERLYN, P. S.
21858	Rfm. BETH, D.
23320	Rfm. BLONDIN, A.
	Pte. BLOOM, E.
29843	Rfm. BLOOM, J.
19040	Rfm. BLOOM, H., 9th Bn.
13/1699	Rfm. BROD, H.
45994	Rfm. BROWN, H.
42637	Rfm. BRONARD, C., 9th Bn.
15816	Rfm. BURROWS, G., 5th Bn.
	Rfm. BIRNSTEIN, P.
14196	Rfm. BROWN, A., 8th Bn.
	Rfm. BROWN, M.
	Rfm. BARRISH, C., 2nd Bn.
	Rfm. BEAVER, M.
33809	Rfm. BERLIN, S., 7th Bn.
15730	Rfm. BERMEL, J., 9th Bn.
19738	Rfm. BELKIN, B. (M.M.), 13th Bn.
3115681	Rfm. BENG, M., 10th Bn.
6/1220	L/Cpl. BRESLAU, H., 8th Bn.
A.390	Rfm. BLACK, L., 7th Bn.
8008	Rfm. BROMBERG, D., 18th Bn.
2976	Rfm. BLAIN, S.* (M.M.), 1st Bn.
35596	Rfm. BLAUPAPER, D., 1st Bn.
15121	Rfm. BLASKI, Z., 20th Bn.
201147	Rfm. BOWMAN, D., 16th Bn.
R/25438	Rfm. BOSTLE, I., 11th Bn.
23184	Rfm. BLOCK, D., 8th Bn.
3551	Rfm. BLACKER, B., 17th Bn.
40932	Rfm. BILL, J., 1st Bn.
R/35834	Rfm. BURTON, D., 2nd Bn.
28702	Rfm. BROCKMAN, M.
	Rfm. BRESH, S., 1st Bn.
	Rfm. BRESLOW, 1st Bn.
11193	Rfm. BOVRISH, C., 2nd Bn.
201604	Rfm. BLACK, N., 20th Bn.
	Rfm. BLUMBERG, I., 4th Bn.
R/25853	Rfm. BLANES, A., 6th Bn.
R/29365	Rfm, BIERMAN, J., 6th Bn.
60779	Rfm. BIRBOCK, S.
11656	Rfm. CLARE, F., 1st Bn.
R/4843	Rfm. CLEVE, P., 13th Bn.
22023	Rfm. CROSS, A., 7th Bn.
A/200041	Rfm. COOPMAN, A.,* 17th Bn.
200185	Rfm. CLAFF, M., 17th Bn.
64460	L/Cpl. COHN, C., 16th Bn.
C/7067	Rfm. COHEN, H., 18th Bn.
14613	L/Cpl. COHEN, E., 18th Bn.
517515	L/Cpl. COHEN, H., 25th Bn.
R/28621	L/Cpl. COHEN, G., 6th Bn.
200123	Rfm. COHEN, A. J.,* 17th Bn.
4280	Rfm. COHEN, A., 17th Bn.
13469	Rfm. COHEN, M.,* 19th Bn.
30078	Rfm. COHEN, I., 18th Bn.
201255	Rfm. COHEN, S.,* 16th Bn.
R/21903	Rfm. COHEN, L., 12th Bn.
R/32264	Rfm. COHEN, R., 18th Bn.
R/32885	Rfm. COHEN, A., 2nd Bn.
17224	Rfm. COHEN, D., 18th Bn.
39170	Rfm. COHEN, L., 20th.
6915	Rfm. COHEN, M., 3rd Bn.
C/9650	Rfm. COHEN, J., 20th Bn.
R/14615	Rfm. COHEN, H., 6th Bn.
R/22204	Rfm. COHEN, M., 5th Bn.
R/32464	Rfm. COOTS, H., 5th Bn.
R/32224	Rfm. COHEN, J., 5th Bn.
6660	Rfm. COHEN, A., 15th Bn.
R/31671	Rfm. COHEN, P., 6th Bn.
	L/Cpl. COHEN, H. O. (D.C.M.).
R/41862	Rfm. COHEN, H., 5th Bn.
30416	Rfm. COHEN, A., 18th Bn.
393332	Rfm. COHEN, D., 52nd Bn.
37796	Rfm. COHEN, S., 18th Bn.
18656	L/Cpl. COHEN, C., 16th Bn.
39650	Rfm. COHEN, J., 10th Bn.
23316	Rfm. COHEN, A., 15th Bn.
21904	Rfm. COHEN, A.
30577	Rfm. COHEN, B.
30739	Rfm. COHEN, H., 15th Bn.
80114	Pte. COHEN, L.
29233	Rfm. COFMAN, N.
38733	Rfm. COHEN, J., 5th Bn.
32778	Rfm. COHEN, L.
32706	Rfm. COHEN, J.
37525	Rfm. COHEN, H., 6th Bn.
38006	Rfm. COHEN, I.
27704	Rfm. COHEN, M.
24496	Rfm. COHEN, M.
30576	Rfm. CROSPUL, E.
4879	Rfm. CRUGMAN, S.

King's Royal Rifle Corps.—*Continued.*

841651	Rfm. COHEN, M., 9th Bn.
62900	Rfm. CIBBAL, 20th Bn.
14087	Rfm. COFF, 14th Bn.
91611	Rfm. COOPER, F.
25423	Rfm. CROWTHER, W., 16th Bn.
R/32139	Rfm. CLARKE, H., 5th Bn.
202466	Rfm. CHERRY, M., 21st Bn.
R/45099	Rfm. CHITRIN, H.,* 2nd Bn.
345056	Rfm. CHAYTOW, M., 2nd Bn.
535488	Rfm. COSTA, J., 2nd Bn.
37373	Rfm. CRUTZMAN, M., 8th Bn.
A/202958	Rfm. CAPLAN, H., 17th Bn.
R/31760	Rfm. COOPER, H., 5th Bn.
62901	Rfm. COLEMAN, H., 20th Bn.
	L/Cpl. COHEN, R. (M.M.).
94148	Rfm. CREME, M., 1/7th Bn.
25376	Rfm. COEL, S., 18th Bn.
	Rfm. CHODICK, M.
393189	Rfm. CHARNEICH, H., 52nd Bn.
	Rfm. DAVIS, G., 1st Bn.
1261	Rfm. DAVIS, H., 8th Bn.
	Rfm. DAVIS, I., 7th Bn.
516127	Rfm. DAVIS, M. D., 25th Bn.
	Rfm. DAVIS, J., 1st Bn.
R/30174	Rfm. DAVIS, J., 6th Bn.
R/30255	Rfm. DAVIS, I., 6th Bn.
15167	Rfm. DAVIS, J.,* 13th Bn.
8505	Rfm. DAVIES, S., 9th Bn.
23232	Rfm. DAVIDS, A., 15th Bn.
	Rfm. DAVIDS, H. H., 15th Bn.
38734	Rfm. DANIEL, A., 17th Bn.
62118	Rfm. DENDE, M., 52nd Bn.
S/17755	Rfm. DEUTCH, E., 12th Bn.
19008	Rfm. DELAFWENTE, J., 4th Bn.
14439	Rfm. DEANE, E., 20th Bn.
28089	Rfm. de GROOT, J., 12th Bn.
	Rfm. DE MESQUITA, J. B.,
R/22271	L/Cpl. DIAMOND, H., 18th Bn.
R/31517	Rfm. DIAMOND, A.,* 16th Bn.
37122	L/Cpl. DONSKY, H., 6th Bn.
R/39923	Rfm. DOODOVITCH, I., 5th Bn.
R/27253	Rfm. DRESON, A., 7th Bn.
14613	L/Cpl. EDEN
38299	L/Cpl. EDGAR, L., 13th Bn.
29918	Rfm. ELIAS, E., 15th Bn.
17456	Rfm. ELLIS, M.
30326	Rfm. ELLISON, S.
332516	Rfm. ELSNER, M., 2/9th Bn.
R/39340	L/Cpl. ELIASCHEFF, H., 13th Bn.
	Drm. ENGLEMAN, J.
1393	Rfm. EPSTEIN, H., 9th Bn.
23793	Rfm. EPSTEIN, J.
17225	Rfm. ERIERA, J.
45954	Rfm. FALK, M., 1st Bn.
240066	L/Cpl. FELDMAN, H., 6th Bn.
	C.Q.M.S. FREEMAN, H. S., 18th Bn.
27218	Rfm. FREEMAN, H.
R/12202	Rfm. FREEDMAN, M.,* 13th Bn.
31945	Rfm. FREEDMAN, M., 2nd Bn.
87450	Rfm. FREEDMAN, D., 20th Bn.
43046	Rfm. FREEDMAN, H., 7th Bn.
17570	Rfm. FRIEDMAN, B., 13th Bn.
R/18607	Rfm. FRANKS, M., 5th Bn.
C/3249	Rfm. FRANKS, A.,* 17th Bn.
26050	Rfm. FRANKS, L., 1st Bn.
38511	Rfm. FRANKS, I., 13th Bn.
R/39500	Rfm. FOX, L., 6th Bn.
35481	Rfm. FRIEND, J.
36876	Rfm. FINKLESTEIN, M., 6th Bn.
40632	Rfm. FUGLER, M.
30803	Rfm. FINSKY, M., 15th Bn.
29844	Rfm. FINKLE, H.
18657	Rfm. FLEX, L., 15th Bn.
23325	Rfm. FRIEDBERG, R., 15th Bn.
23186	Rfm. FLASHMAN, S.,* 9th Bn.
200110	Rfm. FRAZER, H., 17th Bn.
21018	Rfm. FINEBERG, M., 17th Bn.
32392	Rfm. FLEISHER, L., 9th Bn.
R/31272	Rfm. FINKLESTEIN, H., 17th Bn.
37908	Rfm. FRESCOE, E., 13th Bn.
A/204438	Rfm. FRIEDLANDER, L., 13th Bn.
R/15062	Rfm. FISHER, H., 13th Bn.
R/13208	Rfm. FLAXMAN, H., 6th Bn.
R/10924	Rfm. FIELD, J., 5th Bn.
R/32243	Rfm. FRAM, J., 5th Bn.
C/13011	L/Cpl. FLATOW, E. W., 21st Bn.
K/20939	Rfm. FROM, M., 1st Bn.
9638	Rfm. GARDNER, H., 3rd Bn.
33763	Rfm. GARCIA, J., 13th Bn.
201861	Rfm. GARRETT, S., 18th Bn.
18058	Rfm. GALINSKY, H.
A/202488	Rfm. GALINSKY, A.,* 16th Bn.
A/201807	Rfm. GREENBLATT, H., 2nd Bn.
18166	Rfm. GREENBERG, L., 17th Bn.
C/12695	L/Cpl. GOLDBERG, H.,* 21st Bn.
201119	Rfm. GOLDBERG, J., 9th Bn.
9711	Rfm. GOLDBERG, B., 4th Bn.
R/32245	Rfm. GOLDSTEIN, J., 5th Bn.
R/19597	Rfm. GOLDSTEIN, M., 7th Bn.
21007	Rfm. GOLDSTEIN, D., 9th Bn.
9043	Rfm. GOLDSTEIN, P.,* 9th Bn.
20955	Rfm. GOBLONSKY, A., 1st Bn.
58690	Rfm. GOLLOND, J.
29842	Rfm. GROSS, J.
28216	Rfm. GOLDFORB, M., 19th Bn.
4038	Rfm. GOLDRING, H.
18361	Rfm. GOLDSTEIN, L.
30159	Rfm. GOLDSTON, A. B., 6th Bn.
42807	Rfm. GILLMAN, P., 5th Bn.
13083	Rfm. GOTTLIEB, A. 13th Bn.
	Cpl. GOODMAN, J. (D.C.M.).
25393	Rfm. GOLDRICH, L., 1st Bn.
32821	Rfm. GINSBERG, G., 16th Bn.
5149	Rfm. GOLDSMITH, L., 1st Bn.

King's Royal Rifle Corps.—*Continued.*

	Rfm. GOLDSTONE, A., 8th Bn.
14872	Rfm. GOLDMAN, J., 16th Bn.
12/23870	Rfm. GOLD, A., 17th Bn.
	Rfm. GOLDSMITH, A., 4th Bn.
205498	Rfm. GOLDRING, M.
642	Rfm. GOLDSTON, R. B.
R/25444	Rfm. GREENBAUM, E.
41779	Rfm. GOODMAN, E., 16th Bn.
43982	Rfm. GLUCKSTEIN, S., 18th Bn.
	Rfm. GROSSER, C., 1st Bn.
R/14956	Rfm. GELDER, H., 6th Bn.
	Rfm. GOLD, N., 5th Bn.
32221	Rfm. GINSBERG, J., 5th Bn.
R/31557	Rfm. GREEN, A.,
R/32244	Rfm. GORDON, J., 5th Bn.
13061	Rfm. GORDON, D., 6th Bn.
	Rfm. GORDON, H., 2nd Bn.
29342	Rfm. HARRIS, A., 5th Bn.
	Rfm. HARRIS, I.
29424	Rfm. HARRIS, P., 7th Bn.
1205	Rfm. HARRIS, J., 4th Bn.
39434	Rfm. HARRIS, H., 6th Bn.
30699	Rfm. HARRIS, H., 15th Bn.
1023	L/Cpl. HARRIS, J., 2nd Bn.
R/41731	Rfm. HARRIS, E., 5th Bn.
27754	Rfm. HARRIS, L. B., 5th Bn.
30138	Rfm. HARRIS, H., 17th Bn.
41792	Rfm. HART, M., 5th Bn.
R/21696	Rfm. HART, D.,* 10th Bn.
R/38768	L/Cpl. HART, J., 2nd Bn.
32265	Rfm. HART, J.,* 8th Bn.
6827	Rfm. HAYMAN, M., 2nd Bn.
25301	Rfm. HARING, M., 8th Bn.
25399	Rfm. HAMBURG, D., 8th Bn.
26715	Rfm. HALTER, M. D. S., 8th Bn.
393337	Rfm. HAND, H. B., 52nd Bn.
	Rfm. HENT, S., 10th Bn.
38974	Rfm. HEFTEL, L., 5th Bn.
22515	Rfm. HELLER, D., 5th Bn.
19831	Rfm. HERMAN, S.
R/32465	Rfm. HELLER, H., 5th Bn.
A/1498	Rfm. HERTZBURG, N.,* 8th Bn.
19691	Rfm. HERMAN, M., 13th Bn.
A/202491	Rfm. HERMAN, J., 21st Bn.
3230	Sgt. HEINBERG, J. S., 17th Bn.
R/3817	Rfm. HENRY, M., 13th Bn.
R/29981	Rfm. HOUSE, S.
31871	Rfm. HOENDERKOPPER, M., 17th Bn
23330	Rfm. HONIGMAN, S., 8th Bn.
545010	Rfm. HOLLANDER, S., 2nd Bn.
22056	Rfm. HYMAN, I. J.
14716	Rfm. HYMAN, G. I., 9th Bn.
R/14915	Rfm. HYMAN, M., 6th Bn.
35759	Rfm. HYMAN, M., 1st Bn.
39494	Rfm. HYMAN, A. A., 1st Bn.
37301	Rfm. HYAMS, B., 13th Bn.
9569	Rfm. HYAMS, P., 20th Bn.
23324	Rfm. ISAACS, H., 15th Bn.
22102	Rfm. ISAACS, H.
23187	Rfm. ISAACS, M., 15th Bn.
6/1122	Rfm. ISAACS, H., 7th Bn.
34007	Rfm. ISAACS, B.,* 16th Bn.
R/19103	Rfm. ISAACS, J.,* 21st Bn.
23865	Rfm. ISAACS, D. B., 10th Bn.
	Rfm. ISAACS, B., 16th Bn.
373345	Rfm. ISENSTARK, M., 52nd Bn.
35911	Rfm. ISHBITSKY, W. M., 10th Bn.
31860	Rfm. INDICK, W., 12th Bn.
1541	Rfm. JACOBS, M., 8th Bn.
1306	Rfm. JACOBS, M., 12th Bn.
1227	Rfm. JACOBS, B., 13th Bn.
3060	Rfm. JACOBS (JAY), M.,* 17th Bn.
19438	Rfm. JACOBS, D.,* 2nd Bn.
8733	Rfm. JACOBS, L.,* 5th Bn.
19154	Rfm. JACOBS, H.,* 1st Bn.
38426	Rfm. JACOBS, S.
28138	Rfm. JACOBS, D., 6th Bn.
21859	Rfm. JACOBS, L. H., 10th Bn.
23322	Rfm. JACOBS, J., 15th Bn.
	Rfm. JACOBS, R., "C" Coy.
	Rfm. JACOBS, N., 6th Bn.
46716	Rfm. JACOBSON, I., 5th Bn.
	L/Cpl. JACOBSON, A. E.
31870	Rfm. JAFFE, D., 5th Bn.
14667	Rfm. JAFFE, J.,* 20th Bn.
	Rfm. JACKS, M., 8th Bn.
26423	Rfm. JOSEPH, G.
	L/Cpl. JOSEPH, W.
11583	Rfm. JOSEPH, B., 8th Bn.
397793	Rfm. JOSEPH, S., 25th Bn.
12551	Rfm. JOSEPH, L., 11th Bn.
133966	Rfm. JOSEPHSON, A.
20955	Rfm. JOBLONSKY, A., 1st Bn.
	Rfm. JOEL, H., 3rd Bn.
R/38280	Rfm. JONAS, S.,* 9th Bn.
36617	Rfm. JUDALSON, D., 5th Bn.
38643	Rfm. KAPLAN, T. S.
12601	Rfm. KAUFMAN, L.,* 7th Bn.
300937	Rfm. KAY, I. M.,* 16th Bn.
37869	Rfm. KATZ, I., 7th Bn.
R/22100	Rfm. KAAS, W., 21st Bn.
A/27681	Rfm. KATZ, A., 1st Bn.
C/7146	Rfm. KEMP, S.,* 18th Bn.
21578	Rfm. KEEN, T. G., 6th Bn.
62908	Rfm. KIELBEG, N., 20th Bn.
32221	Rfm. KINSBERG, J., 1st Bn.
R/18620	Rfm. KINGSTONE, J. W.,* 16th Bn.
38569	Rfm. KISBERG, L., 18th Bn.
23815	Rfm. KLEIN, L., 14th Bn.
46682	Rfm. KLEIN, I.
17782	Rfm. KOSSICK, R.,* 13th Bn.
	Sgt. KOHN, H. D. (D.C.M.).
34020	Rfm. KRONENBERG, M., 10th Bn.
6827	Rfm. KONYM, M.,* 2nd Bn.
5/5074	Rfm. KOSKY, R.,* 2nd Bn.

King's Royal Rifle Corps.—*Continued.*

23818	Rfm. KRONEMBERG, M., 14th Bn.
32227	Rfm. KUTCHINSKY, A.,* 9th Bn.
23319	Rfm. KUTNER, B., 15th Bn.
25394	Rfm. LACHRAN, E., 5th Bn.
21008	Rfm. LAMPTEAR, T. W., 1st Bn.
68371	L/Cpl. LAZARUS, 52nd Bn.
R/15455	Rfm. LAZARUS, L., 6th Bn.
6/1156	Rfm. LAZARUS, J., 6th Bn.
393318	Pte. LAZAROFF, L., 52nd Bn.
R/18835	Rfm. LANSNER, E., 7th Bn.
40631	Rfm. LEVY, L. J., 6th Bn.
40427	Rfm. LEVY, P., 5th Bn.
33582	Rfm. LEVY, D.
29330	Rfm. LEVY, 6th Bn.
25423	Rfm. LEVY, W.
R/28813	Rfm. LEVY, A., 19th Bn.
21901	Rfm. LEVY, A. J., 7th Bn.
19731	Rfm. LEVY, C.
205537	Rfm. LEVY, L., 13th Bn.
205537	Rfm. LEVY, D., 17th Bn.
17976	Rfm. LEVY, S., 6th Bn.
	Rfm. LEVY, V. C.,
	Rfm. LEVY, H., 17th Bn.
1218	Sgt. LEVY, A. I.,* 2nd Bn.
201248	Rfm. LEVY, I., 16th Bn.
21902	Rfm. LEVY, L., 17th Bn.
37294	Rfm. LEVY, M., 11th Bn.
A/201797	Rfm. LEVY, C., 18th Bn.
23321	Rfm. LEVY, E., 13th Bn.
A/358	Rfm. LEVI, J., 8th Bn.
202322	Rfm. LEVY, J., 17th Bn.
880240	Rfm. LEVEY, E. B., 34th Bn.
	Rfm. LEVENE, S.,* 1st Bn.
596005	Rfm. LEVENE, M., 25th Bn.
Y/1163	Rfm. LEVENE, S.,* 8th Bn.
18854	Sig. LEVENSTON, C., 2nd Bn.
12764	Rfm. LEVITT, B., 6th Bn.
22795	Rfm. LEWIS, F. E., 14th Bn.
12551	Rfm. LEWIS, F. J., 15th Bn.
R/9463	Rfm. LEWIS, J.,* 9th Bn.
A/410	Rfm. LEWIS, W.,* 4th Bn.
17965	Rfm. LEWIS, M. P., 6th Bn.
R/32222	Rfm. LEWIS, H., 5th Bn.
21652	Rfm. LEO, K.
59681	L/Cpl. LEYMAN, H., 52nd Bn.
27540	Rfm. LERNER, W., 18th Bn.
18213	Rfm. LE BOSSE, T., 20th Bn.
18882	Rfm. LEE, A., 11th Bn.
2107	Rfm. LEIBHART, 8th Bn.
21885	Rfm. LETTER, S., 12th Bn.
R/32421	Rfm. LENA, J., 5th Bn.
R/36615	Rfm. LEBOVITCH, B., 5th Bn.
29415	Rfm. LIPSCHITZ, M.
30486	Rfm. LISSACK, H.
14008	Rfm. LIPMAN, J., 4th Bn.
26691	Rfm. LIZERBRAM, R., 16th Bn.
A/493	Rfm. LING, N., 13th Bn.
71413	Rfm. LONDON, D.
54370	Rfm. LYONS, L. S., 2nd Bn.
14737	Rfm. LOBER, S., 21st Bn.
R/13164	Rfm. LOWRY, M., 5th Bn.
202055	Rfm. LUBETSKY, J., 2nd Bn.
23859	Rfm. LYONS, A.
37474	Rfm. LYONS, A., 2nd Bn.
41899	Rfm. LEVEY, T., 1st Bn.
R/32217	Rfm. MARKS, G., 5th Bn.
R/27249	Rfm. MARKS, D., 5th Bn.
R/15142	Rfm. MARKS, J., 7th Bn.
13163	Rfm. MARKS, J.,* 2nd Bn.
36125	Rfm. MARKS, J., 5th Bn.
R/23364	Rfm. MARMELSTEIN, S.,* 9th Bn.
C/38767	Rfm. MAISEL, M., 2nd Bn.
1848	Rfm. MARCUS, H., 20th Bn.
201512	Rfm. MARCUS, S., 9th Bn.
34919	L/Cpl. MAGNUS, M., 9th Bn.
R/4274	Cpl. MARTINEZ, A., 13th Bn.
21826	Rfm. MARGOLLIS, A., 15th Bn.
34853	Rfm. MARGOLLIS, A., 10th Bn.
60824	Rfm. MADALYER, J., 52nd Bn.
R/27602	Rfm. MAZIN, J., 6th Bn.
8765	Rfm. MELLINS, J., 2nd Bn.
18765	Rfm. MECHULAM, I., 9th Bn.
37802	Rfm. MENDELSOHN, H. T., 18th Bn.
44661	Rfm. MEDNIKOFF, M., 16th Bn.
19732	Rfm. MERRIAN, D., 16th Bn.
36830	Rfm. MERBER, J.,* 2nd Bn.
2831	L/Sgt. MICHAEL, M. S., 10th Bn.
N/13130	L/Cpl. MIRON, G. (M.M.), 7th Bn.
A/379	Rfm. MILLER, E.,* 7th Bn.
30484	Rfm. MICHAELS, H., 17th Bn.
27229	Rfm. MILION, M., 20th Bn.
R/27538	Rfm. MOSELEY, L., 16th Bn.
21017	Rfm. MOROWITZ, A., 8th Bn.
30466	Rfm. MORIS, J., 1st Bn.
30079	Rfm. MORDECAI, L., 21st Bn.
33234	Rfm. MONTLACK, A., 18th Bn.
	Rfm. MYERS, T. (M.M.).
13810	Rfm. MOSS, J., 21st Bn.
23124	Rfm. MOSES, B., 15th Bn.
203569	Rfm. MORGON, L., 17th Bn.
R/32623	Rfm. MONTAGUE, C., 5th Bn.
23234	Rfm. MONTLACK, A., 18th Bn.
41730	Rfm. MYERS, A.,* 16th Bn.
38899	Rfm. MYERS, M., 9th Bn.
11266	Rfm. MYERS (MORDECAI), J.,* 1st Bn.
9462	Rfm. MYERS, J., 3rd Bn.
1710	Rfm. NATHAN, S., 5th Bn.
R/18161	Rfm. NATHAN,
39567	Rfm. NATALSKY, J., 5th Bn.
34244	Rfm. NANBROOK, S., 13th Bn.
323670	Rfm. NASILLSKI, D., 2nd Bn.
202587	Rfm. NEEDLEMAN, M., 18th Bn.
C/6683	Rfm. NEWMAN, S.,* 17th Bn.
	Rfm. NEWMAN, F., 14th Bn.
1186	Cpl. NEWMAN, A., 2nd Bn.

King's Royal Rifle Corps.—*Continued.*

8055	Rfm. NEWALKI, A., 52nd Bn.
R/300444	Rfm. NEWHOUSE, D. L.
7071	Rfm. NEWSTEAD, L., 20th Bn.
R/19178	L/Cpl. NEWROCK, M., 4th Bn.
	Rfm. NICHOLSON, M., 16th Bn.
R/21015	Rfm. NIEBERG, J. S., 17th Bn.
38233	Rfm. NICORESTI, G. C., 2nd Bn.
R/14550	Rfm. NIMAN S., 5th Bn.
14737	Rfm. NOBER, S., 21st Bn.
35759	Rfm. NYMAN, M., 1st Bn.
22102	Rfm. NYMAN, I., 11th Bn.
21196	Rfm. OSARVITCH, I., 5th Bn.
9761	Rfm. OLASKY, I., 20th Bn.
127166	Rfm. OWENS, S., 2nd Bn.
534269	Rfm. OGUS, G. H., 1st Bn.
R/30139	Rfm. OPPENHEIM, B., 6th Bn.
27277	Rfm. PAMPEL, A.,* 11th Bn.
14742	Rfm. PARKER, M., 7th Bn.
266968	Rfm. PRICE, B., 25th Bn.
R/38684	Rfm. PEREZ, I., 21nd Bn.
18059	Rfm. PEREZ, E., 16th Bn.
62116	Rfm. PEARL, L., 51st Bn.
20601	Rfm. PEARLSON, H., 1/60th Bn.
29433	Rfm. PERKOFF, B., 8th Bn.
22321	Rfm. PERETZ, J., 14th Bn.
2/5833	Rfm. PEATER, N.
21019	Rfm. PETLOCK, J.
60828	Rfm. PRICEMAN, L., 52nd Bn.
TR13/47207	Rfm. PHILLIPS, H., 51st Bn.
R/20310	Rfm. POLISHOFSKY, 19th Bn.
317507	Sgt. PRAG, J., 25th Bn.
R/8411	Rfm. PICKOLTZ, M., 9th Bn.
R/10640	Rfm. PYE, A., 3rd Bn.
21023	Rfm. PADLOFSKY, J.,* 9th Bn.
C/7178	Rfm. PRESTON, E., 18th Bn.
15089	Rfm. POLAKOFF, J.,* 2nd Bn.
37685	Rfm. PHILLIPS, S.,* 8th Bn.
18070	Rfm. POSNER, D., 5th Bn.
22918	Rfm. POLAK, P., 6th Bn.
393316	Rfm. PINKOPSKY, H., 52nd Bn.
	Rfm. RAPHAEL, S., 8th Bn.
	Rfm. RAPHAEL, L., 8th Bn.
32223	Rfm. RAPPERPORT, S., 9th Bn.
R/29413	Rfm. RABINOWITZ, B.,* 8th Bn.
35774	Rfm. ROSENBERG, J.
23335	Rfm. ROSENBERG, L.
13468	Rfm. ROSENBERG, J., 9th Bn.
23797	Rfm. ROSENBERG, G., 14th Bn.
205198	Rfm. ROSENBERG, A.,* 1st Bn.
R/29089	Rfm. ROSENBERG, B., 6th Bn.
38035	Rfm. ROSENBERG, T., 10th Bn.
A/201818	Rfm. ROSENBERG, L., 18th Bn.
23798	Rfm. ROSENTHAL, S., 14th Bn.
34242	Rfm. ROSENTHAL, S., 13th Bn.
	Rfm. ROSE, A., 1st Bn.
35170	Rfm. ROSE, S., 5th Bn.
R/32020	Rfm. ROSE, F., 5th Bn.
TR13/62226	L/Cpl. ROWBOTTOM, C., 51st Bn.
30020	Rfm. ROBUTTUM, A.
21749	Rfm. ROSEN, A., 10th Bn.
8411	Rfm. RICKHOLTZ, M., 7th Bn
23362	Rfm. REICHENBERG, D.
R/28695	Rfm. ROGERS, G., 19th Bn.
10470	Rfm. RUBENS, H., 2nd Bn.
R/146431	Rfm. ROSE, H., 11th Bn.
20966	Rfm. RICHMAN, W., 9th Bn.
41858	Rfm. RUBENSTEIN, B.,* 12th Bn.
29446	Rfm. RAPHAEL, N., 17th Bn.
	Rfm. REUBEN, B., 2nd Bn.
R/14769	Rfm. ROCKSHIA, P., 7th Bn.
	Rfm. ROSENTHAL, S., 13th Bn.
58870	Rfm. ROSSLYN, M., 2nd Bn.
3715	Rfm. SAMUELS, I., 2/5th Bn.
33120	Rfm. SAMUELS, J., 7th Bn.
	Rfm. SAMUELS, P., 5th Bn.
R/20985	Rfm. SAMUELS, A.,* 7th Bn.
53894	Rfm. SAMSON, I. S.,* 2nd Bn.
	Rfm. SAUL, S., 8th Bn.
31726	Rfm. SAUNDERS, J., 8th Bn.
	Rfm. SAVITZ, A., 11th Bn.
	Rfm. SAPP, F.
18058	Rfm. SALINSKY, H., 7th Bn.
21015	Rfm. SANDGROUND, H., 6th Bn.
31957	Rfm. SAX, V., 18th Bn.
28814	Rfm. SCHLANDOVER, D., 19th Bn.
37786	Rfm. SCHLINGBAUM, J., 6th Bn.
177676	Rfm. SCHNEIDER, J., 5th Bn.
32624	Rfm. SCHULTZ, P., 9th Bn.
R/37727	Rfm. SCHNEIDERMAN, L.,* 11th Bn.
R/39352	Rfm. SCHWEITZER, W., 13th Bn.
R/35577	Rfm. SCHWARTZMAN, D.,* 17th Bn.
32624	Rfm. SCHELTZ, P., 9th Bn.
33266	Rfm. SCHRADSKY, P., 7th Bn.
18853	Rfm. SCHWARTZ, S., 10th Bn.
939	Rfm. SCHLEICH, J., 8th Bn.
R/22227	Rfm. SCHILLING, R.,* 8th Bn.
522605	Rfm. SCHECKTER, M.. 3rd Bn.
60310	Rfm. SELINGBAUM, N., 52nd Bn.
51500	Rfm. SEIGENBAUM, H., 2nd Bn.
	Sig. SESSEL, G. H., 1st Bn.
22054	Rfm. SEGAL, I., 8th Bn.
R/15629	Rfm. SEGAL, J., 8th Bn.
R/18840	Rfm. SEGAL, G., 16th Bn.
3041	Rfm. SHERMAN, R.
897177	Rfm. SHARP, M.
R/18460	L/Cpl. SHAAP, M., 6th Bn.
33887	Rfm. SHAW, J.* 17th Bn.
204507	Rfm. SHURANCE, H., 12th Bn.
25049	Rfm. SIMMONS, H., 14th Bn.
23192	Rfm. SIMMONS, H., 15th Bn.
	Rfm. SIMMONS, E., 17th Bn.
41881	Rfm. SIMONS, A., 1st Bn.
201704	Rfm. SIMONS, P.,* 10th Bn.
18850	Rfm. SIMONS, A.
23948	Rfm. SIMONS, P., 14th Bn.

King's Royal Rifle Corps.—*Continued.*

30323	Rfm. SIMMONDS, S.	
4360	Rfm. SIMMONDS, C., 17th Bn.	
27350	Rfm. SILVER, B., 18th Bn.	
	Rfm. SILVER, R.	
7352	L/Cpl. SILVER, B.,* 1st Bn	
3908	Rfm. SILVER, T., 17th Bn.	
29466	Rfm. SILVERSTEIN, A., 19th Bn.	
2176	Rfm. SILVERSTEIN, L., 19th Bn.	
R/22093	Rfm. SILVERSTONE, L.,* 9th Bn.	
61896	Rfm. SILVERSTONE, M., 6th Bn.	
R/25266	Rfm. SILVERMAN, P.,* 18th Bn.	
A/1496	Cpl. SILVERMAN, E., 8th Bn.	
	Rfm. SILVERMAN, H., 8th Bn.	
57600	Rfm. SLAMER, E., 51st Bn.	
	Rfm. SIEV, J., 1st Bn.	
201704	Rfm. SIONS, P.,* 10th Bn.	
R/30988	Rfm. SINGER, N., 17th Bn.	
11884	Rfm. SINGER, P., 9th Bn.	
14614	Rfm. SIMON, G., 8th Bn.	
	Rfm. SIMPSON, D., 9th Bn.	
44502	Rfm. SLAVNER, E., 1st Bn.	
42053	Rfm. SMITH, C., 9th Bn.	
37643	Rfm. SMITH, J., 13th Bn.	
1921	L/Cpl. SMITH, F., 6th Bn.	
R/22022	Rfm. SMITH, N., 11th Bn.	
R/32018	Rfm. SMITH, M., 5th Bn.	
62522	Rfm. SOLOMON, A., 52nd Bn.	
22018	Rfm. SOLOMON, A., 1st Bn.	
	Rfm. SOLOMON, E. H., 9th Bn.	
A/1990	Rfm. SOLOMAN, B., 2nd Bn.	
23327	Rfm. SOLOMON, H., 18th Bn.	
58407	Rfm. SOLOMON, J., 25th Bn.	
6011	Rfm. SOLOMON, C., 13th Bn.	
203216	Rfm. SOLOMON, J., 16th Bn.	
21021	Rfm. SOLOMON, D., 16th Bn.	
23189	L/Cpl. SOLOMON, F.,* 9th Bn.	
2730	Rfm. SOLOMON, J., 12th Bn.	
14872	Rfm. SOLOMON, J., 16th Bn.	
R/32266	Rfm. SOLOMONS, R., 5th Bn.	
27226	Rfm. SOLOMONS, M.,* 2nd Bn.	
R/9593	Rfm. SOLOMONS, L.,* 1st Bn.	
18061	Rfm. SOLOMONS, H., 1st Bn.	
9801	Rfm. SOLOMONS, P., 6th Bn.	
34857	Rfm. SOLOMONS, D., 10th Bn.	
R/18848	Rfm. SOLOMONS, A., 21st Bn.	
R/33819	Rfm. SOLOMONS, H., 21st Bn.	
	Rfm. SNYDER, H., 8th Bn.	
15797	Rfm. SOPHER, R., 15th Bn.	
R/35663	Rfm. SPEVACK, J., 13th Bn.	
20986	Rfm. SPRINGERS, H. J., 7th Bn.	
61276	Rfm. SPRINGER, A. A., 20th Bn.	
A/204188	Rfm. SPRINGER, M.,* 13th Bn.	
	Rfm. STEREK, H.	
	Rfm. STEIN, H.	
R/30272	Rfm. STEIN, J., 17th Bn.	
R/19682	L/Cpl. STODEL, I. A.,* 16th Bn.	
517514	Rfm. STONE, H., 25th Bn.	
12145	Rfm. STEINBERG, L., 21st Bn.	
34075	Rfm. STAAL, M., 16th Bn.	
1129	Rfm. SUSSMAN, M., 2nd Bn.	
C/3283	Sgt. SUSMAN, D., 17th Bn.	
R/32260	Rfm. SUGARMAN, L., 5th Bn.	
21857	Rfm. SYMONS, A.	
325219	Rfm. SYMONS, H., 3rd Bn.	
	Rfm. SYMONS, L., 3rd Bn.	
	Cpl. SILVER, E., 1st Bn.	
R/26719	Rfm. TALTZBERG, L., 5th Bn.	
7251	Rfm. TAYLOR, S., 1st Bn.	
21856	Rfm. TETLER, S.	
A/204520	Rfm. TEACHER, A., 2nd Bn.	
201763	Rfm. TEINMAN, J., 18th Bn.	
21578	Rfm. THOMAS, G. K., 6th Bn.	
32823	Rfm. TOBIAS, H., 5th Bn.	
23188	Rfm. TREEP, J., 15th Bn.	
23317	Rfm. TREVES, M., 15th Bn.	
34859	Rfm. TREVES, H., 12th Bn.	
R/8107	Rfm. TUMPOWSKY, J., 5th Bn.	
39422	Rfm. UNGER, S., 13th Bn.	
200064	Rfm. VAN PRAAGH, L., 17th Bn.	
36653	L/Cpl. VALENTINE, G., 12th Bn.	
34244	Rfm. VANBROOK, S., 13th Bn.	
R/19644	Rfm. VALENCIA, R., 16th Bn.	
34820	Rfm. VELGEROSKY, J., 6th Bn.	
R/30391	Rfm. VEIN, N.	
59228	Rfm. VERBER, R.	
3318	Rfm. VOSS, C. 17th Bn.	
20987	Rfm. VOLCOVITCH, L., 9th Bn.	
40167	Rfm. WALKERWITCH, M., 1st Bn.	
42852	Rfm. WANSKER, H., 6th Bn.	
4887	Rfm. WEINSTEIN, P., 2/6th Bn.	
R/14108	Rfm. WEINSTEIN, G., 11th Bn.	
	Rfm. WERNER, M., 8th Bn.	
60821	Rfm. WIGMAN, A., 51st Bn.	
2331	Rfm. WINTINSKY, W., 16th Bn.	
	Rfm. WINTINSKY, A., 18th Bn.	
55979	Rfm. WINER, H., 5th Bn.	
12740	Rfm. WISE, M., 6th Bn.	
18845	Rfm. WOOLF, J.,* 16th Bn.	
C/3059	Rfm. WOOLF, S.,* 17th Bn.	
A/204003	Rfm. WOLF, B. J.,* 13th Bn.	
59655	Rfm. WOOLF, G. E., 3rd Bn.	
32718	Rfm. WOOLF, A., 5th Bn.	
C/6043	Rfm. WOOLFE, 18th Bn.	
R/13007	Rfm. WOOD, L., 1st B.	
23323	Rfm. WYNOCHENK, 15th Bn.	
20998	Rfm. YARITZKY, J., 5th Bn.	
60826	Rfm. YESSOLOVITCH, M., 52nd Bn.	
423222	Rfm. ZIMMERMAN, 13th Bn.	
C/6123	Rfm. ZIMMERMAN, J.,* 16th Bn.	
21855	Rfm. ZETTRE, S., 10th Bn.	
18825	Rfm. ZAUSMAN, E., 7th Bn.	
32966	A/Sgt. ZEELAND, W., 21st Bn.	

* Killed in Action or died on Active Service.

THE DUKE OF EDINBURGH'S (WILTSHIRE REGIMENT).

OFFICERS.

Lieut. EMANUEL, O.,* 1st Bn.
2nd Lieut. FALK, C. J. (M.C.), 7th Bn.
2nd Lieut. POSENER, P. J.,* 2nd Bn.

N.C.O.'s AND MEN.

31931	Pte. ASH, S., 2nd Bn.	
402126	Pte. AARONOVITCH, L., 6th Bn.	
31720	Pte. BLAUPAPER, N., 6th Bn.	
47903	L/Cpl. BLAU, N., 6th Bn.	
9908	Pte. BERKMAN, M., 5th Bn.	
204037	Pte. BRACKSTONE, A. W.	
	Pte. BARNETT, J. S.	
17119	Pte. COHEN, J., 7th Bn.	
17710	Pte. COLLIER, H., 6th Bn.	
33237	L/Cpl. COHEN, J.,* 2nd Bn.	
40082	Pte. COHEN, W., 6th Bn.	
	Pte. CRASH, M., 3rd Bn.	
189960	Pte. CONFIDERI, H., 2nd Bn.	
41638	Pte. COHEN, J., 1st Bn.	
27481	Pte. DE FRIEND, S., 1st Bn.	
26218	Pte. DEAN, C., 3rd Bn.	
36541	Pte. DUNNERSTEIN, A., 3rd Bn.	
8585	Pte. EHRENBERG, N., 1st Bn.	
17719	Pte. ENGLEMAN, A., 6th Bn.	
25360	Pte. EDELSTEIN, I., 8th Bn.	
27859	Pte. FIFER, G.,* 6th Bn.	
40089	Pte. FRIEDLANDER, L., 6th Bn.	
208893	Pte. GOODFRIEND, J., 6th Bn.	
43906	Pte. GRANITE, J.	
17745	Pte. HARRIS, S., 6th Bn.	
33	Pte. HYAMS, M., 2nd Bn.	
26973	Pte. HIRSCHMAN, S., 2nd Bn.	
32351	Pte. HURRENS, C. S., 3rd Bn.	
204204	Pte. ISRAEL, D., 2nd Bn.	
25646	Pte. ISAACS, A., 3rd Bn.	
127	Pte. JACKSON, S., 6th Bn.	
25508	Pte. JESKI, A., 6th Bn.	
27858	Pte. JESKI, R. L.,* 2nd Bn.	
	Pte. JACOBSON, S., 3rd Bn.	
33403	Pte. KUMOLICK, J., 5th Bn.	
26805	C.Q.M.S. LANDAW, M., 1/4th Bn.	
	Pte. LEVY, L.	
11925	Pte. LEVY, H., 5th Bn.	
30228	Pte. LEVENSON, W. H., 7th Bn.	
2354	Pte. LEVY, S., 3rd Bn.	
	Pte. MARKS, S.	
32426	Pte. MERMELSTEIN, G., 7th Bn.	
25405	Pte. MARKSON, H., 2nd Bn.	
616	Pte. MAZFIER, H.	
8599	Pte. NASH, W., 5th Bn.	
31747	Pte. PULVERMACHER, A., 2nd Bn.	
32974	Pte. RICHLAND, S., 2nd Bn.	
40154	Pte. RACHMULLIS, L., 6th Bn.	
33238	L/Cpl. ROTENBERG, B.,* 2nd Bn.	
25173	Pte. ROSENBERG, G., 5th Bn.	
39819	Pte. ROOD, B., 1st Bn.	
34367	Pte. RITCHIE, H., 3rd Bn.	
16082	Pte. SYMONDS, B., 2nd Bn.	
	Pte. SILVERMAN, E., 3rd Bn.	
	Pte. SHOTLAND, M.	
46788	Pte. SNIDER, D., 4th Res. Bn.	
29661	Pte. SYMONDS, B., 2nd Bn.	
4817	Pte. SHAPIRO, H., 7th Bn.	
87042	Pte. SILVERSTONE, J., 2nd Bn.	
312	Pte. TUCKER, E., 1st Bn.	
24753	Pte. ZIMMERMAN, E., 2nd Bn.	

* Killed in Action or died on Active Service.

THE MANCHESTER REGIMENT.

OFFICERS.

2nd Lieut. BERNSTEIN, J., 23rd Bn.
2nd Lieut. BESSO, A., 1st Bn.
2nd Lieut. BENOLIEL, S. H., 6th Bn.
2nd Lieut. CANSINO, J. H.,* 22nd Bn.
2nd Lieut. DRUCQUER, M. W., 2nd Bn.
2nd Lieut. DAVIS, L. E.,* 5th Bn.
2nd Lieut. DANZIGER, C. W. J.,* 21st Bn.
Capt. DRESCHFIELD, H. T.,* 13th Bn.
Capt. FRANKENBURG, S. S., 1/8th Bn.
2nd Lieut. FREEDMAN, B.,* 1/9th Bn.
Lieut. GROS, H. S., 20th Bn.
2nd Lieut. GOLDSTEIN, H., 2nd Bn.
Lieut. HENRIQUES, G. G., 16th Bn.
2nd Lieut. HARRIS, A. J., 21st Bn.
2nd Lieut. ISAACS, B. C.
2nd Lieut. JACOBS, J., 5th Bn.
Lieut. KLUGMAN, J. V., 22nd Bn.
Capt. KOHNSTAMM, N.,* 18th Bn.
Capt. KROLICK, P. D., 2nd Bn.
2nd Lieut. KAY, W., 11th Bn.
Lieut. KERSHAW, G., 9th Bn.
2nd Lieut. LEWIN, I., 2/10th Bn.
2nd Lieut. LYONS, A., 12th Bn.
Lieut. LEVINSTEIN, G. E.,* 26th Bn.
Lieut. MOSES, B., 12th Bn.
2nd Lieut. NATHAN, F. H. (M.C.), 11th Bn.
Capt. ROTHBAND, J. E.,* 23rd Bn.
2nd Lieut. RAPAPORT, L., 9th Bn.
Capt. SALOMON, S., 1/8th Bn.
Capt. SPIELMAN, H. L. I.,* 10th Bn.
2nd Lieut. SINGTON, A. J. C., 1st Bn.
2nd Lieut. SELIGMAN, L. B. (M.C.), 18th Bn.
Lieut. TUCKMAN, M. J., 12th Bn.
2nd Lieut. VANDYKE, P.
2nd Lieut. WALTERS, 11th Bn.

The Manchester Regt.—*Continued.*
N.C.O.'s AND MEN.

- 2177 L/Cpl. ABRAMS, B., 11th Bn.
- 49431 Pte. ABRAHAMS, I., 19th Bn.
- 252495 Pte. AKIN, 2/6th Bn.
- 277711 Pte. ANNISKI, J., 2/7th Bn.
- 52839 Pte. ASH, M., 20th Bn.
- Pte. ALMOND, S., 1st Bn.
- 23007 Pte. ANNETT, E., 3rd Bn.
- 55309 Pte. ARONBERG, S.,* 12th Bn.
- 34123 Pte. AINSKY, E., 4th Bn.
- 45137 Pte. ASKINS, J., 4th Bn.
- 38766 Pte. ABRAMOVITZ, I., 1st Bn.
- 400974 Pte. ABRAHAM, B., 3/8th Bn.
- 252492 Pte. ARTHUR, J., 2/6th Bn.
- 94669 Pte. ABRAHAMS, D.
- Pte. ALEX, M., 4th Bn.
- 201390 Pte. ABRAHAMS, J. W., 1st Bn.
- 10609 Pte. BERNSTEIN, M., 17th Bn.
- 8405 Pte. BERLYN, C. S., 17th Bn.
- 3860 Pte. BEROFSYI, J., 23rd Bn.
- 25747 Pte. BERNSTEIN, S., 24th Bn.
- 40738 Pte. BAKER, D.,* 22nd Bn.
- Pte. BLOOM, H., 22nd Bn.
- 28639 Pte. BERNSTEIN, J., 19th Bn.
- 30095 L/Cpl. BROOKE-FOX, H., 16th Bn.
- 34528 Pte. BARNETT, H., 2nd Bn.
- 7537 Pte. BROWN, J., 2nd Bn.
- 40547 Pte. BARNETT, M., 12th Bn.
- 377371 Pte. BERLINSKI, A., 2/10th Bn.
- 400294 Pte. BELL, D., 2/5th Bn.
- 277076 Pte. BLACK, I., 2/7th Bn.
- 2367 Pte. BENZIMRA, W., 1/6th Bn.
- 202681 Pte. BARNETT, L., 16th Bn.
- 49099 Pte. BARNETT, F., 22nd Bn.
- 4984 Pte. BENJAMIN, W., 6th Bn.
- 4189 Pte. BERKS, J., 7th Bn.
- 858 Sgt. BENJAMIN, L., 11th Bn.
- 9070 Pte. BARNARD, S., 7th Bn.
- Pte. BASS, J., 1st Bn.
- 1862 Pte. BURMAN, A., 2nd Bn.
- 25128 Cpl. BROOK, B., 3rd Bn.
- 47659 Pte. BLASER, M., 18th Bn.
- 2403 Pte. BALON, J. E.,* 1/7th Bn.
- 62272 Pte. BLACK, E., 22nd Bn.
- 351858 Pte. BENSON, M., 1/6th Bn.
- 57556 Pte. BLUMENTHAL, J.
- 281850 Pte. BERKSON, M., 1/6th Bn.
- 250462 Pte. BENZIMRA, S., 6th Bn.
- 39229 Pte. BLACK, S., 1st Bn.
- 36786 Pte. BERTLESTEIN, S., 1st Bn.
- 80159 Pte. BROWN, J., 16th Bn.
- Pte. BRODIE, L., 9th Bn.
- 55856 Pte. BARRITZ, C.
- 1345 Cpl. BOODSON, L.,* 6th Bn.
- 36336 Pte. BARRETT, H., 13th Bn.
- 25601 Pte. BARNETT, H., 22nd Bn.
- 34265 Pte. BARNETT, L., 3rd Bn.
- 4770 Pte. BARNETT, M., 3/6th Bn.
- 5664 Pte. BERENBAUM, I., 3/8th Bn.
- 5658 Pte. BERENBAUM, S., 8th Bn.
- 1607 Sgt. BOODSON, D., 6th Bn.
- 35754 Pte. BRAZIL, J., 25th Bn.
- Sgt. Major BROOKS, H. (D.C.M., M.S.M.), 1/5th Bn.
- 46573 Pte. BARNETT, M., 3rd Bn.
- 82754 Pte. BALKIN, I., 53rd Bn.
- 1839 Pte. BLUMENTHAL, E., 6th Bn.
- 25455 Pte. BARFHAPSKY, E., 11th Bn.
- Pte. BENTATA, J. T., 6th Bn.
- Pte. BLOOM, L., 7th Bn.
- Pte. BINNS, H., 3rd Bn.
- 1824 Pte. COHEN, A., 1st Bn.
- 1891 Pte. COHEN, J., 1st Bn.
- 6494 Pte. COHEN, S.,* 16th Bn.
- 6851 Pte. COHEN, M., 16th Bn.
- 11514 Pte. COWAN, A. G., 19th Bn.
- 20015 Pte. COHEN, A., 22nd Bn.
- 26196 Pte. COHEN, B.,* 21st Bn.
- 4024 Pte. COHEN, D.,* 21st Bn.
- 11514 Pte. COWEN, A., 19th Bn.
- 9393 Pte. COPELAND, A., 16th Bn.
- 32958 Pte. CANTER, H., 16th Bn.
- 5220 Pte. COHEN, N., 18th Bn.
- 34134 Pte. CROOP, M.,* 18th Bn.
- 46612 Pte. CARLIPH, S.,* 12th Bn.
- 203057 Pte. CLAYMAN, A., 2/10th Bn.
- 42905 Pte. COHEN, S.,* 2/5th Bn.
- 252663 Pte. COHEN, J.,* 2/6th Bn.
- 4843 Pte. COHEN, M., 1/5th Bn.
- 4176 L/Cpl. CLASSIE, E., 1/6th Bn.
- 77402 Pte. COPITCH, B., 16th Bn.
- 51163 Pte. CHARIG, A., 19th Bn.
- 3786 Pte. COHEN, A., 3/7th Bn.
- 2204 Pte. COHEN, M., 53rd Bn.
- 47245 Pte. COHEN, H., 23rd Bn.
- 47800 Pte. COHEN, S., 23rd Bn.
- 32242 L/Cpl. COHEN, H., 23rd Bn.
- 32497 Pte. COHEN, H., 3rd Bn.
- 32704 Pte. COHEN, M., 3rd Bn.
- 32644 Pte. COWEN, S., 3rd Bn.
- 48748 Pte. COOPER, I., 3rd Bn.
- 39087 Pte. COHEN, D., 3rd Bn.
- 78109 Pte. COHEN, J., 22nd Bn.
- 1827 Pte. COHEN, B., 1st Bn.
- 44073 Sgt. COMER, D., 52nd Bn.
- 2292 Pte. CLIFFORD, 7th Bn.
- 2582 Pte. COHEN, D., 7th Bn.
- 60100 Pte. CHADWICK, P., 3rd Bn.
- 5718 Pte. COHEN, M., 2nd Bn.
- 19759 Pte. CHINDLER, L., 21st Bn.
- 36777 Pte. COHEN, H., 26th Bn.
- 7800 Pte. COHEN, S., 23rd Bn.
- 34045 Pte. CORAL, I., 24th Bn.
- 54103 Pte. COHEN, H., 4th Bn.
- 110140 Pte. COHEN, M., 53rd Bn.

The Manchester Regt.—*Continued.*

49096	Pte. COHEN, W., 22nd Bn.
5245	Pte. CIVEL, H., 3/7th Bn.
44141	Pte. COHEN, N.
3323	Pte. COPELAND, R., 1/8th Bn.
33981	Pte. COLLINS, H., 3rd Bn.
4713	Pte. COHEN, S., 6th Bn.
343231	Pte. COHEN, I.
34532	L/Cpl. DRUCE, L., 17th Bn.
16379	Pte. DRILSMAN, J., 16th Bn.
377515	Pte. DANIELS, L., 2/10th Bn.
1747	Pte. DAVIDSON, S.,* 1/7th Bn.
5584	Pte. DYSON, J., 2nd Bn.
27011	L/Cpl. DAVIES, C. A., 4th Bn.
34559	Pte. DELACOVITCH, H., 20th Bn.
303225	Pte. DAVIS, J., 2nd Bn.
	L/Cpl. DAVIES, W., 2nd Bn.
31937	L/Cpl. EDELSTON, S.,* 23rd Bn.
38716	Pte. EPSTEIN, H., 3rd Bn.
37352	Pte. EVENTHAL, H. ,3rd Bn.
45293	Pte. EVENTHAL, J., 3rd Bn.
302039	Pte. ELLIS, L., 9th Bn.
352776	Pte. ERDMAN, A., 1st Bn.
	Pte. ELLINGER, G. C., 1st Bn.
	Pte. EPSTEIN, B.
25762	Pte. FINBERG, H., 23rd Bn.
34953	Pte. FLOX, M., 22nd Bn.
29881	Pte. FRANKS, H., 11th Bn.
3200	Pte. FINK, S.,* 12th Bn.
50206	Pte. FLOWERS, J., 11th Bn.
34314	Pte. FREEDMAN, H., 1,th Bn.
25358	Pte. FINEBERG, H., 11th Bn.
40616	Pte. FEITLEBAUM, N., 21st Bn.
37338	Pte. FRIEND, J., 3rd Bn.
49889	Pte. FAUST, A. E.
39987	Pte. FINK, N., 4th Bn.
55595	Pte. FRIEDLAND, H., 3rd Bn.
35306	Pte. FRANKLIN, L., 1st Bn.
	Pte. FREEDMAN, A., 24th Bn.
27363	Pte. FIFER, J.
24935	Pte. FINKLESTEIN, P.
56012	Pte. FINKLESTEIN, N., 3rd Bn.
56009	Pte. FINKLESTEIN, L., 2nd Bn.
7295	Pte. FISHER, E., 8th Bn.
25040	Pte. FIRESTONE, M., 1st Bn.
4373	Pte. FINKEL, A., 7th Bn.
60281	Pte. FERBER, C., 53rd Bn.
48015	Pte. FLITTLEMAN, D., 18th Bn.
53428	Pte. FIGENBAUM, 9th Bn.
3095	Sgt. FOX, B., 16th Bn.
	Pte. FREEMAN, D. B., 7th Bn.
	Pte. FISHLER, W., 8th Bn.
62439	Pte. GOODMAN, M., 21st Bn.
	L/Cpl. GLYNN, S. (M.M.), 22nd Bn.
63558	Pte. GOODALL, L., 1/6th Bn.
39072	Pte. GERBER, J.
39073	Pte. GERBER, M.
86255	Pte. GOULD, H., 52nd Bn.
85723	Pte. GORDON, B., 51st Bn.
35144	Pte. GORDON, S.
7498	Pte. GOLDSTONE, A., 16th Bn.
57252	L/Cpl. GOLDING, J.,* 1/7th Bn.
35887	Pte. GREAGER, E., 17th Bn.
12083	Pte. GLASKIE, C., 19th Bn.
	C.S.M. GILBERT, J. (D.C.M.), 19th Bn.
18987	Pte. GOODMAN, W., 21st Bn.
	Sgt. GOLDMAN, S., 23rd Bn.
32801	Pte. GOLDFISH, S., 22nd Bn.
35386	Pte. GOODMAN, G., 21st Bn.
39687	Pte. GREENOVITCH, I., 24th Bn.
34499	Pte. GLAZIER, H., 20th Bn.
25440	Pte. GOLDBERG, M., 19th Bn.
35171	Pte. GOODMAN, J., 16th Bn.
277767	Pte. GUSTAFF, B., 16th Bn.
277121	Pte. GOLDSTONE, H., 16th Bn.
34468	Pte. GOLDSTONE, G., 2nd Bn.
29430	Pte. GLASS, F.,* 2nd Bn.
203335	Pte. GOLDSTONE, M., 2/5th Bn.
33950	Pte. GLASBERG, J.,* 12th Bn.
I/45307	Pte. GOLDBERG, N., 12th Bn.
245380	Pte. GILMAN, H., 22nd Bn.
36669	Pte. GOLDSTONE, J., 14th Bn.
36888	Pte. GOLDSTONE, J.
9283	Pte. GOLDSTEIN, M., 17th Bn.
	Pte. GREEN, 3rd Bn.
2127	Pte. GRANT, L., 3rd Bn.
23300	Pte. GREENBERG, 3rd Bn.
46962	Pte. GOLDBERG, J., 3rd Bn.
22461	C.S.M. GOLDMAN, S., 23rd Bn.
53431	Pte. GOODBREAD, G. M., 2/9th Bn.
45307	Pte. GOLDBERG, M., 12th Bn.
39132	Pte. GOLDSTONE, J., 13th Bn.
5717	Pte. GOLDSTON, E., 28th Bn.
87155	Pte. GOLDSTEIN, N., 1/7th Bn.
276787	Pte. GOLDBERG, H. L., 1st Bn.
295176	Pte. GOLDSTEIN, B., 2/7th Bn.
400869	Pte. GRINDER, H.
	Pte. GREEN, H., 1st Bn.
	Pte. GOLDSTONE, A.
62350	Pte. GARDIE, P., 4th Bn.
94452	Pte. GILLMAN, S., 53rd Bn.
215171	Pte. GOODMAN, J., 25th Bn.
36478	Pte. GORDON, T., 26th Bn.
2503	L/Cpl. GOULD, M., 18th Bn.
97246	Pte. GOLDBERG, S., 53rd Bn.
22461	C.S.M. GOLDMAN, M., 23rd Bn.
59104	Pte. GERBER, J., 3rd Bn.
44060	Pte. GWILLIAN, A. E., 1/6th Bn.
295176	Pte. GOLDSTEIN, B., 2/7th Bn.
9444	Pte. HANSELL, A.,* 17th Bn.
19995	Pte. HERBERT, M., 21st Bn.
1255	Pte. HYMAN, I.* (PIVANSKI), 7th Bn.
19860	Pte. HARRIS, I. H., 21st Bn.
47879	Pte. HAFT, I. G.,* 18th Bn.
202298	Pte. HOREWITZ, J., 2/5th Bn.

The Manchester Regt.—*Continued.*

203077 Pte. HARMAN, E. J., 2/7th Bn.
36478 Pte. HOFFENBERG, I.
       Sig. HAMANI, E. E.
 4943 Sgt. HARRIS, F., 4th Bn.
27140 Sgt. HARPER, L. L., 1st Bn.
45156 Pte. HYMAN, S., 4th Bn.
30875 Pte. HARRIS, A., 1st Bn.
20088 Pte. HALPERN, B., 1st Bn.
36466 Pte. HYMAN, H., 26th Bn.
36782 Pte. HYMAN, M., 26th Bn.
303729 Pte. HERWALD, M., 8th Bn.
35526 Pte. HARRIS, P., 14th Bn.
19784 Pte. HALPER, G.
55981 Pte. HOREVITZ, N.
48015 Pte. HITTLEMAN, D., 18th Bn.
77837 Pte. HOLSTEIN, L., 1st Bn.
       Pte. HALL, H., 8th Bn.
53887 Pte. ISRAEL, A., 2/7th Bn.
38124 Pte. ISAACS, S., 3rd Bn.
55005 Pte. ISAACS, J., 4th Bn.
303755 Pte. ISAACS, A., 8th Bn.
30124 Pte. ISAACS, S., 23rd Bn.
12/4174 Sgt. JACKSON, S., 12th Bn.
27325 Pte. JACOBS, H., 16th Bn.
34481 Sgt. JACOBS, R. B.,* 12th Bn.
276292 Pte. JAFFE, D., 1/7th Bn.
276343 Pte. JAFFE, S., 1/7th Bn.
29818 Pte. JACOBS, D., 14th Bn.
110140 Pte. JAPINSKY, L., 53rd Bn.
 2618 Pte. JACOBS, A., 2nd Bn.
20037 Pte. JACOBS, R., 1st Bn.
35196 Pte. JACOBS, J., 1st Bn.
85743 Pte. JACOBS, B., 51st Bn.
51043 Pte. JACOBS, I. L., 10th Bn.
303588 L/Cpl. JOSEPH, M., 8th Bn.
       Pte. JACOBSON, W., 6th Bn.
30872 Pte. JACOBS, E.
       Pte. JACOBS, H., 4th Bn.
       Pte. JACOBS, R., 22nd Bn.
       Pte. JOSEPH, B., 6th Bn.
12/7945 Pte. KWARTZ, J., 12th Bn.
48653 Pte. KERSH, P., 19th Bn.
 4943 Pte. KITOFSKI, W.,* 2/7th Bn.
33854 Pte. KENDLE, G., 16th Bn.
352653 Sgt. KAY, S., 2/9th Bn.
       Sgt. KAUFMAN, H. (M.M.).
 4883 Pte. KESSLER, L., 1/6th Bn.
245524 Pte. KERSHAW, R., 12th Bn.
       Sgt. KUTNER, P., 2nd Bn.
 2206 Pte. KRELL, J.,* 1/7th Bn.
37349 Pte. KEISH, H., 3rd Bn.
55838 Pte. KUIT, M., 4th Bn.
80488 Pte. KOSTORIS, L., 5th Bn.
14/34530 Pte. KORNOFSKY, L., 14th Bn.
14/32377 Pte. KEADANSKY, M., 14th Bn.
       Pte. KRUPP, L., 5th Bn.
       Pte. KRAM, E., 7th Bn.
27881 Pte. LYONS, R., 2nd Bn.
22533 L/Cpl. LEVY, M.,* 23rd Bn.
 9172 Pte. LIGHT, L., 17th Bn.
12561 Pte. LIZAR, L., 19th Bn.
18937 Pte. LEWIS, H., 21stB Bn.
20101 Dmr. LEVY, L., 22nd Bn.
40670 Pte. LEVI, J., 21st Bn.
47971 Pte. LUDWIG, H., 22nd Bn.
47701 Pte. LAZARUS, S., 22nd Bn.
35426 Pte. LEWIS, B., 16th Bn.
 2667 L/Cpl. LEVY, L. 2nd Bn.
327367 Pte. LIPMAN, S., 2/9th Bn.
377550 Pte. LAWRENCE, M., 2/10th Bn.
203082 Pte. LEVINE, W., 2/10th Bn.
302783 Pte. LEVY, A., 2/8th Bn.
252218 Pte. LEWIS, L., 2/6th Bn.
       Sgt. LEON, A., 6th Bn.
53863 Pte. LEVY, R., 2/6th Bn.
251486 Pte. LIVINGSTONE, J.,* 1/6th Bn.
 2621 Pte. LOBEL, E., 1/7th Bn.
 4311 Pte. LEE, B., 1/7th Bn.
 3709 Pte. LEVY, F., 1/7th Bn.
295047 Cpl. LATTER, B., 1/7th Bn.
282013 Pte. LERMAN, A., 1/7th Bn.
49830 Pte. LAZARUS, H., 1/7th Bn.
38955 Pte. LAWRENCE, J., 23rd Bn.
21012 Pte. LAZARUS, R., 23rd Bn.
203306 Pte. LEVY, B., 2nd Bn.
61927 Pte. LEMBERGER, 2n dBn.
53252 Pte. LAZARUS, J., 11th Bn.
28586 Pte. LEVY, R., 23rd Bn.
       Pte. LEWIS, M., 2nd Bn.
33171 Pte. LEES, S., 3rd Bn.
27731 Pte. LEWIS, J., 3rd Bn.
35170 L/Cpl. LEVY, H., 3rd Bn.
46652 Pte. LEVY, I.,* 16th Bn.
46780 Pte. LEWIS, N., 3rd Bn.
 5719 Pte. LEVY, L., 3rd Bn.
27918 Pte. LEWIS, C., 3rd Bn.
38640 Pte. LEWIS, M.
47667 Pte. LIZARS, H,
14889 Pte. LEES, H., 22nd Bn.
63558 Pte. LEWIS, J., 1/6th Bn.
32437 L/Cpl. LUDWIG, D., 3rd Bn.
61471 Pte. LIPMAN, 12th Bn.
 5198 Pte. LEVY, A.,* 21st Bn.
48266 Pte. LASERSON, A.
       Pte. LEVY, L. (M.M.).
59098 Pte. LEVIN, M., 3rd Bn.
 2661 Pte. LEVY, T., 1st Bn.
48020 Pte. LEVENE, H., 10th Bn.
 6192 Pte. LEA, M., 5th Bn.
34479 Pte. LEWIS, T., 12th Bn.
 4854 Pte. LASCISON, A., 5th Bn.
49771 Pte. LESSER, M., 4th Bn.
276200 Pte. LEVY, F.

The Manchester Regt.—*Continued.*

42067 L/Cpl. LECHS, S., 22nd Bn.
34477 Pte. LEWIS, A., 3rd Bn.
36423 Pte. LIPMAN, H., 4th Bn.
34538 Pte. LOPPER, J. E., 14th Bn.
4794 Pte. LEVY, J., 3/5th Bn.
1845 Pte. LEVY, G. D., 22nd Bn.
5302 Pte. LEVY, A., 2/5th Bn.
C.S.M. LEBELSKI, I. (M.M.).
2579 Pte. LEVY, A., 7th Bn.
66332 Pte. LEVINSKY, S., 53rd Bn.
250374 Pte. LORRES, J., 1/6th Bn.
4468 Pte. LABOVITZ, M., 1/7th Bn.
48020 Pte. LEVENE, H., 18th Bn.
22925 Pte. MASSING, J., 23rd Bn.
12150 Cpl. MILLER, D. (D.C.M., M.M.), 19th Bn.
25461 Pte. MAYERS, R., 18th Bn.
9467 Pte. MORRIS, P., 17th Bn.
24679 L/Cpl. MARKS L., 17th Bn.
12156 Pte. MOSCO, A., 19th Bn.
34072 Pte. MORRIS, N.,* 19th Bn.
18948 Pte. MARKS, M., 21st Bn.
47938 Pte. MICHELSON, H.,* 22nd Bn.
276503 Pte. MYERS, H., 22nd Bn.
2598 Pte. MATTHEWS, A., 22nd Bn.
3618 Pte. McKENNELL, J., 11th Bn.
34535 Pte. MALLON, G.,1 6th Bn.
Pte. MILLER, T.
39982 Pte. MORRIS, H., 17th Bn.
3307 Cpl. MASON, A., 18th Bn.
31986 Pte. MARKS, W.,* 2nd Bn.
53764 Pte. MICHAELS, M., 2/6th Bn.
250216 Sgt. MORRIS, M., 2/6th Bn.
252255 Pte. MORRIS, 2/6th Bn.
400238 Pte. MARKS, J., 2/7th Bn.
42302 Pte. MARKS, H.,* 16th Bn.
377411 Pte. MARKS, H., 2/10th Bn.
202284 Pte. MORYOSEPH, S.,* 2/5th Bn.
344837 Pte. MICHAEL, H., 2/9th Bn.
276612 Pte. MILLWARD, A.,* 1/7th Bn.
46536 Pte. MICHAELOVITCH, M., 23rd Bn.
29136 Pte. MORRIS, M., 23rd Bn.
245350 Pte. MORRIS, J., 2nd Bn.
57538 Pte. MYBERG, J., 11th Bn.
4389 Pte. MOSS, H., 6th Bn.
2752 Pte. MILLER, H., 2nd Bn.
1429 Pte. MARKS, S.,* 1st Bn.
39873 Pte. MISELL, W., 11th Bn.
36331 Pte. MISTOVSKI, M., 23rd Bn.
1643 Pte. MARLOW, H., 2nd Bn.
25291 Pte. MENDICK, A., 3rd Bn.
2004 Pte. MARKS, J., 3rd Bn.
45245 Pte. MARKS, L.
245397 Pte. MOSCOVITCH, I., 22nd Bn.
93873 Pte. MISSELL, W. G., 4th Bn.
39982 Pte. MORRIS, H., 4th Bn.
45245 Pte. MARKS, L., 4th Bn.

50276 Pte. MISTOVSKI, J.
5880 Pte. MARKS, H., 2/8th Bn.
25174 Pte. MANCHAR, H. N., 25th Bn.
14/29549 Pte. MARKS, H., 14th Bn.
12146 Pte. MILLS, D.
235422 Pte. MITCHELSON, S., 2nd Bn.
14/29403 Pte. MARKS, M., 14th Bn.
36762 Pte. MEYERS, H., 25th Bn.
5453 Pte. MORRIS, S., 2/6th Bn.
33628 Pte. MYERS, W., 26th Bn.
245350 Pte. MORRIS, H., 2nd Bn.
401158 Pte. MORRIS, S., 28th Bn.
3904 L/Cpl. NIMNI, J., 12th Bn.
53456 Pte. NATHAN, G., 2/7th Bn.
23378 Pte. NICHICK, J., 11th Bn.
32712 Pte. NATHAN, A., 3rd Bn.
57538 Pte. NYBERG, I., 11th Bn.
47938 L/Cpl. NICHOLSON, H., 22nd Bn.
9113 Pte. NARRENBERG, A. G., 1/7th Bn.
4981 Pte. NATHAN, H., 6th Bn.
377855 Pte. OPPENHEIM, E., 1/10th Bn.
51232 Pte. OPPENHEIM, E.,* 19th Bn.
29619 Pte. OPPENHEIM, P., 3rd Bn.
57543 Pte. OBENSTEIN, A., 11th Bn.
40653 Pte. PAYMAN, L., 21st Bn.
25462 Pte. PHILLIPS, L., 18th Bn.
40171 Pte. PAREEZER, S., 21st Bn.
378011 Pte. POVELSKY, H., 2/10th Bn.
2700 Pte. PRESS, M., 1st Bn.
25496 Pte. POVIDLER, A., 3rd Bn.
45241 Pte. POVELSKY, I,. 4th Bn.
203190 Pte. PORTNER, 5th Bn.
6617 Pte. POLLICK, S., 3/8th Bn.
6674 Pte. POSNER, B., 2/8th Bn.
30872 Pte. PERSIMMON, J., 1st Bn.
105336 Pte. PAUSE, M.
2483 Pte. POSNER, C.
Pte. PHILLIPS, S., 7th Bn.
12194 Sgt. ROSENBERG, A., 19th Bn.
47993 Pte. ROSENTHAL, J,. 2nd Bn.
45240 Pte. RAZEL, H., 16th Bn.
34038 Pte. ROSENSON, J., 17th Bn.
45042 Pte. ROSENBERG, N., 17th Bn.
47203 Pte. ROSENBLOOM, H.,* 12th Bn.
352816 Pte. RUBNER, S., 2/9th Bn.
2045 Pte. RASKY, L. S.,* 2/5th Bn.
37108 Pte. ROSENSON, H. U., 2/7th Bn.
251467 Pte. ROSENBLOOM, J., 1/6th Bn.
628 L/Cpl. ROSENTHAL, H.,* 2nd Bn.
49131 Pte. ROSEN, L., 3rd Bn.
34041 Pte. RUBENSTEIN, M.,* 19th Bn.
37108 Pte. ROSEN, H., 2/7th Bn.
45042 Pte. ROSENBERG M., 4th Bn.
57567 Pte. RUMDOMSKY, 1/8th Bn.
75890 Pte. RABJOHUS, A., 4th Bn.
400859 L/Cpl. ROSENBAUM, H.
268406 Pte. ROSENBLOOM, L., 1/7th Bn.

The Manchester Regt.—*Continued.*

36732 Pte. Rabin, A., 25th Bn.
4818 Pte. Reuben, E., 5th Bn.
203502 Pte. Roland, L., 5th Bn.
14/29536 Pte. Rickler, J. L., 14th Bn.
36487 Pte. Rosenberg, S., 26th Bn.
44837 Pte. Rosenthal, 9th Bn.
84942 Pte. Rose, E. V., 52nd Bn.
53428 Pte. Rosenthal,
2172 Pte. Shire, M., 2nd Bn.
2534 Pte. Stillman, A., 2nd Bn.
10713 Cpl. Stahl, M. E., 18th Bn.
31302 Pte. Silverstein, S., 18th Bn.
34538 L/Cpl. Soffer, J. S., 17th Bn.
27829 L/Cpl. Sugarman, M.* 17th Bn.
18039 Pte. Simons, N., 20th Bn.
20117 Pte. Shippen, L., 22nd Bn.
20727 Pte. Segal, M., 22nd Bn.
168 Sgt. Smith, I., (V.C.) 1st Bn.
28874 Pte. Sniderman, J., 20th Bn.
35802 Pte. Solomons, M., 22nd Bn.
19757 Pte. Shindler, L., 21st Bn.
33294 Pte. Shiers, S., 21st Bn.
42067 Pte. Secks, S., 22nd Bn.
47264 Pte. Solomon, M., 19th Bn.
34189 Pte. Sternberg, N., 16th Bn.
33847 Pte. Smullen, H.,* 16th Bn.
47904 Pte. Silverman, S., 18th Bn.
36832 Pte. Stone, J., 16th Bn.
352814 Pte. Swordlow, L., 2/9th Bn.
202947 Pte. Saker, L., 2/5th Bn.
240813 Pte. Spero, A., 2/5th Bn.
31243 Pte. Stone, H., 2/7th Bn.
251908 Pte. Solomon, B.,* 1/6th Bn.
1683 Cpl. Seideman, C., 1/7th Bn.
276557 Pte. Seideman, R., 1/7th Bn.
302579 Pte. Simon, J., 2nd Bn.
2152 Pte. Scheer, J., 2nd Bn.
2151 Pte. Sher, S., 2nd Bn.
756 Pte. Sternshine, H., 1st Bn.
5007 Pte. Symons, A., 8th Bn.
33502 Pte. Stone, R.,* 16th Bn.
23174 Pte. Scholes, J. W., 3rd Bn.
38661 L/Cpl. Samuels, D., 3rd Bn.
36897 Pte. Strauss, W. H., 3rd Bn.
48665 Pte. Sniderman, B., 3rd Bn.
203189 Pte. Singer, M., 21st Bn.
51784 Pte. Shapiro, I., 22nd Bn.
203843 Pte. Suchard, S., 18th Bn.
35082 Pte. Solomon, M., 28th Bn.
85807 Pte. Stoloff, J., 51st Bn.
39123 Pte. Sonnenberg, I., 13th Bn.
56023 Pte. Stein, M., 3rd Bn.
31243 Pte. Strong, H., 12th Bn.
94949 Pte. Solomons, S., 3rd Bn.
59627 Pte. Senofsky, H., 53rd Bn.
202947 Pte. Saiker, L., 2/5th Bn.
303862 Pte. Sackier, I., 8th Bn.

34089 Pte. Sheratsky, H., 14th Bn.
Sgt. Stahl, J., 22nd Bn.
272950 Pte. Sterling, L., 5th Bn.
56023 Pte. Stein, S., 3rd Bn.
Pte. Salzedo, S., 3rd Bn.
75752 Pte. Solden, J., 1st Bn.
Pte. Serevitch, J.
Pte. Stark, S., 8th Bn.
Cpl. Stahl, F., 27th Bn.
Pte. Silverstone, J.
Pte. Steinberg, F., 19th Bn.
59875 Pte. Stone, H.,* 1/6th Bn.
40616 Pte. Teitelbaum, M., 21st Bn.
35887 Pte. Treager, E., 17th Bn.
202442 Pte. Teulmin, 2/5th Bn.
302635 Pte. Tavill, E., 2nd Bn.
295129 Pte. Taylor, J., 1/7th Bn.
350374 Cadet Torres, J., 2/7th Bn.
10844 Sgt. Taylor, S., 22nd Bn.
7278 Pte. Tabhurst, V., 8th Bn.
6458 Pte. Tovill, S., 2/8th Bn.
30834 Pte. Treager, J., 1st Bn.
6181 Pte. Tuckman, J., 8th Bn.
36676 Pte. Tobias, J., 26th Bn.
36344 Pte. Toff, G., 14th Bn.
56003 L/Cpl. Tuckman, L., 1st Bn.
33620 Pte. Viner, B., 17th Bn.
33612 Pte. Vingan, P., 21st Bn.
25455 Pte. Vershofsky, E,, 11th Bn.
21570 Pte. Velensky, B., 2/6th Bn.
64616 L/Cpl. Verber, R., 16th Bn.
506 Pte. Valentine, A. H., 1st Bn.
26554 Pte. White, L., 19th Bn.
49096 Pte. Wise, M. C., 22nd Bn.
Cpl. White, L. W. (M.M.), 10th Bn.
42050 Pte. Williams, H., 22nd Bn.
23252 Pte. Wilchenski, H., 21st Bn.
29874 Pte. Weisberg, J., 11th Bn.
36340 Pte. Weinberg, D., 16th Bn.
42284 Pte. Wolff, A., 2/9th Bn.
377616 Pte. Weiss, N., 2/10th Bn.
377288 Pte. Wolfe, R., 2/10th Bn.
251776 Pte. Weintraub, 2/6th Bn.
377288 Pte. Wolfe, P., 1/6th Bn.
3689 Pte. Wise, J., 1/7th Bn.
245283 Pte. Williams, B., 2nd Bn.
3569 Pte. Warn, L., 7th Bn.
25215 Pte. Wolfe, M., 25th Bn.
23023 Pte. Weingard, A. J., 3rd Bn.
37111 Pte. Weitzman, D., 3rd Bn.
32690 Pte. Weiner, T. D., 3rd Bn.
29874 Pte. Wiseberg, J., 11th Bn.
23023 Pte. Weingard, A. I., 23rd Bn.
627564 Pte. Wiseman, S., 1st Bn.
39439 Pte. Weinberg, M., 1st Bn.
35757 Pte. Weinberg, H.,* 1st Bn.
30964 Pte. Waters, J., 1st Bn.

The Manchester Regt.—*Continued.*

41537 Pte. WEINOW, B., 13th Bn.
303276 Pte. WILKINS, M., 5th Bn.
4321 Pte. WYNE, 6th Bn.
17391 Pte. WAXMAN, J., 5th Bn.
60472 Pte. WHITE, E., 4th Bn.
47208 Pte. WYNE, J. B.,* 19th Bn.
29821 Pte. YESNER, S., 14th Bn.
400517 Pte. YENNSHOWSKY, P., 1/6th Bn.
276292 Pte. YAFFE, W., 7th Bn.
276343 Pte. YAFFE, S.
45118 Pte. ZUTNER, W., 4th Bn.
203193 Pte. ZANCONY, J., 5th Bn.

* Killed in Action or died on Active Service.

THE PRINCE OF WALES'S (NORTH STAFFORDSHIRE REGIMENT).

OFFICERS.

2nd Lieut. BIERNSTEIN, A. E., 1st Bn.
2nd Lieut. COOK, N. G.,* 1/6th Bn.
2nd Lieut. EPSTEIN, S., 2/6th Bn.
2nd Lieut. FISHER, S. G., 3rd Bn.
2nd Lieut. JOSEPH,, N. C., 6th Bn.
2nd Lieut. KRAUSS, D. E.,* 1/5th Bn.
2nd Lieut. KOHNSTAMM, O. J. C., attd. M.G.C.
2nd Lieut. MARKS, J. A.,* 10th Bn.
Major MYER, H. D., 6th Lond. Regt., att. 4th Bn.
2nd Lieut. REISS, J.

N.C.O.'s AND MEN.

240546 L/Cpl. ASTELL, F., 6th Bn.
S/23870 Pte. ANKER, V., 1st Bn.
123329 Pte. ASLEY, 2nd Bn.
49209 Pte. BERG, M., 12th Bn.
242242 Pte. BLOOM, S.
40591 Pte. BOSTON, F., 1st Bn.
49309 Pte. BERRY, M., 12th Bn.
27614 L/Sgt. BENOLIEL, D., 4th Bn.
2724 Pte. COPPERMAN, 2/5th Bn.
7979 Pte. COHEN, H., 12th Bn.
19316 Pte. COHEN, A., 12th Bn.
42698 Pte. COHEN, I., 12th Bn.
41854 Cpl. CREMER, A.
242113 Pte. COHEN, M.
42697 Pte. COHEN, G., 12th Bn.
44285 Pte. COHEN, I., 12th Gar. Bn.
17428 Pte. CAPLAN, H., 9th Bn.
43506 Pte. CAPLAN, A., 2nd Bn.
42215 Pte. COLEMAN, J., 2/10th Bn.
43468 L/Cpl. DAVIS, H., 1st Gar. Bn.
4967 Pte. EPSTEIN, E., 2/5th Bn.

6097 Pte. ERDBERG, N. J., 2/5th Bn.
43194 Pte. ELLENBOGEN, H., 1st Bn.
53420 Pte. FIGENBAUM, H., 12th Bn.
55242 Pte. FREEMAN, J., 13th Bn.
37653 Pte. GATOFF, M., 1st Gar. Bn.
41107 Pte. GOLDBERG, J., 5th Bn.
41116 Pte. HYAM, A. L., 9th Bn.
43562 Pte. HYMAN, M., 1st Bn.
103423 Pte. HILL, S. C., 12th Bn.
41573 Pte. HARRIS, H., 2/6th Bn.
8830 Pte. JOSEPH, A.
46576 Pte. JACOBS, D., 4th Bn.
24224 Pte. JOSEPH, M., 4th Bn.
50859 Pte. KIRK, S., 8th Bn.
48712 Pte. KAMINTZKY, M., 8th Bn.
42130 Pte. KAPUSTENSKY, L.
35698 Pte. KAY, L. H., 2nd Bn.
32160 Pte. LEWIS, A., 2/6th Bn.
32999 Pte. LASSMAN, A., 5th Bn.
50895 Pte. LUBEL, H.,* 8th Bn.
477058 Pte. LEVI, E., 12th Bn.
202616 Pte. LANDAU, J. R.
48552 Pte. MORRIS, W., 1st Bn.
28710 Pte. MUSAPHIA, 2nd Bn.
383538 Pte. NEWMAN, A., 12th Bn.
25009 Cpl. PHILLIPS, M., 8th Bn.
43736 Pte. PEARLMAN, M.
42163 Pte. REUBENS, A., 4th Bn.
48712 Pte. RAMINITZ, M., 8th Bn.
60391 Pte. REUBEN, H., 6th Bn.
43438 Pte. RUBINSTEIN, B., 13th Bn.
32432 Pte. RABINOVITCH, H., 2nd Bn.
53420 Pte. SIGENBAUM, H., 12th Bn.
42372 Pte. SAPPERSTONE, H., 9th Bn.
41110 Pte. SUGARMAN, H.
45382 Pte. STERNE, R., 4th Bn.
39441 Pte. SILVERSTEIN, 7th Bn.
25414 Pte. SILVERBERG, C., 1st Bn.
Pte. SMITH, A. M., 5th Bn.
43163 Pte. TAYLOR, H., 8th Bn.
43042 Pte. WARM, L., 12th Bn.

* Killed in Action or died on Active Service.

THE YORK AND LANCASTER REGIMENT.

OFFICERS.

2nd Lieut. BLUMBERG, M., 8th Bn.
2nd Lieut. HART, V. D., 2/4th Bn.
Lieut. HIGHAM, W., 2/4th Bn.
2nl Lieut. KAPLIN, I., 10th Bn.
Lieut. NEWTON, C. B., 7th Bn.
Lieut. SCHAVERINE, S., 2nd Bn.

York and Lancaster Regt.—*Continued.*
N.C.O.'s AND MEN.

24484	Pte. APPEL, D., 8th Bn.
34243	Pte. ABRAHAMS, M., 8th Bn.
676	Pte. ASHER, S.,* 9th Bn.
53224	Pte. AARON, H., 1st Bn.
3903	Pte. BROWN, H., 1/4th Bn.
202600	Pte. BRONKS, D., 2/4th Bn.
34249	Pte. BLOOMBERG, M., 8th Bn.
32647	Pte. BOAM, C.,* 8th Bn.
62193	Pte. BERNSTEIN, E., 18th Bn.
	L/Cpl. BETHELL, H. S., 2nd Bn.
55741	Pte. BASSICK, J., 2/4th Bn.
84667	Pte. BEBROVSKY, 1st Bn.
33612	Pte. BUTLER, J., 1/4th Bn.
	L/Cpl. BLOOMBERG, G. (M.M.).
5418	Pte. COHEN, J., 1/4th Bn.
3/37619	Pte. COHEN, H., 7th Bn.
33335	Pte. CARP, L.,* 1/4th Bn.
62215	Pte. COHEN, J., 18th Bn.
53617	L/Cpl. COHEN, A., 18th Bn.
6546	Pte. COHN, J., 1/5th Bn.
35777	Pte. COHEN, L.
55811	Pte. COLEMAN, P., 9th Bn.
	Pte. COLEMAN, H., 13th Bn.
241888	Pte. COHEN, S., 2/5th Bn.
242560	Pte. COHEN, J., 8th Bn.
21299	Pte. DAVISON, G., 10th Bn.
10138	Pte. DAWSON, R. H.,* 2nd Bn.
39960	Pte. DIAMOND, E., 6th Bn.
33142	Pte. DAVIES, J., 4th Bn.
5787	Pte. DAVIES, S., 5th Bn.
263058	Pte. EPSTEIN, I., 2/4th Bn.
18465	Pte. FREEMAN, W., 7th Bn.
28711	Pte. FRITZ, P., 12th Bn.
242751	Pte. FELDSTEIN, A., 2/4th Bn.
2161	Cpl. FREEDMAN, A., 1st Bn.
64319	Pte. FREEDMAN, M. S., 3rd Bn.
19191	Pte. GRIMSTONE, M., 9th Bn.
5184	Pte. GERSH, A., 2/4th Bn.
34257	Pte. GOLDBERG, E., 8th Bn.
33653	Pte. GOLDBERG, S., 1/4th Bn.
47094	Pte. GONSHAW, J., 1/4th Bn.
47095	Pte. GREENGROSS, J. G., 1/4th Bn.
25200	C.Q.M.S. GOLDSTON, R. J., 16th Bn.
260074	Pte. HART, E., 1/5th Bn.
62064	Pte. HARRIS, S., 18th Bn.
8270	Pte. HARRIS, J., 4th Bn.
34682	Pte. HUSH, G., 9th Bn.
29848	Pte. HARRIS, M., 16th Bn.
41597	Pte. HILL, H., 9th Bn.
	Pte. ISAACS, C., 10th Bn.
39924	Pte. JACOBS, S., 6th Bn.
36888	Sgt. JUDD, A., 16th Bn.
4536	L/Cpl. JOSEPH, M.,* 1st Bn.
16835	Pte. KORPANDER, H., 6th Bn.
2477	Pte. LAZARUS, H., 1/4th Bn.
6107	Pte. LOWENBERG, B., 1/4th Bn.
31092	Pte. LEVY, H., 2nd Bn.
20604	L/Cpl. LEFTON, L., 6th Bn.
33247	Pte. LEVESON, R., 6th Bn.
32837	Pte. LYNES, C., 6th Bn.
30887	L/Cpl. LANDY, S.
16836	Pte. LEVISON, E. S., 4th Bn.
55743	Pte. LEVY, A., 2/4th Bn.
3212	Pte. MENDOZA, A., 7th Bn.
35933	Pte. MYERS, S.,* 1/5th Bn.
	Pte. MORRIS, H., 12th Bn.
242775	Pte. MARKS, W.,* 2/5th Bn.
235326	Pte. MYERSON, S., 8th Bn.
62282	Pte. MARKS, J., 18th Bn.
42702	Pte. MENDELSON, A., 18th Bn.
62433	Pte. NUNAR, I., 18th Bn.
22401	Pte. NEEDLER, M., 14th Bn.
33403	Pte. OLSWANG, M., 1/4th Bn.
9439	Cpl. PHILLIPS, M. W., 2nd Bn.
9884	Pte. PHILLIPS, A., 1st Bn.
26861	Pte. PIZER, B., 16th Bn.
	Pte. ROSENBERG, H., 2nd Bn.
9888	L/Cpl. ROBSON, J.,* 2nd Bn.
5/5284	Pte. ROSENBLUM, L., 4th Bn.
47038	Pte. REECE, M., 2nd Bn.
12/2087	Pte. ROSE, S. L., 15th Bn.
34268	Pte. SOLOMON, M. (M.M.), 8th Bn.
62135	Pte. SELWYN, M., 18th Bn.
204380	Pte. SILVER, J.,* 2/4th Bn.
62149	Pte. SAUL, I., 18th Bn.
62134	Pte. SPEAR, H., 18th Bn.
62130	Pte. SAVILLE, R., 18th Bn.
20604	Cpl. SEFTON, L. (M.M.), 6th Bn.
34462	Pte. SHALGOSKY, B.,* 9th Bn.
6170	Pte. SUGARMAN, J., 1/4th Bn.
39515	L/Cpl. SHINBERG, N., 8th Bn.
14/221	Pte. SEGAL, S., 9th Bn.
55577	Pte. STEPNITSKY, B., 7th Bn.
41534	Pte. SIMMONS, I., 1st Bn.
79815	Pte. SHERMAN, M., 18th Bn.
27904	Pte. SPIGAL, L., 12th Bn.
54104	Pte. SAMUELS, R., 2nd Bn.
41233	Pte. SONENBERG, W. W., 17th Bn.
5696	Pte. SPINK, J., 4th Bn.
33415	Pte. TROTSKY, D., 1/4th Bn.
29313	Pte. THOMPSON, H., 1st Bn.
8207	Pte. VALENCIA, A., 4th Bn.
41811	Pte. WOLF, B., 7th Bn.
35951	Pte. WEINTROB, L., 12th Bn.
7173	Pte. YAFFE, A., 4th Bn.
21899	Pte. ZISSMAN, S., 7th Bn.
204673	Pte. ZOTNICK, M.,* 2/5th Bn.
7056	Pte. ZOTNICK, S., 4th Bn.
38632	Pte. ZACKS, S., 3rd Bn.

* Killed in Action or died on Active Service.

THE DURHAM LIGHT INFANTRY.

OFFICERS.

2nd Lieut. COHEN, M.* (M.M.), 2nd Bn.
Lieut. DAVIS, L., 5th Bn.
Lieut. JESSELL, V. A. Z.,* 15th Bn.
Lieut. LEVESON, R. M.,* 10th Bn.
Capt. LYONS, M. A.
Capt. JOSEPH, H., 7th Bn.
Lieut. MARKS, H. H. (M.C.), 10th Bn.
Lieut. MARKS, J.,* 15th Bn.
2nd Lieut. MARKS, G. D., 12th Bn.
Lieut. NATHAN, G., 22nd Bn.
Capt. PHILLIPS, H. M., 14th Bn.
Lieut. ROTHFIELD, A. (M.C. & Bar), 14th Bn.
Lieut. SHRAGER, A.
2nd Lieut. SAMUEL, G. B.,* att. R.A.F.

N.C.O.'s AND MEN.

676 Pte. ASHER, S., 20th Bn.
52971 Pte. ALEXANDER, H., 13th Bn.
30167 Pte. ASHER, G., 15th Bn.
20405 Pte. ABRAHAMS, M.
252458 Sgt. ANGELL, S., 2/6th Bn.
Pte. ABRAHAMSON, N., 2/6th Bn.
326372 Pte. ABRAHAMS, P., 2/9th Bn.
326477 Pte. ANZURAT, J., 2/9th Bn.
74364 Pte. ABRAHAMS, A. L., 2/5th Bn.
Cpl. ABRAHAMS, L. O. (D.C.M.).
326161 Pte. ABRAHAMS, H., 2/9th Bn.
326425 L/Cpl. ABRAHAMS, K., 2/9th Bn.
326347 Pte. ADLER, M., 2/9th Bn.
245409 Pte. ANDERSON, C., 10th Bn.
251875 Pte. ABRAHAMS, M., 2/4th Bn.
170246 Pte. AARONS, A., 53rd Bn.
83559 Pte. AARONS, 1st Bn.
2317 Sgt. BLACK, D. (D.C.M.), 7th Bn.
194 Pte. BARNETT, N., 22nd Bn.
916 Pte. BIERMAN, J., 22nd Bn.
23209 Pte. BERNSTEIN, J., 19th Bn.
53313 Pte. BLASCHKEY, J., 19th Bn.
52664 L/Cpl. BLOOMBAUM, M., 12th Bn.
31454 Pte. BLACOVITCH, S., 10th Bn.
5113 Pte. BREWER, I., 5th Bn.
58289 Pte BLOOM, P., 25th Bn.
37882 Pte. BAKER, A., 25th Bn.
10658 Pte. BARNETT, M. J., 5th Bn.
40462 L/Cpl. BASS, J., 25th Bn.
56720 Pte. BAKER, J.
326481 Pte. BLUESTONE, M., 5th Bn.
326393 L/Cpl. BLACKMAN, J., 2/9th Bn.
326489 Pte. BLOOM, M., 2/9th Bn.
326336 L/Cpl. BOMBERG, M. H., 2/9th Bn.
326469 Pte. BRILL, E., 2/9th Bn.
326460 Pte. BERNSTEIN, H., 2/9th Bn.
240989 Pte. BRAMSON, H.

242256 Pte. BEST, J., 26th Bn.
21990 Pte. BAKER, I., 2/6th Bn.
6257 Pte. BANKOFSKY, A., 2/7th Bn.
42854 Pte. COHEN, A., 22nd Bn.
6166 Pte. COHEN, H., 5th Bn.
104107 Pte. COLLINS, L., 29th Bn.
35314 Pte. CODDLE, A., 25th Bn.
53052 Pte. COHEN, S., 15th Bn.
53062 Pte. CRUSKAL, E., 19th Bn.
11046 Pte. COHEN, L., 2nd Bn.
52971 Pte. COLEMAN, T., 13th Bn.
11346 Cpl. COHEN, 1st Bn.
198015 Pte. COHEN, H., 2/8th Bn.
51466 Pte. COHEN, J., 25th Bn.
47854 Pte. COHEN, L., 25th Bn.
5/7804 Pte. COHEN, J.
302955 Pte. COHEN, S., 2/6th Bn.
302953 Pte. COHEN, J., 2/6th Bn.
302954 Pte. COHEN, H., 2/6th Bn.
252220 Pte. COHEN, M., 2/6th Bn.
326476 Pte. CAPLAN, M., 2/9th Bn.
326274 L/Cpl. COHEN, W., 2/9th Bn.
326377 Pte. COHEN, S. C., 2/9th Bn.
326494 Pte. COHEN, S. L., 2/9th Bn.
326177 Pte. COHEN, A., 2/9th Bn.
326473 Pte. COHEN, W., 2/9th Bn.
326478 Pte. COPELAND, S., 2/9th Bn.
74367 Pte. COHEN, J., 2/5th Bn.
326493 Pte. COHEN, M., 2/9th Bn.
6518 Pte. COHEN, M., 2/9th Bn.
4706 Pte. COHEN, A., 6th Bn.
4077 Pte. COHEN, I., 8th Bn.
85668 Pte. CALITSKY, J., 29th Bn.
6542 Pte. COHEN, S., 2/9th Bn.
118137 Pte. CALLER, P., 3rd Bn.
351153 Pte. COHEN, J., 25th Bn.
6396 Pte. COHEN, A., 22nd Bn.
75970 Pte. CAXNER, G., 2/7th Bn.
40144 Pte. COHEN, M., 3rd Bn.
59619 Pte. COLEMAN, H., 26th Bn.
6118 Pte. COHEN, S., 2nd Bn.
52969 Pte. COHEN, P.,* 13th Bn.
43542 Pte. DAVIS, J., 22nd Bn.
6069 Pte. DAVIES, J., 8th Bn.
85699 Pte. DAVIES, H. M., 29th Bn.
82374 Pte. DALINSKY, L., 20th Bn.
63886 Pte. DAVIS, D., 5th Bn.
23/192 Pte. DENNIS, H., 23rd Bn.
10772 Pte. DAVIS, M., 5th Bn.
75841 Pte. DAVIES, F., 2/6th Bn.
252336 Pte. DAGGERS, D., 2/6th Bn.
59371 Pte. DAVIS, E., 7th Bn.
74370 Pte. DEITCH, J., 2/5th Bn.
326482 L/Cpl. DAVIS, H., 2/9th Bn.
326497 Pte. DANZIGER, M., 2/9th Bn.
21959 Pte. DEITCH, S. S., 2/6th Bn.
35375 Pte. DAVID, I., 25th Bn.
38645 Pte. DEIUBRUA, R., 4th Bn.

Durham Light Infantry.—*Continued.*

5859 Pte. DISHKIN, H., 9th Bn.
301733 Pte. DAVIS, J., 8th Bn.
38848 Pte. ERNSTON, A.
50196 Pte. EPSTINE, M.
21678 Pte. FREEDMAN, H., 14th Bn.
82264 Pte. FARBER, H. H.,* 20th Bn.
85766 Pte. FREEMAN, J., 2/6th Gar. Bn.
81266 L/Cpl. FISHKIN, M., 15th Bn.
Pte FISHER.
29388 Pte. FINKLESTEIN, G., 25th Bn.
47999 Pte. FREEDMAN, H., 25th Bn.
326468 Pte. FIELD, P., 2/9th Bn.
326036 Pte. FRANCO, W., 2/9th Bn.
202451 Pte. FREEDMAN, I., 2/5th Bn.
326346 Pte. FELLERMAN, H., 2/9th Bn.
327455 Pte. FERNANDEZ, V., 2/9th Bn.
50921 Pte. FROMANCHICK, D., 17th Bn.
331111 Pte. FINEGOLD, M., 18th Bn.
75841 L/Cpl. FRANK, D., 2/6th Bn.
245927 Pte. FREEDMAN, J., 20th Bn.
50203 Pte. FRENDENBERG, B., 25th Bn.
203727 Pte. FRIEND, A., 7th Bn.
243798 Pte. FREEMAN, S., 2/6th Bn.
9340 Pte. GUTERMAN, A.,* 5th Bn.
43621 Pte. GOLDSTEIN, J., 19th Bn.
277098 Pte. GOLDBERG, H., 20th Bn.
85151 Pte. GOLDSTONE, P., 11th Bn.
85152 Pte. GOLDSTONE, B., 11th Bn.
351369 Pte. GREEN, G., 2/6th Gar. Bn.
168906 Pte. GOLDBERG, H., 25th Bn.
39562 Pte. GALLEWSKI, R., 3rd Bn.
Pte. GOMPERTZ, E., 3rd Bn.
10790 Pte. GREENBAUM, J., 5th Bn.
9893 Pte. GOLDSTEIN, N., 5th Bn.
10664 Pte. GOLDSTEIN, H., 5th Bn.
29235 Pte. GOLDBERG, E., 25th Bn.
41231 Pte. GOLDSTEIN, J., 25th Bn.
277088 Pte. GOODMAN, J., 25th Bn.
6235 Pte. GOLDSTEIN, M., 2/7th Bn.
6276 Pte. GOLDBERG, H., 2/7th Bn.
6265 Pte. GOODMAN, J., 2/7th Bn.
201680 Pte. GOLDMAN, S. A.
326139 Pte. GARCIA, D., 2/9th Bn.
326471 Pte. GLASS, M., 2/9th Bn.
326496 Pte. GRAJEWSKY, B., 2/9th Bn.
326119 L/Cpl. GREENBAUM, J., 2/9th Bn.
201686 L/Cpl. GOLDMAN, I., 2/5th Bn.
9391 Pte. GOLDSLEY, N.
23241 Pte. GRATZ, H., 1/5th Bn.
6067 Pte. GOULD, M., 2/19th Bn.
327400 Pte. GOLDSMITH, L., 2/9th Bn.
27739 Pte. GATOFF, M., 4th Bn.
27738 Pte. GATOFF, W., 4th Bn.
327526 Pte. GOLD, M., 2/9th Bn.
45365 Pte. GOLDSTEIN, L., 18th Bn.
53081 Pte. HYAMS, A., 15th Bn.
99326 Sgt HUSH, P. A., 2/6th Gar. Bn.

10749 Pte. HERMAN, J., 5th Bn.
57346 Pte. HERMAN, H., 25th Bn.
10720 Pte. HIRSH, S., 5th Bn.
59435 Cpl. HARRIS, A., 7th Bn.
74378 Pte. HARRIS, S., 2/5th Bn.
326499 Pte. HYAMS, H., 2/9th Bn.
80035 Pte. HARRIS, J., 2/9th Bn.
492610 Pte. HARTSILVER, J., 2/5th Bn.
52978 Pte. HYAMS, B., 15th Bn.
11090 Pte. HARRIS, I., 12th Bn.
74379 Pte. ISRAEL, G. L., 2/5th Bn.
326352 Pte. ISRAEL, N., 2/9th Bn.
38809 Pte. ISAACS, M., 2nd Bn.
326356 Pte. ISAACS, A., 2/5th Bn.
376736 Pte. ISAACS, F., 27th Bn.
Pte. ISAACS, D., 3rd Bn.
2579 Cpl. JACOBY, H., 7th Bn.
10454 L/Cpl. JACKSON, H., 10th Bn.
2578 Pte. JACKSON, I.,* 7th Bn.
74381 Pte. JOSEPH, E., 2/5th Bn.
Sgt. JACOBS, G. H. (M.M.).
326491 Pte. JACOBS, M., 2/9th Bn.
326490 Pte. JEFF, J., 2/9th Bn.
52216 Pte. JACOBS, L.
Pte. JACKSON, A., 6th Bn.
MS/4163 Pte. KARET, B., 22nd Bn.
345006 Pte. KRATOSKY, L., 8th Bn.
79267 Pte. KAUFMAN, J., 2nd Bn.
74831 Pte. KOHLER, W., 2/6th Gar. Bn.
10669 Pte. KRONENBERG, A., 5th Bn.
10670 Pte. KRATOSKY, L., 5th Bn.
6225 Pte. KERN, P., 2/7th Bn.
6226 Pte. KAZENOSKI, H., 2/7th Bn.
50938 Pte. KLINEBERG, S., 17th Bn.
7517 Pte. KRANZ, D., 2/6th Bn.
73556 Pte. KLEINMAN, M., 3rd Bn.
Pte. KEMPNER, J., 2nd Bn.
8421 Pte. LETSKY, C.,* 2nd Bn.
26990 Pte. LEVINSON, N., 20th Bn.
T2/11091 Dvr. LEVY, J., 22nd Bn.
30809 Pte. LEVINSON, A., 2nd Bn.
1065 Pte. LEVY,, D., 18th Bn.
273090 Pte. LELYVELD, L., 9th Bn.
53191 Cpl. LEWIS, E. F.,* 15th Bn.
85592 L/Cpl. LEWIS, A., 29th Bn.
38538 Pte. LEVY, D., 18th Bn.
168936 Pte. LAVINE, J., 25th Bn.
168944 Pte. LEVY, H., 25th Bn.
201437 Pte. LEVY, L., 10th Bn.
22421 Pte. LETSKY, M., 12th Bn.
44363 Pte. LAZARUS, S., 13th Bn.
17873 Pte. LEVY, 5th Bn.
10672 Pte. LESCHINSKY, M., 5th Bn.
3263 Pte. LEVY, M., 2/9th Bn.
73088 Pte. LEVINE, H., 4th Bn.
252343 Pte. LAZARUS, J., 2/6th Bn.
50066 Pte. LINKSY, L., 2/6th Bn.
326228 Pte. LESLIE, E., 2/9th Bn.

Durham Light Infantry.—*Continued.*

326470 Pte. LAZARUS, M., 2/9th Bn.
326349 Pte. LEADER, M., 2/9th Bn.
326480 Pte. LEVI, J., 2/9th Bn.
326538 Pte. LEVY, A., 2/5th Bn.
326475 Pte. LEVY, L., 2/9th Bn.
202472 Pte. LEA, P., 2/5th Bn.
21/524 Pte. LEVY, H., 21st Bn.
5743 Pte. LUTMAN, P., 2/9th Bn.
39161 Pte. LINSKILL, B., 4th Bn.
6607 Pte. LEVY, A., 2/9th Bn.
10605 Cpl. MERKEL, A., 15th Bn.
45807 Pte. MIRSKY, H., 20th Bn.
Pte. MINCOTT, H., 19th Bn.
53106 Pte. MICHAEL, H., 15th Bn.
70736 Pte. MATTATIA, R., 5th Bn.
3351 Pte. McKENNEL, N., 2nd Bn
L/Cpl. MOSES, D. (M.M.).
302633 Pte. MINSK, S., 28th Bn.
10798 Pte. MORRIS, W., 5th Bn.
37995 Pte. MOSES, L., 25th Bn.
32895 Cpl. MILLER, S., 26th Bn.
251875 Pte. MOSS, A., 2/6th Bn.
6261 Pte. MARCUSON, H., 2/9th Bn.
326083 Pte. MANTLE, I., 2/9th Bn.
74384 Pte. MORDECAI, L., 2/9th Bn.
326344 Pte. MARKS, H., 2/9th Bn.
326536 Pte. MOSCO, B., 2/9th Bn.
327289 Pte. MOSCO, L., 2/9th Bn.
327285 Pte. MARCUSON, N., 2/5th Bn.
202269 Pte. MYERS, P., 26th Bn.
277198 Pte. MOSS, I., 20th Bn.
76020 Pte. MENDOZA, J., 2/7th Bn.
69776 Pte. MARKS, I.
59663 Pte. MARKS, I. I., 26th Bn.
7931 Pte. MASSING, M., 52nd Bn.
Staff-Sgt. MORRIS, A., 15th Bn.
778 Sig. NOVINSKI, S., 20th Bn.
640 Pte. NINCOFF, H., 19th Bn.
326486 Pte. NATHAN, P., 2/9th Bn.
28505 Pte. NIMAN, H., 16th Bn.
331259 Pte. NORMAN, E., 26th Bn.
44634 Pte. NATHAN, A., 20th Bn.
85668 Pte. OLANITSKIE, J., 29th Bn.
53517 Pte. PENER, N., 11th Bn.
21984 Cpl. PHILLIPS, J., 14th Bn.
10568 Pte. PEARSON, J., 2nd Bn.
168974 Pte. PYZER, J., 2nd Bn.
325988 Pte. POLACK, L.,* 9th Bn.
6266 Pte. PULCOVITCH, R., 2/7th Bn.
527489 Pte. PYSER, I., 2/9th Bn.
74386 L/Cpl. PASSES, A., 2/5th Bn.
74387 Pte. PRESTON, B., 2/5th Bn.
326078 L/Cpl. PETERMAN, A., 2/5th Bn.
326357 Pte. POWER, W. W., 2/9th Bn.
326495 Pte. PALENBAUM, E., 2/9th Bn.
31943 Pte. POLLACK, A., 4th Bn.

200956 Pte. RICKAZEN, H. S.,* 9th Bn.
868 L/Cpl. RUBEN, J., 20th Bn.
16786 Cpl. ROSE, A. H., 14th Bn.
53358 Pte. REUBEN, E., 11th Bn.
26300 Pte. ROSENBERG, D., 22nd Bn.
80465 Pte. ROSENBERG, L., 2/6th Bn.
11140 Pte. REECE, D., 2nd Bn.
168985 Pte. ROCKMAN, M., 25th Bn.
26847 Pte. RUBENSTEIN, B., 2nd Bn.
10677 L/Cpl. RUBENSTEIN, I., 5th Bn.
48108 L/Sgt. ROSENFIELD.
Cpl. RAYMAN, M., 1st Bn.
74804 Pte. REFSON, L., 19th Bn.
21974 Pte. ROSE, J., 2/6th Bn.
203732 Cpl. RUBENSTEIN, C., 5th Bn.
326092 Pte. ROSENBLOOM, A., 2/9th Bn.
326348 Pte. ROSENBERG, S., 2/9th Bn.
326411 Pte. ROGIES, S., 2/9th Bn.
326345 Pte. ROSEMAN, N., 2/9th Bn.
4908 Pte. RAISMAN, J., 27th Bn.
28629 Pte. RUBENSTEIN, E., 1st Bn.
24845 Pte. SPEAKER, J., 14th Bn.
52957 Pte. SANDALL, D.,* 13th Bn.
23/394 Pte. SOLBERG, B.,* 10th Bn.
23708 Pte. STEINBURG, E.,* 15th Bn.
245056 Pte. SOLOMONS, L., 8th Bn.
53185 Pte. SHANES, H., 15th Bn.
1078 Pte. STEINBERG, A., 7th Bn.
252458 Sgt. SMITH, A., 2/6th Bn.
99241 Pte. SWERSKI, A. (M.M.), 2/6th Bn.
277099 Pte. SONSKY, S., 2/6th Bn.
5088 Pte. SABIN, B.
169003 Pte. SIMONS, J.
89148 Pte. SCHULTZ, J. L., 12th Bn.
44403 Pte. SHAW, H., 13th Bn.
44415 Pte. SOLOMONS, L., 13th Bn.
52973 Pte. SANDERSON, S., 13th Bn.
110766 Pte. SORKIN, C., 3rd Bn.
10682 Pte. SMOLENSKY, B., 5th Bn.
10734 Pte. STOCK, P., 5th Bn.
48676 Pte. SAMUELS, M., 25th Bn.
14114 Pte. SAGAR, G., 2/6th Bn.
277086 Pte. SCHAVERIEN.
80064 Pte. SILVERMAN, S. J., 2/9th Bn.
316698 Pte. STEVENSON, I., 28th Bn.
251860 Pte. STRONG, 2/6th Bn.
74912 Pte. SAFFER, B., 2/6th Bn.
251874 Pte. SILVERMAN, W., 2/6th Bn.
98694 Pte. SOLOMON, J., 2/6th Bn.
223883 Pte. SORKIN, A., 5th Bn.
204483 Sgt. SMOLE, B., 9th Bn.
21986 Pte. SILVERMAN, W.
6231 Pte SAPLER, M., 2/7th Bn.
6277 Pte. SONSKY, I., 2/7th Bn.
21976 Pte. SHULTZ, A., 2/6th Bn.
326492 Pte. SEGAL, I., 2/9th Bn.
74389 Pte. SNACKS, V., 2/5th Bn.

Durham Light Infantry.—*Continued.*

74390 Pte. SCHWALBE, M., 2/5th Bn.
326206 Pte. SILVER, S., 2/9th Bn.
326483 Pte. STERNE, J. L., 2/9th Bn.
326350 Pte. SYDNEY, S., 2/9th Bn.
6526 Pte. SYKES, W., 2/9th Bn.
326084 L/Cpl. SALTIEL, E., 2/9th Bn.
327395 Pte. SAMUELS, I., 2/9th Bn.
17678 Pte. SUGAR, D., 2/9th Bn.
221470 Pte. SAPERIA, H.
85238 Pte. SPIWACK, W., 7th Bn.
6051 Pte. SOLOMONS, L., 2/9th Bn.
6337 Pte. SORIN, C., 2/9th Bn.
166900 Pte. SOLOMONS, S., 2/7th Bn.
6532 Pte. SAUNDERS, I.
76062 Pte. SAPERIA, H., 17th Bn.
205207 Pte. SALLEY, L., 2/7th Bn.
6055 Pte. SOLOMON, S., 2/7th Bn.
326487 Pte. SAUNDERS, I., 5th Bn.
6571 Pte. SOMERFIELD, W. E., 2/9th Bn.
59692 Pte. SEUEL, I., 26th Bn.
19304 Pte. SIMMONS, H., 2/9th Bn.
40068 Pte. SHARE, L.
5055 Pte. SANSKY, J., 2/9th Bn.
24775 Pte. SOLOMONS, H., 26th Bn.
24845 Pte. SPATER, J., 1st Bn.
73591 Pte. SPICKER, I., 3rd Bn.
81195 Pte. SEITZ, M., 19th Bn.
326470 Pte. TEFF, B., 2/9th Bn.
74397 Pte. TASS, J., 2/5th Bn.
50968 Pte. TAYLOR, S., 17th Bn.
30367 Pte. TUFLE, S., 4th Bn.
6229 Pte. TILL, H., 2/7th Bn.
50969 Pte. TAYLOR, J., 10th Bn.
53146 Sgt. VAN PRAAG, B.,* 15th Bn.
240625 Pte. VALINSKY, I., 26th Bn.
326482 Pte. VINGHAM, M., 2/9th Bn.
51206 Pte. VENENSKY, A., 53rd Bn.
76876 Pte. VINER, N., 11th Bn.
21290 Pte. WOOLMAN, A.,* 15th Bn.
53296 Pte. WARSHAWSKY, B., 13th Bn.
64156 Pte. WOLFSON, 1st Bn.
10764 L/Cpl. WEISBERG, W., 5th Bn.
326472 Pte. WAGNER, J., 2/9th Bn.
326217 Pte. WISEMAN, B., 2/9th Bn.
326488 Pte. WEINSTEIN, J., 2/9th Bn.
202241 Pte. WOODNICK, M., 26th Bn.
5/170207 Pte. WOLSON, H., 53rd Bn.
109370 Pte. WOLFE, B., 2/6th Bn.
173146 Pte. WEIL, M.
113704 Pte. YARMOVINSKY, F., 53rd Bn.
75038 Pte. YOUNGMAN, H., 2/5th Bn.
52797 Pte. ZIMMERMAN, E., 19th Bn.

* Killed in Action or died on Active Service.

THE HIGHLAND LIGHT INFANTRY.

OFFICERS.

Lieut. HARRIS, S.
2nd Lieut. NEWMAN, N.,* 10th Bn.

N.C.O.'s AND MEN.

356387 Pte. ABRAHAMS, M., 21st Bn.
280346 Cpl. ABRAHAMS, B., 7th Bn.
44103 Pte. ACKERMAN, J., 10th Bn.
53806 Pte. AIGEN, D., 15th Bn.
40036 Pte. ARVEIGH, 1st Bn.
355917 Pte. ANSIL, J., 10th Bn.
5987 Pte. BARNETT, J., 2/9th Bn.
B/30774 Pte. BARNETT, B., 2nd Bn.
39509 Pte. BARRON, H., 3rd Bn.
7913 Pte. BERMAN, L., 12th Bn.
27007 Pte. BERNSTEIN, M., 16th Bn.
73758 L/Cpl. BERNSTEIN, S. H.
241803 Pte. BENJAMIN, H., 1/9th Bn.
28400 Pte. BENJAMIN, A., 20th Bn.
67243 Pte. BENJAMIN, J., 15th Bn.
50773 Pte. BENSTOCK, F., 2nd Bn.
51294 Pte. BEMBAY, 1st Bn.
23007 Pte. BLACK, M., 17th Bn.
8495 Sgt. BLACK, D.,* 1st Bn.
2619 Sgt. BLACK, C., 2/7th Bn.
34790 Pte. BLASHKEY, A., 6th Bn.
35042 Pte BLINT, L., 18th Bn.
42615 Pte. BLINT, R., 12th Bn.
30193 Bglr. BLINT, C., 16th Bn.
41923 Pte. BLIEVERS, C.,* 10/11th Bn.
203426 Pte. BLOCK, M., 14th Bn.
51792 Pte. BLOOM, M., 3rd Bn.
4422 L/Cpl. BLOOMFIELD, E.,* 1/9th Bn.
333001 Pte. BOBBIE, R., 9th Bn.
Pte. BOYLE, A., 4th Bn.
31646 Pte. CAMBERG, H., 2nd Bn.
27094 Pte. CHURIE, M., 17th Bn.
198015 Pte. COHEN, H., 2/8th Bn.
29374 Pte. COHEN, I., 14th Bn.
356282 Pte. COHEN, H., 21st Bn.
1113 Pte. COHEN, S., 15th Bn.
14998 Pte. COHEN, L. M., 16th Bn.
15841 Sgt. COHEN, A. M., 17th Bn.
37484 Pte. COHEN, J., 5th Bn.
38073 Pte. COWAN, J., 12th Bn.
75826 Pte. COPELAND, M., 1st Bn.
203667 Pte. DAVIDSON, M. L.
332622 Pte. DISHKIN, H., 1/9th Bn.
27134 Pte. DISHKIN, M., 16th Bn.
2763 Pte. DICKSON, J., 6th Bn.
31826 Cpl. DORFMAN, M., 9th Bn.
38399 Pte. FACTOR, I., 12th Bn.
36350 Pte. FACTOR, P., 1/9th Bn.
356056 Pte. FELDMAN, N., 21st Bn.
Pte. FELIX, R., 17th Bn.

Highland Light Infantry.—*Continued.*

73587 Pte. FELL, H., 51st Bn.
33001 Pte. FERRA, P., 16th Bn.
16058 Pte. FINN, J., 17th Bn.
31408 Pte. FISHMAN, M.
      Pte. FLICK, I., 2/9th Bn.
4269 Pte. FRANKLIN, L., 3/5th Bn.
15579 Pte. FREEMAN, M.,* 17th Bn.
15579 Pte. FREEMAN, I.,* 17th Bn.
353623 Pte. FREEDMAN, H., 21st Bn.
52309 Cpl. FREEDMAN, J., 15th Bn.
37143 Pte FREEDMAN, L., 9th Bn.
4463 Pte. FRIEDMAN, C., 2/7th Bn.
16038 Pte. FRIEND, J., 17th Bn.
41676 Pte. FRIEZE, A., 10/11th Bn.
25812 Pte. GLICKMAN, A., 10/11th Bn.
37492 Pte. GOLDBERG, H., 5th Bn.
298 Pte. GOLDBERG, J., 2/6th Bn.
37906 Pte. GOLDBERG, S., 17th Bn.
202912 Pte. GOLDSTEIN, A., 21st Bn.
184120 Pte. GOLDSTEIN, G., 2nd Bn.
333546 Pte. GOLDSTEIN, J., 1/9th Bn.
34963 Pte. GOODMAN, J., 4th Bn.
17592 Pte. GOODMAN, L., 52nd Bn.
201708 Pte. GOODMAN, M.
356100 Pte. GOODMAN, W., 21st Bn.
356473 Pte. GRAYTON, J., 21st Bn.
332434 Pte. GREEN, D., 9th Bn.
6071 Pte. GREEN, L., 52nd Bn.
14887 Pte. GROUNDLEN, M., 16th Bn.
16168 Sgt. HAFT, J., 17th Bn.
2922 Cpl. HAFT, S.,* 17th Bn.
356392 Pte. HARRIS, B., 21st Bn.
2686 Pte. HARRIS, E., 17th Bn.
31695 Pte. HARRIS, G.,* 2nd Bn.
38961 Pte. HARRIS, J.
1730 Pte. HARRIS, J., 1/5th Bn.
2232 Cpl. HARRIS, M., 9th Bn.
356261 Pte. HARRISON, A.
39064 Pte. HAINES, W., 15th Bn.
356134 Pte. HECKER, M., 10th Bn.
333904 Pte. HILL, W. J., 2/9th Bn.
28734 Pte. HOPPENSTEIN, M., 17th Bn.
52093 Pte. HUDSON, G. H.
      Pte. ISAACS, M., 7th Bn.
210701 Sgt. JACOBS, J., 5th Bn.
2756 Pte. JACOBS, L.,* 6th Bn.
31677 Pte. JACOBSON, E., 2nd Bn.
4465 Pte. JACKSON, 2/7th Bn.
21580 Pte. JAFFE, J., 15th Bn.
28632 Pte. JOELS, A.
57799 Pte. JOSEPH, A., 12th Bn.
72325 Pte. KAPLAN, L., 15th Bn.
13971 Pte. KAPLIN, N., 52nd Bn.
13871 Pte. KOPLAN, L., 52nd Bn.
356244 Pte. KREITZMAN, H., 21st Bn.
5880 L/Cpl LANGDON, W. L., 12th Bn.

38320 Pte. LAWRENCE, A., 10/11th Bn.
356395 Pte. LAZARUS, W., 21st Bn.
281438 Pte. LEFKOVITCH, A., 7th Bn.
16250 Cpl. LEVY, B., 17th Bn.
29006 Pte. LEVY, J.,* 14th Bn.
38187 Pte. LEVI, M., 16th Bn.
44151 Pte. LEVINE, H., 10th Bn.
55769 Pte. LEVENE, L., 16th Bn.
45900 Pte. LEVENE, J., 2/7th Bn.
41324 L/Cpl. LEVISON, H., 15th Bn.
356099 Pte. LEVINSON, M., 21st Bn.
11131 Pte. LENT, J., 16th Bn.
11605 Pte. LEVENTHAL, M.,* 1st Bn.
41941 Pte. LIZAR, H., 52nd Bn.
27094 Pte. LURIE, M., 17th Bn.
27162 Pte. LURIE, J., 19th Bn.
353636 Pte. MARKS, A., 10th Bn.
70642 Pte. MEDVIDOFF, J., 16th Bn.
331159 Pte. MENDELSOHN, M.,* 9th Bn.
356121 Pte. MILLER, J., 10th Bn.
      Pte. MICHAELSON, H., 2/7th Bn.
40036 Pte. MORWEIGH, 3rd Bn.
27134 Pte. MORRIS, D., 1st Bn.
14497 Pte. MOFSHOWITZ, H., 16th Bn.
29374 L/Cpl. MUSGRAVE, F., 14th Bn.
      Pte. MUSCOVITCH, 10/11th Bn.
281561 Pte. NETTLER, H., 7th Bn.
3309 Pte. NELSON, C., 2/7th Bn.
2077 Pte. OAKES, A., 9th Bn.
356057 Pte. PAYNE, H., 21st Bn.
      Pte. PEARLMAN, L., 2/5th Bn.
4754 Pte. PHILLIPS, A., 9th Bn.
22426 Pte. PINTO, L.,* 16th Bn.
21935 Pte. PRISE, H., 5th Bn.
4415 Pte. PRICEMAN, M., 2/6th Bn.
29544 Sgt. PROX, J., 14th Bn.
16168 L/Cpl. RACIONZER, J. L., 17th Bn.
2923 Pte. ROSENBLOOM, H., 17th Bn.
29430 Pte. ROSS, L., 14th Bn.
1267 Pte. RUBENSTEIN, J., 1st Bn.
1852 Sgt. SAXON, M.,* 12th Bn.
1355097 Sig. SAMUELS, J., 21st Bn.
27062 Pte. SALBERG, S., 2nd Bn.
47227 Pte. SKLANOWITZ, T., 2/6th Bn.
6709 Pte. SHAPIRO, J., 52nd Bn.
356100 Pte. SUGARMAN, I., 21st Bn.
366299 Pte. SCHAAPWOOL, J., 21st Bn.
356455 Pte. STOLERVITSKY, I., 21st Bn.
356189 Pte. STEPHENS, A., 21st Bn.
5288 Pte. SCHNEIDERMAN, I., 2/7th Bn.
7141 Pte. SEGAL, J., 2/9th Bn.
2947 Pte. SHATENSTEIN, W., 2/9th Bn.
38669 Pte. SHATZ, M., 1st Bn.
      Pte. SILVERSTONE, J., 3/7th Bn.
2077 Sgt. SPILG, G. (M.M. and Bar), 9th Bn.
330253 Pte. SPILG, W.,* 9th Bn.

Highland Light Infantry.—*Continued.*

34927 Pte. STONMAN, H., 16th Bn.
203130 Pte. SNOOK, W., 16th Bn.
281273 Pte. SMITH, H., 7th Bn.
10589 L/Cpl. STRELITZ, P., 1st Bn.
53527 L/Cpl. SAGEL, R., 1/7th Bn.
Cpl. STANLEY, H. L. (M.M.), 5th Bn.
6709 Pte. SHAPERS, A. J., 52nd Bn.
51422 Pte. SLESS, L., 15th Bn.
18602 Pte. TAYLOR, D.,* 12th Bn.
56414 Pte. TERRY, M.
52346 Pte. TURBIN, H., 15th Bn.
356459 Pte. VANDERMALA, S., 21st Bn.
39342 Pte. WEINSTEIN, H., 6th Bn.
51294 Pte. WEINBERG, 1st Bn.
33187 Pte. ZIVE, M., 16th Bn.

* Killed in Action or died on Active Service.

SEAFORTH HIGHLANDERS (THE DUKE OF ALBANY'S).

OFFICERS.

2nd Lieut. ASHER, F., 1/6th Bn.
2nd Lieut. HART. A. M.
2nd Lieut. SIMON, H., 1/6th Bn.

N.C.O.'s AND MEN.

201904 Pte. BERNSTEIN, A., 1/4th Bn.
10770 Pte. BLACKSTONE, M.,* 7th Bn.
5/13686 Pte. BROWN, B., 3rd Bn.
Pte. BARCLAY, M. A., 6th Bn.
15584 Pte. BOYD, G., 1st Bn.
3176 Pte. COHEN, H., 1/5th Bn.
4176 Pte. CUCKLE, L.,* 1/4th Bn.
10983 Pte. COHEN, S.,* 7th Bn.
10894 Pte. COHEN, H., 7th Bn.
4703 Pte. COHEN, M., 3/5th Bn.
4607 Pte. CROOK, M. M., 5th Bn.
4775 Pte. CLAPHAM, P.,* 4th Bn.
241285 Pte. COHEN, M., 5th Bn.
5/11262 Pte. CANSINO, D., 10th Bn.
241285 Pte. COHEN, M.
10870 Pte. DEAN, H., 8th Bn.
5289 L/Cpl. FINN, J., 1/5th Bn.
5288 Pte. FINN, H., 1/5th Bn.
4696 Pte. FREEMAN, C., 5th Bn.
267731 Pte. FINBERG, M., 1/6th Bn.
4167 Pte. GOLD, S., 2nd Bn.
13073 Pte. GOODSTON, J., 9th Bn.
33760 Pte. GREEN, A., 3rd Bn.
4791 Pte. GROLL, H., 1/4th Bn.
4708 Pte. GABRIEL, L., 5th Bn.
Pte. GOLBERG, F.
Pte. GOLDIN, W., 8th Bn.
241285 Pte. HARRIS, M., 1/6th Bn.
203810 Pte. HART, A. J., 2nd Bn.
23523 Pte. HARRIS, J., 1st Bn.
Pte. HERMAN, G., 2nd Bn.
241688 Pte. JOELS, H., 8th Bn.
41891 Pte. JOELS, S., 7th Bn.
S/15379 Pte. JOSEPH, H., 1st Gar. Bn.
Pte. JOELS, A., 2nd Bn.
10591 Pte. LINSKIE, A., 8th Bn.
2137 Pte. LEHMANN, R. R.,* 1/6th Bn.
266780 Pte. LEWIS, D., 1/6th Bn.
253667 Pte. LATMAN, B., 5th Bn.
1252 Pte. LEVENTHAL, L.,* 1st Bn.
S/15189 Pte. LEVY, A., 1st Bn.
203653 Pte. LEFCOVITCH, P., 2/4th Bn.
14651 Pte. LIVINGSTONE, D., 3rd Bn.
43664 Pte. MIRANDA, M., 1/5th Bn.
9389 Sgt. MACK, W.,* 2nd Bn.
16440 Sgt. MEAKIN, P., 1st Bn.
200338 L/Cpl. MILLER, J., 7th Bn.
8792 L/Cpl. MILLER, L., 8th Bn.
10669 Pte. TAYLOR, D., 10th Bn.
240672 Sgt. NATHAN, A. L., 1/5th Bn.
S/8014 Pte. PAYMAN, S.,* 1st Bn.
2728 Pte. PELLER, I., 1/4th Bn.
201896 Pte. ROSENBLOOM, N., 1/4th Bn.
Pte. RUSSELL, A. M., 7th Bn.
4951 Pte. ROSENBLOOM, M., 1/4th Bn.
5098 L/Cpl. SOLOMON, C., 1/4th Bn.
267275 Sig. SOLOMON, J.,* 1/4th Bn.
40406 Pte. SOLOMONS, C.,* 1/6th Bn.
42335 Pte. SHANEY, W., 8th Bn.
S/43226 Pte. STEIN, B., 2nd Bn.
23811 Pte. SAFFER, J., 1st Bn.
23543 Pte. SILVERMAN, J., 1st Bn.
2047 Pte. WELLS, A., 1st Bn.
636707 Pte. YELLIN, N., 3rd Bn.

* Killed in Action or died on Active Service.

THE GORDON HIGHLANDERS.

OFFICERS.

Lieut.-Col. LEVEY, J. H. (D.S.O., O.B.E.).
Capt. LOEWE, L.

N.C.O.'s AND MEN.

Pte. AARONSON, M.
40587 Pte. BARNES, I. (M.M.), 2nd Bn.
517141 Pte. BERMAN, B., 1/5th Bn.
290742 Pte. BURMAN, E., 4th Bn.
16903 L/Cpl. CAPLAN, P. I.
3643 Pte. CLIFFE, I., 1/6th Bn.
203087 Pte. CREME, L., 4th Bn.

Gordon Highlanders.—Continued.

12300 Pte. DUBB, J., 9th Bn.
55789 L/Cpl. FLEIGENBAUM, A., 16th Bn.
60496 Pte. FRANKS, A., 10th Bn.
77772 Pte. FRANKS, J., 1/4th Bn.
202985 Pte. FREEDMAN, A.
42286 Pte. FREEDMAN, C., 4th Bn.
7474 Sgt. FRIESNER, W., 2nd Bn.
S/13990 Pte. GORDON, A., 9th Bn.
29974 Pte. GORDON.
29973 Pte. GOLDSTEIN.
29468 Pte. GOLDSTEIN, B.
40922 Pte. HARRIS, J.,* 1/6th Bn.
202277 Pte. HYAMS, E., 2/5th Bn.
9/25100 Pte. KEILL, B., 1/7th Bn.
203228 Pte. KISSIN, H., 4th Bn.
14193 L/Cpl. ISAACS, S.,* 1st Bn.
11207 L/Cpl. JABLONSKY, A., 2/10th Bn.
11183 Pte. KURLANDER, L., 8/10th Bn.
263663 Pte. LATTER, A., 4th Bn.
Pte. LEVY, I., 1st Bn.
272042 Pte. LIPETZ, S., 2/7th Bn.
241564 Pte. LYONS, J., 1st Bn.
17235 Pte. MARTIN, J.
31750 Pte. MORRIS, A., 3rd Bn.
24027 Pte. METCHICK, B.
372 Pte. PHILLIPS, S., 2/7th Bn.
40443 Cpl. PATERSON, R. F.,* 8/10th Bn.
24015 Pte. RUBENSTEIN, A., 52nd Bn.
263455 Pte. RIFFKIN, 1st Bn.
238081 Pte. TAYLOR, S., 1/4th Bn.
24001 Pte. WALLACK, H.
S/14252 Pte. WEINSHEL, J., 9th Bn.
292134 Pte. WEDECLEFSKY, H. E., 2/15th Bn.
Pte. WOOLF, P., 23rd Bn.
291018 Pte. YABLONSKI, A., 1/7th Bn.

* Killed in Action or died on Active Service.

220167 Pte. FREEMAN, C., 6th Bn.
220244 Pte. FREEDMAN, I., 7th Bn.
29436 Pte. GLEEK, M., 2nd Bn.
17710 Pte. GOLDSTEIN, H., 6th Bn.
27855 Pte. GOLDSTEIN, I., 1st Bn.
9021 Sgt. HARRIS, S., 5th Bn.
30499 L/Cpl. HARRIS, S., 6th Bn.
7411 Pte. HARRIS, N.,* 1st Bn.
20603 Pte. HALLSIDE, H., 7th Bn.
21756 Pte. HENES, S., 5th Bn.
201403 Pte. HEILBRON, T., 2/4th Bn.
220066 Pte. HIRSHALL, A., 6th Bn.
29833 Pte. HYMAN, R., 9th Bn.
Sgt. HYMAN, S., 7th Bn.
21460 L/Cpl. JACOBSON, R., 7th Bn.
41527 Pte. JULIUS, M., 5th Bn.
15037 Pte. KASTAIN, M.
27860 Pte. KERNOFSKY, L., 1st Bn.
23830 Pte. LEVER, A., 5th Bn.
27843 Pte. LEWIS, J., 1st Bn.
39040 Pte. LUBINSKY, L., 2/4th Bn.
43344 Pte. MAISSEL, C., 5th Bn.
28193 Pte. MEYERS, L., 1st Bn.
40648 Pte. MYERS, A., 1/6th Bn.
41641 Sig. PINTO, H.,* 1st Bn.
15603 Pte. SANDYS, J.,* 3rd Bn.
Pte. SLOWMAN, W.
41910 Pte. SELBERG, A., 1st Bn.
203208 Pte. SHAFFENSTEIN, L., 7th Bn.
33437 Pte. SIGERT, M., 3rd Bn.
403296 Sgt. SPIRO, A., 16th Bn.
40287 Pte. STEINBERG, I.,* 1st Bn.
91767 L/Cpl. STEWARD, J., 2nd Bn.
16634 Pte. THOMPSON, S., 7th Bn.
33945 Pte. WALLIS, A., 4th Bn.
Pte. WEITZMAN, M., 1st Bn.
Pte. WEITZMAN, P., 1st Bn.
16630 Pte. WOOLF, S., 7th Bn.

* Killed in Action or died on Active Service.

(THE QUEEN'S OWN) CAMERON HIGHLANDERS.

N.C.O.'s AND MEN.

3753 Pte. ADELSON, H., 14th Bn.
21609 Pte. BARON, B., 7th Bn.
21608 Pte. COHEN, H., 6th Bn.
50726 Cpl. COHEN, J. M., 11th Bn.
7780 Pte. COHEN, D., 1/4th Bn.
3740 Cpl. COHEN, W.
4843 Cpl. COHEN, J. A., 11th Bn.
Pte. COHEN, I., 2nd Bn.
11189 Sgt. COPELAND, P., 5th Bn.
359450 Pte. COPPELOR, A., 5th Bn.
8269 Pte. DAVIES, D., 6th Bn.
Pte. DAVIES, E., 6th Bn.
4075 Pte. DEUTSHMAN, J., 5th Bn.

THE ROYAL IRISH RIFLES.

OFFICERS.

2nd Lieut. BERLYN, B. H.
2nd Lieut. GORFUNCLE, P., 10th Bn.
Major LORIE, R. M., 1st Bn.
Lieut. PHILLIPS, H., 5th Bn.
Capt. WOLFE, E. M.

N.C.O.'s AND MEN.

16165 L/Cpl. ALEXANDER, A., 14th Bn.
22964 Rfm. ALTMAN, D., 7/8th Bn.

Royal Irish Rifles.—*Continued.*

- 9756 Cpl. ALTMAN, J.,* 1st Bn.
- 43525 Rfm. ANSELL, S., 9th Bn.
- 41807 Rfm. AZEN, J., 7th Bn.
- 18007 Rfm. ABRAHAMS, J., 2nd Bn.
- 8/12603 Rfm. BAKER, J., 8th Bn.
- 634130 L/Cpl. BERRY, H., 15th Bn.
- 42637 Rfm. BERNARD, C., 2nd Bn.
- 42202 Rfm. BENJAMIN, B., 12th Bn.
- 44425 Rfm. BLUMENTHAL, H., 15th Bn.
- 45134 Rfm. BROOKARCH, D., 10th Bn.
- 47352 Rfm. BELEVITCH, 1st Bn.
- 42638 Rfm. BROD, H., 2nd Bn.
- 45457 Rfm. BLACK, B., 8th Bn.
- 20664 Rfm. BOXTON, D., 3rd Bn.
- 44508 Rfm. CHAMPANY, L., 16th Bn.
- 42388 Rfm. COHEN, 1st Bn.
- 45425 Rfm. CHYTE, H., 1/8th Bn.
- 8252 Rfm. COHEN, H.,* 1st Bn.
- 42388 Rfm. COHEN, S.,* 1st Bn.
- 41976 Rfm. DOBKIN, M., 16th Bn.
- 45096 Rfm. DAVIS, M. R., 10th Bn.
- Rfm. DAVIS, I., 1st Bn.
- Rfm. DUNCAN, J., 2nd Bn.
- Rfm. ENLANDER, H., 3rd Bn.
- 43505 Rfm. FALK, M., 9th Bn.
- 47111 Rfm. FAIRMAN, P., 15th Bn.
- Rfm. FEIGELSTEIN, I.
- 14630 Rfm. FREEMAN, J., 14th Bn.
- 68 Rfm. FREEMAN, D., 16th Bn.
- 41788 Cpl. FRANKLIN, M., 7th Bn.
- 43314 L/Cpl. FURFANSKY, M. T., 9th Bn.
- 44748 Rfm. GOLDSTONE, L. (M.M.), 12th Bn.
- 42612 Rfm. GOLD, J.
- 43239 L/Cpl. GOODMAN, L., 15th Bn.
- 45082 Rfm. GOLDRING, P., 12th Bn.
- 47093 Rfm. GOTLOP, E.,* 13th Bn.
- 44195 Rfm. GREEN, A.
- 42551 Rfm. HARRIS, J.,* 14th Bn.
- 44344 Rfm. HANBURY, A., 11th Bn.
- Rfm. HOFFMAN, S. (M.M.)
- 5317 Rfm. HYMAN, A., 2nd Bn.
- 45762 Rfm. HYAMS, M., 9th Bn.
- 43873 Rfm. HART, M., 18th Bn.
- 5054 Rfm. ISAACS, S., 2nd Bn.
- 43213 Rfm. ISAACS, A.,* 15th Bn.
- 9600 Rfm. ISAACS, 3rd Bn.
- 4311 L/Cpl. JACOBS, A., 7th Bn.
- 8974 Rfm. JACKSON, F., 15th Bn.
- 41813 Rfm. JAFFE, D., 7th Bn.
- 43890 Rfm. JOSEPH, 1st Bn.
- 45021 Rfm. JOSEPH, A., 16th Bn.
- 519 Rfm JOSEPH, 19th Bn.
- 42141 Rfm. JOSEPHS, W., 9th Bn.
- 42246 Rfm. KIRSTEIN, H., 9th Bn.
- 42561 Rfm. KLEIN, H., 14th Bn.
- Rfm. KARASECK, M., 18th Bn.
- 45473 Rfm. LANDON, D., 1/18th Bn.
- 2080 Rfm. LEVY, A.,* 10th Bn.
- 42408 Rfm. LEVY, J., 1st Bn.
- 45104 Pte. LEVY, E. J.
- 42353 Rfm. LEVY, J.,* 12th Bn.
- 11640 Rfm. LEVENSTON, A., 2nd Bn.
- 42322 Rfm. LEVIN, S., 10th Bn.
- 45083 Rfm. LEWIS, H.,* 10th Bn.
- 11 Sgt. LEWIS, F., 16th Bn.
- 8456 Rfm. LUBINSKY, M., 2nd Bn.
- D/23902 Rfm. LESSER, P., 18th Bn.
- 42248 Rfm. LION, W. M., 9th Bn.
- 15546 Rfm. MARCUS, C., 14th Bn.
- 43595 Rfm. MONASTIRSKY, J. S., 13th Bn.
- 43679 Rfm. MERCADO, B., 9th Bn.
- 44661 Rfm. MEDNIKOFF, M., 16th Bn.
- 44662 Rfm. MORRIS, P., 16th Bn.
- 16426 Rfm. NATHAN, N., 2nd Bn.
- 593546 Rfm. NATHAN, J., 11th Bn.
- 5532 Rfm. NOAH, C. A., 13th Bn.
- 7214 Rfm. PALOFFSKY, L., 16th Bn.
- 50138 Rfm. PHILLIPS, 12th Bn.
- Rfm. PINKER, J., 1st Bn.
- 42742 Rfm. PLOSKEY, 6th Bn.
- 43379 Rfm. ROSENBAUM, I., 12th Bn.
- 575886 Rfm. RUBIN, D., 18th Bn.
- 47598 Rfm. ROSS, D., 3rd Bn.
- 10272 Rfm. ROGERS, F., 6th Bn.
- 32411 Rfm. ROSIN, M., 2nd Bn.
- 41042 Rfm. SCHNEIDER, E., 10th Bn.
- Rfm. SCHWEIM, H., 2nd Bn.
- 9894 Rfm. SHAULMAN, 5th Bn.
- 7154 L/Cpl. SHUMAN, D., 10th Bn.
- 32351 Rfm. SHRIMSKY, S., 1st Bn.
- Rfm. SHERESKI, R., 2nd Bn.
- 10257 Rfm. SILVERSTEIN, A., 6th Bn.
- Rfm. SILVER, S.
- 16176 Rfm. SIMONS, S., 2nd Bn.
- Rfm. SIMONS, A.
- 25379 Rfm. SLOURNY, D.
- 42053 Rfm. SMITH, C. C.
- 8620 Rfm. SOLOMON, A., 11th Bn.
- 592430 Rfm. SOLOMON, J., 15th Bn.
- 44997 Rfm. SOLOMONS, A., 3rd Bn.
- 43302 Rfm. STAAL, L., 10th Bn.
- 43410 Rfm SUSMAN, J., 12th Bn.
- 43599 Rfm. VAN BOOLEN, B., 13th Bn.
- 43307 Rfm. WARSHAWSKY, M., 10th Bn.
- 9526 Rfm. WILLIAMS, F.,* 2nd Bn.
- 43305 Rfm. WOOLF, H.,* 15th Bn.
- 8603 Rfm. WOOLF, J., 15th Bn.
- 5891 Rfm. WOOLF, S., 13th Bn.
- 43510 Rfm. WARREN, I., 13th Bn.
- 44982 Rfm. WOLFF, S., 12th Bn.
- 43389 Rfm. WOOLF, J.,* 9th Bn.

* Killed in Action or died on Active Service.

PRINCESS VICTORIA'S (ROYAL IRISH FUSILIERS).

OFFICERS.
2nd Lieut. CULLEN, R. N.,* 5th Bn.
Major BEDDINGTON, F. M., 10th Bn.
Lt.-Col. ELKAN, C. J. (D.S.O., O.B.E.), 1st Bn.

N.C.O.'s AND MEN.
22964 Pte. ALTMAN, D., 7th Bn.
 1903 Pte. ARKURZ, M., F. Coy.
43314 L/Cpl. FURFANSAFSKY, M. T., 9th Bn.
40011 Pte. FREEDMAN, E., 9th Bn.
 3514 Pte. GOLDIE, B.,* 1st Bn.
45672 Pte. HYAMS, M., 9th Bn.
43852 Pte. ISAACS, M.
42141 Pte. JOSEPHS, W., 9th Bn.
 8974 Pte. JACKSON, F.,1 5th Bn.
19135 Pte. KING, S. J., 7/8th Bn.
26039 Pte. KOSKY, L., 5th Bn.
      Sgt. LEAN, J., 7/8th Bn.
43679 Pte. MERCADO, B., 9th Bn.
      Pte. MYERS, C. (M.M.).
41690 Pte. MOSS, H., 1st Bn.
40025 Pte. ROSENBERG, B.,* 9th Bn.
31142 L/Cpl. RAMUS, A.
      L/Cpl. SILVERMAN, A.
 7159 Rfm. STAAL, L., 10th Bn.
43314 Pte. TUKANOFSKY, M., 9th Bn.
 6182 Pte. WOOLF, G., 9th Bn.
392574 Pte. WOOLF, J., 9th Bn.
42035 Pte. WOOLF, M.

* Killed in Action or died on Active Service.

THE CONNAUGHT RANGERS.

N.C.O.'s AND MEN.
 9660 Pte. BERNSTEIN, C.,* 1st Bn.
      Pte. GORDON, A., 2nd Bn.
      Pte. HARRIS, B., 2nd Bn.
 4662 Sgt. JACOBS, A., 3rd Bn.
      Pte. JOFFE, D.
 9793 Sgt. LEVY, B. M.,* 3rd Bn.
 4868 Pte. MARKS, M.
 2439 Pte. MARKS, S.
10114 Pte. MINSK, H.,* 1st Bn.
18184 L/Cpl. NATHAN, S., 6th Bn.

* Killed in Action or died on Active Service.

PRINCESS LOUISE'S (ARGYLL AND SUTHERLAND HIGHLANDERS).

OFFICERS.
2nd Lieut. CAMPBELL, N. M., 3rd Bn.
2nd Lieut. GOTTSCHALK, M., 4th Bn.

N.C.O.'s AND MEN.
  6041 Pte. AITKEN, L., 11th Bn.
  5479 Cpl. ARONSON, M.P., 2nd Bn.
301764 Pte. ABRAM, J., 10th Bn.
       Pte. BERMAN, B., 1/7th Bn.
202337 Pte. BREMEN, S., 1/8th Bn.
212260 Pte. BLOOMFIELD, N.
  4471 Pte. BIEM, S.
351167 Pte. BURNS, M., 16th Bn.
278755 Pte. BERMAN, C., 5th Bn.
351155 Pte. BRODSKY, L., 16th Bn.
301820 Pte. BROWN, H., 2/8th Bn.
S/6479 Pte. COWAN, H., 12th Bn.
       Pte. COHEN, L.
S/19429 Pte. COHEN, E., 2/6th Bn.
 29272 Pte. CALLER, P., 16th Bn.
 99055 Pte. COHEN, R., 2/8th Bn.
 22507 Dvr. DAVIDSON, S., 3rd Bn.
278755 Dvr. DERLAN, T., 7th Bn.
303466 Pte. ELISON, M., 2/8th Bn.
 13546 Pte. FRASER, M., 14th Bn.
 13351 Pte. FREEMAN, H., 10th Bn.
 18333 Pte. FREEDMAN, T., 10th Bn.
326781 Pte. FREEMAN, C., 1/8th Bn.
301907 Pte. FREEMAN, L., 14th Bn.
276977 Pte. FACTOR, B., 2/6th Bn.
327117 Pte. FREEMAN, J., 2/8th Bn.
279127 Pte. FREEDMAN, A.
407370 Pte. FRANK, P., 14th Bn.
  5102 Pte. FRANK, D., 7th Bn.
  3072 Pte. GLEEK, M., 1/8th Bn.
  3266 Pte. GERBER, J.,* 1/8th Bn.
 10312 Pte. GERSON, P., 10th Bn.
302536 Pte. GINSBERG, I. L., 2/8th Bn.
253070 Pte. GLICKMAN, D.
  5110 Pte. GOLDENBERG, M., 7th Bn.
253536 Pte. GOLDWATER, P., 2/6th Bn.
  6105 Pte. HARRIS, M., 11th Bn.
  3084 Pte. HALL, H., 1/8th Bn.
202487 Pte. HIRSHALL, D., 1/8th Bn.
202814 Pte. HIRSHALL, A., 1/7th Bn.
301907 Pte. HEEMAN, L., 14th Bn.
 29619 Pte. HYMAN, D., 5th Bn.
       Pte. HORACE, M.
  5944 L/Cpl. HYMAN, E. H., 13th Bn.
 21756 Pte. HINES, 13th Bn.
351159 Pte. JACOBS, M., 14th Bn.
253173 Pte. JONES, S., 2/6th Bn.
       Pte. KAYE, A., 1st Bn.
2500/8 L/Cpl. KAYE, C., 5th Bn.
  6972 Pte. LEMON, W., 1/1st Bn.

Argyll and Sutherland Highlanders.—Con.

2940	Pte. LEVY, R.,* 8th Bn.
278729	Pte. LEWIS, N.,* 7th Bn.
350253	Pte. LEVINE, H., 16th Bn.
276956	L/Cpl. LEVINSON, A. M., 2/6th Bn.
253667	Pte. LATMAR, B., 2/6th Bn.
30134	Pte. LUCAS, J. L., 2/8th Bn.
6967	Pte. LATMAN, B., 2/6th Bn.
350807	Pte. MARKS, A., 1/7th Bn.
326892	Pte. MANDLESTON, J., 2/8th Bn.
17059	Pte. MILLAN, L., 14th Bn.
	Sgt. MATZ, A., 4th Bn.
15478	Pte. MYRON, M.,* 13th Bn.
351119	Pte. NOVITSKY, M., 1/17th Bn.
28469	Pte. PLARTUS, N., 14th Bn.
3274	Pte. ROSENTHAL, B., 1/8th Bn.
43841	L/Cpl. ROTENBERG, 14th Bn.
16148	Pte. RUSSELL, W., 2nd Bn.
11455	Pte. RUSSELL, A. C.
28868	Dvr. RABINOVITCH, G., 3rd Bn.
3417	Pte. SIMONS, E., 1/8th Bn.
301185	Pte. SIMMONS, J., 1/8th Bn.
11456	Pte. SOLOMAN, A., 2nd Bn.
12079	Pte. SHOTLAND, M., 3rd Bn.
47438	Pte. SHANCUP, L., 3rd Bn.
326787	Pte. SALMON, D., 2/8th Bn.
277900	Pte. SHABBAS, L., 2/8th Bn.
302660	Pte. SMITH, S., 2/8th Bn.
35069	Pte. SMOLENSKY, A., 3rd Bn.
6101	Pte. SHULMAN, B., 2/6th Bn.
20130	Pte. SWART, A.
3004	Pte. SILVERMAN, H.
7302	L/Cpl. VALLANCE, L., 1st Bn.
32648	Pte. WOLFSON, P., 12th Bn.
301701	Pte. WOOLF, S., 2/8th Bn.
4041	Pte. WOLF, L., 2/8th Bn.
6209	Pte. WANDELSTON, J., 2/9th Bn.
361148	Pte. ZACK S.

* Killed in Action or died on Active Service.

THE PRINCE OF WALES'S LEINSTER REGIMENT (ROYAL CANADIANS).

OFFICERS.

Lieut. ESINGER, S. B., 5th Bn.
2nd Lieut. KAHN, E.,* 1st Bn.

N.C.O.'s AND MEN.

5922	Pte. BURNARD.
5977	Pte. BENJAMIN.
	Pte. DRUKKER, A.
9036	Pte. ELKIN, J., 1st Bn.
	L/Cpl. GREENFIELD, H., 2nd Bn.
	Cpl. GOLDBERG, A., 10th Bn.
5866	Pte. GREEN, I., 6th Bn.

5338	Pte. ISAACS, T. W., 2nd Bn.
8243	Pte. JACKSON, S.
5586	L/Cpl. LEVENSTINE, 3rd Bn.
5619	Pte. MILLER, F., 6th Bn.
18225	Pte. MARKS, L., 2nd Bn.
28199	Pte. MOSES, L., 1st Bn.
5618	Pte. MARCUS, 6th Bn.
15285	Pte. NATHAN, N., 2nd Bn.
1095	L/Cpl. NATHAN, 3rd Bn.
27710	Pte. SUMMERFIELD, A., 2nd Bn.
4950	Pte. SONNENFIELD, I., 1st Bn.
5487	L/Cpl. SALOMONS, G., 2nd Bn.

* Killed in Action or died on Active Service.

THE ROYAL MUNSTER FUSILIERS.

N.C.O.'s AND MEN.

9070	L/Cpl. BARNARD, S.,* 1st Bn.
9232	Pte. COHEN, L., 2nd Bn.
2909	Pte. DION, J.,* 6th Bn.
G/2116	Pte. GOLDIE, D., 2nd Bn.
7676	C.Q.M.S. JACKS, I. (D.C.M.), 2nd Bn
	Pte. KELLER, H., 2nd Bn.
7770	Pte. LEVI, J., 2nd Bn.
10691	Pte. McGUIRE, J., 1st Bn.
2457	Pte. WOLFE, J., 7th Bn.

* Killed in Action or died on Active Service.

THE ROYAL DUBLIN FUSILIERS.

OFFICERS.

Lieut. JACOBS, G. L., 1st Bn.
Lieut. LELAND,* W. A., 1st Bn.

N.C.O.'s AND MEN.

17718	Pte. ARTHUR, J., 2nd Bn.
332650	Pte. ABRAHAMS, G., 1st Bn.
40885	Pte. ABRAHAMS, F., 8th Bn.
26520	Pte. BENJAMIN, M., 10th Bn.
4606	Pte. BLOOMBAUM, E., 10th Bn.
43172	Pte. BLOSTEIN,* P., (M.M.), 2nd Bn.
	Pte. BURN, G.
	Pte. BETTS, E., 11th Bn.
26722	Pte. COLEMAN, 11th Bn.
16635	L/Cpl. CAIDENZ, 3rd Bn.
19748	Pte. CASSELL,* E., 1st Bn.
19126	Pte. DAVIS, A. V., 2nd Bn.
	Pte. DAVIES, S., 3rd Bn.
17848	Pte. DREEZER,* J., 1st Bn.
	Pte. DAVIES, L., 3rd Bn.
5617	Pte. FREEMAN, L., 10th Bn.
3/17150	Pte. FALK,* N., 1st Bn.

Royal Dublin Fusiliers.—*Continued.*

7/13809	Pte. GREENBLATT, N., 7th Bn.
	Cpl. GOLDBERG, H., 2nd Bn.
40214	Pte. HARRIS, H., 1st Bn.
26398	Pte. ISAACS, M., 10th Bn.
26651	Pte. ISAACS, I. H., 10th Bn.
21755	Pte. ISAACS, J., 8th Bn.
	Pte. KAUFFMAN, S., 4th Bn.
5526	Pte. LEWIS, S.
3/16635	L/Sgt. LAIDEN, 3rd Bn.
40419	Pte. LEVENSTON, M.
41016	Cpl. MARKS, D., 1st Bn.
	Pte. MORDECAI, R., 2nd Bn.
28857	Pte. MOSES, L., 6th Bn.
7/24154	Pte. MUCKLESTONE, C., 7th Bn.
29154	Pte. RICHMOND, J., 10th Bn.
18011	Pte. SAUNDERSON, R., 2nd Bn.
5473	Pte. SOLOMONS, A., 10th Bn.
29116	Pte. SOLOMONS, T.,* 7th Bn.
15898	Pte. SIMPSON, H., 9th Bn.
10648	Pte. SOLOMON, P. M., 1st Bn.
10642	Pte. SOLOMONS, B., 1st Bn.
27324	Pte. SMITH, 11th Bn.
52072	Pte. WOOLFE, L.
15003	Pte. SKINNER, S., 7th Bn.

* Killed in Action or died on Active Service.

THE RIFLE BRIGADE (THE PRINCE CONSORT'S OWN).

OFFICERS.

Major ABRAHAMS, M. N.,* 16th Bn.
Lieut. COHEN, H. W., 4th Bn.
2nd Lieut. DAVIES, C. S., 33rd Bn
2nd Lieut. DE PASS, D. A.
2nd Lieut. FRANKAU, P. E.,* 20th Bn.
Capt. KROLICK, E.* (M.C.), 16th Bn.
Capt. LEZARD, A. G.,* 13th Bn.
2nd Lieut. STEPHANY, M., 3rd Bn.
2nd Lieut. SONNENTHAL, A., 10th Bn.
Lieut. SOMAN, D., 3rd Bn.
2nd Lieut. WEIL, A.,* 1st Bn.

N.C.O.'s AND MEN.

B/200150	Rfm. ATKINS, L., 11th Bn.
27758	Rfm. ABRAHAMS, C.,* 11th Bn.
3546	Sgt. ABRAHAMS, D. (M.M.), 16th Bn.
28438	Rfm. ALTER, J., 8th Bn.
S/17926	Rfm. ABRAHAMS, W.,* 1st Bn.
17388	Rfm. ABRAHAMS, S.,* 12th Bn.
17544	Rfm. AARONS, L.. 16th Bn.
8120	Rfm. ABRAHAM, J., 9th B.
15260	Rfm. ABRAHAMS, H., 7th Bn.
23979	L/Cpl. ALLEN, L., 6th Bn.
	Cpl. ARBEID, A. (M.M.).
32025	Rfm. AZEN, E., 12th Bn.
28589	Rfm. ABRAHAMS, A., 5th Bn.
27021	Rfm. ABRAHAMS, 23rd Bn.
209002	L/Cpl. ASHFIELD, J., 25th Bn.
17830	Rfm. ABRAHAMS, R., 1st Bn.
209116	Rfm. ALBERT, H., 27th Bn.
210640	Rfm. ABRAHAMS, D., 25th Bn.
210068	Rfm. ABRAHAMS, E., 25th Bn.
203245	Rfm. ARGUSH, M.
209824	Rfm. ABRAHAMS, M., 25th Bn.
18364	Rfm. ANDREWS, B., 14th Bn.
3531	Rfm. ALTMAN, A.
32244	Rfm. ATCHER, G.
	Rfm. ALEXANDER, H. L., 35th Bn.
33824	Rfm. ABRAHAMS, I., 12th Bn.
14778	Rfm. ANGEL, M., 5th Bn.
621	Rfm. BLOOMBERG, J., 7th Bn.
434	Rfm. BENSUSAN, J., 3rd Bn.
16788	Cpl. BLOOM, A. A., 13th Bn.
374684	Rfm. BARNETT, E., 2nd Bn.
S/7822	Cpl. BARNETT, S.,* 1st Bn.
S/30729	Rfm. BERNSTEIN, S.,* 1st Bn.
I/27385	Rfm. BROCKMAN, M., 1st Bn.
17429	Rfm. BERWALD, A., 9th Bn.
B/200176	Rfm. BRILLESLYPER, J., 11th Bn.
200163	Rfm. BERNARD, A.,* 11th Bn.
28264	Rfm. BURMAN, J., 11th Bn.
S/28102	Rfm. BENSUSAN, D., 10th Bn.
200663	Rfm. BUTLER, A.,* 7th Bn.
S/27291	Rfm. BIERMAN, A., 16th Bn.
S/23860	Rfm. BLOOMBERG, A., 16th Bn.
27214	Rfm. BLOOM, J., 16th Bn.
17776	Rfm. BLUMENTHAL, J.,* 1st Bn.
28228	Rfm. BERNSTEIN, A. F., 8th Bn.
27273	Rfm. BERLINSKI, R., 9th Bn.
Z/2891	Rfm. BRAND, H., 1st Bn.
R/4553	Rfm. BERNSTEIN, M., 11th Bn.
23972	Rfm. BARWICKE, D., 10th Bn.
23319	Rfm. BARNOVITCH, M., 12th Bn.
36826	Rfm. BARON, I., 16th Bn.
5509	Rfm. BARNETT, R.,* 1st Bn.
	Rfm. BERNS, H., 1st Bn.
1851	Rfm. BLOOM, J.,* 4th Bn.
61300	Rfm. BERNSTEIN, S., 85th Bn.
24273	Rfm. BEBLUSKI, 9th Bn.
27385	Rfm. BROCKMAN, M., 1st Bn.
S/23808	Pte. BEAGLE, W., 4th Bn.
S/16322	Rfm. BEERMAN, A., 15th Bn.
Z/2891	L/Cpl. BRAND, H., 5th Bn.
S/15112	Rfm. BLOOMBAUM, B., 5th Bn.
37703	Rfm. BENJAMIN, H ,.5th Bn.
23972	Rfm. BARUCH, D., 5th Bn.
57911	Rfm. BALIECK, M., 5th Bn.
17775	Rfm. BARBITSKY, H. (M.M.), 9th Bn.
33310	Rfm. BARNETT, E., 2nd Bn.
23581	Rfm. BENJAMIN, M., 2nd Bn.
302202	Cpl. BERNSTEIN, A., 1st Bn.
62057	Rfm. BOTCHAM, C., 51st Bn.

Rifle Brigade.—*Continued.*

210658	Rfm. Barbash, J.
	Rfm. Bloom, H. (M.M.).
15990	Rfm. Bernstein, M., 3rd Bn.
9686	Rfm. Berlyn, W., 4th Bn.
7008	Rfm. Booker, J.,* 1st Bn.
3008	Rfm. Bomberg, D., 1st Bn.
210154	Rfm. Bloomfield, I., 25th Bn.
210480	Rfm. Bloom, J., 25th Bn.
210178	Rfm. Bernard, R.
210611	Rfm. Bloom, R., 25th Bn.
210602	Rfm. Bird, C.
208606	Rfm. Blake, M., 25th Bn.
208607	Rfm. Berg, M., 25th Bn.
13621	Rfm. Bloomberg, G., 5th Bn.
210943	Rfm. Bronstein, D.
29940	Rfm. Berger, H., 6th Bn.
S/36689	Rfm. Bisberg, C., 25th Bn.
78228	Rfm. Bernstein, I. I., 1st Bn.
745698	Rfm. Berkman, 37th Bn.
210726	Rfm. Begmen, M., 25th Bn.
9979	Rfm. Barnett, J.
O/359	Rfm. Biton, H.
2891	Rfm. Brand, H.
211447	Rfm. Black, M., 25th Bn.
210483	Rfm. Blendis, S., 25th Bn.
203240	Rfm. Benabo, L.,
R/35596	Rfm. Blaupapier, D., 5th Bn.
50785	Rfm. Brookman, W. W., 2nd Bn.
21466	Rfm. Berman, A., 12th Bn.
	Rfm. Burman, R.
9466	Rfm. Benjamin, A.,* 1st Bn.
	Cpl. Benjamin, J., 5th Bn.
	Rfm. Benson, S.
	Rfm. Barnett, H. J.
	Cpl. Barrett, S.
	Rfm. Bresh, A., 14th Bn.
	Rfm. Breslam, H.
26185	Rfm. Bogard, J.,* 8th Bn.
5467	Rfm. Cohen, J.,* 1st Bn.
9611	Rfm. Cohen, H., 9th Bn.
8166	Rfm. Cohen, C., 9th Bn.
S/6116	Rfm. Cohen, B., 7th Bn.
S/8293	Cpl. Clompers, J., 8th Bn.
S/2213	Rfm. Cohen, J., 12th Bn.
S/8103	Rfm. Conn, D., 12th Bn.
1646	Cpl. Cowan, S., 4th Bn.
17909	Rfm. Cohen, J.,* 1st Bn.
C/200569	Rfm. Cohen, S., 1st Bn.
B/1908	Rfm. Cohen, .H, 7th Bn.
2166	Rfm. Cohen, W., 9th Bn.
S/28932	Rfm. Cohen, H., 3rd Bn.
B/200158	Rfm. Cohen, B., 11th Bn.
B/200155	Rfm. Cohen, J., 11th Bn.
B/200167	Rfm. Carter, J., 11th Bn.
J/177617	Rfm. Cohen, J., 11th Bn.
30637	Rfm. Cohen, D., 1st Bn.
200942	Rfm. Cohen, J.,* 13th Bn.
S/23931	Rfm. Cohen, N., 3rd Bn.
2040	Rfm. Cox, E., 2nd Bn.
274416	Rfm Cohen, A., 13th Bn.
14647	Rfm. Cohen, S., 14th Bn.
23709	Rfm. Cooper, A., 17th Bn.
200569	Rfm. Cohen, S., 1st Bn.
2132	Sgt. Cohen, H., 4th Bn.
16390	Sig. Cavalsky, 10th Bn.
6243	Rfm. Cope, W., 13th Bn.
32772	Rfm. Caplin, P., 3rd Bn.
19063	Rfm. Carstin, H., 3rd Bn.
S/17475	Rfm. Cohen, S., 15th Bn.
S/25368	Rfm. Cohen, W., 5th Bn.
16546	Rfm. Cohen, S., 15th Bn.
S/2525	Sgt. Cook, S., 5th Bn.
15605	Rfm. Cormick, S., 5th Bn.
302535	Rfm. Cohen, L.
S/34024	Rfm. Caplan, F.,* 1st Bn.
209754	Rfm. Cohen, E., 22nd Bn.
S/18656	Rfm. Cohn, C., 12th Bn.
6220	Rfm. Caplin, M.
4172	Rfm. Cohen, R., 25th Bn.
210429	Rfm. Cohen, L., 25th Bn.
17817	Rfm. Cohen, I.
27291	Rfm. Cosham, N., 16th Bn.
33117	Rfm. Cohen, P., 6th Bn.
13/51578	Rfm. Caplin, A.
211357	Rfm. Cohen, H., 2nd Bn.
210156	Rfm. Cleak, W., 25th Bn.
210644	Rfm. Cohen, M., 25th Bn.
21680	Rfm. Cregor, C., 15th Bn.
8103	Rfm. Coun, D., 4th Bn.
41866	Rfm. Cohen, A. J., 5th Bn.
72135	Rfm. Cohen, M., 49th Bn.
45716	Rfm. Curzon, J., 12th Bn.
37786	Rfm. Chillingbaum, N., 13th Bn.
3243	Rfm. Cope, W., 13th Bn.
5/221	Rfm. Cohn, E.,* 1st Bn.
B/200356	Rfm. Dancyger, W., 11th Bn.
S/19776	Rfm. Da Costa, J.,* 2nd Bn.
32173	Rfm. Dudinsky, J.,* 2nd Bn.
18186	Rfm. Druke, S., 9th Bn.
B/1200173	Rfm. Daum, J., 11th Bn.
B/1200161	Rfm. Davis, M., 11th Bn.
S/17757	Rfm. Davis,. D.,* 11th Bn.
17755	Rfm. Deutch, E., 10th Bn.
29910	Rfm. Davis, N., 11th Bn.
29934	Rfm. Davis, I., 11th Bn.
17795	Rfm. Diamond, J., 9th Bn.
23977	Cpl. Defries, B., 8th Bn.
860991	Rfm. Davis, A., 33rd Bn.
S/25772	Cpl. Davids, A., 2nd Bn.
21395	Rfm. Deswarte, T. A., 6th Bn.
S/15170	Rfm. Davis, H., 5th Bn.
S/25013	Rfm. Deutchman, M., 5th Bn.
55535	Rfm. Didyachate, 8th Bn.
5/434	Rfm. Davis, H.,* 1st Bn.
S/28901	Rfm. Dalter, S., 12th Bn.

Rifle Brigade.—*Continued.*

210470	Rfm. Davis, M., 25th Bn.	
210881	Rfm. Defries, E., 25th Bn.	
16319	Rfm. Dertz, F. L., 14th Bn.	
18782	Rfm. Dosovitch, S.	
316873	Rfm. Davis, J., 6th Bn.	
	Rfm. Dexter, A. R., 5th Bn.	
	Rfm. Delew, J., 7th Bn.	
B/200358	Rfm. Ereira, J., 11th Bn.	
23746	Rfm. Epstein, J., 7th Bn.	
S/13897	Cpl. Ellis, W., 8th Bn.	
2911	Rfm. Ereira, A., 8th Bn.	
27227	Rfm. Elias, E., 8th Bn.	
59662	Rfm. Edwards, H., 5th Bn.	
80942	Rfm. Edgart, L., 52nd Bn.	
210068	Rfm. Eckstein, A., 23rd Bn.	
210472	Rfm. Edelman, M., 25th Bn.	
	Rfm. Egelnick, M., 14th Bn.	
	Rfm. Egelnick, A., 14th Bn.	
277	Rfm. Freeman, H., 1st Bn.	
2606	Rfm. Figgins, J.,* 2nd Bn.	
B/377	Rfm. Franklin, F.,* 11th Bn.	
23540	Rfm. Freedman, S., 13th Bn.	
18647	Rfm. Flix, L., 13th Bn.	
19811	Rfm. Franklin, A., 13th Bn.	
30733	Rfm. Fish, H., 1st Bn.	
19028	Rfm. Flaum, M., 13th Bn.	
7234	Rfm. Feld, R. (M.M.), 7th Bn.	
200679	Rfm. Flack, W., 8th Bn.	
17828	Rfm. Finklestein, W., 2nd Bn.	
375	Rfm. Fox, S.,* 2nd Bn.	
O/359	Cpl. Freedman, S., 1st Bn.	
1328	Rfm. Flarman, H.	
21716	Rfm. Fisher, T., 6th Bn.	
23932	L/Cpl. Fineberg, J., 6th Bn.	
110	Rfm. Freeman, I., 1st Bn.	
27291	Rfm. Flowre, J., 16th Bn.	
211221	Rfm. Foot, H.	
209202	Rfm. Falk, M., 25th Bn.	
52392	Rfm. Fleisher, L., 5th Bn.	
203245	Rfm. Firth, F.	
209939	Rfm. Finegold, A.	
209756	Rfm. Falk, W., 25th Bn.	
	Rfm. Fieldman, H., 25th Bn.	
30733	Rfm. Fisher, H., 1st Bn.	
39015	Rfm. Fishman, L., 3rd Bn.	
23641	Rfm. Finkelstein, J., 17th Bn.	
58524	Rfm. Freedman, J.,* 7th Bn.	
S/35069	Rfm. Fidler, M.,* 16th Bn.	
S/23819	Rfm. Goldberg, B., 5th Bn.	
24020	Rfm. Guralnisk, D., 6th Bn.	
306905	Rfm. Getter, H., 5th Bn.	
15344	Rfm. Gotlop, E., 7th Bn.	
23277	Rfm. Gregory, J., 16th Bn.	
50207	Rfm. Godfrey, G., 1st Bn.	
S/8623	Rfm. Goldstein, B., 8th Bn.	
S/5743	Cpl. Goldsmith, V., 11th Bn.	
203302	L/Cpl. Goldstein, S., 13th Bn.	
1877	Cpl. Gordon, C.,* 13th Bn.	
574732	Rfm. Garcia, A., 2nd Bn.	
25727	Rfm. Gordon, J., 1st Bn.	
17797	Rfm. Gordon, B.,* 8th Bn.	
S/19758	L/Cpl. Green, N., 11th Bn.	
200168	Rfm. Goldberg, M.,* 11th Bn.	
S/14721	Rfm. Goldsmith, L., 12th Bn.	
S/19802	L/Cpl. Goodman, L.,* 12th Bn.	
S/27032	Rfm. Gausten, A., 8th Bn.	
23106	Rfm. Gordon, S., 8th Bn.	
17667	Sig. Goldberg, I., 8th Bn.	
48614	Rfm. Goldstein, B.,* 13th Bn.	
48960	Rfm. Golenska, J., 13th Bn.	
861194	Rfm. Gusofsky, G., 33rd Bn.	
29430	Pte. Glass, F., 25th Bn.	
15588	Rfm. Golden, A., 1st Bn.	
5167	Rfm. Goldstein, H., 3rd Bn.	
8294	Rfm. Goodman, H., 4th Bn.	
S/5743	Rfm. Goldsmith, F., 11th Bn.	
S/28001	Rfm. Golizky, J.,* 10th Bn.	
16320	Rfm. Gresofsky, P., 12th Bn.	
S/8623	Rfm. Goldstein, W., 6th Bn.	
38312	Rfm. Goldstein, D., 6th Bn.	
17342	Rfm. Goldberg, H., 7th Bn.	
14445	Rfm. Garfinkle, J., 12th Bn.	
34150	Rfm. Garbett, B., 2nd Bn.	
59810	Rfm. Gardiner, 23rd Bn.	
200345	Rfm. Goldstein, 8th Bn.	
S/8078	Rfm. Gluck, A.,* 12th Bn.	
S/24196	Rfm. Goldstein, D.,* 1st Bn.	
19802	L/Cpl. Goodman, L.,* 12th Bn.	
83328	Rfm. Goldstone, H., 52nd Bn.	
82475	Rfm. Goodman, C., 52nd Bn.	
218434	Rfm. Goldman, I., 25th Bn.	
32638	Rfm. Gassman, S., 5th Bn.	
210914	Rfm. Goorwich, M.	
31281	Rfm. Green, A., 6th Bn.	
30810	Rfm. Greenberg, A., 11th Bn.	
210927	Rfm. Gurivitch, M., 25th Bn.	
17760	Rfm. Galinsky, L., 14th Bn.	
18787	Rfm. Goldberg, A., 14th Bn.	
24195	Rfm. Greenberg, B., 5th Bn.	
19802	L/Cpl. Gootman, R.	
17785	Rfm. Goldstein, J.	
54339	Rfm. Gold, H., 53rd Bn.	
30018	Rfm. Geller, M., 31st Bn.	
	Rfm. Gerald, J., 2nd Bn.	
485	Rfm. Goldman, N.,* 21st Bn.	
10112	Rfm. Harris, J., 9th Bn.	
9076	Rfm. Harvey, A., 9th Bn.	
S/7393	Cpl. Harris, L., 7th Bn.	
S/7391	Sgt. Harris, C., 7th Bn.	
1024	Cpl. Herman, S.,* 10th Bn.	
S/7885	Rfm. Harris, S.,* 11th Bn.	
S/5992	Rfm. Hyman, H., 11th Bn.	
18852	Rfm. Hyams, M., 13th Bn.	
S/2650	Rfm. Hyams, L.,* 13th Bn.	

Rifle Brigade.—*Continued.*

28004	Rfm. HYAMS, J., 10th Bn.		210558	Rfm. ISAACS, N., 22nd Bn.
S/16543	Rfm. HYMAN, M., 3rd Bn.		210375	Rfm. ISAACMAN, A., 22nd Bn.
S/26352	Rfm. HARRIS, D., 7th Bn.		210728	Rfm. ISAACS, C., 23rd Bn.
S/15318	Rfm. HENRIQUES, B., 7th Bn.		20795	Rfm. ISAACS, L. (M.M.).
S/27241	Rfm. HOUSE, S., 16th Bn.		445068	Rfm. ISAACS, M., 9th Bn.
S/34005	Rfm. HONIGMAN, A., 11th Bn.		31091	Rfm. ISAACSON, R., 9th Bn.
861194	Rfm. HUNT, H., 33rd Bn.		276	Rfm. ISRAEL, S.
860821	Rfm. HERSHAFT, W., 33rd Bn.		26795	Rfm. ISAACS, S., 2nd Bn.
5598	Rfm. HYMAN, S. H., 11th Bn.		S/23824	Rfm. ISRAEL, H., 5th Bn.
34725	Rfm. HARRIS, S., 12th Bn.		B/200154	Rfm. JACOBS, S., 11th Bn.
13002	Rfm. HARRIS, L.		B/200165	Rfm. JACOBS, J.,* 11th Bn.
5396	Rfm. HARRIS, M.,* 4th Bn.		16075	Rfm. JOEL, S., 10th Bn.
S/29916	Rfm. HARRIS, S., 3rd Bn.		S/14771	Cpl. JACOBS, M., 8th Bn.
16543	Rfm. HYAM, M., 12th Bn.		23980	Cpl. JAFFE, S., 8th Bn.
17504	Rfm. HARRIS, H.		46890	Rfm. JOSEPH, A., 3rd Bn.
17796	Rfm. HARRIS, G.		46701	Rfm. JOHNSON, W., 12th Bn.
17773	Rfm. HARRIS I., 6th Bn.		S/31870	Rfm. JAFFE, D.
31714	Rfm. HARRIS, H., 1st Bn.		S/8525	Sgt. JOSEPHS, J., 6th Bn.
12970	L/Cpl. HALPERN, 11th Bn.		28138	Rfm. JACOBS, D., 10th Bn.
210874	Rfm. HARING, B., 20th Bn.		213768	Rfm. JACOBS, S., 25th Bn.
202018	Rfm. HOLSTEIN, M., 19th Bn.		17789	Rfm. JACOBS, A., 6th Bn.
S/16064	Rfm. HARRIS, S.,* 1st Bn.		742345	Rfm. JACOBS, I.
16284	Rfm. HIZER, L.,* 3rd Bn.		58429	Rfm. JEFFRIES, J., 52nd Bn.
S/8770	Rfm. HAYMAN, J.		210364	Rfm. JOSEPH, H., 22nd Bn.
210605	Rfm. HOFFMAN, I., 25th Bn.		29011	C.Q.M.S. JACOB, M.
210436	Rfm. HYAMS, H., 25th Bn.		65409	Rfm. JACKSON, L., 3rd Bn.
210409	Rfm. HARRIS, J., 25th Bn.		211231	Rfm. JACOBS, L., 25th Bn.
203385	Rfm. HARRIS, M.		18223	Rfm. JACOBS, H., 14th Bn.
21696	Rfm. HART, D., 7th Bn.		3/18184	Rfm. JACOBSON, H., 25th Bn.
32270	Rfm. HELLER, 6th Bn.		22180	Rfm. JANETSKY, H.
174769	Rfm. HIRSHKOWITZ, J., 6th Bn.		1853	L/Cpl. KASS, A., 7th Bn.
211103	Rfm. HEMMINGS, L.		S/15121	Rfm. KARASEK, H.,* 16th Bn.
211171	Rfm. HARTOG, A.		17748	Rfm. KOSMINSKY, L., 12th Bn.
29933	Rfm. HELLINGER, P., 6th Bn.		28385	Rfm. KLEPS, L.,* 12th Bn.
31872	Cpl. HOFFMAN, T., 16th Bn.		24986	Rfm. KALINSKY, A., 8th Bn.
202157	Rfm. HARRIS, H., 7th Bn.		24021	Rfm. KRATOSKY, D.,* 8th Bn.
210517	Rfm. HILLMAN, J., 25th Bn.		S/22343	Rfm. KOPINSKY, J.,* 8th Bn.
830505	Rfm. HILL, E., 25th Bn.		18568	Rfm. KIRSCH, H.,* 8th Bn.
8770	Rfm. HYMAN, J.		62478	Rfm. KLEINBERG, H., 53rd Bn.
23440	Rfm. HARRIS, S., 6th Bn.		17484	Rfm. KRAYER, A.
21678	Rfm. HOFFMAN, S.		19063	Rfm. KERSTEIN, H., 6th Bn.
19456	Rfm. HARDING, H.		31201	Rfm. KINSLER, S., 8th Bn.
25399	Rfm. HAMBURG, H.		210362	Rfm. KUTCHINSKY, P., 22nd Bn.
3/23928	Cpl. HAMBERGER, J., 7th Bn.		S/8808	Rfm. KAYES, L., 4th Bn.
21872	Rfm. HOFFMAN, I., 16th Bn.		210848	Rfm. KRONENBERG, D.
202157	Rfm. HARRIS, H., 7th Bn.		211127	Rfm. KORINSKY, A.
71632	Rfm. HERTZ, S., 25th Bn.		210696	Rfm. KRAUSE, S., 25th Bn.
64242	Rfm. HARRIS, J., 3rd Bn.		S/18784	Rfm. KAPILOFF, V., 14th Bn.
	Rfm. HERNE, S., 9th Bn.		15605	Rfm. KORNICK, S., 6th Bn.
	Rfm. HARRIS, A., 5th Bn.		17494	Rfm. KRUGER, A.
24014	Rfm. HARRIS, A. J., 6th Bn.		14882	Rfm. KING, S., 2nd Bn.
6044	Rfm. ISAACS, A.,* 9th Bn.		8170	Rfm. KELOFSKY, 1st Bn.
17747	Rfm. ISAACS, D., 7th Bn.		341	Rfm. LYONS, W., 7th Bn.
19759	Rfm. ISAACS, A., 11th Bn.		5062	Rfm. LYONS, H., 7th Bn.
860565	Rfm. ILIAN, H., 33rd Bn.		991	Rfm. LEWIS, S., 8th Bn.
764	Rfm. ISAACS, H., 10th Bn.		8260	Rfm. LEVY, D., 8th Bn.
28137	Rfm. ISAACS, S. M., 10th Bn.		S/750	Sgt. LEVY, S.,* 12th Bn.
			304476	Rfm. LEVY, L. G., 13th Bn.

Rifle Brigade.—*Continued.*

203220	Rfm. LEVY, P., 13th Bn.
17756	Rfm. LEVI, A., 1st Bn.
17746	Rfm. LEVISON, I., 1st Bn.
17754	Rfm. LEVY, J., 1st Bn.
25776	Rfm. LAZARUS, H., 1st Bn.
S/13857	Rfm. LAVANDER, H., 8th Bn.
18416	Rfm. LEVEY, L. N., 9th Bn.
S/11583	Rfm. LEVENSON, H.,* 7th Bn.
B/200157	Rfm. LEVY, S., 11th Bn.
200153	Rfm. LUBINSKY, H.,* 11th Bn.
29936	Rfm. LIBERMAN, H., 10th Bn.
S/21652	Rfm. LEE, H., 7th Bn.
21725	Rmf. LANSHINSKI, A., 7th Bn.
71578	Rfm. LEVY, C., 7th Bn.
24674	Rfm. LANSBERG, N.,* 8th Bn.
32161	Rfm. LEAPMAN, B., 9th Bn.
16496	Rfm. LEVY, J.,* 16th Bn.
S/18729	Rfm. LAZARAWITCH, S., 16th Bn.
46555	Rfm. LEVY, A., 12th Bn.
29716	Rfm. LEWIS, A.,* 11th Bn.
27809	Rfm. LEVY, A.
24/2025	Rfm. LEVY, B., 3rd Bn.
115	Rfm. LIMBERG, M., 1st Bn.
B/1550	Cpl. LANGER, S.,* 9th Bn.
7640	Rfm. LION, A. J.,* 9th Bn.
16524	Rfm. LEVY, C.,* 2nd Bn.
34890	Rfm. LAZARUS, N., 1st Bn.
19975	Rfm. LEVY, C., 16th Bn.
35378	Rfm. LYNCH, E., 9th Bn.
24072	Rfm. LEVY, H., 1st Bn.
2241	Rfm. LISSACK, A., 9th Bn.
210820	Rfm. LUBOTSKY, 24th Bn.
211696	Pte. LEVENE, H., 19th Bn.
28657	Rfm. LEVY, L., 8th Bn.
200374	Rfm. LYONS, 18th Bn.
36184	Rfm. LAZARUS, J., 6th Bn.
S/34416	Rfm. LANGLEBEN, M., 5th Bn.
51694	Rfm. LEVY, W., 5th Bn.
46707	Rfm. LYONS, L. S., 12th Bn.
401	Rfm. LYONS, H., 3rd Bn.
207675	Rfm. LAMPERT, J., 19th Bn.
Z36	Rfm. LAZARUS, R.,* 1st Bn.
15629	Rfm. LEHMANN, L. C.,* 2nd Bn.
17441	Rfm. LEVY, A.,* 7th Bn.
48240	Rfm. LIGHTSTONE, L.,* 2nd Bn.
S/22846	Rfm. LIPMAN, H.,* 3rd Bn.
11922	Rfm. LYONS, S.,* 9th Bn.
83667	L/Cpl. LAWRENCE, M., 52nd Bn.
84042	L/Cpl. LEVENE, M. P., 52nd Bn.
209172	Rfm. LOSKY, G., 22nd Bn.
17647	Rfm. LESSER, E., 13th Bn.
210359	Rfm. LEVY, B., 25th Bn.
210418	Rfm. LESME, P., 25th Bn.
210155	Rfm. LEVY, B., 25th Bn.
102435	Rfm. LANTENBURY, M., 25th Bn.
210391	Rfm. LEVY, S. L., 25th Bn.
210114	Rfm. LEVY, P., 25th Bn.
209000	Rfm. LEBOFSKI, A., 25th Bn.
38150	Rfm. LEVY, F., 5th Bn.
12764	Rfm. LEVITT, B.
211235	Rfm. LEVY, S., 25th Bn.
210696	Rfm. LISTER, J., 25th Bn.
215702	Rfm. LAZARUS, L., 25th Bn.
81612	Rfm. LEWBITZ, I., 7th Bn.
403220	Rfm. LEVY, P., 13th Bn.
208961	Rfm. LESS, L.
200854	Rfm. LEVY, E. B., 8th Bn.
47887	Rfm. LEWIS, J., 11th Bn.
32022	Rfm. LEVY, I.,* 11th Bn.
10368	Rfm. MILLER, N.,* 7th Bn.
10641	Rfm. MUSAPHIA, S., 8th Bn.
S/8601	Cpl. MAGNUS, R., 11th Bn.
B/200359	Rfm. MICHEALS, J. M., 11th Bn.
3722	Rfm. MORTIMER, R., 13th Bn.
B/72	Rfm. MANDLE, M., 16th Bn.
15816	Rfm. MYERS, A.,* 1st Bn.
B/200159	Rfm. MOSSBAUM, A., 11th Bn.
B/200171	Rfm. MOLDOFSKY, S.,* 11th Bn.
32917	Rfm. MYERS, J.,* 11th Bn.
17831	Rfm. MICOFSKY, H., 9th Bn.
15570	Rfm. MYERS, R., 9th Bn.
32098	Rfm. MARTIN, J., 9th Bn.
305041	Rfm. MOSS, A., 1st Bn.
28859	Cpl. MAYER, G. (M.M.), 1st Bn.
S/19698	Rfm. MORRIS, C., 3rd Bn.
41136	Rfm. MEERLOO, B., 11th Bn.
B/200664	Rfm. MENDOZA, N., 2nd Bn.
5798	Rfm. MARKS, J., 1st Bn.
16585	Rfm. MILENOFSKY, W., 10th Bn.
200610	L/Cpl. MOSCOW, P., 2nd Bn.
17752	Rfm. MICHAELSON, J., 8th Bn.
31286	Rfm. MARCUS, I.,* 3rd Bn.
	Rfm. MORRIS, H. J., 1st Bn.
31296	L/Cpl. MALINA, D,. 11th Bn.
516029	Rfm. MENDOZA, H., 6th Bn.
S/24125	Rfm. MARKS, S. M., 5th Bn.
29935	Rfm. MARKOFSKY, H., 8th Bn.
B/203750	Rfm. MOSS, H., 2nd Bn.
O/302	Cpl. MIDDLEMAN, H., 51st Bn.
204263	Rfm. MERCADO, A., 21st Bn.
S/9979	Rfm. MAGNUS, M.,* 7th Bn.
4673	Rfm. MORRIS, H.,* 2nd Bn.
17981	Rfm. MYERS, J.,* 8th Bn.
83957	L/Cpl. MARKS, H., 52nd Bn.
S/16722	Rfm. MAGNUS, P., 4th Bn.
210446	Rfm. MENDOZA, P., 25th Bn.
210170	Rfm. MILLER, S., 25th Bn.
34919	Cpl. MAGNUS, M., 8th Bn.
210162	Rfm. MARKS, W., 25th Bn.
210368	Rfm. MICHAELS, A., 25th Bn.
210707	Rfm. MOORE, W., 25th Bn.
210700	Rfm. MORDECAR, J., 25th Bn.
15576	Rfm. MYERS, L., 22nd Bn.
20577	Rfm. MARIENSTRAUSS, L., 5th Bn.

Rifle Brigade.—*Continued.*

S/17667	Rfm. MICHAELS, S., 6th Bn.
23378	Rfm. MISHIC, J., 25th Bn.
14461	Rfm. MOCOVITCH, A.
2227	Rfm. MILLWAN, 4th Bn.
40030	Rfm. MATHERMAN, S.
	Rfm. MILLER, J., 7th Bn.
21198	Rfm. MARCUS, S., 23rd Bn.
3657	Rfm. MICHAILIFSKY, W., 25th Bn.
35826	Rfm. MATTER, S.
S/26880	Rfm. NYMAN, J.,* 2nd Bn.
76543	Rfm. NAYMAN, 12th Bn.
S/10358	Rfm. NACHAN, M., 11th Bn.
1710	Rfm. NATHAN, S., 3rd Bn.
S/19086	Rfm. NUNES, VAZ, L.,* 10th Bn.
319006	L/Cpl. NATKEIL, S., 12th Bn.
	Cpl. NORMAN, H., 1st Bn.
1710	Rfm. NATHAN, S., 13th Bn.
10358	Rfm. NATHAN, M., 4th Bn.
B/200164	Rfm. OVERS, M., 11th Bn.
S/23780	Rfm. OLIVER, A., 1st Bn.
3/17493	Rfm. OESTERMAN, J., 25th Bn.
728435	Pte. OPOS, J., 19th Bn.
17493	Rfm. OTTERLANGER, M., 4th Bn.
196	Rfm. OBENEY, J. C.
164002	Rfm. ODDIER, W., 3rd Bn.
200156	Rfm. OSOSKI, N.,* 11th Bn.
200597	Rfm. PARK, J., 2nd Bn.
S/23292	Rfm. PEARLMAN, D. W., 2nd Bn.
200997	Rfm. PARKER, A., 10th Bn.
203978	Rfm. POSENER, A., 8th Bn.
423676	Rfm. PLOTZKER, J., 13th Bn.
28001	Rfm. POLINSKI, 10th Bn.
32182	Rfm. PARLEY, G., 2nd Bn.
5411	Rfm. PULVERMACHER, 4th Bn.
29939	Rfm. PHILLIPS, H., 13th Bn.
P/166	Rfm. PHILLIPS, S. M., 1st Bn.
15989	Rfm. PRICE, H., 6th Bn.
24021	Rfm. PRATOSKY, D., 8th Bn.
209209	Rfm. PERRY, L., 20th Bn.
13789	Rfm. PARKER, S.,* 11th Bn.
3407	Rfm. PISSARIO, T., 2nd Bn.
209829	Rfm. PHILLIPS, N., 25th Bn.
34071	Rfm. PEARSON, N., 6th Bn.
207775	Rfm. PHILLIPS, B. E., 2nd Bn.
21375	Rfm. PERRILLY, S.
30528	Rfm. PEARLSTONE, M.
3119	Rfm. PHILLIPS, E., 25th Bn.
3754	Rfm. RODRIGUES, J. L., 13th Bn.
6372	Rfm. ROSENBAUM, H., 2nd Bn.
S/14578	Rfm. ROSE, A., 7th Bn.
7186	Rfm. RIPPS, L., 7th Bn
21749	Rfm. ROSEN, A., 7th Bn.
B/200166	Rfm. ROSENBERG, J., 11th Bn.
S/13937	Rfm. RAPHAEL, L., 3rd Bn.
S/16186	Rfm. ROSEN, B., 3rd Bn.
200953	L/Cpl. RACHKIN, F., 9th Bn.
B/203654	Rfm. ROSEN, A., 2nd Bn.
32973	Rfm. REZKER, M., 9th Bn.
53431	Rfm. ROSEN, M., 2nd Bn.
24809	Rfm. ROBERTS, D., 6th Bn.
19066	Rfm. ROSOFF, J.,* 3rd Bn.
32218	Rfm. RUBINSKY, H., 51st Bn.
591224	Rfm. RADSTONE, D., 5th Bn.
S/28547	Rfm. ROSENBERG, B.,* 2nd Bn.
209284	Rfm. ROSE, S., 25th Bn.
211442	Rfm. REISTER, A. I., 25th Bn.
211234	Rfm. ROZELAAR, I.
24021	Rfm. RATOSKY, D., 8th Bn.
210823	Rfm. ROSENBLOOM, E., 25th Bn.
	Rfm. RUDA, M.
309939	Rfm. RHINEGOLD, M.
211248	Rfm. ROSEN, P., 25th Bn.
492786	Rfm. ROSENBURG, H.
40205	Rfm. ROSENTHALL, L.
24126	Rfm. ROGEL, H., 12th Bn.
438	L/Cpl. SINGER, P.,* 2nd Bn.
13370	Rfm. SCOBLE, S., 9th Bn.
629	Rfm. SILVER, L. (M.M.), 7th Bn.
1855	Rfm. SPERO, M., 8th Bn.
18849	Rfm. SILVERSTONE, A., 13th Bn.
12145	Rfm. STERNBERG, L., 13th Bn.
20413	L/Cpl. SHERWIN, M. (M.M.), 13th Bn.
203240	Rfm. SIMONS, A., 13th Bn.
3/17006	Rfm. SILVERMAN, M., 2nd Bn.
S/1768	Rfm. SAMUELS, M.* (M.M.), 1st Bn.
17788	Rfm. SLASBERG, I., 1st Bn.
15485	Rfm. SOLOMONS, L., 3rd Bn.
31438	Rfm. SCHWARTZ, M., 3rd Bn.
S/24430	Rfm. SOLOMAN, A., 11th Bn.
18853	Rfm. SCHWARTZ, S., 10th Bn.
S/17195	Rfm. SILVER, J., 7th Bn.
24629	Rfm. SOKEL, M., 7th Bn.
30546	Rfm. STEINHART, A., 7th Bn.
24630	Rfm. SIROTKIN, T., 7th Bn.
29447	Sgt. SAUNDERS, M., 9th Bn.
S/24051	Rfm. SACKSHIVER, J.,* 9th Bn.
S/8174	L/Cpl. SANDREICH, L., 9th Bn.
28185	Rfm. STRONG, J., 9th Bn.
27269	Rfm. SACKROVITCH, I., 16th Bn.
5/8830	Rfm. SOLOMONS, J.* (KNOWLES), 1st Bn.
13560	Rfm. SOLOMONS, 1st Bn.
S/28895	Rfm. SOLOMONS, N., 3rd Bn.
25276	Rfm. SYMONDS, L., 12th Bn.
S/14646	Rfm. SELIGMAN, S., 14th Bn.
S/9487	Sgt. SINGER, J., 2nd Bn.
355	Rfm. SINGER, E.,* 1st Bn.
1471	Cpl. SCHULMAN, S., 5th Bn.
S/13934	Rfm. SIMMONDS, H., 15th Bn.
9325	Rfm. SMITH, A., 5th Bn.
19757	Rfm. SOLOMONS, L., 10th Bn.
210912	Rfm. SICKMAN, 24th Bn.
17809	Rfm. SPURLING, S.,* 1st Bn.
S/25179	Rfm. SOLOMONS, S., 5th Bn.
S/25000	Rfm. SHRIER, M., 5th Bn.
S/21746	Rfm. SIMMS, H., 5th Bn.

Rifle Brigade.—Continued.

S/25379	Rfm. STAVNY, D., 5th Bn.
S/14615	Rfm. SELSON, J., 5th Bn.
17786	Rfm. SOLOMON, A., 6th Bn.
19757	Rfm. SOLOMON, J., 6th Bn.
24631	Rfm. SIROTKIN, S., 6th Bn.
59461	Rfm. SUGAR, A., 5th Bn.
24640	Rfm. SOROTKIN, 7th Bn.
210604	Rfm. SMITH, J., 25th Bn.
30871	Rfm. SAMUEL, S.,* 3rd Bn.
S/355	Rfm. SINGER, E.,* 1st Bn.
S/17055	Rfm. STRELITZ, L.,* 16th Bn.
209774	Rfm. SILVER, H., 23rd Bn.
210083	L/Cpl. SAMPSON, A. A., 23rd Bn.
	Rfm. SAMUEL, S.
B/13	L/Cpl. STONE, J.
7718	L/Cpl. SMITH, H., 3rd Bn.
210525	Rfm. STEINBERG, H., 25th Bn.
210430	Rfm. SALOMONS, A., 25th Bn.
210164	Rfm. SAMUEL, A., 25th Bn.
210582	Rfm. SAMPSON, F., 25th Bn.
210543	Rfm. SAMPSON, C., 25th Bn.
22186	Rfm. SYMONS, S.
31400	Rfm. SOLOMONS, M.
211334	Rfm. SINGER, M., 25th Bn.
210048	Rfm. SHENKER, L.
33086	Rfm. SAMUELS, A.
210914	Rfm. SILMAN, M.
31295	Rfm. SCHWARTZMAN, L., 6th Bn.
209137	Rfm. SANKERWITZ, A., 25th Bn.
211297	Rfm. SAMUEL, E., 25th Bn.
30024	Rfm. SHALINSKY, L., 6th Bn.
32239	Rfm. SCHWARSEREIN, L.
14872	Rfm. SOLOMON, J., 5th Bn.
	Rfm. SINGER, S.
	Rfm. SILVER, J., 2nd Bn.
	Rfm. SPERO, L.
1549	Rfm. TIEMAN, H., 9th Bn.
8/397	Rfm. TOBIAS, J.,* 1st Bn.
33643	Rfm. TEMPLE, T., 2nd Bn.
23823	Rfm. TOBIAS, H., 3rd Bn.
S/22428	Rfm. TRUEFITT, E., 5th Bn.
775	Rfm. TRAVERS, E.,* 8th Bn.
S/17779	Rfm. THEOBALD, J.,* 1st Bn.
28901	Rfm. TAITER, S.
50428	Pte. TANNIN, I., 51st Bn.
2641	Rfm. VAN THAL, M.,* 2nd Bn.
594436	Rfm. VALENCIA, M., 13th Bn.
17751	Rfm. VAN GELDER, M., 1st Bn.
29937	Rfm. VISHNICK, J., 3rd Bn.
S/16648	Rfm. VITOW, H., 12th Bn.
17770	Cpl. VOS, S., 1st Bn.
19070	Rfm. VALINSKY, H., 10th Bn.
S/23818	Rfm. VANCLIFF, J., 5th Bn.
A/17758	Rfm. WURMS, A., 1st Bn.
17440	Rfm. WINTERMAN, G., 9th Bn.
B/200162	Rfm. WARSHAWSKY, B., 11th Bn.
25201	L/Cpl. WALTERS, A., 10th Bn.
30810	Rfm. WEINBERG, A., 11th Bn.
15036	Sig. WARSHAWSKY, M., 1st Bn.
S/27276	Rfm. WOLFBERG, C., 16th Bn.
S/26011	Rfm. WILKS, A., 8th Bn.
24594	Rfm. WAGENHOUSEN, B., 7th Bn.
5798	Rfm. WOLB, L., 5th Bn.
210037	Rfm. WERNER, I., 24th Bn.
S/25382	Rfm. WEISSMAN, L., 5th Bn.
8207	Sgt. WATERFIELD, A., 52nd Bn.
209253	Rfm. WERSCHKER, S., 25th Bn.
209042	Rfm. WEINGOTT, I.
209810	Rfm. WALTERS, H., 25th Bn.
210082	Rfm. WEIN, B.
210088	Rfm. WILLIAMS, N.
210093	Rfm. WEXLER, N.
210721	Rfm. WEITZMAN, H.
29937	Rfm. WISHNICK, J.
118621	Rfm. WAXMAN, H., 2nd Bn.
423222	Rfm. ZIMMERMAN, L. (M.M.), 13th Bn.
209994	Rfm. ZIMMERMAN, K., 22nd Bn.
3777	Rfm. ZIMMERMAN, W., 25th Bn.
2715	Rfm. ZUCKER, W. H., 19th Bn.
23930	Rfm. ZAUSMER, J., 9th Bn.

* Killed in Action or died on Active Service.

ARMY CYCLIST CORPS.

OFFICERS.

Major GINSBURG, 2nd Bn.
Lieut. JOSEPH, E. G., 12th Div. Cyclists Coy.
Capt. WALEY, A. C.
2nd Lieut. WOOLF, A. S., 18th Cyclists Bn.
2nd Lieut. WEBER, J., 17th Corps, Cy. Bn.

N.C.O.'s AND MEN.

	Cyc. ALEXANDER, J.
260913	Cyc. ABRAHAMS, J.
3065	Cyc. ABRAHAMS, L., 2/1st Northern C.
17433	Pte. ABRAMS, S., 53rd Div.
538856	Pte. ABRAHAMS, H.
	Pte. ALEXANDER, H., 2/1st West Lancs. Cycling Co.
	Pte. ALEXANDER, L., 2/1st West Lancs. Cycling Co.
	Pte. ABRAHAMS, B., 2/1st West Lancs. Cycling Co.
1466	Pte. BENSON, J., 55th Div. Cyc. Coy.
48	Pte. BAKER, A., 62nd Div. Cyclists.
5173	Pte. BAMFORD, C., 6th Cyclists Bn.
4551	Pte. BAKER, S., Cyclists Bn.
20388	Pte. BAKER, A., Cyclists Bn.
21456	Pte. BAKER, L. S.
19618	Cyc. BARNETT, A.,
22366	Pte. BARNETT, M., 67th Coy.

Cyclist Battalion.—*Continued.*

	Pte. Barnett, S., 2/1st West Lancs. Cyc.
355148	L/Cpl. Berns, J., 9th Bn.
18148	Pte. Bernstein, E. F., Cyc. Bn., 2nd Co.
2876	Cyc. Bennett, J., 2/1st Northern Cy. Bn.
17615	Cyc. Black, B.
90703	Pte. Black, M.
12517	Pte. Bloom, J.
50254	L/Cpl. Campani, S., 7th Bn.
10523	Cpl. Coleman, P. N., 32nd Div. Cyc. Co.
76259	Pte. Cohen, S.
234	Pte. Cohen, W. M.
202	Pte. Cohen, R. J.
18156	L/Cpl. Cohen, C. L., 1st Corps Cyclists.
19536	Cyc. Cohen, M., 2nd Corps.
	Pte. Cohen, A., W. Lancs. Cyc. Corps.
	Pte. Cohen, P., 2/1st West Lancs. C. C.
26773	Pte. Conrade, E., 2/1st Kent Cyclists.
19502	Pte. Davies, I., 15th Corps.
1449	Pte. Davies, M., 1/1st W.L.D. Cyc. Cps.
7879	L/Cpl. Davis, A., 14th Div.
190	Cpl. Davis, B. B., 46th Div.
74264	Cyc. Davis, D., 2/25th Bn.
1640	Pte. Davies, J., 55th Div. Cyc. Coy.
26622	Cyc. Daniels, L., 1/6th Bn.
76324	Cyc. De Groot, I., 6th Bn.
18804	Cyc. Diamond, W., 19th Bn.
18160	Cyc. Donn, P., 19th Bn.
741954	Cyc. Dreyfus, W. A., 2/25th Bn.
17725	Pte. Ellman, J., 71st.
1444	Cyc. Falk, A., 25th Bn.
265704	Cyc. Feinstein, A.
215	Pte. Frankel, B., 56th Div. Cyc. Coy.
6594	Pte. Friedlander, J., 17th Cyclists Corps.
14165	Pte. Flowers, J., 10th Corps, Cyclists.
20754	Cyc. Finestone, J., 15th Bn.
76876	Cyc. Finer, M., 11th Bn.
3433	Cyc. Friedlander, B., 1/16th Bn.
16159	Pte. Gale, Cyclists Corps.
506	Cyc. Gale, N., 3/2nd.
34443	Cyc. Gasdon, A., 1/6th Bn.
	Pte. Gill, R., W. Lancs. Cyc. Corps.
741878	Cyc. Gold, M., 2/25th Bn.
19479	Cyc. Goldstone, S., 5th Corps, Cyclists.
215268	Pte. Goldman, J., 1st Cyc. Bde.
21824	Pte. Goodman, A., 67th Coy.
34424	Cyc. Gorden, A.
16819	Pte. Greenbaum, L. W.
34788	Pte. Grossman, J. D., 1/6th Bn.
	Cyc. Harris, C.
	Pte. Hecker, M.
366685	Cyc. Harris, L., 2/1st N. C. Bn.
11090	Cyc. Harris, I.
742265	Cyc. Halter, S., 2/25th Bn.
2528	Pte. Helber, J.
742218	Cyc. Hill, P., 2/25th Bn.
503	Cyc. Hill, W., 3/2nd Bn.
1423	L/Cpl. Hunter, A., 8th Div. Cyc. Coy.
422517	Pte. Isaacs, C. S., 25th Bn.
245	Pte. Iynas, H.
1423	Pte. Jacobs, A.
366661	Cyc. Jacobs, B., 2/1st N.C. Bn.
741956	Cyc. Jacobs, J. D., 2/25th Bn.
741781	Cyc. Jacobs, S. D., 2/25th Bn.
742345	Cyc. Jacobs, I., 2/25th Bn.
23539	Pte. Jeffries, H.
290939	Cyc. Josephs, W., 2/1st N. C. Bn.
26644	Pte. Joseph, J., 2/1st Bn.
12859	Pte. Joseph.
741945	Cyc. Karlish, H., 2/25th Bn.
4966	L/Cpl. Kaufman, H., 6th Cyclists Bn.
16901	Pte. Krebsman, B. J.
16936	Pte. Kirstein, A.
742263	Cyc. King, P., 2/25th Bn.
3087	Cyc. Krasny, A., 2/1st Northern C. Bn.
2340	Pte. Lazarus, 1/6th Bn.
742283	Cyc. Lazarus, E., 2/25th Bn.
22306	Cyc. Levi, A., 65th Bn.
3923	L/Cpl. Levy, L., 14th.
8240	Pte. Lelyveld, H., 6th Cyclists Bn.
18205	Cyc. Lipton, B., 19th Bn.
48821	L/Cpl. Lewis, A., 1/1st Hants. Cyclists.
22361	Pte. Lewis, H., 67th Coy.
10141	Pte. Martell, E., 31st Div. Cyc. Coy.
13265	Cyc. Myers, A.,* 8th Corps Cyclists.
19129	Pte. Myner, A., Cyclists Bn.
12755	Pte. Maidart, H., 10th Corps, Cyclists.
10141	Pte. Marshall, E., 8th Corps, Cyclists.
027308	Pte. Marks, N.
11594	Pte. Markson, L.
	L/Cpl. Marx, C., 18th Div. Cyclists.
	Cyc. Mendis, A., 3/2nd Bn.
	Cyc. Mercado, W., 9th Bn.
266463	L/Cpl. Mear, J., 2/1st Bn.
61542	Pte. Mercado, S., 2/6th Cyc. Bn. Suffolk.
11693	Pte. Mercado, J.
367184	Cyc. Moses, P. L., 2/1st N. C. Bn.
741526	Cyc. Molin, N., 2/25th Bn.
	Pte. Muscovitch, A.
	Cpl. Mocatta, C. H.
17695	Pte. Morris, A. Z., 67th Coy
8727	L/Cpl. Morgenstein, J.
1015	Cyc. Natkiel, S., 2/25th Bn.
8145	Pte. Newman, S., 33rd Div. Cyc. Coy.
741344	Cyc. Norden, H., 2/25th Bn.
34445	Cyc. Press, L.
22241	Pte. Phillips, A.
3563	Pte. Phillips, J., 15th Div.
291002	Pte. Pims, B.
19529	Cyc. Pollack, A., 11th Bn.
16876	Pte. Perrily, L.
12572	Cyc. Rackind, S.
266663	Cyc. Reininger, P., 2/1st Kent Cyclists.
4434	Pte. Rose, H. B., 20th Div. Cyc. Coy.
20252	Cyc. Rose, J.
52835	Pte. Rosenberg, D.

Cyclist Battalion.—*Continued.*

741581 L/Cpl. ROSENBERG, M., 2/25th Bn.
367114 Cyc. ROSENBERG, D., 2/1st N. C. Bn.
       Pte. ROSENSTEIN, M., 8th Bn.
74614 Pte. ROUSGA, H., 2/25th Bn.
2908 Cpl. ROSENTHAL, D., 41st Div. Cyc.
13621 Pte. ROSENTHAL, H. W., 5th Cyc. Bn.
       Pte. ROVINSKY, W., Motor Cycle Corps.
34488 Cyc. RUBINSTEIN, I. M.
40976 Pte. RUBENSTEIN, J., 8th Bn.
366334 Cyc. SALINSKY, J., 2/1st Bn.
741458 Cyc. SALAMAN, W., 2/25th Bn.
3238 Cyc. SALAMONS, W., 3/25th Bn.
168 Cyc. SANDALL, D.
292179 Cyc. SAVINSON, B., 1/7th Bn.
8751 Cpl. SAMUEL, H. L.
13728 Pte. SCHWARTZ, E.,* 6th Cyclists Bn.
321 Pte. SCHWARTZ, S., 6th Cyclists Bn.
2507 Sgt. SCHOENTAL, H.
59521 Cyc. SHINEMAN, L. J., 1/7th Bn.
12874 Pte. SHACKMAN, D.
1185 Cyc. SHIERR, J., 5th Bn.
46066 Cyc. SILVERMAN, J., 1/1st Bn.
34205 Cyc. SIMONS, J.
3898 Cyc. SIMMONDS, M., 2/25th Bn.
3938 Pte. SINGER, S., 14th.
17484 Cyc. SOLOMONS, H.
       Pte. SOLOMON, A., 20th.
46742 Cyc. STALANSKY, I., 3/25th Bn.
16352 Cyc. STEIN, J., 11th Corps, Cyclists.
367210 Pte. SURAFAS, I., 2/1st Bn.
39729 Cyc. SUGARMAN, L.
12880 Pte. SUGARMAN, S.
3111 Cyc. SUGERMAN, M., 2/1st Northern C. B.
245 Cyc. SYMES, H., 68th Bn.
4896 Pte. TAYLOR, M., 18th Div. Cyclists.
16358 Pte. VANCLIFFE, J., 72nd Div.
34454 Cyc. VENITSKY, N.
223 Pte. WARSHAWSKY, B., Cyclists Corps.
7800 Cyc. WAGNER, H.,* 18th Corps Cyclists.
       Pte. WEBER, J., 52nd Coy.
741600 Cyc. WISEMAN, H., 2/25th Bn.
1914 Cyc. WOOLF, M., 47th Lond. Div. Cyc.
290939 Pte. WOLFS, J.

* Killed in Action or died on Active Service.

MACHINE GUN CORPS.

OFFICERS.

Lieut. ABRAHAMS, A., 59th M.G.C.
Capt. BENZECRY, A. (M.C.), 164th
Lieut. BARTON, G. H. R., 124th
Lieut. BURNS, S. H., 16th
Lieut. BENZIMRA, F. J. (M.C.).
2nd Lieut. BLOOM, I., 37th.
2nd Lieut. BENZIMIRA, A.
Lieut. COLLINS, A. C., 104th
2nd Lieut. COHEN, M., 184th
Lieut. COLLINS, G. S. V.
Lieut. DAVIS, A., 115th
Lieut. DAVIS, D. L.
2nd Lieut. DURLACHER, P. A. (M.C.).
Lieut. FIELD, G. F.
Lieut. FOA, A. H., 21st
2nd Lieut. GOLDMAN, J. W., 109th
Lieut. GORDON, C. J.
Capt. GOLDBERG, R. (M.C.).
2nd Lieut. GOSLING, H. E., 2nd
Lieut. HART, W. A., 1st
Lieut. HARRIS, G., 58th
Capt. HENRIQUES, W. A
Capt. HART, S. H. R.
Lieut. HENRIQUES, B. L. Q.
Lieut. HALLENSTEIN, D., 14th
2nd Lieut. HENOCHSBERG, D. E., 153rd
2nd Lieut. ISAACS, B. C.,* 89th
2nd Lieut. JACOBS, H. W.
2nd Lieut. KRAKO, G., 93rd
Lieut. KAUFMANN, B., 216th
2nd Lieut. KEMP, B. H., 55th
2nd Lieut. KOHNSTAMM, J.,* 54th
2nd Lieut. LEWIS,* L. W., 165th
2nd Lieut. LEWY, S. W., 31st
2nd Lieut. LEVY, B. H., 102nd
2nd Lieut. LESSER, A. C., 198th
Major LAZARUS, K. M., 178th
Lieut. LEVY, A.
Lieut. LEVY, B., 47th
2nd Lieut. LUBELSKI, W. W. (M.C.), 4th
Capt. LOWY, J. E., 2nd
Lieut. MARSDEN, E., 117th
Lieut. MILINSKY, M. M., 95th
Lieut. MUSCOVITCH, J. A., 200th.
Lieut. NEWMAN, A. D., 95th
Lieut. NATHAN, L. P.
2nd Lieut. NATHAN, G. (M.C.).
2nd Lieut. OPPENHEIMER, H., 234th
Lieut. POLLAK, L. A. (M.C. and Bar).
2nd Lieut. PRINS, L., 40th
Capt. PHILLIPS, G. G.
2nd Lieut. ROSKIN, N., 40th
Major RICHARDSON, A. N. (D.S.O., M.C.), 164th
2nd Lieut. ROSE, D., 56th
2nd Lieut. SCHLOSS,* L. E., 44th
Lieut. SCHONFIELD, G., 124th
Lieut. SAUNDERS, A., 37th
2nd Lieut. SAQUI, H. J., 30th
Lieut. SASSOON, A. M., 2nd M.G. Squad.
Lieut. SASSOON, H. W., 4th
Lieut. SAUNDERS, J., 112th
Lieut. SAQUI, L. V. H.
Lieut. VANDYKE, P. R,. 119th
2nd Lieut. WHITE, A. A., 29th

Machine Gun Corps.—*Continued.*

N.C.O.'s AND MEN.

104377 Pte. AARON, H., 109th
67327 Pte. ARONSON, L., 220th
154391 Pte. ALEXANDER, S., 9th
152844 Pte. ABRAHAMS, H., 2nd
164303 Pte. ASH, R., 2nd
159383 Pte. ABRAHAMS, 6th
265017 Pte. ABRAHAMS, A., 6th
67911 Pte. ABRAHAMS, I., 2nd
67327 Pte. AARONSON, L., 2nd
86955 Pte. ASH, R., 1st
81010 Pte. APPLEBAUM, J., 48th
78462 Gnr. ANNETT, H., 1st
163750 Pte. ABRAHAMS, S., 24th
5639 Pte. ABRAHAMS, H. A.
93083 Pte. ABRAHAMS, L. N.
Sgt. BARNETT, L. F. (M.M.)
31090 Gnr. BLACKMAN,* J., 56th
60863 Pte. BERKIS, M., 111th
10523 Pte. BROMBERG, D., 25th
6318 Pte. BENNETT, J., 180th
54901 Pte. BRAHAM, S., 192nd
39034 Pte. BENJAMIN, L., 11th
39399 Cpl. BLOOM, J., 11th
21673 Pte. BERNSTEIN, H., 53rd
26425 Pte. BABBIN, B., 54th
84555 Pte. BLUMTHAL, A., 100th
2310 Gnr. BERIRO, A., 13th
85152 Pte. BENJAMIN, D., 31st
86981 Pte. BERNSTEIN, S., 103rd
81979 Pte. BENJAMIN, R., 44th
85174 Pte. BEAR, C.,* 118th
59047 Pte BROWN, M. G., 59th
90670 Pte. BLOOM, J., 27th
552547 Rfm. BORGZINNER, E. C., 169th
106683 Pte. BENJAMIN, J., 254th
55856 Pte. BROOKE, S., 24th
104187 Pte. BLACK, B., 41st
131464 Pte. BERNSTEIN, S., 58th
141406 Pte. BLACKMAN, A., 58th
130140 Pte. BLACK, P., 61st
60863 Pte. BERKINGOFF, M., 37th
131940 Pte. BERNSTEIN, E. M., 19th
153597 Pte. BERGER, J.
5020 Pte. BLOCH, C., 184th
100834 Tpr. BOWMAN, M. L., 11th
126272 Pte. BENSUSAN, S. A., 224th
90475 Pte. BERNSTEIN, M., 228th
89941 Pte. BERGER, H., 202nd
107007 Pte. BARNARD, L., 182nd
45507 A/Cpl. BLONDIN, A., 1st
152644 Pte. BENOLIEL, K., 2nd
Pte. BENOLIEL, M. H., 8th
Dvr. BADER, M.
90659 Pte. BARRON, J., 5th
123821 Pte. BOSS, S., 6th
28496 Sgt./Instr. BENJAMIN, D.,
82935 L/Cpl. BLOMBERG, R.,
14198 Pte BROWN, H., 36th
83336 Pte. BURSKI, L., 1st
341 Pte. BRITAIN, S., 11th
153 Pte. BERG, B.,
89832 Pte. BLACK, I., 5th
81841 Pte. BARNETT, T., 2nd
57664 L/Cpl. BLOOM, I., 5th
86765 Pte. BROWN, S., 4th
98420 Pte. BERNSTEIN, E.,
98872 Pte. BLASKEY, I., 3rd
89941 Pte. BERGER, H., 2nd
67528 Cpl. BARWELL, B. C., 2nd
59947 Pte. BROWN, M., 174th
81700 Pte. BERMAN, V., 54th
12063 Dvr. BERNSTEIN, H., 53rd
528347 Gnr. BAKER, H.,
86981 Pte. BERNSTEIN, S., 35th
147578 Pte. BLACK, M., 37th
140626 Pte. BROOKER, S.,
1397309 Pte. BLOOMBERG, L., 123rd
132624 Pte. BROWN, J., 5th
32717 Gnr. BARNETT, B., 1st
2671710 Pte. BERGAMAN, A., 105th
173798 Pte. BARNETT, J. V.
Pte. BARON, J. B. (M.M.)
114734 L/Cpl. BAUM, H., 39th
144165 Pte. BLOOMBERG, G., 2nd
73397 Pte. BOSWORTH, S. C., 5th
159 Pte. BERG, J.
58397 Pte. BLACK, J., 5th Bn.
191230 Pte. BAGLEY, J.
64776 Pte. BLANK, G., 89th
31090 Pte. BLACKMAN, J.
41331 Pte. BURMAN, M.
67526 Pte. BEHRENS, H. J.
54776 Pte. BLANK, G.
88420 Pte. BERNSTEIN, W.
27046 L/Cpl. COLLOTT, L., 114th
7933 Pte. COHEN, A., 114th
88393 Pte. COHEN, S., 100th
7965 Pte. COHEN, J., 28th
103545 Pte. COHEN, N., 193rd
36163 Dvr. COLLINS, G., 50th
68521 Pte. COOTS, H., 46th
45952 Sgt. COHEN, S., 170th
55959 L/Cpl. COHEN, A., 170th
72970 Pte. COSHER, W., 47th
58722 Pte. COHEN, H., 3rd
51753 Cpl. COHEN, J., 3rd M.G. Sq.
37119 Sig. COHEN, J., 31st Bn.
116821 Pte. COHEN, J., 11th
127929 Pte. COHEN, H., 34th
136868 Pte. COHEN, P., 19th
107802 Pte. COHEN, J. O., 19th
105068 S/Sgt. CAMINER, M., 4th M.G. Sq. Cav.

Machine Gun Corps.—*Continued.*

138031	Cpl.	COSTA, S., 6th
155583	Pte.	COHEN, C., 62nd
159022	Pte.	COHEN, M., 2nd
144967	Pte.	COHEN, D., 6th
8902	Cpl.	COHEN, S
13973	Pte.	COHEN, H.
68635	Cpl	COHEN, N., 26th
87838	Pte.	COHEN, M., 4th
88393	Pte.	COHEN, S.
89535	Pte.	COHEN, W., 3rd
32464	Pte.	COOTES, H. H., 3rd
321587	Pte.	CASSILL, C., Signals
116686	Pte.	COHEN, E.
12249	Pte.	COHEN, H., 6th
86317	Pte.	CHILD, W. (M.M.), 1st
31446	L/Cpl.	COHEN, D., 1st
34693	Gnr.	CHAPMAN, F., 5th
67740	Cpl.	CLASPER, F., 249th
2672472	Pte.	COHEN, M., 105th
69535	Gnr.	COHEN, H., 1st
141385	Pte.	COLLINS, B., 51st
86	Pte.	CASSIER, J.,
58735	Pte.	COHEN, J., 57th
678064	Pte.	COOPER, S., 45th
89133	Pte.	CHRENBURG, A., 8th
5679	Pte.	COHEN, M.
	Sgt.	CORIAT, P. M. (D.C.M.).
123905	Pte.	COHEN, J.
100918	Pte.	CAPLAN, M.
148351	Sgt.	COHEN, J., 2nd
473684	Pte.	COHEN, I., 19th Bn.
78490	Gnr.	COHEN, G.
28796	Pte.	COHEN, J.
128121	Pte.	COHEN, E. H., 36th
36163	Dvr.	COLLINS, E. C., 15th
1203187	Pte.	COOPER, E., 105th
7806	Pte.	COLEMAN, J., 5th
89	Cpl.	CRAWCOUR, S., 8th Bn.
114524	Pte.	COHEN, H., 43rd
	Cpl.	DAVIS, P. (M.M.), 36th
23687	Pte.	DURLACHER, G., 113th
89827	Pte.	DAVIS, L., 114th
67248	Pte.	DEMBOVSKY, L., 172nd
64645	Pte.	DAGUL, M., 39th
64069	Pte.	DIAS, D., 219th
87832	Pte.	DAVIES, B., 111th
57979	Pte.	DIAMOND, B. D., 178th
115200	Pte.	DOBIAS, J., 24th
193956	Pte.	DAMELRICH, J., 35th
36984	Pte.	DAVIDSON, M., 198th
123909	Pte.	DA COSTA, G., 46th
17122	Pte.	DORSMAN, D., A.C.C.
79236	Gnr.	DANS, B.
85312	Pte.	DAVIES, M., 3rd
121901	Pte.	DUBENSKY, J.,
98905	Pte.	DIAMOND, W., 2nd
68847	Gnr.	DIGGOTTS, A., 6th
69263	Gnr.	DAVIES, B. A., 6th
10541	Pte.	DAVIES, H., 1st
28644	Pte.	DAVIS, N., 1st
36984	Pte.	DAVIDSON, M., 9th
118822	Pte.	DAVIDSON, M.
58821	Pte.	DAVIS, L., 36th
158830	Pte.	DAVIES, S., 6th
149271	Pte.	DE POWER, J., 4th
115002	Pte.	DEFRIES, B., 3rd
54054	Pte.	DEEPROSE, E., 192nd
624294	Pte.	DAVIS, J.
749	Sgt.	DIAMOND, S., 114th
115176	Pte.	DELAFUENTA, M., 15th
704394	Pte.	DONOLOVITCH, H., 2/4th
10541	Pte.	ESTREYACK, B., 244th
139335	Pte.	EPSTEIN, D., 37th
	Sgt.	ENOCH, E. A. (M.S.M.).
64478	Pte.	ELLISON, S., 214th
181	Pte.	EPSTANE, L.
89133	Pte.	EHRENBERG, A., 2nd
30177	Pte.	ELLIS, J. H., 2nd
31937	Pte.	EDELSTONE, S.,
45709	Pte.	ESTREYACK, B.,
27317	Pte.	FISKIN, F., 121st
44737	Pte.	FOX, J., 27th
131170	Pte.	FROMBERG, S., 47th
87450	Pte.	FREEDMAN, D., 8th
115594	Pte.	FASCENDA, J., 11th
28108	Pte.	FELDMAN, J., 216th
129239	Pte.	FISHMAN, B., 30th
123946	Pte.	FALK, J., 2nd
81533	Pte.	FRAM, J., 1st
157668	Pte.	FRANKLIN, J., 5th
89853	Pte.	FISHTAL, S.
59143	Pte.	FITELSON, A., 4th
115602	Pte.	FIELD, J.
82064	Pte.	FIFER, M. H., 1st
220167	Pte.	FREEMAN, C., att. 5th
66184	Pte.	FRASER, W., 200th
65864	Pte.	FANNENBAUM, S., 66th
509184	Pte.	FEDERMAN,
2672315	Pte.	FLATTS, S.
122652	Pte.	FRANKS, L., 4th
49882	L/Cpl.	FRESHWATER, L.
115602	Pte.	FINSTERFIELD, I.
7152	Dvr.	GREEN, H., 72nd
82448	Gnr.	GILLES, J., 40th
81666	Pte.	GOLDBERG, S., 30th
65114	L/Cpl.	GROGINSKI, G., 89th
14887	Pte.	GROUNDLEN, M., 97th
81666	Pte.	GOLDBERG, S., 101st
26860	Pte.	GOLD, J., 114th
81981	Pte.	GOODMAN, J.,* 44th
82468	Pte.	GILLMAN, J., 37th
122577	Pte.	GARDNER, J.,* 8th
98017	Pte.	GOLDMAN, J., 14th
65621	L/Cpl.	GOLDSMITH, S., 208th
13083	Pte.	GOTTLIEB, A., 111th

Machine Gun Corps.—*Continued.*

89224 Pte. GOLDSTEIN, M., 95th
71903 Pte. GOLDSTONE, B., 254th
1778 Pte. GORDON, J., 218th
149854 Pte. GOODMAN, W., 51st
13271 Pte. GOLDBERG, D., 20th
66707 Pte. GLUCK, J., 93rd
28514 Pte. GOLDSTEIN, D
85378 Pte. GARFINKLE, L., 195th
7512 Dvr. GRERU, H., 76th
10564 Pte. GANCE, B., 1st
57332 Pte. GOLDSTEIN, S., 2nd
46442 Pte. GREEN, H., 5th
98077 Pte. GOLDMAN, J., 5th
45038 Sgt. GOLDBERG, D., 1st
31348 Pte. GOLDSTEIN, R., 1st
7512 Pte. GREEN, W., 1st
55767 Pte. GERSHONBLATT, I., 2nd
29920 L/Cpl. GOODSTON, W., 3rd
89936 Pte. GREEN, A.,* 25th
90516 Pte. GOLDMAN, H., 2nd
67333 Pte. GOLD, S., 2nd
103010 Pte. GLANTZ, J., 5th
10452 Pte. GOLD, J., 1st
148974 Pte. GLAZIER, H., 7th
100042 Dvr. GRABER, J., 228th
202676 Pte. GOODMAN, V. E., 18th
78465 Gnr. GOLDBERG, M., 19st
47692 Pte. GOLDMAN, F., 4th Coy.
M/272440 Pte. GOLDMAN, M.
142659 Pte. GOODMAN, V. E.
87519 Pte. GOODMAN, E.,* 62nd
120172 Pte. GOLDBERG, F.
15116 Pte. GARTMAN, J.
67909 Pte. GORDON, J., 8th
153915 Pte. GORDON, A., 4th
143297 Pte. GROSS, H. R., 4th
52809 Pte. GREENBAUM, A., 138th
54903 Pte. GROBINER, A., 192nd
9182 Pte. GORSMAN, D., 199th
132715 Pte. GOLDEBRG, M., 20th
243276 Pte. GOLDSTONE, I., 42nd
123849 Pte. GRABINER, I., 42nd
153915 Pte. GORION, A., 29th
72689 Pte. GINN, H.
10042 Gnr. GRABER, G.
78726 Pte. GONSHAW, L.
24795 Pte. GOLDSTEIN, R.
61768 Cpl. GOLDSTEIN, I.
201542 Dvr. GOLDSTEIN, P., 15th
353746 Pte. GINSBERG, J.,* 58th
Sgt. GOOD, J.
87426 Pte. HARRIS, L., 111th
35755 Pte. HEYBURNE, I., 100th
38376 Pte. HARRIS, H., 13th
81496 Pte. HUNT, M., 46th
26859 Pte. HARBOUR, S., 11th
57687 Pte. HARRIS, B., 59th
39084 Pte. HAINES, W., 14th
54899 Pte. HARRIS, J., 192nd
106770 Pte. HARVEY, M., 232nd
R/37301 Pte. HYAMS, B., 111th
140143 Pte. HERMAN, B., 104th
43274 Pte. HILL, A. W.,* 50th
99362 Cpl. HART, D., 47th
115509 Pte. HOFFMAN, C., 31st
89697 Pte. HELLER, J., 74th
144153 Pte. HARRIS, A., 30th
136474 Pte. HARRISON, M., 19th
144316 Pte. HARRIS, E., 15th
87715 Pte. HENRY, J., 138th
270 Pte. HART, 2nd
14069 Pte. HARRIS, S. H. R.,
132599 Pte. HYAMS, B., 1st
108737 Pte. HYMAN, H., 5th
129442 L/Cpl. HOGGARD, M., 6th
101726 Sgt. HARRISON, A. T.
23074 L/Cpl. HOBSON, H. J.
81496 L/Cpl. HART, M.,* 46th
Sgt. HERBERTS, J.*
87526 Pte. HERMAN, H., 5th
104910 Pte. HYMAN, C., 2nd
123911 Pte. HELMAN, I.
34904 Sig. HERMAN, A., 1st
16334 Pte. HARRIS, J., 7th
126978 Pte. HART, M.,* 19th
26352 Pte. HARRIS, A. D., 14th
9076 Pte. HARVEY, A., 14th
148003 Pte. HAINES, W., 32nd
119448 Pte. HILLMAN, I., 4th
56808 Pte. HART, A., 7th
38487 L/Cpl. HYMAN, W.
37382 Sgt. HERBERTS, G.
87086 Gnr. HIRSHMAN, H.
38487 Pte. HYMAN, W.
92587 Pte. HYAMS, S. H.
95387 Pte. HATTER, E.
22797 Cpl. HALLIDAY, H.
141003 Dvr. ISAACS, J., 11th
67362 Pte. ISAACS, R., 220th
151475 Pte. ISAACS, N., 104th
106677 Pte. ISAACS, S. H., 61st
13309 Pte. ISAACS, L.,* 48th
144205 Pte. ISAACS, J., 19th
145321 Pte. ISAACS, J., 8th
138839 Pte. ISAACS, M., 6th
54266 Pte. ISAACS, D., 2nd
54391 Pte. ISAAC, J. H., 2nd
44940 Cadet ISAACS, H. I., 2nd
30558 Pte. ISRAEL, T., 41st
13306 Pte. ISAACS, M.
107164 Pte. ISAACS, M., 2nd
1183 Pte. JACOBS, B., 114th
25052 L/Cpl. JOSEPH, M., 5th
98302 Pte. JACOBS, L. H., 235th
149795 Gnr. JACOBS, S., 15th

Machine Gun Corps.—*Continued.*

67362 Pte. JACOBS, R., 220th
132600 Pte. JAFFRATO, J., 1st
30087 Pte. JEPHSON, H., 1st
63340 Pte. JACOBS, H., 4th
89938 Pte. JACOBS, J., 2nd
85641 L/Cpl. JOSEPH, L., 4th
130564 Pte. JOCKLESON, M., 58th
       Pte. JACOBS, C. (M.M.).
129594 Pte. JANOWSKY, M.
35580 Pte. JOSEPH, B., 8th
129286 Pte. JESSON, S., 36th
4082 Pte. JACOBS, H., 4th
       Cpl. JACOBS, S. F. (M.M.).
S/15379 Pte. JOSEPH, H.
78216 Gnr. JACOBY, J.
133966 Pte. JOSEPHSON, A., 19th
5215 Pte. JOSEPH, J., 141st
92896 Gnr. JOSEPHS, A.
78929 Gnr. JACOBS, H.
154 Bdr. JACOBSON, R.,
123285 Pte. JACOBS, H. M.
3600 Pte. JOSEPH, J.
81508 Pte. JACOBS, N.
83018 Pte. KRONENBERG, J., 11th
83103 Pte. KYTE, A.,* 55th
83749 Pte. KLEIN, A., 31st
53826 Pte. KLEIN, I.,* 171st
62936 Pte. KONTROVITCH, T., 199th
67885 Pte. KANTRONITZ, E., 212th
147690 Pte. KREITZMAN, H., 51st
87157 Pte. KRISCH, H., 2nd
90892 Pte. KESLER, E., 5th
117005 Pte. KISSIN, H
88549 Pte. KRANGOLD, S. S., 5th
267274 Pte. KING, D.,
16865 Pte. KOCH, D., 4th
       Pte. KOSOFSKY, H., 3rd
125963 Pte. KEMP, L., 2nd
136846 Pte. KALMOVITZ, I., 3rd
45747 Gnr. KREYER, A.
3038 Pte. KLINGER, M.
78730 Gnr. KASHERBAUM, H., 1st
11187 Pte. LEWIS, H., 74th
       Pte. LEVINE, J., 115th
S/3992 Pte. LEVY, M., 191st
62893 Pte. LEWIS, J., 53rd
82084 Pte. LANDSBERG, H., 54th
86607 Pte. LYONS, A., 90th
2430 Pte. LEVY, L., 72nd
81590 Pte. LEVY, P., 191st
67743 Pte. LAZARUS, S., 217th
82367 Pte. LEVY, H., 166th
82563 Pte. LANDAY, J., 19th
69433 Pte. LEVY, L., 14th
54122 Pte. LEVEY, J., 150th
67908 Pte. LEWIS, H.,* 51st
66928 Pte. LAVINE, L., 144th

53864 Pte. LEVY, N., 171st
30378 Cpl. LEWIN, W. (M.M.), 109th
90503 Pte. LEVY, E., 37th
85555 Pte. LANDEY, I., 3rd
86935 Pte. LIVINGSTONE, B., 197th
98373 Pte. LEVI, S.,* 206th
1877 Pte. LELYVELD, L., 16th
106816 Dvr. LESSER, S., 62nd
73055 Pte. LYONS, M., 112th
107475 Pte. LANDAU, H., 3rd
115026 Pte. LEVY, M., 237th
147125 Pte. LEVY, M.,* 4th
129443 Pte. LEVENSOHN, A., 37th
97859 Pte. LEVI, J., 29th
101056 Pte. LEWIS, A., 18th
145752 Pte. LYONS, H., 8th
52771 Pte. LEWINSTEIN, M., 14th M.G. Sq.
12294 Pte. LEVINE, H., 115th
138878 Pte. LEVENE, R., 1st
43830 Sgt. LEAPMAN, B., 1st
15109 Cpl. LEWIS, J., 2nd
153666 Pte. LEVINE, H., 2nd
145752 Pte. LYONS, E., 2nd
123950 Pte. LEVENE, L., 2nd
73371 Cpl. LANDSLER, J., 5th
10849 Pte. LEVY, L., 5th
30537 Pte. LIPMAN, S.,
87657 Pte. LEVY, J., 1st
87459 Pte. LEVY, L., 2nd
8367 Pte. LEVY, H., 4th
88510 Pte. LAVENSTEIN, S., 5th
1876 Gnr. LEWIS, H., 6th
48399 Sgt. LENSKY, P.,* 214th
118739 Pte. LEWIS, S., 7th
34122 Pte. LEVY, T., 150
101793 Pte. LEVENE, E., 6th
9880 Pte. LILLIMAN, C., 240th
10849 Dvr. LEVY, L., 233rd
73371 Pte. LANCASTER, J., 5th
267362 Gnr. LAZERUS, 1st
367553 Gnr. LYTTLESTON, M. E., 1st
98810 Pte. LIPMAN, C., 16th
156183 Pte. LAZARUS, N., 3rd
PS/1845 Pte. LEVY, G.,
107235 Pte. LEVINE, S., 4th
156183 Pte. LAZARUS, H., 8th
40670 Pte. LIN, J., 8th
125293 Pte. LATTER, A.,* 25th Bn.
78270 Pte. LEVY, D., 3rd
115109 L/Cpl. LEWIS, J., 2nd
124230 Pte. LEVY, L., 2nd
66705 Pte. LEMON, J., 3rd
67838 Pte. LISSNER, H.
191217 Pte. LEVY, J.
6989 Pte. LEVINE, L.
184994 Pte. LOVAINE, I., 5th
4667 Gnr. LEWIS, P.

Machine Gun Corps.—*Continued.*

60997	Pte. LEVINE, C.,*	112th
179383	Pte. LEVY, J.	
81496	Pte. LICHTENSTEIN, M.,*	46th
2367	Gnr. MARKS, J.,	5th
72453	Pte. MORRIS, J.,	113th
57991	Pte. MICHAELSON, L.,	227th
99839	Pte. MIDDLEMAN, S.,	233rd
116860	Pte. MOSS, B.,	1st
141837	Pte. MARKS, J.,	56th
122711	Pte. MILLER, H.,	58th
140350	Pte. MARKS, L.,	61st
67907	Pte. MARKS, P.,	203rd
53867	Cpl. MORRIS, C.,*	63rd
100464	Pte. MARKS, R.,	8th M.G. Sq.
64405	L/Cpl. MARKS, M.,	225th
64433	L/Cpl. MARKSON, L.,	248th
931	Dvr. MALATZKI, L.,	7th
127728	Pte. MENDLEBAUM, J.,	1st
145337	Pte. MAGNUS, B.,	6th
10774	Pte. MELINSKI, A.,	36th
37160	Pte. MARKS, B.,	1st
67502	Pte. MANFORD, H.,	1st
66100	Pte. MONCHER, H.,	207th
86851	Pte. MILLER, A.,	2nd
115692	Pte. MARSHALL, H.,	1st
29	Pte. MALATZKY, H.,	7th
101396	Pte. MUSCOVITCH, M.,	11th
140350	Pte. MARKS, L.	
122761	Pte. MILLER, H.,	50th
3734	Pte. MENDELSOHN, M.	
127319	Pte. MONITZ, S. L.,	5th
69934	Gnr. MENDICK, A.,	3rd
273165	Pte. MAZERKOFF, J.,	3rd
100398	Pte. MYRON,	5th
2263	Pte. MARKS, B.,	4th
28236	Pte. MORTON, G.	
129286	Pte. MESSON, S.	
100068	Pte. MELLER, A.,	9th
153285	Pte. MALNICK, C.,	4th
70881	Pte. MILLER, E.,	4th
146442	Pte. MIDDLEMAN, L.,	4th
	Pte. MIDDLEBAUM, S.	
	Trp. MYERS, A. M.	
	Pte. MENDEL, G. H.	
91306	Gnr. MARKS, S.	
19976	Pte. MARKS, B.	
6190	Pte. MARKS, M.,	5th
7064	Pte. MAW, B.	
43282	Pte. MARKS, W.	
30778	Pte. MYERS, L.	
64340	Pte. MARTIN, G.	
	Pte. MORRIS, C.,	3rd
25047	Pte. MARKS, J.	
5503	Pte. NEWMAN, A.,	68th
87055	Pte. NIMAN, M.,	19th
37279	Cpl. NATHAN, E. D.,	178th
18194	Pte. NATHAN, J.	
103024	Pte. NEYMOVITCH, M.	
89881	Pte. NOCHOVITCH, A.,	36th
86943	Pte. NEWMAN, I.,	10th
161921	Pte. NISSENBAUM, J.,	62nd
84714	Pte. NOSEVITCH, S.,	
30742	Pte. NOCTOVITCH, A.,	3rd
86944	Pte. NATHAN, M. L.,	2nd
117245	Pte. NEWMAN, M.,	
8823	Pte. NICKLESBURG, J.,	2nd
5503	Pte. NEWMAN, P.,	68th
127266	Cpl. NETTLER, M.	
	Sgt. NEWCRON, B.	
78469	Gnr. NATHAN, A.	
78841	Gnr. NEWMARK, M.	
130691	Gnr. NATHAN, J.,	17th
45768	Pte. OTTOLANGUI, M.,	18th
102205	Gnr. OLINSKI, A.,	232nd
129800	Pte. OSTERLENSKY, B.,	62nd
65809	Pte. OTTO, H.,	111th
126263	Pte. ORCHANT, L.,	2nd
69241	Gnr. OPPENHEIM, M.,	2nd
2671612	Pte. OPPENHEIM, J.,	106th
116204	Pte. OSSOSKI, D.,	58th
191076	Pte. OGNALL, H. H.	
16237	Pte. POGRUND, S.,	13th
9665	Pte. PEARLMAN, L.,	35th
245	Pte. PHILLIPS, D.,	7th
14563	Pte. PULCOVITCH, S.,	191st
68426	Pte. PARIS, A.,	53rd
43846	Pte. PHILLIPS, N.,	26th
68426	Pte. PARIS, A.,	51st
9600	Pte. PRICE, S.,	113th
53863	Pte. PHILLIPS, B.,	173rd
4448	Pte. PEARLMAN, W.,	35th
9976	Pte. POLLICK, J.,	233rd
81910	Pte. PAMPLE, A.,	206th
70451	Pte. PLOTTS, A.,	95th
64658	Pte. POLLACK, A.,*	216th
55762	Pte. POSLOW, A.,	41st
153287	Pte. PITMAN, H.,	58th
123766	L/Cpl. PIZER, J. L.,	34th
972	Gnr. PEARLMAN, J.,	12th
159479	Pte. PALLEY, B.,	6th
104965	Pte. PHILLIPS, I.,	36th
104349	Pte. PAGE, T. G.,	4th
51258	Pte. PLATER, J.,	
69772	Gnr. PRIMACK, H.,	3rd
69935	Gnr. PROVIDLER, A.,	3rd
155983	Pte. PHILLIPS, B.,	34th
118645	Pte. PERKINS,	222nd
31557	Cpl. PETERSON,	19th M.G. Bty.
149243	Pte. PATINOVITZ,	24th
133928	Pte. POTTSTEIN, J.	
151625	Pte. PETERS, P.	
145869	Pte. PELEKANSKY, J.,	3rd
	Cpl. PHILLIPSON, L. G. (M.M.)	

Machine Gun Corps.—*Continued.*

153920	Pte. POLLOWAY, M., 4th
172099	Pte. PADOLSKY, H.
2961	Pte. PHILLIPS, C.
1177	Cpl. PHILLIPS, H.
43846	Pte. PHILLIPS, N.
10424	Pte. ROSENBERG, A., 113th
34242	Rfm. ROSENTHAL, S., 111th
22004	Pte. ROSENBAUM, A., 13th
87456	Gnr. RABINOWITZ, M., 5th
17052	Pte. REUBENS, H., 1st Div.
53196	Pte. ROSENTHAL, D.,* 41st
102412	Pte. REUBENS, J., 114th
54093	Pte. ROSENTHAL, M., 173rd
57656	Pte. ROSENSTON, L., 178th
34958	Pte. ROSENBERG, H.,* 51st
67416	L/Cpl. ROSENBURG, S., 148th
82111	Pte. ROBERTS, D., 11th
149243	Pte. RABBINOWITZ, H., 24th
45494	Pte. ROSENFIELD, D., 152nd
162166	Pte. ROSENTHAL, H., 1st
80311	Gnr. RIDZ, S., 6th
17052	Pte. RUBEN, H., 1st
35729	Pte. ROSENBURG, S., 2nd
57355	Pte. ROSE, H., 2nd
69144	Gnr. ROWEN, D.,
81272	Pte. ROSENTHAL, H., 3rd
10424	Pte. ROSENBURG, A., 2nd
82830	Pte. ROSE, W. G., 1st
83700	Pte. RAMUS, N. J., 1st Cadet Bn.
23104	Pte. ROSENBLOOM, 45th
57656	Pte. ROSENSTEIN, L., 2nd
27818	Pte. ROGERS, J.
117110	Pte. ROSENBERG, J.
52835	Pte. ROSENBERG, D.
2670315	Pte. RABINOVITZ, A., 107th
1216159	Sgt.-Major ROSENBERG, H., 106th
M/381198	Pte. ROSENTHAL, H. H., 9th
155154	Pte. ROBINS, A. F., 3rd
69381	Pte. ROSNICK, V.
38059	Gnr. ROSENBERG, D.
133928	L/Cpl. ROTTSTEIN, G., 55th Bn.
1478	Pte. SIMONS, L. J.,* 20th
67192	Pte. SOLOMONS, R.
531210	Pte. SILVERHAMMER, E., 2nd
71711	Pte. SHIRE, J., 5th
139227	Pte. STONE, J., 5th
159481	Pte. SHEVANSKY, E., 6th
5040	Pte. SCHIEVERT, R.,
57749	Pte. SIMMONS, S., 2nd
57334	Pte. SHIRE, J., 2nd
6751	Pte. STERNSHIRE, H., 2nd
66200	Pte. SIGER, P.,
66562	Pte. SARABOUSKI, E., 204th
37210	Pte. SACKS, V., 204th
103314	Pte. SCHWARTZ, L., 4th
103016	Pte. SOLOMONS, M., 2nd
66734	Pte. SADKIE, J., 3rd
82262	Pte. SOLOMONS, I., 3rd.
48286	Pte. SEFF, H.
	Pte. SAMUELS, H. (D.C.M., M.M.).
36177	L/Cpl. SHOOP, H., 6th
5040	Pte. SCHIVERT, R.,
116130	Pte. SCHNEIDER, J., 7th
33866	Pte. SYMONS, I., 48th
204488	Pte. SOLOMONS, A., 206th
66911	Pte. SELINGER, H., 38th
1890426	Pte. SHMOOKLER, B., 320th
38023	Cpl. STRAUSS, S. G., 3rd
155693	Pte. SAUNDERS, M.
62924	Gnr. SELTZAR, H., 249th
79495	Gnr. SIMONS, H.
491154	Spr. SAMUELS.
114504	Pte. SOLOMON, M., 17th
26501	L/Cpl. SALKIE, L. H., 139th
13604	Gnr. SILVER, L., 22nd
73302	Pte. SULKIN, M.,* 184th
82262	Pte. SOLOMON, J., 33rd
52735	Dvr. SCHATZEN, B., 11th
36263	Pte. SCHWARTZ, A., 68th
85279	Pte. SPIRO, M., 30th
87042	Pte. SILVERSTONE, J., 30th
62927	Pte. SALTER, H., 149th
204389	Pte. SHILCO, E., 52nd
90527	Pte. SEIGEL, A., 42nd
37161	Pte. SOLOMONS, J., 234th
29352	Pte. SHINEMAN, D., 119th
57360	Pte. SIMON, W., 178th
67910	Pte. SUGARMAN, L., 212th
37162	Pte. SNOOK, I., 213th
151666	Cpl. SIMPSON, V., 10th
30749	Gnr. SULTAN, J.,* 90th
132092	Pte. SHATCOFSKY, H.,* 8th
79638	Sgt. SOBER, M.*
118093	Pte. SANKERWITZ, A., 51st
98988	Pte. STERNBERG, N., 57th
139696	Cpl. SALAMAN, E., 61st
73303	Pte. SALTMAN, M., 61st
48286	L/Cpl. SEFF, H., 34th
133730	Pte. SILVER, J., 30th
34927	Pte. STONEMAN, A. H., 97th
73651	Pte. SILVERMAN, D., 246th
66971	Pte. SELIGMAN, H., 38th
47392	Pte. SINGER, J.
13965	Pte. SPERO, P.
130572	Pte. SOLOMONS, M.
40735	Pte. SOLOMONS, A.
125620	Pte. SHAPIRO, S. M.
123172	Pte. SMITH, L.
276183	Pte. STROSS, G.
	Cpl. SAGAR, H. (M.M.).
60877	Pte. SANDLER, S.
68876	Gnr. STOLLER, E.

Machine Gun Corps.—Continued.

- 10734 Pte. STOCK, P.
- 32647 Pte. SANDERS, I.
- 20013 Pte. SNOOKS, J.
- 19917 Pte. SOLOMONS, J.
- 36124 Pte. SOLOMON, J.
- L/Cpl. SOLOMONS, M. (M.M.).
- 14250 Pte. SABLOVSKI, S.
- 95167 Pte. SIMONS, L.
- 96127 Pte. SAMSON, E.*
- 17495 Pte. SILVER, J., 17495
- 19495 Pte. SILVER, J.
- 115200 Pte. TOBIAS, J.,* 8th
- 58645 Pte. TOFF, G., 2nd
- 65804 Pte. TANNERBAUM, A. S.
- 97711 Pte. TOBBUSH, V., 5th
- 225040 Pte. TURNER, J., 56th
- 65367 Pte. TAYLOR, M.
- 36280 Pte. ULPH, C. H. T., 2nd
- 58735 Pte. VEDENBOHM, I., 173rd
- 64530 Pte. VEIN, M., 32nd M.G.
- 78474 Gnr. VALLENSKY, E., 1st
- 30241 Pte. VELLMAN, D.
- 88839 Pte. WHITEFIELD, L.,* 152nd
- 66535 Pte. WOOLF, P., 108th
- 115620 Pte. WOLLMAN, M.,* 227th
- 300670 Pte. WOOD, S.
- 146097 Pte. WOLF, J., 35th
- 132810 Pte. WARSCHAWSKY, B., 35th
- 79105 Pte. WEBBER, M., 74th
- 99197 Pte. WALMAN, L., 37th
- 1148 Pte. WHITE, 2nd M.G. Squad.
- 105273 L/Cpl. WINDER, J., 14th
- 1752 Pte. WEIS, A., 36th
- 104079 Pte. WEINBERG, S., 3rd
- 88368 Pte. WOLFE, S., 4th
- 46738 Pte. WEBER, J., 2nd
- 86255 Pte. WILLIAMS, J., 2nd
- 36546 Pte. WALCHOLDER, B., 1st
- 118621 Pte. WAXMAN, H., 7th
- 66535 Pte. WOOLF, P., 2nd
- 164015 Pte. WASSERMAN, J., 29th
- 332676 Pte. WOOLFE, B.
- 137470 Pte. WISE, J., 62nd
- 124803 Pte. WALLIS, A., 3rd
- 111705 Pte. WISE, I.
- 69527 Gnr. WOOLFE, C.
- 22837 Pte. WOOLF, S. P.
- 2883 Gnr. WOLFMAN, A.
- 108845 Gnr. WHITTIER, J.
- 103036 Gnr. WATERMAN, H.
- 141430 Gnr. WILLIAMS, N. A., 206th
- 28768 Pte. YEGLIS, N., 180th
- 129286 Pte. YESSON, S., 36th
- 66971 Pte. ZELIGMAN, H., 59th
- 2956 Gnr. ZIMMERMAN, K.
- 125076 Pte. ZETTER, B., 2nd
- 91451 Pte. ZAUSMER, M.

* Killed in Action or died on Active Service.

TANK CORPS.

OFFICERS.

- Lieut. ABRAHAMS, D., 2nd Bn.
- Lieut. BARTON, G. H. R. (M.C.), 26th Bn.
- 2nd Lieut. COHEN, L. H.
- 2nd Lieut. DE PASS, C. A.,* 2nd Bn.
- Capt. DAVIS, O.
- Capt. DAVIS, R. G. (M.C.).
- Capt. ENOCH, A. J. (M.C.).
- 2nd Lieut. FRANKENSTEIN, C. J.,*
- Lieut. FINSBERG, G. N. (M.C.).
- 2nd Lieut. GOLDSTEIN, A. A., 7th Bn.
- Capt. HENRIQUES, B. L. Q., 7th Bn.
- 2nd Lieut. HARRIS, S. H. R.
- Lieut. HARRIS, S. J.
- Lieut. HARRIS, C. E.
- Capt. HARRISON, A.
- 2nd Lieut. INGRAM, E. S.
- Capt. JACOBS, H. W.
- Capt. JACOBS, A. C.
- 2nd Lieut. JACOBS, S. J.
- Lieut. LEVY, A.
- Lieut. LEVY, S.
- 2nd Lieut. LAWTON, A. E.
- 2nd Lieut. MYERS, R. A.
- Major MARKS, E. S.
- 2nd Lieut. MORTON, M. S.
- 2nd Lieut. PEARLMAN, J.
- Lieut. SOMPER, J. J.
- 2nd Lieut. TOM, L.
- Capt. WOOLF, B. M. (M.C.), 9th Bn.
- Capt. WOLF, E. M.(M.C.),

N.C.O.'s AND MEN.

- 201475 Pte. ADLER, P. B., 7th Bn.
- 78483 Pte. ADLER, S.
- 76188 Pte. ABRAHAMS, R.
- 317878 Pte. ALEXANDER, B. C.
- 307973 Pte. AROTSKY, L.
- 308600 Pte. AARONS, M., 17th Bn.
- 91331 Pte. BERMAN, N., 5th Bn.
- 69526 Cpl. BEHRENS.
- 40294 Cpl. BEREN, B.
- Cpl. BARDER, M. D.
- 306571 Pte. BERNSTONE, M., 9th Bn.
- 69535 Gnr. COHEN, H., 12th Heavy Bn.
- 77006 L/Cpl. CONN, L., 2nd Bn.
- 76326 Gnr. COHEN, H., 2rd Bn.
- 110302 Sgt. COHEN, S.
- 78490 Pte. COHEN, G., H.Q.
- 309875 Pte. CHAYTOW, A., 16th Bn.

Tank Corps.—Continued.

97226 Pte. COEN, H.
41879 Pte. COHEN, 5th Bn.
317365 Pte. COLP, B.
303056 Pte. COHEN, N.
205304 Gnr. DAVIS, B. A., 10th Bn.
91874 Gnr. DAVIS, A., 8th Bn.
310348 Pte. DEGGOTS, A.
75504 L/Cpl. EPSTEIN, M., 2nd Bn.
11831 Gnr. FINE, P. J., 10th Bn.
312581 Pte. FRIEDMAN, M.
316592 Pte. FAUGH, H., 9th Bn.
76180 Sgt. GLUCKSTEIN, C.
Pte. GOLDMAN, M., 3rd Bde.
318474 Pte. GEBER, C., 5th Bn.
205211 Pte. GERSTEIN, H., 9th Bn.
313402 Pnr. GOLDMAN, J., 2nd Sig. Coy.
5503084 Pnr. GOLDENBERG, M. M., 5th S. Coy.
78726 Gnr. GONSHAW, L.
309557 A/Cpl. GOLDWATER, S. P.
308384 Pte. GLICK, J.
112042 Gnr. HARDY, V. I., 8th Bn.
109783 Pte. HUNT, A.,* 11th Bn.
47626 Pte. HARRIS, A., 2nd Bn.
95387 L/Cpl. HARRIS, S. H. R,
201113 L/Cpl. HYMAN, W., 2nd Adv. Wks.
S/440091 Pte. HART, D.
317402 Pte. HILSUM, B.
26651 Pte. ISAACS, J., 9th Bn.
301823 Pte. ISRAEL, A., 14th Bn.
78216 Pte. JACOBY, J. M., 5th Bn.
78928 Pte. JACOBS, H., 5th Bn.
205748 Ptet. JOHNSON, W. R.,
309064 Pte. JACKSON, F.
109509 L/Cpl. KAY, H. F.
074309 Pte. KIRSCHNER, W. J.
309922 Pte. KAUFMAN, S.
78836 Gnr. LITTLESTONE, M. E., 8th Bn.
91649 Pte. LEVY, H., 6th Bn.
307909 Pte. LEVY, J.,* 16th Bn.
302235 Pte. LYONS, J. C.
112642 Cpl. LEVY, S., H.Q.
308995 Pte. LEVI, J.
95634 Pte. LEVI, M., 13th Bn.
317876 Pte. LAYMAN, L., 25th Bn.
305308 L/Cpl. LEWIS, H., 21st Bn.
08995 Pte. LEVEY, S.
40356 Pte. MOSES, J. C. L., 4th Bn.
0/18383 Sgt. MONAET.
710557 Pte. MARKS, S., 2nd Bn.
318613 Pte. MYERS, S., 5th Bn.
318756 Pte. MYERS, A., 11th Bn.
311474 Pte. MICHAELSON, B., 22nd Bn.
317987 Pte. MIDGEN, S., 20th Bn.
69934 L/Cpl. MENDICK, A.
78841 Gnr. NEWMARK, M., 8th Bn.
78469 Gnr. NATHAN, A.
69241 Pte. OPPENHEIM, M., Reinf. Depot.

200938 Sgt. PHILLIPS, H., 5th Bn.
69935 Pte. POVIDLER, A. 4th, Bn.
95389 L/Cpl. PHILLIPS, R.
2961 Gnr. PHILLIPS, C.
32307 Gnr. PROTHERSE, J. H.
318915 Gnr. POLREK, I.
308479 Pte. POSENOR, A.,* 11th Bn.
201530 Pte. ROSENBERG D.,
200513 Pte. ROSE, A. M.
302699 Pte RING, R., 4th Bn.
161342 Pnr. REBUCK, 5th Sig. Coy.
69381 Gnr. ROSNICK, V.
311492 Pte. ROSEN, D., 22nd Bn.
312197 Pte. RUBINOWITZ, 20th Bn.
306301 Pte. ROSENBERG, M.
Pte. RAPPAPORT, C.
95168 Cpl. SIMONS, L., 11th Bn.
91388 Gnr. STOCK, P., 9th Bn.
302209 Pte. SCHWARTZ, J.
76493 Pte. SCHATT, D.
311887 Pte. STONFIELD, J., 23rd Bn.
312198 Pte. SIMONS, J., 20th Bn.
320488 Pte. SILVER, M.
317676 Pte. SEFF, S.
320236 Pte. SIMONS, L. 2nd Bn.
309735 Pte. SAMPSON, F.
205093 Pte. STRAUS, S. G.,
1112651 L/Cpl. VAUGHAN, R.
Pte. WEINBERG, M.
307685 Pte. WINESTEIN, L.
2883 L/Cpl. WOLFMAN, A.
309808 Pte. WEINBERG, S. W.
38189 Gnr. WOLFINEGER, L., 13th Bn.
310371 Pte. WOLFFE, S.
92696 Gnr. YAFFE, S. D.
91451 Gnr. ZAUSMER, M., 9th Bn.
307690 A/C.Q.M.S. ZISKIND, L.
31876 Pte. ZEFF, S.
205666 Pte. ZIMMERMAN, E.
309833 Pte. ZEFF, L.

* Killed in Action or died on Active Service.

TRAINING RESERVE.*

OFFICERS.

Capt. ARON, F. R., 51st Bn.
Lieut. FRIEND, L. M., 85th Bn.
Lieut. REISS, J. M., 15th Bn.

N.C.O.'s AND MEN.

16014 Pte. ACKSTONE, S., 15th Bn.
17648 Pte. ABRAHAMS, J., 15th Bn.

* A large proportion of this list is included in the units to which they were afterwards transferred.

Training Reserve.—*Continued.*

76165 Cpl. ABRAHAMS, S., 89th Bn.
38926 Pte. ABLESON, W., 73rd Bn.
3/469 Pte. ADDIS, I., 48th Bn.
62383 Pte. ASH, S., 50th Bn.
71114 Pte. AROZKIN, P., 49th Bn.
3/7337 Pte. ABRAHAMS, H., 49th Bn.
3/72999 Pte. AGREER, L., 49th Bn.
44170 Pte. AIGEBAND, M., 27th Bn.
13/25 Pte. ABRAHAMS, S., 14th Bn.
33442 Pte. AARON, H., 71st Bn.
9/20763 Pte. ADELSON, A., 44th Bn.
17327 Pte. AROTSKY, V., 43rd Bn.
6618 Pte. ALFANKARY, A., 26th Bn.
13/76553 Pte. ABRAMOVITCH, B.
42644 Pte. ALLEN, L., 99th Bn.
42313 Pte. ABRAHAMS, D., 99th Bn.
72895 L/Cpl. ABRAHAM, L., 111th Bn.
32897 Pte. ALEXANDER, A., 71st Bn.
28744 Pte. ALEX, L., 70th Bn.
90978 Pte. ABRAHAMS, M., 7th Bn.
5759 Pte. ABRAHAMS, A., 16th Bn.
42733 Pte. ALLEN, S., 99th Bn.
39972 Pte. APPLEBOAM, J., 98th Bn.
39539 Pte. ANTEN, P., 98th Bn.
71278 Rfm. ASHER, H., 109th Bn.
76789 Pte. ABRAHAMS, E., 111th Bn.
39507 Pte. ABRAHAMS, M., 98th Bn.
7636 Pte. ABRAHAMS, S., 49th Bn.
128763 Pte. ABRAHAMS, B., 102nd Bn.
27206 Pte. APPELL, J., 46th Bn.
29765 Pte. AARONS, I. S., 46th Bn.
29205 Pte. ALCO, J., 46th Bn.
50287 Pte. ABRAHAMS, S. M., 18th Bn.
91337 Pte. ALLEN, B., 25th Bn.
22814 Pte. ADLER, D., 6th Bn.
57354 Pte. ABRAHAMS, E., 103rd Bn.
25271 Pte. ALTMAN, D., 78th Bn.
3204362 Sgt. ALEXANDER, R. L., 65th Bn.
274307 Pte. APPLEBAUM, A., 4th Bn.
21168 L/Cpl. AARONHEIM, S., 44th Bn.
14571 Pte. ANSELL, D., 19th Bn.
13/72895 Pte. ABRAHAMS, L. P., 111th Bn.
29155 Pte. ABRAHAMS, A., 46th Bn.
296552 Pte. ABRAHAMS, A., 4th Bn.
192769 Pte. AGRODBITCH, A.
62448 Pte. ANDREWS, R., 104th Bn.
Pte. ARNOTT, D., 47th Bn.
51369 Pte. ASH, M., 233rd Bn.
75524 Cpl. ABECASES, B.
2420 Pte. ADELSON, A., 206th Bn.
50287 Pte. ABRAHAMS, S. M., 237th Bn.
13245 Pte. ALFRED, R., 24th Bn.
26180 Pte. BERNSTEIN, I., 45th Bn.
25373 Pte. BARNETT, S. E., 45th Bn.
28727 L/Cpl. BOGOD, M., 46th Bn.
4686 Pte. BENJAMIN, H., 93rd Bn.
16779 Pte. BROWN, S., 14th Bn.

96261 Pte. BRANSKEY, S., 85th Bn.
89129 Pte. BALOFSKY, B., 24th Bn.
30451 Pte. BRAMZIL, W., 110th Bn.
36858 L/Cpl. BRIGG, M., 18th Bn.
34028 Pte. BROZEL, J., 97th Bn.
37869 Pte. BERNBAUM, M., 73rd Bn.
28926 Pte. BLOOM, R., 73rd Bn.
44917 Pte. BARNETT, 74th Bn.
44869 Pte. BOWMAN, H., 74th Bn.
45088 Pte. BRASS, D., 74th Bn.
48522 Pte. BLACK, S., 75th Bn.
38541 Pte. BURMAN, M., 76th Bn.
12273 L/Cpl. BEAVER, J., 48th Bn.
2268 Pte. BAKER, M., 48th Bn.
3,4043 Pte. BLACK, M., 49th Bn.
5686 Pte. BLACK, H., 49th Bn.
12272 L/Cpl. BRANCO, J., 49th Bn.
6336 Pte. BERNSTEIN, H., 49th Bn.
6953 Pte. BLACK, N., 49th Bn.
62785 Pte. BARNETT, L., 50th Bn.
63006 Pte. BROWNSTEIN, B., 50th Bn.
63868 Pte. BAKER, M., 50th Bn.
3/12273 Sgt. BRANCO, 51st Bn.
5929 Pte. BENNETT, I., 49th Bn.
9/82543 Pte. BRODSKY, H., 25th Bn.
82531 Pte. BROMBERG, H., 25th Bn.
82530 Pte. BARON, A., 25th Bn.
363650 Pte. BRIGHT, W., 25th Bn.
3/70578 Pte. BOLSER, R., 49th Bn.
1484 Pte. BERENBAUM, J., 49th Bn.
70901 Pte. BRUCKS, A., 49th Bn.
3/72593 Pte. BLOCK, G., 49th Bn.
3/72739 Pte. BLUESTEIN, S., 49th Bn.
3/73327 Pte. BLOOM, S., 49th Bn.
3/73333 Pte. BROOKSTONE, S., 49th Bn.
108453 Pte. BULL, A., 31st Bn.
34038 Pte. BENJAMIN, N. H., 209th Bn.
34456 Pte. BELASCO, S., 209th Bn.
34028 Pte. BROZEL, J., 209th Bn.
75101 Pte. BENJAMIN, B., 112th Bn.
45715 Pte. BARON, H., 100th Bn.
74492 Pte. BENJAMIN, J., 109th Bn.
74523 Pte. BERGMAN, H., 112th Bn.
76359 Pte. BALLABON, S. H., 110th Bn.
74482 Pte. BERNSTEIN, J., 109th Bn.
74615 Pte. BENJAMIN, H., 109th Bn.
15158 Pte. BENSUSAN, H., 18th Bn.
14773 Pte. BRETZFELDER, M. H., 19th Bn.
14721 Pte. BERNSTEIN, A., 19th Bn.
34630 Pte. BROWN, J. H., 49th Bn.
29771 Pte. BARNETT, B., 46th Bn.
12648 Pte. BERNSTEIN, B., 60th Bn.
91382 Pte. BRIGHT, W., 25th Bn.
91458 Pte. BENCHOWSKY, S., 25th Bn.
108466 Pte. BARDONI, M., 97th Bn.
6/15307 L/Cpl. BARNETT, B., 12th Bn.
Pte. BARAK, 110th Bn.
55507 Pte. BARNETT, B., 74th Bn.

Training Reserve.—*Continued.*

70482 Pte. BROOKS, D. B., 111th Bn.
5/29954 Pte. BLASKEY, D., 8th Bn.
21181 Pte. BAUM, C., 6th Bn.
2771 Pte. BRAHAMS, H., 11th Bn.
30843 Pte. BROOD, N., 18th Bn.
30760 Pte. BIERMAN, A., 18th Bn.
2959 Pte. BAKESEF, I., 103rd Bn.
29161 Pte. BAYHAM, H. L., 66th Bn.
36256 Cpl. BLASENSTEIN, C., 66th Bn.
14765 Pte. BLACK, B., 4th Bn.
14720 Pte. BLOOM, J., 19th Bn.
21021 Pte. BENSUSAN, I., 44th Bn.
19452 Pte. BIRD, J., 5th Bn.
71650 Pte. BERNSTEIN, B., 108th Bn.
21407 Pte. BERLOFSKY, I., 108th Bn.
75587 Pte. BASS, L., 108th Bn.
26244 Pte. BOORMAN, D., 25th Bn.
74052 Pte. BRONITZSKI, D., 110th Bn.
76113 Pte. BAYNARD, S., 111th Bn.
56169 Pte. BARNESS, M., 20th Bn.
13639 Pte. BARBACK, 55th Bn.
45708 Pte. BARNETT, I., 100th Bn.
46211 Pte. BERNSTEIN, M. N., 100th Bn.
42387 Pte. BEECHAN, J., 99th Bn.
126166 Pte. BICKLER, S., 7th Bn.
10/50585 Pte. BRESLAU, A., 101st Bn.
36186 Pte. BOWDEN, W., 98th Bn.
42654 Pte. BOBER, H., 99th Bn.
10/50668 Pte. BOSSICK, J., 101st Bn.
45707 Pte. BROOKSTON, H., 100th Bn.
49820 Pte. BUITEKANT, M., 101st Bn.
77621 Pte. BAUM, I., 108th Bn.
17671 L/Cpl. BROOKS, H., 67th Bn.
42729 Pte. BRESLAU, D., 99th Bn.
21301 Pte. BERGSON, S., 68th Bn.
75393 Pte. BARNETT, S., 108th Bn.
75639 Pte. BIERMAN, S., 111th Bn.
33662 Pte. BENJAMIN, B., 111th Bn.
73777 Pte. BERG, A., 112th Bn.
21685 Pte. BLACK, L., 77th Bn.
29979 Pte. BLOMFIELD, C., 46th Bn.
41235 Pte. BLOCK, M., 59th Bn.
108453 Pte. BULL, J., 97th Bn.
73032 Pte. BUTLER, J., 110th Bn.
5/93235 Pte. BERGSON, I., 8th Bn.
73770 L/Cpl. BLACK, 112th Bn.
70992 Pte. BRITZ, S., 112th Bn.
98338 Pte. BERNSTEIN, E., 84th Bn.
13/1898 Pte. BALANOFF, S., 16th Bn.
8850 Sgt. BLOCK, H., 18th Bn.
8527 Pte. BETH, B., 18th Bn.
12641 Pte. BEST, B., 19th Bn.
81604 Pte. BLISS, M., 90th Bn.
36933 L/Cpl. BERNSTEIN, S., 10th Bn.
16994 Pte. BROD, H., 20th Bn.
16906 Pte. BERNARD, C., 20th Bn.
12505 Pte. BARNETT, J. S.

28702 Pte. BROCKMAN, M., 106th Bn.
12222 Pte. BAKER, J., 41st Bn.
25603 Pte. BARNETT, L., 69th Bn.
24884 Pte. BERMAN, S., 45th Bn.
5097 Pte. BURNS, F., 34th Bn.
76819 Pte. BAUM, J., 111th Bn.
76952 Pte. BIERMAN, L., 111th Bn.
29771 Pte. BARRET, B., 46th Bn.
73053 Pte. BIGLIZION, H., 110th Bn.
15242 Pte. BAKER, H., 14th Bn.
54459 Pte. BAUMGART, M., 103rd Bn.
49132 Pte. BUSNACK, M., 101st Bn.
70433 Pte. BENJAMIN, B., 26th Bn.
70431 Pte. BERNSTEIN, W., 26th Bn.
38644 L/Cpl. BARNETT, J., 111th Bn.
10/66487 Pte. BERGER, D.
615654 Pte. BOURNISH, B., 3rd Bn.
28146 L/Cpl. BENJAMIN, A., 79th Bn.
Pte. BOLSERI, R. B., 49th Bn.
74617 Pte. BERNSTEIN, I., 107th Bn.
74167 Pte. BROWN, S. C., 108th Bn.
112267 Pte. BORSTEIN, W., 98th Bn.
128520 Pte. BARON, J. A. H., 102nd Bn.
54954 Pte. BARNETT, P.
29930 Pte. BODESKY, J. E.
76393 Pte. BARNETT, S., 108th Bn.
75494 Pte. BLOOM, H., 109th Bn.
77733 Pte. BOHN, B.
75393 Pte. BARNETT, S., 108th Bn.
21781 Pte. BARBUK, M., 44th Bn.
33644 Pte. BARNETT, J., 111th Bn.
91427 Pte. BAUM, R., 25th Bn.
33856 Pte. BECKERMAN, B., 47th Bn.
Pte. BAINSTOCK, A., 24th Bn.
33786 Pte. BERKENSTADT, S., 47th Bn.
242799 Pte. BURMAN, I., 208th Bn.
14457 Pte. BLOCK, A., 245th Bn.
42654 Pte. BOBER, H., 253rd Bn.
3263 Pte. BEHAR, J., 249th Bn.
14874 Pte. BLOODSTEIN, B., 244th Bn.
35474 L/Cpl. BRISCOL, M., 208th Bn.
32059 Sgt. CHADWICK, R., 47th Bn.
30027 Pte. COHEN, B., 4th Bn.
7/8184 Pte. CASALMAN, L., 94th Bn.
5/29268 Pte. COHEN, V., 8th Bn.
17920 Pte. COLEMAN, A. M., 15th Bn.
16412 Pte. COHEN, D., 15th Bn.
5/68925 Pte. COHEN, H., 87th Bn.
17523 Pte. COLEMAN, L., 43rd Bn.
13/51272 Pte. COHEN, H., 16th Bn.
1326 Pte. COHEN, B., 206th Bn.
17161 Pte. CHERRY, M.
30028 Pte. COHEN, J., 46th Bn.
8902 Cpl. COHEN, S., 27th Bn.
38685 Pte. COHEN, H., 73rd Bn.
44072 L/Cpl. COMER, D., 74th Bn.
45454 Pte. CAPLAN, S., 74th Bn.
3704 Pte. COHEN, J., 74th Bn.

Training Reserve.—*Continued.*

38685 Pte. COHEN, S., 76th Bn.
38596 Pte. COHEN, C., 76th Bn.
39288 Pte. COVEL, J., 76th Bn.
46836 Pte. COLLACK, H., 48th Bn.
7534 Pte. COHEN, S., 49th Bn.
7384 Pte. COHEN, M., 49th Bn.
7550 Pte. COHEN, S., 49th Bn.
7750 Pte. COHEN, E., 49th Bn.
9781 Pte. CHAWICK, A., 50th Bn.
3/62007 Pte. COCKLIN, S., 50th Bn.
62525 Pte. COHEN, J., 50th Bn.
3/12076 Pte. CANTOR, J. I., 51st Bn.
132710 Pte. COHEN, C., 85th Bn.
70920 Pte. COHEN, A., 49th Bn.
70706 Pte. COHEN, A., 49th Bn.
3/72135 Pte. COHEN, N., 49th Bn.
3/72926 Pte. COLE, S., 49th Bn.
3/73012 Pte. CAPLAN, S., 49th Bn.
27934 Pte. COOPER, M., 31st Bn.
21914 Pte. CLAPPER, J., 30th Bn.
34227 Pte. CASH, P., 209th Bn.
6/4733 Cpl. COUPLAND, A., 270th Bn.
8476 Pte. COHEN, B., 18th Bn.
13085 Pte. COHEN, J., 19th Bn.
66807 Pte. CHURNER, M., 6th Bn.
17103 L/Cpl. CREGOR, C., 20th Bn.
68554 Pte. COHEN, H., 106th Bn.
68189 Sgt. COHEN, S., 106th Bn.
55542 Pte. CLYNES, L.
33461 Pte. CRANGLE, S., 71st Bn.
5986 Pte. COHEN, J. E., 49th Bn.
5328 Pte. COSTA, M., 26th Bn.
8184 Pte. CASSELMAN, 94th Bn.
TR/76552 Pte. CLEMENTS, J., 111th Bn.
77001 Pte. CLIFF, M., 111th Bn.
77283 Pte. COHEN, S., 111th Bn.
57578 Pte. CAPLIN, A., 18th Bn.
25887 Pte. CAPLAN, M., 63rd Bn.
38729 Pte. CALMUS, J., 98th Bn.
75151 Pte. CHESTER, H., 108th Bn.
22099 Pte. CAPLIN, H., 108th Bn.
20272 Pte. COHEN, H., 26th Bn.
21396 Pte. COOPER, S., 44th Bn.
33375 Pte. COHEN, S. W., 71st Bn.
51269 L/Cpl. CLARE, S. H., 18th Bn.
32736 Pte. CHAPLIN, W., 97th Bn.
56516 Pte. COHEN, M., 20th Bn.
73479 Pte. COHEN, M., 110th Bn.
74639 Pte. CAPLIN, I., 108th Bn.
42656 Pte. CAVE, A. G., 99th Bn.
21972 Pte. COHEN, J., 108th Bn.
17977 Pte. COHEN, A., 43rd Bn.
55837 Pte. COHEN, M., 2nd Bn.
28421 Pte. COWEN, J., 70th Bn.
74626 Pte. COHEN, H., 109th Bn.
6225 Pte. CANIN, M., 49th Bn.
112144 Pte. COHEN, H., 98th Bn.

7804 Pte. COHEN, J., 2nd Bn.
5206 Pte. COHEN, H., 16th Bn.
6453 Pte. COLIVING, M., 49th Bn.
74955 Pte. COSTA, S., 110th Bn.
27539 Pte. CANTOR, C., 7th Bn.
75071 Pte. COHEN, J., 111th Bn.
75246 Pte. CAPLIN, G., 110th Bn.
58326 Pte. COHEN, M., 20th Bn.
10924 Pte. COLLINS, W., 97th Bn.
10171 Pte. CARDAN, H., 27th Bn.
8711 Sgt. CONTILE, H., 27th Bn.
36189 Cpl. COHEN, C. G., 10th Bn.
29763 Pte. CHRUST, J., 46th Bn.
73633 Pte. CHYTE, H.
21777 Pte. COHEN, D., 44th Bn.
31568 Pte. COHEN, S., 17th Bn.
S/17475 Cpl. COHEN, S., 20th Bn.
30762 Rfm. CORPER, A., 18th Bn.
33438 Pte. CAMBERG, J., 77th Bn.
91411 Pte. CORNBLAUM, A., 25th Bn.
80538 Pte. COHEN, L., 25th Bn.
108346 Pte. CLEMENTS, J., 97th Bn.
2/17279 Pte. COHEN, E., 43rd Bn.
34363 Pte. COLEMAN, H., 71st Bn.
5909 Pte. COLLICK, J., 49th Bn.
21143 Pte. CLYNES, L., 65th Bn.
38013 Pte. CANTER, S., 10th Bn.
12831 Pte. COHEN, H., 36th Bn.
71456 Pte. COHEN, H., 36th Bn.
71456 Pte. COHEN, S., 110th Bn.
25033 L/Cpl. CORRINGTON, J., 78th Bn.
200155 Pte. COHEN, J., 11th Bn.
73982 Pte. CASIMIR, L., 109th Bn.
58310 Pte. COHEN, H., 20th Bn.
70191 Pte. COLE, R. E., 112th Bn.
77876 Pte. COHEN, J., 108th Bn.
34497 Pte. CIRSCH, H., 49th Bn.
42731 L/Cpl. CAKLAN, D., 99th Bn.
42655 Pte. CAPLAN, M., 99th Bn.
38780 Pte. CRITZMAN, W., 98th Bn.
55855 Pte. COHEN, B., 102nd Bn.
38476 Pte. COHEN, M., 98th Bn.
39253 Pte. COHEN, D., 98th Bn.
39621 Pte. COHEN, M., 98th Bn.
42518 Pte. COHEN, N., 99th Bn.
42675 L/Cpl. COHEN, S., 99th Bn.
46662 Pte. COHEN, D., 100th Bn.
46664 Pte. COHEN, H., 100th Bn.
77810 Pte. COHEN, D., 100th Bn.
46663 Pte. COHEN, S., 100th Bn.
45656 Pte. COHEN, J., 100th Bn.
45653 Pte. COHEN, C., 100th Bn.
46514 Pte. COHEN, H., 100th Bn.
77879 Pte. COHEN, H., 100th Bn.
46164 Pte. COHEN, S., 100th Bn.
49903 Pte. COHEN, M., 101st Bn.
38778 Pte. CUTLEVOVITCH, W., 98th Bn.
73692 Pte. CRAWFORD, M., 111th Bn.

Training Reserve.—*Continued.*

34764 Pte. CHAPMAN, C., 9th Bn.
38965 Pte. CANTOR, L., 66th Bn.
75612 Pte. CALTON, L., 111th Bn.
46500 Pte. COHEN, A., 81st Bn.
108518 Pte. CLARK, L., 97th Bn.
14989 L/Cpl. COHEN, Z., 14th Bn.
57657 Pte. COHEN, B., 16th Bn.
52090 Pte. COHEN, A., 16th Bn.
10151 Pte. CHARNEZ, B., 62nd Bn.
38538 Pte. CAKLAN, J., 72nd Bn.
28784 Pte. CASHER, B., 46th Bn.
26817 Pte. COHEN, V., 17th Bn.
28686 Pte. COMBLATT, G., 46th Bn.
21087 Pte. CONFEDRA, I., 44th Bn.
9278 Pte. COHEN, H., 27th Bn.
72014 Pte. COHEN, S., 110th Bn.
17428 Pte. CAPLAN, A., 43rd Bn.
26164 Pte. COHL, L. P., 63rd Bn.
Pte. COHEN, L., 61st Bn.
91780 Pte. CREEGOR, J., 24th Bn.
145601 Pte. COHEN, W. M.
9871 Pte. COPELAND, L., 104th Bn.
10151 Pte. CHARNEY, B., 62nd Bn.
36497 Pte. CIRSCH, H., 47th Bn.
51269 Pte. CLARE, S., 18th Bn.
51578 Pte. CAPLAN, 18th Bn.
128364 Pte. CUTNEROVITCH, M., 86th Bn.
39288 Pte. COVELL, J., 76th Bn.
71091 Pte. COLE, R., 112th Bn.
351153 Pte. COHEN, J., 222nd Bn.
242800 Pte. CARTZ, L., 208th Bn.
241614 Pte. COHEN, J., 208th Bn.
86996 Cpl. COUPLAN, L., 270th Bn.
30184 Pte. COHEN, J., 237th Bn.
45656 Pte. COHEN, J., 256th Bn.
49903 Pte. COHEN, N., 215th Bn.
13882 Cpl. COHEN, S., 237th Bn.
12427 Pte DAVIS, H., 95th Bn.
13/35151 Pte. DOBKINS, M., 11th Bn.
41236 Pte. DAVIES, M., 73rd Bn.
46754 Pte. DELACOVITCH, M., 73rd Bn.
42414 Pte. DONOF, H., 73rd Bn.
38484 Pte. DALINSKY, L., 74th Bn.
54124 Pte. DRIBBIN, H., 76th Bn.
13717 Pte. DENBY, L., 51st Bn.
3/73084 Pte. DRABIN, J., 49th Bn.
5/66556 Pte. DONNE, J., 273rd Bn.
13430 Pte. DOSAVITCH, S., 19th Bn.
13661 Pte. DEITZ, W., 19th Bn.
17221 L/Cpl. DAVIS, J., 20th Bn.
13/76684 Pte. DOLLMAN, J.
76953 Pte. DISTELMAN, A.
77214 Pte. DARER, D.
73161 Pte. DOSAVITCH, J., 110th Bn.
29261 Pte. DAVIDS, L., 46th Bn.
38015 Pte. DUNN, I., 10th Bn.
74848 Pte. DEMOVITZ, M., 109th Bn.

5301 L/Cpl. DAVIS, J., 57th Bn.
148023 Pte. DAVIS, J., 107th Bn.
76468 Pte. DONSKIE, A., 112th Bn.
67928 Pte. DAITZ B., 16th Bn.
42144 Pte. DRAPKIN, A. A., 99th Bn.
46092 Pte. DAVISON, S., 100th Bn.
55836 Pte. DA COSTA, E., 102nd Bn.
55557 Pte. DAVIS, G., 102nd Bn.
52238 Pte. DAVIS, J., 102nd Bn.
49597 Pte. DRILSMA, B., 101st Bn.
55865 Pte. DOMBROSKY, N., 102nd Bn.
75657 Pte. DAVIS, J., 111th Bn.
56387 Pte. DULOVSKY, S., 20th Bn.
77274 Pte. DRAGOVITCH, A.
74752 Pte. DAVIS, M., 112th Bn.
74646 Pte. DEFRIES, I., 111th Bn.
17935 Pte. DUNNE, A., 5th Bn.
93125 Pte. DAVIS, I., 8th Bn.
75657 Pte. DAVIS, J., 112th Bn.
112030 Pte. DAVIS, R., 100th Bn.
10719 Pte. DAVIS, A., 23rd Bn.
339698 Pte. DONIGER, S., 98th Bn.
2579 Pte. DONNE, I., 11th Bn.
5/23228 Pte. DAVIS, J., 6th Bn.
33927 Pte. DAVE, A., 47th Bn.
71600 Pte. DAVIS, H., 110th Bn.
26845 Pte. DE SWARTE, R., 31st Bn.
19429 Pte. DIETCH, D., 15th Bn.
28869 Pte. DA COSTA, M., 46th Bn.
30641 Pte. DORSHT, M., 64th Bn.
9/21299 Pte. DAVIS, D., 44th Bn.
21104 Pte. DIAMONDSTEIN, W., 44th Bn.
76739 Pte. DOFFMAN, H., 26th Bn.
2276 Pte. DAVILS, 76th Bn.
12261 Pte. DEITZ, L. F., 19th Bn.
47896 Pte. EMANUEL, H., 74th Bn.
44082 Pte. ELLIS, I., 74th Bn.
55393 Pte. EDGART, L., 86th Bn.
13/509 Pte. EPSTEIN, J., 16th Bn.
81236 Pte. EISNER, J., 90th Bn.
13/76739 Pte. ELF,
194328 Pte. ELKAN, D., 73rd Bn.
73627 Pte. EDWARDS, S., 49th Bn.
22704 Pte. ECKER, E., 30th Bn.
39921 Pte. EVANS, A. A., 98th Bn.
76137 Pte. ELLIS, D., 110th Bn.
74337 Pte. ELLIS, M.
76505 Pte. ENDLEMAN, D., 111th Bn.
49944 Pte. EDWARDS, J., 62nd Bn.
128619 Pte. ELLIS, S., 102nd Bn.
30004 Pte. EDGAR, L., 18th Bn.
18747 Pte. ELLIGER, H., 5th Bn.
78231 Drm. ELSBERG, H., 87th Bn.
10066 Pte. EDELMAN, M., 54th Bn.
28789 Pte. EPSTEIN, M.
10/2703 Pte. EMANUEL, J., 21st Bn.
22567 Pte. EMANUEL, A., 6th Bn.
12578 Pte. ESTERMAN, J., 24th Bn.

Training Reserve.—*Continued.*

242009 Pte. EDGAR, L., 208th Bn.
17688 Pte. FREEDMAN, J., 15th Bn.
25941 Pte. FREEMAN, E., 7th Bn.
13/35227 Pte. FRESCO, E. 11th Bn.
76315 Pte. FRIEZE, M., 89th Bn.
34963 L/Cpl. FINKLESTEIN, W., 47th Bn.
127503 Pte. FREEMAN, J. M
40082 Pte FREEMAN, H., 73rd Bn.
41493 Pte. FRANKS, H., 73rd Bn.
1973 Pte. FRANKS, 73rd Bn.
42317 Pte. FRIEND, R., 73rd Bn.
66281 Pte. FERBER, C., 74th Bn.
48518 Pte. FREEDMAN, J., 74th Bn.
38915 Pte. FARBER, H., 74th Bn.
54040 Pte. FINKLESTEIN, J., 76th Bn.
2638 Pte. FRIEDLANDER, C. L., 48th Bn.
59312 Pte. FINMAN, A. L., 49th Bn.
62377 Pte. FROINBERG, S., 50th Bn.
1221/4 L/Cpl. FINK, 51st Bn.
62219 Pte. FREEMAN, S., 50th Bn.
82232 Pte. FREEDMAN, J., 25th Bn.
129690 Pte. FREED, I., 86th Bn.
509235 Pte. FREDLEWSKY, A., 115th Bn.
70452 Pte. FISHEL, M., 49th Bn.
71102 Pte. FIDLER, S., 49th Bn.
71548 Pte. FRIESER, S. J., 49th Bn.
72113 Pte. FLETCHER, H., 49th Bn.
3/72594 Pte. FRANKLIN, H., 49th Bn.
34175 Pte. FELDMAN, T. S., 209th Bn.
35541 Pte. FRANKS, D., 209th Bn.
42923 Pte. FINKLE, D., 45th Bn.
89292 Pte. FLATOW, F., 6th Bn.
112232 Pte. FRIEDLANDER, R., 98th Bn.
128262 Pte. FRESHWATER, L., 102nd Bn.
76822 Pte. FINEBERG, B.
73211 Pte. FINKLESTEIN, A., 110th Bn.
76366 Pte. FRIEDMAN, A., 110th Bn.
51828 Pte. FOOTRING, A., 18th Bn.
34964 Pte. FINEBERG, S., 47th Bn.
27100 Pte. FRIED, J., 43rd Bn.
8049 A/Cpl. FRANKS, J., 22nd Bn.
18191 Pte. FREEDMAN, A., 5th Bn.
70452 Pte. FISHEL, M., 49th Bn.
91413 Pte. FLEXER, B., 25th Bn.
73877 Pte. FREEMAN, S., 88th Bn.
34750 Sdlr. FARBER, M., 71st Bn.
72299 Pte. FELDMAN, J., 25th Bn.
28694 Pte. FELL, H., 79th Bn.
65022 Pte. FINEBERG, P., 103rd Bn.
51646 Pte. FISHER, J.
21531 Pte. FRIETAG, W., 30th Bn.
29527 Pte. FAIRSTEINFELD, J., 46th Bn.
26818 Pte. FAIRBURN, H. M., 7th Bn.
51825 Pte. FALK, J., 20th Bn.
50337 Pte. FINN, O., 19th Bn.
29220 Pte. FREEDMAN, S., 46th Bn.
36289 L/Cpl. FOX, L. H., 66th Bn.

74077 Pte. FLOWERS, A. S., 112th Bn.
57454 Pte. FISHTELL, M., 16th Bn.
56377 Pte. FREEMAN, A.
12825 Pte. FELD, N., 102nd Bn.
705 Pte. FRANKS, A., 57th Bn.
18430 Pte. FRIEDMAN, E., 20th Bn.
17308 Pte. FELDMAN, H., 20th Bn.
21709 Pte. FINBERG, S., 108th Bn.
6539 Pte. FRIEDENBERG, D., 111th Bn.
76822 Pte. FINEBERG, B., 111th Bn.
76929 Pte. FELDMAN, O., 111th Bn.
77302 Pte. FOGEL, I., 111th Bn.
29348 L/Cpl. FRIEDMAN, D., 26th Bn.
8281 Pte. FICKLE, B., 111th Bn.
796078 Pte. FREEDAN, S., 21st Bn.
29172 Pte. FRANKS, J., 46th Bn.
29129 Pte. FRESCO, D., 46th Bn.
17877 Pte. FLIEGELMAN, S., 43rd Bn.
71489 Pte. FRIEDMAN, H.
73780 Pte. FREEDMAN, M., 112th Bn.
26900 Pte. FRANKS, M., 69th Bn.
22148 L/Cpl. FLANKLIN, J., 112th Bn.
74032 Pte. FALLON, S., 112th Bn.
45923 L/Cpl. FRANKS, M., 100th Bn.
74742 Pte. FRANKS, B. G., 109th Bn.
41867 Pte. FREEDMAN, B., 99th Bn.
34175 Pte. FIELDMAN, S., 97th Bn.
39206 Pte. FINSGOLD, A., 98th Bn.
41869 Pte. FINKLE, J., 99th Bn.
46790 Pte. FRIEDPANDER, R., 100th Bn.
49735 Pte. FISHERBOAM, H., 101st Bn.
39856 Pte. FISHMAN, B., 98th Bn.
5/58071 Pte. FRANKS, M., 84th Bn.
77399 Pte. FREEDMAN.
78042 Pte. FELT, J.
75851 Pte. FORREST, B., 110th Bn.
25964 Pte. FINKLESTEIN, L., 45th Bn.
34965 Pte. FELTHEIM, N., 47th Bn.
6772 Pte. FREEDMAN, P., 49th Bn.
34590 Pte. FREEDMAN, J., 111th Bn.
13018 Pte. FLYNBERG, H., 49th Bn.
44502 Sgt. FLIGELSTONE, 61st Bn.
125470 Pte. FRANKS, E., 5th Bn.
92868 Pte. FALK, H., 49th Bn.
356050 Pte. FELDMAN, N., 221st Bn.
50343 Pte. FRIEDLANDER, L., 237th Bn.
13410 Pte. FRIEDMAN, B., 245th Bn.
3501 Sgt. FRIEDLANDER, B., 253rd Bn.
41869 Pte. FINKLE, J., 253rd Bn.
26239 Pte. GOLDSTEIN, J., 45th Bn.
29843 Pte. GREENBERG, I., 45th Bn.
25646 Pte. GOLDSTEIN, P., 45th Bn.
25552 Pte. GOLDSTEIN, R., 45th Bn.
25997 Pte. GREENWOOD, I., 45th Bn.
26240 Pte. GOLD, S., 45th Bn.
872 Pte. GREENFIELD, 92nd Bn.
873 Pte. GRAHAM, J. H., 92nd Bn.
4417 L/Cpl. GREENBERG, J., 93rd Bn.

Training Reserve.—*Continued.*

       Sgt. GOLDSTEIN, J. D., 47th Bn.
29221 Pte. GINSBERG, W., 46th Bn.
9/25417 Pte. GOLDSTEIN, J., 45th Bn.
10467 Pte. GORDEN, J., 35th Bn.
5/22248 Pte. GOODSON, S., 6th Bn.
30280 Pte. GOLDBERG, M.
13/642 Rfm. GOLDSTON, A. B.
10900 Pte. GATES, B., 27th Bn.
40159 Pte. GRIMSHAW, H., 73rd Bn.
45348 Pte. GINSBURG, D., 74th Bn.
45517 Pte. GALINSKY, 74th Bn.
46152 Pte. GLAZIER, D., 74th Bn.
39042 Pte. GLASS, S., 76th Bn.
54032 Pte. GOODALL, H., 76th Bn.
53555 Pte. GOLDMAN, J., 76th Bn.
192529 Pte. GOODMAN, W.,* 24th Bn.
2530 Pte. GORDON, A., 76th Bn.
2766 Pte. GERBER, M. C., 48th Bn.
3291 Pte. GLASSER, B., 48th Bn.
6127 Pte. GROSSMAN, H., 49th Bn.
7551 Pte. GIRVANNETTI, J., 49th Bn.
6285 Pte GLASBERG, E., 49th Bn.
9589 Pte. GOLDING, J., 50th Bn.
82409 Pte. GREENHAM, L., 25th Bn.
61768 L/Cpl. GOLDSTEIN, I., 85th Bn.
37519 Pte. GOODMAN, E., 86th Bn.
53577 Pte. GOLDMAN, J., 49th Bn.
70971 Pte. GOLDENFIELD, M., 49th Bn.
70912 Pte. GOULD, J., 49th Bn.
70965 Pte. GUISE, H., 49th Bn.
71101 Pte. GOLDSTONE, M., 49th Bn.
3/72809 Pte. GOULD, E., 49th Bn.
3/73328 Pte. GOLDMAN, M., 49th Bn
27969 Pte GOLDSTEIN, A., 31st Bn.
34055 Pte. GLUCKSTEIN, J., 209th Bn.
35379 L/Cpl. GOULD, J., 209th Bn.
34085 L/Cpl. GOLDBERG, H., 209th Bn.
5/65274 Pte. GOLDSTEIN, L., 273rd Bn.
25866 Pte. GANETSKY, S., 45th Bn.
25221 Pte. GOLDBERG, L., 45th Bn.
49536 Pte. GASTER, A. E., 101st Bn.
42590 Pte. GARFINKLE, J., 99th Bn.
46754 Pte. GENYON, L., 100th Bn.
52242 Pte. GRADIST, E., 102nd Bn.
54484 Pte. GREEN, J., 102nd Bn.
55351 Pte. GORDON, I., 102nd Bn.
55570 Pte. GOLDMAN, H., 102nd Bn.
42732 Pte. GROSSMAN, M., 99th Bn.
42434 Pte. GOLDBERG, M., 99th Bn.
45770 Pte. GOROWITZ, S., 100th Bn.
34055 Pte. GLUCKSTEIN, I. C., 97th Bn.
74341 Pte. GOLDSTEIN, H., 108th Bn.
75152 Pte. GREENBAUM, L., 108th Bn.
61327 Pte. GRAFFINSKY, M., 85th Bn.
76168 Pte. GOLD, M., 111th Bn.
12923 Pte. GOLDSTON, J., 14th Bn.
76432 Pte. GOLDBERG, M., 112th Bn.
3202 Pte. GOLDSTONE, I., 3/59th Bn.
39843 Pte. GREENBERG, A. A., 45th Bn.
25417 Pte. GOLDSTEIN, J., 45th Bn.
25157 Pte. GREENSTEIN, I., 45th Bn.
25160 Pte. GOLDMAN, S., 45th Bn.
108843 Pte. GREENBAUM, L., 87th Bn.
319988 Pte. GREEN, D., 111th Bn.
77328 Pte. GROSSE, J., 108th Bn.
128264 Pte. GARCIA, P., 102nd Bn.
74341 Pte. GOLDSTEIN, H., 108th Bn.
74239 Pte. GORDON, S., 109th Bn.
75536 Pte. GOWLER, M., 112th Bn.
46440 Pte. GATOFF, N., 8th Bn.
98832 Pte. GOLDSTEIN, S., 84th Bn.
9052 Pte. GOLDMAN, M., 18th Bn.
13195 L/Sgt. GOLDSMITH, V., 19th Bn.
36978 Pte. GREENFIELD, H., 10th Bn.
72237 Pte. GOLDRING, H., 107th Bn.
38977 Pte. GOLDBERG, D., 112th Bn.
25424 Pte. GOLDBERG, I., 69th Bn.
17144 Pte. GOLDSTEIN, S., 43rd Bn.
29225 Pte. GLICK, H., 46th Bn.
3/6217 Pte. GROSSMAN, H., 49th Bn.
10900 Pte. GATES, B., 27th Bn.
13/76551 Pte. GOLDING, J.
13/76595 Pte. GORDON, A. E.
62788 Pte. GAUTMAN, S., 107th Bn.
22215 Pte. GERSHBERG, A., 108th Bn.
21581 Pte. GORDON, A., 108th Bn.
70627 Pte. GREENSPAN, L., 109th Bn.
70723 Pte. GATES, A., 111th Bn.
44677 Pte. GOLDSTEIN, J., 100th Bn.
44667 Pte. GOLDBERG, R., 100th Bn.
45164 Pte. GREEN, J., 100th Bn.
10/48369 Pte. GREENHOLTZ, J., 101st Bn.
33308 Pte. GREENFIELD, S., 71st Bn.
25261 Pte. GOLDSTONE, A., 69th Bn.
28697 Pte. GOODMAN, M., 46th Bn.
74376 Pte. GOLDBURG, F., 112th Bn.
74575 Pte. GARFINKLE, A., 108th Bn.
73303 L/Cpl. GOLLAND, J.
26291 Pte. GERSHON, S., 78th Bn.
33861 Pte. GOLDENFELD, H., 47th Bn.
5811 Pte. GOLDBERG, J., 112th Bn.
74741 Pte. GOODMAN, S., 109th Bn.
75093 Pte. GOLD, S., 111th Bn.
75930 Pte. GOLDSTEIN, R., 110th Bn.
74613 Pte. GOLDBERG, S., 109th Bn.
58175 Pte. GOODMAN, M., 20th Bn.
57496 Pte. GEMBESKI, H., 20th Bn.
128321 Pte. GOLDSTEIN, N., 102nd Bn.
42436 Pte. GREEN, L. J., 99th Bn.
108480 Pte. GOLD, R., 96th Bn
75958 Pte. GREENBERG, J., 110th Bn.
74594 Pte. GREENBERG, I., 109th Bn.
29222 Pte. GOLDSTEIN, D., 46th Bn.
21840 Pte. GOLDMAN, S. D., 20th Bn.
28900 Rfm. GOLD, A., 18th Bn.

Training Reserve.—*Continued.*

8959 Pte. GOLDWATER, H. J., 3rd Bn.
12923 Pte. GOLDSTON, I., 14th Bn.
91412 Pte. GREENBAUM, I., 25th Bn.
45728 Pte. GUGGENHEIM, E., 100th Bn.
25791 Pte. GERSKOWITCH, J., 78th Bn.
17668 Pte. GOLDMAN, C., 5th Bn.
26617 Pte. GLASS, J., 78th Bn.
61327 Pte. GRAFF, M., 85th Bn.
35000 Pte. GERLINSKY, A., 71st Bn.
9489 Pte. GORDON, N., 13th Bn.
17511 Pte. GOLDBERG, 5th Bn.
5591 Pte. GOLDBERG, J., 6th Bn.
57422 L/Cpl. GOLDMAN, H. L., 103rd Bn.
25027 Pte. GOLDBERG, B., 78th Bn.
12966 Pte. GOLDMAN, E., 60th Bn.
5/29730 Pte. GREENFIELD, H., 8th Bn.
13419 Pte. GOLDMAN, M. C., 4th Bn.
33298 Pte. GOLDBERG, A., 6th Bn.
5/29367 Pte. GERSTEIN, H., 8th Bn.
14592 Pte. GOLDWIN, M.
14729 Pte. GALINSKY, A., 19th Bn.
26610 Pte. GREENFIELD, H., 7th Bn.
14727 Pte. GILBERT, J., 19th Bn.
14659 Pte. GOLENCKA, J., 19th Bn.
51831 Pte. GREENBERG, S., 18th Bn.
52263 Pte. GREENBLATT, H., 16th Bn.
39173 Pte. GULLEN, H., 46th Bn.
28898 Pte. GRIZZARD, S., 46th Bn.
21399 L/Cpl. GERSTEIN, S., 44th Bn.
23377 Pte. GOLDBERG, R. B., 6th Bn.
72569 Pte. GITTER, I., 109th Bn.
71082 Pte. GARRETT, I., 112th Bn.
29224 Pte. GORDON, J., 46th Bn.
90162 Pte. GLASS, J., 7th Bn.
Pte. GRETZHANDLER, 24th Bn.
33871 Pte. GOLDBERG, A., 47th Bn.
66993 Pte. GOLDMAN, H., 87th Bn.
29976 Pte. GOLDMAN, A., 46th Bn.
50352 Pte. GRIEW, H., 236th Bn.
42436 Pte. GREEN, L. J., 263rd Bn.
51095 Pte. GREEN, I., 20th Bn.
51093 Pte. GORDON, H., 250th Bn.
241504 Pte. GOLDBERG, J., 208th Bn.
242575 Pte. GOLDSTEIN, S., 208th Bn.
12195 L/Sgt. GOLDSMITH, V., 237th Bn.
22161 Pte. HOFFMAN, A., 44th Bn.
25538 Pte. HURLANDER, H., 45th Bn.
25550 Pte. HOFFMAN, B., 45th Bn.
27026 Pte. HYAMS, S., 45th Bn.
17703 Pte. HERSON, H., 14th Bn.
2113 Pte. HYMAN, L. E., 30th Bn.
5/26267 Pte. HARRIS, S., 7th Bn.
10/1444 Pte. HARTSTONE, N., 7th Bn.
569310 Pte. HYMAN, L., 87th Bn.
263549 L/Cpl. HAROWITZ, H., 1st Bn.
2267 Pte. HYMAN, M., 73rd Bn.
38084 Pte. HYMAN, D., 73rd Bn.
44168 Sgt. HILLISON, E., 74th Bn.
44774 Pte. HYMNA, L. M., 74th Bn.
45315 Pte. HALFORD, H., 74th Bn.
63010 Pte. HAVELITZ, J., 74th Bn.
53740 Pte. HARRIS, J., 76th Bn.
39722 Pte. HALPERIN, J., 76th Bn.
70114 Pte. HALPERN, S. P., 49th Bn.
9788 Pte. HARRISON, J., 50th Bn.
63010 Pte. HURWITZ, J., 50th Bn.
82540 Pte. HERMAN, B., 25th Bn.
70327 Pte. HURWITZ, N., 49th Bn.
34643 Pte. HIRSHOWITZ, E., 209th Bn.
75490 Pte. HAMBURG, B., 109th Bn.
39504 Pte. HARRIS, J., 98th Bn.
34643 Pte. HIRSCHOWITZ, F., 97th Bn.
38494 Pte. HIMELFARB, J., 98th Bn.
46170 Pte. HOFFMAN, H., 100th Bn.
42756 Pte. HYMAN, S., 99th Bn.
75547 Pte. HANDEL, H., 111th Bn.
76091 Pte. HANNU, M., 110th Bn.
35902 Pte. HYMAN, H., 9th Bn.
74225 Pte. HARRIS, P., 111th Bn.
29889 Pte. HARRIS, J., 70th Bn.
34858 Pte. HORWICK, J., 71st Bn.
6025 Pte. HALKERN, C.,* 57th Bn.
78022 Pte. HYMAN, D., 108th Bn.
45811 Pte. HART, L., 100th Bn.
39003 Pte. HILION, B., 98th Bn.
51592 Pte. HART, M., 16th Bn.
25622 Pte. HART, S., 45th Bn.
54803 Pte. HARRIS, E., 16th Bn.
109501 Pte. HILL, H. D., 97th Bn.
71632 Pte. HERTZ, S., 112th Bn.
38278 Pte. HALPERN, S., 66th Bn.
76181 Pte. HECKER, J., 112th Bn.
74336 Pte. HART, N., 109th Bn.
74366 Pte. HART, S., 109th Bn.
74455 Pte. HARRIS, D., 109th Bn.
74597 Pte. HARRIS, M., 109th Bn.
74722 Pte. HARRINGMAN, M., 109th Bn.
74728 Pte. HALPER, J., 109th Bn.
24855 Pte. HARRIS, J., 45th Bn.
14003 Pte. HARRIS, S., 19th Bn.
30494 Pte. HYMANS, A., 17th Bn.
26910 Pte. HALTER, H., 63rd Bn.
30470 Pte. HALSBAND, H., 17th Bn.
7133 Pte. HARRIS, M., 18th Bn.
5984 Pte. HARRIS, A., 53rd Bn.
82540 Pte. HERMAN, B.
322542 Bandsman HILDERSHEIMER, D., 30th Bn.
13480 Pte. HOFFMAN, S., 19th Bn.
13/17748 Cpl. HARRIS, H., 20th Bn.
17276 Pte. HYAMS, F., 5th Bn.
13/27053 Pte. HORNE, G. E.
18384 Pte. HONIGBAUM, L., 20th Bn.
2/685 Pte. HARRIS, A., 52nd Bn.
61109 Pte. HYMAN, G., 104th Bn.
10/64351 Pte. HYAMS, J., 105th Bn.

Training Reserve.—*Continued.*

29097 Pte. HERMAN, H., 70th Bn.
24832 Pte. HANOVER, J., 45th Bn.
24903 Pte. HYAMS, S., 45th Bn.
17292 Pte. HYAMS, M., 43rd Bn.
6625 Pte. HAL, W., 26th Bn.
53098 Pte. HARRIS, A., 106th Bn.
13/76554 Pte. HYMAN, D., 111th Bn.
13/76561 Pte. HABERFIELD, G.
76926 Pte. HORNSTEIN, L., 111th Bn.
75150 Pte. HARRIS, H., 108th Bn.
13082 Pte. HUNT, W., 60th Bn.
4626 Pte. HIRSCHMAN, S., 34th Bn.
25653 Pte. HERSCHAFT, W. M., 45th Bn.
63322 Pte. HARRIS, L., 97th Bn.
75150 Pte. HARRIS, P., 108th Bn.
74154 Pte. HYMAN, A., 25th Bn.
5954 Pte. HIGGS, W. I., 63rd Bn.
74326 Pte. HARRIS, H., 110th Bn.
14594 Pte. HERSHMAN, P. J., 14th Bn.
54629 Pte. HARRIS, I., 16th Bn.
51227 Pte. HONIGMAN, A., 19th Bn.
53931 Pte. HARRISON, A., 17th Bn.
57836 Pte. HITNER, H., 103rd Bn.
685 Pte. HARRIS, A., 52nd Bn.
26616 Pte. HOROWITZ, S., 55th Bn.
9551 Pte. HARRIS, B., 59th Bn.
36304 Cpl. HARRIS, S., 66th Bn.
33183 Pte. HOFFMAN, L., 9th Bn.
851 Pte. HAINES, W., 52nd Bn.
21113 Pte. HYMAN, L. E., 30th Bn.
50037 Pte. HARRIS, D., 19th Bn.
50104 Pte. HYMAN, H., 19th Bn
14852 Pte. HYAMS, I., 19th Bn.
51592 Pte. HART, M., 18th Bn.
51998 Pte. HARRIS, S., 18th Bn.
13885 Pte. HALPERTS, S., 19th Bn.
30449 Pte. HARDLEY, M. B., 40th Bn.
70841 Pte. HELPER, A.
73945 Pte. HYAMS, I.
2683 Pte. HECHTKOSKY, L., 77th Bn.
57944 Pte. HEMP, J.
Pte. HECKER, J., 111th Bn.
50820 Pte. HARRIS, J., 250th Bn.
L/Cpl. HUGO, L., 287th Bn.
9551 Pte. HARRIS, B., 234th Bn.
241380 Pte. HYAMS, L. A., 208th Bn.
Pte. HICKMAN, L., 6th Bn.
Pte. HARRISON, D., 6th Bn.
711 Pte. ISAACS, M., 92nd Bn.
16364 L/Cpl. ISAACS, J., 15th Bn.
41295 Pte. ISAACS, J. 73rd Bn.
7278 Pte. ISENBERG, E., 49th Bn.
35401 Pte. ISADORE, T., 209th Bn.
16364 Cpl. ISAACS, J., 267th Bn.
98825 Pte. ISAACS, J., 4th Bn.
13/1984 Pte. ISAACS, S. E., 16th Bn.
70506 Pte. ISAACS, B. P., 109th Bn.
74061 Pte. ISAACS, A., 112th Bn.
2149 Pte. ISAACS, H.
39797 Pte. ISAACS, M., 98th Bn.
55093 Pte. ISADORE, B., 102nd Bn.
46686 Pte. ISAACS, H. A., 100th Bn.
74419 Pte. ISAACS, M., 111th Bn.
56500 Pte. ISAACS, G., 20th Bn.
56337 Pte. ILIAN, H., 20th Bn.
6635 Pte. ISENBERG, L., 49th Bn.
21372 Pte. ISAACS, C., 108th Bn.
74419 Pte. ISAACS, C., 112th Bn.
50227 Pte. ISRAEL, S., 19th Bn.
72047 Sgt. ISAACS, A., 107th Bn.
72891 Pte. ISRAEL, J., 88th Bn.
29394 Pte. ISAACS, M., 8th Bn.
28799 Pte. ISAACS, E. E., 46th Bn.
242010 Pte. ISAACS, J., 208th Bn.
50227 Pte. ISAACS, S., 237th Bn.
7/80 Sgt. JOSEPH, H., 92nd Bn.
569092 Pte. JACKSON, M., 87th Bn.
5/68091 Pte. JACKSON, S., 87th Bn.
Pte. JOSEPH, H., 111th Bn.
76711 Pte. JOSEPH, G., 89th Bn.
76712 Pte. JOSEPH, J., 89th Bn.u
57281 Pte. JACOBSON, S., 16th Bn.
77390 Pte. JACOBS, R. E.
40640 L/Cpl. JOSEPH, J., 73rd Bn.
51224 Pte. JACOBS, F., 75tho Bn.
52318 Pte. JACOBS, F., 76th Bn.
54066 Pte. JACOBS, A., 76th Bn.
3681 Pte. JACOBS, E., 48th Bn.
552006 Pte. JAY, P. S., 50th Bn.
129749 Pte. JOSEPH, E., 86th Bn.
723616 Pte. JENKNS, M., 49th Bn.
34541 Pte. JACOBSON, N., 209th Bn.
86963 Pte. JACOBS, W., 270th Bn.
574499 Pte. JONAS, 274th Bn.
1987 Pte. JACOBS, F., 16th Bn.
8444 L/Cpl. JACOBS, A. A., 14th Bn.
13/17583 Pte. JANETSKY, H., 20th Bn.
12433 Pte. JOSEPH, L., 36th Bn.
225 Sgt. JONAS, B., 9th Bn.
44673 Pte. JACOBS, C., 100th Bn.
TR6/282 Pte. JACOBS, M., 11th Bn.
22380 Pte. JAY, J. J., 30th Bn.
52708 Pte. JACOB, D., 102nd Bn.
128532 Pte. JACOBS, J., 102nd Bn.
339692 Pte. JACQUES, J., 88th Bn.
74074 L/Cpl. JACOBS, D., 112th Bn.
7637 Pte. JOHANNESBERG, A., 12th Bn.
7172 Pte. JOSEPH, A.
52807 Pte. JACOBS, D., 102nd Bn.
24541 Pte. JACOBSON, M., 97th Bn.
25244 Pte. JOEL, I., 97th Bn.
74781 Pte. JACOBS, I., 111th Bn.
22827 Pte. JACOBS, A., 62nd Bn.
74658 Pte. JACOBS, J., 111th Bn.

Training Reserve.—*Continued.*

19798 Pte. JACKSON, S., 5th Bn.
1353 Pte. JACOBS, S., 66th Bn.
7185 Pte. JACOBS, W., 12th Bn.
29009 L/Cpl. JACOBSON, H., 32nd Bn.
64980 Pte. JACOBS, H., 105th Bn.
12624 Pte. JACOBS, D., 60th Bn.
51844 Pte. JACOBS, J., 18th Bn.
24955 Pte. JESSEL, H., 45th Bn.
23376 Pte. JOSEPH, M., 6th Bn.
21098 Pte. JACOBS, I., 44th Bn.
8189 Cpl. JENKINS, S., 59th Bn.
28703 Pte. JOSEPH, J., 46th Bn.
29405 Pte. JOSEPHSON, L., 8th Bn.
     Pte. JACOBS, F. W., 20th Bn.
282 Pte. JACOBS, M., 11th Bn.
85901 Pte. JACOBS, W., 270th Bn.
44673 Pte. JACOBS, G., 356th Bn.
26241 Pte. KOENIGSBERG, A., 45th Bn.
29328 Pte. KENT, C. G., 46th Bn.
26261 Pte. KOSNER, M., 45th Bn.
25589 Pte. KAPLAN, J., 45th Bn.
16397 Pte. KING, H. M., 15th Bn.
13/35144 Pte. KIRSTEIN, H., 111th Bn.
13/35145 Pte. KIRSCH, H., 111th Bn.
25171 Pte. KARCREK, M., 4th Bn.
     Pte. KOCHINSKY, S., 40th Bn.
12890 Pte. KASENBAUM, H., 36th Bn.
8711 L/Sgt. KONTILI, H., 27th Bn.
1973 Pte. KLETZ, B., 73rd Bn.
52678 Pte. KARASELCHIK, 76th Bn.
46776 Pte. KAVARSKY, J., 48th Bn.
70000 Pte. KROLOSKY, D., 49th Bn.
3/12399 C.Q.M.S. KAUFMAN, R., 51st Bn.
536389 Pte. KERSLAU, L., 25th Bn.
71047 Pte. KOSLOFF, G., 49th Bn.
34107 Pte. KROLL, D., 209th Bn.
14040 Pte. KUTCHINSKY, A., 19th Bn.
81535 Pte. KROHN, R. J., 90th Bn.
13/937 Pte. KLEIN, L., 16th Bn.
73009 Pte. KERR, M., 107th Bn.
68861 Pte. KONOPOLA, S., 106th Bn.
77004 Pte. KRIETZMAN, M., 111th Bn.
76988 Pte. KAFFEN, S., 111th Bn.
77128 Pte. KRAFCHICK, S., 111th Bn.
77139 Pte. KNIGHTS, A., 111th Bn.
20877 Pte. KAPFEROTH, H., 44th Bn.
57836 Pte. KITNER, H., 103rd Bn.
12689 Pte. KREMER, I., 60th Bn.
70724 Pte. KOSSOFF, H., 111th Bn.
21825 Pte. KEYZOR, H. S. A., 108th Bn.
74958 Pte. KALMOVITZ, I., 110th Bn.
73122 Pte. KOSKY, H., 110th Bn.
74048 Pte. KIMMELBERG, M., 111th Bn.
56536 Pte. KLEIN, I., 20th Bn.
26261 Pte. KOSNER, M., 45th Bn.
38499 Pte. KASHERBAUM, L., 98th Bn.
49745 Pte. KARSTADT, D., 101st Bn.

39376 Pte. KAFTON, I., 98th Bn.
42382 Pte. KRIEGER, J., 99th Bn.
46144 Pte. KELLER, J., 100th Bn.
34107 Pte. KROLL, D., 97th Bn.
75506 Pte. KLEIN, B., 109th Bn.
17434 Pte. KAPUSTISKY, L., 67th Bn.
8586 L/Cpl. KOHEN, A., 26th Bn.
29789 Pte. KREPPS, S., 46th Bn.
77131 Pte. KARBRITZ, L., 109th Bn.
75553 Pte. KLEIN, I., 111th Bn.
76342 Pte. KROSKAFSKY, S., 112th Bn.
4278 Pte. KAY, J., 99th Bn.
59428 Pte. KANGDON, S., 72nd Bn.
77263 Pte. KRASNY, C., 138th Bn.
25538 Pte. KURLANDER, H., 45th Bn.
108796 Pte. KADISHEARTY, R., 97th Bn.
108984 Pte. KRISMAN, N., 97th Bn.
109619 Pte. KIRSCH, A., 97th Bn.
76986 Pte. KAFFIN, L., 111th Bn.
109060 Pte. KOSKY, J., 97th Bn.
75073 Pte. KERSTEIN, J., 112th Bn.
34304 Pte. KAHN, E., 47th Bn.
29789 Pte. KIRPS, S., 46th Bn.
33681 Pte. KLINE, I., 9th Bn.
33183 Pte. KOFFMAN, L., 9th Bn.
30435 Pte. KAVARSKY, G., 64th Bn.
30187 Pte. KREISBERG, L., 32nd Bn.
91398 Pte. KATZ, S., 25th Bn.
91319 Pte. KORMORNICK, M., 25th Bn.
74148 Pte. KESLER, H., 107th Bn.
71049 Pte. KROTOSKY, R., 87th Bn.
45738 Pte. KRISKY, S., 100th Bn.
72564 L/Cpl. KAUER, I.
13971 Pte. KAPLAN, L., 55th Bn.
12890 Pte. KASHENBAUM, H., 36th Bn.
64976 Pte. KIEGER, H., 105th Bn.
39273 Pte. KATZ, I., 112th Bn.
51230 Pte. KATZ, A., 18th Bn.
29478 Pte. KRACKER, E., 64th Bn.
     Pte. KILMAN, I., 53rd Bn.
8170 Pte. KITOFSKY, S., 101st Bn.
38716 Pte. KLEPS, L., 112th Bn.
13/30 Pte. KRATCHINSKY, A.
42382 Pte. KREEGER, L., 253rd Bn.
50374 Pte. KROVITZ, J., 237th Bn.
33021 Pte. KOPPLEMAN, J., 208th Bn.
49745 Pte. KARSTADT, D., 208th Bn.
25873 Pte. LEVY, A., 45th Bn.
26183 Pte. LACKMAKER, D., 45th Bn.
163 Pte. LEVENE, I., 92nd Bn.
17170 Pte. LANG P., 15th Bn.
16414 Pte. LUSTGARTEN, M., 15th Bn
5/69124 Pte. LEADER, M., 87th Bn.
76413 Pte. LEWIS, 89th Bn.
26179 Pte. LELOFSKY, A., 45th Bn.
5/127488 Pte. LEVINE, J.
38164 Pte. LANDSMAN, D., 73rd Bn.
38760 Pte. LIVINGSTONE, F., 73rd Bn.

Training Reserve.—*Continued.*

44423 Pte. LEWIS, H., 74th Bn.
45320 Pte. LOOKER, J. R., 74th Bn.
46102 Pte. LEWIS, E. G., 48th Bn.
26238 Pte. LIPSHITZ, B., 48th Bn.
5429 Pte. LANDEY, I., 49th Bn.
3/7580 Pte. LEWIS, F., 49th Bn.
70221 Pte. LANDE, J. H., 49th Bn.
9636 Pte. LIPMAN, S., 50th Bn.
70688 Pte. LANGER, D., 49th Bn.
3/72853 Pte. LEVY, A., 49th Bn.
3/73100 Pte. LAZARUS, J. M., 49th Bn.
3/73154 Pte. LISTINSKI, B., 49th Bn.
34375 Pte. LUATENBERG, H. J., 209th Bn.
34458 Pte. LEVY, J., 209th Bn.
86431 Pte. LINSKY, L., 270th Bn.
46238 Pte. LIPSCHITZ, B., 48th Bn.
75383 Pte. LEVISON, M., 108th Bn.
75479 Pte. LEVY, A. S., 109th Bn.
75929 Pte. LEVY, I., 110th Bn.
30122 Pte. LEARER, S., 46th Bn.
73778 Pte. LEVY, M., 112th Bn.
77383 Pte. LAZARUS, B.
35391 Pte. LACKMAKER, G., 47th Bn.
24360 Pte. LEVY, J., 57th Bn.
25871 Pte. LANGEN, M., 45th Bn.
109142 Pte. LETTMAN, M., 97th Bn.
73312 L/Cpl. LAZARUS, M. D., 112th Bn.
74392 Pte. LEVY, A., 108th Bn.
77775 Pte. LEVI.
56401 Pte. LIPMAN, F., 20th Bn.
57665 Pte. LEVY, I., 20th Bn.
53561 Pte. LEWIS, N., 102nd Bn.
13067 Pte. LAZARUS, E., 24th Bn.
4189 Pte. LYONS, L., 58th Bn.
1310 Pte. LEWIS, J., 52nd Bn.
36679 Pte. LEVENE, J., 78th Bn.
74313 L/Cpl. LEVY, L., 54th Bn.
26384 Pte. LAZARUS, L., 69th Bn.
34360 Pte. LEWIS, P., 71st Bn.
7796 Pte. LEVENSON, W., 22nd Bn.
34755 Pte. LEVY, E., 71st Bn.
71578 Pte. LEVY, S. C., 110th Bn.
903 Pte. LYONS, J., 57th Bn.
4247 Cpl. LUDZKEE, A., 58th Bn.
36007 Pte. LYONS, H., 10th Bn.
14404 Pte. LEVINE, N. S., 4th Bn.
71612 Pte. LAWBITZ, I., 110th Bn.
44625 Pte. LIPMAN, J., 81st Bn.
108886 Pte. LEVY, D., 97th Bn.
10286 Pte. LEVINE, S., 18th Bn.
10288 Pte. LIVINGSTONE, E., 18th Bn.
14369 Pte. LEVY, E., 19th Bn.
14397 Pte. LAVETSKY, H., 19th Bn.
14370 Pte. LEVY, J., 19th Bn.
17298 Pte. LEVY, M., 5th Bn.
12074 Pte. LESSAR, M., 14th Bn.
81542 Pte. LECHEM, L., 90th Bn.

81432 Pte. LEWIS, H. P., 90th Bn.
81538 Pte. LEVINSON, A. D., 90th Bn.
E7681 Pte. LYONS, A., 20th Bn.
32589 Pte. LEVY, S., 71st Bn.
32443 Pte. LEVY, M., 64th Bn.
33749 Dvr. LEWIS, H., 43rd Bn.
38796 Pte. LAURENCE, M., 72nd Bn.
52273 Pte. LYONS, B., 102nd Bn.
76794 Pte. LAZARUS, L., 111th Bn.
21502 Pte. LAZARUS, I., 111th Bn.
10025 Pte. LAZARUS, J., 3rd Bn.
5037 L/Cpl. LEHMAN, H., 22nd Bn.
39393 Pte. LEVY, L., 26th Bn.
70695 Pte. LION, W. M., 111th Bn.
53141 Pte. LEVERSON, S., 102nd Bn.
24794 Pte. LIVINGSTONE, M., 68th Bn.
33430 Pte. LEZECOVITCH, P., 71st Bn.
22653 Pte. LYLE, C., 6th Bn.
37756 Pte. LEVITT, J., 10th Bn.
50741 Pte. LASKER, L. J., 75th Bn.
6078 Pte. LEVINE, B., 53rd Bn.
65956 Pte. LYONS, H., 105th Bn.
32999 Pte. LASSMAN, A., 46th Bn.
8120 Pte. LEVY, J., 59th Bn.
74400 Pte. LEVY, H., 112th Bn.
108848 Pte. LASSMAN, B., 97th Bn.
73441 Pte. LILLIMAN, S., 112th Bn.
74684 Pte. LAZARUS, S., 108th Bn.
73847 Pte. LEWIS, J., 112th Bn.
72611 L/Cpl. LEVY, C., 112th Bn.
74051 Pte. LANDSMAN, H., 110th Bn.
74959 Pte. LAMKIN, R., 110th Bn.
75834 Pte. LEWIS, B., 110th Bn.
71413 Pte. LANDAU, D., 111th Bn.
57097 Pte. LEROCHINSKI, J., 20th Bn.
53561 Pte. LEWIS, M., 102nd Bn.
34562 Pte. LEVY, L., 85th Bn.
38501 Pte. LEVY, L., 98th Bn.
26211 Pte. LACHINSKY, S., 45th Bn.
26148 Pte. LEAFSCHITZ, I., 45th Bn.
76172 Pte. LEWIS, H., 112th Bn.
49487 Pte. LAURENCE, H., 101st Bn.
34375 Pte. LAWTON, H., 97th Bn.
38592 Pte. LEVY, H., 98th Bn.
39799 Pte. LEVY, W., 98th Bn.
49747 Pte. LIPMAN, H., 101st Bn.
42658 Pte. LUBINSKY, A., 99th Bn.
76301 Pte. LAZARUS, J., 110th Bn.
3204 Pte. LOBINSKY, N., 57th Bn.
25607 Pte. LEVY, S., 45th Bn.
29923 Pte. LEVY, M., 46th Bn.
76449 Pte. LYONS, H., 112th Bn.
15140 Pte. LEVY, S., 14th Bn.
39474 Pte. LUSTGARTEN, L., 66th Bn.
78278 Pte. LAMPERT, D., 108th Bn.
77884 Pte. LEWIS, M.
78180 Pte. LEVISON, S.
56292 Pte. LEWIS, H., 20th Bn.

Training Reserve.—*Continued.*

42264 Pte. LEIF, B., 99th Bn.
71613 Pte. LEVY, J., 110th Bn.
24433 Pte. LURIE, J., 78th Bn.
52754 Pte. LEVY, L., 76th Bn.
31084 Pte. LEVY, J., 110th Bn.
39275 Pte. LAPSEIN, J. H., 112th Bn.
13439 Pte. LAZARUS, J., 2nd Bn.
56301 Pte. LEVY, A., 19th Bn.
14893 Pte. LEVY, A. L.
51325 Pte. LANGLABEN, M., 18th Bn.
33911 Pte. LEVY, M., 47th Bn.
14241 Pte. LETSKY, M., 4th Bn.
6413 Pte. LEVY, N., 2nd Bn.
51706 Pte. LEMBERGER, J., 18th Bn.
51854 Pte. LEVINE, L., 20th Bn.
6280 Pte. LANCH, M., 2nd Bn.
21100 Pte. LEVINE, I. S., 44th Bn.
70695 Pte. LION, W. M., 111th Bn.
109356 Pte. LEWIS, S.
75082 Pte. LISSACK, M., 111th Bn.
10103 Pte. LAZARUS, A., 110th Bn.
76340 Pte. LYONS, L., 112th Bn.
29654 Pte. LIST, S., 46th Bn.
17229 Pte. LEVY, L., 5th Bn.
88215 Pte. LEVINE, S., 6th Bn.
17742 Pte. LISTER, E., 43rd Bn.
77356 Pte. LORD, F., 26th Bn.
        Pte. LASSMAN, M., 24th Bn.
17726 Pte. LESSER, J., 83rd Bn.
72895 Pte. LEWIS, H., 111th Bn.
50381 Pte. LEVY, A., 237th Bn.
241636 L/Cpl. LUBEL, J., 208th Bn.
242338 Pte. LUSTIG, N., 208th Bn.
243091 Pte. LEBROVITCH, N., 208th Bn.
36503 Pte. LONG, P., 274th Bn.
87250 Pte. LABOFSKY, P., 270th Bn.
37758 Pte. LIPMAN, S., 261st Bn.
51325 Pte. LANGLEBEN, M., 237th Bn.
50402 Pte. LEVINE, M., 237th Bn.
14736 Pte. LEVY, T., 237th Bn.
51117 Pte. LEVY, S., 250th Bn.
241847 Pte. LANDO, B., 208th Bn.
28661 Pte. LANE, H., 208th Bn.
29515 Pte MIDGEN, J., 56th Bn.
25999 Pte. MORRIS, D. E., 45th Bn.
17175 Pte. MILBERG, J., 15th Bn.
34919 Cpl. MAGNUS, M., 111th Bn. atd 8th R.B
41237 Pte. MARKS, J., 73rd Bn.
2214 Pte. MARSHALL, M., 76th Bn.
39912 Pte. MARKS, L., 48th Bn.
9376 Pte. MENDELSON, R., 48th Bn.
9481 Pte. MOSES, M. R., 48th Bn.
8648 Pte. MARKS, H. R., 49th Bn.
6948 Pte. MARCUS, J., 49th Bn.
59086 Pte. MELZER, S., 49th Bn.
3/8648 Pte. MARK, H., 50th Bn.
9113 Pte. MARIENBERG, A. G., 50th Bn.

9481 Pte. MOSES, R., 50th Bn.
170147 Pte. MENDOZA, I., 25th Bn.
509278 Pte. MANNELL, S., 115th Bn.
185180 Pte. MARKS, I., 115th Bn.
70990 Pte. MICHAELSON, J., 49th Bn.
70966 Pte. MARKS, E., 49th Bn.
71100 Pte. MISIERIEZSKY, B., 49th Bn.
3/72729 Pte. MODLENSKI, H., 49th Bn.
3/72828 Pte. MILLER, H., 49th Bn.
3/72746 Pte. MARKS, I., 49th Bn.
3/73265 Pte. MORRIS, J., 49th Bn.
100002 Pte. MAURICE, L., 31st Bn.
34125 Pte. MIRANDA, D., 209th Bn.
35416 Pte. MILLER, M., 209th Bn.
35594 Pte. MULLER, C., 209th Bn.
33279 Pte. MALOFSKI, L., 209th Bn.
202619 Pte. MOSSESSION, 274th Bn.
107382 Pte. MICKLER, S., 242nd Bn.
132318 Pte. MENDELSOHN, A., 45th Bn.
13/1998 Pte. MILLER, L. A., 16th Bn.
13349 Cpl. MORRIS, E., 19th Bn.
13/17748 Pte. MENDLESON, J., 20th Bn.
17759 L/Cpl. MORRIS, M., 20th Bn.
9/32024 C.Q.M.S. MARKS, R., 47th Bn.
17595 Pte. MEARS, M., 35th Bn.
13/9437 Pte. MARGOLLIS, A., 18th Bn.
24905 Pte. MORRIS, H., 45th Bn.
17278 Pte. MEASURES, L., 43rd Bn.
76569 Pte. MEELOO, M., 111th Bn.
76661 Pte. MILAKSKY, H., 111th Bn.
77002 Pte. MOROVITCH, J., 111th Bn.
69938 Pte. MALAMED, I., 106th Bn.
44071 Pte. MANSFIELD, J., 100th Bn.
20255 Pte. MYERS, B., 68th Bn.
61360 Pte. MARKOVITCH, L., 85th Bn.
21896 Pte. MALNICK, C., 30th Bn.
74070 Pte. MOSS, B., 112th Bn.
112060 Pte. MAGNUS, H., 98th Bn.
14041 Pte. MARGOLYES, J., 55th Bn.
74771 L/Cpl. MENDESS, H., 102nd Bn.
7615 Pte. MANDLESON, S. C., 12th Bn.
3020 Pte. MICHELON, M., 13th Bn.
35760 Pte. MORRIS, G., 9th Bn.
75031 Pte. MONTSOFF, H., 110th Bn.
84991 Pte. MOORE, S., 91st Bn.
25147 Pte. MYERS, H., 69th Bn.
45747 L/Cpl. MYEROVITZ, I., 100th Bn.
340969 Pte. MYERS, B., 111th Bn.
46363 Pte. MAGNUS, 100th Bn.
38430 Pte. MAISEL, C., 98th Bn.
55658 Pte. MARGOLIS, S., 102nd Bn.
50544 Pte. MICHAELSON, J., 110th Bn.
49855 Pte. MOSOE, S., 101st Bn.
4595 Pte. MICHER, J., 100th Bn.
42730 Pte. MOSES, L., 99th Bn.
38716 Pte. MOSCOVSKY, H., 98th Bn.
39801 Pte. MORRIS, M., 98th Bn.
75532 Pte. MASSOBY, W. I., 111th Bn.

Training Reserve.—*Continued.*

75011	Pte. MARKILL, A., 110th Bn.
56539	Pte. MENDOZA, J., 20th Bn.
76256	Pte. MENDELSOHN, H., 110th Bn.
62232	Pte. MICHAEL, H., 85th Bn.
62560	Pte. MORRIS, J., 104th Bn.
75145	Pte. MARKS, L., 108th Bn.
48950	Pte. MOSES, I., 75th Bn.
73402	Pte. MOSCOVITCH, A., 88th Bn.
25916	Pte MORGENSTEIN, B., 45th Bn.
93068	Pte. MYERS, J., 8th Bn.
50807	Pte. MYERS, A., 16th Bn.
74076	Pte. MISHELOVE, J., 112th Bn.
73914	Pte. MORRIS, J., 108th Bn.
108851	Pte. MERENBERG, H., 97th Bn.
74587	Pte. MARKS, J., 109h Bn.
49702	Pe. MARKS, I., 12th Bn.
18877	Pte. MICHAELSON, D., 2nd Bn.
88584	Pte. MICKLER, S., 6th Bn.
54733	Pte. MILOFSKY, L., 102nd Bn.
50399	Pte. MOSS, J. S., 19th Bn.
91343	Pte. MINEVSKY, A., 25th Bn.
29516	Pte. MARKS, M., 71st Bn.
91240	Pte. MARKINSON, H., 7th Bn.
3523	Pte. MENDELSON, E., 57th Bn.
58971	Pte. MARKS, L., 64th Bn.
9127	Pte. MORRIS, L., 59th Bn.
	Pte. MOSS, C., 64th Bn.
53408	Pte. MARTIN, D., 102nd Bn.
74718	Pte. MARKS, F., 19th Bn.
57610	L/Cpl. MERCH, M., 103rd Bn.
12232	Pte. MUSCOVITCH, S., 60th Bn.
29332	Pte. MYERS, J., 46th Bn.
17204	Pte. MARKS, M., 43rd Bn.
5941	Pte. MARKS, J., 2nd Bn.
57604	Pte. MICHAELS, L., 20th Bn.
30610	Pte. MARKINSON, H., 8th Bn.
33760	Pte. MILLER, A., 43rd Bn.
52186	Pte. MAPPEN, S., 18th Bn.
65023	Pte. MORRIS, S., 105th Bn.
	Pte. MARKOVITCH, M., 24th Bn.
5961	Pte. MARKS, J., 2nd Bn.
22773	Pte. MORRIS, S.
72913	Pte. MORRIS, J., 108th Bn.
68415	Pte. MICKLOPKE, J., 109th Bn.
14030	Pte. MARRIS, P., 203rd Bn.
9113	Pte. MARIENBERG, G., 225th Bn.
14824	Pte. MARKS, H., 245th Bn.
2463	Pte. MORRIS, H., 206th Bn.
9127	Pte. MORRIS, L., 214th Bn.
14738	Pte. MIDDLEMAN, H., 237th Bn.
13349	L/Sgt. MORRIS, E., 237th Bn.
14/22401	Pte. NEEDLER, M., 7th Bn.
5/69130	Pte. NATHAN, N., 87th Bn.
76151	L/Cpl. NATHAN, M., 89th Bn.
72303	Pte. NAFTALIN, H. M., 109th Bn.
127515	Pte. NEWMAN, B.
13786	Pte. NOAH, H., 73rd Bn.
46987	Pte. NEWMAN, H., 74th Bn.
6846	Pte. NEWMAN, L., 49th Bn.
71346	Pte. NABUM, H. V., 49th Bn.
10322	Pte. NAMEN, M., 18th Bn.
10324	Pte. NEWMAN, S., 18th Bn.
10325	Pte. NATHAN, M. L., 18th Bn.
24898	Pte. NELSON, B., 45th Bn.
24906	Pte. NACOWITZ, J., 45th Bn.
4391	Pte. NOBLE, S., 26th Bn.
37677	Pte. NATHAN, A., 28th Bn.
	Pte. NOVERGROTSKI, E., 4th Bn.
21604	Pte. NAGUS, S., 68th Bn.
22518	L/Cpl. NEWFIELD, H., 108th Bn.
74326	Pte. NATHANSON, M., 110th Bn.
5832	Pte. NIEMAN, L., 49th Bn.
77477	Pte. NATHAN, A., 111th Bn.
35438	Pte. NATHAN, W., 47th Bn.
55373	Pte. NATHAN, H., 102nd Bn.
4279	Pte. NATELSKI, A., 99th Bn.
56530	Pte. NYBERG, M., 20th Bn.
120240	L/Cpl. NATHAN, W., 8th Bn.
305846	Rfm. NATHAN, J., 100th Bn.
12815	Pte. NAGELKOP, L.
29955	Pte. NEIMAN, E., 18th Bn.
91303	Pte. NODBOLSKY, H., 25th Bn.
13111	Pte. NEWMAN, H., 60th Bn.
71751	Pte. NIEBERG, I., 109th Bn.
28900	Pte. NELSON, R., 46th Bn.
28552	Pte. NEWMAN, S., 60th Bn.
22106	Pte. NIMAN, J., 68th Bn.
50956	Pte. NATHAN, H., 253rd Bn.
17510	L/Cpl. NATHAN, J. Z., 258th Bn.
7099	Pte. OLANDSKI, I., 49th Bn.
76593	Pte. OSTILENSKY, P., 111th Bn.
291041	Pte. OSNOWITZ, I., 6th Bn.
12995	Pte. ORGEL, S., 19th Bn.
17132	Pte. OLINSKI, A., 58th Bn.
53498	Pte. OBERSTEIN, A., 18th Bn.
26220	Pte. PALACHE, A., 45th Bn.
21099	Pte. PHILLIPS, D., 44th Bn.
12510	Pte. PELLMAN, W., 95th Bn.
76722	Pte. PHILLIPS, J. S., 89th Bn.
76496	Pte. PHILLIPS, L., 89th Bn.
	Pte. PALLEY, B., 4th Bn.
40660	Pte. PALENBAUM, J. L., 73r Bn.
38600	Pte. POLSHNASKY, F., 73rd Bn.
45006	Pte. PEVAIVSKI, A., 74th Bn.
46104	Pte. PHILLIPS, M., 74th Bn.
49809	Pte. PODGER, .W, 75th Bn.
46104	Pte. PHILLIPS, H. M., 48th Bn.
5909	Pte. POLLICK, I., 49th Bn.
7581	Pte. PISTKER, B., 39th Bn.
7654	Pte. PRESSMAN, I., 49th Bn.
70197	Pte. PHILLIPS, D., 49th Bn.
3/49809	Pte. PODGER, W., 51st Bn.
24947	Pte. PHILLIPS, B., 85th Bn.
35438	Pte. PROSNER, E., 209th Bn.

Training Reserve.—Continued.

13060 Cpl. PINKOFSKY, M., 19th Bn.
17892 Pte. PARKUS, A., 20th Bn.
　　　 Pte. PEARCE, J., 110th Bn.
38378 Pte. PINTO, H., 98th Bn.
13/54300 Pte. PLASKOW, S., 16th Bn.
72049 Pte. PLARTUS, N., 88th Bn.
　262 L/Cpl. POSOLOSKY, S., 57th Bn.
25872 Pte. POLISTOFSKY, I., 26th Bn.
21410 Pte. PASSES, A., 108th Bn.
22151 Pte. PEARSON, M., 108th Bn.
57149 Pte. PEARSE, S., 16th Bn.
74153 Pte. PHILLIPS, B., 112th Bn.
42645 Pte. PRINCE, F., 99th Bn.
9776 Pte. PATTIE, H. J., 54th Bn.
75349 Pte. PINKUS, S., 111th Bn.
76222 Pte. PRESS, L., 69th Bn.
18273 Pte. PEARLMAN, S., 5th Bn.
14730 Pte. PERES, H., 14th Bn.
53148 Pte. PORTNER, J., 18th Bn.
38747 Pte. PRICE, N., 48th Bn.
42645 Pte. PRINCE, T., 99th Bn.
55106 Pte. POSENER, S., 102nd Bn.
76852 Pte. POLLACK, J., 111th Bn.
91525 Pte. PRESSMAN, D., 7th Bn.
7825 Pte. PLOTZKIN, I., 49th Bn.
128656 Pte. PEREZ, L., 102nd Bn.
15586 Sgt. PEARCE, H., 111th Bn.
70513 Pte. PLOSKY, I., 109th Bn.
52148 Pte. PORMER, J. M., 18th Bn.
29853 Pte. PERSSECRE, A. H., 46th Bn.
74085 Pte. PUTSMAN, H.
20884 Pte. PERILLY, 30th Bn.
29189 Pte. PAGE, T. G., 5th Bn.
91402 Pte. PASSMAN, A., 25th Bn.
80545 Pte. PETERMAN, M., 25th Bn.
108751 Pte. POSENER, M., 97th Bn.
13730 Pte. PELIKANSKY, J., 55th Bn.
38031 Pte. PHILLIPS, E., 66th Bn.
64971 Pte. PHILLIPS, S., 105th Bn.
33868 Pte PRESS, M., 44th Bn.
76173 Pte. PRICE, N., 111th Bn.
　　　 Pte. PROOPS, H., 30th Bn.
26908 Pte. PUSHKIN, L., 109th Bn.
25849 Pte. PRAGUE, P., 45th Bn.
41767 Pte. PAMPEL, H., 59th Bn.
9621 Pte. PENER, M., 18th Bn.
26181 Pte. ROSENBERG, J. A., 45th Bn.
16/127 Pte. RICHMAN, M., 86th Bn.
4/26225 Pte. ROSENBURG, A., 12th Bn.
40181 Pte. ROBINSON, J., 73rd Bn.
42257 Pte. ROSSFIELD, S., 73rd Bn.
44753 Pte. ROSENTHAL, L., 74th Bn.
45595 Pte. ROSENBERG, A., 75th Bn.
44753 Pte. ROSENTHAL, S., 76th Bn.
1925 Pte. ROSENTHAL, S. H., 48th Bn.
7165 Pte. RICHMAN, T., 49th Bn.
7377 Pte. RICKLESS, I., 49th Bn.
9798 Pte. ROCKETER, A., 50th Bn.
62265 Pte. ROBINSON, H., 50th Bn.
62299 Pte. ROSENBLOOM, J. V., 50th Bn.
M/403736 Pte. ROSEN, H., 25th Bn.
71180 Pte. ROBINSON, A., 49th Bn.
107647 Pte. ROSENBLOOM, R., 242nd Bn.
11393 Pte. ROSENBERG, R.
10395 Pte. ROSENBURG, S., 18th Bn.
10397 Pte. ROOD, S., 18th Bn.
10410 Pte. ROCKING, F., 18th Bn.
81220 Pte. ROBENBLUM, A., 90th Bn.
9900 Pte. RIFSON, L., 15th Bn.
37031 Pte. RUDSTEIN, S., 10th Bn.
18/286 Cpl. RICHE, S., 6th Bn.
13/21766 L/Cpl. ROSENTHALL, H. H.
32625 Pte. ROSENFELDT, A., 68th Bn.
36161 Pte. ROSENTHALL, J., 10th Bn.
6/12568 L/Cpl. RECKLER, I. L., 14th Bn.
31365 L/Cpl. RASKY, D., 69th Bn.
54312 Pte. ROSE, W., 102nd Bn.
76594 Pte. RUBENSTEIN, J. N., 111th Bn.
76734 Pte. RABBINOVITCH, J., 111th Bn.
76925 Pte. ROSENBERG, M., 111th Bn.
52122 Pte. RICADO, H., 18th Bn.
34765 Pte. ROSENTHAL, S., 99th Bn.
2852 Pte. ROSENBLUM, H., 4th Bn.
1308 Pte. ROSENTHAL, S., 16th Bn.
74305 Pte. REUBENS, L., 112th Bn.
74565 Pte. REDLIRSH, G. L., 108th Bn.
80412 Pte. RABBINOWITZ, J., 19th Bn.
62461 Pte. ROSENBLOOM, N., 50th Bn.
35397 Pte. RUBINSTEIN, W., 47th Bn.
42542 Pte. RAPPAPORT, P., 99th Bn.
41911 Pte. ROSENBLOOM, H., 99th Bn.
39490 Pte. ROSELAAR, A., 98th Bn.
39892 Pte. ROBINSON, A. J., 98th Bn.
39922 L/Cpl. ROTTSTEIN, J., 98th Bn.
34764 Pte. ROSENBERG, J., 97th Bn.
54796 Pte. RUTER, 102nd Bn.
75658 Pte. ROSENTHAL, J., 111th Bn.
32625 Pte. ROSENFELD, A.
40514 Pte. RUDOFSKI, G., 9th Bn.
74617 Pte. ROSENSTEIN, L., 109th Bn.
203282 Pte. ROSENBERG, L.
39459 Pte. REUBENS, A., 98th Bn.
38993 Pte. ROSEN, I., 98th Bn.
39273 Pte. ROSENBERG, R., 98th Bn.
75789 Pte. ROTHSTEIN, M., 110th Bn.
15651 Pte. REEVES, J., 14th Bn.
13776 Pte. RIBEIRO, J., 24th Bn.
52033 Pte. RUBINSTEIN, B., 16th Bn.
22576 Pte. RUBINSTEIN, A., 44th Bn.
57299 Pte. ROSENBERG, S., 16th Bn.
58319 Pte. ROSEN, J., 20th Bn.
57776 Pte. ROSE, L., 16th Bn.
75927 Pte. ROSENTHAL, A., 110th Bn.
73955 Pte. ROGERS, S., 109th Bn.
75942 Pte. ROSENBLOOM, H., 110th Bn.

Training Reserve.—*Continued.*

- 15117 Pte. ROSENBERG, H., 19th Bn.
- 23853 Pte. RICHMAN, L., 6th Bn.
- 71261 Pte. ROOMS, N., 15th Bn.
- 71671 Pte. REEVES, I. J.
- 9214 L/Cpl. RAPATOFF, A., 54th Bn.
- 34683 Pte. RABINOVITZ, A., 71st Bn.
- 13127 Pte. ROSENBLATT, A., 58th Bn.
- 21145 Pte. ROSENTHAL, J., 62nd Bn.
- 51551 Pte. RUBENSTEIN, R., 18th Bn.
- 51253 Pte. ROSENFELD, J., 18th Bn.
- 6522 Pte. REUBEN, L., 5th Bn.
- 23587 Pte. ROSENBLOOM, R., 6th Bn.
- 9278 Pte. RICHMAN, J., 27th Bn.
- 71456 Pte. ROSENBERG, L., 110th Bn.
- 20878 Pte. RAPHAEL, J., 44th Bn.
- 28712 Pte. ROSE, W. J., 46th Bn.
- 91427 Pte. RAMBERGER, H., 25th Bn.
- 26449 Pte. RIFKIN, S.
- 22589 Pte. RUSSLANDER, L., 44th Bn.
- 7001 Pte. ROSENTHAL, 2nd Bn.
- 36610 Pte. ROSENTHALL, J., 10th Bn.
- 21161 Pte. RUBENSTEIN, M., 64th Bn.
- Pte. RAPSTONE, J., 7th Bn.
- 24286 Pte. ROSENBERG, M., 208th Bn.
- 242772 Pte. ROSENFIELD, H., 208th Bn.
- Pte. RUDA H.
- 13761 Pte. RABINOVITZ, N., 245th Bn.
- 13245 Pte. REUBEN, A., 245th Bn.
- 3060 L/Sgt. RINKOFSKY, M., 237th Bn.
- 50412 Pte. RABBINOWITZ, I.,* 18th Bn.
- 30019 Pte. SOLOMON, 46th Bn.
- 25976 Pte. STEINFIELD, B., 45th Bn.
- 26000 Pte. SCHMERKIN, H., 45th Bn.
- 25548 Pte. SILVERSTONE, M., 45th Bn.
- 25500 Pte. SAFFER, T., 45th Bn.
- 25924 Pte. SELLAR, J., 45th Bn.
- 25995 Pte. SILVERMAN, J., 45th Bn.
- 7/4648 Pte. SOLOMON, D., 22nd Bn.
- 12421 Pte. SILVERMAN, S., 22nd Bn.
- 18099 Pte. SILVERSTEIN, M., 15th Bn.
- 17833 Pte. SCHAVERIEN, J., 15th Bn.
- 18094 Pte. SKLANOWITZ, L., 15th Bn.
- 5/25929 Pte. SIMON, L., 7th Bn.
- 5/64510 Pte. SCHVALBA, M. G., 86th Bn.
- 76541 Pte. SLOMSON, L., 89th Bn.
- 30014 Pte. SHOCKER, I., 46th Bn.
- 1808 Pte. SIMONS, M., 52nd Bn.
- Pte. SAUVERS, S., 49th Bn.
- 10528 Pte. SIMPSON, H. L., 27th Bn.
- 127514 Pte. SUGARMAN, J.
- 44761 Pte. SUGARMAN, L., 74th Bn.
- 46514 Pte. SOLOMON, E., 74th Bn.
- 45966 Pte. STONE, M., 74th Bn.
- 45800 Pte. SHAPIRA, L., 74th Bn.
- 47039 Pte. SOHL, A. H., 74th Bn.
- 59627 Pte. SANOFSKY, .H, 74th Bn.
- 50190 Pte. SILVER, J., 75th Bn.
- 54800 Pte. SHAPIRA, L., 76th Bn.
- 3/507 Pte. SOLOMONS, J., 48th Bn.
- 2352 Pte. SAMUELS, M., 48th Bn.
- 5457 Pte. SADJOFF, A., 49th Bn.
- 5809 Pte. SIMONOVITCH, M., 49th Bn.
- 8283 Pte. SIMLO, S., 49th Bn.
- 7371 Pte. SENIE, N., 49th Bn.
- 7836 Pte. SOLOMAN, D., 49th Bn.
- 8977 Pte. STERN, L., 50th Bn.
- 70518 Pte. SHEDLETSKY, I., 49th Bn.
- 63365 Pte. SNIDER, D., 49th Bn.
- 3/72333 Pte. SARNS, M., 49th Bn.
- 3/72692 Pte. SEIGLE, I., 49th Bn.
- 3/73336 Pte. SAMUELS, G., 49th Bn.
- 3/72718 Pte. SHANNON, M., 49th Bn
- 3/73302 Pte. SAVELESKI, M., 49th Bn.
- 3/73040 Pte. SAMUEL, L., 49th Bn.
- 23209 Pte. SUSMAN, N., 49th Bn.
- 35453 Pte. SOCKER, H., 209th Bn.
- 35650 Pte. SOLOMON, J., 209th Bn.
- 35664 Pte. SHOLMAN, M., 209th Bn.
- 34172 Pte. SIMMONS, H., 209th Bn.
- 18/27373 Pte. STONE, H., 21st Bn.
- 76549 Pte. SASSIENIE, A.
- 76558 Pte. SOLOMONS, E., 111th Bn.
- 76682 Pte. SAMUELS, D., 111th Bn.
- 77003 Pte. SALINCOURT, R. S., 111th Bn.
- 77051 Pte. SHAOVITZ, I., 111th Bn.
- 74031 Pte. SHALGOSKY, H., 107th Bn.
- 53964 Pte. SHINEROCK, H., 102nd Bn.
- 17166 Pte. STECKLYN, H., 29th Bn.
- 13/35078 Pte. SOLOMONS, S., 111th Bn.
- 52664 Pte. STROON, I., 76th Bn.
- 50190 L/Cpl. SILVER, J., 75th Bn.
- 28322 Pte. SIMONS, I., 70th Bn.
- 16352 Pte. STONE, H., 68th Bn.
- 51245 Pte. SIMONS, A., 16th Bn.
- 30003 Pte. SCHNEIDER, B., 18th Bn.
- 26183 Pte. SACKMAKER, D., 45th Bn.
- 70917 Pte. STACTVAGNOR, I., 49th Bn.
- 74561 Pte. SIMONS, S., 108th Bn.
- 75405 Pte. SQUARSKY, L., 108th Bn.
- 74446 Pte. SMEJIROVITCH,* 111th Bn.
- 76017 L/Cpl. SCHINDLER, P., 108th Bn.
- 75828 Pte. SILVERSTONE, J., 107th Bn.
- 98776 Pte. SHERMAN, J., 84th Bn.
- 75262 Pte. SARAFSKY, L. D., 110th Bn.
- 75066 Pte. SACKLOVITCH, J., 111th Bn.
- 90451 Pte. STONE, A., 7th Bn.
- 35401 Pte. SHEINBANN, J., 47th Bn.
- 30485 Pte. SHANES, H., 17th Bn.
- 32059 Sgt. SHADWICK, I., 47th Bn.
- 35440 Pte. SOLOMON, B., 47th Bn.
- 24923 Pte. SYMONS, A., 45th Bn.
- 25539 Pte. SIVERNER, H., 45th Bn.
- 54630 Pte. SIMMONS, P., 16th Bn.
- 93907 L/Cpl. SHATCOFSKY, H., 98th Bn.
- 36377 Sgt. SHIFIREEN, R., 66th Bn.

Training Reserve.—*Continued.*

36379 Cpl. SCHLARFMAN, A., 66th Bn.
13516 Pte. SLINERSON, M., 19th Bn.
33888 Pte. SOLOMON, B., 47th Bn.
29371 Pte. SNAJE, M., 46th Bn.
68288 Sgt. SALJEDO, S. L., 106th Bn.
        Pte. SCHWARTZMAN, M.
30965 Pte. SEGAL, A., 110th Bn.
30455 Pte. SILVERMAN, J., 110th Bn.
16027 Pte. SPIRO, A., 61st Bn.
 5557 Pte. SAGOFF, A., 29th Bn.
21588 Pte. STEINBARK, L., 30th Bn.
21288 Pte. SOLOMONS, C., 44th Bn.
 6627 Pte. SAUNDERS, A., 5th Bn.
17695 Pte. SILVERMAN, D., 63rd Bn.
13765 Pte. SIMONS, D.
14925 Drm. SAPERA, W., 4th Bn.
13516 Pte. SLIMERSON, M., 18th Bn.
28854 Pte. SILVERMAN, C., 46th Bn.
25699 Pte. SULLMAN, C., 63rd Bn.
19341 Pte. SILVERSTONE, A., 15th Bn.
5/30612 Pte. SILVER, P., 8th Bn.
21114 Pte. STICKLER, J., 44th Bn.
71362 Pte. STODEL, L. 111th Bn.
29292 Pte. SINGER, J., 46th Bn.
21793 Pte. SMOLLAN, D., 5th Bn.
17546 Pte. SHILSO, S., 61st Bn.
51875 Pte. SPEAR, H., 18th Bn.
44761 Pte. SUGARMAN, N., 74th Bn.
85958 Pte. SORKIN, J., 270th Bn.
4/141052 S/Sgt. SWEVE, L., 226th Bn.
86963 Pte. SAUNDERS, P., 270th Bn.
13066 L/Sgt. SHEPHARD, S., 270th Bn.
12861 Cpl. SELIGMAN, S., 232nd Bn.
50419 Pte. SHURANCE, A., 232nd Bn.
98837 Pte. SOLOMONS, H., 84th Bn.
99129 Pte. SIMMONS, P., 84th Bn.
98829 Pte. SOBILL, J., 84th Bn.
38978 Pte. STONEFIELD, S., 87th Bn.
38976 Pte. STONE, J., 84th Bn.
75066 Pte. SAKLOVITCH, J., 112th Bn.
10412 Pte. SCOTT, D. S., 18th Bn.
 9858 Pte. SMITH, E., 18th Bn.
13156 Pte. SHMERELSON, J., 19th Bn.
14426 Pte. SMITH, H., 19th Bn.
12861 L/Cpl. SELIGMAN, S., 19th Bn.
14438 Pte. SILVERSTONE, J., 19th Bn.
14439 Pte. STEINBERG, N., 19th Bn.
13/27117 Pte. SCHNEIDER, A., 109th Bn.
13/27091 Pte. SCHAVINSKY, A., 109th Bn.
81644 Pte. STEIN, J., 90th Bn.
13/18080 Pte. SIMMOCK, I., 20th Bn.
13/18044 Pte. SYMONS, S., 20th Bn.
 4176 Pte. SLAZER, J., 39th Bn.
69007 L/Cpl. SALZEDO, S., 106th Bn.
24582 Pte. SAMUEL, N., 10th Bn.
21953 Pte. SAACKS, V., 108th Bn.
13/25988 Pte. SPLADOVER, D., 109th Bn.

68065 Sgt. SAMUELS, J., 106th Bn.
24399 Pte. SHINDLER, L., 69th Bn.
21408 Cpl. SIMPSON, C., 108th Bn.
32117 Cpl. STAAL, F., 71st Bn.
16849 Pte. SWEDE, J. A., 67th Bn.
17454 Pte. SHONIAK, J., 43rd Bn.
24892 Pte. SYMONS, A., 45th Bn.
17508 Pte. SCHWEITZER, J. H., 43rd Bn.
24893 Pte. SCHWARTZ, H., 45th Bn.
17453 Pte. SOLOMONS, J., 43rd Bn.
53964 Pte. SHINROOK, H., 102nd Bn.
46380 Pte. SOLOMONS, J., 100th Bn.
        Sgt. SAMUELS, J., 106th Bn.
75948 Pte. SPEAR, S., 110th Bn.
77313 Pte. SEGAL, 108th Bn.
136124 Pte. SHANN, I., 7th Bn.
13734 Pte. SCHNEIDER, S., 24th Bn.
46867 Pte. SILKMAN, A., 100th Bn.
35403 Pte. SIMMONDS, S., 47th Bn.
128107 Pte. SHULMAN, S., 102nd Bn.
74311 Pte. SAVAGE, R., 112th Bn.
74339 Pte. SIMMONS, J., 108th Bn.
27384 Pte. STEINBERG, J., 7th Bn.
60738 Pte. SHULFINE, M., 104th Bn.
74751 Pte. SIMONS, S., 109th Bn.
74325 Pte. SILVERSTEIN, 112th Bn.
74592 Pte. SILVERMAN, S., 109th Bn.
74593 Pte. STEBBING, I., 109th Bn.
74727 Pte. SILVERSTEIN, J., 109th Bn.
72569 Pte. SITTER, J., 109th Bn.
37875 Pte. SPIER, H., 18th Bn.
24960 Pte. SHAVEREIN, C., 43rd Bn.
21780 Pte. SACKROVITCH, H., 44th Bn.
5/6295 Pte. SPITZ, M., 2nd Bn.
 6979 Pte. SAUNDERS, P., 12th Bn.
49916 Pte. SOLOMONS, L., 24th Bn.
26467 Pte. STEELE, C. S., 69th Bn.
108767 Pte. SAUNDERS, B., 97th Bn.
108271 Pte. SOLOWAY, W., 97th Bn.
42264 Pte. SERF, B, 99th Bn.
 2588 Pte. SURIMANER, 22nd Bn.
 9228 L/Cpl. SAGAL, R., 54th Bn.
 5873 Pte. SILVERSTEIN, H., 53rd Bn.
34621 Pte. SMOLENSKY, C., 71st Bn.
 9129 Pte. SOLOMON, H., 59th Bn.
  988 Pte. SHEINKER, K., 57th Bn.
38524 Pte. SAMUELS, B., 98th Bn.
49758 Pte. SPECTEROFSKY, S., 101st Bn.
46410 Pte. SHEFFERBLATT, B., 100th Bn.
39912 Pte. SIMMONS, H., 98th Bn.
54526 Pte. SIMMONS, 102nd Bn.
34173 Pte. SOLOMONS, S. I., 102nd Bn.
42725 Pte. SUMMERFIELD, N., 99th Bn.
74339 Pte. SIMMONS, J., 108th Bn.
74944 Pte. SOLOMONS, M., 109th Bn.
74774 Pte. SOLOMONS, I., 111th Bn.
75983 Pte. SILVERSTEIN, H., 110th Bn.
76158 Pte. SCHNEIDER, M., 110th Bn.

Training Reserve.—*Continued.*

7204 Pte. SILBERG, B., 67th Bn.
30004 Pte. SAGON, M., 70th Bn.
74486 Pte. SOLOMONS, C., 110th Bn.
76203 Pte. SOLOSKY, M., 110th Bn.
75638 Pte. STOOLMARK, J., 111th Bn.
76365 Pte. SAMUEL, D. L., 110th Bn.
15350 Pte. SHIBKO, M., 14th Bn.
40302 Pte. SANTER, C., 59th Bn.
76550 Pte. SCHLOSS, L., 111th Bn.
70518 Pte. SHERLESKY, I., 49th Bn.
45928 Pte. SCHNEIDER, H., 102nd Bn.
55385 Pte. SHOLMAN, M., 102nd Bn.
3210 Pte. SELCOVITCH, H., 2/59th Bn.
131401 Pte. STAAL, M., 16th Bn.
76201 Pte. SOLOMONS, A. V., 112th Bn.
17328 Pte. SHUSK, M., 67th Bn.
22734 Pte. SAUL, M., 62nd Bn.
46372 Pte. SILVERSTEIN, S., 100th Bn.
46131 Pte. SHAEL, J. M., 100th Bn.
41938 Pte. SILVERMAN, J., 99th Bn.
41920 Pte. SILVERMAN, J., 99th Bn.
49811 Pte. SOLOMONS, B., 101st Bn.
61738 Pte. SHULFINE, M., 104th Bn.
4588 Pte. SURIANAMER, B., 22nd Bn.
77448 Pte. STONE, G., 111th Bn.
58296 Pte. SOKOLOFF, C., 20th Bn.
Pte. SHEDLETSKY, L., 59th Bn.
8406 Pte. SOLOMONS, A., 23rd Bn.
52664 Pte. STROOM, I., 76th Bn.
24923 Pte. SIMONS, A., 45th Bn.
33769 Pte. SACKSHIVER, A., 47th Bn.
112532 Pte. SUMROY, B., 86th Bn.
Pte. SHIRLEY, W., 20th Bn.
Pte. SANDRONITZ, D., 24th Bn.
Pte. STEINWOLD, 49th Bn.
29979 Pte. SHARE, 78th Bn.
1728 Pte. SCHNEIDER, F., 256th Bn.
9228 L/Cpl. SAGEL, R., 201st Bn.
9129 Rfm. SOLOMONS, H., 213rd Bn.
241541 Pte. SUGARMAN, H. W., 208th Bn.
24364 Pte. SELT, M., 208th Bn.
Pte. TOBIAS, S., 49th Bn.
10656 Pte. TEW, C., 27th Bn.
46238 Pte. TYSTITZ, B., 74th Bn.
46433 Pte. TYNAS, H., 74th Bn.
38761 Pte. TRAY, M., 76th Bn.
5812 Pte. TERRIS, H., 49th Bn.
62381 Pte. TOBE, N., 50th Bn.
81095 L/Cpl. THOMAS, G., 86th Bn.
3/72982 Pte. TOBIAS, A., 49th Bn.
3/72644 Pte. TEIGER, W., 49th Bn.
32090 Cpl. TOMLINSON, J. H., 209th Bn.
Pte. TANBURN, H. S.
32420 Pte. TESCOFFREY, A., 68th Bn.
29246 Pte. TUCKER, I., 46th Bn.
76916 Pte. TABILOF, G., 111th Bn.
73672 Pte. TOBIAS, J., 112th Bn.

45884 Pte. TABRISBY, D., 100th Bn.
49360 Pte. TAYLOR, H., 101st Bn.
73363 Pte. TEMPLE, M., 111th Bn.
75475 Pte. TUCKER, B., 109th Bn.
74681 L/Cpl. TANKLESON, P.
45905 Pte. TUSSMAN, M., 100th Bn.
21779 Pte. TERNOFSKY, M., 44th Bn.
50428 Pte. TANNAN, I., 18th Bn.
79114 Pte. THOMAS, C., 59th Bn.
13146 Pte. TANNERBAUM, S., 60th Bn.
72182 Pte. TEIMAN, J., 109th Bn.
30603 Pte. TAYLOR, S., 8th Bn.
Pte. TSURILLOFF, B. M.
15132 Pte. TEACHER, A., 237th Bn.
53763 Pte. USDEN, M., 76th Bn.
108464 Pte. USHERWICH, J., 97th Bn.
41190 Pte. VALLENSKY, I., 73rd Bn.
34138 Pte. VINSLOVSKY, H., 209th Bn.
10027 L/Cpl. VALENTINE, G. D., 18th Bn.
13/27062 Pte. VIGNISKI, N. M., 109th Bn.
76834 Pte. VINITSKY, N., 111th Bn.
9516 Pte. VINESTOCK, H., 54th Bn.
22080 Pte. VOLLENBERG, J., 44th Bn.
39542 Pte. VAN DANN, 98th Bn.
39481 Pte. VENISON, D., 98th Bn.
38939 Pte. VOUSNEY, D., 66th Bn.
89877 Pte. VANGROVE, H., 24th Bn.
74565 Pte. VELTMEN, I., 109th Bn.
4785 Pte. VINER, H., 106th Bn.
30783 Pte. VANDENBERG, A., 18th Bn.
91384 Pte. VINETSKY, S.
77378 Pte. VEISBLATT, H., 111th Bn.
90168 Pte. VINEGARD, D., 7th Bn.
480755 Pte. VYON, P., 237th Bn.
25343 Pte. WISEMAN, G., 45th Bn.
68349 Pte. WOLFE, A. H., 87th Bn.
10454 Pte. WILDES, H., 35th Bn.
42399 Pte. WEINER, F., 73rd Bn.
52205 Pte. WILLIAMSON, H., 76th Bn.
8723 Pte. WATSKI, J., 49th Bn.
70228 Pte. WEINBERG, H., 49th Bn.
63016 Pte. WEISS, L., 50th Bn.
9/82449 Pte. WHITE, S., 25th Bn.
82544 Pte. WERCH, S., 25th Bn.
70591 Pte. WEISSBERG, N., 49th Bn.
3/72247 Pte. WINE, M., 49th Bn.
72508 Pte. WALDAM, S., 49th Bn.
3/72594 Pte. WALTERS, A., 49th Bn.
3/73338 Pte. WOODMAN, A., 49th Bn.
3/53110 Pte. WALDMAN, S., 49th Bn.
22671 Pte. WEIN, M., 86th Bn.
34596 Pte. WARMBARDT, R., 209th Bn.
99133 Pte. WARSHAWSKY, B., 84th Bn.
14494 Pte. WOCFF, H., 19th Bn.
13/27089 Pte. WITONSKI, A., 109th Bn.
8503 Pte. WEINER, S., 3rd Bn.
17218 Pte. WOOLFSON, W., 2nd Bn.
21819 Pte. WRIGHT, R., 6th Bn.

Training Reserve—Continued.

18200 Pte. WHITE, A., 20th Bn.
18474 Pte. WOOD, A., 20th Bn.
77028 Pte. WALTERS, L., 111th Bn.
77123 Pte. WHITE, M., 111th Bn.
76555 Pte. WOODWICK, I., 111th Bn.
76666 Pte. WAXKIRSH, E., 111th Bn.
13/53857 Pte. WEINBERG, 17th Bn.
30046 Pte. WEINBERG, T., 79th Bn.
28742 Pte. WEINOW, B., 70th Bn.
25689 Pte. WISE, M. C., 69th Bn.
53522 Pte. WOOD, G. R., 102nd Bn.
1644 Pte. WILK, A., 16th Bn.
34453 Pte. WISE, I.
73772 Pte. WOOLFE, H., 112th Bn.
25890 Pte. WISEMAN, G., 45th Bn.
75146 Pte. WEINBERG, H., 108th Bn.
65100 Pte. WEXLEY, C.
76647 Pte. WEINSTEIN, S., 111th Bn.
75928 Pte. WILLIAMS, H., 110th Bn.
76223 Pte. WEISBORG, A., 110th Bn.
17391 Pte. WAXMAN, J., 67th Bn.
9280 Pte. WARMER, A. G., 98th Bn.
42676 Pte. WOLFE, H., 99th Bn.
75409 Pte. WINETROPE, H., 108th Bn.
25512 Pte. WISE, M., 45th Bn.
76226 Pte. WEISBORD, A., 110th Bn.
34401 Pte. WEINSTEIN, P., 65th Bn.
50443 Pte. WOOLF, J., 19th Bn.
53857 Pte. WEINBERG, S. W.
39280 Pte. WAINES, A. G., 98th Bn.
30064 Pte. WOLFBERG, C., 18th Bn.
30360 Pte. WISHNEVSKY, I.
22941 Pte. WOOLFSON, I.
64872 Pte. WEISS, H. J., 105th Bn.
36402 Pte. WEINBERG, D., 66th Bn.
13673 Pte. WALMAN, S., 34th Bn.
29200 Pte. WILDER, H.
20898 Pte. WINCHINSKY, R.
23379 Pte. WOLFSON, H., 6th Bn.
28861 Pte. WEINBERG, W., 46th Bn.
74076 L/Cpl. WALLEN, C., 112th Bn.
26767 Pte. WOLFSON, S., 63rd Bn.
64898 Pte. WOOLF, V., 106th Bn.
         Pte. WHITE, A., 20th Bn.
52202 Pte. WOOLF, L., 102nd Bn.
29840 Pte. WEINBURG, 113th Bn.
75535 Pte. WOOLLEY, L. C., 112th Bn.
44680 Pte. WOOLF, W., 100th Bn.
6182 Pte. WOLLFE, J., 9th Bn.
42857 Pte. WEISS, D., 253rd Bn.
50443 Pte. WOOLF, B. J., 237th Bn.
88963 Pte. WARNS, J.
5/64520 Pte. YOUNGMAN, 86th Bn.
12627 Pte. YESNER, S., 14th Bn.
6/538 Pte. YZORSKY, S. D., 11th Bn.
16843 Pte. YOUNG, D., 67th Bn.
21256 Pte. YASOVITCH, H., 44th Bn.

30153 Pte. YOUNG, O., 70th Bn.
29945 Pte. ZAUSMER, M., 92nd Bn.
25678 Pte. ZIMMERMAN, N., 7th Bn.
3/72747 Pte. ZEFFERTT, J., 49th Bn.
3/72681 Pte. ZAIVE, R., 49th Bn.
32737 Pte. ZEIFF, C., 209th Bn.
54909 Pte. ZETTER, H., 102nd Bn.
22119 Pte. ZIMMERMAN, P., 44th Bn.
45905 Pte. ZUSMAN, J., 100th Bn.
25462 Pte. ZIMMERMAN, M., 45th Bn.
1606 Pte. ZIVE, M., 52nd Bn.

LABOUR CORPS.

OFFICERS.

2nd Lieut. AFRIAT, J., E.L.C.
2nd Lieut. BARNETT, A., 188th Lab. Coy.
Lieut. BLOCH, R. A., 12th Lincoln Lab. Coy.
Capt. COHEN, S., Egyptian Labour Corps.
2nd Lieut. DAVIS, K. J., 192nd Lab. Coy.
2nd Lieut. GERSON, J. L.
Lieut. GOLDBERG, P., 390th Coy.
Capt. HANSFORD, B., 298th Coy.
2nd Lieut. JOSEPH, E., 199th Lab. Coy.
2nd Lieut. JESSEL, R. W. A.
Lieut. KESSING, G. S., 12th Coy.
2nd Lieut. LEYTON, R., E.L.C.
2nd Lieut. MARCUS, J. L., 3rd Mx. Lab. Coy.
Lieut. Col. MARKS, J. S., 5th Lab. Coy. Devons.
2nd Lieut. PHILLIPS, J. M., 713th Lab. Coy.
2nd Lieut. ROSENFELD, E., 111th Lab. Coy.
2nd Lieut. ROSS, N., 303rd Lab. Coy.
2nd Lieut. SASSOON, D.
Capt. SOLOMON, A., 128th L. Coy.
Lieut. SOLOMONS, 675th Lab. Coy.
Lieut.-Col. WOLFF, H. P. (O.B.E.).

N.C.O.'s AND MEN.

651289 Pte. ABRAMS, E. B., 274th Area Employment Coy.
143073 Pte. ABRAHAM, A., 191st Lab. Coy.
373103 Pte. ABRAHAMS, J., 749th A.E. Coy.
67238 Pte. ABRAHAMS, R., 763rd A.E. Coy.
74248 Pte. ALBAN, P., 7th Inf. Lab. Coy.
93211 Pte. ASCHER, E., 7th Inf. Lab. Coy.
96787 Pte. AARONS, A., 7th Inf. Lab. Coy.
93498 Pte. AARONSON, J., 7th Inf. Lab. Coy.
35794 Pte. AARONS, S., 2nd Inf. Lab. Coy.
31203 Pte. AARONS, S. C., 2nd Inf. Lab. Coy.
37248 Pte. ABRAHAMS, J., 2nd Inf. Lab. Coy.
31543 Pte. ALPER, L., 2nd Inf. Lab. Coy.
41856 Cpl. ALBERT, 5th Lab. Coy., Devons.
G/80338 Pte. ALLBROOK, W.
46300 Pte. AMSTERDAM, H., 28th Lab. Coy.
33463 Pte. ALBERGE, G., 11th Lab. Bn.
74068 Pte. AZA, E., 1st Inf. Lab. Coy., Mx.

Labour Corps.—Continued.

74310 Pte. ANSELL, G., 1st Inf. Lab. Coy.
74305 Pte. ASKINS, J., 1st Inf. Lab. Coy.
24380 Cpl. ANSELL, B. S., att. 7th Corps.
74055 L/Cpl. ADLER, M. A., att. 7th Corps.
48575 Pte. ALBAN, W. A., att. 7th Corps.
37372 Pte. ALBAN, A., att. 7th Corps.
48448 Pte. ALPER, H., att. 7th Corps.
G/35085 Pte. ALEXANDER, H. L., att. 7th Corps.
20405 Pte. ABRAHAMS, M., 35th Lab. Coy.
103236 Pte. ABRAMOVITCH, A., 173rd Lab. Coy.
432697 Pte. ALBERT, L. H., 22nd Lab. Coy.
569103 Pte. ABRAHAMS, A., 63rd Lab. Coy.
551783 Pte. ABRAHAMS, H. G., 79th Lab. Coy.
72475 Pte. AARONS, J., 121st Lab. Coy.
88917 Pte. AARONS, S., 149th Lab. Coy.
143961 Pte. ANGEL, J., 188th Lab. Coy.
208661 L/Cpl. ARONOWITCH, R., 746th L. Coy.
480167 Pte. ALLUM, J. W., 918th Lab. Coy.
75635 Pte. AMSTERDAM, H., 127th Lab. Coy.
75641 Pte. ARLICK, M., 127th Lab. Coy.
64205 Pte. ALEXANDER, D., 108th Lab. Coy.
307494 Pte. AARONS, M., 727th Lab. Coy.
G/84186 Pte. ABRAHAMS, H., 4th Lab. Coy.
23888 Pte. ANNOVITCH, J., 40th Lab. Coy.
384586 Pte. AARONS, S., 19th Lab. Coy.
67813 Pte. ANTINE, M., 114th Lab. Coy.
55812 Pte. AARONS, M., 94th Lab. Coy.
82846 Pte. ARMGLASS, J., 139th Lab. Coy.
G/93610 Pte. ABRAHAM, W., 5th Mx. Lab. Coy.
G/93476 Pte. ALFANDARY, R., 5th Mx. Lab. Coy.
G/83037 Pte. ARNFIELD, R., 5th Mx. Lab. Coy.
G/93183 Pte. ARNFIELD, V. J., 5th Mx. Lab. Co.
G/35980 Pte. ARRON, D., 5th Mx. Lab. Coy.
141441 Pte. ABRAHAMS, I., 67th Lab. Coy.
523423 Pte. ADLER, A., 60th Lab. Coy.
402783 Pte. ALEXANDER, A.,
83093 Pte. ALBAN, L., 6th Mx. Lab. Coy.
74491 Pte. ADLER, S., 6th Mx. Lab. Coy.
80260 Pte. ADLER, D., 6th Mx. Lab. Coy.
84304 Pte. ALTARUS, J., 6th Mx. Lab. Coy.
74368 Pte. ALBAN, W., 4th Inf. Lab. Coy.
74206 Pte. ANWOOD, L., 1st Mx. Lab. Coy.
80334 Pte. ADLER,* W., 3rd Mx. Lab. Coy.
522598 Pte. ARONOVITCH, M., 341st Lab. Coy.
103246 Pte. APPEL, A., 173rd Lab. Coy.
70836 Pte. ABRAHAMS, S., 119th Lab. Coy.
84604 Pte. ALTMAN, P., 150th Lab. Coy.
375763 L/Cpl. ABRAHAMS, J., 758th Lab. Coy.
579218 Pte. ABRAHAMS, N. H., 389th Lab. Coy.
556593 Cpl. ABRAHAMOVITCH, E.
37179 Cpl. ALBERT, H., 14th Devon. Regt.
39868 Pte. AARONS, G. H., 14th Devon. Regt.
38238 Pte. ALEXANDER, D., 37th Lab. Coy.
92851 Pte. AARONS, H., 155th Lab. Coy.
525016 Pte. ALEXANDER, R., 171st Lab. Coy.
401630 Pte. ADDIS, M., 891st A.E. Coy.
557380 Pte. ALMONOFF, J., 1001st Lab. Coy.
46457 Pte. ALEXANDER, M., 2nd Mx. Lab. Coy.
48499 Pte. ARRAM, R. M., 3rd Mx. Lab. Coy.
45639 Pte. ARONOVITCH, B., 3rd Mx. Lab. Coy.
75849 Pte. AARON, G., 21st Lab. Coy.
506 Pte. ABRAHAMS, H., 935th A.E. Coy.
828438 Pte. ALTER, J., Lab. Coy.
33832 Pte. ANNOWITCH,
41856 Pte. ALBERT, N., 5th Lab. Coy.
40935 Pte. AARONS, 14th Lab. Coy.
266793 Pte. AARONS, M., 6th Lab. Coy.
204109 Pte. AARONS, S., 11th Lab. Coy.
132 Sgt. ASKINAZI, A., 72nd Lab. Coy.
396 Cpl. AZOOZ, E., 72nd Lab. Coy.
139 Cpl. ABRADY, E., 72nd Lab. Coy.
157 Pte. AARONIOS, A., 72nd Lab. Coy.
387494 Pte. AARONS, W., 727th Lab. Coy.
663449 Pte. ABRAHAMS, J. H., Labour Centre.
G/93241 Pte. AARONSON, S., 5th Mx. Lab. Coy.
93161 Pte. ALMOND, J., 8th Mx. Lab. Coy.
93405 Pte. ALBAN, G., 8th Mx. Lab. Coy.
558134 Pte. ALLINSON, A., 1002nd Lab. Coy.
74095 Pte. ABRAHAMSON, J., 8th Mx. Lab. Coy.
74092 Pte. ASCHERBERG, S., 8th Mx. Lab. Coy.
97526 Pte. ARTZT, D., 8th Mx. Lab. Coy.
557670 Pte. ANVONER, J., 1002nd Lab. Coy.
557750 Pte. ADLEMAN, J., 1002nd Lab. Coy.
558541 Pte. ABELL, B., 1002nd Lab. Coy.
557772 Pte. ASHER, S., 1002nd Lab. Coy.
557868 Pte. ANSLZVITCH, J., 1002nd Lab. Coy.
557688 Pte. ABRAMSON, J., 1002nd Lab. Coy.
557075 Pte. ABRAHAMSON, A., 1001st Lab. Coy.
557564 Pte. ANSCHELVITZ, S., 1001st Lab. Coy.
557146 Pte. ALSCHWANG, H., 1001st Lab. Coy.
557553 Pte. ABEL, J., 1001st Lab. Coy.
82978 Pte. ADDISMAN, B.
391780 Pte. ATLAS, B., 365th Res. Emp. Coy.
541824 Pte. ABRAHAMS, B., 677th H.S. Coy.
483929 Pte. ASKE, E., 678th Res. Emp. Coy.
409739 Sgt. AFLER, H. S., 884th A.E. Coy.
319812 Pte. ANISKY, E., 506th A.E. Coy.
564650 Pte. ANCILL, N.
36409 Pte. ABRAHAMS, A., 113th Lab. Coy.
422336 Pte. ADDIS, M., 169th Lab. Coy.
84108 Cpl. ANSELL, P., Inf. Lab. Coy.
273770 Pte. AKSELROD, M., 8th A.E. Coy.
72475 Pte. ARONE, J., 121st Lab. Coy.
1064 Pte. ALGHAZI, N., E.L.C.
011033 Cpl. AXELROUND, S., E.L.C.
371 L/Cpl. ADDES, P., E.L.C.
011043 Cpl. AMZALAK, R., E.L.C.
08749 Cpl. AMIEL, M., E.L.C.
459 Sgt. ARONOVITCH, H., E.L.C.
V/308 Sgt. ARWAS, B. S., E.L.C.
011006 Cpl. AZOULAI, F. E., E.L.C.
02857 Cpl. ALMON, M., E.L.C.
21073 L/Sgt. AZUELOS, V., E.L.C.
180963 Pte. ABRAHAMS, D., 341st Lab. Coy.

Labour Corps.—*Continued.*

126316	Pte. ADAMS, L. A.	
498003	Pte. AUSTIN, J., 54th Lab. Coy.	
525209	Pte. ABRAHAMS, S., 54th Lab. Coy.	
45639	Pte. AARONOVITZ, B., 3rd Lab. Coy.	
97607	Pte. AARON, S. A., 7th Lab. Coy.	
82978	Pte. ADDESMAN,	
272820	Pte. ALLENSTEIN, A., 371st Lab. Coy.	
14868	Pte. ABRAHAMSON, 4th Lab. Coy.	
130073	Pte. ANSELL, R., 1st Lab. Coy.	
48449	Pte. ARRAM, A. M., 124th Lab. Coy.	
522603	Pte. ADAMSBAUM, M.	
525211	Pte. ALEXANDER, A., 554th Lab. Coy.	
556553	Pte. ABRAHAMOVITCH, A., 9th Lab. Coy.	
20405	Pte. ABRAHAMS, A., 35th Lab. Coy.	
51016	Pte. AARON, G., 86th Lab. Coy.	
261317	Pte. ALEX, L., 478th Lab. Coy.	
523409	Pte. ADLER, M., 628th Lab. Coy.	
2886	Pte. ANTONY, J., 7th Lab. Coy.	
48841	L/Cpl. ADLER, Mx. Lab. Coy.	
460725	Pte. AXELROD, H., S.C.L.C.	
128065	Pte. ALVEREZ, C.	
52603	Pte. ABRAHAMSON, S., 527th Lab. Coy.	
38771	Pte. ALLCHILD, L., R.W.S. Lab. Coy.	
162182	Pte. ADLER, A., 6th Lab. Coy.	
382430	Pte. ALBERT, G.	
375763	L/Cpl. ABRAHAMS, G., 758th Lab. Coy.	
525274	Pte. ABRAHAMS, 4th Lab. Coy.	
134643	Pte. ABRAHAMS, E. L., S.C.L.C.	
127494	Pte. ANDERS, A., S.C.L.C.	
190856	Pte. BANKOFSKY, A.,* 258th Area E. Coy.	
379320	Pte. BERGSON, M., 258th Area Emp. Coy.	
162720	Pte. BRAMZEL, W., 259th Area Em. Coy.	
79865	Pte. BERNSTEIN, M., 134th Lab. Coy.	
410989	Pte. BLUESTEIN, A., 4th Lab. Coy.	
79843	Pte. BENJAMIN, H., 134th Lab. Coy.	
432418	Pte. BASSICK, J., 154th Lab. Coy.	
202056	Pte. BINDEL, E., 154th Lab. Coy.	
30297	Pte. BARTH, F., 7th Inf Lab. Coy.	
80062	Pte. BICKLES, L., 7th Inf. Lab. Coy.	
93261	Pte. BAKER, J., 7th Inf. Lab. Coy.	
93735	Pte. BLOOMENFIELD, P., 7th Inf. Lab. Co.	
93552	Pte. BUCHLER, W., 7th Inf. Lab. Coy.	
93350	Pte. BERGMAN, P., 7th Inf. Lab. Coy.	
98071	Pte. BISHOP, H., 7th Inf. Lab. Coy.	
200574	Pte. BISHOP, J., 27th Emp. Coy.	
126519	Pte. BOGARD, E., 234th Emp. Coy.	
510287	Pte. BRANDON, H., 247th Emp. Coy.	
142758	Cpl. BERNITZ, S., 211th Emp. Coy.	
580676	Pte. BALL, G., 243rd Emp. Coy.	
207064	Pte. BENZIMRA, J., 259th Area Emp. Coy.	
14521	Pte. BRADLEY, H., 25th Lab. Coy.	
518019	Pte. BIRLINSKI, R., 73rd Lab. Coy.	
37527	Pte. BARNES, H., 2nd Inf. Lab. Coy.	
37024	Pte. BASS, H. J., 2nd Inf. Lab. Coy.	
80318	Pte. BELLON, M., 2nd Inf. Lab. Coy.	
37545	Pte. BERGMANN, D. B., 2nd Inf. Lab. Co.	
37447	Pte. BREM, G. H., 2nd Inf. Lab. Coy.	
74261	Pte. BUCHLER, E., 2nd Inf. Lab. Coy.	
49099	Pte. BURNETT, F., 191st Lab. Coy.	
237623	Pte. BERLIN, D., 744th A.E. Coy.	
357742	Pte. BARNET, G., 801st A.E. Coy.	
407726	Pte. BUTLER, J.	
G/3531	Pte. BEHAR, J., 5th Lab. Coy.	
40823	Pte. BEHERSON, L., 119th Lab. Coy.	
407729	Pte. BENNETT, I., 871st A.E. Coy.	
140058	Pte. BEAVER, D., 221st Lab. Coy.	
19272	Pte. BARANOFSKY, U., 32nd Lab. Coy.	
60074	Pte. BLUESTONE,* M., 101st Lab. Coy.	
526119	Pte. BUENOS DE MESQUITA, J.	
298880	Cpl. BERNSTEIN, G., 714th Lab. Coy.	
40823	Pte. BAKERSON, L., 69th Lab. Coy.	
9654	L/Cpl. BAKER, I., M.F.P.	
663650	Pte. BRIGHT, W., 389th Lab. Coy.	
393296	Pte. BEST, D., 766th A.E. Coy.	
558520	Pte. BEUCHOWSKY, 8th Lab. Co.	
551125	Pte. BECKER, A.	
51014	Pte. BARON, M., 5th Lab. Coy.	
36538	Pte. BECKER, S., 2nd Lab. Coy. R.S.	
	Pte. BERWICK, P., Lab. Corps.	
234414	Pte. BROADY, C., 247th Div. Emp. Coy.	
224408	L/Cpl. BURGESS, M.	
76251	Pte. BELL, D., 128th Lab. Coy.	
45883	Pte. BROWN, C., 1st Mx. Lab. Coy.	
80163	Pte. BERLIN, J. J., 3rd Mx. Lab. Coy.	
74442	Pte. BOXER, B., 3rd Mx. Lab. Coy.	
74351	Pte. BERGMAN, B., 1st Mx. Lab. Coy.	
49166	Sgt. BELL, 28th Lab. Coy.	
33596	Pte. BROTSKY, E., 2nd Lab. Coy.	
34654	Pte. BERMAN, H., 4th Lab. Coy.	
33610	Pte. BLOOM, S., 1st Lab. Coy.	
74376	Pte. BERNSTEIN, L., 4th Mx. Lab. Coy.	
31564	Sgt. BROWN, J., 1st Inf. Lab. Coy.	
16261	Pte. BASSOVITCH, H., 44th Lab. Coy.	
8279	Pte. BLOOMBERG, A., 14th Lab. Coy.	
101470	Pte. BARON, M., 170th Lab. Coy.	
16267	Pte. BLACK, I., 28th Lab. Coy.	
280922	Pte. BLOOM, R., 1/4th Lab. Coy.	
87052	Pte. BERNSTEIN, M., 173rd Lab. Coy.	
31477	L/Cpl. BURSON, M., 16th Lab. Coy.	
119605	L/Cpl. BRIGHTMAN, S. H., 7th Lab. Coy.	
39849	Pte. BERNSTONE, H., 14th Lincolns.	
25747	Pte. BERNSTEIN, S., Employ. Det.	
	Pte. BLANKENSER, A., Employ. Det.	
635	Sgt. BLUMENTHAL, S.	
37635	Cpl. BREST, R., 18th Cheshire Regt.	
36661	Pte. BLOOM, J., 14th Devon Regt.	
48575	Pte. BLACK, I., 20th Lab. Coy.	
27114	Pte. BROWN, H., 12th Lab. Coy.	
30300	Rfm. BROOKS, J., 2nd Lab. Coy.	
2103	Pte. BRADLEY, H., 12th Lab. Coy.	
29774	Pte. BARNETT, M., 37th Lab. Coy.	
551123	Pte. BLOOM, S.	
557678	Pte. BRASS, S., 1002nd Lab. Coy.	
116291	Pte. BROWN, B., 194th Lab. Coy.	
33249	Sgt. BREST, L., 56th Lab. Coy.	

Labour Corps.—*Continued.*

Number	Rank/Name	Unit
224408	L/Cpl. BURGESS, M.,	248th Lab. Coy.
69041	Pte. BRILE, H.,	99th Lab. Coy.
567787	Pte. BERNBAUM, L.,	109th Lab. Coy.
53044	Pte. BERNSTEIN, S.,	186th Lab. Coy.
76221	L/Cpl. BEST, M.,	128th Lab. Coy.
443025	Pte. BERMAN, N.,	236th Lab. Coy.
544	Pte. BROGALL, H.,	1021st Lab. Coy.
40823	Pte. BAKERSON, L.	
391680	Pte. BLAIBERG, M.,	829th Lab. Coy.
303541	Pte. BOSGOLD, S.,	716th Lab. Coy.
93856	Pte. BENOLIEL, M. H.,	244th Emp. Coy.
307033	Pte. BARNARD, L.,	729th Lab. Coy.
19852	Pte. BAKER, I.,	34th Lab. Coy.
656315	Gnr. BARNETT, S.,	7th Lab. Coy.
557051	Pte. BEECHER, E. L.,	29th Lab. Coy.
44282	Pte. BADER, C.,	1st Mx. Lab. Coy.
84362	Pte. BADER, G.,	1st Mx. Lab. Coy.
74050	Pte. BADER, M.,	1st Mx. Lab. Coy.
73485	Pte. BARBASH, W.,	1st Mx. Lab. Coy.
84271	Pte. BARD, S.,	1st Mx. Lab. Coy.
21667	Pte. BLACK, B.,	37th Lab. Coy.
39652	Pte. BERSON, M.,	67th Lab. Coy.
27676	Pte. BOOKSTEIN,* J.,	76th Lab. Coy.
64238	L/Cpl. BENJAMIN, L.,	108th Lab. Coy.
567787	Pte. BERNBAUM, L.,	109th Lab. Coy.
78603	Sgt. BELL, H.,	132nd Lab. Coy.
79300	Pte. BARNETT, P.,	133rd Lab. Coy.
79865	Pte. BERNSTEIN, M.,	134th Lab. Coy.
79843	Pte. BENJAMIN, H.,	134th Lab. Coy.
571300	Pte. BYE, E.,	139th Lab. Coy.
87665	Pte. BETH, M.,	147th Lab. Coy.
650952	Pte. BURNS,	152nd Lab. Coy.
252056	Pte. BINDEL, E.,	154th Lab. Coy.
111340	Pte. BARNETT, M. J.,	186th Lab. Coy.
338953	Pte. BLASKEY, Z.,	188th Lab. Coy.
85858	Pte. BLOOM, S.,	735th Lab. Coy.
310737	Pte. BERGSON, M.,	735th Lab. Coy.
199045	Pte. BIGOFSKI,* E.,	746th A.E. Coy.
273811	Pte. BASS, M.,	991st Lab. Coy.
441299	Pte. BARNETT, J.,	833rd Lab. Coy.
377661	Pte. BIRD, J.,	833rd A.E. Coy.
452408	Pte. BYE, M.,	122nd Lab. Coy.
279283	Pte. BERKSON, J.,	179th Lab. Coy.
75670	Pte. BROMBERG, M.,	127th Lab. Coy.
101470	Pte. BARON, M.,	170th Lab. Coy.
77483	Pte. BLOCK, J.,	130th Lab. Coy.
13238	L/Cpl. BURSON, M.,	23rd Lab. Coy.
71424	Pte. BARAK, J.,	120th Lab. Coy.
112892	Pte. BYE, J.,	718th Lab. Coy.
80069	Pte. BARMACK, J.,	1st Mx. Lab. Coy.
70086	Pte. BARNETT, M.,	1st Mx. Lab. Coy.
70087	Pte. BARNETT, S.,	1st Mx. Lab. Coy.
38994	Pte. BARNETT, N.,	1st Mx. Lab. Coy.
38231	Pte. BARNETT, A.,	1st Mx. Lab. Coy.
84386	Pte. BEAR, E.,	1st Mx. Lab. Coy.
74047	Pte. BERGNER, F. A.,	1st Mx. Lab. Coy.
74351	Pte. BERGMANN, B.,	1st Mx. Lab. Coy.
74234	Pte. BESSO, V.,	1st Mx. Lab. Coy.
74256	Pte. BLASENSTEIN, H.,	1st Mx. Lab. Coy.
71399	Cpl. BROWN, A.,	3rd Mx. Lab. Coy.
72080	Pte. BERGER, P. W.,	3rd Mx. Lab. Coy.
38838	Pte. BERGMAN, H.,	3rd Mx. Lab. Coy.
72079	Pte. BIBER, B.,	3rd Mx. Lab. Coy.
48984	Pte. BLASBERG, I.,	3rd Mx. Lab. Coy.
36730	Pte. BLOOMFIELD, D.,	3rd Mx. Lab. Coy.
71562	Pte. BRESLAUER, B.,	3rd Mx. Lab. Coy.
46436	Pte. BARNETT, L.,	3rd Mx. Lab. Coy.
G/74435	Pte. BROTMAN, H.,	4th Mx. Lab. Coy.
G/80188	Pte. BLAUSTEIN, A.,	4th Mx. Lab. Coy.
G/80262	Pte. BRANDSTATER, B.,	4th Mx. Lab. Co.
G/74376	Pte. BERNSTEIN, L.,	4th Mx. Lab. Coy.
G/83003	Pte. BIRNBAUM, N.,	4th Mx. Lab. Coy.
G/74678	Pte. BILANTZ, D.,	4th Mx. Lab. Coy.
6684	Pte. BERNSTEIN, M.,	12th Mx. Lab. Coy.
39652	Pte. BERSON, M.,	67th Lab. Coy.
	Pte. BELL,	93rd Lab. Coy.
15040	Pte. BROWN, H.,	26th Lab. Coy.
517556	Pte. BLOOM, J.,	793rd A.E. Coy.
629041	Pte. BENSUSAN, D.,	281st A.E. Coy.
302638	A/Sgt. BARNETT, A. L.,	77th Lab. Coy.
509167	Pte. BADDERMAN, W.,	509th A.E. Coy.
601860	Pte. BURNETT, A.,	282nd A.E. Coy.
513494	Pte. BRESLAW, M.,	941st A.E. Coy.
93531	Pte. BEHAR, T.,	5th Lab. Coy.
31281	Pte. BERNSTONE, H.,	53rd Lab. Coy.
347423	Pte. BERKOFSKY, B.,	733rd Lab. Coy.
374475	Pte. BERMAN, G.,	754th A.E. Coy.
G/80163	Pte. BERLIN, J. J.,	4th Lab. Coy.
G/84076	Pte. BILGORA, S.,	4th Lab. Coy.
116714	Pte. BERNSTEIN, J.,	195th Lab. Coy.
10903	Pte. BRANKS, J.,	19th Lab. Coy.
70689	Pte. BERNSTEIN, M.,	118th Lab. Coy.
198554	Pte. BENJAMIN, L.,	143rd Lab. Coy.
35481	Pte. BENNIS, A. A.,	1st Lab. Coy.
45883	Pte. BROWN, B.,	1st Lab. Coy.
31189	Pte. BARD, L.,	2nd Mx. Lab. Coy.
279399	Pte. BURNS, A.,	581st A.E. Coy.
500942	Pte. BERNSTEIN, H.,	621st Lab. Coy.
G/93218	Pte. BAZAR, L.,	5th Mx. Lab. Coy.
G/80280	Pte. BECKER, D.,	5th Mx. Lab. Coy.
G/93513	Pte. BEIN, C.,	5th Mx. Lab. Coy.
G35784	Pte. BENNIS, R.,	5th Mx. Lab. Coy.
36220	Pte. BISHOP, H.,	5th Mx. Lab. Coy.
G/74337	Pte. BLOOMBERG, A.,	5th Mx. Lab. Coy.
G/93793	Pte. BLASER, B.,	5th Mx. Lab. Coy.
G/93679	Pte. BOXER, J.,	5th Mx. Lab. Coy.
G/93822	Pte. BRATSBIES, I.,	5th Mx. Lab. Coy.
G/93291	Pte. BRAND, J. A.,	5th Mx. Lab. Coy.
G/93782	Pte. BRUNOWSKY, J. M.,	5th Mx. L. Co.
G/93643	Pte. BACKNER, J.,	5th Mx. Lab. Coy.
643790	Pte. BOWMAN, C.,	79th Lab. Coy.
68431	Pte. BARNETT, M.,	115th Lab. Coy.
78603	Sgt. BELL, H.,	1932nd Lab. Coy.
624615	Pte. BERNSTEIN, H.,	155th Lab. Coy.

Labour Corps.—*Continued.*

370010	Pte. BARNETT, H., 285th A.E. Coy.
610820	Pte. BERGSEN, A., 712nd Lab. Coy.
629041	Pte. BENSUSAN, D., 995th A.E. Coy.
372287	Pte. BARNETT, S., 16th Lab. Group.
74365	Pte. BARNETT, H. D., 6th Mx. Lab. Coy.
208024	Pte. BREWER, P., 6th Mx. Lab. Coy.
80429	Pte. BROWN, H., 6th Mx. Lab. Coy.
80483	Pte. BENAZON, J., 6th Mx. Lab. Coy.
80317	Pte. BEEKMAN, N., 6th Mx. Lab. Coy.
74403	Pte. BOXER, M., 6th Mx. Lab. Coy.
71699	Pte. BADER, J., 6th Mx. Lab. Coy.
71576	Pte. BERMAN, S., 6th Mx. Lab. Coy.
71644	Pte. BRUCKMAN, J., 6th Mx. Lab. Coy.
80090	Pte. BERNSTEIN, H., 6th Mx. Lab. Coy.
83076	Pte. BROWN, E., 6th Mx Lab. Coy.
92194	Pte. BAUN, H., 6th Mx. Lab. Coy.
84615	Pte. BERMAN, H., 6th Mx. Lab. Coy.
71422	Pte. BERNSTEIN, M., 6th Mx. Lab. Coy.
581876	Pte. BOTOSHAW, S., 991st Lab. Coy.
651459	Pte. BICKLER, E., 6th A.E. Coy.
418203	Pte. BENJAMIN, J., 251st A.E. Coy.
506760	Pte. BORSTEIN, J., A.E. Coy.
541827	Pte. BELSON, D., A.E. Coy.
393354	Pte. BERNSTEIN, M., 389th H.S. Coy.
371794	Pte. BLOOM, J.,
601535	Pte. BERGE, C., 269th A.E. Coy.
411468	Pte. BLACK, L., 78th Lab. Coy.
508366	Pte. BOGISH, G., 527th Emp. Coy.
509194	Pte. BELISKIR, J., 527th Emp. Coy.
530141	Pte. BLACK, H., 527th Emp. Coy.
575955	Pte. BROOKS, E., 849th A.E. Coy.
30454	Pte. BIRGOLDS, Z., 716th Lab. Coy.
40823	Pte. BAKERSON, Z., 716th Lab. Coy.
27083	Pte. BENAZAROF, L. J., Lab. Coy.
645869	Pte. BENJAMIN, S., Lab. Coy.
670728	Pte. BENICI, F., Lab. Coy.
681800	Cpl. BURNSTOCK, J. H., Lab. Coy.
31564	Cpl. BROWN, J.,
399	Cpl. BROWN, A., 3rd Lab. Coy.
8585	Pte. BOXER, S., 3rd Lab. Coy.
	Pte. BARNETT, M., 7th Lab. Coy.
	Pte. BENDERSKY, A., 11th Lab. Coy.
46568	Pte. BROMBERG, B., 19th Lab. Coy.
50816	Pte. BITTON, J., 28th Lab. Coy.
88271	Pte. BERLINER,* H., 148th Coy.
7243	Pte. BREM,* J., 13th Lab. Coy.
64247	Pte. BOTASHANI, M., 4th Lab. Coy.
64388	Pte. BURMAN, E., 9th Lab. Co.
65665	Pte. BARRETT, J., 9th Lab. Coy.
68052	Pte. BRODY, I., 9th Lab. Coy.
68589	Pte. BARNETT, B., 10th Lab. Coy.
193856	Pte. BENOLIEL, 7th Lab. Coy.
4855	Pte. BECKER, S., 9th Lab. Coy.
18830	Pte. BREM, B., 2nd Lab. Coy.
61829	Pte. BARONOTSKI, V. W., 2nd Lab. Coy.
36661	Pte. BLOOM, J., 14th Lab. Coy.
141	Cpl. BARUKH, M., 72nd Lab. Coy.
281359	Pte. BERLINER, B., 738th A.E. Coy.
418742	Pte. BROMBEVO, N., 776th A.E. Coy.
125055	Pte. BOROWSKY,
624615	Pte. BERNSTEIN, H., 155th Lab. Coy.
525121	Pte. BAZANOKI, D., 183rd Lab. Coy.
44942	Pte. BRICHZE, S. R., 6th Mx. Lab. Coy.
93557	Pte. BECKER, A. S., 8th Mx. Lab. Coy.
74480	Pte. BIRN, J., 8th Mx. Lab. Coy.
93434	Pte. BLOOM, H., 8th Mx. Lab. Coy.
100160	Pte. BEIN, E. B., 8th Mx. Lab. Coy.
74194	Pte. BAMBERGER, H., 8th Mx. Lab. Coy.
98223	Pte. BIBER, S., 8th Mx. Lab. Coy.
93450	Pte. BISCHOFSWERDER, M., 8th Mx. Lab. Coy.
93389	Pte. BERNSTEIN, S., 8th Mx. Lab. Coy.
45884	Pte. BROWN, J., 8th Mx. Lab. Coy.
557062	L/Cpl. BOWMAN, M., 1002nd Lab. Coy.
557956	Pte. BEROGOFSKY, J., 1002nd Lab. Coy.
557605	Pte. BOBROVSKY, A., 1002nd Lab. Coy.
557634	Pte. BERNSTEIN, L., 1002nd Lab. Coy.
557927	Pte. BELFER, L., 1002nd Lab. Coy.
557938	Pte. BUSCOVITCH, H., 1002nd Lab. Coy.
558173	Pte. BRAGMAN, M., 1002nd Lab. Coy.
558089	Pte. BENSON, L., 1002nd Lab. Coy.
558165	Pte. BERENBAUM, D., 1002nd Lab. Coy.
558109	Pte. BESRODNES, J., 1002nd Lab. Coy.
557055	Pte. BROODY, S., 1002nd Lab. Coy.
557472	Pte. BRAUNER, M., 1002nd Lab. Coy.
557494	Pte. BRAND, J., 1002nd Lab. Coy.
557292	Pte. BOOTIN, M., 1002nd Lab. Coy.
557913	Pte. BURMAN, W., 1002nd Lab. Coy.
557880	Pte. BASS, M., 1002nd Lab. Coy.
557905	Pte. BERNSTEIN, H., 1002nd Lab. Coy.
557800	Pte. BLOOMSTEIN, I., 1002nd Lab. Coy.
557904	Pte. BLOOM, S., 1002nd Lab. Coy.
557877	Pte. BERNSTEIN, J., 1002nd Lab. Coy.
557863	Pte. BENJAMIN, E., 1002nd Lab. Coy.
558080	Pte. BERNSTEIN, J., 1002nd Lab. Coy.
558101	Pte. BERNSTEIN, M., 1002nd Lab. Coy.
557183	Pte. BREATMAN, J., 1002nd Lab. Coy.
558207	Pte. BEER, F., 1002nd Lab. Coy.
558147	Pte. BURMAN, H., 1002nd Lab. Coy.
558133	Pte. BIRCHWALD, A., 1002nd Lab. Coy.
557287	Pte. BRESH, A., 1002nd Lab. Coy.
558077	Pte. BERNSTEIN, J., 1002nd Lab. Coy.
558156	Pte. BLOOM, B., 1002nd Lab. Coy.
558186	Pte. BLOOM, A., 1002nd Lab. Coy.
557683	Pte. BOORMAN, J., 1002nd Lab. Coy.
557994	Pte. BIERNASKI, J., 1002nd Lab. Coy.
557310	Pte. BRUKNER, N., 1001st Lab. Coy.
557392	Pte. BRODCOVITCH, A., 1001st Lab. Coy.
557420	Pte. BIDDER, J., 1001st Lab. Coy.
557466	Pte. BAKER, C., 1001st Lab. Coy.
557372	Pte. BLOOM, R. G., 1001st Lab. Coy.
557446	Pte. BERLINER, J., 1001st Lab. Coy.
557443	Pte. BASS, H., 1001st Lab. Coy.
557231	Pte. BECKER, M. N., 1001st Lab. Coy.
557205	Pte. BARTECK, S., 1001st Lab. Coy.

Labour Corps.—*Continued.*

558681 Pte. BLOOZER, J., 1001st Lab. Coy.
558633 Pte. BERGER, F., 1001st Lab. Coy.
557259 Pte. BUKAWASKI, J., 1001st Lab. Coy.
557154 Pte. BEZINSKI, M., 1001st Lab. Coy.
557204 Pte. BYER, J., 1001st Lab. Coy.
557164 Pte. BALCOVITCH, S., 1001st Lab. Coy.
557252 Pte. BLAKE, L., 1001st Lab. Coy.
557384 Pte. BLUMSTEIN, L., 1001st Lab. Coy.
557071 Pte. BURSTEIN, W., 1001st Lab. Coy.
557064 Pte. BERKOFFSKY, M., 1001st Lab. Coy.
557449 Pte. BIGIT, G., 1001st Lab. Coy.
557327 Pte. BURNSTEIN, D., 1001st Lab. Coy.
557534 Pte. BERNARD, L., 1001st Lab. Coy.
557596 Pte. BERG, P., 1001st Lab. Coy.
557574 Pte. BENKOFFSKI, M., 1001st Lab. Coy.
557536 Pte. BLOOM, S., 1001st Lab. Coy.
557051 Pte. BREECHER, E. L., 1001st Lab. Coy.
557156 Pte. BARGET, T., 1001st Lab. Coy.
557569 Pte. BROOKNER, A., 1001st Lab. Coy.
557254 Pte. BENCE, E., 1001st Lab. Coy.
557303 Pte. BROCKHUME, M., 1001st Lab. Coy.
557015 Pte. BOOKMIS, H., 1001st Lab. Coy.
557123 Pte. BERN, A., 1001st Lab. Coy.
575303 Pte. BARNETT, P., 886th A.E. Coy.
557605 Pte. BOBOROWSKY,
120048 Pte. BARNETT, J., 14th Lab. Bn.
57039 Pte. BOOKEY, I., 96th Lab. Coy.
391687 Pte. BRANDEA, S.
586160 Pte. BARBEROFSKY, H., Lab. Centre.
638585 Pte. BARNETT, A., 365th Res. Emp. Coy.
447248 Pte. BLUESTONE, H., 365th Res. Em. Coy.
391715 Pte. BALKIND, A., 365th Res. Emp. Coy.
506726 Pte. BOWMAN, M., 673rd H.S. Em. Coy.
391781 Pte. BESSER, B., 365th Res. Emp. Coy.
662963 Pte. BLOOMBERG, J., 365th Res. Em. Coy.
134495 Pte. BROOK, A., 675th H.S. Emp. Coy.
391794 Pte. BLOOM, I., 365th Res. Emp. Coy.
507907 Pte. BAKER, J., 300th Rese. Lab. Coy.
125055 Pte. BERNSTEIN, J. M., Lab. Centre.
250165 Pte. BURMAN, E., Lab. Centre.
357043 Pte. BRAVE, D. B., 537th H.S. Emp. Coy.
32968 Pte. BURMAN, M., 1st Lab. Centre.
507685 Pte. BERKOWITZ, M., Lab. Centre.
498089 Pte. BARNETT, J., Lab. Centre.
498081 Pte. BLUESTEIN, S., Lab. Centre.
92193 Pte. BARBASH, J. M., 2nd Inf. Lab. Coy.
93107 Pte. BARNETT, L., 5th Lab. Coy.
177570 Pte. BARNETT, J., 170th Lab. Coy.
46996 Pte. BARNETT, H., 128th Lab. Coy.
30296 Cpl. BARTH, J., 2nd Inf. Lab. Coy.
224408 L/Cpl. BERGER, M. L., 248th Emp. Coy.
48090 Pte. BLOOM, J., 82nd Lab. Coy.
62608 Pte. BOWMAN, H., 58th Lab. Coy.
40256 Pte. BOWMAN, H., 68th Lab. Coy.
279578 Pte. BLOOMFIELD, J., 93rd Lab. Coy.
79330 Pte. BARNETT, J., 133rd Lab. Coy.
72479 Pte. BERLOVITCH, L., 121st Lab. Coy.

376963 Pte. BENSON, J., 763rd Emp. Coy.
256952 Pte. BENDAL, R., 154th Lab. Coy.
350941 Pte. BARNES, L., 215th Div. E. Coy.
V/418 Pte. BENBAYER, E.L.C.
913 Sgt. BARDA, G., E.L.C.
VO/50 Pte. BABANI, M., E.L.C.
458 Pte. BALESTRA, D., E.L.C.
3130 Pte. BENDAVID, S., E.L.C.
Pte. BERO, M., E.L.C.
07275 Pte. BETITO, M., E.L.C.
08746 Pte. BENVENISTE, J., E.L.C.
288602 Pte. BARNARD, B., 689th Lab. Coy.
272822 L/Cpl. BELOSKY, H., 689th Lab. Coy.
393266 Pte. BEAN, L.
108205 Pte. BRATT, H., 166th Lab. Coy.
194225 Pte. BERENBAUM, S., 393rd Lab. Coy.
333632 Pte. BECHORASCHVILLE, M. L., 301st L.C.
179753 Pte. BOSS, J., 337th Lab. Coy.
265216 Pte. BERNSTEIN, B.
210221 Pte. BEBER, I. M., 366th Lab. Coy.
762181 Pte. BEN, D., 718th Lab. Coy.
45884 Pte. BROWN, J., 1st Lab. Coy.
72388 Pte. BROWN, H., 1st Lab. Coy.
40823 Pte. BAKERSON, S., 69th Lab. Coy.
131977 Rfm. BRESLAW, H., 566th Lab. Coy.
134495 Pte. BROOK, A., 2nd Lab. Coy.
372287 Pte. BARNETT, S., 294th Lab. Coy.
195728 Cpl. BRODIE, M.,* 520th Lab. Coy.
397702 Pte. BEROFSKI, M., 786th Lab. Coy.
8279 Cpl. BLOOMBERG, A., 718th Lab. Coy.
391680 Pte. BLAEBERG, M., 829th Lab. Coy.
85858 Pte. BLOOM, S., 717th Lab. Coy.
203505 Pte. BLATTSTONE, S.
Sgt. BAMBERGER, A. E. (M.S.M.).
507907 Pte. BAKER, J.
525150 Pte. BERNSTEIN, J.
507670 Pte. BORNSTEIN, J.
88271 Pte. BERLINER, W.
352302 Pte. BERNARD, H., 364th Lab. Coy.
257930 Pte. BERNSTEIN, H., 542nd Lab. Coy.
373133 Pte. BRADLAW, L., 8th Lab. Coy.
207664 Pte. BENZIMRA, R., 259th Lab. Coy.
471179 Pte. BERNETT, S., 848th Lab. Coy.
87052 Pte. BERNSTEIN, M., 146th Lab. Coy.
26261 Pte. BASSOVITCH, H., 44th Lab. Coy.
19272 Pte. BARONOFSKY, B. W., 33rd Lab. Coy.
69041 Pte. BRILL, H., 116th Lab. Coy.
69052 Pte. BURNS, L.
46778 Pte. BELL, D., 20th Lab. Coy.
74435 Pte. BROTMAN, H., 4th Lab. Coy.
30297 Pte. BARTH, F.
394560 Pte. BALLABON, S. N., 369th Lab. Coy.
208734 Pte. BLASTIN, J., 369th Lab. Coy.
357652 Pte. BLOOM, M., 262nd Lab. Coy.
48690 Pte. BLOOM, J., 82nd Lab. Coy.
45883 Pte. BROWN, C., 1st Lab. Coy.
80121 Pte. BROWN, S., 1st Lab. Coy.

Labour Corps.—*Continued.*

19877	Pte. BLASKY, M., 34th Lab. Coy.
74678	Pte. BLANTZ, D.
19852	Pte. BAKER, J., 34th Lab. Coy.
133521	Pte. BUSMARCK, M., 2nd Lab. Coy.
509464	Pte. BROGENSKI, L., 298th Lab. Coy.
70877	Pte. BENDESOSKY, A.
347341	Pte. BLAND, J.
101470	Pte. BARON, M., 107th Lab. Coy.
128796	Pte. BOGARD, I.
452408	Pte. BYE, M., 299th Lab. Coy.
556554	Pte. BROSGALL, H., 9th Lab. Coy.
556570	Pte. BANKS, H., 9th Lab. Coy.
10698	Pte. BENJAMIN, S., 583rd Lab. Coy.
71424	Pte. BARAK, J., 275th Lab. Coy.
40256	Pte. BOWMAN, H.
400990	Pte. BENJAMIN, H., 799th Lab. Coy.
557789	Pte. BARNETT, A., 8th Lab. Coy.
307033	Pte. BARNARD, L., 729th Lab. Coy.
325589	Pte. BELINFORT, J.
80069	Pte. BARMACK, J., 4th Lab. Coy.
446681	Pte. BERGMAN, S., 838th Lab. Coy.
27974	Pte. BROWN, I., 370th Lab. Coy.
31477	Pte. BURSON, M., 6th Lab. Coy.
6684	Pte. BERNSTEIN, M.
53044	Pte. BERNSTEIN, S.
31189	Pte. BARD, L., 2nd Lab. Coy.
226971	Pte. BLACKMAN, S., 4/62nd Lab. Coy.
81107	Pte. BITTON, J., 136th Lab. Coy.
163522	Pte. BUCOVITCH, G., 370th Lab. Coy.
47039	Pte. BOOKY, I., 96th Lab. Coy.
	Pte. BENDELL, B., 360th Lab. Coy.
237506	Pte. BEVERLEY, 836th Lab. Coy.
16267	Pte. BLACK, I., 28th Lab. Coy.
21667	Pte. BLACK, B., 37th Lab. Coy.
370	Pte. BIRNSTEIN.
379624	Pte. BIRD, C., 364th Lab. Coy.
509167	Pte. BEADMAN, R.
393295	Pte. BLOOMBERG, W., 612th Lab. Coy.
472988	Pte. BEER, M., 945th Lab. Coy.
532077	Pte. BAUM, L., 366th Lab. Coy.
273790	Pte. BRIGHTSTEIN, B.
	Pte. BESKOVSKY, P., 306th Lab. Coy.
498080	Pte. BARNETT, I.
38585	L/Cpl. BOXER, S., 3rd Lab. Coy.
461026	Pte. BOROVITCH, I., 303rd Lab. Coy.
38994	Pte. BARNETT, M., 1st Lab. Coy.
64238	L/Cpl. BENJAMIN, L., 108th Lab. Coy.
461082	Pte. BLOOM, H., 303rd Lab. Coy.
273863	Pte. BARNETT, P.
461067	Pte. BAYLIN, P.
515758	Pte. BROWN, 169th Lab. Coy.
460792	Pte. BERNSTEIN, S.C.L.C.
273784	Pte. BELKIN, 108th Lab. Coy.
87055	Pte. BERGER, L., 146th Lab. Coy.
279283	Pte. BERKSON, J., 179th Lab. Coy.
80069	Pte. BARMAS, J.
	Pte. BABOT, S., 8th Lab. Coy.
523417	Pte. BROMBERG, G., S.C.L.C.
523433	Pte. BADEGU, M., S.C.L.C.
134783	Pte. BOSMAN, J., S.C.L.C.
09275	Pte. BETITO, M., E.L.C.
506731	Pte. COHEN, J., 787th Area Employ. Coy.
525216	Pte. COHEN, A., 131st Lab. Coy.
79904	Pte. COHEN, B., 134th Lab. Coy.
79896	Pte. COHEN, J., 134th Lab. Coy.
189258	Pte. COHEN, A., 143rd Lab. Coy.
65532	Cpl. CITRON, L., 110th Lab. Coy.
81133	L/Cpl. COHEN, S., 136th Lab. Coy.
82292	Sgt. COHEN, J. J., 138th Lab. Coy.
91833	Pte. COHEN, J., 154th Lab. Coy.
421896	Pte. CORPER, J., 744th A.E. Coy.
459754	Pte. COHEN, J., 764th A.E. Coy.
93361	Pte. COHEN, D., 7th Mx. Lab. Coy.
97575	Pte. CHADWICK, A., 7th Mx. Lab. Coy.
93154	Pte. COHEN, A. I., 7th Mx. Lab. Coy.
97545	Pte. CLEMENT, L., 7th Mx. Lab. Coy.
193940	Pte COHEN, L., 232nd Div. Emp. Coy.
510297	Pte. CROSIER, H., 247th Emp. Coy.
250060	Pte. CHERNICK, J., 14th Div., 215th E. Co.
272847	Pte. COHEN, L., 213th Emp. Coy.
473684	Pte. COHEN, I., 220th Emp. Coy.
266438	Pte. COHEN, J., 212th Div. Emp. Coy.
581729	Pte. COHEN, I., 25th Lab. Coy.
30677	Pte. CLINE, H., 52nd Lab. Coy.
31295	Pte. CORNBERG, I., 2nd Inf. Lab. Coy.
25975	Pte. COHEN, J., 44th Lab. Coy.
76296	Pte. COHEN, L., 128th Lab. Coy.
79882	Pte. COHEN, A., 134th Lab. Coy.
49268	Pte. CAPLIN, J., 5th Lab. Coy., Devons.
33874	Pte. COHEN, S., 1st Lab. Coy., N. Hants.
80114	Pte. COHEN, L., 2nd Lab. Coy., Middlx.
42698	Pte. COHEN, I., 72nd Lab. Coy.
15316	Pte. COHEN, M., 26th Lab. Coy.
107462	L/Cpl. COHEN, S., 108th Lab. Coy.
47656	Pte. CLAYMAN, M., 63rd Lab. Coy.
565001	Rfm. COHEN, P. W., 247th E.C.
201844	Pte. COHEN, L., 6th Lab. Coy.
84674	Pte. COHEN, J., 142nd Lab. Coy.
104509	Pte. COHEN, H., 175th Lab. Coy.
70924	Pte. COHEN, A., 119th Lab. Coy.
42697	Pte. COHEN, G., 72nd Lab. Coy.
622159	Pte. CLIFF, R., 801st A.E. Coy.
187826	Pte. COHEN, H.
470632	Pte. COHEN, M.,
118575	Pte. CHEEK, E., 198th Lab. Coy.
479333	Rfm. COHEN, A., 45th Lab. Coy.
25654	Pte. COHEN, A., 182nd Lab. Coy.
87099	Pte. COHEN, D., 146th Lab. Coy.
90093	Pte. COHEN, S. S., 151st Lab. Coy.
	Pte. CONNER, W. B., 5th Lab. Coy.
525213	Pte. CAPLIN, S., 150th Lab. Coy.
60109	Pte. COSTER,* H., 101st Lab. Coy.
21112	Pte. CANTOR, H., 36th Lab. Coy.
88311	Pte. COHEN, M., 148th Lab. Coy.
7660	Pte. COWAN, J., 6th Lab. Coy.

Labour Corps.—*Continued.*

557439 Pte. CHIPKIN, D., 1001st Lab. Coy.
17301 Pte. COHEN, J., 24th Lab. Coy.
45663 Pte. COHEN, S. W.
510287 Pte. CROSIER, H., 247th Lab. Coy.
558556 Pte. COOK, M., 8th Lab. Coy.
82292 Sgt. COHEN, A., 138th Lab. Coy.
556417 Pte. CAPLAN, S., 9th Lab. Coy.
563825 Pte. COPELAND, S., 475th Lab. Coy.
37134 Pte. COHEN, H., 18th Cheshire Regt.
Pte. COHEN, S., 21st Cheshire Regt.
24113 Pte. COHEN, S., 10th R. Berks.
5412 Pte. COHEN, P., 2nd Durham L.I.
61836 Pte. COHEN, P., 2nd Durham L.I.
40931 Pte. COHEN, J., 14th Devon Regt.
52425 Pte. COSHNSKY, A., 12th Devon Regt.
50700 Pte. COHEN, A., 12th Devon Regt.
48681 Pte. COWAN, J., 20th Lab. Coy.
1771 L/Cpl. COHEN, J., 20th Lab. Coy.
575080 Pte. CALISHER, D., 189th Lab. Coy.
460763 Pte. COHEN, B., 721st Lab. Coy.
512872 Pte. COHEN, L., 249th D.E. Coy.
70261 Pte. COHEN, M., 118th Lab. Coy.
215134 Pte. CORNBERG, 86th Lab. Coy.
557126 Pte. COHEN, S., 1001st Lab. Coy.
558611 Pte. CHEGAN, W., 1001st Lab. Coy.
558518 Pte. CABEL, A., 1001st Lab. Coy.
581729 Pte. COHEN, I., 23rd Lab. Coy.
125053 Pte. COPELAND, C., 77th Lab. Coy.
46898 Pte. COHEN, M., 79th Lab. Coy.
65532 Cpl. CITRON, L., 110th Lab. Coy.
72120 Pte. COHEN, J., 121st Lab. Coy.
525216 Pte. COHEN, A., 131st Lab. Coy.
79313 Pte. COHEN, J., 133rd Lab. Coy.
79318 Pte. COHEN, J., 133rd Lab. Coy.
79904 Pte. COHEN, B., 134th Lab. Coy.
79896 Pte. COHEN, J., 134th Lab. Coy.
82292 Sgt. COHEN, J. J., 138th Lab. Coy.
91833 Pte. COHEN, J., 154th Lab. Coy.
G/19865 Pte. CEDERBAUM, J., 991st Lab. Coy.
273859 Pte. CITRON, A., 991st Lab. Coy.
273640 Pte. COHEN, A., 991st Lab. Coy.
273798 Pte. COHEN, S., 991st Lab. Coy.
273807 Pte. COOPER, B., 991st Lab. Coy.
393300 Pte. CARMEL,* M., 302nd Lab. Coy.
650691 Pte. COSTA, M., 822nd Lab. Coy.
54476 Sgt. COHEN, B., 9th Lab. Coy.
10310 Pte. COHEN, M., 18th Lab. Coy.
10944 Pte. COHEN, A., 19th Lab. Coy.
404050 Pte. CAMBERG, J., 19th Lab. Coy.
460763 Pte. COHEN, B., 721st Lab. Coy.
88933 Pte. CHALK, H., 149th Lab. Coy.
112939 Pte. COHEN, H., 189th Lab. Coy.
273854 Pte. COHEN, S., 827th Lab. Coy.
75704 Pte. COHEN, C., 127th Lab. Coy.
198574 Pte. COHEN, S., 127th Lab. Coy.
101529 Pte. CAPLIN, J., 180th Lab. Coy.
81718 Pte. COHEN, A., 137th Lab. Coy.
476986 Pte. COHEN, A., 182nd Lab. Coy.
556492 Pte. CARLICK, S., 1021st Lab. Coy.
70222 Pte. CARACO, L., 6th Lab. Coy.
558389 Pte. CHASKALOVITCH, L., 1022nd Lab. Co.
7666 Pte. COWAN, J., 6th Lab. Coy.
523407 Pte. CAPLIN, B.
44261 Pte. COHEN, B., 1st Mx. Lab. Coy.
75090 Pte. COHEN, J., 1st Mx. Lab. Coy.
74176 Pte. CYPRUS, L., 1st Mx. Lab. Coy.
84101 Pte. CYPRUS, M., 1st Mx. Lab. Coy.
44347 Pte. COHEN, J., 3rd Mx. Lab. Coy.
38984 Pte. COHEN, P. V., 3rd Mx. Lab. Coy.
72988 Pte. CORNREICH, H., 3rd Mx. Lab. Coy.
37346 Pte. CORNREICH, P., 3rd Mx. Lab. Coy.
G/801991 Pte. COHEN, J. L., 4th Mx. Lab. Coy.
G/74434 Pte. COHEN, A., 4th Mx. Lab. Coy.
G/74369 Pte. CLIPSTEIN, H. H., 4th Mx. Lab. C.
G/80038 Pte. COMOR, W., 4th Mx. Lab. Coy.
G/46974 Pte. CARLEBACH, A., 4th Mx. Lab. Coy.
G/70082 Pte. COHEN, P., 4th Mx. Lab. Coy.
G/84238 Pte. CAMINER, F., 4th Mx. Lab. Coy.
G/92164 Pte. CHECKLER, J., 4th Mx. Lab. Coy.
55315 Pte. COHEN, S., 93rd Lab. Coy.
439754 Pte. COHEN, J., 92nd Lab. Coy.
8471 Cpl. COHEN, J. N., 92nd Chin. Lab.
10944 Pte. COHEN, A., 19th Lab. Coy.
54476 Sgt. COHEN, B., 91st Lab. Coy.
54380 Pte. CANTER, J., 91st Lab. Co.y
54248 Pte. COTTON, J., 91st Lab. Coy.
263048 Pte. COOPERSMITH, R., 4th Mx. Lab. Co.
105700 Pte. COHEN, A., 45th Lab. Coy.
391784 Pte. CHASTER, M., 51st Lab. Coy.
446359 Pte. COHN, J., 837th A.E. Coy.
23891 Pte. COHEN, A.,* 1st Lincoln Lab. Coy.
09054 Sgt. CASVENIR, R.,* E.L.C.
506731 Pte. COHEN, J., 787th A.E. Coy.
331715 Cpl. COWAN, S. S., 282nd A.E. Coy.
132948 Pte. COHEN, S., 62nd Lab. Coy.
446703 Cpl. COHEN, B., 838th A.E. Coy.
112004 Pte. COHEN, B., 187th Lab. Coy.
80814 Pte. CHOINE, J., 135th Lab. Coy.
65532 Cpl. CITRON, L., 110th Lab. Coy.
110468 Pte. CAPLAN, S., 185th Lab. Coy.
19316 Pte. COHEN, P., 33rd Lab. Coy.
81335 Pte. COHEN, S., 136th Lab. Coy.
85321 Pte. CHOREWITZ, H., 143rd Lab. Coy.
189258 Pte. COHEN, A., 143rd Lab. Coy.
4522 Pte. COHEN, I., 153rd Lab. Coy.
91319 Pte. COHEN, L., 153rd Lab. Coy.
636394 Pte. COHEN, M., 72nd Lab. Coy.
G/74299 Pte. CLAIR, J., 5th Mx. Lab. Coy.
G/93428 Pte. COHEN, J., 5th Mx. Lab. Coy.
G/72577 Pte. COHEN, H., 5th Mx. Lab. Coy.
G/93285 Pte. CONNOR, W. B., 5th Mx. Lab. Co.
314711 Sgt. COOPER, D. L., 70th Lab. Coy.
46898 Pte. COHEN, M., 79th Lab. Coy.
496148 Pte. COLEMAN, J., 155th Lab. Coy.
563630 Pte. COHEN, J., 169th Lab. Coy.

Labour Corps.—*Continued.*

569658	Pte. CEDERBAUM, J. M.,	991st Lab. Coy.
98211	Pte. CARO, E.,	3rd Inf. Lab. Coy.
49193	Pte. COHEN, I.,	49th Lab. Coy.
118494	Pte. COHEN, S.	
523437	Pte. CHARINSKI, S.,	784th A.E. Coy.
206601	Pte. COHEN, I.,	784th A.E. Coy.
90926	Pte. COHEN, D.,	716th Lab. Coy.
353995	Pte. COHEN, H.,	385th H.S. Lab. Coy.
446703	Cpl. COHEN, B.,	838th A.E. Coy.
334922	Pte. CRAMEN, P.,	Lab. Coy.
568660	Pte. COHEN, L.,	871st A.E. Coy.
31592	Pte. COOK, G.,	2nd Lab. Coy.
46256	Pte. COHEN, C.,	19th Lab. Coy.
43968	Pte. COHEN, A.,	26th Coy.
50258	Pte. COHEN, I.,	27th Lab. Coy.
50048	Pte. COHEN, J.,	26th Lab. Coy.
49740	Pte. COHEN, B.,	26th Lab. Coy.
50842	Pte. COHEN, S.,	28th Lab. Coy.
51421	Pte. COHEN, A.,	29th Lab. Coy.
50658	Pte. CHOINE, I.,	27th Lab. Coy.
42697	Pte. COHEN, G.,	7th Lab. Coy.
42698	Pte. COHEN, I.,	7th Lab. Coy.
68838	Pte. CRAMMER, S.,	11th Lab. Coy.
75562	Pte. COHEN, L.,	21st Lab. Coy.
33100	Pte. CLASS, S.,	1st Lab. Coy.
33101	Pte. COHEN, A.,	1st Lab. Coy.
7919	Pte. COHEN, H.,	3rd Lab. Coy.
61745	Pte. CLEET, B.,	2nd Lab. Coy.
61836	Pte. COHEN, D.,	2nd Lab. Coy.
36462	L/Cpl. COHEN, S.,	3rd Lab. Coy.
91319	Pte. COHEN, L.,	12th Lab. Coy.
39868	Pte. COHEN,	14th Lab. Coy.
34826	Pte. COHEN, J.,	4th Lab. Coy.
89077	Pte. COHEN, D.,	8th Lab. Coy.
204146	Pte. CANTER, H.,	11th Lab. Coy.
37421	Pte. CHALK, H.,	11th Lab. Coy.
444755	Pte. COHEN, M. E.,	35th Lab. Coy.
118575	Pte. CHEEK, S.,	198th Lab. Coy.
118494	Pte. COHEN, S.,	198th Coy.
375518	Pte. COOPER, I.,	200th Lab. Coy.
53879	Pte. CRISTOL, H. S.,	11th Lab. Coy.
210366	Pte. COHEN, J.,	62nd Lab. Coy.
34231	Pte. COHEN, J.,	146th Lab. Coy.
28846	Pte. COWAN, B. J.,	125th Coy.
200155	Pte. COHEN, J.,	81st Lab. Coy.
671876	Pte. COHEN, S.,	88th Lab. Coy.
101912	Pte. CLARE, E.,	5th Mx. Lab. Coy.
35080	Cpl. COHEN, C.,	8th Mx. Lab. Coy.
100072	Pte. COHEN, H. C.,	8th Mx. Lab. Coy.
93536	Pte. COHEN, A.,	8th Mx. Lab. Coy.
93563	Pte. COHEN, J.,	8th Mx. Lab. Coy.
84009	Pte. COHEN, M. D.,	8th Mx. Lab. Coy.
98299	Pte. CASTELETTE, B.,	8th Mx. Lab. Coy.
101903	Pte. CAPLAN, S.,	8th Mx. Lab. Coy.
98036	Pte. CONREICH, A.,	8th Mx. Lab. Coy.
80175	Pte. COHN, G.,	8th Mx. Lab. Coy.
93813	Pte. COHN, H.,	8th Mx. Lab. Coy.
557689	Pte. CAPLIN, M.,	1002nd Lab. Coy.
557085	Pte. COHEN, J.,	1002nd Lab. Coy.
558567	Pte. CLAPPER, S.,	1002nd Lab. Coy.
558195	Pte. COHEN, I.,	1002nd Lab. Coy.
558136	Pte. CHERNINOFSKY, D.,	1002nd Lab. Coy.
557609	Pte. CAPLIN, J.,	1002nd Lab. Coy.
557620	Pte. COHEN, H.,	1002nd Lab. Coy.
557645	Pte. COHEN, I.,	1002nd Lab. Coy.
557663	Pte. COHEN, H.,	1002nd Lab. Coy.
557638	Pte. CHODICK, S.,	1002nd Lab. Coy.
557458	Pte. CAPLIN, D.,	1002nd Lab. Coy.
557505	Pte. COHEN, I.,	1002nd Lab. Coy.
558012	Pte. COHEN, H.,	1002nd Lab. Coy.
558123	Pte. COHEN, V.,	1002nd Lab. Coy.
557506	Pte. CAPELOW, M.,	1002nd Lab. Coy.
557540	Pte. CZARKANSKY, M.,	1002nd Lab. Coy.
557884	Pte. COSHERER, I.,	1002nd Lab. Coy.
558579	Pte. CROWN, I.,	1002nd Lab. Coy.
557275	Pte. COHEN, D.,	1002nd Lab. Coy.
557512	Pte. COOKS, A.,	1002nd Lab. Coy.
557874	Pte. COSSAK, C.,	1002nd Lab. Coy.
557756	Pte. COHEN, I.,	1002nd Lab. Coy.
557823	Pte. COHEN, M.,	1002nd Lab. Coy.
557796	Pte. COHEN, W.,	1002nd Lab. Coy.
557557	Pte. COHEN, V.,	1002nd Lab. Coy.
557756	Pte. CHOPP, S.,	1002nd Lab. Coy.
557833	Pte. CHERNOFSKY, L.,	1002nd Lab. Coy.
558174	Pte. CREEGER, J.,	1002nd Lab. Coy.
558154	Pte. COHEN, M.,	1002nd Lab. Coy.
558185	Pte. COHEN, B.,	1002nd Lab. Coy.
558146	Pte. CORDENFELT, B.,	1002nd Lab. Coy.
557963	Pte. CANTER, M.,	1002nd Lab. Coy.
558017	Pte. COHEN, M.,	1002nd Lab. Coy.
557964	Pte. COMMISSAR, M.,	1002nd Lab. Coy.
557662	Pte. CLINGBINE, A.,	1002nd Lab. Coy.
558263	Pte. CAPLAN, M.,	1002nd Lab. Coy.
558558	Pte. CONBOYSKY, M.,	1002nd Lab. Coy.
557124	Pte. COHEN, J.,	1001st Lab. Coy.
557249	Pte. CHARLES, J.,	1001st Lab. Coy.
557180	Pte. COHEN, A.,	1001st Lab. Coy.
557152	Pte. COHEN, J.,	1001st Lab. Coy.
557125	Pte. CHAPLIER, W.,	1001st Lab. Coy.
557216	Pte. COHEN, S.,	1001st Lab. Coy.
557453	Pte. CASHMAN, J.,	1001st Lab. Coy.
557007	Pte. COHEN, D.,	1001st Lab. Coy.
557439	Pte. CHIPKIN, D.,	1001st Lab. Coy.
557395	Pte. CYMERMAN, M.,	1001st Lab. Coy.
557611	Pte. CHEZAN, W.,	1001st Lab. Coy.
558570	Pte. CAPLAN, M.,	1001st Lab. Coy.
557542	Pte. CEDAR, M.,	1001st Lab. Coy.
557596	Pte. CHACTOW, I.,	1001st Lab. Coy.
557589	Pte. CHESTER, L.,	1001st Lab. Coy.
557213	Pte. CRONCHMAN, A.,	1001st Lab. Coy.
557039	Pte. CAPLAN, J.,	1001st Lab. Coy.
557083	Pte. CURZON, A.,	1001st Lab. Coy.
558639	Pte. CAPLAN, J.,	1001st Lab. Coy.
557227	Pte. COHEN, E.,	1001st Lab. Coy.
558594	Pte. CRAVITZ, A.,	1001st Lab. Coy.

Labour Corps.—*Continued.*

557473	Pte. COOPER, J., 1001st Lab. Coy.
80114	Pte. COHEN, L., 4th Lab. Coy.
47175	Pte. COHEN, L., 128th Lab. Coy.
70082	Pte. COHEN, P., 4th Mx. Lab. Coy.
250060	Pte. CHIRNICK, J. M., 215th Emp. Coy.
520470	Pte. CHABROVITCHY, M., 27th Lab. Coy.
36193	Pte. CLEVE, P., 113th Lab. Coy.
75710	Pte. COHEN, B., 127th Lab. Coy.
102718	L/Cpl. COHEN, A., 172nd Lab. Coy.
34307	Pte. COHEN, S., 58th Lab. Coy.
411973	Pte. COHEN, I., 49th Lab. Coy.
386173	Pte. CASSON, D., 144th Lab. Coy.
25975	Pte. COHEN, J., 144th Lab. Coy.
609028	Pte. COHEN, H., 139th Lab. Coy.
209056	Pte. COHEN, J., 365th Res. Emp. Coy.
391654	Pte. CORKSON, B., 365th H.E. Emp. Coy.
553141	Pte. CARN, J., Lab. Centre.
104680	Pte. CONN, P., 365th Res. Emp. Coy.
391784	Pte. CHASLER, M., 365th Res. Emp. Coy.
391720	Pte. COHEN, S., 672nd Res. Emp. Coy.
265074	Pte. COPITCH, B., 535th H.S. E. Coy.
525062	Pte. CARNSTEIN, S., 535th H.S. E. Coy.
344112	Pte. CHAPLAIN, J., 535th H.S. E. Coy.
46796	Cpl. COHEN, S. S., Lab. Centre.
45663	Pte. COHEN, S. W., Lab. Centre.
462837	Pte. COHEN, J., Lab. Centre.
525411	Pte. COHEN, A., 300th Lab. Coy.
525215	Pte. CITREN, M., Lab. Centre.
357672	Pte. CHEEK, D., Lab. Centre.
38970	Pte. COHEN, J., 1st Lab. Bn.
43988	Pte. COHEN, I., 1st Lab. Bn.
55052	L/Cpl. COHEN, A., 1st Lab. Bn.
216751	Pte. COHEN, B., 362nd E. Coy.
216765	Pte. COHEN, H., 362nd Lab. Centre.
507614	Pte. COLOMBERG, I., Lab. Centre.
507721	Pte. COHEN, B., Lab. Centre.
58297	L/Cpl. COHEN, J., 98th Coy.
544803	Pte. COHEN, I., 525 A.E. Coy.
196857	Pte. COHEN, I.
564626	Sgt. COSSACK, S.
485455	Pte. COHEN, D.
85878	Pte. COHEN, S., 144th Lab. Coy.
17301	Pte. COHEN, I., 24th Lab. Coy.
557606	Pte. CIOLKOVSKY, P., 9th Lab. Coy.
66058	Pte. CORSEL, H., 153rd Lab. Coy.
6243	Pte. COPE, W. J., E.L.C.
219	Pte. CHALOM, I., E.L.C.
237	Pte. COHEN, M., E.L.C.
078	Pte. COHEN, A., E.L.C.
1068	Pte. COHEN, M. Y., E.L.C.
3477	Pte. COHEN, I., E.L.C.
321	Cpl. COHEN, I., E.L.C.
3138	Pte. COBER, C., E.L.C.
130143	L/Cpl. COHEN, A., 1st Lab. Coy.
153491	Pte. CHERNOFSKY, S., 5th Lab. Coy.
V/329	Pte. COHEN, J. S., E.L.C.
380300	Pte. COMM, R., 2/5th Lab. Coy.
162219	Pte. COOPER, L., 689th Lab. Coy.
163103	Pte. COLE, M., 389th Lab. Coy.
2731122	Pte. COHEN, S., 689th Lab. Coy.
525240	Pte. COHEN, I.
365243	Pte. COHEN, J.
99116	Pte. CROCHINSKY, A., 166th Lab. Coy.
187539	Pte. CODDLE, A. H., 3rd Lab. Coy.
80492	Pte. CROSKY, M., 135th Lab. Coy.
204066	Pte. COHEN, I.
84832	Pte. CAMINER, I.
120279	Pte. COHEN, M., 12th Lab. Coy.
58297	Cpl. COHEN, J., 98th Lab. Coy.
344028	Pte. COHEN, B.
42404	Pte. CAMPLIN, P. H., 45th Lab. Coy.
24113	Pte. COHEN, S., 10th Lab. Coy.
171113	Pte. COHEN, S., 13th Lab. Coy.
515343	Pte. COLLINS, J., 552nd Lab. Coy.
216751	Bds. COHEN, B., 1st Lab. Coy.
235310	Pte. CARNOVITZ, J.
198169	Sgt. COHEN, O. H., 299th Lab. Coy.
407515	Pte. CORBY, B.
216751	Pte. COHEN, B., 540th Lab. Coy.
418219	Pte. CAIN, N., 930th Lab. Coy.
485783	Pte. COOPER, D., 120th Lab. Coy.
72343	Pte. CANTER, H., 8th Lab. Coy. ...
76296	Pte. COHEN, L., 128th Lab. Coy.
17301	Pte. COHEN, I., 24th Lab. Coy.
70082	Pte. COHEN, P., 41st Lab. Coy.
19316	Pte. COHEN, P., 33rd Lab. Coy.
12079	Pte. COHEN, M., 12th Lab. Coy.
153003	Pte. COHEN, L., 5th Lab. Coy.
42697	L/Cpl. COHEN, C., 72nd Lab. Coy.
169828	Pte. COHEN, L., N.C.L.C.
39511	Pte. CAMPLIN, B. H., 35th Lab. Coy.
54248	Pte. COTTON, J., 91st Lab. Coy.
279581	Pte. COHEN, D., 642nd Lab. Coy.
357579	Pte. COHEN, L., 299th Lab. Coy.
357466	Pte. COHEN, H. E., 299th Lab. Coy.
	Sgt.-Major COHEN, H. (M.M.).
890999	Pte. CAPALOFF, B., S.C.L.C.
470419	Pte. COHEN, A., 660th Lab. Coy.
80471	Pte. COHEN, J., 135th Lab. Coy.
462087	Pte. COHEN, J., 546th Lab. Coy.
593514	Pte. COHEN, H.
431051	Pte. COHEN, H., 362nd Lab. Coy.
452479	Pte. CAPLIN, M. R., 299th Lab. Coy.
125053	Pte. COPELAND, C., 77th Lab. Coy.
183472	Pte. COHEN, D.
393308	Pte. COHEN, H., 332nd Lab. Coy.
491676	Pte. COVEL, G., 556th Lab. Coy.
54130	Pte. COHEN, L.
51098	Pte. COHEN, C., 86th Lab. Coy.
70926	Pte. COHEN, D., 119th Lab. Coy.
509197	Pte. CRUSKIN, W., 635th Lab. Coy.
140680	Pte. CONN, P.
312100	Pte. COLLINSON, J., 364th Lab. Coy.
446598	Pte. CANTER, P., 839th Lab. Coy.

Labour Corps.—*Continued.*

163491	Pte. Costa, S., 686th Lab. Coy.
37787	Pte. Cohen, J., 15th Lab. Coy.
180278	Pte. Calo, L., 340th Lab. Coy.
85297	Cpl. Cohen, A., 143rd Lab. Coy.
691696	Pte. Covell, J., 6th Lab. Coy.
526082	Pte. Cleven, J., 527th Lab. Coy.
273754	Pte. Chait, S., 363rd Lab. Coy.
273871	Pte. Caplan, A.
460815	Pte. Cooper, J., 304th Lab. Coy.
85878	Pte. Cohen, S., 144th Lab. Coy.
549868	Pte. Capland, A. H., 279th Lab. Coy.
391720	Pte. Cohen, S., 672nd Lab. Coy.
47063	Pte. Cohen, M., 833rd Lab. Coy.
79882	Pte. Cohen, A.
118494	Pte. Cohen, S.
88064	Pte. Cohen, J., 157th Lab. Coy.
466759	Pte. Chenelnitsky, S., 379th Lab. Coy.
91780	Pte. Crugas, J., E.C.L.C.
145337	Pte. Cohen, H., 380th Lab. Coy.
72988	Pte. Conreick, H., 3rd Lab. Coy.
409010	Pte. Cottlieb, E.
560079	Pte. Cohen, A.
60052	Pte. Cohen, H.
273819	Pte. Cohen, J.
75704	Pte. Cohen, C.
386173	Pte. Casson, D.
650692	Pte. Costa, H., 822nd Lab. Coy.
86279	Pte. Cohen, G., 150th Lab. Coy.
155091	Pte. Cutner, A., E.C.L.C.
489205	Pte. Catts, 480th Lab. Coy.
77832	Pte. Cohen, I., 134th Lab. Coy.
150408	Pte. Clapp, N., E.C.L.C.
460815	Pte. Cooperstaff, J., 400th Lab. Coy.
101903	Pte. Chaplan, S., 8th Lab. Coy.
321986	Pte. Cheshner, J.
197903	Pte. Cohen, D.
1879	Pte. Davis, C., 4th Lab. Coy.
181016	Pte. Da Costa, A., 744th A.E. Coy.
73466	Pte. Desser, I., 7th Mx. Lab. Coy.
35779	Pte. Danenberg, I., 7th Mx. Lab. Coy.
193956	Pte. Danielowitch, I., 232nd Div. E. Co.
87128	Pte. Diamond, S., 272nd Emp. Coy.
134194	Pte. Davis, H., 213th Emp. Coy.
35928	Pte. De Jung, W. E., 2nd Inf. Lab. Coy.
125194	Pte. Davidson, S., 253rd Emp. Coy.
64309	Pte. Decker, S., 108th Lab. Coy.
89542	Pte. Davies, A., 782nd Emp. Coy.
30144	Pte. Delau, M., 51st Lab. Coy.
392606	Pte. Davis J., 72nd Lab. Coy.
346408	Pte. De Leevo, A., 249th A.E. Coy.
323231	Pte. Davis, P., 156th Lab. Coy.
433493	Pte. De Friend, L.,
33993	Pte. Davis, E., 1st Lab. Coy.
668823	Pte. Diamond, E., Labour Centre.
551704	L/Cpl. De Salla, B., 363rd Lab. Coy.
86833	Pte. Dubinsky, F., 1021st Lab. Coy.
203560	Pte. Daniels, G., 24th Lab. Coy.
304904	L/Cpl. Drulu, M., 724th Lab. Coy.
87428	Pte. Dresman, H. J., 146th Lab. Coy.
84225	Pte. Dresner, M., 1st Mx. Lab. Coy.
G/83011	Pte. Dornfest, F., 4th Mx. Lab. Coy.
475936	Pte. Davies, H., 91st Lab. Coy.
273990	Pte. Duzzy, S., 29th Lab. Coy.
516931	Pte. Drukker, C., 56th Lab. Coy.
45126	Pte. Delacovitch, H., 76th Lab. Coy.
45698	Pte. Dobonsky, S., 77th Lab. Coy.
475936	Pte. Davis, H., 91st Lab. Coy.
69123	Pte. Diamondstein, B., 116th Lab. Coy.
88940	Pte. Davis, J., 149th Lab. Coy.
536191	Pte. Devekslogham, 178th Lab. Coy.
525198	Pte. Dansky, C., 721st Lab. Coy.
65322	Pte. Delgovitch, M., 991st Lab. Coy.
266461	Pte. Dolinsky, J., 20th Lab. Coy.
31826	Cpl. Dorfman, M., 54th Lab. Coy.
532160	Pte. Dashefsky, L., 54th Lab. Coy.
81746	Pte. Deutch, M., 137th Lab. Coy.
127700	Pte. Deutch, D., 137th Lab. Coy.
419652	Pte. De Haan, E., 123rd Lab. Coy.
273828	Pte. Diamond, J., 120th Lab. Coy.
189317	Pte. Davis, J., 745th A.E. Coy.
26706	Pte. Defries, A., A.E. Coy.
80493	Pte. De Carte, D., 135th Lab. Coy.
50527	Pte. Davies, M., 85th Lab. Coy.
31061	Pte. De Hann, E., 123rd Lab. Coy.
92867	Pte. Drinker, E., 3rd Lab. Coy.
616974	Pte. Dore, A., 67th Lab. Coy.
483562	Pte. Dragovitch, A., 72nd Lab. Coy.
G/93334	Pte. Danzig, C., 5th Mx. Lab. Coy.
83067	Pte. Dublon, H., 6th Mx. Lab. Coy.
84382	Pte. Dannenberg, A., 6th Mx. Lab. Coy.
653854	Pte. Dorsman, A., 35th Lab. Group.
601888	Pte. Dombey, F., 35th Labour Group.
582014	Pte. Delacovitch, S., 991st Lab. Coy.
35475	Pte. Dilbner, J., 4th Inf. Lab. Coy.
95779	Pte. Dannenberg, J., 7th Inf. Lab. Coy.
585876	Pte. Dehann, R., 610th Lab. Coy.
483482	Pte. Davies, R., Employ. Coy.
63750	Pte. Dufresney, A., Res. Employ. Coy.
304904	L/Cpl. Driver, M., 716th Lab. Coy.
353806	Pte. Davis, J., Labour Corps.
134194	Pte. Davis, H., Div. Employ. Coy.
37891	Pte. Dameron, D., 2nd Lab. Coy.
35024	Pte. Davis, A., 4th Lab. Coy.
51269	Pte. Deutch, M., 27th Lab. Coy.
75282	Pte. Davies, M., 20th Lab. Coy.
8075	Pte. Delew, M., 12th Lab. Coy.
87128	Pte. Diamond, M., 8th Lab. Coy.
208825	Cpl. Diamond, W., 255th A.E. Coy.
214163	Pte. Davies, J., 288th A.E. Coy.
375425	Pte. Daniels, G., 200th Lab. Coy.
583285	Pte. Damary, C., 148th Lab. Coy.
557665	L/Cpl. Davis, M., 1002nd Lab. Coy.
558187	Pte. Davis, S., 1002nd Lab. Coy.
558270	Pte. Dembrinsky, J., 1002nd Lab. Coy.
557881	Pte. Dickens, M., 1002nd Lab. Coy.

Labour Corps.—*Continued.*

557570	Pte. Distleman, R., 1002nd Lab. Coy.
557857	Pte. Daggers, A., 1002nd Lab. Coy.
558257	Pte. Dobkins, P., 1002nd Lab. Coy.
558234	Pte. Darer, M., 1002nd Lab. Coy.
557393	Pte. Dorn, J., 1001st Lab. Coy.
557517	Pte. Droshman, J., 1001st Lab. Coy.
557568	Pte. Danovitch, I., 1001st Lab. Coy.
557576	Pte. Drunberg, R., 1001st Lab. Coy.
557313	Pte. Drodoff, J. C., 1001st Lab. Coy.
557220	Pte. Dobroshitski, M., 1001st Lab. Coy.
557218	Pte. Decknofski, N., 1001st Lab. Coy.
557155	Pte. Dunitz, S., 1001st Lab. Coy.
557233	Pte. Dove, J., 1001st Lab. Coy.
557285	Pte. Duke, H., 1001st Lab. Coy.
558698	Pte. Dovidov, C., 1001st Lab. Coy.
391785	Pte. Deincovitch, S., 365th Emp. Coy.
457128	Pte. Diamond, B., 572nd H.S. Emp. Coy.
428727	Pte. Davies, J., 679th H.S. Emp. Coy.
	Pte. Daniels, G.
594644	Pte. Davies, I., Lab. Centre.
444707	Pte. Diamond, I., Lab. Centre.
37305	Pte. Davies, I., 1st Lab. Coy.
44941	Pte. Doun, D., 1st Lab. Bn.
498003	Pte. Divorman, I., 707th Lab. Coy.
71424	Pte. Daruk, J., 120th Lab. Centre.
87751	Pte. Dobre, A., 147th Lab. Coy.
48390	L/Cpl. Donnor, 2nd Inf. Lab. Coy.
79334	Pte. Dragovitch, R. P., 133rd Lab. Coy.
256952	Pte. Dendel, B., 154th Lab. Coy.
349	Sgt. Diskin, A., E.L.C.
011009	Cpl. Davidson, M. C., E.L.C.
011008	Pte. Dvoupoloff, M., E.L.C.
V/770	Pte. Drubin, E., E.L.C.
134032	Pte. Da Costa, A., 2nd Lab. Coy.
275692	Pte. Denny, S.
498003	Pte. Divorman, J., 549th Lab. Coy.
391785	Pte. Dinkavitch, S.
63886	Pte. Davis, D., 5th Lab. Coy.
392606	Pte. Davis, J., 76th Lab. Coy.
282459	Pte. Davis, N.
28785	Pte. Da Costa, A., 29th Lab. Coy.
204904	Pte. Druler, M., 725th Lab. Coy.
31826	Cpl. Darfman, M., 54th Lab. Coy.
83011	Pte. Darnfarb, M., 4th Lab. Coy.
79334	Pte. Dragowitz, P., 133rd Lab. Coy.
163247	Pte. Danalt, P., 689th Lab. Coy.
525198	Pte. Dansky, A.
129159	Pte. Dembovitch, M., 662nd Lab. Coy.
322149	Pte. Duinkerk,
596557	Pte. Da Costa, E., A.E. Coy.
208825	Cpl. Diamond, W., 366th Lab. Coy.
35518	Pte. Diamond, M., 35th Lab. Coy.
304704	Pte. Denler, M., 725th Lab. Coy.
354437	Pte. Davidson, A., 385th Lab. Coy.
77357	Pte. Dannenberg, I.
31218	Pte. Ditofsky, H., 64th Lab. Coy.
397979	Pte. Dufresnoy, A., 290th Lab. Coy.
87052	Pte. Dernstein, M.
260218	Pte. Davies, A., E.C.L.C.
38809	Pte. Duffey, J.
V/042	Cpl. Douek, J., E.L.C.
193232	Pte. Donns, P.
385780	Pte. Davis, L.
35806	Pte. Davis, J., 654th Lab. Coy.
29455	Pte. Dessert, E., 246th Lab. Coy.
509195	Pte. Dinkle, A., 486th Lab. Coy.
163253	Pte. Davis, M.
66745	Pte. Davis, A., 112th Lab. Coy.
461058	Pte. Didbrofsky, A.
134902	Sgt. Delcanho, E., S.C.L.C.
93043	Pte. Elkan, E. H., 7th Inf. Lab. Coy.
74122	Pte. Epstein, M., 2nd Inf. Lab. Coy.
249321	Pte. Evans, G. R., 744th A.E. Coy.
381679	Pte. Ellis, E. B., 185th Lab. Coy.
193734	Pte. Estry, H., 243rd Div. Emp. Coy.
10337	Pte. Epstein, L., 173rd Lab. Coy.
126249	Pte. Edelstein, D., 76th Lab. Coy.
3491	Pte. Erenberg, S., 13th Lab. Coy.
273276	Pte. Elephant, P., A.E. Coy.
443597	Pte. Elinger, M., 82nd A.E. Coy.
445234	Sgt. Emanuel, M., 14th Lab. Coy.
307053	Rfm. Ellinger, M., 828th A.E. Coy.
G/70026	L/Cpl. Englander, M., 4th Mx. L. Co.
G/80082	Pte. Eisenberg, 4th Mx. Lab. Coy.
34229	Cpl. Elfinbaum, H., 58th Lab. Coy.
430015	Pte. Edwards, 6th A.E. Coy.
G/80314	Pte. Emanuel, V., 4th Lab. Coy.
60927	Pte. Elion, R., 102nd Lab. Coy.
67971	Pte. Etgart, G., 114th Lab. Coy.
G/93483	Pte. Ellena, M., 5th Mx. Lab. Coy.
G/93920	Pte. Eldod, H., 5th Mx. Lab. Coy.
80034	Pte. Eintrcht, P. S., 35th Lab. Coy.
92085	Pte. Epstein, M., 35th Lab. Coy.
67918	Pte. Ellis, I., 75th Lab. Coy.
75844	Pte. Ephraim, L., 21st Lab. Coy.!
444868	L/Cpl. Esterman, S., 21st Lab. Coy.
34546	Pte. Erdberg, J., 7th Lab. Coy.
34579	Pte. Epstine, J., 7th Lab. Coy.
52279	Pte. Elkan, H., 6th Lab. Coy.
125539	Pte. Erenberg, S., 222nd D.E. Coy.
	Pte. Epstein, B., Lab. Corps.
93411	Pte. Ernest, E., 8th Mx. Lab. Coy.
100073	Pte. Elkan, A., 8th Mx. Lab. Coy.
100071	Pte. Elkan, S., 8th Mx. Lab. Coy.
100134	Pte. Ettlinger, C., 8th Mx. Lab. Coy.
557641	L/Cpl. Ehrenberg, J., 1002nd Lab. Coy.
558168	Pte. Enoch, A., 1002nd Lab. Coy.
558072	Pte. Ezrush, L., 1002nd Lab. Coy.
557165	Pte. Eigelnick, J., 1001st Lab. Coy.
557263	Pte. Emma, D., 1001st Lab. Coy.
557063	Pte. Eldat, W., 1001st Lab. Coy.
557390	Pte. Eigenberg, M., 1001st Lab. Coy.
557086	Pte. Engelbratt, J., 1001st Lab. Coy.
557482	Pte. Elson, L., 1001st Lab. Coy.
557168	Pte. Elevitsky, S., 1001st Lab. Coy.

Labour Corps.—*Continued.*

557364	Pte. EPSTEIN, J., 1001st Lab. Coy.
523155	Pte. ELKINSON, H., 365th H.S. E. Coy.
133194	Pte. EDLESTEIN, J., 672nd H.E. Coy.
134352	Pte. EMANUEL, J., Lab. Centre.
407774	Pte. ESTERSON, P., 365th Res. Em. Coy.
224856	Pte. ELLIS, W., 365th Res. Emp. Coy.
132721	Pte. EPSTEIN, G., 677th H.S. Emp. Coy.
627066	Pte. EPHRAIM, H., 68th Lab. Coy.
374251	Pte. EPSTEIN, H., 764th A.E. Coy.
216	Cpl. ELIEL, D., E.L.C.
432	Pte. ESPERANCE, E., E.L.C.
102132	L/Cpl. ELKIN, H., 303rd Lab. Coy.
51142	Pte. EPHRAIM, L., 86th Lab. Coy.
34958	Pte. ERENBERG, S., 902nd Lab. Coy.
452399	Pte. EDELS, R., 362nd Lab. Coy.
273276	Pte. ELEPHANT, R., 368th Lab. Coy.
516294	Pte. ELIMAN, D., 279th Lab. Coy.
133194	Pte. EDELSTEIN, I.
217881	Pte. ELLIS, G., 300th Lab. Coy.
509172	Pte. EUIBENDER, I., 8th Lab. Coy.
615714	Pte. EDELMAN, M., 304th Lab. Coy.
415969	Pte. EMES, C. M.,
273836	Pte. EAGLE, W.
393169	Pte. ELBY, L.
20805	Pte. FILEMAN, H., 29th Div. Lab. Coy.
378701	Pte. FLIEGELMAN, S., 258th Area Em. Co.
79956	Pte. FREEDMAN, L., 134th Lab. Coy.
72983	Pte. FIELDMAN, C., 7th Mx. Lab. Coy.
97541	Pte. FREEDMAN, W., 7th Mx. Lab. Coy.
74229	Cpl. FINESTEIN, M., 7th Mx. Lab. Coy.
74222	Pte. FLEISHER, J., 7th Mx. Lab. Coy.
280173	Pte. FAIRMAN, W., 247th Emp. Coy.
74541	Pte. FREDMAN, S., 243rd Emp. Coy.
211586	Pte. FRANKS, B., 240th Emp. Coy.
205188	Pte. FAUST, M., 244th Emp. Coy.
198311	Pte. FINEBURG, S., att. 1st Army Em. Co.
85085	Pte. FELBERT, R., c/o Labour Coy.
31212	Pte. FAULHABER, O., 2nd Inf. Lab. Coy.
92039	Pte. FELBER, B., 2nd Inf. Lab. Coy.
84387	Pte. FERBER, B., 2nd Inf. Lab. Coy.
84266	Pte. FINK, D., 2nd Inf. Lab. Coy.
84283	Pte. FIRESTONE, H., 2nd Inf. Lab. Coy.
35853	Pte. FIRESTONE, L., 2nd Inf. Lab. Coy.
80053	Pte. FLOWER, S., 2nd Inf. Lab. Coy.
93698	Pte. FOWNES, M., 2nd Inf. Lab. Coy.
74016	Pte. FRIEBERG, I., 2nd Inf. Lab. Coy.
84141	Pte. FRIEDMANN, E., 2nd Inf. Lab. Coy.
86572	Pte. FIELDMAN, P., 145th Lab. Coy.
51760	Pte. FREDMAN, B. J., 87th Lab. Coy.
181688	Pte. FREEDMAN, S., 744th Area Em. Coy.
224450	Pte. FELLAR, A. H., 249th Div. Em. Coy.
94370	Pte. FIFER,* D., 158th Lab. Coy.
	Pte. FREEMAN, L., 2nd Lab. Coy.
48056	Pte. FREEDMAN, F., 28th Lab. Coy.
30040	Pte. FIELDMAN, P., 1st Lab. Coy.
33879	Pte. FINKLE, P., 1st Lab. Coy.
74215	Pte. FLEISIG, N., 1st Mx. Lab. Bn.
64341	Pte. FRANKS, H., 108th Lab. Coy.
44599	Pte. FREEMAN, S., 75th Lab. Coy.
79976	Pte. FREEMAN, L., 134th Lab. Coy.
192758	Pte. FORDONSKY, H., 196th Lab. Coy.
35154	Pte. FREDLAND, W., 3rd Lab. Coy.
363225	Pte. FROCKMAN, B., 76th Lab. Coy.
31376	Pte. FREEDMAN, C., 14th Lab. Coy.
132983	Pte. FOX, H. 210th Div. Emp. Coy.
74542	Pte. FREDMAN, S., 210th Div. Emp. Coy.
622118	Pte. FEINGOLD, S., 800th A.E. Coy.
521917	Pte. FOX, S.
5821	S/S.M. FEIGENBAUM, S. S., Mil. Lab. Co.
452444	Pte. FUSS, H., 122nd Lab. Coy.
273881	Pte. FINKLE, F., 29th Lab. Coy.
522849	Pte. FELLERMAN, S., 389th Lab. Coy.
454583	Pte. FRANKEL, I., Works Coy.
285220	Pte. FELDMAN, S.,
495885	Pte. FLETCHER, H.
509184	Pte. FEDERMAN, M.,
599738	Cpl. FORD, A. G., 475th Lab. Coy.
29245	Pte. FELDHEIM, M. E., 13th Lab. Coy.
36313	Pte. FISHER, E., 14th Devon Regt.
	Pte. FINEBERG, M., 19th Lab. Coy.
18358	Pte. FISHER, J., 1st Lab. Coy.
55943	Pte. FISCHLER, A., 32nd Lab. Coy.
393327	Pte. FOX, M., 22nd Lab. Coy.
273881	Pte. FINKEL, T., 29th Lab. Coy.
39163	Pte. FONESTONE, H., 66th Lab. Coy.
656979	Pte. FEDDY, F., 76th Lab. Coy.
54308	L/Cpl. FAJAN, H., 91st Lab. Coy.
54755	Pte. FRIEDLAND, S., 92nd Lab. Coy.
656877	Pte. FIN, A., 100th Lab. Coy.
64665	Pte. FRANKLIN, S., 102nd Lab. Coy.
380995	Pte. FREEDMAN, M., 116th Lab. Coy.
452500	Pte. FREEDMAN, G., 122nd Lab. Coy.
452444	Pte. FASS, H., 122nd Lab. Coy.
73927	Sgt. FREEMAN, M., 124th Lab. Coy.
78759	Pte. FRESHWATER, A., 132nd Lab. Coy.
79367	Pte. FAW, J., 133rd Lab. Coy.
79676	Pte. FREDMAN, G., 133rd Lab. Coy.
79956	Pte. FREDMAN, L., 134th Lab. Coy.
42895	Pte. FELDMAN, A., 991st Lab. Coy.
5181963	Pte. FINE, B., 991st Lab. Coy.
273847	Pte. FARBER, M., 737th A.E. Coy.
26562	Pte. FREEDMAN, H., 822nd A.E. Coy.
273772	Pte. FINKLESTEIN, J., 12th Lab. Coy.
198371	Pte. FINEBERG, S., 827th Lab. Coy.
39141	Pte. FREEDMAN, M., 54th Lab. Coy.
85085	Pte. FELBER, R., 127th Lab. Coy.
66784	Pte. FREEDMAN, H., 112nd Lab. Coy.
669	Pte. FINEBERG, M., 2nd Lab. Coy.
47525	Pte. FISHER, J. L., 80th Lab. Coy.
85953	Pte. FINKLE, P., 835th A.E. Coy.
273793	Pte. FAUST, 244th A.E. Coy.
558031	Pte. FREEDMAN, D., 966th A.E. Coy.
69749	Pte. FISHMAN, S., 117th A.E. Coy.
372889	Pte. FISHER, B., 748th A.E. Coy.
192708	Pte. FRASER, I., 1st Lab. Coy.

Labour Corps.—*Continued.*

456912	Pte. FREEDMAN, R.,	Labour Centre.
644368	Pte. FINEBERG, R.,	67th Lab. Coy.
205188	Pte. FAUST, M.,	244th Lab. Coy.
64341	Pte. FRANKS, J.,	846th A.E. Coy.
472428	Pte. FRIEZE, B.,	943rd A.E. Coy.
79966	Pte. FINKLESTEIN, C.,	846th A.E. Coy.
93560	Pte. FONENFIELD, H.,	5th Lab. Coy.
31376	Pte. FRIEDMAN, C.,	53rd Lab. Coy.
391473	Pte. FINTUCK, S.,	225th A.E. Coy.
201747	Pte. FRENDT, B.,	225th A.E. Coy.
557669	Pte. FARS, L.,	1002nd Lab. Coy.
74069	Pte. FREEMAN, M.,	1st Mx. Lab. Coy.
80227	Pte. FRIEDMAN, M.,	1st Mx. Lab. Coy.
F/2511	Pte. FIFER, S.,	1st Mx. Lab. Coy.
45430	L/Cpl. FRANK, M.,	3rd Mx. Lab. Coy.
45451	L/Cpl. FRANK, A. S.,	3rd Mx. Lab. Coy.
45357	Pte. FEIGENBAUM, J.,	3rd Mx. Lab. Coy.
74034	Pte. FINEGOLD, N.,	3rd Mx. Lab. Coy.
48893	Pte. FINEGOLD, P.,	3rd Mx. Lab. Coy.
48829	Pte. FINESTEIN, B. J.,	3rd Mx. Lab. Coy.
92092	Pte. FRENDENBERG, B.,	3rd Mx. Lab. Co.
45801	Pte. FRIEDBERG, L. W.,	3rd Mx. Lab. C.
G/37347	Cpl. FRIEDNER, E.,	4th Mx. Lab. Co.
G/71290	Pte. FREY, E.,	4th Mx. Lab. Coy.
G/84470	Pte. FRANKLIN, F.,	4th Mx. Lab. Coy.
273772	Pte. FINKLESTEIN, J.,	12th Lab. Coy.
54755	Pte. FRIEDLAND, S.,	92nd Lab. Coy.
54308	L/Cpl. FAGAN, H.,	91st Lab. Coy.
6780	Pte. FISHER, J.,	17th Lab. Coy.
128296	Pte. FRANKAL, F.,	Labour Centre.
348325	Pte. FRANKEL, L.,	Lab. Coy.
645916	Pte. FALKSON, H.,	Lab. Coy.
54749	Pte. FINBERG, M.,	92nd Lab. Coy.
6780	Pte. FISHER, T.,	12th Lab. Coy.
49275	Pte. FRIEDMAN, J.,	83rd Lab. Coy.
19370	Pte. FLUGALMAN, I.,	33rd Lab. Coy.
92093	Pte. FRENDENBERG, M.,	3rd Lab. Coy.
81193	Pte. FREEDMAN, L.,	136th Lab. Coy.
280173	Pte. FAIRMAN, W.,	247th A.E. Coy.
74251	Pte. FISHER, J.,	1st Mx. Lab. Coy.
652320	Pte. FRESHWATER, L.,	72nd Lab. Coy.
G/7425	Pte. FEIGENBAUM, I.,	5th Mx. Lab. Coy.
G/92474	Pte. FISCHOF, J.,	5th Mx. Lab. Coy.
G/93082	Pte. FRIEDMAN, L.,	5th Mx.L ab. Coy.
G/60811	Pte. FREEMAN, J.,	5th Mx. Lab. Coy.
G/45357	Pte. FEIGANBAUM, J.,	5th Mx. Lab. Coy.
G/74098	Pte. FLEISCHER, A.,	5th Mx. Lab. Coy.
G/80449	Pte. FRENDENBERG, I.,	5th Mx. Lab. Co.
273861	Pte. FERDONSKY, S.,	69th Lab. Coy.
84412	Pte. FERBER, H. D.,	35th Lab. Coy.
48840	L/Cpl. FALK, L.,	35th Lab. Coy.
28834	Sgt. FEUERMAN, S.,	35th Lab. Coy.
74395	Pte. FRIESNER, J.,	35th Lab. Coy.
71497	Pte. FINESTEIN, P. J.,	35th Lab. Coy.
92094	Pte. FRENDENBERG, L.,	35th Lab. Coy.
74452	Pte. FRANKEL, P. M.,	35th Lab. Coy.
581985	Pte. FELDMAN, N.,	991st Lab. Coy.
581963	Pte. FINE, B.,	991st Lab. Coy.
98245	Pte. FRENDENBERG, H.,	4th Inf. Lab. Co.
44834	Pte. FERSTEIN, E.,	1st Inf. Lab. Coy.
43037	Pte. FIELD, W.,	1st Inf. Lab. Coy.
88365	Pte. FRANKS, J.,	32nd Lab. Coy.
273881	L/Cpl. FINKIE, L.,	29th Lab. Coy.
259814	Pte. FINKLESTEIN, L.,	Res. Emp. Coy.
443771	Pte. FRANKS, A.,	829th A.E. Coy.
35110	Pte. FREEDMAN, J.,	5th Lab. Coy.
69749	Pte. FISHMAN, S.,	9th Lab. Coy.
	Pte. FRANKS, J.,	10th Lab. Coy.
44185	Sgt. FREEMAN, M.,	16th Lab. Coy.
48010	Pte. FREEDMAN, S.,	17th Lab. Coy.
	Pte. FREEDMAN, M.,	17th Lab. Coy.
	Pte. FRIEND, W.,	17th Lab. Coy.
50055	L/Cpl. FINE, T.,	26th Lab. Coy.
51603	Pte. FORDER, A.,	29th Lab. Coy.
51431	Pte. FRANKLIN, G.,	29th Lab. Coy.
68039	Pte. FREEMAN, S.,	9th Lab. Coy.
74743	Pte. FIGGELSTONE, J.,	20th Lab. Coy.
34371	Pte. FREEMAN, H.,	6th Lab. Coy.
4955	Pte. FREEDMAN, L.,	9th Lab. Coy.
1997	Pte. FREEDMAN, H.,	39th Lab. Coy.
181688	Pte. FREEDMAN, S.,	735th Lab. Coy.
169333	Pte. FINKLESTEIN, J.,	Labour Centre.
588583	Pte. FISHMAN, M.,	221st D.E. Coy.
93357	Pte. FRIEDMAN, W.,	5th Mx. Lab. Coy.
97760	Pte. FRANKS, S.,	5th Mx. Lab. Coy.
363225	L/Cpl. FROCKMAN, B.,	162nd C.L. Coy.
97553	Pte. FINGLESTEIN, H.,	8th Mx. Lab. Coy.
93069	Pte. FELDMAN, E.,	8th Mx. Lab. Coy.
93692	Pte. FRIESNER, E.,	8th Mx. Lab. Coy.
101932	Pte. FISH, J.,	8th Mx. Lab. Coy.
557657	Pte. FRANKS, J.,	1002nd Lab. Coy.
557669	Pte. FOW, L.,	1002nd Lab. Coy.
557926	Pte. FISHER, J.,	1002nd Lab. Coy.
557951	Pte. FEDERMAN, B.,	1002nd Lab. Coy.
557744	Pte. FLEISCHER, D.,	1002nd Lab. Coy.
558072	Pte. FACALSON, F.,	1002nd Lab. Coy.
558040	Pte. FINKLESTEIN, J.,	1002nd Lab. Coy.
558189	Pte. FREEDMAN, S.,	1002nd Lab. Coy.
557308	Pte. FRIEDMAN, H.,	1002nd Lab. Coy.
557845	Pte. FOXMAN, M.,	1002nd Lab. Coy.
558024	Pte. FAGAN, N.,	1002nd Lab. Coy.
558143	Pte. FOX, H.,	1002nd Lab. Coy.
558074	Pte. FRIER, D.,	1002nd Lab. Coy.
557470	Pte. FINE, S.,	1002nd Lab. Coy.
557532	Pte. FINE, A.,	1002nd Lab. Coy.
557762	Pte. FRANKS, J.,	1002nd Lab. Coy.
557851	Pte. FOX, L.,	1002nd Lab. Coy.
558605	Pte. FRIDKIN, M.,	1002nd Lab. Coy.
557848	Pte. FRIEDMAN, J.,	1002nd Lab. Coy.
557801	Pte. FIREMAN, S.,	1002nd Lab. Coy.
557834	Pte. FOXMAN, M.,	1002nd Lab. Coy.
557962	Pte. FLEISHMAN, M.,	1002nd Lab. Coy.
557730	Pte. FELT, A.,	1002nd Lab. Coy.
557274	Pte. FIZON, J.,	1002nd Lab. Coy.
557244	Pte. FRIEDBERG, N.,	1002nd Lab. Coy.

Labour Corps.—*Continued.*

557317 L/Cpl Fisher, H., 1101st Lab. Coy.
557301 Pte. Finklestein, H., 1001st Lab. Coy.
557556 Pte. Friberg, A., 1001st Lab. Coy.
557588 Pte. Fell, N., 1001st Lab. Coy.
558591 Pte. Freedman, T., 1001st Lab. Coy.
557545 Pte. Feldman, M., 1001st Lab. Coy.
557406 Pte. Fridkin, A., 1001st Lab. Coy.
557653 Pte. Fox, I., 1001st Lab. Coy.
557178 Pte. Fox, J., 1001st Lab. Coy.
557182 Pte. Fox, S., 1001st Lab. Coy.
557250 Pte. Freedlander, A., 1001st Lab. Coy.
557117 Pte. Fine, N., 1001st Lab. Coy.
557251 Pte. Fox, H., 1001st Lab. Coy.
557005 Pte. Freedman, H., 1001st Lab. Coy.
557380 Pte. Fireman, N., 1001st Lab. Coy.
259931 Pte. Fottring, 673rd H.S. E. Coy.
192758 Pte. Fordansky, H., 365th Res. E. Coy.
551728 Pte. Freed, A., 677th H.S. E. Coy.
391472 Pte. Finetuck, S., 365th Res. Em. Coy.
550681 Pte. Foxley, L. M., 365th Res. E. Coy.
507869 Pte. Fox, D., Lab. Centre.
597794 Pte. Franks, I., Lab. Centre.
597758 Pte. Freedman, A., Lab. Centre.
456912 Pte. Freedman, R., Lab. Centre.
452500 Pte. Freedman, G., 299th Res. Lab. Coy.
78205 Pte. Fynburg, H., Lab. Centre.
24091 Pte. Freeman, N., 1st Lab. Bn.
169833 Pte. Finklestein, J., Lab. Centre.
342325 Pte. Franks, L.
72502 Pte. Foreman, S., 121st Lab. Coy.
85950 Pte. Franks, M., 144th Lab. Coy.
558074 Pte. Frever, D., Lab. Coy.
79681 Pte. Faltinovitch, N., 133th Lab. Coy.
977 Pte. Farbe, L., E.L.C.
011188 Cpl. Ferman, A., E.L.C.
60839 Pte. Freeman, S., 75th Lab. Coy.
155892 Sgt. Finer, S., 301st Lab. Coy.
209705 Pte. Fimberg, J., 685th Lab. Coy.
487728 Pte. Freeder, J.
184544 Pte. Fromanchick, D., 506th Lab. Coy.
79681 Pte. Flatlinovitch, N.
Pte. Fix, S., 304th Lab. Coy.
461066 Pte. Feinsilva, H., 8th Lab. Coy.
163384 Pte. Franklin, 686th Lab. Coy.
37347 Cpl. Friedver, E., 4th Lab. Coy.
65359 L/Cpl. Finestone, H.
127049 Pte. Ferari, U., 124th Lab. Coy.
194329 Pte. Freedman, B., 133rd Lab. Coy.
48570 Pte. Fairland, I., 628th Lab. Coy.
462087 Pte. Forsanger, J., 546th Lab. Coy.
556237 Pte. Fineberg, E., 9th Lab. Coy.
158844 Pte. Franklin, R., 5th Lab. Coy.
42748 Pte. Faust, H., 72nd Lab. Coy.
129181 Pte. Fineberg, S.
389767 Pte. Feinstein, M., 622nd Lab. Coy.
89570 Pte. Finland, I., 150th Lab. Coy.
117810 Pte. Fitelson, P., 11th Lab. Coy.

496885 Pte. Fletcher, H., E.C.L.C.
49275 Pte. Freedman, P., 829th Lab. Coy.
273869 Pte. Frank, S.
208709 Pte. Frankenstein, S., 366th Lab. Coy.
50553 L/Cpl. Fliegelstone, J., 85th Lab. Coy.
80449 Pte. Freideberg, J., 1st Lab. Coy.
74222 Pte. Flesher, J.
273682 Pte. Frost, M., 212th Lab. Coy.
509235 Pte. Fredlewsky, N., 512th Lab. Coy.
509189 Pte. Faderman, M., 207th Lab. Coy.
460956 Pte. Feldman, M., 615th Lab. Coy.
452145 Pte. Forrest, C., 694th Lab. Coy.
588583 Pte. Fishman, M., 22nd Lab. Coy.
52760 Spr. Goldstein, M., No. 1 Section.
76336 Pte. Goldman, B., 927th A.E. Coy.
518912 Pte. Gershon, S., 930th Area Emp. Coy.
37354 Pte. Goldman, J., 134th Lab. Coy.
81218 Pte. Gilbert, H., 136th Lab. Coy.
81226 Pte. Gold, J., 136th Lab. Coy.
90181 Pte. Gardner, I., 151st Lab. Coy.
276737 Pte. Goldberg, H. L., 749th A.E. Coy.
37623 Pte. Gould, E. H., 7th Mx. Lab. Coy.
93749 Pte. Green, G., 7th Mx. Lab. Coy.
93911 Pte. Gottlieb, I., 7th Mx. Lab. Coy.
97574 Pte. Greenberg, M., 7th Mx. Lab. Coy.
30977 Pte. Gellman, J., 7th Mx. Lab. Coy.
97758 Pte. Gluck, J., 7th Mx. Lab. Coy.
93884 Pte. Goldwasser, A., 7th Mx. Lab. Coy.
93049 Pte. Gross, M., 7th Mx. Lab. Coy.
93237 Pte. Guttentag, S., 7th Mx. Lab. Coy.
365200 Pte. Gold, M., 224th Div. Emp. Coy.
192768 Pte. Greenberg, H., 214th Emp. Coy.
379323 Pte. Gordon, L., 240th Emp. Coy.
216474 Pte. Gotliffe, J., 209th Emp. Coy.
125842 Pte. Gleek, S., 172nd Lab. Coy.
2611 Pte. Goldwater, T., 5th Lab. Coy.
84322 Pte. Goldberg, H., 2nd Inf. Lab. Coy.
208033 Pte. Goldenberg, M., 2nd Inf. Lab. Coy.
30976 Pte. Gellman, D., 2nd Inf. Lab. Coy.
84406 Pte. Goldstein, S., 2nd Inf. Lab. Coy.
31937 Pte. Greenspan, A. S., 2nd Inf. Lab. Co.
31602 Pte. Groship, M., 2nd Inf. Lab. Coy.
61967 Pte. Goldberg, E., 104th Lab. Coy.
51767 Pte. Goldman, M., 87th Lab. Coy.
79989 Pte. Goldstone, C. D., 134th Lab. Coy.
198427 Pte. Gottlieb, W., 249th Div. Emp. Co.
87933 Pte. Groship, L., 1st Mx. Lab. Coy.
53117 Pte. Goldstein, S., 1st Lab. Coy.
58543 Pte. Galefsky, J., 9th Lab. Coy.
36534 Pte. Grossky, H., 3rd Lab. Coy.
37574 Pte. Groundland, H. S., 1st Lab. Coy.
204582 Pte. Goodman, M., 1st Lab. Coy.
81013 Cpl. Greenholtz, J., 136th Lab. Coy.
201997 Pte. Greenburg, I., 23rd Lab. Coy.
30220 Pte. Gorson, M., 51st Lab. Coy.
258188 Pte. Goldberg, N., 223rd E. Coy.
210395 Pte. Gellam, M., 62nd Lab. Coy.
7842 Pte. Goodson, S., 14th Lab. Coy.

Labour Corps.—*Continued.*

202730	Pte. GINSBERG, S., 246th Emp. Coy.
87155	Pte. GOLDSTEIN, M., 146th Lab. Coy.
8269	Pte. GREEN, A., 14th Lab. Coy.
671847	Pte. GOLDBERG, J., 641st A.E. Coy.
557011	Pte. GRABENER, D., 8th Lab. Coy.
134997	Pte. GOLDMAN, S., 3rd Labour Corps.
156839	Cpl. GOLDSTEIN, N., 5th Lab. Coy.
134398	Pte. GREEN, A., 675th E. Coy.
S/8679	Pte. GOLDBERG, J.
11797	Pte. GOLDSTONE, H., 4th Lab. Coy.
192725	Pte. GREENBERG, J., 151st Lab. Coy.
48477	Pte. GILLMAN, S. C., 3rd Lab. Coy.
69624	Pte. GORDON, M., 718th Lab. Coy.
G/93185	Pte. GRADE, A. E., 5th Mx. Lab. Coy.
522787	Pte. GOODMAN, M., 102nd Lab. Coy.
215253	Pte. GOLDMAN, H., 758th A.E. Coy.
682523	Pte. GOLDBLATT, L., 389th Lab. Coy.
524550	Pte. GREEN, J., 389th Lab. Coy.
551135	Pte. GARDATSKY, B., 337th H.S.
7842	Pte. GOODSON, S., 14th Lab. Coy.
556236	Pte. GREENSPAN, 8th Lab. Coy.
129466	Pte. GOODMAN, H., Employ. Coy.
37413	Pte. GAFFIN, J., 18th Cheshire Regt.
47667	Pte. GOLDMAN, E., 21st Cheshire Regt.
34817	Sgt. GLASSMAN, M., 13th Lab. Coy.
39926	Pte. GRYSPAN, J., 14th Devon Regt.
39927	Pte. GREEN, H., 14th Devon Regt.
39923	Pte. GREENFIELD, H., 14th Devon Regt.
24295	Pte. GRONARD, J., 12th Devon Regt.
	Pte. GREEN, M., 19th Lab. Coy.
559065	Pte. GOLDING, M., 8th Lab. Coy.
558410	Pte. GOLDBERG, I., 1001st Lab. Coy.
558711	Pte. GRODINSKY, N., 1001st Lab. Coy.
277509	Cpl. GREEN, I., 726th Lab. Coy.
274066	Pte. GOLDBERG, J., 69th Lab. Coy.
357672	Pte. GLEEK, D., 299th Lab. Coy.
409010	Pte. GOTTLIEB, E., 206th A.E. Coy.
194023	Pte. GOLDSTONE, H., 4th Lab. Coy.
183487	Pte. GOLDSTEIN, N.
207082	Pte. GADIAN, A., 9th Lab. Coy.
273621	Pte. GRADUS, S. M., 723rd Lab. Coy.
531191	Pte. GOLDBERG, A.
55849	Pte. GEDULD, P.
556873	Pte. GOLDMAN, L., 122nd Lab. Coy.
74298	Pte. GELLMAN, L., 1st Mx. Lab. Coy.
44196	Pte. GELLMAN, L., 1st Mx. Lab. Coy.
84100	Pte. GLATZ, M., 1st Mx. Lab. Coy
263054	Pte GLATZ, N., 1st Mx. Lab. Coy.
37933	Pte. GROSHIP, L., 1st Mx. Lab. Coy.
38000	Pte. GARBNER, H., 3rd Mx. Lab. Coy.
45163	Pte. GECOFSKY, F. G., 3rd Mx. Lab. Coy.
48477	Pte. GELLMAN, S. C., 3rd Mx. Lab. Coy.
38256	Pte. GOLDSCHNEIDER, W., 3rd Mx. L. Co.
70226	Pte. GOTTLIEB, M., 3rd Mx. Lab. Coy.
84393	Pte. GRILL, M., 3rd Mx. Lab. Coy.
35903	Pte. GRILL, L., 3rd Mx. Lab. Coy.
G/80197	Pte. GREENWOOD, J. M., 4th Mx. L. Co.
G/74111	Pte. GOLDSMITH, M., 4th Mx. Lab. Coy.
G/84309	Pte. GOLDBERG, H., 4th Mx. Lab. Coy.
G/74377	Pte. GOLDBERG, P., 4th Mx. Lab. Coy.
G/84199	Pte. GOTTLIEB, L., 4th Mx. Lab. Coy.
216056	Pte. GOLDSMITH, M., 35th Lab. Coy.
504443	Cpl. GLASS, J., 58th Lab. Coy.
16874	Pte. GOLDMAN, S., 29th Lab. Coy.
273989	Pte. GOLDBERG, T., 29th Lab. Coy.
273786	Pte. GREEN, N., 29th Lab. Coy.
516934	Pte. GARRETT, D., 56th Lab. Coy.
64358	Pte. GOLDSTEIN, S., 108th Lab. Coy.
87173	Pte. GREEN, A., 118th Lab. Coy.
452481	Pte. GREENBERG, J., 122nd Lab. Coy.
78775	Pte. GOLDSTEIN, F., 132nd Lab. Coy.
78779	Pte. GROSSMAN, M., 132nd Lab. Coy.
79678	Pte. GHENKIN, C., 133rd Lab. Coy.
37354	Pte. GOLDMAN, J., 134th Lab. Coy.
81218	Pte. GILBERT, H., 136th Lab. Coy.
81226	Pte. GOLD, J., 136th Lab. Coy.
82826	Sgt. GOLDSTEIN, G., 139th Lab. Coy.
189554	Pte. GOLDSTEIN, B., 143rd Lab. Coy.
90181	Pte. GARDNER, I., 151st Lab. Coy.
125842	Pte. GLEEK, S., 172nd Lab. Coy.
591992	Pte. GABRIEL, J., 991st Lab. Coy.
274006	Pte. GREEN, J., 991st Lab. Coy.
274016	Pte. GORDON, M., 991st Lab. Coy.
273791	Pte. GRODENTZ, S., 991st Lab. Coy.
G/19904	Pte. GREENBAUM, J., 991st Lab. Coy.
274025	Pte. GERSHOVITCH, M., 991st Lab. Coy.
273789	Pte. GERGULSKY, S., 991st Lab. Coy.
390619	Pte. GOODSTONE, N., 12th A.E. Coy.
276737	Pte. GOLDBERG, H. L., 729th A.E. Coy.
75198	Pte. GROSS, M., 833rd A.E. Coy.
421830	Pte. GOUDEKET, J., 927th A.E. Coy.
424919	Pte. GROWS, H., 947th A.E. Coy.
2164747	Pte. GOTLIFFE, J., 209th Div. Emp. Coy.
516450	Pte. GOLDBERG, W., 141st Lab. Coy.
480871	Pte. GERSHON, S., 22nd Lab. Coy.
66814	Pte. GROOSHKY, B., 112nd Lab. Coy.
392832	Pte. GOLDBERG, L., 47th Lab. Coy.
574592	Pte. GERLINSKY, A., 137th Lab. Coy.
125384	Pte. GRAJEWSKY, J., 149th Lab. Coy.
516934	Pte. GARRETT, D., 56th Lab. Coy.
71585	Pte. GOODSON, B., 120th Lab. Coy.
71599	Pte. GOODMAN, M., 120th Lab. Coy.
273825	Pte. GOLDSTEIN, M., 192nd Lab. Coy.
518912	Pte. GERSHON, S., 930th A.E. Coy.
558182	Pte. GWARTZMAN, 8th Lab. Coy.
557858	Pte. GREEN, P., 9th Lab. Coy.
393285	Pte. GOLD, 584th Lab. Coy.
31395	Pte. GREEN, J., 53rd Lab. Coy.
374529	Pte. GOODMAN, M., 754th A.E. Coy.
G/80283	Pte. GORTZ, F. B., 4th Lab. Coy.
G/74440	Pte. GREENBAUNS, G., 4th Lab. Coy.
G/84200	Pte. GOTTLIEB, S., 4th Lab. Coy.
69771	Pte. GORDON, D., 117th Lab. Coy.
69776	Pte. GODINSKI, J., 117th Lab. Coy.
114155	Pte. GOLDBLUN, H., 31st Lab. Coy.

Labour Corps.—*Continued.*

68078	Pte. GAISBERG, D., 114th Lab. Coy.
68244	Pte. GOLDSTEIN, J. D., 114th Lab. Coy.
192725	Pte. GREENBERG, J., 151st Lab. Coy.
49363	Pte. GLICK, A., 83rd Lab. Coy.
80089	Pte. GOLDSTEIN, S. D., 134th Lab. Coy.
30998	Pte. GOLDMAN, A., 2nd Mx. Lab. Coy.
70994	Pte. GILBERT, H., 119th Lab. Coy.
91421	Pte. GRANARD, I., 153rd Lab. Coy.
273826	Pte. GROSS, L., 707th Lab. Coy.
435301	Pte. GOLDBERG, H., 579th A.E. Coy.
154829	Pte. GORDON, J.
157450	Pte. GOLDMAN, A.
607166	Pte. GOODMAN, H., 72nd Lab. Coy.
213917	Pte. GRESCU, A., 280th A.E. Coy.
G/35954	Pte. GREENHOTZ, L. E., 5th Mx. Lab. C.
G/84080	Pte. GELERNTER, M., 5th Mx. Lab. Coy.
G/93388	Pte. GROSHOFF, L., 5th Mx. Lab. Coy.
G/93763	Pte. GROBLER, G., 5th Mx. Lab. Coy.
G/93035	Pte. GREEN, M., 5th Mx. Lab. Coy.
G/93061	Pte. GEWIRTZ, L., 5th Mx. Lab. Coy.
G/35594	Pte. GOLDSMITH, L., 5th Mx. Lab. Coy.
G/74041	Pte. GLASS, H., 5th Mx. Lab. Coy.
93185	Pte. GRAD, A. E. C., 5th Mx. Lab. Coy.
208049	Pte. GALIZER, H., 5th Mx. Lab. Coy.
G/93946	Pte. GOODMAN, A., 5th Mx. Lab. Coy.
G/93325	Pte. GOODMAN, A., 5th Mx. Lab. Coy.
G/93186	Pte. GRAD, O., 5th Mx. Lab. Coy.
535339	Pte. GOLDSTEIN, A., 155th Lab. Coy.
515949	Sgt. GOBER, A., 141st C.L.C.
48744	Cpl. GERSON, V., 35th Lab. Group.
74492	Pte. GOTTLIEB, M., 35th Lab. Group.
92169	Pte. GREENSTEIN, P., 35th Lab. Group.
84479	L/Cpl. GROSSMAN, E. A., 35th Lab. Grp.
84334	Pte. GERBER, S. C., 35th Lab. Group.
84323	Pte. GOLDBERG, S., 35th Lab. Group.
84199	Pte. GOTTLIEB, L., 35th Lab. Group.
97574	Pte. GREENBERG, M., 35th Lab. Group.
577802	Pte. GREENFIELD, D., 35th Lab. Group.
581992	Pte. GABRIEL, J. M., 991st Lab. Group.
273791	Pte. GRODENTZ, S. M., 991st Lab. Coy.
274006	Pte. GREEN, J., 991st Lab. Coy.
274025	Pte. GERSHOVITZ, M. S., 991st Lab. Coy.
103396	Pte. GREENBAUM, A. M., 991st Lab. Coy.
273789	Pte. GERGULSKY, S. M., 991st Lab. Coy.
G/93963	Pte. GOODMAN, J., 5th Mx. Lab. Coy.
80197	Pte. GREENWOOD, J. M., 4th Inf. Lab. C.
84309	Pte. GOLDBERG, H., 4th Inf. Lab. Coy.
43284	Pte. GOLDBLUM, H., 1st Inf. Lab. Coy.
74404	Pte. GREENBERG,* G., 6th Mx. Lab. Coy.
234169	Pte. GREENBERG,* R., 488th Lab. Coy.
669218	Pte. GLUCKSTEIN, A., 153rd Lab. Coy.
91421	Pte. GRANARD, I., 153rd Lab. Coy.
16974	Pte. GOLDMAN, S., 29th Lab. Coy.
597063	Pte. GOLDBERG, N.
557011	Pte. GRABINER, D., 8th Lab. Coy.
168906	Pte. GOLDBERG, H., 377th H.S. Lab. Coy.
81226	Pte. GOLD, J., 849th A.E. Coy.
426498	L/Cpl. GREEN, M., 935th A.E. Coy.
645403	Pte. GREENBERG, I., Lab. Coy.
682222	Pte. GIMSBERG, P., Lab. Coy.
216474	Pte. GOTCLIFFE, J., 209th D.E. Coy
8000	Pte. GARTNER, H., 3rd Lab. Coy.
70994	Pte. GILBERT, H., 11th Lab. Coy.
	Pte. GOLDSTEIN, H., 11th Lab. Coy.
46611	Pte. GARCIA, D., 19th Lab. Coy.
49955	Pte. GREEN, B., 26th Lab. Coy.
50009	Pte. GALSTON, C., 26th Coy.
125103	Pte. GREENBERG, B., 15th Coy.
44268	L/Sgt. GREENSTONE, M. H., 20th Lab. C.
36210	Pte. GORDON, M., 51st Lab. Coy.
36534	Pte. GROSSHOP, H. C., 3rd Lab. Coy.
183487	Pte. GOLDSTEIN, N., 36th Lab. Coy.
99195	Pte. GOLDSTEIN, S., 1st Lab. Coy.
34791	Pte. GOLDBERG, J., 4th Lab. Coy.
465462	Pte. GOLDBERG, B., 593rd A. Coy.
557758	Pte. GRABOUSKY,
31937	Pte. GREENFAN, S.,
551302	Pte. GOLDMAN, I., 386th H.S. Lab. Coy.
70902	Pte. GILBERT, H., 119th Lab. Coy.
208154	Sgt. GERSHON, S., 8th Mx. Lab. Coy.
93710	L/Cpl. GERSHON, J., 8th Mx. Lab. Coy.
93409	Pte. GREENBERG, B., 8th Mx. Lab. Coy.
97778	Pte. GOLDBLUM, L., 8th Mx. Lab. Coy.
100116	Pte. GOTTLIEB, J. L., 8th Mx. Lab. Coy.
101908	Pte. GROSSMAN, P., 8th Mx. Lab. Coy.
93888	Pte. GILBERT, E., 8th Mx. Lab. Coy.
98106	Pte. GATTENBERG, J., 8th Mx. Lab. Coy.
557129	Cpl. GOLDBERG, H., 1002nd Lab. Coy.
557940	Pte. GEDULOVITCH, L., 1002nd Lab. Coy.
557655	Pte. GRIER, L., 1002nd Lab. Coy.
557737	Pte. GOTTFRIED, F., 1002nd Lab. Coy.
557702	Pte. GOLDSTEIN, J., 1002nd Lab. Coy.
557738	Pte. GELLERY, M., 1002nd Lab. Coy.
557408	Pte. GORGIN, I., 1002nd Lab. Coy.
558178	Pte. GOLDBERG, M., 1002nd Lab. Coy.
571618	Pte. GITTER, E., 1002nd Lab. Coy.
557743	Pte. GELLER, S., 1002nd Lab. Coy.
557084	Pte. GOTTFRIED, B., 1002nd Lab. Coy.
557428	Pte. GATHER, I., 1002nd Lab. Coy.
558672	Pte. GROSSMOUND, I., 1002nd Lab. Coy.
558114	Pte. GREENFIELD, H., 1002nd Lab. Coy.
558038	Pte. GOLDSTEIN, B., 1002nd Lab. Coy.
558112	Pte. GALINSKY, H., 1002nd Lab. Coy.
558073	Pte. GOLDBERG, T., 1002nd Lab. Coy.
557187	Pte. GOLDSTEIN, J., 1002nd Lab. Coy.
557513	Pte. GEETES, M., 1002nd Lab. Coy.
557999	Pte. GERITZMAN, S., 1002nd Lab. Coy.
558002	Pte. GORDON, M., 1002nd Lab. Coy.
558020	Pte. GRAFF, J., 1002nd Lab. Coy.
558037	Pte. GOLD, J., 1002nd Lab. Coy.
558160	Pte. GOLDBERG, I., 1002nd Lab. Coy.
558041	Pte. GAYER, M., 1002nd Lab. Coy.
557762	Pte. GAUCHANSKY, M., 1002nd Lab. Coy.
557760	Pte. GREENFIELD, B., 1002nd Lab. Coy.
557788	Pte. GOLDMAN, H., 1002nd Lab. Coy.

Labour Corps.—*Continued.*

557829 Pte. GOTTHELF, H., 1002nd Lab. Coy.
558310 Pte. GERITZER, H., 1002nd Lab. Coy.
557850 Pte. GITLEMAN, M., 1002nd Lab. Coy.
558254 Pte. GOLDSTEIN, B., 1002nd Lab. Coy.
558247 Pte. GRUNDMAN, J., 1002nd Lab. Coy.
558842 Pte. GRINBLATT, M., 1002nd Lab. Coy.
557717 Pte. GRODENTZ, J., 1002nd Lab. Coy.
557705 Pte. GLICENSTEIN, H., 1002nd Lab. Coy.
558167 Pte. GLADSTONE, D., 1002nd Lab. Coy.
558977 Pte. GINGOLD, S., 1002nd Lab. Coy.
558980 Pte. GROCHINSKY, J., 1002nd Lab. Coy.
557985 Pte. GUETCOVSKY, L., 1002nd Lab. Coy.
557560 Pte. GARFINKLEF, S., 1002nd Lab. Coy.
557210 L/Cpl. GROSSMAN, L., 1001st Lab. Coy.
557153 Pte. GINSBERG, M., 1001st Lab. Coy.
557243 Pte. GOTTFRIED, M., 1001st Lab. Coy.
558682 Pte. GLOBUS, S., 1001st Lab. Coy.
557654 Pte. GILBERT, S., 1001st Lab. Coy.
557631 Pte. GROSSMAN, N., 1001st Lab. Coy.
557262 Pte. GOLDSTEIN, M., 1001st Lab. Coy.
557612 Pte. GUANSKY, T., 1001st Lab. Coy.
557340 Pte. GOLDING, S., 1001st Lab. Coy.
557539 Pte. GABLOFSKY, M., 1001st Lab. Coy.
557551 Pte. GOLDSTEIN, S., 1001st Lab. Coy.
557451 Pte. GOLDBERG, J. M., 1001st Lab. Coy.
557412 Pte. GINSBERG, A., 1001st Lab. Coy.
557094 Pte. GOLD, S., 1001st Lab. Coy.
557476 Pte. GREENBERG, I., 1001st Lab. Coy.
557068 Pte. GOWAN, J., 1001st Lab. Coy.
557474 Pte. GREEN, S., 1001st Lab. Coy.
557424 Pte. GOTTMAN, C., 1001st Lab. Coy.
557084 Pte. GOTTFRIED, B., 1001st Lab. Coy.
557421 Pte. GOLDSTEIN, H., 1001st Lab. Coy.
557477 Pte. GRUNDBERG, A., 1001st Lab. Coy.
557032 Pte. GREEN, I., 1001st Lab. Coy.
557429 Pte. GOLDMAN, H., 1001st Lab. Coy.
557495 Pte. GRAYMAN, B., 1001st Lab. Coy.
557020 Pte. GOLDSTEIN, M., 1001st Lab. Coy.
557464 Pte. GOLLOP, H., 1001st Lab. Coy.
557403 Pte. GOTTLIEB, H., 1001st Lab. Coy.
557379 Pte. GOLDSTEIN, P. M., 1001st Lab. Coy.
557320 Pte. GOLDSTEIN, M., 1001st Lab. Coy.
557375 Pte. GINSBERG, T., 1001st Lab. Coy.
557559 Pte. GOLD, I., 1001st Lab. Coy.
558587 Pte. GINSBERG, H., 1001st Lab. Coy.
557096 Pte. GARFINKLE, I., 1001st Lab. Coy.
506735 Pte. GOLDBERG, N., 677th H.S. E. Coy.
461532 Pte. GLASS, J., 671st H.S. E. Coy.
123308 Pte. GOLD, J., 365th Res. Emp. Coy.
235153 Pte. GOLDSTEIN, M., 365th Res. E. Coy.
134420 Pte. GOLDSTEIN, J., 673rd H.S. E. Coy.
506723 Pte. GOLDSTEIN, D., 671st H.S. E. Co.y
391738 Pte. GOLDENBERG, J., 365th Res. E. Coy.
391773 Pte. GILBERT, H., 365th Res. Emp. Coy.
391786 Pte. GOLBOURNE, W., 365th Res. E. Coy.
49810 L/Sgt. GOLDSTONE, H., Lab. Centre.
593493 Pte. GOODMAN, H., Lab. Centre.
216474 Pte. GOTCLIFFE, J., 375th Lab. Coy.
507731 Pte. GERANSKY, J., Lab. Centre.
45191 Pte. GOODMAN, H., 1st Lab. Bn.
38964 Pte. GOLDBERG, T., 1st Lab. Bn.
129091 Pte. GAROM, J. S., 362nd Emp. Coy.
122630 Pte. GREEN, H., 42nd Coy.
531191 Pte. GODFREY, M., 527th Coy.
414773 Pte. GOODMAN, S.
545600 Pte. GOLDBERG, M., 305th Lab. Coy.
38286 Pte. GOLDSTEIN, C., 139th Lab. Coy.
76366 Pte. GOLDMAN, B., 128th Lab. Coy.
39641 Pte. GOLDMAN, A., 3rd Lab. Coy.
72507 Pte. GALINSKY, M., 121st Lab. Coy.
40384 Pte. GOULD, H., 68th Lab. Coy.
78776 Pte. GOLDSTEIN, M. A., 132nd Lab. Coy.
79679 Pte. GOLDSTEIN, S., 133rd Lab. Coy.
V/604 Cpl. GREENBERG, C., E.L.C.
087743 Cpl. GRUNBERH, O., E.L.C.
V/1028 Cpl. GUERSHON, V., E.L.C.
1048 Pte. GEBALI, V., E.L.C.
93 Pte. GAAN, F., E.L.C.
143 Pte. GAAN, A., E.L.C.
09095 Pte. GRINBERG, J., E.L.C.
192725 Pte. GREENBERG, J., 151st Lab. Coy.
425252 Pte. GWILLIAN, A. E., 127th Lab. Coy.
134420 Pte. GOLDSTEIN, J., 675th Lab. Coy.
162919 Pte. GREEN, S., 187th Lab. Coy.
198500 Pte. GOLDBERG, S., 366th Lab. Coy.
198606 Pte. GREENFIELD, A., 6th Lab. Coy.
162934 Pte. GREENSTEIN, H., 687th Lab. Coy.
365200 Pte. GOLD, M.
190608 Pte. GLASS, A., 236th Lab. Coy.
47942 Pte. GOLLAND, A.
461351 Pte. GRASS, J.
7842 Pte. GOODSAN, S., 14th Lab. Coy.
79406 Pte. GOLDSTEIN, H., 782nd Lab. Coy.
344021 Pte. GREENBERG, S., 5th Lab. Coy.
446380 Pte. GUINESS, S., 37th Lab. Coy.
94148 Pte. GLAISNER, A., 4th Lab. Coy.
193285 Pte. GLASS,
202730 Pte. GINSBERG, S., 246th Lab. Coy.
558708 Pte. GOLDRONS, J.
235513 Pte. GOLDSTEIN, M.
452465 Pte. GOODMAN, B.
39338 Pte. GOLDBERG, E., 35th Lab. Coy.
103967 Pte. GALEFSKY, J., 902nd A.E. Coy.
357462 Pte. GLUCKMAN, C.
45737 Pte. GROSE, A., 77th Lab. Coy.
210395 Pte. GELLMAN, H., 21st Lab. Coy.
Pte. GROSSMAN, D.
258188 Pte. GOLDBERG, N., 223rd Lab. Coy.
204051 Pte. GORDON, B., 1st Lab. Coy.
231718 Pte. GOULD, J., N.C.L.C.
84199 Pte. GOTTLIEB, L.
392832 Pte. GOLDBERG, L., 195th Lab. Coy.
79679 Pte. GOLDSTEIN, S., 133rd Lab. Coy.
11797 Pte. GOLDSTONE, H., 4th Lab. Coy.
79667 Pte. GOLDSTEIN, J., 689th Lab. Coy.

Labour Corps.—*Continued.*

78119	Pte. GROSSMAN, M., 132nd Lab. Coy.
460777	Pte. GERCHICK, A.
822687	Pte. GOLDMAN, M.
207082	Pte. GADION, 9th Lab. Coy.
556291	Pte. GREEN, H., 9th Lab. Coy.
556290	Pte. GLANZ, B., 9th Lab. Coy.
556277	Pte. GOLONBOCK, W., 9th Lab. Coy.
567131	Pte. GERANSKY, J.
556538	Pte. GOULDING, 9th Lab. Coy.
556485	Pte. GOODMAN, M., 9th Lab. Coy.
556504	Pte. GOLDBERG, H., 9th Lab. Coy.
268080	Pte. GAFFIN, J., 659th Lab. Coy.
50198	Pte. GOLDMAN, B., 20th Lab. Coy.
82828	Pte. GOLDSTEIN, G., 139th Lab. Coy.
365421	Pte. GOLDBERG, M.
562645	Pte. GLEEK, M.
558120	Pte. GEARALB, F., 8th Lab. Coy.
70998	Pte. GOLDSTEIN,
465462	Pte. GOLDBERG, W.
377833	Pte. GOLDMAN, A., 769th A.E. Coy.
35520	Pte. GORDON, A., 35th Lab. Coy.
596924	Pte. GOLDBERG, E., 28th Lab. Coy.
399548	Pte. GREENBERG, I., 369th Lab. Coy.
162922	Pte. GEDULD, M. A., 366th Lab. Coy.
66814	Pte. GROOSKY, B.
74492	Pte. GOTLIEB, M.
593159	Pte. GIRSH, H., 641st Lab. Coy.
273869	Pte. GREENBAUM, B.
509171	Pte. GREENBLATT, S., 298th Lab. Coy.
273876	Pte. GLAZER, H.
589199	Pte. GLORER, J., 373rd Lab. Coy.
58953	Pte. GODINSKY, J.
81013	Pte. GREENHOLTZ, 136th Lab. Coy.
366776	Pte. GORDON, P., 512th Lab. Coy.
434184	Pte. GOLDSTEIN, S., 536th Lab. Coy.
460743	Pte. GREENBAUM, F.
460955	Pte. GARSON,
274014	Pte. GOODMAN, H.
208713	Pte. GOLDBERG, I.
535575	Pte. GREENBOAM, E.
357672	Pte. GLICK, W., 393rd Lab. Coy.
429927	Pte. GOLDSTEIN, C.
	C.S.M. HARRIS, G. S. (M.S.M.).
368684	Sgt. HOFFMAN, H., 280th Area Em. Coy.
80018	Pte. HERMAN, H., 134th Lab. Coy.
417523	Pte. HOFFENBERG, M., 706th Lab. Coy.
93628	Pte. HEILBRON, I., 7th Mx. Lab. Coy.
93269	Pte. HEMPEL, K. V. R., 7th Mx. Lab. Co.
33890	Pte. HARTSTEIN, S. C., 7th Mx. Lab. Co.
98234	Pte. HAAS, M., 7th Mx. Lab. Coy.
272505	Pte. HARRIS, B., 234th Emp. Coy.
80416	Pte. HOLT, N., 4th Mx. Lab. Coy.
84093	Pte. HALPERN, B., 2nd Inf. Lab. Coy.
70081	Pte. HATTENSTEIN, I., 2nd Inf. Lab. Coy.
35798	Pte. HAUPT, S. L., 2nd Inf. Lab. Coy.
25908	Pte. HYMAN, S., 44th Lab. Coy.
30401	Pte. HERZL, H., 2nd Mx. Inf. Coy.
76222	Pte. HARRISON, F. G., 128th Lab. Coy.
76400	Pte. HIBBS, G. T., 128th Lab. Coy.
62000	Pte. HASSNOVITCH, J. J., 104th Lab. Coy.
92880	Pte. HESSER, N., 155th Lab. Coy.
80047	Pte. HARRIS, I., 134th Lab. Coy.
461638	Pte. HOFFBERG, L., 247th Div. Em. Coy.
47697	Pte. HEILBUT, A., 1st Mx. Lab. Coy.
28828	Cpl. HOUPT, A., 1st Mx. Lab. Coy.
75469	Pte. HARRIS, D., 1st Lab. Coy.
56404	Pte. HERMAN, J., 19th Lab. Coy.
51611	Pte. HYAMS, M., 29th Lab. Coy.
4993	Pte. HARRIS, D., 3rd Lab. Coy.
171362	L/Cpl. HYAMS, E., 192nd Lab. Coy.
143304	Cpl. HARRIS, A., 245th Lab. Coy.
233155	Pte. HART, H., 2nd Lab. Coy.
103441	Pte. HYAMS, S., 173th Lab. Coy.
68697	Cpl. HERWALD, R., 7th Lab. Coy.
311525	Gnr. HISHMAN, J., 641st A.E. Coy.
93555	Pte. HILNER, M., 5th Lab. Coy.
208945	Pte. HYAMS, E., 746th A.E.C.
282376	Pte. HANDLE, S., 90th Lab. Coy.
208119	Pte. HART, S., 6th Lab. Cov.
391492	L/Cpl. HARRIS, M. C., 75th Lab. Coy.
551080	Pte. HYAMS, J., 610th Lab. Coy.
511594	Pte. HARRIS, S. S., 9th Lab. Coy.
492772	Pte. HARRIS, H., 377th Lab. Coy.
494799	Pte. HARRIS, M., 389th Lab. Coy.
27148	Pte. HILLON, J., 46th Lab. Coy.
461538	Pte. HOFFBERG, L., 247th Emp. Coy.
684294	Pte. HAUFFMAN, J.
486796	Pte. HONIGMAN, S.
261089	Pte. HIRSCH, L.
42535	Pte. HERSKOVITCH, I., 9th Lab. Coy.
682275	Pte. HIMMELFALB, S., Labour Centre.
69211	Pte. HERMAN, D., 116th Lab. Coy.
27818	Pte. HARRISON, N. L., 849th Lab. Coy.
307400	Sgt. HARRIS, H., 729th Lab. Coy.
197980	Pte. HOFFBERG, J., 67th Lab. Coy.
530057	Pte. HALSEN, B., 512th H.S.E.C.
74272	L/Cpl. HARBURG, H., 1st Mx. Lab. Coy.
70000	Pte. HITNER, H. J., 1st Mx. Lab. Coy.
48521	Pte. HIRSCH, B. L., 1st Mx. Lab. Coy.
18555	Pte. HYMAN, W., 1st Mx. Lab. Coy.
44575	Pte. HIRSHALL, D., 1st Mx. Lab. Coy.
44574	Pte. HIRSHALL, A., 1st Mx. Lab. Coy.
44726	Pte. HILL, A., 1st Mx. Lab. Coy.
36756	L/Cpl. HAAS, A., 3rd Mx. Lab. Coy.
36752	Pte. HALLE, A., 3rd Lab. Coy.
80403	Pte. HAUOT, S., 3rd Mx. Lab. Coy.
45609	Pte. HERBST, G., 3rd Mx. Lab. Coy.
G/74437	Pte. HERTZBERG, J., 4th Mx. Lab. Coy.
G/80166	Pte. HAMMER, M., 4th Mx. Lab. Coy.
G/71397	Pte. HERRMANN, L., 4th Mx. Lab. Coy.
G/80068	Pte. HIRSCH, H., 4th Mx. Lab. Coy.
G/70127	Pte. HERRMANN, N., 4th Mx. Lab. C.
G/44730	Pte. HEILBRON, G., 4th Mx. Lab. Coy.
523644	Pte. HOEDEMAKER, J., 71st Lab. Coy.
585688	Pte. HOBITS, S., 109th Lab. Coy.

Labour Corps.—*Continued.*

69211	Pte. HERMAN, D., 116th Lab. Coy.
78807	Pte. HOFFMAN, R., 132nd Lab. Coy.
87808	Pte. HARRIS, J., 147th Lab. Coy.
417523	Pte. HOFFENBERG, M., 706th Lab. Coy.
273823	Pte. HOCHBERG, A., 947th A.E.
1912	Cpl. HARRIS, M., 4th Lab. Coy.
273822	Pte. HERSHCOVITCH, H., 991st Lab. Coy.
272420	Pte. HART, B., 86th Lab. Coy.
452697	Pte. HALBERT, L., 22nd Lab. Coy.
75793	Pte. HERMAN, J,. 127th Lab. Coy.
75883	Pte. HENRIQUES, J., 127th Lab. Coy.
81848	Pte. HYAMS, M., 137th Lab. Coy.
47558	Pte. HARRIS, M., 80th Lab. Coy.
461325	Pte. HAAS, A., 170th Lab. Coy.
69211	Pte. HERMAN, W., 116th Lab. Coy.
27826	Pte. HARRIS, N., 47th Lab. Coy.
442055	Pte. HERBERT, M., 939th A.E. Coy.
561554	Pte. HONSE, S., 713rd Coy.
442055	Pte. HERBERT, M., 939th A.E. Coy.
208119	Pte. HART, V., 6th Lab. Coy.
80508	Pte. HIRSCH, L., 135th Lab. Coy.
G/80087	L/Cpl. HOLT, D., 4th Lab. Coy.
G/80416	Pte. HOLT, F., 4th Lab. Coy.
69812	Pte. HERSCOVITCH, J., 117th Lab. Coy.
800487	Pte. HARRIS, I., 134th Lab. Coy.
800183	Pte. HERMAN, H., 83rd Lab. Coy.
28823	Cpl. HAPT, A., 1st Mx. Lab. Coy.
74272	L/Cpl. HARBURG, H. W., 1st Mx. L. Co.
84093	Pte. HALPERN, B., 2nd Mx. Lab. Coy.
31158	Pte. HART, H., 2nd Mx. Lab. Coy.
70081	Pte. HATTENSTEIN, I., 2nd Mx. Lab. Coy.
145317	Pte. HYAMS, J., 91st Lab. Coy.
87857	Pte. HUTCHINSKY, A., 91st Lab. Coy.
91435	Pte. HEMMINGS, B. A., 153rd Lab. Coy.
279595	Pte. HARRIS, D., 641st A.E. Coy.
311525	Pte. HIRSCHMAN, J., 641st A.E. Coy.
436796	Pte. HONIGMAN, S., 650th Lab. Coy.
651642	Pte. HAMBLING, H., 156th Lab. Coy.
G/35612	Pte. HELLER, S., 5th Mx. Lab. Coy.
G/74028	Pte. HIRSCH, M., 5th Mx. Lab. Coy.
G/84092	Pte. HENICH, C., 5th Mx. Lab. Coy.
G/84194	Pte. HUDIS, M., 5th Mx. Lab. Coy.
G/933994	Pte. HOBERMAN, B., 5th Mx. Lab. Co.
G/93423	Pte. HYMAN, A., 5th Mx. Lab. Coy.
G/36828	Pte. HEMPEL, S., 5th Mx. Lab. Coy.
G/31307	Pte. HOFFMAN, M., 5th Mx. Lab. Coy.
G/93033	Pte. HUDIS, P., 5th Mx. Lab. Coy.
G/74172	Pte. HUDIS, J., 5th Mx. Lab. Coy.
G/72617	Pte. HIRSCH, M., 5th Mx. Lab. Coy.
G/47888	Pte. HALLE, L., 5th Mx. Lab. Coy.
G/93306	Pte. HATTENA, I., 5th Mx. Lab. Coy.
G/93555	Pte. HITNER, A., 5th Mx. Lab. Coy.
G/80068	Pte. HIRSCH, H., 5th Mx. Lab. Coy.
79688	Pte. HILLEL, Z., 69th Lab. Coy.
171449	Pte. HART, S. L., 70th Lab. Coy.
74362	L/Cpl. HERZ, P. J., 35th Lab. Coy.
80006	Pte. HOCHMAN, L., 35th Lab. Coy.
84360	Pte. HARRIS, S., 35th Lab. Coy.
208035	Pte. HEIMAN, H. P., 35th Lab. Coy.
105827	Pte. HERNBERG, S., 35th Lab. Coy.
273822	Pte. HERSHOVITZ, H. M., 991st Lab. Co.
44831	Pte. HALPERN, H., 4th Mx. Inf. Lab. Coy.
461118	Pte. HEISER, J.,
40411	Cpl. HYAM, M. L., 203rd P. & W. Coy.
71397	Pte. HERMAN, L., 4th Lab. Coy.
577109	Pte. HAFTEL, L., 964th A.E. Coy.
55114	Pte. HARRIS, J., 844th A.E. Coy.
31172	Pte. HABERER, S., 2nd Coy.
36662	Pte. HAMBERG, J., 7th Lab. Coy.
69812	Pte. HERSKOVITCH, J., 117th Lab. Coy.
396352	Pte. HIRSHKOVITCH, N., 42nd Lab. Coy.
61666	Pte. HAWKBERG, H., 2nd Lab. Coy.
99264	Pte. HUSCOVITCH, H. S., 1st Lab. Coy.
89870	Pte. HENRIQUIES, A., 12th Lab. Coy.
34593	Pte. HARRIS, L., 4th Lab. Coy.
34378	Pte. HILSURN, S., 4th Lab. Coy.
199888	Pte. HART, S. R., 735th Lab. Coy.
561554	Pte. HOUSE, S., 713rd Lab. Coy.
282376	Pte. HANDEL, S., 86th Lab. Coy.
98243	Cpl. HAMILTON, H., 8th Mx. Lab. Coy.
100800	Pte. HUDIS, J. P., 8th Mx. Lab. Coy.
100060	Pte. HARRIS, H., 8th Mx. Lab. Coy.
100785	Pte. HEXTER, S., 8th Mx. Lab. Coy.
74398	Pte. HAKIM, R., 8th Mx. Lab. Coy.
93563	Pte. HIPSHMAN, C. M., 8th Mx. Lab. Coy.
93342	Pte. HOROWITZ, G., 8th Mx. Lab. Coy.
93155	Pte. HALPERN, J.,e 8th Mx. Lab. Coy.
93545	Pte. HARRIS, L. O., 8th Mx. Lab. Coy.
98202	Pte. HIRSCHHORN, C., 8th Mx. Lab. Coy.
93676	Pte. HELLER, H., 8th Mx. Lab. Coy.
557827	L/Cpl. HARRIS, H., 1002nd Lab. Coy.
557649	Pte. HEINSDROFF, L., 1002nd Lab. Coy.
557734	Pte. HASKIN, L., 1002nd Lab. Coy.
557222	Pte. HARRIS, H., 1002nd Lab. Coy.
558132	Pte. HARRIS, H., 1002nd Lab. Coy.
557603	Pte. HUBERMAN, I., 1002nd Lab. Coy.
557832	Pte. HODDES, J., 1002nd Lab. Coy.
557582	Pte. HADDERMAN, H., 1002nd Lab. Coy.
557578	Pte. HELMAN, D., 1002nd Lab. Coy.
557778	Pte. HENDRICK, M., 1002nd Lab. Coy.
557886	Pte. HOFFMAN, J., 1002nd Lab. Coy.
557586	Pte. HALBER, P., 1002nd Lab. Coy.
557809	Pte. HYMAN, H., 1002nd Lab. Coy.
557923	Pte. HOROWITZ, M., 1002nd Lab. Coy.
558004	Pte. HARRIS, M., 1002nd Lab. Coy.
558158	Pte. HYAMS, L., 1002nd Lab. Coy.
557693	Pte. HORNE, S., 1002nd Lab. Coy.
557374	Pte. HIRSCH, D., 1001st Lab. Coy.
557080	Pte. HARRIS, F., 1001st Lab. Coy.
558523	Pte. HANSTEAD, L. V., 1001st Lab. Coy.
557399	Pte. HUNTER, P., 1001st Lab. Coy.
557079	Pte. HYMAN, S., 1001st Lab. Coy.
558657	Pte. HATINSKY, S., 1001st Lab. Coy.
557145	Pte. HIRSCHBERG, A., 1001st Lab Coy.

Labour Corps.—*Continued.*

557270	Pte. HUBERMAN, M., 1001st Lab. Coy.
557120	Pte. HALPERIN, M., 1001st Lab. Coy.
557147	Pte. HARRIS, L., 1001st Lab. Coy.
557261	Pte. HERTZBERG, A., 1001st Lab. Coy.
557701	Pte. HENNICK, A., 1001st Lab. Coy.
558555	Pte. HECHT, S., 1001st Lab. Coy.
557324	Pte. HOCKMAN, A., 1001st Lab. Coy.
557366	Pte. HASKIN, M., 1001st Lab. Coy.
557363	Pte. HARRIS, I., 1001st Lab. Coy.
557498	Pte. HAMMERMAN, A., 1001st Lab. Coy.
557271	Pte. HYMANOVITCH, A., 1001st Lab. Coy.
461253	Pte. HEISER, A., 672nd Emp. Coy
235471	Pte. HART, A., Emp. Coy.
134138	Pte. HARRIS, A., 675th Res. Emp. Coy.
428498	Pte. HANELLA, A., 365th Res. Emp. Coy.
193328	Pte. HARRIS, S., 362nd Emp. Coy.
	Pte. HYMANSON, D., Lab. Centre.
948160	Pte. HARRIS, A., Lab. Centre.
393045	Pte. HORNICK, P., Lab. Centre.
31981	Pte. HARRIS, I., Lab. Centre.
412189	Cpl. HARRIS, L., 893rd A.E. Coy.
322542	Pte. HILDESHEIMER, D., 527th Coy.
605942	L/Cpl. HARRIS, L.
645848	Pte. HARRIS, J.
39376	Pte. HASSNOVITCH, J. J., 35th Lab. Coy.
219695	Pte. HINICH, J., 738th Lab. Coy.
87832	Pte. HART, A., 147th Lab. Coy.
79843	Pte. HYMAN, B., 134th Lab. Coy.
563761	Pte. HYMAN, J., 298th Lab. Coy.
353	Pte. HAROUCH, I., E.L.C.
100	Sgt. HAIM, F., E.L.C.
155	Pte. HAKIM, I., E.L.C.
09069	Pte. HAZZEM, I. S., E.L.C.
139475	Pte. HIMMY, J., E.L.C.
011038	Cpl. HELOU, J., E.L.C.
338	Cpl. HEMMI, A., E.L.C.
43967	Pte. HARRIS, B.
272420	Pte. HART, B., 186th Lab. Coy.
6198163	Pte. HARRIS, P., 689th Lab. Coy.
353098	Pte. HARRIS, A.
209911	Pte. HACKMAN, A.
88087	Pte. HYAMS, A.
551964	Pte. HORWICK.
68613	Pte. HOMBERG, J.
44575	Pte. HERSHEL, D., 1st Lab. Coy.
355165	Pte. HARRIS, G.
525612	Pte. HAVERLACK, J., 305th Lab. Coy.
482429	Pte. HOFFENBERG, I.
80166	Pte. HAMMER, M., 4th Lab. Coy.
80416	Pte. HOLT, M., 4th Lab. Coy.
80087	L/Cpl. HOLT, D., 4th Lab. Coy.
461263	Pte. HEISER, A.
75759	Pte. HARMAN, J.
800117	Pte. HARRIS, J., 134th Lab. Coy.
273279	Pte. HOFFMAN, M.
103110	Pte. HYAMS, S., 162nd Lab. Coy.
31172	Pte. HARBERER, S., 2nd Lab. Coy.
88419	Pte. HILLSON, B., 366th Lab. Coy.
636911	Pte. HYMAN, S.
27826	Pte. HARRIS, W., 47th Lab. Coy.
27818	Pte. HARRISON, N. L., 99th Lab. Coy.
41387	Pte. HAYHURST, S.
556550	Pte. HYMANS, H., 9th Lab. Coy.
407534	Pte. HARVEY, 375th Lab. Coy.
171362	L/Cpl. HYAMS, E., 824th Lab. Coy.
31952	Pte. HENRY, N., 54th Lab. Coy.
40411	Pte. HYAM, M.,* 230th P.O.W. Lab. Coy.
430796	Pte. HONIGMAN, S., 650th Lab. Coy.
261689	Pte. HIRSCH, L., 650th Lab. Coy.
307400	Sgt. HARRIS, H., 729th Lab. Coy.
208945	Pte. HYAMS, C., 746th Lab. Coy.
537987	Pte. HOVIDLER, W.
219695	Pte. HITCHICH, J., 738th Lab. Coy.
209841	Pte. HARRIS, H. P., 685th Lab. Coy.
39332	Pte. HENRIQUES, A.
36865	Pte. HILSURN, B., 10th Lab. Coy.
197980	Pte. HOFFBERG, H. J., 368th Lab. Coy.
1912	Pte. HARRIS, M., 4th Lab. Coy.
166388	L/Sgt. HARRIS, J. M., N.C.L.C.
150939	Pte. HILLIER, L., 389th Lab. Coy.
161040	Pte. HARRIS, G.
15459	Pte. HYMAN, J., 585th Lab. Coy.
62676	L/Cpl. HYAMS, D., 105th Lab. Coy.
39376	Pte. HASSNOVITCH, J. J., 35th Lab. Coy.
27148	Pte. HILTON, G., 46th Lab. Coy.
51243	Pte. HIRSH, L., 739th Lab. Coy.
42620	Cpl. HERWALD, R.
87819	Pte. HERMAN, E., 147th Lab. Coy.
363717	Pte. HILL, W., 7th Lab. Coy.
31781	L/Cpl. HARRIS, I., 18th Lab. Coy.
175338	Pte. HARRIS, J., 322nd Lab. Coy.
103409	Pte. HARIS, L., 173rd Lab. Coy.
457638	Pte. HERZFIELD, S., 547th Lab. Coy.
530057	Pte. HALSON, B., 512th Lab. Coy.
153592	Pte. HYMAN, W., 339th Lab. Coy.
206353	Pte. HARPER, A., 524th Lab. Coy.
49521	Pte. HIRSCH, B. L., 1st Lab. Coy.
192919	Pte. HOCKER, M.
272973	Pte. ISENBERG, F., 287th A.E. Coy.
109823	Pte. ISRAEL, A. I., 184th Lab. Coy.
127859	Pte. ISAACS, J., 161st Lab. Coy.
62826	L/Cpl. ISAACS, 109th Lab. Coy.
356801	Pte. ISAACS, R.
67432	Pte. ISAACS, G., 729th Lab. Coy.
425486	Pte. IDMAS, G., 113th Lab. Coy.
G/80154	Pte. ISENSTEIN, L., 4th Mx. Lab. Coy.
78824	Pte. ISAACMAN, S., 132nd Lab. Coy.
433989	Pte. ISAACS, M., 189th Lab. Coy.
449541	Pte. ISAACS, M., 822nd Lab. Coy.
51774	Pte. ISAACS, M., 20th Lab. Coy.
	Pte. IDELS, H.
629528	Pte. ISRAEL, D., 108th Lab. Coy.
392438	Pte. ISAACS, S., 39th Lab. Coy.
89198	Pte. ISAACS, W. D., 149th Lab. Coy.
80516	Pte. ISAAC, R., 135th Lab. Coy.

Labour Corps.—*Continued.*

209051	Pte. ISAACS, C., 706th Lab. Coy.
377733	Pte. ISAACS, M., 165th Lab. Coy.
50320	Pte. ISAACS, R. J., 27th Lab. Coy.
38124	Pte. ISAACS, 1st Lab. Coy.
116	Pte. INGIAN, H., 72nd Lab. Coy.
375165	Pte. ISAACS, W,. 56th A.E. Coy.
36488	Pte. ISAACS, 51st Lab. Coy.
558262	Pte. IZZARD, M., 1002nd Lab. Coy.
558019	Pte. ITSKOWITCH, H., 1002nd Lab. Coy.
557010	Pte. ISAACSON, S., 1002nd Lab. Coy.
557557	Pte. ISBITSKY, S., 1001st Lab. Coy.
557018	Pte. ISEN, H., 1001st Lab. Coy.
557144	Pte. ISAACS, S., 1001st Lab. Coy.
209051	Pte. ISAACS, C., 365th Res. Emp. Coy.
235036	Pte. ISAACS, S., 673rd Res. H.S. Coy.
45004	Pte. ISAACSON, M., 1st Lab. Bn.
125965	Pte. ISAAC, R., 375th Lab. Coy.
48839	Pte. ISAACS, I., 82nd Lab. Coy.
210697	Pte. ISAACS, D., 127th Lab. Coy.
36359	Pte. ISAACS, G., 113th Lab. Coy.
10295	Pte. ISRAEL, L.
201183	Pte. ISAACS, A., 301st Lab. Coy.
323777	Pte. ISAACS, H., 604th Lab. Coy.
407542	Pte. ISAACS, G., 875th Lab. Coy.
36359	Pte. ISAACS, G., 5th Lab. Coy.
48839	Pte. ISAACS, A., 82nd Lab. Coy.
477298	Pte. INESKY, N. J., 110th Lab. Coy.
89876	Pte. ISAACS, J., 712th Lab. Coy.
378621	Pte. JACOBS, J., 258th Area Emj. Coy.
226703	Pte. JACOBSON, R., 259th Area Emp. C.
83658	Pte. JOSEPH, B,. 140th Lab. Coy.
3174	Pte. JACOBSON, B., 6th Lab. Coy.
93142	Pte. JACOB, E. E. A., 7th Inf. Lab. Coy.
93368	Pte. JULIUS, J., 7th Inf. Lab. C. Mx. R.
76422	Pte. JOEL, B., 128th Lab. Coy.
413412	Pte. JACOBS, A., 211th (Divl.) E. Coy.
55739	Pte. JERICHOWER, N., 1st Mx. Lab. Coy.
39124	Pte. JACOBS, M., 6th Lab. Coy.
105216	Pte. JACOBS, M., 176th Lab. Coy.
71040	Pte. JACOBS, E., 119th Lab. Coy.
272729	Sgt. JOSEPH, W. G., Lond. Dist.
397882	Cpl. JACKSON, C., 796th A.E. Coy.
81853	Pte. JACOBSON, L., 723rd Lab. Coy.
864044	Pte. JACOBS, M., 144th Lab. Coy.
217736	Pte. JACOBS, A., 539th Lab. Coy.
13592	Pte. JACOBSON, B., 12th Black Watch.
226703	Pte. JACOBSON, R., 257th A.E. Coy.
561836	Pte. JOFFE, D., 240th A.E. Coy.
397793	Pte. JOSEPH, S., 786th A.E. Coy.
557225	Pte. JAFFERBAUM, B., 686th Lab. Coy.
58448	Pte. JACOBSON, S.
36229	Pte. JERICHOWER, S., 1st Mx. Lab. Coy.
48456	Pte. JACOBSEN, H., 3rd Mx. Lab. Coy.
47692	Pte. JASON, J., 3rd Mx. Lab. Coy.
G/80128	Pte. JOURADO, V., 4th Mx. Lab. Coy.
G/71494	Pte. JOURADO, F. E., 4th Mx. Lab. Coy.
G/80279	Pte. JOSEPH, I., 4th Mx. Lab. Coy.
69247	Pte. JACOBS, B., 116th Lab. Coy.
78838	Pte. JOEL, J., 132nd Lab. Coy.
609012	Pte. JOLOFSKY, S., 139th Lab. Coy.
83658	Pte. JOSEPH, B., 140th Lab. Coy.
516438	Pte. JASPER, H., 141st Lab. Coy.
107108	Pte. JOSEPH, J., 179th Lab. Coy.
473727	Pte. JOSEPH, L., 991st Lab. Coy.
657712	Pte. JONESCU, A., 991st Lab. Coy.
377339	Pte. JACKSON, F., 832nd A.E. Coy.
3174	Pte. JACOBSON, B., 6th Lab. Coy.
177570	Pte. JACOBS, B., 170th Lab. Coy.
69247	Pte. JACOBS, B., 116th Lab. Coy.
525256	Pte. JACOBSON, A., 281st A.E. Coy.
634136	Pte. JACOBS, D., 7th Lab. Coy.
G/89279	Pte. JOSEPH, I., 4th Lab. Coy.
69841	Pte. JUDGE, J. A., 117th Lab. Coy.
19458	Pte. JACOBS, B. M., 33rd Lab. Coy.
476471	Pte. JACOBS, D., 10th Lab. Coy.
440871	Pte. JACOBS, M., 621st Lab. Coy.
197988	Pte. JACOBS, E., 69th Lab. Coy.
88428	Pte. JACOBS, A., 70th Lab. Coy.
84465	L/Cpl. JERICHOWER, M., 35th Lab. Coy.
421950	Pte. JACOBS, L.,
444890	Cpl. JOSEPHS, A., 56th Chin. Lab. Coy.
357564	Pte. JULIUS, J., A.E. Coy.
409896	A/Sgt. JACOBS, G., 888th A.E. Coy.
673827	Pte. JOSEPHSON, J.
406723	Pte. JACOBS, H. L., 871st A.E. Coy.
626975	Pte. JACOBOVITCH, H., 871st A.E. Coy.
67436	Pte. JATTA, S., 5th Lab. Coy.
71042	Pte. JACOBS, I., 11th Lab. Coy.
71041	Pte. JACOBS, N., 11th Lab. Coy.
51531	Pte. JACOBSON, L., 29th Lab. Coy.
61946	Pte. JACOBS, E. W., 2nd Lab. Coy.
108507	Pte. JOSEPH, H., 4th Lab. Coy.
558103	Pte. JOSEPH, A., 1002nd Lab. Coy.
558137	Pte. JACOBS, J., 1002nd Lab. Coy.
558238	Pte. JACOBSON, A., 1002nd Lab. Coy.
557718	Pte. JACOBOWITZ, H., 1002nd Lab. Coy.
557709	Pte. JOSEPHSON, H., 1002nd Lab. Coy.
558139	Pte. JOSEPHS, H., 1002nd Lab. Coy.
557238	L/Cpl. JOIBELSON, A., 1001st Lab. Coy.
557054	Pte. JACOBS, N., 1001st Lab. Coy.
557116	Pte. JEFF, I., 1001st Lab. Coy.
557201	Pte. JACOBS, G., 1001st Lab. Coy.
391833	Pte. JACOBS, P., 672nd H.S. E. Coy.
552841	Pte. JACOBS, S. D., 572nd H.S. E. Coy.
525130	Pte. JACOBS, H., Lab. Centre.
456783	L/Cpl. JACOBS, J., Lab. Centre.
409896	Sgt. JACOBS, G. S., 888th A.E. Coy.
58448	Pte. JACOBS, S., 98th Coy.
589890	Pte. JACOBSON, H.
33313	Pte. JACKSON, A., 139th Lab. Coy.
35274	Pte. JAFFA, A., 113th Lab. Coy.
586264	Pte. JAHANSBERG, L., 181st Lab. Coy.
	Chief Clerk JOSEPH, A. (M.S.M.).
417959	Pte. JEFFREYS, A., 94th Lab. Coy.
111	Pte. JERUSALEM, A., E.L.C.

Labour Corps.—Continued.

09046 Pte. JACKMAN, D., E.L.C.
19616 Pte. JACOBS, A., 1st Lab. Coy.
         Sgt. JACOBS, W. T. G. (M.S.M.).
31995 Pte. JACOBS, M., 54th Lab. Coy.
202762 Pte. JACOBSON, H., 376th Lab. Coy.
36099 Pte. JACOBS, H.
64444 Pte. JACOBSON, 22nd Lab. Coy.
17455 Pte. JACOBS, G., 13th Lab. Coy.
398133 Pte. JACOBS, P.
397793 L/Cpl. JOSEPH, S., 786th Lab. Coy.
79414 Pte. JOURADO, F. E., 4th Lab. Coy.
19458 Pte. JACOBS, V. M., 33rd Lab. Coy.
69247 Pte. JACOBS, B., 116th Lab. Coy.
491827 Pte. JACOBS, A.
452477 Pte. JOSEPH, A., 362nd Lab. Coy.
38054 Pte. JIBERSON,
452439 Pte. JOSEPH, A.
152669 Pte. JACOBS, J. W., 5th Lab. Coy.
236350 Pte. JOSEPH, M.
357538 Pte. JAFFA, M., 1st Lab. Coy.
528936 Pte. JACOBS, A., 30th Lab. Coy.
556270 Pte. JACKSON, D., 9th Lab. Coy.
357671 Pte. JOFFE, S., 362nd Lab. Coy.
86044 Pte. JACOBS, M., 144th Lab. Coy.
192638 Pte. JOSEPH, I., 25th Lab. Coy.
527140 Pte. JONES, A., 723rd Lab. Coy.
36624 Pte. JAFFE, A., 525th Lab. Coy.
273352 Pte. JACKOVITCH, P.
15776 Pte. JOEL, J.
31472 Pte. JUBESKI, I., 480th Lab. Coy.
552458 Pte. JEW, A., S.C.L.C.
47043 Pte. KAUFFMAN, R., 258th Area Em. Cy.
379261 Pte. KAYLES, M., 258th Area Emp. Coy.
342732 Pte. KLEINS, S., 154th Lab. Coy.
74214 Pte. KEIL, A., 7th Inf. Mx. Lab. Coy.
98048 Pte. KOBER, N., 7th Inf. Mx. Lab. Coy.
36048 Pte. KLEIN, M. A., 7th Mx. Lab. Coy.
84116 Pte. KATZNER, I., 7th Mx. Lab. Coy.
191968 Pte. KOBIESKY, M., 246th Emp. Coy.
197696 L/Cpl. KALISKI, H., 746th A.E. Coy.
30993 Pte. KRENDLE, M., 2nd Inf. Lab. Coy.
84351 Pte. KURASCH, L., 110th Lab. Coy.
889 Pte. KALISKER, A.,* 80th Egyp. Lab. Co.
86651 Pte. KRESOVSKY, B., 145th Lab. Coy.
92771 Pte. KOSKI, M., 155th Lab. Coy.
512104 Pte. KLINE, J., 185th Lab. Coy.
73499 Pte. KERNER, W., 1st Mx. Lab. Coy.
36098 Pte. KIRSHNER, A., 1st Mx. Lab. Coy.
39062 Pte. KOSKY, C., 6th Lab. Coy.
104636 Pte. KANTOVITCH, J., 175th Lab. Coy.
80361 Pte. KOHN, B., 4th Lab. Coy.
633053 Pte. KEFFER, M., 4th Lab. Coy.
103458 Pte. KNIAGER, J., 173rd Lab. Coy.
103455 Pte. KAPLAN, W., 173rd Lab. Coy.
88828 Pte. KRAFSOFF, 807th A. E. Coy.
80068 Pte. KIRSH, F., 4th Lab. Coy.
558483 Pte. KRIEMAN, 8th Lab. Coy.

326609 Pte. KLIEMAN, A.
55787 Pte. KELLY, D., 13th Lab. Coy.
40935 Pte. KASHKEN, B., 14th Devon L.C.
7009 Pte. KELLY, S., 1st Lab. Coy.
639640 Pte. KING H., Labour Centre.
1087022 Pte. KAUFMAN, S., 21st Lab. Coy.
49629 Pte. KUDISH, J.
38579 Pte. KAUFMAN, G., 1st Mx. Lab. Coy.
73482 Pte. KANTZ, H., 1st Mx. Lab. Coy.
74213 Pte. KIEL, H., 1st Mx. Lab. Coy.
37241 Pte. KALINSKY, V., 3rd Mx. Lab. Coy.
4519 Pte. KAUFMANN, F., 3rd Mx. Lab. Coy.
38591 Pte. KIRSCHBAUM, J., 3rd Mx. Lab. Coy.
83030 Pte. KITZBERG, L., 3rd Mx. Lab. Coy.
48468 Pte. KRANTISCH, M., 3rd Mx. Lab. Coy.
G/80147 Pte. KLEIN, A., 4th Mx. Lab. Coy.
G/72020 Pte. KLAUSNER, M., 4th Mx. Lab. Coy.
G/47698 Pte. KAYE, A. E., 4th Mx. Lab. Coy.
630381 Pte. KATZ, E., 108th Lab. Coy.
583787 Pte. KERSH, P., 108th Lab. Coy.
78848 Pte. KLEIN, D. D., 132nd Lab. Coy.
79448 Pte. KLAN, M., 133rd Lab. Coy.
78757 Pte. KULCHINSKY, A., 147th Lb. Coy.
461076 Pte. KLUNMAN, 178th Lab. Coy.
512140 Pte. KLINE, J., 185th Lab. Coy.
         Pte. KRISHEK, I. S., 708th Lab. Coy.
393320 Pte. KRAVETZ, L., 715th Lab. Coy.
655245 Pte. KOHEN, H., 735th Lab. Coy.
581986 Pte. KEPELMAN, A., 991st Lab. Coy.
153152 Pte. KOLINSKY, J., 991st Lab. Coy.
461076 Pte. KLEINMAN, N., 991st Lab. Coy.
197696 L/Cpl. KALISKY, H., 746th Lab. Coy.
48653 Pte. KERSH, P., 108th Lab. Coy.
108839 Pte. KELLY, S., 278th A.E. Coy.
197566 Pte. KOOPER, M. H., 256th A.E. Coy.
44710 Pte. KAROVITCH, J., 281st A.E. Coy.
525233 Pte. KELMAN, M., 745th A.E. Coy.
519341 Pte. KAVONIS, I., 9th Lab. Coy.
98048 Pte. KOBER, N., 7th Lab. Coy.
G/74408 Pte. KRAMBACK, J., 4th Lab. Coy.
G/84134 Pte. KLEIN, J., 5th Mx. Lab. Coy.
G/93376 Pte. KOMAILSE, O. M., 5th Lab. Coy.
G/93086 Pte. KEIL, J., 5th Mx. Lab. Coy.
G/93491 Pte. KRENGEL, S., 5th Mx. Lab. Coy.
G/73372 Pte. KLETZ, W., 5th Mx. Lab. Coy.
G/97766 Pte. KLAPISH, J., 5th Mx. Lab. Coy.
G/92121 Pte. KLAPISH, S., 5th Mx. Lab. Coy.
G/90843 Pte. KAISER, G. B., 5th Mx. Lab. Coy.
108839 Pte. KELLY, S., 278th A.E. Coy.
208000 L/Cp. KRAM, E., 35th Lab. Coy.
208021 L/Cpl. KENNEDY, K. A., 35th Lab. Coy.
84343 Pte. KUTTNER, E. H., 35th Lab. Coy.
71564 Pte. KANE, H. A., 35th Lab. Coy.
84292 Pte. KATS, J., 35th Lab. Coy.
74471 Pte. KIRSCH, M., 35th Lab. Coy.
61585 Pte. KEPPER, E., 35th Lab. Coy.
581986 Pte. KEPELMAN, N. S., 991st Lab. Coy.
15352 Pte. KOLINSKY, J. M., 991st Lab. Coy.

Labour Corps.—*Continued.*

Pte. KOOPCHICK, I., Lab. Coy.
Pte. KROKHINLICK, A.
L/Cpl. KRAMAR, J.
461076 Pte. KLEINMAN, M. M., 991st Lab. Coy.
36095 Pte. KIRSCHMAN, A., 1st Inf. Lab. Coy.
629745 Pte. KATZ, A., Lab. Centre.
72615 Pte. KRAKAUER, J., 1st Lab. Coy.
67452 Pte. KING, F., 5th Lab. Coy.
46649 Pte. KLIPP, L., 19th Lab. Coy.
33928 Pte. KLEIN, L., 2nd Lab. Coy.
2002673 Pte. KENNELL, M., 12th Lab. Coy.
34643 Pte. KOSKY, A., 7th Lab. Coy.
Pte. KINAGER, J., 8th Lab. Coy.
Pte. KAMONOVITCH, M., 8th Lab. Coy.
39923 Pte. KOSKI, 14th Lab. Coy.
40190 Pte. KASHDEN, 14th Lab. Coy.
80651 Pte. KRESOVSKY, B., 145th Lab. Coy.
204285 Pte. KRATSOFF, A., 11th Lab. Coy.
254 Pte. KNAWAN, A., 72nd Lab. Coy.
G/93436 Pte. KOPIESKIE, N., 5th Lab. Coy.
93379 Pte. KINSLER, M., 8th Mx. Lab. Coy.
73473 Pte. KINSLER, A., 8th Mx. Lab. Coy.
100175 Pte. KLAR, M., 8th Mx. Lab. Coy.
98109 Pte. KAHN, R., 8th Mx. Lab. Coy.
93673 Pte. KIMMERHART, M., 8th Mx. Lab. Coy.
557226 Pte. KNOPP, B., 1002nd Lab. Coy.
557937 Pte. KITCHENOFF, R., 1002nd Lab. Coy.
557952 Pte. KONSOHN, N., 1002nd Lab. Coy.
558106 Pte. KLEIN, T., 1002nd Lab. Coy.
558200 Pte. KASHKET, S., 1002nd Lab. Coy.
558286 Pte. KOSKY, H., 1002nd Lab. Coy.
558081 Pte. KITE, J., 1002nd Lab. Coy.
558199 Pte. KUSHNER, M., 1002nd Lab. Coy.
557751 Pte. KRESNER, J., 1002nd Lab. Coy.
557575 Pte. KUSHNER, J., 1002nd Lab. Coy.
557867 Pte. KAFFERBAUM, M., 1002nd Lab. Coy.
557822 Pte. KOMINSKY, B., 1002nd Lab. Coy.
557852 Pte. KLEIN, M., 1002nd Lab. Coy.
557099 Pte. KLEINMAN, J., 1002nd Lab. Coy.
557256 Pte. KREPSKY, G., 1002nd Lab. Coy.
557990 Pte. KRIGER, M., 1002nd Lab. Coy.
557953 Pte. KIRCHENBAUM, D., 1002nd Lab. Coy.
557956 Pte. KAMLISH, H., 1002nd Lab. Coy.
558144 Pte. KOVLER, M., 1002nd Lab. Coy.
557703 Pte. KASONOFSKY, J., 1002nd Lab. Coy.
558150 Pte. KASONOFSKY, I., 1002nd Lab. Coy.
557687 Pte. KAISER, C., 1002nd Lab. Coy.
558092 Pte. KRANT, S., 1002nd Lab. Coy.
558390 Pte. KOMINSKY, H., 1002nd Lab. Coy.
557372 L/Cpl. KLEINADT, S., 1001st Lab. Coy.
557565 Pte. KLEPFISH, A., 1001st Lab. Coy.
557571 Pte. KATZ, J., 1001st Lab. Coy.
557332 Pte. KLOWANSKY, P., 1001st Lab. Coy.
558642 Pte. KRONER, L., 1001st Lab. Coy.
557161 Pte. KERCHINSKY, M., 1001st Lab. Coy.
558699 Pte. KLUGMAN, H., 1001st Lab. Coy.
557242 Pte. KAPLAN, S., 1001st Lab. Coy.
557114 Pte. KAUFMAN, A. W., 1001st Lab. Coy.
557483 Pte. KURLAND, I., 1001st Lab. Coy.
557436 Pte. KANARICK, A., 1001st Lab. Coy.
557059 Pte. KOWALSKY, A. L., 1001st Lab. Coy.
557368 Pte. KERIEVSKY, M., 1001st Lab. Coy.
557382 Pte. KREMHOLTZ, R., 1001st Lab. Coy.
557417 Pte. KAUFMAN, I., 1001st Lab. Coy.
557467 Pte. KOTZ, H., 1001st Lab. Coy.
557176 Pte. KAPOTA, H., 1001st Lab. Coy.
557479 Pte. KALASKY, J., 1001st Lab. Coy.
558652 Pte. KERKUT, L., 1001st Lab. Coy.
557433 Pte. KLINGER, S., 19001st Lab. Coy.
557396 Pte. KLEIN, S., 1001st Lab. Coy.
391656 Pte. KOSKI, L., 673rd H.S. E. Coy.
132769 Pte. KRASTEN, A., 673rd H.S. E. Coy.
235310 Pte. KARENOVITZ, G., 677th H.S. E. Coy.
171479 Pte. KUTNER, N., Lab. Centre.
636940 Pte. KING, H., Lab. Centre.
39778 C.S.M.R. KINT, R., 1st Lab. Bn.
252066 Pte. KAYLE, H., Lab. Centre.
554479 Pte. KOLASKY, L.
533947 Pte. KALISKY.
79449 Pte. KUDISH, J.
378930 Pte. KAMINSKY, S. D., 246th A.E. Coy.
87857 Pte. KUTCHIVSKY, A., 147th Lab. Coy.
597497 Pte. KONENSKY, L. H., 188th Lab. Coy.
396833 Pte. KESLER, L., 171st Lab. Coy.
49629 Pte. KUDISH, J., 25th Lab. Coy.
567879 Pte. KERDANSKY, I.
124383 Pte. KLEIN, G. A., 4th Lab. Coy.
134445 Pte. KELLY, W. J., 2nd Lab. Coy.
171199 Pte. KLINE, D., 308th Lab. Coy.
50986 Sgt. KLEIN, D., 389th Lab. Coy.
204078 Pte. KONIFF, E., 185th Lab. Coy.
70293 Pte. KELLY, J., 366th Lab. Coy.
132768 Pte. KRASTEIN, A., 2nd Lab. Coy.
42533 Pte. KURASCH, J., 3rd Lab. Coy.
525370 Pte. KAMINSKY, S., 562nd Lab. Coy.
391656 Pte. KOSKI, L., 1st Lab. Coy.
171479 Pte. KUTNER, I., 67th Lab. Coy.
296833 Pte. KISLER, L., 171st Lab. Coy.
197563 Pte. KLICHEWSKI, L., 369th Lab. Coy.
394485 Pte. KONTISH, A.
273912 Pte. KALINSKI, A.
163004 Pte. KRISTEIN, J., 689th Lab. Coy.
460746 Pte. KALINSKI, M., 628th Lab. Coy.
460754 Pte. KAISRE, M.
65130 Pte. KANMINSKY, S., 5th Lab. Coy.
93523 Pte. KATCHNIK, I.
274015 Pte. KLEIN, J., 49th Lab. Coy.
461083 Pte. KAUFFIES, S., 303rd Lab. Coy.
48468 Pte. KRAMRISCH, M. W., 3rd Lab. Coy.
171479 Pte. KUTNER, N.
432029 Pte. KAFFEN, S., 366th Lab. Coy.
598517 Pte. KAMMINSKY, S., 546th Lab. Coy.
163499 Pte. KLEINBERG, J., 68th Lab. Coy.
532057 Pte. KAUFMAN, A., 368th Lab. Coy.
344485 Pte. KOSTICK, A., 304th Lab. Coy.

Labour Corps.—*Continued.*

378672	Pte. LIFTON, A., 258th Area Emp. Coy.
65675	Pte. LEVENE, D., 110th Lab. Coy.
81308	Pte. LEARY, R., 136th Lab. Coy.
81309	Pte. LEWIN, S., 136th Lab. Coy.
80689	Pte. LENSKY,* N., 257th Lab. Coy.
74402	Pte. LEVY, M., 7th Mx. Lab. Coy.
31590	Pte. LEVY, J., 7th Mx. Lab. Coy.
98241	Pte. LAWSON, J., 7th Mx. Lab. Coy.
97679	Pte. LEVY, J., 7th Mx. Lab. Coy.
97688	Pte. LEWIN, H., 7th Mx. Lab. Coy.
98250	Pte. LEIPTZ, R., 7th Mx. Lab. Coy.
130773	Pte. LANG, S., 205th Emp. Coy.
471984	L/Cpl. LESLIE, M., 247th Emp. Coy.
150557	Pte. LEVY, W. E., 772nd Div. Emp. Coy.
518401	Pte. LEWBITZ, F., 230th Div. Emp. Coy.
350941	Pte. LAZARUS, B., 14th Div. Emp. Coy.
416583	Pte. LEVENTHAL, A., 240th Emp. Coy.
201466	C.Q.M.S. LEVY, A., 224th Div. Emp. Co.
51868	Pte. LEVENTHAL, M., 87th Lab. Coy.
219623	Pte. LIPMAN, S., 172nd Lab. Coy.
198401	Cpl. LEVY, W., 746th A.E. Coy.
198715	Pte. LEVY, J., 746th A.E. Coy.
30441	Pte. LEFTKOVITZ, S., 2nd Mx. Lab. Coy.
93254	Pte. LANGEMANN, S., 2nd Mx. Lab. Coy.
92068	Pte. LEIDER, J., 2nd Mx. Lab. Coy.
80386	Pte. LUNZER, F., 2nd Mx. Lab. Coy.
86661	Pte. LEVEY, F., 145th Lab. Coy.
86674	Pte. LEVEY, L., 145th Lab. Coy.
80083	Pte. LEVY, C., 134th Lab. Coy.
123979	Pte. LEVIN, A., 255th Emp. Coy.
35643	Pte. LIPMAN, B., 1st Mx. Lab. Coy.
55744	Cpl. LAZARUS, M., 24th Lab. Coy.
81735	Pte. LUBETZKI, J.
95651	Pte. LIMBURG, J., 160th Lab. Coy.
71081	Pte. LEVY, S., 119th Lab. Coy.
72138	Pte. LEVY, M., 3rd Mx. Lab. Coy.
472499	Pte. LENNENS, J., 12th Lab. Coy.
103467	Pte. LEVASCHIVILLY, A., 173rd Lab. Coy.
30873	Pte. LEVINSTONE.
39797	Pte. LUBESKY, 14th Lab. Coy.
31472	Pte. LUBESKI, I., 53rd Lab. Coy.
69279	Pte. LEVY, J., 116th Lab. Coy.
197003	Pte. LEWIS, J., 162nd Lab. Coy.
394583	Pte. LYONS, H., 228th Lab. Coy.
67480	Pte. LANCASTER, M., 259th Area E. Coy.
69860	Pte. LUSH, P., 117th Lab. Coy.
71080	Pte. LEVY, M., 119th Lab. Coy.
546585	Pte. LIPMAN, A., 389th Lab. Coy.
470984	Pte. LESLIE, M., 247th Emp. Coy.
86661	Pte. LEVY, E., 45th Lab. Coy.
42414	L/Cpl. LEVY, M., 20th Cheshire Regt.
680052	Pte. LEE, E., 475th Lab. Coy.
01268	Pte. LEAVY, M. L., 21st Lab. Coy.
G/83007	Pte. LANDESBERG, N., 4th Mx. Lab. C.
G/80268	Pte. LANDSMAN, B., 4th Mx. Lab. Coy.
G/74425	Pte. LICHTENSTEIN, F., 4th Mx. L. Coy.
G/80100	Pte. LOBSENGER, I., 4th Mx. Lab. Coy.
G/80499	Pte. LANG, A., 4th Mx. Lab. Coy.
G/70681	Pte. LEVY, E., 4th Mx. Lab. Coy.
18367	Cpl. LANDY, S., 31st Lab. Coy.
20653	Pte. LEVEY, J., 35th Lab. Coy.
51869	Pte. LEVY, S., 38th Lab. Coy.
461023	Pte. LIPMAN,* I., 84th Lab. Coy.
11124	Pte. LANDSMAN, H., 19th Lab. Coy.
11131	Pte. LEVI, J., 19th Lab. Coy.
475870	L/Cpl. LEVY, D., 91st Lab. Coy.
72584	Pte. LEVI, A., 1st Mx. Lab. Coy.
425743	Pte. LURIE, M., 29th Lab. Coy.
18367	Cpl. LANDY, S., 31st Lab. Coy.
51869	Pte. LEVY, S., 38th Lab. Coy.
39267	Pte. LAZARUS, F., 66th Lab. Coy.
45823	Pte. LAZARUS, B., 77th Lab. Coy.
325370	Pte. LEVINE, A., 36th Lab. Coy.
61011	Cpl. LONSDALE, J., 102nd Lab. Coy.
60750	Pte. LEBERMAN, G., 102nd Lab. Coy.
65675	Pte. LAVINE, D., 110th Lab. Coy.
69279	Pte. LEVY, A., 116th Lab. Coy.
400664	Pte. LEVY, A., 130th Lab. Coy.
78616	Cpl. LAZARUS, H., 132nd Lab. Coy.
79494	Pte. LENINSTEIN,* B., 133rd Lab. Coy.
422003	Pte. LAVINSTEIN, S., 133rd Lab. Coy.
260413	Pte. LEVINE, C., 149th Lab. Coy.
614619	Pte. LEVINE, B., 162nd Lab. Coy.
506732	Pte. LEWIS. M., 176th Lab. Coy.
157790	Pte. LIPMAN, A., 189th Lab. Coy.
46933	L/Cpl. LEBERSON, S., 13th Lab. Coy.
64647	L/Cpl. LIBERMAN, R., 3rd Lab. Coy.
41857	Pte. LESSER, N., 14th Lab. Coy.
	Pte. LEZARBRAM, R., 19th Lab. Coy.
507910	Pte. LANDSMAN, W., Labour Corps.
556278	Pte. LOTNICOFF, J.
640452	Pte. LEVY, H., 67th Lab. Coy.
567460	Pte. LECIDER, M., 173rd Lab. Coy.
210034	Pte. LEVINSON, K., 724th Lab. Coy.
17748	Pte. LUCKER, A., 5th Lab. Coy.
421375	Pte. LASSMAN, I., 846th A.E. Coy.
48237	Pte. LEVI, J., 81st Lab. Coy.
51868	Pte. LEVENTHAL, M., 700th A.E. Coy.
93107	Pte. LEVI, B., 5th Lab. Coy.
304542	Pte. LEVY, M., 725th Lab. Coy.
586361	Pte. LEVI, S., 512 Emp. Coy.
557864	Pte. LEWIS, S.,
44720	L/Cpl. LICHTENSTEIN, M., 1st Mx. L. Co.
74341	Pte. LENG, J., 1st Mx. Lab. Coy.
28213	Pte. LEVY, A., 1st Mx. Lab. Coy.
71806	Pte. LICHBLOW, H., 1st Mx. Lab. Coy.
74267	Pte. LICHTENBERG, E., 1st Mx. Lab. Coy.
35643	Pte. LIPMAN, B., 1st Mx. Lab. Coy.
44571	Pte. LANSBERG, H., 1st Mx. Lab. Coy.
208025	Pte. LABINSKY, W., 3rd Mx. Lab. Coy.
48832	Pte. LASKY, H., 3rd Mx. Lab. Coy.
45434	Pte. LEFKOVITZ, J., 3rd Mx. Lab. Coy.
45373	Pte. LEVINGER, A. S., 3rd Mx. Lab. Coy.
74183	Pte. LEVINGER, P., 3rd Mx. Lab. Coy.
71553	Pte. LEVY, A., 3rd Mx. Lab. Coy.

Labour Corps.—*Continued.*

80442	Pte. LEWIN, E. R., 3rd Mx. Lab. Coy.
70978	Pte. LIPPMANN, H., 3rd Mx. Lab. Coy.
G/48842	C.Q.M.S. LANG, A., 4th Mx. Lab. Coy.
392355	Pte. LEBOUFSKI, L., 715th Lab. Coy.
304542	Pte. LEVY, M., 725th Lab. Coy.
53675	Pte. LIGHT,* J., 90th Lab. Coy.
461023	Pte. LIPMAN, J.,* 84th Lab. Coy.
272782	Pte LEDERMAN, D., 991st Lab. Coy.
480165	Pte. LEVENE, H., 918th A.E. Coy.
475870	L/Cpl. LEVY, D., 9th Lab. Coy.
10498	Pte. LESTCHICK, J., 18th Lab. Coy.
2456	Pte. LEVY, R., att. A.S.C.
	Pte. LEWIS, J., 11th Lab. Coy.
440118	Pte. LUBESKI, L., 715th Lab. Coy.
95651	Pte. LIMBERG, G., 733rd Lab. Coy.
192701	Pte. LEVINE, S., 122nd Lab. Coy.
75864	Pte. LEVENE, R., 127th Lab. Coy.
75880	Pte. LEVY, M., 127th Lab. Coy.
26107	Pte. LEWIS, J., 170th Lab. Coy.
477058	Pte. LEVY, T., 112th Lab. Coy.
400664	Pte. LEVY, A., 130th Lab. Coy.
13464	Pte. LEVINSON, T., 23rd Lab. Coy.
71669	Pte. LEVY, M., 120th Lab. Coy.
71667	Pte. LAZARUS, H., 120th Lab. Coy.
584184	Pte. LIEBERT, J., 181st Lab. Coy.
7213	Cpl. LYONS, B., 79th Chinese Lab. Coy.
594600	Pte. LIEBSCHUTZ, I., 835th A.E. Coy.
273890	Pte. LITVIN, B., 78th Lab. Group.
567460	Pte. LEADER, M., 787th A.E. Coy.
550121	Pte. LEVY, A., 589th A.E. Coy.
157791	Pte. LIPMAN, D., 104th Lab. Coy.
124636	Pte. LEVY, F., 81st Lab. Coy.
12280	Pte. LANG, P., 21st Lab. Coy.
69866	Pte. LEVY, A., 117th Lab. Coy.
27258	Pte. LEVINE, I., 46th Lab. Coy.
21270	Pte. LEES, H., 40th Lab. Coy.
21273	Pte. LEVY, H., 40th Lab. Coy.
61479	Pte. LEVY, A. L., 103rd Lab. Coy.
54616	Cpl. LEVI, A., 92nd Lab. Coy.
67954	Pte. LESTER, W., 92nd Lab. Coy.
381765	Pte. LEVINSON, H., 92nd Lab. Coy.
81308	Pte. LEVY, S., 136th Lab. Coy.
81309	Pte. LEWIN, S., 136th Lab. Coy.
38054	Pte. LIBERSON, S., 64th Lab. Coy.
525485	Pte. LEVY, J., 91st Lab. Coy.
452756	Pte. LAWRENCE, B., 67th Lab. Coy.
71070	Pte. LUBRINSKY, M., 67th Lab. Coy.
154831	Pte. LEWIS, D., 368th Lab. Coy.
655612	Pte. LEE, H., 90th Lab. Coy.
G/48169	Cpl. LIPMAN, D., 5th Mx. Lab. Coy.
G/84235	Pte. LITCHMAN, M., 5th Mx. Lab. Coy.
G/83549	Pte. LIGHTSTEIN, B., 5th Mx. Lab. Co.
G/39294	Pte. LEVY, M., 5th Mx. Lab. Coy.
G/74219	Pte. LEVY, B., 5th Mx. Lab. Coy.
G/93107	Pte. LEVY, B., 5th Mx. Lab. Coy.
273905	Pte. LEVY, H., 69th Lab. Coy.
74638	Pte. LIPMAN, H., 57th Lab. Coy.
346511	Pte. LAZARUS, L. N., 70th Lab. Coy.
627163	Cpl. LAZARUS, J., 111th Chin. Lab. Coy.
35734	L/Cpl. LEVY, 157th Lab. Coy.
83084	L/Cpl. LION, B. L., 35th Lab. Group.
80421	Pte. LEVY, H. L., 35th Lab. Group.
84045	Pte. LIEBLING, N., 35th Lab. Group.
80430	Pte. LEAF, M., 35th Lab. Group.
48822	Pte. LIEBLING, H., 35th Lab. Group.
92170	Pte. LEVI, J., 35th Lab. Group.
44828	Pte. LEVY, J., 35th Lab. Group.
72138	Pte. LEVY, M., 35th Lab. Group.
413718	Pte. LEVINE, I., 35th Lab. Group.
105863	Pte. LYONS, I., 35th Lab. Group.
656656	Pte. LUDWIN, N. S., 991st Lab. Group.
567460	Pte. LEDER, M., 7/8th Lab. Coy.
149612	Pte. LIMBLER, D., H.S. Coy.
664098	Pte. LEVY, E., Emp. Coy.
523851	Pte. LEWIS, A. J.
130773	Pte. LANG, S., 205th D.E. Coy.
518401	Pte. LEMBETZ, F., 230th D.E. Coy.
168944	Pte. LEVY, H., 377th H.S. Lab. Coy.
406474	Pte. LEVY, J., 870th A.E. Coy.
577140	Pte. LEVIN, B., 964th A.E. Coy.
44728	Pte. LIPSHAW, C., 784th A.E. Coy.
210034	Pte. LEVINSON, A., 724th Lab. Coy.
421375	Pte. LASSMAN, F., 846th Lab. Coy.
89665	Pte. LEVY, M., 884th Lab. Coy.
516732	Cpl. LUPER, J., 887th Lab. Coy.
217161	Pte. LEOPOLD, L., 17th Lab. Coy.
618	Pte. LEVY, A., 935th A.E .Coy.
616152	Pte. LADD, A., 4th Lab. Group.
535313	Pte. LAZARUS, P., Lab. Centre.
535188	Pte. LAZYAH, M., Lab. Centre.
644843	Pte. LITWICK, N., Lab. Centre.
98251	Pte. LANDSMAN, R., 8th Lab. Coy
38213	Pte. LEVY, A., 1st Lab. Coy.
69860	Pte. LUSH, P., 117th Lab. Coy.
69865	Pte. LEVY, H., 117th Lab. Coy.
69851	Pte. LEVY, I., 117th Lab. Coy.
43619	Pte. LEVY, A., 117th Lab. Coy.
51862	Pte. LEWIS, A. E., 17th Lab. Coy.
48755	Pte. LEVY, M., 19th Lab. Coy.
46443	Pte. LEVENE, R., 19th Lab. Coy.
50108	Pte. LEY, C., 26th Lab. Coy.
51620	Pte. LEVY, B., 29th Lab. Coy.
51052	Pte. LEVY, S. 28th Lab. Coy.
51050	Pte. LOSOWSKY, D., 28th Lab. Coy.
51054	Pte. LEWIN, S., 29th Lab. Coy.
51686	Pte. LYONS, B., 29th Lab. Coy.
53028	Pte. LEAPMAN, R., 29th Lab. Coy.
	Pte. LEVEY, J., 70th Lab. Coy.
64355	Cpl. LEVY, E., 9th Lab. Coy.
34644	Pte. LEVENE, I., 7th Lab. Coy.
7213	Cpl. LYONS, B., 2nd Lab. Coy.
49024	Pte. LANG, P., 21st Lab. Coy.
3885	Pte. LAMBERT, M., 7th Lab. Coy.
201693	Pte. LARNA, J., 692nd Lab. Coy.
35734	L/Cpl. LEVY, M., 60th Lab. Coy.

Labour Corps.—*Continued.*

563725	Pte. LEVY, M., Labour Centre.
273890	Pte. LITVIN, B., 78th Lab. Coy.
551021	Pte. LEVY, A., 589th Lab. Coy.
93101	Cpl. LINDER, N., 8th Mx. Lab. Coy.
93251	Pte. LANDSMAN, R., 8th Mx. Lab. Coy.
93024	Pte. LEVY, J., 8th Mx. Lab. Coy.
97763	Pte. LEVY, H., 8th Mx. Lab. Coy.
35780	L/Cpl. LEWISOHN, V., 8th Mx. Lab. Coy.
93706	Pte. LANDSBERG, S. E., 8th Mx. Lab. Coy.
98087	Pte. LEHMAN, J., 8th Mx. Lab. Coy.
557969	Pte. LEIPTSHITZ, J., 1002nd Lab. Coy.
557933	Pte. LEVOFSKY, S., 1002nd Lab. Coy.
557209	Pte. LAKUMSKY, T., 1002nd Lab. Coy.
558226	Pte. LEWIS, L., 1002nd Lab. Coy.
557643	Pte. LITKIN, H., 1002nd Lab. Coy.
557041	Pte. LEVOFSKY, J., 1002nd Lab. Coy.
557523	Pte. LAZINESKOFF, L., 1002nd Lab. Coy.
558015	Pte. LAKUMSKY, M., 1002nd Lab. Coy.
558039	Pte. LAVENDOFSKY, B., 1002nd Lab. Coy.
557117	Pte. LEVEY, H., 1002nd Lab. Coy.
558141	Pte. LINSTONE, S., 1002nd Lab. Coy.
557502	Pte. LEWIS, J., 1002nd Lab. Coy.
558245	Pte. LEVENE, M., 1002nd Lab. Coy.
557314	Pte. LANDSMAN, D., 1002nd Lab. Coy.
557802	Pte. LIPPIN, J., 1002nd Lab. Coy.
557564	Pte. LAWRENCE, J., 1002nd Lab. Coy.
557786	Pte. LUNN, S., 1002nd Lab. Coy.
557828	Pte. LIEBMAN, P., 1002nd Lab. Coy.
557798	Pte. LANCAFF, J., 1002nd Lab. Coy.
557566	Pte. LACHINSKY, S., 1002nd Lab. Coy.
557708	Pte. LOFFMAN, J., 1002nd Lab. Coy.
558128	Pte. LEVY, S., 1002nd Lab. Coy.
557957	Pte. LEWIS, H., 1002nd Lab. Coy.
557968	Pte. LISHACK, S., 1002nd Lab. Coy.
558190	Pte. LAIBGLIT, H., 1002nd Lab. Coy.
5581907	Pte. LUNTZ, J., 1002nd Lab. Coy.
558720	Pte. LEVY, M., 1002nd Lab. Coy.
558320	Pte. LEVY, J., 1002nd Lab. Coy.
558288	Pte. LANDSMAN, J., 1002nd Lab. Coy.
557091	Pte. LAKUMSKY, D., 1001st Lab. Coy.
557427	Pte. LEFCOVITCH, B., 1001st Lab. Coy.
557162	Pte. LEFCO, H., 1001st Lab. Coy.
558663	Pte. LEVY, C., 1001st Lab. Coy.
557127	Pte. LEVY, B., 1001st Lab. Coy.
557222	Pte. LASSERSON, H., 1001st Lab. Coy.
557140	Pte. LIEW, L., 1001st Lab. Coy.
557656	Pte. LEVITSKY, M., 1001st Lab. Coy.
558688	Pte. LEVY, H., 1001st Lab. Coy.
557166	Pte. LEDERMAN, A., 1001st Lab. Coy.
557349	Pte. LUBITSKY, M., 1001st Lab. Coy.
557529	Pte. LEVINE, M., 1001st Lab. Coy.
557351	Pte. LAZARUS, H., 1001st Lab. Coy.
558566	Pte. LIPSCHITZ, S., 1001st Lab. Coy.
557266	Pte. LICHTENBERG, M., 1001st Lab. Coy.
557333	Pte. LEVIN, S., 1001st Lab. Coy.
33819	Pte. LEVASCHVILLY, J., 1001st Lab. Coy.
171350	Cpl. LEVINE, L., 672nd H.S. E. Coy.
36607	Pte. LEWIS, J., Res. Emp. Coy.
523851	Pte. LEWIS, G. J., 676th H.S. E. Coy.
391667	Pte. LEVISON, A., Emp. Coy.
251767	Pte. LEVINE, L., 365th Res. Emp. Coy.
478436	Pte. LUCAS, N., 365th Res. Emp. Coy.
	Cpl. LEVINE, D., 309th Works Coy.
218012	Pte. LEWIN, H., 537th H.S. E. Coy.
325199	Pte. LEVY, M., 300th Lab. Coy.
218108	Pte. LEWIS, H., 375th Lab. Coy.
217771	Pte. LEVY, I., 375th Lab. Coy.
452482	Pte. LERMAN, I., 375th Lab. Coy.
452309	Pte. LEVY, H., 375th Lab. Coy.
507719	Pte. LEE, D., Lab. Centre.
45037	Pte. LANCHIN, J., 1st Lab. Bn.
37320	Pte. LIGHT, J., 1st Lab. Bn.
89665	Pte. LEVY, M., 884th A.E. Coy.
57208	Pte. LEVINE, J., 96th Coy.
29147	Pte. LEVEY, A.,
53267	Pte. LEVY, B., 363rd A.E. Coy.
616872	Pte. LEVENE, S., 252nd A.E. Coy.
557314	Pte. LANDUSAN, I.
1026	Pte. LEVI, J., 81st Lab. Coy.
54853	Pte. LEVEY, E., 92nd Lab. Coy.
73370	Pte. LEAKE, A. C., 82nd Lab. Coy.
201466	Pte. LEVY, A., 224th D.E. Coy.
551116	Pte. LAZAROVITCH, M., 719th Lab. Coy.
320341	Pte. LANKIFF, L., 53rd Lab. Coy.
280843	Pte. LEVY, D. W., Lab. Coy.
352022	Pte. LEVY, A., 10th Lab. Coy.
376516	Pte. LEVY, M., 144th Lab. Coy.
340565	Pte. LEVY, G., 25th Lab. Coy.
71081	Pte. LEVY, S., 11th Lab. Coy.
460754	Pte. LOUIS, J.
640745	Pte. LIRKOFF, M., 642nd Lab. Coy.
245774	Pte. LEWIS, P., 448th Lab. Coy.
452422	Pte. LEVY, M., 362nd Lab. Coy.
430426	Pte. LEWIS, F., 299th Lab. Coy.
268105	Pte. LEVY, H., 659th Lab. Coy.
8188	Pte. LEVY, D., 137th Lab. Coy.
381315	Pte. LEVY, C., 364th Lab. Coy.
273785	Pte. LITMANOVITCH, S., 185th Lab. Coy.
525288	Pte. LEGINSKY, I.
186554	Pte. LIPMAN, H., 385th Lab. Coy.
280155	Cpl. LEVY, A.
86661	Pte. LEAVY F., 145th Lab. Coy.
525171	Pte. LEADER, A., H.S.L.C.
357140	Pte. LIEW, L.
506754	Pte. LEVISON, S., 176th Lab. Coy.
517232	Pte. LEVY, L., 177th Lab. Coy.
523555	Pte. LEVY, H., 299th Lab. Coy.
217161	Pte. LEOPOLD, L.
461037	Pte. LEVENS, L., S.C.L.C.
460769	Pte. LEVENE, H., S.C.L.C.
77494	Pte. LIVENSTEIN, A., 133rd Lab. Coy.
951	Cpl. LANGYAVO, A., E.L.C.
08734	Cpl. LIPMAN, A., E.L.C.
433	Pte. LEVY, Y. L., E.L.C.
552	Pte. LEVY, S., E.L.C.

Labour Corps.—*Continued.*

21191 Sgt. LIBERMAN, M., E.L.C.
712 Cpl. LEVY, J. R., E.L.C.
383 Pte. LUBA, I., E.L.C.
0831 Sgt. LEVY, V. C. D., E.L.C.
326 Cpl. LELAS, J., E.L.C.
42856 Pte. LEVY, H., 72nd Lab. Coy.
421036 Pte. LEVY, S., 38th Lab. Coy.
207871 Pte. LAMB, J. R., 71st Lab. Coy.
82543 Pte. LOSSOON, D., 138th Lab. Coy.
Pte. LANCE, M.
73890 Pte. LITRIN, B., 133rd Lab. Coy.
0/11052 Cpl. LEVY, J., E.L.C.
422002 Pte. LARENSTEIN, S., 133rd Lab. Coy.
218304 Pte. LEOPOLD, A., 119th Lab. Coy.
51862 Pte. LEWIS, A. E., 126th Lab. Coy.
42202 Pte. LAVENSTEIN, S., 133rd Lab. Coy.
33819 Pte. LAVISCHIVILLY, J., 165th Lab. Coy.
496 L/Cpl. LEVY, D., E.L.C.
31868 Pte. LEVENTHAL, M., 89th Lab. Coy.
135437 Pte. LIMBERG, M., 385th Lab. Coy.
186650 Pte. LAUTENBERG, S., 212th Lab. Coy.
461414 Pte. LAZARUS, 635th Lab. Coy.
18791 Lte. LEVY, A.
27258 Pte. LEVENE, M., 46th Lab. Coy.
43874 Pte. LIPMAN, P., 2nd Lab. Coy.
152689 L/Cpl. LAZARUS, A.
163551 Pte. LUBETSKI, I., 6th Lab. Coy.
18367 Cpl. LANDY, S., 31st Lab. Coy.
340565 Pte. LEVY, D., 25th Lab. Coy.
543571 Pte. LERMAN, S.
164151 Pte. LEVY, L.
3465511 Pte. LAZARUS, L.
29439 Pte. LEVY, A. L., 35th Lab. Coy.
156045 Pte. LEVY, P., 614th Lab. Coy.
150557 Pte. LEVY, W. E.
237545 Pte. LEVY, B.
71070 Pte. LUBINSKY, N., 119th Lab. Coy.
58326 Pte. LEVIACHVILLE, J., 8th Lab. Coy.
57208 Pte. LEVINE, J., 96th Lab. Coy.
365180 Pte. LISSACK, M., 908th Lab. Coy.
171350 Cpl. LEVINE, L., 4th Lab. Coy.
314834 Pte. LEVY, A., 395th Lab. Coy.
452676 Pte. LECHERMAN, 362nd Lab. Coy.
525274 Pte. LEVY, A.
78868 Pte. LEVY, L., 5th Lab. Coy.
296244 Pte. LEVY, A., 133rd Lab. Coy.
79465 Pte. LEVEY, E., 4th Lab. Coy.
97560 Pte. LASMAN, J., 369th Lab. Coy.
48237 Pte. LEVI, J., 81st Lab. Coy.
398306 Pte. LANSMAN, S., 601st Lab. Coy.
25754 Pte. LEVY, J., 20th Lab. Coy.
430421 Pte. LEWIS, F., 299th Lab. Coy.
74341 Pte. LANG, J., 1st Lab. Coy.
673132 Pte. LYONS, J. L.
394583 Pte. LYONS, H.
70681 Pte. LEVY, E., 4th Lab. Coy.
48842 C.Q.M.S. LAND, A., 4th Lab. Coy.

80499 Pte. LANG, A., 4th Lab. Coy.
130744 Pte. LEA, M., 1st Lab. Coy.
54616 Cpl. LEVI, A., 92nd Lab. Coy.
48616 Pte. LAZARUS, M., 132nd Lab. Coy.
199461 Sgt. LIEBERMAN, R. (M.S.M.).
198717 Pte. LEBERMAN, J., 366th Lab. Coy.
279579 Pte. LEVY, B.
452421 Pte. LEVY, I., 362nd Lab. Coy.
9909 Pte. LAZARUS, A., 6th Lab. Coy.
29430 Pte. LEVY, S. L., 35th Lab. Coy.
273890 Pte. LETRIN, B.
499414 Pte. LEVY, M., 689th Lab. Coy.
69320 Pte. MICHAELS, D. M., attd. H.Q.
128919 Pte. MOSSES, J., 291st Area Emp. Coy.
331389 Pte. MYERS, P., 259th Area Emp. Coy.
85540 Cpl. MORRIS, H., 143rd Lab. Coy.
92231 Pte. MECHANIC, H., 7th Mx. Lab. Coy.
194055 Pte. MOSS, J., 232nd Div. Emp. Coy.
20388 Pte. MOSS, H., 204th Emp. Coy.
511466 Pte. MENDOZA, M., 214th Emp. Coy.
196379 Pte. MASSER, S., 256th Emp. Coy.
31591 Pte. MANDEL, M., 2nd Lab. Coy.
30992 Pte. METZGER, C., 2nd Lab. Coy.
92098 Pte. MICHAEL, M., 2nd Lab. Coy.
76472 Pte. MISCHER, N., 128th Lab. Coy.
82659 Cpl. MOSES,* I., 257th Area Emp. Coy.
124663 Pte. MOSS, H., 204th Div. Emp. Coy.
35508 Pte. MILLER, M., 1st Mx. Lab. Coy.
45201 Pte. MILLER, S., 1st Mx. Lab. Coy.
52321 Pte. MUSCOVITCH, S. J., 1st Dev. L. C.
Pte. MOSES, D., 3rd Lab. Coy.
33219 Pte. MISTOFSKI, S., 1st N. Hants. L.C.
39136 Pte. MYERS, J., 6th N. Hants. Lab. Coy.
44180 L/Cpl. MORRIS, L., 4th Mx. Lab. Coy.
74396 Pte. MAYER, H. B., 11th Mx. Lab. Coy.
8077 Pte. MENDEZ, F. W., 776th A.E. Coy.
46224 Sgt. MICHALOVITCH, D., 78th Lab. Coy.
79485 Pte. MORRIS, M., 133rd Lab. Coy.
89672 Pte. MARGOFSKY, D., 15th Lab. Coy.
89686 Pte. MOSES, M., 150th Lab. Coy.
258151 Pte. MORRIS, J., 223rd Emp. Coy.
621640 Pte. MELNICK, Labour Corp.
393367 Pte. MARTIN, A., 766th Area Emp. Coy.
105216 Pte. MYERS, J., 176th Lab. Coy.
596012 Pte. MANTLERS, H.
89672 Pte. MARGOLSKY, D., 288th Lab. Coy.
443493 Pte. MARKUSON, L., Area Emp. Coy.
28474 Pte. MEINTZ, A. W., 148th Lab. Coy.
100483 Pte. MOSES, W., 168th Lab. Coy.
76472 Pte. MIRCHER, N., 128th Lab. Coy.
196609 Pte. MARCUS, H., 249th Area Emp. Coy
332038 Pte. MILLER, G., 539th Lab. Coy.
180578 Pte. MERKELL, S. M.
Pte. MICHAELS, D. M., 116th Lab. Coy.
88483 Pte. MARGOLSKY,* J., 148th Lab. Coy.
509274 Pte. MEDWEDINER, 695th Lab. Coy.
558368 Pte. MOSHENSKY, A., 8th Lab. Coy.
465098 L/Cpl. MARKS, L. A.

Labour Corps.—*Continued.*

546130 Pte. MARUS, B.
43167 L/Cpl. MELLOR, R., 20th Cheshire Regt.
40909 Pte. MECHANIC, H., 14th Lab. Coy.
6373337 Pte. MALINOWSKI, M., Labour Centre.
29105 Pte. MARGARIT, A., 49th Lab. Coy.
100464 Pte. MORGANSTINSKY, H., 168th L. Coy.
71116 Pte. MOSES, M., 119th Lab. Coy.
36003 C.Q.M.S. MARX, H., 1st Mx. Lab. Coy.
74296 Pte. MARKS, M. F., 1st Mx Lab. Coy.
79989 Pte. MARKOVITCH, J., 1st Mx. Lab. Coy.
72982 Pte. MILLER, M., 1st Mx. Lab. Coy.
35508 Pte. MILLET, M., 1st Mx. Lab. Coy.
80116 Pte. MILLET, J., 1st Mx. Lab. Coy.
80379 Pte. MORGAN-BESSER, B., 3rd Mx. L. Co.
G/80422 Pte. MICHAELIS, H., 4th Mx. Lab. Coy.
G/44180 Pte. MORRIS, L., 4th Mx. Lab. Coy.
G/84325 Pte. MINTZ, S., 4th Mx. Lab. Coy.
601105 Pte. MARCUS, J., 13th Lab. Coy.
34206 Cpl. Moscow, H., 58th Lab. Coy.
124663 Pte. Moss, H., 204th Employ. Coy.
509444 Pte. MYERS, A., 30th Lab. Coy.
42290 Pte. MISTOSKI, H., 71st Lab. Coy.
24310 Pte. MARCUS, M., 102nd Lab. Coy.
234554 Pte. MYERKERZER, H., 108th Lab. Coy.
65109 Pte. MARKS, A., 109th Lab. Coy.
69324 Pte. MILESTOEN, M., 116th Lab. Coy.
79479 Pte. MOSCOW, L., 133rd Lab. Coy.
79683 Pte. MALKOLLY, M., 133rd Lab. Coy.
79684 Pte. MIKHARLOFF, M., 133rd Lab. Coy.
85540 Cpl. MORRIS, H., 143rd Lab. Coy.
87876 Pte. MYERS, A., 147th Lab. Coy.
273992 Pte. MILLER, J., 149th Lab. Coy.
90638 Cpl. MARKSON, P., 152nd Lab. Coy.
92231 Pte. MECHANIC, H., 154th Lab. Coy.
273790 Pte. MONDSHEIN, W., 164th Lab. Coy.
11259 L/Cpl. MOSES, H. N., 186th Lab. Coy.
581972 Pte. MOOCHNIK, L., 991st Lab. Coy.
581979 Pte. MYEROVITZ, J., 991st Lab. Coy.
581993 Pte. MILLER, M., 991st Lab. Coy.
45858 Pte. MARCOVITCH, J., 822nd A.E. Coy.
451537 Pte. MYERS, J., 946th A.E. Coy.
601105 Pte. MARCUS, J., 13th Lab. Coy.
13484 Pte. MARKS, H., 23rd Lab. Coy.
13495 Pte. MARKS, H., 23rd Lab. Coy.
26676 Pte. MARKS, A., 45th Lab. Coy.
71691 Pte. MARKS, S., 120th Lab. Coy.
196379 Pte. MAISER, S., 256th A.E. Coy.
470660 Pte. MOROWITZ, A., 837th A.E. Coy.
194055 Pte. MOSS, J., 281st A.E. Coy.
274012 L/Cpl. MENDELSOHN, A., 877th A.E. Co.
G/80281 Pte. MYER, R. M., 4th Lab. Coy.
273580 Sgt. MAURICE, P., 32nd Chin. Lab. Coy.
100483 Pte. MOSES, D., 168th Lab. Coy.
19479 Pte. MORRIS, I., 33rd Lab. Coy.
31381 Pte. MAACK, H., 3rd Lab. Coy.
83116 Pte. MISTOFSKI, S., 139th Lab. Coy.
273882 Pte. MIRCOVITCH, G., 67th Lab. Coy.
71098 Pte. MARANEY, D., 67th Lab. Coy.
71116 Pte. MOSES, M., 67th Lab. Coy.
593042 Pte. MARKOVITCH, H., 67th Lab. Coy.
465098 L/Cpl. MARKS, L., 621st Lab. Coy.
G/93886 Pte. MYERS, B., 5th Mx. Lab. Coy.
G/93439 Pte. MULLER, M., 5th Mx. Lab. Coy.
G/93391 Pte. MARKS, S., 5th Mx. Lab. Coy.
G/93266 Pte. MANTEL, A., 5th Mx. Lab. Coy.
65102 Pte. MARCOVITZ, L., 155th Lab. Coy.
81916 Pte. MUSICKANSKY, J., 955th A.E. Coy.
84111 L/Cpl. MARTIN, H. J., 35th Lab. Coy.
83083 Pte. MARKBRIDE, A., 35th Lab. Coy.
84013 Pte. MORRIS, H., 35th Lab. Coy.
72164 Pte. MARTIN, S., 35th Lab. Coy.
86095 Pte. MYERS, I., 69th Lab. Coy.
31591 Pte. MANDEL, M., 2nd Inf. Lab. Coy.
30992 Pte. MELTZGER, C., 2nd Inf. Lab. Coy.
92098 Pte. MICHAEL, M., 2nd Inf. Lab. Coy.
59080 Pte. MINDEN, J., 29th Lab. Coy.
461151 Pte. MIRANDA, J.
565234 Pte. MENDOZA, H.
132798 Pte. MORDEN, L.
507273 Pte. MARGOLIS, R., 527th Emp. Coy.
509278 Pte. MANNEL, S., 527th Emp. Coy.
516688 Pte. MORRIS, F., 887th A.E. Coy.
51342 Pte. MUSICHANSKY, T., 29th Lab. Coy.
L/Cpl. MICHAELOVITCH, D., 13th L. Coy.
58186 Pte. MARKS, H., 9th Lab. Coy.
75301 Pte. MARKSON, T., 20th Lab. Coy.
33313 Pte. MARCUS, M., 2nd Lab. Coy.
Pte. MARGALOS, 2nd Lab. Coy.
61820 Pte. MORRIS, J., 2nd Lab. Coy.
180579 Pte. MIRSHOFSKY,* A., 723rd Lab. Coy.
506693 Pte. MARKS,* L., 222nd A.E. Coy.
87874 Pte. MOSES,* H., 147th Lab. Coy.
128577 Pte. MYERSON, B., 12th Lab. Coy.
452518 Pte. MIRSKY, M., 4th Lab. Coy.
710 Pte. MAMON, S., 72nd Lab. Coy.
64462 Pte. MELTZER,* S., 108th Lab. Coy.
Pte. MARKS, H., R.M. Lab.
158919 Pte. MOSSES, I., 740th A.E. Coy.
41471 Pte. MARGERITE, G. B., 8th Lab. Coy.
563830 Pte. MARKS, J., Labour Centre.
551137 Pte. MILLER, H., 386th H.S. Lab. Coy.
98271 Pte. MANDEL, N., 8th Mx. Lab. Coy.
98291 Pte. MANDEL, K., 8th Mx. Lab. Coy.
93667 Pte. MORGAN-BESSER, H., 8th Mx. Lab. Coy.
100035 Pte. MORIANO, S., 8th Mx. Lab. Coy.
93526 Pte. MARTIN, S., 8th Mx. Lab. Coy.
557712 L/Cpl. MYDAT, H., 1002nd Lab. Coy.
557627 Pte. MYERS, M., 1002nd Lab. Coy.
557667 Pte. MALINOWITZ, G., 1002nd Lab. Coy.
558042 Pte. MAGAZINER, S., 1002nd Lab. Coy.
558309 Pte. MUSCOVITCH, L., 1002nd Lab. Coy.
558278 Pte. MICHAELS, S., 1002nd Lab. Coy.
558007 Pte. MALLINA, B., 1002nd Lab. Coy.
558097 Pte. MIGDOL, H., 1002nd Lab. Coy

Labour Corps.—*Continued.*

558127 Pte. MAKLER, A., 1002nd Lab. Coy.
557998 Pte. MALINA, L., 1002nd Lab. Coy.
558153 Pte. MALAVA, L., 1//2nd Lab. Coy.
557500 Pte. MORRIS, A., 1002nd Lab. Coy.
558239 Pte. MORDSKY, A., 1002nd Lab. Coy.
557872 Pte. MILROOD, D., 1002nd Lab. Coy.
557577 Pte. MINTZ, Z., 1002nd Lab. Coy.
557561 Pte. MANDELOFSKY, E., 1002nd Lab. Coy.
557803 Pte. MATTHEWS, B., 1002nd Lab. Coy.
557777 Pte. MARKOVITCH, J., 1002nd Lab. Coy.
558285 Pte. MADALYER, J., 1002nd Lab. Coy.
558258 Pte. MARKOVITCH, M., 1002nd Lab. Coy.
557728 Pte. MARKOVITZ, W., 1002nd Lab. Coy.
557972 Pte. MARKOVITCH, S., 1002nd Lab. Coy.
558076 Pte. MARKOVITCH, M., 19002nd Lab. Coy.
       Pte. MILLER, A.
557610 Pte. MANGALOFSKY, S., 1001st Lab. Coy.
557334 Pte. MILLER, I., 1001st Lab. Coy.
557548 Pte. MALAFSTRY, I. A., 1001st Lab. Coy.
557119 Pte. MORRIS, S., 1001st Lab. Coy.
558651 Pte. MEDNICK, A., 1001st Lab. Coy.
558649 Pte. MENDELSON, A., 1001st Lab. Coy.
558628 Pte. MORRIS, M., 1001st Lab. Coy.
558650 Pte. MARDER, I., 1001st Lab. Coy.
558660 Pte. MAYLE, L., 1001st Lab. Coy.
558696 Pte. MARDER, A. N., 1001st Lab. Coy.
558666 Pte. MARKOVITCH, S., 1001st Lab. Coy.
558692 Pte. MORRISON, J., 1001st Lab. Coy.
557398 Pte. MENDELOVITCH, I., 1001st Lab. Coy.
557269 Pte. MOSS, M., 1001st Lab. Coy.
557350 Pte. MILLER, P., 1001st Lab. Coy.
39672 Pte. MARGOFSKY, D., 672nd Emp. Coy.
506693 Pte. MARKS, L., 365th Res. Emp. Coy.
134457 Pte. MOSS, M., 675th H.S. Emp. Coy.
235786 Pte. MIRCHER, L., 365th Res. Emp. Coy.
391523 Pte. MIRANDA, F., 367th Res. Emp. Coy.
29118 Pte. MILLINGS, M., 367th Res. Emp. Coy.
204739 Pte. MARKS, P., 300th Lab. Coy.
191639 Pte. MARKS, H., 300th H.S. Emp. Coy.
637296 Pte. MYERSTONE, J., 40th Lab. Bn.
637317 Pte. MICHAELS, I., Lab. Coy.
637061 Pte. MIDGEON, S., Lab. Centre.
507613 Pte. MINTZ, M., Lab. Centre.
507616 Pte. MARKS, M., Lab. Centre.
507751 Pte. MAURER, J., Lab. Centre.
45235 Pte. MENTEL, M., 1st Lab. Bn.
20630 Pte. MOSES, J., 14th Lab. Bn.
       Pte. MICHAELS, D. M., 116th Lab. Bn.
195180 Pte. MARKS, I., Lab. Centre.
413566 Cpl. MOSS, C.,
99264 Pte. MUSCOVITCH, S. J., 166th Lab. Coy.
44751 Pte. MARKS, H., 75th Lab. Coy.
610345 Pte. MEYERS, A., 151st Lab. Coy.
182021 Pte. MORRIS, J., 622nd H.S.E. Coy.
203 Pte. MINAHAM, S., E.L.C.
297 Cpl. MIZRAHI, S., E.L.C.
191 L/Cpl. MIZRAHY, J., E.L.C.

1011 Cpl. MIZRAHY, M., E.L.C.
159 Pte. MENASCHE, E., E.L.C.
483 Pte. MALKA, J., E.L.C.
156 Pte. MESSICA, S., E.L.C.
V/509 Pte. MANDELOBITZ, M., E.L.C.
327 Pte. MASTUK, I. B., E.L.C.
154599 Pte. MYER, J., 5th Lab. Coy.
48587 Pte. MARKOVITCH, I., 77th Lab. Coy.
39307 Pte. MOSS, R., 66th Lab. Coy.
65109 Pte. MARKS, A., 109th Lab. Coy.
507749 Pte. MICHAELSON, J.
301871 Pte. MAGNUS, E. D., 524th Lab. Coy.
289934 Pte. MUSLUCK, A., 370th Lab. Coy.
423360 Pte. MILLER, H., 848th Lab. Coy.
237810 Pte. MYERS, E., 743rd Lab. Coy.
87672 Pte. MARGOFSKY, D.
184438 Pte. MARSOVITCH, L., 349th Lab. Coy.
74466 Pte. MOSS, M., 125th Lab. Coy.
84224 Pte. MORRIS, M., 775th Lab. Coy.
43110 Pte. MOSES, V., 74th Lab. Coy.
31000 Pte. MORRIS, J., 2nd Lab. Coy.
21149 Pte. MOSES, I., 1st Lab. Coy.
534371 Pte. MOSES, R.
209755 Cpl. MOSS, J. L.
210100 Pte. MORGURGO, S., 266th Lab. Coy.
134435 Pte. MARKS, A., 2nd Lab. Coy.
134457 Pte. MORS, M., 2nd Lab. Coy.
203875 Pte. MILLER, G.
125327 Pte. MARKOFF, M., 1st Lab. Coy.
103483 Pte. MARSELS, N.
248379 Pte. MILLER, S., 405th Lab. Coy.
134207 Pte. MAUGNUS, I., 2nd Lab. Coy.
208650 Pte. MYERS, M., 6th Lab. Coy.
34532 Pte. MAISELS, N., 8th Lab. Coy.
293195 Pte. MORRIS, H.
443493 Pte. MARCUSSON, L., 828th Lab. Coy.
134457 Pte. MOSS, M.
51918 Pte. MYERS, M., 229th Lab. Coy.
56712 Pte. MARKOWN, L., 718th Lab. Coy.
507932 Pte. MILLER, W.
507904 Pte. MARGOLIS.
365288 Pte. MACOBY, W. I., 686th Lab. Coy.
74072 Pte. MOSSBAUM, A., 41st Lab. Coy.
79479 Pte. MOWCOW, L., 7th Lab. Coy.
94/128557 Dvr. MYERSON, 4th Lab. Coy.
42290 Pte. MISTOVSKI, H., 71st Lab. Coy.
62754 Pte. MARKOVITCH, J., 77th Lab. Coy.
637061 Pte. MIDGER, N. L., 300th Lab. Coy.
661034 Pte. MARKS, J., 8th Lab. Coy.
452439 Pte. MORRIS, A., 299th Lab. Coy.
27736 Pte. MORRIS, L., 4th Lab. Coy.
80116 Pte. MILLETT, I., 4th Lab. Coy.
80287 Pte. MEYEN, R. N., 4th Lab. Coy.
19479 Pte. MORRIS, I., 33rd Lab. Coy.
69329 Pte. MORRIS, P., 116th Lab. Coy.
180823 Pte. MORRIS, J., 371st Lab. Coy.
31799 Pte. MARKS, H., 16th Lab. Coy.
31493 Pte. MARKS, H., 16th Lab. Coy.

Labour Corps.—Continued.

103499	Pte. MISELL, B.	
373914	Pte. MONCEL, J., 366th Lab. Coy.	
393267	Pte. MUNDELACK, A., 576th Lab. Coy.	
23605	Pte. MYERS, C., N.C.L.C.	
50712	Pte. MARKSON, L.	
	C.S.M. MINTZ, J. D. (M.S.M.).	
46079	Pte. MORTFIELD, H., 62nd Lab. Coy.	
229507	Cpl. MOSELY, S., 658th Lab. Coy.	
88474	Pte. MUNTZ, A. W., 148th Lab. Coy.	
522595	Pte. MORRIS, H., 363rd Lab. Coy.	
235514	Pte. MORRIS, S., 678th Lab. Coy.	
15607	Pte. MARCHINSKY, S.	
273885	Pte. MARKS, K., 34th Lab. Coy.	
460788	Pte. MALDOFSKY, A., 34th Lab. Coy.	
460741	Pte. MOSCOVITCH, J.	
93667	Pte. MORGAN, B., 8th Lab. Coy.	
235789	Pte. MIRCHER, N., 721st Lab. Coy.	
273875	Pte. MARCOWITZ, L., 732nd Lab. Coy.	
359	Pte. MOSSERI, I., E.L.C.	
158	Pte. MAKIN, E.L.C.	
266	Pte. MOSES, Y., E.L.C.	
343650	Pte. MARGOLSKY, W., 365th Lab. Coy.	
31500	Pte. McFARLANE, A. L., 53rd Lab. Coy.	
84276	Pte. MARCUS, C., 720th Lab. Coy.	
460824	Pte. MEREDEEN, A., 304th Lab. Coy.	
29105	Pte. MARGARET, A., 49th Lab. Coy.	
105077	Pte. MENDES, R. A., 117th Lab. Coy.	
182021	Pte. MORRIS, J., 522nd Lab. Coy.	
250710	Pte. MARGOLIS, S.	
560155	Pte. MENZIE, A.	
456621	Pte. NEWMAN, L., 739th Area Emp. Coy.	
97552	Pte. NOUSOKAFF, H., 7th Mx. Lab. Coy.	
363707	Pte. NEIBERG, A., 224th Div. Emp. Coy.	
31595	Pte. NYMAN, N., 2nd Lab. Coy.	
79511	Pte. NATHAN, A., 133rd Lab. Coy.	
450024	Pte. NELSON, B., 27th Lab. Coy.	
88064	Pte. NATHAN, J., 147th Lab. Coy.	
544325	Pte. NEVISSKI, S., 389th Lab. Coy.	
251793	Pte. NIMAN, F., 389t hLab. Coy.	
191738	Pte. NATHAN, A., Labour Centre.	
	L/Cpl. NEWMAN, D., 8th Lab. Coy.	
37351	Pte. NEWMAN, A., 160th Lab. Coy.	
25908	Pte. NYMA, S., 44th Lab. Coy.	
84276	Pte. NEWMAN, N.	
	Pte. NORMAN, M. (M.M.).	
44722	Pte. NETTLER, M., 1st Mx. Lab. Coy.	
80432	Pte. NERVITZK, P., 3rd Mx. Lab. Coy.	
36744	Pte. NEWSTADT, M., 3rd Mx. Lab. Coy.	
G/80352	Pte. NATHAN, B., 4th M.x Lab. Coy.	
506757	Pte. NYMAN, H., 37th Lab. Coy.	
304569	Sgt. NATHAN, R., 725th Lab. Coy.	
370217	Pte. NOLET, H., 286th Area Emp. Coy.	
456621	Pte. NEWMAN, L., 27th Lab. Coy.	
10550	Pte. NIMAN, P., 18th Lab. Coy.	
48453	Pte. NETTRAM, A., 7th Lab. Coy.	
219695	Pte. NICHNICK, J., 738th Area Emp. Coy.	
38218	Pte. NITOFSKY, H., 64th Lab. Coy.	
G/31146	Sgt. NEWTON, H. H., 5th Mx. L. Coy.	
G/74024	Pte. NORTON, R., 5th Mx. Lab. Coy.	
67529	Pte. NEWMAN, L., 69th Lab. Coy.	
84176	Pte. NEWNEAU, M., 35th Lab. Coy.	
74072	Pte. NUSSBAUM, H., 7th Lab. Coy.	
G/74476	Pte. NEVITSKI, M., 4th Lab. Coy.	
G/80352	Pte. NATHAN, M., 4th Lab. Coy.	
51095	Pte. NEGUES, D., 27th Lab. Coy.	
220414	Pte. NATHAN, S., 1st Lab. Coy.	
34804	L/Cpl. NEWMAN, A., 4th Lab. Coy.	
132978	Pte. NOORDEN, L.	
293230	Pte. NOVOGREDSKI, A., 386th H.S. L. C.	
100831	Pte. NYMAN, F., 8th Mx. Lab. Coy.	
557021	L/Cpl. NEWMAN, D., 1002nd Lab. Coy.	
557624	Pte. NOSSICK, M., 1002nd Lab. Coy.	
557997	Pte. NEWFIELD, W., 1002nd Lab. Coy.	
558295	Pte. NYMAN, A., 1002nd Lab. Coy.	
558203	Pte. NEAR, E., 1002nd Lab. Coy.	
558201	Pte. NEHARD, S., 1002nd Lab. Coy.	
558144	Pte. NEIMARK, H., 1002nd Lab. Coy.	
557407	Pte. NATHAN, L., 1001st Lab. Coy.	
557487	Pte. NEEDLE, H., 1001st Lab. Coy.	
557546	Pte. NYMAN, M., 1001st Lab. Coy.	
506734	Pte. NASH, B., 672nd H.S. E. Coy.	
452397	Pte. NATHAN, I., 299th Res. Lab. Bn.	
31952	Pte. NATHAN, H., 54th Lab. Coy.	
30423	Pte. NATHAN, S., 51st Lab. Coy.	
554	Pte. NENUE, S., E.L.C.	
580	Cpl. NAHARY, E., E.L.C.	
210918	Pte. NERDON, J., 265th Lab. Coy.	
460759	Pte. NURENBERG, B., 623rd Lab. Coy.	
272476	Cpl. NOSCOVITCH, H., 366th Lab. Coy.	
166869	Pte. NERMAN, M., 525th Lab. Coy.	
356620	Pte. NEWMAN,	
1989	Pte. OCKRENT, H., 4th Lab. Coy.	
97624	Pte. OLIVER, S. A., 7th Mx. Lab. Coy.	
32221	Pte. OSTERMAN, R., Lincoln Bn.	
559285	Pte. OSTRICK, D., 8th Lab. Coy.	
41165	Pte. OSBORNE, A., 20th Chshire Regt.	
122364	Pte. OKONOFSKY, I., 892nd A.E. Coy.	
74206	Pte. ORWOOD, L., 1st Mx. Lab. Coy.	
80346	Pte. OETINGER, M., 1st Mx. Lab. Coy.	
G/74147	Pte. OPPER, H., 4th Mx. Lab. Coy.	
381680	Pte. OLLIS, B., 185th Lab. Coy.	
47849	Pte. OESBER, S., 80th Lab. Coy.	
80346	Pte. ORGAL, S., 3rd Lab. Coy.	
465100	Pte. OPPENHEIM, H., 621st Lab. Coy.	
G/72918	Pte. OFFER, E., 5th Mx. Lab. Coy.	
45199	Pte. ORONARD, D., 5th Lab. Coy.	
50390	Pte. OVERS, S., 27th Lab. Coy.	
34656	Pte. OTTOLANGUI, D., 4th Lab. Coy.	
204078	Pte. OKOUNER, E., 11th Lab. Coy.	
006	Cpl. OUSIZE, M., 72nd Lab. Coy.	
557563	Pte. OBRANT, L., 1002nd Lab. Coy.	
558121	Pte. OGUS, J., 1002nd Lab. Coy.	
557949	Pte. OZAROFF, A., 1002nd Lab. Coy.	
557014	Pte. OLSHANITZKY, P., 1002nd Lab. Coy.	
557121	Pte. OSSIN, E., 1001st Lab. Coy.	

Labour Corps.—*Continued.*

557426	Pte. OFULLSKY, A., 1001st Lab. Coy.
557081	Pte. OSTROI, S., 1001st Lab. Coy.
557223	Pte. OPOLION, M., 1001st Lab. Coy.
557456	Pte. OLESHEVSKY, A., 1001st Lab. Coy.
526402	Pte. OBERSTEIN, A., 676th H.S. E. Coy.
57927	Pte. OSCAR, T., 97th Coy.
383993	Pte. OLINSKY, M., 917th Lab. Coy.
99620	Pte. OLIVER, S. A., 7th Lab. Coy.
45698	Pte. ORBINSKY, L.
93683	Pte. OAKES, A., 7th Lab. Coy.
45639	Pte. OROMOVITZ, B., 3rd Lab. Coy.
523460	Pte. ORDER, H., 364th Lab. Coy.
461073	Pte. ORNER, I., 304th Lab. Coy.
G/26878	Pte. OSOSKI, L., 170th Lab. Coy.
135270	Pte. OSTRER, M., S.C.L.C.
270928	Pte. PHILLIPS, H., 259th A.E. Coy.
475984	Pte. POST, N., 207th Emp. Coy.
39316	Pte. PETERKOVSKY, D., 209th Emp. Coy.
31952	Pte. PLENDER, A., 2nd Inf. Lab. Coy.
92852	Pte. PAUPLE, S., 155th Lab. Coy.
224830	Pte. PETERKOVSKY, R., 232nd Div. E. C.
483334	Pte. PEARL, H., A.E. Collecting Depot.
87324	Pte. PYZER, A., 146th Lab. Coy.
29851	Pte. PARKER, J., 34th Lab. Coy.
162030	Pte. PROOFS, H. J., 237th Emp. Coy.
87339	Pte. POU, S., 146th Lab. Coy.
87917	Pte. POLLACK, J., 147th Lab. Coy.
64526	Pte. PADRANSKY, D., 108th Lab. Coy.
392841	Pte. PADOLSKY, M., 74th Lab. Coy.
71140	Pte. PEZARO, I., 119th Lab. Coy.
273776	Pte. PUCHYER, S., 105th Lab. Coy.
87324	L/Cpl. PYZER, A., 146th Lab. Coy.
452464	Pte. PLATT, M., 142nd Lab. Coy.
393186	Pte. PERKINS, M., 281st A.E. Coy.
24369	Pte. PYZER, N., 41st Lab. Coy.
366612	Pte. PARKINSON, W., 298th Lab. Coy.
352335	Pte. PELLER, I., 350th Res. Emp. Coy.
534972	Pte. PARTRIA, S.
36288	Pte. PESTKA,* L., 61st Lab. Coy.
37748	Q.M.S. PHILLIPS, J., 18th Cheshire Rgt.
40936	Pte. PAMPLE, M. S., 14th Lab. Coy.
282947	Pte. PEARLSTONE, A., 3rd Lab. Coy.
47736	Pte. PASKIN, H., Labour Centre.
529801	Pte. PRUZANSKY, B., Labour Centre.
84435	Pte. PILVERNITZ, A., 3rd Mx. Lab. Coy.
G/71813	Pte. PHILIP, E., 4th Mx. Lab. Coy.
G/37451	Pte. PARNES, M., 4th Mx. Lab. Coy.
64526	Pte. PODBRANSKY, D., 22nd Lab. Coy.
521370	Pte. PLOTKIN, H., 30th Lab. Coy.
42326	Pte. PYMAN, L., 71st Lab. Coy.
522771	Pte. PEROWITZ, J., 102nd Lab. Coy.
87922	Pte. POLSKI, J., 147th Lab. Coy.
610766	Pte. PHILLIPS, J., 162nd Lab. Coy.
14360	Pte. PYNT, F., 186th Lab. Coy.
521369	Pte. PEARLMAN, A., 721st Lab. Coy.
10566	Pte. PHILLIPS, J., 18th Lab. Coy.
111360	Pte. PYNT, J., 186th Lab. Coy.
75935	Pte. PEZARS, B., 127th Lab. Coy.
75948	Pte. PROUT, M., 127th Lab. Coy.
75956	Pte. POLACK, N., 127th Lab. Coy.
47622	Pte. PETERS, H., 80th Lab. Coy.
26716	Pte. PRICE, A. L., 45th Lab. Coy.
189568	Pte. PRICE, H., 837th A.E. Coy.
273817	Pte. PLOTSKY, M., 787th A.E. Coy.
266461	Pte. POLINSKY, J., 733rd Lab. Coy.
G/80319	Pte. PUCKATCH, H., 4th Lab. Coy.
12333	Pte. PEER, A., 21st Lab. Coy.
69938	Pte. PAZEBWISKI, J., 117th Lab. Coy.
84318	Pte. PARKS, A., 141st Lab. Coy.
68264	L/Cpl. PASS, C., 114th Lab. Coy.
633258	Pte. PELLAR, G., 707th Lab. Coy.
	Pte. POLINSKY, H., 5th Lab. Coy.
279437	Pte. PIZER, W., 581st Area Emp. Coy.
G/84234	Pte. PRESS, B., 5th Mx. Lab. Coy.
273699	Pte. POLINSKY, M., 5th Lab. Coy.
92852	Pte. PAMPEL, S., 155th Lab. Coy.
669	Pte. PINEBERG, M., 45th Lab. Coy.
92108	Pte. PARMAN, W., 35th Lab. Coy.
71689	Pte. PECH, J. M., 35th Lab. Coy.
	Pte. PINCUS, H.
299258	Pte. PHILLIPS, N., 716th Lab. Coy.
508145	Pte. PLOTKA, S., 779th Area Emp. Coy.
285062	Sgt. PHILLIPS, F., Labour Centre.
378612	Pte. PHILLIPS, M., 8th Lab. Coy.
	Cpl. PICKERCHICK, J., 11th Lab. Coy.
46160	Pte. PROUT, M., 19th Lab. Coy.
48786	Pte. POLAK, B., 19th Lab. Coy.
46478	Pte. PEZARO, B., 19th Lab. Coy.
79685	Pte. PADVA,* S., 133rd Lab. Coy.
47736	Pte. PASKIN, H., 15th Lab. Coy.
44095	Pte. PETERS, H., 16th Lab. Coy.
34528	Pte. PRICE, A. L., 6th Lab. Coy.
34646	Pte. PHILLIPS, A., 7th Lab. Coy.
39525	Pte. PHILLIPS, L., 12th Lab. Coy.
35596	Pte. PEER, A., 21st Lab. Coy.
285047	Pte. POSNESKY, A., 1st Lab. Coy.
452464	Pte. PLATT, M., 4th Lab. Coy.
493247	Pte. PHILLIPS, D., 4th Lab. Coy.
534972	Pte. PARTNOIR, S., 643rd H.S. Emp. C.
93315	Pte. PERLMUTTER, J., 8th Mx. Lab. Coy.
557692	Cpl. PACKER, S., 1002nd Lab. Coy.
557753	Pte. PATERCHINSKY, P., 1002nd Lab. Coy.
558206	Pte. PERGRISHT, D., 1002nd Lab. Coy.
557515	Pte. POBEREVSKY, M., 1002nd Lab. Coy.
558023	Pte. PINKUS, M., 1002nd Lab. Coy.
557783	Pte. POLLICK, A., 1002nd Lab. Coy.
557847	Pte. POBEREVSKY, H., 1002nd Lab. Coy.
558256	Pte. PILER, L., 1002nd Lab. Coy.
558232	Pte. POPPMACHER, B., 1002nd Lab. Coy.
557056	L/Cpl. PRICE, J., 1001st Lab. Coy.
557247	Pte. PETER, H., 1001st Lab. Coy.
557253	Pte. PLIOPLIS, V., 1001st Lab. Coy.
557219	Pte. PLATER, H., 1001st Lab. Coy.
557163	Pte. PEDRO, M., 1001st Lab. Coy.
557206	Pte. PLUSKWA, H., 1001st Lab. Coy.

Labour Corps.—Continued.

557016	Pte.	PYNT, L., 1001st Lab. Coy.
557065	Pte.	PUSHKIN, P., 1001st Lab. Coy.
557478	Pte.	PINSKER, M., 1001st Lab. Coy.
557432	Pte.	PEISSEL, J., 1001st Lab. Coy.
557330	Pte.	PEDLOFSKY, J., 1001st Lab. Coy.
557297	Pte.	PUSZACK, I., 1001st Lab. Coy.
557331	Pte.	POTASHNICK, B., 1001st Lab. Coy.
557497	Pte.	POLLEN, H., 1001st Lab. Coy.
557095	Pte.	PLEVATSKY, S., 1001st Lab. Coy.
391812	Pte.	POLASHERIK, 365th Res. E. Coy.
134177	Pte.	PRICEMAN, M., 675th H.S. Lab. Coy.
507911	Pte.	POLENSKY, Lab. Centre.
130993	Pte.	PRENSKI, I., 300th Lab. Coy.
452471	Pte.	PEARL, A., 300th Lab. Coy.
193667	Pte.	PETERS,* A., 376th Lab. Coy.
507783	Pte.	PLOTKIN, A., 535th H.S. Emp. Coy.
636907	Pte.	PAMPEL, H., Lab. Bn.
43065	L/Cpl.	PASERSKI, A., 1st Lab. Bn.
55084	Pte.	POLLICK, J., 1st Lab. Bn.
34926	Pte.	PYSER, F.
58862	Pte.	PEARL, H., 947th A.E. Coy.
631254	Pte.	PENNER, A., 991st Lab. Coy.
484664	Pte.	POLIWANSKY, N., 227th D.E. Coy.
179484	Pte.	PHILLIPS, A., Lab. Coy.
36288	L/Cpl.	PESTKA,* L., 61st Lab. Coy.
136	Pte.	PERES, M. J., E.L.C.
011005	Cpl.	PASVOLSKY, B., E.L.C.
011017	Cpl.	POLLACK, S., E.L.C.
89716	Pte.	PORTRATE, G., 150th Lab. Coy.
71149	Pte.	PINKUS, M., 119th Lab. Coy.
151384	Pte.	PERELLY, S., 587th Lab. Coy.
213965	Pte.	PYZER, J., 62nd Lab. Coy.
79685	Pte.	PADON, S.
71140	Pte.	PEZARO, I., 119th Lab. Coy.
162791	Pte.	PRECLINE, S., 369th Lab. Coy.
1905	Pte.	PHILLIPS, H.
60606	Pte.	PEARSON, F., 3rd Lab. Coy.
87917	Pte.	POLLAK, J., 147th Lab. Coy.
198334	Pte.	POLISHOFSKY, I., 6th Lab. Coy.
134177	Pte.	PRICEMAN, M., 2nd Lab. Coy.
273776	Pte.	PRACHNER, F., 165th Lab. Coy.
452663	Pte.	POLLACK, B., 362nd Lab. Coy.
75342	Pte.	PRIMHACK, M.
250788	Pte.	PETERS, P., 301st Lab. Coy.
269636	Pte.	POLENBAUM, J., 299th Lab. Coy.
273158	Pte.	PENNAMACONE, J., 366th Lab. Coy.
90353	Pte.	PERRICK, N.
134322	Pte.	PINKUS, A., 675th Lab. Coy.
8795	Pte.	PHILLIPS, H., R. Marine Lab. Crps.
87324	Pte.	PYZERS, A., 146th Lab. Co.y.
125052	Pte.	PEARLMAN, H. E., 89th Lab. Coy.
507911	Pte.	POLINSKY, S.
162030	Pte.	PROOPS, H. J., 237th Lab. Coy.
209838	Pte.	POLACK, A., 368th Lab. Coy.
254243	Pte.	PESCOVITCH, A., 364th Lab. Coy.
509282	Pte.	POLESHOOK, I., 480th Lab. Coy.
460813	Pte.	POLLOCK, J.
619537	Pte.	PERLSTEIN, M., 303rd Lab. Coy.
354343	Pte.	PESCOVITCH, A., 364th Lab. Coy.
87326	Pte.	POLLITTI, R.
458718	Pte.	PICKHOLT, W.
209838	Pte.	POLLACK, N., 268th Lab. Coy.
84435	Pte.	PEELRERNITZ, A.
352335	Pte.	PELLAR, I.
465260	Pte.	PEARLMAN.
524257	Pte.	PYZER, H.
24369	Pte.	POGSON, M., 41st Lab. Coy.
G/70556	Pte.	QUASTEL, H., 4th Mx. Lab. Coy.
	Pte.	QUESKEY, R. I., 110th Lab. Coy.
G/93985	Pte.	QUADRATSTEIN, M., 5th Mx. L. C.
46558	Pte.	QUINT, H., 13th Lab. Coy.
477298	Pte.	QUISKEY, J., 110th Lab. Coy.
377205	L/Cpl.	RICHMAN, M., 764th A.E. Coy.
93510	Pte.	RICHARDS, M., 7th Mx. Lab. Coy.
93730	Pte.	ROSENTHAL, S., 7th Mx. Lab. Coy.
92511	Pte.	ROSENTHAL, H., 7th Mx. Lab. Coy.
93809	Sgt.	ROSSENGER, L., 7th Mx. Lab. Coy.
69396	Pte.	RUSSELL, G., 261st Emp. Coy.
190359	Pte.	ROSENBERG, M., 161st Lab. Coy.
30908	Sgt.	REICHENBERG, E. H., 2nd Inf. L. Co.
48397	L/Cpl.	REICHENBERG, S., 2nd Inf. L. Co.
74241	Pte.	RAPP,* L., 2nd Inf. Lab. Coy.
35803	Pte.	ROSENBLOOM, M., 2nd Inf. Lab. Co.
48157	Pte.	ROSENBLOOM, H., 2nd Inf. Lab. Co.
35797	Pte.	ROSENFELD, F., 2nd Inf. Lab. Coy.
31954	Pte.	ROSENWEG, W., 2nd Inf. Lab. Coy.
44368	Pte.	ROTTESMANN, J., 2nd Inf. Lab. Coy.
76541	Pte.	ROSANKY, S., 128th Lab. Coy.
128034	Pte.	RUTENBERG, H., 161st Lab. Coy.
51960	Pte.	ROBISON, S., 87th Lab. Coy.
161953	Pte.	ROSENTHAL, S., 744th A.E. Coy.
373770	Pte.	ROFOFSKIE, P., 751st A.E. Coy.
581838	Pte.	RAPHAEL, J., 249th Div. Emp. Coy.
512885	Pte.	ROSENBLOOM, S., 249th Div. Em. Co.
481219	Pte.	ROSENTHAL,* A., 250th Div. Lab. Co.
38457	Pte.	ROSE, O. N., 3rd Mx. Lab. Coy.
50876	Pte.	RAHICK, D., 5th Lab. Coy.
19628	Pte.	RAPHAEL, P., 28th Lab. Coy.
8179	Pte.	ROAT, S., 114th Lab. Coy.
201853	Pte.	ROSEN, H., 233rd Emp. Coy.
87365	Pte.	ROTHSTEIN, H., 146th Lab. Coy.
310714	Pte.	RIBOSKY, J., 735th Lab. Coy.
396380	Pte.	ROSENTHAL, S., 42nd Lab. Coy.
131107	Pte.	RHINE, L., 223rd Employ. Coy.
160131	Pte.	RABINOVITZ, S.
135350	Pte.	RAPHAEL, J., 3rd Lab. Corps.
273829	Pte.	ROSENTHAL, M., 876th A.E. Coy.
37680	Pte.	ROSENSTEIN, D., 146th Lab. Coy.
210637	Pte.	ROSENBAUM, A., 255th Lab. Coy.
69392	Pte.	RUBINSTEIN, M., 116th Lab. Coy.
243623	Pte.	RABINOVITCH, I., 36th Lab. Coy.
366920	Pte.	ROSEN, M., 522nd Lab. Coy.
491223	Pte.	ROWLAND, L., 475th Lab. Coy.
42276	Pte.	ROSENBERG, S., 20th Lab. Coy.
24376	L/Cpl.	ROSEMAN, B., 9th Lab. Coy.

Labour Corps.—*Continued.*

36283 Pte. ROSENBERG, M., 14th Lab. Coy.
48137 Pte. RHUDSTEIN, H., 20th Lab. Coy.
451871 Pte. ROSENBAUM, E., Labour Centre.
383748 Pte. RABINOWITCH, A., Labour Centre.
557883 Pte. ROSENFELD, B.
27576 Pte. ROSENTHAL, S., 41st Lab. Coy.
655314 Pte. ROEK, A., 24th A.E. Coy.
197771 Pte. ROSENBERG, E., 892nd A.E. Coy.
31406 Pte. RABINSTEIN, O., 1st Mx. Lab. Coy.
38753 Pte. ROSS, H., 1st Mx. Lab. Coy.
45074 Pte. ROSENTHAL, A., 3rd Mx. Lab. Coy.
47884 Pte. RUBEN, P., 3rd Mx. Lab. Coy.
G80226 Pte. RYMER, L., 4th Mx. Lab. Coy.
G/80235 Pte. RIBANOVITCH, M., 4th Mx. Lab. C.
G/71552 Pte. REINSTEIN, M., 4th Mx. Lab. Coy.
G/74148 Pte. RAUCHMAN-GALIZER, A., 4th Mx.
G/70679 Pte. RAUCHWERK, A., 4th Mx. Lab. Co.
G/71563 Pte. ROSENBAUM, A., 4th Mx. Lab. Co.
G/80286 Pte. ROTH, M., 4th Mx. Lab. Coy.
G/80424 Pte. RAPP, J., 4th Mx. Lab. Coy.
6981 Pte. ROSENBAUM, S., 12th Lab. Coy.
525116 Pte. ROSENBAUM, A., 55th Lab. Coy.
39956 Pte. ROSENFIELD, A., 84th Lab. Coy.
161953 Pte. ROSENTHAL, S., 93rd Lab. Coy.
56116 Pte. RUBENSTEIN, I., 94th Lab. Coy.
34607 Cpl. RASHMAN, S. G., 58th Lab. Coy.
393093 Pte. ROAT, T., 22nd Lab. Coy.
163115 Pte. REVENSKY, H., 37th Lab. Coy.
419797 Pte. ROSENSTEIN, B., 54th Lab. Coy.
39375 Pte. RUBENS, F., 66th Lab. Coy.
441721 Pte. RUDOLF, B., 109th Lab. Coy.
79558 Pte. ROSENBLOOM, A., 118th Lab. Coy.
79559 Pte. RUTSTEIN, I., 133rd Lab. Coy.
88055 Pte. ROSENBAUM, M., 147th Lab. Coy.
208106 L/Cpl. RUBENSTEIN, J., 733rd Lab. Coy.
393346 Pte. ROSENWEIG, M., 991st Lab. Coy.
581961 Pte. RAPSTOFF, A., 991st Lab. Coy.
377205 L/Cpl. RICHMAN, M., 764th A.E. Coy.
69396 Pte. RUSSELL, G., 822nd A.E. Coy.
70558 Pte. ROSENBLOOM, A., 118th Lab. Coy.
559017 Pte. ROGALEK,* M., 1001st Lab. Coy.
26423 Cpl. RUDSTEIN, M., 45th Lab. Coy.
339634 Pte. REUBEN, E., 116th Lab. Coy.
14197 Pte. ROSEATHALL, M., 941st A.E. Coy.
472328 Pte. RADAM, H., 787th Area Emp. Coy.
38596 Pte. RADVANT, P., 3rd Lab. Coy.
84179 Pte. RAPPAPORT, L., 3rd Lab. Coy.
6981 Pte. ROSENBLOOM, S., 12th Lab. Coy.
39956 Pte. ROSENFIELD, A., 67th Lab. Coy.
317258 Pte. ROSENBERG, S., 579th A.E. Coy.
655583 Pte. ROSEN, L., 72nd Lab. Coy.
568739 Pte. RICH, S., 90th Lab. Coy.
273870 Pte. ROSENBURGH, H., 156th Lab. Coy.
G/30909 C.Q.M.S. ROTHERSTEIN, L., 5th Mx. Lab. Coy.
G.93403 Pte. ROTHAMN, D., 5th Mx. Lab. Coy.
G/93153 Pte. ROSENBERG, I., 5th Mx. Lab. Coy.
G/93017 Pte. ROSENBERG, I., 5th Mx. Lab. Coy.
G/93233 Pte. ROTH, B., 5th Mx. Lab. Coy.
G/93199 Pte. ROSE, J., 5th Mx. Lab. Coy.
G/90089 Pte. ROUSSE, V., 5th Mx. Lab. Coy.
35577 Pte. ROSENBERG, S., 60th Lab. Coy.
80033 Pte. ROSSMAN, J. J., 35th Lab. Coy.
80003 Pte. RADZVILLA, L., 35th Lab. Coy.
80391 Pte. ROSE, H., 35th Lab. Coy.
84132 Pte. ROTHMER, S., 35th Lab. Coy.
48845 Pte. ROSE, I., 4th Lab. Coy.
572868 Pte. ROSENKRANTZ, J., Area Emp. Coy.
168985 Pte. ROCKMAN, W., 377th H.S. Lab. C.
509331 Pte. ROSENSTEIN, J., 527th A.E. Coy.
567915 Pte. ROSENBERG, G., 893th A.E. Coy.
79568 Pte. RAPHAEL, P. J., 846th A.E. Coy.
198771 Pte. ROSENBERG, E., 887th A.E. Coy.
92852 Pte. RAMPEL, S., 17th Lab. Coy.
14197 Pte. ROSENTHALL, M., 941st A.E. Coy.
S/361809 Pte. ROTHFIELD, M. L., 30th L. of C.
20442 Pte. ROSEWOOD, M., Labour Centre.
51465 Pte. ROGERS, A., 29th Lab. Coy.
50876 Pte. RATTISK, 5th Lab. Coy.
 L/Cpl. RUBIN, P. B., 46th Coy.
87353 Pte. RAPHAEL, S., 146th Lab. Coy.
204300 Cpl. ROSE, S. S., 11th Lab. Coy.
4221 L/Cpl. ROSEMAN, B. N., 8th Lab. Coy.
52670 Pte. ROTAPPLE, J., 2nd Lab. Coy.
26847 Pte. RUBENSTEIN, B., 37th Lab. Coy.
460719 Pte. ROTHSTONE, 633rd Emp. Coy.
461012 Pte. RUTMAN, M., 633rd Emp. Coy.
80378 Pte. RICHER, I., 5th Mx. Lab. Coy.
98164 Pte. RADVANT, M., 5th Mx. Lab. Coy.
101906 Pte. RUBENSTEIN, M., 5th Mx. Lab. Coy.
71689 Pte RECH, J. M., 18th Lab. Group.
93329 Pte. ROSENGARTEN, S., 8th Mx. Lab. Coy.
98143 Pte. ROTHFIELD, J., 8th Mx. Lab. Coy.
93419 Pte. RUBINSTEIN, J., 8th Mx. Lab. Coy.
97539 Pte. RADIVAN, A., 8th Mx. Lab. Coy.
93496 Pte. ROSNER, J., 8th Mx. Lab. Coy.
93612 Pte. REICHENBERG, H., 8th Mx. Lab. Coy.
100028 Pte. RAPPAPORT, S., 8th Mx. Lab. Coy.
93762 Pte. ROSENBLOOM, S., 8th Mx. Lab. Coy.
93819 Pte. ROTHFIELD, 8th Mx. Lab. Coy.
92040 Pte. ROSNER, A., 8th Mx. Lab. Coy.
35933 Pte. ROSENBERG, W., 8th Mx. Lab. Coy.
557696 Pte. RUBINSKY, 1002nd Lab. Coy.
557740 Pte. REIDLER, 1002nd Lab. Coy.
557929 Pte. ROSE, M., 1002nd Lab. Coy.
557716 Pte. ROSEN, M., 1002nd Lab. Coy.
558220 Pte. RECHINSKY, M., 1002nd Lab. Coy.
558094 Pte. RIFFCHIN, S., 1002nd Lab. Coy.
558142 Pte. RINGART, A., 1002nd Lab. Coy.
558028 Pte. ROSENSWAIG, A., 1002nd Lab. Coy
558188 Pte. RINDER, M,. 1002nd Lab. Coy.
557488 Pte. RENACH, S., 1002nd Lab. Coy.
557050 Pte. ROITH, L., 1002nd Lab. Coy.
557530 Pte. RAPAPORT, I., 1002nd Lab. Coy.
558005 Pte. RUBIN, M., 1002nd Lab. Coy.

Labour Corps.—*Continued.*

557890	Pte. RABBINOWITZ, H., 1002nd Lab. Coy.
557909	Pte. ROSENBLOOM, Z., 1002nd Lab. Coy.
557775	Pte. ROSENCRANTZ, H., 1002nd Lab. Coy.
557773	Pte. ROSEN, S., 1002nd Lab. Coy.
558265	Pte. RUBIN, H., 1002nd Lab. Coy.
558249	Pte. RUBIN, S., 1002nd Lab. Coy.
558140	Pte. RICHMOND, D., 1002nd Lab. Coy.
557966	Pte. ROACH, J., 1002nd Lab. Coy.
557987	Pte. ROSEMAN, J., 1002nd Lab. Coy.
557967	Pte. RICHENBERG, M., 1002nd Lab. Coy.
557199	Pte. ROSENBAUM, J. M., 1001st Lab. Coy.
557370	Pte. ROSE, M., 1001st Lab. Coy.
557409	Pte. ROSEN, A., 1001st Lab. Coy.
557489	Pte. RETSCH, R. C., 1001st Lab. Coy.
557455	Pte. RATZKER, J., 1001st Lab. Coy.
557480	Pte. RUBINSTEIN, I., 1001st Lab. Coy.
557538	Pte. ROSENBERG, S., 1001st Lab. Coy.
557296	Pte. ROSENBAUM, A., 1001st Lab. Coy.
557290	Pte. RAYOFSKY, H., 1001st Lab. Coy.
557081	Pte. RUDZEVIZ, C., 1001st Lab. Coy.
152812	Pte. RADSTONE, S., 673rd H.S. E. Coy.
171244	Pte. ROSE, S., 309th Works Coy.
525241	Pte. ROTHBARR, D., Lab. Centre.
452575	Pte. ROWLAND, A., 300th Lab. Bn.
452407	Pte. RUBIN, M., 299th Res. Lab. Coy.
556081	Pte. RITZMAN, A., Lab. Bn.
45951	L/Cpl. RUEBEN, M., 1st Lab. Bn.
44667	Pte. ROBESKY, M., 1st Lab. Bn.
366612	Pte. RAKINSON, W., 266th A.E. Coy.
39024	Pte. ROBINS, H., 266th A.E. Coy.
534155	Pte. ROSE, G. E., 527th A.E. Coy.
519053	Pte. RONSYA, H.
605007	Pte. ROSENBERG, D.
53217	Pte. ROSE, C., 89th Lab. Coy.
273827	Pte. ROSEN, L., 824th A.E. Coy.
86152	Pte. ROTHSCHILD, H., 144th Lab. Coy.
19431	Pte. ROSENTHAL, A., 764th A.E. Coy.
56116	Pte. RUBENSTEIN, I., 94th Lab. Coy.
011054	Cpl. RAZAK, K. E. A., E.L.C.
05124	Pte. ROSENBLOOM, S., E.L.C.
419797	Pte. ROSENSTEIN, B., 54th Lab. Coy.
392210	Pte. ROSENBERG, H.
460808	Pte. ROSENBERG, H.
69392	Pte. RUBENSTEIN, M., 116th Lab. Coy.
53786	Pte. ROSENBAND, 96th Lab. Coy.
56108	Pte. ROSENBERG, I.
210367	Pte. ROSENBAUM, A., 366th Lab. Coy.
56116	Pte. RUBENSTEIN, I.
163146	Pte. RUBENSTEIN, A., 687th Lab. Coy.
70825	Pte. ROSENBERG, H.
273610	Pte. RABINOVITCH, S.
35410	Pte. RAPHAEL, S., 35th Lab. Coy.
39656	Pte. ROUNDSTEIN, H., 35th Lab. Coy.
174229	Pte. RAGVINOFSKY, E., 3/19th Lab. Coy
352816	Pte. RUVENS, S., 198th Lab. Coy.
135369	Pte. REVENSKY, M., 3rd Lab. Coy.
157886	Pte. RANDALL, M., 301st Lab. Coy.
132819	Pte. RADSTONE, S. H.
37680	Pte. ROSENSTEIN, G., 8th Lab. Coy.
202950	L/Cpl. RUBEN, M., 299th Lab. Coy.
53217	Pte. ROSE, C., 89th Lab. Coy.
16285	Pte. RUEBEN, H., 369th Lab. Coy.
24376	Pte. ROSENTHAL, S., 41st Lab. Coy.
74148	Pte. RAUCHMAN, A., 4th Lab. Coy.
30236	Pte. ROBINS, H., 299th Lab. Coy.
87365	Pte. RORKSTEIN, H., 146th Lab. Coy.
64607	Pte. RICHMAN, G., 68th Lab. Coy.
389366	Pte. ROSENBERG, H., 818th Lab. Coy.
460799	Pte. RICHGINSKY, A.
527250	Pte. ROSE, N.
556287	Pte. ROME, S., 9th Lab. Coy.
452484	Pte. ROSENTHAL, S., 299th Lab. Coy.
241782	Pte. ROSENTHAL, S.
69392	Pte. RUBENSTEIN, M., 100th Lab. Coy.
544627	Pte. RUBENSTEIN, B., 106th Lab. Coy.
42589	Pte. RUBENSTEIN, R., 8th Lab. Coy.
86152	Pte. ROTHSCHILD, I., 83rd Lab. Coy.
264723	Pte. RAPAPORT, A., 561st Lab. Coy.
422049	Pte. ROSENTHAL, H., 464th Lab. Coy.
39969	Pte. ROSENTHAL, S., 67th Lab. Coy.
92003	Pte. REICH, 3rd Lab. Coy.
46559	Pte. ROBINSON, B., 78th Lab. Coy.
509350	Pte. ROSENWATER, S., 512th Lab. Coy.
9778	Pte. RADZWILLER, G. J., 8th Lab. Coy.
523879	Pte. ROSENBERG, S.
273843	Pte. ROSENBERG, J., 876th Lab. Coy.
274002	Pte. RENDERLICK, A.
132383	Pte. SAVITZ, L., 7th Lab .Coy.
128664	Pte. SUGERMAN, N., 291st Area Emp. C.
425602	Pte. SIMONOVITCH, M., 834th Artizan C.
379113	Pte. SIMMONS, S., 259th Area Emp. Coy.
274023	Pte. SAKOVITCH, P., 787th A.E. Coy.
90419	Pte. SINGER, H., 151st Lab. C. VII Cps.
90388	L/Cpl. STRELITZ, J., 151st L. C. VII Cps.
104174	Pte SCHILLING, P., 174th L. C. VII Cps.
97585	Pte. SPIER, L., 7th Mx. Lab. Coy.
93456	Pte. SILVERMAN, L., 7th Mx. Lab. Coy.
93687	Pte. STERN, A., 7th Mx. Lab. Coy.
74080	Pte. SPERBER, J. A., 7th Mx. Lab. Coy.
97663	Pte. SCHULKIND, M., 7th Mx. Lab. Coy.
97596	Pte. SANTHAUSE, B., 7th Mx. Lab. Coy.
93252	Pte. SPITZER, H., 7th Mx. Lab. Coy.
93732	Pte. SHNEIDER, H. P., 7th Mx. Lab. C.
83052	Pte. STEIN, H., 7th Mx. Lab. Coy.
93141	Pte. SEFTON, I., 7th Mx. Lab. Coy.
97518	Pte. STEINLOFT, J., 7th Mx. Lab. Coy.
93684	Pte. SHNEIDERS, H., 7th Mx. Lab. Coy.
192830	Pte. SCHWARTZ, S., 214th Emp. Coy.
130777	Pte. SHEFFER, S., 205th Emp. Coy.
125901	Pte. SWIRLING, H., 205th Emp. Coy.
126700	Pte. SAILSBURY, H., 234th Emp. Coy.
208109	Pte. SOLOMON, D., 251st Emp. Coy.
201639	Pte. SHILCO, A., 224th Div. Emp. Coy.
36690	Pte. SYMONS, R., 147th Lab. Coy.
36690	Pte. SYMONS, R., 147th Lab. Coy.

Labour Corps.—*Continued.*

258236 Pte. SOLOMONS, H., 218th Emp. Coy.
65803 Pte. SLIFKIN, S., 110th Lab. Coy.
30914 Pte. SCHEIER A., 2nd Lab. Coy.
84099 Pte. SCHINDLER, E., 2nd Lab. Coy.
31969 Pte. SCHLOSS, E. P., 2nd Lab. Coy.
84162 Pte. SCHNEIDERS, J., 2nd Lab. Coy.
37373 Pte. SCHREIBER, R., 2nd Lab. Coy.
84072 Pte. SCHWARTZ, J., 2nd Lab. Coy.
31488 Pte. SCHWARTZ, B., 2nd Lab. Coy.
74335 Pte. SELINGER, A., 2nd Lab. Coy.
31147 Pte. SHEAR, M., 2nd Lab. Coy.
30924 Pte. SMITH, M., 2nd Lab. Coy.
74228 Pte. SNELL, J., 2nd Lab. Coy.
86797 Pte. SOLOMONS, B., 735th Lab. Coy.
98786 Pte. SIMONS, J., 165th Lab. Coy.
67812 Pte. SHONA, 742nd Area Emp. Coy.
220625 Pte. SKLAIR, M., 752nd Area Emp. Coy.
762418 Pte. SEYMOUR, S. J., 63rd Div. Emp. C.
73472 Pte. SHULKIND, N., 1st Mx. Lab. Coy.
31722 Pte. STERN, A., 1st Mx. Lab. Coy.
74131 Pte. SCHNITTLINGER, B. H., 1st Mx. L.C
70470 Pte. SAMUEL, T., 1st Mx. Lab. Coy.
72917 Pte. STERNSTEIN, S., 1st Mx. Lab. Coy.
80602 Pte. STRATTON, S. A., 1st Mx. Lab. Coy.
47728 L/Cpl. SIMON, .H, 1st Mx. Lab. Coy.
53070 Pte. SHELLER, 1st Dev. Lab. Coy.
Pte. SOLOMONS, A., 3rd Dev. Lab. Coy.
37993 Pte SIMONS, M., 2nd R.S.F. Lab. Coy.
39642 Pte. SELLARS, H., 2nd R.S.F. Lab. Coy.
35951 Pte. SHERMAN, S., 6th N. Hants. L. Coy.
80815 Pte. SILVER, S., 135th Lab. Coy.
163534 Pte. SAKS, M., 17th Lab. Coy.
102374 Pte. SCHWEEITZER, S., 177th Lab. Coy.
202947 Pte. SAKER, L., 146th Lab. Coy.
444784 Pte. STEIN, H., 15th Lab. Coy.
42978 Pte. SKEIN, I., 72nd Lab. Coy.
191529 Pte. SPYERS, S., 196th Lab. Coy.
34947 Pte. SOLOMONS, L., 273rd A.E. Coy.
622922 L/Cpl. SALAANT, J., 806th A.E. Coy.
548681 Pte. SILBERSTON, L., 802nd Lab. Corps.
93204 Pte. SOULAM, I., Labour Corps.
522585 Pte. SINGER, J., 363rd Labour Corps.
67812 Pte. SHOUL, S., 42nd Lab. Coy.
393326 Pte. SUGAR, L., 281st Lab. Coy.
22660 Pte. SHUNDLER, H., 246th Lab. Coy.
192818 Pte. SHANKS, J., 217th A.E. Coy.
71208 Pte. SOLET, I., 119th Lab. Coy.
89449 Cpl. SIMONS, I., 150th Lab. Coy.
103574 Pte. SCHEKTER, D., 173rd Lab. Coy.
65803 Pte. SLIFKIN, S., 19th Lab. Coy.
46023 Pte. STOMAFF, 846th Lab. Coy.
87968 Pte. SANK, H., 147th Lab. Coy.
274009 Pte. SILVER, S., 104th Lab. Coy.
309268 Pte. SAMUELS, A., 83rd Lab. Coy.
29783 Pte. SHORNSTEIN, 41st Lab. Coy.
89783 Pte. SHORNSTEIN, S., 44th Lab. Coy.
639052 Pte. SILVER, S., 390th Lab. Coy.

317293 Pte. SMUCKLER, A., 390th Lab. Coy.
273765 Pte. SOLOMON, M., 389th Lab. Coy.
457377 Pte. SALAMON, E.
5801 Pte. SIMONS, M., 10th Lab. Coy.
70834 L/Cpl. SCHULMOVITCH, S. (M.S.M.), 119th Lab. Coy.
510287 Pte. SOLOMON, H., 247th Emp. Coy.
558367 Pte. SILVER, L., 8th Lab. Coy.
597750 Pte. STROON, I., 207th Lab. Coy.
558113 Pte. SANDEMAN, 8th Lab. Coy.
273684 Pte. SCARMARLINSKY, 366th A.E. Coy.
149612 Pte. SIMPLER, D.
524176 Pte. STERNBERG, M.
55593 Pte. SHROOT, M., 93rd Lab. Coy.
91010 Pte. SHULTOSKY, M., 123rd Lab. Coy.
79028 Pte. STODEL, M., 132nd Lab. Coy.
80815 Pte. SILVER, S., 135th Lab. Coy.
84381 Pte. SCHUSTER, H., 141st Lab. Coy.
87968 Pte. SANK, H., 147th Lab. Coy.
87987 Pte. SAMUELS, S., 1947th Lab. Coy.
197815 Pte. SOLOMON, S., 147th Lab. Coy.
88975 Pte. SPRINGER, S., 149th Lab. Coy.
90419 Pte. SINGER, H., 151st Lab. Coy.
90388 L/Cpl. STRELITZ, J., 151st Lab. Coy.
273820 Pte. SCHWARTZ, M., 164th Lab. Coy.
104174 Pte. SCHILLING, P., 174th Lab. Coy.
107142 Pte. SOLOMON, N., 179th Lab. Coy.
640946 Pte. STIRZAKER, T., 715th Lab. Coy.
614112 Pte. SOLOMONS, W., 725th Lab. Coy.
273848 Pte. SKUZONS, D., 991st Lab. Coy.
273794 Pte. SKUKERVITSKY, S., 991st Lab. Coy.
582004 Pte. SELTZER, S., 991st Lab. Coy.
460960 Pte. SILVER, L., 991st Lab. Coy.
274007 Pte. SHRIER, S., 991st Lab. Coy.
281209 Pte. SAMUELS, H., 833rd A.E. Coy.
387142 Pte. SOLOMONS, N., 918th A.E. Coy.
346570 Sgt. SAUNDERS, H., 47th Chin. Lab. Coy.
10615 Pte. SAMOFSKI, J., 18th Lab. Coy.
11788 Pte. SPINK, D., 20th Lab. Coy.
529964 L/Cpl. SAIET, C., 122nd Lab. Coy.
32145 Pte. SUCHALL, A., 54th Lab. Coy.
75987 Pte. SECAL, H., 127th Lab. Coy.
27967 Pte. SLIFKIN, J., 47th Lab. Coy.
190860 Pte. SOLOMON, K., 182nd Lab. Coy.
67035 Pte. SCHWATLING, J., 112th Lab. Coy.
88975 Pte. SPRINGER, S., 149th Lab. Coy.
523420 Pte. SCHWARTZBERG, A.
356610 Pte. SETON, A. W., Employ. Coy.
682989 Pte. SIMONS, att. Military Col. Stat.
41133 Pte. SILVERMAN, J., 20th Cheshire Regt.
14973 Pte. SILVERMAN, G., 12th Black Watch.
31437 Pte. SHORE, H., 13th Lab. Coy.
51472 Pte. STERN, G., 1st Lab. Coy.
37993 Pte. SIMONS, M., 2nd Lab. Coy.
556639 Pte. SMITH, L.
565572 Pte. SAX, V., 76th Lab. Coy.
143598 Pte. SWART, M., 72nd Lab. Coy.

Labour Corps.—*Continued.*

74494 Pte. SOLOMONS, G., 179th Lab. Coy.
61616 Pte. SHELBERT, J., 892nd A.E. Coy.
365411 Pte. SILBERG, B., 483rd A.E. Coy.
577561 Cpl. SEIGAL, I., 967th A.E. Coy.
419966 Pte. SIMPSON, N. L., 931st Lab. Coy.
100590 Pte. SOLOMONS, A., 168th Lab. Coy.
130777 Pte. SHEFTER, S., 205th Lab. Coy.
80186 Pte. SOLOMONS, Q., 134th Lab. Coy.
480685 Pte. SCHAPIRO, M.,
74076 Pte. SAMUEL, V., 1st Mx. Lab. Coy.
74358 Pte. SHIER, M., 1st Mx. Lab. Coy.
74084 Pte. SILVERFIELD, H., 1st Mx. Lab. Coy.
74295 Pte. SPICER, L., 1st Mx. Lab. Coy.
74221 Pte. SPIELBERG, M., 1st Mx. Lab. Coy.
48847 Pte. SWAGER, H., 1st Mx. Lab. Coy.
38532 Pte. SUCKLEY, C., 1st Mx. Lab. Coy.
84462 Pte. SAND, M., 3rd Mx. Lab. Coy.
30978 Pte. SCHREERER, A. J., 3rd Mx. Lab. Co.
72162 Pte. SEELIG, C., 3rd Mx. Lab. Coy.
70020 Pte. SCHWARTZ, J., 3rd Mx. Lab. Coy.
208001 Pte. SEINWELLS, J., 3rd Mx. Lab. Coy.
48843 Pte. SEYNER, M., 3rd Mx. Lab. Coy.
45340 Pte. SHEERE, H., 3rd Mx. Lab. Coy.
48349 Pte. SINGER, A., 3rd Mx. Lab. Coy.
38890 Pte. SINGER, M., 3rd Mx. Lab. Coy.
G/74344 Sgt. STROUD, E. Y., 4th Mx. Lab. C.
G/80173 Pte. STEIN, S., 4th Mx. Lab. Coy.
G/74433 Pte. SHINE,, A. J., 4th Mx. Lab Coy.
G/80304 Pte. SWANGER,* C., 4th Mx. Lab. Coy.
G/83043 L/Cpl. SUSSWEIN, P., 4th Mx. Lab. C.
G/80333 Pte. STRAWSON, A. W., 4th Mx. L. C.
G/80364 Pte. SHAPIRA, P., 4th Mx. Lab. Coy.
G/83074 Pte. SCHARFF, S., 4th Mx. Lab. Coy.
G/93921 L/Cpl. STRAUSS, B. N., 5th Mx. L.C.
G/93171 Pte. SENEFFT, S., 5th Mx. Lab. Coy.
G/74266 Pte. SMITH, L., 5th Mx. Lab. Coy.
G/74294 Pte. SPICER, W., 5th Mx. Lab. Coy.
G/83013 Pte. SUNDERLAND, G., 5th Mx. Lab. C.
G/93560 Pte. SONENFIELD, A., 5th Mx. Lab. C.
G/93251 Pte. SCHALLER, H., 5th Mx. Lab. C.
G/93290 Pte. SANGER, M., 5th Mx. Lab. Coy.
G/93926 Pte. SCHWADRON, L., 5th Mx. Lab. C.
G/72963 Pte. SUMMERFIELD, J., 5th Mx. Lab. C.
G/35981 Pte. STEIN, S. A., 5th Mx. Lab. Coy.
G/94237 Pte. STERN, J., 5th Mx. Lab. Coy.
G/93804 Pte. SCHAZ, A., 5th Mx. Lab. Coy.
G/93839 Pte. STEINBERG, H., 5th Mx. Lab. Coy.
G/94272 Pte. SCHLOFF, S., 5th Mx. Lab. Coy.
G/73449 Pte. SMITH, F. A., 5th Mx. Lab. Coy.
88975 Pte. SPRINGER, S., 57th Mx. Lab. Coy.
79028 Pte. STODEL, M., 132nd Lab. Coy.
87419 Pte. SIMMONS, M., 2nd Lab. Coy.
84426 Pte. SCHNEIDER, I., 35th Lab. Coy.
84280 Pte. SCHNEIDERMAN, 35th Lab .Coy.
80234 Pte. SEGALMAN, I., 35th Lab. Coy.
48347 L/Cpl. STEIN, I., 35th Lab. Coy.
80457 Pte. SEGAL, I., 35th Lb. Coy.
80021 Pte. STERN, S., 35th Lab. Coy.
92023 Pte. SHOWMAN, C. L., 35th Lab. Coy.
84279 Pte. STERNBERG, H., 35th Lab. Coy.
92126 Pte. SANTER, G. H., 35th Lab. Coy.
74494 Pte. SHINE, T., 35th Lab. Coy.
71812 Pte. SWERLENG, H., 35th Lab. Coy.
84296 Pte. SILVERMAN, L., 35th Lab. Coy.
84416 Pte. SHOBEN, D. L., 35th Lab. Coy.
74433 Pte. SHINE, H. J., 35th Lab. Coy.
48392 Pte. SENEN, J., 35th Lab. Coy.
47134 Pte. SAYLOR, T., 35th Lab. Coy.
80455 Pte. SENENBAUM, M., 35th Lab. Coy.
568398 Pte. SAGER, S., 35th Lab. Coy.
273848 Pte. SHUJONS, A. M., 991st Lab. Coy.
272795 Pte. SHUKERVITCH, S. M., 991st Lab. C.
460960 Pte. SILVER, S., 991st Lab. Coy.
274007 Pte. SHIER, S., 991st Lab. Coy.
98217 Pte. SEGALMAN, G., 7th Lab. Coy.
132383 Pte. SAVITZ, L., 209th A.E. Coy.
233800 Pte. SOSNOVSKEY, M., 153rd Lab. Coy.
493962 Pte. SHIRLEG, J., 714th Lab. Coy.
498827 Pte. STONEFIELD.
2799 Pte. SOLOSKY, J., Emp. Coy.
132829 Pte. SILK, J., Emp. Coy.
208109 Pte. SOLOMO, D., 251st A.E. Coy.
509336 Pte. SINGER, J., 527th A.E. Coy.
68712 Pte. SHONE, S., 527th A.E. Coy.
76023 Pte. STOMOFF, J., 784th A.E. Coy.
117828 Pte. SOLOMON, G., 197th Lab. Coy
365411 Pte. SILBERG, B., 783rd A.E .Coy.
397093 Pte. SHEETER, M. H., 949th A.E. Coy.
60815 Pte. SEIGENBERG, B., 887th A.E. Coy.
446033 Pte. SCHAVERIEN, J., 835th A.E. Coy.
139528 Pte. SPERBER, M., 835th A.E. Coy.
653200 Pte. SCHATZEN, L., 577th A.E. Coy.
535314 Pte. SOFIER, I., Labour Centre.
681868 Pte. STANLEY, J. H., Labour Centre.
89782 Pte. SCHNIERDERMAN, J., 41st Lab. Coy.
68820 Pte. SAPPERCHINSKY, E., 63rd Lab. Coy.
35729 Pte. SCHWATLING, J., 4th Lab. Coy.
70834 Pte. SCHULMAVITCH, S., 10th Lab. Coy.
48816 Pte STROMOFF, T., 19th Lab. Coy.
46500 Pte. SEGAL, H., 19th Lab. Coy.
65700 Pte. SPIER, S., 9th Lab. Coy.
69607 Pte. SILVERMAN, S., 76th Lab. Coy.
45803 Pte. SITKIN, S., 14th Lab. Coy.
74771 Pte. SILNER, H., 20th Lab. Coy.
59081 Pte. STEIN, B., 2nd Lab. Coy.
57806 Pte. SHILLING, H., 173rd Lab. Coy.
58353 Pte. SCHWEITZER, S., 111th Coy.
35732 Pte. SPINK, D., 21st Lab. Coy.
461379 L/Cpl. SAGON, M., Labour Centre.
97527 Pte. SMITH, D., 5th Mx. Lab. Coy.
93744 Pte. SMER, I., 5th Mx. Lab. Coy.
93969 Pte. SHAPERO, I., 5th Mx. Lab. Coy.
99375 Pte. SHELLER, M., 166th Lab. Coy.
31082 C.Q.M.S. SCHWABACHER, R., 8th Mx. Lab. Coy.

Labour Corps.—*Continued.*

93384	Pte. STARSOLLA, R., 8th Mx. Lab. Coy.
97745	Pte. STYSBERG, M., 8th Mx. Lab. Coy.
93038	Pte. SALTMAN, A., 8th Mx. Lab. Coy.
93265	Pte. SLOTWINER, H., 8th Mx. Lab. Coy.
98208	Pte. SCHNEIDER, H., 8th Mx. Lab. Coy.
93705	Pte. SALPETER, S., 8th Mx. Lab. Coy.
93810	Pte. SCHWARTZ, L., 8th Mx. Lab. Coy.
98287	Pte. SCHNEIDER, S., 8th Mx. Lab. Coy.
93083	Pte. SINGER, I., 8th Mx. Lab. Coy.
97675	Pte. SPIELMAN, H., 8th Mx. Lab. Coy.
97794	Pte. STAMM, B., 8th Mx. Lab. Coy.
98088	Pte. SILVERMAN, A., 8th Mx. Lab. Coy.
92219	Pte. SPICKER, J., 8th Mx. Lab. Coy.
83072	Pte. SMITH, E. B., 8th Mx. Lab. Coy.
93059	Pte. SHERMAN, M., 8th Mx. Lab. Coy.
100041	Cpl. STEINER, J., 8th Mx. Lab. Coy.
93206	Pte. SOLDINGER, 8th Mx. Lab. Coy.
558612	Pte. SPITALNICK, A., 1002nd Lab. Coy.
558611	Pte. STONE, J., 1002nd Lab. Coy.
558690	Pte. SNOW, 1002nd Lab. Coy.
558664	Pte. SCAVRONSKY, M., 1002nd Lab. Coy.
558944	Pte. SLAVID, S., 1002nd Lab. Coy.
558945	Pte. SPIRO, L., 1002nd Lab. Coy.
558742	Pte. SCHFRON, H., 1002nd Lab. Coy.
558707	Pte. STIRN, J., 1002nd Lab. Coy.
558746	Pte. SMIDT, S., 1002nd Lab. Coy.
557697	Pte. STORCH, M., 1002nd Lab. Coy.
558745	Pte. SEGAL, 1002nd Lab. Coy.
557735	Pte. SIDAK, 1002nd Lab. Coy.
557686	Pte. SHROOT, 1002nd Lab. Coy.
558170	Pte. SHILKOFF, S., 1002nd Lab. Coy.
558171	Pte. SHILKOFF, E., 1002nd Lab. Coy.
525157	Pte. SCHULTZ, W., 1002nd Lab. Coy.
558223	Pte. STERN, M., 1002nd Lab. Coy.
557595	Pte. STEIN, A., 1002nd Lab. Coy.
557391	Pte. SIRENSTEIN, S., 1002nd Lab. Coy.
557509	Pte. SMHERKOVITCH, M., 1002nd Lab. Coy
558000	Pte. SCHAFFIER, M., 1002nd Lab. Coy.
558006	Pte. STIRN, S., 1002nd Lab. Coy.
G/70023	Pte. SCHNEIDER, K., 4th Mx. Lab. C.
G/48846	Pte. STERN, M. I., 4th Mx. Lab. Coy.
G/84274	Pte. STERNSHINE, H., 4th Mx. Lab. C.
G/84352	Pte. SHEERE, S., 4th Mx. Lab. Coy.
531210	Pte. SILVERHAMMER, E., Lab. Corps.
238201	Pte. SHIER, S., 4th Mx. Lab. Coy.
208047	Pte. STEINLOFT, I., 4th Mx. Lab. Coy.
273750	Pte. SHAFFER, J., 12th Lab. Coy.
273803	Pte. SEGAL, M., 38th Lab. Coy.
8794	Pte. STEIN, B., 38th Lab. Coy.
27381	Pte. SAMUEL, J., 46th Lab. Coy.
36364	Pte. SILVERMAN, L., 61st Lab. Coy.
55593	Pte. SHROOT, M., 93rd Lab. Coy.
112245	Pte. SWOLEWSKIE, M., 40th Lab. Coy.
416738	L/Cpl. SAUNDERS, H., 3rd Mx. Lab. C.
45105	Pte. SCOTTIE, J. P., 3rd Mx. Lab. Coy.
509332	Pte. SORKI, P., 30th Lab. Coy.
30972	Pte. SOLOMONS, M., 52nd Lab. Coy.
235823	Pte. SILKMAN, D. A., 54th Lab. Coy.
199226	Pte. SWABE, W., 63rd Lab. Coy.
47180	Pte. SHIRES, L., 79th Lab. Coy.
574110	Pte. STEMBERG, N., 988th Lab. Coy.
53240	Pte. SONENBERG, R., 89th Lab. Coy.
71795	Cpl. STEINGOLD, B., 120th Lab. Coy.
526514	Pte. SCHNEIDER, D., 50th Lab. Coy.
526378	Pte. SCOLNICK, R., 50th Lab. Coy.
30423	Pte. SIMON, N., 51st Lab. Coy.
399276	Pte. SOLMAN, M., 792nd A.E. Coy.
446033	Pte. SCHAVERIEN, J., 835th A.E. Coy.
139523	Pte. SPERBER, M., 835th A.E. Coy.
68820	Pte. SAPERCHINSKY, E., 936th A.E. Coy.
466770	Pte. SWATSKY, L., 8th Lab. Coy.
	Pte. SOODY, 7th Lab. Coy.
574993	Dmr. SAMUELS, N., 22nd Lab. Coy.
202302	Pte. SCOBLE, S., 5th Lab. Coy.
G/80463	Pte. STEIN, J., 4th Lab. Coy.
G/70660	Pte. SERENS, M., 4th Lab. Coy.
50796	Pte. SILVER, M., 85th Lab. Coy.
18449	Pte. SONNENBERG, W., 31st Bn.
61628	L/Cpl. STEWART, H., 103rd Lab. Coy.
39990	Pte. SILVERSTONE, A., 67th Lab. Coy.
90419	Pte. SINGER, H., 123rd Lab. Coy.
100590	Pte. SOLOMON, A., 168th Lab. Coy.
G/45105	L/Cpl. SCOTTIE, P., 3rd Lab. Coy.
L/16738	Cpl. SAUNDERS, H., 3rd Bn.
445012	Cpl. SLENDER, H., 85th Chin. Lab. Coy.
83197	Pte. SCHARTZ, F. 139th Lab. Coy.
51419	Pte. SILVERSTONE, A., 38th Lab. Coy.
73472	Pte. SCHULKIND, N., 1st Mx. Lab. Coy.
72584	Pte. SERI, A., 1st Mx. Lab. Coy.
31722	Pte. STEIN, H., 1st Mx. Lab. Coy.
72917	Pte. STERNSTEIN, S., 1st Mx. Lab. Coy.
80602	Pte. STRATTON, F. A., 1st Mx. Lab. C.
74228	Pte. SNELL, J., 2nd Mx. Lab. Coy.
71218	Pte. SHYACK, A. H., 135rd Lab. Coy.
88614	Pte. SIMMONS, L., 707th Lab. Coy.
317293	Pte. SCHMOKER, A., 579th A.E. Coy.
88411	Pte. SOLOMON, N., 5th Lab. Coy.
157541	Pte. SOLOMON, A., 5th Lab. Coy.
42978	Pte. SKEIN, I., 72nd Lab. Coy.
71206	Pte. SIMONS, D. A., 706th Lab. Coy.
417215	Pte. SINCLAIR, M., 293rd A.E. Coy.
G/31305	Cpl. STRAUSS, R. L., 5th Mx. Lab. Coy.
G/36055	L/Cpl. STERN, L., 5th Mx. Lab. Coy.
558025	Pte. SONENFELD, H., 1002nd Lab. Coy.
558036	Pte. SHAPIRO, M., 1002nd Lab. Coy.
558181	Pte. SILVERMAN, M., 1002nd Lab. Coy.
558145	Pte. SCHULMAN, A., 1002nd Lab. Coy.
557520	Pte. STOCKFEDER, D., 1002nd Lab. Coy.
557001	Pte. SCHWARTZ, S., 1002nd Lab. Coy.
557873	Pte. SHEEKA, S., 1002nd Lab. Coy.
557854	Pte. SERKES, M., 1002nd Lab. Coy.
557817	Pte. SILVERMAN, A., 1002nd Lab. Coy.
557870	Pte. SPIELMAN, M., 1002nd Lab. Coy.
557831	Pte. STRAUZER, Z., 1002nd Lab. Coy.
557808	Pte. SILVERMAN, L., 1002nd Lab. Coy.

Labour Corps.—*Continued.*

557965	Pte. SILVER, A., 1002nd Lab. Coy.
557198	Pte. SEENER, S., 1002nd Lab. Coy.
558271	Pte. SIMON, P., 1002nd Lab. Coy.
558231	Pte. SPITALNICK, H., 1002nd Lab. Coy.
558230	Pte. SCHNEIDER, A., 1002nd Lab. Coy.
557059	Pte. SHERMAN, G., 1002nd Lab. Coy.
557713	Pte. SHIRIER, W., 1002nd Lab. Coy.
558125	Pte. SAXE, A., 1002nd Lab. Coy.
558126	Pte. SCHWARTZ, R., 1002nd Lab. Coy.
558192	Pte. SNOPKOPSKY, J., 1002nd Lab. Coy.
557028	Pte. SHERMAN, J., 1002nd Lab. Coy.
558626	Pte. STEINMAN, J., 1002nd Lab. Coy.
557352	Pte. SINGER, N., 1002nd Lab. Coy.
557553	Pte. SUNDLER, H., 1001st Lab. Coy.
557537	Pte. SCHUTZ, M., 1001st Lab. Coy.
557354	Pte. SHATZ, A., 1001st Lab. Coy.
557367	Pte. SCHLAGER, B., 1001st Lab. Coy.
558658	Pte. SEGAL, I., 1001st Lab. Coy.
557544	Pte. SILVERMAN, S., 1001st Lab. Coy.
557607	Pte. SEDAR, H., 1001st Lab. Coy.
557329	Pte. SILBERMAN, N., 1001st Lab. Coy.
557552	Pte. SMYDCIENSKY, J., 1001st Lab. Coy.
557337	Pte. SCHRIER, F., 1001st Lab. Coy.
557460	Pte. SPURGIN, M., 1001st Lab. Coy.
557194	Pte. SCHNIDER, I., 1001st Lab. Coy.
557172	Pte. SPURLING, S., 1001st Lab. Coy.
557142	Pte. SCHULMAN, P., 1001st Lab. Coy.
557190	Pte. SIDDLER, I., 1001st Lab. Coy.
558645	Pte. SLENOFF, I., 1001st Lab. Coy.
557914	Pte. SAKOLOVITZ, H., 1001st Lab. Coy.
557234	Pte. SCHULTZ, S., 1001st Lab. Coy.
557191	Pte. SINGER, D., 1001st Lab. Coy.
557169	Pte. SACK, H., 1001st Lab. Coy.
558670	Pte. SPEVACH, M., 1001st Lab. Coy.
558644	Pte. STAHL, V., 1001st Lab. Coy.
558655	Pte. SOLOMON, A., 1001st Lab. Coy.
557133	Pte. SHAW, H., 1001st Lab. Coy.
	Pte. SASOFSKY, L.
136334	Pte. SAMUELS, W. S., S.C.L.C.
557139	Pte. SILVER, L., 1001st Lab. Coy.
557221	Pte. STEINBERG, A. W., 1001st Lab. Coy.
558697	Pte. SALZMAN, S., 1001st Lab. Coy.
557195	Pte. SPERO, H., 1001st Lab. Coy.
558675	Pte. SIMBOLIST, M., 1001st Lab. Coy.
557115	Pte. SUNASKY, S., 1001st Lab. Coy.
558677	Pte. SCHERMAN, S., 1001st Lab. Coy.
557405	Pte. SCHRIER, D., 1001st Lab. Coy.
557438	Pte. SCHRIER, I., 1001st Lab. Coy.
557078	Pte. SILLMANS, M., 1001st Lab. Coy.
557048	Pte. SHIPERO, S., 1001st Lab. Coy.
557486	Pte. SHLOFFMAN, H., 1001st Lab. Coy.
557447	Pte. SEGAL, L., 1001st Lab. Coy.
557072	Pte. STILLER, J. A. R., 1001st Lab. Coy.
557441	Pte. SLOTNICK, J., 1001st Lab. Coy.
557418	Pte. SULLIVAN, W., 1001st Lab. Coy.
557435	Pte. SILKOFF, L., 1001st Lab. Coy.
557017	Pte. SATANOVSKY, S., 1001st Lab. Coy.
557440	Pte. SCHUSTER, C., 1001st Lab. Coy.
557215	Pte. SCHEDLOVITCH, A., 1001st Lab. Coy.
557192	Pte. SILVERWORG, J., 1001st Lab. Coy.
557415	Pte. SINGER, J., 1001st Lab. Coy.
558516	Pte. SOLCOVITCH, S., 1001st Lab. Coy.
557389	Pte. SHAPIRO, M., 1001st Lab. Coy.
103574	Pte. SCHEKHTER, D., 1001st Lab. Coy.
509333	Pte. SPIZER, S., Lab. Coy.
433420	Pte. SCHWARTZBERG, I.
305237	Pte. STREAK, A. E.
57756	Pte. SEIGAL, G.
89782	Pte. SCHNEIDERMAN, A., 198th Lab. Coy.
55593	Pte. SHROOT, M., 93rd Lab. Coy.
480271	Pte. SOLOMON, G., 22nd Lab. Coy.
441302	Pte. SEGAL, J., 144th Lab. Coy.
577971	Pte. SARNA, J., 912nd A.E. Coy.
50803	Pte. SANDLER, J. H., 31st Lab. Coy.
592501	Pte. SILVERMAN, M., 719th Lab. Coy.
551066	Pte. STEIN, H., 188th Lab. Coy.
11788	Pte. SPINK, D., 20th Lab. Coy.
	Pte. SELKIN, J., 365th Res. Emp. Coy.
	Pte. SHARP, B., 365th Res. Emp. Coy.
326705	Pte. SACHS, A., 365th Res. Emp. Coy.
391469	Pte. SAMPSON, H., 365th Res. Emp. Coy.
506721	Pte. SOLSTEIN, J., Lab. Bn.
640042	Pte. STEINBERG, H., 675th Res. Em. Coy.
254338	Pte. STEINBERG, H., 675th Lab. Coy.
235332	Pte. SCHAPER, L., 676th H.S. Emp. Coy.
357231	Pte. SNIPPER, J., 537th H.S. Emp. Coy.
452484	Pte. STEIN, B., Lab. Centre.
525157	Pte. SCHULTZ, W., Lab. Centre.
637060	Pte. SOESAN, H., Lab. Centre.
525230	Pte. SEGAL, E., Lab. Cntre.
668811	Pte. SAGINSKY, B., Lab. Centre.
131558	Pte. SHERMAN, J., Lab. Centre.
525946	Pte. SAIET, I., Lab. Centre.
45261	Pte. SILVERMAN, I., 1st Lab. Bn.
6/4850	Pte. SANTER, L., 1st Lab. Bn.
32968	Pte. SUSSMAN, L., 1st Lab. Bn.
128664	Pte. SUGARMAN, N., 362nd Emp. Coy.
593047	Pte. SALDINACK, F., Lab. Centre.
509321	Pte. SHAPERS, S., Lab. Centre.
273999	Pte. SHEROTSKY, A., Lab. Centre.
19986	Pte. SANDERS, M., Lab. Centre.
26613	L/Cpl. SOLOSKY, H. S., Lab. Centre.
56794	Pte. SIGENFIELD' S., 95th Lab. Coy.
274023	Pte. SAKOVITCH, P., Lab. Coy.
509335	Pte. SOLOMON, H., 512th Lab. Coy.
139464	Pte. SOLOMON, J., E.L.C.
804	Pte. SYON, J., E.L.C.
139465	Cpl. SHEMMA, D., E.L.C.
280	Pte. SHEWEIKA, C., E.L.C.
V/806	Pte. SOUROUR, D., E.L.C.
367	Cpl. SHAAR, E. E., E.L.C.
V/273	Pte. SALANA, I., E.L.C.
07299	Sgt. SALFATT, G., E.L.C.
V/391	Sgt. SHIFF, S., E.L.C.
V/902	Pte. SEIAMA, E. J., E.L.C.

Labour Corps.—*Continued.*

09088 Pte. SINDLER, M., E.L.C.
747 Sgt. STESKOVITCH, G., E.L.C.
V/457 Cpl. SORIANO, M., E.L.C.
V/474 Pte. SHOUSHA, A., E.L.C.
202947 Pte. SAKER, L., 146th Lab. Coy.
105377 Cpl. SAMUELS, F. B.
421060 Pte. STEIN, V., 38th Lab. Coy.
27967 Pte. SLIFKIN, J., 47th Lab. Coy.
274449 Pte. SILVERMAN, G., 769th Lab. Coy.
64826 Pte. SAACHAS, L., 109th Lab. Coy.
273801 Pte. STEINBURGH, L., 56th A.E. Coy.
162374 Pte. SCHWEITZER, S., 177th Lab. Coy.
262539 Pte. STAAL, M., 134th Lab. Coy.
312745 Pte. SAERTZ, H., 685th H.S. Coy.
424716 Pte. SHESSRIM, A., 252nd A.E. Coy.
122824 Pte. SLAGER, J.,
27769 Pte. SHINE, M., 282nd Lab. Coy.
491841 Pte. SMITH, S., 362nd Lab. Coy.
452878 Pte. SIMONS, M., 546th Lab. Coy.
50793 Pte. SIMONS, H.
404092 Pte. SLIMMER, H., 860th Lab. Coy.
208734 Pte. SHISKA, A., 689th Lab. Coy.
883197 Pte. SCHWARTZ, F., 139th Lab. Coy.
82543 Pte. SASSOON, D., 138th Lab. Coy.
42476 Pte. SHEFFRIN, B., 125th Lab. Coy.
312745 Pte. SAVITZ, H., 635th Lab. Coy.
523694 Pte. SCHREIBER, H. B., 635th Lab. Coy.
535624 Pte. SCHNEIDER, A., 635th Lab. Coy.
452582 Pte. SILVERMAN, P., 306th H.S. Coy.
71490 Pte. SCHRIEBER, J., 41st Lab. Coy.
79686 Pte. SEGALL, E., 133rd Lab. Coy.
79659 Pte. SCHWURMAN, 758th Lab. Coy.
76023 Pte. STOMOFF, J.
84072 Pte. SCHWARTZ, C., 2nd Lab. Coy.
204079 Pte. SILVERMAN, B.
37425 Pte. SLAYER, J., 10th Lab. Coy.
7429 Pte. SOLOMON, 2nd Lab. Coy.
23312 Pte. STEINBERG, H., 13th Lab. Coy.
65803 Pte. SLIFTON, S., 19th Lab. Coy.
525298 Pte. SIMONS, I.
16738 Cpl. SAUNDERS, H.,* Lab. Coy.
Pte. SCHEIN, S.
460770 Pte. SWATSKY, L., S.C.L.C.
273799 Pte. SUSLOVITCH, H., 366th Lab. Coy.
198174 Pte. SILVERSTONE, I.
19764 Pte. STONE, A., 13th Lab. Coy.
19986 Pte. SANDERS, M., 14th Lab. Coy.
26613 L/Cpl. SOLOSKY, H. S., 14th Lab. Coy.
134504 Pte. SOLOMONS, J., 2nd Lab. Coy.
235024 Pte. STONS, P., 676th Lab. Coy.
36794 Pte. SIGENFIELD, S., 95th Lab. Coy.
199258 L/Cpl. STERMAN, J., 6th Lab. Coy.
336303 Pte. SARNA, A. J., 397th Lab Co.y.
55593 Pte. SHIRT, M., 92nd Lab. Coy.
201055 Pte. SCHILLIER, H., 298th Lab. Coy.
64826 Pte. SAACHES, L., 109th Lab. Coy.
192830 Pte. SCHWAN, S.

103574 Pte. SCHEDTER, D., 173rd Lab. Coy.
44223 Pte. SPIER, S., 7th Lab. Coy.
117828 Pte. SOLOMONS, G., 197th Lab. Coy.
525230 Pte. SEGAL, E., 229th Lab. Coy.
525126 Pte. SEGAL, I., 300th Lab. Coy.
525168 Pte. SCHVEL, E., 305th Lab. Coy.
792645 Pte. STONE, S., 299th Lab. Coy.
393339 Pte. SHATZER, P., 607th Lab. Coy.
452485 Pte. SUSMAN, M., 299th Lab. Coy.
235823 Pte. SILKMAN, D. A., 54th Lab. Coy.
154662 Pte. SCHIFF, B., 612th Lab. Coy.
193879 Pte. SOLOMON, M., 82nd Lab. Coy.
11734 Pte. SARENS, M., 4th Lab. Coy.
20099 Pte. SACKS, J., 150th Lab. Coy.
13024 Pte. SAMUELS, R., 22nd Lab. Coy.
54237 Pte. SIMONS, W., 5/6th Lab. Coy.
153451 Pte. SOLOMONS, I., 5th Lab Coy.
126700 Pte. SALISBURY, H. B., 234th Lab. Coy.
74084 Pte. SILVERFIELD, H., 1st Lab. Coy.
73885 Pte. SPICER, L., 1st Lab. Coy.
351947 Pte. SHIN, J., 8th Lab. Coy.
393270 Pte. SOMERS, L., 386th Lab. Coy.
163534 Pte. SACKS, M., 17th Lab. Coy.
79868 Pte. SCHKURMAN, F.
556276 Pte. SAMUELS, J., 9th Lab. Coy.
282376 Pte. SYDNEY, H., 90th Lab. Coy.
504999 Pte. SHINKOVSKOE, S.
556552 Pte. SIMBLER, H., 9th Lab. Coy.
556374 Pte. SIMON, N., 9th Lab. Coy.
79698 Pte. SAVITSKY, G., 133rd Lab. Coy.
1013192 Pte. SIMON, A., 230th Lab. Coy.
352882 Pte. SPECTOR, J., 364th Lab. Coy.
342491 Pte. SOLOMONS, A., 643rd Lab. Coy.
461243 Pte. SHARP, B., 365th Lab. Coy.
27679 Pte. SHINE, M., 282nd Lab. Coy.
197680 Pte. STONE, J., 6th Lab. Coy.
163581 Pte. SMOYAS, J.
214611 Pte. SILVERSTONE, 297th Lab. Coy.
273758 Pte. STERMAN, S.
345861 Pte. SCHLESSERMAN, R., 717th Lab. Coy.
14527 Pte. SYMONS, S., 364th Lab. Coy.
39425 Pte. SAMUELS, H. E., 66th Lab. Coy.
25924 Pte. SELLAR, J., 264th Lab. Coy.
273802 Pte. SILVERMAN, H., 271st Lab. Coy.
74784 Pte. STEIN, H., 15th Lab. Coy.
202302 Pte. SCOBLE, S.
461077 Pte. SYATT, B., 303rd Lab. Coy.
35692 Pte. SCHILLER, H., 13th Lab. Coy.
198612 Pte. SAMUELS, L., 368th Lab. Coy.
140890 Pte. STEBBE, J., 3rd Lab. Coy.
5801 Pte. SIMONS, M., 10th Lab. Coy.
49643 Pte. SIMONS, I., 83rd Lab. Coy.
509348 Pte. SKIMGOLSKY, M., 360th Lab. Coy.
393326 Pte. SUGAR, L.
33611 Pte. SIDMAN, D., 30th Lab. Coy.
22660 Pte. SCHINDLER, H., 246th Lab. Coy.
273840 Pte. SHERMAN, J., 754th Lab. Coy.
293275 Pte. SATTEL, J., 386th Lab. Coy.

Labour Corps.—*Continued.*

273063 Pte. STEINBERG, J.
186548 Pte. SOLOMON, J.
460794 Pte. STEAN, H., 279th Lab. Coy.
424948 Pte. SAKER, L.
524176 Pte. STERNBERG, M., 368th Lab. Coy.
273806 Pte. SALSBY, H.
93265 Pte. SLOTWINER, H., Lab. Coy.
93705 Pte. SALPETER, S.
98287 Pte. SCHNEIDER, S., 8th Lab. Coy.
273999 Pte. SHEROTSKY, D., 748th Lab. Coy.
137351 Pte. SCHNEIDER, H., 724th Lab. Coy.
273808 Pte. SHARMAN, M.
273729 Pte. SEXER, H., 100th Lab. Coy.
273272 Pte. SHAPIRO, J., 255th Lab. Coy.
447761 Pte. SOLOMON, S.
93477 Pte. STEINLOFF, M., 7th Lab. Coy.
452532 Pte. SILVERMAN, R., 306th Lab. Coy.
198266 Pte. SCHINEBERG, M.
661852 Pte. SIMMONS, L., 58th Lab. Coy.
84272 Pte. SCHLAFF, S., 6th Lab. Coy.
274009 Pte. SILVER, S., 104th Lab. Coy.
273802 Pte. SILVERMAN, H., 366th Lab. Coy.
506512 Pte. SOLOMON, P., 368th Lab. Coy.
480685 Pte. SCHAPIRO, N.
60303 Pte. STEINGOLD, N., 486th Lab. Coy.
093732 Pte. SCHNEIDER, H., 7th Lab. Coy.
2991157 Pte. SPECTERMAN, M., E.C.L.C.
Pte. SAXE, I., 8th Lab. Coy.
57595 Pte. SIMON, A., 8th Lab. Coy.
164573 L/Cpl. SYMONS,
Pte. STERN, H.
533834 Pte. SOLOMON, S.
127828 Pte. SOLOMON, G., 197th Lab. Coy.
680962 Pte. SELIGMAN, J.
127287 Pte. SOMFIELD, H. S.
129572 Pte. TAYLOR, S., 291st Area Emp. Coy.
98033 Pte. TISCH, M., 7th Mx. Lab. Coy.
31972 Pte. TITLE, J. B., 2nd Lab. Coy.
35645 Pte. TRIBICH, J., 1st Mx. Lab. Coy.
53832 Pte. TIKTIN, M., 90th Lab. Coy.
460775 Pte. TEACHER, J., 668th Lab. Coy.
445207 Pte. TUCKER, I., 165th Lab. Coy.
558116 Pte. TANNER, A., 225th A.E. Coy.
36166 Pte. TRESMAN, H. J., 146th Lab. Coy.
G/84326 Pte. TABUSH, V., 4th Mx. Lab. Coy.
69447 Pte. TUSHINSKI, S., 116th Lab. Coy.
78626 Cpl. TAYLOR, W. M. L., 132nd Lab. C.
491977 Pte. TIMPOFSKY, J., 991st Lab. Coy.
G/74373 Pte. TOPALIAN, H. D., 4th Lab. Coy.
74074 L/Cpl. TEMBAUNE, A., 1st Mx. Lab. Coy.
35852 Pte. TUCKLEY, C., 1st Mx. Lab. Coy.
72478 L/Cpl. TITLEBOAM, S., 5th Lab. Coy.
G/93747 Pte. TISCH, S., 5th Mx. Lab. Coy.
G/35968 Pte. TROMER, A., 5th Mx. Lab. Coy.
G/93630 Pte. TRACHMAN, L., 5th Mx. Lab. Coy.
G/93447 Pte. TOPER, D., 5th Mx. Lab. Coy.
G/93855 Pte. TENNENBAUM, J., 5th Mx. Lab. C.
G/93685 Pte. TAFFEL, A., 5th Mx. Lab. Coy.
G/35345 Pte. THIEL, A., 5th Mx. LIab. Coy.
G/93976 Pte. TISCHLER, M., 5th Mx. Lab. Coy.
G/37934 Pte. THIEL, H., 5th Mx. Lab. Coy.
533115 Pte. TYLER, A., A.E. Coy.
87428 Pte. TRIESMAN, H., 146th Lab. Coy.
Sgt. TEBBITT, A., 101st Lab. Coy.
879 Pte. TROTSKY, D., 39th Lab. Coy.
393273 Pte. TAPPER, J., 386th H.S. Lab. Coy.
93551 Pte. TILLES, M., 386th H.S. Lab. Coy.
80455 Pte. TENNENBAUM, M., 6th Mx. Lab. C.
93937 Pte. TAUBER, F. A., 8th Mx. Lab. Coy.
100059 Pte. TUCHVERDERBER, H., 8th Mx. Lab. Coy.
557915 L/Cpl. TONNISSON, A., 1002nd Lab. Coy.
557679 Pte. TEIZINOWSKI, 1002nd Lab. Coy.
558116 Pte. TANNER, H., 1002nd Lab. Coy.
557507 Pte. TEITZ, A., 1002nd Lab. Corps.
557813 Pte. TREDLER, E., 1002nd Lab. Coy.
557785 Pte. TOUCHE, 1002nd Lab. Coy.
557958 Pte. TONDOFSKY, J., 1002nd Lab. Coy.
558110 Pte. TASH, B., 1002nd Lab. Coy.
557200 Pte. TEPPER, H., 1001st Lab. Coy.
557185 Pte. TULERWITCH, R., 1001st Lab. Coy.
557043 Pte. TETTON, J., 1001st Lab. Coy.
557067 Pte. TOBIN, H., 1001st Lab. Coy.
557326 Pte. TANNENBAUM, A., 1001st Lab. Coy.
557369 Pte. TEMFEL, J., 1001st Lab. Coy.
557462 Pte. TROUBE, A., 1001st Lab. Coy.
452648 Pte. TEMPOFSKI, H., 300th Res. Lab. Cy.
47134 Pte. TAYLOR, J., 6th Mx. Lab. Coy.
16033 Pte. TAYLOR, P., 27th Lab. Coy.
56282 Pte. TOBIAS, V.
6521 Pte. TAYLOR, H.
53832 Pte. TIKTIN, M.
367054 Pte. TURERGO, G.
196339 Pte. THOMAS, C.
306728 Pte. TRAEGER, H., 365th Lab. Coy.
35645 Pte. TUBITCH, J., 1st Lab. Coy.
341773 Pte. TOTLETHWAITE, T.
393273 Pte. TAPPER, J., 386th Lab. Coy.
325343 Pte. TAYLOR, S., 562nd Lab. Coy.
21819 Pte. TANNENBAUM, S., 376th Lab. Coy.
40092 Pte. TRICKINSKY, 621st Lab. Coy.
273747 Pte. TENENBAUM, J., 366th Lab. Coy.
293293 Pte. TASNICK, M.
273763 Pte. TIBTILSKY, L., 366th Lab. Coy.
98110 Pte. UNGER, H., 7th Mx. Lab. Coy.
G/92015 Pte. UNGER, P., 4th Mx. Lab. Coy.
G/30532 C.S.M. UMLAUF, S., 5th Mx. Lab. Coy.
74463 L/Cpl. ULLMAN, L., 35th Lab. Coy.
36280 Pte. ULPH, 2nd Lab. Coy.
460763 Pte. USAM, S., 385th Lab. Coy.
90449 Pte. VAN WEZEL, M., 7th Mx. Lab. Coy.
199890 L/Cpl. VINEFSKI,* A., 70th Lab. Coy.
86840 Pte. VRIGON, J., 720th Lab. Coy.
47825 Pte. VALENTINE, C. S., 17th R.W.S. L.C.

Labour Corps.—*Continued.*

606413	Pte. VERBLOSKI, H., 210th Div. Emp. C.
159408	Pte. VALENCIA, R.
50846	Pte. VELTMAN, L., 85th Lab. Coy.
130663	Pte. VOS, E.
30476	Pte. VALENTINE, I., 135th Lab. Coy.
67075	Pte. VAN LOCHEN, H., 716th Lab. Coy.
G/48393	Pte. VOSS, A., 4th Mx. Lab. Coy.
404672	Pte. VERBER, R., 108th Lab. Coy.
70642	Sgt. VOS, L., 11th Lab. Coy.
79692	Pte. VINIK, F., 133rd Lab. Coy.
483568	Pte. VALENTINE, M. D., 947th A.E. Coy.
445058	Cpl. VINEFSKY, H., 26th Chin. Lab. Coy.
80476	Pte. VALENTINE, J., 135th Lab. Coy.
80138	Pte. VINE, J., 4th Lab. Coy.
G/93704	Pte. VAN CLEGG, J., 5th Mx. Lab. Coy.
G/74271	Pte. VIDLER, P., 5th Mx. Lab. Coy.
74781	Pte. VALENTINE, C., 57th Lab. Coy.
83086	Pte. VILKA, M., 35th Lab. Coy.
304565	Pte. VANDERSTEIN, A., 17th Lab. Coy.
35742	Pte. VAN LOCHEN, H., 4th Lab. Coy.
51570	Pte. VOITCASH, B., 29th Lab. Coy.
47849	Pte. VERBER, L., 19th Lab. Coy.
19153	L/Cpl. VINICOTT, B., 13th Lab. Coy.
30988	Pte. VILKA, I., 8th Mx. Lab. Coy.
557132	Pte. VANEG, I., 1001st Lab. Coy.
557113	Pte. VINSKY, T., 1001st Lab. Coy.
557541	Pte. VOLTAISH, H., 1001st Lab. Coy.
365023	Pte. VANCIFFE, A., 365th Res. Emp. Coy.
452557	Pte. VINESTONE, S., 300th Lab. Coy.
557846	Pte. VANGROSKY, M., 1002nd Lab. Coy.
V/365	Sgt. VAISS, E., E.L.C.
7559	L/Cpl. VENICOFF, B.
82052	Pte. VOLTCASH, B., 137th Lab. Coy.
161639	Pte. VANDERMOOT, E., 602nd Lab. Coy.
270931	Pte. VITKURSKI, M.
29800	Pte. VAN GELDEN, G.
268152	Pte. VENSLOFSKY, W., 658th Lab. Coy.
59408	Pte. VALANCIA, T., 390th Lab. Coy.
88015	Pte. VANCLYLE, B.
38218	Pte. VITOFSKI, H., 64th Lab. Coy.
509040	Pte. VRUNER, B., 480th Lab. Coy.
86840	Pte. VIGON, I., 730th Lab. Coy.
274067	Pte. VOLINSKY, L., 366th Lab. Coy.
463490	Pte. VIGRON, M.
379058	Pte. WOLFE, B., 259th A.E. Coy.
573718	C.S.M. WILKINSON, R., 915th A.E. C.
2058	Pte. WOLFSON, 4th Lab. Coy. VII Cps.
114459	L/Cpl. WALTERS, J., 191st Lab. Coy.
97775	Pte. WEHL, J. H., 7th Mx. Lab. Coy.
93418	Pte. WEINROBE, P., 7th Mx. Lab. Coy.
97741	Pte. WALLACH, H. L., 7th Mx. Lab. C.
93314	Pte. WARZAGER, H., 7th Mx. Lab. Coy.
98092	Pte. WITTENBERG, M., 7th Mx. Lab. C.
97759	Pte. WEINER, J., 7th Mx. Lab. Coy.
97676	Pte. WOLFMAN, S., 7th Mx. Lab. Coy.
93235	Pte. WALTUCK, N., 7th Mx. Lab. Coy.
224733	Pte. WOLFE, A., 254th Div. Emp. Coy.
80351	Pte. WISBERG, J., 4th Lab. Coy.
84027	Pte. WEISS, W., 2nd Lab. Coy.
35902	Pte. WEISER, H., 2nd Lab. Coy.
30994	Pte. WHITE, M., 2nd Lob. Coy.
31438	Pte. WILDER, H., 2nd Lab. Coy.
92593	Pte. WOLFSON, A., 155th Lab. Coy.
265196	Pte. WEINBERG, H., 259th A.E. Coy.
374437	Pte. WOLFSON, I., 753rd A.E. Coy.
544847	Pte. WOODS, H., 248th Div. Emp. Coy.
74257	Pte. WEINSTEIN, L., 1st Mx. Lab. Coy.
74015	Pte. WEISENBLOOM, M., 1st Mx. Lab. C.
41191	Cpl. WARSCHDUER, A., 1st Mx. Lab. C.
74170	Pte. WEITZMAN, F., 1st Mx. Lab. Coy.
63286	Pte. WEITZMAN, S., 1st Mx. Lab. Coy.
74153	Pte. WEISS, E., 1st Mx. Lab. Coy.
23776	Pte. WHITE, H., 1st Mx. Lab. Coy.
79258	Pte. WALKANBRIGHT, L., 3rd Mx. L. C.
80477	Pte. WECHSLER, B., 3rd Mx. Lab. Coy.
55233	Pte. WILLIAMS, F., 7th Lab. Coy.
100676	Pte. WILLIAMS, F., 776th A.E. Coy.
54243	Pte. WOOLF, F. J, 37th R.F.
70075	Pte. WILSON, S. B., 117th Lab. Coy.
200192	Pte. WERNER, L., 9th Lab. Coy.
48355	Pte. WISBERG, J., 3rd Lab. Coy.
45203	Pte. WEBB, H., 3rd Lab. Coy.
29840	Pte. WINEBERG, V. 50th Lab. Coy.
460663	Pte. WINTER, E., 641st A.E. Coy.
319636	Pte. WEINBERG, S., 285th A.E. Coy.
452557	Pte. WINESTONE, S., 294th Lab. Coy.
93562	Pte. WEINROBE, A., 5th Lab. Coy.
106080	Pte. WOOLF, I., 177th Lab. Coy.
251801	Pte. WINEBERG, G., 6th Lab. Coy.
558281	Pte. WISEMAN, M., 1002nd Lab. Coy.
557583	Pte. WILKOFSKY, 8th Lab. Coy.
3007	Pte. WILLIAMS, J. J., 13th Lab. Coy.
40910	Pte. WOLFSTON, A., 14th Lab. Coy.
33812	Pte. WEINSTEIN, B., 1st Lab. Coy.
46707	Pte. WEINTROBE, L., 19th Lab. Coy.
80452	Pte. WEBBER, J. M., 4th Lab. Coy.
38805	L/Cpl. WARSHOWSKY, 91st Lab. Coy.
106080	Cpl. WOOLF, J., 75th Lab. Coy.
331230	Pte. WERTGAME, L., 829th Lab. Coy.
64666	Pte. WONDEROVITCH, B., 108th Lab. C.
557481	L/Cpl. WACKS, I., 8th Lab. Coy.
558361	Pte. WOOLFOVITCH, M.
41991	Cpl. WARCHAUER, 1st Mx. Lab. Coy.
74153	L/Cpl. WISE, E., 1st Mx. Lab. Coy.
81331	Pte. WALTERS, W., 1st Mx. Lab Coy.
74039	Pte. WEIDLING, S., 1st Mx. Lab. Coy.
73478	Pte. WEINSTEIN, H., 1st Mx. Lab. Coy.
74257	Pte. WEINSTEIN, L., 1st Mx. Lab. Coy.
74015	Pte. WEISENBLOOM, M., 1st Mx. Lab. C.
28801	Pte. WEITZMAN, L., 1st Mx. Lab. Coy.
80382	Pte. WASSERBERG, D., 3rd Mx. Lab. C.
208002	Pte. WILDER, W., 3rd Mx. Lab. Coy.
48834	Pte. WOOLF, J., 3rd Mx. Lab. Coy.

Labour Corps.—*Continued.*

G/74446 Pte. WEINER, I., 4th Mx. Lab. Coy.
G/31589 Pte. WEINER, L., 4th Mx. Lab. Coy.
G/80494 Pte. WERMAN, H., 4th Mx. Lab. Coy.
G/84324 Pte. WINFIELD, M., 4th Mx. Lab. Coy.
263050 Pte. WEITZMAN, H., 4th Mx. Lab. Coy.
418453 C.Q.M.S. WOOLF, M., 35th Lab. Coy.
40036 Pte. WEINBERG, B., 67th Lab. Coy.
Pte. WINBERG, D., 93rd Lab. Coy.
506719 Pte. WELSMAN, J., 64th Lab. Coy.
77435 Cpl. WYLDE, J., 130th Lab. Coy.
79066 Pte. WEISBLATT, S., 132nd Lab. Coy.
28032 Pte. WOOF, L., 147th Lab. Coy.
88980 Pte. WOOLF, W., 149th Lab. Coy.
105462 Pte. WINSTEIN, H., 176th Lab. Coy.
134555 L/Cpl. WEBBER, S., 189th Lab. Coy.
114459 L/Cpl. WALTERS, J., 191st Lab. Coy.
89098 L/Cpl. WISE, R., 737th A.E. Coy.
53261 Pte. WOLFSON, J., 822nd A.E. Coy.
84289 Pte. WINKEL, S., 832nd A.E. Coy.
47884 Pte. WOOLF, J., 80th Lab. Coy.
67101 Pte. WOLF, S., 936th A.E. Coy.
187869 Pte. WEINBERG, N., 745th A.E. Coy.
624155 Pte. WOOLF, B., 787th A.E. Coy.
92593 Pte. WOLFSON, A., A.E. Coy.
74352 Pte. WISBERG, P., 941st Lab. Coy.
G/80131 Pte. WEDALL, S., 4th Lab. Coy.
G/80477 Pte. WECHSLER, B., 4th Lab. Coy.
23877 Pte. WEINSTEIN, S., 40th Lab. Coy.
4/040 Pte. WALLACE, D., 67th Lab. Coy.
80289 Pte. WINKER, S., 134th Lab. Coy.
55653 Pte. WEYNBERG, D., 93rd Lab. Coy.
4036 Pte. WEINBERG, B., 67th Lab. Coy.
319363 Cpl. WOOLF, F. J., 579th A.E. Coy.
G/35900 Cpl. WEIL, S. E. C., 5th Mx. Lab. C.
G/93099 Pte. WOLOSKY, E. L., 5th Mx. Lab. C.
G/35935 Pte. WECHSLER, L., 5th Mx. Lab. Coy.
G/93781 Pte. WHITEMAN, J., 5th Mx. Lab. Coy.
G/3592 Pte. WEISS A., 5th Mx. Lab. Coy.
G/74352 Pte. WYSBERG, P., 5th Mx. Lab. Coy.
G/93562 Pte. WEINRABE, A., 5th Mx. Lab. Coy.
G/31606 Pte. WRITZMAN, A., 5th Mx. Lab. Coy.
G/74115 Pte. WEINBERG, A., 5th Mx. Lab. Coy.
G/93143 Pte. WEISENBLOOM, C., 5th Mx. L. C.
Pte. WENDER, I.
G/93402 Pte. WEINTROUB, H., 5th Mx. Lab. C.
G393037 Pte. WASSERMAN, J., 5th Mx. Lab. C.
G/92101 Pte. WEBBER, G., 5th Mx. Lab. Coy.
164776 Pte. WAITE, P., 115th Lab. Coy.
319636 Pte. WEINBERG, S., 285th A.E. Coy.
84371 Pte. WEEKSTER, D., 35th Lab. Coy.
84431 Pte. WEIL, D., 35th Lab. Coy.
31595 Pte. WYMAN, N., 2nd Lab. Coy.
225653 L/Cpl. WEINBERG, A., A.E. Coy.
234597 Pte. WINDISH, M.
13340 Sgt WOOD, L. G.
525779 Pte. WOOD, J., 527th A.E. Coy.
371230 Pte. WERTGAME, L., 829th A.E. Coy.
411729 Pte. WIST, A., 891st A.E. Coy.
187869 Pte. WEINBERG, N., 78th Lab. Group.
Pte. WALMAN, S., 870th A.E. Coy.
655419 Pte. WERSOFF, N., 50th Div.
35651 Pte. WOLF, S., 4th Lab. Coy.
49995 Pte. WINKLE, J., 29th Lab. Coy.
47884 Pte. WOOLFE, J., 15th Lab. Coy.
40684 Pte. WOLFSON, 14th Coy.
37420 Pte. WOOLF, A., 11th Coy.
204200 Pte. WISE, R., 11th Lab. Coy.
204240 Pte. WALKOVITCH, M., 11th Lab. Coy.
445088 Cpl. WINEFSKY, H., 26th Lab. Coy.
53296 Pte. WEINBAUM, I., 11th Lab. Coy.
361090 Pte. WAXKARSH, 633rd Emp. Coy.
92593 Pte. WOLFSON, A..E Coy.
41866 Pte. WHITE,* J., 70th Lab. Coy.
557816 Pte. WANGER,* N., 1002nd Lab. Coy.
97615 Pte. WEISGARD, L., 8th Mx. Lab. Coy.
80210 Pte. WOOLF, M., 8th Mx. Lab. Coy.
93084 Pte. WOLFSHAUT, J., 8th Mx. Lab. Coy.
93173 Pte. WEIL, V., 8th Mx. Lab. Coy.
557642 Pte. WEINSTEIN, D., 1002nd Lab. Coy.
557640 Pte. WEBBER, H., 1002nd Lab. Coy.
558643 Pte. WHITE, J., 1002nd Lab. Coy.
558193 Pte. WEINSTEIN, L., 1002nd Lab. Coy.
558012 Pte. WEINER, J., 1002nd Lab. Coy.
558157 Pte. WEINBERG, W., 1002nd Lab. Coy.
558810 Pte. WANKOVITCH, A., 1002nd Lab. Coy.
557717 Pte. WORTSKY, S., 1002nd Lab. Coy.
557869 Pte. WAROCHAUSKY, H., 1002nd Lab. Coy.
557596 Pte. WEINGERTNER, J., 1002nd Lab. Coy.
558266 Pte. WRESTLER, M., 1002nd Lab. Coy.
558246 Pte. WARSCHAWSKY, D., 1002nd Lab. Coy.
558212 Pte. WISEMAN, P., 1002nd Lab. Coy.
558199 Pte. WOOLF, J., 1002nd Lab. Coy.
557295 Pte. WARRITSKY, M., 1001st Lab. Coy.
557561 Pte. WEISBLATT, H., 1001st Lab. Coy.
557591 Pte. WEISS, A., 1001st Lab. Coy.
558559 Pte. WEINSTEIN, S., 1001st Lab. Coy.
557046 Pte. WEXLER, H., 1001st Lab. Coy.
557060 Pte. WALTER, N., 1001st Lab. Coy.
557493 Pte. WAGNER, J., 1001st Lab. Coy.
557131 Pte. WOOLFIN, J., 1001st Lab. Coy.
557211 Pte. WOOLFSTEIN, I., 1001st Lab. Coy.
557267 Pte. WOLKOVITCH, D., 1001st Lab. Coy.
558635 Pte. WAGNER, S., 1001st Lab. Coy.
557112 Pte. WILFORT, M., 1001st Lab. Coy.
557414 Pte. WINSKY, M., 1001st Lab. Coy.
557090 Pte. WEISBARD, M., 1001st Lab. Coy.
118339 Pte. WOOD, G., 365th Lab. Coy.
461132 Pte. WINEGARTEN, E., 672nd H.E.E. Coy.
132862 Pte. WEINRICH, 677th H.S. E. Coy.
56850 Pte. WANDER, M., Lab. Coy.
88032 Pte. WOOLF, L., 147th Lab. Coy.
40036 Pte. WEINBURG, B., 67th Lab. Coy.

Labour Corps.—*Continued.*

318 Pte. WEIBER, H., E.L.C.
09093 Pte. WEINBERG, S., E.L.C.
46951 Pte. WINEBERG, V., 50th Lab. Coy.
92593 Pte. WOOLFSON, A.
461080 Pte. WAAKIRSH, M., 635th Lab. Coy.
48471 Pte. WHITE, E., 81st Lab. Coy.
80452 Pte. WEBBER, J. M., 4th Lab. Coy.
106080 Pte. WOOLF, I., 117th Lab. Coy.
132682 Pte. WEINRICH, E.
35824 Pte. WOSMITZER, F., 1st Lab. Coy.
210185 Pte. WELT, I., 365th Lab. Coy.
71290 Pte. WOOLF, T., 301st Lab. Coy.
56850 Pte. WANDER, M., 95th Lab. Coy.
133124 Pte. WOOLF, M., 2nd Lab. Coy.
73133 Pte. WEITZRUSARY, M., 82nd Lab. Coy.
47884 Pte. WOLF, J., 40th Lab. Coy.
642 Sgt. WOLFSON, H., 395th Lab. Coy.
33812 Pte. WEINSTEIN, S., 1st Lab. Coy.
10075 Pte. WILSON, S. B., 585th Lab. Coy.
39062 Pte. WEITZMAN, S., 35th Lab. Coy.
461116 Pte. WEISS, B.
47874 Pte. WOOLF, J., 18th Lab. Coy.
210185 Pte. WILT, I., 366th Lab. Coy.
460753 Pte. WEITZ, P.
545697 Pte. WOOLFE, L., 300th Lab Coy.
452486 Pte. WINSTEIN, 299th Lab. Coy.
461741 Pte. WAXMAN, I., 450th Lab. Coy.
70089 Pte. WISBERG, J., 6th Lab. Coy.
251801 Pte. WINBERG, G., 6th Lab. Coy.
481 Pte. WITTENBERG, H., 4th Lab. Coy.
393241 Pte. WEIDENGARTEN, J. A.
273830 Pte. WEXLER, R.
075695 Pte. WOOLFSON, W.
54237 Pte. WOOLF, S.
44816 Pte. WILDER, W., 3rd Lab. Coy.
322289 Pte. WILLING, M., 595th Lab. Coy.
135577 Cpl. WOOLF, G., S.C.L.C.
48453 Pte. YETTRAM, A., 7th Mx. Lab. Coy.
31204 Pte. YETTRAM, V., 2nd Lab. Coy.
46674 Pte. YANOKOVITCH, M., 78th Lab. Coy.
35738 Pte. YAFFA, M., 539th Lab. Coy.
63717 Pte. YESNER, S., 5th Durham Lab. Coy.
46736 Pte. YUREY, P., 20th Lab. Coy.
Pte. YANKOVITCH, W., 13th Lab. Coy.
Pte. YELIN, N., 3rd Lab. Coy.
21470 Pte. YESNER, S., 36th Lab. Coy.
176 Pte. YOUSEF, I., 72nd Lab. Coy.
366002 Pte. YOUNG, O. A., Labour Centre.
557698 Pte. YANALOVITCH, A., 1002nd Lab. Coy.
558216 Pte. YARROW, B., 1002nd Lab. Coy.
557626 Pte. YESHIN, A., 1002nd Lab. Coy.
557532 Pte. YELLOW, H., 1001st Lab. Coy.
557572 Pte. YAFFE, J., 1001st Lab. Coy.
557346 Pte. YADZICK, J., 1001st Lab. Coy.
507616 Pte. YAFFE, E., Lab. Bn.
124201 Pte. YOUNG, D., 172nd Lab. Coy.

V/622 Cpl. YAKUB, Y., E.L.C.
129091 Pte. YARSON, J. S., 1st Lab. Coy.
46762 Pte. YUSAN S., 628th Lab. Coy.
509328 Pte. YARBITCH, M., 524th Lab. Coy.
593594 Pte. YENERSHEVITZ, J.
273293 Pte. YESNICK, S.
84040 Pte. ZEMLA, H., 2nd Lab. Coy.
31980 Pte. ZOLTY, N., 2nd Lab. Coy.
70018 Pte. ZIMMER, D., 3rd Mx. Lab. Coy.
56062 Pte. ZISSLIN, T., 24th R.W.S. Lab. Coy.
153544 Pte. ZAMERIN, I.
393246 Pte. ZAVADSKY, J., 390th Lab. Coy.
149223 Pte. ZEALEY, A., 390th Lab. Coy.
74074 L/Cpl. ZENBORNE, A., 1st Mx. Lab. Coy.
80311 Pte. ZUNG, L., 3rd Mx. Lab. Coy.
G/71406 Pte. ZICKEL, J., 4th Mx. Lab. Coy.
G/84455 Pte. ZEMBA, L., 4th Mx. Lab. Coy.
G/44723 Pte. ZEIGLER, A., 4th Mx. Lab. Coy.
G/69499 Pte. ZETTER, I., 116th Lab. Coy.
79693 Pte. ZAYTOUN, S., 133rd Lab. Coy.
506190 Pte. ZELEPOUKIN, 178th Lab. Coy.
69499 Pte. ZELTER, J., 116th Lab. Coy.
G/74402 Pte. ZEMBA, A., 4th Lab. Coy.
G/84361 Pte. ZUCKER, A., 4th Lab. Coy.
G/72227 L/Cpl. ZEILINSKY, J. G., 5th Lab. Coy.
452381 Pte. ZAGERMA, M., 706th Lab. Coy.
78769 Pte. ZISSLIN, I., 132nd Lab. Coy.
92057 Pte. ZACKIE, N., 35th Lab. Coy.
44817 Pte. ZEMMEL, H., 2nd Lab. Coy.
46344 Pte. ZANG, C., 78th Lab. Coy.
89866 Pte. ZEEGAN, L., 32nd Lab. Coy.
509236 Pte. ZALICKS, J., 527th A.E. Coy.
53887 Pte. ZEFFERT, M., 10th Lab. Coy.
37894 Pte. ZEEGAN, L., 12th Lab. Coy.
35787 Pte. ZACKIS, A., 8th Mx. Lab. Coy.
98089 Pte. ZITZNITZKY, 8th Mx. Lab. Coy.
93587 Pte. ZELLER, R., 8th Mx. Lab. Coy.
83016 Pte. ZEMLA, B., 8th Mx. Lab. Coy.
557733 Pte. ZELINSKY, 1002nd Lab. Coy.
557928 Pte. ZEMBER, A., 1002nd Lab. Coy.
558103 Pte. ZAGGER, S., 1002nd Lab. Coy.
557811 Pte. ZAIDERMAN, L., 1002nd Lab. Coy.
557761 Pte. ZUPRANSKY, H., 1002nd Lab. Coy.
557922 Pte. ZALKOWITZ, M., 1002nd Lab. Coy.
558264 Pte. ZACHINSKY, M., 1002nd Lab. Coy.
557430 Pte. ZAIDE, K., 1001st Lab. Coy.
557402 Pte. ZABNER, S., 1001st Lab. Coy.
557149 Pte. ZLOTY, H., 1001st Lab. Coy.
452557 Pte. ZAMBLOVSKY, H., 300th Lab. Coy.
596819 Pte. ZERETSKY, M. H., 46th Lab. Coy.
011053 Sgt. ZILBER, W., E.L.C.
3091 Pte. ZIGMON, Y., E.L.C.
53887 Pte. ZEFFERT, W., 90th Lab. Coy.
163560 Pte. ZWART, S., 368th Lab. Coy.
4523581 Pte. ZAGERMAN, M., 299th Lab. Coy.
212343 Pte. ZEID, L.
460165 Pte. ZITNICK, H., 303rd Lab. Coy.
274008 Pte. ZASSHOLZ, C.

Labour Corps.—Continued.

	Pte. ZEITEL, M., 629th Lab. Coy.
509328	Pte. ZURIBITCH, M., 524th Lab. Coy.
98089	Pte. ZITUITTSHI, M., 8th Lab. Coy.
691	L/Cpl. ZARER, M.

* Killed in Action or died on Active Service.

THE MONMOUTHSHIRE REGIMENT.

OFFICERS.

Lieut. ROSENBAUM, L. B.,* 2nd Bn.
Lieut. SELINE, A., 1st Bn.

N.C.O.'s AND MEN.

- 291108 Pte. ARINSKY, L., 2nd Bn.
- 226892 Pte. ABELSON, A., 2nd Bn.
- 226896 Pte. ABELSON, M., 1st Bn.
- 228196 Pte. BRAVO, D. B., 1st Bn.
- 226901 Pte. CORB, L., 1st Bn.
- 292226 Pte. COHEN, L., 2nd Bn.
- 292019 Pte. COHEN, I., 1st Bn.
- 4261 Pte. COHEN, M., 2/3rd Bn.
- 230187 Pte. COHEN, A. B., 2/1st Bn.
- 4485 Pte. CLOMPUS, B., 2/1st Bn.
- 267372 Pte. CLOMPUS, S., 2nd Bn.
- Pte. CUNISKY, W., 2/2nd Bn.
- 291144 Pte. FRENDT, N., 2nd Bn.
- 4704 Pte. FINE, M., 2/1st Bn.
- 228691 L/Cpl. FINKLE, A., 2nd Bn.
- 5652 Pte. FREEDMAN, M., 2/3rd Bn.
- 276977 Pte. FACTOR, B., 4th Bn.
- 44 Sgt. FOX, M., 2nd Bn.
- 1/5472 Pte. GOLDBERG, B., 2nd Bn.
- 227285 Pte. GOLDBERG, B., 1st Bn.
- 228852 Pte. GORBEY, L., 1st Bn.
- 4479 Pte. GRUPMAN, R. B., 1st Bn.
- 228352 L/Cpl. GRANT, L., 2nd Bn.
- 267212 Pte. GLOSSIN, S., 2/2nd Bn.
- 318354 Pte. GREENBAUM, H., 4th Bn.
- 53646 Pte. GLASS, 4th Bn.
- 3/2299 Cpl. HARRIS, A. H., 1st Bn.
- 1/25711 L/Cpl. HARRIS, R. B., 1st Bn.
- 281978 Pte. HARRIS, H., 1st Bn.
- 315957 Pte. HARRIS, M. J., 1st Bn.
- 316684 Pte. ISAACS, T. C., 4th Bn.
- 266291 Pte. KAPLAN, A., 1st Bn.
- 42486 Pte. KERDANSKI, J. D., 1st Bn.
- 266610 Pte. KAUFMAN, J., 2/2nd Bn.
- 285041 Pte. LEVY, A. H., 2nd Bn.
- 291059 Pte. LEVY, S., 2/3rd Bn.
- 30477 Pte. LITTLESTONE, 4th Bn.
- 230056 Pte. LEVINE, S., 4th Bn.
- 4296 Pte. LERMAN, L., 2/3rd Bn.
- 31060 Pte. MICHAELSON, 4th Bn.
- 228413 Pte. MEYERS, J., 1st Bn.
- 4902 Pte. MARKS, A., 2/2nd Bn.
- 228415 Pte. MARCHINSKY, G., 2/1st Bn.
- 291953 Pte. NATHAN, B., 2nd Bn.
- 30773 Pte. ORMAN, J., 4th Bn.
- 41912 Pte. PHILLIPS, S., 1/2nd Bn.
- 41937 Pte. POLICOVSKY, B., 1/2nd Bn.
- 4309 Pte. PAUL, D., 2/3rd Bn.
- 314727 Pte. PETERS, J., 1st Bn.
- 291160 Pte. ROTHBLATT, S.
- 227982 Pte. SIMONS, M., 1st Bn.
- 4755 Pte. SIMPSON, H., 3rd Bn.
- 35816 Pte. SWATTS, F. G., 4th Bn.
- 36011 Pte. SAXSHIVER, 4th Bn.
- 4721 Pte. TAGERMAN, H., 1st Bn.
- 4320 Pte. TRAGENHEIM, H., 2/3rd Bn.
- 290933 Pte. WEINGLASS, I., 1st Bn.
- 290437 C.Q.M.S. WOLFSON, J., 1st Bn.
- 303610 Pte. WISHNEVSKY, I.
- 285089 Pte. ZAGERMAN, H., 2nd Bn.

* Killed in Action or died on Active Service.

THE CAMBRIDGESHIRE REGIMENT.

N.C.O.'s AND MEN.

- 327616 Pte. BARNARD, N. D., 4/1st Bn.
- 6115 Pte. BERNBERG, H., 2/1st Bn.
- 329016 Pte. BERNSTEIN, 2/1st Bn.
- 5617 Pte. BERMAN, H., 2/1st Bn.
- 91331 Pte. BERMAN, N., 1/1st Bn.
- 47004 L/Cpl. BRISCOE, M., 4/1st Bn.
- 327352 Pte. GILBERT, J., 2/1st Bn.
- 5303 Pte. COLSTER, L., 2/1st Bn.
- 6139 Pte. COHEN, I., 2/1st Bn.
- Pte. COHEN, B., 1st Bn.
- 9463 Pte. COHEN, J.
- 330947 Pte. COHEN, S., 4/1st Bn.
- 327240 Pte. COHEN, D., 2/1st Bn.
- 41879 Pte. COHEN, P., 11th Bn.
- 330071 Pte. COLEMAN, J., 4/1st Bn.
- 238555 Pte. CRISTOL, J., 4/1st Bn.
- 328992 Pte. DAVIS, I., 4/1st Bn.
- 5552 Pte. DAVIS, O., 2/1st Bn.
- 328504 Pte. DE FRIEND, L., 4/1st Bn.
- 5492 Pte. FREEDMAN, M., 2/1st Bn.
- 9409 Pte. GREEN, H., 4/1st Bn.
- 5432 Pte. GROOSKY, E., 2/1st Bn.
- 330407 Pte. HARRINGMAN, S., 4/1st Bn.
- 5268 Pte. HERMAN, S., 2/1st Bn.
- 34639 Pte. HOFFBERG, L., 4/1st Bn.
- 327431 Pte. HOEPELMAN, G., 4/1st Bn.
- 329055 Pte. ISAACS, B., 4/1st Bn.
- 328913 Pte. JACOBS, R. P., 4/1st Bn.
- 327836 Pte. JACOB, B., 2/1st Bn.
- 5272 Pte. JACKSON, A., 2/1st Bn.

Cambridgeshire Regt.—*Continued.*

302517 Pte. KAKLAN, S., 4/1st Bn.
328445 Pte. KOSSOFF, H., 2/1st Bn.
37569 Pte. LABOR, S.,* 1st Bn.
327780 Cpl. LEWIS, B., 4/1st Bn.
327325 L/Cpl. LESSER, C., 2/1st Bn.
48822 Pte. LEVINE, M., 1st Bn.
Pte. LEBE, A., 2/1st Bn.
242338 Pte. LUSTIG, N., 1st Bn.
5529 Pte. MORGAN, M., 2/1st Bn.
345042 Pte. OTTOLANGI, 1st Bn.
330074 Pte. PITMAN, H., 2/1st Bn.
252682 Pte. RAPPORT, I., 4/1st Bn.
5511 Pte. RACKLIN, M., 2/1st Bn.
327254 Pte. ROSE, E., 2/1st Bn.
330817 Pte. ROSENBERG, 2/1st Bn.
5829 Pte. RUBINSKY, S., 2/1st Bn.
242796 Pte. SAUNDERS, M., 1st Bn.
328842 Cpl. SNIDERS, A., 4/1st Bn.
5564 Pte. SAPERCHIVSKY, E., 2/1st Bn.
327424 Pte. SOLOMONS, I., 2/1st Bn.
6135 Pte. SOLOMONS, J., 2/1st Bn.
327837 Pte. SOLOMON, S., 2/1st Bn.
328391 Pte. STODEL, L., 2/1st Bn.
151925 Pte. SNYDER, N.
328478 Pte. STEIN, M., 4/1st Bn.
5610 Pte. VIGOR, M., 2/1st Bn.
329028 Pte. WITTEY, N., 2/1st Bn.

* Killed in Action or died on Active Service.

THE LONDON REGIMENT.

OFFICERS.

2nd Lieut. ARON, D. J., 2/3rd Bn.
2nd Lieut. ARNOLD, A. L.,* 9th Bn.
2nd Lieut. ABRAHAMS, M., 19th Bn.
Lieut. ALBERGA, E. M., 10th Bn.
Capt. BERLINER, P. B. (M.C.), 2/7th Bn.
2nd Lieut. BROWN, S., 1/13th Bn.
Lieut. BERNHEIM, H., 1/3rd Bn.
2nd Lieut. BARNETT, C. E. (M.C.).
Capt. BARNETT, H. W.,* 13th Bn.
Capt. BASWITZ, A.* (M.C.), 1/22nd Bn.
2nd Lieut. BENCHER, G. A.,* 2/19th Bn.
2nd Lieut. BARNETT, S., 18th Bn.
2nd Lieut. BENJAMIN, A. F., 11th Bn.
2nd Lieut. CARO, J. P.,* 2/17th Bn.
Lieut.-Col. COHEN, J. WALEY- (C.M.G., D.S.O.), 1/16th Bn.
2nd. Lieut. COOTE, P. E.* 8th Bn.
Capt. COHEN, L. L., 1/13th Bn.
2nd Lieut. COHEN, S. M.,* 1/12th Bn.
2nd Lieut. CUMMINS, T. D.,* 2/3rd Bn.
2nd Lieut. CHART, A., 16th Bn.
Col. CARLEBACH, P. (C.M.G.), 2nd Bn.
2nd Lieut. CARO, J. P.,* 2/17th Bn.
2nd Lieut. COHEN, M.,* 21st Bn.
Lieut. CRICHTON, C. A.,* 3rd Bn.
Capt. DAVIS, F. M., 1/7th Bn.
Major DAVIS, E. J., 1/19th Bn.
Capt. DE MEZA, J.* (M.C.), 1/19th Bn.
Capt. DAVIS, L. J.,* 1/19th Bn.
2nd Lieut. DE PINNA, C. D., 2/3rd Bn.
Capt. DAVIS, S. (M.C.), 2/4th Bn.
2nd Lieut. DURLACHER, H. W. (M.C.), 2/1st Bn.
Lieut. DUPARC, I. M., 1/21st Bn.
2nd Lieut. DAVIS, C. S., 19th Reserve Bn.
2nd Lieut. DAVIS, B. C.,* 2/12th Bn.
Lieut. DREYFUS, 6th Bn.
Major ENOCH, C. D., 1/7th Bn.
Capt. ELKAN, A. E.
Lieut. EHRMANN, A., 2nd Bn.
Capt. FRANK, J. L., 1/19th Bn.
Lieut. FREEDMAN, A. H. D., 13th Bn.
Lieut. GROSSMAN, E. E., 1/12th Bn.
Capt. GREEN, S. M., 2/13th Bn.
Capt. GLUCKSTEIN, I. M., 2/10th Bn.
Lieut. GLUCKMAN, P.,* 1/3rd Bn.
2nd Lieut. GORDON, A., 3/1st Bn.
2nd Lieut. GOLDSMITH, W. C., 2/17th Bn.
Capt. GINSBURG, J. W., 2nd Bn.
2nd Lieut. GREENLAND, A. E., 8th Bn.
2nd Lieut. GODWIN, S. W., 1/9th Bn.
Capt. GOLDSTON, J. J., 10th Bn.
2nd Lieut. HICKMAN, S. H., 1/6th Bn.
Lieut. HART, L. H., 2/15th Bn.
2nd Lieut. HARRIS, G., 2/19th Bn.
2nd Lieut. HYAMS, D. H. (M.C.), 1/23rd Bn.
2nd Lieut. HARRIS, J., 2/6th Bn
Lieut. HOLT, G. N., 2/10th Bn.
Capt. HOLT, L.,* 2/10th Bn.
Major HENRIQUES, J. Q., 1/16th Bn.
Capt. HEUMANN, R.,* 2nd Bn.
Lieut. HARRIS, A.,* 13th Bn.
2nd Lieut. ISAACS, F. H., 2/1st Bn.
Major INFELD, H. (M.C.), 1/12th Bn.
Lieut. ISAACS, G. H., 23rd Bn.
Lieut. ISRAEL, N. V., 19th Bn.
Col. JESSEL, Sir H. M. (C.M.G.), 1st Bn.
2nd Lieut. JOSEPHS, J.,* 12th Bn.
Lieut. JACOBS, L. E., 1/13th Bn.
Lieut. JAY, S. C., 1/19th Bn.
2nd Lieut. JOSEPH, L. E. A., 1/13th Bn.
Capt. JOSEPH, C. L., 1/13th Bn.
2nd Lieut. JOSEPH, C. I. J., 21st Bn.
2nd Lieut. JOSEPH, G., 17th Bn.
Lieut. JACOBS, P., 19th Bn.
Capt. KISCH, E. R. (M.C.), 2/13th Bn.
2nd Lieut. LYNES, J., 1/23rd Bn.
2nd Lieut. LEON, E. J.,* 8th Bn.
Lieut. LISSACK, S. M., 2/13th Bn.
Capt. LEWIS, W. (M.C.), 1/23rd Bn.

London Regt.—*Continued.*

Lieut. LEVY, F. D., 2/21st Bn.
Lieut. LIPSEY, S. M., 13th Bn.
Lieut. LAZARUS, J. P., 17th Bn.
Lieut. LOEWY, J. E., 1/6th Bn.
Lieut. LYONS, E., 1/4th Bn.
2nd Lieut. LAWRENCE, A. P., 1/10th Bn.
2nd Lieut. LELYVELD, H., 1/6th Bn.
2nd Lieut. LEVY, N. B. L. (M.C.).
Capt. LESSER, A., 13th Bn.
Lieut. LEAPMAN, L. C. (M.C.), 6th Bn.
Capt. MONTAGU, H. S., 2/7th Bn.
2nd Lieut. MENDES, E. G., 1/15th Bn.
2nd Lieut. MENDL, R. H. J., 2/1st Bn.
2nd Lieut. MILLER, S. L., 2/15th Bn.
Capt. MARKS, O. S. (M.C. and Bar), 2/23rd Bn.
Lieut. MOSELEY, E. P. M., 1/4th Bn.
Lieut. MELHADO, C. S. H., 10th Bn.
Capt. MYER, H. D., 1/6th Bn.
2nd Lieut. MICHAEL, E. (D.C.M.), 1/18th Bn.
2nd Lieut. MYER, M. A., 1/6th Bn.
Lieut. MOSELY, M., 1/25th Bn.
Major MARIANS, R. I., 1/2nd Bn.
Major MARKS, N.,* 1/23 Bn.
Major MYER, E. A.,* 6th Bn.
2nd Lieut. MARTINEZ, H. E. N.
2nd Lieut. MENDL, C., 10th Bn.
Capt. MEREDITH, H., 18th Bn.
Lieut. MOSES, P., 19th Bn.
2nd Lieut. MENDES-CHUMACEIRO, I., 13th Bn.
Capt. MOSS-VERNON, S. R. (M.C.), 12th Bn.
2nd Lieut. NORMAN, J., 2/17th Bn.
Capt. NEWTON, L. H., 1/11th Bn.
Major NATHAN, H. L., 1/1st Bn.
2nd Lieut. OPET, T. H.,* 8th Bn.
Major PHILLIPS, H., 1/19th Bn.
Capt. PHILLIPS, E. L., 1/6th Bn.
2nd Lieut. PHILLIPS, H. F., 2nd Bn.
2nd Lieut. PHILLIPS, I. G., 3/4th Bn.
Capt. POLLAK, L. A., 19th Bn.
2nd Lieut. PHILLIPS, J. J. E., 5th Bn.
Major ROTHSCHILD, M. C., 2/10th Bn.
2nd Lieut. RAPHAEL, G. G., 8th Bn.
2nd Lieut. RAPHAEL, O. P., 8th Bn.
2nd Lieut. RICHARDSON, 1/11th Bn.
2nd Lieut. ROSEN, W. (M.C.).
Lieut. SIMON, H. J. B., 2/3rd Bn.
Lieut.-Col. SAMUEL, F. D. (D.S.O. and Bar), 1/3rd Bn.
Capt. SALMON, B. A., 2/17th Bn.
Capt. SCHONFIELD, E.,* 2/19th Bn.
Major SCHONFIELD, W., 1/19th Bn.
Capt. SOLOMON, H., 2/24th Bn.
2nd Lieut. SOLOMON, G. D., 2/10th Bn.
Capt. STEIN, L. J., 2/12th Bn.
2nd Lieut. SHENOW, E., 1/13th Bn.
2nd Lieut. SLATTERY, J., 2/2nd Bn.
Capt. SOLOMON, A. M.,* 2/10th Bn.

2nd Lieut. STERN, L. H.,* 1/13th Bn.
Capt. SPIELMAN, E. R. M., 25th Bn.
Major SWEARS, M. H., 6th Bn.
Capt. SHAW, E., 10th Bn.
Lieut. SOLOMON, S. M., 10th Bn.
Lieut. SAMUEL, E., 10th Bn.
2nd Lieut. SELIGSOHN, H. L. (M.C. and Bar).
2nd Lieut. SAMUEL, H., 20th Bn.
2nd Lieut. SCHONFIELD, G. H., 19th Bn.
Lieut. SOMAN, H. D., 5th Bn.
Capt. SUTTON, D. (M.C.), 7th Bn.
2nd Lieut. SOLOMAN, A., 10th Bn.
2nd Lieut. SALAMAN, J., 16th Bn.
2nd Lieut. SOLOMON, J. C., 24th Bn.
Lieut. SHANNER, L. C. G., 24th Bn.
2nd Lieut. SELBY, M. G.,* 5th Bn.
Lieut. SOLOMON, C. S., 7th Bn.
2nd Lieut. SAMUEL, T. A. S. (M.C.).
2nd Lieut. TEBBITT, I. L.,* 1/19th Bn.
2nd Lieut. VANDERLINDE, M. J. T.,* 9th Bn.
Lieut. VANDYK, A., 3/24th Bn.
Capt. VAN GELDER, L., 23rd Bn.
Capt. WALTERS, A. B., 1/17th Bn.
Lieut. WALEY, S. D. (M.C.), 1/22nd Bn.
Major WALEY, E. G. S. (O.B.E.), 1/16th Bn.
2nd Lieut. WOLBRANCH, V. M., 4/1st Bn.
Lieut. WALFORD, L. N., 12th Bn.
2nd Lieut. WEENER, P., 6th Bn.
2nd Lieut. WEENAN, A. L., 9th Bn.
Capt. ZEFFERT, H. M., 3/11th Bn.

N.C.O.'s AND MEN.

1881	Rfm. ALBERGA, E. M., 1/9th Bn.
4636	Rfm. ABRAHAMS, J. R., 1/6th Bn.
2268	Rfm. ABRAHAMS, S.,* 1/16th Bn.
5154	Pte. ABRAHAMS, M., 1/20th Bn.
5639	Pte. ABRAHAMS, H., 1/23rd Bn.
5634	Pte. ADDERMAN, S., 1/19th Bn.
5187	Pte. ABRAHAMS, L., 1/17th Bn.
5175	Pte. ADOLPHUS, B. (M.M.), 1/17th Bn.
4326	Pte. ABRAHAMS, S.,* 1/4th Bn.
	Rfm. ADLER, D. (D.C.M.), 1/13th Bn.
4646	Pte. ARONIN, D., 1/2nd Bn.
2703	Rfm. AARONS, S. L., 1/5th Bn.
4952	Rfm. ARNOLD, B., 1/5th Bn.
4374	Rfm. AUSHUL, S., 1/5th Bn.
570489	L/Cpl. ABRAHAMS, A., 2/17th Bn.
1444	Rfm. ABRAHAMS, J., 2/18th Bn.
5876	Rfm. ABLEMAN, J., 2/21st Bn.
5754	L/Cpl. ABRAHAMS, A., 2/24th Bn.
5529	Pte. ALTMAN, A., 2/22nd Bn.
280443	Pte. ABRAHAMS, C., 1/4th Bn.
7177	Pte. ALLENSTEIN, J., 1/4th Bn.
4908	Pte. ASHBERRY, B.,* 1/13th Bn.
8483	Pte. AARONS, M.,* 1/14th Bn.
5438	Rfm. ARIA, C. D., 1/5th Bn.
315048	Rfm. ANGEL, R., 1/5th Bn.

London Regt.—Continued.

6026	L./Cpl. APPELBAUM, S., 2/1st Bn.
8342	Pte. AARONS, J., 2/2nd Bn.
5697	Pte. ABRAHAMS, H., 2/3rd Bn.
5587	Pte. ABRAHAMS, N., 2/4th Bn.
345020	Rfm. AMSTELL, S., 2/6th Bn.
1767	L/Cpl. ALBERT, J.,* 2/10th Bn.
538856	Pte. ABRAHAMS, H., 2/15th Bn.
35765	Pte. ABRAHAMS, L., 1/19th Bn.
373703	Pte. ABRAHAMS, E., 1/8th Bn.
4449	L./Cpl. ABRAHAMS, H., 2/10th Bn.
422969	Pte. ABRAHAMS, B., 2/10th Bn.
5638	Pte. ABRAHAMS, I.,* 2/10th Bn.
5780	Pte. ABRAHAMS, H., 2/10th Bn.
5374	Rfm. ADELSON, S., 2/12th Bn.
6817	Rfm. ABRAHAM, I., 1/8th Bn.
374321	Rfm. ARONOW, H.,* 1/8th Bn.
495441	Rfm. ALVAREZ, J., 1/18th Bn.
632317	Rfm. ABRAHAMS, M., 1/20th Bn.
54111	Pte. ABRAMS, J., 1/15th Bn.
275260	Pte. ABRAHAMS, S., 2/3rd Bn.
491298	Pte. ALDENS, L. F., 2/6th Bn.
425520	Pte. ACKERMAN, A., 2/10th Bn.
701884	Pte. ABRAHAMS, J., 2/23rd Bn.
4600	Pte. ATKINS, L., 1/22nd Bn.
375767	Pte. ABRAHAMS, I., 1/13th Bn.
497127	Pte. ANDERS, I., 1/13th Bn.
2156	Pte. ABRAHAMS, H., 1/4th Bn.
4522	Pte. ALBOZ, J., 1/21st Bn.
42006	Pte. ABRAHAMS, R., 2/10th Bn.
252639	Pte. ABRAHAMS, H., 1/3rd Bn.
608829	Pte. ALVERY, J., 1/18th Bn.
2190	Pte. ABRAHAMS, C., 1/3rd Bn.
8006	Rfm. AARONSON, L., 2/17th Bn.
540236	Pte. ABRAHAMS, E.,* 6th Bn.
3007	Pte. ABRAHAMS, H. A.,* 13th Bn.
576157	Rfm. ABRAHAMS, S.,* 1/17th Bn.
1685	Pte. ANDRADE, W. A.,* 4th Bn.
6817	Pte. ABRAHAMS, J., 8th Bn.
280443	Pte. ABRAHAMS, C. E.
281753	Pte. ABRAHAMS, S.,* 1/4th Bn.
12012	Pte. AMSTELL, S., 1st Bn.
18400	Pte. ABELSTON, A.
554774	Pte. ABRAHAM, L. I.
555683	Pte. ABELSON, L. I.
204867	Pte. AARONS, M., 1st Bn.
375121	Pte. ALEXANDER, B. K., 8th Bn.
354999	Pte. AVERS, 3/7th Bn.
303777	L/Cpl. ARNOLD, M. P., 5th Bn.
260913	Pte. ABRAHAMS, J., 2/4th Bn.
233751	Pte. AARONS, J.,* 2/2nd Bn.
652710	Rfm. AVELMAN, J., 2/21st Bn.
632317	Pte. ABRAHAMS, M., 1/20th Bn.
41358	Pte. AHRINGULD, L., 2/1st Bn.
595991	Pte. ALTER, S., 18th Bn.
302603	Pte. ANSCHULL, R., 2/5th Bn.
421721	Pte. ARBITER, J., 1/10th Bn.
200951	Pte. ARBIS, A.
1091	Pte. ABRAHAMS, J., 2nd Bn.
590326	Pte. ABRAHAMS, J., 2/18th Bn.
2903	Pte. ANGEL, H. B., 11th Bn.
71799	Pte. ABRAHAMOVITCH, A., 1/9th Bn.
5025	Pte. AARONS, J., 13th Bn.
3295	Pte. ABLER, J., 3/7th Bn.
4036	Pte. ABRAHAMS, I. L., 3/6th Bn.
3319	Pte. ADELMAN, T., 3/6th Bn.
4548	Pte. AMSTELL, S., 3/10th Bn.
3250	Pte. ARBITER, J., 3/10th Bn.
23224	Cpl. ANGEL, A. B., 10th Bn.
4962	Pte. ANGEL, H., 7th Bn.
	Pte. AARONS, G. V., 8th Bn.
	Pte. ALBERT, I., 2/10th Bn.
	Pte. ABRAHAMS, B., 17th Bn.
4374	Rfm. ANSCHELL, L., 5th Bn.
252639	Pte. ABRAHAMS, H., 2/3rd Bn.
354936	Pte. ABRAHAMS, S. M., 3/7th Bn.
495578	Pte. ANDERS, J.
392298	L/Cpl. ADLER, L., 9th Bn.
472255	Rfm. ANDLESON, L., 2/12th Bn.
496648	Pte. ARNOLD, N.
282594	Pte. ABRAHAMS, N., 2/4th Bn.
28197	Pte. ABRAHAMS, H., 1/17th Bn.
612062	Pte. ADDESMAN, S., 1/19th Bn.
514271	Pte. AARONS, M. J.,* 1/14th Bn.
423036	Pte. ABRAHAMS, I.,* 2/10th Bn.
2268	Pte. ABRAHAMS, S.,* 16th Bn.
228173	Pte. ABRAHAMS, H. S.
48058	Pte. ABRAHAMS, D., 2/23rd Bn.
492044	Pte. AARONS, J., 2/18th Bn.
722627	L/Cpl. ABRAHAMS, A., 2/24th Bn.
492038	Pte. ABRAHAMS, L., 13th Bn.
422512	Cpl. ABRAHAMS, H., 10th Bn.
721412	Sig. ABRAHAMS, S., 24th Bn.
701884	Pte. ABRAHAMS, J., 2/23rd Bn.
540489	Cpl. ABRAHAMS, A., 2/17th Bn.
570489	Cpl. ABRAHAMS, A., 2/17th Bn.
5816	Rfm. ARNOLD, M. L., 3rd Bn.
5530	Pte. ABRAHAMS, P., 10th Bn.
5454	Pte. ASH, A., 10th Bn.
11/2633	Rfm. AZEN, J., 16th Bn.
426520	Pte. ABRAMS, P. B., 10th Bn.
282594	Pte. ABRAHAMS, N., 3rd Bn.
6026	L/Cpl. APPLEBAUM, S., 2/1st Bn.
8342	Pte. AARONS, J., 2/2nd Bn.
557258	Rfm. ALFREDS, G., 1/16th Bn.
801299	Pte. ABRAHAMS, H., 30th Bn.
722612	L/Cpl. ABRAHAMS, J., 2/24th Bn.
492044	Dvr. AARONS, J., 2/31st Bn.
801410	Pte. ABRAHAMS, E. V., 38th Bn.
573521	Rfm. ANGEL, I., 3/17th Bn.
572377	Pte. ABRAHAMS, L., 17th Bn.
6949	Pte. APTER, G., 3/20th Bn.
699007	Pte. BERMAN, P.,* 1/22nd Bn.
225	Rfm. H. BEYFUS,* L. R. B.
5411	Pte. BARNETT, E.,* 24th Bn.

London Regt.—*Continued.*

532898	Pte. BARNETT, G.,*	15th Bn.
1751	Cpl. BLACKMAN, M.,*	4th Bn.
6244	Pte. BLUESTEIN, J.,*	1/1st Bn.
534120	Pte. BUCK, A. I.,	1/12th Bn.
203065	Pte. BERGMAN, H.,	3rd Bn.
653984	Pte. BRONSTEIN, W.	
615572	Pte. BENEVITZ, D.,	1/19th Bn.
536931	Pte. BARENTZ, J. L.,	3/10th Bn.
32398	Pte. BERLIN, I. J.,	2/6th Bn.
741804	Pte. BECLER, M.,	2/10th Bn.
	Pte. BARON, H.	
	Pte. BENAZON, J.,	13th Bn.
	Cpl. BAKER, M.,	12th Bn.
	Pte. BLANKENSEE, G. E.,	28th Bn.
	Pte. BLOOMFIELD, E.,	16th Bn.
	Bgl. BERKOFF, G.,	13th Bn.
	Pte. BROGILL, F. B.,	2nd Bn.
	Pte. BOGGIN, E.,	4th Bn.
4330	Pte. BEVERLEY, L. G.,	9th Bn.
634130	Rfm. BERRY, H.,	20th Bn.
283037	Pte. BAKER,	21st Bn.
232601	Pte. BLOOM, T.,	1st Bn.
324270	Rfm. BLOOM, P.,	2/6th Bn.
204305	Pte. BARNETT, S.,*	2/1st Bn.
3246	Rfm. BARNETT, A.,	2/6th Bn.
323698	Pte. BERLEW,	2/6th Bn.
334946	Rfm. BERMAN,	6th Bn.
304270	Cpl. BLUM,	2/6th Bn.
422522	Cpl. BERG, S.,	2/10th Bn.
253325	Pte. BENJAMIN, C.,	1st Bn.
54622	Pte. BARNETT, J.,	7th Bn.
391794	Pte. BLOOM, J.	
295205	Rfm. BRODY, D. M.,	9th Bn.
738237	Pte. BERGER, J.,	1/24th Bn.
40972	Pte. BAKER, I.	
203752	Pte. BLAIKLOCK, E.	
61564	Pte. BAVON, B.,	19th Bn.
1752	Pte. BLOCK, A.	
4947	Pte. BETH, J.,	1/18th Bn.
7432	Pte. BLACHER, J.,	3/7th Bn.
423037	Pte. BROOKS, H.,	10th Bn.
534120	Pte. BUCK, A. I.,*	1/12th Bn.
452180	Pte. BARNETT, M.,	2/11th Bn.
302535	Rfm. BLON, R.,	2/6th Bn.
73776	Pte. BERGER, R.,	21st Bn.
591970	Pte. BROWN, R.,	2/22nd Bn.
6401	Pte. BAKER, M.,	1/4th Bn.
283967	Pte. BENJAMIN, H.,	2/3rd Bn.
225508	Cpl. BLUM, E.	
354968	Pte. BEAR, M.,	7th Bn.
204878	Pte. BRICK, M.,	1st Bn.
556827	Pte. BOSS, N.,	16th Bn.
204305	Pte. BARNETT, G.,	2/1st Bn.
L/12410	Pte. BLOOM, J.,	2nd Bn.
41007	Pte. BLOOM, S.	
698131	Pte. BENSUSAN, R.,	1/22nd Bn.
452294	L/Cpl. BOSS, A. E.,	2/11th Bn.
653852	Pte. BENJAMIN, C.,	1/21st Bn.
761387	Pte. BERGMAN, S.,	2/8th Bn.
653560	Pte. BISHOP, M.,	21st Bn.
452842	Rfm. BEBBER, S.,	9th Bn.
424379	Rfm. BERNSTOCK, G.,	15th Bn.
557139	Rfm. BERGER, J. A.,	3/16th Bn.
2489	Pte. BENJAMIN, N.,	13th Bn.
7193	Pte. BERNSTEIN, S.,	1/4th Bn.
767286	Pte. BAGEL, J.	
613861	Pte. BLUMENTHAL, J.	
683908	Pte. BARNARD,	2/22nd Bn.
700573	Pte. BATCHELDER, S.,	23rd Bn.
1607	Cpl. BRUNSTARB, J. H.,	3rd Bn.
324120	Rfm. BERMAN, L.,	6th Bn.
25/4027	Rfm. BEDER, M.,	10th Bn.
10/16421	Rfm. BARNETT, M.,	10th Bn.
10/6634	Pte. BLOWER, L.,	10th Bn.
763119	L/Cpl. BERG, E. C.,	2nd Bn.
	Pte. BERNSTEIN, H.,	31st Bn.
4472	Pte. BARNETT, J.	
4163	Pte. BAMBERGER, A. G.,	3/10th Bn.
6191	Pte. BARNETT, S.,	4/4th Bn.
5334	Pte. BASS, A. I.,	2/17th Bn.
2242	L/Sgt. BOWELL, H.,	2/10th Bn.
4511	Rfm. BERNITZ, S. S.,	3/18th Bn.
3672	Rfm. BLOCK, M.,	3/6th Bn.
4606	Rfm. BLOOMBAUM, E.,	3/12th Bn.
4173	Rfm. BODGIN,	3/2nd Bn.
6201	Rfm. BRAHAM, S.,	17th Bn.
5562	Rfm. BROUER, A.,	17th Bn.
3171	Rfm. BROUETT, W.,	7th Bn.
2468	Rfm. BUCKMASTER, H.,	6th Bn.
3319	Rfm. BURNS, H.,	3/10th Bn.
4152	Rfm. BURNS R.,	3/10th Bn.
614179	Rfm. BARNETT, H.,	19th Bn.
6975	Rfm. BORISOFF, M.,	3/20th Bn.
6940	Rfm. BEER, A.,	3/20th Bn.
6981	Rfm. BEHORASHVILE, B.,	3/20th Bn.
8047	Rfm. BENDER, J.,	3/20th Bn.
8016	Rfm. BACK, S.,	3/20th Bn.
6980	Rfm. BONDINE, A.,	3/20th Bn.
6983	Rfm. BOGATCH, H. L.,	3/20th Bn.
8023	Sgt. BOBROV, J.,	3/20th Bn.
8046	L/Sgt. BLUESTEIN, A.,	3/20th Bn.
5989	Pte. BROWN, M.	
282842	Pte. BLOCK, M.,	1st Bn.
158409	Rfm. BERGARD, A. V.,	5th Bn.
315129	Pte. BERMAN, S.,	5th Bn.
57911	Pte. BAILECK, M.,	5th Bn.
348162	L/Cpl. BUIRSKI, J.,	6th Bn.
935783	Gnr. BALCON, R.,	3/3rd Bn.
5954	Rfm. BARNETT, B.,	12th Bn.
2901	Cyc. BEARMAN, I.,	2/25th Bn.
	Sig. BEAUMONT, G. S.,	1/1st Bn.
615572	Pte. BENEVITZ, B.,	1/19th Bn.
45457	Rfm. BLACK, B.,	1/18th Bn.
494071	Pte. BROWN, S.,	1/13th Bn.

London Regt.—*Continued.*

30450	Pte. BERBALOFF, 29th Bn.	
4152	Pte. BURNS, R., 29th Bn.	
683768	L/Cpl. BEAGLE, T. 22nd Bn.	
615654	Pte. BOURNISH, B., 3/19th Bn.	
822097	Pte. BERNSTEIN, H., 31st Bn.	
822150	Pte. BERNARD, H., 31st Bn.	
822179	Pte. BLOND, H., 31st Bn.	
1664	Pte. BLUCHER, M., 31st Bn.	
525273	Pte. BERNSTEIN, B., 3/15th Bn.	
9096	Pte. BOGARD, I., 3/th Bn.	
42466	Pte. BLUMENKRANTZ, G., 13th Bn.	
45457	Rfm. BLACK, B., 18th Bn.	
452953	Rfm. BROWN, L., 2/11th Bn.	
27172	Rfm. BETH, H., 2/17th Bn.	
574540	Rfm. BROOKMARSH, G., 3/17th Bn.	
614183	Rfm. BALL, E., 2/19th Bn.	
535542	Rfm. BERNSTEIN, S., 15th Bn.	
577113	Rfm. BRANDON, S.	
	Pte. BRESLAU, M., 17th Bn.	
6382	Pte. BONSTROF, S., 4th Bn.	
633856	Pte. BENNETT, I., 2/29th Bn.	
383706	Cpl. BEARMAN, M., 2/4th Bn.	
39475	Pte. BISBERG, C., 23rd Bn.	
548059	Pte. BENJAMIN, 15th Bn.	
38085	Pte. BENGNIAT, P. J., 8th Bn.	
353704	Pte. BLACKER, B., 2/7th Bn.	
614200	Pte. BENNETT, H. S., 19th Bn.	
7419	Pte. BURCAN, 1/25th Bn.	
703945	Pte. BERNSTEIN, J., 2/20th Bn.	
5688	Rfm. BLOOM, I. H.	
6820	Rfm. BENNETT, P., 9th Bn.	
4082	Rfm. BORNE, A. 3rd Bn.	
	Rfm. BLUCHER, W., 6th Bn.	
8246	Rfm. BEAR, S., 6th Bn.	
9/6915	Rfm. BLUMENTHAL, H., 9th Bn.	
12/5204	Rfm. BURNE, L., 9th Bn.	
25/3958	Pte. BATTON, S., 10th Bn.	
10/14527	Pte. BEDER, M., 10th Bn.	
5151	Rfm. BERNSTEIN, E., 10th Bn.	
8293	Rfm. BARON, M., 17th Bn.	
324292	Rfm. BELOFEKI, S., 6th Bn.	
422389	Pte. BERGER, B., 10th Bn.	
614293	Pte. BERMAN, P., 19th Bn.	
425856	Pte. BILLING, I., 10th Bn.	
625101	Pte. BARNES, L., 19th Bn.	
G/72205	Pte. BERG, A. A., 1st Bn.	
5722	L/Cpl. BARNETT, H.,* 2/4th Bn.	
2002	Rfm. BENJAMIN, P.,* 17th Bn.	
4748	Pte. BLOOM, J.,* 2/4th Bn.	
523486	Rfm. BENTLEY, J.,* (M.M.), 6th Bn.	
3194	L./Sgt. BENTLEY, H., 2/24th Bn.	
5957	Pte. BERNARD, M., 1/1st Bn.	
5636	Pte. BROWN, A., 1/3rd Bn.	
7505	Pte. BERMAN, M., 1/4th Bn.	
6397	Pte. BARNETT, F., 1/4th Bn.	
6401	Pte. BAKER, M., 1/4th Bn.	
1799	Pte. BLOOM, L., 1/4th Bn.	
5949	Pte. BROWN, M., 1/4th Bn.	
7654	Rfm. BARNETT, M.,* 1/12th Bn.	
472596	Rfm. BARNETT, B.,* 1/12th Bn.	
8026	Pte. BREWER, H., 1/2nd Bn.	
3699	Cpl. BERNSTEIN, A., 1/5th Bn.	
1752	Pte. BLOCK, R., 1/2nd Bn.	
315129	Rfm. BERMAN, B., 1/5th Bn.	
393106	Rfm. BERNSTEIN, C. N.,* 9th Bn.	
565099	Rfm. BRAER, A.,* 1/16th Bn.	
204305	Pte. BARNETT, S.,* 2/1st Bn.	
253569	Cpl. BERNSTEIN, L., 2/3rd Bn.	
5722	L/Cpl. BARNETT, H.,* 2/4th Bn.	
4748	Pte. BLOOM, J.,* 2/4th Bn.	
6916	Rfm. BERLIN, I. J., 2/6th Bn.	
6784	Rfm. BLACKMAN, A., 2/6th Bn.	
3246	Rfm. BARNETT, A., 2/6th Bn.	
6003	Pte. BARNETT, H., 2/7th Bn.	
3255	Rfm. BIRNSTINGL, C. D., 2/9th Bn.	
4462	Pte. BERG, S., 2/10th Bn.	
4463	Pte. BLOOMBERG, J., 2/10th Bn.	
741804	Pte. BEDER, M., 2/10th Bn.	
7379	Pte. BELL, S., 2/10th Bn.	
5047	L./Cpl. BOSS, A. E., 2/11th Bn.	
6303	Rfm. BARKMAN, C. B., 2/11th Bn.	
452180	Rfm. BARNETT, M.,* 2/11th Bn.	
6899	Rfm. BROWN, L., 2/11th Bn.	
322804	Rfm. BELL, I.,* 1/6th Bn.	
5921	Pte. BARNETT, G., 1/15th Bn.	
6671	Rfm. BANUS, H., 1/17th Bn.	
592426	Rfm. BETH, J., 1/18th Bn.	
8667	Rfm. BAZINSKI, S.,* 1/21st Bn.	
653560	Rfm. BISHOP, M., 1/21st Bn.	
305721	Pte. BENJAMIN, J., 1/15th Bn.	
678045	Rfm. BROWN, L., 1/21st Bn.	
653852	Rfm. BENJAMIN, C., 1/21st Bn.	
678049	Rfm. BARKMAN, C.,* 1/21st Bn.	
702371	Pte. BUITEKANT, M., 1/23rd Bn.	
208033	Pte. BERGER, J., 1/24th Bn.	
47075	Rfm. BERNARD, L., 1/17th Bn.	
225508	Pte. BLUM, E., 2/1st Bn.	
324270	Rfm. BLAIN, R., 2/6th Bn.	
423034	Pte. BROOKS, H., 2/10th Bn.	
283165	Pte. BERGMAN, H., 1/1st Bn.	
203522	L./Cpl. BERG, F. R., 1/2nd Bn.	
623486	Rfm. BENTLEY, J., 1/6th Bn.	
6537	Pte. BERGMAN, S., 1/28th Bn.	
2424	L./Sgt. BOLASCO, S., 1/17th Bn.	
2933	C.S.M. BITTON, B. (M.M.), 1/6th Bn.	
2153	Pte. BURROWS, G., 1/7th Bn.	
3036	Rfm. BEAGLE, S., 1/17th Bn.	
2002	Rfm. BENJAMIN, P.,* 1/17th Bn.	
1493	Cpl. BLOM, H., 1/17th Bn.	
2623	Pte. BYRNE, A. M., 1/23rd Bn.	
6043	Pte. BIRNBAUM, M.,* 15th Bn.	
5921	Pte. BARNETT, G., 1/15th Bn.	
611863	Pte. BARZOLOI, L.,* 1/19th Bn.	
6471	Pte. BLUMENTHAL, H., 1/13th Bn.	

London Regt.—*Continued.*

2926	Pte. BRAHAM, C.,*	1/1st Bn.
2318	Pte. BARTLETT, S.,	1/4th Bn.
2400	Pte. BASS, A.,	1/4th Bn.
4656	Pte. BLUSTIN, J. A.,*	4th Bn.
280174	Cpl. BERNSTOCK, J. H.,	1/4th Bn.
2489	Rfm. BENJAMIN, N.,	1/13th Bn.
7007	L/Cpl. BEARMAN, L.,	1/9th Bn.
5674	Rfm. BENJAMIN, E.,	1/16th Bn.
2502	L./Cpl. BROADY, A.,	2/13th Bn.
3227	Pte. BRILLIANT, N. M.,	2/15th Bn.
4965	Pte. BROWN, A.,	2/15th Bn.
5676	Pte. BERG, J. G.,	2/15th Bn.
550719	L/Sgt. BERNSTEIN, P. V.,	2/16th Bn.
4658	Rfm. BERG, A.,	2/16th Bn.
1392	Rfm. BALL, H. J.,	2/17th Bn.
2872	Rfm. BENSON, R. C.,	2/17th Bn.
4294	Rfm. BROWN, R.,	2/18th Bn.
2570	Pte. BRAHAM, J. H.,	2/20th Bn.
7034	Pte. BARNARD, H. D.,	2/22nd Bn.
4477	Pte. BRILLESLIPER, S.,	1/22nd Bn.
4534	Pte. BENARD, A.,	1/22nd Bn.
5699	Pte. BARNETT, A.,	3/15th Bn.
2390	Pte. BELL, H.,	1/4th Bn.
2230	Pte. BLACK, H.,	1/2nd Bn.
556827	Rfm. BOSS, N.,*	1/16th Bn.
1445	Pte. BAKER, S.,	1/4th Bn.
6513	Rfm. BELOVITZ, S.,	1/17th Bn.
6987	Pte. BRODY, S.,	1/7th Bn.
472385	Rfm. BROWN, H.,*	12th Bn.
6053	Pte. BLUESTEIN, I.,	1/2nd Bn.
634130	Pte. BOSY, H.,	1/20th Bn.
574684	Rfm. BARNETT, E.,	1/17th Bn.
741980	Pte. BENDON,	1/25th Bn.
545273	Pte. BERNSTEIN, B.,	3/15th Bn.
592374	Rfm. BERGY,	1/18th Bn.
615654	Pte. BOWRUSH, B.,	1/19th Bn.
698131	Pte. BENSUSAN, R.,	1/22nd Bn.
81245	Pte. BERNSTOFF, S.,	2/4th Bn.
5602	Rfm. BARNETT, J.,	1/17th Bn.
6731	Pte. BEBBER,	2/11th Bn.
5633	Pte. BURMAN, J.,	2/10th Bn.
6419	Pte. BUSHKOS, A.,	2/10th Bn.
6890	Pte. BERMEL, D.,	1/3rd Bn.
4/6628	Pte. BROOKMAN, S.,	1/3rd Bn.
10411	Pte. BENEDICTUS, J. H.,	1/28th Bn.
61965	Rfm. BENJAMIN, E.,	8th Res. Bn.
125071	Pte. BEER, M.,	8th Reserve Bn.
39034	Pte. BENJAMIN,	3rd Reserve Bn.
494071	Pte. BROWN, S.,	1/13th Bn.
202361	Pte. BALHAM, W.,	1/1st Bn.
2336	Rfm. COHEN, C. E.,	1/9th Bn.
2216	Rfm. COHEN, B. H.,	1/9th Bn.
2765	Rfm. COSHER, W.,	1/6th Bn.
3054	Rfm. COHEN, D.,	1/17th Bn.
2142	L/Cpl. COHEN, J.* (M.M.),	1/17th Bn.
2731	Pte. CONSTABLE, A.,	1/24th Bn.
2787	Rfm. COLE, M.,	1/6th Bn.
4249	Rfm. CROOK, A.,*	16th Bn.
5106	Pte. COHEN, M.,	1/7th Bn.
4607	Pte. CHARING, J.,	1/7th Bn.
5462	Pte. COOPER, M.,	1/6th Bn.
4583	Pte. CUSHNER, J.,	1/6th Bn.
5300	Pte. COHEN, W.,	1/6th Bn.
5376	Pte. COHEN, L.,	1/19th Bn.
5564	Pte. COHEN, M.,	1/21st Bn.
5006	Pte. COLSTER, A.,	1/22nd Bn.
5304	Pte. COHEN, M.,	1/19th Bn.
5363	Pte. COHEN, P.,	1/22nd Bn.
5956	Pte. COHEN, A.,	1/13th Bn.
5931	Pte. COHEN, H.,	1/13th Bn.
1985	Pte. CHART, B.,*	1/4th Bn.
1839	Pte. COHEN, J.,	1/4th Bn.
2635	Pte. CROOK, S.,*	1/4th Bn.
6394	Pte. COHEN, A.,	1/4th Bn.
5613	Rfm. COHEN, M.,	1/22nd Bn.
6177	Rfm. CAHN, R. J.,	1/16th Bn.
5660	Pte. COPLANS, S. H.	2/13th Bn.
5440	Pte. COHEN, M.,	2/16th Bn.
4784	Rfm. COHEN, L.,	2/16th Bn.
5662	Pte. CARO, M.,*	2/13th Bn.
7068	Rfm. COHEN, A.,	2/18th Bn.
7093	Pte. COHEN, J.,	2/22nd Bn.
3227	Rfm. COHEN, I. R.,	1/12th Bn.
474343	Rfm. COLLINS, D.,	1/12th Bn.
2703	Pte. COHEN, S.,	1/13th Bn.
493113	Pte. CHALFEN, J.,*	1/13th Bn.
8177	Rfm. COHEN, M.,	1/12th Bn.
8176	Rfm. CASHSTEIN, J.,	1/12th Bn.
6549	Pte. COHEN, J.,	1/2nd Bn.
6039	Pte. COHEN, S. B.,*	1/2nd Bn.
7138	Rfm. COHEN, H.,	1/9th Bn.
303264	Rfm. CAPALOFSKY, A.,	1/5th Bn.
472220	Pte. COLLINS, A.,	1/9th Bn.
39396	Pte. CORNICK, J.,	1/9th Bn.
8805	Rfm. CONN, L.,	1/16th Bn.
865001	Rfm. COHEN, R. W.,	1/16th Bn.
9006	Pte. COHEN, E.,	2/1st Bn.
9066	Pte. COHEN, L.,	2/1st Bn.
5691	Pte. COHEN, M.,*	2/2nd Bn.
8287	Pte. CLARK, W. J.,	2/2nd Bn.
8353	Pte. COHEN, R. L.,	2/2nd Bn.
4100	Pte. COHEN, L.,*	2/2nd Bn.
8107	Pte. COHEN, J.,	2/3rd Bn.
252426	Pte. COHEN, B.,*	2/3rd Bn.
4251	Rfm. COHEN, L.,	2/5th Bn.
6763	Rfm. COHEN, E. (M.M.),	2/6th Bn.
4120	Rfm. COHEN, L.,*	2/9th Bn.
223048	L/Cpl. COHEN, J.,*	2nd Bn.
8254	Pte. COWEN, M. M.,	1/7th Bn.
8252	Pte. COHEN, M.,	1/7th Bn.
5783	Rfm. COHEN, E.,	1/17th Bn.
573511	Rfm. COHEN, Z.,	1/17th Bn.
5405	Pte. COHEN, H.,	1/20th Bn.

London Regt.—*Continued.*

4887	L/Cpl. COHEN, S., 1/21st Bn.
3116	Pte. COHEN, C., 1/22nd Bn.
4759	Pte. COHEN, J., 1/23rd Bn.
204946	Pte. COHEN, L., 1/15th Bn.
614298	Rfm. COHEN, I., 1/19th Bn.
322588	Pte. CATS, L. V.,* 1/23rd Bn.
718318	Pte. COHEN, A., 1/23rd Bn.
203246	Cpl. COHEN, D.,* 2/1st Bn.
821405	Rfm. COOPER, S., 2/11th Bn.
424077	Pte. COHEN, L., 2/10th Bn.
88880	Pte. CANTOR, I., 2/2nd Bn.
423003	Sig. COLEMAN, M., 2/10th Bn.
468011	Rfm. COOPER, S., 2/11th Bn.
704506	Pte. COHEN, M., 2/23rd Bn.
533720	Pte. COHEN, A., 2/15th Bn.
881641	Rfm. COHEN, 1/34th Bn.
9983	Pte. CLARK, W., 1/28th Bn.
5689	Rfm. COHEN, G., 1/9th Bn.
4393	Rfm. COHEN, G., 1/22nd Bn.
4484	Pte. CARTER, J., 1/22nd Bn.
4474	Pte. COHEN, B., 1/22nd Bn.
6352	Pte. COOPER, D., 3/20th Bn.
4393	Pte. COHEN, J., 1/22nd Bn.
4291	Rfm. COOPMAN, H., 1/1st Bn.
4197	Rfm. CLAFF, N., 1/1st Bn.
4183	Rfm. COHEN, A. J., 1/1st Bn.
938	Sgt. COHEN, D. H., 1/9th Bn.
2330	Pte. COHEN, H., 1/4th Bn.
1839	Pte. COHEN, J., 1/4th Bn.
245067	Pte. CROWN, S., 2/2nd Bn.
820405	Rfm. COHEN, J. H., 1/16th Bn.
281979	Pte. COHEN, D., 1/4th Bn.
532630	Pte. CAMRASS, E.,* 1/15th Bn.
615663	Pte. COHEN, M.,* 1/19th Bn.
45425	Rfm. CHYTE, H., 1/18th Bn.
225012	Pte. COHEN, M. G., 1/1st Bn.
374467	Rfm. COHEN, R. W., 1/8th Bn.
683581	Pte. COHEN, F., 2/22nd Bn.
4768	Pte. COLE, A., 1/10th Bn.
574162	Rfm. COHEN, H., 1/17th Bn.
5269	Pte. COOPER, S., 1/7th Bn.
4472	Pte. CRISTOL, J., 1/1st Bn.
3741	Pte. COHEN, L., 1/22nd Bn.
324022	Rfm. COHEN, A., 1/6th Bn.
323653	Rfm. COHEN, E., 1/6th Bn.
5635	Pte. CARTZ, L., 2/10th Bn.
5661	Pte. COHEN, L., 2/10th Bn.
4/6381	Pte. COHEN, A. S., 1/3rd Bn.
4/5587	Pte. COHEN, H., 1/3rd Bn.
1849	Pte. CASHMAN, M., 1/3rd Bn.
2330	Pte. COHEN, H., 1/3rd Bn.
10191	Pte. COWAN, A., 1/28th Bn.
13873	Pte. COHEN, 1/3rd Res. Bn.
	Rfm. COHEN, P., 1/10th Bn.
	Rfm. COHEN, R., 1/12th Bn.
2818	Rfm. COHEN, S., 1/16th Bn.
472437	Rfm. CATES, A.,* 1/12th Bn.
6728	Rfm. COHEN, A.,* 17th Bn.
6310	Pte. COHEN, S.,* 13th Bn.
302535	Rfm. COHEN, L., 5th Bn.
140411	Rfm. COHEN, L., 8th Bn.
426440	Pte. COLLINS, D. G., 10th Bn.
G/96382	Pte. CLIFF, M., 19th Bn.
R/48117	Rfm. COHEN, J., 6th Bn.
318333	Rfm. COHEN, H., 5th Bn.
329725	Pte. COHEN, R. J., 1st Bn.
5775	Pte. COHEN, L., 2/2nd Bn.
5423	Pte. COHEN, B., 2/3rd Bn.
56661	Pte. COHEN, L., 2/10th Bn.
537533	Pte. CIVVAL, J.
537677	Rfm. COLEMAN, H.
3352	C.S.M. CARMELL, J. R., 20th Bn.
6352	Pte. COOPER, D., 20th Bn.
5024	Pte. CALO, A., 13th Bn.
5861	Pte. CARTER, F., 20th Bn.
4525	Pte. CHAPMAN, A. A., 28th Bn.
6824	Pte. CHAPLIN, D., 2nd Bn.
3948	Pte. CHARRIGE, S., 3/10th Bn.
3642	Pte. CLAPPISH, P., 10th Bn.
3372	Pte. CLARK, J., 3/6th Bn.
456303	Pte. COHEN, A., 3/7th Bn.
6027	Pte. COHEN, E., 4/2nd Bn.
4783	Pte. COHEN, E., 7th Bn.
4885	Pte. COHEN, H., 7th Bn.
4020	Pte. COHEN, H. R., 3/6th Bn.
3911	Pte. COHEN, I., 3/3rd Bn.
615813	Pte. COHEN, L., 3/19th Bn.
780494	Pte. COHEN, H., 29th Bn.
781516	Pte. COHEN, M., 29th Bn.
801446	Pte. COHEN, L., 30th Bn.
801497	Pte. COFFER, D., 30th Bn.
613997	Pte. CHARING, J. S., 2/19th Bn.
5738	Pte. COHEN, D., 30th Bn.
G/23551	Pte. CLEMENTS, J., 29th Bn.
12148	Pte. COHEN, H.
766855	Pte. COOPMAN, L. B., 2/28th Bn.
295367	Pte. COHEN, J., 2/4th Bn.
253970	Pte. CANTOR, W., 3rd Bn.
253969	Pte. CANTOR, S. B., 3rd Bn.
534597	Pte. COSTA, A., 26th Bn.
392228	Pte. COHEN, G., 9th Bn.
254175	Pte. COHEN, H., 3rd Bn.
280272	Pte. COHEN, C., 3rd Bn.
2669	Pte. COHEN, D., 1/4th Bn.
574778	Pte. CORB, I., 17th Bn.
592287	Pte. COHEN, P., 2/18th Bn.
703556	Pte. COHEN, M., 2/23rd Bn.
492921	Pte. COHEN, L. W., 2/13th Bn.
252426	Pte. COHEN, B., 2/4th Bn.
470823	Pte. COHEN, R., 12th Bn.
3492	Pte. COHEN, J., 17th Bn.
1499	Pte. COHEN, L., 7th Bn.
4394	Pte. COHEN, P., 3/2nd Bn.
5030	Pte. COHEN, W., 7th Bn.

London Regt.—*Continued.*

6690	Pte. COHEN, Z., 17th Bn.		492921	Pte. COHEN, L. W., 2/13th Bn.
2375	Pte. COMER, H., 4/4th Bn.		42555	Cpl. CRAVAT, H., 8th Bn.
5988	Pte. CAPLANS, 28th Bn.		535488	Pte. COSTA, J. J., 15th Bn.
2999	Pte. CORNBLAT, S., 4/1st Bn.		36704	Pte. CRABB, M., 2/20th Bn.
19116	Pte. COSTA, H., 20th Bn.		614409	Pte. COHEN, E. L., 1/19th Bn.
3546	Pte. COWAN, N., 3/1st Bn.		26872	Pte. COHEN, H., 29th Bn.
4472	Pte. CRISTOL, J., 4/1st Bn.		6112	Pte. COHEN, H., 29th Bn.
2601	Pte. CRAVETY, M., 11th Bn.		741995	Pte. COHEN, 1/25th Bn.
4350	Pte. CROSS, I., 2/3rd Bn.		574162	Rfm. COHEN, H., 2/17th Bn.
35644	Pte. CAPLIN, A., 7th Bn.		533720	Pte. COHEN, A., 2/15th Bn.
7003	Pte. CHARRY, S., 1/20th Bn.		683966	Pte. COHEN, J., 2/22nd Bn.
4097	Pte. COHEN, J.		2/6043	Rfm. COLE, M., 1st Bn.
6552	Pte. COHEN, W., Q.W.R.		2/5406	Pte. CANTER, H. J., 1st Bn.
551918	Pte. COHEN, L., 2/10th Bn.		4098	Rfm. CUTNER, B., 3rd Bn.
322529	Pte. COHEN, J., 6th Bn.		5600	Rfm. COHEN, H., 3rd Bn.
49294	Pte. COHEN, L. W., 2/13th Bn.		8249	Pte. COHEN, A., 6th Bn.
633619	Pte. CRASSOFF, A. M.		6470	Pte. COHEN, H., 7th Bn.
574606	Rfm. COHEN, J., 17th Bn.		8277	Pte. COHEN, H., 8th Bn.
53548	Pte. COSTA, J. J., 15th Bn.		8282	Rfm. CUTLER, M., 8th Bn.
597473	Rfm. CLAYTON, M., 3/17th Bn.		12/3227	Rfm. COHEN, R., Q.V.R.
280513	Pte. COHEN, A., 3rd Bn.		12/6169	Rfm. COHEN, D., Q.V.R.
11585	Pte. CONNECK, M., 20th Bn.		6546	Pte. COOPER, H., 3/19th Bn.
551501	Pte. CLAPPER, W., 14th Bn.		5956	Pte. COHEN, A., 13th Bn.
573934	Pte. COHEN, M., 17th Bn.		6728	Rfm. COHEN, A., 17th Bn.
683168	Pte. COHEN, W., 22nd Bn.		493113	Pte. CHALFEN, J.,* 13th Bn.
17433	Pte. COHEN, W., 22nd Bn.		576508	Rfm. COHEN, L., 17th Bn.
374227	Rfm. COHEN, H.		24507	Rfm. CROWN, S. S., 2/2nd Bn.
7139	Rfm. COSTA, H., 8th Bn.		474341	Rfm. COSHSTEIN, J., 1/12th Bn.
225012	Pte. COHEN, M. G., 1st Bn.		681268	Pte. COHEN, C., 1/22nd Bn.
4461	L/Cpl. CROWSON, J., 13th Bn.		678064	Rfm. COOPER, S., 1/21st Bn.
424077	Pte. COHEN, L., 10th Bn.		515501	Rfm. CLAPPER, B.
614409	Pte. COHEN, E. J., 19th Bn.		393352	Rfm. COHEN, H., 1/5th Bn.
574573	Pte. CHAYTOW, M., 17th Bn.		81268	Pte. COHEN, C., 1/28th Bn.
253568	Pte. COHEN, J.		82715	Pte. COHEN, S., 2/2nd Bn.
1985	Sig. CHART, B., 1/4th Bn.		29146	Pte. COHEN, L., 23rd Bn.
632485	Pte. COHEN, H., 20th Bn.		88429	Pte. CLAPHAM, D., 30th Bn.
3227	Pte. COHEN, R. I., 1/12th Bn.		354370	Pte. COHEN, M., 1/7th Bn.
25125	Pte. COHEN, M., 4/7th Bn.		5030	Pte. COHEN, G., 7th Bn.
203246	Cpl. COHEN, D., 2nd Bn.		474342	Rfm. COHEN, M., 1/12th Bn.
782222	Pte. COHEN, D., 29th Bn.		200569	Rfm. COHEN, S., 1st Bn.
474342	Pte. COHEN, M., 1/12th Bn.		2703	Rfm. COHEN, 13th Bn.
163405	Pte. COHEN, L., 32nd Bn.		6075	Rfm. COHEN, L. W., 2/13th Bn.
233755	Pte. COHEN, R., 2/2nd Bn.		574416	L/Cpl. COHEN, A., 1/17th Bn.
533728	Pte. COHEN, A., 2/15th Bn.		5688	Pte. COHEN, H., 5th Bn.
703536	Pte. COHEN, M., 2/23rd Bn.		3227	Pte. COHEN, J. R.
611922	Pte. COHEN, L., 19th Bn.		5691	Pte. COHEN, M.,* 2/2nd Bn.
374227	Rfm. COHEN, H., 8th Bn.		253709	Pte. CLEVE, M.,* 3rd Bn.
354372	L/Cpl. COWAN, M. M.		1985	Pte. CHART, B.,* 4th Bn.
2934	L/Cpl. CHISSICK, S., 1/11th Bn.		252426	Pte. COHEN, B.,* 2/3rd Bn.
6546	Pte. COOPER, H., 19th Bn.		203246	Cpl. COHEN, D.,* 2nd Bn.
254797	Pte. CRUGMAN, B.		2142	L/Cpl. COHEN, J.,* 17th Bn.
318533	Rfm. COHEN, H., 5th Bn.		2635	Pte. CROOK, S.,* 4th Bn.
766591	Pte. COHEN, A. H., 28th Bn.		370132	Q.M.S. DEFRIEND, M., 1/17th Bn.
652077	Rfm. COHEN, S., 21st Bn.		2237	Rfm. DAVIS, M., 1/17th Bn.
426550	Pte. COOKSON, J.		4180	Rfm. DAVID, J.,* 1/16th Bn.
				Rfm. DANIN, E., 1/6th Bn.
50679	Rfm. COHEN, A. E., 5th Bn.		5379	L./Cpl. DRUCKER, E., 1/15th Bn.
651919	Pte. COHEN, N. M., 2/21st Bn.		4693	Rfm. DE GROOT, B., 1/6th Bn.

London Regt.—*Continued.*

1933	Pte. DEFRIES, G., 1/17th Bn.
3124	Pte. DE SOLLA, G., 1/3rd Bn.
1905	Pte. DAVIS, C., 1/4th Bn.
5994	Pte. DIAS, L., 1/4th Bn.
3962	L/Cpl. DRUKKER, J. B., 1/16th Bn.
4724	Rfm. DAVIS, E., 2/21st Bn.
5997	Pte. DE KEYSER, A., 2/13th Bn.
203876	Pte. DAVIS, S., 1/1st Bn.
282873	Pte. DAVIES, B.,* 1/4th Bn.
5575	Rfm. DAVIS, J., 1/12th Bn.
452575	Pte. DEMBINA, J., 1/13th Bn.
505090	Pte. DAVIS, D. K.,* 13th Bn.
9362	Sgt. DAVIS, K. J., 1/5th Bn.
631	Rfm. DAVISON, J., 2/6th Bn.
423062	Pte. DAVIS, M.,* 2/10th Bn.
453048	Rfm. DOBKIN, J.,* 2/11th Bn.
5038	Rfm. DAVIS, G., 2/12th Bn.
8019	Rfm. DEMBENSKI, A., 1/17th Bn.
472439	Pte. DAVIES, J., 1/15th Bn.
6454	Rfm. DROBNER, A., 1/17th Bn.
1777	Pte. DEVINE, G., 1/20th Bn.
23268	L/Cpl. DE SOLLA, B. B., 2/2nd Bn.
7072	Rfm. DE WOLF, F., 1/8th Bn.
245238	Pte. DRIMAN, L., 1/2nd Bn.
64877	Pte. DAINOW, G.,* 2/4th Bn.
375185	Rfm. DAVIS, D., 2/8th Bn.
760221	Cpl. DAVIS, C., 1/28th Bn.
760338	Pte. DAVIDSON, E. H. L.,* 1/28th Bn.
4499	Pte. DAVIS, M., 1/22nd Bn.
4497	Pte. DAUM, J., 1/22nd Bn.
5606	Pte. DANCYGER, M., 3/15th Bn.
5412	Pte. DAVIS, S., 1/19th Bn.
63471	Pte. DAINOW, D., 3/20th Bn.
1140	Pte. DEVEREUX, C., 1/28th Bn.
4565	Pte. DEHAAN, J., 1/22nd Bn.
423828	Pte. DAVIES, J. H., 1/8th Bn.
492787	Pte. DAVIS, 1/13th Bn.
741999	Pte. DAVIES, 1/25th Bn.
742000	Pte. DAVIS, S., 1/25th Bn.
741999	Pte. DAVIS, I., 1/25th Bn.
231481	Pte. DOMBERG, F., 1/4th Bn.
573525	Pte. DAVIS, B., 1/8th Bn.
8119	Pte. DELMONTE, J., 1/3rd Bn.
67248	Pte. DEMBOSKI, S., 1/1st Res. Bn.
115002	Pte. DEFRIES, B., 1/3rd Bn.
6997	L/Cpl. DELTONZ, M., 3/20th Bn.
495582	Pte. DELOW, M., 13th Bn.
5275	Rfm. DE LIEW, A., 1/5th Bn.
425475	Rfm. DIAMOND, B., 10th Bn.
5146	Rfm. DAVIS, 3/17th Bn.
453048	Rfm. DOBKIN, H.
20445	Rfm. DAVIES, H., 1st Bn.
354830	Rfm. DRIVER, 7th Bn.
394578	Rfm. DE SAXE, M., 9th Bn.
5991	Rfm. DAVIS, B., 4th Bn.
655745	Rfm. DAVIS, J., 21st Bn.
801251	Rfm. DAVIS, A., 30th Bn.
282949	Rfm. DE FRESNEY, A., 1/4th Bn.
612022	Rfm. DAVIS, N., 2/19th Bn.
630422	Pte. DIVINE, G., 2/20th Bn.
472439	Rfm. DAVIS, J.
472063	Pte. DAVIS, G., 2/12th Bn.
556677	Pte. DRUSKIN, S., 17th Bn.
5038	Pte. DAVIES, J., 2/13th Bn.
4350	Pte. DAVIS, G., 2/7th Bn.
5921	L/Cpl. DAVIS, M., 13th Bn.
5523	Pte. DE LOLLIO, M., 2/19th Bn.
324416	Pte. DAVIS, J., 6th Bn.
322159	Pte. DAVIS, H., 6th Bn.
633648	L/Cpl. DEITZ, M., 20th Bn.
	Pte. DIAMONDSTEIN, A., 10th Bn.
	Pte. DANIELS, 7th Bn.
	L/Cpl. DAVEY, D., 11th Bn.
	Rfm. DAVID, F., 16th Bn.
	Rfm. DUPARC, H., 16th Bn.
763927	Pte. DEFRIES, D., 1st Bn.
576999	Rfm. DIAMOND, A.
769182	Pte. DAVAN, C. W., 28th Bn.
616162	Pte. DIAMOND, H.
472063	Pte. DAVIS, G.
493054	Pte. DAVIS, A., 2/13th Bn.
492852	Pte. DE KEYSER, A., 2/13th Bn.
424055	Pte. DE SOLLA, A., 1/10th Bn.
4724	Pte. DAVIES, E., 2/21st Bn.
238592	Cpl. DE GROOTS, D., 58th Bn.
860991	Rfm. DAVIS, A., 33rd Bn.
3180	Pte. DREYFUSS, H. W., 2nd Q.V.R.
2/6979	Pte. DRAGOVITCH, R., 1st Bn.
5938	Rfm. DAVIS, J., 6th Bn.
4889	L/Cpl. DAVIS, H., 6th Bn.
1717	Rfm. DANIM, E., 6th Bn.
6947	Pte. DOVAN, J., 7th Bn.
12/5523	Rfm. DE WILDS, M., Q.V.R.
6707	Rfm. DAVIS, B., 17th Bn.
306755	Rfm. DAVIS, C. M., 5th Bn.
228166	Cpl. DAVIS, P. A., 1st Bn.
8910	Pte. DAVIS, H., 2/1st Bn.
6723	Pte. DECARTE, W.
594419	Rfm. DE MESQUITA, J. B., 1/18th Bn.
5570	Pte. DAVIS, N., 1/19th Bn.
7161	Pte. DAVIS, H., 1/4th Bn.
5724	Rfm. DAVIES, J., 12th Bn.
7076	Pte. DE KOVNICK, A., 19th Bn.
3861	Rfm. DAVIS, D., 5th Bn.
7310	Col./Sgt. DAVIS, R. G., 29th Bn.
613798	Pte. DAVIS, C. S., 19th Bn.
780359	Pte. DAVIS, A. A., 29th Bn.
801359	Pte. DAVIS, B., 30th Bn.
4786	Pte. DAVIS, A., 29th Bn.
301251	Pte. DAVIS, A., 30th Bn.
574571	Pte. DEUTCH, D., 17th Bn.
8074	Pte. DEGTAI, M., 3/20th Bn.
5994	Pte. DIAS, L., 4th Bn.
203870	Pte. DAVIS, S.
570375	Rfm. DEFRIES, S., 17th Bn.

London Regt.—*Continued.*

324416	Rfm. DAVIS, J., 6th Bn.
375185	Pte. DAVIS, D., 2/8th Bn.
231481	Pte. DOMBERG, F., 4th Bn.
5724	Rfm. DAVIES, I., 1/12th Bn.
5759	Rfm. DE FRIEND, L., 17th Bn.
4565	Pte. DE HAAN, J., 22nd Bn.
5563	Pte. EDELSTEIN, A., 1/17th Bn.
468	Pte. EMDEN, H., 1/3rd Bn.
5947	Pte. ERIERA, J., 1/4th Bn.
513770	Pte. EPRILE, C. J., 1/14th Bn.
5203	Rfm. EHRENBERG, J.,* 2/6th Bn.
5368	Pte. EISEN, D., 3/19th Bn.
4532	Pte. ELBOZ, J., 1/21st Bn.
425463	Rfm. ERIERA, A., 2/10th Bn.
8408	Rfm. ERLINSKY, 1/9th Bn.
740461	Pte. ELKAM, 1/25th Bn.
	Pte. EZRA, J. M., 1/19th Bn.
2150	Pte. EDWARDS, R.,* 24th Bn.
8771	Pte. ELLIS, A. A., 29th Bn.
9/6513	Rfm. EHRENBAUM, L. J., Q.V.R.
B/96547	Pte. EPSTEIN, M., 19th Bn.
	Sgt. EHRLICK, M., 3rd Bn.
G/19965	Pte. EPSTEIN, Z., 20th Bn.
1144	Pte. ERAD, S., 4th Bn.
6978	Pte. EISSENSTADT, H., 3/20th Bn.
615724	Pte. EDELMAN, M., 3/19th Bn.
392429	Rfm. EMANUEL, M., 1/9th Bn.
202362	Sgt. EMDEN, J., 1st Bn.
3047	Rfm. EAGLE, N., 15th Bn.
3319	Rfm. EDELMAN, I., 3/6th Bn.
2071	Rfm. ELIAS, A., 3/3rd Bn.
5164	Rfm. ENDERCOTT, F., 3/17th Bn.
	Rfm. ENOCH, D., 11th Bn.
	Cpl. ELLEN, S., 17th Bn.
	Rfm. EMANUEL, J., 7th Bn.
	Rfm. ELSTER, M., 7th Bn.
	Rfm. EMANUEL, H., 6th Bn.
3861	Rfm. FINN, J., 1/6th Bn.
4271	Pte. FOX, B.,* 1/15th Bn.
1736	Cpl. FRIEDLANDER, R., 1/7th Bn.
2268	Rfm. FRANKEL, F., 1/17th Bn.
1934	Rfm. FERN, J., 1/17th Bn.
4924	Pte. FAIRMAN, A., 1/4th Bn.
5973	Pte. FRANKLIN, H.,* 1/4th Bn.
2818	Rfm. FRASER, A.,* 1/5th Bn.
5899	Rfm. FURST, E.,* 1/9th Bn.
4158	Pte. FRAZER, H., 1/5th Bn.
2702	Pte. FERNANDEZ, B. H., 2/13th Bn.
7059	Rfm. FERSHT, J., 2/18th Bn.
5773	Pte. FIGOV, H., 2/24th Bn.
6858	Pte. FRANKS, B., 1/1st Bn.
6397	Pte. FELLER, B., 1/4th Bn.
5968	Sgt. FINKLE, B., 1/4th Bn.
	Cadet FRANKS, B., Artist Rifles.
7568	Pte. FOGELMAN, L.,* 1/4th Bn.
7124	Pte. FISHER, G., 1/4th Bn.
5944	Pte. FRANKS, M., 1/4th Bn.
5242	Rfm. FRESHFIELD, M. M., 1/12th Bn.
5108	Pte. FRIEDLANDER, M., 1/13th Bn.
514552	Pte. FOX, M., 1/14th Bn.
474352	Rfm. FRESCO, M.,* 1/12th Bn.
7460	Pte. FELTBROAT, H., 1/9th Bn.
3433	Rfm. FRIEDBERG, B., 1/16th Bn.
204325	Pte. FOREMAN, M.,* 2/1st Bn.
202842	Pte. FIRSHT, J.,* 2/1st Bn.
9032	Pte. FELLER, H. A., 2/1st Bn.
3722	Pte. FELLERMAN, C., 2/2nd Bn.
8318	Pte. FELTZER, J., 2/2nd Bn.
8345	Pte. FELD, A., 2/2nd Bn.
128680	Pte. FALK, L., 2/4th Bn.
282370	Pte. FRANKS, I.,* 2/4th Bn.
6994	Rfm. FISTAL, S., 2/6th Bn.
553936	Rfm. FORDER, M., 2/6th Bn.
5637	Pte. FREEDMAN, B., 2/10th Bn.
4315	Pte. FRANKS, S., 2/10th Bn.
4929	Rfm. FELDMAN, N., 2/11th Bn.
6450	Pte. FREELAND, M., 1/7th Bn.
354910	Pte. FEDER, M.,* 7th Bn.
4479	Pte. FISHER, M., 1/22nd Bn.
72281	Rfm. FISHTALL, M., 1/17th Bn.
36024	Rfm. FREEDMAN, M., 1/21st Bn.
G/37324	Pte. FORESTER, S., 1/23rd Bn.
415050	Cpl. FRANKLIN, M., 1/9th Bn.
415138	Rfm. FAUGH, H., 1/9th Bn.
40534	Rfm. FRIEDMAN, H.,* 1/9th Bn.
A/202171	Rfm. FREEMAN, J., 2/12th Bn.
280173	Pte. FAIRMAN, W., 1/4th Bn.
881047	Sgt. FLATAU, W. P., 1/34th Bn.
1840	Pte. FREEMAN, J., 1/1st Bn.
G/59534	Pte. FITZPATRICK, C., 2/19th Bn.
705202	Pte. FORREN, B., 1/23rd Bn.
5034	Pte. FINKLESTEIN, D., 1/23rd Bn.
6249	Pte. FISHMAN, J., 1/1st Bn.
6859	Pte. FEARD, A., 1/2nd Bn.
5977	Pte. FOREMAN, A., 1/3rd Bn.
5950	Pte. FOREMAN, J., 1/3rd Bn.
10233	Pte. FERMO, L., 1/28th Bn.
10234	Pte. FERMO, R., 1/28th Bn.
	Pte. FERNANDES, J., 1/17th Bn.
	Rfm. FINSBERG, A. H., 1/17th Bn.
702819	Sgt. FRIEDLANDER, C., 21st Bn.
61508	L/Cpl. FALCON, S.
574588	Pte. FREEDMAN, M., 17th Bn.
43046	Rfm. FREEDMAN, H., 12th Bn.
26894	Pte. FEINSTEIN, H., 3rd Bn.
	Pte. FOOTE, J., 4th Bn.
	Pte. FONSECA, P., 17th Bn.
26859	Pte. FORSTEEN, J., 29th Bn.
26895	Pte. FAGELSON, S., 29th Bn.
143012	Pte. FERN, A., 1/25th Bn.
4034	L/Sgt. FREEDMAN, L., 7th Bn.
6841	Pte. FELDMAN, I., 7th Bn.
6681	Rfm. FRANKEL, A., 8th Bn.
12/4206	Sgt. FRANKLIN, G., Q.V.R.
11/6207	Rfm. FAINLIGHT, A. P., Q.V.R.

London Regt.—*Continued.*

4144	Pte. Falk, A., 10th Bn.
6196	Rfm. Fleishman, J., 10th Bn.
R/46647	Rfm. Freedman, M., 6th Bn.
781880	Pte. Forstein, J., 1st Bn.
254434	Pte. Fisher, C., 1st Bn.
424281	Pte. Friedman, J., 10th Bn.
395189	Rfm. Freedman, J., 9th Bn.
426337	Pte. Flack, J., 10th Bn.
39688	Pte. Friedman, J., 7th Bn.
8672	Pte. Foreman. H., 2/1st Bn.
8600	Pte. Finklestein, J., 2/1st Bn.
8218	Pte. Fickler, B., 2/2nd Bn.
6858	Pte. Franks, B., 1/1st Bn.
633653	Rfm. Flamberg, S., 1/21st Bn.
5227	Cpl. Firth, M., 19th Bn.
5749	L/Cpl. Freeman, S., 19th Bn.
34690	Pte. Freedman, J., 20th Bn.
7059	Rfm. Fersht, J., 2/18th Bn.
R/233736	Pte. Flatzer, J.
801481	Pte. Franklin, L., 38th Bn.
574494	Rfm. Finegold, H., 3/17th Bn.
10/5353	Rfm. Faugh, H., 10th Bn.
574588	Rfm. Freedman, M., 17th Bn.
6974	Rfm. Frog, I., 3/20th Bn.
8008	Rfm. Feldman, I., 3/20th Bn.
6986	Rfm. Faltinovitch, M., 3/20th Bn.
7468	Rfm. Felbrodt, H., 1/9th Bn.
422396	Rfm. Franks, S., 2/10th Bn.
323767	Rfm. Fistol, S., 2/6th Bn.
280173	Rfm. Fairman, W.
	Rfm. Friend.
352965	Rfm. Freedman, M.
684048	Rfm. Flowers, A. S., 22nd Bn.
491637	Rfm. Federishern, E., 23rd Bn.
254033	Rfm. Frank, M., 3rd Bn.
422396	Rfm. Franks, S., 10th Bn.
353533	Rfm. Falkenstein, M., 3rd Bn.
425585	Rfm. Fisher, B., 10th Bn.
233753	Rfm. Feld, A., 2/2nd Bn.
722631	Rfm. Figov, H., 2/24th Bn.
424281	Rfm. Freedman, I.
254032	Rfm. Frank, M. J., 3rd Bn.
452551	L/Cpl. Flaxman, C., 9th Bn.
6630	Pte. Falk, S., 25th Bn.
5440	Cpl. Finglestein, W., 4/1st Bn.
2281	Pte. Flack, I. W., 19th Bn.
5932	Pte. Follis, D., 4/1st Bn.
4625	Pte. Foreman, H., 3/7th Bn.
2872	Pte. Frankel, B., 12th Bn.
4924	Pte. Freedman, 3/7th Bn.
5617	Pte. Freeman, L., 3/17th Bn.
594119	Pte. Ferth, J., 18th Bn.
3433	Pte. Friedberg, S., 3/16th Bn.
	Pte. Fishman, I.
	Pte. Flaum, M., 7th Bn.
6859	S/Sgt. Ford, J., 5th Bn.
	Pte. Freedman, F., 18th Bn.
	Pte. Freedman, J., 22nd Bn.
	Pte. Freedman, M., 17th Bn.
	Pte. Fink, D., 13th Bn.
	Pte. Frankoff, H.
6692	Pte. Furize, A., 3/16 Bn.
6917	Pte. Fellerman, I., 2/3rd Bn.
6450	Pte. Friedman, M., 3/7th Bn.
6859	Pte. Ford, J., 2nd Bn.
7123	Pte. Fagelstone, S., 4th Bn.
233736	Pte. Feltzer, M., 2/3rd Bn.
42053	Pte. Freeman, A., 9th Bn.
3592965	Pte. Freedman, M.
322585	Pte. Fox, M.
71274	Pte. Fingelstone, C. E.
203265	Pte. Franklyn, H. O.,* 1st Bn.
205	Rfm. Green, P., 1/9th Bn.
52	Cpl. Gabriel, M., 1/24th Bn.
6204	Pte. Goldman, L., 1/7th Bn.
7122	Rfm. Goldman, M. J., 1/8th Bn.
5572	Pte. Godfrey, J., 1/19th Bn.
7555	Pte. Greenwald, L.,* 1/22nd Bn.
5537	Pte. Grodner, M., 1/19th Bn.
4491	L./Cpl. Gowson, J., 1/13th Bn.
5493	Pte. Glass, H., 1/13th Bn.
5022	Pte. Green, A.,* 1/6th Bn.
1144	Pte. Grad, S., 1/4th Bn.
6144	Pte. Gudeket, J., 1/4th Bn.
5970	Pte. Greenberg, L., 1/4th Bn.
4905	Pte. Goldstein, L., 1/2nd Bn.
4421	L./Cpl. Gilbert, S.,* 1/2nd Bn.
1375	Rfm. Griew, S., 1/5th Bn.
2520	Rfm. Gordon, M.,* 1/5th Bn.
1398	Rfm. Griew, B.,* 1/5th Bn.
4338	Rfm. Green, J., 1/9th Bn.
5673	Pte. Geffen, E.,* 2/13th Bn.
4763	Pte. Greenberg, S., 2/13th Bn.
6402	Pte. Goldman, L., 2/20th Bn.
5478	Pte. Goldman, J., 2/22nd Bn.
3165	Pte. Gluckstein, C., 1/1st Bn.
8015	Pte. Goldstein, J., 1/1st Bn.
5959	Pte. Glass, A., 1/1st Bn.
4823	Pte. Galizer, H., 1/3rd Bn.
275106	Pte. Gold, D., 1/3rd Bn.
202952	Pte. Gold, H., 1/1st Bn.
280268	Pte. Gilbert, S.,* 1/4th Bn.
5983	Pte. Gunter, I., 1/4th Bn.
7585	Pte. Goldstein, I., 1/4th Bn.
8041	Rfm. Goldstone, L., 1/12th Bn.
485001	Rfm. Gold, A., 1/12th Bn.
8015	Rfm. Goldstone, J., 1/12th Bn.
472406	Rfm. Gosschalk, E., 1/12th Bn.
7662	Rfm. Goldstein, H., 1/2nd Bn.
301825	Rfm. Gulliver, A. P., 1/5th Bn.
374193	Rfm. Green, W.,* 1/8th Bn.
8690	Pte. Glassberg, L., 2/1st Bn.
8192	Pte. Goldstein, A. (M.M.), 2/2nd Bn.
8531	Pte. Goldberg, J., 2/2nd Bn.
252638	Pte. Goldstein, R.,* 1/3rd Bn.

London Regt.—*Continued.*

281362	Pte. GOLDSTEIN, F., A.,*	2/4th Bn.
6957	Pte. GORDON, H. I.,*	2/4th Bn.
7263	Pte. GREENBAUM, L.,	2/4th Bn.
3990	Rfm. GLUCK, J.,	2/5th Bn.
2659	Rfm. GOLDSWORTHY, A. J. V.,	2/5th Bn.
302726	Rfm. GOSSCHALK, L.,*	2/5th Bn.
7412	Pte. GOLDSECHER, L.,	2/7th Bn.
5379	Pte. GROSS, B.,	2/7th Bn.
7516	Pte. GINSBERG, J.,	2/7th Bn.
6810	Rfm. GREENBERG, D. C.,	2/6th Bn.
5262	Pte. GOLDMAN, A.,	2/9th Bn.
5784	Pte. GLAMBOTSKY, M.,	2/10th Bn.
422404	Pte. GOLDSTEIN, A.,*	2/10th Bn.
5631	Pte. GOODMAN, A. C.,	2/10th Bn.
4306	Pte. GLANTZ,	2/10th Bn.
472368	Rfm. GOLDSHAFT, J.,	2/11th Bn.
5519	Rfm. GOLDBERG, A.,	2/12th Bn.
5817	Pte. GREENLAND, E. G.,	1/7th Bn.
353488	Pte. GOLD, A.,	1/7th Bn.
374949	Rfm. GOLDBERG, I.,	1/8th Bn.
3873	L./Cpl. GROOSHKY, S.,	1/15th Bn.
573510	Rfm. GOODFRIEND, H.,*	1/17th Bn.
6520	Rfm. GOLDSTEIN, H.,	1/17th Bn.
6573	Rfm. GOLDBERGH, M.,	1/18th Bn.
5572	Pte. GODFREY, J.,	1/19th Bn.
41643	Rfm. GOLDSTEIN, R.,	1/18th Bn.
G/19964	Rfm. GREENBAUM, I.,	1/20th Bn.
682052	L./Cpl. GOLDING, M.,	1/22nd Bn.
5004	Rfm. GOLDSTEIN, J.,*	1/12th Bn.
472000	Rfm. GOLDSTEIN, L.,	1/12th Bn.
324469	Rfm. GINSBERG, B.,	1/9th Bn.
373528	Pte. GOLDSTEIN, B.,*	2/8th Bn.
298072	Pte. GREEN, J.,	1/4th Bn.
275424	Pte. GOLDBERG, J.,	1/3rd Bn.
G/84066	Pte. GREENSPAN, L.,	1/3rd Bn.
392023	Rfm. GOLDMAN, A.,	1/9th Bn.
202389	Pte. GOLDSTEIN, A. B.,	2/11th Bn.
465124	Pte. GOLD, C.,	2/11th Bn.
702586	Pte. GOODMAN, M.,	2/23rd Bn.
4579	Pte. GOLDBERG, M.,	1/22nd Bn.
1786	Pte. GLEITZMAN, A.,	1/7th Bn.
6152	Pte. GORDON, L.,	1/16th Bn.
6672	Rfm. GREENBERG, J.,	1/17th Bn.
4948	Rfm. GALINSKY, J.,	1/18th Bn.
2130	Rfm. GOLDSTON, L. E.,*	1/21st Bn.
302435	Rfm. GLUCK, F.,	2/5th Bn.
376949	Rfm. GOLDBERG, J.,	1/8th Bn.
423861	Pte. GOLDRING, P.,	1/10th Bn.
574732	Rfm. GARCIA, A.,	1/17th Bn.
8242	Rfm. GREEN,	1/7th Bn.
743023	Pte. GOLDSTEIN, B.,	1/25th Bn.
557324	Pte. GROSE, H.,	1/16th Bn.
452186	Rfm. GOLDSTEIN, S.,	2/11th Bn.
	Pte. GOLD, G.,	1/17th Bn.
A/202236	Rfm. GITTER, E.,	2/9th Bn.
576100	Rfm. GRODINSKY, H.,	1/17th Bn.
28388	Pte. GOLDSTEIN, J.,	1/4th Bn.
320966	Sgt. GOLD, A. (D.C.M., M.M.),	1/6th Bn.
352299	Pte. GROOS, S.,	1/2nd Bn.
5519	Rfm. GOLDBERG, A.,	2/12th Bn.
5674	Pte. GOLDSTEIN, C.,	2/10th Bn.
4/6388	Pte. GREEN, M.,	1/3rd Bn.
6199	Pte. GORDON, J.,	1/3rd Bn.
4226	Pte. GOLDSTEIN, J.,	1/3rd Bn.
142659	Pte. GOODMAN,	1/3rd Res. Bn.
153915	Pte. GORDON, A.,	1/1st Res. Bn.
635686	Pte. GALINSKY, H.,*	2/20th Bn.
1540	Pte. GINSBERG, D.,*	13th Bn.
353746	Pte. GINSBERG, S.,*	2/7th Bn.
298021	Pte. GINSBURG, B.,*	1/4th Bn.
3499	Pte. GOLDBAUM, P.,*	1/10th Bn.
472346	L/Cpl. GOLDBERG, A.,*	12th Bn.
5429	Rfm. GOLDBERG, L.,*	17th Bn.
2130	Rfm. GOLDSTON, L. E.,*	21st Bn.
625006	Pte. GOODMAN, M.,*	1/19th Bn.
1891	Sgt. GORDON, M. M.,*	17th Bn.
303855	Rfm. GREEN, M. M.,*	1/5th Bn.
204717	Pte. GROUSE, A.,*	1st Bn.
295215	Pte. GROWER, A.,*	1/4th Bn.
515568	Pte. GREEN, A.,	14th Bn.
514945	Pte. GOLD, G.,	17th Bn.
8022	Pte. GARODENTSCHICK, Z.,	3/20th Bn.
8020	Pte. GOBINDER, O.,	3/20th Bn.
8087	Pte. GHENKIN, S.,	3/20th Bn.
6965	Pte. GARODENSCHLICK, A.,	3/20th Bn.
6987	Pte. GARNSTEIN, M.,	3/20th Bn.
6984	Pte. GOLDENBERG, M.,	3/20th Bn.
6954	Pte. GOLDSTEIN, J.,	3/20th Bn.
6752	Pte. GOLDSBERG, M.,	3rd Bn.
282868	Pte. GUNTER, J.	
415039	Pte. GOLDINSKY, J.	
282959	Pte. GOUDEKETE, L.,	1/4th Bn.
5671	Pte. GOODFRIEND, H. A.,	1/17th Bn.
282861	Pte. GREENBERGH,	3rd Bn.
5544	Pte. GLAZER, S.,	3/10th Bn.
70784	Pte. GUTTERIDGE, F.,	1/23rd Bn.
	Pte. GOLDSTEIN.	
323602	Pte. CRUMBERG,	2/6th Bn.
574552	Pte. GOLDBERG, M.,	3/22nd Bn.
531488	Pte. GOVOOSHKY, S.,	1/15th Bn.
821808	Pte. GRISACK, I.	
2936	Pte. GINSBERG, G.,	1/10th Bn.
576488	Pte. GOLDSTEIN, L.,	17th Bn.
782586	Pte. GOODMAN, M.,	2/23rd Bn.
682674	Pte. GOLDMAN, J.,	2/22nd Bn.
422404	Pte. GOLDSTEIN, A.,	2/10th Bn.
557324	Pte. GROSS, H.	
57100	Pte. GRODGINSKY, H.	
42571	Pte. GEFFEN, E.,	2/13th Bn.
424247	Pte. GOLDSTEIN, J.,	3/10th Bn.
233853	Pte. GOLDBERG, J.,	2/2nd Bn.
781478	Pte. GOLDBERG, S.,	1st Bn.
491858	Pte. GREENBERG, S.,	2/13th Bn.
485001	Rfm. GOLDSTEIN, A.	
233425	Pte. GOLDSTEIN, H.	

London Regt.—*Continued.*

374949	Rfm. GOLDBERG, J.	
306711	Rfm. GREENBERG, S.	
421487	Pte. GINSBERG, S.	
194211	Pte. GOLDSTEIN, J., 2/13th Bn.	
722816	Pte. GOLD, B., 1/10th Bn.	
19964	Pte. GREENBAUM, F., 20th Bn.	
92897	Pte. GOLLON, T., 2/2nd Bn.	
	Pte. GREEN, L., 10th Bn.	
	Pte. GOLD, R., 9th Bn.	
30466	Pte. GORDON, A., 29th Bn.	
8850	Pte. GREEN, H., 29th Bn.	
742024	Pte. GOLDSTEIN, H., 1/25th Bn.	
742026	Pte. GREENSTONE, 1/25th Bn.	
720080	Pte. GOLD, M., 2/24th Bn.	
	Rfm. GOLDSMITH, L., 2/17th Bn.	
65213	Rfm. GOLDMAN, H., 2/21st Bn.	
702627	Rfm. GOLDSTEIN, S., 2/23rd Bn.	
5262	Rfm. GOLDMAN, A., 9th Bn.	
2/6003	Pte. GOLDSTEIN, L., 1st Bn.	
1579332	Pte. GOLDSTEIN, S., 1st Bn.	
46101	Cadet GROSSMAN, P., 28th Bn.	
7160	Pte. GOLD, A., 7th Bn.	
12/5759	Pte. GOLDINSKY, I., Q.V.R.	
11/5970	Pte. GLASSMAN, C., Q.V.R.	
5256	Pte. GERSHON, S., 10th Bn.	
5977	Pte. GOLD, I., 17th Bn.	
21/5421	Rfm. GOLDSTEIN, H. T., 21st Bn.	
21/5422	Rfm. GOLDSTEIN, S., 21st Bn.	
21/6251	Rfm. GOLDSTEIN, F. J., 21st Bn.	
2407	Rfm. GOTLEY, M., 17th Bn.	
425762	Pte. GREENBERG, H., 10th Bn.	
134420	Pte. GOLDSTEIN, J. M., 1st Bn.	
306711	Rfm. GREENBERG, S. V., 5th Bn.	
205790	Pte. GORDON, H., 1st Bn.	
485001	Rfm. GOLDSTEIN, N., 9th Bn.	
R/41010	Rfm. GLUCK, E., 9th Bn.	
426727	Pte. GREEN, H., 10th Bn.	
6654	Rfm. GILBERT, 2/11th Bn.	
4905	Rfm. GOLDSTEIN, S., 2/11th Bn.	
765447	Pte. GRODLE, W., 28th Bn.	
861194	Pte. GUSOFSKY, P., 33rd Bn.	
4178	Pte. GOLD, M., 2/25th Bn.	
6128	Rfm. GLAZER, M., 31st Bn.	
683806	Pte. GOLDWATER, P. S., 3/22nd Bn.	
801161	Pte. GREENBERG, A., 30th Bn.	
801254	Pte. GREEN, I., 30th Bn.	
801348	Pte. GOLDSTEIN, J., 30th Bn.	
801368	Pte. GOMPERTZ, J., 30th Bn.	
425570	Pte. GREATEREK, J., 5th Bn.	
8049	Cpl. GOODMAN, D., 32nd Bn.	
830623	Pte. GLAZER, G., 18th Bn.	
358577	Pte. GREENBAUM, S., 2/10th Bn.	
52809	Pte. GREENBAUM, A., 17th Bn.	
2682674	L/Cpl. GOLDMAN, J., 2/22nd Bn.	
422816	Pte. GOLD, B., 1/10th Bn.	
7936	Pte. GLASS, H., 13th Bn.	
763949	Pte. GERSON, C., 2/28th Bn.	
652136	Pte. GOLDMAN, H., 2/21st Bn.	
8048	Pte. GLUCKSTEIN, S., 18th Bn.	
613762	Pte. GROWER, A.	
612004	Pte. GRODNER, W. E., 2/19th Bn.	
682674	L/Cpl. GOLDMAN, J., 2/12th Bn.	
485001	Pte. GOLDSTEIN, J., 1/12th Bn.	
633955	Pte. GRODENZICK, S., 3/20th Bn.	
4024	Pte. GILBERT, H., 3/17th Bn.	
6697	Pte. GOLD, S., 3/15th Bn.	
5003	Pte. GOLDMAN, H., 3/31st Bn.	
3471	Pte. GOLDMAN, I., 3/5th Bn.	
6257	Pte. GOLDSTEIN, S., 3/21st Bn	
4565	Pte. GOLDSTEIN, S., 9th Bn.	
4508	Pte. GOODMAN, H. E., 3/19th Bn.	
4566	Pte. GOODMAN, M., 2/2nd Bn.	
4116	Pte. GOZLIN, M., 3/12th Bn.	
7555	Pte. GREENWALD, L., 12th Bn.	
3697	Pte. GRIDNER, F., 3/10th Bn.	
280268	Pte. GILBERT, S.	
	Pte. GOODMAN, N., 3/9th Bn.	
	Pte. GERSHON, M., 24th Bn.	
	Pte. GLASCOE, R. F., 1/10th Bn.	
	Pte. GILLITZEN, G., 2nd Bn.	
573438	Pte. GOLD, J., 17th Bn.	
630060	Pte. GALDER, H., 2/20th Bn.	
423174	Pte. GAMBOTSKY, 2/10th Bn.	
57314	Pte. GREENBAUM, D., 17th Bn.	
31488	Pte. GROSHKY, S., 1/15th Bn.	
452186	Pte. GOLDSTEIN, S., 2/11th Bn.	
612034	Pte. GODFREY, 19th Bn.	
202799	Pte. GLASS, I., 2/4th Bn.	
204341	Pte. GLASSBERG, L.	
	Pte. GALLOWITZ, S., 34th Bn.	
281362	Pte. GOLDSTEIN, F.	
92857	Pte. GALLON, T., 1/2nd Bn.	
37397	Pte. GOLDMAN, N. J.*	
5004	Pte. GOLDSTEIN, J.,* 12th Bn.	
252638	Pte. GOLDSTEIN, R.,* 1/3rd Bn.	
2258	Rfm. HOLTZ, P. M., 1/9th Bn.	
1391	Rfm. HARRIS, B. B., 1/17th Bn.	
531103	Rfm. HAINES, L.,* 1/15th Bn.	
3683	Rfm. HARRIS, S., 1/15th Bn.	
2212	Rfm. HYAMS, H., 1/17th Bn.	
2719	Rfm. HERNBERG, D. (M.M.), 1/17th Bn.	
5505	Rfm. HAAGMAN, E. (M.M.), 1/8th Bn.	
	Pte. HENISON, M.,* 1/13th Bn.	
6236	Pte. HARRIS, E., 1/13th Bn.	
6238	Pte. HIMMELFOLD, J., 1/13th Bn.	
6417	Pte. HYAMS, L. H., 1/13th Bn.	
4789	Sgt.Maj HARRIS, R., 1/4th Bn.	
1401	Pte. HART, S., 1/4th Bn.	
4739	Pte. HART, M., 1/2nd Bn.	
6031	Pte. HANKIN, H., 1/2nd Bn.	
301	Rfm. HOLTZ, L. A., 1/5th Bn.	
9521	Rfm. HART, S.,* 1/5th Bn.	
4916	Rfm. HOFFMAN, J., 1/16th Bn.	
5720	Pte. HARTSILVER, J., 2/13th Bn.	
1905	Pte. HYMAN, J., 2/15th Bn.	

London Regt.—*Continued.*

6748	Rfm. Hymans, F. A., 2/16th Bn.		5432	Pte. Harris, W., 1/24th Bn.
4828	Pte. Hyams, W. E., 2/13th Bn.		545010	Rfm. Hollander, S., 1/15th Bn.
5111	Pte. Harris, J., 2/19th Bn.		485041	Rfm. Hyams, H., 1/12th Bn.
7597	Pte. Harris, F., 2/22nd Bn.		2318811	Pte. Hart, B., 1/1st Bn.
3164	L./Cpl. Harrison, W., 1/1st Bn.		6658	Pte. Hirsch, H., 1/3rd Bn.
5971	Pte. Hyman, J., 1/1st Bn.		493751	Pte. Henison, M.,* 13th Bn.
7008	Sgt. Harris, D., 1/3rd Bn.		6857	Pte. Houtman, J., 1/3rd Bn.
204053	Pte. Hollander, M., 1/1st Bn.		6952	Pte. Hyam, J., 1/14th Bn.
7321	Pte. Harriman, M., 1/4th Bn.		613308	Pte. Harris, R. H., 2/17th Bn.
5779	Rfm. Herman, J., 1/12th Bn.		252255	Pte. Harris, A., 2/3rd Bn.
	Rfm. Hyams, B., 1/12th Bn.		2583	Pte. Hayman, H. A., 1/15th Bn.
231881	Pte. Hart, B., 1/2nd Bn.		554283	Pte. Harris, H. I., 1/13th Bn.
204434	Pte. Harris, M.,* 2/1st Bn.		202780	L/Cpl. Hart, J.,* 1st Bn.
5936	Pte. Hart, J., 2/1st Bn.		41283	Pte. Heller, D.,* 1/28th Bn.
5937	Pte. Hart, H. L., 2/3rd Bn.		6874	Rfm. Herman, J.,* 9th Bn.
283366	Pte. Hamburg, N.,* 2/4th Bn.		2/30116	Pte. Holbrook, M.,* 1/6th Bn.
3250	Rfm. Hill, J. M., 2/5th Bn.			Pte. Hamberger, H., 22nd Bn.
2934	Sgt. Henry, H., 2/7th Bn.			Pte. Haicke, T., 6th Bn.
1492	C.S.M. Hart, J., 2/10th Bn.			Pte. Hamberg, L.
452475	Rfm. Hyman, 1/6th Bn.			Rfm. Hacovitch, J.
7201	Pte. Hyams, L. E., 1/7th Bn.			Pte. Haggman, A., 1st Bn.
2919	Pte. Harris, J., 1/7th Bn.		252826	Pte. Hart, H. L., 2/3rd Bn.
5755	Rfm. Harris, E., 1/17th Bn.		302047	L/Cpl. Hill, J., 2/5th Bn.
573826	Rfm. Hart, W.,* 1/17th Bn.		350927	Pte. Henry, H., 7th Bn.
4894	L./Cpl. Hart, H., 1/19th Bn.		315622	Sgt. Harris, L., 2nd Bn.
30088	Rfm. Hyams, N., 1/20th Bn.		496717	Pte. Hart, J., 13th Bn.
470330	Rfm. Hershon, J. J., 1/12th Bn.		273233	Pte. Hoffman, M., 2/16th Bn.
531269	Sgt. Hertz, A.,* 1/15th Bn.		2934	Sgt. Henry, H.
203842	Pte. Himmelstein, H.,* 2/2nd Bn.		233155	Pte. Hart, H.
252825	Pte. Hyman, G. N., 2/3rd Bn.			Cpl. Hassan, V. (M.M.).
570828	Rfm. Hernberg, W., 2/5th Bn.		202806	Sgt. Hyman, J.
493789	L/Cpl. Hymans, L. H.,* 2/6th Bn.		426579	Pte. Hyams, J.
373346	Rfm. Hart, H.,* 1/8th Bn.		119448	Pte. Hillman, I., 17th Bn.
424088	Pte. Hyams, H., 2/10th Bn.		44911	Pte. Herner, A., 2/10th Bn.
224736	Pte. Hyams, L., 2/1st Bn.		653632	Pte. Hamberg, S., 23rd Bn.
225688	Pte. Harris, J., 2/1st Bn.		50514	Sgt. Hyman, H., 8th Bn.
880131	Rfm. Harris, 1/34th Bn.		225688	Pte. Harris, J. W., 3rd Bn.
232728	Pte. Harris, W., 1/2nd Bn.		530294	Pte. Hyman, I., 2/15th Bn.
232825	Pte. Harris, H., 1/2nd Bn.		2568	Cpl. Harris, H. P., 13th Bn.
305055	Pte. Hill, E., 1/28th Bn.		554990	Rfm. Harris, B., 2nd Q.W.R.
4941	Rfm. Hyams, N., 1/9th Bn.		861194	Rfm. Hunt, H., 33rd Bn.
7071	Pte. Harbour, L., 2nd Bn.		860821	Rfm. Hershaft, W., 33rd Bn.
198806	Pte. Harris, A., 1/13th Bn.		2407	Pte. Harris, E., 30th Bn.
2350	Pte. Harris, C., 1/4th Bn.		742037	Pte. Herschman, 1/25th Bn.
1797	Pte. Harris, A, 1/12th Bn.		485041	Pte. Hiles, H., 1/12th Bn.
4828	Rfm. Hyams, D., 1/13th Bn.		2/6054	Rfm. Hatten, E., 1st Bn.
635562	Pte. Hart, T., 1/20th Bn.		1/2407	Pte. Harris, E., 1st Bn.
1926	Rfm. Heron, J.,* 1/21st Bn.		739	Sgt. Howard, M. (Hyams), 3rd Bn.
1651	Rfm. Hyams, P., 1/21st Bn.		8291	Rfm. Hyams, B., 6th Bn.
611617	Cpl. Hart, H., 1/19th Bn.		8222	Rfm. Harris, A., 6th Bn.
373703	Pte. Harris, L., 1/8th Bn.		4500	Sgt. Harris, L., 6th Bn.
742009	Pte. Hoffman, 1/25th Bn.		6203	Pte. Harris, N., 7th Bn.
741747	L./Sgt. Hill, 1/25th Bn.		7330	Pte. Harris, S. A., 7th Bn.
740467	L./Cpl. Hirschland, 1/25th Bn.		11/4945	Rfm. Hyams, H., Q.V.R.
491908	Sgt. Hyams, 2/13th Bn.		5083	Pte. Hyams, B., 10th Bn.
538119	Pte. Harty, H., 2/16th Bn.		422131	Pte. Heiser, A., 10th Bn.
7868	Pte. Hyman, L. H., 1/13th Bn.		615938	Pte. Harris, I., 19th Bn.
			253249	Sgt. Harris, D., 1st Bn.

London Regt.—*Continued.*

355924	Pte. Hirschon, H., 7th Bn.
424088	Pte. Hyman, H., 10th Bn.
306421	Rfm. Hyams, P. J., 5th Bn.
5936	Pte. Hart, J., 2/1st Bn.
8889	Pte. Harris, M., 2/1st Bn.
5232	Pte. Harris, A., 2/3rd Bn.
22/683784	Pte. Hyams, M., 22nd Bn.
545081	Pte. Hart, E., 2/15th Bn.
860821	Pte. Herstraff, W., 33rd Bn.
633612	Pte. Hayman, H., 3/20th Bn.
780719	Pte. Harris, A., 29th Bn.
252826	Pte. Hart, H. L., 7th Bn.
204434	Pte. Harris, M., 2/11th Bn.
6901	Pte. Hillier, 29th Bn.
42495	Pte. Hartog, A., 13th Bn.
530294	Pte. Hyman, I., 2/15th Bn.
9521	Pte. Hart, S., 1/5th Bn.
3171	Cpl. Hess, F. J., 16th Bn.
4941	Pte. Hyams, N., 3rd Bn.
17769	Pte. Hirschovitz, B., 3rd Bn.
57255	Pte. Harris, J., 17th Bn.
57499	Pte. Herschman, J., 3/17th Bn.
733654	Pte. Handel, S., 15th Bn.
2407	Pte. Harris, E. S., 30th Bn.
781350	Pte. Hellier, A., 29th Bn.
253856	Pte. Harris, H., 3rd Bn.
8291	Pte. Hyams, B., 6th Bn.
614195	Pte. Hyams, L., 3/19th Bn.
53011	Pte. Holtz, A., 17th Bn.
614527	Pte. Harris, M. S., 3/19th Bn.
8017	Pte. Halpern, B., 3/20th Bn.
6961	Pte. Hammanx H., 3/20th Bn.
8003	Pte. Hillel, Z., 3/20th Bn.
8020	Pte. Horwitz, M., 3/20th Bn.
8051	Pte. Hornstein, D., 3/20th Bn.
235471	Pte. Hart, A.
6406	Pte. Hart, H., 8th Bn.
23181	Pte. Hart, B.
7330	Pte. Harris, B., 7th Bn.
205100	Pte. Hillman, J., 1st Bn.
635562	Pte. Hart, T.
	L/Cpl. Hart, W. H. (M.M.)
280124	Pte. Hart, S., 3rd Bn.
1054121	Pte. Herman, S., 23rd Bn.
201024	Pte. Harrison, D.
354903	Pte. Hack, M., 3/7th Bn.
204660	Pte. Hirschkowitz, H.
203842	Pte. Himmelstein, H.
452475	Pte. Hyman, H. C., 9th Bn.
614527	Pte. Harris, M. S., 3/19th Bn.
474396	Pte. Hyams, B., 1/10th Bn.
3267	Pte. Hurst, H., 1/11th Bn.
782302	Pte. Hack, M., 29th Bn.
560282	L/Cpl. Hernberg, D., 2/5th Bn.
373346	Pte. Hart, M., 8th Bn.
722375	Pte. Harris, W.
760923	Pte. Hecht, H. J., 2/28th Bn.
767398	Pte. Harris, C. L. R., 28th Bn.
765124	Pte. Hayman, H. L.
570525	Pte. Hyams, H., 17th Bn.
253856	Pte. Harris, A., 3/10th Bn.
7825	Pte. Hennison, M., 13th Bn.
7820	Pte. Harris, 1st Bn.
8191	Pte. Hyams, 1/4th Bn.
511617	Cpl. Hart, H,
2568	Pte. Harris, L., 3/7th Bn.
4791	Cpl. Hart, E., 3/19th Bn.
2233	Pte. Hart, M., 13th Bn.
	Pte. Harris, D. (M.M.).
4122	Pte. Heiser, A., 13th Bn.
2141	Pte. Hart, S.
3363	Cpl. Henry, W., 3/7th Bn.
5632	Pte. Hyman, H. C., 3/11th Bn.
633963	Pte. Horovitz, M., 20th Bn.
	Pte. Hoffman, J., 5th Bn.
	Rfm. Hearman, J. S., 21st Bn.
	S/Sgt. Hernberg, H., 15th Bn.
	Pte. Hewine, H., 15th Bn.
	Pte. Hales, H.
	Pte. Hill A. I., 5th Bn.
	Sgt. Herwitz. S., 10th Bn.
	Pte. Hyams, G., 28th Bn.
	Pte. Hyam, C. E., 7th Bn.
	Pte. Hyam, C., 13th Bn.
	Pte. Hyman, M., 12th Bn.
	Pte. Hyman, R., 18th Bn.
	Pte. Hyman, F. A., 12th Bn.
	Pte. Hyman, E. H., 12th Bn.
	Pte. Hyman, C., 18th Bn.
	Rfm. Hymans, H. D., 28th Bn.
	Rfm. Herbert, B., 7th Bn.
	Rfm. Harris, A., 17th Bn.
	Rfm. Herne, H., 15th Bn.
	Rfm. Harris, S., 15th Bn.
	Rfm. Hart, 28th Bn.
	Rfm. Harris, P., 10th Bn.
	Rfm. Harris, J., 17th Bn.
	Rfm. Harris, A., 12th Bn.
353620	Rfm. Harris, A., 9th Bn.
36756	Rfm. Harris, A., 17th Bn.
5835	Pte. Isaacs, A.,* 1/16th Bn.
2692	Rfm. Isaacs, J.,* 2/15th Bn.
4729	Rfm. Isaacs, N., 2/18th Bn.
5186	Rfm. Isaacs, F. I., 2/21st Bn.
8018	Rfm. Isaacs, F. J., 1/1st Bn.
415019	Rfm. Isbit, A., 1/16th Bn.
5406	Pte. Isaacs, L., 2/4th Bn.
3872	Rfm. Isaacs, L. G., 2/5th Bn.
4456	Pte. Isaacs, S., 2/10th Bn.
5981	Pte. Isaacs, J., 2/10th Bn.
5528	Rfm. Isaacs, H., 2/12th Bn.
4769	Rfn. Isaacs, E. A., 2/12th Bn.
6779	Rfm. Isaacs, S., 2/12th Bn.

London Regt.—*Continued.*

610553	Pte. ISAACS, W., 1/19th Bn.
722600	Pte. ISRAEL, S., 1/24th Bn.
374235	Pte. ISAACS, M., 1/8th Bn.
495314	Rfm. ISAACS, L., 2/11th Bn.
375033	Rfm. ISRAEL, L., 1/28th Bn.
5339	Pte. ISAACS, F., 3/19th Bn.
5824	Pte. ISRAEL, E., 1/8th Bn.
422517	Rfm. ISAACS, C. S., 2/5th Bn.
1716	Pte. ISAACS, A. V.,* 12th Bn.
473221	Rfm. ISAACS, S.,* 1/12th Bn.
704015	Rfm. ILIAN, H., 2/3rd Bn.
4923	Rfm. ISAACS, A., 29th Bn.
491966	Rfm. ISAACS, I. E.,* 2/13th Bn.
5285	Pte. ISAACS, N., 8th Bn.
12/4725	Pte. ISAACS, M., Q.V.R.
203734	Pte. ISAACS, J., 1st Bn.
445063	Pte. ISAACS, M., 10th Bn.
306167	Rfm. ISRAEL, R., 5th Bn.
21/6608	Rfm. ISRAEL, N.
5764	Pte. ISAACS, J., 1/4th Bn.
615818	Pte. ISAACS, S., 19th Bn.
781865	Pte. ISAACS, A., 29th Bn.
8005	Pte. ISRAEL, A., 3/20th Bn.
423319	Pte. ISRAEL, B., 6th Bn.
65339	Pte. ISAACS, L., 2/19th Bn.
471856	Pte. ISAACS, E., 2/12th Bn.
253828	Pte. ISAACS, J.
495314	Pte. ISAACS, L. A., 3/16th Bn.
472354	Pte. ISAACS, H., 2/12th Bn.
611892	Pte. ISAACS, F., 2/19th Bn.
282449	L/Cpl. ISAACS, L.
8018	Pte. ISAACS, J., 1st Bn.
424225	Pte. ISAACS, S., 10th Bn.
723600	Pte. ISRAEL, S., 24th Bn.
282857	Pte. ISAACS, J., 2/4th Bn.
5339	Pte. ISAACS, F., 19th Bn.
2512	Pte. ISAACS, H. L., 2/1st Bn.
5692	Pte. ISAACS, L., 3/15th Bn.
41456	Pte. ISAACS, G., 10th Bn.
4725	Pte. ISAACS, S., 2/11th Bn.
	Pte. INKER, H., 12th Bn.
	Pte. ISAACS, D., 17th Bn.
	Pte. ISAACS, H., 13th Bn.
423263	Pte. ISAACS, J., 2/10th Bn.
8402	Rfm. ISAACS, M., 18th Bn.
655918	Rfm. ISAACS, E., 23rd Bn.
634466	Pte. ISAACS, S. E., 2/20th Bn.
2789	Rfm. JACOBS, S.,* 1/18th Bn.
2886	Rfm. JACOBS, A.,* 1/7th Bn.
1473	L/Cpl. JACOBS, J., 1/6th Bn.
1771	Rfm. JACOBS, T., 1/16th Bn.
3282	Rfm. JACOBS, J. A., 1/16th Bn.
4771	Pte. JACOBS, J., 1/7th Bn.
4471	Rfm. JUDELSON, J., 1/5th Bn.
2378	Pte. JOSEPH, B., 1/4th Bn.
4649	Rfm. JACOBSON D., 1/13th Bn.
4910	L/Cpl. JOSEPH, J. O.,* 1/14th Bn.
4950	L/Cpl. JACOBS, L. E.,* 2/16th Bn.
492399	Rfm. JACOBS, L.,* 2/13th Bn.
6109	Rfm. JACOBS, H., 2/16th Bn.
2652	L/Cpl. JACOBS, H., 2/17th Bn.
7047	Pte. JONES, S., 2/22nd Bn.
6139	Pte. JACOBS, A., 1/1st Bn.
8395	Pte. JACOBS, R., 1/1st Bn.
474177	Rfm. JACOBS, B.,* 1/12th Bn.
5519	Pte. JONES, W., 2/2nd Bn.
8445	Pte. JACOBS, J.,* 2/2nd Bn.
8112	Pte. JORDAN, H., 2/3rd Bn.
3930	Rfm. JOSEPH, J. R., 2/5th Bn.
7857	Pte. JOSEPH, W., 2/7th Bn.
3562	Pte. JACOBS, L., 2/10th Bn.
5375	Rfm. JACOBS, H., 2/12th Bn.
3616	L/Cpl. JACOBS, H., 1/6th Bn.
5068	Pte. JOSEPHS, H., 1/19th Bn.
	Cpl. JACOBS, H. (D.C.M.).
675025	Rfm. JACOBS, P.,* 1/21st Bn.
611717	Rfm. JOSEPH, H., 1/19th Bn.
574296	Rfm. JACOBS, W., 1/17th Bn.
573091	Rfm. JACOBSON, N., 2/8th Bn.
G/82640	L./Cpl. JACOBS, A. H., 2/2nd Bn.
555357	Rfm. JONES, B., 2/16th Bn.
4529	Pte. JACOBS, S., 1/22nd Bn.
4491	Pte. JACOBS, J., 1/22nd Bn.
7092	Cadet JOSEPHS, S. S., 1/28th Bn.
5500	Pte. JUWEILER, 1/5th Bn.
415089	Pte. JAFFE, D., 1/9th Bn.
684369	Pte. JAFFE, E., 1/22nd Bn.
742041	Pte. JACOBS, M., 1/25th Bn.
2262	Pte. JAY, A., 1/5th Bn.
7514	Dvr. JACOBS, A., 1/1st Bn.
88434	Pte. JACOB, N., 1/7th Bn.
74234	Pte. JACOBS, I., 2/10th Bn.
320189	Cpl. JACOBS, J., 1/6th Bn.
253573	L./Cpl. JORDON, H., 2/4th Bn.
421950	Pte. JACOBS, L. J., 2/10th Bn.
742345	Rfm. JACOBS, J., 1/6th Bn.
4260	L./Cpl. JOSEPHS, A., 1/3rd Bn.
450560	Cpl. JAMESON, J. G., 1/11th Bn.
570757	L/Cpl. JACOBS, H., 1/17th Bn.
530525	Pte. JOFFE, M.,* 1/15th Bn.
472256	Rfm. JACOBS, H., 12th Bn.
766757	Pte. JACOBS, G. A., 28th Bn.
614423	Pte. JACKSON, A., 2/19th Bn.
570757	Pte. JACOLES, N., 2/17th Bn.
	C.S.M. JACOBS, H., 2/16th Bn.
572496	Pte. JACOBS, D., 17th Bn.
552859	Rfm. JACOBS, H., 9th Bn.
3676	L/Sgt. JOSEPHS, E., 13th Bn.
5375	Rfm. JACOBS, H., 2/12th Bn.
5500	Rfm. JEURLER, A., 3rd Bn.
7092	Cadet JOSEPHS, I., 28th Bn.
8266	Rfm. JOSEPHS, O. M., 6th Bn.
4771	Pte. JACOBS, J., 7th Bn.
23/5986	Pte. JUDGE, J., 21st Bn.
741781	Pte. JACOBS, S. D., 10th Bn.

London Regt.—*Continued.*

35794	Pte. JACOBS, M., 1st Bn.
235087	Pte. JACOBS, D., 1st Bn.
801420	Pte. JACOBS, H., 30th Bn.
302648	Pte. JUDELSON, J., 5th Bn.
611717	Pte. JOSEPH, H., 19th Bn.
68370	Pte. JACOBS, J., 17th Bn.
57429	Pte. JACOBS, E., 17th Bn.
57499	Pte. JONAS, J., 17th Bn.
8315	Pte. JACOBS, I., 6th Bn.
613697	Pte. JACOBS, P., 3/19th Bn.
6971	Pte. JANIASHBILI, J., 3/20th Bn.
420134	Dvr. JACOBS, E., 1/10th Bn.
354707	Pte. JAY, H.
280531	Pte. JOSEPHS, B., 2nd Bn.
415089	Pte. JAFFE, D., 1/9th Bn.
232483	Pte. JONES, W., 2/2nd Bn.
683921	Pte. JONES, S., 2/22nd Bn.
35058	Pte. JOSEPHSON, S., 15th Bn.
1346	Pte. JACOBS, H., 10th Bn.
204573	Pte. JACOBS, R., 3/1st Bn.
253573	L/Cpl. JORDON, H., 2/3rd Bn.
251673	Cpl. JOSEPHS, A., 3rd Bn.
4950	L/Cpl. JACOBS, L. E., 2nd Bn.
5480	Pte. JACOBS, A., 3/7th Bn.
5297	Pte. JACOBS, E., 4/1st Bn.
3746	Pte. JACOBS, N., 3/17th Bn.
5171	Pte. JAFFA, M., 20th Bn.
3663	Pte. JONES, A. R., 3/9th Bn.
4495	Pte. JOSEPH, I., 22nd Bn.
4468	Pte. JOSEPH, L. E. A., 3/16th Bn.
145318	Pte. JOSEPH, J., 1st Bn.
	Pte. JACOB, H. J., 6th Bn.
	Pte. JOSEPHS, S., 10th Bn.
4581	Pte. JACOBS, H. J., 3/9th Bn.
	Pte. JACOBS, I. M., 16th Bn.
	Pte. JEWELL, H., 2nd Bn.
2339	Cpl. JESSEL, G., 2/6th Bn.
	Pte. JACOBSON, I., 18th Bn.
7562	Pte. JARSHY, J., 14th Bn.
266530	Pte. JACKSON, G., 13th Bn.
321361	L/Cpl. JACOBS, H., 6th Bn.
252779	L/Cpl. JOEL, L., 2/3rd Bn.
	Pte. JACOBS, A. A. (M.M.).
283086	L/Cpl. JAFFA, L., 3rd Bn.
280531	Pte. JOSEPHS, D., 1/4th Bn.
424109	Pte. JACOBS, J., 10th Bn.
91960	Pte. JULIUS, J., 21st Bn.
4589	Pte. KANAPKIN, A., 1/6th Bn.
1834	Pte. KARET, H., 1/20th Bn.
3040	Pte. KAUFMAN, A., 1/20th Bn.
2659	Pte. KING, D. S., 1/23rd Bn.
3935	Pte. KENNER, F., 1/19th Bn.
5663	Rfm. KAUFMAN, J., 1/22nd Bn.
6800	Pte. KYZOR, J., 1/22nd Bn.
5306	Pte. KAUFMAN, A., 1/21st Bn.
2456	Pte. KATZ, C.,* 1/4th Bn.
5191	Pte. KLEINFELD, C., 2/20th Bn.
4727	Rfm. KARSTADT, N., 2/18th Bn.
5765	Pte. KALMS, C., 2/24th Bn.
204072	Pte. KAISSER, S. L.,* 1/1st Bn.
5939	Pte. KARMULSTEIN, J., 1/4th Bn.
5972	Pte. KREITZMAN, B., 1/4th Bn.
4051	Rfm. KAY, M., 1/5th Bn.
6783	Rfm. KASANOSKI, W., 2/6th Bn.
6018	Pte. KOZMINSKY, M., 2/7th Bn.
6799	Rfm. KRONJUIST, O. G., 2/6th Bn.
6755	Rfm. KLEIN, E., 2/6th Bn.
614298	Pte. KOHEN, I., 1/19th Bn.
5072	Pte. KITZBERG, J., 1/24th Bn.
385113	Rfm. KLEIN, M., 2/8th Bn.
80518	Pte. KESLER, H., 1/1st Bn.
230372	Pte. KING, J. A., 1/1st Bn.
650823	Rfm. KRANGLE, A., 2/11th Bn.
573	Rfm. KOBINSKY,
551579	Pte. KOSKY, A., 2/16th Bn.
204905	Pte. KADISH, M., 1/4th Bn.
575001	Rfm. KARUSH, L., 1/17th Bn.
30525	Pte. KOBRIN, J. H., 2/8th Bn.
42296	Rfm. KALIKMAN, A. L., 1/10th Bn.
421961	Sgt. KATIM, M., 1/8th Bn.
4/6093	Pte. KATZ, J. J., 1/3rd Bn.
88549	Pte. KRANGOLD, S., 1/1st Res. Bn.
395147	Rfm. KLEINER, D.,* 9th Bn.
625457	Pte. KATZOVITZ, N.,* 20th Bn.
1975	Pte. KOSMAN, G. E.,* 2nd Bn.
44911	Pte. KESNER, A., 2/10th Bn.
92565	Pte. KLEIN, A., 2nd Bn.
633619	Pte. KRAFSOFF, A. M., 20th Bn.
305325	Pte. KOBORIN, J., 5th Bn.
8746	Pte. KOSOFSKY, H., 29th Bn.
254292	Pte. KRAUSE, S.
706359	Pte. KRAFSHIG, A., 23rd Bn.
3843	Cpl. KLINE, J., 10th Bn.
8171	Rfm. KOLINSKY, J., 17th Bn.
9/6525	Rfm. KINSLER, A., Q.V.R.
134445	Pte. KELLY, W. J., 3rd Bn.
255214	Pte. KRUGER, J., 3rd Bn.
612944	Pte. KANTOVITCH, I., 19th Bn.
5868	Pte. KRAMER, A., 2/3rd Bn.
2741	Rfm. KENGALL, A., 2/11th Bn.
5529	Pte. KLEENBERG, F., 19th Bn.
537526	Rfm. KIELBIG, M.
	Rfm. KAUFMAN, C., 1/16th Bn.
325644	Rfm. KLEINBURG, H.
5367	Pte. KURASCH, J., 20th Bn.
822094	Rfm. KRONENBERG, M., 31st Bn.
822176	Rfm. KOSKER, H., 31st Bn.
781765	Pte. KESOFSKY, H., 29th Bn.
55473	Pte. KAUFMAN, C., 2/6th Bn.
420709	Pte. KONIGWINTER, L., 1/10th Bn.
1964	Pte. KLOOT, H., 25th Bn.
324107	Pte. KONTISH, A., 3/6th Bn.
6956	Pte. KROCKSHMALNICK, 3/20th Bn.
6945	Pte. KAHAM, C., 3/20th Bn.

London Regt.—*Continued.*

3829	Pte. Kravitz, H., 29th Bn.		5327	Rfm. Lenzberg, J., 2/12th Bn.
25/5134	Pte. Kanutan, J., 10th Bn.		473006	Rfm. List, H.,* 2/12th Bn.
6994	Pte. Kemmelman, H., 3/20th Bn.		353069	Pte. Lawrence, A., 1/7th Bn.
6995	Pte. Kretchmann, S., 3/20th Bn.		8203	Rfm. Leviensky, S., 1/17th Bn.
6973	Pte. Krasinatsky, E., 3/20th Bn.		573957	Rfm. Levy, E., 2/17th Bn.
8074	Pte. Krasinatsky, M., 3/20th Bn.		2540	Sgt. Levi, M., 1/18th Bn.
6958	Pte. Kravaschaff, M., 3/20th Bn.		45472	Rfm. Landau, D., 1/18th Bn.
6955	Pte. Krasmiatsky, D., 3/20th Bn.		5031	Pte. Lazarus, P. (M.M.), 1/23rd Bn.
534747	Rfm. Kauffman, C., 3/16th Bn.		4291	Rfm. Levy, M., 1/6th Bn.
354803	Rfm. Kresman, B., 3/7th Bn.		4528	Pte. Levy, S., 1/7th Bn.
574500	Pte. Konmise, M., 17th Bn.		3973	Pte. Lewis, B., 1/23rd Bn.
	Rfm. Kain, I., 1/6th Bn.		3099	Rfm. Lazarus, I., 1/17th Bn.
425572	Pte. Klein, J. J., 3rd Bn.		2640	Rfm. Lyons, S., 1/18th Bn.
894	Pte. Kaufman, A., 21st Bn.		2437	Pte. Lewis, H., 1/19th Bn.
3295	Pte. Kain, F., 6th Bn.		2473	Pte. Littman, J., 1/23rd Bn.
4626	Pte. Kaufman, W., 20th Bn.		5610	Pte. Levy, L., 1/7th Bn.
2410	Pte. Kent, M., 4/4th Bn.		1552	Rfm. Levy, H., 1/8th Bn.
5164	Pte. Keslofski, A., 4/4th Bn.		1598	Pte. Levy, H., 1/17th Bn.
324107	Pte. Kostick, A., 6th Bn.		4340	Pte. Lee, A., 1/17th Bn.
635467	Pte. Kassovitch, M., 20th Bn.		3826	Pte. Levy, A. M., 1/17th Bn.
4106	Pte. Kopenhagen, M., 3/28th Bn.		1537	Pte. Levy, J., 1/17th Bn.
1145	Pte. Kantorovitch, V., 19th Bn.		5921	Pte. Lazarus, L., 1/19th Bn.
573391	Pte. Krobinsky, 2/17th Bn.		5035	Pte. Leux, J., 1/23rd Bn.
92565	Pte. Klein, I. A., 3rd Bn.		5007	Pte. Levene, H., 1/23rd Bn.
2/6981	Pte. Kalinsky, 1st Bn.		3475	L./Cpl. Leslie, M., 1/12th Bn.
6392	Pte. Karrovitz, J., 1/4th Bn.		2271	Rfm. Lappin, J.,* 1/12th Bn.
	Pte. Kramer, M. (M.M.).		6652	Rfm. Lelyveld, J., 1/14th Bn.
4248	Pte. Karlish, H., 2/25th Bn.		4824	Pte. Louis, P.,* 1/2nd Bn.
	Pte. Klapfish, P., 23rd Bn.		7689	L/Cpl. Lipschitz, D., 1/2nd Bn.
473310	Rfm. Lawson, F. D., 1/12th Bn.		6149	Pte. Levey, A., 1/4th Bn.
302019	Rfm. Libstein, M., 1/5th Bn.		5074	Pte. Levy, J., 2/13th Bn.
6026	Rfm. Lipman, C., 1/9th Bn.		530998	Pte. Lumer, J.,* 2/15th Bn.
415226	Rfm. Levy, L., 1/9th Bn.		3386	L/Cpl. Lipman, A., 2/17th Bn.
4735	Rfm. Levy, A. B., 1/16th Bn.		472393	Pte. Levine, M., 1/15th Bn.
2487	Sgt. Lewis, H., 1/16th Bn.		37361	Rfm. Levy, I.,* 1/21st Bn.
8891	Pte. Levy, L., 2/1st Bn.		353069	Rfm. Lawrence, A., 1/19th Bn.
8667	Pte. Leibert, M., 21/st Bn.		576096	Rfm. Levy, S., 1/17th Bn.
5421	Pte. Lubinsky, G. S., 2/2nd Bn.		698063	Rfm. Levine, A., 1/22nd Bn.
3701	Pte. Levy, M., 2/2nd Bn.		282194	Pte. Lee, V., 1/4th Bn.
253570	Pte. Lubertz, C.,* 2/3rd Bn.		231946	Pte. Levy, A., 1/2nd Bn.
5780	Pte. Lappin, T., 2/3rd Bn.		205708	Pte. Lazarus, J. E.,* 1/2nd Bn.
5322	Pte. Lipman, R., 2/4th Bn.		554946	Rfm. Levy, S., 1/16th Bn.
2507	Pte. Levy, L., 2/4th Bn.		510507	Pte. Lappin, S., 2/3rd Bn.
5581	Pte. Levy, P., 2/4th Bn.		492038	Cpl. Lewis, A., 2/6th Bn.
5525	Pte. Lyons, B., 2/4th Bn.		392325	Rfm. Litchfield, E., 2/6th Bn.
2671	Rfm. Leapman, L. C., 2/5th Bn.		370204	Rfm. Levy, H., 2/8th Bn.
8052	Rfm. Levy, R., 2/6th Bn.		452313	Rfm. Levene, H., 2/11th Bn.
6728	Rfm. Lackmacker, J., 2/6th Bn.		738305	Rfm. Levy, L., 2/24th Bn.
322327	Rfm. Levy, P.,* 2/6th Bn.		21902	Rfm. Levy, F., 1/12th Bn.
5378	Rfm. Levy, E., 2/9th Bn.		551833	Rfm. Lawson, R. W., 2/6th Bn.
	Pte. Lipman, A. (M.M.).		881389	Rfm. Lawson, 1/34th Bn.
2699	Sgt. Lewis, G., 2/10th Bn.		881609	Rfm. Levy, 1/34th Bn.
3633	L./Cpl. Lewis, C. A., 2/10th Bn.		881607	Rfm. Lee, 1/34th Bn.
5715	Pte. Lifchitz, J., 2/10th Bn.		764780	Pte. Logette, B., 1/28th Bn.
5825	Pte. Labofsky, S., 2/10th Bn.		764440	Pte. Lazarus, M. A., 1/28th Bn.
5971	Rfm. Levene, H., 2/10th Bn.		4947	Pte. Levy, D.,* 1/9th Bn.
6734	Rfm. Levey, E., 2/11th Bn.		6435	Pte. Lipsey, S., 1/16th Bn.
			4593	Pte. Levy, S., 1/22nd Bn.

London Regt.—*Continued.*

4535	Pte. LUBINSKY, H., 1/22nd Bn.
496298	Pte. LUX, S., 1/13th Bn.
2245	Rfm. LEVY, G., 2/17h Bn.
5477	Rfm. LEVY, M., 2/17th Bn.
7076	Rfm. LIPMAN, H., 2/18th Bn.
7646	Rfm. LOWENBERG, A., 2/18th Bn.
4832	Pte. LENNARD, W., 2/19th Bn.
4730	Rfm. LEWIS, P., 2/18th Bn.
7062	Rfm. LEVY, A., 2/18th Bn.
7023	Pte. LAZARUS, M., 2/22nd Bn.
4908	Pte. LEVY, H., 2/23rd Bn.
5776	Pte. LAMBERT, H., 2/23rd Bn.
4926	Pte. LEVY, J., 1/13th Bn.
6295	Pte. LASSMAN, G., 1/1st Bn.
8144	Pte. LAZARUS, H., 1/1st Bn.
203660	Pte. LEVENE, L., 1/1st Bn.
253865	Pte. LEVENE, B., 1/3rd Bn.
282588	Pte. LEVY, P., 1/3rd Bn.
253655	Pte. LUBINSKY, J., 1/3rd Bn.
5963	Pte. LEVINSKI, L., 1/4th Bn.
6147	Pte. LEVY, J.,* 1/4th Bn
6115	Pte. LOUISSON, L., 1/4th Bn.
6085	Pte. LEBOTT, S., 1/4th Bn.
5969	Pte. LAZARUS, H., 1/4th Bn.
5508	Ptt. LYONS, L., 1/4th Bn.
4400	Pte. LEVETT, N., 1/4th Bn.
5958	Pte. LEVENE, L., 1/4th Bn.
283783	Pte. LESSMAN, H., 1/4th Bn.
5821	L./Cpl. LEWIS, R., 1/12th Bn.
5630	Rfm. LEVENE, M., 1/12th Bn.
5017	Pte. LEWIS, A., 1/13th Bn.
492311	Pte. LEVI, N., 1/13th Bn.
2436	Pte. LEWIS, A. A., 1/20th Bn.
2085	Pte. LESSMAN, S., 1/3rd Bn.
	Pte. LEVY, B. H., 1/28th Bn.
8735	Pte. LEVY, B., 2/1st Bn.
2329	Pte. LYON, H. M., 1/2nd Bn.
5407	Rfm. LEVY, I., 2/9th Bn.
452198	Rfm. LETTER, H., 2/11th Bn.
415172	Rfm. LEE, L., 1/9th Bn.
574075	Rfm. LEVINSKY, A., 1/17th Bn.
701908	Rfm. LEVY, J., 1/23rd Bn.
652133	Rfm. LEVY, E., 1/21st Bn.
7172	Pte. LORENSTEIN, 1/1st Bn.
798	Sgt./Instr. LEVY, S., 1/17th Bn.
354089	Pte. LEVY, L., 1/7th Bn.
3161	Pte. LIDESTEIN, M., 1/5th Bn.
304476	Rfm. LEVY, G. L., 1/5th Bn.
125863	Pte. LEWIS, H., 1/10th Bn.
742051	Rfm. LEVENE, S., 1/25th Bn.
742050	Pte. LEVENE, B., 1/25th Bn.
741240	Pte. LEVY, M., 1/25th Bn.
4994	Pte. LEVY, E., 1/21st Bn.
39735	Rfm. LAZAROVITCH, L., 1/11th Bn.
583368	Pte. LANDAU, P., 2/17th Bn.
424870	Pte. LEVY, A., 1/13th Bn.
761905	Pte. LAZARUS, P., 1/23rd Bn.
422461	Cpl. LYONS, J., 1/10th Bn.
492080	Pte. LEVY, J., 1/13th Bn.
1598	Rfm. LEVY, J., 1/17th Bn.
6392	Rfm. LEVY, D., 1/4th Bn.
370204	L./Cpl. LEVY, H., 2/8th Bn.
365012	Pte. LEVENE, M., 1/10th Bn.
906449	Pte. LAZARUS, I., 1/20th Bn.
4/5915	Pte. LEVY, A., 1/3rd Bn.
4/6594	Pte. LERNER, B., 1/3rd Bn.
5521	Pte. LEVENE, B., 1/3rd Bn.
4/6692	Pte. LEMBERG, H., 1/3rd Bn.
4400	Pte. LEVITT, A., 1/3rd Bn.
6375	Pte. LEVINE, L., 2/10th Bn.
5905	Pte. LEVY, A., 2/10th Bn.
139716	Pte. LEWIS, S., 1/1st Res. Bn.
67248	Cpl. LISSNER, H., 1/1st Res. Bn.
534807	L./Cpl. LYONS, M., 1/15th Bn.
282856	Pte. LEVINSKY, B., 1/4th Bn.
251374	Cpl. LANE, S.,* 2/3rd Bn.
615654	Pte. LEVY, B.,* 1/19th Bn.
415193	Rfm. LEVY, G.,* 1/9th Bn.
324458	Rfm. LEVY, H.,* 6th Bn.
37361	Pte. LEVY, J.,* 1/20th Bn.
4532	Pte. LEVY, M.,* 22nd Bn.
1584	Pte. LEWIS, H. R.,* 12th Bn.
5820	Pte. LIPMAN, H.,* 23rd Bn.
5978	Rfm. LIPMAN, W. R.,* 17th Bn.
351517	Pte. LIPSACK, J.,* 1/7th Bn.
683036	Pte. LUBINSKY, M.,* 2/22nd Bn.
72465	Pte. LUDSKI, C.,* 7th Bn.
232394	Pte. LUPINSKY, L.,* 2/2nd Bn.
2/8261	Pte. LEWIS, E., 1st Bn.
5259	Rfm. LEWIS, H., 3rd Bn.
6628	Pte. LIPMAN, H., 7th Bn.
6847	Pte. LEWIS, P., 7th Bn.
6668	Pte. LAWRENCE, A., 7th Bn.
7168	Pte. LEWIN, A., 7th Bn.
7891	Cadet LUDSKI, J. C., 28th Bn.
4528	Pte. LEVY, S., 7th Bn.
11/6108	Rfm. LEVENE, H., Q.V.R.
11/5289	Rfm. LEVY, W. J., 10th Bn.
8056	Rfm. LENT, J., 17th Bn.
8384	Rfm. LANDSBERG, H., 17th Bn.
G/97194	Pte. LIGHTER, H. S., 7th Bn.
355168	Pte. LEE, P., 7th Bn.
423723	Pte. LEVY, I., 10th Bn.
305734	Rfm. LEWIS, H., 5th Bn.
283660	Pte. LEVY, A., 1st Bn.
230488	L/Cpl. LYONS, N., 1st Bn.
92465	Pte. LUDSKI, E., 7th Bn.
324661	Rfm. LEVY, J., 6th Bn.
G/96449	Pte. LAZARUS, L., 19th Bn.
614217	Pte. LEWIS, J., 7th Bn.
56565	Rfm. LEVI, E. N., 5th Bn.
110720	Pte. LUBOROFF, S. W., 7th Bn.
323826	Rfm. LEVY, R., 6th Bn.
G/97059	Pte. LEVI, W., 19th Bn.
231310	Cpl. LEVY, M., 1st Bn.

London Regt.—*Continued.*

158428	Rfm. Levy, A., 5th Bn.
425856	Pte. Levy, M., 10th Bn.
304476	Rfm. Levy, G., 5th Bn.
8814	Pte. Lubicit, I., 29th Bn.
30448	Pte. Levene, L., 29th Bn.
205806	Pte. Lewis, J.
51694	Rfm. Levy, W.
45492	Rfm. Levy, C. S., 2/18th Bn.
101133	Pte. Lipman, 2/23rd Bn.
724545	Pte. Lesnie, S., 2/27th Bn.
36469	Rfm. Levy, S., 6th Bn.
92288	Pte. Levy, W., 3rd Bn.
243864	Pte. Levene, V., 1/2nd Bn.
350321	Pte. Levy, F., 7th Bn.
573306	Pte. Laderman, D., 3/17th Bn.
1552	Rfm. Levy, N., 8th Bn.
	Dmr. Lazarus, M., 17th Bn.
423205	Pte. Labofsky, T., 2/10th Bn.
	L/Cpl. Landsberg, J., 13th Bn.
1863	Pte. Loffren, 4th Bn.
577005	Rfm. Levy, I.
282535	Pte. Lyons, I.,* 1/4th Bn.
701822	Pte. Levy, H., 2/23rd Bn.
570200	Rfm. Levy, J., 2/17th Bn.
742053	Pte. Lewis, 1/25th Bn.
683307	Pte. Leschinsky, E., 2/22nd Bn.
6059	Rfm. Levenston, A., 2/18th Bn.
594122	Rfm. Levy, A., 2/18th Bn.
530959	Sgt. Levy, D., 2/15th Bn.
701266	Rfm. Lewis, B., 2/21st Bn.
5016	Cadet Lewis, S., 28th Bn.
5327	Rfm. Lenzberg, W., 2/12th Bn.
2/4790	Pte. Levy, S., 1st Bn.
	Pte. Lansky, J., 13th Bn.
395344	Pte. Lewis, A. L., 9th Bn.
422461	Cpl. Lyons, H. J. (M.M.), 10th Bn.
8667	Pte. Leibert, M., 2/1st Bn.
8891	Pte. Levy, L., 2/1st Bn.
8286	Pte. Levin, J. E., 2/2nd Bn.
5525	Pte. Lyons, B., 2/4th Bn.
6375	Pte. Lavine, L., 2/10th Bn.
4778	Pte. Lipman, I., 2/23rd Bn.
4678	Pte. Liggi, A., 1/15th Bn.
553679	Cpl. Lewis, H., 1/16th Bn.
7587	Pte. Lessman, M., 1/4th Bn.
4914	Rfm. Lederer, R., 1/18th Bn.
537778	L/Cpl. Lazarus.
4494	Pte. Levy, S., 22nd Bn.
571245	Rfm. Lipman, A., 2/17th Bn.
4470	Pte. Lazarus, M., 2/25th Bn.
683682	Pte. Landau, G. G., 22nd Bn.
822143	Pte. Lipshitz, S., 31st Bn.
782048	Pte. Levene, L., 29th Bn.
782070	Pte. Levy, D., 29th Bn.
801339	Pte. Lyons, D. A., 30th Bn.
801342	Pte. Levy, J. A., 30th Bn.
115	Pte. Labin, C.
2972	Cpl. Lambert, H., 7th Bn.
253660	Pte. Levy, A., 3rd Bn.
5407	Pte. Levy, J., 2/9th Bn.
750591	Pte. Lisser, W. C., 2nd Bn.
140546	Pte. Lyons, J., 3/20th Bn.
30474	Pte. Levy, D., 29th Bn.
8747	Pte. Levy, H., 29th Bn.
594122	Rfm. Levy, A., 2/18th Bn.
551833	Rfm. Lawson, R. W., 2/16th Bn.
683898	Pte. Lazarus, 2/22nd Bn.
5709	Pte. Levy, N., 1/19th Bn.
8434	Pte. Luskin, I., 1/1st Bn.
8144	Pte. Lazarus, H., 1/1st Bn.
5630	Pte. Levine, M., 1/12th Bn.
492038	Pte. Lewis, A., 13th Bn.
204320	Pte. Leibert, M., 2/1st Bn.
9871	Rfm. Landsberg, G. G.,* 1st L.R.B.
203845	Pte. Lazarus, H., 1/1st Bn.
282929	Pte. Leboff, S.
282588	Pte. Levy, P.
376096	Pte. Levy, S., 17th Bn.
742052	Cyc. Lavanthar, H., 1/25th Bn.
341250	Pte. Lewis, M., 13th Bn.
2640	Pte. Lyons, S., 1/18th Bn.
29439	Pte. Levy, F. L., 35th Bn.
154115	Pte. Levene, M., 3rd Bn.
301753	L/Cpl. Leapman, L. L., 5th Bn.
283754	L/Cpl. Louisson, L. F., 3rd Bn.
355002	Pte. Lyons, L., 3/7th Bn.
392691	Pte. Levy, E., 2/9th Bn.
633994	Pte. Lyons, J., 3/20th Bn.
27444	Pte. Lewis, S., 2nd Bn.
781805	Pte. Levy, L. L., 29th Bn.
574770	Pte. Levy, J., 17th Bn.
2389	Pte. Ludmansky, G., 6th Bn.
1777	Pte. Lyons, A., 3/6th Bn.
4913	Pte. Lyons, M., 3/6th Bn.
4208	Sgt. Lewis, W. M., 7th Bn.
473310	Pte. Lawson, F., 1/12th Bn.
682027	Pte. Levy, M., 2/22nd Bn.
5181	Pte. Levey, B., 20th Bn.
5021	Pte. Levy, E., 13th Bn.
5998	Pte. Levy, G., 16th Bn.
2578	L/Sgt. Levy, J., 2/19th Bn.
4132	Pte. Lewis, J., 1/10th Bn.
	Rfm. Levy, E. (M.M.).
324458	Rfm. Levy, H., 1/6th Bn.
593833	Pte. Levenson, A., 2/18th Bn.
611582	Pte. Lennard, W., 2/19th Bn.
701822	Pte. Levy, H., 2/23rd Bn.
92525	Pte. Lichfield, E., 2/6th Bn.
3995	Pte. Levy, A., 3rd Bn.
590879	L/Cpl. Lyons, S., 18th Bn.
8055	Pte. Levy, E., 3/17th Bn.
6432	Pte. Leschinsky, I.
8194	Pte. Lubinsky, J. L., 3rd Bn.
1/6242	Dvr. Levy, 1st Bn.
5074	Pte. Levy, J., 2/14th Bn.

London Regt.—*Continued.*

5708	Pte. Levy, 3/14th Bn.
4528	Pte. Levy, S., 3/7th Bn.
25/5376	Pte. Levy, L., 10th Bn.
25/4019	Pte. Lazarus, H., 10th Bn.
25/6621	Pte. Levene, J., 10th Bn.
25/6585	Pte. Lee, L., 10th Bn.
5318	Pte. Lesitsky, J., 10th Bn.
8977	L/Cpl. Lyons, M., 2nd Bn.
554946	Rfm. Levy, S., 16th Bn.
2133	Sgt. Levy, D., 2/15th Bn.
	Pte. Lewis, P., 3/7th Bn.
594136	Rfm. Lipman, H., 18th Bn.
571856	Rfm. Lee, A., 17th Bn.
574927	Pte. Levine, A., 17th Bn.
472499	Rfm. Lennens, J., 1/12th Bn.
8203	Rfm. Levensky, A., 17th Bn.
2180	Rfm. Lyons, A. A., 2nd Bn.
798	Sgt. Levy, S.
6574	Pte. Levy, L., 2nd Bn.
3701	Pte. Levy, M., 2/2nd Bn.
28182	Pte. Levy, S., 1st Bn.
5010	Pte. Levy., H., 13th Bn.
4837	Pte. Levy, P., 4/3rd Bn.
1751	Pte. Levy, T., 7th Bn.
	Sgt. Levy, B. (D.C.M.).
4970	Pte. Lipman, J., 13th Bn.
2473	Pte. Littman, I., 23rd Bn.
5762	Pte. Lockern, J., 21st Bn.
633830	Cpl. Lensberg, A., 2/20th Bn.
101133	Pte. Lipman, 2/23rd Bn.
724545	Pte. Lesnie, S., 2/24th Bn.
	C.S.M. Levey, S. M. (M.M.).
282194	Pte. Lee, V., 1/4th Bn.
4294	L/Sgt. Levy, 4/1st Bn.
2935	Pte. Levy, G., 3/10th Bn.
492039	Pte. Lewis, A., 2/6th Bn.
203660	Pte. Levene, R., 1st Bn.
841250	Pte. Lewis, N., 32nd Bn.
473006	Rfm. List, H.,* 2/12th Bn.
576096	Rfm. Levy, S., 17th Bn.
452845	Rfm. Levy, S., 2/11th Bn.
351800	Rfm. Levy, S., 1/17th Bn.
201722	L/Sgt. Levy, J., 1st Bn.
4735	Pte. Levy, A., 16th Bn.
472511	Pte. Lewis, R., 1/12th Bn.
204436	Pte. Levy, L., 1st Bn.
557095	Rfm. Ladd, A. E., 3/16th Bn.
254192	Rfm. Lazarus, R., 3rd Bn.
354982	Rfm. Levy, M., 3/7th Bn.
425457	Pte. Lewis, D., 3/10th Bn.
421998	Pte. Lewis, C., 3/10th Bn.
7320	Pte. Lewis, H., 1/16th Bn.
8451	Rfm. Lazarus, B.
422886	Rfm. Lesitsky, J.
576498	Rfm. Lewis, A., 17th Bn.
472393	L/Cpl. Levine, M.
573306	Sgt. Laderman, D., 17th Bn.
204436	Pte. Levy, L., 2/1st Bn.
3036	Pte. Langer, R. B., 12th Bn.
4019	Pte. Lazarus, H., 3/10th Bn.
701908	Pte. Levy, J., 23rd Bn.
8867	Pte. Leibert, M., 21st Bn.
633904	Pte. Lyons, J., 3/20th Bn.
302019	Pte. Lipstein, M., 1/5th Bn.
282375	Pte. Lipman, R., 2/4th Bn.
46178	Pte. Ligge, A., 1/15th Bn.
5007	Pte. Levine, H., 23rd Bn.
	Pte. Labenoff, L., 17th Bn.
	Pte. Littaur, C., 10th Bn.
	Pte. Littaur, J., 10th Bn.
97413	Pte. Levy, I., 2nd Bn.
42047	Rfm. Lazarus, J., 9th Bn.
46707	Rfm. Lyons, L., 17th Bn.
354071	Rfm. Lelyveld, B., 7th Bn.
51694	Pte. Levy, W.
2944	L/Cpl. Littman, M.,* 1/11th Bn.
	C.S.M. Levey, O. S. H. (M.S.M.).
204441	Pte. Myerovitz, R.,* 2/1st Bn.
5419	Pte. Miller, A., 2/2nd Bn.
5813	Pte. Michaels, M., 2/2nd Bn.
3431	Pte. Moses, S., 2/3rd Bn.
4033	L./Cpl. Mendoza, D., 2/3rd Bn.
2014	Cpl. Morris, H., 2/4th Bn.
5557	Pte. Miller, J., 2/7th Bn.
8975	Rfm. Malofsky, S., 2/8th Bn.
4261	Rfm. Morris, H., 2/9th Bn.
2556	Sgt. Murray, H., 2/10th Bn.
2083	Sgt. Monty, J.,* 2/10th Bn.
424087	Pte. Meister, S., 2/10th Bn.
6645	Rfm. Marmulstein, J., 2/11th Bn.
3287	Rfm. Morris, J., 2/11th Bn.
5064	Rfm. Markovitch, S., 2/11th Bn
4896	Rfm. Morrell, W. H., 2/11th Bn.
5520	Rfm. Myers, H., 2/12th Bn.
4105	Pte. Marks, J., 1/7th Bn.
6593	Pte. Moses, M., 1/7th Bn.
572682	Rfm. Marks, L., 1/17th Bn.
594693	Rfm. Myers, M., 1/18th Bn.
678117	Rfm. Morrell, W., 1/21st Bn.
36135	Rfm. Mishlove, F., 1/21st Bn.
232682	Rfm. Michaels, M., 1/18th Bn.
53651	Rfm. Marks, H., 1/19th Bn.
611400	Rfm. Metless, L., 1/19th Bn.
698019	Pte. Marmulstein, I., 1/22nd Bn.
39470	Pte. Marks, J., 1/23rd Bn.
37293	Pte. Montsatt, H., 1/23rd Bn.
68858	Pte. Marks, H., 1/24th Bn.
	Pte. Myers, J. M. (M.M.).
25205	Pte. Marcus, H., 1/8th Bn.
350445	Cpl. Morris, H., 2/7th Bn.
385111	Rfm. Myers, M., 2/8th Bn.
552658	Rfm. Margerite, W., 2/12th Bn.
472341	Rfm. Myers, P. M., 2/12th Bn.
552648	Rfm. Morris, A. B., 2/12th Bn.

London Regt.—*Continued.*

304822	Pte. MENDOZA, G. H., 1/28th Bn.		6229	Pte. MCHAELS, W., 1/13th Bn.
767387	Pte. MARCHANT, H., 1/28th Bn.		5418	Pte. MARTIN, A., 1/7th Bn.
415206	Pte. MYERS, S., 1/6th Bn.		6208	Pte. MATHER, J., 1/7th Bn.
275217	Pte. MOSELY, A.,* 1/3rd Bn.		6765	Pte. MELTZER, G.,* 1/7th Bn.
375055	Rfm. MORRIS, A., 1/5th Bn.		1805	Pte. MARKS, J., 1/4th Bn.
70130	L/Cpl. MARIS, L. G., 1/28th Bn.		2216	Rfm. MARCUS, D. H.,* 1/12th Bn.
762908	Pte. MOSS, M. A.,* 1/28th Bn.		4052	Cpl. MARKS, H., 1/12th Bn.
4486	Pte. MOSSBAUM, A., 1/22nd Bn.		4653	Pte. MALNICK, J., 1/12th Bn.
4516	Pte. MYERS, L., 1/22nd Bn.		2505	Rfm. MARSH, H. W., 1/5th Bn.
4500	Pte. MOLDASKY, A., 1/22nd Bn.		5337	Rfm. MARKS, C. B., 1/16th Bn.
	Rfm. MOSES, I., 1/11th Bn.		5421	Rfm. MILLER, J. D., 1/9th Bn.
4442	L/Cpl. MERVISH, G., 1st Bn.		5767	Rfm. MORRIS, A., 1/16th Bn.
2414	Pte. MOSS, M. C., 1/12th Bn.		553877	Pte. MAIN, M., 2/16th Bn.
244	Rfm. MOSS, H., 1/5th Bn.			Sgt. MENDEL, F. W. (M.S.M.).
245009	L/Cpl. MANDELBAUM, M., 1/5th Bn.		422077	Pte. MYERS, S., 1/10th Bn.
8275	Rfm. MERCADO, B., 1/9th Bn.		453750	Rfm. MINDEL, B., 1/11th Bn.
423003	Sgt. MORRIS, C., 1/10th Bn.		259189	Pte. MERBY, S., 1/18th Bn.
742060	Pte. MORRIS, C., 1/25th Bn.		468	Pte. MORRIS, J., 1/1st Bn.
5734	Pte. MEEK, H., 2/13th Bn.		771	Sgt. MOSS, J. H., 2/2nd Bn.
5698	Pte. MARKS, R., 2/15th Bn.		43968	Pte. MARKS, J., 1/4th Bn.
5320	Rfm. MARKS, S., 2/16th Bn.		41185	Pte. MEDNICK, M., 1/2nd Bn.
2858	Rfm. MARKS, G. H., 2/21st Bn.			Cpl. MYERS, P. (M.M.).
5960	Pte. MORRELL, J.,* 2/24th Bn.		493100	Pte. MOSS, W. G., 1/13th Bn.
6965	Pte. MOSES, J.,* 1/3rd Bn.		253821	Pte. MARKASKY, M., 1/3rd Bn.
20047	L/Cpl. MINNIS, J., 1/1st Bn.		391425	Pte. MORRIS, H., 1/9th Bn.
204732	Pte. MILLER, N., 1/1st Bn.		4/5940	Pte. MARSHBAUM, J., 1/3rd Bn.
8202	Pte. MENDOZA, L., 1/1st Bn.		4/5946	Pte. MILOFSKY, L., 1/3rd Bn.
282867	Pte. MODLYN, S., 1/3rd Bn.		6280	Pte. MAZZIER, M., 2/10th Bn.
6396	Pte. MORRIS, A., 1/4th Bn.		5522	Pte. MUSAPHIA, E., 2/4th Bn.
6398	Pte. MICHAELS, B.,* 1/4th Bn.		5377	Pte. MAGNUS, B., 1/14th Bn.
4396	Pte. MARKS, J.,* 1/4th Bn.		64741	Pte. MONTSOFF, H.,* 1/23rd Bn.
5989	Pte. MARKOFSKY, M., 1/4th Bn.		305127	Pte. MANHOFF, J.,* 2/10th Bn.
8501	Pte. MOSES I., 1/9th Bn.		3790	Pte. MARKS, S.,* 3rd Bn.
245009	L/Cpl. MENDELBAUM, M., 1/2nd Bn.		204583	Pte. MAZZIER, M.,* 1/2nd Bn.
232820	Pte. MUSCOVITCH, L., 1/2nd Bn.		64741	Pte. MONTSOFF, H.,* 1/7th Bn.
233337	Cpl. MYERS, P., 1/2nd Bn.		2083	Sgt. MONTY, J., 2/10th Bn.
305452	Rfm. MALIN, A., 1/5th Bn.		6965	Pte. MOSES, J.,* 3rd Bn.
375055	Rfm. MINIS, A., 1/5th Bn.		353020	Pte. MOSES, N.,* 7th Bn.
392730	Rfm. MORDECAI, H., 1/9th Bn.		572484	Rfm. MYERS, M.* (M.M.), 1/17th Bn.
392499	Rfm. MICHAELS, M., 1/9th Bn.		5900	Pte. MYERS, S.,* 2nd Bn.
5181	Rfm. MARGRETE, E., 1/16th Bn.		766484	Pte. MYERS, J. W., 28th Bn.
552609	Rfm. MILLEM, H.,* 1/16th Bn.		454451	Rfm. MENAKES, A.
8730	Pte. MOSS, J., 2/1st Bn.		3261	Pte. MAURICE, E.
202744	Pte. MORRIS, B.,* 2/1st Bn.		37293	Pte. MONTSOFF, H., 1/23rd Bn.
2002	Rfm. MILLER, S., 1/9th Bn.		493744	Pte. MICHAELS, M., 2/12th Bn.
2657	Rfm. MORRIS, S., 1/6th Bn.		485099	Pte. MICHAELS, G., 12th Bn.
4291	Rfm. MONTHUNE, M., 1/6th Bn.		471571	L/Cpl. MORRIS, A., 9th Bn.
3292	Rfm. MARKS, H.,* 1/6th Bn.		34686	Pte. MYERS, H., 29th Bn.
2250	Pte. MYERS, G.,* 1/7th Bn.		552341	Rfm. MARKS, S., 2/16th Bn.
1536	Rfm. MORRIS, R., 1/17th Bn.			Pte. MICHAELS, J. M., 15th Bn.
2718	Rfm. MINSK, M.,* 1/17th Bn.		4190	Pte. MORVERAI, J., 19th Bn.
3712	Rfm. MORRIS, J., 1/18th Bn.		574199	Pte. MICHAELS, S.
1251	Cpl. MORRIS, A., 1/24th Bn.		742057	Pte. MARKS, 1/25th Bn.
181	Sgt. MAAS, A., 1/16th Bn.		652854	Rfm. MORRIS, M., 2/21st Bn.
5370	Rfm. MYERS, J., 1/17th Bn.		5520	Rfm. MYERS, P., 2/12th Bn.
652298	Sgt. MYERS, J.,* 1/21st Bn.		4261	Rfm. MORRIS, H., 9th Bn.
5540	Pte. MARKS, A., 1/24th Bn.		10532	Rfm. MAYERS, L., 3rd Bn.
			6593	Pte. MOSES, N., 7th Bn.

London Regt.—*Continued.*

7195	Pte. Meltzer, D. B., 7th Bn.
8340	Rfm. Michaels, S., 17th Bn.
425889	Pte. Manoff, S., 10th Bn.
8011341	Pte. Montagues, M., 1st Bn.
426395	Pte. Michael, G., 10th Bn.
426448	Pte. Marks, J., 10th Bn.
283072	Pte. Marcus, M., 3rd Bn.
205015	Pte. Miller, W., 1st Bn.
282426	L/Cpl. Maguis, B., 3rd Bn.
306166	Rfm. Marks, H., 5th Bn.
426703	Pte. Marks, H., 10th Bn.
36731	Rfm. Michaelofsky, W., 8th Bn.
252853	Pte. Markosky, M., 3rd Bn.
5892	Pte. Morris, B., 2/1st Bn.
3431	Pte. Moses, S., 2/3rd Bn.
21/5107	Cpl. Muslin, R.
715045	Pte. Marcus, 2/23rd Bn.
275217	Pte. Moseley, A., 2/3rd Bn.
55346	Pte. Marks, S., 2/16th Bn.
822161	Pte. Michaels, A., 31st Bn.
801341	Pte. Montague, M., 30th Bn.
38968	Pte. Mendoza, J., 18th Bn.
55264	Rfm. Morris, A. S., 9th Bn.
452805	Rfm. Maisner, J.
452805	Rfm. Marmelstein, I., 2/11th Bn.
6713	Pte. Moss, M. B., 2/18the Bn.
	Rfm. Marks, H.
532754	Rfm. Marks, R., 2/15th Bn.
682967	Pte. Morris, M. D., 2/22nd Bn.
204441	Pte. Myerovitz, R.,* 2/4th Bn.
840953	Pte. Mendoza, J., 32nd Bn.
4961	Pte. Mason, D., 4/2nd Bn.
6952	Pte. Mikhialoll, M., 3/20th Bn.
6808	L/Cpl. Mendlebaum, M., 19th Bn.
8541	Pte. Marks, J., 2/1st Bn.
801183	Pte. Michaels, J., 29th Bn.
861179	Pte. Moses, L., 30th Bn.
763709	Sgt. Markheim, P., 2nd Bn.
762908	Pte. Moss, M. A.,* 28th Bn.
5337	Rfm. Marks, C., 16th Bn.
6998	Pte. Maklifka, V., 3/20th Bn.
6967	Pte. Malkoff, N., 3/20th Bn.
8011	Pte. Milbastien, P., 3/20th Bn.
425587	Pte. Mester, F.
204583	Pte. Mazzier, M.,* 1/2nd Bn.
5592	Pte. Monk, R., 2/17th Bn.
7048	Pte. Moses, S., 1/1st Bn.
282426	L/Cpl. Magnus, B., 2/4th Bn.
471370	Cpl. Marks, H., 1/12th Bn.
555611	Rfm. Margovsky, H., 3/16th Bn.
251532	Cpl. Mendoza, M., 2/3rd Bn.
92499	Rfm. Michaels, M., 1/9th Bn.
820483	Sgt. Maisden, D., 31st Bn.
6396	Pte. Morris, A., 4th Bn.
372730	Rfm. Mordecai, H., 1/9th Bn.
490	Pte. Mordecai, 19th Bn.
2672	Rfm. Morris, 2/5th Bn.
4421	Pte. Martin, M., 4/4th Bn.
3598	L/Cpl. Mellin, J., 3/10th Bn.
3583	C.Q.M.S. Mayes, B. V., 19th Bn.
5380	Pte. Mendoza, M., 3/19th Bn.
3720	Rfm. Mayers, L., 3/6th Bn.
22878	Pte. Marlinsky, B., 1st Bn
532754	Pte. Marks, R., 2/15th Bn.
394264	Rfm. Moses, J.
3693	Rfm. Magasiner, M., 3/11th Bn.
5064	Pte. Marcovitch, 2/11th Bn.
1752	Pte. Marks, A., 10th Bn.
7877	Pte. Marks, A., 3/21st Bn.
4052	Cpl. Marks, H., 3/12th Bn.
3292	Pte. Marks, H., 6th Bn.
552609	Rfm. Millem, H.,* 1/16th Bn.
42437	Rfm. Marks, D., 16th Bn.
24645	Pte. Moss, H., 3rd Bn.
	Pte. Myers, P. (D.C.M.).
285072	Pte. Marcus, M., 1/4th Bn.
253821	Pte. Markasky, M., 3rd Bn.
232682	Pte. Michaels, M.
493744	Pte. Michaels, M., 2/12th Bn.
4757	Pte. Morris, J., 4/1st Bn.
4511	Pte. Morris, S., 3/22nd Bn.
3911	Pte. Morris, V., 3/10th Bn.
374059	Pte. Manofsky, S., 2/8th Bn.
3737	Pte. Myers, S., 3/10th Bn.
760130	Cpl. Muris, G.
842083	Pte. Mendoza, D., 32nd Bn.
L/172433	Pte. Miller, H., 3rd Bn.
426391	Pte. Michaels, G.
201818	Pte. Mervish, G., 1st Bn.
8501	Pte. Moses, L., 9th Bn.
233638	Pte. Malinsky, S.,* 2/2nd Bn.
6292	Pte. Moss, W. C., 13th Bn.
594419	Rfm. Mesquita, J., 18th Bn.
552346	Rfm. Marks, M., 2/16th Bn.
4653	Rfm. Malnick, J.,* 1/12th Bn.
493100	Rfm. Moss, E., 1/13th Bn.
39470	Pte. Marks, J., 1/22nd Bn.
352851	Pte. Mather, I.
	Sgt. Milcovitch, M. (M.M.).
653280	Pte. Makerwith, 21st Bn.
4480	Pte. Magnus, A., 3/22nd Bn.
	Pte. McOwen, M., 24th Bn.
	Pte. Millenger, E., 1st Bn.
	Pte. Martinez, H., 20th Bn.
304822	Pte. Mendoza, G., 1/28th Bn.
76309	Sgt. Markham, P., 1st Bn.
301621	Pte. Marsh, H. W., 5th Bn.
64741	Pte. Montsoff, H., 7th Bn.
493100	Pte. Moss, W. C., 6th Bn.
5522	Pte. Musaphia, E., 2/4th Bn.
452203	Pte. Michaelberg, A., 2/11th Bn.
55509	Pte. Meeloo, M., 17th Bn.
682386	Pte. Moss, W., 1/22nd Bn.
	Pte. Martin, J., 20th Bn.

London Regt.—*Continued.*

5781	Pte. MARGERITE, W.	
2216	Rfm. MARCUS, D. H.,* 1/12th Bn.	
2016	Sgt. NATHAN, L. (M.M.), 1/9th Bn.	
3368	Rfm. NASHLER, J., 1/17th Bn.	
5126	Pte. NUSBORNE, A., 1/19th Bn.	
5624	Pte. NATHAN, N., 1/15th Bn.	
4573	Pte. NATHAN, J. J., 1/23rd Bn.	
2191	Pte. NORMAN, A. E.,* 1/23rd Bn.	
1974	Rfm. NORTON, M., 2/17th Bn.	
7554	Pte. NATALI, H.,* 1/4th Bn.	
5957	Pte. NATHAN, H., 1/4th Bn.	
4271	Rfm. NORMAN, G. F., 1/5th Bn.	
8088	Pte. NYMAN, D., 2/3rd Bn.	
5063	Rfm. NYKERK, M., 2/11th Bn.	
4928	Rfm. NICKLESBURG, A., 2/11th Bn.	
8209	Pte. NATHAN, E., 1/7th Bn.	
707718	L/Cpl. NATHAN, J., 1/23rd Bn.	
29818	Rfm. NATHAN, A., 1/20th Bn.	
574556	Rfm. NATHAN, A., 2/8th Bn.	
422402	Pte. NOVITZKY, H.,* 2/10th Bn.	
9462	Pte. NEWMAN, N. B., 1/5th Bn.	
240015	L/Cpl. NATHAN, 1/25th Bn.	
453594	Rfm. NACOVITCH, J., 1/11th Bn.	
254176	Pte. NATHAN, C.,* 1/1st Bn.	
452306	Rfm. NYKERK, M., 1/15th Bn.	
4/6626	Pte. NEEDLEMAN, H., 1/3rd Bn.	
741115	Pte. NATHAN, O., 1/25th Bn.	
354327	Pte. NATHAN, E., 1/7th Bn.	
491980	Pte. NAPHTALI, H.,* 1/13th Bn.	
	Cpl. NEWFIELD, M., 13th Bn.	
6885	Rfm. NASSELLSKI, D. A., 6th Bn.	
5509	Rfm. NATHAN, M., 17th Bn.	
254393	Pte. NATHAN, J., 3rd Bn.	
323670	Rfm. NASELSKI, W., 6th Bn.	
305846	Rfm. NATHAN, J., 5th Bn.	
282846	Rfm. NILOFSKY, 3rd Bn.	
26/2618	L/Sgt. NATHAN, O., 10th Bn.	
763206	Pte. NATHAN, M., 2nd Bn.	
495646	Pte. NECUS, I., 3/16th Bn.	
244176	Pte. NATHAN, C., 3rd Bn.	
202908	Pte. NYMAN, A., 1st Bn.	
424087	Pte. NEISTER, S., 2/10th Bn.	
11/821457	Pte. NOVOSESKY, M., 32nd Bn.	
254393	Pte. NATHAN, J.	
5018	Pte. NATHAN, A., 4/3rd Bn.	
351259	Pte. NORMAN, E., 23rd Bn.	
574971	Pte. NEGIN, 17th Bn.	
4813	L/Cpl. OPET, A. H., 1/5th Bn.	
5044	Rfm. OSTERLENSKY, S., 2/12th Bn.	
4521	Pte. OSOSKY, M., 1/22nd Bn.	
4523	Pte. OVERS, H., 1/22nd Bn.	
415094	Rfm. OZEN, J., 1/9th Bn.	
534269	Pte. OGUS, G. H., 1/15th Bn.	
5874	Pte. OLEMBOSKY, H., 2/10th Bn.	
2088	Pte. OSTROFF, M., 7th Bn.	
683811	Pte. OESTERMAN, J., 3/22nd	
822130	Rfm. OPPENHEIM, H., 31st Bn.	
354743	Rfm. OLIVER, M., 7th Bn.	
8004	Rfm. OKENOFF, E., 3/20th Bn.	
574591	Rfm. OPPENHEIM, S., 3/20th Bn.	
1536	Rfm. OKOWSFSKI, H., 10th Bn.	
3212	Rfm. OLSEN, C., 3/22nd Bn.	
	Rfm. ORNSTEIN, L., 24th Bn.	
	Rfm. OSBORNE, L., 17th Bn.	
4035	Pte. PHILLIPS, J., 1/7th Bn.	
2288	Rfm. POTTER, P., 1/17th Bn.	
2208	Rfm. PYE, A. J., 1/21st Bn.	
5479	Pte. PENDRY, H., 1/7th Bn.	
3991	Pte. PRAAGH, B., 1/15th Bn.	
7636	Sgt. PRINS, L., 2/22nd Bn.	
5415	Rfm. PEPPER, W., 1/22nd Bn.	
5222	Pte. PHILLIPS, S., 1/1st Bn.	
2142	Pte. PHILLIPS, R., 1/2nd Bn.	
2380	Rfm. PECKAR, C., 1/5th Bn.	
5050	Rfm. PASS, J., 1/5th Bn.	
4723	Rfm. POLITZER, E., 1/9th Bn.	
2106	Rfm. PHILLIPS, W., 2/17th Bn.	
5280	Pte. PAMPLE, P. A., 2/19th Bn.	
7029	Rfm. PEISTER, H., 2/18th Bn.	
200930	Pte. PHILLIPS, G., 1/1st Bn.	
5986	Pte. POLLACK, M.,* 1/4th Bn.	
2495	Pte. PRICE, S., 1/4th Bn.	
5953	Pte. PINKUS, A., 1/4th Bn.	
2785	Rfm. POSNER, H. L., 1/12th Bn.	
492788	Pte. POMERANCE, S.,* 1/13th Bn.	
2458	Rfm. PLATSKY, M., 1/12th Bn.	
493927	Cpl. PARKER, A., 1/13th Bn.	
5412	Pte. PARK, L., 2/2nd Bn.	
4363	Pte. PRESTON, W., 2/7th Bn.	
4461	L./Cpl. PARK, S., 2/10th Bn.	
423036	Pte. PAYNE, A.,* 2/10th Bn.	
4658	Rfm. POSENER, J. B., 2/11th Bn.	
574995	Rfm. PHILLIPS, H., 1/17th Bn.	
7588	Rfm. POSENER, C. B., 1/21st Bn.	
7570	Pte. PEPPER, W., 1/22nd Bn.	
701906	Pte. PHILLIPS, J., 1/23rd Bn.	
303870	Rfm. PYSER, L., 2/5th Bn.	
5001	Pte. PALMER, H., 2/4th Bn.	
570224	L./Cpl. PIETERS, J., 1/17th Bn.	
608491	Rfm. PYSER, L., 1/18th Bn.	
684011	Pte. PARK, H., 1/22nd Bn.	
46721	Rfm. PLOTKINE, M., 1/17th Bn.	
232850	Pte. PRICE, B.,* 2/2nd Bn.	
203266	Pte. PODOBRANSKY, M., 2/1st Bn.	
570751	Rfm. PORTER, P., 17th Bn.	
353566	Pte. PHILLIPS, L. L., 2/7th Bn.	
421424	Pte. PRINCE, D., 2/10th Bn.	
425471	Pte. PETRUSHKIN, M., 2/10th Bn.	
5281	Pte. PAMPLE, S., 3/19th Bn.	
4239	Rfm. PHILLIPS, H. F., 3/12th Bn.	
3119	Pte. PHILLIPS, E., 1/17th Bn.	
7148	Pte. PRINS, B., 1/1st Bn.	
437	Rfm. POSNER, M., 1/12th Bn.	
574464	Rfm. PISMARA, T., 1/17th Bn.	
304601	Rfm. PHILLIPS, A., 1/5th Bn.	

London Regt.—*Continued.*

742070	Pte. Peskoff, 1/25th Bn.
614395	Pte. Pearlstein, L.,* 2/19th Bn.
453792	Rfm. Perry, L., 1/11th Bn.
4489	Pte. Putman, W., 1/22nd Bn.
452004	L./Cpl. Posener, 2/11th Bn.
615821	Pte. Phillips, N., 1/19th Bn.
282947	Pte. Pearlstone, A., 2/4th Bn.
5002	Pte. Ponska, W. C., 1/14th Bn.
4/6600	Pte. Paris, G., 1/3rd Bn.
10452	Pte. Phillips, E. L., 1/28th Bn.
4501	Pte. Pollard, J. A., 1/3rd Bn.
761869	Sgt. Phillips, W. L., 1/28th Bn.
423036	Pte. Payne, A., 2/10th Bn.
203864	Pte. Pepper, M.,* 2/4th Bn.
5032	Pte. Phillips, B.,* 1/23rd Bn.
351517	Pte. Phillips, J.,* 7th Bn.
5801	Pte. Prins, A.,* 4th Bn.
766448	Pte. Prager, B., 28th Bn.
608491	Rfm. Pyser, S., 1/13th Bn.
421424	Pte. Priner, D., 2/10th Bn.
354911	Pte. Phillips, A. I., 7th Bn.
656580	Pte. Pye, F., 2/2nd Bn.
5029	Pte. Pyser, I., 2/23rd Bn.
702694	Pte. Porte, H., 2/23rd Bn.
7261	Pte. Phillips, L., 7th Bn.
12/5833	Rfm. Plater, M., Q.V.R.
23/6026	Pte. Porte, H. H., 21st Bn.
254955	Pte. Phillips, J., 3rd Bn.
375053	Pte. Pallatz, R., 1/5th Bn.
6347	Pte. Painon, D., 20th Bn.
615821	Pte. Phillips, N., 3/19th Bn.
801324	Pte. Poluski, G., 30th Bn.
5222	Pte. Phillips, S., 4/1st Bn.
6964	L/Cpl. Panico, J., 3/20th Bn.
8010	Pte. Papisinedashvili, M., 3/20th Bn.
8031	Pte. Padva, S., 3/20th Bn.
514737	Pte. Perlmutter, H., 14th Bn.
514336	Pte. Phillips, H. G., 3/14th Bn.
25/6666	Pte. Plotzker, J., 10th Bn.
35/4594	Pte. Pamet, F., 10th Bn.
6115	Pte. Perlsfoul, A., 4th Bn.
7158	Pte. Park, S., 4th Bn.
2944	Pte. Phillips, G., 1/1st Bn.
683560	Pte. Phillios, A., 22nd Bn.
493927	Pte. Parker, M. A.
304291	Rfm. Pass, J. J., 5th Bn.
27594	Pte. Peter, P.
282161	Pte. Palmer, H., 2/4th Bn.
422521	L/Cpl. Partt, S., 2/10th Bn.
20932	Pte. Phillips, S., 1st Bn.
G/23390	Pte. Posner, M., 29th Bn.
574464	L/Cpl. Pisaro, T.
202778	Pte. Pepper, A.
324724	Pte. Poresky, M.
180130	Pte. Posener, H., 30th Bn.
1023	Pte. Phillips, C. J., 21st Bn.
4259	Pte. Palmer, M., 2nd Bn.
4781	Pte. Pelster, H., 13th Bn.
5048	Pte. Phillips, L., 3/7th Bn.
	Pte. Phillips, P. F., 5th Bn.
5657	Pte. Polinsky, J., 3/12th Bn.
2815	Pte. Pollack, A., 11th Bn.
3855	Pte. Pollack, J., 3/10th Bn.
4284	Pte. Pool, L. M., 28th Bn.
5038	Pte. Preshman, A., 3/7th Bn.
128140	Pte. Preeman, G., 20th Bn.
	Pte. Perlman, D., 19th Bn.
100619	Pte. Pariser, C., 19th Bn.
472458	Pte. Platsky, 1/12th Bn.
	Pte. Proops, H.
1443	Sgt. Ramus, S. L., 1/9th Bn.
2808	Rfm. Rosenberg, C. A., 1/6th Bn.
2389	Rfm. Rudmanski, S., 1/6th Bn.
4179	Pet. Rose, J., 1/6th Bn.
5460	Pte. Rosenthal, B., 1/17th Bn.
5310	L/Cpl. Rich, J., 1/20th Bn.
5412	Pte. Rich, W., 1/20th Bn.
4505	Pte. Rosenberg, H., 1/22nd Bn.
4488	Pte. Rutman, D., 1/22nd Bn.
4976	Pte. Rapport, J., 1/3rd Bn.
6251	Pte. Ross, A., 1/3rd Bn.
2285	Cpl. Raperport, E., 1/4th Bn.
3904	Pte. Rozelaar, P., 1/2nd Bn.
4849	Pte. Ross, E., 1/2nd Bn.
4979	Pte. Rebak, D., 1/2nd Bn.
5069	Pte. Rubinstein, H., 1st Bn.
2785	Pte. Rosener, H., 1/12th Bn.
5636	Pte. Rosenberg, J., 2/20th Bn.
4585	Rfm. Rose, S., 2/21st Bn.
282930	Pte. Redhouse, B., 1/4th Bn.
283682	Pte. Rothman, M., 1/4th Bn.
283552	Pte. Rosenbloom, L., 1/4th Bn.
282852	Pte. Roundstein, H., 1/4th Bn.
472437	Rfm. Rates, A., 1/12th Bn.
5208	Pte. Rotman, A., 1/9th Bn.
415150	Pte. Rubinstein, E., 1/9th Bn.
5108	Pte. Raphael, J., 2/1st Bn.
233855	L/Cpl. Rosenberg, L.,* 2/2nd Bn.
6778	Pte. Rosenbloom, S., 2/4th Bn.
5516	Pte. Romaine, P., 2/4th Bn.
8321	Pte. Rubenstein, G., 1/7th Bn.
535203	Pte. Rose, H., 1/15th Bn.
209284	Pte. Rose, S., 1/17th Bn.
6542	Rfm. Rosenthal, 1/17th Bn.
595886	Rfm. Rubin, D., 1/18th Bn.
576580	Pte. Rosenthal, H., 1/17th Bn.
203657	Pte. Rebark, C., 2/2nd Bn.
534614	Rfm. Rosenberg, H., 2/6th Bn.
741581	Pte. Rosenberg, M., 2/10th Bn.
742167	Pte. Rousga, H., 2/10th Bn.
415024	Rfm. Ramet, P., 2/9th Bn.
5873	Rfm. Ramus, R. A., 1/9th Bn.
4524	Pte. Rosenberg, J., 1/22nd Bn.
6145	Dmr. Rose, W. R., 1/20th Bn.
2317	Pte. Rosenthal, C.,* 1/4th Bn.

London Regt.—Continued.

7015	Pte. RICHLAND, G. F., 1/20th Bn.
471298	Rfm. REDSTONE, D., 1/12th Bn.
742113	Pte. ROBINSON, 1/25th Bn.
616778	Pte. RAPHAEL, I.
44195	Pte. ROTHSTEIN, L., 1/22nd Bn.
322647	Rfm. ROME, L.,* 1/6th Bn.
425589	Rfm. ROBINSON, P., 1/8th Bn.
419008	Pte. RUBIN, 1/9th Bn.
6300	Pte. RAMET, A., 1/3rd Bn.
5951	Pte. ROSENTHAL, H., 1/3rd Bn.
5769	Pte. ROSENFELD, H., 2/10th Bn.
28228	Pte. ROSENBERG, M., 1/3rd Res. Bn.
1599	Cpl. RAMUS, E. J.,* 9th Bn.
2401	Pte. RAMUS, J.,* 8th Bn.
203115	Pte. ROSENBAUM, S.,* 1st Bn.
612000	Pte. ROSENBERG, I.,* 1/19th Bn.
7292	Pte. ROSENBERG, J.,* 8th Bn.
88368	Pte. ROSENBERG, M.,* 1st Bn.
6215	Rfm. ROWSON, D.,* 16th Bn.
6993	L/Cpl. RIBKIS, S., 3/20th Bn.
5531	Pte. ROSENBERG, 2/19th Bn.
10/5680	Pte. RUDHOF, S. E., 10th Bn.
25/5770	Pte. RUBENSTEIN, C., 10th Bn.
8107	Pte. ROSENBERG, J., 3/17th Bn.
4495	Pte. ROTHSTEIN, L., 22nd Bn.
5467	Pte. ROSENTHAL, B., 17th Bn.
801266	Pte. ROWLANDS, E. A., 30th Bn.
6990	Pte. RAZBINOFSKY, E., 3/20th Bn.
6957	Pte. RODKAMINSKI, 3/20th Bn.
8049	Pte. RUSSIN, J., 3/20th Bn.
324747	Pte. ROSENBERG, A. E.
208749	L/Cpl. RUBNER, C., 2/4th Bn.
354438	Pte. RUBENSTEIN, C., 1/7th Bn.
573398	Pte. ROSENTHAL, P.
204057	Pte. ROSENBERG, M., 1st Bn.
536829	Pte. RABINOWITZ, E., 15th Bn.
	S.M. ROSENBERG, W. F. H. (M.S.M.).
534614	Pte. ROSENBERG, H., 2/6th Bn.
320601	Pte. RUDANSKI, T., 30th Bn.
82331	Pte. ROSEN, S., 31st Bn.
4998	Pte. RACK, M., 4/1st Bn.
4739	Pte. REBACK, B., 4/2nd Bn.
5567	Pte. REIS, V. C., 3/15th Bn.
533392	Pte. RUTER, L., 2/1st Bn.
40976	Pte. RUBENSTEIN, J., 2/1st Bn.
5108	Pte. RABEL, I., 3/1st Bn.
4965	Pte. RABENSKY, H., 20th Bn.
3010	Pte. ROAT, A., 7th Bn.
3450	Pte. ROSEN, J., 2nd Bn.
	Pte. ROTHSTEIN, L.
820476	Pte. RODRIQUES, A., 31st Bn.
651814	Rfm. ROSE, S. A., 2/21st Bn.
	Pte. ROTHFIELD, B. H., 15th Bn.
780004	Pte. ROOD, S., 29th Bn.
6093	Pte. RANDOLPH, A., 29th Bn.
355924	Pte. RAITZ, H.
682035	Pte. ROSENGRAD, A., 2/22nd Bn.
5470	Pte. ROSENTHAL, M., 16th Bn.
497633	Pte. ROSENBERG, M.
767160	Pte. REED, R. M. P.
682005	Pte. ROSENGARD, A., 2/22nd Bn.
373206	Rfm. ROSENBAUM, H., 8th Bn.
8443	Rfm. ROSENBERG, E., 8th Bn.
5538	Rfm. REUBEN, M., 6th Bn.
420164	Sgt. ROME, S., 10th Bn.
351781	Pte. ROGERS, J., 7th Bn.
392367	Rfm. RAMUS, R. A., 9th Bn.
320889	Rfm. ROSENBERG, J., 6th Bn.
8362	Rfm. RUBENSTEIN, A., 2/2nd Bn.
1628	Rfm. ROSE, A. H., 15th Bn.
6713	Rfm. ROSEN, S., 13th Bn.
780004	Rfm. ROOD, S., 24th Bn.
822129	Pte. RONTAL, B. A., 31st Bn.
357781	Pte. ROGERS, G., 1/7th Bn.
322870	Pte. RODKER, J.
3197	Pte. ROSENBERG, A.
635478	Pte. RUBIN, L.
233855	Pte. ROSENBERG, L., 2/2nd Bn.
4497	Pte. ROGERS, 7th Bn.
20963	Pte. RYDZ, R., 3rd Bn.
	L/Cpl. REECE, W. (M.M.).
653563	Pte. ROSENBERG, J., 2/20th Bn.
6942	Pte. RABIN, B., 3/20th Bn.
840284	Pte. RUBENSTEIN, B., 32nd Bn.
556035	Pte. ROSENBERGER, W., 16th Bn.
282591	Pte. ROMAIN, P.
7137	Pte. ROSENBLOOM, L., 1/4th Bn.
35405	Pte. RABINOVITCH, J., 17th Bn.
69059	Pte. RUTTISK, D., 22nd Bn.
8278	Pte. ROSENBERG, M., 1st Bn.
2389	Pte. RUDMANSKY, S., 1/6th Bn.
5531	Pte. ROSENBERG, 2/19th Bn.
8107	Pte. ROSENBERG, J., 3/17th Bn.
322870	Pte. RODKERN, J., 6th Bn.
601670	Pte. RICHLAND, A.
	Pte. RICKERSON, H., 18th Bn.
	Pte. ROSENBLATT, H., 12th Bn.
573398	Pte. ROSENTHAL, P., 1/7th Bn.
311560	Pte. REUBENS, P., 7th Bn.
650475	Pte. RYE, S., 21st Bn.
1889	Qmr.-Sgt. SOMERS, R. J., 1/9th Bn.
4287	Rfm. SCORA, S., 1/6th Bn.
3497	Pte. STOCKFIS, R., 1/7th Bn.
4991	Rfm. SALISBURY, S., 1/17th Bn.
3060	Pte. SARNER, J., 1/7th Bn.
2250	Pte. SAMSON, J., 1/7th Bn.
2807	Pte. SPIELMAN I., 1/7th Bn.
2176	Cpl. SCHIFF, W., 1/17th Bn.
1991	Rfm. STRONG, B., 1/17th Bn.
2408	Rfm. SELMAN, B., 1/17th Bn.
3190	Rfm. SOLOMON, J., 1/17th Bn.
2178	Rfm. SALBERG, V., 1/18th Bn.
303327	Rfm. SPERO, C. N., 1/16th Bn.
6234	Pte. STERN, M., 1/13th Bn.

London Regt.—*Continued.*

3912	Rfm. SCHLEICH, C. S., 1/6th Bn.
4952	Pte. STAAL, J., 1/7th Bn.
5159	Pte. SWEDLOFF, S.,* 1/7th Bn.
4851	Pte. SCHRIEBER, J., 1/7th Bn.
2267	Pte. SHILLING, H.,* 1/7th Bn.
6550	Rfm. STOTT, J.,* 1/8th Bn.
5540	Rfm. SOLOMONS, H.,* 1/6th Bn.
4142	Pte. SIMMONS, L., 1/15th Bn.
4488	Rfm. SALMON, S., 1/18th Bn.
4949	Rfm. SAFFER, L., 1/18th Bn.
6691	Pte. SOLOMON, N., 1/15th Bn.
572559	Pte. SIMMONS, S.,* 1/17th Bn.
7159	Pte. STAAL, L., 1/17th Bn.
3637	Pte. SCHOOL, J., 1/22nd Bn.
4478	Pte. SMITH, S., 1/22nd Bn.
7575	Pte. SIMONS, A., 1/22nd Bn.
5151	Pte. SIMMONDS, M., 1/24th Bn.
5358	Pte. SANTEN A., 1/24th Bn.
6504	Pte. SMOYAS, J. I., 1/1st Bn.
6045	Pte. SOLOMAN, W., 1/3rd Bn.
203518	Pte. SCHORENSTEIN, M., 1/1st Bn.
7046	Pte. SCHAVERIN, S., 1/4th Bn.
5965	Pte. SHERKOSKY, S., 1/4th Bn.
5974	Pte. SOLOMONS, J., 1/4th Bn.
7148	Pte. SILVER, S., 1/4th Bn.
5323	Rfm. SOLOMONS, I., 1/12th Bn.
6054	Pte. SAVILLE, 1/13th Bn.
493028	Pte. SCHREIR, A., 1/13th Bn.
474071	Rfm. SOLOMONS, H.,* 1/12th Bn.
493983	Pte. SPECTOR, M., 1/13th Bn.
	Sgt. SAMUELS, M. (M.S.M.), 1/2nd Bn.
6221	Pte. SPANIER, G., 1/2nd Bn.
7099	Pte. SUSKIN, I., 1/2nd Bn.
5322	Rfm. SPERO, L. H., 1/5th Bn.
4274	Rfm. SILKOWITCH, L., 1/5th Bn.
5961	Rfm. SHOOLMAN, C., 1/9th Bn.
315024	Rfm. SIMMONDS, A. W., 1/5th Bn.
303905	Rfm. SACHS, I., 1/5th Bn.
394297	Rfm. SHELKIN, I., 1/9th Bn.
415206	Rfm. SKITTEN, M., 1/9th Bn.
8969	Pte. SOLOMANS, A., 2/1st Bn.
202776	Pte. SPEAR, H.,* 2/1st Bn.
204687	Pte. STONE, W.,* 2/1st Bn.
5405	Pte. SHAFRANSKY, T., 2/2nd Bn.
5513	Pte. SOLOMONS, M.,* 13th Bn.
5549	Pte. SHAPIRO, L., 2/3rd Bn.
5540	Pte. SOLOMONS, J., 2/3rd Bn.
6939	Pte. SCOLNICK, R., 2/3rd Bn.
1848	Pte. SAMUELS, H., 1/4th Bn.
4144	Pte. SUGARMAN, M.,* 1/4th Bn.
6096	Pte. SLACKMAN, S., 1/4th Bn.
5980	Pte. STRELSOFF, W.,* 1/4th Bn.
3752	Pte. SOLOMONS, H., 1/2nd Bn.
1471	Cpl. SCHUMAN, A., 1/5th Bn.
302933	Pte. SPURLING, M. W.,* 1/5th Bn.
5627	Rfm. SACKS, A. M., 1/9th Bn.
1635	Rfm. SYMONS, B. V., 1/9th Bn.
3715	Cpl. SAMUELS, M. T., 2/13th Bn.
5566	L./Cpl. SAMUELS, H. B., 2/13th Bn.
2921	Sgt. SILVERSTONE, A., 2/15th Bn.
6901	Rfm. SCHLESINGER, B. E., 2/16th Bn.
5966	Rfm. SELLER, J., 2/17th Bn.
4950	Rfm. SONENFELD, I., 2/18th Bn.
2532	Sgt. SAUNDERS, M., 2/19th Bn.
5508	Pte. SILBERSTON, L., 2/19th Bn.
5536	Pte. SOLOMON, A. L., 2/19th Bn.
3721	Pte. SALKIN, S., 2/19th Bn.
5629	Pte. SILOW, L., 2/20th Bn.
6452	Pte. SPINDLER, J., 2/17th Bn.
5687	Pte. SPECTERMAN, R., 2/17th Bn.
7071	Pte. SUGARMAN, L., 2/18th Bn.
4545	Rfm. SEIGENBERG, J., 2/21st Bn.
4539	Pte. SLOMAR, M., 2/23rd Bn.
5478	Pte. SOLOMON, S.,
6364	Pte. SAIPE, L., 1/15th Bn.
412068	Pte. SWERDLEN, H.,* 1/19th Bn.
5068	Pte. SHINE, J., 2/4th Bn.
300003	C.Q.M.S. SCHONEWALD, S.,* 2/5th Bn.
2673	Rfm. SIMONS, J., 2/5th Bn.
5874	Rfm. SIMONS, K. J., 2/6th Bn.
6787	Rfm. SAMPSON, S., 2/6th Bn.
6031	Pte. SOLOMON, D., 2/7th Bn.
2624	Rfm. SMART, S., 2/6th Bn.
3075	L/Cpl. SANKEMITZ, P. (M.M.), 12th Bn.
6167	Rfm. SHAPIRO, M., 1/6th Bn.
6329	Rfm. SOLERTI, A., 1/6th Bn.
6691	Pte. SOLOMON, L., 1/15th Bn.
8439	Rfm. SCHNEIDERMAN, M., 1/17th Bn.
5641	Pte. SVORDLIN, K., 1/19th Bn.
5257	Rfm. SILVERMAN, H.,* 1/21st Bn.
616149	Rfm. SUCKLING, H.,* 1/19th Bn.
R/30272	Pte. STEIN, I., 1/15th Bn.
51155	Rfm. SPEAR, S., 1/17th Bn.
573380	Rfm. STARHOPH, H., 1/17th Bn.
392425	Rfm. SCHOOLMAN, S., 1/9th Bn.
7033	L/Cpl. SUGARE, E. J., 1/3rd Bn.
203932	Pte. SUGAR, H., 2/3rd Bn.
252903	Pte. SIMONS, J., 2/3rd Bn.
572594	Rfm. SOLOMONS, L., 2/5th Bn.
492904	Rfm. SAVILLE, S., 2/9th Bn.
741458	Sgt. SALAMAN, W., 2/10th Bn.
3325	Pte. STRAUSS, R. A.,* 2nd Bn.
321787	Rfm. SCORA, S., 2/11th Bn.
766906	Pte. SELBY, M. G.,* 1/28th Bn.
252524	Cpl. SOLOMONS, J.
20488	Rfm. SINGER, M.
384825	Rfm. SHENKER, J., 1/9th Bn.
723543	Pte. SMITH, J. J., 2/24th Bn.
295387	Pte. SAMUELS, A., 2/4th Bn.
283184	Pte. SALTER, F., 2/4th Bn.
572627	L/Cpl. SINNOCK, A., 2/17th Bn.
203520	Pte. SHORNSHEIM, M., 1/1st Bn.
1091	Pte. STERN, E., 1/4th Bn.
37786	Rfm. SHILLINGBOURNE, N., 2/17th Bn.
762418	Pte. SEYMOUR, L. J., 1/28th Bn.

London Regt.—*Continued.*

6508	Pte. SILVERSTONE, M.,* 1/1st Bn.
3238	Pte. SALAMAN, W., 3/25th Bn.
273765	Pte. SOLOMONS, J., 1/13th Bn.
2748	Pte. STAHL, R., 1/12th Bn.
3190	Pte. SAQUI, L. V. H., 1/28th Bn.
1939	Pte. SAMPSON, J., 1/7th Bn.
3145	Pte. STERN, S., 1/9th Bn.
1427	Pte. SAMPSON, E., 1/4th Bn.
1863	Pte. SAFRON, I., 1/4th Bn.
7584	Pte. SOLOMONS, M., 1/4th Bn.
6117	Pte. SADOW, A., 1/13th Bn.
6835	Pte. SALKIND, R., 1/3rd Bn.
282858	Pte. SHERKOSKY, P., 1/4th Bn.
570657	L/Cpl. SELMAN, B.,* 1/17th Bn.
611876	Pte. SILVER, H., 1/9th Bn.
6096	Pte. SLACKMAN, S., 1/4th Bn.
5301	Sig. SILVER, H., 1/19th Bn.
8620	Rfm. SOLOMONS, A., 1/9th Bn.
8534	Pte. SHELKIN, I., 1/9th Bn.
204187	Pte. SCHIFF, B., 1/1st Bn.
233640	Pte. SIMMONS, I., 1/1st Bn.
	L/Cpl. SOLOMONS, G. (M.M. and Bar).
742081	Pte. SILVERMAN, I., 1/25th Bn.
742082	Cpl. SILVERMAN, S., 1/25th Bn.
	Pte. SOESAN, 1/25th Bn.
742083	Pte. SILVERSTONE, J., 1/25th Bn.
492310	Pte. STEINBERG, F. J., 2/13th Bn.
45628	Rfm. SHIREWITZ, D., 1/11th Bn.
203932	Pte. SINGER, H., 1/1st Bn.
72220	Pte. SIMMONDS, M., 1/24th Bn.
370148	Sgt. SIMMONS, P., 1/8th Bn.
44502	Rfm. SLAVENER, E., 1/6th Bn.
42480	Pte. SOLOMON, M., 1/10th Bn.
8021	Pte. SCHINEBERG, N., 1/19th Bn.
1586	Pte. SILVERMAN, A., 1/4th Bn.
352699	Pte. SOLOMON, D., 3/7th Bn.
232378	L./Cpl. SHAFRINSKY, J., 2/2nd Bn.
820217	Pte. SCHAVINSKY, I., 1/13th Bn.
635464	Pte. SOLOMONS, H., 1/20th Bn.
422886	Pte. SESITSKY, J., 2/10th Bn.
538285	L./Cpl. SYMONS, H., 1/6th Bn.
6646	Rfm. SCHNEIDER, M., 2/11th Bn.
4/4930	Pte. SAMUEL, F. B., 1/3rd Bn.
4798	Pte. SAUNDERS, J., 1/3rd Bn.
4/5943	Pte. SOLOMON, N., 1/3rd Bn.
5610	Pte. SAUNDERS, M., 2/10th Bn.
5725	Pte. SCHWACHMANN, N., 2/10th Bn.
5644	Pte. SHEFFRIN, J., 1/14th Bn.
44364	Pte. SHIRT, A., 1/3rd Bn.
36177	L/Cpl. SHOOP, H., 1/6th Bn.
252530	Pte. SHAPIRO, L., 1/3rd Bn.
9261	Cpl. SCHONBERG, B.,* 5th Bn.
63232	L/Cpl. SELMAN, H.,* 1/19th Bn.
2267	Pte. SHILLING, H.,* 7th Bn.
652267	Rfm. SILVERMAN, H.,* 1/21st Bn.
2176	Pte. SILVERSTEIN, L. B.,* 23rd Bn.
8456	Rfm. SIMONS, A.,* 17th Bn.
5540	Rfm. SOLOMONS, H.,* 6th Bn.
572664	Rfm. SOLOMONS, S.,* 17th Bn.
3141	Rfm. SPERO, M.,* 17th Bn.
2869	Rfm. STRAUSS, A. L.,* 17th Bn.
3518	Cadet STYER, W. B.,* 28th Bn.
5159	Pte. SWEDLOFF, S., 1/7th Bn.
2/6827	Pte. SYKES, R.,* 2nd Bn.
395002	Rfm. STEINBERG, J., 9th Bn.
325024	Pte. STONE, P., 9th Bn.
29553	Rfm. SILVER, D., 9th Bn.
575834	Pte. SHILLINGBOURN, J., 1/17th Bn.
5930	Pte. SPEAR, H., 2/1st Bn.
8969	Pte. SOLOMONS, A., 2/1st Bn.
6939	Pte. SCHOLNICK, R., 2/3rd Bn.
21/5024	L/Cpl. STITCHER, P.
24/6593	Pte. SAKIN, R.
111843	Dvr. STONEFIELD, L., 4th Bn.
592428	Rfm. SAFFER, S., 1/18th Bn.
533425	Rfm. SOLOMON, N., 2/11th Bn.
204507	Rfm. SHURRANCE, A., 2/16th Bn.
6793	Pte. SCHWEITZER, M., 4th Bn.
615748	Pte. SAMUELS, A., 3/19th Bn.
801318	Pte. SHAPIRO, M., 30th Bn.
801345	Pte. SIMONS, A. C., 30th Bn.
801382	Pte. SCHLOSBERG, M., 30th Bn.
801401	Pte. SOLOMONS, N., 30th Bn.
801454	Pte. SPURLINGS, S. R., 30th Bn.
6176	Pte. SHORE, S., 8th Bn.
211297	Pte. SAMUELS, E., 21st Bn.
30254	Pte. SILKOVITCH, L., 5th Bn.
253402	Pte. SCOLNICK.
5687	Pte. SPECTERMAN, R.
611988	Pte. SILVERSTEIN, J., 2/19th Bn.
323582	Pte. SAMPSON, S., 2/6th Bn.
590651	L/Cpl. SALEMAN, D., 1/7th Bn.
553782	Pte. SAINES, I.
780356	Pte. SAFFNOVITCH, M., 29th Bn.
354656	Pte. SCHNEIDERMAN, 7th Bn.
3243	Pte. SIMMONS, M., 28th Bn.
356058	Pte. SWYERS, J.
572627	L/Cpl. SIMMOCK, A., 2/17th Bn.
301755	L/Cpl. SIMONS, F.
39813	Pte. SCHUIT, L., 1/11th Bn.
553783	Pte. SAENS, I., 2/16th Bn.
323123	Pte. SPERO, M., 1/15th Bn.
614161	Pte. SCHWATLING, F., 3/19th Bn.
422886	Pte. SEBITSKY, G., 2/28th Bn.
3117	L/Cpl. SAQUI, H., 15th Bn.
232386	Pte. SOLOMON, M., 3rd Bn.
635464	Pte. SOLOMONS, H. S., 5th Bn.
252907	Pte. SOLOMONS, W., 2nd Bn.
4459	Pte. SAFNOVITCH, C., 29th Bn.
801158	Pte. SCHWARTZ, W., 30th Bn.
766624	Pte. SILVERSTONE, N., 28th Bn.
7016	Pte. STEIN, H. K., 1/28th Bn.
325628	Rfm. SHAAPWOL, G.
739546	Pte. SILVERMAN, J., 28th Bn.
572452	Pte. STERN, S., 2/17th Bn.

London Regt.—*Continued.*

684347	Pte. SIMONS, A., 2/22nd Bn.
6552	Pte. STEPHENSON, F., 2/23rd Bn.
6647	Pte. SCHISKA, A., 7th Bn.
7924	Pte. SKITTRE, M., 7th Bn.
6825	Pte. SCHWAICENBERG, H., 7th Bn.
3497	Pte. STOCKFIS, R., 7th Bn.
8056	Pte. SALKIN, I., 8th Bn.
5789	Rfm. SOLOMONS, A., Q.V.R.
6651	Rfm. SHINE, A. J., 2/12th Bn.
6799	Rfm. STONE, W., 2/12th Bn.
1/8434	Pte. SUSKIN, J., 1st Bn.
2/1985	Pte. SAVILLE, E., 1st Bn.
8418	Sgt. SOMAN, L. L., 3rd Bn.
8088	Rfm. SOLOMON, M., 6th Bn.
393	C.Q.M.S. SALMON, H., 6th Bn.
4894	Pte. SOLOMON, L., 7th Bn.
10/4065	Pte. SAMUELS, P., 10th Bn.
5780	Rfm. SWART, W., 17th Bn.
21/6555	Rfm. SOLOMON, H., 21st Bn.
23/6293	Pte. SAMUELS, I., 21st Bn.
616031	Pte. SCHAFTER, F., 19th Bn.
231337	Pte. SOLOMONS, H., 1st Bn.
283753	Pte. SCHATT, H., 1st Bn.
205377	Pte. SMITH, M., 1st Bn.
322940	Rfm. SIMONS, R. I., 6th Bn.
254436	Pte. STOCKLAND, M., 1st Bn.
741458	Pte. SALAMAN, H., 10th Bn.
425865	Rfm. SELIGMAN, B., 10th Bn.
204488	Pte. SOLOMANS, A., 1st Bn.
225374	Pte. SYMONS, A., 1st Bn.
295585	Pte. SIMMONS, A., 1st Bn.
472224	Rfm. SOLOMONS, J., 9th Bn.
301755	L/Cpl. SIMONS, F., 5th Bn.
301869	Rfm. SACKS, A. C., 5th Bn.
282864	Pte. SOLOMONS, J., 1st Bn.
306111	Rfm. SEPEL, S., 5th Bn.
024172	Pte. SOLOMONS, M., 1st Bn.
203639	Pte. SCHNEIDER, D., 1st Bn.
527	Sgt. SAMUEL, J. M., 1st Bn.
	Cpl. SLOMAN, 1st Bn.
285238	Boy SIMMONS, M., 3rd Bn.
255154	Pte. SUGAR, M., 3rd Bn.
303905	Pte. SACKS, J. H., 5th Bn.
300027	S/Sgt. SOMAN, L. L., 5th Bn.
616615	Pte. SOLOMONS, S., 19th Bn.
781055	Pte. SOLOMONS, H. N., 29th Bn.
10/5073	Pte. SHEROTSKY, L., 10th Bn.
581	Pte. SCHWARTZ, I., 3/2nd Bn.
6386	Pte. SCHLOSBERG, T., 17th Bn.
7819	Pte. STERN, M., 13th Bn.
8021	Pte. STEPHANSKY, M., 3/20th Bn.
8019	Pte. SCHWARTZ, M., 3/20th Bn.
6963	Pte. SHITITZINLINITSKY, 3/20th Bn.
8012	Pte. SAPARSVILLE, M., 3/20th Bn.
6999	Pte. SCHAUB, J., 3/20th Bn.
6988	Pte. SCHIFF, S., 3/20th Bn.
6950	Pte. SHOKLET, J., 3/20th Bn.
6979	Pte. SEGAL, G., 3/20th Bn.
6991	Pte. STOCKLIN, D., 3/20th Bn.
282844	L/Cpl. SCHLOMM, N.
611876	Rfm. SILVER, H., 1/9th Bn.
4951	Rfm. SOLOMONS, J., 1/18th Bn.
6197	Rfm. SCHRIER, A., 1/13th Bn.
6034	Rfm. SAVILLE, F., 1/13th Bn.
575080	Rfm. STARKOP, H., 17th Bn.
5557	Cpl. SUMMERS, J., 1/17th Bn.
282211	Pte. SHINE, J., 2/4th Bn.
251975	Pte. SAUNDERS, J.
703265	Pte. SOLOMON, G.
351210	Pte. STOCKFIS, R.
197650	Pte. STONE, J., 3rd Bn.
495647	Pte. STRATTON, 16th Bn.
553871	L/Cpl. SANIG, S., 3/16th Bn.
324492	Rfm. STAAL, M., 6th Bn.
204303	Pte. SAMUEL, B., 1st Bn.
3298	Pte. SOLOMONS, A., 3/1st Bn.
652267	Pte. SILVERMAN, H., 2nd Bn.
74255	Pte. SUPERFINE, L., 1/10th Bn.
30428	Pte. SEGAL, M.
5318	Pte. SADISKY, K., 3/10th Bn.
474341	Pte. SACKSTEIN, J., 12th Bn.
5961	Pte. SCHOOLMAN, C., 1/9th Bn.
7556	Pte. SCHUTT, H., 1/4th Bn.
881400	Pte. SCHIFNER, J., 38th Bn.
553871	Cpl. SANIG, S., 16th Bn.
634157	Pte. SILVERMAN, A., 22nd Bn.
635571	Pte. STEMPEL, E., 3/20th Bn.
	Cpl. SEGAL, L.
	Pte. SILVERSTEIN, M.
	Pte. SILVERBERG, L., 17th Bn.
	Pte. SKIFF, A., 17th Bn.
	Pte. SHEARN, A., 17th Bn.
	Pte. SHORTS, A., 4th Bn.
	Pte. SILVER, J., 17th Bn.
	Pte. SHEREK, H., 16th Bn.
	Pte. STUART, D., 9th Bn.
	Pte. SUSWIN, L., 7th Bn.
	Pte. SOBITKI, D., 11th Bn.
612068	Pte. SWERDLEN, H.,* 1/19th Bn.
	Pte. SCHWARTZ, S., 7th Bn.
	Cpl. SHINDLER, P., 1/12th Bn.
	Pte. SOLOMONS, J., 10th Bn.
324414	Rfm. SOLOMON, H.,* 1/6th Bn.
	Pte. SOLOMONS, K. M., 18th Bn.
	Pte. SMOLLY, N., 7th Bn.
	Pte. SOLOMONS, J. B., 28th Bn.
2685	Rfm. STAHL E. F.,* 21st Bn.
	Pte. STAENBERG, M., 10th Bn.
	Pte. SINGER, P., 5th Bn.
	Pte. SINGER, I., 5th Bn.
	Pte. SOLOMONS, R., 1st Bn.
	Pte. SOMPER, H. R., 10th Bn.
	Pte. SIMSON, H., 12th Bn.
	Pte. STRAUSS, A. L., 17th Bn.
	Pte. STOOLMARK, J., 10th Bn.

London Regt.—*Continued.*

	Pte. Steinberg, G., 12th Bn.	
	Pte. Schofield, W., 1st Bn.	
	Pte. Stein, H., 7th Bn.	
	Cpl. Strong, B.	
	Pte. Schineberg, M.	
	Cpl. Shindler, E., 12th Bn.	
5615	Pte. Solomon, I., 17th Bn.	
4065	Pte. Samuels, 10th Bn.	
6742	Pte. Solomons, S. S., 2/4th Bn.	
3678	Pte. Smith, J., 22nd Bn.	
354656	Pte. Schneiderman, J., 7th Bn.	
353191	Pte. Schwartenberg, H., 7th Bn.	
4142	Pte. Simmons, L., 15th Bn.	
55605	Pte. Shuill, J., 20th Bn.	
254338	Pte. Steinberg, H., 1st Bn.	
395003	Pte. Steinberg, J., 9th Bn.	
204320	Pte. Seihart, M., 2/1st Bn.	
4511	Pte. Sidnery, M., 3/22nd Bn.	
3060	Pte. Sarner, J., 7th Bn.	
2323617	Pte. Shear, M., 2nd Bn.	
351210	Pte. Stockfis, R., 1/7th Bn.	
282937	Pte. Stackman, S., 1/4th Bn.	
354750	Pte. Silverstone, I., 2/7th Bn.	
324723	Pte. Segal, M., 6th Bn.	
554321	Pte. Silverproof, B., 16th Bn.	
495715	Pte. Shemberg, J., 3/13th Bn.	
27978	Pte. Sonenthal, 3rd Bn.	
685586	Pte. Smith, J., 22nd Bn.	
298026	Pte. Shulman, C., 14th Bn.	
374701	Rfm. Salkin, J., 8th Bn.	
374882	Rfm. Schweitzer, I., 8th Bn.	
324414	Rfm. Solomons, H., 6th Bn.	
3455	Pte. Steinberg, 3/10th Bn.	
5363	Pte. Steinberg, I. J., 13th Bn.	
5311	Pte. Stern, S., 2/17th Bn.	
5780	Pte. Smart, M., 17th Bn.	
1435	Pte. Simons, B., 9th Bn.	
841210	Pte. Stitcher, B., 32nd Bn.	
722326	Pte. Santer, A., 1/24th Bn.	
613960	Pte. Salpin, S., 2/19th Bn.	
6041	Pte. Shenow, E., 13th Bn.	
2921	Sgt. Silverstein, A., 2/15th Bn.	
4446	Pte. Smith, J., 3/11th Bn.	
3678	Pte. Smith, J., 3/22nd Bn.	
6874	Pte. Salter, H., 3/19th Bn.	
2302	Pte. Simpson, V.	
766850	Pte. Stodel, J. H., 2nd Bn.	
430854	Sgt. Silverstone, A., 2/15th Bn.	
4032	Pte. Sarafsky, W., 2/1st Bn.	
251079	Pte. Solomon, S.	
762963	Pte. Stross, A., 28th Bn.	
	Sgt. Simons, P. (M.M.).	
76642	Pte. Silverstone, M., 28th Bn.	
232903	Pte. Spanier, G., 1/2nd Bn.	
2799	Pte. Speyer, J., 17th Bn.	
593326	Pte. Spindler, J., 2/17th Bn.	
3804	Pte. Schaverein, L., 3/2nd Bn.	

4856	Pte. Schreiber, J., 3/7th Bn.	
4652	Pte. Simons, A., 13th Bn.	
422115	Pte. Simmons, M., 13th Bn.	
4951	Pte. Solomons, I., 4/1st Bn.	
37796	Pte. Schillingbaum, M., 2/7th Bn.	
530794	Sgt. Spielman, I., 1/15th Bn.	
987177	Pte. Sharp, M., 34th Bn.	
553348	Pte. Schlessinger, B. E., 2/16th Bn.	
2764	Sgt. Taylor, D. J.,* 1/6th Bn.	
2346	Rfm. Turner, A., 2/21st Bn.	
282922	Pte. Tobias, R., 1/4th Bn.	
472499	Rfm. Tennens, J.,* 1/12th Bn.	
2526	Rfm. Tucker, C., 1/16th Bn.	
493415	Rfm. Tannen, P.,* 2/6th Bn.	
3200	Sgt. Terry, D., 2/7th Bn.	
2552	Pte. Teitelbaum, A.,* 2/10th Bn.	
534866	Rfm. Tomlinson, A., 2/12th Bn.	
225014	Pte. Turner, J., 1/1st Bn.	
5573	Pte. Tavaloff, N., 32nd Bn.	
7111	Pte. Trobe, G., 1/2nd Bn.	
7460	Rfm. Talbrodt, H., 1/9th Bn.	
614813	Pte. Turner, A., 2/19th Bn.	
5976	L./Cpl. Tanner, B., 1/3rd Bn.	
4/6387	Pte. Tanner, H. D., 1/3rd Bn.	
21/5008	Pte. Tennenbaum, J.,* 2nd Bn.	
415019	Pte. Tabet, A., 1/9th Bn.	
1/6817	Pte. Throle, J., 1st Bn.	
4485	Rfm. Tichner, P. J., 3rd Bn.	
6768	Pte. Tentscher, J., 7th Bn.	
6481	Rfm. Tyler, M., 10th Bn.	
822117	Pte. Tuchinski, A., 31st Bn.	
4904	Rfm. Tischer, A., 31st Bn.	
50017	Rfm. Turiansky, C., 3/10th Bn.	
36944	Rfm. Timofsky, I., 4th Bn.	
840666	Rfm. Tavaloff, N., 32nd Bn.	
6947	Pte. Tishenka, A., 3/20th Bn.	
8025	Rfm. Tovla, E., 3/20th Bn.	
282865	L/Cpl. Tauner, B., 3/20th Bn.	
4042	Cpl. Teisheff, S., 25th Bn.	
6816	Pte. Tryanowsky, S., 7th Bn.	
4188	Pte. Turner, J., 2/2nd Bn.	
51455	Pte. Taylor, S., 14th Bn.	
2526	Pte. Tucker, C., 1/16th Bn.	
38785	Pte. Toffler, B., 20th Bn.	
4455	Pte. Vine J., 1/19th Bn.	
5276	Pte. Vogel, M., 1/22nd Bn.	
5971	Pte. Vangrove, F., 1/4th Bn.	
6879	Rfm. Vorst, S. F., 2/16th Bn.	
5762	Pte. Van Locken, J. N.,* 2/1st Bn.	
202834	Pte. Verblowsky, H.,* 2/1st Bn.	
7229	Pte. Van Gelder, B., 1/7th Bn.	
6347	Pte. Van Gelder, S., 2/10th Bn.	
202869	L/Cpl. Van Biene, M., 2/2nd Bn.	
4854	Rfm. Vignesky, S. M., 2/12th Bn.	
4318	Rfm. Van Praagh, W. J., 1/1st Bn.	
592572	Pte. Vanroogen, W. C., 1/18th Bn.	
10107	Pte. Vermont, J., 1/28th Bn.	
204079	Pte. Valencia, H.,* 1/2nd Bn.	

London Regt.—*Continued.*

3448	Rfm. VAN RYN, D.,* 9th Bn.
8820	Pte. VAN GELDER, I., 29th Bn.
376439	Rfm. VALENTINE, J. E., 8th Bn.
6922	Pte. VELDER, S., 3/20th Bn.
6950	Pte. VINEICK, J., 3/20th Bn.
	Pte. VAN CLEEF, A. (D.C.M.), 14th Bn.
12817	Pte. VAN ROLT, A. A., 5th Bn.
57	Rfm. VANDRIVILDE, J. H., 1/26th Bn.
5818	Rfm. VOGEL, I., 17th Bn.
764105	Rfm. VERMONT, J., 2nd Bn.
422402	Pte. VOVITSKY, H., 2/10th Bn.
5276	Pte. VOGEL, M., 1/19th Bn.
766321	Pte. VOS, H., 28th Bn.
766368	Pte. VANDER LINDE, S., 28th Bn.
553226	Pte. VORR, F., 2/16th Bn.
4923	Pte. WOOLF, R., 1/7th Bn.
1914	Rfm. WOOLF, G., 1/6th Bn.
524	Sgt. WALLENSTEIN, L. J., 1/15th Bn.
2355	Rfm. WILSON, G., 1/17th Bn.
1155	Rfm. WALMSLEY, H., 1/21st Bn.
2520	Rfm. WOOLF, N.,* 1/17th Bn.
1853	Rfm. WINTER, M., 1/2nd Bn.
5344	Pte. WOOLF, M., 1/6th Bn.
4744	Pte. WOLFERS, J., 1/7th Bn.
6575	Rfm. WOOLF, C., 1/21st Bn.
2538	Rfm. WEINER, J. D * 1/5th Bn.
5924	Pte. WINDISH, M., 1/9th Bn.
4225	Rfm. WEINSTEIN, P., 1/9th Bn.
2041	Rfm. WINSTON, S., 1/9th Bn.
6391	Pte. WEINTROP, J., 2/17th Bn.
6397	Pte. WEINSTEIN, S., 2/17th Bn.
5989	Rfm. WEINBERG, G., 2/21st Bn.
4076	Pte. WERSCHKER, D., 2/23rd Bn.
3204	Pte. WEIDER, M., 1/3rd Bn.
5800	L/Cpl. WACKS, S., 1/12th Bn.
2641	Pte. WEINER, S., 1/12th Bn.
8892	Pte. WARMAN, A. A., 2/1st Bn.
204304	Pte. WOLFSBERGEN, H.,* 2/1st Bn.
252388	Cpl. WHITE, G. B.,* 2/3rd Bn.
283399	Pte. WEINER, P.,* 2/4th Bn.
423246	Pte. WISEMAN, M., 2/10th Bn.
6846	Rfm. WATTLESTONE, H. A., 1/21st Bn.
35430	Rfm. WEINSTEIN, C., 1/17th Bn.
67100	Pte. WHITE, M., 1/22nd Bn.
700575	L/Cpl. WALTERS, L. P., 1/21st Bn.
G/37333	Pte. WILLIAMS, H., 1/23rd Bn.
33602	Rfm. WYLER, J. M.,* 1/15th Bn.
452953	Rfm. WARZARSKI, T. M., 2/11th Bn.
27276	Rfm. WOLFBERG, C. 1/8th Bn.
225727	Pte. WILLIAMS, N., 2/1st Bn.
555644	Pte. WOOLF, L., 2/9th Bn.
252058	Pte. WEIDER, W. W., 1/3rd Bn.
470515	Rfm. WEINER, G. W., 1/12th Bn.
4481	Pte. WARSHAWSKY, B., 1/22nd Bn.
3209	Pte. WEINBERG, G., 1/5th Bn.
1497	Pte. WAGNER, M., 1/4th Bn.
9810	L/Cpl. WEILL, A., 1/5th Bn.
6934	Pte. WYLER, J. M., 1/15th Bn.
6182	Pte. WOOLF, J., 1/9th Bn.
322529	Rfm. WOOLF, 1/6th Bn.
742104	Pte. WERNSTEIN, C., 1/25th Bn.
426653	Pte. WORMS, H.,
630043	Pte. WOOLF, D. (M.M.), 1/20th Bn.
6043	Pte. WAGENHUISEN, S., 4/3rd Bn.
702422	Pte. WOOLFE, F. E., 1/23rd Bn.
40167	Rfm. WABRICH, 1/6th Bn.
5870	Pte. WISEMAN, M., 2/10th Bn.
6959	Pte. WEINER, T., 1/14th Bn.
137470	Pte. WISE, J., 1/6th Res. Bn.
6029	Rfm. WEIL, R. C.,* 9th Bn.
324771	Rfm. WOLLMAN, E.,* 1/17th Bn.
G/68446	Pte. WOOLF, H. B.,* 2/2nd Bn.
303905	Pte. WEIDES, J., 5th Bn.
614481	Pte. WEINER, L., 19th Bn.
	Sgt. WINTER, M. (M.M.), 10th Bn.
	Rfm. WRIGHT, G., 2/11th Bn.
205188	Pte. WEITZMAN, M., 16th Bn.
12/3003	Rfm. WOLFF, J., Q.V.R.
9/7041	Rfm. WINSTON, S., Q.V.R.
1/8649	Pte. WOLFBERGEN, H. M., 1st Bn.
5543	Rfm. WEINBERG, A., 6th Bn.
6642	Pte. WOOLF, A., 7th Bn.
8051	Rfm. WINEHOUSE, A., 17th Bn.
303093	Rfm. WORTMAN, A. G., 5th Bn.
306112	Pte. WARSHAWSKY, J., 5th Bn.
306037	Pte. WOLF, H., 5th Bn.
306860	Pte. WOLF, S., 5th Bn.
6436	Pte. WELLS, H. A., 2/10th Bn.
4771	Pte. WARGARSKI, 2/11th Bn.
255653	Pte. WEINBERG, A.
6113	Pte. WARREN, I., 13th Bn.
3181	Pte. WILDER, H., 3rd Bn.
3958	Pte. WEINSTOCK, M., 3/6th Bn.
6246	Pte. WEITZMAN, W., 4/1st Bn.
449	Pte. WOLFE, E., 1st Bn.
3986	Pte. WOLFF, H., 25th Bn.
5544	Pte. WEISENFIEL, 2/7th Bn.
4864	Pte. WOLFSON, W., 13th Bn.
322697	Pte. WEINBERG, A., 6th Bn.
324371	Pte. WATTS, A., 6th Bn.
322529	Pte. WOOLF, 6th Bn.
573274	Pte. WEINTROP, J., 2/17th Bn.
	Pte. WEISBERG, T. (M.M. and Bar).
552658	Pte. WOOLF, N., 1/16th Bn.
573280	Pte. WEINSTEIN, S., 2/17th Bn.
8006	Pte. WHER, A., 3/20th Bn.
8013	Pte. WEISSBLAND, S., 3/20th Bn.
254306	Pte. WEITZMAN, H.
570616	Pte. WILSON, J., 17th Bn.
6029	Pte. WEIL, R. C., 1/9th Bn.
41057	Pte. WOLF, M., 2nd Bn.
702761	Pte. WEYNBERG, J., 3/23rd Bn.
65323	Pte. WOOLF, C., 2nd Bn.
204587	Pte. WOOLF, J., 2/12th Bn.
8088	Pte. WYMAN, D., 2/3rd Bn.

London Regt.—*Continued.*

2880	Pte. WOOLF, G. E., 3/18th Bn.
4913	Pte. WRIGHT, J., 3/25th Bn.
42799	Pte. WINDSHANK, B., 1/13th Bn.
318064	L/Cpl. WACKS, S.
5366	Pte. WYNICK, 3/11th Bn.
4482	Dvr. WINBERG, 3rd Bn.
5680	Pte. WOOLF, P., 23rd Bn.
4779	Pte. WINSTONE, 9th Bn.
702422	Pte. WOOLF, P., 3/23rd Bn.
6391	Pte. WEINTROP, J., 2/17th Bn.
353046	Pte. WOOLF, 7th Bn.
395122	Pte. WILLIAMS, 9th Bn.
22429	Pte. WINESTEIN, T., 23rd Bn.
2538	Pte. WEINER, J. D., 1st Bn.
570616	Pte. WILSON, J., 17th Bn.
1354	Pte. WOOLF, J. L.,* 6th Bn.
7028	Pte. YUTKOVITCH, M.,* 1/1st Bn.
6300	Pte. ZEALANDER, N., 1/13th Bn.
6094	Pte. ZELTZER, M. B., 1/4th Bn.
4920	Rfm. ZETTA, H., 2/11th Bn.
6650	Rfm. ZETTA, A., 2/11th Bn.
324486	Rfm. ZEEGEN, H., 1/9th Bn.
5015	Pte. ZELIGMAN, T., 10th Bn.
5842	Pte. ZIMMERMAN, L., 10th Bn.
133345	Pte. ZIMMERMAN, E., 1st Bn.
423346	Pte. ZEIGELMAN, S.,* 2/10th Bn.
422753	Pte. ZELIGMAN, J., 1/10th Bn.
576146	Pte. ZIGGLES, A., 17th Bn.
472763	Pte. ZISS, J. B., 18th Bn.
282935	Pte. ZALTER, M., 1/4th Bn.
678134	Pte. ZELTER, A., 23rd Bn.

267712 Pte. FALKSON, J., 4/1st Bn.
277713 Pte. FALKSON, S., 4/1st Bn.
7973 Pte. GLENOVITCH, L., 1/1st Bn.
48715 Pte. GOODMAN, M., 1/1st Bn.
271101 Pte. GOLDSTEIN, L., 4/1st Bn.
270245 L/Cpl. GOLLAND, J., 2/1st Bn.
269421 Pte. GOLDMAN, D., 2/1st Bn.
5082 Pte. GREEN, H., 2/1st Bn.
7450 Pte. GOULSTON, G., 4/12th Bn.
10694 Pte. HYMAN, J., 4/1st Bn.
267718 Cpl. ISAACS, B., 4/1st Bn.
267514 L/Cpl. JACOBS, B., 4/1st Bn.
267720 L/Cpl. JACOBS, H., 4/1st Bn.
267513 L/Cpl. JOEL, S. L., 4/1st Bn.
10391 Pte. LAZARUS, J., 2/1st Bn.
270258 Pte. LAZARUS, H.
7285 Pte. LEVY, A., 4/1st Bn.
270530 Pte. LEVENE, H.
10701 Pte. LEVENSON, A.
6800 Pte. LEVENBERG, V., 4/1st Bn.
7984 Pte. LEWIS, S.
10481 Pte. LIPMAN, B., 2/1st Bn.
268282 Pte. MORRIS, D., 2/1st Bn.
6950 Pte. PHILLIPS, R., 4/1st Bn.
267873 Pte. RICHES, H., 4/1st Bn.
270691 Pte. ROZELAAR, P.
267741 Pte. RYNER, M., 4/1st Bn.
268188 Pte. SAMUELS, A., 1st Bn.
10727 Pte. SERLIN, M., 4/1st Bn.
267836 Cpl. SHALSON, R. A., 4/1st Bn.
271444 Pte. SYMON, A., 4/1st Bn.
271421 Pte. SILVERMAN, M.

* Killed in Action or died on Active Service.

THE HERTFORDSHIRE REGIMENT.

OFFICERS.

Lieut. ARNHOLZ, R. H. P.,* 1st Bn.
2nd Lieut. FREEDMAN, E.
2nd Lieut. HARVEY-SAMUEL, F. K.

N.C.O.'s AND MEN.

267495 Pte. ANSELL, I., 1st Bn.
270818 Pte. ABRAHAMS, J., 2/1st Bn.
41885 Pte. BUIRSKI, S., 1st Bn.
7491 Pte. BERWALD, J.
7240 Pte. BAUM, E., 4/1st Bn.
     Pte. BERGE, G., 4/1st Bn.
268255 L/Cpl. CAPLAN, B., 2/1st Bn.
     Pte. CARMEL, L., 2/1st Bn.
267500 Pte. COHEN, J., 4/1st Bn.
     Pte. COHEN, N., 4/1st Bn.
270322 Pte. COHEN, S., 2/1st Bn.
7249 Pte. DAVIS, H., 4/1st Bn.

THE HEREFORDSHIRE REGIMENT.

N.C.O.'s AND MEN.

5035 Pte. ALEXANDER, J., 2/1st Bn.
41885 Pte. BUIRSTIR, S., 1st Bn.
6058 Pte. COHEN, A., 2/1st Bn.
6059 Pte. COHEN, H., 2/1st Bn.
6550 Pte. COHEN, L., 2/1st Bn.
6496 Pte. EFFERMAN, E., 2/1st Bn.
6715 Pte. FREIDEL, L., 2/1st Bn.
4373 Pte. FINKLE, A., 2/1st Bn.
6058 Pte. FREEMAN, B., 2/1st Bn.
48715 Pte. GOODMAN, M., 1st Bn.
28813 Pte. GLICK, H., 1/1st Bn.
1812 Pte. CRAWCOUR, J. H.
29323 Pte. GORDON, B., 2/1st Bn.
236655 Pte. ISAACS, H., 1/1st Bn.
6495 Pte. KINGS, H., 2/1st Bn.
239528 Pte. LIVINGSTONE, J., 1/1st Bn.
5157 Pte. LEVY, B., 2/1st Bn.
239625 Pte. ROBINSON, J. R., 1st Bn.
6120 Pte. WEINSTEIN, P., 2/1st Bn.

ROYAL DEFENCE CORPS.

OFFICERS.

Lieut. JAY, D., 213th Protect. Coy.
Major MAGNUS, L., att. War Office Staff.
2nd Lieut. MARCUS, L. G., 265th Coy.
2nd Lieut. SCHLESINGER, A. S., 6th Bn.

N.C.O.'s AND MEN.

37613 Pte. ALEXANDER, L.
18007 L/Cpl. ABRAHAMS, G.
46932 Pte. APPELBOOM, S.
38463 Pte. ANGEL, H. B.
27411 Pte. ABRAHAMS, H.
40437 Pte. ALEXANDER, J.
34980 Cpl. APPLETON, W.
36391 Pte. ADAMS, N.
193013 Pte. ARCHER, J., 24th Bn.
91864 Pte. ABRAHAMS, D., 24th Bn.
192371 Sgt. ALEXANDER, L., 24th Bn.
96731 Pte. BOHM, B.
T/18/9/82530 Pte. BARON, A., 25th Coy.
192552 Pte. BALICK, M.
192407 Pte. BLACK, J. J.
41971 Pte. BARNETT, M., 268th Protect. Coy.
85356 Pte. BERMAN, L., 300th Coy.
351298 Pte. BEST, J.
Pte. BORNSTEIN.
36205 Pte. BENJAMIN, D., 17th Bn.
46211 Pte. BERNARD, H.
47510 Pte. BERENBAUM, L.
68425 Pte. BARRETT, M., 4th Bn.
64849 Pte. BENJAMIN, A., 19th Bn.
90115 Pte. BLOCK, L. I., 24th Bn.
192509 Pte. BORSTEIN, J.
L/Cpl. COHEN, A.
91415 Pte. COHEN, S.
65748 Pte. COLTON, L.
32238 Pte. COHEN, A.
22883 Pte. COHEN, H.
33969 Pte. COHEN, H.
91714 Pte. CANNEL, C.
64133 Pte. CAMPBELL, H., 10th Bn.
41606 Pte. COHEN, E.
68244 Pte. COHEN, F., 4th Bn.
1673 Pte. COHEN, H.
62020 Pte. CITROEN, C.
15390 Pte. COHEN, M., 24th Bn.
91659 Pte. COPPERMAN, J., 24th Bn.
Pte. COBLENZ, J., 24th Bn.
91780 Pte. CREEGOR, J., 24th Bn.
192689 Pte. CHASSIS, H., 24th Bn.
192571 Pte. COHEN, L., 24th Bn.
90474 Pte. CIRSCH, H., 24th Bn.
58907 Pte. DAVIS, I.*
26482 A/Sgt. DAVIES, J., 4th Bn.

201663 Pte. DE COSTA, B.
91957 Gnr. DISLER, D., 24th Bn.
192292 Pte. DROSHMAN, J., 24th Bn.
39029 Pte. EDELSTEIN, J.
68118 Pte. EVENTHALL, T. V., 4th Bn.
35743 L/Cpl. ENOCH, D.
192503 Pte. FINEMAN, G. S. J.
41112 Pte. FORREST, A., 258th Coy.
40988 Pte. FRASER, M.
741854 Pte. FALK, A.
78005 Pte. FIERSTEIN, S. M.
29688 Pte. FRIEDMAN, M.
39688 Pte. FREEDMAN, J., 150th Coy.
4113 Pte. FORREST, A., 258th Coy.
Pte. FRIEDMAN, N., 24th Bn.
192330 Pte. FLAMBERG, J. F., 24th Bn.
192450 Pte. GORDON, H.
192518 Pte. GOLDBROOM, J.
48924 Pte. GRODZINSKY, H.*
48883 Pte. GOLDBERG, J., 2/5th Bn.
18091 Pte. GOLDSTEIN, J.
63581 Pte. GOLSTEIN, L., 165th Coy.
Pte. GOLDSTEIN, A., 24th Bn.
22077 Pte. GOLDSTEIN, S., 5th Bn.
06555 Pte. GOLDSTEIN, S., 5th Bn.
91976 Pte. GOLDSTEIN, R., 24th Bn.
192077 Pte. GORBATIZ, C., 24th Bn.
192540 Pte. GOLDBERG, M., 24th Bn.
192254 Pte. GRABINSKI, A., 24th Bn.
192176 Pte. GLASSMAN, L., 24th Bn.
192064 Pte. GREEN, D., 24th Bn.
19944 Pte. HART, L., 72nd Coy.
Pte. HAMBERG, J.
192266 Pte. HYMAN, M.
48565 Pte. HARRIS, L., 13th Bn.
36731 L/Cpl. HESS, F. J.
49575 Pte. HYAMS, I.
91625 Pte. HARRIS, L., 24th Bn.
192554 Pte. HAMPTUAN, M., 24th Bn.
350053 Pte. HAYES, M., 24th Bn.
91953 Pte. HORNIOCK, F., 24th Bn.
69258 Pte. ISENBERG, L., 315th Coy.
192582 Pte. ISAACS, S.
91527 Pte. ISAACSON, W., 24th Bn.
50377 Pte. JACOBS, H., 62nd Coy.
78556 Pte. JACOBS, G., 258th Coy.
38931 Pte. JONES, H.
69328 Pte. JOSEPH, S.
46006 Pte. KORSHOR, H.
36892 Pte. KLAPISH, S.
65756 Pte. KROSNEFSKY, S., 14th Bn.
11/91908 Pte. KREEMAN, P.
91312 Pte. KAUFFMAN, J., 24th Bn.
91400 Pte. KOFFMAN, C., 24th Bn.
192553 Pte. KRANSHOLTZ, H., 24th Bn.
91711 Pte. KREPSEY, G., 24th Bn.
Pte. KLEIMAN, A., 24th Bn.
33984 Pte. LEVY, J., 2nd Bn.

Royal Defence Corps.—Continued.

- 38396 Pte. LEVY, A., 2nd Bn.
- 33794 Pte. LOUIS, M.
- 91891 Pte. LYONS, A.
- 56565 Pte. LEVI, N.
- 38590 Cpl. LEWIS, J.
- 49648 L/Cpl. LEWIS, M. P., 13th Bn.
- 10/91613 Pte. LEVY, L.
- 45633 Pte. LEWIS, J.
- Dvr. LABSOFSKY, D., 24th Bn.
- 91543 Pte. LICHENSTEIN, M., 24th Bn.
- 91226 Pte. LIEBET, J., 24th Bn.
- 192663 Pte. LAMBERT, B., 24th Bn.
- 193642 Pte. LAZARUS, H., 24th Bn.
- 192305 Pte. LEWIS, M., 24th Bn.
- 192361 Pte. LEFCOVITCH, M., 24th Bn.
- Pte. MERMBERG, H., 68th Coy.
- 39245 Pte. MORRIS, S.
- 33950 Pte. MOSELEY, A.
- 69426 Pte. MORRIS, H., 4th Bn.
- 39381 Pte. MARCOVITCH, M.
- 29755 Pte. MARSHALL, H.
- 192050 Pte. MERCADO, S., 24th Bn.
- 192266 Pte. MERRON, H., 24th Bn.
- 19156 Pte. MARCOVITCH, H., 24th Bn.
- 192440 Pte. MILLAR, M., 24th Bn.
- 28013 Pte. NYMAN, D.
- 65032 A/Sgt. NINIAN, D., 4th Bn.
- 91546 Pte. OESTERMAN, D.
- 39215 Pte. OLSBERG, W.
- 192358 Pte. PAIN, G.
- 2/5262 L/Cpl. PHILLIPS, H. G., 28th Coy.
- 48619 Pte. PHILLIPS, C.
- 632420 Pte. RICH, J.
- 61874 Pte. ROSEN, B., 6th Coy.
- 91258 Pte. ROSENFIELD, L.
- 913111 Pte. ROTHBERG, A.
- 46035 Pte. RUBINSTEIN, B.
- 78782 Pte. ROSEN, J., 268th Coy.
- 19099 Pte. ROSEN, E.
- 82483 Pte. ROSENBAUM, J.
- 84580 Pte. RALLING G.
- 30020 Pte. ROBOTKIN, A.
- 69050 Pte. ROSSFIELD, 3rd Bn.
- 48067 Pte. SCHEIDER, B.
- 65942 Pte. SAGAR, J., 166th Coy.
- 19023 Pte. SUMMERS, A.
- 192483 Pte. SCHWARTZ, S.
- 91951 Pte. SINGER, S. 24th Bn.
- 80669 Pte. SIMONS, S., 300th Coy.
- 40173 Pte. STEINBERG, J.
- 48624 Pte. SEGALOVITCH, A.
- 36749 Pte. SHEYER, J.
- 39628 Pte. SESSELBERG, M.
- 2797 Pte. SPEYER, I.
- Pte. SPURGIA, N.
- Pte. SHATZ, A.
- 43440 Pte. SOLOMONS, A.,* 10th Bn.
- 91975 Pte. SCHWARTZ, N., 24th Bn.
- 192488 Pte. SCHWARTZ, C., 24th Bn.
- 192103 Pte. SWAGER, J., 24th Bn.
- 91526 Pte. SEGAL, I., 24th Bn.
- 192310 Pte. SOLKOVITCH, 24th Bn.
- 192141 Pte. SKUZER, A., 24th Bn.
- Pte. SPURGIN, M., 24th Bn.
- 109121 Pte. TAMPOUSKY, 106th Coy.
- 91952 Pte. TOBIN, J., 24th Bn.
- Pte. USHERAVITCH, J., 72nd Coy.
- Pte. VOLINSKI, S. C.
- 83839 Pte. VATES, I., 257th Coy.
- 22267 Pte. VIRGO, S.
- 192167 Pte. VITOFSKY, A., 24th Bn.
- 68324 Pte. WARMS, J., 164th Coy.
- 306327 Pte. ZAIDE, J.
- 91181 Pte. ZISKIND, H., 24th Bn.

* Killed in Action or died on Active Service.

ROYAL ARMY SERVICE CORPS.

OFFICERS.

- Capt. ADLER, H. M. (M.B.E.).
- Lieut. ABRAHAMS, A.
- Lieut. ALVAREZ, N.
- Major BAMBERGER, A. P. W. (D.S.O.).
- Capt. BENDIT, A. C., 24th Divisional Train.
- 2nd Lieut. BENJAMIN, H. E. B., 2nd Cav. Div.
- 2nd Lieut. BARNETT, L., 47th D.M.T. Coy.
- Major BLAIRMAN, S. I., 9th Reserve Park.
- Capt. BRASH, A., Transport Officer.
- Major BARNETT, M.
- Capt. BARNETT, G. (M.C.).
- Lieut. BARNETT, S.
- Lieut. COHEN, E. V., 8th G.H.Q. Amn. Pk.
- Lieut. CARLISH, E
- Lieut.-Col. COHEN, C. WALEY- (C.M.G., C.B.E.).
- 2nd Lieut. COHEN, M.
- 2nd Lieut. COHEN, S. B.
- Lieut. CHAPMAN, E. J. (M.C.).
- Lieut. DE CORDOVA, M., Army Supply & Trans.
- Lieut. DU PARC, S., R.T.O., Arquata.
- Major DAVIS, H. E., 2nd London Divisional.
- Capt. DAVIS, F. G., O.B.E.
- 2nd Lieut. ESPIR, I. J., 60th Aux. Steam Coy.
- Capt. ESPIR, H.
- Lieut. FRANKS, I. A., 20th D.S.C.
- Lieut. FREDMAN, S.
- Lieut. FAY, S. J., M.T.
- Capt. FRISHER, L. M.
- 2nd Lieut. FREEMAN, J. N.
- Lieut.-Col. GOLDSMID, O. D'AVIGDOR.
- Capt. GREEN, A. A.
- Lieut. GARLISH.
- 2nd Lieut. GOLDMAN, J. I. (M.B.E.)

Royal Army Service Corps.—*Continued.*

Major HARRIS, A. I., 28th Div. Train.
2nd Lieut. HYAM, F. J., 58th Am. Sub. Pk.
Lieut. HARDING, A.
Lieut. HARRIS, L. W., c/o A.D.G.T.
Capt. HORE-BELISHA, J. L.
Lieut. HITNER, V. J.*
Lieut. Col. HEILBRON, I. M. (D.S.O.).
Capt. ISAAC, H., 38th Div. Train.
Major ISAACS, I. B. (O.B.E.), 1st Reserve Park.
Capt. ISAACS, E. D.
2nd Lieut. ISAACS, N. H.
Lieut. JACOBS, R., 2nd Water Tank Coy.
2nd Lieut. JACOBS, L.
Lieut. JOSEPH, E. G.
Lieut. JACOBS, G. J.
2nd Lieut. KAUFFMAN, E.*
Lieut. KLINGENSTEIN, G., M.T.
Major LEVY, W. H. (D.S.O.), 28th Div. Train.
Major LANGDON, P. H.
Capt. LANDAUER, A. M.
2nd Lieut. LINDE, H., 9th Div.
Major LEON, J. (O.B.E.), D.A.O.T., 5th Army.
Lieut. LEE, V.
2nd Lieut. LEVY, C., 5th Aux. Corps.
2nd Lieut. LOGETTE, M., M.T.
Capt. MOSS, C. E., 60th Div.
2nd Lieut. MAYER, H. S.
2nd Lieut. MOCATTA, O. E., M.T.
Lieut. MARX, B., 4th Coy.
Lieut. MYERS, W., 116th Aux. Petrol Coy.
2nd Lieut. MASON, W. B., M.T. 33rd Div. Train.
2nd Lieut. MONTAGUE, G. W.
2nd Lieut. MINDELSOHN, M. G.
2nd Lieut. MINDEL, J.
Lieut. NATHAN, F.
Capt. NATHAN, A.
Lieut. NUROCK, M.
2nd Lieut. PRINCE, G. A.
Lieut.-Col. ROSE, E. A. (C.B.E.), 358th Coy. M.T.
Lieut. ROLFE, C.
Lieut. ROSSELLI, J. E.
2nd Lieut. ROTHSCHILD, S.
2nd Lieut. SAMUEL, A. D.*
Capt. SABEL, P. P. E., 47th Div. Train.
Lieut. STERN, A. S., 636th Coy.
Lieut. SELIGMAN, V. J.
Capt. SASSOON, H. W., 17th Div. Train.
2nd Lieut. SHAER, J., H.Q., No. 2 A.S.D.
Lieut.-Col. SOLOMON, H. (D.S.O., M.C., O.B.E.).
Capt. SIMON, C. E.
2nd Lieut. SIMON, F.
2nd Lieut. SOMAN, G. S.
2nd Lieut. SEFTON, C. A.
Lieut. SPRING, A.
Capt. TYLER, B. M., H.Q., 5th Cav. Div.
2nd Lieut. TEBBITT, D., 14th M.T. Coy.
2nd Lieut. TREN, R.
Lieut. VAN DEN BERG, D. S., R.T.O.
2nd Lieut. WOOLF, G., 47th Div. Train.
Lieut. WOOLF, H. I., 35th Div. Train.
Capt. WOOLF, H. M.
Lieut. WALFORD, H. H.
Lieut. WALTER, A.
Capt. WILKS, A. S.
2nd Lieut. WOOLF, H. S.
2nd Lieut. WOOLF, J.
2nd Lieut. WOOLF, G. F. S.
2nd Lieut. WILLIAMS, A.
Lieut. WOLFE, C. F.
Major WOOLF, E. S. (O.B.E.).

N.C.O.'s AND MEN.

T/20920 Dvr. ABRAHAMS, H., 7th Div. Train.
129605 Pte. ALVAREZ, A., 17th D.S.C.
M/2/137293 Pte. APPELBOOM, M., 39th D.S.C.
SS/1345 Cpl. ALEXANDER, H., 16th Div. Train.
078917 Cpl. AMOSS, W., attd. 14th Field Amb.
689 Pte. ABRAHAMS, S. D., 60th Div.
M3/034177 Cpl. ADLER, B., M.T., att. G.H.Q.
M2/187065 Pte. ALGE, A. J., 562nd M.T. Coy.
S/4215605 Pte. ABRAHAMS, W. S., 19th H.Q.
M2/050809 Pte. ABRAMS, J., 1st Mob. Rep. Unit.
103236 Pte. ABRAMOVITZ, A., Laundry 3rd Corp.
T/2371 Dvr. ABRAMS, J., 29th Div. Train.
MT/183166 L/Cpl. ABRAHAMS, H. V.
MT/183166 L/Cpl. ABRAHAMS, H. V.
S/368410 Pte. AVNER, M.*
Pte. ABRAHAMS, L.
M2/203680 Pte. ALEXANDER, J., attd. 97th F. Am.
M/397419 Pte. ALION, N., 68th Aux. M.T. Co.
M/336950 Pte. ABRAHAMSON, A., 5th A.T. M.T.
324103 Pte. ABRAHAMS, S. C., 15th G.H.Q. Res.
M2/188627 Pte. ABRAHAMS, J. S., 71st S.B.A.C.
SS/2846 Dvr. ANTHONY, J.
048053 Pte. ABRAM, B., 49th W.R. Am. Pk.
SS/3883 C.Q.M.S. ASHER, A.
2/133501 Pte. ADLER, H. M.
DM2/164098 Pte. ABRAHAMS, A., M.T.
T/3/292598 Pte. ABRAHAMS, S., 212th Coy.
T/325497 Pte. ASHER, M. J., 1124 M.T.
T4/216734 Pte. ARONHEIM, A., M.T.
T/413908 Pte. ABRAHAMS, H., M.T.
T4/263424 Dvr. APPEL, P., 212th Coy.
T4/219266 Pte. ALEXANDER, M., Base Depot.
M/426234 Pte. ABRAHAMS, M.
T/307740 Pte. ASH, V., 274th M.T.C.
134098 Pte. ALLEN, A.
T/423588 L/Cpl. APFEL, 620th M.T.C.
M/408590 Dvr. ALTMAN, E. N.
306090 Pte. ABRAHAMS, H.
DM/163857 Dvr. ANGEL, E.
2244 Cadet ABRAHAMS, A.
325497 Pte. ASBER, M. J.
548124 Pte. ABRAHAMS, B.
275462 Dvr. ABRAHAMS, L.

Royal Army Service Corps.—*Continued.*

385744 Pte. ARONWYCH, B.
T/3074 Pte. ABRAHAMS, S.
1874 Pte. ASHER, F.
M2/228873 Pte. ABRAHAMS, F.
DM/271029 Pte. APPEL, H.
2/6177 Pte. ASHER, S.
292726 Pte. AARONS, J.
316885 Pte. APPLEBAUM,
M/318344 Pte. AARONS, A. P.
T/328077 Pte. AARONS, A.
M/303729 Pte. ASHER, M.
M/302444 Pte. ARMSTRONG, C.
199661 Pte. ANGEL, A.
M2/048053 Artificer ABRAHAMS, B.
305721 Pte. ARGEL, H.
26144 Pte. ABRAHAMS, H.
354955 Pte. ABRAHAMS, M.
439849 Pte. ABRAHAMS, H.
M/322702 Pte. ASHKENAZA, N.
S4/215605 Pte. ABRAHAMS, W.
302803 Pte. ANGEL, S.
S/48 S.Q.M.S. ABRAHAMS, C.
DM2/180153 Pte. ASSENHEIM, W.
1641 Dvr. ABRAHAMS, F.
M2/188627 Pte. ABRAHAMS, I. S.
10663 Pte. BERNSTEIN, G., 20th Coy.
142467 Pte. BERGSON, M., M.T.
197219 Pte. BLOM, H., 365th M.T.C.
DM2/208718 Pte. BOSTON, H., M.T.
M2/222997 Cpl. BARNETT, L., M.T.
22257 Sgt. BEDFORD, B.
164616 Pte. BLUM, N.
T2/10929 Pte. BRED, L.
259924 Dvr. BRUSKE, C.
259923 Dvr. BRUSKE, J.
T/260313 Dvr. BORGEN, B., T.T.S.
T/329493 Dvr. BERNSTEIN, S., T.T.S.
2/135512 Pte. BECK, H., M.T.
M1/052527 Dvr. BYARTT, W., M.T.
M/336758 Pte. BEAVER, C. D., M.T.
M/339490 Pte. BARRS, T. M., M.T.
189979 L/Cpl. BROWN, M.
54/140227 Pte. BEHEINS, M.T.
185418 Pte. BOWMAN, L.
184661 Pte. BAUM, A. I.
179069 Pte. BARNET, E.
M/315702 Pte. BERNSTEIN, S.
325990 Pte. BLUMENTHAL,
Pte. BARROW, A.
T/325041 Dvr. BLUMENFIELD, L.
T4/235478 Dvr. BAKER, I.
T4/219956 Pte. BELINSKEY, J., D.S.C.
T4/219647 Pte. BILLITZ, A., 12th D.M.T. Coy.
M/396346 Pte. BLACK, S.
DM2/189631 Pte. BAGEL, M., 118th S.B.A.C.
M2/168147 Pte. BEST, J., 152nd S.B.A.C.
326650 Dvr. BLOOM, H., 52nd Div. Train.

SS/803 S/Sgt. BARNETT, J., 14th Div. Train.
346000 Pte. BERWALD, A., 14th Div. Train.
M2/268631 Pte. BORRIS, E., "R" Siege Park.
Pnr. BERNSTEIN, Forway Tram. Depot.
M2/178747 Cpl. BLOMMEKOPER, A., att. 4th Ar. Intell. Office.
169543 Pte. BRACKUP, A. W., 70th Aux. Pet. Cy.
285255 Pte. BARNES, E., M.T.
T/307863 Pte. BARKER, S. G., 23rd D.S.C.
DM2/138307 Pte. BENJAMIN, G., M.T., No. 5, G.H.Q.
46436 Pte. BARNETT, L., 2nd Fld. Supply Depot.
S4/086034 L/Cpl. BROADY, H., 8th Fld. S. Coy.
189461 Pte. BLASHKEY, P., 88th S.B. Amn. Col.
219025 Pte. BERG, J., 12th L.C. Supply Col.
184661 Pte. BAUM, A. A.
162452 Pte. BENJAMIN, J., 269th M.T.
T2/16526 Pte. BERLIN, J., 2nd Lab. Coy.
16620 Pte. BARON, H., M.T.
SS/4259 Pte. BUSNACH, H.*
Pte. BRESH, L., 9th Res. Pk.
M2/074359 Pte. BARNETT, H., M.T.
485759 Pte. BLACK, 20th Coy.
098496 L/Cpl. BENJAMIN, H., 24th D.S.C.
SS/16 Cpl. BLUSH, L., 56th Div. Train.
138491 Pte. BLACK, W., 1st D.S.C.
S4/064829 S/Sgt. BARNETT, C. H., 32nd Div.
M2/184294 Cpl. BARNETT, H., 562nd M.T. Coy.
S4/072383 Sgt. BESCHEN-KOWSKY, R. G., Corps Troops Supply Col.
T/812889 Dvr. BARNETT, L., 25th Aux. H.T. Co.
103256 Pte. BARNSTEIN, B., Laundry 3rd Corps.
T4/247912 Sgt. BARDER, W., att. 1/1st E.L.F. Amb.
M/298699 Pte. BELCHER, G.
292445 Pte. BUTLER, A., 33rd Res. Park.
285255 Pte. BARNETT, E., 2nd Anzac T.S.C.
135032 Pte. BLOOMBERG, S., 60th S.B.A.C.
M/304463 Pte. BERGER, B. C., 19th C.C.S.
M/279663 Pte. BENABO, L., D. Corps S. Park.
369909 Pte. BERG, A., No. 1 Amn. Sub. Park.
M5346046 Pte. BOCHINSKY, H. I., 494th S.B.A.C.
83336 Sdlr. BUIRSKI, L., 1st Sub. Sec. A.H.T.D.
M/320586 Pte. BENSON, I., 18th Aux. Bus Coy.
140058 Pte. BEAVER, D., 20th Div. Train.
SS/803 S/Sgt. BARNETT, J., 14th Div. Train.
T/330429 Pte. BYNOFSKY, D., 49th D.S.C.
M/376703 Pte. BERNARD, M., 2nd Aux. Bus Coy.
T4/275479 Pte. BLUMENTHAL, M., 5th A.A. Workshop M.T.
T4/071132 Pte. BARNETT, S., 24th Div. M.T. Co.
DM2/189979 Pte. BROWN, M., 47th Bde.
M/228541 Pte. BERNSTEIN, W., "C" Siege Pk. Workshop.
M/320590 Pte. BESSER, S., 1124th M.T.
M/225132 Pte. BRANDVAIN, L., 1124th M.T.
225552 Pte. BENNOSON, J. H., 776th M.T.
M/316183 Pte. BENJAMIN, H., 1st Res. M.T.

Royal Army Service Corps.—*Continued.*

M/376335 Pte. BAYNARD, S., 1st Res. M.T.
M/427926 Pte. BLACK, B., M.T.
S/262501 Cpl. BLAKE, A., M.T.
S/368436 Pte. BURN, M. M., M.T.
234343 Dvr. BERNSTEIN, H.
369716 Pte. BARCHEFSKI, L.
S4/061213 Cpl. BENSHER, A. M.
M/286972 Pte. BRAVERMAN, D.
S/255260 Pte. BECKER, T., 58th Field Bakery.
M/336085 Cpl. BRODIE, J.*
Pte. BENSUSAN, J.
509164 Pte. BERNSTEIN, M.
260001 Pte. BRODSKY, S.
69831 Pte. BLOOM, P.
M/339590 Pte. BARRS, T. M.
390808 Pte. BECKLER, S.
M2/286408 Pte. BENNETT, L.
19785 L/Cpl. BERMAN, M.
M/283650 Pte. BERLINSKI, G.
169443 Gnr. BERLINER, F.
306055 A/Cpl. BENJAMIN, G. V.
S4/125987 Cpl. BENSON, J.
T4/252808 Dvr. BRESLAVSKY, E.
331152 Dvr. BADEN, H.
330610 Dvr. BLACK, L.
383714 Pte. BIGLIZION, S.
M/395669 Pte. BRANSKEY, S.
M2/319301 Pte. BANDELL, J.
172905 Pte. BELEVITCH, L.
Pte. BANTAM, H.
T/369909 Pte. BERG, A.
107475 Dvr. BERLANSKY, S.
M2/227496 Pte. BARNARD, L.
M2/227739 Pte. BELIAVSKY, J.
M2/268031 Pte. BERMAN, N.
M2/272264 Pte. BEERMAN M.
DM/228451 Pte. BURNSTEIN, W.
M2/194446 Pte. BENSON, J.
M2/269352 Pte. BRILLIANT, J. S.
DM2/169130 Cpl. BEVIN, L. J. B.
M2/229595 Pte. BLOOMBERG, R.
M2/268721 Pte. BRAYHAM, H. L.
DM2/266925 Pte. BERNSTEIN, A.
T/41052 Cpl. BAKER, D.
T/4/234343 Dvr. BERNSTINE, H.
26952 Pte. BEROLOWICH, S.
126519 Pte. BOGARD, E.
M2/299564 Pte. BECKLER, J.
M/300787 Pte. BENJAMIN, C. H.
M/225552 Pte. BENNOSON, J. N.
DM2/189978 Pte. BROWN, M.
MS/4519 Pte. BUCKLER, J.
M/303118 Dvr. BLOOM, L.
DM2/189148 Pte. BARNETT, M.
M/333585 Pte. BECK, H. L.
DM2/207926 Pte. BERNSTEIN S.
DM2/112479 Pte. BROWN, W.

M/334497 Pte. BARNETT, L.
M/2282528 Pte. BENJAMIN, S.
220090 Pte. BENJAMIN, I.
112479 Pte. BUTLER, J.
316183 Pte. BENJAMIN, H.
328127 Pte. BERMAN, W.
L/Cpl. BARNETT, R. C. S. (M.S.M.).
280046 Pte. BLOOM, L.
138491 Pte. BLACK, M.
28543 Pte. BLOOMENTHAL, J.
286223 Pte. BENJAMIN, M.
5231 Pte. BONNEY, E.
315702 Pte. BERENSTEIN, M.
283650 Pte. BERL, G.
230363 Pte. BERMAN, M.
Pte. BARROW, A. (M.M.).
M/281540 Pte. BARNETT, R.
216577 Pte. BROAKES, N.
382611 Pte. BEAGLE, J.
460792 Pte. BERNSTEIN.
M/285255 Pte. BARNETT, E.
M/38869 Pte. BLACKMAN, A.
247965 Pte. BALANBAN, H.
292865 Pte. BLOOM, B.
162433 Pte. BROWN, R.
S4/125987 Cpl. BENSON, J.
358694 Sgt. BENJAMIN, H.
197649 Pte. BITTAN, H.
188942 Pte. BENJAMIN, S.
184661 Cpl. BAUM, A.
73560855 Pte. BRODIE, J.
315378 Pte. BRINSKY, S.
54/197199 Pte. BLITZ, J.
T4/248031 Dvr. BARNETT, N.
T4/571132 Dvr. BARNETT, D.
365911 Dvr. BABINSKY, J.
S4/143593 Dvr. BALSANN, D.
S4/124569 Cpl. BERG, R.
20663 Dvr. BERNSTEIN, G.
DM2/162430 Dvr. BERSON, B.
168982 Dvr. BLASHKY, A.
171014 Dvr. BOORMAN, A.
178747 Dvr. BLOOMEKOPER, A.
S/342739 Dvr. BERNBRG, B.
4519 Dvr. BROWN, M.
169148 Dvr. BARNETT, J.
299524 Dvr. BIRNES, P.
Sgt. BARNETT, A.
Pte. BENN, B.
Pte. BENDITT, S.
Pte. BENABO, S.
Pte. BROADY, A.
Pte. BATES, P.
Pte. BAUMAN, L.
Pte. BERNARD, C.
Pte. BENSTOCK, H.
Pte. BLOOMFIELD, I.
Pte. BENJAMIN, H.*

Royal Army Service Corps.—*Continued.*

M/283650 Pte. BERLINSKY, G.
DM2/138307 Pte. BENJAMIN, G. L.
DM2/138491 Pte. BLACK, W.
T4/219698 Pte. COHEN, J., "R" Siege Pk.
  72988 Pte. CONREICH, H., No. 2 F. Sup. Depot.
  37346 Pte. CONREICH, P., No. 2 F. Sup. Depot.
162880 Pte. COFFMAN, D., 15th Corps, S.A.P.
162959 Pte. COHEN, M., 97th Sge. Bty., S.A.P.
07761 Pte. CONSTAD, H.
088925 Pte. COHEN, W., 3rd Coy.
25936 Cpl. COSTA, A., M.T.
046778 Dvr. CARLISH, A., M.T.
083705 Pte. COHEN, D., M.T.
33188 Pte. CARSON, J., M.T.
333358 Pte. COEN, R.
  Pte. CRAYE, L.
T4/159317 Pte. COHEN, J. L.
074857 Pte. COHEN, S. H., 265th Coy.
285917 Pte. CONN, J.,* 706th Coy., M.T.
MS/803 Cpl. COSH, E. R.
155962 Pte. COHEN, S., M.T.
306925 Pte. COHEN, S. A., M.T.
  802 Pte. COHEN, N. C., M.T.
34273 Dvr. COHEN, S., M.T.
M/284689 Pte. COHEN, H., No. 5, G.H.Q. Col.
M2/227161 Pte. COHEN, C. J., M.T.
DM/162465 Pte. CORNBERG, A.
  Sgt. CROSSLEY, A., Base Depot.
M2/227269 Pte. CARSON, P., 1st Base.
M2/192365 Pte. COHEN, H.
T/294223 Dvr. CAPLAN, H., No. 3 Depot Coy.
  Pte. COHEN, R. P.
271595 Pte. COHEN, M., M.T.
296349 Dvr. COHEN, B., 57th Division.
113551 Pte. COHEN, B. A., Sup. Col. 306th Coy.
T3/029414 Dvr. CAPLAN, S., 26th Div. Train.
T2/015965 Dvr. CLIFFORD, F. C., 17th Div. Tn.
M2/081756 S/Sgt. CAPPER, S. M., 34th Div. S.C.
M2/081930 L/Cpl. COHEN, H., 34th D.S.C.
M2/136781 Pte. COHEN, S., 39th D.S.C.
T4/140838 Pte. COZERBRIET, J., 18th D.S.C.
T3/029306 L/Cpl. COHEN, B., 33rd Div. Train.
DM2/168501 Pte. COHEN, A.
M2/131338 Sgt. COHEN, L., Siege Art. Park.
M2/079821 Pte. COWAN, M., Siege Art. Park.
SS/15107 L/Cpl. COFFER, P., H.Q.
T2/249554 Dvr. CALLER, H., 50th Div. Train.
111809 Gnr. COHEN, H., 7th Div. Train.
M2/192365 Pte. COHEN, J., 57th D.S.C.
M1/08098 Pte. COHEN, J., 21st Amn. Sub. Pk.
327194 Dvr. CHEAL, L., H.T., 5th Res. Park.
335546 Pte. CONRIDGE, H., 12th S. 1. BaseM.T.
M/206379 Pte. COHEN, A. J., 4th Div. M.T. Cy.
T/291835 Dvr. COUSINS, S., 3rd Div. Train.
M/296349 Pte. COHEN, B., 20th Div. M.T. Coy.
M/296867 Pte. COHEN, S., 16th Aux. Bus. Coy.

M/283133 Pte. COHEN, H. Y., 60th Aux. S. Cy.
M/320858 Pte. COHEN, L. L., 377th M.T. Coy.
DM2/112308 Pte. CRAMER, H.
M2/031877 Pte. COLLINS, W. G., No. 1 Water Tank M.T. Coy.
A/490 Dvr. COHEN, R., attd. 4th C.F.A.
M2/201146 Pte. COHEN, V., 261st S.B.A.C.
M2/200271 Pte. COHEN, L., 261st S.B.A.C.
016254 Pte. COHEN, H., 10th Ord. Mob. Wks.
54/179896 S/Sgt. COHEN, V. L.
T/261078 Dvr. CRAVITZ, H., 3rd Depot Coy.
M/352205 Pte. COOPER, H. A., 1124th M.T.
M/414854 Pte. COHEN, J., M.T.
M2/269467 Pte. CLAYMAN, H., M.T.
M/318092 Pte. CROWN, A., M.T.
M/345844 Pte. COHEN, L., M.T.
M/316961 Pte. CHETHAM, E., M.T.
T/311532 Pte. COHEN, H., M.T.
T/356419 Dvr. COHEN, H., M.T.
M/298976 Pte. CRAIG, I., 274th M.T.
156677 Pte. COHEN, A., 709th Coy.
  Pte. COMES, C., Field Park Reserve.
T4/216232 Pte. COUTERCHO
7/365401 Pte. CHRISTOL, J.
DM2/171017 Pte. CAPLAN, M., M.T.
256445 Pte. COHEN, S., 4th.
345087 Pte. COLGOWSKI, H.
M2/193041 Pte. COHEN, M., 620th M.T.
236842 A/Cpl. COHEN, J.
D/79821 Pte. COWAN, M.
M/347117 Pte. COHEN, S. L.
375337 Pte. CHUDICK, P.
446196 Dvr. CLASS, R.
236842 Cpl. COHEN, J.
77365 Sgt. COWAN, C.
M2/201146 Pte. COHEN, J.
285917 Pte. CORON, J.
M2/193041 Pte. COHEN, N.
M/274351 Pte. CLAYTON, C.*
DM2/189657 Pte. COHEN, J. A.
219871 Pte. COOPER, S.
385837 Pte. COHEN, C.
254886 Pte. COHEN, I.
21630 L/Cpl. COHEN, L.
M2/195986 Pte. CORRIE, B.
M2/271861 Pte. COLMAN, A. M.
DM3/0054 Pte. CAHILL, J.
DM/227037 Pte. COHEN, M.
DM/227161 Pte. COHEN, C. J.
M2/273025 Pte. COHEN, N.
S/15107 Pte. COFFER, P.
M2/081930 Pte. COHEN, H.
17301 Pte. COHEN, I.
159317 Pte. COHEN, I. L.
R/277307 Pte. COHEN, L.
M2/268147 Sgt. COHEN, P.
M/296442 Pte. COHEN, C.
M/273025 Pte. COHEN, M.

Royal Army Service Corps.—*Continued.*

DM2/154771 Pte. COLLINS, F. N.
M/333934 Pte. COHEN, J.
M/297530 Pte. CROSBY, P.
M/334838 Pte. COHEN, M.
280038 Pte. COHEN, A.
M/333853 Pte. COHEN, H.
DM2/228295 L/Cpl. COHEN, S. R.
179247 Pte. CROWN, M.
317426 Pte. COLGOSKI, B.
5/342851 Pte. COWAN, J. W.
54399 Pte. CROMER, C.
204304 Pte. COPENHAGEN, F.
6670 Pte. COHEN, C. L.
141613 Pte. COHEN, A.
315778 Pte. COHEN, M.
T4/145833 Pte. COLTON, M.
DM2171027 Pte. COPLIN, R.
M/274351 Pte. CLAYTON, M.
376366 Pte. COHEN, E.
353549 Pte. CREMER, J. A.
DM2/202346 Pte. COHEN, S.
525255 Pte. CARASON, A.
310780 Pte. CARSELL, C.
259533 Pte. COLLINS, R.
170395 Pte. COHEN, S.
171035 Pte. COHEN, S.
291704 Pte. COHEN, R. S.
34399 Pte. COMER, C.
M/298976 Pte. CRAIG, I.
DM2/208693 Pte. COHEN, N.
273272 Pte. COHEN, M.
M2/200699 Sgt. CARRE, J.
316961 Pte. CHATHAM, E.
334363 Pte. COLEMAN, H. C.
37706 Pte. CLASS, S.
306925 Pte. COHEN, S. A.
898 Cpl. COOK, E. R.
259533 Pte. COLLINS, R.
257836 Pte. CHIVELL, W. S.
298530 Pte. CROSBY, P.
345844 Pte. COHEN, L.
Sgt. CAMM, H. (M.M.).
113551 Pte. COHEN, B. A.
352299 Pte. CROMWELL, B.
232809 Pte. CASTELL, L.
227161 Pte. COHEN, C. J.
454237 Pte. COHEN, S.
47658 Pte. CLAYMEN, N.
307838 Pte. CHAMANSKY, J.
296442 Pte. COHEN, C.
198619 Pte. COHEN, S.
M2/136701 Pte. COHN, S.
M/28478 Pte. COHEN, H.
M/2097653 Pte. DE FRIEND, H., 19th D.S.C.
S4/128123 Pte. DAVIS, S., 320th Div. Supply C.
M2/200988 Pte. DAVIS, H.

T/4/219570 Pte. DELINSKY, I.* 51st Supply Col.
162367 Cpl. DRESHER, E., 141st Sect.
Pte. DA COSTA, J.
Pte. DAVIDOFF, P.
M2/231334 Pte. DIGHT, L. L., 20th Div. M.T.C.
M/346126 Pte. DAVIS, J. E., No. 2 G.H.Q.
351668 Pte. DAVIS, A. I., 15th G.H.Q.
M/324706 Pte. de HAAN, M., 68th Aux. M.T. C.
M/323456 Pte. DA COSTA, A.
M2/178057 Sgt. DALTROFF, A. C.
310350 Pte. DONNE, D. P., No. 56 Supply Col.
877 Pte. DIAMOND, J., H. Aux. Bus Coy.
1632 Pte. DE FRIEND, L., 7th Div. Amn. Pk
18910 Cpl. DAVIS, S.
225 Pte. DANIELS, B.
172831 Pte. DA COSTA, R.
653884 Pte. DAVIS, L., 365th M.T. Coy.
M5/930 Pte. DETMOLD, G. W., 317th Coy.
053885 Pte. DAVIS, A., 336th Coy.
M3/16230 Pte. DAVISON, D., M.T.
M1/09076 Pte. DEURDON, W., M.T.
Pte. DIXON, C. L.
281185 Pte. DANS, A., M.T.
WR/280081 Pte. DUKE, A.
392333 Dvr. DAVIS, M.
316230 Pte. DAVISON, D., M.T. 91st Coy.
232331 Dvr. DAVIS, G., 878th Coy.
327575 Pte. DRIFF, P. J., Supply Depot.
156266 Sdlr. DONNE, L., 166th Bn.
T/260737 Dvr. DRESSLER, N., 3rd Depot Coy.
M/371862 Pte. DUTCH, L., M.T.
M/316120 Pte. DAWSON, A., M.T.
355580 Pte. DICKSON, W.
175738 Cpl. DINEHOUSE, S., M.T.
371467 Pte. DAVIS, B.
395110 Pte. DAVIS, H.
353806 Pte. DAVIS, J.
Pte. DREMER, E.
231099 Pte. DAVIDOFF, P.
DM2/189329 Pte. DAVIS, M.
T4/232805 Dvr. DOUBROVITCH, K.
M2/178429 Pte. DIAMOND, H.
438157 Pte. DITCH, S.
375185 Pte. DAVIES, D.
347993 Pte. DE GROOT, P.
12087 Pte. DRIVER, M.
M2/116920 Pte. DE GROOT, D.
M2/228895 Pte. DREEZER, M.
M2/267754 Pte. DE WINTER, C.
DM2/231515 Pte. DEFRIES, A.
272325 Pte. DOLBERG, B.
M2/273065 Pte. DAVIS, M.
M/299682 Pte. DA COSTA, H.
M2/229191 Pte. DALTROFF, L.
237326 Pte. DAVID, J. H.
Sgt. DAVIS, I. (M.M.).
171704 Pte. DE KRONME, J.

Royal Army Service Corps.—*Continued.*

330250 Pte. DELMONT, S.
281970 Pte. DA COSTA, H.
321040 Pte. DUMB, B.
1951 Pte. DINKENOR, D.
6/1890 Pte. COSTA, E.
309616 Pte. DEFRIES, M.
M2/052918 Pte. DINSWANTH, T.
282684 Pte. DAVISON, E.
326038 Pte. DICKLER, B.
021173 Pte. DAVIES, R. G.
366425 Pte. DAVISON, I.
321750 Pte. DAVIS, S.
327575 Pte. DRUIFF, J. P.
38146 Pte. DAVIS, H.
105885 Pte. DAVIS, H.
837 Pte. DE HAAN,
71890 A/Sgt. DA COSTA, E.
Pte. DRESNER, A.
Pte. DAVIS, A.
Pte. DAVIDS, G. E.
Pte. DARAN, P.
125539 Pte. ERENBERG, S., 182nd Coy. 21st D.T.
278678 Pte. ERENBERG, Z., 182nd Coy. 21st D.T.
T4/096090 Pte. EREIRA, J., 18th Light Ord. Mobile Workshop.
103367 Pte. EPSTEIN, Z., Laundry 3rd Corps.
DM2/209276 Cpl. ELIAS, B.,* att. Tank Corps.
193734 Pte. ESTRY, H., 49th Div. Train.
M2/205642 Pte. ELIPOWSKY, M., 80th H.A.G.
T4/199029 Pte. EISENBERG, L., 63rd D.S.C.
350338 Pte. ELLIS, F. E., 15th G.H.Q. Res.
DM2/171870 Cpl. ELKIN, M., 325th S.B.A.C.
S4/218005 Cpl. ERENBURG, M. E.
278025 Pte. ELDELBURGH,
M/314479 Pte. ETTLINGER, L. D.
151595 Pte. EMANUEL, L.
427251 Pte. ELLIS, A.
M2/177069 S/Sgt. EMANUEL, E. (M.S.M.).
M/428031 Pte. ELSNER, M., M.T.
T/405465 Sgt. EDWARDS, E. F., M.T.
444098 Pte. ELLIS, J.
T4/241166 Sgt. EDWARDS, H.*
M/231477 Pte. ELLIS, L., 620th M.T.C.
M2/113605 L/Cpl. EPSTEIN, H. A.
167934 Pte. EMANUEL, H.
T/4/241166 Pte. EDWARDS, H.
S/4/084922 Pte. ELIAS, H.
M2/195904 Pte. ELKIN, S.
M/296222 Pte. ESCHWERZE, H.
M/317421 Pte. EPSTEIN, H.
S4/070793 A/Cpl. EVANS, W. P.
221302 Pte. EMANUEL, J.
S4/278023 Pte. EDELBERG, E.
S/294993 Pte. ETOFF, B.
266979 Pte. EPSTEIN, S.
218005 Pte. EISENBERG, J.
218393 Pte. ENGLISH, D.

321477 Pte. ELLIS, L.
309154 Cpl. ELLISON, M.
Pte. ELLIS, M.
Pte. EDELLS, A.
13340 Dvr. FOX, J., attd. 46th Field Amb.
T/2136 Dvr. FISHMAN, M., 47th Div. Train.
DM2/117615 Pte. FRIEDLANDER, N.
Pte. FREEDMAN, R., 59th D.S.C.
M/300716 Pte. FRANKLE, L. H., 39th D.M.T.C.
M/283424 Pte. FINE, R. J., 326th S.B.A.C.
DM2/162777 Pte. FREEDMAN, J., 350th S.B.A.C.
M/08466 Sgt. FLEMING, W. G., att. 149th F.A.
M2/116175 Pte. FOUNTAIN, G., 3rd Mob. Repair Unit.
088296 Dvr. FAITH, J., 3rd Coy.
4719 L/Sgt. FRANKLIN, D.
Pte. FOOT, D. S., Motor Transport.
Dvr. FOOTE, S., 52nd Coy.
S.M. FREEMAN, B.
291130 Pte. FREEDMAN, S.
Pte. FALKNER, J.
M/295655 Pte. FLIGELSTONE, P.
T4/261388 Dvr. FINEBERG, A. E., 212th Coy.
676 Pte. FRANK, F., 13th Coy.
257671 Pte. FINBURG, E.
R/259177 Pte. FISHMAN, R.
M/317513 Pte. FRY, A.*
189949 Cpl. FREEDMAN, D., M.T.
198352 Dvr. FUTERMAN, K., 502nd Coy.
DM2/223274 Pte. FLATOW, L. W.
259764 Dvr. FREEDMAN, B., 3rd Depot Coy.
T4/234688 Pte. FELSESTEIN, J., M.T.
M/316325 Cpl. FREEDMAN, S., M.T.
267872 Pte. FELDMAN, B., M.T.
T3/025369 Dvr. FRANKS, J., 17th Div. Train.
316167 Dvr. FREEMAN, H., 11th Res. Park.
180698 Pte. FALO, E.
M/164072 Pte. FIFER, J.
286315 Pte. FREEDMAN, S.
T/420832 Pte. FREEDMAN, S.
350602 Pte. FLITMAN, I.
BM2/130298 A/Sgt. FREEMAN, C.
R/257681 Pte. FEINBERG, P.
301098 Pte. FELTZ, D.
137782 Pte. FINE, L.
25621 Pte. FISHER, J.
511514 Pte. FRED, J.
205485 Pte. FRIEZE, S.
M/196810 Pte. FINE, P. J.
274500 Pte. FRENCH, L.
DM2/195295 Pte. FACTOR, M.
198207 Pte. FREEDMAN, S.
DM2/102664 Pte. FINERMAN, S.
216358 Cpl. FELTBRODT, J.
225553 Cpl. FREDLER, W.
208308 Pte. FEAT, A.
361872 Pte. FRUMPKIN, J.
198207 Pte. FREEMAN, J.

Royal Army Service Corps.—*Continued.*

Pte. FINERMAN, H.
Pte. FONSECT, A. B.
L/Cpl. FOX, D.
Pte. FRIEDLANDER, D. N.
DM2/130398 A/Sgt. FREEMAN, J. C.
M/282546 Pte. FOX, P.
255204 Pte. FABIN, S.
S4/090729 Pte. FREEDMAN, L.
Pte. FOX, C.
M3/029563 Pte. FINEBERG, A.
302600 Pte. FINESTONE, H. G.
171030 Pte. FITTON, N.
T4/216358 Pte. FELTBRODT, J.
T4/143098 Pte. FREEMAN, G.
405176 Pte. FROMBERG, D.
016455 Pte. FENN.
208238 L/Cpl. FEIT, A.
207227 Pte. FAITH, D.
M2/222157 Pte. FEIT, D.
M2/130012 Pte. FRANKS, J.
DM2/196164 Pte. FREEMAN, I.
DM2/196204 Pte. FREEDMAN, E.
DM2/189950 Pte. FREEDMAN, H. G.
DM2/190100 Pte. FLYMAN, S.
DM2/270150 Pte. FRIEZE, E.
N/302017 Sgt. FRIEND, N.
M/317313 Pte. FRY, A.
M/302494 Pte. FLUGELMAN, A. S.
M/300607 Pte. FINBURGH, A.
128125 Pte. FERMINS, J.
215 Pte. FRANKAL, B.
Pte. FRANKENSTEIN, C. J.
13908 Pte. FREEMAN, H.
301823 Pte. FOOTRING, S.
M/316270 Pte. FEATHERM, P.
327410 Pte. FELSTEIN, L.
M/288275 Pte. FINEBERG, J.
46320 Pte. FRIEND, L.
T4/41591117 Pte. GITTLESON, A.
M/350788 Pte. GOLD, L., 8th Div. M.T. Coy.
M/346929 Pte. GREEN, F.
M2/074322 Pte. GARCIA, P., M.T.
Dvr. GOLDBERG, C.
Pte. GOLDSTEIN, R., A. Coy.
31426 Pte. GABRIEL, H., 50th Coy.
15266 Pte. GREEN, I.
9042 Pte. GREENSTONE, P.
303420 Pte. GOLD, I., 650th Coy.
T/358565 Pte. GOLDSTEIN, N., M.T.
M/307078 Pte. GOLDCRON, A. M.T.
268906 Dvr. GROSS, M.
420573 Pte. GINSBERG, S.
T/294022 Dvr. GOLDWATER, M., No. 3 Dep. Coy.
T/294019 Dvr. GOODMAN, D., No. 3 Depot. Cy.
180555 Cpl. GROSBERG, M.T.
257089 Dvr. GREEN, L., 878th Coy.
27240 Pte. GOLDMAN, M.

220084 Pte. GOLDMAN, D., M.T. 650th Coy.
446567 Pte. GORDEN, I., 321st Coy.
M/277444 Pte. GOLDSTEIN, M.
T4/197966 Dvr. GOLDSTEIN, H.
34352 Pte. GOLDBLUM, E.
T/291178 Dvr. GOLDBERG, W. W., 3rd Dpt. C.
M/396576 Pte. GOLDMAN, H. A., M.T.
M/267455 Pte. GLIKSTEIN, L., M.T.
DM2/178593 Cpl. GERSHON, B., M.T.
DM2/228898 Pte. GRIZARD, A., M.T.
M/300294 Pte. GOLDMAN, M., M.T.
T/438390 Dvr. GOLDSTONE, M., M.T.
M/3523142 Pte. GERSHUNY, A., M.T.
T3/029421 Cpl. GARBUTT, L.,* 199th Coy.
T/35676 Dvr. GADD, J., 25th Div. Train.
T/076509 Cpl. GOLDSTEIN, H., 345th Coy.
M2/073447 A/Q.M.S. GILES, A. W., 358th Cy.
161340 Pte. GORDON, H., 31st Div. Train.
M2/120835 Pte. GREENBURGH, C., Sge. Art. P.
14171 Dvr. GOLDBERG, Z., 577th A.H.T. Coy.
M/188942 Pte. GARCIA, B., Siege Art. Park.
DM2/135348 Pte. GOLDBERG, R., Army W. Col.
T/23887 L/Cpl. GOLDSTEIN, J., 15th Div. Train.
T2/61659 Pte. GALES, J. S., 59th D.S.C.
M2/081715 Pte. GALACIAN, S., 4th Corps.
T/368604 Pte. GINSBERG, J., 40th D.S.C.
170369 Dvr. GOLDBERG, H.
M/317098 Pte. GOLDCROWN, H., 245th S.B.A.C.
T4/219701 Pte. GOLDSTEIN, B., Cav. S. Col.
T4/276729 Dvr. GALINSKY, B., 5th Res. Park.
M/351893 Pte. GINSBURG, M.
M/319771 Pte. GILLINGS, C. D.
M2/192304 Pte. GOLDMAN, M., No. 2 G.H.Q.
M/298978 Pte. GREENFIELD, H., 68th Aux. Coy.
4/127735 Dvr. GOODMAN, J., 59th Div. Train.
073506 Pte. GOODCHILD, S. G.
145924 Pte. GOODMAN, J., 49th Div.
155281 Pte. GELLMAN, M., 80th H.A.G. .M.T.
319 Pte. GARFINCLE, R., M.T. Rep. Shops.
166246 Pte. GOLDBERG, M.
T/326622 Dvr. GLADSTONE, H., 46th Div. Trn.
407331 Pte. GOLDBERG, P.*
1981 Pte. GOLDBERG, I.
098541 Pte. GERALD, L.
052842 Pte. GARSON, M.
T4/159204 Pte. GALLER, J.
T2/14171 Pte. GOLDBERG, Z., 2nd Ind. Sup. C.
M/271918 Pte. GOLDBERG, M.
52/153204 Pte. GOODMAN, S.
052842 Pte. GAVSON, M., 320th Coy.
168460 Pte. GOLDBERG, S.
3/343375 Pte. GLOSS, G.
DM2/171218 Pte. GEFFEN, M.
M/345597 Pte. GREEN, S.
M2/267764 Pte. GOLDBERG, I.
331048 Pte. GOLDHILL, W. J.
414110 Pte. GOLDWATER, B., 900th Coy.
M2/222686 Pte. GARFINKLE, H.

Royal Army Service Corps.—*Continued.*

T4/197644 Pte. GOULD, S.
229941 Pte. GONSHAW, L.
M/206061 Pte. GOODMAN, G.
M/334944 Pte. GALLOP, C.
M/321952 Pte. GOLDSTEIN, H.
M/318460 Pte. GREY, E.
M/317801 Pte. GOLDENBURG, S. J.
M/512814 Pte. GREENBURG, H. J.
M/316785 Pte. GOLDSTEIN, F.
M/274275 Pte. GREENFIELD, H.
M/301614 Pte. GOLDIE, S.
M/206437 Pte. GOLDSTEIN, N.
283248 Pte. GREEN, P.
282519 Pte. GOLD, J.
309021 Dvr. GOLDBERG, A.
236506 Pte. GROSSBAUM, S.
328920 Pte. GOLDSTEIN, H.
T4/240737 Sgt. GOODMAN, H.
352849 Pte. GUNDER, H.
9042 Pte. GOLDSTONE, P.
358540 Pte. GELPRE, H.
259574 Pte. GLUCK, D.
M/301780 Pte. GOLDSTEIN, H.
315232 Pte. GREENBERG, L.
228744 Pte. GREENSTEIN, P.
D7/224511 Pte. GATES, J.
378075 Pte. GREENSPAN, A. J.
371385 Pte. GARRISH, J.
378675 Pte. GOODMAN, G.
353525 Pte. GROSSMAN, C.
S/363775 Pte. GOLDING, H.
359970 Pte. GOLDFINE, H.
326365 Pte. GOLDBERG, S.
324467 Pte. GOLDSTEIN, S.
162919 Pte. GOLDSTEIN, H.
369825 Pte. GOLDSTEIN, A.
551082 Dvr. GOLDSTEIN, M.
353981 Pte. GRIVER, M.
385611 Pte. GOLDRING, A.
281946 Pte. GOLDFLAM, A. H.
06344 Pte. GABEL, C. S.
152935 Pte. GREISMAN, B.
T4/232804 Dvr. GRUNSTEIN, M.
334898 Pte. GOLDSTON, J.
171218 Pte. GAFFIN, M.
M2/155307 Dvr. GOODFIELD, H.
M2/155440 L/Cpl. GINSBURG, J.
DM2/195047 Pte. GOODMAN, M.
DM2/168679 Pte. GOLFSKY, B.
DM2/162436 Pte. GOLDBERG, M.
DM2/162760 Pte. GORSDEN, S.
446675 Pte. GARCIA, A.
46648 Pte. GREENBERG, S.
382612 Dvr. GALPERT, S.
336831 Pte. GOLDSTONE, J.
DM2/228002 Pte. GOLDBERG, P. J.
M2/229959 Pte. GOLDMAN, H. L.

Dvr. GREEN, M.
M2/195047 Pte. GOODMAN, M.
DM/156591 Cpl. GOLDMAN, J. U.
DM2/190027 Pte. GREENBERG, H.
DM/206446 Pte. GALLEWISKI, J.
DM2/207169 Pte. GOLTMAN, W.
DM2/26733 Pte. GREENBOAM, J.
M2/267567 Pte. GREENBERG, A.
M2/267184 Pte. GOLDBERG, J.
DM2/274275 Pte. GREENFIELD, S.
363274 Pte. GORDON, J.
261235 Pte. GARCIA, H.
M/345087 Pte. GALFOROSKY, H.
S4/25302 Sgt. GOLDBERG.
261799 Pte. GLUCKSTEIN, L.
121566 Pte. GOODMAN, L.
S4/215988 Pte. GREENHILL, J.
311025 Pte. GOLDWERG, M.
298413 Pte. GOLDWATER, L.
081715 Pte. GALICKMAN, S.
79427 Pte. GREENBERG, B.
1100 Pte. GOODMAN.
165753 Pte. GOULD, S.
169180 Pte. GRIEZE, H.
165869 Pte. GROSSMAN, L.
170369 Pte. GOLDBERG, H.
S4/13408 Pte. GOLDMAN, R.
S4/064628 Pte. GOODENAY, N.
304375 Pte. GRUSHKOFSKY, M.
278520 Pte. GRYPSON, D.
308152 Pte. GREENBERG, J.
173022 Pte. GOLDBERG, M. S.
311025 Dvr. GOLDZWIG, M.
352189 Pte. GOOREBECH, M.
152935 Dvr. GROSSMAN, B.
230908 Dvr. GRAHAM, J.
356044 Dvr. GRANEEK, J.
219697 Dvr. GRIEFER, B.
396241 Dvr. GRONNER, B.
207169 Dvr. GOLDMAN, M.
390808 Dvr. GOLDSTEIN, M.
M2/153204 L/Cpl. GOODMAN, S.
M2/188942 Pte. GARCIA, B.
T4/160717 Dvr. HAMBURGER, E. B., 27th D.T.
M2/112343 Pte. HARRIS, S.
T4/083658 Pte. HART, J., 5th Div. Supply Col.
M2/114939 Pte. HYAMS, J., attd. 87th Siege By.
M2/194012 Pte. HARRIS, P., Siege Art. Park.
M2/100259 Pte. HOWARD, L., 6th Div. H.Q.
T/211328 Dvr. HYAMS, A.
133439 Cpl. HESS, A. J., 58th Mot. Airline Hec.
MS/1708 Sgt. HENRY, C. A.
103341 Pte. HYAMS, S., Laundry 3rd Corps.
M2/121752 L/Cpl. HARRIS, J., 18th Aux. B.C.
T/4172541 Pte. HYAM, A. A., 55th D.S.C.
M2/6385 Cpl. HARRISON, A., 363rd Coy.
T/293312 Pte. HART, A., 49th Div. Train.
M4/090158 Pte. HULLES, H., No. 2 G.H.Q. Res.
M/273642 Pte. HURWICH, S., 61st Aux. M.T. Coy.

Royal Army Service Corps.—*Continued.*

DM2/190110 Pte. HYMAN, E., 154th S.B.A.C
111919 Bdr. HARRIS, J., 168th Coy. 32nd D.T.
13220 Pte. HARRIS, L., 15th R. Pk. 162nd Coy.
2146 Pte. HARRIS, J., Remount Depot.
S/4070887 Pte. HARTSILVER, H., No. 4. Coy. B.D.T.
151440 C.Q.M.S. HUMPHREYS, H., M.T.
Pte. HARRS, J., Remount Depot.
6003 Pte. HERSHMAN, J., M.T.
M3/2516 Pte. HYMAN, M., M.T.
Sgt. HART, S. D., 149th D.V.S.
T4/172541 Dvr. HYMAN, A., 8th Div. Train.
1085 Pte. HELLER, M., 4th Cav. Supply Col.
S/29200 Pte. HENES, H.
4224 Dvr. HARRIS D., Remount Depot.
T/313477 Pte. HASSAN, M., No. 1 Centre M.T.
T4/292613 Dvr. HIGHBLOOM, S., 212th Coy.
16727 Cpl. HART, L. A. V.
255263 Pte. HARRIS, M.
129969 Pte. HYMAN, A.
M2/229611 Pte. HARTFIELD, H., M.T.
M/322533 Pte. HYAMS, E. S.
169289 Dvr. HYMAN, H.
M2/266918 Pte. HARTSTONE, L., M.T.
231005 Pte. HYMAN, H.
1085 Pte. HELLER, 4th M.T. Depot.
T/446293 Pte. HART, L., 776th M.T.
T/419583 Pte. HARRIS, J., M.T.
S/420086 Pte. HYMAN, A. R., M.T.
M/287336 Pte. HARRIS A., M.T.
M/305721 Pte. HARRIS, A., M.T.
S/443273 Pte. HYMAN, H. C.
L/Cpl. HIRSCH, M.
T2/73589 Pnr. HADDERWITCH, B.
T2/11328 Dvr. HYAMS, 108th Coy.
DM2/207237 L/Cpl. HYMAN, S., M.T.
461016 Pte. HAMBERGER, J.
M2/114939 Pte. HYAMS, H., 620th M.T.C.
M/299969 Pte. HEXTER, B., 710th M.T.C.
M2/090012 Pte. HARRY, P.
46165 Pte. HYMES, J. K.
11328 Pte. HYAM, A.
40003 Pte. HARRIS, N.
9765 Pte. HYAMS, J.
M/360640 Pte. HYMAN, H.
42/152443 Pte. HART, J.
M/314612 Pte. HARRISON, H.
T4/232815 Dvr. HAZAN, J.
215746 Pte. HARRISBURG, M.
Pte. HYAMS, E.
M2/191633 Pte. HARENBERG, I.
331244 Pte. HART, J.
T4/239315 L/Cpl. HARRIS, L.
326699 Dvr. HYAMS, D.
270504 Cadet HYAM, F. J.
769289 Pte. HYMAN, I.
M/2/051925 Dvr. HARRIS, H.

TS/478 Pte. HARRISON, L.
M2/193408 Pte. HOLFORD, H.
DM2/195974 Pte. HASSAN, R.
M4/060334 Pte. HUMPHREYS, B. A.
DM2/231886 Pte. HIRSCHMAN, H.
207237 Pte. HYMAN, S.
267271 Pte. HIRSCHMANN, S.
TS/478 Pte. HARRISON, L.
M/320762 Pte. HERSON, M.
M/280151 Pte. HARRIS, J.
M/321249 Pte. HILLS, J.
M/273620 Pte. HART, B.
M/300030 Pte. HART, M. I.
DM2/224416 Pte. HARRIS, L.
T/328121 Pte. HARRIS, H.
175415 Pte. HYATT, A.
285754 Dvr. HERSHMAN, M.
T/263319 Pte. HARRIS, J.
S4/072603 Sgt. HART, S. T.
M/296620 Pte. HERSKOWITZ, H.
5920 Pte. HYAMS, E.
11221 L/Cpl. HARRIS, J.
2552630 Pte. HARRIS, H. C.
394351 Pte. HYMAN, J.
20772 Pte. HYAMS, D.
15715 A/Sgt. HARRIS, H.
3589 Dvr. HADDONICK, P.
303712 Pte. HIMMELL, J.
M/318121 Pte. HESS, J. T.
261736 Pte. HART, H.
S/965 Pte. HERTZFELD, S.
T4/14124 Pte. HAZWELL, H.
265454 Pte. HELLER, M.
147620 Cpl. HELLER, E.
323112 Pte. HARRIS, D.
371127 Pte. HABER, M.
414827 Cpl. HARRINGTON, B.
232815 Pte. HORWITZ, M.
1288 Pte. HYAM, B. L.
Pte. HARVEY, A.
Pte. HOROWITZ, G.
Pte. HYMAN, B. L.
M/251713 Pte. HARRIS, M.
Pte. HIMMELL, L.
M2/090158 Pte. HULLES, H.
T/36657 Dvr. HYAM, L. W.*
187564 Pte. ISRAELSON, M.
36005 Pte. ISAACS, S.
M2/264959 Pte. ISAACS, H., 76th Bde.
M/272657 Pte. ISAACS, W. H. T., No. 1 Tank M.T. Coy.
053278 Pte. ISAACS, C., M.T.
SS/8936 Pte. ISAACS, W., 10th L. Coy.
941 Pte. ISAACS, A., 49th Coy.
M/302200 Pte. ISAACS, J.*
S/Sgt.Maj. ISAACS, G. (M.S.M.).
M401612 Pte. ISAACS, L., No. 1 Centre M.T.

Royal Army Service Corps.—*Continued.*

22787 Pte. ISRAELSON.
T/354595 Pte. ISAACS, D.
DM2/209992 Pte. IZCHAKIN, K., M.T.
M/377612 Pte. ISAACS, E., M.T.
M2/271928 Pte. ISAACS, H., M.T. Train. Schl.
385953 Pte. ISAACS, A.
M2/316969 Pte. ISAACS, J. A.
M2/194443 Pte. ISAACS, S.
Pte. ISENBERG, L.
407770 Pte. IKEN, H. D.
A/293926 Pte. ISAACS, A.
DM2/289994 Pte. ISAACS, N. H.
DM2/169407 Pte. ISENBERG, H.
Sgt. ISAACS, C. (M.S.M.).
DM2/231296 Pte. ISAACS, H. B.
DM2/270115 Pte. ISAACS, S. E.
T/306007 Pte. ISAACS, S. H.
M/99380 Pte. ISRAEL, H. F.
M2/271928 Pte. ISAACS, H. H.
231900 Pte. ISRAEL, L.
8936 Pte. ISAACS, W.
14402 Dvr. ISEN, B.
275061 Pte. ISAACS, R.
274481 Pte. ISRAEL, M.
T4/292424 Pte. ISAACS, L.
391029 Pte. ISAACS, M. A.
302200 Pte. ISAACS, J.
M2/054035 Cpl. JACOBS, P. M., 47th Div. Tn.
3316 Dvr. JACOBS, W., 102nd Coy.
M2/049473 Pte. JACOBS, R. A., 14th D.S.C.
M3/045709 Pte. JACOBS, A. K., M.T. Scl. of In.
T2/024526 Dvr. JACOBS, F. R., 12th Div. Tn.
T4/085585 Pte. JACOBS, R., 41st D.S.C.
DM2/164041 Pte. JACOBS, R. C., 33rd A.M.T.C.
SS/5248 S.Q.M.S. JELLIN, J. (M.S.M.)., H.Q.
207423 Pte. JACOBS, E., 396th M.T. Coy.
S4/277977 Pte. JULIUS, J., attd. H.Q.
176486 Dvr. JACOBS, H. W., G.H.Q.
M/273254 Pte. JOSEPH, M. M.
275061 Pte. JACOBS, D., 4th Base Rmts. 24th Sq.
M/318331 Dvr. JACOBS, J., 375th S.B.A.C.
M/273712 A/L/Cpl. JACKSON, R. M., 2nd Aux. Bus Coy.
233209 Dvr. JOSEPH, J., 74th Div. Train.
229177 Pte. JACOBS, M., 41st Div. M.T. Coy.
T4/060846 Dvr. JOSEPH, S., attd. 135th F. Amb.
3/34125 Pte. JACOBS, L., M.T.
28542 Pte. JOSEPH, V., attd Siege Bty.
2630 Pte. JACOBS, E., 539th Coy.
163031 Pte. JOSEPH, A., 3rd M.T.C.
T4/243836 Dvr. JACOBS, M., 46th Div. Train.
T4/159088 Pte. JACKSON, B., 29th Div.
T4/172937 Pte. JACOBS, M., 52nd R.H.S.O.
SS/3301 Sgt. JEWELL, J., attd. 31st Lab. Coy.
19134 Pte. JACOBS, G., 13th Lab. Coy.
216257 Pte. JOSEPHS, W.
T/309616 Dvr. JEFRIES, M.

259780 Pte. JACKSON, M. M.
273254 Pte. JOSEPH, W.
2392 L/Cpl. JUDELL, C.
M2/045709 Pte. JACOBS, K.
171942 Pte. JACOBS, A. E.
340019 Pte. JACOBS, H.
328382 Pte. JACOBS, M.
Pte. JACOBY, B.
205438 Pte. JACOBS, L.
164860 Pte. JOSEPH, A. D.
T4/245311 Pte. JACOBS, E.
346019 Pte. JACOBS, H.
328302 Pte. JACOBS, M.
DM2/162892 Pte. JACOBS, A.
M2/193996 Pte. JACOBS, S.
3/1525813 Pte. JACOBS, G. P.
25813 Pte. JACOBS, E. P.
M/205652 Pte. JOSEPHS, A.
M2/338168 Pte. JACOBSON, I.
104584 Pte. JACOBS, N.
T4/243836 Dvr. JACOBS, M.
24623 Dvr. JOSEPH, R.
M2/196024 Pte. JAFFA, L.
M2/204007 Pte. JOSEPH, C.
DM2/163783 Pte. JACOBS, B.
DM2/232022 Pte. JACOBS, H.
R/275061 Pte. JACOBS, D.
DM2/190947 Cpl. JACOBS, P. J.
M/300358 Pte. JONES, J.
M/271605 Pte. JACOBS, F. W.
197988 Pte. JACOBS, E.
317820 Pte. JOEL, D.
282979 Pte. JACOBS, D., M.T.
M2/269400 Pte. JACOBS, A. J.*
3060 Pte. JACOBOVITCH, M.
T/259780 Dvr. JACKSON, M. M., 3rd Depot Cy.
DM2/154010 Cpl. JACOBS, M.T.
S/394268 Pte. JUDELSON, J., M.T.
M/282047 Cpl. JACKSON, A.
T/369936 Pte. JACOBS, A., 206th M.T.
T4/17377 Pte. JACOBS, J. (M.M.).
21859 Rfm. JACOBS, H. L.
S/525813 Pte. JACOBS, E. P.
301665 Pte. JAY, S., M.T.
T/391067 Pte. JOEL, D., 620th M.T.C.
M/404282 Pte. JACOBS, D., M.T.
T/406482 Pte. JACOBSON, G.
M2/213365 Pte. JACOBS, L.
M2/285424 Pte. JOSEPH, V.
301665 Pte. JAY, S.
M/316929 Pte. JACOBS, J.
T4/161180 Dvr. JACKSON, H.
M2/193996 Pte. JACOBS, S.
DM2/163032 Pte. JOSEPH, S.
269131 Cadet JACOBS, L.
R.T.S/272 Pte. JACOBS, S.
164860 L/Cpl. JOSEPH, A. D.
SS/21395 Pte. JOSEPH, H.

Royal Army Service Corps.—*Continued.*

82833 Cpl. JOSEPH.
3622 R.Q.M.S. JACOBSON.
    Pte. JONAS, M.
    Pte. JACOBS, A. C.
117026 Pte. JACOBS, C. A.
    Pte. JACOBS, P. M.
M/213365 Pte. JACOBS, L.
M2/285424 Pte. JOSEPHS, V.
MS/4163 Dvr. KARET, B., 8th Div. Train.
T/3025678 Dvr. KING, S., 290th Coy.
S/1181 Pte. KING, J. K., 47th Div. Train.
872 Pte. KIRSTEIN, M., No. 3 Coy. 60th Div.
103758 Pte. KNAIGER, Y., Laundry 3rd Corps.
S/126286 Pte. KOSKIE, D., 24th Div. Sply Col.
208905 Pte. KAY, J., 42nd Div. Supply Col.
M2/204304 Pte. KOPPENHAGEN, F., 1st G.H.Q. Ammunition Column.
M2/202548 Pte. KROTOSKI, S., attd. 7th Bde. R.G.A.
DM2/117717 Cpl. KRISKY, H., "G" Siege Pk.
DM2/165067 Pte. KANTOROVITCH, L., No.3 C.H.Q
M/345539 Pte. KAY, H., 76th Bde.
M/332189 Pte. KALMINSKY, J.*
S4/145939 Sgt. KITCHING, M.
45190 Pte. KAUFMAN, F., No. 2 Fld. Sply Dept.
187227 Cpl. KOOPMAN, J., A.C. 4th Sge. Bey.
14413 Pte. KING, S., H.T.
S4/064810 Sgt. KANZELL, M., 243rd D.S.U.
074309 Pte. KIRSCHNER, W. I.
    Pte KRAMMER, M., 13th Coy.
52/370586 Dvr. KLOOS, E. P., atd 33rd F. Amb.
317280 Dvr. KYTE, M., M.T.
301110 Pte. KAUFMAN, J. B.
M/302241 Pte. KAYLIS, H., M.T., 150th Coy.
M/393658 Pte. KLEIN, H.
T/260997 Dvr. KAUFFMAN, J. I., 3rd Dept. Coy.
M/288949 Pte. KUTTNER, E. H., M.T.
M/322681 Pte. KING, M. M., M.T.
M2/206130 Pte. KINGSLEY, C. H., M.T.
T/419510 Pte. KRAMER, N., M.T.
S/360639 Pte. KOPLOVITCH, J., M.T.
24755 Pte. KERSH, J., M.T.
339132 Pte. KROHN, A., M.T.
5620 Pte. KROHN, S., M.T.
404534 Pte. KESTER, H.
2/259528 Pte. KAY, J. A.
385728 Pte. KOWALSKI.
313645 Pte. KAYE, A. L.
186307 Sig. KEMP, M., 65th Sge. Bty.
T/292180 Dvr. KINSKI, I., 223rd Inf. Bde. Tn.
10994 Pte. KISCH,
198207 Dvr. KORODKIN, A.
275017 Pte. KRANGOLD, S.
348003 Pte. KONOPLA.
208728 Pte. KUTTNER, J.
352125 Pte. KRAVITSKY, I.
DM2/195729 Pte. KAISER, T. B.

DM/203780 Pte. KROHN, R. J.
DM2/195549 L/Cpl. KEITH, A. C.
DM/122147 Pte. KEPPER, M.
099088 Cpl. KANDT, G. G.
RT/4458 S/Sgt.-Maj. KEY, L.
T/307805 Pte. KATZ, B.
S/393507 Cpl. KAHN, S.
M/346443 Pte. KLEIN, J.
S4/072383 Sgt. KOWSKY, R. A. G. B.
292718 Pte. KUTNER, A.
25936 Pte. KOSTA, A.
385289 Pte. KOSKY, A.
    Pte. KACHKI, B.
136709 Pte. KASTONBERG,
189956 Pte. KRONENBERG, J.
259523 Pte. KAY, G. H.
385728 Pte. KOWALSKY.
292713 Pte. KLEIN, M.
292180 Pte. KENSKI, I.
288949 Pte. KUTMAN, E. H.
311154 Pte. KALEPH, D.
M1/5620 Pte. KROHN, S. L.
M2/202548 Pte. KROTSKY, S.
M/274351 Pte. KOSKI, C.* (CLAYTON), M.T.
DM2/118389 Pte. LEVY, S., 2nd Ind. Sup. Col.
DM2/097318 Pte. LEWIS, B., 2nd Ind. Sup Col.
2180 Pte. LYONS, H.
    Pte. LEVER, H.
    Pte. LEVY, G.
    Pte. LEVY, J., G.H.Q.
    Pte. LEVINSON, F., No. 2 Sect. H.T.
T4/109356 Pte. LEWIS, S., Lahore Res. Park.
T/277429 Dvr. LEVY, S., 8th Div. Train.
    Pte. LARKEY, A.
T/27563 Cpl. LEVY, M., 169th Coy. 21st D. Tn.
DMR/163915 Pte. LUDZKER, M.
14693 Dvr. LEE, M.
112116 Cpl. LUCAS, J.
15723 Pte. LEVY, G.
204642 Pte. LOPOUSKY, M. E.
M/285278 Pte. LEVY, S., M.T.
M2/135670 Pte. LEVY, N., 23rd Div. M.T. Coy.
M333244 Pte LOWY, A. E., 41st M.A.C.
M/345548 Pte. LEE, J., Base Depot.
T/363901 Pte. LAZARUS, C.
190275 Pte. LEIBMAN, M.
309313 Dvr. LEVY, A., 6th Section.
131075 Pte. LEVY, L.
S/385839 Pte. LITTMAN, S.
352190 Pte. LEVINSON, A.
M2/221775 Pte. LEVY, M., M.T.
S/255041 Pte. LEVY, W., 531st Coy.
268221 Pte. LEVY, L. E., M.T. 348th Coy.
315702 Pte. LEMON, B., M.T.
DMF/163082 Pte. LEVER, M.
8/4/088813 Dvr. LEVI, A.
M/296088 Pte. LIPMAN, J.

Royal Army Service Corps.—*Continued.*

S/S/1568 L/Cpl. LOVEGUARD, C.*
M2/077901 Cpl. LIBGOTT, H., 267th Cy. D.S.C.
63499 Dvr. LEVY, W., 5th Amm. Sub. Park.
T2/11091 Dvr. LEVY, J., 8th Div. Train.
    Sgt.Maj. LEVY, M., 213th Coy.
    Pte. LEWIS, B., 35th Div. Supply Col.
T1/3075 Dvr. LEVER, J., attd. Hqrs. R.F.A.
M3/074037 Cpl. LIPMAN, D. L., M.T. S. of Ins.
14573 Dvr. LUPER, M., 3rd Div. Amm. Col.
689 Cpl. LYONS, C. R., No. 3 Coy. 60th Div.
MS/4094 S/M/Sgt. LEVEY, C., 30th D.S.C.
M2/19263 Pte. LEVY, H., 562nd M.T. Coy.
M2/194581 Pte. LEVY, J., 562nd M.T. Coy.
M2/034016 Pte. LEVY, A. G., 562nd M.T. Coy.
09282 Pte. LEWIS, S., 46th Light Ord. M.W.
M2/101634 Pte. Pte. LEVY, R., M.T. 13th Corps.
M2/047714 L/Cpl. LEVY, A., No. 3 M.A.C.
AH2/11839 L/Cpl. LEVY, S., 1. O.M.
DM/097318 Pte. LEWIS, B., Sge. Art. Park.
M2/2654 Pte. LUCAS, D., 1st Mob. Rep. Unit.
M2/121954 Pte. LEVY, S., 18th Aux. Bus Coy.
T4/037174 Dvr. LATNER, J., 38th Div. Train.
260277 Dvr. LANGER, R.
74360 L/Cpl. LIVINGSTONE, H., 35th A.L.S.
155083 Pte. LYONS, M., attd. 44th H.A.G.
M/301800 Pte. LEO, P., 358th Coy.
080193 Pte. LYONS, M., 163rd S.B.A.C.
T/327194 Dvr. LAWRENCE, C., 5th Res. Park.
T/364137 Dvr. LEWIS, H., 1st Cav. Res. Park.
T/014693 Dvr. LEE, H., attd. 110th Fld. Amb.
M1/08389 L/Cpl. LINTZ, M. B.
M2/048634 Pte. LEVY, H., 2nd Aux. Bus Coy.
M/351846 Pte. LASSMAN, J., M.T.
M/321068 Pte. LILLY, A. C., 47th Bde.
5/255612 Pte. LUSTIG, E., D.S.C.
M/303065 Pte. LEVY, H., 194th S.B.A.C.
M2/116219 Pte. LIPOWSKY, J.
M2/201348 Pte. LEVENSTEIN, A.
DM2/228195 Pte. LEVY, J. J.
S4/238186 Pte. LEVY, H. G., Div. Train.
DM2/221328 Pte. LEON, E., "R" Siege Park.
266337 Spr. LURINGTON, I. L., F. Tramy. Dpt.
M/318517 Pte. LEVY, L., 325th S.B.A.C.
M/273185 Pte. LIPMAN, I.,* 25th S.B.A.C.
T4/220091 Pte. LESKEY, J., 177th S.B.A.C.
163082 Pte. LEVER, M., 7th G.H.Q. Amm. Pk.
DM2/151595 Pte. LEWIS, E., Y.M.T.C
171817 Pte LEVY, M. A., M.T.
    Pte. LITTLE, A., Lab. Coy.
27890 Pte. LOSBAN, I.
2456 Pte. LEVY, R.
1263 Pte. LEWIS, S.
    Pte. LEVY, E., 2nd Amm. Park, G.H.Q.
8055 Pte. LEVY, M., No. 6 G.H.Q.
55928 Pte. LOGETTE, A.
3753 Pte. LEWIS, E. S., M.T.
751 Pte. LEVY, E., M.T.

09222 Pte. LEVY, J., M.T.
061933 Pte. LEVINSON, F., A.H.T.D.
33572 Pte. LUBRICK, J., 6th Res. Park .
DM2/134848 Pte. LITCHFIELD, F.
S/383074 Pte. LEVENE, A., M.T.
M/413782 Pte. LYONS H., M.T.
M/267362 Pte. LAZARUS, J., M.T.
M/427655 Pte. LANGER, J., M.T.
M/345325 Pte. LEON, R., M.T.
T/291244 Dvr. LEUSKY, M., 3rd Coy.
T4/188176 Pte. LEVER, A., M.T.
M/282467 Pte. LEWIS, A., M.T.
281925 Pte. LEVY, I., M.T.
356903 Pte. LEVY, A.
62076 Pte. LURVEM, J.
136156 Pte. LANDEN, L.
1/4618 Dvr. LEE, D.
T/392230 Dvr. LUKEMAN, L.
315781 Pte. LEVENTHAL, I.
48447 Dvr. LEE, H.,
T4/263923 L/Cpl LEVY, S.
166669 Pte. LEVY, H. E.
S/329731 Pte. LEVY, L., attd. A.V.C.
M316595 Pte. LEDEVER, F., M.T.
268724 Pte. LEVENSTEIN, I.
M2/120178 Pte. LAURENCE, B., 58th.
172839 Gnr. LESTER, S., att. 164th Siege Bty.
39267 Pte. LAZARUS, H.
24513e Pte. LEVY, M., 2nd Amm. Park.
    Pte. LEVER, T., 13th Div. Train.
3/026287 Pte. LEWIS, A.
T4/21917 Cpl. LEVY, G.
67972 Pte. LIBERMAN, A. N., 243rd Sge. Bty.
M/255612 Pte. LUSTIG, E., M.T.
DM2/266109 Pte. LEVY, M., M.T.
290951 L/Cpl. LOVETT, S.
    Cadet LIGHTSTONE, I.
365367 Pte. LYAMEN, L.
523935 Pte. LEVY, A.
427264 Pte. LAZARUS, I.
227107 Pte. LATSKY, W. J.
CMT/751 Pte. LEVY, E.
DM2/155083 Pte. LYONS, M.
M/273185 Pte. LIPMAN, I.
712116 Pte. LUCAS, G.
371259 Pte. LEVY, D.
290068 Pte. LEWIS, J.
312606 Pte. LEE, H.
277429 Pte. LEVY, S.
    L/Cpl. LOWY, A. E.
132876 Dvr. LEWIS, H.
M/348537 Pte. LEVINSON, J.
T4/216255 Cpl. LEVY, C.
363079 Pte. LEVY, J.
M2/080193 Pte. LYONS, M.
T/331122 Pte. LEWIS, A. J.
225150 Pte. LEZ, H. F.
T1/3075 Dvr. LEVER, J.

Royal Army Service Corps.—*Continued.*

213074 Dvr. LAVENSTEIN, C.
207580 Pte. LEVIN, S.
039723 L/Cpl. LEVY, C.
356903 Pte. LEVY, A.
117885 Pte. LAZARUS, A.
M2/202391 Pte. LOUISSON, J. E.
T/313129 Dvr. LEVY, A. J.
272850 Pte. LEVINE, E. C.
SS/17167 S/Sgt. LEHMAN, E.
331122 Dvr. LEWIS, E. J.
Cadet LIGHTSTONE, H.
93213 Dvr. LIBERMAN, E.
M2/271743 Pte. LESHGOLD, S.
M2/207580 Pte. LEWIN, S.,
M2/228140 Pte. LANGBART, R. V.
DM2/180100 Pte. LYONS, J.
DM2/179461 Pte. LEACHEM, L.
DM22/66349 Pte. LEVIN, S.
366431 Pte. LULLSON, C.
366426 Pte. LAZARUS, M.
216754 Pte. LINKE, M.
366431 Pte. LUBBER, C.
M/379213 Pte. LIPCHITZ, W.
16483 Pte. LEVER, A.
112259 Pte. LEVITSKY, M.
M2/221775 Pte. LEVY, M.
10118 Pte. LEWIS, J.
M/083839 Pte. LINZ, M. B.
260600 Pte. LEVINE, J.
273696 Pte. LOMS, H.
295731 Pte. LEWIS, M.
M2/10634 Pte. LEVY, M.
2034016 Pte. LEVY, I.
62493 Pte. LEVY, W.
335693 Pte. LE SAIRE, M. A.
278360 Pte. LIEVE, M.
24662 Pte. LIVINGSTONE, J.
185817 Pte. LEVER, A.
225150 Pte. LEZ, H. F.
345556 Pte. LEVI, J.
T4/259931 Pte. LIND, S.
36235 Pte. LANDER, R.
T4/249931 Pte. LINDER, L.
7205642 Pte. LIPOWSKY, M.
M/516595 Pte. LEDERER, F.
273255 Pte. LEWIS, J. A.
668 Pte. LEVY, S.
T4/029723 Pte. LEVY, C.
19873 Pte. LEWIS, M.
288949 Pte. LEVISON, H.
32973 Pte. LEVY, M. L.
2921 Pte. LEVY, J. R.
DM2/266109 Pte. LEVY, H.
DM2/230693 Pte. LEVY, E. B.
DM2/231632 Pte. LANGLEBEN, N.
DM2/232090 Pte. LYNES, C.
M2/267553 Pte. LITTLESTON, M. E.

DM/195289 Pte. LEVITT, N.
DM2/171817 Pte. LEVY, M. A.
T4/172686 Pte. LESSER, A.
M2/055128 Pte. LANGER, W.
313129 Dvr. LEVY, A. J.
187026 Pte. LERNER, W.
DM2/169130 Cpl. LEVIN, L. J. B.
M/296068 Pte. LAZARUS, A. H.
M/282467 Pte. LEWIS, A.
M/296108 Pte. LEVY, M.
302644 Pte. LEVY, L.
T/328026 Pte. LEWIS, M.
M/285278 Pte. LEVY, S.
300396 Pte. LEVENSHON, A.
328121 Pte. LEVISON, H.
226912 Pte. LOWENBERG, A.
273696 Pte. LOUIS, H.
272787 Pte. LAZARUS, C.
330639 Dvr. LEBERMAN, B.
315781 Pte. LEVENTHAL, L. L.
6819 Pte. LEVY.
Pte. LUBIN, N.
215255 Pte. LEVY, C.
269593 Pte. LEVINE, E.
260600 Dvr. LEVINE, J.
227107 Pte. LATSKY, W. J.*
215560 Pte. LOTSKY, J.
371259 Pte. LEVY, D. D.
T/14767 Dvr. MORGAN, H., 9th Div. Train.
T1/4764 Dvr. MORRIS, A., 9th Div. Sup. Col.
M2/034153 Pte. MORRIS, G. G., 12th D.S.C.
18202 Pte. MASTERMAN, C., 15th D.S.C.
M2/048719 Pte. MARKS, G., 14th D.S.C.
082972 Cpl. MORRIS, H. I., atttd. A.S.P. G. D.
164707 Pte. MARGOLIN, A., 1st D.S.C.
T/1653 Dvr. MALINSKI, B., 523rd Coy. Div. Tn.
T/1481 Dvr. MALINSKI, T., 524th Coy. Div. Tn.
103499 Pte. MISEL, B., Laundry Corps.
112254 Pte. MESSIAS, S., 32nd Div. Tn. No. 4 C.
M2/171755 Pte. MENDLESON, L., Sge. Art. Pk.
M2/051925 Pte. MORRIS, H., Sge. Art. Park.
180534 Pte. MUENDE, P., Sge. Art. Park.
M2/076664 Sgt. MINDELSOHN, M. G., Corps Troops Supply Column.
M1/07026 Sgt. MYERS, R. A., Aux. Pet. Coy.
M3/3651 L/Cpl. MARCUSSEN, M.
P4/128577 Dvr. MYERSON, B.
T4/251760 Dvr. MOSS, J. H., 50th Div. Train.
M2/05156 Pte. MILES, A., No. 47 Div. Sply Col.
M2/269538 Pte. MORRIS, A., attd M.G.C.
279300 Pte. MARKS, E.
M/33689 Pte. MARKS, H., 42nd S.B.A.C.
T2/017113 Dvr. MARKS, L., Aux. H.T. Coy.
139551 Cpl. MYERS, L., 8th Div. M.T. Coy.
T/391304 Pte. MOSS, W., 70th Aux. Pet. Coy.
297262 Pte. MILLER, I., 15th G.H.Q. Res. M.T. Cov.

Royal Army Service Corps.—*Continued.*

049637 Cpl. MANHAM, A., 15th G.H.Q. Coy.
M/281462 Pte. MARTIN, J., 450th S.B.A.C.
M2/131258 Pte. MANNY, L., 287th S.B.A.C.
M2/0428719 Pte. MARKS, G. C.*
0121300 Cpl. MARKS, A., M.T.
171823 Pte. MENCOFSKY, I., M.T.
557147 Pte. MORRIS, J., 3rd Coy.
169238 Pte. MILLER, S., M.T.C.
019102 Pte. MORDECAI, A. B., M.T.
42055 Pte. MARKS, A., Tramway Section.
166108 Pte. MARKS, H., attd. 31st Lab. Coy.
DM2/196211 Pte. MARCUSSON, J., M.T.
520 L/Cpl. MIKENER, S., 3rd Coy.
T4/260588 Pte. MARTIN, D., 554th H.T. Coy..
M/273242 Sgt. MARGOLIS, M. L.
T/368188 Pte. MERCADO, M., No. 1 Centre M.T.
257160 Dvr. MOSS, I.
12084 Dvr. MORRIS.
288507 Pte. MENDOZA, S.
254734 Pte. MAEROVITZ, D., M.T.
S/38545 Pte. MORRIS, J.
19621 Pte. MARCUSON, L. C.
368509 Pte. MOSESON, M.
5508 Pte. MYERS, E.F.C.
391283 Pte. MUSAPHIA, E.
Pte. MANDELL, J., Div. Amm. Train.
136154 Pte. MANDER, A.
73353 Pte. MARKSON,
M2/156779 Pte. MYERS, C., M.T
M/350916 Pte. MILLER, J.
T/260745 Dvr. MOSES, M., 3rd Depot Coy.
T/260997 Dvr. MORRIS, A., 3rd Depot Coy.
M/285072 Pte. MYERS, J., 606th M.T.C.
M/287818 Sgt. MANSON, B., M.T.
M229132 Pte. MOSES, S. H., M.T.
M/296638 Pte. MARKS, S., M.T.
S/363371 Pte. MARKS, W., M..T
S/441247 Pte. MYERS, M., M.T.
9183 Pte. MORRIS, V. A., M.T.
23553 Pte. MARKSON, H.
S5/25810 Pte. MENDOZA, M.
S/343467 Pte. MORRIS, P.
368491 Pte. MILSTEIN,
M2/047550 Cpl. MYERS, R., M.T.
M/300450 Pte. MICHAELS, A., 620th M.T.C.
299300 Pte. MARKS, E.
419927 Pte. MORRIS, M.
291422 Pte. MARKS, B.
407990 Pte. MATTERIN, B.
Mech.S/Sgt. MYERS, S. W. (M.S.M.).
460746 Pte. MOSCOVITCH, J.
3881 Dvr. MORRIS, L.
190077 Pte. MOSS, E.
31457 Pte. MARKS, G.
S/278024 Cpl. MEERSON, K.
M/347475 Pte. MILCH, M.
500 Dvr. MARTIN, J.

245 Dvr. MATOOK, A.
SS/1066 Pte. MARKS, H. G.
T4/232811 Dvr. MATINIFEA, I.
M2/019102 Cpl. MORDECAI, A.
1223 Dvr. MOSS, A.
133850 Pte. MARKS, A.
270553 Cadet MARKS, T.
S4/125619 Cadet MILLINGS, N.
T/1481 Dvr. MALINSKY, A.
112688 Pte. MAJERAN, N. J.
M2/228657 Pte. MARDELL, E.
STA/204 Pte. MORRIS, L.
DM2/192077 Pte. MOSS, H.
M2/265811 Pte. MAYER, H.
DM2/231698 Pte. MILLER, L.
082972 Cpl. MORRIS, H.
258022 Pte. MILLER, A.
STA/204 Pte. MORRIS, L.
M/231416 Pte. MYER, W.
M/305102 Pte. MINDEN, V. S.
DM2/190077 Pte. MOSS, S.
M/315431 Pte. MARKS, D.
M/286808 Pte. MAY, S.
M2/156779 Pte. MYER, C.
M2/119068 Pte. MAGNER, M.
220045 Pte. MORDECAI, L.
291315 Pte. MARGOLINS, N.
M/225088 Pte. MORDICAI, A.
32630 Pte. MAXWELL, T. S.
M/347110 Pte. MORRIS, C.
359 Pte. MOLLIN, H.
DM2/89597 Pte. MARKS, L.
254734 Pte. MELCOVITZ, D.
62608 Pte. MIDDLESBROOK, L. B.
J/368509 Pte. MOSESON, M.
112259 Pte. MARKS, L.
63094 Pte. MILLER, J.
8146 Pte. MERSKY, J.
DM2/196211 Pte. MARCUSON.
278944 Pte. MALOFSKY, N.
300684 Pte. MARTIN, H.
208469 Pte. MICHAEL, A.
359373 Pte. MORRIS, M.
303952 Pte. MENDES, J.
355251 Pte. METSELAAN, M.
337141 Pte. MENDOZA.
Pte. MARIENTHAL, W. S.
383054 Pte. MORRIS, M.
138025 Pte. MORDICAI, I.
419210 Pte. MYERS, H.
2184 Pte. MYERS, W. J.
155413 Pte. MICHAELS,
297262 Pte. MILLER, T.
T4/037603 Pte. NORDON, C., attd 22nd Fld. A.
T1/1424 Dvr. NEEDLE, M., 15th Div. Train.
M2/018921 Pte. NATHAN, N.
278923 Dvr. NEWMAN, D., 42nd Div. Train.
DM2/224488 Pte. NEWMAN, J., 1st Div. M.T. C.

Royal Army Service Corps.—*Continued.*

M2/182241 Pte. NATHAN, L., No. 6 M.A.C.
M2/073490 Pte. NEWMAN, T. W., 15th Corps
DM2/178185 Pte. NEWMAN, A., 15th Corps
S/327558 Pte. NATHAN, J.
M2/204122 A/Sgt. NEWMAN, M., 182 S.B.A.C.
Pte. NATHAN, M.
Pte. NIMAN, J., att. E.F.C.
S4/146889 Cpl. NIMAN, N., Claims Comm. and Reg. G.H.Q.
Pte. NAHUM, H. V.
377342 Pte. NIMITZ, B.
DM2/169070 Cpl. NORMAN, M.
M/335558 L/Cpl. NATHAN, H. D.
M/298673 Pte. NATHAN, J., M.T.
34/276079 Pte. NEWMAN, H.
223808 Dvr. NATANIELOR,
M2/272850 Pte. NEVIN, E. C.
DM2/230748 Pte. NEWMAN, N.
169070 Cpl. NORMAN, M.
S4/146889 Pte. NIMAN, M.
133756 Pte. NATHAN, A.
DM2/129648 Pte. NABARRO, B.
327558 Pte. NATHAN, I.
S4/276079 Pte. NEWMAN, H.
335558 Pte. NATHAN, H.
301109 Pte. NORMAN, R. J.
4030 Pte. NATHAN, D.
2671 Dvr. NAFTALIN, H. M.
MD2/267077 Pte. NATHAN, J.
284404 Pte. NATHAN, J.
342407 Pte. NATHAN, D.
DM2/224488 Pte. NEWMAN, J.
207798 Pte. OFSTEIN, H., att. 264th Siege Bty.
208504 Pte. OCKER, J., M.T.
163086 Pte. ORLITSKY, M.
207 Pte. OSPIASH, A.
SR/75 Dvr. POLLOCK, J., 7th Div. Train.
T/26368 Dvr. POTT, J., 1st Div. Train.
M2/206244 L/Cpl. PHILLIPS, S. F., 363rd Coy
DM2/154238 Pte. PELICAYN, R., attd. 22nd M.A.C.
292559 Pte. PHILLIPS, H., 44th Aux. Steam Co
M20114170 Pte. PHILLIPS, L., Cav. Corps Tps. Supply Column.
M/339932 Cpl. PITCHFORTH, T. C., 194th S.B.A.C.
263302 Pte. POLOCK, M., No. 2 Ar. Remt. Sqd.
T/326451 Dvr. PERCIVAL, J. W., 9th Res. Park.
2961 Pte. POWELL, B., Anti Aircraft Wkps.
T4/199695 Pte. PREVOST, S., 168th S.B.A.C.
11340 Pte. PHILLIPS, S., 13th Coy.
159243 Pte. PERLMUTTER, N.
1173 Pte. PEET, A.
SS/77 Pte. PINTO, E.
1905 Pte. PHILLIPS, H., M.T.
M2/034884 Sgt. POLLACK, M. M., M.T.
SS/2552 Pte. PHILLIPS, J., 4th Lab. Coy.

11340 Pte. PHILLIPS, L., 13th Lab. Coy.
085381 Pte. POMER, J., 131st Coy.
11612 Pte. PHILLIPS, J., M.T.
7558 Pte. PHILLIPS, E.
296625 Pte. PHILLIPS, H.
T/4276143 Pte. POLLOCK, H. M., 776th M T.
DM2/129561 Pte. PROCKSHIRE, M.
M/286980 Pte. PHILLIPS, F.
M/284404 Pte. PAUL, C.
M/274381 Pte. PHILLIPS, S.
673114 Pte. PLOTSKER, L.
199695 Pte. PROVOST, J., 255th Bn.
36007 Pte. PIZER, H.
299258 Pte. PHILLIPS, Z.
296657 Pte. PLOTIZKER, L.
46182 Pte. PEARLSTEIN, M.
DMS/164054 Cpl. PHILLIPS, H.
DM2/266432 Pte. PHILLIPS, S.
DM2/231931 Pte. POLINSKY, H.
220352 Pte. PHILLIPS, S.
M/293660 Pte. POLMSKY, P.
M/225544 Pte. PEARLMAN, D.
1905 Pte. PHILLIPS, H.
299258 Pte. PHILLIPS, L.
170475 Pte. PLASKI, N. W.
M/274244 Pte. POLATCHIE, S.
T4/087657 Pte. PHILLIPS, H.
T/276143 Pte. POLLACK, H. M.
T/39144 Pte. PELTZ, J.
T/39726 Pte. PERETZ, M.
T/325489 Pte. PYZER, W.
6039 Pte. POLLOCK, J.
M/274381 Pte. PHILLIPS, S.
3/360642 Pte. PRAVERMAN, H.
597 Pte. PAGET, A. L.
131314 Pte. PHILLIPS, A.
8096 Pte. PHILLIPS, M.
130569 Pte. PHILLIPS, M.
T1/2017 Cpl. POINTING F.
T4/085381 Pte. POSNER, C.
23394 Pte. PRESSMAN, I.
M2/232561 L/Cpl. PHILLIPS, I. P.
MT/131615 Pte. PHILLIPS, A.,* att. 99th Fld. A.
13732 L/Cpl. RICHFIELD, A., 116th Coy.
034159 Pte. ROSOMAN, E., 12th D.S.C.
1251 Dvr. ROTHFIELD, D., N. Div. Train.
054935 Dvr. ROSENTHAL, I., 335th Coy.
M2/138703 Pte. ROSENTHAL, A., Sgt. Art. Pk.
T4/198534 Pte. ROSENBERG, A., H.A.
SS/25820 Pte. REES, J., Branch Registry Office H.Q.
SS/15104 L/Cpl. REGARDIE, B., H.Q.
M2/099627 Pte. ROSENBAUM, S., 15th Aux. B.C.
M2/150346 Pte. ROSENTHAL, L. A., 25th M.A.C.
DM2/207807 Pte. RUBEN, T., 657th M.T. Coy.
M2/266847 Pte. RUBENSTEIN, J., 20th Aux. P. Co.
M/318356 Pte. RICH, D.

Royal Army Service Corps.—*Continued.*

M2/182639 Pte. RODNINSKY, B. B., 5th G.H.Q. Reserve M.T. Coy.
T/259911 Dvr. RUBENSTEIN, J., 1st Cav. Res. P.
M2/269087 Sgt. RUBENS, H. I., att. 117th Sge. Bty.
M2/031999 Pte. ROSENTHAL, M., 89th Bde.
M/324059 Pte. RODIQUES, A. M., 96th S.B. A.C.
S/361809 Pte. ROTHFIELD, M. L.
DM2/29824 Cpl. RAINSBURY, M. N., "R" Sge. Park.
M/316732 Pte. RADEZKY, R.
088317 Pte. RANDALL, M. E., 208th Coy.
164446 Pte. ROSENBERG, A., M.T.
4208 Pte. READING, P., M.T.
1386 Sgt. ROSEN, H., 32nd Coy.
M2/054195 Pte. RICH, C. J., 32nd Coy.
S4/061022 Pte. ROSENBLOOM, J., 32nd Coy.
1614 Pte. ROSE, T., M.T.
129561 Pte. ROCKSHINE, M., M.T.
T4/159014 Pte. REUBEN, J.
172828 Pte. RICHARDSON, A. M.
159213 Pte. ROSENBERG, A., 365th M.T. Coy.
M/6761 Cpl. RUFFELL, R., M.T.
M/281540 Pte. RICHARDS, B., No. 1 Ctre. M.T.
T/422361 Pte. ROGERGINSKY, M., No. 1 C.M.T.
S4/278023 Pte. REIDELBERG.
R/327362 Pte. RAPKIN, M., attd. 5th Pontoon Park, R.E.
T/309358 Dvr. ROSENFIELD, B., T.T.S.
343808 Pte. ROSENTHAL, M.*
M/350916 Pte. ROTENBERG, J.
S/405459 Cpl. RUBENSTEIN, A.
S/Sgt.-Maj. RABINOWITZ, H. J., 96th D.V.S.
M/215646 Pte. ROSENBLATT, E.
M/296802 Pte. ROSENBERG, D.
M/287161 Pte. RICHARDS, H.
M/2225267 Pte. ROSENBAUM, A.
19713 Sgt. RONEAN, J.
352557 Pte. RUBITSKI, A.
T/449108 Pte. RUBENSTEIN, J.
398420 Pte. ROSOFSKY, S.
T/345691 Pte. RACKOW, J.
335 Pte. ROSENTHAL, I.
343808 Pte. ROSENTHAL, D. W.
447230 Pte. RICHMOND, P.
35233 Dvr. ROSEN, J.
T4/232814 Dvr. RAPOPORT, M.
R4/106875 Pte. ROSS, E.
T4/232810 Pte. RABINOWITZ, P.
DM2/195087 Pte. RAKENSON, M.
Pte. RUDDOCK, I.
294851 Sgt. ROSS, D.
276608 Dvr. RIBKOFF, W.
389543 Pte. ROSENTHAL, I.
129511 Pte. ROCKSTENA, M.
6003 Sgt. REGAL, P.
13848 Pte. RHODES, B.
S/M. RABINOWICZ, H. J.
M2/208977 Pte. ROSEN, A.
M/17589 S/M. RUMBALL, G.
DM2/154420 L/Cpl. RUDELSHEIM, L. H.
O4/242496 Pte. ROBERTSON, W. C.
DM2/138502 L/Cpl. REISS, F.
T4/274573 Pte. RAYNER, A.
M2/274270 Pte. ROSE, A.
M2/229685 Pte. ROSENBLATT, A. D.
M2/195087 Pte. RAKNSEN, N.
M2/169025 Pte. RAKNSEN, W.
DM/266831 Pte. ROSENBERG, T.
M/334307 Pte. ROSENBERG, M.
M/215885 Pte. RAY, H. C.
M/315187 Pte. ROSS, N.
M2/270086 Pte. ROSENFELD, A.
M/314972 Pte. ROSENTHAL, I.
M2/227272 Pte. REUBENROTH, H.
DM2/208977 Pte. ROSEN, A.
DM2/224412 Pte. RUBINSTEIN,
T4/276008 Dvr. REBEKOFF, W.
315865 Dvr. RAY, A.
DM2/195109 Pte. ROSOLOSKY, M. J.
6681 Pte. ROSE, A.
324075 Pte. RAPPORT, J.
2/251 Pte. ROTHFIELD, D.
2417 Cpl. ROSE, D.
533922 Pte. RUTER, L.
38 Pte. ROSENBAUM, A.
159213 Pte. ROSENBERG,
371693 Pte. ROSSELOWSKY, H.
M/389918 Pte. ROSENTHAL, H. H.
162398 Pte. ROCKETER, M.
165026 Pte. RICKMAN, B.
165145 Pte. ROSEN, A.
1614 Pte. ROSEN, M.
385778 Pte. RAINGOLD, H.
303118 Pte. ROBSON, L.
221509 Pte. RIBATZKIE, A.
106875 Pte. ROSS, E.
1343 Pte. ROSEN, A.
M2/154523 Pte. ROSENBERG, J.
229973 Pte. RHUDSTEIN, S.
2/5603 Pte. REUBEN, L.
2431 Pte. ROSENBERG, A.
227272 Pte. REUBENROTH,
14/17288 Pte. RICHARDSON, A. M.
163032 Pte. SIM, J., M.T.C.
170126 Pte. SCHWARTZ, B.
904 Pte. SILVER, J., M.T.C.
2549 Pte. STONE, H.
112225 Pte. SHAER, J., 19th Aux. M.T.C.
26721 Pte. SPICKER, F., 32nd Coy.
SS/3719 Pte. SPERO, J.
081034 Pte. SCHWEITZER, S.
073105 Pte. SPIRO, C. H.

Royal Army Service Corps.—*Continued.*

2087 Pte. SPRINGER, A., 4th Amm. Park.
SS/2535 Cpl. SAUNDERS, M., 4th Lab. Coy.
8589 Pte. STREAK, A. E., attd. 8th Lab. Coy
S2/13066 Sgt. SHEPHERD, S., attd. Guards. Div
6684 Pte. SOLOMON, C., Troops Supply Col.
S4/128388 Pte. SAUNDERS, M., 13th Fld. Bakery.
4379 Pte. SMITH, H.
018574 Pte. SELINE, M., M.T.C.
14873 Pte. SAMUEL, A.
T/422351 Pte. SCHRAM, M., 8th Div. M.T. Coy.
M/316798 Pte. STEINBERG, M.
M/298360 Pte. SEIVE, M.
M3/17798 Pte. SAFIER, S.
M2/020128 Dvr. SOLOMON, V.
Dvr. SUMMERFIELD, M., 2nd Div. M.T.
MS/1675 Cpl. SCHNORE, F. J.
Pte. STOLLER, S.
M2/272324 Dvr. SANDGROUND, W. W.
S/26721 Cpl. SPICKER, F., 26th Depot.
T/356172 Dvr. SILVER, D., 872nd Coy.
TS/781 Pte. SILVERMAN, S., No. 1 Ctre. M.T.
3124 Pte. SANDGROUND.
192367 Pte. SCHWARTZ, S., M.T.
198783 Pte. SCULSKY, S., M.T.
273035 Pte. SAIFE, A. M.
M/318641 Dvr. SHIENBERG.
16453 Pte. SOLOMON, D. A.
23692 Pte. SILVERSTONE, J.
OM2/118391 Pte. SEGAL, H.
M/252777 Pte. STEINBERG, M. L.,* 1st B. Depot, M.T.
383824 Pte. STOLARSKY, I.
220313 Pte. SOLOMONS, J.
273765 Pte. SOLOMON, M., att. 3/13th Lon. Regt.
Pte. STAUL, M.
314944 Pte. SOLOMON.
317762 Pte. SANDGROUND, M.
M/341065 Pte. SELWIN, A.
Dvr. SOLOMON, P.
337276 Pte. SELIGSON, T.
319489 Pte. STERNHEIM, A. H.*
M/341065 Pte. SELVRIN, H.
231507 Pte. SUNSHEIN, L.
347375 Pte. SCHWARTZ, J., 57th Div.
301704 Pte. STONE, S.
179655 Pte. SANDOWN, M. L.
MS/5753 Pte. SANDYS, W.
55113 L/Sgt. SAPIRA, S., B.T.F. Depot.
S/407182 Pte. SHEINBAUM, L.
M2/268411 Pte. SCHWARTZ, I.
S/441399 Sgt. SYDNEY, H. C.
M2/180961 Pte. STODEL,
S/419601 Cpl. SONENFIELD, C. C.T.
118479 Dvr. STILLMAN, A., 4th D.S.C.
CMT/888 Pte. SCHORNSHINE, R., 5th D.S.C.
M/37206 Pte. SMITH, J. W., 8th D.S.C.
M2/073469 L/Cpl. SHARP, L. M., 12th D.S.C.

T/23702 L/Cpl. SAMUEL, M., 46th Div Train.
T/1603 Dvr. STEWART, L., 47th Div. Train.
T/30410 Sgt. SOLOMON, L., 51st Div. Train.
10967 Dvr. SEGALL, A., attd. 106th Fld. Amb.
029839 Pte. STARR, I., att. 105th Fld. Amb.
204578 Dvr. SHEPHERD, H. O., 57th Div. Train.
621 Svr. SAMUEL, B. D., attd 2/2nd Ln. F.A.
M3/162964 Pte. SABLOVSKI, H., M.T. Scl of In.
2507 Sgt. SOLOMON, H. G., attd 2/1st West Lancs. Fld. Amb.
2546 Pte. SHEPHERD, H. D., 60th Dvi. Train.
103585 Pte. SINGER, S., Laundry 3rd Corps.
103517 Pte. SHEKHTER, D., Laundry 3rd Corps.
M2/162983 Pte. SOLOMON, L., 11th Div.
M2/019988 Pte. SHARP, W., 47th D.S.C.
M2/175515 Cpl. SAMUELS, E., 54th A.A. Bty.
09282 Pte. SIDNEY, L., 46th Ord. Mob. Workshop (Light).
MS/3085 S/Sgt. SILVERSTONE, D. (M.M.), No. 4 G.H.Q., Amm. Park.
T4/237875 Dvr. SMITH, S. A., 58th Div. Train.
M2/118391 Pte. SEGAL, H., 57th Div. Train.
M2/073661 Pte. SAMUELS, E., 57th Div. Train.
M2/192856 Pte. SILVER, E.
T/307752 Pte. SHANNON, H., 63rd D.S.C.
T/254279 Pte. SCHIFF, J., 40th D.S.C.
171715 L/Cpl. SOLOMON, J.
M2/265197 Pte. SAXON, J.
272971 L/Cpl. SYMONS, I., 66th D.S.C.
276729 Dvr. SALINSKY, B., H.T., 5th Res. Park.
T/382633 Dvr. SYMONS, E., 15th Div. Train.
M2/203672 Dvr. SHILKOFF, P., attd. 20th S. By.
258236 Dvr. SOLOMONS, H., 17th Div. Train.
M2/080344 Pte. STEADMAN, B. J., 66th Aux. Bus.
DM2/169285 Pte. SCHILLER, S., 15th Aux. B. C.
M2/272324 Pte. SILVERMAN, J., att. 65th A.F.A.
DM/190955 Pte. SAMSON, J., 76th Bde.
T/382612 Pte. SEGAL, G., 4th Div. Train.
274023 Pte. SAKOVITCH, P.
T/32313 Dvr. SAUNDERS, M., Aux. H.T. Coy.
S3/21867 Pte. SAMPSON, L., 35th Div. Train.
M/285329 Pte. SNIPPER, S., 3rd Mob. Repair Unit.
M/6684 Pte. SOLOMON, C., "R" Siege Park.
T/314393 Pte. SMITH, B., 62nd Aux. Pet. Coy.
M2/050443 Sgt. SPARLING, R., No. 1 M.A.C.
221089 Gnr. SOLOMONS, L., 32nd Div.
G/47728 L/Cpl. SIMON, H., No. 2 Fld. Sp. Dpt.
3801 Pte. SEINWELL, J., No. 2 Fld. Sply Dpt.
S4/184742 L/Cpl. SMITH, J. H., 409th S.B.A.C.
M/318708 Pte. STUNGO, S.
260232 Pte. STANLEY, M.
52735 Pte. SCHATZIN, B., att. Cav. M.G.C.
M2/264333 Pte. SEGAR, H.
M2/287333 Pte. SWAEBE, B. D.
S/301368 Cpl. SALOMON, H.
S/308977 Pte. SAHAL, J. F.
Sgt. SHOCK, C. H. (M.M.).

Royal Army Service Corps.—*Continued.*

T/438835 Pte. SIMONS, H.
298299 Pte. SIMON, B.,* 59th Aux. Pet. Coy.
285329 Pte. SNIPPERS, S.
100544 Pte. SALOMO, H.
3805 Pte. SOLOMON, I.
388680 Pte. STAAL, L.
773246 Pte. STEIN, F., 398th M.T.C.
384341 Pte. SILK, B. D.
216239 Pte. SAMUELS, W.
S4/145851 Pte. SAMUELS, H. L.
5263 Pte. SALOMON, B., M.T.
T/308603 Dvr. SASKIN, L.
T4/237875 Dvr. SMITH, S. F., 58th Div. Train.
M2/296659 Pte. STONE, H. M., 710th M.T.C.
387983 Pte. SHABINSKY, I.
311517 Pte. SILVERSTON, H.
M2/263174 Pte. SIMONS, E.
M/2265197 Pte. SAXON, J.
DM2/162701 Pte. SAMPSON, L.
Sgt.-Maj. STEPHANY, M.
117711 Pte. SCHNIDER, M.
T/062812 Dvr. SOLOMON, I.
2392 Pte. SIMMONS, M.
T4/216107 Pte. SPECTERMAN, J. J.
261577 Dvr. STODELL, J.
301704 Pte. STONE, S.
DM2/162983 Pte. SOLOMON, S.
DM2/168980 Pte. SLUIFKO, S. A.
T4/244783 Dvr. SUNDERLAND, B.
232802 Dvr. SHMIDT, M.
115829 Pte. SOLOMONS, M.
SS/5263 Pte. SALMON, B.
M2/190286 Pte. SILVER, A.
2920 Pte. SAHS, S.
T/308603 Dvr. SACKER.
S4/218245 Pte. STODALL.
Cadet SINGER, E. C.
Cadet SOLOMON, S. A.
35636 Pte. SCHINDLER, H.
169285 Pte. SCHILLER, S.
MS/1675 Cpl. SCHNARE, F. J.
300673 Pte. SCHWARTZMAN, I.
S4/232727 Pte. STILLER, A.
M2/229554 Pte. SINCLAIR, M.
DM2/178761 Pte. SIMONS, B.
35580 Pte. SOKEL, J.
DM2/227492 Pte. SLOMNIKI, E.
DM2/267067 Pte. SHERIDAN, H. L.
DM/231456 Pte. SCOTT, D. S.
M2/273510 Pte. SLINDER, H.
M2/266757 Pte. STICKLYN, H.
283098 Pte. STEIN, J.
276437 Pte. SOLOMONS, S.
57949 Pte. STERN, H. G.
M/274147 Cpl. SWART, J. M.
M/296083 Pte. SCHNEIDER, S.

DM2/207817 Pte. SLOMICKI, J.
DM2/190241 Pte. SLAWEIT, M.
M/283318 Pte. SHEA, J.
M/281289 Pte. STEINHEIM, H.
M/288270 Pte. SCHEFF, N.
M/225315 Pte. STOLIER, H. V.
M/296361 Pte. SILVERBERG, H.
M/298299 Pte. SIMON B.
M/333692 Pte. SINGER, H.
M2/267510 Pte. SAMUEL, J. C.
M/394944 Pte. SOLOMONS, S.
288497 Pte. SILVERMAN, H.
M/298481 Pte. STEPHENSON, W. H.
145851 Pte. SIMONS.
257836 Pte. SCHIVELL, W. S.
336618 L/Cpl. SAX, L.
673105 Pte. SPIRO, S. H.
260464 Pte. SELLER, B.
M/319489 Pte. STERNHEIM, A.
222084 Pte. SMITH, A.
296003 Pte. SCHWARTZ.
C.Q.M.S. SOMPER, J. (M.S.M.).
331143 Pte. SILVERMAN, S.
123633 Pte. STONE, J.
140283 Pte. SACKS, S.
621 Pte. SAMUELS, B. D.
41114 Pte. SYMELANSKY, L. C.
326301 Pte. SCHIEFFER, M.
SS/3719 Pte. SPERO, J.
349859 Pte. SHAPIRO, W.
350421 Pte. STONE, H.
T/307995 Pte. SILVER, S.
356171 Pte. SOROKA, M.
DM2/16980 Pte. SLUIFKI, S. A.
S/294295 Pte. SINGER, J.
207816 Pte. SHINASKY, W.
326301 Pte. SCHEIFFER, M. T.
342868 Pte. SOLOMON, E.
273035 Pte. SOIPRE, A. M.
165209 Pte. SILVERMAN, I.
296361 Pte. SILVERBERG, M.
307838 Pte. SHYMENSKY, H.
54707 Pte. SIMONDS, L.
178761 Pte. SIMONS, B.
5/69523 Pte. SCHULTZ, L.
2163239 Pte. SAMUELS, H.
49450 Pte. SCHMIDT, M.
3061 Pte. SASIENE, H.
369643 Pte. SKIN, J.
292598 Pte. SAMUEL, A.
175745 Pte. SILVÉRSTONE, J.
155413 Pte. STONE, H.
382378 Pte. SACKLOVE, J.
366969 Pte. SMITH, M.
385937 Pte. SIMONOFF, J.
391163 Pte. STATEMAN, F.
188339 Pte. SUNSHINE,

Royal Army Service Corps.—*Continued.*

3413203 Pte. SHAMROCK, H.
44425 Pte. SOLIDINSKY.
287333 Pte. SWAEBE, B. D.
020128 Pte. SALOMON, E. M.
55439 Pte. STANLEY, P.
366430 Pte. STEVENSON, J.
311294 Pte. SOSKIN, E.
Pte. SIDERMAN, W. W. (M.M.).
308134 Pte. SPECTERMAN, S.
274069 Pte. SPANBOK, M.
330239 Pte. STERN, D.
Pte. SIMMONS, A.
Pte. SCHNEIDERS, G.
Pte. STEMM, S.
Pte. SWEET, L.
DM2/162704 Pte. SAMPSON, L.
M2/175515 Cpl. SAMUELS, E.
M2/66317 Gnr. SIMONS, E.
3750 Dvr. TAYLOR, P., 102nd Coy.
T4/084984 Dvr. TEBBITT, M., 37th Div. Train.
138170 Pte. TAYLOR, S., 27th M.A.C.
Dvr. TOTT, J., 1st Div. Train.
T4/172991 Pte. TEIGER, S., 36th Railhead S.D
923 Pte. TAYLOR, J., Supply Col.
5911 Pte. TUSH, L., M.T. Coy.
Pte. TRAVERS, J., 256th Coy.
8404 Pte. TASMINSKY, I.
394534 Pte. TUBB, A.
M/2H96364 Pte. TOBIAS, D.
294993 Pte. TEFF, B.
M/40680 Pte. TUBB, J.,* 1144th Coy.
255204 Pte. TUBEN, S., 23rd Field Bakery.
316167 Pte. TRUMAN, H., M.T.
M/335765 Pte. TAUBER, S., 620th M.T.C.
350962 Pte. TAYLOR, H.
DM2/228243 Pte. TCHOUDNOSKY, S.
366427 Pte. TRIEGMAN, S.
909 Pte. TEIGER, S.
1497 Pte. TAYLOR, D.
DM2/269651 Pte. TITLEBOAM, M.
DM2/178021 Pte. TARTAKOVER, T. B.
DM/168535 Pte. TEEMAN, A.
M/322406 Pte. TEBBITT, D.
M2/202763 Pte. TARARSKY, S.
SS/21591 Pte. TOBIAS, T. A.
348135 Pte. TOITZE, J.
225134 Pte. TCHATCHASRURLY, P.
185109 Pte. TRUVERS, J.
288275 Pte. TEINMESSER, A. G.
031790 Pte. TRAVERS, J. M.
M/284619 Pte. ULANSKY, L., 7th Corps Troops
202819 Pte. UPLAND, H.
M2/073632 Pte. VINESTOCK, M., 9th Div. S. C.
261716 Pte. VAN GELDER, P., 3rd Corps Troops
M2/269103 Pte. VANPRAAGH, I., 377th M.T Cy.
365 Dvr. VALENTINE, J.
228267 Pte. VERIBY, H.

T/292686 Pte. VIDOFSKY, S., 555th H.T. Coy.
M/399512 Pte. VINER, M.T.
M/288629 Pte. VAN DER LINDE, H.
0172/169234 Pte. VOOK, A. E.
34751 Pte. VALENTINE.
T/306078 Pte. VERBER, A.
112540 Pte. VOS, B. B.
228267 Pte. VERITZ, H.
T4/396175 Pte. VAN COLLE, M.
SS/1108 S/Sgt. WELFARE, C., 17th Div. Train.
T2/017580 L/Cpl. WOOLF, S., 56th Div. Train.
221372 Pte. WOLFSON, S., 128th Sn. H.A.M.T.
T4/249561 Dvr. WALTERS, J., 50th Div. Train.
DM2/208731 Pte. WOLF, T., attd. 349th S.B. R.G.A.
142184 Pte. WOLFE, B., 4th Cav. Supply Col.
M2/223068 Pte. WATSSMAN, J., 77th Aux. Pet. Coy. M.T.
T2/13327 Pte. WOOLER, L., 88th Coy.
T/418517 Dvr. WATTS, A., 14th Div. Train.
M/345001 Pte. WEINBERG, A., Div. M.T. Coy.
M/315232 Pte. WEINBERG, L., 11th M.T. Coy.
M/302426 Pte. WEISBLATT, M., No. 3 Water Tank Coy.
M2/048639 Pte. WOLINSKY, V., 89th Bde.
M2/175738 Cpl. WEINHOUSE, S., 6th G.H.Q. Reserve M.T. Coy.
T3/031013 Dvr. WOLFSON, L., Aux. H.T. Coy.
80200 Dvr. WOLFSON, J., Rmt. Dpt. Boulogne.
075965 Pte. WOLFSON, W., 358th M.T. Coy.
065555 Cpl. WOLLMAN, R. C., 3rd Ech.
Pte. WOLKIN, V., 318th Coy.
169281 Pte. WOLFE, A.
162281 Pte. WISELMAN, H., "I" Coy. M.T.
2772 Pte. WALSH, L., Remount Squad.
Sgt. WILLETTS, H., Remount Squad.
22578 L/Cpl. WHITBREAD, H. G., Sup. Col.
3803 Pte. WITMOND, L., 73rd M.T.C.
Pte. WALTON, J.
2554 Pte. WOLFSON, J., M.T.C.
159349 Pte. WOOLF, H., 34th Lab. Coy.
M/347908 Sgt. WARSCHARSKY, I. H.
T/328997 Dvr. WEINER, S., T.T.S.
T/313964 Dvr. WOLFE, S., T.T.S
21798 Pte. WEYASTA, M.
T/421319 Pte. WAGNER, H.
M2/166950 Pte. WOLLRANCH, J.
DM2/208732 Pte. WOLK, T.
400836 Pte. WINSLOW, W.
T/449592 Pte. WINE, M., M.T.
2616 Sgt. WOOLRAUCH, W.
S4/260251 Cpl. WATSON, M.
338468 Pte. WATTERSON, N.
328391 Pte. WALTERS, L. K.
065555 Cpl. WOLLMAN, R. C.
355580 Pte. WOLF, D.
92593 Pte. WOLFSON, A., 72nd Coy.
M/272094 Pte. WEISBERG, H.

Royal Army Service Corps.—*Continued.*

S4/260251 A/Cpl. WATSON, M.
DM2/162797 Pte. WHITE, M.
M/409464 Pte. WOOLF, S., 606th M.T. Coy.
S4/128797 Pte. WOOD, H.
291684 Pte. WOOLF, H.
        Pte. WOOLF, A.
M/348010 Pte. WISEMAN, H.
162423 Pte. WOLFE, S.
T/355739 Pte. WINE, C.
395951 Pte. WATERS, S.
119068 Pte. WAGNER, M.
513614 Pte. WARSTEIN, L. B.
31594 Pte. WINDISH, H.
296332 Pte. WOOLF, H.
3804 Pte. WITMAN, L.
338468 Cpl. WATERSON, H.
63130 Cpl. WEINBERG, S.
DM2/16928 Sgt. WOLFE, A.
        Dvr. WASS, B.
223068 Pte. WATSMAN, J.
T4/261964 Dvr. WONDER, T.
DM2/171901 Pte. WYNICK, J.
M2/191573 Pte. WAGENHEIM, L.
180392 Pte. WILLIAMS, J.
DM2/176092 Pte. WISE, S.
S/368087 Pte. WEYNBERG, I.
M2/116935 Pte. WINSTON, H.
2772 Pte. WALSH, L.
M2/228423 Pte. WOLFFE, A.
M2/228477 Pte. WEISS, H. J.
M2/268030 Pte. WOOLF, V.
35605 Pte. WINTER, H.
35637 Pte. WEITZMAN, E.

DM2/189086 Pte. WOLFE, L.
DM2/190505 Pte. WALL, S.
M2/269035 Pte. WOLFF, A. N.
DM2/231692 Pte. WISEPART, M.
302426 Pte. WEISBLATT, C.
282161 Pte. WOOLFSON, S. J.
R/277500 Pte. WILLIAMS, G.
M/116950 Pte. WALBRANCH, J.
M/317993 Pte. WEINBURG, J.
        Dvr. WOOLF, H.
93140 Dvr. WOLFENSOHN, M.
298260 Dvr. WOTTSPAN.
220431 Dvr. WONESHANK, J.
355739 Dvr. WINE, S.
3031013 Dvr. WOLFSON, L.
371870 Pte. WALLACE, H.
276352 Pte. WERSHKER, A.
135577 L/Cpl. WOOLF, C.
46106 Pte. WEINBERGER, G.
165129 Pte. YOUNGMAN, S., M.T.C.
S/256000 Pte. YABLONSKI, D.
5/345 Pte. ZUCKER, M., Northumbrian D. Tn.
M/303957 Dvr. ZIMMERMAN, L., M.T.
341694 Pte. ZIFF, M.T.
M/305556 Pte. ZEITLIN, W.
291187 Dvr. ZACKRINSKIE, J.
T/327248 Dvr. ZACKLIN, J.
M/377489 Pte. ZANSHUR, H.
M2/267082 Pte. ZANAMER, M.
M2/231719 Pte. ZIMMERMAN, W.
742075 Pte. ZACHAYESH, I. C.
M/377489 Pte. ZANSMER, W.

* Killed in Action or died on Active Service.

Zion Mule Corps.

(See page 60).

Lieut.-Col. J. H. PATTERSON, D.S.O., Officer Commanding.

Officers.

Capt. TRUMPELDOR, JOSEF
Med. Off. LEVONTIN, MESHULAM.
Lieut. ROLO, I.

Lieut. ROLO, C. J.
Lieut. BEROUL, SHALOMO.
2nd Lieut. AVERBUCH, WOLFF.

2nd Lieut. GOULDIN, JACOB.
2nd Lieut. MER, GERONIM.
2nd Lieut. ZLOTINE, S. Z.

N.C.O.'s and Men.

1 O.R.S.M. (later 2nd Lieut.) GORODISSKY, ALEX.*
2 Int. Sgt. AMZALAK, MOSES.
3 O.R.Sgt. BACHNER, CESAR.
4 O.R.Sgt. CAPLAN, NATAN.

5 Pte. COHEN, A.
6 Pte. COHEN, ELIE.
7 Sgt. ROUSSIN, ISRAEL.
8 Pte. BACK, SHAYA.
9 Sgt. COGON, ECHIEL.

10 Sgt.-Maj. HALIF, MAX.
11 Sgt. HASSIN, JOSHUA.
12 Sgt. ITSCOVITZ, JACOB.
13 Sgt. KAMINTSKY, JOSHUA.
14 Sgt.-Maj. KATZNELSON, R.

Zion Mule Corps.—*Continued.*

15	Sgt. Koffman, Arie.	77	Pte. Bravesman, Joel.	137	Pte. Heber, Mordehay.
16	Sgt. Kriksonof, Samuel.	78	Pte. Brodski, David.	138	Pte. Ichlonis, H.
17	Cpl. Monte, Abram.	79	Pte. Zelnik, Israel.	139	Pte. Hemmo Salomon.
18	Sgt. Mouchkatine, Isaie.	80	Pte. Hitritt, Joseph.	140	Pte. Hodorov, Eliezer.
19	Pte. Polani, Abram.	81	Pte. Cohen, Z.	141	Pte. Hodorov, Gershon.
20	Sgt. Pavzner, Volf.	82	Pte. Cohen, Reubin.	142	Pte. Horovitz, Moshe.
22	Sgt. Shender, David.	83	Pte. Cohen, Isaac.	143	Pte. Jacobson, Haim.
23	Sgt. Volkovitch, Haym.	84	Pte. Cohen, Zewi.	144	Pte. Janovski, Simon.
25	Cpl. Astrovosky, Isaac.	85	Pte. Dogbani, Abram.	145	Sgt.-Maj. Jassinski.
26	Sgt. Bobror, Einoch.	86	S.-Maj. Aboulafia, Rafael.	146	Pte. Zatchmenik, Samuel.
27	Pte. Cogon, Zalman.	87	Pte. Daniel, Shaoul.	147	Pte. Jehoudis, Mehemia.
28	Sgt. Dar. David Victor.	88	Pte. Darmon, Shalom.	148	Pte. Javtshinovski, Israel.
29	Cpl. Esersky, Josef.	89	Pte. Donskay, Haskel.	149	Cpl. Jatovitch, Moshe.
30	Cpl. Hildesheim, Elie.	90	Pte. Doubovi, Isaac.	150	Pte. Eni, Salomon.
32	Cpl. Kohn, Berish.	91	Pte. Doubrovitz, K.	151	Pte. Joffe, Abram.
33	Sgt. Kozlovsky, Efraim.	92	Pte. Elbag, Jacob.	152	Pte. Enousca, Abram.
34	Pte. Mischelson, —.	93	Pte. Elkaim, Isaac.	153	Pte. Kaffech, Salomon.
35	Cpl. Mizrahi, Jhié.	94	Pte. Engelman, Arie.	154	Pte. Kastel, E.
36	Cpl. Monsargi, Moses.	95	Cpl. Enpert, Simon.	155	Pte. Katz, Jacob.
37	Sgt. Rachmilof, Ben.	96	Pte. Inchstein, Elia.	156	Pte. Katzap, Mordehay.
38	Pte. Rosenbaum, Abram.	97	Pte. Epstein, Mordoh.	157	Pte. Katzinelsohn, B.*
39	Sgt. Sid, Jacob.	98	Pte. Epstein, Mordehay.	158	Pte. Kirzner, Jacob.
40	Cpl. Volodarsky, I.	99	Sgt. Erchcovitz, Mayer (D.C.M.).	159	Pte. Kirzner, I.*
41	Pte. Abadi, J.			160	Pet. Kirzner, Simon.
42	Pte. Abramovitch, Abram.	100	Pte. Faltinovitch, Nahum.	161	Pte. Kleinbaum, Jeshua.
43	Pte. Aizen, A.	101	Pte. Farber, Samuel.	162	Pte. Kablenz, Peivel.
44	Pte. Aizen, S.	102	Pte. Flato, Israel.	163	Farr.-Cpl. Capp, Isaac.
45	Pte. Albert, Jehouda.	103	Pte. Feinberg, Joseph.	164	Pte. Karman, Israel.
46	Pte. Alhatef, Mosche.	104	Pte. Fichef, Mosche.	165	Pte. Kravtzov, Abram.
47	Pte. Alcaley, Joseph.	106	Pte. Fogelson, Mendel.	166	Pte. Krivosheiff, Naoum.
48	Cpl. Alshinsky, Raoul.	108	Pte. Frishberg, Isaac.	167	Pte. Krouk, Shlomo.
49	Pte. Ansi, Shalom.	109	Pte. Froug, Isaac.	168	Pte. Kaizserman, Volf.
50	Pte. Ankari, H.	110	Pte. Gabrilovitz, Enoch.	169	Pte. Lacrieff, Mamon.
51	Pte. Apter, Jacob.	111	Pte. Galkerin, Joseph.	170	Farr.-Sgt. Shoub, Leib.
52	Pte. Apter, Pinhas.	112	Pte. Glouskin, Jeshoua.	171	Pte. Leibovitz, Moshe.
53	Pte. Aronaf, Leib.	113	Pte. Goldberg, Moshe.	172	Pte. Leibovitz, Shaoul.
54	Pet. Ashri, Zecharia.	114	Pte. Holdman, Joseph.	173	Pte. Leibovitz, G.
55	Pte. Ashkenzi, Nissem.	115	Pte. Goldenberg, Barouch.	174	Pte. Leventan, Moshe.
56	Pte. Akhalkassichvily, J.	117	Pte. Goloubov, Moshe.	175	Pte. Levi, Abel.
57	Pte. Azrilant, Pessach.	118	Pte. Gorban, Falik.	176	Pte. Levi, Isaac.
58	Pte. Averbuch, Efraim.	119	Pte. Horastein, Wolf.	177	Pte. Levi, Joseph.
60	Pte. Bargman, Samuel.*	120	Cpl. Goroditsky, Jeshua.	178	Pte. Levichvily, Jacob.
61	Pte. Bedawi, Abram.	121	Pte. Hornstein, Moshe.	179	Pte. Leberman, NNaoum.
62	Pte. Bahtboul, Moshe.	122	Pte. Goss, David.	180	Pte. Lichman, Naoum.
63	Pte. Baloul, Joseph.	123	Pte. Hornstein, Sam.	181	Pte. Lipman, Abram.
64	Pte. Berouch, Jehouda.	124	Pte. Grandapel, Aron.	182	Pte. Maizlin, Ben.
65	Pte. Bardan, Mordehay.	125	Pte. Grinberg, Mordehay.	183	Pte. Makievsky, Joseph.
66	Pte. Barouch, Massoud.	126	Pte. Groushcovsky, M.	184	Pte. Maman, H.
67	Pte. Behar, Isaac.	127	Pte. Gelman, Moshe.	185	Pte. Menshirof, J.
68	Pte. Behar, Nissim.	128	Pte. Genkin, Sam.	186	Pte. Marcous, Mordehay.
69	Pte. Behar, Samuel.	129	Pte. Herzenstein, M.	187	Pte. Margaulis, Jonah.
70	Sgt. Benshakar, Jacob.	130	Pte. Hadad, Shalom.	188	Pte. Margoulis, Zoussi.
71	Pte. Bernstein, Isaac.	131	Pte. Halivy, Mcrdehay.	190	Pte. Mosseri, Isaac.
72	Pte. Berstein, Leon.	132	Pte. Haliff, David.	191	Pte. Menasce, Ben.
73	Pte. Bedawi, Shalom.	133	Pte. Halif, Jeshoua.	192	Pte. Mertzel, Salomon.
74	Pte. Elkaim, Haim.	134	Pte. Harvon, Abram.	193	Pte. Mesholam, Israel.
75	Pte. Boudnic, Peretz.	135	Pte. Harrin, Jacob.	195	Pte. Michailov, Michael.
76	Pte. Breslahsky, Abram.	136	Pte. Hafkin, Levi.	196	Pte. Milshtein, Menasce.

Zion Mule Corps—*Continued.*

#	Name	#	Name	#	Name
197	Sgt.-Maj. MORENS, JOSEPH.	265	L/Cpl. MESHOULAM, TERAM.	327	Pte. PERETZ, MORDEHAY.
198	Pte. MUSCOVITZ, DAVID.*	266	Pte. TOPOLINSKY, NISH.	328	Pte. REGINE, BEN.
199	Pte. NAGAR, ELIA.	267	Cpl. TOURKENITZ, MORDEH.	329	Pte. RAUP, HAIM.
200	Pte. NATANILOFF, NISSIM.	268	Pte. TAURAK, JESHOUA.	330	Pte. SAKIRSKY, JACOB.
201	Pte. NASHLITZ, JOSEPH.	269	Pte. TROPER, MOSHE.	331	Pte. SABAA, ISAAC.
202	Pte. NAZAROF, ELIA.	270	Pte. VEINBERG, JULIAN.	332	Pte. SABITAY, ABRAM.
203	Pte. NISSIMBAUM, SAM.	271	Pte. VARSHAYSKY, ISAAC.	333	Pte. SION, LEBEL.
204	Pte. NOVAK, SALOMON.	272	Pte. VELDER, SHLOMO.	334	Pte. SHMIT, MOSHE,
205	Cpl. NOGNITSKY, ISAAC.	273	Pte. VERTHEIM, ABRAM.	335	Pte. SHVARTZE'AN, HAIM.
206	Pte. ORTASS, LEON.	274	Pte. VILDAVSKY, S.	336	Pte. VERTHEIM, DAVID.
207	Pte. OSSIAH, ABRAM.	275	Pte. VINDMAN, VOLF.	338	Pte. ZISMAN, JOSEPH.
208	Pte. PAPLAVSKY, J.	276	Pte. ZABRI, HAYM.	339	Pte. AMIEL, DAVID.
209	Pte. PEISSEL JEHOUDA.	277	Pte. ZAGAG, ARIL.	340	Pte. BENSOUR, RAPHAEL.
210	Pte. PLICH, ZEWI.	278	Pte. ZAGOURI, JACOB.	341	Pte. BOUDNIC, ARON.
212	Pte. PROCOPETZ, JACOB.	279	Pte. ZALMAN, DAVID.	342	Pte. BRENDMAN, ISRAEL.
213	Pte. RABINOSVITZ, JACOB.	280	Pte. ZARAMATI, ISAAC.	343	Pte. COHEN, DAVID.
215	Sgt. RAHMILOFF, RAHMIEL.	281	Pte. ZEBOUL, ABRAM.	344	Pte. COHEN, SHALOM.
216	Pte. RAVIDOVITZ, JACOB.	283	Pte. ZLOTNIC, SHEMOUL.	345	Pte. COHEN, BENJAMIN.
217	Pte. RAZVINOVSKY, HAIM.	284	Pte. PAGISSIMIDI, MORDHAY.	346	Pte. COHEN, BENZION.
218	Pte. RAPAPORT, MORDEHAY.	285	Cpl. DVONPOLOV, MICHEL.	347	Pte. COHEN, HAYM.
219	Pte. ROSANER, JACOB.	286	Pte. BACHKOURINSKY, L.	348	Pte. COHEN, ABRAM.
220	Pte. ROSENBERG, ISAAC.	287	Pte. MARGOLIS, ABRAM.	349	Pte. DEPASS, MICHEL.
221	Sgt. ROSENBERG, NISSEL.	288	Farr.-Cpl. FRANK, ABRAM.*	350	Pte. DEPASS, SAL.
223	Pte. RATTENBERG, MORDEH.	289	Pte. RABLIN, Z.	351	Pte. GRINBERG, SAM
224	Pte. ROUSI, HAIM.	290	Pte. ROUBLINSKY, MOSES.	352	Pte. HANDEL, ROUBEN.
225	Pte. SHAVITSKY, ISAAC.	291	Pte. TIDGI, SION.	353	Pte. ISRAEL, ABRAM.
227	Pte. SHAOUL, ISAAC.	293	Pte. JORISH, ISAAC.	354	Pte. KAGLAN, ISAAC.
232	Pte. SHEHLER, DAVID.	294	Pte. ZAGOURI, MOSCHE.	355	Pte. KIKI, JACOB.
233	Pte. SHOHET, BEN.	295	Pte. BACHARI, ABRAM.	356	Pte. LEVI, NISSIM.
234	Pte. SHOUL, ISAAC.	296	Pte. BEHAR, LEON.	357	Pte. LEVI, SALOMON.
235	Pte. STER, NETZEMENIA.	297	BEHAR, MOSHÉ.	358	Pte. MIZRAHI, NISSIM.
236	Pte. SPREGEL, EIN.	299	Pte. BRESLER, ABRAM.	359	Pte. MOLLIM, HAIM.
237	Sgt. SHVARTZER, ELIHON.	300	Pte. COHEN, ELI.	360	Pte. PAGHIR, MORIS.
238	Pte. STILVASSIR, DAVID.	301	Pte. COHEN, GERSHON.	361	Pte. REDLICH, GERSHON.
239	Pte. SPRELBERG, ZALMAN.	302	Pte. DAVIDOVITCH, B.	363	Pte. ROTTMAN, JACOB.*
240	Pte. SHMIDT, ELIESEN.	303	Pte. ESPERENCE, ELIE.	364	Pte. SIBERI, JEHOUDA.
241	Pte. SHAVRTZEN, MENARZE.	304	Pte. FARHI, JOSEPH.	365	Pte. VERSLER, SHALOM.
242	Pte. SHVARTZ MOSHE.	305	Pte. FARSI, JEHOUDA.	366	Pte. WERTHEIMER, BEN.*
243	Pte. SENDEROFF MORDEH.	306	Pte. FISHBEIN, MOSHE.	367	Pte. ZALMAN, MOSHE.
244	Pte. ZAVLANSVITZ, ABRAM.	307	Pte. GOULAK, ELIE.	368	Pte. AZOUZ, ELIE.
245	Pte. SIBUSHNIK, JACOB.	308	Pte. HAFKIN, ISAAC.	369	Pte. AZOUZ, ISAAC.
246	Pte. SIMONTOV, ABRAM.	309	Pte. HAZAN, SCHLOMS.	370	Pte. ASHKENAZI, NATHAN.
248	Pte. SION, MOSHE.	310	Pte. HOURVITZ, DAVID.	371	Pte. ARAZI, JACOB.
249	L/Cpl. SIRKES, JACOB.	311	Pte. HAYON, HAIM.	372	Pte. AMIEL, GABRIEL.
250	Pte. SISKEL, DAVID.	312	Pte. LABOK, JACOB.	373	Pte. ACOUCA, MATTATIA.
251	Pte. SIDKOF, MORDEHAY.	313	Pte. LEVI, SIMON.	374	Pte. HARRARI, ELIE.
252	Pte. SKALETSKY, MAROUCH.	314	Pte. LEVI, JOEPH.	375	Pte. CHERBIT, MATOUL.
253	Pte. SKALETSKY, MOSHE.	315	Pte. MARGOULIS, ABRAM.	376	Pte. COHEN, JOSEF.
254	Cpl. SCOROBOGATS, ABRAM.	316	Pte. MACOVER, ABRAM.	377	Pte. COHEN, FELIX.
255	Pte. SMOROVINSKY, ROUBIN.	317	Pte. MIZRAKI, HAIM.	378	Pte. EPSTEIN, ZALMON.
256	Pte. SAUMLOVITZ, ARON.	318	Pte. MELTZER, SHELOMS.	379	Pte. GITTER, ISAAC.
257	Pte. STERN, HIRSH.*	319	Pte. MASSAUD, SHOUSHA.	381	Pte. JDELOVITZ, ISAIE.
259	Pte. STIKOVITZ, GIRSHON.	320	Pte. MORDOCH, JACOB.	382	Pte. JAPOSHVILY, ELIE.
260	Pte. STILERMAN, SHMILL.	321	Pte. MIZRAHI, JEHOUDA.	383	Pte. KRETCHMER, SALOMON.
261	Pte. STOUKILIN, DAVID.	322	Pte. MELEMED, MOSHE.	384	Pte. KOFFMAN, HANANIA.
262	Pte. TARATETSKY, ABRAM.	323	Pte. MIZRAKI, ABRAM.	385	Pte. PERETZ, MAYER.
263	Pte. TOHASKA, MOSHE.	324	Pte. MIZRAKI, JACOB.	387	Pte. SAADIEF, ABRAM.
264	Pte. TOHINIO, ALBERT.	326	Pte. POLLAK, ARON.	388	Pte. SLONIN, JACOB.

Zion Mule Corps—Continued.

No.	Name	No.	Name	No.	Name
389	Pte. SUID, NESSIM.	461	Pte. COHEM, SIMON ELIE.	540	Pte. MILIS, OVADIA.
390	Pte. SABAN, ISAAC.	464	Pte. LENNER, ABRAM.	541	Pte. MOSHE, ARON.
392	Pte. ZELIG, SAMUEL.	465	Pte. LEVY, SHALOM.	542	Pte. MAHUIFEA, WOLF.
393	Pte. ABOUTBOUL, ALBERT.	466	Pte. NINI, FELIX.	543	Pte. MAHUIFEA, ISRAEL.
394	Pte. AROUSSI, MASSOUD.	467	Pte. PINCHEVER, LEIB.	544	Pte. MIZRAHI, SALOMON.
395	Pte. ALICOS, SALVADOR.	468	Pte. SIBONI, ELIE.	545	Pte. MENASHI, EZRA.
396	Pte. BARUCH, MOUSSA.	470	Pte. COHEN, ABRAM.	546	Pte. NEHARI, EZRA.
397	Pte. BONAN, MARES.	471	Pte. B'URCHAN, ARON.	547	Pte. ZAGDOUN, ABRAM.
399	Pte. COHEN, ISAAC.	472	Pte. MOYAL, RAFAEL.	548	Pte. OBADIA, DAVID.
400	Pte. COHEN, MORDEKAY.	473	Pte. ROUMI, MENASCE.	549	Pte. PALACCI, LEON.
403	Pte. ISRAEL, ELIE.	474	Pte. SHOUSHANA, VICTOR.	550	Pte. ROZANES, RAFAEL.
404	Pte. JOUDANI, LEON.	475	Pte. AMIEL, MOSHE ELIE.	551	Cpl. RABIN, LEVY.
405	Pte. KEMELMAN, HAIM.	476	Pte. COHEN, ABRAM.	552	Pte. MAARABI, MOUSSA.
406	Pte. MALET, DAVID.	478	Pte. AZRIEL, RAPHAEL.	553	Pte. MECHAN, ISAAC.
407	Pte. MATZA, ELIE.	480	Pte. ROUAH, JOSEPH.	554	Pte. SHAOUL, ISAAC.
408	Pte. MESSEKA, SAUL.	481	Pte. GELINDER, SHAOUL.	555	Pte. SFORMES, VICTOR.
409	Pte. MORHI, ARON JOUSSEF.	482	Pte. KRIMSKY, ELIHIN.	556	Pte. SHOUSHAN, MASSOUD.
410	Pte. NEHARI, EZRA SHALOM.	483	Pte. KOVOS, JACOB.	557	Pte. SION, MOSHE M.
411	Pte. OBED, RICHARD.	500	Pte. AZIZ, JAOUB.	558	Pte. STIFOUSKY, ROB.
412	Pte. RAZANOVSKY, EFRAIM.	501	Pte. MARGOCHEZ, JOSEPH.	559	Cpl. SINTO, ISAAC.
413	Pte. SAAL, MORDEKAY.	502	Pte. BEN, MAJOR ALBERT.	560	Pte. SHAUNCHEHATA, S.
414	Pte. SHOUNE, JOSEPH.	503	Pte. HELEWA, MOUSSA.	561	Pte. STERN, NAHAMIA.
415	Pte. SAPIROFF, MOSHE.	504	Pte. SIVISSA, DAVID.	562	Pte. SAYED, HAIM WAHBA.
416	Pte. SITTON, SIOMN.	505	Pte. COHEN, MOISE.	563	Pte. SAUVEUR, SAMAMA.
417	Pte. VALP, RAUBIN.	506	Pte. COHEN, DANIEL.	564	Pte. SALEM, DAVID.
418	Pte. ZILBERMAN, ISAAC.	507	Pte. COHEN, HAIM.	565	Pte. SALEM, YEHIA.
419	Pte. BRASLARSKY, ISAAC.	508	Pte. CHIPROUT, NESSIM.	566	Pte. HOUNA, FARAG JACOUB.
420	Pte. ELKAIM, ABRAM.	509	Pte. COHEN, JACOB.	567	Pte. YAFET, JEHOUDA.
421	Pte. FARHI, ARON.	510	Pte. DASSA, DANIEL.	568	Pte. JOHAY, JOSEPH.
422	Pte. GOLDESTEIN, SALOMON.	511	Pte. RENKEVITZ, HATZKEL.	569	Pte. JEHIA, SHALOM.
423	Pte. GORODENTZIG, ZALMAN.	512	Pte. DAHAN, ZAKI.	570	Pte. ZAGDOUN, VICTOR.
424	Pte. GERTNER, ARON.	513	Sgt.-Maj. ABOULAFIA, R.	571	Pte. MIZRAHI, BENJAMIN.
425	Pte. HAKIM, ABOO.	514	Pte. GOLDSTEIN, ARON.	572	Pte. AMIEL, JACOUB.
426	Pte. LEDES, DAVID.	515	Pte. GREENBERG, ZIAS.	573	Pte. COHEN, DAVID.
427	Pte. LIFSHITZ, JOSEPH.	516	Pte. GAAN, FELIX.	574	Pte. LEVY, SIMON.
428	Pte. MALLAK, DAVID.	517	Pte. GOLDSTEIN, MOISE.	575	Pte. MIZRAHI SOLOMON.
430	Pte. MIZRAHI, SALOMON.	518	Pte. HAZAN, VICTOR.	576	Pte. MAMAN RALIMOZ.
431	Pte. MOSHHAIEFF, LEON.	519	Pte. ZAKI, SIMON LEVY.	577	Pte. OBBI, MASSOUD.
432	Pte. ROUSI, JOSEPH.	520	Pte. HABIL, DAVID.	578	Pte. COHEN, ELIAHOU.
433	Pte. SHIFF, SALOMON.	521	Pte. KAFFECH, SALOMON.	579	Pte. BRIMATI, ISRAEL.
434	Pte. JOUSEFF, ARON.	522	Pte. KISS, MOUSSA.	580	Pte. TARANTO, JOSEPH.
435	Pte. ZAIDMAN, J.	523	Pte. KHODR, JOUSSEF.	581	Pte. COHEN, JOUSSEF ISAAC.
436	Pte. GRINBERG, DAVID.	524	Pte. KHADR, JOUSSEF J.	582	Pte. ROUSSO, SHALOM.
437	Pte. AMIEL, MOSHE.	525	Pte. KRASMONSKY, DAVID.	583	Pte. HALAWANI, ABRAM.
438	Pte. FREINDLICH, JACOB.	526	Pte. KHOBA, SHILIBI.	584	Pte. DANIEL, SHAOUL.
439	Cpl. SHULMAN, ISAAC.	527	Pte. YEMAIN, JOUSSEF.	585	Pte. CAMHI, NESSIM.
440	Pte. VEINBERG, LEIZER.	528	Pte. LEVY, MOUSSA.	586	Pte. CHERBIT, MATOUK.
441	Pte. HOURVITZ, HAIM.	529	Pte. LIBRESCO, MOISE.	587	Pte. NOUSSERI, JEHIA JOE.
444	Pte. MATVEILFF, ABRAM.	530	Pte. LEVY, JAOUB.	588	Pte. HOROVITZ, HAIM.
448	Pte. ARIER, LEIB.	531	Pte. LEVY, MEIR.	589	Pte. HARARI, ELIE.
451	Pte. LEVY, ISAAC.	532	Pte. LEVY, JOSEPH SHALOM.	590	Pte. MANSOW, MOISE.
454	Pte. BAJAAIEV, ABRAM.	533	Pte. ASLAN, MOUSSA.	591	Pte. MOYAL, RAFAEL.
455	Pte. KATZ, JOE.	534	Pte. SAUARES, PINHAS.	592	Pte. TERAM, MESHIELAM.
456	Pte. LEVY, DAVID MOSHE.	535	Pte. FEDEDA, NESSIM.	593	Pte. MEKAIECH, ABRAM.
457	Pte. LEVY, DAVID.	536	Pte. MEZRAHI, RAFOUL.	594	Pte. VOLINSKY, LEVI.
458	Pte. SAPIROFF, JACQUES.	537	Pte. ENOUCA, SHRIVLY G.	595	Pte. BIDOUVI, ABRAM.
459	Pte. SOLIMANOFF, MAMON.	538	Pte. ATTOUN, ARON.	596	Pte. SKIFF, SALOMON.
460	Pte. BOURSHTEIN, ARON.	539	Pte. MIZRAHI, JEOUDA.	597	Pte. BOUBLI, ABRAM.

Zion Mule Corps—*Continued.*

598 Pte. BEN, SOUSSAN MEIR.
599 Pte. ICHBIA, JOUSSEF.
600 Pte. FATHI, EFRAIM.
601 Pte. DUEK, HAIM.
602 Pte. COHEN, LIETO S.
603 Pte. TIDRI, SION.
604 Pte. PEREZ, VICTOR.
605 Pte. GREENSTEIN, MOISE.
606 Pte. LEVI, SALOMON DAVID.
607 Pte. AZOULAY, NESSIM.
608 Pte. MIZRAHI, VITA.
609 Pte. SUSSO, VICTOR.
610 Pte. MENASHE, EZRA.
611 Pte. CAMHI, HAIM.
612 Pte. ROSETHAL, ELIE.
613 Pte. MENASHE, BENJAMIN.
614 Pte. SITTON, RAHMIN.
615 Pte. AZOULAY, NESSIM.
616 Pte. HAY, SASSON.
617 Pte. SALAMA, FARAG.
618 Pte. SOUCCAR, VITA.
619 Pte. MEDIAN, ELIA.
620 Pte. HAUSUCAIAFF, H.
621 Pte. ZAVLONOVITCH, A.
622 Pte. BRESLAVSKY, ISAAC.
623 Pte. HARMCHIN, OZIA.
624 Pte. SORINO, SALOMON.
625 Pte. HAZAN, JOUSSEF.
626 Pte. SAADA, LIETO.
627 Pte. ISCAKI, JOUSSEF.
628 Pte. SOUROUR, DAVID.
629 Pte. ELLIS, MICHAEL.
630 Pte. LEVY, JOUSSEF HAIM.
631 Pte. SERGANI, BAROUCH.
632 Pte. BAROUCH, MOUSSA.
633 Pte. MIZRAHI, JONA.
634 Pte. MESSALI, RAFAEL.
635 Pte. SHAMA, DANIEL.
636 Pte. ABOURBI, JEOUDA.
637 Pte. LEVY, JACQUES M.
638 Pte. GHEBALI, VITA.
639 Pte. FISHER, ISRAEL.
640 Pte. BONFIL, BAROUCH.
641 Pte. VEINTROL, DAVID.
642 Pte. PESSACHOVITZ, G.
643 Pte. ESPERANCE, ELIE.
644 Pte. MESSALI, RAFAEL.
645 Pte. KASSANTO, ISAAC.
646 Pte. GRINBERG, JOSEPH.
647 Pte. SHEHIB, HAIM.
648 Pte. MALKI, DAVID.
649 Pte. SCONIN, LEIB.
650 Pte. COHEN, SHABETAI.
651 Pte. LEVY, ISAAC.
652 Pte. HAZAK, SALOMON.
653 Pte. HADSI, SALOMON.
654 Pte. ISIMBERG, ABRAM.
655 Pte. VARON, ISAAC.
656 Pte. BAROS, MOISE.
657 Pte. BEN, BACHIR VITA.
658 Pte. KASSAR, DAHOUD.
659 Pte. FRANKO, MARCO.
660 Pte. EDMOND, ELIE.
661 Pte. ZETOUNA, SION.
662 Pte. SALAMA, RAHMIN.
663 Pte. ABRAHAM, JAISI.
664 Cpl. ZEEDMAN, EFFIN.
665 Pte. SABRI, HAIM.
666 Pte. HIMMI, ELIE.
667 Pte. ELIAOU, MOUSSA.
668 Pte. BENISTI, SOUA.
669 Pte. HANOUCAEF, HAIM.
670 Pte. LALOUSH, MOISE.
671 Pte. BOURLA, DAVID.
672 Pte. GROS, HERMAN.
673 Pte. FIDLER, ADOLPHE.
674 Pte. CATLAN, ELIE.
675 Pte. FARAG, SALIM.
676 Pte. KHADR, SALOMON.
677 Pte. KHADR, ZAKI.
678 Pte. BAROUCH, DAVID.
679 Pte. BAROUCH, MOUSSA.
680 Pte. JOANA, ZAKARYE.
681 Pte. MEIZES, NOAH.
682 Pte. ABDALLA, JAUOB.
683 Pte. SMITH, MOISE.
684 Pte. CAMHI, JOUSSEF.
685 Pte. MUNIR, ABRAM.
686 Pte. NAIM, KHALIFA.
687 Pte. POLLAK, SHALLOM.
688 Pte. LIPSON, RUBEN.
689 Pte. EISENCHTAD, ELIE.
690 Pte. PENSO, DAVID.
691 Pte. GRELER, JACOUB.
692 Pte. BEHAR, SAMUEL.
693 Pte. EZRA, DAVID.
694 Pte. TARANTO, DAVID.
695 Pte. COHEN, ZEVI.
696 Pte. PIVKO, ISAAC.
697 Pte. DAHAN, DAVID.
698 Pte. KRIVIN, ABRAM.
699 Pte. SAADA, HAIM.
700 Pte. MOUSSA, JOHAN.
701 Pte. BRISLOVSKY, EHIEL.
702 Pte. ABOUTBOUL, JACOB.
703 Pte. ROUBEN, JACOB.
704 Pte. MANSOUR, SALIM.
705 Pte. JOUSSEF, SALAMON.
706 Pte. SALAMA, IBRAHIM.
707 Pte. MIZRAHI, JOUSSEF.
708 Pte. ANSI, SHALOM.
709 Pte. ZISMAN, JOUSSEF.
710 Pte. CASTEL, ISAAC.
711 Pte. SAMPOUN, MRAD.
712 Pte. ROUSSO, SIMON.
713 Pte. OVERBOUCH, ISAAC.
714 Pte. SLIMAN, IBRAHIM.
715 Pte. KHAMRI, ABDALLA A.
716 Pte. BAROUCH, JEHOUDA.
717 Pte. NAZAREFF, ELISHA.
718 Pte. MATREEF, ABRAM.
719 Pte. SHALOM, HARON.
720 Pte. HOROVITZ, MOSHE.
721 Pte. ACHALKATZ, HAZKEL.
722 Pte. SHEHTER, DAVID.
723 Pte. GOLDSVEIG M.
724 Pte. DAVARNOFF ISAAC.
725 Pte. GOLDSTEIN, SALAMON.
726 Pte. MIZRAHI, SHEHATA.
727 Pte. LEVY, RAPHAEL.

ROYAL ARMY MEDICAL CORPS.

OFFICERS.

Major ABRAHAMS, A. C. (C.B.E.).
Capt. ABRAHAMS, R. G., 10th Stat. Hosp.
Lieut. ABRAHAMS, G., No. 1 Stationary Hosp.
Major ABRAHAMS, A. (O.B.E.).
Capt. AFLALO, F. G.
Lieut. ANSELL.
Lieut. ALLAUN, I.
Capt. ABRAHAM, E. C. (M.C.).
Capt. ANCILL, S. J.
Capt. BLASHKI, E. P. (M.C.), att. 7th Yorks.
Lieut. BRIDGE, L. D., O.C. 35th Div. San. Sect.
Lieut. BALKIN, J. J., 13th Field Amb.
Capt. BLOOM, A., 250th Bde. R.F.A.
Lieut. BRISCOE, M.
Lieut. BARNETT, P.
Lieut. BERNSTEIN, J. B.
Lieut. BLOCK, I. M.

Royal Army Medical Corps.—*Continued.*

Capt. BURN, R.
Lieut. and Qmr. COHEN, M., 3rd Nor. Field Amb.
Lieut. COHEN, A. S.,* att. 8th Somerset L.I.
Lieut. COHEN, B.*
Capt. COHEN, M., 77th Field Amb.
Lieut. COHEN, B. W., att. 7th York and Lancs.
Lieut. COLT, M., att. 16th R.W. Fusiliers.
Capt. COHEN, C. K., 64th Field Amb.
Major COPLANS, M. (D.S.O., O.B.E.).
Lieut. CLARKE, W.
Capt. COHEN, L. D.
Lieut. COHEN, L. C., No. 5 Stationary Hosp.
Lieut. CLARKE, D. S., 113th Field Amb.
Lieut. CANTER, M. W.
Lieut. COPLANS, J. M.
Lieut. CAPLAN, H.
Capt. COPLANS, E.
Capt. CIVELSTAM, D. A.
Capt. CHAIKIN, B.
Lieut. COHEN, J.
Capt. COHEN, B.
Capt. COHEN, M. M.
Lieut. DUVEEN, E. E., G.H.Q., B.R.C.
Capt. DELGADO, A. E.
Capt. DULBERG, J.
Capt. DAVIS, H.
Capt. ECCLES, O.
Capt. DUPARC, S.
Lieut. ELLENBOGEN, J.
Capt. EMANUEL, J. G.
Major EHRMANN, A. (O.B.E.).
Lieut. EDER, M. D.
Capt. FELDMAN, J., 21st Field Amb.
Capt. FARMER, H. L., 74th Sanitary Sect.
Capt. FINZI, N. S.
Capt. FRANKS, L. L., 11th C.C.S.
Lieut. GOLDSMID, H., No. 1 Red Cross Hosp.
Capt. GIDEON, C. I., att. 7th K. Shropshire L.I.
Capt. GUEST, L. H. (M.C.), O.C. 29th San. Sect.
Major GREEN, M.
Capt. GEFFEN, M. D.
Capt. GOLDING, M.
Capt. GROSS, M.
Capt. GOODMAN, H.
Capt. HARRIS, S.
Lieut. HARRIS, C. M.,* att. 7th R. Scots Fus.
Lieut. HILTON, M. J.
Lieut. HARRIS, J. M.
Capt. JACOBS, C. (M.C. and Bar), att. 1st Lincoln.
Capt. JAFFE, J.,* att. 2/4th Somerset L.I.
Capt. JOSEPH, H. M. (M.C.), 93rd Field Amb.
Capt. JONES, E. B.
Lieut. KALICHMAN, C., 2nd N.M. Field Amb.
Lieut. LUCAS, N. S., att. 48th Div. R.E.
Capt. LEVINE, L., 2/1st West Lancs. Fld. Amb.
Lieut.-Col. LIGHTSTONE, H. (D.S.O., M.C.).
Capt. LEVY, L., 42nd C.C.S.
Capt. LAZARUS, L., 2nd Field Amb.
Capt. LEON, J. T.*
Capt. LEVENTON, J.
Capt. LEVY, A. G.
Lieut. and Qr. LEWIS, J.
Lieut. LEVY, V.
Lieut. LURIER.
Lieut. LEWIS, I. M. J.
Capt. LUMLEY, E. A.
Lieut. MARGOLLIS, 39th Stat. Hosp.
Lieut. MOSES, D. A. H. (M.C.), att. 17th Welsh Regt.
Lieut.-Col. MYERS, C. S. (C.B.E.).
Lieut. MENDELSON, B., 30th C.C.S.
Capt. MORRIS, N., 62nd General Hosp.
Capt. MAYERS, L. M.
Lieut. MORLEY, A. S.,
Capt. MONTAGUE, S. A.
Capt. MOSSERI, R.
Major MUSSEN, A. A.
Lieut. MOSES, P.
Capt. NATHAN, S.
Lieut. Col. PHILLIPS, S. P.
Capt. RICH, V. M., 90th Field Amb.
Lieut. ROSE, D., Allied Forces Base Hosp.
Capt. REECE, L. N.
Capt. ROSSDALE, G. H.
Capt. ROSENTHAL, J.
Capt. ROSENCWIGE, J. (M.B.).
Capt. STEVENS, A. R.
Lieut. SIMONS, S., 90th Field Amb.
Lieut. SMITH, I. R., 2nd General Hosp.
Lieut. SILINGER, E.
Lieut. SACOSCHANSKY, E.
Lieut. SHOCKETT, H. C.
Dr. SCHLESINGER, E. G.
Capt. SALAMAN, R. N.
Capt. SAMUEL, B. B.
Lieut. SAMUEL, S.
Lieut. SANDLESON, A. E. W.
Lieut. SHEROWITZ, C. G.
Lieut. SIMON, I B.
Capt. SINGER, C.
Lieut. SOROKIEWITCH, H.
Capt. SINSON, J. B.
Capt. SMITH, I. R.
Lieut. TURIANSKY, M.C., 12th Stationary Hosp.
Lieut. TYLER, S.
Capt. WOOLF, A. E. M.
Lieut. WOOLF, M. S.
Lieut. WYLER, E. J. (M.C.).

N.C.O.'s AND MEN.

5001 Pte. ALEXANDER, H. M., 3rd Field Amb.
1738 L/Cpl. ABRAHAMS, J. (M.M.), 4th Lond. Field Amb.

Royal Army Medical Corps—*Continued.*

1490	Pte. ABRAHAMS, S., 5th Field Amb.
3116	Pte. ABELSON, I., 60th Div. San. Sect.
50123	Pte. ALEXANDER, B., 45th C.C.S.
112622	Pte. ABRAHAMS, I., 50th Field Amb.
122060	Pte. ABRAHAMS, M.*
112629	Pte. AMSDORF, C., 5th Native Lab. Hp.
117613	Pte. APPLEBAUM, M., 30th S.H.P.
75524	Pte. ABECASIS, V. B.
112906	Pte. AJULNICK, J.,
114093	Pte. APPELBOAM, H., 7th Stat. Hosp.
18904	Cpl. AARONS, S., 13th Gen. Hosp.
11044	Pte. ALEXANDER, A. J.
545682	L./Cpl. ABELSON, P.
117971	Pte. ANGLEVITZ, H.
105076	Cpl. ANGEL, S. P.
4090	Pte. ABRAHAMS, S.
132362	Pte. ABRAHAMS, L.
137655	Pte. ALLSCHWANG.
136217	Pte. ABRAMS, H.
153661	Pte. ARONSBERG, H.
130981	Pte. ABELSON, L., No. 3 Gen. Hosp.
136342	Pte. ARONWITCH, S.
118499	Pte. ABRAHAMS, H.
86300	Pte. AIZEN, M.
570	Pte. ALTARAS, W.
	Pte. AARONS, I. A.
97372	Pte. AUERBACH, J.
543096	Pte. ABRAHAMS, A.
98459	Pte. ABELSON, J.
98186	Pte. AIZEN, J.
13251	Pte. AARONS, L.
1645	Pte. ARONOVITCH, S.
2/G.H.141	Pte. ARON, J.
114252	Pte. ALFERT, R.
113219	Pte. ALEXANDER.
554182	L./Cpl. ABRAHAMS, J.
118655	Pte. ALBERGE, C. E.
35701	Pte. ALLEN, M.
136342	Pte. ASONWITCH, S.
118499	Pte. ABRAHAMS, H.
	Pte. ALTARAS, W.
83275	Pte. ABRAHAMS, H.
5210	Sgt. BURKE, S. (M.M.), 7th Field Amb.
53841	Pte. BLACK, J., 46th Field Amb.
40004	Sgt. BARNETT, H., 57th Field Amb.
41618	Cpl. BLOOM, J., 57th Field Amb.
592	Pte. BARNETT, S., 37th Div. San. Sect.
1750	Pte. BROWN, H., 4th Lond. Field Amb.
337	Pte. BRAND, W., att. 9th London Regt.
508505	Pte. BOSWELL, R. H., 2/1st Lond. F.A.
	Pte. BLOOM, A., 4th Stat. Hosp.
56500	
59168	Pte. BERNSTEIN, L.,* 22nd Field Amb.
2306	Pte. BARDER, K., 2/6th Lond. Fld. Am.
86009	Pte. BOGDANOR, S., 59th Field Amb.
47677	Sgt.-Maj. BOWMAN, A. J., 60th Fld. Am.
64915	Pte. BLOOM, P., 29th Field Amb.
1963	Pte. BLACK, R., 3/2nd W. Lancs.
450008	Pte. BERNER, C. P., 74th Field Amb.
115658	Pte. BENJAMIN, L., 44th Field Amb.
47678	Q.M.S. BENJAMIN, J., M.A.C.
546168	L./Cpl. BARENTS, A. J., 33rd San. Sect.
36764	Pte. BARTLETT, C. E., 2/3rd N.M.F.A.
247912	Sgt. BARDER, W., 1/1st E.L. Field Am.
8711	Sgt. BASWITZ, J.
142712	Pte. BENJAMIN, D.
	Pte. BARNETT, A.
33635	Cpl. BLOOM, M., 30th Field Amb.
117242	Pte. BERMAN, I., 8th Stat. Hosp.
6738	Pte. BENNETT, B., 10th Mob. Lab.
524015	Pte. BALCON, I., 12th Stat. Hosp.
	Pte. BENNETT, D., 14th Gen. Hosp.
2843	L./Cpl. BROWN, A., 9th Amb. Train.
9545	Dvr. BOAS, C., B.R.C.S.
	Pte. BURNARD, D.
93085	Pte. BARR, M., 11th Gen. Hosp.
6223	Pte. BALDRY, J. W.
96991	Pte. BOOTMAN, M.
350192	Sgt. BEVION, H.
85975	L/Cpl. BERG, A.
63165	Pte. BAKER, J.
S/106	Pte. BERNERS, G., 8th Field Amb.
1717	L/Cpl. BLAIBERG, S., 3/6th Field Amb.
40004	Cpl. BARNETT.
	Staff Sgt.-Maj. BAMBERGER, F. O. W., 74th San. Sect.
139182	Pte. BLASHKEY, A.*
105270	Pte. BLACK, L., 34th Field Amb.
58259	Pte. BIRD, C.
135464	Pte. BARNETT, B.
96505	Pte. BACHRACH, S. E.
116722	Pte. BIEGLE, W.
528414	Pte. BARDER, K. C.
126780	Pte. BLAIN, J.
123865	Pte. BOYERS, H.
99185	Pte. BERKOVITCH, I., 311th Field Amb.
2GH/183	Pte. BRAHAM, D. H.
113950	Pte. BROWN, I.
94968	Pte. BARNETT, J.
126779	Pte. BLACK, P.
126862	Pte. BENNETT, L.
118612	Pte. BELENFORTE, J. E.
114098	Pte. BARIAN, S.
121646	Pte. BARNETT, A.
27346	Pte. BOLLAND, L.
75524	Pte. BRANDON, V.
10500	Pte. BOKIOKIE.
63163	Pte. BAKER, J.
47006	Pte. BELINFANTE, A.
98997	Pte. BLOCK, A.
112535	Pte. BLACK, H.
113306	Pte. BERGER, S.
524015	Pte. BALLON, I.
541287	Pte. BERCOVITCH, B.
125317	Pte. BLACKMAN, S.
114096	Pte. BEAGLE, J.

Royal Army Medical Corps—*Continued.*

24330	Pte. BLOOM, L.
115880	Pte. BEST, J.
376027	Pte. BOLLAND, L.
1672	Pte. BRILL, S.
1142106	Pte. BANN, E.
541287	Pte. BERCOVITCH, B.
112933	Pte. BERNSTEIN, H.
113206	Pte. BERGEE, S.
112291	Pte. BLUMENTHAL, L.
112689	Pte. BROOKS, K.
116722	Pte. BERGEL, W.
128218	Pte. BROWN, G. E.
139225	Pte. BROWN, I.
128183	Pte. BROWN, R. J.
139297	Pte. BLACK, L.
121743	Pte. BENJAMIN, E.
105000	Pte. BOLASKIE, J.
431008	Pte. BERNSTEIN, T. H.
113306	Pte. BERGER, S., 44th Stat. Hosp.
113825	Pte. BLACK, H., 44th Stat. Hosp.
111627	Pte. BLOOM, B.
	Sgt. Dispenser BEST, B.
	Pte. BROSKY, A., 49th Fld. Amb.
116495	Pte. BROWN, M., 68th C.C.S.
125527	Pte. BERG, J.
125407	Pte. BERNSTONE, H.
600	Pte. BOCK, B.
136742	Pte. BELLMAN, A.
	Pte. BAKER, J. C.
91331	Pte. BEREN, J.
527091	L/Cpl. BRAHAM, M.
538178	Pte. BLAIBERG, S.
67558	Pte. BORGEN, P.
	Pte. BERLYN, M.
4606	Pte. BURNARD, D.
86832	Pte. BERNSTEIN, A.
114267	Pte. BOAS, A., 95th Fld. Amb.
516297	Pte. BRANDON, H., 2/2nd Lond. F. Am
98883	Pte. BOAS, B.
6738	Pte. BENNETT, D.
126253	Pte. BRESLAU, H.
119113	Pte. BOOKMAN, S.
11507	Pte. BERNSTEIN, H.
	Pte. BACHRACH, S. E. (M.S.M.).
135537	Pte. BROOKSTEIN, W.
130257	Pte. BEBBER, M.
	Sgt. BLOOM, I. (M.M.).
98997	Pte. BLOCK, L.
66450	Pte. BLASHKEY, A.
13929	Pte. BENJAMIN, E.
	Pte. BALKIND, E.
	Pte. BENSUSAN, J.
	Pte. BURKE, A. J.
	Orderly BULL, S. L.
	Pte. BERLOWITZ, P. B.
	Pte. BARNETT, G. (D.C.M.).

	Pte. BROSGARTH, S.
	Pte. BRISCO, H.
	Pte. BRILLIANT, N. S.
	Pte. BENSON, J., 1st W. Lancs. F.A.
	Pte. BENSAUDE, V.
9705	Pte. COWAN, H., 23rd Field Amb.
41519	Pte. CANIN, M., 52nd Field Amb.
47784	Pte. COWEN, L., 73rd Field Amb.
1906	Pte. COLEMAN, P., 1st S.M. Field Amb.
318	Pte. CIPKIN, M., 1st W.R. Field Amb.
48227	Sgt. COHEN, L. C., 130th Field Amb.
508273	Pte. COWEN, R., 2/1st Field Amb.
83627	Pte. COHEN, V. S., 88th Field Amb.
6462	Pte. COHEN, H. V., 12th Field Amb.
28029	Pte. CRIETZMAN, M., 33rd Field Amb.
60119	Pte. COCK, J. R., 35th Field Amb.
545560	Sgt. CRULEY, G. D., 25th San. Sect.
2796	L/Cpl. COHEN, L., 45th C.C.S.
774	Pte. COPPERSMITH, R., 2/1st E. Lancs.
92332	Sgt. COHEN, P., 44th Field Amb.
116898	Pte. COHEN, J. E., 1/1st N.M. F. Amb.
116898	Pte. COHEN, J. E., 1/1st N.M. F. Amb.
343144	Pte. CURLANDER, A., 57th C.C.S.
29476	Sgt. CROCKER, S.
	Pte. COHEN, L., No. 7 Gen. Hosp.
113080	Pte. COHEN, A., 72nd Gen. Hospital.
202	Pte. COHEN, S., Ldn. San. Coy.
	Pte. CLIVE, L.,
95288	Pte. COHEN, I.,
64069	Pte. CHAPMAN, H., 69th Field Amb.
55463	Pte. CADMAN, P. J., 1/2nd (S.M.) F. A.
116395	Pte. COHEN, J. N. 9 C.C.S.
1812	Pte. CRAUCOUR, J., 1/3rd Field Amb.
118812	Pte. COLLAR, H.,
70076	Pte. COHEN, H.,
23514	Pte. CIEMAN, S.,
S/22810	Pte. COVERMAN, C.,
91893	Pte. CUTNER, J.,
337897	Pte. COHEN, L.
112766	Pte. COHEN, J.
114264	Pte. COHEN, H.
76	Pte. COHEN, S.,
113821	Pte. COHEN, B.
112185	Pte. COHEN, S.
511	Pte. CLYNES, I.
118580	Pte. COHEN, P.
136516	Pte. COHEN, D.
99204	Pte. CLEMENTS, H., 311th Lon. Fld. Am.
94986	Pte. COHEN, I., 311th Lon. Fld. Amb.
98288	Pte. COHEN, M., 11th Stat. Hosp.
130363	Pte. CLUMPUS, R.
95098	Pte. CRAMMER, L. J.
122579	Pte. COHEN, B.
118367	Pte. COHEN, A., 70th Gen. Hosp.
	Pte. CHAIKIN, B.
93521	Pte. COHEN, M.
63090	Pte. CLAYMAN, I.

Royal Army Medical Corps—*Continued.*

96904	Pte. COHEN, H.
135212	Pte. COHEN, J.
960423	Gnr. COHEN, A.
44711	Pte. COHEN, J.
112624	Pte. COHEN, E.
83820	Pte. COHEN, S.
110013	Pte. COSTA, B.
35528	Pte. COHEN, A.
80090	Pte. COHEN, B.
99055	Pte. COHEN, R.
85100	Pte. COTTON, S.
115581	Pte. COHEN, J.
119515	Pte. COHEN, J.
119515	Pte. COHEN, R. A.
114102	Pte. CROSKY, C.
93521	Pte. COHEN, M.
98228	Pte. COHEN, W.
113185	Pte. COHEN, S.
113538	Pte. COHEN, M.
118624	Pte. COHEN, J.
77331	Pte. COHEN, G.
112766	Pte. COHEN, J.
54560	Sgt. CRULEY, G.
112901	Pte. COHEN, I.
85098	Pte. CRAMMER, L. J.
122577	Pte. COWAN, H.
41656	Pte. CLAYMAN, M.
83820	Pte. COHEN, S.
60674	Sgt. COWAN, S.
45103	Pte. CRAMMINS, S.
45656	Pte. COHEN, J.
50403	Pte. CLAYTON, L.
48227	Sgt. COHEN, L. C.
63121	Q.M.S. CONQUY,* J. S.
33033	Pte. COOPER, J.
95098	Pte. CRAMMER, L. J.
117153	Pte. COHEN, J.
280	Pte. CANNON, F.
124558	L/Cpl. COHEN, I.
132637	Pte. CAPLAN, J.
126828	Pte. COUSINS, J.
63090	Pte. CLAYMAN, J.
35730	Pte. COOKLIN, B.
116547	Pte. COHEN, S.
1710	Pte. COHEN, M.
205126	Pte. COHEN, G.
35749	S/Sgt. CANTON, J. (COHEN),* 142nd F.A.
39027	Pte. DE YOUNG, R., 53rd Field Amb.
61963	Pte. DANTZIC, S. C., 9th Field Amb.
32744	Pte. DYAS, B., 4th Stat. Hosp.
77196	Pte. DREESDE, S., 16th Field Amb.
42929	Pte. DAVIS, H. R., 7th Field Amb.
401346	Pte. DANIELS, J., 1/1st W.R. Fld. Amb.
18459	Pte. DANIEL, V., t7h Stat. Hosp.
217480	Pte. DAVIS, M. V.
77134	Pte. DISHKIN, 9th C.C.S.
	Pte. DAVIS, P., 3rd Lond. Field Amb.
119014	Pte. DAVIS, B.
37	Pte. DEANS, J.
112336	Pte. DE GROOT, M.
508048	Pte. DA SILVER, L. D.
44233	Pte. DOODEWOOD, W.
	Sgt./Major DUTCH, H.
93	Sgt. DAVIS, J.
124277	Pte. DIAS, M.
96617	Pte. DAVIS, R.
8025	Pte. DE SAXE, H. L.
	Pte. DERTSHMAN, C.
1199	Pte. DA SILVA, L. N.
61824	Pte. DAVIS, B. A.
374036	Pte. DEANSGERTIE, J.
32806	Pte. DAVIS, L.
120889	Pte. DANSKY, D.
99297	Pte. DA COSTA.
37	Pte. DEAULFENTIE, J.
3190	Pte. DELEFSKY, M.
98821	Pte. DREEZER, S.
115905	Pte. DIAMOND, L.
120228	Pte. DIAMONSTEIN, W.
99297	Pte. DA COSTA, D.
40025	L/Sgt. DE SAXE, H.
	Pte. DEVON, E.
	Pte. DEVON, H.
	Pte. DIGHT, R.
	Pte. DALY, A. O. S.
	Pte. DAITZ, S.
2611	Sgt. ECKER, R., 21st Div. San. Sect.
24632	Pte. ENGLEBERY, N., 12th Field Amb.
538228	Pte. ELLIS, A. M., 5th Lond. Fld. Amb.
2064	Pte. EDWARD, M.
	Pte. ELWY, L.
78628	Pte. ELLIS, S.
144465	Pte. EISNER, J.
76786	Pte. ESTERMAN, M.
83461	Pte. ENDLER, L.
13627	Orderly ELKAN, V. B.
140015	Pte. ELION, R.
60822	Sgt. EPSTEIN, J.
	Sgt./Maj. EHRMAN, E.
357248	Cpl. ELLIS, M., 1/2nd E.L. Fld. Amb.
85322	L/Cpl. ELKAN, J.
116673	Pte. EASTERMAN, J.
22	Pte. EDWARDS, H.
83845	Cpl. ELKAN, M.
40107	Pte. ELLIS, H.
14795	Pte. EMANUEL, F.
23698	Pte. ESTERMAN, J.
116673	Pte. ESTERMAN, J.
13040	Pte. ELLISON, A.
47629	Pte. EMERY, J. A.

Royal Army Medical Corps—*Continued.*

83845	Cpl. ELKAN, M.	
112627	Pte. EPRILE, B.	
31860	Sgt. FRANKEL, G., 29th Field Amb.	
49575	Pte. FREEMAN, L., 55th Field Amb.	
1683	Pte. FRANKS, L., 2/1st W. Lancs. F.A.	
58673	Pte. FREEMAN, A., 12th Field Amb.	
69509	Pte. FRAZER, I., 136th Field Amb.	
403093	L/Cpl. FORSTER, G., 2/2nd W. Riding Field Amb.	
	Staff Sgt. FRANKS, S. R. B., 58th Div.	
85407	Pte. FISHER, A., 131st H.C. Fld. Amb.	
117	Pte. FRITZ, J., 2nd W.R. Field Amb.	
528253	A./L./Cpl. FINERMAN, L., 8th San. Sec.	
	Sgt. FRANKS, M.	
	Pte. FREEMAN, G., Red Cross.	
	Pte. FOX, J., 46th Field Amb.	
36824	Pte. FISHER, M., 13th Gen. Hosp.	
	Pte. FRESHWATER, N. (D.C.M.).	
126972	Pte. FRIEDBERGER, H., 51st Stat. Hosp.	
80340	Pte. FIRESON, C.	
112771	Pte. FELDMAN, D.	
113222	Pte. FINER, J.	
139130	Pte. FREEMAN, N.	
99357	Pte. FELDMAN, J.	
125072	Pte. FELDMAN, J.	
A/202171	Pte. FREEMAN, J.	
128260	Pte. FINEBURG, M.	
137865	Pte. FRENSTEIN, A.	
120586	Pte. FRANKS, G.	
75752	Pte. FELDMAN, W.	
	Pte. FAGIN, M.	
133719	Pte. FINE, I.	
125174	Pte. FLETCHER, I.	
22691	Pte. FREEDMAN, J.	
112823	Pte. FELDMAN.	
125072	Pte. FELDMAN, J.	
113888	Pte. FALK, I.	
390430	Pte. FINBERG, D.	
130298	Pte. FRENKEL, I.	
3067	L/Cpl. FAY, A. M.	
61047	Pte. FOX, S.	
97417	Pte. FRITZ, C.	
98151	Pte. FEINGOLD, D.	
113140	Pte. FANSKY, L. S.	
85954	Pte. FLAX, S.	
95159	Pte. FINEGOLD, G.	
75752	Pte. FELDMAN, W.	
125470	Pte. FRANKS, D.	
49575	Pte. FREEMAN, L.	
1365	Pte. FINERMAN, L.	
848001	Pte. FOREST, J.	
1921	Pte. FINBURG, D.	
36824	Cpl. FISHER, M.	
61047	Pte. FOX, S. S.	
32470	Sgt. FRANKS, H.	
9276	Pte. FREEDMAN, F.	
123127	Pte. FELDMAN, T.	
	Pte. FINN, R.	
	Pte. FRANKLIN, H.	
	Pte. FEDDY, F.	
	Pte. FLANCEBAUM, D.	
	Pte. FINE, L.	
23802	Pte. FRIEDLANDER,* H.	
5744	Pte. GORDON, H., 95th Field Amb.	
77705	Pte. GOLDMAN, A., 47th Field Amb.	
41542	Pte. GLUCKSTEIN, C. S.* (M.M.), 52nd Field Amb.	
49083	Pte. GOLDBERG, M., 66th Field Amb.	
47936	Pte. GOMPERTZ, A., 73rd Field Amb.	
69528	Pte. GOLDBERG, G., 138th Field Amb.	
30421	Pte. GORDON, M., 78th Field Amb.	
1569	L/Cpl. GOODMAN, S. F., 98th Fld Amb.	
64548	L/Cpl. GALLEWSKI, M.* (M.M.), 100th Field Amb.	
502	L/Cpl. GOLDSTEIN, S., 2/1st Field Amb.	
492	Pte. GABRIEL, M., 43rd Field Amb.	
1969	Pte. GOUGH, D., 3/2nd W. Lancs.	
82510	Pte. GARSDEN, H., 48th Field Amb.	
508188	Pte. GOSSCHALK, R. J., 72nd F. Amb.	
21150	Pte. GORDON, V., 19th C.C.S.	
114425	Pte. GOLDMAN, B., 6th Stat. Hospital.	
44415	A/Cpl. GANTZ, S., 81st Gen. Hospital.	
116630	Pte. GOLDSTEIN, J., 81st Gen. Hospital.	
112507	Pte. GRIMSTONE, J., 2/2nd F. F. Amb.	
51034	Pte. GOLDSTONE, T. C., 1/1st N, F. A.	
393347	L/Cpl. GLASS, M.*	
28029	Pte. GREITZMAN, M., 33rd Field Amb.	
438001	C.Q.M.S. GILT, H., E. Lancs. Fld. Am.	
S/3994	Pte. GREEN, B., 1st R. N. Field Amb.	
105169	Pte. GOLDSTONE, H.	
79574	Pte. GAFFIN, M.	
114425	Pte. GOLDMAN, B., 6th Stat. Hospt.	
4634	Pte. GREEN, H.	
	Cpl. GOLDSTONE, S.	
40617	Sgt. GOODMAN, R.	
8958	Pte. GORDON, E.	
42941	Pte. GOLDSTUK, N.	
	Pte. GREEN, J., B. Red Cross.	
	Pte. GILBERT, A.	
8770	S/Sgt. GROSSMAN, J., 1st Lon. San. Cy.	
24736	Cpl. GOODMAN, M., 11th Gen. Hosp.	
12056	Pte. GORLIFFE, I. L., B.R.C.S.	
125941	Pte. GOLDSTEIN, L., 62nd Field Amb.	
120172	Pte. GOLDBERG, G., 73rd Field Amb.	
125769	Pte. GOLDBAUM.	
116550	Pte. GREEN, H.	
	Pte. GAFFIN, M.	
135142	Pte. GROOSKY, D.	
115548	Pte. GOLDSTEIN, L.	
	Pte. GREEN, G., 51st Hosp. Train.	
138005	Pte. GERBER, H.	
67851	Pte. GOLDBERG, I.	
143494	Pte. GOLD, M.	
41519	Pte. GLUCKSTEIN, S., 52nd Field Amb.	

Royal Army Medical Corps—*Continued.*

	Pte. GABRIELSON, M.
127400	Pte. GOLDSTONE, I.
143329	Pte. GOLDBERG, M.
125790	Pte. GINSBERG, N.
115548	Pte. GOLDSTEIN, I.
21830	Pte. GARDNER, S.
	Pte. GOODMAN, S., 2nd W. Lancs. F.A.
	Pte. GOLDSTONE, S.
135660	Pte. GOLLARD, S.
125941	Pte. GOLDSTEIN, L.
125769	Pte. GOLDBAUM, M.
461	Pte. GOLDSTONE, M.
390442	Pte. GREENBAUM, V.
91333	Pte. GRONOSKY, A.
24736	Pte. GOODMAN, H.
113502	Pte. GOODMAN, M.
104577	Pte. GOLDBERG, W.
85067	Pte. GOODMAN, H.
96996	Pte. GOLDSTEIN, A.
116550	Pte. GREEN, H.
24	Pte. GOLD, J.
1899	Pte. GOLDBERG, P.
126395	Pte. GOODMAN, L.
1938	Pte. GREENBAUM, V.
126774	Pte. GOLDSTEIN, J.
126986	Pte. GORED, A. V.
1009	Pte. GREENLEAF, H.
536298	Pte. GATER, L.
85982	Pte. GOLDBERG, J.
124095	Pte. GOLDBERG, P.
116630	Pte. GOLDSTEIN.
26960	Pte. GOLDBERG, H.
63374	Pte. GOLDSTEIN, D.
49083	Pte. GOLDBERG, M.
91333	Pte. GRONOSKY.
126443	Pte. GREENBERG, H.
67851	Pte. GOLDBERG.
121443	Pte. GILBERT, J.
510327	Pte. GABRIEL, M. P.
	Pte. GAUTRY, S.
126973	Pte. GRODNER, H.
	Cpl. GROSSMAN, J.
	Pte. GINN, L.
140	L/Cpl. HANDS, S., 6th San. Sect.
31509	Pte. HARRIS, J., 44th Field Amb.
31241	Cpl. HARRIS, M., 69th Field Amb.
40039	Cpl. HARRIS, F. H., 76th Field Amb.
7534	Pte. HENRY, L., 19th Field Amb.
90917	Pte. HYMANS, A.,* 23rd Field Amb.
1629	Pte. HARTZ, H., 2/6th Field Amb.
2737	Cpl. HYMAN, L. A., 41st C.C.S.
510233	Pte. HYMAN, M., 2/3rd Lond. Fld. Amb.
2983	Pte. HARRIS, S., 71st San. Sect.
36186	Pte. HART, H., 34th Field Amb.
5353	Pte. HARRIS, J., 27th Field Amb.
67436	Pte. HARRIS, A.,* 25th W.R. Fld. Amb.
2207	Pte. HAMMERSON, M., 5th Lond. F.A.
98152	Pte. HARRIS, S., 42nd Stat. Hosp.
99907	Pte. HARRIS, S., 2nd Lond. San. Sect.
112123	Pte. HASS, H., 68th Gen. Hosp.
2528	Pte. HELLER, J., 10th Gen. Hosp.
8420	Sgt. HART, L., 8th Stat. Hosp.
	Pte. HARRIS, J., 45th C.C.S.
	Qr.-Mr. HYMAN, A. E., Red Cross.
178	Pte. HART, L., 84th Field Amb.
7523	Pte. HARRIS, G., 4th C.C.S.
114228	Pte. HANRECK, L.
44042	Pte. HYMAN, L., 51st Stat. Hosp.
LC/343023	Pte. HART, S.
60548	Pte. HOBSBAUM, S. B.
1592	Pte. HARRIS, B. M.
100885	L/Cpl. HERSCH.
MR/166401	L/Cpl. HARRIS, 22nd Motor Amb.
128039	Pte. HENNEMAN, J.
90088	Pte. HARRISON, E. A.
125182	Pte. HERWALD, M.
96215	Pte. HARRIS, J., 328th Field Amb.
527144	Pte. HANDS, S.
	L/Cpl. HARRIS, M. (M.M.).
93152	Pte. HARRIS, I.
526055	Pte. HYMAN, J.
1848	Pte. HEILBUT, 2nd W. Lancs. F. Amb.
	Pte. HERMAN, S.
128123	Pte. HUMMELBLAN, L.
86145	Pte. HOFFBERG, D.
113219	Pte. HYMAN, A.
97028	Pte. HARRIS, J. D.
492610	Pte. HARTSILVER, J.
71965	Pte. HYMANS, I.
105667	L/Cpl. HYAMS, M., 47th San. Section.
96215	Pte. HARRIS, J.
356051	Pte. HAMAUL, E.
99448	Pte. HILSUN, A.
113226	Pte. HIMMEL, I.
91508	Pte. HYMAN, H.
29164	Pte. HEIMAN, S.
8008	S/Sgt. HAYMAN, P. G.
	Pte. HERWALD, D.
128009	Pte. HENRY, J.
331	Pte. HYMAN, N.
94845	Pte. HARRIS, D.
99907	Cpl. HARRIS, S. P.
	Pte. HAMANI, E. E.
98152	Pte. HARRIS, S.
646	Pte. HUMBER, P.
47436	Pte. HARRIS.
99	Sgt. HENOCHSBERG, G. S.
113235	Pte. HABER, H.
526021	Pte. HUMBER, E.
97028	Pte. HARRIS, D. E.
91508	Pte. HYMAN, H.
100933	L/Cpl. HARTOG, S.
11820	Pte. HAYES, J. A.

Royal Army Medical Corps—*Continued.*

11741	Sgt. Hyman, S.	
2539	Dvr. Hamburger, E. B.	
330	Pte. Hyman, I.	
273074	Pte. Harris, H.	
59381	L/Sgt. Hyman, L. A.	
121123	Pte. Hyman, L.	
	Pte. Heller, F., 4th Lond. Fld. Amb.	
	Pte. Herman, S.	
	Sgt. Hoppinskin, S.	
133420	Pte. Horton, B.	
32336	Pte. Isaacs, S., 62nd Field Amb.	
116544	Pte. Isaacs, H., 39th E. Hosp.	
75934	Pte. Irons, L., 30th C.C.S.	
	Pte. Isaacs, D.	
115688	Pte. Iken, S., 22nd Gen. Hospt.	
12055	Pte. Isaacs, M., B.R.C.S.	
124009	Pte. Israel, M.	
142023	Pte. Irsofsky, M.	
837	Pte. Isaacs, P.	
1243	Cpl. Israel, H.	
96243	Pte. Israel, H.	
123791	Pte. Isaacs, I.	
99455	Pte. Isaacs, L.	
80128	Pte. Isaacs, E.	
497372	Pte. Isaacs, M.	
	Pte. Isaacs, C.	
	Pte. Isaacson, F.	
39538	Pte. Japp, W., 36th Field Amb.	
39928	Sgt. Jacobs, G.* (D.C.M.), 47th F. Am.	
3622	Pte. Jacob, M. J. (D.C.M., M.M.), 82nd Field Amb.	
42722	Q.M.S. Jacob, S. (M.S.M.), 79th Fld. A.	
38806	Pte. Jonas, A., 47th Field Amb.	
62180	Pte. Jackson, J., 19th Field Amb.	
79474	Pte. Jacobs, I. Z., 45th C.C.S.	
764	Pte. Jacobs, H., 2/2nd E.L. Field Amb.	
L/3316	Dvr. Jacobs, W., 43rd Field Amb.	
78437	Sgt. Johnson, D.	
114712	Pte. Jacobs, J.*	
28033	Sgt. Jacobs, H., 40th B. Gen. Hospt.	
	Pte. Jacobs, A.	
1098	Pte. Joseph, J.	
	Q.M.S. Jewell, J.	
110204	Pte. Joseph, L., 323rd Field Amb.	
73689	Pte. Josephs, B., 70th Field Amb.	
2262	Pte. Jay, A., 5th Field Amb.	
59169	Pte. Joseph, J. H.	
144968	Pte. Joel, B.	
114257	Pte. Jacobs, M.	
117737	Pte. Jacobs, M.	
512264	Pte. Joseph, C. F., 3rd City of London.	
143147	Pte. Jacobs, S.	
117725	Pte. Josephs, J.	
	Pte. Jacobs, E.	
	Cpl. Joseph, L.	
112527	Pte. Jackson, H.	
495108	Pte. Jacob, M. J.	
144968	Pte. Joel, B.	
495108	Pte. Jacobs, R. G.	
536528	Pte. Jay, A.	
114742	Pte. Jacobs, J. D.	
112618	Pte. Joseph, A. E.	
91372	Pte. Joseph, M.	
224	Pte. Jaffe, L.	
122183	Pte. Jacobs, L.	
352459	Pte. Jacobs, H.	
	Pte. Julius, W.	
	Pte. Jaffe, W.	
588	Pte. Klein, G. L., 37th Div. San. Sect.	
17	Sgt. Krakauer, M., 49th D. San. Sect.	
16390	Pte. Kovalesky, J., 137th Field Amb.	
27270	Pte. Klein, H., 38th Field Amb.	
19097	Sgt. Koftoff, A., 57th Field Amb.	
313645	Pte. Kaye, A. L., 2/1st London Fld. A.	
113531	Pte. Kaitiff, J.	
110186	Pte. Kadish, I., 323rd Field Amb.	
700885	L./Cpl. Kersch.	
75377	Pte. Krantz, B. B.	
115202	Pte. Klein, E.	
118370	Pte. Kerschenbaum.	
129010	Pte. Knight, F. G.	
143741	Pte. Kirstein, H.	
94269	Pte. Koski, A., 328th Field Amb.	
94188	Pte. Kosky, L., 328th Field Amb.	
126043	Pte. Koski, I.	
	S/M. Kaufman, A. (M.C.).	
134649	Pte. Kletsell, A., 26th Gen. Hosp.	
99673	Pte. Kosofski, A.	
135460	Cpl. Kossick, A.	
545512	Pte. Kartz, S.	
	L/Cpl. Kavish.	
118370	Pte. Kuschancam, P.	
32	Dvr. Karns, F. D.	
115202	Pte. Klein, G.	
122389	Pte. Kessing, N.	
75049	Pte Kimbler, J.	
198000	Pte. Kolensky, L.	
11475	Pte. King, W. K.	
891	Pte. Luxemberg, A., 6th Field Amb.	
	Sgt. Lion, H. M., 3rd Sanitary Sect.	
35139	Pte. Levin, H. V., 16th Field Amb.	
32112	Pte. Levy, J., 27th Field Amb.	
47435	Pte. Levy, S., 37th Field Amb.	
1534	Pte. Lewis, C., att. 1st. K.E.H.	
39044	Pte. Levy, A., 53rd Field Amb.	
38831	Pte. Lipton, S., 56th Field Amb.	
59009	Pte. Levy, C.,* 70th Field Amb.	
58950	Pte. Lipson, E. J., 70th Field Amb.	
2028	Pte. Lavine, B., 1st S.M. Field Amb.	
2198	Pte. Leapman, A., 5th Lond. Fld. Amb.	
47437	Pte. Leek, R., 78th Field Amb.	
1505	Pte. Liberson, M., 98th Field Amb.	

Royal Army Medical Corps—*Continued.*

61927	Pte. LEMBERGER, A., 90th Field Amb.
61901	Pte. LIPPMAN, T., 91st Field Amb.
64793	Pte. LEVI, D., 100th Field Amb.
4589	Pte. LAZARUS, S. J., 10th Stat. Hosp.
214592	Pte. LEVI, J., 10th Stat. Hosp.
75923	Pte. LUBELL, J., 136th Field Amb.
2174	Pte. LYONS, S., 2/5th Lond. Fld. Amb.
1931	L/Cpl. LOTHEIM, J., 21st S.M. Fld. Am.
1306	Pte. LEWIS, J., 72nd Field Amb.
527299	Cpl. LEVY, A. (M.M.), 42nd San. Sect.
454	Pte. LIZAR, I. C., 2/3rd E.L. Field Am.
56870	Pte. LUTZES, A., 12th Field Amb.
S/3992	Pte. LEVY, M., 148th Field Amb.
116541	Pte. LITKIN, J., 39th Stat. Hosp.
39044	Pte. LEVY, A,. 34th Field Amb.
75250	Pte. LEVY, A.
	S/Sgt. LEVIN, R. B., 4th Gen. Hospt.
82587	Pte. LEVI, E., 50th Gen. Sal.
86329	Pte. LUXEMBURG, J., 3rd Stat. Hospt.
86007	Pte. LOFTUS, A.,* 134th Field Amb.
82553	Pte. LEVY, M., 25th Amb. Train.
99908	Pte. LEWBITZ, A., 82nd Sanitary Sect.
68919	Pte. LEVENE, M., 54th C.C.S.
51136	Pte. LEVY, N., No. 23rd G.H.P.
94405	Pte. LEWINSKY, J., No. 39 C.C.S.
10600	Dvr. LAZAW, B., B.R.C.S.
2456	Pte. LEVY, R.
52737	Pte. LEWIS, G.
27367	Pte. LUSH, H.
4830	Pte. LEVY, D. W., 3/6th Field Amb.
19803	Cpl. LEVY, A.
75250	Pte. LEVY, A.
113130	L/Cpl. LEVY, H.
120459	Pte. LEVENSON, S.
105152	Pte. LEWIS, T.
121123	Pte. LEVEY, H.
139086	Pte. LEWIS, J.
144781	Pte. LYONS, L. A.
4589	Cpl. LAZARUS, S. J., 10th Stat. Hosp.
139540	Pte. LEE, D.
98078	Pte. LAZARUS, M.
119359	Pte. LIPMAN, S.
1846	Pte. LANGER, R. B.
455039	Cpl. LISSMAN.
454	Pte. LIZER, J. C.
208950	Pte. LEVY, M.
124654	Pte. LEVY, N.
112766	Pte. LEVY, J.
112310	Pte. LEWIS, I.
94405	Pte. LEVINSKY, J.
98078	Pte. LAZARUS, M.
34334	Pte. LEVY, E.
119045	Pte. LEVY, A.
113787	Pte. LEFTWICH, J.
96946	Pte. LATHOVITCH, H.
844352	Pte. LEE, J.
527683	Pte. LEVEY, L. H.
4830	Pte. LEVY, D. W.
2361	Pte. LEVY, L.
2341	Pte. LEVY, M.
105752	Pte. LEWIS, A. J.
62162	Pte. LIEBERMAN, J.
89650	Pte. LAZARUS, B.
112091	Pte. LABOVITCH, H.
112824	Pte. LAZARUS, L.
112310	Pte. LEWIS, J.
112610	Pte. LEWIS, I.
117010	Pte. LEVY, C.
27399	Cpl. LAYTON, R.
54319	Pte. LEVY, L.
117069	Pte. LEMAN, D.
113041	Pte. LIPMAN, H.
60496	Pte. LAWSON, S. W.
96941	Pte. LATHOVITCH, M.
117061	Pte. LEVY, C.
123850	Pte. LEVY, B. B.
110269	Pte. LEVY, C.
125216	Pte. LEVY, R.
117010	Pte. LEVY, C.
201	Sgt. LEVINSON, B.
94657	Pte. LEWIS, A.
135017	Pte. LEWIS, W.
121123	Pte. LEVY, H.
114562	Pte. LYONS, F.
114562	Pte. LYONS, F.
140426	Pte. LIBERSON, S.
1255266	Pte. LEVEY, L., No. 3 Gen. Hosp.
128086	Pte. LEVEY, E.
113120	Pte. LANDAU, J.
133490	Pte. LEVI, D.
27563	Cpl. LEVY, M.
112169	Pte. LIFTSHUTZ, W., 49th Stat. Hosp.
91144	Pte. LEVIN, A.
84352	Pte. LEE, C. G.
99904	Pte. LEVY, I. J.
82587	Pte. LEVI, E.
103099	Pte. LIPMAN, B.
68031	Pte. LEVY, I.
8338	Pte. LENT.
97413	Pte. LEVY, I.
99904	Pte. LEVY, I. J.
113787	Pte. LEFTWICH, J.
67545	Pte. LEVY, J.
119045	Pte. LEVY, L.
510507	Pte. LAPPIN, S.
12274	Pte. LEVENSON, M.
114563	Pte. LIEBERMAN, I.
408331	Pte. LEVINE, G.
86056	Pte. LEVY, E.
136457	Pte. LATNER, S.
	Pte. LEVINE, M.
98862	Pte. LIEBERMAN, H.
106298	Pte. LEVENSON, E.
11853	Pte. LIPSON, A. V.

Royal Army Medical Corps—*Continued.*

	Cpl. Loskey, C.
14176	Pte. Livingstone, H.
39087	Pte. Levinsky, S.
	S./M. Levy, J. (M.B.E.).
7319	A/Sgt. Marcus, L., No. 1 Field Amb.
4689	Cpl. Myers, S., 4th Field Amb.
30545	Sgt. Mordecai, M. J., 67th F. Amb.
407	Pte. Morris, H., 84th Field Amb.
1839	Pte. Mears, S., 4th Lon. Field Amb.
36560	Pte. Morris, L., 80th Field Amb.
67443	Pte. Morris, L., 96th Field Amb.
67357	Pte. Morris, S., 97th Field Amb.
78798	Pte. Magnus, S., 105th Field Amb.
1740	Pte. Morris, P., 2/1st W. L. F. Amb.
771	Cpl. Moss, J. H., 2/2nd Lon. F. Amb.
497531	Pte. Morris, H., 2/3rd H. C. F. Amb.
1970	Pte. Marks, M., 3/2nd W. Lancs.
2002	Pte. Marks, J., 3/2nd W. Lancs.
1786	Pte. McTigue, O.,
76377	Pte. Morgan, I., 19th Field Amb.
81855	Pte. Muscat, N., Welsh Coy.
2126	Pte. Main, S., 3/6th Lon. Field Amb
	Dvr. Myers C., D. of W. Hospital.
6634	Pte. Marks, S.,
	Pte. Marks, I., St. John's Amb.
	Cpl. Myers, A. P., 1st M.A.C.
35470	Pte. Miller, M. G., No. 13 G.H.P.
4873	Sgt. Mortimer, L. C. W., 1st Corps.
115200	Pte. Miller, H.
16156	A/Sgt. Morris, J., 79th Gen. Hospt.
118900	L/Sgt. Mathews, K. E., 79th G. Hospt.
117777	Pte. Myers, 2/1st West. Lancs. F.A.
15032	Pte. Myers, L. J., 5th Field Amb.
118190	L./Cpl. Mullin, N.
29053	Pte. Morris.
96446	Pte. Madolney, W.
67522	Pte. Morris, D.
683707	Pte. Morris, F.
11779	Pte. Moss, H.
12041	Pte. Moss, H.
127468	Pte. Manson, S.
29563	Pte. Morris, S.
2064	Pte. Morris, E. J.
89571	Pte. Miller, H. M., 97th San. Sect.
77964	Pte. Marcus, A.
114532	Pte. Moscow, J.
118624	Pte. Moss, L.
123802	Pte. Mazzier, H.
112754	Pte. Mersiers, S.
376051	Pte. Marfalinski, L.
510279	Pte. Morris, I.
99665	Pte. Manus, N.
	Pte. Moses, H. D. (M.S.M.).
85772	Pte. Mass, M.
114620	Pte. Myers, B.
112940	Pte. Margolis, D.
116871	Pte. Manbock, P.

	Staff Sgt. Moss, H. L. (M.S.M.).
112309	Pte. Morris, A.
113713	Pte. Markson, M.
2486	Pte. Mathews, A.
98284	Pte. Minkin, J.
68735	Pte. Marcovitch, H.
11872	Pte. Magnus, D.
51935	Pte. Miller, M.
7831	Pte. Miller, S.
1228	Pte. Moss, J.
771	Cpl. Moss, J. H.
475	Pte. Marks, J.
113836	Pte. Moses, H. W.
95445	Tpr. Myron, H.
84276	Pte. Marcus, C.
62522	Pte. Morris, D.
527740	Pte. Miller, H.
27304	Pte. Marks, M.
2064	Pte. Morris, E. J.
457912	Pte. Morris, J.
133730	Pte. Miskie, M.
	S./S.M. Myers, O. B. (M.S.M.).
126107	Pte. Marks, M.
132365	Pte. Margofsky, H.
125965	Pte. Mendelbaum, J.
357248	Cpl. Michael, E. M.
142795	Pte. Michaels, M.
113836	Clerk Moses, H. P., M. Special Hosp.
	Pte. Morris, H. J., W. Lancs. Fld. Am.
14731	Pte. Misrahi, E. S.
113713	Pte. Martson, M.
99342	Pte. Myers, P.
12552	Pte. Marks, P.
444	Cpl. Michaels, E.
112309	Pte. Morniz, A.
130184	Pte. Marks, M.
10157	Pte. Moss, I.
510279	Pte. Morris, H.
62522	Pte. Morris, D.
339526	Pte. Marks, J., 3/2nd N.L. Fld. Amb.
91617	Pte. Marquis, S.
3351	Pte. McKinnill, N.
136342	Pte. Muslin, C.
303	Pte. Marco, L.
113184	Pte. Marks, B.
98284	Pte. Martin, J.
	S./S.M. Moss, W. F. (M.S.M.).
112389	Pte. Myers, L. J.
276051	Pte. Manglinski, L.
98285	Pte. Minkin, J.
19850	Pte. Margo, L.
115111	Pte. Mindel, B.
114099	Pte. Millman, S.
113795	Pte. Morison, J.
112778	Pte. Mendleson, H.
472	Pte. Mellor, H.
461585	Pte. Morrison, A.
139432	Pte. Maurer, J.

Royal Army Medical Corps—*Continued.*

1599	S/Sgt.	MILLENGER, C.
126931	Cpl.	MOSCOVITCH, A. L.
112677	Pte.	MORRIS, M.
205863	Pte.	MANZIG, N.
	Pte.	METTERSON, T.
	Pte.	MEERGINSKY, S.
112317	Pte.	MANUEL, B.
336820	Pte.	MORRIS, P.
68397	Pte.	NASH, E., 91st Field Amb.
72852	Pte.	NEWMAN, I., 60th Field Amb.
116548	Pte.	NEWMARK, H., Lahore Ind. Gen. H.
91183	Pte.	NEWMAN, A., Marseilles Stat. Hos.
	Pte.	NORTON, M.
87432	Pte.	NABARRO, H. L.
35156	Pte.	NIEMAN, M.
145295	Pte.	NIMNI, M.
96459	Pte.	NEWMAN, M.
128572	Pte.	NATHAN, A. N.
35438	Pte.	NATHAN, M.
31369	A/Cpl.	NETHERSON, C.
55142	Pte.	NATHAN, L.
	Pte.	NEWMEGEN, A. L.
131968	Pte.	NERDEN, J.
112526	Pte.	ORLAMS, M., 46th Field Amb.
131240	Pte.	OESTERMAN, L., Marseilles Stat. H.
113089	L./Cpl.	ORNSTEIN, E., 328th Field Am.
1254912	Pte.	OGINSKY, M.
84820	Pte.	OLIVER, R.
125033	Pte.	OXELRED, M.
325	Pte.	PAIBA, G., 84th Field Amb.
58125	Pte.	PHILLIPS, F., 142nd Field Amb.
131614	Pte.	PHILLIPS, A., 99th Field Amb.
69569	Pte.	PEREZ, I., 138th Field Amb.
2316	Pte.	PATER, L. M., 2/5th Lond. Fld. A.
1676	Sgt.-Maj.	PULVERMACHER, T. B., 2/6th Lond. Field Amb.
375053	Pte.	PALLATZ, R., 5th Lond. Field Amb.
395	Sgt.	PAVION, H., 2/1st E. Lancs.
350774	Pte.	POLUVANSKY, M., 129th Fld. Amb.
	Pte.	PARKE, J., St. John's Fld. Amb.
45184	Pte.	PHILLIPS, H., 35th Field Amb.
393279	Pte.	PRICE, L.
123713	Pte.	PINKUS, L.
124868	Pte.	PELTZ, C. N.
125829	Pte.	PYZER, E.
138938	Pte.	PERSSECNE, A. H.
	Sgt.	POLLOCK, M.
11875	Pte.	PLOMPER, H.
543188	Pte.	POLITI, V. A.
75782	Pte.	PRESSMAN, J.
119244	Pte.	PYSER, N.
116687	Pte.	PHILLIPS, R.
114268	Pte.	PROUT, A.
37966	Cpl.	POLLOCK, H.
1721	Pte.	PRICE, H.
1767	Pte.	PRICE, B.
9867	Ass. S/M.	PHILLIPS, D. S.
123713	Pte.	PINKISS, L.
118793	Pte.	PRUZAMSKI, B.
375053	Pte.	PALLATZ, R.
	Pte.	PINKUS, J.
31293	Pte.	RICHARDS, A., 43rd Field Amb.
39856	Pte.	ROMAIN, J., 51st Field Amb.
2199	Pte.	ROSENTHAL, A., 5th Field Amb.
42864	Pte.	ROSEN, L., 80th Field Amb.
68814	Pte.	ROSENTHAL, H., 90th Field Amb.
33257	Cpl.	ROMAIN, L., 15th Field Amb.
	Pte.	RAITIFF, J.
2014	Pte.	ROSENBERG, I., 2/4th Lond. F. Am.
90569	Pte.	ROSENTHAL, S., 92nd Field Amb.
2053	Pte.	ROSENSTONE, P. P., 2/2nd Nth. Field Amb.
2202	Pte.	ROTHENBERG, H.
150346	Pte.	ROSENTHAL, L. A., 25th M.A.C.
10716	Pte.	ROSENBERG, C., 102nd Field Amb.
92706	Pte.	ROBINSON, L., 109th Field Amb.
3035	Pte.	ROSBUCK, T., 8th Field Amb.
115659	Pte.	RAISMAN, H., 39th Stat. Hosp.
95251	Pte.	ROSENBLATT, M., 92nd Field Amb.
79095	Pte.	ROSENBAUM, H. J.
137834	Pte.	ROSENBERG, A., 26th Field Amb.
112865	Pte.	ROSE, H., 26th Amb. Train.
	Pte.	ROBERTS, S., 2nd General Hospt.
86127	Pte.	ROSENTHAL, S., 38th Stat. Hospt.
69089	Pte.	ROBINSON, W., 51st Stat. Hospt.
382030	Pte.	ROSATSKY, S., 11th Field Amb.
495223	Pte.	RODWELL, J.
117789	Pte.	ROSEN, M.
23262	Pte.	ROSENBERG, L.
	Pte.	RUBENSTEIN, J.
350391	Pte.	RUSHMAN, J.,* 2/1st E. Lancs. F.A.
85293	Pte.	REIS.
30797	Pte.	ROTH, S. W.
98933	Pte.	RESSER, S.
508543	Pte.	RODGERS, G.
31293	Pte.	RUBENSTEIN, A.
138539	Pte.	RICHMOND, H.
117416	Pte.	RUBENSTEIN, L.
128204	Pte.	RUBINSTEIN, H. T.
96092	Pte.	ROSENSTEIN, R.
117318	Pte.	ROUT, S.
239265	Pte.	ROBINSON, R., 3rd Welsh F.A.
390534	Pte.	ROSENSTON, P. H.
121016	Pte.	ROKENSON, B.
78314	Pte.	ROEG, J. N.
23263	Pte.	ROSENBERG, M.
510262	Pte.	ROSE, S.
86773	Pte.	RICH, S., 7th Gen. Hosp.
541229	Pte.	RADIN, H.
91249	Pte.	RAPHAEL, S.
534270	Sgt.	ROMAIN, H. E.
339523	Pte.	ROSE, E.
96461	Pte.	ROSE, I.
112311	Pte.	REES, C.
56882	Pnr.	REED, A.

Royal Army Medical Corps—*Continued.*

28042	Pte. Rosen, A.
10224	Pte. Rosengarten, A.
1724	Sgt. Robinson, R.
81	Pte. Rothe, M. A.
25481	Pte. Rubinstein, L.
1905	Pte. Rubinstein, L.
378	Pte. Rose, S.
2014	Pte. Rosenberg, R.
70888	Pte. Rosenthal, E.
2412	Pte. Robinson, L.
1724	Sgt. Robinson, R.
531721	Pte. Reinbron, C. G.
114318	Pte. Rosenberg, H.
118386	Pte. Rosenbloom, J.
28642	Pte. Rosen, A.
121816	Pte. Robinson, B.
1476	Pte. Rose, J.
14253	Pte. Reuben, A.
14299	Pte. Rosenthall, K.
117395	Pte. Rosenberg, S.
10716	Pte. Rosenberg, C.
62971	L/Cpl. Rabinovitch, H.
	Pte. Rich, B.
	Pte. Rosenblatt, J.
1520	Pte. Schulman, B., 14th Stat. Hosp.
35494	Pte. Smith, N., 24th Gen. Hosp.
4754	Pte. Saunders, H., 5th C.C.S.
	Pte. Solomons, E., 2nd M.A.C.,
45374	Pte. Saphir, M., 45th C.C.S.
	Pte. Silverman, L. S.
	Pte. Spicer, M.
86043	Pte. Shalinsky, J., 38th Stat. Hosp.
98989	Pte. Stevenson, L., 100th Field Amb.
	Pte. Shopnick, M., 12th Field Amb.
86366	Pte. Solomons, A.
546014	L/Cpl. Sampson, H.
99905	Pte. Speigal, H., 4th San. Sect.
62779	Pte. Shapiro, M.
103906	Pte. Spiro, 16th C.
86366	Pte. Solomons, A.
83732	Pte. Simons, A. C.
85683	Pte. Stockland.
	Pte. Sierer.
79609	Sgt. Sarfaty, J.*
144488	Pte. Salmon, D.
6217	Cpl. Schoenthal, C.
139469	Pte. Solomon, M.
143790	Pte. Stone, 19th Coy.
128039	Pte. Stenneman, I.
97148	Pte. Solomon, H.
357371	Pte. Sugarman, D.
23274	Staff Sgt. Solomon, W.
	Pte. Spanier, R. F.
127787	Pte. Sagar, M.
2368	Pte. Symons, L., 2nd Field Amb.
31150	S/Sgt. Simons, J., 53rd Field Amb.
1931	L/Cpl. Symons, H. (M.M.), 6th Fld. A.
30886	Pte. Symons, F. M., 78th Field Amb.
31112	Pte. Swart, A., 78th Field Amb.
39948	Pte. Saunders, A., 79th Field Amb.
62775	Pte. Sharman, S., 91st Field Amb.
75238	Pte. Sidman, E., 101st Field Amb.
3077	L./Cpl. Saffa, M. A., 82nd San. Sect.
3048	Pte. Samuel, P., 60th Div. San. Sect.
8758	Pte. Smith, W. G.
201	Pte. Saffer, J., 2/1st W. Riding F.A.
290	L./Cpl. Solomon, Z., 36th San. Sect.
400	L./Cpl. Sorsky, J. M., 1/1st E.L. F.A.
12097	Pte. Shotland, M., 2/2nd E.L. Fld. A.
541167	Pte. Spiner, R. F., 1/1st S.M. Fld. Am.
41619	Pte. Solomon, M., 1/2nd S.M. Fld. A.
337544	Pte. Stoner, B., 87th Field Amb.
117711	Pte. Schneider, M., 58th Field Amb.
2261	L./Cpl. Sagman, J., Marseilles Stat. H.
T4/253430	Sgt. Solomon, H. G., 2/1st West Lancs. Field Amb.
S/4345	Pte. Sack, S. R. N.D.
82061	Pte. Shapira, L.
	Pte Shnitzer, S., 2/1st S.M. C.C.S.
	Pte. Simons, J., 10th C.C.S.
89572	Pte. Schwartz, C., 48th C.C.S.
324304	Pte. Schecter, A., 10th Can. G.H.
6985	Pte. Simmons, R., 8th Gen. Hosp.
4382	Pte. Sidney, J., 8th Gen. Hosp.
1196	Pte. Shaverin, C.
393	Pte. Shinwell, J.
63000	Pte. Silvert, I.
75638	Pte. Stoolmark, J.
116641	Pte. Simons, S.
121572	Pte. Schweitzer, G.
213967	Pte. Simons, J.
123434	Pte. Silverman, J. D.
120893	Pte. Smith, J.
61890	Pte. Smith, M. A.
98989	Pte. Stevenson.
350192	Sgt. Swion, H.
112320	Pte. Shepherd, J.
113086	Pte. Steinberg, H.
62775	Pte. Sharman, S.
127645	Pte. Sagaloff, M.
86408	Pte. Solomon, S.
114105	Pte. Sellars, M.
527278	L/Cpl. Solomon, L.
130219	Pte. Stack, A.
	Pte. Samuel, B.
113140	Pte. Smutanski, L.
	Pte. Smith, B.
545996	Pte. Samuel, P.
266558	Pte. Stanton, C. S.
137064	Pte. Sweet, P.
130213	Pte. Segal, J.
75705	Pte. Steinhart, S.
92334	Pte. Schneiderman, H.
70547	Pte. Solomon, H.
142158	Pte. Sampson, R.

Royal Army Medical Corps—*Continued.*

6217	Cpl. SCHOENTHAL, S.
29544	Pte. SOLOMONS, A.
23274	S/Sgt. SOLOMONS, W.
77624	Pte. SILVERMAN, P.
200614	Pte. STANTON, S. C.
86141	Pte. SUGARMAN, A.
541240	Pte. SHENKER, A.
20886	Pte. SYMONS, M.
127067	Pte. STEINBERG, W.
1848	Pte. SPANIER, R. F.
12	Pte. SCHIFF, S. A.
82977	Pte. SHECKMAN, L.
62779	Pte. SHAPIRO, M.
86299	Pte. SCHAFFER, P.
386214	Pte. SIGER, P.
117710	Pte. SILVERMAN, T.
3786	Pte. SYMONS, E.
18862	Pte. SILVERMAN, H.
83627	Pte. SOLOMON, V.
492921	Pte. SOLOMON, H.
68899	Pte. SAMEL, C.
124653	Pte. SUNNERY, I.
847	Pte. SLUERS, H.
	Sgt. SYMMONS, L. F. A. (M.M.).
99083	Pte. SOLOMONS, H.
99040	Pte. SEELIG, A.
105154	Pte. SAMTON, B.
125301	Pte. SOLOMONS, A.
85423	Pte. SALKIE, G.
240125	Pte. SAMUEL, B.
97671	Pte. SHWEVITZ, D.
4382	Pte. SYDNEY, J.
35499	Pte. SMITH, M.
5667	Cpl. SPIERS, I.
9	Pte. SALTMAN, I.
9882	Sgt./Maj. SELINGER, E.
52051	Pte. SAMPSON, M.
99083	Pte. SOLOMON, H.
	Pte. SAMS, S. L.
29545	Pte. SALTIEL.
133360	Pte. SHAETZEN, H. F., 26th Gen. Hosp
146791	Pte. SAUGER, I.
93758	Pte. SHIMWELL, J., 30th Field Amb.
	Pte. SANDERSON, S., 3/5th W. L. F.A
125214	Pte. SYMONS, S.
125114	Pte. SHINDLER, J.
125734	Pte. SKERUPA, J.
13140	Pte. SMETHANSKI, L.
115112	Pte. SAUNDERS, S.
115829	Pte. SCHONBERG, J. M.
84468	Pte. STANSFIELD, D.
115008	Pte. SKINNER, J.
	Staff. Sgt. SIMONS, G. (D.C.M.).
97627	Pte. SLOMS,
617	Pte. SILVERMAN, J.
629	Pte. SUGARMAN, D.
847	Pte. SHIERS, H.
116477	Pte. SWERDLOW, S.
98732	Pte. SIMMONS, R.
35996	L/Cpl. SORSKY, I. M.
133016	Pte. SIDNEY, B.
401127	Pte. SAFFER, J. H.
2368	Pte. SIMONS, L.
97376	Pte. SILVERSTEIN, M.
118491	Pte. SILVER, S.
39948	Pte. SAUNDERS, A.
120893	Pte. SMITH, J.
61890	Pte. SMITH, M. A.
79607	Pte. SARFATZ, J.
94938	Pte. SILVER, M.
93758	Pte. SHINWELL, J.
	Pte. SELCOW, H., E. Lancs. F.A.
	Pte. SILVERSTONE, T.
	Pte. SIMONS, A.
	Pte. SOLOMON, A.
	Pte. SYMONS, I.
	Pte. STOKES, A. J.
34327	Pte. TROTSKEY, S. R.,* 7th Field Amb.
34334	Pte. TAYLOR, I., 58th Field Amb.
99041	Pte. TOBIAS, S., 100th Field Amb.
138170	Pte. TAYLOR, S., 27th M.A.C.
118764	Pte. TAYLOUR, S. C.
95715	Sgt. TAYLOR, S.
83633	Pte. TOBINS, B.
126838	Pte. TURANSKY, S.
533115	Pte. TYLER,
116819	Pte. TILLER, J.
123255	Pte. TAYLOR.
136	S./Sgt. UNGAR, I. I. (M.S.M.), 6th San. Section.
	Pte. VELLEMAN, H.
91896	Pte. VALENCIA, L., No. 10 Ital. R.C. Trn.
112360	Pte. VANCLIFFE, L., No. 10 Ital. R.C. Tn.
86333	Pte. VALENTINE, P.
27744	Pte. VELLEMAN, 40th B.G.H.
127480	Pte. VINICOFF, B.
143694	Pte. VINEGRAD, G.
99906	Pte. VEZAN, A.
128408	Pte. VALLENTINE, P. N.
94130	Pte. VELINSKI, W.
97709	Pte. VOSS, S.
28045	L/Cpl. VAN GELDER, L. M.
43756	Pte. VANDERLIND, M. S.*
7604	Pte. WOLFE, D., 5th Field Amb.
10470	Pte. WAND, A., 21st Field Amb.
734	Pte. WOOLF, A. J., 41st San. Sect.
69508	Pte. WAGENHEIM, S., 136th Field Amb.
527684	Pte. WOOLF, A. I., 41st San. Sect.
45428	Pte. WOOLF, L., 11th C.C.S.
	L./Cpl. WERTHEIMER, F., 1st City of London San. Coy.
11415	Pte. WISTFIELD, M., 14th Am. Train.
36195	Pte. WERNER, G. G.
113405	Pte. WOLITSKY, J.

Royal Army Medical Corps—Continued.

364209	Pte. WISELMAN, J.
29474	Pte. WILSON, W.
119108	Pte. WINE, H.
136010	Pte. WOOLF, C.
155271	Pte. WOLFSON, J.
99900	Pte. WEINGLASS, J.
	S./Sgt. WOOLF, I. (M.S.M.).
357336	Pte. WILLIAMSON, P.
118687	Pte. WOOLF, J., 72nd Gen. Hosp.
	Sgt./Maj. WASS, M.
122002	Pte. WOLFSON, E.
1887	Pte. WARSON, L.
79422	Pte. WACHALDER, A.
82171	Pte. WOLF, A. S.
117923	Pte. WALTERS, M.
1853	Pte. WINTER, M.
	Pte. WARD, G.
271	Pte. WINEROPE, S.
597	Pte. WOOLFE, H.
37097	Pte. WILLIAMS, N.
14258	Pte. WOOD, L.
26219	Pte. YATES, T. C. F., 24th C.C.S.
1875	Sgt. YOUNG, A. H. E.,
39027	Pte. YOUNG, R., 53rd Fld. Amb.
1642	Cpl. ZISSMAN, G. G. (D.C.M.).
82300	Pte. ZEITLIN, G., 1/3rd Field Amb.
435039	Cpl. ZISSMANN, B.
124102	Pte. ZIMMERMAN, S.
75049	Pte. ZIMLER, J.
120961	Pte. ZOWLOWSKY, B.
	Pte. ZIMMERMAN, W.

*Killed in Action or died on Active Service.

ROYAL ARMY ORDNANCE CORPS.

OFFICERS.

Capt. GOLDHILL, L. J.
Lieut. GOODMAN, H. J.
Major JOEL, H. C. (O.B.E.), C.O.O. Gloucester Docks.
Lieut. JOSEPHS, F. C.
Lieut. LOEBL, A.
Lieut. MICHAELS, C.
Major ROTH, A. A. (O.B.E.).
Capt. MORRIS, F. (M.C.).
Lieut. SELIGMAN, G.
Lieut. SINGLETON, L.
Lieut. SOMERS, R. G.
Lieut. SPRING, A.

N.C.O.'s AND MEN.

010534	Pte. ABRAHAMS, A.
029908	Pte. ABRAHAMS, A.
048828	Pte. ABRAHAMS, B.
038445	Pte. ABRAHAMS, H.
025610	Pte. ABRAHAMS, I.*
015834	L./Cpl. ABRAHAMS, J.,
027402	Pte. ABRAHAMS, T. I.
015272	Sgt. ABRAHAMSON, A.
05175	Pte. ADLER, W.
027262	Pte. ALTER, H.
	Pte. ANDERS, J.
032062	Pte. ANGEL, D.
024400	Pte. APPLE, M.
019816	Pte. APPLETON, E.
023578	Pte. ASH, A.
040028	Pte. AXELROD, J.
024207	Pte. BARNETT, A.
023125	Pte. BELOFSKY, J.
027418	L/Cpl. BENJAMIN, D.
025986	Pte. BENJAMIN, B.
030695	Pte. BENJAMIN, L.
020452	Cpl. BENNETT, J.
019138	Pte. BENNETT, J.
031233	Pte. BENNY, H. B.
017758	Pte. BERLIN, J. N.
	Pte. BERMAN, N.
	Cpl. BERMEL, H.
026977	Pte. BERNBAUM, J.
2829	Sgt. BERNSTEIN.
24562	Pte. BETTAN, S.
031899	Pte. BIERMAN, L.
024562	Pte. BITTERS,
020514	Pte. BLACK, E.
016024	Pte. BLITZ, M.
028317	Cpl. BLOOM, H.
028854	Pte. BLOOMFIELD, H.
036367	Pte. BOURNE, A.
034455	Pte. BRANDON, P.
027963	Pte. BRIODNER, H.
	Pte. BRISKI, S.
7561	Pte. BROWN, J.
	Pte. BROWN, J.
040595	Pte. BULVER, C.
02660	Cpl. CHARLES, I.
026796	Pte. CHEIFETZ, M.
03224	Sgt. CITREON, M. J.
023393	Pte. COHEN, B.
034496	Pte. COHEN, S.
043161	Pte. COHEN, J.
028633	L/Cpl. COHEN, R.
039723	Pte. COHEN, I.
021468	Staff/Sgt. COHEN, B.
030625	Pte. COHEN, P.
023999	Pte. COHEN, C.
03937	Pte. COHEN, E.
039929	Pte. COHEN, D.
04857	Pte. COHEN, S.
03744	Pte. COHEN, C.
019767	Pte. COHEN, P. G.*
016254	Pte. COHEN, H.

Royal Army Ordnance Corps.—*Continued.*

06136	Pte. COHEN, H.		0196256	Pte. GOLDSTEIN, J.
016260	Pte. COHEN, A.		025085	Cpl. GOLDSTEIN, D. H.
015864	Pte. CITRON, L.		019698	Pte. GOODMAN, L.
018159	Pte. COHEN, N.		041546	Pte. GOODMAN, G.
025038	Staff/Sgt. COHEN, P.		021369	Pte. GOODMAN, S.
016251	Pte. COHEN, A.		023060	Pte. GORDON, S.
018436	Pte. COHEN, M.		02425	Sgt. GORDON, A.
021121	Pte. COPPLEMAN, A.		326351	Pte. GOULD, M.
030361	Pte. COHEN, D.		028815	Pte. GREENBAUM, H.
016316	Pte. COHEN, S.		04568	Staff/Sgt. GREENBAUM.
026013	Pte. COHEN, H.		025568	Pte. GROSSMAN, J. P.
016722	L./Cpl. COPELAND, J.		021743	Pte. HARRIS, E. N.
030497	Pte. CORNBERG, A.		013891	Pte. HARRIS, H.
027928	Pte. CRYSTAL, I.		030897	Pte. HARRIS, S.
028600	Pte. DA COSTA, J.		A/2182	Sgt. HARRIS, J.
027889	Pte. DAVIS, A.		03867	L./Cpl. HARRIS, H.
026451	Pte. DAVIS, I.		032789	Pte. HARRIS, A.
035584	Pte. DAVIS, M.		035110	Pte. HARRIS, M.
2996	A/Staff-Sgt. DAVIS, G.		016101	Pte. HARRIS, W.
025336	Pte. DEFRIES, N.		033224	Pte. HARRIS.
024713	Pte. DE GROOT, D.			Pte. HARRIS, B.
014761	Pte. DE POWER, S.		02124	Pte. HART, M.
626757	Pte. DAVIDSON, J.		015143	Pte. HART, A.
1030	S/Sgt. DORIN, S.		024894	Pte. HAYMAN, B.
038713	Pte. ELLIS, F.		024894	Pte. HAYMAN, B. H.
022889	Pte. ENGELL, A.		031346	Pte. HENRY, I.
	Pte. ENGLISHMAN, H.		016370	Pte. HIMMELFELT, H.
025489	Pte. EZRA, A.		026235	L/Cpl. HILL, S.
07286	Pte. FELD, S. M.		020226	Pte. HILTMAN, S.
016455	Pte. FENN, M.		024080	Pte. HOELPELMAN.*
023603	Pte. FINBURG, M.		019025	Pte. HYMAN, D. S.
026165	Pte. FINKLESTEIN, G.		028233	Pte. HYMAN, A.
029526	Pte. FISHERMAN, J.		02660	S./Sgt. ISAACS, C. (M.S.M.).
034890	Pte. FOGEL, W.		030396	Pte. ISAACS, L.
034411	Pte. FRYDE, M.		033963	Pte. ISAACMAN, J.
017951	Pte. FRANKS, W.			Pte. JACOBS, H.
	L./Cpl. FINK, H.		5838	Pte. JACOBS, J. P.
031616	Pte. FREEDMAN, H.		021652	Pte. JACOBS, L. E.
021462	Pte. FREEDMAN, W.			Pte. JACOBS, B.
016259	Pte. FREEDMAN, L.		021595	Pte. JACOBS, I.
025055	Pte. FREEDMAN, M.			Cpl. JACOBS, J.
032420	Pte. FREEMAN, D.		058448	Pte. JACOBS, S.
035358	Pte. FREEDMAN, R.		022652	Pte. JACOBS, R.
021415	Pte. FREEDMAN, W.		010975	Pte. JACOBS, H.
019164	Pte. FREEDMAN, S.		011982	Pte. JACOBS, F.
039759	Pte. FUKUWEIZ, S.			Pte. JEFFREYS, A.
7334	L./Cpl. GIBBON, J. A.,		024494	Pte. JONES, A. J.
16257	Pte. GINSBERG, J.		016026	Pte. JOSEPH, S.
031470	Pte. GLATT, S.		7620	Pte. KAISSER, S. C.
014565	Pte. GOLD, B.		230734	Pte. KATZ, B.
025557	Pte. GOLDBERG, M.		023215	Pte. KERSH, J.
038218	Pte. GOLDENBURG, J.		023577	Pte. KITTER, S.
020189	Pte. GOLDMAN, I.		015726	Pte. LANCHIN, H.
010548	Cpl. GOLDSMID, J.		034417	Pte. LANDAU, D.,,
031026	Pte. GOLDSTEIN, L.		01748	Pte. LANG, P.
027038	Pte. GOLDSTEIN, M.		037174	Pte. LATNER, J.
016256	Pte. GOLDSTEIN, J.		020199	Pte. LATNER, B.
			034176	Pte. LAWTON, J.

Royal Army Ordnance Corps— *Continued.*

031005	Pte. LETTER, E.
03521	Pte. LEVEY, R. N.
016261	Pte. LEVI, L.
026737	Pte. LEVISON, M.
023106	Pte. LEVINSON, A.
016148	Pte. LEVINSTEIN, C.,
03521	Pte. LEVY, M. D.
031734	Pte. LEVY, B.
016517	L/Cpl. LEVY, L.
016149	Pte. LEVY, B. H.,
022900	Pte. LEVY, M.,
014517	L/Cpl. LEVY, R.,
09494	Pte. LEWIS, A.
	A/Staff-Sgt. LEWIS, H.
09282	L/Cpl. LEWIS, S.
048275	Pte. LEWIS, R.,
038793	Pte. LIFFMAN, E.
013399	L/Cpl. LIPMAN, B.
035663	Pte. LITTMAN, G.
	Pte. LITTMAN, J.
021720	Pte. LOWENTHAL, J.,
034455	Pte. LUPINSKY, P.
016733	2nd/Cpl. LEWIS, J.
021120	Pte. LUBEL, H.,
021768	Pte. LYONS, J.
033547	Pte. LYSMAN, C.
016455	Pte. MAGNUS, F.
03884	Pte. MAICHINSKY, I.
016611	Pte. MANKIN, J.
016275	Pte. MARONOVITCH, M.
027038	Pte. MARKS, N.
033043	Pte. MARKS, I.
030391	Pte. MARCOSKY, J.
029533	Pte. MATTHEWS, A.
027886	Pte. MAYERS, A. A.
019137	Pte. MARKSON, B.
4673	Pte. MENDOZA, V. M.*
015836	Pte. MILBERG, J.
034327	Pte. MILLER, L.
07608	Pte. MILLER, H.
024098	Pte. MISTLIN, D.
017713	Pte. MISTOFSKIE, M.
028664	Pte. MONITZ, S. L.
018386	Pte. MORAET, L.
034638	Pte. MORRIS, S.
04249	Pte. MORRIS, S. D.
035800	Pte. MOSLENSKY, I.
026832	Pte. MOSS, D.
030733	Pte. MOSS, D.
021673	Pte. MOSS, H.
031036	Pte. MYER, E.
030672	Pte. MYERS, E.
S/3361	Conductor MYERS, W. D.
022652	Pte. MYERS, E.
039577	Pte. PAIORSKY, D.
039356	Pte. PANE, G.
031712	Pte. PAPERDORF.
043402	Pte. PATNICK, A.
020514	Pte. PEARL, H.
024052	Pte. PORASHNER, I.
016362	Pte. PORTER, L.
014761	Pte. POWER, S.
019720	Pte. PRICE.
024001	Pte. PRICEMAN, C.
015835	Pte. PRINCE, J.
035049	Pte. QUIRK, J.
11630	Pte. RAINSBURY, S.
026234	Pte. RASCH, N.
035554	Pte. REICHENSTEIN, J.
036681	Pte. RICH, B.
025157	Pte. RICHARD, D. F.
018628	Pte. RITTER, J.
024584	Pte. RODEN, H.
021188	Pte. ROSE, A.
027670	Sgt. ROSE, I. J.
024985	Pte. ROSEN, S.
016696	Pte. ROSENBERG, I.
037410	Pte. ROSENBERG.
020505	L/Cpl. ROSENBERG, H.
021141	Pte. ROSENBERG, I.
026113	Pte. ROSENBLATT, E.
033291	Pte. RUBENSTEIN, A.
032386	Pte. ROSENTHAL, J.
022083	Pte. SAGAR, R.
025721	Pte. SALONT, M.
021825	Pte. SAMUELS, S.
041600	Pte. SCHWARCENBERG.
016253	Pte. SCHWARTZ, I.
030604	Pte. SELTZER, L.
027560	Pte. SHAPERO, D.
02979	Pte. SIDEMAN, Y.
016437	Pte. SILBERG, M.
	S./Sgt. SILVERBERG, A. E. (M.S.M.).
033699	Pte. SILVERSTEIN, H.
	Pte. SIMMONS, L. H.
016313	Pte. SIMONS, S.
017772	Pte. SIMONS, B.
016026	Pte. SIMONS, J.
016375	Pte. SIMONS, L.
019469	L/Cpl. SINCLAIR, L.
025009	Pte. SKUDDER, G.
021544	Pte. SLONIMSKY, W.
020794	L/Cpl. SMITH, R.
031502	L/Cpl. SMITH, J.
038579	Pte. SMOLLEN, B.
027013	Pte. SOKEL, J.
019230	Pte. SOLL, M.
018230	Pte. SOLLS, M.
034549	Pte. SOLOMON, S.
035538	Pte. SOLOMON, C.
034639	Pte. SOLOMON, H.
025861	Pte. SOLOMON, L.
027172	Pte. SOLOMONS, M.
032593	Pte. SOLOMONS, P.

Royal Army Ordnance Corps—*Continued.*

03042	Sgt.	SOLOMONS, A. G.
031075	Pte.	SOLOMONS, I.
035050	Pte.	SOLOMONS, J.
024901	Cpl.	SONFIELD, C.
019483	Gnr.	SPEAKMASTER, E.
042467	Pte.	SPECTERMAN, A.
016904	Cpl.	SPRINGER, J. H.
	Pte.	SPYERS,
7101	Pte.	STEINBERG, Z.
	Pte.	STEINBERG, S.
027905	Pte.	STERN, J.
027888	Pte.	STIBBING, A.
020730	Pte.	STRATTON, S. A.
032315	Pte.	STUMP, A.
	Pte.	SUGARMAN, N.
022958	L/Cpl.	SUGARMAN, L.
025769	Pte.	SUMMERFIELD, S.
017726	Pte.	SUNON, N.
09769	S./Condr.	SUSSMAN, J.
023062	Pte.	SYMONS, M.
	Pte.	TAYLOR, S.
025334	Pte.	TEMPLE, M.
08455	Pte.	TERRY, H.
034455	Pte.	THOMAS, B.
025767	L/Sgt.	WALLER, H.
020182	Cpl.	WANSKER, R.
017482	L/Cpl.	WARSHOWSKY.
029534	Pte.	WEBER, H.,
022486	Pte.	WEINER, H.
031092	Pte.	WEINRABE, J.
034428	Pte.	WHITE, H.
018305	Pte.	WIENER, H.
029892	Pte.	WIENER, L.
022874	Pte.	WINTEROCK, E.
019960	Pte.	WISEMAN, J.
023227	Pte.	WISEMAN, D.
016101	Pte.	WOOLF, H.
010385	Pte.	WOOLF, J.
827760	L/Cpl.	WORMS, S.
019333	Pte.	WILCHINSKY, M.
	Pte.	WILSON, S.,
	Pte.	WILSON, E.,
010628	Cpl.	YULES, M. A.
048451	Pte.	ZAIDE, J.
016227	Pte.	ZEALANDER, M.
22252	Pte.	ZEFFRYS, A.,
027472	Pte.	ZELTZER, M.

* Killed in Action or died on Active Service.

ROYAL ARMY VETERINARY CORPS.

OFFICERS.

Capt. SOMERS, H. L., 22nd Vet. Hosp.

N.C.O.'s AND MEN.

	Pte.	ABRAHAM, J., 18th F. Vet. Sect.
22670	Pte.	AVNER, S.
24443	Pte.	AARONS, L.
34351	Pte.	ABRAHAMS, A.
RX4/276177	Pte.	ASHER, S.
27036	Pte.	ALPER, D.
30141	Pte.	ABRAHAMS, L.
15631	Pte.	BLUSVILLE, M.
8592	Sgt.	BRANDON, I.
19956	Pte.	BERGSON, D., 17th Vet. Hosp.
26362	Pte.	BECK, J.
30640	Pte.	BERNSTEIN,
R/311271	Pte.	BELLOTTI, A. A.
29162	Pte.	BENJAMIN, H.
27913	Pte.	BURMAN.
SE/312	Pte.	COHEN, L., 48th Mob. Vet. Sect.
18030	Pte.	COHEN, A., 24th A.V.C.
15141	Pte.	CASH, J., No. 1 Con. "A" Depot.
31343	Pte.	COHEN, D.
T/312668	Dvr.	COHEN, A.
R/277307	Pte.	COHEN, L.
19872	Pte.	COWAN, M. L.
21857	Pte.	CARR, H.
551139	Pte.	COHEN, I.
SE/27987	Pte.	CLINE, A., No. 8 Vet. Hosp.
24253	A/Cpl.	COHEN, A., 3rd Reserve Sect.
14891	Pte.	DUNN, M.
SE/15209	Pte.	DAVIDSON, 41st Mob. Vet. Sect.
SE/27828	Pte.	DAVIDSON, S., No. 7 Vet. Hosp.
33876	Pte.	DE HAAN, M.
161	Pte.	EPSTANE
23852	Pte.	EMANUEL, P.
R/310823	Pte.	FOOTRING, S. I.
17727	Pte.	FINK, H.
22691	Pte.	FREEDMAN, L., 9th A.V.C. Hosp.
30312	Pte.	FELDMAN, J.
TT/03082	Pte.	FREEDMAN, B.
24301	Pte.	FINEBERG, B.
	Pte.	GOODMAN, L.
581082	Pte.	GOLDSTONE, M.
24898	Pte.	GODFREY, A., 3rd Vet. Hosp.
16786	Pte.	GILDER, J., 14th Vet. Hosp.
389	Cpl.	GELLER, A., 5th Vet. Hosp.
26924	Pte.	GALLEWSKI, L.
24260	Pte.	GOODSTONE, A.
SE/23876	Pte.	HELINGER, D.
27513	Pte.	IKEN, E.
15108	Pte.	JACOBS, H., No. 4 Vet. Hosp.
28729	Pte.	JACOB, D. A.
13240	Pte.	JOSEPHS, M., 17th Vet. Hosp.
R4/106603	Pte.	JOSEPHS, N. L.

Royal Army Veterinary Corps.—*Continued.*

- 27496 Pte. Kurtz, L.
- RTS/4458 S.S.M. Key, L.
- 34276 Pte. Kans, A.
- 19721 Pte. Levene, H., No. 9 A.V.C. Hosp.
- 26737 Pte. Levison, M., 13th Vet. Hosp.
- 21842 Pte Levy, M.
- 17921 Pte. Levine, M.
- 29028 Pte. Levine, H., No. 5 Vet. Hosp.
- 31006 Pte. Levy, J.
- R/390958 Pte. Lubinsky, D.
- R/367086 Pte. Lazarus, B.
- 28763 Pte. Landy, J.
- 534898 Pte. Levy, L.
- 8004 Pte. Moss, S., 35th Mobile Vet. Sect.
- 21832 Pte. Morris, A., 19th A.V.C. Hosp.
- 21852 Pte. Miranda, M., 9th A.V.C. Hosp.
- 14499 L/Cpl. Mendelson, H.
- 15228 Pte. Mitchell.
- 1148 Pte. Myers, I. M.
- 1443 Pte. Muslin.
- SE/24533 Cpl. Nathan, V. N.
- 26740 Pte. O'Ginsky, S. A.
- 23852 Pte. Phillips, E.
- 109155 Pte. Pearlman, N.
- Pte. Pearlman, A.
- 1292 Pte. Pearl, L.
- Pte. Phillips, A.
- 23084 Pte. Polack, M. M.
- 24276 Pte. Posner, J.
- 20089 Pte. Rosenberg, J., 24th Vet. Hosp.
- 20809 Pte. Richman, A.
- 31994 Pte. Raphael, V.
- 18194 Pte. Refson, R.
- 29091 Pte. Rose, N.
- 25971 Pte. Reece, J.
- R/1446 Pte. Rosenthall, J.
- 23107 Pte. Sado, G., 9th A.V.C. Hosp.
- 10967 Pte. Segal, A., No. 9 Vet. Hosp.
- 23706 Pte. Simmons, J., 22nd Vet. Hosp.
- 16868 Pte. Solomons, S., 7th Vet. Hosp.
- 24680 Pte. Stone, B.
- 162964 Pte. Sablovski, H.
- R/366989 Pte. Solomon, D.
- R/366969 Pte. Smith, M.
- R/311294 Pte. Soskin, E.
- 17600 Pte. Tuffrey, F.
- 627643 Pte. Thomas, E.
- 19726 Pte. Volinski, M.
- 348691 Pte. Vetofski, J.
- 7679 Pte. Wiggins, H. W.
- 28552 Pte. Wingarten, D.
- 16411 Pte. Wenzerul, A., 23rd A.V.C. Hosp.
- 15254 Sadd. Wiseman, H.
- R/388443 Pte. Zausmer, M.

ROYAL ARMY PAY CORPS.

OFFICERS.

- Capt. Levene, L.
- Capt. Sandleson, D. I. (M.B.E.).

N.C.O.'s AND MEN.

- Pte. Abrahams, B.
- 8772 Pte. Abrahams, B. A.
- Pte. Abrahams, L. M.
- 12669 L/Cpl. Adler, L.
- 4524 Pte. Alfred, R.
- 298941 Pte. Appleby, E. J.
- 18910 Pte. Assenheim, H.
- 4651 Sgt. Back, E.
- 12710 Cpl. Barnett, M.
- 19706 A/Cpl. Barnett, J.
- 6377 Pte. Barnett, I.
- Pte. Barnett, W. L.
- 5537 Pte. Bebei, A.
- 193392 Pte. Beckoff, A. J.
- 5552 Pte. Bernstein, F.
- 19166 L/Cpl. Bill, D.
- 3917 Cpl. Black, W. C.
- Pte. Bradstock.
- 16452 Cpl. Bromberg, A.
- 15816 Pte. Burrows, G. E.
- 4660 L/Cpl. Cheek, E.
- 18493 Pte. Clarke, M.
- 15752 Cpl. Cohen, S.
- 14496 Pte. Cohen, B.
- 8122 Pte. Cohen, J. E.
- 23105 Pte. Cohen, H.
- 14895 Pte. Cohen, H.
- 3424 Pte. Compani, S.
- 9044 Pte. Da Costa, B.
- 13099 Pte. Daniels, B.
- 9147 Cpl. Davis, B.
- 14787 Cpl. De Groot, L.
- 9888 Pte. De Meza, A.
- 11238 Pte. De Smith, J.
- Pte. De Wilde, M.
- 10477 L/Cpl. Ellis, H.
- 236788 Pte. Felsenstein, J.
- Pte. Field, E.
- 10866 Pte. Fineberg, S.
- 10311 Pte. Finklestein, J.
- C/44078 Pte. Finklestein, G.
- Pte. Freedman, E.
- L/Cpl. Green, L.
- 15643 Pte. Garber, E.
- 11993 Pte. Gelman, R.
- 18912 Pte. Gilbert, G. G.
- Pte. Goldfield.
- 10508 Cpl. Gold, I.
- 11130 Pte. Goldberg, J.
- 64326 Pte. Goldberg, I.

Royal Army Pay Corps.—*Continued.*

8326	Pte.	GOLDBLOOM.
12080	Pte.	GOLDSTEIN, B.
1942	Pte.	GOLDSTONE, D.
12989	Cpl.	GOLDSTONE, M.
18014	Pte.	GOLTMANN, L.
10120	L/Cpl.	GOODSON, E.
2388	Pte.	GOULD, J.
10692	Pte.	GREEN, M.
16331	Pte.	GOLDMAN, H.
3643	Pte.	GREEN, F.
8292	Cpl.	GREENBAUM, S.
	Pte.	GREENFIELD, A.
2626	Sgt.	GROSSMAN, W.
13268	Pte.	GUTTERMAN, I.
9029	Cpl.	HALPERIN, I.
2753	Pte.	HARCOURT, S. B.
22605	Pte.	HARMAN, A.
15674	Cpl.	HARRIS, D.
9110	Pte.	HARRISON, L.
841033	Pte.	HARRYMAN, J.
6964	Sgt.	HART, H. H.
11166	Pte.	HELLEMAN, H.
5439	Pte.	HERSCHOP, C.
285757	Pte.	HERSCHMAN.
17052	Pte.	HOREWITZ, M.
	Pte.	HYMAN, S.
23114	Pte.	ISAACS, L.
	Pte.	JACOBS, S.
	Pte.	JACOBS, D.
	Pte.	JACOBS, C. M.
23054	Pte.	JACOBSON, J.
	S./Sgt.-Major	JACOBS, H. W. (M.S.M.).
1434	L/Cpl.	JOEL, W.
	L/Cpl.	JOSEPH, M.
	Pte.	JOSEPH, J. R.
	Pte.	JOSEPH, S.
	Pte.	JOSEPH, L.
3614	Pte.	JOSEPHS, G. M.
15412	Pte.	KEERLSING, H.
22552	Pte.	KLANURT, I.
18472	Cpl.	KUTNER, M.
21058	Pte.	LAGERMAN, C.
14500	Pte.	LANDY, S.
2633	Pte.	LAZARUS, M.
23079	Pte.	LEWIS, M.
55100	Pte.	LEWIS, S.
29526	Sgt.	LEWIS, S.
17238	L/Cpl.	LEWIS, H.
21842	Pte.	LEVY, D.
626163	Pte.	LEVY.
22287	Pte.	LEVY, R.
8854	Pte.	LEVY, T.
2348	Pte.	LEVY, E.
12493	Pte.	LEVY, M.
11279	Pte.	LEVY, H. C.
11551	Pte.	LEVINSON, E.
43865	Pte.	LIEMAN, A. E.
43821	Pte.	LIPERT, S.
1751	Pte.	LISSMAN, M. L.
6709	Pte.	MAGNUS, A.
1440	Pte.	MARKS, L.
73835	Pte.	MARKS, N.
5705	Pte.	MAYERS, A.
17098	Cpl.	MILLER, S.
24901	L/Cpl.	MILLER, M.
9183	Cpl.	MORRIS, V. A.
	Pte.	MORRIS, W. E.
7438	Pte.	MOSES, H.
22551	Pte.	MUNDEL, J.
11051	Pte.	NEWMARK, P. L.
	S/Sgt.	ORAM, W. F.
15304	Cpl.	PERLMUTTER, M.
9733	Pte.	PHILLIPS, P. E.
23657	Pte.	POPPLEDORF, A.
21855	Pte.	POSNER, D.
107496	Sgt.	PYSER, R.
7879	Pte.	RAINSBERG, A.
392367	Pte.	RAMUS, R. A.
2308	Pte.	REGARDIE, A.
5225	Pte.	RIDZ, A. S.
11765	Pte.	ROGERS, S.
12931	Pte.	ROSE, E.
23430	Pte.	ROSENBAUM, J. D.
11595	Cpl.	ROSENBERG, I. N.
71678	Pte.	ROSENTHAL, N.
9132	Pte.	ROSS, S.
23658	Pte.	RUBENSTEIN, A.
11674	Pte.	RUD, L.
11278	Pte.	SAMUELS, A. T.
	Pte.	SAMUELS, J. E.
9757	Pte.	SAMUELS, H. L.
14976	Pte.	SANDISVITCH, I.
	Pte.	SCHILLING, L.
56988	Pte.	SCHOOLBERG, L.
	Pte.	SCHWADRON, O.
4705	Pte.	SHREIDER, A. W.
18125	Pte.	SHULEBERG, E.
8424	L/Cpl.	SILVERBERG, J.
11888	S/Sgt.	SIMONS, H.
11194	L/Cpl.	SIMMONS, J.
	Sgt.	SINCLAIRE, D. A.
10412	Pte.	SMITH, P.
17912	Pte.	SNAPPER, W. M.
11758	Cpl.	SOLOMON, A.
80527	Pte.	SOLOMON, E.
1371	Cpl.	SOLOMONS,
	Pte.	SOLOMONS, B.
4450	Pte.	SPECULAND, J.
6657	Pte.	SPIERS, I.
8562	L/Cpl.	STEINER, J.
	Pte.	STONE, T.
12930	Cpl.	SUMMERAY, J.
	L/Cpl.	TAYLOR, S.
18610	Cpl.	TEACHER, S. M.
11990	Cpl.	WAX, B.

Royal Army Pay Corps—*Continued.*

- 11029 Cpl. WEITZMAN, D.
- Pte. WERNER, D.
- 16598 Cpl. WESANSKY, M.
- 57150 Pte. WHITEMAN, A. E.
- 2811 Pte. WILLIAMS, S.
- Pte. WINTER, E.
- 1304 S/Sgt. WOLFE, F.
- 13030 Pte. WOOLF, S.
- 19552 Pte. WOOLFE, H.
- 2616 Pte. WOLLRAUCH.
- Pte. ZNEIMER, N.

ROYAL AIR FORCE.

OFFICERS.

- 2nd Lieut. ADLER, J. H.
- 2nd Lieut. ALSTON, D.
- 2nd Lieut. ABRAHAMS, F.
- 2nd Lieut. ABECASIS, L. D.
- 2nd Lieut. ABRAHAMS, C. R. G.
- 2nd Lieut. ABRAHAMS, G.
- Lieut. ALBER, W. G.
- Lieut. ARONSON, J. G.
- Lieut. ASERMAN, A.
- Lieut. AUERBACH, H. W.
- 2nd Lieut. BUCKNER, H.
- Capt. BAUER, D. C.* (D.F.C.).
- 2nd Lieut. BENJAMIN, N. A. (M.C.)
- 2nd Lieut. BERNSTEIN, J. J.
- 2nd Lieut. BARNETT, D. E.
- 2nd Lieut. BENNETT, J. D.
- Lieut. BERNARD, H.
- 2nd Lieut. BESCHEN-KOWSKY, R.A.G.
- 2nd Lieut. BAMBERGER, M. De W.
- Lieut. BEDDINGTON, F. B.
- 2nd Lieut. BENJAMIN, A. L.
- Lieut. BENJAMIN, C. M.
- Lieut. BENJAMIN, L.
- Lieut. BENJAMIN, M. A.
- Lieut. BENSUSAN, K. E.
- Lieut. BENVENISTI, J. L.
- Lieut. BERLYN, R. C.
- Lieut. BESSO, M.
- 2nd Lieut. BRODZIAK, P. H.
- 2nd Lieut. BEILING, N.
- Lieut. BAUMAN, E.
- Lieut. BRECKMAN, J.
- Capt. BARNATO, J. I.*
- 2nd Lieut. BODENHEIMER, B.
- 2nd Lieut. BENDELSTEIN, A.
- Capt. BARNATO, I. H. W.
- 2nd Lieut. CHAPMAN, L. L.
- 2nd Lieut. COHEN, A. E.
- Capt. COHEN, B. S.
- Lieut. COHEN, E. S.
- 2nd Lieut. COHEN, F.
- 2nd Lieut. COHEN, H.
- 2nd Lieut. COHEN, M.
- 2nd Lieut. COHEN, R.
- 2nd Lieut. COHEN, B.
- 2nd Lieut. COHEN, S.
- Lieut. CRESNER, V. A.
- Lieut. DAVIS, G.
- Lieut. DAVIS, B. R.*
- Lieut. DIAMOND, J.*
- 2nd Lieut. DENDLESTEIN, A.
- 2nd Lieut. DAVIS, A. D. S.
- Lieut. DAVIES, C. M.
- Major DEFRIES, C.
- Lieut. DE MEZA, B.
- 2nd Lieut. DE PINNA, C. D.
- Capt. DE PASS, E. A.
- 2nd Lieut. DE PASS, E. S.
- Lieut. DE PASS, K.
- 2nd Lieut. DE SAXE, M. R.
- Lieut. DRESCHFIELD, S. E.
- Capt. DRESCHFIELD, V. (D.F.C.).
- Capt. DRESCHFIELD, W. G.
- Capt. DE PASS, A.
- 2nd Lieut. DE SAXE, M. R.
- Capt. DAVIS, S.
- 2nd Lieut. ELLIS, S.
- Lieut. EPSTEIN, M. G.
- Lieut. EICHHOLZ, H. O.
- 2nd Lieut. FRIDJOHN, H. M.
- 2nd Lieut. FINE, S.*
- Lieut. FINZI, E.*
- 2nd Lieut. FRECE, C. R.
- 2nd Lieut. FRASER, H.
- Lieut. FALCK, L. L.
- Lieut. FONSECA, G. G.
- Capt. FALKENBERG, F. C. (D.F.C. and Bar).
- 2nd Lieut. FONSECA, L. A.
- 2nd Lieut. FUTERMAN, L.
- 2nd Lieut. FLEET, L.*
- 2nd Lieut. GROSSBERG, S.
- Lieut. GLUCKSTEIN, I. V.
- 2nd Lieut. GROS, H. S.
- 2nd Lieut. GEIGER, A. D.
- 2nd Lieut. GEIGER, G. F.
- 2nd Lieut. GOLDMAN, R.
- Lieut. GREEN, F. M.
- 2nd Lieut. GLAZER, D. P.
- 2nd Lieut. GOLDING, A.
- 2nd Lieut. GOTTLIEB, D.
- Capt. HYAMS, G. G. (D.F.C.).
- Major HALFORD, E. S. (O.B.E.).
- 2nd Lieut. HENRIQUES, E.
- Lieut. HYMAN, M.
- 2nd Lieut. HARRIS, J. M.
- 2nd Lieut. HELLER, V.
- Lieut. HAYDESS, S.
- Sub.-Lieut. HYMAN, E.
- Lieut. ISAAC, K. J.
- 2nd Lieut. ISAACS, J. B.
- Capt. ISAACS, J. C.
- 2nd Lieut. ISAACS, R.
- 2nd Lieut. ISAACS, M. J.
- Capt. ISAACS, A. D.
- 2nd Lieut. JOYCE, P. S.*
- 2nd Lieut. JACOBS, B.
- Lieut. JACOBS, E. S.
- 2nd Lieut. JACOBS, F. T.
- 2nd Lieut. JACOBS, H. J. V.
- Lieut. JACOBS, J.
- 2nd Lieut. JACOBS, L.
- 2nd Lieut. JACOBS, M. R.
- Capt. JACOBS, V. J. B.
- 2nd Lieut. JACOBSON, S. N.
- 2nd Lieut. JACOBUS, S. H.
- 2nd Lieut. JACOBY, A. H. M.
- 2nd Lieut. JOSEPH, M. B.
- Capt. JOSEPH, S. C. (D.F.C. and Bar).
- Lieut. JOSEPH, W. E.
- Lieut. JOSEPH, W. L.
- 2nd Lieut. JACKSON, C. F.
- Lieut. KLINGENSTEIN, G. K.
- Major KEMPER, J. (M.B.E.).
- Lieut. KRAKO, I.
- 2nd Lieut. KAYE, M. M.
- Capt. KAHN, L. V.
- Lieut. KAIZER, M. M.
- Lieut. KESTON, W. S.
- Lieut. LEVY, F. D.
- Lieut. LEWIN, M. S.
- 2nd Lieut. LOWENSTEIN, J. C.*
- 2nd Lieut. LUBELSKI, W. W.
- 2nd Lieut. LEVI, B. L.
- 2nd Lieut. LEVY, E. I.
- 2nd Lieut. LEVY, S. W.
- 2nd Lieut. LESSER, A. C.
- Lieut. LEVINSON, A. V.
- 2nd Lieut. LEVINE, M. G.*

Royal Air Force.—*Continued.*
2nd Lieut. LEVY, H. W.
2nd Lieut. LEVY, J.
2nd Lieut. LEVY, A. G.*
Capt. LEVY, J. G.
Capt. LEVY, J. M. D'A.
2nd Lieut. LEVY, M. H.
Lieut. LEVY, V. I.
2nd Lieut. LAZARUS, M.
Flight Lieut. LAN-DAVIS, C. F.*
Capt. LEVY, J. S.
2nd Lieut. LEVEY, B. A. (M.B.E.).
2nd Lieut. MYERS, M.
Lieut. MARKS, L. T.*
Capt. MARKS, C. H.*
2nd Lieut. MARTINSON, K. L.*
2nd Lieut. MYERS, F. M.* (M.C.).
Lieut. MYERS, M. I.
Lieut. MARKS, L. C.
Lieut. MARCUS, S. P.
Major MARIX, R. L. G.
Lieut. MARKS, A. E.
Lieut. MARKS, G. I. D.
2nd Lieut. MAYBAUM, A.
Capt. MANZER, R. (D.F.C.).
Lieut. MAYER, C. E.
Lieut. MAYER, J. L.
Lieut. MENDELSSOHN, L.
2nd Lieut. MENDOZA, P.
Lieut. MESSULAM, R.
2nd Lieut. MICHAELIS, R.
2nd Lieut. MORDECAI, J. J.
Capt. NATHAN, C. H.
Capt. NATHAN, A. A.
Lieut. NATHAN, C. F. (M.C.).
Lieut. NATHAN, E.
2nd Lieut. NATHAN, W. M.
2nd Lieut. NATHAN, E. L.
F./Sub.-Lieut. NEIL, L. M. B.
2nd Lieut. PELL, C. J.
2nd Lieut. PAIBA, R. I.
Capt. PARKER, G. A. (D.S.O., M.C.).
Lieut. PONSER, H.
Major POLLAK, E. R. H. (M.C. and Bar).
Lieut. PRINCE, G.
Lieut. ROSE, W.
2nd Lieut. ROSENTHAL, A.*
Lieut. ROBINSON, A. A. (D.F.C., M.C. and Bar).
Lieut. ROSE, B.
2nd Lieut. ROSKIN, N.
Lieut. ROSENBLATT, M. A.
2nd Lieut. ROSENTHAL, R. H.
2nd Lieut. ROTHFIELD, A.
Lieut. ROTHSCHILD, L. V.

2nd Lieut. ROTHSCHILD, J.
Lieut. RUBINOVICH, T. J.
Lieut. RACIODGER, J. Z.
2nd Lieut. ROBSON, W. A.
Lieut. ROSELLI, J. E.
Lieut. RAPHAEL, C. G.
Capt. SOLOMON, G. B.
Capt. SHEREK, P.*
Capt. SILVERSTEIN, H.
Capt. SIMONSON, E. L.
Lieut. SONNENBERG, M.C.*
2nd Lieut. SALOMON, F. R.
2nd Lieut. SAMUEL, G. B.*
Capt. SOLOMONS, G. B.
Lieut. STUART-SMITH, P. J.*
2nd Lieut. SILVERSTON, C. J.
Lieut. SIMMONS, D. H.
Lieut. SOLOMON, B.*
2nd Lieut. SHUMER, C.
Lieut. STRAUSS, V. A.*
Lieut. SAQUI, L. V. H.
2nd Lieut. STARFIELD, B.*
Major SOLOMON, J. H. (M.C.).
Lieut. SAMUELS, B. J.
2nd Lieut. SAMUELS, H.
Capt. SASSOON, E. V.
2nd Lieut. SCHULMAN, A. A.
2nd Lieut. SHEROWITZ, J.
2nd Lieut. SOLOMAN, B.
Capt. SOLOMON, D. R. (D.F.C.).
2nd Lieut. SOLOMON, E. V.
2nd Lieut. SOLOMON, F. H.
Lieut. SOLOMON, S. A. R.
Lieut. SPERO, W. P.
2nd Lieut. STERN, L. G.
2nd Lieut. STIEBEL, R.
Lieut. STROSS, D.*
2nd Lieut. SUGARMAN, C.
2nd Lieut. SOLOMON, G. H.
Lieut. SYLVESTA, G. H.
2nd Lieut. SALZBERG, S. S.
2nd Lieut. SHERATTEN, S.
2nd Lieut. SUSSMAN, W.
Lieut. SOLZBERG, S.
Lieut. STERN, A.
2nd Lieut. SONDHEIM, W.*
Lieut. STERN, S. L.*
Capt. TUCK, D.
Lieut. TELLERMAN, K.
2nd Lieut. TORRES, H. D.
Lieut. VANDYKE, P. R.
2nd Lieut. VAN PRAAGH, F.
Lieut. VINEBERG, H. A. (D.F.C.).
2nd Lieut. VENTURA, G. M. V.
Lieut. VALLENTINE, P.
2nd Lieut. WEIL, L.*
2nd Lieut. WOLFF, H. S.

Lieut. WISNEKOWITZ, H. (M.C.).
2nd Lieut. WILLIAMS, A. T.
Lieut. WEISS, E. S.*
Capt. WEIL, B.
2nd Lieut. WEINBERG, L.
Lieut. WEINBERG, M.
Liet. WEINER, L. DE V.
2nd Lieut. WEINGOTT, F. F.
2nd Lieut. WINKLER, M. H.
Lieut. WIGDEN, L.
2nd Lieut. YOUNGLESON, A. H. R.
Lieut. ZIEMAN, J. R.

N.C.O.'s AND MEN.

49947 2/A.M. ABRAHAMS, J.
18117 1/A.M. ABRAHAMS, B.
30748 2/A.M. ABRAMS, M.
58144 3/A.M. ABRAHAM, M.
18727 1/Pte. APPLETON, H.
64342 1/Pte. ASHER, G. K.
64245 2/A.M. AARONS, P.
48376 1/A.M. ABRAHAMS, M.
92411 2/A.M. ABRAHAM, S.
81707 2/Pte. ALEXANDER, M.
44107 2/A.M. ARONHEIM, D.
66704 3/A.M. APPEL, O.
10249 2/A.M. AUSTIN, J.
361317 3/A.M. ALEN, L.
237792 1/Pte. ABRAHAMS, I.
111847 2/A.M. ACKSTINE, P.
24114 2/A.M. ABRAHAMS, B.
44423 2/A.M. ADLER, A.
229981 Sgt. ABRAHAMS, H.
213956 1/Pte. ABRAHAMS, J.
       Cpl. ARNOPLIN, S.
       Pte. ABRAMS, R. E.
       Pte. ALLONOFF, L.
66218 2/A.M. ALKEVITCH, W.
111922 2/A.M. ABRAHAMS, H.
33902 2/A.M. AUSTRICK, M.
30040 2/A.M. ALEXANDER.
60611 2/A.M. ABRAHAMS, T.
91598 2/A.M. ARONSON.
98020 3/A.M. ALEXANDER, G.
167157 2/A.C. AUSTEN.
62251 Cpl./Clerk AMSTELL, A.
298941 Pte. APPLEBY, E. J.
50698 2/A.M. ABRAHAMS, I.
177989 1/A.M. AARONS, J.
37727 Fl.Cad. ABRAHAMS, B. B.
219241 La.C. ABRAHAMS, I.
76027 3/A.M. ABRAHAMS, N.
37238 2/A.M. ARNOLD, I.
40287 2/A.M. ABRAHAMS, P. G.
122470 3/A.M. ARBUS, L.
277575 1/A.M. ANGEL, F.
109951 3/A.M. AGULSKY, I.

Royal Air Force.—*Continued.*

86157	Cadet ASERMAN, D.		
33902	2/A.M. ANSTRICK, M.		
96355	2/A.M. ABRAHAMSON, H.		
34658	1/A.M. ABRAHAMS, B.		
408628	A/Sgt. AFRIGAN, A.		
134249	Pte. ARMSTRONG,		
24521	2/A.M. ABRAHAMS, B.		
36863	2/A.M. ABRAHAMS, G.		
79515	2/A.M. ASHER, H. M.		
76027	3/A.M. ABRAHAMS, N.		
59551	3/A.M. ABRAHAMS, S.		
43979	2/A.M. ATHERTON,		
301748	2/A.M. ABRAHAMS, M.		
64596	2/A.M. ARGEBARD, W.		
131136	2/A.M. APPELL, I.		
31075	2/A.M. ABRAHAMS, S.		
9367	Cpl. ASHLEY, J. R.		
17186	2/A.M. AMBERRY, A. E.		
65735	2/A.M. ARENHEIM, W.		
77996	2/A.M. ABRAHAMS, A.		
31075	2/A.M. ABRAHAMS, S.		
80073	3/A.M. ALEXANDER, A.		
2414	2/A.M. ABRAHAMS,		
77898	Cpl. ALBURG, S.		
33270	1/A.M. ALDERMAN, S.		
116312	3/A.M. AARON, A.		
50698	2/A.M. ABRAHAMS, I.		
147797	3/A.M. ALECZETZ.		
33270	Pte. ADELSON, S.		
23710	1/A.M. ANSELL, E.		
	P.F.O. AARONSON, N.		
26942	1/A.M. AMSTER, J. J.		
38787	Pte. ABRAHAMS, I.		
100845	2/A.M. BARNETT, I.		
41107	2/A.M. BUSKIN, D.		
41182	2/A.M. BERNSTEIN, I.		
17174	2/A.M. BORSTEIN.		
35183	2/A.M. BERGER, R.		
82894	3/A.M. BECKER, A.		
23418	2/A.M. BAUM, J.		
76480	3/A.M. BENSON.		
22812	2/A.M. BRINE, J.		
23422	Pte. BLAKE, J.		
	3/A.M. BRESLAW, L.		
138331	Pte. BLATT, J.		
18937	L.A.C. BRAIDMAN.		
156837	A.C.2 BLASHKY, J. B.		
65206	2/A.M. BENSON, L.		
87514	Pte. BETH, B.		
7352	2/A.M. BARNARD, E. G.		
11742	2/A.M. BERNEY, C.		
7761	2/A.M. BAKER, A.		
31429	2/A.M. BARNETT, A.		
31433	2/A.M. BAKER, N.		
31330	2/A.M. BLACK, B.		
17872	2/A.M. BURNS, J.		

39069	Cpl. BRAIDMAN, S.
42998	2/A.M. BILLING, B.
492095	2/Pte. BERGSON, S.
103418	2/A.M. BERKOVITCH, H.
57868	1/Pte. BERBALOFF, L.
108111	1/Pte. BIRTLESTEEN, J.
33103	1/Pte. BLACK, H.
57770	3/A.M. BLOOMBERG, A.
243243	2/A.M. BARUCH, S.
19824	Pte. BAKER, M.
36998	Sgt. BAUMWELL, M. B.
36964	Pte. BECKER, M.
68332	3/A.M. BERNSTEIN, J.
106245	1/Pte. BORSTEIN, A.
133471	2/Pte. BARDOFSKY, R.
52144	1/Pte. BARNETT, L.
37130	2/A.M. BROADY, H. E.
104695	2/Pte. BOWMANN, A. M.
59301	3/A.M. BRANDON, A.
50362	2/A.M. BENABO, A.
45076	2/A.M. BRODSKI, J.
59199	2/A.M. BERG, J.
27868	1/A.M. BRENNER, H.
P/4945	3/A.M. BLOOMBERG, M.
111792	3/A.M. BERSHACK, L.
78541	2/A.M. BENSON, J.
98175	2/A.M. BARNETT, M.
45565	2/A.M. BENJAMIN, M.
P/47492	2/A.M. BRODIE, A.
50613	2/A.M. BERNSTEIN, M.
43452	A./M. BURMAN, E. H.
36006	2/A.M. BROSGILL, H.
16948	Cpl. BARNARD, R. D.
22812	2/A.M. BIRNE, J.
47121	Cpl. BERG, S.
41120	2/A.M. BROSGILL, W.
4505	A./M. BENOLIEL, J.
18941	2/A.M. BERG, S.
75448	Sgt. Maj. BIRLEY, O.
130271	2/A.M. BRENZSKI, C.
86866	3/A.M. BENJAMIN, E.
58588	2/A.M. BROSNALL, N.
531017	Pte. BRILLIANT, N. M.
301860	2/Pte. BELLINFANTE, A.
82935	Sgt. BLOOMBERG, M. S.
98872	Pte. BLASHKEY, N.
35339	2/A.M. BERG, A. A.
32928	2/A.M. BLITSTEIN, H. H.
36000	2/A.M. BLUESTEIN, H.
53068	2/A.M. BALKING, H.
11503	2/A.M. BENSON, C.
14596	2/A.M. BURNS, N.
45287	2/A.M. BARNETT, S. I.
58825	2/A.M. BLOOM, J.
	Pte. BONNY, E.
43769	2/A.M. BOSKIN, A.
43451	Pte. BUTTLE,
24345	2/Pte. BEETLE, C. R.

33343	2/A.M. BRENNER, S.
497930	3/A.M. BESSO, G. E.
344037	3/A.M. BERNSTEIN, A.
138856	3/A.M. BELINFANTE, J.
229225	Pte. BUCKS, I.
99604	1/A.M. BOBET, M.
92981	3/A.M. BLOOM, W.
215978	1/Pte. BEAVER, J. J.
193392	2/Pte. BECKHOFF, A. J.
135544	2/A.M. BRISLOW, A.
392364	Pte. BASS, R.
147801	2/Pte. BLANK, I.
166904	2/Pte. BRAIDMAN, S.
40335	2/A.M. BORWEIN, J.
60502	2/A.M. BROWN, C.
301790	2/A.M. BLAND, J.
31328	2/A.M. BERNSTEIN, A.
35343	2/A.M. BERMAN, L.
42314	Dvr. BENSON, A.
17652	2/A.M. BARNET, M.
23434	2/A.M. BERNBAUM, H.
16876	2/A.M. BRICKMAN, R.
80826	3/A.M. BLOCK, N. B.
46833	2/A.M. BOWMAN, B. A.
137526	Cadet BARNES, E.
88973	2/A.M. BARNETT, I.
35176	2/A.M. BRAGAMAN, A.
55427	2/A.M. BARRETT, P.
110957	Pte. BLOOM, J.
241669	2/A.M. BRESLAU, M. A.
31428	2/A.M. BERNSTEIN, E.
522	2/A.M. BENJAMIN, L.
44751	2/A.M. BOWMAN, J.
298527	3/Clk. BYRENS, L.
82709	3/A.M. BLOOM, S.
62033	2/A.M. BOWMAN, S.
125509	Pte. BARNETT, B.
	Pte. BIRD, E.
47916	3/A.M. BLOCH, E.
92237	3/A.M. BURSTEIN, L. H.
122987	3/A.M. BLOOMBERG, J. H.
16694	3/A.M. BRAIDMAN, S.
7362	1/A.M. BARNARD, E. G.
279264	Pte. BIRD, C.
144091	3/A.M. BARUCH.
97677	2/A.M. BARNETT, C.
10035	2/A.M. BERLINSKY, J.
60765	1/A.M. BOLSON, H. A.
290579	2/Pte. BAIN, J.
53084	2/A.M. BLASKEY, A.
59372	2/A.M. BLOOMBLATT, R. Z.
	Cadet BANKS, B. L.
88963	Cadet BERSON, S.
110927	Cadet BARNARD, H. P.
41446	2/A.M. BALON, M. N.
19618	2/A.M. BARNETT, A.

Royal Air Force.—*Continued.*

60762	2/A.M. Bolson, H.	61689	3/A.M. Cohen, A.	227126	A/Cpl. Coronel, S. H.
66676	3/A.M. Brand, H. M.	37008	1/A.M. Charik, H.	62690	2/A.M. Cook, E. A.
53084	2/A.M. Blaskey, A.	129501	Pte. Canter, P.	107318	A.C.2. Cohen, L.
67442	3/A.M. Beaver, S.	61024	1/Pte. Cooper, H.	223929	A.C.1. Cohen, J.
39020	2/A.M. Berger, S.	58213	2/A.M. Cohen, M.	96675	2/A.M. Cohen, J. K.
75448	1/A.M. Birby, O.	33271	2/A.M. Cohen, N.	11424	F./Sgt. Cidder, S.
124256	2/A.M. Berenstein, H.	44250	2/A.M. Coleman, G.	36888	2/A.M. Cohen, J.
497930	3/A.M. Besso, G. E.	36898	2/A.M. Cohen, P.	59099	2/A.M. Cohen, D.
53068	2/A.M. Balkind, H.		2/A.M. Cohen, D. (M.M.).	175111	Cadet Coopman, B. F.
60201	1/A.M. Bloom, M.	40649	2/A.M. Charles, C.	43558	2/A.M. Crystol, L. M.
97677	2/A.M. Barnet, C.	47382	2/A.M. Cohen, J.	35759	2/A.M. Cohen, C.
72584	Pte. Black, I.	44750	2/A.M. Cohen, A.	91580	3/A.M. Cowan, A.
79419	2/A.M. Berrick, J. W.	44239	2/A.M. Clusky, P.	66938	2/A.M. Clow, R. W.
50317	1/A.M. Barnett, E.	75783	2/A.M. Carman, J.	33981	1/A.M. Cregor.
66938	2/A.M. Blow, W. R.	105052	2/A.M. Cohen, D.	84503	A/Cpl. Cohen, F.
55427	2/A.M. Barnett, H.	267195	2/A.M. Cohen, P.	91529	2/A.M. Cohen, A.
81473	3/A.M. Berstine, A.	18603	1/A.M. Ciring, S.	97841	2/A.M. Cohen, M.
67911	2/A.M. Barnett, S.	92410	3/A.M. Cohen, I.	34619	3/A.M. Cohen, M.
19122	2/A.M. Barnett, D.	98114	2/A.M. Cohen, B.	208934	2/A.M. Cohen, M.
66846	2/A.M. Bernstein, R. L.	54436	2/A.M. Cohen, J.	92591	2/A.M. Crown, M.
40621	2/A.M. Blankstone, C.	113541	2/A.M. Click, J.	95752	A.M. Courlander, I.
69794	2/A.M. Bianeo, M.	38794	2/A.M. Coleman, A.	132187	3/A.M. Cooper, A. M.
36289	A.M. Binns, W.	96423	Pte. Cohen, A.	44862	2/A.M. Crooks, A.
273295	2/A.M. Barnett, B.	75614	Cpl. Cohen, E.	16965	1/A.M. Coleman, S.
30390	A.M. Bland, J.	59565	2/A.M. Crook, A.	109598	3/A.M. Cohen, E.
28615	Cadet Banks, B. L.	105279	3/A.M. Cohen, B.	50050	2/A.M. Cutuer, D.
54113	Pte. Baker, H.	244460	2/Pte. Cohen, H.	23248	A/Sgt. Cowan, M.
13554	2/A.M. Breslow, A.	29683	1/Pte. Cass, T.	101383	3/A.M. Cohen, L.
	3/A.M. Broomberg, H.	289302	3/Clk. Chesney, M.	265001	2/Pte. Cohen, H. P.
16709	A.C.2. Barnett, L. S.	292085	2/Pte. Caro, L.	59752	A.M. Cooper, M.
715979	G.L.A. Beaver, J.	303525	3/Clk. Cohen, B. L.	36870	2/A.M. Cohen, J.
33972	1/A.M. Barder, H.	75917	Cpl./Clk. Cohen, S.	31687	1/A.M. Coleman, A.
25478	A.C.1. Brilliant, V.	38208	2/A.M. Cohen, M.	48832	2/A.M. Cohn, H.
47642	2/A.M. Chishelsky, J.		Pte. Crystal, S.	49060	3/A.M. Celner, L.
7992	2/A.M. Cohen, H.	45952	Sgt. Cohen, S.	45077	2/A.M. Charig, A. V.
7098	2/A.M. Cohen, S.	45116	Pte. Cocking.	44349	2/A.M. Colinsky, J.
32720	2/A.M. Cohen, J.	83617	L/Cpl. Child, W. (M.M.)	55785	3/A.M. Cohen, A.
23798	2/A.M. Castenburg, M.	44728	2/A.M. Cohen, S.	166111	2/A.M. Cohen, J.
18375	2/A.M. Cohen, G. M.	60390	2/A.M. Cohen, A.	24050	1/A.M. Cohen, I.
20932	2/A.M. Crook, E.	44849	2/A.M. Colinsky, J.*	53027	F/Cadet Cresner, V. A.
38811	2/A.M. Charnak, M.	51914	1/Pte. Cooper, E.	54105	Pte. Carrasic, H. S.
30627	2/A.M. Caplan, J.	49557	2/A.M. Cohen, G.	123536	Pte. Cohen, M.
22020	2/A.M. Caplan, H.	34748	2/A.M. Cohen, D.	80639	2/A.M. Clements, H.
13/40301	2/A.M. Crook, S.	40627	2/A.M. Cohen, E.	57396	3/A.M. Cohen, A.
29975	1/A.M. Caplan, L.	75783	3/A.M. Carman, J.	27704	Pte. Cohen, M.
51818	2/Pte. Cohen, J.	6109	Cpl. Crook, M.*	59546	3/A.M. Cohen, R.
123737	2/Pte. Chesses, S.	58523	Pte. Cohen, H. A.*	36888	2/A.M. Cohen, A.
20767	1/Pte. Coyne, D.	7848	Pte. Cohen, M.	26868	2/A.M. Cohen, H.
27385	Cpl./M. Cohen, N. E.	64535	Pte. Cohen, J.	67207	2/A.M. Calo, H.
53849	1/Pte. Cohen, D.	146538	2/A.C. Cohen, H.	64370	2/A.M. Comras, M.
61088	1/Pte. Cohen, A. S.	222276	Clerk Caplan, M.	62344	A/Cpl. Collins, D.
58760	2/A.M. Cohen, S.	89690	Cpl./Clerk Cohen, F. C.	53212	2/A.M. Coopenberg, M.
94904	2/A.M. Cantor, M.	95766	3/A.M. Clayton, J.	59752	2/A.M. Cooper, M.
19239	1/Pte. Cornberg, J.	22126	A/Cpl. Cook, S.	49507	2/A.M. Cohen, M.
50379	2/A.M. Constadt, S.	32434	1/A.M. Cush, B.	2066	3/A.M. Cowan, S.
130960	2/A.M. Cohen, A.	11214	3/A.M. Cohen, V.	86938	3/A.M. Chubertz,
46264	1/A.M. Cooper, J. C. W.	35080	L/Cpl. Cohen, C.	26842	2/A.M. Cornofski, L.
				36870	2/A.M. Cohen, J.

Royal Air Force.—*Continued.*

115687	3/A.M. COHEN, D.	180172	Cpl. DAVIS, B.		Sgt. DAVIS, D. T. (M.S.M.).
112771	3/A.M. COHEN, J.	76031	3/A.M. DODDS, R.	236127	2/A.M. DANSER, S.
44862	2/A.M. CROOKS, A.	289943	2/Pte. DAVIDSON, J.	801380	A.M. DAVIS, G.
58656	1/A.M. COLEMAN, V. I.	155881	3/A.M. DAVIES, E.	5035	2/A.M. DIAMOND, R.
224930	2/A.M. COTT, C.	28698	2/A.M. DANZIGER, H.	118777	Pte. DAVIS, H.
9729	2/A.M. CHER, J.	20274	1/A.M. DA COSTA.	23015	A.C.2. DEANE, A.
59549	2/A.M. COHEN, R.	16834	1/A.M. DAVIES, J.		3/A.M. DIBBELL, H.
98491	2/A.M. CANTOR, S.	15979	2/A.M. DORFMAN, I.		A.C.2. DA COSTA, H.
94333	Pte. COHEN, H.	60427	3/A.M. DE CASSIERES.		A.C.1. DONN, A.
101713	2/A.M. CORBETT, J.		1/A.M. DANZYER, H.	245291	A.C.2. DAVIS, S.
49507	2/A.M. COHEN, M.	37177	L/Cpl. DAVIS, A. A.	235127	A.C.1 DANSER, S.
40301	2/A.M. CROOK, S.		Pte. DODDS, A. M.	9801	2/A.M. ELISHA, S. B.
278297	2/A.M. COHEN, I.	134655	2/A.M. DAVIDSON, J.	17199	2/A.M. ECKSTEIN, L.
493112	3/A.M. COHEN, E.	98142	2/A.M. DAVIS, A.	68624	1/Clerk ELAND, E.
7221	1/A.M. CONN, A.	38776	2/A.M. DENCYGER, L.	44872	2/A.M. EREIRA, H.
48834	2/A.M. COHEN, H.	52707	3/A.M. DANCYGER, H.	51914	2/A.M. ELL, C.
23787	1/A.M. CLIFTON, H.	405091	2/A.M. DAVIS, C.		2/A.M. ENGLANDER.
27798	2/A.M. CASTENBERG, A.		2/A.M. DIGHTMAKER, D.	95779	3/A.M. ELLIS, J.
254175	2/A.M. COHEN, H.	17258	2/A.M. DE YOUNG, M.	50440	2/A.M. EDELSTEIN, J.
62344	Cpl. COLLINS, B.	267695	2/Pte. DAVIS, D. G.	32273	2/A.M. ELLIS, S. I.
53344	2/A.M. CLIVE, S.	29817	1/A.M. DOVER, H. H.	2180	Cpl. EMANUEL, R.
	Cadet COHEN, H.	106281	2/A.M. DAGGERS, R.	136283	3/A.M. ELLISON, M.
78150	A.M. COWAN, A.	81220	2/A.M. DRUIOFF, H.	105133	2/A.M. ESTERSON, E.
40634	1/A.M. CALMANSON.	51758	2/A.M. DAVIES, H.	75191	2/A.M. ENOCH, R.
82270	Pte. COOPER, M.	23426	1/A.M. DURDAN, J.	43234	2/A.M. EPSTEIN, A.
111691	3/A.M. COHEN, C. B.	55233	3/A.M. DELMONTE, H.	41855	Pte. ELLENBERG,
94928	2/A.M. COHEN, J.	47694	2/A.M. DIAMOND, S.	54666	2/A.M. EXCISA, S.
57396	Pte. COHEN, A.	56107	1/Pte. DONNE, L.	2490741	2/A.M. EDELSTEIN, M.
185201	Pte. COHEN, S.	32446	1/A.M. DAVIES, H.	91413	2/A.M. ELIAS, J.
261724	Pte. CUTISS, J.	89992	1/A.M. DAVIES, J.	40320	2/A.M. ELBERT, D.
123536	3/A.M. COHEN, M.	145291	2/Pte. DAVIS, S.	31685	2/A.M. EPSTEIN, M.
50050	3/A.M. CUTNER, S.	169735	Pte. DAVIS, C.	32293	2/A.M. EEL, I.
26531	3/A.M. CAUL.	52517	3/A.M. DA COSTA, A.	17087	2/A.M. FRANKLIN, M.
40649	2/A.M. CLARENCE, C.	7249	2/A.M. DAVIS, H.	271317	2/A.M. FLATAU, J. C.
64535	3/A.M. COHEN, J.	19784	1/A.M. DE WINTER, L.	20187	2/A.M. FIBER, J.
27492	A.M. COHEN, L.	1586	A.M. DAVIS, S.	17742	Cpl. FERSHT, M.
	A.M.1. CHARLATON, A.	57417	2/A.M. DE GROOT, J.	32332	2/A.M. FLIGENBAUM, W.
24495	A.M. COHEN, I.	36896	2/A.M. DAVID, B.	100472	2/A.M. FREEMAN, F.
23305	2/A.M. DICKEY, S.	58838	3/A.M. DAVIS, P.	22964	Cpl. FISHER, M. C.
6091	1/A.M. DAVIS, E. S.	64283	2/A.M. DAVISON, A.	50429	2/A.M. FITZPATRICK, P.
20834	2/A.M. DAVIS, M.	32446	2/A.M. DAVIS, S. S.	53366	2/Pte. FRIEDLANDER, J.
23010	2/A.M. DAVIS, R. M.	81226	2/A.M. DINOFF, H.	49237	Cpl./M. FELLERMAN, L.
32445	2/A.M. DAGGERS, M.	2490882	Pte. DARNASTADER, A.	111403	2/Pte. FRIEND, R.
36623	2/A.M. DAVIS, E. D.	88728	3/A.M. DIX, M.	78528	1/A.M. FRIEDBERG, B.
35930	2/A.M. DAWSON, A. B.	91641	2/A.M. DESMITH, L.	22196	2/A.M. FISHER, A.
45066	1/Pte. DAVIS, N.	1396	Dvr. DAVIS, J.	43268	3/A.M. FRANKENSTEIN, L.
19842	Pte. DAY, H.	79286	3/A.M. DA COSTA, H.	75773	3/A.M. FREDMAN, V. A.
15923	1/A.M. DUMOSCH, D. C.	66939	3/A.M. DAVIS, C.	64719	3/A.M. FRANKLIN, A.
16834	2/A.M. DAVIS, J.	31699	3/A.M. DURHAM, F. C.	P/472194	2/A.M. FRESHFIELD, M.
22742	1/Pte. DA COSTA, S.	59498	2/A.M. DE POWER, M.	38192	2/A.M. FRANKLIN, W.
62237	3/A.M. DE JONGH, B.	101791	2/A.M. DYSEH, S. J.	23952	2/A.M. FREEDMAN, H.
6631	1/A.M. DUKE, W.	89992	2/A.M. DAVIS, H.	13323	Dvr. FREEMAN, F.
51989	3/A.M. DAVID, I.	23426	2/A.M. DUNDEN, I.	44237	2/A.M. FREEMAN, J.
66851	2/A.M. DEMPSEY, G.	23010	2/A.M. DAVIS, R.	290327	2/Pte. FOX, C.
52075	2/A.M. DRYER, W.	82178	2/A.M. DIAMOND, G.	130619	3/A.M. FEINBURGH, S.
101791	2/A.M. DYSCH, S. J.	55341	2/A.M. DAVID, J.	59430	2/A.M. FRANKEL, A.
29817	2/A.M. DOVER, H. W.	81226	2/A.M. DENOFF, H.		

Royal Air Force.—*Continued.*

91793	2/A.M. Freedman, M.
	Pte. Frank, W. C.
235362	A.C.M.L. Fraser, L.
20945	2/A.M. Field, W.
80579	2/A.M. Farra, J.
17259	1/Pte. Folb, L.
57428	1/A.M. Freedman, L.
11874	2/A.M. Frais, A.
23653	2/A.M. Finious.
31288	2/A.M. Feddy, B.
33095	2/A.M. Franks, H.
47361	2/A.M. Foreman, L.
28589	2/A.M. Fishman, M.
13901	2/A.M. Fisher, P.
	2/A.M. Fasht, J. B.
114830	2/A.M. Finley, J.
61737	A./C. Franks.
157250	Boy Felpin, M.
93035	2/A.M. Flacks, M.
114830	3/A.M. Finberg, J.
34261	3/A.M. Fink, M.
126212	3/A.M. Foreman, H.
36469	2/A.M. Foreman, A.
35529	2/A.M. Freedman, M.
112124	3/A.M. Freedman, L.
48989	2/A.M. Fishberg, A.
56504	2/A.M. Frank, I. J.
53214	2/A.M. Fieldman, R.
101916	2/A.M. Freedman, P.
53210	2/A.M. Freedman, J.
52780	2/A.M. Frankenstein, A.
129661	3/A.M. Finberg, I.
42875	1/A.M. Foster, R.
67137	2/A.M. Franks, L.
408726	2/A.M. Freedman, J.
91753	2/A.M. Freedman, M.
35167	2/A.M. Fogel, B.
1148	2/A.M. Finky, J.
30589	2/A.M. Fishman, M.
35010	2/A.M. Freeman, M.
35058	2/A.M. Flowers, A.
37264	2/A.M. Fallau, S.
822212	2/A.M. Foreman, A.
58826	2/A.M. Freeman, H.
56993	2/A.M. Friedman, M.
86990	2/A.M. Freedman, H. D.
33890	2/A.M. Franburg, S.
122178	2/A.M. Ferber, A.
492685	Pte. Factor, P.
57428	1/A.M. Freeman, T.
33564	2/A.M. Friedlander, G.
27187	1/A.M. Finkelblech, H.
20308	2/A.M. Frais, S.
8304	A.C.1. Fobell, D.
493014	3/A.M. Foreman, H.
35713	2/A.M. Friezman, A.
31680	2/A.M. Frieze, E.
18255	2/A.M. Freeman, W.
139704	3/A.M. Fickler, B.
89823	2/A.M. Freedman, L.
109528	3/A.M. Frankell, L.
157250	A.M. Felperin, M.*
109555	2/A.M. Frieze, B.
34060	2/A.M. Freeman, A.
1045098	Pte. Frankel, E. S.
140066	2/A.M. Finklestein,
34640	2/A.M. Flashtig, L. S.
31679	2/A.M. Fishberg, S. S.
162312	2/Pte. Franklin, J.
50403	2/A.M. Feldman, M.
33214	2/A.M. Feldman, H.
137834	Cadet Futerman, L.
253311	Cadet Field, L.
20309	1/A.M. Fogal, P.
130515	3/A.M. Fisher, S.
22193	2/A.M. Feldman, I.
20308	2/A.M. Frais, S.
50200	2/A.M. Finberg, P.
50399	2/A.M. Fram, J.
50549	3/A.M. Farbey, C. S.
89136	C/Clk. Franks, J.
60478	2/A.M. Fynsong, M.
34519	2/A.M. Freeman, A.
79938	2A/.M. Feldman, D.
144484	3/A.M. Franklin, J.
114476	3/A.M. Finegold, M.
761175	Pte. Frarnby, T.
27187	2/A.M. Finkelblech, M.
82511	2/A.M. Feinstein, T.
48919	1/A.M. Fishberg, A.
36831	A.M. Friedlander, S.
33095	2/A.M. Franks, H.
493014	3/A.M. Foreman, H.
101096	2/A.M. Friedman, P.
	A.M. Fligelstone, D.
56504	2/A.M. Frank, F. A.
55241	3/A.M. Freeman, D.*
34451	A.C.2. Freedman, S.
23027	A.C.2. Fedderman, J.
11950	A.M. Fraiz.
402943	1/Pte. Goldman, B.
22013	2/A.M. Goldman, S.
44223	Cpl./Clerk Gallop, L.
75780	1/Pte. Glazier, D.
56619	1/A.M. Goodman, P.
53455	2/A.M. Goldfarb, H.
61156	2/Pte. Greenfield, P. H.
77711	2/A.M. Greenberg, M.
53022	2/Pte. Goldstein, M.
50522	2/Pte. Goldstein, D.
144195	3/A.M. Gordon, B.
38850	2/Pte. Goodstein, B.
37129	1/A.M. Greenleaf, I.
112387	3/A.M. Glazer, L.
50709	2/Clerk Goldstein, S.
79200	3/A.M. Green, H.
126118	2/Pte. Glazier, H.
60337	2/Pte. Goldberg, H.
32263	2/A.M. Goldberg, L.
19266	1/A.M. Goodman, J. S.
23724	1/A.M. Goodman, E.
43561	2/A.M. Goldstein, D.
57822	3/A.M. Goldberg, D.
89619	2/A.M. Ginsberg, H.
93012	2/A.M. Goodfield, H.
64018	2/A.M. Grad, H.
103302	2/A.M. Grafinski, M.
101138	3/A.M. Gwin, H.
49072	2/A.M. Gilston, J.
61558	3/A.M. Goldman, B.
25672	2/A.M. Gudelsky, S. G
31523	2/A.M. Goodman, H.
2230	2/A.M. Gilbert, H.
289065	2/A.M. Gluckstein, M.
16821	2/A.M. Glass, G.
4503	Sgt. Goldberg, D.
33596	Pte. Gershon, A.
58223	2/A.M. Goldsmith, R.
22126	2/A.M. Gamp, S.
29269	2/A.M. Godlove.
17972	2/A.M. Gold, H.
B/32439	2/A.M. Goldberg, L.
22121	2/A.M. Goodman, A.
4209	Cpl. Geller, H.
82045	2/A.M. Greenspan, J.
41120	3/A.M. Gozlan, M.
93622	1/A.C. Greenberg, J.
48318	L./A. Goodman, L.
36871	2/A.C. Goldinsky, S.
100035	1/Pte. Goldenberg, T.
235651	2/A.M. Gabriel, S.
10452	Pte. Gold, J.
16337	1/A.M. Goodman, H.
10662	2/A.M. Griver, M.
7891	2/A.M. Gulland, W.
20935	2/A.M. Gurney, W.
34346	2/A.M. Goldwater, W.
18116	2/A.M. Gemblitski, S.
35427	2/A.M. Goodman, S.
17858	2/A.M. Gilberg, S.
43978	2/A.M. Glazer, S.
18265	2/A.M. Golding, S. R.
4209	Cpl. Geller, H.*
16561	2/A.M. Green, S. C.
22013	2/A.M. Goldman, S.
20944	2/A.M. Goldman, M.
19184	2/A.M. Goldberg, J.
9729	2/A.M. Gehr, G.
31343	2/A.M. Gilman, P.
19476	2/A.M. Goldberg, B. S.
22069	2/Pte. Goldstein, H.

Royal Air Force.—*Continued.*

79638	2/Pte. GREENBAUM, M.	31679	2/A.M. GOLDSTONE, I.	218987	2/A.M. HARRIS, D.		
111377	2/A.M. GLAZIER, S.	84033	2/A.M. GOODSTONE, M.	22998	1/Pte. HARRIS, W.		
75770	2/Pte. GOULD, L.	22121	2/A.M. GOODMAN, A.	103440	2/A.M. HYMAN, M.		
40391	2/A.M. GOODAK, L.	11836	2/A.M. GOLDSTEIN, M.	20958	Sgt./Mech. HYMANS, M.		
53833	A./Cpl. GAMBINSKY, W.	84033	3/A.M. GOODSTEIN, M.	64839	Pte. HARING, D.		
125953	2/Pte. GATOFF, N.	82215	2/A.M. GALINISKY, H.	45286	2/A.M. HOLMAN, W.		
120334	1/Pte. GREENBERG, R.	602404	2/A.M. GOLDSTEIN, M.	68386	2/A.M. HALFLICK, H.		
35016	1/A.M. GLEITZMAN, M.	801380	3/A.M. GRIVER, S. D.	53319	3/A.M. HYAMS, S.		
3927	3/A.M. GOODMAN, M.	53558	Pte. GREEN, M.	34978	2/A.M. HUFTEL, W.		
113641	2/A.M. GLICK, J.	99575	3/A.M. GOODMAN, J.	82001	2/A.M. HARRIS, K.		
92656	2/A.M. GOLDSTONE, A.	16821	2/A.M. GITTLESON, J. B.	17876	2/A.M. HAMBURY, A. E		
33981	1/A.M. GREGOR, B.	36516	2/A.M. GOLDMAN, I.	23441	2/A.M. HARRIS, W.		
98639	2/A.M. GOLDBERG, H.	44898	2/A.M. GOODMAN, H.	289728	2/Pte. HORKINS, S.		
104894	2/A.M. GLAZER, R.	59373	3/A.M. GREENBLATT, R. J.	290530	2/Pte. HARRIS, J.		
81596	2/A.M. GOODSTONE, A.	06029	1/A.M. GOLDSTEIN, S.	305462	2/Pte. HARRIS, J.		
54015	1/A.M. GOLDSTEIN, M.	78641	2/A.M. GRIEW, S.	85929	1/A.M. HARRIS, C. L.		
83076	3/A.M. GREENBAUM, J.	75770	A.M. GOULD, L.		Pte. HERTZFIELD, G. C.		
42718	3/A.M. GREEN, M.	72591	Pte. GOLDBERG, L.	104910	L./Cpl. HYMAN, C.		
108855	2/A.M. GOLDENBERG, T.	456880	3/A.M. GLUCK, S.	45781	2/A.M. HARRIS, H.		
62860	2/A.M. GOLDSTONE, M.	36897	2/A.M. GREENBERG, P.	54893	1/A.M. HARRIS, G.		
36516	Cpl. GOLDMAN, I.	98175	3/A.M. GEFFERT, W.		2/A.M. HERBERT, L. P.		
55118	3/A.M. GOLDBERG, H.	42599	Cpl. GOLDWATER, S. H.	20957	2/A.M. HARRIS.		
11961	2/A.M. GOLDBERG, D.	48137	Pte. GARCIA, P.	24089	2/A.M. HARRIS, L. M.		
75888	2/A.M. GILSTON, T.	107938	2/A.M. GARBLATT, J.	37841	1/A.M. HAMBERGER, J.		
204151	3/A.M. GORDON, G.	385939	Pte. GATTOFF, A.	34768	2/A.M. HERMAN, L.		
122141	3/A.M. GREENBLATT, S.	19326	1/A.M. GARCIA, H.	33079	1/A.M. HARRIS.		
421998	3/A.M. GORDON, E.	60701	2/A.M. GOLDENBERG, M.		Pte. HATFORD, C. F.		
131162	2/Pte. GORDON, E.	85468	2/A.M. GOODMAN, A.	54026	2/A.M. HUFFEL.		
19326	1/A.M. GARCIA, H.	245628	2/A.M. GLASS, P.	30847	Clerk HYAMS, A.		
61640	2/A.M. GOTZ, S.	91530	2/A.M. GOLDRING, S.	116221	2/Pte. HARRIS, B.		
31679	3/A.M. GOLDSTONE, J.	112718	3/A.M. GREEN, M.	92740	2/A.M. HARRIS, L.		
53558	3/A.M. GREEN, M.	59184	2/A.M. GOLD, R.	185116	Pte. HOFFMAN, S.		
303461	2/Pte. GOODMAN, R.	64019	3/A.M. GOLDHILL, B.M.	41721	2/A.M. HART, C.		
29204	1/A.M. GARBUTT.		2/A.M. GREYSTONE, L.	46329	1/A.M. HARRISON, H.		
406880	3/A.M. GLUCK.	148753	A.M. GASSON, M.	18980	1/A.M. HOUPT, E.		
87765	2/A.M. GRIVER, S. C.	309591	2/A.M. GROSS, D.	37361	2/A.M. HARRIS, H.		
84584	Cadet GREENBERG, M.	81596	2/A.M. GOODSTONE, J.	54662	2/A.M. HAROLD, J.		
17146	Cadet GOLDSMITH, I.	20218	2/A.M. GINSBERG, G.	19203	Cpl. HOKOIS, M.		
81940	Cadet GORDON, V.	93847	2/A.M. GOLDBONE, S.	69185	3/A.M. HARRIS, F.		
35016	1/A.M. GLITZMAN, J.	62353	2/A.M. GELDMAN, M.	52146	2/A.M. HORSEMAN, M. E.		
36871	2/A.M. GOLDINSKY, J.	Z/65887	Sig. GILBERT, I.	53556	3/A.M. HEKT, H. T.		
56840	2/A.M. GERALD, M.	32389	A.C.2. GOLDHILL, S.	93488	2/A.M. HANN, B.		
88104	2/A.M. GLASS, P.	19266	Pte. GOODMAN, J. S.	109170	2/A.M. HYAMS.		
58287	2/A.M. GOLDSHACKEN, J. L.	17444	A.C.2. GOLDSMITH, S.	34971	2/A.M. HATTER, D.		
		108835	Pte. GOLDENBERG, 1/L.A. GOODMAN, E.	2617	2/A.M. HIELMAN, H.		
23562	A.M. GOODMAN, J. J.			41270	2/A.M. HEFTEL, D.		
43317	2/A.M. GREEN, H.	18977	2/A.M. HARRISON, H.	67356	2/A.M. HAYMAN, J.		
75192	2/A.M. GOLD, M.	54740	3/A.M. HYAMS, N.	43819	Sgt. HENRY, N.		
79526	2/A.M. GOLDSMITH, L.	22523	2/A.M. HARRIS, S.	91566	2/A.M. HIRSHOWITZ, J. L.		
300845	3/A.M. GRIEW, S.	34215	2/A.M. HARRIS, W.				
38850	2/A.M. GOODSTEIN, B.	12747	1/A.M. HOROWITZ, N.	50319	2/A.M. HARRIS, S.		
55426	2/A.M. GOULDSTON, M.	31685	2/A.M. HOFSTEIN, M.	98248	2/A.M. HARRIS, N.		
32870	2/A.M. GOLDSTEIN, D.	17133	2/A.M. HARRIS, H. I.	111849	2/A.M. HARRIS, I.		
55426	1/Pte. GOLDSTEIN, M.	36586	2/A.M. HARRIS, S.	22523	2/A.M. HARRIS, I.		
230208	1/Pte. GOLDMAN, J.	93448	2/A.M. HANN, B. E.	67986	2/A.M. HARRIS, A. J.		
125475	1/A.M. GORDON, J.	224618	2/Clerk HART, E. J.	64839	3/A.M. HARING, D.		
31697	2/A.M. GAMP, J.	20131	1/A.M. HARRIS, H.	33588	2/A.M. HILSON, B.		

Royal Air Force.—*Continued.*

34184	A/Cpl. HART, M.	90159	2/A.M. ISAACS, V.	107938	2/A.M. JACBUTT, J.
55807	2/A.M. HEYMAN, N. B.*	53575	3/A.M. ISAACS, S.	81675	3/A.M. JACOBS, S.
30849	A/Cpl. HYAMS, A. A.	79380	2/A.M. ISAACS, M.	68599	3/A.M. JOSEPHS.
37841	F/Sgt. HAMBERGER, J.	251691	3/A.M. ISAACS, S.	35887	2/A.M. JACOBS, W. J.
108408	3/A.M. HART, A.	85276	Cadet ISAACS, J. B.	276441	2/Pte. JACOBS, C. A.
34978	3/A.M. HARRIS, N.	137409	Cadet ISAACS, M. A.	741956	2/A.M. JACOBS, J. L.
106904	2/A.M. HASSONOVITCH, J.	175444	Cadet ISAACS, L. G. H.	106563	2/A.M. JACOBS, E.
		82066	2/A.M. ISRAEL, S.		Rect. JACOBS, N.
		22371	1/A.M. ISAACS, L. J.	237732	3/A.M. JOSEPHS, F.
88227	2/A.M. HARRINGMAN, M.	50242	1/A.M. ISAACS, L.	763427	Cadet JOSEPH, B.
112035	3/A.M. HERTZBERG, J.	219856	1/Pte. ISAACS, H.	491125	2/A.M. JOSEPHS, E.
35359	2/A.M. HYMAN, J.	56267	2/A.M. ISAACS, I.	145797	Pte. JACOBS, A.
34184	Cpl. HART, M.	22371	2/A.M. ISAACS, L. J.	55926	2/A.M. JACOBS, S.
12876	Q.A.M. HAMBERG, A. E.	63330	2/A.M. ISAACS, J. C.	37861	2/A.M. JOSEPH, M.
20957	Cpl. HARRIS, I.	59267	2/Pte. ISAACS, I.	35778	2/A.M. JACOBS, W. J.
29943	2/A.M. HARRIS, T.	38189	2/A.M. IVERDFOFF, L.	50148	2/A.M. JACOBS, H.
59063	2/A.M. HANSER, A.	125939	2/A.M. ISAACS, F.	75867	2/A.M. JOSEPH, L.
55053	2/A.M. HART, C.	22371	2/A.M. ISAACS, J.	336871	A.M. JACOBS, A.
660481	2/A.M. HUBBERSGILT, I.	10786	2/A.M. ISAACS, A.	94718	3/A.M. JACOBS, M.
91466	3/A.M. HARRIS, H.	83515	3/A.M. ISAACS, E.	93823	2/A.M. JACOBS, J. L.
32028	A.M. HARRIS, J.		ISRAEL, B.	41147	2/A.M. JACOBS, L.
159331	2/A.M. HYAMS, J.		ISAACSON, A. C.	69435	3/A.M. JONAS, D. G.
147798	Pte. HASSMAN, L.		ISAACS, P.	78470	2/A.M. JONES, A. C.
139909	3/A.M. HEMMING, C.	15619	2/A.M. JOSEPH, A. D.	80222	2/A.M. JACOBS, M.
59276	Cadet HARTMAN, J.	22719	2/A.M. JOEL, A.	92823	2/A.M. JACOBS, J.
18977	1/A.M. HARRISON, H.	29136	2/A.M. JACOBS, H.	98133	3/A.M. JOSEPH, D.
40828	2/A.M. HOFFMAN, J.	11219	F/Sgt. JACOBS, J. J.	88846	3/A.M. JACOBS, J.
8841	Pte. HART.	24757	2/A.M. JACOBY, E. H.		Fl.Sgt. JACOBS, J. (M.M.)
	Seaman HYMAN, I.	23531	2/A.M. JOSEPHSON, H.	132177	2/A.M. JOSEPH, E.
23727	A.C. HYMAN, M.	37979	2/A.M. JAY, A. S.	41865	2/A.M. JOSEPH, M.
	A.C.2. HARRIS, L. A.	7072	Pte. JACOB, M. D.	54662	2/A.M. JOSEPH, H.
9759	P.O. HYAMS, I.	50414	2/Pte. JACOBS, H.	58936	2/A.M. JOSEPH, I.
1945	P.O. HELLER, L.	57758	2/Pte. JACOBS, J.	145797	3/A.M. JACOBS, A.
	A.B. HART, E. J.	19609	1/A.M. JACOBSON, J.		2/A.M. JACKSON, A.
	A.C.2. HYMES, D.	91561	2/A.M. JACOBS, S.	33374	A.C.2 JACOBS, J.
	Petty O. HASSAN, S.	38180	2/A.M. JOSEPHS, S.	26635	A.M.1 JOSEPH, H.
15182	2/A.M. ISAACS, G.	29637	1/A.M. JAFFE, L. H.		A.C.2 JACOBS, F.
17744	2/A.M. ISRAEL, J.	277389	1/A.M. JORDON, L. M.		O/S.3 JACOBS, J.
11853	2/A.M. ISAACS, C.	69952	3/A.M. JACOBS, L.		Pte. JACOBSON, L.
13103	2/A.M. ISAACS, C.	122135	3/A.M. JACOBS, A.	38948	2/A.M. KOLSKI, J. H.
13068	2/A.M. ISAACS, C.	198711	2/Pte. JOSEPH, A.	24120	2/A.M. KIRSCH, I.
31456	2/A.M. ISAACS, H.		Pte. JAPHA, H.	303074	2/A.C. KARET, G. P.
45287	2/A.M. ISAACS, B.	20766	2/A.M. JACOBOVITCH, G.	77486	1/A.M. KENT, M.
1310	1/A.M. ISAACS, C.	107753	Pte. JACOBS, A.	403733	Pte. KENDLE, G.
18267	Cpl./Clk. INFIELD, H.	80349	Pte. JOSEPH, H.	38236	2/A.M. KRISMAN, L.
81854	2/Pte. ISAACS, M.	51189	1/A.C. JACOBS, S.	16526	2/A.M. KARET, S.
51989	1/Pte. ISAACS, D.	115491	Pte. JOEL, L.	23819	2/A.M. KOSTER, B.
50119	2/A.M. ISAACS, S.	80458	2/A.M. JACOBS, J.	20141	2/A.M. KONSKIER, H.
107807	2/Pte. ISAACS, B.	77677	2/A.M. JACOBS, D.	7221	1/A.M. KORN, S.
64540	3/A.M. ISAACS, G.	27957	Pte. JACOBS, S.	7542	Sgt. KLEIN, P.
B/41106	2/A.M. ISENSTONE, I.	62757	1/A.M. JACOBS, G.	16877	2/A.M. KOSKI, P.
23425	2/A.M. ISRAEL, J.	36691	2/A.M. JARTSKY, J.	17363	2/A.M. KEMPNER, A.
37919	2/A.M. ISENBERG, M. H.		2/Pte. JAFFE, M.	40849	2/A.M. KING, J.
106295	Pte. ISAACS, H.			57136	Clk. KAZENELLENBOGEN, H. L.
40679	2/A.M. ISAACS, M.	252563	Pte. JACOBS,		
217286	2/A.C. ISAACS, L.	54662	2/A.M. JOSEPH, H.	23433	Cpl.Mech. KUPLAN, A.
87245	3/A.M. ISAACS, J.	53448	2/A.M. JOSEPH, N.	52076	1/Pte. KAHL, R.
305143	3/A.M. ISRAEL, A.	486293	3/A.M. JAYES, J.	43695	2/A.M. KORITSKY, J.

Royal Air Force.—*Continued.*

17870	1/Pte. KLIENFIELD, D.	11582	2/A.M. LIBERMAN, W.	36517	2/A.M. LEVY, J.
59297	2/A.M. KLIMAN.	31143	2/A.M. LEWIS, J.	37301	2/A.M. LIBENTAL, D.
44566	2/A.M. KLEMIN, J. H.	130959	2/A.M. LEWIS, L.	31647	2/A.M. LINNEWIEL, J.
47753	2/A.M. KRAMER, L. E.	23818	1/A.M. LEWIS, S.	59209	2/A.M. LUBINSKY, M.
50750	2/A.M. KRAM, J.	4166	F./Sgt. LEVIN, E. M.	33555	1/Pte. LUBINSKY, J.*
44357	2/A.M. KANAPKIN, J. S.	353761	2/Pte. LANGUI, M.	49108	2/A.M. LEARNER.
44107	2/A.M. KAISER, S.	27852	1/A.M. LEVY, P.	45812	2/A.M. LEVY, J.
44675	A.M. KAPLANSKY, W. M.*	52372	1/Pte. LEVY, J.	26599	1/A.M. LEWIS, B.
50246	2/A.M. KUTCHINSKY, S.	82514	1/Pte. LEIBSHUTZ, J.	51867	2/A.M. LEVY, L.
59160	2/A.M. KLOSS. L.	20773	1/Pte. LEVI, M.	20775	Cpl. LEWIS.
129391	2/Pte. KARBRITZ, L.	26815	1/A.M. LEWIS, L.	1009	2/A.M. LEVY, S.
130880	3/A.M. KATZNELSON, G.	47696	3/A.M. LEVEY, A.	11101	2/A.M. LEWIS, P. H.
164407	3/A.M. KRAMRISH, E.	20762	2/Pte. LYONS, J.	29962	2/A.M. LEWIS, J.
119489	2/A.M. KISSIN, S.	53147	3/A.M. LOUFER, M. H.	16974	2/A.M. LAZARUS.
7543	1/A.M. KEENE, A.	126119	2/Pte. LEWIS, M.	18388	2/A.M. LEVENE, J.
20763	1/A.M. KLEIN, W.	67377	3/A.M. LEVY, D.	34751	2/A.M. LANDA, H.
40634	2/A.M. KELMANSON, A.		C./Mech. LONSDALE, R.	8056	2/A.M. LENT.
35714	2/A.M. KRUGER, H.	37113	Cpl./Clk. LEVY, E. H.*	25497	Pte. LACKMAKER.
109416	3/A.M. KANTRY, P.	67972	1/A.M. LIBERMAN, A. M.	28499	Pte. LAZARUS, M.
108984	2/A.M. KREISMAN, W.	26044	2/A.M. LEVY, J.	2401	3/A.M. LAZARUS, N.
91532	2/A.M. KEWRICK, R.	50397	2/A.M. LEVY, S.	64854	2/A.M. LEVEY, M. D.
264376	2/Pte. KATZ, R.	23818	Sgt. LEWIS, S.	130431	2/A.M. LEVENE, T.*
139645	3/A.M. KAY, M.	106125	1/Pte. LIVINGSTONE, D.	32007	1/A.M. LABOVITCH.
102345	2/A.M. KING, S.	75389	3/A.M. LESSAR, P.	81722	2/A.C. LOBENZ, A. L.
93328	2/A.M. KAPLAN, M.	61015	1/Pte. LOCKITCH, M.	43672	2/A.M. LEVY, E.
137916	Cadet KLEINOT, J. H.	84938	2/A.M. LUMBARTZ, C.	273991	3/A.M. LEVY, I.
165283	Pte. KOFFLER, L.	50373	2/A.M. LUX, A.	56479	Pte. LYONS, A.
82001	2/A.M. KUVAL, H.	17636	2/A.M. LEVY, C.	34767	Pte. LEVY, W.
107945	2/A.M. KRISMAN, N.	37468	2/A.M. LEVIN, R.	124251	2/A.M. LEVIN, J.
47362	2/A.M. KAAS, I.	55442	3/A.M. LION, L. D.	66264	3/A.M. LEDCRIMAN, E.
43695	2/A.M. KONTZSKY, J.	30188	2/A.M. LIGHTER, J.	43914	A.M. LAZARUS, L.
27202	2/A.M. KUTNER, E.	50534	2/A.M. LEVY, L.	52407	1/A.M. LEVY, W.
51916	2/A.M. KAPLAN, A.	43979	2/A.M. LITTLESTONE, A.	85699	2/A.M. LEVY, S.
109991	2/A.M. KRESNER, H. R.	55834	3/A.M. LEVY, J.	48217	2/A.M. LEVY, F.
108229	2/A.M. KILBANOV, J.	19178	2/A.M. LESS, R.	32227	2/A.M. LEVENE, M.
35714	2/A.M. KREEGER, H.	81894	Pte. LYONS, B.	38626	2/A.M. LEITZ, D.
33558	2/A.M. KOSKY, W.	78227	2/A.M. LOOKEV, J.		Cadet LEWIN, S.
7164	1/A.M. KEAN, J....	P/13497	2/A.M. LAVETSKY, H.	52621	Cadet LEVY, M.
97087	2/A.M. KUTNER, M.	56844	2/A.M. LEWIS, A. M.	281482	1/A.M. LEVINE, H.
95285	2/A.M. KERKOFF, N.	39609	2/A.M. LEWIS, B. A.	18388	2/A.M. LEVENE, J.
89198	2/A.M. KIEFF, J.	98128	2/A.M. LEVY, A.*	29962	2/A.M. LEWIS, J.
33908	2/A.M. KASMER, N.	34519	1/A.M. LEVY, E.	17743	1/A.M. LEWIS, C. J.
66555	2/A.M. KOOLOSKI.	111288	3/A.M. LEVI, H. S.	56072	2/A.M. LEVY, E.
64915	2/A.M. KOSILOV, S.	17427	2/A.M. LAZARUS, S.	79532	2/A.M. LAZARUS, I.
19375	2/A.M. KORN, M.	91566	2/A.M. LEWIS, J.	59589	2/A.M. LEVY, M.
53074	2/A.M. KAUFMAN, L.	40829	3/A.M. LEWIS, C.	58883	3/A.M. LYONS, I. A.
62497	2/A.M. KATZORN, N.	295351	3/A.M. LEVY, A.	4679	A.M. LEE, M.
64915	2/A.M. KASILOVITCH, S.	12955	Sgt.-Maj. LEVESON, W.	33117	2/A.M. LEVY,
33866	2/A.M. KING, M.	121555	3/Clk. LEVINE, I.	33551	2/A.M. LEFAVITCH, H.
27303	2/A.M. KAHN, W.	33544	1/A.M. LIPMAN, E.	112574	2/A.M. LEVISON, J.
20763	2/A.M. KLEIN, W.	99528	3/A.M. LAZARUS, J.	148708	2/Pte. LEVI, J. A.
11224	2/A.M. KAMOFSKI, J.	111602	3/A.M. LEVY, C.	142940	2/Pte. LEWIN, H.
28079	3/A.M. KAYE,		Pte. LEVEY, L. C.	46147	3/A.M. LAVENSTEIN, S.
17743	2/A.M. LEWIS, G.		Pte. LASTICK, L.	31067	1/A.M. LEVINE, B.
5415	2/A.M. LEVY, P.	12294	Pte. LEVINE.	23397	2/A.M. LEVY, S. D.
16531	2/A.M. LEVY, B.	115026	Pte. LEVY, M.	63523	3/A.M. LANDSBERG, B.
7071	2/A.M. LAZARUS, E.	35340	2/A.M. LEVY, M.	56844	2/A.M. LEWIS, M.
		34767	2/A.M. LEVI, W.	35333	2/A.M. LANTWORTH, W.

Royal Air Force.—*Continued.*

24358	2/A.M. Leavy, L.
63310	2/A.M. Lipman, I.
59580	2/A.M. Leveson, A.
63310	2/A.M. Lipman, J.
65801	2/A.M. Levy, M.
75383	2/A.M. Levinson, H.
80756	2/A.M. Lubinsky, H. L.
86616	3/A.M. Levy, J.
61844	1/A.M. Leaman, S. J.
421998	A.M. Lewis, C.
108963	3/A.M. Lett, F.
124521	3/A.M. Levin, I.
77723	2/A.M. Livingstone, J.
35715	2/A.M. Levy, J.
32747	2/A.M. Levy, A.
33552	2/A.M. Legar, J.
293747	2/A.C. Levy, H.
7796	2/A.M. Levenson, D.
98128	3/A.M. Levy, A.
79532	3/A.M. Lazarus, S.
53216	2/A.M. Losberg, T.
52452	2/A.M. Levy, R.
112225	3/A.M. Lubin, M.
62076	2/A.M. Lurie, J.
41171	2/A.M. Lipman, E.
64002	2/A.M. Levinson, B.
17427	1/A.M. Lazarus, F.
45918	2/A.M. Lewis, E.
24016	1/A.M. Lazarus, H.
105921	3/A.M. Lewis.
39460	2/A.M. Leopold, B.
61844	1/A.M. Leaman, J.
33884	2/A.M. Lighter, M.
281482	3/A.M. Levine,
293747	Pte. Levy, H.
26857	2/A.M. Lisky, H.
67992	3/A.M. Liberman, J.
53216	2/A.M. Losberg, E.
33555	2/A.M. Lubinsky, J.
23397	2/A.M. Levy, S. D.
31331	2/A.M. Levenson, M.
65998	2/A.M. Levy, L.
75771	3/A.M. Logette.
22023	2/A.M. Lester, H.
33117	2/A.M. Levy, S.
23397	2/A.M. Levy, S.
62525	2/A.M. Levy, I.
93178	2/A.M. Lubin, J.
35715	2/A.M. Levy, J.
56483	2/A.M. Lacovsky, P.
7357	2/A.M. Lazarus, H.
26599	3/A.M. Lewis, R.
14444	2/A.M. Levy, J.
147748	3/A.M. Lewin, H.
26842	2/A.M. Lazarus, C.
32818	3/A.M. Lazarus, M.
111848	2/A.M. Lewis, L.
191965	2/A.M. Ligensky, S.
35414	2/A.M. Loofe, L.
17636	2/A.M. Levy, C.
30628	2/A.M. Labovitch, L.
36228	2/A.M. Lilleman, S.
7272	2/A.M. Leaman, S. I.
58559	2/A.M. Lewis, A.
	Fl.-Sgt. Levy, E. (M.S.M.).
20235	2/A.M. Lyons, A.
10529	3/A.M. Lewis.
71828	2/A.M. Lagerman, C.
8254	2/A.M. Leinstein, S.
33535	2/A.M. Labinsky, J.
84193	3/A.M. Lapin, M.
55834	3/A.M. Levy, J.
64854	3/A.M. Levy, M.
139679	Pte. Levin, A.
130869	3/A.M. Lloyd, R. J.
375435	2/A.M. Levison, H.
23444	A.C.1 Lazarus, H.
17456	Pte. Lyons, I.
30942	A.C.2 Lipman, H.
23101	A.C.2 Lewis, B.
18554	A.C.2 Levy, M.
22443	A.C.1 Levy, M.
55123	3/A.M. Marks, C.
7071	2/A.M. Mazerus, E.
43361	2/A.M. Mazzier, J.
63288	1/A.M. Morris, S.
282287	3/Clk. Miron, J.
159913	Boy Matchman, H.
290525	2/Pte. Morris, J.
293345	2/Pte. Maynard, A.
289352	3/A.M. Messing, M.
135251	2/Clk. Mendoza, E.
47495	Cpl./Clk. Marchant, M.
225739	Cpl. Mellor, F. D. M.
	Pte. Movel, J.
30019	2/A.M. Messias, S.
50356	Pte. Michelson, W.
75772	3/A.M. Mantus, J.
36185	2/A.M. Molofsky, N.
	1/A.M. Marks, J. S.
36914	2/A.M. Markson.
B/30845	2/A.M. Miller, J.
23404	2/A.M. Moss, C.
32754	2/A.M. Myers.
23881	2/A.M. Mendelsohn, H. G.
23856	Pte. Matz, A.
32847	3/A.M. Mason, M.
71100	Pte. Marks, B.
48126	2/A.M. Moss, J.
23001	2/A.M. Marks, D.
17871	2/A.M. Marks, A.
22997	2/A.M. Miller, H.
12140	2/A.M. Mendoza, H.
16966	1/A.M. Morris, A.
35411	2/A.M. Mindel, L.
40859	2/A.M. Marks, H.
48917	2/A.M. Mogilinsky, S.
59345	2/A.M. Magnus, J. I.
98847	2/Clk. Morgenstein, I.
78485	1/Pte. Myers, A.
37106	1/Pte. Mintz, E.
64536	1/Pte. Mendoza, S.
19643	1/Pte. Morris, H.
54681	3/A.M. Myers, A.
98986	3/A.M. Marks, J.
43913	2/Pte. Myers, M.
63309	2/Pte. Miller, J.
67947	2/A.M. Miller, C.
50366	3/A.M. Margolis, H.
51410	1/Pte. Marcovitch, C.
50331	1/A.M. Moses, C. S.
62435	2/A.M. Muscovitch, A.
66350	2/A.M. Michaels, I.
20913	1/A.M. Maizel, S.
50669	2/A.M. Moses, M.
82159	2/A.M. Musickensky, A.
48536	2/A.M. Marks, A. A.
82499	3/A.M. Myers, M.
407560	2/A.M. Milinsky, A.
97509	L./Cpl. Muscovitch, D.
109090	2/Pte. Mendels, L.
51913	1/A.M. Malinski, E.
100794	2/Pte. Myers, H.
52365	2/A.M. Myers, J.
24171	2/A.M. Michaels, H.
69023	3/A.M. Mendleowitz, A.
36466	2/A.M. Mendlesohn, S.
32431	2/A.M. Myers, M.
57075	3/A.M. Myron,
55954	2/A.M. Mandelbon,
10190	3/A.M. Marks, A.
p/21805	Cpl. Myers, L.
56015	2/A.M. Marks, D.
30039	1/A.M. Martin, L.
97173	2/A.M. Mather, G.
72576	Pte. Morris, H.
69565	2/A.M. Mitchaels, C.
644152	2/A.M. Michaels, J.
40228	2/A.M. Milevitch, H.
55152	2/A.M. Morris, E. M.
89799	2/A.M. Mendelbaum.
197979	Dvr. Mech. Magone, S.
46703	2/A.M. Malitzski, L.
43819	Sgt. Marcus, H.
91817	3/A.M. McQuillen.
60048	2/A.M. May, G.
7728	3/A.M. Michaels, L. L.
66861	2/A.M. Monell, A.
20913	1/A.M. Maizel, S.
9344	Pte. Mer, J.

Royal Air Force.—*Continued.*

37448	Pte. MAURITZ, A.	85058	3/A.M. NATHAN, A. A.	86594	3/A.M. PINKUS, B.
89839	2/A.M. MARKOVITCH, J.	76179	2/A.M. NATHAN, J.	MS/2961	Pte. POWELL, B.
147750	Pte. MEIZELS, N.	64564	2/A.M. NATHAN, H.	41833	2/Pte. PARK, S.
40597	2/A.M. MORRIS, M.	44745	2/A.M. NATHAN, W.	58672	2/A.M. POLLAK, J.
144943	3/A.M. MARKS, B.	75232	3/A.M. NIMEROSKY, L.	50428	2/A.M. PEARLSTONE, M.
51950	2/A.M. MILLER, B.	50356	Pte. NICHOLSON, D.	62922	2/A.M. PHILLIPS, M.
147658	3/A.M. MELETSKI, E.		Pte. NEWSTEIN, J.	69572	3/A.M. POLLOCK, H.
	Cadet MEDOFSKI, S.	5503	Cpl. NEWMAN, P.	56839	2/A.M. PRAGUE, A.
05007	A.M. MANNING, P. E.	8823	Pte. NICKLESBURG, S.	36512	2/A.M. PRICE, N.
39061	2/A.M. MUSCOVITCH, C.	34654	2/A.M. NEWTON, S. N.	87674	2/A.M. PATINSKY, H.
56918	2/A.M. MEIVOLSKY, L.	407615	3/A.M. NEWMAN.	41811	1/A.M. POSIMENSKY, A.
219528	A.C.2 MYERS, H.	38185	2/A.M. NEWMAN.	105435	3/A.M. PROSHANSKY, H.
33554	3/A.M. MAYOVER, M.	147658	Pte. NORRISH, F. C.	281606	3/A.M. PHILLIPS, D.
214923	Sgt. MARKS, J. D.	275261	Pte. NEWMARK, I.	35511	1/A.M. PATEMAN.
90010	3/A.M. MILLER, H.	58873	Pte. NAGELKOP, I.	193710	3/A.M. PHILLIPS, P. J.
631521	2/A.M. MYERS, A.		3/A.M. NATHAN, N. S.		2/A.M. PEARL, A.
1922	2/A.M. MARKS, R.	79012	3/A.M. NATHAN.		Pte. POKIDILE, H.
67203	2/A.M. MAUDELIVITZ, A.	114672	3/A.M. NADOLNICH, H. J.		Pte. PORTNAY, J. Z.
104139	2/A.M. MYERS.	55725	2/A.M. NATHAN, S.	99766	Pte. POLLICK, J.
97066	2/A.M. MARKS, H.	52331	2/A.M. NATHAN, C.	27541	2/A.M. PALDERNASKI, S.
60429	2/A.M. MATTHEWS, A.	5725	2/A.M. NATHAN, S.	12144	Sgt./Clk. POSNER, B. B.
200013	Dvr. MENDELSOHN, M.	3669	1/A.M. NIELFIELD, A.	F/33460	2/A.M. PHILLIPS, G.
144943	3/A.M. MARKS,	79112	2/A.M. NATHAN, S.		2/A.M. PYKE, R. L.
265911	2/Pte. MARKS, P.	58489	2/A.M. NATHAN, N.	81513	2/A.M. PHILLIPS, S. S.
87070	3/A.M. MYERS, H.	122857	2/A.M. NEWMAN, L.	229683	Pte. PARKER, E.
58542	3/A.M. MEKELBERG, S.	12325	2/A.M. NAPTHALI, H.	64669	Pte. PAYNE, D.
91627	Cadet MILLER, J. J.	91532	2/A.M. NEWRICH, C.	147846	Clerk PRAG, L.
93093	Cadet MARKS, L. C.	56918	2/A.M. NIEWOLSKY,	27017	Pte. PELINSKY, N.
49801	Cadet MILNER, J.	64001	2/A.M. NATHAN, M.	129660	Pte. PEARLBERG, M.*
176585	Cadet MAGID, H. L.	82017	3/A.M. NELSON, J.	121381	L/Cpl. PERLMAN, M. C.
137809	Cadet MAR, S.	56484	2/A.M. NELMAN, L.	20188	1/A.M. PARKER, E. A.
166868	2/A.M. MORRIS, J.	12255	Pte. NEWMAN, L.	705	2/A.M. PRUSS, I.
33554	2/A.M. MARJOVER, M.	227263	Pte. NUNES-VAZ, I. W.	219948	1/A.M. PHILLIPS, M. M.
35360	2/A.M. MARKOVITCH, D.	125311	Obsvr. NAGUS, S.	213289	Pte. PHILLIPS, A.
68500	2/A.M. MICHAELS, A. J		A.M. NATKIEL, L.	59674	2/A.M. PADWELL, H.
104518	A.M. MENDESS, M.		Pte. NATHAN, C.	23077	Sgt. PRAAGH, S. V.
39061	2/A.M. MUSCOVITCH, C.	11219	2/A.M. OVERS, H.	136576	3/A.M. PADOLSKY, H.
103783	3/A.M. MAISELS, M. N.	34649	2/A.M. OLIVER, C.	50393	2/A.M. PEARL, B.
166868	2/A.M. MORRIS, J.	47495	2/A.M. OESTERMAN, I.	12932	2/A.M. PESKOFF, J.
32421	2/A.M. MYERS, M.	26715	Sgt. OVERS, H.	30367	2/A.M. PHILLIPS, L.
54435	2/A.M. MICHAELS, J.	88029	3/A.M. OSIAKOWSKI, I.	116448	3/A.M. POLLACK, J.
96542	Pte. MERSKY, A.	36465	2/A.M. OPPENHEIM, H.	343040	3/A.M. PASS, J.
69850	A.M. MICHAELSON, A.	95154	1/A.M. OBRART, I.	280663	2/Pte. PARLOW, L.
101188	2/A.M. MOSS,	64550	1/A.M. OSOSKI, H.	34250	1/A.M. PEARL, I.
279547	Pte. MARTIN, W.	43930	2/A.M. OPPENHEIM, J.	130905	3/A.M. POREDLEY, W.
196841	3/A.M. MILLER, J.	64010	2/A.M. OFSTEIN, J.	113950	3/A.M. PHILLIPS, M.
	A.C.M.1 MELLER, F. D	54424	2/A.M. OLIVER, S.		Cadet PEARCE, H.
23047	A.C.1 MYERS, H.	31685	1/A.M. OFSTEIN, M.	14686	Cadet POPPER, D. H.
L/3/2231	A.B. MARAPHIA, J.	49354	2/A.M. OLSWANG, H. E.	64806	2/A.M. PRAGER, H.
	Pte. MARCHANT, M.		Pte. OLIPHANT, O. I.	26531	2/A.M. PAUL, B.
	Pte. MARCHANT, M.	44667	2/A.M. PIZER, H.	59185	2/A.M. POLINSKI, E.
	A.M. MENDOZA, M.	16105	2/A.M. PYSER, M. G.	37965	Cpl. PHILLIPS, J.
17927	2/A.M. NATHAN, I.	35511	2/A.M. PATEMAN, A.	68461	3/A.M. PINKUS, B.
23591	2/A.M. NEWDALL, M.	B/41709	2/A.M. PHILLIPS, S.	50380	2/A.M. PHILLIPS, S.
1291661	Pte. NIMAN, H.	19385	2/A.M. POSNER, N.	224866	Pte. POLLOCK, L. L.
79510	1/Pte. NORDEN, C.	31459	1/A.M. PHILLIPS, H.	49295	Cpl. PENSO, R.
22372	1/A.M. NATHAN, A.	45776	3/A.M. PLOTZKER, J.	56839	2/A.M. PRAGELL, A.
				93756	2/A.M. PHILLIPS, L.

35

Royal Air Force.—*Continued.*

44349	2/A.M. POLINSKY, J.	22901	2/A.M. RAYMOND.	31696	2/A.M. STEINGOLD, B.
72706	Pte. PROVIDLE, L.		Cpl. RABINOVITCH, I. J.	47624	2/A.M. SOLOMONS, H.
75836	3/A.M. PEREZ, R.	132547	2/A.M. ROSS, H.	29919	1/A.M. SCHNEIDERS, A.*
113675	3/A.M. PEARCE, S.	57559	Sgt. REINISH, H.	35129	2/Pte. SMITH, W. T.
84005	3/A.M. PARK, I.	38459	2/A.M. RACK, A.	22017	1/A.M. SAFFER, S.
493474	2/A.M. PEARLSTEIN, H.	27203	A/Cpl. ROASE, N.	93312	2/A.M. SILVER, B. B.
1881	1/A.M. PARRUS, P.	63311	2/A.M. ROSENBLOOM, B.	45691	2/A.M. SMITH, C.
64500	2/A.M. PRIMHACK, N.	114058	2/A.M. RUBINSTEIN, J.	100708	2/Pte. SCHWEITZER, L.
2364	2/A.M. PELL, J. C.		2/A.M. RAPHAEL, A.	38797	1/A.M. SALMON, J.
91967	2/A.M. PLOWSKY, H.	495830	3/A.M. RUSLANDER, H.	129677	2/Pte. SOLOMON, D.
331702	A.C.2 PEBURG, S.	109272	3/A.M. RUBINSTEIN, J.	23030	1/Pte. STONEFIELD, I.
91533	2/A.M. PEARLMAN, A.	47540	2/A.M. ROSENBLOOM, N.	98938	1/Pte. SCHNEIDER, H.
85897	2/A.M. PALKOWSKI,	111314	1/Pte. ROSENBERG, J.	107001	2/Pte. SILVERMAN, L.
84005	3/A.M. PARK, I.	52491	2/A.M. ROSE, H.	118340	2/Pte. SIMMONS, I. J.
37287	2/A.M. PLOTKIN, K.	35630	2/A.M. RABINOVITCH, E.	82002	2/Pte. SIMONS, L.
41313	2/A.M. PHILLIPS, H. I.		Cadet ROWE, F.	93633	1/Pte. SMITH, S.
66664	Cpl. PHILLIPS, G.	84603	Cadet ROBINSTONE, N.	79231	3/Clk. SHUBSACHS, A. D.
218274	Pte. PRAGOFF, J.	206138	Cadet RAPHAEL, A.	57859	2/Pte. SIRENSTEIN, S.
18881	Pte. PAUS, E.	137816	Cadet ROBINSON, P.	23653	Cpl. SIMONS, S.
			2/A.M. ROBINSON, A.	106936	3/A.M. SEFF, A.
19543	A.M.1 PHILLIPS, S.	36127	2/A.M. ROSENBERG, M.	69889	1/Pte. SIMONS, B.
35575	A.C.2 PHILLIPS, S.	121296	3/A.M. ROWLANDS, E. A.	90788	2/A.M. SILVERMAN, S.
	Pte. POPPER, D.			109950	1/Pte. SAMUELS, R.
24308	2/A.M. RUBENS, L.	80773	A.M. ROCHMAN,	37725	2/A.M. SAUNDERS, M. W.
11907	1/A.M. ROMOFF, H.	87215	2/A.M. RABIN, S.		
11906	1/A.M. ROSEN, L.	383279	Pte. RUSSELL, R.		Pte. SELTZER, M. B.
31672	2/A.M. ROSEN, A.	23898	2/A.M. ROSENBLAM, S.		Pte. SCHMUKLER, M.
16276	2/A.M. RUBENSTEIN, J.	13455	2/A.M. ROSENBERG, L.	13604	Pte. SILVER, L.
42247	2/A.M. ROSENBERG, W.	12513	2/A.M. ROGOFF, P.	67912	Pte. SOLOMONS, R.
36039	2/A.M. RYNER, J.		2/A.M. ROSKIN, E.	47152	2/A.M. SLOMSON, J.
24090	2/A.M. ROSENBAUM, H.	19389	2/A.M. RUEBENSON, S.	27157	2/A.M. SAFFAR, A.
53831	2/A.M. RAPPORT, H.	59373	2/A.M. ROTHSCHILD, B.	24253	2/A.M. SMALINSKY, J.
67291	1/Pte. ROSENTHAL, A.	35398	2/A.M. ROSENBERG, I.	45617	2/A.M. SIMON, E.
19813	Pte. RICHMAN, W.	44021	2/A.M. ROSENTHAL, A.	39215	1/A.C. SOLOMON, H. A.
81738	2/Pte. ROSENBAUM, S.	78497	2/A.M. ROSENBERG, R.	20153	2/A.M. SILVER, M.
65209	3/A.M. ROSE, H.	13384	3/A.M. REUBEN, N.	43275	2/A.M. SNIPPER, M.
94972	3/A.M. RUDOFSKI, E.	14859	2/Pte. RICHMAN, S.	P/22280	2/A.M. SIMONS, E.
35511	2/A.M. RITEMAN, A.	62297	2/Pte. ROBINSON, A.	46398	2/A.M. SADKIE, J.
44340	2/A.M. REINSTEIN, L.	111314	2/A.M. ROSENBERG, I.	10302	Pte. SOMERS, S.
57855	3/A.M. ROZELAAR, A.	36029	3/A.M. RYNER, J.	27858	2/A.M. STOMACHIEN.
95034	3/A.M. ROSEN, D. M.	80422	Cadet ROWE, F.	80232	Pte. SAGER, C.
101037	3/A.M. ROSEWOOD, I.	80773	3/A.M. RATHMAN,	16346	2/A.M. SAGER, A.
P/269506	3/A.M. ROSENBERG, J.	83047	2/A.M. ROTHBERG, W. L.	130074	3/A.M. SHONFELD, M.
89628	2/A.M. ROSEN, S.				2/A.M. SOLOMON, L. B.
31495	2/A.M. ROSENBLOOM, M.	78497	2/A.M. ROSENBERG, L.	56040	2/A.M. SULMAN, M.
124365	3/A.M. ROSENTHAL, J. J.	100941	2/A.M. REUBEN, M.	72880	3/A.M. SAVITCH, H.
	Cpl. RAPPOPORT, J. A.		Cadet ROSENTHAL, S.		Cpl. SARNER, A.
	Pte. ROTH, J. A.		A.C.2 RANDOLPH, E. F.	52540	2/A.M. SCHWARCENBERG, M.
	Pte. ROSEN, H.	32730	A.C.2 RICHMAN, I.		
117540	Pte. ROSENBLOOM, M. R.		A.C. ROSENTHAL, E.	129763	Cpl. SOLOMON, D.
143262	Pte. RENOVITCH, D.	17302	2/A.M. SHIMBERG, W.	88285	2/A.C. STEBBINGS, I.
59174	2/A.M. ROSENBERG, L.	27452	2/A.M. SAMUELS, J.	63502	Cpl. STERNHEIM, A.
42513	2/A.M. ROGOFF, P.	7220	1/A.M. STONEFIELD, G.	37161	Pte. SOLOMON, J.
43757	2/A.M. RAKUSEN, C.	45033	2/A.M. SADKIE, B.	419985	Dvr. SIMMONS, J.
24009	1/A.M. ROSENBAUM, J. B.	22304	2/A.M. STONE, M.	280714	A./Sgt. SYLVESTON, I.
22212	2/A.M. ROSENGRANT, M.	20156	2/A.M. SYDNEY, P.	77228	2/A.M. SCHORNHEIM, S.
36084	1/A.M. ROSENBAUM, V.	19024	2/A.M. SYMONS, L.		2/A.M. SHEERE, N.
83118	3/A.M. ROSS, W. A.	31331	2/A.M. SEVENSON, M.	32089	2/A.M. SIMONS, H.

Royal Air Force.—*Continued.*

19017	A.M. SMOLINSKY, S. D.	
31434	2/A.M. STEIN, M.	
375739	2/A.M. SOLWAY, J.	
52562	2/A.M. SMOLENSKI, H. W.	
50658	2/A.M. STOCKMAN, G.	
53202	2/A.M. SEGELL, A.	
P/204251	3/A.M. STRELITZ, E.	
54873	2/A.M. SAUNDERS, H.	
56040	2/A.M. SELMAN, M.	
49060	3/A.M. SELNER, L.	
93443	2/A.M. SOLOMON, P. S.	
54863	2/A.M. SOLOMONS, J.*	
78614	2/A.M. STEINBERG, A.	
23664	2/A.M. SILVERMAN, M.	
36980	Pte. STONE, D.	
53267	2/A.M. SUGARMAN, S.	
138320	2/Pte. SHAER, H.	
40348	2/A.M. STEYNBERG, B.	
282216	2/A.M. SAPIER.	
Z/461	2/A.M. STIERI, E.	
Z/144	F/Sgt. SOLOMONS, A. L.	
75729	1/A.M. SIMONS, G.	
214044	Sgt./Clk. SNAPPER, N. A.	
86052	Pte. SHURE, L.	
P/161275	1/A.M. SPIRE, V. B.	
131065	3/A.M. SAGAR, A.	
34313	3/A.M. SPERO, H.	
23661	Cpl. SABEL, J.	
131201	3/A.M. STONE, E.	
64501	2/A.M. SILVERBERG, R. H.	
40628	2/A.M. SILVERSTONE, L.	
712188	Pte. STERN, J. E.	
147916	3/A.M. SOBEL, S.	
22924	1/A.M. SHEERE, M.	
21775	2/A.M. SIDMAN, L.	
91089	3/A.M. SPELLMAN, S.	
89425	Cadet SHULMAN, M. J.	
	Cadet SEGATER, L.	
175152	Cadet SAMUEL, A.	
20153	2/A.M. SILVER, M.	
31707	2/A.M. SAMPSON, V.	
33552	2/A.M. SEGAR, T.	
445991	3/A.M. STRINGER, M.	
59210	2/A.M. SMITH, H.	
69227	2/A.M. SIMONS, T.	
50796	2/A.M. SILVER, H.	
69407	2/A.M. SERASKY, I.	
93013	2/A.M. SCHNEIDER, A.	
53025	1/A.M. SAUNDERS, S. S.	
64817	2/A.M. SALAMON, L. L.	
64619	2/A.M. SADOFSYK, J.	
56483	2/A.M. SACOFSKY, P.	
54734	3/A.M. SCHEWEITZER, R.	
83011	3/A.M. SOBELL, D.	
50380	2/A.M. SAMUEL, P.	
44244	2/A.M. SIMMONDS, H.	
133986	2/Pte. SPECTOR, M.
025009	Pte. SKUDDER, G.
38258	2/A.M. SOLLE, T.
239	A.M. SPIER, E. E.
90284	2/A.M. SHERKOSKY, S.
33104	2/A.M. SILVER, A.
56483	2/A.M. SACOFSKY, S.
91230	3/A.M. SANTEN, M.
80217	2/A.M. SPRINGER, L.
116644	2/A.M. SAMPSON, C.
32911	2/A.M. SILVER, G.
136332	3/A.M. SEGAL, B.
137948	Cadet SIMON, H.
17365	2/A.M. SAMPSON, J.
52209	2/A.M. SOLOMON, M.
33096	2/A.M. SUTCLIFFE, B.
46376	2/A.M. SILVERBERG, C.
62899	2/A.M. SCHREIBEN, M.
52709	2/A.M. SOLOMON, M.
59550	L.A.C. SOLOMON, J.
52562	2/A.M. SMOLENSKI, H.
37559	2/A.M. SAMUEL, R.
17746	2/A.M. SAMUEL, L.
238138	Pte. SAUNDERS, S.
175515	Sgt. SAMUELS, E.
9129	3/A.M. SOLOMON, H. R.
65057	3/A.M. SOLOMON, J.
60055	2/A.M. SHORE.
90483	Cadet SCIANA, E. J.
198249	2/Pte. SPIERS, C.
245936	3/A.M. SIMONS, M.
92729	3/A.M. SILVER, S.
120541	3/A.M. SOLOMON, D.
58686	2A/.M. SPIERMAN, H.
110149	Cadet SPIERS, A. J.
99359	3/A.M. SOLOMON, L.
123151	2/A.M. SOLOMON, A.
38286	2/A.M. SIMONS, M.
23209	2/A.M. SUSSMAN, P.
111577	2/A.M. SOLOMONS, A.
300121	Cpl. SOLOMON, B.
20885	Spr. SOLOMONS, S. J.
41938	2/A.M. SILVERMAN, J.
22115	2/A.M. SHIPKO, M.
13266	2/A.M. SPIERS, C.
10623	2/A.M. SPIER, J.
72583	Pte. SHEVLOFF, I.
76970	2/A.M. SOLOMONS, J.
	A.M. SAMP, P.
2490850	Pte. SHAPIRO, R.
80813	3/A.M. SLOWMAN, B.
50723	2/A.M. SPERO, A.
229790	Pte. SOLOMONS, J.
66872	2/A.M. SILVER, M.
14476	2/A.M. SAMUEL, L.
139763	2/A.M. SOLOMONS, I.
43275	1/A.M. SNAPPER, N. M.
48786	2/A.M. SILVERMAN, S.
39011	2/A.M. SCHULMAN, J.
24253	2/A.M. SMALINSKY, J.
4209	Pte. SELLER, H.
23107	2/A.M. SIMMONDS, L.
68876	Gnr. STOLLER, E.
92737	2/A.M. SPERO, J.
95542	2/A.M. STEVENS, S.
2958	Dvr. SHENKIN, A.
21774	2/A.M. SIDMAN, L.
242129	2/A.M. SIMONS, A. S.
24389	2/A.M. SINCLAIRE, H.
81619	2/A.M. SCHAAPPOOL, J.
32911	2/A.M. SILVER, G.
56114	3/A.M. SHILKOFF, J.
57611	1/A.M. SIMON, M.
52709	2/A.M. SOLOMON, M.
62526	2/A.N. STABINSKY, I.*
33958	2/A.M. SIMON, L.
19385	3/A.M. SMITH, J.
33892	A.M. SHINBERG, J.
	1/A.M. SANKER, J.
46398	2/A.M. SADKIE, J.
107425	2/A.M. SOLOMON, A.
68096	1/A.M. SELIGMAN, A.
68543	2/A.M. SELMAN, E. J.
58686	2/A.M. SPIERMAN, H.
143238	Pte. SIRESKY, I.
59550	Pte. SOLOMONS, J.
41832	Pte. STEINBERG, A.
128513	2/A.M. SOLOMON, G.
131201	2/A.M. STONE, E.
148753	Pte. SASSON, S.
	2/A.M. SHUTSKE, L.
30696	A.C.2 SOLOMON, H.
29380	A.M.2 STONE, E.
19725	A.M. STINE, E.
30637	A.M. SOLOMONS, H.
	A.C. SAPER, H.
220907	Sgt. SIMONS, H.
	2/A.M. STONE, M.
235936	A.M. SIMONS, N.
	Pte. SIMONS, S.
	Pte. SOLOMONS, S.
27348	A/Sgt. STEINBERG, J. I.*
50333	2/Pte. TEACHER, S.
36636	2/A.M. TAYLOR, J.
2084	1/A.M. TEITELBAUM, L.
66093	3/A.M. TRAPPLER, A. E.*
34519	1/A.M. TEEMAN, A.
29943	2/A.M. TOBIAS, H.
285043	2/Pte. TAYLOR, D.
65367	Cpl. TAYLOR, M.
66990	3/A.M. TALBOT, A.
34519	2/A.M. TEEMAN, A.
32332	1/A.M. TEIGENBAUM, W.
15979	2/A.M. TEITLEBAUM, L.
98009	Pte. TOFT, J.
58697	3/A.M. THOMAS, A.

Royal Air Force.—*Continued.*

99448	3/A.M. TOBIAS, D.	87659	1/Pte. WOLFE, H.	20164	Sgt. WOOLF, E.
106582	3/A.M. TOBIAS, B.	41679	2/Pte. WOOLF, B.	60654	3/A.M. WEINTROP, S.
176835	Cadet THOMAS, S.	52376	2/Pte. WALLEN, S.	16887	2/A.M. WEIL, M.
19069	2/A.M. TAWIFF, L.	32722	1/Pte. WALKEX, A.	52796	2/A.M. WELTERDEN, J.
42416	2/A.M. TOBIAS, I.	169909	3/Clk. WOLFERS, L.	200192	2/A.M. WERNER, L.
38258	2/A.M. TYMANS, T.	22915	2/A.M. WIGGIN, J.	63522	3/A.M. WOOLF, P.
66168	2/A.M. TEFF, W.	22202	2/A.M. WOLFE, M.	124598	3/A.M. WEISBLATT, H.
144851	2/A.M. TEEMAN, M.	51858	2/A.M. WEINER, J.	122243	2/A.M. WASSERMAN, A.
33890	2/A.M. TRAMBERG, S.	87216	2/A.M. WEINSTEIN, D.	58378	2/A.M. WESIL, J.
	A.M. TERRY, P.	3472	3/A.M. WALTERS, G.	83869	3/A.M. WRIGHT, J.
		56476	2/A.M. WOOLF, L.	17633	3/A.M. WISCH,
20390	2/A.M. VALENTINE, A. H.	P/26164	3/A.M. WARMBARDT, R.	39301	2/A.M. WIGNAL, G.
17050	2/A.M. VENTURA, A.	31009	2/A.M. WALDMAN, M.	31730	2/A.M. WEINER, H.
16877	2/A.M. VANGELDER, L.	20464	2/A.M. WOOLF, E.	43094	2/A.M. WINEBAUM, G. C.
67784	1/Pte. VAN WEZEL, H.	23911	1/A.M. WINSHANK, H.		
68601	2/A.M. VAN RAALTE, G. F.	294454	3/A.M. WINTER, A. B.	140145	2/A.M. WINSTON, G.
		287474	2/A.M. WORTMAN, A.	98184	3/A.M. WEINSTONE, R.
62433	2/A.M. VALENTINE, L.	186325	3/A.M. WEINBERG, J.	27413	A.M. WHITMOND, G.
76424	3/A.M. VERBY, B.	115826	2/A.M. WILLIAMS, S.	159358	2/Cpl. WAXKUSCHEN, M.
16967	2/A.M. VAN NIEROP, E.	45006	Pte. WOOLFE, M.	55238	2/Cpl. WOLFBERG, J.
18713	2/A.M. VANDERLINDE, G.	103036	Pte. WATTMAN, H.	98184	3/A.M. WINSTONE, L.
41057	2/A.M. VALINSKY, L.	32104	2/A.M. WOOLF, D.	60642	Pte. WINETROP, C.
23474	Pte. VALENTINE, R.	89220	2/.AM. WINTER, C. S.	31720	2/A.M. WINER, H.
158110	2/Pte. VICTOR, L.	35481	2/A.M. WORTHY, C.	892270	A.M. WINTER, C. S.
92371	2/A.M. VALENSKI, J.	37475	Sgt./Mech. WURZAL, J.	88728	3/A.M. WIX, M.
85479	2/A.M. VALLINS, L.	23246	2/A.M. WOOLF, H. E.	24536	2/A.M. WHITE, P.
48968	3/A.M. VOGEL, J.	23460	2/A.M. WHITE, G. M.	23911	2/A.M. WINDSHANK, H.
186720	3/A.M. VANDERVELDE,	40223	2/A.M. WEINER, J. W.	48670	2/A.M. WEIBER, H.
198711	Pte. VOLSKI, E. H.	64480	2/A.M. WILLIAMS, T.	35411	2/A.M. WINDMILL, L.
23667	A.C.2 VALENTINE, S.	42466	1/A.M. WEINBERG, L.	10785	2/A.M. WOOLF, W.
	A.C.2 VEN GELDER, I.	222909	S.M. WEINGOTT, H. S.	17633	2/A.M. WYSE, L.
20466	Pte. VAN SLUIS, L.	90053	Boy WAEKS, R.	57645	2/A.M. WANSKER, H.
184984	F/Cadet VALENTINE, J.*	113826	3/Clk. WILLIAMS, S.	38078	1/A.M. WELLINS, L.
44340	2/A.M. WEINSTEIN, L.	76590	2/A.M. WEISWELL, H. M.	16887	2/A.M. WEIL, M.
32066	2/A.M. WINTER, L.			87216	2/A.M. WEINSTEIN, D.
36027	2/A.M. WEINER, C.	36704	2/A.M. WILSON, A.	112939	3/A.M. WAINSTEIN, L.
34721	2/A.M. WALTERS, J.	81672	3/A.M. WOLFSBERGER, H.	87659	Cpl. WOOLF, H.
22466	2/A.M. WERNER, B. E.				2/A.M. WOOLF, J. D.
17597	2/A.M. WATKINS, J.	159126	Pte. WOOLF, A.		2/A.M. WOOLF, S.
34266	2/A.M. WOOLF, H.	55533	Boy WALLINETS, H.	89117	2/A.M. YULES, I.
22868	Cpl. WARSHAWSKI, W.	38078	1/A.M. WELKINS, L.	19041	2/A.M. ZEIDENBERG, A.
27413	1/A.M. WITMOND, S.	18363	2/A.M. WOSEMAN, J.	34452	2/A.M. ZOOLANDER, J.
16573	2/A.M. WEIKS.	160462	3/A.M. WHITE, C.	38814	2/A.M. ZEFF, S.
22601	3/A.M. WOLFSON, J.	39368	2/A.M. WESIL, J.	98175	3/A.M. ZEFFERTT, W.
53213	2/A.M. WARSHAWSKY, M.	112939	3/A.M. WEINSTEIN, L.	89840	2/A.M. ZAUMAN, M. M.
		266809	2/Pte. WOOLF, F. A.	37388	2/A.M. ZASS, E.
20805	Cpl./Mech. WALTERS, L.	176147	Cadet WOOLF, P. J.	34769	2/A.M. ZIMMACH, H.
133255	2/Pte. WINEBERG, H.	20805	1/A.M. WALTERS, L.	59379	1/A.M. ZEMMELL, A.
87816	2/Pte. WEIL, I.	129081	Pte. WOOLF, B.	40653	2/A.M. ZISKINA, L.
129671	2/Pte. WINER, S.	379058	Pte. WOLFE, B.	108914	3/A.M. ZELLER, A.
79418	1/Pte. WALTERS, W.	54791	3/A.M. WILLIAMS, N.	36691	2/A.M. ZANITSKY, J.
44108	2/A.M. WODISLAWSKY, S. E.	48670	3/A.M. WEBER, H.	89840	2/A.M. ZZAIMAN, N. N.
		101241	2/Pte. WHIL, J.	147797	2/A.M. ZETZ.

* Killed in Action or died on Active Service.

AUSTRALIAN CORPS.

OFFICERS.

Capt. AARONS, D. S. (M.C. and Bar), 16th Bn.
Lieut. AARONS, T. H., 39th Bn.
2nd Lieut. ABRAHAM, L.
Lieut. ADES, S. A.,* 35th Bn.
Capt. ALLEN, S. H.
2nd Lieut. ALSTON, D., A.F.C.
Lieut. ANSELL, A.,* 52nd Bn.
Lieut. ANSELL, H. A., 8th M.G.C.
Lieut. ASHER, F., 5th Seaforth Highlanders.
Capt. ASHER, G. B., 4th Div. H.Q.
Lieut. ASHER, J. H.,* 11th Bn.
Lieut. BARNETT, R., 5th D.A.C.
Lieut. BASSER, M., 19th Bn.
Capt. BENJAMIN, G. S., 21st Bn.
Lieut. BEAVER, W. M.,* 60th Bn.
Capt. BEHREND, O., Dental Corps.
Lieut. BOAS, H., A. Y.M.C.A.
Capt. BRAHAM, B., Dental Unit.
Lieut. BRASCH, C. H., A.F.C.
Major BRODZIAK, A., 33rd Bn.
Major BRODZIAK, C. E. M.* (D.S.O.), M.G.C.
Capt. BENJAMIN, H. A., A.S.C.
Lieut. BENJAMIN, L., A.F.C.
Lieut. BENPORATH, C. W., 16th Bn.
Capt. BENNETT, G. B., Dental Unit A.A.M.C.
Lieut. BROWN, W. H., 4th Div. Sig. Coy.
Capt. BICKART, W. D., A.M.C.
Capt. BLASHKI, R. H.,* 58th Bde. Arty.
Capt. BLASHKI, E., A.M.C.
Major BLAUBAUM, I., S.M.O., A.A.M.C.
Capt. BLAUBAUM, O., 83rd Bn.
Capt. CARO, P. (M.B.E.), 1st Tun. Coy.
Capt. CANTOR, S. J., A.M.C.
Capt. COHEN, A. F., 2nd Tun. Coy.
Rabbi COHEN, F. L., Chaplain.
Capt. COHEN, A. M., 56th Bn.
Capt. COHEN, C. A. K., 33rd Bn.
Lieut. COHEN, C. K., 30th Bn.
2nd Lieut. COHEN, B. H., A.O.C.
Lieut. COLES, A. W., 8th Bn.
Major COPPELSON, V. M., 14th Field Amb.
Capt. CRAWCOUR, S., 4th F. Amb., A.M.C.
Lieut. COHEN, E. G., 5th L.H.
Lieut.-Col. COHEN, H. E. (C.M.G., D.S.O.), A.F.A.
Capt. COHEN, H. F., 5th F.C.
Lieut. COHEN, R. P., A.M.C.
Lieut. COHEN, S. L., A.A.M.C.
Lieut. COHEN, S. E., 5th Bn.
2nd Lieut. DARE, H. S., 3rd Bn.
2nd Lieut. DARE, J., 24th Bn.
Capt. DANGLOW, J., Chaplain.
Capt. DAVIS, W. E., 39th Bn.
Capt. DAVIS, C. I., 5th Field Amb.
Lieut. DAVIS, M., 17th Bn.
Lieut. DE SAXE, R., 18th Bn.
Capt. DAVIS, N., A.M.C.
Lieut. DIAMOND, A., 19th Bn.
Lieut. DIAMOND, S. (D.C.M.), 60th Bn.
2nd Lieut. DREWITT, G. E., 10th F.A.B.
Lieut. DYTE, N. V.
Lieut. ENGEL, G. H. F. (M.C.), Engineers.
Capt. ELLIS (Dr.), O. J., A.A.M.C.
Lieut. FRANKEL, R. C. J., 2nd Div. Train.
Major FREEDMAN, D. I., Chaplain.
Lieut. FREEDMAN, Z. E.,* A.F.C.
Lieut. FREDMAN, G. H., 51st Bn.
Lieut. FREDMAN, H. S., 14th Bn.
Lieut. FREIMAN, N. B., A.F.C.
Capt. FRYBERG, L., A.F.C.
Lieut. FREDMAN, H. S., 14th Bn.
Lieut. GARCIA, L., 14th Bn.
2nd Lieut. GLASS, S. B., 24th Bn.
Lieut. GOLDFINCH, G. M., 12th F.A.B.
Capt. GOLDRING, E. C., 3rd Bn.
Lieut. GOLDRING, W. H., 3rd Bn.
Lieut. GOLDSMITH, S. R., 46th Bn.
Lieut. GOLDSMITH, H., 51st Battery.
Capt. GOLDSTEIN, P. H., 17th Bn.
Lieut. GOLDSTEIN, L. J., 16th Bn.
Lieut. GOLDSTEIN, G., A.M.C.
Major GOLDSTEIN, A., A.A.M.C.
Major GOULD, D. Sig. Coy.
Lieut. GRIFFEN, 45th Bn.
Lieut. HAGGAR, E. N.,* 21st Bn.
Capt. HAINS, C. C.,* 13th F.A.B.
Lieut. HALLENSTEIN, D.,* 12th M.G.C.
Lieut. HARRINGTON, A., 46th Bn.
Lieut. HARRIS, J. M., A.F.C.
Lieut. HARRIS, P. L., 23rd Bn.
Capt. HARRIS, I. M., A.M.C.
Lieut. HART, B. (M.C.), 49th Bn.
2nd Lieut. HART, B., 7th Bn.
Lieut. HORWITZ, M., 11th Bn.
Capt. HOLLANDER, P. E.
Capt. HARRIS, H., A.A.M.C.
Lieut. HOLLAND, J. F., 14th L.H.
Capt. HYMAN E. M. (D.S.O., M.C.), 12th L.H.
Major HENRY, A., 14th Bn.
2nd Lieut. HERTZBERG, 7th Bn.
Lieut. HART, H. L., 7th Engineers.
Lieut. HATFIELD, E. K., 57th Bn.
Major HYMAN, A. E. W. (O.B.E.).
Lieut. HATFIELD, A. V., 46th Bn.
Lieut. HEUGH, A. B., 56th Bn.
Major ISAACSON, I., 3rd Div. Train.
S/Nurse ISAACS, N., A.M.C.
Lieut. IKEN, D. B. B., 2nd Div. Artil.
Capt. IKEN, H. C., A.I.F. Depôts.
Capt. ISAAC, A. S., Infantry.
2nd Lieut. ISAACS, A. G., 17th Bn.
Capt. ISAACS, D. W. (M.C.), 4th Bn.
Lieut. ISAACS, R. M. (M.C.), 8th F.C.E.
Lieut. ISAACSON, A., 17th A.S.C.

Australian Corps.—*Continued.*
2nd Lieut. ISAACSON, T. L., 49th Bn.
Lieut. ISAACSON, J.
Lieut. ISRAEL, N. (D.C.M.).
Lieut. ISRAEL, H., 6th Bn.
2nd Lieut. ISRAEL, L. P., 19th Bn.
Lieut. JACOBS, C. J., 21st Bn.
Lieut. JACOBS, D. C., 10th Bn.
Lieut. JACOBS, F. A., 1st F.A.B.
Capt. JACOBS, H. G., 56th Bn.
Major JACOBS, H., 1st Bn.
Lieut. JACOBS, H. L. (M.C.), A.F.A.
Capt. JACOBS, H. S., A.A.M.C.
Lieut. JACOBS, L. W.
Capt. JACOBS, R. E., 23rd L.H.
Capt. JOEL, J. C.
Capt. JONA, J., A.A.M.C.
Lieut. JONES, M. (M.C.), 49th Bn.
2nd Lieut. JONES, S. J., 60th Bn.
Major JOSEPH, C. E., 4th D.S.C.
Lieut. JOSEPH, E. F., 25th A.S.C.
Lieut. JOSEPH, H. E.,* 5th Bn.
Capt. JOSEPH, C. H. (M.C.), Inf.
Lieut. JONES, M. (M.M.), Inf.
Capt. JOSEPH, W.
Lieut. JOSEPHS, J. R., 5th Bn.
2nd Lieut. KAYE, J. H., 8th Bn.
Capt. KATZ, L. S.
Capt. KEESING, G. S., 12th F.C.E.
Lieut. KEYZOR, L. (V.C.), 42nd Bn.
Lieut. KING, A., 14th Bn.
2nd Lieut. KOHN, J. (M.C.), Inf.
Lieut. KOSMINSKY, M. E.,* 7th Bn.
Major LAZARUS, J. S., 22nd Bn.
Lieut. LANDSBERG, G., 14th Bn.
Lieut. LAWRENCE, A.P.C.
Lieut. LAZER, H. J.,* 33rd Bn.
Capt. LEON, J. H., A.M.C.
Capt. LEEDMAN, C. H. (M.C.), 54th Bn.
Capt. LENZER, R., A.M.C.
Capt. LEVI, K. M.,* A.A.M.C.
Lieut. LEVI, R. N., 23rd Bn.
Capt. LEVINSON, E.
Capt. LEVY, 9th Field Amb.
Lieut. LEVY, H. S.,* 35th Bn.
2nd Lieut. LEVY, F., 17th L.H.
Major LEVY, F., 12th F.A.B.
Lieut. LEVY, R. N., 23rd Bn.
Capt. LEVY, L., 5th Bn.
Capt. LAZARUS, S. L. (O.B.E.), A.P.S.
Capt. LEVY, T. H., A.P.C.
Capt. LEWIS, M. R. (M.C.), 44th Bn.
Lieut. LIPSHITZ, S.
Lieut. LIPMAN, A. A., 52nd Bn.
Lieut. LIPSHUT, L., 38th Bn.
Lieut. LOBASCHER, L. D., 29th Bn.
Lieut. LUSCOMBE, E. L.,* 19th Bn.
Lieut.-Col. MARGOLIN, E. A. (D.S.O.), 16th **Bn.**

2nd Lieut. MIERS, V. D., 60th Bn.
Capt. MICHAELSON, A. C., Sea Trans. Service.
Lieut. MIELS, R. L., A.F.A.
Lieut. MITCHELL, E. M., 4th Bn.
Lt.-Gen. MONASH, Sir J., K.C.B., V.D., G.C.M.G.,
Col. MARKS, D. G. (D.S.O., M.C.), 13th Bn.
Q-M. and Hon. Capt. MARKS, R.
Capt. MARKS, R. M., 38th Bn.
Lieut. MOSS, J.,* 11th Bn.
Capt. MOSS, A. M., 3rd Div.
Lieut. MOSS, A. H.,* 15th Bn.
Lieut. MEYERS, E. H. W. (M.C. & 2 Bars), 9th Bn.
Lieut. MYER, C. B., 13th Bn.
Lieut. MEARS, C. K., 35th Bn.
Capt. MENDELSOHN, H. (M.C.), A.A.M.C.
Lieut. MENDELSON, B. H.,* 55th Bn.
Lieut. MENDOZA, C. L., 47th Bn.
Col. MARKS, A. H. (C.B.E., D.S.O.).
Lieut. MENDOZA, H. K.,* 52nd Bn.
Lieut. MEYER, A. H., 48th Bn.
Lieut. MYERS, H. A., 11th A.M.C.
Major MEYERS, E. S., A.A.M.C.
Capt. NATHAN, L. P., 1st M.G.C.
2nd Lieut. NICOL, J. G., 11th Bn.
Lieut. NORDIN, W. L., 27th Bn.
2nd Lieut. NETTHEIM, E. L., 27th Bn.
Lieut. ORBUCK, L., 37th Bn.
Capt. ORNSTEIN, S. P., 39th Bn.
Lieut. PARKER, S. W., 46th Bn.
Capt. PHILLIPS, P. D.,
Lieut. PHILLIPS, P.,
Capt. PHILLIPS, L. D., 7th L. H.
Major PHILLIPS, A. M., 11th Bn.
Lieut. PHILLIPS, E. A., 34th Bn.
2nd Lieut. PHILLIPS, J. A., 22nd Bn.
Capt. PYKE, C. A. (M.C.), Q.M.G., A.S.C.
Lieut. PYKE, G. J., 3rd Div. Train.
Lieut. PRICE, H .C., 7th L. H.
Lieut. RAPHAEL, H., Cylists Bn.
Lieut. RIGAL,
Lieut. RINTEL, H. L.,* 8th Bn.
Lieut. ROSEN, L. W. (M.C.), Inf.
Major ROSENTHAL, R. L., A.M.C.
Lieut. ROSENGARTEN, L. J., 6th F.A.B.
Capt. ROSENTHAL, C. P., 33rd Bn.
Sister ROSENTHAL.
Capt. ROSENTHAL, J., A.M.C.
Lieut. ROSENTHAL, S.,* 58th Bn.
Lieut. ROXBURGH, K. G., 12th Bn.
Lieut. ROCKSTEIN, F. S.,
Capt. RUBINOWICH, A. S.,
Lieut. ROY.
Capt. SAMUEL, P.,
Capt. SAMUEL, S. G., 6th Bn.
Capt. SAMUELSON, G. S.,
Lieut. SAMUELS, (M.C.), L., 101st H. Bty
Lieut. SAMUELS, R. O., 1st Bn.
2nd Lieut. SAMUELS, E., 24th Bn.

Australian Corps.—*Continued.*

Capt. SOROKIEWITCH, M. N., A.M.C.
Lieut. SAUNDERS, M. G., 32nd Bn.
Lieut. SOLOMONS, M., 32nd Bn.
2nd Lieut. SELIG, H.,
Lieut. SHALBERY, J. R.,* 23rd Bn.
Lieut. SHAPPERE, C. S.,* 3rd Bn.
Lieut. SHAPPERE, H.,
Lieut. STERNBERG, O. J., 3rd Tun. Coy.
Lieut. SUSMAN, H. S., 33rd Bn.
Capt. SYMONDS, H., A.A.M.C.
Capt. SILVERBERG, M. D., A.M.C.
Lieut. SILVERSTON, L. I., 48th Bn.
Capt. SIMONSEN, P. W. (O.B.E.), 3rd Div.
2nd Lieut. SIMMONS, S. J. L., 3rd Aust. Tun. Coy.
Lieut. SMITH, K. A., 1st M.G. Bn.
Lieut. SOLOMON, H., 26th Bn.
Lieut. SHAPIRA, F. C., A.F.C.
Lieut. SCHONHEIMER, R., 26th Bn.
Lieut. TOFLER, L. J., 53rd Bn.
Lieut. VOGLER, H. H., 23rd Bn.
Major VAN GELDEN, 2nd Bn.
Major WALTERS, H. B., Sea Transport Service.
Lieut.-Col. WALL, G. (C.M.G.), A.Q.M.G.
Lieut. WERTHEIMER, A. T.,* 12th Bn.
Capt. WOLFS, O. F. J., 4th Bn.
Capt. ZANDER, W. H., 30th Bn.

N.C.O.'s AND MEN.

2281	Pte. AARONS, M. L.,* 16th Bn.
1325	Pte. AARONS, 14th Field Amb.
776	Tpr. AARONS, H.,* 4th L.H.
2868	Pte. AARONS, J. F.,* 16th Bn.
3	Sgt. AARONSON, M., A.A.M.S.
2026	Pte. ABELSON, C.,* 40th Bn.
1910	Cpl. ABRAHAM, G., 1st Bn.
4356	Pte. ABRAHAMS, B., 2nd Bn.
2362	Pte. ABRAHAMS, H., 9th Bn.
33941	Dvr. ABRAHAMS, J., A.F.A.
7051	Pte. ABRAHAMS, G., 2nd Bn.
	Pte. ABRAHAMS, L. C., 16th Bn.
468	Pte. ABRAHAMS, S. V., 13th Bn.
3103	Pte. ABRAHAMS, M., 45th Bn.
65903	Pte. ABRAHAMS, L. J., 3rd Bn.
7073	Pte. ABRAHAMS, R. W., 1st Bn.
11633	Dvr. ABRAHAMS, L. H., A.S.C.
33	Pte. ABRAHAM, B. H., 1st M.G.C.
6764	Pte. ABRAHAM, L., 26th Bn.
5029	Pte. ABRAHAMS, A. T., 14th Bn.
4057	Pte. ABRAHAMS, J. H., Cycling Co.
15227	Pte. ABRAMOVITCH, E. D.
6708	Pte. ABRAHAMS, G. F., 6th Bn.
52549	Cpl. ABRAMOVITCH, P.* (M.M.), Sig. Cy.
6028	Pte. ABRAHAMS, F. W.,* 17th Bn.
60586	Pte. ABRAMOVITCH, A., A.S.C.
14962	Pte. ABRAHAMS, W. S., A.A.S.C.
5646	Pte. ABRAHAMS, E., 46th Bn.
13135	Pte. ADLER, H. C., 1st Bn.
6646	Spr. ADLER, J. F., 7th F.C.E.
86	L/Cpl. AHBUL, L. E.* (M.M.), 41st Bn.
	Pte. ALMAN, L.
	Sgt. ABRAHAMS, G. (M.M.).
2776	Pte. ALMAN, T., 44th Bn.
814	Sgt. ALMOND, L., 24th Bn.
2700	Spr. ALEXANDER, L., 7th F.C.E.
5291	L/Cpl. ADOLFSON, A. S., 24th Bn.
2872	Sgt. ALEXANDER, J. A., 17th Bn.
897	Spr. ALEXANDER, G.
	Pte. ALEXANDER, R.
3847	Pte. ALEXANDER, M. M., 51st Bn.
3382	Pte. ALEXANDER, B., 2nd Field Amb.
7843	Cpl. ALEXANDER, E. B., 1st Aust. Aux. Hos.
61345	Pte. ALEXANDER, J. S., 14th Bn.
2196	Pte. ALEXANDER, A.,* 36th Bn.
328	Pte. ALEXANDER, E., 40th Bn.
4651	Pte. ALEXANDER, S., 24th Bn.
3020	S/Sgt. ALEXANDER, E. G., 44th Bn.
2619	Pte. ALLEN, B. H., 60th Bn.
401	Pte. ALLEN, D. C.,* 58th Bn.
1134	Pte. ALTMANN, C.,* 24th Bn.
6953	Pte. ALTMAN, S., 14th Bn.
	Q.M.S. ALSTON, B., 14th Bn.
4728	Cpl. AMBROSE, C. P., 46th Bn.
1023	Pte. ANDERSON, W., 9th Bn.
22299	Spr. ANDET, L., Engineers.
4429	Sgt. ASCHMAN, R., 50th Bn.
4495	Pte. ASH, C., 29th Bn.
4494	Pte. ASH, S., 29th Bn.
2149	Pte. ASHER, S.,* 36th Bn.
6276	Dvr. ASHER, C., 20th Bn.
16778	S/Sgt. ASHER, R., 2nd Field Amb.
607	Dvr. ASHER, D. H., 9th Bn.
3576	Pte. ASHER, M., A.S.C.
	Sgt. ABRAHAMS, J. J. (M.S.M.), A.I.F.
1776	Pte. ASHER, J., 1st Bn.
4099	Pte. ASIAH, D., Anzac Cyclists.
	Pte. ASSENHEIM, A. I.
65730	Pte. ABRAHAMS, S. Y., 3rd Bn.
6851	Pte. ALEXANDER, B. P., 17th Bn.
268	Pte. ALTHAM, J., 11th Bn.
	Nurse BENNETT.
3969	Pte. BALL, A. M., 6th M.G.C.
4943	Cpl. BALKIND, J., 4th Pioneers.
	Pte. BARCOUTZ, M.
713	Pte. BARFIELD, L. W., 36th Bn.
3231	Pte. BARKMAN, H., 7th Bn.
13661	Pte. BARKOWITZ, B., 28th Bn.
495	Pte. BARNARD, L. L., 27th Bn.
3233	L/Cpl. BARNARD, S. C., 50th Bn.
5044	Pte. BARNARD, R. H., 1st Bn.
1748	Gnr. BARMES, W.,* 11th A.F.A.
1747	Gnr. BARMES, F. M., A.F.A.
1291	Pte. BARNETT, J. W., 33rd Bn.
	Pte. BARNETT, J. L., 30th Bn.
1026	Cpl. BARNETT, J., 42nd Bn.
732	Pte. BARNETT, W., 35th Bn.

Australian Corps.—*Continued.*

6767	L/Cpl. BARNETT, D. D., 24th Bn.
3362	Cpl. BANNETT, N., 4th. Div. Sig. Coy.
5935	Pte. BARNETT, S. Y., 22nd Bn.
6712	Pte. BARNETT, M., 5th Bn.
610	Pte. BARNETT, V., 7th Bn.
4134	S/Sgt. BARNETT, M. M., 1st Pioneers.
5339	Pte. BARNETT, C., 45th Bn.
5036	Sgt. BARNETT, F. J., 7th Bn.
6536	Sdlr. BARNETT, P. A., 4th F.A.B.
425	Tpr. BARNETT, J. J., 2nd L.H.
30221	Pte. BARNETT, F. S., A.F.A.
1880	Pte. BARNETT, L., 23rd Bn.
1591	Pte. BARNETT, J. C., 12th Bn.
21	Sgt. BARNETT, J. E. W., 1st M.G.C.
	Pte. BARRINGTON, L. H., 13th Bn.
2417	Pte. BASS, L., 36th Bn.
822	L/Cpl. BENJAMIN, A. L.,* 24th Bn.
6723	Pte. BLOOM, A., 11th Bn.
832	Pte. BLOOMER, H., 40th Bn.
	Pte. BLUM, A., 37th Bn.
3700	Pte. BLUME, J.
1817	Pte. BLOOM, J. S.,* 2nd Bn.
1618	Pte. BLOOM, F. G. C. M., 35th Bn.
19666	Gnr. BLOOM, R. A., 8th Bgde.
	Pte. BOMBERG, W.
5304	Pte. BLOOMFIELD, N., 18th Bn.
4742	Pte. BLOOMFIELD, F., 12th Bn.
230	C.S.M. BOCK, C. E., 56th Bn.
	Sgt. BENJAMIN, J.
	L/Cpl. BENPORATH, F. H.
101	Pte. BOCKELBERG, F. B., 3rd L.H.
3925	Pte. BOROWSKI, L. P.,* 48th Bn.
6217	Pte. BORTNOSKI, L. J., 5th Bn.
1140	Pte. BORTZELL, S., 17th Bn.
1887	Pte. BOURNE, A., 19th Bn.
4375	Pte. BOWMAN, A. W., 21st Bn.
	Pte. BOWMAN, J., 3rd Bn.
13262	Pte. BOWMAN, L. E.,* 4th Field Amb.
5348	Pte. BAUER, O., 11th Bn.
12730	Tpr. BAUMBERG, B., Aust. Res. Cavalry.
8608	Pte. BAUMGARTEN, C., 19th Co., A.S.C.
	Pte. BEARD, M. J., 6th Bn.
89	Pte. BAUMGARTEN, J., 41st Bn.
	Pte. BEAR, S.
2624	Pte. BECKMAN, A., 47th Bn.
12080	Pte. BEHRENS, J., 2nd Pioneers.
4985	Spr. BELKIND, I., 7th F.C.E.
6768	Pte. BELL, I., 21st Bn.
6766	Pte. BELLINSON, A., 22nd Bn.
567	Pte. BEN-ARIE, M., 28th Bn.
15510	Pte. BENDY, A. H., 17th Field Amb.
8819A	Cpl. BENJAMIN, A., A.S.C.
2379	Sgt. BENJAMIN, B., A.S.C.
2224	Spr. BENJAMIN, M., R.O.C.
7372	Pte. BOWSON, A., 3rd Bn.
1114	Pte. BRACY, P. H., 7th Bn.
	Pte. BRACY, D.
3032	Pte. BRADSHAW, S. H., H.Q. A.A.M.C.
2460	Dvr. BRAHAM, M. P., 5th Div. Train.
1009A	Pte. BRAHAM, C. E., 3rd L.H.
2771	L/Cpl. BRAHMS, H., 44th Bn.
2293	Pte. BOXHORN, L., 44th Bn.
2294	Pte. BOXHORN, I., 44th Bn.
1897	Pte. BRAHMS, V., 42nd Bn.
4965	Pte. BREITMAN, J. G.* (M.M.), 3rd Bn.
6924	Pte. BRANDT, C. A., 23rd Bn.
3498	Bdm. BRESSLER, J., 60th Bn.
341A	Pte. BRITAIN, S., 3rd M.G.C.
3109	Pte. BRODSKY, V., 37th Bn.
12877	Pte. BRODZIAK, C., A.S.C.
65950	Pte. BENJAMIN, A. J., 4th Bn.
2098	Sgt. BENJAMIN, C., 18th D.U.S.
171	Sgt. BENJAMIN, E. (M.M.), 2nd Pioneers.
3002	2/A.M. BENJAMIN, E., A.F.C.
8772	Gnr. BENJAMIN, E. L., 53rd Siege Battery.
3959	Bdr. BENJAMIN, S. O.,* 21st D.H.C.
2795	Sgt. BENJAMIN, D. H., Army Pay Corps.
20021	Pte. BENJAMIN, V. M. J., 55th Bn.
7978	Sgt. BENJAMIN, O. D., 6th F.A.B.
2321	Pte. BENJAMIN, L., 5th Pioneers.
4992	L/Cpl. BENJAMIN, M. H., 20th Bn.
	L/Cpl. BENPORATH, F. H.
1660	Pte. BENN, I. I., 57th Bn.
26429	Pte. BENNETT, P., 1st M.B.
381	Pte. BENNETT, G., A.F.C.
5927	Pte. BENTWICH, J. H., 4th Bn.
1914	Sgt. BENTWICH, S. B., 6th Bn.
6730	Pte. BROMBERG, J. M., 16th Bn.
3257	Pte. BROWN, A., 1st Bn.
1160	Spr. BROWN, A., 1st L.H.
2572	Pte. BROWN, R. W., 54th Bn.
3687	Pte. BROWN, L., 13th Bn.
13034	Gnr. BROWNE, L. H., 4th F.H.B.
370	Dvr. BROWNE, R. G., 14th M.G.C.
5059	Pte. BUCHNER, H., 59th Bn.
1339	Pte. BUCHNER, W., 59th Bn.
	Pte. BUCKINGHAM, W., 3rd Brig.
6151	Pte. BURNS, R., 19th Bn.
5661	Drv. BURT, H., 3rd Army Bde. A.F.A.
3762	Pte. BUTTEL, F. A., Aust. Corps.
230363	Pte. BURMAN, M., A.S.C.
1030	Cpl. BUTTELL, M. A., 13th Bn.
T/742	Dvr. BYFORD, J., 1st Div. Train.
	Pte. BIER, B., A.M.C.
4380	Gnr. BENJAMIN, E. J., A.F.A.
	Pte. BLOUSTEIN, A., 22nd Bn.
1310	Pte. BLACK, E., 10th Bn.
1518	Pte. BRILLIANT, N., 8th Bn.
11	Pte. BARRINGTON, L. H., 13th Bn.
5337	Pte. BERKOVITCH, M., 16th Bn.
942	Pte. BERMAN, J. S., New Guinea Guard.
799	Pte. BERMAN, H. W., 4th Bn.
13661	Pte. BERCOWITZ, B., 3rd Bn.
7214	Spr. BERGER, J., Engineers.
452	Pte. BERG, C. A., 20th Bn.

Australian Corps.—*Continued.*

2786	Pte. BERLINSKY, J., 39th Bn.
908	Pte. BERNAYS, R. M.,* 3rd Bn.
	Pte. BERNSTEIN, B.
501	Pte. BERNSTEIN, H., 23rd Bn.
5552	L/Cpl. BERNSTEIN, A. H.
699	Pte. BERNSTEIN, A. B., 29th Bn.
1659A	Pte. BERNARD, F. H.,* 17th Bn.
	Pte. BARNARD, S.
3757	Pte. BETH, M., 29th Bn.
2980	2/A.M. BERNER, L., Aus. Air Force.
9387	Pte. BICKART, J., 12th Field Amb.
3356	Sgt. BIER, A., 57th Bn.
9	R.S.M. BIER, E. W., 7th Bn.
6724	Pte. BIRNBERG, L., 10th Bn.
1187	Pte. BISHOP, S.,* 5th Bn.
7845	Pte. BITTON, W. E., 6th Field Amb.
33274	Gnr. BLASKI, B. H., 38th Bn.
290	C.Q.M.S. BLAINE, C. N., 23rd Bn.
34944	Gnr. BLOCH, F. L.,* A.F.A.
8496	Pte. BLOCH, H. S., 106th H. Battery.
614	C.Q.M.S. BLOUSTEIN, H. M. (M.S.M.), 5th Bn.
1574	Pte. BLOCK, N. S.,* 14th Bn.
18861	Cpl. BLOOM, H. M., F.C., Eng.
230	Tpr. BLOUSTEIN, S., 9th L.H.
3415	Pte. BLOOM, A. T. H., 16th Bn.
1641	Pte. BLOOM, A., A.A.M.C.
28121	Gnr. BLOOM, G. A., A.F.A.
1542	Tpr. BLOOM, A., 7th L.H.
2871	Pte. BLOOM, H. W., 31st Bn.
201	Pte. BLOOM, L. R.,* 16th Bn.
5351	Cpl. CANTOR, A. C., 14th Bn.
993	Sgt. CANTOR, B.,* A.F.A.
11928	Gnr. CALDICOTT, H. L., 1st D.A.C.
18848	Dvr. CAMP, H.,* 12th A.F.A.
6043	Pte. CAPLAN, J., 3rd Bn.
1246	Tpr. CAREY, P. J., A.A.V.C.
6058	Cpl. CARO, M., H.Q.
14028	L/Cpl. CARO, G. A., No. 3 Aust. C.C.S.
18625	Pte. CARSON, A., A.A.M.C.
3272	Pte. CASHMAN, W. A., 32nd Bn.
5067	Pte. CHAIN, J., 4th Bn.
	Cpl. CHAPMAN, H., A.M.C.
1522	Sgt. CHART, A. T., 11th Bn.
3555	Pte. CHERRY, J., 59th Bn.
3934	Pte. CHOMEL, L., 48th Bn.
1311	Sgt. CLIFFORD, L., 11th Bn.
1290	Pte. CLIFFORD, D. L., A.M.C.
373	A/Cpl. COATE, J. C., 7th M.G.C.
2452	Cpl. COENORDEN, M., 1st Pioneers.
	Sig COHEN, A. V., 7th Bn.
3065	Pte. COHEN, P. S. (M.M.), A.V. Hosp.
4939	Rfm. COHEN, 3/2nd Vict. Rifles.
43	Pte. COHEN, W.,* 14th Bn.
	Pte. COHEN, L. G.
797A	Pte. COHEN, A., 22nd Bn.
3280	Pte. COHEN, A. A., 6th Bn.
5072	Pte. COHEN, H. L., 4th Bn.
6228	Pte. COHEN, A., 23rd Bn.
7215	Pte. COHEN, A. H., 8th Bn.
3128	Pte. COHEN, A., 47th Bn.
280	Pte. COHEN, A., 32nd Bn.
6739	Pte. COHEN, A.,* 16th Bn.
882	Cpl. COHEN, B. A., 4th G.R.O.C.
4087	Pte. COHEN, B. C., 19th Bn.
4391	Pte. COHEN, B., 21st Bn.
3025	S/Sgt. COHEN, B. D., 35th Bn.
20024	Cpl. COHEN, C. L., A.A.M.C.
	Pte. COHEN, C.
6240	Pte. COPELAND, G., 6th Bn.
4082	Pte. COPELAND, C. L., 22nd Bn.
32343	Gnr. COPPELL, V. S., 14th F.A. Bgde.
285	Pte. COHN, W. A., 2nd M.G.C.
9295	Dvr. COLLEY, J., 1st D.A.C.
477	Pte. COLLEY, A. W., 44th Bn.
6014	Pte. COLEY, R. H., 11th Bn.
619	Cpl. COLLINS, H. E., 68th Squad. A.F.C.
16924	Gnr. COLLINS, A., A.F.A.
936	Pte. COLLINS, L.,* 2nd Bn.
	Pte. COLLINS, S. G., 4th Bn.
3784	Pte. COLLINS, M. B., 2nd Bn.
7854	Gnr. COPPEL, E. G., 2nd D.A.C.
1594	Gnr. COLLINS, H., 54th Battery.
5420	Pte. CONNOR, R., 19th Bn.
3704	Pte. COOPER, H., 3rd Bn.
6787	Cpl. COOPERSMITH, H., 23rd Bn.
12419	Dvr. COPELAND, N., A.M.T.S.
	Pte. COPPELSON, R.
1904	Cpl. CORROL, J., 21st Bn.
5670	Pte. De COSTA, D., 8th Bn.
32365	Dvr. DA COSTA, I., 54th Battery.
3282	Pte. COSTELLO, F. J., 6th Bn.
6141	Pte. COTTEN, L., 11st Bn.
	Sgt. COTTON, C. W., A.O.C.
517	Pte. COX, F. C. A., 19th Bn.
89	Pte. CRAWCOUR, S. L., 8th M.G.C.
39732	Gnr. CRAWCOUR, H. R., 4th Battery.
16661	Pte. CRAWCOUR, I. V., A.A.M.C.
54170	Pte. COHEN, H. C., A.M.T.S.
16331	Pte. COHEN, E., A.M.C.
3027A	Pte. COHEN, C. P., 35th Bn.
21	Pte. COHEN, C. K., 1st Bn.
211	S/Sgt. COHEN, C. W., H.Q.
4153	Cpl. COHEN, K.M., 6th F.C.E.
3136	Pte. COHEN, D., 51st Bn.
	Sgt. COHEN, E. D.
2637	Bugler COHEN, F. J., 33rd Bn.
619	Pte. COHEN, F. L., 31st Bn.
6300	Pte. COHEN, G.,* 28th Bn.
54170	Pte. COHEN, H., 33rd Bn.
2359	Pte. COHEN, H., 9th Bn.
3706	Pte. COHEN, H., 3rd Bn.
	Pte. COHEN, H. D. V., 4th Bn.
2126	Pte. COHEN, H. L., 22nd Bn.
6540	Pte. COHEN, H.,* 19th Bn.

Australian Corps.—*Continued.*

3024	Pte. COHEN, H., 8th Bn.
2212	Pte. COHEN, F., 6th Bn.
2590	Pte. COHEN, R. G. S., 1st Pioneers.
5967	Spr. COHEN, J. A., 4th Tun. Coy.
1578	Cpl. COHEN, J., 1st A.A.S.C.
6229	Pte. COHEN, J. V., 1st Bn.
397	Sgt. COHEN, J. H., 14th Field Amb.
1630	Pte. COHEN, J.,* 59th Bn.
6043	Pte. COHEN, J., 19th Bn.
1333	Pte. COHEN, J., 33rd Bn.
5985	Pte. COHEN, T.,* 2nd Bn.
35	Cpl. COHEN, A. V., A.B.P.O.
3518	Pte. COHEN, M. C., 41st Bn.
6309	Pte. CROMER, S., 27th Bn.
2622A	Pte. CROOK, L., 9th Bn.
6057	Pte. CROOT, H., 22nd Bn.
1911	Pte. CULLEN, K. J., 1st Pioneers.
14028	Pte. CARL, G., C.C.S.
4322	Pte. COHEN, H. E., 11th Bn.
3467	Pte. CORRINHAM, W., 37th Bn.
2389	Pte. COHEN, A. V., 57th Bn.
1122	Bdr. CRAWFORD, S., 17th L.T.M.B.
33897	Gnr. COUSINS, E. G., 13th Bn.
	Pte. CONROW, D., 4th Bn.
951	Pte. CYFER, H., 2nd Bn.
708	Pte. CONROY, D.,* 4th Bn.
22252	Gnr. COHEN, R. M., 8th F.A.B.
	S.S.M. COHEN, M.,* 21st Bn.
3500	Cpl. COHEN, J.,* 24th Bn.
1864	Cpl. COHEN, N. S., 4th M.G.C.
325	Pte. COHEN, K. L., 13th M.G.C.
5666	L/Cpl. COHEN, L. L., 8th Bn.
216	Pte. COHEN, L. L., 8th Bn.
2346	Pte. COHEN, L. J., 56th Bn.
3359	Spr. COHEN, L., 54th Bn.
16795	Pte. COHEN, M., A.M.C.
3421	Pte. COHEN, M. S., 36th Bn.
5106	Pte. COHEN, M., 2nd Tun. Coy.
1894	Pte. COHEN, M., 23rd Bn.
5324	Sgt. COHEN, N. K., 19th Bn.
	Pte. COHEN, N. P., 30th Bn.
29254	Gnr. COHEN, O. E. M., 5th Battery.
4257	Pte. COHEN, R. I., A.A.M.C.
3711	Pte. COHEN, R. C., 8th Bn.
6052	Pte. COHEN, R. G., 17th Bn.
2590	Pte. COHEN, R. G. S., 1st Pioneer Bn.
	Pte. COHEN, S. A.
2895	Pte. COHEN, S., 30th Bn.
34720	Gnr. COHEN, S. H., 4th F.A.B.
3378	Pte. COHEN, S. I.,* 55th Bn.
276	Cpl. COHEN, S., M.G.C.
427	Sgt. COHEN, D. G., 3rd F.C.E.
957	Pte. COHEN, S. V., 5th Bn.
5552	Cpl. COHEN, V. H., 20th Bn.
18198	Pte. COHEN, V., A.A.M.C.
6294	Pte. COHEN, V., 21st Bn.
3026	Pte. COHEN, V., 35th Bn.

3279	Pte. COHEN, W. R., 4th Bn.
6476	Pte. COHN, C.,* 4th Bn.
6002	Pte. COHEN, W. F., 16th Bn.
	Pte. DALHAM, J. A.,
4357	Pte. DALMER, F., 35th Bn.
478	Pte. DANIELS, A., 44th Bn.
259	Pte. DAVEY, W., 37th Bn.
6486	Sgt. DAVID, T. J.,* 15th Bn.
	Sgt. DAVID, L. E. 6th Bn.
2412	Pte. DAVIDSON, A. B., 52nd Bn.
6498	Pte. DAVIDSON, C., 16th Bn.
2180	Pte. DAVIES, H. I., 46th Bn.
435	Pte. DAVIES, D. T. M., 27th Bn.
2535	Pte. DAVIES, C. H., 27th Bn.
4595	Pte. DAVIES, J., 16th Bn.
5010	Pte. DAVIS, J. H., 29th Bn.
6072	Pte. DAVIS, R., 25th Bn.
6247	Pte. DAVIS, R., 6th Bn.
1480	Pte. DAVIS, A.,* 22nd Bn.
139	Pte. DAVIS, H. A., 18th Bn.
3044	Pte. DAVIS, C. F., 33rd Bn.
2104A	Pte. DAVIES, F. J., 29th Battery.
7832	Pte. DAVIS, C., 1st Bn.
5372	Pte. DAVIS, D. W., 11th Bn.
1463	Gnr. DAVIS, W. E., 1st A.S. Battery.
4099	Pte. DAVIS, O. H., 21st Bn.
20482	Pnr. DAVIES, R. W., Tun. Coy.
6804	Pte. DAVIS, E. P.,* 28th Bn.
3741	Pte. DAVIS, J., 3rd Bn.
1662	Spr. DAVIS, H. E., 5th F.C.E.
935	Spr. DAVIS, F. D., 49th Bn.
2694	Gnr. DAVIS, S., 3rd A. Artil.
774	Pte. DAVIS, E. P.,* 11th Bn.
20	Cpl. DAVIS, F. J., 1st Field Amb.
1070	Cpl. DIAMOND, S. W., 12th A. Bgde.
362	Pte. DEFRIES, S. H., 56th Bn.
9300	Pte. DIAMOND, S. L., 2nd D.A.C.
5807	Drv. DIAMOND, B. H., 1st F.A.B.
	Pte. DOMINSKI, O. E.
1947	Pte. DOEL, B. F., 33rd Bn.
	Gnr. DEFRIES, H., A.G.A.
	Pte. DREYFUS, C.
	Dispenser DRYEN, M., A.M.S.
2687	Pte. DONIZER, S.
625862	Dvr. DIAMOND, A. A., A.F.A.
1113	Pte. DEAS, E. D.,* 54th Bn.
3288	Pte. DAVIS, C. E., 41st Bn.
3280	Pte. DAVIS, R., 6th Bn.
5817	Pte. DEATKER, E. F., 25th Bn.
1630	Pte. DEGARVILLIERES, E., 25th Bn.
3639	Pte. DE GROEN, L. S., 18th Bn.
7079	Pte. DENNISON, H., 1st Bn.
14861	Pte. DENNERSTEIN, W., 1st C.C.S.
260	Bglr. DENNERSTEIN, A., 37th Bn.
1420	Pte. DENTON, E. P., 44th Bn.
225	Pte. DENTON, E. P., 4th Bn.
2571A	Pte. DEVORETSKY, F., 4th D.A.C.
9683	Pte. DIMDORE, S., 14th Field Amb.

Australian Corps.—*Continued.*

2912	Pte. DONIGER, H., 30th Bn.
4477	Pte. DORFMAN, W., 54th Bn.
3045	Dvr. DOTGER, E., 4th D.A.C.
614	Pte. DOCURA, A. L. J., 2nd Bn.
2471	Pte. DREW, 16th Bn.
2363	Pte. DURLACHER, L.,* 4th M.G.C.
34	Pte. DRING, A., 2nd M.G.C.
3278	Pte. DUMISKI, O. E., 47th Bn.
6014	Pte. DUSENBERG, H. A., 16th Bn.
1021	Spr. DYMOND, L., 13th Fld. Coy. R.E.
1874	Pte. DETINOULD, Aus. D.A.P.
1645	Dvr. DETMOLD, F. J., 1st A.S. Park.
317	Pte. DELMAR, 1st D.A.C.
5600	Pte. DAVIES, G. C., 25th Bn.
3039	Pte. DAVIDSON, A. E., 34th Bn.
2062	Pte. EDELSTEIN, H. V.,* 37th Bn.
4682	Cpl. EDMONDS, A. T., 20th Bn.
725	Sgt. EHRENBERG, S. M.,* 5th Bn.
5667	Pte. EITELBERG, W., 14th Bn.
1646	Pte. EISENTRAGER, M. E. C., 49th Bn.
5022	Pte. EKLUND, C., 32nd Bn.
6753	Q.M.S. ELLICE, A. Y. R., 11th Bn.
5836	Pte. ELLICE, B. E.,* 11th Bn.
53717	A/Cpl. ELLIS, V. B., 13th Bn.
8177	Sgt. EILENBERG, E. G., A.M.C.
29267	Gnr. ELLISON, H. H., A.F.A.
7576	Bdr. ELLIOTT, S., 1st F.A.B.
2646	Pte. ELY, N. 21st Bn.
1115	Pte. EMANUEL, F. B., 34th Bn.
8360	Pte. EMANUEL, H. L., 5th Field Amb.
26426	Dvr. ESSERMAN, E., 2nd D.A.C.
	Pte. EDWARDS, A. S., 4th Bn.
5573	Sig. EDWARDS, A. T., 25th Bn.
	Pte. EPSTEIN, M.
	Pte. ELSSNER, A. L., 37th Bn.
	Sgt. EMANUEL, J. (M.M.), Inf.
34739	Gnr. FADER, M. A., A.F.A.
12	Pte. FALK, A.,* 1st Anzac Bn.
219	Pte. FALK, C. J., 10th Bn.
1623	Pte. FALK, G. E., 6th Bn.
1014	Pte. FAY, A. H., 12th Bn.
3380	Pte. FEILMAN, H. B., 51st Bn.
3158	Pte. FELDMAN, I., 51st Bn.
599	Cpl. FELDMAN, N., 7th M.G.C.
2163	Pte. FELDT, A., 56th Bn.
4113	Pte. FELDT, I., 19th Bn.
2164	Pte. FELDT, M., 56th Bn.
3299	Pte. FELDT, D., 34th Bn.
3379	Pte. FELDT, S., 51st Bn.
6715	L/Cpl. FERNANDEZ, A., A.A.M.C.
4789	Pte. FERNANDEZ, J. F.,* 45th Bn.
1639	Pte. FERNDALE, D., 45th Bn.
1997	Pte. FERSTAT, A., 16th Bn.
20129	Dvr. FERSTAT, A., A.F.A.
3745	Sgt. FIENBERG, L. M., 47th Bn.
9101	Pte. FINEBERT, E., A.S.C.
33148	Gnr. FINK, T., A.F.A.
674	Pte. FINK, G.,* 16th Bn.
450	Cpl. FINKELSTEIN, H. C.,* 20th Bn.
5819	Pte. FISCHER, P., 20th Bn.
5269	Pte. FISCHER, H., 31st Bn.
5679	Pte. FITZALAN, J., 17th Field Amb.
6165	Pte. FLACK, J. A., 24th Bn.
1147	Pte. FLEGELTAUB, A., 3rd Mines Corps.
1539	Pte. FLEGELTAUB, B., 11th Bn.
	Pte. FLEGELTAUB, G.
1596	Pte. FLESEMOOR, J., 5th Pioneers.
58294	Pte. FLITTERMAN, F., 34th Bn.
7230	Pte. FOLLICK, A. C., A.A.S.C.
20289	Pte. FOX, L., 3rd D.S.C
4807	Pte. FRANCES, S., 38th Bn.
106	S./M. FRANKFORD, E. (M.S.M.), 2nd L.H.
382	Pte. FRANKEL, A. P., 49th Bn.
2027A	Cpl. FRANKEL, S.,* 24th Bn.
6953	Pte. FRANKEL, L. B., 10th Bn.
4786	Pte. FRANKENBERG, E., 32nd Bn.
33022	Gnr. FRANKLIN, C. L., 4th D.A.C.
27325	Dvr. FRANKS, J., 1st D.A.A.C.
	Pte. FRANKS, S., 3rd Bn.
2313	Pte. FRANKS, R.,* 38th Bn.
7244	Pte. FREEDMAN, A.,* 13th Bn.
907	Gnr. FREDMAN, L. W., 36th A.H.A.
909	Gnr. FREEDMAN, S., 1st A.S. Battery.
	Pte. FREADMAN, E., 4th Bn.
53020	Gnr. FREEMAN, A., 42nd Bn.
39976	Pte. FREEMAN, D., Sig. Sec.
	Sgt. FREEMAN, L.
108	W.O. FREIDMAN, L., A.F.A.
1913A	Pte. FRIBERG, C. C., 46th Bn.
20956	Gnr. FRIEDLANDER, W. G., A.F.A.
3501	Cpl. FREEDLANDER, B., 53rd Bn.
4304A	Pte. FRIEND, Y., 51st Bn.
1504	Sgt. FROMER, H., 24th Bn.
2896	Pte. FRUEDENBERG, B. C.,* 49th Bn.
2898	Pte. FRUEDENSTEIN, W. I., 19th Bn.
14017	Cpl. FREEDMAN, E., C.C.S.
1506	Pte. FARCHY, L., 3rd Bn.
2304	Pte. FRYBERG, H. H., 6th Bn.
2323	Pte. FITTISOFF, M., 48th Bn.
2936	Pte. FREUDENTHAL, I., 46th Bn.
1002	Spr. FLEGELTAUB, A., 3rd Aust. Tun. Coy.
585	Pte. FELB, F. R., 37th Bn.
	Pte. FELS, S., 13th Bn.
880	Sgt. FIERMAN, N. B., 3rd Div. Art.
676	Pte. FRANK, E., 1st Field Bakery.
1504	Pte. FROMER, H.,* 24th Bn.
	Pte. GABRIEL, F. G.
3516	Pte. GABRIEL, A. F., 13th Bn.
2309	Pte. GABRIEL, V., 34th Bn.
2659	Pte. GABRIELSON, H., 16th Bn.
7006	Sgt. GALLAND, B., 18th Bn.
37551	Bdr. GARCIA, G. M., Art.
461	Pte. GARDINER, H., 2nd Bn.
38496	Cpl. GEORGE, F., 3rd D.A.C.
5307	Cpl. GEORGE, L., 8th F.A.B.

Australian Corps.—*Continued.*

7742	Pte. GERSHEN, M., 16th Bn.
19425	Pte. GERSON, J., A.A.M.C.
52292	Pte. GANANBURG, C. W., 40th Bn.
4243	Sgt. GILD, S., 32nd Bn.
5461	Pte. GENSBURG, J., A.V.C.
2470	Sgt. GLANCE, A. M., 29th Bn.
3465	Pte. GLANCE, A., 16th Bn.
594	Pte. GLASS, M. H., 37th Bn.
101349	Gnr. GLASSER, M., A.F.A.
387	Pte. GLASSER, H., 40th Bn.
3976	Cpl. GLUCK, M. B., 51st Bn.
6425	Pte. GLICK, H. W., 28th Bn.
2058	Pte. GLOVER, P., 33rd Bn.
42	Pte. GLUCK, L. J.,* 11th Bn.
5014	Pte. GOFFIN, B., 22nd Bn.
118	Pte. GOLDBERG, C., 39th Bn.
3055	Pte. GOLDBERG, J., 36th Bn.
5591	Pte. GOLDBERG, J., 22nd Bn.
5103	Pte. GOLDBERG, B., 14th Bn.
50182	Pte. GOLDBERG, H., 22nd Bn.
62312	Pte. GOLDBERG, J., 27th Bn.
27487	Gnr. GOLDBERG, J. C., 2nd Amb. Sub. Park.
8867	Pte. GOLDENBERG, A., 5th Field. Amb.
10931	Pte. GOLDEN, R., 1st R.M.T.C.
2386	Pte. GOLDING, A., 2nd Pioneers.
15313	Spr. GOLDING, S. A., 12th F.C.E.
66	Cpl. GOLDMAN, A., 30th Bn.
4421	Pte. GOLDMAN, V. J., 30th Bn.
1704	Spr. GOLDMAN, L., 2nd Pioneers.
227	Bmb./Sgt. GOLDRING, L., 12th F.A.B.
	Pte. GOLDRING, C., 9th Bn.
140	Pte. GOLDRING, G.,* 15th Bn.
4194	Pte. GOLDSMITH, W. D., 14th Bn.
236	Pte. GOLDSMITH, H. T., 34th Bn.
5025	Pte. GOLDSTEIN, E., 30th Bn.
5096	Pte. GOLDSMITH, Y. A., 44th Bn.
5338	Pte. GOLDSTEIN, R., 21st Bn.
3118	Pte. GOLDSTEIN. A., 8th Bn.
3746	Sgt. GOLDSTEIN, D. H., 54th Bn.
16565	Spr. GOLDSTEIN, P., A.R.S.U.
6153	Pte. GOLDSTEIN, F., 23rd Bn.
2701	A.M. GOLDSTEIN, O. T., A.F.C.
1548	Pte. GOLDSTEIN, L. N., 16th Bn.
6249	Pte. GOLDSTEIN, L., 9th Bn.
887	Sgt. GOLDSTON, A.,* 37th Bn.
333	Cpl. GOLDWATER, N.,* 4th Bn.
2573	Pte. GOODMAN, G. W., 44th Bn.
3408	Pte. GOODMAN, R. G.,* 55th Bn.
4501	A/C.S.M. GOODMAN, D. W., 4th Bn.
2373	Pte. GOODMAN, C. W., 17th Bn.
435	Sgt. GOODMAN, R., 3rd Pioneers.
2045	Pte. GOODMAN, M., 30th Bn.
595	Dvr. GOODRICK, A., 21st H. Battery.
10766	Gnr. GORDON, A. L.R., 6th F.A.B.
61	Pte. GORDON, D., Cyclists Corps.
2671	Pte. GORFINE, S., 21st Bn.
1792	Pte. GOTHARD, W., 6th Bn.
2797	Pte. GOTTLIEB, H. A. (M.M., D.C.M.), 16th Bn.
53585	Pte. GOULD, N., 56th Bn.
20469	Spr. GOULD, B., 18/5th Engineers.
5059	Pte. GOULDSTON, V. S., 52nd Bn.
3173	Pte. GRANGER, J., 39th Bn.
1540	Pte. GRANSAUSKY, F., 3rd M.G.C.
3291	Cpl. GREEN, S., 46th Bn.
9609	Pte. GREEN, S. M., 15th Field Amb.
3342	Cpl. GREEN, S., 1st Pioneers.
2157	Pte. GREEN, L. H. S., 25th M.G.C.
4363	Pte. GREEN, S., 25th M.G.C.
6006	Pte. GREEN, T. R.,* 4th Bn.
20172	Gnr. GREEN, J. M., 8th F.A.
4223	Pte. GREEN, I., 1st Pioneers.
53582	Pte. GREEN, J., 56th Bn.
5377	Pte. GREEN, M. S., 13th Bn.
3109	Pte. GREENBAUM, S. E., 8th Bn.
514	Pte. GREENBERG, J. S., 17th Bn.
4776	Pte. GREENBURY, I., 15th Bn.
6057	Pte. GREENBERG, W., 23rd Bn.
5829	Pte. GREENBERG, P., 2nd M.T. Coy.
5677	Pte. GREENFIELD, A. C., 3rd Bn.
60562	Pte. GREENSTEIN, W., 2nd Bn.
6314	Spr. GREENWALD, S., 4th F.C.E.
7777	Pte. GRIEF, P., 11th Bn.
9958	L/Cpl. GRIMMISH, L. J., 3rd A.G.H.
1748	Cpl. GRIMISH, A. B.,* 9th Bn.
15806	Pte. GREENWOOD, A., 2nd Field Amb.
	Pte. GRIMMICH, J. J., 6th L.H.
1139	Pte. GRIMMISH, J. P., 9th Bn.
275	Pte. GRIMBLATT, S., A.M.C.
246	Cpl. GROSSMAN, S., 14th L.H.
1827	Cpl. GROUSE, R. C.,* 36th Bn.
2308	Pte. GUBBAY, J. M.,* 36th Bn.
1130	Pte. GUILFOYLE, J., 35th Bn.
2019	Pte. GUINSBERG, A., 23rd Bn.
6029	Pte. GLUSHNER, E., 39th Bn.
2569	Pte. GOOD, L., 39th Bn.
2291	L/Cpl. GOLDENBERG, L., 12th L.T.M.B.
7484	Pte. GOLDBERG, L., 5th Bn.
2079	C.Q.M.S. GEISE, F., 42nd Bn.
	Pte. GROSS, A., 22nd Bn.
	Pte. GROSS, D., A.M.C.
275	Pte. GRINBLAT, S., A.M.C.
	Cpl. GILBERT, A., Motor Cyclists.
2705	Gnr. GURR, H. S.,* 13th F.A.B.
6057	Pte. GROAT, J. W. S., 20th Bn.
	Pte. GROSSMAN, R., 7th Bn.
L/37706	Dvr. GLASS, S., N.Z. A.S.P.
	Pte. GOTTLIEB, H. A. (D.C.M., M.M.), In.
563	Pte. HAINSON, D., 23rd Bn.
3166	Pte. HAIFF, S., 53rd Bn.
1136	Pte. HAINS, C. L., 9th L.H.
578	Pte. HAINS, H. J., A.A.M.C.
2150	Pte. HAINS, M.,* 3rd Bn.
14634	Sgt. HAINS, P., Div. Cyclist Corps.
1558	Pte. HAMBURGER, C. W., 54th Bn.

Australian Corps.—*Continued.*

68	Cpl. HAMBURGER, S., 38th Bn.
14561	Pte. HANMEL, W., A.S.C.
2604	Pte. HAMMERSBERG, R. M.,* 14th Bn.
4710	Pte. HAVENSTEIN, C., 23rd Bn.
2578	Pte. HANSMAN, H. J.,* 37th Bn.
883	A.M. HANSMAN, E. E.,* A.F.C.
2173	Pte. HARBERT, G.,* 59th Bn.
6824	L/Cpl. HARLEM, B. J., 21st Bn.
19850	Pte. HARLEM, J. D., A.M.C.
2707	2/A.M. HARLEM, D. E., A.F.C.
2611	Pte. HARLEIN, E., 60th Bn.
1098	Tpr. HARLAP, L., 10th L.H.
36097	Gnr. HARBARD, C. S., F.A.B.
1592	Pte. HARRIS, B. M., 17th A.M.C.
4799	Pte. HARRIS, J., 43rd Bn.
3406	L/Cpl. HARRIS, A., 59th Bn.
3372	Pte. HARRIS, R. L., 49th Bn.
8281	Dvr. HARRIS, H., 5th Div. Train.
18426	Pte. HARRIS, M., A.A.M.C.
1592	Pte. HARRIS, B., 7th Field Amb.
13789	Pte. HARRIS, C. D., 16th Field Amb.
6604	Cpl. HARRIS, B., 8th F.A.B.
8070	Sgt. HARRIS, P. L., D.A.P.
1354	L/Cpl. HART, H.,* 7th Bn.
1815	Bdr. HARRIS, E. B., 14th F.A.B.
15341	Spr. HARRIS, J. D., 9th Engineers.
53835	Pte. HARRIS, B., 7th Bn.
35353	Gnr. HARRIS, J. C., 7th F.A.B.
6444	Cpl. HARRIS, S. W.,* 20th Bn.
4811	Bdr. HARRIS, W. K., 1st D.A.C.
4454	A/Cpl. HARRIS, R. L., 22nd Bn.
2187	Tpr. HARRIS, W., 7th L.H.
1937	Pte. HARRIS, M. H., 18th Bn.
15	Cpl. HARRIS, E. O. 2nd Div. H.Q.
3158	Pte. HARRIS, M., 45th Bn.
1559	Pte. HARRISON, R. J., 7th Bn.
6032	Pte. HART, E. J., 11th Field Amb.
6582	Pte. HART, J. H., 7th Field Amb.
2056	Pte. HART, O. R., 3rd A.L.T.M.B.
4486	Cpl. HART, H. S., 10th Bn.
3104	Pte. HART, L., 57th Bn.
21354	Pte. HART, W. N., 3rd D.A.C.
2785	Pte. HART, H., 58th Bn.
1227	Pte. HART, H. J., 17th Bn.
1943	Sgt. HART, C. A. H.,* 18th Bn.
190	Pte. HART, J.,* 30th Bn.
1010	Dvr. HART, W. Y., 14th F.A.B.
3131	Pte. HART, J., 28th Bn.
267	Pte. HART, L.,* 7th Bn.
559	Pte. HART, R. J., 40th Bn.
6465	Pte. HART, J.,* 7th Bn.
3131	Pte. HART, J., 28th Bn.
14324	Pte. HART, H., A.M.C.
71	Cpl. HART, H. A.,* 8th Bn.
4138	Pte. HEILMAN, R., 19th Bn.
2635	Cpl. HEILMAN, N., 4th Bn.
2617	2/A.M. HIELMAN, H., A.F.C.
570	Pte. HILL, G., 7th Bn.
17115	Gnr. HIMMELHOCK, A., 53rd Battery.
2296	Cpl. HINES, J., 45th Bn.
47	L/Cpl. HINES, M. G., 31st Bn.
1728	Pte. HIRSCHFIELD, F. B., 27th Bn.
168	Pte. HOARE, F., 22nd Bn.
1661	Pte. HOFFMAN, G., 49th Bn.
92	Pte. HOFFMAN, R. W., 36th Bn.
3334	Pte. HOFFMAN, W., 9th Field Amb.
5028	Pte. HOFFMAN, J. A., 28th Bn.
14610	Pte. HOFFMAN, W., 2nd A.F.A.
1633	Pte. HOFFMAN, J., 28th Bn.
16052	Gnr. HONEY, S., Art.
11987	Pte. HOLTZBAUM, W., 9th Field Amb
2063	Pte. HOLTZBAUM, T. R.,* 33rd Bn.
3363	Pte. HOULDER, W. R., 38th Bn.
913	Pte. HUGHES, H. N., M.G.C.
4138	Pte. HEILMAN, R., 19th Bn.
6625	Dvr. HUSSIES, W. R., 21st Bn.
16053	Gnr. HUMBERLD, J. H., 3rd Battery.
5359	Pte. HYAMS, W.,* 24th Bn.
2334	Pte. HYAMS, M. H., 36th Bn.
4519	Pte. HYLAND, A., 14th Bn.
3925	Dvr. HYMAN, J., 53rd Battery.
574	Pte. HECKSNER, B. H., 43nd Bn.
886	Pte. HYAMS, F. M., 4th Tropical Force.
7021	Pte. HYMAN, A., 2nd Bn.
3059	Spr. HOLLEBONE, S. T., 1st A.L.R.O. Coy.
896	Sgt. HART, M. P., 20th Bn.
	Spr. HAST, H. L., Aus. Eng.
1227	Pte. HART, H. J., 17th Bn.
3661	Pte. HATFIELD, H., 49th Bn.
6747	Pte. HATFIELD, J. W., 2nd Bn.
1663	L/Cpl. HATFIELD, E. H., 47th Bn.
6354	Pte. HATFIELD, C., 22nd Bn.
2635	L/Cpl. HIELMANN, N. N., 4th Bn.
50403	Gnr. HELMETT, P. W., 6th F.C.E.
18647	Pte. HENRY, A. S., A.M.C.
6265	Pte. HEPLEIN, M., 9th Bn.
2617	2/A.M. HIELMAN, H., A.F.C.
6833A	Pte. HERMAN, G. H. N., 24th Bn.
2910	Pte. HERMAN, C.,* 58th Bn.
1770	Pte. HERMAN, E., 7th Bn.
445	Pte. HEMAN, W., 34th Bn.
8072	Sgt. HERMAN, L. C., 5th Div. Train.
16165	Pte. HERMAN, A. E., 4th Field Amb.
1706	Pte. HERMAN, H. E.,* 17th Bn.
4370	Pte. HERMAN, M. P.,* 30th Bn.
3800	Pte. HERMAN, J., 4th Div. H.Q.
5602	Pte. HERMAN, W. R.,* 26th Bn.
3852	Pte. HERMAN, F. L., 5th Pioneers.
2198	Pte. HERMAN, F., 26th Bn.
476	Pte. HERRMAN, H. J., 39th Bn.
6356	Pte. HERZ, M. L. S., 22nd Bn.
1597	Spr. HESSION, J. J., 13th F.C.E.
22328	Gnr. HYMAN, L., 6th Bgde. A.F.A.
400	Pte. HICKMAN, L., 2nd Pioneers.
10307	Dvr. ISAACS, E. H., A.S.C.

Australian Corps.—*Continued.*

982	Pte. Isaacs, H., 9th Bn.
2173	Pte. Idstein, V. F.,* 35th Bn.
27513	Pte. Iken, E., A.V.C.
14904	Pte. Iken, J. E., A.S.C.
5666	Pte. Illfield, J.,* 20th Bn.
2315	Dvr. Ipp, J., 1st Bty. A.F.A.
3161	Pte. Isaac, A. E., 14th Field Amb.
6536	2/A.M. Isaac, L. G., A.F.C.
4959	Gnr. Isaac, V. H., 1st F.A.B.
2828	Sgt. Isaacs, L. D., 2nd Bn.
4838	Sgt. Isaacs, S., 7th Bn.
7514	Pte. Isaacs, R. L., 14th Bn.
4757	Pte. Isaac, R. S., 18th Bn.
4138	Pte. Isaacs, W.,* 22nd Bn.
3655	Pte. Isaacs, P., 32nd Bn.
505A	C.Q.M.S. Isaacs, D. J. (M.S.M.), 3rd M.G. Bn.
751	Pte. Isaacs, H., 23rd Bn.
5400	Pte. Isaacs, S. W., 7th Bn.
1288	Spr. Isaacs, M. T., 1st Bn. Mines.
2398	Pte. Isaacs, F. W., 49th Bn.
3626	Sgt. Isaacs, L. E., 40th Bn.
2936	Pte. Israel, R., 50th Bn.
867	Gnr. Israel, G., 1st A.S. Bty.
5131	Pte. Israel, H. R., 56th Bn.
2543	Sgt. Israel, H., 6th Bn.
3076	Pte. Israel, A.,* 33rd Bn.
595	Cpl. Israel, M. S., 3rd Sig. Troop.
2704	L/Cpl. Israel, L. C. M.,* 20th Bn.
2389	Sgt. Israel, N. J., 58th Bn.
22649	Spr. Israel, L., 4th Div. Sig. Coy.
458	L/Cpl. Jacobs, C. J. (M.M.), 3rd Pion. Bn.
1938	Pte. Jacobs, J. D., 22nd Bn.
101	Pte. Jacobs, W., 7th Bn.
13262	Dvr. Jacobs, F. W., A.M.C.
1934a	Pte. Jacobs, H., 43rd Bn.
15343	Pte. Jacobs, F. M., A.S.C.
23762	Gnr. Jacobs, C. N., 3rd Battery.
2286	Pte. Jacobs, M., 22nd Bn.
4453	Cpl. Jacobs, A. M.,* 27th Bn.
2197	Pte. Jacobs, G. C., 50th Bn.
2853	Pte. Jacobs, J. T., 53rd Bn.
2105	Dvr. Jacobs, L., 1st D.A.C.
795	Pte. Jacobs, H. W., 33rd Bn.
	Pte. Jacobs, S. T., 13th Bn.
7269	Pte. Jacobs, A. E., 1st Bn.
4807	Pte. Jacobs, M. E., 32nd Bn.
1148	Pte. Jacobs, W. S., 43rd Bn.
	Pte. Jacobs, A. N. (M.M.), 4th Bn.
2168	Pte. Jacobs, E. H., 5th Bn.
952	Dvr. Jacobs, H. E., 10th Bn.
833	Dvr. Jacobson, A. E., 44th Bn.
4171	Pte. Jacobson, L. B., 2nd Field Amb.
3706	Pte. Jacobson, B. C., 1st Pioneers.
6042	Pte. Jacobson, F. J., 16th Bn.
3718	Pte. Jacobson, L., 18th Bn.
18881	Sgt. Jaques, H., 25th Battery.
25	Spr. Jacobson, A. H., L.H.
1945	Spr. Jennings, W., 2nd F.C.E.
1968	Spr. Jenetzky, O., 2nd L.R.O.C.
1246	L/Cpl. Jew, W., 5th Bn.
489	Pte. Joel, M. S., 39th Bn.
1850	Sgt. Joel, J., 4th Bn.
1382	Pte. Jacob, M., 54th Bn.
31824	Gnr. Jacob, N. F., 1st Div. Artillery.
3387	Pte. Jacks, A.,* 49th Bn.
	Pte. Jabinsky, A.
5130	Pte. Jacobs, A. J., 46th Bn.
3421	Pte. Jacobs, H. J., 5th Bn.
6566	Cpl. Jacobs, S., 27th Bn.
2662	Pte. Jacobs, W. G., 36th Bn.
3556	Pte. Jacobs, F. W., 58th Bn.
1674	Pte. Jacobs, F., 6th B.I.R.O. Coy.
324	Pte. Jacobs, L. G., 43rd Bn.
3421	Pte. Jacobs, H. J., 29th Bn.
1694	Pte. Jacobs, J. G., 50th Bn.
2363	Tpr. Jacobs, M. J., 10th L.H.
7853	Sgt. Jacobs, L., Cyclists' Coy.
3264	Pte. Jacobs, S., 32nd Bn.
4524	Pte. Jacobs, R. J., 34th Bn.
1459	Pte. Jacobs, S. A.,* 1st L.H.
1685	Pte. Jacobs, H., 16th Bn.
6378	L/Cpl. Jacobs, C. A., 4th A.M.T.
6046	Pte. Jacobs, V. N.,* 16th Bn.
325	Pte. Jacobs, P. K.,* 43rd Bn.
13438	Dvr. Jacobs, S., 2nd D.S.
33641	Pte. Jacobs, J. L., 8th L.T.M.B.
3144	Pte. Jacobs, E. W., 5th Bn.
1566	Pte. Jacob, R. C., 53rd Bn.
4359	L/Cpl. Jacobs, B., 3rd A.F.A.
357	Pte. Jacobs, T. E., 27th Bn.
	Cpl. Jacobs, H., 9th Bn.
	Dvr. Jacobs, C., 2nd F.A. Bde.
4357	Pte. Johnstone, F.
2681	Pte. Jonas, E.,* 1st Pioneers.
2278	Pte. Jonas, A. R. B.,* 48th Bn.
225	Sgt. Jonas, B.,* 33rd Bn.
	Pte. Jonas, C., 16th Bn.
2837	Sgt. Jonas, G. M., 46th Bn.
14262	Dvr. Jones, B. G., 2nd A. Siege Bde., A.C.
48	Pte. Jones, A. C., 1st Field Amb.
7261	Pte. Jones, H. M., 2nd Bn.
8731	Pte. Jonsen, O. C., 7th Field Amb.
8730	Pte. Jonsen, W. S., 7th Field Amb.
4589	Pte. Joseph, F. H., 22nd Bn.
7079	Pte. Josephs, J., 19th Bn.
1070	Gnr. Joseph, A., 12th F.A.B.
6522	Pte. Joseph, S. A.,* 7th Bn.
666	Pte. Joseph, B. A., 12th Bde., H.Q.
24386	Gnr. Josephs, W. S., 3rd By., D.A.C.
1220	Dvr. Joseph, F., 17th Bn.
548	Pte. Joseph, H. A., 8th Bde., H.Q.
1841	Pte. Joseph, E., 12th Bn.
	Cpl. Jacobson, A. (M.M.), Inf.
2794	Pte. Joseph, M. C. C., A.F.C.

Australian Corps.—*Continued.*

2699	Pte. Joseph, O. H., 46th Bn.
8760	Pte. Joseph, I., 6th Field Amb.
10629	Dvr. Joseph, E. F., 25th A.A.S.C.
500	Cpl. Josephs, W. C.,* 43rd Bn.
3660	S/Sgt. Joseph, L. C., Dental Corps.
1055	Pte. Joseph, J. D.,* 31st Bn.
	Pte. Jacobs, A. N. (M.M.), A.A.M.C.
6399	Pte. Joseph, F. R., 17th Bn.
2736	Dvr. Joseph, A., 45th Battery.
	Dvr. Joseph, C., 6th Field Amb.
6643	Pte. Joseph, M., 63rd Bn.
6758	Pte. Josephson, J., 1st Bn.
2392	Sgt. Judell, C., 30th Bn.
213	Q.M.S. Judell, E. M.,* 9th L.H.
2435	Pte. Jenkins, O. M., 57th Bn.
66	Pte. Jacoby, 10th Bn.
905	Pte. Jacobs, B. H., 26th Bn.
31011	Pte. Jackson, C. M.,* 10th Field Amb.
1772	Pte. Jacobs, L. W.,* 7th Bn.
19303	Gnr. Jacobson, R. E.,* 7th Field Art.
130	Tpr. Kaiser, S. T., 1st L.H.
134	Pte. Kafer, F.,* 53rd Bn.
1783	Bdr. Kalik, L., 5th L.H.
1684	Pte. Kamesaroff, P., 56th Bn.
7021	Pte. Karmel, E. M., 7th Bn.
5389	Pte. Katzberg, E. W., 48th Bn.
1329	L/Cpl. Kaufman, C.,* 15th Bn.
2220	Pte. Kaufman, K.,* 58th Bn.
48	Pte. Katz, L. S., 13th Bn.
2411	Pte. Kaufmann, M. O., 14th Bn.
54006	Pte. Kersh, A., 3rd Bn.
475	Pte. Kessell, R., 34th Bn.
4450	Cpl. Kessel, I., 1st Bn.
	Pte. Keesing, A., A.M.C.
2617	Pte. Keesing, R. A., 51st Bn.
	Pte. Keesing, H., 20th Bn.
5057	Pte. Keizer, N. D., 18th Bn.
	Sgt. Keswell, I. (D.C.M.), Inf.
2190	Pte. Keppel, T. J., 48th Bn.
6996	Pte. King, H. J., 2nd Bn.
62	Sgt. King, T., 1st Field Amb.
38642	Gnr. Kino, W. P., 12th A. Bde.
110	Pte. Kirchener, G., 36th Bn.
3529	Spr. Kirk, R., 4th Coy.
6556	Gnr. Kirk, T. E., 4th A.F.A.
3088	Sgt. Kirvalidge, P. I., 54th Bn.
3070	Pte. Klein, A., 56th Bn.
2133	Pte. Klein, J.,* 26th Bn.
7020	Pte. Klein, C. H., 3rd Bn.
31593	Gnr. Klinberg, H. T.,* 4th Art. Bde.
3539	Pte. Kloot, P. P., 5th Bn.
1711	L/Cpl. Kohn, S. E., 60th Bn.
6299	Pte. Kohn, E. R., 7th Bn.
3174	Pte. Kohn, C., 37th Bn.
66	Pte. Kohn, S.,* 24th Bn.
5421	Pte. Kohen, H. J., 6th Bn.
4465	Pte. Kosky, J. J., 27th Bn.
3833	L/Cpl. Kospit, A. S., 5th Bn.
6460	W./O. Kott, M., 13th Bn.
1235	Bgl. Kotton, M.,* 4th Bn.
463	Pte. Krausman, N., 3rd Pioneer Bn.
2345	Pte. Kramer, H. M., 34th Bn.
953	Pte. Krantz, H. A., 17th Bn.
	Tpr. Krantz, H. B., 8th L.H.
2281	Cpl. Krantz, S. H., 43rd Bn.
4161	Pte. Kreisman, J. H.,* 25th Bn.
7714	Gnr. Kresner, H., 2nd D.A.C.
19067	Pte. Kresner, E., A.A.M.C.
978	Pte. Krug, D.,* 44th Bn.
216894	Gnr. Kloot, A., A.F.A.
	Pte. Klein, F. W. (M.M.), Inf.
5043	Pte. Kunin, J.,* 22nd Bn.
11154	Pte. Kurtz, D. M., 11th F. Amb.
6265	Pte. Keplein, M. B., 9th Bn.
	Pte. Kopit, W. L., 4th Bn.
19838	Pte. Kosminsky, C. S., No. 2 Hosp. Ship.
	Spr. Krakower, S., 3rd Tunnelling Coy.
1063	Pte. Krakouer, F., 3rd Bn.
	Pte. Krakouer, R., 3rd Bn.
	Pte. Lakovsky, E., 10th Bn.
	Pte. Laredo, D., 14th Bn.
12633	Pte. Langley, J., 11th Field Amb.
330	Pte. Lambert, D., 43rd Bn.
256	Pte. Lacey, R., 18th Bn.
5661	Pte. Landes, L. S., 19th Bn.
	Gnr. Landes, L., 1st H. Siege Battery.
1304	Gnr. Lakovsky, D., Field Artillery.
2662	Pte. Lundberg, M. O. W., 32nd Bn.
3336	Pte. Landsler, E. L.,* 53rd Bn.
718	Pte. Langley, J. V., 33rd Bn.
3089	Pte. Langley, S. A., 30th Bn.
31532	Dvr. Langley, J. M., A.F.A.
3836	Pte. Langford, L., 6th Bn.
723	Pte. Latzer, H., 6th Bn.
6436	Pte. Lawrence, K. F., 6th Field Amb.
56360	Pte. Lawrence, H. S., 12th Bn.
2942	Pte. Lawrence, N. I., 48th Bn.
2707	Pte. Lazarus, T. H., 46th Bn.
3836	Pte. Lazarus, R. R., 12th Bn.
1599	Pte. Lazarus, M., 4th L.H.
2379	Pte. Lazarus, M. M., 1st Pioneer Bn.
33305	Dvr. Lazarus, A. M., A.F.A.
31204	Pte. Lazarus, J., 11th F.A.B.
56358	Pte. Lazarus, S. E., 11th Bn.
4830	Pte. Lazarus, L., 31st Bn.
3968	L/Cpl. Lazarus, F. H., 20th Bn.
2351	Sgt. Lazarus, W., 38th Bn.
378	Pte. Lazarus, I.,* 7th Bn.
3404	Pte. Lazarus, I., 58th Bn.
6838	Pte. Lazarus, L., 23rd Bn.
7531	Pte. Lazer, L.,* 8th Bn.
7002	Pte. Lebovitch, M.,* 2nd Bn.
	Tpr. Lebovitch, S., 10th L.H.

Australian Corps.—*Continued.*

1275	Pte. LEE, D.,* 14th Bn.	2956	Pte. LEVY, S., 2nd Pioneer Bn.
2607	Pte. LEVAN, F., 4th Bn.	2209	Pte. LEVY, L.,* 56th Bn.
	Pte. LEVIN, R., 8th Bn.		Pte. LEVY, H. S. (M.M.), A.A.M.C.
	Pte. LEVY, G. I., 29th Bn.	115	L/Cpl. LEVY, M. S., 36th Bn.
	Cpl. LEVY, T. (M.B.E.), Mounted Police.	27041	Dvr. LEVY, S. M., 113th How. Bty.
	Pte. LEMISH, D., 37th Bn.	18867	Pte. LEWIS, A., A.M.C.
	Pte. LENZER, S.	1793	2/A.M. LEVY, A., A.F.C.
908	Dvr. LEBOVITCH, E., 28th Bn.	6853	Spr. LEWIS, G. W., 17th Bn.
7264	Pte. LENNEBERG, F. B.,* 16th Bn.	5130	Pte. LEWIS, D., 52nd Bn.
6383	Pte. LENNEBERG, H. G., 22nd Bn.	2090	Pte. LEWIS, D. E., 33rd Bn.
2828	Pte. LENTZ, L., 36th Bn.	2346	Pte. LEWIS, F. I., 41st Bn.
3857	Pte. LESHKEBITCH, F., 24th Bn.	20043	Pte. LEWIS, I., A.A.M.C.
2458	Pte. LESSING, F. E., 58th Bn.	4527	Pte. LEWIS, A., 9th Bn.
14991	Dvr. LEVI, N. L., A.A.S.	5078	Pte. LEWIS, W. E., 33rd Bn.
	Pte. LEWIN, A.,* 1st Bn.	77	Dvr. LEWIS, M., 1st Field Amb.
1775	Pte. LEVEY, E. C.,* 2nd Bn.	314	Pte. LEWIS, L.,* 8th Bn.
2706	Gnr. LEVEN, H. H., 24th Heavy Bty.	6291	Pte. LEWIS, A. F., 11th Bn.
2927	Pte. LEVINSKI, J., 14th Bn.	2178	Pte. LOUIS, G. E., 54th Bn.
650	Tpr. LEVISON, A. H., 2nd L.H.	2627	Pte. LEWIS, S. S., 60th Bn.
6342	Pte. LEVISON, B., 25th Bn.	1749	Pte. LEWIS, A. M., 6th Field Amb.
2660	L/Cpl. LEVINSON, E. G.	6648	Pte. LEWIS, G. E., 8th Bn.
2707	Pte. LEVINSOHN, H. A., 17th Bn.	L/3297	Dvr. LEWIS, H., N.Z. A.S.P.
2850	Sgt. LEVOI, J. P., 5th Pioneer Bn.	6582	Pte. LEWIS, R., 17th Bn.
668	Sgt. LEVY, S., 6th Bn.	2627	Pte. LEWIS, S., 60th Bn.
5314	Spr. LEVY, E. W., 2nd D.S.C.	6087	Pte. LEWIS, V. G., 24th Bn.
752	Pte. LEVY, R. C., 10th M.G.C.	3589	Pte. LEWIS, V., 57th Bn.
60243	Pte. LEVY, M., 1st Bn.	6582	Pte. LEWIS, R., 17th Bn.
505	Sgt. LEVY, A.* (M.M.), 39th Bn.	424	Spr. LEWIS, R., 1st Tunnelling Coy.
3179	Pte. LEVY, H. A.,* 60th Bn.	3850	Pte. LEWIS, W. S., 2nd Bn.
114	Pte. LEVY, F., 1st Anzac Corps.	147	Pte. LIEFMAN, L. D., 14th Field Amb.
15535	Pte. LEVY, R. L.,* 3rd Field Amb.	2608	Pte. LIPMAN, S. F., 33rd Bn.
1750	L/Cpl. LEVY, C. G., 2nd A.G.H.	56103	Gnr. LIPERT, L., Sig. Bty.
4128	Gnr. LEAVER, G. J., 53rd Battery.	12632	Pte. LIPMAN, A. E., 11th Field Amb.
6893	Pte. LEVY, F. W., 5th Bn.	1792	Pte. LIONE, E. A., 1st Bn.
2870	Pte. LEVY, L. S.,* 53rd Bn.	2199	Pte. LEHMAN, A.,* 27th Bn.
2904	Cpl. LEVY, C. H., 2nd Pioneer Bn.	18654	Pte. LIPMAN, H., A.A.M.C.
1491	Tpr. LEVY, L. L., 2nd Anzac M. Regt.	13266	Dvr. LIPMAN, A., 2nd A.M.T.S.
1141	Pte. LEVY, L., 3rd Bn.	948	W./O. LIPMAN, L. B. (M.S.M.), 3rd Bn.
2956	Pte. LEVY, S., 2nd Pioneer Bn.	2547	Sgt. LIPSHUT, D., 56th Bn.
6274	Pte. LEVY, H., 1st Bn.	3282a	Sgt. LISSNER, H., 1st Pioneer Bn.
121	S./Sgt. LEVY, R., A.A.D.C.	2403	Pte. LITTMAN, S.* (M.M.), 51st Bn.
7087	Pte. LEVY, R. D., 18th Bn.	2406	Pte. LIVINGSTONE, J., 46th Bn.
25562	Pte. LEVY, C.,* 55th Bn.	4837	Pte. LOEWE, S.,* 15th Bn.
3980	Pte. LEVY, G., 1st Pioneer Bn.	6340	Pte. LOEWE, L. O., 26th Bn.
4812	Pte. LEVY, E. M.,* 50th Bn.	11283	Pte. LOEWENTHAL, A., 24th A.S.C.
18892	Cpl. LEVY, D. A., 61st Bn.	4480	Pte. LUBLIN, V. B., 19th Bn.
7000	Pte. LEVY, G. N.,* 11th Bn.		Bdr. LOUSADA, A. P., 1st F.A.
1726	Sgt. LEVY, G. S., 17th Bn.	2172	Pte. LUSCOMBE, S. J., 19th Bn.
7365	Pte. LEVY, H.,* 11th Bn.	3975	L/Cpl. LUSCOMBE, B. T.,* 4th Bn.
2633	Pte. LEVY, S., 2nd A.F.A.	2660	Pte. LYONS, M., 45th Bn.
7995	Cpl. LEVY, J. A., 16th Bn.	259	Pte. LYNES, A.,* 18th Bn.
3531	Pte. LEVY, H. M.,* 8th Bn.	150	Pte. LYONS, J., 3rd Bn.
4643	Pte. LEVY, H. H., 14th Bn.	3510	Pte. LOFFMAN, P., 16th Bn.
5732	Dvr. LEVY, L. H., 4th F.A.B.	1984	Gnr. LEVER, W., D.A.C.
1045	Pte. LEVY, L. V., 25th Bn.	13839	Pte. LUTCLIFFE, L., A.M.C.
7515	Cpl. LEVY, L., 6th Bn.	256	Pte. LEVY, R., 18th Bn.
174	W./O. LEVY, J. M., 23rd Bn.	124	Pte. LYONS, S.,* 17th Bn.
			Pte. LUBRANSKY, H.

Australian Corps.—*Continued.*

7	Sgt. Liggi, R.,* L.H.
	L/Cpl. Lazarus, D. (D.C.M., M.M.), A.M.G.C.
	L/Cpl. Lewis, M. (M.M.), Inf.
5372	Pte. McKenzie, G. B., 24th Bn.
146	Pte. McWatt, D., 3rd Eng.
2052	Cpl. Muchomes, S., 4th D.A.C.
28418	Gnr. Magino, B. H., 3rd D.A.C.
4190	Pte. Magodrick, D., 20th Bn.
931	Pte. Malatzki, L., 2nd M. G. Bn.
219	L/Cpl. Malatzky, H., 2nd M.G.C.
3987	Pte. Mandelson, F., 1st F. Amb.
658	Pte. Mandelson, H.,* 28th Bn.
3972	Gnr. Mandelsohn, C., M.T.M.B.
5125	Pte. Manuel, J. E. 49th Bn.
732	Pte. Marcus, R.,* 31st Bn.
4217	Pte. Marcus, B. T. J., 50th Bn.
3350	L/Cpl. Marcus, R.. 52nd Bn.
72	Pte. Mark, J. M., 1st F. Amb.
2667	Sgt. Mark, J. E. 2nd Pion.
4418	Pte. Marker, H. A., 1st Bn.
1577	Pte. Marquis, G.,* 13th Bn.
3083	Pte. Marks, R. G., 7th Bn.
49	Dvr. Marks, R. H.. 1st F. Amb.
658	Sgt. Marks, A.,* 5th Bn.
155	Pte. Marks, J. J., 35th Bn.
1922	2/A.M. Marks, R., A.F.C.
	Sgt. Marks, L. M. B., 13th Bn.
156	Pte. Marks, J., 3rd Bn.
2111	Pte. Marks, H. H.,* 41st Bn.
1102	Spr. Marks, M., 2nd Sig. Coy.
25838	Gnr. Marks, D., A.F.A.
31586	Gnr. Michaelis, F. M.,* Art.
1731	Pte. Michaelis, M., 18th Bn.
55507	Pte. Michaelson, J. F., 6th Bn.
4646	Pte. Michaelson, M, 3rd Bn
3830	Cpl. Middlemas, A. R., 1st Bn.
35645	Gnr. Milewsky, H., 3rd Btty.
1874	Pte. Millingen. A. C., 42nd Bn.
1688	Pte. Millingen, H. S., A.I.F., Hqrs. Ldn.
1599	Sgt. Millingen, C., 14th Amb.
20974	Cpl. Millar, J., A.F.A
3984	Sgt. Miller, J.* (D.C.M.), 21st Bn.
2613	Pte. Miller, W., 36th Bn.
2350	Pte. Miller, T. F., 32nd Bn.
6051	Pte. Minor, D.,* 1st Bn.
371	Cpl. Mirls, A., 31st Bn.
1323	Cpl. Mitchell, A. D.,* 1st Bn.
6320	Cpl. Mitchell, A. K., 7th Bn.
3411	Pte. Mulgrave, R. B., 8th Bn.
3181	Pte. Moore, J.,* 5th Pioneers.
2330	Pte. Morris, J. R., 39th Bn.
7118	L/Cpl. Morris, A. L., 14th Bn.
4498	Pte. Morris, H. A., 22nd Bn.
32323	Gnr. Morris, G. A., 12th Bty.
742	Pte. Morris, B., 22nd Bn.
14505	Pte. Morris. L., 1st L. H. F. Amb.
3547	L/Cpl. Morris, M., 8th Bn.
7099	Pte. Marks, M.,* 35th Bn.
1957	Pte. Marks, H. E. (M.M.), 48th Bn.
2394	Sgt. Marks, G. A., 1st Bn.
1655	Pte. Marks, H. A. A., A.M.C.
4843	Pte. Marks, A., 7th Bn.
895	Gnr. Marks, H. E. C., 22nd Bn.
3075	Sgt. Marks, H. W.,* 5th Bn.
351	Pte. Marks, A.. 3rd Pios.
857	Pte. Marks, F. H., 3rd Pion.
1568	Cpl. Marks, A. G.,* 1st Bn.
3111	Pte. Marks, M. J., 38th Bn.
3576	Pte. Marks, A., A.M.C.
5729	Cpl. Marks, C. M., 5th Bn.
1586	Pte. Marks, A., 1st Bn.
1671	Pte. Marks, W. O., 35th Bn.
2681	Pte. Marks, C. (M.M.), 2nd Pion.
4553	Pte. Marks, J., 13th F.A.B.
	Cpl. Marks, R. (D.C.M.), A.F.C.
6346	Pte. Marks, C., 25th Bn.
2667	Pte. Marks, J. E., 2nd Pion.
2723	L/Cpl. Marks, H. R., 46th Bn.
28	Bdr. Marks, B., 2nd D.H.Q.
1858a	Pte. Marks, R., 3rd M.G.C.
3547	Bgl. Marks, J. H., 2nd Pion.
7992	Dvr. Marks, J., A.F.A.
6537	Pte. Marks, E. E., 1st A.M.V.S.
7888	Pte. Marks, M. L.,* 1st Field Amb.
413	Sgt. Marks, L. D.,* 13th Bn.
5633	Pte. Marks, E. P., 1st Field Amb.
1128	Cpl. Marks, J. G., 23rd Bn.
469	Pte. Marks, R. J., 47th Bn.
2431	Cpl. Marks, L., 37th Bs.
1948	Pte. Marks, A. E., 50th Bn.
176	Cpl. Marryat, F. A., Lon : H. Q.
10440	Sgt. Marsden, A. E.. Dental Unit.
3435	Pte. Marshal, L. T., M.G.C.
246	Pte. Marks, B. E.,* 10th Bn.
2878	Pte. Marzan, W.,* 35th Bn.
2873	Pte. Mayer, H.,* 55th Bn.
1205	Pte. Morris, F., 3rd Bn.
5307	Cpl. Morris. L. G., 14th Field Amb.
4352	Sgt. Morris, R. A., 27th Bn.
4557	Pte. Morris, H., 6th Bn.
1598	Sgt. Morris, C., 11th Bn.
2436	Pte. Morris, F. D., A.M.C.
5435	Pte. Morris, F. L., 19th Bn.
7168	Pte. Moses, J. M., 17th Bn.
497	L/Cpl. Moses, H. L.,* 44th Bn.
3387	Pte. Moses, J. M, 30th Bn.
2685	Pte. Moses, W., 15th Bn.
7438	Dvr. Moses, H. E., 19th A.P.O.C.
413	Cpl. Mosley, W. E., 5th Bn.
2350	Pte. Moss, E. J., 42nd Bn.
130	Pte. Moss, D. V., 33rd Bn.
2397	1/A.M. Moss, L., A.F.C.
3107	Pte. Moss, E. H., 11th Bn.

Australian Corps.—*Continued.*

7768	Pte. Moss, H., 35th Bs.	
1573	L/Cpl. Moss, H., 1st Field Bakery.	
1871	Pte. Moss, L., A.A.M.C.	
707	Pte. Moss, R., M.G. Dtls.	
13667	Pte. Moss, L., Tunnelers.	
17	Spr. Mowitz, L. B., 2nd L. H.	
6783	Pte. Myall, A., 5th Bn.	
28348	Dvr. Myer, N., 1st D.A.C.	
1571a	Cpl. Meyer, O. W., 17th Bn.	
6519	Pte. Myers, J. L., 4th Bn.	
21828	Spr. Myers, I. Field Engineers.	
1612	Pte. Moss, A.,* 6th Bn.	
	Pte. Moss, H. S., 9th Bn.	
1585	Pte. Moss, E. C.,* 4th Bn.	
8146	Pte. Mersky, J., 5th Field Bakery.	
433	Cpl. Massarovitch, M. Y., 38th Bn.	
3584	Tpr. Mathias, I. W., 3rd A.G.H.	
6606	Pte. Mayer, R., 28th Bn.	
926	Pte. Mayer, C. E., 33rd Bn.	
3185	Pte. Meyer, W. H., 38th Bn.	
1571a	Cpl. Meyer, O. W., 17th Bn.	
2873	Pte. Meyer, W., 35th Bn.	
5853	Pte. Medina, A. E., 19th Bs.	
3864	Pte. Meintath, J. E., 1st Pion.	
4086	Pte. Mendelowitz, A., 32nd Bn.	
3347	Pte. Mendezy, I., 36th Bn.	
7500	Pte. Meuser, H. M., 34th Bn.	
2525	Sgt. Menser, L. M.,* 55th Bn.	
4742	Pte. Merkulski, J. B., 5th Bty.	
7531	Pte. Mercer, H., 1st Bn.	
4522a	Cpl. Meyer, W. J., 50th Bn.	
6313	Pte. Meyer, H. J., 7th Bn.	
1321	Pte. Meyer, R., 51st Bn.	
20561	Pte. Meyer, R., A.A.M.C.	
6606	Pte. Meyer, R., 28th Bn.	
1575	Pte. Meyer, C., 59th Bn.	
2184	Pte. Meyer, L. H., 19th Bn.	
2924	Pte. Michael, L., 58th Bn.	
1954	Pte. Michael, J. R., 50th Bn.	
3377	Pte. Michael, J. S., 5th Pion.	
1965	Pte. Michael, R. F.,* 18th Bn.	
12808	L/Cpl. Michael, N. B., A.A.S.C.	
12807	Dvr. Michael, C., Aus. Eng. Coy.	
1731	Pte. Michaels, J., 18th Bn.	
7019	Pte. Myers, W., 4th Bn.	
3743	Pte. Meyers, F. H., 2nd Pion.	
2640	Pte. Myers, J. H., 2nd Bn.	
2125	Pte. Myers, F., 44th Bn.	
96	Cpl. Myers, R., 10th M.G.C.	
1704	Pte. Myers, C. E., 54th Bn.	
2184	Pte. Meyers, L. H., 19th Bn.	
3881	Sgt. Myers, E. L., 1st Bn.	
1225	Cpl. Myers, J. A., 11th A.L.T.M.B.	
6850a	Pte. Myers, D. M., 21st Bn.	
3582	Pte. Myers, W. J., 4th Bn.	
33197	Pte. Myers, W. G., 5th F.A.B.	
3480	Pte. Myers, C. W., 7th Bn.	
681	Pte. Myers, G. E., 39th Bn.	
3157	Bglr. Myers, L., 25th Bn.	
2387a	Pte. Myers, L., 1st Pion.	
6301	Pte. Meyers, A. H., 8th Bn.	
1148	Tpr. Myers, J. M., A.V.C.	
3881	Sgt. Myers, E. L., 2nd Bn.	
58605	Gnr Myers, H. M., Art.	
2401	Pte. Meyers, A. W., 5th Pion.	
3848	Pte. Myers, M.,* 4th Bn.	
2455	Pte. Myers, F. L., 55th Bn.	
6117	Pte. Meyers, H. L.,* 10th Bn.	
902	Dvr. Myslis, H. S., A.P.C.	
1044	Spr. Myslis, M., 5th D.A.C.	
2052	Pte. Muckomel, S., 10th L.H.	
6396	Pte. Morris, H., 4th Bn.	
146	Spr. Mowatt, D., F.C.E.	
DM2/112688	Pte. Mazaran, N. J., N.Z. A.S.P.	
7768	Pte. Nable, H., 1st Bn.	
12213	L/Sgt. Napthali, W., 5th A.F.A.	
13821	Pte. Narr, R., 16th Field Amb.	
2201	Dvr. Nation, E., 10th Bn.	
12213	Bdr. Nathan, E., 34th Bn.	
4909	Pte. Nathan, A.,* 60th Bn.	
33159	Gnr. Nathan, A. Y., 1st D.A.C.	
2829b	Pte. Nathan, E., 34th Bn.	
2025	Sgh. Nathan, B. V., 24th Btty.	
	Pte. Nathan, H., 17th Bn.	
1258	Cpl. Nathan, E. W., 38th Bn.	
6553	Sgt. Nathan, B., A.I.F., Hqrs.	
6858a	Pte. Nathan, M., 24th Bn.	
2368	Pte. Nathan, R., 33rd Bn.	
3325	Pte. Nathan, H., 28th Bn.	
972	Pte. Nathan, P. J., 6th Bn.	
1021	Pte. Neimann, A., 2nd Bn.	
6322	Pte. Nelkin, F. A., 7th Bn.	
2050	Pte. Nesbit, R. G., 19th Bn.	
4865	Pte. Nemerousky, M., 19th Bn.	
725	Pte. Netter, H., 43rd Bn.	
22827	Gnr. Newman, Y. H., 107th H. Bty.	
6799	Pte. Nield, J., 14th Bn.	
9406	Pte. Nimenski, C. F., 21st A.A.S.C.	
11266	Pte. Nimenski, M., A.A.S.C.	
3104	Pte. Nyeman, G., 4th Pioneers.	
7021	Pte. Nyman, A.,* 2nd Bn.	
5400	Pte. Nyman, S., 24th Bn.	
2250	Pte. Nyman, J. E., 49th Bn.	
5401	Cpl. Nyman, W., 24th Bn.	
3882	Pte. Nyman, C.,* 8th Bn.	
112	Sgt. Neelson, A. F. G., 3rd D.A.C.	
3410	W.O. Nathan, G. A., Camel Corps.	
13823	Pte. Nathan, L., A.M.C.	
3925	Dvr. Nyman, J., A.FA.	
1883	Pte. Nicholls, H., A.S.C.	
1142	Sgt. Nenstadt, J. L., Aus. H. Q.	
1303	Sgt. Norman, A. S.,* 4th Bn.	
1366	Sgt. Norman, A. E., 15th Bn	
	L/Cpl. Nimon, J., 8th Bn.	

Australian Corps.—*Continued.*

6090	Pte. OBERMAN, E., 11th Bn.
2831b	Pte. ODDY, R. G., 2nd Bn.
11881	Gnr. OPITZ, H., 105th H. Bty.
3267	Pte. ORAM, L. D. A., 38th Bn.
5450	Pte. ORLOFF, C., 6th Bn.
2372	Pte. ORMISTON, J. H.,* 35th Bn
3890	Pte. ORMSTON, G. W.,* 6th Bn.
944	Tpr. OSMOND, A.,3rd Bn.
2179	Pte. PARKER, B. A., 56th Bn.
3861	Pte. PASCOE, W. B., 32nd Bn.
2531	Pte. PARNEMAN, H. A., 49th Bn.
4872	Pte. PASVALSKY, L.,* 51st Bn.
4200	Pte. PAYTON, F., 28th Bn.
2723	Pte. PEAK, S. H. J., 53rd Bn.
1799	Pte. PEREIRA, E. M.,* 48th Bn.
4505	Pte. PEIRCE, L., 54th Bn.
6803	Bdr. PERLSTEIN, A., 4th F.A.B.
4056	Pte. PETERSEN, S., 12th Bn.
12041	Pte. PESMANY, T., 9th Field Amb.
1041	Pte. PHILLIPS, E. Y., 19th Bn.
6858	Pte. PHILLIPS, A. H., 17th Bn.
15429	Dvr. PHILLIPS, E. M., A.M.T.S.
3103	Sgt. PHILLIPS, M., 56th Bn.
22561	Sgt. PHILLIPS, P. D., 8th F.A.B.
6567	Pte. PHILLIPS, P. F., 16th Bn.
2654	L/Cpl. PHILLIPS, J. W., 5th Bn.
6563	Pte. PHILLIPS, H. B., 7th Bn.
245	Pte. PHILLIPS, D., 2nd M.G. Bn.
3899	Pte. PHILLIPS, S., 22nd Bn.
2898	Cpl. PHILLIPS, W., 1st Bn.
3227	Pte. PHILLIPS, C., 59th Bn.
5885	Cpl. PHILLIPS, A. J.,* 20th Bn.
20190	Sgt. PHILLIPS, W. H., 108th Bty.
4758	Cpl. PHILLIPS, D. A., 20th Bn.
4498	L/Cpl. PICKERING, G. W., 24th Bn.
1756	Pte. PHILLIPS, P., 21st Bn.
498	Dvr. PHILLIPS, J., 6th L. H.
11594	Gnr. PHILLIPS, S., 106th H. Bty.
15938	Pte. PIMENTEL, M. P., 7th Field Amb.
3531	Pte. PINKEVITCH, C., 7th Field Amb.
4443	Pte. PINTO, R., 48th Bn.
218	Pte. PIRANI, C. S., 16th Bn.
3924	Pte. PIRANI, J., 11th Bn.
5433	Pte. PIZER, E.,* 14th Bn.
37448	Gnr. PLATKIN, H., 2nd Bty.
2747	Pte. POLLOCK, E., 23rd Bn.
3707	Pte. POLLOCK, B. N., 13th Bn.
4775	Pte. POLLOCK, L., 21st Bn.
2893	A/Cpl. PRESHNER, M., 37th Bn.
705	2/A.M. PRUSS, I., A.F.C.
480	Pte. PYKE, O., 39th Bn.
1990	Pte. PYKE, A., 2nd Pioneers.
2704	Pte. PHILLIPS, G. G., 45th Bn.
304	Pte. PHILLIPS, W. R., 19th Bn.
6866	Pte. PASTIC, P. T., 48th Bn.
987	Pte. POOL, F. M., Aus. Eng Coy.
983	Cpl. PECK, A., 21st Bn.

	Pte PINCUS, A., 1st Div. Train, A.S.C.
5427	Pte. PINCUS, F.,
6108	Gnr. POLAK, G. E.* (M.M.), A.F.A.
2925	Bdr. POOL, M. C., A.F.A.
4322	Pte. PLATT, 1st Bn.
	Pte RAPKIN, T., 8th Bn.
	Pte. RAPPEPORT, J., 7th M.G.C.
1798	Pte. RABINOVITCH, B.,* 59th Bn.
17708	Pte. RABINOVITCH, E. H., A.A.M.C.
9731	Pte. RABINOVITCH, L., 1st Bn.
1890	Pte. RAPHAEL, F. J.,* 21st Bn.
	Dvr. RAPHAEL, 2nd D.S.C.
13448	Dvr. RAPHAEL, K. S., 3rd A.A.M.T.
13008	Pte. RAPHAEL, A. J., 2nd Field Amb.
2659	Pte. RAPPEPORT, S., 43rd Bn.
6815	Pte. REGAN, L. W., 7th Bn.
1617	L/Cpl. RIBEIRO, M.,* 4th Bn.
1963	Pte. RICH, F. P.,* 38th Bn.
15321	Gnr. RICHARD, J. B., 1st D.A.C.
18530	Cpl. RICHARDS, C. S.,* 25th Bty.
28	Spr. RICHARDS, J., 13th L. H.
3001	Spr. RISCHIN, P., 14th Pioneers.
6816	Bglr. RISCHIN, 37th Bn.
2002	Pte. ROBIN, D. K.,* 18th Bn.
204	Sgt. ROBINSON, A., 46th Bn.
2034	L/Cpl. RODGERS, J., 45th Bn.
6893	C/S/M. ROMAIN, H. A., 24th Bn.
4035	Pte. ROMAIN, H., 24th Bn.
7541	Spr. ROSEBERG, M., Tun. Coy
1328	Pte ROSEMAN, A, 37th Bn.
20104	Gnr. ROSEN, M. L., 12th F.A.B.
6582	Pte. ROSEN, J., 14th Bn.
2868	Pte. ROSENBERG, S., 33rd Bn.
3446	Pte. ROSENBAUM, D., 58th Bn.
2431	Dvr. ROSENBERG, A., 1st D. T.,
2074	Pte. ROSENTHAL, J. L., 2nd Camel Corps.
1678	Spr. ROSENBERG, L. M.,* 2nd L.H.
4737	Pte. ROSENBERG, J. M. (M.M.), 16th Bn.
1024	Pte. ROSENGARTEN, A L., A.M.C.
3618	Pte. ROSENTHAL, C. H. R., 32nd Bn.
10385	Pte. ROSENTHAL, J., 2nd Field Amb.
116/1814	S/Sgt. ROSENTHAL, S., 18th Bn.
7780	Pte. ROSENTHAL, M., 11th Bn.
	Sgt. REINOVITCH, M. (D.C.M.).
	A./M. RAPHAEL, H. S. (M.M.).
	Sister ROSENTHAL, L. (R.R.C.).
	Pte. ROSENTHAL, H., 1st Bn.
641	Pte. ROSENTHAL, A. C., 14th Bn.
1819	Pte. ROSENTHAL, S., 11th Bn.
50	Tpr. ROSENTHAL, A. K.,* 1st L.H.
2236	Pte. ROSENWAX, C. H.,* 19th Bn.
1676	Pte. ROSSOGSKY, I. P.,* 34th Bn.
530	Pte. ROTH, S., 60th Bn.
537	Sgt. ROTH, K. C., 22nd Bn.
7730	Pte. ROTHBERG, H. R., 2nd A.C.C.S.
21859	Pte. ROTHBERG, M., Eng.
6388	Pte ROTHSTEIN, M., A.S.C.
3425	Gnr ROTHSTEIN, M., 10th F.A.B.

Australian Corps.—*Continued.*

No.	Name
2442	Pte. ROTHBAUM, H. I., 32nd M.G.C.
18729	Pte. RUBINOWITCH, L. J., A.A.M.C.
3427	Pte. RUBENACH, T. J., t4h Pioneers.
402	Pte. RUDOVSKY, J., 1st Tun. Coy.
4197	Bglr. RUSSELL, H.,* 26th Bn.
1132	Pte. RUSCHIN, L., 14th Bn.
2613	Pte. ROLBIN, H.,* 3rd Bn.
	Pte. ROSENBROOK, R., 5th Bn.
1177	Pte. SALAMON, J. H., 5th Field Ab.
3154	Pte. SALEK, L., 4th F.C.E.
126	Dvr. SAMUELS, J., 1st A.S.C.
6479	Pte. SABER, K. W., 14th Bn.
2880	Pte. SACKETT, H., 41stBn.
712	L/Cpl. SACKLOVE, N B., 24th Bn.
4341	Spr. SACKS, C.,* 13th Field Coy. Eng.
4804	Pte. SAFFAR, M., 51st Bn.
1762	Cpl. SALDERN, G. F., 19th Bn
21295	Gnr. SELIG, R. R., A.F.A.
1735	Cpl. SALMOND, A. G., 26th Bn.
2736	L/Cpl. SALMON, B. P., 50th Bn.
35587	Gnr. SAMINS, A., 18th Bty.
2146	Pte. SAMUEL, W., 44th Bn.
3911	Pte. SAMUEL, E.,* 59th Bn.
11408	Gnr. SAMUELS, L., 21st H. Bty.
1444	Tpr. SAMUELS, H., 9th L. H.
12728	Cpl. SAMUELS, H., A.A.S.C.
1132	Pte. SAMUEL, A. G., A.A.S.C.
5423	Cpl. SAMUEL, G.,* 16th Bn.
254	Gnr. SAMUEL, H., 36th A. A. B.
2410	Pte. SAMUELS, W., 45th Bn.
4214	Pte. SAMUEL, A. D.,
2835a	Pte. SAMUELS, B .T., 13th L.T.M.B.
5938	Pte. SAMUELS, W. F., 24th Bn.
589	Pte. SAMUELS, E.,* 39th Bn.
2604	Cpl. SANDER, C., 20th Bn.
7902	Pte. SANDERS, A. B., 6th Field Amb.
2450	Pte. SAPPIR, A., 11th Bn.
321	Pte. SOLOMON, H. O., 13th Bn.
15765	Cpl. SOLOMON, V., Engrs.
2647	Pte. SOLOMON, J. N., 9th Bn.
6393	Pte. SOLOMON, C. S., 4th M.G. Bn.
5407	Pte. SOLOMON, W. E., 25th Bn.
214	Pte. SOLOMON, L. V.,
16589	Dvr. SOLOMON, P. J., A.S.C.
1367	Pte. SOLOMON, M.,* 32nd Bn.
16228	Pte. SOLOMON, H. A., A.S.C.
2375	Spr. SOLOMON, S., 5th D.S.C.
33483	Pte. SOLOMON, S. R., 2nd F.A.B.
26942	Gnr. SOLOMON, E. L., 37th Bty.
2418	Pte. SOLOMON, L., 44th Bn.
976	C/Q.M.S. SOLOMONS, S., 21st Bn.
6101a	L/Cpl. SOLOMON, S. G., 27th Bn.
1071	Pte. SOLOMONS, M., 4th D.S.C.
304	Sgt. SOLOMONS, J. H., 4th Bn.
2902	Cpl. SOLOMON, A. Y., 43rd Bn.
513	Pte. SOLOMON, C., 56th Bn.
1825	Pte. SOLOMON, J. H., 6th Bn.
3415a	Pte. SOLOMON, M., 19th Bn.
522	Cpl. SOLOMON, J. C.,* 41st Bn.
	Gnr. SOLOMON, 21st B.A.C.
3947	Pte. SOLTAIR, H., 2nd Pioneers.
1810	Pte. SOLTEIR, W., 2nd Pioneers.
418	Sgt. SPANGER, H., A.O.D./3rd Bn.
6681	Spr. SPIERS, J., 6th T.C.E.
6566	Pte. SPIGELL, J. K., 13th Bn.
239	2nd/A.M. SPEAR, E. E., A.F.C.
11914	L/Cpl. SPIERS, F. (M.S.M.), A.S.C.
147	Pte. SAUNDERS, M., 7th Bn.
7901	Pte. SANDERS, F. R., 6th Field Amb.
1898	Pte. SARASOR, S., 37th Bn.
5022	Spr. SARFATY, A. Engrs.
2531	Cpl. SATINOVER, Y., 16th Bn.
	Sgt. SARFATY, Y., A.M.C.
35	Cpl. SAUNDERS, A. S., 3rd L. H.,
6627a	L/Cpl. SAUNDERS, A., 17th Bn.
6831	Sgt. SAUNDERS, S. A.,* 14th M.G. Bn.
5467	Pte. SAUL, H. J.,* 9th Bn.
4308	Pte. SAUNDERS, G. E., 7th Bn.
4901	Gnr. SAUNDERS, W. H., 4th D.A.C.
1005	Pte. SAUNDERS, H., 17th Bn.
2630	Pte. SAUNDERS, M. D., 44th Bn.
173	Pte. SCHAFFER, T. J.,* 33rd Bn.
2141	Pte. SCHNEIDER, R. E., 39th Bn.
1326	Pte. SCHNEIDER, A., 4th Bn.
5676	Pte. SCHNEIDER, W. H., 22nd Bn.
2691	Cpl. SCHOFMAN, L. H., 57th Bn.
55220	Pte. SCHWARTZ, H., 8th Bn.
7323	Pte. SCHWARTZ, C. F.,* 23rd Bn.
3633	Pte. SCOTT, Y. W., 2nd Pioneer Bn.
33065	Gnr. SCOTT, H. L., Artillery.
3903	Pte. SEEBOHN, A. J., 10th Bn.
4130	Pte. SEELIGSON, J. H., 32nd Bn.
2865	Pte. SEELIGSON, C. E., 48th Bn.
3459	Pte. SEIGEL, W. W., 45th Bn.
3917	Pte. SELIG, O. M. (M.M.), 13th Bn.
5665	Pte. SELIG, M., 19th Bn.
	Pte. SELIG, L., 3rd Bn.
357	Pte. SHALBERG, J. R., 8th Bn.
3925	Pte. SHAPIRO, R., 24th Bn.
261	Pte. STEINBERG, S.
6884	Pte. SPRINGER, S., 35th Bn.
2778	L/Cpl. STEIN, W.,* 58th Bn.
7081	Pte. STEIN, S. E., 13th Bn.
2218A	Pte. STEINBERG, A. J.,* 9th Bn.
2887	Pte. STEINBERG, L. S., 44th Bn.
	Pte. STONE, B. E., 9th Bn.
7903	A/Sgt. STERNBERG, S. H., 6th F.A.B.
2904	Pte. STERNHEIM, A., 5th Bn.
324	Pte. STIEBEL, L.,* 13th Bn.
4111	Pte. SWIFT, W. F., 30th Bn.
1020	Spr. SYMOND, L., 13th F.C.E.
2540	Cpl. SYMONS, J.W., 45th Bn.
2371	Pte. SYMONS, E.,* 22nd Bn

Australian Corps.—*Continued.*

1970	Pte. SEINLITZKY, J. R., 35th Field Amb.
154	Pte. SIMBERG, A., 44th Bn.
4611	Pte. SHINEBERfi, L. S., 44th Bn.
5197	Pte. STEIN, P., 29th Bn.
3376	Pte. SACKS, B.S., 46th Bn.
50	Pte. SOLNICK, A. I., A.F.C.
	Pte. SUSMAN, E. L., 13th Bn.
	Cpl. SHAPIRO, A.C., 18th Bn.
5763	Pte. SHARP, L., 13th Bn.
19102	Spr. SHARP, S. S., Engineers.
1914	Gnr. SHARP, W., 101st Bty.
3258	Pte. SHARPE, J., 33rd Bn.
	Pte. SHELODOWSKY, M., 13th Bn.
6880	Pte. SHERICK, J., 28th Bn.
206	Pte. SHERMAN, G. J.,* 9th Bn.
5108A	Pte. SHERMAN, I., 33rd Bn.
19629	Pte. SHILONY, J., A.A.M.C.
2139	Cpl. SHINEBERG, J., 29th Bn.
5611	Pte. SHEINBERG, H., A.M.C
16203	Dvr. SHMITH, A. V., 5th A.M.T. Coy.
7774	Pet. SHONTHALL, J., 2nd Bn.
3646	Sgt. SHUTER, S. C., 57th Bn.
30440	Dvr. SIEDEKUM, F. W., 14th D.A.C.
1798	Sgt. SIEGER, F., 12th Bn.
6365	Pte. SILBERTHAU, R. S., 1st. Bn.
6311	Pte. SILBERTHAU, R.,* 1st Bn.
2881	Pte. SILVER, H. J., 35th Bn.
2815	Pte. SILVERMAN, A.,* 20th Bn.
14994	Pte. SILVERMAN, J., 14th Field Ahb.
6248	Pte. SILVERSTONE, F., A.A.M.C.
6152	Pte. SIMMONDS, D. M. B. 26th Bn.
12402	Pte. SIMMONS, V. E., 10th Field Amb.
105	Pte. SIMON, O.,* 9th Bn.
4809	Pte. SIMONS, L. J.,* 18th Bn.
7549	Pte. SIMONSEN, J. M., 15th Bn.
4242	Cpl. SIMONSON, C., 45th Bn.
1419	L/Cpl. SIMONSEN, M., 14th Bn.
566	Pte. SIMONS, S., 13th Bn.
3168	A/Sgt. SIMON, A. A., 35th Bn.
3469	Pte. SIMMONDS, D. J.,* 55th Bn.
2438	Pte. SIMMONS, A. E.,* 50th Bn.
960	Pte. SIMMONS, E., 29th Bn.
14015	Sgt. SIMMONS, A. M., No. 3. Aus. C.C.S.
50157	Pte. SIMMONS, L., 22nd Bn.
4905	Pte. SIMMONS, P., 57th Bn.
12402	Gnr. SIMMONS, V. E., 10th Field Art.
6416	Pte. SIMMONS, P.,* 20th Bn.
5868	Pte. SIMMONS, R. W., 12th Bn.
2513	Pte. SIMMONS, T., 54th Bn.
1086	Pte. SIMMONS, N. H., 7th Bn.
2455	Pte. SIMMONS, J. R.* (M.M.), 23rd Bn.
8223	Pte. SIMPSON, A., 3rd Aus. Tun. Coy.
53555	Pte. SIMPSON, B., 54th Bn.
1621	Pte. SINGER, S.,* 2nd Bn.
2499	Pte. SINGER, J., 47th Bn.
3432	Pte. SINGER, A., 53rd Bn.
558	Sgt. STOMAN, L., 45th Bn.
136	Gnr. SLAPOFFSKY, C. L., 36th HA.B.
16203	Dvr. SMITH, A. H,. A.S.C.
1428	Pte. SMITH, W. C., 9th Bn.
1345	Cpl. SOLE, L. C., 24th Bn.
1999	Pte. SOLNICK, E.,* 2nd Bn.
685	Pte. SOLOMON, M., 3rd Bn.
11406	Gnr. SOLOMON, E., 1st Bn.
	Cpl. SCHIMKOVITZ, E. (M.M.), Inf.
	L/Cpl. SCHUMANN, J. D. (M.M.), Inf.
11911	Dvr. SOLOMON, R. P., 2nd D.S.C.
31183	Dvr. SOLOMON, M., 25th Bty
34830	Cpl. SOLOMON, A. H., Artillery.
5641	Pte. SOLOMON, A., 20th Bn.
15218	Gnr. SOLOMON, L., 51st Bty.
1004	Pte. SOLOMON, P. M., 17th Bn.
	Pte. SOLOMON, D., 10th Bn.
1103	Sgt. SOLOMON, J., 3rd Bn.
1391	Sgt. TAUBMAN, F. C., 3rd Bn.
328	Sgt. TAYLOR, H. E., 3rd Pioneers.
5925	Pte. TAYLOR, H.,* 25th Bn.
967	Pte. THOMAS, W. H., 9th Bn.
2466	Gnr. THOMAS, H. L., 2nd Bty.
7092	Pte. THOMPSON, V., 66th Bn.
487	Pte. THORLEY, C. D., 42nd Bn.
613a	Pte. TOEBELMAN, A., 8th Bn.
6127	Pte. TORTSON, M., 1st Bn.
8483	Cpl. TOWNSEND, E. J., 31st A.S.C.
2952	Pte. TRIGGER, F. W., 4th Pioneers.
909	Pte. TRIGGER, S., A.M.C.
54999	Pte. TRAUB, A., 58th Bn.
3894	Pte. TURNER, J. A., 11th Bn.
1750	Pte. TRIGGER, S. W.,* 50th Bn.
1054	B/S.M. THOMPSON, A. W., 12th Art. Bde.
	Tpr. TOPAL, I., Light Horse.
1898	Pte. TARASOV, S.,* 34th Bn.
1506	Cpl. TARDY, 3rd Bn.
1639	Pte. TARDY, J. A., 1st Div. M. T. Bty.
6897	Pte. VAN EMDEN, J., 19th Bn.
2500	Pte. VANDENBERG, J. W., 56th Bn.
53826	Pte. VERNON, M. H.,
9751	Pte. VERNON, H. E., 30th Bn.
2109	Pte. VISBORD, J., 22nd Bn.
249	Pte. VANCE, R. E., 47th Bn.
	Pte. VALENTINE, S. H., 15th Bn.
6814	Sgt. WAGNER, J., 4th Bn.
1881	Pte. WATCHMAN, N., 6th Bn.
2	Tpr. WACHMAN, 3rd L. H.
826	Pte. WATCHMAN, S. D., 44th Bn.
4451	Cpl. WACHMAN, R.,* 48th Bn.
3923	Pte. WATCHMAN, A. E.,* 50th Bn.
395	Pte. WAKELING, W. N., 19th Bn.
3304	Pte. WALLIS, F., 8th Bn.
6835	Pte. WALTERS, I., 11th Bn.
1066	Cpl. WALTERS, J., 32nd Bn.
6763	Sgt. WALTERS, P., 28th Bn.
13341	Dvr. WARNER, J., 6th A.A.M.T.
3969	Sgt. WAXMAN, C. R., 22nd Bn.
5905	L/Cpl. WAXMAN, S., 24th Bn.

Australian Corps.—*Continued.*

4250	Sgt. WAXMAN, E., 21st Bn.
6341	Pte. WEBBER, J. J., 4th Bn.
11120	Gnr. WEINBERG, R., 1st D.A.C.
4597	Pte. WEINBERG, W., 4th Engineers.
4003	Pte. WEINBERG, O., 2nd Bn.
4517	Pte. WEINER, S., 23rd Bn.
121860	Pte. WEINER, C., 24th Bn.
695	Pte. WEINGOTT, A. A.,* 13th Bn.
127	Pte. WEINGOTT, S.,* 1st Bn.
7741	Dvr. WEINGOTT, B., 16th F.C.E.
2494	Pte. WEINTABE, F. L. B., 55th Bn.
6739	Pte. WEISS, A., 16th Bn.
3730	Pte. WEISS, I., 51st Bn.
7091	Pte. WEISS, J., 16th Bn.
4620	Pte. WEISS, T. H., 49th Bn.
	Pte. WERTHEIM, R., 22nd Bn.
12429	Pte. WERNER, L. R. C., 10th Field Amb.
3491	Bglr. WERTHEIM, J., 56th Bn.
1022	Pte. WESTERBERG, E. A.,* 38th Bn.
2134	Q.M.S. WHITEHILL, T., 3rd F.A.B.
2749	Sgt. WHITE, W. B., 56th Bn.
1106	Pte. WHITE, J., 50th Bn.
545	Pte. WHITE, M.,* 51st Bn.
355	Bglr. WHORTON, G. E., 6th Bn.
2311	Pte. WILLIAMS, J., 2nd Pioneers.
2269A	Pte. WILSON, B. G.,* 57th Bn.
5470	Pte. WINEBERG, J. M., 16th Bn.
58912	Pte. WISHMAN, D., 35th Bn.
55012	Pte. WITTNER, M. B., 59th Bn.
3963	Cpl. WITTNER, H.,* 22nd Bn.
53832	Dvr. WOLFSON, J., 4th Bty.
221	Pte. WOLFSON, H., 32nd Bn.
2318	Pte. WOODS, L.,* 3rd Bn.
2898	L/Cpl. WOLFS, H., A.P.C.
5216	Pte. WOLFE, D. H., 47th Bn.
14853	Pte. WOLFE, P. P. A., 5th Field Amb.
300	Pte. WOOLFE, H. E., 59th Bn.
270	Dvr. WRIGHT, H., 1st Bn.
4033	Pte. WEINBERG, A., 11th Bn.
834	Pte. WYMAS, G. H., 8th Bn.
6616a	Pte. WYNDHAM, E., 21st Bn.
238	Pte. WEBBER, J. W., 35th Bn.
4928	Pte. WIGHT, W. J., 51st Bn.
1792	Sgt. WHITEFIELD, C. S.* (M.S.M.), 4th B.
7062	Pte. WHITWORTH, J., 15th Fld. Coy. A.E.
	Pte. WOLENSKI, J. H.,
	Pte. WALKAWITZ, K., 16th Bn.
6906	Pte. WOODWARD, P., 28th Bn.
5095	Cpl. WOOLFF, H. S., 25th Bn.
66699	Gnr. WHITEHOUSE, A. E., A.F.A.
138	Pte. WOOLMAN, S., 9th M.G. Coy.
612	Pte. YOUNG, C. G., 2nd M.G. Bn.
3345	Pte. YOUNG, L., 59th Bn.
6203	Sgt. YAKO, B., 20th Bn.
804	Pte. ZANDER, C. O.,* 10th Bn.
1589	Tpr. ZANDER, L. H., 12th L. H.
2175a	Pte. ZIMMEBERG, J., 3rd Pioneers.
5793	Pte. ZINOOD, W., 2nd Bn.
3546	Pte. ZEFFERETT, S. W., 49th Bn.
16202	Dvr. ZELTZER, I., A.S.C.
1435	Pte. ZINES, J. M., 52nd Bn.
2612a	Sgt. ZEFFERT, M. E., 51st Bn.
322	Pte. ZICHOWSKI, R. A., 47th Bn.
12442	Dvr. ZEENG, W., 10th Field Amb.

* Killed in Action or died on Active Service.

NEW ZEALAND DIVISION.

OFFICERS.

Lieut. ABEL, J., Div. Amm. Col.
Capt. BERNSTEIN, A., N.Z. Amb. Col.
2nd Lieut. FISHER, C. B., N.Z. Div. Train.
Capt. GOLDSTEIN, H. M. (M.C.), N.Z.M.C.
2nd Lieut. HERMAN, R. P.,* 1st Bn. Cant. Regt
Capt. ISAACS, D. N. (M.B.E.), N.Z. Stat. Hosp.
Lieut. JACOBS, B. J., 2nd B.M.R.B.
Capt. KEESING, H. M., (M.C.) 2nd N.Z.R.B.
Lieut. LEVIEN, E. (M.C.).
Lieut. LEVY, T. H. (M.B.E.).
Lieut. MARKS, E. (D.C.M.), Inf.
Lieut. MAYER, J. (M.C.), N.Z.F.A.
Capt. MARKS, J. D. (M.C.), N.Z.M.C.
Capt. MYERS D., N.Z. Medical Corps.
Major SAMUELS, M.R. Regt.

N.C.O.'s AND MEN.

	Sgt. ANSELL, L. G.
	B/Sgt.-Maj. ASHER, C. (M.M.), Div. Am. Col. No. 4. S.
	Pte. ABRAHAMS, S.
4/933	Dvr. ABRAHAMS, H., 1st Fld. Cy. N.Z.E.
35230	Dvr. ABER, I., N.Z. Field Art.
12/14	Pte. ANKER, A.,* 3rd Auckland Inf.
19444	Pte. ASHER, G. N., 12th Maori Rifles.
12116	Rfm. BERKER, M., 3rd N.Z. Rifle Bde.
8/3495	Pte. BOWDEN, E.,* 2nd Otago Regt.
	Pte. BRAHAM, S., 16th Waikaita Regt. 2nd Brigade.
24772	Pte. BARLIN, R. O., 1st Otago Regt.
3/563	Sgt. BENJAMIN, A. R., N.Z. Stat. Hos.
54637	Rfm. BARNETT, E., 4th Bn. N.Z.R.B.
3/2612	Pte. BOOCK, H. J., N.Z. Med. Corps.
23/369	L/Cpl. BRODZIAK, H. J., Auckland Rgt.
40495	Pte. BLACK, S., 3rd N.Z.R.B.
	Staff Sgt. BERG, L. A. (D.C.M., M.M.).
79012	Rfm. BROADY, J. I., N.Z.R.B.
12/2039	Gnr. BLOWES, W., 1st Bde. Fld. Art.
	Pte. BLACK, J. T.
	Pte. BELESKY, A. M., Otago Bn.
	Pte. BLOOMFIELD, R. M.
	Pte. BLANKENSEE, C. R. B., Mounted Rifles.

New Zealand Division.—*Continued.*

8/3495 Pte. BLAUBAUM, E.*
23/2535 Pte. COOK, E., 1st R.B.
871 Pte. COHEN, S., Div. Hqrs. A.S.C.
2/1176A Cpl. COHEN, L., 4th N.Z.R.B.
46292 Spr. CASSRELS, N., 2nd Fld. Coy. N.Z.E.
53478 Pte. COHEN, L., 4th N.Z.R.B.
Spr. CASTLEBERG, A. L. (D.C.M.), N.Z.R.B.
18230 Dvr. COHEN, A. E., N.Z.F.A.
6/2096 Pte. COHEN, H. R., 1st Canterbury Inf.
3/1008 Pte. CANTOR, W. (M.M.), Mtd. Bde., Field Amb.
6/2118 Pte. DOMB, L., 1st Bn. Cant. Regt.
13/2317 Pte. DAVIS, B., 2nd Auckland Regt.
16/529 Pte. EMANUEL, R., N.Z. Med. Corps.
27/1984 Pte. FREEMAN, R., 3rd Rifle Bde.
9/1166 Pte. FAIGAN, A., 2nd Otago Regt.
Gnr. FELS, H. H., 1st Bde. N.Z.F.A
39976 Pte FREEMAN, D., 2nd Bn. Otago Regt.
585 Pte. FEDEDA, N., N.Z.M.C.
Pte. FRIEDLANDER, L., N.Z. Infantry.
Pte. FRIEDLANDER, J.
12/1421 Sgt. GREEN, H., Auckland Regt.
44932 Dvr. GOLDWATER, D. L., N.Z. A.S.C.
29162 Pte. GOLDSMITH, T. J., 2nd Cant. Regt.
098541 Pte. GERALD, L., N.Z. A.S.C.
Pte. GREENWALD. E.
Pte. GOODMAN, D.
8/578 Pte. GOLDSACK, A. A.,* 1st Bn.
12/1047 Pte. HAYMAN, E. P.,* 1st Auckland Rgt.
3/1892 Pte. HARRIS, A., 1st N.Z. Field Amb.
45378 Rfm. HOFFER, E., 2nd Bn. N.Z.R.B.
Sgt. HAYMAN, P. J., Samoa E.F.
11036 Rfm. HICKMAN, A., Rifle Bde.
13913 Pte. HARBEVITCH, M. J., 2nd Otago Inf.
25515 Cpl. HAINES, B., 1st Wellington Regt.
33359 Pte. HART, H. E.,* N.Z. Inf.
Pte. HERMAN, P.
Pte. HAYMAN, L., N.Z. Infantry.
Sgt. HAYMAN, H. S., N.Z.M.C.
58019 Pte. HYMAN, S.
Sgt. HAYMAN, H. M.
Drm. ISAACS, M., Samoa E.F.
Pte. JOSEPH, M.
Pte. JACOBSON, Canterbury Bn.
87821 Pte. JACOBS, H. N., 1st C.I.B.
50549 Dvr. JACOBS, B. C., Amb. Col.
33028 Rfm. JOSEPHSON, A., 1st Rifle Bde.
45409 Rfm. JACKSON, L., 2nd R.B.
69243 Pte. JACOBS, C. H., 35th Rfts. W.I.R.
55980 Rfm. KUTNER, I., Rifle Bde.
13/2047 Dvr. KINDER, L. E., 2nd Cant. Inf. R.
36155 T/Sgt. KAY, M., N.Z.R.B.
72773 L/Cpl KESSING, P., N.Z.R.B.
50967 Dvr. KRABIS, H.,* N.Z.A.S.C.
Pte. KLINGENBERG, A., Canterbury Bn.
11688 Pte. LEWIS, B., 2nd Cant. Regt.

12/2021 Sgt. LURY, G. H., 1st Auckland Regt.
2/54 Pte. LEVY, I. J., 2nd Wellington Regt.
36749 C.S.M. LEVY, E.,* 1st Rifle Bde.
Pte. LEVY, A., Div. Train.
Pte. LEWIS, M., No. 1 N.Z. Fld. Amb.
59359 Pte. LEVY, M. A., N.Z.Div. Emp. Coy.
25903 Pte. LYONS, L. E., 1. Coy. 17th Reinf.
24/2025 Rfm. LEVY, B., 4th Rifle Brigade.
3/3382 Pte. LEES, H., Medical Corps.
53903 Pte. LYONS, J., 1st O.R.
82537 Pte. LEVY, W., Otago Regt.
42351 Pte. LEES, P., 1st Bn.
66244 Sgt. LYONS, R., A.O.C.
56158 L/Cpl. LAURENCE, A., N.Z.R.B.
Sgt. LEVIEN, N. J.
2nd Lieut. LURY, G. H.,* 15th Bn.
Pte. LEVY, J.
10/2498 Sgt. MANOY, R. L.,* 1st Wellington R.
21295 Pte. MILLGREW, H., 1st Otago Regt.
27/1745 Pte. MELTZER, J., No. 2. N.Z. Fld. Am.
21295 Pte. MELTZER, H., 2nd Auckland Bn.
53234 Sgt. MOSS, E. S., Rifle Bde.
76355 Rfm. MELTZER, S., Rifle Bde.
44503 Pte. MARKS, A., 2nd Wellongton Regt.
10/2498 Sgt. MANDY, R. L., 1st Wellington R.
3/2819 Pte. MYERS, H. E., N.Z.M.C.
72077 Rfm. MILLER, T. F., 37th Rfts. N.Z.R.B.
11514 Pte. NATHAN, C., 2nd Auckland Regt.
3/1069 Pte. NEWMEGAN, A. L., No. 3 Con. N.Z. Field Ambulance.
3/610 L/Cpl. NATHAN, S. D., N.Z. Stat. Hos.
45378 Rfm. NEFFER, E., 2nd Bn.
5/613 Dvr. ORNSTEIN, P., Div. Train.
33664 Pte. PHILLIPS, L., 1st Wellington Regt.
2/925 A/Sgt. POOL, M. P., 1st Bde. N.Z.F.A.
77445 Rfm. PEZARO, S. A., Rifle Bde.
Pte. PONTAWERA, J., N.Z.I.
3/3846 Pte. POSSENUISKIE, H. L.
46242 Sig. PEZARO, M. G.
3/3517 Pte. PHILIPS, I., F.A.
2/724 Sgt. ROTHSCHILD, L. C., Div. Train.
70728 Cpl. RATHBONE, A., Wellington Regt.
23/1818 Pte. SOLOMON, N., 2n Cant Regt
26/970 Rfm. SOLOMON, P., 4th N.Z.R.B.
L/Cpl. SAMUELS, V., 2nd Auck. Regt.
10/3995 Pte. SAMUELS, J., 1st Otago Regt.
31373 Pte. SPIRO, J., 1st Wellington Regt.
Dvr. SEATON, W. L., 3rd Bde. N.Z.F.A.
14/23 L/Cpl. SKYNNER, A., A.S.C.
26184 Sgt. SAMUEL, A. M., N.Z. Rifle Bde.
2/2407 Gnr. SELS, H. H., 1st Bde. Fld. Art.
74350 Pte. SAMPSON, I., 4th N.Z. Inf. Res. B.
43550 L/Cpl. SALEK, A. M., N.Z.A.S.C.
8/2893 Pte. SAMUEL, 1st Bn.
Dvr. SYTNER, A.
Pte. SELIG, I., N.Z.A.M.C.
52820 Sgt. THEOMIN, E. M., Wellington Regt.

New Zealand Division.—*Continued.*
39645 Pte. VANSTAVERN, I., 2nd Cant. Regt.
23/1882 Pte. WOOLF, S. S., 2nd Wellington R.
21366 Pte. WOLFE, S.,* 2nd Otago Regt.
　　　 Cpl. WITTNER, 3rd Bde. N.Z. Fld. Art.
　　　 Dvr. WITTNER, H, No. 1 N.Z. Fld. Amb.
4668 Rfm. WILFORD, D. H., 2nd Rifle Bde.
60243 Pte. WILLIAMS, H., Wellington Regt.

* Killed in Action or died on Active Service.

SOUTH AFRICAN FORCES.

OFFICERS.

Lieut. ADLER, F. B., S.A.A.
Lieut. BERNSTEIN, I. L., 3rd Bn.
Staff Sister BERNSTEIN, D.,* S.A.M.S.
Capt. BLOOMENTHAL, H., S.A.A.
2nd Lieut. BRISCOE, A. J., S.A.M.C.
Capt. BLOCK, I., S.A.M.C.
Capt. BLOCK, J., S.A.M.C.
Lieut. BASCH, E., S.A.M.C.
Major COHEN, L. (D.S.O., M.C.), S.A. Horse.
Capt. COLB, M., S.A.M.C.
Capt. COHEN, J. M., S.A.A.S.C.
Capt. COHEN, J., S.A.A.S.C.
Lieut. COHEN, M., S.A.R.F.A.
Capt. COHEN, A., S.A.M.C.
Lieut. CAZES, P. J. (M.C.).
Lieut. EXSTEIN, E.A. Mounted Rifles.
2nd Lieut. FRIEND, M., 1st Rhod. Rifles.
Lieut. FEIGENBAUM, S., E.A. Pay Corps.
2nd Lieut. FRANK, I., Namaqualand Command.
Lieut. FALKE, J., R.F.A.
Lieut. FRIEDLANDER, D., Namaqualand Comd.
Lieut. FORMAN, M., 8th B.L.R.
Lieut. GOLDBERG, R., S.A.M.G.C.
Lieut. GORDON, I., 10th Mounted Brigade.
Lieut. GREENBERG, S.A.M.C.
Capt. GOLDBERG, I., S.A.M.G.C.
Capt. GREENBURG, N., S.A.M.C.
Capt. GALGUT, E., S.A.M.C.
Lieut. GORDON, J.
Capt. GREENBERG, M., S.A.M.C.
Col. HARRIS, Sir D. (K.C.M.G.), 1st Kimb. Regt.
2nd Lieut. HELLER, V.
Major HIRSCH, H. A. (D.S.O.)
Major HORWICH, D., S.A.M.C.
2nd Lieut HIRSCHBERG, A., 75th Sge. Bty., Hy. Arty., S.A.F.A.

Lieut. ISAACS, A., G.W.A. and G.E.A.
Capt. ISAACS, L. I., 1st Bn.
Capt. & Adjt. JACOBS, B., S. A. Lichenburg Com.
Capt. JACOBS, L. M. (D.S.O.), S.A. Inf.
Lieut. KING, B. L., S.A.I. Rhodesia.
Capt. KOSSICK, J., Defence Force.
2nd Lieut. LAZARUS, R. H., 2nd Bn.
Lieut. LAZARUS, B., Namaqualand Command.
Lieut. LURIE, G., S.A.M.C.
2nd Lieut. LAVINE, B., S.A.M.C.
Lieut. LOWENSTEIN, H., G.W.A.
Capt. LIEBSON, S.* (M.C.), S.A.M.C.
Capt. LEVISEUR, E. A., S.A.M.C.
Lieut. MYERS, S. T., G.E.A.
Lieut. OSHRY, C., Namaqualand Command.
Lieut. OSRIN, J., Rand. L.I., S.A.
OPPENHEIMER, Sir F. (K.C.M.G.), S.A.D.F.
Lieut. PHILLIPS, F., 2nd Rhodesian Regt.
Capt. PEARLMAN, A., Vryheid Command.
2nd Lieut. RIGAL, G., S.A.S.C.
Lieut. RIGAL, G., 1st S.A.I.
Lieut. ROSEN, A., S.A.D.R.
Lieut. SAGAR, H., 1st Kimberley Regt. S.A.
Major SCHLOM, S.A. Forces.
Lieut. SOLOMON, A. C. (M.C.).
Lieut. SUSKIND, F., Rand L.I.
Capt. SAUNDERS, S.A.M.C.
Capt. SIMON, M., S.A.S.C.
Lieut. SIMONS, J. S.A. R.E.
Lieut. SOLOMON, I.M., W.P.M. Rifles.
2nd Lieut. SOLOMON, I., 17th Mounted Rifles.
Lieut. SILBERT, S.
Lieut. SCHERATA, S., S.A.I.
Lieut.-Col. SOLOMON, S., Staff, Kimberley.
Lieut. STERN, S.,* King's African Rifles.
Lieut. VAN PRAAGH, J., S.A.R.
Lieut. WEITZMANN, S.A.D.C.
Lieut. WILLERGRO, B. L., S.A.S.C.
Capt. WOOLF, C., Staff, S.A.
Capt. WOLFF, J. V. C., S.A.D.C.
Capt. ZEFFERT, H. L.

N.C.O.'s AND MEN.

19576 Pte. AARON, H., 2nd Bn.
2054 Pte. AARON, W.
　　　 Pte. AARONSOHN, S., Cape Gar. Artil.
1012 Sgt. AARONS, L. L., 1st Bn.
　　　 Pte. ABGEL, A., Pnrs. Bn.

ABBREVIATIONS.

S.A.A. = S. African Artillery. S.A.M.C. = S. African Medical Corps. S.A.A.S.C. = S. African Army Service Corps. G.W.A. = Served in German West African Campaign. G.E.A. = Served in German East African Campaign. S.A.D.F. = South African Defence Force. S.A.I. = South African Infantry. W.P.M. = Western Province Mounted Rifles. C.P.G.R. = Cape Peninsular Garrison Regt. C.P.R. = Cape Peninsular Rifles. S.A.N.L.C. = S. African Native Labour Corps. S.A.H.A. = S. African Heavy Artillery. RR. = Rhodesian Rifles. E.A.M.S. = E. African Medical Service.

South African Forces.—*Continued.*

- Pte. ABELRAN, L., Rand Rifles.
- 4019 Pte. ABRAHAMS, J., 1st S.A.I.
- 12348 Pte. ABRAHAMS, W., 7th Inf.
- Cpl. ABRAHAMS, J. E., S.A. Horse.
- 13689 Pte. ABRAHAMS, A., Inf.
- 1952 Pte. ABRAHAMS, E., S.A.I.
- Pte. ABRAHAMS, H. L., S.A.M.C.
- Pte. ABRAHAMS, M.
- 11505 Cpl. ABRAHAMS, A., 3rd Bn.
- 17937 Pte. ABRAHAMS, H., 2nd Bn.
- Pte. ABRAHAMS, H. W. (D.C.M.), Inf.
- Pte. ADAMSTEIN, C.
- 659 Sgt. ADLER, M., S.A.N.L.C.
- Pte. ADLER, L., Rand Rifles.
- Tpr. ADLER, P., 3rd Horse.
- 13135 Pte. ADLER, H. L., 1st Bn.
- 2504 Pte, ARONSON, N., 3rd Bn.
- Pte. AHRENSON, A., 9th Inf.
- 15157 L/Cpl. AICHURTZ, E.
- 1999 Pte. ALBU, A.
- Pte. ALEXANDER, B., 3rd Horse.
- Pte ALEXANDER, E. V., C.P.G.R.
- Pte. ALEXANDER, J., C.P.G.R.
- Pte. ALEXANDER, K., C.P.G.R.
- Pte. ALEXANDER, M., K.C., M.L.A. C.P.G.R.
- Pte. ALGE, W., 2nd Horse.
- Tpr. ALGE, A. D.
- Pte. ALLIN, J., S.A.M.C.
- Pte. AMBROSE, S., S.A.M.C.
- Pte. ARENSTEIN, A., P.G.
- 7201 Pte. AVEL, J., Inf.
- Pte. ARENSHEN, F., Transvaal Scots.
- Pte. ANGEL, M., 9th Sportsman Bn.
- Pte. ANGISTA, J., Cronje's Commando.
- Pte. ANGER, S., 2nd S.A. Rifles.
- Pte. ARONSEN, H., C.C.A.
- Pte. ARENSOHN, M., C.P.R.
- Pte. ARONOWITZ, R., C.P.R.
- Pte. ARENSTEIN, F. F., 1st Transvaal Sc.
- Pte. ASCHMAN, I., 9th L.A. Horse.
- Pte. ASHER, H., S.A.M.C.
- Pte. ASHER, H. M., King Edward Horse
- P/Nurse ASHMAN, V., S.A.M.N.S.
- 5163 Pte. ABELSON, J.,* 7th S.A. Inf.
- 1146 Pte. BAKER, H. R.,* 1st Bn.
- 2827 Pte. BANKS, R., 2nd Bn.
- Pte. BARKER, S., 4th Bn.
- 117 Gnr. BECKMAN, S., 71st Bty. H. Art.
- 171 Gnr. BERMAN, R.,* 74th Bty. H. Art.
- 439 Gnr. BENDLESTEIN, A., 74th Bty. H. Art.
- 167 Gnr. BROWN, H., 75th Bty. H. Art.
- 4266 Pte. BLASHKER, A., 1st Bn.
- 8286 Pte. BAKER, M., 1st Bn.
- 6907 Sgt. BLOOM, H., 1st Bn.
- 369 Pte. BERKER, S., 2nd Bn.
- 5704 Pte. BLOOM, B., 2nd Bn.
- 803 Pte. BROOKSTONE, M., 2nd Bn.
- 7746 Pte. BROWN, J., 4th Bn.
- 15876 Pte. BERNSTEIN, B., 1st Bn.
- 16337 Pte. BARNETT, M., 3rd Bn.
- 15895 Pte. BUSKEY, A. I.
- 5927 Bglr. BROOKSTONE, M. S., 9th Bn.
- 1776 Pte. BROOKSTONE, A. H., 10th Bn.
- 15098 Pte. BEAVER, C., S.A.M.C.
- 66 Sgt. BONUS, F. L., S.A.N.L.
- 1146 Pte. BAKER, H. R.,* 1st Bn.
- 12843 Pte. BARNES, J.,* 3rd Bn.
- 584 Sgt. BADER, M., S.A.N.L.C.
- 317 Cpl. BERNITZ, A., S.A.M.C.
- 20694 Pte. BECKER, G. H., S.A.
- 1799 Pte. BANSKIN, S.A.F.A.
- 1799 Pte. BARKOWITZ, B., 1st Brigade S.A.R.
- 13661 Pte. BARNETT, B., 1st Bde. S.A.I.
- 15985 Pte. BERNSON, S., 1st Bde. S.A.I.
- 16959 Pte. BEHR, A. H., 1st Bde. S.A.I.
- 16859 Pte. BELLIS, J. H., C.P.G.R.
- Pte. BENDER, W. J., C.P.G.R.
- Pte. BERNSTEIN, L., C.P.G.R.
- Pte. BERNSTEIN, M. B., C.P.G.R.
- Pte. BRIN, M., C.P.G.R.
- Pte. BROOKSTEIN, I., S.A.I.
- Pte. BERGER, A., 5th I.A.I.
- Pte. BLUMBERG, E.
- Pte. BLUMBERG, S.
- Pte. BLUMBERG, H.
- Pte. BAUMGARTEN, B.
- Pte. BLUMENTHAL, H., S.A.F.A.
- Cpl. BLECH, A. L., Brit. East Africa.
- Tpr. BRANITZKY, S., B.E.A.
- Pte. BOND, A. S.A.F.
- Sgt. BECKER, P., Inf.
- Pte. BRANCH, F., B.D.F.N.R.
- Pte. BERGER, S., S.A. D.E.F. A.C.
- Rfm. BENNIE, J., Rand Rifles.
- Tpr. BARRETT, L., S.A.F.
- Cpl. BLOOM, E., S.A.I.
- Pte. BARIOM, V., F.A.C.
- Pte. BUNTMAN, S., K.M.C.
- Pte. BUNTMAN, B., I.L.H.
- 113355 Pte. BRAUDE, W. H., S.A.I.
- Pte. BATLIN, I., G.E.A.
- Pte. BLOOM, T., G.E.A.
- Pte. BLOOM, I. J., G.E.A.
- Pte. BECKER, M., Defence Force.
- Pte. BROOK, J.
- Sgt. Maj. BARNETT, M., 18th Mtd. Rifles.
- 12069 Pte. BASS, A. H.
- X/283 Pte. BARNETT, H. R.
- 16262 Pte. BREST, H.
- 7751 Pte. BROOKSTEIN, R.
- 17870 Pte. BERNSTEIN, D. S.
- 18107 Pte. BRITSTONE, S.
- 21043 Pte. BRESLER, J.,
- 6938 Pte. BLOM, S.

South African Forces.—*Continued.*

Pte. BANET, L., S. Rhodesian Vol.
Pte. BLOOM, B., S. Rhodesian Vol.
Pte. BROWN, L., 2nd Rhodesian Rifles.
6018 Sgt. BERGER, C. H., Uganda Med. Ser., G.E.A.
Pte. BORWEIN, J. N., Transvaal Rifles.
Pte. BALDACHIN, S., S.A. Motor Trans.
13786 Pte. BAKER, H., S.A.I.
11595 Pte. BITCH, A., 2nd Res. Infantry.
1093 Pte. BROWNE, R., S.A.H.A.
Pte. BOWMAN, J., S.A.C.S.
Pte. BERNSTEIN, A.
Pte. BOWMAN, E., 9th Infantry.
Pte. BARNARD, A., 7th Sportsman's Bn.
Pte. BERNSTEIN, M., S.A.M.C.
S/Major BRUCE, J., S.A.S.C.
Pte. BARNETT, B., S.A.M.C.
Pte. BLOOM, S., S.A.S.C.
Pte. BLOOM, S., S.A.M.C.
Pte. BLOOM, J., S.A.M.C.
Sgt. BERNSTEIN, J.
Pte. BRIN, S., S.A.M.C.
Pte. BAIMAN, B., 9th S.A.I.
Sgt. BERNSTEIN, P., 8th Bn.
Pte. BRANDE, W., 11th Bn.
Gnr. BERKOVITZ, J., S.A.M.R.
11584 Pte. BEITSCH, A., 1st Bde. S.A.R.
12178 Pte. BROWNSTEIN, M., 1st Bde. S.A.R.
11957 Pte. BLOOMENTHAL, F., 1st Bde. S.A.R.
372 Pte. BRAZIL, L., S.A.M.C.
Pte. BENN, I. L., C.H.M.R.
Pte. BERTZ, J., G.W.A.
Pte. BORWIN, J., G.S.W.A.
Pte. BERMAN, J., D.E.O.R., G.W.A.
Pte. BLOCH, L., C.T.H., G.W.A.
Pte. BERKOWITZ, J., S.A.M.R., G.W.A.
1110 Dvr. BERKOWITCH, D., Mounted Trans.
Pte. BLOCH, S., R.L.I.
Pte. BEROCHOWITZ, C.P.R.
Pte. BROWN, H., H.A.
Pte. BUCHELTZ, H., 4th Bty., S.A.R.
Pte. BROWN, M. L., 2nd R.R.
Pte. BERMAN, S.A.M.C.
Dvr. BERMAN, M. T.
81108 Sgt. BERNFIELD, I., S.A.A.
Trp. BENJAMIN, M.A., Imperial Light. I.
Trp. BLUMENFELD, A., Zulu M.R.
Trp. BENN, I. L., Hanover M.R.
17 Pte. BURROWS, N.
11802 Pte. BERMAN, B.,* 4th S.A. Inf.
Pte. BRONKHORST, M. J., S.A.M.C.
1110 Pte. COHEN, E., 1st Bn.
1167 Pte. COOPER, L.,* 1st Bn.
1777 Pte. CRISTEL, M., 1st Bn.
1564 L/Sgt. CHART, A., 2nd Bn.
3174 Pte. COLLY, H. D.,* 2nd Bn.
362 Pte. COHEN, A. E.,* 2nd Bn.
362 L/Sgt. COHEN, A. E.,* 2nd Bn.
1393 Cpl. CROSS, L. A., 3rd Bn.
878 Cpl. CLINE, D.,* 4th Bn.
926 Pte. CLINE, J.,* 4th Bn.
448 Gnr. COHEN, N., 73rd Bty. Art.
182 Gnr. COHEN, S. G. de, 73rd Bty. Art.
1151 Gnr. CANARD, H., 74th Bty. Art.
8734 Pte. COHEN, N., 2nd Bn.
9006 Pte. COHEN, A., 3rd Bn.
9011 Pte. COHEN, J., 3rd Bn.
12118 Pte. CHITMAN, S., 1st Bn.
12081 Pte. CHAIMOWITZ, M.,* 1st Bn.
12359 Pte. CAMINSKY, L., 2nd Bn.
7065 Pte. COHEN, J., 3rd Bn.
469 Pte. COLEMAN, J. H., 1st Bn.
19538 Pte. COHEN, S., S.A.I.
19381 Pte. CHAIT, B., S.A.I.
201317 Pte. COBB, E., S.A.I.
726 Sgt. CRANKS, H., 9th Bn.
Gnr. COHEN, M., 71st Siege Bty.
20008 Pte. CUGAUF, S., S.A.I.
1736 Pte. CHITRIN, H.
1369 Pte. COHEN, B.
798 Pte. CAINARIE, J.
20008 Pte. CAGANOFF, S.
A/288 Pte. CAMAROFF, H.,* Brit. S.A. Police.
Pte. COHEN, B., 2nd Rand Rifles.
Pte. CRISTOL, L., A.S.C.
Pte. COHEN, A., S.A.M.
Pte. COHEN, A., Nyasaland N. Border.
Sgt. COLWIN, A., E.A.MS.
6639 Sgt. COHEN, M., S.A.R.E.
1101 Gnr. CLAER, H., S.A.H.A.
Tpr. COHEN, V., Aubrey's Horse.
9690 Dv. CAPLAN, L., S.A. Signals.
Cpl. COHN, L. J., I.L.H.
2545 Pte. COHEN, R., S.A.S.C.
Pte. CIPEN, K., S.A.M.C.
6282 Pte. COHEN, R., S.A.I.
Pte. COHEN, J., Transvaal Scts.
Pte. COWAN, F., Transvaal Scts.
Pte. COHEN, L., S.A.M.C.
757 Pte. CROSS, W., 3rd Bde. Inf.
3681 Pte. COLMAN, H. V., 2nd Inf.
15638 Pte. COHEN, N. B., 1st Bde. Inf.
12536 Pte. COTTLER D. I., 1st Bde. Inf.
11306 Pte. CANSTIC, J., 1st Bde. Inf.
12858 Pte. COWAN, B. B., 1st Bde. Inf.
13308 Pte. COHEN, A., 1st Bde. Inf.
Pte. CERFF, G., C.P.G.R.
Pte. COHEN, G., C.P.G.R.
Pte. COHEN, J. E., C.P.G.R.
Pte. COHEN, R., C.P.G.R.
Pte. COHEN, P., G.W.A.
Pte. CLANKE, B.
Tpr. CLANKE, A., Botha's Horse.
Pte. CRAMER, S.A.D.F.
Sgt. CHAIN, A., R.S.A.F.

South African Forces.—*Continued.*

      Cpl. CANIEL COHEN, I.L.H.
      Pte. CAPLAN, M., S.A.M.C.
234 Pte. CHAPMAN, B., S.A.M.C.
      Pte. CLAIN, H., S.A.H.A.
1775 Pte. CARNOFSKY, M., F.A.P.A.C.
      Pte. CINAMON, A., 2nd R.R. G.E.A.
      Pte. COHEN, S. H.
      Pte. COHEN, G., Sig. Corps.
      Pte. CHESLER, S., S.C.G.A.
      Pte. COHEN, B., R.S.A.P.
      Cpl. CURRIE, M., R.A.M.C.
      Pte. COLWIN, E., B.S.A.P.
      Pte. COHEN, H., S.A.I. G.E.A.
      Cpl. COHEN, M.T. A.S.C. N. & R. B. Rgt.
17215 Pte. COHEN, A. H.
2390 Gnr. CINNAMON, N., S.A. Hy. Artil.
      Pte. CANARICK, C.,* S.A. Inf.
      Pte. COHEN, H., Rhod. Light Horse.
18068 Pte. DAVIS, L.
      Pte. DELVET, A.
      Pte. DAITCH, H., Infantry.
      Pte. DAITSH, I., Infantry.
      A/Sgt. DAVIS, J., 3rd Inf. Bde.
      Pte. DANZIGER, H., 9th Inf. Bde.
      Pte. DAVIS, B., 8th Inf. Bde.
10791 Pte. DRUKER, E., 1st Inf. Bde.
      Dmr. DYNE, N. H., 1st. Inf. Bde.
      Pte. DAVIDOFF, J., 12th Inf. Bde.
      Pte. DEMBOVSKY, A., C.P.G.R.
      Sgt. DRUIFF, L. J., C.P.G.R.
      Pte. DVOLITZKY, P.R., S.A.F.
      Pte. DIAMOND, W. H.
      Pte. DIAMOND, L. S.
      Pte. DIAMOND, A. B., B.D.F.
      Pte. DAVIS, A. R., S.A.I.
      Pte. DONNIGER, S., P.A.G.
203 Pte. DIAMOND, J., S.A.M.C.
7760 Pte. DAVIS, J., S.A.M.C.
      Pte. DAVIS, I., S.A.F.
1428 Cpl. DOITSH, E., 1st Bn.
12925 Pte. DUMAS, N.,* 1st Bn.
6684 Pte. DAVIS, C. D., 3rd Bn.
2255 Pte. DAVIS, A. A., 3rd Bn.
3849 Pte. DRUION, A. I., 3rd Bn.
1430 Gnr. DAVIS, C., S.A.H.A.
10737 Spr. DANILER, H. J.,* Engineers.
18714 Pte. DEVRIES, A., S.A.
10006 Pte. ELIAS, H. F.
      Rfm. ESTERMAN, H., N.R.R.
      Pte. EHMKE, C., C.P.G.R.
      Pte. ELIASOV, C., C.P.G.R.
      Pte. ELIASON, C.
2436 Pte. ELIASON, S.
      Pte. ELKANOWITZ, J., S.A.F.
      Bugler EPSTEIN, S.A.M.C.
      Pte. EPSTEIN, M., S.A.M.C.
      Pte. ELION, S., 2nd S.A.I.

      Pte. EDELSTEIN, C.
2860 Pte. EMANUEL, J., 2nd Bn.
4499 Pte. EPPEL, A., 2nd Bn.
3455 Pte. ELMAN, N.,* 4th Bn.
      Pte. ELMAN, B., 4th Bn.
1980 Pte. EMANUEL, B., 4th Bn.
12619 Pte. ERLSTEIN, H., 2nd Bn.
13185 Pte. ESTERMAN, A.,* 3rd Bn.
19430 Pte. EPTSEIN, L., A.S.I.
620722 Sgt. EMANUEL, M., 21st Bn.
6292 Pte. FIGG, S., 2nd Bn .
8402 Pte. FREEMAN, I.,* 1st Bn.
172 Pte. FRANKLIN, S.,* 1st Bn.
7502 Pte. FEINBERG, M.,* 2nd Bn.
13114 Pte. FINE, G., 2nd Bn.
12434 Pte. FREEDMAN, B.,* 2nd Bn.
13298 Pte. FUCHS, R., 2nd Bn.
424 Pte. FINE, L., S.A. (Comp.) Bn.
S/Nurse FROMBERG, B., S.A.M.N.S.
20183 Pte. FINEBERG, A., S.A.I.
14794 Pte. FERRERS, L.
4395 Pte. FISH, F.
18939 Pte. FEINSTEIN, L.
16 Pte. FRANKENSTEIN, A.
      Pte. FINKLESTEIN, D., S.A.M.C.
      Pte. FINKLESTEIN, J., S.A.M.C.
12619 Pte. FRUNSTEIN, H., 1st Inf. Bde.
12057 Pte. FEIGENBAUM, M., 1st Inf. Bde.
9861 Pte. FREEDMAN, D., 1st Inf. Bde.
926 Pte. FISHER, P., S.A.M.C.
      Pte. FENDEL, G. H., Cronje's Command.
      Pte. FINE, J., S.A.H.
      Pte. FISHER, J., 7th Inf. Bde.
      Pte. FALK, 5th Inf. Bde.
      Pte. FREEDMAN, L., 4th S.A.M.C.
      Pte. FISHER, I., S.A.M.C.
      Pte. FUCHS, S., 12th Inf. Bde.
      Spr. FINE, B., S.A. Horse.
      Sgt. FINEBERG, A. (M.S.M.), S.A. A.S.C.
      Pte. FLAX, S., S.A.M.C.
      Pte. FISHER, F. T., C.P.G.R.
      Pte. FREEDMAN, J., C.P.G.R.
      L/Cpl. FEINBERG, D., W.R., S.A.F.
      Pte. FRIDJOHN, L.,* S.A.M.C.
      Pte. FISHER, D., Victoria West Comd.
      Pte. FRIEDLANDER, H., S.A.A., G.W.A.
      Pte. FRIEDMAN, F., G.E.A.
      Pte. FREEDMAN, L., G.E.A.
      Tpr. FRANKLIN, L., Natal Carbineers.
      Cpl. FIELD, B.E.A.
      Pte. FREEMAN, B., S.A.I.
      Pte. FELDMAN, J., G.W.A.
      Pte. FISHER, B., 1st City Volunteers.
371 Pte. FLETCHBERG, P., S.A.M.C.
      Pte. FELDMAN, J., C.T.A.
      Pte. FEIGENBAUM, S., E.A. Pay Corps.
      Pte. FREEMAN, P., S.A.I. G.E.A.
2250 Q.M.S. FREEDMAN, M. D., N. & R.B. Rg.

South African Forces.—*Continued.*

Dvr. FREEDMAN, D., A.S.C. N. and R.B. Regt.
Pte. FINSTEIN.
Pte. FRITZ, Pretoria Regt.
Pte. FLORENSTEIN, W. K., S.A.S.C.
2704 Pte. GOLDBLATT, G. M.,* 2nd Bn.
634 Pte. GLASS, C., 3rd Bn.
5886 Pte. GOLDHILL, H., 3rd Bn.
2183 Pte. GABRIELSON, S. L. P., 4th Bn.
1109 Pte. GOSSCHALK, M., 125th S. Bty. S.A.H.A.
214 Pte. GLASS, S., 1st Bn.
8195 L/Cpl. GOLDSTEIN, A., 2nd Bn.
7439 Pte. GRASS, M., 2nd Bn.
9213 Pte. GOLDBERG, H., 2nd Bn.
8718 Pte. GREEN, A. B.,* 3rd Bn.
7670 Pte. GLUCKMAN, B., 3rd Bn.
6171 Pte. GLUCKMAN, S.,* 3rd Bn.
4901 Pte. GOLDSTEIN, D. M., 3rd Bn.
11176 Pte. GOSCHEN, S., 4th Bn.
7773 Pte. GREEN, C. G., S.A. (Comp.) Bn.
16945 Pte. GAIS, M. S., S.A. (Comp.) Bn.
345 Sgt. GREENBERG, I.
20325 Pte. GOLDWASSER, H., S.A.I.
Pte. GLAZER, B., W.R.
Rfm. GOORMAN, H., W.R.
Sgt. GOLDSTEIN, J., C.M.R.
Gnr. GOLDRICH, C., M.G.C. S.A.I.
Pte. GLASSMAN, J., S.A.I.
Pte. GORDON, A., Defence Force.
Pte. GORDON, J., Defence Force.
Cpl. GREENBERG, M., South R.G.W.A.
Pte. GABRIEL, L., S.A.I.
Cpl. GOLDBERG, A., Artillery.
Pte. GOLDMAN, H., S.A.M.C.
Tpr. GREEN, I., V.C.T.A.
Cpl. GINSBERG, L., P.A.G.
Sgt. GORDON, P., 18th Mtd. Rfls B.S.W.
Sgt. GREENBLATT, M., K.H. G.W.A.
Pte. GOLDMAN, J., 2nd S.A.M.C. G.S.W.A.
1681 Pte. GOTTSMAN, J., S.A.M.C.
Pte. GILLIS, J., P.A.G. G.W.& G.E.A.
5283 Pte. GERBER, P., 5th S.A.I. G.E.A.
Pte. GEFFEN, J., D.E.O.R. G.W.A.
Cpl. GROMLAND, A. D., S.A.M.C.
Pte. GOTSMAN, C. P. R.
Pte. GOLDMAN, H. J.
Pte. GLUCKMAN, P.
Pte. GARB, M., M.G.S. C.P.R.
Pte. GOLDMAN, B., C.P.R.
Pte. GERSOHN, B.
Pte. GLATT, S.A.F.A.
Pte. GREEN, A., W. Rifles.
L/Cpl. GABRIEL, W., W. Rifles.
16748 Pte. GROSSMAN, L., S.A.M.C.
Pte. GOODMAN, N., I. Light Horse.
Pte. GINSBERG, M., N. Command.
Pte. GLADSTONE, W., Witwat. Rifles.
Pte. GUTCHEN, M., 12th Pretoria.
259 Gnr. GRANGER, F., G.S.W.
1844 Pte. GUIGUE, D., 2nd Rhodesian Rifles.
1638 Pte. GOULD, H., 2nd Rhodesian Rifles.
1825 Pte. GERSBACK, A. J., 2nd Rhod. Rifles.
16882 Pte. GINSBERG, I., 2nd Rhodesian Rifles.
Pte. GINSBERG, B., S. Rhodesian Vol.
Pte. GLICK, J., 7th S.A.I.
Sgt. GREENSPAN, M., N. Regt. N. Border.
Gnr. GRANGER, F., M.M.G.
Pte. GOLDMAN, J., 2nd S.A.M.C.
245139 Gnr. GOLDMAN, M., 3rd S.A.A.
14052 Pte. GIELICK, M. H., 2nd Inf. Bde.
7564 Pte. GLUCKMAN, L., Inf. Bde.
Pte. GOLDSTEIN, A.
2163 Tpr. GOODMAN, R. B., S.A. Horse.
198 Pte. GROSBERG, B., B.S.A.P.
8871 Pte. GIHBERG, C., 2nd Inf. Bde.
15346 Pte. GOLDRING, H., 2nd Inf. Bde.
Pte. GUDVIS, S., S.A.M.C.
Pte. GOODMAN, M., 9th Inf. Bn.
Pte. GREENBERG, A. B., S.A.M.C.
Pte. GOLDSTEIN, L., S.A.M.C.
Pte. GOODMAN, H., 9th Bn.
12767 Pte. GINSBERG, M., 1st Bde. S.A.I.
12815 Pte. GALE, R., 1st Bde. S.A.I.
11953 Pte. GOLDBERG, S., 1st Bde. S.A.I.
11285 Pte. GOLDBERG, M., 1st Bde. S.A.I.
595071 Pte. GROSE, M., S.A.I.
Pte. GIBBERT, S., C.P.G.R.
Pte. GOLDSTEIN, J., C.P.G.R.
Pte. GOLDSTEIN, S., C.P.G.R.
S/Major GOLDBERG, S.,* S.A. Service C.
751 L/Cpl. HENOCHSBERG, D. H., 1st S.A.M.C.
99 Gnr. HIRSCHBERG, A., 74th Bty. Art.
127 Gnr. HILL, S., 72nd Bty. Art.
1116 Pte. HAYES, J., 1st Bn.
4342 Pte. HERSON, B., 1st Bn.
1946 L/Cpl. HARRIS, J., 1st Bn.
8011 Pte. HYAMS, P.,* 2nd Bn.
8701 Pte. HANRICK, I., 2nd Bn.
1421 Pte. HOFFMAN, J.,* 3rd Bn.
8509 Pte. HARRIS, E., 3rd Bn.
6925 Pte. HELLER, B., 4th Bn.
11115 Pte. HERSON, I., 1st Bn.
16101 Pte. HIDES, A., 3rd Bn.
13139 Pte. HURWITZ, I., 1st Bn.
9769 Pte. HOFFBRAND, L., 3rd Bn.
749 Pte. HYAMS, L., 3rd Bn.
6265 Pte. HENLEIN, B., 9th Bn.
3438 Pte. HALBREACE, J. E., 3rd Bn.
15900 Pte. HARRIS, J., S.A.M.C.
12672 Pte. HYMAN, L., S.A.I.
454 Sgt. HENOCHSBERG, A. J.
Sgt. HENOCHSBERG, E. M.
14106 Pte. HART, V. Y., 3rd Bn.

South African Forces.—*Continued.*

371	Pte. HAHN, A., S.A.M.C.
9765	Sgt. HYAMS, J., S.A.R.B.
21474	Pte. HYMAN, E. B., S.A.I.
9780	Pte. HAMMERSCHLAG, H.
	Pte. HIRSCHON, H., A.S.C., G.E.A.
	Pte. HARRIS, A. H., Scouts, G.E.A.
	Pte. HERSHOWITZ, A., A.S.C.
7376	Pte. HARRIS, E., 3rd Bn.
389	Gnr. HERSCHBERG, A., S.A.H.A.
16140	Pte. HARRIS, W., 1st Bn.
	Bmd. HART, J., S.A.R.E.
426	Pte. HARRISBERG, S., S.A. Motor Cyclists.
	S/Sgt. HESSE, S.A.S.C.
	Sgt. HYMAN, J. H., 5th Bn.
	Pte. HERTZBERG, G. J., S.A.H.
	Pte. HERTZBERG, H., 12th Bn.
	Spr. HOLLANDER, A., S.A. Forces.
5579	Gnr. HERRING, H., 10th Bn.
11862	Pte. HARRIS, M., 1st Bde. S.A.I.
16438	Pte. HOFFBRAND, J., 1st Bde. S.A.I.
14542	Pte. HARRIS, A., 1st Bde. S.A.I.
	Pte. HORWITZ, J., C.P.G.R.
	Pte. HARTSTONE, J., C.P.G.R.
	Pte. HOLLINGTON, J., C.P.G.R.
	Pte. HEIMAN, E., S.A.F.F.
	Pte. HASSES, J., Defence Force.
	Pte. HERSCHMAN, J. C., S.A.I.
	Pte. HORWITZ, M., Victoria West Co.
	Pte. HERSCHON, N., G.S.W.A.
8329	Pte. HARRIS, H. V., O.I.
	Pte. HARRIS, A., G.W.A.
	Pte. HARRIS, S., G.W.A.
	Pte. HORWITZ, H., C.T.H., G.W.A.
	Pte. HOFFMAN, R., D.E.O.R., G.W.A.
	Pte. HOFFMAN, B., S.A.S.C.
	Pte. HANDLER, D.E.O.R., G.W.A.
	Pte. HERMAN, L., S.A.I., G.E.A.
	Pte. HUYS, J., S.A.I.
	Pte. HOFFMAN, A., R.F.C.
1995574	Pte. HOLTZMAN, I., S.A.I.
	Pte. HARRIS, E., Bethal Commando.
	Pte. HODES, L., S.A.D. Corps.
	Pte. HYMAN, S., Transvaal Scott.
4999	L/Cpl. ISRAEL, G. R.,* 3rd Bn.
9381	Pte. ISRAEL, R., 1st Bn.
7511	Pte. ISAACS, S. W., 2nd Bn.
X/252	Pte. ISRAEL, P., S.A. (Comp.) Bn.
17763	Pte. ISHLOVE, A., C. Coy. 1st Bn.
295285	Dvr. ISRAEL, B., S.A. Artillery.
19957	Pte. ISAACSON, C., 2nd Res. Bn.
20249	Pte. INGEL, J. H., 2nd Res. Bn.
	Pte. ISAACS, H., M.M.G.
	Pte. ISAACS, Medical Corps, G.E.A.
1590	Tpr. ISAACS, I., 1st S.A. Horse.
	Cpl. ISAACS, S., S.A.M.C.
	Pte. ISAACSON, S., Kimberley Regt.
	Pte. ISAACS, J., C.P.G.R.

	Pte. ISRAEL, C., C.P.G.R.
	Rfm. ISRITZ, S., W.R.
	Pte. ISAACSON, G., 1st Kimberley Regt.
	Pte. ISAACS, S., 1st S.A.H. G.E.A.
	Pte. ISAACS, G. T., S.A.I.
	Pte. ISRAEL, G., S.A.I.
	Pte. ISAACSOHN, I., Kimber. Rgt. G.W.A.
	Pte. ISANOWITZ, J., S.A.M.C.
	Pte. ISSEROW, L., Simonstown C.P.R.
	Staff/Sgt. ISAACSON, C., G.E.A.
	Q.M.S. ISAACS, P., Botha's Own.
	Pte. ISRITZ, S., Witwaters. Rand Rfls.
	Q.M.S. JACOBS, A.
2846	Pte. JACOBS, A. N.,* 2nd Bn.
3462	L/Cpl. JACOBS, H. M.,* 3rd Bn.
123	Pte. JACOBS, C. I. (M.M.), 1st S.A. F.A.
7042	Pte. JOFFE, J., 1st Bn.
8219	Pte. JACOBSON, D. M., 2nd Bn.
7555	Pte. JACOBSON, A.
10648	Pte. JACOB, P., 2nd Bn.
1592	Pte. JACOB, M., 2nd Bn.
227	Pte. JACOBSON, M.
13527	Pte. JACOBS, P.
4156	Pte. JOSHUA, A.
	Pte. JACOB, H.
	Pte. JONES, J., 2nd Bn. Rhodesian Rfls.
	Pte. JOFFEY, M., 12th S.A.I., G.E.A.
	Pte. JONES, H., E.A. Pay Corps.
10407	Pte. JACOBS, S., 2nd Bn.
421	Pte. JACOBSON, H., S.A.M.C.
CM/524	Pte. JACOBS, E., S.A.M.C.
2462	Pte. JACOBSEN, S., 7th Bn.
	Pte. JACOBS, J., 7th Bn.
	Cpl. JACOBS, I., 7th Bn.
	S/Maj JUDALSON, H., Botha's H.
	Pte. JACOBS, S. S., 7th Bn.
10898	Pte. JACOBS, M., 1st Bde. S.A.I.
13209	Pte. JOEL, L., 1st Bde. S.A.I.
	Pte. JACOBS, A., C.P.G.R.
	Pte. JACOBSOHN, L. B., C.P.G.R.
	Pte. JOFFE, J., C.P.G.R.
	Pte. JONAS, A. J., C.P.G.R.
	Pte. JUDELSOHN, J. H., C.P.G.R.
	Pte. JOSEPHSON, S., Namaqua Command.
	Tpr. JOSEPH, C. J., S.R.
	Sgt. JORSH, L. H., P.R. S.A.F.
	Pte. JEWELL, R., S.A.I.
	Pte. JANKOWITZ, S., S.A.I.
	Pte. JACOBSOHN, S., S.A.I.
	Pte. JOSOPHSON, B., S.A.M.C.
	Sgt. JACKSON, S., C.P.R.
	Pte. JACOBSOHN, I., P.A.G.
	Pte. JULIOUS, B., S.A.F.A.
	Pte. JAFFE, I., 17th Mtd. Rifles, G.E.A.
	Pte. JONES, J., 2nd R.R.
	Sgt. KING, I.
20582	Pte. KAHN, S.
	Pte. KING, I., S. Rhodesian Vol.

South African Forces.—*Continued.*

	Pte. KIRKLER, H. A., S. Rhodesian Vol.
	Cpl. KLEMPTMER, H., 1st Rhodesian Rfls.
	Pte. KUHN, S., S.A.M.C., E.A. Pay C.
	Pte. KLEMPTER, A., Motor Cycl. G.E.A.
878	Cpl. KLEIN, D., 4th S.A. Scottish.
1066	Gnr. KATZEN, H., S.A.H.A.
	Rfm. KLEMPTNER, W., Rhodesian Rifles.
14162	Pte. KIDOH, I., 3rd Bn.
	Cpl. KALMS, J., 9th Bn.
	Dvr. KASSEL, J., S.A.S.C.
	Pte. KAPLAN, J., Transvaal Scottish.
	Pte. KIRSCH, H., 9th Bn.
	Pte. KEMP, S.A.V. Corps.
8209	Sgt. KLASS, B., 11th Bn.
	Sgt. KLASS, Botha's Horse.
14549	Pte. KRINKEN, 1st Bde. S.A.I.
11925	Pte. KLEIN, A., 1st Bde. S.A.I.
13366	Pte. KARP, N., 1st Bde. S.A.I.
13359	Pte. KAMINSKY, A., 1st Bde. S,A.I.
10815	Pte. KAHN, S. L., 1st Bde. S.A.I.
	Pte. KREIGER, J., 1st Bde. S.A.I.
	Pte. KAHN, L., C.P.G.R.
	Pte. KOSSICK, J., C.P.G.R.
	Pte. KRUYER, H., C.P.G.R.
	Rfm. KAKLAN, C., W.R.
	Rfm. KARELSTEIN, B., W.R.
	Rfm. KRESER, L., W.R.
	Rfm. KRESER, S., W.R. S.A.F.
	Rfm. KING, I., S.R.V.
	Sgt. KREASKY, M., Bech. Rifles.
	Cpl. KARK, B., Trans. Scott., G.W.A.
	Pte. KRIKLER, H. A., S.R.V.C., B.S.A.P. E.A.
	Sgt. KLUGMAN, J. S., Trans. Scott.
	Pte. KLUGMAN, R. S., S.A. Service Cps.
	Cpl. KAROUS, L. L., 1st S.A.I.
	Sgt. KAPLAN, H., P.A.G.
	Pte. KAPLAN, M., C.M.C.
202098	Pte. KAHN, J., Witwters Rifles,
	Pte. KLEMPTNER, H., 1st Rhod. Regt.
	Pte. KAPLAN, M., Mech. Trans., E.A.
	Pte. KRISTAL, A., G.C.
B/149	Sig. KAPLAN, P., S.A.F.F., P.C., G.W.A.
	Pte. KROLL, B., G.E.A.
	Gnr. KOZAN, T. H. A.
	Pte. KIRSCHON, H., S. Scouts.
	Pte. KATZLER, Brit. E.A. Force.
	Pte. KARET, C.,* S.A.S.C.
	Cpl. KAPLAN, H., P.A. Guards.
	Pte. KOHEN, D.
	Pte. KRESER, S., W. Rifles.
790	Pte. KAHN, A. A., 1st Bn.
5565	Pte. KLONOWSKI, T. J., 2nd Bn.
5951	Pte. KAPELUSNIK, A. J.,* 3rd Bn.
2217	Pte. KNOPF, D.,* 4th Bn.
2856	Pte. KOSSICK, P., 4th Bn.
8676	Pte. KAPPAN, V., 2nd Bn.

9194	Pte. KATZENSTEIN, M.,* 2nd Bn.
7036	Pte. KESEL, O., 4th Bn.
11295	Pte. KOLLENBERG, D., 2nd Bn.
8676	Pte. KAPLAN, V.,* 2nd Bn.
14163	Pte. KADISH, J., 3rd Bn.
15646	Pte. KIBEL, L., 1st Bn.
21583	Pte. KAHN, S., S.A.I.
371	Pte. KAHN, A., S.A.M.C.
9690	Pte. KAPLAN, L., Sig. Coy.
11115	Pte. KERSON, I., 1st Bn.
21805	Pte. KAUFMAN, J., S.A.I.
3987	Pte. LOWENTHAL, F. K., 1st Bn.
3757	Pte. LASKER, L., 2nd Bn.
3632	Pte. LAZARUS, J. B., 2nd Bn.
5612	Pte. LAZARUS, S. C., 2nd Bn.
2660	Pte. LEVISON, E. E., 2nd Bn.
2656	Pte. LEVINSON, L.* (M.M.), 2nd Bn.
172	Pte. LIPMAN, S., 3rd Bn.
5001	Pte. LEVINE, A., 3rd Bn.
5067	Pte. LURIE, I.,* 4th Bn.
3540	Pte. LEVY, D., 4th Bn.
297	Gnr. LEVEN, R., 75th Bty. S.A. Art.
7843	Pte. LAZARUS, C. M. (M.M.), 2nd Bn.
8874	Pte. LAZARUS, R. H., 2nd Bn.
10817	Pte. LEINHARD, I. M., 2nd Bn
9548	Pte. LEVIN, R., 2nd Bn.
7171	Pte. LEVY, H. L., 2nd Bn.
6359	Pte. LOWRIE, W. J., 2nd Bn.
7221	Pte. LEVIN, M.,* 3rd Bn.
7201	Pte. LEVY, A. V., 1st Bn.
13115	Pte. LANGBART, S. H., 1st Bn.
358	Pte. LENZ, F. A., 3rd Bn.
7602	Pte. LEMCHEM,* Comp. Bn.
17594	Pte. LEZARD, S., S.A.I.
1836	Pte. LITHANER, L. J., C. Coy. 1st Bn.
	S/Maj. LEVY, B., 5th Bn.
16983	Pte. LINDE, H. H., S.A.
41312	Sgt. LYONS, A. I., 29th S.A.N.L.C.
868	Sgt. LYONS, E. H., 29th S.A.N.L.C.
18078	Pte. LEVINSON, A., 2nd Bn.
18164	Pte. LACK, L.,* Medical Corps.
18928	Pte. LIPINSKI, H., S.A.
16131	Pte. LAVENSKIE, H. J., S.A.I.
20516	Pte. LEMKIN, S., S.A.I.
510044	Pte. LEVO, G., S.A.M.C.
18937	Pte. LAVINSKIE, L.
20405	Pte. LAZAURS, P., 2nd Res. Bn.
16102	Pte. LEVI, H. J., 1st Bn.
16100	Pte. LEVI, F.
13628	Pte. LEVENTHAL, S., 2nd Bn.
17569	Pte. LEVIN, S.
836	Pte. LITTAUER, L. J., 1st Res. Bn.
20516	Pte. LEINHUIS, S.
15157	Pte. LITCHWITZ, E., 2nd Bn.
	Pte. LANDAN, E., S. Rhodesian Vol.
691	Pte. LEVY, H., 2nd Bn. Rhod. Rifles.
	Pte. LANENSTEIN, M., 2nd Rhod. Rifles.
	Pte. LYONS, A., S.A.N.L.C.

South African Forces.—*Continued.*

S/Major Levy, B., Union Troops, G.E.A.
12276 Pte. Levi, M., 1st R.S.A.I.
236 Pte. Landau, E., B.S.A.P.
5186 Pte. Lewis, A., S.A.I.
1573 Pte. Lewis, E., 3rd Bn.
Rfm. Live, J., 1st Rhod. Rifles.
2395 Pte. Lester, B., 6th S.A.I.
Cpl. Lorie, S. W.,* S.A.S.C.
Pte. Livingstone, D., 9th S.A.I.
Pte. Livingstone, J., 9th S.A.I.
Pte. Levy, D., S.A.M.C.
Pte. Lipman, J., Burgher Forces.
Pte. Lipman, M., Burgher Forces.
6206 Sgt. Lynn, J., 2nd S.A. Force.
Sgt. Levene, M., S.A.S.C.
Pte. Leon, J., 4th S.A.M.C.
Pte. Lieberman, J., S.A.M.C.
Pte. Losky, M., 9th S.A.I.
Pte. Lee, D. E., 1st Trans. Scots.
Pte. Levi, I., Inf.
Cpl. Levison, M., 7th Inf.
Sgt. Lipman, L.
Cpl. Lipman, B., S.A.I.
Gnr. Liwinsky, S., S.A.H.A.
Tpr. Lazaraw, B., 1st S.A.H.
13115 Pte. Longforth, S., 1st Bde. S.A.I.
1075 Pte. Levy, B. L., 1st Bde. S.A.I.
12443 Pte. Levy, M. S., 1st Bde. S.A.I.
3754 Pte. Leeper, J., 4th Bde. S.A.I.
Pte. Levin, H., C.P.G.R.
Pte. Levitt, S., C.P.G.R.
Pte. Levy, S. A., C.P.G.R.
Rfm. Levine, H., W. R.
Gnr. Lighter, H., 3rd Res. Bn.
S/Major Lewis, J., S.A.F.F.
Pte. Levine, C., S.A. Defence Force.
Pte. Lowenstein, H., G.E.A.
Pte. Levein, M., G.W.A.
Pte. Lewin, L., Kimberley Regt.
Pte. Leveson, B.E.A.
Pte. Lowenstein, J., S.A.I.
Pte. Levin, M., S.A.I.
Sgt. Levoi, I. P., S.A. Inf. Force.
Pte. Levitt, H., Despatch Rider.
Sgt. Lerner, A., G.W.A.
Pte. Lapin, P., P.A.G., G.S.W.A.
Pte. Lapin, A., P.A.G.
4205 Pte. Liebson, H., 1st L.G.W. Sq.
Pte. Levin, J., C.T.H., G.S.W.A.
Pte. Lezerblum, H., C.P.R.L. Bn.
Pte. Lipschitz, J. R.F.A.
Pte. Liering, S., Cyclists' Bn.
1101 Pte. Lurie, I., 2nd Rhod. Regt.
Pte. Levinsohn, E., E.L. Kaff. Regt.
Pte. Lewenson, M., 2nd Rhod. Regt.
Pte. Leizerowitz, S., G.W.A.
Pte. Liss, W., C.P.R.

1292 L/Cpl. Lurie, A., C.P.R.
Pte. Livingston, M., S.A.M.R.
Pte. Lappin, P., 3rd Bn.
Pte. Levy, H., 2nd R.R.
Pte. Lapping, M., 2nd R.R.
Pte. Lepowsky, R.A. Corps, G.W.A.
Sgt. Levinkind, L., C.P.R.
Pte. Lewis, P., S.A.I. G.W.A.
Pte. Lorie, S. E., S.A.I. G.E.A.
Pte. Lurie, A., S.A.I., G.S.W.A.
Dvr. Leventhal, M.T. A.S.C.
4196 Pte. Loggie, A., 4th Bn.
S/Sgt. Levin, B., S.A.M.C.
Pte. Lehmann, D., S.A.I.
151 Pte. Levenski, A.
3632 L/Cpl. Lazarus, J. B.,* 2nd Bn.
152 Pte. Michaels, H.,* 2nd Bn.
4648 Pte. Myers, S. S., 2nd Bn.
2126 Pte. Myers, M. H.,* 2nd Bn.
333 Pte. Myerson, W., 3rd Bn.
111 Pte. Margolis, H. J., 4th Bn.
Pte. Morris, C., 4th Bn.
278 Pte. Maudelstein, B., 9th D. S.A.F.A.
8001 Pte. Margolis, W., 4th Bn.
6879 Pte. Maash, C., 4th Bn.
277 Pte. Mark, J., 1st Bn.
11278 Pte. Mintz, M. A. L., 4th Bn.
R/1812 Pte. Mathews, H. A., S.A.(Comp.)Bn.
12245 Pte. Mackinson, S., 3rd Bn.
25435 Pte. Marks, F., 4th Bn.
12333 Pte. Mann, A.
215340 Sgt. Morris, S. F., 2nd M.C.
Pte. Mandelstom, S., Rhod. Light H.
701 Spr. Miller, M., 93rd Bde.
950 Pte. Matlen, E.
189 Gnr. Moss, J., S.A.H.A.
18761 Pte. Mizroch, E., S.A.I.
21100 Pte. Marcusson, I., S.A.I.
22605 Pte. Martin, M., S.A.I.
21256 Pte. Marles, I. B., S.A.I.
21344 Pte. Michel, S., S.A.I.
15657 Pte. Marks, F., 2nd Bn.
17509 L/Cpl. Marks, L., 2nd Res. Bn.
15935 Pte. Marks, J.
1245 Sgt. Maurer, D., 1st Bn.
22881 Pte. Malin, D., 2nd Res. Bn.
Pte. Matthews, A. J., 2nd Bn. Rhod. R.
Tpr. Mendelsohn, F.,* S.A. Motor Tr.
Sgt. Marks, J., Pay Corps, G.E.A.
13814 Pte. Meun, A., 1st S.A.I.
Cpl. Merver, J., Rhodesian Platoon.
Pte. Maisel, M., Kimberley Rgt.
Pte. Max, H., 8th S.A.I.
Pte. Marks, H., 2nd Rhodesian Platoon.
Pte. Markin, 9th S.A.I.
Pte. Millin, E., S.A.A.
Pte. Marcus, M., S.A.M.C.
Cpl. Myers, J., 7th 7th S.A.H.

South African Forces.—*Continued.*

	Pte. METTER, J., S.A.M.C.
	Pte. MORRISON, J., 8th S.A.I.
	Pte. MORRIS, R., S.A.I.
	Pte. MICHAELS, O., 9th Inf.
	Pte. MOSS-MORRIS, B., 9th Inf.
	Pte. MANNE, B., 7th Inf.
	Pte. MANNE, R., 7th Inf.
	Pte. MANNE, W., 7th Inf.
	Pte. MANNE, N., 7th Inf.
	Pte. MINSKY, P., Cronje's Command
	Pte. MULLAMED, Cronje's Command.
14106	Pte. MART, Y. V., 1st Bde. Inf.
	Pte. MARKS, T. J., C.P.G.R.
	L/Cpl. MARKS, L. B., C.P.G.R.
	Cpl. MANN, A., C.P.G.R.
	Rfm. MERKEL, I., Witwat. Rifles.
216	Pte. MEYROWITZ, L., G.W.A.
	Pte. MICHAELSON, S., Scots. Horse, G.W.
	Pte. MOUSENBAUM, S.A.M.R.
	Sgt. MOSCOW, I., B.E.A.
	Rfm. MANUE, W., Witwat. Rifles.
	Rfm. MANUE, M., Witwat. Rifles.
	Pte. MARKS, E. P., S.A.I.
	Pte. MORRIS, H., M.T. Corps.
	Pte. MEYER, S.R.
	Pte. MENDELSOHN, F., G.S.W.A.
	Pte. MILLER, S., M.B.H.
	Pte. MAUGELDORF, S.
	Pte. MICHEL, M., Kimberley Regt.
1355	Pte. MOSS, D., S.A.I.
1121	Pte. MATHESON, S., E.A.
	Cpl. MARKS, D., 1st W.P.M.R., G.W.A.
	Pte. MENN, L., S.A.M.C., G.W.A.
	Pte. MEYERSOM, A., Signal Section.
453	Pte. MUSKOWITZ, J., S.E.O.R., G.W.A.
	Pte. MUSKOWITZ, J., S.A.E.C., G.W.A.
	Pte. MARCUS, E., S.A.I., G.E.A.
	Pte. MARCUS, H., S.A.I., G.E.A.
5718	Rfm. MOSENBAUM, S., S.A.M.R.
	Rfm. MENDELSON, W., S.A.M.C.
	Pte. MISEL, M., Kimberley Regt.
	Pte. MARKET, I., Wit. Rifles.
17831	Pte. NOOLL, B.
13898	Pte. NATHAN, A., 1st Inf. Bde.
14767	Pte. NACHENSON, J., 1st Inf. Bde.
13378	Pte. NEIMEN, M., 1st Inf. Bde.
	Pte. NOAR, I. W., C.P.G.R.
	Pte. NAIMAN, H.
	Sgt. NEUFLIES, F.
	Pte. NOCHAMSOHN, H., 6th S.A.I.
	Pte. NIMKIN, A., S.A.M.C.
A/197	Pte. NATHAN, M., S.A.M.C.
	Pte. NATHAN, H., G.S.W.A.
	Pte. NATHAN, G., R.A.M.C., G.S.W.A.
	Pte. NETTER, N., Rand L. Inf.
	Pte. NARGAOKER, R. E., R. Rifles.
	Pte. NETTER, I., S.A. M.C.
4799	Pte. NATHAN, N., 1st Bn.
2107	Pte. NORMAN, H.
20034	Pte. ODDES, J., 2nd Res. Bn.
13986	Pte. OLIVER, L. H.
20224	Pte. OZROVITCH, 2nd Res. Bn.
	Pte. OSRIN, J., S.A.H.
	Gnr. OSRIN, A., 6th Inf. Bde.
	Pte. ORKIN, I., Kimberley Regt.
3319	Pte. OLINSKY, R. C., 3rd Bn., G.W.A.
3390	Pte. OLINSKY, L. C., 3rd Bn., G.W.A.
	Pte. OPPENHEIM, D., Inf.
494	Gnr. OPPENHEIM, H., 74th Bty. Art.
7612	Pte. OLIVER, J., 2nd Bn.
14542	Pte. ORDANG, I., 1st Bn.
540	L/Bdr. OPPENHEIMER, O., 71st S. Bty. S.A.H.A.
16074	Pte. PAULSAR, E.
7299	Pte. PIPER, A.
	Pte. PINKUS, M., 12th Inf. Bde.
	Ptc. PLOTKIN, L., Inf.
2364	Pte. PHILLIPS, S., S.A. Horse.
	Sgt. PHILLIPS, I., Inf.
13154	Pte. PHILLIPS, L., 1st Inf. Bde.
	Pte. PENCHANZ, M., Transport Section.
	Pte. PINN, L., C.P.G.R.
	Pte. POGRUND, S., C.P.G.R.
	Pte. PRIEM, G., C.P.G.R.
	Tpr. PEARLMAN, S.
	Pte. PETROVSKY, N., 1st S.A.M.R.
	Pte. PRICE, N., P.A.G.
	Pte. PANENSKY, G., S.R.
P4	Pte. POKROY, H., S.A.M.C.
	Pte. PRISMAN, D., C.P.R.
	Pte. PEARL, C.P.R.
	Pte. POTASH, R., Cycle Corps.
A/454	Pte. PINK, J., D.E.O.R., G.W.A.
	Pte. PRESS, B., M.T., A.S.C.
6031	Spr. PURCELL, I., Engineers.
6580	Pte. PRAGER, H., 2nd Bn.
10475	Pte. POLSKY, J. 2nd Bn.
12233	Pte. POLLACK, S., S.A. (Comp.) Bn.
20470	Pte. PHILLIPS, W., S.A.A.
16362	Pte. PRICE, A., 1st S.A.I.
17029	Pte. PROOPS, J., 2nd S.A.I.
2314	Pte. QOITOWITZ, H., 4th Bn.
1277	Pte. RAPHAEL, H. C.,* 1st Bn.
1407	Pte. ROSENTHAL, S., 1st Bn.
1107	Pte. ROTHKUGEL, H.,* 1st Bn.
4017	Pte. RIGAL, G., 1st Bn.
2971	Pte. ROSE, M., 1st Bn.
1273	Sgt. RAPHAEL, S. F.,* 1st Bn.
2721	Pte. RIFFKIN, L., 2nd Bn.
3737	Pte. RABINOWITZ, C., 3rd Bn.
6510	Pte. ROSEN, E., 4th Bn.
7039	Pte. ROSE, R., 4th Bn.
273	Pte. RAPP, L., 2nd Bn.
3084	Sgt. RUBENSON, J., 2nd Bn.
4583	Pte. RUBIN, J.,* 1st Bn.

South African Forces.—*Continued.*

11166	Pte. ROBINS, P., 2nd Bn.
13190	Pte. RAPPAPORT, M., 2nd Bn.
11028	Pte. ROSENBERG, S., 3rd Bn.
6683	Pte. ROSEMAN, N., 3rd Bn.
6003	Sgt. RIGAL, P., 2nd Bn.
9731	Sgt. RABINOWITZ, L., 1st Bn.
1555	Pte. RUBENSTEIN, F., 1st Bn.
1654	Gnr. RANKOW, Horse Artillery.
17036	Pte. ROTTENBURG, J., S.A.I.
956	Pte. ROSENBLOOM, D., S.A.I.
18915	Pte. ROTSKIN, D., S.A.I.
493	Cpl. RAPP, S., 4th Bn.
234	Pte. RYGOR, H., 84th S.A.M.C.
R/1451	Pte. ROTHSTEIN, L., 1st Res. Bn.
18915	Pte. ROTHSTEIN, D., 2nd Res. Bn.
10703	Pte. REINGOLD, J.
21171	Pte. REGAL, J., 1st Res. Bn.
	Pte. ROBERTS, H. I.
	Pte. RICHMAN, I., S. Rhodesian Vol.
	Pte. ROBINSON, A., S. Rhodesian Vol.
	Pte. RABINSON, A., S. Rhodesian Vol.
956	Pte. ROSENBLUM, D., 2nd Bn. Rhod. Rs.
	Pte. ROTSTEIN, L., 2nd Bn. Rhod. Rs.
623	Pte. RUBINSTEIN, H., 2nd Bn. Rhod. Rs.
	Pte. RABINSON, B.,* 1st Bn. Rhod. Rs.
	Pte. ROLLNICK, J., Uganda Rifles.
	Pte. ROSEN, S.A.M.C.
	Pte. ROSEN, S., Wit. Rifles, G.S.W.
	Pte. RUBENSTEIN, R., G.S.W.
10946	Pte. RAFIELD, J., 1st Res. Inf.
12159	Pte. ROSENTHAL, S., 1st Inf.
	Pte. RUBEN, S., 2nd Rhod. Rifles.
	Pte. ROSENBERG, L., 9th Inf. Bde.
	Cpl. ROSENBERG, W., 3rd Res. Bn.
	Pte. RUBIN, A., Grissel's Command.
	Pte. RAPPAPORT, N., 1st Rhod. Regt.
	Bmd. ROM, T.H.A.
	Tpr. RITCH, E., 1st Horse.
	Pte. ROTHQUAL, 1st Inf. Bde.
4583	Pte. RUBIN, J.,* 1st Inf.
11830	Pte. ROCH, L. N., 9th Inf. Bde.
	Pte. REUBEN, M., 1st Inf. Bde.
	Pte. REICH, H., Cronje's Command.
13647	Pte. RETERS, M., 1st Inf. Bde.
12244	Pte. RATHBONE, H. M., 1st Inf. Bde.
16612	Pte. ROSENBERG, S., 1st Inf. Bde.
14638	Pte. RUSKIN, M., 1st Inf. Bde.
	Pte. ROSE, H. A., C.P.G.R.
	Pte. ROTHENBURG, R. C.P.G.R.
	Pte. ROTHUGEL, B., C.P.G.R.
	Pte. ROTHUGEL, M., C.P.G.R.
	Pte. ROYTOWSKI, S., C.P.G.R.
	Pte. RISE, V., 7th S.A.I.
1118	Pte. RUBINSTEIN, J., S.A.F.A. E.A.
	Pte. RIETOFF, I., Defence Corps.
	Pte. ROSENTHAL, S., S.A.I.
	Pte. RIFKIN, E., B.E.A.
	Pte. RIFKIN, J., B.E.A.
	Pte. ROLLNICK, B.E.A.
	Cpl. ROSENDORFF, M., Defence Force.
	L/Cpl. RUBIN, H., B.E.A.
	Pte. ROTHMAN, I. W., S.A.I.
	Pte. RIFKIN, B., 2nd S.A.I. S.A.O.E.F.
	Tpr. ROBINSON, P., S.A.F. E.A.
	Pte. RUDNICK, A., B.E.A. E.F.
	Pte. RUBENS, H.
1334	Pte. RICHENBERG, A. M., 3rd F.A. M.C.
	Pte. ROSEN, S. E., Witwat. R. G.S.W.A.
	Pte. RUTHENBERG, C., Oriels Comm.
	Pte. ROSENWEIG, A., S.A.M.C.
	Pte. ROSENTHAL, D., 5th S.A.I. G.E.A.
	Pte. ROTHERBERG, M., S.A.M.C.
	Pte. RAPHAEL, W., C.P.R.
9608	Pte. RAPHEN, S. W., S.A.S.S. R.E.
	Pte. ROSENBERG, M., G.W.A.
	Pte. ROSEN, H., R.A.M.C.
	Cpl. ROSENTHAL, L., M.T. A.S.C.
	Sgt. ROSENTHAL, M.T. A.S.C.
	Pte. RABE, E., N Command.
	Cpl. ROSENDORFF, M., S.A. U. Def. F.
4049	Pte. SAGAR, N., 1st Bn.
5913	Pte. SIMON, M.,* 3rd Bn.
3381	Pte. SCHWARTZ, L., 3rd Bn.
5712	Cpl. SASIENI, D., 3rd Bn.
5711	Pte. SCHERGER, B., 3rd Bn.
7169	Pte. SAMUELS, J., 3rd Bn.
5198	Pte. SHERMAN, A., 3rd Bn.
514	Gnr. SHRADER, H. U., 74th Bty. Art.
198	L/Cpl. SOLOMON, H. J., 1st S.A. F. Am.
7673	Pte. SCHLOMOOSKY, P., 1st Bn.
9527	Pte. SCHUR, L., 1st Bn.
10653	Pte. SEGAL, M., 1st Bn.
8231	Pte. SALBERG, I. M., 2nd Bn.
10157	Pte. SMITH, A., 2nd Bn.
7321	Pte. SUSSMAN, N., 3rd Bn.
8118	Pte. SCHATZ, M.,* 3rd Bn.
14799	A/Sgt. SHALL, I.,* 1st Bn.
9897	Pte. SOLOMON, A., 1st Bn.
12082	Pte. SUGARMAN, S., 1st Bn.
10346	Pte. SERATKIN, H., 3rd Bn.
7547	Pte. SUPER, E. S., 4th Bn.
11802	Pte. SAVILLE, H.,* 4th Bn.
754	Pte. SAMUELS, R., 2nd R.R.
16110	Pte. SIMMONDS H., 1st Bn.
13106	Pte. SHUR, M., 3rd Bn.
708	Pte. SANDLER, D. M.C.
19891	Pte. SCHUSTER, M., A.S.I.
17226	Pte. SHAPER, A., 1st Bn.
427	Pte. SAUL, J., S.A.M.C.
1045	Gnr. SULMAN, S., S.A.H.A.
18253	Pte. SHELLER, H. J., 2nd Bn.
547	Pte. SAMUEL, E., 4th Bn.
17226	Pte. SHAPER, J., S.A.S.
505	Sgt. SIDCRADSKI, J., 2nd Bn.
660	Sgt. STERN, R., 3rd Bn.

South African Forces.—*Continued.*

407	Pte. SALOMON, A. V., Medical Corps.
198266	Gnr. SHINEBERG, N., S.A.R.B.
15042	Pte. SOLLER, J., S.A.L.C.
20486	Pte. SHIERS, J., S.A.I.
	Spr. SHULMAN, B., 7th Bn.
	Spr. SHAPIRO, B., Cronje's Command.
	Spr. SUMMERS, H., 3rd S.A.H.
7127	Pte. SUSELL, O. N., 9th Bn.
9645	Pte. SULVER, P., 7th Bn.
14229	Pte. STALL, I., 1st Bde. Inf.
14840	Pte. SHORT, J., 1st Bde. Inf.
15337	Pte. SEVER, H., 1st Bde. Inf.
15245	Pte. SCRAIGO, D., 1st Bde. Inf.
15931	Pte. SCHLES, J. I., 2nd Bde. Inf.
16242	Pte. SACK, H., 1st Bde. Inf.
16620	Pte. STEIN, J., 1st Bde. Inf.
16137	Pte. SONG, 1st Bde. Inf.
11638	Pte. SHANDLER, H., 1st Bde. Inf.
C/288	Sgt. STERN. 1st Bde. Inf.
V.392	Spr. SCHLYER, N., S.A.I.
	Pte. SAFRO, A. J., C.P.G.R.
	Pte. SEGAL, J., C.P.G.R.
	Pte. SILVER, I., C.P.G.R.
	Pte. SIMENHOFF, L., C.P.G.R.
	Pte. SOLOMON, L. S., C.P.G.R
	Pte. SURITZ, F., C.P.G.R.
	Pte. SYMONS, M., C.P.G.R.
	Pte. SCHUMAN, B. F., C.P.G.R.
	Pte. SHAPIRO, H., C.P.G.R.
	Pte. SHER, C. M., C.P.G.R.
	Pte. SMITH, I. B., C.P.G.R.
	Pte. STODEL, H. J., C.P.G.R.
	Rfm. SYMONS, M. M., Witwat. Regt.
	Rfm. SLEVANSKY, S., Witwat. Rifles.
	Rfm. SCHUSMAN, I., Witwat. Regt.
	Pte. SAMUELS, S. L., S.A.H.
	Pte. SANDLER, D., S.A.M.C.
	Pte. SAMUEL, M., G.E.A.
	Pte. SAMUEL, F., Defence Force.
	Pte. SHRAUBAUM, B., 1st Kimberley, G.W.A. and G.E.A.
	Pte. STEINWEISS, J., Transvaal Scott., G.W.A. and G.E.A.
	Rfm. SAMUELS, A., Witwat. Rifles.
	Pte. SERAWBAUM, S., S.A. Def. Force.
	Pte. SARIF, M., E.S.A.P., E.A.
	Pte. SARIERS, D., S.A.I.
	Pte. STEIN, P., Midd. Mounted Rifles.
	Pte. SANDLER, S., S.A.M.C.
	Dvr. SIMON, E., 2nd S.M. Corps.
	Gnr. SONNANFELD, H., C.G. Artillery.
	Pte. STERN, A., C. Pen. Rifles.
	Pte. SYFNER, A., H.A.
	Pte. SAINFIELD, G.E.A.
	Pte. SMITH, M., M.T. G.E.A.
A/620	Pte. SHATTENSTEIN, E., C.T.H., G.S.W.A.
	Pte. SILOWITZ, L.

	Pte. SONNENBERG, F., Vryburg Comm.
	Pte. SOLOMON, S., Vryburg Command.
	Pte. SIMON, I., 2nd W.P.R.
	Pte. SCHNEIDER, A., Hay Command.
B/3346	Pte. SARFLENEWITZ, Z., 17th Mtd. Rifles.
	Pte. STUSSER, J., 82nd Rand Rifles.
	Pte. STUSSER, B., 12th Regt., 3rd Bde.
	Pte. SOLOMOVSKY, H., G.W.A.
	Pte. SHULMAN, L., G.S.W.A.
	Pte. STEIN, L., Defence Force, G.W.A.
	Pte. STEIN, J., G.E.A.
	Pte. SCHNEIDER, B., Defence Force.
	Pte. SURAT, H., Mounted Bde., G.W.A.
	Pte. SINDLER, I., 17th Mounted Rifles.
	Pte. SOLOMON, T., 1st W.P.R., G.W.A.
6625	Sig. SESSEL, G. H., 1st R.R.
19980	Pte. SWEKE, E., 2nd Res. Bn.
13627	Pte. SOLOMON, L. A.
14723	Pte. SOLOMONS, L.
20482	Pte. SOLOMON, H., 1st Bn. Inf.
22187	Pte. SCHONBERG, M. M., 2nd Bn. Inf.
20485	Pte. SHIEN, J., 2nd Bn. Inf.
	Pte. SARIF, N., S. Rhodesian Vol.
	Pte. SUSSMAN, O., 2nd Bn. Rhod. Rifles.
1129	Pte. SUSSMAN, M., 2nd Bn. Rhod. Rifles.
	Pte. STONE, H., 2nd Bn. Rhod. Rifles.
	Pte. SIVE, J., 1st Bn. Rhod. Rifles.
	Pte. SIFF, L., 1st L.H., G.S.W.
	Pte. SYMMONS, H., G.E.A.
	Pte. SKOP, J., G.S.W.
	Pte. SPARK, J., Motor Section, G.S.W.
235857	Pte. SHIELL, H., S.A. Field Art.
11684	Pte. SONNENBERG, M. C., 2nd Res. Inf.
6580	Pte. SAGAR, H., Inf.
	Pte. SHERMAN, H. (M.M.), Inf.
15893	Pte. SAUNDERS, H., 2nd Res. Inf.
	Pte. SMITH, I., R.L.I.
	Pte. SOLOMON, M., Grissel's Command.
	Pte. SACKES, 7th Bn.
	Pte. SHOOM, E., 8th Bn.
	Sgt. SEWANSKY, H., S.A.M.C.
	Pte. SCHONBERG, S., S.A.S.C.
	Bugl. SILVERMAN, L. E., S.A.M.C.
	Pte. SEIGELBERG, M., 9th Bn.
	Pte. SANDGROUND, S., S.A.M.C.
	Gnr. SMITH, S., S.A.F.A.
	Pte. SHULMAN, J., 7th Bn.
9314	Spr. SABER, F., S.A. Signal Depot, R.E.
	Pte. SAMUELS, E., 8th Bn.
	Pte. SILBERT, I., 9th Water Sect. G.E.A.
	Sgt./Maj. SILBERT, E., G.W.A. & G.E.A.
	Pte. SHENKER, S.
	Pte. SAMUEL, L., S.A.M.C. G.S.A.W.
	Pte. SEBBA, J., C.P.R.
	Pte. SOLOMONS, B., M.T. G.W.A.
	Pte. SHER, H., 1st R.R.
	Pte. SONNENFIELD, J., C.G.A.
	Pte. SIERADSKI, P., S.A.H.A.

South African Forces.—*Continued.*

Sgt. SIERADSKI, J., Cape Corps.
Pte. SIMONHOFF, E., S.A.H.A. G.E.A.
Pte. SIMONHOFF, L., Mech. Tr. G.E.A.
Pte. SMITH, M., Mech. Trans. G.E.A.
2249 Sgt. SCANLON, M. J., N. & R. Border Rgt.
Pte. SKOLNICK, I., Namaqualand Comm.
Pte. STODEL, J. H., Cape Town High.
7550 Pte. TAPUACH, J., 2nd Bn.
11046 Pte. TOUYZ, T., 2nd Bn.
1670 Pte. TYLER, A.,* 4th Bn.
16882 Pte. THORNTON, J., 2nd Bn.
Pte. TRIPLER, H., 2nd Bn. Rhodesian R.
Pte. TRIPLER, M., 2nd Bn. Rhodesian R.
8895 Pte. TUSKA, J. G., 4th Bn.
10105 Pte. TOBIANSKY, 3rd Bn.
Rfm. TEBBITT, I., 1st Rhodesian Rifles.
Rfm. TOBIAS, J., 11th Bn.
Pte. TULE, L., S.A.I.
Pte. TAFELSTEIN, E., C.P.G.R.
Pte. TEPERSON.
Pte. TRAPPLER, M., 2nd R. Rifles.
Pte. TRAPPLER, H., 2nd R. Rifles.
8069 Sgt. TAYFIELD, E., S.A.I.
Pte. TYLER, S., G.E.A.
Pte. TYLER, L., G.E.A. and G.W.A.
Pte. TYLER, A., G.E.A.
16433 Pte. TUMBLETT, 2nd Bn.
15441 Pte. TAYLOR, B., 4th Bn.
8895 Pte. TUCKER, D. J., 4th S.A.I.
14542 Pte. URDANY, I., 1st Bn.
16140 Pte. URDANG, J., 1st Res. Bn.
10728 Pte. URDANG, H., 1st Bde. S.A.I.
Pte. URDANG, M., G.W.A.
Pte. URDANG, A.
1620 Pte. VALENTINE, J., 3rd Horse.
Pte. VALENTINE, P., C.P.G.R.
Pte. VILENSKY, B., 1st W.P.R.
Sgt. VENIKER, D.
2166 S/Sgt. VAN THAL, J., 2nd Bn.
7453 Pte. VAN DER HEIM, H., 2nd Bn.
17877 S/Sgt. VOLPERT, J., 1st M.C.
1967 Pte. WOCFSON, H. P., 4th Bn.
X/225 Pte. WEINBERG, A.,* 1st S.A. Fld. Amb.
3754 Cpl. WEINER, J., 2nd Bn.
Cpl. WERBESOFF, S.A.N. Troops.
10710 Pte. WALKER, S., 4th Bn.
18775 Pte. WOOLFSON, A., S.A.I.
14589 Pte. WOOLF, S. H., 3rd Bn.
992 Gnr. WEINRICH, M., S.A.H.A.
16101 Pte. WIDES, A., S.A.I.
16346 Pte. WINDISH, H., S.A.I.
17831 Pte. WOOL, B.
Pte. WEITZMAN, C., 2nd Bn.
494 C.Q.M.S. WHITESMAN, L., 35th Bn.
10703 Pte. WEINMAN.
21401 Pte. WOLK, H. R., 1st Bn.
18371 Pte. WINDSOR, T. G., 2nd Res. Bn.

Pte. WITENBERG, B. M., 2nd Rhodes. R.
Sgt. WOOLF, A. M., E.A. Pay Corps.
11933 Pte. WEST, J. H., 1st Bde. Inf.
Pte. WEINER, D., 7th Bn.
Pte. WASKY, V., Inf.
Pte. WOOD, L., 9th Bn.
13320 Sgt. WOOLF, H., 3rd Bde. Inf.
Pte. WEINER, B., S.A.M.C.
791 Pte. WETLENSKY, B. (D.C.M.), Inf.
Spr. WASSERBERG, H., S.A.H.
Spr. WASSERBERG, J., Natal Carbineers.
Spr. WILSON, H., 6th Inf.
251 A/M. WIMBORNE, S., Flying Corps.
1144 Gnr. WOOLF, J., S.A.H.A.
Pte. WITTEN, W., C.P.G.R.
5469 Pte. WHITE, J. R.,* 4th S.A. Inf.
Pte. YOUNGELSON, S., S.A.M.T.
Cpl. YOUNGELSON, I., Rand Rifles.
Sgt. YOUNGELSON, T., 8th Inf.
Pte. YOUNGELSON, R.
Pte. YOFFE, M., C.P.G.R.
7604 Pte. YULE, L., 2nd Bn.
Pte. ZIMMERMAN, H., Cronje's Commando
Pte. ZUCKERMAN, D., C.P.G.R.

* Killed in Action or died on Active Service.

CANADIAN DIVISION.

OFFICERS.

Lieut. ANSELL, E. (M.C.), Ontario Regt.
Lieut. AARONSON, B., 79th Bn.
Lieut. ABENDANA, E. M.,* Div. Eng.
Lieut. BAUM. H., 6th Can. Hussars.
Major BENJAMIN, E. V. (M.C.), Inf.
Lieut. COWAN, W. J. (M.C.), 41st Bn.
Lieut. COHEN, M. T.,* (M.C.), 42nd Bn.
Capt. COHEN, H. R., 10th Res. Bn.
Lieut. COHEN, B., 20th Res. Bn.
Lieut. COHEN, H. B., 14th Inf. Bn.
Lieut. COHEN, J., C.A.M.C.
Lieut. COHEN, J. B., 10th Res. Bn.
Lieut. COHEN, W. N., Fort Garry Horse.
Lieut. COHEN, N.
2nd Lieut. COHEN, B., Can. Air Force.
Capt. COHEN, H., 163rd Bn.
Lieut. COHEN, N., 2nd Bn.
Lieut. COHEN, G., Can. Air Force.
Capt. DOVER, H., C.A.M.C.
Capt. FREEDMAN, Dr., C.A.M.C.
Lieut. FRANKS, N. (M.C.), Inf.
Capt. FREEDMAN, A., Intelligence Dept.
Capt. FREEDMAN, I., Inf.
2nd Lieut. GOLDMAN, E., Training Corps.
Capt. GOLDSTINE, S. L., 152nd Coy.
Capt. GROSS, L. (Dr.), C.A.M.C.

Canadian Division.—*Continued.*
Lieut. GOFT, M., Can. Air Force.
Major GOLDSTEIN, S., Can. Air Force.
Lieut. GOLDSTEIN, J., Tank Bn.
Capt. GELDZALER, B., Can. Engrs.
Lieut. HAVDES, S., Can. Air Force.
Capt. HALPERN, H. (Dr.), C.A.D.C.
Lieut. HYMAN, E. M.,* Inf.
Capt. ILLIEVITZ, Dr., C.A.M.C.
Lieut. JACOM, M. (M.M. and Bar, M.C.).
Major JENNINGS, S. (M.C.), Inf.
Capt. LEVY, J., 12th Fld Coy. Eng.
Lieut. LESSER, C., 87th Bn.
Lieut. LUCY, W. J.
Lieut. LEVY, A. L. (M.C.), 7th Bn.
Capt. LEAVITT, J., A.M.C. attd 18th Can. Inf.
2nd Lieut. LYONS, E. L., Engineers.
Lieut.-Col. LIGHTSTONE, H. H. (D.S.O., M.C.).
Capt. LEVISON, E. R., Can. Militia.
Lieut. LYON, R., Inf.
Lieut. LERNER, M., Inf.
Lieut. Col. LERNER, L., C.A.M.C.
Lieut. LIGHTSTONE, A.
Capt. LEVY, S., 5th Bn.
Lieut. LEO M., R.A.F.
Lieut. LIPSEY, R., R.A.F.
Lieut. LEVY, M., M.G.C.
Lieut. LYONS, A., Inf.
Lieut. MICHAELSON, A., C.A.S.C.
Lieut. MOSELY, G. H., 14th M.G.C.
Lieut. MOSS, C.
Capt. MOSES, H. C. (M.C. and Bar).
Capt. MOSS, H.
Lieut. MYERS, J., Inf.
Lieut. MICHAELSOHN, C.A.F.
Capt. NATHAN, L. (M.C.), Inf.
2nd Lieut. NELSON, H., Can. Air Force.
Capt. NEWHOUSE, P., Can. H. Q. Staff.
Lieut. OPPENHEIM, A. E., Can. Horse.
Lieut. PEARCE, R. M.
Capt. PHILLIPS, G. G., Army Medical Corps.
Lieut. ROTHCHILD, J. A. E., 5th Can. Div.
Capt. ROSS, E. M., 10th Bn.
Capt. ROSENBAUM, J., C.A.M.C.
Lieut. RUBIN, S., 29th Bn.
Lieut. ROSE, 24th Bn.
Lieut. RUBINOVITCH, I. J., Can. Air Force.
Capt. RAPHAEL, F. M., Inf.
Lieut. SOLOMAN, H. K.
Lieut. SPENCER, A., Cavalry.
Lieut. SAMUEL, A., Inf.
Lieut. SOLOMAN, A.,* 87th Bn.
2nd Lieut. SUSMAN, W., C.A.F.
Lieut. STUART-SMITH, P. J., Can. Air Force.
Lieut. SCHAFFER, H.,* 7th Engineers.
Lieut. SOLOMON, A.,* 87th Bn.
Capt. TRITSCH, A. A., 5th C.M.R.
Lieut. TOBIAS, W. V., 54th Bn.

Lieut. ULLMAN, V. R. (M.C.).
Lieut. VINEBERG, H., Can. Air Force.
Lieut. WORKMAN, M. J.,* 75th Bn.
Capt. WHITEHOUSE, Gen. Hosp. C.A.M.C.
Lieut.-Col. WOOLF, M. A. (O.B.E.), 3rd Bn.
Lieut. WOOLF, M., 16th Bn.
Lieut. WORKMAN, E., Tank Bn.
Lieut. WENDER, L., P.P.C.L.I.
Lieut. YOUKLES, I.,* 87th Bn.

N.C.O.'s AND MEN.

2509 Pte. ANDERSON, S. L., Lord S. Horse.
65013 Pte. ALMOND, S., 24th Bn.
412016 Pte. ADLER, M., 24th Bn.
91272 Gnr. ANNIS, H. 1th Bde.
2152437 Gnr. AARONSON, B., 2nd Bde. C.F.A.
8679 Cpl. AGRANOVITCH, N., 2nd Bn.
294481 Pte. AARONS, M., 27th Bn.
104544 Pte. ALECH, A., 5th M.G.C.
1027186 Pte. ADLER, J., 123rd Pioneer Bn.
524112 Pte. ACHIEZER, E. L., 6th C. F. Amb.
P/1312 Gnr. ABRAHAM, P., 1st S. Bty. Am. Col.
660312 Spr. ASTROF, M., 6th Bn. C.R.T.
1018262 Pte. ALYEA, A., 52nd Coy. For. Corps.
201475 Pte. ADLER, B., 7th Bn.
1001182 Spr. ADAMS, J. A., Can. Rail. Troops.
34425 Cpl. ALBERT, D., C.A.M.C.
302870 Gnr. ABINOVITCH, P., 107th C. S. Bty.
3231280 Cpl. ABRAMS, N., Inf.
3036962 Pte. AARON, R., Inf.
1763323 Pte. ADELSON, H. J., Can. Res. Bn.
2595856 Pte. ASHLEY, W., 21st Bn.
2381523 Pte. ANDRE, M., 11th Can. Res. Bn.
4537411 Pte. AARONS, M. V., Can. Res. Cyc.
2522557 Dvr. ADLER, B., C.R.A.
2304485 Pte. ANOLIK, I.
445201 L/Cpl. ABRAHAMSON, C. O.,* 54th Bn.
2765852 L/Cpl. AXELROD, W., 1st Can. T. Bn.
2379943 Spr. ANGEL, G.
Pte. ALTMAN, G. G., 14th Bn.
2393399 Pte. ANKER, M., 12th Res. Bn.
2100161 Gnr. ARBEAN, F. A., Artillery.
323639 Pte. ASSKIN, W., 12th Res. Bn.
524112 Pte. ACHEIZER, L. E., 12th C. Gen. Hosp.
2204581 Pte. ABRAMS, P., Can. Forestry Corps.
2178345 Pte. AECHENSTEIN, B., Can. For. Corps.
1105241 Pte. ADOLPH, F., 23rd Res. Bn.
249195 L/Cpl. ATKINS, J., 5th Can. Div.
261364 Pte. ARONOVITCH, M. E.
3257608 Gnr. ADELSTEIN, M., Res. Artillery.
256390 Spr. ABRAMSKY, R., 12th Bn.
1039936 Pte. ABRAMS, S., 10th Bn.
475004 Pte. AARONOVITCH, M., 11th Bn.
13245 Pte. ALFRED, R., 245th Bn.
Pte. AARON, S., C.A.M.C.
Tpr. ADLER, L., R.C.H.
207214 Pte. ABRAHAMSON, 97th Bn.
Pte. ABELL, A., 5th Bn.

Canadian Division.—*Continued.*

Sgt.-Maj. ABELSON, F. (D.C.M.), 13th Bn.
Pte. ANTEL, S., 42nd Bn.
2139484 Pte. AARONSON, J., 1st Bn.
216762 Pte. ABRAHAMSON, A.
Pte. ALPERT, J., 216th Bn.
323370 Pte. ALTER, L. I.
3234663 Pte. ACKERMAN, Y.
3235360 Pte. ALSPECTOR, J.
174974 Pte. BERG, M., 14th Bn.
217241 Pte. BLACKBURN, B., 19th Bn.
70698 Pte. BLACK, A., 29th Bn.
431008 Pte. BURNS, S. H., 3rd Pioneer Bn.
31847 Pte. BALKIN, W., 255th Tun. Coy.
1057191 Pte. BROMBERG, H., 1st Entr. Bn.
70417 Pte. BROWN, M., 169th S. Bty.
3033490 Pte. BOKOFSKI, J., 7th Bn. C.R.T.
2498320 Pte. BALLEN, I. S., 47th Coy. For. Cps.
441299 Pte. BARNETT, J., 47th Coy. For. Cps.
214195 Pte. BAMBURY, H. J., 12th Coy. For. C.
197417 Pte. BELL, J. R., 1st Can. M.G.C.
1427 Pte. BARNARD, L.,* 8th Bn.
256354 Pte. BECKERMAN, H., 3rd Bn. C.R.T.
3232072 Spr. BECHNER, L. L., 3rd Bn. C.R.T.
153317 Gnr. BROWN, T., 326th Siege Bty.
M/270725 Pte. BENABO, A., Can. Cps. S. Park.
850609 Pte. BAKER, H. J.,* 20th Bn.
3085349 Pte. BEN, L., Inf.
3084082 Pte. BUSSACK, S., Inf.
2365764 Pte. BLUMENTHAL, J. J., Inf.
295454 Pte. BRONDY, L., Inf.
3233961 Pte. BRODIE, M., Inf.
3036488 Spr. BUCKSTEIN, L. L. J., Engineers.
3110622 Pte. BUCKSTEIN, J. M., Inf.
268261 Pte. BERNER, I. E., 15th Res. Bn.
3084082 Pte. BURACK, S., 20th Res. Bn.
61209 Pte. BIRENSOHN, G., Army Med. Cps.
87102 Sgt.-Maj. BEARD, M. (D.C.M.), C.F.A.
491462 Pte. BELAN, N., 24th Bn.
9651 Cpl. BROWN, H. B., 3rd Bn.
26056 Cpl. BARNETT, S. G., 14th Bn.
42446 Gnr. BREGMAN, S., 9th Bty. 3rd Bde.
41745 Dvr. BONAPARTE, L., 2nd Bde. Amm. C.
46814 Pte. BURNSTEIN, J.,* 13th Bn.
59067 Pte. BIND, E., 21st Bn.
474065 Pte. BERG, N., R.C.R.
527148 Pte. BERNSTEIN, W. S., 1st Field Amb.
175 Pte. BRITT, A., Div. Cyclist Coy.
1205 Cpl. BRODERSON, S., 2nd Can. R. S. D.
457100 Pte. BROMET, M. J.,* 60th Bn.
457193 Pte. BROWN, J., 60th Bn.
457900 Pte. BRUSSELL, H., 60th Bn.
404789 Pte. BAKER, A., 35th Bn.
11556 Pte. BASKIN, F., 4th Bn.
424569 Sct. BERCOVITCH, B., 1st C.M.R.
457900 Pte. BRUSSELL, N., 60th Bn.
46814 Pte. BURNSTEIN, J.,* 13th Bn. atd. D. T.
197417 Pte. BONDEER, J., 1st Bn.

Spr. BLOOM, C., 1st Div. Signals.
35343 Dvr. BLACKMAN, H., 1st Can. Res. P.
27043 S/Sgt. BERNARD, L.,* 15th Bn.
2152530 Gnr. BECKOWITZ, H., 1st D.A.C.
310756 Dvr. BREGMAN, A., 5thu D.A.C.
177483 Pte. BLACK, I., 1st Bn.
198235 Pte. BERNSTOCK, H. C., 5th Bn.
6712 Pte. BARNETO, M., 5th Bn.
491487 Pte. BLUMENTHAL, P. G., 24th Bn.
706198 Pte. BLOCK, A. L., 29th Bn.
524054 Pte. BARNETT, L., 6th Field Amb.
746301 Pte. BABBINGTON, I. R., 116th Bn.
871006 Pte. BARNETT, S., 44th Bn.
737078 Cpl. BARNETT, A., 16th C. Inf.
803977 Cpl. BAUM, R. W. (M.M. & Bar), 4th Bn.
268261 Pte. BERNER, J. E., 15th Res. Bn.
528347 Gnr. BAKER, H., M.G.C.
2273322 Pte. BRODSKY, I.
344176 Dvr. BENEDICT, M. W., Inf.
1016011 Pte. BENDZ, I. W., C.A.M.C.
3037035 Pte. BROWN, W. J., Inf.
542516 Pte. BEST, D., Inf.
2273372 Pte. BELIPOLSKY, H., Inf.
3037918 Pte. BACHRACH, H., Inf.
2520465 Pte. BOXINBAUM, M., Inf.
41010 Gnr. BLANK, 5th Bn.
2765029 Pte. BLOOM, S. V., 1st Can. Tanks.
14081 Pte. BENJAMIN, H. E.,* 5th C.M.R.
Pte. BENJAMIN, L., Inf.
2009118 Sap. BLUMBERGH, M., Can. Eng.
836330 Pte. BERNSTEIN, L.
2304342 Pte. BLACK, H., C.A.M.C.
3231804 Pte. BARRON, S., 2nd Bn. 1st. Coy.
3232501 Pte. BRAFMEN, A., M.G.C.
2356305 Pte. BLACK, R., M.G.C.
3036494 Pte. BURNSTEIN, L., 1st Bn.
2356293 Pte. BEAR, R. C.M.G.C.
2500058 Pte. BLUMFELD, H., Ry. Con. Depot.
3039080 Pte. BOWMAN, H., 1st Con. Bn.
303697 Pte. BELYEA, Y., 1st Con. Bn.
3036485 Pte. BERNSTEIN, E. P., 1st Con. Bn.
2498298 Sgt. BLACK, K. B., 1st Con. Bn.
681167 Pte. BENNETT, R., 170th Bn.
Pte. BLOOMBERG, H., Inf.
Dvr. BLACKMORE, H., C.A.S.C.
Cad. BALD, M., C. Air Force.
Pte. BERSON, H., Inf.
Cpl. BENJAMIN, C., E. Ontario Regt.
Spr. BRAHINSKY, M., Can. Eng.
341544 Gnr. BOULD, B., Can. F.A.
282005 Pte. BLUMENTHAL, B., 219th Bn.
Pte. BOW, C., 97th O.S. Bn.
3082908 Pte. BLOOMBERG, S.
Cad. BROTMAN, C. Air Force.
Gnr. BLUMENTHAL, M., C.F.A.
Pte. BRADY, J., Inf.
20865 Pte. BERGMAN, S., 97th Bn.
Pte. BERG, B. L., Can. Rly. Troops.

Canadian Division.—*Continued.*

	Bglr. BERG, A.
527260	Spr. BLOOM, S., Can. Eng.
	Pte. BERGER, M., Inf.
111031	Pte. BENJAMIN, H. E.,* 5th Mt. Rifles.
	Pte. BLACK, E., Inf.
	Pte. BROWN, S., Inf.
	Pte. BURMAN, E., Inf.
	Pte. BERNARD, S., 1st Tank Bn.
72910	1/A.M. Ob. BARNETT, J., Can. Air Force.
163534	Pte. BERKOVITZ, I. M.,* 1st Inf.
1427	Pte. BARNARD, L., 8th Bn.
201128	Cpl. BUSSIN, S., 95th Bn.
201014	Pte. BLACK, S., 95th Bn.
	Pte. BARNETT, J. (M.M.).
201013	Pte. BLACK, J. L., 95th Bn.
669028	Pte. BERKOWITZ, S., 95th Bn.
200296	Spr. BERG, B.
2500910	Spr. BIRD, M.
3259310	Spr. BERGER, H.
3084804	Spr. BERNSTEIN, H.
2304342	Spr. BLACK, H.
	Pte. BRUNNING, M.
3036644	Pte. BEDER, E.
334390	Gnr. BURGERS, N. J., Can. Arty.
288030	Pte. BERSIM, D., Can. For. Corps.
3033522	Gnr. BOSSIN, M., Can. Arty.
3036644	Pte. BEDEX, E. A.
3032831	Pte. BERNSTEIN, S.
2497934	Pte. BLOOMBERG, J., 3rd Bn.
310904	Gnr. BRAHINSKY, M., C.F.A.
3105906	Pte. BERKOWITZ, A., 8th Bn.
157016	Pte. BOYD, D.
177417	Pte. BONDER, J.
186362	Pte. BLOOM, M.
17058	Dvr. BRACKMAN, J.
3084442	Pte. BRODY, M.
5272260	Pte. BLOOM, S., C.A.M.C.
	Cadet BARISH, H., C.A.F.
	Pte. BERGER, H., 1st Bn.
	Cpl. BOOTH, M., 1st Bn.
	Pte. BLUM, S., C.A.M.C.
	Tpr. BARIS, H., R.C. Dragoons.
	Gnr. BLANKENSEE, M.
	Pte. BOND, J. (M.M.).
	Pte. BARNETT, H., 52nd Bn.
	Pte. BERZIN, A., Inf.
81625	Pte. CHEYENEE, I. M., 2nd Bn.
9458	Pte. COHEN, I., 3rd Bn.
19113	Sgt. CAMINER, H. (D.C.M., M.M.), 10th B.
42297	Gnr. COMROE, H., 3rd Bde. F.A.
69145	Sgt. COHEN, L., 26th Bn.
452059	Pte. COUTS, I., 58th Bn.
147120	Pte. COHEN P., 5th Bn.
110087	Pte. CHARATAN, R., 5th C.M.R.
718059	Dvr. COHEN, R., 5th D.A.C.
875033	Pte. COHEN, A., 107th Pioneers.
101493	Pte. COHEN, A. E., 31st Bn.
871344	Pte. CORDEN, A., 1st C.M.R.
552903	Pte. COHEN, H., P.P.C.L.I.
524007	Pte. CARP, L., 12th Field Amb.
347688	Pte. COHEN, J.,* Div. Amm. Col.
739062	Pte. COHEN, M., 19th Bn.
296349	Pte. COHEN, B., 3rd D.S.C.
162880	Pte. COFFMAN, D., 1st S. Bty. Amm. C.
476287	Pte. CRAMER, D. A., Fort Garry Horse.
106130	Cpl. COHEN, E,, O. Spec. Coy. R.E.
1082235	Spr. CROSSMAN, R. D., 2nd Bn. C.R.T.
3105435	Spr. COHEN, D.
279259	Spr. COHEN, M. A., 8th C.R.T.
871913	Spr. CRAF, C., 10th C.R.T.
210186	Dvr. COHEN, J., 2nd Bn. C.R.T.
2498380	Pte. COHEN, A., 26th Coy. F.F.C.
264576	Spr. CEGEL, H., 8th Can. Rail. Troops.
3180886	Pte. COHEN, L., 87th Bn.
2006425	Spr. COHEN, A., 11th C..E
69535	Gnr. COHEN, H., 12th Heavy Bn.
460919	Pte. COHEN, F.,* C.A.M.C.
661337	Gnr. COHEN, J., 383rd Bty. 179th Bde.
1670	A/Sgt. CHAPLAIN, M. H., 8th Bn.
829837	Pte. COHEN, S., 44th Bn.
65187	Pte. COHEN, 24th Bn.
543	Pte. COHEN, I., Inf.
3085098	Pte. COHER, F., Inf.
3083959	Pte. COHEN, R., Inf.
3084958	Pte. CROWN, I., Inf.
3084047	Pte. CHINAN, B., Inf.
3035443	Pte. CROWN, A., Inf.
3158854	Pte. CARLAU, A., Inf.
3037459	Pte. COHEN, H., Inf.
3158854	Cpl. CAPLAN, A., 20th Res. Bn.
3172557	Pte. COHEN, H., 23rd Res. Bn.
475295	Pte. COHEN, J., Fort Garry Horse.
18330	Pte. CLARKE, H.,* 1st Bn.
226896	Pte. COHEN, G., Can. Inf.
2075402	Pte. COHEN, L., Inf.
	Pte. COHEN, A. (M.M.), Inf.
122276	Sgt. COPPLEMAN, A., Inf.
277380	Spr. COHEN, P., C.R.E.
65187	Pte. COHEN, M., 2nd Bn.
2503178	Dvr. CREAMER, A. C., C.A.M.C.
2378581	Pte. COHEN, E., C.F.C.
2393376	Pte. CARR, M., Inf.
7746	Pte. COHN, L.,* 5th C.M.R.
	Pte. CLIMAN, A., 1st Bn.
	Pte. CAPLAN, B., 1st Bn.
	Pte. COHEN, R., 1st Bn.
	Sgt. COLLE, C., C.A.M.C.
	Pte. COHEN, M., 2nd Bn.
	Pte. CHAPIN, J., 8th Bn.
	Pte. CODRESCZ, R.
	Pte. COHEN, J., 3rd Bn.
	Pte. COHEN, H. (M.M.), Can. High.
	Sgt. COHEN, S., 26th Bn.
	Pte. CROWER, A., 57th Bn.
	Pte. COHEN, H., 24th Bn.

Canadian Division.—*Continued.*

- Wire. Op. COHEN, C., R.N.C.V.R.
- 449090 Pte. COUNOS, T., Inf.
- 3207982 Pte. COOPER, Rly. Corps.
- 1467292 Pte. CRESTALL, J., 1st Bn.
- 669517 Pte. CARMAN, J., 166th Bn.
- L/Cpl. COHEN, D., 169th Bn.
- Pte. CAPLAN, S., 169th Bn.
- 862218 Pte. CLINE, H., 180th Bn.
- 2933676 Pte. CARR, M.
- 3030256 Pte. CORKLYN, S.
- 225288 Pte. COWAN, M., C.A.M.C.
- 3035741 Pte. CADESKY, D.
- 3233808 Pte. COHEN, M., 2nd Bn.
- 3233430 Pte. CRASS, H., C.O.R.
- 3036509 Pte. COOPER, M.
- 207659 Pte. CARSON, J.
- 3324657 Spr. COHEN, J., 3rd Coy.
- 201100 Pte. COHN, G., 4th Coy.
- 2791 Pte. COHEN, M. M. H., 48th Bn.
- 207283 Pte. CLARKE, B.
- 467292 Pte. CHRISTALL, T. J., 2nd C.C.D.
- 1027630 Pte. COZENZO, F.
- Pte. COHEN, A. H. (M.M.), Inf.
- 273522 Pte. COWAN, R.
- 273816 Pte. COHN, J.
- 727844 Pte. COHEN, H., C.F.C.
- 235557 Pte. COLITZ, J.
- 261314 Gnr. COYONOW, S., C.F.A.
- 22844 Pte. CRASTER, C.
- 3314534 Pte. COHEN, D.
- 3080127 Pte. COHEN, M. L.
- 344136 Gnr. COHEN, M., C.F.A.
- Cpl. CARFINKLE, M.
- 03788 Pte. COLLEN, D., C.A.M.C.
- 706857 Pte. CHERNIKOFF, L. J., 16th Bn.
- Pte. COSEMATER, C.
- Pte. COHEN, I., 14th Bn.
- Pte. COHEN, E., Inf.
- Pte. COHEN, S., Inf.
- Pte. COHEN, L., 24th Bn.
- Pte. COHEN, B., Inf.
- Pte. CONBISLEY, A. (M.M.), C. Mtd. R.
- 3190 Dvr. DILESKY, M., 2nd Div. Train.
- 457457 Cpl. DAVIDSON, H., 60th Bn.
- 457699 Pte. DAVIS, N., 60th Bn.
- 457927 Pte. DOLGOFF, H., 60th Bn.
- 718573 Pte. DETMOLD, A. H.,* 107th Bn.
- 457978 Pte. DAVIS, C., 60th Bn.
- Pte. DAVIS, B., 1st C.M.R.
- 427099 Pte. DAVIS, L., 28th Bn.
- 470075 Sgt. DAVIS, J. B., 38th Bn.
- 742289 Pte. DEVLIN, T. R., 26th Bn.
- 2043559 Pte. DE TAUBE, S., 4th D.A.C.
- 463053 Pte. DICKSON, W. W. 29th Bn.
- 2075323 Pte. DWORKIN, A., 3rd C. Ent. Bn.
- 2547305 Spr. DAVIDSON, D., 7th C.R.T.
- 2356211 Spr. DAVIS, C., 7th C.R.T.
- 2497473 Spr. DEY, G., 9th C.R.T.
- 1049289 Pte. DULLUCE, J., Hqrs. For. Corps.
- 63262 Pte. DASKEL, A.,* 3rd Bn.
- 3080654 Pte. DAVIDSON, J., 14th Bn.
- 2109957 Pte. DAVIDSON, C., No. 2 C. F. Amb.
- 527559 Pte. DRYER, H., 3rd Bn. Can. Rly Tps.
- 3258695 Pte. DECKER, S. H., Can. Div.
- 2010627 Spr. DAHELBAUM, M., Can. Div.
- 3189209 Pte. DAVID, S., 17th Res. Bn.
- 3091114 Pte. D'ADOLF, O., 20th Res. Bn.
- 681214 Pte. DUDLEY, D., 58th Bn.
- 40122 Pte. DIXON, W., Can. Rail. Troops.
- 2273328 Pte. DIAMOND, B., 3rd Co. atd. L. Coy.
- 850879 Spr. DOLSON, N., 6th Bn.
- 226599 Pte. DONNENBERG, J.
- 3081766 Pte. DOUGLAS, W., Inf.
- 3106289 Pte. DULBERG, M., Inf.
- 20964 Pte. DAVIDS, A., C.F.C.
- 3106332 Pte. DULBERG, H., Inf.
- 3106621 Pte. DE YOUNG, W., 4th Bn.
- 216113 Sgt. DRESNER, J. M., 4th Eng.
- 2009151 Pte. DONALDSON, B., Can. Eng.
- 30817196 Pte. DUBINSKY, D.
- 2356517 Pte. DOMNITZ,
- 3081826 Pte. DEFALCO, A.
- 446354 Pte. DAGUL, S.
- 107179 Cpl. DE PASS, C.
- 345941 Pte. DAWSON, D. L.
- Sgt. DUBNITSKY, C.A.M.C.
- Pte. DUCOFFE, J.
- Pte. DACIES, A.
- Cad. DOCTOR, H.
- Pte. DAVIS, H., 13th Bn.
- Pte. DUBIN, C. Rly. Troops.
- Pte. DEPHAURE, C.A.M.C.
- 442048 Pte. DAVIS, R.,* R.C.R.
- 478841 Pte. DELEIKS, M.
- 3034295 Cpl. DANIELS, P.
- 207595 Cpl. DOMB, L.
- 1440 Pte. ELLISON, L., A.S.C.
- 425584 Pte. ERLICK, L.,* 50th Bn.
- 748980 Pte. ECHENBERG, S., 1st Bde. H. Q.
- 259107 Spr. ENGLE, J. H., 8th C.R.T.
- 2848514 Pte. ELIZER, S. H., 79th Coy. C.F.C.
- 3036522 Pte. ETTENZON, L., Can. Div.
- 344175 Gnr. ENGLEMEN, M., Can. Div.
- 3280241 Sgt. ENDLER, S. D., Can. Div.
- 3189818 Pte. EKER, B., Can. Div.
- 3310342 Spr. EPSTEIN, N., C.R.T.
- 529372 Pte. ERDMAN, M. H., Can. Flying Crps.
- 268275 Spr. ELFINBAUM, A.
- 2204876 Spr. ELLEMSON, I.
- 334442 Sig. EDWARDS, M. I., C.R.A.
- 527078 Pte. EGURIN, A.
- 2503171 Pte. ELGART, H., C.F.C.
- Gnr. EPSTEIN, R.C.H.
- Spr. EISNER, E., Can. Eng.
- 919443 Pte. ELLIS, W., 199th Bn.

Canadian Division.—*Continued.*

Pte. EIDILEFSKY, Inf.
Pte. ERBROFF, R., Inf.
3636522 Pte. ETTENGER, L., C.O.N.
110173 Tpr. FREEDMAN, N. D., C.M.R.
33337 Pte. FRANKESTEIN, M. L., No. 3 F. Amb.
147736 Pte. FRUCHTMAN, P., 28th Bn.
538 Dvr. FRIEZE, M., 2nd Div. Amm. Col.
457193 Pte. FLEISIG, D., 60th Bn.
415258 Sgt. FLEISIG, S., 40th Bn.
110173 Pte. FRIEDMAN, N., 5th C.M.R.
457896 Pte. FABRI, C. B., 60th Bn.
305566 Dvr. FRIEDMAN, G., 3rd Dov. Amm. Col.
511514 Dvr. FREDE, J., 4th Div. Train.
808037 Pte. FLORENCE, J., 31st Bn.
70722 Pte. FREEMAN, H., 54th Bn.
1096286 Pte. FELDMAN, E., 1st Pioneer Bn.
248609 Dvr. FEDER, G., 4th D.A.C.
241 Gnr. FELEX, M., 2nd T.M. Group.
1033237 Pte. FALK, J. L., 38th Bn.
1039089 Spr. FISKE, M. T., 3rd C.T.R.
126080 Spr. FERENBACH, J. J., 10th Can. R. T.
2355837 Spr. FREEMAN, H., 8th Can. R. Tps.
M/283424 Pte. FINE, R. J., Can. Corps. Sge. P.
216103 Pte. FELTON, J., Can. R.E.
50810 Pte. FREEDMAN, J., C.A.M.C.
Pte. FISHER, S., Inf.
3085010 Pte. FINEMAN, H., Inf.
TK/3396 Pte. FOX, B., Inf.
3322330 Pte. FINKLESTEIN, J., Inf.
259270 Pte. FAILBISH, A., 15th Res. Bn.
3084772 Pte. FREEDMAN, H., 20th Res. Bn.
53521 Pte. FREEZE, J., C.A.M.C.
144721 Dvr. FAINER, S., A.S.C.
2266137 Spr. FELDSTEIN, C. L., Can. Eng.
862621 Spr. FINEMARK, J., C.R.A.
3232348 Pte. FRADIN, N., Inf.
1045998 L/Cpl. FRANKEL, S., C.F.C.
3231926 Spr. FARBERMAN, S., C.R.T.
3040343 Pte. FRIEDMAN, M. A., Inf.
3134407 Pte. FOX, P., Inf.
50841 Pte. FRIEDMAN, J., Inf.
862334 Pte. FIELD, M.,* 4th Bn.
3032997 Pte. FELDMAN, J.
3105360 Spr. FREEMAN, H.
859653 Pte. FRANK, M.
L/Cpl. FELDMAN, J. (M.M.).
506627 Pte. FEORDEROFF, E.
2246047 Pte. FENNING, F., C.F.C.
2246824 Pte. FLESCHER, M., C.F.C.
2098824 Pte. FLASHER, S., Special Hospital.
3231028 Pte. FOUGLAR, A.
3036157 Pte. FINE, S.
3036335 Pte. FREEDMAN, I., 12th Res. Bn.
491637 Pte. FEDORISHERE, E., 23rd Res. Bn.
3082315 Pte. FINKLESTEIN, H. J., 2nd C.C.D.
282052 Pte. FREEMAN, G., 3rd Can. Div.
458574 Cpl. FLEISIG, M. (M.M. & Bar), 5th C.M.R.
2537337 Pte. FEGIN, C., P.P.C.L.I.
626078 Pte. FREEDMAN, S.
745374 Pte. FRIED, H.
120271 Pte. FRIEDLEIN, I.
446028 Pte. FRASER, J. M., 2nd C.O.D.
144929 Pte. FIELDS, H. M.
521055 Pte. FLASH, C.
1045188 Pte. FOSTER, D., 164th Bn.
120271 Pte. FRIEDBEL, I.
36469 Pte. FOREMAN, A., C.F.C.
Pte. FREIZE, H., 5th Bn.
Pte. FREIZE, L., 3rd Bn.
Sgt.-Maj. FROMSON, R.C.H.A.
Cad. FEDERMAN, M., C. Air Force.
Gnr. FELSTEIN, H., C.F.A.
Pte. FREIDMAN, N. B., C.A.M.C.
Sgt. Maj. FELDMAN, S., C.O.T.C.
Gnr. FRANKS, F. (M.M.), Inf.
Cpl. FINKLESTEIN, R.
Sgt. Maj. FLORENCE, I., 137th Bn.
Gnr. FIELDS, H., C.F.A.
Pte. FREISMAN, H., Inf.
Pte. FINESTONE, D., Inf.
Sgt. FEINBERG, D.
Cad. FAGLE, M.
Pte. FLAXMAN, R., 15th Bn.
Tpr. FENTON, A., L. Strath. Horse.
Sgt. FLANSBERG, S. (D.C.M.), R.C. Regt.
904107 Spr. FREEDMAN, W., Can. Engineers.
84164 Spr. FLOXZBERG, 24th Bn.
506093 Spr. FLALLER, E.
622936 Pte. GOULDING, B.,* 44th Bn.
458142 Pte. GORBACK, J., 60th Bn.
136469 Pte. GOLDBERG, M., 37th Bn.
10969 Pte. GRONER, R., P.P.C.L.I.
336901 Gnr. GOLDSTEIN, E. H.,* 3rd Bde. Arty.
57831 Pte. GROSSMAN, A.,* 20th Bn.
1995 Pte. GOLDSMITH, B.,* 6th Field Amb.
52 Pte. GOURVITCH, S., 8th Bn.
40412 Dvr. GRIEG, G. O., 1st Bde.
37480 Gnr. GRAEUR, S., 1st Can. Div. Amb.
109356 Sgt. GOLDBERG, M., 4th C.M.R.
145686 Pte. GLAZIER, A. M.,* 45th Bn.
2152463 Gnr. GORBLOOM, J., 14th C.F.A.
347652 Dvr. GITTLESON, H. G., 5th D.A.C.
138291 Pte. GREENFIELD, G., 3rd Bn.
1009907 Pte. GRATCH, W., 5th Bn.
842277 Pte. GOODMAN, H., 13th Bn.
349468 Gnr. GREENBURGH, L., 6th Bde. C.F.A.
34467 Pte. GITTLESON, H., 6th Can. Fld. Amb.
424832 Pte. GOLDENBURG, S., 8th Can. T.M.B.
830623 Pte. GLAZIER, Z., 52nd Bn.
781105 Cpl. GREENBLAT, J., 46th Bn.
745991 Pte. GOLD, J., 2nd Bn.
715842 Pte. GOLDSTEIN, J.,* 25th Bn.
811579 Pte. GALATZ, L., 49th Bn.

Canadian Division.—*Continued.*

718325 Pte. GOLDSTEIN, S. S., Corps School.
136470 Pte. GARFUNKLE, H.,* 42nd Inf.
2321 Pte. GHITTERMAN. M., 3rd Can. C.C.S.
50789 Spr. GOLDSMITH, W. J., 3rd C.R.T.
684459 Spr. GALINSKY, A., 3rd C.R.T.
1081188 Spr. GINSBERG, H., 2nd C.R.T.
3106165 Spr. GOLDSTEIN, A.,* 13th C.R.T.
2498566 Pte. GREY, J., 32nd Coy. For. Corps.
390619 Pte. GOODSTONE, N., 833rd Area Em. C.
2304177 Pte. GOLDMAN, M., 77th Coy. For. C.
2458329 Pte. GOLDBERG, B., 33rd Coy. For. C.
2497837 Pte. GROSSMAN, J., 75th Coy. For. Cps.
2204589 Pte. GABEL, F., 13th Coy. For. Corps.
2498187 Pte. GILBERT, S., 45th Coy. For. Corps.
703634 Pte. GILFORD, D., 71st Coy. For. Corps.
3030436 Pte. GORDON, A. J. (M.M.), 54th Bn.
3230379 Pte. GOLDBERG, L., 4th Bn.
348943 Gnr. GORDON, B.,* 2nd C.F.A.
313402 Pnr. GOLDMAN, J., 1st Bde. Sig. Coy.
432634 S/Sgt. GOLDBERG, S., Can. For. Corps.
25839 Pte. GOODMAN, B.,* 14th Bn.
10650 Pte. GOLDSTEIN, H., 4th Can. Inf.
16892 Pte. GLAZAN, L., C. Div. Cyclist.
129 Pte. GOLDFORBE, J. J., 2nd D.S.C.C.E.
551222 Pte. GREEN, M., Fort Garry Horse.
3039918 Pte. GUNTER, A., Can. Div.
3038123 Pte. GOLDSTEIN, H.. Can. Div.
2378774 Pte. GROSS, M., Can. Div.
349468 Gnr. GREENBERG, L. J., Can. Div.
260606 Pte. GORBACK, M., Can. Div.
1027722 Pte. GROSNISKY, J., 13th R. Bn.
3186120 Pte. GRENDRON, O., 17th Res. Bn.
3186121 Pte. GORDON, R., 17th Res. Bn.
243735 Pte. GREENSPOON, L., 14th Bn.
487385 Pte. GOLDBERG, C., 22nd Bn.
17710 Pte. GOLDSTEIN, H., 6th H.L.
491740 Pte. GETLER, M., 4th Can. Lab. Coy.
Gnr. GILBERT, E., Can. G.A.
Pte. GOODMAN, H., Can. Res. Bn.
12469 Pte. GOODMAN, J., Inf.
261560 Pte. GESS, A., Inf.
226882 Pte. GULFORD, L., Inf.
Pte. GREISMAN, M., Inf.
225238 Pte. GALGERT M., Inf.
Cpl. GOODSON, M. E., Inf.
3005004 Pte. GELDER, T., Can. A.M.C.
334323 Spr. GOLDENBERG, S. A., Can. Eng.
2590828 Pte. GOLDSTEIN, S. J., C.A.S.C.
37480 Gnr. GRANER, S., Div. Amm. Park.
Pte. GEFFIN, G., Snowball Bde.
Cad. GLICKMAN, L., C.A.F.
Cad. GARFINKLE, M., C.A.F.
Cad. GOODMAN, N., Can. Engrs.
Pte. GITTLESON, G., Inf.
Pte. GIBSON.
Pte. GROBESTEIN.
2020279 Spr. GOSBENSKY, M., Can. Engineers.

491473 Pte. GHETTER, M.
Pte. GOLDSTEIN, G., Inf.
Gnr. GALLERT, S., C.F.A.
Pte. GOODMAN, S., 7th Bn.
Pte. GOLDBERG, J., 49th Bn.
Pte. GELLER, C., Inf.
Pte. GREEN, H., Cavalry.
Pte. GUBBINS, W., 23rd Bn.
Cad. GLICKMAN, L., Can. Air Force.
Pte. GHELTER, M., 42nd Bn.
Pte. GINSBERG, J., 146th Bn.
Bugler GOLDBERG, 189th Bn.
Cad. GITTLESON, Can. Air Force.
9351 Pte. GROSOFSKY, B.
Pte. GOLDSTEIN, H., Tank Bn.
Pte. GOLDSTEIN, J., Tank Bn.
2503901 Spr. GOLDSTEIN, N., Can. Eng.
3036544 Pte. GOLLOM, N., 4th Can. Inf. Bn.
2393480 Pte. GREENSIDE, M., M.G.C.
2356305 Pte. GOLDWIN, P.
345323 Gnr. GOULD, B., C.R.A.
847385 Pte. GOLDBERG, C., 150th Bn.
922137 Pte. GOLDBERG, A. S., C.F.C.
3106245 Pte. GARFINKLE, A., 8th Can.
3036450 Pte. GREEDMAN, H. L., C.F.C.
3236105 Pte. GODFREY, H., C.F.C.
2356470 Pte. GOLDBERG, H.
2356111 Pte. GOODMAN, L.
Pte. GOUREVITCH, R. (M.M.), Inf.
3232708 Pte. GRAVER, W. V.
1251843 Pte. GOLDSTEIN, C. H.
3107089 Pte. GOODSTEIN, L.
1102333 Pte. GOLD, J., C.F.C.
2161320 Pte. GINSTER, M., C.F.C.
817268 Pte. GOULD, R.
41510 Pte. GOLDSTONE, I.
M2/081715 Pte. GALICIAN, S.
201172 Pte. GORDON, S.
3317404 Pte. GOLDBERG, W.
1042939 Pte. GAY, M.
563793 Pte. GUITES, T., M.T., C.A.S.C.
820746 Pte. GLASSER, M.
220068 Pte. GIBERMAN, S.
85107 Pte. GINSBERG, S. N., C.F.A.
86051 Pte. GINSBERG, R., C.F.A.
535438 Pte. GOLLON, D., C.A.M.C.
3311566 Cpl. GLASS, G. G.
3311600 Pte. GOLDNER, J.
Sgt.-Maj. GINSBERG, M., C.F.A.
Tpr. GINSBERG, I., 4th C.F.A.
Sgt. GLAZIER, L. (M.M.), C.M.R.
Spr. GOLDSTEIN, J., Rly. Troops.
Pte. GOLDSTEIN, J., 106th Bn.
23520 Pte. GOLDSON, D. A.
Pte. GOLDWATER, S.
1009050 Pte. GANTFORD, A.,* 6th Can. Eng.
410102 Pte. GALOVITCH, A.,* 38th Inf.
38189 Pte. HARRIS, M., 3rd Bn.

Canadian Division.—*Continued.*

416546 Pte. HITTERMAN, B., 41st Bn.
121538 Pte. HOLISCHER, A., 60th Bn.
160123 Pte. HACKMAN, S.,* 4th Bn.
41721 Gnr. HARRIS, L., 2nd Bde. C.F.A.
336948 Gnr. HERSCOVITCH, M., 13th Bd. C.F.E.
186153 Dvr. HANDLEMAN, A., 5th Can. Div. T.
1054778 Pte. HARRISON, C., 14th Bn.
26088 Pte. HIRSHORN, S., 14th Bn.
31872 Pte. HOFFMAN, I., 16th Bn.
718131 C.Q.M.S. HECHTER, F., 107th Bn. C.P.
1078739 Pnr. HIMMEL, S. H., 2nd Pioneer Bn.
491598 Pte. HONINGMAN, A., 5th C.M.R.
2075579 Pte. HENDELMAN, M., 42nd Bn.
644532 Pte. HERSHON, H., 2nd Pioneer Bn.
919519 Pte. HALPERIN, M. C. B., 24th Bn.
746425 Pte. HALTER, N. M., 67th Bn.
112238 Pte. HUNTER, G. T., M. G. Sq.
895409 Pte. HARRIS, J., 8th C.R.T.
237252 Q.M.S. HARRIS, D. L., 21st Coy. F. C.
1099541 Spr. HAWKINS, W., 10th Rail. Troops.
1054121 Pte. HERMAN, S.,* 87th Bn.
410775 Pte. HOFFMAN, S., 87th Bn.
1069760 Pte. HART, A. D., 5th C.M.R.
26088 Pte. HOUCHORIN, S. L., 3rd C.I. Bde. H.
112042 Gnr. HARDY, I., 11th Bn.
109783 Gnr. HUNT, A. J., 11th Bn.
348102 Sdlr. HELLER, S., C.F.A.
763872 Pte. HERSCHFIELD, S. S., Can. For. C.
34480 Pte. HOLTZBERG, S., C.A.M.C.
3085094 Pte. HARRIS, H., Inf.
3232373 Pte. HOFFMAN, M., Inf.
321026 Pte. HYMAN, D., Inf.
2014214 Pte. HANDLEMAN, H. A., 23rd Res. Bn.
3084338 Pte. HAROWITZ, S., Army Pay Corps.
22473 Gnr. HOLDENGRABER, Can. R.A.
775632 Pte. HERMAN, A., 3rd Bn.
536330 Pte. HARRIS, E. D., 12th Res. Bn.
9147113 Pte. HAVELOCK, J., 12th Can. Rail Tps.
192022 Pte. HARRIS, A. A., C.M.G.C.
2098824 Pte. HESHER, S., C.F.A.
919706 Pte. HAFT, D., 24th Bn.
895407 Pte. HARRIS, H., 31st Bn.
678713 Pte. HYMAN, G. H., C.F.A.
3232562 Pte. HART, N., Inf.
Pte. HOLZBERG, R., Can. Med. C.
3083813 Spr. HOLSTEIN, S.
514472 Pte. HAMEL, J., 2nd C.C.D.
200546 Pte. HOFFMAN, V. W. H., 15th Bn.
336227 Gnr. HARRIS, L., Res. Artillery.
2537396 Pte. HARTMAN, J., 8th Res. Bn.
2355637 Pte. HEITSEN, S., 4th Res. Bn.
3231920 Pte. HEIDELSTON, S., 3rd Res. Bn.
3110542 Pte. HART, A., 8th Res. Bn.
3106669 Pte. HELSON, H., 8th Res. Bn.
477389 Pte. HAYWARD, H. F., 17th Res. Bn.
3232562 Pte. HEAD, N., 12th Res. Bn.
1039169 Pte. HIRSCH, M., 3rd C.R.T.

30603 Pte. HARTSIDE, H.
3683 Pte. HARRIS, S.
525093 Pte. HYAMS, H., C.A.M.C.
645508 Cpl. HARRIS, M. J. H. (M.M.), Inf.
Pte. HARRIS, W.
Spr. HERVER, M., 12th C.R.T.
Pte. HOROWITZ, J.
9194769 Pte. HULPIER, M.
Pte. HARRIS, R., 1st Bn.
Pte. HASSAN, F., C.A.M.C.
Gnr. HARRIS, A., C.G.A.
Pte. HEISBERG, R., Inf.
Pte. HARRIS, A., Inf.
892494 Pte. HILLIER, J., 8th Bn.
336227 Pte. HARRIS, J.
3055049 Pte. HANES, S. H., Inf.
Bdr. HARRIS, S., C.F.A.
100390 Pte. HINES, S. C.,* 66th Bn.
602707 Pte. HOLMAN, J.,* 34th Bn.
2500649 Sgt. HENRY, M.
79332 Pte. ISAAC, S. R., 31st Bn.
338542 Pte. ISAAC, S., Can. Div. ?
3186062 Pte. INDESH, M., Can. Div.
1045823 Pte. ISERKOTAKIS, J., 20th Bn.
3085192 Spr. ISBITSKY, W.
40429 Pte. INGRAM, R., 4th C.F.A.
324319 Rfm. ISRAEL, B., 6th C.L.R.
Cpl. IRNSTONE, P., C.A.M.C.
Pte. ISEMAN, J.
Pte. ISEMAN, I., Can. Air Force.
Pte. ISAAC, I.
Pte. ISAACS, R., C.A.M.C.
22882 Pte. ISAACS, E. T.
862334 Pte. ISAACS, M.,* 180th Bn.
603191 Pte. ISAAC, L.,* 34th Bn.
Pte. ISAACS, P. J. (M.M.), Inf.
1668 Pte. JACOBS, S., 5th Field Amb.
71814 Sgt. JACKSON, S., 27th Bn.
474297 Pte. JUDELSON, H., 46th Bn.
190402 Pte. JENKELOVITZ, A., 73rd Bn.
126011 Pte. JOELS, L., 71st Bn.
991519 Cpl. JONAS, L. M. (M.M.), 21st Bn. Inf.
624595 Pte. JACKSON, H., 7th Bn.
910104 Pte. JANVOISH, S., 46th Bn.
139341 Sgt. JOSEPH, A. C., H.Q. 64th H.A.G.
Pte. JACOBS, S., P.P.C.L.I.
34149 Cpl. JACKSON, L., C.A.M.C.
17019 Sgt. JOSEPH, L., 12th Bn.
3083391 Pte. JASLOW, I., Inf.
3189900 Pte. JOSELSON, H., Inf.
2014038 Pte. JONES, A. J., 23rd Res. Bn.
615062 Gnr. JOSEPH, A. A., 72nd Bn.
733511 Pte. JEFFERSON, E. J., Res. Bn.
2085337 Spr. JACOBS, B. B.
1042861 Pte. JACOBS, J.
243629 Pte. JAIS, J.
M2/176486 Pte. JACOBS, H. W., Inf.
922439 Pte. JACOBS, M., C.F.C.

Canadian Division.—*Continued.*

1043061 Pte. JENEROUX, V., C.F.C.
2355665 Pte. JOHNSON, C. A., 4th Res. Bn.
Spr. JACOBSON, A. (M.M.), Eng.
2356427 Pte. JOHNSON, N. J., 4th Res. Bn.
207463 Pte. JALINKE, W. A., Can. Air Force.
527681 Pte. JULIUS, A.
2886 Cpl. JAFFÉ, J.
104 Pte. JOHN, R. L.
Sig. JOSEPHWICH, J., Can. Engrs.
Cad. JACOBS, S., R.C.N.V.R.
Pte. JOSEPH, D., 13th Bn.
Sgt.-Maj. JACOBS, S. (M.S.M.), 10th Bn.
Cpl. JOHNSON, H., Cavalry.
Pte. JONES M., R.C.R.
Pte. JACOBS, E., Inf.
Pte. JACOBS, J., Can. Engrs.
Pte. JACOBS, G., Mt. Rifles.
Pte. JAROSHAW, P., Inf.
Spr. JACOBS, S. (M.M.), Eng.
Cpl. JACOBS, R., Inf.
Pte. JACOBS, F., 77th Bn.
Pte. JACOBS, A., Inf.
Gnr. JOSEPH, H., Siege Bty., **C.G.A.**
Pte. JASBERRY, H.
19935 Pte. JACOBS, W. H.,* 10th Bn.
54175 Pte. KAPLIN, H., 18th Bn.
700789 Pte. KLEINFELD, A., 16th Bn.
427606 Pte. KLEIN, D., 46th Bn.
1093421 Pte. KATES, J., 2nd Bn.
121671 Pte. KURTZMAN, L., 14th Bn.
195143 Pte. KERR, J., 21st Bn.
1087022 Pte. KAUFMAN S., 21st Bn.
916858 Pte. KAUFMAN, J. L., 24th Bn.
449058 Pte. KOZAKUVITCH, L., 3rd Bn.
1013032 Pte. KOFFMAN, J., 24th Coy. C.F.C.
279661 Spr. KEPHART, H. M., 3rd Bn. C.R.T.
258365 Spr. KLINE, L., 8th C.R.T.
3080963 Spr. KAUFMAN, S. P., 9th Bn.
2435819 L/Cpl. KASON, R., 33rd Coy. For. C.
830561 Pte. KOLBASUK, M., 46th Coy. For. C.
1087124 Pte. KATZMAN, H., 46th Coy. For. C.
2100879 Pte. KAPLAN, S., 55th Coy. C.F.C.
510560 Pte. KING. M., 4th Bn.
892404 Pte. KUSHNER, A., 8th Bn.
M1/5620 Pte. KROHN, S., 1st S.B.A.C.
700789 Pte. KLEMFELD, A., 16th Bn.
Pte. KLENMAN, H., 32nd Bn.
TK/5398 Pte. KELLEN, H., Inf.
3083457 Pte. KATZ, J., Inf.
3345295 Pte. KLUNER, A., Inf.
1039169 Sgt. KIRSCH, M., 3rd Bn.
2431330 Sig. KIRSCH, M., C.R.A.
345875 Pnr. KORN, D. R., C.F.A.
2382322 Pte. KAMOSOFSKY, A. Inf.
2246037 Pte. KNOP, M., C.F.C.
514567 Pte. KOLB, B., C.A.S.C.
935 Pte. KRANTZ, A., 17th Bn.

3106995 Pte. KEMP, A. D., Inf.
2356615 Pte. KNIT, M. H., Inf.
Pte. KUTNER, M., Inf.
2020325 Pte. KOPCH, A., Ordnance.
2765183 Pte. KELLER, B., 1st Can. Tank Bn.
3105959 Pte. KASSIN, S.
3039609 Pte. KAPELUCK, M.
3037000 Pte. KEANE, M.
3106331 Pte. KRITZER, H., 8th Res. Bn.
2204563 Pte. KEGGY, H., C.F.C.
2356359 Pte. KIBEL, I. H., 4th Res. Bn.
250112 Pte. KELMAN, M., C.F.C.
3030930 Pte. KORNITZER, B., 8th Res. Bn.
2075423 Pte. KAUFFMAN, A. L., 23rd Res. Bn.
3080260 Pte. KUGNATZ, H., 23rd Res. Bn.
2522503 Gnr. KREVER, M., Res. Arty.
400498 Pte. KORN, J., 4th Res. Bn.
474048 Pte. KOSTNA, J., 46th Bn.
721596 Pte. KINGBERG, S., 14th Bn.
850547 Pte. KUSHNER, B., 58th Bn.
354 Pte. KAPLAN, I.
841878 Pte. KLITZNER, L., 148th Bn.
Cad. KAPLANSKY, W., Can. Air Force.
177280 Spr. KAUFMAN, H., Can. Engrs.
Pte. KEY, S.
313036 Pte. KUEF, J. E.
Cadet KAPLAN, H. W.,* C.R.A.F.
2650509 Sgt. KING, S.
207250 Pte. KING, R. E.
3036087 Pte. KERZMAN, A.
Pte. KUSHNER, L. (M.M.).
3036332 Pte. KAZEL, T. Y.
623195 Pte. LEXIER, M.,* 10th Bn.
458216 Pte. LEWIS, F., 60th Bn.
181 Dvr. LEVINSON. H., 2nd Div. Sig. Coy.
71555 Pte. LYONS, A. M., 27th Bn.
65542 Pte. LANG, S., 54th Bn.
65591 C.Q.M.S. LYON, R. N., 24t hBn.
59580 Pte. LEHBERG. B., 21st Bn.
22955 S/Sgt. LEWIS, J., 2nd Bn.
23407 Sgt. LEVY, A. L., 7th Bn.
32809 Pte. LEWIS, J., No. 1 Field Amb.
150482 Cpl. LION, O. S., 1st C.M.R.
110335 Cpl. LYONS, J., 5th C.M.R.
758 Dvr. LIGHTSTONE, A., 6th C.F.A.
89905 Gnr. LIVINGSTONE, B., 7th C.F..A.
121721 Pte. LEVINSON, S., 14th Bn.
401344 Pte. LAZARUS, M.,* 38th Bn.
132115 Pte. LEVITT, H., 73rd Bn.
504769 Spr. LEVY, L. J., 12th Field Coy. C. E.
532740 Pte. LAIBMAN, B., 13th Can. Fld. Amb.
301124 Bdr. LIGHTER, H., 2nd Bde. C.F.A.
336871 Gnr. LEVI, M. H., 14th Bde. C.F.A.
Sgt. LEVEY, R. (M.M.), Inf.
336949 Gnr. LEVY, I., 14th Bde. C.F.A.
207799 Gnr. LUKON, M. S., 21st Bn.
863152 Pte. LEVINSKY, A., 123rd Pnr. Bn.
2109882 Pte. LEVINE, S., 49th Bn.

Canadian Division.—*Continued.*

102755 Pte. LEVY, B., 54th Bn.
140127 Pte. LUBOSKY, S., 4th Div. Emp. Coy.
146161 Gnr. LEVENE, B., 38th S. Bty.
136486 Pte. LITCHIS, P., 31st Bn.
213754 Pte. LEWIS, B., 2nd C.M.R.
121464 Pte. LEITER, L., 60th Bn.
34940 Pte. LENBIE, E., Can. Scottish.
684862 Spr. LEVINE, I., 6th Bn.
2527357 Spr. LEVEY, F., 13th C.R.T.
2499599 Spr. LEVY, H., 13th C.R.T.
3314354 Spr. LEVINE, J., 8th C.R.T.
1048872 Pte. LEWIS, B., 21st Coy. For. Corps.
415512 L/Cpl. LEVY, A. J.,* 60th Bn.
153929 Pte. LEVY, G. S.,* 43rd Bn.
3034718 Pte. LARVEY, S. L.,* 15th Bn.
3080552 Pte. LEWIS, W., 5th C.M.R. Bn.
02544 Pte. LEVESKY, S., 1st Can. Field Amb.
2293331 Pte. LAVINSON, A.,* L. Strathcona H.
DM2/163915 Pte. LUDZKER, M., Can. C. S. P.
Pte. LINDE. A., 28th Bn.
530563 Pte. LEVY, B., 11th Bde.
Pte. LE FIERRE, H., 10th Bn.
Pte. LAWSON, A., C.A.M.C.
1130 Pte. LEVINE, J., 8th Bn.
3083985 Pte. LURTZGARTEN, I., Inf.
3084154 Pte. LURTZGARTEN, P. P., Inf.
3105173 Pte. LOUIS, S., Inf.
2009934 Spr. LEGONNES, M., Engineers.
491433 Pte. LEITER, W., 20th Res. Bn.
919557 Pte. LEE, J., 24th Bn.
2499599 Spr. LEVY, A.
Dvr. LAWGORSE, D., C.F.A.
213079 Dvr. LUMPS, A., C.F.A.
684862 Spr. LEVINE, A., 6th Bn.
2100687 Pte. LIPSEY, H., C.R.A.
342479 Sgt. LEVITT, P., Inf.
341418 Pte. LIPMAN, J., C.F.C.
2080658 Pte. LOUN, R., Inf.
3040193 Pte. LEVINE, N., Inf.
3106478 Pte. LEIBOVITCH, M.,* 50th Bn.
226912 Pte. LOWENBERG, A., C.F.C.
3080969 Pte. LEIBERVITCH, J., 13th Inf. Bn.
216141 Pte. LEONAR, B., 2nd Inf. Bn.
528976 Pte. LIMBURG, S., 5th Field Amb.
3084445 Pte. LEVENE, I.
3206468 Pte. LAMB, T., 21st Res. Bn.
154775 Pte. LAWSON, H., 2nd C.C.D.
1045931 Pte. LYONS, W., 2nd C.C.D.
1105231 Pte. LESAK, B., 23rd Res. Bn.
3232410 Pte. LEVINE, J., R.D.G.
3040426 Pte. LESHOWRTZ, E., C.F.C.
3036568 Pte. LEWIS, S., C.F.C.
1105212 Pte. LECONSKY, J., 23rd Res. Bn.
2574312 Pte. LABRINSKY, M., C.F.C.
2500328 Pte. LA FARBA, L. F., C.F.C.
2075435 Pte. LEVINE, S., 20th Res. Bn.
2356427 Pte. LEONARDS, N. G., 4th Res. Bn.

542545 Pte. LURIE, W., 7th Res. Bn.
13361 Pte. LEMBERG, C.
43979 Pte. LITTLESTONE, A., 8th Bde.
817099 Pte. LEVENE, M., 26th Bn.
2318 Sdlr. LEVI, J., 306th Bde.
2500707 Pte. LEFKOWITZ, E.
350477 Pte. LITTVICK, M., Can. Dragoons.
500301 Cpl. LYONS, E. L., 5th Can. Sig. Coy.
706280 Cpl. LEE, R., 16th Bn.
55043 Pte. LEVITT, N., Can. Dragoons.
41043 Bdr. LEVINGE, H. A., C.F.A.
550251 Pte. LASHER, H., Can. Dragoons
65866 Scout. LAGAN, S., 24th Bn.
Pte. LERNER, S., C.A.F.
Gnr. LAUTERMAN, J., C.F.A.
Pte. LAZAR, A., C.A.M.C.
Pte. LOZENSKY, E., C.A.M.C.
Spr. LIVINSON, B., Can. Engrs.
Gnr. LIVERMAN, H., C.F.A.
Gnr. LAWRENCE, J., C.F.A.
Pte. LEVERS, J.
844746 Pte. LIGHTMAN, A., 149th Inf.
Pte. LEVY, J., Can. Cav.
470062 Pte. LAMDEN, S., Inf.
233175 Spr. LEVINE, E., Can. Engrs.
Pte. LEVY, G., C.M.R.
Pte. LEVY, N. M., 4th Inf.
303248 Pte. LEVY, C., 2nd C.M.R.
Cpl. LEVY, L., C.A.M.C.
Spr. LIVINGSTONE, L., 5th Pioneers.
Pte. LEWIS, H., 5th Bn.
Pte. LEWIS, W., C.A.M.C.
Sgt. LIVINGSON, B., C.F.A.
l/Cpl. LYONS, A. (M.M.), Inf.
Cpl. LIGHTSTONE, A., C.A.M.C.
Pte. LEON, H., 13th Bn.
Gnr. LIPSEY, H., C.G.A.
Pte. LITZER, L., 148th Bn.
Pte. LEVISON, J., Inf.
Pte. LIPOWSKY, J., 64th Bn.
Pte. LEVY, N. V., Inf.
Cad. LASSER, A., C.A.F.
238092 Pte. LUDWIG, E. C., Inf.
Pnr. LARANTINER, A., Can. Engrs.
Staff Sgt. LEVY, B., 15th Bn.
9800 Pte. LAZOFF, S.,* 3rd Bn.
Cpl. LEVY, J., Inf.
817099 Pte. LEVINE, M., 26th Bn.
874361 Pte. LEONARD, S.
2273304 Pte. LAZELS, S. H.
02571 Pte. LIGHTSTONE, G., C.A.F.A.
2002530 Pte. LEVENE, S., C.A.S.C.
331352 Pte. LEWIS, S., C.A.S.C.
3314584 Pte. LATTNER, D., 2nd Cent. Art.
681619 Pte. LEVINSKY, P., P.P.C.L.I.
3234024 Pte. LEVINE, S.
2500707 Pte. LEFKOWITZ, E.
Pte. LEVY, B. R. (M.M. and Bar), Inf.

Canadian Division.—*Continued.*

3039574 Pte. LEBSKIN, Y.
3311655 Pte. LISNER, A.
159681 Pte. LESTER, H., 81st Bn.
208238 Pte. LINDER, 97th Bn.
3232039 Pte. LIPMAN, A.
3033175 Pte. LEVINE, I.
3230480 Pte. LICHTENSTEIN, A.
         Pte. LIGHTSTONE, I., C.F.A.
41094 Dvr. MARKS, A. (M.M.), 2nd Bty. 1st Bde.
232 L/Cpl. MARCUS, D.,* No. 3 Field Amb.
         Sgt. MORRIS, J. L. (M.M.), C.M.G.C.
454312 Pte. MARKUS, H.,* 19th Bn.
67945 Pte. MICHAELS, P.,* 25th Bn.
4055 Sgt. MECKLINBERG, P., C.A.S.C.
         Arm. Sgt. MYERS, E., Can. Scottish.
404507 Sgt. MARSH, H., 35th Bn.
         Pte. MARKS, J. (M.M.), Inf.
417223 Cpl. MORRIS, J., 41st Bn.
305530 Dvr. MARCOWITZ, M., 3rd Div. Amm. C.
144656 Pte. MARKS, J., 60th Bn.
146375 Pte. MORRIS, L., 47th Bn.
669619 Pte. MARKS, C.,* 3rd Bn.
1054829 Pte. MALLIN, M., 14th Bn.
21 Cpl. MARCUS, J. A., 2nd T.M. Group.
1045623 Pte. MACOD, F., 5th M.G.C.
         Pte. MEYER, P. (M.M.), Inf.
103415 Pte. MAIMAN H, 2nd C.M.R.
825627 Pte. MARCUS, M., 4th C.M.R.
273165 Pte. MAYKRAFF, M., 4th C.M.R.
220341 Pte. METTER, H., 38th Bn.
454573 Pte. MILLAR, S.,* 21st Bn.
769732 Pte. MARKUS, M., 124th Can. Pnr .Bn.
85347 Gnr. MUSICANT, A., 4th Bde. C.F.A.
1081312 Spr. MARTIN, N., 4th Can. C.R.T.
345086 Pte. MUSCOVITZ, M., 7th C..RT.
279677 Pte. MAYER, H., 8th C.R.T.
2499570 Pte. MAISTER, F., 13th C.R.T.
         Sgt. MICHAELS, S. (M.M.), Inf.
2499648 Pte. MAZZE, F., 13th C.R.T.
2499493 Pte. MILLER, S., 13th C.R.T.
56192 Pte. Moss, L. H.,* 19th Bn.
3321015 Spr. MILLER, L., 3rd Bn. Can Rly. T.
2380953 Spr. MUSCOVITZ, H., 3rd Bn. Can. R.T.
6475 Pte. MARKS, H., 1st Bn.
34498 Pte. MARLOW, H., C.A.M.C.
521 Pte. MARTIN, M.,* C.A.M.C.
3031533 Pte. MORRISON, L., Inf.
528143 Gnr. MILON, J. S., Inf.
551137 Pte. MILLER, H., Inf.
3204513 Pte. MURPHY, H., 17th Res. Bn.
42508 Pte. MALLAN, M., 14th C.M.R.
871391 Pte. MYERS, C., Inf.
669635 Pte. MYERS, S. (M.M.), Inf.
2355847 Pte. MAISELLE, D. B., M.G.C.
91803 Gnr. MUNNUTT, M., Can. R.G.A.
3003843 Pte. MILLER, P. L.
3038127 Pte. MORRIS, M.

3036956 Pte. MINEGARTEN, L. H., Inf.
3226432 Pte. MENDELSOHN, J. B., Inf.
3107946 Pte. MENDELS, D. M., Inf.
         Sgt. MENDELSOHN, H.,* 13th C.F.A.
145450 Pte. MYERS, B.,* 77th Bn.
912029 Sgt. MORRIS. J. L. (M.M.), C.M.G.C.
         Pte. MARSDEN, H. A.
273165 Pte. MAZERCOFF, M.,* C.M.G.C.
2204821 Pte. MAVLOSKIE, M. H.
2093459 Pte. MALCOLM, A.
2204821 Pte. MCCLUSKY, A.
766447 Pte. MICHAELSON. J.
2245887 Pte. MILLER, C., C.F.C.
1003631 Pte. MAHID, H., 5th Coy. C.F.C.
2692685 Pte. MALINSKY, S.
3038127 Pte. MEAD, M.
3230923 Pte. MOLAN, H., 3rd Res. Bn.
491463 Pte. MEYERS, W., 23rd Res. Bn.
3083774 Pte. MOROSE, F., 23rd Res. Bn.
3031944 Pte. MORRIS, W., 12th Res. Bn.
3132300 Pte. MAYER, B., C.F.C.
2683752 Pte. MOHR, A., C.F.C.
1105241 Pte. MELEUTOVITCH, C., 23rd Res. Bn.
491467 Pte. MIRENBERG, L.
525501 A/Sgt. MACKENZIE, N. R., Can. Div.
420 Gnr. MAWOULSKY, L., C.F.C.
211199 Pte. MILLER, J., 12th Res. Bn.
628565 Pte. MYERS, P.,* 16th Can. Scottish.
1027664 Pte. MARLIEB, L. M., C.A.M.C.
50082 Pte. MISHMAS, M., C.A.M.C.
200128 Pte. MARKS, T. W., C.A.S.C.
3082868 Pte. MYERS, W.
214222 Spr. MACDONALD, A. W.
         Pte. MICHAELSON, M., Can. Engrs.
         Cad. MARSHALL, C.A.F.
         Cad. MOROSNICK, L., C.A.F.
         Gnr. MARKOVITCH, I., C.F.A.
760217 Staff Sgt. MARSDEN, W. H., C.A.M.C.
         Sgt. MEYERSTEIN, W. (D.C.M.), 7th Bn.
         Pte. MOSES, S., Inf.
         Gnr. MILLER, W., C.F.A.
         Pte. MYERS, C. (M.M.), Inf.
         Pte. MORTIMER. R., Inf.
57260 Pte. NATHAN, J. B., 20th Bn.
420 Pte. NORONLANSKY, L., 6th C Fld. A.
2075432 Pte. NEWTON. H., 42nd Bn.
145375 Pte. NORRIS, L., 47th Bn.
M/2204122 Pte. NEWMAN, M., C.A.S.C.
72076 Bdr. NORWIND, R., 169th S. Bty.
250030 Pte. NODELMAN, M., 13th Coy. For. C.
472160 Pte. NEUFELD, J., 60th Coy. For. Corp.
425697 Pte. NEGAL, J.,* Inf.
208153 Spr. NEMEYER, E., 11th Bn. C.E.
50082 Pte. NISHMAS, N., 7th C.C.F.A.
3181290 Spr. NATHANSON, J. S., 3rd Bn. C.R.T.
2365856 Pte. NEWMAN, R. E., Can. Div.
2356565 Pte. NELSON, J., Can. Div.
3312023 Pte. NORIKOFF, B., Can. Div.

Canadian Division.—*Continued.*

400152	Pte. NATHAN, S., Army Med. Corps.
722038	Pte. NAGDIMON, A., 43rd Bn.
3108716	Pte. NADELL, A., Inf.
98187	Pte. NATHAN, S., 6th Bn.
1087128	Pte. NITKIN, J., C.F.C.
3085570	Spr. NICHELSON, M., 3rd Coy.
	Pte. NIDIVITCH, A.
207419	Pte. NEWMAN, S.
	Pte. NEIDER, A., Inf.
2504000	Pte. NEGRU, N. S., Ry. Con. Depôt.
159156	Pte. NETCHEN, J., 81st Bn.
3031872	Pte. NEIMAN, M.
3231219	Pte. NEEMAN, H., 1st C.O.R.
2769	Pte. OPPENHEIM, A. E., L.S.H.
135203	Pte. OFFREDI, W., 1st C.M.R.
1405724	Pte. OPENBURG, J., 24th Coy. For. C.
8241	Pte. OWEN, C., 2nd Bn.
19771	Pte. OSSOFSKY, H., 10th Bn.
2365190	Pte. OUSKIN, S. H., Can. Div.
2365790	Pte. ORECHKIN, S. H., 13th Bn.
517336	Pte. OZADOWSKY, S., Can. Res. Bn.
2562410	Pte. ORLOVE, H., Inf.
3107009	Pte. OFFSAY, M., 8th Res. Bn.
	Pte. OSTRO, J., 2nd Bn.
	Pte. ORN, J., Inf.
	Spr. OLEYSCHUK, M., Can. Engrs.
669895	Pte. ORGEL, M., 166th Bn.
5231088	Pte. OENSTEIN, A., 2nd Bn.
458476	Pte. PALLETT, S., 60th Bn.
622794	Pte. PERELES, N.,* 10th Bn.
602600	Cpl. PRESSMAN, L., 34th Bn.
198200	Pte. PATTIE, W. D., 5th Bn.
2009289	Gnr. PEZIM, S., Engineers.
348900	Bdr. PHILLIPS, B. G. (M.M.), 2nd Bde. C.F.A.
467312	Pnr. PERLER, A., 2nd Pioneer Bn.
781243	Pte. PLOTKEN, H., 7th T.M.B.
685063	Spr. PELINKOI, J., 3rd Bn. C.R.T.
766681	Pte. PROTES, L., 60th Coy. For. Corps.
3036158	L/Cpl PITLOCK, I., Inf.
FK/5409	Pte. PATTERSEN, H. B., Inf.
3231966	Gnr. PULLEN, J., Inf.
3232730	Pte. PITZER, S., Inf.
3039923	Sgt. PERLMAN, M., Inf.
436741	Pte. PHILLIPS, B. L., 51st Bn.
2522322	Dvr. PLATT, M., C.R.A.
1045188	Pte. POLSTER, D. G., Can. Inf.
3035684	Pte. PAULINE, H., Inf.
2498746	Pte. POLAKOR, J., Can. For. Corps.
345193	Pte. PAUNAMAN, A., Inf.
279632	Pte. PRIMACK, M.,* 49th Bn.
53905	Cpl. PAGE, J.,* 18th Bn.
2013404	Spr. PETROFF, F.
916753	Pte. PRUSSIN, A. N., 5th Can. Div.
3230722	Pte. PAPERMICK, P., 3rd Res. Bn.
3232728	Pte. PLATCHEKA, W., 12th Res. Bn.
2382644	Pte. PRESNER, L. C., C.F.C.
342271	Gnr. PITZELLI, I., C.G.A.
417917	Pte. PHILLIPS, H., 4th Res. Bn.
3233090	Pte. POLKE, L., 12th Res. Bn.
3181411	Pte. PERLIN, I. B., 17th Res. Bn
2356594	Pte. PORIEFMAN, D. J.
	Pte. PASTERNICK, I., 137th Bn.
528119	Pte. PUGACH, E. S., C.A.M.C.
3236722	Pte. PAPERN, S.
	Pte. PECK, B., Inf.
	Pte. POLINSKY, A., 1st Bn.
	Pte. PASNER, H., Inf.
	Sgt. PASCALL, M., Can. Engrs.
	Sgt. Maj. PHILLIPS, L., Inf.
	Cad. PESNER, A., Can. Air Force.
	Pte. PINTO, E., 1st Bn.
	Sgt. PRESS, D., 60th Bn.
	Pte. POVAR, S., Inf.
527118	Pte. PARSKY, M. M., C.A.M.C.
51258	Pte. PLATER, J., 10th Hussars.
3108872	Pte. PAKER, I.
3032850	Pte. PALACE, J.
3037038	Pte. PASSAFIUME.
3039923	Pte. PERLMAN, M. M.
157660	Pte. PETERSON, S. E., 81st Bn.
	Pte. PELLIS, B., 169th Bn.
2528374	Pte. QUATES, B., C.F.C.
16349	Pte. QUINNEY, J. L., 7th Bn.
142062	Pte. RUBENSTEIN, O. A., 37th Bn.
71424	Pte. ROSEN, S., 27th Bn.
148041	Pte. RABINOVITCH, H., 5th Bn.
42377	Gnr. RISSIDORE, F. D.,* 3rd Bde. Arty.
42379	Gnr. RISSIDORE, W. W., 11th By.
1832	Sgt.-Maj. RAMUS, H. R., 1st Div. Hq.
348573	Dvr. RUBEN, F., 45th Bty. 9th Bde.
451296	Pte. ROSENBURGH, A., 4th Bn.
219580	Pte. ROSENTHAL, H.* (M.M.), 50th Bn.
147423	Pte. RODIN, M.,* 78th Bn.
531721	Pte. REINHORN, C. G., 11th C. F. Amb.
874727	Cpl. ROLLES, W., 107th Pioneers.
922594	Pte. RUBENSTEIN, R. H., 27th Bn.
211284	Pte. RODKEVITCH, J., 5th M.G.C.
339315	Spr. ROSE, B., 3rd Div. Sigs.
491495	Pte. RABINOVITCH, J. B., 5th C.M.R.
491714	Pte. ROSEMAN, J., 5th C.M.R.
850736	Pte. RAPORT, M. D.,* 43rd Bn.
104	Pte. RUDOLF, L. J., P.P.C.L.I. —
603294	Spr. ROSE, H. L., 4th Div. Sig. Coy.
157677	Pte. RATTENBERG, L., 1st Bn. —
226645	Pte. ROSEMER, S.,* 18th Bn.
4951	Pte. ROSENBLOOM, M., 1/4th S. High.
M/2031999	Pte. ROSENTHAL, M., Can. A.S.C.
2246099	Pte. ROSEN, B., 12th Coy. For. Corps.
90009	Bdr. RUTENBERG, G., 5th Bty. C.F.A.
	Pte. RAPP, 26th Can. For. Corps.
441	Pte. ROSENTHAL, S., A.M.C.
100535	Sgt. ROBINSON, R., C.M.C.
3234383	Pte. RUBINOFF, J., Inf.
3083970	Pte. RUBIN, D., Inf.

Canadian Division.—*Continued.*

3085152	Pte.	RAWSON, C., Inf.
4082581	Pte.	RUBINOVITZ, S., Inf.
260715	Pte.	RUCKNOT, M., Inf.
2499254	Pte.	RAPP, J., 13th Res. Bn.
	Sgt.	ROSENBAUM, M. (M.S.M.), A.D.H. Sig.
269491	Pte.	ROBERTS, H., 15th Res. Bn.
3091173	Pte.	RHODES, R., 20th Res. Bn.
400309	Pte.	ROSENHEIM, H. B., C.A.M.C.
226634	Pte.	ROSEN, C. 8th Bn. C.E.F.T.
59406	Pte.	ROSEN, J., A.M.C.
3232605	Pte.	ROM, R., Can. For. Corps.
334198	Sig.	ROSENBERG, A. I., C.R.A.
919487	Pte.	RAB, W., Inf.
3022826	Pte.	ROSENTHAL, L., Inf.
2382365	Pte.	ROSEN, M., Inf.
529089	Pte.	RETTIG, L., C.A.M.C.
2100667	Gnr.	ROSENBERG, Inf.
308366	Pte.	RUBIN, R., C.F.C.
3106435	Pte.	ROSE, I., Inf.
3039647	Pte.	RICHMAN, A., Inf.
3030076	Pte.	RUBENSTEIN, A., Inf.
8519	Pte.	REUBEN, A., 2nd Bn.
276443	Pte.	RIPSTEIN, C. K.
2010971	Pte.	ROSENFELD, J.
345181	Dvr.	RUBINOVITCH, L.
3234278	Pte.	RAFARL, M.
2246089	Pte.	ROMAN, M., Can. For. Cor.
3231762	Pte.	ROSENOFF, A. H., 12th Res. Bn.
3031109	Pte.	RICHMAN, S., 8th Res. Bn.
2522494	Gnr.	RIFKIN, G., Res. Artillery.
22708	Pte.	ROTAPPLE, E., 1st Res. Bde.
320690	Pte.	ROTHSCHILD, M., 4th Res. Bn.
2356423	Pte.	RODGERS, S., 4th Res. Bn.
249154	Pte.	RONBACH, H., Y.S. Bn.
721502	Gnr.	ROBBINS, W. A., C.A.R.D.
10969	Gnr.	RALPH, P.P.C.L.I.
39956	Pte.	ROSENFIELD, A., Can. Engrs.
511424	Pte.	RUBENSTEIN, S. Can. Engrs.
237860	Spr.	ROSCOE, P., Can. Engrs.
425048	Pte.	ROBERTSON, G., 1st Coy.
700947	Pte.	ROSENFIELD, H., 17th R. Bn.
454781	Pte.	RAMBESKI, J., 59th Bn.
100230	Pte.	RICTOR, R. M.
523077	Cpl.	REED, S. W.
105918	Cpl.	ROSS, S., 5th Bn.
	Pte.	RUBIN, J.
	Pte.	RUBINOVITCH, I.
	Pte.	RICHSTONE, Inf.
	Sgt.	ROSE, J., Inf.
	Pte.	RUTTENBERG, D.
	Pte.	ROTHENSTEIN, M., 6th Bn.
	Pte.	ROSE, M., 3rd Bn.
	Gnr.	RIDDLER, H., C.G.A.
	Pte.	ROSE, E., Can. Engrs.
875047	Pte.	REEVE, H., 29th Bn.
	Cpl.	ROSS, Railway Troops.
	Pte.	ROSENBERG, E.
48589	Stg.	REDDY, W., C.A.V.C.
	Pte.	RUTTENBERG, S., 53rd Bn.
	Pte.	ROTHENBRG, M., 10th Bn.
18859	Pte.	RADOMAN, B.,* 1st Bn.
130243	Pte.	ROSENBERG, F.,* 72nd Bn.
1043025	Pte.	ROSOPH, R.
105918	Pte.	ROSS, S.
451296	Pte.	ROSENBERG, A.
529246	Pte.	RUBY, D.
323605	Pte.	ROTH, R.
454908	Pte.	RUDY, J.
850736	Pte.	RAPORT, M.
3036612	Pte.	ROSENBERG, I. B.
3036613	Pte.	RASH, S.
3234718	Pte.	ROHER, S.
2606808	Pte.	REUBEN, W.
786	Pte.	RUBENSTEIN, Y.
2500785	Pte.	REID, E.
207630	Pte.	ROBINSON, S.
338451	Pte.	RASHKOFSKY, Y.
3232605	Pte.	RUBINOTH, Y.
13156	Pte.	SANDIFORD, B. E., 5th Bn.
19637	Sgt.	SHULTZ, S. (D.C.M.) 10th Bn.
63810	Pte.	SOLOMONS, R., 15th Bn.
41077	Gnr.	SCHULMAN, J., 5th Bty. 2nd Bde.
5206	Spr.	SAMUELS, S. A., 1st F. Coy. R.E.
33268	Sgt.	STALL, M., No. 3 Field Amb.
491141	Pte.	STAWGKRY, S. M.,* 42nd Scot. Can.
65866	Pte.	SAGAN, S., 24th Bn.
69915	Pte.	SHANNON, J., 26th Bn.
	Dvr.	SNIDERS, A., 2nd Div. Amm. Col.
417822	Pte.	SEMENOWKER, A., 41st Bn.
H/467163	Pte.	SCHLENGER, D., 29th Bn.
42215	Gnr.	SALTROUGH, N., T.M.B. 1st Div.
151925	Pte.	SNYDER, N., 43rd Bn.
135004	Pte.	SHAPIRO, L., 1st C.M.R.
171534	Pte.	SOLOMONS, A., 5th C.M.R.
2152431	Gnr.	SCHULICK, J., 13th Bde. C.F.A.
928302	Pte.	SILVER, J. L., 5th Bn.
1045801	Pte.	SECKER, M. T., 15th Bn.
35309	S/Sgt.	SCHWARTZ, J., 1st Can. Div. T.
771756	Pte.	SIMMONS, B. E.,* 16th Bn.
847575	Pte.	STOLT, S., 24th Bn.
1054736	Pte.	SHAPIRO, P., 24th Bn.
3032326	Pte.	STERN, J., 20th Bn.
157680	Pte.	SAUTMAN, D. W., 8th M.G.C.
264208	Pte.	SADOWSKI, F., 123rd Can. P. Bn.
910058	Pte.	SCHULMAN, L., 1st C.M.R.
2075325	Pte.	SMITH, S. W., 42nd Bn.
136681	Pte.	SILVERSTONE, A., 44th Bn.
911849	Pte.	SEIDELMAN, E. J., 46th Bn.
875392	Pte.	SLUTSKEY, D., 78th Bn.
507371	Spr.	SHEMAN, H., 4th Div. Sig. Coy.
202032	Pte.	SHULMAN, H. M., 3rd Bn.
187174	Pte.	SAGARMAY, A., 16th Bn.
404450	Pte.	SAMUELS, D., 24th Bn.
487434	Pte.	STERNBERG, F. J., P.P.C.L.I.

Canadian Division.—*Continued.*

- 871298 Pte. SAVILLE, E. J.,* 44th Bn.
- 186241 Cadet SILVERSTEIN, H. M.,* 1st C.R.A.F.
- 108294 Spr. SIEGEL, H.,* 2nd Bn. C.R.T.
- 4919 Pte. SOLOMON, J., 1/4th Seaforth H.
- 14606 Pte. SAMUELS, L. H., Fort Garry Horse.
- 2615 Pte. SURTEES, S., Strathcona Horse.
- 491622 Pte. SCOLNUCK, H.,* 24th Bn.
- 264579 Spr. SEGAL, H., 8th C.R.T.
- 1099040 Spr. SMITH, L., 10th C.R.T.
- 3082105 Spr. SMITH, B., 10th C.R.T.
- 490574 Spr. SEAMAN, H., 9th Bn. C.R.T.
- 2498904 Pte. SORBLUM, G., 13th C.R.T.
- 1251331 Spr. STRINSKY, A., 5th C.R.T.
- 2433308 Pte. STARKER, L.. 75th Coy. For. Cps.
- 2020353 Pte. SLOBASKY, L., 72nd Bn.
- 115045 Pte. SPOONER, S., 3rd M.G.C.
- 847569 Pte. SLUTSKY, M., 5th C.M.R. Bn.
- 343054 Sig. SUSMAN, M., C.C.C.R.
- 334275 Spr. SPECTOR, A., 8th Bn. C.R.T.
- 2355647 Spr. SNIDER, W. M., 8th Bn. C.R.T.
- 95168 Cpl. SIMONS, L., 11th Bn.
- 169132 Gnr. SOMAN, S., 127th Hvy. Bty.
- 919830 Pte. SOLCHINSKY, L., 14th Bn.
- 929 Pte. SMITH, B., 42nd Bn.
- 1004207 Pte. SOPHER, B., 54th Bn.
- 15524 Cpl. SILVER, I.,* 8th Bn.
- 887 Pte. SUSMAN, W., C.A.M.C.
- 3084393 Pte. SHATSKY, J., Inf.
- 3036125 Pte. SMITH, H., Inf.
- 3031630 Pte. SANDERS, H., Inf.
- 3230007 Pte. STROM, M., 1st C.O.R.
- 2365852 Pte. SILVERMAN, F., Inf.
- 21924 Pte. SIRWINSKY, J.,* 8th Bn.
- 1060097 Pte. STONE, A.,* R. Can. Regt.
- Pte. SPECTOR, N., 10th Bn.
- 3037097 Pte. SCHATZ, C., 8th Bn.
- Pte. SCHRAM, S. (M.M.), Inf.
- 2701 Pte. SAMUEL, M., 2nd Div. S.C.
- 3034598 Bnds. SILVERMAN, S., 3rd Bn.
- 3084809 Pte. SUNDERLAND, J., Inf.
- 276972 Pte. SHIRLEY, H., 15th Res. Bn.
- 259191 Pte. SILVERMAN, H., 15th Res. Bn.
- 163444 Cpl. SAPLEY, J., 75th Bn.
- 2265959 Spr. SLONEMSKY, J.,* Engineers.
- 685094 Pte. SILVERMAN, H., 13th Bn.
- 2392 S/S/M. SIMMONS, M., C.A.M.C.
- 1013192 Pte. SIMON, A., Can. For. Corps.
- 42297 Dvr. SOMROE, H., C.F.A.
- 1043213 Pte. SILVERMAN, J., Inf.
- 1251757 Pte. SILVER, H. B., C.R.A.
- 2265896 Pte. SHERMAN, H., Inf.
- 3104632 Pte. STEINMANN, J., Inf.
- 5206 Pte. SOFFER, S., 1st Field Coy.
- 4077 Pte. SCHULMAN, J., 2nd Art. Bde.
- 2765342 Pte. STARFIELD, S., 1st Can. Tank Bn.
- 3080073 Pte. SOLNICK, M., 72nd Bn.
- 1013192 Pte. SIMON, A., For. Corps.
- Pte. SCHNEIDER, A., 10th Bn.
- 5956 L/Cpl. SHAFSTEIN, B. A., 3rd Bn.
- 3231967 Gnr. SIMONSKY, C., Canadians.
- 338452 Dvd. SEGLE, J., Res. Artillery.
- 2327626 Gnr. SAMUELS, H., C.R.A.
- 3036617 Pte. STALBERG, S., C.F.C.
- Pte. SIMPSON, J., 14th Can. Div.
- 341655 Gnr. SOLOMON, W. L., Res. Artillery.
- 308603 Dvr. SACKER, L., 61st C.L.C.
- 106038 Pte. SABER, G.
- 46892 Pte. SLAZEN, L.
- 163699 Pte. SNIDER, L., 36th Bn.
- 41372 Sgt. SUVERTY, H., 2nd Bn.
- 467163 Pte. SINGER, D., 29th Bn.
- Cadet SINGER, M., C.A.F.
- Cadet SINGER, B., C.A.F.
- Cadet SCHEVMMER, D., C.A.F.
- Pte. SHAPIRO, J. N., Inf.
- Cadet SIMON, C.A.F.
- Gnr. SLOVES, N., R.C.H.A.
- Gnr. SLOVES, M., R.C.H.A.
- Pte. STANKIEWITZ, S. (D.C.M.), Inf.
- Pte. SHEFLER, H., Mech. R.A.F.
- Pte. STRULOVITCH, 1st Bn.
- Pte. SPELLMAN, R., Inf.
- Cpl. SISSENWAIN, L.,* Inf.
- Pte. SONHEIM, L., Inf.
- 2537400 Pte. STERN, J., P.P.C.L.I.
- 3036615 Pte. SCHWATZ, C.
- 3233461 Pte. SULKES, B.
- 514573 Pte. SPITZEL, M.
- Pte. SOLOMON, M.
- 2488594 Pte. SIEGEL, S. R., Ry. Con. Depôt.
- 4070544 Pte. SCHILLER, S. F., Ry. Con. Depôt.
- 171376 Pte. SHVATS, V., 83rd Bn.
- 201691 Cpl. SHERMAN, C. L., 95th Bn.
- 766703 Pte. SILAMS, P., 123rd Bn.
- 669761 Pte. SAPERIA, L., 166th Bn.
- Pte. STONE, M., 169th Bn.
- 3301828 Pte. SYMONS, L., C.C.O.R.
- 238071 Pte. STORK, L., C.A.M.C.
- 3031959 Pte. SPEILMAN, R., 1st C.O.R.
- 3232279 Pte. SAMPSON, R., 1st C.O.R.
- 338452 Pte. SEGAL, A.
- 3232687 Pte. SANDER, G., 1st C.O.R.
- 3232685 Pte. SANES, L., 1st C.O.R.
- 3231967 Pte. SIMONSNY, C., 67th Battery.
- 3232646 Pte. SNITMAN, R., 1st C.O.R.
- 2606872 Pte. SETZER, S., C.A.M.C.
- 3035883 Pte. STARASHIFSKY, N., 1st C.O.R.
- 3036125 Pte. SMITH, H., 1st Bn.
- 273829 Pte. SALTMAN, L., S.S. Coy.
- 3036603 Pte. SCHAFFER, A.
- 3036744 Pte. SOREN, R., 1st Bn.
- 1051438 Pte. STEINBERG, M., C.A.F.
- 358185 Pte. SONAND, J., 7th C.F.A.
- M1/6684 Pte. SOLOMON, C., Can. Corps, Sge. Pk
- 4327626 Pte. SAMUELS, H.

Canadian Division.—*Continued.*

341655	Dvr.	Solomons, W. L.
	Bomb.	Sniders, E.
2500476	Spr.	Simms, J. B.
3081879	Pte.	Silverman, C., 2nd C.C.D.
2567308	Cpl.	Seidleitz, E., 20th Res. Bn.
2246045	Pte.	Stone, S., C.F.C.
1105213	Pte.	Skorina, W., 23rd Res. Bn.
928946	Pte.	Schechter, 25th Res. Bn.
3233461	Pte.	Sulkey, J., 3rd Res. Bn.
2304472	Pte.	Seigal, D. J., 8th Res. Bn.
345192	Gur.	Slores, M., Res. Artillery.
3031769	Pte.	Sherman, P., 12th Res. Bn.
339776	Gnr.	Smee, W. H., C.R.A.
2075649	Pte.	Sakalove, E., 20th Res. Bn.
3031959	Pte.	Spellman, R., 12th Res. Bn.
3031408	Pte.	Sher, A., 12th Res. Bn.
4070554	A/Cpl.	Schiller, L. F., C.F.C.
525392	Pte.	Steiner, W., C.F.C.
2356044	Pte.	Segal, N., 4th Res. Bn.
527046	Pte.	Sprung, A., C.A.M.C.
2356066	Pte.	Steenberg, H., W.O.R.D.
345065	Gnr.	Staller, W., Res. Artillery.
2233331	Pte.	Silchen, S., 15th Res. Bn.
542330	Pte.	Sampson, M., 5th Div.
2498059	Pte.	Silburn, 3rd Res. Bn.
	Sgt.	Samuels, A., C.A.M.C.
	Pte.	Schwartz, H., C.F.A.
	Gnr.	Shears, J., C.F.A.
	Pte.	Solomans, S., 1st Bn.
	Pte.	Suswein, G., 5th Bn.
3039632	Tpr.	Smith, A., L. Strath. Horse.
3232213	Cpl.	Soloman, H., Inf.
	Pte.	Sloman, H., Inf.
	Pte.	Soloman, A., C.A.M.C.
	Pte.	Solberg, A., Inf.
	Pte.	Schloss, L., Inf.
	Pte.	Segalowitz, H.
	Pte.	Shymansky, L., Inf.
	Cpl.	Sadasky, S., (D.C.M.), Inf.
	Pte.	Suckin, H., Inf.
	Gnr.	Slobes, M.
	Pte.	Schwartz, P.
	Q.M.S.	Soloman, P., 14th Bn.
	Sgt.	Soloman, H., 4th Bn.
	Pte.	Silver, L., Inf.
	Pte.	Samuels, E.
104297	Pte.	Silver, S.
491617	Pte.	Silverman, M.
2378872	Pte.	Sabbut. M.
3032326	Pte.	Stern, D.
2024286	Pte.	Stockinsky, M.
60001	Pte.	Tuckman. E., 21st Bn
439582	Pte	Taylor, S. A., 52nd Bn.
313976	Dvr.	Tarshiss, A., 3rd Can. D. A. C.
T4/084984	Dvr.	Tebbitt, M.. 4th Res. Padk.
257838	Dvr.	Turner, I. M., 10th Bn. C.R.T.
3030132	Dvr.	Travis, C., 12th C.R.T.
1036146	Pte.	Tuckman, B., 14th Coy. For. Cps.
3033202	Spr.	Tenenbaum, A., 8th Bn. Rail. Tps.
50100	Pte.	Tazuk, H.
3085227	Pte.	Taylor, B.. Can. Div.
803997	L/Cpl.	Tobias, R. R. (M.M.).
513508	Pte.	Thompson, C. H., C.A.S.C.
3186062	Pte.	Tudesh, M., Inf.
910090	A/Sgt.	Tobias, H. N.
3233111	Pte.	Tattlebaum, N., 12th Res. Bn.
2250890	Pte.	Toplitsky, B., C.F.C.
336978	Pte.	Therscovitch, M. H., 52nd Bn.
707336	Pte.	Truman, H., 54th Bn.
	Cpl.	Tobias, S., 1st Bn.
	Gnr.	Tivian, C.F.A.
	Cpl.	Taylor, D., C.F.A.
	Pte.	Taylor, H., Inf.
919830	Pte.	Tolinchinlinsky, L., 199th Bn.
506376	Pte.	Thiskin, J., Inf.
	Pte.	Tiptisky, A.
	Cpl.	Taylor, P., 52nd Bn.
	Gnr.	Takefman, M., C.F.A.
42215	Pte.	Trough, S., 1st Can. Artillery.
3036762	Pte.	Thomas, A., 1st C.O.R.
3232422	Pte.	Tawzer, F., 1st C.O.R.
	Cpl.	Ullman, G. D. (M.M.), H.Q.
486282	Pte.	Van Raalte, P., 3rd Div. Sup. Cl.
432016	Pte.	Viner, D.,* 49th Bn.
348605	Gnr.	Vander Hout, J., 45th By. 9th B.
154552	Gnr.	Velinski, I., 337th Sge. Bey ,
3084047	Pte.	Vliman, B., 23rd Res. Bn.
264180	Pte.	Vengene, M., 2nd Can. Eng.
249	Pte.	Vanse, R. E., 48th Can.
1030632	Pte.	Valins, S.,* 13th Bn.
2522552	Gnr.	Vernon, P., C.F.A.
258301	Pte.	Verne, A., Inf.
919557	Pte.	Vanden Berg, A.
473258	Pte.	Viminsky, V., 12th Res. Bn.
	Cpl.	Vosberg, I.
	Cad.	Vineberg, L., C.A.F.
	Cad.	Vineberg. S., P.P.C.L.I.
	Pte.	Vineberg, G.
	A.M.	Vineberg, S., C.A.F.
	Pte.	Voegler, L. G., 97th Bn.
442831	Pte.	Williams, J.,* 2nd Bn.
66029	Pte.	Weinberg, S., 24th Bn.
432550	Pte.	White, H. I., 44th Bn.
22696	Pte.	Waters, C. F., 8th Bn.
110571	Pte.	Wiseman, F., 5th C.M.R.
86050	L/Cpl.	Weber, L., 5th C.F.A.
500598	Spr.	Woolf, H., 2nd Div. Eng.
428574	Pte.	Weissman, M., 7th Bn.
81928	Pte.	Waters, C., 8th Bn.
410668	Pte.	Wisburg, M., 38th Bn.
41711	Q.M.S.	Whitebone, E. A., 2nd C.F.A.
389498	Pte.	Walkoff, A. H., 10th Bn.
184124	Pte.	Wiseman, A., 1st Div. Emp. Coy.
264261	Pnr.	Wedlanski, J., 2nd Pioneer Bn.
862775	Pte.	Wineberg, S., 123rd Pioneer Bn.

Canadian Division.—*Continued.*

144516	Pte.	WEINTROP, J., 72nd Bn.
10095	Pte.	WESSEL, S., 8th Bn.
121440	Pte.	WEINER, C., 24th Bn.
681550	Pte.	WILKES, M., 75th Bn.
300670	Pte.	WOOD, L., M.G. Squad.
1039936	Pte.	WILSON, S., 10th Bn. C.R.T.
3033872	Pte.	WISOTSKY, B., 6th Bn. C.R.T.
3230199	Pte.	WOODROW, A.,* 4th Bn.
225701	Pte.	WHITTIER, M., C.A.M.C.
919443	Pte	WHITMAN, E., 14th Bn.
89964	Pte.	WOLFE, D., 27th Bty.
34179	Pte.	WAXMAN, M., C.A.M.C.
3036962	Pte.	WEBER, B., Can. Div.
3038553	Pte.	WERNSTEIN, H., Can. Div.
3034820	Spr.	WOLFE, B., Can. Div.
3040054	Pte.	WOLFSON, H., 3rd Bn.
C/1304	Gnr.	WOLFSON, M., C.H.M.A.
3033501	Pte.	WEISS, J., Inf.
2327508	Gnr.	WALTERS, H. L., C.F.A.
2014214	Pte.	WANDLESON, H. A., Inf.
3232686	Pte.	WEINER, S., Inf.
325	Pte.	WALTERS, C., 8th Bn.
34179	Pte.	WATMAN, H., Can. A.M.C.
348943	Gnr.	WOOLF, B.* (GORDON), 2nd Art. B.
3131503	Spr.	WINEBERG. B.
3083306	Spr.	WISEGLAT, H.
166729	Pte.	WINSTON, D.
678713	Pte.	WYMAN, A., C.F.C.
400518	Pte.	WOLFOVITZ, 10th Res. Bn.
341408	Sig.	WYNANTS, A. H., Res. Artillery..
121397	Pte.	WEIDER, A., 25th Res. Bn.
3233003	Pte.	WARREN, P. J., 12th Res. Bn.
171713	Pte.	WOLFE, J., 3rd Bn.
1078494	Pte.	WOYSCHOLSKY, 5th Ban. Pioneers.
25780	L/Cpl.	WILLIAMS, M., 23rd Bn.
7741	Dvr.	WEINGOTT, B.
645434	Pte.	WINEBERG, E., 1st Bn.
2265391	Pte.	WEINSTEIN, C., P.P.C.L.I.
	Spr.	WEISBLATT, H., Can. Rly. Tps.
	Sgt.	WAGNER, R.
	Pte.	WEINBERG, D.
	Pte.	WAXMAN, L., C.A.M.C.
	Pte.	WARNER, S., P.P.C.L.I.
	Pte.	WILLIAMS, N., 14th Bn.
	Pte.	WHITEMAN, H., 199th Bn.
1783	Sgt.	WARTMAN, A. E.* (D.C.M.), C.A.M.C.
	Pte.	WOLSTEIN, L. B., Inf.
887364	Pte.	WORTON, A., 46th Bn.
41	Pte.	WENSTONE.
722247	Pte.	WALLOCK, M.
669458	Cpl.	WINEBERG, M.
678440	Pte.	WOBOTH, M., 169th Bn.
3106034	Pte.	WARSALL, M.
3035979	Pte.	WOLFISH, P.
2499637	Sgt.	WEITZ, W., Ry. Con. Depôt.
3233003	Pte.	WARREN, B.
	Pte.	WILLIAMS, S.
3036956	Pte.	WINEGARTEN, L.
207762	Cpl.	WHITE, W.
208037	Pte.	WHITE, J.
461378	Pte.	WASKEY, S.,* 44th Bn.
888273	Pte.	YAMRON, W., 72nd Coy. For. Cps.
474297	Pte.	YUDELSON, H., 46th Can. Inf.
225462	Pte.	YAFFO, M. W., 8th Res. Bn.
478858	Pte.	YANKOSKY, S., 20th Coy.
	Pte.	YOELL, E., Inf.
	Pte.	YEOLL, J., C.A.S.C.
	Pte.	YEOLL, N., Inf.
	Bugler	YEOLL, A., 14th Bn.
273994	Pte.	YECO, G.
766746	Pte.	ZARETINI, A., 123rd Pioneer Bn.
80824	Pte.	ZUIDEMAN, S., 10th Bn.
684707	Pte.	ZARGSKY, P., 60th Coy. For. Cps.
3230208	Pte.	ZASINON, H., Inf.
20924	Cpl.	ZUIDEMA, L. (M.M.), Inf.
294937	Spr.	ZURICH, S., 1st C.E.
742075	Pte.	ZACHAYASH, L., 13th Res. Bn.
829480	Pte.	ZEUTNER, P., 18th C.R. Bn.
42215	Pte.	ZOETOFF, N., Can. F.A.
	Pte.	ZALUDSKI, Inf.
	Pte.	ZEBEN, A., Inf.
	Pte.	ZWEIBEL, J.
2333111	Pte.	ZATELBAUM, M., Inf.
329480	Pte.	ZENTER, P.
3231909	Pte.	ZARETSKY, D.
	Pte.	ZILKA, A., 123rd Bn.
270158	Pte.	ZELINSKY, A.,* Inf.

* Killed in Action or died on Active Service.

FROM JAMAICA, BRITISH WEST INDIES.*

OFFICERS.

Lieut. Col. V. LESLIE DE CORDOVA, King's Own Royal Lancs. Regt. M.C. and Croix de Guerre with Palm Leaf.

Capt. LESLIE ROY MORDECAI, 2/5th Lancashire Fusiliers. Mentioned in Despatches.

Capt. Dr. ALFRED ERROL DELGADO, R.A.M.C. Mentioned in Despatches.

Capt. ROBERT KARL NUNES, British West Indian Regt., and R.A.F.

Lieut. ERIC M. ABENDANA, Canadian Divisional Engineers. Died on Active Service.

Cadet COLIN MELHADO, Canadian A.F.

Capt. THADDEUS R. GIDEON, 6th Lincolnshire Regiment.

Major CYRIL S. GIDEON, R.A.M.C.

Lieut. VERNON RIENZI ANDRADE, 1st Brit. West India Regt., and 39th Royal Fusiliers.

* Compiled by Mr. J. A. P. M. Andrade, Spanish Town, Jamaica.

Jamaica, British West Indies—*Continued.*

2nd Lieut. CARYL FRED JACOBS, British West India Regiment.
Lieut. ARTHUR DE SOUZA JACOBS, British West India Regiment.
2nd Lieut. OWEN S. MELHADO, 11th Yorkshire Regiment. Died on Active Service.
Lieut. DONALD MELHADO, R.H.A. and R.A.F.
Sub-Lieut. ALLAN MELHADO, R.N.A.S.
Capt. VERNON K. MELHADO, 11th British West India Regiment.
Capt. CLIFFORD MELHADO, 2/10th London Regt. and 38th Royal Fusiliers.
Lieut. MICHAEL DE CORDOVA, R.A.S.C.
Capt. LIONEL LAUNCELOT TENNYSON DE CORDOVA, British West India Regiment.
2nd Lieut. DICK DE CORDOVA, British West India Regiment.
Lieut. LOUIS VICTOR COHEN HENRIQUES, 4th British West India Regiment.
Capt. ROBERT CLINTON DE PASS, British West India Regiment.
2nd Lieut. CARYL DANECOURT DE PASS, British West Indian Regiment.
2nd Lieut. EDWARD LESLIE LYONS, Canadian Engineers.
2nd Lieut. GEO. H. ERRINGTON LYON, British West India Regiment.
Lieut. AUBREY H. SPYER, 3rd British West India Regiment.
2nd Lieut. BRIAN LLOYD BRANDON, British West India Regiment and 7th Cheshire Regt. Killed in action in France.
2nd Lieut. ANDREW EARLE DE LISSER, British West India Regiment.
Lieut. L. G. SILVERA, British West India Regt. Died in France.
Lieut. HAROLD KARL SAMUEL, British West India Regiment.
2nd Lieut. KENNETH CORINALDI LEVY, British West India Regiment.
2nd Lieut. FRANK DE MERCADO, British West India Regiment.
2nd Lieut. GORDON STUART LINDO, British West India Regiment.
2nd Lieut. LEANDER LEVY, British West India Regiment.
2nd Lieut. GUY DE CORDOVA, British West India Regiment.
JOSHUA DE CORDOVA, Esq., Volunteer British Motor Transport.
2nd Lieut. KENNETH V. ABENDANA, British West India Regiment.
2nd Lieut. ALAN V. LYONS, British West India Regiment.

N.C.O.'s AND MEN.

Sgt. ALLAN SAMPSON, British West India Regt. Died in France.
Q.M.S. FREDERICK NORCOTT SALMON, British West India Regt. and A.S.C.
Corpl. GEORGE DIGBY DAVID DE PASS, British West India Regiment.
Pte. ALAN BARROW, 142nd F.A. and R.A.S.C. M.M. and Belgian Croix de Guerre.
Bdr. LESTER JACOBS, Royal Field Artillery.
Pte. ERROL COHEN HENRIQUES, British West India Regiment.
Pte. HERBERT IVAN SAMUEL, British West India Regiment.
Sgt. VINCENT CORINALDI LEVY, 10th King's Royal Rifle Corps.
Pte. LIONEL O. CORINALDI, Middlesex Regt.
LESLIE DE LA PENDA, Royal Air Force.

Decorations (in addition to those already mentioned).
Mrs. MICHAEL DE CORDOVA, M.B.E.
ALTAMONT E. DE COSTA, Esq., J.P., M.B.E.

BOMBAY JEWS.

Hon. Maj. DAVID JUDAH, M.D.(Lon.), I.M.S.
Capt. AARON JOSEPH, M.B.B.S. (Bom.), I.M.S. I.M.S.
Capt. JACOB EZEKIEL, L.M. & S. (Bom.), I.M.S. I.M.S.
Capt. J. C. SAMSON, L.M. & S. (Bom.), I.M.S. I.M.S.
Capt. MOSES SOLOMON, L.M. & S. (Bom.), I.M.S. I.M.S.
Capt. NATHAN ELIJAH, L.M. & S. (Bom.), I.M.S. I.M.S.
Sub. Asst. Surg. BENJAMIN, DAVID, I.S.M.D.
Sub. Asst. Surg. BENJAMIN REUBEN, I.S.M.D.
Lieut. ROLFE E. SHALOM, Post and Tel.
Sub. Asst. Surg. ELIJAH ABRAHAM, I.S.M.D.
Sub. Asst. Surg. ARON EZEKIEL, I.S.M.D.
Sgt. S. D. MOSS, Military Accountants.
Sgt. J. SAMSON, Military Accountants.
Sgt. DAVID MORDECAI, Military Accountants.
Sgt. JOHN ABRAHAM, 19th Field Vet. Sec.
Sgt. S. SIMPSON, Military Accountants.
Sgt. ABRAHAM JACOB, Military Accountants.
Sgt. D. J. DANIEL, Military Accountants.
Sgt. M. D. DAVID, Military Accountants.
Sgt. M. SAMUEL, Military Accountants.
Sgt. M. D. DAVID, S. & T.C.
Sgt. ARON ABRAHAM, R.E.
Pte. SAMUEL DANIEL, R.E.
Pte. ARON SAMSON, R.E.
Sgt. ABRAHAM JACOB, Post and Tel.
Elec. Eng. DAVID E. JACOBS, Troop Tpt. S.S. "Ellenga."
3rd Eng. S. BENJAMIN, S.S. "Tayabi."

Bombay Jews—*Continued.*
INDIAN DEFENCE CORPS.

Sgt. W. G. R. ALFREY, Bombay Bn.
Sgt. M. DAVID, Bombay Bn.
Sgt. J. N. REUBEN, Bombay Bn.
Cpl. E. MOSES (Bugler), Bombay Bn.
Cpl. M. S. HIBBA, Bombay Bn.
L/Cpl. E. SOMEK, Bombay Bn.
L/Cpl. M. DAVID, Bombay Bn.
Pte. E. A. F. NISSIM, Bombay Bn.
Pte. M. B. DANIEL, Bombay Bn.
Pte. R. E. BROOKS, Bombay Bn.
Pte. S. DAVID, Bombay Bn.
Pte. S. DAVID, Bombay Bn.
Pte. E. S. EZEKIEL, Bombay Bn.
Pte. A. GEMAL, Bombay Bn.
Pte. H. F. ABRAHAM, Bombay Bn.
Pte. A. M. JACOB, Bombay Bn.
Pte. S. SAMSON, (Bugler).
Pte. E. ABRAHAM, Bombay Bn.
Pte. J. COHEN, Bombay Bn.
Pte. B. JOSEPHS, Bombay Bn.
Pte. F. MYERS, Bombay Bn.
Pte. E. GINDELL, Bombay Bn.
Pte. J. BENJAMIN, Bombay Bn.
Pte. S. DAVID, Bombay Bn.
Pte. M. A. SAMUEL, Bombay Bn.
Pte. E. BENJAMIN, Bombay Bn.
Pte. J. DAVID, Bombay Bn.
Pte. D. ISAAC, Bombay Bn.
Pte. E. JACOB, Bombay Bn.
Pte. I. JUDAH, Bombay Bn.
Pte. M. SAMSON, Bombay Bn.
Pte. N. SAMSON, Bombay Bn.
Pte. M. ABRAHAMS, Bombay Bn.
Pte. H. HERCH, Bombay Bn.
Pte. H. J. SYKES, Bombay Bn.
Pte. MEYER NISSIM, Bombay Bn.
Pte. E. BENJAMIN, Bombay Bn.
Pte. J. J. CASSIER, Bombay Bn.
Pte. ROBERT NAGAVKAR, Bangalore Rifles. (Died on Active Service.)
Pte. JOHN S. REUBEN, Bangalore Rifles.
Pte. S. B. PAYNE, G.I.P. Ry. Bn.
Pte. B. HYAMS, G.I.P. Ry. Bn.
Pte. A. SIMEON, B.B. and C.I. Ry. Bn.
Pte. M. B. SAMUEL, B.B. and C.I. Ry. Bn.
Pte. S. I. BENJAMIN, B.B. and C.I. Ry. Bn.
Cpl. NATHAN AARON, Poona Rifles.
Cpl. E. R. SAMSON, Poona Rifles.
Pte. M. S. JHIRAD, Poona Rifles.
Pte. I. R. SAMSON, Poona Rifles.
Pte. J. S. SAMSON, Poona Rifles.
Pte. ISAAC MORDECCAI, Poona Rifles.
L/Cpl. A. SAMSON, Poona Rifles.
Pte. B. A. AARON, Poona Rifles.
Pte. M. EZEKIEL, Poona Rifles.
Bdr. A. NISSIM, Bombay Gn. Arty.
Gnr. A. RAYMOND, Bombay Gn. Arty.
Gnr. B. D. BENJAMIN, Bombay Gn. Arty.
Gnr. WARHIDE, Bombay Gn. Arty.
Gnr. N. MATHALONE (Signaller), Bombay Gn. A.
Gnr. M. MATHALONE, Bombay Gn. Arty.
Gnr. S. JUDAH, Bombay Gn. Arty.
Gnr. SHELLIM S. D. CORLEY, Bombay Gn. Arty
Gnr. A. CHICK, Bombay Gn. Arty.
Tpr. J. RAYMOND, Bombay Light Horse.
Pte. E. BENJAMIN, Electrical Eng. Coy.
Pte. I. BENJAMIN, Electrical Eng. Coy.
Sgt. M. DANIEL, Sindh Bn.
Cpl. R. A. BENJAMIN, Sindh Bn.
Cpl. D. DANIEL, Sindh Bn.
Cpl. M. SOLOMON, Sindh Bn.
Cpl. M. SOLOMON, Sindh Bn.
Pte. A. G. ISAAC, Sindh Bn.
Pte. Z. JACOB, Sindh Bn.
Pte. I. JACOB, Sindh Bn.
Pte. G. GERSHOME, Sindh Bn.
Pte. S. S. JACOB, Sindh Bn.
Pte. A. D. SOLOMON, Sindh Bn.
Pte. S. D. SOLOMON, Sindh Bn.
Pte. S. ISAAC, Sindh Bn.
Pte. J. SAMSON, Sindh Bn.
Pte. I. AARON, Sindh Bn.
Pte. S. JACOB, Sindh Bn.

ST. JOHN AMBULANCE BRIGADE, BOMBAY.
(Jewish Division.)

Amb. Officer S. E. BAKER.
Amb. Officer M. E. SOLOMON.
Sgt. SAMUEL JUDAH.
Sgt. A. AARON.
Cpl. I. SHALOM.
Cpl. J. EZEKIEL.
Cpl. M. JOSEPH.
L/Cpl. B. S. BENJAMIN.
L/Cpl. H. S. ISAAC.
Pte. P. I. REUBEN.
Pte. MOSES JACOB.
Pte. ISAAC DANIEL.
Pte. D. ABRAHAM.
Pte. S. S. BENJAMIN.
Pte. A. DANIEL.
Pte. R. RAHAMIN.
Pte. R. REUBEN.
Pte. D. BENJAMIN.
Pte. A. BENJAMIN.
Pte. EZEKIEL MOSES.
Pte. A. E. SOLOMON.
Pte. D. A. SAMUEL.
Pte. M. A. MOSES.
Pte. SOLOMON JUDAH.

Bombay Jews—Continued.

Pte. J. David.
Pte. S. I. Reuben.
Pte. Sasoon Benjamin.
Pte. D. I. Taylor.
Pte. S. D. Ezekiel.
Pte. J. B. Aaron, B.A.
Pte. E. Sampson.
Pte. Abraham Daniel.
Pte. Moses Elijah.
Pte. B. M. Benjamin.
Pte. A. Eliajah.
Pte. David Rahamin.
Pte. Isaac Samuel.
Pte. Joseph Howard Mizrahi.
Pte. Benjamin Joseph.

[For additional names of Officers and Men in Indian Army *see* Various Units.]

VARIOUS UNITS.*

2nd Lieut. Aaron, S., Assist. Surgeon, I.M.S.
2nd Lieut. Aaron, E., I.M.S.
Lieut. Abrahams, A., Gen. List.
Surgeon Aaron, R., Indian Army.
Nurse Albury, G. R., 7th Gen. Hospital.
Nurse Angel, R., 30th C.C.S.
Lieut. Attwell, H., General List.
Miss Alvarez, Rachael, V.A.D.
Mrs. Abrahams, R.R.C.
Staff Sister Ashberry (Annenberg), Q.A.N.S.
Nurse Aschman, South African Medical Corps.
Miss Alvarez, Betty, V.A.D.
Mrs. Altman, O. O., V.A.D.
2nd Lieut. Brilliant, L., Indian Army.
Capt. Barnett, F., Adjt. Nat. Reserve.
Lieut. Bronker, E. A., Indian Med. Dept.
Major Barnett, E. S., National Reserve.
2nd Lieut. Brayham, E. F., I.A.R.O.
2nd Lieut. Breckman, S., General List.
Miss Baker, Clara, W.A.A.C.
Sister Baker, Bessie.
Mrs. Bolton, Madge, V.A.D.
Miss Bamberger, Muriel, V.A.D.
Miss Borgzinner, V.A.D.
Miss de Bear, V.A.D.
Mrs. Barnett, Arthur, V.A.D.
Lieut. Cohen, L., 36th Div. Gas Officer.
2nd Lieut. Cohen, H. G., Intelligence Corps.
2nd Lieut. Collings, J. S., Intelligence Corps.
2nd Lieut. Carlish, E., Mob. Sub. Centre.
Capt. Courtland, J., Indian Army.
Capt. Cohen, T. M., A.S.C., Indian Army.
Miss Cohen, Esther, V.A.D.
Mrs. Colman, V.A.D.

Mrs. Cohen, V.A.D.
2nd Lieut. Davis, A. D. S.
Major Davidson, F., 104th Bn., Indian Army.
Major Daniel, A., 104th Bn., Indian Army.
Major Daniel, M., 104th Bn., Indian Army.
Nurse Davis, J., V.A.D., Brit. Red Cross Soc.
Miss Davis, E., V.A.D.
Mrs. Davidson, M.B.E.
Lieut Flatau, A., Army Audit Dept.
Lieut. Freedman, L., Appeal Military Rep.
Sister Eskell, L., 2nd A.I.M.N.S.R.
Nurse Echenberg, R.
Miss Franks, Queenie (Mrs. J. W. Myers), Red Cross Motor Transport.
Miss Franks, Rosie (Mrs. B. Alvarez), V.A.D.
Nursing Sister Froomberg, South African Med. Corps.
2nd Lieut. Grave, J. 5., Special List.
Capt. Goldberg, M., Staff H.Q.
2nd Lieut. Green, A. M., Bombay Artillery.
Miss Greisbach, V.A.D.
Lieut. Holt, H., Claims Office.
2nd Lieut. Henriques, C. G., I.A.R.O.
Nurse Hartman, E.,* V.A.D.
Miss Halford, Hilda, Red Cross.
Miss Harris, Hetty, V.A.D.
Mrs. Hess, Frances, V.A.D.
Miss Hudson, Kitty, V.A.D.
Miss Hess, Minnie, V.A.D.
Miss Hirschland, Doris, V.A.D.
Miss Harris, V.A.D.
Miss Henry, V.A.D.
Capt. Instone, A., Intelligence Corps.
2nd Lieut. Isaac, H., Nat. Reserve.
Miss Isaacs, V.A.D.
Capt. Joseph, M., Indian Army
Lieut. Joseph, A. F., 59th Rifles, Indian Army.
Lieut. Joseph, A., I.A.M.C.
Lieut. Joseph, B., General List.
Capt. Joseph, V., General List.
Lieut. Joseph, F. A., Volunteer Force.
Mrs. Jonas, I. M., V.A.D.
Miss Joseph, V.A.D.
Miss Joseph, Janie, O.B.E., Commandant, Tudor House Hospital.
Nurse Kreemer, R.
Miss Kopenhagen, V.A.D.
Miss Kerman, V.A.D.
Sister Levy, P., 2nd A.I.M.N.S.R.
Lieut Levinson, H., Indian Army.
Sister Levy, D. E., Q.A.I.M.N.S.
Sister Levy, P., V.A.D., 72nd Gen. Hosp.
Capt. Lazarus, J. G., Rand Intelligence Corps
Nurse Levy, D., 24th General Hospital.
Miss Langer, E. S., V.A.D.
Lieut. Lawrence, F. J., P.O.W. Coy.
Miss Lyons, Rosey, V.A.D.
Mrs. Lyons, Julia, V.A.D.

* Including Nurses, Officer Cadet Battalions, Prisoner of War Companies, Indian Army, Military Police, etc.

Various Units—*Continued.*

Miss LUDLOW, AUGUSTA, V.A.D.
Mrs. LONDON, CARRIE, V.A.D.
Mrs. LEVY, V.A.D.
Miss LAZARUS, L., V.A.D.
Miss LAZARUS, H., V.A.D.
Miss LAZARUS, M., V.A.D.
Mrs. LOWENTHAL, V.A.D.
Miss LIPMAN, V.A.D.
Miss LUBIN, V.A.D.
Lieut. MENDOZA, A. 1/7th Rajputs.
2nd Lieut. MOSES, G. O., Indian Army.
2nd Lieut. MYERS, R., Intelligence Officer.
Nurse MUNRO, E. H.,* V.A.D.
Mrs. MARKS, S. JULIAN, British Red Cross.
Miss MAGNUS, KATE, V.A.D.
Mrs. MARX, MAY, V.A.D.
Miss MARKS, A., V.A.D.
Miss MARCS, G., V.A.D.
Mrs. MARSDEN, R.R.C.
Miss MENDEL, V.A.D.
Miss MIDDLETON, V.A.D.
Lieut. NATHAN, G.
Lieut. NISSIM, Indian Army.
2nd Lieut. NATHAN, S. L., 11th Rajputs.
Miss NAHON, JAMILLA, V.A.D.
Miss NATHAN, JEANETTE, V.A.D.
Sister OPPENHEIMER, FLORENCE (Mrs. L. J. Greenberg).
Nursing Sister PIZA, Miss F., No. 1 Red Cross.
Lady PRINCE, V.A.D.
Miss PINTO, SOPHIE, V.A.D.
Miss PINTO, ROSIE, Canteen Worker.
Mrs. PHILLIPS, ROSA, V.A.D.
Mrs. PLATNAUER, ROSE, V.A.D.
Mrs. PHILLIPS, BERTHA, V.A.D.
Lieut. RIFKIN, A. W., Officers' Cadet Unit.
Sister ROSENTHAL, Q.A.N.S.
Cadet REUBEN, E., Sind Vol. Rifles.
Surgeon REUBEN, B.,* Indian Med. Service.
2nd Lieut. ROSSI, R., P.O.W. Coy.
Miss ROE, NITA, V.A.D.
Miss ROSENSTEIN, IRENE, V.A.D.
Miss ROSE, ELLA, V.A.D.
Miss RAINS, ROSE, V.A.D.
Miss REGENSBURG, V.A.D.
Miss ROSENTHAL, V.A.D.
Miss RITCH, S., V.A.D.
Miss RITCH, V.A.D.
Mrs. ROBINSON, V.A.D.
Capt. SALMON, J., Army Staff, Aldershot.
Lieut. SAMUELS, A. D., H.Q. Staff.
Lieut. SAMSON, D., 110th Maharattas.
Lieut. SOFA, E., I.M.S.
Lieut. SOLOMON, J. M., W. Prov. Rifles.
Lieut. STIEBEL, C.,* Indian Med. Corps.
Miss SELBY, ROSE, V.A.D.

Mrs. SPEELMAN, VIOLET, V.A.D.
Miss SAMUELS, V.A.D.
Miss SALOM, V.A.D.
Mrs. STEMBER, V.A.D.
Mrs. SINGER, V.A.D.
Mrs. SIMMONS, V.A.D.
Miss SAMUELS, H., V.A.D.
2nd Lieut. TANBURN, W. L.,* Indian Army.
Sister TONKIN, A. (Mrs.), V.A.D.
Miss VAN GELDER, G., V.A.D.
Sister WOOLMAN, 26th Gen. Hosp.
Lieut. WALLROCK, S., National Reserve.
Capt. WOOLF, C. H., Nigerian Field Force.
Miss WEHL, GRACE F., V.A.D.
Miss WOOLF, KATE A., V.A.D.
Miss WOOLF, A. (Mrs. H. ISAAC), V.A.D.
Miss WOOLF, V.A.D.
Sister WEINER, S.

- 368 W.A.A.C. AARON, E., B.H.Q.
- Dvr. ARNOLD, R.A. Depot.
- Pte. ABRAHAMS, H., Censors Office.
- 419 Pte. AARONS, D., Rang. Vol. Rifles.
- Clerk ABRAHAMS, J., Indian Vety. Hospt.
- 183166 L/Cpl. ABRAHAMS, H. C., Intel. Office.
- 3598 L/Cpl. ABRAHAMS, E., M.F.P.
- 115355 Cadet ABRAHAMS, D., 24th O.C.B.
- 115356 Cadet ABRAHAMS, L. J., 24th O.C.B.
- 42038 Cadet ADLER, S., 17th O.C.B.
- 6676 Cadet ALEXANDER, M. T., 11th O.C.B.
- 21438 Pte. ABRAHAMS, S., 3rd O.C.B.
- 46137 Cadet ALTARAS, H., 17th O.C.B.
- 10140 Cadet ALEXANDER, H. B., O.T.C.
- 4586 Pte. ABRAHAMS, B., 2nd Bn.
- 10141 Pte. ALEXANDRIA, H. B., O.T.C.
- 2872 Sgt. ALEXANDER, J. A., Admin. H.Q.
- Pte. ATTIAS, M., Gibraltar Vol. Force.
- Pte. ATTIAS, I., Gibraltar Vol. Force.
- Pte. ACRIS, I., Gibraltar Vol. Force.
- Pte. ABEL, V., Fiji Defence Force.
- Pte. ABECASIS, L., Gibraltar Vol. Force.
- 676610 Pte. APPLEBAUM, H., 236th P.O.W. Coy.
- 57412 Cpl. ALEXANDER, J., 386th P.O.W. Coy.
- 143073 Pte. ABRAHAMS, A., 106th P.O.W. Coy.
- 676730 Pte. ASH, A. H., 281st P.O.W. Coy.
- 9 63733 Pte. ABRAMS, H., P.O.W. Coy.
- 677030 Pte. AARONS, A., 10th Bn., P.O.W. Coy.
- 267226 Pte. ABRAM, B., 88th P.O.W. Coy.
- 379319 Pte. BLACK, J., 3rd Army Inf. School.
- 379320 Pte. BERGSON, M., 3rd A. Inf. School.
- 130808 Pte. BERMAN, S., Div. Salvage Coy.
- 3498 Pte. BRESLER, J., 60th Dn. Band.
- 7407132 Pte. BARNETT, S., School of Cookery.
- 85611 Gnr. BROWN, I., R.A. Dept.
- S/Sgt. BERNSTEIN, 57th O.M. Wkshop.
- 13125 Pte. BIDES, H. E., O.T.C.
- 5919 Pte. BARNETT, J., E.F.C.
- Pte. BROOKS, A., 19th O.C. Bn.

Various Units—Continued.

P/13407	L/Cpl. BARNETT, H., M.F.P.
302202	Cadet BERNSTEIN, A., 19th O.C. Bn.
	S/Sgt. BLANKFIELD, H., 19th O.C. Bn.
1785	A/Sgt. BERG, L. N., A.G.S.
R/390808	Pte. BECKLER, S., 4th R.D.
1872	A/Sgt. BAROVITCH, W. A., A.G.S.
40004	Cadet BARWELL, H., 11th O.C. Bn.
204021	Cadet BLITZ, J., 11th O.C. Bn.
5929	L/Cpl. BROOKS, D., M.F.P.
P/9654	Pte. BAKER, T., M.F. Police.
	Cadet BLUMBERG, M., 1st O.T.C.
	Cadet BENSUSAN, A., Gibraltar Vol. Cps.
	Cadet BENJUNES, M. A., Gib. Vol. Cps.
	Cadet BELILO, M., Gibraltar Vol. Corps.
	Cadet BLOOM, B., Northern Borderers.
	Cadet BEUDAHON, S., Gib. Vol. Corps.
	Pte. BROCK, C., Plymouth Def. Corps.
	Pte. BHOUKAR, J. A., Indian A.V.C.
50573	Pte. BERLIN, J., 76th P.O.W. Coy.
39652	Pte. BERSON, M., 109th P.O.W. Coy.
676613	Pte. BARON, J., 236th P.O.W. Coy.
	L/Cpl. BARNARD, L. I., M.F.P.
78603	Sgt. BELL, H., 253rd P.O.W. Coy.
84615	Pte. BERMAN, H., 329th P.O.W. Coy.
240	Pte. BEIN, H., 130th P.O.W. Coy.
201078	Rfm. BENYON, M., P.O.W. Coy.
	Interp. BENGHIAT, J., P.O.W. Coy.
	BAKER, Miss C., W.A.A.C.
372287	Pte. BARNETT, S., 214th P.O.W. Coy.
82903	Cpl. BRESLAW, H., 389th P.O.W. Coy.
610820	Pte. BERGSON, A., 240th P.O.W. Coy.
676970	Pte. BERMAN, M., 283rd P.O.W. Coy.
676939	Pte. BOSMAN, L., 259th P.O.W. Coy.
556738	Pte. BURMAN, A., 180th P.O.W. Coy.
556723	Pte. BIAAK, O., 244th P.O.W. Coy.
432418	Pte. BOSSICK, S., 331st P.O.W. Coy.
192864	Pte. CHERNICK, J., Div. H.Q.
593	W.A.A.C. COHEN, R., D.A.P.S.
D/9254	Sgt. R. CASVENIR,* E.L.C.
	Pte. COLLINS, W., E.F.C. —
16903	Pte. CAPLAN, Brigade Office.
79425	Pte. CASSELL, C., Armed Motors.
718	Cpl. CARFUNKEL, J. A., Egypt Lab. Cps.
42824	Pte. CLYLOVITCH, J., 304 Rd. Const. Coy.
260031	Cpl. CARASSO, J., E.L.C.
901	Cadet COLEMAN, L. G., 21st O.C. Bn.
	Pte. COHEN, L. N., 19th O.C. Bn.
26424	Cadet COHEN, C., 11th O.C. Bn.
262483	Cadet CRAFF, H. 10th O.C. Bn.
	Cadet COHEN, A. M., 10th O.C. Bn.
10035	L/Cpl. COSTER, C., M.F.P.
725	L/Cpl. COMOR, M.,* Newfoundland Rgt.
90131	Pte. COHEN, W., 45th P.O.W. Coy.
1053	L/Cpl. CONRAD, P., 396th P.O.W. Coy.
34231	Pte. COHEN, I., 146th P.O.W. Coy.
202808	Pte. COHEN, A., P.O.W. Coy.
200155	Pte. COHEN, J., 81st P.O.W. Coy.
556693	Pte. COHEN, M., 285th P.O.W. Coy.
72343	Pte. CANTOR, 387th P.O.W. Coy.
346252	Pte. COHEN, J. G., 208th P.O.W. Coy.
375518	Pte. COOPER, I., 217th P.O.W. Coy.
535211	Pte. COHEN, J., 192nd P.O.W. Coy.
42251	Pte. COLEMAN, J., 257th P.O.W. Coy.
209056	Pte. COHEN, J., 309th P.O.W. Coy.
87067	Pte. COHEN, L., 259th P.O.W. Coy.
75704	A/L/Cpl. COHEN, C., P.O.W. Coy.
650632	Pte. COHEN, P., 306th P.O.W. Coy.
17334	Pte. COHEN, A., P.O.W. Coy.
	Pte. COHN, O., 147th P.O.W. Coy.
28846	L/Cpl. COWAN, B., 125th P.O.W. Coy.
617015	Bugl. CHAFNER, C., P.O.W. Coy.
5398	Sgt. DE SOLLA, A., 201st Cinema Depot
20141	Pte. DUBOFF, B.
	Pte. DE MEZA, J., Nyasaland Ft. Control.
	Cadet DAVIDS, B., 19th O.C. Bn.
	Pte. DAVIDS, A., 19th O.C. Bn.
	Cadet DRAPKIN, J. A., 19th O.C. Bn.
42929	Cadet DAVIS, H. R., 21st O.C. Bn.
228166	Cadet DAVIES, P. A., 24th O.C. Bn.
9798	Cadet DRUQUER, M. W., O.T.C.
C/225	Pte. DANIELS, B., Mob. Sub. Centre.
601888	Cpl. DOMBEY, F., 329th P.O.W. Coy.
91688	Pte. DAVIES, J., 389th P.O.W. Coy.
625097	Pte. DONNERSTEIN, A., 274th P.O.W. Co.
45106	Pte. DELACOVITCH, H., 314th P.O.W. Co.
	W.A.A.C. ELKIN, Miss. Ass./Adminis.
232725	Gnr. EPSTEIN, L., A/147th Bde.
273276	Pte. ELEPHANT, R., Corps H.Q.
17719	Cadet ENGLEMAN, A., 19th O.C. Bn.
218005	Cpl. ESENBERG, M., P.O.W. Coy.
73627	Pte. EDWARDS, S., 49th P.O.W. Coy.
58335	Pte. ENDELMAN, M., P.O.W. Coy.
474757	Pte. FIOR, L., 3rd Army S. of Cookery.
1412	Pte. FORD, J., E.F.C.
15291	L/Cpl. FRANKS, H., M.M.P.
54260	Pte. FINGARD, J. I.
11660	Pte. FLAXMAN, H., M.F.P.
239	Sgt. FELDMAN, D. M. H., Egypt Lab. C.
39163	Pte. FINESTONE, H. I., Corps. H.Q.
	Cadet FRANKEL, R. H., 21st O.C. Bn.
204732	Cadet FRAMPTON, M., 7th O.C. Bn.
10919	Cadet FISHER, L. G., 7th O.C. Bn.
181699	Cpl. FREEDMAN, S., 96th Chinese L.C.
2508	Pte. FREEMAN, W., 81st Prov. Bn.
1773	Pte. FRIEDBURG, F., 63rd Prov. Bn.
7474	Cadet FRIESNER, W., 14th O.C. Bn.
	Pte. FRANKLIN, H., 2nd Northern Regt.
	Cadet FRANKS, B., O.C. Bn.
38511	Rfm. FRANKS, I., 33rd Bn. P.O.W. Coy.
611429	Pte. FREEMAN, S., P.O.W. Coy.
618471	Pte. FREEDMAN, J., 237th P.O.W. Coy.
676936	Pte. FINKLESTEIN, J., 249th P.O.W. Coy.
522698	Pte. FILEK, A., 250th P.O.W. Coy.
654623	Pte. FIERSTEIN, J., 339th P.O.W. Coy.
27634	Pte. GOLDMAN, N., 33rd Div. H.Q.

Various Units—*Continued.*

19758 A/Cpl. GREEN, M., 20th Div. Wks. Bn.
379323 Pte. GORDON, L., 3rd Army Inf. School.
380213 C.Q.M.S. GOLDMAN, S., 59th D. School.
RL/660 Interp. GOLDSTEIN, M. J.
45240 GOLDBERG, R., Q.M.A.A.C.
47114 Pte. GLICK, A., 16th Officer Cadet Bn.
107492 Cadet GOLDSTEIN, A., 24th O.C. Bn.
Pte. GREEN, A., 19th O.C. Bn.
Cadet GREVILLE, W., 19th O.C. Bn.
811579 Pte. GALETZ, L., 21st Res. Bn.
46101 Cadet GROSSMAN, P., 15th O.C. Bn.
Cadet GOLDSMITH, D., 10th O.C.B.
682674 Cadet GOLDMAN, J., 17th O.C.B.
10054 Cadet GOLDWATER, H. G., O.T.C.
9745 Cadet GOURVITCH, L., O.T.C.
219697 Pte. GREIFER, B.
3746 Pte. GOLDSTEIN, D., Gen. H.Q.
27634 Pte. GOLDMAN, N., Div. H.Q.
2911 Pte. GOLD, J., 102nd Prov. Bn.
2570 Pte. GRAHAM, I., 63rd Prov. Bn.
108118 Pte. GINSBERG, H., Construction Bn.
9745 Bndsman. GOURVICH, L., O.T.C.
P/9902 L/Cpl. GOLDBERG, A., M.F.P.
P/8063 L/Cpl. GOLDBERG, J., M.F.P.
Pte. GOULDSTEIN, F. E., O.T.C.
L/Cpl. GARZON, S., Gibraltar Vol. Force.
20331 Pte. GREENFIELD, 1st P.O.W. Coy.
54307 L/Cpl. GOLDBERG, M., 211th P.O.W. C.
78775 A/Cpl. GOLDSTEIN, D., 253rd P.O.W. C.
578802 Pte. GREENFIELD, 1st P.O.W. Coy.
48960 Rfm. GOLINSKA, J., 375th P.O.W. Coy.
1348 Pte. GERSHON, L., 15th P.O.W. Coy.
620941 Rfm. GOLDBERG, J., 155th P.O.W. Coy.
53364 Cpl. GOLDBERG, A., 397th P.O.W. Coy.
192768 Cpl. GREENBERG, H., 342nd P.O.W. Co.
78779 Cpl. GROSSMAN, M., 261st P.O.W. Coy.
631655 Pte. GOLDBERG, A., 317th P.O.W. Coy.
676938 Pte. GOLDSTEIN, J., 259th P.O.W. Coy.
676940 Pte. GERSON, A., 259th P.O.W. Coy.
32328 Pte. GOLDMAN, F., 314th P.O.W. Coy.
608184 A/Cpl. GREEN, J., 30th P.O.W. Coy.
818 Pte. GORODISKY, H., P.O.W. Coy.
611925 Pte. GOLDSTEIN, A., 21st P.O.W. Coy.
261730 Pte. GROSSMAN, H., 87th P.O.W. Coy.
A/257121 Pte. HAMBURG, J., E.F.C.
S/255263 Pte. HARRIS, M., 23rd Field Bakery.
402 Cpl. HELON, J., E.L.C.
P/4592 L/Cpl. HYMAN, C. D., M.F.P.
Cadet HIRSCH, R. B., R.M.C.
134138 Pte. HARRIS, A., 20th O.C. Bn.
225855 Cadet HARRIS, A. J., 17th O.C. Bn.
Cadet HENRIQUES, L., 10th O.C. Bn.
Cadet HYMAN, E. H., 9th O.C. Bn.
M1/6385 L/Cpl. HARRISON, A., Mob. Sub. Cen.
236780 Pte. HIRSHMAN, S., Mob. Sub. Centre.
230438 Spr. HARTSTONE, A., O.T.C.
50940 Pte. HUFTEL, W., Corps School Staff.

2606 L/Cpl. HILL, L. J., 102nd Prov. Bn.
142628 Pte. HYAMS, J. R., 1st O.T.C.
Pte. HASSAN, S., Gibraltar Volunteer C.
1905 Pte. HYMAN, I., 15th P.O.W. Coy.
40411 Cpl. HYAM, M.,* 230th P.O.W. Coy.
883 Pte. ISAACS, S., 883rd Railroad Con. Coy.
435 Pte. ISRAEL, N., E.L.C.
P/10127 L/Cpl. ISAACS, J., M.F.P.
3584 Pte. ISAACS, S., 106th Prov. Bn.
69258 Pte. ISENBERG, J., 389th P.O.W. Coy.
631510 Pte. ISRAEL, W., 49th P.O.W. Coy.
269687 Pte. ISRAEL, C., 69th P.O.W. Coy.
54223 Pte. JACOBS, A., 6th Salvage Coy.
844 Pte. JACOBS, R. D., 844th Rail. Con. Co.
2706 Sdlr. JESSEL, R.A. Dept.
12930 Pte. JACOBS, B., O.T.C.
Pte. JACOBS, M. J., 19th O.C. Bn.
515159 Cadet JOSEPHS, J. J., 17th O.C. Bn.
321361 Cadet JACOBS, H., 6th O.C. Bn.
9916 Cadet JOLOVICZ, P., O.T.C.
606636 Cpl. JAYE, J. E., 58th P.O.W. Coy.
242192 Pte. JACOBS, D., 67th P.O.W. Coy.
618615 Pte. JACOBS, M., 239th P.O.W. Coy.
78838 Pte. JOEL, J., P.O.W. Coy.
677031 Pte. JONES, B., 301st P.O.W. Coy.
379261 Pte. KAYLES, M., 3rd Army Inf. School.
66632 Pte. KIMER, I., 114th Bde. H.Q.
34674 Pte. KRELL, S., E.F.C.
950 Cpl. KADOURI, A. R., Egypt Lab. Cps.
51345 Pte. KRATOSKY, A.C. Factory Alpine.
Pte. KALISLA, A., Egypt Labour Corps.
Cadet KLEAN, R. M. A., O.T.C.
10994 Pte. KIRSCH, A. N., O.T.C.
620942 Pte. KRAFSOFF, A. M., 155th P.O.W. Co.
676891 Pte. KLIPP, J., 371st P.O.W. Coy.
652052 Pte. KADISHEWITZ, R., 310th P.O.W. C.
614853 Pte. KAUFMAN, 166th P.O.W. Coy.
68896 Pte. KAPSKY, C., 146th P.O.W. Coy.
5194 Sgt. LONDON, E., E.F.C.
45119 Pte. LITMAN, B., Grave, Reg. Unit
Cpl. LEVY, P., Q.M. Strs. 14th Con. Dt.
24765 Cpl. LYONS, R.C. Factory Alpine.
22258 Pte. LEVINE, S., 2nd Army Concen. Cmp.
45240 Pte. LOCKALL, J., M.F.P.
Pte. LOW, D., Belgian Army Motors.
13697 Pte. LYONS, A. L., O.T.C.
47128 Pte. LERMAN, S., Officer Cadet Bn.
130328 Cadet LANGDON, C. L., 20th O.C. Bn.
457990 Cadet LAWRENCE, M., 11th O.C. Bn.
363079 Pte. LEVY, J., 4th R.D.C.
106524 Cadet LEVENSON, S., 11th O.C. Bn.
Cadet LEVY, J., Univ. of Lond. O.T.C.
34899 Cadet LAZARUS, M., 6th O.C. Bn.
Cadet LAZARUS, L., 10th O.C. Bn.
Cadet LEVY, M., 9th Bn.
205768 Cadet LITONI, E. M., 17th O.C. Bn.
546049 Cadet LAWTON, A. E., 24th O.C. Bn.
4790 Pte. LEVY, A., 100th Prov. Bn.

Various Units—Continued.

- 13/027918 Sgt. LEVY, M., Imp. Camel Corps.
- P/10869 L/Cpl. LYONS, S. J.,* M.F.P.
- Cadet LEVENE-DAVIS, J. H.,* O.T.C.
- 71669 Sgt. LEVY, M., 299th P.O.W. Coy.
- 2811 Sgt. LEWIS, D., 51st P.O.W. Coy.
- 199661 Sgt. LIEBERMAN, R., P.O.W. Coy.
- 42408 Pte. LEVY, J., 30th P.O.W. Coy.
- 108404 Pte. LEVI, A., P.O.W. Coy.
- 604790 Sgt. LEWIS, D., P.O.W. Coy.
- 413718 Pte. LEVINE, J., 178th P.O.W. Coy.
- 476574 Pte. LAZARUS, D., 316th P.O.W. Coy.
- 60851 C.S.M. LEVY, S., 143rd P.O.W. Coy.
- 676937 Sgt. LEVY, E., 249th P.O.W. Coy.
- 75880 Pte. LEVY, M., 337th P.O.W. Coy.
- 654621 Pte. LIND, S., 339th P.O.W. Coy.
- 7213 Pte. LYONS, B., P.O.W. Coy.
- 178854 Pte. LEVINE, B., P.O.W. Coy.
- 808202 Pte. LEVY, J., 30th P.O.W. Coy.
- 677032 Pte. LEVINE, M., 10th P.O.W. Coy.
- 603825 Pte. LERMAN, M., 124th P.O.W. Coy.
- 17756 Pte. LEVI, A., 29th P.O.W. Coy.
- 98695 Pte. MEDOLSOHN, A.
- 230186 Pte. MYERS, A. J.
- 75240 L.A.M. MORRIS, N. G. M.
- C/14187 Pte. MORTON, P. D., O.T.C.
- Pte. MORRIS, H. J., West Africa Field Force.
- 9257 L/Cpl. MYERS, A., M.F.P.
- 107748 Cadet MELINSKY, 24th O.C. Bn.
- 134457 Pte. MOSS, M., 20th O.C. Bn.
- 32440 Cadet MILLER, A., 11th O.C. Bn.
- 390258 Cadet MILLER, S., 17th O.C. Bn.
- Cadet MORRIS, H., 6th O.C. Bn.
- Cadet MARKS, J., 7th O.C. Bn.
- 250216 Cadet MORRIS, M., 7th O.C. Bn.
- 10117 Cadet MOSES, C. R., O.T.C.
- 198930 Pte. MENCOPSKI, J., Mob. Sub. Centre.
- M2/269538 Pte. MORRIS, A., Mob. Sub. Centre.
- M2/021300 Pte. MARKS, H., Mob. Sub. Centre.
- P/9587 L/Cpl. MYERS, R., M.F. Police.
- 2863 Pte. MUSLIN, R., 65th Prov. Bn.
- 5501 Pte. MARCHANT, S. N., 100th Prov. Bn.
- 2566 Pte. MICHAEL, 81st Prov. Bn.
- 34206 Cpl. MOSCOW, H., 218th P.O.W. Coy.
- 457917 Pte. MARKS, M., 329th P.O.W. Coy.
- 492 Pte. MAX, M., 99th P.O.W. Coy.
- 565234 A/Sgt. MENDOZA, H., 142nd P.O.W. Co.
- 653060 Pte. MISTOSSKI, S., 214th P.O.W. Coy.
- 46488 Pte. MANDELSTON, J., 399th P.O.W. Coy.
- 523411 Pte. MAYDVSKY, M., 164th P.O.W. Coy.
- 71691 Pte. MARKS, S., 216th P.O.W. Coy.
- 676944 Cpl. MANFORD, H., 286th P.O.W. Coy.
- 79479 Pte. MOSCOW, L., 331st P.O.W. Coy.
- 79684 Pte. MIKHAILOFF, M., 331st P.O.W. Co.
- 1328 Pte. NEWMAN, W., 8th A. Steam.
- 435 Pte. NISOIM, I., Egypt Labour Corps.
- P/9787 L/Cpl. NORWICH, R., M.F.P.
- 62793 Pte. NEWMAN, A., Officer Cadet Bn.
- D/430 Pte. NATHAN, D., E.F.C. Hqrs.
- DM2/220414 Pte. NATHAN, S., Mob. Sub. Cntre.
- 9787 L/Cpl. NORVICK, R., M.F. Police.
- 68896 Pte. NOPSKY, C., 146th P.O.W. Coy.
- 89817 Pte. NOORDEN, 387th P.O.W. Coy.
- 556640 Pte. NEEDOFF, S., 331st P.O.W. Coy.
- 39167 Pte. OCKRENT, L., Salvage Camp.
- 472066 Sgt. OSTERLENSKY, S., P.O.W. Coy.
- 179483 Pte. PHILLIPS, A.
- Pte. PENDRY, R., E.F.C.
- 1095 Pte. PHILLIPS, H., Indian Base.
- 12936 Pte. PEZARO, L., O.T.C.
- 14257 Cadet PIZARO, B., 2nd O.C. Bn.
- Cadet PRINS, L., 14th O.C. Bn.
- 972 Cadet PEARLMAN, J., 24th O.C. Bn.
- DM2/164054 L/Cpl. PHILLIPS, H., Mob. S.C.
- 5560 Pte. PRIVENSON, M., Command Depot.
- 4400 Pte. PHILLIPS, J., 65th Prov. Bn.
- 1728 Pte. PHILLIPS, S., 45th Prov. Bn.
- P/5181 L/Cpl. PINTO, C., M.F. Police.
- 253 Pte. PROCHOWNER, L., 139th P.O.W. Co.
- 90353 Pte. PERRICK, N., 45th P.O.W. Coy.
- 82814 Pte. PICKLES, M., 389th P.O.W. Coy.
- 630258 Pte. PELLER, J., 304th P.O.W. Coy.
- 47125 Pte. QUINT, H., 16th Officer Cadet Bn.
- 142516 L/Cpl. ROSENTHAL, E., No. 3 S. of I.
- 562 Cpl. ROMANS, B., Egypt Labour Corps.
- 13650 Pte. RICKARDS, P. J., O.T.C.
- 73979 Cadet RICHARDSON, J., 11th O.C. Bn.
- Cadet RUDELL, E. A., 19th O.C. Bn.
- Cadet RAPHAEL, C. M., 19th O.C. Bn.
- 27180 Cadet RIFKIN, R., 11th O.C. Bn.
- Cadet ROSENBERG, J., O.T.C.
- 46136 Cadet RAPPAPORT, L., 17th O.T.C.
- 219022 Cadet RICKLOVITCH, S., Mob. Sub. Cen.
- M2/269087 Pte. RUBENS, J. H., Mob. Sub. Cen.
- 5555 Pte. RASCH, J., 85th Prov. Bn.
- 2645 Pte. ROSENBLATT, H., 102nd Prov. Bn.
- 11653 Pte. RATHBONE, M., O.T.C.
- 4497 Pte. ROGERS, C., 65th Prov. B.T.F.
- 5471 Cpl. ROSIN, H., 67th Prov. Bn.
- 12424 Pte. RENTON, B. A., O.T.C.
- 16127 L/Cpl. RICHMAN, M., P.O.W. Coy.
- 534155 Pte. RASE, J., P.O.W. Coy.
- 1720 Pte. ROTHFIELD, A., 15th P.O.W. Coy.
- 1859 Pte. ROTHMAN, W., 15th P.O.W. Coy.
- 605007 Pte. ROSENBERG, D., 123rd P.O.W. Coy.
- 42163 Pte. REUBENS, A., 235th P.O.W. Coy.
- 105857 Pte. ROSSE, J., 240th P.O.W. Coy.
- P/5564 L/Cpl. SÜSS, A., M.M.P.
- 5312 Pte. SOLOMON, S., Corps School.
- 375739 Pte. SAPERIA, N., 8th Corps. Sal. Coy.
- A/357730/6398 Pte. SIMANS, J., E.F.C.
- 379113 Pte. SIMONS, S., 4th Army Mus. School.
- 4450 I/Cpl. SPECULAND, J., Command P.M.
- 4705 Pte. SHERWIN, A. V.
- 1375 Pte. SOLOMONS.

Various Units—Continued.

- 92389 Sgt. SOLOMON, D., Indian.
- 31532 Pte. SCHNEIDER, S., 1st H.Q. Armoured Motor Brigade.
- Pte. SAUNDERS, E., 113th Telegraph Bn.
- 18843 Rfm. SOLOMONS, A., 2nd Army Concen. Camp.
- Med. Stud. SALOMIAC, Egypt Med. Serv.
- Pte. SIBORI, E., E.L..C.
- 190 Pte. SOCONY, I., E.L.C.
- 75752 Pte. SELDEN, J., 16th Officer Cadet Bn.
- 766850 Cadet STODELL, J. H., 24th O.C. Bn.
- 260031 Pte. SOTHALL, N., M.F.P.
- 17874 Cadet SOLOMON, P., 19th O.C. Bn.
- Cadet SIMMONS, E. C., R.M. Col.
- 9876 Cadet SONNENTHAL, A., 20th O.C. Bn.
- 25402 Cadet STONE, L., 15th O.C. Bn.
- Cadet SOLOMONS, L. P., 9th O.C. Bn.
- 19874 Cadet SOLOMONS, P., O.C. Bn.
- 9886 Cadet SAMUEL, S. M., O.T.C.
- T4/217107 Pte. SPECTERMAN, J., Mob. Sub. Cen.
- 175745 Pte. SILVERSTONE, J., Mob. Sub. Centre.
- 5155 L/Cpl. SOLOMAN, S., M.F.P.
- 22018 Rfm. SOLOMONS, A., Command Depot.
- 445012 Cpl. SLINDER, H., Chinese L.C.
- 6213 Pte. SHEERE, B., 4th Army H.Q.
- 2096 Pte. SPITZ, 9th Prov. Bn.
- 5024 Sgt./Ins. STITCHER, P., O.T.C.
- 2731 Pte. SALAMAN, E., 84th Prov. Bn.
- 1659 Pte. SELLAR, I., 63rd Prov. Bn.
- 201736 L/Cpl. SVERSKY, S., Ballykular Com. D.
- 13125 Pte. SIDES, H. E., O.T.C.
- 25805 Pte. SEIGAL, S., No. 1 P.O.W. Coy.
- 614793 Pte. SOLOMONS, N., 165th P.O.W. Coy.
- 47180 Pte. SHIRES, L., 165th P.O.W. Coy.
- 676611 Pte. SILVERMAN, S., 236th P.O.W. Coy.
- Pte. SPIELSINGER, J., 299th P.O.W. Coy.
- 29305 Cpl. SOLOMON, B., P.O.W. Coy.
- 2164 L/Cpl. SEGAL, L., P.O.W. Coy.
- 774 A/Cpl. SHINEBERG, J., P.O.W. Coy.
- 617010 Pte. SHAFFNER, C., 193rd P.O.W. Coy.
- 651998 Pte. SCOTT, J., 309th P.O.W. Coy.
- 55577 Pte. STEPNITZKY, B., 121st P.O.W. Coy.
- 42602 Pte. SHAAPWOL, J., 136th P.O.W. Coy.
- 71795 Sgt. STEINGOLD, B., 302nd P.O.W. Coy.
- 135427 Pte. SIMBERG, M., 224th P.O.W. Coy.
- 573499 Pte. SKLANOFSKI, I., 371st P.O.W. Coy.
- 676957 Pte. SPIELSINGER, J., 299th P.O.W. Coy.
- 613757 Pte. SOLK, E., 180th P.O.W. Coy.
- 619272 Pte. SCHWIETZER, W., 244th P.O.W. Co.
- 34418 Pte. SOLOMONS, H., 18th P.O.W. Coy.
- Pte. TANBURN, H. S., O.T.C.
- 56003 Pte. TUCKMA, L., 16th Officer Cadet Bn.
- 2693 Pte. TABER, M., 45th Prov. Bn.
- 654365 Pte. TAYLOR, M., 334th P.O.W. Coy.
- 615800 Pte. TABRISKY, D., 188th P.O.W. Coy.
- 1136 Pte. VOLST, S., 102nd Prov. Bn.
- 445038 Cpl. VINEFSKY, H., Chinese Labour Cps.
- 67075 Pte. VAN LOCHEN, H., 58th P.O.W. Coy.
- 608327 Pte. VALENCIA, J., 30th P.O.W. Coy.
- 676689 Pte. VALINSKY, I., P.O.W. Coy.
- 79692 Pte. VINICK, P., 41st P.O.W. Coy.
- 43 W.A.A.C. WOOLF, R.
- 2616 Pte. WOLLRAUCH.
- 2615 Pte. WINTERS.
- Pte. WILENSKI, R. H., Cen. Dep. W.O.
- 116935 Cadet WEINSTEIN, H., 11th O.C. Bn.
- 290437 Cadet WOLFSON, J., 16th O.C. Bn.
- Cadet WOLFENSOHN, H., 21st O.C. Bn.
- 2331 Pte. WARSHAWER, A., 63rd Prov. Bn.
- 3002 Rfm. WOLFF, H., 102nd Prov. Bn.
- 3003 Rfm. WOLFF, J., 102nd Prov. Bn.
- 3219 Pte. WEIMAR, F., 9th Prov. Bn.
- 2641 Pte. WEIMAR, S., 102nd Prov. Bn.
- 2335 Cpl. WOOLF, F., 65th Prov. Bn.
- 25280 Pte. WOLFE, S., No. 2 P.O.W. Coy.
- 524 Sgt. WALLERSTEIN, L. D. J., 12th P.O.W. Coy.
- 89214 Pte. WEINBURGH, H., 385th P.O.W. Coy.
- 605089 Pte. WEINBERG, D., 314th P.O.W. Coy.
- 609827 Pte. YELSKI, A., P.O.W. Coy.
- 21470 Sgt. YESNER, S., 294th P.O.W. Coy.
- 234581 Pte. ZAGERMAN, M., A.C Factory Alpine.
- S/23930 Pte. ZAUSMER, J., 375th P.O.W. Coy.

NOMINAL ROLL OF JEWS SERVING WITH 40th (PALESTINIAN) ROYAL FUSILIERS (see p. 66).

Officers.
Lieut. HANBURY, A.
Lieut. SELIGMAN, L. B. (M.C.)
Lieut. JACOBS, P.
Lieut. RICH, J. M.
2nd Lieut. GOODMAN, D.

N.C.O.'s and Men.
J 4007 Pte. ALPER, MAX.
J 1940 Pte. ADLER, L.
J 4590 Pte. ABRAHAM, N.
J 4863 Pte. AFARI, S.
J 5205 Pte. AZUZ, M.
J 4596 Pte. ANTABI, E.
J 457 Pte. ANTABI, M.
J 5113 Pte. ASTER, J.
J 4642 Pte. ALHASID, I.
J 5203 Pte. ALONY, M.
J 5138 Pte. ARUSSI, J.
J 4720 Pte. ASBIL, S.
J 4707 L/Cpl. APTICKMAN, J.
J 4833 Pte. ARLOFF, Z.
J 4918 Pte. ABRAHAMOVITZ, M.
J 4518 Pte. ASHBEL, A.
J 5082 Pte. ALKALI, S.
J 4826 Pte. AARONOVITCH, M.
J 4633 Pte. ALTERMAN, J.
J 4812 Pte. ARBER, A.
J 4905 Pte. AXELROD, H.
J 4580 Sgt. ARBER, M.
J 4689 Pte. ABERMAN, M.
J 4909 Pte. ABRAHOMOVITCH, J.
J 4859 Pte. ABRAMOVITCH, N.
J 4674 Pte. ADIN, M.
J 4964 Pte. ABFLALU, D.
J 4560 Pte. ARBER, J.
J 5040 Pte. ASHHENAZI, M.
J 4879 Pte. ARLOV, A.
J 4572 Pte. ASHKENAZI, R.
J 4570 Pte. ASTA, Z.
J 4544 Pte. AVERBUCH, M.
J 4593 L/Sgt. AVIVI, A.
J 4852 Pte. AZULVY, J.
J 5049 Pte. ARUSSI, Y.
J 5396 Pte. AGEMAN, E.
J 7164 Pte. ABRAHAM, D.
P.W. 18502 Pte. ABRAHAM, D.
P.W. 35631 Pte. AZARIYOH, Y.
P.W. 2809 Pte. ABRAHAM, B.
P.W. 32114 Pte. ABRAHAM, M.

J 5133 Pte. ATTIA, R.
J 4926 Pte. ALKALI, J.
J 5457 Pte. ARONOVITZ, C.
J 5498 Pte. ABNI, D.
J 7020 Pte. ABRAMOVITZ, I.
J 7039 Pte. ABRAHAMSON, T.
J 7050 Pte. ABRAHAMSON, J.
SD/2 Pte. ASHHENAZI, R.
J 5051 Pte. ALSHICH, J.
J 5195 Pte. AMAR, A.
J 5106 Pte. AUBERSMAN, E.
J 4639 Pte. ASTROG, A.
J 5308 Pte. ASHHENAZA, A.
J 4970 Pte. AMDURSHY, S.
J 5197 Pte. ALHUCHIR, C.
J 7092 Pte. ASHKENAZI, J.
J 7100 Pte. ALBALACH, N. M.
J 7103 Pte. ADDATO, S. M.
J 7113 Pte. ASSA, A. J.
J 7155 Pte. ALPANDAH, N. M.
J 7156 Pte. ALBACHERI, J. M.
J 7159 Pte. ARAZI, M.
J 7162 Pte. ARON, K. M.
J 4557 Pte. BADAR, D.
J 4770 Pte. BASKIND, H.
J 4824 Cpl. BENDOR, I.
J 4869 L/Cpl. BLUESTEIN, B.
J 4962 Pte. BELAH, J.
J 4940 Pte. BERACHA, J.
J 4578 Pte. BENVENISTI, I.
J 4637 Pte. BAG-BAG, E.
J 4706 Pte. BUZINOFSKY, M.
J 4908 Pte. BURLA, J.
J 4844 Pte. BETH-HALACHMI, J.
J 4740 Cpl. BACH, I.
J 5161 Pte. BURLA, S.
J 4951 Pte. BANI, Y.
J 5151 Pte. BEKAR, J.
J 4547 Pte. BACHARAV, Z.
J 4754 L/Cpl. BEN YEHUDA, I.
J 5061 L/Cpl. BENVENISTA, A.
J 4845 Pte. BORNSTEIN, B.
J 5192 Pte. BENATTAR, J.
J 4975 Pte. BACHOFF, M.
J 5105 L/Cpl. BARRETT, V.
J 4641 Pte. BEN-ZEVI, D.
J 4601 Pte. BRENMAN, N.
J 4750 Pte. BEN YEHUDA, A.
J 4559 Pte. BARKAY, S.
J 4536 Cpl. BURSTEIN, M.
J 4609 Pte. BERCHENKO, J.
P.W.=Prisoner of War.

J 4683 Sgt. BEN-DAVID, A.
J 4684 Pte. BOLDE, G.
J 4742 L/Cpl. BEN-NISSIM, R.
J 4661 Pte. BREGMAN, J.
J 4761 Pte. BEN DAVID, S.
J 4558 Sgt. BEILIS, P.
J 4980 Pte. BACHOR, J.
J 5080 Pte. BADZANJU, Z.
J 4765 Pte. BARTNICHER, I.
J 4996 Pte. BASS, G.
J 4987 L/Cpl. BASERAVI, M.
J 4900 Pte. BAVLI, N.
J 4787 Pte. BEHAR, A.
J 5019 Pte. BEHAR, B.
J 4561 L/Cpl. BEHAR, J.
J 4938 Pte. BICHAR, M.
J 5206 Pte. BEN-ARYEH, E.
J 4894 L/Cpl. BENVENISTA, D.
af.368 Pte. BIRA, M.
J 4856 L/Cpl. BERNSTEIN, A.
J 4843 Pte. BETH-HALACHMI, J.
J 4790 Pte. BORNSTEIN, A.
J 4915 Pte. BRENNER, B.
J 4884 Pte. BURLA, M.
J 4534 Pte. BURSTEIN, B.
J 5270 Pte. BARUCH, M.
J 5340 Pte. BSCHAR, M.
P.W. 24312 Pte. BEHER, I.
P.W. 28673 Pte. BEHER, S.
P.W. 33243 Pte. BEHER, A.
P.W. 35635 Pte. BEHER, D.
P.W. 37123 Pte. BEHER, I.
P.W. 24129 BARUPH, M.
P.W. 27068 Pte. BEHER, M.
J 5031 Pte. BARADON, M.
J 5011 Pte. BASSON, M.
J 5155 Pte. BETHAR, E.
J 4993 Pte. BEDOVI, A.
J 4739 Pte. BEIFERMAN, I.
J 5065 Pte. BRAVERMAN, M.
J 5438 Pte. BEN-COHAIM, D.
J 5468 Pte. BRAGLEVSKY, S.
J 5476 Pte. BRENNER, M.
J 7005 Pte. BOZANOVSKY, A.
J 7021 Pte. BELACHOVSKY.
J 7032 Pte. BLASHNIKOFF, M.
J 7045 Pte. BIRIAZOFSKY, N.
J 7053 Pte. BOCHLIM, N.
J 7080 Pte. BARZEL, E.
J 5193 Pte. BEZALEL, A.
J 5103 Pte. BONAMI, S.

"Palestinians."—Continued.

N.C.O.'s AND MEN—Continued.

J 4694 Pte. BEN-ZAHAN, M.	J 4925 Pte. CHURGIN, S.	J 4912 Pte. DABA, A.
J 5353 Pte. BARZILAI, D.	J 5231 Pte. CHEN, J.	J 5094 Pte. DABA, J.
J 5034 Pte. BUSANI, J.	J 5233 Pte. COHEN, A.	J 5114 Pte. DADDASHTI, S.
J 5016 Pte. BEVAS, S.	J 5115 Pte. COHEN, H.	J 5497 Cpl. DANIN, D.
J 5111 Pte. BERGER, C.	J 4920 Pte. COHEN, J.	J 7006 L/Cpl. DISKIN, C.
Ter 544 Pte. BABAI, E.	J 5135 Pte. COHEN, S.	J 7009 Pte. DEUTSCH, B.
J 5110 Pte. BUCHARYEH, Y.	J 5436 Pte. COHEN, J.	J 7012 Pte. DASTROFSKY, J.
J 5236 Pte. BEN-ZION, S.	J 5437 Pte. COHEN, J.	J 7040 Pte. DAHAN, E.
J 4950 Pte. BANI, J.	J 5452 Pte. COBLENTZ, J.	J 4041 Pte. DJINO, J.
J 5083 Pte. BENJAMIN, S.	J 5454 Pte. COHEN, S.	J 7061 Pte. DOHAN, S.
J 4870 Pte. BENJAMIN, Z. M.	J 5463 Pte. CANDERON, L.	J 7064 Pte. DRUCKER, S.
J 5053 Pte. BRUZOFSKY, S.	J 5469 Pte. CHALUTZ, S.	J 7086 Pte. DIAMOND, N.
T 532 Pte. BERLATZKY, S.	J 5492 Pte. COHEN, I.	J 4736 Pte. DURANI, J. H.
J 7099 Pte. BEN-EZRAH, S.	J 7035 Pte. COHEN, S.	J 5371 Pte. DUEK, C.
J 7104 Pte. BACHER, J.	J 7073 Pte. COHEN, Z.	J 7102 Pte. DANON, E. N.
J 7107 A./L/Cpl. BEHAR, I.	J 7075 Pte. CHARIT, J.	J 3164 Pte. EISENSTADT, S.
J 7109 Pte. BENADOR, N. A.	J 7078 Pte. COHEN, S.	J 5152 Pte. EZARI, A.
J 7110 Pte. BENBACASTI, I. M.	J 5120 Pte. CHUDODO, E.	J 4828 Pte. EPHRATI, E.
J 7117 Pte. BECHAR, J. A.	J 4985 Pte. COHEN, A.	J 4548 Pte. ELDAD, M.
J 7167 Pte. BECHAR, J. S.	J 5000 Pte. CHUCHA, E.	J 4785 Pte. ESKAYO, A.
J 4069 Pte. COHEN, A.	J 5157 Pte. CHAHASHI, S.	J 4813 L/Cpl. EPSTEIN, D.
J 1988 Pte. COHEN, B.	J 5318 Pte. CONOFINO, M.	J 4819 Pte. EFROTH, J.
J 5554 L/Cpl. COHN, B.	J 5138 Pte. CASSUS, I.	J 4179 Pte. EZROH, A.
J 4713 Pte. CHOINSKY, J.	J 7091 Pte. COHEN, I. S.	J 4983 Pte. ECHT, S.
J 4629 Pte. COHEN, I.	J 5190 Pte. COHEN, I.	J 4730 Pte. ERTZMAN, S.
J 5184 Pte. COHEN, I.	J 5093 Pte. COHEN, M.	J 4666 A/L/Cpl. EIGH, A.
J 4867 Pte. COHEN, A. D.	J 4923 Pte. COHEN, A.	J 4759 Pte. ECHT, J.
J 4868 L/Cpl. CHAVIV, L.	J 4933 Pte. CARUMBIM, A.	J 4872 L/Cpl. ETKIN, A.
J 4721 Pte. COHEN, N.	J 5441 Pte. CASTEL, S.	J 5041 Pte. ELEASHAR, I.
J 5249 Pte. CASTEL, E.	J 1745 Pte. COHEN, W.	J 4784 Pte. EVON-TOB, D.
J 4901 Pte. COHEN, C.	J 5258 Pte. CHAOUL, A.	P.W. 28322 Pte. ELIA, S.
J 4841 Pte. COHEN, J.	J 275 Pte. CARUSO, R.	P.W. 38373 Pte. ELIAN, Y.
J 4717 Pte. COHEN, I.	J 560 Pte. CHICHONOFSKY, E.	J 4864 Pte. EDELMAN, B.
J 5121 Pte. CHADID, J.	J 7089 Pte. CALDERON, B. S.	J 5101 Pte. ERSONI, E.
J 4514 Cpl. CHIRCASHY, D.	J 7090 Pte. CHIPRUTI, R. E.	J 4991 Pte. ETZ-HADAR, C.
J 4513 Pte. CHIRCASHY, M.	J 7106 Pte. CURIEL, M.	J 4941 Pte. ETTINGER, C.
J 5898 L/Sgt. CHAIMSON, M.	J 7112 Pte. CASSAH, J. H.	J 5444 Pte. ELPERN, C.
J 4623 Pte. CHAFKIN, J.	J 7182 L/Cpl. COHEN, B. J.	J 5486 Pte. ERNSTEIN, B.
J 5036 Pte. CHALAF, A.	J 3124 Pte. DEUCH, J.	J 7017 Pte. ERMAN, M.
J 4906 Pte. CHARUBI, S.	J 4751 Pte. DURAN, B.	J 7038 Pte. EHLICH, S.
J 4967 Pte. CHARWSH, E.	J 4535 Pte. DISINGOFF, M.	J 5015 Pte. ELIEZAR, I.
J 4678 L/Cpl. CHAZAN, R.	J 4899 Pte. DICHNEH, M.	J 5156 Pte. EDONAR, C.
J 4114 Pte. CHOMSHY, M.	J 4937 Pte. DASA, B.	J 7145 Pte. ESS, M.
J 4772 Pte. COHEN, A.	J 5199 Pte. DOBRI, S.	J 1433 Pte. FISHER, S.
J 5273 Pte. COHEN, D.	J 4691 Pte. DASA, M.	J 4524 Pte. FISH, N.
J 4795 Pte. COHEN, I.	J 4012 Pte. DASA, R.	J 4939 L/Cpl. FRANKS, R.
J 4888 Pte. COHEN, R.	J 4503 Pte. DRUYAN, M.	P.W. 35328 Pte. FURMANN, M. J.
J 4800 L/Cpl. COHEN, S.	J 4686 Pte. DENKER, M.	J 4567 Cpl. FEILBERG, D.
J 4846 Pte. COHEN, Y.	J 4873 L/Cpl. DOCHNER, D.	J 4725 Pte. FELDMAN, J.
J 5239 Pte. COHEN, M.	J 4959 Pte. DASA, S.	J 4647 Pte. FREIMOVITZ, E.
J 5256 Pte. CHOYGEA, C.	J 5112 Pte. DZAMIN, S.	J 4768 Pte. FEINBERG, H.
J 5286 Pte. COHEN, A.	J 4814 Pte. DOCHMAN, M.	J 4529 Pte. FREEDMAN, A.
CT 27 Pte. CALMY, J.	J 4757 Pte. DURANI, B. Z. M.	J 4660 Pte. FAKTEROFSKY, E.
J 5079 Pte. CHASSON, J.	J 4618 Pte. DRUKARSKY, S.	J 4734 Pte. FINKEL, J.
J 5181 Pte. CHAZAN, J.	P.W. 25647 Pte. DAVID, S.	J 4602 L/Cpl. FISHER, J.
J 4977 Pte. CHEFITZ, A.	P.W. 27063 Pte. DAVID, S.	J 4697 Pte. FUTERMAN, H.
J 5046 Pte. COLDERON, S.	P.W. 37658 Pte. DAVID, J.	J 4651 Pte. FEIGEN, N.

"Palestinians."—Continued.

N.C.O.'s AND MEN—Continued.

J 4571	Pte. FELDSTEIN, M.	J 4832	Pte. GAFECH, S.	P.W. 36084	Pte. HAIM, N.
J 4607	Cpl. FEINSTEIN, L.	J 5073	Pte. GERSHON, E.	J 4543	L/Cpl. HALEVY, I.
J 4669	L/Cpl. FEINERMAN, I.	J 4929	Pte. GIOPEN, S.	J 5194	Pte. HAMELTZKY, S.
J 4508	L/Cpl. FAIMAN, M.	J 5200	Pte. GISSIN, E.	J 4887	Pte. HANUKOH, M.
J 5108	Pte. FREIMAN, M.	J 4886	Pte. GOLDBERG, N.	J 5235	Pte. HASSAN, I.
J 4798	Pte. FEDERMAN, H.	J 4956	Pte. GOLDENBLOOM, J.	J 4850	L/Cpl. HAYUN, D.
J 5038	Pte. FEFERMAN, A.	J 5177	Pte. GREENHOFF, D.	J 5458	Pte. HERTZBERG, N.
J 5432	Pte. FREEDMAN, H.	J 5439	Pte. GREENBERG, N.	J 5474	Pte. HAMBURG, M.
J 5132	Pte. FREEDMAN, J.	J 5459	Pte. GOLDMAN, B.	J 5477	Pte. HARNICH, N.
J 4738	Pte. FERSICKBOIM, A.	J 5461	Pte. GOTHERT, J.	J 7031	Pte. HERTZENSTEIN, J.
J 5451	Pte. FELDMAN, A.	J 5471	Pte. GOLDBERG, Y.	J 7059	Pte. HURVITCH, N.
J 5496	Pte. FAITELSON, M.	J 5475	Pte. GOOTMAN, S.	SD/1	Pte. HARARI, N.
J 7079	Pte. FREEDMAN, F.	J 5484	Pte. GREENBERG, I.	J 4952	Pte. HAMAMI, C.
J 7077	Pte. FINE, J.	J 7001	Pte. GOLDMAN, S.	J 4616	Pte. HERZIK, A.
J 4594	Pte. FISHER, M.	J 7010	Pte. GREENBERG, S.	J 4006	Pte. HAMDI, I.
TS 15	Pte. FLAISHER, J.	J 7014	Pte. GREENSPAN, D.	J 5116	Pte. HELMAN, E.
J 7093	Pte. FTEICHA, N. C.	J 7018	Pte. GREENBERG, S.	J 7161	Pte. HAIM, J.
J 7098	Pte. FISS, S. M.	J 7024	Pte. GUERVITCH, B.	J 5178	Pte. IRANI, J.
J 467	Pte. GREENBERG, M.	J 7034	Pte. GOLDZWEIZ, J.	J 4523	Pte. IHAR, A.
J 4709	Pte. GINSBURG, B.	J 7052	Pte. GABAI, C.	J 4685	Pte. ISENBERG, A. J.,
J 4533	Pte. GELMAN, N.	J 7056	Pte. GLICKSMAN, M.	J 4895	Pte. IDAHAN, M.
J 5217	Pte. GREENBERG, I.	J 7070	Pte. GOLDSTEIN, B.	J 4587	Pte. ISRAEL, Y.
J 4670	Pte. GOLDNAER, A.	J 5075	Pte. GESSEL, J.	J 5173	Pte. IYAN, D.
J 4830	Pte. GOLBOFF, J.	J 4735	Pte. GOLZWEIG, E.	P.W. 2808	Pte. ISAAC, Y.
J 4619	Pte. GLINYENSKY, A.	J 5201	Pte. GOLDSTEIN, J.	J 5070	Pte. ISRAEL, M.
J 4595	Cpl. GARBA, M.	J 5080	Pte. GAYEGO, S.	J 5440	Pte. ITCHKOVITZ, C.
J 4610	Pte. GUVALSKY, B.	J 5165	Pte GALANTI, E.	J 5462	L/Cpl. ISAAC, J.
J 4662	L/Cpl. GOLOVINICK, A.	J 5026	Pte. GAHARAN, A.	J 7172	Pte. IZEN, S. G.
J 4718	Pte. GREENSPAN, J. H.	J 4946	Pte. GANDIL, R.	Jaf. 383	Pte. JACOBSON, S.
J 4505	Pte. GOLOMB, E.	J 5092	Pte. GAGEE, N.	J 4509	Pte. JOFFE, J.
J 4659	L/Cpl. GOLOMB, E.	J 3456	Pte. HARRIS, D.	J 4668	Cpl. JOFFE, D.
J 5134	Pte. GAZOLI, M.	J 912	Pte. HELMAN, J.	J 4762	Pte. JACOBOFSKY, A.
J 4922	Pte. GUZMAN, M.	J 2272	Pte. HARRIS, D.	P.W. 25742	Pte. JERUSALMI, A.
J 4517	Pte. GREENFELD, O.	J 2913	Pte. HOFFMAN, J.	J 4954	Pte. JERUSALMI, I.
J 4786	Pte. GOLDSTEIN, M.	J 4634	Pte. HARTSILVER, C.	J 4794	Pte. JACOBOVITZ, Z.
J 4510	Sgt. GRAZORSKY, A.	J 5148	Pte. HELMAN, R.	J 4957	Pte. JERUSALMI, C.
J 4521	L/Cpl. GINSBURG, A.	J 4775	Pte. HURWITZ, H.	J 5131	Pte. JACOBSON, M.
J 5333	Pte. GINSBERG, G.	J 4764	Pte. HALEVI, S.	J 7180	Pte. JOSEPH, J.
J 3792	Pte. GOLDBERG, S.	J 4849	Pte. HASID, Z.	J 3854	Pte. KEIZERMAN, J.
J 4664	Pte. GLICKMAN, J.	J 4599	Pte. HAFEZ, H.	J 225	Pte. KRETCHMAN.
J 4654	Pte. GAKLIN, M.	J 4663	Pte. HERZENSTEIN, J.	J 4592	Pte. KIPNISS, N.
J 4934	Pte. GALANTI, J.	J 4719	Pte. HENNIGMAN, J.	J 4564	Pte. KISSIN, D.
J 4575	Pte. GARBOVITCH, D.	J 4695	Pte. HAFT, A.	J 4584	Pte. KOFFY, M.
Jaf. 269	L/Cpl. GLASER, J.	J 4780	Pte. HEDGIHICHT, Z.	J 4643	Pte. KLAIZIKIN, S.
J 4612	Pte. GOLDBERG, J.	J 4679	Sgt. HALEVI, J.	J 4728	Pte. KRAMER, C.
J 4965	Pte. GOLDBERG, I.	J 5167	Pte. HAVARI, M.	J 4782	Pte. KANEFSKY, N.
J 4811	Pte. GOLDBERG, J.	J 4649	Pte. HENKIN, A.	J 5084	Pte. KALDARON, B.
J 4665	Pte. GOLDENBERG, M.	Tev. 417	Pte. HILLEL, E.	J 5045	Pte. KALDERON, J.
J 4710	Pte. GOLDENBERG, M.	J 4747	Pte. HERSHFIELD, B. Z.	J 4545	Pte. KRICHEFSKY, A.
J 4743	L/Cpl. GORSTEL, J.	J 5225	Pte. HERSHFIELD, I.	J 4778	Pte. KALODIN, M.
J 4676	Pte. GOTCHEL, H.	J 5124	L/Cpl. HIRSCHIN, M.	J 4717	Pte. KROLL, J.
J 4756	Pte. GROOSHHEVITCH.	J 4506	Sgt. HOSS, D.	J 4632	Pte. KARBEL, S.
J 4608	Pte. GOOTMAN, D.	J 4699	Pte. HURWITCH, J.	J 4705	Pte. KAPLAN, S.
J 5241	L/Cpl. GOOTMAN, J.	4603	L/Cpl. HURWITCH, S. Y.	J 4755	Pte. KASOFSKY, M.
J 5224	Pte. GOOTMAN, N.	J 5324	Pte. HASSAN, S.	J 4822	Pte. KARP, B.
J 4502	Pte. GOODSTEIN, M.	P.W. 25886	Pte. HAIM, A.	J 4628	Pte. KIPNISS, H.
J 5325	Pte. GALLAI, M.	P.W. 38314	Pte. HAIM, B.	J 4803	Pte. KANTROVITZ, D.

"Palestinians."—*Continued.*

J 7160	L/Sgt.	KURIANSKY.
J 4520	Q.S.M.	KRAVASHNI, D.
J 4550	L/Cpl.	KUPERMAN, M.
J 4512	L/Cpl.	KROLL, Z.
J 5209	Pte.	KAUFMAN, C. S.
J 4773	Sgt.	KLEVITZKY, I.
J 5399	Pte.	KAHANI, M.
J 5227	Pte.	KADOSH, J.
J 4621	Pte.	KAHANOVITZ, F.
J 4556	Pte.	KALINSKY, S.
J 4716	Pte.	KALMENOVITZ, E.
J 4677	Cpl.	KANTOR, J.
J 4774	Pte.	KAP, H.
J 4726	Pte.	KASMINSKY, S.
J 4733	Pte.	KATZ, P.
J 4837	Pte.	KATZENLLENSOHN, B.
J 4624	Pte.	KLEIN, C.
J 4874	Pte.	KLATZIN, M.
J 4796	Pte.	KLESS, B.
J 4566	Pte.	KLEWITZKY, N.
J 4875	Pte.	KOCHLANI, M.
J 4555	Pte.	KRAFTZOFF, M.
J 4565	Pte.	KROLL, J.
J 4902	Pte.	KUKER, E.
J 4914	Pte.	KUSHNIR, S.
J 4540	Pte.	KRICHEFSKY, N.
J 4889	L/Cpl.	KASPY, L.
J 5374	Pte.	KISS, M.
J 4936	Pte.	KAPELI, M.
J 4968	Pte.	KRAUSE, A.
J 5163	Pte.	KURASH, C.
TV/6	Pte.	KASTEL, S.
J 7003	Pte.	KATZ, J.
J 7004	Pte.	KAHAN, S.
J 7023	Pte.	KLINCHER, D.
J 7025	Pte.	KOHEN, J.
J 7030	Pte.	KOTLER, Z.
J 7063	Pte.	KILIMNICK, I.
J 7076	Pte.	KROLL, E.
J 5010	Pte.	KASSARLA, S.
J 4911	Pte.	KADOSH, M.
J 4805	Pte.	KAUTROVITZ, E.
J 7084	Pte.	KUSHNER, I.
J 7153	Pte.	KATTAN, J.
J 4574	Pte.	LIZBONA, L.
J 4575	Pte.	LURIA, J.
J 4615	Pte.	LIFSHITZ, H.
J 4763	Pte.	LUSTIGER, E.
J 4767	Pte.	LICHTSHEIN, M.
J 4835	Pte.	LEMPERT, J.
J 4890	Pte.	LEVY, M.
J 5143	Pte.	LEVY, C.
J 5100	Pte.	LEVY, L.
J 4986	Pte.	LANDEAU, I.
J 5183	Pte.	LEVY, M.
J 5007	Pte.	LEVY, A.

N.C.O.'s AND MEN—Continued.

J 5032	Pte.	LEVINROD, M.
J 5172	Pte.	LEISH, E.
J 4605	Pte.	LANDEAU, S.
J 5027	Pte.	LEVY, S.
J 4551	Pte.	LEIBERMAN, S.
J 4672	Pte.	LIFSHITZ, L.
J 4712	Pte.	LEVINE, M.
J 4820	Pte.	LIBERMAN, J.
J 4538	L/Cpl.	LIFSHITZ, J.
J 4537	Cpl.	LIFSHITZ, L.
J 4611	Pte.	LEVINE, M.
J 4776	Pte.	LONDRESS, S. I.
J 4688	Pte.	LEISTNER, A.
J 4853	Pte.	LEMPERT, E.
J 4949	Pte.	LERMAN, M.
J 5096	Pte.	LERMAN, M.
J 4658	Pte.	LERMAN, S.
J 4620	Pte.	LETZ, J.
J 5048	Pte.	LEVY, A.
J 4984	Pte.	LEVY, B.
J 5186	Pte.	LEVY, J.
J 4882	Pte.	LEVY, M.
J 5240	Pte.	LEVY, M.
J 4969	Pte.	LEVY, N.
J 4582	Pte.	LEVY, J.
J 4877	Pte.	LEVINE, I.
J 5069	Pte.	LEVINSON, S.
J 4744	Pte.	LEVITT, I.
J 5154	Pte.	LINDMAN, M.
J 4581	Pte.	LUBARSKY, A.
J 5354	Pte.	LEVY, J.
P.W. 6054	Pte.	LEVY, B.
J 7163	Pte.	LEB, A.
J 7116	Pte.	LOYEA, J.
J 4990	Pte.	LANYADO, A.
J 4916	Pte.	LEFKOVITZ, S.
J 4960	Pte.	LEIBEL, A.
J 5141	Pte.	LEVY, M.
J 5030	Pte.	LEVY, N.
J 5052	Pte.	LEVY, S.
J 5243	Pte.	LISHER, J.
J 5107	Pte.	LURIA, A.
J 5453	Pte.	LIFSHITZ, T.
J 5460	Pte.	LEDERMAN, J.
J 5470	Pte.	LEVY, S.
J 5450	Pte.	LEVY, J.
J 5480	Pte.	LEVY, M.
J 5488	Pte.	LEVY, L.
J 7026	Pte.	LEIZERBAUM, A.
J 7043	Pte.	LEIBOVITCH, M.
J 7068	Pte.	LEVINSON, I.
J 7072	Pte.	LEVITT, M.
J 5074	Pte.	LEVY, S.
J 7085	Pte.	LEVY, I.
J 7154	Pte.	LEVY, I. L.
J 5097	Pte.	LANDAU, J.
J 5285	Pte.	LEVY-KALTAIM, M.

J 5160	Pte.	LEVY, A.
J 3023	Pte.	LEFKOVITCH, JOS.
J 7101	Pte.	LEVY, J.
J 7138	Pte.	LETSCHI, J.
J 7148	Pte.	LEVY, C. J.
J 2169	Pte.	LEVINE, N.
J 4273	Pte.	MIKELSON, A.
J 4738	Pte.	MEDINI, S. A.
J 4966	Pte.	MOIMORANI, M.
J 4897	Pte.	MIZRACHI, M.
J 319	Pte.	MIZRACHI, J.
J 4924	Pte.	MONESHTER, J.
J 4982	Pte.	MEDALIYOH, M.
J 5042	Pte.	MADIMONY, Y.
J 5189	Pte.	MEYUCHAS, C.
J 5245	Pte.	MIZARACHI, A.
J 5014	Pte.	MIZRACH, A.
J 4715	Pte.	MILITKOFSKY, J.
J 367	Pte.	MACHOFSKY, J.
J 4989	Pte.	MARCUS, B.
J 4636	Pte.	MALDOFSKY, E.
J 4690	Pte.	MAHAT, J.
J 4751	Pte.	MOKOSCI, P.
J 4854	Pte.	MALAMED, J.
J 4859	Cpl.	MYROVITCH, B. C.
J 4511	Pte.	MOGALEWSKY, I.
J 4693	Pte.	MIZRACHI, R.
J 5054	Pte.	MAFDELI, S.
J 4638	Pte.	MALK, J.
J 4802	Pte.	MASURI, A.
J 4804	Pte.	MALKA, S.
J 4848	Pte.	MARCUSFELD, B.
J 4722	Pte.	MARGALITH, I.
J 5126	Pte.	MAISEL, S.
J 4858	L/Cpl.	MIRANSKY.
J 5068	Pte.	MERSKY, R.
J 4935	Pte.	MIZRACHI, I.
J 5429	Pte.	MIZRACHI, I. B. N.
J 5035	Pte.	MIZRACHI, J.
J 5191	Cpl.	MIZRACHI, J.
J 4885	Pte.	MIZRACHI, S.
J 5078	Pte.	MIZRACHI, S.
J 5246	Pte.	MIZRACHI, S.
J 5244	Pte.	MIZRACHI, B. L.
J 5279	Pte.	MATHATTA, L.
P.W. 3676	Pte.	MORDE, N.
P.W. 25856	Pte.	MESHE, M.
J 7168	L/Cpl.	MUSHON, S. T.
P.W. 33283	Pte.	MESHEN, S.
P.W. 24617	Pte.	MASLIYAH, J.
P.W. 7174	Pte.	MENTESH, S.
P.W. 7176	Pte.	MISHON, J.
J 4932	Pte.	MALKAH, E.
J 5091	L/Cpl.	MAN, L.
J 4585	Pte.	MELTZER, J.
J 5162	Pte.	MANI, E.
J 4945	Pte.	MARGALITH, A.

"Palestinians."—Continued.

J 4973	Pte. MASHAILI, M.
J 4994	Pte. MASSEOFF, I.
J 5238	Pte. MICKHAH, J.
J 5002	Pte. MINTZ, I.
J 4942	Pte. MINTZ, A.
J 4930	Pte. MIZRACHI, A.
J 5017	Pte. MIZRACHI, J.
J 4931	Pte. MIZRACHI, J.
J 4976	Pte. MIZYAN, I.
J 5008	Pte. MONZON, A.
J 5125	Pte. MONZON, M.
J 5485	L/Cpl. MELIKZT, M.
J 5487	Pte. MALTZIK, A.
J 7007	Pte. MILNER, Y.
J 7008	L/Cpl. MALDOFSKY, M.
J 7011	Pte. MARK, C.
J 7016	Pte. MESSINGER, J.
J 7026	Pte. MARCUS, Y.
J 7047	Pte. MIZRACHI, N. A.
J 7048	Pte. MACHNEIMI, J.
J 7058	Pte. MIZRACHI, S. Y.
J 7060	Pte. MIZRACHI, JAS.
J 7062	Pte. MATTOS, D.
J 7067	Pte. MIZRACHI, D.
J 7071	Pte. MIZRACHI, JOS.
J 4972	Pte. MIZRACHI, A.
J 4921	Pte. MIZRACHI, A.
J 5275	Pte. MIZRACHI, I.
J 7157	Pte. MAYER, M.
J 4992	Pte. MARINO, D.
J 5067	Pte. MALKA, S.
Jef. 379	Pte. MIZRACHI, M.
J 5164	Pte. MORCHA, S.
J 5039	Pte. MIZRACHI, S.
J 5913	Pte. MILSTEIN, T.
1569	Pte. MAIKS, L.
J 7095	Pte. MALKI, A. J.
J 7097	Pte. MASAH, A. E.
J 7111	Pte. MAYAH, E.
J 7119	Pte. MUSOLT, L.
J 7158	Pte. MANDEL, S.
J 7169	Pte. MOSES, A.
Jer. 19	Pte. MIZRACHI, J.
2196	Pte. NEWMAN, H.
J 4648	Pte. NEIHOSS, A.
J 4729	Pte. NATIVI, S.
J 4789	Pte. NADAV, I. S.
J 4839	Pte. NUDLEMAN, I.
J 4635	Pte. NOCHESHET, J.
J 4958	Pte. NECHEMYAH, M.
J 5139	Pte. NACHUMORSKI, B. L.
J 5223	L/Cpl. NORON, C.
J 4539	Pte. NARONSKY, L.
J 5028	Pte. NACHASH, E.
J 4656	Pte. NEHAMIAH, J.
J 5218	Pte. NISSIM, A.
J 4827	Pte. NUTMAN, M.

N.C.O.'s AND MEN—Continued.

P.W. 7166	Pte. NISSIM, M. T.
P.W. 33185	Pte. NISSIM, AB.
P.W. 33338	Pte. NISSIM, AB.
P.W. 35360	Pte. NISSIM, AB.
P.W. 33245	Pte. NISSIM, D.
J 5055	Pte. NACHMIUS, R.
J 5020	Pte. NIGER, J.
J 5187	Pte. NATKIN, A.
J 5064	Pte. NECHEMYAH, R.
J 5433	Pte. NIMCORSKY, I.
J 5491	Pte. NEIMARK, M.
J 7013	Pte. NACHMANI, J.
J 7022	Pte. NACHMANI, V.
J 7054	Pte. NEISTADT, A.
J 5122	Pte. NEDAV, S.
J 5182	Pte. NACHMIUS, D.
J 4818	Pte. NACHAMIR, S. R. T.
J 4675	Pte. NAIMAN, E.
J 4737	Pte. NADAV, S.
J 7088	Pte. NISSIM, L.
J 7177	Pte. NISSIM, A. B.
J 4569	Pte. OMASI, A.
J 4831	Pte. ORKANSHI, H.
J 4500	Pte. ORENSTEIN, M.
J 4881	Pte. OAZIEL, J.
J 4526	Cpl. OLCHANSKY, I.
J 5037	Pte. OSHEROFF, I.
J 5117	Pte. ORODETSKY, I.
J 5085	Pte. ORADIA, D.
J 7046	Pte. OUTSITILO, B.
J 4625	Pte. PELHOWITZ, S.
J 4652	Pte. PERLMAN, S.
J 5044	Pte. POUFFLIS, B.
J 5140	Pte. PINSHER, E.
J 5229	Pte. PUFFLIS, B.
J 4855	Pte. PAKULA, N.
J 4809	Pte. PACHOT, D.
J 4791	L/Sgt. PATT, J.
J 4892	Pte. PAVON, R.
J 4650	Pte. PEARL, M.
J 5210	Pte. PHELER, L.
J 4371	Pte. PINCHEFSKY, I.
J 4948	Pte. PRICE, S.
J 4568	Pte. PRITZKER, E.
Jaf. 223	Pte. PRUZANSKY, J. J.
J 4671	Pte. PROBER, N.
J 5003	Pte. PINDAMINSKY, S.
J 5446	Pte. POPLAVSKY, J.
J 5450	Pte. POLLOCK, L.
J 5465	Pte. PRUZINIM, M.
J 5494	Pte. POLANIA, E.
J 7029	Pte. PORTUGALI, D.
J 7044	Pte. PANKEVITCH, A.
J 7049	Pte. PRICARSHI, J.
J 5025	Pte. PADRO, A.
J 4746	Pte. PINCHEFSKY, J.
J 5089	Pte. PINCHAS, S.
J 4998	Pte. PITSON, S.
J 377	Pte. ROSE, E.
J 4766	Pte. RICHMAN, I.
J 4708	L/Sgt. RUBINSTEIN, M.
J 4541	L/Sgt. RIGAY, M.
J 4626	Pte. RUBINFEIN, S.
J 5219	Pte. ROSENSWEIG, S.
J 4953	Pte. ROTTENBERG, J.
J 4528	Pte. ROSENROCK, J.
J 4840	Pte. ROICHEL, A.
J 5216	Pte. RABINOVITZ, D.
J 4546	Pte. RABBINOWITZ, M.
J 4866	Pte. RASKIN, M.
J 4771	Pte. ROSENBERG, A.
J 5150	Pte. RUBIN, M.
J 4542	Pte. RUBINSKY, J.
J 4680	L/Sgt. RUBINSTEIN, A.
J 4630	Pte. REJCHIN, A.
P.W. 25761	Pte. RAPEEL, S.
J 7165	Pte. RAFOUL, M.
J 5377	Pte. RENOCH, J.
J 5095	L/Cpl. RUSSO, N.
J 5047	Pte. ROHOLD, M.
J 4847	Pte. ROSENBERG, J.
J 4692	Cpl. ROSEN, M.
J 5104	Pte. RUSSO, E.
J 5466	Pte. ROSENBERG, I.
J 5467	Pte. ROSENSWEIG, L.
J 5479	Pte. RUBINSTEIN, C.
J 5490	Pte. RABINOVITZ, B.
J 5499	Pte. RUTEH, A.
J 7002	Pte. RINK, M.
J 7015	Pte. RAVITZKI, B.
J 7028	Pte. RIONICKER, D.
J 7074	L/Cpl. RUDOY, E.
J 5062	Pte. RUSABI, L.
J 4981	Pte. ROBEN, S.
J 4792	Pte. RABAYEV, J.
J 4732	Pte. RESNICK, M.
J 5145	Pte. RECHAVI, E.
J 5259	Pte. RUSSO, M.
J 5043	Pte. RODENSTEIN, E.
J 5128	Pte. ROSENBERG, T.
J 7094	Pte. REFACH, I. J.
J 6100	Sgt. SHINBANE, H.
J 1562	Pte. SADLORSKY, I.
J 558	Pte. SAAD, N.
J 2159	Pte. SHATZ, L.
J 4525	Pte. SHEMION, A.
J 4527	L/Cpl. SEIGAL, J.
J 4724	Pte. SIMSHONI, M.
J 4769	L/Cpl. SHNEERSON, M.
J 4783	Pte. SCHWARTZ, L.
J 4823	Pte. SELHER, D.
J 4862	Pte. SAID, O.
J 4808	Pte. SALINAS, S.
J 4995	Pte. SACHER, M.

"Palestinians."—Continued.

N.C.O.'s AND MEN—Continued.

J 5174	Pte. SAUDER, J.	P.W. 24996	Pte. SEMO, S.	J 7096	Pte. SEREAN, C. I.
J 5119	Pte. SANIA, B. J.	P.W. 33264	Pte. SAMUEL, I.	J 7105	Pte. SOYNAH, H. J.
J 5059	Pte. STERN, E.	P.W. 37312	L/Cpl. SHABETOW, M.	J 7108	Pte. SALEM, JOS.
J 5024	Pte. SARAGOSTA, J.			J 7114	Pte. SONRONJON, J. D.
J 5208	Pte. STERBERG, J.	P.W. 23284	Pte. SHEFOT, M.	J 7118	Pte. SELIM, M.
J 5207	Pte. SHATAL, J.	P.W. 30241	Pte. SOLOMON, N.	J 7150	Pte. SALAMEH, M.
J 5224	Pte. SAUDAL, S.	J 7175	Pte. SHOLO, S. S.	J 7173	Pte. SCHWARTZ, L.
4646	Pte. SHERMAN, M.	J 4799	Pte. SALICH, S.	J 7181	Pte. SEIGAL, H. A.
4687	Pte. SHEVACH, N.	J 5185	Pte. SASSON, L.	J 2195	Pte. TAILAR, A.
4851	Pte. SHACHOM, A.	J 4903	Pte. SCHLANK, M.	4622	Pte. TOLHACHOFF, M.
4655	Pte. STROUNSA, A.	J 4923	Pte. SCHWARTZ, S.	J 4701	Pte. TROYBER, H.
5129	Pte. SALACH, C.	J 4883	Pte. SHOLORM, I.	J 4515	Pte. TASHAV, N.
5204	Pte. SARFIN, S.	J 5159	Pte. SCHREM, A.	J 5086	Pte. TRABLUS, J.
5242	Pte. SPEIGLEMAN, I.	J 5250	Pte. SHREM, A.	J 4549	Pte. TIDHAR, D.
4504	Pte. SWERDLOW, D.	J 5169	Pte. SHAKI, S.	J 4825	L/Cpl. TAL, S.
4563	Pte. SHUGARMAN, A.	J 5018	L/Cpl. SIDAS, M.	J 4810	Pte. TCHONDAKOFF, A.
4645	Pte. SEHEBEL, A.	J 5087	Pte. SITTON, J.	J 4703	Pte. TELEKMAN, J.
4698	Pte. SLISAREFSKY, L.	J 5001	Pte. SIYANI, E.	J 5099	Pte. TINIENI E.
4836	Pte. SPINER, I.	J 4807	Pte. SOPKER, S.	J 4552	Pte. TOOKIN, E.
4860	Pte. SHATZ, L.	J 5237	Pte. SWEKE, B.	J 4519	Pte. TURNER, J.
4753	Pte. SMELENSKY, M.	J 5449	Pte. STEINBERG, I.	J 4553	Cpl. TISNOFSKY, S.
4910	Cpl. SHAPIRO, L.	J 5455	Pte. SHEINBAUM, B.	Tev. 560	Pte. TSCHECHINOWSKY, E.
4598	Cpl. SHASHEN, I.	J 5464	Pte. SHAPIRO, S.		
5435	Pte. SHOPOTCHNICH, J.	J 5473	Pte. SADOVITZ, A.	J 5022	Pte. TAWILE, M.
Jaf. 459	Pte. SHROITMAN, H.	J 5478	Pte. SHTIROPPER, B.	J 5180	Pte. TSARFATTI, C.
4978	Pte. SAADYA, J.	J 5481	Pte. SHAPIRO, Z.	J 4927	Pte. TSOAR, S.
5021	Pte. SABARI, J.	J 5483	Pte. SILBER, J.	J 4988	Pte. TURACH, A.
4586	L/Cpl. SIAS, D.	J 5489	Pte. SIDI, I.	J 5230	Pte. TURGMAN, E.
4781	Pte. SOLOMONOVITCH, S.	J 5493	Pte. SIMKIN, I.	J 5088	Pte. TISHAY, J.
4749	Pte. SAPIRO, J.	J 5495	Pte. SHECHTER, I.	J 5472	Pte. TURKINITZ, I.
4657	Pte. SAIROM, A.	J 7037	Pte. SHECHTER, S.	J 7019	Pte. TSCHAIKOW, M.
4943	Pte. SASSOVAR, M.	J 7042	Pte. SCHINICH, J.	J 7033	Pte. TEITELMAN, M.
4997	Pte. SAVITZKY, M.	J 7055	Pte. STEIN, M.	J 5171	Pte. TIMANI, Y.
4745	Pte. SCHMIDT, M.	J 7065	Pte. SELECTA, L.	J 5166	Pte. TUCHMACHER, H.
4919	Pte. SCHNITZER, A.	J 7066	Pte. SHAPIRO, S.	J 5144	Pte. TEMANI, B.
4842	Pte. SCHWARTZ, E.	SD/4	Pte. SELISS, M.	T3/8	L/Cpl. TRIFON, J.
4928	Pte. SCHWARTMAN, S.	J 5220	Pte. STRICK, E.	J 5050	Pte. UMRANI, C.
4861	Pte. SEIGEL, I.	J 5284	Pte. SCHWARTZ, H.	J 4531	Pte. VEINSHTEIN, E.
4871	Pte. SEIGAL, S.	J 5142	Pte. SHOLOM, D.	J 4834	Pte. VEINSCHTEIN, C.
4777	Pte. SELNER, A.	J 5176	Pte. STRASSBERG, S.	J 5202	Pte. VERSER, S.
4788	Pte. SHOPOTCHNIK, J.	J 4644	Pte. SAMOOSKY, H.	J 5448	Pte. VILHOSHEVITZ, A.
4723	Pte. SHOPSES, D.	J 5196	Pte. SCHVEKI, H.	J 7178	Pte. VANTURA, R. Z.
4667	Pte. SHIDLOFSKY, A.	J 4955	Pte. SAHBACH, M.	J 5968	L/Cpl. WILLIAMS, P.
4696	Pte. SCHKOLNIK, L.	J 5009	Pte. SHEINBAUM, M.	J 4682	L/Cpl. WITKANOVSKY, M.
4562	L/Cpl. SHUR, J.	J 4797	Pte. SLATKIN, L.		
4532	Pte. SIMCHONI, D.	J 5057	Pte. SALIM, S.	J 5398	Pte. WINNICK, M.
5123	Pte. SLONIM, S.	J 4653	Pte. SHOFER, M.	4614	WEISBOARD, E.
4613	Pte. SMELI, M.	J 5232	Pte. SOLOMON, D.	J 4516	Pte. WINNICK, J.
V/412	Pte. SOLOMON, A.	J 5033	Pte. SLIMAN, J.	J 4876	L/Cpl. WILLENCHICK, J.
4507	Cpl. SONIN, N.	J 5248	Pte. SADIA, J.	J 4793	Pte. WINNICK, R.
5251	Pte. STEIN, J.	J 5153	Pte. SUBERRI, J.	J 4530	Cpl. WOLFSON, M.
4817	Pte. STERN, J.	J 4891	Pte. SHIMARYA, R.	5443	Pte. WOLFF, D.
4862	Pte. STUPENSKY, N.	J 7087	Pte. STURMAN, Z.	J 5447	Cpl. WILSON, A.
4963	Pte. SABBA, I.	Ts/43	Pte. SHIMSHELEVITZ.	J 7036	Pte. WEINER, I.
5288	Pte. SAYEG, S.	Ts/242	Pte. SEDLIN, A.	J 7053	Pte. WAGMAN, I.
P.W. 16857	Pte. SHLOMO, B.	J 5330	Pte. SEGALL, J.	J 5127	Pte. WEITENBERG, D.
P.W. 24373	Pte. SAMUELS, B.	J 616	Pte. SHUFLEDER, B.	J 4727	Pte. YOBLOZNICK, I.

"Palestinians."—Continued. N.C.O.'s AND MEN—Continued.

J 5434 Pte. YAFFE, A.	P.W. 25642 Pte. YONSEPH, I.	J 5221 Pte. ZAET, S.
J 5136 Pte. YISHAI, E.	J 5442 Pte. YABLONKIN, A.	J 4971 Pte. ZAHEN, A.
J 5168 Pte. YAISH, A.	J 5445 Pte. YISCHECHAROV, A.	J 4961 Pte. ZAMERO, D.
J 4673 Pte. YELOS, S.	J 5316 Pte. YATTAH, M.	J 4641 L/Sgt. ZELIHOVITZ, E.
J 5274 Pte. YAVNIELI, S.	J 5088 Pte. YISHAY, A.	J 4600 Pte. ZELUDIN, M.
J 4589 Pte. YIMERITSKY, S.	J 1279 Pte. ZUMANOVITCH, I.	J 4606 Pte. ZIFRONI, E.
J 5430 Pte. YIGAEL, M.	J 3272 Pte. ZERNOVITZ, S.	J 4999 Pte. ZIVIRA, M.
J 5247 Pte. YAHIR, J.	J 4821 Pte. ZOAGIN, J.	J 4758 Pte. ZIVONI, M.
J 4501 Pte. YACOBSKIN, I.	J 4904 Pte. ZIMIRI, M.	J 5300 Pte. ZUCARR, V.
J 4604 Pte. YANOVITCH, J.	J 4907 Pte. ZUTA, M.	J 5109 Pte. ZARFATI, S.
J 4588 Pte. YARHONI, I.	J 4597 Pte. ZACKHEIM, E.	J 4947 Pte. ZEVI, P.
J 4554 Pte. YATOM, M.	J 5222 Pte. ZUSSMAN, S.	J 5005 Pte. ZION, M.
J 5158 Pte. YEMANI, Y.	J 4576 Pte. ZELIHOVITZ, L.	J 7051 Pte. ZALMAN, E.
J 5310 Pte. YANOUNON, M.	J 4681 Pte. ZERKIN, D.	J 7069 Pte. ZARCHI, J.
J 7171 Pte. YUSSEF, M. D.	J 5063 Pte. ZUHER, J.	J 5320 Pte. ZONANA, B.
P.W. 26237 Pte. YSANA, S.	J 4704 Pte. ZASLAVSKY, H.	J 4979 Pte. ZARFATI, A.
J 7179 Pte. YOMTOV, A.	J 4627 L/Cpl. ZLOTHOWSKY, M.	J 7115 Pte. ZEVI, N.
P.W. 25228 Pte. YAKO, N.	J 4579 Pte. ZADOH, Y.	

List of Officers, Non-Commissioned Officers, and Men too late for Classification

OFFICERS.

2nd Lieut. ABELSON, E., Royal Air Force.
Sub-Lieut. ABENSUR, R.N.V.R.
Lieut. ALEXANDER, M., R.N.V.R.
Capt. BLAIBERG, E., South Lancs. Regt.
2nd Lieut. CHART, A., 16th Bn. London Regt.
Major DUTCH, H., R.A.M.C.
Capt. FELDMAN, I., R.A.M.C., 40th Royal Fusiliers.
2nd Lieut. FINKLESTONE, M. J., Royal Air Force.
Capt. HARRIS, S. H., R.A.M.C., 40th Royal Fusiliers.
Capt. HYMAN, C. P., R.A.P.C.
Lieut. JOSEPHI, E. H., R.A.S.C.
Capt. KERIN, C. S., 7th Bn. Seaforth Highlanders.
Lieut. LEVY, J., 1/5th Bn. Norfolk Regt.
Capt. MOCATTA, C. H., R.E.
2nd Lieut. MOSENTHAL, B. P., Cape Corps.
Major MOSENTHAL, H. R., Royal Air Force.
Lieut. ROSENBLOOM, H., Royal Fusiliers.
Lieut. ROSENBLOOM, H. C., Highland Light. Inf.
Capt. SALAMAN, R. N., R.A.M.C., 39th Royal Fusiliers.
Capt. SIMONS, S., 1st Bn. Lancs. Fusiliers.
Lieut.-Col. STERN, D., 1st Bn. East Surrey Regt.
Lieut. STUART, A. S., 2nd Grenadier Guards.
2nd Lieut. THOMAS, S., Royal Air Force.

Comt. ABRAHAMS, J. H., B.R.C.S.
Lieut. SCHNEERSON, L. (O.B.E.), Intelligence Corps, E.E.F.
Lieut.-Col. STERN, SIR EDWARD D., East Surrey Volunteers.
Miss SHTITZER, D., V.A.D.
Miss TRENNER, F. J., V.A.D.

N.C.O.'s AND MEN.

23652 Q.M.S. ABRAHAMS, J., Royal Air Force.
A.C.2 ALEXANDER, G., R.N.A.S.
L/Cpl. BAKER, L., R.A.O.C.
Pte. BLOOM, J., A. and S. Highlanders.
Rfm. BROD, H., Rifle Brigade.
Pte. CHART, L., Canadian Division.
Pte. COHEN, M., R.A.S.C.
Pte. DAVIS, J. (SEIGENBERG), Tank Corps.
Pte. FINE, W., Shropshire Light Inf.
Pte. FRANKLIN, E., 2nd Bn. Royal Fusiliers.
Cpl. FRANKLIN, H., R.A.P.C.
C.Q.M.S. GOLDBERG, I. D., 10th Bn. East Lancs. Regt.
Pte. GORDON, N., R.A.M.C.
Cpl. HART, J., R.A.P.C.
M/417770 Pte. HART, S., R.A.S.C.
10909 Pte. HERRING, L., R.A.M.C.
332489 Spr. HYAMS, D., R.E.
Rfm. HOREVITZ, M., 4th Bn. Scottish Rifles.
Sgt. HOROWITZ, H., 15th Bn. Northumberland Fusiliers.
123343 2/A.M. ISRAEL, H., Royal Air Force.
495416 Pte. KOSKY, F., 2/13th Bn. London Regt.
Pte. LEVISON, S., 13th Bn. Suffolk Regt.
Dvr. LOWNE, A., R.A.S.C.
Sgt.-Maj. LYONS, B., R.A.S.C.
30204 Gdsm. MAZARKOFF, S. H., Grenadier Gds.
Sgt. MERVISH, G., K.A. Rifles.
Sgt. MICHAELSON, H., 1st Bn. Welsh Regt.
Pte. MORRIS, C. L., 8th Bn. Northants. Regt.
Pte. NEWHOUSE, M., 14th Bn. Highland Light Inf.
Sig. PARADISE, H., R.N.
Cpl. PERLMUTTER, M., R.E.
4630 Pte. PORTRAIT, S., 1st Bn. Royal Dublin Fusiliers.
Pte. RAPAPORT, A., B.R.C.S.
23019 L/Cpl. ROSEN, H., Machine Gun Corps.
Seaman TOFF, A., Royal Navy.
4879 L/Cpl. SAMUEL, S., R.A.O.C.
Pte. SANDALL, R., Cheshire Regt.
Pte. SCHARFF, S., 6th Bn. Middlesex Regt.
Pte. SHIERS, J., 2nd Bn. East Yorkshire Regt.
Pte. SHTITZER, B., West Kent. Yeo.
351947 Pte. SPIRO, I., King's Liverpool Regt.
31958 Pte. SUCHARD, S., Seaforth Highlanders.
62649 Cpl. THOMAS, C., K.O.S. Borderers.
Sgt. TOFF, E. J., Army G. Staff.
528372 A/Cpl. TRAVIS, H., Canadian A.M.C.
C.S.M. UMLAUF, S., 5th Bn. Middlesex Regt.
S/Sgt. WEINSTEIN, A., Middlesex Regt.
Sgt. WOLFENSOHN, J., 30th Bn. Middlesex Regt.

www.ingramcontent.com/pod-product-compliance
Lightning Source LLC
Chambersburg PA
CBHW080826010526
44111CB00016B/2617